GW00363992

TOP
40
CHARTS

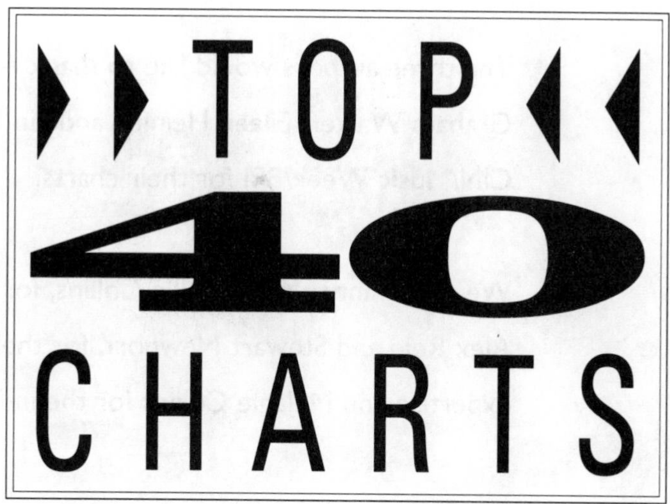

EVERY CHART - EVERY WEEK

PAUL GAMBACCINI • TIM RICE • JONATHAN RICE

GRR Editorial Associate: Tony Brown

GUINNESS PUBLISHING

ACKNOWLEDGEMENTS

The three authors would like to thank Alan Jones, Graham Walker, Eileen Heinink and Jan Rice, and also CIN/Music Week/BPI for their charts.

We also want to thank Sallie Collins, for her typesetting, Alex Reid and Stewart Newport, for their computer expertise and Melanie Collins for the index.

Editor: David Roberts

Deputy Editor: Paola Simoneschi

Published in Great Britain by Guinness Publishing Ltd., 33 London Road, Enfield, Middlesex.

Printed and bound in Great Britain by the Bath Press.

'Guinness' is a registered trade mark of Guinness Publishing Ltd.

A catalogue record for this book is available from The British Library.

ISBN 0-85112-5417

He got it wrong so we could get it right.

A Scottish journalist erroneously reported that we provided a service selling readers copies of the singles chart from any day in history they requested. Our office was deluged with requests for charts from the days the letter writers were born, married, or whatever else they considered important. We realised there was a demand to know not just how high records got on the chart, as can be seen in *Hit Singles*, but what the charts themselves were on any given day.

We then noted, with the obsession for anniversaries that has us constantly aware of how many years have elapsed since 'Rock Around The Clock', the summer of 1967, and 'Anarchy In The UK', that the 40th birthday of the first UK singles chart was approaching. It was the week of 14 November 1952 when the *New Musical Express* printed the first sales chart. As 1991 progressed, we became aware we were heading for the 40th anniversary of that famous issue, when 'Here In My Heart' by Al Martino became for all time the first number one in British chart history. If we could bring out a book around 14 November 1992 with all the charts since that week, we could present *40 Years of the Top 40*!

Well almost. It couldn't be exactly 40 years, since to publish a book for November 1992 we would have to get the manuscript to the printers a few months in advance. *39 and a Fraction Years of the Top 40?* Not even that would be completely accurate, because it wasn't until the week of 10 March 1960 that *Record Retailer* inaugurated its Top 50. Before that, the *NME* printed Top 12s, 20s, 25s and 30s. Even with *Record Retailer* there was only a Top 30 for two weeks in 1973. Should our title therefore be *39 and a Fraction Years of the Top 12? 32 Years of the Top 40 Except for Two Weeks? Nearly Four Decades of Almost 40 Hits?*

We believe in truth in packaging. This book is called *the Top 40 Charts*. It includes every Top 40 chart since the first one was published in 1960. Without a time element in the title, we can honestly publish the book to celebrate the 40th anniversary of the chart without actually having 40 years in it, and we can bring out future editions, if response demands it, without changing the title. *42 Years of the Top 40*, should this volume reappear in 1994, would not sound so sexy.

If you've ever wanted to know what the hits were on your birthday, you now have them at your fingertips. And there's so much more to discover: 'Rock Around The Clock' is credited with beginning the rock era, but what were the other records in the chart the historic week Bill Haley and his Comets went to number one? Was the summer of 1967 all legend has made it out to be?

Who were the artists the Sex Pistols were shaking up when they first poked their gobs into the Top 40 in late 1976?

With a photo of one of the year's leading acts preceding each year of charts, and with commentary in captions and footnotes throughout, you can take a guided tour of Britain's recent musical history. You might want to wade in all on your own and follow the ebb and flow of Frank Sinatra's 'My Way' or the several high water marks of Frankie Goes To Hollywood's 'Relax'. Just don't lose your breath with the charts of the early 1990s, which had the fastest turnover rate to date. Singles have recently tended to enter high and fall fast, dispensing with the long and gradual ascent that traditionally kept fans in suspense for weeks wondering how far their favourite groups would get.

In this book we see clearly how the charts are briefly dominated by artists from every point of the musical spectrum, from Engelbert Humperdinck in 1967 to Madonna in 1985. You can determine the exact chart runs of your favourite singles and the identities of all the hits from the special days in your life.

We thank you for your continued support of *Hit Singles*. We also thank, for the first time in our lives, an inaccurate reporter... the one who caused us such a big postbag and let us know that this book, which we have long desired ourselves, is also wanted by the public.

PAUL GAMBACCINI • TIM RICE • JONATHAN RICE

The New Musical Express Top12 through to Top 30 – 1952-1959

1952

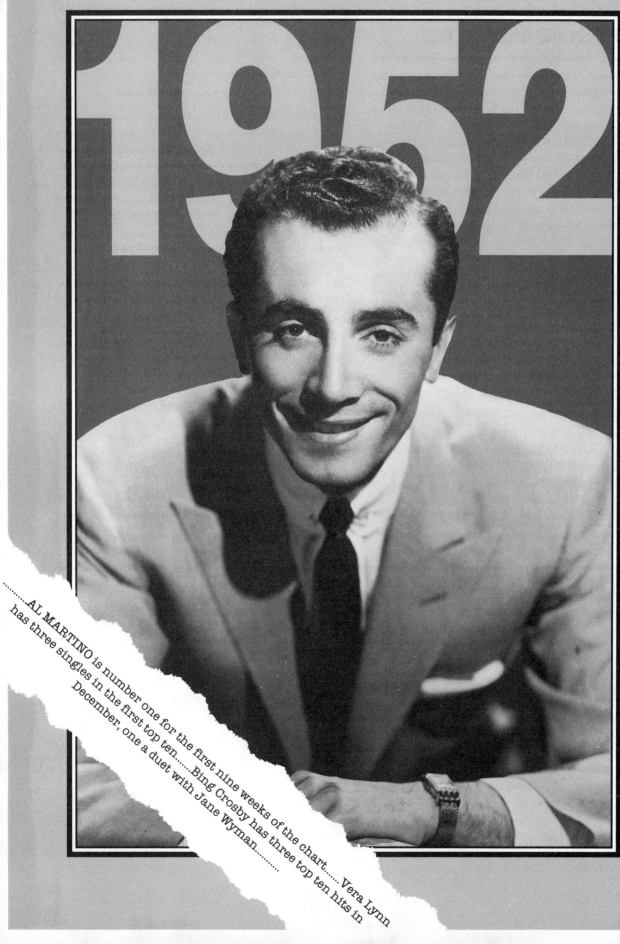

........AL MARTINO is number one for the first nine weeks of the chart...... Vera Lynn has three singles in the first top ten......Bing Crosby has three top ten hits in December, one a duet with Jane Wyman..........

1 9 5 2

The NME Chart is Born

On 14 November 1952, the comparatively new popular music newspaper the *New Musical Express* became the first to print a chart of the best-selling records in Britain. Sheet music charts had existed in Britain on and off since 1936, and *Billboard* magazine in America had been listing the best-selling records on that side of the Atlantic since July 1940, but it was not until after the end of the Second World War that the concept of charts began to be considered important within the British music industry. By the early 50s, it was not so much the song as a particular recording of the song that was the trigger for bringing customers into the shops, so it was inevitable that a record chart should be created. However, the *NME* chart was not so strong that sheet music charts became redundant overnight. For perhaps three more years, the sheet music chart was at least as important to the record industry as the best-selling records chart, and probably more accurately compiled, but the best-selling records chart was the chart of the direction popular music was taking.

The *NME* chart of 14 November 1952 was a Top 12 that was in reality a Top 15 because two records were placed in equal 7th, 8th and 11th places. The sheet music number one since 25 October that year, *Here In My Heart*, also proved to be the number one record, as sung by Al Martino. The two previous sheet music number ones, *Homing Waltz* and *Auf Wiedersehen*, were also on the first record chart, both as recorded by Vera Lynn. The Forces' Sweetheart had a third hit, *Forget-Me-Not*, on that very first chart, thus setting records of chart domination which, although impressive to 1990s eyes, actually only lasted a few months until Frankie Laine swept all before him in 1953. All the same, Vera Lynn was the most successful chart act of the year, even though Al Martino performed the unbeatable feat of staying at number one for every record chart of the year, all seven of them.

The main feature of the first chart is that there were no songs which were hits in two different versions among the Top 12 (or 15), despite the widespread custom of publishers securing as many recorded versions of their most popular songs. The first instance of a song being a hit in two different versions came on 19 December 1952, in the sixth week of the chart's existence, when Nat 'King' Cole's version of *Because You're Mine* joined Mario Lanza's version in the Top 10. Lanza's recording was one of the earliest discs to be issued in the 45rpm format as well as the more usual 78rpm version.

The first chart act to disappear completely from the British charts was Jane Wyman, whose version of *Zing A Little Zong* in duet with Bing Crosby finished its two week run of chart glory on 12 December 1952. Although Bing Crosby went on to many more chart hits, Miss Wyman, ex-wife of Ronald Reagan, never hit our charts again, and thus became the first to be described as a former UK hitmaker.

The Number One Hits

Just one number one single in 1952: **HERE IN MY HEART**: Al Martino (Capitol) for 9 weeks.

1953

..........FRANKIE LAINE sets never- equalled records of twenty-seven weeks at number one in a calendar year and eighteen weeks on top by one disc, 'I Believe'...... the Stargazers are the first British act to reach number one.......for the first time a record goes to number one in two different versions as both Frankie Laine and David Whitfield triumph with 'Answer Me'..........

1953

Laine Leads The Pack

In 1953, Al Martino's *Here In My Heart* began where it had left off at the end of the previous year, at number one, and lasted two more weeks before Jo Stafford, after seven consecutive weeks at number two, enjoyed one week of chart glory with her version of *You Belong To Me.* The big record names of this era were all American, and Eddie Fisher, Perry Como and Guy Mitchell succeeded Jo Stafford before the first British act topped our own charts. They were the Stargazers, whose cover of Art and Dottie Todd's original American hit *Broken Wings* preceded Briton Lita Roza's cover of the American Patti Page's *(How Much Is) That Doggie In The Window* at the top. It would be well over a year before a British song by a British artist would top our charts.

Mario Lanza's hit *Because You're Mine* became the last of the survivors from the first chart to drop out, after 24 weeks, its last week of chart life being the first week at number one for the record which still remains the longest-running number one of all, Frankie Laine's *I Believe.* Guy Mitchell managed to place two hits in the top three during the second week of Laine's domination, but did not manage to knock *I Believe* off the top finally until 11 September, over four months later. By that time *I Believe* had completed 18 weeks at number one, in three runs of nine weeks, six weeks and three weeks. Thus he failed to beat Al Martino's record of nine consecutive weeks on top, but not even Bryan Adams has achieved a total of 18 weeks as number one.

By the end of the year, Laine had also topped our charts with *Hey Joe* and *Answer Me*, becoming the first to achieve three number ones. His total of 27 weeks at the top in 1953 sets a one-year mark that will probably stand for ever. His other major success was in having four hits in the top six in the week ending 30 October, the most spectacular chart domination ever achieved. For the previous two weeks he had had three hits among the top four.

The chart was much less active in those days, of course, which helped Laine achieve these astonishing feats. Doris Day's and Johnnie Ray's duet *Let's Walk That A-Way* spent seven consecutive weeks at number 4 in the autumn, and the Frank Chacksfield Orchestra spent five weeks running at number 5 with their *Theme From 'Limelight'*. This had earlier spent seven weeks at number 2, the most by any record that never hit the very top. On September 25 that year, the top five was unchanged from the previous week, a unique chart occurrence.

By the end of 1953, the *NME* chart was well-established, but it was still reflecting the sheet music traditions of plenty of versions of the hit songs. At one time there were three versions of *Theme From 'Limelight'* in the Top 10. In Coronation week, ending on 5 June, there were two Top 10 versions of *In A Golden Coach*, as well as chart placings for Vera Lynn's *Windsor Waltz* and Winifred Atwell's *Coronation Rag*. But *I Believe* was at number one.

The Number One Hits

In chronological order ■ YOU BELONG TO ME: Jo Stafford (Columbia) 1 week at number one ■ COMES A-LONG A-LOVE: Kay Starr (Capitol) 1 week ■ OUTSIDE OF HEAVEN: Eddie Fisher (HMV) 1 week ■ DON'T LET THE STARS GET IN YOUR EYES: Perry Como (HMV) 5 weeks ■ SHE WEARS RED FEATHERS: Guy Mitchell (Columbia) 4 weeks ■ BROKEN WINGS: Stargazers (Decca) 1 week ■ (HOW MUCH IS) THAT DOGGIE IN THE WINDOW: Lita Roza (Decca) 1 week ■ I BELIEVE: Frankie Laine (Philips) 6 weeks ■ I'M WALKING BEHIND YOU: Eddie Fisher (HMV) 1 week ■ I BELIEVE: Frankie Laine (Philips) 6 weeks ■ MOULIN ROUGE: Mantovani (Decca) 1 week ■ I BELIEVE: Frankie Laine (Philips) 3 weeks ■ LOOK AT THAT GIRL: Guy Mitchell (Philips) 6 weeks ■ HEY JOE: Frankie Laine (Philips) 2 weeks ■ ANSWER ME: David Whitfield (Decca) 2 weeks ■ ANSWER ME: Frankie Laine (Philips) 8 weeks ■

1954

..........FRANK SINATRA has his first number one, 'Three Coins In The Fountain'.......Doris Day has nine weeks on top with 'Secret Love', still the longest-running number one by a female soloist.......David Whitfield and Mantovani, who had number ones of their own the previous year, are together for the ten-week winner 'Cara Mia'..........

1 9 5 4

Rock 'n' Roll Arrives

The year 1954 began as though it would just continue the steady big ballad themes of previous years, but - by the end of the year - changes had taken place that were the first signs of a major shift in popular music. The first new chart-topper of the year was Eddie Calvert's *Oh Mein Papa*. Calvert, billed as 'The Man with the Golden Trumpet', was one of the leading British instrumentalists of the day, and *Oh Mein Papa* was his first chart hit. Other instrumentals, by Mantovani, Frank Chacksfield, Ken Mackintosh, Winifred Atwell, Ted Heath and even Duke Ellington, came on to the charts during Calvert's run at the top, but none could budge him. The vocal version of his hit, by Eddie Fisher, only reached number 9.

One of the long-running hits of the year was the Obernkirchen Children's Choir's *Happy Wanderer*, which spent six months on the chart but failed to reach the very top. It was their only hit. A similar fate also befell Kitty Kallen. Her version of *Little Things Mean A Lot* reached number one in September to make her the first on the list of one-hit wonders, those acts whose only chart hit has climbed to number one. Miss Kallen knocked David Whitfield's *Cara Mia* off the top after a ten week reign - the longest thus far achieved and the first British song by a British artist to reach the pole position.

The year saw the first big hits as soloists by Johnnie Ray and Doris Day, as well as more success for Frankie Laine. At first the charts were as inactive as they had been the previous year, so much so that for five consecutive weeks to mid-June the top three were completely unchanged, but as the weeks passed, something subversive was seen to be happening. On 1 October, the *NME* announced that they were extending the chart from a Top 12 to a Top 20, and, although the top five records that week were by such pillars of conventional music as Frank Sinatra, Nat 'King' Cole, David Whitfield, Frankie Laine and Don Cornell, down at number 16 was a new entry by a new act, *Sh-Boom* by the Crew Cuts. This Canadian foursome of Pat Barrett, Rudi Maugeri and Johnnie and Roy Perkins covered a Chords track that had made number 3 on the US *Rhythm and Blues* charts, and earned themselves immortal fame as the group that brought rock 'n' roll to the British charts. Other hits at the time included Winifred Atwell's *Rachmaninoff's 18th Variation On A Theme By Paganini (The Story Of Three Loves)* and Max Bygraves' novelty *Gilly Gilly Ossenfeffer Katzenellen Bogen By The Sea*, so the Crew Cuts did not have the impact that in retrospect they deserve, if only because their hit title was so short.

Winifred Atwell topped the Christmas chart with a piano medley called *Let's Have Another Party*. This was the only medley disc to go all the way until Jive Bunny's *Swing The Mood* 36 years later. It took over at number one from Rosemary Clooney's version of *This Ole House* which latterday rocker Shakin' Stevens took back to the top in 1981. Nobody thought of Rosemary Clooney as a rock singer, then or now, but by the end of 1954 there was no turning back. Bill Haley and his Comets slipped into the charts at number 13 on 17 December with *Shake Rattle And Roll* and the rock era had begun in earnest.

The Number One Hits

In chronological order ■OH MEIN PAPA: Eddie Calvert (Columbia) 9 weeks ■ I SEE THE MOON: Stargazers (Decca) 5 weeks ■ SECRET LOVE: Doris Day (Philips) 1 week ■ I SEE THE MOON: Stargazers (Decca) 1 week ■ SUCH A NIGHT: Johnnie Ray (Philips) 1 week ■ SECRET LOVE: Doris Day (Philips) 8 weeks ■ CARA MIA: David Whitfield with chorus and Mantovani and his orchestra (Decca) 10 weeks ■ LITTLE THINGS MEAN A LOT: Kitty Kallen (Brunswick) 1 week ■ THREE COINS IN THE FOUNTAIN: Frank Sinatra (Capitol) 3 weeks ■ MY SON MY SON: Vera Lynn (Decca) 2 weeks ■ HOLD MY HAND: Don Cornell (Vogue) 1 week ■ THIS OLD HOUSE: Rosemary Clooney (Philips) 1 week ■ LET'S HAVE ANOTHER PARTY: Winifred Atwell (Philips) 5 weeks

.........RUBY MURRAY, photographed here with dancer Roger Palmer, has five top ten hits in the space of three months...... 'Rock Around The Clock' by Bill Haley and his Comets is the first rock 'n' roll number one......Dickie Valentine has the first Christmas number one actually about Christmas..........

1955

Ruby Reigns

In the first week of the year, the record that did most to change popular music made its entrance. *Rock Around The Clock* by Bill Haley and his Comets lasted only two weeks on our charts, and climbed no higher than number 17, but it brought the word *rock* to Britain. Nine months later, it reappeared in the wake of its inclusion on the soundtrack of the film 'Blackboard Jungle', but for the first half of the year, the charts continued unaware that there was a time bomb ticking away beneath them.

Ruby Murray was the chart star of 1955. The shy Belfast teenager had only made her chart debut in December 1954, but in 1955 she was unstoppable. She had seven different songs in the Top 10, including the number one hit *Softly Softly* and both sides, separately listed, of her third single *Let Me Go Lover* and *Happy Days And Lonely Nights*. Both these songs were also hits for other singers, and the flood of hit songs in more than one version continued throughout the year until rock 'n' roll put emphasis on the performer rather than the song. From 22 April until 15 July, a period of 13 chart weeks, there were at least three songs each with two or more versions on the charts. On 22 May the fifth version of *Unchained Melody* hit the charts, but other songs in multiple hit versions included *Stranger In Paradise, Under The Bridges Of Paris, A Blossom Fell, Tweedle Dee, I Wonder* and the song which became the second to go to number one in two different versions, *Cherry Pink And Apple Blossom White*. By October, there were three versions of the song *Hey There* taking three consecutive chart positions.

It was over all a good year for Britain. Apart from the stunning success of Ruby Murray, who had at least one Top 10 hit throughout every week of the first five months of the year, Jimmy Young became in October the first British artist to top the chart with consecutive singles when his *Man From Laramie* matched the earlier success of his version of *Unchained Melody*. Eddie Calvert, Dickie Valentine, Alma Cogan and the Johnston Brothers were among other British chart-toppers, but the biggest hit of the year came from the American Slim Whitman. His debut hit *Rose Marie* spent 11 consecutive weeks on top, a record which stood until Bryan Adams sustained an even longer run in 1991.

Bill Haley's *Rock Around The Clock* came back on 14 October 1955, and six weeks later was at number one. Throughout the year, a few rock-tinged singles had been brushing the higher reaches of the charts, discs like *Teach Me Tonight* by the deCastro Sisters, which gave the London record label its first UK chart hit, and *Tweedle Dee* by Georgia Gibbs. But Haley opened the floodgates. On 4 November, Britain's proto-rocker Don Lang clocked in with his Frantic Five and *Cloudburst*, and two weeks later the first of the American teenage idols, Pat Boone, charted with his sanitized cover of Fats Domino's *Ain't That A Shame*. But there was still room for novelties like the Stargazers' *Twenty Tiny Fingers*, Alma Cogan's *Never Do A Tango With An Eskimo* and Scottish dance bandleader Jimmy Shand playing his *Bluebell Polka*. Rock was rolling but it wasn't quite king yet.

The Number One Hits

In chronological order ■FINGER OF SUSPICION: Dickie Valentine (Decca) 1 week ■ MAMBO ITALIANO: Rosemary Clooney (Philips) 1 week ■ FINGER OF SUSPICION: Dickie Valentine (Decca) 2 weeks ■ MAMBO ITALIANO: Rosemary Clooney (Philips) 2 weeks ■ SOFTLY SOFTLY: Ruby Murray (Columbia) 3 weeks ■ GIVE ME YOUR WORD: Tennessee Ernie Ford (Capitol) 7 weeks ■ CHERRY PINK AND APPLE BLOSSOM WHITE: Perez Prado (HMV) 2 weeks ■ STRANGER IN PARADISE: Tony Bennett (Philips) 2 weeks ■ CHERRY PINK AND APPLE BLOSSOM WHITE: Eddie Calvert (Columbia) 4 weeks ■ UNCHAINED MELODY: Jimmy Young (Decca) 3 weeks ■ DREAMBOAT: Alma Cogan (HMV) 2 weeks ■ ROSE MARIE: Slim Whitman (London) 11 weeks ■ THE MAN FROM LARAMIE: Jimmy Young (Decca) 2 weeks ■ HERNANDO'S HIDEAWAY: Johnston Brothers (Decca) 2 weeks ■ ROCK AROUND THE CLOCK: Bill Haley and his Comets (Brunswick) 3 weeks ■ THE CHRISTMAS ALPHABET: Dickie Valentine (Decca) 3 weeks ■

1956

..........BILL HALEY AND HIS COMETS return to number one with 'Rock Around The Clock' and set what is still the all-time high of 110 weeks on chart in one year...... Elvis Presley debuts and will be in the top forty in each of twenty-five consecutive years, a record......Johnnie Ray, the Prince of Wails, has his biggest hit, 'Just Walkin' In The Rain'..........

1 9 5 6

Enter Elvis!

In the very first week of the year, the new music tightened its grip. Bill Haley's *Rock Around The Clock* climbed back to number one, and the record it displaced, Dickie Valentine's seasonal *Christmas Alphabet*, tumbled all the way to number 9, the most dramatic fall from the top so far. The next week it was gone completely, after only a seven week stay in the charts. For 35 years that was the briefest chart life of any record that reached number one.

In the first week of the year, the skiffle craze was born. Lonnie Donegan made a record with fellow members of Chris Barber's jazz band mainly as a joke, but *Rock Island Line* became one of the most important records of the decade for the influence it had on getting kids to play pop music and not just listen to it. New songs and new artists began to flood the chart, so much so that by mid-February, none of the records in the Top 20 had spent more than 8 weeks on the chart, the 'newest' chart since the eighth chart week of all. However, the top four that week were all released on that most easy-listening of Fifties labels, Capitol, so it was not just one headlong dash into modernity.

On 13 April, the *New Musical Express* announced that "In response to repeated requests from readers and the trade, we are increasing our list of Best-Selling Records from 20 to 30, as from this week". The record charts had finally overtaken the sheet music charts in both the public's and the trade's eyes, and from now until the start of the *Record Retailer* Top 50 in 1960, the *NME* chart remained the biggest and most accurate in Britain.

In 1956 Bill Haley spent more weeks on the chart with more hits than anybody before or since. His discs spent 110 weeks on the chart, to give him an average of just over two hits a week throughout the year. For nine weeks in the autumn, Haley had five hits on the chart each week, including on one occasion an LP entitled 'Rock And Roll Stage Show'. But probably the most significant event of the chart year took place on 11 May, when a record called *Heartbreak Hotel* by a young Mississippi-born truck driver called Elvis Presley crashed into the chart at number 15. The most prolific chart career of all had begun. Four weeks later he had two hits in the Top 10, but the clean cut Pat Boone prevented Elvis from hitting the very top first time out.

Some new record formats hit the charts for the first time in 1956. On 15 June, two LPs and an EP came onto the lower rungs of the chart ladder, and one of them, Frank Sinatra's 'Songs for Swinging Lovers' went on to reach number 12 on 6 July, the highest placing ever given to an album on the singles charts. The week before, the first charity disc became a hit. The Lord's Taverners sponsored a disc called *All Star Hit Parade*, which featured six Decca stars performing their versions of current hits. It climbed to number two, but it would take Bob Geldof and Midge Ure to take charity all the way to the top, with Band Aid, 28 years later.

The Number One Hits

In chronological order ■ROCK AROUND THE CLOCK: Bill Haley and his Comets (Brunswick) 2 weeks ■ SIXTEEN TONS: Tennessee Ernie Ford (Capitol) 4 weeks ■ MEMORIES ARE MADE OF THIS: Dean Martin (Capitol) 4 weeks ■ IT'S ALMOST TOMORROW: Dreamweavers (Brunswick) 2 weeks ■ ROCK AND ROLL WALTZ: Kay Starr (HMV) 1 week ■ IT'S ALMOST TOMORROW: Dreamweavers (Brunswick) 1 week ■ POOR PEOPLE OF PARIS: Winifred Atwell (Decca) 3 weeks ■ NO OTHER LOVE: Ronnie Hilton (HMV) 6 weeks ■ I'LL BE HOME: Pat Boone (London) 5 weeks ■ WHY DO FOOLS FALL IN LOVE: Teenagers featuring Frankie Lymon (Columbia) 3 weeks ■ WHATEVER WILL BE WILL BE: Doris Day (Philips) 6 weeks ■ LAY DOWN YOUR ARMS: Anne Shelton (Philips) 4 weeks ■ A WOMAN IN LOVE: Frankie Laine (Philips) 4 weeks ■ JUST WALKIN' IN THE RAIN: Johnnie Ray (Philips) 7 weeks ■

1957

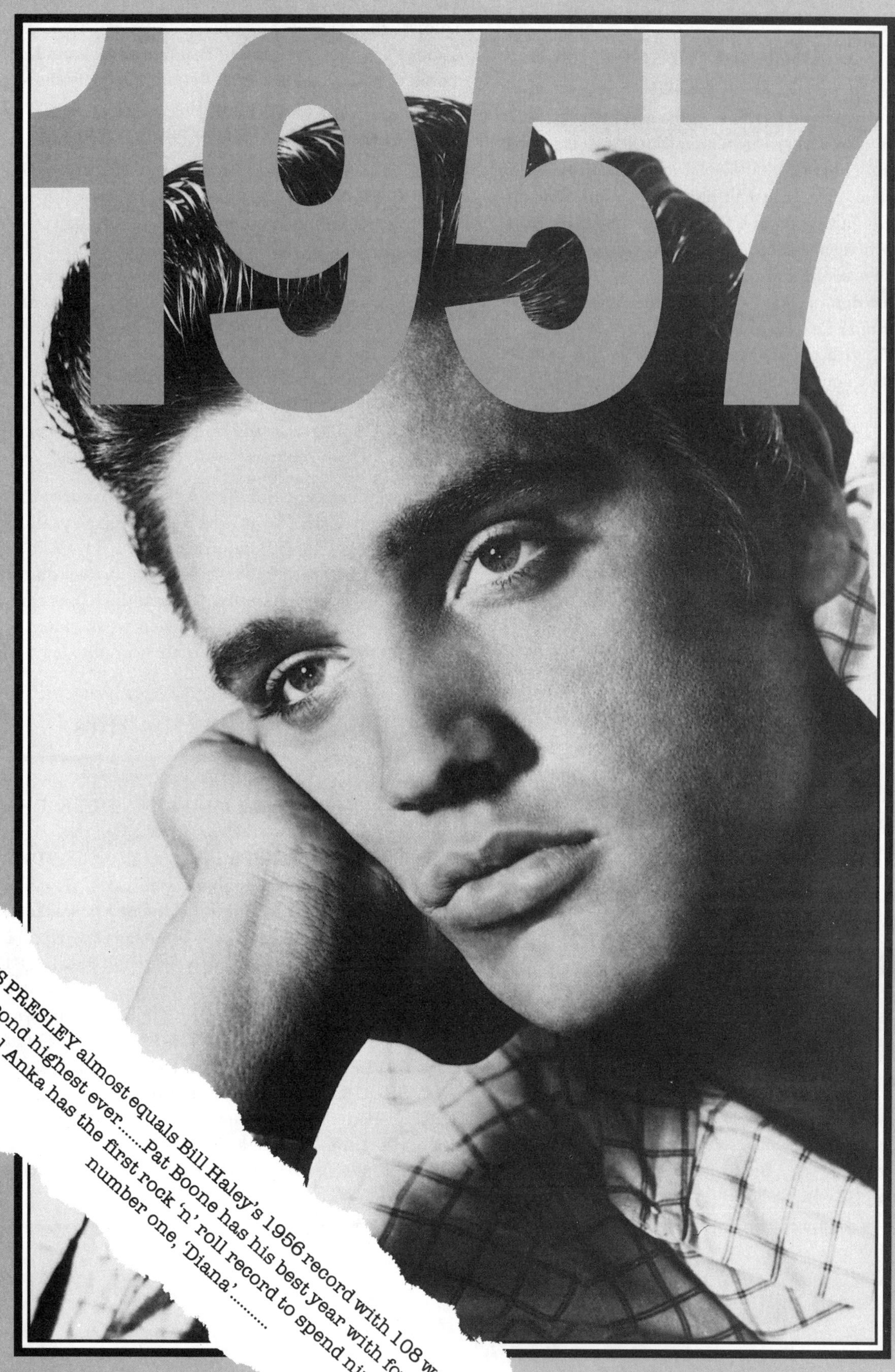

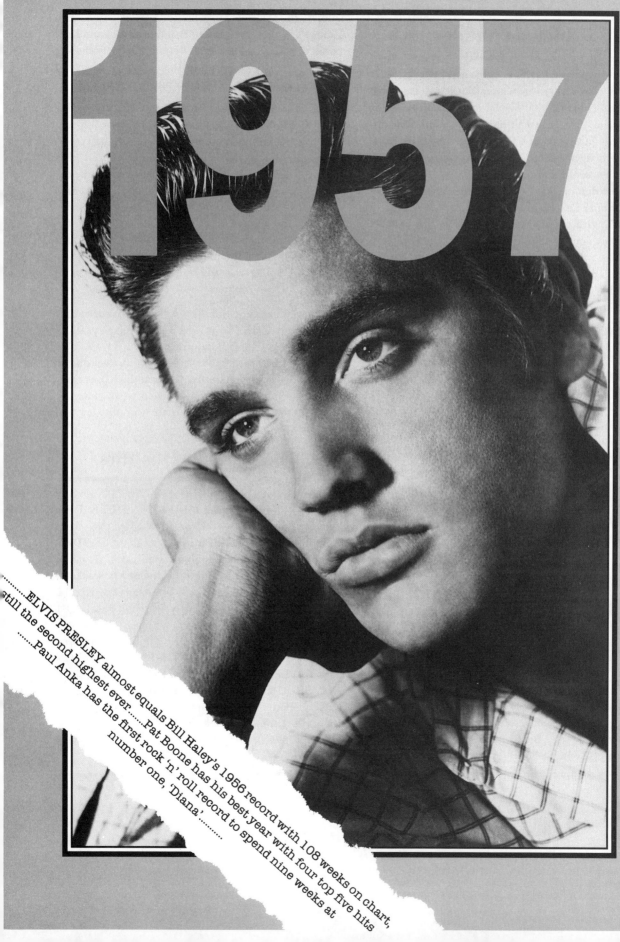

........ELVIS PRESLEY almost equals Bill Haley's 1956 record with 108 weeks on chart, still the second highest ever.......Pat Boone has his best year with four top five hits ....Paul Anka has the first rock 'n' roll record to spend nine weeks at number one, 'Diana'.........

1957

Rock on a Roll

This year belonged to Elvis. To be more exact, it was the first of six years in which Elvis was the most successful chart act, but his achievement in 1957 was phenomenal. He only had one number one hit, *All Shook Up*, but he had no fewer than nine other hits, two of which earned separate chart positions for each side of the record and six of which hit the Top 10. His real chart domination began with his American label RCA forming its own distribution outlet in Britain in mid-1957, with the ultimate result that the first six years' worth of Elvis RCA singles all hit the Top 10. In 1957, RCA only released three Presley records, but the public clamour for Presley product was in part satisfied by HMV releasing back catalogue on singles, giving him hits simultaneously on both labels. On 11 October, he had four hits occupying just three consecutive slots on the chart. *All Shook Up* on HMV was at number 10, *Party* on RCA was at number 11, and *Paralysed* on HMV shared 12th position with *Teddy Bear* on RCA. Three weeks later he had seven hit titles in the Top 30, four on RCA and three on HMV. Elvis ended up with 108 weeks of chart action in the year, just behind Bill Haley's total the year before, but well ahead of all other chart achievers over the next 35 years. Haley himself saw his final chart hit disappear at the end of March 1957, less than 18 months since the sensational reappearance of *Rock Around The Clock* at the end of 1955.

For all his popularity, it was Elvis' first British imitator, Tommy Steele, who reached number one first, six full months before his mentor, with his cover version of Guy Mitchell's *Singing The Blues* in January. Steele's hit was on the Decca label, and when it took over at the top, it ended a line of five consecutive chart-toppers on the Philips label, across a period of 22 weeks, the longest period of ultimate success ever enjoyed by one label.

During the year, the new breed of rock 'n' rollers took their places in the charts. Major stars made their entrances: Chuck Berry (21 June), the Everly Brothers (12 July), Paul Anka (9 August), The Crickets and Jerry Lee Lewis (both 27 September), Jackie Wilson (15 November) and Buddy Holly as a soloist (6 December). Classic records like Tab Hunter's *Young Love*, Harry Belafonte's *Banana Boat Song*, the Diamonds *Little Darlin*, Little Richard's *Long Tall Sally* and Lonnie Donegan's *Cumberland Gap* indicated the way popular music was headed.

There was still room for romantic film themes like *Around The World* to be a Top 10 hit in three different versions, including those by Bing Crosby and Gracie Fields, so the big ballad had not disappeared altogether. The 'beat ballad' was the new phenomenon, with songs like Johnnie Ray's *Yes Tonight Josephine* and Tommy Steele's *Butterfingers* fitting this description, but the biggest of all was the 16-year-old Canadian Paul Anka's multi-million seller *Diana*. This topped the charts for nine weeks, the last record to stay so long at the top until Queen's *Bohemian Rhapsody* 18 years later.

The final number one of the year was the record that for 27 years held the record as the biggest-selling Christmas hit - Harry Belafonte's *Mary's Boy Child*. It still holds the record for most weeks at number one by a Christmas record, helped by hitting the top as early as 22 November. When it fell seven weeks later, it made the biggest drop of all time, straight down to number 12.

The Number One Hits

In chronological order ■ SINGING THE BLUES: Guy Mitchell (Philips) 1 week ■ SINGING THE BLUES: Tommy Steele (Decca) 1 week ■ SINGING THE BLUES: Guy Mitchell (Philips) 2 weeks ■ GARDEN OF EDEN: Frankie Vaughan (Philips) 4 weeks ■ YOUNG LOVE: Tab Hunter (London) 7 weeks ■ CUMBERLAND GAP: Lonnie Donegan (Pye Nixa) 5 weeks ■ ROCK-A-BILLY: Guy Mitchell (Philips) 1 week ■ BUTTERFLY: Andy Williams (London) 2 weeks ■ YES TONIGHT JOSEPHINE: Johnnie Ray (Philips) 3 weeks ■ GAMBLIN' MAN/PUTTING ON THE STYLE: Lonnie Donegan (Pye Nixa) 2 weeks ■ ALL SHOOK UP: Elvis Presley (HMV) 7 weeks ■ DIANA: Paul Anka (Columbia) 9 weeks ■ THAT'LL BE THE DAY: Crickets (Vogue-Coral) 3 weeks ■ MARY'S BOY CHILD: Harry Belafonte (RCA) 7 weeks ■

1958

..........ELVIS PRESLEY is once again chart champ with five top three hits and most weeks on chart, but year's end finds him a US Army Private in Germany.......Perry Como has the year's longest-running number one, 'Magic Moments'.......Connie Francis begins an historic chart career with the number one 'Who's Sorry Now'..........

1 9 5 8

Cliff Crashes in

Elvis Presley continued to dominate the charts in 1958 as he had in 1957. While his tally of weeks on chart, at 70, was well down on the previous year's efforts, he still finished well ahead of the man who had been runner-up to the King in 1957 as well, Pat Boone. Presley began the year by coming straight on to the chart at number one with his classic *Jailhouse Rock* on 24 January, achieving a feat which these days may be comparatively common, but which was at the time unprecedented. Connie Francis, who topped the charts twice, first with *Who's Sorry Now* and then with Neil Sedaka's uptempo novelty *Stupid Cupid*, was the third most successful chart star of the year in her first year of best-selling action, and among the other most successful names of the year were rock acts like Lonnie Donegan, the Everly Brothers, Buddy Holly and the Crickets as well as balladeers like Perry Como, Dean Martin and Michael Holliday.

Marvin Rainwater became the second full-blooded American Indian to top the charts (after Kay Starr) on 25 April. A week later the Mudlarks made their chart debut at number 11 with their cover of the Chordettes' *Lollipop*. This was the highest first chart placing for any British act until neil stormed in at number 5 in July 1984, but it was still one place lower than the American Champs managed on 4 April, when their first hit, *Tequila*, jumped in at number 10. None of these records made it to number one.

The *NME* chart, although the most complete and the most accurate at the time, was still prone to little mistakes. On 5 September they reported that "Inadvertently, the Coasters' *Yakety Yak* was omitted from last week's chart; the position was no. 17". This omission was particularly lucky for Russ Conway. His record *Got A Match* was placed at number 30 for that miscalculated week only, and if the Coasters' record had not been missed out, it would never have made the Top 30 at all.

One week later there was no mistake when Britain's greatest chart star made his first appearance. Cliff Richard's classic *Move It* came on to the charts on 12 September 1958. By 10 October, this record had become the first of his unending string of Top 10 hits, which became the longest of all time when his 56th Top 10 hit, *Saviour's Day*, reached the upper ranks in December 1990. Other acts to make their debuts in 1958 included Sam Cooke (17 January), Ricky Nelson (21 February), Johnny Mathis (23 May), Marty Wilde (11 July), Bobby Darin (1 August), Eddie Cochran (7 November) and the Big Bopper (26 December).

Hit records could still come from all sorts of different directions. The South African Elias and his ZigZag Jive Flutes had a number two hit with *Tom Hark* in May. By late October, there were three versions of *Volare* in the chart, and three versions of *Come Prima* (one in English as *More Than Ever*) giving the charts a very Italian slant. The *Signature Tune Of 'The Army Game'* was a novelty that came from TV, but Sheb Wooley's *Purple People Eater* came from outer space.

The Number One Hits

In chronological order: GREAT BALLS OF FIRE: Jerry Lee Lewis (London) 2 weeks ■ JAILHOUSE ROCK: Elvis Presley (RCA) 3 weeks ■ THE STORY OF MY LIFE: Michael Holliday (Columbia) 2 weeks ■ MAGIC MOMENTS: Perry Como (RCA) 8 weeks ■ WHOLE LOTTA WOMAN: Marvin Rainwater (MGM) 3 weeks ■ WHO'S SORRY NOW: Connie Francis (MGM) 6 weeks ■ ON THE STREET WHERE YOU LIVE: Vic Damone (Philips) 2 weeks ■ ALL I HAVE TO DO IS DREAM/CLAUDETTE: Everly Brothers (London) 7 weeks ■ WHEN: Kalin Twins (Brunswick) 5 weeks ■ CAROLINA MOON/STUPID CUPID: Connie Francis (MGM) 6 weeks ■ IT'S ALL IN THE GAME: Tommy Edwards (MGM) 3 weeks ■ HOOTS MON: Lord Rockingham's XI (Decca) 3 weeks ■ IT'S ONLY MAKE BELIEVE: Conway Twitty (MGM) 5 weeks ■

........CLIFF RICHARD has his first number ones, part of his record of achieving number ones in five different decades......Russ Conway has his two number ones and Shirley Bassey the first of her two......Buddy Holly dies in a plane crash and has a posthumous number one.........

1 9 5 9

Buddy Holly R.I.P.

The day of 3 February 1959 was 'the day the music died'. Buddy Holly's *It Doesn't Matter Any More* became the first in the rather grisly list of posthumous number ones, and Richie Valens became the first person to make his chart debut posthumously, when his *Donna* crept into the bottom of the charts on 6 March. Buddy Holly's number one made him the first person to have a hit as a soloist and as a group member, while the fact that his hit was written by Paul Anka made Anka the first person to have written a number one for himself and for somebody else.

The number one act of the year was the nine-and-a-half-fingered painist, Russ Conway. Thanks to the amazing success of his first number one, *Side Saddle*, and the follow-up, *Roulette*, he led all comers by a vast margin. (His final hit of the year, *Snow Coach*, came into the Top 20 in the same week that Jerry Keller's number one, *Here Comes Summer*, slipped out - an apt comment on the British weather).

The next three most charted acts of the year were also British, Cliff Richard, Marty Wilde and Lonnie Donegan. Elvis Presley, now US Private 53310761 Presley E.A., had only three releases during the year, but two of them hit the very top. Cliff Richard's career moved into overdrive in 1959. His first number one came on July 31 with *Living Doll* and his second came with *Travellin' Light* on 30 October. By that time he was undisputedly Britain's leading pop act, and his success meant that his backing group had to change their name from The Drifters to The Shadows to avoid confusion with the American soul group. *Travellin' Light* was the final record on which they were known as The Drifters.

Billy Fury and Anthony Newley were the two most significant new British acts in the 1959 charts. Billy Fury had his first taste of the charts on 27 February with the self-penned *Maybe Tomorrow*, but his overall impact in 1959 was slight. It would be a couple more years before he established himself as a major force in British pop music. Anthony Newley's first Top 10 hit, *I've Waited So Long*, was also featured on the hit soundtrack EP of his film 'Idle On Parade'. He thus became the only person apart from Elvis to have one recording occupying two chart positions in the same week, but had to wait until 1960 for his two number ones.

Other newcomers in 1959 included Lloyd Price (13 February), Neil Sedaka (24 April), Johnny Kidd and the Pirates (12 June), Dion and the Belmonts (26 June) and Adam Faith (20 November). Adam Faith's *What Do You Want* tied with Emile Ford's *What Do You Want To Make Those Eyes At Me For* at number one on 18 December, the fourth and final time that this happened. At the other end of the career spectrum, Ruby Murray ended her chart life on 9 October, by which time she was the most successful female chart star of all. However she was only able to hold that title for a few weeks into 1960, when Connie Francis overtook her.

There were still problems in producing the charts. The Christmas week *NME* chart, dated 25 December, was actually based on sales over only three days from 16-19 December. No doubt the industry was beginning to see the need for an official chart.

Record Retailer, now *Music Week*, began publication of its Top 50 in their issue dated 10 March 1960. In the early years, the chart day sometimes varied from week to week, so we have followed the date of publication in dating the charts. The chart published in *Record Retailer* dated 10 March was described as the chart for the week ending 5 March 1960, and clearly corresponds to the *NME* chart of 4 March 1960. We therefore discontinue our use of the *NME* charts in *The Guinness Book of British Hit Singles* from 26 February 1960.

The Number One Hits

In chronological order: THE DAY THE RAINS CAME: Jane Morgan (London) 1 week ■ ONE NIGHT/I GOT STUNG: Elvis Presley (RCA) 3 weeks ■ AS I LOVE YOU: Shirley Bassey (Philips) 4 weeks ■ SMOKE GETS IN YOUR EYES: Platters (Mercury) 1 week ■ SIDE SADDLE: Russ Conway (Columbia) 4 weeks ■ IT DOESN'T MATTER ANYMORE: Buddy Holly (Coral) 3 weeks ■ A FOOL SUCH AS I/I NEED YOUR LOVE TONIGHT: Elvis Presley (RCA) 5 weeks ■ ROULETTE: Russ Conway (Columbia) 2 weeks ■ DREAM LOVER: Bobby Darin (London) 4 weeks ■ LIVING DOLL: Cliff Richard and the Drifters (Columbia) 6 weeks ■ ONLY SIXTEEN: Craig Douglas (Top Rank) 4 weeks ■ HERE COMES SUMMER: Jerry Keller (London) 1 week ■ MACK THE KNIFE: Bobby Darin (London) 2 weeks ■ TRAVELLIN' LIGHT: Cliff Richard and the Shadows (Columbia) 5 weeks ■ WHAT DO YOU WANT: Adam Faith (Parlophone) 3 weeks ■ WHAT DO YOU WANT TO MAKE THOSE EYES AT ME FOR: Emile Ford and the Checkmates (Pye) 6 weeks ■ In the two months of 1960 prior to the start of the Top 40, the number one hits were: STARRY EYED: Michael Holliday (Columbia) 1 week ■ WHY: Anthony Newley (Decca) 4 weeks ■

The Top 40 Charts – 1960-1991

PAUL GAMBACCINI • TIM RICE • JONATHAN RICE

1960

..........ADAM FAITH has five top five hits......the Everly Brothers amass seven weeks
t number one with the first release on the Warner Brothers label...... Elvis Presley
returns to civilian life and enjoys his personal best-seller,
'It's Now or Never'.........

March 1960

□ Highest position disc reached ● Act's first ever week on chart

The Top 40 starts here

Record Retailer, now *Music Week,* began publication of a Top 50 on 10 Mar 1960. From this point on their charts are used for *The Guinness Book of TOP 40 CHARTS*

■

The *New Musical Express* Top 30 chart used previously is that of 26 Feb 1960, as the chart published in *Record Retailer* on 10 Mar 1960 was dated 5 Mar and clearly corresponded with the *NME* chart of 4 Mar 1960

■

Other chart changes are highlighted at the point of change in this book with significant dates repeated below

■

3 Jan 63 Top 50 independently audited. 13 Feb 69 Top 50 compiled for *RR* and BBC by British Market Research Bureau. 6 Feb 71 Top 40 only for 7 weeks (postal strikes limited the collection of chart sales information). 27 March 71 Top 50 resumes. 6 Jan 73 Top 30 only, for 1 week. 6 May 78 Top 75 begins. 8 Jan 83 Chart compilation taken over by Gallup, now described as 'The British Record Industry Charts © Social Surveys (Gallup Poll) Ltd'

WEEK ENDING 10 MARCH 1960

LW	TW	Title	Artist	Label	Wks
2	1	POOR ME	Adam Faith	*Parlophone*	7
7	2	RUNNING BEAR	Johnny Preston	*Mercury*	4
6	3	SLOW BOAT TO CHINA	Emile Ford & the Checkmates	*Pye*	5
1	4	WHY	Anthony Newley	*Decca*	8
10	5	SUMMER SET	Mr. Acker Bilk & his Paramount Jazz Band	*Columbia*	7
4	6	PRETTY BLUE EYES	Craig Douglas	*Top Rank*	7
12	7	YOU GOT WHAT IT TAKES	Marv Johnson	*London*	4
24	8	DELAWARE	Perry Como	*RCA*	2
8	9	LA MER (BEYOND THE SEA)	Bobby Darin	*London*	6
4	10	VOICE IN THE WILDERNESS	Cliff Richard & the Shadows	*Columbia*	7
13	11	BE MINE	Lance Fortune	*Pye*	3
3	12	WAY DOWN YONDER IN NEW ORLEANS	Freddie Cannon	*Top Rank*	10
17	13	BONNIE CAME BACK	Duane Eddy	*London*	3
9	14	STARRY EYED	Michael Holliday	*Columbia*	10
-	15	ROYAL EVENT	Russ Conway	*Columbia*	1
-	16	THEME FROM 'A SUMMER PLACE'	Percy Faith ●	*Philips*	1
24	17	WHO COULD BE BLUER	Jerry Lordan	*Parlophone*	2
11	18	HARBOUR LIGHTS	Platters	*Mercury*	6
18	19	LET IT BE ME	Everly Brothers	*London*	4
-	20	WHAT IN THE WORLD'S COME OVER YOU	Jack Scott	*Top Rank*	1
16	21	HEARTACHES BY THE NUMBER	Guy Mitchell	*Philips*	14
-	22	COLETTE	Billy Fury	*Decca*	1
14	23	WHAT DO YOU WANT TO MAKE THOSE EYES AT ME FOR?	Emile Ford & the Checkmates	*Pye*	19
20	24	WHAT DO YOU WANT?	Adam Faith	*Parlophone*	16
15	25	MISTY	Johnny Mathis	*Fontana*	6
-	26	HIT AND MISS	John Barry Seven ●	*Columbia*	1
23	27	TIME AND THE RIVER	Nat 'King' Cole	*Capitol*	3
21	28	RAWHIDE	Frankie Laine	*Philips*	17
26	29	EL PASO	Marty Robbins	*Fontana*	6
-	30	LITTLE WHITE BULL	Tommy Steele	*Decca*	13
-	31	FINGS AIN'T WOT THEY USED T'BE	Max Bygraves	*Decca*	1
22	32	LUCKY DEVIL	Frank Ifield	*Columbia*	3
-	33	CALIFORNIA HERE I COME	Freddy Cannon	*Top Rank*	1
-	34	LOOKING HIGH HIGH HIGH	Bryan Johnson ●	*Decca*	1
-	35	DANCE WITH ME	Drifters	*London*	5
-	36	JOHNNY ROCCO	Marty Wilde	*Philips*	1
-	37	BIG BEAT BOOGIE	Bert Weedon	*Top Rank*	1
-	38	WILD ONE	Bobby Rydell ●	*Columbia*	1
-	39	WILD CAT	Gene Vincent	*Capitol*	4
-	40	STACCATO'S THEME	Elmer Bernstein	*Capitol*	11

WEEK ENDING 17 MARCH 1960

LW	TW	Title	Artist	Label	Wks
2	1	RUNNING BEAR	Johnny Preston	*Mercury*	5
4	2	WHY	Anthony Newley	*Decca*	9
8	3	DELAWARE	Perry Como	*RCA*	3
11	4	BE MINE	Lance Fortune	*Pye*	4
1	5	POOR ME	Adam Faith	*Parlophone*	8
10	6	VOICE IN THE WILDERNESS	Cliff Richard & the Shadows	*Columbia*	8
16	7	THEME FROM 'A SUMMER PLACE'	Percy Faith	*Philips*	2
6	8	PRETTY BLUE EYES	Craig Douglas	*Top Rank*	8
5	9	SUMMER SET	Mr. Acker Bilk & his Paramount Jazz Band	*Columbia*	8
7	10	YOU GOT WHAT IT TAKES	Marv Johnson	*London*	5
3	11	SLOW BOAT TO CHINA	Emile Ford & the Checkmates	*Pye*	6
12	12	WAY DOWN YONDER IN NEW ORLEANS	Freddie Cannon	*Top Rank*	11
19	13	LET IT BE ME	Everly Brothers	*London*	5
22	14	COLETTE	Billy Fury	*Decca*	2
15	15	ROYAL EVENT	Russ Conway	*Columbia*	2
	16	MY HEART	Gene Vincent	*Capitol*	1
20	17	WHAT IN THE WORLD'S COME OVER YOU	Jack Scott	*Top Rank*	2
17	18	WHO COULD BE BLUER	Jerry Lordan	*Parlophone*	3
18	19	HARBOUR LIGHTS	Platters	*Mercury*	7
26	20	HIT AND MISS	John Barry Seven	*Columbia*	2
9	21	LA MER (BEYOND THE SEA)	Bobby Darin	*London*	7
25	22	MISTY	Johnny Mathis	*Fontana*	7
31	23	FINGS AIN'T WOT THEY USED T'BE	Max Bygraves	*Decca*	2
38	24	WILD ONE	Bobby Rydell	*Columbia*	2
34	25	LOOKING HIGH HIGH HIGH	Bryan Johnson	*Decca*	2
-	26	BEATNIK FLY	Johnny & the Hurricanes	*London*	1
13	27	BONNIE CAME BACK	Duane Eddy	*London*	4
14	28	STARRY EYED	Michael Holliday	*Columbia*	11
-	29	HANDY MAN	Jimmy Jones ●	*MGM*	1
36	30	JOHNNY ROCCO	Marty Wilde	*Philips*	2

In these weeks ■ Russ Conway's *Royal Event* was written to celebrate the birth of Prince Andrew on 19 February 1960. Unlike HRH the Duke of York, Russ Conway's record's best week was its first (10.03.60)■

LW	TW	Title	Artist	Label	Wks
23	31	WHAT DO YOU WANT TO MAKE THOSE EYES AT ME FOR?	Emile Ford & the Checkmates	Pye	20
24	32	WHAT DO YOU WANT?	Adam Faith	Parlophone	17
-	[33]	HEART BEAT	England Sisters ●	HMV	1
-	[34]	DARK TOWN STRUTTER'S BALL	Joe Brown ●	Decca	1
21	35	HEARTACHES BY THE NUMBER	Guy Mitchell	Philips	15
-	[36]	THEME FROM 'A SUMMER PLACE'	Norrie Paramor Orchestra	Columbia	1
30	37	LITTLE WHITE BULL	Tommy Steele	Decca	14
29	38	EL PASO	Marty Robbins	Fontana	7
-	39	VALENTINO	Connie Francis	MGM	1
-	40	TEEN ANGEL	Mark Dinning ●	MGM	1

WEEK ENDING 24 MARCH 1960

LW	TW	Title	Artist	Label	Wks
1	[1]	RUNNING BEAR	Johnny Preston	Mercury	6
7	[2]	THEME FROM 'A SUMMER PLACE'	Percy Faith	Philips	3
3	[3]	DELAWARE	Perry Como	RCA	4
5	4	POOR ME	Adam Faith	Parlophone	9
-	5	MY OLD MAN'S A DUSTMAN	Lonnie Donegan	Pye	1
-	6	FALL IN LOVE WITH YOU	Cliff Richard & the Shadows	Columbia	1
24	[7]	WILD ONE	Bobby Rydell	Columbia	3
23	8	FINGS AIN'T WOT THEY USED T'BE	Max Bygraves	Decca	3
14	[9]	COLETTE	Billy Fury	Decca	3
2	10	WHY	Anthony Newley	Decca	10
10	11	YOU GOT WHAT IT TAKES	Marv Johnson	London	6
4	12	BE MINE	Lance Fortune	Pye	5
9	13	SUMMER SET	Mr. Acker Bilk & his Paramount Jazz Band	Columbia	9
8	14	PRETTY BLUE EYES	Craig Douglas	Top Rank	9
-	15	DO YOU MIND?	Anthony Newley	Decca	1
11	16	SLOW BOAT TO CHINA	Emile Ford & the Checkmates	Pye	7
26	17	BEATNIK FLY	Johnny & the Hurricanes	London	2
16	18	MY HEART	Gene Vincent	Capitol	2
17	19	WHAT IN THE WORLD'S COME OVER YOU	Jack Scott	Top Rank	3
29	20	HANDY MAN	Jimmy Jones	MGM	2
20	21	HIT AND MISS	John Barry Seven	Columbia	3
18	22	WHO COULD BE BLUER	Jerry Lordan	Parlophone	4
12	23	WAY DOWN YONDER IN NEW ORLEANS	Freddie Cannon	Top Rank	12
-	24	LUCKY DEVIL	Frank Ifield	Columbia	4
6	25	VOICE IN THE WILDERNESS	Cliff Richard & the Shadows	Columbia	9
25	26	LOOKING HIGH HIGH HIGH	Bryan Johnson	Decca	3
32	27	WHAT DO YOU WANT?	Adam Faith	Parlophone	18
15	28	ROYAL EVENT	Russ Conway	Columbia	3
39	[29]	VALENTINO	Connie Francis	MGM	2
27	30	BONNIE CAME BACK	Duane Eddy	London	5
21	31	LA MER (BEYOND THE SEA)	Bobby Darin	London	8
31	32	WHAT DO YOU WANT TO MAKE THOSE EYES AT ME FOR?	Emile Ford & the Checkmates	Pye	21
22	33	MISTY	Johnny Mathis	Fontana	8
30	34	JOHNNY ROCCO	Marty Wilde	Philips	3
34	35	DARK TOWN STRUTTER'S BALL	Joe Brown	Decca	2
-	36	HE'LL HAVE TO GO	Jim Reeves ●	RCA	1
40	[37]	TEEN ANGEL	Mark Dinning	MGM	2
19	38	HARBOUR LIGHTS	Platters	Mercury	8
-	39	YOU ARE BEAUTIFUL	Johnny Mathis	Fontana	1
-	[40]	MEAN TO ME	Shaye Cogan ●	MGM	1

WEEK ENDING 31 MARCH 1960

LW	TW	Title	Artist	Label	Wks
5	[1]	MY OLD MAN'S A DUSTMAN	Lonnie Donegan	Pye	2
1	2	RUNNING BEAR	Johnny Preston	Mercury	7
2	3	THEME FROM 'A SUMMER PLACE'	Percy Faith	Philips	4
3	4	DELAWARE	Perry Como	RCA	5
4	5	POOR ME	Adam Faith	Parlophone	10
6	6	FALL IN LOVE WITH YOU	Cliff Richard & the Shadows	Columbia	2
8	7	FINGS AIN'T WOT THEY USED T'BE	Max Bygraves	Decca	4
10	8	WHY	Anthony Newley	Decca	11
11	9	YOU GOT WHAT IT TAKES	Marv Johnson	London	7
16	10	SLOW BOAT TO CHINA	Emile Ford & the Checkmates	Pye	8
15	11	DO YOU MIND?	Anthony Newley	Decca	2
7	12	WILD ONE	Bobby Rydell	Columbia	4
17	13	BEATNIK FLY	Johnny & the Hurricanes	London	3
19	14	WHAT IN THE WORLD'S COME OVER YOU	Jack Scott	Top Rank	4
13	15	SUMMER SET	Mr. Acker Bilk & his Paramount Jazz Band	Columbia	10
12	16	BE MINE	Lance Fortune	Pye	6
9	17	COLETTE	Billy Fury	Decca	4
20	18	HANDY MAN	Jimmy Jones	MGM	3
14	19	PRETTY BLUE EYES	Craig Douglas	Top Rank	10
22	20	WHO COULD BE BLUER	Jerry Lordan	Parlophone	5
25	21	VOICE IN THE WILDERNESS	Cliff Richard & the Shadows	Columbia	10
26	22	LOOKING HIGH HIGH HIGH	Bryan Johnson	Decca	4
23	23	WAY DOWN YONDER IN NEW ORLEANS	Freddie Cannon	Top Rank	13
-	24	CLEMENTINE	Bobby Darin	London	1
21	25	HIT AND MISS	John Barry Seven	Columbia	4
-	26	LET IT BE ME	Everly Brothers	London	6
31	27	LA MER (BEYOND THE SEA)	Bobby Darin	London	9
-	28	COUNTRY BOY	Fats Domino	London	1
18	29	MY HEART	Gene Vincent	Capitol	3
34	[30]	JOHNNY ROCCO	Marty Wilde	Philips	4
32	31	WHAT DO YOU WANT TO MAKE THOSE EYES AT ME FOR?	Emile Ford & the Checkmates	Pye	22
30	32	BONNIE CAME BACK	Duane Eddy	London	6
27	33	WHAT DO YOU WANT?	Adam Faith	Parlophone	19
-	34	LITTLE WHITE BULL	Tommy Steele	Decca	14
28	35	ROYAL EVENT	Russ Conway	Columbia	4
33	36	MISTY	Johnny Mathis	Fontana	9
38	37	HARBOUR LIGHTS	Platters	Mercury	9
-	38	FOOTSTEPS	Ronnie Carroll	Philips	1
35	39	DARK TOWN STRUTTER'S BALL	Joe Brown	Decca	3
29	40	VALENTINO	Connie Francis	MGM	3

April 1960

□ Highest position disc reached ● Act's first ever week on chart

WEEK ENDING 7 APRIL 1960

LW	TW	Title	Artist	Label	Wks
1	[1]	MY OLD MAN'S A DUSTMAN	Lonnie Donegan	Pye	3
11	2	DO YOU MIND?	Anthony Newley	Decca	3
6	3	FALL IN LOVE WITH YOU	Cliff Richard & the Shadows	Columbia	3
2	4	RUNNING BEAR	Johnny Preston	Mercury	8
4	5	DELAWARE	Perry Como	RCA	6
3	6	THEME FROM 'A SUMMER PLACE'	Percy Faith	Philips	5
7	7	FINGS AIN'T WOT THEY USED T'BE	Max Bygraves	Decca	5
9	8	YOU GOT WHAT IT TAKES	Marv Johnson	London	8
12	9	WILD ONE	Bobby Rydell	Columbia	5
-	10	STUCK ON YOU	Elvis Presley	RCA	1
14	[11]	WHAT IN THE WORLD'S COME OVER YOU	Jack Scott	Top Rank	5
18	12	HANDY MAN	Jimmy Jones	MGM	4
25	13	HIT AND MISS	John Barry Seven	Columbia	5
13	14	BEATNIK FLY	Johnny & the Hurricanes	London	4
5	15	POOR ME	Adam Faith	Parlophone	11
8	16	WHY	Anthony Newley	Decca	12
24	17	CLEMENTINE	Bobby Darin	London	2
10	18	SLOW BOAT TO CHINA	Emile Ford & the Checkmates	Pye	9
15	19	SUMMER SET	Mr. Acker Bilk & his Paramount Jazz Band	Columbia	11
17	20	COLETTE	Billy Fury	Decca	5
22	21	LOOKING HIGH HIGH HIGH	Bryan Johnson	Decca	5
21	22	VOICE IN THE WILDERNESS	Cliff Richard & the Shadows	Columbia	11
35	23	ROYAL EVENT	Russ Conway	Columbia	5
16	24	BE MINE	Lance Fortune	Pye	7
28	25	COUNTRY BOY	Fats Domino	London	2

■Two new hits crash into the Top Ten in the same week – the only time this happened in 1960. Lonnie Donegan's comedy hit climbed to the very top, but Cliff Richard stalled once again at number two (24.03.60) ■ Two Top Ten hits for writer Lionel Bart – Anthony Newley's *Do You Mind* and Max Bygraves' *Fings Ain't What They Used T'Be* (07.04.60)■

April 1960

□ Highest position disc reached ● Act's first ever week on chart

LW	TW	Title	Artist	Label	Wks
32	26	BONNIE CAME BACK	Duane Eddy	London	7
19	27	PRETTY BLUE EYES	Craig Douglas	Top Rank	11
20	28	WHO COULD BE BLUER	Jerry Lordan	Parlophone	6
29	29	MY HEART	Gene Vincent	Capitol	4
27	30	LA MER (BEYOND THE SEA)	Bobby Darin	London	10
-	31	HE'LL HAVE TO GO	Jim Reeves	RCA	2
40	32	VALENTINO	Connie Francis	MGM	4
-	33	LUCKY DEVIL	Frank Ifield	Columbia	5
23	34	WAY DOWN YONDER IN NEW ORLEANS	Freddie Cannon	Top Rank	14
31	35	WHAT DO YOU WANT TO MAKE THOSE EYES AT ME FOR?	Emile Ford & the Checkmates	Pye	23
34	36	LITTLE WHITE BULL	Tommy Steele	Decca	15
37	37	HARBOUR LIGHTS	Platters	Mercury	10
-	38	WITH THESE HANDS	Shirley Bassey	Columbia	1
-	39	SWEET NOTHIN'S	Brenda Lee ●	Brunswick	1
38	40	FOOTSTEPS	Ronnie Carroll	Philips	2

WEEK ENDING 14 APRIL 1960

LW	TW	Title	Artist	Label	Wks
1	1	MY OLD MAN'S A DUSTMAN	Lonnie Donegan	Pye	4
3	2	FALL IN LOVE WITH YOU	Cliff Richard & the Shadows	Columbia	4
12	3	HANDY MAN	Jimmy Jones	MGM	5
2	4	DO YOU MIND?	Anthony Newley	Decca	4
7	5	FINGS AIN'T WOT THEY USED T'BE	Max Bygraves	Decca	6
10	6	STUCK ON YOU	Elvis Presley	RCA	2
6	7	THEME FROM 'A SUMMER PLACE'	Percy Faith	Philips	6
14	8	BEATNIK FLY	Johnny & the Hurricanes	London	5
4	9	RUNNING BEAR	Johnny Preston	Mercury	9
8	10	YOU GOT WHAT IT TAKES	Marv Johnson	London	9
17	11	CLEMENTINE	Bobby Darin	London	3
13	12	HIT AND MISS	John Barry Seven	Columbia	6
5	13	DELAWARE	Perry Como	RCA	7
9	14	WILD ONE	Bobby Rydell	Columbia	6
11	15	WHAT IN THE WORLD'S COME OVER YOU	Jack Scott	Top Rank	6
31	16	HE'LL HAVE TO GO	Jim Reeves	RCA	3
15	17	POOR ME	Adam Faith	Parlophone	12
39	18	SWEET NOTHIN'S	Brenda Lee	Brunswick	2
25	19	COUNTRY BOY	Fats Domino	London	3
21	20	LOOKING HIGH HIGH HIGH	Bryan Johnson	Decca	6
24	21	BE MINE	Lance Fortune	Pye	8
-	22	CATHY'S CLOWN	Everly Brothers	Warner Brothers	1
18	23	SLOW BOAT TO CHINA	Emile Ford & the Checkmates	Pye	10
-	24	SOMEONE ELSE'S BABY	Adam Faith	Parlophone	1
26	25	BONNIE CAME BACK	Duane Eddy	London	8
28	26	WHO COULD BE BLUER	Jerry Lordan	Parlophone	7
32	27	VALENTINO	Connie Francis	MGM	5
20	28	COLETTE	Billy Fury	Decca	6
27	29	PRETTY BLUE EYES	Craig Douglas	Top Rank	12
-	30	LET IT BE ME	Everly Brothers	London	7
22	31	VOICE IN THE WILDERNESS	Cliff Richard & the Shadows	Columbia	12
-	32	STANDING ON THE CORNER	King Brothers	Parlophone	1
34	33	WAY DOWN YONDER IN NEW ORLEANS	Freddie Cannon	Top Rank	15
37	34	HARBOUR LIGHTS	Platters	Mercury	11
-	35	STAIRWAY TO HEAVEN	Neil Sedaka	RCA	1
40	36	FOOTSTEPS	Ronnie Carroll	Philips	3
-	37	DARK TOWN STRUTTERS' BALL	Joe Brown	Decca	4
16	38	WHY	Anthony Newley	Decca	13
23	39	ROYAL EVENT	Russ Conway	Columbia	6
19	40	SUMMER SET	Mr. Acker Bilk & his Paramount Jazz Band	Columbia	12

WEEK ENDING 21 APRIL 1960

LW	TW	Title	Artist	Label	Wks
1	1	MY OLD MAN'S A DUSTMAN	Lonnie Donegan	Pye	5
4	2	DO YOU MIND?	Anthony Newley	Decca	5
6	3	STUCK ON YOU	Elvis Presley	RCA	3
3	4	HANDY MAN	Jimmy Jones	MGM	6
5	5	FINGS AIN'T WOT THEY USED T'BE	Max Bygraves	Decca	7
9	6	RUNNING BEAR	Johnny Preston	Mercury	10
2	7	FALL IN LOVE WITH YOU	Cliff Richard & the Shadows	Columbia	5
11	8	CLEMENTINE	Bobby Darin	London	4
7	9	THEME FROM 'A SUMMER PLACE'	Percy Faith	Philips	7
12	10	HIT AND MISS	John Barry Seven	Columbia	7
10	11	YOU GOT WHAT IT TAKES	Marv Johnson	London	10
8	12	BEATNIK FLY	Johnny & the Hurricanes	London	6
15	13	WHAT IN THE WORLD'S COME OVER YOU	Jack Scott	Top Rank	7
22	14	CATHY'S CLOWN	Everly Brothers	Warner Brothers	2
24	15	SOMEONE ELSE'S BABY	Adam Faith	Parlophone	2
13	16	DELAWARE	Perry Como	RCA	8
14	17	WILD ONE	Bobby Rydell	Columbia	7
38	18	WHY	Anthony Newley	Decca	14
17	19	POOR ME	Adam Faith	Parlophone	13
-	20	FOOTSTEPS	Steve Lawrence ●	HMV	1
23	21	SLOW BOAT TO CHINA	Emile Ford & the Checkmates	Pye	11
16	22	HE'LL HAVE TO GO	Jim Reeves	RCA	4
20	23	LOOKING HIGH HIGH HIGH	Bryan Johnson	Decca	7
21	24	BE MINE	Lance Fortune	Pye	9
19	25	COUNTRY BOY	Fats Domino	London	4
32	26	STANDING ON THE CORNER	King Brothers	Parlophone	2
31	27	VOICE IN THE WILDERNESS	Cliff Richard & the Shadows	Columbia	13
18	28	SWEET NOTHIN'S	Brenda Lee	Brunswick	3
35	29	STAIRWAY TO HEAVEN	Neil Sedaka	RCA	2
40	30	SUMMER SET	Mr. Acker Bilk & his Paramount Jazz Band	Columbia	13
27	31	VALENTINO	Connie Francis	MGM	6
26	32	WHO COULD BE BLUER	Jerry Lordan	Parlophone	8
-	33	PUPPY LOVE	Paul Anka	Columbia	1
25	34	BONNIE CAME BACK	Duane Eddy	London	9
-	35	MACK THE KNIFE	Ella Fitzgerald	HMV	1
29	36	PRETTY BLUE EYES	Craig Douglas	Top Rank	13
33	37	WAY DOWN YONDER IN NEW ORLEANS	Freddie Cannon	Top Rank	16
-	38	YOU ARE BEAUTIFUL	Johnny Mathis	Fontana	2
-	39	SKYLARK	Michael Holliday	Columbia	1
30	40	LET IT BE ME	Everly Brothers	London	8

WEEK ENDING 28 APRIL 1960

LW	TW	Title	Artist	Label	Wks
2	1	DO YOU MIND?	Anthony Newley	Decca	6
1	2	MY OLD MAN'S A DUSTMAN	Lonnie Donegan	Pye	6
15	3	SOMEONE ELSE'S BABY	Adam Faith	Parlophone	3
14	4	CATHY'S CLOWN	Everly Brothers	Warner Brothers	3
7	5	FALL IN LOVE WITH YOU	Cliff Richard & the Shadows	Columbia	6
4	6	HANDY MAN	Jimmy Jones	MGM	7
3	7	STUCK ON YOU	Elvis Presley	RCA	4
28	8	SWEET NOTHIN'S	Brenda Lee	Brunswick	4
5	9	FINGS AIN'T WOT THEY USED T'BE	Max Bygraves	Decca	8
9	10	THEME FROM 'A SUMMER PLACE'	Percy Faith	Philips	8
17	11	WILD ONE	Bobby Rydell	Columbia	8
26	12	STANDING ON THE CORNER	King Brothers	Parlophone	3
8	13	CLEMENTINE	Bobby Darin	London	4
22	14	HE'LL HAVE TO GO	Jim Reeves	RCA	5
20	15	FOOTSTEPS	Steve Lawrence	HMV	2
6	16	RUNNING BEAR	Johnny Preston	Mercury	11
12	17	BEATNIK FLY	Johnny & the Hurricanes	London	7
13	18	WHAT IN THE WORLD'S COME OVER YOU	Jack Scott	Top Rank	8
16	19	DELAWARE	Perry Como	RCA	9
10	20	HIT AND MISS	John Barry Seven	Columbia	8
-	21	SHAZAM!	Duane Eddy	London	1
19	22	POOR ME	Adam Faith	Parlophone	14
-	23	CRADLE OF LOVE	Johnny Preston	Mercury	1
23	24	LOOKING HIGH HIGH HIGH	Bryan Johnson	Decca	8
25	25	COUNTRY BOY	Fats Domino	London	5

In these weeks ■ This year's Eurovision Song Contest entry is *Looking High High High* sung by the brother and brother-in-law of 1959's Contest entrants, Pearl Carr and Teddy Johnson (14.04.60) ■ The Eurovision Song Contest winner, *Tom Pillibi* by Jacqueline Boyer, peaks only at number 33 (25.04.60) ■ *The Lonely Man Theme* by Cliff Adams is the music from the TV advertisement for Strand cigarettes, the first of many hits to be created by the advertising industry (28.04.60)■

LW	TW	Title	Artist	Label	Wks
29	26	STAIRWAY TO HEAVEN	Neil Sedaka	*RCA*	3
11	27	YOU GOT WHAT IT TAKES	Marv Johnson	*London*	11
18	28	WHY	Anthony Newley	*Decca*	15
21	29	SLOW BOAT TO CHINA	Emile Ford & the Checkmates	*Pye*	12
35	30	MACK THE KNIFE	Ella Fitzgerald	*HMV*	2
32	31	WHO COULD BE BLUER	Jerry Lordan	*Parlophone*	9
24	32	BE MINE	Lance Fortune	*Pye*	10
-	33	TOM PILLIBI	Jacqueline Boyer ●	*Columbia*	1
30	34	SUMMER SET	Mr. Acker Bilk & his Paramount Jazz Band	*Columbia*	14
-	35	HEARTBEAT	Buddy Holly	*Coral*	1
-	36	STANDING ON THE CORNER	Four Lads ●	*Philips*	1
34	37	BONNIE CAME BACK	Duane Eddy	*London*	10
36	38	PRETTY BLUE EYES	Craig Douglas	*Top Rank*	14
-	39	THE LONELY MAN THEME	Cliff Adams Orchestra ●	*Pye*	1
39	40	SKYLARK	Michael Holliday	*Columbia*	2

LW TW *WEEK ENDING* 5 MAY 1960 Wks

LW	TW	Title	Artist	Label	Wks
4	1	CATHY'S CLOWN	Everly Brothers	*Warner Brothers*	4
1	2	DO YOU MIND?	Anthony Newley	*Decca*	7
3	3	SOMEONE ELSE'S BABY	Adam Faith	*Parlophone*	4
12	4	STANDING ON THE CORNER	King Brothers	*Parlophone*	4
5	5	FALL IN LOVE WITH YOU	Cliff Richard & the Shadows	*Columbia*	7
6	6	HANDY MAN	Jimmy Jones	*MGM*	8
8	7	SWEET NOTHIN'S	Brenda Lee	*Brunswick*	5
7	8	STUCK ON YOU	Elvis Presley	*RCA*	5
2	9	MY OLD MAN'S A DUSTMAN	Lonnie Donegan	*Pye*	7
15	10	FOOTSTEPS	Steve Lawrence	*HMV*	3
10	11	THEME FROM 'A SUMMER PLACE'	Percy Faith	*Philips*	9
13	12	CLEMENTINE	Bobby Darin	*London*	5
17	13	BEATNIK FLY	Johnny & the Hurricanes	*London*	8
9	14	FINGS AIN'T WOT THEY USED T'BE	Max Bygraves	*Decca*	9
11	15	WILD ONE	Bobby Rydell	*Columbia*	9
21	16	SHAZAM!	Duane Eddy	*London*	2
14	17	HE'LL HAVE TO GO	Jim Reeves	*RCA*	6
23	18	CRADLE OF LOVE	Johnny Preston	*Mercury*	2
16	19	RUNNING BEAR	Johnny Preston	*Mercury*	12
26	20	STAIRWAY TO HEAVEN	Neil Sedaka	*RCA*	4
22	21	POOR ME	Adam Faith	*Parlophone*	15
20	22	HIT AND MISS	John Barry Seven	*Columbia*	9
18	23	WHAT IN THE WORLD'S COME OVER YOU	Jack Scott	*Top Rank*	9
19	24	DELAWARE	Perry Como	*RCA*	10
27	25	YOU GOT WHAT IT TAKES	Marv Johnson	*London*	12
30	26	MACK THE KNIFE	Ella Fitzgerald	*HMV*	3
-	27	HEART OF A TEENAGE GIRL	Craig Douglas	*Top Rank*	1
24	28	LOOKING HIGH HIGH HIGH	Bryan Johnson	*Decca*	9
28	29	WHY	Anthony Newley	*Decca*	16
35	30	HEARTBEAT	Buddy Holly	*Coral*	2
25	31	COUNTRY BOY	Fats Domino	*London*	6
-	32	THIS LOVE I HAVE FOR YOU	Lance Fortune	*Pye*	1
33	33	TOM PILLIBI	Jacqueline Boyer	*Columbia*	2
36	34	STANDING ON THE CORNER	Four Lads	*Philips*	2
32	35	BE MINE	Lance Fortune	*Pye*	11
29	36	SLOW BOAT TO CHINA	Emile Ford & the Checkmates	*Pye*	13
-	37	DON'T THROW AWAY ALL THOSE TEARDROPS	Frankie Avalon	*HMV*	1
-	38	YOU ARE BEAUTIFUL	Johnny Mathis	*Fontana*	3
-	39	VOICE IN THE WILDERNESS	Cliff Richard & the Shadows	*Columbia*	14
-	40	BEAT FOR BEATNIKS	John Barry Orchestra	*Columbia*	1

LW TW *WEEK ENDING* 12 MAY 1960 Wks

LW	TW	Title	Artist	Label	Wks
1	1	CATHY'S CLOWN	Everly Brothers	*Warner Brothers*	5
2	2	DO YOU MIND?	Anthony Newley	*Decca*	8
3	3	SOMEONE ELSE'S BABY	Adam Faith	*Parlophone*	5
6	4	HANDY MAN	Jimmy Jones	*MGM*	9
7	5	SWEET NOTHIN'S	Brenda Lee	*Brunswick*	6
8	6	STUCK ON YOU	Elvis Presley	*RCA*	6
16	7	SHAZAM!	Duane Eddy	*London*	3

May 1960

□ Highest position disc reached ● Act's first ever week on chart

LW	TW	Title	Artist	Label	Wks
5	8	FALL IN LOVE WITH YOU	Cliff Richard & the Shadows	*Columbia*	8
10	9	FOOTSTEPS	Steve Lawrence	*HMV*	4
9	10	MY OLD MAN'S A DUSTMAN	Lonnie Donegan	*Pye*	8
18	11	CRADLE OF LOVE	Johnny Preston	*Mercury*	3
4	12	STANDING ON THE CORNER	King Brothers	*Parlophone*	5
12	13	CLEMENTINE	Bobby Darin	*London*	6
13	14	BEATNIK FLY	Johnny & the Hurricanes	*London*	9
11	15	THEME FROM 'A SUMMER PLACE'	Percy Faith	*Philips*	10
17	16	HE'LL HAVE TO GO	Jim Reeves	*RCA*	7
14	17	FINGS AIN'T WOT THEY USED T'BE	Max Bygraves	*Decca*	10
22	18	HIT AND MISS	John Barry Seven	*Columbia*	10
15	19	WILD ONE	Bobby Rydell	*Columbia*	10
27	20	HEART OF A TEENAGE GIRL	Craig Douglas	*Top Rank*	2
23	21	WHAT IN THE WORLD'S COME OVER YOU	Jack Scott	*Top Rank*	10
21	22	POOR ME	Adam Faith	*Parlophone*	16
24	23	DELAWARE	Perry Como	*RCA*	11
20	24	STAIRWAY TO HEAVEN	Neil Sedaka	*RCA*	5
19	25	RUNNING BEAR	Johnny Preston	*Mercury*	13
25	26	YOU GOT WHAT IT TAKES	Marv Johnson	*London*	13
-	27	KOOKIE KOOKIE LEND ME YOUR COMB	Eddie Byrnes & Connie Stevens ●	*Warner Brothers*	1
26	28	MACK THE KNIFE	Ella Fitzgerald	*HMV*	4
31	29	COUNTRY BOY	Fats Domino	*London*	7
32	30	THIS LOVE I HAVE FOR YOU	Lance Fortune	*Pye*	2
28	31	LOOKING HIGH HIGH HIGH	Bryan Johnson	*Decca*	10
-	32	THREE STEPS TO HEAVEN	Eddie Cochran	*London*	1
29	33	WHY	Anthony Newley	*Decca*	17
-	34	SUMMER SET	Mr. Acker Bilk & his Paramount Jazz Band	*Columbia*	15
30	35	HEARTBEAT	Buddy Holly	*Coral*	3
39	36	VOICE IN THE WILDERNESS	Cliff Richard & the Shadows	*Columbia*	15
-	37	PUPPY LOVE	Paul Anka	*Columbia*	2
36	38	SLOW BOAT TO CHINA	Emile Ford & the Checkmates	*Pye*	14
-	39	I LOVE THE WAY YOU LOVE	Marv Johnson	*London*	1
-	40	OLD PAYOLA ROLL BLUES	Stan Freberg	*Capitol*	1

LW TW *WEEK ENDING* 19 MAY 1960 Wks

LW	TW	Title	Artist	Label	Wks
1	1	CATHY'S CLOWN	Everly Brothers	*Warner Brothers*	6
3	2	SOMEONE ELSE'S BABY	Adam Faith	*Parlophone*	6
4	3	HANDY MAN	Jimmy Jones	*MGM*	10
2	4	DO YOU MIND?	Anthony Newley	*Decca*	9
5	5	SWEET NOTHIN'S	Brenda Lee	*Brunswick*	7
8	6	FALL IN LOVE WITH YOU	Cliff Richard & the Shadows	*Columbia*	9
7	7	SHAZAM!	Duane Eddy	*London*	4
9	8	FOOTSTEPS	Steve Lawrence	*HMV*	5
11	9	CRADLE OF LOVE	Johnny Preston	*Mercury*	4
10	10	MY OLD MAN'S A DUSTMAN	Lonnie Donegan	*Pye*	9
6	11	STUCK ON YOU	Elvis Presley	*RCA*	7
20	12	HEART OF A TEENAGE GIRL	Craig Douglas	*Top Rank*	3
12	13	STANDING ON THE CORNER	King Brothers	*Parlophone*	6
14	14	BEATNIK FLY	Johnny & the Hurricanes	*London*	10
32	15	THREE STEPS TO HEAVEN	Eddie Cochran	*London*	2
15	16	THEME FROM 'A SUMMER PLACE'	Percy Faith	*Philips*	11
24	17	STAIRWAY TO HEAVEN	Neil Sedaka	*RCA*	6
16	18	HE'LL HAVE TO GO	Jim Reeves	*RCA*	8
28	19	MACK THE KNIFE	Ella Fitzgerald	*HMV*	5
13	20	CLEMENTINE	Bobby Darin	*London*	7
17	21	FINGS AIN'T WOT THEY USED T'BE	Max Bygraves	*Decca*	11
-	22	SIXTEEN REASONS	Connie Stevens ●	*Warner Brothers*	1
21	23	WHAT IN THE WORLD'S COME OVER YOU	Jack Scott	*Top Rank*	11
19	24	WILD ONE	Bobby Rydell	*Columbia*	11
18	25	HIT AND MISS	John Barry Seven	*Columbia*	11
30	26	THIS LOVE I HAVE FOR YOU	Lance Fortune	*Pye*	3

■The first Warner Brothers release becomes their first and biggest hit in Britain – the Everly Brothers' *Cathy's Clown* (05.05.60) ■ Adam Faith, like Cliff Richard a few months earlier, fails by the narrowest margin to have a hat-trick of number one hits when *Someone Else's Baby* stops at number two (19.05.60)■

May 1960

□ Highest position disc reached ● Act's first ever week on chart

LW	TW	Title	Artist	Label	Wks
-	27	TEASE ME	Keith Kelly ●	Parlophone	1
27	28	KOOKIE KOOKIE LEND ME YOUR COMB	Eddie Byrnes & Connie Stevens	Warner Brothers	2
-	29	GREEN JEANS	Flee-Rekkers ●	Triumph	1
22	30	POOR ME	Adam Faith	Parlophone	17
23	31	DELAWARE	Perry Como	RCA	12
25	32	RUNNING BEAR	Johnny Preston	Mercury	14
26	33	YOU GOT WHAT IT TAKES	Marv Johnson	London	14
-	34	MAMA	Connie Francis	MGM	1
39	35	I LOVE THE WAY YOU LOVE	Marv Johnson	London	2
-	36	MY HEART	Gene Vincent	Capitol	5
31	37	LOOKING HIGH HIGH HIGH	Bryan Johnson	Decca	11
-	38	STANDING ON THE CORNER	Four Lads	Philips	3
-	39	LET THE LITTLE GIRL DANCE	Billy Bland ●	London	1
34	40	SUMMER SET	Mr. Acker Bilk & his Paramount Jazz Band	Columbia	16

WEEK ENDING 26 MAY 1960

LW	TW	Title	Artist	Label	Wks
1	1	CATHY'S CLOWN	Everly Brothers	Warner Brothers	7
9	2	CRADLE OF LOVE	Johnny Preston	Mercury	5
3	3	HANDY MAN	Jimmy Jones	MGM	11
8	4	FOOTSTEPS	Steve Lawrence	HMV	6
6	5	FALL IN LOVE WITH YOU	Cliff Richard & the Shadows	Columbia	10
2	6	SOMEONE ELSE'S BABY	Adam Faith	Parlophone	7
4	7	DO YOU MIND?	Anthony Newley	Decca	10
7	8	SHAZAM!	Duane Eddy	London	5
5	9	SWEET NOTHIN'S	Brenda Lee	Brunswick	8
12	10	HEART OF A TEENAGE GIRL	Craig Douglas	Top Rank	4
15	11	THREE STEPS TO HEAVEN	Eddie Cochran	London	3
17	12	STAIRWAY TO HEAVEN	Neil Sedaka	RCA	7
13	13	STANDING ON THE CORNER	King Brothers	Parlophone	7
14	14	BEATNIK FLY	Johnny & the Hurricanes	London	11
22	15	SIXTEEN REASONS	Connie Stevens	Warner Brothers	2
16	16	THEME FROM 'A SUMMER PLACE'	Percy Faith	Philips	12
11	17	STUCK ON YOU	Elvis Presley	RCA	8
18	18	HE'LL HAVE TO GO	Jim Reeves	RCA	9
39	19	LET THE LITTLE GIRL DANCE	Billy Bland	London	2
34	20	MAMA	Connie Francis	MGM	2
21	21	FINGS AIN'T WOT THEY USED T'BE	Max Bygraves	Decca	12
19	22	MACK THE KNIFE	Ella Fitzgerald	HMV	6
23	23	WHAT IN THE WORLD'S COME OVER YOU	Jack Scott	Top Rank	12
20	24	CLEMENTINE	Bobby Darin	London	8
-	25	THAT'S YOU	Nat 'King' Cole	Capitol	1
10	26	MY OLD MAN'S A DUSTMAN	Lonnie Donegan	Pye	10
-	27	THE URGE	Freddie Cannon	Top Rank	1
-	28	I WANNA GO HOME	Lonnie Donegan	Pye	1
26	29	THIS LOVE I HAVE FOR YOU	Lance Fortune	Pye	4
33	30	YOU GOT WHAT IT TAKES	Marv Johnson	London	15
29	31	GREEN JEANS	Flee-Rekkers	Triumph	2
-	32	TRUE LOVE WAYS	Buddy Holly	Coral	1
-	33	THAT'S LOVE	Billy Fury	Decca	1
24	34	WILD ONE	Bobby Rydell	Columbia	12
27	35	TEASE ME	Keith Kelly	Parlophone	2
-	36	LUCKY FIVE	Russ Conway	Columbia	1
28	37	KOOKIE KOOKIE LEND ME YOUR COMB	Eddie Byrnes & Connie Stevens	Warner Brothers	3
-	38	GOT A GIRL	Four Preps	Capitol	1
-	39	YOU'LL NEVER KNOW WHAT YOU'RE MISSING	Emile Ford & the Checkmates	Pye	1
-	40	MUSTAPHA	Bob Azzam & his Orchestra ●	Decca	1

WEEK ENDING 2 JUNE 1960

LW	TW	Title	Artist	Label	Wks
1	1	CATHY'S CLOWN	Everly Brothers	Warner Brothers	8
2	2	CRADLE OF LOVE	Johnny Preston	Mercury	6
11	3	THREE STEPS TO HEAVEN	Eddie Cochran	London	4
9	4	SWEET NOTHIN'S	Brenda Lee	Brunswick	9
6	5	SOMEONE ELSE'S BABY	Adam Faith	Parlophone	8
4	6	FOOTSTEPS	Steve Lawrence	HMV	7
3	7	HANDY MAN	Jimmy Jones	MGM	12
7	8	DO YOU MIND?	Anthony Newley	Decca	11
8	9	SHAZAM!	Duane Eddy	London	6
10	10	HEART OF A TEENAGE GIRL	Craig Douglas	Top Rank	5
5	11	FALL IN LOVE WITH YOU	Cliff Richard & the Shadows	Columbia	11
14	12	BEATNIK FLY	Johnny & the Hurricanes	London	12
12	13	STAIRWAY TO HEAVEN	Neil Sedaka	RCA	8
18	14	HE'LL HAVE TO GO	Jim Reeves	RCA	10
20	15	MAMA/ROBOT MAN	Connie Francis	MGM	3
13	16	STANDING ON THE CORNER	King Brothers	Parlophone	8
15	17	SIXTEEN REASONS	Connie Stevens	Warner Brothers	3
28	18	I WANNA GO HOME	Lonnie Donegan	Pye	2
36	19	LUCKY FIVE	Russ Conway	Columbia	2
17	20	STUCK ON YOU	Elvis Presley	RCA	9
19	21	LET THE LITTLE GIRL DANCE	Billy Bland	London	3
39	22	YOU'LL NEVER KNOW WHAT YOU'RE MISSING	Emile Ford & the Checkmates	Pye	2
22	23	MACK THE KNIFE	Ella Fitzgerald	HMV	7
26	24	MY OLD MAN'S A DUSTMAN	Lonnie Donegan	Pye	11
25	25	THAT'S YOU	Nat 'King' Cole	Capitol	2
27	26	THE URGE	Freddie Cannon	Top Rank	2
33	27	THAT'S LOVE	Billy Fury	Decca	2
31	28	GREEN JEANS	Flee-Rekkers	Triumph	3
37	29	KOOKIE KOOKIE LEND ME YOUR COMB	Eddie Byrnes & Connie Stevens	Warner Brothers	4
16	30	THEME FROM 'A SUMMER PLACE'	Percy Faith	Philips	13
21	31	FINGS AIN'T WOT THEY USED T'BE	Max Bygraves	Decca	13
23	32	WHAT IN THE WORLD'S COME OVER YOU	Jack Scott	Top Rank	13
32	33	TRUE LOVE WAYS	Buddy Holly	Coral	2
35	34	TEASE ME	Keith Kelly	Parlophone	3
24	35	CLEMENTINE	Bobby Darin	London	9
-	36	SING LIKE AN ANGEL	Jerry Lordan	Parlophone	1
40	37	MUSTAPHA	Bob Azzam & his Orchestra	Decca	2
-	38	BABY MY HEART	Crickets	Coral	1
29	39	THIS LOVE I HAVE FOR YOU	Lance Fortune	Pye	5
-	40	BURNING BRIDGES	Jack Scott	Top Rank	1

WEEK ENDING 9 JUNE 1960

LW	TW	Title	Artist	Label	Wks
1	1	CATHY'S CLOWN	Everly Brothers	Warner Brothers	9
2	2	CRADLE OF LOVE	Johnny Preston	Mercury	7
3	3	THREE STEPS TO HEAVEN	Eddie Cochran	London	5
9	4	SHAZAM!	Duane Eddy	London	7
7	5	HANDY MAN	Jimmy Jones	MGM	13
18	6	I WANNA GO HOME	Lonnie Donegan	Pye	3
15	7	MAMA/ROBOT MAN	Connie Francis	MGM	4
6	8	FOOTSTEPS	Steve Lawrence	HMV	8
13	9	STAIRWAY TO HEAVEN	Neil Sedaka	RCA	9
8	10	DO YOU MIND?	Anthony Newley	Decca	12
11	11	FALL IN LOVE WITH YOU	Cliff Richard & the Shadows	Columbia	12
22	12	YOU'LL NEVER KNOW WHAT YOU'RE MISSING	Emile Ford & the Checkmates	Pye	3
5	13	SOMEONE ELSE'S BABY	Adam Faith	Parlophone	9
19	14	LUCKY FIVE	Russ Conway	Columbia	3
4	15	SWEET NOTHIN'S	Brenda Lee	Brunswick	10
10	16	HEART OF A TEENAGE GIRL	Craig Douglas	Top Rank	6
14	17	HE'LL HAVE TO GO	Jim Reeves	RCA	11
26	18	THE URGE	Freddie Cannon	Top Rank	3
17	19	SIXTEEN REASONS	Connie Stevens	Warner Brothers	4
21	20	LET THE LITTLE GIRL DANCE	Billy Bland	London	4
27	21	THAT'S LOVE	Billy Fury	Decca	3
16	22	STANDING ON THE CORNER	King Brothers	Parlophone	9
28	23	GREEN JEANS	Flee-Rekkers	Triumph	4
25	24	THAT'S YOU	Nat 'King' Cole	Capitol	3
30	25	THEME FROM 'A SUMMER PLACE'	Percy Faith	Philips	14
20	26	STUCK ON YOU	Elvis Presley	RCA	10

In these weeks ■ Bob Azzam, one of the many hitmakers with *Mustapha*, is the first Egyptian to hit the British charts (26.05.60) ■ After two weeks of chart action *Robot Man* is listed with *Mama* to give Connie Francis her biggest hit for almost two years (02.06.60) ■ Eddie Cochran becomes the second person to score a posthumous number one with his aptly-titled *Three Steps To Heaven* (23.06.60) ■ Sammy Masters' only hit *Rocking Red Wing* spends three weeks stuck at number 38 (23.06.60)■

June 1960

□ Highest position disc reached ● Act's first ever week on chart

LW	TW	Title	Artist	Label	Wks
33	27	TRUE LOVE WAYS	Buddy Holly	Coral	3
-	28	GOT A GIRL	Four Preps	Capitol	2
-	29	SWEET DREAMS	Dave Sampson ●	Columbia	1
24	30	MY OLD MAN'S A DUSTMAN	Lonnie Donegan	Pye	12
12	31	BEATNIK FLY	Johnny & the Hurricanes	London	13
40	32	BURNING BRIDGES	Jack Scott	Top Rank	2
38	33	BABY MY HEART	Crickets	Coral	2
29	34	KOOKIE KOOKIE LEND ME YOUR COMB	Eddie Byrnes & Connie Stevens	Warner Brothers	5
-	35	AIN'T MISBEHAVIN'	Tommy Bruce ●	Columbia	1
-	36	ANGELA JONES	Michael Cox ●	Triumph	1
32	37	WHAT IN THE WORLD'S COME OVER YOU	Jack Scott	Top Rank	14
-	38	ROCKING RED WING	Sammy Masters ●	Warner Brothers	1
35	39	CLEMENTINE	Bobby Darin	London	10
-	40	PAPER ROSES	Maureen Evans	Oriole	1

WEEK ENDING 16 JUNE 1960

LW	TW	Title	Artist	Label	Wks
1	1	CATHY'S CLOWN	Everly Brothers	Warner Brothers	10
3	2	THREE STEPS TO HEAVEN	Eddie Cochran	London	6
5	3	HANDY MAN	Jimmy Jones	MGM	14
7	4	MAMA/ROBOT MAN	Connie Francis	MGM	5
2	5	CRADLE OF LOVE	Johnny Preston	Mercury	8
6	6	I WANNA GO HOME	Lonnie Donegan	Pye	4
4	7	SHAZAM!	Duane Eddy	London	8
9	8	STAIRWAY TO HEAVEN	Neil Sedaka	RCA	10
15	9	SWEET NOTHIN'S	Brenda Lee	Brunswick	11
8	10	FOOTSTEPS	Steve Lawrence	HMV	9
19	11	SIXTEEN REASONS	Connie Stevens	Warner Brothers	5
12	12	YOU'LL NEVER KNOW WHAT YOU'RE MISSING	Emile Ford & the Checkmates	Pye	4
24	13	THAT'S YOU	Nat 'King' Cole	Capitol	4
10	14	DO YOU MIND?	Anthony Newley	Decca	13
13	15	SOMEONE ELSE'S BABY	Adam Faith	Parlophone	10
20	16	LET THE LITTLE GIRL DANCE	Billy Bland	London	5
14	17	LUCKY FIVE	Russ Conway	Columbia	4
11	18	FALL IN LOVE WITH YOU	Cliff Richard & the Shadows	Columbia	13
18	19	THE URGE	Freddie Cannon	Top Rank	4
21	20	THAT'S LOVE	Billy Fury	Decca	4
35	21	AIN'T MISBEHAVIN'	Tommy Bruce	Columbia	2
17	22	HE'LL HAVE TO GO	Jim Reeves	RCA	12
16	23	HEART OF A TEENAGE GIRL	Craig Douglas	Top Rank	7
26	24	STUCK ON YOU	Elvis Presley	RCA	11
27	25	TRUE LOVE WAYS	Buddy Holly	Coral	4
-	26	DOWN YONDER	Johnny & the Hurricanes	London	1
-	27	RIVER STAY 'WAY FROM MY DOOR	Frank Sinatra	Capitol	1
31	28	BEATNIK FLY	Johnny & the Hurricanes	London	14
25	29	THEME FROM 'A SUMMER PLACE'	Percy Faith	Philips	15
29	30	SWEET DREAMS	Dave Sampson	Columbia	2
36	31	ANGELA JONES	Michael Cox	Triumph	2
22	32	STANDING ON THE CORNER	King Brothers	Parlophone	10
23	33	GREEN JEANS	Flee-Rekkers	Triumph	5
-	34	GOOD TIMIN'	Jimmy Jones	MGM	1
-	35	MUSTAPHA	Bob Azzam & his Orchestra	Decca	3
28	36	GOT A GIRL	Four Preps	Capitol	3
39	37	CLEMENTINE	Bobby Darin	London	11
38	38	ROCKING RED WING	Sammy Masters	Warner Brothers	2
30	39	MY OLD MAN'S A DUSTMAN	Lonnie Donegan	Pye	13
34	40	KOOKIE KOOKIE LEND ME YOUR COMB	Eddie Byrnes & Connie Stevens	Warner Brothers	6

WEEK ENDING 23 JUNE 1960

LW	TW	Title	Artist	Label	Wks
2	1	THREE STEPS TO HEAVEN	Eddie Cochran	London	7
4	2	MAMA/ROBOT MAN	Connie Francis	MGM	6
3	3	HANDY MAN	Jimmy Jones	MGM	15
5	4	CRADLE OF LOVE	Johnny Preston	Mercury	9
6	5	I WANNA GO HOME	Lonnie Donegan	Pye	5
1	6	CATHY'S CLOWN	Everly Brothers	Warner Brothers	11
7	7	SHAZAM!	Duane Eddy	London	9
9	8	SWEET NOTHIN'S	Brenda Lee	Brunswick	12
21	9	AIN'T MISBEHAVIN'	Tommy Bruce	Columbia	3
13	10	THAT'S YOU	Nat 'King' Cole	Capitol	5
8	11	STAIRWAY TO HEAVEN	Neil Sedaka	RCA	11
22	12	HE'LL HAVE TO GO	Jim Reeves	RCA	13
10	13	FOOTSTEPS	Steve Lawrence	HMV	10
31	14	ANGELA JONES	Michael Cox	Triumph	3
16	15	LET THE LITTLE GIRL DANCE	Billy Bland	London	6
26	16	DOWN YONDER	Johnny & the Hurricanes	London	2
11	17	SIXTEEN REASONS	Connie Stevens	Warner Brothers	6
34	18	GOOD TIMIN'	Jimmy Jones	MGM	2
15	19	SOMEONE ELSE'S BABY	Adam Faith	Parlophone	11
23	20	HEART OF A TEENAGE GIRL	Craig Douglas	Top Rank	8
18	21	FALL IN LOVE WITH YOU	Cliff Richard & the Shadows	Columbia	14
12	22	YOU'LL NEVER KNOW WHAT YOU'RE MISSING	Emile Ford & the Checkmates	Pye	5
17	23	LUCKY FIVE	Russ Conway	Columbia	5
19	24	THE URGE	Freddie Cannon	Top Rank	5
24	25	STUCK ON YOU	Elvis Presley	RCA	12
20	26	THAT'S LOVE	Billy Fury	Decca	5
35	27	MUSTAPHA	Bob Azzam & his Orchestra	Decca	4
27	28	RIVER STAY 'WAY FROM MY DOOR	Frank Sinatra	Capitol	2
36	29	GOT A GIRL	Four Preps	Capitol	4
-	30	PISTOL PACKIN' MAMA	Gene Vincent	Capitol	1
28	31	BEATNIK FLY	Johnny & the Hurricanes	London	15
14	32	DO YOU MIND?	Anthony Newley	Decca	14
29	33	THEME FROM 'A SUMMER PLACE'	Percy Faith	Philips	16
25	34	TRUE LOVE WAYS	Buddy Holly	Coral	5
32	35	STANDING ON THE CORNER	King Brothers	Parlophone	11
30	36	SWEET DREAMS	Dave Sampson	Columbia	3
33	37	GREEN JEANS	Flee-Rekkers	Triumph	6
38	38	ROCKING RED WING	Sammy Masters	Warner Brothers	3
-	39	LITTLE CHRISTINE	Dick Jordan ●	Oriole	1
-	40	SHAKING ALL OVER	Johnny Kidd & the Pirates	HMV	1

WEEK ENDING 30 JUNE 1960

LW	TW	Title	Artist	Label	Wks
1	1	THREE STEPS TO HEAVEN	Eddie Cochran	London	8
18	2	GOOD TIMIN'	Jimmy Jones	MGM	3
2	3	MAMA/ROBOT MAN	Connie Francis	MGM	7
9	4	AIN'T MISBEHAVIN'	Tommy Bruce	Columbia	4
4	5	CRADLE OF LOVE	Johnny Preston	Mercury	10
5	6	I WANNA GO HOME	Lonnie Donegan	Pye	6
6	7	CATHY'S CLOWN	Everly Brothers	Warner Brothers	12
-	8	WHEN JOHNNY COMES MARCHING HOME	Adam Faith	Parlophone	1
3	9	HANDY MAN	Jimmy Jones	MGM	16
14	10	ANGELA JONES	Michael Cox	Triumph	4
17	11	SIXTEEN REASONS	Connie Stevens	Warner Brothers	7
12	12	HE'LL HAVE TO GO	Jim Reeves	RCA	14
-	13	WHAT A MOUTH	Tommy Steele	Decca	1
16	14	DOWN YONDER	Johnny & the Hurricanes	London	3
40	15	SHAKING ALL OVER	Johnny Kidd & the Pirates	HMV	2
30	16	PISTOL PACKIN' MAMA	Gene Vincent	Capitol	2
11	17	STAIRWAY TO HEAVEN	Neil Sedaka	RCA	12
7	18	SHAZAM!	Duane Eddy	London	10
26	19	THAT'S LOVE	Billy Fury	Decca	6
15	20	LET THE LITTLE GIRL DANCE	Billy Bland	London	7
-	21	PLEASE DON'T TEASE	Cliff Richard	Columbia	1
28	22	RIVER STAY 'WAY FROM MY DOOR	Frank Sinatra	Capitol	3
13	23	FOOTSTEPS	Steve Lawrence	HMV	11
24	24	THE URGE	Freddie Cannon	Top Rank	6
8	25	SWEET NOTHIN'S	Brenda Lee	Brunswick	13
10	26	THAT'S YOU	Nat 'King' Cole	Capitol	6
22	27	YOU'LL NEVER KNOW WHAT YOU'RE MISSING	Emile Ford & the Checkmates	Pye	6
23	28	LUCKY FIVE	Russ Conway	Columbia	6
36	29	SWEET DREAMS	Dave Sampson	Columbia	4
-	30	HOW DO YOU KNOW IT'S LOVE	Teresa Brewer	Coral	1

■Johnny Kidd's classic *Shaking All Over* becomes the first record to enter the chart at number 40 and climb all the way to number one (23.06.60) ■ Lonnie Donegan is the only British act in the Top Ten (16.06.60) ■ Two Top Ten hits in one week for Jimmy Jones, as *Good Timin'* makes a huge leap towards the top (30.06.60)■

June 1960

□ Highest position disc reached ● Act's first ever week on chart

LW	TW	Title	Artist	Label	Wks
34	31	TRUE LOVE WAYS	Buddy Holly	Coral	6
21	32	FALL IN LOVE WITH YOU	Cliff Richard & the Shadows	Columbia	15
29	33	GOT A GIRL	Four Preps	Capitol	5
32	34	DO YOU MIND?	Anthony Newley	Decca	15
37	35	GREEN JEANS	Flee-Rekkers	Triumph	7
-	36	BILL BAILEY	Bobby Darin	London	1
38	37	ROCKING RED WING	Sammy Masters	Warner Brothers	4
27	38	MUSTAPHA	Bob Azzam & his Orchestra	Decca	5
-	□ 39	CHERRY PIE	Jess Conrad ●	Decca	1
-	40	WALKING THE FLOOR OVER YOU	Pat Boone	London	1

WEEK ENDING 7 JULY 1960

LW	TW	Title	Artist	Label	Wks
2	□ 1	GOOD TIMIN'	Jimmy Jones	MGM	4
1	2	THREE STEPS TO HEAVEN	Eddie Cochran	London	9
7	3	CATHY'S CLOWN	Everly Brothers	Warner Brothers	13
3	4	MAMA/ROBOT MAN	Connie Francis	MGM	8
13	5	WHAT A MOUTH	Tommy Steele	Decca	2
21	6	PLEASE DON'T TEASE	Cliff Richard	Columbia	2
4	7	AIN'T MISBEHAVIN'	Tommy Bruce	Columbia	5
14	□ 8	DOWN YONDER	Johnny & the Hurricanes	London	4
9	9	HANDY MAN	Jimmy Jones	MGM	17
15	10	SHAKING ALL OVER	Johnny Kidd & the Pirates	HMV	3
10	11	ANGELA JONES	Michael Cox	Triumph	5
5	12	CRADLE OF LOVE	Johnny Preston	Mercury	11
18	13	SHAZAM!	Duane Eddy	London	11
6	14	I WANNA GO HOME	Lonnie Donegan	Pye	7
8	15	WHEN JOHNNY COMES MARCHING HOME	Adam Faith	Parlophone	2
17	16	STAIRWAY TO HEAVEN	Neil Sedaka	RCA	13
25	17	SWEET NOTHIN'S	Brenda Lee	Brunswick	14
11	18	SIXTEEN REASONS	Connie Stevens	Warner Brothers	8
22	19	RIVER STAY 'WAY FROM MY DOOR	Frank Sinatra	Capitol	4
12	20	HE'LL HAVE TO GO	Jim Reeves	RCA	15
30	□ 21	HOW DO YOU KNOW IT'S LOVE	Teresa Brewer	Coral	2
16	22	PISTOL PACKIN' MAMA	Gene Vincent	Capitol	3
38	□ 23	MUSTAPHA	Bob Azzam & his Orchestra	Decca	6
19	24	THAT'S LOVE	Billy Fury	Decca	7
-	25	LOVE IS LIKE A VIOLIN	Ken Dodd ●	Decca	1
27	26	YOU'LL NEVER KNOW WHAT YOU'RE MISSING	Emile Ford & the Checkmates	Pye	7
20	27	LET THE LITTLE GIRL DANCE	Billy Bland	London	8
28	28	LUCKY FIVE	Russ Conway	Columbia	7
24	29	THE URGE	Freddie Cannon	Top Rank	7
-	30	PAPER ROSES	Kaye Sisters	Philips	1
23	31	FOOTSTEPS	Steve Lawrence	HMV	12
-	32	WONDERFUL WORLD	Sam Cooke	HMV	1
35	33	GREEN JEANS	Flee-Rekkers	Triumph	8
-	34	THEME FROM 'A SUMMER PLACE'	Percy Faith	Philips	17
31	35	TRUE LOVE WAYS	Buddy Holly	Coral	7
37	□ 36	ROCKING RED WING	Sammy Masters	Warner Brothers	5
26	37	THAT'S YOU	Nat 'King' Cole	Capitol	7
-	38	STUCK ON YOU	Elvis Presley	RCA	13
-	39	GREEN FIELDS	Beverley Sisters	Columbia	1
-	□ 40	GREEN FIELDS	Brothers Four ●	Philips	1

WEEK ENDING 14 JULY 1960

LW	TW	Title	Artist	Label	Wks
1	□ 1	GOOD TIMIN'	Jimmy Jones	MGM	5
6	2	PLEASE DON'T TEASE	Cliff Richard	Columbia	3
4	3	MAMA/ROBOT MAN	Connie Francis	MGM	9
7	4	AIN'T MISBEHAVIN'	Tommy Bruce	Columbia	6
2	5	THREE STEPS TO HEAVEN	Eddie Cochran	London	10
15	6	WHEN JOHNNY COMES MARCHING HOME	Adam Faith	Parlophone	3
11	□ 7	ANGELA JONES	Michael Cox	Triumph	6
5	8	WHAT A MOUTH	Tommy Steele	Decca	3
18	□ 9	SIXTEEN REASONS	Connie Stevens	Warner Brothers	9
10	10	SHAKING ALL OVER	Johnny Kidd & the Pirates	HMV	4
3	11	CATHY'S CLOWN	Everly Brothers	Warner Brothers	14
9	12	HANDY MAN	Jimmy Jones	MGM	18
8	13	DOWN YONDER	Johnny & the Hurricanes	London	5
14	14	I WANNA GO HOME	Lonnie Donegan	Pye	8
22	□ 15	PISTOL PACKIN' MAMA	Gene Vincent	Capitol	4
17	16	SWEET NOTHIN'S	Brenda Lee	Brunswick	15
12	17	CRADLE OF LOVE	Johnny Preston	Mercury	12
19	□ 18	RIVER STAY 'WAY FROM MY DOOR	Frank Sinatra	Capitol	5
24	□ 19	THAT'S LOVE	Billy Fury	Decca	8
-	20	I'M SORRY	Brenda Lee	Brunswick	1
26	21	YOU'LL NEVER KNOW WHAT YOU'RE MISSING	Emile Ford & the Checkmates	Pye	8
20	22	HE'LL HAVE TO GO	Jim Reeves	RCA	16
16	23	STAIRWAY TO HEAVEN	Neil Sedaka	RCA	14
-	24	PAPER ROSES	Anita Bryant ●	London	1
13	25	SHAZAM!	Duane Eddy	London	12
31	26	FOOTSTEPS	Steve Lawrence	HMV	13
21	27	HOW DO YOU KNOW IT'S LOVE	Teresa Brewer	Coral	3
25	28	LOVE IS LIKE A VIOLIN	Ken Dodd	Decca	2
39	□ 29	GREEN FIELDS	Beverley Sisters	Columbia	2
37	30	THAT'S YOU	Nat 'King' Cole	Capitol	8
-	31	ITSY BITSY TEENY WEENY YELLOW POLKA DOT BIKINI	Brian Hyland ●	London	1
23	32	MUSTAPHA	Bob Azzam & his Orchestra	Decca	7
-	□ 33	MOUNTAIN OF LOVE	Kenny Lynch ●	HMV	1
-	□ 34	BILL BAILEY	Bobby Darin	London	2
27	35	LET THE LITTLE GIRL DANCE	Billy Bland	London	9
-	36	WHEN WILL I BE LOVED	Everly Brothers	London	1
32	37	WONDERFUL WORLD	Sam Cooke	HMV	2
33	38	GREEN JEANS	Flee-Rekkers	Triumph	9
-	39	IF SHE SHOULD COME TO YOU	Anthony Newley	Decca	1
-	40	LOOK FOR A STAR	Gary Mills ●	Top Rank	1

WEEK ENDING 21 JULY 1960

LW	TW	Title	Artist	Label	Wks
1	□ 1	GOOD TIMIN'	Jimmy Jones	MGM	6
2	2	PLEASE DON'T TEASE	Cliff Richard	Columbia	4
4	□ 3	AIN'T MISBEHAVIN'	Tommy Bruce	Columbia	7
10	4	SHAKING ALL OVER	Johnny Kidd & the Pirates	HMV	5
6	□ 5	WHEN JOHNNY COMES MARCHING HOME	Adam Faith	Parlophone	4
8	6	WHAT A MOUTH	Tommy Steele	Decca	4
3	7	MAMA/ROBOT MAN	Connie Francis	MGM	10
5	8	THREE STEPS TO HEAVEN	Eddie Cochran	London	11
14	9	I WANNA GO HOME	Lonnie Donegan	Pye	9
7	10	ANGELA JONES	Michael Cox	Triumph	7
31	11	ITSY BITSY TEENY WEENY YELLOW POLKA DOT BIKINI	Brian Hyland	London	2
36	12	WHEN WILL I BE LOVED	Everly Brothers	London	2
20	13	I'M SORRY	Brenda Lee	Brunswick	2
40	14	LOOK FOR A STAR	Gary Mills	Top Rank	2
39	15	IF SHE SHOULD COME TO YOU	Anthony Newley	Decca	2
28	16	LOVE IS LIKE A VIOLIN	Ken Dodd	Decca	3
12	17	HANDY MAN	Jimmy Jones	MGM	19
15	18	PISTOL PACKIN' MAMA	Gene Vincent	Capitol	5
11	19	CATHY'S CLOWN	Everly Brothers	Warner Brothers	15
13	20	DOWN YONDER	Johnny & the Hurricanes	London	6
16	21	SWEET NOTHIN'S	Brenda Lee	Brunswick	16
22	22	HE'LL HAVE TO GO	Jim Reeves	RCA	17
-	23	PAPER ROSES	Kaye Sisters	Philips	2
18	24	RIVER STAY 'WAY FROM MY DOOR	Frank Sinatra	Capitol	6
19	25	THAT'S LOVE	Billy Fury	Decca	9
-	□ 26	LADY IS A TRAMP	Buddy Greco ●	Fontana	1
37	□ 27	WONDERFUL WORLD	Sam Cooke	HMV	3
-	28	BECAUSE THEY'RE YOUNG	Duane Eddy	London	1
27	29	HOW DO YOU KNOW IT'S LOVE	Teresa Brewer	Coral	4
17	30	CRADLE OF LOVE	Johnny Preston	Mercury	13
-	31	TIE ME KANGAROO DOWN SPORT	Rolf Harris ●	Columbia	1
38	32	GREEN JEANS	Flee-Rekkers	Triumph	10
-	33	ALLEY OOP	Hollywood Argyles ●	London	1
25	34	SHAZAM!	Duane Eddy	London	13
-	35	APACHE	Shadows ●	Columbia	1

In these weeks ■ Connie Stevens' only solo hit, *Sixteen Reasons*, has one of the strangest chart careers of all time. Its final six weeks of chart life see it going from 19 to 11, back down to 17, up again to 11, down again to 18, up to its peak of number nine, and then the next week – nowhere! (14.07.60) ■ Fifteen of the Top 40 records are by acts having their first chart hit (28.07.60) ■

LW	TW	Title	Artist	Label	Wks
-	[36]	BANJO BOY	Jan & Kjeld ●	Ember	1
23	37	STAIRWAY TO HEAVEN	Neil Sedaka	RCA	15
21	38	YOU'LL NEVER KNOW WHAT YOU'RE MISSING	Emile Ford & the Checkmates	Pye	9
-	[39]	ROMANTICA	Jane Morgan	London	1
-	40	THEME FROM 'A SUMMER PLACE'	Percy Faith	Philips	18

WEEK ENDING 28 JULY 1960

LW	TW	Title	Artist	Label	Wks
2	[1]	PLEASE DON'T TEASE	Cliff Richard	Columbia	5
1	2	GOOD TIMIN'	Jimmy Jones	MGM	7
4	3	SHAKING ALL OVER	Johnny Kidd & the Pirates	HMV	6
15	[4]	IF SHE SHOULD COME TO YOU	Anthony Newley	Decca	3
12	5	WHEN WILL I BE LOVED	Everly Brothers	London	3
9	6	I WANNA GO HOME	Lonnie Donegan	Pye	10
14	[7]	LOOK FOR A STAR	Gary Mills	Top Rank	3
5	8	WHEN JOHNNY COMES MARCHING HOME	Adam Faith	Parlophone	5
3	9	AIN'T MISBEHAVIN'	Tommy Bruce	Columbia	8
6	10	WHAT A MOUTH	Tommy Steele	Decca	5
28	11	BECAUSE THEY'RE YOUNG	Duane Eddy	London	2
11	12	ITSY BITSY TEENY WEENY YELLOW POLKA DOT BIKINI	Brian Hyland	London	3
10	13	ANGELA JONES	Michael Cox	Triumph	8
35	14	APACHE	Shadows	Columbia	2
7	15	MAMA/ROBOT MAN	Connie Francis	MGM	11
13	16	I'M SORRY	Brenda Lee	Brunswick	3
8	17	THREE STEPS TO HEAVEN	Eddie Cochran	London	12
16	18	LOVE IS LIKE A VIOLIN	Ken Dodd	Decca	4
-	19	MESS OF BLUES	Elvis Presley	RCA	1
19	20	CATHY'S CLOWN	Everly Brothers	Warner Brothers	16
20	21	DOWN YONDER	Johnny & the Hurricanes	London	7
18	22	PISTOL PACKIN' MAMA	Gene Vincent	Capitol	6
17	23	HANDY MAN	Jimmy Jones	MGM	20
31	24	TIE ME KANGAROO DOWN SPORT	Rolf Harris	Columbia	2
23	25	PAPER ROSES	Kaye Sisters	Philips	3
26	[26]	LADY IS A TRAMP	Buddy Greco	Fontana	2
22	27	HE'LL HAVE TO GO	Jim Reeves	RCA	18
21	28	SWEET NOTHIN'S	Brenda Lee	Brunswick	17
33	29	ALLEY OOP	Hollywood Argyles	London	2
-	30	MAIS OUI	King Brothers	Parlophone	1
40	31	THEME FROM 'A SUMMER PLACE'	Percy Faith	Philips	19
24	32	RIVER STAY 'WAY FROM MY DOOR	Frank Sinatra	Capitol	7
27	33	WONDERFUL WORLD	Sam Cooke	HMV	4
-	34	PAPA LOVES MAMA	Joan Regan	Pye	1
25	35	THAT'S LOVE	Billy Fury	Decca	10
-	36	ONLY THE LONELY	Roy Orbison ●	London	1
29	37	HOW DO YOU KNOW IT'S LOVE	Teresa Brewer	Coral	5
32	38	GREEN JEANS	Flee-Rekkers	Triumph	11
36	39	BANJO BOY	Jan & Kjeld	Ember	2
-	[40]	HAPPY GO LUCKY ME/BANJO BOY	George Formby ●	Pye	1

WEEK ENDING 4 AUGUST 1960

LW	TW	Title	Artist	Label	Wks
3	[1]	SHAKING ALL OVER	Johnny Kidd & the Pirates	HMV	7
2	2	GOOD TIMIN'	Jimmy Jones	MGM	8
1	3	PLEASE DON'T TEASE	Cliff Richard	Columbia	6
11	4	BECAUSE THEY'RE YOUNG	Duane Eddy	London	3
9	5	AIN'T MISBEHAVIN'	Tommy Bruce	Columbia	9
5	6	WHEN WILL I BE LOVED	Everly Brothers	London	4
15	7	MAMA/ROBOT MAN	Connie Francis	MGM	12
19	8	MESS OF BLUES	Elvis Presley	RCA	2
12	9	ITSY BITSY TEENY WEENY YELLOW POLKA DOT BIKINI	Brian Hyland	London	4
8	10	WHEN JOHNNY COMES MARCHING HOME	Adam Faith	Parlophone	6
13	11	ANGELA JONES	Michael Cox	Triumph	9
7	12	LOOK FOR A STAR	Gary Mills	Top Rank	4
18	13	LOVE IS LIKE A VIOLIN	Ken Dodd	Decca	5
6	14	I WANNA GO HOME	Lonnie Donegan	Pye	11
14	15	APACHE	Shadows	Columbia	3
4	16	IF SHE SHOULD COME TO YOU	Anthony Newley	Decca	4
10	17	WHAT A MOUTH	Tommy Steele	Decca	6

August 1960

□ Highest position disc reached ● Act's first ever week on chart

LW	TW	Title	Artist	Label	Wks
16	18	I'M SORRY	Brenda Lee	Brunswick	4
17	19	THREE STEPS TO HEAVEN	Eddie Cochran	London	13
25	20	PAPER ROSES	Kaye Sisters	Philips	4
22	21	PISTOL PACKIN' MAMA	Gene Vincent	Capitol	7
20	22	CATHY'S CLOWN	Everly Brothers	Warner Brothers	17
21	23	DOWN YONDER	Johnny & the Hurricanes	London	8
24	24	TIE ME KANGAROO DOWN SPORT	Rolf Harris	Columbia	3
27	25	HE'LL HAVE TO GO	Jim Reeves	RCA	19
-	26	CRADLE OF LOVE	Johnny Preston	Mercury	14
28	27	SWEET NOTHIN'S	Brenda Lee	Brunswick	18
30	28	MAIS OUI	King Brothers	Parlophone	2
34	[29]	PAPA LOVES MAMA	Joan Regan	Pye	2
23	30	HANDY MAN	Jimmy Jones	MGM	21
31	31	THEME FROM 'A SUMMER PLACE'	Percy Faith	Philips	20
32	32	RIVER STAY 'WAY FROM MY DOOR	Frank Sinatra	Capitol	8
-	33	WALKING TO NEW ORLEANS	Fats Domino	London	1
37	34	HOW DO YOU KNOW IT'S LOVE	Teresa Brewer	Coral	6
38	35	GREEN JEANS	Flee-Rekkers	Triumph	12
33	36	WONDERFUL WORLD	Sam Cooke	HMV	5
35	37	THAT'S LOVE	Billy Fury	Decca	11
26	38	LADY IS A TRAMP	Buddy Greco	Fontana	3
-	[39]	WALKING THE FLOOR OVER YOU	Pat Boone	London	2
-	40	AS LONG AS HE NEEDS ME	Shirley Bassey	Columbia	1

WEEK ENDING 11 AUGUST 1960

LW	TW	Title	Artist	Label	Wks
3	[1]	PLEASE DON'T TEASE	Cliff Richard	Columbia	7
1	2	SHAKING ALL OVER	Johnny Kidd & the Pirates	HMV	8
15	3	APACHE	Shadows	Columbia	4
8	4	MESS OF BLUES	Elvis Presley	RCA	3
2	5	GOOD TIMIN'	Jimmy Jones	MGM	9
4	6	BECAUSE THEY'RE YOUNG	Duane Eddy	London	4
6	7	WHEN WILL I BE LOVED	Everly Brothers	London	5
9	[8]	ITSY BITSY TEENY WEENY YELLOW POLKA DOT BIKINI	Brian Hyland	London	5
12	9	LOOK FOR A STAR	Gary Mills	Top Rank	5
5	10	AIN'T MISBEHAVIN'	Tommy Bruce	Columbia	10
16	11	IF SHE SHOULD COME TO YOU	Anthony Newley	Decca	5
24	12	TIE ME KANGAROO DOWN SPORT	Rolf Harris	Columbia	4
18	13	I'M SORRY	Brenda Lee	Brunswick	5
7	14	MAMA/ROBOT MAN	Connie Francis	MGM	13
17	15	WHAT A MOUTH	Tommy Steele	Decca	7
10	16	WHEN JOHNNY COMES MARCHING HOME	Adam Faith	Parlophone	7
14	17	I WANNA GO HOME	Lonnie Donegan	Pye	12
11	18	ANGELA JONES	Michael Cox	Triumph	10
13	19	LOVE IS LIKE A VIOLIN	Ken Dodd	Decca	6
19	20	THREE STEPS TO HEAVEN	Eddie Cochran	London	14
20	21	PAPER ROSES	Kaye Sisters	Philips	5
28	22	MAIS OUI	King Brothers	Parlophone	3
40	23	AS LONG AS HE NEEDS ME	Shirley Bassey	Columbia	2
-	[24]	APACHE	Bert Weedon	Top Rank	1
21	25	PISTOL PACKIN' MAMA	Gene Vincent	Capitol	8
25	26	HE'LL HAVE TO GO	Jim Reeves	RCA	20
-	27	MUSTAPHA	Bob Azzam & his Orchestra	Decca	8
-	28	ALLEY OOP	Hollywood Argyles	London	3
-	[29]	BECAUSE THEY'RE YOUNG	James Darren ●	Pye	1
22	30	CATHY'S CLOWN	Everly Brothers	Warner Brothers	18
-	31	ONLY THE LONELY	Roy Orbison	London	2
31	32	THEME FROM 'A SUMMER PLACE'	Percy Faith	Philips	21
38	33	LADY IS A TRAMP	Buddy Greco	Fontana	4
-	34	PLEASE HELP ME I'M FALLING	Hank Locklin ●	RCA	1
-	35	OLD OAKEN BUCKET	Tommy Sands	Capitol	1
35	36	GREEN JEANS	Flee-Rekkers	Triumph	13
34	37	HOW DO YOU KNOW IT'S LOVE	Teresa Brewer	Coral	7
33	38	WALKING TO NEW ORLEANS	Fats Domino	London	2
32	39	RIVER STAY 'WAY FROM MY DOOR	Frank Sinatra	Capitol	9
-	40	MULE SKINNER BLUES	Rusty Draper ●	Mercury	1

■*Mess of Blues* became the first Elvis Presley single since *Wear My Ring* (over two years before) not to crash straight in to the Top Ten (28.07.60) ■ Anthony Newley's *If She Should Come To You* moves from 15 to four and back down to 16, the biggest variation ever recorded in consecutive weeks. The new Record Retailer chart is still having teething problems (04.08.60) ■ For the first time since January 1957, a record climbs back to number one. Cliff Richard's *Please Don't Tease Me* becomes the tenth record to achieve this feat (11.08.60)■

August 1960

☐ Highest position disc reached ● Act's first ever week on chart

WEEK ENDING 18 AUGUST 1960

LW	TW	Title	Artist	Label	Wks
1	[1]	PLEASE DON'T TEASE	Cliff Richard	*Columbia*	8
3	2	APACHE	Shadows	*Columbia*	5
2	3	SHAKING ALL OVER	Johnny Kidd & the Pirates	*HMV*	9
4	4	MESS OF BLUES	Elvis Presley	*RCA*	4
7	5	WHEN WILL I BE LOVED	Everly Brothers	*London*	6
11	6	IF SHE SHOULD COME TO YOU	Anthony Newley	*Decca*	6
6	7	BECAUSE THEY'RE YOUNG	Duane Eddy	*London*	5
8	[8]	ITSY BITSY TEENY WEENY YELLOW POLKA DOT BIKINI	Brian Hyland	*London*	6
12	[9]	TIE ME KANGAROO DOWN SPORT	Rolf Harris	*Columbia*	5
5	10	GOOD TIMIN'	Jimmy Jones	*MGM*	10
19	11	LOVE IS LIKE A VIOLIN	Ken Dodd	*Decca*	7
13	[12]	I'M SORRY	Brenda Lee	*Brunswick*	6
9	13	LOOK FOR A STAR	Gary Mills	*Top Rank*	6
14	14	MAMA/ROBOT MAN	Connie Francis	*MGM*	14
15	15	WHAT A MOUTH	Tommy Steele	*Decca*	8
21	16	PAPER ROSES	Kaye Sisters	*Philips*	6
16	17	WHEN JOHNNY COMES MARCHING HOME	Adam Faith	*Parlophone*	8
22	18	MAIS OUI	King Brothers	*Parlophone*	4
18	19	ANGELA JONES	Michael Cox	*Triumph*	11
23	20	AS LONG AS HE NEEDS ME	Shirley Bassey	*Columbia*	3
10	21	AIN'T MISBEHAVIN'	Tommy Bruce	*Columbia*	11
17	22	I WANNA GO HOME	Lonnie Donegan	*Pye*	13
31	23	ONLY THE LONELY	Roy Orbison	*London*	3
38	24	WALKING TO NEW ORLEANS	Fats Domino	*London*	3
35	[25]	OLD OAKEN BUCKET	Tommy Sands	*Capitol*	2
37	26	HOW DO YOU KNOW IT'S LOVE	Teresa Brewer	*Coral*	8
-	27	FEEL SO FINE	Johnny Preston	*Mercury*	1
33	28	LADY IS A TRAMP	Buddy Greco	*Fontana*	5
24	29	APACHE	Bert Weedon	*Top Rank*	2
26	30	HE'LL HAVE TO GO	Jim Reeves	*RCA*	21
32	31	THEME FROM 'A SUMMER PLACE'	Percy Faith	*Philips*	22
-	32	EVERYBODY'S SOMEBODY'S FOOL	Connie Francis	*MGM*	1
20	33	THREE STEPS TO HEAVEN	Eddie Cochran	*London*	15
-	[34]	BLUEBERRY HILL	John Barry Orchestra	*Columbia*	1
29	35	BECAUSE THEY'RE YOUNG	James Darren	*Pye*	2
34	36	PLEASE HELP ME I'M FALLING	Hank Locklin	*RCA*	2
-	37	DOWN YONDER	Johnny & the Hurricanes	*London*	9
-	38	HANDY MAN	Jimmy Jones	*MGM*	22
-	39	TRAIN OF LOVE	Alma Cogan	*HMV*	1
27	40	MUSTAPHA	Bob Azzam & his Orchestra	*Decca*	9

WEEK ENDING 25 AUGUST 1960

LW	TW	Title	Artist	Label	Wks
2	[1]	APACHE	Shadows	*Columbia*	6
1	2	PLEASE DON'T TEASE	Cliff Richard	*Columbia*	9
4	3	MESS OF BLUES	Elvis Presley	*RCA*	5
5	[4]	WHEN WILL I BE LOVED	Everly Brothers	*London*	7
3	5	SHAKING ALL OVER	Johnny Kidd & the Pirates	*HMV*	10
7	6	BECAUSE THEY'RE YOUNG	Duane Eddy	*London*	6
6	7	IF SHE SHOULD COME TO YOU	Anthony Newley	*Decca*	7
11	[8]	LOVE IS LIKE A VIOLIN	Ken Dodd	*Decca*	8
10	9	GOOD TIMIN'	Jimmy Jones	*MGM*	11
9	10	TIE ME KANGAROO DOWN SPORT	Rolf Harris	*Columbia*	6
13	11	LOOK FOR A STAR	Gary Mills	*Top Rank*	7
20	12	AS LONG AS HE NEEDS ME	Shirley Bassey	*Columbia*	4
32	13	EVERYBODY'S SOMEBODY'S FOOL	Connie Francis	*MGM*	2
8	14	ITSY BITSY TEENY WEENY YELLOW POLKA DOT BIKINI	Brian Hyland	*London*	7
12	15	I'M SORRY	Brenda Lee	*Brunswick*	7
18	[16]	MAIS OUI	King Brothers	*Parlophone*	5
16	17	PAPER ROSES	Kaye Sisters	*Philips*	7
14	18	MAMA/ROBOT MAN	Connie Francis	*MGM*	15
21	19	AIN'T MISBEHAVIN'	Tommy Bruce	*Columbia*	12
27	20	FEEL SO FINE	Johnny Preston	*Mercury*	2
17	21	WHEN JOHNNY COMES MARCHING HOME	Adam Faith	*Parlophone*	9
23	22	ONLY THE LONELY	Roy Orbison	*London*	4
24	23	WALKING TO NEW ORLEANS	Fats Domino	*London*	4
22	24	I WANNA GO HOME	Lonnie Donegan	*Pye*	14
15	25	WHAT A MOUTH	Tommy Steele	*Decca*	9
-	26	TELL LAURA I LOVE HER	Ricky Valance ●	*Columbia*	1
39	[27]	TRAIN OF LOVE	Alma Cogan	*HMV*	2
31	28	THEME FROM 'A SUMMER PLACE'	Percy Faith	*Philips*	23
25	29	OLD OAKEN BUCKET	Tommy Sands	*Capitol*	3
30	30	HE'LL HAVE TO GO	Jim Reeves	*RCA*	22
-	31	IMAGE OF A GIRL	Mark Wynter ●	*Decca*	1
38	32	HANDY MAN	Jimmy Jones	*MGM*	23
37	33	DOWN YONDER	Johnny & the Hurricanes	*London*	10
-	34	ALLEY OOP	Hollywood Argyles	*London*	4
-	35	PAPA LOVES MAMA	Joan Regan	*Pye*	3
26	36	HOW DO YOU KNOW IT'S LOVE	Teresa Brewer	*Coral*	9
-	[37]	IMAGE OF A GIRL	Nelson Keene ●	*HMV*	1
19	38	ANGELA JONES	Michael Cox	*Triumph*	12
35	39	BECAUSE THEY'RE YOUNG	James Darren	*Pye*	3
-	40	LORELEI	Lonnie Donegan	*Pye*	1

WEEK ENDING 1 SEPTEMBER 1960

LW	TW	Title	Artist	Label	Wks
1	[1]	APACHE	Shadows	*Columbia*	7
2	2	PLEASE DON'T TEASE	Cliff Richard	*Columbia*	10
3	3	MESS OF BLUES	Elvis Presley	*RCA*	6
6	4	BECAUSE THEY'RE YOUNG	Duane Eddy	*London*	7
4	5	WHEN WILL I BE LOVED	Everly Brothers	*London*	8
7	6	IF SHE SHOULD COME TO YOU	Anthony Newley	*Decca*	8
5	7	SHAKING ALL OVER	Johnny Kidd & the Pirates	*HMV*	11
8	[8]	LOVE IS LIKE A VIOLIN	Ken Dodd	*Decca*	9
12	9	AS LONG AS HE NEEDS ME	Shirley Bassey	*Columbia*	5
10	10	TIE ME KANGAROO DOWN SPORT	Rolf Harris	*Columbia*	7
13	11	EVERYBODY'S SOMEBODY'S FOOL	Connie Francis	*MGM*	3
15	[12]	I'M SORRY	Brenda Lee	*Brunswick*	8
17	13	PAPER ROSES	Kaye Sisters	*Philips*	8
26	14	TELL LAURA I LOVE HER	Ricky Valance	*Columbia*	2
22	15	ONLY THE LONELY	Roy Orbison	*London*	5
9	16	GOOD TIMIN'	Jimmy Jones	*MGM*	12
40	17	LORELEI	Lonnie Donegan	*Pye*	2
20	[18]	FEEL SO FINE	Johnny Preston	*Mercury*	3
23	[19]	WALKING TO NEW ORLEANS	Fats Domino	*London*	5
14	20	ITSY BITSY TEENY WEENY YELLOW POLKA DOT BIKINI	Brian Hyland	*London*	8
19	21	AIN'T MISBEHAVIN'	Tommy Bruce	*Columbia*	13
11	22	LOOK FOR A STAR	Gary Mills	*Top Rank*	8
31	23	IMAGE OF A GIRL	Mark Wynter	*Decca*	2
16	24	MAIS OUI	King Brothers	*Parlophone*	6
18	25	MAMA/ROBOT MAN	Connie Francis	*MGM*	16
21	26	WHEN JOHNNY COMES MARCHING HOME	Adam Faith	*Parlophone*	10
24	27	I WANNA GO HOME	Lonnie Donegan	*Pye*	15
-	28	PLEASE HELP ME I'M FALLING	Hank Locklin	*RCA*	3
34	29	ALLEY OOP	Hollywood Argyles	*London*	5
-	30	WHITE CLIFFS OF DOVER	Mr. Acker Bilk	*Columbia*	1
29	31	OLD OAKEN BUCKET	Tommy Sands	*Capitol*	4
-	[32]	LET'S HAVE A PARTY	Wanda Jackson ●	*Capitol*	1
25	33	WHAT A MOUTH	Tommy Steele	*Decca*	10
-	34	I'D DO ANYTHING	Mike Preston	*Decca*	1
39	35	BECAUSE THEY'RE YOUNG	James Darren	*Pye*	4
30	36	HE'LL HAVE TO GO	Jim Reeves	*RCA*	23
28	37	THEME FROM 'A SUMMER PLACE'	Percy Faith	*Philips*	24
38	38	ANGELA JONES	Michael Cox	*Triumph*	13
-	39	MULE SKINNER BLUES	Rusty Draper	*Mercury*	2
37	40	IMAGE OF A GIRL	Nelson Keene	*HMV*	2

WEEK ENDING 8 SEPTEMBER 1960

LW	TW	Title	Artist	Label	Wks
1	[1]	APACHE	Shadows	*Columbia*	8
4	[2]	BECAUSE THEY'RE YOUNG	Duane Eddy	*London*	8
3	3	MESS OF BLUES	Elvis Presley	*RCA*	7
2	4	PLEASE DON'T TEASE	Cliff Richard	*Columbia*	11
5	5	WHEN WILL I BE LOVED	Everly Brothers	*London*	9
7	6	SHAKING ALL OVER	Johnny Kidd & the Pirates	*HMV*	12

In these weeks ■ The Shadows take over from their boss, Cliff Richard, at number one. As they were also playing on Cliff's record, they become the first act ever to supplant themselves at the top of the charts (25.08.60) ■ The top two singles are instrumentals (08.09.60) ■ The surge of new chart talent continues. There are now eighteen chart acts enjoying their first hits (02.09.60)■

LW	TW	Title	Artist	Label	Wks
13	7	PAPER ROSES	Kaye Sisters	Philips	9
11	8	EVERYBODY'S SOMEBODY'S FOOL	Connie Francis	MGM	4
9	9	AS LONG AS HE NEEDS ME	Shirley Bassey	Columbia	6
17	10	LORELEI	Lonnie Donegan	Pye	3
8	11	LOVE IS LIKE A VIOLIN	Ken Dodd	Decca	10
6	12	IF SHE SHOULD COME TO YOU	Anthony Newley	Decca	9
12	13	I'M SORRY	Brenda Lee	Brunswick	9
15	14	ONLY THE LONELY	Roy Orbison	London	6
14	15	TELL LAURA I LOVE HER	Ricky Valance	Columbia	3
10	16	TIE ME KANGAROO DOWN SPORT	Rolf Harris	Columbia	8
23	17	IMAGE OF A GIRL	Mark Wynter	Decca	3
20	18	ITSY BITSY TEENY WEENY YELLOW POLKA DOT BIKINI	Brian Hyland	London	9
18	19	FEEL SO FINE	Johnny Preston	Mercury	4
22	20	LOOK FOR A STAR	Gary Mills	Top Rank	10
16	21	GOOD TIMIN'	Jimmy Jones	MGM	13
19	22	WALKING TO NEW ORLEANS	Fats Domino	London	6
28	23	PLEASE HELP ME I'M FALLING	Hank Locklin	RCA	4
29	24	ALLEY OOP	Hollywood Argyles	London	6
25	25	MAMA/ROBOT MAN	Connie Francis	MGM	17
24	26	MAIS OUI	King Brothers	Parlophone	7
34	27	I'D DO ANYTHING	Mike Preston	Decca	2
37	28	THEME FROM 'A SUMMER PLACE'	Percy Faith	Philips	25
27	29	I WANNA GO HOME	Lonnie Donegan	Pye	16
-	30	THEM THERE EYES	Emile Ford & the Checkmates	Pye	1
30	31	WHITE CLIFFS OF DOVER	Mr. Acker Bilk	Columbia	2
21	32	AIN'T MISBEHAVIN'	Tommy Bruce	Columbia	14
26	33	WHEN JOHNNY COMES MARCHING HOME	Adam Faith	Parlophone	11
32	34	LET'S HAVE A PARTY	Wanda Jackson	Capitol	2
-	35	NICE 'N' EASY	Frank Sinatra	Capitol	1
36	36	HE'LL HAVE TO GO	Jim Reeves	RCA	24
-	37	MULE SKINNER BLUES	Fendermen ●	Top Rank	1
-	38	BROKEN DOLL	Tommy Bruce	Columbia	1
-	39	I JUST GO FOR YOU	Jimmy Jones	MGM	1
-	40	LET'S THINK ABOUT LIVING	Bob Luman ●	Warner Brothers	1

WEEK ENDING 15 SEPTEMBER 1960

LW	TW	Title	Artist	Label	Wks
1	1	APACHE	Shadows	Columbia	9
3	2	MESS OF BLUES	Elvis Presley	RCA	8
2	3	BECAUSE THEY'RE YOUNG	Duane Eddy	London	9
4	4	PLEASE DON'T TEASE	Cliff Richard	Columbia	12
8	5	EVERYBODY'S SOMEBODY'S FOOL	Connie Francis	MGM	5
5	6	WHEN WILL I BE LOVED	Everly Brothers	London	10
15	7	TELL LAURA I LOVE HER	Ricky Valance	Columbia	4
11	8	LOVE IS LIKE A VIOLIN	Ken Dodd	Decca	11
7	9	PAPER ROSES	Kaye Sisters	Philips	10
9	10	AS LONG AS HE NEEDS ME	Shirley Bassey	Columbia	7
12	11	IF SHE SHOULD COME TO YOU	Anthony Newley	Decca	10
13	12	I'M SORRY	Brenda Lee	Brunswick	10
14	13	ONLY THE LONELY	Roy Orbison	London	7
6	14	SHAKING ALL OVER	Johnny Kidd & the Pirates	HMV	13
10	15	LORELEI	Lonnie Donegan	Pye	4
23	16	PLEASE HELP ME I'M FALLING	Hank Locklin	RCA	5
16	17	TIE ME KANGAROO DOWN SPORT	Rolf Harris	Columbia	9
17	18	IMAGE OF A GIRL	Mark Wynter	Decca	4
19	19	FEEL SO FINE	Johnny Preston	Mercury	5
18	20	ITSY BITSY TEENY WEENY YELLOW POLKA DOT BIKINI	Brian Hyland	London	10
20	21	LOOK FOR A STAR	Gary Mills	Top Rank	11
21	22	GOOD TIMIN'	Jimmy Jones	MGM	14
26	23	MAIS OUI	King Brothers	Parlophone	8
-	24	VOLARE	Bobby Rydell	Columbia	1
25	25	MAMA/ROBOT MAN	Connie Francis	MGM	18
-	26	WALK DON'T RUN	Ventures ●	Top Rank	1
24	27	ALLEY OOP	Hollywood Argyles	London	7
35	28	NICE 'N' EASY	Frank Sinatra	Capitol	2
27	29	I'D DO ANYTHING	Mike Preston	Decca	3
36	30	HE'LL HAVE TO GO	Jim Reeves	RCA	25
40	31	LET'S THINK ABOUT LIVING	Bob Luman	Warner Brothers	2
28	32	THEME FROM 'A SUMMER PLACE'	Percy Faith	Philips	26
29	33	I WANNA GO HOME	Lonnie Donegan	Pye	17
30	34	THEM THERE EYES	Emile Ford & the Checkmates	Pye	2

September 1960

□ Highest position disc reached ● Act's first ever week on chart

LW	TW	Title	Artist	Label	Wks
31	35	WHITE CLIFFS OF DOVER	Mr. Acker Bilk	Columbia	3
38	36	BROKEN DOLL	Tommy Bruce	Columbia	2
34	37	LET'S HAVE A PARTY	Wanda Jackson	Capitol	3
33	38	WHEN JOHNNY COMES MARCHING HOME	Adam Faith	Parlophone	12
-	39	HOW ABOUT THAT	Adam Faith	Parlophone	1
-	40	IMAGE OF A GIRL	Nelson Keene	HMV	3

WEEK ENDING 22 SEPTEMBER 1960

LW	TW	Title	Artist	Label	Wks
1	1	APACHE	Shadows	Columbia	10
2	2	MESS OF BLUES	Elvis Presley	RCA	9
3	3	BECAUSE THEY'RE YOUNG	Duane Eddy	London	10
7	4	TELL LAURA I LOVE HER	Ricky Valance	Columbia	5
13	5	ONLY THE LONELY	Roy Orbison	London	8
6	6	WHEN WILL I BE LOVED	Everly Brothers	London	11
4	7	PLEASE DON'T TEASE	Cliff Richard	Columbia	13
5	8	EVERYBODY'S SOMEBODY'S FOOL	Connie Francis	MGM	6
10	9	AS LONG AS HE NEEDS ME	Shirley Bassey	Columbia	8
9	10	PAPER ROSES	Kaye Sisters	Philips	11
18	11	IMAGE OF A GIRL	Mark Wynter	Decca	5
14	12	SHAKING ALL OVER	Johnny Kidd & the Pirates	HMV	14
16	13	PLEASE HELP ME I'M FALLING	Hank Locklin	RCA	6
15	14	LORELEI	Lonnie Donegan	Pye	5
8	15	LOVE IS LIKE A VIOLIN	Ken Dodd	Decca	12
12	16	I'M SORRY	Brenda Lee	Brunswick	11
26	17	WALK DON'T RUN	Ventures	Top Rank	2
39	18	HOW ABOUT THAT	Adam Faith	Parlophone	2
17	19	TIE ME KANGAROO DOWN SPORT	Rolf Harris	Columbia	10
11	20	IF SHE SHOULD COME TO YOU	Anthony Newley	Decca	11
19	21	FEEL SO FINE	Johnny Preston	Mercury	6
24	22	VOLARE	Bobby Rydell	Columbia	2
29	23	I'D DO ANYTHING	Mike Preston	Decca	4
-	24	WALK DON'T RUN	John Barry Seven	Columbia	1
28	25	NICE 'N' EASY	Frank Sinatra	Capitol	3
-	26	NINE TIMES OUT OF TEN	Cliff Richard	Columbia	1
20	27	ITSY BITSY TEENY WEENY YELLOW POLKA DOT BIKINI	Brian Hyland	London	11
-	28	LUCILLE/SO SAD	Everly Brothers	Warner Brothers	1
31	29	LET'S THINK ABOUT LIVING	Bob Luman	Warner Brothers	3
30	30	HE'LL HAVE TO GO	Jim Reeves	RCA	26
32	31	THEME FROM 'A SUMMER PLACE'	Percy Faith	Philips	27
27	32	ALLEY OOP	Hollywood Argyles	London	8
21	33	LOOK FOR A STAR	Gary Mills	Top Rank	12
22	34	GOOD TIMIN'	Jimmy Jones	MGM	15
-	35	I JUST GO FOR YOU	Jimmy Jones	MGM	2
35	36	WHITE CLIFFS OF DOVER	Mr. Acker Bilk	Columbia	4
23	37	MAIS OUI	King Brothers	Parlophone	9
25	38	MAMA/ROBOT MAN	Connie Francis	MGM	19
-	39	WALKING TO NEW ORLEANS	Fats Domino	London	7
-	40	MACDONALD'S CAVE	Piltdown Men ●	Capitol	1

WEEK ENDING 29 SEPTEMBER 1960

LW	TW	Title	Artist	Label	Wks
4	1	TELL LAURA I LOVE HER	Ricky Valance	Columbia	6
1	2	APACHE	Shadows	Columbia	11
2	3	MESS OF BLUES	Elvis Presley	RCA	10
5	4	ONLY THE LONELY	Roy Orbison	London	9
3	5	BECAUSE THEY'RE YOUNG	Duane Eddy	London	11
26	6	NINE TIMES OUT OF TEN	Cliff Richard	Columbia	2
8	7	EVERYBODY'S SOMEBODY'S FOOL	Connie Francis	MGM	7
7	8	PLEASE DON'T TEASE	Cliff Richard	Columbia	14
9	9	AS LONG AS HE NEEDS ME	Shirley Bassey	Columbia	9
18	10	HOW ABOUT THAT	Adam Faith	Parlophone	3
17	11	WALK DON'T RUN	Ventures	Top Rank	3
13	12	PLEASE HELP ME I'M FALLING	Hank Locklin	RCA	7
6	13	WHEN WILL I BE LOVED	Everly Brothers	London	12
10	14	PAPER ROSES	Kaye Sisters	Philips	12

■Ricky Valance becomes the first British one-hit wonder, the fifth of all time. His number one gives producer Norrie Paramor three consecutive chart-toppers, stretching from 11 August to 20 October 1960 (29.09.60) ■ Three singles featuring the Shadows, two with Cliff Richard on vocals, are in the Top Ten (29.09.60) ■ Only *Tell Laura I Love Her*, at number one, was at its peak position this week (29.09.60)■

September 1960

□ Highest position disc reached ● Act's first ever week on chart

LW	TW	Title	Artist	Label	Wks
28	15	LUCILLE/SO SAD	Everly Brothers	Warner Brothers	2
15	16	LOVE IS LIKE A VIOLIN	Ken Dodd	Decca	13
12	17	SHAKING ALL OVER	Johnny Kidd & the Pirates	HMV	15
24	18	WALK DON'T RUN	John Barry Seven	Columbia	2
11	19	IMAGE OF A GIRL	Mark Wynter	Decca	6
20	20	IF SHE SHOULD COME TO YOU	Anthony Newley	Decca	12
29	21	LET'S THINK ABOUT LIVING	Bob Luman	Warner Brothers	4
16	22	I'M SORRY	Brenda Lee	Brunswick	12
19	23	TIE ME KANGAROO DOWN SPORT	Rolf Harris	Columbia	11
14	24	LORELEI	Lonnie Donegan	Pye	6
25	25	NICE 'N' EASY	Frank Sinatra	Capitol	4
21	26	FEEL SO FINE	Johnny Preston	Mercury	7
-	27	PASSING BREEZE	Russ Conway	Columbia	1
-	28	WONDROUS PLACE	Billy Fury	Decca	1
22	29	VOLARE	Bobby Rydell	Columbia	3
-	30	THEM THERE EYES	Emile Ford & the Checkmates	Pye	3
23	31	I'D DO ANYTHING	Mike Preston	Decca	5
-	32	CHAIN GANG	Sam Cooke	RCA	1
-	33	KOOKIE LITTLE PARADISE	Frankie Vaughan	Philips	1
33	34	LOOK FOR A STAR	Gary Mills	Top Rank	13
31	35	THEME FROM 'A SUMMER PLACE'	Percy Faith	Philips	28
30	36	HE'LL HAVE TO GO	Jim Reeves	RCA	27
36	37	WHITE CLIFFS OF DOVER	Mr. Acker Bilk	Columbia	5
40	38	MACDONALD'S CAVE	Piltdown Men	Capitol	2
-	39	LET'S HAVE A PARTY	Wanda Jackson	Capitol	4
-	40	MULE SKINNER BLUES	Fendermen	Top Rank	2

WEEK ENDING 6 OCTOBER 1960

LW	TW	Title	Artist	Label	Wks
1	1	TELL LAURA I LOVE HER	Ricky Valance	Columbia	7
4	2	ONLY THE LONELY	Roy Orbison	London	10
6	3	NINE TIMES OUT OF TEN	Cliff Richard	Columbia	3
3	4	MESS OF BLUES	Elvis Presley	RCA	11
2	5	APACHE	Shadows	Columbia	12
15	6	LUCILLE/SO SAD	Everly Brothers	Warner Brothers	3
10	7	HOW ABOUT THAT	Adam Faith	Parlophone	4
11	8	WALK DON'T RUN	Ventures	Top Rank	4
5	9	BECAUSE THEY'RE YOUNG	Duane Eddy	London	12
32	10	CHAIN GANG	Sam Cooke	RCA	2
9	11	AS LONG AS HE NEEDS ME	Shirley Bassey	Columbia	10
21	12	LET'S THINK ABOUT LIVING	Bob Luman	Warner Brothers	5
12	13	PLEASE HELP ME I'M FALLING	Hank Locklin	RCA	8
7	14	EVERYBODY'S SOMEBODY'S FOOL	Connie Francis	MGM	8
18	15	WALK DON'T RUN	John Barry Seven	Columbia	3
14	16	PAPER ROSES	Kaye Sisters	Philips	13
13	17	WHEN WILL I BE LOVED	Everly Brothers	London	13
8	18	PLEASE DON'T TEASE	Cliff Richard	Columbia	15
19	19	IMAGE OF A GIRL	Mark Wynter	Decca	7
27	20	PASSING BREEZE	Russ Conway	Columbia	2
17	21	SHAKING ALL OVER	Johnny Kidd & the Pirates	HMV	16
16	22	LOVE IS LIKE A VIOLIN	Ken Dodd	Decca	14
25	23	NICE 'N' EASY	Frank Sinatra	Capitol	5
20	24	IF SHE SHOULD COME TO YOU	Anthony Newley	Decca	13
-	25	ROCKING GOOSE	Johnny & the Hurricanes	London	1
29	26	VOLARE	Bobby Rydell	Columbia	4
22	27	I'M SORRY	Brenda Lee	Brunswick	13
31	28	I'D DO ANYTHING	Mike Preston	Decca	6
23	29	TIE ME KANGAROO DOWN SPORT	Rolf Harris	Columbia	12
-	30	DREAMIN'	Johnny Burnette ●	London	1
33	31	KOOKIE LITTLE PARADISE	Frankie Vaughan	Philips	2
24	32	LORELEI	Lonnie Donegan	Pye	7
26	33	FEEL SO FINE	Johnny Preston	Mercury	8
39	34	LET'S HAVE A PARTY	Wanda Jackson	Capitol	5
28	35	WONDROUS PLACE	Billy Fury	Decca	2
30	36	THEM THERE EYES	Emile Ford & the Checkmates	Pye	4
37	37	WHITE CLIFFS OF DOVER	Mr. Acker Bilk	Columbia	6
-	38	MY LOVE FOR YOU	Johnny Mathis	Fontana	1
38	39	MACDONALD'S CAVE	Piltdown Men	Capitol	3
40	40	MULE SKINNER BLUES	Fendermen	Top Rank	3

WEEK ENDING 13 OCTOBER 1960

LW	TW	Title	Artist	Label	Wks
1	1	TELL LAURA I LOVE HER	Ricky Valance	Columbia	8
2	2	ONLY THE LONELY	Roy Orbison	London	11
3	3	NINE TIMES OUT OF TEN	Cliff Richard	Columbia	4
7	4	HOW ABOUT THAT	Adam Faith	Parlophone	5
11	5	AS LONG AS HE NEEDS ME	Shirley Bassey	Columbia	11
4	6	MESS OF BLUES	Elvis Presley	RCA	12
6	7	LUCILLE/SO SAD	Everly Brothers	Warner Brothers	4
5	8	APACHE	Shadows	Columbia	13
13	9	PLEASE HELP ME I'M FALLING	Hank Locklin	RCA	9
9	10	BECAUSE THEY'RE YOUNG	Duane Eddy	London	13
8	11	WALK DON'T RUN	Ventures	Top Rank	5
14	12	EVERYBODY'S SOMEBODY'S FOOL	Connie Francis	MGM	9
10	13	CHAIN GANG	Sam Cooke	RCA	3
12	14	LET'S THINK ABOUT LIVING	Bob Luman	Warner Brothers	6
15	15	WALK DON'T RUN	John Barry Seven	Columbia	4
20	16	PASSING BREEZE	Russ Conway	Columbia	3
23	17	NICE 'N' EASY	Frank Sinatra	Capitol	6
16	18	PAPER ROSES	Kaye Sisters	Philips	14
18	19	PLEASE DON'T TEASE	Cliff Richard	Columbia	16
25	20	ROCKING GOOSE	Johnny & the Hurricanes	London	2
17	21	WHEN WILL I BE LOVED	Everly Brothers	London	14
36	22	THEM THERE EYES	Emile Ford & the Checkmates	Pye	5
19	23	IMAGE OF A GIRL	Mark Wynter	Decca	8
22	24	LOVE IS LIKE A VIOLIN	Ken Dodd	Decca	15
35	25	WONDROUS PLACE	Billy Fury	Decca	3
39	26	MACDONALD'S CAVE	Piltdown Men	Capitol	4
24	27	IF SHE SHOULD COME TO YOU	Anthony Newley	Decca	14
30	28	DREAMIN'	Johnny Burnette	London	2
38	29	MY LOVE FOR YOU	Johnny Mathis	Fontana	2
-	30	NEVER ON SUNDAY	Manuel & his Music of the Mountains	Columbia	1
32	31	LORELEI	Lonnie Donegan	Pye	8
26	32	VOLARE	Bobby Rydell	Columbia	5
-	33	ALL MY LOVE	Jackie Wilson	Coral	1
-	34	RESTLESS	Johnny Kidd & the Pirates	HMV	1
21	35	SHAKING ALL OVER	Johnny Kidd & the Pirates	HMV	17
27	36	I'M SORRY	Brenda Lee	Brunswick	14
33	37	FEEL SO FINE	Johnny Preston	Mercury	9
34	38	LET'S HAVE A PARTY	Wanda Jackson	Capitol	6
-	39	HE'LL HAVE TO GO	Jim Reeves	RCA	28
-	40	SWEETIE PIE	Eddie Cochran	London	1

WEEK ENDING 20 OCTOBER 1960

LW	TW	Title	Artist	Label	Wks
2	1	ONLY THE LONELY	Roy Orbison	London	12
1	2	TELL LAURA I LOVE HER	Ricky Valance	Columbia	9
5	3	AS LONG AS HE NEEDS ME	Shirley Bassey	Columbia	12
7	4	LUCILLE/SO SAD	Everly Brothers	Warner Brothers	5
3	5	NINE TIMES OUT OF TEN	Cliff Richard	Columbia	5
4	6	HOW ABOUT THAT	Adam Faith	Parlophone	6
14	7	LET'S THINK ABOUT LIVING	Bob Luman	Warner Brothers	7
6	8	MESS OF BLUES	Elvis Presley	RCA	13
8	9	APACHE	Shadows	Columbia	14
10	10	BECAUSE THEY'RE YOUNG	Duane Eddy	London	14
15	11	WALK DON'T RUN	John Barry Seven	Columbia	5
11	12	WALK DON'T RUN	Ventures	Top Rank	6
13	13	CHAIN GANG	Sam Cooke	RCA	4
9	14	PLEASE HELP ME I'M FALLING	Hank Locklin	RCA	10
17	15	NICE 'N' EASY	Frank Sinatra	Capitol	7
28	16	DREAMIN'	Johnny Burnette	London	3
12	17	EVERYBODY'S SOMEBODY'S FOOL	Connie Francis	MGM	10
20	18	ROCKING GOOSE	Johnny & the Hurricanes	London	3
26	19	MACDONALD'S CAVE	Piltdown Men	Capitol	5
29	20	MY LOVE FOR YOU	Johnny Mathis	Fontana	3
18	21	PAPER ROSES	Kaye Sisters	Philips	15
34	22	RESTLESS	Johnny Kidd & the Pirates	HMV	2
16	23	PASSING BREEZE	Russ Conway	Columbia	4
22	24	THEM THERE EYES	Emile Ford & the Checkmates	Pye	6
19	25	PLEASE DON'T TEASE	Cliff Richard	Columbia	17
-	26	SHORTNIN' BREAD	Viscounts ●	Pye	1
21	27	WHEN WILL I BE LOVED	Everly Brothers	London	15
25	28	WONDROUS PLACE	Billy Fury	Decca	4

In these weeks ■ All three new entries were by a Johnny – Burnette, Mathis and & the Hurricanes (06.10.60) ■ Roy Orbison's *Only The Lonely* reached number one in its twelfth week of chart life – the slowest climb to the top yet recorded (20.10.60) ■ Four instrumentals occupied consecutive chart positions, at nine, ten, 11 and 12 (20.10.60)■

LW	TW	Title	Artist	Label	Wks
30	[29]	NEVER ON SUNDAY	Manuel & his Music of the Mounains	Columbia	2
23	30	IMAGE OF A GIRL	Mark Wynter	Decca	9
24	31	LOVE IS LIKE A VIOLIN	Ken Dodd	Decca	16
-	[32]	MULE SKINNER BLUES	Fendermen	Top Rank	4
-	33	NEVER ON SUNDAY	Don Costa ●	London	1
-	34	FOUR LITTLE HEELS	Brian Hyland	London	1
39	35	HE'LL HAVE TO GO	Jim Reeves	RCA	29
38	36	LET'S HAVE A PARTY	Wanda Jackson	Capitol	7
35	37	SHAKING ALL OVER	Johnny Kidd & the Pirates	HMV	18
40	[38]	SWEETIE PIE	Eddie Cochran	London	2
-	39	TOP TEEN BABY	Gary Mills	Top Rank	1
-	40	NEVER ON SUNDAY	Makadopoulos & his Greek Serenaders ●	Palette	1

WEEK ENDING 27 OCTOBER 1960

LW	TW	Title	Artist	Label	Wks
1	[1]	ONLY THE LONELY	Roy Orbison	London	13
3	[2]	AS LONG AS HE NEEDS ME	Shirley Bassey	Columbia	13
2	3	TELL LAURA I LOVE HER	Ricky Valance	Columbia	10
6	[4]	HOW ABOUT THAT	Adam Faith	Parlophone	7
4	5	LUCILLE/SO SAD	Everly Brothers	Warner Brothers	6
7	[6]	LET'S THINK ABOUT LIVING	Bob Luman	Warner Brothers	8
5	7	NINE TIMES OUT OF TEN	Cliff Richard	Columbia	6
8	8	MESS OF BLUES	Elvis Presley	RCA	14
13	[9]	CHAIN GANG	Sam Cooke	RCA	5
14	10	PLEASE HELP ME I'M FALLING	Hank Locklin	RCA	11
18	11	ROCKING GOOSE	Johnny & the Hurricanes	London	4
16	12	DREAMIN'	Johnny Burnette	London	4
11	13	WALK DON'T RUN	John Barry Seven	Columbia	6
12	14	WALK DON'T RUN	Ventures	Top Rank	7
17	15	EVERYBODY'S SOMEBODY'S FOOL	Connie Francis	MGM	11
9	16	APACHE	Shadows	Columbia	15
20	17	MY LOVE FOR YOU	Johnny Mathis	Fontana	4
15	18	NICE 'N' EASY	Frank Sinatra	Capitol	8
24	19	THEM THERE EYES	Emile Ford & the Checkmates	Pye	7
10	20	BECAUSE THEY'RE YOUNG	Duane Eddy	London	15
26	21	SHORTNIN' BREAD	Viscounts	Pye	2
22	[22]	RESTLESS	Johnny Kidd & the Pirates	HMV	3
23	23	PASSING BREEZE	Russ Conway	Columbia	5
21	24	PAPER ROSES	Kaye Sisters	Philips	16
19	25	MACDONALD'S CAVE	Piltdown Men	Capitol	6
28	26	WONDROUS PLACE	Billy Fury	Decca	5
39	27	TOP TEEN BABY	Gary Mills	Top Rank	2
33	28	NEVER ON SUNDAY	Don Costa	London	2
25	29	PLEASE DON'T TEASE	Cliff Richard	Columbia	18
-	[30]	NEVER ON SUNDAY	Lynn Cornell ●	Decca	1
-	[31]	I WANT TO BE WANTED	Brenda Lee	Brunswick	1
27	32	WHEN WILL I BE LOVED	Everly Brothers	London	16
29	33	NEVER ON SUNDAY	Manuel & his Music of the Mountains	Columbia	3
31	34	LOVE IS LIKE A VIOLIN	Ken Dodd	Decca	17
35	35	HE'LL HAVE TO GO	Jim Reeves	RCA	30
32	36	MULE SKINNER BLUES	Fendermen	Top Rank	5
30	37	IMAGE OF A GIRL	Mark Wynter	Decca	10
-	38	MILORD	Frankie Vaughan	Philips	1
34	39	FOUR LITTLE HEELS	Brian Hyland	London	2
-	40	LEARNING THE GAME	Buddy Holly	Coral	1

WEEK ENDING 3 NOVEMBER 1960

LW	TW	Title	Artist	Label	Wks
-	[1]	IT'S NOW OR NEVER	Elvis Presley	RCA	1
2	[2]	AS LONG AS HE NEEDS ME	Shirley Bassey	Columbia	14
1	3	ONLY THE LONELY	Roy Orbison	London	14
11	4	ROCKING GOOSE	Johnny & the Hurricanes	London	5
5	5	LUCILLE/SO SAD	Everly Brothers	Warner Brothers	7
12	6	DREAMIN'	Johnny Burnette	London	5
4	7	HOW ABOUT THAT	Adam Faith	Parlophone	8
6	8	LET'S THINK ABOUT LIVING	Bob Luman	Warner Brothers	9
7	9	NINE TIMES OUT OF TEN	Cliff Richard	Columbia	7
3	10	TELL LAURA I LOVE HER	Ricky Valance	Columbia	11
8	11	MESS OF BLUES	Elvis Presley	RCA	15
9	12	CHAIN GANG	Sam Cooke	RCA	6

November 1960

□ Highest position disc reached ● Act's first ever week on chart

LW	TW	Title	Artist	Label	Wks
17	13	MY LOVE FOR YOU	Johnny Mathis	Fontana	5
13	14	WALK DON'T RUN	John Barry Seven	Columbia	7
10	15	PLEASE HELP ME I'M FALLING	Hank Locklin	RCA	12
21	[16]	SHORTNIN' BREAD	Viscounts	Pye	3
25	17	MACDONALD'S CAVE	Piltdown Men	Capitol	7
14	18	WALK DON'T RUN	Ventures	Top Rank	8
16	19	APACHE	Shadows	Columbia	16
15	20	EVERYBODY'S SOMEBODY'S FOOL	Connie Francis	MGM	12
19	21	THEM THERE EYES	Emile Ford & the Checkmates	Pye	8
20	22	BECAUSE THEY'RE YOUNG	Duane Eddy	London	16
18	23	NICE 'N' EASY	Frank Sinatra	Capitol	9
27	[24]	TOP TEEN BABY	Gary Mills	Top Rank	3
-	25	MR. CUSTER	Charlie Drake	Parlophone	1
22	26	RESTLESS	Johnny Kidd & the Pirates	HMV	4
28	[27]	NEVER ON SUNDAY	Don Costa	London	3
-	28	MY HEART HAS A MIND OF ITS OWN	Connie Francis	MGM	1
-	29	BLUE ANGEL	Roy Orbison	London	1
39	30	FOUR LITTLE HEELS	Brian Hyland	London	3
23	31	PASSING BREEZE	Russ Conway	Columbia	6
33	32	NEVER ON SUNDAY	Manuel & his Music of the Mountains	Columbia	4
31	33	I WANT TO BE WANTED	Brenda Lee	Brunswick	2
38	[34]	MILORD	Frankie Vaughan	Philips	2
-	35	MILORD	Edith Piaf ●	Columbia	1
40	[36]	LEARNING THE GAME	Buddy Holly	Coral	2
30	37	NEVER ON SUNDAY	Lynn Cornell	Decca	2
26	38	WONDROUS PLACE	Billy Fury	Decca	6
-	39	SAVE THE LAST DANCE FOR ME	Drifters	London	1
-	40	SORRY ROBBIE	Bert Weedon	Top Rank	1

WEEK ENDING 10 NOVEMBER 1960

LW	TW	Title	Artist	Label	Wks
1	[1]	IT'S NOW OR NEVER	Elvis Presley	RCA	2
2	[2]	AS LONG AS HE NEEDS ME	Shirley Bassey	Columbia	15
3	3	ONLY THE LONELY	Roy Orbison	London	15
4	4	ROCKING GOOSE	Johnny & the Hurricanes	London	6
6	[5]	DREAMIN'	Johnny Burnette	London	6
8	[6]	LET'S THINK ABOUT LIVING	Bob Luman	Warner Brothers	10
5	7	LUCILLE/SO SAD	Everly Brothers	Warner Brothers	8
9	8	NINE TIMES OUT OF TEN	Cliff Richard	Columbia	8
13	[9]	MY LOVE FOR YOU	Johnny Mathis	Fontana	6
7	10	HOW ABOUT THAT	Adam Faith	Parlophone	9
14	[11]	WALK DON'T RUN	John Barry Seven	Columbia	8
28	12	MY HEART HAS A MIND OF ITS OWN	Connie Francis	MGM	2
12	13	CHAIN GANG	Sam Cooke	RCA	7
17	[14]	MACDONALD'S CAVE	Piltdown Men	Capitol	8
10	15	TELL LAURA I LOVE HER	Ricky Valance	Columbia	12
15	16	PLEASE HELP ME I'M FALLING	Hank Locklin	RCA	13
25	17	MR. CUSTER	Charlie Drake	Parlophone	2
21	[18]	THEM THERE EYES	Emile Ford & the Checkmates	Pye	9
16	19	SHORTNIN' BREAD	Viscounts	Pye	4
11	20	MESS OF BLUES	Elvis Presley	RCA	16
39	21	SAVE THE LAST DANCE FOR ME	Drifters	London	2
29	22	BLUE ANGEL	Roy Orbison	London	2
19	23	APACHE	Shadows	Columbia	17
24	[24]	TOP TEEN BABY	Gary Mills	Top Rank	4
-	25	MAN OF MYSTERY/THE STRANGER	Shadows	Columbia	1
35	26	MILORD	Edith Piaf	Columbia	2
18	27	WALK DON'T RUN	Ventures	Top Rank	9
-	28	KOMMOTION	Duane Eddy	London	1
30	[29]	FOUR LITTLE HEELS	Brian Hyland	London	4
40	30	SORRY ROBBIE	Bert Weedon	Top Rank	2
-	31	GOODNESS GRACIOUS ME	Peter Sellers & Sophia Loren ●	Parlophone	1
23	32	NICE 'N' EASY	Frank Sinatra	Capitol	10
20	33	EVERYBODY'S SOMEBODY'S FOOL	Connie Francis	MGM	13
-	34	DON'T BE CRUEL	Bill Black's Combo ●	London	1
27	35	NEVER ON SUNDAY	Don Costa	London	4
26	36	RESTLESS	Johnny Kidd & the Pirates	HMV	5

■Elvis Presley's first post-Army single, *It's Now Or Never*, goes straight to number one, the first record to do that since his *Jailhouse Rock* almost three years before (03.11.60) ■ Several film theme tunes are doing well. *Never On Sunday* is a hit in six versions, *Walk Don't Run* is a hit twice, while *Man Of Mystery* and *Because They're Young* add to the film themes on the chart (10.11.60)■

November 1960

☐ Highest position disc reached ● Act's first ever week on chart

LW	TW	Title	Artist	Label	Wks
22	37	BECAUSE THEY'RE YOUNG	Duane Eddy	London	17
34	38	MILORD	Frankie Vaughan	Philips	3
31	39	PASSING BREEZE	Russ Conway	Columbia	7
32	40	NEVER ON SUNDAY	Manuel & his Music of the Mountains	Columbia	5

LW	TW	*WEEK ENDING* **17 NOVEMBER 1960**			Wks
1	1	IT'S NOW OR NEVER	Elvis Presley	RCA	3
2	2	AS LONG AS HE NEEDS ME	Shirley Bassey	Columbia	16
4	3	ROCKING GOOSE	Johnny & the Hurricanes	London	7
3	4	ONLY THE LONELY	Roy Orbison	London	16
5	5	DREAMIN'	Johnny Burnette	London	7
12	6	MY HEART HAS A MIND OF ITS OWN	Connie Francis	MGM	3
25	7	MAN OF MYSTERY/THE STRANGER	Shadows	Columbia	2
21	8	SAVE THE LAST DANCE FOR ME	Drifters	London	3
6	9	LET'S THINK ABOUT LIVING	Bob Luman	Warner Brothers	11
9	10	MY LOVE FOR YOU	Johnny Mathis	Fontana	7
7	11	LUCILLE/SO SAD	Everly Brothers	Warner Brothers	9
13	12	CHAIN GANG	Sam Cooke	RCA	8
8	13	NINE TIMES OUT OF TEN	Cliff Richard	Columbia	9
17	14	MR. CUSTER	Charlie Drake	Parlophone	3
14	15	MACDONALD'S CAVE	Piltdown Men	Capitol	9
28	16	KOMMOTION	Duane Eddy	London	2
11	17	WALK DON'T RUN	John Barry Seven	Columbia	9
31	18	GOODNESS GRACIOUS ME	Peter Sellers & Sophia Loren	Parlophone	2
10	19	HOW ABOUT THAT	Adam Faith	Parlophone	10
22	20	BLUE ANGEL	Roy Orbison	London	3
19	21	SHORTNIN' BREAD	Viscounts	Pye	5
16	22	PLEASE HELP ME I'M FALLING	Hank Locklin	RCA	14
15	23	TELL LAURA I LOVE HER	Ricky Valance	Columbia	13
-	24	JUST AS MUCH AS EVER	Nat 'King' Cole	Capitol	1
23	25	APACHE	Shadows	Columbia	18
24	26	TOP TEEN BABY	Gary Mills	Top Rank	5
26	27	MILORD	Edith Piaf	Columbia	3
20	28	MESS OF BLUES	Elvis Presley	RCA	17
18	29	THEM THERE EYES	Emile Ford & the Checkmates	Pye	10
-	30	LITTLE DONKEY	Nina & Frederick	Columbia	1
-	31	KICKING UP THE LEAVES	Mark Wynter	Decca	1
34	32	DON'T BE CRUEL	Bill Black's Combo	London	2
32	33	NICE 'N' EASY	Frank Sinatra	Capitol	11
30	34	SORRY ROBBIE	Bert Weedon	Top Rank	3
29	35	FOUR LITTLE HEELS	Brian Hyland	London	5
27	36	WALK DON'T RUN	Ventures	Top Rank	10
-	37	NEVER ON SUNDAY	Lynn Cornell	Decca	3
38	38	MILORD	Frankie Vaughan	Philips	4
39	39	PASSING BREEZE	Russ Conway	Columbia	8
-	40	LONELY PUP (IN A CHRISTMAS SHOP)	Adam Faith	Parlophone	1

LW	TW	*WEEK ENDING* **24 NOVEMBER 1960**			Wks
1	1	IT'S NOW OR NEVER	Elvis Presley	RCA	4
2	2	AS LONG AS HE NEEDS ME	Shirley Bassey	Columbia	17
6	3	MY HEART HAS A MIND OF ITS OWN	Connie Francis	MGM	4
3	4	ROCKING GOOSE	Johnny & the Hurricanes	London	8
5	5	DREAMIN'	Johnny Burnette	London	8
8	6	SAVE THE LAST DANCE FOR ME	Drifters	London	4
7	7	MAN OF MYSTERY/THE STRANGER	Shadows	Columbia	3
18	8	GOODNESS GRACIOUS ME	Peter Sellers & Sophia Loren	Parlophone	3
4	9	ONLY THE LONELY	Roy Orbison	London	17
10	10	MY LOVE FOR YOU	Johnny Mathis	Fontana	8
9	11	LET'S THINK ABOUT LIVING	Bob Luman	Warner Brothers	12
14	12	MR. CUSTER	Charlie Drake	Parlophone	4
16	13	KOMMOTION	Duane Eddy	London	3
12	14	CHAIN GANG	Sam Cooke	RCA	9
15	15	MACDONALD'S CAVE	Piltdown Men	Capitol	10
30	16	LITTLE DONKEY	Nina & Frederick	Columbia	2
20	17	BLUE ANGEL	Roy Orbison	London	4
24	18	JUST AS MUCH AS EVER	Nat 'King' Cole	Capitol	2
19	19	HOW ABOUT THAT	Adam Faith	Parlophone	11
13	20	NINE TIMES OUT OF TEN	Cliff Richard	Columbia	10
17	21	WALK DON'T RUN	John Barry Seven	Columbia	10
21	22	SHORTNIN' BREAD	Viscounts	Pye	6
11	23	LUCILLE/SO SAD	Everly Brothers	Warner Brothers	10
22	24	PLEASE HELP ME I'M FALLING	Hank Locklin	RCA	15
27	25	MILORD	Edith Piaf	Columbia	4
31	26	KICKING UP THE LEAVES	Mark Wynter	Decca	2
40	27	LONELY PUP (IN A CHRISTMAS SHOP)	Adam Faith	Parlophone	2
34	28	SORRY ROBBIE	Bert Weedon	Top Rank	4
26	29	TOP TEEN BABY	Gary Mills	Top Rank	6
-	30	OL' MACDONALD	Frank Sinatra	Capitol	1
25	31	APACHE	Shadows	Columbia	19
35	32	FOUR LITTLE HEELS	Brian Hyland	London	6
29	33	THEM THERE EYES	Emile Ford & the Checkmates	Pye	11
-	34	LIVELY	Lonnie Donegan	Pye	1
-	35	NEVER ON SUNDAY	Manuel & his Music of the Mountains	Columbia	6
37	36	NEVER ON SUNDAY	Lynn Cornell	Decca	4
23	37	TELL LAURA I LOVE HER	Ricky Valance	Columbia	14
33	38	NICE 'N' EASY	Frank Sinatra	Capitol	12
38	39	MILORD	Frankie Vaughan	Philips	5
-	40	NEVER ON SUNDAY	Makadopoulos & his Greek Serenaders	Palette	2

LW	TW	*WEEK ENDING* **1 DECEMBER 1960**			Wks
1	1	IT'S NOW OR NEVER	Elvis Presley	RCA	5
6	2	SAVE THE LAST DANCE FOR ME	Drifters	London	5
4	3	ROCKING GOOSE	Johnny & the Hurricanes	London	9
8	4	GOODNESS GRACIOUS ME	Peter Sellers & Sophia Loren	Parlophone	4
7	5	MAN OF MYSTERY/THE STRANGER	Shadows	Columbia	4
2	6	AS LONG AS HE NEEDS ME	Shirley Bassey	Columbia	18
3	7	MY HEART HAS A MIND OF ITS OWN	Connie Francis	MGM	5
16	8	LITTLE DONKEY	Nina & Frederick	Columbia	3
5	9	DREAMIN'	Johnny Burnette	London	9
11	10	LET'S THINK ABOUT LIVING	Bob Luman	Warner Brothers	13
9	11	ONLY THE LONELY	Roy Orbison	London	18
-	12	STRAWBERRY FAIR	Anthony Newley	Decca	1
10	13	MY LOVE FOR YOU	Johnny Mathis	Fontana	9
12	14	MR. CUSTER	Charlie Drake	Parlophone	5
17	15	BLUE ANGEL	Roy Orbison	London	5
30	16	OL' MACDONALD	Frank Sinatra	Capitol	2
15	17	MACDONALD'S CAVE	Piltdown Men	Capitol	11
34	18	LIVELY	Lonnie Donegan	Pye	2
13	19	KOMMOTION	Duane Eddy	London	4
18	20	JUST AS MUCH AS EVER	Nat 'King' Cole	Capitol	3
27	21	LONELY PUP (IN A CHRISTMAS SHOP)	Adam Faith	Parlophone	3
14	22	CHAIN GANG	Sam Cooke	RCA	10
-	23	I LOVE YOU	Cliff Richard	Columbia	1
26	24	KICKING UP THE LEAVES	Mark Wynter	Decca	3
25	25	MILORD	Edith Piaf	Columbia	5
24	26	PLEASE HELP ME I'M FALLING	Hank Locklin	RCA	16
23	27	LUCILLE/SO SAD	Everly Brothers	Warner Brothers	11
20	28	NINE TIMES OUT OF TEN	Cliff Richard	Columbia	11
28	29	SORRY ROBBIE	Bert Weedon	Top Rank	5
29	30	TOP TEEN BABY	Gary Mills	Top Rank	7
35	31	NEVER ON SUNDAY	Manuel & his Music of the Mountains	Columbia	7
36	32	NEVER ON SUNDAY	Lynn Cornell	Decca	5
-	33	DON'T BE CRUEL	Bill Black's Combo	London	3
21	34	WALK DON'T RUN	John Barry Seven	Columbia	11
-	35	GURNEY SLADE	Max Harris ●	Fontana	1
-	36	EVEN MORE PARTY POPS	Russ Conway	Columbia	1
-	37	POETRY IN MOTION	Johnny Tillotson ●	London	1
-	38	PERFIDIA	Ventures	London	1

In these weeks ■ Peter Sellers, already a Top Ten hitmaker as part of the trio of Goons, climbs back as half of a duo with Sophia Loren. His biggest solo hit was yet to come, although he never made the Top Ten on his own (24.11.60) ■ Twelve instrumentals in the Top 40, including seven between 31 and 40 (01.12.60) ■ Frank Sinatra and the Piltdown Men have versions of the same children's song in consecutive positions. Sinatra's vocal version *Ol'Macdonald* is at number 16, while the Piltdown Men's instrumental version is at number 17 (01.12.60) ■

LW	TW	Title	Artist	Label	Wks
40	39	NEVER ON SUNDAY	Makadopoulos & his Greek Serenaders	Palette	3
33	40	THEM THERE EYES	Emile Ford & the Checkmates	Pye	12

December 1960

☐ Highest position disc reached ● Act's first ever week on chart

WEEK ENDING 8 DECEMBER 1960

LW	TW	Title	Artist	Label	Wks
1	[1]	IT'S NOW OR NEVER	Elvis Presley	RCA	6
2	[2]	SAVE THE LAST DANCE FOR ME	Drifters	London	6
8	[3]	LITTLE DONKEY	Nina & Frederick	Columbia	4
23	4	I LOVE YOU	Cliff Richard	Columbia	2
5	[5]	MAN OF MYSTERY/THE STRANGER	Shadows	Columbia	5
3	6	ROCKING GOOSE	Johnny & the Hurricanes	London	10
4	7	GOODNESS GRACIOUS ME	Peter Sellers & Sophia Loren	Parlophone	5
12	8	STRAWBERRY FAIR	Anthony Newley	Decca	2
6	9	AS LONG AS HE NEEDS ME	Shirley Bassey	Columbia	19
7	10	MY HEART HAS A MIND OF ITS OWN	Connie Francis	MGM	6
16	[11]	OL' MACDONALD	Frank Sinatra	Capitol	3
13	12	MY LOVE FOR YOU	Johnny Mathis	Fontana	10
18	[13]	LIVELY	Lonnie Donegan	Pye	3
9	14	DREAMIN'	Johnny Burnette	London	10
11	15	ONLY THE LONELY	Roy Orbison	London	19
14	16	MR. CUSTER	Charlie Drake	Parlophone	6
15	17	BLUE ANGEL	Roy Orbison	London	6
21	18	LONELY PUP (IN A CHRISTMAS SHOP)	Adam Faith	Parlophone	4
35	19	GURNEY SLADE	Max Harris	Fontana	2
19	20	KOMMOTION	Duane Eddy	London	5
10	21	LET'S THINK ABOUT LIVING	Bob Luman	Warner Brothers	14
37	22	POETRY IN MOTION	Johnny Tillotson	London	2
20	23	JUST AS MUCH AS EVER	Nat 'King' Cole	Capitol	4
17	24	MACDONALD'S CAVE	Piltdown Men	Capitol	12
24	25	KICKING UP THE LEAVES	Mark Wynter	Decca	4
25	26	MILORD	Edith Piaf	Columbia	6
38	27	PERFIDIA	Ventures	London	2
26	28	PLEASE HELP ME I'M FALLING	Hank Locklin	RCA	17
29	29	SORRY ROBBIE	Bert Weedon	Top Rank	6
-	30	APACHE	Shadows	Columbia	20
32	31	NEVER ON SUNDAY	Lynn Cornell	Decca	6
30	32	TOP TEEN BABY	Gary Mills	Top Rank	8
-	33	COUNTING TEARDROPS	Emile Ford & the Checkmates	Pye	1
-	[34]	CHARMING BILLY	Johnny Preston	Mercury	1
22	35	CHAIN GANG	Sam Cooke	RCA	11
27	36	LUCILLE/SO SAD	Everly Brothers	Warner Brothers	12
28	37	NINE TIMES OUT OF TEN	Cliff Richard	Columbia	12
39	38	NEVER ON SUNDAY	Makadopoulos & his Greek Serenaders	Palette	4
34	39	WALK DON'T RUN	John Barry Seven	Columbia	12
-	40	TELL LAURA I LOVE HER	Ricky Valance	Columbia	15

WEEK ENDING 15 DECEMBER 1960

LW	TW	Title	Artist	Label	Wks
1	[1]	IT'S NOW OR NEVER	Elvis Presley	RCA	7
2	[2]	SAVE THE LAST DANCE FOR ME	Drifters	London	7
8	[3]	STRAWBERRY FAIR	Anthony Newley	Decca	3
4	4	I LOVE YOU	Cliff Richard	Columbia	3
6	5	ROCKING GOOSE	Johnny & the Hurricanes	London	11
7	6	GOODNESS GRACIOUS ME	Peter Sellers & Sophia Loren	Parlophone	6
5	7	MAN OF MYSTERY/THE STRANGER	Shadows	Columbia	6
22	8	POETRY IN MOTION	Johnny Tillotson	London	3
3	9	LITTLE DONKEY	Nina & Frederick	Columbia	5
18	10	LONELY PUP (IN A CHRISTMAS SHOP)	Adam Faith	Parlophone	5
10	11	MY HEART HAS A MIND OF ITS OWN	Connie Francis	MGM	7
17	12	BLUE ANGEL	Roy Orbison	London	7
19	13	GURNEY SLADE	Max Harris	Fontana	3
11	14	OL' MACDONALD	Frank Sinatra	Capitol	4
12	15	MY LOVE FOR YOU	Johnny Mathis	Fontana	11
27	16	PERFIDIA	Ventures	London	3
15	17	ONLY THE LONELY	Roy Orbison	London	20
9	18	AS LONG AS HE NEEDS ME	Shirley Bassey	Columbia	20
13	19	LIVELY	Lonnie Donegan	Pye	4
14	20	DREAMIN'	Johnny Burnette	London	11
23	21	JUST AS MUCH AS EVER	Nat 'King' Cole	Capitol	5
16	22	MR. CUSTER	Charlie Drake	Parlophone	7
33	23	COUNTING TEARDROPS	Emile Ford & the Checkmates	Pye	2
-	24	GEORGIA ON MY MIND	Ray Charles ●	HMV	1
20	25	KOMMOTION	Duane Eddy	London	6
26	26	MILORD	Edith Piaf	Columbia	7
25	27	KICKING UP THE LEAVES	Mark Wynter	Decca	5
24	28	MACDONALD'S CAVE	Piltdown Men	Capitol	13
-	29	EVEN MORE PARTY POPS	Russ Conway	Columbia	2
-	30	VIRGIN MARY	Lonnie Donegan	Pye	1
-	31	LIKE STRANGERS	Everly Brothers	London	1
-	32	SWAY	Bobby Rydell	Columbia	1
-	33	BLACK STOCKINGS	John Barry Seven	Columbia	1
32	34	TOP TEEN BABY	Gary Mills	Top Rank	9
21	35	LET'S THINK ABOUT LIVING	Bob Luman	Warner Brothers	15
-	36	BUONA SERA	Mr. Acker Bilk	Columbia	1
-	37	DONALD WHERE'S YOUR TROOSERS?	Andy Stewart ●	Top Rank	1
38	38	NEVER ON SUNDAY	Makadopoulos & his Greek Serenaders	Palette	5
31	39	NEVER ON SUNDAY	Lynn Cornell	Decca	7
-	40	PORTRAIT OF MY LOVE	Matt Monro ●	Parlophone	1

WEEK ENDING 22 DECEMBER 1960

LW	TW	Title	Artist	Label	Wks
1	[1]	IT'S NOW OR NEVER	Elvis Presley	RCA	8
4	2	I LOVE YOU	Cliff Richard	Columbia	4
2	3	SAVE THE LAST DANCE FOR ME	Drifters	London	8
10	[4]	LONELY PUP (IN A CHRISTMAS SHOP)	Adam Faith	Parlophone	6
8	5	POETRY IN MOTION	Johnny Tillotson	London	4
9	6	LITTLE DONKEY	Nina & Frederick	Columbia	6
3	7	STRAWBERRY FAIR	Anthony Newley	Decca	4
6	8	GOODNESS GRACIOUS ME	Peter Sellers & Sophia Loren	Parlophone	7
7	9	MAN OF MYSTERY/THE STRANGER	Shadows	Columbia	7
5	10	ROCKING GOOSE	Johnny & the Hurricanes	London	12
12	[11]	BLUE ANGEL	Roy Orbison	London	8
13	12	GURNEY SLADE	Max Harris	Fontana	4
11	13	MY HEART HAS A MIND OF ITS OWN	Connie Francis	MGM	8
18	14	AS LONG AS HE NEEDS ME	Shirley Bassey	Columbia	21
16	15	PERFIDIA	Ventures	London	4
15	16	MY LOVE FOR YOU	Johnny Mathis	Fontana	12
19	17	LIVELY	Lonnie Donegan	Pye	5
22	18	MR. CUSTER	Charlie Drake	Parlophone	8
14	19	OL' MACDONALD	Frank Sinatra	Capitol	5
23	20	COUNTING TEARDROPS	Emile Ford & the Checkmates	Pye	3
21	21	JUST AS MUCH AS EVER	Nat 'King' Cole	Capitol	6
40	22	PORTRAIT OF MY LOVE	Matt Monro	Parlophone	2
20	23	DREAMIN'	Johnny Burnette	London	12
26	[24]	MILORD	Edith Piaf	Columbia	8
17	25	ONLY THE LONELY	Roy Orbison	London	21
25	26	KOMMOTION	Duane Eddy	London	7
30	[27]	VIRGIN MARY	Lonnie Donegan	Pye	2
24	28	GEORGIA ON MY MIND	Ray Charles	HMV	2
32	29	SWAY	Bobby Rydell	Columbia	2
31	30	LIKE STRANGERS	Everly Brothers	London	2
-	31	LITTLE GIRL	Marty Wilde	Philips	1
29	32	EVEN MORE PARTY POPS	Russ Conway	Columbia	3
28	33	MACDONALD'S CAVE	Piltdown Men	Capitol	14
-	34	STRAWBERRY BLONDE	Frank D'Rone ●	Mercury	1
-	[35]	ONWARD CHRISTIAN SOLDIERS	Harry Simeone Chorale	Ember	1
38	[36]	NEVER ON SUNDAY	Makadopoulos & his Greek Serenaders	Palette	6
-	37	LUCILLE/SO SAD	Everly Brothers	Warner Brothers	13
36	38	BUONA SERA	Mr. Acker Bilk	Columbia	2

■For five consecutive weeks the top three singles have all been records at their peak chart positions. Each week there has been a different record at number three (15.12.60) ■ Andy Stewart's remarkable song *Donald Where's Your Troosers* enters the chart for the first time. Twenty-nine years later, it storms the Top Ten (15.12.60)■

December 1960

□ Highest position disc reached ● Act's first ever week on chart

LW	TW	Title / Artist	Label	Wks
27	39	KICKING UP THE LEAVES Mark Wynter	Decca	6
-	40	LITTLE WHITE BERRY Roy Castle ●	Philips	1

LW	TW	WEEK ENDING 29 DECEMBER 1960	Label	Wks
2	1	I LOVE YOU Cliff Richard	Columbia	5
1	2	IT'S NOW OR NEVER Elvis Presley	RCA	9
7	3	STRAWBERRY FAIR Anthony Newley	Decca	5
6	4	LITTLE DONKEY Nina & Frederick	Columbia	7
3	5	SAVE THE LAST DANCE FOR ME Drifters	London	9
5	6	POETRY IN MOTION Johnny Tillotson	London	5
4	7	LONELY PUP (IN A CHRISTMAS SHOP) Adam Faith	Parlophone	7
10	8	ROCKING GOOSE Johnny & the Hurricanes	London	13
9	9	MAN OF MYSTERY/THE STRANGER Shadows	Columbia	8
13	10	MY HEART HAS A MIND OF ITS OWN Connie Francis	MGM	9
12	11	GURNEY SLADE Max Harris	Fontana	5
15	12	PERFIDIA Ventures	London	5
8	13	GOODNESS GRACIOUS ME Peter Sellers & Sophia Loren	Parlophone	8
20	14	COUNTING TEARDROPS Emile Ford & the Checkmates	Pye	4
17	15	LIVELY Lonnie Donegan	Pye	6
22	16	PORTRAIT OF MY LOVE Matt Monro	Parlophone	3
14	17	AS LONG AS HE NEEDS ME Shirley Bassey	Columbia	22
23	18	DREAMIN' Johnny Burnette	London	13
11	19	BLUE ANGEL Roy Orbison	London	9
19	20	OL' MACDONALD Frank Sinatra	Capitol	6
16	21	MY LOVE FOR YOU Johnny Mathis	Fontana	13
21	22	JUST AS MUCH AS EVER Nat 'King' Cole	Capitol	7
18	23	MR. CUSTER Charlie Drake	Parlophone	9
30	24	LIKE STRANGERS Everly Brothers	London	3
24	25	MILORD Edith Piaf	Columbia	9
31	26	LITTLE GIRL Marty Wilde	Philips	2
32	27	EVEN MORE PARTY POPS Russ Conway	Columbia	4
29	28	SWAY Bobby Rydell	Columbia	3
28	29	GEORGIA ON MY MIND Ray Charles	HMV	3
39	30	KICKING UP THE LEAVES Mark Wynter	Decca	7
38	31	BUONA SERA Mr. Acker Bilk	Columbia	3
27	32	VIRGIN MARY Lonnie Donegan	Pye	3
25	33	ONLY THE LONELY Roy Orbison	London	22
34	34	STRAWBERRY BLONDE Frank D'Rone	Mercury	2
33	35	MACDONALD'S CAVE Piltdown Men	Capitol	15
-	36	LET'S THINK ABOUT LIVING Bob Luman	Warner Brothers	16
-	37	BLACK STOCKINGS John Barry Seven	Columbia	2
-	38	TOP TEEN BABY Gary Mills	Top Rank	10
-	39	BLUE EYED BOY Al Saxon	Fontana	1
-	40	MUST BE SANTA Tommy Steele	Decca	1

In these weeks ■ Anthony Newley's success is not only with *Strawberry Fair* at number three. The theme tune to his TV series, *Gurney Slade* by Max Harris, peaks at number 11 (29.12.60) ■ Only Nina and Frederick and Adam Faith bring Christmas to the Top Ten, although Russ Conway, Lonnie Donegan and Tommy Steele show a little festive spirit lower down (29.12.60)■

1961

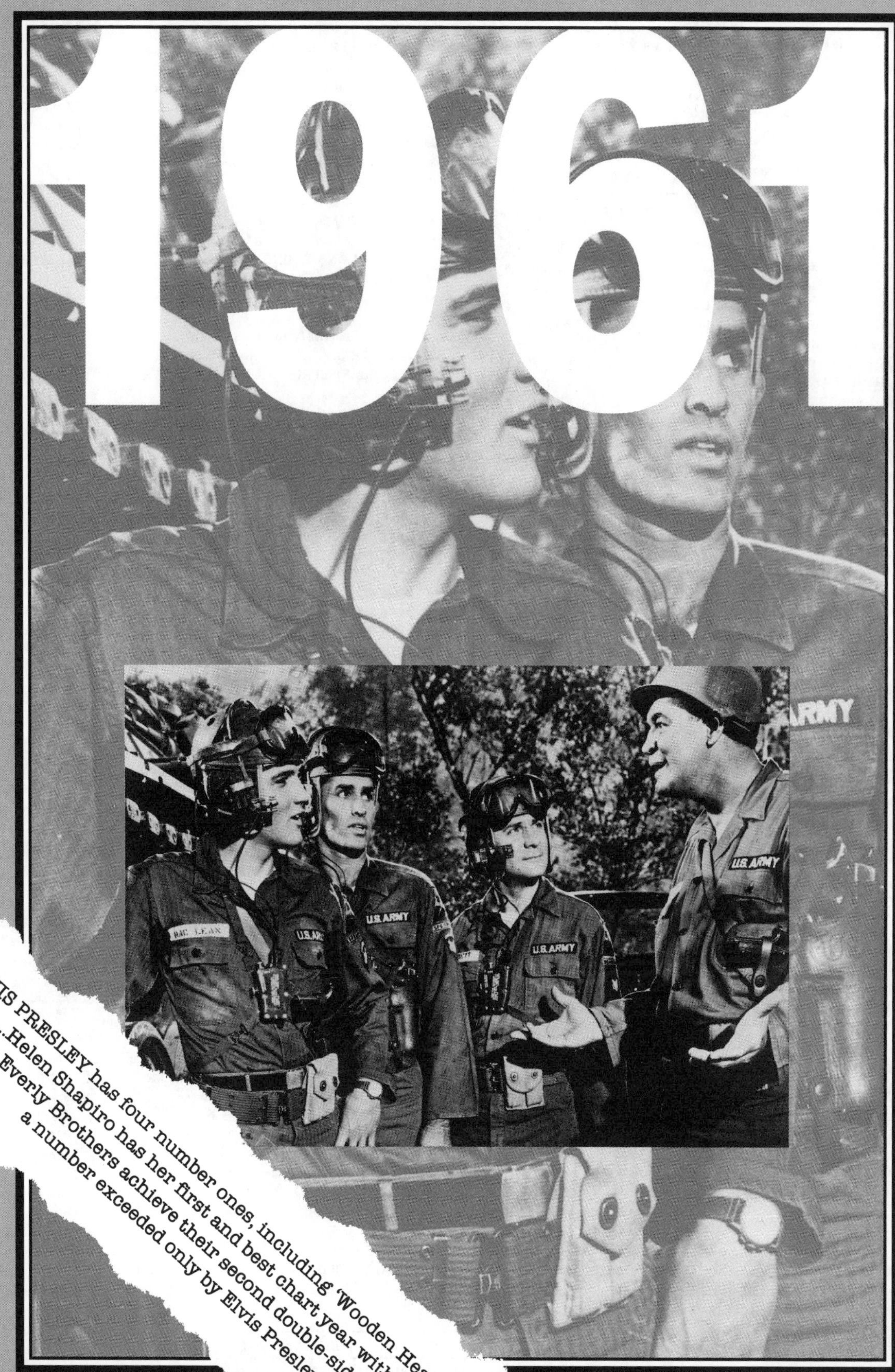

..........ELVIS PRESLEY has four number ones, including 'Wooden Heart' from his film G.I.Blues.......Helen Shapiro has her first and best chart year with two number ones ......the Everly Brothers achieve their second double-sided number one, a number exceeded only by Elvis Presley..........

January 1961

□ Highest position disc reached ● Act's first ever week on chart

LW	TW	*WEEK ENDING* **5 JANUARY 1961**		Wks
1	1	I LOVE YOU Cliff Richard	*Columbia*	6
5	2	SAVE THE LAST DANCE FOR ME Drifters	*London*	10
6	3	POETRY IN MOTION Johnny Tillotson	*London*	6
7	4	LONELY PUP (IN A CHRISTMAS SHOP) Adam Faith	*Parlophone*	8
3	5	STRAWBERRY FAIR Anthony Newley	*Decca*	6
2	6	IT'S NOW OR NEVER Elvis Presley	*RCA*	10
13	7	GOODNESS GRACIOUS ME Peter Sellers & Sophia Loren	*Parlophone*	9
4	8	LITTLE DONKEY Nina & Frederick	*Columbia*	8
12	9	PERFIDIA Ventures	*London*	6
8	10	ROCKING GOOSE Johnny & the Hurricanes	*London*	14
14	11	COUNTING TEARDROPS Emile Ford & the Checkmates	*Pye*	5
16	12	PORTRAIT OF MY LOVE Matt Monro	*Parlophone*	4
9	13	MAN OF MYSTERY/THE STRANGER Shadows	*Columbia*	9
15	14	LIVELY Lonnie Donegan	*Pye*	7
10	15	MY HEART HAS A MIND OF ITS OWN Connie Francis	*MGM*	10
11	16	GURNEY SLADE Max Harris	*Fontana*	6
21	17	MY LOVE FOR YOU Johnny Mathis	*Fontana*	14
24	18	LIKE STRANGERS Everly Brothers	*London*	4
19	19	BLUE ANGEL Roy Orbison	*London*	10
20	20	OL' MACDONALD Frank Sinatra	*Capitol*	7
17	21	AS LONG AS HE NEEDS ME Shirley Bassey	*Columbia*	23
23	22	MR. CUSTER Charlie Drake	*Parlophone*	10
18	23	DREAMIN' Johnny Burnette	*London*	14
28	24	SWAY Bobby Rydell	*Columbia*	4
22	25	JUST AS MUCH AS EVER Nat 'King' Cole	*Capitol*	8
33	26	ONLY THE LONELY Roy Orbison	*London*	23
25	27	MILORD Edith Piaf	*Columbia*	10
27	28	EVEN MORE PARTY POPS Russ Conway	*Columbia*	5
26	29	LITTLE GIRL Marty Wilde	*Philips*	3
31	30	BUONA SERA Mr. Acker Bilk	*Columbia*	4
-	31	KOMMOTION Duane Eddy	*London*	8
30	32	KICKING UP THE LEAVES Mark Wynter	*Decca*	8
34	33	STRAWBERRY BLONDE Frank D'Rone	*Mercury*	3
29	34	GEORGIA ON MY MIND Ray Charles	*HMV*	4
-	35	TILL Tony Bennett	*Philips*	1
-	36	STAY Maurice Williams & the Zodiacs ●	*Top Rank*	1
-	37	LET'S/SERENATA Sarah Vaughan	*Columbia*	1
-	38	ONWARD CHRISTIAN SOLDIERS Harry Simeone Chorale	*Ember*	2
-	39	NEVER ON SUNDAY Makadopoulos & his Greek Serenaders	*Palette*	7
32	40	VIRGIN MARY Lonnie Donegan	*Pye*	4

LW	TW	*WEEK ENDING* **12 JANUARY 1961**		Wks
3	1	POETRY IN MOTION Johnny Tillotson	*London*	7
1	2	I LOVE YOU Cliff Richard	*Columbia*	7
2	3	SAVE THE LAST DANCE FOR ME Drifters	*London*	11
6	4	IT'S NOW OR NEVER Elvis Presley	*RCA*	11
12	5	PORTRAIT OF MY LOVE Matt Monro	*Parlophone*	5
7	6	GOODNESS GRACIOUS ME Peter Sellers & Sophia Loren	*Parlophone*	10
13	7	MAN OF MYSTERY/THE STRANGER Shadows	*Columbia*	10
10	8	ROCKING GOOSE Johnny & the Hurricanes	*London*	15
5	9	STRAWBERRY FAIR Anthony Newley	*Decca*	7
9	10	PERFIDIA Ventures	*London*	7
11	11	COUNTING TEARDROPS Emile Ford & the Checkmates	*Pye*	6
4	12	LONELY PUP (IN A CHRISTMAS SHOP) Adam Faith	*Parlophone*	9
24	13	SWAY Bobby Rydell	*Columbia*	5
30	14	BUONA SERA Mr. Acker Bilk	*Columbia*	5
19	15	BLUE ANGEL Roy Orbison	*London*	11
18	16	LIKE STRANGERS Everly Brothers	*London*	5
8	17	LITTLE DONKEY Nina & Frederick	*Columbia*	9
16	18	GURNEY SLADE Max Harris	*Fontana*	7
15	19	MY HEART HAS A MIND OF ITS OWN Connie Francis	*MGM*	11
29	20	LITTLE GIRL Marty Wilde	*Philips*	4
21	21	AS LONG AS HE NEEDS ME Shirley Bassey	*Columbia*	24
23	22	DREAMIN' Johnny Burnette	*London*	15
17	23	MY LOVE FOR YOU Johnny Mathis	*Fontana*	15
33	24	STRAWBERRY BLONDE Frank D'Rone	*Mercury*	4
36	25	STAY Maurice Williams & the Zodiacs	*Top Rank*	2
14	26	LIVELY Lonnie Donegan	*Pye*	8
-	27	BLACK STOCKINGS John Barry Seven	*Columbia*	3
-	28	DOLL HOUSE King Brothers	*Parlophone*	1
22	29	MR. CUSTER Charlie Drake	*Parlophone*	11
20	30	OL' MACDONALD Frank Sinatra	*Capitol*	8
-	31	PEPE Duane Eddy	*London*	1
28	32	EVEN MORE PARTY POPS Russ Conway	*Columbia*	6
-	33	CHARIOT Rhet Stoller ●	*Decca*	1
25	34	JUST AS MUCH AS EVER Nat 'King' Cole	*Capitol*	9
34	35	GEORGIA ON MY MIND Ray Charles	*HMV*	5
-	36	CAN'T YOU HEAR MY HEART Danny Rivers	*Decca*	1
-	37	BANGERS AND MASH Peter Sellers & Sophia Loren	*Parlophone*	1
-	38	YOU'RE SIXTEEN Johnny Burnette	*London*	1
-	39	MANY TEARS AGO Connie Francis	*MGM*	1
-	40	MY GIRL JOSEPHINE Fats Domino	*London*	1

LW	TW	*WEEK ENDING* **19 JANUARY 1961**		Wks
1	1	POETRY IN MOTION Johnny Tillotson	*London*	8
2	2	I LOVE YOU Cliff Richard	*Columbia*	8
5	3	PORTRAIT OF MY LOVE Matt Monro	*Parlophone*	6
10	4	PERFIDIA Ventures	*London*	8
3	5	SAVE THE LAST DANCE FOR ME Drifters	*London*	12
11	6	COUNTING TEARDROPS Emile Ford & the Checkmates	*Pye*	7
4	7	IT'S NOW OR NEVER Elvis Presley	*RCA*	12
7	8	MAN OF MYSTERY/THE STRANGER Shadows	*Columbia*	11
31	9	PEPE Duane Eddy	*London*	2
6	10	GOODNESS GRACIOUS ME Peter Sellers & Sophia Loren	*Parlophone*	11
16	11	LIKE STRANGERS Everly Brothers	*London*	6
9	12	STRAWBERRY FAIR Anthony Newley	*Decca*	8
8	13	ROCKING GOOSE Johnny & the Hurricanes	*London*	16
15	14	BLUE ANGEL Roy Orbison	*London*	12
25	15	STAY Maurice Williams & the Zodiacs	*Top Rank*	3
20	16	LITTLE GIRL Marty Wilde	*Philips*	5
13	17	SWAY Bobby Rydell	*Columbia*	6
14	18	BUONA SERA Mr. Acker Bilk	*Columbia*	6
-	19	ARE YOU LONESOME TONIGHT? Elvis Presley	*RCA*	1
38	20	YOU'RE SIXTEEN Johnny Burnette	*London*	2
-	21	A SCOTTISH SOLDIER Andy Stewart	*Top Rank*	1
37	22	BANGERS AND MASH Peter Sellers & Sophia Loren	*Parlophone*	2
-	23	PEPE Russ Conway	*Columbia*	1
39	24	MANY TEARS AGO Connie Francis	*MGM*	2
28	25	DOLL HOUSE King Brothers	*Parlophone*	2
33	26	CHARIOT Rhet Stoller	*Decca*	2
18	27	GURNEY SLADE Max Harris	*Fontana*	8
12	28	LONELY PUP (IN A CHRISTMAS SHOP) Adam Faith	*Parlophone*	10
24	29	STRAWBERRY BLONDE Frank D'Rone	*Mercury*	5
-	30	A THOUSAND STARS Billy Fury	*Decca*	1
27	31	BLACK STOCKINGS John Barry Seven	*Columbia*	4
40	32	MY GIRL JOSEPHINE Fats Domino	*London*	2
19	33	MY HEART HAS A MIND OF ITS OWN Connie Francis	*MGM*	12
-	34	PILTDOWN RIDES AGAIN Piltdown Men	*Capitol*	1
-	35	NEW ORLEANS U.S. Bonds ●	*Top Rank*	1
23	36	MY LOVE FOR YOU Johnny Mathis	*Fontana*	16
32	37	EVEN MORE PARTY POPS Russ Conway	*Columbia*	7
21	38	AS LONG AS HE NEEDS ME Shirley Bassey	*Columbia*	25
-	39	NORTH TO ALASKA Johnny Horton	*Philips*	1
-	40	I WISH I COULD SHIMMY LIKE MY SISTER KATE Olympics	*Vogue*	1

LW	TW	*WEEK ENDING* **26 JANUARY 1961**		Wks
19	1	ARE YOU LONESOME TONIGHT? Elvis Presley	*RCA*	2

In these weeks ■ Tony Bennett's *Till* is mistakenly listed as a double-sided hit with *Serenata*. *Serenata* is not the other side of *Till*, it is the other side of Sarah Vaughan's *Let's* (05.01.61) ■ *Are You Lonesome Tonight* jumps from 19 to 1, the first record to jump from a chart position outside the Top 10 straight to number one (26.01.61)■

LW	TW	Title	Artist	Label	Wks
1	2	POETRY IN MOTION	Johnny Tillotson	*London*	9
3	[3]	PORTRAIT OF MY LOVE	Matt Monro	*Parlophone*	7
6	[4]	COUNTING TEARDROPS	Emile Ford & the Checkmates	*Pye*	8
9	5	PEPE	Duane Eddy	*London*	3
2	6	I LOVE YOU	Cliff Richard	*Columbia*	9
4	7	PERFIDIA	Ventures	*London*	9
5	8	SAVE THE LAST DANCE FOR ME	Drifters	*London*	13
18	9	BUONA SERA	Mr. Acker Bilk	*Columbia*	7
20	10	YOU'RE SIXTEEN	Johnny Burnette	*London*	3
7	11	IT'S NOW OR NEVER	Elvis Presley	*RCA*	13
17	[12]	SWAY	Bobby Rydell	*Columbia*	7
11	13	LIKE STRANGERS	Everly Brothers	*London*	7
15	[14]	STAY	Maurice Williams & the Zodiacs	*Top Rank*	4
24	15	MANY TEARS AGO	Connie Francis	*MGM*	3
-	16	RUBBER BALL	Marty Wilde	*Philips*	1
16	17	LITTLE GIRL	Marty Wilde	*Philips*	6
-	18	SAILOR	Petula Clark	*Pye*	1
21	[19]	A SCOTTISH SOLDIER	Andy Stewart	*Top Rank*	2
10	20	GOODNESS GRACIOUS ME	Peter Sellers & Sophia Loren	*Parlophone*	12
25	[21]	DOLL HOUSE	King Brothers	*Parlophone*	3
34	22	PILTDOWN RIDES AGAIN	Piltdown Men	*Capitol*	2
14	23	BLUE ANGEL	Roy Orbison	*London*	13
-	24	RUBBER BALL	Bobby Vee ●	*London*	1
23	25	PEPE	Russ Conway	*Columbia*	2
8	26	MAN OF MYSTERY/THE STRANGER	Shadows	*Columbia*	12
-	27	SAILOR	Anne Shelton	*Philips*	1
30	28	A THOUSAND STARS	Billy Fury	*Decca*	2
13	29	ROCKING GOOSE	Johnny & the Hurricanes	*London*	17
22	30	BANGERS AND MASH	Peter Sellers & Sophia Loren	*Parlophone*	3
29	31	STRAWBERRY BLONDE	Frank D'Rone	*Mercury*	6
39	32	NORTH TO ALASKA	Johnny Horton	*Philips*	2
26	33	CHARIOT	Rhet Stoller	*Decca*	3
12	34	STRAWBERRY FAIR	Anthony Newley	*Decca*	9
27	35	GURNEY SLADE	Max Harris	*Fontana*	9
28	36	LONELY PUP (IN A CHRISTMAS SHOP)	Adam Faith	*Parlophone*	11
-	37	RUBBER BALL	Avons	*Columbia*	1
31	38	BLACK STOCKINGS	John Barry Seven	*Columbia*	5
36	39	MY LOVE FOR YOU	Johnny Mathis	*Fontana*	17
33	40	MY HEART HAS A MIND OF ITS OWN	Connie Francis	*MGM*	13

February 1961

□ Highest position disc reached ● Act's first ever week on chart

WEEK ENDING 2 FEBRUARY 1961

LW	TW	Title	Artist	Label	Wks
1	[1]	ARE YOU LONESOME TONIGHT?	Elvis Presley	*RCA*	3
5	[2]	PEPE	Duane Eddy	*London*	4
2	3	POETRY IN MOTION	Johnny Tillotson	*London*	10
18	4	SAILOR	Petula Clark	*Pye*	2
3	5	PORTRAIT OF MY LOVE	Matt Monro	*Parlophone*	8
10	6	YOU'RE SIXTEEN	Johnny Burnette	*London*	4
4	7	COUNTING TEARDROPS	Emile Ford & the Checkmates	*Pye*	9
6	8	I LOVE YOU	Cliff Richard	*Columbia*	10
24	9	RUBBER BALL	Bobby Vee	*London*	2
9	10	BUONA SERA	Mr. Acker Bilk	*Columbia*	8
16	11	RUBBER BALL	Marty Wilde	*Philips*	2
15	[12]	MANY TEARS AGO	Connie Francis	*MGM*	4
11	13	IT'S NOW OR NEVER	Elvis Presley	*RCA*	14
8	14	SAVE THE LAST DANCE FOR ME	Drifters	*London*	14
12	15	SWAY	Bobby Rydell	*Columbia*	8
13	16	LIKE STRANGERS	Everly Brothers	*London*	8
7	17	PERFIDIA	Ventures	*London*	10
14	18	STAY	Maurice Williams & the Zodiacs	*Top Rank*	5
27	19	SAILOR	Anne Shelton	*Philips*	2
28	20	A THOUSAND STARS	Billy Fury	*Decca*	3
22	21	PILTDOWN RIDES AGAIN	Piltdown Men	*Capitol*	3
25	22	PEPE	Russ Conway	*Columbia*	3
32	[23]	NORTH TO ALASKA	Johnny Horton	*Philips*	3
21	24	DOLL HOUSE	King Brothers	*Parlophone*	4
20	25	GOODNESS GRACIOUS ME	Peter Sellers & Sophia Loren	*Parlophone*	13
19	26	A SCOTTISH SOLDIER	Andy Stewart	*Top Rank*	3
23	27	BLUE ANGEL	Roy Orbison	*London*	14
26	28	MAN OF MYSTERY/THE STRANGER	Shadows	*Columbia*	13
17	29	LITTLE GIRL	Marty Wilde	*Philips*	7
37	[30]	RUBBER BALL	Avons	*Columbia*	2
29	31	ROCKING GOOSE	Johnny & the Hurricanes	*London*	18
-	32	NEW ORLEANS	U.S. Bonds	*Top Rank*	2
-	[33]	SHINE	Joe Brown and his Bruvvers	*Pye*	1
33	34	CHARIOT	Rhet Stoller	*Decca*	4
38	35	BLACK STOCKINGS	John Barry Seven	*Columbia*	6
30	36	BANGERS AND MASH	Peter Sellers & Sophia Loren	*Parlophone*	4
-	37	LET'S JUMP THE BROOMSTICK	Brenda Lee	*Brunswick*	1
-	38	AS LONG AS HE NEEDS ME	Shirley Bassey	*Columbia*	26
39	39	MY LOVE FOR YOU	Johnny Mathis	*Fontana*	18
-	40	FIRST TASTE OF LOVE	Ben E. King ●	*London*	1

WEEK ENDING 9 FEBRUARY 1961

LW	TW	Title	Artist	Label	Wks
1	[1]	ARE YOU LONESOME TONIGHT?	Elvis Presley	*RCA*	4
4	2	SAILOR	Petula Clark	*Pye*	3
3	3	POETRY IN MOTION	Johnny Tillotson	*London*	11
6	4	YOU'RE SIXTEEN	Johnny Burnette	*London*	5
2	5	PEPE	Duane Eddy	*London*	5
5	6	PORTRAIT OF MY LOVE	Matt Monro	*Parlophone*	9
9	7	RUBBER BALL	Bobby Vee	*London*	3
7	8	COUNTING TEARDROPS	Emile Ford & the Checkmates	*Pye*	10
10	9	BUONA SERA	Mr. Acker Bilk	*Columbia*	9
19	[10]	SAILOR	Anne Shelton	*Philips*	3
11	11	RUBBER BALL	Marty Wilde	*Philips*	3
8	12	I LOVE YOU	Cliff Richard	*Columbia*	11
14	13	SAVE THE LAST DANCE FOR ME	Drifters	*London*	15
20	[14]	A THOUSAND STARS	Billy Fury	*Decca*	4
18	15	STAY	Maurice Williams & the Zodiacs	*Top Rank*	6
21	16	PILTDOWN RIDES AGAIN	Piltdown Men	*Capitol*	4
15	17	SWAY	Bobby Rydell	*Columbia*	9
13	18	IT'S NOW OR NEVER	Elvis Presley	*RCA*	15
22	[19]	PEPE	Russ Conway	*Columbia*	4
12	20	MANY TEARS AGO	Connie Francis	*MGM*	5
17	21	PERFIDIA	Ventures	*London*	11
-	22	F.B.I.	Shadows	*Columbia*	1
32	23	NEW ORLEANS	U.S. Bonds	*Top Rank*	3
29	24	LITTLE GIRL	Marty Wilde	*Philips*	8
-	25	EBONY EYES	Everly Brothers	*Warner Brothers*	1
24	26	DOLL HOUSE	King Brothers	*Parlophone*	5
26	27	A SCOTTISH SOLDIER	Andy Stewart	*Top Rank*	4
-	28	THIS IS IT/WHO AM I?	Adam Faith	*Parlophone*	1
-	29	CALENDAR GIRL	Neil Sedaka	*RCA*	1
25	30	GOODNESS GRACIOUS ME	Peter Sellers & Sophia Loren	*Parlophone*	14
16	31	LIKE STRANGERS	Everly Brothers	*London*	9
23	32	NORTH TO ALASKA	Johnny Horton	*Philips*	4
37	33	LET'S JUMP THE BROOMSTICK	Brenda Lee	*Brunswick*	2
-	[34]	WHAT TO DO	Buddy Holly	*Coral*	1
34	35	CHARIOT	Rhet Stoller	*Decca*	5
33	36	SHINE	Joe Brown and his Bruvvers	*Pye*	2
36	37	BANGERS AND MASH	Peter Sellers & Sophia Loren	*Parlophone*	5
40	38	FIRST TASTE OF LOVE	Ben E. King	*London*	2
-	39	GINCHY	Bert Weedon	*Top Rank*	1
-	[40]	MEAN MEAN MAN	Wanda Jackson	*Capitol*	1

WEEK ENDING 16 FEBRUARY 1961

LW	TW	Title	Artist	Label	Wks
1	[1]	ARE YOU LONESOME TONIGHT?	Elvis Presley	*RCA*	5
2	2	SAILOR	Petula Clark	*Pye*	4
4	[3]	YOU'RE SIXTEEN	Johnny Burnette	*London*	6
7	[4]	RUBBER BALL	Bobby Vee	*London*	4
5	5	PEPE	Duane Eddy	*London*	6
22	[6]	F.B.I.	Shadows	*Columbia*	2
9	[7]	BUONA SERA	Mr. Acker Bilk	*Columbia*	10

■Three versions of *Rubber Ball* enter the charts, including the first week of chart action for one of the biggest American stars of the Sixties - Bobby Vee (26.01.61) ■ Two versions each of three different hits in the Top 20 - *Sailor*, *Pepe* and *Rubber Ball* (09.02.61) ■ The Everly Brothers *Ebony Eyes* is listed on its own for one week before becoming a double-sided hit with *Walk Right Back* (09.02.61)■

February 1961

☐ Highest position disc reached ● Act's first ever week on chart

LW	TW	Title	Artist	Label	Wks
25	8	EBONY EYES/WALK RIGHT BACK	Everly Brothers	Warner Bros	2
11	9	RUBBER BALL	Marty Wilde	Philips	4
3	10	POETRY IN MOTION	Johnny Tillotson	London	12
6	11	PORTRAIT OF MY LOVE	Matt Monro	Parlophone	10
10	12	SAILOR	Anne Shelton	Philips	4
28	13	THIS IS IT/WHO AM I?	Adam Faith	Parlophone	2
16	14	PILTDOWN RIDES AGAIN	Piltdown Men	Capitol	5
8	15	COUNTING TEARDROPS	Emile Ford & the Checkmates	Pye	11
12	16	I LOVE YOU	Cliff Richard	Columbia	12
23	17	NEW ORLEANS	U.S. Bonds	Top Rank	4
-	18	WILL YOU LOVE ME TOMORROW?	Shirelles ●	Top Rank	1
20	19	MANY TEARS AGO	Connie Francis	MGM	6
14	20	A THOUSAND STARS	Billy Fury	Decca	5
33	21	LET'S JUMP THE BROOMSTICK	Brenda Lee	Brunswick	3
19	22	PEPE	Russ Conway	Columbia	5
17	23	SWAY	Bobby Rydell	Columbia	10
29	24	CALENDAR GIRL	Neil Sedaka	RCA	2
18	25	IT'S NOW OR NEVER	Elvis Presley	RCA	16
27	26	A SCOTTISH SOLDIER	Andy Stewart	Top Rank	5
21	27	PERFIDIA	Ventures	London	12
15	28	STAY	Maurice Williams & the Zodiacs	Top Rank	7
38	29	FIRST TASTE OF LOVE	Ben E. King	London	3
13	30	SAVE THE LAST DANCE FOR ME	Drifters	London	16
-	31	MYSTERY GIRL	Jess Conrad	Decca	1
24	32	LITTLE GIRL	Marty Wilde	Philips	9
26	33	DOLL HOUSE	King Brothers	Parlophone	6
-	34	GATHER IN THE MUSHROOMS	Benny Hill ●	Pye	1
34	35	WHAT TO DO	Buddy Holly	Coral	2
36	36	SHINE	Joe Brown and his Bruvvers	Pye	3
39	37	GINCHY	Bert Weedon	Top Rank	2
-	38	THE WORLD IN MY ARMS	Nat 'King' Cole	Capitol	1
32	39	NORTH TO ALASKA	Johnny Horton	Philips	5
31	40	LIKE STRANGERS	Everly Brothers	London	10

WEEK ENDING 23 FEBRUARY 1961

LW	TW	Title	Artist	Label	Wks
2	1	SAILOR	Petula Clark	Pye	5
1	2	ARE YOU LONESOME TONIGHT?	Elvis Presley	RCA	6
8	3	EBONY EYES/WALK RIGHT BACK	Everly Brothers	Warner Bros	3
3	4	YOU'RE SIXTEEN	Johnny Burnette	London	7
13	5	WHO AM I?/THIS IS IT	Adam Faith	Parlophone	3
6	6	F.B.I.	Shadows	Columbia	3
4	7	RUBBER BALL	Bobby Vee	London	5
18	8	WILL YOU LOVE ME TOMORROW?	Shirelles	Top Rank	2
5	9	PEPE	Duane Eddy	London	7
24	10	CALENDAR GIRL	Neil Sedaka	RCA	3
7	11	BUONA SERA	Mr. Acker Bilk	Columbia	11
11	12	PORTRAIT OF MY LOVE	Matt Monro	Parlophone	11
9	13	RUBBER BALL	Marty Wilde	Philips	5
12	14	SAILOR	Anne Shelton	Philips	5
10	15	POETRY IN MOTION	Johnny Tillotson	London	13
17	16	NEW ORLEANS	U.S. Bonds	Top Rank	5
14	17	PILTDOWN RIDES AGAIN	Piltdown Men	Capitol	6
19	18	MANY TEARS AGO	Connie Francis	MGM	7
21	19	LET'S JUMP THE BROOMSTICK	Brenda Lee	Brunswick	4
20	20	A THOUSAND STARS	Billy Fury	Decca	6
15	21	COUNTING TEARDROPS	Emile Ford & the Checkmates	Pye	12
34	22	GATHER IN THE MUSHROOMS	Benny Hill	Pye	2
22	23	PEPE	Russ Conway	Columbia	6
-	24	RIDERS IN THE SKY	Ramrods ●	London	1
31	25	MYSTERY GIRL	Jess Conrad	Decca	2
16	26	I LOVE YOU	Cliff Richard	Columbia	13
28	27	STAY	Maurice Williams & the Zodiacs	Top Rank	8
26	28	A SCOTTISH SOLDIER	Andy Stewart	Top Rank	6
23	29	SWAY	Bobby Rydell	Columbia	11
-	30	WHEELS	String-A-Longs ●	London	1
-	31	ARE YOU SURE	Allisons ●	Fontana	1
29	32	FIRST TASTE OF LOVE	Ben E. King	London	4
36	33	SHINE	Joe Brown and his Bruvvers	Pye	4
25	34	IT'S NOW OR NEVER	Elvis Presley	RCA	17
37	35	GINCHY	Bert Weedon	Top Rank	3
33	36	DOLL HOUSE	King Brothers	Parlophone	7
27	37	PERFIDIA	Ventures	London	13
30	38	SAVE THE LAST DANCE FOR ME	Drifters	London	17
-	39	SAMANTHA	Kenny Ball and his Jazz Band ●	Pye	1
35	40	WHAT TO DO	Buddy Holly	Coral	3

WEEK ENDING 2 MARCH 1961

LW	TW	Title	Artist	Label	Wks
3	1	EBONY EYES/WALK RIGHT BACK	Everly Brothers	Warner Bros	4
1	2	SAILOR	Petula Clark	Pye	6
2	3	ARE YOU LONESOME TONIGHT?	Elvis Presley	RCA	7
31	4	ARE YOU SURE	Allisons	Fontana	2
8	5	WILL YOU LOVE ME TOMORROW?	Shirelles	Top Rank	3
5	6	WHO AM I?/THIS IS IT	Adam Faith	Parlophone	4
6	7	F.B.I.	Shadows	Columbia	4
10	8	CALENDAR GIRL	Neil Sedaka	RCA	4
4	9	YOU'RE SIXTEEN	Johnny Burnette	London	8
24	10	RIDERS IN THE SKY	Ramrods	London	2
7	11	RUBBER BALL	Bobby Vee	London	6
22	12	GATHER IN THE MUSHROOMS	Benny Hill	Pye	3
9	13	PEPE	Duane Eddy	London	8
19	14	LET'S JUMP THE BROOMSTICK	Brenda Lee	Brunswick	5
12	15	PORTRAIT OF MY LOVE	Matt Monro	Parlophone	12
30	16	WHEELS	String-A-Longs	London	2
11	17	BUONA SERA	Mr. Acker Bilk	Columbia	12
25	18	MYSTERY GIRL	Jess Conrad	Decca	3
13	19	RUBBER BALL	Marty Wilde	Philips	6
17	20	PILTDOWN RIDES AGAIN	Piltdown Men	Capitol	7
-	21	THEME FOR A DREAM	Cliff Richard	Columbia	1
14	22	SAILOR	Anne Shelton	Philips	6
16	23	NEW ORLEANS	U.S. Bonds	Top Rank	6
39	24	SAMANTHA	Kenny Ball and his Jazz Band	Pye	2
20	25	A THOUSAND STARS	Billy Fury	Decca	7
-	26	JA-DA	Johnny and the Hurricanes	London	1
32	27	FIRST TASTE OF LOVE	Ben E. King	London	5
18	28	MANY TEARS AGO	Connie Francis	MGM	8
28	29	A SCOTTISH SOLDIER	Andy Stewart	Top Rank	7
15	30	POETRY IN MOTION	Johnny Tillotson	London	14
23	31	PEPE	Russ Conway	Columbia	7
26	32	I LOVE YOU	Cliff Richard	Columbia	14
36	33	DOLL HOUSE	King Brothers	Parlophone	8
-	34	AFRICAN WALTZ	Johnny Dankworth	Columbia	1
-	35	76 TROMBONES	King Brothers	Parlophone	1
-	36	THE WORLD IN MY ARMS	Nat 'King' Cole	Capitol	2
34	37	IT'S NOW OR NEVER	Elvis Presley	RCA	18
27	38	STAY	Maurice Williams & the Zodiacs	Top Rank	9
29	39	SWAY	Bobby Rydell	Columbia	12
-	40	C'EST SI BON	Conway Twitty	MGM	1

WEEK ENDING 9 MARCH 1961

LW	TW	Title	Artist	Label	Wks
1	1	WALK RIGHT BACK/EBONY EYES	Everly Brothers	Warner Bros	5
4	2	ARE YOU SURE	Allisons	Fontana	3
2	3	SAILOR	Petula Clark	Pye	7
5	4	WILL YOU LOVE ME TOMORROW?	Shirelles	Top Rank	4
21	5	THEME FOR A DREAM	Cliff Richard	Columbia	2
6	6	WHO AM I?	Adam Faith	Parlophone	5
3	7	ARE YOU LONESOME TONIGHT?	Elvis Presley	RCA	8
7	8	F.B.I.	Shadows	Columbia	5
8	9	CALENDAR GIRL	Neil Sedaka	RCA	5
10	10	RIDERS IN THE SKY	Ramrods	London	3
16	11	WHEELS	String-A-Longs	London	3
14	12	LET'S JUMP THE BROOMSTICK	Brenda Lee	Brunswick	6
9	13	YOU'RE SIXTEEN	Johnny Burnette	London	9
26	14	JA-DA	Johnny and the Hurricanes	London	2
11	15	RUBBER BALL	Bobby Vee	London	7
12	16	GATHER IN THE MUSHROOMS	Benny Hill	Pye	4

In these weeks ■ Ben E. King's first solo hit *First Taste of Love* edges past the final Drifters' hit featuring his lead vocals *Save The Last Dance For Me* (16.02.61) ■ The Allisons' *Are You Sure*, Britains 1961 Eurovision entry, enjoys the first of six weeks at number two (09.03.61)■

LW	TW	Title	Artist	Label	Wks
13	17	PEPE	Duane Eddy	London	9
24	18	SAMANTHA	Kenny Ball and his Jazz Band	Pye	3
34	19	AFRICAN WALTZ	Johnny Dankworth	Columbia	2
17	20	BUONA SERA	Mr. Acker Bilk	Columbia	13
15	21	PORTRAIT OF MY LOVE	Matt Monro	Parlophone	13
-	22	MY KIND OF GIRL	Matt Monro	Parlophone	1
18	23	MYSTERY GIRL	Jess Conrad	Decca	4
-	24	WOODEN HEART	Elvis Presley	RCA	1
23	25	NEW ORLEANS	U.S. Bonds	Top Rank	7
20	26	PILTDOWN RIDES AGAIN	Piltdown Men	Capitol	8
-	27	BABY SITTIN' BOOGIE	Buzz Clifford ●	Fontana	1
25	28	A THOUSAND STARS	Billy Fury	Decca	8
29	29	A SCOTTISH SOLDIER	Andy Stewart	Top Rank	8
35	30	76 TROMBONES	King Brothers	Parlophone	2
22	31	SAILOR	Anne Shelton	Philips	7
27	32	FIRST TASTE OF LOVE	Ben E. King	London	6
-	33	WHAT AM I GONNA DO	Emile Ford & the Checkmates	Pye	1
19	34	RUBBER BALL	Marty Wilde	Philips	7
30	35	POETRY IN MOTION	Johnny Tillotson	London	15
31	36	PEPE	Russ Conway	Columbia	8
32	37	I LOVE YOU	Cliff Richard	Columbia	15
28	38	MANY TEARS AGO	Connie Francis	MGM	9
-	39	NORTH TO ALASKA	Johnny Horton	Philips	6
-	40	MARRY ME	Mike Preston	Decca	1

WEEK ENDING 16 MARCH 1961

LW	TW	Title	Artist	Label	Wks
1	1	WALK RIGHT BACK/EBONY EYES	Everly Brothers	Warner Bros	6
2	2	ARE YOU SURE	Allisons	Fontana	4
5	3	THEME FOR A DREAM	Cliff Richard	Columbia	3
24	4	WOODEN HEART	Elvis Presley	RCA	2
4	5	WILL YOU LOVE ME TOMORROW?	Shirelles	Top Rank	5
8	6	F.B.I.	Shadows	Columbia	6
6	7	WHO AM I?	Adam Faith	Parlophone	6
11	8	WHEELS	String-A-Longs	London	4
10	9	RIDERS IN THE SKY	Ramrods	London	4
22	10	MY KIND OF GIRL	Matt Monro	Parlophone	2
3	11	SAILOR	Petula Clark	Pye	8
9	12	CALENDAR GIRL	Neil Sedaka	RCA	6
7	13	ARE YOU LONESOME TONIGHT?	Elvis Presley	RCA	9
18	14	SAMANTHA	Kenny Ball and his Jazz Band	Pye	4
12	15	LET'S JUMP THE BROOMSTICK	Brenda Lee	Brunswick	7
14	16	JA-DA	Johnny and the Hurricanes	London	3
16	17	GATHER IN THE MUSHROOMS	Benny Hill	Pye	5
19	18	AFRICAN WALTZ	Johnny Dankworth	Columbia	3
13	19	YOU'RE SIXTEEN	Johnny Burnette	London	10
-	20	THEME FROM 'EXODUS'	Ferrante and Teicher ●	London	1
40	21	MARRY ME	Mike Preston	Decca	2
15	22	RUBBER BALL	Bobby Vee	London	8
27	23	BABY SITTIN' BOOGIE	Buzz Clifford	Fontana	2
17	24	PEPE	Duane Eddy	London	10
25	25	NEW ORLEANS	U.S. Bonds	Top Rank	8
29	26	A SCOTTISH SOLDIER	Andy Stewart	Top Rank	9
30	27	76 TROMBONES	King Brothers	Parlophone	3
-	28	AND THE HEAVENS CRIED	Anthony Newley	Decca	1
23	29	MYSTERY GIRL	Jess Conrad	Decca	5
20	30	BUONA SERA	Mr. Acker Bilk	Columbia	14
-	31	GOODNIGHT MRS. FLINTSTONE	Piltdown Men	Capitol	1
26	32	PILTDOWN RIDES AGAIN	Piltdown Men	Capitol	9
-	33	THEME FROM 'EXODUS'	Semprini ●	HMV	1
36	34	PEPE	Russ Conway	Columbia	9
28	35	A THOUSAND STARS	Billy Fury	Decca	9
32	36	FIRST TASTE OF LOVE	Ben E. King	London	7
-	37	DREAM GIRL	Mark Wynter	Decca	1
-	38	BABY ROO/WHERE THE BOYS ARE	Connie Francis	MGM	1
33	39	WHAT AM I GONNA DO	Emile Ford & the Checkmates	Pye	2
39	40	NORTH TO ALASKA	Johnny Horton	Philips	7

WEEK ENDING 23 MARCH 1961

LW	TW	Title	Artist	Label	Wks
4	1	WOODEN HEART	Elvis Presley	RCA	3
1	2	WALK RIGHT BACK/EBONY EYES	Everly Brothers	Warner Bros	7

March 1961

□ Highest position disc reached ● Act's first ever week on chart

LW	TW	Title	Artist	Label	Wks
2	3	ARE YOU SURE	Allisons	Fontana	5
3	4	THEME FOR A DREAM	Cliff Richard	Columbia	4
10	5	MY KIND OF GIRL	Matt Monro	Parlophone	3
5	6	WILL YOU LOVE ME TOMORROW?	Shirelles	Top Rank	6
6	7	F.B.I.	Shadows	Columbia	7
9	8	RIDERS IN THE SKY	Ramrods	London	5
20	9	THEME FROM 'EXODUS'	Ferrante and Teicher	London	2
11	10	SAILOR	Petula Clark	Pye	9
7	11	WHO AM I?	Adam Faith	Parlophone	7
28	12	AND THE HEAVENS CRIED	Anthony Newley	Decca	2
8	13	WHEELS	String-A-Longs	London	5
21	14	MARRY ME	Mike Preston	Decca	3
12	15	CALENDAR GIRL	Neil Sedaka	RCA	7
13	16	ARE YOU LONESOME TONIGHT?	Elvis Presley	RCA	10
14	17	SAMANTHA	Kenny Ball and his Jazz Band	Pye	5
15	18	LET'S JUMP THE BROOMSTICK	Brenda Lee	Brunswick	8
18	19	AFRICAN WALTZ	Johnny Dankworth	Columbia	4
16	20	JA-DA	Johnny and the Hurricanes	London	4
31	21	GOODNIGHT MRS. FLINTSTONE	Piltdown Men	Capitol	2
23	22	BABY SITTIN' BOOGIE	Buzz Clifford	Fontana	3
-	23	LAZY RIVER	Bobby Darin	London	1
27	24	76 TROMBONES	King Brothers	Parlophone	4
17	25	GATHER IN THE MUSHROOMS	Benny Hill	Pye	6
38	26	WHERE THE BOYS ARE/BABY ROO	Connie Francis	MGM	2
33	27	THEME FROM 'EXODUS'	Semprini	HMV	2
-	28	I COUNT THE TEARS	Drifters	London	1
24	29	PEPE	Duane Eddy	London	11
19	30	YOU'RE SIXTEEN	Johnny Burnette	London	11
37	31	DREAM GIRL	Mark Wynter	Decca	2
29	32	MYSTERY GIRL	Jess Conrad	Decca	6
22	33	RUBBER BALL	Bobby Vee	London	9
26	34	A SCOTTISH SOLDIER	Andy Stewart	Top Rank	10
30	35	BUONA SERA	Mr. Acker Bilk	Columbia	15
36	36	FIRST TASTE OF LOVE	Ben E. King	London	8
-	37	TRAMBONE	Krew Kats ●	HMV	1
-	38	DON'T TREAT ME LIKE A CHILD	Helen Shapiro ●	Columbia	1
25	39	NEW ORLEANS	U.S. Bonds	Top Rank	9
-	40	TILL THERE WAS YOU	Peggy Lee	Capitol	1

WEEK ENDING 30 MARCH 1961

LW	TW	Title	Artist	Label	Wks
1	1	WOODEN HEART	Elvis Presley	RCA	4
3	2	ARE YOU SURE	Allisons	Fontana	6
4	3	THEME FOR A DREAM	Cliff Richard	Columbia	5
2	4	WALK RIGHT BACK	Everly Brothers	Warner Bros	8
6	5	WILL YOU LOVE ME TOMORROW?	Shirelles	Top Rank	7
5	6	MY KIND OF GIRL	Matt Monro	Parlophone	4
12	7	AND THE HEAVENS CRIED	Anthony Newley	Decca	3
9	8	THEME FROM 'EXODUS'	Ferrante and Teicher	London	3
8	9	RIDERS IN THE SKY	Ramrods	London	6
23	10	LAZY RIVER	Bobby Darin	London	2
7	11	F.B.I.	Shadows	Columbia	8
13	12	WHEELS	String-A-Longs	London	6
17	13	SAMANTHA	Kenny Ball and his Jazz Band	Pye	6
11	14	WHO AM I?	Adam Faith	Parlophone	8
14	15	MARRY ME	Mike Preston	Decca	4
10	16	SAILOR	Petula Clark	Pye	10
15	17	CALENDAR GIRL	Neil Sedaka	RCA	8
16	18	ARE YOU LONESOME TONIGHT?	Elvis Presley	RCA	11
18	19	LET'S JUMP THE BROOMSTICK	Brenda Lee	Brunswick	9
22	20	BABY SITTIN' BOOGIE	Buzz Clifford	Fontana	4
26	21	WHERE THE BOYS ARE/BABY ROO	Connie Francis	MGM	3
20	22	JA-DA	Johnny and the Hurricanes	London	5
21	23	GOODNIGHT MRS. FLINTSTONE	Piltdown Men	Capitol	3
24	24	76 TROMBONES	King Brothers	Parlophone	5
27	25	THEME FROM 'EXODUS'	Semprini	HMV	3
19	26	AFRICAN WALTZ	Johnny Dankworth	Columbia	5
31	27	DREAM GIRL	Mark Wynter	Decca	3
38	28	DON'T TREAT ME LIKE A CHILD	Helen Shapiro	Columbia	2

■There are eleven instrumentals in the Top 40, plus two other mainly instrumental hits (by Kenny Ball and Mr. Acker Bilk), making this a bad week for lyricists (16.03.61) ■ First week of chart action for the girl who once topped the bill above the Beatles, Helen Shapiro (23.03.61) ■ *Ebony Eyes* no longer listed with *Walk Right Back*, possibly because its tragic tale of death on Flight 1203 denied it airplay on BBC radio (30.03.61)■

March 1961

☐ Highest position disc reached ● Act's first ever week on chart

LW	TW	Title	Artist	Label	Wks
-	29	YOU'RE DRIVING ME CRAZY	Temperance Seven ●	Parlophone	1
29	30	PEPE	Duane Eddy	London	12
28	31	I COUNT THE TEARS	Drifters	London	2
34	32	A SCOTTISH SOLDIER	Andy Stewart	Top Rank	11
-	33	GEE WHIZ IT'S YOU	Cliff Richard	Columbia	1
25	34	GATHER IN THE MUSHROOMS	Benny Hill	Pye	7
-	35	PONY TIME	Chubby Checker ●	Columbia	1
37	36	TRAMBONE	Krew Kats	HMV	2
36	37	FIRST TASTE OF LOVE	Ben E. King	London	9
30	38	YOU'RE SIXTEEN	Johnny Burnette	London	12
-	39	WAR PAINT	Brook Brothers ●	Pye	1
33	40	RUBBER BALL	Bobby Vee	London	10

WEEK ENDING 6 APRIL 1961

LW	TW	Title	Artist	Label	Wks
1	1	WOODEN HEART	Elvis Presley	RCA	5
2	2	ARE YOU SURE	Allisons	Fontana	7
3	3	THEME FOR A DREAM	Cliff Richard	Columbia	6
4	4	WALK RIGHT BACK	Everly Brothers	Warner Bros	9
5	5	WILL YOU LOVE ME TOMORROW?	Shirelles	Top Rank	8
6	6	MY KIND OF GIRL	Matt Monro	Parlophone	5
11	7	F.B.I.	Shadows	Columbia	9
8	8	THEME FROM 'EXODUS'	Ferrante and Teicher	London	4
7	9	AND THE HEAVENS CRIED	Anthony Newley	Decca	4
9	10	RIDERS IN THE SKY	Ramrods	London	7
12	11	WHEELS	String-A-Longs	London	7
10	12	LAZY RIVER	Bobby Darin	London	3
13	13	SAMANTHA	Kenny Ball and his Jazz Band	Pye	7
14	14	WHO AM I?	Adam Faith	Parlophone	9
15	15	MARRY ME	Mike Preston	Decca	5
21	16	WHERE THE BOYS ARE/BABY ROO	Connie Francis	MGM	4
20	17	BABY SITTIN' BOOGIE	Buzz Clifford	Fontana	5
23	18	GOODNIGHT MRS. FLINTSTONE	Piltdown Men	Capitol	4
24	19	76 TROMBONES	King Brothers	Parlophone	6
16	20	SAILOR	Petula Clark	Pye	11
18	21	ARE YOU LONESOME TONIGHT?	Elvis Presley	RCA	12
19	22	LET'S JUMP THE BROOMSTICK	Brenda Lee	Brunswick	10
22	23	JA-DA	Johnny and the Hurricanes	London	6
17	24	CALENDAR GIRL	Neil Sedaka	RCA	9
33	25	GEE WHIZ IT'S YOU	Cliff Richard	Columbia	2
29	26	YOU'RE DRIVING ME CRAZY	Temperance Seven	Parlophone	2
32	27	A SCOTTISH SOLDIER	Andy Stewart	Top Rank	12
25	28	THEME FROM 'EXODUS'	Semprini	HMV	4
26	29	AFRICAN WALTZ	Johnny Dankworth	Columbia	6
-	30	TILL THERE WAS YOU	Peggy Lee	Capitol	2
31	31	I COUNT THE TEARS	Drifters	London	3
39	32	WAR PAINT	Brook Brothers	Pye	2
-	33	I TOLD YOU SO	Jimmy Jones	MGM	1
30	34	PEPE	Duane Eddy	London	13
-	35	I WANNA LOVE MY LIFE AWAY	Gene Pitney ●	London	1
36	36	TRAMBONE	Krew Kats	HMV	3
-	37	ENTRY OF THE GLADIATORS	Nero and the Gladiators ●	Decca	1
28	38	DON'T TREAT ME LIKE A CHILD	Helen Shapiro	Columbia	3
37	39	FIRST TASTE OF LOVE	Ben E. King	London	10
35	40	PONY TIME	Chubby Checker	Columbia	2

WEEK ENDING 13 APRIL 1961

LW	TW	Title	Artist	Label	Wks
1	1	WOODEN HEART	Elvis Presley	RCA	6
2	2	ARE YOU SURE	Allisons	Fontana	8
4	3	WALK RIGHT BACK	Everly Brothers	Warner Bros	10
3	4	THEME FOR A DREAM	Cliff Richard	Columbia	7
12	5	LAZY RIVER	Bobby Darin	London	4
9	6	AND THE HEAVENS CRIED	Anthony Newley	Decca	5
6	7	MY KIND OF GIRL	Matt Monro	Parlophone	6
7	8	F.B.I.	Shadows	Columbia	10
8	9	THEME FROM 'EXODUS'	Ferrante and Teicher	London	5
16	10	WHERE THE BOYS ARE/BABY ROO	Connie Francis	MGM	5
14	11	WHO AM I?	Adam Faith	Parlophone	10
10	12	RIDERS IN THE SKY	Ramrods	London	8
26	13	YOU'RE DRIVING ME CRAZY	Temperance Seven	Parlophone	3
5	14	WILL YOU LOVE ME TOMORROW?	Shirelles	Top Rank	9
13	15	SAMANTHA	Kenny Ball and his Jazz Band	Pye	8
15	16	MARRY ME	Mike Preston	Decca	6
32	17	WAR PAINT	Brook Brothers	Pye	3
25	18	GEE WHIZ IT'S YOU	Cliff Richard	Columbia	3
17	19	BABY SITTIN' BOOGIE	Buzz Clifford	Fontana	6
11	20	WHEELS	String-A-Longs	London	8
24	21	CALENDAR GIRL	Neil Sedaka	RCA	10
29	22	AFRICAN WALTZ	Johnny Dankworth	Columbia	7
20	23	SAILOR	Petula Clark	Pye	12
-	24	BLUE MOON	Marcels ●	Pye	1
18	25	GOODNIGHT MRS. FLINTSTONE	Piltdown Men	Capitol	5
-	26	LITTLE BOY SAD	Johnny Burnette	London	1
19	27	76 TROMBONES	King Brothers	Parlophone	7
21	28	ARE YOU LONESOME TONIGHT?	Elvis Presley	RCA	13
38	29	DON'T TREAT ME LIKE A CHILD	Helen Shapiro	Columbia	4
22	30	LET'S JUMP THE BROOMSTICK	Brenda Lee	Brunswick	11
40	31	PONY TIME	Chubby Checker	Columbia	3
23	32	JA-DA	Johnny and the Hurricanes	London	7
36	33	TRAMBONE	Krew Kats	HMV	4
27	34	A SCOTTISH SOLDIER	Andy Stewart	Top Rank	13
35	35	I WANNA LOVE MY LIFE AWAY	Gene Pitney	London	2
-	36	MORE THAN I CAN SAY/STAYING IN	Bobby Vee	London	1
28	37	THEME FROM 'EXODUS'	Semprini	HMV	5
37	38	ENTRY OF THE GLADIATORS	Nero and the Gladiators	Decca	2
30	39	TILL THERE WAS YOU	Peggy Lee	Capitol	3
-	40	ON THE REBOUND	Floyd Cramer ●	RCA	1

WEEK ENDING 20 APRIL 1961

LW	TW	Title	Artist	Label	Wks
1	1	WOODEN HEART	Elvis Presley	RCA	7
2	2	ARE YOU SURE	Allisons	Fontana	9
5	3	LAZY RIVER	Bobby Darin	London	5
3	4	WALK RIGHT BACK	Everly Brothers	Warner Bros	11
7	5	MY KIND OF GIRL	Matt Monro	Parlophone	7
9	6	THEME FROM 'EXODUS'	Ferrante and Teicher	London	6
4	7	THEME FOR A DREAM	Cliff Richard	Columbia	8
8	8	F.B.I.	Shadows	Columbia	11
6	9	AND THE HEAVENS CRIED	Anthony Newley	Decca	6
13	10	YOU'RE DRIVING ME CRAZY	Temperance Seven	Parlophone	4
10	11	WHERE THE BOYS ARE/BABY ROO	Connie Francis	MGM	6
24	12	BLUE MOON	Marcels	Pye	2
15	13	SAMANTHA	Kenny Ball and his Jazz Band	Pye	9
17	14	WAR PAINT	Brook Brothers	Pye	4
18	15	GEE WHIZ IT'S YOU	Cliff Richard	Columbia	4
14	16	WILL YOU LOVE ME TOMORROW?	Shirelles	Top Rank	10
22	17	AFRICAN WALTZ	Johnny Dankworth	Columbia	8
11	18	WHO AM I?	Adam Faith	Parlophone	11
12	19	RIDERS IN THE SKY	Ramrods	London	9
20	20	WHEELS	String-A-Longs	London	9
29	21	DON'T TREAT ME LIKE A CHILD	Helen Shapiro	Columbia	5
16	22	MARRY ME	Mike Preston	Decca	7
19	23	BABY SITTIN' BOOGIE	Buzz Clifford	Fontana	7
26	24	LITTLE BOY SAD	Johnny Burnette	London	2
27	25	76 TROMBONES	King Brothers	Parlophone	8
28	26	ARE YOU LONESOME TONIGHT?	Elvis Presley	RCA	14
31	27	PONY TIME	Chubby Checker	Columbia	4
35	28	I WANNA LOVE MY LIFE AWAY	Gene Pitney	London	3
36	29	MORE THAN I CAN SAY/STAYING IN	Bobby Vee	London	2
-	30	THEME FROM DIXIE	Duane Eddy	London	1
23	31	SAILOR	Petula Clark	Pye	13
21	32	CALENDAR GIRL	Neil Sedaka	RCA	11
25	33	GOODNIGHT MRS. FLINTSTONE	Piltdown Men	Capitol	6
-	34	100 POUNDS OF CLAY	Craig Douglas	Top Rank	1
40	35	ON THE REBOUND	Floyd Cramer	RCA	2
30	36	LET'S JUMP THE BROOMSTICK	Brenda Lee	Brunswick	12
38	37	ENTRY OF THE GLADIATORS	Nero and the Gladiators	Decca	3
32	38	JA-DA	Johnny and the Hurricanes	London	8
34	39	A SCOTTISH SOLDIER	Andy Stewart	Top Rank	14
37	40	THEME FROM 'EXODUS'	Semprini	HMV	6

In these weeks ■ Cliff Richard's *Gee Whiz It's You* was available only as an import, but it still gave him his twelfth Top 10 hit (30.03.61) ■ Ten of the top fifteen records, including the entire top six, are unchanged from the previous week (06.04.61) ■ Floyd Cramer's future number one comes in at number 40, one of the few records to start at the bottom rung and climb all the way to the top (13.04.61) ■

May 1961

□ Highest position disc reached ● Act's first ever week on chart

LW	TW	WEEK ENDING 27 APRIL 1961		Wks
1	[1]	WOODEN HEART Elvis Presley	*RCA*	8
3	[2]	LAZY RIVER Bobby Darin	*London*	6
2	3	ARE YOU SURE Allisons	*Fontana*	10
10	4	YOU'RE DRIVING ME CRAZY Temperance Seven	*Parlophone*	5
11	[5]	WHERE THE BOYS ARE/BABY ROO Connie Francis	*MGM*	7
15	6	GEE WHIZ IT'S YOU Cliff Richard	*Columbia*	5
12	7	BLUE MOON Marcels	*Pye*	3
4	8	WALK RIGHT BACK Everly Brothers	*Warner Bros*	12
14	9	WAR PAINT Brook Brothers	*Pye*	5
6	10	THEME FROM 'EXODUS' Ferrante and Teicher	*London*	7
7	11	THEME FOR A DREAM Cliff Richard	*Columbia*	9
16	12	WILL YOU LOVE ME TOMORROW? Shirelles	*Top Rank*	11
8	13	F.B.I. Shadows	*Columbia*	12
9	14	AND THE HEAVENS CRIED Anthony Newley	*Decca*	7
21	15	DON'T TREAT ME LIKE A CHILD Helen Shapiro	*Columbia*	6
5	16	MY KIND OF GIRL Matt Monro	*Parlophone*	8
17	17	AFRICAN WALTZ Johnny Dankworth	*Columbia*	9
30	18	THEME FROM DIXIE Duane Eddy	*London*	2
23	19	BABY SITTIN' BOOGIE Buzz Clifford	*Fontana*	8
13	20	SAMANTHA Kenny Ball and his Jazz Band	*Pye*	10
24	21	LITTLE BOY SAD Johnny Burnette	*London*	3
34	22	100 POUNDS OF CLAY Craig Douglas	*Top Rank*	2
35	23	ON THE REBOUND Floyd Cramer	*RCA*	3
22	24	MARRY ME Mike Preston	*Decca*	8
20	25	WHEELS String-A-Longs	*London*	10
28	[26]	I WANNA LOVE MY LIFE AWAY Gene Pitney	*London*	4
19	27	RIDERS IN THE SKY Ramrods	*London*	10
18	28	WHO AM I? Adam Faith	*Parlophone*	12
29	29	MORE THAN I CAN SAY/STAYING IN Bobby Vee	*London*	3
-	30	HOW WONDERFUL TO KNOW Pearl Carr and Teddy Johnson	*Columbia*	1
39	31	A SCOTTISH SOLDIER Andy Stewart	*Top Rank*	15
-	[32]	MUSKRAT RAMBLE Freddie Cannon	*Top Rank*	1
-	[33]	MY BLUE HEAVEN Frank Sinatra	*Capitol*	1
31	34	SAILOR Petula Clark	*Pye*	14
40	35	THEME FROM 'EXODUS' Semprini	*HMV*	7
27	36	PONY TIME Chubby Checker	*Columbia*	5
-	37	EASY GOING ME Adam Faith	*Parlophone*	1
38	38	JA-DA Johnny and the Hurricanes	*London*	9
-	39	ASIA MINOR Kokomo ●	*London*	1
-	40	TRAMBONE Krew Kats	*HMV*	5

LW	TW	WEEK ENDING 4 MAY 1961		Wks
7	[1]	BLUE MOON Marcels	*Pye*	4
1	2	WOODEN HEART Elvis Presley	*RCA*	9
4	3	YOU'RE DRIVING ME CRAZY Temperance Seven	*Parlophone*	6
6	[4]	GEE WHIZ IT'S YOU Cliff Richard	*Columbia*	6
9	[5]	WAR PAINT Brook Brothers	*Pye*	6
3	6	ARE YOU SURE Allisons	*Fontana*	11
15	7	DON'T TREAT ME LIKE A CHILD Helen Shapiro	*Columbia*	7
18	8	THEME FROM DIXIE Duane Eddy	*London*	3
17	[9]	AFRICAN WALTZ Johnny Dankworth	*Columbia*	10
5	10	WHERE THE BOYS ARE/BABY ROO Connie Francis	*MGM*	8
22	11	100 POUNDS OF CLAY Craig Douglas	*Top Rank*	3
2	12	LAZY RIVER Bobby Darin	*London*	7
29	13	MORE THAN I CAN SAY/STAYING IN Bobby Vee	*London*	4
21	14	LITTLE BOY SAD Johnny Burnette	*London*	4
23	15	ON THE REBOUND Floyd Cramer	*RCA*	4
10	16	THEME FROM 'EXODUS' Ferrante and Teicher	*London*	8
11	17	THEME FOR A DREAM Cliff Richard	*Columbia*	10
8	18	WALK RIGHT BACK Everly Brothers	*Warner Bros*	13
14	19	AND THE HEAVENS CRIED Anthony Newley	*Decca*	8
13	20	F.B.I. Shadows	*Columbia*	13
19	21	BABY SITTIN' BOOGIE Buzz Clifford	*Fontana*	9
16	22	MY KIND OF GIRL Matt Monro	*Parlophone*	9
37	23	EASY GOING ME Adam Faith	*Parlophone*	2
20	24	SAMANTHA Kenny Ball and his Jazz Band	*Pye*	11
12	25	WILL YOU LOVE ME TOMORROW? Shirelles	*Top Rank*	12
31	26	A SCOTTISH SOLDIER Andy Stewart	*Top Rank*	16
30	27	HOW WONDERFUL TO KNOW Pearl Carr and Teddy Johnson	*Columbia*	2
-	28	RUNAWAY Del Shannon ●	*London*	1
25	29	WHEELS String-A-Longs	*London*	11
26	30	I WANNA LOVE MY LIFE AWAY Gene Pitney	*London*	5
24	31	MARRY ME Mike Preston	*Decca*	9
27	32	RIDERS IN THE SKY Ramrods	*London*	11
32	33	MUSKRAT RAMBLE Freddie Cannon	*Top Rank*	2
-	34	76 TROMBONES King Brothers	*Parlophone*	9
39	[35]	ASIA MINOR Kokomo	*London*	2
28	36	WHO AM I? Adam Faith	*Parlophone*	13
33	37	MY BLUE HEAVEN Frank Sinatra	*Capitol*	2
-	38	WHAT'D I SAY Jerry Lee Lewis	*London*	1
-	39	BUT I DO Clarence 'Frogman' Henry ●	*Pye*	1
-	[40]	DON'T WORRY Billy Fury	*Decca*	1

LW	TW	WEEK ENDING 11 MAY 1961		Wks
1	[1]	BLUE MOON Marcels	*Pye*	5
3	2	YOU'RE DRIVING ME CRAZY Temperance Seven	*Parlophone*	7
7	[3]	DON'T TREAT ME LIKE A CHILD Helen Shapiro	*Columbia*	8
13	[4]	MORE THAN I CAN SAY Bobby Vee	*London*	5
2	5	WOODEN HEART Elvis Presley	*RCA*	10
15	6	ON THE REBOUND Floyd Cramer	*RCA*	5
8	[7]	THEME FROM DIXIE Duane Eddy	*London*	4
5	8	WAR PAINT Brook Brothers	*Pye*	7
11	[9]	100 POUNDS OF CLAY Craig Douglas	*Top Rank*	4
9	10	AFRICAN WALTZ Johnny Dankworth	*Columbia*	11
4	11	GEE WHIZ IT'S YOU Cliff Richard	*Columbia*	7
14	[12]	LITTLE BOY SAD Johnny Burnette	*London*	5
28	13	RUNAWAY Del Shannon	*London*	2
23	14	EASY GOING ME Adam Faith	*Parlophone*	3
16	15	THEME FROM 'EXODUS' Ferrante and Teicher	*London*	9
12	16	LAZY RIVER Bobby Darin	*London*	8
10	17	WHERE THE BOYS ARE Connie Francis	*MGM*	9
6	18	ARE YOU SURE Allisons	*Fontana*	12
-	19	FRIGHTENED CITY Shadows	*Columbia*	1
20	20	F.B.I. Shadows	*Columbia*	14
38	21	WHAT'D I SAY Jerry Lee Lewis	*London*	2
19	22	AND THE HEAVENS CRIED Anthony Newley	*Decca*	9
27	[23]	HOW WONDERFUL TO KNOW Pearl Carr and Teddy Johnson	*Columbia*	3
24	24	SAMANTHA Kenny Ball and his Jazz Band	*Pye*	12
26	25	A SCOTTISH SOLDIER Andy Stewart	*Top Rank*	17
30	[26]	I WANNA LOVE MY LIFE AWAY Gene Pitney	*London*	6
18	27	WALK RIGHT BACK Everly Brothers	*Warner Bros*	14
39	28	BUT I DO Clarence 'Frogman' Henry	*Pye*	2
17	29	THEME FOR A DREAM Cliff Richard	*Columbia*	11
22	30	MY KIND OF GIRL Matt Monro	*Parlophone*	10
21	31	BABY SITTIN' BOOGIE Buzz Clifford	*Fontana*	10
25	32	WILL YOU LOVE ME TOMORROW? Shirelles	*Top Rank*	13
29	33	WHEELS String-A-Longs	*London*	12
-	34	HAVE A DRINK ON ME Lonnie Donegan	*Pye*	1
37	35	MY BLUE HEAVEN Frank Sinatra	*Capitol*	3
-	36	I STILL LOVE YOU ALL Kenny Ball and his Jazzmen	*Pye*	1
-	[37]	COWBOY JIMMY JOE Alma Cogan	*Columbia*	1
35	38	ASIA MINOR Kokomo	*London*	3
34	39	76 TROMBONES King Brothers	*Parlophone*	10
32	40	RIDERS IN THE SKY Ramrods	*London*	12

LW	TW	WEEK ENDING 18 MAY 1961		Wks
6	[1]	ON THE REBOUND Floyd Cramer	*RCA*	6
2	2	YOU'RE DRIVING ME CRAZY Temperance Seven	*Parlophone*	8
1	3	BLUE MOON Marcels	*Pye*	6
4	[4]	MORE THAN I CAN SAY Bobby Vee	*London*	6
3	5	DON'T TREAT ME LIKE A CHILD Helen Shapiro	*Columbia*	9
5	6	WOODEN HEART Elvis Presley	*RCA*	11

■The Marcels' classic doo-wop version of *Blue Moon* (a song which Elvis Presley had already released on an album) knocks the King from number one (04.05.61) ■ Six artists in the Top 10, including the entire Top Three, are enjoying their first hit (11.05.61) ■ The Shadows feature on four hits in the Top 30 - two of their own and two by Cliff Richard (11.05.61)■

May 1961

□ Highest position disc reached ● Act's first ever week on chart

LW	TW	Title / Artist	Label	Wks
7	7	THEME FROM DIXIE Duane Eddy	London	5
13	8	RUNAWAY Del Shannon	London	3
19	9	FRIGHTENED CITY Shadows	Columbia	2
9	10	100 POUNDS OF CLAY Craig Douglas	Top Rank	5
11	11	GEE WHIZ IT'S YOU Cliff Richard	Columbia	8
14	12	EASY GOING ME Adam Faith	Parlophone	4
8	13	WAR PAINT Brook Brothers	Pye	8
21	14	WHAT'D I SAY Jerry Lee Lewis	London	3
12	15	LITTLE BOY SAD Johnny Burnette	London	6
10	16	AFRICAN WALTZ Johnny Dankworth	Columbia	12
15	17	THEME FROM 'EXODUS' Ferrante and Teicher	London	10
34	18	HAVE A DRINK ON ME Lonnie Donegan	Pye	2
28	19	BUT I DO Clarence 'Frogman' Henry	Pye	3
-	20	YOU'LL NEVER KNOW Shirley Bassey	Columbia	1
18	21	ARE YOU SURE Allisons	Fontana	13
16	22	LAZY RIVER Bobby Darin	London	9
17	23	WHERE THE BOYS ARE Connie Francis	MGM	10
23	24	HOW WONDERFUL TO KNOW Pearl Carr and Teddy Johnson	Columbia	4
20	25	F.B.I. Shadows	Columbia	15
36	26	I STILL LOVE YOU ALL Kenny Ball and his Jazzmen	Pye	2
22	27	AND THE HEAVENS CRIED Anthony Newley	Decca	10
26	28	I WANNA LOVE MY LIFE AWAY Gene Pitney	London	7
-	29	MOTHER-IN-LAW Ernie K-Doe ●	London	1
31	30	BABY SITTIN' BOOGIE Buzz Clifford	Fontana	11
24	31	SAMANTHA Kenny Ball and his Jazz Band	Pye	13
25	32	A SCOTTISH SOLDIER Andy Stewart	Top Rank	18
29	33	THEME FOR A DREAM Cliff Richard	Columbia	12
27	34	WALK RIGHT BACK Everly Brothers	Warner Bros	15
35	35	MY BLUE HEAVEN Frank Sinatra	Capitol	4
-	36	WORDS Allisons	Fontana	1
-	37	LITTLE DEVIL Neil Sedaka	RCA	1
37	38	COWBOY JIMMY JOE Alma Cogan	Columbia	2
32	39	WILL YOU LOVE ME TOMORROW? Shirelles	Top Rank	14
30	40	MY KIND OF GIRL Matt Monro	Parlophone	11

LW	TW	*WEEK ENDING* 25 MAY 1961		Wks
2	1	YOU'RE DRIVING ME CRAZY Temperance Seven	Parlophone	9
3	2	BLUE MOON Marcels	Pye	7
1	3	ON THE REBOUND Floyd Cramer	RCA	7
9	4	FRIGHTENED CITY Shadows	Columbia	3
8	5	RUNAWAY Del Shannon	London	4
4	6	MORE THAN I CAN SAY Bobby Vee	London	7
6	7	WOODEN HEART Elvis Presley	RCA	12
7	8	THEME FROM DIXIE Duane Eddy	London	6
13	9	WAR PAINT Brook Brothers	Pye	9
10	10	100 POUNDS OF CLAY Craig Douglas	Top Rank	6
5	11	DON'T TREAT ME LIKE A CHILD Helen Shapiro	Columbia	10
12	12	EASY GOING ME Adam Faith	Parlophone	5
11	13	GEE WHIZ IT'S YOU Cliff Richard	Columbia	9
20	14	YOU'LL NEVER KNOW Shirley Bassey	Columbia	2
16	15	AFRICAN WALTZ Johnny Dankworth	Columbia	13
14	16	WHAT'D I SAY Jerry Lee Lewis	London	4
18	17	HAVE A DRINK ON ME Lonnie Donegan	Pye	3
17	18	THEME FROM 'EXODUS' Ferrante and Teicher	London	11
19	19	BUT I DO Clarence 'Frogman' Henry	Pye	4
15	20	LITTLE BOY SAD Johnny Burnette	London	7
21	21	ARE YOU SURE Allisons	Fontana	14
25	22	F.B.I. Shadows	Columbia	16
24	23	HOW WONDERFUL TO KNOW Pearl Carr and Teddy Johnson	Columbia	5
26	24	I STILL LOVE YOU ALL Kenny Ball and his Jazzmen	Pye	3
27	25	AND THE HEAVENS CRIED Anthony Newley	Decca	11
23	26	WHERE THE BOYS ARE Connie Francis	MGM	11
-	27	SURRENDER Elvis Presley	RCA	1
22	28	LAZY RIVER Bobby Darin	London	10
32	29	A SCOTTISH SOLDIER Andy Stewart	Top Rank	19
37	30	LITTLE DEVIL Neil Sedaka	RCA	2
-	31	HALFWAY TO PARADISE Billy Fury	Decca	1
34	32	WALK RIGHT BACK Everly Brothers	Warner Bros	16
31	33	SAMANTHA Kenny Ball and his Jazz Band	Pye	14
-	34	WHY NOT NOW?/CAN THIS BE LOVE? Matt Monro	Parlophone	1
36	35	WORDS Allisons	Fontana	2
-	36	I'VE TOLD EVERY LITTLE STAR Linda Scott ●	Columbia	1
33	37	THEME FOR A DREAM Cliff Richard	Columbia	13
-	38	RUNNING SCARED Roy Orbison	London	1
35	39	MY BLUE HEAVEN Frank Sinatra	Capitol	5
29	40	MOTHER-IN-LAW Ernie K-Doe	London	2

LW	TW	*WEEK ENDING* 1 JUNE 1961		Wks
27	1	SURRENDER Elvis Presley	RCA	2
5	2	RUNAWAY Del Shannon	London	5
4	3	FRIGHTENED CITY Shadows	Columbia	4
6	4	MORE THAN I CAN SAY Bobby Vee	London	8
2	5	BLUE MOON Marcels	Pye	8
3	6	ON THE REBOUND Floyd Cramer	RCA	8
11	7	DON'T TREAT ME LIKE A CHILD Helen Shapiro	Columbia	11
14	8	YOU'LL NEVER KNOW Shirley Bassey	Columbia	3
1	9	YOU'RE DRIVING ME CRAZY Temperance Seven	Parlophone	10
16	10	WHAT'D I SAY Jerry Lee Lewis	London	5
19	11	BUT I DO Clarence 'Frogman' Henry	Pye	5
17	12	HAVE A DRINK ON ME Lonnie Donegan	Pye	4
9	13	WAR PAINT Brook Brothers	Pye	10
12	14	EASY GOING ME Adam Faith	Parlophone	6
13	15	GEE WHIZ IT'S YOU Cliff Richard	Columbia	10
7	16	WOODEN HEART Elvis Presley	RCA	13
8	17	THEME FROM DIXIE Duane Eddy	London	7
30	18	LITTLE DEVIL Neil Sedaka	RCA	3
15	19	AFRICAN WALTZ Johnny Dankworth	Columbia	14
18	20	THEME FROM 'EXODUS' Ferrante and Teicher	London	12
10	21	100 POUNDS OF CLAY Craig Douglas	Top Rank	7
20	22	LITTLE BOY SAD Johnny Burnette	London	8
31	23	HALFWAY TO PARADISE Billy Fury	Decca	2
34	24	WHY NOT NOW?/CAN THIS BE LOVE? Matt Monro	Parlophone	2
36	25	I'VE TOLD EVERY LITTLE STAR Linda Scott	Columbia	2
23	26	HOW WONDERFUL TO KNOW Pearl Carr and Teddy Johnson	Columbia	6
38	27	RUNNING SCARED Roy Orbison	London	2
26	28	WHERE THE BOYS ARE Connie Francis	MGM	12
29	29	A SCOTTISH SOLDIER Andy Stewart	Top Rank	20
24	30	I STILL LOVE YOU ALL Kenny Ball and his Jazzmen	Pye	4
40	31	MOTHER-IN-LAW Ernie K-Doe	London	3
-	32	TRAVELIN' MAN/HELLO MARY LOU Ricky Nelson	London	1
22	33	F.B.I. Shadows	Columbia	17
35	34	WORDS Allisons	Fontana	3
28	35	LAZY RIVER Bobby Darin	London	11
-	36	THE BATTLE'S O'ER Andy Stewart	Top Rank	1
21	37	ARE YOU SURE Allisons	Fontana	15
-	38	I WANNA LOVE MY LIFE AWAY Gene Pitney	London	8
-	39	TRANSISTOR RADIO Benny Hill	Pye	1
-	40	BELLS OF AVIGNON Max Bygraves	Decca	1

LW	TW	*WEEK ENDING* 8 JUNE 1961		Wks
1	1	SURRENDER Elvis Presley	RCA	3
2	2	RUNAWAY Del Shannon	London	6
3	3	FRIGHTENED CITY Shadows	Columbia	5
4	4	MORE THAN I CAN SAY Bobby Vee	London	9
11	5	BUT I DO Clarence 'Frogman' Henry	Pye	6
7	6	DON'T TREAT ME LIKE A CHILD Helen Shapiro	Columbia	12
6	7	ON THE REBOUND Floyd Cramer	RCA	9
8	8	YOU'LL NEVER KNOW Shirley Bassey	Columbia	4
5	9	BLUE MOON Marcels	Pye	9
10	10	WHAT'D I SAY Jerry Lee Lewis	London	6
18	11	LITTLE DEVIL Neil Sedaka	RCA	4
12	12	HAVE A DRINK ON ME Lonnie Donegan	Pye	5
16	13	WOODEN HEART Elvis Presley	RCA	14
9	14	YOU'RE DRIVING ME CRAZY Temperance Seven	Parlophone	11

In these weeks ■ George Martin's first number one as a producer is *You're Driving Me Crazy* by the 1920s-style jazz band, the Temperance Seven (25.05.61) ■ In the same week that Elvis Presley's *Surrender* makes the highest leap to number one so far (27 to 1), *You're Driving Me Crazy* takes the second biggest tumble from the top, down to number nine (01.06.61)■

June 1961

☐ Highest position disc reached ● Act's first ever week on chart

LW	TW	Title	Artist	Label	Wks
14	**15**	EASY GOING ME	Adam Faith	Parlophone	7
15	**16**	GEE WHIZ IT'S YOU	Cliff Richard	Columbia	11
13	**17**	WAR PAINT	Brook Brothers	Pye	11
23	**18**	HALFWAY TO PARADISE	Billy Fury	Decca	3
17	**19**	THEME FROM DIXIE	Duane Eddy	London	8
32	**20**	HELLO MARY LOU	Ricky Nelson	London	2
27	**21**	RUNNING SCARED	Roy Orbison	London	3
25	**22**	I'VE TOLD EVERY LITTLE STAR	Linda Scott	Columbia	3
19	**23**	AFRICAN WALTZ	Johnny Dankworth	Columbia	15
21	**24**	100 POUNDS OF CLAY	Craig Douglas	Top Rank	8
39	**25**	TRANSISTOR RADIO	Benny Hill	Pye	2
22	**26**	LITTLE BOY SAD	Johnny Burnette	London	9
24	**27**	WHY NOT NOW?/CAN THIS BE LOVE?	Matt Monro	Parlophone	3
20	**28**	THEME FROM 'EXODUS'	Ferrante and Teicher	London	13
31	**29**	MOTHER-IN-LAW	Ernie K-Doe	London	4
36	**30**	THE BATTLE'S O'ER	Andy Stewart	Top Rank	2
30	**31**	I STILL LOVE YOU ALL	Kenny Ball and his Jazzmen	Pye	5
26	**32**	HOW WONDERFUL TO KNOW	Pearl Carr and Teddy Johnson	Columbia	7
-	**33**	WELL I ASK YOU	Eden Kane ●	Decca	1
29	**34**	A SCOTTISH SOLDIER	Andy Stewart	Top Rank	21
33	**35**	F.B.I.	Shadows	Columbia	18
40	**36**	BELLS OF AVIGNON	Max Bygraves	Decca	2
28	**37**	WHERE THE BOYS ARE	Connie Francis	MGM	13
-	**38**	TAKE GOOD CARE OF HER	Adam Wade	HMV	1
34	**39**	WORDS	Allisons	Fontana	4
37	**40**	ARE YOU SURE	Allisons	Fontana	16

WEEK ENDING 15 JUNE 1961

LW	TW	Title	Artist	Label	Wks
1	**1**	SURRENDER	Elvis Presley	RCA	4
2	**2**	RUNAWAY	Del Shannon	London	7
3	**3**	FRIGHTENED CITY	Shadows	Columbia	6
4	**4**	MORE THAN I CAN SAY	Bobby Vee	London	10
5	**5**	BUT I DO	Clarence 'Frogman' Henry	Pye	7
8	**6**	YOU'LL NEVER KNOW	Shirley Bassey	Columbia	5
6	**7**	DON'T TREAT ME LIKE A CHILD	Helen Shapiro	Columbia	13
12	**8**	HAVE A DRINK ON ME	Lonnie Donegan	Pye	6
18	**9**	HALFWAY TO PARADISE	Billy Fury	Decca	4
22	**10**	I'VE TOLD EVERY LITTLE STAR	Linda Scott	Columbia	4
20	**11**	HELLO MARY LOU	Ricky Nelson	London	3
7	**12**	ON THE REBOUND	Floyd Cramer	RCA	10
11	**13**	LITTLE DEVIL	Neil Sedaka	RCA	5
10	**14**	WHAT'D I SAY	Jerry Lee Lewis	London	7
9	**15**	BLUE MOON	Marcels	Pye	10
14	**16**	YOU'RE DRIVING ME CRAZY	Temperance Seven	Parlophone	12
21	**17**	RUNNING SCARED	Roy Orbison	London	4
33	**18**	WELL I ASK YOU	Eden Kane	Decca	2
13	**19**	WOODEN HEART	Elvis Presley	RCA	15
15	**20**	EASY GOING ME	Adam Faith	Parlophone	8
17	**21**	WAR PAINT	Brook Brothers	Pye	12
16	**22**	GEE WHIZ IT'S YOU	Cliff Richard	Columbia	12
-	**23**	POP GOES THE WEASEL/BEE BOM	Anthony Newley	Decca	1
-	**24**	PASADENA	Temperance Seven	Parlophone	1
27	**25**	WHY NOT NOW?/CAN THIS BE LOVE?	Matt Monro	Parlophone	4
25	**26**	TRANSISTOR RADIO	Benny Hill	Pye	3
-	**27**	TEMPTATION	Everly Brothers	Warner Brothers	1
28	**28**	THEME FROM 'EXODUS'	Ferrante and Teicher	London	14
19	**29**	THEME FROM DIXIE	Duane Eddy	London	9
23	**30**	AFRICAN WALTZ	Johnny Dankworth	Columbia	16
26	**31**	LITTLE BOY SAD	Johnny Burnette	London	10
-	**32**	BREAKING IN A BRAND NEW BROKEN HEART	Connie Francis	MGM	1
-	**33**	EXCLUSIVELY YOURS	Mark Wynter	Decca	1
-	**34**	WEEKEND	Eddie Cochran	London	1
30	**35**	THE BATTLE'S O'ER	Andy Stewart	Top Rank	3
29	**36**	MOTHER-IN-LAW	Ernie K-Doe	London	5
34	**37**	A SCOTTISH SOLDIER	Andy Stewart	Top Rank	22
24	**38**	100 POUNDS OF CLAY	Craig Douglas	Top Rank	9
-	**39**	THEME FROM 'THE MAGNIFICENT SEVEN'	Al Caiola ●	HMV	1
32	**40**	HOW WONDERFUL TO KNOW	Pearl Carr and Teddy Johnson	Columbia	8

WEEK ENDING 22 JUNE 1961

LW	TW	Title	Artist	Label	Wks
1	**1**	SURRENDER	Elvis Presley	RCA	5
2	**2**	RUNAWAY	Del Shannon	London	8
5	**3**	BUT I DO	Clarence 'Frogman' Henry	Pye	8
11	**4**	HELLO MARY LOU	Ricky Nelson	London	4
9	**5**	HALFWAY TO PARADISE	Billy Fury	Decca	5
3	**6**	FRIGHTENED CITY	Shadows	Columbia	7
10	**7**	I'VE TOLD EVERY LITTLE STAR	Linda Scott	Columbia	5
6	**8**	YOU'LL NEVER KNOW	Shirley Bassey	Columbia	6
13	**9**	LITTLE DEVIL	Neil Sedaka	RCA	6
24	**10**	PASADENA	Temperance Seven	Parlophone	2
8	**11**	HAVE A DRINK ON ME	Lonnie Donegan	Pye	7
27	**12**	TEMPTATION	Everly Brothers	Warner Brothers	2
4	**13**	MORE THAN I CAN SAY	Bobby Vee	London	11
17	**14**	RUNNING SCARED	Roy Orbison	London	5
23	**15**	POP GOES THE WEASEL/BEE BOM	Anthony Newley	Decca	2
18	**16**	WELL I ASK YOU	Eden Kane	Decca	3
7	**17**	DON'T TREAT ME LIKE A CHILD	Helen Shapiro	Columbia	14
12	**18**	ON THE REBOUND	Floyd Cramer	RCA	11
14	**19**	WHAT'D I SAY	Jerry Lee Lewis	London	8
19	**20**	WOODEN HEART	Elvis Presley	RCA	16
32	**21**	BREAKING IN A BRAND NEW BROKEN HEART	Connie Francis	MGM	2
15	**22**	BLUE MOON	Marcels	Pye	11
-	**23**	A GIRL LIKE YOU	Cliff Richard	Columbia	1
26	**24**	TRANSISTOR RADIO	Benny Hill	Pye	4
16	**25**	YOU'RE DRIVING ME CRAZY	Temperance Seven	Parlophone	13
25	**26**	WHY NOT NOW?/CAN THIS BE LOVE?	Matt Monro	Parlophone	5
28	**27**	THEME FROM 'EXODUS'	Ferrante and Teicher	London	15
35	**28**	THE BATTLE'S O'ER	Andy Stewart	Top Rank	4
37	**29**	A SCOTTISH SOLDIER	Andy Stewart	Top Rank	23
30	**30**	AFRICAN WALTZ	Johnny Dankworth	Columbia	17
-	**31**	RING OF FIRE	Duane Eddy	London	1
-	**32**	MARCHETA	Karl Denver ●	Decca	1
-	**33**	SHE SHE LITTLE SHEILA	Gene Vincent	Capitol	1
-	**34**	ONCE IN EVERY LIFETIME	Ken Dodd	Decca	1
39	**35**	THEME FROM 'THE MAGNIFICENT SEVEN'	Al Caiola	HMV	2
34	**36**	WEEKEND	Eddie Cochran	London	2
20	**37**	EASY GOING ME	Adam Faith	Parlophone	9
21	**38**	WAR PAINT	Brook Brothers	Pye	13
33	**39**	EXCLUSIVELY YOURS	Mark Wynter	Decca	2
36	**40**	MOTHER-IN-LAW	Ernie K-Doe	London	6

WEEK ENDING 29 JUNE 1961

LW	TW	Title	Artist	Label	Wks
2	**1**	RUNAWAY	Del Shannon	London	9
1	**2**	SURRENDER	Elvis Presley	RCA	6
4	**3**	HELLO MARY LOU	Ricky Nelson	London	5
10	**4**	PASADENA	Temperance Seven	Parlophone	3
12	**5**	TEMPTATION	Everly Brothers	Warner Brothers	3
6	**6**	FRIGHTENED CITY	Shadows	Columbia	8
5	**7**	HALFWAY TO PARADISE	Billy Fury	Decca	6
3	**8**	BUT I DO	Clarence 'Frogman' Henry	Pye	9
14	**9**	RUNNING SCARED	Roy Orbison	London	6
7	**10**	I'VE TOLD EVERY LITTLE STAR	Linda Scott	Columbia	6
8	**11**	YOU'LL NEVER KNOW	Shirley Bassey	Columbia	7
15	**12**	POP GOES THE WEASEL/BEE BOM	Anthony Newley	Decca	3
23	**13**	A GIRL LIKE YOU	Cliff Richard	Columbia	2
13	**14**	MORE THAN I CAN SAY	Bobby Vee	London	12
16	**15**	WELL I ASK YOU	Eden Kane	Decca	4
11	**16**	HAVE A DRINK ON ME	Lonnie Donegan	Pye	8
9	**17**	LITTLE DEVIL	Neil Sedaka	RCA	7
17	**18**	DON'T TREAT ME LIKE A CHILD	Helen Shapiro	Columbia	15

■For the first time, the bottom two places in the chart are taken by the same act, the Allisons (08.06.61) ■ The top four records are all by American male singers (22.06.61) ■ Two hits apiece for Elvis Presley and two lesser chart names, the Temperance Seven and Andy Stewart (22.06.61)■

June 1961

□ Highest position disc reached ● Act's first ever week on chart

LW	TW	Title	Artist	Label	Wks
19	19	WHAT'D I SAY	Jerry Lee Lewis	London	9
31	20	RING OF FIRE	Duane Eddy	London	2
18	21	ON THE REBOUND	Floyd Cramer	RCA	12
21	22	BREAKING IN A BRAND NEW BROKEN HEART	Connie Francis	MGM	3
20	23	WOODEN HEART	Elvis Presley	RCA	17
36	24	WEEKEND	Eddie Cochran	London	3
33	25	SHE SHE LITTLE SHEILA	Gene Vincent	Capitol	2
25	26	YOU'RE DRIVING ME CRAZY	Temperance Seven	Parlophone	14
22	27	BLUE MOON	Marcels	Pye	12
26	28	WHY NOT NOW?/CAN THIS BE LOVE?	Matt Monro	Parlophone	6
29	29	A SCOTTISH SOLDIER	Andy Stewart	Top Rank	24
28	30	THE BATTLE'S O'ER	Andy Stewart	Top Rank	5
24	31	TRANSISTOR RADIO	Benny Hill	Pye	5
34	32	ONCE IN EVERY LIFETIME	Ken Dodd	Decca	2
32	33	MARCHETA	Karl Denver	Decca	2
-	34	GEE WHIZ IT'S YOU	Cliff Richard	Columbia	13
30	35	AFRICAN WALTZ	Johnny Dankworth	Columbia	18
39	36	EXCLUSIVELY YOURS	Mark Wynter	Decca	3
35	37	THEME FROM 'THE MAGNIFICENT SEVEN'	Al Caiola	HMV	3
37	38	EASY GOING ME	Adam Faith	Parlophone	10
27	39	THEME FROM 'EXODUS'	Ferrante and Teicher	London	16
-	40	BELLS OF AVIGNON	Max Bygraves	Decca	3

WEEK ENDING 6 JULY 1961

LW	TW	Title	Artist	Label	Wks
1	[1]	RUNAWAY	Del Shannon	London	10
3	[2]	HELLO MARY LOU	Ricky Nelson	London	6
5	3	TEMPTATION	Everly Brothers	Warner Brothers	4
4	[4]	PASADENA	Temperance Seven	Parlophone	4
13	5	A GIRL LIKE YOU	Cliff Richard	Columbia	3
2	6	SURRENDER	Elvis Presley	RCA	7
7	7	HALFWAY TO PARADISE	Billy Fury	Decca	7
8	8	BUT I DO	Clarence 'Frogman' Henry	Pye	10
6	9	FRIGHTENED CITY	Shadows	Columbia	9
9	10	RUNNING SCARED	Roy Orbison	London	7
15	11	WELL I ASK YOU	Eden Kane	Decca	5
10	12	I'VE TOLD EVERY LITTLE STAR	Linda Scott	Columbia	7
12	13	POP GOES THE WEASEL	Anthony Newley	Decca	4
11	14	YOU'LL NEVER KNOW	Shirley Bassey	Columbia	8
14	15	MORE THAN I CAN SAY	Bobby Vee	London	13
17	16	LITTLE DEVIL	Neil Sedaka	RCA	8
20	[17]	RING OF FIRE	Duane Eddy	London	3
16	18	HAVE A DRINK ON ME	Lonnie Donegan	Pye	9
22	19	BREAKING IN A BRAND NEW BROKEN HEART	Connie Francis	MGM	4
24	20	WEEKEND	Eddie Cochran	London	4
19	21	WHAT'D I SAY	Jerry Lee Lewis	London	10
25	22	SHE SHE LITTLE SHEILA	Gene Vincent	Capitol	3
-	23	WHEELS CHA CHA	Joe Loss ●	HMV	1
18	24	DON'T TREAT ME LIKE A CHILD	Helen Shapiro	Columbia	16
-	25	TIME	Craig Douglas	Top Rank	1
23	26	WOODEN HEART	Elvis Presley	RCA	18
-	27	YOU DON'T KNOW	Helen Shapiro	Columbia	1
21	28	ON THE REBOUND	Floyd Cramer	RCA	13
33	29	MARCHETA	Karl Denver	Decca	3
29	30	A SCOTTISH SOLDIER	Andy Stewart	Top Rank	25
32	31	ONCE IN EVERY LIFETIME	Ken Dodd	Decca	3
36	[32]	EXCLUSIVELY YOURS	Mark Wynter	Decca	4
26	33	YOU'RE DRIVING ME CRAZY	Temperance Seven	Parlophone	15
37	[34]	THEME FROM 'THE MAGNIFICENT SEVEN'	Al Caiola	HMV	4
-	35	MOODY RIVER	Pat Boone	London	1
28	36	WHY NOT NOW?/CAN THIS BE LOVE?	Matt Monro	Parlophone	7
-	37	BABY I DON'T CARE	Buddy Holly	Coral	1
-	[38]	TAKE GOOD CARE OF HER	Adam Wade	HMV	2
30	39	THE BATTLE'S O'ER	Andy Stewart	Top Rank	6
-	[40]	DON'T JUMP OFF THE ROOF DAD	Tommy Cooper ●	Palette	1

WEEK ENDING 13 JULY 1961

LW	TW	Title	Artist	Label	Wks
1	[1]	RUNAWAY	Del Shannon	London	11
2	[2]	HELLO MARY LOU	Ricky Nelson	London	7
3	3	TEMPTATION	Everly Brothers	Warner Brothers	5
7	4	HALFWAY TO PARADISE	Billy Fury	Decca	8
5	5	A GIRL LIKE YOU	Cliff Richard	Columbia	4
8	6	BUT I DO	Clarence 'Frogman' Henry	Pye	11
4	7	PASADENA	Temperance Seven	Parlophone	5
11	8	WELL I ASK YOU	Eden Kane	Decca	6
6	9	SURRENDER	Elvis Presley	RCA	8
9	10	FRIGHTENED CITY	Shadows	Columbia	10
10	11	RUNNING SCARED	Roy Orbison	London	8
13	[12]	POP GOES THE WEASEL	Anthony Newley	Decca	5
14	13	YOU'LL NEVER KNOW	Shirley Bassey	Columbia	9
27	14	YOU DON'T KNOW	Helen Shapiro	Columbia	2
19	15	BREAKING IN A BRAND NEW BROKEN HEART	Connie Francis	MGM	5
12	16	I'VE TOLD EVERY LITTLE STAR	Linda Scott	Columbia	8
20	17	WEEKEND	Eddie Cochran	London	5
17	18	RING OF FIRE	Duane Eddy	London	4
25	19	TIME	Craig Douglas	Top Rank	2
18	20	HAVE A DRINK ON ME	Lonnie Donegan	Pye	10
29	21	MARCHETA	Karl Denver	Decca	4
15	22	MORE THAN I CAN SAY	Bobby Vee	London	14
37	23	BABY I DON'T CARE	Buddy Holly	Coral	2
22	24	SHE SHE LITTLE SHEILA	Gene Vincent	Capitol	4
23	25	WHEELS CHA CHA	Joe Loss	HMV	2
35	26	MOODY RIVER	Pat Boone	London	2
16	27	LITTLE DEVIL	Neil Sedaka	RCA	9
31	[28]	ONCE IN EVERY LIFETIME	Ken Dodd	Decca	4
-	29	NATURE BOY	Bobby Darin	London	1
21	30	WHAT'D I SAY	Jerry Lee Lewis	London	11
30	31	A SCOTTISH SOLDIER	Andy Stewart	Top Rank	26
26	32	WOODEN HEART	Elvis Presley	RCA	19
24	33	DON'T TREAT ME LIKE A CHILD	Helen Shapiro	Columbia	17
-	34	OLD SMOKIE/HIGH VOLTAGE	Johnny & the Hurricanes	London	1
32	35	EXCLUSIVELY YOURS	Mark Wynter	Decca	5
-	36	STAND BY ME	Ben E. King	London	1
-	37	ROMEO	Petula Clark	Pye	1
38	[38]	TAKE GOOD CARE OF HER	Adam Wade	HMV	3
33	39	YOU'RE DRIVING ME CRAZY	Temperance Seven	Parlophone	16
-	40	BOLL WEEVIL SONG	Brook Benton	Mercury	1

WEEK ENDING 20 JULY 1961

LW	TW	Title	Artist	Label	Wks
3	[1]	TEMPTATION	Everly Brothers	Warner Brothers	6
1	2	RUNAWAY	Del Shannon	London	12
5	[3]	A GIRL LIKE YOU	Cliff Richard	Columbia	5
2	4	HELLO MARY LOU	Ricky Nelson	London	8
8	5	WELL I ASK YOU	Eden Kane	Decca	7
7	6	PASADENA	Temperance Seven	Parlophone	6
4	7	HALFWAY TO PARADISE	Billy Fury	Decca	9
6	8	BUT I DO	Clarence 'Frogman' Henry	Pye	12
14	9	YOU DON'T KNOW	Helen Shapiro	Columbia	3
11	10	RUNNING SCARED	Roy Orbison	London	9
9	11	SURRENDER	Elvis Presley	RCA	9
15	[12]	BREAKING IN A BRAND NEW BROKEN HEART	Connie Francis	MGM	6
19	13	TIME	Craig Douglas	Top Rank	3
10	14	FRIGHTENED CITY	Shadows	Columbia	11
17	[15]	WEEKEND	Eddie Cochran	London	6
23	16	BABY I DON'T CARE/VALLEY OF TEARS	Buddy Holly	Coral	3
12	17	POP GOES THE WEASEL	Anthony Newley	Decca	6
18	18	RING OF FIRE	Duane Eddy	London	5
37	19	ROMEO	Petula Clark	Pye	2
26	20	MOODY RIVER	Pat Boone	London	3
16	21	I'VE TOLD EVERY LITTLE STAR	Linda Scott	Columbia	9
-	22	YOU ALWAYS HURT THE ONE YOU LOVE	Clarence 'Frogman' Henry	Pye	1
13	23	YOU'LL NEVER KNOW	Shirley Bassey	Columbia	10
29	[24]	NATURE BOY	Bobby Darin	London	2
20	25	HAVE A DRINK ON ME	Lonnie Donegan	Pye	11

In these weeks ■ For the first time since the chart extended to a top 40, there are no new entries, just two old hits bouncing back (29.06.61) ■ Tommy Cooper's only chart moment is the only week of chart glory for the Palette label (06.07.61) ■ Ricky Nelson achieves the highest chart placing of his career, but is kept off the top by Del Shannon's classic *Runaway* (06.06.61) ■ Ben E. King's *Stand By Me* has to wait another 25 years before hitting number one (13.06.61) ■

LW	TW	Title	Artist	Label	Wks
24	26	SHE SHE LITTLE SHEILA	Gene Vincent	*Capitol*	5
27	27	LITTLE DEVIL	Neil Sedaka	*RCA*	10
25	28	WHEELS CHA CHA	Joe Loss	*HMV*	3
-	29	THAT'S MY HOME	Mr. Acker Bilk	*Columbia*	1
21	30	MARCHETA	Karl Denver	*Decca*	5
31	31	A SCOTTISH SOLDIER	Andy Stewart	*Top Rank*	27
34	32	OLD SMOKIE/HIGH VOLTAGE	Johnny & the Hurricanes	*London*	2
22	33	MORE THAN I CAN SAY	Bobby Vee	*London*	15
40	34	BOLL WEEVIL SONG	Brook Benton	*Mercury*	2
36	35	STAND BY ME	Ben E. King	*London*	2
33	36	DON'T TREAT ME LIKE A CHILD	Helen Shapiro	*Columbia*	18
28	37	ONCE IN EVERY LIFETIME	Ken Dodd	*Decca*	5
-	38	THE BATTLE'S O'ER	Andy Stewart	*Top Rank*	7
-	39	I'LL STEP DOWN	Garry Mills	*Decca*	1
30	40	WHAT'D I SAY	Jerry Lee Lewis	*London*	12

WEEK ENDING 27 JULY 1961

LW	TW	Title	Artist	Label	Wks
1	1	TEMPTATION	Everly Brothers	*Warner Brothers*	7
5	2	WELL I ASK YOU	Eden Kane	*Decca*	8
2	3	RUNAWAY	Del Shannon	*London*	13
9	4	YOU DON'T KNOW	Helen Shapiro	*Columbia*	4
3	5	A GIRL LIKE YOU	Cliff Richard	*Columbia*	6
4	6	HELLO MARY LOU	Ricky Nelson	*London*	9
7	7	HALFWAY TO PARADISE	Billy Fury	*Decca*	10
6	8	PASADENA	Temperance Seven	*Parlophone*	7
13	9	TIME	Craig Douglas	*Top Rank*	4
19	10	ROMEO	Petula Clark	*Pye*	3
10	11	RUNNING SCARED	Roy Orbison	*London*	10
14	12	FRIGHTENED CITY	Shadows	*Columbia*	12
8	13	BUT I DO	Clarence 'Frogman' Henry	*Pye*	13
22	14	YOU ALWAYS HURT THE ONE YOU LOVE	Clarence 'Frogman' Henry	*Pye*	2
16	15	BABY I DON'T CARE/VALLEY OF TEARS	Buddy Holly	*Coral*	4
11	16	SURRENDER	Elvis Presley	*RCA*	10
15	17	WEEKEND	Eddie Cochran	*London*	7
20	18	MOODY RIVER	Pat Boone	*London*	4
12	19	BREAKING IN A BRAND NEW BROKEN HEART	Connie Francis	*MGM*	7
-	20	DON'T YOU KNOW IT?	Adam Faith	*Parlophone*	1
23	21	YOU'LL NEVER KNOW	Shirley Bassey	*Columbia*	11
18	22	RING OF FIRE	Duane Eddy	*London*	6
17	23	POP GOES THE WEASEL	Anthony Newley	*Decca*	7
32	24	OLD SMOKIE/HIGH VOLTAGE	Johnny & the Hurricanes	*London*	3
29	25	THAT'S MY HOME	Mr. Acker Bilk	*Columbia*	2
30	26	MARCHETA	Karl Denver	*Decca*	6
21	27	I'VE TOLD EVERY LITTLE STAR	Linda Scott	*Columbia*	10
-	28	DUM DUM	Brenda Lee	*Brunswick*	1
-	29	QUARTER TO THREE	U.S. Bonds	*Top Rank*	1
34	30	BOLL WEEVIL SONG	Brook Benton	*Mercury*	3
24	31	NATURE BOY	Bobby Darin	*London*	3
31	32	A SCOTTISH SOLDIER	Andy Stewart	*Top Rank*	28
35	33	STAND BY ME	Ben E. King	*London*	3
26	34	SHE SHE LITTLE SHEILA	Gene Vincent	*Capitol*	6
25	35	HAVE A DRINK ON ME	Lonnie Donegan	*Pye*	12
28	36	WHEELS CHA CHA	Joe Loss	*HMV*	4
-	37	REACH FOR THE STARS/CLIMB EV'RY MOUNTAIN	Shirley Bassey	*Columbia*	1
38	38	THE BATTLE'S O'ER	Andy Stewart	*Top Rank*	8
33	39	MORE THAN I CAN SAY	Bobby Vee	*London*	16
27	40	LITTLE DEVIL	Neil Sedaka	*RCA*	11

August 1961

□ Highest position disc reached ● Act's first ever week on chart

WEEK ENDING 3 AUGUST 1961

LW	TW	Title	Artist	Label	Wks
2	1	WELL I ASK YOU	Eden Kane	*Decca*	9
4	2	YOU DON'T KNOW	Helen Shapiro	*Columbia*	5
7	3	HALFWAY TO PARADISE	Billy Fury	*Decca*	11
1	4	TEMPTATION	Everly Brothers	*Warner Brothers*	8
10	5	ROMEO	Petula Clark	*Pye*	4
3	6	RUNAWAY	Del Shannon	*London*	14
8	7	PASADENA	Temperance Seven	*Parlophone*	8
5	8	A GIRL LIKE YOU	Cliff Richard	*Columbia*	7
6	9	HELLO MARY LOU	Ricky Nelson	*London*	10
14	10	YOU ALWAYS HURT THE ONE YOU LOVE	Clarence 'Frogman' Henry	*Pye*	3
9	11	TIME	Craig Douglas	*Top Rank*	5
20	12	DON'T YOU KNOW IT?	Adam Faith	*Parlophone*	2
15	13	BABY I DON'T CARE/VALLEY OF TEARS	Buddy Holly	*Coral*	5
13	14	BUT I DO	Clarence 'Frogman' Henry	*Pye*	14
11	15	RUNNING SCARED	Roy Orbison	*London*	11
17	16	WEEKEND	Eddie Cochran	*London*	8
16	17	SURRENDER	Elvis Presley	*RCA*	11
26	18	MARCHETA	Karl Denver	*Decca*	7
12	19	FRIGHTENED CITY	Shadows	*Columbia*	13
18	20	MOODY RIVER	Pat Boone	*London*	5
29	21	QUARTER TO THREE	U.S. Bonds	*Top Rank*	2
19	22	BREAKING IN A BRAND NEW BROKEN HEART	Connie Francis	*MGM*	8
28	23	DUM DUM	Brenda Lee	*Brunswick*	2
37	24	REACH FOR THE STARS/CLIMB EV'RY MOUNTAIN	Shirley Bassey	*Columbia*	2
25	25	THAT'S MY HOME	Mr. Acker Bilk	*Columbia*	3
-	26	JOHNNY REMEMBER ME	John Leyton ●	*Top Rank*	1
33	27	STAND BY ME	Ben E. King	*London*	4
-	28	CUPID	Sam Cooke	*RCA*	1
32	29	A SCOTTISH SOLDIER	Andy Stewart	*Top Rank*	29
22	30	RING OF FIRE	Duane Eddy	*London*	7
36	31	WHEELS CHA CHA	Joe Loss	*HMV*	5
24	32	OLD SMOKIE/HIGH VOLTAGE	Johnny & the Hurricanes	*London*	4
27	33	I'VE TOLD EVERY LITTLE STAR	Linda Scott	*Columbia*	11
30	34	BOLL WEEVIL SONG	Brook Benton	*Mercury*	4
35	35	HAVE A DRINK ON ME	Lonnie Donegan	*Pye*	13
23	36	POP GOES THE WEASEL	Anthony Newley	*Decca*	8
31	37	NATURE BOY	Bobby Darin	*London*	4
34	38	SHE SHE LITTLE SHEILA	Gene Vincent	*Capitol*	7
-	39	QUITE A PARTY	Fireballs ●	*Pye*	1
-	40	HOW MANY TEARS	Bobby Vee	*London*	1

WEEK ENDING 10 AUGUST 1961

LW	TW	Title	Artist	Label	Wks
2	1	YOU DON'T KNOW	Helen Shapiro	*Columbia*	6
1	2	WELL I ASK YOU	Eden Kane	*Decca*	10
3	3	HALFWAY TO PARADISE	Billy Fury	*Decca*	12
5	4	ROMEO	Petula Clark	*Pye*	5
4	5	TEMPTATION	Everly Brothers	*Warner Brothers*	9
10	6	YOU ALWAYS HURT THE ONE YOU LOVE	Clarence 'Frogman' Henry	*Pye*	4
8	7	A GIRL LIKE YOU	Cliff Richard	*Columbia*	8
9	8	HELLO MARY LOU	Ricky Nelson	*London*	11
11	9	TIME	Craig Douglas	*Top Rank*	6
7	10	PASADENA	Temperance Seven	*Parlophone*	9
6	11	RUNAWAY	Del Shannon	*London*	15
13	12	BABY I DON'T CARE/VALLEY OF TEARS	Buddy Holly	*Coral*	6
12	13	DON'T YOU KNOW IT?	Adam Faith	*Parlophone*	3
24	14	REACH FOR THE STARS/CLIMB EV'RY MOUNTAIN	Shirley Bassey	*Columbia*	3
15	15	RUNNING SCARED	Roy Orbison	*London*	12
21	16	QUARTER TO THREE	U.S. Bonds	*Top Rank*	3
18	17	MARCHETA	Karl Denver	*Decca*	8
26	18	JOHNNY REMEMBER ME	John Leyton	*Top Rank*	2
29	19	A SCOTTISH SOLDIER	Andy Stewart	*Top Rank*	30
20	20	MOODY RIVER	Pat Boone	*London*	6
16	21	WEEKEND	Eddie Cochran	*London*	9
23	22	DUM DUM	Brenda Lee	*Brunswick*	3
14	23	BUT I DO	Clarence 'Frogman' Henry	*Pye*	15
17	24	SURRENDER	Elvis Presley	*RCA*	12
25	25	THAT'S MY HOME	Mr. Acker Bilk	*Columbia*	4
19	26	FRIGHTENED CITY	Shadows	*Columbia*	14
31	27	WHEELS CHA CHA	Joe Loss	*HMV*	6

■Helen Shapiro became the youngest number one hitmaker at 14 years and 310 days, since Frankie Lymon. She remains the youngest female soloist to top the charts (10.08.61) ■ Andy Stewart's *Scottish Soldier* returns to its peak position in its 30th week on the chart, no other record has ever been at its peak after so many weeks on the chart (10.08.61)■

August 1961

☐ Highest position disc reached ● Act's first ever week on chart

LW	TW	Title / Artist	Label	Wks
32	28	OLD SMOKIE/HIGH VOLTAGE Johnny & the Hurricanes	London	5
22	29	BREAKING IN A BRAND NEW BROKEN HEART Connie Francis	MGM	9
28	30	CUPID Sam Cooke	RCA	2
39	31	QUITE A PARTY Fireballs	Pye	2
34	32	BOLL WEEVIL SONG Brook Benton	Mercury	5
30	33	RING OF FIRE Duane Eddy	London	8
40	34	HOW MANY TEARS Bobby Vee	London	2
-	35	YOU'LL NEVER KNOW Shirley Bassey	Columbia	12
-	36	SAN ANTONIO ROSE Floyd Cramer	RCA	1
37	37	NATURE BOY Bobby Darin	London	5
-	38	WHAT KIND OF FOOL AM I? Anthony Newley	Decca	1
-	39	WOODEN HEART Elvis Presley	RCA	20
-	40	GIRLS Johnny Burnette	London	1

WEEK ENDING 17 AUGUST 1961

LW	TW	Title / Artist	Label	Wks
1	1	YOU DON'T KNOW Helen Shapiro	Columbia	7
18	2	JOHNNY REMEMBER ME John Leyton	Top Rank	3
2	3	WELL I ASK YOU Eden Kane	Decca	11
4	4	ROMEO Petula Clark	Pye	6
8	5	HELLO MARY LOU Ricky Nelson	London	12
14	6	REACH FOR THE STARS/CLIMB EV'RY MOUNTAIN Shirley Bassey	Columbia	4
3	7	HALFWAY TO PARADISE Billy Fury	Decca	13
5	8	TEMPTATION Everly Brothers	Warner Brothers	10
6	9	YOU ALWAYS HURT THE ONE YOU LOVE Clarence 'Frogman' Henry	Pye	5
9	10	TIME Craig Douglas	Top Rank	7
10	11	PASADENA Temperance Seven	Parlophone	10
7	12	A GIRL LIKE YOU Cliff Richard	Columbia	9
16	13	QUARTER TO THREE U.S. Bonds	Top Rank	4
11	14	RUNAWAY Del Shannon	London	16
13	15	DON'T YOU KNOW IT? Adam Faith	Parlophone	4
12	16	BABY I DON'T CARE/VALLEY OF TEARS Buddy Holly	Coral	7
21	17	WEEKEND Eddie Cochran	London	10
17	18	MARCHETA Karl Denver	Decca	9
34	19	HOW MANY TEARS Bobby Vee	London	3
20	20	MOODY RIVER Pat Boone	London	7
25	21	THAT'S MY HOME Mr. Acker Bilk	Columbia	5
23	22	BUT I DO Clarence 'Frogman' Henry	Pye	16
15	23	RUNNING SCARED Roy Orbison	London	13
19	24	A SCOTTISH SOLDIER Andy Stewart	Top Rank	31
26	25	FRIGHTENED CITY Shadows	Columbia	15
22	26	DUM DUM Brenda Lee	Brunswick	4
30	27	CUPID Sam Cooke	RCA	3
24	28	SURRENDER Elvis Presley	RCA	13
31	29	QUITE A PARTY Fireballs	Pye	3
33	30	RING OF FIRE Duane Eddy	London	9
32	31	BOLL WEEVIL SONG Brook Benton	Mercury	6
29	32	BREAKING IN A BRAND NEW BROKEN HEART Connie Francis	MGM	10
27	33	WHEELS CHA CHA Joe Loss	HMV	7
35	34	YOU'LL NEVER KNOW Shirley Bassey	Columbia	13
39	35	WOODEN HEART Elvis Presley	RCA	21
38	36	WHAT KIND OF FOOL AM I? Anthony Newley	Decca	2
40	37	GIRLS Johnny Burnette	London	2
37	38	NATURE BOY Bobby Darin	London	6
36	39	SAN ANTONIO ROSE Floyd Cramer	RCA	2
-	40	BABY SITTIN' Bobby Angelo ●	HMV	1

WEEK ENDING 24 AUGUST 1961

LW	TW	Title / Artist	Label	Wks
1	1	YOU DON'T KNOW Helen Shapiro	Columbia	8
2	2	JOHNNY REMEMBER ME John Leyton	Top Rank	4
4	3	ROMEO Petula Clark	Pye	7
3	4	WELL I ASK YOU Eden Kane	Decca	12
6	5	REACH FOR THE STARS/CLIMB EV'RY MOUNTAIN Shirley Bassey	Columbia	5
7	6	HALFWAY TO PARADISE Billy Fury	Decca	14
8	7	TEMPTATION Everly Brothers	Warner Brothers	11
5	8	HELLO MARY LOU Ricky Nelson	London	13
10	9	TIME Craig Douglas	Top Rank	8
9	10	YOU ALWAYS HURT THE ONE YOU LOVE Clarence 'Frogman' Henry	Pye	6
12	11	A GIRL LIKE YOU Cliff Richard	Columbia	10
15	12	DON'T YOU KNOW IT? Adam Faith	Parlophone	5
19	13	HOW MANY TEARS Bobby Vee	London	4
11	14	PASADENA Temperance Seven	Parlophone	11
18	15	MARCHETA Karl Denver	Decca	10
13	16	QUARTER TO THREE U.S. Bonds	Top Rank	5
16	17	BABY I DON'T CARE/VALLEY OF TEARS Buddy Holly	Coral	8
14	18	RUNAWAY Del Shannon	London	17
21	19	THAT'S MY HOME Mr. Acker Bilk	Columbia	6
17	20	WEEKEND Eddie Cochran	London	11
20	21	MOODY RIVER Pat Boone	London	8
27	22	CUPID Sam Cooke	RCA	4
26	23	DUM DUM Brenda Lee	Brunswick	5
22	24	BUT I DO Clarence 'Frogman' Henry	Pye	17
25	25	FRIGHTENED CITY Shadows	Columbia	16
24	26	A SCOTTISH SOLDIER Andy Stewart	Top Rank	32
23	27	RUNNING SCARED Roy Orbison	London	14
33	28	WHEELS CHA CHA Joe Loss	HMV	8
29	29	QUITE A PARTY Fireballs	Pye	4
40	30	BABY SITTIN' Bobby Angelo	HMV	2
-	31	WRITING ON THE WALL Tommy Steele	Decca	1
28	32	SURRENDER Elvis Presley	RCA	14
35	33	WOODEN HEART Elvis Presley	RCA	22
31	34	BOLL WEEVIL SONG Brook Benton	Mercury	7
32	35	BREAKING IN A BRAND NEW BROKEN HEART Connie Francis	MGM	11
34	36	YOU'LL NEVER KNOW Shirley Bassey	Columbia	14
36	37	WHAT KIND OF FOOL AM I? Anthony Newley	Decca	3
30	38	RING OF FIRE Duane Eddy	London	10
-	39	ONCE IN EVERY LIFETIME Ken Dodd	Decca	6
-	40	SAY IT WITH FLOWERS Dorothy Squires & Russ Conway	Columbia	1

WEEK ENDING 31 AUGUST 1961

LW	TW	Title / Artist	Label	Wks
2	1	JOHNNY REMEMBER ME John Leyton	Top Rank	5
1	2	YOU DON'T KNOW Helen Shapiro	Columbia	9
5	3	REACH FOR THE STARS/CLIMB EV'RY MOUNTAIN Shirley Bassey	Columbia	6
4	4	WELL I ASK YOU Eden Kane	Decca	13
6	5	HALFWAY TO PARADISE Billy Fury	Decca	15
3	6	ROMEO Petula Clark	Pye	8
16	7	QUARTER TO THREE U.S. Bonds	Top Rank	6
15	8	MARCHETA Karl Denver	Decca	11
14	9	PASADENA Temperance Seven	Parlophone	12
8	10	HELLO MARY LOU Ricky Nelson	London	14
9	11	TIME Craig Douglas	Top Rank	9
12	12	DON'T YOU KNOW IT? Adam Faith	Parlophone	6
10	13	YOU ALWAYS HURT THE ONE YOU LOVE Clarence 'Frogman' Henry	Pye	7
19	14	THAT'S MY HOME Mr. Acker Bilk	Columbia	7
11	15	A GIRL LIKE YOU Cliff Richard	Columbia	11
7	16	TEMPTATION Everly Brothers	Warner Brothers	12
13	17	HOW MANY TEARS Bobby Vee	London	5
22	18	CUPID Sam Cooke	RCA	5
17	19	BABY I DON'T CARE/VALLEY OF TEARS Buddy Holly	Coral	9
18	20	RUNAWAY Del Shannon	London	18
20	21	WEEKEND Eddie Cochran	London	12
-	22	AIN'T GONNA WASH FOR A WEEK Brook Brothers	Pye	1
28	23	WHEELS CHA CHA Joe Loss	HMV	9
26	24	A SCOTTISH SOLDIER Andy Stewart	Top Rank	33
23	25	DUM DUM Brenda Lee	Brunswick	6
25	26	FRIGHTENED CITY Shadows	Columbia	17
21	27	MOODY RIVER Pat Boone	London	9
24	28	BUT I DO Clarence 'Frogman' Henry	Pye	18
29	29	QUITE A PARTY Fireballs	Pye	5

In these weeks ■ *Time* by Craig Douglas spends three weeks at number 9, but none of them consecutively. This is the second of four consecutive hits by Craig which peak at number 9 (24.08.61) ■ The Fireballs, who also overdubbed backing tracks on some of Buddy Holly's posthumous hits, reach their UK chart peak. Their US number one of 1963 with Jimmy Gilmer will not hit the U.K. Top 40 (17.08.61) ■

LW	TW	Title	Artist	Label	Wks
31	30	WRITING ON THE WALL	Tommy Steele	Decca	2
-	31	SOMEDAY	Kenny Ball & his Jazzmen	Pye	1
34	32	BOLL WEEVIL SONG	Brook Benton	Mercury	8
27	33	RUNNING SCARED	Roy Orbison	London	15
39	34	ONCE IN EVERY LIFETIME	Ken Dodd	Decca	7
-	35	MICHAEL ROW THE BOAT	Lonnie Donegan	Pye	1
32	36	SURRENDER	Elvis Presley	RCA	15
-	37	LET'S TWIST AGAIN	Chubby Checker	Columbia	1
-	38	I'M GOING HOME	Gene Vincent	Capitol	1
-	39	SEA OF HEARTBREAK	Don Gibson ●	RCA	1
37	40	WHAT KIND OF FOOL AM I?	Anthony Newley	Decca	4

LW	TW	WEEK ENDING 7 SEPTEMBER 1961			Wks
1	1	JOHNNY REMEMBER ME	John Leyton	Top Rank	6
2	2	YOU DON'T KNOW	Helen Shapiro	Columbia	10
3	3	REACH FOR THE STARS/CLIMB EV'RY MOUNTAIN	Shirley Bassey	Columbia	7
5	4	HALFWAY TO PARADISE	Billy Fury	Decca	16
4	5	WELL I ASK YOU	Eden Kane	Decca	14
6	6	ROMEO	Petula Clark	Pye	9
14	7	THAT'S MY HOME	Mr. Acker Bilk	Columbia	8
8	8	MARCHETA	Karl Denver	Decca	12
7	9	QUARTER TO THREE	U.S. Bonds	Top Rank	7
10	10	HELLO MARY LOU	Ricky Nelson	London	15
17	11	HOW MANY TEARS	Bobby Vee	London	6
18	12	CUPID	Sam Cooke	RCA	6
12	13	DON'T YOU KNOW IT?	Adam Faith	Parlophone	7
9	14	PASADENA	Temperance Seven	Parlophone	13
13	15	YOU ALWAYS HURT THE ONE YOU LOVE	Clarence 'Frogman' Henry	Pye	8
19	16	BABY I DON'T CARE/VALLEY OF TEARS	Buddy Holly	Coral	10
-	17	WILD IN THE COUNTRY/I FEEL SO BAD	Elvis Presley	RCA	1
15	18	A GIRL LIKE YOU	Cliff Richard	Columbia	12
22	19	AIN'T GONNA WASH FOR A WEEK	Brook Brothers	Pye	2
11	20	TIME	Craig Douglas	Top Rank	10
35	21	MICHAEL ROW THE BOAT/LUMBERED	Lonnie Donegan	Pye	2
16	22	TEMPTATION	Everly Brothers	Warner Brothers	13
23	23	WHEELS CHA CHA	Joe Loss	HMV	10
-	24	KON-TIKI	Shadows	Columbia	1
24	25	A SCOTTISH SOLDIER	Andy Stewart	Top Rank	34
20	26	RUNAWAY	Del Shannon	London	19
21	27	WEEKEND	Eddie Cochran	London	13
31	28	SOMEDAY	Kenny Ball & his Jazzmen	Pye	2
29	29	QUITE A PARTY	Fireballs	Pye	6
26	30	FRIGHTENED CITY	Shadows	Columbia	18
25	31	DUM DUM	Brenda Lee	Brunswick	7
28	32	BUT I DO	Clarence 'Frogman' Henry	Pye	19
39	33	SEA OF HEARTBREAK	Don Gibson	RCA	2
30	34	WRITING ON THE WALL	Tommy Steele	Decca	3
27	35	MOODY RIVER	Pat Boone	London	10
38	36	I'M GOING HOME	Gene Vincent	Capitol	2
-	37	BREAKAWAY	Springfields ●	Philips	1
40	38	WHAT KIND OF FOOL AM I?	Anthony Newley	Decca	5
-	39	HEART AND SOUL	Jan and Dean	London	1
-	40	SAN ANTONIO ROSE	Floyd Cramer	RCA	3

September 1961

□ Highest position disc reached ● Act's first ever week on chart

LW	TW	WEEK ENDING 14 SEPTEMBER 1961			Wks
1	1	JOHNNY REMEMBER ME	John Leyton	Top Rank	7
3	2	REACH FOR THE STARS/CLIMB EV'RY MOUNTAIN	Shirley Bassey	Columbia	8
2	3	YOU DON'T KNOW	Helen Shapiro	Columbia	11
17	4	WILD IN THE COUNTRY/I FEEL SO BAD	Elvis Presley	RCA	2
5	5	WELL I ASK YOU	Eden Kane	Decca	15
4	6	HALFWAY TO PARADISE	Billy Fury	Decca	17
24	7	KON-TIKI	Shadows	Columbia	2
7	8	THAT'S MY HOME	Mr. Acker Bilk	Columbia	9
9	9	QUARTER TO THREE	U.S. Bonds	Top Rank	8
11	10	HOW MANY TEARS	Bobby Vee	London	7
12	11	CUPID	Sam Cooke	RCA	7
6	12	ROMEO	Petula Clark	Pye	10
19	13	AIN'T GONNA WASH FOR A WEEK	Brook Brothers	Pye	3
21	14	MICHAEL ROW THE BOAT/LUMBERED	Lonnie Donegan	Pye	3
14	15	PASADENA	Temperance Seven	Parlophone	14
10	16	HELLO MARY LOU	Ricky Nelson	London	16
15	17	YOU ALWAYS HURT THE ONE YOU LOVE	Clarence 'Frogman' Henry	Pye	9
8	18	MARCHETA	Karl Denver	Decca	13
-	19	MICHAEL	Highwaymen ●	HMV	1
-	20	HATS OFF TO LARRY	Del Shannon	London	1
13	21	DON'T YOU KNOW IT?	Adam Faith	Parlophone	8
16	22	BABY I DON'T CARE/VALLEY OF TEARS	Buddy Holly	Coral	11
20	23	TIME	Craig Douglas	Top Rank	11
-	24	JEALOUSY	Billy Fury	Decca	1
23	25	WHEELS CHA CHA	Joe Loss	HMV	11
18	26	A GIRL LIKE YOU	Cliff Richard	Columbia	13
25	27	A SCOTTISH SOLDIER	Andy Stewart	Top Rank	35
33	28	SEA OF HEARTBREAK	Don Gibson	RCA	3
28	29	SOMEDAY	Kenny Ball & his Jazzmen	Pye	3
-	30	SAY IT WITH FLOWERS	Dorothy Squires & Russ Conway	Columbia	2
22	31	TEMPTATION	Everly Brothers	Warner Brothers	14
-	32	TOGETHER	Connie Francis	MGM	1
-	33	TRUE LOVE	Terry Lightfoot & his New Orleans Jazzmen ●	Columbia	1
27	34	WEEKEND	Eddie Cochran	London	14
-	35	GET LOST	Eden Kane	Decca	1
-	36	YOU'LL ANSWER TO ME	Cleo Laine ●	Fontana	1
-	37	DRIVIN' HOME	Duane Eddy	London	1
38	38	WHAT KIND OF FOOL AM I?	Anthony Newley	Decca	6
37	39	BREAKAWAY	Springfields	Philips	2
39	40	HEART AND SOUL	Jan and Dean	London	2

LW	TW	WEEK ENDING 21 SEPTEMBER 1961			Wks
2	1	REACH FOR THE STARS/CLIMB EV'RY MOUNTAIN	Shirley Bassey	Columbia	9
1	2	JOHNNY REMEMBER ME	John Leyton	Top Rank	8
3	3	YOU DON'T KNOW	Helen Shapiro	Columbia	12
4	4	WILD IN THE COUNTRY/I FEEL SO BAD	Elvis Presley	RCA	3
7	5	KON-TIKI	Shadows	Columbia	3
14	6	MICHAEL ROW THE BOAT/LUMBERED	Lonnie Donegan	Pye	4
11	7	CUPID	Sam Cooke	RCA	8
5	8	WELL I ASK YOU	Eden Kane	Decca	16
6	9	HALFWAY TO PARADISE	Billy Fury	Decca	18
10	10	HOW MANY TEARS	Bobby Vee	London	8
8	11	THAT'S MY HOME	Mr. Acker Bilk	Columbia	10
24	12	JEALOUSY	Billy Fury	Decca	2
20	13	HATS OFF TO LARRY	Del Shannon	London	2
13	14	AIN'T GONNA WASH FOR A WEEK	Brook Brothers	Pye	4
32	15	TOGETHER	Connie Francis	MGM	2
9	16	QUARTER TO THREE	U.S. Bonds	Top Rank	9
19	17	MICHAEL	Highwaymen	HMV	2
12	18	ROMEO	Petula Clark	Pye	11
35	19	GET LOST	Eden Kane	Decca	2
36	20	YOU'LL ANSWER TO ME	Cleo Laine	Fontana	2
25	21	WHEELS CHA CHA	Joe Loss	HMV	12
18	22	MARCHETA	Karl Denver	Decca	14
17	23	YOU ALWAYS HURT THE ONE YOU LOVE	Clarence 'Frogman' Henry	Pye	10
30	24	SAY IT WITH FLOWERS	Dorothy Squires & Russ Conway	Columbia	3
16	25	HELLO MARY LOU	Ricky Nelson	London	17
15	26	PASADENA	Temperance Seven	Parlophone	15
28	27	SEA OF HEARTBREAK	Don Gibson	RCA	4
27	28	A SCOTTISH SOLDIER	Andy Stewart	Top Rank	36
23	29	TIME	Craig Douglas	Top Rank	12
22	30	BABY I DON'T CARE/VALLEY OF TEARS	Buddy Holly	Coral	12
29	31	SOMEDAY	Kenny Ball & his Jazzmen	Pye	4
26	32	A GIRL LIKE YOU	Cliff Richard	Columbia	14
37	33	DRIVIN' HOME	Duane Eddy	London	2

■The top eight singles are by British acts (07.09.61) ■ First chart week as a member of the Springfields, for Dusty Springfield whose chart career will extend into the Nineties (07.09.61) ■ The 36th and final chart week for Andy Stewart's *Scottish Soldier* (21.09.61) ■ Elvis Presley's run of consecutive number ones stops at four, as *Wild In The Country/I Feel So Bad* peaks at number four (14.09.61)■

September 1961

□ Highest position disc reached ● Act's first ever week on chart

LW	TW	Title / Artist	Label	Wks
-	34	ONCE IN EVERY LIFETIME Ken Dodd	Decca	8
21	35	DON'T YOU KNOW IT? Adam Faith	Parlophone	9
39	36	BREAKAWAY Springfields	Philips	3
-	37	I'M GOING HOME Gene Vincent	Capitol	3
40	38	HEART AND SOUL Jan and Dean	London	3
34	39	WEEKEND Eddie Cochran	London	15
33	40	TRUE LOVE Terry Lightfoot & his New Orleans Jazzmen	Columbia	2

WEEK ENDING 28 SEPTEMBER 1961

LW	TW	Title / Artist	Label	Wks
2	[1]	JOHNNY REMEMBER ME John Leyton	Top Rank	9
1	2	REACH FOR THE STARS Shirley Bassey	Columbia	10
3	3	YOU DON'T KNOW Helen Shapiro	Columbia	13
5	4	KON-TIKI Shadows	Columbia	4
4	5	WILD IN THE COUNTRY/I FEEL SO BAD Elvis Presley	RCA	4
12	6	JEALOUSY Billy Fury	Decca	3
17	7	MICHAEL Highwaymen	HMV	3
20	8	YOU'LL ANSWER TO ME Cleo Laine	Fontana	3
7	9	CUPID Sam Cooke	RCA	9
15	10	TOGETHER Connie Francis	MGM	3
6	11	MICHAEL ROW THE BOAT/LUMBERED Lonnie Donegan	Pye	5
19	12	GET LOST Eden Kane	Decca	3
13	13	HATS OFF TO LARRY Del Shannon	London	3
9	14	HALFWAY TO PARADISE Billy Fury	Decca	19
8	15	WELL I ASK YOU Eden Kane	Decca	17
11	16	THAT'S MY HOME Mr. Acker Bilk	Columbia	11
14	17	AIN'T GONNA WASH FOR A WEEK Brook Brothers	Pye	5
10	18	HOW MANY TEARS Bobby Vee	London	9
16	19	QUARTER TO THREE U.S. Bonds	Top Rank	10
27	20	SEA OF HEARTBREAK Don Gibson	RCA	5
18	21	ROMEO Petula Clark	Pye	12
21	22	WHEELS CHA CHA Joe Loss	HMV	13
24	[23]	SAY IT WITH FLOWERS Dorothy Squires & Russ Conway	Columbia	4
38	[24]	HEART AND SOUL Jan and Dean	London	4
-	25	WHO PUT THE BOMP Viscounts	Pye	1
-	26	WALKING BACK TO HAPPINESS Helen Shapiro	Columbia	1
-	27	CRYIN' Roy Orbison	London	1
22	28	MARCHETA Karl Denver	Decca	15
23	29	YOU ALWAYS HURT THE ONE YOU LOVE Clarence 'Frogman' Henry	Pye	11
33	[30]	DRIVIN' HOME Duane Eddy	London	3
36	[31]	BREAKAWAY Springfields	Philips	4
-	[32]	HOLE IN THE BUCKET Harry Belafonte and Odetta ●	RCA	1
34	33	ONCE IN EVERY LIFETIME Ken Dodd	Decca	9
-	34	GRANADA Frank Sinatra	Reprise	1
31	35	SOMEDAY Kenny Ball & his Jazzmen	Pye	5
-	36	YOU DON'T KNOW WHAT YOU'VE GOT Ral Donner ●	Parlophone	1
25	37	HELLO MARY LOU Ricky Nelson	London	18
-	38	I'M GONNA KNOCK ON YOUR DOOR Eddie Hodges ●	London	1
29	39	TIME Craig Douglas	Top Rank	13
26	40	PASADENA Temperance Seven	Parlophone	16

WEEK ENDING 5 OCTOBER 1961

LW	TW	Title / Artist	Label	Wks
4	[1]	KON-TIKI Shadows	Columbia	5
6	2	JEALOUSY Billy Fury	Decca	4
7	3	MICHAEL Highwaymen	HMV	4
1	4	JOHNNY REMEMBER ME John Leyton	Top Rank	10
2	5	REACH FOR THE STARS Shirley Bassey	Columbia	11
5	6	WILD IN THE COUNTRY Elvis Presley	RCA	5
8	7	YOU'LL ANSWER TO ME Cleo Laine	Fontana	4
10	8	TOGETHER Connie Francis	MGM	4
13	9	HATS OFF TO LARRY Del Shannon	London	4
12	[10]	GET LOST Eden Kane	Decca	4
3	11	YOU DON'T KNOW Helen Shapiro	Columbia	14
26	12	WALKING BACK TO HAPPINESS Helen Shapiro	Columbia	2
11	13	MICHAEL ROW THE BOAT/LUMBERED Lonnie Donegan	Pye	6
20	[14]	SEA OF HEARTBREAK Don Gibson	RCA	6
16	15	THAT'S MY HOME Mr. Acker Bilk	Columbia	12
17	16	AIN'T GONNA WASH FOR A WEEK Brook Brothers	Pye	6
34	17	GRANADA Frank Sinatra	Reprise	2
9	18	CUPID Sam Cooke	RCA	10
15	19	WELL I ASK YOU Eden Kane	Decca	18
18	20	HOW MANY TEARS Bobby Vee	London	10
22	[21]	WHEELS CHA CHA Joe Loss	HMV	14
14	22	HALFWAY TO PARADISE Billy Fury	Decca	20
19	23	QUARTER TO THREE U.S. Bonds	Top Rank	11
25	24	WHO PUT THE BOMP Viscounts	Pye	2
-	25	WILD WIND John Leyton	Top Rank	1
-	26	SUCU SUCU Laurie Johnson Orchestra ●	Pye	1
23	27	SAY IT WITH FLOWERS Dorothy Squires & Russ Conway	Columbia	5
27	28	CRYIN' Roy Orbison	London	2
-	29	MUSKRAT Everly Brothers	Warner Brothers	1
28	30	MARCHETA Karl Denver	Decca	16
21	31	ROMEO Petula Clark	Pye	13
33	32	ONCE IN EVERY LIFETIME Ken Dodd	Decca	10
31	33	BREAKAWAY Springfields	Philips	5
-	34	HARD HEARTED HANNAH Temperance Seven	Parlophone	1
24	35	HEART AND SOUL Jan and Dean	London	5
-	36	MY BOOMERANG WON'T COME BACK Charlie Drake	Parlophone	1
-	37	BLESS YOU Tony Orlando ●	Fontana	1
-	38	AMOR Ben E. King	London	1
35	39	SOMEDAY Kenny Ball & his Jazzmen	Pye	6
36	40	YOU DON'T KNOW WHAT YOU'VE GOT Ral Donner	Parlophone	2

WEEK ENDING 12 OCTOBER 1961

LW	TW	Title / Artist	Label	Wks
3	[1]	MICHAEL Highwaymen	HMV	5
12	2	WALKING BACK TO HAPPINESS Helen Shapiro	Columbia	3
1	3	KON-TIKI Shadows	Columbia	6
2	4	JEALOUSY Billy Fury	Decca	5
4	5	JOHNNY REMEMBER ME John Leyton	Top Rank	11
8	[6]	TOGETHER Connie Francis	MGM	5
7	7	YOU'LL ANSWER TO ME Cleo Laine	Fontana	5
6	8	WILD IN THE COUNTRY Elvis Presley	RCA	6
9	9	HATS OFF TO LARRY Del Shannon	London	5
11	10	YOU DON'T KNOW Helen Shapiro	Columbia	15
10	11	GET LOST Eden Kane	Decca	5
25	12	WILD WIND John Leyton	Top Rank	2
26	13	SUCU SUCU Laurie Johnson Orchestra	Pye	2
5	14	REACH FOR THE STARS Shirley Bassey	Columbia	12
14	15	SEA OF HEARTBREAK Don Gibson	RCA	7
13	16	MICHAEL ROW THE BOAT Lonnie Donegan	Pye	7
17	17	GRANADA Frank Sinatra	Reprise	3
36	18	MY BOOMERANG WON'T COME BACK Charlie Drake	Parlophone	2
15	19	THAT'S MY HOME Mr. Acker Bilk	Columbia	13
37	20	BLESS YOU Tony Orlando	Fontana	2
29	21	MUSKRAT/DON'T BLAME ME Everly Brothers	Warner Bros	2
16	22	AIN'T GONNA WASH FOR A WEEK Brook Brothers	Pye	7
18	23	CUPID Sam Cooke	RCA	11
24	24	WHO PUT THE BOMP Viscounts	Pye	3
19	25	WELL I ASK YOU Eden Kane	Decca	19
21	26	WHEELS CHA CHA Joe Loss	HMV	15
20	27	HOW MANY TEARS Bobby Vee	London	11
34	[28]	HARD HEARTED HANNAH Temperance Seven	Parlophone	2
28	29	CRYIN' Roy Orbison	London	3
40	30	YOU DON'T KNOW WHAT YOU'VE GOT Ral Donner	Parlophone	3
32	31	ONCE IN EVERY LIFETIME Ken Dodd	Decca	11
31	32	ROMEO Petula Clark	Pye	14
-	33	SUCU SUCU Nina and Frederick	Columbia	1
22	34	HALFWAY TO PARADISE Billy Fury	Decca	21
27	35	SAY IT WITH FLOWERS Dorothy Squires & Russ Conway	Columbia	6
23	36	QUARTER TO THREE U.S. Bonds	Top Rank	12

In these weeks ■ Four different female vocalists together in the Top 10 (Shirley Bassey, Helen Shapiro, Cleo Laine and Connie Francis), a rare occurence in the early Sixties (28.09.61) ■ For the first and only time, a Lonnie Donegan cover of an American hit fails to outsell the originals, as *Michael* by the Highwaymen tops the chart. Donegan's version peaked at number six three weeks earlier (12.10.61)■

LW	TW	Title	Artist	Label	Wks
33	37	BREAKAWAY	Springfields	Philips	6
-	38	SUCU SUCU	Ted Heath Orchestra	Decca	1
-	39	TRIBUTE TO BUDDY HOLLY	Mike Berry ●	HMV	1
-	40	I'M GONNA KNOCK ON YOUR DOOR	Eddie Hodges	London	2

WEEK ENDING 19 OCTOBER 1961

LW	TW	Title	Artist	Label	Wks
2	1	WALKING BACK TO HAPPINESS	Helen Shapiro	Columbia	4
1	2	MICHAEL	Highwaymen	HMV	6
3	3	KON-TIKI	Shadows	Columbia	7
4	4	JEALOUSY	Billy Fury	Decca	6
7	5	YOU'LL ANSWER TO ME	Cleo Laine	Fontana	6
12	6	WILD WIND	John Leyton	Top Rank	3
9	7	HATS OFF TO LARRY	Del Shannon	London	6
5	8	JOHNNY REMEMBER ME	John Leyton	Top Rank	12
6	9	TOGETHER	Connie Francis	MGM	6
8	10	WILD IN THE COUNTRY	Elvis Presley	RCA	7
20	11	BLESS YOU	Tony Orlando	Fontana	3
11	12	GET LOST	Eden Kane	Decca	6
13	13	SUCU SUCU	Laurie Johnson Orchestra	Pye	3
10	14	YOU DON'T KNOW	Helen Shapiro	Columbia	16
17	15	GRANADA	Frank Sinatra	Reprise	4
14	16	REACH FOR THE STARS	Shirley Bassey	Columbia	13
18	17	MY BOOMERANG WON'T COME BACK	Charlie Drake	Parlophone	3
19	18	THAT'S MY HOME	Mr. Acker Bilk	Columbia	14
15	19	SEA OF HEARTBREAK	Don Gibson	RCA	8
21	20	MUSKRAT/DON'T BLAME ME	Everly Brothers	Warner Bros	3
16	21	MICHAEL ROW THE BOAT	Lonnie Donegan	Pye	8
-	22	WHEN THE GIRL IN YOUR ARMS IS THE GIRL IN YOUR HEART	Cliff Richard	Columbia	1
24	23	WHO PUT THE BOMP	Viscounts	Pye	4
22	24	AIN'T GONNA WASH FOR A WEEK	Brook Brothers	Pye	8
29	25	CRYIN'	Roy Orbison	London	4
-	26	MEXICALI ROSE	Karl Denver	Decca	1
26	27	WHEELS CHA CHA	Joe Loss	HMV	16
28	28	HARD HEARTED HANNAH	Temperance Seven	Parlophone	3
33	29	SUCU SUCU	Nina and Frederick	Columbia	2
39	30	TRIBUTE TO BUDDY HOLLY	Mike Berry	HMV	2
-	31	YOU MUST HAVE BEEN A BEAUTIFUL BABY	Bobby Darin	London	1
30	32	YOU DON'T KNOW WHAT YOU'VE GOT	Ral Donner	Parlophone	4
23	33	CUPID	Sam Cooke	RCA	12
-	34	HOLE IN THE BUCKET	Harry Belafonte and Odetta	RCA	2
35	35	SAY IT WITH FLOWERS	Dorothy Squires & Russ Conway	Columbia	7
38	36	SUCU SUCU	Ted Heath Orchestra	Decca	2
40	37	I'M GONNA KNOCK ON YOUR DOOR	Eddie Hodges	London	3
27	38	HOW MANY TEARS	Bobby Vee	London	12
-	39	AMOR	Ben E. King	London	2
-	40	LET'S GET TOGETHER	Hayley Mills ●	Decca	1

WEEK ENDING 26 OCTOBER 1961

LW	TW	Title	Artist	Label	Wks
1	1	WALKING BACK TO HAPPINESS	Helen Shapiro	Columbia	5
6	2	WILD WIND	John Leyton	Top Rank	4
2	3	MICHAEL	Highwaymen	HMV	7
22	4	WHEN THE GIRL IN YOUR ARMS IS THE GIRL IN YOUR HEART	Cliff Richard	Columbia	2
4	5	JEALOUSY	Billy Fury	Decca	7
7	6	HATS OFF TO LARRY	Del Shannon	London	7
5	7	YOU'LL ANSWER TO ME	Cleo Laine	Fontana	7
11	8	BLESS YOU	Tony Orlando	Fontana	4
13	9	SUCU SUCU	Laurie Johnson Orchestra	Pye	4
3	10	KON-TIKI	Shadows	Columbia	8
26	11	MEXICALI ROSE	Karl Denver	Decca	2
9	12	TOGETHER	Connie Francis	MGM	7
12	13	GET LOST	Eden Kane	Decca	7
10	14	WILD IN THE COUNTRY	Elvis Presley	RCA	8
17	15	MY BOOMERANG WON'T COME BACK	Charlie Drake	Parlophone	4
31	16	YOU MUST HAVE BEEN A BEAUTIFUL BABY	Bobby Darin	London	2
8	17	JOHNNY REMEMBER ME	John Leyton	Top Rank	13
14	18	YOU DON'T KNOW	Helen Shapiro	Columbia	17
-	19	HIT THE ROAD JACK	Ray Charles	HMV	1
15	20	GRANADA	Frank Sinatra	Reprise	5
23	21	WHO PUT THE BOMP	Viscounts	Pye	5
19	22	SEA OF HEARTBREAK	Don Gibson	RCA	9
16	23	REACH FOR THE STARS	Shirley Bassey	Columbia	14
30	24	TRIBUTE TO BUDDY HOLLY	Mike Berry	HMV	3
25	25	CRYIN'	Roy Orbison	London	5
20	26	MUSKRAT/DON'T BLAME ME	Everly Brothers	Warner Bros	4
-	27	TAKE FIVE	Dave Brubeck ●	Fontana	1
32	28	YOU DON'T KNOW WHAT YOU'VE GOT	Ral Donner	Parlophone	5
18	29	THAT'S MY HOME	Mr. Acker Bilk	Columbia	15
21	30	MICHAEL ROW THE BOAT	Lonnie Donegan	Pye	9
-	31	BIG BAD JOHN	Jimmy Dean ●	Philips	1
29	32	SUCU SUCU	Nina and Frederick	Columbia	3
27	33	WHEELS CHA CHA	Joe Loss	HMV	17
33	34	CUPID	Sam Cooke	RCA	13
40	35	LET'S GET TOGETHER	Hayley Mills	Decca	2
34	36	HOLE IN THE BUCKET	Harry Belafonte and Odetta	RCA	3
37	37	I'M GONNA KNOCK ON YOUR DOOR	Eddie Hodges	London	4
-	38	TAKE GOOD CARE OF MY BABY	Bobby Vee	London	1
-	39	THE TIME HAS COME	Adam Faith	Parlophone	1
-	40	I'M A MOODY GUY	Shane Fenton & the Fentones ●	Parlophone	1

November 1961

□ Highest position disc reached ● Act's first ever week on chart

WEEK ENDING 2 NOVEMBER 1961

LW	TW	Title	Artist	Label	Wks
1	1	WALKING BACK TO HAPPINESS	Helen Shapiro	Columbia	6
2	2	WILD WIND	John Leyton	Top Rank	5
4	3	WHEN THE GIRL IN YOUR ARMS IS THE GIRL IN YOUR HEART	Cliff Richard	Columbia	3
-	4	LITTLE SISTER/HIS LATEST FLAME	Elvis Presley	RCA	1
8	5	BLESS YOU	Tony Orlando	Fontana	5
7	6	YOU'LL ANSWER TO ME	Cleo Laine	Fontana	8
19	7	HIT THE ROAD JACK	Ray Charles	HMV	2
11	8	MEXICALI ROSE	Karl Denver	Decca	3
9	9	SUCU SUCU	Laurie Johnson Orchestra	Pye	5
16	10	YOU MUST HAVE BEEN A BEAUTIFUL BABY	Bobby Darin	London	3
3	11	MICHAEL	Highwaymen	HMV	8
6	12	HATS OFF TO LARRY	Del Shannon	London	8
39	13	THE TIME HAS COME	Adam Faith	Parlophone	2
31	14	BIG BAD JOHN	Jimmy Dean	Philips	2
15	15	MY BOOMERANG WON'T COME BACK	Charlie Drake	Parlophone	5
27	16	TAKE FIVE	Dave Brubeck	Fontana	2
5	17	JEALOUSY	Billy Fury	Decca	8
38	18	TAKE GOOD CARE OF MY BABY	Bobby Vee	London	2
12	19	TOGETHER	Connie Francis	MGM	8
13	20	GET LOST	Eden Kane	Decca	8
10	21	KON-TIKI	Shadows	Columbia	9
14	22	WILD IN THE COUNTRY	Elvis Presley	RCA	9
32	23	SUCU SUCU	Nina and Frederick	Columbia	4
24	24	TRIBUTE TO BUDDY HOLLY	Mike Berry	HMV	4
28	25	YOU DON'T KNOW WHAT YOU'VE GOT	Ral Donner	Parlophone	6
18	26	YOU DON'T KNOW	Helen Shapiro	Columbia	18
22	27	SEA OF HEARTBREAK	Don Gibson	RCA	10
17	28	JOHNNY REMEMBER ME	John Leyton	Top Rank	14
20	29	GRANADA	Frank Sinatra	Reprise	6
25	30	CRYIN'	Roy Orbison	London	6
40	31	I'M A MOODY GUY	Shane Fenton & the Fentones	Parlophone	2
35	32	LET'S GET TOGETHER	Hayley Mills	Decca	3
21	33	WHO PUT THE BOMP	Viscounts	Pye	6
33	34	WHEELS CHA CHA	Joe Loss	HMV	18
23	35	REACH FOR THE STARS	Shirley Bassey	Columbia	15

■For the sixth consecutive week, a different record topped the charts each week, the longest such run in chart history (19.10.61) ■ Three songs with men's names in their titles (Michael, Larry and Johnny) stay in the Top 10 together for three weeks (19.10.61) ■ Every record in the Top 10 is either moving up or at its peak (02.11.61) ■ Shane Fenton, later much more successful as Alvin Stardust, makes his chart debut (26.10.61)■

November 1961

□ Highest position disc reached ● Act's first ever week on chart

LW	TW	Title / Artist	Label	Wks
-	36	RUNAROUND SUE Dion ●	Top Rank	1
-	[37]	THE MOUNTAIN'S HIGH Dick and Deedee ●	London	1
30	38	MICHAEL ROW THE BOAT Lonnie Donegan	Pye	10
-	39	STARS AND STRIPES/CREOLE JAZZ Mr. Acker Bilk	Columbia	1
26	40	MUSKRAT/DON'T BLAME ME Everly Brothers	Warner Bros	5

WEEK ENDING 9 NOVEMBER 1961

LW	TW	Title / Artist	Label	Wks
4	[1]	HIS LATEST FLAME Elvis Presley	RCA	2
1	2	WALKING BACK TO HAPPINESS Helen Shapiro	Columbia	7
3	[3]	WHEN THE GIRL IN YOUR ARMS IS THE GIRL IN YOUR HEART Cliff Richard	Columbia	4
14	4	BIG BAD JOHN Jimmy Dean	Philips	3
2	5	WILD WIND John Leyton	Top Rank	6
7	[6]	HIT THE ROAD JACK Ray Charles	HMV	3
13	7	THE TIME HAS COME Adam Faith	Parlophone	3
16	8	TAKE FIVE Dave Brubeck	Fontana	3
8	9	MEXICALI ROSE Karl Denver	Decca	4
5	10	BLESS YOU Tony Orlando	Fontana	6
6	11	YOU'LL ANSWER TO ME Cleo Laine	Fontana	9
9	12	SUCU SUCU Laurie Johnson Orchestra	Pye	6
18	13	TAKE GOOD CARE OF MY BABY Bobby Vee	London	3
10	14	YOU MUST HAVE BEEN A BEAUTIFUL BABY Bobby Darin	London	4
11	15	MICHAEL Highwaymen	HMV	9
15	16	MY BOOMERANG WON'T COME BACK Charlie Drake	Parlophone	6
12	17	HATS OFF TO LARRY Del Shannon	London	9
17	18	JEALOUSY Billy Fury	Decca	9
21	19	KON-TIKI Shadows	Columbia	10
36	20	RUNAROUND SUE Dion	Top Rank	2
32	21	LET'S GET TOGETHER Hayley Mills	Decca	4
31	[22]	I'M A MOODY GUY Shane Fenton & the Fentones	Parlophone	3
-	23	MOON RIVER Danny Williams ●	HMV	1
27	24	SEA OF HEARTBREAK Don Gibson	RCA	11
24	25	TRIBUTE TO BUDDY HOLLY Mike Berry	HMV	5
19	26	TOGETHER Connie Francis	MGM	9
30	27	CRYIN' Roy Orbison	London	7
29	28	GRANADA Frank Sinatra	Reprise	7
23	29	SUCU SUCU Nina and Frederick	Columbia	5
25	30	YOU DON'T KNOW WHAT YOU'VE GOT Ral Donner	Parlophone	7
39	31	STARS AND STRIPES/CREOLE JAZZ Mr. Acker Bilk	Columbia	2
28	32	JOHNNY REMEMBER ME John Leyton	Top Rank	15
20	33	GET LOST Eden Kane	Decca	9
22	34	WILD IN THE COUNTRY Elvis Presley	RCA	10
26	35	YOU DON'T KNOW Helen Shapiro	Columbia	19
34	36	WHEELS CHA CHA Joe Loss	HMV	19
-	37	HOLE IN THE BUCKET Harry Belafonte and Odetta	RCA	4
35	38	REACH FOR THE STARS Shirley Bassey	Columbia	16
-	[39]	MORE MONEY FOR YOU AND ME Four Preps	Capitol	1
37	40	THE MOUNTAIN'S HIGH Dick and Deedee	London	2

WEEK ENDING 16 NOVEMBER 1961

LW	TW	Title / Artist	Label	Wks
1	[1]	HIS LATEST FLAME Elvis Presley	RCA	3
2	2	WALKING BACK TO HAPPINESS Helen Shapiro	Columbia	8
4	3	BIG BAD JOHN Jimmy Dean	Philips	4
3	4	WHEN THE GIRL IN YOUR ARMS IS THE GIRL IN YOUR HEART Cliff Richard	Columbia	5
7	5	THE TIME HAS COME Adam Faith	Parlophone	4
8	[6]	TAKE FIVE Dave Brubeck	Fontana	4
13	7	TAKE GOOD CARE OF MY BABY Bobby Vee	London	4
5	8	WILD WIND John Leyton	Top Rank	7
10	9	BLESS YOU Tony Orlando	Fontana	7
12	10	SUCU SUCU Laurie Johnson Orchestra	Pye	7
9	11	MEXICALI ROSE Karl Denver	Decca	5
11	12	YOU'LL ANSWER TO ME Cleo Laine	Fontana	10
6	13	HIT THE ROAD JACK Ray Charles	HMV	4
16	[14]	MY BOOMERANG WON'T COME BACK Charlie Drake	Parlophone	7
14	15	YOU MUST HAVE BEEN A BEAUTIFUL BABY Bobby Darin	London	5
20	16	RUNAROUND SUE Dion	Top Rank	3
23	17	MOON RIVER Danny Williams	HMV	2
-	18	TOWER OF STRENGTH Frankie Vaughan	Philips	1
21	19	LET'S GET TOGETHER Hayley Mills	Decca	5
15	20	MICHAEL Highwaymen	HMV	10
18	21	JEALOUSY Billy Fury	Decca	10
31	[22]	STARS AND STRIPES/CREOLE JAZZ Mr. Acker Bilk	Columbia	3
17	23	HATS OFF TO LARRY Del Shannon	London	10
22	24	I'M A MOODY GUY Shane Fenton & the Fentones	Parlophone	4
-	25	THIS TIME Troy Shondell ●	London	1
-	26	THE SAVAGE Shadows	Columbia	1
-	27	MIDNIGHT IN MOSCOW Kenny Ball & his Jazzmen	Pye	1
24	28	SEA OF HEARTBREAK Don Gibson	RCA	12
26	29	TOGETHER Connie Francis	MGM	10
30	30	YOU DON'T KNOW WHAT YOU'VE GOT Ral Donner	Parlophone	8
34	31	WILD IN THE COUNTRY Elvis Presley	RCA	11
35	32	YOU DON'T KNOW Helen Shapiro	Columbia	20
27	33	CRYIN' Roy Orbison	London	8
29	34	SUCU SUCU Nina and Frederick	Columbia	6
-	35	BAMBINO Springfields	Philips	1
-	36	RUNAROUND SUE Doug Sheldon ●	Decca	1
-	37	EVERLOVIN' Ricky Nelson	London	1
-	[38]	FOOL NUMBER ONE Brenda Lee	Brunswick	1
-	39	WHO PUT THE BOMP Viscounts	Pye	7
-	40	TOMORROW'S CLOWN Marty Wilde	Philips	1

WEEK ENDING 23 NOVEMBER 1961

LW	TW	Title / Artist	Label	Wks
1	[1]	HIS LATEST FLAME Elvis Presley	RCA	4
3	[2]	BIG BAD JOHN Jimmy Dean	Philips	5
2	3	WALKING BACK TO HAPPINESS Helen Shapiro	Columbia	9
5	[4]	THE TIME HAS COME Adam Faith	Parlophone	5
7	5	TAKE GOOD CARE OF MY BABY Bobby Vee	London	5
4	6	WHEN THE GIRL IN YOUR ARMS IS THE GIRL IN YOUR HEART Cliff Richard	Columbia	6
18	7	TOWER OF STRENGTH Frankie Vaughan	Philips	2
17	8	MOON RIVER Danny Williams	HMV	3
6	9	TAKE FIVE Dave Brubeck	Fontana	5
13	10	HIT THE ROAD JACK Ray Charles	HMV	5
9	11	BLESS YOU Tony Orlando	Fontana	8
8	12	WILD WIND John Leyton	Top Rank	8
26	13	THE SAVAGE Shadows	Columbia	2
11	14	MEXICALI ROSE Karl Denver	Decca	6
16	15	RUNAROUND SUE Dion	Top Rank	4
10	16	SUCU SUCU Laurie Johnson Orchestra	Pye	8
19	[17]	LET'S GET TOGETHER Hayley Mills	Decca	6
15	18	YOU MUST HAVE BEEN A BEAUTIFUL BABY Bobby Darin	London	6
12	19	YOU'LL ANSWER TO ME Cleo Laine	Fontana	11
14	20	MY BOOMERANG WON'T COME BACK Charlie Drake	Parlophone	8
27	21	MIDNIGHT IN MOSCOW Kenny Ball & his Jazzmen	Pye	2
20	22	MICHAEL Highwaymen	HMV	11
25	23	THIS TIME Troy Shondell	London	2
24	24	I'M A MOODY GUY Shane Fenton & the Fentones	Parlophone	5
34	25	SUCU SUCU Nina and Frederick	Columbia	7
22	26	STARS AND STRIPES/CREOLE JAZZ Mr. Acker Bilk	Columbia	4
23	27	HATS OFF TO LARRY Del Shannon	London	11
35	28	BAMBINO Springfields	Philips	2
-	[29]	LET TRUE LOVE BEGIN Nat 'King' Cole	Capitol	1
21	30	JEALOUSY Billy Fury	Decca	11
-	31	YOU'RE THE ONLY GOOD THING Jim Reeves	RCA	1
30	32	YOU DON'T KNOW WHAT YOU'VE GOT Ral Donner	Parlophone	9
28	33	SEA OF HEARTBREAK Don Gibson	RCA	13
-	34	I'LL GET BY Shirley Bassey	Columbia	1
-	35	I LOVE HOW YOU LOVE ME Jimmy Crawford ●	Columbia	1
40	36	TOMORROW'S CLOWN Marty Wilde	Philips	2

In these weeks ■ There are ten new entries in the Top 40, a very high number for the Sixties (16.11.61) ■ Four male/female vocal duets in the Top 40, by Dick and Deedee, Nina and Frederick, Harry Belafonte and Odetta and by Ray Charles and the uncredited Margie Hendrix as *Hit The Road Jack* (09.11.61) ■ Cliff Richard's first hit from his soon-to-be-released film, *The Young Ones* peaks at number three (09.11.61)■

LW	TW	Title / Artist	Label	Wks
36	37	RUNAROUND SUE Doug Sheldon	Decca	2
37	38	EVERLOVIN' Ricky Nelson	London	2
-	39	KON-TIKI Shadows	Columbia	11
-	40	REACH FOR THE STARS Shirley Bassey	Columbia	17

WEEK ENDING 30 NOVEMBER 1961

LW	TW	Title / Artist	Label	Wks
1	1	HIS LATEST FLAME Elvis Presley	RCA	5
7	2	TOWER OF STRENGTH Frankie Vaughan	Philips	3
2	3	BIG BAD JOHN Jimmy Dean	Philips	6
3	4	WALKING BACK TO HAPPINESS Helen Shapiro	Columbia	10
5	5	TAKE GOOD CARE OF MY BABY Bobby Vee	London	6
8	6	MOON RIVER Danny Williams	HMV	4
4	7	THE TIME HAS COME Adam Faith	Parlophone	6
6	8	WHEN THE GIRL IN YOUR ARMS IS THE GIRL IN YOUR HEART Cliff Richard	Columbia	7
9	9	TAKE FIVE Dave Brubeck	Fontana	6
13	10	THE SAVAGE Shadows	Columbia	3
15	11	RUNAROUND SUE Dion	Top Rank	5
10	12	HIT THE ROAD JACK Ray Charles	HMV	6
21	13	MIDNIGHT IN MOSCOW Kenny Ball & his Jazzmen	Pye	3
14	14	MEXICALI ROSE Karl Denver	Decca	7
16	15	SUCU SUCU Laurie Johnson Orchestra	Pye	9
34	16	I'LL GET BY Shirley Bassey	Columbia	2
12	17	WILD WIND John Leyton	Top Rank	9
19	18	YOU'LL ANSWER TO ME Cleo Laine	Fontana	12
18	19	YOU MUST HAVE BEEN A BEAUTIFUL BABY Bobby Darin	London	7
11	20	BLESS YOU Tony Orlando	Fontana	9
17	21	LET'S GET TOGETHER Hayley Mills	Decca	7
31	22	YOU'RE THE ONLY GOOD THING Jim Reeves	RCA	2
23	23	THIS TIME Troy Shondell	London	3
24	24	I'M A MOODY GUY Shane Fenton & the Fentones	Parlophone	6
-	25	MY FRIEND THE SEA Petula Clark	Pye	1
20	26	MY BOOMERANG WON'T COME BACK Charlie Drake	Parlophone	9
25	27	SUCU SUCU Nina and Frederick	Columbia	8
26	28	STARS AND STRIPES/CREOLE JAZZ Mr. Acker Bilk	Columbia	5
29	29	LET TRUE LOVE BEGIN Nat 'King' Cole	Capitol	2
35	30	I LOVE HOW YOU LOVE ME Jimmy Crawford	Columbia	2
22	31	MICHAEL Highwaymen	HMV	12
-	32	STRANGER ON THE SHORE Mr. Acker Bilk	Columbia	1
36	33	TOMORROW'S CLOWN Marty Wilde	Philips	3
38	34	EVERLOVIN' Ricky Nelson	London	3
28	35	BAMBINO Springfields	Philips	3
-	36	THE WAY YOU LOOK TONIGHT Lettermen ●	Capitol	1
39	37	KON-TIKI Shadows	Columbia	12
-	38	MY SUNDAY BABY Dale Sisters ●	Ember	1
-	39	THE COFFEE SONG Frank Sinatra	Reprise	1
-	40	I UNDERSTAND G-Clefs ●	London	1

WEEK ENDING 7 DECEMBER 1961

LW	TW	Title / Artist	Label	Wks
2	1	TOWER OF STRENGTH Frankie Vaughan	Philips	4
1	2	HIS LATEST FLAME Elvis Presley	RCA	6
3	3	BIG BAD JOHN Jimmy Dean	Philips	7
5	4	TAKE GOOD CARE OF MY BABY Bobby Vee	London	7
6	5	MOON RIVER Danny Williams	HMV	5
7	6	THE TIME HAS COME Adam Faith	Parlophone	7
4	7	WALKING BACK TO HAPPINESS Helen Shapiro	Columbia	11
9	8	TAKE FIVE Dave Brubeck	Fontana	7
13	9	MIDNIGHT IN MOSCOW Kenny Ball & his Jazzmen	Pye	4
16	10	I'LL GET BY Shirley Bassey	Columbia	3
10	11	THE SAVAGE Shadows	Columbia	4
8	12	WHEN THE GIRL IN YOUR ARMS IS THE GIRL IN YOUR HEART Cliff Richard	Columbia	8
11	13	RUNAROUND SUE Dion	Top Rank	6
14	14	MEXICALI ROSE Karl Denver	Decca	8
25	15	MY FRIEND THE SEA Petula Clark	Pye	2
32	16	STRANGER ON THE SHORE Mr. Acker Bilk	Columbia	2
12	17	HIT THE ROAD JACK Ray Charles	HMV	7
30	18	I LOVE HOW YOU LOVE ME Jimmy Crawford	Columbia	3
22	19	YOU'RE THE ONLY GOOD THING Jim Reeves	RCA	3

December 1961

□ Highest position disc reached ● Act's first ever week on chart

LW	TW	Title / Artist	Label	Wks
35	20	BAMBINO Springfields	Philips	4
15	21	SUCU SUCU Laurie Johnson Orchestra	Pye	10
23	22	THIS TIME Troy Shondell	London	4
34	23	EVERLOVIN' Ricky Nelson	London	4
21	24	LET'S GET TOGETHER Hayley Mills	Decca	8
24	25	I'M A MOODY GUY Shane Fenton & the Fentones	Parlophone	7
28	26	STARS AND STRIPES/CREOLE JAZZ Mr. Acker Bilk	Columbia	6
17	27	WILD WIND John Leyton	Top Rank	10
19	28	YOU MUST HAVE BEEN A BEAUTIFUL BABY Bobby Darin	London	8
40	29	I UNDERSTAND G-Clefs	London	2
20	30	BLESS YOU Tony Orlando	Fontana	10
-	31	JEANNIE JEANNIE JEANNIE Eddie Cochran	London	1
-	32	TOY BALLOONS Russ Conway	Columbia	1
29	33	LET TRUE LOVE BEGIN Nat 'King' Cole	Capitol	3
26	34	MY BOOMERANG WON'T COME BACK Charlie Drake	Parlophone	10
-	35	SEPTEMBER IN THE RAIN Dinah Washington ●	Mercury	1
38	36	MY SUNDAY BABY Dale Sisters	Ember	2
-	37	SO LONG BABY Del Shannon	London	1
33	38	TOMORROW'S CLOWN Marty Wilde	Philips	4
-	39	CHARLESTON Temperance Seven	Parlophone	1
18	40	YOU'LL ANSWER TO ME Cleo Laine	Fontana	13

WEEK ENDING 14 DECEMBER 1961

LW	TW	Title / Artist	Label	Wks
1	1	TOWER OF STRENGTH Frankie Vaughan	Philips	5
5	2	MOON RIVER Danny Williams	HMV	6
4	3	TAKE GOOD CARE OF MY BABY Bobby Vee	London	8
7	4	WALKING BACK TO HAPPINESS Helen Shapiro	Columbia	12
2	5	HIS LATEST FLAME Elvis Presley	RCA	7
3	6	BIG BAD JOHN Jimmy Dean	Philips	8
9	7	MIDNIGHT IN MOSCOW Kenny Ball & his Jazzmen	Pye	5
15	8	MY FRIEND THE SEA Petula Clark	Pye	3
6	9	THE TIME HAS COME Adam Faith	Parlophone	8
10	10	I'LL GET BY Shirley Bassey	Columbia	4
-	11	JOHNNY WILL Pat Boone	London	1
11	12	THE SAVAGE Shadows	Columbia	5
8	13	TAKE FIVE Dave Brubeck	Fontana	8
16	14	STRANGER ON THE SHORE Mr. Acker Bilk	Columbia	3
13	15	RUNAROUND SUE Dion	Top Rank	7
20	16	BAMBINO Springfields	Philips	5
19	17	YOU'RE THE ONLY GOOD THING Jim Reeves	RCA	4
12	18	WHEN THE GIRL IN YOUR ARMS IS THE GIRL IN YOUR HEART Cliff Richard	Columbia	9
29	19	I UNDERSTAND G-Clefs	London	3
37	20	SO LONG BABY Del Shannon	London	2
18	21	I LOVE HOW YOU LOVE ME Jimmy Crawford	Columbia	4
17	22	HIT THE ROAD JACK Ray Charles	HMV	8
32	23	TOY BALLOONS Russ Conway	Columbia	2
14	24	MEXICALI ROSE Karl Denver	Decca	9
22	25	THIS TIME Troy Shondell	London	5
26	26	STARS AND STRIPES/CREOLE JAZZ Mr. Acker Bilk	Columbia	7
-	27	LET THERE BE DRUMS Sandy Nelson	London	1
-	28	SUCU SUCU Nina and Frederick	Columbia	9
39	29	CHARLESTON Temperance Seven	Parlophone	2
-	30	DON'T BRING LULU Dorothy Provine ●	Warner Brothers	1
-	31	TALL DARK STRANGER Rose Brennan ●	Philips	1
24	32	LET'S GET TOGETHER Hayley Mills	Decca	9
33	33	LET TRUE LOVE BEGIN Nat 'King' Cole	Capitol	4
25	34	I'M A MOODY GUY Shane Fenton & the Fentones	Parlophone	8
-	35	MRS. MILLS MEDLEY Mrs. Mills ●	Parlophone	1
21	36	SUCU SUCU Laurie Johnson Orchestra	Pye	11
23	37	EVERLOVIN' Ricky Nelson	London	5
28	38	YOU MUST HAVE BEEN A BEAUTIFUL BABY Bobby Darin	London	9
34	39	MY BOOMERANG WON'T COME BACK Charlie Drake	Parlophone	11
36	40	MY SUNDAY BABY Dale Sisters	Ember	3

■Acker Bilk's massively long-running hit *Stranger On The Shore* makes its chart debut (30.11.61) ■ The Dale Sisters' *My Sunday Baby* peaks at number 36, one place lower than the only other Ember label hit - the Harry Simeone Chorale *Little Drummer Boy* eleven months earlier (07.12.61) ■ Three ladies who only had one top 40 hit each, all in very different styles, make their chart debuts in the same week - Dorothy Provine, Rose Brennan and Mrs. Mills (14.12.61)■

December 1961

□ Highest position disc reached ● Act's first ever week on chart

WEEK ENDING 21 DECEMBER 1961

LW	TW	Title	Artist	Label	Wks
1	1	TOWER OF STRENGTH	Frankie Vaughan	*Philips*	6
2	2	MOON RIVER	Danny Williams	*HMV*	7
3	3	TAKE GOOD CARE OF MY BABY	Bobby Vee	*London*	9
11	4	JOHNNY WILL	Pat Boone	*London*	2
7	5	MIDNIGHT IN MOSCOW	Kenny Ball & his Jazzmen	*Pye*	6
14	6	STRANGER ON THE SHORE	Mr. Acker Bilk	*Columbia*	4
8	7	MY FRIEND THE SEA	Petula Clark	*Pye*	4
6	8	BIG BAD JOHN	Jimmy Dean	*Philips*	9
4	9	WALKING BACK TO HAPPINESS	Helen Shapiro	*Columbia*	13
5	10	HIS LATEST FLAME	Elvis Presley	*RCA*	8
20	11	SO LONG BABY	Del Shannon	*London*	3
10	12	I'LL GET BY	Shirley Bassey	*Columbia*	5
9	13	THE TIME HAS COME	Adam Faith	*Parlophone*	9
23	14	TOY BALLOONS	Russ Conway	*Columbia*	3
27	15	LET THERE BE DRUMS	Sandy Nelson	*London*	2
12	16	THE SAVAGE	Shadows	*Columbia*	6
18	17	WHEN THE GIRL IN YOUR ARMS IS THE GIRL IN YOUR HEART	Cliff Richard	*Columbia*	10
17	18	YOU'RE THE ONLY GOOD THING	Jim Reeves	*RCA*	5
19	19	I UNDERSTAND	G-Clefs	*London*	4
13	20	TAKE FIVE	Dave Brubeck	*Fontana*	9
-	21	I'D NEVER FIND ANOTHER YOU	Billy Fury	*Decca*	1
15	22	RUNAROUND SUE	Dion	*Top Rank*	8
16	23	BAMBINO	Springfields	*Philips*	6
-	24	HAPPY BIRTHDAY SWEET SIXTEEN	Neil Sedaka	*RCA*	1
30	25	DON'T BRING LULU	Dorothy Provine	*Warner Brothers*	2
21	26	I LOVE HOW YOU LOVE ME	Jimmy Crawford	*Columbia*	5
-	27	MULTIPLICATION	Bobby Darin	*London*	1
29	28	CHARLESTON	Temperance Seven	*Parlophone*	3
25	29	THIS TIME	Troy Shondell	*London*	6
35	30	MRS. MILLS MEDLEY	Mrs. Mills	*Parlophone*	2
28	31	SUCU SUCU	Nina and Frederick	*Columbia*	10
33	32	LET TRUE LOVE BEGIN	Nat 'King' Cole	*Capitol*	5
-	33	THE NIGHT IS YOUNG/THERE GOES THAT SONG AGAIN	Gary Miller	*Pye*	1
-	34	KING KONG	Terry Lightfoot	*Columbia*	1
26	35	STARS AND STRIPES/CREOLE JAZZ	Mr. Acker Bilk	*Columbia*	8
24	36	MEXICALI ROSE	Karl Denver	*Decca*	10
22	37	HIT THE ROAD JACK	Ray Charles	*HMV*	9
31	38	TALL DARK STRANGER	Rose Brennan	*Philips*	2
32	39	LET'S GET TOGETHER	Hayley Mills	*Decca*	10
-	40	THE LION SLEEPS TONIGHT	Tokens ●	*RCA*	1

WEEK ENDING 28 DECEMBER 1961

LW	TW	Title	Artist	Label	Wks
2	1	MOON RIVER	Danny Williams	*HMV*	8
1	2	TOWER OF STRENGTH	Frankie Vaughan	*Philips*	7
5	3	MIDNIGHT IN MOSCOW	Kenny Ball & his Jazzmen	*Pye*	7
15	4	LET THERE BE DRUMS	Sandy Nelson	*London*	3
4	5	JOHNNY WILL	Pat Boone	*London*	3
6	6	STRANGER ON THE SHORE	Mr. Acker Bilk	*Columbia*	5
14	7	TOY BALLOONS	Russ Conway	*Columbia*	4
3	8	TAKE GOOD CARE OF MY BABY	Bobby Vee	*London*	10
7	9	MY FRIEND THE SEA	Petula Clark	*Pye*	5
24	10	HAPPY BIRTHDAY SWEET SIXTEEN	Neil Sedaka	*RCA*	2
27	11	MULTIPLICATION	Bobby Darin	*London*	2
8	12	BIG BAD JOHN	Jimmy Dean	*Philips*	10
10	13	HIS LATEST FLAME	Elvis Presley	*RCA*	9
11	14	SO LONG BABY	Del Shannon	*London*	4
21	15	I'D NEVER FIND ANOTHER YOU	Billy Fury	*Decca*	2
9	16	WALKING BACK TO HAPPINESS	Helen Shapiro	*Columbia*	14
25	17	DON'T BRING LULU	Dorothy Provine	*Warner Brothers*	3
30	18	MRS. MILLS MEDLEY	Mrs. Mills	*Parlophone*	3
12	19	I'LL GET BY	Shirley Bassey	*Columbia*	6
19	20	I UNDERSTAND	G-Clefs	*London*	5
18	21	YOU'RE THE ONLY GOOD THING	Jim Reeves	*RCA*	6
28	22	CHARLESTON	Temperance Seven	*Parlophone*	4
16	23	THE SAVAGE	Shadows	*Columbia*	7
20	24	TAKE FIVE	Dave Brubeck	*Fontana*	10
40	25	THE LION SLEEPS TONIGHT	Tokens	*RCA*	2
-	26	RUN TO HIM	Bobby Vee	*London*	1
13	27	THE TIME HAS COME	Adam Faith	*Parlophone*	10
17	28	WHEN THE GIRL IN YOUR ARMS IS THE GIRL IN YOUR HEART	Cliff Richard	*Columbia*	11
34	29	KING KONG	Terry Lightfoot	*Columbia*	2
-	30	BABY'S FIRST CHRISTMAS	Connie Francis	*MGM*	1
22	31	RUNAROUND SUE	Dion	*Top Rank*	9
23	32	BAMBINO	Springfields	*Philips*	7
29	33	THIS TIME	Troy Shondell	*London*	7
-	34	GOODBYE CRUEL WORLD	James Darren	*Pye*	1
33	35	THE NIGHT IS YOUNG/THERE GOES THAT SONG AGAIN	Gary Miller	*Pye*	2
-	36	ONWARD CHRISTIAN SOLDIERS	Harry Simeone Chorale	Ember	1
-	37	I CRIED FOR YOU	Ricky Stevens ●	*Columbia*	1
35	38	STARS AND STRIPES/CREOLE JAZZ	Mr. Acker Bilk	*Columbia*	9
37	39	HIT THE ROAD JACK	Ray Charles	*HMV*	10
38	40	TALL DARK STRANGER	Rose Brennan	*Philips*	3

In these weeks ■ There are ten instrumentals in the Top 40, of which six are traditional or modern jazz hits (21.12.61) ■ The next week, four of those instrumentals are in the Top 10 - *Midnight In Moscow, Stranger On The Shore, Let There Be Drums* and *Toy Balloons* (28.12.61) ■ Mrs. Mills is the first Top 20 hitmaker to include her own name in the title of her hit - something which becomes common practice in the Eighties and Nineties (28.12.61)■

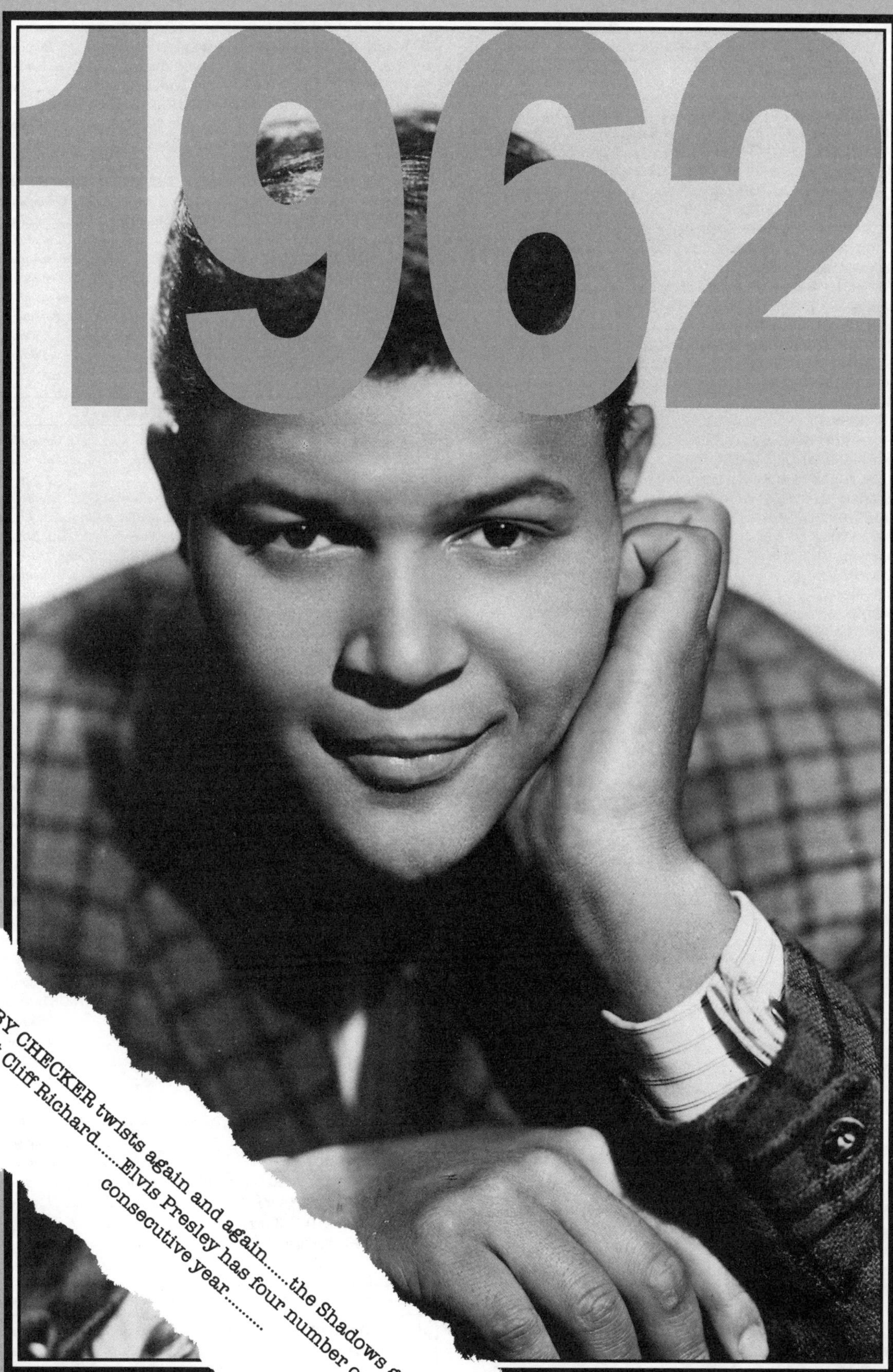

1962

......CHUBBY CHECKER twists again and again......the Shadows get to the top with nd without Cliff Richard......Elvis Presley has four number ones for the second consecutive year.........

January 1962

☐ Highest position disc reached ● Act's first ever week on chart

LW	TW	WEEK ENDING 4 JANUARY 1962			Wks
1	1	MOON RIVER	Danny Williams	*HMV*	9
3	2	MIDNIGHT IN MOSCOW	Kenny Ball & his Jazzmen	*Pye*	8
4	3	LET THERE BE DRUMS	Sandy Nelson	*London*	4
5	4	JOHNNY WILL	Pat Boone	*London*	4
2	5	TOWER OF STRENGTH	Frankie Vaughan	*Philips*	8
10	6	HAPPY BIRTHDAY SWEET SIXTEEN	Neil Sedaka	*RCA*	3
11	7	MULTIPLICATION	Bobby Darin	*London*	3
6	8	STRANGER ON THE SHORE	Mr. Acker Bilk	*Columbia*	6
15	9	I'D NEVER FIND ANOTHER YOU	Billy Fury	*Decca*	3
7	10	TOY BALLOONS	Russ Conway	*Columbia*	5
14	11	SO LONG BABY	Del Shannon	*London*	5
8	12	TAKE GOOD CARE OF MY BABY	Bobby Vee	*London*	11
16	13	WALKING BACK TO HAPPINESS	Helen Shapiro	*Columbia*	15
12	14	BIG BAD JOHN	Jimmy Dean	*Philips*	11
13	15	HIS LATEST FLAME	Elvis Presley	*RCA*	10
25	16	THE LION SLEEPS TONIGHT	Tokens	*RCA*	3
20	17	I UNDERSTAND	G-Clefs	*London*	6
26	18	RUN TO HIM	Bobby Vee	*London*	2
9	19	MY FRIEND THE SEA	Petula Clark	*Pye*	6
23	20	THE SAVAGE	Shadows	*Columbia*	8
17	21	DON'T BRING LULU	Dorothy Provine	*Warner Brothers*	4
21	22	YOU'RE THE ONLY GOOD THING	Jim Reeves	*RCA*	7
18	23	MRS. MILLS MEDLEY	Mrs. Mills	*Parlophone*	4
19	24	I'LL GET BY	Shirley Bassey	*Columbia*	7
22	25	CHARLESTON	Temperance Seven	*Parlophone*	5
24	26	TAKE FIVE	Dave Brubeck	*Fontana*	11
28	27	WHEN THE GIRL IN YOUR ARMS IS THE GIRL IN YOUR HEART	Cliff Richard	*Columbia*	12
32	28	BAMBINO	Springfields	*Philips*	8
-	29	LET'S TWIST AGAIN	Chubby Checker	*Columbia*	2
27	30	THE TIME HAS COME	Adam Faith	*Parlophone*	11
-	31	THE LANGUAGE OF LOVE	John D. Loudermilk ●	*RCA*	1
35	32	THE NIGHT IS YOUNG/THERE GOES THAT SONG AGAIN	Gary Miller	*Pye*	3
33	33	THIS TIME	Troy Shondell	*London*	8
37	34	I CRIED FOR YOU	Ricky Stevens	*Columbia*	2
40	35	TALL DARK STRANGER	Rose Brennan	*Philips*	4
-	36	SON THIS IS SHE	John Leyton	*HMV*	1
-	37	I LOVE HOW YOU LOVE ME	Jimmy Crawford	*Columbia*	6
-	38	COME ALONG PLEASE	Bob Wallis ●	*Pye*	1
-	39	CAN'T YOU HEAR THE BEAT OF A BROKEN HEART	Iain Gregory ●	*Pye*	1
38	40	STARS AND STRIPES/CREOLE JAZZ	Mr. Acker Bilk	*Columbia*	10

LW	TW	WEEK ENDING 11 JANUARY 1962			Wks
-	1	THE YOUNG ONES	Cliff Richard	*Columbia*	1
8	2	STRANGER ON THE SHORE	Mr. Acker Bilk	*Columbia*	7
1	3	MOON RIVER	Danny Williams	*HMV*	10
3	4	LET THERE BE DRUMS	Sandy Nelson	*London*	5
9	5	I'D NEVER FIND ANOTHER YOU	Billy Fury	*Decca*	4
6	6	HAPPY BIRTHDAY SWEET SIXTEEN	Neil Sedaka	*RCA*	4
4	7	JOHNNY WILL	Pat Boone	*London*	5
2	8	MIDNIGHT IN MOSCOW	Kenny Ball & his Jazzmen	*Pye*	9
7	9	MULTIPLICATION	Bobby Darin	*London*	4
11	10	SO LONG BABY	Del Shannon	*London*	6
16	11	THE LION SLEEPS TONIGHT	Tokens	*RCA*	4
5	12	TOWER OF STRENGTH	Frankie Vaughan	*Philips*	9
18	13	RUN TO HIM	Bobby Vee	*London*	3
31	14	THE LANGUAGE OF LOVE	John D. Loudermilk	*RCA*	2
19	15	MY FRIEND THE SEA	Petula Clark	*Pye*	7
12	16	TAKE GOOD CARE OF MY BABY	Bobby Vee	*London*	12
10	17	TOY BALLOONS	Russ Conway	*Columbia*	6
22	18	YOU'RE THE ONLY GOOD THING	Jim Reeves	*RCA*	8
36	19	SON THIS IS SHE	John Leyton	*HMV*	2
17	20	I UNDERSTAND	G-Clefs	*London*	7
21	21	DON'T BRING LULU	Dorothy Provine	*Warner Brothers*	5
29	22	LET'S TWIST AGAIN	Chubby Checker	*Columbia*	3
13	23	WALKING BACK TO HAPPINESS	Helen Shapiro	*Columbia*	16
15	24	HIS LATEST FLAME	Elvis Presley	*RCA*	11
14	25	BIG BAD JOHN	Jimmy Dean	*Philips*	12
-	26	WALK ON BY	Leroy Van Dyke ●	*Mercury*	1
-	27	THE TWIST	Chubby Checker	*Columbia*	1
-	28	GOODBYE CRUEL WORLD	James Darren	*Pye*	2
-	29	YOUR MA SAID YOU CRIED IN YOUR SLEEP LAST NIGHT	Doug Sheldon	*Decca*	1
25	30	CHARLESTON	Temperance Seven	*Parlophone*	6
24	31	I'LL GET BY	Shirley Bassey	*Columbia*	8
27	32	WHEN THE GIRL IN YOUR ARMS IS THE GIRL IN YOUR HEART	Cliff Richard	*Columbia*	13
32	33	THERE GOES THAT SONG AGAIN	Gary Miller	*Pye*	4
34	34	I CRIED FOR YOU	Ricky Stevens	*Columbia*	3
30	35	THE TIME HAS COME	Adam Faith	*Parlophone*	12
37	36	I LOVE HOW YOU LOVE ME	Jimmy Crawford	*Columbia*	7
-	37	KING KONG	Terry Lightfoot	*Columbia*	3
26	38	TAKE FIVE	Dave Brubeck	*Fontana*	12
28	39	BAMBINO	Springfields	*Philips*	9
35	40	TALL DARK STRANGER	Rose Brennan	*Philips*	5

LW	TW	WEEK ENDING 18 JANUARY 1962			Wks
1	1	THE YOUNG ONES	Cliff Richard	*Columbia*	2
2	2	STRANGER ON THE SHORE	Mr. Acker Bilk	*Columbia*	8
4	3	LET THERE BE DRUMS	Sandy Nelson	*London*	6
6	4	HAPPY BIRTHDAY SWEET SIXTEEN	Neil Sedaka	*RCA*	5
8	5	MIDNIGHT IN MOSCOW	Kenny Ball & his Jazzmen	*Pye*	10
5	6	I'D NEVER FIND ANOTHER YOU	Billy Fury	*Decca*	5
3	7	MOON RIVER	Danny Williams	*HMV*	11
9	8	MULTIPLICATION	Bobby Darin	*London*	5
7	9	JOHNNY WILL	Pat Boone	*London*	6
13	10	RUN TO HIM	Bobby Vee	*London*	4
11	11	THE LION SLEEPS TONIGHT	Tokens	*RCA*	5
10	12	SO LONG BABY	Del Shannon	*London*	7
14	13	THE LANGUAGE OF LOVE	John D. Loudermilk	*RCA*	3
27	14	THE TWIST	Chubby Checker	*Columbia*	2
19	15	SON THIS IS SHE	John Leyton	*HMV*	3
22	16	LET'S TWIST AGAIN	Chubby Checker	*Columbia*	4
26	17	WALK ON BY	Leroy Van Dyke	*Mercury*	2
12	18	TOWER OF STRENGTH	Frankie Vaughan	*Philips*	10
-	19	FORGET ME NOT	Eden Kane	*Decca*	1
18	20	YOU'RE THE ONLY GOOD THING	Jim Reeves	*RCA*	9
-	21	CRYIN' IN THE RAIN	Everly Brothers	*Warner Brothers*	1
17	22	TOY BALLOONS	Russ Conway	*Columbia*	7
23	23	WALKING BACK TO HAPPINESS	Helen Shapiro	*Columbia*	17
15	24	MY FRIEND THE SEA	Petula Clark	*Pye*	8
20	25	I UNDERSTAND	G-Clefs	*London*	8
-	26	THE COMANCHEROS	Lonnie Donegan	*Pye*	1
21	27	DON'T BRING LULU	Dorothy Provine	*Warner Brothers*	6
24	28	HIS LATEST FLAME	Elvis Presley	*RCA*	12
16	29	TAKE GOOD CARE OF MY BABY	Bobby Vee	*London*	13
29	30	YOUR MA SAID YOU CRIED IN YOUR SLEEP LAST NIGHT	Doug Sheldon	*Decca*	2
28	31	GOODBYE CRUEL WORLD	James Darren	*Pye*	3
40	32	TALL DARK STRANGER	Rose Brennan	*Philips*	6
-	33	LONESOME	Adam Faith	*Parlophone*	1
-	34	SMALL SAD SAM	Phil McLean ●	*Top Rank*	1
-	35	PEPPERMINT TWIST	Danny Peppermint & the Jumping Jacks ●	*London*	1
38	36	TAKE FIVE	Dave Brubeck	*Fontana*	13
-	37	WHAT A CRAZY WORLD WE LIVE IN	Joe Brown	*Pye*	1
-	38	COME ALONG PLEASE	Bob Wallis	*Pye*	2
34	39	I CRIED FOR YOU	Ricky Stevens	*Columbia*	4
39	40	BAMBINO	Springfields	*Philips*	10

LW	TW	WEEK ENDING 25 JANUARY 1962			Wks
1	1	THE YOUNG ONES	Cliff Richard	*Columbia*	3
2	2	STRANGER ON THE SHORE	Mr. Acker Bilk	*Columbia*	9
4	3	HAPPY BIRTHDAY SWEET SIXTEEN	Neil Sedaka	*RCA*	6

In these weeks ■ Only Cliff Richard crashing in at number one prevents Mr. Acker Bilk from hitting the top. By the time *Stranger On The Shore* drops off the chart, Cliff will have had three more Top 10 hits (11.01.62) ■ This is the peak of the jazz boom. Traditional jazz is represented by Acker Bilk, Kenny Ball, the Temperance Seven, Tony Lightfoot, Dorothy Provine and Bob Wallis, while Dave Brubeck takes the modern route to chart success (11.01.62)■

□ Highest position disc reached ● Act's first ever week on chart

LW	TW	Title	Artist	Label	Wks
3	4	LET THERE BE DRUMS	Sandy Nelson	London	7
8	[5]	MULTIPLICATION	Bobby Darin	London	6
6	6	I'D NEVER FIND ANOTHER YOU	Billy Fury	Decca	6
10	7	RUN TO HIM	Bobby Vee	London	5
19	8	FORGET ME NOT	Eden Kane	Decca	2
5	9	MIDNIGHT IN MOSCOW	Kenny Ball & his Jazzmen	Pye	11
17	10	WALK ON BY	Leroy Van Dyke	Mercury	3
16	11	LET'S TWIST AGAIN	Chubby Checker	Columbia	5
9	12	JOHNNY WILL	Pat Boone	London	7
11	13	THE LION SLEEPS TONIGHT	Tokens	RCA	6
14	[14]	THE TWIST	Chubby Checker	Columbia	3
7	15	MOON RIVER	Danny Williams	HMV	12
13	16	THE LANGUAGE OF LOVE	John D. Loudermilk	RCA	4
12	17	SO LONG BABY	Del Shannon	London	8
21	18	CRYIN' IN THE RAIN	Everly Brothers	Warner Brothers	2
15	19	SON THIS IS SHE	John Leyton	HMV	4
20	20	YOU'RE THE ONLY GOOD THING	Jim Reeves	RCA	10
33	21	LONESOME	Adam Faith	Parlophone	2
25	22	I UNDERSTAND	G-Clefs	London	9
18	23	TOWER OF STRENGTH	Frankie Vaughan	Philips	11
26	24	THE COMANCHEROS	Lonnie Donegan	Pye	2
24	25	MY FRIEND THE SEA	Petula Clark	Pye	9
22	26	TOY BALLOONS	Russ Conway	Columbia	8
-	27	D-DARLING	Anthony Newley	Decca	1
23	28	WALKING BACK TO HAPPINESS	Helen Shapiro	Columbia	18
-	29	JEANNIE	Danny Williams	HMV	1
31	30	GOODBYE CRUEL WORLD	James Darren	Pye	4
27	31	DON'T BRING LULU	Dorothy Provine	Warner Brothers	7
35	32	PEPPERMINT TWIST	Danny Peppermint & the Jumping Jacks	London	2
38	[33]	COME ALONG PLEASE	Bob Wallis	Pye	3
29	34	TAKE GOOD CARE OF MY BABY	Bobby Vee	London	14
36	35	TAKE FIVE	Dave Brubeck	Fontana	14
-	36	THERE GOES THAT SONG AGAIN	Gary Miller	Pye	5
-	[37]	HE'S OLD ENOUGH TO KNOW BETTER	Brook Brothers	Pye	1
30	38	YOUR MA SAID YOU CRIED IN YOUR SLEEP LAST NIGHT	Doug Sheldon	Decca	3
28	39	HIS LATEST FLAME	Elvis Presley	RCA	13
34	40	SMALL SAD SAM	Phil McLean	Top Rank	2

WEEK ENDING 1 FEBRUARY 1962

LW	TW	Title	Artist	Label	Wks
1	[1]	THE YOUNG ONES	Cliff Richard	Columbia	4
11	[2]	LET'S TWIST AGAIN	Chubby Checker	Columbia	6
3	[3]	HAPPY BIRTHDAY SWEET SIXTEEN	Neil Sedaka	RCA	7
8	4	FORGET ME NOT	Eden Kane	Decca	3
2	5	STRANGER ON THE SHORE	Mr. Acker Bilk	Columbia	10
10	6	WALK ON BY	Leroy Van Dyke	Mercury	4
5	7	MULTIPLICATION	Bobby Darin	London	5
4	8	LET THERE BE DRUMS	Sandy Nelson	London	8
6	9	I'D NEVER FIND ANOTHER YOU	Billy Fury	Decca	7
9	10	MIDNIGHT IN MOSCOW	Kenny Ball & his Jazzmen	Pye	12
7	11	RUN TO HIM	Bobby Vee	London	6
-	12	ROCK-A-HULA BABY	Elvis Presley	RCA	1
18	13	CRYIN' IN THE RAIN	Everly Brothers	Warner Brothers	3
14	[14]	THE TWIST	Chubby Checker	Columbia	4
12	15	JOHNNY WILL	Pat Boone	London	8
16	16	THE LANGUAGE OF LOVE	John D. Loudermilk	RCA	5
13	17	THE LION SLEEPS TONIGHT	Tokens	RCA	7
24	18	THE COMANCHEROS	Lonnie Donegan	Pye	3
29	19	JEANNIE	Danny Williams	HMV	2
15	20	MOON RIVER	Danny Williams	HMV	13
19	21	SON THIS IS SHE	John Leyton	HMV	5
21	22	LONESOME	Adam Faith	Parlophone	3
17	23	SO LONG BABY	Del Shannon	London	9
20	24	YOU'RE THE ONLY GOOD THING	Jim Reeves	RCA	11
22	25	I UNDERSTAND	G-Clefs	London	10
32	[26]	PEPPERMINT TWIST	Danny Peppermint & the Jumping Jacks	London	3
27	27	D-DARLING	Anthony Newley	Decca	2
-	28	WIMOWEH	Karl Denver	Decca	1
26	29	TOY BALLOONS	Russ Conway	Columbia	9
-	30	LITTLE BITTY TEAR	Burl Ives ●	Brunswick	1
36	31	THERE GOES THAT SONG AGAIN	Gary Miller	Pye	6
38	32	YOUR MA SAID YOU CRIED IN YOUR SLEEP LAST NIGHT	Doug Sheldon	Decca	4
-	33	DON'T STOP TWIST	Frankie Vaughan	Philips	1
30	34	GOODBYE CRUEL WORLD	James Darren	Pye	5
33	35	COME ALONG PLEASE	Bob Wallis	Pye	4
40	36	SMALL SAD SAM	Phil McLean	Top Rank	3
-	37	NORMAN	Carol Deene ●	HMV	1
31	38	DON'T BRING LULU	Dorothy Provine	Warner Brothers	8
-	39	TALL DARK STRANGER	Rose Brennan	Philips	7
23	40	TOWER OF STRENGTH	Frankie Vaughan	Philips	12

WEEK ENDING 8 FEBRUARY 1962

LW	TW	Title	Artist	Label	Wks
1	[1]	THE YOUNG ONES	Cliff Richard	Columbia	5
2	[2]	LET'S TWIST AGAIN	Chubby Checker	Columbia	7
4	[3]	FORGET ME NOT	Eden Kane	Decca	4
12	4	ROCK-A-HULA BABY/CAN'T HELP FALLING IN LOVE	Elvis Presley	RCA	2
6	[5]	WALK ON BY	Leroy Van Dyke	Mercury	5
3	6	HAPPY BIRTHDAY SWEET SIXTEEN	Neil Sedaka	RCA	8
9	7	I'D NEVER FIND ANOTHER YOU	Billy Fury	Decca	8
5	8	STRANGER ON THE SHORE	Mr. Acker Bilk	Columbia	11
13	9	CRYIN' IN THE RAIN	Everly Brothers	Warner Brothers	4
7	10	MULTIPLICATION	Bobby Darin	London	6
11	11	RUN TO HIM	Bobby Vee	London	7
22	[12]	LONESOME	Adam Faith	Parlophone	4
8	13	LET THERE BE DRUMS	Sandy Nelson	London	9
18	[14]	THE COMANCHEROS	Lonnie Donegan	Pye	4
15	15	JOHNNY WILL	Pat Boone	London	9
19	16	JEANNIE	Danny Williams	HMV	3
14	17	THE TWIST	Chubby Checker	Columbia	5
10	18	MIDNIGHT IN MOSCOW	Kenny Ball & his Jazzmen	Pye	13
30	19	LITTLE BITTY TEAR	Burl Ives	Brunswick	2
28	20	WIMOWEH	Karl Denver	Decca	2
-	21	LITTLE BITTY TEAR	Miki and Griff	Pye	1
17	22	THE LION SLEEPS TONIGHT	Tokens	RCA	8
16	23	THE LANGUAGE OF LOVE	John D. Loudermilk	RCA	6
21	24	SON THIS IS SHE	John Leyton	HMV	6
27	[25]	D-DARLING	Anthony Newley	Decca	3
33	26	DON'T STOP TWIST	Frankie Vaughan	Philips	2
24	27	YOU'RE THE ONLY GOOD THING	Jim Reeves	RCA	12
20	28	MOON RIVER	Danny Williams	HMV	14
31	[29]	THERE GOES THAT SONG AGAIN	Gary Miller	Pye	7
23	30	SO LONG BABY	Del Shannon	London	10
-	31	PIANISSIMO	Ken Dodd	Decca	1
37	32	NORMAN	Carol Deene	HMV	2
25	33	I UNDERSTAND	G-Clefs	London	11
38	34	DON'T BRING LULU	Dorothy Provine	Warner Brothers	9
26	35	PEPPERMINT TWIST	Danny Peppermint & the Jumping Jacks	London	4
-	[36]	IT'S A RAGGY WALTZ	Dave Brubeck	Fontana	1
29	37	TOY BALLOONS	Russ Conway	Columbia	10
-	38	PEPPERMINT TWIST	Joey Dee and the Starliters ●	Columbia	1
-	39	WALK AWAY	Shane Fenton and the Fentones	Parlophone	1
32	40	YOUR MA SAID YOU CRIED IN YOUR SLEEP LAST NIGHT	Doug Sheldon	Decca	5

WEEK ENDING 15 FEBRUARY 1962

LW	TW	Title	Artist	Label	Wks
1	[1]	THE YOUNG ONES	Cliff Richard	Columbia	6
4	2	ROCK-A-HULA BABY	Elvis Presley	RCA	3
3	[3]	FORGET ME NOT	Eden Kane	Decca	5
2	4	LET'S TWIST AGAIN	Chubby Checker	Columbia	8
5	[5]	WALK ON BY	Leroy Van Dyke	Mercury	6
11	[6]	RUN TO HIM	Bobby Vee	London	8
8	7	STRANGER ON THE SHORE	Mr. Acker Bilk	Columbia	12
6	8	HAPPY BIRTHDAY SWEET SIXTEEN	Neil Sedaka	RCA	9
9	9	CRYIN' IN THE RAIN	Everly Brothers	Warner Brothers	5

■Phil McLean's *Small Sad Sam*, a send-up of Jimmy Dean's *Big Bad John* but this time featuring a coward stuck in a lift, does not do anywhere near as well as the original (01.02.62) ■ Karl Denver's *Wimoweh* is the same song as the Tokens' *The Lion Sleeps Tonight* (01.02.62)■

February 1962

□ Highest position disc reached ● Act's first ever week on chart

LW	TW	Title	Artist	Label	Wks
7	10	I'D NEVER FIND ANOTHER YOU	Billy Fury	*Decca*	9
10	11	MULTIPLICATION	Bobby Darin	*London*	7
20	12	WIMOWEH	Karl Denver	*Decca*	3
19	13	LITTLE BITTY TEAR	Burl Ives	*Brunswick*	3
12	14	LONESOME	Adam Faith	*Parlophone*	5
16	15	JEANNIE	Danny Williams	*HMV*	4
17	16	THE TWIST	Chubby Checker	*Columbia*	6
14	17	THE COMANCHEROS	Lonnie Donegan	*Pye*	5
13	18	LET THERE BE DRUMS	Sandy Nelson	*London*	10
21	19	LITTLE BITTY TEAR	Miki and Griff	*Pye*	2
18	20	MIDNIGHT IN MOSCOW	Kenny Ball & his Jazzmen	*Pye*	14
22	21	THE LION SLEEPS TONIGHT	Tokens	*RCA*	9
26	□22	DON'T STOP TWIST	Frankie Vaughan	*Philips*	3
15	23	JOHNNY WILL	Pat Boone	*London*	10
32	□24	NORMAN	Carol Deene	*HMV*	3
31	25	PIANISSIMO	Ken Dodd	*Decca*	2
23	26	THE LANGUAGE OF LOVE	John D. Loudermilk	*RCA*	7
24	27	SON THIS IS SHE	John Leyton	*HMV*	7
27	28	YOU'RE THE ONLY GOOD THING	Jim Reeves	*RCA*	13
-	29	MARCH OF THE SIAMESE CHILDREN	Kenny Ball and his Jazzmen	*Pye*	1
-	30	SOFTLY AS I LEAVE YOU	Matt Monro	*Parlophone*	1
25	31	D-DARLING	Anthony Newley	*Decca*	4
28	32	MOON RIVER	Danny Williams	*HMV*	15
-	33	TELL ME WHAT HE SAID	Helen Shapiro	*Columbia*	1
-	34	TONIGHT	Shirley Bassey	*Columbia*	1
38	35	PEPPERMINT TWIST	Joey Dee and the Starliters	*Columbia*	2
-	36	HOLE IN THE GROUND	Bernard Cribbins ●	*Parlophone*	1
36	37	IT'S A RAGGY WALTZ	Dave Brubeck	*Fontana*	2
39	□38	WALK AWAY	Shane Fenton and the Fentones	*Parlophone*	2
29	39	THERE GOES THAT SONG AGAIN	Gary Miller	*Pye*	8
33	40	I UNDERSTAND	G-Clefs	*London*	12

WEEK ENDING 22 FEBRUARY 1962

LW	TW	Title	Artist	Label	Wks
2	□1	ROCK-A-HULA BABY	Elvis Presley	*RCA*	4
1	2	THE YOUNG ONES	Cliff Richard	*Columbia*	7
4	3	LET'S TWIST AGAIN	Chubby Checker	*Columbia*	9
3	4	FORGET ME NOT	Eden Kane	*Decca*	6
5	□5	WALK ON BY	Leroy Van Dyke	*Mercury*	7
6	□6	RUN TO HIM	Bobby Vee	*London*	9
9	7	CRYIN' IN THE RAIN	Everly Brothers	*Warner Brothers*	6
12	8	WIMOWEH	Karl Denver	*Decca*	4
13	□9	LITTLE BITTY TEAR	Burl Ives	*Brunswick*	4
10	10	I'D NEVER FIND ANOTHER YOU	Billy Fury	*Decca*	10
11	11	MULTIPLICATION	Bobby Darin	*London*	8
7	12	STRANGER ON THE SHORE	Mr. Acker Bilk	*Columbia*	13
8	13	HAPPY BIRTHDAY SWEET SIXTEEN	Neil Sedaka	*RCA*	10
15	□14	JEANNIE	Danny Williams	*HMV*	5
29	15	MARCH OF THE SIAMESE CHILDREN	Kenny Ball and his Jazzmen	*Pye*	2
17	16	THE COMANCHEROS	Lonnie Donegan	*Pye*	6
14	17	LONESOME	Adam Faith	*Parlophone*	6
16	18	THE TWIST	Chubby Checker	*Columbia*	7
30	19	SOFTLY AS I LEAVE YOU	Matt Monro	*Parlophone*	2
19	20	LITTLE BITTY TEAR	Miki and Griff	*Pye*	3
20	21	MIDNIGHT IN MOSCOW	Kenny Ball & his Jazzmen	*Pye*	15
33	22	TELL ME WHAT HE SAID	Helen Shapiro	*Columbia*	2
25	23	PIANISSIMO	Ken Dodd	*Decca*	3
22	24	DON'T STOP TWIST	Frankie Vaughan	*Philips*	4
18	25	LET THERE BE DRUMS	Sandy Nelson	*London*	11
34	26	TONIGHT	Shirley Bassey	*Columbia*	2
27	27	SON THIS IS SHE	John Leyton	*HMV*	8
32	28	MOON RIVER	Danny Williams	*HMV*	16
24	29	NORMAN	Carol Deene	*HMV*	4
21	30	THE LION SLEEPS TONIGHT	Tokens	*RCA*	10
-	31	THE WANDERER	Dion	*HMV*	1
26	32	THE LANGUAGE OF LOVE	John D. Loudermilk	*RCA*	8
28	33	YOU'RE THE ONLY GOOD THING	Jim Reeves	*RCA*	14
-	34	LESSONS IN LOVE	Allisons	*Fontana*	1
35	35	PEPPERMINT TWIST	Joey Dee and the Starliters	*Columbia*	3
36	36	HOLE IN THE GROUND	Bernard Cribbins	*Parlophone*	2
-	37	LESSON ONE	Russ Conway	*Columbia*	1
23	38	JOHNNY WILL	Pat Boone	*London*	11
31	39	D-DARLING	Anthony Newley	*Decca*	5
-	40	I'LL SEE YOU IN MY DREAMS	Pat Boone	*London*	1

WEEK ENDING 1 MARCH 1962

LW	TW	Title	Artist	Label	Wks
1	□1	CAN'T HELP FALLING IN LOVE/ROCK-A-HULA BABY	Elvis Presley	*RCA*	5
2	2	THE YOUNG ONES	Cliff Richard	*Columbia*	8
3	3	LET'S TWIST AGAIN	Chubby Checker	*Columbia*	10
4	4	FORGET ME NOT	Eden Kane	*Decca*	7
8	5	WIMOWEH	Karl Denver	*Decca*	5
7	□6	CRYIN' IN THE RAIN	Everly Brothers	*Warner Brothers*	7
5	7	WALK ON BY	Leroy Van Dyke	*Mercury*	8
15	8	MARCH OF THE SIAMESE CHILDREN	Kenny Ball and his Jazzmen	*Pye*	3
9	□9	LITTLE BITTY TEAR	Burl Ives	*Brunswick*	5
10	10	I'D NEVER FIND ANOTHER YOU	Billy Fury	*Decca*	11
12	11	STRANGER ON THE SHORE	Mr. Acker Bilk	*Columbia*	14
22	12	TELL ME WHAT HE SAID	Helen Shapiro	*Columbia*	3
19	13	SOFTLY AS I LEAVE YOU	Matt Monro	*Parlophone*	3
13	14	HAPPY BIRTHDAY SWEET SIXTEEN	Neil Sedaka	*RCA*	11
6	15	RUN TO HIM	Bobby Vee	*London*	10
16	16	THE COMANCHEROS	Lonnie Donegan	*Pye*	7
20	17	LITTLE BITTY TEAR	Miki and Griff	*Pye*	4
14	18	JEANNIE	Danny Williams	*HMV*	6
11	19	MULTIPLICATION	Bobby Darin	*London*	9
-	20	WONDERFUL LAND	Shadows	*Columbia*	1
23	□21	PIANISSIMO	Ken Dodd	*Decca*	4
36	22	HOLE IN THE GROUND	Bernard Cribbins	*Parlophone*	3
31	23	THE WANDERER	Dion	*HMV*	2
18	24	THE TWIST	Chubby Checker	*Columbia*	8
26	25	TONIGHT	Shirley Bassey	*Columbia*	3
21	26	MIDNIGHT IN MOSCOW	Kenny Ball & his Jazzmen	*Pye*	16
17	27	LONESOME	Adam Faith	*Parlophone*	7
24	28	DON'T STOP TWIST	Frankie Vaughan	*Philips*	5
25	29	LET THERE BE DRUMS	Sandy Nelson	*London*	12
-	30	THEME FROM 'DR. KILDARE'	Johnny Spence ●	*Parlophone*	1
40	31	I'LL SEE YOU IN MY DREAMS	Pat Boone	*London*	2
33	32	YOU'RE THE ONLY GOOD THING	Jim Reeves	*RCA*	15
35	□33	PEPPERMINT TWIST	Joey Dee and the Starliters	*Columbia*	4
34	34	LESSONS IN LOVE	Allisons	*Fontana*	2
-	35	THEME FROM 'Z CARS'	Johnny Keating ●	*Pye*	1
27	36	SON THIS IS SHE	John Leyton	*HMV*	9
30	37	THE LION SLEEPS TONIGHT	Tokens	*RCA*	11
-	□38	WALK AWAY	Shane Fenton and the Fentones	*Parlophone*	3
28	39	MOON RIVER	Danny Williams	*HMV*	17
29	40	NORMAN	Carol Deene	*HMV*	5

WEEK ENDING 8 MARCH 1962

LW	TW	Title	Artist	Label	Wks
1	□1	CAN'T HELP FALLING IN LOVE/ROCK-A-HULA BABY	Elvis Presley	*RCA*	6
2	2	THE YOUNG ONES	Cliff Richard	*Columbia*	9
3	3	LET'S TWIST AGAIN	Chubby Checker	*Columbia*	11
5	□4	WIMOWEH	Karl Denver	*Decca*	6
12	5	TELL ME WHAT HE SAID	Helen Shapiro	*Columbia*	4
8	6	MARCH OF THE SIAMESE CHILDREN	Kenny Ball and his Jazzmen	*Pye*	4
4	7	FORGET ME NOT	Eden Kane	*Decca*	8
7	8	WALK ON BY	Leroy Van Dyke	*Mercury*	9
20	9	WONDERFUL LAND	Shadows	*Columbia*	2
6	10	CRYIN' IN THE RAIN	Everly Brothers	*Warner Brothers*	8
9	11	LITTLE BITTY TEAR	Burl Ives	*Brunswick*	6
13	12	SOFTLY AS I LEAVE YOU	Matt Monro	*Parlophone*	4
11	13	STRANGER ON THE SHORE	Mr. Acker Bilk	*Columbia*	15
14	14	HAPPY BIRTHDAY SWEET SIXTEEN	Neil Sedaka	*RCA*	12
10	15	I'D NEVER FIND ANOTHER YOU	Billy Fury	*Decca*	12
17	□16	LITTLE BITTY TEAR	Miki and Griff	*Pye*	5

In these weeks ■ *Can't Help Falling In Love*, the hit ballad from 'Blue Hawaii', is only listed as a double A-side with *Rock-A-Hula Baby* after the record has reached number one (01.03.62) ■ Television themes begin to fill up the charts. After *Stranger On The Shore* comes *Z Cars* and *Dr. Kildare*, soon there will be more versions of *Z Cars*, the *Maigret* theme and a vocal version of *Dr. Kildare* (01.03.62)■

March 1962

□ Highest position disc reached ● Act's first ever week on chart

LW	TW	Title	Artist	Label	Wks
15	17	RUN TO HIM	Bobby Vee	*London*	11
22	18	HOLE IN THE GROUND	Bernard Cribbins	*Parlophone*	4
18	19	JEANNIE	Danny Williams	*HMV*	7
23	20	THE WANDERER	Dion	*HMV*	3
25	[21]	TONIGHT	Shirley Bassey	*Columbia*	4
21	22	PIANISSIMO	Ken Dodd	*Decca*	5
-	23	LESSON ONE	Russ Conway	*Columbia*	2
35	24	THEME FROM 'Z CARS'	Johnny Keating	*Pye*	2
16	25	THE COMANCHEROS	Lonnie Donegan	*Pye*	8
26	26	MIDNIGHT IN MOSCOW	Kenny Ball & his Jazzmen	*Pye*	17
31	[27]	I'LL SEE YOU IN MY DREAMS	Pat Boone	*London*	3
-	28	DREAM BABY	Roy Orbison	*London*	1
-	29	NEVER GOODBYE	Karl Denver	*Decca*	1
28	30	DON'T STOP TWIST	Frankie Vaughan	*Philips*	6
34	31	LESSONS IN LOVE	Allisons	*Fontana*	3
27	32	LONESOME	Adam Faith	*Parlophone*	8
32	33	YOU'RE THE ONLY GOOD THING	Jim Reeves	*RCA*	16
24	34	THE TWIST	Chubby Checker	*Columbia*	9
19	35	MULTIPLICATION	Bobby Darin	*London*	10
30	36	THEME FROM 'DR. KILDARE'	Johnny Spence	*Parlophone*	2
-	37	TWISTIN' THE NIGHT AWAY	Sam Cooke	*RCA*	1
29	38	LET THERE BE DRUMS	Sandy Nelson	*London*	13
-	[39]	WALK WITH ME MY ANGEL	Don Charles ●	*Decca*	1
33	40	PEPPERMINT TWIST	Joey Dee and the Starliters	*Columbia*	5

WEEK ENDING **15 MARCH 1962**

LW	TW	Title	Artist	Label	Wks
1	[1]	CAN'T HELP FALLING IN LOVE/ROCK-A-HULA BABY	Elvis Presley	*RCA*	7
9	2	WONDERFUL LAND	Shadows	*Columbia*	3
5	3	TELL ME WHAT HE SAID	Helen Shapiro	*Columbia*	5
2	4	THE YOUNG ONES	Cliff Richard	*Columbia*	10
4	5	WIMOWEH	Karl Denver	*Decca*	7
6	6	MARCH OF THE SIAMESE CHILDREN	Kenny Ball and his Jazzmen	*Pye*	5
3	7	LET'S TWIST AGAIN	Chubby Checker	*Columbia*	12
13	8	STRANGER ON THE SHORE	Mr. Acker Bilk	*Columbia*	16
8	9	WALK ON BY	Leroy Van Dyke	*Mercury*	10
7	10	FORGET ME NOT	Eden Kane	*Decca*	9
12	11	SOFTLY AS I LEAVE YOU	Matt Monro	*Parlophone*	5
10	12	CRYIN' IN THE RAIN	Everly Brothers	*Warner Brothers*	9
11	13	LITTLE BITTY TEAR	Burl Ives	*Brunswick*	7
18	14	HOLE IN THE GROUND	Bernard Cribbins	*Parlophone*	5
14	15	HAPPY BIRTHDAY SWEET SIXTEEN	Neil Sedaka	*RCA*	13
28	16	DREAM BABY	Roy Orbison	*London*	2
20	17	THE WANDERER	Dion	*HMV*	4
16	18	LITTLE BITTY TEAR	Miki and Griff	*Pye*	6
19	19	JEANNIE	Danny Williams	*HMV*	8
24	20	THEME FROM 'Z CARS'	Johnny Keating	*Pye*	3
15	21	I'D NEVER FIND ANOTHER YOU	Billy Fury	*Decca*	13
23	22	LESSON ONE	Russ Conway	*Columbia*	3
21	23	TONIGHT	Shirley Bassey	*Columbia*	5
37	24	TWISTIN' THE NIGHT AWAY	Sam Cooke	*RCA*	2
17	25	RUN TO HIM	Bobby Vee	*London*	12
22	26	PIANISSIMO	Ken Dodd	*Decca*	6
36	27	THEME FROM 'DR. KILDARE'	Johnny Spence	*Parlophone*	3
25	28	THE COMANCHEROS	Lonnie Donegan	*Pye*	9
-	[29]	PLEASE DON'T ASK ABOUT BARBARA	Bobby Vee	*Liberty*	1
31	[30]	LESSONS IN LOVE	Allisons	*Fontana*	4
27	31	I'LL SEE YOU IN MY DREAMS	Pat Boone	*London*	4
-	[32]	LETTER FULL OF TEARS	Billy Fury	*Decca*	1
29	33	NEVER GOODBYE	Karl Denver	*Decca*	2
-	34	TOWN WITHOUT PITY	Gene Pitney	*HMV*	1
26	35	MIDNIGHT IN MOSCOW	Kenny Ball & his Jazzmen	*Pye*	18
40	36	PEPPERMINT TWIST	Joey Dee and the Starliters	*Columbia*	6
-	37	FANLIGHT FANNY	Clinton Ford	*Oriole*	1
32	38	LONESOME	Adam Faith	*Parlophone*	9
33	39	YOU'RE THE ONLY GOOD THING	Jim Reeves	*RCA*	17
30	40	DON'T STOP TWIST	Frankie Vaughan	*Philips*	7

WEEK ENDING **22 MARCH 1962**

LW	TW	Title	Artist	Label	Wks
2	[1]	WONDERFUL LAND	Shadows	*Columbia*	4
3	[2]	TELL ME WHAT HE SAID	Helen Shapiro	*Columbia*	6
1	3	CAN'T HELP FALLING IN LOVE/ROCK-A-HULA BABY	Elvis Presley	*RCA*	8
6	[4]	MARCH OF THE SIAMESE CHILDREN	Kenny Ball and his Jazzmen	*Pye*	6
7	5	LET'S TWIST AGAIN	Chubby Checker	*Columbia*	13
5	6	WIMOWEH	Karl Denver	*Decca*	8
4	7	THE YOUNG ONES	Cliff Richard	*Columbia*	11
8	8	STRANGER ON THE SHORE	Mr. Acker Bilk	*Columbia*	17
16	9	DREAM BABY	Roy Orbison	*London*	3
17	[10]	THE WANDERER	Dion	*HMV*	5
11	11	SOFTLY AS I LEAVE YOU	Matt Monro	*Parlophone*	6
14	12	HOLE IN THE GROUND	Bernard Cribbins	*Parlophone*	6
12	13	CRYIN' IN THE RAIN	Everly Brothers	*Warner Brothers*	10
10	14	FORGET ME NOT	Eden Kane	*Decca*	10
9	15	WALK ON BY	Leroy Van Dyke	*Mercury*	11
13	16	LITTLE BITTY TEAR	Burl Ives	*Brunswick*	8
20	17	THEME FROM 'Z CARS'	Johnny Keating	*Pye*	4
24	18	TWISTIN' THE NIGHT AWAY	Sam Cooke	*RCA*	3
18	19	LITTLE BITTY TEAR	Miki and Griff	*Pye*	7
19	20	JEANNIE	Danny Williams	*HMV*	9
22	[21]	LESSON ONE	Russ Conway	*Columbia*	4
15	22	HAPPY BIRTHDAY SWEET SIXTEEN	Neil Sedaka	*RCA*	14
27	23	THEME FROM 'DR. KILDARE'	Johnny Spence	*Parlophone*	4
-	24	HEY LITTLE GIRL	Del Shannon	*London*	1
-	25	HEY BABY	Bruce Channel ●	*Mercury*	1
25	26	RUN TO HIM	Bobby Vee	*London*	13
26	27	PIANISSIMO	Ken Dodd	*Decca*	7
23	28	TONIGHT	Shirley Bassey	*Columbia*	6
-	29	LOVE ME WARM AND TENDER	Paul Anka	*RCA*	1
31	30	I'LL SEE YOU IN MY DREAMS	Pat Boone	*London*	5
29	31	PLEASE DON'T ASK ABOUT BARBARA	Bobby Vee	*Liberty*	2
34	[32]	TOWN WITHOUT PITY	Gene Pitney	*HMV*	2
21	33	I'D NEVER FIND ANOTHER YOU	Billy Fury	*Decca*	14
35	34	MIDNIGHT IN MOSCOW	Kenny Ball & his Jazzmen	*Pye*	19
37	35	FANLIGHT FANNY	Clinton Ford	*Oriole*	2
33	36	NEVER GOODBYE	Karl Denver	*Decca*	3
32	37	LETTER FULL OF TEARS	Billy Fury	*Decca*	2
30	38	LESSONS IN LOVE	Allisons	*Fontana*	5
28	39	THE COMANCHEROS	Lonnie Donegan	*Pye*	10
-	[40]	LONE RIDER	John Leyton	*HMV*	1

WEEK ENDING **29 MARCH 1962**

LW	TW	Title	Artist	Label	Wks
1	[1]	WONDERFUL LAND	Shadows	*Columbia*	5
2	[2]	TELL ME WHAT HE SAID	Helen Shapiro	*Columbia*	7
3	3	CAN'T HELP FALLING IN LOVE/ROCK-A-HULA BABY	Elvis Presley	*RCA*	9
9	4	DREAM BABY	Roy Orbison	*London*	4
5	5	LET'S TWIST AGAIN	Chubby Checker	*Columbia*	14
6	6	WIMOWEH	Karl Denver	*Decca*	9
8	7	STRANGER ON THE SHORE	Mr. Acker Bilk	*Columbia*	18
4	8	MARCH OF THE SIAMESE CHILDREN	Kenny Ball and his Jazzmen	*Pye*	7
12	[9]	HOLE IN THE GROUND	Bernard Cribbins	*Parlophone*	7
11	[10]	SOFTLY AS I LEAVE YOU	Matt Monro	*Parlophone*	7
7	11	THE YOUNG ONES	Cliff Richard	*Columbia*	12
25	12	HEY BABY	Bruce Channel	*Mercury*	2
10	13	THE WANDERER	Dion	*HMV*	6
17	14	THEME FROM 'Z CARS'	Johnny Keating	*Pye*	5
18	15	TWISTIN' THE NIGHT AWAY	Sam Cooke	*RCA*	4
13	16	CRYIN' IN THE RAIN	Everly Brothers	*Warner Brothers*	11
15	17	WALK ON BY	Leroy Van Dyke	*Mercury*	12
24	18	HEY LITTLE GIRL	Del Shannon	*London*	2
23	19	THEME FROM 'DR. KILDARE'	Johnny Spence	*Parlophone*	5
14	20	FORGET ME NOT	Eden Kane	*Decca*	11
36	21	NEVER GOODBYE	Karl Denver	*Decca*	4
16	22	LITTLE BITTY TEAR	Burl Ives	*Brunswick*	9
29	23	LOVE ME WARM AND TENDER	Paul Anka	*RCA*	2
19	24	LITTLE BITTY TEAR	Miki and Griff	*Pye*	8

■The first of five different songs called *Tonight* to hit Top 40, Shirley Bassey's record of the song from 'West Side Story' is the least successful of all the charting *Tonights* peaking at number 21 (08.03.62) ■ The harmonica on Bruce Channel's *Hey Baby*, played by Delbert McClinton will influence both Frank Ifield's *I Remember You* and more importantly, John Lennon on the Beatles' *Love Me Do* (22.03.62)■

March 1962

□ Highest position disc reached ● Act's first ever week on chart

LW	TW	Title	Artist	Label	Wks
-	25	WHEN MY LITTLE GIRL IS SMILING	Craig Douglas	Top Rank	1
20	26	JEANNIE	Danny Williams	HMV	10
27	27	PIANISSIMO	Ken Dodd	Decca	8
22	28	HAPPY BIRTHDAY SWEET SIXTEEN	Neil Sedaka	RCA	15
-	29	WHAT KIND OF FOOL AM I/GONNA BUILD A MOUNTAIN	Sammy Davis Jnr	Reprise	1
-	30	DRUMS ARE MY BEAT	Sandy Nelson	London	1
30	31	I'LL SEE YOU IN MY DREAMS	Pat Boone	London	6
35	32	FANLIGHT FANNY	Clinton Ford	Oriole	3
21	33	LESSON ONE	Russ Conway	Columbia	5
-	34	BRAZILIAN LOVE SONG	Nat 'King' Cole	Capitol	1
31	35	PLEASE DON'T ASK ABOUT BARBARA	Bobby Vee	Liberty	3
28	36	TONIGHT	Shirley Bassey	Columbia	7
32	37	TOWN WITHOUT PITY	Gene Pitney	HMV	3
-	38	THEME FROM 'Z CARS'	Norrie Paramor	Columbia	1
34	39	MIDNIGHT IN MOSCOW	Kenny Ball & his Jazzmen	Pye	20
26	40	RUN TO HIM	Bobby Vee	London	14

WEEK ENDING 5 APRIL 1962

LW	TW	Title	Artist	Label	Wks
1	1	WONDERFUL LAND	Shadows	Columbia	6
2	2	TELL ME WHAT HE SAID	Helen Shapiro	Columbia	8
4	3	DREAM BABY	Roy Orbison	London	5
3	4	CAN'T HELP FALLING IN LOVE/ROCK-A-HULA BABY	Elvis Presley	RCA	10
6	5	WIMOWEH	Karl Denver	Decca	10
7	6	STRANGER ON THE SHORE	Mr. Acker Bilk	Columbia	19
15	7	TWISTIN' THE NIGHT AWAY	Sam Cooke	RCA	5
18	8	HEY LITTLE GIRL	Del Shannon	London	3
9	9	HOLE IN THE GROUND	Bernard Cribbins	Parlophone	8
10	10	SOFTLY AS I LEAVE YOU	Matt Monro	Parlophone	8
14	11	THEME FROM 'Z CARS'	Johnny Keating	Pye	6
12	12	HEY BABY	Bruce Channel	Mercury	3
5	13	LET'S TWIST AGAIN	Chubby Checker	Columbia	15
8	14	MARCH OF THE SIAMESE CHILDREN	Kenny Ball and his Jazzmen	Pye	8
13	15	THE WANDERER	Dion	HMV	7
11	16	THE YOUNG ONES	Cliff Richard	Columbia	13
19	17	THEME FROM 'DR. KILDARE'	Johnny Spence	Parlophone	6
21	18	NEVER GOODBYE	Karl Denver	Decca	5
23	19	LOVE ME WARM AND TENDER	Paul Anka	RCA	3
25	20	WHEN MY LITTLE GIRL IS SMILING	Craig Douglas	Top Rank	2
-	21	THEME FROM 'MAIGRET'	Joe Loss	HMV	1
32	22	FANLIGHT FANNY	Clinton Ford	Oriole	4
16	23	CRYIN' IN THE RAIN	Everly Brothers	Warner Brothers	12
-	24	WHEN MY LITTLE GIRL IS SMILING	Jimmy Justice	Pye	1
27	25	PIANISSIMO	Ken Dodd	Decca	9
29	26	WHAT KIND OF FOOL AM I/GONNA BUILD A MOUNTAIN	Sammy Davis Jnr	Reprise	2
17	27	WALK ON BY	Leroy Van Dyke	Mercury	13
-	28	YOUNG WORLD	Rick Nelson	London	1
22	29	LITTLE BITTY TEAR	Burl Ives	Brunswick	10
24	30	LITTLE BITTY TEAR	Miki and Griff	Pye	9
-	31	WHEN MY LITTLE GIRL IS SMILING	Drifters	London	1
35	32	PLEASE DON'T ASK ABOUT BARBARA	Bobby Vee	Liberty	4
31	33	I'LL SEE YOU IN MY DREAMS	Pat Boone	London	7
30	34	DRUMS ARE MY BEAT	Sandy Nelson	London	2
20	35	FORGET ME NOT	Eden Kane	Decca	12
-	36	LETTER FULL OF TEARS	Billy Fury	Decca	3
33	37	LESSON ONE	Russ Conway	Columbia	6
37	38	TOWN WITHOUT PITY	Gene Pitney	HMV	4
-	39	HER ROYAL MAJESTY	James Darren	Pye	1
26	40	JEANNIE	Danny Williams	HMV	11

WEEK ENDING 12 APRIL 1962

LW	TW	Title	Artist	Label	Wks
1	1	WONDERFUL LAND	Shadows	Columbia	7
3	2	DREAM BABY	Roy Orbison	London	6
2	3	TELL ME WHAT HE SAID	Helen Shapiro	Columbia	9
4	4	CAN'T HELP FALLING IN LOVE/ROCK-A-HULA BABY	Elvis Presley	RCA	11
12	5	HEY BABY	Bruce Channel	Mercury	4
7	6	TWISTIN' THE NIGHT AWAY	Sam Cooke	RCA	6
6	7	STRANGER ON THE SHORE	Mr. Acker Bilk	Columbia	20
5	8	WIMOWEH	Karl Denver	Decca	11
8	9	HEY LITTLE GIRL	Del Shannon	London	4
9	10	HOLE IN THE GROUND	Bernard Cribbins	Parlophone	9
11	11	THEME FROM 'Z CARS'	Johnny Keating	Pye	7
18	12	NEVER GOODBYE	Karl Denver	Decca	6
13	13	LET'S TWIST AGAIN	Chubby Checker	Columbia	16
10	14	SOFTLY AS I LEAVE YOU	Matt Monro	Parlophone	9
17	15	THEME FROM 'DR. KILDARE'	Johnny Spence	Parlophone	7
20	16	WHEN MY LITTLE GIRL IS SMILING	Craig Douglas	Top Rank	3
16	17	THE YOUNG ONES	Cliff Richard	Columbia	14
15	18	THE WANDERER	Dion	HMV	8
19	19	LOVE ME WARM AND TENDER	Paul Anka	RCA	4
14	20	MARCH OF THE SIAMESE CHILDREN	Kenny Ball and his Jazzmen	Pye	9
21	21	THEME FROM 'MAIGRET'	Joe Loss	HMV	2
24	22	WHEN MY LITTLE GIRL IS SMILING	Jimmy Justice	Pye	2
28	23	YOUNG WORLD	Rick Nelson	London	2
25	24	PIANISSIMO	Ken Dodd	Decca	10
-	25	THE PARTY'S OVER	Lonnie Donegan	Pye	1
-	26	SLOW TWISTIN'	Chubby Checker	Columbia	1
22	27	FANLIGHT FANNY	Clinton Ford	Oriole	5
29	28	LITTLE BITTY TEAR	Burl Ives	Brunswick	11
-	29	SPEAK TO ME PRETTY	Brenda Lee	Brunswick	1
23	30	CRYIN' IN THE RAIN	Everly Brothers	Warner Brothers	13
34	31	DRUMS ARE MY BEAT	Sandy Nelson	London	3
26	32	WHAT KIND OF FOOL AM I/GONNA BUILD A MOUNTAIN	Sammy Davis Jnr	Reprise	3
33	33	I'LL SEE YOU IN MY DREAMS	Pat Boone	London	8
35	34	FORGET ME NOT	Eden Kane	Decca	13
-	35	IT'S ALL OVER NOW	Shane Fenton	Parlophone	1
39	36	HER ROYAL MAJESTY	James Darren	Pye	2
-	37	WONDERFUL WORLD OF THE YOUNG	Danny Williams	HMV	1
32	38	PLEASE DON'T ASK ABOUT BARBARA	Bobby Vee	Liberty	5
36	39	LETTER FULL OF TEARS	Billy Fury	Decca	4
31	40	WHEN MY LITTLE GIRL IS SMILING	Drifters	London	2

WEEK ENDING 19 APRIL 1962

LW	TW	Title	Artist	Label	Wks
1	1	WONDERFUL LAND	Shadows	Columbia	8
2	2	DREAM BABY	Roy Orbison	London	7
9	3	HEY LITTLE GIRL	Del Shannon	London	5
5	4	HEY BABY	Bruce Channel	Mercury	5
3	5	TELL ME WHAT HE SAID	Helen Shapiro	Columbia	10
4	6	CAN'T HELP FALLING IN LOVE/ROCK-A-HULA BABY	Elvis Presley	RCA	12
6	7	TWISTIN' THE NIGHT AWAY	Sam Cooke	RCA	7
11	8	THEME FROM 'Z CARS'	Johnny Keating	Pye	8
12	9	NEVER GOODBYE	Karl Denver	Decca	7
16	10	WHEN MY LITTLE GIRL IS SMILING	Craig Douglas	Top Rank	4
8	11	WIMOWEH	Karl Denver	Decca	12
22	12	WHEN MY LITTLE GIRL IS SMILING	Jimmy Justice	Pye	3
7	13	STRANGER ON THE SHORE	Mr. Acker Bilk	Columbia	21
10	14	HOLE IN THE GROUND	Bernard Cribbins	Parlophone	10
13	15	LET'S TWIST AGAIN	Chubby Checker	Columbia	17
14	16	SOFTLY AS I LEAVE YOU	Matt Monro	Parlophone	10
29	17	SPEAK TO ME PRETTY	Brenda Lee	Brunswick	2
15	18	THEME FROM 'DR. KILDARE'	Johnny Spence	Parlophone	8
17	19	THE YOUNG ONES	Cliff Richard	Columbia	15
21	20	THEME FROM 'MAIGRET'	Joe Loss	HMV	3
25	21	THE PARTY'S OVER	Lonnie Donegan	Pye	2
37	22	WONDERFUL WORLD OF THE YOUNG	Danny Williams	HMV	2
18	23	THE WANDERER	Dion	HMV	9
20	24	MARCH OF THE SIAMESE CHILDREN	Kenny Ball and his Jazzmen	Pye	10
19	25	LOVE ME WARM AND TENDER	Paul Anka	RCA	5
23	26	YOUNG WORLD	Rick Nelson	London	3
26	27	SLOW TWISTIN'	Chubby Checker	Columbia	2
24	28	PIANISSIMO	Ken Dodd	Decca	11

In these weeks ■ Three confusingly titled singles by American stars jockey for position below the Shadows: *Dream Baby*, *Hey Baby* and *Hey Little Girl*. It is lucky that Mark Wynter's 1961 hit *Dream Girl* is not up there too (19.04.62) ■ Apart from instrumental groups and orchestras, the only groups in the chart are the duos, the Everly Brothers and Miki and Griff. Within a year, a complete transformation will have taken place (19.04.62)■

LW	TW	Title	Artist	Label	Wks
35	29	IT'S ALL OVER NOW	Shane Fenton	Parlophone	2
27	30	FANLIGHT FANNY	Clinton Ford	Oriole	6
-	31	NUT ROCKER	B. Bumble and the Stingers ●	Top Rank	1
40	32	WHEN MY LITTLE GIRL IS SMILING	Drifters	London	3
-	33	THEME FROM 'Z CARS'	Norrie Paramor	Columbia	2
-	34	LOVE LETTERS	Ketty Lester ●	London	1
-	35	LITTLE BITTY TEAR	Miki and Griff	Pye	10
38	36	PLEASE DON'T ASK ABOUT BARBARA	Bobby Vee	Liberty	6
28	37	LITTLE BITTY TEAR	Burl Ives	Brunswick	12
-	38	EVERYBODY'S TWISTING	Frank Sinatra	Reprise	1
30	39	CRYIN' IN THE RAIN	Everly Brothers	Warner Brothers	14
-	40	KING OF CLOWNS	Neil Sedaka	RCA	1

WEEK ENDING 26 APRIL 1962

LW	TW	Title	Artist	Label	Wks
1	1	WONDERFUL LAND	Shadows	Columbia	9
4	2	HEY BABY	Bruce Channel	Mercury	6
2	3	DREAM BABY	Roy Orbison	London	8
3	4	HEY LITTLE GIRL	Del Shannon	London	6
5	5	TELL ME WHAT HE SAID	Helen Shapiro	Columbia	11
6	6	CAN'T HELP FALLING IN LOVE/ROCK-A-HULA BABY	Elvis Presley	RCA	13
7	7	TWISTIN' THE NIGHT AWAY	Sam Cooke	RCA	8
17	8	SPEAK TO ME PRETTY	Brenda Lee	Brunswick	3
10	9	WHEN MY LITTLE GIRL IS SMILING	Craig Douglas	Top Rank	5
9	10	NEVER GOODBYE	Karl Denver	Decca	8
8	11	THEME FROM 'Z CARS'	Johnny Keating	Pye	9
13	12	STRANGER ON THE SHORE	Mr. Acker Bilk	Columbia	22
12	13	WHEN MY LITTLE GIRL IS SMILING	Jimmy Justice	Pye	4
31	14	NUT ROCKER	B. Bumble and the Stingers	Top Rank	2
14	15	HOLE IN THE GROUND	Bernard Cribbins	Parlophone	11
22	16	WONDERFUL WORLD OF THE YOUNG	Danny Williams	HMV	3
21	17	THE PARTY'S OVER	Lonnie Donegan	Pye	3
18	18	THEME FROM 'DR. KILDARE'	Johnny Spence	Parlophone	9
15	19	LET'S TWIST AGAIN	Chubby Checker	Columbia	18
11	20	WIMOWEH	Karl Denver	Decca	13
16	21	SOFTLY AS I LEAVE YOU	Matt Monro	Parlophone	11
19	22	THE YOUNG ONES	Cliff Richard	Columbia	16
20	23	THEME FROM 'MAIGRET'	Joe Loss	HMV	4
26	24	YOUNG WORLD	Rick Nelson	London	4
25	25	LOVE ME WARM AND TENDER	Paul Anka	RCA	6
34	26	LOVE LETTERS	Ketty Lester	London	2
23	27	THE WANDERER	Dion	HMV	10
27	28	SLOW TWISTIN'	Chubby Checker	Columbia	3
38	29	EVERYBODY'S TWISTING	Frank Sinatra	Reprise	2
40	30	KING OF CLOWNS	Neil Sedaka	RCA	2
24	31	MARCH OF THE SIAMESE CHILDREN	Kenny Ball and his Jazzmen	Pye	11
28	32	PIANISSIMO	Ken Dodd	Decca	12
29	33	IT'S ALL OVER NOW	Shane Fenton	Parlophone	3
30	34	FANLIGHT FANNY	Clinton Ford	Oriole	7
-	35	BIG MAN IN A BIG HOUSE	Leroy Van Dyke	Mercury	1
-	36	CUTTY SARK	John Barry Seven	Columbia	1
-	37	AVE MARIA	Shirley Bassey	Columbia	1
-	38	WHAT KIND OF FOOL AM I/GONNA BUILD A MOUNTAIN	Sammy Davis Jnr	Reprise	4
37	39	LITTLE BITTY TEAR	Burl Ives	Brunswick	13
-	40	DRUMS ARE MY BEAT	Sandy Nelson	London	4

WEEK ENDING 3 MAY 1962

LW	TW	Title	Artist	Label	Wks
1	1	WONDERFUL LAND	Shadows	Columbia	10
4	2	HEY LITTLE GIRL	Del Shannon	London	7
2	3	HEY BABY	Bruce Channel	Mercury	7
14	4	NUT ROCKER	B. Bumble and the Stingers	Top Rank	3
3	5	DREAM BABY	Roy Orbison	London	9
5	6	TELL ME WHAT HE SAID	Helen Shapiro	Columbia	12
8	7	SPEAK TO ME PRETTY	Brenda Lee	Brunswick	4
6	8	CAN'T HELP FALLING IN LOVE/ROCK-A-HULA BABY	Elvis Presley	RCA	14
10	9	NEVER GOODBYE	Karl Denver	Decca	9
12	10	STRANGER ON THE SHORE	Mr. Acker Bilk	Columbia	23
16	11	WONDERFUL WORLD OF THE YOUNG	Danny Williams	HMV	4

May 1962

□ Highest position disc reached ● Act's first ever week on chart

LW	TW	Title	Artist	Label	Wks
7	12	TWISTIN' THE NIGHT AWAY	Sam Cooke	RCA	9
11	13	THEME FROM 'Z CARS'	Johnny Keating	Pye	10
9	14	WHEN MY LITTLE GIRL IS SMILING	Craig Douglas	Top Rank	6
13	15	WHEN MY LITTLE GIRL IS SMILING	Jimmy Justice	Pye	5
17	16	THE PARTY'S OVER	Lonnie Donegan	Pye	4
26	17	LOVE LETTERS	Ketty Lester	London	3
19	18	LET'S TWIST AGAIN	Chubby Checker	Columbia	19
24	19	YOUNG WORLD	Rick Nelson	London	5
18	20	THEME FROM 'DR. KILDARE'	Johnny Spence	Parlophone	10
20	21	WIMOWEH	Karl Denver	Decca	14
15	22	HOLE IN THE GROUND	Bernard Cribbins	Parlophone	12
28	23	SLOW TWISTIN'	Chubby Checker	Columbia	4
21	24	SOFTLY AS I LEAVE YOU	Matt Monro	Parlophone	12
23	25	THEME FROM 'MAIGRET'	Joe Loss	HMV	5
25	26	LOVE ME WARM AND TENDER	Paul Anka	RCA	7
30	27	KING OF CLOWNS	Neil Sedaka	RCA	3
29	28	EVERYBODY'S TWISTING	Frank Sinatra	Reprise	3
33	29	IT'S ALL OVER NOW	Shane Fenton	Parlophone	4
22	30	THE YOUNG ONES	Cliff Richard	Columbia	17
37	31	AVE MARIA	Shirley Bassey	Columbia	2
-	32	LET'S TALK ABOUT LOVE	Helen Shapiro	Columbia	1
31	33	MARCH OF THE SIAMESE CHILDREN	Kenny Ball and his Jazzmen	Pye	12
35	34	BIG MAN IN A BIG HOUSE	Leroy Van Dyke	Mercury	2
36	35	CUTTY SARK	John Barry Seven	Columbia	2
-	36	LAST NIGHT WAS MADE FOR LOVE	Billy Fury	Decca	1
34	37	FANLIGHT FANNY	Clinton Ford	Oriole	8
-	38	PLEASE DON'T ASK ABOUT BARBARA	Bobby Vee	Liberty	7
-	39	DON'T BREAK THE HEART THAT LOVES YOU	Connie Francis	MGM	1
38	40	WHAT KIND OF FOOL AM I/GONNA BUILD A MOUNTAIN	Sammy Davis Jnr	Reprise	5

WEEK ENDING 10 MAY 1962

LW	TW	Title	Artist	Label	Wks
1	1	WONDERFUL LAND	Shadows	Columbia	11
4	2	NUT ROCKER	B. Bumble and the Stingers	Top Rank	4
7	3	SPEAK TO ME PRETTY	Brenda Lee	Brunswick	5
3	4	HEY BABY	Bruce Channel	Mercury	8
2	5	HEY LITTLE GIRL	Del Shannon	London	8
17	6	LOVE LETTERS	Ketty Lester	London	4
5	7	DREAM BABY	Roy Orbison	London	10
11	8	WONDERFUL WORLD OF THE YOUNG	Danny Williams	HMV	5
16	9	THE PARTY'S OVER	Lonnie Donegan	Pye	5
9	10	NEVER GOODBYE	Karl Denver	Decca	10
12	11	TWISTIN' THE NIGHT AWAY	Sam Cooke	RCA	10
15	12	WHEN MY LITTLE GIRL IS SMILING	Jimmy Justice	Pye	6
14	13	WHEN MY LITTLE GIRL IS SMILING	Craig Douglas	Top Rank	7
8	14	CAN'T HELP FALLING IN LOVE/ROCK-A-HULA BABY	Elvis Presley	RCA	15
10	15	STRANGER ON THE SHORE	Mr. Acker Bilk	Columbia	24
-	16	GOOD LUCK CHARM	Elvis Presley	RCA	1
6	17	TELL ME WHAT HE SAID	Helen Shapiro	Columbia	13
13	18	THEME FROM 'Z CARS'	Johnny Keating	Pye	11
19	19	YOUNG WORLD	Rick Nelson	London	6
-	20	DO YOU WANT TO DANCE/I'M LOOKING OUT THE WINDOW	Cliff Richard	Columbia	1
20	21	THEME FROM 'DR. KILDARE'	Johnny Spence	Parlophone	11
25	22	THEME FROM 'MAIGRET'	Joe Loss	HMV	6
-	23	AS YOU LIKE IT	Adam Faith	Parlophone	1
32	24	LET'S TALK ABOUT LOVE	Helen Shapiro	Columbia	2
28	25	EVERYBODY'S TWISTING	Frank Sinatra	Reprise	4
36	26	LAST NIGHT WAS MADE FOR LOVE	Billy Fury	Decca	2
27	27	KING OF CLOWNS	Neil Sedaka	RCA	4
18	28	LET'S TWIST AGAIN	Chubby Checker	Columbia	20
26	29	LOVE ME WARM AND TENDER	Paul Anka	RCA	8
24	30	SOFTLY AS I LEAVE YOU	Matt Monro	Parlophone	13
30	31	THE YOUNG ONES	Cliff Richard	Columbia	18
22	32	HOLE IN THE GROUND	Bernard Cribbins	Parlophone	13

■ *Wonderful Land* by the Shadows completes eight weeks at number one, a record run for an instrumental. The record is still standing thirty years on (10.05.62) ■ *Speak To Me Pretty* is the biggest of four Top 20 hits for Brenda Lee in 1962, to make her the most successful female vocalist of the year (10.05.62) ■ *The Party's Over* is the right title for Lonnie Donegan's 17th and final Top 10 hit. At the time only Elvis, with 27, has had more Top 10 hits (10.05.62) ■

May 1962

□ Highest position disc reached ● Act's first ever week on chart

LW	TW	Title	Artist	Label	Wks
21	33	WIMOWEH	Karl Denver	Decca	15
31	34	AVE MARIA	Shirley Bassey	Columbia	3
-	35	LONELY CITY	John Leyton	HMV	1
-	36	GINNY COME LATELY	Brian Hyland	HMV	1
-	37	CATERINA	Perry Como	RCA	1
23	38	SLOW TWISTIN'	Chubby Checker	Columbia	5
39	39	DON'T BREAK THE HEART THAT LOVES YOU	Connie Francis	MGM	2
-	40	JOHNNY ANGEL	Patti Lynn ●	Fontana	1

WEEK ENDING 17 MAY 1962

LW	TW	Title	Artist	Label	Wks
2	1	NUT ROCKER	B. Bumble and the Stingers	Top Rank	5
16	2	GOOD LUCK CHARM	Elvis Presley	RCA	2
1	3	WONDERFUL LAND	Shadows	Columbia	12
20	4	I'M LOOKING OUT THE WINDOW/DO YOU WANT TO DANCE	Cliff Richard	Columbia	2
3	5	SPEAK TO ME PRETTY	Brenda Lee	Brunswick	6
6	6	LOVE LETTERS	Ketty Lester	London	5
23	7	AS YOU LIKE IT	Adam Faith	Parlophone	2
5	8	HEY LITTLE GIRL	Del Shannon	London	9
12	9	WHEN MY LITTLE GIRL IS SMILING	Jimmy Justice	Pye	7
4	10	HEY BABY	Bruce Channel	Mercury	9
10	11	NEVER GOODBYE	Karl Denver	Decca	11
8	12	WONDERFUL WORLD OF THE YOUNG	Danny Williams	HMV	6
15	13	STRANGER ON THE SHORE	Mr. Acker Bilk	Columbia	25
7	14	DREAM BABY	Roy Orbison	London	11
26	15	LAST NIGHT WAS MADE FOR LOVE	Billy Fury	Decca	3
14	16	CAN'T HELP FALLING IN LOVE/ROCK-A-HULA BABY	Elvis Presley	RCA	16
9	17	THE PARTY'S OVER	Lonnie Donegan	Pye	6
11	18	TWISTIN' THE NIGHT AWAY	Sam Cooke	RCA	11
36	19	GINNY COME LATELY	Brian Hyland	HMV	2
13	20	WHEN MY LITTLE GIRL IS SMILING	Craig Douglas	Top Rank	8
19	21	YOUNG WORLD	Rick Nelson	London	7
25	22	EVERYBODY'S TWISTING	Frank Sinatra	Reprise	5
27	23	KING OF CLOWNS	Neil Sedaka	RCA	5
18	24	THEME FROM 'Z CARS'	Johnny Keating	Pye	12
35	25	LONELY CITY	John Leyton	HMV	2
24	26	LET'S TALK ABOUT LOVE	Helen Shapiro	Columbia	3
28	27	LET'S TWIST AGAIN	Chubby Checker	Columbia	21
-	28	I DON'T KNOW WHY	Eden Kane	Decca	1
-	29	COME OUTSIDE	Mike Sarne ●	Parlophone	1
21	30	THEME FROM 'DR. KILDARE'	Johnny Spence	Parlophone	12
22	31	THEME FROM 'MAIGRET'	Joe Loss	HMV	7
29	32	LOVE ME WARM AND TENDER	Paul Anka	RCA	9
17	33	TELL ME WHAT HE SAID	Helen Shapiro	Columbia	14
-	34	LOVER PLEASE	Vernons Girls ●	Decca	1
31	35	THE YOUNG ONES	Cliff Richard	Columbia	19
-	36	UNSQUARE DANCE	Dave Brubeck	CBS	1
40	37	JOHNNY ANGEL	Patti Lynn	Fontana	2
30	38	SOFTLY AS I LEAVE YOU	Matt Monro	Parlophone	14
34	39	AVE MARIA	Shirley Bassey	Columbia	4
-	40	CLOWN SHOES	Johnny Burnette	Liberty	1

WEEK ENDING 24 MAY 1962

LW	TW	Title	Artist	Label	Wks
2	1	GOOD LUCK CHARM	Elvis Presley	RCA	3
1	2	NUT ROCKER	B. Bumble and the Stingers	Top Rank	6
4	3	I'M LOOKING OUT THE WINDOW/DO YOU WANT TO DANCE	Cliff Richard	Columbia	3
6	4	LOVE LETTERS	Ketty Lester	London	6
7	5	AS YOU LIKE IT	Adam Faith	Parlophone	3
3	6	WONDERFUL LAND	Shadows	Columbia	13
5	7	SPEAK TO ME PRETTY	Brenda Lee	Brunswick	7
8	8	HEY LITTLE GIRL	Del Shannon	London	10
9	9	WHEN MY LITTLE GIRL IS SMILING	Jimmy Justice	Pye	8
19	10	GINNY COME LATELY	Brian Hyland	HMV	3
15	11	LAST NIGHT WAS MADE FOR LOVE	Billy Fury	Decca	4
13	12	STRANGER ON THE SHORE	Mr. Acker Bilk	Columbia	26
12	13	WONDERFUL WORLD OF THE YOUNG	Danny Williams	HMV	7
10	14	HEY BABY	Bruce Channel	Mercury	10
11	15	NEVER GOODBYE	Karl Denver	Decca	12
16	16	CAN'T HELP FALLING IN LOVE/ROCK-A-HULA BABY	Elvis Presley	RCA	17
29	17	COME OUTSIDE	Mike Sarne	Parlophone	2
28	18	I DON'T KNOW WHY	Eden Kane	Decca	2
17	19	THE PARTY'S OVER	Lonnie Donegan	Pye	7
25	20	LONELY CITY	John Leyton	HMV	3
20	21	WHEN MY LITTLE GIRL IS SMILING	Craig Douglas	Top Rank	9
14	22	DREAM BABY	Roy Orbison	London	12
26	23	LET'S TALK ABOUT LOVE	Helen Shapiro	Columbia	4
-	24	GREEN LEAVES OF SUMMER	Kenny Ball and his Jazzmen	Pye	1
-	25	HOW CAN I MEET HER	Everly Brothers	Warner Brothers	1
21	26	YOUNG WORLD	Rick Nelson	London	8
-	27	A PICTURE OF YOU	Joe Brown	Piccadilly	1
18	28	TWISTIN' THE NIGHT AWAY	Sam Cooke	RCA	12
22	29	EVERYBODY'S TWISTING	Frank Sinatra	Reprise	6
23	30	KING OF CLOWNS	Neil Sedaka	RCA	6
36	31	UNSQUARE DANCE	Dave Brubeck	CBS	2
34	32	LOVER PLEASE	Vernons Girls	Decca	2
-	33	FUNNY WAY OF LAUGHIN'	Burl Ives	Brunswick	1
24	34	THEME FROM 'Z CARS'	Johnny Keating	Pye	13
-	35	BESAME MUCHO	Jet Harris ●	Decca	1
-	36	JEZEBEL	Marty Wilde	Philips	1
40	37	CLOWN SHOES	Johnny Burnette	Liberty	2
32	38	LOVE ME WARM AND TENDER	Paul Anka	RCA	10
37	39	JOHNNY ANGEL	Patti Lynn	Fontana	3
27	40	LET'S TWIST AGAIN	Chubby Checker	Columbia	22

WEEK ENDING 31 MAY 1962

LW	TW	Title	Artist	Label	Wks
1	1	GOOD LUCK CHARM	Elvis Presley	RCA	4
3	2	I'M LOOKING OUT THE WINDOW/DO YOU WANT TO DANCE	Cliff Richard	Columbia	4
2	3	NUT ROCKER	B. Bumble and the Stingers	Top Rank	7
11	4	LAST NIGHT WAS MADE FOR LOVE	Billy Fury	Decca	5
5	5	AS YOU LIKE IT	Adam Faith	Parlophone	4
17	6	COME OUTSIDE	Mike Sarne	Parlophone	3
4	7	LOVE LETTERS	Ketty Lester	London	7
18	8	I DON'T KNOW WHY	Eden Kane	Decca	3
6	9	WONDERFUL LAND	Shadows	Columbia	14
10	10	GINNY COME LATELY	Brian Hyland	HMV	4
12	11	STRANGER ON THE SHORE	Mr. Acker Bilk	Columbia	27
9	12	WHEN MY LITTLE GIRL IS SMILING	Jimmy Justice	Pye	9
13	13	WONDERFUL WORLD OF THE YOUNG	Danny Williams	HMV	8
7	14	SPEAK TO ME PRETTY	Brenda Lee	Brunswick	8
8	15	HEY LITTLE GIRL	Del Shannon	London	11
19	16	THE PARTY'S OVER	Lonnie Donegan	Pye	8
24	17	GREEN LEAVES OF SUMMER	Kenny Ball and his Jazzmen	Pye	2
27	18	A PICTURE OF YOU	Joe Brown	Piccadilly	2
25	19	HOW CAN I MEET HER	Everly Brothers	Warner Brothers	2
20	20	LONELY CITY	John Leyton	HMV	4
15	21	NEVER GOODBYE	Karl Denver	Decca	13
32	22	LOVER PLEASE	Vernons Girls	Decca	3
14	23	HEY BABY	Bruce Channel	Mercury	11
31	24	UNSQUARE DANCE	Dave Brubeck	CBS	3
35	25	BESAME MUCHO	Jet Harris	Decca	2
16	26	CAN'T HELP FALLING IN LOVE/ROCK-A-HULA BABY	Elvis Presley	RCA	18
29	27	EVERYBODY'S TWISTING	Frank Sinatra	Reprise	7
26	28	YOUNG WORLD	Rick Nelson	London	9
-	29	DEEP IN THE HEART OF TEXAS	Duane Eddy	RCA	1
36	30	JEZEBEL	Marty Wilde	Philips	2
23	31	LET'S TALK ABOUT LOVE	Helen Shapiro	Columbia	5
28	32	TWISTIN' THE NIGHT AWAY	Sam Cooke	RCA	13
33	33	FUNNY WAY OF LAUGHIN'	Burl Ives	Brunswick	2
-	34	SWINGING IN THE RAIN	Norman Vaughan ●	Pye	1
37	35	CLOWN SHOES	Johnny Burnette	Liberty	3
30	36	KING OF CLOWNS	Neil Sedaka	RCA	7
21	37	WHEN MY LITTLE GIRL IS SMILING	Craig Douglas	Top Rank	10

In these weeks ■ Mike Sarne's *Come Outside* featured the vocal talents of Wendy Richard, later to be a star of 'Are You Being Served?' and 'Eastenders' (17.05.62) ■ For the first time, an instrumental is knocked off the top by another instrumental . It will happen again a year later, and again the Shadows will be the victims (17.05.62)■

LW	TW	Title	Artist	Label	Wks
22	38	DREAM BABY	Roy Orbison	London	13
34	39	THEME FROM 'Z CARS'	Johnny Keating	Pye	14
-	40	THEME FROM 'DR. KILDARE'	Johnny Spence	Parlophone	13

June 1962

□ Highest position disc reached ● Act's first ever week on chart

WEEK ENDING 7 JUNE 1962

LW	TW	Title	Artist	Label	Wks
1	1	GOOD LUCK CHARM	Elvis Presley	RCA	5
2	2	I'M LOOKING OUT THE WINDOW/DO YOU WANT TO DANCE	Cliff Richard	Columbia	5
3	3	NUT ROCKER	B. Bumble and the Stingers	Top Rank	8
6	4	COME OUTSIDE	Mike Sarne	Parlophone	4
5	5	AS YOU LIKE IT	Adam Faith	Parlophone	5
4	6	LAST NIGHT WAS MADE FOR LOVE	Billy Fury	Decca	6
10	7	GINNY COME LATELY	Brian Hyland	HMV	5
9	8	WONDERFUL LAND	Shadows	Columbia	15
8	9	I DON'T KNOW WHY	Eden Kane	Decca	4
18	10	A PICTURE OF YOU	Joe Brown	Piccadilly	3
7	11	LOVE LETTERS	Ketty Lester	London	8
11	12	STRANGER ON THE SHORE	Mr. Acker Bilk	Columbia	28
17	13	GREEN LEAVES OF SUMMER	Kenny Ball and his Jazzmen	Pye	3
19	14	HOW CAN I MEET HER	Everly Brothers	Warner Brothers	3
14	15	SPEAK TO ME PRETTY	Brenda Lee	Brunswick	9
20	16	LONELY CITY	John Leyton	HMV	5
15	17	HEY LITTLE GIRL	Del Shannon	London	12
24	18	UNSQUARE DANCE	Dave Brubeck	CBS	4
13	19	WONDERFUL WORLD OF THE YOUNG	Danny Williams	HMV	9
16	20	THE PARTY'S OVER	Lonnie Donegan	Pye	9
22	21	LOVER PLEASE	Vernons Girls	Decca	4
25	22	BESAME MUCHO	Jet Harris	Decca	3
30	23	JEZEBEL	Marty Wilde	Philips	3
12	24	WHEN MY LITTLE GIRL IS SMILING	Jimmy Justice	Pye	10
21	25	NEVER GOODBYE	Karl Denver	Decca	14
31	26	LET'S TALK ABOUT LOVE	Helen Shapiro	Columbia	6
27	27	EVERYBODY'S TWISTING	Frank Sinatra	Reprise	8
28	28	YOUNG WORLD	Rick Nelson	London	10
29	29	DEEP IN THE HEART OF TEXAS	Duane Eddy	RCA	2
26	30	CAN'T HELP FALLING IN LOVE/ROCK-A-HULA BABY	Elvis Presley	RCA	19
23	31	HEY BABY	Bruce Channel	Mercury	12
-	32	A LITTLE LOVE A LITTLE KISS	Karl Denver	Decca	1
-	33	LET'S TWIST AGAIN	Chubby Checker	Columbia	23
32	34	TWISTIN' THE NIGHT AWAY	Sam Cooke	RCA	14
36	35	KING OF CLOWNS	Neil Sedaka	RCA	8
33	36	FUNNY WAY OF LAUGHIN'	Burl Ives	Brunswick	3
34	37	SWINGING IN THE RAIN	Norman Vaughan	Pye	2
-	38	SOLDIER BOY	Shirelles	HMV	1
-	39	JOHNNY ANGEL	Patti Lynn	Fontana	4
-	40	THEME FROM 'DR. KILDARE' (THREE STARS WILL SHINE TONIGHT)	Richard Chamberlain ●	MGM	1

WEEK ENDING 14 JUNE 1962

LW	TW	Title	Artist	Label	Wks
1	1	GOOD LUCK CHARM	Elvis Presley	RCA	6
2	2	I'M LOOKING OUT THE WINDOW/DO YOU WANT TO DANCE	Cliff Richard	Columbia	6
4	3	COME OUTSIDE	Mike Sarne	Parlophone	5
10	4	A PICTURE OF YOU	Joe Brown	Piccadilly	4
3	5	NUT ROCKER	B. Bumble and the Stingers	Top Rank	9
5	6	AS YOU LIKE IT	Adam Faith	Parlophone	6
9	7	I DON'T KNOW WHY	Eden Kane	Decca	5
6	8	LAST NIGHT WAS MADE FOR LOVE	Billy Fury	Decca	7
7	9	GINNY COME LATELY	Brian Hyland	HMV	6
13	10	GREEN LEAVES OF SUMMER	Kenny Ball and his Jazzmen	Pye	4
12	11	STRANGER ON THE SHORE	Mr. Acker Bilk	Columbia	29
14	12	HOW CAN I MEET HER	Everly Brothers	Warner Brothers	4
11	13	LOVE LETTERS	Ketty Lester	London	9
16	14	LONELY CITY	John Leyton	HMV	6
8	15	WONDERFUL LAND	Shadows	Columbia	16
21	16	LOVER PLEASE	Vernons Girls	Decca	5
18	17	UNSQUARE DANCE	Dave Brubeck	CBS	5
-	18	SHARING YOU	Bobby Vee	Liberty	1
23	19	JEZEBEL	Marty Wilde	Philips	4
32	20	A LITTLE LOVE A LITTLE KISS	Karl Denver	Decca	2
15	21	SPEAK TO ME PRETTY	Brenda Lee	Brunswick	10
19	22	WONDERFUL WORLD OF THE YOUNG	Danny Williams	HMV	10
40	23	THEME FROM 'DR. KILDARE' (THREE STARS WILL SHINE TONIGHT)	Richard Chamberlain	MGM	2
29	24	DEEP IN THE HEART OF TEXAS	Duane Eddy	RCA	3
22	25	BESAME MUCHO	Jet Harris	Decca	4
-	26	FAR AWAY	Shirley Bassey	Columbia	1
20	27	THE PARTY'S OVER	Lonnie Donegan	Pye	10
24	28	WHEN MY LITTLE GIRL IS SMILING	Jimmy Justice	Pye	11
36	29	FUNNY WAY OF LAUGHIN'	Burl Ives	Brunswick	4
-	30	AIN'T THAT FUNNY	Jimmy Justice	Pye	1
17	31	HEY LITTLE GIRL	Del Shannon	London	13
28	32	YOUNG WORLD	Rick Nelson	London	11
35	33	KING OF CLOWNS	Neil Sedaka	RCA	9
-	34	ENGLISH COUNTRY GARDEN	Jimmy Rodgers	Columbia	1
-	35	ORANGE BLOSSOM SPECIAL	Spotnicks ●	Oriole	1
-	36	STRANGER ON THE SHORE	Andy Williams	CBS	1
25	37	NEVER GOODBYE	Karl Denver	Decca	15
27	38	EVERYBODY'S TWISTING	Frank Sinatra	Reprise	9
38	39	SOLDIER BOY	Shirelles	HMV	2
33	40	LET'S TWIST AGAIN	Chubby Checker	Columbia	24

WEEK ENDING 21 JUNE 1962

LW	TW	Title	Artist	Label	Wks
1	1	GOOD LUCK CHARM	Elvis Presley	RCA	7
3	2	COME OUTSIDE	Mike Sarne	Parlophone	6
2	3	I'M LOOKING OUT THE WINDOW/DO YOU WANT TO DANCE	Cliff Richard	Columbia	7
4	4	A PICTURE OF YOU	Joe Brown	Piccadilly	5
9	5	GINNY COME LATELY	Brian Hyland	HMV	7
8	6	LAST NIGHT WAS MADE FOR LOVE	Billy Fury	Decca	8
7	7	I DON'T KNOW WHY	Eden Kane	Decca	6
6	8	AS YOU LIKE IT	Adam Faith	Parlophone	7
5	9	NUT ROCKER	B. Bumble and the Stingers	Top Rank	10
10	10	GREEN LEAVES OF SUMMER	Kenny Ball and his Jazzmen	Pye	5
11	11	STRANGER ON THE SHORE	Mr. Acker Bilk	Columbia	30
23	12	THEME FROM 'DR. KILDARE' (THREE STARS WILL SHINE TONIGHT)	Richard Chamberlain	MGM	3
12	13	HOW CAN I MEET HER	Everly Brothers	Warner Brothers	5
17	14	UNSQUARE DANCE	Dave Brubeck	CBS	6
14	15	LONELY CITY	John Leyton	HMV	7
-	16	I CAN'T STOP LOVING YOU	Ray Charles	HMV	1
16	17	LOVER PLEASE	Vernons Girls	Decca	6
30	18	AIN'T THAT FUNNY	Jimmy Justice	Pye	2
24	19	DEEP IN THE HEART OF TEXAS	Duane Eddy	RCA	4
19	20	JEZEBEL	Marty Wilde	Philips	5
34	21	ENGLISH COUNTRY GARDEN	Jimmy Rodgers	Columbia	2
13	22	LOVE LETTERS	Ketty Lester	London	10
20	23	A LITTLE LOVE A LITTLE KISS	Karl Denver	Decca	3
22	24	WONDERFUL WORLD OF THE YOUNG	Danny Williams	HMV	11
18	25	SHARING YOU	Bobby Vee	Liberty	2
15	26	WONDERFUL LAND	Shadows	Columbia	17
26	27	FAR AWAY	Shirley Bassey	Columbia	2
39	28	SOLDIER BOY	Shirelles	HMV	3
21	29	SPEAK TO ME PRETTY	Brenda Lee	Brunswick	11
35	30	ORANGE BLOSSOM SPECIAL	Spotnicks	Oriole	2
25	31	BESAME MUCHO	Jet Harris	Decca	5
36	32	STRANGER ON THE SHORE	Andy Williams	CBS	2
29	33	FUNNY WAY OF LAUGHIN'	Burl Ives	Brunswick	5
-	34	YES MY DARLING DAUGHTER	Eydie Gormé	CBS	1
28	35	WHEN MY LITTLE GIRL IS SMILING	Jimmy Justice	Pye	12
38	36	EVERYBODY'S TWISTING	Frank Sinatra	Reprise	10
-	37	FOLLOW THAT DREAM (EP)	Elvis Presley	RCA	1
-	38	DON'T EVER CHANGE	Crickets	Liberty	1
27	39	THE PARTY'S OVER	Lonnie Donegan	Pye	11
32	40	YOUNG WORLD	Rick Nelson	London	12

■Elvis Presley is number one not only in the singles charts, but also in the EP and LP charts, for the only time in his entire career (14.06.62) ■ Adam Faith's *As You Like It* is the first of three songs taking Shakespeare plays as their title to hit the charts. All three become Top 10 hits (the others are Dire Straits' *Romeo and Juliet* and David Essex's *Winter's Tale* (07.06.62)■

June 1962

□ Highest position disc reached ● Act's first ever week on chart

LW	TW	WEEK ENDING 28 JUNE 1962		Wks
2	1	COME OUTSIDE Mike Sarne	*Parlophone*	7
4	2	A PICTURE OF YOU Joe Brown	*Piccadilly*	6
1	3	GOOD LUCK CHARM Elvis Presley	*RCA*	8
3	4	I'M LOOKING OUT THE WINDOW/DO YOU WANT TO DANCE Cliff Richard	*Columbia*	8
5	5	GINNY COME LATELY Brian Hyland	*HMV*	8
6	6	LAST NIGHT WAS MADE FOR LOVE Billy Fury	*Decca*	9
21	7	ENGLISH COUNTRY GARDEN Jimmy Rodgers	*Columbia*	3
16	8	I CAN'T STOP LOVING YOU Ray Charles	*HMV*	2
11	9	STRANGER ON THE SHORE Mr. Acker Bilk	*Columbia*	31
9	10	NUT ROCKER B. Bumble and the Stingers	*Top Rank*	11
7	11	I DON'T KNOW WHY Eden Kane	*Decca*	7
10	12	GREEN LEAVES OF SUMMER Kenny Ball and his Jazzmen	*Pye*	6
12	13	THEME FROM 'DR. KILDARE' (THREE STARS WILL SHINE TONIGHT) Richard Chamberlain	*MGM*	4
8	14	AS YOU LIKE IT Adam Faith	*Parlophone*	8
18	15	AIN'T THAT FUNNY Jimmy Justice	*Pye*	3
13	16	HOW CAN I MEET HER Everly Brothers	*Warner Brothers*	6
25	17	SHARING YOU Bobby Vee	*Liberty*	3
14	18	UNSQUARE DANCE Dave Brubeck	*CBS*	7
23	19	A LITTLE LOVE A LITTLE KISS Karl Denver	*Decca*	4
34	20	YES MY DARLING DAUGHTER Eydie Gormé	*CBS*	2
15	21	LONELY CITY John Leyton	*HMV*	8
-	22	HERE COMESTHAT FEELING Brenda Lee	*Brunswick*	1
28	23	SOLDIER BOY Shirelles	*HMV*	4
27	24	FAR AWAY Shirley Bassey	*Columbia*	3
20	25	JEZEBEL Marty Wilde	*Philips*	6
24	26	WONDERFUL WORLD OF THE YOUNG Danny Williams	*HMV*	12
22	27	LOVE LETTERS Ketty Lester	*London*	11
17	28	LOVER PLEASE Vernons Girls	*Decca*	7
38	29	DON'T EVER CHANGE Crickets	*Liberty*	2
32	30	STRANGER ON THE SHORE Andy Williams	*CBS*	3
30	31	ORANGE BLOSSOM SPECIAL Spotnicks	*Oriole*	3
26	32	WONDERFUL LAND Shadows	*Columbia*	18
19	33	DEEP IN THE HEART OF TEXAS Duane Eddy	*RCA*	5
37	34	FOLLOW THAT DREAM (EP) Elvis Presley	*RCA*	2
-	35	OUR FAVOURITE MELODIES Craig Douglas	*Columbia*	1
33	36	FUNNY WAY OF LAUGHIN' Burl Ives	*Brunswick*	6
-	37	CONSCIENCE James Darren	*Pye*	1
31	38	BESAME MUCHO Jet Harris	*Decca*	6
-	39	DRUMMIN' UP A STORM Sandy Nelson	*London*	1
-	40	OLD RIVERS Walter Brennan ●	*Liberty*	1

LW	TW	WEEK ENDING 5 JULY 1962		Wks
1	1	COME OUTSIDE Mike Sarne	*Parlophone*	8
2	2	A PICTURE OF YOU Joe Brown	*Piccadilly*	7
3	3	GOOD LUCK CHARM Elvis Presley	*RCA*	9
8	4	I CAN'T STOP LOVING YOU Ray Charles	*HMV*	3
5	5	GINNY COME LATELY Brian Hyland	*HMV*	9
4	6	I'M LOOKING OUT THE WINDOW/DO YOU WANT TO DANCE Cliff Richard	*Columbia*	9
12	7	GREEN LEAVES OF SUMMER Kenny Ball and his Jazzmen	*Pye*	7
15	8	AIN'T THAT FUNNY Jimmy Justice	*Pye*	4
9	9	STRANGER ON THE SHORE Mr. Acker Bilk	*Columbia*	32
17	10	SHARING YOU Bobby Vee	*Liberty*	4
6	11	LAST NIGHT WAS MADE FOR LOVE Billy Fury	*Decca*	10
7	12	ENGLISH COUNTRY GARDEN Jimmy Rodgers	*Columbia*	4
14	13	AS YOU LIKE IT Adam Faith	*Parlophone*	9
22	14	HERE COMES THAT FEELING Brenda Lee	*Brunswick*	2
11	15	I DON'T KNOW WHY Eden Kane	*Decca*	8
20	16	YES MY DARLING DAUGHTER Eydie Gormé	*CBS*	3
13	17	THEME FROM 'DR. KILDARE' (THREE STARS WILL SHINE TONIGHT) Richard Chamberlain	*MGM*	5
29	18	DON'T EVER CHANGE Crickets	*Liberty*	3
10	19	NUT ROCKER B. Bumble and the Stingers	*Top Rank*	12
19	20	A LITTLE LOVE A LITTLE KISS Karl Denver	*Decca*	5
35	21	OUR FAVOURITE MELODIES Craig Douglas	*Columbia*	2
16	22	HOW CAN I MEET HER Everly Brothers	*Warner Brothers*	7
25	23	JEZEBEL Marty Wilde	*Philips*	7
18	24	UNSQUARE DANCE Dave Brubeck	*CBS*	8
-	25	PALISADES PARK Freddy Cannon	*Stateside*	1
23	26	SOLDIER BOY Shirelles	*HMV*	5
24	27	FAR AWAY Shirley Bassey	*Columbia*	4
21	28	LONELY CITY John Leyton	*HMV*	9
31	29	ORANGE BLOSSOM SPECIAL Spotnicks	*Oriole*	4
37	30	CONSCIENCE James Darren	*Pye*	2
30	31	STRANGER ON THE SHORE Andy Williams	*CBS*	4
-	32	YA YA TWIST Petula Clark	*Pye*	1
27	33	LOVE LETTERS Ketty Lester	*London*	12
28	34	LOVER PLEASE Vernons Girls	*Decca*	8
-	35	AL DI LA Emilio Pericoli ●	*Warner Brothers*	1
-	36	I REMEMBER YOU Frank Ifield	*Columbia*	1
-	37	ADIOS AMIGO Jim Reeves	*RCA*	1
-	38	TEARS Danny Williams	*HMV*	1
38	39	BESAME MUCHO Jet Harris	*Decca*	7
-	40	THE CROWD Roy Orbison	*London*	1

LW	TW	WEEK ENDING 12 JULY 1962		Wks
4	1	I CAN'T STOP LOVING YOU Ray Charles	*HMV*	4
1	2	COME OUTSIDE Mike Sarne	*Parlophone*	9
2	3	A PICTURE OF YOU Joe Brown	*Piccadilly*	8
3	4	GOOD LUCK CHARM Elvis Presley	*RCA*	10
5	5	GINNY COME LATELY Brian Hyland	*HMV*	10
6	6	I'M LOOKING OUT THE WINDOW/DO YOU WANT TO DANCE Cliff Richard	*Columbia*	10
14	7	HERE COMES THAT FEELING Brenda Lee	*Brunswick*	3
12	8	ENGLISH COUNTRY GARDEN Jimmy Rodgers	*Columbia*	5
8	9	AIN'T THAT FUNNY Jimmy Justice	*Pye*	5
16	10	YES MY DARLING DAUGHTER Eydie Gormé	*CBS*	4
36	11	I REMEMBER YOU Frank Ifield	*Columbia*	2
11	12	LAST NIGHT WAS MADE FOR LOVE Billy Fury	*Decca*	11
10	13	SHARING YOU Bobby Vee	*Liberty*	5
18	14	DON'T EVER CHANGE Crickets	*Liberty*	4
7	15	GREEN LEAVES OF SUMMER Kenny Ball and his Jazzmen	*Pye*	8
21	16	OUR FAVOURITE MELODIES Craig Douglas	*Columbia*	3
9	17	STRANGER ON THE SHORE Mr. Acker Bilk	*Columbia*	33
15	18	I DON'T KNOW WHY Eden Kane	*Decca*	9
13	19	AS YOU LIKE IT Adam Faith	*Parlophone*	10
25	20	PALISADES PARK Freddy Cannon	*Stateside*	2
-	21	RIGHT SAID FRED Bernard Cribbins	*Parlophone*	1
20	22	A LITTLE LOVE A LITTLE KISS Karl Denver	*Decca*	6
32	23	YA YA TWIST Petula Clark	*Pye*	2
17	24	THEME FROM 'DR. KILDARE' (THREE STARS WILL SHINE TONIGHT) Richard Chamberlain	*MGM*	6
38	25	TEARS Danny Williams	*HMV*	2
19	26	NUT ROCKER B. Bumble and the Stingers	*Top Rank*	13
24	27	UNSQUARE DANCE Dave Brubeck	*CBS*	9
27	28	FAR AWAY Shirley Bassey	*Columbia*	5
29	29	ORANGE BLOSSOM SPECIAL Spotnicks	*Oriole*	5
-	30	I'M JUST A BABY Louise Cordet ●	*Decca*	1
30	31	CONSCIENCE James Darren	*Pye*	3
-	32	JOHNNY GET ANGRY Carol Deene	*HMV*	1
23	33	JEZEBEL Marty Wilde	*Philips*	8
37	34	ADIOS AMIGO Jim Reeves	*RCA*	2
35	35	AL DI LA Emilio Pericoli	*Warner Brothers*	2
26	36	SOLDIER BOY Shirelles	*HMV*	6
22	37	HOW CAN I MEET HER Everly Brothers	*Warner Brothers*	8
-	38	OLD RIVERS Walter Brennan	*Liberty*	2
-	39	IT KEEPS RIGHT ON A HURTIN' Johnny Tillotson	*London*	1
-	40	SPEEDY GONZALES Pat Boone	*London*	1

LW	TW	WEEK ENDING 19 JULY 1962		Wks
1	1	I CAN'T STOP LOVING YOU Ray Charles	*HMV*	5
11	2	I REMEMBER YOU Frank Ifield	*Columbia*	3
3	3	A PICTURE OF YOU Joe Brown	*Piccadilly*	9
2	4	COME OUTSIDE Mike Sarne	*Parlophone*	10

In these weeks ■ A chart footnote reads: 'Due to difficulties in assessing returns of the Presley EP *Follow That Dream* it has been decided not to include it in the charts' (05.07.62) ■ Four weeks at number five for Brian Hyland's *Ginny Come Lately* (12.07.62) ■ Louise Cordet is Prince Philip's god-daughter (12.07.62) ■ Walter Brennan is a few days short of his 68th birthday in his last week on the chart, the oldest chart soloist to that time (12.07.62)■

LW	TW	Title / Artist	Label	Wks
8	5	ENGLISH COUNTRY GARDEN Jimmy Rodgers	*Columbia*	6
4	6	GOOD LUCK CHARM Elvis Presley	*RCA*	11
7	7	HERE COMES THAT FEELING Brenda Lee	*Brunswick*	4
5	8	GINNY COME LATELY Brian Hyland	*HMV*	11
16	9	OUR FAVOURITE MELODIES Craig Douglas	*Columbia*	4
6	10	I'M LOOKING OUT THE WINDOW/DO YOU WANT TO DANCE Cliff Richard	*Columbia*	11
10	11	YES MY DARLING DAUGHTER Eydie Gormé	*CBS*	5
14	12	DON'T EVER CHANGE Crickets	*Liberty*	5
40	13	SPEEDY GONZALES Pat Boone	*London*	2
12	14	LAST NIGHT WAS MADE FOR LOVE Billy Fury	*Decca*	12
9	15	AIN'T THAT FUNNY Jimmy Justice	*Pye*	6
13	16	SHARING YOU Bobby Vee	*Liberty*	6
21	17	RIGHT SAID FRED Bernard Cribbins	*Parlophone*	2
15	18	GREEN LEAVES OF SUMMER Kenny Ball and his Jazzmen	*Pye*	9
17	19	STRANGER ON THE SHORE Mr. Acker Bilk	*Columbia*	34
23	20	YA YA TWIST Petula Clark	*Pye*	3
19	21	AS YOU LIKE IT Adam Faith	*Parlophone*	11
25	22	TEARS Danny Williams	*HMV*	3
-	23	LITTLE MISS LONELY Helen Shapiro	*Columbia*	1
20	24	PALISADES PARK Freddy Cannon	*Stateside*	3
18	25	I DON'T KNOW WHY Eden Kane	*Decca*	10
22	26	A LITTLE LOVE A LITTLE KISS Karl Denver	*Decca*	7
30	27	I'M JUST A BABY Louise Cordet	*Decca*	2
-	28	CINDY'S BIRTHDAY Shane Fenton	*Parlophone*	1
29	29	ORANGE BLOSSOM SPECIAL Spotnicks	*Oriole*	6
35	30	AL DI LA Emilio Pericoli	*Warner Brothers*	3
24	31	THEME FROM 'DR. KILDARE' (THREE STARS WILL SHINE TONIGHT) Richard Chamberlain	*MGM*	7
26	32	NUT ROCKER B. Bumble and the Stingers	*Top Rank*	14
39	33	IT KEEPS RIGHT ON A HURTIN' Johnny Tillotson	*London*	2
28	34	FAR AWAY Shirley Bassey	*Columbia*	6
27	35	UNSQUARE DANCE Dave Brubeck	*CBS*	10
-	36	LET THERE BE LOVE Nat 'King' Cole with George Shearing	*Capitol*	1
-	37	BREAKING UP IS HARD TO DO Neil Sedaka	*RCA*	1
34	38	ADIOS AMIGO Jim Reeves	*RCA*	3
36	39	SOLDIER BOY Shirelles	*HMV*	7
32	40	JOHNNY GET ANGRY Carol Deene	*HMV*	2

August 1962

□ Highest position disc reached ● Act's first ever week on chart

LW	TW	*WEEK ENDING* 26 JULY 1962		Wks
2	1	I REMEMBER YOU Frank Ifield	*Columbia*	4
1	2	I CAN'T STOP LOVING YOU Ray Charles	*HMV*	6
3	3	A PICTURE OF YOU Joe Brown	*Piccadilly*	10
13	4	SPEEDY GONZALES Pat Boone	*London*	3
7	5	HERE COMES THAT FEELING Brenda Lee	*Brunswick*	5
6	6	GOOD LUCK CHARM Elvis Presley	*RCA*	12
4	7	COME OUTSIDE Mike Sarne	*Parlophone*	11
12	8	DON'T EVER CHANGE Crickets	*Liberty*	6
5	9	ENGLISH COUNTRY GARDEN Jimmy Rodgers	*Columbia*	7
9	10	OUR FAVOURITE MELODIES Craig Douglas	*Columbia*	5
8	11	GINNY COME LATELY Brian Hyland	*HMV*	12
15	12	AIN'T THAT FUNNY Jimmy Justice	*Pye*	7
23	13	LITTLE MISS LONELY Helen Shapiro	*Columbia*	2
20	14	YA YA TWIST Petula Clark	*Pye*	4
17	15	RIGHT SAID FRED Bernard Cribbins	*Parlophone*	3
16	16	SHARING YOU Bobby Vee	*Liberty*	7
11	17	YES MY DARLING DAUGHTER Eydie Gormé	*CBS*	6
19	18	STRANGER ON THE SHORE Mr. Acker Bilk	*Columbia*	35
10	19	I'M LOOKING OUT THE WINDOW/DO YOU WANT TO DANCE Cliff Richard	*Columbia*	12
14	20	LAST NIGHT WAS MADE FOR LOVE Billy Fury	*Decca*	13
18	21	GREEN LEAVES OF SUMMER Kenny Ball and his Jazzmen	*Pye*	10
28	22	CINDY'S BIRTHDAY Shane Fenton	*Parlophone*	2
27	23	I'M JUST A BABY Louise Cordet	*Decca*	3
24	24	PALISADES PARK Freddy Cannon	*Stateside*	4
36	25	LET THERE BE LOVE Nat 'King' Cole with George Shearing	*Capitol*	2
22	26	TEARS Danny Williams	*HMV*	4
37	27	BREAKING UP IS HARD TO DO Neil Sedaka	*RCA*	2
26	28	A LITTLE LOVE A LITTLE KISS Karl Denver	*Decca*	8
-	29	THINGS Bobby Darin	*London*	1
21	30	AS YOU LIKE IT Adam Faith	*Parlophone*	12
-	31	ONCE UPON A DREAM Billy Fury	*Decca*	1
33	32	IT KEEPS RIGHT ON A HURTIN' Johnny Tillotson	*London*	3
25	33	I DON'T KNOW WHY Eden Kane	*Decca*	11
38	34	ADIOS AMIGO Jim Reeves	*RCA*	4
30	35	AL DI LA Emilio Pericoli	*Warner Brothers*	4
34	36	FAR AWAY Shirley Bassey	*Columbia*	7
31	37	THEME FROM 'DR. KILDARE' (THREE STARS WILL SHINE TONIGHT) Richard Chamberlain	*MGM*	8
29	38	ORANGE BLOSSOM SPECIAL Spotnicks	*Oriole*	7
-	39	STRANGER ON THE SHORE Andy Williams	*CBS*	5
35	40	UNSQUARE DANCE Dave Brubeck	*CBS*	11

LW	TW	*WEEK ENDING* 2 AUGUST 1962		Wks
1	1	I REMEMBER YOU Frank Ifield	*Columbia*	5
2	2	I CAN'T STOP LOVING YOU Ray Charles	*HMV*	7
4	3	SPEEDY GONZALES Pat Boone	*London*	4
3	4	A PICTURE OF YOU Joe Brown	*Piccadilly*	11
8	5	DON'T EVER CHANGE Crickets	*Liberty*	7
7	6	COME OUTSIDE Mike Sarne	*Parlophone*	12
5	7	HERE COMES THAT FEELING Brenda Lee	*Brunswick*	6
13	8	LITTLE MISS LONELY Helen Shapiro	*Columbia*	3
9	9	ENGLISH COUNTRY GARDEN Jimmy Rodgers	*Columbia*	8
15	10	RIGHT SAID FRED Bernard Cribbins	*Parlophone*	4
25	11	LET THERE BE LOVE Nat 'King' Cole with George Shearing	*Capitol*	3
10	12	OUR FAVOURITE MELODIES Craig Douglas	*Columbia*	6
6	13	GOOD LUCK CHARM Elvis Presley	*RCA*	13
14	14	YA YA TWIST Petula Clark	*Pye*	5
16	15	SHARING YOU Bobby Vee	*Liberty*	8
29	16	THINGS Bobby Darin	*London*	2
12	17	AIN'T THAT FUNNY Jimmy Justice	*Pye*	8
11	18	GINNY COME LATELY Brian Hyland	*HMV*	13
22	19	CINDY'S BIRTHDAY Shane Fenton	*Parlophone*	3
18	20	STRANGER ON THE SHORE Mr. Acker Bilk	*Columbia*	36
17	21	YES MY DARLING DAUGHTER Eydie Gormé	*CBS*	7
23	22	I'M JUST A BABY Louise Cordet	*Decca*	4
31	23	ONCE UPON A DREAM Billy Fury	*Decca*	2
19	24	I'M LOOKING OUT THE WINDOW/DO YOU WANT TO DANCE Cliff Richard	*Columbia*	13
27	25	BREAKING UP IS HARD TO DO Neil Sedaka	*RCA*	3
21	26	GREEN LEAVES OF SUMMER Kenny Ball and his Jazzmen	*Pye*	11
20	27	LAST NIGHT WAS MADE FOR LOVE Billy Fury	*Decca*	14
-	28	GUITAR TANGO Shadows	*Columbia*	1
34	29	ADIOS AMIGO Jim Reeves	*RCA*	5
24	30	PALISADES PARK Freddy Cannon	*Stateside*	5
32	31	IT KEEPS RIGHT ON A HURTIN' Johnny Tillotson	*London*	4
26	32	TEARS Danny Williams	*HMV*	5
-	33	GOTTA SEE BABY TONIGHT Mr. Acker Bilk	*Columbia*	1
36	34	FAR AWAY Shirley Bassey	*Columbia*	8
28	35	A LITTLE LOVE A LITTLE KISS Karl Denver	*Decca*	9
39	36	STRANGER ON THE SHORE Andy Williams	*CBS*	6
35	37	AL DI LA Emilio Pericoli	*Warner Brothers*	5
-	38	THAT NOISE Anthony Newley	*Decca*	1
30	39	AS YOU LIKE IT Adam Faith	*Parlophone*	13
-	40	VACATION Connie Francis	*MGM*	1

LW	TW	*WEEK ENDING* 9 AUGUST 1962		Wks
1	1	I REMEMBER YOU Frank Ifield	*Columbia*	6
3	2	SPEEDY GONZALES Pat Boone	*London*	5
2	3	I CAN'T STOP LOVING YOU Ray Charles	*HMV*	8
4	4	A PICTURE OF YOU Joe Brown	*Piccadilly*	12
5	5	DON'T EVER CHANGE Crickets	*Liberty*	8
7	6	HERE COMES THAT FEELING Brenda Lee	*Brunswick*	7
28	7	GUITAR TANGO Shadows	*Columbia*	2

■*Our Favourite Melodies* is Craig Douglas' fourth consecutive number nine hit (19.07.62) ■ Three comedy records in the Top 10, *Speedy Gonzales*, *Come Outside* and *Right Said Fred*, and *Ain't That Funny* at number 17 (02.08.62) ■ For the 12th week out of 13, and for the 9th week in a row, the record at number five was at its peak (09.08.62)■

August 1962

□ Highest position disc reached ● Act's first ever week on chart

LW	TW	Title	Artist	Label	Wks
16	8	THINGS	Bobby Darin	London	3
6	9	COME OUTSIDE	Mike Sarne	Parlophone	13
8	10	LITTLE MISS LONELY	Helen Shapiro	Columbia	4
23	11	ONCE UPON A DREAM	Billy Fury	Decca	3
11	12	LET THERE BE LOVE	Nat 'King' Cole with George Shearing	Capitol	4
10	13	RIGHT SAID FRED	Bernard Cribbins	Parlophone	5
9	14	ENGLISH COUNTRY GARDEN	Jimmy Rodgers	Columbia	9
14	15	YA YA TWIST	Petula Clark	Pye	6
22	16	I'M JUST A BABY	Louise Cordet	Decca	5
25	17	BREAKING UP IS HARD TO DO	Neil Sedaka	RCA	4
12	18	OUR FAVOURITE MELODIES	Craig Douglas	Columbia	7
20	19	STRANGER ON THE SHORE	Mr. Acker Bilk	Columbia	37
15	20	SHARING YOU	Bobby Vee	Liberty	9
13	21	GOOD LUCK CHARM	Elvis Presley	RCA	14
19	22	CINDY'S BIRTHDAY	Shane Fenton	Parlophone	4
-	23	ROSES ARE RED	Ronnie Carroll	Philips	1
40	24	VACATION	Connie Francis	MGM	2
-	25	ROSES ARE RED	Bobby Vinton ●	Columbia	1
24	26	I'M LOOKING OUT THE WINDOW/DO YOU WANT TO DANCE	Cliff Richard	Columbia	14
29	27	ADIOS AMIGO	Jim Reeves	RCA	6
33	28	GOTTA SEE BABY TONIGHT	Mr. Acker Bilk	Columbia	2
18	29	GINNY COME LATELY	Brian Hyland	HMV	14
17	30	AIN'T THAT FUNNY	Jimmy Justice	Pye	9
31	[31]	IT KEEPS RIGHT ON A HURTIN'	Johnny Tillotson	London	5
-	32	SEALED WITH A KISS	Brian Hyland	HMV	1
37	33	AL DI LA	Emilio Pericoli	Warner Brothers	6
21	34	YES MY DARLING DAUGHTER	Eydie Gormé	CBS	8
30	35	PALISADES PARK	Freddy Cannon	Stateside	6
38	36	THAT NOISE	Anthony Newley	Decca	2
27	37	LAST NIGHT WAS MADE FOR LOVE	Billy Fury	Decca	15
34	38	FAR AWAY	Shirley Bassey	Columbia	9
26	39	GREEN LEAVES OF SUMMER	Kenny Ball and his Jazzmen	Pye	12
32	40	TEARS	Danny Williams	HMV	6

WEEK ENDING 16 AUGUST 1962

LW	TW	Title	Artist	Label	Wks
1	[1]	I REMEMBER YOU	Frank Ifield	Columbia	7
2	[2]	SPEEDY GONZALES	Pat Boone	London	6
3	3	I CAN'T STOP LOVING YOU	Ray Charles	HMV	9
7	[4]	GUITAR TANGO	Shadows	Columbia	3
8	5	THINGS	Bobby Darin	London	4
4	6	A PICTURE OF YOU	Joe Brown	Piccadilly	13
11	[7]	ONCE UPON A DREAM	Billy Fury	Decca	4
23	8	ROSES ARE RED	Ronnie Carroll	Philips	2
5	9	DON'T EVER CHANGE	Crickets	Liberty	9
10	10	LITTLE MISS LONELY	Helen Shapiro	Columbia	5
12	[11]	LET THERE BE LOVE	Nat 'King' Cole with George Shearing	Capitol	5
6	12	HERE COMES THAT FEELING	Brenda Lee	Brunswick	8
17	13	BREAKING UP IS HARD TO DO	Neil Sedaka	RCA	5
24	14	VACATION	Connie Francis	MGM	3
16	15	I'M JUST A BABY	Louise Cordet	Decca	6
32	16	SEALED WITH A KISS	Brian Hyland	HMV	2
9	17	COME OUTSIDE	Mike Sarne	Parlophone	14
19	18	STRANGER ON THE SHORE	Mr. Acker Bilk	Columbia	38
14	19	ENGLISH COUNTRY GARDEN	Jimmy Rodgers	Columbia	10
25	20	ROSES ARE RED	Bobby Vinton	Columbia	2
13	21	RIGHT SAID FRED	Bernard Cribbins	Parlophone	6
15	22	YA YA TWIST	Petula Clark	Pye	7
27	[23]	ADIOS AMIGO	Jim Reeves	RCA	7
28	[24]	GOTTA SEE BABY TONIGHT	Mr. Acker Bilk	Columbia	3
22	25	CINDY'S BIRTHDAY	Shane Fenton	Parlophone	5
-	26	DANCIN' PARTY	Chubby Checker	Columbia	1
21	27	GOOD LUCK CHARM	Elvis Presley	RCA	15
18	28	OUR FAVOURITE MELODIES	Craig Douglas	Columbia	8
20	29	SHARING YOU	Bobby Vee	Liberty	10
30	30	AIN'T THAT FUNNY	Jimmy Justice	Pye	10
31	[31]	IT KEEPS RIGHT ON A HURTIN'	Johnny Tillotson	London	6
26	32	I'M LOOKING OUT THE WINDOW/DO YOU WANT TO DANCE	Cliff Richard	Columbia	15
33	33	AL DI LA	Emilio Pericoli	Warner Brothers	7
36	[34]	THAT NOISE	Anthony Newley	Decca	3
-	35	PETER AND THE WOLF	Clyde Valley Stompers ●	Parlophone	1
29	36	GINNY COME LATELY	Brian Hyland	HMV	15
34	37	YES MY DARLING DAUGHTER	Eydie Gormé	CBS	9
39	38	GREEN LEAVES OF SUMMER	Kenny Ball and his Jazzmen	Pye	13
38	39	FAR AWAY	Shirley Bassey	Columbia	10
35	40	PALISADES PARK	Freddy Cannon	Stateside	7

WEEK ENDING 23 AUGUST 1962

LW	TW	Title	Artist	Label	Wks
1	[1]	I REMEMBER YOU	Frank Ifield	Columbia	8
2	[2]	SPEEDY GONZALES	Pat Boone	London	7
5	3	THINGS	Bobby Darin	London	5
4	[4]	GUITAR TANGO	Shadows	Columbia	4
8	5	ROSES ARE RED	Ronnie Carroll	Philips	3
3	6	I CAN'T STOP LOVING YOU	Ray Charles	HMV	10
7	[7]	ONCE UPON A DREAM	Billy Fury	Decca	5
16	8	SEALED WITH A KISS	Brian Hyland	HMV	3
13	9	BREAKING UP IS HARD TO DO	Neil Sedaka	RCA	6
9	10	DON'T EVER CHANGE	Crickets	Liberty	10
10	11	LITTLE MISS LONELY	Helen Shapiro	Columbia	6
11	12	LET THERE BE LOVE	Nat 'King' Cole with George Shearing	Capitol	6
6	13	A PICTURE OF YOU	Joe Brown	Piccadilly	14
14	14	VACATION	Connie Francis	MGM	4
20	[15]	ROSES ARE RED	Bobby Vinton	Columbia	3
15	16	I'M JUST A BABY	Louise Cordet	Decca	7
12	17	HERE COMES THAT FEELING	Brenda Lee	Brunswick	9
17	18	COME OUTSIDE	Mike Sarne	Parlophone	15
19	19	ENGLISH COUNTRY GARDEN	Jimmy Rodgers	Columbia	11
26	20	DANCIN' PARTY	Chubby Checker	Columbia	2
-	21	PICK A BALE OF COTTON	Lonnie Donegan	Pye	1
18	22	STRANGER ON THE SHORE	Mr. Acker Bilk	Columbia	39
21	23	RIGHT SAID FRED	Bernard Cribbins	Parlophone	7
24	[24]	GOTTA SEE BABY TONIGHT	Mr. Acker Bilk	Columbia	4
22	25	YA YA TWIST	Petula Clark	Pye	8
-	26	MAIN TITLE THEME FROM 'THE MAN WITH THE GOLDEN ARM'	Jet Harris	Decca	1
-	27	BALLAD OF PALADIN	Duane Eddy	RCA	1
23	28	ADIOS AMIGO	Jim Reeves	RCA	8
-	29	SO DO I	Kenny Ball and his Jazzmen	Pye	1
25	30	CINDY'S BIRTHDAY	Shane Fenton	Parlophone	6
35	31	PETER AND THE WOLF	Clyde Valley Stompers	Parlophone	2
29	32	SHARING YOU	Bobby Vee	Liberty	11
-	[33]	WELCOME HOME BABY	Brook Brothers	Pye	1
33	34	AL DI LA	Emilio Pericoli	Warner Brothers	8
27	35	GOOD LUCK CHARM	Elvis Presley	RCA	16
31	36	IT KEEPS RIGHT ON A HURTIN'	Johnny Tillotson	London	7
28	37	OUR FAVOURITE MELODIES	Craig Douglas	Columbia	9
-	38	MADE TO LOVE (GIRLS GIRLS GIRLS)	Eddie Hodges	London	1
34	39	THAT NOISE	Anthony Newley	Decca	4
30	40	AIN'T THAT FUNNY	Jimmy Justice	Pye	11

WEEK ENDING 30 AUGUST 1962

LW	TW	Title	Artist	Label	Wks
1	[1]	I REMEMBER YOU	Frank Ifield	Columbia	9
2	[2]	SPEEDY GONZALES	Pat Boone	London	8
3	3	THINGS	Bobby Darin	London	6
4	[4]	GUITAR TANGO	Shadows	Columbia	5
8	5	SEALED WITH A KISS	Brian Hyland	HMV	4
5	6	ROSES ARE RED	Ronnie Carroll	Philips	4
7	[7]	ONCE UPON A DREAM	Billy Fury	Decca	6
9	8	BREAKING UP IS HARD TO DO	Neil Sedaka	RCA	7
6	9	I CAN'T STOP LOVING YOU	Ray Charles	HMV	11
14	[10]	VACATION	Connie Francis	MGM	5
11	11	LITTLE MISS LONELY	Helen Shapiro	Columbia	7
12	12	LET THERE BE LOVE	Nat 'King' Cole with George Shearing	Capitol	7

In these weeks ■ Three weeks at number 31 for Johnny Tillotson's *It Keeps Right On A-Hurting* (16.08.62) ■ Four weeks at number two for *Speedy Gonzales*, but Pat Boone can't get past *I Remember You* (30.08.62) ■ The final week in the Top 10 for the leading chart lady of the first ten years of the charts - Connie Francis (30.08.62) ■ By clocking up 37 weeks on the chart, *Stranger On The Shore* overtakes the previous long-running record-holder, Frankie Laine's *I Believe* (09.08.62)■

LW	TW	Title	Artist	Label	Wks
16	13	I'M JUST A BABY	Louise Cordet	Decca	8
29	14	SO DO I	Kenny Ball and his Jazzmen	Pye	2
21	15	PICK A BALE OF COTTON	Lonnie Donegan	Pye	2
13	16	A PICTURE OF YOU	Joe Brown	Piccadilly	15
27	17	BALLAD OF PALADIN	Duane Eddy	RCA	2
10	18	DON'T EVER CHANGE	Crickets	Liberty	11
20	19	DANCIN' PARTY	Chubby Checker	Columbia	3
26	20	MAIN TITLE THEME FROM 'THE MAN WITH THE GOLDEN ARM'	Jet Harris	Decca	2
15	21	ROSES ARE RED	Bobby Vinton	Columbia	4
17	22	HERE COMES THAT FEELING	Brenda Lee	Brunswick	10
22	23	STRANGER ON THE SHORE	Mr. Acker Bilk	Columbia	40
24	24	GOTTA SEE BABY TONIGHT	Mr. Acker Bilk	Columbia	5
31	25	PETER AND THE WOLF	Clyde Valley Stompers	Parlophone	3
18	26	COME OUTSIDE	Mike Sarne	Parlophone	16
-	27	SOME PEOPLE	Carol Deene	HMV	1
19	28	ENGLISH COUNTRY GARDEN	Jimmy Rodgers	Columbia	12
25	29	YA YA TWIST	Petula Clark	Pye	9
28	30	ADIOS AMIGO	Jim Reeves	RCA	9
-	31	SPANISH HARLEM	Jimmy Justice	Pye	1
23	32	RIGHT SAID FRED	Bernard Cribbins	Parlophone	8
33	33	WELCOME HOME BABY	Brook Brothers	Pye	2
-	34	SHE'S NOT YOU	Elvis Presley	RCA	1
34	35	AL DI LA	Emilio Pericoli	Warner Brothers	9
-	36	WILL I WHAT	Mike Sarne	Parlophone	1
38	37	MADE TO LOVE (GIRLS GIRLS GIRLS)	Eddie Hodges	London	2
-	38	WHAT NOW MY LOVE	Shirley Bassey	Columbia	1
-	39	LOVER PLEASE/YOU KNOW WHAT I MEAN	Vernons Girls	Decca	9
32	40	SHARING YOU	Bobby Vee	Liberty	12

LW	TW	*WEEK ENDING* 6 SEPTEMBER 1962			Wks
1	1	I REMEMBER YOU	Frank Ifield	Columbia	10
3	2	THINGS	Bobby Darin	London	7
5	3	SEALED WITH A KISS	Brian Hyland	HMV	5
6	4	ROSES ARE RED	Ronnie Carroll	Philips	5
2	5	SPEEDY GONZALES	Pat Boone	London	9
4	6	GUITAR TANGO	Shadows	Columbia	6
8	7	BREAKING UP IS HARD TO DO	Neil Sedaka	RCA	8
34	8	SHE'S NOT YOU	Elvis Presley	RCA	2
7	9	ONCE UPON A DREAM	Billy Fury	Decca	8
9	10	I CAN'T STOP LOVING YOU	Ray Charles	HMV	12
15	11	PICK A BALE OF COTTON	Lonnie Donegan	Pye	3
17	12	BALLAD OF PALADIN	Duane Eddy	RCA	3
12	13	LET THERE BE LOVE	Nat 'King' Cole with George Shearing	Capitol	8
20	14	MAIN TITLE THEME FROM 'THE MAN WITH THE GOLDEN ARM'	Jet Harris	Decca	3
10	15	VACATION	Connie Francis	MGM	6
14	16	SO DO I	Kenny Ball and his Jazzmen	Pye	3
-	17	IT'LL BE ME	Cliff Richard	Columbia	1
11	18	LITTLE MISS LONELY	Helen Shapiro	Columbia	8
-	19	DON'T THAT BEAT ALL	Adam Faith	Parlophone	1
13	20	I'M JUST A BABY	Louise Cordet	Decca	9
31	21	SPANISH HARLEM	Jimmy Justice	Pye	2
19	22	DANCIN' PARTY	Chubby Checker	Columbia	4
36	23	WILL I WHAT	Mike Sarne	Parlophone	2
18	24	DON'T EVER CHANGE	Crickets	Liberty	12
16	25	A PICTURE OF YOU	Joe Brown	Piccadilly	16
25	26	PETER AND THE WOLF	Clyde Valley Stompers	Parlophone	4
23	27	STRANGER ON THE SHORE	Mr. Acker Bilk	Columbia	41
30	28	ADIOS AMIGO	Jim Reeves	RCA	10
38	29	WHAT NOW MY LOVE	Shirley Bassey	Columbia	2
27	30				
21	31	ROSES ARE RED	Bobby Vinton	Columbia	5
26	32	COME OUTSIDE	Mike Sarne	Parlophone	17
24	33	GOTTA SEE BABY TONIGHT	Mr. Acker Bilk	Columbia	6
33	34	WELCOME HOME BABY	Brook Brothers	Pye	3
22	35	HERE COMES THAT FEELING	Brenda Lee	Brunswick	11
-	36	TELSTAR	Tornados ●	Decca	1
35	37	AL DI LA	Emilio Pericoli	Warner Brothers	10
29	38	YA YA TWIST	Petula Clark	Pye	10
28	39	ENGLISH COUNTRY GARDEN	Jimmy Rodgers	Columbia	13
-	40	TEENAGE IDOL	Rick Nelson	London	1

September 1962

□ Highest position disc reached ● Act's first ever week on chart

LW	TW	*WEEK ENDING* 13 SEPTEMBER 1962			Wks
8	1	SHE'S NOT YOU	Elvis Presley	RCA	3
1	2	I REMEMBER YOU	Frank Ifield	Columbia	11
4	3	ROSES ARE RED	Ronnie Carroll	Philips	6
2	4	THINGS	Bobby Darin	London	8
3	5	SEALED WITH A KISS	Brian Hyland	HMV	6
5	6	SPEEDY GONZALES	Pat Boone	London	10
17	7	IT'LL BE ME	Cliff Richard	Columbia	2
7	8	BREAKING UP IS HARD TO DO	Neil Sedaka	RCA	9
6	9	GUITAR TANGO	Shadows	Columbia	7
12	10	BALLAD OF PALADIN	Duane Eddy	RCA	4
9	11	ONCE UPON A DREAM	Billy Fury	Decca	9
14	12	MAIN TITLE THEME FROM 'THE MAN WITH THE GOLDEN ARM'	Jet Harris	Decca	4
19	13	DON'T THAT BEAT ALL	Adam Faith	Parlophone	2
11	14	PICK A BALE OF COTTON	Lonnie Donegan	Pye	4
16	15	SO DO I	Kenny Ball and his Jazzmen	Pye	4
10	16	I CAN'T STOP LOVING YOU	Ray Charles	HMV	13
36	17	TELSTAR	Tornados	Decca	2
23	18	WILL I WHAT	Mike Sarne	Parlophone	3
13	19	LET THERE BE LOVE	Nat 'King' Cole with George Shearing	Capitol	9
21	20	SPANISH HARLEM	Jimmy Justice	Pye	3
15	21	VACATION	Connie Francis	MGM	7
22	22	DANCIN' PARTY	Chubby Checker	Columbia	5
29	23	WHAT NOW MY LOVE	Shirley Bassey	Columbia	3
-	24	SHEILA	Tommy Roe ●	HMV	1
-	25	THE LOCO-MOTION	Little Eva ●	London	1
18	26	LITTLE MISS LONELY	Helen Shapiro	Columbia	9
30	27	SOME PEOPLE	Carol Deene	HMV	3
20	28	I'M JUST A BABY	Louise Cordet	Decca	10
28	29	ADIOS AMIGO	Jim Reeves	RCA	11
27	30	STRANGER ON THE SHORE	Mr. Acker Bilk	Columbia	42
26	31	PETER AND THE WOLF	Clyde Valley Stompers	Parlophone	5
25	32	A PICTURE OF YOU	Joe Brown	Piccadilly	17
33	33	GOTTA SEE BABY TONIGHT	Mr. Acker Bilk	Columbia	7
-	34	REMINISCING	Buddy Holly	Coral	1
24	35	DON'T EVER CHANGE	Crickets	Liberty	13
-	36	CRY MYSELF TO SLEEP	Del Shannon	London	1
37	37	AL DI LA	Emilio Pericoli	Warner Brothers	11
-	38	THE ROCKET MAN	Spotnicks	Oriole	1
-	39	SWEET LITTLE SIXTEEN	Jerry Lee Lewis	London	1
31	40	ROSES ARE RED	Bobby Vinton	Columbia	5

LW	TW	*WEEK ENDING* 20 SEPTEMBER 1962			Wks
1	1	SHE'S NOT YOU	Elvis Presley	RCA	4
2	2	I REMEMBER YOU	Frank Ifield	Columbia	12
7	3	IT'LL BE ME	Cliff Richard	Columbia	3
3	4	ROSES ARE RED	Ronnie Carroll	Philips	7
4	5	THINGS	Bobby Darin	London	9
5	6	SEALED WITH A KISS	Brian Hyland	HMV	7
8	7	BREAKING UP IS HARD TO DO	Neil Sedaka	RCA	10
6	8	SPEEDY GONZALES	Pat Boone	London	11
13	9	DON'T THAT BEAT ALL	Adam Faith	Parlophone	3
9	10	GUITAR TANGO	Shadows	Columbia	8
17	11	TELSTAR	Tornados	Decca	3
24	12	SHEILA	Tommy Roe	HMV	2
10	13	BALLAD OF PALADIN	Duane Eddy	RCA	5
14	14	PICK A BALE OF COTTON	Lonnie Donegan	Pye	5
12	15	MAIN TITLE THEME FROM 'THE MAN WITH THE GOLDEN ARM'	Jet Harris	Decca	5
11	16	ONCE UPON A DREAM	Billy Fury	Decca	10
25	17	THE LOCO-MOTION	Little Eva	London	2
23	18	WHAT NOW MY LOVE	Shirley Bassey	Columbia	4
15	19	SO DO I	Kenny Ball and his Jazzmen	Pye	5
18	20	WILL I WHAT	Mike Sarne	Parlophone	4
34	21	REMINISCING	Buddy Holly	Coral	2

■*Lover Please* by the Vernons Girls returns after a seven week absence, reactivated by the flip side *You Know What I Mean* (30.08.62) ■ Buddy Holly re-enters the Top 40 three and a half years after his death, one position higher than his former colleagues The Crickets. Tommy Roe, whose style is reminiscent of Holly, debuts ten places higher (13.09.62)■

September 1962

□ Highest position disc reached ● Act's first ever week on chart

LW	TW	Title	Artist	Label	Wks
16	22	I CAN'T STOP LOVING YOU	Ray Charles	*HMV*	14
-	23	YOU DON'T KNOW ME	Ray Charles	*HMV*	1
22	24	DANCIN' PARTY	Chubby Checker	*Columbia*	6
20	25	SPANISH HARLEM	Jimmy Justice	*Pye*	4
19	26	LET THERE BE LOVE	Nat 'King' Cole with George Shearing	*Capitol*	10
29	27	ADIOS AMIGO	Jim Reeves	*RCA*	12
-	28	IT STARTED ALL OVER AGAIN	Brenda Lee	*Brunswick*	1
27	29	SOME PEOPLE	Carol Deene	*HMV*	4
21	30	VACATION	Connie Francis	*MGM*	8
28	31	I'M JUST A BABY	Louise Cordet	*Decca*	11
30	32	STRANGER ON THE SHORE	Mr. Acker Bilk	*Columbia*	43
-	33	PUFF	Kenny Lynch	*HMV*	1
31	34	PETER AND THE WOLF	Clyde Valley Stompers	*Parlophone*	6
-	35	YOUR TENDER LOOK	Joe Brown	*Piccadilly*	1
36	36	CRY MYSELF TO SLEEP	Del Shannon	*London*	2
26	37	LITTLE MISS LONELY	Helen Shapiro	*Columbia*	10
39	38	SWEET LITTLE SIXTEEN	Jerry Lee Lewis	*London*	2
-	39	TEENAGE IDOL	Rick Nelson	*London*	2
38	40	THE ROCKET MAN	Spotnicks	*Oriole*	2

LW	TW	*WEEK ENDING* 27 SEPTEMBER 1962			Wks
1	1	SHE'S NOT YOU	Elvis Presley	*RCA*	5
3	2	IT'LL BE ME	Cliff Richard	*Columbia*	4
11	3	TELSTAR	Tornados	*Decca*	4
2	4	I REMEMBER YOU	Frank Ifield	*Columbia*	13
4	5	ROSES ARE RED	Ronnie Carroll	*Philips*	8
5	6	THINGS	Bobby Darin	*London*	10
6	7	SEALED WITH A KISS	Brian Hyland	*HMV*	8
9	8	DON'T THAT BEAT ALL	Adam Faith	*Parlophone*	4
7	9	BREAKING UP IS HARD TO DO	Neil Sedaka	*RCA*	11
12	10	SHEILA	Tommy Roe	*HMV*	3
10	11	GUITAR TANGO	Shadows	*Columbia*	9
23	12	YOU DON'T KNOW ME	Ray Charles	*HMV*	2
17	13	THE LOCO-MOTION	Little Eva	*London*	3
18	14	WHAT NOW MY LOVE	Shirley Bassey	*Columbia*	5
8	15	SPEEDY GONZALES	Pat Boone	*London*	12
15	16	MAIN TITLE THEME FROM 'THE MAN WITH THE GOLDEN ARM'	Jet Harris	*Decca*	6
13	17	BALLAD OF PALADIN	Duane Eddy	*RCA*	6
14	18	PICK A BALE OF COTTON	Lonnie Donegan	*Pye*	6
20	19	WILL I WHAT	Mike Sarne	*Parlophone*	5
16	20	ONCE UPON A DREAM	Billy Fury	*Decca*	11
21	21	REMINISCING	Buddy Holly	*Coral*	3
28	22	IT STARTED ALL OVER AGAIN	Brenda Lee	*Brunswick*	2
25	23	SPANISH HARLEM	Jimmy Justice	*Pye*	5
-	24	IT MIGHT AS WELL RAIN UNTIL SEPTEMBER	Carole King ●	*London*	1
19	25	SO DO I	Kenny Ball and his Jazzmen	*Pye*	6
22	26	I CAN'T STOP LOVING YOU	Ray Charles	*HMV*	15
24	27	DANCIN' PARTY	Chubby Checker	*Columbia*	7
29	28	SOME PEOPLE	Carol Deene	*HMV*	5
27	29	ADIOS AMIGO	Jim Reeves	*RCA*	13
26	30	LET THERE BE LOVE	Nat 'King' Cole with George Shearing	*Capitol*	11
32	31	STRANGER ON THE SHORE	Mr. Acker Bilk	*Columbia*	44
35	32	YOUR TENDER LOOK	Joe Brown	*Piccadilly*	2
36	33	CRY MYSELF TO SLEEP	Del Shannon	*London*	3
-	34	RAMBLIN' ROSE	Nat 'King' Cole	*Capitol*	1
33	35	PUFF	Kenny Lynch	*HMV*	2
-	36	A FOREVER KIND OF LOVE	Bobby Vee	*Liberty*	1
-	37	BLUE WEEKEND	Karl Denver	*Decca*	1
-	38	LONELY	Mr. Acker Bilk	*Columbia*	1
34	39	PETER AND THE WOLF	Clyde Valley Stompers	*Parlophone*	7
40	40	THE ROCKET MAN	Spotnicks	*Oriole*	3

LW	TW	*WEEK ENDING* 4 OCTOBER 1962			Wks
3	1	TELSTAR	Tornados	*Decca*	5
1	2	SHE'S NOT YOU	Elvis Presley	*RCA*	6
2	3	IT'LL BE ME	Cliff Richard	*Columbia*	5
10	4	SHEILA	Tommy Roe	*HMV*	4
13	5	THE LOCO-MOTION	Little Eva	*London*	4
24	6	IT MIGHT AS WELL RAIN UNTIL SEPTEMBER	Carole King	*London*	2
7	7	SEALED WITH A KISS	Brian Hyland	*HMV*	9
4	8	I REMEMBER YOU	Frank Ifield	*Columbia*	14
12	9	YOU DON'T KNOW ME	Ray Charles	*HMV*	3
8	10	DON'T THAT BEAT ALL	Adam Faith	*Parlophone*	5
5	11	ROSES ARE RED	Ronnie Carroll	*Philips*	9
6	12	THINGS	Bobby Darin	*London*	11
14	13	WHAT NOW MY LOVE	Shirley Bassey	*Columbia*	6
9	14	BREAKING UP IS HARD TO DO	Neil Sedaka	*RCA*	12
11	15	GUITAR TANGO	Shadows	*Columbia*	10
22	16	IT STARTED ALL OVER AGAIN	Brenda Lee	*Brunswick*	3
15	17	SPEEDY GONZALES	Pat Boone	*London*	13
21	18	REMINISCING	Buddy Holly	*Coral*	4
34	19	RAMBLIN' ROSE	Nat 'King' Cole	*Capitol*	2
16	20	MAIN TITLE THEME FROM 'THE MAN WITH THE GOLDEN ARM'	Jet Harris	*Decca*	7
23	21	SPANISH HARLEM	Jimmy Justice	*Pye*	6
19	22	WILL I WHAT	Mike Sarne	*Parlophone*	6
17	23	BALLAD OF PALADIN	Duane Eddy	*RCA*	7
18	24	PICK A BALE OF COTTON	Lonnie Donegan	*Pye*	7
28	25	SOME PEOPLE	Carol Deene	*HMV*	6
20	26	ONCE UPON A DREAM	Billy Fury	*Decca*	12
38	27	LONELY	Mr. Acker Bilk	*Columbia*	2
29	28	ADIOS AMIGO	Jim Reeves	*RCA*	14
33	29	CRY MYSELF TO SLEEP	Del Shannon	*London*	4
27	30	DANCIN' PARTY	Chubby Checker	*Columbia*	8
32	31	YOUR TENDER LOOK	Joe Brown	*Piccadilly*	3
25	32	SO DO I	Kenny Ball and his Jazzmen	*Pye*	7
37	33	BLUE WEEKEND	Karl Denver	*Decca*	2
30	34	LET THERE BE LOVE	Nat 'King' Cole with George Shearing	*Capitol*	12
36	35	A FOREVER KIND OF LOVE	Bobby Vee	*Liberty*	2
35	36	PUFF	Kenny Lynch	*HMV*	3
26	37	I CAN'T STOP LOVING YOU	Ray Charles	*HMV*	16
31	38	STRANGER ON THE SHORE	Mr. Acker Bilk	*Columbia*	45
40	39	THE ROCKET MAN	Spotnicks	*Oriole*	4
-	40	DEVIL WOMAN	Marty Robbins	*CBS*	1

LW	TW	*WEEK ENDING* 11 OCTOBER 1962			Wks
1	1	TELSTAR	Tornados	*Decca*	6
5	2	THE LOCO-MOTION	Little Eva	*London*	5
4	3	SHEILA	Tommy Roe	*HMV*	5
6	4	IT MIGHT AS WELL RAIN UNTIL SEPTEMBER	Carole King	*London*	3
2	5	SHE'S NOT YOU	Elvis Presley	*RCA*	7
3	6	IT'LL BE ME	Cliff Richard	*Columbia*	6
13	7	WHAT NOW MY LOVE	Shirley Bassey	*Columbia*	7
8	8	I REMEMBER YOU	Frank Ifield	*Columbia*	15
9	9	YOU DON'T KNOW ME	Ray Charles	*HMV*	4
10	10	DON'T THAT BEAT ALL	Adam Faith	*Parlophone*	6
19	11	RAMBLIN' ROSE	Nat 'King' Cole	*Capitol*	3
11	12	ROSES ARE RED	Ronnie Carroll	*Philips*	10
12	13	THINGS	Bobby Darin	*London*	12
7	14	SEALED WITH A KISS	Brian Hyland	*HMV*	10
16	15	IT STARTED ALL OVER AGAIN	Brenda Lee	*Brunswick*	4
14	16	BREAKING UP IS HARD TO DO	Neil Sedaka	*RCA*	13
18	17	REMINISCING	Buddy Holly	*Coral*	5
20	18	MAIN TITLE THEME FROM 'THE MAN WITH THE GOLDEN ARM'	Jet Harris	*Decca*	8
17	19	SPEEDY GONZALES	Pat Boone	*London*	14
27	20	LONELY	Mr. Acker Bilk	*Columbia*	3
-	21	LET'S DANCE	Chris Montez ●	*London*	1
-	22	VENUS IN BLUE JEANS	Mark Wynter	*Pye*	1
15	23	GUITAR TANGO	Shadows	*Columbia*	11
21	24	SPANISH HARLEM	Jimmy Justice	*Pye*	7

In these weeks ■ For the second successive release, Cliff Richard is kept from number one by Elvis Presley (27.09.62) ■ Only one new entry in the Top 40 this week, at number 40 (04.10.62) ■ The Spotnicks' *Rocket Man* does much less well than the other space age hit *Telstar*. It manages five weeks on the chart without ever climbing above number 38 (11.10.620■

LW	TW	Title	Artist	Label	Wks
-	25	SHERRY	Four Seasons ●	Stateside	1
40	26	DEVIL WOMAN	Marty Robbins	CBS	2
22	27	WILL I WHAT	Mike Sarne	Parlophone	7
25	28	SOME PEOPLE	Carol Deene	HMV	7
23	29	BALLAD OF PALADIN	Duane Eddy	RCA	8
-	30	IF A MAN ANSWERS	Bobby Darin	Capitol	1
28	31	ADIOS AMIGO	Jim Reeves	RCA	15
24	32	PICK A BALE OF COTTON	Lonnie Donegan	Pye	8
35	33	A FOREVER KIND OF LOVE	Bobby Vee	Liberty	3
29	34	CRY MYSELF TO SLEEP	Del Shannon	London	5
31	35	YOUR TENDER LOOK	Joe Brown	Piccadilly	4
36	36	PUFF	Kenny Lynch	HMV	4
-	37	SEND ME THE PILLOW YOU DREAM ON	Johnny Tillotson	London	1
30	38	DANCIN' PARTY	Chubby Checker	Columbia	9
33	39	BLUE WEEKEND	Karl Denver	Decca	3
39	40	THE ROCKET MAN	Spotnicks	Oriole	5

WEEK ENDING 18 OCTOBER 1962

LW	TW	Title	Artist	Label	Wks
1	1	TELSTAR	Tornados	Decca	7
2	2	THE LOCO-MOTION	Little Eva	London	6
4	3	IT MIGHT AS WELL RAIN UNTIL SEPTEMBER	Carole King	London	4
3	4	SHEILA	Tommy Roe	HMV	6
7	5	WHAT NOW MY LOVE	Shirley Bassey	Columbia	8
5	6	SHE'S NOT YOU	Elvis Presley	RCA	8
11	7	RAMBLIN' ROSE	Nat 'King' Cole	Capitol	4
8	8	I REMEMBER YOU	Frank Ifield	Columbia	16
6	9	IT'LL BE ME	Cliff Richard	Columbia	7
9	10	YOU DON'T KNOW ME	Ray Charles	HMV	5
22	11	VENUS IN BLUE JEANS	Mark Wynter	Pye	2
10	12	DON'T THAT BEAT ALL	Adam Faith	Parlophone	7
21	13	LET'S DANCE	Chris Montez	London	2
20	14	LONELY	Mr. Acker Bilk	Columbia	4
25	15	SHERRY	Four Seasons	Stateside	2
12	16	ROSES ARE RED	Ronnie Carroll	Philips	11
15	17	IT STARTED ALL OVER AGAIN	Brenda Lee	Brunswick	5
13	18	THINGS	Bobby Darin	London	13
-	19	SWISS MAID	Del Shannon	London	1
14	20	SEALED WITH A KISS	Brian Hyland	HMV	11
26	21	DEVIL WOMAN	Marty Robbins	CBS	3
17	22	REMINISCING	Buddy Holly	Coral	6
16	23	BREAKING UP IS HARD TO DO	Neil Sedaka	RCA	14
27	24	WILL I WHAT	Mike Sarne	Parlophone	8
23	25	GUITAR TANGO	Shadows	Columbia	12
30	26	IF A MAN ANSWERS	Bobby Darin	Capitol	2
37	27	SEND ME THE PILLOW YOU DREAM ON	Johnny Tillotson	London	2
28	28	SOME PEOPLE	Carol Deene	HMV	8
18	29	MAIN TITLE THEME FROM 'THE MAN WITH THE GOLDEN ARM'	Jet Harris	Decca	9
24	30	SPANISH HARLEM	Jimmy Justice	Pye	8
19	31	SPEEDY GONZALES	Pat Boone	London	15
-	32	BOBBY'S GIRL	Susan Maughan ●	Philips	1
38	33	DANCIN' PARTY	Chubby Checker	Columbia	10
29	34	BALLAD OF PALADIN	Duane Eddy	RCA	9
-	35	THE PAY OFF	Kenny Ball and his Jazzmen	Pye	1
31	36	ADIOS AMIGO	Jim Reeves	RCA	16
33	37	A FOREVER KIND OF LOVE	Bobby Vee	Liberty	4
40	38	THE ROCKET MAN	Spotnicks	Oriole	6
-	39	STRANGER ON THE SHORE	Mr. Acker Bilk	Columbia	46
35	40	YOUR TENDER LOOK	Joe Brown	Piccadilly	5

WEEK ENDING 25 OCTOBER 1962

LW	TW	Title	Artist	Label	Wks
1	1	TELSTAR	Tornados	Decca	8
2	2	THE LOCO-MOTION	Little Eva	London	7
4	3	SHEILA	Tommy Roe	HMV	7
3	4	IT MIGHT AS WELL RAIN UNTIL SEPTEMBER	Carole King	London	5
7	5	RAMBLIN' ROSE	Nat 'King' Cole	Capitol	5
11	6	VENUS IN BLUE JEANS	Mark Wynter	Pye	3

November 1962

□ Highest position disc reached ● Act's first ever week on chart

LW	TW	Title	Artist	Label	Wks
13	7	LET'S DANCE	Chris Montez	London	3
5	8	WHAT NOW MY LOVE	Shirley Bassey	Columbia	9
6	9	SHE'S NOT YOU	Elvis Presley	RCA	9
19	10	SWISS MAID	Del Shannon	London	2
9	11	IT'LL BE ME	Cliff Richard	Columbia	8
10	12	YOU DON'T KNOW ME	Ray Charles	HMV	6
21	13	DEVIL WOMAN	Marty Robbins	CBS	4
8	14	I REMEMBER YOU	Frank Ifield	Columbia	17
15	15	SHERRY	Four Seasons	Stateside	3
-	16	LOVESICK BLUES	Frank Ifield	Columbia	1
14	17	LONELY	Mr. Acker Bilk	Columbia	5
17	18	IT STARTED ALL OVER AGAIN	Brenda Lee	Brunswick	6
16	19	ROSES ARE RED	Ronnie Carroll	Philips	12
12	20	DON'T THAT BEAT ALL	Adam Faith	Parlophone	8
22	21	REMINISCING	Buddy Holly	Coral	7
18	22	THINGS	Bobby Darin	London	14
32	23	BOBBY'S GIRL	Susan Maughan	Philips	2
26	24	IF A MAN ANSWERS	Bobby Darin	Capitol	3
20	25	SEALED WITH A KISS	Brian Hyland	HMV	12
27	26	SEND ME THE PILLOW YOU DREAM ON	Johnny Tillotson	London	3
25	27	GUITAR TANGO	Shadows	Columbia	13
-	28	OH LONESOME ME	Craig Douglas	Decca	1
35	29	THE PAY OFF	Kenny Ball and his Jazzmen	Pye	2
-	30	NO ONE CAN MAKE MY SUNSHINE SMILE	Everly Brothers	Warner Brothers	1
30	31	SPANISH HARLEM	Jimmy Justice	Pye	9
23	32	BREAKING UP IS HARD TO DO	Neil Sedaka	RCA	15
24	33	WILL I WHAT	Mike Sarne	Parlophone	9
33	34	DANCIN' PARTY	Chubby Checker	Columbia	11
39	35	STRANGER ON THE SHORE	Mr. Acker Bilk	Columbia	47
28	36	SOME PEOPLE	Carol Deene	HMV	9
-	37	BECAUSE OF LOVE	Billy Fury	Decca	1
-	38	HE GOT WHAT HE WANTED	Little Richard	Mercury	1
29	39	MAIN TITLE THEME FROM 'THE MAN WITH THE GOLDEN ARM'	Jet Harris	Decca	10
-	40	KEEP AWAY FROM OTHER GIRLS	Helen Shapiro	Columbia	1

WEEK ENDING 1 NOVEMBER 1962

LW	TW	Title	Artist	Label	Wks
1	1	TELSTAR	Tornados	Decca	9
7	2	LET'S DANCE	Chris Montez	London	4
2	3	THE LOCO-MOTION	Little Eva	London	8
6	4	VENUS IN BLUE JEANS	Mark Wynter	Pye	4
16	5	LOVESICK BLUES	Frank Ifield	Columbia	2
4	6	IT MIGHT AS WELL RAIN UNTIL SEPTEMBER	Carole King	London	6
5	7	RAMBLIN' ROSE	Nat 'King' Cole	Capitol	6
10	8	SWISS MAID	Del Shannon	London	3
3	9	SHEILA	Tommy Roe	HMV	8
9	10	SHE'S NOT YOU	Elvis Presley	RCA	10
15	11	SHERRY	Four Seasons	Stateside	4
13	12	DEVIL WOMAN	Marty Robbins	CBS	5
8	13	WHAT NOW MY LOVE	Shirley Bassey	Columbia	10
12	14	YOU DON'T KNOW ME	Ray Charles	HMV	7
11	15	IT'LL BE ME	Cliff Richard	Columbia	9
17	16	LONELY	Mr. Acker Bilk	Columbia	6
23	17	BOBBY'S GIRL	Susan Maughan	Philips	3
14	18	I REMEMBER YOU	Frank Ifield	Columbia	18
18	19	IT STARTED ALL OVER AGAIN	Brenda Lee	Brunswick	7
30	20	NO ONE CAN MAKE MY SUNSHINE SMILE	Everly Brothers	Warner Brothers	2
26	21	SEND ME THE PILLOW YOU DREAM ON	Johnny Tillotson	London	4
19	22	ROSES ARE RED	Ronnie Carroll	Philips	13
20	23	DON'T THAT BEAT ALL	Adam Faith	Parlophone	9
28	24	OH LONESOME ME	Craig Douglas	Decca	2
37	25	BECAUSE OF LOVE	Billy Fury	Decca	2
21	26	REMINISCING	Buddy Holly	Coral	8

■Carole King and her babysitter, Little Eva, occupy the number two and three positions (18.10.62) ■ The only songs in the Top 20 that do not originate in the States are two instrumentals, *Telstar* at number one and *Lonely* at number 16 (01.11.62) ■ Three song titles beginning with the letters 'She' in consecutive positions at nine, ten and 11 (01.11.62)■

November 1962

□ Highest position disc reached ● Act's first ever week on chart

LW	TW	Title	Artist	Label	Wks
29	27	THE PAY OFF	Kenny Ball and his Jazzmen	*Pye*	3
24	28	IF A MAN ANSWERS	Bobby Darin	*Capitol*	4
25	29	SEALED WITH A KISS	Brian Hyland	*HMV*	13
27	30	GUITAR TANGO	Shadows	*Columbia*	14
-	31	EVER SINCE YOU SAID GOODBYE	Marty Wilde	*Philips*	1
-	32	LOVE ME DO	Beatles ●	*Parlophone*	1
-	33	SUN ARISE	Rolf Harris	*Columbia*	1
22	34	THINGS	Bobby Darin	*London*	15
-	35	SPEEDY GONZALES	Pat Boone	*London*	16
31	36	SPANISH HARLEM	Jimmy Justice	*Pye*	10
-	37	YOU KNOW WHAT I MEAN	Vernons Girls	*Decca*	10
33	38	WILL I WHAT	Mike Sarne	*Parlophone*	10
-	39	MUST BE MADISON	Joe Loss Orchestra	*HMV*	1
35	40	STRANGER ON THE SHORE	Mr. Acker Bilk	*Columbia*	48

WEEK ENDING 8 NOVEMBER 1962

LW	TW	Title	Artist	Label	Wks
5	1	LOVESICK BLUES	Frank Ifield	*Columbia*	3
2	2	LET'S DANCE	Chris Montez	*London*	5
1	3	TELSTAR	Tornados	*Decca*	10
8	4	SWISS MAID	Del Shannon	*London*	4
3	5	THE LOCO-MOTION	Little Eva	*London*	9
4	6	VENUS IN BLUE JEANS	Mark Wynter	*Pye*	5
6	7	IT MIGHT AS WELL RAIN UNTIL SEPTEMBER	Carole King	*London*	7
7	8	RAMBLIN' ROSE	Nat 'King' Cole	*Capitol*	7
11	9	SHERRY	Four Seasons	*Stateside*	5
9	10	SHEILA	Tommy Roe	*HMV*	9
12	11	DEVIL WOMAN	Marty Robbins	*CBS*	6
13	12	WHAT NOW MY LOVE	Shirley Bassey	*Columbia*	11
17	13	BOBBY'S GIRL	Susan Maughan	*Philips*	4
20	14	NO ONE CAN MAKE MY SUNSHINE SMILE	Everly Brothers	*Warner Brothers*	3
14	15	YOU DON'T KNOW ME	Ray Charles	*HMV*	8
18	16	I REMEMBER YOU	Frank Ifield	*Columbia*	19
10	17	SHE'S NOT YOU	Elvis Presley	*RCA*	11
25	18	BECAUSE OF LOVE	Billy Fury	*Decca*	3
24	19	OH LONESOME ME	Craig Douglas	*Decca*	3
33	20	SUN ARISE	Rolf Harris	*Columbia*	2
15	21	IT'LL BE ME	Cliff Richard	*Columbia*	10
16	22	LONELY	Mr. Acker Bilk	*Columbia*	7
27	23	THE PAY OFF	Kenny Ball and his Jazzmen	*Pye*	4
-	24	THE JAMES BOND THEME	John Barry Orchestra	*Columbia*	1
21	25	SEND ME THE PILLOW YOU DREAM ON	Johnny Tillotson	*London*	5
39	26	MUST BE MADISON	Joe Loss Orchestra	*HMV*	2
-	27	LOVE ME TENDER	Richard Chamberlain	*MGM*	1
22	28	ROSES ARE RED	Ronnie Carroll	*Philips*	14
19	29	IT STARTED ALL OVER AGAIN	Brenda Lee	*Brunswick*	8
-	30	A FOREVER KIND OF LOVE	Bobby Vee	*Liberty*	5
26	31	REMINISCING	Buddy Holly	*Coral*	9
23	32	DON'T THAT BEAT ALL	Adam Faith	*Parlophone*	10
40	33	STRANGER ON THE SHORE	Mr. Acker Bilk	*Columbia*	49
31	34	EVER SINCE YOU SAID GOODBYE	Marty Wilde	*Philips*	2
28	35	IF A MAN ANSWERS	Bobby Darin	*Capitol*	5
34	36	THINGS	Bobby Darin	*London*	16
32	37	LOVE ME DO	Beatles	*Parlophone*	2
-	38	WARMED OVER KISSES	Brian Hyland	*HMV*	1
-	39	DANCE WITH THE GUITAR MAN	Duane Eddy	*RCA*	1
-	40	KEEP AWAY FROM OTHER GIRLS	Helen Shapiro	*Columbia*	2

WEEK ENDING 15 NOVEMBER 1962

LW	TW	Title	Artist	Label	Wks
1	1	LOVESICK BLUES	Frank Ifield	*Columbia*	4
2	2	LET'S DANCE	Chris Montez	*London*	6
4	3	SWISS MAID	Del Shannon	*London*	5
3	4	TELSTAR	Tornados	*Decca*	11
6	5	VENUS IN BLUE JEANS	Mark Wynter	*Pye*	6
13	6	BOBBY'S GIRL	Susan Maughan	*Philips*	5
5	7	THE LOCO-MOTION	Little Eva	*London*	10
8	8	RAMBLIN' ROSE	Nat 'King' Cole	*Capitol*	8
9	9	SHERRY	Four Seasons	*Stateside*	6
10	10	SHEILA	Tommy Roe	*HMV*	10
7	11	IT MIGHT AS WELL RAIN UNTIL SEPTEMBER	Carole King	*London*	8
11	12	DEVIL WOMAN	Marty Robbins	*CBS*	9
20	13	SUN ARISE	Rolf Harris	*Columbia*	3
14	14	NO ONE CAN MAKE MY SUNSHINE SMILE	Everly Brothers	*Warner Brothers*	4
16	15	I REMEMBER YOU	Frank Ifield	*Columbia*	20
12	16	WHAT NOW MY LOVE	Shirley Bassey	*Columbia*	12
15	17	YOU DON'T KNOW ME	Ray Charles	*HMV*	9
39	18	DANCE WITH THE GUITAR MAN	Duane Eddy	*RCA*	2
19	19	OH LONESOME ME	Craig Douglas	*Decca*	4
26	20	MUST BE MADISON	Joe Loss Orchestra	*HMV*	3
24	21	THE JAMES BOND THEME	John Barry Orchestra	*Columbia*	2
17	22	SHE'S NOT YOU	Elvis Presley	*RCA*	12
27	23	LOVE ME TENDER	Richard Chamberlain	*MGM*	2
18	24	BECAUSE OF LOVE	Billy Fury	*Decca*	4
22	25	LONELY	Mr. Acker Bilk	*Columbia*	8
23	26	THE PAY OFF	Kenny Ball and his Jazzmen	*Pye*	5
-	27	DESAFINADO	Stan Getz and Charlie Byrd ●	*HMV*	1
25	28	SEND ME THE PILLOW YOU DREAM ON	Johnny Tillotson	*London*	6
37	29	LOVE ME DO	Beatles	*Parlophone*	3
38	30	WARMED OVER KISSES	Brian Hyland	*HMV*	2
33	31	STRANGER ON THE SHORE	Mr. Acker Bilk	*Columbia*	50
30	32	A FOREVER KIND OF LOVE	Bobby Vee	*Liberty*	6
-	33	LITTLE BLACK BOOK	Jimmy Dean	*CBS*	1
-	34	IT ONLY TOOK A MINUTE	Joe Brown	*Piccadilly*	1
21	35	IT'LL BE ME	Cliff Richard	*Columbia*	11
31	36	REMINISCING	Buddy Holly	*Coral*	10
-	37	CAN CAN '62	Peter Jay and the Jaywalkers ●	*Decca*	1
-	38	LIMBO ROCK	Chubby Checker	*Cameo-Parkway*	1
-	39	MY LOVE AND DEVOTION	Matt Monro	*Parlophone*	1
40	40	KEEP AWAY FROM OTHER GIRLS	Helen Shapiro	*Columbia*	2

WEEK ENDING 22 NOVEMBER 1962

LW	TW	Title	Artist	Label	Wks
1	1	LOVESICK BLUES	Frank Ifield	*Columbia*	5
2	2	LET'S DANCE	Chris Montez	*London*	7
3	3	SWISS MAID	Del Shannon	*London*	6
4	4	TELSTAR	Tornados	*Decca*	12
6	5	BOBBY'S GIRL	Susan Maughan	*Philips*	6
5	6	VENUS IN BLUE JEANS	Mark Wynter	*Pye*	7
7	7	THE LOCO-MOTION	Little Eva	*London*	11
9	8	SHERRY	Four Seasons	*Stateside*	7
12	9	DEVIL WOMAN	Marty Robbins	*CBS*	10
18	10	DANCE WITH THE GUITAR MAN	Duane Eddy	*RCA*	3
8	11	RAMBLIN' ROSE	Nat 'King' Cole	*Capitol*	9
11	12	IT MIGHT AS WELL RAIN UNTIL SEPTEMBER	Carole King	*London*	9
14	13	NO ONE CAN MAKE MY SUNSHINE SMILE	Everly Brothers	*Warner Brothers*	5
10	14	SHEILA	Tommy Roe	*HMV*	11
13	15	SUN ARISE	Rolf Harris	*Columbia*	4
19	16	OH LONESOME ME	Craig Douglas	*Decca*	5
15	17	I REMEMBER YOU	Frank Ifield	*Columbia*	21
23	18	LOVE ME TENDER	Richard Chamberlain	*MGM*	3
21	19	THE JAMES BOND THEME	John Barry Orchestra	*Columbia*	3
16	20	WHAT NOW MY LOVE	Shirley Bassey	*Columbia*	13
17	21	YOU DON'T KNOW ME	Ray Charles	*HMV*	10
20	22	MUST BE MADISON	Joe Loss Orchestra	*HMV*	4
29	23	LOVE ME DO	Beatles	*Parlophone*	4
24	24	BECAUSE OF LOVE	Billy Fury	*Decca*	5
34	25	IT ONLY TOOK A MINUTE	Joe Brown	*Piccadilly*	2
22	26	SHE'S NOT YOU	Elvis Presley	*RCA*	13
-	27	THE MAIN ATTRACTION	Pat Boone	*London*	1
25	28	LONELY	Mr. Acker Bilk	*Columbia*	9
32	29	A FOREVER KIND OF LOVE	Bobby Vee	*Liberty*	7
28	30	SEND ME THE PILLOW YOU DREAM ON	Johnny Tillotson	*London*	7

In these weeks ■ Three weeks after entering the Top 50, the Beatles' first hit *Love Me Do* finally creeps into the Top 40 (01.11.62) ■ In the tenth anniversary chart, the only survivor from 14 November 1952 is Nat 'King' Cole, who is still in the Top 10 after a decade of chart action (15.11.62) ■ Mr. Acker Bilk's *Stranger On The Shore* becomes the first record to enjoy 50 weeks of Top 40 success (15.11.62)■

LW	TW	Title	Artist	Label	Wks
27	31	DESAFINADO	Stan Getz and Charlie Byrd	HMV	2
30	32	WARMED OVER KISSES	Brian Hyland	HMV	3
-	[33]	IF ONLY TOMORROW	Ronnie Carroll	Philips	1
39	34	MY LOVE AND DEVOTION	Matt Monro	Parlophone	2
38	35	LIMBO ROCK	Chubby Checker	Cameo-Parkway	2
37	36	CAN CAN '62	Peter Jay and the Jaywalkers	Decca	2
-	37	EVER SINCE YOU SAID GOODBYE	Marty Wilde	Philips	3
26	38	THE PAY OFF	Kenny Ball and his Jazzmen	Pye	6
33	39	LITTLE BLACK BOOK	Jimmy Dean	CBS	2
-	40	DESAFINADO	Ella Fitzgerald	Verve	1

WEEK ENDING 29 NOVEMBER 1962

LW	TW	Title	Artist	Label	Wks
1	[1]	LOVESICK BLUES	Frank Ifield	Columbia	6
3	[2]	SWISS MAID	Del Shannon	London	7
5	[3]	BOBBY'S GIRL	Susan Maughan	Philips	7
2	4	LET'S DANCE	Chris Montez	London	8
9	[5]	DEVIL WOMAN	Marty Robbins	CBS	11
10	6	DANCE WITH THE GUITAR MAN	Duane Eddy	RCA	4
6	7	VENUS IN BLUE JEANS	Mark Wynter	Pye	8
15	8	SUN ARISE	Rolf Harris	Columbia	5
4	9	TELSTAR	Tornados	Decca	13
7	10	THE LOCO-MOTION	Little Eva	London	12
13	[11]	NO ONE CAN MAKE MY SUNSHINE SMILE	Everly Brothers	Warner Brothers	6
11	12	RAMBLIN' ROSE	Nat 'King' Cole	Capitol	10
8	13	SHERRY	Four Seasons	Stateside	8
27	14	THE MAIN ATTRACTION	Pat Boone	London	2
16	[15]	OH LONESOME ME	Craig Douglas	Decca	6
19	16	THE JAMES BOND THEME	John Barry Orchestra	Columbia	4
18	17	LOVE ME TENDER	Richard Chamberlain	MGM	4
12	18	IT MIGHT AS WELL RAIN UNTIL SEPTEMBER	Carole King	London	10
17	19	I REMEMBER YOU	Frank Ifield	Columbia	22
25	20	IT ONLY TOOK A MINUTE	Joe Brown	Piccadilly	3
23	21	LOVE ME DO	Beatles	Parlophone	5
14	22	SHEILA	Tommy Roe	HMV	12
20	23	WHAT NOW MY LOVE	Shirley Bassey	Columbia	14
22	24	MUST BE MADISON	Joe Loss Orchestra	HMV	5
29	25	A FOREVER KIND OF LOVE	Bobby Vee	Liberty	8
-	26	RETURN TO SENDER	Elvis Presley	RCA	1
31	27	DESAFINADO	Stan Getz and Charlie Byrd	HMV	3
32	[28]	WARMED OVER KISSES	Brian Hyland	HMV	4
34	[29]	MY LOVE AND DEVOTION	Matt Monro	Parlophone	3
-	30	ROCKIN' AROUND THE CHRISTMAS TREE	Brenda Lee	Brunswick	1
28	31	LONELY	Mr. Acker Bilk	Columbia	10
35	[32]	LIMBO ROCK	Chubby Checker	Cameo-Parkway	3
36	33	CAN CAN '62	Peter Jay and the Jaywalkers	Decca	3
-	34	WE'RE GONNA GO FISHIN'	Hank Locklin	RCA	1
-	35	NEXT DOOR TO AN ANGEL	Neil Sedaka	RCA	1
30	36	SEND ME THE PILLOW YOU DREAM ON	Johnny Tillotson	London	8
24	37	BECAUSE OF LOVE	Billy Fury	Decca	6
39	38	LITTLE BLACK BOOK	Jimmy Dean	CBS	3
-	39	STRANGER ON THE SHORE	Mr. Acker Bilk	Columbia	51
21	40	YOU DON'T KNOW ME	Ray Charles	HMV	11

WEEK ENDING 6 DECEMBER 1962

LW	TW	Title	Artist	Label	Wks
1	[1]	LOVESICK BLUES	Frank Ifield	Columbia	7
26	2	RETURN TO SENDER	Elvis Presley	RCA	2
2	3	SWISS MAID	Del Shannon	London	8
3	4	BOBBY'S GIRL	Susan Maughan	Philips	8
4	5	LET'S DANCE	Chris Montez	London	9
6	6	DANCE WITH THE GUITAR MAN	Duane Eddy	RCA	5
8	7	SUN ARISE	Rolf Harris	Columbia	6
5	8	DEVIL WOMAN	Marty Robbins	CBS	12
9	9	TELSTAR	Tornados	Decca	14
13	10	SHERRY	Four Seasons	Stateside	9
30	11	ROCKIN' AROUND THE CHRISTMAS TREE	Brenda Lee	Brunswick	2

December 1962

□ Highest position disc reached ● Act's first ever week on chart

LW	TW	Title	Artist	Label	Wks
11	12	NO ONE CAN MAKE MY SUNSHINE SMILE	Everly Brothers	Warner Brothers	7
16	[13]	THE JAMES BOND THEME	John Barry Orchestra	Columbia	5
7	14	VENUS IN BLUE JEANS	Mark Wynter	Pye	9
14	15	THE MAIN ATTRACTION	Pat Boone	London	3
20	16	IT ONLY TOOK A MINUTE	Joe Brown	Piccadilly	4
10	17	THE LOCO-MOTION	Little Eva	London	13
-	18	THE NEXT TIME	Cliff Richard	Columbia	1
17	19	LOVE ME TENDER	Richard Chamberlain	MGM	5
24	[20]	MUST BE MADISON	Joe Loss Orchestra	HMV	6
27	21	DESAFINADO	Stan Getz and Charlie Byrd	HMV	4
25	22	A FOREVER KIND OF LOVE	Bobby Vee	Liberty	9
15	23	OH LONESOME ME	Craig Douglas	Decca	7
12	24	RAMBLIN' ROSE	Nat 'King' Cole	Capitol	11
23	25	WHAT NOW MY LOVE	Shirley Bassey	Columbia	15
21	26	LOVE ME DO	Beatles	Parlophone	6
19	27	I REMEMBER YOU	Frank Ifield	Columbia	23
18	28	IT MIGHT AS WELL RAIN UNTIL SEPTEMBER	Carole King	London	11
35	[29]	NEXT DOOR TO AN ANGEL	Neil Sedaka	RCA	2
37	30	BECAUSE OF LOVE	Billy Fury	Decca	7
-	31	LIKE I DO	Maureen Evans	Oriole	1
22	32	SHEILA	Tommy Roe	HMV	13
-	[33]	IF ONLY TOMORROW	Ronnie Carroll	Philips	2
-	34	HEARTACHES	Patsy Cline ●	Brunswick	1
34	35	WE'RE GONNA GO FISHIN'	Hank Locklin	RCA	2
-	36	ALWAYS YOU AND ME	Russ Conway	Columbia	1
31	37	LONELY	Mr. Acker Bilk	Columbia	11
-	[38]	DESAFINADO	Ella Fitzgerald	Verve	2
32	39	LIMBO ROCK	Chubby Checker	Cameo-Parkway	4
-	40	BABY FACE	Bobby Darin	London	1

WEEK ENDING 13 DECEMBER 1962

LW	TW	Title	Artist	Label	Wks
2	[1]	RETURN TO SENDER	Elvis Presley	RCA	3
1	2	LOVESICK BLUES	Frank Ifield	Columbia	8
7	[3]	SUN ARISE	Rolf Harris	Columbia	7
4	4	BOBBY'S GIRL	Susan Maughan	Philips	9
18	5	THE NEXT TIME	Cliff Richard	Columbia	2
3	6	SWISS MAID	Del Shannon	London	9
5	7	LET'S DANCE	Chris Montez	London	10
9	8	TELSTAR	Tornados	Decca	15
6	9	DANCE WITH THE GUITAR MAN	Duane Eddy	RCA	6
8	10	DEVIL WOMAN	Marty Robbins	CBS	13
11	11	ROCKIN' AROUND THE CHRISTMAS TREE	Brenda Lee	Brunswick	3
15	[12]	THE MAIN ATTRACTION	Pat Boone	London	4
21	13	DESAFINADO	Stan Getz and Charlie Byrd	HMV	5
16	14	IT ONLY TOOK A MINUTE	Joe Brown	Piccadilly	5
14	15	VENUS IN BLUE JEANS	Mark Wynter	Pye	10
19	16	LOVE ME TENDER	Richard Chamberlain	MGM	6
22	17	A FOREVER KIND OF LOVE	Bobby Vee	Liberty	10
10	18	SHERRY	Four Seasons	Stateside	10
26	19	LOVE ME DO	Beatles	Parlophone	7
12	20	NO ONE CAN MAKE MY SUNSHINE SMILE	Everly Brothers	Warner Brothers	8
20	21	MUST BE MADISON	Joe Loss Orchestra	HMV	7
13	22	THE JAMES BOND THEME	John Barry Orchestra	Columbia	6
17	23	THE LOCO-MOTION	Little Eva	London	14
-	24	DANCE ON!	Shadows	Columbia	1
25	25	WHAT NOW MY LOVE	Shirley Bassey	Columbia	16
27	26	I REMEMBER YOU	Frank Ifield	Columbia	24
31	27	LIKE I DO	Maureen Evans	Oriole	2
30	28	BECAUSE OF LOVE	Billy Fury	Decca	8
24	29	RAMBLIN' ROSE	Nat 'King' Cole	Capitol	12
23	30	OH LONESOME ME	Craig Douglas	Decca	8
34	[31]	HEARTACHES	Patsy Cline	Brunswick	2
29	32	NEXT DOOR TO AN ANGEL	Neil Sedaka	RCA	3
36	[33]	ALWAYS YOU AND ME	Russ Conway	Columbia	2

■Having already established the record for biggest jump to number one, Elvis breaks the record for biggest jump to number two. Both records will eventually be broken, in 1982 and 1968 respectively (06.12.62) ■ *Swiss Maid* is written by Roger Miller, who almost three years later will have a record that goes one place higher than Del Shannon's record (29.11.62)■

December 1962

□ Highest position disc reached ● Act's first ever week on chart

LW	TW	Title	Artist	Label	Wks
35	34	WE'RE GONNA GO FISHIN'	Hank Locklin	*RCA*	3
-	35	CAN CAN '62	Peter Jay and the Jaywalkers	*Decca*	4
-	36	BABY TAKE A BOW	Adam Faith	*Parlophone*	1
-	37	STRANGER ON THE SHORE	Mr. Acker Bilk	*Columbia*	52
-	38	GO AWAY LITTLE GIRL	Mark Wynter	*Pye*	1
-	39	SUSIE DARLIN'	Tommy Roe	*HMV*	1
-	40	UP ON THE ROOF	Kenny Lynch	*HMV*	1

WEEK ENDING 20 DECEMBER 1962

LW	TW	Title	Artist	Label	Wks
1	[1]	RETURN TO SENDER	Elvis Presley	*RCA*	4
5	2	THE NEXT TIME	Cliff Richard	*Columbia*	3
2	3	LOVESICK BLUES	Frank Ifield	*Columbia*	9
3	4	SUN ARISE	Rolf Harris	*Columbia*	8
4	5	BOBBY'S GIRL	Susan Maughan	*Philips*	10
9	6	DANCE WITH THE GUITAR MAN	Duane Eddy	*RCA*	7
11	7	ROCKIN' AROUND THE CHRISTMAS TREE	Brenda Lee	*Brunswick*	4
6	8	SWISS MAID	Del Shannon	*London*	10
8	9	TELSTAR	Tornados	*Decca*	16
10	10	DEVIL WOMAN	Marty Robbins	*CBS*	14
24	11	DANCE ON!	Shadows	*Columbia*	2
7	12	LET'S DANCE	Chris Montez	*London*	11
14	13	IT ONLY TOOK A MINUTE	Joe Brown	*Piccadilly*	6
12	14	THE MAIN ATTRACTION	Pat Boone	*London*	5
16	15	LOVE ME TENDER	Richard Chamberlain	*MGM*	7
22	16	THE JAMES BOND THEME	John Barry Orchestra	*Columbia*	7
18	17	SHERRY	Four Seasons	*Stateside*	11
13	18	DESAFINADO	Stan Getz and Charlie Byrd	*HMV*	6
17	19	A FOREVER KIND OF LOVE	Bobby Vee	*Liberty*	11
27	20	LIKE I DO	Maureen Evans	*Oriole*	3
20	21	NO ONE CAN MAKE MY SUNSHINE SMILE	Everly Brothers	*Warner Brothers*	9
19	22	LOVE ME DO	Beatles	*Parlophone*	8
15	23	VENUS IN BLUE JEANS	Mark Wynter	*Pye*	11
21	24	MUST BE MADISON	Joe Loss Orchestra	*HMV*	8
-	25	YOUR CHEATING HEART	Ray Charles	*HMV*	1
40	26	UP ON THE ROOF	Kenny Lynch	*HMV*	2
34	27	WE'RE GONNA GO FISHIN'	Hank Locklin	*RCA*	4
23	28	THE LOCO-MOTION	Little Eva	*London*	15
28	29	BECAUSE OF LOVE	Billy Fury	*Decca*	9
36	30	BABY TAKE A BOW	Adam Faith	*Parlophone*	2
35	[31]	CAN CAN '62	Peter Jay and the Jaywalkers	*Decca*	5
-	32	ME AND MY SHADOW	Frank Sinatra and Sammy Davis Jnr ●	*Reprise*	1
29	33	RAMBLIN' ROSE	Nat 'King' Cole	*Capitol*	13
-	34	ISLAND OF DREAMS	Springfields	*Philips*	1
31	35	HEARTACHES	Patsy Cline	*Brunswick*	3
26	36	I REMEMBER YOU	Frank Ifield	*Columbia*	25
-	37	LIMBO ROCK	Chubby Checker	*Cameo-Parkway*	5
-	38	GOSSIP CALYPSO	Bernard Cribbins	*Parlophone*	1
38	39	GO AWAY LITTLE GIRL	Mark Wynter	*Pye*	2
-	40	HE'S A REBEL	Crystals ●	*London*	1

WEEK ENDING 27 DECEMBER 1962

LW	TW	Title	Artist	Label	Wks
1	[1]	RETURN TO SENDER	Elvis Presley	*RCA*	5
2	2	THE NEXT TIME	Cliff Richard	*Columbia*	4
11	3	DANCE ON!	Shadows	*Columbia*	3
6	[4]	DANCE WITH THE GUITAR MAN	Duane Eddy	*RCA*	8
3	5	LOVESICK BLUES	Frank Ifield	*Columbia*	10
7	[6]	ROCKIN' AROUND THE CHRISTMAS TREE	Brenda Lee	*Brunswick*	5
4	7	SUN ARISE	Rolf Harris	*Columbia*	9
9	8	TELSTAR	Tornados	*Decca*	17
5	9	BOBBY'S GIRL	Susan Maughan	*Philips*	11
12	10	LET'S DANCE	Chris Montez	*London*	12
18	[11]	DESAFINADO	Stan Getz and Charlie Byrd	*HMV*	7
8	12	SWISS MAID	Del Shannon	*London*	11
25	[13]	YOUR CHEATING HEART	Ray Charles	*HMV*	2
10	14	DEVIL WOMAN	Marty Robbins	*CBS*	15
13	15	IT ONLY TOOK A MINUTE	Joe Brown	*Piccadilly*	7
14	16	THE MAIN ATTRACTION	Pat Boone	*London*	6
22	[17]	LOVE ME DO	Beatles	*Parlophone*	9
27	[18]	WE'RE GONNA GO FISHIN'	Hank Locklin	*RCA*	5
19	19	A FOREVER KIND OF LOVE	Bobby Vee	*Liberty*	12
32	[20]	ME AND MY SHADOW	Frank Sinatra and Sammy Davis Jnr	*Reprise*	2
24	21	MUST BE MADISON	Joe Loss Orchestra	*HMV*	9
26	22	UP ON THE ROOF	Kenny Lynch	*HMV*	3
30	23	BABY TAKE A BOW	Adam Faith	*Parlophone*	3
34	24	ISLAND OF DREAMS	Springfields	*Philips*	2
17	25	SHERRY	Four Seasons	*Stateside*	12
40	26	HE'S A REBEL	Crystals	*London*	2
15	27	LOVE ME TENDER	Richard Chamberlain	*MGM*	8
39	28	GO AWAY LITTLE GIRL	Mark Wynter	*Pye*	3
20	29	LIKE I DO	Maureen Evans	*Oriole*	4
36	30	I REMEMBER YOU	Frank Ifield	*Columbia*	26
16	31	THE JAMES BOND THEME	John Barry Orchestra	*Columbia*	8
23	32	VENUS IN BLUE JEANS	Mark Wynter	*Pye*	12
37	33	LIMBO ROCK	Chubby Checker	*Cameo-Parkway*	6
35	34	HEARTACHES	Patsy Cline	*Brunswick*	4
38	35	GOSSIP CALYPSO	Bernard Cribbins	*Parlophone*	2
-	[36]	THE MADISON	Ray Ellington ●	*Ember*	1
-	[37]	SUSIE DARLIN'	Tommy Roe	*HMV*	2
-	38	ONWARD CHRISTIAN SOLDIERS	Harry Simeone Chorale	*Ember*	1
-	39	DEAR LONELY HEARTS	Nat 'King' Cole	*Capitol*	1
-	[40]	JINGLE BELL ROCK	Chubby Checker and Bobby Rydell ●	*Cameo-Parkway*	1

In these weeks ■ *Stranger On The Shore* spends its 52nd and final week on the chart (13.12.62) ■ Three songs with the word *Dance* in their titles in the Top 10, as well as four other dance titles in the 40, *Desafinado*, *Limbo Rock*, *Must Be Madison* and *The Madison* (27.12.62) ■ Only twelve new number ones all year, the fewest since 1954 when there were only eleven, and the second lowest number in any year (27.12.62)■

1963

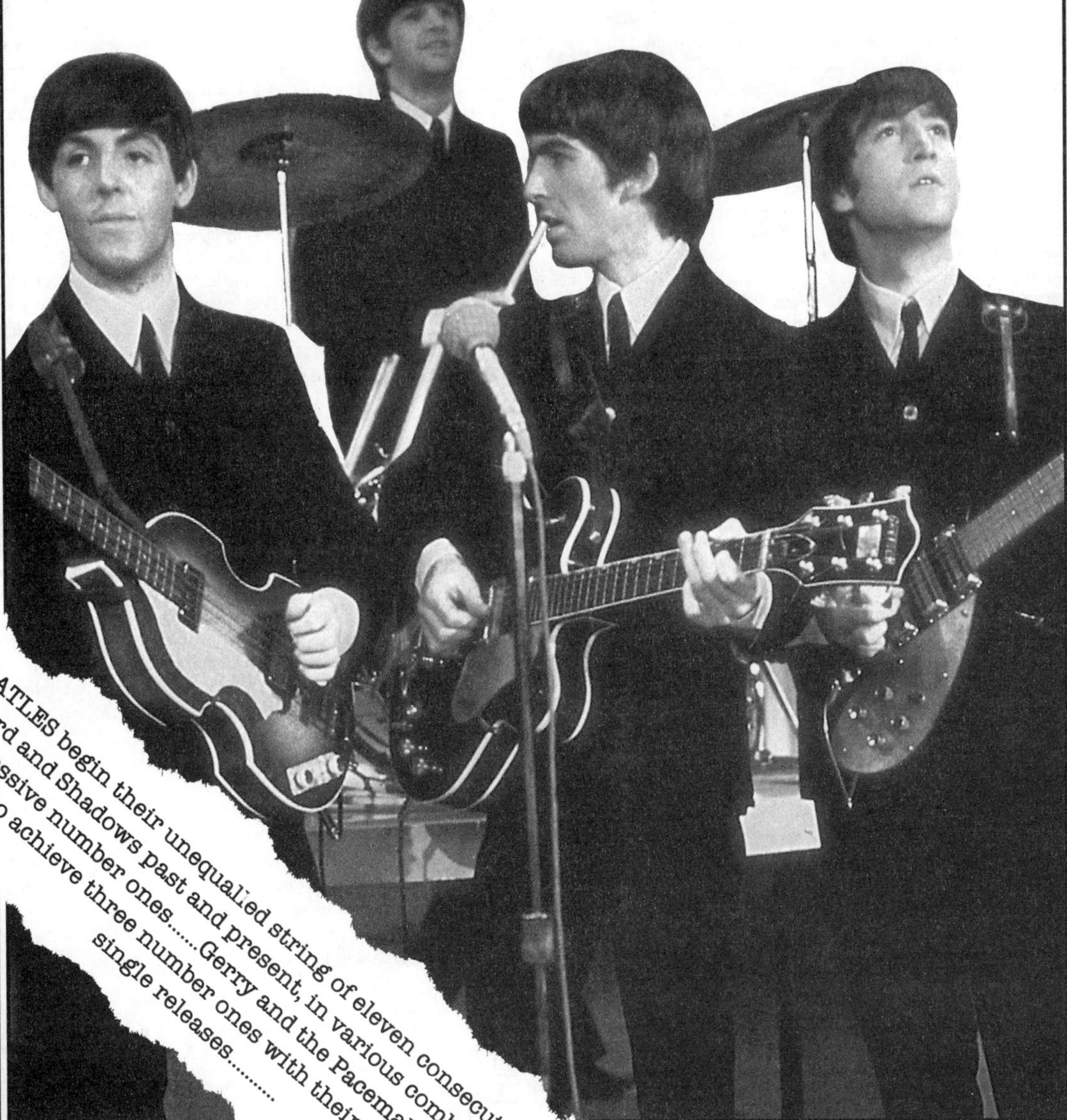

........THE BEATLES begin their unequalled string of eleven consecutive number ones ......Cliff Richard and Shadows past and present, in various combinations, have five of six successive number ones......Gerry and the Pacemakers are the first act to achieve three number ones with their first three single releases..........

January 1963

□ Highest position disc reached ● Act's first ever week on chart

LW	TW	*WEEK ENDING* **3 JANUARY 1963**	Wks
2	[1]	THE NEXT TIME Cliff Richard ... *Columbia*	5
1	2	RETURN TO SENDER Elvis Presley ... *RCA*	6
5	3	LOVESICK BLUES Frank Ifield ... *Columbia*	11
7	4	SUN ARISE Rolf Harris ... *Columbia*	10
4	5	DANCE WITH THE GUITAR MAN Duane Eddy ... *RCA*	9
9	6	BOBBY'S GIRL Susan Maughan ... *Philips*	12
3	7	DANCE ON! Shadows ... *Columbia*	4
15	8	IT ONLY TOOK A MINUTE Joe Brown ... *Piccadilly*	8
8	9	TELSTAR Tornados ... *Decca*	18
10	10	LET'S DANCE Chris Montez ... *London*	13
12	11	SWISS MAID Del Shannon ... *London*	12
6	12	ROCKIN' AROUND THE CHRISTMAS TREE Brenda Lee ... *Brunswick*	6
19	[13]	A FOREVER KIND OF LOVE Bobby Vee ... *Liberty*	13
22	14	UP ON THE ROOF Kenny Lynch ... *HMV*	4
13	15	YOUR CHEATING HEART Ray Charles ... *HMV*	3
14	16	DEVIL WOMAN Marty Robbins ... *CBS*	16
28	17	GO AWAY LITTLE GIRL Mark Wynter ... *Pye*	4
11	18	DESAFINADO Stan Getz and Charlie Byrd ... *HMV*	8
29	19	LIKE I DO Maureen Evans ... *Oriole*	5
16	20	THE MAIN ATTRACTION Pat Boone ... *London*	7
20	21	ME AND MY SHADOW Frank Sinatra and Sammy Davis Jnr ... *Reprise*	3
23	22	BABY TAKE A BOW Adam Faith ... *Parlophone*	4
21	23	MUST BE MADISON Joe Loss Orchestra ... *HMV*	10
17	24	LOVE ME DO Beatles ... *Parlophone*	10
35	[25]	GOSSIP CALYPSO Bernard Cribbins ... *Parlophone*	3
24	26	ISLAND OF DREAMS Springfields ... *Philips*	3
25	27	SHERRY Four Seasons ... *Stateside*	13
27	28	LOVE ME TENDER Richard Chamberlain ... *MGM*	9
18	29	WE'RE GONNA GO FISHIN' Hank Locklin ... *RCA*	6
26	30	HE'S A REBEL Crystals ... *London*	3
-	31	DON'T YOU THINK IT'S TIME Mike Berry & the Outlaws ... *HMV*	1
-	32	LET'S GO Routers ● ... *Warner Brothers*	1
-	33	UP ON THE ROOF Julie Grant ● ... *Pye*	1
30	34	I REMEMBER YOU Frank Ifield ... *Columbia*	27
-	35	ALWAYS YOU AND ME Russ Conway ... *Columbia*	3
-	36	CAN CAN '62 Peter Jay and the Jaywalkers ... *Decca*	6
39	[37]	DEAR LONELY HEARTS Nat 'King' Cole ... *Capitol*	2
37	38	SUSIE DARLIN' Tommy Roe ... *HMV*	3
33	39	LIMBO ROCK Chubby Checker ... *Cameo-Parkway*	7
-	40	KEEP YOUR HANDS OFF MY BABY Little Eva ... *London*	1

LW	TW	*WEEK ENDING* **10 JANUARY 1963**	Wks
1	[1]	THE NEXT TIME/BACHELOR BOY Cliff Richard ... *Columbia*	6
2	2	RETURN TO SENDER Elvis Presley ... *RCA*	7
7	3	DANCE ON! Shadows ... *Columbia*	5
5	[4]	DANCE WITH THE GUITAR MAN Duane Eddy ... *RCA*	10
3	5	LOVESICK BLUES Frank Ifield ... *Columbia*	12
8	[6]	IT ONLY TOOK A MINUTE Joe Brown ... *Piccadilly*	9
4	7	SUN ARISE Rolf Harris ... *Columbia*	11
17	8	GO AWAY LITTLE GIRL Mark Wynter ... *Pye*	5
6	9	BOBBY'S GIRL Susan Maughan ... *Philips*	13
19	10	LIKE I DO Maureen Evans ... *Oriole*	6
9	11	TELSTAR Tornados ... *Decca*	19
14	12	UP ON THE ROOF Kenny Lynch ... *HMV*	5
10	13	LET'S DANCE Chris Montez ... *London*	14
11	14	SWISS MAID Del Shannon ... *London*	13
18	15	DESAFINADO Stan Getz and Charlie Byrd ... *HMV*	9
15	16	YOUR CHEATING HEART Ray Charles ... *HMV*	4
24	[17]	LOVE ME DO Beatles ... *Parlophone*	11
13	18	A FOREVER KIND OF LOVE Bobby Vee ... *Liberty*	14
30	[19]	HE'S A REBEL Crystals ... *London*	4
20	20	THE MAIN ATTRACTION Pat Boone ... *London*	8
31	21	DON'T YOU THINK IT'S TIME Mike Berry & the Outlaws ... *HMV*	2
-	[22]	THE LONELY BULL Tijuana Brass ● ... *Stateside*	1
21	23	ME AND MY SHADOW Frank Sinatra and Sammy Davis Jnr ... *Reprise*	4
-	24	COMING HOME BABY Mel Tormé ... *London*	1
16	25	DEVIL WOMAN Marty Robbins ... *CBS*	17
26	26	ISLAND OF DREAMS Springfields ... *Philips*	4
23	27	MUST BE MADISON Joe Loss Orchestra ... *HMV*	11
-	28	GLOBE-TROTTER Tornados ... *Decca*	1
22	29	BABY TAKE A BOW Adam Faith ... *Parlophone*	5
40	[30]	KEEP YOUR HANDS OFF MY BABY Little Eva ... *London*	2
25	31	GOSSIP CALYPSO Bernard Cribbins ... *Parlophone*	4
29	32	WE'RE GONNA GO FISHIN' Hank Locklin ... *RCA*	7
32	33	LET'S GO Routers ... *Warner Brothers*	2
33	34	UP ON THE ROOF Julie Grant ... *Pye*	2
-	35	JUST FOR KICKS Mike Sarne ... *Parlophone*	1
12	36	ROCKIN' AROUND THE CHRISTMAS TREE Brenda Lee ... *Brunswick*	7
28	37	LOVE ME TENDER Richard Chamberlain ... *MGM*	10
27	38	SHERRY Four Seasons ... *Stateside*	14
-	39	FUNNY ALL OVER Vernons Girls ... *Decca*	1
36	40	CAN CAN '62 Peter Jay and the Jaywalkers ... *Decca*	7

LW	TW	*WEEK ENDING* **17 JANUARY 1963**	Wks
1	[1]	THE NEXT TIME/BACHELOR BOY Cliff Richard ... *Columbia*	7
3	2	DANCE ON! Shadows ... *Columbia*	6
2	3	RETURN TO SENDER Elvis Presley ... *RCA*	8
5	4	LOVESICK BLUES Frank Ifield ... *Columbia*	13
10	5	LIKE I DO Maureen Evans ... *Oriole*	7
8	[6]	GO AWAY LITTLE GIRL Mark Wynter ... *Pye*	6
4	7	DANCE WITH THE GUITAR MAN Duane Eddy ... *RCA*	11
7	8	SUN ARISE Rolf Harris ... *Columbia*	12
28	9	GLOBE-TROTTER Tornados ... *Decca*	2
11	10	TELSTAR Tornados ... *Decca*	20
6	11	IT ONLY TOOK A MINUTE Joe Brown ... *Piccadilly*	10
-	12	DIAMONDS Jet Harris and Tony Meehan ● ... *Decca*	1
12	13	UP ON THE ROOF Kenny Lynch ... *HMV*	6
9	14	BOBBY'S GIRL Susan Maughan ... *Philips*	14
21	15	DON'T YOU THINK IT'S TIME Mike Berry & the Outlaws ... *HMV*	3
13	16	LET'S DANCE Chris Montez ... *London*	15
16	17	YOUR CHEATING HEART Ray Charles ... *HMV*	5
24	18	COMING HOME BABY Mel Tormé ... *London*	2
26	19	ISLAND OF DREAMS Springfields ... *Philips*	5
14	20	SWISS MAID Del Shannon ... *London*	14
19	21	HE'S A REBEL Crystals ... *London*	5
35	[22]	JUST FOR KICKS Mike Sarne ... *Parlophone*	2
15	23	DESAFINADO Stan Getz and Charlie Byrd ... *HMV*	10
18	24	A FOREVER KIND OF LOVE Bobby Vee ... *Liberty*	15
20	25	THE MAIN ATTRACTION Pat Boone ... *London*	9
22	26	THE LONELY BULL Tijuana Brass ... *Stateside*	2
25	27	DEVIL WOMAN Marty Robbins ... *CBS*	18
17	28	LOVE ME DO Beatles ... *Parlophone*	12
23	29	ME AND MY SHADOW Frank Sinatra and Sammy Davis Jnr ... *Reprise*	5
32	30	WE'RE GONNA GO FISHIN' Hank Locklin ... *RCA*	8
39	[31]	FUNNY ALL OVER Vernons Girls ... *Decca*	2
-	32	RUBY ANN Marty Robbins ... *CBS*	1
33	33	LET'S GO Routers ... *Warner Brothers*	3
30	34	KEEP YOUR HANDS OFF MY BABY Little Eva ... *London*	3
-	35	BECAUSE OF LOVE Billy Fury ... *Decca*	10
27	36	MUST BE MADISON Joe Loss Orchestra ... *HMV*	12
-	37	IT'S UP TO YOU Rick Nelson ... *London*	1
31	38	GOSSIP CALYPSO Bernard Cribbins ... *Parlophone*	5
-	[39]	DON'T HANG UP Orlons ● ... *Cameo-Parkway*	1
-	40	ALL ALONE AM I Brenda Lee ... *Brunswick*	1

LW	TW	*WEEK ENDING* **24 JANUARY 1963**	Wks
2	[1]	DANCE ON! Shadows ... *Columbia*	7
1	2	THE NEXT TIME/BACHELOR BOY Cliff Richard ... *Columbia*	8
5	[3]	LIKE I DO Maureen Evans ... *Oriole*	8
12	4	DIAMONDS Jet Harris and Tony Meehan ... *Decca*	2

In these weeks ■ Bachelor Boy is only credited as a double A-side with *The Next Time* from this week (10.01.63) ■ Two Top Ten hits for the Tornados in what proves to be Pat Boone's final week of chart action (17.01.63) ■ *Like I Do* is the biggest ever hit on the Oriole label (24.01.63) ■

LW	TW	Title	Artist	Label	Wks
9	5	GLOBE-TROTTER	Tornados	*Decca*	3
3	6	RETURN TO SENDER	Elvis Presley	*RCA*	9
6	7	GO AWAY LITTLE GIRL	Mark Wynter	*Pye*	7
15	8	DON'T YOU THINK IT'S TIME	Mike Berry & the Outlaws	*HMV*	4
7	9	DANCE WITH THE GUITAR MAN	Duane Eddy	*RCA*	12
13	10	UP ON THE ROOF	Kenny Lynch	*HMV*	7
4	11	LOVESICK BLUES	Frank Ifield	*Columbia*	14
19	12	ISLAND OF DREAMS	Springfields	*Philips*	6
18	13	COMING HOME BABY	Mel Tormé	*London*	3
-	14	LITTLE TOWN FLIRT	Del Shannon	*London*	1
8	15	SUN ARISE	Rolf Harris	*Columbia*	13
-	16	SOME KINDA FUN	Chris Montez	*London*	1
40	17	ALL ALONE AM I	Brenda Lee	*Brunswick*	2
-	18	BIG GIRLS DON'T CRY	Four Seasons	*Stateside*	1
14	19	BOBBY'S GIRL	Susan Maughan	*Philips*	15
10	20	TELSTAR	Tornados	*Decca*	21
11	21	IT ONLY TOOK A MINUTE	Joe Brown	*Piccadilly*	11
-	22	SUKIYAKI	Kenny Ball and his Jazzmen	*Pye*	1
21	23	HE'S A REBEL	Crystals	*London*	6
32	24	RUBY ANN	Marty Robbins	*CBS*	2
22	25	JUST FOR KICKS	Mike Sarne	*Parlophone*	3
16	26	LET'S DANCE	Chris Montez	*London*	16
26	27	THE LONELY BULL	Tijuana Brass	*Stateside*	3
37	28	IT'S UP TO YOU	Rick Nelson	*London*	2
-	29	WAYWARD WIND	Frank Ifield	*Columbia*	1
17	30	YOUR CHEATING HEART	Ray Charles	*HMV*	6
23	31	DESAFINADO	Stan Getz and Charlie Byrd	*HMV*	11
-	32	A TASTE OF HONEY	Mr. Acker Bilk	*Columbia*	1
-	33	PLEASE PLEASE ME	Beatles	*Parlophone*	1
-	34	CHARMAINE	Bachelors ●	*Decca*	1
20	35	SWISS MAID	Del Shannon	*London*	15
31	36	FUNNY ALL OVER	Vernons Girls	*Decca*	3
28	37	LOVE ME DO	Beatles	*Parlophone*	13
-	38	MY LITTLE GIRL	Crickets	*Liberty*	1
30	39	WE'RE GONNA GO FISHIN'	Hank Locklin	*RCA*	8
-	40	LOO-BE-LOO	Chucks ●	*Decca*	1

LW	TW	*WEEK ENDING* **31 JANUARY 1963**			Wks
4	1	DIAMONDS	Jet Harris and Tony Meehan	*Decca*	3
2	2	THE NEXT TIME/BACHELOR BOY	Cliff Richard	*Columbia*	9
3	3	LIKE I DO	Maureen Evans	*Oriole*	9
1	4	DANCE ON!	Shadows	*Columbia*	8
5	5	GLOBE-TROTTER	Tornados	*Decca*	4
8	6	DON'T YOU THINK IT'S TIME	Mike Berry & the Outlaws	*HMV*	5
14	7	LITTLE TOWN FLIRT	Del Shannon	*London*	2
6	8	RETURN TO SENDER	Elvis Presley	*RCA*	10
29	9	WAYWARD WIND	Frank Ifield	*Columbia*	2
16	10	SOME KINDA FUN	Chris Montez	*London*	2
7	11	GO AWAY LITTLE GIRL	Mark Wynter	*Pye*	8
10	12	UP ON THE ROOF	Kenny Lynch	*HMV*	8
18	13	BIG GIRLS DON'T CRY	Four Seasons	*Stateside*	2
12	14	ISLAND OF DREAMS	Springfields	*Philips*	7
17	15	ALL ALONE AM I	Brenda Lee	*Brunswick*	3
33	16	PLEASE PLEASE ME	Beatles	*Parlophone*	2
9	17	DANCE WITH THE GUITAR MAN	Duane Eddy	*RCA*	13
13	18	COMING HOME BABY	Mel Tormé	*London*	4
22	19	SUKIYAKI	Kenny Ball and his Jazzmen	*Pye*	2
11	20	LOVESICK BLUES	Frank Ifield	*Columbia*	15
32	21	A TASTE OF HONEY	Mr. Acker Bilk	*Columbia*	2
40	22	LOO-BE-LOO	Chucks	*Decca*	2
38	23	MY LITTLE GIRL	Crickets	*Liberty*	2
28	24	IT'S UP TO YOU	Rick Nelson	*London*	3
15	25	SUN ARISE	Rolf Harris	*Columbia*	14
34	26	CHARMAINE	Bachelors	*Decca*	2
19	27	BOBBY'S GIRL	Susan Maughan	*Philips*	16
23	28	HE'S A REBEL	Crystals	*London*	7
-	29	LOOP-DE-LOOP	Frankie Vaughan	*Philips*	1
20	30	TELSTAR	Tornados	*Decca*	22
24	31	RUBY ANN	Marty Robbins	*CBS*	3
-	32	THE ALLEY CAT SONG	David Thorne ●	*Stateside*	1
25	33	JUST FOR KICKS	Mike Sarne	*Parlophone*	4

February 1963

□ Highest position disc reached ● Act's first ever week on chart

LW	TW	Title	Artist	Label	Wks
21	34	IT ONLY TOOK A MINUTE	Joe Brown	*Piccadilly*	12
27	35	THE LONELY BULL	Tijuana Brass	*Stateside*	4
37	36	LOVE ME DO	Beatles	*Parlophone*	14
31	37	DESAFINADO	Stan Getz and Charlie Byrd	*HMV*	12
30	38	YOUR CHEATING HEART	Ray Charles	*HMV*	7
-	39	WALK RIGHT IN	Rooftop Singers ●	*Fontana*	1
-	40	WHAT NOW	Adam Faith	*Parlophone*	1

LW	TW	*WEEK ENDING* **7 FEBRUARY 1963**			Wks
1	1	DIAMONDS	Jet Harris and Tony Meehan	*Decca*	4
2	2	THE NEXT TIME/BACHELOR BOY	Cliff Richard	*Columbia*	10
16	3	PLEASE PLEASE ME	Beatles	*Parlophone*	3
9	4	WAYWARD WIND	Frank Ifield	*Columbia*	3
3	5	LIKE I DO	Maureen Evans	*Oriole*	10
5	6	GLOBE-TROTTER	Tornados	*Decca*	5
7	7	LITTLE TOWN FLIRT	Del Shannon	*London*	3
6	8	DON'T YOU THINK IT'S TIME	Mike Berry & the Outlaws	*HMV*	6
4	9	DANCE ON!	Shadows	*Columbia*	9
14	10	ISLAND OF DREAMS	Springfields	*Philips*	8
15	11	ALL ALONE AM I	Brenda Lee	*Brunswick*	4
10	12	SOME KINDA FUN	Chris Montez	*London*	3
13	13	BIG GIRLS DON'T CRY	Four Seasons	*Stateside*	3
19	14	SUKIYAKI	Kenny Ball and his Jazzmen	*Pye*	3
29	15	LOOP-DE-LOOP	Frankie Vaughan	*Philips*	2
21	16	A TASTE OF HONEY	Mr. Acker Bilk	*Columbia*	3
8	17	RETURN TO SENDER	Elvis Presley	*RCA*	11
12	18	UP ON THE ROOF	Kenny Lynch	*HMV*	9
23	19	MY LITTLE GIRL	Crickets	*Liberty*	3
11	20	GO AWAY LITTLE GIRL	Mark Wynter	*Pye*	9
39	21	WALK RIGHT IN	Rooftop Singers	*Fontana*	2
24	22	IT'S UP TO YOU	Rick Nelson	*London*	4
22	23	LOO-BE-LOO	Chucks	*Decca*	3
18	24	COMING HOME BABY	Mel Tormé	*London*	5
17	25	DANCE WITH THE GUITAR MAN	Duane Eddy	*RCA*	14
-	26	HAVA NAGILA	Spotnicks	*Oriole*	1
26	27	CHARMAINE	Bachelors	*Decca*	3
20	28	LOVESICK BLUES	Frank Ifield	*Columbia*	16
32	29	THE ALLEY CAT SONG	David Thorne	*Stateside*	2
-	30	THE NIGHT HAS A THOUSAND EYES	Bobby Vee	*Liberty*	1
31	31	RUBY ANN	Marty Robbins	*CBS*	4
-	32	BLAME IT ON THE BOSSA NOVA	Eydie Gormé	*CBS*	1
35	33	THE LONELY BULL	Tijuana Brass	*Stateside*	5
40	34	WHAT NOW	Adam Faith	*Parlophone*	2
28	35	HE'S A REBEL	Crystals	*London*	8
25	36	SUN ARISE	Rolf Harris	*Columbia*	15
-	37	TELL HIM	Billie Davis ●	*Decca*	1
27	38	BOBBY'S GIRL	Susan Maughan	*Philips*	17
30	39	TELSTAR	Tornados	*Decca*	23
33	40	JUST FOR KICKS	Mike Sarne	*Parlophone*	5

LW	TW	*WEEK ENDING* **14 FEBRUARY 1963**			Wks
1	1	DIAMONDS	Jet Harris and Tony Meehan	*Decca*	5
4	2	WAYWARD WIND	Frank Ifield	*Columbia*	4
3	3	PLEASE PLEASE ME	Beatles	*Parlophone*	4
7	4	LITTLE TOWN FLIRT	Del Shannon	*London*	4
2	5	THE NEXT TIME/BACHELOR BOY	Cliff Richard	*Columbia*	11
15	6	LOOP-DE-LOOP	Frankie Vaughan	*Philips*	3
5	7	LIKE I DO	Maureen Evans	*Oriole*	11
8	8	DON'T YOU THINK IT'S TIME	Mike Berry & the Outlaws	*HMV*	7
11	9	ALL ALONE AM I	Brenda Lee	*Brunswick*	5
14	10	SUKIYAKI	Kenny Ball and his Jazzmen	*Pye*	4
9	11	DANCE ON!	Shadows	*Columbia*	10
10	12	ISLAND OF DREAMS	Springfields	*Philips*	9
6	13	GLOBE-TROTTER	Tornados	*Decca*	6

■Ten new entries in the Top 40, including 3 in the Top 20, make this one of the most active charts yet published (24.01.63) ■ Ex-Shadows Jet Harris and Tony Meehan take over at number one from their erstwhile colleagues, in the final example of one instrumental replacing another at the top (31.01.63) ■ In the Beatles' first week in the Top 10, there are nine British records there, with only Del Shannon holding out for America at number seven (07.02.63)■

February 1963

□ Highest position disc reached ● Act's first ever week on chart

LW	TW	Title	Artist	Label	Wks
30	14	THE NIGHT HAS A THOUSAND EYES	Bobby Vee	*Liberty*	2
13	15	BIG GIRLS DON'T CRY	Four Seasons	*Stateside*	4
16	16	A TASTE OF HONEY	Mr. Acker Bilk	*Columbia*	4
19	17	MY LITTLE GIRL	Crickets	*Liberty*	4
21	18	WALK RIGHT IN	Rooftop Singers	*Fontana*	3
26	19	HAVA NAGILA	Spotnicks	*Oriole*	2
12	20	SOME KINDA FUN	Chris Montez	*London*	4
29	21	THE ALLEY CAT SONG	David Thorne	*Stateside*	3
27	22	CHARMAINE	Bachelors	*Decca*	4
17	23	RETURN TO SENDER	Elvis Presley	*RCA*	12
22	24	IT'S UP TO YOU	Rick Nelson	*London*	5
23	25	LOO-BE-LOO	Chucks	*Decca*	4
-	26	THAT'S WHAT LOVE WILL DO	Joe Brown	*Piccadilly*	1
37	27	TELL HIM	Billie Davis	*Decca*	2
18	28	UP ON THE ROOF	Kenny Lynch	*HMV*	10
20	29	GO AWAY LITTLE GIRL	Mark Wynter	*Pye*	10
24	30	COMING HOME BABY	Mel Tormé	*London*	6
34	31	WHAT NOW	Adam Faith	*Parlophone*	3
32	32	BLAME IT ON THE BOSSA NOVA	Eydie Gormé	*CBS*	2
-	33	QUEEN FOR TONIGHT	Helen Shapiro	*Columbia*	1
-	34	LIKE I'VE NEVER BEEN GONE	Billy Fury	*Decca*	1
31	35	RUBY ANN	Marty Robbins	*CBS*	5
-	36	BOSS GUITAR	Duane Eddy	*RCA*	1
-	37	I SAW LINDA YESTERDAY	Doug Sheldon	*Decca*	1
39	38	TELSTAR	Tornados	*Decca*	24
40	39	JUST FOR KICKS	Mike Sarne	*Parlophone*	6
-	40	HEY PAULA	Paul and Paula ●	*Philips*	1

WEEK ENDING 21 FEBRUARY 1963

LW	TW	Title	Artist	Label	Wks
2	1	WAYWARD WIND	Frank Ifield	*Columbia*	5
3	2	PLEASE PLEASE ME	Beatles	*Parlophone*	5
1	3	DIAMONDS	Jet Harris and Tony Meehan	*Decca*	6
14	4	THE NIGHT HAS A THOUSAND EYES	Bobby Vee	*Liberty*	3
4	5	LITTLE TOWN FLIRT	Del Shannon	*London*	5
6	6	LOOP-DE-LOOP	Frankie Vaughan	*Philips*	4
9	7	ALL ALONE AM I	Brenda Lee	*Brunswick*	6
12	8	ISLAND OF DREAMS	Springfields	*Philips*	10
5	9	THE NEXT TIME/BACHELOR BOY	Cliff Richard	*Columbia*	12
10	10	SUKIYAKI	Kenny Ball and his Jazzmen	*Pye*	3
18	11	WALK RIGHT IN	Rooftop Singers	*Fontana*	4
26	12	THAT'S WHAT LOVE WILL DO	Joe Brown	*Piccadilly*	2
8	13	DON'T YOU THINK IT'S TIME	Mike Berry & the Outlaws	*HMV*	8
7	14	LIKE I DO	Maureen Evans	*Oriole*	12
19	15	HAVA NAGILA	Spotnicks	*Oriole*	3
13	16	GLOBE-TROTTER	Tornados	*Decca*	7
16	17	A TASTE OF HONEY	Mr. Acker Bilk	*Columbia*	5
15	18	BIG GIRLS DON'T CRY	Four Seasons	*Stateside*	5
17	19	MY LITTLE GIRL	Crickets	*Liberty*	5
20	20	SOME KINDA FUN	Chris Montez	*London*	5
11	21	DANCE ON!	Shadows	*Columbia*	11
34	22	LIKE I'VE NEVER BEEN GONE	Billy Fury	*Decca*	2
22	23	CHARMAINE	Bachelors	*Decca*	5
27	24	TELL HIM	Billie Davis	*Decca*	3
24	25	IT'S UP TO YOU	Rick Nelson	*London*	6
40	26	HEY PAULA	Paul and Paula	*Philips*	2
-	27	SUMMER HOLIDAY	Cliff Richard	*Columbia*	1
21	28	THE ALLEY CAT SONG	David Thorne	*Stateside*	4
25	29	LOO-BE-LOO	Chucks	*Decca*	5
36	30	BOSS GUITAR	Duane Eddy	*RCA*	2
31	31	WHAT NOW	Adam Faith	*Parlophone*	4
32	32	BLAME IT ON THE BOSSA NOVA	Eydie Gormé	*CBS*	3
23	33	RETURN TO SENDER	Elvis Presley	*RCA*	13
28	34	UP ON THE ROOF	Kenny Lynch	*HMV*	11
33	35	QUEEN FOR TONIGHT	Helen Shapiro	*Columbia*	2
37	36	I SAW LINDA YESTERDAY	Doug Sheldon	*Decca*	2
30	37	COMING HOME BABY	Mel Tormé	*London*	7
-	38	HI-LILI HI-LO	Richard Chamberlain	*MGM*	1
-	39	FROM A JACK TO A KING	Ned Miller ●	*London*	1
29	40	GO AWAY LITTLE GIRL	Mark Wynter	*Pye*	11

WEEK ENDING 28 FEBRUARY 1963

LW	TW	Title	Artist	Label	Wks
1	1	WAYWARD WIND	Frank Ifield	*Columbia*	6
2	2	PLEASE PLEASE ME	Beatles	*Parlophone*	6
4	3	THE NIGHT HAS A THOUSAND EYES	Bobby Vee	*Liberty*	4
3	4	DIAMONDS	Jet Harris and Tony Meehan	*Decca*	7
6	5	LOOP-DE-LOOP	Frankie Vaughan	*Philips*	5
12	6	THAT'S WHAT LOVE WILL DO	Joe Brown	*Piccadilly*	3
27	7	SUMMER HOLIDAY	Cliff Richard	*Columbia*	2
5	8	LITTLE TOWN FLIRT	Del Shannon	*London*	6
8	9	ISLAND OF DREAMS	Springfields	*Philips*	11
10	10	SUKIYAKI	Kenny Ball and his Jazzmen	*Pye*	4
11	11	WALK RIGHT IN	Rooftop Singers	*Fontana*	5
7	12	ALL ALONE AM I	Brenda Lee	*Brunswick*	7
15	13	HAVA NAGILA	Spotnicks	*Oriole*	4
22	14	LIKE I'VE NEVER BEEN GONE	Billy Fury	*Decca*	3
14	15	LIKE I DO	Maureen Evans	*Oriole*	13
9	16	THE NEXT TIME/BACHELOR BOY	Cliff Richard	*Columbia*	13
26	17	HEY PAULA	Paul and Paula	*Philips*	3
23	18	CHARMAINE	Bachelors	*Decca*	6
13	19	DON'T YOU THINK IT'S TIME	Mike Berry & the Outlaws	*HMV*	9
16	20	GLOBE-TROTTER	Tornados	*Decca*	8
24	21	TELL HIM	Billie Davis	*Decca*	4
17	22	A TASTE OF HONEY	Mr. Acker Bilk	*Columbia*	6
19	23	MY LITTLE GIRL	Crickets	*Liberty*	6
18	24	BIG GIRLS DON'T CRY	Four Seasons	*Stateside*	6
38	25	HI-LILI HI-LO	Richard Chamberlain	*MGM*	2
20	26	SOME KINDA FUN	Chris Montez	*London*	6
21	27	DANCE ON!	Shadows	*Columbia*	12
25	28	IT'S UP TO YOU	Rick Nelson	*London*	7
30	29	BOSS GUITAR	Duane Eddy	*RCA*	3
39	30	FROM A JACK TO A KING	Ned Miller	*London*	2
28	31	THE ALLEY CAT SONG	David Thorne	*Stateside*	5
32	32	BLAME IT ON THE BOSSA NOVA	Eydie Gormé	*CBS*	4
29	33	LOO-BE-LOO	Chucks	*Decca*	6
-	34	CUPBOARD LOVE	John Leyton	*HMV*	1
35	35	QUEEN FOR TONIGHT	Helen Shapiro	*Columbia*	3
36	36	I SAW LINDA YESTERDAY	Doug Sheldon	*Decca*	3
31	37	WHAT NOW	Adam Faith	*Parlophone*	5
-	38	TROUBLE IS MY MIDDLE NAME	Brook Brothers	*Pye*	1
-	39	PIED PIPER (THE BEEJE)	Steve Race ●	*Parlophone*	1
-	40	SATURDAY NIGHT AT THE DUCK POND	Cougars ●	*Parlophone*	1

WEEK ENDING 7 MARCH 1963

LW	TW	Title	Artist	Label	Wks
1	1	WAYWARD WIND	Frank Ifield	*Columbia*	7
7	2	SUMMER HOLIDAY	Cliff Richard	*Columbia*	3
2	3	PLEASE PLEASE ME	Beatles	*Parlophone*	7
3	4	THE NIGHT HAS A THOUSAND EYES	Bobby Vee	*Liberty*	5
6	5	THAT'S WHAT LOVE WILL DO	Joe Brown	*Piccadilly*	4
14	6	LIKE I'VE NEVER BEEN GONE	Billy Fury	*Decca*	4
4	7	DIAMONDS	Jet Harris and Tony Meehan	*Decca*	8
5	8	LOOP-DE-LOOP	Frankie Vaughan	*Philips*	6
9	9	ISLAND OF DREAMS	Springfields	*Philips*	12
11	10	WALK RIGHT IN	Rooftop Singers	*Fontana*	6
17	11	HEY PAULA	Paul and Paula	*Philips*	4
18	12	CHARMAINE	Bachelors	*Decca*	7
8	13	LITTLE TOWN FLIRT	Del Shannon	*London*	7
21	14	TELL HIM	Billie Davis	*Decca*	5
12	15	ALL ALONE AM I	Brenda Lee	*Brunswick*	8
13	16	HAVA NAGILA	Spotnicks	*Oriole*	5
10	17	SUKIYAKI	Kenny Ball and his Jazzmen	*Pye*	5
-	18	ONE BROKEN HEART FOR SALE	Elvis Presley	*RCA*	1
16	19	THE NEXT TIME/BACHELOR BOY	Cliff Richard	*Columbia*	14
25	20	HI-LILI HI-LO	Richard Chamberlain	*MGM*	3
30	21	FROM A JACK TO A KING	Ned Miller	*London*	3
20	22	GLOBE-TROTTER	Tornados	*Decca*	9
34	23	CUPBOARD LOVE	John Leyton	*HMV*	2

In these weeks ■ Frank Ifield completes the first hat-trick of number ones by a British artist when *Wayward Wind* matches the achievement of his previous releases, *I Remember You* and *Lovesick Blues* (21.02.63) ■ For three weeks, two artists with acute accents in their names are in the charts - Mel Tormé and Eydie Gormé (21.02.63) ■ Edyie Gormé spends four weeks at number 32 (28.02.63)■

March 1963

□ Highest position disc reached ● Act's first ever week on chart

LW	TW	Title	Artist	Label	Wks
15	24	LIKE I DO	Maureen Evans	Oriole	14
-	25	FOOT TAPPER	Shadows	Columbia	1
19	26	DON'T YOU THINK IT'S TIME	Mike Berry & the Outlaws	HMV	10
29	27	BOSS GUITAR	Duane Eddy	RCA	4
22	28	A TASTE OF HONEY	Mr. Acker Bilk	Columbia	7
24	29	BIG GIRLS DON'T CRY	Four Seasons	Stateside	7
-	30	RHYTHM OF THE RAIN	Cascades ●	Warner Brothers	1
27	31	DANCE ON!	Shadows	Columbia	13
23	32	MY LITTLE GIRL	Crickets	Liberty	7
26	33	SOME KINDA FUN	Chris Montez	London	7
28	34	IT'S UP TO YOU	Rick Nelson	London	8
-	35	MY KIND OF GIRL	Frank Sinatra with Count Basie	Reprise	1
39	36	PIED PIPER (THE BEEJE)	Steve Race	Parlophone	2
-	37	SAY WONDERFUL THINGS	Ronnie Carroll	Philips	1
-	38	IN DREAMS	Roy Orbison	London	1
-	39	TOWN CRIER	Craig Douglas	Decca	1
40	40	SATURDAY NIGHT AT THE DUCK POND	Cougars	Parlophone	2

WEEK ENDING 14 MARCH 1963

LW	TW	Title	Artist	Label	Wks
2	1	SUMMER HOLIDAY	Cliff Richard	Columbia	4
3	2	PLEASE PLEASE ME	Beatles	Parlophone	8
5	3	THAT'S WHAT LOVE WILL DO	Joe Brown	Piccadilly	5
6	4	LIKE I'VE NEVER BEEN GONE	Billy Fury	Decca	5
4	5	THE NIGHT HAS A THOUSAND EYES	Bobby Vee	Liberty	6
9	6	ISLAND OF DREAMS	Springfields	Philips	13
1	7	WAYWARD WIND	Frank Ifield	Columbia	8
11	8	HEY PAULA	Paul and Paula	Philips	5
25	9	FOOT TAPPER	Shadows	Columbia	2
14	10	TELL HIM	Billie Davis	Decca	6
12	11	CHARMAINE	Bachelors	Decca	8
18	12	ONE BROKEN HEART FOR SALE	Elvis Presley	RCA	2
8	13	LOOP-DE-LOOP	Frankie Vaughan	Philips	7
7	14	DIAMONDS	Jet Harris and Tony Meehan	Decca	9
10	15	WALK RIGHT IN	Rooftop Singers	Fontana	7
21	16	FROM A JACK TO A KING	Ned Miller	London	4
30	17	RHYTHM OF THE RAIN	Cascades	Warner Brothers	2
13	18	LITTLE TOWN FLIRT	Del Shannon	London	8
15	19	ALL ALONE AM I	Brenda Lee	Brunswick	9
17	20	SUKIYAKI	Kenny Ball and his Jazzmen	Pye	6
37	21	SAY WONDERFUL THINGS	Ronnie Carroll	Philips	2
23	22	CUPBOARD LOVE	John Leyton	HMV	3
16	23	HAVA NAGILA	Spotnicks	Oriole	6
20	24	HI-LILI HI-LO	Richard Chamberlain	MGM	4
19	25	THE NEXT TIME/BACHELOR BOY	Cliff Richard	Columbia	15
-	26	LET'S TURKEY TROT	Little Eva	London	1
24	27	LIKE I DO	Maureen Evans	Oriole	15
38	28	IN DREAMS	Roy Orbison	London	2
36	29	PIED PIPER (THE BEEJE)	Steve Race	Parlophone	3
27	30	BOSS GUITAR	Duane Eddy	RCA	5
22	31	GLOBE-TROTTER	Tornados	Decca	10
-	32	BROWN-EYED HANDSOME MAN	Buddy Holly	Coral	1
40	33	SATURDAY NIGHT AT THE DUCK POND	Cougars	Parlophone	3
32	34	MY LITTLE GIRL	Crickets	Liberty	8
35	35	MY KIND OF GIRL	Frank Sinatra with Count Basie	Reprise	2
39	36	TOWN CRIER	Craig Douglas	Decca	2
26	37	DON'T YOU THINK IT'S TIME	Mike Berry & the Outlaws	HMV	11
29	38	BIG GIRLS DON'T CRY	Four Seasons	Stateside	8
-	39	HOW DO YOU DO IT?	Gerry and the Pacemakers ●	Columbia	1
28	40	A TASTE OF HONEY	Mr. Acker Bilk	Columbia	8

WEEK ENDING 21 MARCH 1963

LW	TW	Title	Artist	Label	Wks
1	1	SUMMER HOLIDAY	Cliff Richard	Columbia	5
9	2	FOOT TAPPER	Shadows	Columbia	3
3	3	THAT'S WHAT LOVE WILL DO	Joe Brown	Piccadilly	6
4	4	LIKE I'VE NEVER BEEN GONE	Billy Fury	Decca	6
2	5	PLEASE PLEASE ME	Beatles	Parlophone	9
5	6	THE NIGHT HAS A THOUSAND EYES	Bobby Vee	Liberty	7
6	7	ISLAND OF DREAMS	Springfields	Philips	14
11	8	CHARMAINE	Bachelors	Decca	9
8	9	HEY PAULA	Paul and Paula	Philips	6
7	10	WAYWARD WIND	Frank Ifield	Columbia	9
10	11	TELL HIM	Billie Davis	Decca	7
12	12	ONE BROKEN HEART FOR SALE	Elvis Presley	RCA	3
16	13	FROM A JACK TO A KING	Ned Miller	London	5
17	14	RHYTHM OF THE RAIN	Cascades	Warner Brothers	3
13	15	LOOP-DE-LOOP	Frankie Vaughan	Philips	8
21	16	SAY WONDERFUL THINGS	Ronnie Carroll	Philips	3
15	17	WALK RIGHT IN	Rooftop Singers	Fontana	8
14	18	DIAMONDS	Jet Harris and Tony Meehan	Decca	10
32	19	BROWN-EYED HANDSOME MAN	Buddy Holly	Coral	2
39	20	HOW DO YOU DO IT?	Gerry and the Pacemakers	Columbia	2
26	21	LET'S TURKEY TROT	Little Eva	London	2
22	22	CUPBOARD LOVE	John Leyton	HMV	4
19	23	ALL ALONE AM I	Brenda Lee	Brunswick	10
24	24	HI-LILI HI-LO	Richard Chamberlain	MGM	5
28	25	IN DREAMS	Roy Orbison	London	3
20	26	SUKIYAKI	Kenny Ball and his Jazzmen	Pye	7
23	27	HAVA NAGILA	Spotnicks	Oriole	7
18	28	LITTLE TOWN FLIRT	Del Shannon	London	9
-	29	END OF THE WORLD	Skeeter Davis ●	RCA	1
29	30	PIED PIPER (THE BEEJE)	Steve Race	Parlophone	4
-	31	THE FOLK SINGER	Tommy Roe	HMV	1
-	32	ROBOT	Tornados	Decca	1
31	33	GLOBE-TROTTER	Tornados	Decca	11
30	34	BOSS GUITAR	Duane Eddy	RCA	6
25	35	THE NEXT TIME/BACHELOR BOY	Cliff Richard	Columbia	16
-	36	MR. BASS MAN	Johnny Cymbal ●	London	1
27	37	LIKE I DO	Maureen Evans	Oriole	16
-	38	GOOD GOLLY MISS MOLLY	Jerry Lee Lewis	London	1
36	39	TOWN CRIER	Craig Douglas	Decca	3
35	40	MY KIND OF GIRL	Frank Sinatra with Count Basie	Reprise	3

WEEK ENDING 28 MARCH 1963

LW	TW	Title	Artist	Label	Wks
2	1	FOOT TAPPER	Shadows	Columbia	4
1	2	SUMMER HOLIDAY	Cliff Richard	Columbia	6
4	3	LIKE I'VE NEVER BEEN GONE	Billy Fury	Decca	7
13	4	FROM A JACK TO A KING	Ned Miller	London	6
7	5	ISLAND OF DREAMS	Springfields	Philips	15
8	6	CHARMAINE	Bachelors	Decca	10
5	7	PLEASE PLEASE ME	Beatles	Parlophone	10
3	8	THAT'S WHAT LOVE WILL DO	Joe Brown	Piccadilly	7
14	9	RHYTHM OF THE RAIN	Cascades	Warner Brothers	4
20	10	HOW DO YOU DO IT?	Gerry and the Pacemakers	Columbia	3
16	11	SAY WONDERFUL THINGS	Ronnie Carroll	Philips	4
9	12	HEY PAULA	Paul and Paula	Philips	7
6	13	THE NIGHT HAS A THOUSAND EYES	Bobby Vee	Liberty	8
12	14	ONE BROKEN HEART FOR SALE	Elvis Presley	RCA	4
11	15	TELL HIM	Billie Davis	Decca	8
19	16	BROWN-EYED HANDSOME MAN	Buddy Holly	Coral	3
10	17	WAYWARD WIND	Frank Ifield	Columbia	10
21	18	LET'S TURKEY TROT	Little Eva	London	3
31	19	THE FOLK SINGER	Tommy Roe	HMV	2
25	20	IN DREAMS	Roy Orbison	London	4
15	21	LOOP-DE-LOOP	Frankie Vaughan	Philips	9
22	22	CUPBOARD LOVE	John Leyton	HMV	5
23	23	ALL ALONE AM I	Brenda Lee	Brunswick	11
29	24	END OF THE WORLD	Skeeter Davis	RCA	2
36	25	MR. BASS MAN	Johnny Cymbal	London	2
18	26	DIAMONDS	Jet Harris and Tony Meehan	Decca	11
17	27	WALK RIGHT IN	Rooftop Singers	Fontana	9
-	28	SO IT WILL ALWAYS BE	Everly Brothers	Warner Brothers	1
24	29	HI-LILI HI-LO	Richard Chamberlain	MGM	6
32	30	ROBOT	Tornados	Decca	2
27	31	HAVA NAGILA	Spotnicks	Oriole	8
26	32	SUKIYAKI	Kenny Ball and his Jazzmen	Pye	8
38	33	GOOD GOLLY MISS MOLLY	Jerry Lee Lewis	London	2
30	34	PIED PIPER (THE BEEJE)	Steve Race	Parlophone	5

■Two hits based on classical tunes *Like I Do* and *Saturday Night At The Duckpond* mix with two hits based on old folk tunes, *Hava Nagila* from Israel and *Sukiyaki* from Japan in the Top 40 (07.03.60) ■ When *How Do You Do It* first enters the chart, the act is so unknown that the name is mis-spelt 'Jerry' (14.03.63) ■ Sensation as Elvis Presley's *One Broken Heart For Sale* stops at number 12, ending a string of 23 consecutive Top Ten hits for the King (21.03.63)■

March 1963

□ Highest position disc reached ● Act's first ever week on chart

LW	TW	Title	Artist	Label	Wks
-	35	CAN'T GET USED TO LOSING YOU	Andy Williams	CBS	1
-	36	CAN YOU FORGIVE ME	Karl Denver	Decca	1
-	37	DON'T SET ME FREE	Ray Charles	HMV	1
-	38	SAY I WON'T BE THERE	Springfields	Philips	1
37	39	LIKE I DO	Maureen Evans	Oriole	17
34	40	BOSS GUITAR	Duane Eddy	RCA	7

WEEK ENDING 4 APRIL 1963

LW	TW	Title	Artist	Label	Wks
2	1	SUMMER HOLIDAY	Cliff Richard	Columbia	7
10	2	HOW DO YOU DO IT?	Gerry and the Pacemakers	Columbia	4
4	3	FROM A JACK TO A KING	Ned Miller	London	7
1	4	FOOT TAPPER	Shadows	Columbia	5
3	5	LIKE I'VE NEVER BEEN GONE	Billy Fury	Decca	8
11	6	SAY WONDERFUL THINGS	Ronnie Carroll	Philips	5
9	7	RHYTHM OF THE RAIN	Cascades	Warner Brothers	5
6	8	CHARMAINE	Bachelors	Decca	11
16	9	BROWN-EYED HANDSOME MAN	Buddy Holly	Coral	4
8	10	THAT'S WHAT LOVE WILL DO	Joe Brown	Piccadilly	8
7	11	PLEASE PLEASE ME	Beatles	Parlophone	11
12	12	HEY PAULA	Paul and Paula	Philips	8
19	13	THE FOLK SINGER	Tommy Roe	HMV	3
18	14	LET'S TURKEY TROT	Little Eva	London	4
5	15	ISLAND OF DREAMS	Springfields	Philips	16
15	16	TELL HIM	Billie Davis	Decca	9
20	17	IN DREAMS	Roy Orbison	London	5
13	18	THE NIGHT HAS A THOUSAND EYES	Bobby Vee	Liberty	9
14	19	ONE BROKEN HEART FOR SALE	Elvis Presley	RCA	5
17	20	WAYWARD WIND	Frank Ifield	Columbia	11
24	21	END OF THE WORLD	Skeeter Davis	RCA	3
38	22	SAY I WON'T BE THERE	Springfields	Philips	2
-	23	WALK LIKE A MAN	Four Seasons	Stateside	1
30	24	ROBOT	Tornados	Decca	3
25	25	MR. BASS MAN	Johnny Cymbal	London	3
22	26	CUPBOARD LOVE	John Leyton	HMV	6
28	27	SO IT WILL ALWAYS BE	Everly Brothers	Warner Brothers	2
35	28	CAN'T GET USED TO LOSING YOU	Andy Williams	CBS	2
23	29	ALL ALONE AM I	Brenda Lee	Brunswick	12
-	30	COUNT ON ME	Julie Grant	Pye	1
33	31	GOOD GOLLY MISS MOLLY	Jerry Lee Lewis	London	3
29	32	HI-LILI HI-LO	Richard Chamberlain	MGM	7
21	33	LOOP-DE-LOOP	Frankie Vaughan	Philips	10
31	34	HAVA NAGILA	Spotnicks	Oriole	9
-	35	LOSING YOU	Brenda Lee	Brunswick	1
26	36	DIAMONDS	Jet Harris and Tony Meehan	Decca	12
-	37	CODE OF LOVE	Mike Sarne	Parlophone	1
36	38	CAN YOU FORGIVE ME	Karl Denver	Decca	2
-	39	OUR DAY WILL COME	Ruby and the Romantics ●	London	1
27	40	WALK RIGHT IN	Rooftop Singers	Fontana	10

WEEK ENDING 11 APRIL 1963

LW	TW	Title	Artist	Label	Wks
2	1	HOW DO YOU DO IT?	Gerry and the Pacemakers	Columbia	5
3	2	FROM A JACK TO A KING	Ned Miller	London	8
4	3	FOOT TAPPER	Shadows	Columbia	6
9	4	BROWN-EYED HANDSOME MAN	Buddy Holly	Coral	5
7	5	RHYTHM OF THE RAIN	Cascades	Warner Brothers	6
1	6	SUMMER HOLIDAY	Cliff Richard	Columbia	8
6	7	SAY WONDERFUL THINGS	Ronnie Carroll	Philips	6
8	8	CHARMAINE	Bachelors	Decca	12
5	9	LIKE I'VE NEVER BEEN GONE	Billy Fury	Decca	9
13	10	THE FOLK SINGER	Tommy Roe	HMV	4
22	11	SAY I WON'T BE THERE	Springfields	Philips	3
17	12	IN DREAMS	Roy Orbison	London	6
14	13	LET'S TURKEY TROT	Little Eva	London	5
10	14	THAT'S WHAT LOVE WILL DO	Joe Brown	Piccadilly	9
15	15	ISLAND OF DREAMS	Springfields	Philips	17
23	16	WALK LIKE A MAN	Four Seasons	Stateside	2
11	17	PLEASE PLEASE ME	Beatles	Parlophone	12
12	18	HEY PAULA	Paul and Paula	Philips	9
24	19	ROBOT	Tornados	Decca	4
21	20	END OF THE WORLD	Skeeter Davis	RCA	4
28	21	CAN'T GET USED TO LOSING YOU	Andy Williams	CBS	3
26	22	CUPBOARD LOVE	John Leyton	HMV	7
27	23	SO IT WILL ALWAYS BE	Everly Brothers	Warner Brothers	3
25	24	MR. BASS MAN	Johnny Cymbal	London	4
16	25	TELL HIM	Billie Davis	Decca	10
30	26	COUNT ON ME	Julie Grant	Pye	2
35	27	LOSING YOU	Brenda Lee	Brunswick	2
19	28	ONE BROKEN HEART FOR SALE	Elvis Presley	RCA	6
18	29	THE NIGHT HAS A THOUSAND EYES	Bobby Vee	Liberty	10
-	30	NOBODY'S DARLIN' BUT MINE	Frank Ifield	Columbia	1
37	31	CODE OF LOVE	Mike Sarne	Parlophone	2
38	32	CAN YOU FORGIVE ME	Karl Denver	Decca	3
20	33	WAYWARD WIND	Frank Ifield	Columbia	12
-	34	FIREBALL	Don Spencer ●	HMV	1
29	35	ALL ALONE AM I	Brenda Lee	Brunswick	13
32	36	HI-LILI HI-LO	Richard Chamberlain	MGM	8
31	37	GOOD GOLLY MISS MOLLY	Jerry Lee Lewis	London	4
34	38	HAVA NAGILA	Spotnicks	Oriole	10
39	39	OUR DAY WILL COME	Ruby and the Romantics	London	2
33	40	LOOP-DE-LOOP	Frankie Vaughan	Philips	11

WEEK ENDING 18 APRIL 1963

LW	TW	Title	Artist	Label	Wks
1	1	HOW DO YOU DO IT?	Gerry and the Pacemakers	Columbia	6
2	2	FROM A JACK TO A KING	Ned Miller	London	9
4	3	BROWN-EYED HANDSOME MAN	Buddy Holly	Coral	6
10	4	THE FOLK SINGER	Tommy Roe	HMV	5
5	5	RHYTHM OF THE RAIN	Cascades	Warner Brothers	7
3	6	FOOT TAPPER	Shadows	Columbia	7
11	7	SAY I WON'T BE THERE	Springfields	Philips	4
7	8	SAY WONDERFUL THINGS	Ronnie Carroll	Philips	7
6	9	SUMMER HOLIDAY	Cliff Richard	Columbia	9
12	10	IN DREAMS	Roy Orbison	London	7
9	11	LIKE I'VE NEVER BEEN GONE	Billy Fury	Decca	10
8	12	CHARMAINE	Bachelors	Decca	13
16	13	WALK LIKE A MAN	Four Seasons	Stateside	3
30	14	NOBODY'S DARLIN' BUT MINE	Frank Ifield	Columbia	2
21	15	CAN'T GET USED TO LOSING YOU	Andy Williams	CBS	4
15	16	ISLAND OF DREAMS	Springfields	Philips	18
19	17	ROBOT	Tornados	Decca	5
13	18	LET'S TURKEY TROT	Little Eva	London	6
20	19	END OF THE WORLD	Skeeter Davis	RCA	5
27	20	LOSING YOU	Brenda Lee	Brunswick	3
14	21	THAT'S WHAT LOVE WILL DO	Joe Brown	Piccadilly	10
17	22	PLEASE PLEASE ME	Beatles	Parlophone	13
-	23	FROM ME TO YOU	Beatles	Parlophone	1
18	24	HEY PAULA	Paul and Paula	Philips	10
22	25	CUPBOARD LOVE	John Leyton	HMV	8
26	26	COUNT ON ME	Julie Grant	Pye	3
24	27	MR. BASS MAN	Johnny Cymbal	London	5
23	28	SO IT WILL ALWAYS BE	Everly Brothers	Warner Brothers	4
25	29	TELL HIM	Billie Davis	Decca	11
31	30	CODE OF LOVE	Mike Sarne	Parlophone	3
-	31	HE'S SO FINE	Chiffons ●	Stateside	1
32	32	CAN YOU FORGIVE ME	Karl Denver	Decca	4
29	33	THE NIGHT HAS A THOUSAND EYES	Bobby Vee	Liberty	11
34	34	FIREBALL	Don Spencer	HMV	2
33	35	WAYWARD WIND	Frank Ifield	Columbia	13
28	36	ONE BROKEN HEART FOR SALE	Elvis Presley	RCA	7
-	37	SOME OTHER GUY	Big Three ●	Decca	1
39	38	OUR DAY WILL COME	Ruby and the Romantics	London	3
36	39	HI-LILI HI-LO	Richard Chamberlain	MGM	9
-	40	MY LITTLE BABY	Mike Berry and the Outlaws	HMV	1

WEEK ENDING 25 APRIL 1963

LW	TW	Title	Artist	Label	Wks
1	1	HOW DO YOU DO IT?	Gerry and the Pacemakers	Columbia	7
2	2	FROM A JACK TO A KING	Ned Miller	London	10
23	3	FROM ME TO YOU	Beatles	Parlophone	2

In these weeks ■ A return to the Top Ten by Buddy Holly, four years after his death and almost as long since *It Doesn't Matter Anymore* gave him his previous Top Ten hit (04.04.63) ■ A week after becoming the thirteenth record to climb back to the number one spot, *Summer Holiday* becomes the seventh to fall from the top right out of the top five (11.04.63)■

LW	TW	Title	Artist	Label	Wks
4	[4]	THE FOLK SINGER	Tommy Roe	*HMV*	6
7	[5]	SAY I WON'T BE THERE	Springfields	*Philips*	5
14	6	NOBODY'S DARLIN' BUT MINE	Frank Ifield	*Columbia*	3
5	7	RHYTHM OF THE RAIN	Cascades	*Warner Brothers*	8
10	8	IN DREAMS	Roy Orbison	*London*	8
6	9	FOOT TAPPER	Shadows	*Columbia*	8
3	10	BROWN-EYED HANDSOME MAN	Buddy Holly	*Coral*	7
15	11	CAN'T GET USED TO LOSING YOU	Andy Williams	*CBS*	5
13	[12]	WALK LIKE A MAN	Four Seasons	*Stateside*	4
9	13	SUMMER HOLIDAY	Cliff Richard	*Columbia*	10
8	14	SAY WONDERFUL THINGS	Ronnie Carroll	*Philips*	8
12	15	CHARMAINE	Bachelors	*Decca*	14
20	16	LOSING YOU	Brenda Lee	*Brunswick*	4
11	17	LIKE I'VE NEVER BEEN GONE	Billy Fury	*Decca*	11
19	[18]	END OF THE WORLD	Skeeter Davis	*RCA*	6
18	19	LET'S TURKEY TROT	Little Eva	*London*	7
16	20	ISLAND OF DREAMS	Springfields	*Philips*	19
17	21	ROBOT	Tornados	*Decca*	6
31	22	HE'S SO FINE	Chiffons	*Stateside*	2
28	[23]	SO IT WILL ALWAYS BE	Everly Brothers	*Warner Brothers*	5
26	[24]	COUNT ON ME	Julie Grant	*Pye*	4
27	25	MR. BASS MAN	Johnny Cymbal	*London*	6
21	26	THAT'S WHAT LOVE WILL DO	Joe Brown	*Piccadilly*	11
25	27	CUPBOARD LOVE	John Leyton	*HMV*	9
24	28	HEY PAULA	Paul and Paula	*Philips*	11
30	[29]	CODE OF LOVE	Mike Sarne	*Parlophone*	4
22	30	PLEASE PLEASE ME	Beatles	*Parlophone*	14
-	31	SCARLETT O'HARA	Jet Harris and Tony Meehan	*Decca*	1
34	[32]	FIREBALL	Don Spencer	*HMV*	3
32	33	CAN YOU FORGIVE ME	Karl Denver	*Decca*	5
-	34	YOUNG LOVERS	Paul and Paula	*Philips*	1
-	35	DECK OF CARDS	Wink Martindale	*London*	1
40	36	MY LITTLE BABY	Mike Berry and the Outlaws	*HMV*	2
-	37	ALL ALONE AM I	Brenda Lee	*Brunswick*	14
-	38	TWO KINDS OF TEARDROPS	Del Shannon	*London*	1
38	39	OUR DAY WILL COME	Ruby and the Romantics	*London*	4
37	40	SOME OTHER GUY	Big Three	*Decca*	2

May 1963

□ Highest position disc reached ● Act's first ever week on chart

WEEK ENDING 2 MAY 1963

LW	TW	Title	Artist	Label	Wks
3	[1]	FROM ME TO YOU	Beatles	*Parlophone*	3
1	2	HOW DO YOU DO IT?	Gerry and the Pacemakers	*Columbia*	8
2	3	FROM A JACK TO A KING	Ned Miller	*London*	11
6	[4]	NOBODY'S DARLIN' BUT MINE	Frank Ifield	*Columbia*	4
5	[5]	SAY I WON'T BE THERE	Springfields	*Philips*	6
11	6	CAN'T GET USED TO LOSING YOU	Andy Williams	*CBS*	6
8	7	IN DREAMS	Roy Orbison	*London*	9
7	8	RHYTHM OF THE RAIN	Cascades	*Warner Brothers*	9
10	9	BROWN-EYED HANDSOME MAN	Buddy Holly	*Coral*	8
9	10	FOOT TAPPER	Shadows	*Columbia*	9
4	11	THE FOLK SINGER	Tommy Roe	*HMV*	7
12	[12]	WALK LIKE A MAN	Four Seasons	*Stateside*	5
16	13	LOSING YOU	Brenda Lee	*Brunswick*	5
13	14	SUMMER HOLIDAY	Cliff Richard	*Columbia*	11
31	15	SCARLETT O'HARA	Jet Harris and Tony Meehan	*Decca*	2
14	16	SAY WONDERFUL THINGS	Ronnie Carroll	*Philips*	9
38	17	TWO KINDS OF TEARDROPS	Del Shannon	*London*	2
22	18	HE'S SO FINE	Chiffons	*Stateside*	3
17	19	LIKE I'VE NEVER BEEN GONE	Billy Fury	*Decca*	12
18	20	END OF THE WORLD	Skeeter Davis	*RCA*	7
15	21	CHARMAINE	Bachelors	*Decca*	15
19	22	LET'S TURKEY TROT	Little Eva	*London*	8
21	23	ROBOT	Tornados	*Decca*	7
34	24	YOUNG LOVERS	Paul and Paula	*Philips*	2
20	25	ISLAND OF DREAMS	Springfields	*Philips*	20
23	26	SO IT WILL ALWAYS BE	Everly Brothers	*Warner Brothers*	6
24	27	COUNT ON ME	Julie Grant	*Pye*	5
-	28	CASABLANCA	Kenny Ball and his Jazzmen	*Pye*	1
35	29	DECK OF CARDS	Wink Martindale	*London*	2
25	30	MR. BASS MAN	Johnny Cymbal	*London*	7
30	31	PLEASE PLEASE ME	Beatles	*Parlophone*	15
29	32	CODE OF LOVE	Mike Sarne	*Parlophone*	5
26	33	THAT'S WHAT LOVE WILL DO	Joe Brown	*Piccadilly*	12
28	34	HEY PAULA	Paul and Paula	*Philips*	12
27	35	CUPBOARD LOVE	John Leyton	*HMV*	10
36	36	MY LITTLE BABY	Mike Berry and the Outlaws	*HMV*	3
-	37	PIPELINE	Chantays ●	*London*	1
-	38	MY WAY	Eddie Cochran	*Liberty*	1
-	39	WOE IS ME	Helen Shapiro	*Columbia*	1
-	40	JUST LISTEN TO MY HEART	Spotnicks	*Oriole*	1

WEEK ENDING 9 MAY 1963

LW	TW	Title	Artist	Label	Wks
1	[1]	FROM ME TO YOU	Beatles	*Parlophone*	4
2	2	HOW DO YOU DO IT?	Gerry and the Pacemakers	*Columbia*	9
3	3	FROM A JACK TO A KING	Ned Miller	*London*	12
4	[4]	NOBODY'S DARLIN' BUT MINE	Frank Ifield	*Columbia*	5
6	5	CAN'T GET USED TO LOSING YOU	Andy Williams	*CBS*	7
7	[6]	IN DREAMS	Roy Orbison	*London*	10
15	7	SCARLETT O'HARA	Jet Harris and Tony Meehan	*Decca*	3
5	8	SAY I WON'T BE THERE	Springfields	*Philips*	7
17	9	TWO KINDS OF TEARDROPS	Del Shannon	*London*	3
13	[10]	LOSING YOU	Brenda Lee	*Brunswick*	6
9	11	BROWN-EYED HANDSOME MAN	Buddy Holly	*Coral*	9
8	12	RHYTHM OF THE RAIN	Cascades	*Warner Brothers*	10
11	13	THE FOLK SINGER	Tommy Roe	*HMV*	8
12	14	WALK LIKE A MAN	Four Seasons	*Stateside*	6
10	15	FOOT TAPPER	Shadows	*Columbia*	10
18	[16]	HE'S SO FINE	Chiffons	*Stateside*	4
-	17	DO YOU WANT TO KNOW A SECRET?	Billy J. Kramer and the Dakotas ●	*Parlophone*	1
24	18	YOUNG LOVERS	Paul and Paula	*Philips*	3
14	19	SUMMER HOLIDAY	Cliff Richard	*Columbia*	12
16	20	SAY WONDERFUL THINGS	Ronnie Carroll	*Philips*	10
-	21	LUCKY LIPS	Cliff Richard	*Columbia*	1
29	22	DECK OF CARDS	Wink Martindale	*London*	3
19	23	LIKE I'VE NEVER BEEN GONE	Billy Fury	*Decca*	13
22	24	LET'S TURKEY TROT	Little Eva	*London*	9
20	25	END OF THE WORLD	Skeeter Davis	*RCA*	8
21	26	CHARMAINE	Bachelors	*Decca*	16
28	27	CASABLANCA	Kenny Ball and his Jazzmen	*Pye*	2
23	28	ROBOT	Tornados	*Decca*	8
38	29	MY WAY	Eddie Cochran	*Liberty*	2
27	30	COUNT ON ME	Julie Grant	*Pye*	6
25	31	ISLAND OF DREAMS	Springfields	*Philips*	21
37	32	PIPELINE	Chantays	*London*	2
26	33	SO IT WILL ALWAYS BE	Everly Brothers	*Warner Brothers*	7
36	[34]	MY LITTLE BABY	Mike Berry and the Outlaws	*HMV*	4
39	[35]	WOE IS ME	Helen Shapiro	*Columbia*	2
40	[36]	JUST LISTEN TO MY HEART	Spotnicks	*Oriole*	2
-	37	IF YOU GOTTA MAKE A FOOL OF SOMEBODY	Freddie and the Dreamers ●	*Columbia*	1
32	38	CODE OF LOVE	Mike Sarne	*Parlophone*	6
-	39	LITTLE BAND OF GOLD	James Gilreath	*Pye*	1
33	40	THAT'S WHAT LOVE WILL DO	Joe Brown	*Piccadilly*	13

WEEK ENDING 16 MAY 1963

LW	TW	Title	Artist	Label	Wks
1	[1]	FROM ME TO YOU	Beatles	*Parlophone*	5
5	[2]	CAN'T GET USED TO LOSING YOU	Andy Williams	*CBS*	8
7	3	SCARLETT O'HARA	Jet Harris and Tony Meehan	*Decca*	4
2	4	HOW DO YOU DO IT?	Gerry and the Pacemakers	*Columbia*	10
9	[5]	TWO KINDS OF TEARDROPS	Del Shannon	*London*	4
6	[6]	IN DREAMS	Roy Orbison	*London*	11
3	7	FROM A JACK TO A KING	Ned Miller	*London*	13
4	8	NOBODY'S DARLIN' BUT MINE	Frank Ifield	*Columbia*	6
21	9	LUCKY LIPS	Cliff Richard	*Columbia*	2
17	10	DO YOU WANT TO KNOW A SECRET?	Billy J. Kramer and the Dakotas	*Parlophone*	2
10	11	LOSING YOU	Brenda Lee	*Brunswick*	7
8	12	SAY I WON'T BE THERE	Springfields	*Philips*	8
11	13	BROWN-EYED HANDSOME MAN	Buddy Holly	*Coral*	10

■The first cover of a Lennon-McCartney song to hit the charts is Billy J. Kramer's *Do You Want To Know A Secret?* (09.05.63) ■ Frank Ifield's attempt to clock up four consecutive number ones fails when *Nobody's Darlin' But Mine* stops at number four (02.05.63)■

May 1963

□ Highest position disc reached ● Act's first ever week on chart

LW	TW	Title	Artist	Label	Wks
18	14	YOUNG LOVERS	Paul and Paula	Philips	4
12	15	RHYTHM OF THE RAIN	Cascades	Warner Brothers	11
16	16	HE'S SO FINE	Chiffons	Stateside	5
13	17	THE FOLK SINGER	Tommy Roe	HMV	9
14	18	WALK LIKE A MAN	Four Seasons	Stateside	7
22	19	DECK OF CARDS	Wink Martindale	London	4
15	20	FOOT TAPPER	Shadows	Columbia	11
27	21	CASABLANCA	Kenny Ball and his Jazzmen	Pye	3
32	22	PIPELINE	Chantays	London	3
29	23	MY WAY	Eddie Cochran	Liberty	3
19	24	SUMMER HOLIDAY	Cliff Richard	Columbia	13
20	25	SAY WONDERFUL THINGS	Ronnie Carroll	Philips	11
23	26	LIKE I'VE NEVER BEEN GONE	Billy Fury	Decca	14
25	27	END OF THE WORLD	Skeeter Davis	RCA	9
-	28	WHEN WILL YOU SAY I LOVE YOU	Billy Fury	Decca	1
26	29	CHARMAINE	Bachelors	Decca	17
28	30	ROBOT	Tornados	Decca	9
37	31	IF YOU GOTTA MAKE A FOOL OF SOMEBODY	Freddie and the Dreamers	Columbia	2
24	32	LET'S TURKEY TROT	Little Eva	London	10
33	33	SO IT WILL ALWAYS BE	Everly Brothers	Warner Brothers	8
31	34	ISLAND OF DREAMS	Springfields	Philips	22
39	35	LITTLE BAND OF GOLD	James Gilreath	Pye	2
36	36	JUST LISTEN TO MY HEART	Spotnicks	Oriole	3
34	37	MY LITTLE BABY	Mike Berry and the Outlaws	HMV	5
30	38	COUNT ON ME	Julie Grant	Pye	7
-	39	CASANOVA/CHARIOT	Petula Clark	Pye	1
35	40	WOE IS ME	Helen Shapiro	Columbia	3

WEEK ENDING 23 MAY 1963

LW	TW	Title	Artist	Label	Wks
1	1	FROM ME TO YOU	Beatles	Parlophone	6
3	2	SCARLETT O'HARA	Jet Harris and Tony Meehan	Decca	5
10	3	DO YOU WANT TO KNOW A SECRET?	Billy J. Kramer and the Dakotas	Parlophone	3
9	4	LUCKY LIPS	Cliff Richard	Columbia	3
2	5	CAN'T GET USED TO LOSING YOU	Andy Williams	CBS	9
5	6	TWO KINDS OF TEARDROPS	Del Shannon	London	5
6	7	IN DREAMS	Roy Orbison	London	12
4	8	HOW DO YOU DO IT?	Gerry and the Pacemakers	Columbia	11
14	9	YOUNG LOVERS	Paul and Paula	Philips	5
11	10	LOSING YOU	Brenda Lee	Brunswick	8
8	11	NOBODY'S DARLIN' BUT MINE	Frank Ifield	Columbia	7
7	12	FROM A JACK TO A KING	Ned Miller	London	14
19	13	DECK OF CARDS	Wink Martindale	London	5
12	14	SAY I WON'T BE THERE	Springfields	Philips	9
28	15	WHEN WILL YOU SAY I LOVE YOU	Billy Fury	Decca	2
16	16	HE'S SO FINE	Chiffons	Stateside	6
15	17	RHYTHM OF THE RAIN	Cascades	Warner Brothers	12
13	18	BROWN-EYED HANDSOME MAN	Buddy Holly	Coral	11
17	19	THE FOLK SINGER	Tommy Roe	HMV	10
22	20	PIPELINE	Chantays	London	4
-	21	TAKE THESE CHAINS FROM MY HEART	Ray Charles	HMV	1
18	22	WALK LIKE A MAN	Four Seasons	Stateside	8
31	23	IF YOU GOTTA MAKE A FOOL OF SOMEBODY	Freddie and the Dreamers	Columbia	3
21	24	CASABLANCA	Kenny Ball and his Jazzmen	Pye	4
23	25	MY WAY	Eddie Cochran	Liberty	4
20	26	FOOT TAPPER	Shadows	Columbia	12
24	27	SUMMER HOLIDAY	Cliff Richard	Columbia	14
25	28	SAY WONDERFUL THINGS	Ronnie Carroll	Philips	12
-	29	ANOTHER SATURDAY NIGHT	Sam Cooke	RCA	1
-	30	HARVEST OF LOVE	Benny Hill	Pye	1
29	31	CHARMAINE	Bachelors	Decca	18
30	32	ROBOT	Tornados	Decca	10
27	33	END OF THE WORLD	Skeeter Davis	RCA	10
-	34	OUT OF MY MIND	Johnny Tillotson	London	1
33	35	SO IT WILL ALWAYS BE	Everly Brothers	Warner Brothers	9
35	36	LITTLE BAND OF GOLD	James Gilreath	Pye	3
32	37	LET'S TURKEY TROT	Little Eva	London	11
34	38	ISLAND OF DREAMS	Springfields	Philips	23
26	39	LIKE I'VE NEVER BEEN GONE	Billy Fury	Decca	15
36	40	JUST LISTEN TO MY HEART	Spotnicks	Oriole	4

WEEK ENDING 30 MAY 1963

LW	TW	Title	Artist	Label	Wks
1	1	FROM ME TO YOU	Beatles	Parlophone	7
3	2	DO YOU WANT TO KNOW A SECRET?	Billy J. Kramer and the Dakotas	Parlophone	4
2	3	SCARLETT O'HARA	Jet Harris and Tony Meehan	Decca	6
4	4	LUCKY LIPS	Cliff Richard	Columbia	4
5	5	CAN'T GET USED TO LOSING YOU	Andy Williams	CBS	10
6	6	TWO KINDS OF TEARDROPS	Del Shannon	London	6
15	7	WHEN WILL YOU SAY I LOVE YOU	Billy Fury	Decca	3
7	8	IN DREAMS	Roy Orbison	London	13
9	9	YOUNG LOVERS	Paul and Paula	Philips	6
13	10	DECK OF CARDS	Wink Martindale	London	6
11	11	NOBODY'S DARLIN' BUT MINE	Frank Ifield	Columbia	8
10	12	LOSING YOU	Brenda Lee	Brunswick	9
8	13	HOW DO YOU DO IT?	Gerry and the Pacemakers	Columbia	12
21	14	TAKE THESE CHAINS FROM MY HEART	Ray Charles	HMV	2
12	15	FROM A JACK TO A KING	Ned Miller	London	15
23	16	IF YOU GOTTA MAKE A FOOL OF SOMEBODY	Freddie and the Dreamers	Columbia	4
16	17	HE'S SO FINE	Chiffons	Stateside	7
14	18	SAY I WON'T BE THERE	Springfields	Philips	10
20	19	PIPELINE	Chantays	London	5
30	20	HARVEST OF LOVE	Benny Hill	Pye	2
18	21	BROWN-EYED HANDSOME MAN	Buddy Holly	Coral	12
-	22	I LIKE IT	Gerry and the Pacemakers	Columbia	1
24	23	CASABLANCA	Kenny Ball and his Jazzmen	Pye	5
17	24	RHYTHM OF THE RAIN	Cascades	Warner Brothers	13
19	25	THE FOLK SINGER	Tommy Roe	HMV	11
22	26	WALK LIKE A MAN	Four Seasons	Stateside	9
25	27	MY WAY	Eddie Cochran	Liberty	5
29	28	ANOTHER SATURDAY NIGHT	Sam Cooke	RCA	2
-	29	FORGET HIM	Bobby Rydell	Cameo-Parkway	1
26	30	FOOT TAPPER	Shadows	Columbia	13
36	31	LITTLE BAND OF GOLD	James Gilreath	Pye	4
27	32	SUMMER HOLIDAY	Cliff Richard	Columbia	15
-	33	FALLING	Roy Orbison	London	1
28	34	SAY WONDERFUL THINGS	Ronnie Carroll	Philips	13
34	35	OUT OF MY MIND	Johnny Tillotson	London	2
32	36	ROBOT	Tornados	Decca	11
33	37	END OF THE WORLD	Skeeter Davis	RCA	11
31	38	CHARMAINE	Bachelors	Decca	19
-	39	JUST LIKE ME	Hollies ●	Parlophone	1
-	40	FOOLISH LITTLE GIRL	Shirelles	Stateside	1

WEEK ENDING 6 JUNE 1963

LW	TW	Title	Artist	Label	Wks
1	1	FROM ME TO YOU	Beatles	Parlophone	8
2	2	DO YOU WANT TO KNOW A SECRET?	Billy J. Kramer and the Dakotas	Parlophone	5
7	3	WHEN WILL YOU SAY I LOVE YOU	Billy Fury	Decca	4
3	4	SCARLETT O'HARA	Jet Harris and Tony Meehan	Decca	7
14	5	TAKE THESE CHAINS FROM MY HEART	Ray Charles	HMV	3
6	6	TWO KINDS OF TEARDROPS	Del Shannon	London	7
22	7	I LIKE IT	Gerry and the Pacemakers	Columbia	2
4	8	LUCKY LIPS	Cliff Richard	Columbia	5
10	9	DECK OF CARDS	Wink Martindale	London	7
5	10	CAN'T GET USED TO LOSING YOU	Andy Williams	CBS	11
8	11	IN DREAMS	Roy Orbison	London	14
16	12	IF YOU GOTTA MAKE A FOOL OF SOMEBODY	Freddie and the Dreamers	Columbia	5
9	13	YOUNG LOVERS	Paul and Paula	Philips	7
11	14	NOBODY'S DARLIN' BUT MINE	Frank Ifield	Columbia	9
13	15	HOW DO YOU DO IT?	Gerry and the Pacemakers	Columbia	13
19	16	PIPELINE	Chantays	London	6
15	17	FROM A JACK TO A KING	Ned Miller	London	16
12	18	LOSING YOU	Brenda Lee	Brunswick	10
33	19	FALLING	Roy Orbison	London	2

In these weeks ■ Eddie Cochran's *My Way* is not, of course, the same song as the Frank Sinatra hit of six years later, but it is his final new chart hit (16.05.63) ■ *He's So Fine*, the song that George Harrison apparently copied in composing his 1971 chart topper *My Sweet Lord*, peaks at number 16 while Harrison and his colleagues stay at number one (23.05.63)■

LW	TW	Title / Artist	Label	Wks
17	20	HE'S SO FINE Chiffons	*Stateside*	8
29	21	FORGET HIM Bobby Rydell	*Cameo-Parkway*	2
18	22	SAY I WON'T BE THERE Springfields	*Philips*	11
20	23	HARVEST OF LOVE Benny Hill	*Pye*	3
21	24	BROWN-EYED HANDSOME MAN Buddy Holly	*Coral*	13
28	25	ANOTHER SATURDAY NIGHT Sam Cooke	*RCA*	3
27	26	MY WAY Eddie Cochran	*Liberty*	6
-	27	ATLANTIS Shadows	*Columbia*	1
23	28	CASABLANCA Kenny Ball and his Jazzmen	*Pye*	6
31	29	LITTLE BAND OF GOLD James Gilreath	*Pye*	5
26	30	WALK LIKE A MAN Four Seasons	*Stateside*	10
39	31	JUST LIKE ME Hollies	*Parlophone*	2
25	32	THE FOLK SINGER Tommy Roe	*HMV*	12
30	33	FOOT TAPPER Shadows	*Columbia*	14
-	34	ICE CREAM MAN Tornados	*Decca*	1
-	35	BO DIDDLEY Buddy Holly	*Coral*	1
32	36	SUMMER HOLIDAY Cliff Richard	*Columbia*	16
-	37	HEY PAULA Paul and Paula	*Philips*	13
24	38	RHYTHM OF THE RAIN Cascades	*Warner Brothers*	14
37	39	END OF THE WORLD Skeeter Davis	*RCA*	12
-	40	HE'S THE ONE Billie Davis	*Decca*	1

WEEK ENDING **13 JUNE 1963**

LW	TW	Title / Artist	Label	Wks
1	1	FROM ME TO YOU Beatles	*Parlophone*	9
7	2	I LIKE IT Gerry and the Pacemakers	*Columbia*	3
2	3	DO YOU WANT TO KNOW A SECRET? Billy J. Kramer and the Dakotas	*Parlophone*	6
3	4	WHEN WILL YOU SAY I LOVE YOU Billy Fury	*Decca*	5
4	5	SCARLETT O'HARA Jet Harris and Tony Meehan	*Decca*	8
8	6	LUCKY LIPS Cliff Richard	*Columbia*	6
12	7	IF YOU GOTTA MAKE A FOOL OF SOMEBODY Freddie and the Dreamers	*Columbia*	6
5	8	TAKE THESE CHAINS FROM MY HEART Ray Charles	*HMV*	4
9	9	DECK OF CARDS Wink Martindale	*London*	8
11	10	IN DREAMS Roy Orbison	*London*	15
13	11	YOUNG LOVERS Paul and Paula	*Philips*	8
27	12	ATLANTIS Shadows	*Columbia*	2
6	13	TWO KINDS OF TEARDROPS Del Shannon	*London*	8
10	14	CAN'T GET USED TO LOSING YOU Andy Williams	*CBS*	12
14	15	NOBODY'S DARLIN' BUT MINE Frank Ifield	*Columbia*	10
35	16	BO DIDDLEY Buddy Holly	*Coral*	2
19	17	FALLING Roy Orbison	*London*	3
21	18	FORGET HIM Bobby Rydell	*Cameo-Parkway*	3
16	19	PIPELINE Chantays	*London*	7
15	20	HOW DO YOU DO IT? Gerry and the Pacemakers	*Columbia*	14
18	21	LOSING YOU Brenda Lee	*Brunswick*	11
17	22	FROM A JACK TO A KING Ned Miller	*London*	17
20	23	HE'S SO FINE Chiffons	*Stateside*	9
23	24	HARVEST OF LOVE Benny Hill	*Pye*	4
34	25	ICE CREAM MAN Tornados	*Decca*	2
31	26	JUST LIKE ME Hollies	*Parlophone*	3
25	27	ANOTHER SATURDAY NIGHT Sam Cooke	*RCA*	4
28	28	CASABLANCA Kenny Ball and his Jazzmen	*Pye*	7
29	29	LITTLE BAND OF GOLD James Gilreath	*Pye*	6
-	30	SHY GIRL Mark Wynter	*Pye*	1
26	31	MY WAY Eddie Cochran	*Liberty*	7
24	32	BROWN-EYED HANDSOME MAN Buddy Holly	*Coral*	14
22	33	SAY I WON'T BE THERE Springfields	*Philips*	12
36	34	SUMMER HOLIDAY Cliff Richard	*Columbia*	17
-	35	LONELY BOY LONELY GUITAR Duane Eddy	*RCA*	1
33	36	FOOT TAPPER Shadows	*Columbia*	15
-	37	DON'T TRY TO CHANGE ME Crickets	*Liberty*	1
-	38	FOOLISH LITTLE GIRL Shirelles	*Stateside*	2
30	39	WALK LIKE A MAN Four Seasons	*Stateside*	11
-	40	IT'S BEEN NICE Everly Brothers	*Warner Brothers*	1

WEEK ENDING **20 JUNE 1963**

LW	TW	Title / Artist	Label	Wks
2	1	I LIKE IT Gerry and the Pacemakers	*Columbia*	4
1	2	FROM ME TO YOU Beatles	*Parlophone*	10
7	3	IF YOU GOTTA MAKE A FOOL OF SOMEBODY Freddie and the Dreamers	*Columbia*	7

June 1963

☐ Highest position disc reached ● Act's first ever week on chart

LW	TW	Title / Artist	Label	Wks
3	4	DO YOU WANT TO KNOW A SECRET? Billy J. Kramer and the Dakotas	*Parlophone*	7
4	5	WHEN WILL YOU SAY I LOVE YOU Billy Fury	*Decca*	6
8	6	TAKE THESE CHAINS FROM MY HEART Ray Charles	*HMV*	5
5	7	SCARLETT O'HARA Jet Harris and Tony Meehan	*Decca*	9
9	8	DECK OF CARDS Wink Martindale	*London*	9
12	9	ATLANTIS Shadows	*Columbia*	3
6	10	LUCKY LIPS Cliff Richard	*Columbia*	7
10	11	IN DREAMS Roy Orbison	*London*	16
17	12	FALLING Roy Orbison	*London*	4
16	13	BO DIDDLEY Buddy Holly	*Coral*	3
14	14	CAN'T GET USED TO LOSING YOU Andy Williams	*CBS*	13
13	15	TWO KINDS OF TEARDROPS Del Shannon	*London*	9
18	16	FORGET HIM Bobby Rydell	*Cameo-Parkway*	4
11	17	YOUNG LOVERS Paul and Paula	*Philips*	9
15	18	NOBODY'S DARLIN' BUT MINE Frank Ifield	*Columbia*	11
20	19	HOW DO YOU DO IT? Gerry and the Pacemakers	*Columbia*	15
24	20	HARVEST OF LOVE Benny Hill	*Pye*	5
22	21	FROM A JACK TO A KING Ned Miller	*London*	18
25	22	ICE CREAM MAN Tornados	*Decca*	3
27	23	ANOTHER SATURDAY NIGHT Sam Cooke	*RCA*	5
21	24	LOSING YOU Brenda Lee	*Brunswick*	12
19	25	PIPELINE Chantays	*London*	8
-	26	WELCOME TO MY WORLD Jim Reeves	*RCA*	1
26	27	JUST LIKE ME Hollies	*Parlophone*	4
30	28	SHY GIRL Mark Wynter	*Pye*	2
23	29	HE'S SO FINE Chiffons	*Stateside*	10
28	30	CASABLANCA Kenny Ball and his Jazzmen	*Pye*	8
29	31	LITTLE BAND OF GOLD James Gilreath	*Pye*	7
31	32	MY WAY Eddie Cochran	*Liberty*	8
40	33	IT'S BEEN NICE Everly Brothers	*Warner Brothers*	2
-	34	IT'S MY PARTY Lesley Gore ●	*Mercury*	1
-	35	RONDO Kenny Ball and his Jazzmen	*Pye*	1
-	36	INDIAN LOVE CALL Karl Denver	*Decca*	1
-	37	DA DOO RON RON Crystals	*London*	1
33	38	SAY I WON'T BE THERE Springfields	*Philips*	13
35	39	LONELY BOY LONELY GUITAR Duane Eddy	*RCA*	2
32	40	BROWN-EYED HANDSOME MAN Buddy Holly	*Coral*	15

WEEK ENDING **27 JUNE 1963**

LW	TW	Title / Artist	Label	Wks
1	1	I LIKE IT Gerry and the Pacemakers	*Columbia*	5
9	2	ATLANTIS Shadows	*Columbia*	4
3	3	IF YOU GOTTA MAKE A FOOL OF SOMEBODY Freddie and the Dreamers	*Columbia*	8
2	4	FROM ME TO YOU Beatles	*Parlophone*	11
6	5	TAKE THESE CHAINS FROM MY HEART Ray Charles	*HMV*	6
13	6	BO DIDDLEY Buddy Holly	*Coral*	4
4	7	DO YOU WANT TO KNOW A SECRET? Billy J. Kramer and the Dakotas	*Parlophone*	8
8	8	DECK OF CARDS Wink Martindale	*London*	10
12	9	FALLING Roy Orbison	*London*	5
5	10	WHEN WILL YOU SAY I LOVE YOU Billy Fury	*Decca*	7
7	11	SCARLETT O'HARA Jet Harris and Tony Meehan	*Decca*	10
10	12	LUCKY LIPS Cliff Richard	*Columbia*	8
11	13	IN DREAMS Roy Orbison	*London*	17
16	14	FORGET HIM Bobby Rydell	*Cameo-Parkway*	5
26	15	WELCOME TO MY WORLD Jim Reeves	*RCA*	2
15	16	TWO KINDS OF TEARDROPS Del Shannon	*London*	10
37	17	DA DOO RON RON Crystals	*London*	2
22	18	ICE CREAM MAN Tornados	*Decca*	4
14	19	CAN'T GET USED TO LOSING YOU Andy Williams	*CBS*	14
17	20	YOUNG LOVERS Paul and Paula	*Philips*	10
18	21	NOBODY'S DARLIN' BUT MINE Frank Ifield	*Columbia*	12
-	22	BOBBY TOMORROW Bobby Vee	*Liberty*	1
-	23	CONFESSIN' Frank Ifield	*Columbia*	1
34	24	IT'S MY PARTY Lesley Gore	*Mercury*	2
27	25	JUST LIKE ME Hollies	*Parlophone*	5
33	26	IT'S BEEN NICE Everly Brothers	*Warner Brothers*	3

■Six different records are at number two during the seven week run at number one by the Beatles first chart topper *From Me To You*. No Beatles' single will ever spend longer at the top (13.06.63) ■ The top four acts are all from Liverpool (13.06.63)■

June 1963

□ Highest position disc reached ● Act's first ever week on chart

LW	TW	Title / Artist	Label	Wks
19	27	HOW DO YOU DO IT? Gerry and the Pacemakers	Columbia	16
35	28	RONDO Kenny Ball and his Jazzmen	Pye	2
23	29	ANOTHER SATURDAY NIGHT Sam Cooke	RCA	6
-	30	HEY MAMA Frankie Vaughan	Philips	1
-	31	YOU CAN NEVER STOP ME LOVING YOU Kenny Lynch	HMV	1
25	32	PIPELINE Chantays	London	9
28	33	SHY GIRL Mark Wynter	Pye	3
36	34	INDIAN LOVE CALL Karl Denver	Decca	2
20	35	HARVEST OF LOVE Benny Hill	Pye	6
21	36	FROM A JACK TO A KING Ned Miller	London	19
24	37	LOSING YOU Brenda Lee	Brunswick	13
29	38	HE'S SO FINE Chiffons	Stateside	11
-	39	SWING THAT HAMMER Mike Cotton's Jazzmen ●	Columbia	1
32	40	MY WAY Eddie Cochran	Liberty	9

LW	TW	WEEK ENDING 4 JULY 1963		Wks
1	1	I LIKE IT Gerry and the Pacemakers	Columbia	6
2	2	ATLANTIS Shadows	Columbia	5
23	3	CONFESSIN' Frank Ifield	Columbia	2
3	4	IF YOU GOTTA MAKE A FOOL OF SOMEBODY Freddie and the Dreamers	Columbia	9
8	5	DECK OF CARDS Wink Martindale	London	11
5	6	TAKE THESE CHAINS FROM MY HEART Ray Charles	HMV	7
6	7	BO DIDDLEY Buddy Holly	Coral	5
4	8	FROM ME TO YOU Beatles	Parlophone	12
15	9	WELCOME TO MY WORLD Jim Reeves	RCA	3
9	10	FALLING Roy Orbison	London	6
7	11	DO YOU WANT TO KNOW A SECRET? Billy J. Kramer and the Dakotas	Parlophone	9
10	12	WHEN WILL YOU SAY I LOVE YOU Billy Fury	Decca	8
14	13	FORGET HIM Bobby Rydell	Cameo-Parkway	6
24	14	IT'S MY PARTY Lesley Gore	Mercury	3
13	15	IN DREAMS Roy Orbison	London	18
17	16	DA DOO RON RON Crystals	London	3
11	17	SCARLETT O'HARA Jet Harris and Tony Meehan	Decca	11
18	18	ICE CREAM MAN Tornados	Decca	5
12	19	LUCKY LIPS Cliff Richard	Columbia	9
16	20	TWO KINDS OF TEARDROPS Del Shannon	London	11
22	21	BOBBY TOMORROW Bobby Vee	Liberty	2
31	22	YOU CAN NEVER STOP ME LOVING YOU Kenny Lynch	HMV	2
20	23	YOUNG LOVERS Paul and Paula	Philips	11
28	24	RONDO Kenny Ball and his Jazzmen	Pye	3
19	25	CAN'T GET USED TO LOSING YOU Andy Williams	CBS	15
21	26	NOBODY'S DARLIN' BUT MINE Frank Ifield	Columbia	13
-	27	DEVIL IN DISGUISE Elvis Presley	RCA	1
32	28	PIPELINE Chantays	London	10
33	29	SHY GIRL Mark Wynter	Pye	4
26	30	IT'S BEEN NICE Everly Brothers	Warner Brothers	4
30	31	HEY MAMA Frankie Vaughan	Philips	2
34	32	INDIAN LOVE CALL Karl Denver	Decca	3
-	33	NATURE'S TIME FOR LOVE Joe Brown	Piccadilly	1
29	34	ANOTHER SATURDAY NIGHT Sam Cooke	RCA	7
-	35	SUKIYAKI Kyu Sakamoto ●	HMV	1
39	36	SWING THAT HAMMER Mike Cotton's Jazzmen	Columbia	2
25	37	JUST LIKE ME Hollies	Parlophone	6
-	38	AIN'T THAT A SHAME Four Seasons	Stateside	1
-	39	SWEETS FOR MY SWEET Searchers ●	Pye	1
27	40	HOW DO YOU DO IT? Gerry and the Pacemakers	Columbia	17

LW	TW	WEEK ENDING 11 JULY 1963		Wks
1	1	I LIKE IT Gerry and the Pacemakers	Columbia	7
3	2	CONFESSIN' Frank Ifield	Columbia	3
2	3	ATLANTIS Shadows	Columbia	6
7	4	BO DIDDLEY Buddy Holly	Coral	6
6	5	TAKE THESE CHAINS FROM MY HEART Ray Charles	HMV	8
9	6	WELCOME TO MY WORLD Jim Reeves	RCA	4
5	7	DECK OF CARDS Wink Martindale	London	12
4	8	IF YOU GOTTA MAKE A FOOL OF SOMEBODY Freddie and the Dreamers	Columbia	10
14	9	IT'S MY PARTY Lesley Gore	Mercury	4
27	10	DEVIL IN DISGUISE Elvis Presley	RCA	2
10	11	FALLING Roy Orbison	London	7
16	12	DA DOO RON RON Crystals	London	4
8	13	FROM ME TO YOU Beatles	Parlophone	13
11	14	DO YOU WANT TO KNOW A SECRET? Billy J. Kramer and the Dakotas	Parlophone	10
13	15	FORGET HIM Bobby Rydell	Cameo-Parkway	7
12	16	WHEN WILL YOU SAY I LOVE YOU Billy Fury	Decca	9
39	17	SWEETS FOR MY SWEET Searchers	Pye	2
22	18	YOU CAN NEVER STOP ME LOVING YOU Kenny Lynch	HMV	3
-	19	TWIST AND SHOUT Brian Poole and the Tremeloes ●	Decca	1
15	20	IN DREAMS Roy Orbison	London	19
21	21	BOBBY TOMORROW Bobby Vee	Liberty	3
18	22	ICE CREAM MAN Tornados	Decca	6
17	23	SCARLETT O'HARA Jet Harris and Tony Meehan	Decca	12
19	24	LUCKY LIPS Cliff Richard	Columbia	10
35	25	SUKIYAKI Kyu Sakamoto	HMV	2
31	26	HEY MAMA Frankie Vaughan	Philips	3
33	27	NATURE'S TIME FOR LOVE Joe Brown	Piccadilly	2
20	28	TWO KINDS OF TEARDROPS Del Shannon	London	12
24	29	RONDO Kenny Ball and his Jazzmen	Pye	4
-	30	IT'S TOO LATE NOW Swinging Blue Jeans ●	HMV	1
26	31	NOBODY'S DARLIN' BUT MINE Frank Ifield	Columbia	14
34	32	ANOTHER SATURDAY NIGHT Sam Cooke	RCA	8
23	33	YOUNG LOVERS Paul and Paula	Philips	12
32	34	INDIAN LOVE CALL Karl Denver	Decca	4
25	35	CAN'T GET USED TO LOSING YOU Andy Williams	CBS	16
-	36	FARAWAY PLACES Bachelors	Decca	1
-	37	WALKIN' TALL Adam Faith	Parlophone	1
37	38	JUST LIKE ME Hollies	Parlophone	7
29	39	SHY GIRL Mark Wynter	Pye	5
28	40	PIPELINE Chantays	London	11

LW	TW	WEEK ENDING 18 JULY 1963		Wks
2	1	CONFESSIN' Frank Ifield	Columbia	4
1	2	I LIKE IT Gerry and the Pacemakers	Columbia	8
10	3	DEVIL IN DISGUISE Elvis Presley	RCA	3
3	4	ATLANTIS Shadows	Columbia	7
12	5	DA DOO RON RON Crystals	London	5
5	6	TAKE THESE CHAINS FROM MY HEART Ray Charles	HMV	9
17	7	SWEETS FOR MY SWEET Searchers	Pye	3
4	8	BO DIDDLEY Buddy Holly	Coral	7
9	9	IT'S MY PARTY Lesley Gore	Mercury	5
7	10	DECK OF CARDS Wink Martindale	London	13
19	11	TWIST AND SHOUT Brian Poole and the Tremeloes	Decca	2
6	12	WELCOME TO MY WORLD Jim Reeves	RCA	5
11	13	FALLING Roy Orbison	London	8
8	14	IF YOU GOTTA MAKE A FOOL OF SOMEBODY Freddie and the Dreamers	Columbia	11
15	15	FORGET HIM Bobby Rydell	Cameo-Parkway	8
13	16	FROM ME TO YOU Beatles	Parlophone	14
25	17	SUKIYAKI Kyu Sakamoto	HMV	3
14	18	DO YOU WANT TO KNOW A SECRET? Billy J. Kramer and the Dakotas	Parlophone	11
16	19	WHEN WILL YOU SAY I LOVE YOU Billy Fury	Decca	10
18	20	YOU CAN NEVER STOP ME LOVING YOU Kenny Lynch	HMV	4
26	21	HEY MAMA Frankie Vaughan	Philips	4
20	22	IN DREAMS Roy Orbison	London	20
21	23	BOBBY TOMORROW Bobby Vee	Liberty	4
24	24	LUCKY LIPS Cliff Richard	Columbia	11
37	25	WALKIN' TALL Adam Faith	Parlophone	2
27	26	NATURE'S TIME FOR LOVE Joe Brown	Piccadilly	3
29	27	RONDO Kenny Ball and his Jazzmen	Pye	5
22	28	ICE CREAM MAN Tornados	Decca	7
23	29	SCARLETT O'HARA Jet Harris and Tony Meehan	Decca	13
-	30	I WONDER Brenda Lee	Brunswick	1
32	31	ANOTHER SATURDAY NIGHT Sam Cooke	RCA	9
-	32	THE CRUEL SEA Dakotas ●	Parlophone	1
34	33	INDIAN LOVE CALL Karl Denver	Decca	5

In these weeks ■ The top four singles are all on the Columbia label (04.07.63) ■ Frank Ifield becomes the seventh act in chart history to have at least four number ones. Two of the seven, Elvis Presley and the Shadows, are at numbers three and four (18.07.63) ■ Billy J. Kramer's backing group, the Dakotas, debut with their own instrumental hit, *The Cruel Sea*. Like Kenny Ball's *Casablanca* which dropped off the charts three weeks before, it has nothing to do with the film of the same name (18.07.63)■

LW	TW	Title	Artist	Label	Wks
38	34	JUST LIKE ME	Hollies	Parlophone	8
30	35	IT'S TOO LATE NOW	Swinging Blue Jeans	HMV	2
-	36	BY THE WAY	Big Three	Decca	1
-	37	THE GOOD LIFE	Tony Bennett	CBS	1
36	38	FARAWAY PLACES	Bachelors	Decca	2
-	39	IF YOU WANNA BE HAPPY	Jimmy Soul ●	Stateside	1
-	40	ONE FINE DAY	Chiffons	Stateside	1

WEEK ENDING 25 JULY 1963

LW	TW	Title	Artist	Label	Wks
1	1	CONFESSIN'	Frank Ifield	Columbia	5
3	2	DEVIL IN DISGUISE	Elvis Presley	RCA	4
7	3	SWEETS FOR MY SWEET	Searchers	Pye	4
4	4	ATLANTIS	Shadows	Columbia	8
11	5	TWIST AND SHOUT	Brian Poole and the Tremeloes	Decca	3
5	6	DA DOO RON RON	Crystals	London	6
2	7	I LIKE IT	Gerry and the Pacemakers	Columbia	9
6	8	TAKE THESE CHAINS FROM MY HEART	Ray Charles	HMV	10
9	9	IT'S MY PARTY	Lesley Gore	Mercury	6
10	10	DECK OF CARDS	Wink Martindale	London	14
12	11	WELCOME TO MY WORLD	Jim Reeves	RCA	6
17	12	SUKIYAKI	Kyu Sakamoto	HMV	4
8	13	BO DIDDLEY	Buddy Holly	Coral	8
13	14	FALLING	Roy Orbison	London	9
16	15	FROM ME TO YOU	Beatles	Parlophone	15
14	16	IF YOU GOTTA MAKE A FOOL OF SOMEBODY	Freddie and the Dreamers	Columbia	12
15	17	FORGET HIM	Bobby Rydell	Cameo-Parkway	9
20	18	YOU CAN NEVER STOP ME LOVING YOU	Kenny Lynch	HMV	5
18	19	DO YOU WANT TO KNOW A SECRET?	Billy J. Kramer and the Dakotas	Parlophone	12
30	20	I WONDER	Brenda Lee	Brunswick	2
21	21	HEY MAMA	Frankie Vaughan	Philips	5
19	22	WHEN WILL YOU SAY I LOVE YOU	Billy Fury	Decca	11
25	23	WALKIN' TALL	Adam Faith	Parlophone	3
24	24	LUCKY LIPS	Cliff Richard	Columbia	12
-	25	THEME FROM 'THE LEGION'S LAST PATROL'	Ken Thorne ●	HMV	1
32	26	THE CRUEL SEA	Dakotas	Parlophone	2
23	27	BOBBY TOMORROW	Bobby Vee	Liberty	5
-	28	I'LL NEVER GET OVER YOU	Johnny Kidd and the Pirates	HMV	1
-	29	WIPE OUT	Surfaris ●	London	1
22	30	IN DREAMS	Roy Orbison	London	21
28	31	ICE CREAM MAN	Tornados	Decca	8
26	32	NATURE'S TIME FOR LOVE	Joe Brown	Piccadilly	4
40	33	ONE FINE DAY	Chiffons	Stateside	2
-	34	TRUE LOVE	Richard Chamberlain	MGM	1
36	35	BY THE WAY	Big Three	Decca	2
37	36	THE GOOD LIFE	Tony Bennett	CBS	2
27	37	RONDO	Kenny Ball and his Jazzmen	Pye	6
-	38	GO GO GO	Chuck Berry	Pye	1
-	39	COME ON HOME	Springfields	Philips	1
31	40	ANOTHER SATURDAY NIGHT	Sam Cooke	RCA	10

WEEK ENDING 1 AUGUST 1963

LW	TW	Title	Artist	Label	Wks
2	1	DEVIL IN DISGUISE	Elvis Presley	RCA	5
1	2	CONFESSIN'	Frank Ifield	Columbia	6
3	3	SWEETS FOR MY SWEET	Searchers	Pye	5
5	4	TWIST AND SHOUT	Brian Poole and the Tremeloes	Decca	4
6	5	DA DOO RON RON	Crystals	London	7
7	6	I LIKE IT	Gerry and the Pacemakers	Columbia	10
4	7	ATLANTIS	Shadows	Columbia	9
12	8	SUKIYAKI	Kyu Sakamoto	HMV	5
11	9	WELCOME TO MY WORLD	Jim Reeves	RCA	7
9	10	IT'S MY PARTY	Lesley Gore	Mercury	7
8	11	TAKE THESE CHAINS FROM MY HEART	Ray Charles	HMV	11
18	12	YOU CAN NEVER STOP ME LOVING YOU	Kenny Lynch	HMV	6
10	13	DECK OF CARDS	Wink Martindale	London	15
20	14	I WONDER	Brenda Lee	Brunswick	3
25	15	THEME FROM 'THE LEGION'S LAST PATROL'	Ken Thorne	HMV	2

August 1963

□ Highest position disc reached ● Act's first ever week on chart

LW	TW	Title	Artist	Label	Wks
13	16	BO DIDDLEY	Buddy Holly	Coral	9
15	17	FROM ME TO YOU	Beatles	Parlophone	16
14	18	FALLING	Roy Orbison	London	10
-	19	IN SUMMER	Billy Fury	Decca	1
29	20	WIPE OUT	Surfaris	London	2
28	21	I'LL NEVER GET OVER YOU	Johnny Kidd and the Pirates	HMV	2
26	22	THE CRUEL SEA	Dakotas	Parlophone	3
16	23	IF YOU GOTTA MAKE A FOOL OF SOMEBODY	Freddie and the Dreamers	Columbia	13
17	24	FORGET HIM	Bobby Rydell	Cameo-Parkway	10
21	25	HEY MAMA	Frankie Vaughan	Philips	6
-	26	SO MUCH IN LOVE	Tymes ●	Cameo-Parkway	1
35	27	BY THE WAY	Big Three	Decca	3
23	28	WALKIN' TALL	Adam Faith	Parlophone	4
24	29	LUCKY LIPS	Cliff Richard	Columbia	13
19	30	DO YOU WANT TO KNOW A SECRET?	Billy J. Kramer and the Dakotas	Parlophone	13
34	31	TRUE LOVE	Richard Chamberlain	MGM	2
-	32	COME ON	Rolling Stones ●	Decca	1
39	33	COME ON HOME	Springfields	Philips	2
-	34	BAD TO ME	Billy J Kramer and the Dakotas	Parlophone	1
22	35	WHEN WILL YOU SAY I LOVE YOU	Billy Fury	Decca	12
27	36	BOBBY TOMORROW	Bobby Vee	Liberty	6
-	37	EIGHTEEN YELLOW ROSES	Bobby Darin	Capitol	1
31	38	ICE CREAM MAN	Tornados	Decca	9
36	39	THE GOOD LIFE	Tony Bennett	CBS	3
30	40	IN DREAMS	Roy Orbison	London	22

WEEK ENDING 8 AUGUST 1963

LW	TW	Title	Artist	Label	Wks
3	1	SWEETS FOR MY SWEET	Searchers	Pye	6
2	2	CONFESSIN'	Frank Ifield	Columbia	7
1	3	DEVIL IN DISGUISE	Elvis Presley	RCA	6
4	4	TWIST AND SHOUT	Brian Poole and the Tremeloes	Decca	5
5	5	DA DOO RON RON	Crystals	London	8
8	6	SUKIYAKI	Kyu Sakamoto	HMV	6
7	7	ATLANTIS	Shadows	Columbia	10
19	8	IN SUMMER	Billy Fury	Decca	2
6	9	I LIKE IT	Gerry and the Pacemakers	Columbia	11
12	10	YOU CAN NEVER STOP ME LOVING YOU	Kenny Lynch	HMV	7
34	11	BAD TO ME	Billy J Kramer and the Dakotas	Parlophone	2
10	12	IT'S MY PARTY	Lesley Gore	Mercury	8
20	13	WIPE OUT	Surfaris	London	3
15	14	THEME FROM 'THE LEGION'S LAST PATROL'	Ken Thorne	HMV	3
9	15	WELCOME TO MY WORLD	Jim Reeves	RCA	8
21	16	I'LL NEVER GET OVER YOU	Johnny Kidd and the Pirates	HMV	3
11	17	TAKE THESE CHAINS FROM MY HEART	Ray Charles	HMV	12
14	18	I WONDER	Brenda Lee	Brunswick	4
22	19	THE CRUEL SEA	Dakotas	Parlophone	4
17	20	FROM ME TO YOU	Beatles	Parlophone	17
16	21	BO DIDDLEY	Buddy Holly	Coral	10
27	22	BY THE WAY	Big Three	Decca	4
13	23	DECK OF CARDS	Wink Martindale	London	16
26	24	SO MUCH IN LOVE	Tymes	Cameo-Parkway	2
25	25	HEY MAMA	Frankie Vaughan	Philips	7
24	26	FORGET HIM	Bobby Rydell	Cameo-Parkway	11
18	27	FALLING	Roy Orbison	London	11
32	28	COME ON	Rolling Stones	Decca	2
-	29	ONE FINE DAY	Chiffons	Stateside	3
31	30	TRUE LOVE	Richard Chamberlain	MGM	3
23	31	IF YOU GOTTA MAKE A FOOL OF SOMEBODY	Freddie and the Dreamers	Columbia	14
28	32	WALKIN' TALL	Adam Faith	Parlophone	5
33	33	COME ON HOME	Springfields	Philips	3
-	34	I'M TELLING YOU NOW	Freddie and the Dreamers	Columbia	1
-	35	ONLY THE HEARTACHES	Houston Wells ●	Parlophone	1

■ Kyu Sakamoto's *Sukiyaki* reaches number six, out performing Kenny Ball's instrumental version earlier in the year, which peaked at number ten. Nevertheless, it becomes one of only a handful of songs to have been a Top Ten hit in both vocal and instrumental versions (08.08.63) ■ The Rolling Stones make their chart debut, with a Chuck Berry song (01.08.63) ■

August 1963

☐ Highest position disc reached ● Act's first ever week on chart

LW	TW	Title	Artist	Label	Wks
-	36	YOU DON'T HAVE TO BE A BABY TO CRY	Caravelles ●	Decca	1
29	37	LUCKY LIPS	Cliff Richard	Columbia	14
-	38	JUST LIKE EDDIE	Heinz ●	Decca	1
-	39	BLUE GIRL	Bruisers ●	Parlophone	1
36	40	BOBBY TOMORROW	Bobby Vee	Liberty	7

WEEK ENDING 15 AUGUST 1963

LW	TW	Title	Artist	Label	Wks
1	[1]	SWEETS FOR MY SWEET	Searchers	Pye	7
2	2	CONFESSIN'	Frank Ifield	Columbia	8
11	3	BAD TO ME	Billy J Kramer and the Dakotas	Parlophone	3
4	[4]	TWIST AND SHOUT	Brian Poole and the Tremeloes	Decca	6
3	5	DEVIL IN DISGUISE	Elvis Presley	RCA	7
8	6	IN SUMMER	Billy Fury	Decca	3
14	7	THEME FROM 'THE LEGION'S LAST PATROL'	Ken Thorne	HMV	4
5	8	DA DOO RON RON	Crystals	London	9
6	9	SUKIYAKI	Kyu Sakamoto	HMV	7
13	10	WIPE OUT	Surfaris	London	4
7	11	ATLANTIS	Shadows	Columbia	11
16	12	I'LL NEVER GET OVER YOU	Johnny Kidd and the Pirates	HMV	4
15	13	WELCOME TO MY WORLD	Jim Reeves	RCA	9
34	14	I'M TELLING YOU NOW	Freddie and the Dreamers	Columbia	2
10	15	YOU CAN NEVER STOP ME LOVING YOU	Kenny Lynch	HMV	8
9	16	I LIKE IT	Gerry and the Pacemakers	Columbia	12
18	17	I WONDER	Brenda Lee	Brunswick	5
17	18	TAKE THESE CHAINS FROM MY HEART	Ray Charles	HMV	13
12	19	IT'S MY PARTY	Lesley Gore	Mercury	9
36	20	YOU DON'T HAVE TO BE A BABY TO CRY	Caravelles	Decca	2
24	[21]	SO MUCH IN LOVE	Tymes	Cameo-Parkway	3
19	22	THE CRUEL SEA	Dakotas	Parlophone	5
22	23	BY THE WAY	Big Three	Decca	5
23	24	DECK OF CARDS	Wink Martindale	London	17
28	25	COME ON	Rolling Stones	Decca	3
38	26	JUST LIKE EDDIE	Heinz	Decca	2
20	27	FROM ME TO YOU	Beatles	Parlophone	18
-	28	THE GOOD LIFE	Tony Bennett	CBS	4
35	29	ONLY THE HEARTACHES	Houston Wells	Parlophone	2
29	30	ONE FINE DAY	Chiffons	Stateside	4
33	[31]	COME ON HOME	Springfields	Philips	4
39	32	BLUE GIRL	Bruisers	Parlophone	2
21	33	BO DIDDLEY	Buddy Holly	Coral	11
-	[34]	SURFIN' U.S.A.	Beach Boys ●	Capitol	1
26	35	FORGET HIM	Bobby Rydell	Cameo-Parkway	12
-	[36]	I'LL CUT YOUR TAIL OFF	John Leyton	HMV	1
-	[37]	CHRISTINE	Miss X ●	Ember	1
25	38	HEY MAMA	Frankie Vaughan	Philips	8
-	39	SURF CITY	Jan and Dean	Liberty	1
30	40	TRUE LOVE	Richard Chamberlain	MGM	4

WEEK ENDING 22 AUGUST 1963

LW	TW	Title	Artist	Label	Wks
3	[1]	BAD TO ME	Billy J Kramer and the Dakotas	Parlophone	4
1	2	SWEETS FOR MY SWEET	Searchers	Pye	8
14	3	I'M TELLING YOU NOW	Freddie and the Dreamers	Columbia	3
2	4	CONFESSIN'	Frank Ifield	Columbia	9
6	[5]	IN SUMMER	Billy Fury	Decca	4
7	6	THEME FROM 'THE LEGION'S LAST PATROL'	Ken Thorne	HMV	5
4	7	TWIST AND SHOUT	Brian Poole and the Tremeloes	Decca	7
8	8	DA DOO RON RON	Crystals	London	10
12	9	I'LL NEVER GET OVER YOU	Johnny Kidd and the Pirates	HMV	5
10	10	WIPE OUT	Surfaris	London	5
5	11	DEVIL IN DISGUISE	Elvis Presley	RCA	8
20	12	YOU DON'T HAVE TO BE A BABY TO CRY	Caravelles	Decca	3
13	13	WELCOME TO MY WORLD	Jim Reeves	RCA	10
9	14	SUKIYAKI	Kyu Sakamoto	HMV	8
17	15	I WONDER	Brenda Lee	Brunswick	6
11	16	ATLANTIS	Shadows	Columbia	12
15	17	YOU CAN NEVER STOP ME LOVING YOU	Kenny Lynch	HMV	9
26	18	JUST LIKE EDDIE	Heinz	Decca	3
18	19	TAKE THESE CHAINS FROM MY HEART	Ray Charles	HMV	14
16	20	I LIKE IT	Gerry and the Pacemakers	Columbia	13
22	21	THE CRUEL SEA	Dakotas	Parlophone	6
19	22	IT'S MY PARTY	Lesley Gore	Mercury	10
23	23	BY THE WAY	Big Three	Decca	6
25	24	COME ON	Rolling Stones	Decca	4
-	25	IT'S ALL IN THE GAME	Cliff Richard	Columbia	1
21	26	SO MUCH IN LOVE	Tymes	Cameo-Parkway	4
-	27	DANCE ON	Kathy Kirby ●	Decca	1
29	28	ONLY THE HEARTACHES	Houston Wells	Parlophone	3
24	29	DECK OF CARDS	Wink Martindale	London	18
39	30	SURF CITY	Jan and Dean	Liberty	2
32	[31]	BLUE GIRL	Bruisers	Parlophone	3
28	32	THE GOOD LIFE	Tony Bennett	CBS	5
-	33	STILL	Karl Denver	Decca	1
34	[34]	SURFIN' U.S.A.	Beach Boys	Capitol	2
30	35	ONE FINE DAY	Chiffons	Stateside	5
-	36	I WANT TO STAY HERE	Steve and Eydie ●	CBS	1
27	37	FROM ME TO YOU	Beatles	Parlophone	19
-	38	ACAPULCO 1922	Kenny Ball and his Jazzmen	Pye	1
31	39	COME ON HOME	Springfields	Philips	5
37	40	CHRISTINE	Miss X	Ember	2

WEEK ENDING 29 AUGUST 1963

LW	TW	Title	Artist	Label	Wks
1	[1]	BAD TO ME	Billy J Kramer and the Dakotas	Parlophone	5
3	[2]	I'M TELLING YOU NOW	Freddie and the Dreamers	Columbia	4
2	3	SWEETS FOR MY SWEET	Searchers	Pye	9
6	[4]	THEME FROM 'THE LEGION'S LAST PATROL'	Ken Thorne	HMV	6
10	[5]	WIPE OUT	Surfaris	London	6
9	6	I'LL NEVER GET OVER YOU	Johnny Kidd and the Pirates	HMV	6
12	7	YOU DON'T HAVE TO BE A BABY TO CRY	Caravelles	Decca	4
5	8	IN SUMMER	Billy Fury	Decca	5
4	9	CONFESSIN'	Frank Ifield	Columbia	10
25	10	IT'S ALL IN THE GAME	Cliff Richard	Columbia	2
18	11	JUST LIKE EDDIE	Heinz	Decca	4
-	12	SHE LOVES YOU	Beatles	Parlophone	1
7	13	TWIST AND SHOUT	Brian Poole and the Tremeloes	Decca	8
8	14	DA DOO RON RON	Crystals	London	11
11	15	DEVIL IN DISGUISE	Elvis Presley	RCA	9
14	16	SUKIYAKI	Kyu Sakamoto	HMV	9
27	17	DANCE ON	Kathy Kirby	Decca	2
13	18	WELCOME TO MY WORLD	Jim Reeves	RCA	11
36	19	I WANT TO STAY HERE	Steve and Eydie	CBS	2
21	20	THE CRUEL SEA	Dakotas	Parlophone	7
16	21	ATLANTIS	Shadows	Columbia	13
17	22	YOU CAN NEVER STOP ME LOVING YOU	Kenny Lynch	HMV	10
24	23	COME ON	Rolling Stones	Decca	5
23	24	BY THE WAY	Big Three	Decca	7
33	25	STILL	Karl Denver	Decca	2
28	26	ONLY THE HEARTACHES	Houston Wells	Parlophone	4
32	[27]	THE GOOD LIFE	Tony Bennett	CBS	6
30	28	SURF CITY	Jan and Dean	Liberty	3
20	29	I LIKE IT	Gerry and the Pacemakers	Columbia	14
15	30	I WONDER	Brenda Lee	Brunswick	7
19	31	TAKE THESE CHAINS FROM MY HEART	Ray Charles	HMV	15
38	32	ACAPULCO 1922	Kenny Ball and his Jazzmen	Pye	2
26	33	SO MUCH IN LOVE	Tymes	Cameo-Parkway	5
31	34	BLUE GIRL	Bruisers	Parlophone	4
22	35	IT'S MY PARTY	Lesley Gore	Mercury	11
29	36	DECK OF CARDS	Wink Martindale	London	19
-	37	TWO SILHOUETTES	Del Shannon	London	1
34	38	SURFIN' U.S.A.	Beach Boys	Capitol	3
-	39	I WANNA STAY HERE	Mike and Griff	Pye	1
-	40	WHISPERING	Bachelors	Decca	1

In these weeks ■ In the same week that the Tornados drop out of the Top 40 for the final time, group member Heinz makes his chart debut with his tribute to Eddie Cochran, *Just Like Eddie* (08.08.63) ■ Steve and Eydie are Steve Lawrence and Eydie Gormé, who thus become the first, but not the last, married couple to have hits both separately and together (22.08.63)■

September 1963

☐ Highest position disc reached ● Act's first ever week on chart

LW	TW	WEEK ENDING 5 SEPTEMBER 1963			Wks
1	☐1	BAD TO ME	Billy J Kramer and the Dakotas	Parlophone	6
2	☐2	I'M TELLING YOU NOW	Freddie and the Dreamers	Columbia	5
12	3	SHE LOVES YOU	Beatles	Parlophone	2
10	4	IT'S ALL IN THE GAME	Cliff Richard	Columbia	3
6	5	I'LL NEVER GET OVER YOU	Johnny Kidd and the Pirates	HMV	7
3	6	SWEETS FOR MY SWEET	Searchers	Pye	10
7	7	YOU DON'T HAVE TO BE A BABY TO CRY	Caravelles	Decca	5
5	8	WIPE OUT	Surfaris	London	7
11	9	JUST LIKE EDDIE	Heinz	Decca	5
19	10	I WANT TO STAY HERE	Steve and Eydie	CBS	3
4	11	THEME FROM 'THE LEGION'S LAST PATROL'	Ken Thorne	HMV	7
9	12	CONFESSIN'	Frank Ifield	Columbia	11
8	13	IN SUMMER	Billy Fury	Decca	6
17	14	DANCE ON	Kathy Kirby	Decca	3
13	15	TWIST AND SHOUT	Brian Poole and the Tremeloes	Decca	9
14	16	DA DOO RON RON	Crystals	London	12
25	17	STILL	Karl Denver	Decca	3
20	☐18	THE CRUEL SEA	Dakotas	Parlophone	8
16	19	SUKIYAKI	Kyu Sakamoto	HMV	10
15	20	DEVIL IN DISGUISE	Elvis Presley	RCA	10
18	21	WELCOME TO MY WORLD	Jim Reeves	RCA	12
26	☐22	ONLY THE HEARTACHES	Houston Wells	Parlophone	5
39	☐23	I WANNA STAY HERE	Mike and Griff	Pye	2
23	24	COME ON	Rolling Stones	Decca	6
21	25	ATLANTIS	Shadows	Columbia	14
28	☐26	SURF CITY	Jan and Dean	Liberty	4
32	☐27	ACAPULCO 1922	Kenny Ball and his Jazzmen	Pye	3
22	28	YOU CAN NEVER STOP ME LOVING YOU	Kenny Lynch	HMV	11
40	29	WHISPERING	Bachelors	Decca	2
24	30	BY THE WAY	Big Three	Decca	8
27	31	THE GOOD LIFE	Tony Bennett	CBS	7
30	32	I WONDER	Brenda Lee	Brunswick	8
37	33	TWO SILHOUETTES	Del Shannon	London	2
31	34	TAKE THESE CHAINS FROM MY HEART	Ray Charles	HMV	16
-	35	WISHING	Buddy Holly	Coral	1
38	36	SURFIN' U.S.A.	Beach Boys	Capitol	4
33	37	SO MUCH IN LOVE	Tymes	Cameo-Parkway	6
-	38	SEARCHIN'	Hollies	Parlophone	1
29	39	I LIKE IT	Gerry and the Pacemakers	Columbia	15
-	40	STILL	Ken Dodd	Columbia	1

LW	TW	WEEK ENDING 12 SEPTEMBER 1963			Wks
3	☐1	SHE LOVES YOU	Beatles	Parlophone	3
4	☐2	IT'S ALL IN THE GAME	Cliff Richard	Columbia	4
1	3	BAD TO ME	Billy J Kramer and the Dakotas	Parlophone	7
5	☐4	I'LL NEVER GET OVER YOU	Johnny Kidd and the Pirates	HMV	8
2	5	I'M TELLING YOU NOW	Freddie and the Dreamers	Columbia	6
7	☐6	YOU DON'T HAVE TO BE A BABY TO CRY	Caravelles	Decca	6
10	7	I WANT TO STAY HERE	Steve and Eydie	CBS	4
8	8	WIPE OUT	Surfaris	London	8
9	9	JUST LIKE EDDIE	Heinz	Decca	6
11	10	THEME FROM 'THE LEGION'S LAST PATROL'	Ken Thorne	HMV	8
14	☐11	DANCE ON	Kathy Kirby	Decca	4
6	12	SWEETS FOR MY SWEET	Searchers	Pye	11
17	☐13	STILL	Karl Denver	Decca	4
13	14	IN SUMMER	Billy Fury	Decca	7
12	15	CONFESSIN'	Frank Ifield	Columbia	12
-	16	APPLEJACK	Jet Harris and Tony Meehan	Decca	1
15	17	TWIST AND SHOUT	Brian Poole and the Tremeloes	Decca	10
35	18	WISHING	Buddy Holly	Coral	2
18	19	THE CRUEL SEA	Dakotas	Parlophone	9
16	20	DA DOO RON RON	Crystals	London	13
29	21	WHISPERING	Bachelors	Decca	3
24	22	COME ON	Rolling Stones	Decca	7
22	23	ONLY THE HEARTACHES	Houston Wells	Parlophone	6
23	24	I WANNA STAY HERE	Mike and Griff	Pye	3
19	25	SUKIYAKI	Kyu Sakamoto	HMV	11
26	☐26	SURF CITY	Jan and Dean	Liberty	5
33	27	TWO SILHOUETTES	Del Shannon	London	3
27	28	ACAPULCO 1922	Kenny Ball and his Jazzmen	Pye	4
21	29	WELCOME TO MY WORLD	Jim Reeves	RCA	13
20	30	DEVIL IN DISGUISE	Elvis Presley	RCA	11
31	31	THE GOOD LIFE	Tony Bennett	CBS	8
38	32	SEARCHIN'	Hollies	Parlophone	2
-	33	DO YOU LOVE ME?	Brian Poole and the Tremeloes	Decca	1
-	34	FRANKIE AND JOHNNY	Sam Cooke	RCA	1
25	35	ATLANTIS	Shadows	Columbia	15
-	36	IF I HAD A HAMMER	Trini Lopez ●	Reprise	1
40	37	STILL	Ken Dodd	Columbia	2
36	38	SURFIN' U.S.A.	Beach Boys	Capitol	5
28	39	YOU CAN NEVER STOP ME LOVING YOU	Kenny Lynch	HMV	12
30	40	BY THE WAY	Big Three	Decca	9

LW	TW	WEEK ENDING 19 SEPTEMBER 1963			Wks
1	☐1	SHE LOVES YOU	Beatles	Parlophone	4
2	☐2	IT'S ALL IN THE GAME	Cliff Richard	Columbia	5
3	3	BAD TO ME	Billy J Kramer and the Dakotas	Parlophone	8
7	4	I WANT TO STAY HERE	Steve and Eydie	CBS	5
4	5	I'LL NEVER GET OVER YOU	Johnny Kidd and the Pirates	HMV	9
5	6	I'M TELLING YOU NOW	Freddie and the Dreamers	Columbia	7
6	7	YOU DON'T HAVE TO BE A BABY TO CRY	Caravelles	Decca	7
9	8	JUST LIKE EDDIE	Heinz	Decca	7
16	9	APPLEJACK	Jet Harris and Tony Meehan	Decca	2
8	10	WIPE OUT	Surfaris	London	9
10	11	THEME FROM 'THE LEGION'S LAST PATROL'	Ken Thorne	HMV	9
33	12	DO YOU LOVE ME?	Brian Poole and the Tremeloes	Decca	2
18	13	WISHING	Buddy Holly	Coral	3
11	14	DANCE ON	Kathy Kirby	Decca	5
13	15	STILL	Karl Denver	Decca	5
36	16	IF I HAD A HAMMER	Trini Lopez	Reprise	2
12	17	SWEETS FOR MY SWEET	Searchers	Pye	12
21	☐18	WHISPERING	Bachelors	Decca	4
14	19	IN SUMMER	Billy Fury	Decca	8
15	20	CONFESSIN'	Frank Ifield	Columbia	13
22	☐21	COME ON	Rolling Stones	Decca	8
-	22	THEN HE KISSED ME	Crystals	London	1
27	☐23	TWO SILHOUETTES	Del Shannon	London	4
24	24	I WANNA STAY HERE	Mike and Griff	Pye	4
17	25	TWIST AND SHOUT	Brian Poole and the Tremeloes	Decca	11
32	26	SEARCHIN'	Hollies	Parlophone	3
19	27	THE CRUEL SEA	Dakotas	Parlophone	10
-	28	HELLO MUDDAH! HELLO FADDUH!	Allan Sherman ●	Warner Bros	1
26	29	SURF CITY	Jan and Dean	Liberty	6
34	☐30	FRANKIE AND JOHNNY	Sam Cooke	RCA	2
-	31	IT'S LOVE THAT REALLY COUNTS	Merseybeats ●	Fontana	1
-	32	SHINDIG	Shadows	Columbia	1
-	33	HELLO HEARTACHE GOODBYE LOVE	Little Peggy March ●	RCA	1
20	34	DA DOO RON RON	Crystals	London	14
31	35	THE GOOD LIFE	Tony Bennett	CBS	9
-	36	HELLO LITTLE GIRL	Fourmost ●	Parlophone	1
37	37	STILL	Ken Dodd	Columbia	3
23	38	ONLY THE HEARTACHES	Houston Wells	Parlophone	7
25	39	SUKIYAKI	Kyu Sakamoto	HMV	12
-	40	NO ONE	Ray Charles	HMV	1

LW	TW	WEEK ENDING 26 SEPTEMBER 1963			Wks
1	☐1	SHE LOVES YOU	Beatles	Parlophone	5
2	☐2	IT'S ALL IN THE GAME	Cliff Richard	Columbia	6

■The Beatles are top of the singles, EP and LP charts for three weeks from this week. In all, they will top all three charts at once 21 times between now and 6 May 1965 (12.09.63) ■ Three new chart acts all debut with titles beginning with the word 'Hello' (19.09.63)■

September 1963

☐ Highest position disc reached ● Act's first ever week on chart

LW	TW	Title	Artist	Label	Wks
4	3	I WANT TO STAY HERE	Steve and Eydie	*CBS*	6
9	4	APPLEJACK	Jet Harris and Tony Meehan	*Decca*	3
8	5	JUST LIKE EDDIE	Heinz	*Decca*	8
5	6	I'LL NEVER GET OVER YOU	Johnny Kidd and the Pirates	*HMV*	10
12	7	DO YOU LOVE ME?	Brian Poole and the Tremeloes	*Decca*	3
16	8	IF I HAD A HAMMER	Trini Lopez	*Reprise*	3
22	9	THEN HE KISSED ME	Crystals	*London*	2
13	10	WISHING	Buddy Holly	*Coral*	4
3	11	BAD TO ME	Billy J Kramer and the Dakotas	*Parlophone*	9
7	12	YOU DON'T HAVE TO BE A BABY TO CRY	Caravelles	*Decca*	8
10	13	WIPE OUT	Surfaris	*London*	10
6	14	I'M TELLING YOU NOW	Freddie and the Dreamers	*Columbia*	8
32	15	SHINDIG	Shadows	*Columbia*	2
14	16	DANCE ON	Kathy Kirby	*Decca*	6
-	17	BLUE BAYOU/MEAN WOMAN BLUES	Roy Orbison	*London*	1
15	18	STILL	Karl Denver	*Decca*	6
11	19	THEME FROM 'THE LEGION'S LAST PATROL'	Ken Thorne	*HMV*	10
26	20	SEARCHIN'	Hollies	*Parlophone*	4
18	21	WHISPERING	Bachelors	*Decca*	5
21	22	COME ON	Rolling Stones	*Decca*	9
28	23	HELLO MUDDAH! HELLO FADDUH!	Allan Sherman	*Warner Bros*	2
17	24	SWEETS FOR MY SWEET	Searchers	*Pye*	13
-	25	THE FIRST TIME	Adam Faith	*Parlophone*	1
19	26	IN SUMMER	Billy Fury	*Decca*	9
36	27	HELLO LITTLE GIRL	Fourmost	*Parlophone*	2
20	28	CONFESSIN'	Frank Ifield	*Columbia*	14
33	29	HELLO HEARTACHE GOODBYE LOVE	Little Peggy March	*RCA*	2
29	30	SURF CITY	Jan and Dean	*Liberty*	7
25	31	TWIST AND SHOUT	Brian Poole and the Tremeloes	*Decca*	12
23	32	TWO SILHOUETTES	Del Shannon	*London*	5
31	33	IT'S LOVE THAT REALLY COUNTS	Merseybeats	*Fontana*	2
27	34	THE CRUEL SEA	Dakotas	*Parlophone*	11
30	35	FRANKIE AND JOHNNY	Sam Cooke	*RCA*	3
40	36	NO ONE	Ray Charles	*HMV*	2
-	37	EVERYBODY	Tommy Roe	*HMV*	1
38	38	ONLY THE HEARTACHES	Houston Wells	*Parlophone*	8
35	39	THE GOOD LIFE	Tony Bennett	*CBS*	10
24	40	I WANNA STAY HERE	Mike and Griff	*Pye*	5

WEEK ENDING 3 OCTOBER 1963

LW	TW	Title	Artist	Label	Wks
1	1	SHE LOVES YOU	Beatles	*Parlophone*	6
7	2	DO YOU LOVE ME?	Brian Poole and the Tremeloes	*Decca*	4
9	3	THEN HE KISSED ME	Crystals	*London*	3
2	4	IT'S ALL IN THE GAME	Cliff Richard	*Columbia*	7
8	5	IF I HAD A HAMMER	Trini Lopez	*Reprise*	4
3	6	I WANT TO STAY HERE	Steve and Eydie	*CBS*	7
5	7	JUST LIKE EDDIE	Heinz	*Decca*	9
15	8	SHINDIG	Shadows	*Columbia*	3
17	9	BLUE BAYOU/MEAN WOMAN BLUES	Roy Orbison	*London*	2
6	10	I'LL NEVER GET OVER YOU	Johnny Kidd and the Pirates	*HMV*	11
4	11	APPLEJACK	Jet Harris and Tony Meehan	*Decca*	4
10	12	WISHING	Buddy Holly	*Coral*	5
25	13	THE FIRST TIME	Adam Faith	*Parlophone*	2
18	14	STILL	Karl Denver	*Decca*	7
11	15	BAD TO ME	Billy J Kramer and the Dakotas	*Parlophone*	10
12	16	YOU DON'T HAVE TO BE A BABY TO CRY	Caravelles	*Decca*	9
20	17	SEARCHIN'	Hollies	*Parlophone*	5
27	18	HELLO LITTLE GIRL	Fourmost	*Parlophone*	3
14	19	I'M TELLING YOU NOW	Freddie and the Dreamers	*Columbia*	9
23	20	HELLO MUDDAH! HELLO FADDUH!	Allan Sherman	*Warner Bros*	3
16	21	DANCE ON	Kathy Kirby	*Decca*	7
13	22	WIPE OUT	Surfaris	*London*	11
21	23	WHISPERING	Bachelors	*Decca*	6
19	24	THEME FROM 'THE LEGION'S LAST PATROL'	Ken Thorne	*HMV*	11
37	25	EVERYBODY	Tommy Roe	*HMV*	2
22	26	COME ON	Rolling Stones	*Decca*	10
-	27	I WHO HAVE NOTHING	Shirley Bassey	*Columbia*	1
-	28	SOMEBODY ELSE'S GIRL	Billy Fury	*Decca*	1
-	29	MEMPHIS TENNESSEE	Dave Berry and the Cruisers ●	*Decca*	1
29	30	HELLO HEARTACHE GOODBYE LOVE	Little Peggy March	*RCA*	3
33	31	IT'S LOVE THAT REALLY COUNTS	Merseybeats	*Fontana*	3
28	32	CONFESSIN'	Frank Ifield	*Columbia*	15
24	33	SWEETS FOR MY SWEET	Searchers	*Pye*	14
-	34	SALLY ANN	Joe Brown	*Piccadilly*	1
36	35	NO ONE	Ray Charles	*HMV*	3
26	36	IN SUMMER	Billy Fury	*Decca*	10
34	37	THE CRUEL SEA	Dakotas	*Parlophone*	12
30	38	SURF CITY	Jan and Dean	*Liberty*	8
35	39	FRANKIE AND JOHNNY	Sam Cooke	*RCA*	4
31	40	TWIST AND SHOUT	Brian Poole and the Tremeloes	*Decca*	13

WEEK ENDING 10 OCTOBER 1963

LW	TW	Title	Artist	Label	Wks
2	1	DO YOU LOVE ME?	Brian Poole and the Tremeloes	*Decca*	5
3	2	THEN HE KISSED ME	Crystals	*London*	4
1	3	SHE LOVES YOU	Beatles	*Parlophone*	7
5	4	IF I HAD A HAMMER	Trini Lopez	*Reprise*	5
9	5	BLUE BAYOU/MEAN WOMAN BLUES	Roy Orbison	*London*	3
8	6	SHINDIG	Shadows	*Columbia*	4
13	7	THE FIRST TIME	Adam Faith	*Parlophone*	3
4	8	IT'S ALL IN THE GAME	Cliff Richard	*Columbia*	8
11	9	APPLEJACK	Jet Harris and Tony Meehan	*Decca*	5
12	10	WISHING	Buddy Holly	*Coral*	6
6	11	I WANT TO STAY HERE	Steve and Eydie	*CBS*	8
17	12	SEARCHIN'	Hollies	*Parlophone*	6
27	13	I WHO HAVE NOTHING	Shirley Bassey	*Columbia*	2
18	14	HELLO LITTLE GIRL	Fourmost	*Parlophone*	4
7	15	JUST LIKE EDDIE	Heinz	*Decca*	10
25	16	EVERYBODY	Tommy Roe	*HMV*	3
20	17	HELLO MUDDAH! HELLO FADDUH!	Allan Sherman	*Warner Bros*	4
28	18	SOMEBODY ELSE'S GIRL	Billy Fury	*Decca*	2
14	19	STILL	Karl Denver	*Decca*	8
10	20	I'LL NEVER GET OVER YOU	Johnny Kidd and the Pirates	*HMV*	12
15	21	BAD TO ME	Billy J Kramer and the Dakotas	*Parlophone*	11
-	22	YOU'LL NEVER WALK ALONE	Gerry and the Pacemakers	*Columbia*	1
21	23	DANCE ON	Kathy Kirby	*Decca*	8
23	24	WHISPERING	Bachelors	*Decca*	7
-	25	LET IT ROCK/MEMPHIS TENNESSEE	Chuck Berry	*Pye*	1
31	26	IT'S LOVE THAT REALLY COUNTS	Merseybeats	*Fontana*	4
22	27	WIPE OUT	Surfaris	*London*	12
29	28	MEMPHIS TENNESSEE	Dave Berry and the Cruisers	*Decca*	2
16	29	YOU DON'T HAVE TO BE A BABY TO CRY	Caravelles	*Decca*	10
26	30	COME ON	Rolling Stones	*Decca*	11
19	31	I'M TELLING YOU NOW	Freddie and the Dreamers	*Columbia*	10
30	32	HELLO HEARTACHE GOODBYE LOVE	Little Peggy March	*RCA*	4
34	33	SALLY ANN	Joe Brown	*Piccadilly*	2
24	34	THEME FROM 'THE LEGION'S LAST PATROL'	Ken Thorne	*HMV*	12
-	35	STILL	Ken Dodd	*Columbia*	4
35	36	NO ONE	Ray Charles	*HMV*	4
39	37	FRANKIE AND JOHNNY	Sam Cooke	*RCA*	5
32	38	CONFESSIN'	Frank Ifield	*Columbia*	16
-	39	TWO SILHOUETTES	Del Shannon	*London*	6
-	40	THE GOOD LIFE	Tony Bennett	*CBS*	11

WEEK ENDING 17 OCTOBER 1963

LW	TW	Title	Artist	Label	Wks
1	1	DO YOU LOVE ME?	Brian Poole and the Tremeloes	*Decca*	6
2	2	THEN HE KISSED ME	Crystals	*London*	5
3	3	SHE LOVES YOU	Beatles	*Parlophone*	8

In these weeks ■ Brian Poole and the Tremeloes might have climbed higher than number four with *Twist And Shout* if that song had not also been the title track on the Beatles' first EP. They gain their revenge when they knock the Beatles off the top with their next single *Do You Love Me* (10.10.63)■

November 1963

□ Highest position disc reached ● Act's first ever week on chart

LW	TW	Title	Artist	Label	Wks
5	4	BLUE BAYOU/MEAN WOMAN BLUES	Roy Orbison	London	4
7	[5]	THE FIRST TIME	Adam Faith	Parlophone	4
4	6	IF I HAD A HAMMER	Trini Lopez	Reprise	6
22	7	YOU'LL NEVER WALK ALONE	Gerry and the Pacemakers	Columbia	2
6	8	SHINDIG	Shadows	Columbia	5
16	[9]	EVERYBODY	Tommy Roe	HMV	4
13	10	I WHO HAVE NOTHING	Shirley Bassey	Columbia	3
14	11	HELLO LITTLE GIRL	Fourmost	Parlophone	5
9	12	APPLEJACK	Jet Harris and Tony Meehan	Decca	6
12	13	SEARCHIN'	Hollies	Parlophone	7
11	14	I WANT TO STAY HERE	Steve and Eydie	CBS	9
10	15	WISHING	Buddy Holly	Coral	7
8	16	IT'S ALL IN THE GAME	Cliff Richard	Columbia	9
15	17	JUST LIKE EDDIE	Heinz	Decca	11
17	18	HELLO MUDDAH! HELLO FADDUH!	Allan Sherman	Warner Bros	5
18	19	SOMEBODY ELSE'S GIRL	Billy Fury	Decca	3
19	20	STILL	Karl Denver	Decca	9
25	21	LET IT ROCK/MEMPHIS TENNESSEE	Chuck Berry	Pye	2
23	22	DANCE ON	Kathy Kirby	Decca	9
20	23	I'LL NEVER GET OVER YOU	Johnny Kidd and the Pirates	HMV	13
21	24	BAD TO ME	Billy J Kramer and the Dakotas	Parlophone	12
28	25	MEMPHIS TENNESSEE	Dave Berry and the Cruisers	Decca	3
24	26	WHISPERING	Bachelors	Decca	8
26	27	IT'S LOVE THAT REALLY COUNTS	Merseybeats	Fontana	5
33	[28]	SALLY ANN	Joe Brown	Piccadilly	3
30	29	COME ON	Rolling Stones	Decca	12
29	30	YOU DON'T HAVE TO BE A BABY TO CRY	Caravelles	Decca	11
27	31	WIPE OUT	Surfaris	London	13
-	32	BE MY BABY	Ronettes ●	London	1
-	33	DO YOU LOVE ME?	Dave Clark Five ●	Columbia	1
-	[34]	PRETTY THING	Bo Diddley ●	Pye	1
-	35	MISS YOU	Jimmy Young	Columbia	1
35	36	STILL	Ken Dodd	Columbia	5
-	[37]	I'LL TAKE YOU HOME	Drifters	London	1
32	38	HELLO HEARTACHE GOODBYE LOVE	Little Peggy March	RCA	5
-	39	GIRL SANG THE BLUES	Everly Brothers	Warner Brothers	1
-	40	FOOLS RUSH IN	Rick Nelson	Brunswick	1

WEEK ENDING 24 OCTOBER 1963

LW	TW	Title	Artist	Label	Wks
1	[1]	DO YOU LOVE ME?	Brian Poole and the Tremeloes	Decca	7
7	2	YOU'LL NEVER WALK ALONE	Gerry and the Pacemakers	Columbia	3
3	3	SHE LOVES YOU	Beatles	Parlophone	9
2	4	THEN HE KISSED ME	Crystals	London	6
4	5	BLUE BAYOU/MEAN WOMAN BLUES	Roy Orbison	London	5
10	[6]	I WHO HAVE NOTHING	Shirley Bassey	Columbia	4
6	7	IF I HAD A HAMMER	Trini Lopez	Reprise	7
5	8	THE FIRST TIME	Adam Faith	Parlophone	5
11	[9]	HELLO LITTLE GIRL	Fourmost	Parlophone	6
21	10	LET IT ROCK/MEMPHIS TENNESSEE	Chuck Berry	Pye	3
9	11	EVERYBODY	Tommy Roe	HMV	5
8	12	SHINDIG	Shadows	Columbia	6
13	13	SEARCHIN'	Hollies	Parlophone	8
18	[14]	HELLO MUDDAH! HELLO FADDUH!	Allan Sherman	Warner Bros	6
12	15	APPLEJACK	Jet Harris and Tony Meehan	Decca	7
15	16	WISHING	Buddy Holly	Coral	8
20	17	STILL	Karl Denver	Decca	10
32	18	BE MY BABY	Ronettes	London	2
16	19	IT'S ALL IN THE GAME	Cliff Richard	Columbia	10
17	20	JUST LIKE EDDIE	Heinz	Decca	12
14	21	I WANT TO STAY HERE	Steve and Eydie	CBS	10
35	22	MISS YOU	Jimmy Young	Columbia	2
40	23	FOOLS RUSH IN	Rick Nelson	Brunswick	2
19	24	SOMEBODY ELSE'S GIRL	Billy Fury	Decca	4
-	25	MULE TRAIN	Frank Ifield	Columbia	1
27	26	IT'S LOVE THAT REALLY COUNTS	Merseybeats	Fontana	6
39	27	GIRL SANG THE BLUES	Everly Brothers	Warner Bros	2
-	28	BLOWING IN THE WIND	Peter Paul and Mary ●	Warner Bros	1
-	29	SUGAR AND SPICE	Searchers	Pye	1
33	[30]	DO YOU LOVE ME?	Dave Clark Five	Columbia	2
25	31	MEMPHIS TENNESSEE	Dave Berry and the Cruisers	Decca	4
22	32	DANCE ON	Kathy Kirby	Decca	10
-	33	BOSSA NOVA BABY	Elvis Presley	RCA	1
-	34	GUILTY	Jim Reeves	RCA	1
28	35	SALLY ANN	Joe Brown	Piccadilly	4
23	36	I'LL NEVER GET OVER YOU	Johnny Kidd and the Pirates	HMV	14
37	[37]	I'LL TAKE YOU HOME	Drifters	London	2
26	38	WHISPERING	Bachelors	Decca	9
36	39	STILL	Ken Dodd	Columbia	6
-	40	LOVE OF THE LOVED	Cilla Black ●	Parlophone	1

WEEK ENDING 31 OCTOBER 1963

LW	TW	Title	Artist	Label	Wks
2	[1]	YOU'LL NEVER WALK ALONE	Gerry and the Pacemakers	Columbia	4
3	2	SHE LOVES YOU	Beatles	Parlophone	10
1	3	DO YOU LOVE ME?	Brian Poole and the Tremeloes	Decca	8
5	4	BLUE BAYOU/MEAN WOMAN BLUES	Roy Orbison	London	6
4	5	THEN HE KISSED ME	Crystals	London	7
7	6	IF I HAD A HAMMER	Trini Lopez	Reprise	8
6	7	I WHO HAVE NOTHING	Shirley Bassey	Columbia	5
29	8	SUGAR AND SPICE	Searchers	Pye	2
10	9	LET IT ROCK/MEMPHIS TENNESSEE	Chuck Berry	Pye	4
8	10	THE FIRST TIME	Adam Faith	Parlophone	6
18	11	BE MY BABY	Ronettes	London	3
9	12	HELLO LITTLE GIRL	Fourmost	Parlophone	7
33	[13]	BOSSA NOVA BABY	Elvis Presley	RCA	2
14	[14]	HELLO MUDDAH! HELLO FADDUH!	Allan Sherman	Warner Bros	7
11	15	EVERYBODY	Tommy Roe	HMV	6
23	16	FOOLS RUSH IN	Rick Nelson	Brunswick	3
22	17	MISS YOU	Jimmy Young	Columbia	3
12	18	SHINDIG	Shadows	Columbia	7
13	19	SEARCHIN'	Hollies	Parlophone	9
17	20	STILL	Karl Denver	Decca	11
28	21	BLOWING IN THE WIND	Peter Paul and Mary	Warner Bros	2
15	22	APPLEJACK	Jet Harris and Tony Meehan	Decca	8
16	23	WISHING	Buddy Holly	Coral	9
31	24	MEMPHIS TENNESSEE	Dave Berry and the Cruisers	Decca	5
27	[25]	GIRL SANG THE BLUES	Everly Brothers	Warner Bros	3
25	26	MULE TRAIN	Frank Ifield	Columbia	2
20	27	JUST LIKE EDDIE	Heinz	Decca	13
26	28	IT'S LOVE THAT REALLY COUNTS	Merseybeats	Fontana	7
34	[29]	GUILTY	Jim Reeves	RCA	2
-	30	SUE'S GONNA BE MINE	Del Shannon	London	1
24	31	SOMEBODY ELSE'S GIRL	Billy Fury	Decca	5
21	32	I WANT TO STAY HERE	Steve and Eydie	CBS	11
19	33	IT'S ALL IN THE GAME	Cliff Richard	Columbia	11
-	34	SWEET IMPOSSIBLE YOU	Brenda Lee	Brunswick	1
40	[35]	LOVE OF THE LOVED	Cilla Black	Parlophone	2
30	36	DO YOU LOVE ME?	Dave Clark Five	Columbia	3
39	37	STILL	Ken Dodd	Columbia	7
37	38	I'LL TAKE YOU HOME	Drifters	London	3
32	39	DANCE ON	Kathy Kirby	Decca	11
35	40	SALLY ANN	Joe Brown	Piccadilly	5

WEEK ENDING 7 NOVEMBER 1963

LW	TW	Title	Artist	Label	Wks
1	[1]	YOU'LL NEVER WALK ALONE	Gerry and the Pacemakers	Columbia	5
2	2	SHE LOVES YOU	Beatles	Parlophone	11
4	[3]	BLUE BAYOU/MEAN WOMAN BLUES	Roy Orbison	London	7
8	4	SUGAR AND SPICE	Searchers	Pye	3
3	5	DO YOU LOVE ME?	Brian Poole and the Tremeloes	Decca	9
11	6	BE MY BABY	Ronettes	London	4

■Jimmy Young is back in the charts for the first time since May 1957 (17.10.63) ■ Nine weeks after Buddy Holly's version of his autobiographical song drops off the chart, Bo Diddley makes his chart debut in his own right (17.10.63) ■ The first Bob Dylan song hits the chart - Peter, Paul and Mary's version of his *Blowing In The Wind* (24.10.63) ■ Gerry and the Pacemakers achieve a hat-trick of number ones with their first three releases, a feat which will not be duplicated until 1984 (31.10.63)■

November 1963

□ Highest position disc reached ● Act's first ever week on chart

LW	TW	Title	Artist	Label	Wks
9	7	LET IT ROCK/MEMPHIS TENNESSEE	Chuck Berry	*Pye*	5
7	8	I WHO HAVE NOTHING	Shirley Bassey	*Columbia*	6
5	9	THEN HE KISSED ME	Crystals	*London*	8
6	10	IF I HAD A HAMMER	Trini Lopez	*Reprise*	9
10	11	THE FIRST TIME	Adam Faith	*Parlophone*	7
16	[12]	FOOLS RUSH IN	Rick Nelson	*Brunswick*	4
12	13	HELLO LITTLE GIRL	Fourmost	*Parlophone*	8
13	14	BOSSA NOVA BABY	Elvis Presley	*RCA*	3
17	[15]	MISS YOU	Jimmy Young	*Columbia*	4
21	16	BLOWING IN THE WIND	Peter Paul and Mary	*Warner Bros*	3
15	17	EVERYBODY	Tommy Roe	*HMV*	7
18	18	SHINDIG	Shadows	*Columbia*	8
24	[19]	MEMPHIS TENNESSEE	Dave Berry and the Cruisers	*Decca*	6
20	20	STILL	Karl Denver	*Decca*	12
30	[21]	SUE'S GONNA BE MINE	Del Shannon	*London*	2
26	[22]	MULE TRAIN	Frank Ifield	*Columbia*	3
-	23	DON'T TALK TO HIM	Cliff Richard	*Columbia*	1
28	[24]	IT'S LOVE THAT REALLY COUNTS	Merseybeats	*Fontana*	8
25	[25]	GIRL SANG THE BLUES	Everly Brothers	*Warner Bros*	4
14	26	HELLO MUDDAH! HELLO FADDUH!	Allan Sherman	*Warner Bros*	8
19	27	SEARCHIN'	Hollies	*Parlophone*	10
-	28	MARIA ELENA	Los Indios Tabajaras ●	*RCA*	1
29	[29]	GUILTY	Jim Reeves	*RCA*	3
-	30	SECRET LOVE	Kathy Kirby	*Decca*	1
22	31	APPLEJACK	Jet Harris and Tony Meehan	*Decca*	9
33	32	IT'S ALL IN THE GAME	Cliff Richard	*Columbia*	12
34	33	SWEET IMPOSSIBLE YOU	Brenda Lee	*Brunswick*	2
-	34	I'LL KEEP YOU SATISFIED	Billy J Kramer and the Dakotas	*Parlophone*	1
27	35	JUST LIKE EDDIE	Heinz	*Decca*	14
23	36	WISHING	Buddy Holly	*Coral*	10
39	37	DANCE ON	Kathy Kirby	*Decca*	12
31	38	SOMEBODY ELSE'S GIRL	Billy Fury	*Decca*	6
-	39	YOU WERE MADE FOR ME	Freddie and the Dreamers	*Columbia*	1
-	40	BUSTED	Ray Charles	*HMV*	1

WEEK ENDING 14 NOVEMBER 1963

LW	TW	Title	Artist	Label	Wks
1	[1]	YOU'LL NEVER WALK ALONE	Gerry and the Pacemakers	*Columbia*	6
4	[2]	SUGAR AND SPICE	Searchers	*Pye*	4
2	3	SHE LOVES YOU	Beatles	*Parlophone*	12
3	4	BLUE BAYOU/MEAN WOMAN BLUES	Roy Orbison	*London*	8
6	5	BE MY BABY	Ronettes	*London*	5
7	[6]	LET IT ROCK/MEMPHIS TENNESSEE	Chuck Berry	*Pye*	6
23	7	DON'T TALK TO HIM	Cliff Richard	*Columbia*	2
5	8	DO YOU LOVE ME?	Brian Poole and the Tremeloes	*Decca*	10
8	9	I WHO HAVE NOTHING	Shirley Bassey	*Columbia*	7
9	10	THEN HE KISSED ME	Crystals	*London*	9
34	11	I'LL KEEP YOU SATISFIED	Billy J Kramer and the Dakotas	*Parlophone*	2
30	12	SECRET LOVE	Kathy Kirby	*Decca*	2
10	13	IF I HAD A HAMMER	Trini Lopez	*Reprise*	10
11	14	THE FIRST TIME	Adam Faith	*Parlophone*	8
12	15	FOOLS RUSH IN	Rick Nelson	*Brunswick*	5
28	16	MARIA ELENA	Los Indios Tabajaras	*RCA*	2
16	17	BLOWING IN THE WIND	Peter Paul and Mary	*Warner Bros*	4
14	18	BOSSA NOVA BABY	Elvis Presley	*RCA*	4
15	19	MISS YOU	Jimmy Young	*Columbia*	5
13	20	HELLO LITTLE GIRL	Fourmost	*Parlophone*	9
21	[21]	SUE'S GONNA BE MINE	Del Shannon	*London*	3
39	22	YOU WERE MADE FOR ME	Freddie and the Dreamers	*Columbia*	2
17	23	EVERYBODY	Tommy Roe	*HMV*	8
40	24	BUSTED	Ray Charles	*HMV*	2
19	25	MEMPHIS TENNESSEE	Dave Berry and the Cruisers	*Decca*	7
27	26	SEARCHIN'	Hollies	*Parlophone*	11
18	27	SHINDIG	Shadows	*Columbia*	9
33	[28]	SWEET IMPOSSIBLE YOU	Brenda Lee	*Brunswick*	3
26	29	HELLO MUDDAH! HELLO FADDUH!	Allan Sherman	*Warner Bros*	9
25	30	GIRL SANG THE BLUES	Everly Brothers	*Warner Bros*	5
24	31	IT'S LOVE THAT REALLY COUNTS	Merseybeats	*Fontana*	9
-	32	IT'S ALMOST TOMORROW	Mark Wynter	*Pye*	1
20	33	STILL	Karl Denver	*Decca*	13
-	[34]	RED SAILS IN THE SUNSET	Fats Domino	*HMV*	1
-	35	DEEP PURPLE	Nino Tempo and April Stevens ●	*London*	1
22	36	MULE TRAIN	Frank Ifield	*Columbia*	4
-	[37]	WHAT DO YOU SAY	Chubby Checker	*Cameo-Parkway*	1
31	38	APPLEJACK	Jet Harris and Tony Meehan	*Decca*	10
-	39	LOVE OF THE LOVED	Cilla Black	*Parlophone*	3
35	40	JUST LIKE EDDIE	Heinz	*Decca*	15

WEEK ENDING 21 NOVEMBER 1963

LW	TW	Title	Artist	Label	Wks
1	[1]	YOU'LL NEVER WALK ALONE	Gerry and the Pacemakers	*Columbia*	7
3	2	SHE LOVES YOU	Beatles	*Parlophone*	13
2	3	SUGAR AND SPICE	Searchers	*Pye*	5
5	[4]	BE MY BABY	Ronettes	*London*	6
7	5	DON'T TALK TO HIM	Cliff Richard	*Columbia*	3
12	6	SECRET LOVE	Kathy Kirby	*Decca*	3
4	7	BLUE BAYOU/MEAN WOMAN BLUES	Roy Orbison	*London*	9
9	8	I WHO HAVE NOTHING	Shirley Bassey	*Columbia*	8
11	9	I'LL KEEP YOU SATISFIED	Billy J Kramer and the Dakotas	*Parlophone*	3
6	10	LET IT ROCK/MEMPHIS TENNESSEE	Chuck Berry	*Pye*	7
22	11	YOU WERE MADE FOR ME	Freddie and the Dreamers	*Columbia*	3
8	12	DO YOU LOVE ME?	Brian Poole and the Tremeloes	*Decca*	11
16	13	MARIA ELENA	Los Indios Tabajaras	*RCA*	3
10	14	THEN HE KISSED ME	Crystals	*London*	10
13	15	IF I HAD A HAMMER	Trini Lopez	*Reprise*	11
15	16	FOOLS RUSH IN	Rick Nelson	*Brunswick*	6
17	17	BLOWING IN THE WIND	Peter Paul and Mary	*Warner Bros*	5
19	18	MISS YOU	Jimmy Young	*Columbia*	6
14	19	THE FIRST TIME	Adam Faith	*Parlophone*	9
18	20	BOSSA NOVA BABY	Elvis Presley	*RCA*	5
24	[21]	BUSTED	Ray Charles	*HMV*	3
32	22	IT'S ALMOST TOMORROW	Mark Wynter	*Pye*	2
20	23	HELLO LITTLE GIRL	Fourmost	*Parlophone*	10
21	24	SUE'S GONNA BE MINE	Del Shannon	*London*	4
33	25	STILL	Karl Denver	*Decca*	14
23	26	EVERYBODY	Tommy Roe	*HMV*	9
-	27	FROM RUSSIA WITH LOVE	Matt Monro	*Parlophone*	1
25	28	MEMPHIS TENNESSEE	Dave Berry and the Cruisers	*Decca*	8
35	29	DEEP PURPLE	Nino Tempo and April Stevens	*London*	2
27	30	SHINDIG	Shadows	*Columbia*	10
28	31	SWEET IMPOSSIBLE YOU	Brenda Lee	*Brunswick*	4
-	32	I WANNA BE YOUR MAN	Rolling Stones	*Decca*	1
26	33	SEARCHIN'	Hollies	*Parlophone*	12
30	34	GIRL SANG THE BLUES	Everly Brothers	*Warner Bros*	6
34	35	RED SAILS IN THE SUNSET	Fats Domino	*HMV*	2
31	36	IT'S LOVE THAT REALLY COUNTS	Merseybeats	*Fontana*	10
36	37	MULE TRAIN	Frank Ifield	*Columbia*	5
-	38	GLAD ALL OVER	Dave Clark Five	*Columbia*	1
-	39	IF I RULED THE WORLD	Harry Secombe	*Philips*	1
38	40	APPLEJACK	Jet Harris and Tony Meehan	*Decca*	11

WEEK ENDING 28 NOVEMBER 1963

LW	TW	Title	Artist	Label	Wks
2	[1]	SHE LOVES YOU	Beatles	*Parlophone*	14
1	2	YOU'LL NEVER WALK ALONE	Gerry and the Pacemakers	*Columbia*	8
5	3	DON'T TALK TO HIM	Cliff Richard	*Columbia*	4
9	[4]	I'LL KEEP YOU SATISFIED	Billy J Kramer and the Dakotas	*Parlophone*	4
6	5	SECRET LOVE	Kathy Kirby	*Decca*	4
3	6	SUGAR AND SPICE	Searchers	*Pye*	6
11	7	YOU WERE MADE FOR ME	Freddie and the Dreamers	*Columbia*	4

In these weeks ■ Harry Secombe's first solo hit since December 1955 enters the chart. It is the hit song from his successful London musical 'Pickwick' (21.11.63) ■ The Beatles set further chart records by climbing back to number one with *She Loves You* after a seven week gap, a gap not beaten until 1991 (28.11.63)■

December 1963

□ Highest position disc reached ● Act's first ever week on chart

LW	TW	Title	Artist	Label	Wks
4	8	BE MY BABY	Ronettes	London	7
7	9	BLUE BAYOU/MEAN WOMAN BLUES	Roy Orbison	London	10
13	10	MARIA ELENA	Los Indios Tabajaras	RCA	4
8	11	I WHO HAVE NOTHING	Shirley Bassey	Columbia	9
10	12	LET IT ROCK/MEMPHIS TENNESSEE	Chuck Berry	Pye	8
17	[13]	BLOWING IN THE WIND	Peter Paul and Mary	Warner Bros	6
22	14	IT'S ALMOST TOMORROW	Mark Wynter	Pye	3
15	15	IF I HAD A HAMMER	Trini Lopez	Reprise	12
12	16	DO YOU LOVE ME?	Brian Poole and the Tremeloes	Decca	12
14	17	THEN HE KISSED ME	Crystals	London	11
16	18	FOOLS RUSH IN	Rick Nelson	Brunswick	7
38	19	GLAD ALL OVER	Dave Clark Five	Columbia	2
27	[20]	FROM RUSSIA WITH LOVE	Matt Monro	Parlophone	2
29	21	DEEP PURPLE	Nino Tempo and April Stevens	London	3
18	22	MISS YOU	Jimmy Young	Columbia	7
19	23	THE FIRST TIME	Adam Faith	Parlophone	10
21	24	BUSTED	Ray Charles	HMV	4
-	25	I ONLY WANT TO BE WITH YOU	Dusty Springfield ●	Philips	1
25	26	STILL	Karl Denver	Decca	15
26	27	EVERYBODY	Tommy Roe	HMV	10
20	28	BOSSA NOVA BABY	Elvis Presley	RCA	6
-	29	STAY	Hollies	Parlophone	1
32	30	I WANNA BE YOUR MAN	Rolling Stones	Decca	2
-	31	MONEY	Bern Elliott and the Fenmen ●	Decca	1
-	32	HUNGRY FOR LOVE	Johnny Kidd and the Pirates	HMV	1
24	33	SUE'S GONNA BE MINE	Del Shannon	London	5
23	34	HELLO LITTLE GIRL	Fourmost	Parlophone	11
39	35	IF I RULED THE WORLD	Harry Secombe	Philips	2
31	36	SWEET IMPOSSIBLE YOU	Brenda Lee	Brunswick	5
30	37	SHINDIG	Shadows	Columbia	11
34	38	GIRL SANG THE BLUES	Everly Brothers	Warner Bros	7
35	39	RED SAILS IN THE SUNSET	Fats Domino	HMV	3
-	40	YESTERDAY'S GONE	Chad Stuart and Jeremy Clyde ●	Ember	1

WEEK ENDING 5 DECEMBER 1963

LW	TW	Title	Artist	Label	Wks
1	[1]	SHE LOVES YOU	Beatles	Parlophone	15
3	[2]	DON'T TALK TO HIM	Cliff Richard	Columbia	5
7	[3]	YOU WERE MADE FOR ME	Freddie and the Dreamers	Columbia	5
2	4	YOU'LL NEVER WALK ALONE	Gerry and the Pacemakers	Columbia	9
5	5	SECRET LOVE	Kathy Kirby	Decca	5
4	6	I'LL KEEP YOU SATISFIED	Billy J Kramer and the Dakotas	Parlophone	5
10	7	MARIA ELENA	Los Indios Tabajaras	RCA	5
19	8	GLAD ALL OVER	Dave Clark Five	Columbia	3
25	9	I ONLY WANT TO BE WITH YOU	Dusty Springfield	Philips	2
-	10	I WANT TO HOLD YOUR HAND	Beatles	Parlophone	1
8	11	BE MY BABY	Ronettes	London	8
14	[12]	IT'S ALMOST TOMORROW	Mark Wynter	Pye	4
6	13	SUGAR AND SPICE	Searchers	Pye	7
9	14	BLUE BAYOU/MEAN WOMAN BLUES	Roy Orbison	London	11
11	15	I WHO HAVE NOTHING	Shirley Bassey	Columbia	10
30	16	I WANNA BE YOUR MAN	Rolling Stones	Decca	3
21	[17]	DEEP PURPLE	Nino Tempo and April Stevens	London	4
12	18	LET IT ROCK/MEMPHIS TENNESSEE	Chuck Berry	Pye	9
13	19	BLOWING IN THE WIND	Peter Paul and Mary	Warner Bros	7
32	[20]	HUNGRY FOR LOVE	Johnny Kidd and the Pirates	HMV	2
20	21	FROM RUSSIA WITH LOVE	Matt Monro	Parlophone	3
15	22	IF I HAD A HAMMER	Trini Lopez	Reprise	13
31	23	MONEY	Bern Elliott and the Fenmen	Decca	2
-	24	DOMINIQUE	Singing Nun ●	Philips	1
16	25	DO YOU LOVE ME?	Brian Poole and the Tremeloes	Decca	13
24	26	BUSTED	Ray Charles	HMV	5
29	27	STAY	Hollies	Parlophone	2
-	28	GERONIMO	Shadows	Columbia	1
18	29	FOOLS RUSH IN	Rick Nelson	Brunswick	8
22	30	MISS YOU	Jimmy Young	Columbia	8
35	31	IF I RULED THE WORLD	Harry Secombe	Philips	3
17	32	THEN HE KISSED ME	Crystals	London	12
-	33	TWENTY FOUR HOURS FROM TULSA	Gene Pitney	United Artists	1
-	34	AT THE PALACE (PARTS 1 AND 2)	Wilfred Brambell and Harry H Corbett ●	Pye	1
-	35	SWINGING ON A STAR	Big Dee Irwin ●	Colpix	1
-	36	I CAN DANCE	Brian Poole and the Tremeloes	Decca	1
-	37	ALL I WANT FOR CHRISTMAS IS A BEATLE	Dora Bryan ●	Fontana	1
-	38	COUNTRY BOY	Heinz	Decca	1
33	39	SUE'S GONNA BE MINE	Del Shannon	London	6
-	40	MEMPHIS TENNESSEE	Dave Berry and the Cruisers	Decca	9

WEEK ENDING 12 DECEMBER 1963

LW	TW	Title	Artist	Label	Wks
10	[1]	I WANT TO HOLD YOUR HAND	Beatles	Parlophone	2
1	2	SHE LOVES YOU	Beatles	Parlophone	16
3	[3]	YOU WERE MADE FOR ME	Freddie and the Dreamers	Columbia	6
5	[4]	SECRET LOVE	Kathy Kirby	Decca	6
7	[5]	MARIA ELENA	Los Indios Tabajaras	RCA	6
2	6	DON'T TALK TO HIM	Cliff Richard	Columbia	6
9	7	I ONLY WANT TO BE WITH YOU	Dusty Springfield	Philips	3
4	8	YOU'LL NEVER WALK ALONE	Gerry and the Pacemakers	Columbia	10
8	9	GLAD ALL OVER	Dave Clark Five	Columbia	4
24	10	DOMINIQUE	Singing Nun	Philips	2
6	11	I'LL KEEP YOU SATISFIED	Billy J Kramer and the Dakotas	Parlophone	6
15	12	I WHO HAVE NOTHING	Shirley Bassey	Columbia	11
28	13	GERONIMO	Shadows	Columbia	2
12	14	IT'S ALMOST TOMORROW	Mark Wynter	Pye	5
16	15	I WANNA BE YOUR MAN	Rolling Stones	Decca	4
14	16	BLUE BAYOU/MEAN WOMAN BLUES	Roy Orbison	London	12
27	17	STAY	Hollies	Parlophone	3
17	18	DEEP PURPLE	Nino Tempo and April Stevens	London	5
23	19	MONEY	Bern Elliott and the Fenmen	Decca	3
33	20	TWENTY FOUR HOURS FROM TULSA	Gene Pitney	United Artists	2
11	21	BE MY BABY	Ronettes	London	9
31	22	IF I RULED THE WORLD	Harry Secombe	Philips	4
20	23	HUNGRY FOR LOVE	Johnny Kidd and the Pirates	HMV	3
37	24	ALL I WANT FOR CHRISTMAS IS A BEATLE	Dora Bryan	Fontana	2
13	25	SUGAR AND SPICE	Searchers	Pye	8
21	26	FROM RUSSIA WITH LOVE	Matt Monro	Parlophone	4
35	27	SWINGING ON A STAR	Big Dee Irwin	Colpix	2
19	28	BLOWING IN THE WIND	Peter Paul and Mary	Warner Bros	8
22	29	IF I HAD A HAMMER	Trini Lopez	Reprise	14
-	30	NOT TOO LITTLE - NOT TOO MUCH	Chris Sandford ●	Decca	1
36	[31]	I CAN DANCE	Brian Poole and the Tremeloes	Decca	2
18	32	LET IT ROCK/MEMPHIS TENNESSEE	Chuck Berry	Pye	10
29	33	FOOLS RUSH IN	Rick Nelson	Brunswick	9
38	34	COUNTRY BOY	Heinz	Decca	2
26	35	BUSTED	Ray Charles	HMV	6
30	36	MISS YOU	Jimmy Young	Columbia	9
25	37	DO YOU LOVE ME?	Brian Poole and the Tremeloes	Decca	14
34	38	AT THE PALACE (PARTS 1 AND 2)	Wilfred Brambell and Harry H Corbett	Pye	2
-	39	YESTERDAY'S GONE	Chad Stuart and Jeremy Clyde	Ember	2
32	40	THEN HE KISSED ME	Crystals	London	13

WEEK ENDING 19 DECEMBER 1963

LW	TW	Title	Artist	Label	Wks
1	[1]	I WANT TO HOLD YOUR HAND	Beatles	Parlophone	3
2	2	SHE LOVES YOU	Beatles	Parlophone	17
3	[3]	YOU WERE MADE FOR ME	Freddie and the Dreamers	Columbia	7
9	4	GLAD ALL OVER	Dave Clark Five	Columbia	5
4	5	SECRET LOVE	Kathy Kirby	Decca	7
7	6	I ONLY WANT TO BE WITH YOU	Dusty Springfield	Philips	4
5	7	MARIA ELENA	Los Indios Tabajaras	RCA	7
10	8	DOMINIQUE	Singing Nun	Philips	3

■By hitting the top three with each of their first three singles, Freddie and the Dreamers enjoy the best chart start by any act which never hit the very top (05.12.63) ■ Predating the success of 'Neighbours' stars by a quarter of a century, 'Coronation Street's Chris Sandford becomes the first soap star to chart (12.12.63) ■ The Beatles become the first act to knock themselves off the top, and the first act to hold the top two positions (12.12.63)■

December 1963

□ Highest position disc reached ● Act's first ever week on chart

LW	TW	Title / Artist	Label	Wks
20	9	TWENTY FOUR HOURS FROM TULSA Gene Pitney	*United Artists*	3
6	10	DON'T TALK TO HIM Cliff Richard	*Columbia*	7
13	[11]	GERONIMO Shadows	*Columbia*	3
8	12	YOU'LL NEVER WALK ALONE Gerry and the Pacemakers	*Columbia*	11
15	13	I WANNA BE YOUR MAN Rolling Stones	*Decca*	5
19	[14]	MONEY Bern Elliott and the Fenmen	*Decca*	4
27	15	SWINGING ON A STAR Big Dee Irwin	*Colpix*	3
11	16	I'LL KEEP YOU SATISFIED Billy J Kramer and the Dakotas	*Parlophone*	7
30	[17]	NOT TOO LITTLE - NOT TOO MUCH Chris Sandford	*Decca*	2
22	[18]	IF I RULED THE WORLD Harry Secombe	*Philips*	5
17	19	STAY Hollies	*Parlophone*	4
14	20	IT'S ALMOST TOMORROW Mark Wynter	*Pye*	6
24	21	ALL I WANT FOR CHRISTMAS IS A BEATLE Dora Bryan	*Fontana*	3
12	22	I WHO HAVE NOTHING Shirley Bassey	*Columbia*	12
16	23	BLUE BAYOU/MEAN WOMAN BLUES Roy Orbison	*London*	13
23	24	HUNGRY FOR LOVE Johnny Kidd and the Pirates	*HMV*	4
-	25	KISS ME QUICK Elvis Presley	*RCA*	1
34	[26]	COUNTRY BOY Heinz	*Decca*	3
-	27	HIPPY HIPPY SHAKE Swinging Blue Jeans	*HMV*	1
25	28	SUGAR AND SPICE Searchers	*Pye*	9
21	29	BE MY BABY Ronettes	*London*	10
28	30	BLOWING IN THE WIND Peter Paul and Mary	*Warner Bros*	9
26	31	FROM RUSSIA WITH LOVE Matt Monro	*Parlophone*	5
38	32	AT THE PALACE (PARTS 1 AND 2) Wilfred Brambell and Harry H Corbett	*Pye*	3
31	33	I CAN DANCE Brian Poole and the Tremeloes	*Decca*	3
18	34	DEEP PURPLE Nino Tempo and April Stevens	*London*	6
-	35	WE ARE IN LOVE Adam Faith	*Parlophone*	1
35	36	BUSTED Ray Charles	*HMV*	7
-	[37]	WALKING ALONE Richard Anthony ●	*Columbia*	1
-	38	WHAT TO DO Buddy Holly	*Coral*	1
-	39	RUN RUDOLPH RUN Chuck Berry	*Pye*	1
36	40	MISS YOU Jimmy Young	*Columbia*	10

LW	TW	*WEEK ENDING* **26 DECEMBER 1963**		Wks
1	[1]	I WANT TO HOLD YOUR HAND Beatles	*Parlophone*	4
2	2	SHE LOVES YOU Beatles	*Parlophone*	18
3	[3]	YOU WERE MADE FOR ME Freddie and the Dreamers	*Columbia*	8
5	[4]	SECRET LOVE Kathy Kirby	*Decca*	8
6	5	I ONLY WANT TO BE WITH YOU Dusty Springfield	*Philips*	5
4	6	GLAD ALL OVER Dave Clark Five	*Columbia*	6
8	[7]	DOMINIQUE Singing Nun	*Philips*	4
10	8	DON'T TALK TO HIM Cliff Richard	*Columbia*	8
9	9	TWENTY FOUR HOURS FROM TULSA Gene Pitney	*United Artists*	4
7	10	MARIA ELENA Los Indios Tabajaras	*RCA*	8
11	[11]	GERONIMO Shadows	*Columbia*	4
12	12	YOU'LL NEVER WALK ALONE Gerry and the Pacemakers	*Columbia*	12
16	13	I'LL KEEP YOU SATISFIED Billy J Kramer and the Dakotas	*Parlophone*	8
13	14	I WANNA BE YOUR MAN Rolling Stones	*Decca*	6
15	15	SWINGING ON A STAR Big Dee Irwin	*Colpix*	4
25	16	KISS ME QUICK Elvis Presley	*RCA*	2
19	17	STAY Hollies	*Parlophone*	5
17	18	NOT TOO LITTLE - NOT TOO MUCH Chris Sandford	*Decca*	3
14	19	MONEY Bern Elliott and the Fenmen	*Decca*	5
21	[20]	ALL I WANT FOR CHRISTMAS IS A BEATLE Dora Bryan	*Fontana*	4
18	21	IF I RULED THE WORLD Harry Secombe	*Philips*	6
20	22	IT'S ALMOST TOMORROW Mark Wynter	*Pye*	7
27	23	HIPPY HIPPY SHAKE Swinging Blue Jeans	*HMV*	2
24	24	HUNGRY FOR LOVE Johnny Kidd and the Pirates	*HMV*	5
22	25	I WHO HAVE NOTHING Shirley Bassey	*Columbia*	13
23	26	BLUE BAYOU/MEAN WOMAN BLUES Roy Orbison	*London*	14
35	27	WE ARE IN LOVE Adam Faith	*Parlophone*	2
26	28	COUNTRY BOY Heinz	*Decca*	4
38	29	WHAT TO DO Buddy Holly	*Coral*	2
28	30	SUGAR AND SPICE Searchers	*Pye*	10
30	31	BLOWING IN THE WIND Peter Paul and Mary	*Warner Bros*	10
32	32	AT THE PALACE (PARTS 1 AND 2) Wilfred Brambell and Harry H Corbett	*Pye*	4
34	33	DEEP PURPLE Nino Tempo and April Stevens	*London*	7
33	34	I CAN DANCE Brian Poole and the Tremeloes	*Decca*	4
-	[35]	KANSAS CITY Trini Lopez	*Reprise*	1
31	36	FROM RUSSIA WITH LOVE Matt Monro	*Parlophone*	6
-	[37]	YESTERDAY'S GONE Chad Stuart and Jeremy Clyde	*Ember*	3
29	38	BE MY BABY Ronettes	*London*	11
-	[39]	FROM RUSSIA WITH LOVE John Barry Orchestra	*Ember*	1
36	40	BUSTED Ray Charles	*HMV*	8

In these weeks ■ The Shadow's thirteenth hit, *Geronimo* is their first to miss the Top Ten (19.12.63) ■ *At The Palace* is Wilfred Brambell and Harry H. Corbett's appearance at the 1963 Royal Variety Performance as Steptoe and Son. It is the only all-spoken hit single (26.12.63)■

1964

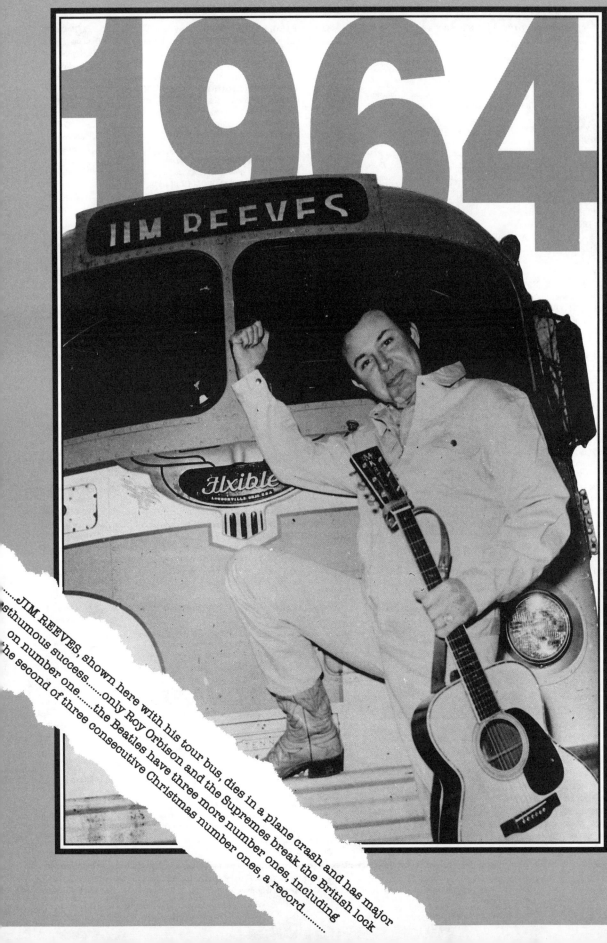

......JIM REEVES, shown here with his tour bus, dies in a plane crash and has major sthumous success......only Roy Orbison and the Supremes break the British lock on number one......the Beatles have three more number ones, including he second of three consecutive Christmas number ones, a record........

January 1964

□ Highest position disc reached ● Act's first ever week on chart

LW	TW	*WEEK ENDING* **2 JANUARY 1964**	Artist	Label	Wks
1	□ 1	I WANT TO HOLD YOUR HAND	Beatles	*Parlophone*	5
6	2	GLAD ALL OVER	Dave Clark Five	*Columbia*	7
2	3	SHE LOVES YOU	Beatles	*Parlophone*	19
3	4	YOU WERE MADE FOR ME	Freddie and the Dreamers	*Columbia*	9
9	□ 5	TWENTY FOUR HOURS FROM TULSA	Gene Pitney	*United Artists*	5
5	6	I ONLY WANT TO BE WITH YOU	Dusty Springfield	*Philips*	6
7	□ 7	DOMINIQUE	Singing Nun	*Philips*	5
10	8	MARIA ELENA	Los Indios Tabajaras	*RCA*	9
4	9	SECRET LOVE	Kathy Kirby	*Decca*	9
8	10	DON'T TALK TO HIM	Cliff Richard	*Columbia*	9
15	11	SWINGING ON A STAR	Big Dee Irwin	*Colpix*	5
11	12	GERONIMO	Shadows	*Columbia*	5
23	13	HIPPY HIPPY SHAKE	Swinging Blue Jeans	*HMV*	3
16	□ 14	KISS ME QUICK	Elvis Presley	*RCA*	3
14	15	I WANNA BE YOUR MAN	Rolling Stones	*Decca*	7
12	16	YOU'LL NEVER WALK ALONE	Gerry and the Pacemakers	*Columbia*	13
17	17	STAY	Hollies	*Parlophone*	6
18	18	NOT TOO LITTLE - NOT TOO MUCH	Chris Sandford	*Decca*	4
19	19	MONEY	Bern Elliott and the Fenmen	*Decca*	6
27	20	WE ARE IN LOVE	Adam Faith	*Parlophone*	3
13	21	I'LL KEEP YOU SATISFIED	Billy J Kramer and the Dakotas	*Parlophone*	9
21	22	IF I RULED THE WORLD	Harry Secombe	*Philips*	7
26	23	BLUE BAYOU/MEAN WOMAN BLUES	Roy Orbison	*London*	15
20	24	ALL I WANT FOR CHRISTMAS IS A BEATLE	Dora Bryan	*Fontana*	5
25	25	I WHO HAVE NOTHING	Shirley Bassey	*Columbia*	14
32	26	AT THE PALACE (PARTS 1 AND 2)	Wilfred Brambell and Harry H Corbett	*Pye*	5
28	27	COUNTRY BOY	Heinz	*Decca*	5
29	28	WHAT TO DO	Buddy Holly	*Coral*	3
36	29	FROM RUSSIA WITH LOVE	Matt Monro	*Parlophone*	7
22	30	IT'S ALMOST TOMORROW	Mark Wynter	*Pye*	8
24	31	HUNGRY FOR LOVE	Johnny Kidd and the Pirates	*HMV*	6
-	32	I'M IN LOVE	Fourmost	*Parlophone*	1
34	33	I CAN DANCE	Brian Poole and the Tremeloes	*Decca*	5
33	34	DEEP PURPLE	Nino Tempo and April Stevens	*London*	8
31	35	BLOWING IN THE WIND	Peter Paul and Mary	*Warner Bros*	11
-	□ 36	RUN RUDOLPH RUN	Chuck Berry	*Pye*	2
-	37	DO YOU REALLY LOVE ME TOO	Billy Fury	*Decca*	1
30	38	SUGAR AND SPICE	Searchers	*Pye*	11
37	39	YESTERDAY'S GONE	Chad Stuart and Jeremy Clyde	*Ember*	4
-	40	WALKING ALONE	Richard Anthony	*Columbia*	2

LW	TW	*WEEK ENDING* **9 JANUARY 1964**	Artist	Label	Wks
1	□ 1	I WANT TO HOLD YOUR HAND	Beatles	*Parlophone*	6
2	2	GLAD ALL OVER	Dave Clark Five	*Columbia*	8
13	3	HIPPY HIPPY SHAKE	Swinging Blue Jeans	*HMV*	4
6	□ 4	I ONLY WANT TO BE WITH YOU	Dusty Springfield	*Philips*	7
3	5	SHE LOVES YOU	Beatles	*Parlophone*	20
5	6	TWENTY FOUR HOURS FROM TULSA	Gene Pitney	*United Artists*	6
4	7	YOU WERE MADE FOR ME	Freddie and the Dreamers	*Columbia*	10
11	8	SWINGING ON A STAR	Big Dee Irwin	*Colpix*	6
9	9	SECRET LOVE	Kathy Kirby	*Decca*	10
7	10	DOMINIQUE	Singing Nun	*Philips*	6
17	11	STAY	Hollies	*Parlophone*	7
15	□ 12	I WANNA BE YOUR MAN	Rolling Stones	*Decca*	8
8	13	MARIA ELENA	Los Indios Tabajaras	*RCA*	10
10	14	DON'T TALK TO HIM	Cliff Richard	*Columbia*	10
14	15	KISS ME QUICK	Elvis Presley	*RCA*	4
20	16	WE ARE IN LOVE	Adam Faith	*Parlophone*	4
16	17	YOU'LL NEVER WALK ALONE	Gerry and the Pacemakers	*Columbia*	14
12	18	GERONIMO	Shadows	*Columbia*	6
18	19	NOT TOO LITTLE - NOT TOO MUCH	Chris Sandford	*Decca*	5
37	20	DO YOU REALLY LOVE ME TOO	Billy Fury	*Decca*	2
22	21	IF I RULED THE WORLD	Harry Secombe	*Philips*	8
21	22	I'LL KEEP YOU SATISFIED	Billy J Kramer and the Dakotas	*Parlophone*	10
19	23	MONEY	Bern Elliott and the Fenmen	*Decca*	7
31	24	HUNGRY FOR LOVE	Johnny Kidd and the Pirates	*HMV*	7
26	□ 25	AT THE PALACE (PARTS 1 AND 2)	Wilfred Brambell and Harry H Corbett	*Pye*	6
27	□ 26	COUNTRY BOY	Heinz	*Decca*	6
28	□ 27	WHAT TO DO	Buddy Holly	*Coral*	4
25	28	I WHO HAVE NOTHING	Shirley Bassey	*Columbia*	15
-	29	AS USUAL	Brenda Lee	*Brunswick*	1
30	30	IT'S ALMOST TOMORROW	Mark Wynter	*Pye*	9
32	31	I'M IN LOVE	Fourmost	*Parlophone*	2
23	32	BLUE BAYOU/MEAN WOMAN BLUES	Roy Orbison	*London*	16
34	33	DEEP PURPLE	Nino Tempo and April Stevens	*London*	9
33	34	I CAN DANCE	Brian Poole and the Tremeloes	*Decca*	6
38	35	SUGAR AND SPICE	Searchers	*Pye*	12
29	36	FROM RUSSIA WITH LOVE	Matt Monro	*Parlophone*	8
-	37	THERE I'VE SAID IT AGAIN	Bobby Vinton	*Columbia*	1
-	38	DON'T BLAME ME	Frank Ifield	*Columbia*	1
35	39	BLOWING IN THE WIND	Peter Paul and Mary	*Warner Bros*	12
-	40	BABY I LOVE YOU	Ronettes	*London*	1

LW	TW	*WEEK ENDING* **16 JANUARY 1964**	Artist	Label	Wks
2	□ 1	GLAD ALL OVER	Dave Clark Five	*Columbia*	9
1	2	I WANT TO HOLD YOUR HAND	Beatles	*Parlophone*	7
3	3	HIPPY HIPPY SHAKE	Swinging Blue Jeans	*HMV*	5
4	□ 4	I ONLY WANT TO BE WITH YOU	Dusty Springfield	*Philips*	8
5	5	SHE LOVES YOU	Beatles	*Parlophone*	21
6	6	TWENTY FOUR HOURS FROM TULSA	Gene Pitney	*United Artists*	7
8	□ 7	SWINGING ON A STAR	Big Dee Irwin	*Colpix*	7
11	□ 8	STAY	Hollies	*Parlophone*	8
7	9	YOU WERE MADE FOR ME	Freddie and the Dreamers	*Columbia*	11
10	10	DOMINIQUE	Singing Nun	*Philips*	7
13	11	MARIA ELENA	Los Indios Tabajaras	*RCA*	11
9	12	SECRET LOVE	Kathy Kirby	*Decca*	11
16	13	WE ARE IN LOVE	Adam Faith	*Parlophone*	5
12	14	I WANNA BE YOUR MAN	Rolling Stones	*Decca*	9
15	15	KISS ME QUICK	Elvis Presley	*RCA*	5
29	16	AS USUAL	Brenda Lee	*Brunswick*	2
20	17	DO YOU REALLY LOVE ME TOO	Billy Fury	*Decca*	4
19	18	NOT TOO LITTLE - NOT TOO MUCH	Chris Sandford	*Decca*	6
38	19	DON'T BLAME ME	Frank Ifield	*Columbia*	2
17	20	YOU'LL NEVER WALK ALONE	Gerry and the Pacemakers	*Columbia*	15
14	21	DON'T TALK TO HIM	Cliff Richard	*Columbia*	11
18	22	GERONIMO	Shadows	*Columbia*	7
-	23	I'M THE ONE	Gerry and the Pacemakers	*Columbia*	1
23	24	MONEY	Bern Elliott and the Fenmen	*Decca*	8
21	25	IF I RULED THE WORLD	Harry Secombe	*Philips*	9
-	26	NEEDLES AND PINS	Searchers	*Pye*	1
40	27	BABY I LOVE YOU	Ronettes	*London*	2
24	28	HUNGRY FOR LOVE	Johnny Kidd and the Pirates	*HMV*	8
27	29	WHAT TO DO	Buddy Holly	*Coral*	5
25	30	AT THE PALACE (PARTS 1 AND 2)	Wilfred Brambell and Harry H Corbett	*Pye*	7
22	31	I'LL KEEP YOU SATISFIED	Billy J Kramer and the Dakotas	*Parlophone*	11
26	32	COUNTRY BOY	Heinz	*Decca*	7
31	33	I'M IN LOVE	Fourmost	*Parlophone*	3
37	□ 34	THERE I'VE SAID IT AGAIN	Bobby Vinton	*Columbia*	2
-	35	WHISPERING	Nino Tempo and April Stevens	*London*	1
36	36	FROM RUSSIA WITH LOVE	Matt Monro	*Parlophone*	9
28	37	I WHO HAVE NOTHING	Shirley Bassey	*Columbia*	16
32	38	BLUE BAYOU/MEAN WOMAN BLUES	Roy Orbison	*London*	17
-	39	ALL MY LOVING	Dowlands ●	*Oriole*	1
39	40	BLOWING IN THE WIND	Peter Paul and Mary	*Warner Bros*	13

In these weeks ■ After eighteen weeks in the top three, *She Loves You* drops to number five (09.01.64) ■ Dusty Springfield's *I Only Want To Be With You* is the first of three versions of the song to peak at number four (09.01.64) ■ For the third consecutive week, *I Can Dance* and *Deep Purple* swap places at numbers 33 and 34 (09.01.64) ■

February 1964

□ Highest position disc reached ● Act's first ever week on chart

LW	TW	WEEK ENDING 23 JANUARY 1964		Wks
1	[1]	GLAD ALL OVER Dave Clark Five	Columbia	10
3	[2]	HIPPY HIPPY SHAKE Swinging Blue Jeans	HMV	6
2	3	I WANT TO HOLD YOUR HAND Beatles	Parlophone	8
4	[4]	I ONLY WANT TO BE WITH YOU Dusty Springfield	Philips	9
6	[5]	TWENTY FOUR HOURS FROM TULSA Gene Pitney	United Artists	8
26	6	NEEDLES AND PINS Searchers	Pye	2
7	[7]	SWINGING ON A STAR Big Dee Irwin	Colpix	8
5	8	SHE LOVES YOU Beatles	Parlophone	22
16	9	AS USUAL Brenda Lee	Brunswick	3
23	10	I'M THE ONE Gerry and the Pacemakers	Columbia	2
13	[11]	WE ARE IN LOVE Adam Faith	Parlophone	6
8	12	STAY Hollies	Parlophone	9
19	13	DON'T BLAME ME Frank Ifield	Columbia	3
15	[14]	KISS ME QUICK Elvis Presley	RCA	6
14	15	I WANNA BE YOUR MAN Rolling Stones	Decca	10
10	16	DOMINIQUE Singing Nun	Philips	8
17	17	DO YOU REALLY LOVE ME TOO Billy Fury	Decca	5
12	18	SECRET LOVE Kathy Kirby	Decca	12
11	19	MARIA ELENA Los Indios Tabajaras	RCA	12
9	20	YOU WERE MADE FOR ME Freddie and the Dreamers	Columbia	12
33	21	I'M IN LOVE Fourmost	Parlophone	4
20	22	YOU'LL NEVER WALK ALONE Gerry and the Pacemakers	Columbia	16
27	23	BABY I LOVE YOU Ronettes	London	3
22	24	GERONIMO Shadows	Columbia	8
18	25	NOT TOO LITTLE - NOT TOO MUCH Chris Sandford	Decca	7
21	26	DON'T TALK TO HIM Cliff Richard	Columbia	12
-	27	5 4 3 2 1 Manfred Mann ●	HMV	1
24	28	MONEY Bern Elliott and the Fenmen	Decca	9
-	29	I THINK OF YOU Merseybeats	Fontana	1
25	30	IF I RULED THE WORLD Harry Secombe	Philips	10
35	31	WHISPERING Nino Tempo and April Stevens	London	2
31	32	I'LL KEEP YOU SATISFIED Billy J Kramer and the Dakotas	Parlophone	12
39	[33]	ALL MY LOVING Dowlands	Oriole	2
34	[34]	THERE I'VE SAID IT AGAIN Bobby Vinton	Columbia	3
30	35	AT THE PALACE (PARTS 1 AND 2) Wilfred Brambell and Harry H Corbett	Pye	8
36	36	FROM RUSSIA WITH LOVE Matt Monro	Parlophone	10
37	37	I WHO HAVE NOTHING Shirley Bassey	Columbia	17
-	[38]	FEVER Helen Shapiro	Columbia	1
-	[39]	SONG OF MEXICO Tony Meehan ●	Decca	1
-	40	DIANE Bachelors	Decca	1

LW	TW	WEEK ENDING 30 JANUARY 1964		Wks
6	[1]	NEEDLES AND PINS Searchers	Pye	3
1	2	GLAD ALL OVER Dave Clark Five	Columbia	11
2	3	HIPPY HIPPY SHAKE Swinging Blue Jeans	HMV	7
10	4	I'M THE ONE Gerry and the Pacemakers	Columbia	3
4	5	I ONLY WANT TO BE WITH YOU Dusty Springfield	Philips	10
3	6	I WANT TO HOLD YOUR HAND Beatles	Parlophone	9
5	7	TWENTY FOUR HOURS FROM TULSA Gene Pitney	United Artists	9
12	[8]	STAY Hollies	Parlophone	10
9	9	AS USUAL Brenda Lee	Brunswick	4
13	10	DON'T BLAME ME Frank Ifield	Columbia	4
11	[11]	WE ARE IN LOVE Adam Faith	Parlophone	7
7	12	SWINGING ON A STAR Big Dee Irwin	Colpix	9
17	[13]	DO YOU REALLY LOVE ME TOO Billy Fury	Decca	6
27	14	5 4 3 2 1 Manfred Mann	HMV	2
14	15	KISS ME QUICK Elvis Presley	RCA	7
8	16	SHE LOVES YOU Beatles	Parlophone	23
15	17	I WANNA BE YOUR MAN Rolling Stones	Decca	11
23	18	BABY I LOVE YOU Ronettes	London	4
29	19	I THINK OF YOU Merseybeats	Fontana	2
21	20	I'M IN LOVE Fourmost	Parlophone	5
18	21	SECRET LOVE Kathy Kirby	Decca	13
40	22	DIANE Bachelors	Decca	2
19	23	MARIA ELENA Los Indios Tabajaras	RCA	13
16	24	DOMINIQUE Singing Nun	Philips	9
20	25	YOU WERE MADE FOR ME Freddie and the Dreamers	Columbia	13
31	26	WHISPERING Nino Tempo and April Stevens	London	3
22	27	YOU'LL NEVER WALK ALONE Gerry and the Pacemakers	Columbia	17
30	28	IF I RULED THE WORLD Harry Secombe	Philips	11
24	29	GERONIMO Shadows	Columbia	9
-	30	FOR YOU Rick Nelson	Brunswick	1
28	31	MONEY Bern Elliott and the Fenmen	Decca	10
26	32	DON'T TALK TO HIM Cliff Richard	Columbia	13
25	33	NOT TOO LITTLE - NOT TOO MUCH Chris Sandford	Decca	8
34	[34]	THERE I'VE SAID IT AGAIN Bobby Vinton	Columbia	4
33	35	ALL MY LOVING Dowlands	Oriole	3
-	36	MY SPECIAL DREAM Shirley Bassey	Columbia	1
-	37	POISON IVY Paramounts ●	Parlophone	1
35	38	AT THE PALACE (PARTS 1 AND 2) Wilfred Brambell and Harry H Corbett	Pye	9
-	39	WHAT TO DO Buddy Holly	Coral	6
-	40	LOUIE LOUIE Kingsmen ●	Pye	1

LW	TW	WEEK ENDING 6 FEBRUARY 1964		Wks
1	[1]	NEEDLES AND PINS Searchers	Pye	4
4	[2]	I'M THE ONE Gerry and the Pacemakers	Columbia	4
3	3	HIPPY HIPPY SHAKE Swinging Blue Jeans	HMV	8
2	4	GLAD ALL OVER Dave Clark Five	Columbia	12
9	[5]	AS USUAL Brenda Lee	Brunswick	5
7	6	TWENTY FOUR HOURS FROM TULSA Gene Pitney	United Artists	10
6	7	I WANT TO HOLD YOUR HAND Beatles	Parlophone	10
22	8	DIANE Bachelors	Decca	3
14	9	5 4 3 2 1 Manfred Mann	HMV	3
10	10	DON'T BLAME ME Frank Ifield	Columbia	5
5	11	I ONLY WANT TO BE WITH YOU Dusty Springfield	Philips	11
8	12	STAY Hollies	Parlophone	11
18	13	BABY I LOVE YOU Ronettes	London	5
13	14	DO YOU REALLY LOVE ME TOO Billy Fury	Decca	7
19	15	I THINK OF YOU Merseybeats	Fontana	3
12	16	SWINGING ON A STAR Big Dee Irwin	Colpix	10
20	[17]	I'M IN LOVE Fourmost	Parlophone	6
11	18	WE ARE IN LOVE Adam Faith	Parlophone	8
16	19	SHE LOVES YOU Beatles	Parlophone	24
26	[20]	WHISPERING Nino Tempo and April Stevens	London	4
30	21	FOR YOU Rick Nelson	Brunswick	2
-	22	CANDY MAN Brian Poole and the Tremeloes	Decca	1
-	23	I'M THE LONELY ONE Cliff Richard	Columbia	1
17	24	I WANNA BE YOUR MAN Rolling Stones	Decca	12
15	25	KISS ME QUICK Elvis Presley	RCA	8
28	26	IF I RULED THE WORLD Harry Secombe	Philips	12
21	27	SECRET LOVE Kathy Kirby	Decca	14
-	28	ANYONE WHO HAD A HEART Cilla Black	Parlophone	1
24	29	DOMINIQUE Singing Nun	Philips	10
25	30	YOU WERE MADE FOR ME Freddie and the Dreamers	Columbia	14
23	31	MARIA ELENA Los Indios Tabajaras	RCA	14
27	32	YOU'LL NEVER WALK ALONE Gerry and the Pacemakers	Columbia	18
-	33	BOYS CRY Eden Kane	Fontana	1
40	34	LOUIE LOUIE Kingsmen	Pye	2
34	35	THERE I'VE SAID IT AGAIN Bobby Vinton	Columbia	5
36	36	MY SPECIAL DREAM Shirley Bassey	Columbia	2
37	37	POISON IVY Paramounts	Parlophone	2
29	38	GERONIMO Shadows	Columbia	10
35	39	ALL MY LOVING Dowlands	Oriole	4
-	40	EIGHT BY TEN Ken Dodd	Columbia	1

■ *Needles And Pins* is co-written by Sonny Bono, giving him a first taste of the number one position eighteen months before he is there as a performer with wife Cher (30.01.64) ■ Bobby Vinton's *There I've Said It Again* spends three weeks at its peak of number 34. In America it is the record which is knocked off the top by the Beatles' first US number one *I Want To Hold Your Hand* (30.01.64) ■

February 1964

☐ Highest position disc reached ● Act's first ever week on chart

WEEK ENDING 13 FEBRUARY 1964

LW	TW	Title	Artist	Label	Wks
1	[1]	NEEDLES AND PINS	Searchers	*Pye*	5
2	[2]	I'M THE ONE	Gerry and the Pacemakers	*Columbia*	5
8	3	DIANE	Bachelors	*Decca*	4
3	4	HIPPY HIPPY SHAKE	Swinging Blue Jeans	*HMV*	9
9	[5]	5 4 3 2 1	Manfred Mann	*HMV*	4
4	6	GLAD ALL OVER	Dave Clark Five	*Columbia*	13
5	7	AS USUAL	Brenda Lee	*Brunswick*	6
10	[8]	DON'T BLAME ME	Frank Ifield	*Columbia*	6
15	9	I THINK OF YOU	Merseybeats	*Fontana*	4
28	10	ANYONE WHO HAD A HEART	Cilla Black	*Parlophone*	2
6	11	TWENTY FOUR HOURS FROM TULSA	Gene Pitney	*United Artists*	11
13	12	BABY I LOVE YOU	Ronettes	*London*	6
22	13	CANDY MAN	Brian Poole and the Tremeloes	*Decca*	2
23	14	I'M THE LONELY ONE	Cliff Richard	*Columbia*	2
7	15	I WANT TO HOLD YOUR HAND	Beatles	*Parlophone*	11
21	16	FOR YOU	Rick Nelson	*Brunswick*	3
11	17	I ONLY WANT TO BE WITH YOU	Dusty Springfield	*Philips*	12
17	18	I'M IN LOVE	Fourmost	*Parlophone*	7
12	19	STAY	Hollies	*Parlophone*	12
16	20	SWINGING ON A STAR	Big Dee Irwin	*Colpix*	11
19	21	SHE LOVES YOU	Beatles	*Parlophone*	25
14	22	DO YOU REALLY LOVE ME TOO	Billy Fury	*Decca*	8
20	23	WHISPERING	Nino Tempo and April Stevens	*London*	5
33	24	BOYS CRY	Eden Kane	*Fontana*	2
18	25	WE ARE IN LOVE	Adam Faith	*Parlophone*	9
34	[26]	LOUIE LOUIE	Kingsmen	*Pye*	3
24	27	I WANNA BE YOUR MAN	Rolling Stones	*Decca*	13
26	28	IF I RULED THE WORLD	Harry Secombe	*Philips*	13
31	29	MARIA ELENA	Los Indios Tabajaras	*RCA*	15
25	30	KISS ME QUICK	Elvis Presley	*RCA*	9
40	31	EIGHT BY TEN	Ken Dodd	*Columbia*	2
27	32	SECRET LOVE	Kathy Kirby	*Decca*	15
29	33	DOMINIQUE	Singing Nun	*Philips*	11
36	34	MY SPECIAL DREAM	Shirley Bassey	*Columbia*	3
37	35	POISON IVY	Paramounts	*Parlophone*	3
32	36	YOU'LL NEVER WALK ALONE	Gerry and the Pacemakers	*Columbia*	19
38	37	GERONIMO	Shadows	*Columbia*	11
-	[38]	FEVER	Helen Shapiro	*Columbia*	2
39	39	ALL MY LOVING	Dowlands	*Oriole*	5
-	40	MONEY	Bern Elliott and the Fenmen	*Decca*	11

WEEK ENDING 20 FEBRUARY 1964

LW	TW	Title	Artist	Label	Wks
3	[1]	DIANE	Bachelors	*Decca*	5
10	2	ANYONE WHO HAD A HEART	Cilla Black	*Parlophone*	3
1	3	NEEDLES AND PINS	Searchers	*Pye*	6
2	4	I'M THE ONE	Gerry and the Pacemakers	*Columbia*	6
5	[5]	5 4 3 2 1	Manfred Mann	*HMV*	5
4	6	HIPPY HIPPY SHAKE	Swinging Blue Jeans	*HMV*	10
7	7	AS USUAL	Brenda Lee	*Brunswick*	7
14	[8]	I'M THE LONELY ONE	Cliff Richard	*Columbia*	3
9	9	I THINK OF YOU	Merseybeats	*Fontana*	5
6	10	GLAD ALL OVER	Dave Clark Five	*Columbia*	14
13	11	CANDY MAN	Brian Poole and the Tremeloes	*Decca*	3
8	12	DON'T BLAME ME	Frank Ifield	*Columbia*	7
12	13	BABY I LOVE YOU	Ronettes	*London*	7
16	[14]	FOR YOU	Rick Nelson	*Brunswick*	4
15	15	I WANT TO HOLD YOUR HAND	Beatles	*Parlophone*	12
11	16	TWENTY FOUR HOURS FROM TULSA	Gene Pitney	*United Artists*	12
17	17	I ONLY WANT TO BE WITH YOU	Dusty Springfield	*Philips*	13
24	18	BOYS CRY	Eden Kane	*Fontana*	3
-	19	BITS AND PIECES	Dave Clark Five	*Columbia*	1
18	20	I'M IN LOVE	Fourmost	*Parlophone*	8
19	21	STAY	Hollies	*Parlophone*	13
31	[22]	EIGHT BY TEN	Ken Dodd	*Columbia*	3
21	23	SHE LOVES YOU	Beatles	*Parlophone*	26
25	24	WE ARE IN LOVE	Adam Faith	*Parlophone*	10
23	25	WHISPERING	Nino Tempo and April Stevens	*London*	6
20	26	SWINGING ON A STAR	Big Dee Irwin	*Colpix*	12
-	[27]	NADINE	Chuck Berry	*Pye*	1
22	28	DO YOU REALLY LOVE ME TOO	Billy Fury	*Decca*	9
26	29	LOUIE LOUIE	Kingsmen	*Pye*	4
-	30	STAY AWHILE	Dusty Springfield	*Philips*	1
27	31	I WANNA BE YOUR MAN	Rolling Stones	*Decca*	14
34	[32]	MY SPECIAL DREAM	Shirley Bassey	*Columbia*	4
-	33	BORNE ON THE WIND	Roy Orbison	*London*	1
28	34	IF I RULED THE WORLD	Harry Secombe	*Philips*	14
29	35	MARIA ELENA	Los Indios Tabajaras	*RCA*	16
-	36	LET ME GO LOVER	Kathy Kirby	*Decca*	1
-	[37]	MY BABY LEFT ME	Dave Berry	*Decca*	1
33	38	DOMINIQUE	Singing Nun	*Philips*	12
30	39	KISS ME QUICK	Elvis Presley	*RCA*	10
-	[40]	UM UM UM UM UM UM	Major Lance ●	*Columbia*	1

WEEK ENDING 27 FEBRUARY 1964

LW	TW	Title	Artist	Label	Wks
2	[1]	ANYONE WHO HAD A HEART	Cilla Black	*Parlophone*	4
1	2	DIANE	Bachelors	*Decca*	6
3	3	NEEDLES AND PINS	Searchers	*Pye*	7
19	4	BITS AND PIECES	Dave Clark Five	*Columbia*	2
9	[5]	I THINK OF YOU	Merseybeats	*Fontana*	6
4	6	I'M THE ONE	Gerry and the Pacemakers	*Columbia*	7
5	7	5 4 3 2 1	Manfred Mann	*HMV*	6
11	8	CANDY MAN	Brian Poole and the Tremeloes	*Decca*	4
7	9	AS USUAL	Brenda Lee	*Brunswick*	8
8	10	I'M THE LONELY ONE	Cliff Richard	*Columbia*	4
13	[11]	BABY I LOVE YOU	Ronettes	*London*	8
6	12	HIPPY HIPPY SHAKE	Swinging Blue Jeans	*HMV*	11
18	13	BOYS CRY	Eden Kane	*Fontana*	4
10	14	GLAD ALL OVER	Dave Clark Five	*Columbia*	15
12	15	DON'T BLAME ME	Frank Ifield	*Columbia*	8
14	16	FOR YOU	Rick Nelson	*Brunswick*	5
15	17	I WANT TO HOLD YOUR HAND	Beatles	*Parlophone*	13
30	18	STAY AWHILE	Dusty Springfield	*Philips*	2
16	19	TWENTY FOUR HOURS FROM TULSA	Gene Pitney	*United Artists*	13
-	20	OVER YOU	Freddie and the Dreamers	*Columbia*	1
33	21	BORNE ON THE WIND	Roy Orbison	*London*	2
22	[22]	EIGHT BY TEN	Ken Dodd	*Columbia*	4
20	23	I'M IN LOVE	Fourmost	*Parlophone*	9
36	24	LET ME GO LOVER	Kathy Kirby	*Decca*	2
17	25	I ONLY WANT TO BE WITH YOU	Dusty Springfield	*Philips*	14
-	26	I LOVE YOU BECAUSE	Jim Reeves	*RCA*	1
27	[27]	NADINE	Chuck Berry	*Pye*	2
23	28	SHE LOVES YOU	Beatles	*Parlophone*	27
-	29	NOT FADE AWAY	Rolling Stones	*Decca*	1
29	30	LOUIE LOUIE	Kingsmen	*Pye*	5
21	31	STAY	Hollies	*Parlophone*	14
28	32	DO YOU REALLY LOVE ME TOO	Billy Fury	*Decca*	10
25	33	WHISPERING	Nino Tempo and April Stevens	*London*	7
-	34	LITTLE CHILDREN	Billy J Kramer and the Dakotas	*Parlophone*	1
24	35	WE ARE IN LOVE	Adam Faith	*Parlophone*	11
31	36	I WANNA BE YOUR MAN	Rolling Stones	*Decca*	15
26	37	SWINGING ON A STAR	Big Dee Irwin	*Colpix*	13
32	38	MY SPECIAL DREAM	Shirley Bassey	*Columbia*	5
-	39	JUST ONE LOOK	Hollies	*Parlophone*	1
-	40	YOU WERE THERE	Heinz	*Decca*	1

WEEK ENDING 5 MARCH 1964

LW	TW	Title	Artist	Label	Wks
1	[1]	ANYONE WHO HAD A HEART	Cilla Black	*Parlophone*	5
4	[2]	BITS AND PIECES	Dave Clark Five	*Columbia*	3
2	3	DIANE	Bachelors	*Decca*	7
3	4	NEEDLES AND PINS	Searchers	*Pye*	8
5	[5]	I THINK OF YOU	Merseybeats	*Fontana*	7
8	[6]	CANDY MAN	Brian Poole and the Tremeloes	*Decca*	5
6	7	I'M THE ONE	Gerry and the Pacemakers	*Columbia*	8

In these weeks ■ Helen Shapiro's chart career finishes at the age of 17 years and 138 days. She has already achieved ten Top 40 hits and two number ones (13.02.64) ■ After 19 consecutive top five hits, Cliff Richard's *I'm The Lonely One* breaks the string by stopping at number eight (20.02.64) ■

March 1964

□ Highest position disc reached ● Act's first ever week on chart

LW	TW	Title	Artist	Label	Wks
7	8	5 4 3 2 1	Manfred Mann	HMV	7
34	9	LITTLE CHILDREN	Billy J Kramer and the Dakotas	Parlophone	2
9	10	AS USUAL	Brenda Lee	Brunswick	9
29	11	NOT FADE AWAY	Rolling Stones	Decca	2
13	12	BOYS CRY	Eden Kane	Fontana	5
20	[13]	OVER YOU	Freddie and the Dreamers	Columbia	2
10	14	I'M THE LONELY ONE	Cliff Richard	Columbia	5
11	15	BABY I LOVE YOU	Ronettes	London	9
18	16	STAY AWHILE	Dusty Springfield	Philips	3
21	17	BORNE ON THE WIND	Roy Orbison	London	3
24	18	LET ME GO LOVER	Kathy Kirby	Decca	3
16	19	FOR YOU	Rick Nelson	Brunswick	6
39	20	JUST ONE LOOK	Hollies	Parlophone	2
26	21	I LOVE YOU BECAUSE	Jim Reeves	RCA	2
22	[22]	EIGHT BY TEN	Ken Dodd	Columbia	5
12	23	HIPPY HIPPY SHAKE	Swinging Blue Jeans	HMV	12
14	24	GLAD ALL OVER	Dave Clark Five	Columbia	16
17	25	I WANT TO HOLD YOUR HAND	Beatles	Parlophone	14
15	26	DON'T BLAME ME	Frank Ifield	Columbia	9
19	27	TWENTY FOUR HOURS FROM TULSA	Gene Pitney	United Artists	14
-	28	THAT GIRL BELONGS TO YESTERDAY	Gene Pitney	United Artists	1
40	29	YOU WERE THERE	Heinz	Decca	2
27	30	NADINE	Chuck Berry	Pye	3
30	31	LOUIE LOUIE	Kingsmen	Pye	6
-	[32]	IT'S AN OPEN SECRET	Joy Strings ●	Regal-Zonophone	1
28	33	SHE LOVES YOU	Beatles	Parlophone	28
23	34	I'M IN LOVE	Fourmost	Parlophone	10
31	35	STAY	Hollies	Parlophone	15
-	36	THEME FOR YOUNG LOVERS	Shadows	Columbia	1
25	37	I ONLY WANT TO BE WITH YOU	Dusty Springfield	Philips	15
-	38	I LOVE HOW YOU LOVE ME	Maureen Evans	Oriole	1
32	39	DO YOU REALLY LOVE ME TOO	Billy Fury	Decca	11
-	[40]	A FOOL NEVER LEARNS	Andy Williams	CBS	1

WEEK ENDING 12 MARCH 1964

LW	TW	Title	Artist	Label	Wks
1	[1]	ANYONE WHO HAD A HEART	Cilla Black	Parlophone	6
2	[2]	BITS AND PIECES	Dave Clark Five	Columbia	4
9	3	LITTLE CHILDREN	Billy J Kramer and the Dakotas	Parlophone	3
3	4	DIANE	Bachelors	Decca	8
11	5	NOT FADE AWAY	Rolling Stones	Decca	3
20	6	JUST ONE LOOK	Hollies	Parlophone	3
4	7	NEEDLES AND PINS	Searchers	Pye	9
5	8	I THINK OF YOU	Merseybeats	Fontana	8
12	9	BOYS CRY	Eden Kane	Fontana	6
18	[10]	LET ME GO LOVER	Kathy Kirby	Decca	4
6	11	CANDY MAN	Brian Poole and the Tremeloes	Decca	6
7	12	I'M THE ONE	Gerry and the Pacemakers	Columbia	9
16	[13]	STAY AWHILE	Dusty Springfield	Philips	4
21	14	I LOVE YOU BECAUSE	Jim Reeves	RCA	3
17	[15]	BORNE ON THE WIND	Roy Orbison	London	4
28	16	THAT GIRL BELONGS TO YESTERDAY	Gene Pitney	United Artists	2
10	17	AS USUAL	Brenda Lee	Brunswick	10
13	18	OVER YOU	Freddie and the Dreamers	Columbia	3
15	19	BABY I LOVE YOU	Ronettes	London	10
8	20	5 4 3 2 1	Manfred Mann	HMV	8
14	21	I'M THE LONELY ONE	Cliff Richard	Columbia	6
36	22	THEME FOR YOUNG LOVERS	Shadows	Columbia	2
19	23	FOR YOU	Rick Nelson	Brunswick	7
25	24	I WANT TO HOLD YOUR HAND	Beatles	Parlophone	15
22	25	EIGHT BY TEN	Ken Dodd	Columbia	6
29	[26]	YOU WERE THERE	Heinz	Decca	3
23	27	HIPPY HIPPY SHAKE	Swinging Blue Jeans	HMV	13
26	28	DON'T BLAME ME	Frank Ifield	Columbia	10
-	29	TELL ME WHEN	Applejacks ●	Decca	1
24	30	GLAD ALL OVER	Dave Clark Five	Columbia	17
27	31	TWENTY FOUR HOURS FROM TULSA	Gene Pitney	United Artists	15
-	32	MY WORLD OF BLUE	Karl Denver	Decca	1
30	33	NADINE	Chuck Berry	Pye	4
38	[34]	I LOVE HOW YOU LOVE ME	Maureen Evans	Oriole	2
33	35	SHE LOVES YOU	Beatles	Parlophone	29
-	[36]	I WONDER	Crystals	London	1
32	37	IT'S AN OPEN SECRET	Joy Strings	Regal-Zonophone	2
-	38	MOVE OVER DARLING	Doris Day	CBS	1
-	39	WORLD WITHOUT LOVE	Peter and Gordon ●	Columbia	1
31	40	LOUIE LOUIE	Kingsmen	Pye	7

WEEK ENDING 19 MARCH 1964

LW	TW	Title	Artist	Label	Wks
3	[1]	LITTLE CHILDREN	Billy J Kramer and the Dakotas	Parlophone	4
2	[2]	BITS AND PIECES	Dave Clark Five	Columbia	5
1	3	ANYONE WHO HAD A HEART	Cilla Black	Parlophone	7
5	4	NOT FADE AWAY	Rolling Stones	Decca	4
6	5	JUST ONE LOOK	Hollies	Parlophone	4
4	6	DIANE	Bachelors	Decca	9
8	7	I THINK OF YOU	Merseybeats	Fontana	9
9	[8]	BOYS CRY	Eden Kane	Fontana	7
14	9	I LOVE YOU BECAUSE	Jim Reeves	RCA	4
7	10	NEEDLES AND PINS	Searchers	Pye	10
10	11	LET ME GO LOVER	Kathy Kirby	Decca	5
16	12	THAT GIRL BELONGS TO YESTERDAY	Gene Pitney	United Artists	3
13	[13]	STAY AWHILE	Dusty Springfield	Philips	5
22	14	THEME FOR YOUNG LOVERS	Shadows	Columbia	3
11	15	CANDY MAN	Brian Poole and the Tremeloes	Decca	7
18	16	OVER YOU	Freddie and the Dreamers	Columbia	4
15	17	BORNE ON THE WIND	Roy Orbison	London	5
29	18	TELL ME WHEN	Applejacks	Decca	2
12	19	I'M THE ONE	Gerry and the Pacemakers	Columbia	10
17	20	AS USUAL	Brenda Lee	Brunswick	11
19	21	BABY I LOVE YOU	Ronettes	London	11
20	22	5 4 3 2 1	Manfred Mann	HMV	9
25	23	EIGHT BY TEN	Ken Dodd	Columbia	7
21	24	I'M THE LONELY ONE	Cliff Richard	Columbia	7
24	25	I WANT TO HOLD YOUR HAND	Beatles	Parlophone	16
26	[26]	YOU WERE THERE	Heinz	Decca	4
23	27	FOR YOU	Rick Nelson	Brunswick	8
-	28	I BELIEVE	Bachelors	Decca	1
-	29	VIVA LAS VEGAS	Elvis Presley	RCA	1
28	30	DON'T BLAME ME	Frank Ifield	Columbia	11
-	31	IF HE TELLS YOU	Adam Faith	Parlophone	1
27	32	HIPPY HIPPY SHAKE	Swinging Blue Jeans	HMV	14
31	33	TWENTY FOUR HOURS FROM TULSA	Gene Pitney	United Artists	16
38	34	MOVE OVER DARLING	Doris Day	CBS	2
34	35	I LOVE HOW YOU LOVE ME	Maureen Evans	Oriole	3
39	36	WORLD WITHOUT LOVE	Peter and Gordon	Columbia	2
32	37	MY WORLD OF BLUE	Karl Denver	Decca	2
30	38	GLAD ALL OVER	Dave Clark Five	Columbia	18
-	39	GOOD GOLLY MISS MOLLY	Swinging Blue Jeans	HMV	1
37	40	IT'S AN OPEN SECRET	Joy Strings	Regal-Zonophone	3

WEEK ENDING 26 MARCH 1964

LW	TW	Title	Artist	Label	Wks
1	[1]	LITTLE CHILDREN	Billy J Kramer and the Dakotas	Parlophone	5
5	[2]	JUST ONE LOOK	Hollies	Parlophone	5
4	[3]	NOT FADE AWAY	Rolling Stones	Decca	5
3	4	ANYONE WHO HAD A HEART	Cilla Black	Parlophone	8
9	[5]	I LOVE YOU BECAUSE	Jim Reeves	RCA	5
2	6	BITS AND PIECES	Dave Clark Five	Columbia	6
12	[7]	THAT GIRL BELONGS TO YESTERDAY	Gene Pitney	United Artists	4
-	8	CAN'T BUY ME LOVE	Beatles	Parlophone	1
8	9	BOYS CRY	Eden Kane	Fontana	8
6	10	DIANE	Bachelors	Decca	10
28	11	I BELIEVE	Bachelors	Decca	2
18	12	TELL ME WHEN	Applejacks	Decca	3
14	13	THEME FOR YOUNG LOVERS	Shadows	Columbia	4

■For the first time since 2 November 1961, and for only the second time since a Top 40 began, none of the top twenty records have been on the charts for ten weeks or more (05.03.64) ■ The top thirteen records are by British acts, and there are only eleven American records in the Top 40 (12.03.64) ■ The Joy Strings are a Salvation Army pop group (05.03.64)■

□ Highest position disc reached ● Act's first ever week on chart

LW	TW	Title	Artist	Label	Wks
7	14	I THINK OF YOU	Merseybeats	Fontana	10
11	15	LET ME GO LOVER	Kathy Kirby	Decca	6
36	16	WORLD WITHOUT LOVE	Peter and Gordon	Columbia	3
13	17	STAY AWHILE	Dusty Springfield	Philips	6
10	18	NEEDLES AND PINS	Searchers	Pye	11
15	19	CANDY MAN	Brian Poole and the Tremeloes	Decca	8
29	20	VIVA LAS VEGAS	Elvis Presley	RCA	2
16	21	OVER YOU	Freddie and the Dreamers	Columbia	5
17	22	BORNE ON THE WIND	Roy Orbison	London	6
39	23	GOOD GOLLY MISS MOLLY	Swinging Blue Jeans	HMV	2
20	24	AS USUAL	Brenda Lee	Brunswick	12
19	25	I'M THE ONE	Gerry and the Pacemakers	Columbia	11
34	26	MOVE OVER DARLING	Doris Day	CBS	3
23	27	EIGHT BY TEN	Ken Dodd	Columbia	8
-	28	MY BOY LOLLIPOP	Millie ●	Fontana	1
37	[29]	MY WORLD OF BLUE	Karl Denver	Decca	3
21	30	BABY I LOVE YOU	Ronettes	London	12
22	31	5 4 3 2 1	Manfred Mann	HMV	10
25	32	I WANT TO HOLD YOUR HAND	Beatles	Parlophone	17
31	33	IF HE TELLS YOU	Adam Faith	Parlophone	2
27	34	FOR YOU	Rick Nelson	Brunswick	9
-	[35]	MARY JANE	Del Shannon	Stateside	1
40	36	IT'S AN OPEN SECRET	Joy Strings	Regal-Zonophone	4
-	37	EVERYTHING'S ALRIGHT	Mojos ●	Decca	1
-	38	NEW ORLEANS	Bern Elliott and the Fenmen	Decca	1
24	39	I'M THE LONELY ONE	Cliff Richard	Columbia	8
26	40	YOU WERE THERE	Heinz	Decca	5

WEEK ENDING 2 APRIL 1964

LW	TW	Title	Artist	Label	Wks
8	[1]	CAN'T BUY ME LOVE	Beatles	Parlophone	2
1	2	LITTLE CHILDREN	Billy J Kramer and the Dakotas	Parlophone	6
2	3	JUST ONE LOOK	Hollies	Parlophone	6
3	4	NOT FADE AWAY	Rolling Stones	Decca	6
5	[5]	I LOVE YOU BECAUSE	Jim Reeves	RCA	6
11	6	I BELIEVE	Bachelors	Decca	3
6	7	BITS AND PIECES	Dave Clark Five	Columbia	7
10	8	DIANE	Bachelors	Decca	11
7	9	THAT GIRL BELONGS TO YESTERDAY	Gene Pitney	United Artists	5
4	10	ANYONE WHO HAD A HEART	Cilla Black	Parlophone	9
12	11	TELL ME WHEN	Applejacks	Decca	4
9	12	BOYS CRY	Eden Kane	Fontana	9
16	13	WORLD WITHOUT LOVE	Peter and Gordon	Columbia	4
13	14	THEME FOR YOUNG LOVERS	Shadows	Columbia	5
14	15	I THINK OF YOU	Merseybeats	Fontana	11
21	16	OVER YOU	Freddie and the Dreamers	Columbia	6
15	17	LET ME GO LOVER	Kathy Kirby	Decca	7
20	18	VIVA LAS VEGAS	Elvis Presley	RCA	3
17	19	STAY AWHILE	Dusty Springfield	Philips	7
23	20	GOOD GOLLY MISS MOLLY	Swinging Blue Jeans	HMV	3
18	21	NEEDLES AND PINS	Searchers	Pye	12
19	22	CANDY MAN	Brian Poole and the Tremeloes	Decca	9
26	23	MOVE OVER DARLING	Doris Day	CBS	4
22	24	BORNE ON THE WIND	Roy Orbison	London	7
33	[25]	IF HE TELLS YOU	Adam Faith	Parlophone	3
27	26	EIGHT BY TEN	Ken Dodd	Columbia	9
28	27	MY BOY LOLLIPOP	Millie	Fontana	2
25	28	I'M THE ONE	Gerry and the Pacemakers	Columbia	12
24	29	AS USUAL	Brenda Lee	Brunswick	13
38	30	NEW ORLEANS	Bern Elliott and the Fenmen	Decca	2
37	31	EVERYTHING'S ALRIGHT	Mojos	Decca	2
29	32	MY WORLD OF BLUE	Karl Denver	Decca	4
31	33	5 4 3 2 1	Manfred Mann	HMV	11
39	34	I'M THE LONELY ONE	Cliff Richard	Columbia	9
35	[35]	MARY JANE	Del Shannon	Stateside	2
40	36	YOU WERE THERE	Heinz	Decca	6
34	37	FOR YOU	Rick Nelson	Brunswick	10
36	38	IT'S AN OPEN SECRET	Joy Strings	Regal-Zonophone	5
-	39	TWENTY FOUR HOURS FROM TULSA	Gene Pitney	United Artists	17
-	40	JULIET	Four Pennies ●	Philips	1

WEEK ENDING 9 APRIL 1964

LW	TW	Title	Artist	Label	Wks
1	[1]	CAN'T BUY ME LOVE	Beatles	Parlophone	3
2	2	LITTLE CHILDREN	Billy J Kramer and the Dakotas	Parlophone	7
6	3	I BELIEVE	Bachelors	Decca	4
13	4	WORLD WITHOUT LOVE	Peter and Gordon	Columbia	5
3	5	JUST ONE LOOK	Hollies	Parlophone	7
4	6	NOT FADE AWAY	Rolling Stones	Decca	7
5	7	I LOVE YOU BECAUSE	Jim Reeves	RCA	7
9	8	THAT GIRL BELONGS TO YESTERDAY	Gene Pitney	United Artists	6
11	9	TELL ME WHEN	Applejacks	Decca	5
7	10	BITS AND PIECES	Dave Clark Five	Columbia	8
10	11	ANYONE WHO HAD A HEART	Cilla Black	Parlophone	10
14	[12]	THEME FOR YOUNG LOVERS	Shadows	Columbia	6
8	13	DIANE	Bachelors	Decca	12
20	14	GOOD GOLLY MISS MOLLY	Swinging Blue Jeans	HMV	4
23	15	MOVE OVER DARLING	Doris Day	CBS	5
27	16	MY BOY LOLLIPOP	Millie	Fontana	3
18	[17]	VIVA LAS VEGAS	Elvis Presley	RCA	4
31	18	EVERYTHING'S ALRIGHT	Mojos	Decca	3
17	19	LET ME GO LOVER	Kathy Kirby	Decca	8
15	20	I THINK OF YOU	Merseybeats	Fontana	12
12	21	BOYS CRY	Eden Kane	Fontana	10
16	22	OVER YOU	Freddie and the Dreamers	Columbia	7
19	23	STAY AWHILE	Dusty Springfield	Philips	8
30	[24]	NEW ORLEANS	Bern Elliott and the Fenmen	Decca	3
25	[25]	IF HE TELLS YOU	Adam Faith	Parlophone	4
22	26	CANDY MAN	Brian Poole and the Tremeloes	Decca	10
21	27	NEEDLES AND PINS	Searchers	Pye	13
24	28	BORNE ON THE WIND	Roy Orbison	London	8
26	29	EIGHT BY TEN	Ken Dodd	Columbia	10
-	30	MOCKING BIRD HILL	Migil Five ●	Pye	1
32	31	MY WORLD OF BLUE	Karl Denver	Decca	5
28	32	I'M THE ONE	Gerry and the Pacemakers	Columbia	13
29	33	AS USUAL	Brenda Lee	Brunswick	14
-	34	HI-HEEL SNEAKERS	Tommy Tucker ●	Pye	1
-	35	I LOVE HOW YOU LOVE ME	Maureen Evans	Oriole	4
40	36	JULIET	Four Pennies	Philips	2
-	37	GONE	Shirley Bassey	Columbia	1
38	38	IT'S AN OPEN SECRET	Joy Strings	Regal-Zonophone	6
-	39	ONLY YOU	Mark Wynter	Pye	1
-	40	I WANT TO HOLD YOUR HAND	Beatles	Parlophone	18

WEEK ENDING 16 APRIL 1964

LW	TW	Title	Artist	Label	Wks
1	[1]	CAN'T BUY ME LOVE	Beatles	Parlophone	4
4	2	WORLD WITHOUT LOVE	Peter and Gordon	Columbia	6
3	3	I BELIEVE	Bachelors	Decca	5
2	4	LITTLE CHILDREN	Billy J Kramer and the Dakotas	Parlophone	8
7	[5]	I LOVE YOU BECAUSE	Jim Reeves	RCA	8
5	6	JUST ONE LOOK	Hollies	Parlophone	8
9	[7]	TELL ME WHEN	Applejacks	Decca	6
6	8	NOT FADE AWAY	Rolling Stones	Decca	8
8	9	THAT GIRL BELONGS TO YESTERDAY	Gene Pitney	United Artists	7
16	10	MY BOY LOLLIPOP	Millie	Fontana	4
14	[11]	GOOD GOLLY MISS MOLLY	Swinging Blue Jeans	HMV	5
15	12	MOVE OVER DARLING	Doris Day	CBS	6
18	13	EVERYTHING'S ALRIGHT	Mojos	Decca	4
10	14	BITS AND PIECES	Dave Clark Five	Columbia	9
11	15	ANYONE WHO HAD A HEART	Cilla Black	Parlophone	11
13	16	DIANE	Bachelors	Decca	13
30	17	MOCKING BIRD HILL	Migil Five	Pye	2
17	18	VIVA LAS VEGAS	Elvis Presley	RCA	5
12	19	THEME FOR YOUNG LOVERS	Shadows	Columbia	7
-	20	DON'T THROW YOUR LOVE AWAY	Searchers	Pye	1
20	21	I THINK OF YOU	Merseybeats	Fontana	13
19	22	LET ME GO LOVER	Kathy Kirby	Decca	9

In these weeks ■ Two early ska hits enter the chart, Millie's *My Boy Lollipop* and the Migil Five's odd version of *Mocking Bird Hill* (09.04.64) ■ *Viva Las Vegas*, the title track from Elvis Presley's fifteenth film, becomes his least successful RCA single so far (09.04.64) ■

May 1964

□ Highest position disc reached ● Act's first ever week on chart

LW	TW	Title	Artist	Label	Wks
21	23	BOYS CRY	Eden Kane	*Fontana*	11
24	[24]	NEW ORLEANS	Bern Elliott and the Fenmen	*Decca*	4
22	25	OVER YOU	Freddie and the Dreamers	*Columbia*	8
25	26	IF HE TELLS YOU	Adam Faith	*Parlophone*	5
-	27	THINK	Brenda Lee	*Brunswick*	1
23	28	STAY AWHILE	Dusty Springfield	*Philips*	9
-	29	HUBBLE BUBBLE TOIL AND TROUBLE	Manfred Mann	*HMV*	1
26	30	CANDY MAN	Brian Poole and the Tremeloes	*Decca*	11
-	31	DON'T LET THE SUN CATCH YOU CRYING	Gerry and the Pacemakers	*Columbia*	1
36	32	JULIET	Four Pennies	*Philips*	3
34	33	HI-HEEL SNEAKERS	Tommy Tucker	*Pye*	2
28	34	BORNE ON THE WIND	Roy Orbison	*London*	9
35	35	I LOVE HOW YOU LOVE ME	Maureen Evans	*Oriole*	5
29	36	EIGHT BY TEN	Ken Dodd	*Columbia*	11
37	37	GONE	Shirley Bassey	*Columbia*	2
27	38	NEEDLES AND PINS	Searchers	*Pye*	14
-	39	BABY LET ME TAKE YOU HOME	Animals ●	*Columbia*	1
32	40	I'M THE ONE	Gerry and the Pacemakers	*Columbia*	14

WEEK ENDING 23 APRIL 1964

LW	TW	Title	Artist	Label	Wks
2	[1]	WORLD WITHOUT LOVE	Peter and Gordon	*Columbia*	7
1	2	CAN'T BUY ME LOVE	Beatles	*Parlophone*	5
3	3	I BELIEVE	Bachelors	*Decca*	6
20	4	DON'T THROW YOUR LOVE AWAY	Searchers	*Pye*	2
10	5	MY BOY LOLLIPOP	Millie	*Fontana*	5
5	6	I LOVE YOU BECAUSE	Jim Reeves	*RCA*	9
7	[7]	TELL ME WHEN	Applejacks	*Decca*	7
8	8	NOT FADE AWAY	Rolling Stones	*Decca*	9
4	9	LITTLE CHILDREN	Billy J Kramer and the Dakotas	*Parlophone*	9
6	10	JUST ONE LOOK	Hollies	*Parlophone*	9
12	11	MOVE OVER DARLING	Doris Day	*CBS*	7
13	12	EVERYTHING'S ALRIGHT	Mojos	*Decca*	5
17	13	MOCKING BIRD HILL	Migil Five	*Pye*	3
11	14	GOOD GOLLY MISS MOLLY	Swinging Blue Jeans	*HMV*	6
9	15	THAT GIRL BELONGS TO YESTERDAY	Gene Pitney	*United Artists*	8
29	16	HUBBLE BUBBLE TOIL AND TROUBLE	Manfred Mann	*HMV*	2
31	17	DON'T LET THE SUN CATCH YOU CRYING	Gerry and the Pacemakers	*Columbia*	2
32	18	JULIET	Four Pennies	*Philips*	4
15	19	ANYONE WHO HAD A HEART	Cilla Black	*Parlophone*	12
19	20	THEME FOR YOUNG LOVERS	Shadows	*Columbia*	8
16	21	DIANE	Bachelors	*Decca*	14
18	22	VIVA LAS VEGAS	Elvis Presley	*RCA*	6
14	23	BITS AND PIECES	Dave Clark Five	*Columbia*	10
-	24	DON'T TURN AROUND	Merseybeats	*Fontana*	1
-	25	WALK ON BY	Dionne Warwick ●	*Pye*	1
27	[26]	THINK	Brenda Lee	*Brunswick*	2
24	27	NEW ORLEANS	Bern Elliott and the Fenmen	*Decca*	5
33	28	HI-HEEL SNEAKERS	Tommy Tucker	*Pye*	3
39	29	BABY LET ME TAKE YOU HOME	Animals	*Columbia*	2
22	30	LET ME GO LOVER	Kathy Kirby	*Decca*	10
23	31	BOYS CRY	Eden Kane	*Fontana*	12
21	32	I THINK OF YOU	Merseybeats	*Fontana*	14
-	[33]	TELL IT ON THE MOUNTAIN	Peter Paul and Mary	*Warner Bros*	1
25	34	OVER YOU	Freddie and the Dreamers	*Columbia*	9
26	35	IF HE TELLS YOU	Adam Faith	*Parlophone*	6
37	[36]	GONE	Shirley Bassey	*Columbia*	3
-	37	A LITTLE LOVING	Fourmost	*Parlophone*	1
-	38	ONLY YOU	Mark Wynter	*Pye*	2
-	39	IF I LOVED YOU	Richard Anthony	*Columbia*	1
-	40	STAND BY ME	Kenny Lynch	*HMV*	1

WEEK ENDING 30 APRIL 1964

LW	TW	Title	Artist	Label	Wks
1	[1]	WORLD WITHOUT LOVE	Peter and Gordon	*Columbia*	8
4	2	DON'T THROW YOUR LOVE AWAY	Searchers	*Pye*	3
3	3	I BELIEVE	Bachelors	*Decca*	7
2	4	CAN'T BUY ME LOVE	Beatles	*Parlophone*	6
5	5	MY BOY LOLLIPOP	Millie	*Fontana*	6
6	6	I LOVE YOU BECAUSE	Jim Reeves	*RCA*	10
17	7	DON'T LET THE SUN CATCH YOU CRYING	Gerry and the Pacemakers	*Columbia*	3
11	[8]	MOVE OVER DARLING	Doris Day	*CBS*	8
12	[9]	EVERYTHING'S ALRIGHT	Mojos	*Decca*	6
13	[10]	MOCKING BIRD HILL	Migil Five	*Pye*	4
16	[11]	HUBBLE BUBBLE TOIL AND TROUBLE	Manfred Mann	*HMV*	3
18	12	JULIET	Four Pennies	*Philips*	5
8	13	NOT FADE AWAY	Rolling Stones	*Decca*	10
7	14	TELL ME WHEN	Applejacks	*Decca*	8
25	15	WALK ON BY	Dionne Warwick	*Pye*	2
9	16	LITTLE CHILDREN	Billy J Kramer and the Dakotas	*Parlophone*	10
24	17	DON'T TURN AROUND	Merseybeats	*Fontana*	2
10	18	JUST ONE LOOK	Hollies	*Parlophone*	10
37	19	A LITTLE LOVING	Fourmost	*Parlophone*	2
14	20	GOOD GOLLY MISS MOLLY	Swinging Blue Jeans	*HMV*	7
29	[21]	BABY LET ME TAKE YOU HOME	Animals	*Columbia*	3
15	22	THAT GIRL BELONGS TO YESTERDAY	Gene Pitney	*United Artists*	9
28	[23]	HI-HEEL SNEAKERS	Tommy Tucker	*Pye*	4
20	24	THEME FOR YOUNG LOVERS	Shadows	*Columbia*	9
-	[25]	ANGRY AT THE BIG OAK TREE	Frank Ifield	*Columbia*	1
21	26	DIANE	Bachelors	*Decca*	15
26	27	THINK	Brenda Lee	*Brunswick*	3
39	28	IF I LOVED YOU	Richard Anthony	*Columbia*	2
22	29	VIVA LAS VEGAS	Elvis Presley	*RCA*	7
-	30	CONSTANTLY	Cliff Richard	*Columbia*	1
-	31	IT'S OVER	Roy Orbison	*London*	1
-	32	THE SPARTANS	Sounds Incorporated ●	*Columbia*	1
23	33	BITS AND PIECES	Dave Clark Five	*Columbia*	11
27	34	NEW ORLEANS	Bern Elliott and the Fenmen	*Decca*	6
19	35	ANYONE WHO HAD A HEART	Cilla Black	*Parlophone*	13
-	36	NON HO L'ETA PER AMARTI	Gigliola Cinquetti ●	*Decca*	1
33	37	TELL IT ON THE MOUNTAIN	Peter Paul and Mary	*Warner Bros*	2
-	38	I WILL	Billy Fury	*Decca*	1
-	39	BABY IT'S YOU	Dave Berry	*Decca*	1
30	40	LET ME GO LOVER	Kathy Kirby	*Decca*	11

WEEK ENDING 7 MAY 1964

LW	TW	Title	Artist	Label	Wks
2	[1]	DON'T THROW YOUR LOVE AWAY	Searchers	*Pye*	4
3	[2]	I BELIEVE	Bachelors	*Decca*	8
5	3	MY BOY LOLLIPOP	Millie	*Fontana*	7
1	4	WORLD WITHOUT LOVE	Peter and Gordon	*Columbia*	9
12	5	JULIET	Four Pennies	*Philips*	6
7	[6]	DON'T LET THE SUN CATCH YOU CRYING	Gerry and the Pacemakers	*Columbia*	4
4	7	CAN'T BUY ME LOVE	Beatles	*Parlophone*	7
8	[8]	MOVE OVER DARLING	Doris Day	*CBS*	9
15	[9]	WALK ON BY	Dionne Warwick	*Pye*	3
6	10	I LOVE YOU BECAUSE	Jim Reeves	*RCA*	11
19	11	A LITTLE LOVING	Fourmost	*Parlophone*	3
10	12	MOCKING BIRD HILL	Migil Five	*Pye*	5
17	[13]	DON'T TURN AROUND	Merseybeats	*Fontana*	3
31	14	IT'S OVER	Roy Orbison	*London*	2
11	15	HUBBLE BUBBLE TOIL AND TROUBLE	Manfred Mann	*HMV*	4
30	16	CONSTANTLY	Cliff Richard	*Columbia*	2
9	17	EVERYTHING'S ALRIGHT	Mojos	*Decca*	7
28	[18]	IF I LOVED YOU	Richard Anthony	*Columbia*	3
14	19	TELL ME WHEN	Applejacks	*Decca*	9
38	20	I WILL	Billy Fury	*Decca*	2
13	21	NOT FADE AWAY	Rolling Stones	*Decca*	11
16	22	LITTLE CHILDREN	Billy J Kramer and the Dakotas	*Parlophone*	11
21	23	BABY LET ME TAKE YOU HOME	Animals	*Columbia*	4
39	[24]	BABY IT'S YOU	Dave Berry	*Decca*	2
25	[25]	ANGRY AT THE BIG OAK TREE	Frank Ifield	*Columbia*	2

■Doris Day's first Top Ten hit since the 50s is the theme from her hit film co-starring Rock Hudson (30.04.64) ■ Three number ones in a row with the word 'Love' in the title (07.05.64) ■ Kenny Lynch's version of Ben E. King's 1961 hit *Stand By Me* sneaks into the bottom of the chart, beating out another version by the heavyweight boxer then known as Cassius Clay (23.04.64)■

May 1964

□ Highest position disc reached ● Act's first ever week on chart

LW	TW	Title	Artist	Label	Wks
23	26	HI-HEEL SNEAKERS	Tommy Tucker	Pye	5
20	27	GOOD GOLLY MISS MOLLY	Swinging Blue Jeans	HMV	8
36	28	NON HO L'ETA PER AMARTI	Gigliola Cinquetti	Decca	2
18	29	JUST ONE LOOK	Hollies	Parlophone	11
-	30	YOU'RE MY WORLD	Cilla Black	Parlophone	1
27	31	THINK	Brenda Lee	Brunswick	4
22	32	THAT GIRL BELONGS TO YESTERDAY	Gene Pitney	United Artists	10
26	33	DIANE	Bachelors	Decca	16
32	34	THE SPARTANS	Sounds Incorporated	Columbia	2
-	35	CAN'T BUY ME LOVE	Ella Fitzgerald	Verve	1
-	36	YOU'RE THE ONE	Kathy Kirby	Decca	1
-	37	RISE AND FALL OF FLINGEL BUNT	Shadows	Columbia	1
24	38	THEME FOR YOUNG LOVERS	Shadows	Columbia	10
-	39	STAND BY ME	Kenny Lynch	HMV	2
29	40	VIVA LAS VEGAS	Elvis Presley	RCA	8

WEEK ENDING 14 MAY 1964

LW	TW	Title	Artist	Label	Wks
1	1	DON'T THROW YOUR LOVE AWAY	Searchers	Pye	5
5	2	JULIET	Four Pennies	Philips	7
3	3	MY BOY LOLLIPOP	Millie	Fontana	8
2	4	I BELIEVE	Bachelors	Decca	9
4	5	WORLD WITHOUT LOVE	Peter and Gordon	Columbia	10
14	6	IT'S OVER	Roy Orbison	London	3
16	7	CONSTANTLY	Cliff Richard	Columbia	3
10	8	I LOVE YOU BECAUSE	Jim Reeves	RCA	12
6	9	DON'T LET THE SUN CATCH YOU CRYING	Gerry and the Pacemakers	Columbia	5
11	10	A LITTLE LOVING	Fourmost	Parlophone	4
9	11	WALK ON BY	Dionne Warwick	Pye	4
30	12	YOU'RE MY WORLD	Cilla Black	Parlophone	2
7	13	CAN'T BUY ME LOVE	Beatles	Parlophone	8
12	14	MOCKING BIRD HILL	Migil Five	Pye	6
8	15	MOVE OVER DARLING	Doris Day	CBS	10
13	16	DON'T TURN AROUND	Merseybeats	Fontana	4
20	17	I WILL	Billy Fury	Decca	3
17	18	EVERYTHING'S ALRIGHT	Mojos	Decca	8
15	19	HUBBLE BUBBLE TOIL AND TROUBLE	Manfred Mann	HMV	5
18	20	IF I LOVED YOU	Richard Anthony	Columbia	4
37	21	RISE AND FALL OF FLINGEL BUNT	Shadows	Columbia	2
19	22	TELL ME WHEN	Applejacks	Decca	10
23	23	BABY LET ME TAKE YOU HOME	Animals	Columbia	5
28	24	NON HO L'ETA PER AMARTI	Gigliola Cinquetti	Decca	3
25	25	ANGRY AT THE BIG OAK TREE	Frank Ifield	Columbia	3
-	26	NO PARTICULAR PLACE TO GO	Chuck Berry	Pye	1
22	27	LITTLE CHILDREN	Billy J Kramer and the Dakotas	Parlophone	12
21	28	NOT FADE AWAY	Rolling Stones	Decca	12
24	29	BABY IT'S YOU	Dave Berry	Decca	3
36	30	YOU'RE THE ONE	Kathy Kirby	Decca	2
34	31	THE SPARTANS	Sounds Incorporated	Columbia	3
26	32	HI-HEEL SNEAKERS	Tommy Tucker	Pye	6
27	33	GOOD GOLLY MISS MOLLY	Swinging Blue Jeans	HMV	9
-	34	SOMEONE SOMEONE	Brian Poole and the Tremeloes	Decca	1
29	35	JUST ONE LOOK	Hollies	Parlophone	12
31	36	THINK	Brenda Lee	Brunswick	5
33	37	DIANE	Bachelors	Decca	17
35	38	CAN'T BUY ME LOVE	Ella Fitzgerald	Verve	2
-	39	SUSPICION	Terry Stafford ●	London	1
-	40	ANYONE WHO HAD A HEART	Cilla Black	Parlophone	14

WEEK ENDING 21 MAY 1964

LW	TW	Title	Artist	Label	Wks
2	1	JULIET	Four Pennies	Philips	8
3	2	MY BOY LOLLIPOP	Millie	Fontana	9
1	3	DON'T THROW YOUR LOVE AWAY	Searchers	Pye	6
12	4	YOU'RE MY WORLD	Cilla Black	Parlophone	3
6	5	IT'S OVER	Roy Orbison	London	4
4	6	I BELIEVE	Bachelors	Decca	10
9	7	DON'T LET THE SUN CATCH YOU CRYING	Gerry and the Pacemakers	Columbia	6
10	8	A LITTLE LOVING	Fourmost	Parlophone	5
7	9	CONSTANTLY	Cliff Richard	Columbia	4
8	10	I LOVE YOU BECAUSE	Jim Reeves	RCA	13
11	11	WALK ON BY	Dionne Warwick	Pye	5
5	12	WORLD WITHOUT LOVE	Peter and Gordon	Columbia	11
21	13	RISE AND FALL OF FLINGEL BUNT	Shadows	Columbia	3
17	14	I WILL	Billy Fury	Decca	4
13	15	CAN'T BUY ME LOVE	Beatles	Parlophone	9
16	16	DON'T TURN AROUND	Merseybeats	Fontana	5
15	17	MOVE OVER DARLING	Doris Day	CBS	11
14	18	MOCKING BIRD HILL	Migil Five	Pye	7
20	19	IF I LOVED YOU	Richard Anthony	Columbia	5
26	20	NO PARTICULAR PLACE TO GO	Chuck Berry	Pye	2
19	21	HUBBLE BUBBLE TOIL AND TROUBLE	Manfred Mann	HMV	6
24	22	NON HO L'ETA PER AMARTI	Gigliola Cinquetti	Decca	4
23	23	BABY LET ME TAKE YOU HOME	Animals	Columbia	6
18	24	EVERYTHING'S ALRIGHT	Mojos	Decca	9
-	25	I LOVE YOU BABY	Freddie and the Dreamers	Columbia	1
34	26	SOMEONE SOMEONE	Brian Poole and the Tremeloes	Decca	2
25	27	ANGRY AT THE BIG OAK TREE	Frank Ifield	Columbia	4
30	28	YOU'RE THE ONE	Kathy Kirby	Decca	3
22	29	TELL ME WHEN	Applejacks	Decca	11
31	30	THE SPARTANS	Sounds Incorporated	Columbia	4
-	31	SHOUT	Lulu and the Luvvers ●	Decca	1
29	32	BABY IT'S YOU	Dave Berry	Decca	4
28	33	NOT FADE AWAY	Rolling Stones	Decca	13
38	34	CAN'T BUY ME LOVE	Ella Fitzgerald	Verve	3
32	35	HI-HEEL SNEAKERS	Tommy Tucker	Pye	7
27	36	LITTLE CHILDREN	Billy J Kramer and the Dakotas	Parlophone	13
-	37	MY GUY	Mary Wells ●	Stateside	1
39	38	SUSPICION	Terry Stafford	London	2
-	39	WALKIN' THE DOG	Dennisons ●	Decca	1
-	40	DON'T LET THE RAIN COME DOWN	Ronnie Hilton	HMV	1

WEEK ENDING 28 MAY 1964

LW	TW	Title	Artist	Label	Wks
4	1	YOU'RE MY WORLD	Cilla Black	Parlophone	4
1	2	JULIET	Four Pennies	Philips	9
2	3	MY BOY LOLLIPOP	Millie	Fontana	10
5	4	IT'S OVER	Roy Orbison	London	5
9	5	CONSTANTLY	Cliff Richard	Columbia	5
8	6	A LITTLE LOVING	Fourmost	Parlophone	6
13	7	RISE AND FALL OF FLINGEL BUNT	Shadows	Columbia	4
3	8	DON'T THROW YOUR LOVE AWAY	Searchers	Pye	7
6	9	I BELIEVE	Bachelors	Decca	11
20	10	NO PARTICULAR PLACE TO GO	Chuck Berry	Pye	3
11	11	WALK ON BY	Dionne Warwick	Pye	6
10	12	I LOVE YOU BECAUSE	Jim Reeves	RCA	14
26	13	SOMEONE SOMEONE	Brian Poole and the Tremeloes	Decca	3
14	14	I WILL	Billy Fury	Decca	5
7	15	DON'T LET THE SUN CATCH YOU CRYING	Gerry and the Pacemakers	Columbia	7
16	16	DON'T TURN AROUND	Merseybeats	Fontana	6
28	17	YOU'RE THE ONE	Kathy Kirby	Decca	4
-	18	HERE I GO AGAIN	Hollies	Parlophone	1
17	19	MOVE OVER DARLING	Doris Day	CBS	12
22	20	NON HO L'ETA PER AMARTI	Gigliola Cinquetti	Decca	5
25	21	I LOVE YOU BABY	Freddie and the Dreamers	Columbia	2
15	22	CAN'T BUY ME LOVE	Beatles	Parlophone	10
12	23	WORLD WITHOUT LOVE	Peter and Gordon	Columbia	12
31	24	SHOUT	Lulu and the Luvvers	Decca	2
37	25	MY GUY	Mary Wells	Stateside	2
18	26	MOCKING BIRD HILL	Migil Five	Pye	8
19	27	IF I LOVED YOU	Richard Anthony	Columbia	6
40	28	DON'T LET THE RAIN COME DOWN	Ronnie Hilton	HMV	2
23	29	BABY LET ME TAKE YOU HOME	Animals	Columbia	7
24	30	EVERYTHING'S ALRIGHT	Mojos	Decca	10
27	31	ANGRY AT THE BIG OAK TREE	Frank Ifield	Columbia	5

In these weeks ■ *Juliet* is the first girl's name at number one since *Tell Laura I Love Her* in October 1960 (21.05.64) ■ A good week for teenage girl vocalists. Millie is at number two, Italian Eurovision winner Gigliola Cinquetti is beginning her climb up the charts and Scottish fifteen year old Lulu makes her chart debut (21.05.64)■

LW	TW	Title / Artist	Label	Wks
-	32	CAN'T YOU SEE THAT SHE'S MINE Dave Clark Five	Columbia	1
38	33	SUSPICION Terry Stafford	London	3
21	34	HUBBLE BUBBLE TOIL AND TROUBLE Manfred Mann	HMV	7
30	35	THE SPARTANS Sounds Incorporated	Columbia	5
32	36	BABY IT'S YOU Dave Berry	Decca	5
-	[37]	STOP LOOK AND LISTEN Wayne Fontana and the Mindbenders ●	Fontana	1
-	38	I LOVE BEING IN LOVE WITH YOU Adam Faith	Parlophone	1
-	39	THINK Brenda Lee	Brunswick	6
-	[40]	YOU'VE GOT LOVE Buddy Holly and the Crickets	Coral	1

LW	TW	*WEEK ENDING* **4 JUNE 1964**		Wks
1	[1]	YOU'RE MY WORLD Cilla Black	Parlophone	5
4	2	IT'S OVER Roy Orbison	London	6
2	3	JULIET Four Pennies	Philips	10
5	[4]	CONSTANTLY Cliff Richard	Columbia	6
7	[5]	RISE AND FALL OF FLINGEL BUNT Shadows	Columbia	5
10	6	NO PARTICULAR PLACE TO GO Chuck Berry	Pye	4
3	7	MY BOY LOLLIPOP Millie	Fontana	11
13	8	SOMEONE SOMEONE Brian Poole and the Tremeloes	Decca	4
6	9	A LITTLE LOVING Fourmost	Parlophone	7
11	10	WALK ON BY Dionne Warwick	Pye	7
18	11	HERE I GO AGAIN Hollies	Parlophone	2
25	12	MY GUY Mary Wells	Stateside	3
12	13	I LOVE YOU BECAUSE Jim Reeves	RCA	15
9	14	I BELIEVE Bachelors	Decca	12
8	15	DON'T THROW YOUR LOVE AWAY Searchers	Pye	8
14	16	I WILL Billy Fury	Decca	6
24	17	SHOUT Lulu and the Luvvers	Decca	3
20	18	NON HO L'ETA PER AMARTI Gigliola Cinquetti	Decca	6
17	19	YOU'RE THE ONE Kathy Kirby	Decca	5
21	20	I LOVE YOU BABY Freddie and the Dreamers	Columbia	3
32	21	CAN'T YOU SEE THAT SHE'S MINE Dave Clark Five	Columbia	2
16	22	DON'T TURN AROUND Merseybeats	Fontana	7
28	23	DON'T LET THE RAIN COME DOWN Ronnie Hilton	HMV	3
15	24	DON'T LET THE SUN CATCH YOU CRYING Gerry and the Pacemakers	Columbia	8
22	25	CAN'T BUY ME LOVE Beatles	Parlophone	11
19	26	MOVE OVER DARLING Doris Day	CBS	13
23	27	WORLD WITHOUT LOVE Peter and Gordon	Columbia	13
26	28	MOCKING BIRD HILL Migil Five	Pye	9
-	29	RAMONA Bachelors	Decca	1
27	30	IF I LOVED YOU Richard Anthony	Columbia	7
33	[31]	SUSPICION Terry Stafford	London	4
-	32	HOLD ME P.J. Proby ●	Decca	1
31	33	ANGRY AT THE BIG OAK TREE Frank Ifield	Columbia	6
-	34	YOU'RE NO GOOD Swinging Blue Jeans	HMV	1
38	35	I LOVE BEING IN LOVE WITH YOU Adam Faith	Parlophone	2
-	[36]	WALKIN' THE DOG Dennisons	Decca	2
-	37	HELLO DOLLY Louis Armstrong	London	1
29	38	BABY LET ME TAKE YOU HOME Animals	Columbia	8
-	39	NOBODY I KNOW Peter and Gordon	Columbia	1
37	40	STOP LOOK AND LISTEN Wayne Fontana and the Mindbenders	Fontana	2

LW	TW	*WEEK ENDING* **11 JUNE 1964**		Wks
1	[1]	YOU'RE MY WORLD Cilla Black	Parlophone	6
2	2	IT'S OVER Roy Orbison	London	7
6	[3]	NO PARTICULAR PLACE TO GO Chuck Berry	Pye	5
8	4	SOMEONE SOMEONE Brian Poole and the Tremeloes	Decca	5
3	5	JULIET Four Pennies	Philips	11
4	6	CONSTANTLY Cliff Richard	Columbia	7
5	7	RISE AND FALL OF FLINGEL BUNT Shadows	Columbia	6
11	8	HERE I GO AGAIN Hollies	Parlophone	3
12	9	MY GUY Mary Wells	Stateside	4
17	10	SHOUT Lulu and the Luvvers	Decca	4
21	11	CAN'T YOU SEE THAT SHE'S MINE Dave Clark Five	Columbia	3
13	12	I LOVE YOU BECAUSE Jim Reeves	RCA	16

June 1964

□ Highest position disc reached ● Act's first ever week on chart

LW	TW	Title / Artist	Label	Wks
10	13	WALK ON BY Dionne Warwick	Pye	8
9	14	A LITTLE LOVING Fourmost	Parlophone	8
7	15	MY BOY LOLLIPOP Millie	Fontana	12
20	[16]	I LOVE YOU BABY Freddie and the Dreamers	Columbia	4
18	[17]	NON HO L'ETA PER AMARTI Gigliola Cinquetti	Decca	7
37	18	HELLO DOLLY Louis Armstrong	London	2
29	19	RAMONA Bachelors	Decca	2
16	20	I WILL Billy Fury	Decca	7
23	[21]	DON'T LET THE RAIN COME DOWN Ronnie Hilton	HMV	4
19	22	YOU'RE THE ONE Kathy Kirby	Decca	6
39	23	NOBODY I KNOW Peter and Gordon	Columbia	2
14	24	I BELIEVE Bachelors	Decca	13
34	25	YOU'RE NO GOOD Swinging Blue Jeans	HMV	2
15	26	DON'T THROW YOUR LOVE AWAY Searchers	Pye	9
22	27	DON'T TURN AROUND Merseybeats	Fontana	8
-	28	HELLO DOLLY Frankie Vaughan	Philips	1
-	29	BAMA LAMA BAMA LOO Little Richard	London	1
25	30	CAN'T BUY ME LOVE Beatles	Parlophone	12
32	31	HOLD ME P.J. Proby	Decca	2
24	32	DON'T LET THE SUN CATCH YOU CRYING Gerry and the Pacemakers	Columbia	9
-	33	HELLO DOLLY Kenny Ball and his Jazzmen	Pye	1
30	34	IF I LOVED YOU Richard Anthony	Columbia	8
31	35	SUSPICION Terry Stafford	London	5
26	36	MOVE OVER DARLING Doris Day	CBS	14
27	37	WORLD WITHOUT LOVE Peter and Gordon	Columbia	14
35	38	I LOVE BEING IN LOVE WITH YOU Adam Faith	Parlophone	3
28	39	MOCKING BIRD HILL Migil Five	Pye	10
36	40	WALKIN' THE DOG Dennisons	Decca	3

LW	TW	*WEEK ENDING* **18 JUNE 1964**		Wks
1	[1]	YOU'RE MY WORLD Cilla Black	Parlophone	7
2	2	IT'S OVER Roy Orbison	London	8
4	3	SOMEONE SOMEONE Brian Poole and the Tremeloes	Decca	6
8	[4]	HERE I GO AGAIN Hollies	Parlophone	4
9	[5]	MY GUY Mary Wells	Stateside	5
3	6	NO PARTICULAR PLACE TO GO Chuck Berry	Pye	6
10	[7]	SHOUT Lulu and the Luvvers	Decca	5
7	8	RISE AND FALL OF FLINGEL BUNT Shadows	Columbia	7
6	9	CONSTANTLY Cliff Richard	Columbia	8
18	10	HELLO DOLLY Louis Armstrong	London	3
11	11	CAN'T YOU SEE THAT SHE'S MINE Dave Clark Five	Columbia	4
19	12	RAMONA Bachelors	Decca	3
5	13	JULIET Four Pennies	Philips	12
23	14	NOBODY I KNOW Peter and Gordon	Columbia	3
12	15	I LOVE YOU BECAUSE Jim Reeves	RCA	17
25	16	YOU'RE NO GOOD Swinging Blue Jeans	HMV	3
13	17	WALK ON BY Dionne Warwick	Pye	9
17	18	NON HO L'ETA PER AMARTI Gigliola Cinquetti	Decca	8
14	19	A LITTLE LOVING Fourmost	Parlophone	9
16	20	I LOVE YOU BABY Freddie and the Dreamers	Columbia	5
15	21	MY BOY LOLLIPOP Millie	Fontana	13
31	22	HOLD ME P.J. Proby	Decca	3
20	23	I WILL Billy Fury	Decca	8
21	24	DON'T LET THE RAIN COME DOWN Ronnie Hilton	HMV	5
29	25	BAMA LAMA BAMA LOO Little Richard	London	2
28	26	HELLO DOLLY Frankie Vaughan	Philips	2
22	27	YOU'RE THE ONE Kathy Kirby	Decca	7
24	28	I BELIEVE Bachelors	Decca	14
-	[29]	AIN'T SHE SWEET Beatles	Polydor	1
33	[30]	HELLO DOLLY Kenny Ball and his Jazzmen	Pye	2
-	31	DIMPLES John Lee Hooker ●	Stateside	1
-	32	LIKE DREAMERS DO Applejacks	Decca	1
38	[33]	I LOVE BEING IN LOVE WITH YOU Adam Faith	Parlophone	4
-	34	NEAR YOU Migil Five	Pye	1
-	35	WHY NOT TONIGHT Mojos	Decca	1
26	36	DON'T THROW YOUR LOVE AWAY Searchers	Pye	10

■ *You've Got Love* is the only hit credited to Buddy Holly and the Crickets. All the others were either by 'The Crickets' or else credited to Holly alone (28.05.64) ■ Three consecutive titles beginning with the word *Don't* surrounded by two beginning with the word *Can't* between positions 21 and 25 (04.06.64) ■ Three versions of *Hello Dolly* chase each other up the charts (11.06.64)■

June 1964

☐ Highest position disc reached ● Act's first ever week on chart

LW	TW	Title / Artist	Label	Wks
-	37	I WON'T FORGET YOU Jim Reeves	RCA	1
30	38	CAN'T BUY ME LOVE Beatles	Parlophone	13
34	39	IF I LOVED YOU Richard Anthony	Columbia	9
-	40	CHAPEL OF LOVE Dixie Cups ●	Pye	1

WEEK ENDING 25 JUNE 1964

LW	TW	Title / Artist	Label	Wks
2	1	IT'S OVER Roy Orbison	London	9
3	2	SOMEONE SOMEONE Brian Poole and the Tremeloes	Decca	7
1	3	YOU'RE MY WORLD Cilla Black	Parlophone	8
10	4	HELLO DOLLY Louis Armstrong	London	4
5	5	MY GUY Mary Wells	Stateside	6
12	6	RAMONA Bachelors	Decca	4
4	7	HERE I GO AGAIN Hollies	Parlophone	5
16	8	YOU'RE NO GOOD Swinging Blue Jeans	HMV	4
7	9	SHOUT Lulu and the Luvvers	Decca	6
11	10	CAN'T YOU SEE THAT SHE'S MINE Dave Clark Five	Columbia	5
6	11	NO PARTICULAR PLACE TO GO Chuck Berry	Pye	7
14	12	NOBODY I KNOW Peter and Gordon	Columbia	4
8	13	RISE AND FALL OF FLINGEL BUNT Shadows	Columbia	8
15	14	I LOVE YOU BECAUSE Jim Reeves	RCA	18
13	15	JULIET Four Pennies	Philips	13
9	16	CONSTANTLY Cliff Richard	Columbia	9
22	17	HOLD ME P.J. Proby	Decca	4
26	18	HELLO DOLLY Frankie Vaughan	Philips	3
17	19	WALK ON BY Dionne Warwick	Pye	10
25	20	BAMA LAMA BAMA LOO Little Richard	London	3
18	21	NON HO L'ETA PER AMARTI Gigliola Cinquetti	Decca	9
32	22	LIKE DREAMERS DO Applejacks	Decca	2
23	23	I WILL Billy Fury	Decca	9
37	24	I WON'T FORGET YOU Jim Reeves	RCA	2
31	25	DIMPLES John Lee Hooker	Stateside	2
21	26	MY BOY LOLLIPOP Millie	Fontana	14
24	27	DON'T LET THE RAIN COME DOWN Ronnie Hilton	HMV	6
20	28	I LOVE YOU BABY Freddie and the Dreamers	Columbia	6
19	29	A LITTLE LOVING Fourmost	Parlophone	10
29	30	AIN'T SHE SWEET Beatles	Polydor	2
-	31	HOUSE OF THE RISING SUN Animals	Columbia	1
35	32	WHY NOT TONIGHT Mojos	Decca	2
-	33	KISSIN' COUSINS Elvis Presley	RCA	1
30	34	HELLO DOLLY Kenny Ball and his Jazzmen	Pye	3
27	35	YOU'RE THE ONE Kathy Kirby	Decca	8
28	36	I BELIEVE Bachelors	Decca	15
34	37	NEAR YOU Migil Five	Pye	2
33	38	I LOVE BEING IN LOVE WITH YOU Adam Faith	Parlophone	5
40	39	CHAPEL OF LOVE Dixie Cups	Pye	2
36	40	DON'T THROW YOUR LOVE AWAY Searchers	Pye	11

WEEK ENDING 2 JULY 1964

LW	TW	Title / Artist	Label	Wks
1	1	IT'S OVER Roy Orbison	London	10
2	2	SOMEONE SOMEONE Brian Poole and the Tremeloes	Decca	8
8	3	YOU'RE NO GOOD Swinging Blue Jeans	HMV	5
6	4	RAMONA Bachelors	Decca	5
17	5	HOLD ME P.J. Proby	Decca	5
31	6	HOUSE OF THE RISING SUN Animals	Columbia	2
3	7	YOU'RE MY WORLD Cilla Black	Parlophone	9
4	8	HELLO DOLLY Louis Armstrong	London	5
5	9	MY GUY Mary Wells	Stateside	7
12	10	NOBODY I KNOW Peter and Gordon	Columbia	5
10	11	CAN'T YOU SEE THAT SHE'S MINE Dave Clark Five	Columbia	6
24	12	I WON'T FORGET YOU Jim Reeves	RCA	3
9	13	SHOUT Lulu and the Luvvers	Decca	7
7	14	HERE I GO AGAIN Hollies	Parlophone	6
13	15	RISE AND FALL OF FLINGEL BUNT Shadows	Columbia	9
14	16	I LOVE YOU BECAUSE Jim Reeves	RCA	19
33	17	KISSIN' COUSINS Elvis Presley	RCA	2
18	18	HELLO DOLLY Frankie Vaughan	Philips	4
11	19	NO PARTICULAR PLACE TO GO Chuck Berry	Pye	8
22	20	LIKE DREAMERS DO Applejacks	Decca	3
16	21	CONSTANTLY Cliff Richard	Columbia	10
20	22	BAMA LAMA BAMA LOO Little Richard	London	4
25	23	DIMPLES John Lee Hooker	Stateside	3
15	24	JULIET Four Pennies	Philips	14
-	25	IT'S ALL OVER NOW Rolling Stones	Decca	1
39	26	CHAPEL OF LOVE Dixie Cups	Pye	3
32	27	WHY NOT TONIGHT Mojos	Decca	3
21	28	NON HO L'ETA PER AMARTI Gigliola Cinquetti	Decca	10
30	29	AIN'T SHE SWEET Beatles	Polydor	3
27	30	DON'T LET THE RAIN COME DOWN Ronnie Hilton	HMV	7
-	31	ON THE BEACH Cliff Richard	Columbia	1
19	32	WALK ON BY Dionne Warwick	Pye	11
34	33	HELLO DOLLY Kenny Ball and his Jazzmen	Pye	4
37	34	NEAR YOU Migil Five	Pye	3
29	35	A LITTLE LOVING Fourmost	Parlophone	11
23	36	I WILL Billy Fury	Decca	10
-	37	LOVE ME WITH ALL YOUR HEART Karl Denver	Decca	1
-	38	TOUS LES GARCONS ET LES FILLES Françoise Hardy ●	Pye	1
-	39	SWEET WILLIAM Millie	Fontana	1
26	40	MY BOY LOLLIPOP Millie	Fontana	15

WEEK ENDING 9 JULY 1964

LW	TW	Title / Artist	Label	Wks
6	1	HOUSE OF THE RISING SUN Animals	Columbia	3
25	2	IT'S ALL OVER NOW Rolling Stones	Decca	2
5	3	HOLD ME P.J. Proby	Decca	6
2	4	SOMEONE SOMEONE Brian Poole and the Tremeloes	Decca	9
1	5	IT'S OVER Roy Orbison	London	11
4	6	RAMONA Bachelors	Decca	6
3	7	YOU'RE NO GOOD Swinging Blue Jeans	HMV	6
12	8	I WON'T FORGET YOU Jim Reeves	RCA	4
8	9	HELLO DOLLY Louis Armstrong	London	6
17	10	KISSIN' COUSINS Elvis Presley	RCA	3
10	11	NOBODY I KNOW Peter and Gordon	Columbia	6
9	12	MY GUY Mary Wells	Stateside	8
31	13	ON THE BEACH Cliff Richard	Columbia	2
11	14	CAN'T YOU SEE THAT SHE'S MINE Dave Clark Five	Columbia	7
7	15	YOU'RE MY WORLD Cilla Black	Parlophone	10
14	16	HERE I GO AGAIN Hollies	Parlophone	7
13	17	SHOUT Lulu and the Luvvers	Decca	8
-	18	I JUST DON'T KNOW WHAT TO DO WITH MYSELF Dusty Springfield	Philips	1
15	19	RISE AND FALL OF FLINGEL BUNT Shadows	Columbia	10
18	20	HELLO DOLLY Frankie Vaughan	Philips	5
20	21	LIKE DREAMERS DO Applejacks	Decca	4
26	22	CHAPEL OF LOVE Dixie Cups	Pye	4
16	23	I LOVE YOU BECAUSE Jim Reeves	RCA	20
23	24	DIMPLES John Lee Hooker	Stateside	4
27	25	WHY NOT TONIGHT Mojos	Decca	4
22	26	BAMA LAMA BAMA LOO Little Richard	London	5
28	27	NON HO L'ETA PER AMARTI Gigliola Cinquetti	Decca	11
19	28	NO PARTICULAR PLACE TO GO Chuck Berry	Pye	9
29	29	AIN'T SHE SWEET Beatles	Polydor	4
-	30	WISHIN' AND HOPIN' Merseybeats	Fontana	1
34	31	NEAR YOU Migil Five	Pye	4
21	32	CONSTANTLY Cliff Richard	Columbia	11
39	33	SWEET WILLIAM Millie	Fontana	2
-	34	(THEY CALL HER) LA BAMBA Crickets	Liberty	1
32	35	WALK ON BY Dionne Warwick	Pye	12
24	36	JULIET Four Pennies	Philips	15
33	37	HELLO DOLLY Kenny Ball and his Jazzmen	Pye	5
-	38	CALL UP THE GROUPS Barron Knights ●	Columbia	1
37	39	LOVE ME WITH ALL YOUR HEART Karl Denver	Decca	2
30	40	DON'T LET THE RAIN COME DOWN Ronnie Hilton	HMV	8

WEEK ENDING 16 JULY 1964

LW	TW	Title / Artist	Label	Wks
2	1	IT'S ALL OVER NOW Rolling Stones	Decca	3
1	2	HOUSE OF THE RISING SUN Animals	Columbia	4

In these weeks ■ Roy Orbison's *It's Over* is the first American record to top the British charts since *Devil In Disguise* 46 weeks earlier. It will be another 32 weeks before any American act apart from Orbison tops our charts (25.06.64) ■ Another Continental female teenage vocalist, French sensation Françoise Hardy hits our charts (02.07.64) ■ Elvis Presley's only week in the Top 10 in all of 1964 (09.07.64) ■

August 1964

□ Highest position disc reached ● Act's first ever week on chart

LW	TW	Title	Artist	Label	Wks
-	3	A HARD DAY'S NIGHT	Beatles	Parlophone	1
8	4	I WON'T FORGET YOU	Jim Reeves	RCA	5
3	5	HOLD ME	P.J. Proby	Decca	7
18	6	I JUST DON'T KNOW WHAT TO DO WITH MYSELF	Dusty Springfield	Philips	2
5	7	IT'S OVER	Roy Orbison	London	12
7	8	YOU'RE NO GOOD	Swinging Blue Jeans	HMV	7
13	9	ON THE BEACH	Cliff Richard	Columbia	3
4	10	SOMEONE SOMEONE	Brian Poole and the Tremeloes	Decca	10
10	11	KISSIN' COUSINS	Elvis Presley	RCA	4
6	12	RAMONA	Bachelors	Decca	7
9	13	HELLO DOLLY	Louis Armstrong	London	7
11	14	NOBODY I KNOW	Peter and Gordon	Columbia	7
14	15	CAN'T YOU SEE THAT SHE'S MINE	Dave Clark Five	Columbia	8
12	16	MY GUY	Mary Wells	Stateside	9
38	17	CALL UP THE GROUPS	Barron Knights	Columbia	2
30	18	WISHIN' AND HOPIN'	Merseybeats	Fontana	2
17	19	SHOUT	Lulu and the Luvvers	Decca	9
15	20	YOU'RE MY WORLD	Cilla Black	Parlophone	11
21	21	LIKE DREAMERS DO	Applejacks	Decca	5
-	22	SOME DAY WE'RE GONNA LOVE AGAIN	Searchers	Pye	1
19	23	RISE AND FALL OF FLINGEL BUNT	Shadows	Columbia	11
16	24	HERE I GO AGAIN	Hollies	Parlophone	8
23	25	I LOVE YOU BECAUSE	Jim Reeves	RCA	21
-	26	TOBACCO ROAD	Nashville Teens ●	Decca	1
25	27	WHY NOT TONIGHT	Mojos	Decca	5
22	28	CHAPEL OF LOVE	Dixie Cups	Pye	5
24	29	DIMPLES	John Lee Hooker	Stateside	5
-	30	DO WAH DIDDY DIDDY	Manfred Mann	HMV	1
20	31	HELLO DOLLY	Frankie Vaughan	Philips	6
-	32	I GET AROUND	Beach Boys	Capitol	1
34	33	(THEY CALL HER) LA BAMBA	Crickets	Liberty	2
27	34	NON HO L'ETA PER AMARTI	Gigliola Cinquetti	Decca	12
33	35	SWEET WILLIAM	Millie	Fontana	3
-	36	THE FERRIS WHEEL	Everly Brothers	Warner Bros	1
32	37	CONSTANTLY	Cliff Richard	Columbia	12
-	38	I FOUND OUT THE HARD WAY	Four Pennies	Philips	1
26	39	BAMA LAMA BAMA LOO	Little Richard	London	6
-	40	TOUS LES GARCONS ET LES FILLES	Françoise Hardy	Pye	2

WEEK ENDING 23 JULY 1964

LW	TW	Title	Artist	Label	Wks
3	[1]	A HARD DAY'S NIGHT	Beatles	Parlophone	2
1	2	IT'S ALL OVER NOW	Rolling Stones	Decca	4
6	[3]	I JUST DON'T KNOW WHAT TO DO WITH MYSELF	Dusty Springfield	Philips	3
4	4	I WON'T FORGET YOU	Jim Reeves	RCA	6
2	5	HOUSE OF THE RISING SUN	Animals	Columbia	5
17	6	CALL UP THE GROUPS	Barron Knights	Columbia	3
5	7	HOLD ME	P.J. Proby	Decca	8
9	8	ON THE BEACH	Cliff Richard	Columbia	4
30	9	DO WAH DIDDY DIDDY	Manfred Mann	HMV	2
7	10	IT'S OVER	Roy Orbison	London	13
11	11	KISSIN' COUSINS	Elvis Presley	RCA	5
26	12	TOBACCO ROAD	Nashville Teens	Decca	2
22	13	SOME DAY WE'RE GONNA LOVE AGAIN	Searchers	Pye	2
8	14	YOU'RE NO GOOD	Swinging Blue Jeans	HMV	8
10	15	SOMEONE SOMEONE	Brian Poole and the Tremeloes	Decca	11
18	16	WISHIN' AND HOPIN'	Merseybeats	Fontana	3
13	17	HELLO DOLLY	Louis Armstrong	London	8
12	18	RAMONA	Bachelors	Decca	8
16	19	MY GUY	Mary Wells	Stateside	10
32	20	I GET AROUND	Beach Boys	Capitol	2
15	21	CAN'T YOU SEE THAT SHE'S MINE	Dave Clark Five	Columbia	9
21	22	LIKE DREAMERS DO	Applejacks	Decca	6
38	23	I FOUND OUT THE HARD WAY	Four Pennies	Philips	2
29	24	DIMPLES	John Lee Hooker	Stateside	6
31	25	HELLO DOLLY	Frankie Vaughan	Philips	7
14	26	NOBODY I KNOW	Peter and Gordon	Columbia	8
20	27	YOU'RE MY WORLD	Cilla Black	Parlophone	12
19	28	SHOUT	Lulu and the Luvvers	Decca	10
25	29	I LOVE YOU BECAUSE	Jim Reeves	RCA	22
28	30	CHAPEL OF LOVE	Dixie Cups	Pye	6
-	31	IT'S ONLY MAKE BELIEVE	Billy Fury	Decca	1
33	32	(THEY CALL HER) LA BAMBA	Crickets	Liberty	3
-	[33]	I SHOULD CARE	Frank Ifield	Columbia	1
27	34	WHY NOT TONIGHT	Mojos	Decca	6
-	35	THE GIRL FROM IPANEMA	Stan Getz & Joao Gilberto ●	Verve	1
40	[36]	TOUS LES GARCONS ET LES FILLES	Françoise Hardy	Pye	3
34	37	NON HO L'ETA PER AMARTI	Gigliola Cinquetti	Decca	13
-	38	FROM A WINDOW	Billy J Kramer and the Dakotas	Parlophone	1
35	39	SWEET WILLIAM	Millie	Fontana	4
23	40	RISE AND FALL OF FLINGEL BUNT	Shadows	Columbia	12

WEEK ENDING 30 JULY 1964

LW	TW	Title	Artist	Label	Wks
1	[1]	A HARD DAY'S NIGHT	Beatles	Parlophone	3
2	2	IT'S ALL OVER NOW	Rolling Stones	Decca	5
3	[3]	I JUST DON'T KNOW WHAT TO DO WITH MYSELF	Dusty Springfield	Philips	4
6	4	CALL UP THE GROUPS	Barron Knights	Columbia	4
9	5	DO WAH DIDDY DIDDY	Manfred Mann	HMV	3
7	6	HOLD ME	P.J. Proby	Decca	9
5	7	HOUSE OF THE RISING SUN	Animals	Columbia	6
8	8	ON THE BEACH	Cliff Richard	Columbia	5
4	9	I WON'T FORGET YOU	Jim Reeves	RCA	7
12	10	TOBACCO ROAD	Nashville Teens	Decca	3
20	11	I GET AROUND	Beach Boys	Capitol	3
13	12	SOME DAY WE'RE GONNA LOVE AGAIN	Searchers	Pye	3
16	[13]	WISHIN' AND HOPIN'	Merseybeats	Fontana	4
10	14	IT'S OVER	Roy Orbison	London	14
11	15	KISSIN' COUSINS	Elvis Presley	RCA	6
15	16	SOMEONE SOMEONE	Brian Poole and the Tremeloes	Decca	12
14	17	YOU'RE NO GOOD	Swinging Blue Jeans	HMV	9
31	18	IT'S ONLY MAKE BELIEVE	Billy Fury	Decca	2
18	19	RAMONA	Bachelors	Decca	9
17	20	HELLO DOLLY	Louis Armstrong	London	9
32	[21]	(THEY CALL HER) LA BAMBA	Crickets	Liberty	4
38	22	FROM A WINDOW	Billy J Kramer and the Dakotas	Parlophone	2
29	23	I LOVE YOU BECAUSE	Jim Reeves	RCA	23
19	24	MY GUY	Mary Wells	Stateside	11
23	25	I FOUND OUT THE HARD WAY	Four Pennies	Philips	3
22	26	LIKE DREAMERS DO	Applejacks	Decca	7
-	27	THE FERRIS WHEEL	Everly Brothers	Warner Bros	2
26	28	NOBODY I KNOW	Peter and Gordon	Columbia	9
24	29	DIMPLES	John Lee Hooker	Stateside	7
39	[30]	SWEET WILLIAM	Millie	Fontana	5
21	31	CAN'T YOU SEE THAT SHE'S MINE	Dave Clark Five	Columbia	10
35	32	THE GIRL FROM IPANEMA	Stan Getz and Joao Gilberto	Verve	2
34	33	WHY NOT TONIGHT	Mojos	Decca	7
-	34	HAVE I THE RIGHT?	Honeycombs ●	Pye	1
27	35	YOU'RE MY WORLD	Cilla Black	Parlophone	13
30	36	CHAPEL OF LOVE	Dixie Cups	Pye	7
33	37	I SHOULD CARE	Frank Ifield	Columbia	2
25	38	HELLO DOLLY	Frankie Vaughan	Philips	8
-	39	HAPPINESS	Ken Dodd	Columbia	1
-	[40]	HURT BY LOVE	Inez Foxx	Sue	1

WEEK ENDING 6 AUGUST 1964

LW	TW	Title	Artist	Label	Wks
1	[1]	A HARD DAY'S NIGHT	Beatles	Parlophone	4
5	2	DO WAH DIDDY DIDDY	Manfred Mann	HMV	4
4	[3]	CALL UP THE GROUPS	Barron Knights	Columbia	5
2	4	IT'S ALL OVER NOW	Rolling Stones	Decca	6
3	5	I JUST DON'T KNOW WHAT TO DO WITH MYSELF	Dusty Springfield	Philips	5
10	[6]	TOBACCO ROAD	Nashville Teens	Decca	4
8	[7]	ON THE BEACH	Cliff Richard	Columbia	6
7	8	HOUSE OF THE RISING SUN	Animals	Columbia	7

■Only the number one record is at its peak (16.07.64) ■ *A Hard Day's Night* becomes the Beatles' fifth consecutive number one, equalling the record set by Elvis Presley at the end of 1962. It knocks *It's All Over Now* off the top, a record which proves to be the first of five consecutive number ones by the Rolling Stones (23.07.64) ■ Five past, present and future number ones in the Top Ten (23.07.64)■

August 1964

☐ Highest position disc reached ● Act's first ever week on chart

LW	TW	Title	Artist	Label	Wks
9	9	I WON'T FORGET YOU	Jim Reeves	RCA	8
11	10	I GET AROUND	Beach Boys	Capitol	4
12	[11]	SOME DAY WE'RE GONNA LOVE AGAIN	Searchers	Pye	4
18	12	IT'S ONLY MAKE BELIEVE	Billy Fury	Decca	3
6	13	HOLD ME	P.J. Proby	Decca	10
13	14	WISHIN' AND HOPIN'	Merseybeats	Fontana	5
22	15	FROM A WINDOW	Billy J Kramer and the Dakotas	Parlophone	3
15	16	KISSIN' COUSINS	Elvis Presley	RCA	7
14	17	IT'S OVER	Roy Orbison	London	15
34	18	HAVE I THE RIGHT?	Honeycombs	Pye	2
17	19	YOU'RE NO GOOD	Swinging Blue Jeans	HMV	10
16	20	SOMEONE SOMEONE	Brian Poole and the Tremeloes	Decca	13
19	21	RAMONA	Bachelors	Decca	10
20	22	HELLO DOLLY	Louis Armstrong	London	10
25	23	I FOUND OUT THE HARD WAY	Four Pennies	Philips	4
21	24	(THEY CALL HER) LA BAMBA	Crickets	Liberty	5
-	25	YOU'LL NEVER GET TO HEAVEN	Dionne Warwick	Pye	1
23	26	I LOVE YOU BECAUSE	Jim Reeves	RCA	24
24	27	MY GUY	Mary Wells	Stateside	12
-	28	IT'S FOR YOU	Cilla Black	Parlophone	1
27	29	THE FERRIS WHEEL	Everly Brothers	Warner Bros	3
26	30	LIKE DREAMERS DO	Applejacks	Decca	8
39	[31]	HAPPINESS	Ken Dodd	Columbia	2
28	32	NOBODY I KNOW	Peter and Gordon	Columbia	10
29	33	DIMPLES	John Lee Hooker	Stateside	8
30	34	SWEET WILLIAM	Millie	Fontana	6
-	[35]	SPANISH HARLEM	Sounds Incorporated	Columbia	1
-	[36]	HANDY MAN	Del Shannon	Stateside	1
37	37	I SHOULD CARE	Frank Ifield	Columbia	3
32	38	THE GIRL FROM IPANEMA	Stan Getz and Joao Gilberto	Verve	3
31	39	CAN'T YOU SEE THAT SHE'S MINE	Dave Clark Five	Columbia	11
35	40	YOU'RE MY WORLD	Cilla Black	Parlophone	14

WEEK ENDING 13 AUGUST 1964

LW	TW	Title	Artist	Label	Wks
2	[1]	DO WAH DIDDY DIDDY	Manfred Mann	HMV	5
1	2	A HARD DAY'S NIGHT	Beatles	Parlophone	5
3	[3]	CALL UP THE GROUPS	Barron Knights	Columbia	6
4	4	IT'S ALL OVER NOW	Rolling Stones	Decca	7
9	5	I WON'T FORGET YOU	Jim Reeves	RCA	9
6	[6]	TOBACCO ROAD	Nashville Teens	Decca	5
5	7	I JUST DON'T KNOW WHAT TO DO WITH MYSELF	Dusty Springfield	Philips	6
10	8	I GET AROUND	Beach Boys	Capitol	5
7	9	ON THE BEACH	Cliff Richard	Columbia	7
12	[10]	IT'S ONLY MAKE BELIEVE	Billy Fury	Decca	4
18	11	HAVE I THE RIGHT?	Honeycombs	Pye	3
15	12	FROM A WINDOW	Billy J Kramer and the Dakotas	Parlophone	4
8	13	HOUSE OF THE RISING SUN	Animals	Columbia	8
23	[14]	I FOUND OUT THE HARD WAY	Four Pennies	Philips	5
14	15	WISHIN' AND HOPIN'	Merseybeats	Fontana	6
11	16	SOME DAY WE'RE GONNA LOVE AGAIN	Searchers	Pye	5
28	17	IT'S FOR YOU	Cilla Black	Parlophone	2
13	18	HOLD ME	P.J. Proby	Decca	11
26	19	I LOVE YOU BECAUSE	Jim Reeves	RCA	25
25	[20]	YOU'LL NEVER GET TO HEAVEN	Dionne Warwick	Pye	2
-	21	THE CRYING GAME	Dave Berry	Decca	1
29	[22]	THE FERRIS WHEEL	Everly Brothers	Warner Bros	4
16	23	KISSIN' COUSINS	Elvis Presley	RCA	8
17	24	IT'S OVER	Roy Orbison	London	16
20	25	SOMEONE SOMEONE	Brian Poole and the Tremeloes	Decca	14
21	26	RAMONA	Bachelors	Decca	11
-	27	AS TEARS GO BY	Marianne Faithfull ●	Decca	1
19	28	YOU'RE NO GOOD	Swinging Blue Jeans	HMV	11
22	29	HELLO DOLLY	Louis Armstrong	London	11
38	30	THE GIRL FROM IPANEMA	Stan Getz and Joao Gilberto	Verve	4
-	31	THINKING OF YOU BABY	Dave Clark Five	Columbia	1
24	32	(THEY CALL HER) LA BAMBA	Crickets	Liberty	6
31	33	HAPPINESS	Ken Dodd	Columbia	3
-	34	YOU REALLY GOT ME	Kinks ●	Pye	1
-	35	SHE'S NOT THERE	Zombies ●	Decca	1
35	36	SPANISH HARLEM	Sounds Incorporated	Columbia	2
30	37	LIKE DREAMERS DO	Applejacks	Decca	9
-	38	WHY NOT TONIGHT	Mojos	Decca	8
27	39	MY GUY	Mary Wells	Stateside	13
-	40	HOW CAN I TELL HER	Fourmost	Parlophone	1

WEEK ENDING 20 AUGUST 1964

LW	TW	Title	Artist	Label	Wks
1	[1]	DO WAH DIDDY DIDDY	Manfred Mann	HMV	6
2	2	A HARD DAY'S NIGHT	Beatles	Parlophone	6
11	3	HAVE I THE RIGHT?	Honeycombs	Pye	4
5	4	I WON'T FORGET YOU	Jim Reeves	RCA	10
3	5	CALL UP THE GROUPS	Barron Knights	Columbia	7
6	[6]	TOBACCO ROAD	Nashville Teens	Decca	6
4	7	IT'S ALL OVER NOW	Rolling Stones	Decca	8
8	8	I GET AROUND	Beach Boys	Capitol	6
7	9	I JUST DON'T KNOW WHAT TO DO WITH MYSELF	Dusty Springfield	Philips	7
12	[10]	FROM A WINDOW	Billy J Kramer and the Dakotas	Parlophone	5
9	11	ON THE BEACH	Cliff Richard	Columbia	8
10	12	IT'S ONLY MAKE BELIEVE	Billy Fury	Decca	5
17	13	IT'S FOR YOU	Cilla Black	Parlophone	3
14	[14]	I FOUND OUT THE HARD WAY	Four Pennies	Philips	6
34	15	YOU REALLY GOT ME	Kinks	Pye	2
19	16	I LOVE YOU BECAUSE	Jim Reeves	RCA	26
15	17	WISHIN' AND HOPIN'	Merseybeats	Fontana	7
16	18	SOME DAY WE'RE GONNA LOVE AGAIN	Searchers	Pye	6
27	19	AS TEARS GO BY	Marianne Faithfull	Decca	2
21	20	THE CRYING GAME	Dave Berry	Decca	2
-	21	I WOULDN'T TRADE YOU FOR THE WORLD	Bachelors	Decca	1
13	22	HOUSE OF THE RISING SUN	Animals	Columbia	9
20	23	YOU'LL NEVER GET TO HEAVEN	Dionne Warwick	Pye	3
18	24	HOLD ME	P.J. Proby	Decca	12
-	25	THE WEDDING	Julie Rogers ●	Mercury	1
31	[26]	THINKING OF YOU BABY	Dave Clark Five	Columbia	2
22	27	THE FERRIS WHEEL	Everly Brothers	Warner Bros	5
35	28	SHE'S NOT THERE	Zombies	Decca	2
30	[29]	THE GIRL FROM IPANEMA	Stan Getz and Joao Gilberto	Verve	5
23	30	KISSIN' COUSINS	Elvis Presley	RCA	9
-	31	SUCH A NIGHT	Elvis Presley	RCA	1
24	32	IT'S OVER	Roy Orbison	London	17
40	[33]	HOW CAN I TELL HER	Fourmost	Parlophone	2
33	34	HAPPINESS	Ken Dodd	Columbia	4
25	35	SOMEONE SOMEONE	Brian Poole and the Tremeloes	Decca	15
26	36	RAMONA	Bachelors	Decca	12
28	37	YOU'RE NO GOOD	Swinging Blue Jeans	HMV	12
29	38	HELLO DOLLY	Louis Armstrong	London	12
-	39	I SHOULD HAVE KNOWN BETTER	Naturals ●	Parlophone	1
-	40	I'M INTO SOMETHING GOOD	Herman's Hermits ●	Columbia	1

WEEK ENDING 27 AUGUST 1964

LW	TW	Title	Artist	Label	Wks
3	[1]	HAVE I THE RIGHT?	Honeycombs	Pye	5
1	2	DO WAH DIDDY DIDDY	Manfred Mann	HMV	7
4	[3]	I WON'T FORGET YOU	Jim Reeves	RCA	11
15	4	YOU REALLY GOT ME	Kinks	Pye	3
2	5	A HARD DAY'S NIGHT	Beatles	Parlophone	7
6	[6]	TOBACCO ROAD	Nashville Teens	Decca	7
8	[7]	I GET AROUND	Beach Boys	Capitol	7
13	8	IT'S FOR YOU	Cilla Black	Parlophone	4
7	9	IT'S ALL OVER NOW	Rolling Stones	Decca	9
5	10	CALL UP THE GROUPS	Barron Knights	Columbia	8
21	11	I WOULDN'T TRADE YOU FOR THE WORLD	Bachelors	Decca	2
20	12	THE CRYING GAME	Dave Berry	Decca	3
9	13	I JUST DON'T KNOW WHAT TO DO WITH MYSELF	Dusty Springfield	Philips	8
16	14	I LOVE YOU BECAUSE	Jim Reeves	RCA	27
11	15	ON THE BEACH	Cliff Richard	Columbia	9
19	16	AS TEARS GO BY	Marianne Faithfull	Decca	3
12	17	IT'S ONLY MAKE BELIEVE	Billy Fury	Decca	6

In these weeks ■ The first nonsense title to top the charts is *Do Wah Diddy Diddy* (13.08.64) ■ The death of Jim Reeves in a plane crash on 31 July 64 pushes his singles back up the charts. His ironically titled *I Won't Forget You* is the first example of a single being in the Top 10 when the artist dies (13.08.64) ■ Four weeks at number six for the Nashville Teens' *Tobacco Road* (27.08.64)■

LW	TW	Title	Artist	Label	Wks
14	18	I FOUND OUT THE HARD WAY	Four Pennies	Philips	7
10	19	FROM A WINDOW	Billy J Kramer and the Dakotas	Parlophone	6
31	20	SUCH A NIGHT	Elvis Presley	RCA	2
28	21	SHE'S NOT THERE	Zombies	Decca	3
23	22	YOU'LL NEVER GET TO HEAVEN	Dionne Warwick	Pye	4
25	23	THE WEDDING	Julie Rogers	Mercury	2
17	24	WISHIN' AND HOPIN'	Merseybeats	Fontana	8
40	25	I'M INTO SOMETHING GOOD	Herman's Hermits	Columbia	2
27	26	THE FERRIS WHEEL	Everly Brothers	Warner Bros	6
39	27	I SHOULD HAVE KNOWN BETTER	Naturals	Parlophone	2
18	28	SOME DAY WE'RE GONNA LOVE AGAIN	Searchers	Pye	7
-	29	RAG DOLL	Four Seasons	Philips	1
22	30	HOUSE OF THE RISING SUN	Animals	Columbia	10
-	31	YOU NEVER CAN TELL	Chuck Berry	Pye	1
26	32	THINKING OF YOU BABY	Dave Clark Five	Columbia	3
24	33	HOLD ME	P.J. Proby	Decca	13
34	34	HAPPINESS	Ken Dodd	Columbia	5
29	35	THE GIRL FROM IPANEMA	Stan Getz and Joao Gilberto	Verve	6
33	36	HOW CAN I TELL HER	Fourmost	Parlophone	3
-	37	TWELVE STEPS TO LOVE	Brian Poole and the Tremeloes	Decca	1
32	38	IT'S OVER	Roy Orbison	London	18
-	39	MOVE IT BABY	Simon Scott ●	Parlophone	1
-	40	EVERYBODY LOVES SOMEBODY	Dean Martin	Reprise	1

LW	TW	*WEEK ENDING* 3 SEPTEMBER 1964			Wks
1	[1]	HAVE I THE RIGHT?	Honeycombs	Pye	6
4	2	YOU REALLY GOT ME	Kinks	Pye	4
3	[3]	I WON'T FORGET YOU	Jim Reeves	RCA	12
2	4	DO WAH DIDDY DIDDY	Manfred Mann	HMV	8
12	[5]	THE CRYING GAME	Dave Berry	Decca	4
5	6	A HARD DAY'S NIGHT	Beatles	Parlophone	8
8	[7]	IT'S FOR YOU	Cilla Black	Parlophone	5
11	8	I WOULDN'T TRADE YOU FOR THE WORLD	Bachelors	Decca	3
7	9	I GET AROUND	Beach Boys	Capitol	8
9	10	IT'S ALL OVER NOW	Rolling Stones	Decca	10
10	11	CALL UP THE GROUPS	Barron Knights	Columbia	9
14	12	I LOVE YOU BECAUSE	Jim Reeves	RCA	28
20	[13]	SUCH A NIGHT	Elvis Presley	RCA	3
6	14	TOBACCO ROAD	Nashville Teens	Decca	8
16	15	AS TEARS GO BY	Marianne Faithfull	Decca	4
21	16	SHE'S NOT THERE	Zombies	Decca	4
29	17	RAG DOLL	Four Seasons	Philips	2
25	18	I'M INTO SOMETHING GOOD	Herman's Hermits	Columbia	3
23	19	THE WEDDING	Julie Rogers	Mercury	3
13	20	I JUST DON'T KNOW WHAT TO DO WITH MYSELF	Dusty Springfield	Philips	9
17	21	IT'S ONLY MAKE BELIEVE	Billy Fury	Decca	7
19	22	FROM A WINDOW	Billy J Kramer and the Dakotas	Parlophone	7
15	23	ON THE BEACH	Cliff Richard	Columbia	10
18	24	I FOUND OUT THE HARD WAY	Four Pennies	Philips	8
27	25	I SHOULD HAVE KNOWN BETTER	Naturals	Parlophone	3
22	26	YOU'LL NEVER GET TO HEAVEN	Dionne Warwick	Pye	5
31	27	YOU NEVER CAN TELL	Chuck Berry	Pye	2
26	28	THE FERRIS WHEEL	Everly Brothers	Warner Bros	7
40	29	EVERYBODY LOVES SOMEBODY	Dean Martin	Reprise	2
24	30	WISHIN' AND HOPIN'	Merseybeats	Fontana	9
30	31	HOUSE OF THE RISING SUN	Animals	Columbia	11
-	32	WHERE DID OUR LOVE GO	Supremes ●	Stateside	1
-	33	RHYTHM AND GREENS	Shadows	Columbia	1
37	34	TWELVE STEPS TO LOVE	Brian Poole and the Tremeloes	Decca	2
34	35	HAPPINESS	Ken Dodd	Columbia	6
35	36	THE GIRL FROM IPANEMA	Stan Getz and Joao Gilberto	Verve	7
-	[37]	WHAT AM I TO YOU	Kenny Lynch	HMV	1
-	38	IT'S GONNA BE ALL RIGHT	Gerry & the Pacemakers	Columbia	1
-	39	TOGETHER	P.J. Proby	Decca	1
33	40	HOLD ME	P.J. Proby	Decca	14

September 1964

□ Highest position disc reached ● Act's first ever week on chart

LW	TW	*WEEK ENDING* 10 SEPTEMBER 1964			Wks
2	[1]	YOU REALLY GOT ME	Kinks	Pye	5
1	2	HAVE I THE RIGHT?	Honeycombs	Pye	7
3	[3]	I WON'T FORGET YOU	Jim Reeves	RCA	13
8	[4]	I WOULDN'T TRADE YOU FOR THE WORLD	Bachelors	Decca	4
5	[5]	THE CRYING GAME	Dave Berry	Decca	5
4	6	DO WAH DIDDY DIDDY	Manfred Mann	HMV	9
18	7	I'M INTO SOMETHING GOOD	Herman's Hermits	Columbia	4
17	8	RAG DOLL	Four Seasons	Philips	3
15	[9]	AS TEARS GO BY	Marianne Faithfull	Decca	5
6	10	A HARD DAY'S NIGHT	Beatles	Parlophone	9
7	11	IT'S FOR YOU	Cilla Black	Parlophone	6
16	[12]	SHE'S NOT THERE	Zombies	Decca	5
13	[13]	SUCH A NIGHT	Elvis Presley	RCA	4
12	14	I LOVE YOU BECAUSE	Jim Reeves	RCA	29
9	15	I GET AROUND	Beach Boys	Capitol	9
19	16	THE WEDDING	Julie Rogers	Mercury	4
10	17	IT'S ALL OVER NOW	Rolling Stones	Decca	11
32	18	WHERE DID OUR LOVE GO	Supremes	Stateside	2
11	19	CALL UP THE GROUPS	Barron Knights	Columbia	10
14	20	TOBACCO ROAD	Nashville Teens	Decca	9
29	21	EVERYBODY LOVES SOMEBODY	Dean Martin	Reprise	3
33	[22]	RHYTHM AND GREENS	Shadows	Columbia	2
27	[23]	YOU NEVER CAN TELL	Chuck Berry	Pye	3
25	[24]	I SHOULD HAVE KNOWN BETTER	Naturals	Parlophone	4
39	25	TOGETHER	P.J. Proby	Decca	2
20	26	I JUST DON'T KNOW WHAT TO DO WITH MYSELF	Dusty Springfield	Philips	10
23	27	ON THE BEACH	Cliff Richard	Columbia	11
38	28	IT'S GONNA BE ALL RIGHT	Gerry & the Pacemakers	Columbia	2
21	29	IT'S ONLY MAKE BELIEVE	Billy Fury	Decca	8
-	30	IS IT TRUE?	Brenda Lee	Brunswick	1
24	31	I FOUND OUT THE HARD WAY	Four Pennies	Philips	9
26	32	YOU'LL NEVER GET TO HEAVEN	Dionne Warwick	Pye	6
35	33	HAPPINESS	Ken Dodd	Columbia	7
34	34	TWELVE STEPS TO LOVE	Brian Poole and the Tremeloes	Decca	3
22	35	FROM A WINDOW	Billy J Kramer and the Dakotas	Parlophone	8
-	36	OH PRETTY WOMAN	Roy Orbison	London	1
-	[37]	MOVE IT BABY	Simon Scott	Parlophone	2
31	38	HOUSE OF THE RISING SUN	Animals	Columbia	12
-	39	BREAD AND BUTTER	Newbeats ●	Hickory	1
-	40	THE LETTER	Long And The Short ●	Decca	1

LW	TW	*WEEK ENDING* 17 SEPTEMBER 1964			Wks
1	[1]	YOU REALLY GOT ME	Kinks	Pye	6
2	2	HAVE I THE RIGHT?	Honeycombs	Pye	8
7	3	I'M INTO SOMETHING GOOD	Herman's Hermits	Columbia	5
3	4	I WON'T FORGET YOU	Jim Reeves	RCA	14
8	5	RAG DOLL	Four Seasons	Philips	4
5	6	THE CRYING GAME	Dave Berry	Decca	6
4	7	I WOULDN'T TRADE YOU FOR THE WORLD	Bachelors	Decca	5
6	8	DO WAH DIDDY DIDDY	Manfred Mann	HMV	10
18	9	WHERE DID OUR LOVE GO	Supremes	Stateside	3
9	10	AS TEARS GO BY	Marianne Faithfull	Decca	6
14	11	I LOVE YOU BECAUSE	Jim Reeves	RCA	30
12	[12]	SHE'S NOT THERE	Zombies	Decca	6
16	13	THE WEDDING	Julie Rogers	Mercury	5
13	14	SUCH A NIGHT	Elvis Presley	RCA	5
10	15	A HARD DAY'S NIGHT	Beatles	Parlophone	10
21	16	EVERYBODY LOVES SOMEBODY	Dean Martin	Reprise	4
36	17	OH PRETTY WOMAN	Roy Orbison	London	2
11	18	IT'S FOR YOU	Cilla Black	Parlophone	7
25	19	TOGETHER	P.J. Proby	Decca	3
17	20	IT'S ALL OVER NOW	Rolling Stones	Decca	12
15	21	I GET AROUND	Beach Boys	Capitol	10
22	[22]	RHYTHM AND GREENS	Shadows	Columbia	3
30	23	IS IT TRUE?	Brenda Lee	Brunswick	2
28	[24]	IT'S GONNA BE ALL RIGHT	Gerry & the Pacemakers	Columbia	3
23	25	YOU NEVER CAN TELL	Chuck Berry	Pye	4

■Diana Ross makes her first chart appearance as lead singer of the Supremes (03.09.64) ■ P.J. Proby emulates the feat of Millie nine weeks earlier by holding the two anchor positions in the Top 40 (03.09.64) ■ Simon Scott is the first chart star managed by Robert Stigwood, later to make his name with the Bee Gees and then 'Jesus Christ Superstar', 'Grease' and 'Saturday Night Fever' (10.09.64)■

September 1964

□ Highest position disc reached ● Act's first ever week on chart

LW	TW	Title	Artist	Label	Wks
19	26	CALL UP THE GROUPS	Barron Knights	Columbia	11
20	27	TOBACCO ROAD	Nashville Teens	Decca	10
24	28	I SHOULD HAVE KNOWN BETTER	Naturals	Parlophone	5
39	29	BREAD AND BUTTER	Newbeats	Hickory	2
-	30	SEVEN DAFFODILS	Mojos	Decca	1
33	31	HAPPINESS	Ken Dodd	Columbia	8
34	32	TWELVE STEPS TO LOVE	Brian Poole and the Tremeloes	Decca	4
-	33	WALK AWAY	Matt Monro	Parlophone	1
29	34	IT'S ONLY MAKE BELIEVE	Billy Fury	Decca	9
40	35	THE LETTER	Long And The Short	Decca	2
26	36	I JUST DON'T KNOW WHAT TO DO WITH MYSELF	Dusty Springfield	Philips	11
27	37	ON THE BEACH	Cliff Richard	Columbia	12
-	38	SEVEN DAFFODILS	Cherokees ●	Columbia	1
-	39	LOVE'S MADE A FOOL OF YOU	Buddy Holly	Coral	1
-	40	I'M CRYING	Animals	Columbia	1

WEEK ENDING 24 SEPTEMBER 1964

LW	TW	Title	Artist	Label	Wks
3	1	I'M INTO SOMETHING GOOD	Herman's Hermits	Columbia	6
5	2	RAG DOLL	Four Seasons	Philips	5
2	3	HAVE I THE RIGHT?	Honeycombs	Pye	9
9	4	WHERE DID OUR LOVE GO	Supremes	Stateside	4
1	5	YOU REALLY GOT ME	Kinks	Pye	7
7	6	I WOULDN'T TRADE YOU FOR THE WORLD	Bachelors	Decca	6
4	7	I WON'T FORGET YOU	Jim Reeves	RCA	15
17	8	OH PRETTY WOMAN	Roy Orbison	London	3
10	9	AS TEARS GO BY	Marianne Faithfull	Decca	7
6	10	THE CRYING GAME	Dave Berry	Decca	7
13	11	THE WEDDING	Julie Rogers	Mercury	6
16	12	EVERYBODY LOVES SOMEBODY	Dean Martin	Reprise	5
19	13	TOGETHER	P.J. Proby	Decca	4
11	14	I LOVE YOU BECAUSE	Jim Reeves	RCA	31
8	15	DO WAH DIDDY DIDDY	Manfred Mann	HMV	11
12	16	SHE'S NOT THERE	Zombies	Decca	7
23	17	IS IT TRUE?	Brenda Lee	Brunswick	3
14	18	SUCH A NIGHT	Elvis Presley	RCA	6
15	19	A HARD DAY'S NIGHT	Beatles	Parlophone	11
40	20	I'M CRYING	Animals	Columbia	2
-	21	WHEN YOU WALK IN THE ROOM	Searchers	Pye	1
29	22	BREAD AND BUTTER	Newbeats	Hickory	3
18	23	IT'S FOR YOU	Cilla Black	Parlophone	8
24	24	IT'S GONNA BE ALL RIGHT	Gerry & the Pacemakers	Columbia	4
22	25	RHYTHM AND GREENS	Shadows	Columbia	4
33	26	WALK AWAY	Matt Monro	Parlophone	2
-	27	WE'RE THROUGH	Hollies	Parlophone	1
20	28	IT'S ALL OVER NOW	Rolling Stones	Decca	13
25	29	YOU NEVER CAN TELL	Chuck Berry	Pye	5
21	30	I GET AROUND	Beach Boys	Capitol	11
28	31	I SHOULD HAVE KNOWN BETTER	Naturals	Parlophone	6
32	32	TWELVE STEPS TO LOVE	Brian Poole and the Tremeloes	Decca	5
38	33	SEVEN DAFFODILS	Cherokees	Columbia	2
30	34	SEVEN DAFFODILS	Mojos	Decca	2
31	35	HAPPINESS	Ken Dodd	Columbia	9
26	36	CALL UP THE GROUPS	Barron Knights	Columbia	12
-	37	MAYBE I KNOW	Lesley Gore	Mercury	1
35	38	THE LETTER	Long And The Short	Decca	3
-	39	HOW SOON?	Henry Mancini Orchestra ●	RCA	1
-	40	COME TO ME	Julie Grant	Pye	1

WEEK ENDING 1 OCTOBER 1964

LW	TW	Title	Artist	Label	Wks
1	1	I'M INTO SOMETHING GOOD	Herman's Hermits	Columbia	7
2	2	RAG DOLL	Four Seasons	Philips	6
4	3	WHERE DID OUR LOVE GO	Supremes	Stateside	5
8	4	OH PRETTY WOMAN	Roy Orbison	London	4
6	5	I WOULDN'T TRADE YOU FOR THE WORLD	Bachelors	Decca	7
7	6	I WON'T FORGET YOU	Jim Reeves	RCA	16
11	7	THE WEDDING	Julie Rogers	Mercury	7
3	8	HAVE I THE RIGHT?	Honeycombs	Pye	10
9	9	AS TEARS GO BY	Marianne Faithfull	Decca	8
5	10	YOU REALLY GOT ME	Kinks	Pye	8
13	11	TOGETHER	P.J. Proby	Decca	5
12	12	EVERYBODY LOVES SOMEBODY	Dean Martin	Reprise	6
10	13	THE CRYING GAME	Dave Berry	Decca	8
16	14	SHE'S NOT THERE	Zombies	Decca	8
20	15	I'M CRYING	Animals	Columbia	3
21	16	WHEN YOU WALK IN THE ROOM	Searchers	Pye	2
14	17	I LOVE YOU BECAUSE	Jim Reeves	RCA	32
17	18	IS IT TRUE?	Brenda Lee	Brunswick	4
22	19	BREAD AND BUTTER	Newbeats	Hickory	4
27	20	WE'RE THROUGH	Hollies	Parlophone	2
18	21	SUCH A NIGHT	Elvis Presley	RCA	7
26	22	WALK AWAY	Matt Monro	Parlophone	3
25	23	RHYTHM AND GREENS	Shadows	Columbia	5
19	24	A HARD DAY'S NIGHT	Beatles	Parlophone	12
23	25	IT'S FOR YOU	Cilla Black	Parlophone	9
24	26	IT'S GONNA BE ALL RIGHT	Gerry & the Pacemakers	Columbia	5
15	27	DO WAH DIDDY DIDDY	Manfred Mann	HMV	12
37	28	MAYBE I KNOW	Lesley Gore	Mercury	2
29	29	YOU NEVER CAN TELL	Chuck Berry	Pye	6
31	30	I SHOULD HAVE KNOWN BETTER	Naturals	Parlophone	7
39	31	HOW SOON?	Henry Mancini Orchestra	RCA	2
28	32	IT'S ALL OVER NOW	Rolling Stones	Decca	14
35	33	HAPPINESS	Ken Dodd	Columbia	10
30	34	I GET AROUND	Beach Boys	Capitol	12
34	35	SEVEN DAFFODILS	Mojos	Decca	3
-	36	MECCA	Cheetahs ●	Philips	1
-	37	SUMMER IS OVER	Frank Ifield	Columbia	1
-	38	NO-ONE TO CRY TO	Ray Charles	HMV	1
38	39	THE LETTER	Long And The Short	Decca	4
40	40	COME TO ME	Julie Grant	Pye	2

WEEK ENDING 8 OCTOBER 1964

LW	TW	Title	Artist	Label	Wks
4	1	OH PRETTY WOMAN	Roy Orbison	London	5
1	2	I'M INTO SOMETHING GOOD	Herman's Hermits	Columbia	8
3	3	WHERE DID OUR LOVE GO	Supremes	Stateside	6
2	4	RAG DOLL	Four Seasons	Philips	7
7	5	THE WEDDING	Julie Rogers	Mercury	8
5	6	I WOULDN'T TRADE YOU FOR THE WORLD	Bachelors	Decca	8
6	7	I WON'T FORGET YOU	Jim Reeves	RCA	17
11	8	TOGETHER	P.J. Proby	Decca	6
16	9	WHEN YOU WALK IN THE ROOM	Searchers	Pye	3
15	10	I'M CRYING	Animals	Columbia	4
12	11	EVERYBODY LOVES SOMEBODY	Dean Martin	Reprise	7
9	12	AS TEARS GO BY	Marianne Faithfull	Decca	9
8	13	HAVE I THE RIGHT?	Honeycombs	Pye	11
20	14	WE'RE THROUGH	Hollies	Parlophone	3
19	15	BREAD AND BUTTER	Newbeats	Hickory	5
10	16	YOU REALLY GOT ME	Kinks	Pye	9
22	17	WALK AWAY	Matt Monro	Parlophone	4
18	18	IS IT TRUE?	Brenda Lee	Brunswick	5
17	19	I LOVE YOU BECAUSE	Jim Reeves	RCA	33
14	20	SHE'S NOT THERE	Zombies	Decca	9
13	21	THE CRYING GAME	Dave Berry	Decca	9
28	22	MAYBE I KNOW	Lesley Gore	Mercury	3
31	23	HOW SOON?	Henry Mancini Orchestra	RCA	3
21	24	SUCH A NIGHT	Elvis Presley	RCA	8
23	25	RHYTHM AND GREENS	Shadows	Columbia	6
26	26	IT'S GONNA BE ALL RIGHT	Gerry & the Pacemakers	Columbia	6
27	27	DO WAH DIDDY DIDDY	Manfred Mann	HMV	13
24	28	A HARD DAY'S NIGHT	Beatles	Parlophone	13
-	29	ONE WAY LOVE	Cliff Bennett and the Rebel Rousers ●	Parlophone	1
-	30	TWELFTH OF NEVER	Cliff Richard	Columbia	1
-	31	(THERE'S) ALWAYS SOMETHING THERE TO REMIND ME	Sandie Shaw ●	Pye	1
37	32	SUMMER IS OVER	Frank Ifield	Columbia	2
35	33	SEVEN DAFFODILS	Mojos	Decca	4
-	34	UM UM UM UM UM UM	Wayne Fontana and the Mindbenders	Fontana	1

In these weeks ■ Herman's Hermits' *I'm Into Something Good* is the only number one written by Carole King, although co-writer and then husband Gerry Goffin will hit number one again in 1988 as co-writer of Glenn Medeiros' chart-topper (24.09.64) ■ Eleven weeks of chart action for Ken Dodd's *Happiness* without ever climbing higher than number 31 (08.10.64)■

October 1964

□ Highest position disc reached ● Act's first ever week on chart

LW	TW	Title / Artist	Label	Wks
32	35	IT'S ALL OVER NOW Rolling Stones	Decca	15
33	36	HAPPINESS Ken Dodd	Columbia	11
40	37	COME TO ME Julie Grant	Pye	3
29	38	YOU NEVER CAN TELL Chuck Berry	Pye	7
25	39	IT'S FOR YOU Cilla Black	Parlophone	10
30	40	I SHOULD HAVE KNOWN BETTER Naturals	Parlophone	8

WEEK ENDING 15 OCTOBER 1964

LW	TW	Title / Artist	Label	Wks
1	[1]	OH PRETTY WOMAN Roy Orbison	London	6
2	2	I'M INTO SOMETHING GOOD Herman's Hermits	Columbia	9
3	[3]	WHERE DID OUR LOVE GO Supremes	Stateside	7
5	4	THE WEDDING Julie Rogers	Mercury	9
4	5	RAG DOLL Four Seasons	Philips	8
6	6	I WOULDN'T TRADE YOU FOR THE WORLD Bachelors	Decca	9
9	7	WHEN YOU WALK IN THE ROOM Searchers	Pye	4
10	[8]	I'M CRYING Animals	Columbia	5
14	9	WE'RE THROUGH Hollies	Parlophone	4
7	10	I WON'T FORGET YOU Jim Reeves	RCA	18
31	11	(THERE'S) ALWAYS SOMETHING THERE TO REMIND ME Sandie Shaw	Pye	2
17	12	WALK AWAY Matt Monro	Parlophone	5
11	13	EVERYBODY LOVES SOMEBODY Dean Martin	Reprise	8
8	14	TOGETHER P.J. Proby	Decca	7
12	15	AS TEARS GO BY Marianne Faithfull	Decca	10
30	16	TWELFTH OF NEVER Cliff Richard	Columbia	2
23	17	HOW SOON? Henry Mancini Orchestra	RCA	4
13	18	HAVE I THE RIGHT? Honeycombs	Pye	12
15	19	BREAD AND BUTTER Newbeats	Hickory	6
16	20	YOU REALLY GOT ME Kinks	Pye	10
22	21	MAYBE I KNOW Lesley Gore	Mercury	4
18	22	IS IT TRUE? Brenda Lee	Brunswick	6
29	23	ONE WAY LOVE Cliff Bennett and the Rebel Rousers	Parlophone	2
21	24	THE CRYING GAME Dave Berry	Decca	10
32	[25]	SUMMER IS OVER Frank Ifield	Columbia	3
19	26	I LOVE YOU BECAUSE Jim Reeves	RCA	34
20	27	SHE'S NOT THERE Zombies	Decca	10
-	28	REACH OUT FOR ME Dionne Warwick	Pye	1
34	29	UM UM UM UM UM UM Wayne Fontana and the Mindbenders	Fontana	2
25	30	RHYTHM AND GREENS Shadows	Columbia	7
37	[31]	COME TO ME Julie Grant	Pye	4
-	32	REMEMBER (WALKIN' IN THE SAND) Shangri-Las ●	Red Bird	1
26	33	IT'S GONNA BE ALL RIGHT Gerry & the Pacemakers	Columbia	7
-	34	GOLDFINGER Shirley Bassey	Columbia	1
-	[35]	DO I LOVE YOU Ronettes	London	1
27	36	DO WAH DIDDY DIDDY Manfred Mann	HMV	14
-	37	THREE LITTLE WORDS Applejacks	Decca	1
-	[38]	BYE BYE BABY Tony Jackson and the Vibrations ●	Pye	1
-	[39]	QUESTIONS I CAN'T ANSWER Heinz	Columbia	1
24	40	SUCH A NIGHT Elvis Presley	RCA	9

WEEK ENDING 22 OCTOBER 1964

LW	TW	Title / Artist	Label	Wks
11	[1]	(THERE'S) ALWAYS SOMETHING THERE TO REMIND ME Sandie Shaw	Pye	3
1	2	OH PRETTY WOMAN Roy Orbison	London	7
7	[3]	WHEN YOU WALK IN THE ROOM Searchers	Pye	5
3	4	WHERE DID OUR LOVE GO Supremes	Stateside	8
2	5	I'M INTO SOMETHING GOOD Herman's Hermits	Columbia	10
4	6	THE WEDDING Julie Rogers	Mercury	10
12	7	WALK AWAY Matt Monro	Parlophone	6
9	8	WE'RE THROUGH Hollies	Parlophone	5
8	9	I'M CRYING Animals	Columbia	6
17	[10]	HOW SOON? Henry Mancini Orchestra	RCA	5
6	11	I WOULDN'T TRADE YOU FOR THE WORLD Bachelors	Decca	10
5	12	RAG DOLL Four Seasons	Philips	9
16	13	TWELFTH OF NEVER Cliff Richard	Columbia	3
10	14	I WON'T FORGET YOU Jim Reeves	RCA	19
23	15	ONE WAY LOVE Cliff Bennett and the Rebel Rousers	Parlophone	3
14	16	TOGETHER P.J. Proby	Decca	8
13	17	EVERYBODY LOVES SOMEBODY Dean Martin	Reprise	9
-	18	SHA LA LA Manfred Mann	HMV	1
15	19	AS TEARS GO BY Marianne Faithfull	Decca	11
21	[20]	MAYBE I KNOW Lesley Gore	Mercury	5
19	21	BREAD AND BUTTER Newbeats	Hickory	7
29	22	UM UM UM UM UM UM Wayne Fontana and the Mindbenders	Fontana	3
28	[23]	REACH OUT FOR ME Dionne Warwick	Pye	2
-	24	BABY LOVE Supremes	Stateside	1
18	25	HAVE I THE RIGHT? Honeycombs	Pye	13
20	26	YOU REALLY GOT ME Kinks	Pye	11
34	27	GOLDFINGER Shirley Bassey	Columbia	2
22	28	IS IT TRUE? Brenda Lee	Brunswick	7
-	29	HE'S IN TOWN Rockin' Berries ●	Pye	1
25	30	SUMMER IS OVER Frank Ifield	Columbia	4
32	31	REMEMBER (WALKIN' IN THE SAND) Shangri-Las	Red Bird	2
37	32	THREE LITTLE WORDS Applejacks	Decca	2
-	33	ANYWAY YOU WANT IT Dave Clark Five	Columbia	1
-	34	GOOGLE EYE Nashville Teens	Decca	1
-	35	WALK TALL Val Doonican ●	Decca	1
-	[36]	IT HURTS TO BE IN LOVE Gene Pitney	United Artists	1
24	37	THE CRYING GAME Dave Berry	Decca	11
-	38	LOSING YOU Dusty Springfield	Philips	1
26	39	I LOVE YOU BECAUSE Jim Reeves	RCA	35
-	40	IS IT BECAUSE? Honeycombs	Pye	1

WEEK ENDING 29 OCTOBER 1964

LW	TW	Title / Artist	Label	Wks
1	[1]	(THERE'S) ALWAYS SOMETHING THERE TO REMIND ME Sandie Shaw	Pye	4
2	2	OH PRETTY WOMAN Roy Orbison	London	8
6	[3]	THE WEDDING Julie Rogers	Mercury	11
3	4	WHEN YOU WALK IN THE ROOM Searchers	Pye	6
4	5	WHERE DID OUR LOVE GO Supremes	Stateside	9
7	6	WALK AWAY Matt Monro	Parlophone	7
8	[7]	WE'RE THROUGH Hollies	Parlophone	6
13	[8]	TWELFTH OF NEVER Cliff Richard	Columbia	4
15	[9]	ONE WAY LOVE Cliff Bennett and the Rebel Rousers	Parlophone	4
5	10	I'M INTO SOMETHING GOOD Herman's Hermits	Columbia	11
18	11	SHA LA LA Manfred Mann	HMV	2
10	12	HOW SOON? Henry Mancini Orchestra	RCA	6
24	13	BABY LOVE Supremes	Stateside	2
9	14	I'M CRYING Animals	Columbia	7
11	15	I WOULDN'T TRADE YOU FOR THE WORLD Bachelors	Decca	11
12	16	RAG DOLL Four Seasons	Philips	10
14	17	I WON'T FORGET YOU Jim Reeves	RCA	20
29	18	HE'S IN TOWN Rockin' Berries	Pye	2
17	19	EVERYBODY LOVES SOMEBODY Dean Martin	Reprise	10
22	20	UM UM UM UM UM UM Wayne Fontana and the Mindbenders	Fontana	4
27	[21]	GOLDFINGER Shirley Bassey	Columbia	3
16	22	TOGETHER P.J. Proby	Decca	9
32	[23]	THREE LITTLE WORDS Applejacks	Decca	3
23	24	REACH OUT FOR ME Dionne Warwick	Pye	3
20	25	MAYBE I KNOW Lesley Gore	Mercury	6
34	26	GOOGLE EYE Nashville Teens	Decca	2
33	27	ANYWAY YOU WANT IT Dave Clark Five	Columbia	2
35	28	WALK TALL Val Doonican	Decca	2
31	29	REMEMBER (WALKIN' IN THE SAND) Shangri-Las	Red Bird	3
38	30	LOSING YOU Dusty Springfield	Philips	2
19	31	AS TEARS GO BY Marianne Faithfull	Decca	12
-	32	AIN'T THAT LOVING YOU BABY Elvis Presley	RCA	1
30	33	SUMMER IS OVER Frank Ifield	Columbia	5
-	34	DON'T BRING ME DOWN Pretty Things ●	Fontana	1
-	35	TOKYO MELODY Helmut Zacharias ●	Polydor	1
21	36	BREAD AND BUTTER Newbeats	Hickory	8

■ Ex-Searcher Tony Jackson enters the chart while his erstwhile colleagues enjoy life 31 places higher (15.10.64) ■ A chart full of uncertainty: five questions, three doubtful answers (*Um Um Um Um Um Um, Maybe I Know* and *You Really Got Me*) and Heinz's *Questions I Can't Answer* (15.10.64) ■ For two weeks, Jim Reeves holds the unique distinction of having two simultaneous chart hits, each of which have lasted for at least 20 weeks on the chart (29.10.64) ■

October 1964

□ Highest position disc reached ● Act's first ever week on chart

LW	TW	Title / Artist	Label	Wks
39	37	I LOVE YOU BECAUSE Jim Reeves	RCA	36
40	38	IS IT BECAUSE? Honeycombs	Pye	2
-	39	NOW WE'RE THRU Poets ●	Decca	1
28	40	IS IT TRUE? Brenda Lee	Brunswick	8

WEEK ENDING 5 NOVEMBER 1964

LW	TW	Title / Artist	Label	Wks
1	1	(THERE'S) ALWAYS SOMETHING THERE TO REMIND ME Sandie Shaw	Pye	5
2	2	OH PRETTY WOMAN Roy Orbison	London	9
3	3	THE WEDDING Julie Rogers	Mercury	12
6	4	WALK AWAY Matt Monro	Parlophone	8
11	5	SHA LA LA Manfred Mann	HMV	3
4	6	WHEN YOU WALK IN THE ROOM Searchers	Pye	7
13	7	BABY LOVE Supremes	Stateside	3
8	8	TWELFTH OF NEVER Cliff Richard	Columbia	5
5	9	WHERE DID OUR LOVE GO Supremes	Stateside	10
7	10	WE'RE THROUGH Hollies	Parlophone	7
12	11	HOW SOON? Henry Mancini Orchestra	RCA	7
9	12	ONE WAY LOVE Cliff Bennett and the Rebel Rousers	Parlophone	5
20	13	UM UM UM UM UM UM Wayne Fontana and the Mindbenders	Fontana	5
18	14	HE'S IN TOWN Rockin' Berries	Pye	3
10	15	I'M INTO SOMETHING GOOD Herman's Hermits	Columbia	12
26	16	GOOGLE EYE Nashville Teens	Decca	3
32	17	AIN'T THAT LOVING YOU BABY Elvis Presley	RCA	2
-	18	ALL DAY AND ALL OF THE NIGHT Kinks	Pye	1
17	19	I WON'T FORGET YOU Jim Reeves	RCA	21
15	20	I WOULDN'T TRADE YOU FOR THE WORLD Bachelors	Decca	12
35	21	TOKYO MELODY Helmut Zacharias	Polydor	2
14	22	I'M CRYING Animals	Columbia	8
16	23	RAG DOLL Four Seasons	Philips	11
21	24	GOLDFINGER Shirley Bassey	Columbia	4
27	25	ANYWAY YOU WANT IT Dave Clark Five	Columbia	3
29	26	REMEMBER (WALKIN' IN THE SAND) Shangri-Las	Red Bird	4
23	27	THREE LITTLE WORDS Applejacks	Decca	4
30	28	LOSING YOU Dusty Springfield	Philips	3
34	29	DON'T BRING ME DOWN Pretty Things	Fontana	2
28	30	WALK TALL Val Doonican	Decca	3
24	31	REACH OUT FOR ME Dionne Warwick	Pye	4
19	32	EVERYBODY LOVES SOMEBODY Dean Martin	Reprise	11
-	33	THERE'S A HEARTACHE FOLLOWING ME Jim Reeves	RCA	1
25	34	MAYBE I KNOW Lesley Gore	Mercury	7
22	35	TOGETHER P.J. Proby	Decca	10
-	36	BLACK GIRL Four Pennies	Philips	1
33	37	SUMMER IS OVER Frank Ifield	Columbia	6
39	38	NOW WE'RE THRU Poets	Decca	2
37	39	I LOVE YOU BECAUSE Jim Reeves	RCA	37
-	40	DANCING IN THE STREET Martha & the Vandellas ●	Stateside	1

WEEK ENDING 12 NOVEMBER 1964

LW	TW	Title / Artist	Label	Wks
2	1	OH PRETTY WOMAN Roy Orbison	London	10
1	2	(THERE'S) ALWAYS SOMETHING THERE TO REMIND ME Sandie Shaw	Pye	6
5	3	SHA LA LA Manfred Mann	HMV	4
4	4	WALK AWAY Matt Monro	Parlophone	9
7	5	BABY LOVE Supremes	Stateside	4
14	6	HE'S IN TOWN Rockin' Berries	Pye	4
18	7	ALL DAY AND ALL OF THE NIGHT Kinks	Pye	2
13	8	UM UM UM UM UM UM Wayne Fontana and the Mindbenders	Fontana	6
3	9	THE WEDDING Julie Rogers	Mercury	13
16	10	GOOGLE EYE Nashville Teens	Decca	4
6	11	WHEN YOU WALK IN THE ROOM Searchers	Pye	8
21	12	TOKYO MELODY Helmut Zacharias	Polydor	3
8	13	TWELFTH OF NEVER Cliff Richard	Columbia	6
12	14	ONE WAY LOVE Cliff Bennett and the Rebel Rousers	Parlophone	6
17	15	AIN'T THAT LOVING YOU BABY Elvis Presley	RCA	3
9	16	WHERE DID OUR LOVE GO Supremes	Stateside	11
29	17	DON'T BRING ME DOWN Pretty Things	Fontana	3
26	18	REMEMBER (WALKIN' IN THE SAND) Shangri-Las	Red Bird	5
33	19	THERE'S A HEARTACHE FOLLOWING ME Jim Reeves	RCA	2
10	20	WE'RE THROUGH Hollies	Parlophone	8
11	21	HOW SOON? Henry Mancini Orchestra	RCA	8
28	22	LOSING YOU Dusty Springfield	Philips	4
19	23	I WON'T FORGET YOU Jim Reeves	RCA	22
15	24	I'M INTO SOMETHING GOOD Herman's Hermits	Columbia	13
30	25	WALK TALL Val Doonican	Decca	4
24	26	GOLDFINGER Shirley Bassey	Columbia	5
-	27	I UNDERSTAND Freddie and the Dreamers	Columbia	1
20	28	I WOULDN'T TRADE YOU FOR THE WORLD Bachelors	Decca	13
22	29	I'M CRYING Animals	Columbia	9
25	30	ANYWAY YOU WANT IT Dave Clark Five	Columbia	4
36	31	BLACK GIRL Four Pennies	Philips	2
38	32	NOW WE'RE THRU Poets	Decca	3
-	33	WILD SIDE OF LIFE Tommy Quickly ●	Pye	1
-	34	I'M GONNA BE STRONG Gene Pitney	Stateside	1
-	35	MARCH OF THE MODS Joe Loss Orchestra	HMV	1
23	36	RAG DOLL Four Seasons	Philips	12
27	37	THREE LITTLE WORDS Applejacks	Decca	5
40	38	DANCING IN THE STREET Martha and the Vandellas	Stateside	2
31	39	REACH OUT FOR ME Dionne Warwick	Pye	5
-	40	LAST NIGHT Merseybeats	Fontana	1

WEEK ENDING 19 NOVEMBER 1964

LW	TW	Title / Artist	Label	Wks
5	1	BABY LOVE Supremes	Stateside	5
7	2	ALL DAY AND ALL OF THE NIGHT Kinks	Pye	3
6	3	HE'S IN TOWN Rockin' Berries	Pye	5
1	4	OH PRETTY WOMAN Roy Orbison	London	11
3	5	SHA LA LA Manfred Mann	HMV	5
8	6	UM UM UM UM UM UM Wayne Fontana and the Mindbenders	Fontana	7
2	7	(THERE'S) ALWAYS SOMETHING THERE TO REMIND ME Sandie Shaw	Pye	7
4	8	WALK AWAY Matt Monro	Parlophone	10
12	9	TOKYO MELODY Helmut Zacharias	Polydor	4
17	10	DON'T BRING ME DOWN Pretty Things	Fontana	4
19	11	THERE'S A HEARTACHE FOLLOWING ME Jim Reeves	RCA	3
9	12	THE WEDDING Julie Rogers	Mercury	14
10	13	GOOGLE EYE Nashville Teens	Decca	5
18	14	REMEMBER (WALKIN' IN THE SAND) Shangri-Las	Red Bird	6
11	15	WHEN YOU WALK IN THE ROOM Searchers	Pye	9
34	16	I'M GONNA BE STRONG Gene Pitney	Stateside	2
22	17	LOSING YOU Dusty Springfield	Philips	5
13	18	TWELFTH OF NEVER Cliff Richard	Columbia	7
15	19	AIN'T THAT LOVING YOU BABY Elvis Presley	RCA	4
-	20	DOWNTOWN Petula Clark	Pye	1
21	21	HOW SOON? Henry Mancini Orchestra	RCA	9
14	22	ONE WAY LOVE Cliff Bennett and the Rebel Rousers	Parlophone	7
25	23	WALK TALL Val Doonican	Decca	5
-	24	LITTLE RED ROOSTER Rolling Stones	Decca	1
16	25	WHERE DID OUR LOVE GO Supremes	Stateside	12
20	26	WE'RE THROUGH Hollies	Parlophone	9
31	27	BLACK GIRL Four Pennies	Philips	3
26	28	GOLDFINGER Shirley Bassey	Columbia	6
27	29	I UNDERSTAND Freddie and the Dreamers	Columbia	2
28	30	I WOULDN'T TRADE YOU FOR THE WORLD Bachelors	Decca	14
32	31	NOW WE'RE THRU Poets	Decca	4
38	32	DANCING IN THE STREET Martha and the Vandellas	Stateside	3
23	33	I WON'T FORGET YOU Jim Reeves	RCA	23
-	34	PRETTY PAPER Roy Orbison	London	1
33	35	WILD SIDE OF LIFE Tommy Quickly	Pye	2
35	36	MARCH OF THE MODS Joe Loss Orchestra	HMV	2
29	37	I'M CRYING Animals	Columbia	10

In these weeks ■ The Poets are the only Scottish beat group to hit the charts until Marmalade a few years later (29.10.64) ■ Four *Walk* records in the chart, and also a little *Dancing In The Street* (05.11.64) ■ For the eighth consecutive week, the record at number three is at its peak, and for one of the very few times in chart history, there is a total change in the top three singles (19.11.64) ■

LW	TW	Title	Artist	Label	Wks
24	38	I'M INTO SOMETHING GOOD	Herman's Hermits	*Columbia*	14
-	39	SHOW ME GIRL	Herman's Hermits	*Columbia*	1
-	40	WHEN I GROW UP TO BE A MAN	Beach Boys	*Capitol*	1

December 1964

□ Highest position disc reached ● Act's first ever week on chart

WEEK ENDING 26 NOVEMBER 1964

LW	TW	Title	Artist	Label	Wks
1	[1]	BABY LOVE	Supremes	*Stateside*	6
2	[2]	ALL DAY AND ALL OF THE NIGHT	Kinks	*Pye*	4
24	3	LITTLE RED ROOSTER	Rolling Stones	*Decca*	2
3	4	HE'S IN TOWN	Rockin' Berries	*Pye*	6
6	[5]	UM UM UM UM UM UM	Wayne Fontana and the Mindbenders	*Fontana*	8
16	6	I'M GONNA BE STRONG	Gene Pitney	*Stateside*	3
11	7	THERE'S A HEARTACHE FOLLOWING ME	Jim Reeves	*RCA*	4
4	8	OH PRETTY WOMAN	Roy Orbison	*London*	12
20	9	DOWNTOWN	Petula Clark	*Pye*	2
17	10	LOSING YOU	Dusty Springfield	*Philips*	6
5	11	SHA LA LA	Manfred Mann	*HMV*	6
9	12	TOKYO MELODY	Helmut Zacharias	*Polydor*	5
10	13	DON'T BRING ME DOWN	Pretty Things	*Fontana*	5
8	14	WALK AWAY	Matt Monro	*Parlophone*	11
14	15	REMEMBER (WALKIN' IN THE SAND)	Shangri-Las	*Red Bird*	7
7	16	(THERE'S) ALWAYS SOMETHING THERE TO REMIND ME	Sandie Shaw	*Pye*	8
23	17	WALK TALL	Val Doonican	*Decca*	6
12	18	THE WEDDING	Julie Rogers	*Mercury*	15
34	19	PRETTY PAPER	Roy Orbison	*London*	2
27	[20]	BLACK GIRL	Four Pennies	*Philips*	4
13	21	GOOGLE EYE	Nashville Teens	*Decca*	6
19	22	AIN'T THAT LOVING YOU BABY	Elvis Presley	*RCA*	5
18	23	TWELFTH OF NEVER	Cliff Richard	*Columbia*	8
15	24	WHEN YOU WALK IN THE ROOM	Searchers	*Pye*	10
39	25	SHOW ME GIRL	Herman's Hermits	*Columbia*	2
29	26	I UNDERSTAND	Freddie and the Dreamers	*Columbia*	3
25	27	WHERE DID OUR LOVE GO	Supremes	*Stateside*	13
21	28	HOW SOON?	Henry Mancini Orchestra	*RCA*	10
28	29	GOLDFINGER	Shirley Bassey	*Columbia*	7
32	30	DANCING IN THE STREET	Martha and the Vandellas	*Stateside*	4
22	31	ONE WAY LOVE	Cliff Bennett and the Rebel Rousers	*Parlophone*	8
30	32	I WOULDN'T TRADE YOU FOR THE WORLD	Bachelors	*Decca*	15
40	33	WHEN I GROW UP TO BE A MAN	Beach Boys	*Capitol*	2
-	34	MESSAGE TO MARTHA (KENTUCKY BLUEBIRD)	Adam Faith	*Parlophone*	1
35	35	WILD SIDE OF LIFE	Tommy Quickly	*Pye*	3
-	[36]	MESSAGE TO MARTHA (KENTUCKY BLUEBIRD)	Lou Johnson ●	*London*	1
-	[37]	WHAT'CHA GONNA DO ABOUT IT	Doris Troy ●	*Atlantic*	1
33	38	I WON'T FORGET YOU	Jim Reeves	*RCA*	24
-	39	TERRY	Twinkle ●	*Decca*	1
31	40	NOW WE'RE THRU	Poets	*Decca*	5

WEEK ENDING 3 DECEMBER 1964

LW	TW	Title	Artist	Label	Wks
3	[1]	LITTLE RED ROOSTER	Rolling Stones	*Decca*	3
6	[2]	I'M GONNA BE STRONG	Gene Pitney	*Stateside*	4
1	3	BABY LOVE	Supremes	*Stateside*	7
9	4	DOWNTOWN	Petula Clark	*Pye*	3
2	5	ALL DAY AND ALL OF THE NIGHT	Kinks	*Pye*	5
-	6	I FEEL FINE	Beatles	*Parlophone*	1
5	7	UM UM UM UM UM UM	Wayne Fontana and the Mindbenders	*Fontana*	9
7	8	THERE'S A HEARTACHE FOLLOWING ME	Jim Reeves	*RCA*	5
10	[9]	LOSING YOU	Dusty Springfield	*Philips*	7
4	10	HE'S IN TOWN	Rockin' Berries	*Pye*	7
17	11	WALK TALL	Val Doonican	*Decca*	7
19	12	PRETTY PAPER	Roy Orbison	*London*	3
13	13	DON'T BRING ME DOWN	Pretty Things	*Fontana*	6
11	14	SHA LA LA	Manfred Mann	*HMV*	7
12	15	TOKYO MELODY	Helmut Zacharias	*Polydor*	6
8	16	OH PRETTY WOMAN	Roy Orbison	*London*	13
26	17	I UNDERSTAND	Freddie and the Dreamers	*Columbia*	4
14	18	WALK AWAY	Matt Monro	*Parlophone*	12
25	[19]	SHOW ME GIRL	Herman's Hermits	*Columbia*	3
20	[20]	BLACK GIRL	Four Pennies	*Philips*	5
34	21	MESSAGE TO MARTHA (KENTUCKY BLUEBIRD)	Adam Faith	*Parlophone*	2
18	22	THE WEDDING	Julie Rogers	*Mercury*	16
15	23	REMEMBER (WALKIN' IN THE SAND)	Shangri-Las	*Red Bird*	8
16	24	(THERE'S) ALWAYS SOMETHING THERE TO REMIND ME	Sandie Shaw	*Pye*	9
21	25	GOOGLE EYE	Nashville Teens	*Decca*	7
22	26	AIN'T THAT LOVING YOU BABY	Elvis Presley	*RCA*	6
33	[27]	WHEN I GROW UP TO BE A MAN	Beach Boys	*Capitol*	3
30	[28]	DANCING IN THE STREET	Martha and the Vandellas	*Stateside*	5
23	29	TWELFTH OF NEVER	Cliff Richard	*Columbia*	9
39	30	TERRY	Twinkle	*Decca*	2
-	[31]	SO DEEP IS THE NIGHT	Ken Dodd	*Columbia*	1
24	32	WHEN YOU WALK IN THE ROOM	Searchers	*Pye*	11
29	33	GOLDFINGER	Shirley Bassey	*Columbia*	8
-	34	GENIE WITH THE LIGHT BROWN LAMP	Shadows	*Columbia*	1
-	35	BABY I NEED YOUR LOVIN'	Fourmost	*Parlophone*	1
27	36	WHERE DID OUR LOVE GO	Supremes	*Stateside*	14
36	37	MESSAGE TO MARTHA (KENTUCKY BLUEBIRD)	Lou Johnson	*London*	2
35	38	WILD SIDE OF LIFE	Tommy Quickly	*Pye*	4
38	39	I WON'T FORGET YOU	Jim Reeves	*RCA*	25
37	40	WHAT'CHA GONNA DO ABOUT IT	Doris Troy	*Atlantic*	2

WEEK ENDING 10 DECEMBER 1964

LW	TW	Title	Artist	Label	Wks
6	[1]	I FEEL FINE	Beatles	*Parlophone*	2
2	[2]	I'M GONNA BE STRONG	Gene Pitney	*Stateside*	5
1	3	LITTLE RED ROOSTER	Rolling Stones	*Decca*	4
4	4	DOWNTOWN	Petula Clark	*Pye*	4
11	5	WALK TALL	Val Doonican	*Decca*	8
8	[6]	THERE'S A HEARTACHE FOLLOWING ME	Jim Reeves	*RCA*	6
5	7	ALL DAY AND ALL OF THE NIGHT	Kinks	*Pye*	6
3	8	BABY LOVE	Supremes	*Stateside*	8
12	9	PRETTY PAPER	Roy Orbison	*London*	4
7	10	UM UM UM UM UM UM	Wayne Fontana and the Mindbenders	*Fontana*	10
9	11	LOSING YOU	Dusty Springfield	*Philips*	8
17	12	I UNDERSTAND	Freddie and the Dreamers	*Columbia*	5
10	13	HE'S IN TOWN	Rockin' Berries	*Pye*	8
21	14	MESSAGE TO MARTHA (KENTUCKY BLUEBIRD)	Adam Faith	*Parlophone*	3
15	15	TOKYO MELODY	Helmut Zacharias	*Polydor*	7
-	16	NO ARMS COULD EVER HOLD YOU	Bachelors	*Decca*	1
13	17	DON'T BRING ME DOWN	Pretty Things	*Fontana*	7
18	18	WALK AWAY	Matt Monro	*Parlophone*	13
19	[19]	SHOW ME GIRL	Herman's Hermits	*Columbia*	4
-	20	I COULD EASILY FALL	Cliff Richard	*Columbia*	1
20	21	BLACK GIRL	Four Pennies	*Philips*	6
34	22	GENIE WITH THE LIGHT BROWN LAMP	Shadows	*Columbia*	2
14	23	SHA LA LA	Manfred Mann	*HMV*	8
30	24	TERRY	Twinkle	*Decca*	3
22	25	THE WEDDING	Julie Rogers	*Mercury*	17
-	26	BLUE CHRISTMAS	Elvis Presley	*RCA*	1
-	27	WHAT HAVE THEY DONE TO THE RAIN	Searchers	*Pye*	1
16	28	OH PRETTY WOMAN	Roy Orbison	*London*	14
23	29	REMEMBER (WALKIN' IN THE SAND)	Shangri-Las	*Red Bird*	9
-	30	SOMEWHERE	P.J. Proby	*Liberty*	1
28	31	DANCING IN THE STREET	Martha and the Vandellas	*Stateside*	6
25	32	GOOGLE EYE	Nashville Teens	*Decca*	8
31	33	SO DEEP IS THE NIGHT	Ken Dodd	*Columbia*	2
-	34	CAST YOUR FATE TO THE WIND	Sounds Orchestral ●	*Piccadilly*	1
-	35	GO NOW	Moody Blues ●	*Decca*	1
-	[36]	GONE GONE GONE	Everly Brothers	*Warner Bros*	1
27	37	WHEN I GROW UP TO BE A MAN	Beach Boys	*Capitol*	4

■ For the second time, the Rolling Stones are knocked off the top after only one week by the new Beatles' single (10.12.64) ■ Gene Pitney is kept from the top by first the Rolling Stones and then by the Beatles (10.12.64) ■ Surrey teenager Twinkle's motorbike death saga *Terry* hits the charts a few weeks before the better-known American hit on the same grisly theme, the Shangri-Las' *Leader Of The Pack* (26.11.64) ■

December 1964

□ Highest position disc reached ● Act's first ever week on chart

LW	TW	Title	Artist	Label	Wks
-	38	GIRL DON'T COME	Sandie Shaw	*Pye*	1
26	39	AIN'T THAT LOVING YOU BABY	Elvis Presley	*RCA*	7
38	40	WILD SIDE OF LIFE	Tommy Quickly	*Pye*	5

WEEK ENDING 17 DECEMBER 1964

LW	TW	Title	Artist	Label	Wks
1	1	I FEEL FINE	Beatles	*Parlophone*	3
4	2	DOWNTOWN	Petula Clark	*Pye*	5
5	3	WALK TALL	Val Doonican	*Decca*	9
2	4	I'M GONNA BE STRONG	Gene Pitney	*Stateside*	6
3	5	LITTLE RED ROOSTER	Rolling Stones	*Decca*	5
9	6	PRETTY PAPER	Roy Orbison	*London*	5
12	7	I UNDERSTAND	Freddie and the Dreamers	*Columbia*	6
16	8	NO ARMS COULD EVER HOLD YOU	Bachelors	*Decca*	2
20	9	I COULD EASILY FALL	Cliff Richard	*Columbia*	2
8	10	BABY LOVE	Supremes	*Stateside*	9
6	11	THERE'S A HEARTACHE FOLLOWING ME	Jim Reeves	*RCA*	7
14	12	MESSAGE TO MARTHA (KENTUCKY BLUEBIRD)	Adam Faith	*Parlophone*	4
26	13	BLUE CHRISTMAS	Elvis Presley	*RCA*	2
30	14	SOMEWHERE	P.J. Proby	*Liberty*	2
24	15	TERRY	Twinkle	*Decca*	4
7	16	ALL DAY AND ALL OF THE NIGHT	Kinks	*Pye*	7
11	17	LOSING YOU	Dusty Springfield	*Philips*	9
38	18	GIRL DON'T COME	Sandie Shaw	*Pye*	2
27	19	WHAT HAVE THEY DONE TO THE RAIN	Searchers	*Pye*	2
19	20	SHOW ME GIRL	Herman's Hermits	*Columbia*	5
22	21	GENIE WITH THE LIGHT BROWN LAMP	Shadows	*Columbia*	3
18	22	WALK AWAY	Matt Monro	*Parlophone*	14
13	23	HE'S IN TOWN	Rockin' Berries	*Pye*	9
10	24	UM UM UM UM UM UM	Wayne Fontana and the Mindbenders	*Fontana*	11
15	25	TOKYO MELODY	Helmut Zacharias	*Polydor*	8
-	26	YEH YEH	Georgie Fame ●	*Columbia*	1
23	27	SHA LA LA	Manfred Mann	*HMV*	9
17	28	DON'T BRING ME DOWN	Pretty Things	*Fontana*	8
25	29	THE WEDDING	Julie Rogers	*Mercury*	18
28	30	OH PRETTY WOMAN	Roy Orbison	*London*	15
34	31	CAST YOUR FATE TO THE WIND	Sounds Orchestral	*Piccadilly*	2
35	32	GO NOW	Moody Blues	*Decca*	2
21	33	BLACK GIRL	Four Pennies	*Philips*	7
33	34	SO DEEP IS THE NIGHT	Ken Dodd	*Columbia*	3
-	35	A STARRY NIGHT	Joy Strings	*Regal-Zonophone*	1
36	36	GONE GONE GONE	Everly Brothers	*Warner Bros*	2
-	37	FERRY CROSS THE MERSEY	Gerry and the Pacemakers	*Columbia*	1
-	38	CHRISTMAS WILL BE JUST ANOTHER LONELY DAY	Brenda Lee	*Brunswick*	1
-	39	LIKE A CHILD	Julie Rogers	*Mercury*	1
32	40	GOOGLE EYE	Nashville Teens	*Decca*	9

WEEK ENDING 24 DECEMBER 1964

LW	TW	Title	Artist	Label	Wks
1	1	I FEEL FINE	Beatles	*Parlophone*	4
2	2	DOWNTOWN	Petula Clark	*Pye*	6
4	3	I'M GONNA BE STRONG	Gene Pitney	*Stateside*	7
3	4	WALK TALL	Val Doonican	*Decca*	10
7	5	I UNDERSTAND	Freddie and the Dreamers	*Columbia*	7
6	6	PRETTY PAPER	Roy Orbison	*London*	6
8	7	NO ARMS COULD EVER HOLD YOU	Bachelors	*Decca*	3
5	8	LITTLE RED ROOSTER	Rolling Stones	*Decca*	6
9	9	I COULD EASILY FALL	Cliff Richard	*Columbia*	3
14	10	SOMEWHERE	P.J. Proby	*Liberty*	3
13	11	BLUE CHRISTMAS	Elvis Presley	*RCA*	3
15	12	TERRY	Twinkle	*Decca*	5
18	13	GIRL DON'T COME	Sandie Shaw	*Pye*	3
12	14	MESSAGE TO MARTHA (KENTUCKY BLUEBIRD)	Adam Faith	*Parlophone*	5
10	15	BABY LOVE	Supremes	*Stateside*	10
19	16	WHAT HAVE THEY DONE TO THE RAIN	Searchers	*Pye*	3
26	17	YEH YEH	Georgie Fame	*Columbia*	2
11	18	THERE'S A HEARTACHE FOLLOWING ME	Jim Reeves	*RCA*	8
16	19	ALL DAY AND ALL OF THE NIGHT	Kinks	*Pye*	8
22	20	WALK AWAY	Matt Monro	*Parlophone*	15
17	21	LOSING YOU	Dusty Springfield	*Philips*	10
23	22	HE'S IN TOWN	Rockin' Berries	*Pye*	10
31	23	CAST YOUR FATE TO THE WIND	Sounds Orchestral	*Piccadilly*	3
39	24	LIKE A CHILD	Julie Rogers	*Mercury*	2
20	25	SHOW ME GIRL	Herman's Hermits	*Columbia*	6
24	26	UM UM UM UM UM UM	Wayne Fontana and the Mindbenders	*Fontana*	12
32	27	GO NOW	Moody Blues	*Decca*	3
21	28	GENIE WITH THE LIGHT BROWN LAMP	Shadows	*Columbia*	4
38	29	CHRISTMAS WILL BE JUST ANOTHER LONELY DAY	Brenda Lee	*Brunswick*	2
25	30	TOKYO MELODY	Helmut Zacharias	*Polydor*	9
37	31	FERRY CROSS THE MERSEY	Gerry and the Pacemakers	*Columbia*	2
29	32	THE WEDDING	Julie Rogers	*Mercury*	19
-	33	BABY I NEED YOUR LOVIN'	Fourmost	*Parlophone*	2
34	34	SO DEEP IS THE NIGHT	Ken Dodd	*Columbia*	4
35	35	A STARRY NIGHT	Joy Strings	*Regal-Zonophone*	2
28	36	DON'T BRING ME DOWN	Pretty Things	*Fontana*	9
-	37	RINGO	Lorne Greene ●	*RCA*	1
-	38	FOR MAMA	Matt Monro	*Parlophone*	1
36	39	GONE GONE GONE	Everly Brothers	*Warner Bros*	3
27	40	SHA LA LA	Manfred Mann	*HMV*	10

WEEK ENDING 31 DECEMBER 1964

(no chart compiled: chart for 24 December repeated)

LW	TW	Title	Artist	Label	Wks
1	1	I FEEL FINE	Beatles	*Parlophone*	5
2	2	DOWNTOWN	Petula Clark	*Pye*	7
3	3	I'M GONNA BE STRONG	Gene Pitney	*Stateside*	8
4	4	WALK TALL	Val Doonican	*Decca*	11
5	5	I UNDERSTAND	Freddie and the Dreamers	*Columbia*	8
6	6	PRETTY PAPER	Roy Orbison	*London*	7
7	7	NO ARMS COULD EVER HOLD YOU	Bachelors	*Decca*	4
8	8	LITTLE RED ROOSTER	Rolling Stones	*Decca*	7
9	9	I COULD EASILY FALL	Cliff Richard	*Columbia*	4
10	10	SOMEWHERE	P.J. Proby	*Liberty*	4
11	11	BLUE CHRISTMAS	Elvis Presley	*RCA*	4
12	12	TERRY	Twinkle	*Decca*	6
13	13	GIRL DON'T COME	Sandie Shaw	*Pye*	4
14	14	MESSAGE TO MARTHA (KENTUCKY BLUEBIRD)	Adam Faith	*Parlophone*	6
15	15	BABY LOVE	Supremes	*Stateside*	11
16	16	WHAT HAVE THEY DONE TO THE RAIN	Searchers	*Pye*	4
17	17	YEH YEH	Georgie Fame	*Columbia*	3
18	18	THERE'S A HEARTACHE FOLLOWING ME	Jim Reeves	*RCA*	9
19	19	ALL DAY AND ALL OF THE NIGHT	Kinks	*Pye*	9
20	20	WALK AWAY	Matt Monro	*Parlophone*	16
21	21	LOSING YOU	Dusty Springfield	*Philips*	11
22	22	HE'S IN TOWN	Rockin' Berries	*Pye*	11
23	23	CAST YOUR FATE TO THE WIND	Sounds Orchestral	*Piccadilly*	4
24	24	LIKE A CHILD	Julie Rogers	*Mercury*	3
25	25	SHOW ME GIRL	Herman's Hermits	*Columbia*	7
26	26	UM UM UM UM UM UM	Wayne Fontana and the Mindbenders	*Fontana*	13
27	27	GO NOW	Moody Blues	*Decca*	4
28	28	GENIE WITH THE LIGHT BROWN LAMP	Shadows	*Columbia*	5
29	29	CHRISTMAS WILL BE JUST ANOTHER LONELY DAY	Brenda Lee	*Brunswick*	3
30	30	TOKYO MELODY	Helmut Zacharias	*Polydor*	10
31	31	FERRY CROSS THE MERSEY	Gerry and the Pacemakers	*Columbia*	3
32	32	THE WEDDING	Julie Rogers	*Mercury*	20
33	33	BABY I NEED YOUR LOVIN'	Fourmost	*Parlophone*	3
34	34	SO DEEP IS THE NIGHT	Ken Dodd	*Columbia*	5
35	35	A STARRY NIGHT	Joy Strings	*Regal-Zonophone*	3
36	36	DON'T BRING ME DOWN	Pretty Things	*Fontana*	10
37	37	RINGO	Lorne Greene	*RCA*	2
38	38	FOR MAMA	Matt Monro	*Parlophone*	2
39	39	GONE GONE GONE	Everly Brothers	*Warner Bros*	4
40	40	SHA LA LA	Manfred Mann	*HMV*	11

In these weeks ■ Lorne Greene's hit has nothing to do with the Beatles' drummer. It is a ballad of the Old West, inspired by the success of Greene's role as Pa Cartwright in the TV series 'Bonanza' (24.12.64) ■ The Beatles become the first act to be number one at Christmas twice (31.12.64)■

1965

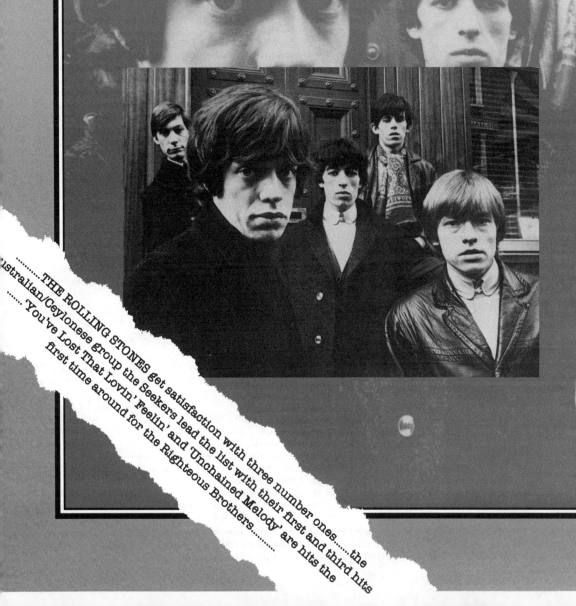

..........THE ROLLING STONES get satisfaction with three number ones......the ustralian/Ceylonese group the Seekers lead the list with their first and third hits ...... 'You've Lost That Lovin' Feelin' and 'Unchained Melody' are hits the first time around for the Righteous Brothers..........

January 1965

□ Highest position disc reached ● Act's first ever week on chart

LW	TW	WEEK ENDING 7 JANUARY 1965			Wks
1	1	I FEEL FINE	Beatles	Parlophone	6
17	2	YEH YEH	Georgie Fame	Columbia	4
2	3	DOWNTOWN	Petula Clark	Pye	8
12	4	TERRY	Twinkle	Decca	7
4	5	WALK TALL	Val Doonican	Decca	12
3	6	I'M GONNA BE STRONG	Gene Pitney	Stateside	9
13	7	GIRL DON'T COME	Sandie Shaw	Pye	5
10	8	SOMEWHERE	P.J. Proby	Liberty	5
9	9	I COULD EASILY FALL	Cliff Richard	Columbia	5
27	10	GO NOW	Moody Blues	Decca	5
7	11	NO ARMS COULD EVER HOLD YOU	Bachelors	Decca	5
5	12	I UNDERSTAND	Freddie and the Dreamers	Columbia	9
16	13	WHAT HAVE THEY DONE TO THE RAIN	Searchers	Pye	5
31	14	FERRY CROSS THE MERSEY	Gerry and the Pacemakers	Columbia	4
14	15	MESSAGE TO MARTHA (KENTUCKY BLUEBIRD)	Adam Faith	Parlophone	7
8	16	LITTLE RED ROOSTER	Rolling Stones	Decca	8
23	17	CAST YOUR FATE TO THE WIND	Sounds Orchestral	Piccadilly	5
18	18	THERE'S A HEARTACHE FOLLOWING ME	Jim Reeves	RCA	10
19	19	ALL DAY AND ALL OF THE NIGHT	Kinks	Pye	10
28	20	GENIE WITH THE LIGHT BROWN LAMP	Shadows	Columbia	6
15	21	BABY LOVE	Supremes	Stateside	12
6	22	PRETTY PAPER	Roy Orbison	London	8
20	23	WALK AWAY	Matt Monro	Parlophone	17
11	24	BLUE CHRISTMAS	Elvis Presley	RCA	5
24	25	LIKE A CHILD	Julie Rogers	Mercury	4
37	26	RINGO	Lorne Greene	RCA	3
33	27	BABY I NEED YOUR LOVIN'	Fourmost	Parlophone	4
21	28	LOSING YOU	Dusty Springfield	Philips	12
26	29	UM UM UM UM UM UM	Wayne Fontana and the Mindbenders	Fontana	14
25	30	SHOW ME GIRL	Herman's Hermits	Columbia	8
-	31	MARCH OF THE MODS	Joe Loss Orchestra	HMV	3
22	32	HE'S IN TOWN	Rockin' Berries	Pye	12
30	33	TOKYO MELODY	Helmut Zacharias	Polydor	11
34	34	SO DEEP IS THE NIGHT	Ken Dodd	Columbia	6
32	35	THE WEDDING	Julie Rogers	Mercury	21
38	36	FOR MAMA	Matt Monro	Parlophone	3
-	37	THREE BELLS	Brian Poole and the Tremeloes	Decca	1
-	38	BLACK GIRL	Four Pennies	Philips	8
-	39	BABY PLEASE DON'T GO	Them ●	Decca	1
-	40	TRIBUTE TO JIM REEVES	Larry Cunningham and the Mighty Avons ●	King	1

LW	TW	WEEK ENDING 14 JANUARY 1965			Wks
2	1	YEH YEH	Georgie Fame	Columbia	5
1	2	I FEEL FINE	Beatles	Parlophone	7
10	3	GO NOW	Moody Blues	Decca	6
4	4	TERRY	Twinkle	Decca	8
7	5	GIRL DON'T COME	Sandie Shaw	Pye	6
8	6	SOMEWHERE	P.J. Proby	Liberty	6
5	7	WALK TALL	Val Doonican	Decca	13
3	8	DOWNTOWN	Petula Clark	Pye	9
14	9	FERRY CROSS THE MERSEY	Gerry and the Pacemakers	Columbia	5
17	10	CAST YOUR FATE TO THE WIND	Sounds Orchestral	Piccadilly	6
9	11	I COULD EASILY FALL	Cliff Richard	Columbia	6
6	12	I'M GONNA BE STRONG	Gene Pitney	Stateside	10
11	13	NO ARMS COULD EVER HOLD YOU	Bachelors	Decca	6
12	14	I UNDERSTAND	Freddie and the Dreamers	Columbia	10
13	15	WHAT HAVE THEY DONE TO THE RAIN	Searchers	Pye	6
15	16	MESSAGE TO MARTHA (KENTUCKY BLUEBIRD)	Adam Faith	Parlophone	8
20	17	GENIE WITH THE LIGHT BROWN LAMP	Shadows	Columbia	7
16	18	LITTLE RED ROOSTER	Rolling Stones	Decca	9
39	19	BABY PLEASE DON'T GO	Them	Decca	2
18	20	THERE'S A HEARTACHE FOLLOWING ME	Jim Reeves	RCA	11
25	21	LIKE A CHILD	Julie Rogers	Mercury	5
26	22	RINGO	Lorne Greene	RCA	4
19	23	ALL DAY AND ALL OF THE NIGHT	Kinks	Pye	11
27	24	BABY I NEED YOUR LOVIN'	Fourmost	Parlophone	5
21	25	BABY LOVE	Supremes	Stateside	13
-	26	COME TOMORROW	Manfred Mann	HMV	1
37	27	THREE BELLS	Brian Poole and the Tremeloes	Decca	2
-	28	YOU'VE LOST THAT LOVIN' FEELIN'	Cilla Black	Parlophone	1
22	29	PRETTY PAPER	Roy Orbison	London	9
-	30	KEEP SEARCHIN'	Del Shannon	Stateside	1
-	31	ET MEME	Françoise Hardy	Pye	1
-	32	I'M LOST WITHOUT YOU	Billy Fury	Decca	1
-	33	I'LL NEVER FIND ANOTHER YOU	Seekers ●	Columbia	1
-	34	GETTING MIGHTY CROWDED	Betty Everett ●	Fontana	1
-	35	YOU'VE LOST THAT LOVIN' FEELIN'	Righteous Brothers ●	London	1
23	36	WALK AWAY	Matt Monro	Parlophone	18
28	37	LOSING YOU	Dusty Springfield	Philips	13
24	38	BLUE CHRISTMAS	Elvis Presley	RCA	6
-	39	GOIN' OUT OF MY HEAD	Dodie West ●	Decca	1
40	40	TRIBUTE TO JIM REEVES	Larry Cunningham and the Mighty Avons	King	2

LW	TW	WEEK ENDING 21 JANUARY 1965			Wks
1	1	YEH YEH	Georgie Fame	Columbia	6
3	2	GO NOW	Moody Blues	Decca	7
5	3	GIRL DON'T COME	Sandie Shaw	Pye	7
4	4	TERRY	Twinkle	Decca	9
10	5	CAST YOUR FATE TO THE WIND	Sounds Orchestral	Piccadilly	7
6	6	SOMEWHERE	P.J. Proby	Liberty	7
2	7	I FEEL FINE	Beatles	Parlophone	8
9	8	FERRY CROSS THE MERSEY	Gerry and the Pacemakers	Columbia	6
7	9	WALK TALL	Val Doonican	Decca	14
8	10	DOWNTOWN	Petula Clark	Pye	10
19	11	BABY PLEASE DON'T GO	Them	Decca	3
28	12	YOU'VE LOST THAT LOVIN' FEELIN'	Cilla Black	Parlophone	2
11	13	I COULD EASILY FALL	Cliff Richard	Columbia	7
26	14	COME TOMORROW	Manfred Mann	HMV	2
12	15	I'M GONNA BE STRONG	Gene Pitney	Stateside	11
13	16	NO ARMS COULD EVER HOLD YOU	Bachelors	Decca	7
15	17	WHAT HAVE THEY DONE TO THE RAIN	Searchers	Pye	7
14	18	I UNDERSTAND	Freddie and the Dreamers	Columbia	11
30	19	KEEP SEARCHIN'	Del Shannon	Stateside	2
35	20	YOU'VE LOST THAT LOVIN' FEELIN'	Righteous Brothers	London	2
27	21	THREE BELLS	Brian Poole and the Tremeloes	Decca	3
16	22	MESSAGE TO MARTHA (KENTUCKY BLUEBIRD)	Adam Faith	Parlophone	9
17	23	GENIE WITH THE LIGHT BROWN LAMP	Shadows	Columbia	8
22	24	RINGO	Lorne Greene	RCA	5
24	25	BABY I NEED YOUR LOVIN'	Fourmost	Parlophone	6
18	26	LITTLE RED ROOSTER	Rolling Stones	Decca	10
-	27	LEADER OF THE PACK	Shangri-Las	Red Bird	1
20	28	THERE'S A HEARTACHE FOLLOWING ME	Jim Reeves	RCA	12
32	29	I'M LOST WITHOUT YOU	Billy Fury	Decca	2
21	30	LIKE A CHILD	Julie Rogers	Mercury	6
-	31	TIRED OF WAITING FOR YOU	Kinks	Pye	1
33	32	I'LL NEVER FIND ANOTHER YOU	Seekers	Columbia	2
23	33	ALL DAY AND ALL OF THE NIGHT	Kinks	Pye	12
-	34	PROMISED LAND	Chuck Berry	Pye	1
34	35	GETTING MIGHTY CROWDED	Betty Everett	Fontana	2
36	36	WALK AWAY	Matt Monro	Parlophone	19
-	37	THE SPECIAL YEARS	Val Doonican	Decca	1
29	38	PRETTY PAPER	Roy Orbison	London	10
-	39	DANCE DANCE DANCE	Beach Boys	Capitol	1
25	40	BABY LOVE	Supremes	Stateside	14

In these weeks ■ From 12 March 1964 until this week, there is at least one Jim Reeves single in the Top 20 every week (14.01.65) ■ Seven of the Top Ten are at their peak, as the Moody Blues continue to climb to their highest position with their first chart offering (21.01.65)■

LW	TW	WEEK ENDING 28 JANUARY 1965			Wks
2	[1]	GO NOW	Moody Blues	*Decca*	8
12	[2]	YOU'VE LOST THAT LOVIN' FEELIN'	Cilla Black	*Parlophone*	3
20	3	YOU'VE LOST THAT LOVIN' FEELIN'	Righteous Brothers	*London*	3
1	4	YEH YEH	Georgie Fame	*Columbia*	7
14	5	COME TOMORROW	Manfred Mann	*HMV*	3
31	6	TIRED OF WAITING FOR YOU	Kinks	*Pye*	2
4	7	TERRY	Twinkle	*Decca*	10
3	8	GIRL DON'T COME	Sandie Shaw	*Pye*	8
8	9	FERRY CROSS THE MERSEY	Gerry and the Pacemakers	*Columbia*	7
5	10	CAST YOUR FATE TO THE WIND	Sounds Orchestral	*Piccadilly*	8
11	11	BABY PLEASE DON'T GO	Them	*Decca*	4
19	12	KEEP SEARCHIN'	Del Shannon	*Stateside*	3
7	13	I FEEL FINE	Beatles	*Parlophone*	9
6	14	SOMEWHERE	P.J. Proby	*Liberty*	8
9	15	WALK TALL	Val Doonican	*Decca*	15
10	16	DOWNTOWN	Petula Clark	*Pye*	11
21	[17]	THREE BELLS	Brian Poole and the Tremeloes	*Decca*	4
13	18	I COULD EASILY FALL	Cliff Richard	*Columbia*	8
32	19	I'LL NEVER FIND ANOTHER YOU	Seekers	*Columbia*	3
27	20	LEADER OF THE PACK	Shangri-Las	*Red Bird*	2
37	21	THE SPECIAL YEARS	Val Doonican	*Decca*	2
16	22	NO ARMS COULD EVER HOLD YOU	Bachelors	*Decca*	8
15	23	I'M GONNA BE STRONG	Gene Pitney	*Stateside*	12
29	24	I'M LOST WITHOUT YOU	Billy Fury	*Decca*	3
17	25	WHAT HAVE THEY DONE TO THE RAIN	Searchers	*Pye*	8
34	[26]	PROMISED LAND	Chuck Berry	*Pye*	2
25	27	BABY I NEED YOUR LOVIN'	Fourmost	*Parlophone*	7
18	28	I UNDERSTAND	Freddie and the Dreamers	*Columbia*	12
35	[29]	GETTING MIGHTY CROWDED	Betty Everett	*Fontana*	3
23	30	GENIE WITH THE LIGHT BROWN LAMP	Shadows	*Columbia*	9
39	31	DANCE DANCE DANCE	Beach Boys	*Capitol*	2
-	32	COME SEE ABOUT ME	Supremes	*Stateside*	1
-	33	WHAT IN THE WORLD'S COME OVER YOU	Rockin' Berries	*Piccadilly*	1
24	34	RINGO	Lorne Greene	*RCA*	6
26	35	LITTLE RED ROOSTER	Rolling Stones	*Decca*	11
-	36	YES I WILL	Hollies	*Parlophone*	1
22	37	MESSAGE TO MARTHA (KENTUCKY BLUEBIRD)	Adam Faith	*Parlophone*	10
-	38	EVERYBODY KNOWS	Dave Clark Five	*Columbia*	1
-	[39]	SOLDIER BOY	Cheetahs	*Philips*	1
28	40	THERE'S A HEARTACHE FOLLOWING ME	Jim Reeves	*RCA*	13

February 1965

☐ Highest position disc reached ● Act's first ever week on chart

LW	TW	WEEK ENDING 4 FEBRUARY 1965			Wks
3	[1]	YOU'VE LOST THAT LOVIN' FEELIN'	Righteous Brothers	*London*	4
6	2	TIRED OF WAITING FOR YOU	Kinks	*Pye*	3
1	3	GO NOW	Moody Blues	*Decca*	9
5	[4]	COME TOMORROW	Manfred Mann	*HMV*	4
2	5	YOU'VE LOST THAT LOVIN' FEELIN'	Cilla Black	*Parlophone*	4
12	6	KEEP SEARCHIN'	Del Shannon	*Stateside*	4
10	7	CAST YOUR FATE TO THE WIND	Sounds Orchestral	*Piccadilly*	9
4	8	YEH YEH	Georgie Fame	*Columbia*	8
8	9	GIRL DON'T COME	Sandie Shaw	*Pye*	9
7	10	TERRY	Twinkle	*Decca*	11
11	11	BABY PLEASE DON'T GO	Them	*Decca*	5
9	12	FERRY CROSS THE MERSEY	Gerry and the Pacemakers	*Columbia*	8
21	13	THE SPECIAL YEARS	Val Doonican	*Decca*	3
19	14	I'LL NEVER FIND ANOTHER YOU	Seekers	*Columbia*	4
14	15	SOMEWHERE	P.J. Proby	*Liberty*	9
24	[16]	I'M LOST WITHOUT YOU	Billy Fury	*Decca*	4
17	[17]	THREE BELLS	Brian Poole and the Tremeloes	*Decca*	5
20	18	LEADER OF THE PACK	Shangri-Las	*Red Bird*	3
13	19	I FEEL FINE	Beatles	*Parlophone*	10
16	20	DOWNTOWN	Petula Clark	*Pye*	12
18	21	I COULD EASILY FALL	Cliff Richard	*Columbia*	9
15	22	WALK TALL	Val Doonican	*Decca*	16
33	[23]	WHAT IN THE WORLD'S COME OVER YOU	Rockin' Berries	*Piccadilly*	2
31	[24]	DANCE DANCE DANCE	Beach Boys	*Capitol*	3
36	25	YES I WILL	Hollies	*Parlophone*	2
26	[26]	PROMISED LAND	Chuck Berry	*Pye*	3
-	27	GAME OF LOVE	Wayne Fontana and the Mindbenders	*Fontana*	1
22	28	NO ARMS COULD EVER HOLD YOU	Bachelors	*Decca*	9
32	29	COME SEE ABOUT ME	Supremes	*Stateside*	2
29	30	GETTING MIGHTY CROWDED	Betty Everett	*Fontana*	4
25	31	WHAT HAVE THEY DONE TO THE RAIN	Searchers	*Pye*	9
28	32	I UNDERSTAND	Freddie and the Dreamers	*Columbia*	13
-	33	DON'T LET ME BE MISUNDERSTOOD	Animals	*Columbia*	1
27	34	BABY I NEED YOUR LOVIN'	Fourmost	*Parlophone*	8
34	35	RINGO	Lorne Greene	*RCA*	7
23	36	I'M GONNA BE STRONG	Gene Pitney	*Stateside*	13
38	[37]	EVERYBODY KNOWS	Dave Clark Five	*Columbia*	2
30	38	GENIE WITH THE LIGHT BROWN LAMP	Shadows	*Columbia*	10
-	39	FUNNY HOW LOVE CAN BE	Ivy League ●	*Piccadilly*	1
-	[40]	LONG AFTER TONIGHT IS ALL OVER	Jimmy Radcliffe ●	*Stateside*	1

LW	TW	WEEK ENDING 11 FEBRUARY 1965			Wks
1	[1]	YOU'VE LOST THAT LOVIN' FEELIN'	Righteous Brothers	*London*	5
2	2	TIRED OF WAITING FOR YOU	Kinks	*Pye*	4
6	[3]	KEEP SEARCHIN'	Del Shannon	*Stateside*	5
3	4	GO NOW	Moody Blues	*Decca*	10
14	5	I'LL NEVER FIND ANOTHER YOU	Seekers	*Columbia*	5
4	6	COME TOMORROW	Manfred Mann	*HMV*	5
13	[7]	THE SPECIAL YEARS	Val Doonican	*Decca*	4
7	8	CAST YOUR FATE TO THE WIND	Sounds Orchestral	*Piccadilly*	10
5	9	YOU'VE LOST THAT LOVIN' FEELIN'	Cilla Black	*Parlophone*	5
11	[10]	BABY PLEASE DON'T GO	Them	*Decca*	6
18	[11]	LEADER OF THE PACK	Shangri-Las	*Red Bird*	4
12	12	FERRY CROSS THE MERSEY	Gerry and the Pacemakers	*Columbia*	9
33	13	DON'T LET ME BE MISUNDERSTOOD	Animals	*Columbia*	2
27	14	GAME OF LOVE	Wayne Fontana and the Mindbenders	*Fontana*	2
8	15	YEH YEH	Georgie Fame	*Columbia*	9
16	[16]	I'M LOST WITHOUT YOU	Billy Fury	*Decca*	5
10	17	TERRY	Twinkle	*Decca*	12
9	18	GIRL DON'T COME	Sandie Shaw	*Pye*	10
39	19	FUNNY HOW LOVE CAN BE	Ivy League	*Piccadilly*	2
-	20	IT HURTS SO MUCH	Jim Reeves	*RCA*	1
17	21	THREE BELLS	Brian Poole and the Tremeloes	*Decca*	6
25	22	YES I WILL	Hollies	*Parlophone*	3
23	[23]	WHAT IN THE WORLD'S COME OVER YOU	Rockin' Berries	*Piccadilly*	3
15	24	SOMEWHERE	P.J. Proby	*Liberty*	10
19	25	I FEEL FINE	Beatles	*Parlophone*	11
24	26	DANCE DANCE DANCE	Beach Boys	*Capitol*	4
29	[27]	COME SEE ABOUT ME	Supremes	*Stateside*	3
22	28	WALK TALL	Val Doonican	*Decca*	17
20	29	DOWNTOWN	Petula Clark	*Pye*	13
21	30	I COULD EASILY FALL	Cliff Richard	*Columbia*	10
26	31	PROMISED LAND	Chuck Berry	*Pye*	4
30	32	GETTING MIGHTY CROWDED	Betty Everett	*Fontana*	5
-	33	STOP FEELING SORRY FOR YOURSELF	Adam Faith	*Parlophone*	1
28	34	NO ARMS COULD EVER HOLD YOU	Bachelors	*Decca*	10
-	35	MARY ANNE	Shadows	*Columbia*	1
-	36	GOODNIGHT	Roy Orbison	*London*	1
-	37	PAPER TIGER	Sue Thompson ●	*Hickory*	1
-	38	WHAT'CHA GONNA DO ABOUT IT?	Doris Troy	*Atlantic*	3
-	39	IT'S NOT UNUSUAL	Tom Jones ●	*Decca*	1
-	40	WINDMILL IN OLD AMSTERDAM	Ronnie Hilton	*HMV*	1

■Two versions of *You've Lost That Lovin' Feelin'* in the top three (28.01.65) ■ *Mary Anne* is the first vocal hit by the Shadows (11.02.65) ■ Tom Jones' debut hit is the sixth consecutive new entry at number 39. It is the only one that will climb all the way to number one (11.02.65)■

February 1965

☐ Highest position disc reached ● Act's first ever week on chart

LW	TW	WEEK ENDING 18 FEBRUARY 1965		Wks
2	[1]	TIRED OF WAITING FOR YOU Kinks	Pye	5
5	2	I'LL NEVER FIND ANOTHER YOU Seekers	Columbia	6
1	3	YOU'VE LOST THAT LOVIN' FEELIN' Righteous Brothers	London	6
3	4	KEEP SEARCHIN' Del Shannon	Stateside	6
14	5	GAME OF LOVE Wayne Fontana and the Mindbenders	Fontana	3
13	6	DON'T LET ME BE MISUNDERSTOOD Animals	Columbia	3
7	[7]	THE SPECIAL YEARS Val Doonican	Decca	5
6	8	COME TOMORROW Manfred Mann	HMV	6
19	9	FUNNY HOW LOVE CAN BE Ivy League	Piccadilly	3
4	10	GO NOW Moody Blues	Decca	11
20	11	IT HURTS SO MUCH Jim Reeves	RCA	2
8	12	CAST YOUR FATE TO THE WIND Sounds Orchestral	Piccadilly	11
9	13	YOU'VE LOST THAT LOVIN' FEELIN' Cilla Black	Parlophone	6
11	14	LEADER OF THE PACK Shangri-Las	Red Bird	5
22	15	YES I WILL Hollies	Parlophone	4
10	16	BABY PLEASE DON'T GO Them	Decca	7
36	17	GOODNIGHT Roy Orbison	London	2
12	18	FERRY CROSS THE MERSEY Gerry and the Pacemakers	Columbia	10
39	19	IT'S NOT UNUSUAL Tom Jones	Decca	2
16	20	I'M LOST WITHOUT YOU Billy Fury	Decca	6
15	21	YEH YEH Georgie Fame	Columbia	10
17	22	TERRY Twinkle	Decca	13
21	23	THREE BELLS Brian Poole and the Tremeloes	Decca	7
-	24	I MUST BE SEEING THINGS Gene Pitney	Stateside	1
35	25	MARY ANNE Shadows	Columbia	2
-	26	COME AND STAY WITH ME Marianne Faithfull	Decca	1
26	27	DANCE DANCE DANCE Beach Boys	Capitol	5
23	28	WHAT IN THE WORLD'S COME OVER YOU Rockin' Berries	Piccadilly	4
24	29	SOMEWHERE P.J. Proby	Liberty	11
40	30	WINDMILL IN OLD AMSTERDAM Ronnie Hilton	HMV	2
18	31	GIRL DON'T COME Sandie Shaw	Pye	11
33	32	STOP FEELING SORRY FOR YOURSELF Adam Faith	Parlophone	2
27	33	COME SEE ABOUT ME Supremes	Stateside	4
28	34	WALK TALL Val Doonican	Decca	18
32	35	GETTING MIGHTY CROWDED Betty Everett	Fontana	6
37	36	PAPER TIGER Sue Thompson	Hickory	2
-	[37]	YOUR HURTIN' KIND OF LOVE Dusty Springfield	Philips	1
25	38	I FEEL FINE Beatles	Parlophone	12
31	39	PROMISED LAND Chuck Berry	Pye	5
29	40	DOWNTOWN Petula Clark	Pye	14

LW	TW	WEEK ENDING 25 FEBRUARY 1965		Wks
2	[1]	I'LL NEVER FIND ANOTHER YOU Seekers	Columbia	7
5	[2]	GAME OF LOVE Wayne Fontana and the Mindbenders	Fontana	4
6	[3]	DON'T LET ME BE MISUNDERSTOOD Animals	Columbia	4
3	4	YOU'VE LOST THAT LOVIN' FEELIN' Righteous Brothers	London	7
1	5	TIRED OF WAITING FOR YOU Kinks	Pye	6
4	6	KEEP SEARCHIN' Del Shannon	Stateside	7
7	[7]	THE SPECIAL YEARS Val Doonican	Decca	6
11	[8]	IT HURTS SO MUCH Jim Reeves	RCA	3
9	9	FUNNY HOW LOVE CAN BE Ivy League	Piccadilly	4
19	10	IT'S NOT UNUSUAL Tom Jones	Decca	3
24	11	I MUST BE SEEING THINGS Gene Pitney	Stateside	2
15	12	YES I WILL Hollies	Parlophone	5
-	13	SILHOUETTES Herman's Hermits	Columbia	1
17	[14]	GOODNIGHT Roy Orbison	London	3
26	15	COME AND STAY WITH ME Marianne Faithfull	Decca	2
8	16	COME TOMORROW Manfred Mann	HMV	7
-	17	I'LL STOP AT NOTHING Sandie Shaw	Pye	1
10	18	GO NOW Moody Blues	Decca	12
12	19	CAST YOUR FATE TO THE WIND Sounds Orchestral	Piccadilly	12
25	20	MARY ANNE Shadows	Columbia	3
16	21	BABY PLEASE DON'T GO Them	Decca	8
13	22	YOU'VE LOST THAT LOVIN' FEELIN' Cilla Black	Parlophone	7
14	23	LEADER OF THE PACK Shangri-Las	Red Bird	6
32	24	STOP FEELING SORRY FOR YOURSELF Adam Faith	Parlophone	3
18	25	FERRY CROSS THE MERSEY Gerry and the Pacemakers	Columbia	11
20	26	I'M LOST WITHOUT YOU Billy Fury	Decca	7
21	27	YEH YEH Georgie Fame	Columbia	11
22	28	TERRY Twinkle	Decca	14
30	29	WINDMILL IN OLD AMSTERDAM Ronnie Hilton	HMV	3
23	30	THREE BELLS Brian Poole and the Tremeloes	Decca	8
-	31	GOLDEN LIGHTS Twinkle	Decca	1
-	32	HONEY I NEED Pretty Things	Fontana	1
-	33	I APOLOGISE P.J. Proby	Liberty	1
36	34	PAPER TIGER Sue Thompson	Hickory	3
31	35	GIRL DON'T COME Sandie Shaw	Pye	12
-	36	CAN'T YOU HEAR MY HEART BEAT Goldie and the Gingerbreads ●	Decca	1
34	37	WALK TALL Val Doonican	Decca	19
28	38	WHAT IN THE WORLD'S COME OVER YOU Rockin' Berries	Piccadilly	5
27	39	DANCE DANCE DANCE Beach Boys	Capitol	6
-	40	I CAN'T EXPLAIN Who ●	Brunswick	1

LW	TW	WEEK ENDING 4 MARCH 1965		Wks
1	[1]	I'LL NEVER FIND ANOTHER YOU Seekers	Columbia	8
10	2	IT'S NOT UNUSUAL Tom Jones	Decca	4
2	3	GAME OF LOVE Wayne Fontana and the Mindbenders	Fontana	5
13	4	SILHOUETTES Herman's Hermits	Columbia	2
3	5	DON'T LET ME BE MISUNDERSTOOD Animals	Columbia	5
11	[6]	I MUST BE SEEING THINGS Gene Pitney	Stateside	3
7	[7]	THE SPECIAL YEARS Val Doonican	Decca	7
9	[8]	FUNNY HOW LOVE CAN BE Ivy League	Piccadilly	5
15	9	COME AND STAY WITH ME Marianne Faithfull	Decca	3
5	10	TIRED OF WAITING FOR YOU Kinks	Pye	7
17	11	I'LL STOP AT NOTHING Sandie Shaw	Pye	2
8	12	IT HURTS SO MUCH Jim Reeves	RCA	4
4	13	YOU'VE LOST THAT LOVIN' FEELIN' Righteous Brothers	London	8
12	14	YES I WILL Hollies	Parlophone	6
14	15	GOODNIGHT Roy Orbison	London	4
6	16	KEEP SEARCHIN' Del Shannon	Stateside	8
20	[17]	MARY ANNE Shadows	Columbia	4
33	18	I APOLOGISE P.J. Proby	Liberty	2
16	19	COME TOMORROW Manfred Mann	HMV	8
19	20	CAST YOUR FATE TO THE WIND Sounds Orchestral	Piccadilly	13
32	21	HONEY I NEED Pretty Things	Fontana	2
31	22	GOLDEN LIGHTS Twinkle	Decca	2
24	[23]	STOP FEELING SORRY FOR YOURSELF Adam Faith	Parlophone	4
29	24	WINDMILL IN OLD AMSTERDAM Ronnie Hilton	HMV	4
36	[25]	CAN'T YOU HEAR MY HEART BEAT Goldie and the Gingerbreads	Decca	2
23	26	LEADER OF THE PACK Shangri-Las	Red Bird	7
18	27	GO NOW Moody Blues	Decca	13
-	28	THE 'IN' CROWD Dobie Gray ●	London	1
21	29	BABY PLEASE DON'T GO Them	Decca	9
34	[30]	PAPER TIGER Sue Thompson	Hickory	4
-	31	THE LAST TIME Rolling Stones	Decca	1
22	32	YOU'VE LOST THAT LOVIN' FEELIN' Cilla Black	Parlophone	8
40	33	I CAN'T EXPLAIN Who	Brunswick	2
-	34	IN THE MEANTIME Georgie Fame	Columbia	1
-	35	CONCRETE AND CLAY Unit Four Plus Two ●	Decca	1
25	36	FERRY CROSS THE MERSEY Gerry and the Pacemakers	Columbia	12
-	[37]	YOUR HURTIN' KIND OF LOVE Dusty Springfield	Philips	2
26	38	I'M LOST WITHOUT YOU Billy Fury	Decca	8
27	39	YEH YEH Georgie Fame	Columbia	12
37	40	WALK TALL Val Doonican	Decca	20

In these weeks ■ For two consecutive weeks, records jump from 14 to 5 and from 39 to 19 (18.02.65) ■ Plenty of contradictory coming and going in the charts, from *Come Tomorrow* and *Go Now* to *Girl Don't Come* and *Baby Please Don't Go* (18.02.65) ■ After the scandal of his trousers splitting on stage, it seems only right that P.J. Proby's fourth hit should be *I Apologise*, following *Hold Me*, *Together* and *Somewhere* (25.02.65) ■ Four weeks at number 7 for *The Special Years* (04.03.65) ■

LW	TW	WEEK ENDING 11 MARCH 1965		Wks
2	[1]	IT'S NOT UNUSUAL Tom Jones	*Decca*	5
1	2	I'LL NEVER FIND ANOTHER YOU Seekers	*Columbia*	9
4	[3]	SILHOUETTES Herman's Hermits	*Columbia*	3
11	[4]	I'LL STOP AT NOTHING Sandie Shaw	*Pye*	3
3	5	GAME OF LOVE Wayne Fontana and the Mindbenders	*Fontana*	6
31	6	THE LAST TIME Rolling Stones	*Decca*	2
9	7	COME AND STAY WITH ME Marianne Faithfull	*Decca*	4
5	8	DON'T LET ME BE MISUNDERSTOOD Animals	*Columbia*	6
6	9	I MUST BE SEEING THINGS Gene Pitney	*Stateside*	4
14	10	YES I WILL Hollies	*Parlophone*	7
8	11	FUNNY HOW LOVE CAN BE Ivy League	*Piccadilly*	6
7	12	THE SPECIAL YEARS Val Doonican	*Decca*	8
-	13	GOODBYE MY LOVE Searchers	*Pye*	1
15	[14]	GOODNIGHT Roy Orbison	*London*	5
10	15	TIRED OF WAITING FOR YOU Kinks	*Pye*	8
18	16	I APOLOGISE P.J. Proby	*Liberty*	3
12	17	IT HURTS SO MUCH Jim Reeves	*RCA*	5
17	18	MARY ANNE Shadows	*Columbia*	5
21	19	HONEY I NEED Pretty Things	*Fontana*	3
16	20	KEEP SEARCHIN' Del Shannon	*Stateside*	9
22	[21]	GOLDEN LIGHTS Twinkle	*Decca*	3
13	22	YOU'VE LOST THAT LOVIN' FEELIN' Righteous Brothers	*London*	9
24	[23]	WINDMILL IN OLD AMSTERDAM Ronnie Hilton	*HMV*	5
34	24	IN THE MEANTIME Georgie Fame	*Columbia*	2
28	[25]	THE 'IN' CROWD Dobie Gray	*London*	2
33	26	I CAN'T EXPLAIN Who	*Brunswick*	3
35	27	CONCRETE AND CLAY Unit Four Plus Two	*Decca*	2
23	28	STOP FEELING SORRY FOR YOURSELF Adam Faith	*Parlophone*	5
19	29	COME TOMORROW Manfred Mann	*HMV*	9
-	30	I KNOW A PLACE Petula Clark	*Pye*	1
25	31	CAN'T YOU HEAR MY HEART BEAT Goldie and the Gingerbreads	*Decca*	3
-	32	DO THE CLAM Elvis Presley	*RCA*	1
20	33	CAST YOUR FATE TO THE WIND Sounds Orchestral	*Piccadilly*	14
-	[34]	FIND MY WAY BACK HOME Nashville Teens	*Decca*	1
30	35	PAPER TIGER Sue Thompson	*Hickory*	5
26	36	LEADER OF THE PACK Shangri-Las	*Red Bird*	8
-	37	I DON'T WANT TO GO ON WITHOUT YOU Moody Blues	*Decca*	1
-	38	THE MINUTE YOU'RE GONE Cliff Richard	*Columbia*	1
-	39	I BELONG Kathy Kirby	*Decca*	1
32	40	YOU'VE LOST THAT LOVIN' FEELIN' Cilla Black	*Parlophone*	9

April 1965

□ Highest position disc reached ● Act's first ever week on chart

LW	TW	WEEK ENDING 18 MARCH 1965		Wks
6	[1]	THE LAST TIME Rolling Stones	*Decca*	3
1	2	IT'S NOT UNUSUAL Tom Jones	*Decca*	6
3	[3]	SILHOUETTES Herman's Hermits	*Columbia*	4
2	4	I'LL NEVER FIND ANOTHER YOU Seekers	*Columbia*	10
7	5	COME AND STAY WITH ME Marianne Faithfull	*Decca*	5
13	6	GOODBYE MY LOVE Searchers	*Pye*	2
9	7	I MUST BE SEEING THINGS Gene Pitney	*Stateside*	5
4	8	I'LL STOP AT NOTHING Sandie Shaw	*Pye*	4
10	[9]	YES I WILL Hollies	*Parlophone*	8
5	10	GAME OF LOVE Wayne Fontana and the Mindbenders	*Fontana*	7
16	[11]	I APOLOGISE P.J. Proby	*Liberty*	4
8	12	DON'T LET ME BE MISUNDERSTOOD Animals	*Columbia*	7
19	[13]	HONEY I NEED Pretty Things	*Fontana*	4
14	[14]	GOODNIGHT Roy Orbison	*London*	6
12	15	THE SPECIAL YEARS Val Doonican	*Decca*	9
17	16	IT HURTS SO MUCH Jim Reeves	*RCA*	6
11	17	FUNNY HOW LOVE CAN BE Ivy League	*Piccadilly*	7
27	18	CONCRETE AND CLAY Unit Four Plus Two	*Decca*	3
32	[19]	DO THE CLAM Elvis Presley	*RCA*	2
18	20	MARY ANNE Shadows	*Columbia*	6
30	21	I KNOW A PLACE Petula Clark	*Pye*	2
24	[22]	IN THE MEANTIME Georgie Fame	*Columbia*	3
26	23	I CAN'T EXPLAIN Who	*Brunswick*	4
23	24	WINDMILL IN OLD AMSTERDAM Ronnie Hilton	*HMV*	6
15	25	TIRED OF WAITING FOR YOU Kinks	*Pye*	9
38	26	THE MINUTE YOU'RE GONE Cliff Richard	*Columbia*	2
25	27	THE 'IN' CROWD Dobie Gray	*London*	3
21	28	GOLDEN LIGHTS Twinkle	*Decca*	4
20	29	KEEP SEARCHIN' Del Shannon	*Stateside*	10
-	30	REELIN' AND ROCKIN' Dave Clark Five	*Columbia*	1
-	31	YOU'RE BREAKIN' MY HEART Keely Smith ●	*Reprise*	1
-	32	FOR YOUR LOVE Yardbirds ●	*Columbia*	1
37	[33]	I DON'T WANT TO GO ON WITHOUT YOU Moody Blues	*Decca*	2
31	34	CAN'T YOU HEAR MY HEART BEAT Goldie and the Gingerbreads	*Decca*	4
-	35	KING OF THE ROAD Roger Miller ●	*Philips*	1
39	[36]	I BELONG Kathy Kirby	*Decca*	2
22	37	YOU'VE LOST THAT LOVIN' FEELIN' Righteous Brothers	*London*	10
-	38	I'M LOST WITHOUT YOU Billy Fury	*Decca*	9
-	[39]	HEY GOOD LOOKIN' Bo Diddley	*Chess*	1
-	[40]	STRANGER IN TOWN Del Shannon	*Stateside*	1

LW	TW	WEEK ENDING 25 MARCH 1965		Wks
1	[1]	THE LAST TIME Rolling Stones	*Decca*	4
2	2	IT'S NOT UNUSUAL Tom Jones	*Decca*	7
3	[3]	SILHOUETTES Herman's Hermits	*Columbia*	5
5	[4]	COME AND STAY WITH ME Marianne Faithfull	*Decca*	6
6	5	GOODBYE MY LOVE Searchers	*Pye*	3
4	6	I'LL NEVER FIND ANOTHER YOU Seekers	*Columbia*	11
8	7	I'LL STOP AT NOTHING Sandie Shaw	*Pye*	5
18	8	CONCRETE AND CLAY Unit Four Plus Two	*Decca*	4
7	9	I MUST BE SEEING THINGS Gene Pitney	*Stateside*	6
26	10	THE MINUTE YOU'RE GONE Cliff Richard	*Columbia*	3
9	11	YES I WILL Hollies	*Parlophone*	9
11	12	I APOLOGISE P.J. Proby	*Liberty*	5
32	13	FOR YOUR LOVE Yardbirds	*Columbia*	2
10	14	GAME OF LOVE Wayne Fontana and the Mindbenders	*Fontana*	8
23	15	I CAN'T EXPLAIN Who	*Brunswick*	5
15	16	THE SPECIAL YEARS Val Doonican	*Decca*	10
21	[17]	I KNOW A PLACE Petula Clark	*Pye*	3
13	18	HONEY I NEED Pretty Things	*Fontana*	5
12	19	DON'T LET ME BE MISUNDERSTOOD Animals	*Columbia*	8
19	20	DO THE CLAM Elvis Presley	*RCA*	3
14	21	GOODNIGHT Roy Orbison	*London*	7
-	22	CATCH THE WIND Donovan ●	*Pye*	1
31	23	YOU'RE BREAKIN' MY HEART Keely Smith	*Reprise*	2
22	24	IN THE MEANTIME Georgie Fame	*Columbia*	4
24	25	WINDMILL IN OLD AMSTERDAM Ronnie Hilton	*HMV*	7
17	26	FUNNY HOW LOVE CAN BE Ivy League	*Piccadilly*	8
20	27	MARY ANNE Shadows	*Columbia*	7
30	28	REELIN' AND ROCKIN' Dave Clark Five	*Columbia*	2
16	29	IT HURTS SO MUCH Jim Reeves	*RCA*	7
28	30	GOLDEN LIGHTS Twinkle	*Decca*	5
-	31	I'LL BE THERE Gerry and the Pacemakers	*Columbia*	1
-	32	HERE COMES THE NIGHT Them	*Decca*	1
33	[33]	I DON'T WANT TO GO ON WITHOUT YOU Moody Blues	*Decca*	3
27	34	THE 'IN' CROWD Dobie Gray	*London*	4
35	35	KING OF THE ROAD Roger Miller	*Philips*	2
-	36	THE TIMES THEY ARE A-CHANGIN' Bob Dylan ●	*CBS*	1
-	37	LITTLE THINGS Dave Berry	*Decca*	1
25	38	TIRED OF WAITING FOR YOU Kinks	*Pye*	10
-	39	BIRDS AND THE BEES Jewel Akens ●	*London*	1
-	40	WITHOUT YOU Matt Monro	*Parlophone*	1

LW	TW	WEEK ENDING 1 APRIL 1965		Wks
1	[1]	THE LAST TIME Rolling Stones	*Decca*	5
8	2	CONCRETE AND CLAY Unit Four Plus Two	*Decca*	5
2	3	IT'S NOT UNUSUAL Tom Jones	*Decca*	8
5	[4]	GOODBYE MY LOVE Searchers	*Pye*	4
13	5	FOR YOUR LOVE Yardbirds	*Columbia*	3
10	6	THE MINUTE YOU'RE GONE Cliff Richard	*Columbia*	4

■A different record at number 3 every week of the year until *Silhouettes* stays for three weeks (11.03.65) ■ Bob Dylan and his British 'rival' Donovan both make their first chart appearances in the same week (25.03.65) ■ Del Shannon's final week on the U.K. Singles chart (18.03.65)■

April 1965

□ Highest position disc reached ● Act's first ever week on chart

LW	TW	Title	Artist	Label	Wks
22	7	CATCH THE WIND	Donovan	*Pye*	2
4	8	COME AND STAY WITH ME	Marianne Faithfull	*Decca*	7
3	9	SILHOUETTES	Herman's Hermits	*Columbia*	6
6	10	I'LL NEVER FIND ANOTHER YOU	Seekers	*Columbia*	12
7	11	I'LL STOP AT NOTHING	Sandie Shaw	*Pye*	6
15	12	I CAN'T EXPLAIN	Who	*Brunswick*	6
9	13	I MUST BE SEEING THINGS	Gene Pitney	*Stateside*	7
32	14	HERE COMES THE NIGHT	Them	*Decca*	2
36	15	THE TIMES THEY ARE A-CHANGIN'	Bob Dylan	*CBS*	2
23	16	YOU'RE BREAKIN' MY HEART	Keely Smith	*Reprise*	3
11	17	YES I WILL	Hollies	*Parlophone*	10
17	18	I KNOW A PLACE	Petula Clark	*Pye*	4
31	19	I'LL BE THERE	Gerry and the Pacemakers	*Columbia*	2
12	20	I APOLOGISE	P.J. Proby	*Liberty*	6
14	21	GAME OF LOVE	Wayne Fontana and the Mindbenders	*Fontana*	9
20	22	DO THE CLAM	Elvis Presley	*RCA*	4
-	23	STOP IN THE NAME OF LOVE	Supremes	*Tamla Motown*	1
16	24	THE SPECIAL YEARS	Val Doonican	*Decca*	11
18	25	HONEY I NEED	Pretty Things	*Fontana*	6
37	26	LITTLE THINGS	Dave Berry	*Decca*	2
28	27	REELIN' AND ROCKIN'	Dave Clark Five	*Columbia*	3
24	28	IN THE MEANTIME	Georgie Fame	*Columbia*	5
-	29	EVERYBODY'S GONNA BE HAPPY	Kinks	*Pye*	1
19	30	DON'T LET ME BE MISUNDERSTOOD	Animals	*Columbia*	9
21	31	GOODNIGHT	Roy Orbison	*London*	8
-	32	POP GO THE WORKERS	Barron Knights	*Columbia*	1
-	33	ALL OVER THE WORLD	Françoise Hardy	*Pye*	1
25	34	WINDMILL IN OLD AMSTERDAM	Ronnie Hilton	*HMV*	8
35	35	KING OF THE ROAD	Roger Miller	*Philips*	3
-	36	NOWHERE TO RUN	Martha and the Vandellas ●	*Tamla Motown*	1
40	37	WITHOUT YOU	Matt Monro	*Parlophone*	2
33	38	I DON'T WANT TO GO ON WITHOUT YOU	Moody Blues	*Decca*	4
34	39	THE 'IN' CROWD	Dobie Gray	*London*	5
39	40	BIRDS AND THE BEES	Jewel Akens	*London*	2

WEEK ENDING 8 APRIL 1965

LW	TW	Title	Artist	Label	Wks
2	1	CONCRETE AND CLAY	Unit Four Plus Two	*Decca*	6
1	2	THE LAST TIME	Rolling Stones	*Decca*	6
5	3	FOR YOUR LOVE	Yardbirds	*Columbia*	4
6	4	THE MINUTE YOU'RE GONE	Cliff Richard	*Columbia*	5
7	5	CATCH THE WIND	Donovan	*Pye*	3
14	6	HERE COMES THE NIGHT	Them	*Decca*	3
3	7	IT'S NOT UNUSUAL	Tom Jones	*Decca*	9
8	8	COME AND STAY WITH ME	Marianne Faithfull	*Decca*	8
9	9	SILHOUETTES	Herman's Hermits	*Columbia*	7
12	10	I CAN'T EXPLAIN	Who	*Brunswick*	7
4	11	GOODBYE MY LOVE	Searchers	*Pye*	5
23	12	STOP IN THE NAME OF LOVE	Supremes	*Tamla Motown*	2
15	13	THE TIMES THEY ARE A-CHANGIN'	Bob Dylan	*CBS*	3
16	14	YOU'RE BREAKIN' MY HEART	Keely Smith	*Reprise*	4
10	15	I'LL NEVER FIND ANOTHER YOU	Seekers	*Columbia*	13
19	16	I'LL BE THERE	Gerry and the Pacemakers	*Columbia*	3
26	17	LITTLE THINGS	Dave Berry	*Decca*	3
29	18	EVERYBODY'S GONNA BE HAPPY	Kinks	*Pye*	2
32	19	POP GO THE WORKERS	Barron Knights	*Columbia*	2
11	20	I'LL STOP AT NOTHING	Sandie Shaw	*Pye*	7
13	21	I MUST BE SEEING THINGS	Gene Pitney	*Stateside*	8
18	22	I KNOW A PLACE	Petula Clark	*Pye*	5
25	23	HONEY I NEED	Pretty Things	*Fontana*	7
27	24	REELIN' AND ROCKIN'	Dave Clark Five	*Columbia*	4
22	25	DO THE CLAM	Elvis Presley	*RCA*	5
35	26	KING OF THE ROAD	Roger Miller	*Philips*	4
17	27	YES I WILL	Hollies	*Parlophone*	11
33	28	ALL OVER THE WORLD	Françoise Hardy	*Pye*	2
20	29	I APOLOGISE	P.J. Proby	*Liberty*	7
28	30	IN THE MEANTIME	Georgie Fame	*Columbia*	6
-	31	HAWAIIAN WEDDING SONG	Julie Rogers	*Mercury*	1
36	32	NOWHERE TO RUN	Martha and the Vandellas	*Tamla Motown*	2
40	33	BIRDS AND THE BEES	Jewel Akens	*London*	3
-	34	BRING IT ON HOME TO ME	Animals	*Columbia*	1
-	35	TRUE LOVE FOR EVERMORE	Bachelors	*Decca*	1
38	36	I DON'T WANT TO GO ON WITHOUT YOU	Moody Blues	*Decca*	5
-	37	YOU CAN HAVE HIM	Dionne Warwick	*Pye*	1
24	38	THE SPECIAL YEARS	Val Doonican	*Decca*	12
-	39	TRUE LOVE WAYS	Peter and Gordon	*Columbia*	1
34	40	WINDMILL IN OLD AMSTERDAM	Ronnie Hilton	*HMV*	9

WEEK ENDING 15 APRIL 1965

LW	TW	Title	Artist	Label	Wks
4	1	THE MINUTE YOU'RE GONE	Cliff Richard	*Columbia*	6
1	2	CONCRETE AND CLAY	Unit Four Plus Two	*Decca*	7
3	3	FOR YOUR LOVE	Yardbirds	*Columbia*	5
5	4	CATCH THE WIND	Donovan	*Pye*	4
6	5	HERE COMES THE NIGHT	Them	*Decca*	4
2	6	THE LAST TIME	Rolling Stones	*Decca*	7
12	7	STOP IN THE NAME OF LOVE	Supremes	*Tamla Motown*	3
10	8	I CAN'T EXPLAIN	Who	*Brunswick*	8
13	9	THE TIMES THEY ARE A-CHANGIN'	Bob Dylan	*CBS*	4
19	10	POP GO THE WORKERS	Barron Knights	*Columbia*	3
-	11	TICKET TO RIDE	Beatles	*Parlophone*	1
17	12	LITTLE THINGS	Dave Berry	*Decca*	4
7	13	IT'S NOT UNUSUAL	Tom Jones	*Decca*	10
26	14	KING OF THE ROAD	Roger Miller	*Philips*	5
16	15	I'LL BE THERE	Gerry and the Pacemakers	*Columbia*	4
14	16	YOU'RE BREAKIN' MY HEART	Keely Smith	*Reprise*	5
34	17	BRING IT ON HOME TO ME	Animals	*Columbia*	2
11	18	GOODBYE MY LOVE	Searchers	*Pye*	6
15	19	I'LL NEVER FIND ANOTHER YOU	Seekers	*Columbia*	14
8	20	COME AND STAY WITH ME	Marianne Faithfull	*Decca*	9
9	21	SILHOUETTES	Herman's Hermits	*Columbia*	8
18	22	EVERYBODY'S GONNA BE HAPPY	Kinks	*Pye*	3
28	23	ALL OVER THE WORLD	Françoise Hardy	*Pye*	3
39	24	TRUE LOVE WAYS	Peter and Gordon	*Columbia*	2
20	25	I'LL STOP AT NOTHING	Sandie Shaw	*Pye*	8
32	26	NOWHERE TO RUN	Martha and the Vandellas	*Tamla Motown*	3
21	27	I MUST BE SEEING THINGS	Gene Pitney	*Stateside*	9
22	28	I KNOW A PLACE	Petula Clark	*Pye*	6
24	29	REELIN' AND ROCKIN'	Dave Clark Five	*Columbia*	5
25	30	DO THE CLAM	Elvis Presley	*RCA*	6
27	31	YES I WILL	Hollies	*Parlophone*	12
-	32	I'M GONNA GET THERE SOMEHOW	Val Doonican	*Decca*	1
31	33	HAWAIIAN WEDDING SONG	Julie Rogers	*Mercury*	2
40	34	WINDMILL IN OLD AMSTERDAM	Ronnie Hilton	*HMV*	10
-	35	AT THE CLUB	Drifters	*Atlantic*	1
33	36	BIRDS AND THE BEES	Jewel Akens	*London*	4
23	37	HONEY I NEED	Pretty Things	*Fontana*	8
35	38	TRUE LOVE FOR EVERMORE	Bachelors	*Decca*	2
-	39	NOT UNTIL THE NEXT TIME	Jim Reeves	*RCA*	1
-	40	OH NO NOT MY BABY	Manfred Mann	*HMV*	1

WEEK ENDING 22 APRIL 1965

LW	TW	Title	Artist	Label	Wks
11	1	TICKET TO RIDE	Beatles	*Parlophone*	2
5	2	HERE COMES THE NIGHT	Them	*Decca*	5
1	3	THE MINUTE YOU'RE GONE	Cliff Richard	*Columbia*	7
2	4	CONCRETE AND CLAY	Unit Four Plus Two	*Decca*	8
12	5	LITTLE THINGS	Dave Berry	*Decca*	5
4	6	CATCH THE WIND	Donovan	*Pye*	5
3	7	FOR YOUR LOVE	Yardbirds	*Columbia*	6
14	8	KING OF THE ROAD	Roger Miller	*Philips*	6
6	9	THE LAST TIME	Rolling Stones	*Decca*	8
10	10	POP GO THE WORKERS	Barron Knights	*Columbia*	4
17	11	BRING IT ON HOME TO ME	Animals	*Columbia*	3
7	12	STOP IN THE NAME OF LOVE	Supremes	*Tamla Motown*	4
9	13	THE TIMES THEY ARE A-CHANGIN'	Bob Dylan	*CBS*	5
16	14	YOU'RE BREAKIN' MY HEART	Keely Smith	*Reprise*	6
8	15	I CAN'T EXPLAIN	Who	*Brunswick*	9
15	16	I'LL BE THERE	Gerry and the Pacemakers	*Columbia*	5
22	17	EVERYBODY'S GONNA BE HAPPY	Kinks	*Pye*	4
13	18	IT'S NOT UNUSUAL	Tom Jones	*Decca*	11

In these weeks ■ A third week at number 35 for Roger Miller's *King Of The Road* before it finally takes off and climbs all the way to number one (01.04.65) ■ The first two Tamla Motown singles to chart in Britain are the first two releases on the UK label, by the Supremes and by Martha and the Vandellas (01.04.65) ■ The highest chart position ever achieved by Eric Clapton is as a Yardbird on *For Your Love* (08.04.65) ■

LW	TW	Title	Artist	Label	Wks
-	19	WORLD OF OUR OWN	Seekers	Columbia	1
24	20	TRUE LOVE WAYS	Peter and Gordon	Columbia	3
20	21	COME AND STAY WITH ME	Marianne Faithfull	Decca	10
21	22	SILHOUETTES	Herman's Hermits	Columbia	9
18	23	GOODBYE MY LOVE	Searchers	Pye	7
19	24	I'LL NEVER FIND ANOTHER YOU	Seekers	Columbia	15
32	25	I'M GONNA GET THERE SOMEHOW	Val Doonican	Decca	2
40	26	OH NO NOT MY BABY	Manfred Mann	HMV	2
23	27	ALL OVER THE WORLD	Françoise Hardy	Pye	4
37	28	HONEY I NEED	Pretty Things	Fontana	9
36	29	BIRDS AND THE BEES	Jewel Akens	London	5
28	30	I KNOW A PLACE	Petula Clark	Pye	7
26	31	NOWHERE TO RUN	Martha and the Vandellas	Tamla Motown	4
25	32	I'LL STOP AT NOTHING	Sandie Shaw	Pye	9
30	33	DO THE CLAM	Elvis Presley	RCA	7
38	34	TRUE LOVE FOR EVERMORE	Bachelors	Decca	3
-	35	WHERE ARE YOU NOW (MY LOVE)	Jackie Trent ●	Pye	1
34	36	WINDMILL IN OLD AMSTERDAM	Ronnie Hilton	HMV	11
-	37	A LITTLE YOU	Freddie and the Dreamers	Columbia	1
39	37	NOT UNTIL THE NEXT TIME	Jim Reeves	RCA	2
29	39	REELIN' AND ROCKIN'	Dave Clark Five	Columbia	6
33	40	HAWAIIAN WEDDING SONG	Julie Rogers	Mercury	3

WEEK ENDING 29 APRIL 1965

LW	TW	Title	Artist	Label	Wks
1	1	TICKET TO RIDE	Beatles	Parlophone	3
3	2	THE MINUTE YOU'RE GONE	Cliff Richard	Columbia	8
2	3	HERE COMES THE NIGHT	Them	Decca	6
8	4	KING OF THE ROAD	Roger Miller	Philips	7
10	5	POP GO THE WORKERS	Barron Knights	Columbia	5
5	6	LITTLE THINGS	Dave Berry	Decca	6
11	7	BRING IT ON HOME TO ME	Animals	Columbia	4
4	8	CONCRETE AND CLAY	Unit Four Plus Two	Decca	9
6	9	CATCH THE WIND	Donovan	Pye	6
12	10	STOP IN THE NAME OF LOVE	Supremes	Tamla Motown	5
7	11	FOR YOUR LOVE	Yardbirds	Columbia	7
9	12	THE LAST TIME	Rolling Stones	Decca	9
13	13	THE TIMES THEY ARE A-CHANGIN'	Bob Dylan	CBS	6
20	14	TRUE LOVE WAYS	Peter and Gordon	Columbia	4
19	15	WORLD OF OUR OWN	Seekers	Columbia	2
14	16	YOU'RE BREAKIN' MY HEART	Keely Smith	Reprise	7
26	17	OH NO NOT MY BABY	Manfred Mann	HMV	3
15	18	I CAN'T EXPLAIN	Who	Brunswick	10
24	19	I'LL NEVER FIND ANOTHER YOU	Seekers	Columbia	16
27	20	ALL OVER THE WORLD	Françoise Hardy	Pye	5
16	21	I'LL BE THERE	Gerry and the Pacemakers	Columbia	6
18	22	IT'S NOT UNUSUAL	Tom Jones	Decca	12
17	23	EVERYBODY'S GONNA BE HAPPY	Kinks	Pye	5
35	24	WHERE ARE YOU NOW (MY LOVE)	Jackie Trent	Pye	2
21	25	COME AND STAY WITH ME	Marianne Faithfull	Decca	11
-	26	WONDERFUL WORLD	Herman's Hermits	Columbia	1
37	27	A LITTLE YOU	Freddie and the Dreamers	Columbia	2
25	28	I'M GONNA GET THERE SOMEHOW	Val Doonican	Decca	3
22	29	SILHOUETTES	Herman's Hermits	Columbia	10
37	30	NOT UNTIL THE NEXT TIME	Jim Reeves	RCA	3
-	31	I'VE BEEN WRONG BEFORE	Cilla Black	Parlophone	1
23	32	GOODBYE MY LOVE	Searchers	Pye	8
31	33	NOWHERE TO RUN	Martha and the Vandellas	Tamla Motown	5
29	34	BIRDS AND THE BEES	Jewel Akens	London	6
-	35	SUBTERRANEAN HOMESICK BLUES	Bob Dylan	CBS	1
-	36	LOVE HER	Walker Brothers ●	Philips	1
36	37	WINDMILL IN OLD AMSTERDAM	Ronnie Hilton	HMV	12
30	38	I KNOW A PLACE	Petula Clark	Pye	8
-	39	SOMETHING BETTER BEGINNING	Honeycombs	Pye	1
-	40	COME ON OVER TO MY PLACE	Drifters	Atlantic	1

May 1965

□ Highest position disc reached ● Act's first ever week on chart

WEEK ENDING 6 MAY 1965

LW	TW	Title	Artist	Label	Wks
1	1	TICKET TO RIDE	Beatles	Parlophone	4
4	2	KING OF THE ROAD	Roger Miller	Philips	8
3	3	HERE COMES THE NIGHT	Them	Decca	7
15	4	WORLD OF OUR OWN	Seekers	Columbia	3
14	5	TRUE LOVE WAYS	Peter and Gordon	Columbia	5
5	6	POP GO THE WORKERS	Barron Knights	Columbia	6
2	7	THE MINUTE YOU'RE GONE	Cliff Richard	Columbia	9
7	8	BRING IT ON HOME TO ME	Animals	Columbia	5
9	9	CATCH THE WIND	Donovan	Pye	7
6	10	LITTLE THINGS	Dave Berry	Decca	7
17	11	OH NO NOT MY BABY	Manfred Mann	HMV	4
10	12	STOP IN THE NAME OF LOVE	Supremes	Tamla Motown	6
8	13	CONCRETE AND CLAY	Unit Four Plus Two	Decca	10
26	14	WONDERFUL WORLD	Herman's Hermits	Columbia	2
24	15	WHERE ARE YOU NOW (MY LOVE)	Jackie Trent	Pye	3
13	16	THE TIMES THEY ARE A-CHANGIN'	Bob Dylan	CBS	7
35	17	SUBTERRANEAN HOMESICK BLUES	Bob Dylan	CBS	2
11	18	FOR YOUR LOVE	Yardbirds	Columbia	8
12	19	THE LAST TIME	Rolling Stones	Decca	10
20	20	ALL OVER THE WORLD	Françoise Hardy	Pye	6
18	21	I CAN'T EXPLAIN	Who	Brunswick	11
19	22	I'LL NEVER FIND ANOTHER YOU	Seekers	Columbia	17
16	23	YOU'RE BREAKIN' MY HEART	Keely Smith	Reprise	8
31	24	I'VE BEEN WRONG BEFORE	Cilla Black	Parlophone	2
21	25	I'LL BE THERE	Gerry and the Pacemakers	Columbia	7
27	26	A LITTLE YOU	Freddie and the Dreamers	Columbia	3
30	27	NOT UNTIL THE NEXT TIME	Jim Reeves	RCA	4
22	28	IT'S NOT UNUSUAL	Tom Jones	Decca	13
-	29	THAT'S WHY I'M CRYING	Ivy League	Piccadilly	1
23	30	EVERYBODY'S GONNA BE HAPPY	Kinks	Pye	6
33	31	NOWHERE TO RUN	Martha and the Vandellas	Tamla Motown	6
-	32	ONCE UPON A TIME	Tom Jones	Decca	1
36	33	LOVE HER	Walker Brothers	Philips	2
25	34	COME AND STAY WITH ME	Marianne Faithfull	Decca	12
-	35	THAT'LL BE THE DAY	Everly Brothers	Warner Brothers	1
-	36	AT THE CLUB	Drifters	Atlantic	2
28	37	I'M GONNA GET THERE SOMEHOW	Val Doonican	Decca	4
34	38	BIRDS AND THE BEES	Jewel Akens	London	7
-	39	THIS LITTLE BIRD	Marianne Faithfull	Decca	1
-	40	THE CLAPPING SONG	Shirley Ellis ●	London	1

WEEK ENDING 13 MAY 1965

LW	TW	Title	Artist	Label	Wks
2	1	KING OF THE ROAD	Roger Miller	Philips	9
1	2	TICKET TO RIDE	Beatles	Parlophone	5
4	3	WORLD OF OUR OWN	Seekers	Columbia	4
5	4	TRUE LOVE WAYS	Peter and Gordon	Columbia	6
15	5	WHERE ARE YOU NOW (MY LOVE)	Jackie Trent	Pye	4
3	6	HERE COMES THE NIGHT	Them	Decca	8
8	7	BRING IT ON HOME TO ME	Animals	Columbia	6
6	8	POP GO THE WORKERS	Barron Knights	Columbia	7
7	9	THE MINUTE YOU'RE GONE	Cliff Richard	Columbia	10
17	10	SUBTERRANEAN HOMESICK BLUES	Bob Dylan	CBS	3
14	11	WONDERFUL WORLD	Herman's Hermits	Columbia	3
11	12	OH NO NOT MY BABY	Manfred Mann	HMV	5
39	13	THIS LITTLE BIRD	Marianne Faithfull	Decca	2
9	14	CATCH THE WIND	Donovan	Pye	8
10	15	LITTLE THINGS	Dave Berry	Decca	8
12	16	STOP IN THE NAME OF LOVE	Supremes	Tamla Motown	7
24	17	I'VE BEEN WRONG BEFORE	Cilla Black	Parlophone	3
27	18	NOT UNTIL THE NEXT TIME	Jim Reeves	RCA	5
13	19	CONCRETE AND CLAY	Unit Four Plus Two	Decca	11
16	20	THE TIMES THEY ARE A-CHANGIN'	Bob Dylan	CBS	8
20	21	ALL OVER THE WORLD	Françoise Hardy	Pye	7
29	22	THAT'S WHY I'M CRYING	Ivy League	Piccadilly	2
18	23	FOR YOUR LOVE	Yardbirds	Columbia	9
19	24	THE LAST TIME	Rolling Stones	Decca	11
40	25	THE CLAPPING SONG	Shirley Ellis	London	2
22	26	I'LL NEVER FIND ANOTHER YOU	Seekers	Columbia	18
23	27	YOU'RE BREAKIN' MY HEART	Keely Smith	Reprise	9
-	28	POOR MAN'S SON	Rockin' Berries	Piccadilly	1
21	29	I CAN'T EXPLAIN	Who	Brunswick	12
35	30	THAT'LL BE THE DAY	Everly Brothers	Warner Brothers	2
33	31	LOVE HER	Walker Brothers	Philips	3

■Two records tie at number 37 (22.04.65) ■ Twelve weeks of chart life for Ronnie Hilton's final hit, even though it never climbed higher than number 23 (29.04.65) ■ The Walker Brothers are the first 'brothers' to chart who are not really brothers at all. None of them are even really called Walker (29.04.65) ■ Five records on the Columbia label take consecutive positons in the Top Ten (06.05.65)■

May 1965

□ Highest position disc reached ● Act's first ever week on chart

LW	TW	Title	Artist	Label	Wks
32	[32]	ONCE UPON A TIME	Tom Jones	*Decca*	2
-	33	LONG LIVE LOVE	Sandie Shaw	*Pye*	1
26	34	A LITTLE YOU	Freddie and the Dreamers	*Columbia*	4
25	35	I'LL BE THERE	Gerry and the Pacemakers	*Columbia*	8
28	36	IT'S NOT UNUSUAL	Tom Jones	*Decca*	14
31	37	NOWHERE TO RUN	Martha and the Vandellas	*Tamla Motown*	7
-	38	YOU'VE NEVER BEEN IN LOVE LIKE THIS BEFORE	Unit Four Plus Two	*Decca*	1
-	39	IKO IKO	Dixie Cups	*Red Bird*	1
36	40	AT THE CLUB	Drifters	*Atlantic*	3

WEEK ENDING 20 MAY 1965

LW	TW	Title	Artist	Label	Wks
5	[1]	WHERE ARE YOU NOW (MY LOVE)	Jackie Trent	*Pye*	5
4	[2]	TRUE LOVE WAYS	Peter and Gordon	*Columbia*	7
2	3	TICKET TO RIDE	Beatles	*Parlophone*	6
1	4	KING OF THE ROAD	Roger Miller	*Philips*	10
3	5	WORLD OF OUR OWN	Seekers	*Columbia*	5
13	[6]	THIS LITTLE BIRD	Marianne Faithfull	*Decca*	3
11	[7]	WONDERFUL WORLD	Herman's Hermits	*Columbia*	4
33	8	LONG LIVE LOVE	Sandie Shaw	*Pye*	2
10	[9]	SUBTERRANEAN HOMESICK BLUES	Bob Dylan	*CBS*	4
8	10	POP GO THE WORKERS	Barron Knights	*Columbia*	8
12	[11]	OH NO NOT MY BABY	Manfred Mann	*HMV*	6
7	12	BRING IT ON HOME TO ME	Animals	*Columbia*	7
28	13	POOR MAN'S SON	Rockin' Berries	*Piccadilly*	2
25	14	THE CLAPPING SONG	Shirley Ellis	*London*	3
18	15	NOT UNTIL THE NEXT TIME	Jim Reeves	*RCA*	6
14	16	CATCH THE WIND	Donovan	*Pye*	9
9	17	THE MINUTE YOU'RE GONE	Cliff Richard	*Columbia*	11
21	18	ALL OVER THE WORLD	Françoise Hardy	*Pye*	8
6	19	HERE COMES THE NIGHT	Them	*Decca*	9
17	20	I'VE BEEN WRONG BEFORE	Cilla Black	*Parlophone*	4
16	21	STOP IN THE NAME OF LOVE	Supremes	*Tamla Motown*	8
20	22	THE TIMES THEY ARE A-CHANGIN'	Bob Dylan	*CBS*	9
22	23	THAT'S WHY I'M CRYING	Ivy League	*Piccadilly*	3
15	24	LITTLE THINGS	Dave Berry	*Decca*	9
19	25	CONCRETE AND CLAY	Unit Four Plus Two	*Decca*	12
-	[26]	WE SHALL OVERCOME	Joan Baez ●	*Fontana*	1
-	27	TRAINS AND BOATS AND PLANES	Burt Bacharach ●	*London*	1
24	28	THE LAST TIME	Rolling Stones	*Decca*	12
-	29	THE PRICE OF LOVE	Everly Brothers	*Warner Brothers*	1
31	30	LOVE HER	Walker Brothers	*Philips*	4
23	31	FOR YOUR LOVE	Yardbirds	*Columbia*	10
38	32	YOU'VE NEVER BEEN IN LOVE LIKE THIS BEFORE	Unit Four Plus Two	*Decca*	2
26	33	I'LL NEVER FIND ANOTHER YOU	Seekers	*Columbia*	19
32	34	ONCE UPON A TIME	Tom Jones	*Decca*	3
-	35	TRAINS AND BOATS AND PLANES	Billy J Kramer and the Dakotas	*Parlophone*	1
39	36	IKO IKO	Dixie Cups	*Red Bird*	2
27	37	YOU'RE BREAKIN' MY HEART	Keely Smith	*Reprise*	10
37	38	NOWHERE TO RUN	Martha and the Vandellas	*Tamla Motown*	8
-	39	MARIE	Bachelors	*Decca*	1
34	40	A LITTLE YOU	Freddie and the Dreamers	*Columbia*	5

WEEK ENDING 27 MAY 1965

LW	TW	Title	Artist	Label	Wks
8	[1]	LONG LIVE LOVE	Sandie Shaw	*Pye*	3
1	2	WHERE ARE YOU NOW (MY LOVE)	Jackie Trent	*Pye*	6
2	3	TRUE LOVE WAYS	Peter and Gordon	*Columbia*	8
5	4	WORLD OF OUR OWN	Seekers	*Columbia*	6
4	5	KING OF THE ROAD	Roger Miller	*Philips*	11
6	[6]	THIS LITTLE BIRD	Marianne Faithfull	*Decca*	4
3	7	TICKET TO RIDE	Beatles	*Parlophone*	7
13	8	POOR MAN'S SON	Rockin' Berries	*Piccadilly*	3
9	[9]	SUBTERRANEAN HOMESICK BLUES	Bob Dylan	*CBS*	5
14	10	THE CLAPPING SONG	Shirley Ellis	*London*	4
7	11	WONDERFUL WORLD	Herman's Hermits	*Columbia*	5
27	12	TRAINS AND BOATS AND PLANES	Burt Bacharach	*London*	2
11	13	OH NO NOT MY BABY	Manfred Mann	*HMV*	7
15	14	NOT UNTIL THE NEXT TIME	Jim Reeves	*RCA*	7
10	15	POP GO THE WORKERS	Barron Knights	*Columbia*	9
12	16	BRING IT ON HOME TO ME	Animals	*Columbia*	8
18	17	ALL OVER THE WORLD	Françoise Hardy	*Pye*	9
39	18	MARIE	Bachelors	*Decca*	2
29	19	THE PRICE OF LOVE	Everly Brothers	*Warner Brothers*	2
35	20	TRAINS AND BOATS AND PLANES	Billy J Kramer and the Dakotas	*Parlophone*	2
17	21	THE MINUTE YOU'RE GONE	Cliff Richard	*Columbia*	12
32	22	YOU'VE NEVER BEEN IN LOVE LIKE THIS BEFORE	Unit Four Plus Two	*Decca*	3
24	23	LITTLE THINGS	Dave Berry	*Decca*	10
-	24	CRYING IN THE CHAPEL	Elvis Presley	*RCA*	1
19	25	HERE COMES THE NIGHT	Them	*Decca*	10
36	26	IKO IKO	Dixie Cups	*Red Bird*	3
20	27	I'VE BEEN WRONG BEFORE	Cilla Black	*Parlophone*	5
33	28	I'LL NEVER FIND ANOTHER YOU	Seekers	*Columbia*	20
26	29	WE SHALL OVERCOME	Joan Baez	*Fontana*	2
16	30	CATCH THE WIND	Donovan	*Pye*	10
23	31	THAT'S WHY I'M CRYING	Ivy League	*Piccadilly*	4
30	32	LOVE HER	Walker Brothers	*Philips*	5
-	33	COME HOME	Dave Clark Five	*Columbia*	1
21	34	STOP IN THE NAME OF LOVE	Supremes	*Tamla Motown*	9
-	35	ANYWAY ANYHOW ANYWHERE	Who	*Brunswick*	1
22	36	THE TIMES THEY ARE A-CHANGIN'	Bob Dylan	*CBS*	10
-	37	SET ME FREE	Kinks	*Pye*	1
25	38	CONCRETE AND CLAY	Unit Four Plus Two	*Decca*	13
-	39	THIS LITTLE BIRD	Nashville Teens	*Decca*	1
-	[40]	IF I RULED THE WORLD	Tony Bennett	*CBS*	1

WEEK ENDING 3 JUNE 1965

LW	TW	Title	Artist	Label	Wks
1	[1]	LONG LIVE LOVE	Sandie Shaw	*Pye*	4
2	2	WHERE ARE YOU NOW (MY LOVE)	Jackie Trent	*Pye*	7
4	[3]	WORLD OF OUR OWN	Seekers	*Columbia*	7
3	4	TRUE LOVE WAYS	Peter and Gordon	*Columbia*	9
8	[5]	POOR MAN'S SON	Rockin' Berries	*Piccadilly*	4
6	[6]	THIS LITTLE BIRD	Marianne Faithfull	*Decca*	5
10	7	THE CLAPPING SONG	Shirley Ellis	*London*	5
12	8	TRAINS AND BOATS AND PLANES	Burt Bacharach	*London*	3
5	9	KING OF THE ROAD	Roger Miller	*Philips*	12
7	10	TICKET TO RIDE	Beatles	*Parlophone*	8
19	11	THE PRICE OF LOVE	Everly Brothers	*Warner Brothers*	3
9	12	SUBTERRANEAN HOMESICK BLUES	Bob Dylan	*CBS*	6
14	[13]	NOT UNTIL THE NEXT TIME	Jim Reeves	*RCA*	8
24	14	CRYING IN THE CHAPEL	Elvis Presley	*RCA*	2
11	15	WONDERFUL WORLD	Herman's Hermits	*Columbia*	6
17	[16]	ALL OVER THE WORLD	Françoise Hardy	*Pye*	10
18	17	MARIE	Bachelors	*Decca*	3
22	18	YOU'VE NEVER BEEN IN LOVE LIKE THIS BEFORE	Unit Four Plus Two	*Decca*	4
20	19	TRAINS AND BOATS AND PLANES	Billy J Kramer and the Dakotas	*Parlophone*	3
16	20	BRING IT ON HOME TO ME	Animals	*Columbia*	9
33	21	COME HOME	Dave Clark Five	*Columbia*	2
37	22	SET ME FREE	Kinks	*Pye*	2
-	23	I'M ALIVE	Hollies	*Parlophone*	1
26	24	IKO IKO	Dixie Cups	*Red Bird*	4
15	25	POP GO THE WORKERS	Barron Knights	*Columbia*	10
35	26	ANYWAY ANYHOW ANYWHERE	Who	*Brunswick*	2
13	27	OH NO NOT MY BABY	Manfred Mann	*HMV*	8
32	28	LOVE HER	Walker Brothers	*Philips*	6
29	29	WE SHALL OVERCOME	Joan Baez	*Fontana*	3
31	30	THAT'S WHY I'M CRYING	Ivy League	*Piccadilly*	5
21	31	THE MINUTE YOU'RE GONE	Cliff Richard	*Columbia*	13
-	32	COLOURS	Donovan	*Pye*	1
-	33	HELP ME RHONDA	Beach Boys	*Capitol*	1
27	34	I'VE BEEN WRONG BEFORE	Cilla Black	*Parlophone*	6
-	35	IT AIN'T ME BABE	Johnny Cash ●	*CBS*	1
-	36	ENGINE ENGINE NUMBER NINE	Roger Miller	*Philips*	1
30	37	CATCH THE WIND	Donovan	*Pye*	11

In these weeks ■ This is the only week in British chart history when one British female vocalist replaces another at number one (27.05.65) ■ The top three singles all have titles featuring the word 'Love' (27.05.65) ■ Two versions of *Trains And Boats And Planes* in the Top 20, and two versions of *This Little Bird* in the Top 40 (27.05.65)■

LW	TW	Title	Artist	Label	Wks
39	[38]	THIS LITTLE BIRD	Nashville Teens	Decca	2
-	[39]	NO REGRETS	Shirley Bassey	Columbia	1
25	40	HERE COMES THE NIGHT	Them	Decca	11

June 1965

□ Highest position disc reached ● Act's first ever week on chart

WEEK ENDING 10 JUNE 1965

LW	TW	Title	Artist	Label	Wks
1	[1]	LONG LIVE LOVE	Sandie Shaw	Pye	5
14	2	CRYING IN THE CHAPEL	Elvis Presley	RCA	3
3	[3]	WORLD OF OUR OWN	Seekers	Columbia	8
11	4	THE PRICE OF LOVE	Everly Brothers	Warner Brothers	4
5	[5]	POOR MAN'S SON	Rockin' Berries	Piccadilly	5
8	6	TRAINS AND BOATS AND PLANES	Burt Bacharach	London	4
7	7	THE CLAPPING SONG	Shirley Ellis	London	6
6	8	THIS LITTLE BIRD	Marianne Faithfull	Decca	6
2	9	WHERE ARE YOU NOW (MY LOVE)	Jackie Trent	Pye	8
23	10	I'M ALIVE	Hollies	Parlophone	2
17	11	MARIE	Bachelors	Decca	4
19	[12]	TRAINS AND BOATS AND PLANES	Billy J Kramer and the Dakotas	Parlophone	4
4	13	TRUE LOVE WAYS	Peter and Gordon	Columbia	10
10	14	TICKET TO RIDE	Beatles	Parlophone	9
18	15	YOU'VE NEVER BEEN IN LOVE LIKE THIS BEFORE	Unit Four Plus Two	Decca	5
9	16	KING OF THE ROAD	Roger Miller	Philips	13
22	17	SET ME FREE	Kinks	Pye	3
13	18	NOT UNTIL THE NEXT TIME	Jim Reeves	RCA	9
15	19	WONDERFUL WORLD	Herman's Hermits	Columbia	7
12	20	SUBTERRANEAN HOMESICK BLUES	Bob Dylan	CBS	7
32	21	COLOURS	Donovan	Pye	2
21	22	COME HOME	Dave Clark Five	Columbia	3
24	[23]	IKO IKO	Dixie Cups	Red Bird	5
26	24	ANYWAY ANYHOW ANYWHERE	Who	Brunswick	3
16	25	ALL OVER THE WORLD	Françoise Hardy	Pye	11
28	26	LOVE HER	Walker Brothers	Philips	7
-	27	STINGRAY	Shadows	Columbia	1
-	28	LOOKING THROUGH THE EYES OF LOVE	Gene Pitney	Stateside	1
25	29	POP GO THE WORKERS	Barron Knights	Columbia	11
20	30	BRING IT ON HOME TO ME	Animals	Columbia	10
33	31	HELP ME RHONDA	Beach Boys	Capitol	2
-	32	ON MY WORD	Cliff Richard	Columbia	1
-	33	FROM THE BOTTOM OF MY HEART	Moody Blues	Decca	1
35	34	IT AIN'T ME BABE	Johnny Cash	CBS	2
36	35	ENGINE ENGINE NUMBER NINE	Roger Miller	Philips	2
-	36	MY CHILD	Connie Francis	MGM	1
29	37	WE SHALL OVERCOME	Joan Baez	Fontana	4
30	38	THAT'S WHY I'M CRYING	Ivy League	Piccadilly	6
27	39	OH NO NOT MY BABY	Manfred Mann	HMV	9
-	[40]	BACK IN MY ARMS AGAIN	Supremes	Tamla Motown	1

WEEK ENDING 17 JUNE 1965

LW	TW	Title	Artist	Label	Wks
2	[1]	CRYING IN THE CHAPEL	Elvis Presley	RCA	4
4	[2]	THE PRICE OF LOVE	Everly Brothers	Warner Brothers	5
1	3	LONG LIVE LOVE	Sandie Shaw	Pye	6
10	4	I'M ALIVE	Hollies	Parlophone	3
6	5	TRAINS AND BOATS AND PLANES	Burt Bacharach	London	5
5	6	POOR MAN'S SON	Rockin' Berries	Piccadilly	6
7	7	THE CLAPPING SONG	Shirley Ellis	London	7
3	8	WORLD OF OUR OWN	Seekers	Columbia	9
11	[9]	MARIE	Bachelors	Decca	5
21	10	COLOURS	Donovan	Pye	3
24	11	ANYWAY ANYHOW ANYWHERE	Who	Brunswick	4
8	12	THIS LITTLE BIRD	Marianne Faithfull	Decca	7
17	13	SET ME FREE	Kinks	Pye	4
12	14	TRAINS AND BOATS AND PLANES	Billy J Kramer and the Dakotas	Parlophone	5
13	15	TRUE LOVE WAYS	Peter and Gordon	Columbia	11
15	16	YOU'VE NEVER BEEN IN LOVE LIKE THIS BEFORE	Unit Four Plus Two	Decca	6
28	17	LOOKING THROUGH THE EYES OF LOVE	Gene Pitney	Stateside	2
9	18	WHERE ARE YOU NOW (MY LOVE)	Jackie Trent	Pye	9
22	19	COME HOME	Dave Clark Five	Columbia	4
26	[20]	LOVE HER	Walker Brothers	Philips	8
32	21	ON MY WORD	Cliff Richard	Columbia	2
18	22	NOT UNTIL THE NEXT TIME	Jim Reeves	RCA	10
27	23	STINGRAY	Shadows	Columbia	2
14	24	TICKET TO RIDE	Beatles	Parlophone	10
16	25	KING OF THE ROAD	Roger Miller	Philips	14
20	26	SUBTERRANEAN HOMESICK BLUES	Bob Dylan	CBS	8
25	27	ALL OVER THE WORLD	Françoise Hardy	Pye	12
34	[28]	IT AIN'T ME BABE	Johnny Cash	CBS	3
33	29	FROM THE BOTTOM OF MY HEART	Moody Blues	Decca	2
31	30	HELP ME RHONDA	Beach Boys	Capitol	3
36	31	MY CHILD	Connie Francis	MGM	2
-	32	HEART FULL OF SOUL	Yardbirds	Columbia	1
35	[33]	ENGINE ENGINE NUMBER NINE	Roger Miller	Philips	3
23	34	IKO IKO	Dixie Cups	Red Bird	6
19	35	WONDERFUL WORLD	Herman's Hermits	Columbia	8
-	36	I'LL STAY BY YOU	Kenny Lynch	HMV	1
-	37	SHE'S ABOUT A MOVER	Sir Douglas Quintet ●	London	1
-	38	MR. TAMBOURINE MAN	Byrds ●	CBS	1
37	39	WE SHALL OVERCOME	Joan Baez	Fontana	5
-	40	MAGGIE'S FARM	Bob Dylan	CBS	1

WEEK ENDING 24 JUNE 1965

LW	TW	Title	Artist	Label	Wks
4	[1]	I'M ALIVE	Hollies	Parlophone	4
1	2	CRYING IN THE CHAPEL	Elvis Presley	RCA	5
2	3	THE PRICE OF LOVE	Everly Brothers	Warner Brothers	6
5	[4]	TRAINS AND BOATS AND PLANES	Burt Bacharach	London	6
10	5	COLOURS	Donovan	Pye	4
7	[6]	THE CLAPPING SONG	Shirley Ellis	London	8
3	7	LONG LIVE LOVE	Sandie Shaw	Pye	7
6	8	POOR MAN'S SON	Rockin' Berries	Piccadilly	7
13	[9]	SET ME FREE	Kinks	Pye	5
17	10	LOOKING THROUGH THE EYES OF LOVE	Gene Pitney	Stateside	3
9	11	MARIE	Bachelors	Decca	6
8	12	WORLD OF OUR OWN	Seekers	Columbia	10
11	13	ANYWAY ANYHOW ANYWHERE	Who	Brunswick	5
16	[14]	YOU'VE NEVER BEEN IN LOVE LIKE THIS BEFORE	Unit Four Plus Two	Decca	7
12	15	THIS LITTLE BIRD	Marianne Faithfull	Decca	8
19	[16]	COME HOME	Dave Clark Five	Columbia	5
21	17	ON MY WORD	Cliff Richard	Columbia	3
15	18	TRUE LOVE WAYS	Peter and Gordon	Columbia	12
23	[19]	STINGRAY	Shadows	Columbia	3
32	20	HEART FULL OF SOUL	Yardbirds	Columbia	2
20	21	LOVE HER	Walker Brothers	Philips	9
29	[22]	FROM THE BOTTOM OF MY HEART	Moody Blues	Decca	3
14	23	TRAINS AND BOATS AND PLANES	Billy J Kramer and the Dakotas	Parlophone	6
18	24	WHERE ARE YOU NOW (MY LOVE)	Jackie Trent	Pye	10
-	25	LEAVE A LITTLE LOVE	Lulu	Decca	1
31	[26]	MY CHILD	Connie Francis	MGM	3
37	27	SHE'S ABOUT A MOVER	Sir Douglas Quintet	London	2
30	28	HELP ME RHONDA	Beach Boys	Capitol	4
36	[29]	I'LL STAY BY YOU	Kenny Lynch	HMV	2
25	30	KING OF THE ROAD	Roger Miller	Philips	15
34	31	IKO IKO	Dixie Cups	Red Bird	7
24	32	TICKET TO RIDE	Beatles	Parlophone	11
38	33	MR. TAMBOURINE MAN	Byrds	CBS	2
28	34	IT AIN'T ME BABE	Johnny Cash	CBS	4
40	35	MAGGIE'S FARM	Bob Dylan	CBS	2
39	36	WE SHALL OVERCOME	Joan Baez	Fontana	6
-	37	GOODBYEE	Peter Cook and Dudley Moore ●	Decca	1
-	38	JUST A LITTLE BIT TOO LATE	Wayne Fontana and the Mindbenders	Fontana	1
26	39	SUBTERRANEAN HOMESICK BLUES	Bob Dylan	CBS	9
-	[40]	BACK IN MY ARMS AGAIN	Supremes	Tamla Motown	2

■In a great week for the ladies, there are four female vocalists in the Top Ten, not counting hits by the Seekers and Burt Bacharach which feature female lead vocals. Even Connie Francis is back for what proves to be her final Top 40 hit (10.06.65) ■ Elvis and the Everly Brothers at numbers one and two for the first time since the 1950s (17.06.65)■

July 1965

□ Highest position disc reached ● Act's first ever week on chart

LW	TW	WEEK ENDING 1 JULY 1965		Wks
2	[1]	CRYING IN THE CHAPEL Elvis Presley	RCA	6
1	2	I'M ALIVE Hollies	Parlophone	5
3	3	THE PRICE OF LOVE Everly Brothers	Warner Brothers	7
5	[4]	COLOURS Donovan	Pye	5
10	5	LOOKING THROUGH THE EYES OF LOVE Gene Pitney	Stateside	4
4	6	TRAINS AND BOATS AND PLANES Burt Bacharach	London	7
7	7	LONG LIVE LOVE Sandie Shaw	Pye	8
6	8	THE CLAPPING SONG Shirley Ellis	London	9
9	[9]	SET ME FREE Kinks	Pye	6
13	[10]	ANYWAY ANYHOW ANYWHERE Who	Brunswick	6
20	11	HEART FULL OF SOUL Yardbirds	Columbia	3
17	[12]	ON MY WORD Cliff Richard	Columbia	4
25	13	LEAVE A LITTLE LOVE Lulu	Decca	2
12	14	WORLD OF OUR OWN Seekers	Columbia	11
-	15	TO KNOW YOU IS TO LOVE YOU Peter and Gordon	Columbia	1
11	16	MARIE Bachelors	Decca	7
8	17	POOR MAN'S SON Rockin' Berries	Piccadilly	8
14	18	YOU'VE NEVER BEEN IN LOVE LIKE THIS BEFORE Unit Four Plus Two	Decca	8
33	19	MR. TAMBOURINE MAN Byrds	CBS	3
16	20	COME HOME Dave Clark Five	Columbia	6
-	21	TOSSING AND TURNING Ivy League	Piccadilly	1
35	[22]	MAGGIE'S FARM Bob Dylan	CBS	3
-	23	IN THE MIDDLE OF NOWHERE Dusty Springfield	Philips	1
22	24	FROM THE BOTTOM OF MY HEART Moody Blues	Decca	4
27	25	SHE'S ABOUT A MOVER Sir Douglas Quintet	London	3
23	26	TRAINS AND BOATS AND PLANES Billy J Kramer and the Dakotas	Parlophone	7
19	27	STINGRAY Shadows	Columbia	4
38	28	JUST A LITTLE BIT TOO LATE Wayne Fontana and the Mindbenders	Fontana	2
-	29	WOOLY BULLY Sam The Sham and the Pharaohs ●	MGM	1
26	30	MY CHILD Connie Francis	MGM	4
29	31	I'LL STAY BY YOU Kenny Lynch	HMV	3
15	32	THIS LITTLE BIRD Marianne Faithfull	Decca	9
28	33	HELP ME RHONDA Beach Boys	Capitol	5
18	34	TRUE LOVE WAYS Peter and Gordon	Columbia	13
34	35	IT AIN'T ME BABE Johnny Cash	CBS	5
37	36	GOODBYEE Peter Cook and Dudley Moore	Decca	2
21	37	LOVE HER Walker Brothers	Philips	10
36	38	WE SHALL OVERCOME Joan Baez	Fontana	7
-	39	WHEN THE SUMMERTIME IS OVER Jackie Trent	Pye	1
-	40	ALL OVER THE WORLD Françoise Hardy	Pye	13

LW	TW	WEEK ENDING 8 JULY 1965		Wks
2	[1]	I'M ALIVE Hollies	Parlophone	6
1	2	CRYING IN THE CHAPEL Elvis Presley	RCA	7
5	[3]	LOOKING THROUGH THE EYES OF LOVE Gene Pitney	Stateside	5
11	4	HEART FULL OF SOUL Yardbirds	Columbia	4
15	[5]	TO KNOW YOU IS TO LOVE YOU Peter and Gordon	Columbia	2
3	6	THE PRICE OF LOVE Everly Brothers	Warner Brothers	8
4	7	COLOURS Donovan	Pye	6
19	8	MR. TAMBOURINE MAN Byrds	CBS	4
13	9	LEAVE A LITTLE LOVE Lulu	Decca	3
21	10	TOSSING AND TURNING Ivy League	Piccadilly	2
10	11	ANYWAY ANYHOW ANYWHERE Who	Brunswick	7
6	12	TRAINS AND BOATS AND PLANES Burt Bacharach	London	8
23	13	IN THE MIDDLE OF NOWHERE Dusty Springfield	Philips	2
9	14	SET ME FREE Kinks	Pye	7
7	15	LONG LIVE LOVE Sandie Shaw	Pye	9
8	16	THE CLAPPING SONG Shirley Ellis	London	10
12	17	ON MY WORD Cliff Richard	Columbia	5
14	18	WORLD OF OUR OWN Seekers	Columbia	12
25	19	SHE'S ABOUT A MOVER Sir Douglas Quintet	London	4
28	[20]	JUST A LITTLE BIT TOO LATE Wayne Fontana and the Mindbenders	Fontana	3
16	21	MARIE Bachelors	Decca	8
17	22	POOR MAN'S SON Rockin' Berries	Piccadilly	9
29	23	WOOLY BULLY Sam The Sham and the Pharaohs	MGM	2
22	24	MAGGIE'S FARM Bob Dylan	CBS	4
18	25	YOU'VE NEVER BEEN IN LOVE LIKE THIS BEFORE Unit Four Plus Two	Decca	9
24	26	FROM THE BOTTOM OF MY HEART Moody Blues	Decca	5
33	[27]	HELP ME RHONDA Beach Boys	Capitol	6
36	28	GOODBYEE Peter Cook and Dudley Moore	Decca	3
20	29	COME HOME Dave Clark Five	Columbia	7
35	30	IT AIN'T ME BABE Johnny Cash	CBS	6
27	31	STINGRAY Shadows	Columbia	5
-	32	THERE BUT FOR FORTUNE Joan Baez	Fontana	1
-	33	LET THE WATER RUN DOWN P.J. Proby	Liberty	1
-	[34]	SOMEONE'S TAKEN MARIA AWAY Adam Faith	Parlophone	1
30	35	MY CHILD Connie Francis	MGM	5
31	36	I'LL STAY BY YOU Kenny Lynch	HMV	4
-	37	YOU'VE GOT YOUR TROUBLES Fortunes ●	Decca	1
-	38	THAT'S THE WAY LOVE GOES Charles Dickens ●	Pye	1
37	39	LOVE HER Walker Brothers	Philips	11
32	40	THIS LITTLE BIRD Marianne Faithfull	Decca	10

LW	TW	WEEK ENDING 15 JULY 1965		Wks
1	[1]	I'M ALIVE Hollies	Parlophone	7
4	[2]	HEART FULL OF SOUL Yardbirds	Columbia	5
8	3	MR. TAMBOURINE MAN Byrds	CBS	5
3	4	LOOKING THROUGH THE EYES OF LOVE Gene Pitney	Stateside	6
2	5	CRYING IN THE CHAPEL Elvis Presley	RCA	8
5	6	TO KNOW YOU IS TO LOVE YOU Peter and Gordon	Columbia	3
10	7	TOSSING AND TURNING Ivy League	Piccadilly	3
9	[8]	LEAVE A LITTLE LOVE Lulu	Decca	4
6	9	THE PRICE OF LOVE Everly Brothers	Warner Brothers	9
13	10	IN THE MIDDLE OF NOWHERE Dusty Springfield	Philips	3
7	11	COLOURS Donovan	Pye	7
11	12	ANYWAY ANYHOW ANYWHERE Who	Brunswick	8
17	13	ON MY WORD Cliff Richard	Columbia	6
23	14	WOOLY BULLY Sam The Sham and the Pharaohs	MGM	3
19	[15]	SHE'S ABOUT A MOVER Sir Douglas Quintet	London	5
32	16	THERE BUT FOR FORTUNE Joan Baez	Fontana	2
15	17	LONG LIVE LOVE Sandie Shaw	Pye	10
37	18	YOU'VE GOT YOUR TROUBLES Fortunes	Decca	2
28	19	GOODBYEE Peter Cook and Dudley Moore	Decca	4
14	20	SET ME FREE Kinks	Pye	8
16	21	THE CLAPPING SONG Shirley Ellis	London	11
12	22	TRAINS AND BOATS AND PLANES Burt Bacharach	London	9
-	[23]	I CAN'T HELP MYSELF Four Tops ●	Tamla Motown	1
33	24	LET THE WATER RUN DOWN P.J. Proby	Liberty	2
26	25	FROM THE BOTTOM OF MY HEART Moody Blues	Decca	6
18	26	WORLD OF OUR OWN Seekers	Columbia	13
24	27	MAGGIE'S FARM Bob Dylan	CBS	5
20	28	JUST A LITTLE BIT TOO LATE Wayne Fontana and the Mindbenders	Fontana	4
27	29	HELP ME RHONDA Beach Boys	Capitol	7
21	30	MARIE Bachelors	Decca	9
-	31	HE'S GOT NO LOVE Searchers	Pye	1
25	32	YOU'VE NEVER BEEN IN LOVE LIKE THIS BEFORE Unit Four Plus Two	Decca	10
-	33	WITH THESE HANDS Tom Jones	Decca	1
-	34	CRY TO ME Pretty Things	Fontana	1
-	35	BALLAD OF SPOTTY MULDOON Peter Cook ●	Decca	1
36	36	I'LL STAY BY YOU Kenny Lynch	HMV	5
29	37	COME HOME Dave Clark Five	Columbia	8
-	38	CATCH US IF YOU CAN Dave Clark Five	Columbia	1
22	39	POOR MAN'S SON Rockin' Berries	Piccadilly	10
31	40	STINGRAY Shadows	Columbia	6

LW	TW	WEEK ENDING 22 JULY 1965		Wks
3	[1]	MR. TAMBOURINE MAN Byrds	CBS	6
2	[2]	HEART FULL OF SOUL Yardbirds	Columbia	6

In these weeks ■ The end of Cliff Richard's all-time record run of 26 consecutive Top Ten hits comes to a close when *On My Word* peaks at number 12 (01.07.65) ■ *Crying In The Chapel* is Elvis Presley's fifteenth number one. Since 3 November 1960 he has been the outright leader on the list of Most Number Ones, and he will stay there until 11 September 1968, when the Beatles equal his tally (01.07.65)■

LW	TW	Title	Artist	Label	Wks
7	3	TOSSING AND TURNING	Ivy League	Piccadilly	4
1	4	I'M ALIVE	Hollies	Parlophone	8
6	5	TO KNOW YOU IS TO LOVE YOU	Peter and Gordon	Columbia	4
5	6	CRYING IN THE CHAPEL	Elvis Presley	RCA	9
4	7	LOOKING THROUGH THE EYES OF LOVE	Gene Pitney	Stateside	7
8	8	LEAVE A LITTLE LOVE	Lulu	Decca	5
10	9	IN THE MIDDLE OF NOWHERE	Dusty Springfield	Philips	4
18	10	YOU'VE GOT YOUR TROUBLES	Fortunes	Decca	3
16	11	THERE BUT FOR FORTUNE	Joan Baez	Fontana	3
11	12	COLOURS	Donovan	Pye	8
14	13	WOOLY BULLY	Sam The Sham and the Pharaohs	MGM	4
12	14	ANYWAY ANYHOW ANYWHERE	Who	Brunswick	9
9	15	THE PRICE OF LOVE	Everly Brothers	Warner Brothers	10
15	16	SHE'S ABOUT A MOVER	Sir Douglas Quintet	London	6
-	17	WE GOTTA GET OUT OF THIS PLACE	Animals	Columbia	1
31	18	HE'S GOT NO LOVE	Searchers	Pye	2
19	19	GOODBYEE	Peter Cook and Dudley Moore	Decca	5
13	20	ON MY WORD	Cliff Richard	Columbia	7
33	21	WITH THESE HANDS	Tom Jones	Decca	2
24	22	LET THE WATER RUN DOWN	P.J. Proby	Liberty	3
38	23	CATCH US IF YOU CAN	Dave Clark Five	Columbia	2
23	24	I CAN'T HELP MYSELF	Four Tops	Tamla Motown	2
17	25	LONG LIVE LOVE	Sandie Shaw	Pye	11
21	26	THE CLAPPING SONG	Shirley Ellis	London	12
20	27	SET ME FREE	Kinks	Pye	9
34	28	CRY TO ME	Pretty Things	Fontana	2
22	29	TRAINS AND BOATS AND PLANES	Burt Bacharach	London	10
29	30	HELP ME RHONDA	Beach Boys	Capitol	8
26	31	WORLD OF OUR OWN	Seekers	Columbia	14
25	32	FROM THE BOTTOM OF MY HEART	Moody Blues	Decca	7
27	33	MAGGIE'S FARM	Bob Dylan	CBS	6
35	34	BALLAD OF SPOTTY MULDOON	Peter Cook	Decca	2
28	35	JUST A LITTLE BIT TOO LATE	Wayne Fontana and the Mindbenders	Fontana	5
30	36	MARIE	Bachelors	Decca	10
-	37	THIS WORLD IS NOT MY HOME	Jim Reeves	RCA	1
-	38	IN THOUGHTS OF YOU	Billy Fury	Decca	1
-	39	THAT'S THE WAY LOVE GOES	Charles Dickens	Pye	2
-	40	THIS STRANGE EFFECT	Dave Berry	Decca	1

WEEK ENDING 29 JULY 1965

LW	TW	Title	Artist	Label	Wks
1	1	MR. TAMBOURINE MAN	Byrds	CBS	7
2	2	HEART FULL OF SOUL	Yardbirds	Columbia	7
10	3	YOU'VE GOT YOUR TROUBLES	Fortunes	Decca	4
3	4	TOSSING AND TURNING	Ivy League	Piccadilly	5
-	5	HELP!	Beatles	Parlophone	1
17	6	WE GOTTA GET OUT OF THIS PLACE	Animals	Columbia	2
4	7	I'M ALIVE	Hollies	Parlophone	9
9	8	IN THE MIDDLE OF NOWHERE	Dusty Springfield	Philips	5
5	9	TO KNOW YOU IS TO LOVE YOU	Peter and Gordon	Columbia	5
11	10	THERE BUT FOR FORTUNE	Joan Baez	Fontana	4
23	11	CATCH US IF YOU CAN	Dave Clark Five	Columbia	3
13	12	WOOLY BULLY	Sam The Sham and the Pharaohs	MGM	5
7	13	LOOKING THROUGH THE EYES OF LOVE	Gene Pitney	Stateside	8
6	14	CRYING IN THE CHAPEL	Elvis Presley	RCA	10
8	15	LEAVE A LITTLE LOVE	Lulu	Decca	6
18	16	HE'S GOT NO LOVE	Searchers	Pye	3
21	17	WITH THESE HANDS	Tom Jones	Decca	3
19	18	GOODBYEE	Peter Cook and Dudley Moore	Decca	6
22	19	LET THE WATER RUN DOWN	P.J. Proby	Liberty	4
15	20	THE PRICE OF LOVE	Everly Brothers	Warner Brothers	11
16	21	SHE'S ABOUT A MOVER	Sir Douglas Quintet	London	7
37	22	THIS WORLD IS NOT MY HOME	Jim Reeves	RCA	2
20	23	ON MY WORD	Cliff Richard	Columbia	8
-	24	SUMMER NIGHTS	Marianne Faithfull	Decca	1
24	25	I CAN'T HELP MYSELF	Four Tops	Tamla Motown	3
12	26	COLOURS	Donovan	Pye	9
14	27	ANYWAY ANYHOW ANYWHERE	Who	Brunswick	10
-	28	WALK IN THE BLACK FOREST	Horst Jankowski ●	Mercury	1
38	29	IN THOUGHTS OF YOU	Billy Fury	Decca	2
-	30	(SAY) YOU'RE MY GIRL	Roy Orbison	London	1

August 1965

☐ Highest position disc reached ● Act's first ever week on chart

LW	TW	Title	Artist	Label	Wks
28	31	CRY TO ME	Pretty Things	Fontana	3
-	32	ZORBA'S DANCE	Marcello Minerbi ●	Durium	1
25	33	LONG LIVE LOVE	Sandie Shaw	Pye	12
31	34	WORLD OF OUR OWN	Seekers	Columbia	15
34	35	BALLAD OF SPOTTY MULDOON	Peter Cook	Decca	3
-	36	TOO MANY RIVERS	Brenda Lee	Brunswick	1
39	37	THAT'S THE WAY LOVE GOES	Charles Dickens	Pye	3
30	38	HELP ME RHONDA	Beach Boys	Capitol	9
40	39	THIS STRANGE EFFECT	Dave Berry	Decca	2
-	40	EVERYONE'S GONE TO THE MOON	Jonathan King ●	Decca	1

WEEK ENDING 5 AUGUST 1965

LW	TW	Title	Artist	Label	Wks
5	1	HELP!	Beatles	Parlophone	2
1	2	MR. TAMBOURINE MAN	Byrds	CBS	8
3	3	YOU'VE GOT YOUR TROUBLES	Fortunes	Decca	5
6	4	WE GOTTA GET OUT OF THIS PLACE	Animals	Columbia	2
4	5	TOSSING AND TURNING	Ivy League	Piccadilly	6
2	6	HEART FULL OF SOUL	Yardbirds	Columbia	8
11	7	CATCH US IF YOU CAN	Dave Clark Five	Columbia	4
10	8	THERE BUT FOR FORTUNE	Joan Baez	Fontana	5
8	9	IN THE MIDDLE OF NOWHERE	Dusty Springfield	Philips	6
7	10	I'M ALIVE	Hollies	Parlophone	10
12	11	WOOLY BULLY	Sam The Sham and the Pharaohs	MGM	6
16	12	HE'S GOT NO LOVE	Searchers	Pye	4
17	13	WITH THESE HANDS	Tom Jones	Decca	4
14	14	CRYING IN THE CHAPEL	Elvis Presley	RCA	11
24	15	SUMMER NIGHTS	Marianne Faithfull	Decca	2
9	16	TO KNOW YOU IS TO LOVE YOU	Peter and Gordon	Columbia	6
13	17	LOOKING THROUGH THE EYES OF LOVE	Gene Pitney	Stateside	9
40	18	EVERYONE'S GONE TO THE MOON	Jonathan King	Decca	2
28	19	WALK IN THE BLACK FOREST	Horst Jankowski	Mercury	2
29	20	IN THOUGHTS OF YOU	Billy Fury	Decca	3
15	21	LEAVE A LITTLE LOVE	Lulu	Decca	7
32	22	ZORBA'S DANCE	Marcello Minerbi	Durium	2
18	23	GOODBYEE	Peter Cook and Dudley Moore	Decca	7
22	24	THIS WORLD IS NOT MY HOME	Jim Reeves	RCA	3
19	25	LET THE WATER RUN DOWN	P.J. Proby	Liberty	5
30	26	(SAY) YOU'RE MY GIRL	Roy Orbison	London	2
25	27	I CAN'T HELP MYSELF	Four Tops	Tamla Motown	4
21	28	SHE'S ABOUT A MOVER	Sir Douglas Quintet	London	8
36	29	TOO MANY RIVERS	Brenda Lee	Brunswick	2
26	30	COLOURS	Donovan	Pye	10
27	31	ANYWAY ANYHOW ANYWHERE	Who	Brunswick	11
20	32	THE PRICE OF LOVE	Everly Brothers	Warner Brothers	12
-	33	I WANT CANDY	Brian Poole and the Tremeloes	Decca	1
31	34	CRY TO ME	Pretty Things	Fontana	4
35	35	BALLAD OF SPOTTY MULDOON	Peter Cook	Decca	4
38	36	HELP ME RHONDA	Beach Boys	Capitol	10
23	37	ON MY WORD	Cliff Richard	Columbia	9
39	38	THIS STRANGE EFFECT	Dave Berry	Decca	3
-	39	SEE MY FRIEND	Kinks	Pye	1
-	40	DON'T MAKE MY BABY BLUE	Shadows	Columbia	1

WEEK ENDING 12 AUGUST 1965

LW	TW	Title	Artist	Label	Wks
1	1	HELP!	Beatles	Parlophone	3
4	2	WE GOTTA GET OUT OF THIS PLACE	Animals	Columbia	3
3	3	YOU'VE GOT YOUR TROUBLES	Fortunes	Decca	6
2	4	MR. TAMBOURINE MAN	Byrds	CBS	9
7	5	CATCH US IF YOU CAN	Dave Clark Five	Columbia	5
5	6	TOSSING AND TURNING	Ivy League	Piccadilly	7
18	7	EVERYONE'S GONE TO THE MOON	Jonathan King	Decca	3
8	8	THERE BUT FOR FORTUNE	Joan Baez	Fontana	6
20	9	IN THOUGHTS OF YOU	Billy Fury	Decca	4
15	10	SUMMER NIGHTS	Marianne Faithfull	Decca	3
6	11	HEART FULL OF SOUL	Yardbirds	Columbia	9

■The Kinks issue two consecutive singles, each with three words in the title and the initial letters of each title are the same. In each case, only the final letter is different in the first and second words. But they sound quite different and both reach the Top Ten (05.08.65) ■ For a fifth consecutive week, the number 8 record is by a feamle vocalist and is at the peak of its chart run (12.08.65)■

August 1965

□ Highest position disc reached ● Act's first ever week on chart

22	12	ZORBA'S DANCE	Marcello Minerbi	Durium	3
13	13	WITH THESE HANDS	Tom Jones	Decca	5
19	14	WALK IN THE BLACK FOREST	Horst Jankowski	Mercury	3
11	15	WOOLY BULLY	Sam The Sham and the Pharaohs	MGM	7
9	16	IN THE MIDDLE OF NOWHERE	Dusty Springfield	Philips	7
12	17	HE'S GOT NO LOVE	Searchers	Pye	5
10	18	I'M ALIVE	Hollies	Parlophone	11
14	19	CRYING IN THE CHAPEL	Elvis Presley	RCA	12
40	20	DON'T MAKE MY BABY BLUE	Shadows	Columbia	2
16	21	TO KNOW YOU IS TO LOVE YOU	Peter and Gordon	Columbia	7
24	22	THIS WORLD IS NOT MY HOME	Jim Reeves	RCA	4
26	23	(SAY) YOU'RE MY GIRL	Roy Orbison	London	3
39	24	SEE MY FRIEND	Kinks	Pye	2
29	25	TOO MANY RIVERS	Brenda Lee	Brunswick	3
-	26	ALL I REALLY WANT TO DO	Byrds	CBS	1
25	27	LET THE WATER RUN DOWN	P.J. Proby	Liberty	6
33	28	I WANT CANDY	Brian Poole and the Tremeloes	Decca	2
21	29	LEAVE A LITTLE LOVE	Lulu	Decca	8
-	30	I GOT YOU BABE	Sonny and Cher ●	Atlantic	1
17	31	LOOKING THROUGH THE EYES OF LOVE	Gene Pitney	Stateside	10
34	32	CRY TO ME	Pretty Things	Fontana	5
-	33	LIKE WE USED TO BE	Georgie Fame	Columbia	1
-	34	THAT'S THE WAY	Honeycombs	Pye	1
23	35	GOODBYEE	Peter Cook and Dudley Moore	Decca	8
27	36	I CAN'T HELP MYSELF	Four Tops	Tamla Motown	5
38	37	THIS STRANGE EFFECT	Dave Berry	Decca	4
-	38	UNCHAINED MELODY	Righteous Brothers	London	1
32	39	THE PRICE OF LOVE	Everly Brothers	Warner Brothers	13
28	40	SHE'S ABOUT A MOVER	Sir Douglas Quintet	London	9

WEEK ENDING 19 AUGUST 1965

LW	TW				Wks
1	1	HELP!	Beatles	Parlophone	4
3	2	YOU'VE GOT YOUR TROUBLES	Fortunes	Decca	7
2	3	WE GOTTA GET OUT OF THIS PLACE	Animals	Columbia	4
30	4	I GOT YOU BABE	Sonny and Cher	Atlantic	2
14	5	WALK IN THE BLACK FOREST	Horst Jankowski	Mercury	4
7	6	EVERYONE'S GONE TO THE MOON	Jonathan King	Decca	4
5	7	CATCH US IF YOU CAN	Dave Clark Five	Columbia	6
4	8	MR. TAMBOURINE MAN	Byrds	CBS	10
12	9	ZORBA'S DANCE	Marcello Minerbi	Durium	4
9	10	IN THOUGHTS OF YOU	Billy Fury	Decca	5
10	11	SUMMER NIGHTS	Marianne Faithfull	Decca	4
8	12	THERE BUT FOR FORTUNE	Joan Baez	Fontana	7
6	13	TOSSING AND TURNING	Ivy League	Piccadilly	8
26	14	ALL I REALLY WANT TO DO	Byrds	CBS	2
13	15	WITH THESE HANDS	Tom Jones	Decca	6
24	16	SEE MY FRIEND	Kinks	Pye	3
20	17	DON'T MAKE MY BABY BLUE	Shadows	Columbia	3
15	18	WOOLY BULLY	Sam The Sham and the Pharaohs	MGM	8
17	19	HE'S GOT NO LOVE	Searchers	Pye	6
11	20	HEART FULL OF SOUL	Yardbirds	Columbia	10
-	21	WHAT'S NEW PUSSYCAT	Tom Jones	Decca	1
25	22	TOO MANY RIVERS	Brenda Lee	Brunswick	4
16	23	IN THE MIDDLE OF NOWHERE	Dusty Springfield	Philips	8
34	24	THAT'S THE WAY	Honeycombs	Pye	2
28	25	I WANT CANDY	Brian Poole and the Tremeloes	Decca	3
23	26	(SAY) YOU'RE MY GIRL	Roy Orbison	London	4
22	27	THIS WORLD IS NOT MY HOME	Jim Reeves	RCA	5
19	28	CRYING IN THE CHAPEL	Elvis Presley	RCA	13
38	29	UNCHAINED MELODY	Righteous Brothers	London	2
18	30	I'M ALIVE	Hollies	Parlophone	12
-	31	MAKE IT EASY ON YOURSELF	Walker Brothers	Philips	1
21	32	TO KNOW YOU IS TO LOVE YOU	Peter and Gordon	Columbia	8
27	33	LET THE WATER RUN DOWN	P.J. Proby	Liberty	7
29	34	LEAVE A LITTLE LOVE	Lulu	Decca	9
33	35	LIKE WE USED TO BE	Georgie Fame	Columbia	2
36	36	I CAN'T HELP MYSELF	Four Tops	Tamla Motown	6
32	37	CRY TO ME	Pretty Things	Fontana	6
31	38	LOOKING THROUGH THE EYES OF LOVE	Gene Pitney	Stateside	11
37	39	THIS STRANGE EFFECT	Dave Berry	Decca	5
-	40	ALL I REALLY WANT TO DO	Cher ●	Liberty	1

WEEK ENDING 26 AUGUST 1965

LW	TW				Wks
4	1	I GOT YOU BABE	Sonny and Cher	Atlantic	3
1	2	HELP!	Beatles	Parlophone	5
5	3	WALK IN THE BLACK FOREST	Horst Jankowski	Mercury	5
6	4	EVERYONE'S GONE TO THE MOON	Jonathan King	Decca	5
14	5	ALL I REALLY WANT TO DO	Byrds	CBS	3
3	6	WE GOTTA GET OUT OF THIS PLACE	Animals	Columbia	5
9	7	ZORBA'S DANCE	Marcello Minerbi	Durium	5
2	8	YOU'VE GOT YOUR TROUBLES	Fortunes	Decca	8
7	9	CATCH US IF YOU CAN	Dave Clark Five	Columbia	7
17	10	DON'T MAKE MY BABY BLUE	Shadows	Columbia	4
10	11	IN THOUGHTS OF YOU	Billy Fury	Decca	6
16	12	SEE MY FRIEND	Kinks	Pye	4
11	13	SUMMER NIGHTS	Marianne Faithfull	Decca	5
8	14	MR. TAMBOURINE MAN	Byrds	CBS	11
-	15	(I CAN'T GET NO) SATISFACTION	Rolling Stones	Decca	1
21	16	WHAT'S NEW PUSSYCAT	Tom Jones	Decca	2
12	17	THERE BUT FOR FORTUNE	Joan Baez	Fontana	8
31	18	MAKE IT EASY ON YOURSELF	Walker Brothers	Philips	2
-	19	LIKE A ROLLING STONE	Bob Dylan	CBS	1
13	20	TOSSING AND TURNING	Ivy League	Piccadilly	9
15	21	WITH THESE HANDS	Tom Jones	Decca	7
40	22	ALL I REALLY WANT TO DO	Cher	Liberty	2
22	23	TOO MANY RIVERS	Brenda Lee	Brunswick	5
24	24	THAT'S THE WAY	Honeycombs	Pye	3
29	25	UNCHAINED MELODY	Righteous Brothers	London	3
19	26	HE'S GOT NO LOVE	Searchers	Pye	7
-	27	THE TIME IN BETWEEN	Cliff Richard	Columbia	1
18	28	WOOLY BULLY	Sam The Sham and the Pharaohs	MGM	9
20	29	HEART FULL OF SOUL	Yardbirds	Columbia	11
25	30	I WANT CANDY	Brian Poole and the Tremeloes	Decca	4
23	31	IN THE MIDDLE OF NOWHERE	Dusty Springfield	Philips	9
-	32	LAUGH AT ME	Sonny ●	Liberty	1
26	33	(SAY) YOU'RE MY GIRL	Roy Orbison	London	5
27	34	THIS WORLD IS NOT MY HOME	Jim Reeves	RCA	6
35	35	LIKE WE USED TO BE	Georgie Fame	Columbia	3
30	36	I'M ALIVE	Hollies	Parlophone	13
28	37	CRYING IN THE CHAPEL	Elvis Presley	RCA	14
33	38	LET THE WATER RUN DOWN	P.J. Proby	Liberty	8
-	39	PARADISE	Frank Ifield	Columbia	1
-	40	IL SILENZIO	Nini Rosso ●	Durium	1

WEEK ENDING 2 SEPTEMBER 1965

LW	TW				Wks
1	1	I GOT YOU BABE	Sonny and Cher	Atlantic	4
2	2	HELP!	Beatles	Parlophone	6
15	3	(I CAN'T GET NO) SATISFACTION	Rolling Stones	Decca	2
5	4	ALL I REALLY WANT TO DO	Byrds	CBS	4
3	5	WALK IN THE BLACK FOREST	Horst Jankowski	Mercury	6
7	6	ZORBA'S DANCE	Marcello Minerbi	Durium	6
4	7	EVERYONE'S GONE TO THE MOON	Jonathan King	Decca	6
18	8	MAKE IT EASY ON YOURSELF	Walker Brothers	Philips	3
19	9	LIKE A ROLLING STONE	Bob Dylan	CBS	2
12	10	SEE MY FRIEND	Kinks	Pye	5
16	11	WHAT'S NEW PUSSYCAT	Tom Jones	Decca	3
6	12	WE GOTTA GET OUT OF THIS PLACE	Animals	Columbia	6
22	13	ALL I REALLY WANT TO DO	Cher	Liberty	3
8	14	YOU'VE GOT YOUR TROUBLES	Fortunes	Decca	9
10	15	DON'T MAKE MY BABY BLUE	Shadows	Columbia	5
11	16	IN THOUGHTS OF YOU	Billy Fury	Decca	7
9	17	CATCH US IF YOU CAN	Dave Clark Five	Columbia	8
24	18	THAT'S THE WAY	Honeycombs	Pye	4
32	19	LAUGH AT ME	Sonny	Liberty	2
13	20	SUMMER NIGHTS	Marianne Faithfull	Decca	6
25	21	UNCHAINED MELODY	Righteous Brothers	London	4
14	22	MR. TAMBOURINE MAN	Byrds	CBS	12

In these weeks ■ After climbing one place a week for four weeks, Dave Berry's long range assault on the number one position comes to an end at number 37 (12.08.65) ■ Four past or future number ones occupy four consecutive chart positons, from 28 to 31 (19.08.65) ■ As in February, for two consecutive weeks, a record jumps from 14 to 5 (26.08.65) ■ In consecutive weeks, Sonny and Cher, Cher and finally Sonny hit the chart to become the second husband and wife team to have hits both separately and together (26.08.65)■

LW	TW	Title	Artist	Label	Wks
27	23	THE TIME IN BETWEEN	Cliff Richard	*Columbia*	2
17	24	THERE BUT FOR FORTUNE	Joan Baez	*Fontana*	9
21	25	WITH THESE HANDS	Tom Jones	*Decca*	8
20	26	TOSSING AND TURNING	Ivy League	*Piccadilly*	10
23	27	TOO MANY RIVERS	Brenda Lee	*Brunswick*	6
40	28	IL SILENZIO	Nini Rosso	*Durium*	2
28	29	WOOLY BULLY	Sam The Sham and the Pharaohs	*MGM*	10
-	30	JUST A LITTLE BIT BETTER	Herman's Hermits	*Columbia*	1
39	31	PARADISE	Frank Ifield	*Columbia*	2
-	32	LOOK THROUGH ANY WINDOW	Hollies	*Parlophone*	1
26	33	HE'S GOT NO LOVE	Searchers	*Pye*	8
33	34	(SAY) YOU'RE MY GIRL	Roy Orbison	*London*	6
30	35	I WANT CANDY	Brian Poole and the Tremeloes	*Decca*	5
29	36	HEART FULL OF SOUL	Yardbirds	*Columbia*	12
-	37	TEARS	Ken Dodd	*Columbia*	1
-	38	I'LL NEVER GET OVER YOU	Everly Brothers	*Warner Bros*	1
34	39	THIS WORLD IS NOT MY HOME	Jim Reeves	*RCA*	7
-	[40]	YOU'RE MY GIRL	Rockin' Berries	*Piccadilly*	1

LW	TW	*WEEK ENDING* **9 SEPTEMBER 1965**			Wks
3	[1]	(I CAN'T GET NO) SATISFACTION	Rolling Stones	*Decca*	3
1	2	I GOT YOU BABE	Sonny and Cher	*Atlantic*	5
8	3	MAKE IT EASY ON YOURSELF	Walker Brothers	*Philips*	4
5	4	WALK IN THE BLACK FOREST	Horst Jankowski	*Mercury*	7
2	5	HELP!	Beatles	*Parlophone*	7
9	6	LIKE A ROLLING STONE	Bob Dylan	*CBS*	3
4	7	ALL I REALLY WANT TO DO	Byrds	*CBS*	5
6	8	ZORBA'S DANCE	Marcello Minerbi	*Durium*	7
13	[9]	ALL I REALLY WANT TO DO	Cher	*Liberty*	4
19	10	LAUGH AT ME	Sonny	*Liberty*	3
32	11	LOOK THROUGH ANY WINDOW	Hollies	*Parlophone*	2
11	12	WHAT'S NEW PUSSYCAT	Tom Jones	*Decca*	4
18	13	THAT'S THE WAY	Honeycombs	*Pye*	5
21	[14]	UNCHAINED MELODY	Righteous Brothers	*London*	5
7	15	EVERYONE'S GONE TO THE MOON	Jonathan King	*Decca*	7
37	16	TEARS	Ken Dodd	*Columbia*	2
15	17	DON'T MAKE MY BABY BLUE	Shadows	*Columbia*	6
10	18	SEE MY FRIEND	Kinks	*Pye*	6
14	19	YOU'VE GOT YOUR TROUBLES	Fortunes	*Decca*	10
12	20	WE GOTTA GET OUT OF THIS PLACE	Animals	*Columbia*	7
30	21	JUST A LITTLE BIT BETTER	Herman's Hermits	*Columbia*	2
23	[22]	THE TIME IN BETWEEN	Cliff Richard	*Columbia*	3
28	23	IL SILENZIO	Nini Rosso	*Durium*	3
17	24	CATCH US IF YOU CAN	Dave Clark Five	*Columbia*	9
16	25	IN THOUGHTS OF YOU	Billy Fury	*Decca*	8
20	26	SUMMER NIGHTS	Marianne Faithfull	*Decca*	7
31	27	PARADISE	Frank Ifield	*Columbia*	3
24	28	THERE BUT FOR FORTUNE	Joan Baez	*Fontana*	10
-	29	HANG ON SLOOPY	McCoys ●	*Immediate*	1
27	30	TOO MANY RIVERS	Brenda Lee	*Brunswick*	7
22	31	MR. TAMBOURINE MAN	Byrds	*CBS*	13
-	32	CALIFORNIA GIRLS	Beach Boys	*Capitol*	1
-	33	WHATCHA GONNA DO ABOUT IT	Small Faces ●	*Decca*	1
26	34	TOSSING AND TURNING	Ivy League	*Piccadilly*	11
38	[35]	I'LL NEVER GET OVER YOU	Everly Brothers	*Warner Bros*	2
-	36	IT'S ALL OVER NOW BABY BLUE	Joan Baez	*Fontana*	1
29	37	WOOLY BULLY	Sam The Sham and the Pharaohs	*MGM*	11
25	38	WITH THESE HANDS	Tom Jones	*Decca*	9
-	39	EVE OF DESTRUCTION	Barry McGuire ●	*RCA*	1
35	40	I WANT CANDY	Brian Poole and the Tremeloes	*Decca*	6

LW	TW	*WEEK ENDING* **16 SEPTEMBER 1965**			Wks
1	[1]	(I CAN'T GET NO) SATISFACTION	Rolling Stones	*Decca*	4
2	2	I GOT YOU BABE	Sonny and Cher	*Atlantic*	6
3	3	MAKE IT EASY ON YOURSELF	Walker Brothers	*Philips*	5
6	[4]	LIKE A ROLLING STONE	Bob Dylan	*CBS*	4
11	5	LOOK THROUGH ANY WINDOW	Hollies	*Parlophone*	3
4	6	WALK IN THE BLACK FOREST	Horst Jankowski	*Mercury*	8
16	7	TEARS	Ken Dodd	*Columbia*	3
5	8	HELP!	Beatles	*Parlophone*	8
10	[9]	LAUGH AT ME	Sonny	*Liberty*	4

September 1965

□ Highest position disc reached ● Act's first ever week on chart

LW	TW	Title	Artist	Label	Wks
8	10	ZORBA'S DANCE	Marcello Minerbi	*Durium*	8
9	11	ALL I REALLY WANT TO DO	Cher	*Liberty*	5
7	12	ALL I REALLY WANT TO DO	Byrds	*CBS*	6
13	13	THAT'S THE WAY	Honeycombs	*Pye*	6
12	14	WHAT'S NEW PUSSYCAT	Tom Jones	*Decca*	5
14	15	UNCHAINED MELODY	Righteous Brothers	*London*	6
21	16	JUST A LITTLE BIT BETTER	Herman's Hermits	*Columbia*	3
23	17	IL SILENZIO	Nini Rosso	*Durium*	4
39	18	EVE OF DESTRUCTION	Barry McGuire	*RCA*	2
15	19	EVERYONE'S GONE TO THE MOON	Jonathan King	*Decca*	8
29	20	HANG ON SLOOPY	McCoys	*Immediate*	2
17	21	DON'T MAKE MY BABY BLUE	Shadows	*Columbia*	7
36	[22]	IT'S ALL OVER NOW BABY BLUE	Joan Baez	*Fontana*	2
22	23	THE TIME IN BETWEEN	Cliff Richard	*Columbia*	4
-	24	BABY DON'T GO	Sonny and Cher	*Reprise*	1
20	25	WE GOTTA GET OUT OF THIS PLACE	Animals	*Columbia*	8
27	[26]	PARADISE	Frank Ifield	*Columbia*	4
-	27	ALMOST THERE	Andy Williams	*CBS*	1
19	28	YOU'VE GOT YOUR TROUBLES	Fortunes	*Decca*	11
33	29	WHATCHA GONNA DO ABOUT IT	Small Faces	*Decca*	2
18	30	SEE MY FRIEND	Kinks	*Pye*	7
32	31	CALIFORNIA GIRLS	Beach Boys	*Capitol*	2
24	32	CATCH US IF YOU CAN	Dave Clark Five	*Columbia*	10
-	33	TRY TO UNDERSTAND	Lulu	*Decca*	1
30	34	TOO MANY RIVERS	Brenda Lee	*Brunswick*	8
26	35	SUMMER NIGHTS	Marianne Faithfull	*Decca*	8
25	36	IN THOUGHTS OF YOU	Billy Fury	*Decca*	9
-	37	IF YOU GOTTA GO GO NOW	Manfred Mann	*HMV*	1
-	38	RUN TO MY LOVIN' ARMS	Billy Fury	*Decca*	1
-	39	RIDE AWAY	Roy Orbison	*London*	1
31	40	MR. TAMBOURINE MAN	Byrds	*CBS*	14

LW	TW	*WEEK ENDING* **23 SEPTEMBER 1965**			Wks
3	[1]	MAKE IT EASY ON YOURSELF	Walker Brothers	*Philips*	6
1	2	(I CAN'T GET NO) SATISFACTION	Rolling Stones	*Decca*	5
7	3	TEARS	Ken Dodd	*Columbia*	4
2	4	I GOT YOU BABE	Sonny and Cher	*Atlantic*	7
5	5	LOOK THROUGH ANY WINDOW	Hollies	*Parlophone*	4
4	6	LIKE A ROLLING STONE	Bob Dylan	*CBS*	5
6	7	WALK IN THE BLACK FOREST	Horst Jankowski	*Mercury*	9
10	8	ZORBA'S DANCE	Marcello Minerbi	*Durium*	9
18	9	EVE OF DESTRUCTION	Barry McGuire	*RCA*	3
9	10	LAUGH AT ME	Sonny	*Liberty*	5
37	11	IF YOU GOTTA GO GO NOW	Manfred Mann	*HMV*	2
13	[12]	THAT'S THE WAY	Honeycombs	*Pye*	7
8	13	HELP!	Beatles	*Parlophone*	9
17	14	IL SILENZIO	Nini Rosso	*Durium*	5
16	[15]	JUST A LITTLE BIT BETTER	Herman's Hermits	*Columbia*	4
20	16	HANG ON SLOOPY	McCoys	*Immediate*	3
11	17	ALL I REALLY WANT TO DO	Cher	*Liberty*	6
27	18	ALMOST THERE	Andy Williams	*CBS*	2
15	19	UNCHAINED MELODY	Righteous Brothers	*London*	7
14	20	WHAT'S NEW PUSSYCAT	Tom Jones	*Decca*	6
12	21	ALL I REALLY WANT TO DO	Byrds	*CBS*	7
29	22	WHATCHA GONNA DO ABOUT IT	Small Faces	*Decca*	3
24	23	BABY DON'T GO	Sonny and Cher	*Reprise*	2
22	24	IT'S ALL OVER NOW BABY BLUE	Joan Baez	*Fontana*	3
33	[25]	TRY TO UNDERSTAND	Lulu	*Decca*	2
31	[26]	CALIFORNIA GIRLS	Beach Boys	*Capitol*	3
19	27	EVERYONE'S GONE TO THE MOON	Jonathan King	*Decca*	9
26	28	PARADISE	Frank Ifield	*Columbia*	5
23	29	THE TIME IN BETWEEN	Cliff Richard	*Columbia*	5
38	30	RUN TO MY LOVIN' ARMS	Billy Fury	*Decca*	2
21	31	DON'T MAKE MY BABY BLUE	Shadows	*Columbia*	8
-	32	SOME OF YOUR LOVIN'	Dusty Springfield	*Philips*	1
-	33	TAKE A HEART	Sorrows ●	*Piccadilly*	1
39	[34]	RIDE AWAY	Roy Orbison	*London*	2
34	35	TOO MANY RIVERS	Brenda Lee	*Brunswick*	9

■Sonny and Cher break new ground by having Top Ten hits as a duo and as solo artists in the same week. No combination of artists, whether married or not, has ever matched this unique achievement (09.09.65) ■ *Hang On Sloopy* is the first hit on the Immediate label (09.09.65) ■ Bob Dylan climbs to his highest ever chart placing. In the same week, five other records written by him are in the Top 40 (16.09.65)■

September 1965

□ Highest position disc reached ● Act's first ever week on chart

LW	TW	Title	Artist	Label	Wks
25	36	WE GOTTA GET OUT OF THIS PLACE	Animals	Columbia	9
-	37	IT'S THE SAME OLD SONG	Four Tops	Tamla Motown	1
28	38	YOU'VE GOT YOUR TROUBLES	Fortunes	Decca	12
30	39	SEE MY FRIEND	Kinks	Pye	8
32	40	CATCH US IF YOU CAN	Dave Clark Five	Columbia	11

WEEK ENDING 30 SEPTEMBER 1965

LW	TW	Title	Artist	Label	Wks
3	1	TEARS	Ken Dodd	Columbia	5
1	2	MAKE IT EASY ON YOURSELF	Walker Brothers	Philips	7
2	3	(I CAN'T GET NO) SATISFACTION	Rolling Stones	Decca	6
5	4	LOOK THROUGH ANY WINDOW	Hollies	Parlophone	5
11	5	IF YOU GOTTA GO GO NOW	Manfred Mann	HMV	3
9	6	EVE OF DESTRUCTION	Barry McGuire	RCA	4
4	7	I GOT YOU BABE	Sonny and Cher	Atlantic	8
6	8	LIKE A ROLLING STONE	Bob Dylan	CBS	6
7	9	WALK IN THE BLACK FOREST	Horst Jankowski	Mercury	10
14	10	IL SILENZIO	Nini Rosso	Durium	6
16	11	HANG ON SLOOPY	McCoys	Immediate	4
18	12	ALMOST THERE	Andy Williams	CBS	3
12	13	THAT'S THE WAY	Honeycombs	Pye	8
10	14	LAUGH AT ME	Sonny	Liberty	6
15	15	JUST A LITTLE BIT BETTER	Herman's Hermits	Columbia	5
8	16	ZORBA'S DANCE	Marcello Minerbi	Durium	10
23	17	BABY DON'T GO	Sonny and Cher	Reprise	3
13	18	HELP!	Beatles	Parlophone	10
22	19	WHATCHA GONNA DO ABOUT IT	Small Faces	Decca	4
17	20	ALL I REALLY WANT TO DO	Cher	Liberty	7
19	21	UNCHAINED MELODY	Righteous Brothers	London	8
32	22	SOME OF YOUR LOVIN'	Dusty Springfield	Philips	2
-	23	MESSAGE UNDERSTOOD	Sandie Shaw	Pye	1
20	24	WHAT'S NEW PUSSYCAT	Tom Jones	Decca	7
25	25	TRY TO UNDERSTAND	Lulu	Decca	3
33	26	TAKE A HEART	Sorrows	Piccadilly	2
30	27	RUN TO MY LOVIN' ARMS	Billy Fury	Decca	3
26	28	CALIFORNIA GIRLS	Beach Boys	Capitol	4
24	29	IT'S ALL OVER NOW BABY BLUE	Joan Baez	Fontana	4
21	30	ALL I REALLY WANT TO DO	Byrds	CBS	8
-	31	IN THE MIDNIGHT HOUR	Wilson Pickett ●	Atlantic	1
28	32	PARADISE	Frank Ifield	Columbia	6
-	33	YOU'VE GOT TO HIDE YOUR LOVE AWAY	Silkie ●	Fontana	1
37	34	IT'S THE SAME OLD SONG	Four Tops	Tamla Motown	2
34	35	RIDE AWAY	Roy Orbison	London	3
-	36	PAPA'S GOT A BRAND NEW BAG	James Brown ●	London	1
27	37	EVERYONE'S GONE TO THE MOON	Jonathan King	Decca	10
31	38	DON'T MAKE MY BABY BLUE	Shadows	Columbia	9
-	39	THAT MEANS A LOT	P.J. Proby	Liberty	1
29	40	THE TIME IN BETWEEN	Cliff Richard	Columbia	6

WEEK ENDING 7 OCTOBER 1965

LW	TW	Title	Artist	Label	Wks
1	1	TEARS	Ken Dodd	Columbia	6
5	2	IF YOU GOTTA GO GO NOW	Manfred Mann	HMV	4
2	3	MAKE IT EASY ON YOURSELF	Walker Brothers	Philips	8
6	4	EVE OF DESTRUCTION	Barry McGuire	RCA	5
12	5	ALMOST THERE	Andy Williams	CBS	4
11	6	HANG ON SLOOPY	McCoys	Immediate	5
4	7	LOOK THROUGH ANY WINDOW	Hollies	Parlophone	6
3	8	(I CAN'T GET NO) SATISFACTION	Rolling Stones	Decca	7
10	9	IL SILENZIO	Nini Rosso	Durium	7
8	10	LIKE A ROLLING STONE	Bob Dylan	CBS	7
17	11	BABY DON'T GO	Sonny and Cher	Reprise	4
23	12	MESSAGE UNDERSTOOD	Sandie Shaw	Pye	2
9	13	WALK IN THE BLACK FOREST	Horst Jankowski	Mercury	11
7	14	I GOT YOU BABE	Sonny and Cher	Atlantic	9
19	15	WHATCHA GONNA DO ABOUT IT	Small Faces	Decca	5
13	16	THAT'S THE WAY	Honeycombs	Pye	9
15	17	JUST A LITTLE BIT BETTER	Herman's Hermits	Columbia	6
16	18	ZORBA'S DANCE	Marcello Minerbi	Durium	11
22	19	SOME OF YOUR LOVIN'	Dusty Springfield	Philips	3
14	20	LAUGH AT ME	Sonny	Liberty	7
26	21	TAKE A HEART	Sorrows	Piccadilly	3
31	22	IN THE MIDNIGHT HOUR	Wilson Pickett	Atlantic	2
18	23	HELP!	Beatles	Parlophone	11
21	24	UNCHAINED MELODY	Righteous Brothers	London	9
27	25	RUN TO MY LOVIN' ARMS	Billy Fury	Decca	4
20	26	ALL I REALLY WANT TO DO	Cher	Liberty	8
29	27	IT'S ALL OVER NOW BABY BLUE	Joan Baez	Fontana	5
28	28	CALIFORNIA GIRLS	Beach Boys	Capitol	5
25	29	TRY TO UNDERSTAND	Lulu	Decca	4
33	30	YOU'VE GOT TO HIDE YOUR LOVE AWAY	Silkie	Fontana	2
-	31	IT'S GOOD NEWS WEEK	Hedgehoppers Anonymous ●	Decca	1
-	32	SHE NEEDS LOVE	Wayne Fontana and the Mindbenders	Fontana	1
36	33	PAPA'S GOT A BRAND NEW BAG	James Brown	London	2
24	34	WHAT'S NEW PUSSYCAT	Tom Jones	Decca	8
34	35	IT'S THE SAME OLD SONG	Four Tops	Tamla Motown	3
39	36	THAT MEANS A LOT	P.J. Proby	Liberty	2
32	37	PARADISE	Frank Ifield	Columbia	7
35	38	RIDE AWAY	Roy Orbison	London	4
-	39	DOWN IN THE BOONDOCKS	Billy Joe Royal ●	CBS	1
30	40	ALL I REALLY WANT TO DO	Byrds	CBS	9

WEEK ENDING 14 OCTOBER 1965

LW	TW	Title	Artist	Label	Wks
1	1	TEARS	Ken Dodd	Columbia	7
5	2	ALMOST THERE	Andy Williams	CBS	5
2	3	IF YOU GOTTA GO GO NOW	Manfred Mann	HMV	5
4	4	EVE OF DESTRUCTION	Barry McGuire	RCA	6
6	5	HANG ON SLOOPY	McCoys	Immediate	6
3	6	MAKE IT EASY ON YOURSELF	Walker Brothers	Philips	9
7	7	LOOK THROUGH ANY WINDOW	Hollies	Parlophone	7
9	8	IL SILENZIO	Nini Rosso	Durium	8
12	9	MESSAGE UNDERSTOOD	Sandie Shaw	Pye	3
8	10	(I CAN'T GET NO) SATISFACTION	Rolling Stones	Decca	8
11	11	BABY DON'T GO	Sonny and Cher	Reprise	5
13	12	WALK IN THE BLACK FOREST	Horst Jankowski	Mercury	12
19	13	SOME OF YOUR LOVIN'	Dusty Springfield	Philips	4
15	14	WHATCHA GONNA DO ABOUT IT	Small Faces	Decca	6
14	15	I GOT YOU BABE	Sonny and Cher	Atlantic	10
10	16	LIKE A ROLLING STONE	Bob Dylan	CBS	8
22	17	IN THE MIDNIGHT HOUR	Wilson Pickett	Atlantic	3
16	18	THAT'S THE WAY	Honeycombs	Pye	10
17	19	JUST A LITTLE BIT BETTER	Herman's Hermits	Columbia	7
18	20	ZORBA'S DANCE	Marcello Minerbi	Durium	12
31	21	IT'S GOOD NEWS WEEK	Hedgehoppers Anonymous	Decca	2
-	22	EVIL HEARTED YOU/STILL I'M SAD	Yardbirds	Columbia	1
23	23	HELP!	Beatles	Parlophone	12
20	24	LAUGH AT ME	Sonny	Liberty	8
21	25	TAKE A HEART	Sorrows	Piccadilly	4
33	26	PAPA'S GOT A BRAND NEW BAG	James Brown	London	3
25	27	RUN TO MY LOVIN' ARMS	Billy Fury	Decca	5
30	28	YOU'VE GOT TO HIDE YOUR LOVE AWAY	Silkie	Fontana	3
-	29	HERE IT COMES AGAIN	Fortunes	Decca	1
24	30	UNCHAINED MELODY	Righteous Brothers	London	10
-	31	YESTERDAY MAN	Chris Andrews ●	Decca	1
26	32	ALL I REALLY WANT TO DO	Cher	Liberty	9
28	33	CALIFORNIA GIRLS	Beach Boys	Capitol	6
32	34	SHE NEEDS LOVE	Wayne Fontana and the Mindbenders	Fontana	2
27	35	IT'S ALL OVER NOW BABY BLUE	Joan Baez	Fontana	6
29	36	TRY TO UNDERSTAND	Lulu	Decca	5
36	37	THAT MEANS A LOT	P.J. Proby	Liberty	3
39	38	DOWN IN THE BOONDOCKS	Billy Joe Royal	CBS	2
34	39	WHAT'S NEW PUSSYCAT	Tom Jones	Decca	9
-	40	I LEFT MY HEART IN SAN FRANCISCO	Tony Bennett	CBS	1

WEEK ENDING 21 OCTOBER 1965

LW	TW	Title	Artist	Label	Wks
1	1	TEARS	Ken Dodd	Columbia	8
2	2	ALMOST THERE	Andy Williams	CBS	6
3	3	IF YOU GOTTA GO GO NOW	Manfred Mann	HMV	6

In these weeks ■ In the week when Jonathan King's first hit drops from the Top 40, the first of his many hit productions, *It's Good News Week*, makes its chart entrance (07.10.65) ■ For a fifth week there are three continental instrumentals in the Top 20, each featuring a different instrument. German Horst Jankowski plays the piano, while Italians Marcello Minerbi and Nini Rosso have hits with bouzouki and trumpet respectively (14.10.65)■

LW	TW	Title	Artist	Label	Wks
4	4	EVE OF DESTRUCTION	Barry McGuire	*RCA*	7
5	5	HANG ON SLOOPY	McCoys	*Immediate*	7
9	6	MESSAGE UNDERSTOOD	Sandie Shaw	*Pye*	4
6	7	MAKE IT EASY ON YOURSELF	Walker Brothers	*Philips*	10
13	8	SOME OF YOUR LOVIN'	Dusty Springfield	*Philips*	5
22	9	EVIL HEARTED YOU/STILL I'M SAD	Yardbirds	*Columbia*	2
21	10	IT'S GOOD NEWS WEEK	Hedgehoppers Anonymous	*Decca*	3
8	11	IL SILENZIO	Nini Rosso	*Durium*	9
17	12	IN THE MIDNIGHT HOUR	Wilson Pickett	*Atlantic*	4
11	13	BABY DON'T GO	Sonny and Cher	*Reprise*	6
7	14	LOOK THROUGH ANY WINDOW	Hollies	*Parlophone*	8
10	15	(I CAN'T GET NO) SATISFACTION	Rolling Stones	*Decca*	9
12	16	WALK IN THE BLACK FOREST	Horst Jankowski	*Mercury*	13
29	17	HERE IT COMES AGAIN	Fortunes	*Decca*	2
31	18	YESTERDAY MAN	Chris Andrews	*Decca*	2
14	19	WHATCHA GONNA DO ABOUT IT	Small Faces	*Decca*	7
15	20	I GOT YOU BABE	Sonny and Cher	*Atlantic*	11
20	21	ZORBA'S DANCE	Marcello Minerbi	*Durium*	13
16	22	LIKE A ROLLING STONE	Bob Dylan	*CBS*	9
18	23	THAT'S THE WAY	Honeycombs	*Pye*	11
25	24	TAKE A HEART	Sorrows	*Piccadilly*	5
26	25	PAPA'S GOT A BRAND NEW BAG	James Brown	*London*	4
-	26	YESTERDAY	Matt Monro	*Parlophone*	1
19	27	JUST A LITTLE BIT BETTER	Herman's Hermits	*Columbia*	8
28	28	YOU'VE GOT TO HIDE YOUR LOVE AWAY	Silkie	*Fontana*	4
23	29	HELP!	Beatles	*Parlophone*	13
24	30	LAUGH AT ME	Sonny	*Liberty*	9
37	31	THAT MEANS A LOT	P.J. Proby	*Liberty*	4
27	32	RUN TO MY LOVIN' ARMS	Billy Fury	*Decca*	6
34	33	SHE NEEDS LOVE	Wayne Fontana and the Mindbenders	*Fontana*	3
-	34	I LOVE YOU YES I DO	Merseybeats	*Fontana*	1
-	35	WHEN I GET HOME	Searchers	*Pye*	1
-	36	UNTIL IT'S TIME FOR YOU TO GO	Four Pennies	*Philips*	1
33	37	CALIFORNIA GIRLS	Beach Boys	*Capitol*	7
30	38	UNCHAINED MELODY	Righteous Brothers	*London*	11
38	39	DOWN IN THE BOONDOCKS	Billy Joe Royal	*CBS*	3
40	40	I LEFT MY HEART IN SAN FRANCISCO	Tony Bennett	*CBS*	2

WEEK ENDING 28 OCTOBER 1965

LW	TW	Title	Artist	Label	Wks
1	1	TEARS	Ken Dodd	*Columbia*	9
2	2	ALMOST THERE	Andy Williams	*CBS*	7
4	3	EVE OF DESTRUCTION	Barry McGuire	*RCA*	8
9	4	EVIL HEARTED YOU/STILL I'M SAD	Yardbirds	*Columbia*	3
18	5	YESTERDAY MAN	Chris Andrews	*Decca*	3
10	6	IT'S GOOD NEWS WEEK	Hedgehoppers Anonymous	*Decca*	4
3	7	IF YOU GOTTA GO GO NOW	Manfred Mann	*HMV*	7
5	8	HANG ON SLOOPY	McCoys	*Immediate*	8
17	9	HERE IT COMES AGAIN	Fortunes	*Decca*	3
26	10	YESTERDAY	Matt Monro	*Parlophone*	2
8	11	SOME OF YOUR LOVIN'	Dusty Springfield	*Philips*	6
6	12	MESSAGE UNDERSTOOD	Sandie Shaw	*Pye*	5
12	13	IN THE MIDNIGHT HOUR	Wilson Pickett	*Atlantic*	5
11	14	IL SILENZIO	Nini Rosso	*Durium*	10
7	15	MAKE IT EASY ON YOURSELF	Walker Brothers	*Philips*	11
13	16	BABY DON'T GO	Sonny and Cher	*Reprise*	7
-	17	GET OFF OF MY CLOUD	Rolling Stones	*Decca*	1
19	18	WHATCHA GONNA DO ABOUT IT	Small Faces	*Decca*	8
14	19	LOOK THROUGH ANY WINDOW	Hollies	*Parlophone*	9
15	20	(I CAN'T GET NO) SATISFACTION	Rolling Stones	*Decca*	10
16	21	WALK IN THE BLACK FOREST	Horst Jankowski	*Mercury*	14
-	22	LOVE IS STRANGE	Everly Brothers	*Warner Bros*	1
34	23	I LOVE YOU YES I DO	Merseybeats	*Fontana*	2
36	24	UNTIL IT'S TIME FOR YOU TO GO	Four Pennies	*Philips*	2
25	25	PAPA'S GOT A BRAND NEW BAG	James Brown	*London*	5
21	26	ZORBA'S DANCE	Marcello Minerbi	*Durium*	14
23	27	THAT'S THE WAY	Honeycombs	*Pye*	12
22	28	LIKE A ROLLING STONE	Bob Dylan	*CBS*	10
-	29	BUT YOU'RE MINE	Sonny and Cher	*Atlantic*	1
31	30	THAT MEANS A LOT	P.J. Proby	*Liberty*	5
-	31	BABY I'M YOURS	Peter and Gordon	*Columbia*	1
24	32	TAKE A HEART	Sorrows	*Piccadilly*	6
27	33	JUST A LITTLE BIT BETTER	Herman's Hermits	*Columbia*	9

November 1965

□ Highest position disc reached ● Act's first ever week on chart

LW	TW	Title	Artist	Label	Wks
28	34	YOU'VE GOT TO HIDE YOUR LOVE AWAY	Silkie	*Fontana*	5
20	35	I GOT YOU BABE	Sonny and Cher	*Atlantic*	12
33	36	SHE NEEDS LOVE	Wayne Fontana and the Mindbenders	*Fontana*	4
-	37	IT'S MY LIFE	Animals	*Columbia*	1
35	38	WHEN I GET HOME	Searchers	*Pye*	2
-	39	POSITIVELY 4TH STREET	Bob Dylan	*CBS*	1
29	40	HELP!	Beatles	*Parlophone*	14

WEEK ENDING 4 NOVEMBER 1965

LW	TW	Title	Artist	Label	Wks
17	1	GET OFF OF MY CLOUD	Rolling Stones	*Decca*	2
1	2	TEARS	Ken Dodd	*Columbia*	10
4	3	EVIL HEARTED YOU/STILL I'M SAD	Yardbirds	*Columbia*	4
5	4	YESTERDAY MAN	Chris Andrews	*Decca*	4
6	5	IT'S GOOD NEWS WEEK	Hedgehoppers Anonymous	*Decca*	5
9	6	HERE IT COMES AGAIN	Fortunes	*Decca*	4
2	7	ALMOST THERE	Andy Williams	*CBS*	8
10	8	YESTERDAY	Matt Monro	*Parlophone*	3
3	9	EVE OF DESTRUCTION	Barry McGuire	*RCA*	9
37	10	IT'S MY LIFE	Animals	*Columbia*	2
8	11	HANG ON SLOOPY	McCoys	*Immediate*	9
7	12	IF YOU GOTTA GO GO NOW	Manfred Mann	*HMV*	8
-	13	THE CARNIVAL IS OVER	Seekers	*Columbia*	1
22	14	LOVE IS STRANGE	Everly Brothers	*Warner Bros*	2
39	15	POSITIVELY 4TH STREET	Bob Dylan	*CBS*	2
11	16	SOME OF YOUR LOVIN'	Dusty Springfield	*Philips*	7
29	17	BUT YOU'RE MINE	Sonny and Cher	*Atlantic*	2
13	18	IN THE MIDNIGHT HOUR	Wilson Pickett	*Atlantic*	6
12	19	MESSAGE UNDERSTOOD	Sandie Shaw	*Pye*	6
24	20	UNTIL IT'S TIME FOR YOU TO GO	Four Pennies	*Philips*	3
15	21	MAKE IT EASY ON YOURSELF	Walker Brothers	*Philips*	12
31	22	BABY I'M YOURS	Peter and Gordon	*Columbia*	2
23	23	I LOVE YOU YES I DO	Merseybeats	*Fontana*	3
14	24	IL SILENZIO	Nini Rosso	*Durium*	11
16	25	BABY DON'T GO	Sonny and Cher	*Reprise*	8
18	26	WHATCHA GONNA DO ABOUT IT	Small Faces	*Decca*	9
-	27	SOMETHING	Georgie Fame	*Columbia*	1
20	28	(I CAN'T GET NO) SATISFACTION	Rolling Stones	*Decca*	11
21	29	WALK IN THE BLACK FOREST	Horst Jankowski	*Mercury*	15
19	30	LOOK THROUGH ANY WINDOW	Hollies	*Parlophone*	10
-	31	1-2-3	Len Barry ●	*Brunswick*	1
-	32	IN THE CHAPEL IN THE MOONLIGHT	Bachelors	*Decca*	1
-	33	MY GENERATION	Who	*Brunswick*	1
30	34	THAT MEANS A LOT	P.J. Proby	*Liberty*	6
-	35	YOU'RE THE ONE	Petula Clark	*Pye*	1
25	36	PAPA'S GOT A BRAND NEW BAG	James Brown	*London*	6
-	37	SHAME AND SCANDAL IN THE FAMILY	Lance Percival ●	*Parlophone*	1
-	38	SINS OF THE FAMILY	P.F. Sloan ●	*RCA*	1
-	39	A LOVER'S CONCERTO	Toys ●	*Stateside*	1
-	40	YESTERDAY	Marianne Faithfull	*Decca*	1

WEEK ENDING 11 NOVEMBER 1965

LW	TW	Title	Artist	Label	Wks
1	1	GET OFF OF MY CLOUD	Rolling Stones	*Decca*	3
2	2	TEARS	Ken Dodd	*Columbia*	11
4	3	YESTERDAY MAN	Chris Andrews	*Decca*	5
6	4	HERE IT COMES AGAIN	Fortunes	*Decca*	5
3	5	EVIL HEARTED YOU/STILL I'M SAD	Yardbirds	*Columbia*	5
5	6	IT'S GOOD NEWS WEEK	Hedgehoppers Anonymous	*Decca*	6
10	7	IT'S MY LIFE	Animals	*Columbia*	3
8	8	YESTERDAY	Matt Monro	*Parlophone*	4
7	9	ALMOST THERE	Andy Williams	*CBS*	9
13	10	THE CARNIVAL IS OVER	Seekers	*Columbia*	2
14	11	LOVE IS STRANGE	Everly Brothers	*Warner Bros*	3
15	12	POSITIVELY 4TH STREET	Bob Dylan	*CBS*	3
9	13	EVE OF DESTRUCTION	Barry McGuire	*RCA*	10

■The Top Five records remain unchanged (21.10.65) ■ By taking her version of *Yesterday* into the charts, Marianne Faithfull becomes the first act, apart from the Rolling Stones themselves, to chart with songs written by Lennon-McCartney and Jagger-Richard (04.11.65) ■ Two 'family' hits peaking at 37 and 38. Lance Percival gained fame from television, and P.F. Sloan from Barry McGuire's version of his doom-laden song *Eve Of Destruction* (04.11.65)■

November 1965

□ Highest position disc reached ● Act's first ever week on chart

LW	TW	Title	Artist	Label	Wks
33	14	MY GENERATION	Who	Brunswick	2
31	15	1-2-3	Len Barry	Brunswick	2
11	16	HANG ON SLOOPY	McCoys	Immediate	10
12	17	IF YOU GOTTA GO GO NOW	Manfred Mann	HMV	9
16	18	SOME OF YOUR LOVIN'	Dusty Springfield	Philips	8
22	[19]	BABY I'M YOURS	Peter and Gordon	Columbia	3
20	20	UNTIL IT'S TIME FOR YOU TO GO	Four Pennies	Philips	4
17	21	BUT YOU'RE MINE	Sonny and Cher	Atlantic	3
23	[22]	I LOVE YOU YES I DO	Merseybeats	Fontana	4
39	23	A LOVER'S CONCERTO	Toys	Stateside	2
19	24	MESSAGE UNDERSTOOD	Sandie Shaw	Pye	7
18	25	IN THE MIDNIGHT HOUR	Wilson Pickett	Atlantic	7
27	26	SOMETHING	Georgie Fame	Columbia	2
24	27	IL SILENZIO	Nini Rosso	Durium	12
32	28	IN THE CHAPEL IN THE MOONLIGHT	Bachelors	Decca	2
-	29	WIND ME UP (LET ME GO)	Cliff Richard	Columbia	1
-	[30]	TREAT HER RIGHT	Roy Head ●	Vocalion	1
-	31	PRINCESS IN RAGS	Gene Pitney	Stateside	1
26	32	WHATCHA GONNA DO ABOUT IT	Small Faces	Decca	10
35	33	YOU'RE THE ONE	Petula Clark	Pye	2
25	34	BABY DON'T GO	Sonny and Cher	Reprise	9
-	35	CRAWLIN' BACK	Roy Orbison	London	1
40	[36]	YESTERDAY	Marianne Faithfull	Decca	2
21	37	MAKE IT EASY ON YOURSELF	Walker Brothers	Philips	13
-	38	DON'T BRING ME YOUR HEARTACHES	Paul and Barry Ryan ●	Decca	1
29	39	WALK IN THE BLACK FOREST	Horst Jankowski	Mercury	16
-	40	TELL ME WHY	Elvis Presley	RCA	1

WEEK ENDING 18 NOVEMBER 1965

LW	TW	Title	Artist	Label	Wks
1	[1]	GET OFF OF MY CLOUD	Rolling Stones	Decca	4
10	2	THE CARNIVAL IS OVER	Seekers	Columbia	3
3	[3]	YESTERDAY MAN	Chris Andrews	Decca	6
2	4	TEARS	Ken Dodd	Columbia	12
14	5	MY GENERATION	Who	Brunswick	3
15	6	1-2-3	Len Barry	Brunswick	3
7	[7]	IT'S MY LIFE	Animals	Columbia	4
4	8	HERE IT COMES AGAIN	Fortunes	Decca	6
5	9	EVIL HEARTED YOU/STILL I'M SAD	Yardbirds	Columbia	6
12	10	POSITIVELY 4TH STREET	Bob Dylan	CBS	4
8	11	YESTERDAY	Matt Monro	Parlophone	5
6	12	IT'S GOOD NEWS WEEK	Hedgehoppers Anonymous	Decca	7
9	13	ALMOST THERE	Andy Williams	CBS	10
11	14	LOVE IS STRANGE	Everly Brothers	Warner Bros	4
23	15	A LOVER'S CONCERTO	Toys	Stateside	3
29	16	WIND ME UP (LET ME GO)	Cliff Richard	Columbia	2
13	17	EVE OF DESTRUCTION	Barry McGuire	RCA	11
31	18	PRINCESS IN RAGS	Gene Pitney	Stateside	2
20	[19]	UNTIL IT'S TIME FOR YOU TO GO	Four Pennies	Philips	5
21	20	BUT YOU'RE MINE	Sonny and Cher	Atlantic	4
19	21	BABY I'M YOURS	Peter and Gordon	Columbia	4
40	22	TELL ME WHY	Elvis Presley	RCA	2
26	[23]	SOMETHING	Georgie Fame	Columbia	3
16	24	HANG ON SLOOPY	McCoys	Immediate	11
33	25	YOU'RE THE ONE	Petula Clark	Pye	3
38	26	DON'T BRING ME YOUR HEARTACHES	Paul and Barry Ryan	Decca	2
28	[27]	IN THE CHAPEL IN THE MOONLIGHT	Bachelors	Decca	3
-	28	IS IT REALLY OVER?	Jim Reeves	RCA	1
17	29	IF YOU GOTTA GO GO NOW	Manfred Mann	HMV	10
30	[30]	TREAT HER RIGHT	Roy Head	Vocalion	2
18	31	SOME OF YOUR LOVIN'	Dusty Springfield	Philips	9
35	32	CRAWLIN' BACK	Roy Orbison	London	2
22	33	I LOVE YOU YES I DO	Merseybeats	Fontana	5
-	34	TURQUOISE	Donovan	Pye	1
25	35	IN THE MIDNIGHT HOUR	Wilson Pickett	Atlantic	8
24	36	MESSAGE UNDERSTOOD	Sandie Shaw	Pye	8
-	37	THE RIVER	Ken Dodd	Columbia	1
-	38	LET'S HANG ON	Four Seasons	Philips	1
-	39	TURN! TURN! TURN!	Byrds	CBS	1
27	40	IL SILENZIO	Nini Rosso	Durium	13

WEEK ENDING 25 NOVEMBER 1965

LW	TW	Title	Artist	Label	Wks
2	[1]	THE CARNIVAL IS OVER	Seekers	Columbia	4
5	[2]	MY GENERATION	Who	Brunswick	4
1	3	GET OFF OF MY CLOUD	Rolling Stones	Decca	5
6	4	1-2-3	Len Barry	Brunswick	4
4	5	TEARS	Ken Dodd	Columbia	13
3	6	YESTERDAY MAN	Chris Andrews	Decca	7
7	[7]	IT'S MY LIFE	Animals	Columbia	5
16	8	WIND ME UP (LET ME GO)	Cliff Richard	Columbia	3
8	9	HERE IT COMES AGAIN	Fortunes	Decca	7
10	10	POSITIVELY 4TH STREET	Bob Dylan	CBS	5
15	11	A LOVER'S CONCERTO	Toys	Stateside	4
18	12	PRINCESS IN RAGS	Gene Pitney	Stateside	3
11	13	YESTERDAY	Matt Monro	Parlophone	6
9	14	EVIL HEARTED YOU/STILL I'M SAD	Yardbirds	Columbia	7
14	15	LOVE IS STRANGE	Everly Brothers	Warner Bros	5
13	16	ALMOST THERE	Andy Williams	CBS	11
12	17	IT'S GOOD NEWS WEEK	Hedgehoppers Anonymous	Decca	8
22	18	TELL ME WHY	Elvis Presley	RCA	3
37	19	THE RIVER	Ken Dodd	Columbia	2
26	20	DON'T BRING ME YOUR HEARTACHES	Paul and Barry Ryan	Decca	3
28	21	IS IT REALLY OVER?	Jim Reeves	RCA	2
19	22	UNTIL IT'S TIME FOR YOU TO GO	Four Pennies	Philips	6
25	[23]	YOU'RE THE ONE	Petula Clark	Pye	4
20	24	BUT YOU'RE MINE	Sonny and Cher	Atlantic	5
21	25	BABY I'M YOURS	Peter and Gordon	Columbia	5
32	26	CRAWLIN' BACK	Roy Orbison	London	3
17	27	EVE OF DESTRUCTION	Barry McGuire	RCA	12
23	28	SOMETHING	Georgie Fame	Columbia	4
24	29	HANG ON SLOOPY	McCoys	Immediate	12
27	30	IN THE CHAPEL IN THE MOONLIGHT	Bachelors	Decca	4
34	31	TURQUOISE	Donovan	Pye	2
35	32	IN THE MIDNIGHT HOUR	Wilson Pickett	Atlantic	9
30	33	TREAT HER RIGHT	Roy Head	Vocalion	3
39	34	TURN! TURN! TURN!	Byrds	CBS	2
38	35	LET'S HANG ON	Four Seasons	Philips	2
31	36	SOME OF YOUR LOVIN'	Dusty Springfield	Philips	10
-	37	MARIA	P.J. Proby	Liberty	1
-	38	WALK HAND IN HAND	Gerry and the Pacemakers	Columbia	1
-	39	HOW CAN YOU TELL	Sandie Shaw	Pye	1
29	40	IF YOU GOTTA GO GO NOW	Manfred Mann	HMV	11

WEEK ENDING 2 DECEMBER 1965

LW	TW	Title	Artist	Label	Wks
1	[1]	THE CARNIVAL IS OVER	Seekers	Columbia	5
2	[2]	MY GENERATION	Who	Brunswick	5
4	[3]	1-2-3	Len Barry	Brunswick	5
3	4	GET OFF OF MY CLOUD	Rolling Stones	Decca	6
11	[5]	A LOVER'S CONCERTO	Toys	Stateside	5
5	6	TEARS	Ken Dodd	Columbia	14
8	7	WIND ME UP (LET ME GO)	Cliff Richard	Columbia	4
10	[8]	POSITIVELY 4TH STREET	Bob Dylan	CBS	6
12	[9]	PRINCESS IN RAGS	Gene Pitney	Stateside	4
6	10	YESTERDAY MAN	Chris Andrews	Decca	8
19	11	THE RIVER	Ken Dodd	Columbia	3
7	12	IT'S MY LIFE	Animals	Columbia	6
20	[13]	DON'T BRING ME YOUR HEARTACHES	Paul and Barry Ryan	Decca	4
37	14	MARIA	P.J. Proby	Liberty	2
18	[15]	TELL ME WHY	Elvis Presley	RCA	4
13	16	YESTERDAY	Matt Monro	Parlophone	7
21	[17]	IS IT REALLY OVER?	Jim Reeves	RCA	3
9	18	HERE IT COMES AGAIN	Fortunes	Decca	8
26	[19]	CRAWLIN' BACK	Roy Orbison	London	4
35	20	LET'S HANG ON	Four Seasons	Philips	3
39	[21]	HOW CAN YOU TELL	Sandie Shaw	Pye	2

In these weeks ■ The Who reach their highest ever chart placing. They will return to number 2 in 1966, but never manage that final step (25.11.65) ■ Paul and Barry Ryan, twin sons of 50s hitmaker Marion Ryan, are the first sons of a hitmaking mother to chart (11.11.65) ■ The very high figure of 14 records are at their chart peak, including ten of the Top 20 (02.12.65) ■

December 1965

□ Highest position disc reached ● Act's first ever week on chart

LW	TW	Title	Artist	Label	Wks
14	22	EVIL HEARTED YOU/STILL I'M SAD	Yardbirds	Columbia	8
15	23	LOVE IS STRANGE	Everly Brothers	Warner Bros	6
16	24	ALMOST THERE	Andy Williams	CBS	12
23	25	YOU'RE THE ONE	Petula Clark	Pye	5
34	26	TURN! TURN! TURN!	Byrds	CBS	3
22	27	UNTIL IT'S TIME FOR YOU TO GO	Four Pennies	Philips	7
17	28	IT'S GOOD NEWS WEEK	Hedgehoppers Anonymous	Decca	9
38	29	WALK HAND IN HAND	Gerry and the Pacemakers	Columbia	2
31	30	TURQUOISE	Donovan	Pye	3
25	31	BABY I'M YOURS	Peter and Gordon	Columbia	6
-	32	TO WHOM IT CONCERNS	Chris Andrews	Decca	1
-	33	RESCUE ME	Fontella Bass ●	Chess	1
-	34	TILL THE END OF THE DAY	Kinks	Pye	1
27	35	EVE OF DESTRUCTION	Barry McGuire	RCA	13
24	36	BUT YOU'RE MINE	Sonny and Cher	Atlantic	6
33	37	TREAT HER RIGHT	Roy Head	Vocalion	4
-	38	MY SHIP IS COMING IN	Walker Brothers	Philips	1
-	39	WAR LORD	Shadows	Columbia	1
28	40	SOMETHING	Georgie Fame	Columbia	5

WEEK ENDING 9 DECEMBER 1965

LW	TW	Title	Artist	Label	Wks
1	1	THE CARNIVAL IS OVER	Seekers	Columbia	6
-	2	DAY TRIPPER/WE CAN WORK IT OUT	Beatles	Parlophone	1
2	3	MY GENERATION	Who	Brunswick	6
7	4	WIND ME UP (LET ME GO)	Cliff Richard	Columbia	5
5	5	A LOVER'S CONCERTO	Toys	Stateside	6
3	6	1-2-3	Len Barry	Brunswick	6
11	7	THE RIVER	Ken Dodd	Columbia	4
6	8	TEARS	Ken Dodd	Columbia	15
4	9	GET OFF OF MY CLOUD	Rolling Stones	Decca	7
9	10	PRINCESS IN RAGS	Gene Pitney	Stateside	5
8	11	POSITIVELY 4TH STREET	Bob Dylan	CBS	7
14	12	MARIA	P.J. Proby	Liberty	3
38	13	MY SHIP IS COMING IN	Walker Brothers	Philips	2
12	14	IT'S MY LIFE	Animals	Columbia	7
13	15	DON'T BRING ME YOUR HEARTACHES	Paul and Barry Ryan	Decca	5
20	16	LET'S HANG ON	Four Seasons	Philips	4
15	17	TELL ME WHY	Elvis Presley	RCA	5
33	18	RESCUE ME	Fontella Bass	Chess	2
10	19	YESTERDAY MAN	Chris Andrews	Decca	9
16	20	YESTERDAY	Matt Monro	Parlophone	8
32	21	TO WHOM IT CONCERNS	Chris Andrews	Decca	2
19	22	CRAWLIN' BACK	Roy Orbison	London	5
21	23	HOW CAN YOU TELL	Sandie Shaw	Pye	3
17	24	IS IT REALLY OVER?	Jim Reeves	RCA	4
18	25	HERE IT COMES AGAIN	Fortunes	Decca	9
34	26	TILL THE END OF THE DAY	Kinks	Pye	2
26	27	TURN! TURN! TURN!	Byrds	CBS	4
25	28	YOU'RE THE ONE	Petula Clark	Pye	6
-	29	DON'T FIGHT IT	Wilson Pickett	Atlantic	1
-	30	KEEP ON RUNNING	Spencer Davis Group ●	Fontana	1
29	31	WALK HAND IN HAND	Gerry and the Pacemakers	Columbia	3
39	32	WAR LORD	Shadows	Columbia	2
22	33	EVIL HEARTED YOU/STILL I'M SAD	Yardbirds	Columbia	9
24	34	ALMOST THERE	Andy Williams	CBS	13
27	35	UNTIL IT'S TIME FOR YOU TO GO	Four Pennies	Philips	8
-	36	MY GIRL	Otis Redding ●	Atlantic	1
23	37	LOVE IS STRANGE	Everly Brothers	Warner Bros	7
31	38	BABY I'M YOURS	Peter and Gordon	Columbia	7
30	39	TURQUOISE	Donovan	Pye	4
-	40	I LEFT MY HEART IN SAN FRANCISCO	Tony Bennett	CBS	3

WEEK ENDING 16 DECEMBER 1965

LW	TW	Title	Artist	Label	Wks
2	1	DAY TRIPPER/WE CAN WORK IT OUT	Beatles	Parlophone	2
1	2	THE CARNIVAL IS OVER	Seekers	Columbia	7
4	3	WIND ME UP (LET ME GO)	Cliff Richard	Columbia	6
6	4	1-2-3	Len Barry	Brunswick	7
3	5	MY GENERATION	Who	Brunswick	7
7	6	THE RIVER	Ken Dodd	Columbia	5
8	7	TEARS	Ken Dodd	Columbia	16
12	8	MARIA	P.J. Proby	Liberty	4
5	9	A LOVER'S CONCERTO	Toys	Stateside	7
13	10	MY SHIP IS COMING IN	Walker Brothers	Philips	3
18	11	RESCUE ME	Fontella Bass	Chess	3
10	12	PRINCESS IN RAGS	Gene Pitney	Stateside	6
16	13	LET'S HANG ON	Four Seasons	Philips	5
21	14	TO WHOM IT CONCERNS	Chris Andrews	Decca	3
11	15	POSITIVELY 4TH STREET	Bob Dylan	CBS	8
9	16	GET OFF OF MY CLOUD	Rolling Stones	Decca	8
19	17	YESTERDAY MAN	Chris Andrews	Decca	10
15	18	DON'T BRING ME YOUR HEARTACHES	Paul and Barry Ryan	Decca	6
24	19	IS IT REALLY OVER?	Jim Reeves	RCA	5
17	20	TELL ME WHY	Elvis Presley	RCA	6
14	21	IT'S MY LIFE	Animals	Columbia	8
30	22	KEEP ON RUNNING	Spencer Davis Group	Fontana	2
26	23	TILL THE END OF THE DAY	Kinks	Pye	3
23	24	HOW CAN YOU TELL	Sandie Shaw	Pye	4
20	25	YESTERDAY	Matt Monro	Parlophone	9
25	26	HERE IT COMES AGAIN	Fortunes	Decca	10
32	27	WAR LORD	Shadows	Columbia	3
36	28	MY GIRL	Otis Redding	Atlantic	2
28	29	YOU'RE THE ONE	Petula Clark	Pye	7
29	30	DON'T FIGHT IT	Wilson Pickett	Atlantic	2
40	31	I LEFT MY HEART IN SAN FRANCISCO	Tony Bennett	CBS	4
22	32	CRAWLIN' BACK	Roy Orbison	London	6
34	33	ALMOST THERE	Andy Williams	CBS	14
27	34	TURN! TURN! TURN!	Byrds	CBS	5
33	35	EVIL HEARTED YOU/STILL I'M SAD	Yardbirds	Columbia	10
-	36	MERRY GENTLE POPS	Barron Knights	Columbia	1
-	37	SPANISH FLEA	Herb Alpert and the Tijuana Brass	Pye	1
37	38	LOVE IS STRANGE	Everly Brothers	Warner Bros	8
31	39	WALK HAND IN HAND	Gerry and the Pacemakers	Columbia	4
-	40	IF I NEEDED SOMEONE	Hollies	Parlophone	1

WEEK ENDING 23 DECEMBER 1965

LW	TW	Title	Artist	Label	Wks
1	1	DAY TRIPPER/WE CAN WORK IT OUT	Beatles	Parlophone	3
3	2	WIND ME UP (LET ME GO)	Cliff Richard	Columbia	7
6	3	THE RIVER	Ken Dodd	Columbia	6
2	4	THE CARNIVAL IS OVER	Seekers	Columbia	8
7	5	TEARS	Ken Dodd	Columbia	17
10	6	MY SHIP IS COMING IN	Walker Brothers	Philips	4
5	7	MY GENERATION	Who	Brunswick	8
4	8	1-2-3	Len Barry	Brunswick	8
9	9	A LOVER'S CONCERTO	Toys	Stateside	8
13	10	LET'S HANG ON	Four Seasons	Philips	6
11	11	RESCUE ME	Fontella Bass	Chess	4
8	12	MARIA	P.J. Proby	Liberty	5
14	13	TO WHOM IT CONCERNS	Chris Andrews	Decca	4
23	14	TILL THE END OF THE DAY	Kinks	Pye	4
22	15	KEEP ON RUNNING	Spencer Davis Group	Fontana	3
12	16	PRINCESS IN RAGS	Gene Pitney	Stateside	7
15	17	POSITIVELY 4TH STREET	Bob Dylan	CBS	9
27	18	WAR LORD	Shadows	Columbia	4
36	19	MERRY GENTLE POPS	Barron Knights	Columbia	2
17	20	YESTERDAY MAN	Chris Andrews	Decca	11
19	21	IS IT REALLY OVER?	Jim Reeves	RCA	6
28	22	MY GIRL	Otis Redding	Atlantic	3
16	23	GET OFF OF MY CLOUD	Rolling Stones	Decca	9
18	24	DON'T BRING ME YOUR HEARTACHES	Paul and Barry Ryan	Decca	7
31	25	I LEFT MY HEART IN SAN FRANCISCO	Tony Bennett	CBS	5
40	26	IF I NEEDED SOMEONE	Hollies	Parlophone	2
24	27	HOW CAN YOU TELL	Sandie Shaw	Pye	5
21	28	IT'S MY LIFE	Animals	Columbia	9
20	29	TELL ME WHY	Elvis Presley	RCA	7
37	30	SPANISH FLEA	Herb Alpert and the Tijuana Brass	Pye	2
-	31	TAKE ME FOR WHAT I'M WORTH	Searchers	Pye	1

■One of the greatest of the British white soul singers, Steve Winwood of the Spencer Davis Group, charts for the first time in the same week that one of the greatest of the American black soul singers, Otis Redding, also makes his debut (09.12.65) ■ Two hits in the top five for Britain's most successful singing funny man, Ken Dodd (23.12.65)■

December 1965

□ Highest position disc reached ● Act's first ever week on chart

LW	TW	Title	Artist	Label	Wks
25	32	YESTERDAY	Matt Monro	*Parlophone*	10
-	33	A MUST TO AVOID	Herman's Hermits	*Columbia*	1
26	34	HERE IT COMES AGAIN	Fortunes	*Decca*	11
30	35	DON'T FIGHT IT	Wilson Pickett	*Atlantic*	3
-	36	IT WAS EASIER TO HURT HER	Wayne Fontana	*Fontana*	1
-	37	A HARD DAY'S NIGHT	Peter Sellers	*Parlophone*	1
29	38	YOU'RE THE ONE	Petula Clark	*Pye*	8
-	39	THE VERY THOUGHT OF YOU	Tony Bennett	*CBS*	1
33	40	ALMOST THERE	Andy Williams	*CBS*	15

LW TW *WEEK ENDING* **30 DECEMBER 1965** **Wks**

(no chart compiled: chart for 23 December repeated)

LW	TW	Title	Artist	Label	Wks
1	1	DAY TRIPPER/WE CAN WORK IT OUT	Beatles	*Parlophone*	4
2	2	WIND ME UP (LET ME GO)	Cliff Richard	*Columbia*	8
3	3	THE RIVER	Ken Dodd	*Columbia*	7
4	4	THE CARNIVAL IS OVER	Seekers	*Columbia*	9
5	5	TEARS	Ken Dodd	*Columbia*	18
6	6	MY SHIP IS COMING IN	Walker Brothers	*Philips*	5
7	7	MY GENERATION	Who	*Brunswick*	9
8	8	1-2-3	Len Barry	*Brunswick*	9
9	9	A LOVER'S CONCERTO	Toys	*Stateside*	9
10	10	LET'S HANG ON	Four Seasons	*Philips*	7
11	11	RESCUE ME	Fontella Bass	*Chess*	5
12	12	MARIA	P.J. Proby	*Liberty*	6
13	13	TO WHOM IT CONCERNS	Chris Andrews	*Decca*	5
14	14	TILL THE END OF THE DAY	Kinks	*Pye*	5
15	15	KEEP ON RUNNING	Spencer Davis Group	*Fontana*	4
16	16	PRINCESS IN RAGS	Gene Pitney	*Stateside*	8
17	17	POSITIVELY 4TH STREET	Bob Dylan	*CBS*	10
18	18	WAR LORD	Shadows	*Columbia*	5
19	19	MERRY GENTLE POPS	Barron Knights	*Columbia*	3
20	20	YESTERDAY MAN	Chris Andrews	*Decca*	12
21	21	IS IT REALLY OVER?	Jim Reeves	*RCA*	7
22	22	MY GIRL	Otis Redding	*Atlantic*	4
23	23	GET OFF OF MY CLOUD	Rolling Stones	*Decca*	10
24	24	DON'T BRING ME YOUR HEARTACHES	Paul and Barry Ryan	*Decca*	8
25	25	I LEFT MY HEART IN SAN FRANCISCO	Tony Bennett	*CBS*	6
26	26	IF I NEEDED SOMEONE	Hollies	*Parlophone*	3
27	27	HOW CAN YOU TELL	Sandie Shaw	*Pye*	6
28	28	IT'S MY LIFE	Animals	*Columbia*	10
29	29	TELL ME WHY	Elvis Presley	*RCA*	8
30	30	SPANISH FLEA	Herb Alpert and the Tijuana Brass	*Pye*	3
31	31	TAKE ME FOR WHAT I'M WORTH	Searchers	*Pye*	2
32	32	YESTERDAY	Matt Monro	*Parlophone*	11
33	33	A MUST TO AVOID	Herman's Hermits	*Columbia*	2
34	34	HERE IT COMES AGAIN	Fortunes	*Decca*	12
35	35	DON'T FIGHT IT	Wilson Pickett	*Atlantic*	4
36	36	IT WAS EASIER TO HURT HER	Wayne Fontana	*Fontana*	2
37	37	A HARD DAY'S NIGHT	Peter Sellers	*Parlophone*	2
38	38	YOU'RE THE ONE	Petula Clark	*Pye*	9
39	39	THE VERY THOUGHT OF YOU	Tony Bennett	*CBS*	2
40	40	ALMOST THERE	Andy Williams	*CBS*	16

In these weeks ■ Wayne Fontana's first solo he since his split with his backing group, the Mindbenders, just sneaks into the Top 40 (23.12.65) ■ The Beatles are at number one for a third Christmas in a row (30.12.65) ■ Chris Andrews only ever has two Top 20 hits, but for three weeks they are both in the Top 20 together (30.12.65) ■

1966

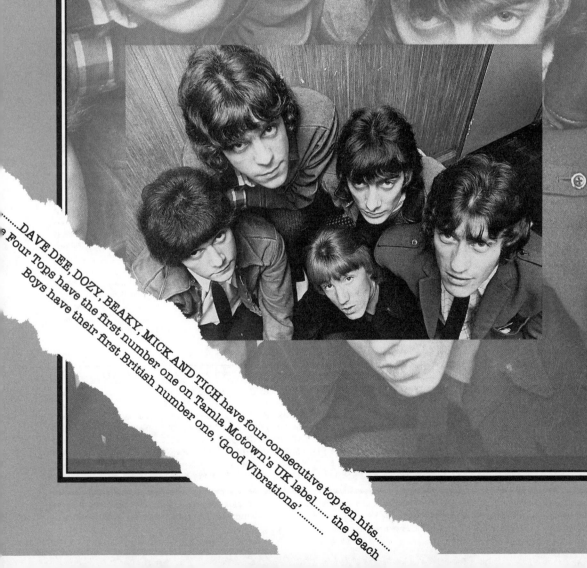

......**DAVE DEE, DOZY, BEAKY, MICK AND TICH** have four consecutive top ten hits...... e Four Tops have the first number one on Tamla Motown's UK label...... the Beach Boys have their first British number one, 'Good Vibrations'..........

January 1966

□ Highest position disc reached ● Act's first ever week on chart

LW	TW	*WEEK ENDING* **6 JANUARY 1966**			Wks
1	[1]	DAY TRIPPER/WE CAN WORK IT OUT	Beatles	*Parlophone*	5
2	[2]	WIND ME UP (LET ME GO)	Cliff Richard	*Columbia*	9
4	3	THE CARNIVAL IS OVER	Seekers	*Columbia*	10
3	4	THE RIVER	Ken Dodd	*Columbia*	8
15	5	KEEP ON RUNNING	Spencer Davis Group	*Fontana*	5
6	6	MY SHIP IS COMING IN	Walker Brothers	*Philips*	6
5	7	TEARS	Ken Dodd	*Columbia*	19
10	8	LET'S HANG ON	Four Seasons	*Philips*	8
19	[9]	MERRY GENTLE POPS	Barron Knights	*Columbia*	4
14	10	TILL THE END OF THE DAY	Kinks	*Pye*	6
8	11	1-2-3	Len Barry	*Brunswick*	10
7	12	MY GENERATION	Who	*Brunswick*	10
11	13	RESCUE ME	Fontella Bass	*Chess*	6
12	14	MARIA	P.J. Proby	*Liberty*	7
13	15	TO WHOM IT CONCERNS	Chris Andrews	*Decca*	6
37	16	A HARD DAY'S NIGHT	Peter Sellers	*Parlophone*	3
9	17	A LOVER'S CONCERTO	Toys	*Stateside*	10
16	18	PRINCESS IN RAGS	Gene Pitney	*Stateside*	9
33	19	A MUST TO AVOID	Herman's Hermits	*Columbia*	3
22	20	MY GIRL	Otis Redding	*Atlantic*	5
30	21	SPANISH FLEA	Herb Alpert and the Tijuana Brass	*Pye*	4
26	22	IF I NEEDED SOMEONE	Hollies	*Parlophone*	4
18	23	WAR LORD	Shadows	*Columbia*	6
20	24	YESTERDAY MAN	Chris Andrews	*Decca*	13
25	[25]	I LEFT MY HEART IN SAN FRANCISCO	Tony Bennett	*CBS*	7
39	26	THE VERY THOUGHT OF YOU	Tony Bennett	*CBS*	3
31	27	TAKE ME FOR WHAT I'M WORTH	Searchers	*Pye*	3
17	28	POSITIVELY 4TH STREET	Bob Dylan	*CBS*	11
23	29	GET OFF OF MY CLOUD	Rolling Stones	*Decca*	11
21	30	IS IT REALLY OVER?	Jim Reeves	*RCA*	8
-	31	ENGLAND SWINGS	Roger Miller	*Philips*	1
27	32	HOW CAN YOU TELL	Sandie Shaw	*Pye*	7
-	33	BYE BYE BLUES	Bert Kaempfert ●	*Polydor*	1
32	34	YESTERDAY	Matt Monro	*Parlophone*	12
-	[35]	FAREWELL ANGELINA	Joan Baez	*Fontana*	1
35	36	DON'T FIGHT IT	Wilson Pickett	*Atlantic*	5
-	37	GIRLS! GIRLS! GIRLS!	Fourmost	*Parlophone*	1
24	38	DON'T BRING ME YOUR HEARTACHES	Paul and Barry Ryan	*Decca*	9
-	[39]	I HEAR A SYMPHONY	Supremes	*Tamla-Motown*	1
36	40	IT WAS EASIER TO HURT HER	Wayne Fontana	*Fontana*	3

LW	TW	*WEEK ENDING* **13 JANUARY 1966**			Wks
1	[1]	DAY TRIPPER/WE CAN WORK IT OUT	Beatles	*Parlophone*	6
5	2	KEEP ON RUNNING	Spencer Davis Group	*Fontana*	6
2	3	WIND ME UP (LET ME GO)	Cliff Richard	*Columbia*	10
3	4	THE CARNIVAL IS OVER	Seekers	*Columbia*	11
6	5	MY SHIP IS COMING IN	Walker Brothers	*Philips*	7
4	6	THE RIVER	Ken Dodd	*Columbia*	9
8	7	LET'S HANG ON	Four Seasons	*Philips*	9
10	[8]	TILL THE END OF THE DAY	Kinks	*Pye*	7
19	9	A MUST TO AVOID	Herman's Hermits	*Columbia*	4
9	10	MERRY GENTLE POPS	Barron Knights	*Columbia*	5
7	11	TEARS	Ken Dodd	*Columbia*	20
21	12	SPANISH FLEA	Herb Alpert and the Tijuana Brass	*Pye*	5
11	13	1-2-3	Len Barry	*Brunswick*	11
13	14	RESCUE ME	Fontella Bass	*Chess*	7
16	15	A HARD DAY'S NIGHT	Peter Sellers	*Parlophone*	4
12	16	MY GENERATION	Who	*Brunswick*	11
20	17	MY GIRL	Otis Redding	*Atlantic*	6
15	18	TO WHOM IT CONCERNS	Chris Andrews	*Decca*	7
17	19	A LOVER'S CONCERTO	Toys	*Stateside*	11
22	[20]	IF I NEEDED SOMEONE	Hollies	*Parlophone*	5
14	21	MARIA	P.J. Proby	*Liberty*	8
27	22	TAKE ME FOR WHAT I'M WORTH	Searchers	*Pye*	4
23	23	WAR LORD	Shadows	*Columbia*	7
31	24	ENGLAND SWINGS	Roger Miller	*Philips*	2
18	25	PRINCESS IN RAGS	Gene Pitney	*Stateside*	10
33	26	BYE BYE BLUES	Bert Kaempfert	*Polydor*	2
26	27	THE VERY THOUGHT OF YOU	Tony Bennett	*CBS*	4
-	28	YOU WERE ON MY MIND	Crispian St. Peters ●	*Decca*	1
-	29	TAKE ME TO YOUR HEART AGAIN	Vince Hill ●	*Columbia*	1
-	30	YOU MAKE IT MOVE	Dave Dee Dozy Beaky Mick and Tich ●	*Fontana*	1
25	31	I LEFT MY HEART IN SAN FRANCISCO	Tony Bennett	*CBS*	8
24	32	YESTERDAY MAN	Chris Andrews	*Decca*	14
37	[33]	GIRLS! GIRLS! GIRLS!	Fourmost	*Parlophone*	2
-	34	GROOVY KIND OF LOVE	Mindbenders ●	*Fontana*	1
29	35	GET OFF OF MY CLOUD	Rolling Stones	*Decca*	12
-	36	MICHELLE	Overlanders ●	*Pye*	1
28	37	POSITIVELY 4TH STREET	Bob Dylan	*CBS*	12
-	[38]	HELLO DOLLY	Bachelors	*Decca*	1
-	39	MICHELLE	David and Jonathan ●	*Columbia*	1
32	40	HOW CAN YOU TELL	Sandie Shaw	*Pye*	8

LW	TW	*WEEK ENDING* **20 JANUARY 1966**			Wks
2	[1]	KEEP ON RUNNING	Spencer Davis Group	*Fontana*	7
1	2	DAY TRIPPER/WE CAN WORK IT OUT	Beatles	*Parlophone*	7
5	[3]	MY SHIP IS COMING IN	Walker Brothers	*Philips*	8
7	[4]	LET'S HANG ON	Four Seasons	*Philips*	10
3	5	WIND ME UP (LET ME GO)	Cliff Richard	*Columbia*	11
12	6	SPANISH FLEA	Herb Alpert and the Tijuana Brass	*Pye*	6
4	7	THE CARNIVAL IS OVER	Seekers	*Columbia*	12
9	8	A MUST TO AVOID	Herman's Hermits	*Columbia*	5
6	9	THE RIVER	Ken Dodd	*Columbia*	10
8	10	TILL THE END OF THE DAY	Kinks	*Pye*	8
36	11	MICHELLE	Overlanders	*Pye*	2
17	12	MY GIRL	Otis Redding	*Atlantic*	7
29	[13]	TAKE ME TO YOUR HEART AGAIN	Vince Hill	*Columbia*	2
15	[14]	A HARD DAY'S NIGHT	Peter Sellers	*Parlophone*	5
11	15	TEARS	Ken Dodd	*Columbia*	21
10	16	MERRY GENTLE POPS	Barron Knights	*Columbia*	6
13	17	1-2-3	Len Barry	*Brunswick*	12
14	18	RESCUE ME	Fontella Bass	*Chess*	8
24	19	ENGLAND SWINGS	Roger Miller	*Philips*	3
22	[20]	TAKE ME FOR WHAT I'M WORTH	Searchers	*Pye*	5
27	[21]	THE VERY THOUGHT OF YOU	Tony Bennett	*CBS*	5
16	22	MY GENERATION	Who	*Brunswick*	12
20	23	IF I NEEDED SOMEONE	Hollies	*Parlophone*	6
39	24	MICHELLE	David and Jonathan	*Columbia*	2
26	25	BYE BYE BLUES	Bert Kaempfert	*Polydor*	3
18	26	TO WHOM IT CONCERNS	Chris Andrews	*Decca*	8
28	27	YOU WERE ON MY MIND	Crispian St. Peters	*Decca*	2
30	28	YOU MAKE IT MOVE	Dave Dee Dozy Beaky Mick and Tich	*Fontana*	2
34	29	GROOVY KIND OF LOVE	Mindbenders	*Fontana*	2
-	30	LIKE A BABY	Len Barry	*Brunswick*	1
-	31	LOVE'S JUST A BROKEN HEART	Cilla Black	*Parlophone*	1
19	32	A LOVER'S CONCERTO	Toys	*Stateside*	12
-	33	GIRL	St. Louis Union ●	*Decca*	1
21	34	MARIA	P.J. Proby	*Liberty*	9
-	[35]	THUNDERBALL	Tom Jones	*Decca*	1
23	36	WAR LORD	Shadows	*Columbia*	8
31	37	I LEFT MY HEART IN SAN FRANCISCO	Tony Bennett	*CBS*	9
-	[38]	I STAND ACCUSED	Merseybeats	*Fontana*	1
38	39	HELLO DOLLY	Bachelors	*Decca*	2
-	40	MIRROR MIRROR	Pinkerton's Assorted Colours ●	*Decca*	1

LW	TW	*WEEK ENDING* **27 JANUARY 1966**			Wks
11	[1]	MICHELLE	Overlanders	*Pye*	3
1	2	KEEP ON RUNNING	Spencer Davis Group	*Fontana*	8
6	[3]	SPANISH FLEA	Herb Alpert and the Tijuana Brass	*Pye*	7
2	4	DAY TRIPPER/WE CAN WORK IT OUT	Beatles	*Parlophone*	8
4	5	LET'S HANG ON	Four Seasons	*Philips*	11
8	[6]	A MUST TO AVOID	Herman's Hermits	*Columbia*	6
3	7	MY SHIP IS COMING IN	Walker Brothers	*Philips*	9
10	[8]	TILL THE END OF THE DAY	Kinks	*Pye*	9

In these weeks ■ Six new acts debut in the Top 40 (13.01.66) ■ For a third consecutive week, a record moves from 22 to 20, and for two of those weeks, the record in question hits its peak (20.01.66) ■ Tony Bennett's *The Very Thought Of You* reaches a higher chart position than his far better known *I Left My Heart In San Francisco*, which peaked at number 25 two weeks earlier (20.01.66)■

□ Highest position disc reached ● Act's first ever week on chart

LW	TW	Title	Artist	Label	Wks
9	9	THE RIVER	Ken Dodd	Columbia	11
27	10	YOU WERE ON MY MIND	Crispian St. Peters	Decca	3
12	11	MY GIRL	Otis Redding	Atlantic	8
24	12	MICHELLE	David and Jonathan	Columbia	3
19	13	ENGLAND SWINGS	Roger Miller	Philips	4
7	14	THE CARNIVAL IS OVER	Seekers	Columbia	13
31	15	LOVE'S JUST A BROKEN HEART	Cilla Black	Parlophone	2
5	16	WIND ME UP (LET ME GO)	Cliff Richard	Columbia	12
-	17	CAN YOU PLEASE CRAWL OUT YOUR WINDOW	Bob Dylan	CBS	1
29	18	GROOVY KIND OF LOVE	Mindbenders	Fontana	3
15	19	TEARS	Ken Dodd	Columbia	22
14	20	A HARD DAY'S NIGHT	Peter Sellers	Parlophone	6
30	21	LIKE A BABY	Len Barry	Brunswick	2
13	22	TAKE ME TO YOUR HEART AGAIN	Vince Hill	Columbia	3
21	23	THE VERY THOUGHT OF YOU	Tony Bennett	CBS	6
33	24	GIRL	St. Louis Union	Decca	2
25	25	BYE BYE BLUES	Bert Kaempfert	Polydor	4
28	26	YOU MAKE IT MOVE	Dave Dee Dozy Beaky Mick and Tich	Fontana	3
20	27	TAKE ME FOR WHAT I'M WORTH	Searchers	Pye	6
40	28	MIRROR MIRROR	Pinkerton's Assorted Colours	Decca	2
18	29	RESCUE ME	Fontella Bass	Chess	9
17	30	1-2-3	Len Barry	Brunswick	13
16	31	MERRY GENTLE POPS	Barron Knights	Columbia	7
23	32	IF I NEEDED SOMEONE	Hollies	Parlophone	7
26	33	TO WHOM IT CONCERNS	Chris Andrews	Decca	9
-	34	SECOND HAND ROSE	Barbra Streisand ●	CBS	1
-	35	RECOVERY	Fontella Bass	Chess	1
-	36	ATTACK	Toys	Stateside	1
-	37	BREAKIN' UP IS BREAKIN' MY HEART	Roy Orbison	London	1
-	38	THESE BOOTS ARE MADE FOR WALKIN'	Nancy Sinatra ●	Reprise	1
-	39	DON'T MAKE ME OVER	Swinging Blue Jeans	HMV	1
-	40	TCHAIKOVSKY ONE	Second City Sound ●	Decca	1

WEEK ENDING 3 FEBRUARY 1966

LW	TW	Title	Artist	Label	Wks
1	1	MICHELLE	Overlanders	Pye	4
2	2	KEEP ON RUNNING	Spencer Davis Group	Fontana	9
3	3	SPANISH FLEA	Herb Alpert and the Tijuana Brass	Pye	8
10	4	YOU WERE ON MY MIND	Crispian St. Peters	Decca	4
15	5	LOVE'S JUST A BROKEN HEART	Cilla Black	Parlophone	3
6	6	A MUST TO AVOID	Herman's Hermits	Columbia	7
4	7	DAY TRIPPER/WE CAN WORK IT OUT	Beatles	Parlophone	9
5	8	LET'S HANG ON	Four Seasons	Philips	12
7	9	MY SHIP IS COMING IN	Walker Brothers	Philips	10
8	10	TILL THE END OF THE DAY	Kinks	Pye	10
12	11	MICHELLE	David and Jonathan	Columbia	4
9	12	THE RIVER	Ken Dodd	Columbia	12
11	13	MY GIRL	Otis Redding	Atlantic	9
18	14	GROOVY KIND OF LOVE	Mindbenders	Fontana	4
14	15	THE CARNIVAL IS OVER	Seekers	Columbia	14
21	16	LIKE A BABY	Len Barry	Brunswick	3
13	17	ENGLAND SWINGS	Roger Miller	Philips	5
38	18	THESE BOOTS ARE MADE FOR WALKIN'	Nancy Sinatra	Reprise	2
24	19	GIRL	St. Louis Union	Decca	3
16	20	WIND ME UP (LET ME GO)	Cliff Richard	Columbia	13
28	21	MIRROR MIRROR	Pinkerton's Assorted Colours	Decca	3
20	22	A HARD DAY'S NIGHT	Peter Sellers	Parlophone	7
17	23	CAN YOU PLEASE CRAWL OUT YOUR WINDOW	Bob Dylan	CBS	2
25	24	BYE BYE BLUES	Bert Kaempfert	Polydor	5
19	25	TEARS	Ken Dodd	Columbia	23
22	26	TAKE ME TO YOUR HEART AGAIN	Vince Hill	Columbia	4
40	27	TCHAIKOVSKY ONE	Second City Sound	Decca	2
27	28	TAKE ME FOR WHAT I'M WORTH	Searchers	Pye	7
34	29	SECOND HAND ROSE	Barbra Streisand	CBS	2
23	30	THE VERY THOUGHT OF YOU	Tony Bennett	CBS	7
-	31	LITTLE BY LITTLE	Dusty Springfield	Philips	1
35	32	RECOVERY	Fontella Bass	Chess	2
37	33	BREAKIN' UP IS BREAKIN' MY HEART	Roy Orbison	London	2
29	34	RESCUE ME	Fontella Bass	Chess	10
26	35	YOU MAKE IT MOVE	Dave Dee Dozy Beaky Mick and Tich	Fontana	4
30	36	1-2-3	Len Barry	Brunswick	14
-	37	HAVE PITY ON THE BOY	Paul and Barry Ryan	Decca	1
-	38	THUNDERBALL	Tom Jones	Decca	2
36	39	ATTACK	Toys	Stateside	2
-	40	UPTIGHT	Stevie Wonder ●	Tamla-Motown	1

WEEK ENDING 10 FEBRUARY 1966

LW	TW	Title	Artist	Label	Wks
1	1	MICHELLE	Overlanders	Pye	5
4	2	YOU WERE ON MY MIND	Crispian St. Peters	Decca	5
3	3	SPANISH FLEA	Herb Alpert and the Tijuana Brass	Pye	9
18	4	THESE BOOTS ARE MADE FOR WALKIN'	Nancy Sinatra	Reprise	3
5	5	LOVE'S JUST A BROKEN HEART	Cilla Black	Parlophone	4
2	6	KEEP ON RUNNING	Spencer Davis Group	Fontana	10
14	7	GROOVY KIND OF LOVE	Mindbenders	Fontana	5
6	8	A MUST TO AVOID	Herman's Hermits	Columbia	8
21	9	MIRROR MIRROR	Pinkerton's Assorted Colours	Decca	4
16	10	LIKE A BABY	Len Barry	Brunswick	4
19	11	GIRL	St. Louis Union	Decca	4
13	12	MY GIRL	Otis Redding	Atlantic	10
7	13	DAY TRIPPER/WE CAN WORK IT OUT	Beatles	Parlophone	10
-	14	NINETEENTH NERVOUS BREAKDOWN	Rolling Stones	Decca	1
8	15	LET'S HANG ON	Four Seasons	Philips	13
11	16	MICHELLE	David and Jonathan	Columbia	5
9	17	MY SHIP IS COMING IN	Walker Brothers	Philips	11
37	18	HAVE PITY ON THE BOY	Paul and Barry Ryan	Decca	2
-	19	TOMORROW	Sandie Shaw	Pye	1
10	20	TILL THE END OF THE DAY	Kinks	Pye	11
31	21	LITTLE BY LITTLE	Dusty Springfield	Philips	2
27	22	TCHAIKOVSKY ONE	Second City Sound	Decca	3
17	23	ENGLAND SWINGS	Roger Miller	Philips	6
12	24	THE RIVER	Ken Dodd	Columbia	13
24	25	BYE BYE BLUES	Bert Kaempfert	Polydor	6
29	26	SECOND HAND ROSE	Barbra Streisand	CBS	3
23	27	CAN YOU PLEASE CRAWL OUT YOUR WINDOW	Bob Dylan	CBS	3
20	28	WIND ME UP (LET ME GO)	Cliff Richard	Columbia	14
15	29	THE CARNIVAL IS OVER	Seekers	Columbia	15
-	30	SHA LA LA LA LEE	Small Faces	Decca	1
40	31	UPTIGHT	Stevie Wonder	Tamla-Motown	2
26	32	TAKE ME TO YOUR HEART AGAIN	Vince Hill	Columbia	5
33	33	BREAKIN' UP IS BREAKIN' MY HEART	Roy Orbison	London	3
-	34	GET OUT OF MY LIFE WOMAN	Lee Dorsey	Stateside	1
-	35	MY LOVE	Petula Clark	Pye	1
-	36	GIRL	Truth ●	Pye	1
-	37	THINK	Chris Farlowe and the Thunderbirds ●	Immediate	1
25	38	TEARS	Ken Dodd	Columbia	24
32	39	RECOVERY	Fontella Bass	Chess	3
-	40	YOU'VE COME BACK	P.J. Proby	Liberty	1

WEEK ENDING 17 FEBRUARY 1966

LW	TW	Title	Artist	Label	Wks
4	1	THESE BOOTS ARE MADE FOR WALKIN'	Nancy Sinatra	Reprise	4
14	2	NINETEENTH NERVOUS BREAKDOWN	Rolling Stones	Decca	2
2	3	YOU WERE ON MY MIND	Crispian St. Peters	Decca	6
3	4	SPANISH FLEA	Herb Alpert and the Tijuana Brass	Pye	10
1	5	MICHELLE	Overlanders	Pye	6
7	6	GROOVY KIND OF LOVE	Mindbenders	Fontana	6
5	7	LOVE'S JUST A BROKEN HEART	Cilla Black	Parlophone	5
6	8	KEEP ON RUNNING	Spencer Davis Group	Fontana	11
19	9	TOMORROW	Sandie Shaw	Pye	2
9	10	MIRROR MIRROR	Pinkerton's Assorted Colours	Decca	5
8	11	A MUST TO AVOID	Herman's Hermits	Columbia	9
11	12	GIRL	St. Louis Union	Decca	5

■Apart from their own double-sided former number one, Beatles compositions are at numbers one, 12, 20, 24 and 32. The man who first recorded them in Germany, Bert Kaempfert, is at number 25 (27.01.66) ■ *Girl*, a Beatles cover, peaks at number 11 (10.02.66) ■ Two Jagger, Richard compositions enter the chart, one by the Rolling Stones and one by Chris Farlowe (10.02.66)■

February 1966

□ Highest position disc reached ● Act's first ever week on chart

LW	TW	Title	Artist	Label	Wks
10	13	LIKE A BABY	Len Barry	Brunswick	5
26	[14]	SECOND HAND ROSE	Barbra Streisand	CBS	4
35	15	MY LOVE	Petula Clark	Pye	2
12	16	MY GIRL	Otis Redding	Atlantic	11
21	[17]	LITTLE BY LITTLE	Dusty Springfield	Philips	3
30	18	SHA LA LA LA LEE	Small Faces	Decca	2
18	19	HAVE PITY ON THE BOY	Paul and Barry Ryan	Decca	3
16	20	MICHELLE	David and Jonathan	Columbia	6
15	21	LET'S HANG ON	Four Seasons	Philips	14
33	[22]	BREAKIN' UP IS BREAKIN' MY HEART	Roy Orbison	London	4
32	23	TAKE ME TO YOUR HEART AGAIN	Vince Hill	Columbia	6
22	24	TCHAIKOVSKY ONE	Second City Sound	Decca	4
27	25	CAN YOU PLEASE CRAWL OUT YOUR WINDOW	Bob Dylan	CBS	4
31	26	UPTIGHT	Stevie Wonder	Tamla-Motown	3
13	27	DAY TRIPPER/WE CAN WORK IT OUT	Beatles	Parlophone	11
20	28	TILL THE END OF THE DAY	Kinks	Pye	12
34	29	GET OUT OF MY LIFE WOMAN	Lee Dorsey	Stateside	2
28	30	WIND ME UP (LET ME GO)	Cliff Richard	Columbia	15
17	31	MY SHIP IS COMING IN	Walker Brothers	Philips	12
36	32	GIRL	Truth	Pye	2
25	33	BYE BYE BLUES	Bert Kaempfert	Polydor	7
23	34	ENGLAND SWINGS	Roger Miller	Philips	7
-	35	BARBARA ANN	Beach Boys	Capitol	1
-	36	MAKE THE WORLD GO AWAY	Eddy Arnold ●	RCA	1
-	37	DON'T MAKE ME OVER	Swinging Blue Jeans	HMV	2
-	38	INSIDE - LOOKING OUT	Animals	Decca	1
-	39	THIS GOLDEN RING	Fortunes	Decca	1
40	40	YOU'VE COME BACK	P.J. Proby	Liberty	2

WEEK ENDING 24 FEBRUARY 1966

LW	TW	Title	Artist	Label	Wks
1	[1]	THESE BOOTS ARE MADE FOR WALKIN'	Nancy Sinatra	Reprise	5
2	[2]	NINETEENTH NERVOUS BREAKDOWN	Rolling Stones	Decca	3
6	3	GROOVY KIND OF LOVE	Mindbenders	Fontana	7
3	4	YOU WERE ON MY MIND	Crispian St. Peters	Decca	7
15	5	MY LOVE	Petula Clark	Pye	3
4	6	SPANISH FLEA	Herb Alpert and the Tijuana Brass	Pye	11
18	7	SHA LA LA LA LEE	Small Faces	Decca	3
35	8	BARBARA ANN	Beach Boys	Capitol	2
9	[9]	TOMORROW	Sandie Shaw	Pye	3
7	10	LOVE'S JUST A BROKEN HEART	Cilla Black	Parlophone	6
5	11	MICHELLE	Overlanders	Pye	7
10	12	MIRROR MIRROR	Pinkerton's Assorted Colours	Decca	6
38	13	INSIDE - LOOKING OUT	Animals	Decca	2
14	[14]	SECOND HAND ROSE	Barbra Streisand	CBS	5
-	15	BACKSTAGE	Gene Pitney	Stateside	1
12	16	GIRL	St. Louis Union	Decca	6
17	[17]	LITTLE BY LITTLE	Dusty Springfield	Philips	4
26	18	UPTIGHT	Stevie Wonder	Tamla-Motown	4
13	19	LIKE A BABY	Len Barry	Brunswick	6
8	20	KEEP ON RUNNING	Spencer Davis Group	Fontana	12
36	21	MAKE THE WORLD GO AWAY	Eddy Arnold	RCA	2
29	[22]	GET OUT OF MY LIFE WOMAN	Lee Dorsey	Stateside	3
16	23	MY GIRL	Otis Redding	Atlantic	12
19	24	HAVE PITY ON THE BOY	Paul and Barry Ryan	Decca	4
40	[25]	YOU'VE COME BACK	P.J. Proby	Liberty	3
11	26	A MUST TO AVOID	Herman's Hermits	Columbia	10
32	[27]	GIRL	Truth	Pye	3
22	28	BREAKIN' UP IS BREAKIN' MY HEART	Roy Orbison	London	5
24	29	TCHAIKOVSKY ONE	Second City Sound	Decca	5
-	30	WHAT NOW MY LOVE	Sonny and Cher	Atlantic	1
37	[31]	DON'T MAKE ME OVER	Swinging Blue Jeans	HMV	3
39	32	THIS GOLDEN RING	Fortunes	Decca	2
-	33	BLUE RIVER	Elvis Presley	RCA	1
33	34	BYE BYE BLUES	Bert Kaempfert	Polydor	8
25	35	CAN YOU PLEASE CRAWL OUT YOUR WINDOW	Bob Dylan	CBS	5
-	36	JENNY TAKE A RIDE	Mitch Ryder and the Detroit Wheels ●	Stateside	1
21	37	LET'S HANG ON	Four Seasons	Philips	15
-	38	TROUBLE IS MY MIDDLE NAME	Four Pennies	Philips	1
-	39	YOU DON'T LOVE ME	Gary Walker ●	CBS	1
-	40	LIGHTNING STRIKES	Lou Christie ●	MGM	1

WEEK ENDING 3 MARCH 1966

LW	TW	Title	Artist	Label	Wks
1	[1]	THESE BOOTS ARE MADE FOR WALKIN'	Nancy Sinatra	Reprise	6
2	[2]	NINETEENTH NERVOUS BREAKDOWN	Rolling Stones	Decca	4
3	3	GROOVY KIND OF LOVE	Mindbenders	Fontana	8
5	[4]	MY LOVE	Petula Clark	Pye	4
7	5	SHA LA LA LA LEE	Small Faces	Decca	4
8	6	BARBARA ANN	Beach Boys	Capitol	3
15	7	BACKSTAGE	Gene Pitney	Stateside	2
6	8	SPANISH FLEA	Herb Alpert and the Tijuana Brass	Pye	12
4	9	YOU WERE ON MY MIND	Crispian St. Peters	Decca	8
21	10	MAKE THE WORLD GO AWAY	Eddy Arnold	RCA	3
9	11	TOMORROW	Sandie Shaw	Pye	4
13	[12]	INSIDE - LOOKING OUT	Animals	Decca	3
10	13	LOVE'S JUST A BROKEN HEART	Cilla Black	Parlophone	7
18	[14]	UPTIGHT	Stevie Wonder	Tamla-Motown	5
16	15	GIRL	St. Louis Union	Decca	7
40	16	LIGHTNING STRIKES	Lou Christie	MGM	2
12	17	MIRROR MIRROR	Pinkerton's Assorted Colours	Decca	7
-	18	I CAN'T LET GO	Hollies	Parlophone	1
11	19	MICHELLE	Overlanders	Pye	8
17	20	LITTLE BY LITTLE	Dusty Springfield	Philips	5
14	21	SECOND HAND ROSE	Barbra Streisand	CBS	6
30	22	WHAT NOW MY LOVE	Sonny and Cher	Atlantic	2
33	23	BLUE RIVER	Elvis Presley	RCA	2
22	24	GET OUT OF MY LIFE WOMAN	Lee Dorsey	Stateside	4
25	[25]	YOU'VE COME BACK	P.J. Proby	Liberty	4
-	26	THE SUN AIN'T GONNA SHINE ANYMORE	Walker Brothers	Philips	1
19	27	LIKE A BABY	Len Barry	Brunswick	7
-	28	SHAPES OF THINGS	Yardbirds	Columbia	1
27	29	GIRL	Truth	Pye	4
39	30	YOU DON'T LOVE ME	Gary Walker	CBS	2
32	31	THIS GOLDEN RING	Fortunes	Decca	3
38	[32]	TROUBLE IS MY MIDDLE NAME	Four Pennies	Philips	2
36	[33]	JENNY TAKE A RIDE	Mitch Ryder and the Detroit Wheels	Stateside	2
-	34	DEDICATED FOLLOWER OF FASHION	Kinks	Pye	1
-	[35]	I'LL NEVER QUITE GET OVER YOU	Billy Fury	Decca	1
31	36	DON'T MAKE ME OVER	Swinging Blue Jeans	HMV	4
23	37	MY GIRL	Otis Redding	Atlantic	13
-	[38]	FLOWERS ON THE WALL	Statler Brothers ●	CBS	1
24	39	HAVE PITY ON THE BOY	Paul and Barry Ryan	Decca	5
-	40	MAY EACH DAY	Andy Williams	CBS	1

WEEK ENDING 10 MARCH 1966

LW	TW	Title	Artist	Label	Wks
1	[1]	THESE BOOTS ARE MADE FOR WALKIN'	Nancy Sinatra	Reprise	7
3	[2]	GROOVY KIND OF LOVE	Mindbenders	Fontana	9
6	[3]	BARBARA ANN	Beach Boys	Capitol	4
7	[4]	BACKSTAGE	Gene Pitney	Stateside	3
8	5	SPANISH FLEA	Herb Alpert and the Tijuana Brass	Pye	13
5	6	SHA LA LA LA LEE	Small Faces	Decca	5
18	7	I CAN'T LET GO	Hollies	Parlophone	2
2	8	NINETEENTH NERVOUS BREAKDOWN	Rolling Stones	Decca	5
4	9	MY LOVE	Petula Clark	Pye	5
26	10	THE SUN AIN'T GONNA SHINE ANYMORE	Walker Brothers	Philips	2
11	11	TOMORROW	Sandie Shaw	Pye	5
12	[12]	INSIDE - LOOKING OUT	Animals	Decca	4
9	13	YOU WERE ON MY MIND	Crispian St. Peters	Decca	9
16	14	LIGHTNING STRIKES	Lou Christie	MGM	3
31	[15]	THIS GOLDEN RING	Fortunes	Decca	4
10	16	MAKE THE WORLD GO AWAY	Eddy Arnold	RCA	4

In these weeks ■ The Rolling Stones spend three weeks at number two behind Nancy Sinatra. A few months later they will spend two more weeks at number two behind her father Frank (03.03.66) ■ Gary Walker's first solo hit is swamped by the success of the Walker Brothers' fourth hit (03.03.66) ■ The Mindbenders prove to be more successful chartwise than their erstwhile boss, Wayne Fontana (10.03.66)■

LW	TW	Title	Artist	Label	Wks
28	17	SHAPES OF THINGS	Yardbirds	Columbia	2
14	18	UPTIGHT	Stevie Wonder	Tamla-Motown	6
22	19	WHAT NOW MY LOVE	Sonny and Cher	Atlantic	3
34	20	DEDICATED FOLLOWER OF FASHION	Kinks	Pye	2
21	21	SECOND HAND ROSE	Barbra Streisand	CBS	7
23	22	BLUE RIVER	Elvis Presley	RCA	3
17	23	MIRROR MIRROR	Pinkerton's Assorted Colours	Decca	8
13	24	LOVE'S JUST A BROKEN HEART	Cilla Black	Parlophone	8
15	25	GIRL	St. Louis Union	Decca	8
30	26	YOU DON'T LOVE ME	Gary Walker	CBS	3
24	27	GET OUT OF MY LIFE WOMAN	Lee Dorsey	Stateside	5
20	28	LITTLE BY LITTLE	Dusty Springfield	Philips	6
-	29	WOMAN	Peter and Gordon	Columbia	1
25	30	YOU'VE COME BACK	P.J. Proby	Liberty	5
-	31	HOLD TIGHT	Dave Dee Dozy Beaky Mick and Tich	Fontana	1
19	32	MICHELLE	Overlanders	Pye	9
-	33	SUBSTITUTE	Who	Reaction	1
32	34	TROUBLE IS MY MIDDLE NAME	Four Pennies	Philips	3
33	35	JENNY TAKE A RIDE	Mitch Ryder and the Detroit Wheels	Stateside	3
40	36	MAY EACH DAY	Andy Williams	CBS	2
27	37	LIKE A BABY	Len Barry	Brunswick	8
29	38	GIRL	Truth	Pye	5
-	39	I GOT YOU	James Brown	Pye	1
-	40	TAKE ME TO YOUR HEART AGAIN	Vince Hill	Columbia	7

WEEK ENDING 17 MARCH 1966

LW	TW	Title	Artist	Label	Wks
10	1	THE SUN AIN'T GONNA SHINE ANYMORE	Walker Brothers	Philips	3
7	2	I CAN'T LET GO	Hollies	Parlophone	3
6	3	SHA LA LA LA LEE	Small Faces	Decca	6
2	4	GROOVY KIND OF LOVE	Mindbenders	Fontana	10
3	5	BARBARA ANN	Beach Boys	Capitol	5
17	6	SHAPES OF THINGS	Yardbirds	Columbia	3
4	7	BACKSTAGE	Gene Pitney	Stateside	4
20	8	DEDICATED FOLLOWER OF FASHION	Kinks	Pye	3
1	9	THESE BOOTS ARE MADE FOR WALKIN'	Nancy Sinatra	Reprise	8
16	10	MAKE THE WORLD GO AWAY	Eddy Arnold	RCA	5
14	11	LIGHTNING STRIKES	Lou Christie	MGM	4
8	12	NINETEENTH NERVOUS BREAKDOWN	Rolling Stones	Decca	6
5	13	SPANISH FLEA	Herb Alpert and the Tijuana Brass	Pye	14
9	14	MY LOVE	Petula Clark	Pye	6
19	15	WHAT NOW MY LOVE	Sonny and Cher	Atlantic	4
15	16	THIS GOLDEN RING	Fortunes	Decca	5
12	17	INSIDE - LOOKING OUT	Animals	Decca	5
33	18	SUBSTITUTE	Who	Reaction	2
36	19	MAY EACH DAY	Andy Williams	CBS	3
13	20	YOU WERE ON MY MIND	Crispian St. Peters	Decca	10
-	21	ELUSIVE BUTTERFLY	Bob Lind ●	Fontana	1
21	22	SECOND HAND ROSE	Barbra Streisand	CBS	8
31	23	HOLD TIGHT	Dave Dee Dozy Beaky Mick and Tich	Fontana	2
18	24	UPTIGHT	Stevie Wonder	Tamla-Motown	7
11	25	TOMORROW	Sandie Shaw	Pye	6
22	26	BLUE RIVER	Elvis Presley	RCA	4
26	27	YOU DON'T LOVE ME	Gary Walker	CBS	4
29	28	WOMAN	Peter and Gordon	Columbia	2
39	29	I GOT YOU	James Brown	Pye	2
-	30	A MAN WITHOUT LOVE	Kenneth McKellar ●	Decca	1
23	31	MIRROR MIRROR	Pinkerton's Assorted Colours	Decca	9
-	32	HEARTACHES	Vince Hill	Columbia	1
24	33	LOVE'S JUST A BROKEN HEART	Cilla Black	Parlophone	9
27	34	GET OUT OF MY LIFE WOMAN	Lee Dorsey	Stateside	6
-	35	ELUSIVE BUTTERFLY	Val Doonican	Decca	1
25	36	GIRL	St. Louis Union	Decca	9
28	37	LITTLE BY LITTLE	Dusty Springfield	Philips	7
-	38	I MET A GIRL	Shadows	Columbia	1
-	39	SOUND OF SILENCE	Bachelors	Decca	1
30	40	YOU'VE COME BACK	P.J. Proby	Liberty	6

WEEK ENDING 24 MARCH 1966

March 1966

□ Highest position disc reached ● Act's first ever week on chart

LW	TW	Title	Artist	Label	Wks
1	1	THE SUN AIN'T GONNA SHINE ANYMORE	Walker Brothers	Philips	4
2	2	I CAN'T LET GO	Hollies	Parlophone	4
6	3	SHAPES OF THINGS	Yardbirds	Columbia	4
3	4	SHA LA LA LA LEE	Small Faces	Decca	7
5	5	BARBARA ANN	Beach Boys	Capitol	6
8	6	DEDICATED FOLLOWER OF FASHION	Kinks	Pye	4
4	7	GROOVY KIND OF LOVE	Mindbenders	Fontana	11
21	8	ELUSIVE BUTTERFLY	Bob Lind	Fontana	2
7	9	BACKSTAGE	Gene Pitney	Stateside	5
10	10	MAKE THE WORLD GO AWAY	Eddy Arnold	RCA	6
11	11	LIGHTNING STRIKES	Lou Christie	MGM	5
9	12	THESE BOOTS ARE MADE FOR WALKIN'	Nancy Sinatra	Reprise	9
15	13	WHAT NOW MY LOVE	Sonny and Cher	Atlantic	5
23	14	HOLD TIGHT	Dave Dee Dozy Beaky Mick and Tich	Fontana	3
18	15	SUBSTITUTE	Who	Reaction	3
14	16	MY LOVE	Petula Clark	Pye	7
12	17	NINETEENTH NERVOUS BREAKDOWN	Rolling Stones	Decca	7
35	18	ELUSIVE BUTTERFLY	Val Doonican	Decca	2
13	19	SPANISH FLEA	Herb Alpert and the Tijuana Brass	Pye	15
39	20	SOUND OF SILENCE	Bachelors	Decca	2
17	21	INSIDE - LOOKING OUT	Animals	Decca	6
19	22	MAY EACH DAY	Andy Williams	CBS	4
22	23	SECOND HAND ROSE	Barbra Streisand	CBS	9
16	24	THIS GOLDEN RING	Fortunes	Decca	6
20	25	YOU WERE ON MY MIND	Crispian St. Peters	Decca	11
38	26	I MET A GIRL	Shadows	Columbia	2
26	27	BLUE RIVER	Elvis Presley	RCA	5
32	28	HEARTACHES	Vince Hill	Columbia	2
-	29	SOMEBODY HELP ME	Spencer Davis Group	Fontana	1
24	30	UPTIGHT	Stevie Wonder	Tamla-Motown	8
27	31	YOU DON'T LOVE ME	Gary Walker	CBS	5
29	32	I GOT YOU	James Brown	Pye	3
30	33	A MAN WITHOUT LOVE	Kenneth McKellar	Decca	2
28	34	WOMAN	Peter and Gordon	Columbia	3
-	35	BLUE TURNS TO GREY	Cliff Richard	Columbia	1
-	36	634-5789	Wilson Pickett	Atlantic	1
25	37	TOMORROW	Sandie Shaw	Pye	7
-	38	SOMEDAY ONE DAY	Seekers	Columbia	1
-	39	YOU WON'T BE LEAVIN'	Herman's Hermits	Columbia	1
-	40	TIJUANA TAXI	Herb Alpert and the Tijuana Brass	Pye	1

WEEK ENDING 31 MARCH 1966

LW	TW	Title	Artist	Label	Wks
1	1	THE SUN AIN'T GONNA SHINE ANYMORE	Walker Brothers	Philips	5
2	2	I CAN'T LET GO	Hollies	Parlophone	5
3	3	SHAPES OF THINGS	Yardbirds	Columbia	5
6	4	DEDICATED FOLLOWER OF FASHION	Kinks	Pye	5
8	5	ELUSIVE BUTTERFLY	Bob Lind	Fontana	3
18	6	ELUSIVE BUTTERFLY	Val Doonican	Decca	3
4	7	SHA LA LA LA LEE	Small Faces	Decca	8
10	8	MAKE THE WORLD GO AWAY	Eddy Arnold	RCA	7
5	9	BARBARA ANN	Beach Boys	Capitol	7
29	10	SOMEBODY HELP ME	Spencer Davis Group	Fontana	2
14	11	HOLD TIGHT	Dave Dee Dozy Beaky Mick and Tich	Fontana	4
20	12	SOUND OF SILENCE	Bachelors	Decca	3
13	13	WHAT NOW MY LOVE	Sonny and Cher	Atlantic	6
15	14	SUBSTITUTE	Who	Reaction	4
7	15	GROOVY KIND OF LOVE	Mindbenders	Fontana	12
9	16	BACKSTAGE	Gene Pitney	Stateside	6
12	17	THESE BOOTS ARE MADE FOR WALKIN'	Nancy Sinatra	Reprise	10
11	18	LIGHTNING STRIKES	Lou Christie	MGM	6
35	19	BLUE TURNS TO GREY	Cliff Richard	Columbia	2
19	20	SPANISH FLEA	Herb Alpert and the Tijuana Brass	Pye	16
38	21	SOMEDAY ONE DAY	Seekers	Columbia	2
26	22	I MET A GIRL	Shadows	Columbia	3
22	23	MAY EACH DAY	Andy Williams	CBS	5
16	24	MY LOVE	Petula Clark	Pye	8

■Nancy Sinatra's spectacular plummet from the top equals the fall inflicted on the Temperance Seven five years earlier as the biggest drop since the Top 40 began. Harry Belafonte's all time record with *Mary's Boy Child* (one to 12 in January 1958) is unchallenged (17.03.66) ■ For a third consecutive week, the record at number four falls to number seven, and the record at number 12 drops to number 17 (31.03.6)■

March 1966

□ Highest position disc reached ● Act's first ever week on chart

LW	TW	Title	Artist	Label	Wks
39	25	YOU WON'T BE LEAVIN'	Herman's Hermits	Columbia	2
-	26	BALLAD OF THE GREEN BERETS	S/Sgt Barry Sadler ●	RCA	1
23	27	SECOND HAND ROSE	Barbra Streisand	CBS	10
28	[28]	HEARTACHES	Vince Hill	Columbia	3
-	29	HOMEWARD BOUND	Simon and Garfunkel ●	CBS	1
21	30	INSIDE - LOOKING OUT	Animals	Decca	7
-	31	SUPERGIRL	Graham Bonney ●	Columbia	1
27	32	BLUE RIVER	Elvis Presley	RCA	6
25	33	YOU WERE ON MY MIND	Crispian St. Peters	Decca	12
-	34	ALFIE	Cilla Black	Parlophone	1
24	35	THIS GOLDEN RING	Fortunes	Decca	7
17	36	NINETEENTH NERVOUS BREAKDOWN	Rolling Stones	Decca	8
40	[37]	TIJUANA TAXI	Herb Alpert and the Tijuana Brass	Pye	2
-	38	I PUT A SPELL ON YOU	Alan Price Set ●	Decca	1
-	39	BANG BANG	Cher	Liberty	1
-	40	A LEGAL MATTER	Who	Brunswick	1

WEEK ENDING 7 APRIL 1966

LW	TW	Title	Artist	Label	Wks
1	[1]	THE SUN AIN'T GONNA SHINE ANYMORE	Walker Brothers	Philips	6
10	2	SOMEBODY HELP ME	Spencer Davis Group	Fontana	3
2	3	I CAN'T LET GO	Hollies	Parlophone	6
4	[4]	DEDICATED FOLLOWER OF FASHION	Kinks	Pye	6
5	[5]	ELUSIVE BUTTERFLY	Bob Lind	Fontana	4
11	6	HOLD TIGHT	Dave Dee Dozy Beaky Mick and Tich	Fontana	5
6	7	ELUSIVE BUTTERFLY	Val Doonican	Decca	4
3	8	SHAPES OF THINGS	Yardbirds	Columbia	6
12	9	SOUND OF SILENCE	Bachelors	Decca	4
8	10	MAKE THE WORLD GO AWAY	Eddy Arnold	RCA	8
14	11	SUBSTITUTE	Who	Reaction	5
7	12	SHA LA LA LA LEE	Small Faces	Decca	9
34	13	ALFIE	Cilla Black	Parlophone	2
9	14	BARBARA ANN	Beach Boys	Capitol	8
19	[15]	BLUE TURNS TO GREY	Cliff Richard	Columbia	3
-	16	YOU DON'T HAVE TO SAY YOU LOVE ME	Dusty Springfield	Philips	1
13	17	WHAT NOW MY LOVE	Sonny and Cher	Atlantic	7
39	18	BANG BANG	Cher	Liberty	2
21	19	SOMEDAY ONE DAY	Seekers	Columbia	3
17	20	THESE BOOTS ARE MADE FOR WALKIN'	Nancy Sinatra	Reprise	11
25	21	YOU WON'T BE LEAVIN'	Herman's Hermits	Columbia	3
16	22	BACKSTAGE	Gene Pitney	Stateside	7
15	23	GROOVY KIND OF LOVE	Mindbenders	Fontana	13
38	24	I PUT A SPELL ON YOU	Alan Price Set	Decca	2
18	25	LIGHTNING STRIKES	Lou Christie	MGM	7
-	26	PIED PIPER	Crispian St. Peters	Decca	1
29	27	HOMEWARD BOUND	Simon and Garfunkel	CBS	2
22	28	I MET A GIRL	Shadows	Columbia	4
26	29	BALLAD OF THE GREEN BERETS	S/Sgt Barry Sadler	RCA	2
20	30	SPANISH FLEA	Herb Alpert and the Tijuana Brass	Pye	17
24	31	MY LOVE	Petula Clark	Pye	9
31	32	SUPERGIRL	Graham Bonney	Columbia	2
28	33	HEARTACHES	Vince Hill	Columbia	4
40	34	A LEGAL MATTER	Who	Brunswick	2
-	35	TWINKLE TOES	Roy Orbison	London	1
-	36	FRANKIE AND JOHNNY	Elvis Presley	RCA	1
23	37	MAY EACH DAY	Andy Williams	CBS	6
-	38	SATISFACTION	Otis Redding	Atlantic	1
30	39	INSIDE - LOOKING OUT	Animals	Decca	8
37	40	TIJUANA TAXI	Herb Alpert and the Tijuana Brass	Pye	3

WEEK ENDING 14 APRIL 1966

LW	TW	Title	Artist	Label	Wks
2	[1]	SOMEBODY HELP ME	Spencer Davis Group	Fontana	4
1	2	THE SUN AIN'T GONNA SHINE ANYMORE	Walker Brothers	Philips	7
9	[3]	SOUND OF SILENCE	Bachelors	Decca	5
6	[4]	HOLD TIGHT	Dave Dee Dozy Beaky Mick and Tich	Fontana	6
11	[5]	SUBSTITUTE	Who	Reaction	6
7	6	ELUSIVE BUTTERFLY	Val Doonican	Decca	5
5	7	ELUSIVE BUTTERFLY	Bob Lind	Fontana	5
10	8	MAKE THE WORLD GO AWAY	Eddy Arnold	RCA	9
4	9	DEDICATED FOLLOWER OF FASHION	Kinks	Pye	7
16	10	YOU DON'T HAVE TO SAY YOU LOVE ME	Dusty Springfield	Philips	2
19	[11]	SOMEDAY ONE DAY	Seekers	Columbia	4
24	12	I PUT A SPELL ON YOU	Alan Price Set	Decca	3
18	13	BANG BANG	Cher	Liberty	3
8	14	SHAPES OF THINGS	Yardbirds	Columbia	7
26	15	PIED PIPER	Crispian St. Peters	Decca	2
15	16	BLUE TURNS TO GREY	Cliff Richard	Columbia	4
27	17	HOMEWARD BOUND	Simon and Garfunkel	CBS	3
13	18	ALFIE	Cilla Black	Parlophone	3
14	19	BARBARA ANN	Beach Boys	Capitol	9
21	[20]	YOU WON'T BE LEAVIN'	Herman's Hermits	Columbia	4
20	21	THESE BOOTS ARE MADE FOR WALKIN'	Nancy Sinatra	Reprise	12
17	22	WHAT NOW MY LOVE	Sonny and Cher	Atlantic	8
-	23	DAYDREAM	Lovin' Spoonful ●	Pye	1
12	24	SHA LA LA LA LEE	Small Faces	Decca	10
3	25	I CAN'T LET GO	Hollies	Parlophone	7
36	26	FRANKIE AND JOHNNY	Elvis Presley	RCA	2
32	27	SUPERGIRL	Graham Bonney	Columbia	3
29	28	BALLAD OF THE GREEN BERETS	S/Sgt Barry Sadler	RCA	3
35	[29]	TWINKLE TOES	Roy Orbison	London	2
22	30	BACKSTAGE	Gene Pitney	Stateside	8
30	31	SPANISH FLEA	Herb Alpert and the Tijuana Brass	Pye	18
34	[32]	A LEGAL MATTER	Who	Brunswick	3
38	[33]	SATISFACTION	Otis Redding	Atlantic	2
25	34	LIGHTNING STRIKES	Lou Christie	MGM	8
-	35	HIGHWAY CODE	Master Singers ●	Parlophone	1
-	36	THAT'S NICE	Neil Christian ●	Strike	1
23	37	GROOVY KIND OF LOVE	Mindbenders	Fontana	14
-	38	PLEASE STAY	Cryin' Shames ●	Decca	1
-	39	(YOU'RE MY) SOUL AND INSPIRATION	Righteous Brothers	Verve	1
-	40	WALKING MY CAT NAMED DOG	Norma Tanega ●	Stateside	1

WEEK ENDING 21 APRIL 1966

LW	TW	Title	Artist	Label	Wks
1	[1]	SOMEBODY HELP ME	Spencer Davis Group	Fontana	5
10	2	YOU DON'T HAVE TO SAY YOU LOVE ME	Dusty Springfield	Philips	3
3	[3]	SOUND OF SILENCE	Bachelors	Decca	6
4	[4]	HOLD TIGHT	Dave Dee Dozy Beaky Mick and Tich	Fontana	7
6	[5]	ELUSIVE BUTTERFLY	Val Doonican	Decca	6
13	6	BANG BANG	Cher	Liberty	4
2	7	THE SUN AIN'T GONNA SHINE ANYMORE	Walker Brothers	Philips	8
5	8	SUBSTITUTE	Who	Reaction	7
12	[9]	I PUT A SPELL ON YOU	Alan Price Set	Decca	4
15	10	PIED PIPER	Crispian St. Peters	Decca	3
7	11	ELUSIVE BUTTERFLY	Bob Lind	Fontana	6
18	12	ALFIE	Cilla Black	Parlophone	4
9	13	DEDICATED FOLLOWER OF FASHION	Kinks	Pye	8
11	14	SOMEDAY ONE DAY	Seekers	Columbia	5
17	15	HOMEWARD BOUND	Simon and Garfunkel	CBS	4
8	16	MAKE THE WORLD GO AWAY	Eddy Arnold	RCA	10
23	17	DAYDREAM	Lovin' Spoonful	Pye	2
16	18	BLUE TURNS TO GREY	Cliff Richard	Columbia	5
14	19	SHAPES OF THINGS	Yardbirds	Columbia	8
20	[20]	YOU WON'T BE LEAVIN'	Herman's Hermits	Columbia	5
36	21	THAT'S NICE	Neil Christian	Strike	2
-	22	PRETTY FLAMINGO	Manfred Mann	HMV	1
26	23	FRANKIE AND JOHNNY	Elvis Presley	RCA	3
27	24	SUPERGIRL	Graham Bonney	Columbia	4
28	25	BALLAD OF THE GREEN BERETS	S/Sgt Barry Sadler	RCA	4
25	26	I CAN'T LET GO	Hollies	Parlophone	8
21	27	THESE BOOTS ARE MADE FOR WALKIN'	Nancy Sinatra	Reprise	13

In these weeks ■ The Hollies' *I Can't Let Go* tumbles from number three to number 25, the biggest ever drop from one of the top three positions, and the only time a record has fallen out of the Top 20 from the top three (14.04.66) ■ The *Elusive Butterfly* battle between writer Bob Lind and Ireland's Val Doonican ends in a tie, when Doonican's version matches the peak of number five achieved by Lind three weeks before (21.04.66) ■

LW	TW	Title	Artist	Label	Wks
22	28	WHAT NOW MY LOVE	Sonny and Cher	Atlantic	9
29	29	TWINKLE TOES	Roy Orbison	London	3
19	30	BARBARA ANN	Beach Boys	Capitol	10
38	31	PLEASE STAY	Cryin' Shames	Decca	2
39	32	(YOU'RE MY) SOUL AND INSPIRATION	Righteous Brothers	Verve	2
40	33	WALKING MY CAT NAMED DOG	Norma Tanega	Stateside	2
35	34	HIGHWAY CODE	Master Singers	Parlophone	2
32	35	A LEGAL MATTER	Who	Brunswick	4
-	36	SLOOP JOHN B	Beach Boys	Capitol	1
24	37	SHA LA LA LA LEE	Small Faces	Decca	11
33	38	SATISFACTION	Otis Redding	Atlantic	3
31	39	SPANISH FLEA	Herb Alpert and the Tijuana Brass	Pye	19
-	40	I FOUGHT THE LAW	Bobby Fuller Four ●	London	1

WEEK ENDING 28 APRIL 1966

LW	TW	Title	Artist	Label	Wks
2	1	YOU DON'T HAVE TO SAY YOU LOVE ME	Dusty Springfield	Philips	4
22	2	PRETTY FLAMINGO	Manfred Mann	HMV	2
1	3	SOMEBODY HELP ME	Spencer Davis Group	Fontana	6
6	4	BANG BANG	Cher	Liberty	5
4	5	HOLD TIGHT	Dave Dee Dozy Beaky Mick and Tich	Fontana	8
17	6	DAYDREAM	Lovin' Spoonful	Pye	3
3	7	SOUND OF SILENCE	Bachelors	Decca	7
10	8	PIED PIPER	Crispian St. Peters	Decca	4
9	9	I PUT A SPELL ON YOU	Alan Price Set	Decca	5
12	10	ALFIE	Cilla Black	Parlophone	5
8	11	SUBSTITUTE	Who	Reaction	8
15	12	HOMEWARD BOUND	Simon and Garfunkel	CBS	5
36	13	SLOOP JOHN B	Beach Boys	Capitol	2
7	14	THE SUN AIN'T GONNA SHINE ANYMORE	Walker Brothers	Philips	9
14	15	SOMEDAY ONE DAY	Seekers	Columbia	6
5	16	ELUSIVE BUTTERFLY	Val Doonican	Decca	7
16	17	MAKE THE WORLD GO AWAY	Eddy Arnold	RCA	11
18	18	BLUE TURNS TO GREY	Cliff Richard	Columbia	6
24	19	SUPERGIRL	Graham Bonney	Columbia	5
13	20	DEDICATED FOLLOWER OF FASHION	Kinks	Pye	9
21	21	THAT'S NICE	Neil Christian	Strike	3
11	22	ELUSIVE BUTTERFLY	Bob Lind	Fontana	7
23	23	FRANKIE AND JOHNNY	Elvis Presley	RCA	4
25	24	BALLAD OF THE GREEN BERETS	S/Sgt Barry Sadler	RCA	5
32	25	(YOU'RE MY) SOUL AND INSPIRATION	Righteous Brothers	Verve	3
20	26	YOU WON'T BE LEAVIN'	Herman's Hermits	Columbia	6
33	27	WALKING MY CAT NAMED DOG	Norma Tanega	Stateside	3
-	28	SHOTGUN WEDDING	Roy C ●	Island	1
19	29	SHAPES OF THINGS	Yardbirds	Columbia	9
34	30	HIGHWAY CODE	Master Singers	Parlophone	3
29	31	TWINKLE TOES	Roy Orbison	London	4
-	32	COMMUNICATION	David McCallum ●	Capitol	1
40	33	I FOUGHT THE LAW	Bobby Fuller Four	London	2
31	34	PLEASE STAY	Cryin' Shames	Decca	3
-	35	ONE OF US MUST KNOW	Bob Dylan	CBS	1
35	36	A LEGAL MATTER	Who	Brunswick	5
-	37	HOW DOES THAT GRAB YOU DARLIN'	Nancy Sinatra	Reprise	1
-	38	TAKE IT OR LEAVE IT	Searchers	Pye	1
27	39	THESE BOOTS ARE MADE FOR WALKIN'	Nancy Sinatra	Reprise	14
-	40	COME ON HOME	Wayne Fontana	Fontana	1

May 1966

□ Highest position disc reached ● Act's first ever week on chart

WEEK ENDING 5 MAY 1966

LW	TW	Title	Artist	Label	Wks
2	1	PRETTY FLAMINGO	Manfred Mann	HMV	3
6	2	DAYDREAM	Lovin' Spoonful	Pye	4
4	3	BANG BANG	Cher	Liberty	6
1	4	YOU DON'T HAVE TO SAY YOU LOVE ME	Dusty Springfield	Philips	5
13	5	SLOOP JOHN B	Beach Boys	Capitol	3
8	6	PIED PIPER	Crispian St. Peters	Decca	5
5	7	HOLD TIGHT	Dave Dee Dozy Beaky Mick and Tich	Fontana	9
7	8	SOUND OF SILENCE	Bachelors	Decca	8
10	9	ALFIE	Cilla Black	Parlophone	6
12	10	HOMEWARD BOUND	Simon and Garfunkel	CBS	6
3	11	SOMEBODY HELP ME	Spencer Davis Group	Fontana	7
11	12	SUBSTITUTE	Who	Reaction	9
9	13	I PUT A SPELL ON YOU	Alan Price Set	Decca	6
15	14	SOMEDAY ONE DAY	Seekers	Columbia	7
16	15	ELUSIVE BUTTERFLY	Val Doonican	Decca	8
21	16	THAT'S NICE	Neil Christian	Strike	4
17	17	MAKE THE WORLD GO AWAY	Eddy Arnold	RCA	12
18	18	BLUE TURNS TO GREY	Cliff Richard	Columbia	7
25	19	(YOU'RE MY) SOUL AND INSPIRATION	Righteous Brothers	Verve	4
28	20	SHOTGUN WEDDING	Roy C	Island	2
23	21	FRANKIE AND JOHNNY	Elvis Presley	RCA	5
27	22	WALKING MY CAT NAMED DOG	Norma Tanega	Stateside	4
14	23	THE SUN AIN'T GONNA SHINE ANYMORE	Walker Brothers	Philips	10
19	24	SUPERGIRL	Graham Bonney	Columbia	6
30	25	HIGHWAY CODE	Master Singers	Parlophone	4
34	26	PLEASE STAY	Cryin' Shames	Decca	4
37	27	HOW DOES THAT GRAB YOU DARLIN'	Nancy Sinatra	Reprise	2
-	28	SORROW	Merseys ●	Fontana	1
20	29	DEDICATED FOLLOWER OF FASHION	Kinks	Pye	10
40	30	COME ON HOME	Wayne Fontana	Fontana	2
38	31	TAKE IT OR LEAVE IT	Searchers	Pye	2
24	32	BALLAD OF THE GREEN BERETS	S/Sgt Barry Sadler	RCA	6
35	33	ONE OF US MUST KNOW	Bob Dylan	CBS	2
-	34	CALIFORNIA DREAMIN'	Mamas and the Papas ●	RCA	1
32	35	COMMUNICATION	David McCallum	Capitol	2
-	36	CAN'T LIVE WITH YOU (CAN'T LIVE WITHOUT YOU)	Mindbenders	Fontana	1
-	37	RHAPSODY IN THE RAIN	Lou Christie	MGM	1
22	38	ELUSIVE BUTTERFLY	Bob Lind	Fontana	8
26	39	YOU WON'T BE LEAVIN'	Herman's Hermits	Columbia	7
31	40	TWINKLE TOES	Roy Orbison	London	5

WEEK ENDING 12 MAY 1966

LW	TW	Title	Artist	Label	Wks
1	1	PRETTY FLAMINGO	Manfred Mann	HMV	4
2	2	DAYDREAM	Lovin' Spoonful	Pye	5
5	3	SLOOP JOHN B	Beach Boys	Capitol	4
3	4	BANG BANG	Cher	Liberty	7
6	5	PIED PIPER	Crispian St. Peters	Decca	6
4	6	YOU DON'T HAVE TO SAY YOU LOVE ME	Dusty Springfield	Philips	6
7	7	HOLD TIGHT	Dave Dee Dozy Beaky Mick and Tich	Fontana	10
8	8	SOUND OF SILENCE	Bachelors	Decca	9
10	9	HOMEWARD BOUND	Simon and Garfunkel	CBS	7
20	10	SHOTGUN WEDDING	Roy C	Island	3
9	11	ALFIE	Cilla Black	Parlophone	7
28	12	SORROW	Merseys	Fontana	2
-	13	WILD THING	Troggs ●	Fontana	1
16	14	THAT'S NICE	Neil Christian	Strike	5
19	15	(YOU'RE MY) SOUL AND INSPIRATION	Righteous Brothers	Verve	5
11	16	SOMEBODY HELP ME	Spencer Davis Group	Fontana	8
13	17	I PUT A SPELL ON YOU	Alan Price Set	Decca	7
12	18	SUBSTITUTE	Who	Reaction	10
27	19	HOW DOES THAT GRAB YOU DARLIN'	Nancy Sinatra	Reprise	3
14	20	SOMEDAY ONE DAY	Seekers	Columbia	8
15	21	ELUSIVE BUTTERFLY	Val Doonican	Decca	9
22	22	WALKING MY CAT NAMED DOG	Norma Tanega	Stateside	5
-	23	HEY GIRL	Small Faces	Decca	1
17	24	MAKE THE WORLD GO AWAY	Eddy Arnold	RCA	13
30	25	COME ON HOME	Wayne Fontana	Fontana	3
-	26	PROMISES	Ken Dodd	Columbia	1
21	27	FRANKIE AND JOHNNY	Elvis Presley	RCA	6
18	28	BLUE TURNS TO GREY	Cliff Richard	Columbia	8
34	29	CALIFORNIA DREAMIN'	Mamas and the Papas	RCA	2

■Cher reaches her highest chart placing as a soloist for 25 years, until her version of *The Shoop Shoop Song* gives her a number one hit in 1991 (05.05.66) ■ For the fourth consecutive week, the record at number nine is at its chart peak. Paul Simon is the writer of both the number eight and the number nine ranked records (12.05.66)■

May 1966

□ Highest position disc reached ● Act's first ever week on chart

LW	TW	Title	Artist	Label	Wks
25	30	HIGHWAY CODE	Master Singers	Parlophone	5
-	31	MONDAY MONDAY	Mamas and the Papas	RCA	1
-	32	RAINY DAY WOMEN NOS. 12 AND 35	Bob Dylan	CBS	1
36	33	CAN'T LIVE WITH YOU (CAN'T LIVE WITHOUT YOU)	Mindbenders	Fontana	2
31	34	TAKE IT OR LEAVE IT	Searchers	Pye	3
24	35	SUPERGIRL	Graham Bonney	Columbia	7
-	36	I FEEL A CRY COMING ON	Hank Locklin	RCA	1
23	37	THE SUN AIN'T GONNA SHINE ANYMORE	Walker Brothers	Philips	11
32	38	BALLAD OF THE GREEN BERETS	S/Sgt Barry Sadler	RCA	7
-	39	YOU CAN'T SIT DOWN	Phil Upchurch Combo ●	Sue	1
-	40	STRANGERS IN THE NIGHT	Frank Sinatra	Reprise	1

WEEK ENDING 19 MAY 1966

LW	TW	Title	Artist	Label	Wks
1	1	PRETTY FLAMINGO	Manfred Mann	HMV	5
3	2	SLOOP JOHN B	Beach Boys	Capitol	5
2	3	DAYDREAM	Lovin' Spoonful	Pye	6
13	4	WILD THING	Troggs	Fontana	2
-	5	PAINT IT, BLACK	Rolling Stones	Decca	1
10	6	SHOTGUN WEDDING	Roy C	Island	4
6	7	YOU DON'T HAVE TO SAY YOU LOVE ME	Dusty Springfield	Philips	7
5	8	PIED PIPER	Crispian St. Peters	Decca	7
12	9	SORROW	Merseys	Fontana	3
32	10	RAINY DAY WOMEN NOS. 12 AND 35	Bob Dylan	CBS	2
4	11	BANG BANG	Cher	Liberty	8
40	12	STRANGERS IN THE NIGHT	Frank Sinatra	Reprise	2
7	13	HOLD TIGHT	Dave Dee Dozy Beaky Mick and Tich	Fontana	11
26	14	PROMISES	Ken Dodd	Columbia	2
23	15	HEY GIRL	Small Faces	Decca	2
9	16	HOMEWARD BOUND	Simon and Garfunkel	CBS	8
31	17	MONDAY MONDAY	Mamas and the Papas	RCA	2
8	18	SOUND OF SILENCE	Bachelors	Decca	10
15	19	(YOU'RE MY) SOUL AND INSPIRATION	Righteous Brothers	Verve	6
11	20	ALFIE	Cilla Black	Parlophone	8
19	21	HOW DOES THAT GRAB YOU DARLIN'	Nancy Sinatra	Reprise	4
25	22	COME ON HOME	Wayne Fontana	Fontana	4
14	23	THAT'S NICE	Neil Christian	Strike	6
27	24	FRANKIE AND JOHNNY	Elvis Presley	RCA	7
16	25	SOMEBODY HELP ME	Spencer Davis Group	Fontana	9
29	26	CALIFORNIA DREAMIN'	Mamas and the Papas	RCA	3
22	27	WALKING MY CAT NAMED DOG	Norma Tanega	Stateside	6
20	28	SOMEDAY ONE DAY	Seekers	Columbia	9
17	29	I PUT A SPELL ON YOU	Alan Price Set	Decca	8
-	30	I LOVE HER	Paul and Barry Ryan	Decca	1
33	31	CAN'T LIVE WITH YOU (CAN'T LIVE WITHOUT YOU)	Mindbenders	Fontana	3
21	32	ELUSIVE BUTTERFLY	Val Doonican	Decca	10
-	33	EIGHT MILES HIGH	Byrds	CBS	1
-	34	WHEN A MAN LOVES A WOMAN	Percy Sledge ●	Atlantic	1
24	35	MAKE THE WORLD GO AWAY	Eddy Arnold	RCA	14
18	36	SUBSTITUTE	Who	Reaction	11
36	37	I FEEL A CRY COMING ON	Hank Locklin	RCA	2
30	38	HIGHWAY CODE	Master Singers	Parlophone	6
-	39	CONFUSION	Lee Dorsey	Stateside	1
34	40	TAKE IT OR LEAVE IT	Searchers	Pye	4

WEEK ENDING 26 MAY 1966

LW	TW	Title	Artist	Label	Wks
5	1	PAINT IT, BLACK	Rolling Stones	Decca	2
4	2	WILD THING	Troggs	Fontana	3
12	3	STRANGERS IN THE NIGHT	Frank Sinatra	Reprise	3
1	4	PRETTY FLAMINGO	Manfred Mann	HMV	6
9	5	SORROW	Merseys	Fontana	4
2	6	SLOOP JOHN B	Beach Boys	Capitol	6
6	7	SHOTGUN WEDDING	Roy C	Island	5
17	8	MONDAY MONDAY	Mamas and the Papas	RCA	3
10	9	RAINY DAY WOMEN NOS. 12 AND 35	Bob Dylan	CBS	3
15	10	HEY GIRL	Small Faces	Decca	3
3	11	DAYDREAM	Lovin' Spoonful	Pye	7
14	12	PROMISES	Ken Dodd	Columbia	3
8	13	PIED PIPER	Crispian St. Peters	Decca	8
7	14	YOU DON'T HAVE TO SAY YOU LOVE ME	Dusty Springfield	Philips	8
34	15	WHEN A MAN LOVES A WOMAN	Percy Sledge	Atlantic	2
11	16	BANG BANG	Cher	Liberty	9
16	17	HOMEWARD BOUND	Simon and Garfunkel	CBS	9
13	18	HOLD TIGHT	Dave Dee Dozy Beaky Mick and Tich	Fontana	12
19	19	(YOU'RE MY) SOUL AND INSPIRATION	Righteous Brothers	Verve	7
30	20	I LOVE HER	Paul and Barry Ryan	Decca	2
22	21	COME ON HOME	Wayne Fontana	Fontana	5
21	22	HOW DOES THAT GRAB YOU DARLIN'	Nancy Sinatra	Reprise	5
26	23	CALIFORNIA DREAMIN'	Mamas and the Papas	RCA	4
18	24	SOUND OF SILENCE	Bachelors	Decca	11
-	25	NOTHING COMES EASY	Sandie Shaw	Pye	1
-	26	ONCE THERE WAS A TIME/NOT RESPONSIBLE	Tom Jones	Decca	1
23	27	THAT'S NICE	Neil Christian	Strike	7
31	28	CAN'T LIVE WITH YOU (CAN'T LIVE WITHOUT YOU)	Mindbenders	Fontana	4
20	29	ALFIE	Cilla Black	Parlophone	9
37	30	I FEEL A CRY COMING ON	Hank Locklin	RCA	3
33	31	EIGHT MILES HIGH	Byrds	CBS	2
-	32	I'M COMIN' HOME CINDY	Trini Lopez	Reprise	1
24	33	FRANKIE AND JOHNNY	Elvis Presley	RCA	8
25	34	SOMEBODY HELP ME	Spencer Davis Group	Fontana	10
28	35	SOMEDAY ONE DAY	Seekers	Columbia	10
27	36	WALKING MY CAT NAMED DOG	Norma Tanega	Stateside	7
29	37	I PUT A SPELL ON YOU	Alan Price Set	Decca	9
39	38	CONFUSION	Lee Dorsey	Stateside	2
35	39	MAKE THE WORLD GO AWAY	Eddy Arnold	RCA	15
32	40	ELUSIVE BUTTERFLY	Val Doonican	Decca	11

WEEK ENDING 2 JUNE 1966

LW	TW	Title	Artist	Label	Wks
3	1	STRANGERS IN THE NIGHT	Frank Sinatra	Reprise	4
1	2	PAINT IT, BLACK	Rolling Stones	Decca	3
2	3	WILD THING	Troggs	Fontana	4
5	4	SORROW	Merseys	Fontana	5
8	5	MONDAY MONDAY	Mamas and the Papas	RCA	4
6	6	SLOOP JOHN B	Beach Boys	Capitol	7
9	7	RAINY DAY WOMEN NOS. 12 AND 35	Bob Dylan	CBS	4
12	8	PROMISES	Ken Dodd	Columbia	4
15	9	WHEN A MAN LOVES A WOMAN	Percy Sledge	Atlantic	3
10	10	HEY GIRL	Small Faces	Decca	4
7	11	SHOTGUN WEDDING	Roy C	Island	6
4	12	PRETTY FLAMINGO	Manfred Mann	HMV	7
-	13	DON'T BRING ME DOWN	Animals	Decca	1
25	14	NOTHING COMES EASY	Sandie Shaw	Pye	2
11	15	DAYDREAM	Lovin' Spoonful	Pye	8
13	16	PIED PIPER	Crispian St. Peters	Decca	9
14	17	YOU DON'T HAVE TO SAY YOU LOVE ME	Dusty Springfield	Philips	9
21	18	COME ON HOME	Wayne Fontana	Fontana	6
20	19	I LOVE HER	Paul and Barry Ryan	Decca	3
26	20	ONCE THERE WAS A TIME/NOT RESPONSIBLE	Tom Jones	Decca	2
-	21	OVER UNDER SIDEWAYS DOWN	Yardbirds	Columbia	1
16	22	BANG BANG	Cher	Liberty	10
23	23	CALIFORNIA DREAMIN'	Mamas and the Papas	RCA	5
18	24	HOLD TIGHT	Dave Dee Dozy Beaky Mick and Tich	Fontana	13
19	25	(YOU'RE MY) SOUL AND INSPIRATION	Righteous Brothers	Verve	8
17	26	HOMEWARD BOUND	Simon and Garfunkel	CBS	10
-	27	TWINKIE-LEE	Gary Walker	CBS	1
32	28	I'M COMIN' HOME CINDY	Trini Lopez	Reprise	2
22	29	HOW DOES THAT GRAB YOU DARLIN'	Nancy Sinatra	Reprise	6
31	30	EIGHT MILES HIGH	Byrds	CBS	3

In these weeks ■ The Rolling Stones' sixth number one, *Paint It Black* is the third of those six to spend only one week on top (26.05.66) ■ *Pretty Flamingo* is the first number one hit with an animal in the title since *Little Red Rooster* and the last until *Albatross* in 1969. No four-legged beast tops the chart between *Running Bear* in 1960 and *Puppy Love* in 1972 (19.05.66)■

LW	TW	Title / Artist	Label	Wks
28	31	CAN'T LIVE WITH YOU (CAN'T LIVE WITHOUT YOU) Mindbenders	Fontana	5
27	32	THAT'S NICE Neil Christian	Strike	8
24	33	SOUND OF SILENCE Bachelors	Decca	12
30	34	I FEEL A CRY COMING ON Hank Locklin	RCA	4
-	35	STOP HER ON SIGHT (S.O.S.) Edwin Starr ●	Polydor	1
-	36	MERCI CHERIE Vince Hill	Columbia	1
29	37	ALFIE Cilla Black	Parlophone	10
38	38	CONFUSION Lee Dorsey	Stateside	3
-	39	WATER Geno Washington and his Ram Jam Band ●	Piccadilly	1
-	40	WHATCHA GONNA DO NOW Chris Andrews	Decca	1

LW	TW	*WEEK ENDING* **9 JUNE 1966**		Wks
1	1	STRANGERS IN THE NIGHT Frank Sinatra	Reprise	5
2	2	PAINT IT, BLACK Rolling Stones	Decca	4
3	3	WILD THING Troggs	Fontana	5
4	4	SORROW Merseys	Fontana	6
5	5	MONDAY MONDAY Mamas and the Papas	RCA	5
8	6	PROMISES Ken Dodd	Columbia	5
9	7	WHEN A MAN LOVES A WOMAN Percy Sledge	Atlantic	4
13	8	DON'T BRING ME DOWN Animals	Decca	2
6	9	SLOOP JOHN B Beach Boys	Capitol	8
7	10	RAINY DAY WOMEN NOS. 12 AND 35 Bob Dylan	CBS	5
10	11	HEY GIRL Small Faces	Decca	5
11	12	SHOTGUN WEDDING Roy C	Island	7
12	13	PRETTY FLAMINGO Manfred Mann	HMV	8
14	14	NOTHING COMES EASY Sandie Shaw	Pye	3
21	15	OVER UNDER SIDEWAYS DOWN Yardbirds	Columbia	2
18	16	COME ON HOME Wayne Fontana	Fontana	7
19	17	I LOVE HER Paul and Barry Ryan	Decca	4
20	18	ONCE THERE WAS A TIME/NOT RESPONSIBLE Tom Jones	Decca	3
17	19	YOU DON'T HAVE TO SAY YOU LOVE ME Dusty Springfield	Philips	10
15	20	DAYDREAM Lovin' Spoonful	Pye	9
16	21	PIED PIPER Crispian St. Peters	Decca	10
22	22	BANG BANG Cher	Liberty	11
24	23	HOLD TIGHT Dave Dee Dozy Beaky Mick and Tich	Fontana	14
30	24	EIGHT MILES HIGH Byrds	CBS	4
-	25	DON'T ANSWER ME Cilla Black	Parlophone	1
23	26	CALIFORNIA DREAMIN' Mamas and the Papas	RCA	6
25	27	(YOU'RE MY) SOUL AND INSPIRATION Righteous Brothers	Verve	9
27	28	TWINKIE-LEE Gary Walker	CBS	2
34	29	I FEEL A CRY COMING ON Hank Locklin	RCA	5
28	30	I'M COMIN' HOME CINDY Trini Lopez	Reprise	3
-	31	SUNNY AFTERNOON Kinks	Pye	1
31	32	CAN'T LIVE WITH YOU (CAN'T LIVE WITHOUT YOU) Mindbenders	Fontana	6
-	33	RIVER DEEP MOUNTAIN HIGH Ike and Tina Turner ●	London	1
-	34	OPUS 17 Four Seasons	Philips	1
29	35	HOW DOES THAT GRAB YOU DARLIN' Nancy Sinatra	Reprise	7
26	36	HOMEWARD BOUND Simon and Garfunkel	CBS	11
-	37	NOBODY NEEDS YOUR LOVE Gene Pitney	Stateside	1
-	38	HIDEAWAY Dave Dee Dozy Beaky Mick and Tich	Fontana	1
35	39	STOP HER ON SIGHT (S.O.S.) Edwin Starr	Polydor	2
39	40	WATER Geno Washington and his Ram Jam Band	Piccadilly	2

June 1966

□ Highest position disc reached ● Act's first ever week on chart

LW	TW	*WEEK ENDING* **16 JUNE 1966**		Wks
1	1	STRANGERS IN THE NIGHT Frank Sinatra	Reprise	6
-	2	PAPERBACK WRITER Beatles	Parlophone	1
5	3	MONDAY MONDAY Mamas and the Papas	RCA	6
4	4	SORROW Merseys	Fontana	7
7	5	WHEN A MAN LOVES A WOMAN Percy Sledge	Atlantic	5
2	6	PAINT IT, BLACK Rolling Stones	Decca	5
8	7	DON'T BRING ME DOWN Animals	Decca	3
6	8	PROMISES Ken Dodd	Columbia	6
3	9	WILD THING Troggs	Fontana	6
15	10	OVER UNDER SIDEWAYS DOWN Yardbirds	Columbia	3
25	11	DON'T ANSWER ME Cilla Black	Parlophone	2
33	12	RIVER DEEP MOUNTAIN HIGH Ike and Tina Turner	London	2
9	13	SLOOP JOHN B Beach Boys	Capitol	9
31	14	SUNNY AFTERNOON Kinks	Pye	2
10	15	RAINY DAY WOMEN NOS. 12 AND 35 Bob Dylan	CBS	6
14	16	NOTHING COMES EASY Sandie Shaw	Pye	4
11	17	HEY GIRL Small Faces	Decca	6
37	18	NOBODY NEEDS YOUR LOVE Gene Pitney	Stateside	2
18	19	ONCE THERE WAS A TIME/NOT RESPONSIBLE Tom Jones	Decca	4
16	20	COME ON HOME Wayne Fontana	Fontana	8
38	21	HIDEAWAY Dave Dee Dozy Beaky Mick and Tich	Fontana	2
13	22	PRETTY FLAMINGO Manfred Mann	HMV	9
12	23	SHOTGUN WEDDING Roy C	Island	8
17	24	I LOVE HER Paul and Barry Ryan	Decca	5
34	25	OPUS 17 Four Seasons	Philips	2
28	26	TWINKIE-LEE Gary Walker	CBS	3
24	27	EIGHT MILES HIGH Byrds	CBS	5
-	28	I AM A ROCK Simon and Garfunkel	CBS	1
19	29	YOU DON'T HAVE TO SAY YOU LOVE ME Dusty Springfield	Philips	11
-	30	IT'S A MAN'S MAN'S MAN'S WORLD James Brown	Pye	1
-	31	LANA Roy Orbison	London	1
-	32	SWEET TALKIN' GUY Chiffons	Stateside	1
20	33	DAYDREAM Lovin' Spoonful	Pye	10
-	34	TO MAKE A BIG MAN CRY P.J. Proby	Liberty	1
-	35	LADY JANE David Garrick ●	Piccadilly	1
23	36	HOLD TIGHT Dave Dee Dozy Beaky Mick and Tich	Fontana	15
26	37	CALIFORNIA DREAMIN' Mamas and the Papas	RCA	7
-	38	SITTIN' ON A FENCE Twice As Much ●	Immediate	1
21	39	PIED PIPER Crispian St. Peters	Decca	11
39	40	STOP HER ON SIGHT (S.O.S.) Edwin Starr	Polydor	3

LW	TW	*WEEK ENDING* **23 JUNE 1966**		Wks
2	1	PAPERBACK WRITER Beatles	Parlophone	2
1	2	STRANGERS IN THE NIGHT Frank Sinatra	Reprise	7
3	3	MONDAY MONDAY Mamas and the Papas	RCA	7
5	4	WHEN A MAN LOVES A WOMAN Percy Sledge	Atlantic	6
14	5	SUNNY AFTERNOON Kinks	Pye	3
7	6	DON'T BRING ME DOWN Animals	Decca	4
11	7	DON'T ANSWER ME Cilla Black	Parlophone	3
12	8	RIVER DEEP MOUNTAIN HIGH Ike and Tina Turner	London	3
4	9	SORROW Merseys	Fontana	8
10	10	OVER UNDER SIDEWAYS DOWN Yardbirds	Columbia	4
18	11	NOBODY NEEDS YOUR LOVE Gene Pitney	Stateside	3
6	12	PAINT IT, BLACK Rolling Stones	Decca	6
8	13	PROMISES Ken Dodd	Columbia	7
21	14	HIDEAWAY Dave Dee Dozy Beaky Mick and Tich	Fontana	3
9	15	WILD THING Troggs	Fontana	7
13	16	SLOOP JOHN B Beach Boys	Capitol	10
16	17	NOTHING COMES EASY Sandie Shaw	Pye	5
19	18	ONCE THERE WAS A TIME/NOT RESPONSIBLE Tom Jones	Decca	5
-	19	BUS STOP Hollies	Parlophone	1
25	20	OPUS 17 Four Seasons	Philips	3
17	21	HEY GIRL Small Faces	Decca	7
20	22	COME ON HOME Wayne Fontana	Fontana	9
28	23	I AM A ROCK Simon and Garfunkel	CBS	2
30	24	IT'S A MAN'S MAN'S MAN'S WORLD James Brown	Pye	2
22	25	PRETTY FLAMINGO Manfred Mann	HMV	10
33	26	DAYDREAM Lovin' Spoonful	Pye	11
15	27	RAINY DAY WOMEN NOS. 12 AND 35 Bob Dylan	CBS	7
-	28	GET AWAY Georgie Fame and the Blue Flames	Columbia	1
31	29	LANA Roy Orbison	London	2
23	30	SHOTGUN WEDDING Roy C	Island	9
-	31	NO ONE WILL EVER KNOW Frank Ifield	Columbia	1
32	32	SWEET TALKIN' GUY Chiffons	Stateside	2
35	33	LADY JANE David Garrick	Piccadilly	2
-	34	THE MORE I SEE YOU Joy Marshall ●	Decca	1
38	35	SITTIN' ON A FENCE Twice As Much	Immediate	2

■ *River Deep Mountain High* becomes the fourth record in the Top 40 which will enjoy at least two separate spells of chart action. *When A Man Loves A Woman* will return in 1987, *Shotgun Wedding* will be a Top Ten hit again in 1972, and *Stop Her On Sight (SOS)* will reappear in 1968 (09.06.66) ■ *Paperback Writer* comes in at number two, the highest new chart entry since *The Young Ones* crashed in at number one in January 1962 (16.06.66) ■

June 1966

□ Highest position disc reached ● Act's first ever week on chart

LW	TW	Title	Artist	Label	Wks
-	36	OUT OF TIME	Chris Farlowe and the Thunderbirds	Immediate	1
-	37	THIS DOOR SWINGS BOTH WAYS	Herman's Hermits	Columbia	1
24	38	I LOVE HER	Paul and Barry Ryan	Decca	6
26	39	TWINKIE-LEE	Gary Walker	CBS	4
40	40	STOP HER ON SIGHT (S.O.S.)	Edwin Starr	Polydor	4

WEEK ENDING 30 JUNE 1966

LW	TW	Title	Artist	Label	Wks
1	1	PAPERBACK WRITER	Beatles	Parlophone	3
2	2	STRANGERS IN THE NIGHT	Frank Sinatra	Reprise	8
5	3	SUNNY AFTERNOON	Kinks	Pye	4
8	4	RIVER DEEP MOUNTAIN HIGH	Ike and Tina Turner	London	4
11	5	NOBODY NEEDS YOUR LOVE	Gene Pitney	Stateside	4
7	6	DON'T ANSWER ME	Cilla Black	Parlophone	4
4	7	WHEN A MAN LOVES A WOMAN	Percy Sledge	Atlantic	7
3	8	MONDAY MONDAY	Mamas and the Papas	RCA	8
19	9	BUS STOP	Hollies	Parlophone	2
14	10	HIDEAWAY	Dave Dee Dozy Beaky Mick and Tich	Fontana	4
6	11	DON'T BRING ME DOWN	Animals	Decca	5
28	12	GET AWAY	Georgie Fame and the Blue Flames	Columbia	2
10	13	OVER UNDER SIDEWAYS DOWN	Yardbirds	Columbia	5
13	14	PROMISES	Ken Dodd	Columbia	8
9	15	SORROW	Merseys	Fontana	9
12	16	PAINT IT, BLACK	Rolling Stones	Decca	7
23	17	I AM A ROCK	Simon and Garfunkel	CBS	3
15	18	WILD THING	Troggs	Fontana	8
16	19	SLOOP JOHN B	Beach Boys	Capitol	11
29	20	LANA	Roy Orbison	London	3
24	21	IT'S A MAN'S MAN'S MAN'S WORLD	James Brown	Pye	3
20	22	OPUS 17	Four Seasons	Philips	4
37	23	THIS DOOR SWINGS BOTH WAYS	Herman's Hermits	Columbia	2
17	24	NOTHING COMES EASY	Sandie Shaw	Pye	6
31	25	NO ONE WILL EVER KNOW	Frank Ifield	Columbia	2
22	26	COME ON HOME	Wayne Fontana	Fontana	10
18	27	ONCE THERE WAS A TIME/NOT RESPONSIBLE	Tom Jones	Decca	6
33	28	LADY JANE	David Garrick	Piccadilly	3
35	29	SITTIN' ON A FENCE	Twice As Much	Immediate	3
21	30	HEY GIRL	Small Faces	Decca	8
32	31	SWEET TALKIN' GUY	Chiffons	Stateside	3
25	32	PRETTY FLAMINGO	Manfred Mann	HMV	11
36	33	OUT OF TIME	Chris Farlowe and the Thunderbirds	Immediate	2
-	34	I COULDN'T LIVE WITHOUT YOUR LOVE	Petula Clark	Pye	1
-	35	BLACK IS BLACK	Los Bravos ●	Decca	1
30	36	SHOTGUN WEDDING	Roy C	Island	10
-	37	MAMA	Dave Berry	Decca	1
26	38	DAYDREAM	Lovin' Spoonful	Pye	12
-	39	THE MORE I SEE YOU	Chris Montez	Pye	1
27	40	RAINY DAY WOMEN NOS. 12 AND 35	Bob Dylan	CBS	8

WEEK ENDING 7 JULY 1966

LW	TW	Title	Artist	Label	Wks
3	1	SUNNY AFTERNOON	Kinks	Pye	5
1	2	PAPERBACK WRITER	Beatles	Parlophone	4
4	3	RIVER DEEP MOUNTAIN HIGH	Ike and Tina Turner	London	5
5	4	NOBODY NEEDS YOUR LOVE	Gene Pitney	Stateside	5
2	5	STRANGERS IN THE NIGHT	Frank Sinatra	Reprise	9
9	6	BUS STOP	Hollies	Parlophone	3
12	7	GET AWAY	Georgie Fame and the Blue Flames	Columbia	3
6	8	DON'T ANSWER ME	Cilla Black	Parlophone	5
7	9	WHEN A MAN LOVES A WOMAN	Percy Sledge	Atlantic	8
10	10	HIDEAWAY	Dave Dee Dozy Beaky Mick and Tich	Fontana	5
8	11	MONDAY MONDAY	Mamas and the Papas	RCA	9
13	12	OVER UNDER SIDEWAYS DOWN	Yardbirds	Columbia	6
21	13	IT'S A MAN'S MAN'S MAN'S WORLD	James Brown	Pye	4
11	14	DON'T BRING ME DOWN	Animals	Decca	6
20	15	LANA	Roy Orbison	London	4
14	16	PROMISES	Ken Dodd	Columbia	9
17	17	I AM A ROCK	Simon and Garfunkel	CBS	4
23	18	THIS DOOR SWINGS BOTH WAYS	Herman's Hermits	Columbia	3
19	19	SLOOP JOHN B	Beach Boys	Capitol	12
33	20	OUT OF TIME	Chris Farlowe and the Thunderbirds	Immediate	3
34	21	I COULDN'T LIVE WITHOUT YOUR LOVE	Petula Clark	Pye	2
15	22	SORROW	Merseys	Fontana	10
16	23	PAINT IT, BLACK	Rolling Stones	Decca	8
22	24	OPUS 17	Four Seasons	Philips	5
35	25	BLACK IS BLACK	Los Bravos	Decca	2
39	26	THE MORE I SEE YOU	Chris Montez	Pye	2
29	27	SITTIN' ON A FENCE	Twice As Much	Immediate	4
18	28	WILD THING	Troggs	Fontana	9
24	29	NOTHING COMES EASY	Sandie Shaw	Pye	7
-	30	GOING BACK	Dusty Springfield	Philips	1
28	31	LADY JANE	David Garrick	Piccadilly	4
25	32	NO ONE WILL EVER KNOW	Frank Ifield	Columbia	3
27	33	ONCE THERE WAS A TIME/NOT RESPONSIBLE	Tom Jones	Decca	7
37	34	MAMA	Dave Berry	Decca	2
26	35	COME ON HOME	Wayne Fontana	Fontana	11
31	36	SWEET TALKIN' GUY	Chiffons	Stateside	4
-	37	LOVE LETTERS	Elvis Presley	RCA	1
30	38	HEY GIRL	Small Faces	Decca	9
32	39	PRETTY FLAMINGO	Manfred Mann	HMV	12
-	40	CAN I TRUST YOU	Bachelors	Decca	1

WEEK ENDING 14 JULY 1966

LW	TW	Title	Artist	Label	Wks
1	1	SUNNY AFTERNOON	Kinks	Pye	6
4	2	NOBODY NEEDS YOUR LOVE	Gene Pitney	Stateside	6
3	3	RIVER DEEP MOUNTAIN HIGH	Ike and Tina Turner	London	6
7	4	GET AWAY	Georgie Fame and the Blue Flames	Columbia	4
6	5	BUS STOP	Hollies	Parlophone	4
5	6	STRANGERS IN THE NIGHT	Frank Sinatra	Reprise	10
2	7	PAPERBACK WRITER	Beatles	Parlophone	5
21	8	I COULDN'T LIVE WITHOUT YOUR LOVE	Petula Clark	Pye	3
20	9	OUT OF TIME	Chris Farlowe and the Thunderbirds	Immediate	4
10	10	HIDEAWAY	Dave Dee Dozy Beaky Mick and Tich	Fontana	6
25	11	BLACK IS BLACK	Los Bravos	Decca	3
8	12	DON'T ANSWER ME	Cilla Black	Parlophone	6
9	13	WHEN A MAN LOVES A WOMAN	Percy Sledge	Atlantic	9
37	14	LOVE LETTERS	Elvis Presley	RCA	2
11	15	MONDAY MONDAY	Mamas and the Papas	RCA	10
15	16	LANA	Roy Orbison	London	5
30	17	GOING BACK	Dusty Springfield	Philips	2
26	18	THE MORE I SEE YOU	Chris Montez	Pye	3
13	19	IT'S A MAN'S MAN'S MAN'S WORLD	James Brown	Pye	5
18	20	THIS DOOR SWINGS BOTH WAYS	Herman's Hermits	Columbia	4
19	21	SLOOP JOHN B	Beach Boys	Capitol	13
16	22	PROMISES	Ken Dodd	Columbia	10
17	23	I AM A ROCK	Simon and Garfunkel	CBS	5
12	24	OVER UNDER SIDEWAYS DOWN	Yardbirds	Columbia	7
34	25	MAMA	Dave Berry	Decca	3
14	26	DON'T BRING ME DOWN	Animals	Decca	7
-	27	(BABY) YOU DON'T HAVE TO TELL ME	Walker Brothers	Philips	1
27	28	SITTIN' ON A FENCE	Twice As Much	Immediate	5
-	29	WITH A GIRL LIKE YOU	Troggs	Fontana	1
22	30	SORROW	Merseys	Fontana	11
-	31	A PLACE IN THE SUN	Shadows	Columbia	1
23	32	PAINT IT, BLACK	Rolling Stones	Decca	9
24	33	OPUS 17	Four Seasons	Philips	6
40	34	CAN I TRUST YOU	Bachelors	Decca	2
31	35	LADY JANE	David Garrick	Piccadilly	5
28	36	WILD THING	Troggs	Fontana	10
33	37	ONCE THERE WAS A TIME/NOT RESPONSIBLE	Tom Jones	Decca	8
-	38	YOU GAVE ME SOMEBODY TO LOVE	Manfred Mann	HMV	1
36	39	SWEET TALKIN' GUY	Chiffons	Stateside	5
32	40	NO ONE WILL EVER KNOW	Frank Ifield	Columbia	4

In these weeks ■ James Brown reaches number 13, his highest chart placing in Britain until *Living In America* hits the Top Ten almost 20 years later (07.07.66) ■ A *Black* week as Los Bravos enter the chart, the Rolling Stones slip a little, but Cilla's seventh Top Ten hit is at its peak (30.06.66) ■

LW	TW	WEEK ENDING 21 JULY 1966			Wks
4	[1]	GET AWAY	Georgie Fame and the Blue Flames	Columbia	5
1	2	SUNNY AFTERNOON	Kinks	Pye	7
9	3	OUT OF TIME	Chris Farlowe and the Thunderbirds	Immediate	5
3	4	RIVER DEEP MOUNTAIN HIGH	Ike and Tina Turner	London	7
2	5	NOBODY NEEDS YOUR LOVE	Gene Pitney	Stateside	7
11	6	BLACK IS BLACK	Los Bravos	Decca	4
8	7	I COULDN'T LIVE WITHOUT YOUR LOVE	Petula Clark	Pye	4
5	8	BUS STOP	Hollies	Parlophone	5
14	9	LOVE LETTERS	Elvis Presley	RCA	3
29	10	WITH A GIRL LIKE YOU	Troggs	Fontana	2
6	11	STRANGERS IN THE NIGHT	Frank Sinatra	Reprise	11
17	12	GOING BACK	Dusty Springfield	Philips	3
18	13	THE MORE I SEE YOU	Chris Montez	Pye	4
7	14	PAPERBACK WRITER	Beatles	Parlophone	6
10	15	HIDEAWAY	Dave Dee Dozy Beaky Mick and Tich	Fontana	7
16	16	LANA	Roy Orbison	London	6
12	17	DON'T ANSWER ME	Cilla Black	Parlophone	7
25	18	MAMA	Dave Berry	Decca	4
13	19	WHEN A MAN LOVES A WOMAN	Percy Sledge	Atlantic	10
15	20	MONDAY MONDAY	Mamas and the Papas	RCA	11
27	21	(BABY) YOU DON'T HAVE TO TELL ME	Walker Brothers	Philips	2
19	22	IT'S A MAN'S MAN'S MAN'S WORLD	James Brown	Pye	6
20	23	THIS DOOR SWINGS BOTH WAYS	Herman's Hermits	Columbia	5
31	[24]	A PLACE IN THE SUN	Shadows	Columbia	2
23	25	I AM A ROCK	Simon and Garfunkel	CBS	6
34	[26]	CAN I TRUST YOU	Bachelors	Decca	3
28	27	SITTIN' ON A FENCE	Twice As Much	Immediate	6
-	28	SUMMER IN THE CITY	Lovin' Spoonful	Kama Sutra	1
-	29	VISIONS	Cliff Richard	Columbia	1
22	30	PROMISES	Ken Dodd	Columbia	11
24	31	OVER UNDER SIDEWAYS DOWN	Yardbirds	Columbia	8
-	32	I WANT YOU	Bob Dylan	CBS	1
21	33	SLOOP JOHN B	Beach Boys	Capitol	14
-	34	HI-LILI HI-LO	Alan Price Set	Decca	1
-	35	LOVERS OF THE WORLD UNITE	David and Jonathan	Columbia	1
38	[36]	YOU GAVE ME SOMEBODY TO LOVE	Manfred Mann	HMV	2
26	37	DON'T BRING ME DOWN	Animals	Decca	8
-	[38]	YOUNGER GIRL	Critters ●	London	1
-	39	MY LOVER'S PRAYER	Otis Redding	Atlantic	1
33	40	OPUS 17	Four Seasons	Philips	7

LW	TW	WEEK ENDING 28 JULY 1966			Wks
3	[1]	OUT OF TIME	Chris Farlowe and the Thunderbirds	Immediate	6
6	[2]	BLACK IS BLACK	Los Bravos	Decca	5
10	3	WITH A GIRL LIKE YOU	Troggs	Fontana	3
1	4	GET AWAY	Georgie Fame and the Blue Flames	Columbia	6
2	5	SUNNY AFTERNOON	Kinks	Pye	8
7	[6]	I COULDN'T LIVE WITHOUT YOUR LOVE	Petula Clark	Pye	5
13	7	THE MORE I SEE YOU	Chris Montez	Pye	5
9	8	LOVE LETTERS	Elvis Presley	RCA	4
4	9	RIVER DEEP MOUNTAIN HIGH	Ike and Tina Turner	London	8
12	[10]	GOING BACK	Dusty Springfield	Philips	4
5	11	NOBODY NEEDS YOUR LOVE	Gene Pitney	Stateside	8
8	12	BUS STOP	Hollies	Parlophone	6
21	[13]	(BABY) YOU DON'T HAVE TO TELL ME	Walker Brothers	Philips	3
18	14	MAMA	Dave Berry	Decca	5
11	15	STRANGERS IN THE NIGHT	Frank Sinatra	Reprise	12
28	16	SUMMER IN THE CITY	Lovin' Spoonful	Kama Sutra	2
15	17	HIDEAWAY	Dave Dee Dozy Beaky Mick and Tich	Fontana	8
29	18	VISIONS	Cliff Richard	Columbia	2
14	19	PAPERBACK WRITER	Beatles	Parlophone	7
16	20	LANA	Roy Orbison	London	7
34	21	HI-LILI HI-LO	Alan Price Set	Decca	2
32	22	I WANT YOU	Bob Dylan	CBS	2
17	23	DON'T ANSWER ME	Cilla Black	Parlophone	8
24	[24]	A PLACE IN THE SUN	Shadows	Columbia	3

August 1966

□ Highest position disc reached ● Act's first ever week on chart

LW	TW				Wks
27	[25]	SITTIN' ON A FENCE	Twice As Much	Immediate	7
19	26	WHEN A MAN LOVES A WOMAN	Percy Sledge	Atlantic	11
35	27	LOVERS OF THE WORLD UNITE	David and Jonathan	Columbia	2
25	28	I AM A ROCK	Simon and Garfunkel	CBS	7
-	29	I LOVE HOW YOU LOVE ME	Paul and Barry Ryan	Decca	1
26	30	CAN I TRUST YOU	Bachelors	Decca	4
20	31	MONDAY MONDAY	Mamas and the Papas	RCA	12
23	32	THIS DOOR SWINGS BOTH WAYS	Herman's Hermits	Columbia	6
22	33	IT'S A MAN'S MAN'S MAN'S WORLD	James Brown	Pye	7
-	34	GOD ONLY KNOWS	Beach Boys	Capitol	1
30	35	PROMISES	Ken Dodd	Columbia	12
33	36	SLOOP JOHN B	Beach Boys	Capitol	15
39	[37]	MY LOVER'S PRAYER	Otis Redding	Atlantic	2
-	38	I SAW HER AGAIN	Mamas and the Papas	RCA	1
-	39	AIN'T TOO PROUD TO BEG	Temptations ●	Tamla Motown	1
36	40	YOU GAVE ME SOMEBODY TO LOVE	Manfred Mann	HMV	3

LW	TW	WEEK ENDING 4 AUGUST 1966			Wks
3	[1]	WITH A GIRL LIKE YOU	Troggs	Fontana	4
1	2	OUT OF TIME	Chris Farlowe and the Thunderbirds	Immediate	7
2	3	BLACK IS BLACK	Los Bravos	Decca	6
7	4	THE MORE I SEE YOU	Chris Montez	Pye	6
4	5	GET AWAY	Georgie Fame and the Blue Flames	Columbia	7
8	[6]	LOVE LETTERS	Elvis Presley	RCA	5
14	7	MAMA	Dave Berry	Decca	6
6	8	I COULDN'T LIVE WITHOUT YOUR LOVE	Petula Clark	Pye	6
5	9	SUNNY AFTERNOON	Kinks	Pye	9
10	[10]	GOING BACK	Dusty Springfield	Philips	5
9	11	RIVER DEEP MOUNTAIN HIGH	Ike and Tina Turner	London	9
16	12	SUMMER IN THE CITY	Lovin' Spoonful	Kama Sutra	3
13	[13]	(BABY) YOU DON'T HAVE TO TELL ME	Walker Brothers	Philips	4
11	14	NOBODY NEEDS YOUR LOVE	Gene Pitney	Stateside	9
18	15	VISIONS	Cliff Richard	Columbia	3
34	16	GOD ONLY KNOWS	Beach Boys	Capitol	2
21	17	HI-LILI HI-LO	Alan Price Set	Decca	3
22	18	I WANT YOU	Bob Dylan	CBS	3
12	19	BUS STOP	Hollies	Parlophone	7
15	20	STRANGERS IN THE NIGHT	Frank Sinatra	Reprise	13
19	21	PAPERBACK WRITER	Beatles	Parlophone	8
23	22	DON'T ANSWER ME	Cilla Black	Parlophone	9
17	23	HIDEAWAY	Dave Dee Dozy Beaky Mick and Tich	Fontana	9
38	24	I SAW HER AGAIN	Mamas and the Papas	RCA	2
28	25	I AM A ROCK	Simon and Garfunkel	CBS	8
29	26	I LOVE HOW YOU LOVE ME	Paul and Barry Ryan	Decca	2
20	27	LANA	Roy Orbison	London	8
27	28	LOVERS OF THE WORLD UNITE	David and Jonathan	Columbia	3
24	29	A PLACE IN THE SUN	Shadows	Columbia	4
26	30	WHEN A MAN LOVES A WOMAN	Percy Sledge	Atlantic	12
39	31	AIN'T TOO PROUD TO BEG	Temptations	Tamla Motown	2
25	32	SITTIN' ON A FENCE	Twice As Much	Immediate	8
30	33	CAN I TRUST YOU	Bachelors	Decca	5
-	34	MORE THAN LOVE	Ken Dodd	Columbia	1
31	35	MONDAY MONDAY	Mamas and the Papas	RCA	13
35	36	PROMISES	Ken Dodd	Columbia	13
-	37	JUST LIKE A WOMAN	Manfred Mann	Fontana	1
-	[38]	HANKY PANKY	Tommy James and the Shondells ●	Roulette	1
33	39	IT'S A MAN'S MAN'S MAN'S WORLD	James Brown	Pye	8
37	40	MY LOVER'S PRAYER	Otis Redding	Atlantic	3

LW	TW	WEEK ENDING 11 AUGUST 1966			Wks
1	[1]	WITH A GIRL LIKE YOU	Troggs	Fontana	5
2	2	OUT OF TIME	Chris Farlowe and the Thunderbirds	Immediate	8
4	[3]	THE MORE I SEE YOU	Chris Montez	Pye	7

■Mick Jagger and Keith Richards hit the top as writers for another artist for the only time (28.07.66) ■ The Temptations' ninth American Top 40 success gives them their first taste of chart action in Britain (28.07.66) ■ For the ninth week in 11, the record at number ten is at its peak (04.08.66)■

August 1966

☐ Highest position disc reached ● Act's first ever week on chart

LW	TW	Title	Artist	Label	Wks
3	4	BLACK IS BLACK	Los Bravos	*Decca*	7
16	5	GOD ONLY KNOWS	Beach Boys	*Capitol*	3
7	6	MAMA	Dave Berry	*Decca*	7
6	7	LOVE LETTERS	Elvis Presley	*RCA*	6
-	8	YELLOW SUBMARINE/ELEANOR RIGBY	Beatles	*Parlophone*	1
12	9	SUMMER IN THE CITY	Lovin' Spoonful	*Kama Sutra*	4
8	10	I COULDN'T LIVE WITHOUT YOUR LOVE	Petula Clark	*Pye*	7
5	11	GET AWAY	Georgie Fame and the Blue Flames	*Columbia*	8
15	12	VISIONS	Cliff Richard	*Columbia*	4
9	13	SUNNY AFTERNOON	Kinks	*Pye*	10
10	14	GOING BACK	Dusty Springfield	*Philips*	6
17	15	HI-LILI HI-LO	Alan Price Set	*Decca*	4
18	[16]	I WANT YOU	Bob Dylan	*CBS*	4
24	17	I SAW HER AGAIN	Mamas and the Papas	*RCA*	3
11	18	RIVER DEEP MOUNTAIN HIGH	Ike and Tina Turner	*London*	10
14	19	NOBODY NEEDS YOUR LOVE	Gene Pitney	*Stateside*	10
20	20	STRANGERS IN THE NIGHT	Frank Sinatra	*Reprise*	14
26	[21]	I LOVE HOW YOU LOVE ME	Paul and Barry Ryan	*Decca*	3
34	22	MORE THAN LOVE	Ken Dodd	*Columbia*	2
13	23	(BABY) YOU DON'T HAVE TO TELL ME	Walker Brothers	*Philips*	5
28	24	LOVERS OF THE WORLD UNITE	David and Jonathan	*Columbia*	4
30	25	WHEN A MAN LOVES A WOMAN	Percy Sledge	*Atlantic*	13
19	26	BUS STOP	Hollies	*Parlophone*	8
37	27	JUST LIKE A WOMAN	Manfred Mann	*Fontana*	2
23	28	HIDEAWAY	Dave Dee Dozy Beaky Mick and Tich	*Fontana*	10
31	29	AIN'T TOO PROUD TO BEG	Temptations	*Tamla Motown*	3
21	30	PAPERBACK WRITER	Beatles	*Parlophone*	9
-	31	THEY'RE COMING TO TAKE ME AWAY HA-HAA	Napoleon XIV ●	*Warner Brothers*	1
25	32	I AM A ROCK	Simon and Garfunkel	*CBS*	9
29	33	A PLACE IN THE SUN	Shadows	*Columbia*	5
22	34	DON'T ANSWER ME	Cilla Black	*Parlophone*	10
33	35	CAN I TRUST YOU	Bachelors	*Decca*	6
-	36	BAREFOOTIN'	Robert Parker ●	*Island*	1
-	37	GIVE ME YOUR WORD	Billy Fury	*Decca*	1
-	38	LOVING YOU IS SWEETER THAN EVER	Four Tops	*Tamla Motown*	1
-	39	ALL OR NOTHING	Small Faces	*Decca*	1
38	40	HANKY PANKY	Tommy James and the Shondells	*Roulette*	2

LW	TW	*WEEK ENDING* 18 AUGUST 1966			Wks
8	[1]	YELLOW SUBMARINE/ELEANOR RIGBY	Beatles	*Parlophone*	2
1	2	WITH A GIRL LIKE YOU	Troggs	*Fontana*	6
5	3	GOD ONLY KNOWS	Beach Boys	*Capitol*	4
4	4	BLACK IS BLACK	Los Bravos	*Decca*	8
6	[5]	MAMA	Dave Berry	*Decca*	8
3	6	THE MORE I SEE YOU	Chris Montez	*Pye*	8
12	[7]	VISIONS	Cliff Richard	*Columbia*	5
9	[8]	SUMMER IN THE CITY	Lovin' Spoonful	*Kama Sutra*	5
2	9	OUT OF TIME	Chris Farlowe and the Thunderbirds	*Immediate*	9
31	10	THEY'RE COMING TO TAKE ME AWAY HA-HAA	Napoleon XIV	*Warner Brothers*	2
7	11	LOVE LETTERS	Elvis Presley	*RCA*	7
15	12	HI-LILI HI-LO	Alan Price Set	*Decca*	5
10	13	I COULDN'T LIVE WITHOUT YOUR LOVE	Petula Clark	*Pye*	8
24	14	LOVERS OF THE WORLD UNITE	David and Jonathan	*Columbia*	5
17	15	I SAW HER AGAIN	Mamas and the Papas	*RCA*	4
22	16	MORE THAN LOVE	Ken Dodd	*Columbia*	3
16	17	I WANT YOU	Bob Dylan	*CBS*	5
27	18	JUST LIKE A WOMAN	Manfred Mann	*Fontana*	3
14	19	GOING BACK	Dusty Springfield	*Philips*	7
39	20	ALL OR NOTHING	Small Faces	*Decca*	2
11	21	GET AWAY	Georgie Fame and the Blue Flames	*Columbia*	9
13	22	SUNNY AFTERNOON	Kinks	*Pye*	11
20	23	STRANGERS IN THE NIGHT	Frank Sinatra	*Reprise*	15
19	24	NOBODY NEEDS YOUR LOVE	Gene Pitney	*Stateside*	11
-	25	TOO SOON TO KNOW	Roy Orbison	*London*	1
38	26	LOVING YOU IS SWEETER THAN EVER	Four Tops	*Tamla Motown*	2
36	27	BAREFOOTIN'	Robert Parker	*Island*	2
37	28	GIVE ME YOUR WORD	Billy Fury	*Decca*	2
29	29	AIN'T TOO PROUD TO BEG	Temptations	*Tamla Motown*	4
23	30	(BABY) YOU DON'T HAVE TO TELL ME	Walker Brothers	*Philips*	6
18	31	RIVER DEEP MOUNTAIN HIGH	Ike and Tina Turner	*London*	11
21	32	I LOVE HOW YOU LOVE ME	Paul and Barry Ryan	*Decca*	4
-	33	DISTANT DRUMS	Jim Reeves	*RCA*	1
-	34	WORKING IN THE COAL MINE	Lee Dorsey	*Stateside*	1
-	35	GOT TO GET YOU INTO MY LIFE	Cliff Bennett and the Rebel Rousers	*Parlophone*	1
25	36	WHEN A MAN LOVES A WOMAN	Percy Sledge	*Atlantic*	14
26	37	BUS STOP	Hollies	*Parlophone*	9
40	[38]	HANKY PANKY	Tommy James and the Shondells	*Roulette*	3
-	39	WARM AND TENDER LOVE	Percy Sledge	*Atlantic*	1
30	40	PAPERBACK WRITER	Beatles	*Parlophone*	10

LW	TW	*WEEK ENDING* 25 AUGUST 1966			Wks
1	[1]	YELLOW SUBMARINE/ELEANOR RIGBY	Beatles	*Parlophone*	3
3	[2]	GOD ONLY KNOWS	Beach Boys	*Capitol*	5
2	3	WITH A GIRL LIKE YOU	Troggs	*Fontana*	7
10	[4]	THEY'RE COMING TO TAKE ME AWAY HA-HAA	Napoleon XIV	*Warner Brothers*	3
5	[5]	MAMA	Dave Berry	*Decca*	9
4	6	BLACK IS BLACK	Los Bravos	*Decca*	9
7	[7]	VISIONS	Cliff Richard	*Columbia*	6
6	8	THE MORE I SEE YOU	Chris Montez	*Pye*	9
20	9	ALL OR NOTHING	Small Faces	*Decca*	3
14	10	LOVERS OF THE WORLD UNITE	David and Jonathan	*Columbia*	6
12	[11]	HI-LILI HI-LO	Alan Price Set	*Decca*	6
8	12	SUMMER IN THE CITY	Lovin' Spoonful	*Kama Sutra*	6
15	13	I SAW HER AGAIN	Mamas and the Papas	*RCA*	5
16	[14]	MORE THAN LOVE	Ken Dodd	*Columbia*	4
9	15	OUT OF TIME	Chris Farlowe and the Thunderbirds	*Immediate*	10
18	16	JUST LIKE A WOMAN	Manfred Mann	*Fontana*	4
25	17	TOO SOON TO KNOW	Roy Orbison	*London*	2
17	18	I WANT YOU	Bob Dylan	*CBS*	6
11	19	LOVE LETTERS	Elvis Presley	*RCA*	8
13	20	I COULDN'T LIVE WITHOUT YOUR LOVE	Petula Clark	*Pye*	9
19	21	GOING BACK	Dusty Springfield	*Philips*	8
33	22	DISTANT DRUMS	Jim Reeves	*RCA*	2
35	23	GOT TO GET YOU INTO MY LIFE	Cliff Bennett and the Rebel Rousers	*Parlophone*	2
29	24	AIN'T TOO PROUD TO BEG	Temptations	*Tamla Motown*	5
27	25	BAREFOOTIN'	Robert Parker	*Island*	3
26	26	LOVING YOU IS SWEETER THAN EVER	Four Tops	*Tamla Motown*	3
23	27	STRANGERS IN THE NIGHT	Frank Sinatra	*Reprise*	16
21	28	GET AWAY	Georgie Fame and the Blue Flames	*Columbia*	10
34	29	WORKING IN THE COAL MINE	Lee Dorsey	*Stateside*	2
28	30	GIVE ME YOUR WORD	Billy Fury	*Decca*	3
22	31	SUNNY AFTERNOON	Kinks	*Pye*	12
-	32	BIG TIME OPERATOR	Zoot Money and the Big Roll Band ●	*Columbia*	1
24	33	NOBODY NEEDS YOUR LOVE	Gene Pitney	*Stateside*	12
39	[34]	WARM AND TENDER LOVE	Percy Sledge	*Atlantic*	2
31	35	RIVER DEEP MOUNTAIN HIGH	Ike and Tina Turner	*London*	12
32	36	I LOVE HOW YOU LOVE ME	Paul and Barry Ryan	*Decca*	5
30	37	(BABY) YOU DON'T HAVE TO TELL ME	Walker Brothers	*Philips*	7
-	38	BLOWIN' IN THE WIND	Stevie Wonder	*Tamla Motown*	1
-	[39]	HEADLINE NEWS	Edwin Starr	*Polydor*	1
38	40	HANKY PANKY	Tommy James and the Shondells	*Roulette*	4

LW	TW	*WEEK ENDING* 1 SEPTEMBER 1966			Wks
1	[1]	YELLOW SUBMARINE/ELEANOR RIGBY	Beatles	*Parlophone*	4
2	[2]	GOD ONLY KNOWS	Beach Boys	*Capitol*	6

In these weeks ■ With the entry of *Distant Drums* there are nine past, present or future number ones in the Top 40. Four of them occupy positions 20 to 23 (18.08.66) ■ The Beatles occupy the pole and anchor positions, heading the lists with the first of their singles to be taken from an already recorded album (18.08.66) ■ For the ninth consecutive week, the record at number 19 is falling down the charts (25.08.66)■

LW	TW	Title	Artist	Label	Wks
9	3	ALL OR NOTHING	Small Faces	*Decca*	4
4	[4]	THEY'RE COMING TO TAKE ME AWAY HA-HAA	Napoleon XIV	*Warner Brothers*	4
3	5	WITH A GIRL LIKE YOU	Troggs	*Fontana*	8
5	6	MAMA	Dave Berry	*Decca*	10
7	[7]	VISIONS	Cliff Richard	*Columbia*	7
17	8	TOO SOON TO KNOW	Roy Orbison	*London*	3
10	9	LOVERS OF THE WORLD UNITE	David and Jonathan	*Columbia*	7
12	10	SUMMER IN THE CITY	Lovin' Spoonful	*Kama Sutra*	7
13	[11]	I SAW HER AGAIN	Mamas and the Papas	*RCA*	6
11	12	HI-LILI HI-LO	Alan Price Set	*Decca*	7
16	13	JUST LIKE A WOMAN	Manfred Mann	*Fontana*	5
8	14	THE MORE I SEE YOU	Chris Montez	*Pye*	10
14	15	MORE THAN LOVE	Ken Dodd	*Columbia*	5
6	16	BLACK IS BLACK	Los Bravos	*Decca*	10
22	17	DISTANT DRUMS	Jim Reeves	*RCA*	3
23	18	GOT TO GET YOU INTO MY LIFE	Cliff Bennett and the Rebel Rousers	*Parlophone*	3
29	19	WORKING IN THE COAL MINE	Lee Dorsey	*Stateside*	3
18	20	I WANT YOU	Bob Dylan	*CBS*	7
24	[21]	AIN'T TOO PROUD TO BEG	Temptations	*Tamla Motown*	6
26	22	LOVING YOU IS SWEETER THAN EVER	Four Tops	*Tamla Motown*	4
15	23	OUT OF TIME	Chris Farlowe and the Thunderbirds	*Immediate*	11
25	[24]	BAREFOOTIN'	Robert Parker	*Island*	4
32	[25]	BIG TIME OPERATOR	Zoot Money and the Big Roll Band	*Columbia*	2
27	26	STRANGERS IN THE NIGHT	Frank Sinatra	*Reprise*	17
30	[27]	GIVE ME YOUR WORD	Billy Fury	*Decca*	4
19	28	LOVE LETTERS	Elvis Presley	*RCA*	9
-	29	ASHES TO ASHES	Mindbenders	*Fontana*	1
21	30	GOING BACK	Dusty Springfield	*Philips*	9
20	31	I COULDN'T LIVE WITHOUT YOUR LOVE	Petula Clark	*Pye*	10
-	32	HOW SWEET IT IS	Junior Walker and the All-Stars ●	*Tamla Motown*	1
-	33	I CAN'T TURN YOU LOOSE	Otis Redding	*Atlantic*	1
34	[34]	WARM AND TENDER LOVE	Percy Sledge	*Atlantic*	3
31	35	SUNNY AFTERNOON	Kinks	*Pye*	13
-	[36]	STOP THAT GIRL	Chris Andrews	*Decca*	1
38	37	BLOWIN' IN THE WIND	Stevie Wonder	*Tamla Motown*	2
-	38	WHEN I COME HOME	Spencer Davis Group	*Fontana*	1
39	[39]	HEADLINE NEWS	Edwin Starr	*Polydor*	2
40	40	HANKY PANKY	Tommy James and the Shondells	*Roulette*	5

September 1966

☐ Highest position disc reached ● Act's first ever week on chart

WEEK ENDING 8 SEPTEMBER 1966

LW	TW	Title	Artist	Label	Wks
1	[1]	YELLOW SUBMARINE/ELEANOR RIGBY	Beatles	*Parlophone*	5
3	2	ALL OR NOTHING	Small Faces	*Decca*	5
2	3	GOD ONLY KNOWS	Beach Boys	*Capitol*	7
4	[4]	THEY'RE COMING TO TAKE ME AWAY HA-HAA	Napoleon XIV	*Warner Brothers*	5
8	5	TOO SOON TO KNOW	Roy Orbison	*London*	4
17	6	DISTANT DRUMS	Jim Reeves	*RCA*	4
9	[7]	LOVERS OF THE WORLD UNITE	David and Jonathan	*Columbia*	8
6	8	MAMA	Dave Berry	*Decca*	11
5	9	WITH A GIRL LIKE YOU	Troggs	*Fontana*	9
19	10	WORKING IN THE COAL MINE	Lee Dorsey	*Stateside*	4
13	11	JUST LIKE A WOMAN	Manfred Mann	*Fontana*	6
7	12	VISIONS	Cliff Richard	*Columbia*	8
11	13	I SAW HER AGAIN	Mamas and the Papas	*RCA*	7
12	14	HI-LILI HI-LO	Alan Price Set	*Decca*	8
18	15	GOT TO GET YOU INTO MY LIFE	Cliff Bennett and the Rebel Rousers	*Parlophone*	4
15	16	MORE THAN LOVE	Ken Dodd	*Columbia*	6
10	17	SUMMER IN THE CITY	Lovin' Spoonful	*Kama Sutra*	8
14	18	THE MORE I SEE YOU	Chris Montez	*Pye*	11
16	19	BLACK IS BLACK	Los Bravos	*Decca*	11
-	20	I'M A BOY	Who	*Reaction*	1
22	[21]	LOVING YOU IS SWEETER THAN EVER	Four Tops	*Tamla Motown*	5
29	22	ASHES TO ASHES	Mindbenders	*Fontana*	2
38	23	WHEN I COME HOME	Spencer Davis Group	*Fontana*	2
24	[24]	BAREFOOTIN'	Robert Parker	*Island*	5
21	25	AIN'T TOO PROUD TO BEG	Temptations	*Tamla Motown*	7
20	26	I WANT YOU	Bob Dylan	*CBS*	8
32	27	HOW SWEET IT IS	Junior Walker and the All-Stars	*Tamla Motown*	2
25	28	BIG TIME OPERATOR	Zoot Money and the Big Roll Band	*Columbia*	3
26	29	STRANGERS IN THE NIGHT	Frank Sinatra	*Reprise*	18
23	30	OUT OF TIME	Chris Farlowe and the Thunderbirds	*Immediate*	12
-	31	WALK WITH ME	Seekers	*Columbia*	1
33	32	I CAN'T TURN YOU LOOSE	Otis Redding	*Atlantic*	2
27	33	GIVE ME YOUR WORD	Billy Fury	*Decca*	5
-	34	LAND OF A THOUSAND DANCES	Wilson Pickett	*Atlantic*	1
-	35	LITTLE MAN	Sonny and Cher	*Atlantic*	1
36	[36]	STOP THAT GIRL	Chris Andrews	*Decca*	2
37	37	BLOWIN' IN THE WIND	Stevie Wonder	*Tamla Motown*	3
-	38	YOU CAN'T HURRY LOVE	Supremes	*Tamla Motown*	1
34	39	WARM AND TENDER LOVE	Percy Sledge	*Atlantic*	4
28	40	LOVE LETTERS	Elvis Presley	*RCA*	10

WEEK ENDING 15 SEPTEMBER 1966

LW	TW	Title	Artist	Label	Wks
2	[1]	ALL OR NOTHING	Small Faces	*Decca*	6
6	2	DISTANT DRUMS	Jim Reeves	*RCA*	5
1	3	YELLOW SUBMARINE/ELEANOR RIGBY	Beatles	*Parlophone*	6
5	4	TOO SOON TO KNOW	Roy Orbison	*London*	5
3	5	GOD ONLY KNOWS	Beach Boys	*Capitol*	8
15	[6]	GOT TO GET YOU INTO MY LIFE	Cliff Bennett and the Rebel Rousers	*Parlophone*	5
4	7	THEY'RE COMING TO TAKE ME AWAY HA-HAA	Napoleon XIV	*Warner Brothers*	6
10	[8]	WORKING IN THE COAL MINE	Lee Dorsey	*Stateside*	5
7	9	LOVERS OF THE WORLD UNITE	David and Jonathan	*Columbia*	9
11	[10]	JUST LIKE A WOMAN	Manfred Mann	*Fontana*	7
8	11	MAMA	Dave Berry	*Decca*	12
35	12	LITTLE MAN	Sonny and Cher	*Atlantic*	2
38	13	YOU CAN'T HURRY LOVE	Supremes	*Tamla Motown*	2
20	14	I'M A BOY	Who	*Reaction*	2
23	15	WHEN I COME HOME	Spencer Davis Group	*Fontana*	3
22	16	ASHES TO ASHES	Mindbenders	*Fontana*	3
13	17	I SAW HER AGAIN	Mamas and the Papas	*RCA*	8
16	18	MORE THAN LOVE	Ken Dodd	*Columbia*	7
12	19	VISIONS	Cliff Richard	*Columbia*	9
14	20	HI-LILI HI-LO	Alan Price Set	*Decca*	9
9	21	WITH A GIRL LIKE YOU	Troggs	*Fontana*	10
27	[22]	HOW SWEET IT IS	Junior Walker and the All-Stars	*Tamla Motown*	3
31	23	WALK WITH ME	Seekers	*Columbia*	2
18	24	THE MORE I SEE YOU	Chris Montez	*Pye*	12
34	25	LAND OF A THOUSAND DANCES	Wilson Pickett	*Atlantic*	2
-	26	WINCHESTER CATHEDRAL	New Vaudeville Band ●	*Fontana*	1
19	27	BLACK IS BLACK	Los Bravos	*Decca*	12
17	28	SUMMER IN THE CITY	Lovin' Spoonful	*Kama Sutra*	9
28	29	BIG TIME OPERATOR	Zoot Money and the Big Roll Band	*Columbia*	4
32	30	I CAN'T TURN YOU LOOSE	Otis Redding	*Atlantic*	3
21	31	LOVING YOU IS SWEETER THAN EVER	Four Tops	*Tamla Motown*	6
-	32	SUNNY	Bobby Hebb ●	*Philips*	1
-	33	RUN	Sandie Shaw	*Pye*	1
25	34	AIN'T TOO PROUD TO BEG	Temptations	*Tamla Motown*	8
24	35	BAREFOOTIN'	Robert Parker	*Island*	6
37	[36]	BLOWIN' IN THE WIND	Stevie Wonder	*Tamla Motown*	4
-	37	BEND IT!	Dave Dee Dozy Beaky Mick and Tich	*Fontana*	1
29	38	STRANGERS IN THE NIGHT	Frank Sinatra	*Reprise*	19
-	[39]	SUMMERTIME	Billy Stewart ●	*Chess*	1
-	40	I DON'T CARE	Los Bravos	*Decca*	1

■Five weeks of chart action for Tommy James' *Hanky Panky* without ever climbing higher than number 38 (01.09.66) ■ For the ninth consecutive week, the records at number 30 and at number 40 are falling down the charts (08.09.66) ■ The final week of Top 40 listing for the man who had more hits than anybody without ever hitting number one - the late Billy Fury (08.09.66)■

September 1966

□ Highest position disc reached ● Act's first ever week on chart

LW	TW	*WEEK ENDING* **22 SEPTEMBER 1966**		Wks
2	1	DISTANT DRUMS Jim Reeves	*RCA*	6
1	2	ALL OR NOTHING Small Faces	*Decca*	7
4	3	TOO SOON TO KNOW Roy Orbison	*London*	6
14	4	I'M A BOY Who	*Reaction*	3
3	5	YELLOW SUBMARINE/ELEANOR RIGBY Beatles	*Parlophone*	7
12	6	LITTLE MAN Sonny and Cher	*Atlantic*	3
13	7	YOU CAN'T HURRY LOVE Supremes	*Tamla Motown*	3
5	8	GOD ONLY KNOWS Beach Boys	*Capitol*	9
6	9	GOT TO GET YOU INTO MY LIFE Cliff Bennett and the Rebel Rousers	*Parlophone*	6
8	10	WORKING IN THE COAL MINE Lee Dorsey	*Stateside*	6
9	11	LOVERS OF THE WORLD UNITE David and Jonathan	*Columbia*	10
15	12	WHEN I COME HOME Spencer Davis Group	*Fontana*	4
37	13	BEND IT! Dave Dee Dozy Beaky Mick and Tich	*Fontana*	2
16	14	ASHES TO ASHES Mindbenders	*Fontana*	4
11	15	MAMA Dave Berry	*Decca*	13
7	16	THEY'RE COMING TO TAKE ME AWAY HA-HAA Napoleon XIV	*Warner Brothers*	7
23	17	WALK WITH ME Seekers	*Columbia*	3
26	18	WINCHESTER CATHEDRAL New Vaudeville Band	*Fontana*	2
-	19	ALL I SEE IS YOU Dusty Springfield	*Philips*	1
10	20	JUST LIKE A WOMAN Manfred Mann	*Fontana*	8
32	21	SUNNY Bobby Hebb	*Philips*	2
25	22	LAND OF A THOUSAND DANCES Wilson Pickett	*Atlantic*	3
18	23	MORE THAN LOVE Ken Dodd	*Columbia*	8
22	24	HOW SWEET IT IS Junior Walker and the All-Stars	*Tamla Motown*	4
29	25	BIG TIME OPERATOR Zoot Money and the Big Roll Band	*Columbia*	5
40	26	I DON'T CARE Los Bravos	*Decca*	2
19	27	VISIONS Cliff Richard	*Columbia*	10
17	28	I SAW HER AGAIN Mamas and the Papas	*RCA*	9
30	29	I CAN'T TURN YOU LOOSE Otis Redding	*Atlantic*	4
20	30	HI-LILI HI-LO Alan Price Set	*Decca*	10
-	31	GUANTANAMERA Sandpipers ●	*Pye*	1
33	32	RUN Sandie Shaw	*Pye*	2
-	33	ANOTHER TEAR FALLS Walker Brothers	*Philips*	1
21	34	WITH A GIRL LIKE YOU Troggs	*Fontana*	11
24	35	THE MORE I SEE YOU Chris Montez	*Pye*	13
31	36	LOVING YOU IS SWEETER THAN EVER Four Tops	*Tamla Motown*	7
28	37	SUMMER IN THE CITY Lovin' Spoonful	*Kama Sutra*	10
-	38	SUNNY Georgie Fame	*Columbia*	1
-	39	IN THE ARMS OF LOVE Andy Williams	*CBS*	1
-	40	BORN A WOMAN Sandy Posey ●	*MGM*	1

LW	TW	*WEEK ENDING* **29 SEPTEMBER 1966**		Wks
1	1	DISTANT DRUMS Jim Reeves	*RCA*	7
4	2	I'M A BOY Who	*Reaction*	4
7	3	YOU CAN'T HURRY LOVE Supremes	*Tamla Motown*	4
6	4	LITTLE MAN Sonny and Cher	*Atlantic*	4
3	5	TOO SOON TO KNOW Roy Orbison	*London*	7
13	6	BEND IT! Dave Dee Dozy Beaky Mick and Tich	*Fontana*	3
18	7	WINCHESTER CATHEDRAL New Vaudeville Band	*Fontana*	3
2	8	ALL OR NOTHING Small Faces	*Decca*	8
5	9	YELLOW SUBMARINE/ELEANOR RIGBY Beatles	*Parlophone*	8
17	10	WALK WITH ME Seekers	*Columbia*	4
19	11	ALL I SEE IS YOU Dusty Springfield	*Philips*	2
11	12	LOVERS OF THE WORLD UNITE David and Jonathan	*Columbia*	11
10	13	WORKING IN THE COAL MINE Lee Dorsey	*Stateside*	7
21	14	SUNNY Bobby Hebb	*Philips*	3
9	15	GOT TO GET YOU INTO MY LIFE Cliff Bennett and the Rebel Rousers	*Parlophone*	7
8	16	GOD ONLY KNOWS Beach Boys	*Capitol*	10
-	17	HAVE YOU SEEN YOUR MOTHER BABY STANDING IN THE SHADOW Rolling Stones	*Decca*	1
31	18	GUANTANAMERA Sandpipers	*Pye*	2
12	19	WHEN I COME HOME Spencer Davis Group	*Fontana*	5
14	20	ASHES TO ASHES Mindbenders	*Fontana*	5
26	21	I DON'T CARE Los Bravos	*Decca*	3
38	22	SUNNY Georgie Fame	*Columbia*	2
33	23	ANOTHER TEAR FALLS Walker Brothers	*Philips*	2
22	24	LAND OF A THOUSAND DANCES Wilson Pickett	*Atlantic*	4
15	25	MAMA Dave Berry	*Decca*	14
24	26	HOW SWEET IT IS Junior Walker and the All-Stars	*Tamla Motown*	5
16	27	THEY'RE COMING TO TAKE ME AWAY HA-HAA Napoleon XIV	*Warner Brothers*	8
20	28	JUST LIKE A WOMAN Manfred Mann	*Fontana*	9
23	29	MORE THAN LOVE Ken Dodd	*Columbia*	9
-	30	LADY GODIVA Peter and Gordon	*Columbia*	1
25	31	BIG TIME OPERATOR Zoot Money and the Big Roll Band	*Columbia*	6
28	32	I SAW HER AGAIN Mamas and the Papas	*RCA*	10
29	33	I CAN'T TURN YOU LOOSE Otis Redding	*Atlantic*	5
-	34	SOMEWHERE MY LOVE Mike Sammes Singers ●	*HMV*	1
27	35	VISIONS Cliff Richard	*Columbia*	11
-	36	DEAR MRS. APPLEBEE David Garrick	*Piccadilly*	1
-	37	SUNNY Cher	*Liberty*	1
40	38	BORN A WOMAN Sandy Posey	*MGM*	2
32	39	RUN Sandie Shaw	*Pye*	3
39	40	IN THE ARMS OF LOVE Andy Williams	*CBS*	2

LW	TW	*WEEK ENDING* **6 OCTOBER 1966**		Wks
1	1	DISTANT DRUMS Jim Reeves	*RCA*	8
6	2	BEND IT! Dave Dee Dozy Beaky Mick and Tich	*Fontana*	4
2	3	I'M A BOY Who	*Reaction*	5
3	4	YOU CAN'T HURRY LOVE Supremes	*Tamla Motown*	5
4	5	LITTLE MAN Sonny and Cher	*Atlantic*	5
7	6	WINCHESTER CATHEDRAL New Vaudeville Band	*Fontana*	4
17	7	HAVE YOU SEEN YOUR MOTHER BABY STANDING IN THE SHADOW Rolling Stones	*Decca*	2
5	8	TOO SOON TO KNOW Roy Orbison	*London*	8
11	9	ALL I SEE IS YOU Dusty Springfield	*Philips*	3
18	10	GUANTANAMERA Sandpipers	*Pye*	3
10	11	WALK WITH ME Seekers	*Columbia*	5
14	12	SUNNY Bobby Hebb	*Philips*	4
8	13	ALL OR NOTHING Small Faces	*Decca*	9
23	14	ANOTHER TEAR FALLS Walker Brothers	*Philips*	3
22	15	SUNNY Georgie Fame	*Columbia*	3
21	16	I DON'T CARE Los Bravos	*Decca*	4
-	17	I CAN'T CONTROL MYSELF Troggs	*Page One*	1
9	18	YELLOW SUBMARINE/ELEANOR RIGBY Beatles	*Parlophone*	9
13	19	WORKING IN THE COAL MINE Lee Dorsey	*Stateside*	8
19	20	WHEN I COME HOME Spencer Davis Group	*Fontana*	6
16	21	GOD ONLY KNOWS Beach Boys	*Capitol*	11
12	22	LOVERS OF THE WORLD UNITE David and Jonathan	*Columbia*	12
15	23	GOT TO GET YOU INTO MY LIFE Cliff Bennett and the Rebel Rousers	*Parlophone*	8
30	24	LADY GODIVA Peter and Gordon	*Columbia*	2
24	25	LAND OF A THOUSAND DANCES Wilson Pickett	*Atlantic*	5
20	26	ASHES TO ASHES Mindbenders	*Fontana*	6
36	27	DEAR MRS. APPLEBEE David Garrick	*Piccadilly*	2
34	28	SOMEWHERE MY LOVE Mike Sammes Singers	*HMV*	2
-	29	I'VE GOT YOU UNDER MY SKIN Four Seasons	*Philips*	1
25	30	MAMA Dave Berry	*Decca*	15
38	31	BORN A WOMAN Sandy Posey	*MGM*	3
37	32	SUNNY Cher	*Liberty*	2
40	33	IN THE ARMS OF LOVE Andy Williams	*CBS*	3
26	34	HOW SWEET IT IS Junior Walker and the All-Stars	*Tamla Motown*	6
-	35	NO MILK TODAY Herman's Hermits	*Columbia*	1
-	36	SUMMER WIND Frank Sinatra	*Reprise*	1
-	37	THERE WILL NEVER BE ANOTHER YOU Chris Montez	*Pye*	1
28	38	JUST LIKE A WOMAN Manfred Mann	*Fontana*	10
33	39	I CAN'T TURN YOU LOOSE Otis Redding	*Atlantic*	6
27	40	THEY'RE COMING TO TAKE ME AWAY HA-HAA Napoleon XIV	*Warner Brothers*	9

In these weeks ■ Jim Reeves hits number one over two years after his death (22.09.66) ■ For the first time ever, after 11 number one hits, the Beatles occupy the number nine position in the charts (29.09.66) ■ For three weeks, three versions of *Sunny* battle for chart supremacy. Composer Bobby Hebb achieves the highest placing (06.10.66)■

November 1966

□ Highest position disc reached ● Act's first ever week on chart

LW	TW	WEEK ENDING 13 OCTOBER 1966		Wks
1	1	DISTANT DRUMS Jim Reeves	*RCA*	9
2	2	BEND IT! Dave Dee Dozy Beaky Mick and Tich	*Fontana*	5
3	3	I'M A BOY Who	*Reaction*	6
6	4	WINCHESTER CATHEDRAL New Vaudeville Band	*Fontana*	5
7	5	HAVE YOU SEEN YOUR MOTHER BABY STANDING IN THE SHADOW Rolling Stones	*Decca*	3
4	6	YOU CAN'T HURRY LOVE Supremes	*Tamla Motown*	6
10	7	GUANTANAMERA Sandpipers	*Pye*	4
5	8	LITTLE MAN Sonny and Cher	*Atlantic*	6
17	9	I CAN'T CONTROL MYSELF Troggs	*Page One*	2
9	10	ALL I SEE IS YOU Dusty Springfield	*Philips*	4
11	11	WALK WITH ME Seekers	*Columbia*	6
14	12	ANOTHER TEAR FALLS Walker Brothers	*Philips*	4
15	13	SUNNY Georgie Fame	*Columbia*	4
8	14	TOO SOON TO KNOW Roy Orbison	*London*	9
12	15	SUNNY Bobby Hebb	*Philips*	5
24	16	LADY GODIVA Peter and Gordon	*Columbia*	3
16	17	I DON'T CARE Los Bravos	*Decca*	5
29	18	I'VE GOT YOU UNDER MY SKIN Four Seasons	*Philips*	2
-	19	REACH OUT I'LL BE THERE Four Tops	*Tamla Motown*	1
35	20	NO MILK TODAY Herman's Hermits	*Columbia*	2
13	21	ALL OR NOTHING Small Faces	*Decca*	10
27	22	DEAR MRS. APPLEBEE David Garrick	*Piccadilly*	3
20	23	WHEN I COME HOME Spencer Davis Group	*Fontana*	7
19	24	WORKING IN THE COAL MINE Lee Dorsey	*Stateside*	9
21	25	GOD ONLY KNOWS Beach Boys	*Capitol*	12
18	26	YELLOW SUBMARINE/ELEANOR RIGBY Beatles	*Parlophone*	10
-	27	STOP STOP STOP Hollies	*Parlophone*	1
31	28	BORN A WOMAN Sandy Posey	*MGM*	4
25	29	LAND OF A THOUSAND DANCES Wilson Pickett	*Atlantic*	6
28	30	SOMEWHERE MY LOVE Mike Sammes Singers	*HMV*	3
23	31	GOT TO GET YOU INTO MY LIFE Cliff Bennett and the Rebel Rousers	*Parlophone*	9
22	32	LOVERS OF THE WORLD UNITE David and Jonathan	*Columbia*	13
33	33	IN THE ARMS OF LOVE Andy Williams	*CBS*	4
-	34	TIME DRAGS BY Cliff Richard	*Columbia*	1
-	35	BEAUTY IS ONLY SKIN DEEP Temptations	*Tamla Motown*	1
26	36	ASHES TO ASHES Mindbenders	*Fontana*	7
32	37	SUNNY Cher	*Liberty*	3
36	38	SUMMER WIND Frank Sinatra	*Reprise*	2
-	39	HIGH TIME Paul Jones ●	*HMV*	1
-	40	ALL THAT I AM Elvis Presley	*RCA*	1

LW	TW	WEEK ENDING 20 OCTOBER 1966		Wks
1	1	DISTANT DRUMS Jim Reeves	*RCA*	10
19	2	REACH OUT I'LL BE THERE Four Tops	*Tamla Motown*	2
2	3	BEND IT! Dave Dee Dozy Beaky Mick and Tich	*Fontana*	6
9	4	I CAN'T CONTROL MYSELF Troggs	*Page One*	3
3	5	I'M A BOY Who	*Reaction*	8
4	6	WINCHESTER CATHEDRAL New Vaudeville Band	*Fontana*	6
7	7	GUANTANAMERA Sandpipers	*Pye*	5
5	8	HAVE YOU SEEN YOUR MOTHER BABY STANDING IN THE SHADOW Rolling Stones	*Decca*	4
6	9	YOU CAN'T HURRY LOVE Supremes	*Tamla Motown*	7
27	10	STOP STOP STOP Hollies	*Parlophone*	2
10	11	ALL I SEE IS YOU Dusty Springfield	*Philips*	5
11	12	WALK WITH ME Seekers	*Columbia*	7
8	13	LITTLE MAN Sonny and Cher	*Atlantic*	7
13	14	SUNNY Georgie Fame	*Columbia*	5
14	15	TOO SOON TO KNOW Roy Orbison	*London*	10
16	16	LADY GODIVA Peter and Gordon	*Columbia*	4
20	17	NO MILK TODAY Herman's Hermits	*Columbia*	3
12	18	ANOTHER TEAR FALLS Walker Brothers	*Philips*	5
17	19	I DON'T CARE Los Bravos	*Decca*	6
18	20	I'VE GOT YOU UNDER MY SKIN Four Seasons	*Philips*	3
34	21	TIME DRAGS BY Cliff Richard	*Columbia*	2
15	22	SUNNY Bobby Hebb	*Philips*	6
22	23	DEAR MRS. APPLEBEE David Garrick	*Piccadilly*	4
28	24	BORN A WOMAN Sandy Posey	*MGM*	5
35	25	BEAUTY IS ONLY SKIN DEEP Temptations	*Tamla Motown*	2
40	26	ALL THAT I AM Elvis Presley	*RCA*	2
30	27	SOMEWHERE MY LOVE Mike Sammes Singers	*HMV*	4
39	28	HIGH TIME Paul Jones	*HMV*	2
-	29	IF I WERE A CARPENTER Bobby Darin	*Atlantic*	1
26	30	YELLOW SUBMARINE/ELEANOR RIGBY Beatles	*Parlophone*	11
25	31	GOD ONLY KNOWS Beach Boys	*Capitol*	13
23	32	WHEN I COME HOME Spencer Davis Group	*Fontana*	8
21	33	ALL OR NOTHING Small Faces	*Decca*	11
24	34	WORKING IN THE COAL MINE Lee Dorsey	*Stateside*	10
33	35	IN THE ARMS OF LOVE Andy Williams	*CBS*	5
29	36	LAND OF A THOUSAND DANCES Wilson Pickett	*Atlantic*	7
38	37	SUMMER WIND Frank Sinatra	*Reprise*	3
-	38	A FOOL AM I Cilla Black	*Parlophone*	1
-	39	I LOVE MY DOG Cat Stevens ●	*Deram*	1
31	40	GOT TO GET YOU INTO MY LIFE Cliff Bennett and the Rebel Rousers	*Parlophone*	10

LW	TW	WEEK ENDING 27 OCTOBER 1966		Wks
2	1	REACH OUT I'LL BE THERE Four Tops	*Tamla Motown*	3
4	2	I CAN'T CONTROL MYSELF Troggs	*Page One*	4
1	3	DISTANT DRUMS Jim Reeves	*RCA*	11
10	4	STOP STOP STOP Hollies	*Parlophone*	3
6	5	WINCHESTER CATHEDRAL New Vaudeville Band	*Fontana*	7
3	6	BEND IT! Dave Dee Dozy Beaky Mick and Tich	*Fontana*	7
7	7	GUANTANAMERA Sandpipers	*Pye*	6
5	8	I'M A BOY Who	*Reaction*	9
17	9	NO MILK TODAY Herman's Hermits	*Columbia*	4
8	10	HAVE YOU SEEN YOUR MOTHER BABY STANDING IN THE SHADOW Rolling Stones	*Decca*	5
11	11	ALL I SEE IS YOU Dusty Springfield	*Philips*	6
9	12	YOU CAN'T HURRY LOVE Supremes	*Tamla Motown*	8
21	13	TIME DRAGS BY Cliff Richard	*Columbia*	3
20	14	I'VE GOT YOU UNDER MY SKIN Four Seasons	*Philips*	4
28	15	HIGH TIME Paul Jones	*HMV*	3
12	16	WALK WITH ME Seekers	*Columbia*	8
16	17	LADY GODIVA Peter and Gordon	*Columbia*	5
29	18	IF I WERE A CARPENTER Bobby Darin	*Atlantic*	2
14	19	SUNNY Georgie Fame	*Columbia*	6
15	20	TOO SOON TO KNOW Roy Orbison	*London*	11
25	21	BEAUTY IS ONLY SKIN DEEP Temptations	*Tamla Motown*	3
26	22	ALL THAT I AM Elvis Presley	*RCA*	3
38	23	A FOOL AM I Cilla Black	*Parlophone*	2
13	24	LITTLE MAN Sonny and Cher	*Atlantic*	8
24	25	BORN A WOMAN Sandy Posey	*MGM*	6
18	26	ANOTHER TEAR FALLS Walker Brothers	*Philips*	6
19	27	I DON'T CARE Los Bravos	*Decca*	7
23	28	DEAR MRS. APPLEBEE David Garrick	*Piccadilly*	5
39	29	I LOVE MY DOG Cat Stevens	*Deram*	2
27	30	SOMEWHERE MY LOVE Mike Sammes Singers	*HMV*	5
22	31	SUNNY Bobby Hebb	*Philips*	7
-	32	SEMI-DETACHED SUBURBAN MR. JAMES Manfred Mann	*Fontana*	1
30	33	YELLOW SUBMARINE/ELEANOR RIGBY Beatles	*Parlophone*	12
-	34	WRAPPING PAPER Cream ●	*Reaction*	1
35	35	IN THE ARMS OF LOVE Andy Williams	*CBS*	6
-	36	HELP ME GIRL Eric Burdon and the Animals ●	*Decca*	1
-	37	RIDE ON BABY Chris Farlowe and the Thunderbirds	*Immediate*	1
-	38	A LOVE LIKE YOURS Ike and Tina Turner	*London*	1
37	39	SUMMER WIND Frank Sinatra	*Reprise*	4
36	40	LAND OF A THOUSAND DANCES Wilson Pickett	*Atlantic*	8

LW	TW	WEEK ENDING 3 NOVEMBER 1966		Wks
1	1	REACH OUT I'LL BE THERE Four Tops	*Tamla Motown*	4
4	2	STOP STOP STOP Hollies	*Parlophone*	4
2	3	I CAN'T CONTROL MYSELF Troggs	*Page One*	5
3	4	DISTANT DRUMS Jim Reeves	*RCA*	12

■As Manfred Mann's first single with Mike d'Abo as lead vocalist drops off the chart, his predecessor Paul Jones makes his solo debut (13.10.66) ■ Another previous member of Manfred Mann, Jack Bruce, makes his first entrance with ex-Yardbird Eric Clapton and ex-Acker Bilk drummer Ginger Baker, as Cream (27.10.66)■

November 1966

□ Highest position disc reached ● Act's first ever week on chart

LW	TW	Title	Artist	Label	Wks
5	5	WINCHESTER CATHEDRAL	New Vaudeville Band	Fontana	8
15	6	HIGH TIME	Paul Jones	HMV	4
9	7	NO MILK TODAY	Herman's Hermits	Columbia	5
7	8	GUANTANAMERA	Sandpipers	Pye	7
6	9	BEND IT!	Dave Dee Dozy Beaky Mick and Tich	Fontana	8
13	10	TIME DRAGS BY	Cliff Richard	Columbia	4
32	11	SEMI-DETACHED SUBURBAN MR. JAMES	Manfred Mann	Fontana	2
14	12	I'VE GOT YOU UNDER MY SKIN	Four Seasons	Philips	5
18	13	IF I WERE A CARPENTER	Bobby Darin	Atlantic	3
23	14	A FOOL AM I	Cilla Black	Parlophone	3
-	15	GOOD VIBRATIONS	Beach Boys	Capitol	1
8	16	I'M A BOY	Who	Reaction	10
11	17	ALL I SEE IS YOU	Dusty Springfield	Philips	7
22	18	ALL THAT I AM	Elvis Presley	RCA	4
10	19	HAVE YOU SEEN YOUR MOTHER BABY STANDING IN THE SHADOW	Rolling Stones	Decca	6
12	20	YOU CAN'T HURRY LOVE	Supremes	Tamla Motown	9
20	21	TOO SOON TO KNOW	Roy Orbison	London	12
21	22	BEAUTY IS ONLY SKIN DEEP	Temptations	Tamla Motown	4
17	23	LADY GODIVA	Peter and Gordon	Columbia	6
16	24	WALK WITH ME	Seekers	Columbia	9
-	25	HOLY COW	Lee Dorsey	Stateside	1
-	26	GIMME SOME LOVING	Spencer Davis Group	Fontana	1
36	27	HELP ME GIRL	Eric Burdon and the Animals	Decca	2
29	28	I LOVE MY DOG	Cat Stevens	Deram	3
30	29	SOMEWHERE MY LOVE	Mike Sammes Singers	HMV	6
19	30	SUNNY	Georgie Fame	Columbia	7
25	31	BORN A WOMAN	Sandy Posey	MGM	7
38	32	A LOVE LIKE YOURS	Ike and Tina Turner	London	2
24	33	LITTLE MAN	Sonny and Cher	Atlantic	9
37	34	RIDE ON BABY	Chris Farlowe and the Thunderbirds	Immediate	2
34	35	WRAPPING PAPER	Cream	Reaction	2
28	36	DEAR MRS. APPLEBEE	David Garrick	Piccadilly	6
26	37	ANOTHER TEAR FALLS	Walker Brothers	Philips	7
-	38	PAINTER MAN	Creation ●	Planet	1
-	39	FRIDAY ON MY MIND	Easybeats ●	United Artists	1
27	40	I DON'T CARE	Los Bravos	Decca	8

WEEK ENDING 10 NOVEMBER 1966

LW	TW	Title	Artist	Label	Wks
1	1	REACH OUT I'LL BE THERE	Four Tops	Tamla Motown	5
2	2	STOP STOP STOP	Hollies	Parlophone	5
11	3	SEMI-DETACHED SUBURBAN MR. JAMES	Manfred Mann	Fontana	3
6	4	HIGH TIME	Paul Jones	HMV	5
15	5	GOOD VIBRATIONS	Beach Boys	Capitol	2
3	6	I CAN'T CONTROL MYSELF	Troggs	Page One	6
4	7	DISTANT DRUMS	Jim Reeves	RCA	13
26	8	GIMME SOME LOVING	Spencer Davis Group	Fontana	2
7	9	NO MILK TODAY	Herman's Hermits	Columbia	6
5	10	WINCHESTER CATHEDRAL	New Vaudeville Band	Fontana	9
10	11	TIME DRAGS BY	Cliff Richard	Columbia	5
8	12	GUANTANAMERA	Sandpipers	Pye	8
13	13	IF I WERE A CARPENTER	Bobby Darin	Atlantic	4
14	14	A FOOL AM I	Cilla Black	Parlophone	4
9	15	BEND IT!	Dave Dee Dozy Beaky Mick and Tich	Fontana	9
25	16	HOLY COW	Lee Dorsey	Stateside	2
12	17	I'VE GOT YOU UNDER MY SKIN	Four Seasons	Philips	6
22	18	BEAUTY IS ONLY SKIN DEEP	Temptations	Tamla Motown	5
16	19	I'M A BOY	Who	Reaction	11
27	20	HELP ME GIRL	Eric Burdon and the Animals	Decca	3
23	21	LADY GODIVA	Peter and Gordon	Columbia	7
19	22	HAVE YOU SEEN YOUR MOTHER BABY STANDING IN THE SHADOW	Rolling Stones	Decca	7
17	23	ALL I SEE IS YOU	Dusty Springfield	Philips	8
18	24	ALL THAT I AM	Elvis Presley	RCA	5
20	25	YOU CAN'T HURRY LOVE	Supremes	Tamla Motown	10
32	26	A LOVE LIKE YOURS	Ike and Tina Turner	London	3
21	27	TOO SOON TO KNOW	Roy Orbison	London	13
28	28	I LOVE MY DOG	Cat Stevens	Deram	4
29	29	SOMEWHERE MY LOVE	Mike Sammes Singers	HMV	7
24	30	WALK WITH ME	Seekers	Columbia	10
-	31	WHAT WOULD I BE	Val Doonican	Decca	1
31	32	BORN A WOMAN	Sandy Posey	MGM	8
39	33	FRIDAY ON MY MIND	Easybeats	United Artists	2
34	34	RIDE ON BABY	Chris Farlowe and the Thunderbirds	Immediate	3
-	35	GREEN GREEN GRASS OF HOME	Tom Jones	Decca	1
38	36	PAINTER MAN	Creation	Planet	2
35	37	WRAPPING PAPER	Cream	Reaction	3
-	38	IT'S LOVE	Ken Dodd	Columbia	1
40	39	I DON'T CARE	Los Bravos	Decca	9
33	40	LITTLE MAN	Sonny and Cher	Atlantic	10

WEEK ENDING 17 NOVEMBER 1966

LW	TW	Title	Artist	Label	Wks
5	1	GOOD VIBRATIONS	Beach Boys	Capitol	3
3	2	SEMI-DETACHED SUBURBAN MR. JAMES	Manfred Mann	Fontana	4
1	3	REACH OUT I'LL BE THERE	Four Tops	Tamla Motown	6
8	4	GIMME SOME LOVING	Spencer Davis Group	Fontana	3
4	5	HIGH TIME	Paul Jones	HMV	6
16	6	HOLY COW	Lee Dorsey	Stateside	3
2	7	STOP STOP STOP	Hollies	Parlophone	6
6	8	I CAN'T CONTROL MYSELF	Troggs	Page One	7
13	9	IF I WERE A CARPENTER	Bobby Darin	Atlantic	5
35	10	GREEN GREEN GRASS OF HOME	Tom Jones	Decca	2
7	11	DISTANT DRUMS	Jim Reeves	RCA	14
9	12	NO MILK TODAY	Herman's Hermits	Columbia	7
14	13	A FOOL AM I	Cilla Black	Parlophone	5
10	14	WINCHESTER CATHEDRAL	New Vaudeville Band	Fontana	10
12	15	GUANTANAMERA	Sandpipers	Pye	9
31	16	WHAT WOULD I BE	Val Doonican	Decca	2
20	17	HELP ME GIRL	Eric Burdon and the Animals	Decca	4
11	18	TIME DRAGS BY	Cliff Richard	Columbia	6
15	19	BEND IT!	Dave Dee Dozy Beaky Mick and Tich	Fontana	10
33	20	FRIDAY ON MY MIND	Easybeats	United Artists	3
26	21	A LOVE LIKE YOURS	Ike and Tina Turner	London	4
17	22	I'VE GOT YOU UNDER MY SKIN	Four Seasons	Philips	7
23	23	ALL I SEE IS YOU	Dusty Springfield	Philips	9
-	24	WHAT BECOMES OF THE BROKEN HEARTED?	Jimmy Ruffin ●	Tamla Motown	1
18	25	BEAUTY IS ONLY SKIN DEEP	Temptations	Tamla Motown	6
29	26	SOMEWHERE MY LOVE	Mike Sammes Singers	HMV	8
24	27	ALL THAT I AM	Elvis Presley	RCA	6
-	28	JUST ONE SMILE	Gene Pitney	Stateside	1
-	29	MY MIND'S EYE	Small Faces	Decca	1
21	30	LADY GODIVA	Peter and Gordon	Columbia	8
28	31	I LOVE MY DOG	Cat Stevens	Deram	5
34	32	RIDE ON BABY	Chris Farlowe and the Thunderbirds	Immediate	4
30	33	WALK WITH ME	Seekers	Columbia	11
27	34	TOO SOON TO KNOW	Roy Orbison	London	14
25	35	YOU CAN'T HURRY LOVE	Supremes	Tamla Motown	11
19	36	I'M A BOY	Who	Reaction	12
-	37	I CAN'T MAKE IT ALONE	P.J. Proby	Liberty	1
32	38	BORN A WOMAN	Sandy Posey	MGM	9
22	39	HAVE YOU SEEN YOUR MOTHER BABY STANDING IN THE SHADOW	Rolling Stones	Decca	8
38	40	IT'S LOVE	Ken Dodd	Columbia	2

WEEK ENDING 24 NOVEMBER 1966

LW	TW	Title	Artist	Label	Wks
1	1	GOOD VIBRATIONS	Beach Boys	Capitol	4
4	2	GIMME SOME LOVING	Spencer Davis Group	Fontana	4
10	3	GREEN GREEN GRASS OF HOME	Tom Jones	Decca	3
3	4	REACH OUT I'LL BE THERE	Four Tops	Tamla Motown	7
2	5	SEMI-DETACHED SUBURBAN MR. JAMES	Manfred Mann	Fontana	5
5	6	HIGH TIME	Paul Jones	HMV	7
6	7	HOLY COW	Lee Dorsey	Stateside	4
7	8	STOP STOP STOP	Hollies	Parlophone	7
16	9	WHAT WOULD I BE	Val Doonican	Decca	3

In these weeks ■ *I Love My Dog* by Cat Stevens is the second hit this year to link cats and dogs. Norma Tanega's *Walking My Cat Named Dog* reached number 22 in May (10.11.66) ■ *Good Vibrations* is the third consecutive American number one single, the first time that three U.S. discs in a row have topped our charts since 20 July 1961 (17.11.66) ■

LW	TW	Title	Artist	Label	Wks
9	10	IF I WERE A CARPENTER	Bobby Darin	*Atlantic*	6
8	11	I CAN'T CONTROL MYSELF	Troggs	*Page One*	8
11	12	DISTANT DRUMS	Jim Reeves	*RCA*	15
28	13	JUST ONE SMILE	Gene Pitney	*Stateside*	2
17	□ 14	HELP ME GIRL	Eric Burdon and the Animals	*Decca*	5
29	15	MY MIND'S EYE	Small Faces	*Decca*	2
21	□ 16	A LOVE LIKE YOURS	Ike and Tina Turner	*London*	5
20	17	FRIDAY ON MY MIND	Easybeats	*United Artists*	4
12	18	NO MILK TODAY	Herman's Hermits	*Columbia*	8
15	19	GUANTANAMERA	Sandpipers	*Pye*	10
13	20	A FOOL AM I	Cilla Black	*Parlophone*	6
24	21	WHAT BECOMES OF THE BROKEN HEARTED?	Jimmy Ruffin	*Tamla Motown*	2
14	22	WINCHESTER CATHEDRAL	New Vaudeville Band	*Fontana*	11
18	23	TIME DRAGS BY	Cliff Richard	*Columbia*	7
19	24	BEND IT!	Dave Dee Dozy Beaky Mick and Tich	*Fontana*	11
26	25	SOMEWHERE MY LOVE	Mike Sammes Singers	*HMV*	9
22	26	I'VE GOT YOU UNDER MY SKIN	Four Seasons	*Philips*	8
25	27	BEAUTY IS ONLY SKIN DEEP	Temptations	*Tamla Motown*	7
-	28	WHITE CLIFFS OF DOVER	Righteous Brothers	*London*	1
23	29	ALL I SEE IS YOU	Dusty Springfield	*Philips*	10
27	30	ALL THAT I AM	Elvis Presley	*RCA*	7
32	□ 31	RIDE ON BABY	Chris Farlowe and the Thunderbirds	*Immediate*	5
30	32	LADY GODIVA	Peter and Gordon	*Columbia*	9
-	33	DEAD END STREET	Kinks	*Pye*	1
31	34	I LOVE MY DOG	Cat Stevens	*Deram*	6
-	35	MORNINGTOWN RIDE	Seekers	*Columbia*	1
-	36	FA-FA-FA-FA-FA (SAD SONG)	Otis Redding	*Atlantic*	1
-	37	THINK SOMETIMES ABOUT ME	Sandie Shaw	*Pye*	1
40	38	IT'S LOVE	Ken Dodd	*Columbia*	3
34	39	TOO SOON TO KNOW	Roy Orbison	*London*	15
-	40	96 TEARS	? (Question Mark) and the Mysterians ●	*Cameo Parkway*	1

LW	TW	*WEEK ENDING* 1 DECEMBER 1966			Wks
3	□ 1	GREEN GREEN GRASS OF HOME	Tom Jones	*Decca*	4
1	2	GOOD VIBRATIONS	Beach Boys	*Capitol*	5
2	3	GIMME SOME LOVING	Spencer Davis Group	*Fontana*	5
9	4	WHAT WOULD I BE	Val Doonican	*Decca*	4
5	5	SEMI-DETACHED SUBURBAN MR. JAMES	Manfred Mann	*Fontana*	6
7	□ 6	HOLY COW	Lee Dorsey	*Stateside*	5
4	7	REACH OUT I'LL BE THERE	Four Tops	*Tamla Motown*	8
15	8	MY MIND'S EYE	Small Faces	*Decca*	3
13	9	JUST ONE SMILE	Gene Pitney	*Stateside*	3
6	10	HIGH TIME	Paul Jones	*HMV*	8
17	11	FRIDAY ON MY MIND	Easybeats	*United Artists*	5
12	12	DISTANT DRUMS	Jim Reeves	*RCA*	16
8	13	STOP STOP STOP	Hollies	*Parlophone*	8
21	14	WHAT BECOMES OF THE BROKEN HEARTED?	Jimmy Ruffin	*Tamla Motown*	3
10	15	IF I WERE A CARPENTER	Bobby Darin	*Atlantic*	7
33	16	DEAD END STREET	Kinks	*Pye*	2
16	17	A LOVE LIKE YOURS	Ike and Tina Turner	*London*	6
35	18	MORNINGTOWN RIDE	Seekers	*Columbia*	2
11	19	I CAN'T CONTROL MYSELF	Troggs	*Page One*	9
14	20	HELP ME GIRL	Eric Burdon and the Animals	*Decca*	6
20	21	A FOOL AM I	Cilla Black	*Parlophone*	7
25	□ 22	SOMEWHERE MY LOVE	Mike Sammes Singers	*HMV*	10
18	23	NO MILK TODAY	Herman's Hermits	*Columbia*	9
19	24	GUANTANAMERA	Sandpipers	*Pye*	11
28	25	WHITE CLIFFS OF DOVER	Righteous Brothers	*London*	2
22	26	WINCHESTER CATHEDRAL	New Vaudeville Band	*Fontana*	12
23	27	TIME DRAGS BY	Cliff Richard	*Columbia*	8
36	28	FA-FA-FA-FA-FA (SAD SONG)	Otis Redding	*Atlantic*	2
-	29	YOU KEEP ME HANGIN' ON	Supremes	*Tamla Motown*	1
27	30	BEAUTY IS ONLY SKIN DEEP	Temptations	*Tamla Motown*	8
31	□ 31	RIDE ON BABY	Chris Farlowe and the Thunderbirds	*Immediate*	6
37	□ 32	THINK SOMETIMES ABOUT ME	Sandie Shaw	*Pye*	2
24	33	BEND IT!	Dave Dee Dozy Beaky Mick and Tich	*Fontana*	12
26	34	I'VE GOT YOU UNDER MY SKIN	Four Seasons	*Philips*	9
30	35	ALL THAT I AM	Elvis Presley	*RCA*	8
38	□ 36	IT'S LOVE	Ken Dodd	*Columbia*	4

December 1966

□ Highest position disc reached ● Act's first ever week on chart

LW	TW	Title	Artist	Label	Wks
40	□ 37	96 TEARS	? (Question Mark) and the Mysterians	*Cameo Parkway*	2
39	38	TOO SOON TO KNOW	Roy Orbison	*London*	16
-	39	THERE WON'T BE MANY COMING HOME	Roy Orbison	*London*	1
-	40	IF EVERY DAY WAS LIKE CHRISTMAS	Elvis Presley	*RCA*	1

LW	TW	*WEEK ENDING* 8 DECEMBER 1966			Wks
1	□ 1	GREEN GREEN GRASS OF HOME	Tom Jones	*Decca*	5
2	2	GOOD VIBRATIONS	Beach Boys	*Capitol*	6
4	3	WHAT WOULD I BE	Val Doonican	*Decca*	5
8	□ 4	MY MIND'S EYE	Small Faces	*Decca*	4
3	5	GIMME SOME LOVING	Spencer Davis Group	*Fontana*	6
18	6	MORNINGTOWN RIDE	Seekers	*Columbia*	3
5	7	SEMI-DETACHED SUBURBAN MR. JAMES	Manfred Mann	*Fontana*	7
9	□ 8	JUST ONE SMILE	Gene Pitney	*Stateside*	4
11	9	FRIDAY ON MY MIND	Easybeats	*United Artists*	6
6	10	HOLY COW	Lee Dorsey	*Stateside*	6
16	11	DEAD END STREET	Kinks	*Pye*	3
14	12	WHAT BECOMES OF THE BROKEN HEARTED?	Jimmy Ruffin	*Tamla Motown*	4
7	13	REACH OUT I'LL BE THERE	Four Tops	*Tamla Motown*	9
12	14	DISTANT DRUMS	Jim Reeves	*RCA*	17
29	15	YOU KEEP ME HANGIN' ON	Supremes	*Tamla Motown*	2
10	16	HIGH TIME	Paul Jones	*HMV*	9
15	17	IF I WERE A CARPENTER	Bobby Darin	*Atlantic*	8
17	18	A LOVE LIKE YOURS	Ike and Tina Turner	*London*	7
13	19	STOP STOP STOP	Hollies	*Parlophone*	9
40	20	IF EVERY DAY WAS LIKE CHRISTMAS	Elvis Presley	*RCA*	2
25	□ 21	WHITE CLIFFS OF DOVER	Righteous Brothers	*London*	3
22	□ 22	SOMEWHERE MY LOVE	Mike Sammes Singers	*HMV*	11
28	□ 23	FA-FA-FA-FA-FA (SAD SONG)	Otis Redding	*Atlantic*	3
20	24	HELP ME GIRL	Eric Burdon and the Animals	*Decca*	7
19	25	I CAN'T CONTROL MYSELF	Troggs	*Page One*	10
39	26	THERE WON'T BE MANY COMING HOME	Roy Orbison	*London*	2
21	27	A FOOL AM I	Cilla Black	*Parlophone*	8
24	28	GUANTANAMERA	Sandpipers	*Pye*	12
26	29	WINCHESTER CATHEDRAL	New Vaudeville Band	*Fontana*	13
-	30	WALK WITH FAITH IN YOUR HEART	Bachelors	*Decca*	1
-	31	SUNSHINE SUPERMAN	Donovan	*Pye*	1
-	32	SAVE ME	Dave Dee Dozy Beaky Mick and Tich	*Fontana*	1
23	33	NO MILK TODAY	Herman's Hermits	*Columbia*	10
-	34	UNDER NEW MANAGEMENT	Barron Knights	*Columbia*	1
32	35	THINK SOMETIMES ABOUT ME	Sandie Shaw	*Pye*	3
30	36	BEAUTY IS ONLY SKIN DEEP	Temptations	*Tamla Motown*	9
27	37	TIME DRAGS BY	Cliff Richard	*Columbia*	9
-	38	I'M READY FOR LOVE	Martha and the Vandellas	*Tamla Motown*	1
31	39	RIDE ON BABY	Chris Farlowe and the Thunderbirds	*Immediate*	7
37	40	96 TEARS	? (Question Mark) and the Mysterians	*Cameo Parkway*	3

LW	TW	*WEEK ENDING* 15 DECEMBER 1966			Wks
1	□ 1	GREEN GREEN GRASS OF HOME	Tom Jones	*Decca*	6
3	□ 2	WHAT WOULD I BE	Val Doonican	*Decca*	6
6	3	MORNINGTOWN RIDE	Seekers	*Columbia*	4
4	□ 4	MY MIND'S EYE	Small Faces	*Decca*	5
2	5	GOOD VIBRATIONS	Beach Boys	*Capitol*	7
9	□ 6	FRIDAY ON MY MIND	Easybeats	*United Artists*	7
11	7	DEAD END STREET	Kinks	*Pye*	4
5	8	GIMME SOME LOVING	Spencer Davis Group	*Fontana*	7
15	9	YOU KEEP ME HANGIN' ON	Supremes	*Tamla Motown*	3
12	□ 10	WHAT BECOMES OF THE BROKEN HEARTED?	Jimmy Ruffin	*Tamla Motown*	5

■*If Every Day Was Like Christmas* is Elvis Presley's third consecutive single to spend at least one week at number 40 (01.12.66) ■ For the second time this year, a weekday makes the Top Ten. *Friday On My Mind* does not quite match the number three position reached by *Monday Monday* earlier in the year. In 1967 *Ruby Tuesday* will be a third Top Ten hit for the days of the week (15.12.66)■

December 1966

□ Highest position disc reached ● Act's first ever week on chart

LW	TW	Title	Artist	Label	Wks
8	11	JUST ONE SMILE	Gene Pitney	*Stateside*	5
7	12	SEMI-DETACHED SUBURBAN MR. JAMES	Manfred Mann	*Fontana*	8
31	13	SUNSHINE SUPERMAN	Donovan	*Pye*	2
14	14	DISTANT DRUMS	Jim Reeves	*RCA*	18
10	15	HOLY COW	Lee Dorsey	*Stateside*	7
20	16	IF EVERY DAY WAS LIKE CHRISTMAS	Elvis Presley	*RCA*	3
32	17	SAVE ME	Dave Dee Dozy Beaky Mick and Tich	*Fontana*	2
13	18	REACH OUT I'LL BE THERE	Four Tops	*Tamla Motown*	10
26	19	THERE WON'T BE MANY COMING HOME	Roy Orbison	*London*	3
16	20	HIGH TIME	Paul Jones	*HMV*	10
34	21	UNDER NEW MANAGEMENT	Barron Knights	*Columbia*	2
30	[22]	WALK WITH FAITH IN YOUR HEART	Bachelors	*Decca*	2
17	23	IF I WERE A CARPENTER	Bobby Darin	*Atlantic*	9
21	24	WHITE CLIFFS OF DOVER	Righteous Brothers	*London*	4
22	25	SOMEWHERE MY LOVE	Mike Sammes Singers	*HMV*	12
19	26	STOP STOP STOP	Hollies	*Parlophone*	10
23	27	FA-FA-FA-FA-FA (SAD SONG)	Otis Redding	*Atlantic*	4
18	28	A LOVE LIKE YOURS	Ike and Tina Turner	*London*	8
29	29	WINCHESTER CATHEDRAL	New Vaudeville Band	*Fontana*	14
-	30	HAPPY JACK	Who	*Reaction*	1
28	31	GUANTANAMERA	Sandpipers	*Pye*	13
38	32	I'M READY FOR LOVE	Martha and the Vandellas	*Tamla Motown*	2
24	33	HELP ME GIRL	Eric Burdon and the Animals	*Decca*	8
-	34	PAMELA PAMELA	Wayne Fontana	*Fontana*	1
25	35	I CAN'T CONTROL MYSELF	Troggs	*Page One*	11
-	36	IN THE COUNTRY	Cliff Richard and the Shadows	*Columbia*	1
37	37	TIME DRAGS BY	Cliff Richard	*Columbia*	10
27	38	A FOOL AM I	Cilla Black	*Parlophone*	9
-	39	ANYWAY THAT YOU WANT ME	Troggs	*Page One*	1
-	40	DEADLIER THAN THE MALE	Walker Brothers	*Philips*	1

WEEK ENDING 22 DECEMBER 1966

LW	TW	Title	Artist	Label	Wks
1	[1]	GREEN GREEN GRASS OF HOME	Tom Jones	*Decca*	7
3	[2]	MORNINGTOWN RIDE	Seekers	*Columbia*	5
2	3	WHAT WOULD I BE	Val Doonican	*Decca*	7
13	4	SUNSHINE SUPERMAN	Donovan	*Pye*	3
7	[5]	DEAD END STREET	Kinks	*Pye*	5
17	6	SAVE ME	Dave Dee Dozy Beaky Mick and Tich	*Fontana*	3
6	7	FRIDAY ON MY MIND	Easybeats	*United Artists*	8
9	[8]	YOU KEEP ME HANGIN' ON	Supremes	*Tamla Motown*	4
5	9	GOOD VIBRATIONS	Beach Boys	*Capitol*	8
4	10	MY MIND'S EYE	Small Faces	*Decca*	6
8	11	GIMME SOME LOVING	Spencer Davis Group	*Fontana*	8
10	12	WHAT BECOMES OF THE BROKEN HEARTED?	Jimmy Ruffin	*Tamla Motown*	6
16	[13]	IF EVERY DAY WAS LIKE CHRISTMAS	Elvis Presley	*RCA*	4
14	14	DISTANT DRUMS	Jim Reeves	*RCA*	19
12	15	SEMI-DETACHED SUBURBAN MR. JAMES	Manfred Mann	*Fontana*	9
11	16	JUST ONE SMILE	Gene Pitney	*Stateside*	6
30	17	HAPPY JACK	Who	*Reaction*	2
19	[18]	THERE WON'T BE MANY COMING HOME	Roy Orbison	*London*	4
15	19	HOLY COW	Lee Dorsey	*Stateside*	8
21	20	UNDER NEW MANAGEMENT	Barron Knights	*Columbia*	3
36	21	IN THE COUNTRY	Cliff Richard and the Shadows	*Columbia*	2
18	22	REACH OUT I'LL BE THERE	Four Tops	*Tamla Motown*	11
22	23	WALK WITH FAITH IN YOUR HEART	Bachelors	*Decca*	3
20	24	HIGH TIME	Paul Jones	*HMV*	11
39	25	ANYWAY THAT YOU WANT ME	Troggs	*Page One*	2
25	26	SOMEWHERE MY LOVE	Mike Sammes Singers	*HMV*	13
27	27	FA-FA-FA-FA-FA (SAD SONG)	Otis Redding	*Atlantic*	5
23	28	IF I WERE A CARPENTER	Bobby Darin	*Atlantic*	10
32	[29]	I'M READY FOR LOVE	Martha and the Vandellas	*Tamla Motown*	3
29	30	WINCHESTER CATHEDRAL	New Vaudeville Band	*Fontana*	15
24	31	WHITE CLIFFS OF DOVER	Righteous Brothers	*London*	5
-	32	(I KNOW) I'M LOSING YOU	Temptations	*Tamla Motown*	1
28	33	A LOVE LIKE YOURS	Ike and Tina Turner	*London*	9
31	34	GUANTANAMERA	Sandpipers	*Pye*	14
34	35	PAMELA PAMELA	Wayne Fontana	*Fontana*	2
40	36	DEADLIER THAN THE MALE	Walker Brothers	*Philips*	2
-	[37]	EAST WEST	Herman's Hermits	*Columbia*	1
-	38	MUSTANG SALLY	Wilson Pickett	*Atlantic*	1
-	39	ISLAND IN THE SUN	Righteous Brothers	*Verve*	1
-	40	I FEEL FREE	Cream	*Reaction*	1

WEEK ENDING 29 DECEMBER 1966

(no chart compiled: chart for 22 December repeated)

LW	TW	Title	Artist	Label	Wks
1	[1]	GREEN GREEN GRASS OF HOME	Tom Jones	*Decca*	8
2	[2]	MORNINGTOWN RIDE	Seekers	*Columbia*	6
3	3	WHAT WOULD I BE	Val Doonican	*Decca*	8
4	4	SUNSHINE SUPERMAN	Donovan	*Pye*	4
5	[5]	DEAD END STREET	Kinks	*Pye*	6
6	6	SAVE ME	Dave Dee Dozy Beaky Mick and Tich	*Fontana*	4
7	7	FRIDAY ON MY MIND	Easybeats	*United Artists*	9
8	[8]	YOU KEEP ME HANGIN' ON	Supremes	*Tamla Motown*	5
9	9	GOOD VIBRATIONS	Beach Boys	*Capitol*	9
10	10	MY MIND'S EYE	Small Faces	*Decca*	7
11	11	GIMME SOME LOVING	Spencer Davis Group	*Fontana*	9
12	12	WHAT BECOMES OF THE BROKEN HEARTED?	Jimmy Ruffin	*Tamla Motown*	7
13	[13]	IF EVERY DAY WAS LIKE CHRISTMAS	Elvis Presley	*RCA*	5
14	14	DISTANT DRUMS	Jim Reeves	*RCA*	20
15	15	SEMI-DETACHED SUBURBAN MR. JAMES	Manfred Mann	*Fontana*	10
16	16	JUST ONE SMILE	Gene Pitney	*Stateside*	7
17	17	HAPPY JACK	Who	*Reaction*	3
18	[18]	THERE WON'T BE MANY COMING HOME	Roy Orbison	*London*	5
19	19	HOLY COW	Lee Dorsey	*Stateside*	9
20	20	UNDER NEW MANAGEMENT	Barron Knights	*Columbia*	4
21	21	IN THE COUNTRY	Cliff Richard and the Shadows	*Columbia*	3
22	22	REACH OUT I'LL BE THERE	Four Tops	*Tamla Motown*	12
23	23	WALK WITH FAITH IN YOUR HEART	Bachelors	*Decca*	4
24	24	HIGH TIME	Paul Jones	*HMV*	12
25	25	ANYWAY THAT YOU WANT ME	Troggs	*Page One*	3
26	26	SOMEWHERE MY LOVE	Mike Sammes Singers	*HMV*	14
27	27	FA-FA-FA-FA-FA (SAD SONG)	Otis Redding	*Atlantic*	6
28	28	IF I WERE A CARPENTER	Bobby Darin	*Atlantic*	11
29	[29]	I'M READY FOR LOVE	Martha and the Vandellas	*Tamla Motown*	4
30	30	WINCHESTER CATHEDRAL	New Vaudeville Band	*Fontana*	16
31	31	WHITE CLIFFS OF DOVER	Righteous Brothers	*London*	6
32	32	(I KNOW) I'M LOSING YOU	Temptations	*Tamla Motown*	2
33	33	A LOVE LIKE YOURS	Ike and Tina Turner	*London*	10
34	34	GUANTANAMERA	Sandpipers	*Pye*	15
35	35	PAMELA PAMELA	Wayne Fontana	*Fontana*	3
36	36	DEADLIER THAN THE MALE	Walker Brothers	*Philips*	3
37	[37]	EAST WEST	Herman's Hermits	*Columbia*	2
38	38	MUSTANG SALLY	Wilson Pickett	*Atlantic*	2
39	39	ISLAND IN THE SUN	Righteous Brothers	*Verve*	2
40	40	I FEEL FREE	Cream	*Reaction*	2

In these weeks ■ *In The Country* is the last single to feature Cliff Richard and the Shadows together for almost two years. It will prove to be their final Top Ten single together (15.12.66) ■ Four weeks at number fourteen for the still-echoing *Distant Drums* (29.12.66) ■

1967

........The man who began the year at number one, TOM JONES (left), and the man who spent the most weeks at number one this year, ENGELBERT HUMPERDINCK (right), spend royalties together.......Sandie Shaw has her third number one, which will remain the record for a female soloist for twenty years ......the Summer of Love is dominated by Procol Harum, the Beatles and Scott McKenzie.........

January 1967

☐ Highest position disc reached ● Act's first ever week on chart

LW	TW	WEEK ENDING 5 JANUARY 1967			Wks
1	[1]	GREEN GREEN GRASS OF HOME	Tom Jones	*Decca*	9
2	[2]	MORNINGTOWN RIDE	Seekers	*Columbia*	7
4	3	SUNSHINE SUPERMAN	Donovan	*Pye*	5
6	[4]	SAVE ME	Dave Dee, Dozy, Beaky, Mick and Tich	*Fontana*	5
17	5	HAPPY JACK	Who	*Reaction*	4
5	6	DEAD END STREET	Kinks	*Pye*	7
3	7	WHAT WOULD I BE	Val Doonican	*Decca*	9
8	[8]	YOU KEEP ME HANGIN' ON	Supremes	*Tamla Motown*	6
21	9	IN THE COUNTRY	Cliff Richard and the Shadows	*Columbia*	4
10	10	MY MIND'S EYE	Small Faces	*Decca*	8
9	11	GOOD VIBRATIONS	Beach Boys	*Capitol*	10
7	12	FRIDAY ON MY MIND	Easybeats	*United Artists*	10
25	13	ANYWAY THAT YOU WANT ME	Troggs	*Page One*	4
14	12	WHAT BECOMES OF THE BROKEN HEARTED	Jimmy Ruffin	*Tamla Motown*	8
20	[15]	UNDER NEW MANAGEMENT	Barron Knights	*Columbia*	5
35	16	PAMELA PAMELA	Wayne Fontana	*Fontana*	4
14	17	DISTANT DRUMS	Jim Reeves	*RCA*	21
16	18	JUST ONE SMILE	Gene Pitney	*Stateside*	8
-	19	SITTING IN THE PARK	Georgie Fame	*Columbia*	1
22	20	REACH OUT I'LL BE THERE	Four Tops	*Tamla Motown*	13
11	21	GIMME SOME LOVING	Spencer Davis Group	*Fontana*	10
13	22	IF EVERY DAY WAS LIKE CHRISTMAS	Elvis Presley	*RCA*	6
32	23	(I KNOW) I'M LOSING YOU	Temptations	*Tamla Motown*	3
18	24	THERE WON'T BE MANY COMING HOME	Roy Orbison	*London*	6
40	25	I FEEL FREE	Cream	*Reaction*	3
23	26	WALK WITH FAITH IN YOUR HEART	Bachelors	*Decca*	5
19	27	HOLY COW	Lee Dorsey	*Stateside*	10
15	28	SEMI DETACHED SUBURBAN MR JAMES	Manfred Mann	*Fontana*	11
-	29	CALL HER YOUR SWEETHEART	Frank Ifield	*Columbia*	1
38	30	MUSTANG SALLY	Wilson Pickett	*Atlantic*	3
29	31	I'M READY FOR LOVE	Martha and the Vandellas	*Tamla Motown*	5
-	32	NIGHT OF FEAR	Move ●	*Deram*	1
30	33	WINCHESTER CATHEDRAL	New Vaudeville Band	*Fontana*	17
36	[34]	DEADLIER THAN THE MALE	Walker Brothers	*Philips*	4
26	35	SOMEWHERE MY LOVE	Mike Sammes Singers	*HMV*	15
39	[36]	ISLAND IN THE SUN	Righteous Brothers	*Verve*	3
24	37	HIGH TIME	Paul Jones	*HMV*	13
37	38	EAST WEST	Herman Hermits	*Columbia*	3
27	39	FA-FA-FA-FA-FA (SAD SONG)	Otis Redding	*Atlantic*	7
-	40	HEART	Rita Pavone ●	*RCA Victor*	1

LW	TW	WEEK ENDING 12 JANUARY 1967			Wks
1	[1]	GREEN GREEN GRASS OF HOME	Tom Jones	*Decca*	10
2	[2]	MORNINGTOWN RIDE	Seekers	*Columbia*	8
3	[2]	SUNSHINE SUPERMAN	Donovan	*Pye*	6
-	4	I'M A BELIEVER	Monkees ●	*RCA Victor*	1
4	5	SAVE ME	Dave Dee, Dozy, Beaky, Mick and Tich	*Fontana*	6
5	6	HAPPY JACK	Who	*Reaction*	5
9	7	IN THE COUNTRY	Cliff Richard and the Shadows	*Columbia*	5
13	[8]	ANYWAY THAT YOU WANT ME	Troggs	*Page One*	5
6	9	DEAD END STREET	Kinks	*Pye*	8
7	10	WHAT WOULD I BE	Val Doonican	*Decca*	10
8	11	YOU KEEP ME HANGIN' ON	Supremes	*Tamla Motown*	7
16	12	PAMELA PAMELA	Wayne Fontana	*Fontana*	5
19	13	SITTING IN THE PARK	Georgie Fame	*Columbia*	2
12	14	FRIDAY ON MY MIND	Easybeats	*United Artists*	11
11	15	GOOD VIBRATIONS	Beach Boys	*Capitol*	11
12	16	WHAT BECOMES OF THE BROKEN HEARTED	Jimmy Ruffin	*Tamla Motown*	9
32	17	NIGHT OF FEAR	Move	*Deram*	2
15	18	UNDER NEW MANAGEMENT	Barron Knights	*Columbia*	6
23	[19]	(I KNOW) I'M LOSING YOU	Temptations	*Tamla Motown*	4
10	20	MY MIND'S EYE	Small Faces	*Decca*	9
25	21	I FEEL FREE	Cream	*Reaction*	4
17	22	DISTANT DRUMS	Jim Reeves	*RCA*	22
-	23	STANDING IN THE SHADOWS OF LOVE	Four Tops	*Tamla Motown*	1
18	24	JUST ONE SMILE	Gene Pitney	*Stateside*	9
20	25	REACH OUT I'LL BE THERE	Four Tops	*Tamla Motown*	14
26	26	WALK WITH FAITH IN YOUR HEART	Bachelors	*Decca*	6
29	27	CALL HER YOUR SWEETHEART	Frank Ifield	*Columbia*	2
24	28	THERE WON'T BE MANY COMING HOME	Roy Orbison	*London*	7
30	29	MUSTANG SALLY	Wilson Pickett	*Atlantic*	4
21	30	GIMME SOME LOVING	Spencer Davis Group	*Fontana*	11
31	31	I'M READY FOR LOVE	Martha and the Vandellas	*Tamla Motown*	6
-	32	HEY JOE	Jimi Hendrix ●	*Polydor*	1
-	33	MATTHEW AND SON	Cat Stevens	*Deram*	1
-	34	NASHVILLE CATS	Lovin' Spoonful	*Kama Sutra*	1
34	35	DEADLIER THAN THE MALE	Walker Brothers	*Philips*	5
-	36	SINGLE GIRL	Sandy Posey	*MGM*	1
27	37	HOLY COW	Lee Dorsey	*Stateside*	11
40	38	HEART	Rita Pavone	*RCA Victor*	2
36	39	ISLAND IN THE SUN	Righteous Brothers	*Verve*	4
39	40	FA-FA-FA-FA-FA (SAD SONG)	Otis Redding	*Atlantic*	8

LW	TW	WEEK ENDING 19 JANUARY 1967			Wks
4	[1]	I'M A BELIEVER	Monkees	*RCA Victor*	2
1	2	GREEN GREEN GRASS OF HOME	Tom Jones	*Decca*	11
6	[3]	HAPPY JACK	Who	*Reaction*	6
2	4	MORNINGTOWN RIDE	Seekers	*Columbia*	9
2	5	SUNSHINE SUPERMAN	Donovan	*Pye*	7
7	[6]	IN THE COUNTRY	Cliff Richard and the Shadows	*Columbia*	6
17	7	NIGHT OF FEAR	Move	*Deram*	3
5	8	SAVE ME	Dave Dee, Dozy, Beaky, Mick and Tich	*Fontana*	7
8	9	ANYWAY THAT YOU WANT ME	Troggs	*Page One*	6
23	10	STANDING IN THE SHADOWS OF LOVE	Four Tops	*Tamla Motown*	2
33	11	MATTHEW AND SON	Cat Stevens	*Deram*	2
13	[12]	SITTING IN THE PARK	Georgie Fame	*Columbia*	3
21	13	I FEEL FREE	Cream	*Reaction*	5
12	14	PAMELA PAMELA	Wayne Fontana	*Fontana*	6
9	15	DEAD END STREET	Kinks	*Pye*	9
32	16	HEY JOE	Jimi Hendrix	*Polydor*	2
11	17	YOU KEEP ME HANGIN' ON	Supremes	*Tamla Motown*	8
10	18	WHAT WOULD I BE	Val Doonican	*Decca*	11
19	[19]	(I KNOW) I'M LOSING YOU	Temptations	*Tamla Motown*	5
-	20	A PLACE IN THE SUN	Stevie Wonder	*Tamla Motown*	1
14	21	FRIDAY ON MY MIND	Easybeats	*United Artists*	12
16	22	WHAT BECOMES OF THE BROKEN HEARTED	Jimmy Ruffin	*Tamla Motown*	10
15	23	GOOD VIBRATIONS	Beach Boys	*Capitol*	12
27	[24]	CALL HER YOUR SWEETHEART	Frank Ifield	*Columbia*	3
22	25	DISTANT DRUMS	Jim Reeves	*RCA*	23
-	26	LET'S SPEND THE NIGHT TOGETHER	Rolling Stones	*Decca*	1
36	27	SINGLE GIRL	Sandy Posey	*MGM*	2
29	[28]	MUSTANG SALLY	Wilson Pickett	*Atlantic*	5
18	29	UNDER NEW MANAGEMENT	Barron Knights	*Columbia*	7
34	30	NASHVILLE CATS	Lovin' Spoonful	*Kama Sutra*	2
26	31	WALK WITH FAITH IN YOUR HEART	Bachelors	*Decca*	7
20	32	MY MIND'S EYE	Small Faces	*Decca*	10
38	33	HEART	Rita Pavone	*RCA Victor*	3
25	34	REACH OUT I'LL BE THERE	Four Tops	*Tamla Motown*	15
24	35	JUST ONE SMILE	Gene Pitney	*Stateside*	10
28	36	THERE WON'T BE MANY COMING HOME	Roy Orbison	*London*	8
-	[37]	TELL IT TO THE RAIN	Four Seasons	*Philips*	1
-	38	I'VE BEEN A BAD BAD BOY	Paul Jones	*HMV*	1
31	39	I'M READY FOR LOVE	Martha and the Vandellas	*Tamla Motown*	7
-	40	SUGAR TOWN	Nancy Sinatra	*Reprise*	1

LW	TW	WEEK ENDING 26 JANUARY 1967			Wks
1	[1]	I'M A BELIEVER	Monkees	*RCA Victor*	3
7	[2]	NIGHT OF FEAR	Move	*Deram*	4
11	3	MATTHEW AND SON	Cat Stevens	*Deram*	3

In these weeks ■ Donovan's best ever chart position is second equal, but Tom Jones and the new TV sensation the Monkees prevent him from reaching the very top (12.01.67) ■ The Walker Brothers' theme to the spy movie *Deadlier Than The Male* is, like the film, not a great success (12.01.67) ■ Three towns (Morning town, Sugar town and Nashville), a park, a street, *A Place In The Sun* and the joys of being *In The Country* all contribute to a geographically varied chart (19.06.67)■

2 4 GREEN GREEN GRASS OF HOME Tom Jones *Decca* 12
3 5 HAPPY JACK Who *Reaction* 7
10 6 STANDING IN THE SHADOWS OF LOVE Four Tops *Tamla Motown* 3
26 7 LET'S SPEND THE NIGHT TOGETHER Rolling Stones *Decca* 2
4 8 MORNINGTOWN RIDE Seekers *Columbia* 10
16 9 HEY JOE Jimi Hendrix *Polydor* 3
6 10 IN THE COUNTRY Cliff Richard and the Shadows *Columbia* 7
13 11 I FEEL FREE Cream *Reaction* 6
12 12 SITTING IN THE PARK Georgie Fame *Columbia* 4
9 13 ANYWAY THAT YOU WANT ME Troggs *Page One* 7
5 14 SUNSHINE SUPERMAN Donovan *Pye* 8
14 15 PAMELA PAMELA Wayne Fontana *Fontana* 7
8 16 SAVE ME Dave Dee, Dozy, Beaky, Mick and Tich *Fontana* 8
38 17 I'VE BEEN A BAD BAD BOY Paul Jones *HMV* 2
18 18 WHAT WOULD I BE Val Doonican *Decca* 12
27 19 SINGLE GIRL Sandy Posey *MGM* 3
15 20 DEAD END STREET Kinks *Pye* 10
19 21 (I KNOW) I'M LOSING YOU Temptations *Tamla Motown* 6
40 22 SUGAR TOWN Nancy Sinatra *Reprise* 2
20 23 A PLACE IN THE SUN Stevie Wonder *Tamla Motown* 2
17 24 YOU KEEP ME HANGIN' ON Supremes *Tamla Motown* 9
24 25 CALL HER YOUR SWEETHEART Frank Ifield *Columbia* 4
30 26 NASHVILLE CATS Lovin' Spoonful *Kama Sutra* 3
33 27 HEART Rita Pavone *RCA Victor* 4
22 28 WHAT BECOMES OF THE BROKEN HEARTED Jimmy Ruffin *Tamla Motown* 11
\- 29 YOU ONLY YOU Rita Pavone *RCA Victor* 1
\- 30 SNOOPY VS THE RED BARON Royal Guardsmen ● *Stateside* 1
21 31 FRIDAY ON MY MIND Easybeats *United Artists* 13
\- 32 LET ME CRY ON YOUR SHOULDER Ken Dodd *Columbia* 1
25 33 DISTANT DRUMS Jim Reeves *RCA* 24
\- 34 I'M A MAN Spencer Davis Group *Fontana* 1
28 35 MUSTANG SALLY Wilson Pickett *Atlantic* 6
23 36 GOOD VIBRATIONS Beach Boys *Capitol* 13
37 37 TELL IT TO THE RAIN Four Seasons *Philips* 2
\- 38 98.6 Keith ● *Mercury* 1
\- 39 RELEASE ME Engelbert Humperdinck ● *Decca* 1
31 40 WALK WITH FAITH IN YOUR HEART Bachelors *Decca* 8

LW TW *WEEK ENDING* **2 FEBRUARY 1967** Wks

1 1 I'M A BELIEVER Monkees *RCA Victor* 4
3 2 MATTHEW AND SON Cat Stevens *Deram* 4
2 3 NIGHT OF FEAR Move *Deram* 5
7 4 LET'S SPEND THE NIGHT TOGETHER Rolling Stones *Decca* 3
4 5 GREEN GREEN GRASS OF HOME Tom Jones *Decca* 13
9 6 HEY JOE Jimi Hendrix *Polydor* 4
17 7 I'VE BEEN A BAD BAD BOY Paul Jones *HMV* 3
6 8 STANDING IN THE SHADOWS OF LOVE Four Tops *Tamla Motown* 4
5 9 HAPPY JACK Who *Reaction* 8
8 10 MORNINGTOWN RIDE Seekers *Columbia* 11
15 11 PAMELA PAMELA Wayne Fontana *Fontana* 8
11 12 I FEEL FREE Cream *Reaction* 7
12 13 SITTING IN THE PARK Georgie Fame *Columbia* 5
22 14 SUGAR TOWN Nancy Sinatra *Reprise* 3
19 15 SINGLE GIRL Sandy Posey *MGM* 4
10 16 IN THE COUNTRY Cliff Richard and the Shadows *Columbia* 8
30 17 SNOOPY VS THE RED BARON Royal Guardsmen *Stateside* 2
32 18 LET ME CRY ON YOUR SHOULDER Ken Dodd *Columbia* 2
34 19 I'M A MAN Spencer Davis Group *Fontana* 2
13 20 ANYWAY THAT YOU WANT ME Troggs *Page One* 8
29 21 YOU ONLY YOU Rita Pavone *RCA Victor* 2
16 22 SAVE ME Dave Dee, Dozy, Beaky, Mick and Tich *Fontana* 9
39 23 RELEASE ME Engelbert Humperdinck *Decca* 2
\- 24 I WON'T COME IN WHILE HE'S THERE Jim Reeves *RCA Victor* 1
14 25 SUNSHINE SUPERMAN Donovan *Pye* 9
38 26 98.6 Keith *Mercury* 2
18 27 WHAT WOULD I BE Val Doonican *Decca* 13
27 28 HEART Rita Pavone *RCA Victor* 5
\- 29 IT TAKES TWO Marvin Gaye and Kim Weston ● *Tamla Motown* 1
25 30 CALL HER YOUR SWEETHEART Frank Ifield *Columbia* 5

February 1967

□ Highest position disc reached ● Act's first ever week on chart

26 31 NASHVILLE CATS Lovin' Spoonful *Kama Sutra* 4
\- 32 PEEK-A-BOO New Vaudeville Band *Fontana* 1
\- 33 LAST TRAIN TO CLARKSVILLE Monkees *RCA Victor* 1
\- 34 HERE COMES MY BABY Tremeloes ● *CBS* 1
21 35 (I KNOW) I'M LOSING YOU Temptations *Tamla Motown* 7
23 36 A PLACE IN THE SUN Stevie Wonder *Tamla Motown* 3
24 37 YOU KEEP ME HANGIN' ON Supremes *Tamla Motown* 10
20 38 DEAD END STREET Kinks *Pye* 11
37 39 TELL IT TO THE RAIN Four Seasons *Philips* 3
33 40 DISTANT DRUMS Jim Reeves *RCA Victor* 25

LW TW *WEEK ENDING* **9 FEBRUARY 1967** Wks

1 1 I'M A BELIEVER Monkees *RCA Victor* 5
2 2 MATTHEW AND SON Cat Stevens *Deram* 5
4 3 LET'S SPEND THE NIGHT TOGETHER Rolling Stones *Decca* 4
3 4 NIGHT OF FEAR Move *Deram* 6
7 5 I'VE BEEN A BAD BAD BOY Paul Jones *HMV* 4
6 6 HEY JOE Jimi Hendrix *Polydor* 5
5 7 GREEN GREEN GRASS OF HOME Tom Jones *Decca* 14
\- 8 THIS IS MY SONG Petula Clark *Pye* 1
19 9 I'M A MAN Spencer Davis Group *Fontana* 3
14 10 SUGAR TOWN Nancy Sinatra *Reprise* 4
18 11 LET ME CRY ON YOUR SHOULDER Ken Dodd *Columbia* 3
23 12 RELEASE ME Engelbert Humperdinck *Decca* 3
8 13 STANDING IN THE SHADOWS OF LOVE Four Tops *Tamla Motown* 5
17 14 SNOOPY VS THE RED BARON Royal Guardsmen *Stateside* 3
24 15 I WON'T COME IN WHILE HE'S THERE Jim Reeves *RCA Victor* 2
12 16 I FEEL FREE Cream *Reaction* 8
32 17 PEEK-A-BOO New Vaudeville Band *Fontana* 2
11 18 PAMELA PAMELA Wayne Fontana *Fontana* 9
15 19 SINGLE GIRL Sandy Posey *MGM* 5
13 20 SITTING IN THE PARK Georgie Fame *Columbia* 6
9 21 HAPPY JACK Who *Reaction* 9
29 22 IT TAKES TWO Marvin Gaye and Kim Weston *Tamla Motown* 2
10 23 MORNINGTOWN RIDE Seekers *Columbia* 12
34 24 HERE COMES MY BABY Tremeloes *CBS* 2
21 25 YOU ONLY YOU Rita Pavone *RCA Victor* 3
26 26 98.6 Keith *Mercury* 3
33 27 LAST TRAIN TO CLARKSVILLE Monkees *RCA Victor* 2
16 28 IN THE COUNTRY Cliff Richard and the Shadows *Columbia* 9
20 29 ANYWAY THAT YOU WANT ME Troggs *Page One* 9
27 30 WHAT WOULD I BE Val Doonican *Decca* 14
30 31 CALL HER YOUR SWEETHEART Frank Ifield *Columbia* 6
28 32 HEART Rita Pavone *RCA Victor* 6
22 33 SAVE ME Dave Dee, Dozy, Beaky, Mick and Tich *Fontana* 10
25 34 SUNSHINE SUPERMAN Donovan *Pye* 10
\- 35 INDESCRIBABLY BLUE Elvis Presley *RCA Victor* 1
31 36 NASHVILLE CATS Lovin' Spoonful *Kama Sutra* 5
\- 37 MELLOW YELLOW Donovan *Pye* 1
\- 38 I'VE PASSED THIS WAY BEFORE Jimmy Ruffin *Tamla Motown* 1
\- 39 RUN TO THE DOOR Clinton Ford *Piccadilly* 1
\- 40 EDELWEISS Vince Hill *Columbia* 1

LW TW *WEEK ENDING* **16 FEBRUARY 1967** Wks

8 1 THIS IS MY SONG Petula Clark *Pye* 2
1 2 I'M A BELIEVER Monkees *RCA Victor* 6
3 3 LET'S SPEND THE NIGHT TOGETHER Rolling Stones *Decca* 5
12 4 RELEASE ME Engelbert Humperdinck *Decca* 4
2 5 MATTHEW AND SON Cat Stevens *Deram* 6
5 6 I'VE BEEN A BAD BAD BOY Paul Jones *HMV* 5
4 7 NIGHT OF FEAR Move *Deram* 7
10 8 SUGAR TOWN Nancy Sinatra *Reprise* 5
14 9 SNOOPY VS THE RED BARON Royal Guardsmen *Stateside* 4

■Just over three years after his fourth number one in five singles, Frank Ifield's final Top 40 hit drops from the charts (09.02.67) ■ Petula Clark's second number one, almost six years after her first, becomes the only number one hit written by Charlie Chaplin. His other big hit, the theme from his film *Limelight*, peaked at number two fourteen years earlier (16.02.67)■

February 1967

□ Highest position disc reached ● Act's first ever week on chart

LW	TW	Title	Artist	Label	Wks
24	10	HERE COMES MY BABY	Tremeloes	*CBS*	3
17	11	PEEK-A-BOO	New Vaudeville Band	*Fontana*	3
7	12	GREEN GREEN GRASS OF HOME	Tom Jones	*Decca*	15
15	13	I WON'T COME IN WHILE HE'S THERE	Jim Reeves	*RCA Victor*	3
6	14	HEY JOE	Jimi Hendrix	*Polydor*	6
11	15	LET ME CRY ON YOUR SHOULDER	Ken Dodd	*Columbia*	4
9	16	I'M A MAN	Spencer Davis Group	*Fontana*	4
37	17	MELLOW YELLOW	Donovan	*Pye*	2
22	18	IT TAKES TWO	Marvin Gaye and Kim Weston	*Tamla Motown*	3
19	19	SINGLE GIRL	Sandy Posey	*MGM*	6
40	20	EDELWEISS	Vince Hill	*Columbia*	2
35	[21]	INDESCRIBABLY BLUE	Elvis Presley	*RCA Victor*	2
13	22	STANDING IN THE SHADOWS OF LOVE	Four Tops	*Tamla Motown*	6
27	[23]	LAST TRAIN TO CLARKSVILLE	Monkees	*RCA Victor*	3
26	[24]	98.6	Keith	*Mercury*	4
39	[25]	RUN TO THE DOOR	Clinton Ford	*Piccadilly*	2
-	[26]	STAY WITH ME BABY	Walker Brothers	*Philips*	1
16	27	I FEEL FREE	Cream	*Reaction*	9
20	28	SITTING IN THE PARK	Georgie Fame	*Columbia*	7
38	[29]	I'VE PASSED THIS WAY BEFORE	Jimmy Ruffin	*Tamla Motown*	2
25	30	YOU ONLY YOU	Rita Pavone	*RCA Victor*	4
18	31	PAMELA PAMELA	Wayne Fontana	*Fontana*	10
-	32	THERE'S A KIND OF HUSH	Herman's Hermits	*Columbia*	1
23	33	MORNINGTOWN RIDE	Seekers	*Columbia*	13
-	34	ON A CAROUSEL	Hollies	*Parlophone*	1
-	35	BEAT GOES ON	Sonny and Cher	*Atlantic*	1
21	36	HAPPY JACK	Who	*Reaction*	10
34	37	SUNSHINE SUPERMAN	Donovan	*Pye*	11
-	38	DETROIT CITY	Tom Jones	*Decca*	1
30	39	WHAT WOULD I BE	Val Doonican	*Decca*	15
-	40	MICHAEL	Geno Washington	*Piccadilly*	1

WEEK ENDING 23 FEBRUARY 1967

LW	TW	Title	Artist	Label	Wks
1	[1]	THIS IS MY SONG	Petula Clark	*Pye*	3
4	2	RELEASE ME	Engelbert Humperdinck	*Decca*	5
2	3	I'M A BELIEVER	Monkees	*RCA Victor*	7
10	[4]	HERE COMES MY BABY	Tremeloes	*CBS*	4
-	5	PENNY LANE/STRAWBERRY FIELDS FOREVER	Beatles	*Parlophone*	1
3	6	LET'S SPEND THE NIGHT TOGETHER	Rolling Stones	*Decca*	6
11	[7]	PEEK-A-BOO	New Vaudeville Band	*Fontana*	4
9	[8]	SNOOPY VS THE RED BARON	Royal Guardsmen	*Stateside*	5
5	9	MATTHEW AND SON	Cat Stevens	*Deram*	7
17	10	MELLOW YELLOW	Donovan	*Pye*	3
6	11	I'VE BEEN A BAD BAD BOY	Paul Jones	*HMV*	6
13	[12]	I WON'T COME IN WHILE HE'S THERE	Jim Reeves	*RCA Victor*	4
20	13	EDELWEISS	Vince Hill	*Columbia*	3
8	14	SUGAR TOWN	Nancy Sinatra	*Reprise*	6
34	15	ON A CAROUSEL	Hollies	*Parlophone*	2
18	[16]	IT TAKES TWO	Marvin Gaye and Kim Weston	*Tamla Motown*	4
7	17	NIGHT OF FEAR	Move	*Deram*	8
12	18	GREEN GREEN GRASS OF HOME	Tom Jones	*Decca*	16
32	19	THERE'S A KIND OF HUSH	Herman's Hermits	*Columbia*	2
19	20	SINGLE GIRL	Sandy Posey	*MGM*	7
38	21	DETROIT CITY	Tom Jones	*Decca*	2
16	22	I'M A MAN	Spencer Davis Group	*Fontana*	5
14	23	HEY JOE	Jimi Hendrix	*Polydor*	7
15	24	LET ME CRY ON YOUR SHOULDER	Ken Dodd	*Columbia*	5
21	25	INDESCRIBABLY BLUE	Elvis Presley	*RCA Victor*	3
23	26	LAST TRAIN TO CLARKSVILLE	Monkees	*RCA Victor*	4
-	27	GIVE IT TO ME	Troggs	*Page One*	1
26	28	STAY WITH ME BABY	Walker Brothers	*Philips*	2
29	[29]	I'VE PASSED THIS WAY BEFORE	Jimmy Ruffin	*Tamla Motown*	3
-	30	GEORGY GIRL	Seekers	*Columbia*	1
35	31	BEAT GOES ON	Sonny and Cher	*Atlantic*	2
24	32	98.6	Keith	*Mercury*	5
22	33	STANDING IN THE SHADOWS OF LOVE	Four Tops	*Tamla Motown*	7
25	34	RUN TO THE DOOR	Clinton Ford	*Piccadilly*	3
33	35	MORNINGTOWN RIDE	Seekers	*Columbia*	14
27	36	I FEEL FREE	Cream	*Reaction*	10
28	37	SITTING IN THE PARK	Georgie Fame	*Columbia*	8
30	38	YOU ONLY YOU	Rita Pavone	*RCA Victor*	5
40	[39]	MICHAEL	Geno Washington	*Piccadilly*	2
31	40	PAMELA PAMELA	Wayne Fontana	*Fontana*	11

WEEK ENDING 2 MARCH 1967

LW	TW	Title	Artist	Label	Wks
2	[1]	RELEASE ME	Engelbert Humperdinck	*Decca*	6
5	[2]	PENNY LANE/STRAWBERRY FIELDS FOREVER	Beatles	*Parlophone*	2
1	3	THIS IS MY SONG	Petula Clark	*Pye*	4
4	[4]	HERE COMES MY BABY	Tremeloes	*CBS*	5
3	5	I'M A BELIEVER	Monkees	*RCA Victor*	8
13	6	EDELWEISS	Vince Hill	*Columbia*	4
15	7	ON A CAROUSEL	Hollies	*Parlophone*	3
10	[8]	MELLOW YELLOW	Donovan	*Pye*	4
7	9	PEEK-A-BOO	New Vaudeville Band	*Fontana*	5
8	10	SNOOPY VS THE RED BARON	Royal Guardsmen	*Stateside*	6
19	11	THERE'S A KIND OF HUSH	Herman's Hermits	*Columbia*	3
6	12	LET'S SPEND THE NIGHT TOGETHER	Rolling Stones	*Decca*	7
21	13	DETROIT CITY	Tom Jones	*Decca*	3
12	14	I WON'T COME IN WHILE HE'S THERE	Jim Reeves	*RCA Victor*	5
9	15	MATTHEW AND SON	Cat Stevens	*Deram*	8
16	[16]	IT TAKES TWO	Marvin Gaye and Kim Weston	*Tamla Motown*	5
20	17	SINGLE GIRL	Sandy Posey	*MGM*	8
30	18	GEORGY GIRL	Seekers	*Columbia*	2
14	19	SUGAR TOWN	Nancy Sinatra	*Reprise*	7
11	20	I'VE BEEN A BAD BAD BOY	Paul Jones	*HMV*	7
18	21	GREEN GREEN GRASS OF HOME	Tom Jones	*Decca*	17
27	22	GIVE IT TO ME	Troggs	*Page One*	2
24	23	LET ME CRY ON YOUR SHOULDER	Ken Dodd	*Columbia*	6
25	24	INDESCRIBABLY BLUE	Elvis Presley	*RCA Victor*	4
17	25	NIGHT OF FEAR	Move	*Deram*	9
28	[26]	STAY WITH ME BABY	Walker Brothers	*Philips*	3
23	27	HEY JOE	Jimi Hendrix	*Polydor*	8
22	28	I'M A MAN	Spencer Davis Group	*Fontana*	6
31	29	BEAT GOES ON	Sonny and Cher	*Atlantic*	3
26	30	LAST TRAIN TO CLARKSVILLE	Monkees	*RCA Victor*	5
-	31	THIS IS MY SONG	Harry Secombe	*Philips*	1
-	32	I'LL TRY ANYTHING	Dusty Springfield	*Philips*	1
29	33	I'VE PASSED THIS WAY BEFORE	Jimmy Ruffin	*Tamla Motown*	4
-	34	SO GOOD	Roy Orbison	*London*	1
34	35	RUN TO THE DOOR	Clinton Ford	*Piccadilly*	4
32	36	98.6	Keith	*Mercury*	6
-	37	MEMORIES ARE MADE OF THIS	Val Doonican	*Decca*	1
-	[38]	COLD LIGHT OF DAY	Gene Pitney	*Stateside*	1
-	40	THEN YOU CAN TELL ME GOODBYE	Casinos ●	*President*	1

WEEK ENDING 9 MARCH 1967

LW	TW	Title	Artist	Label	Wks
1	[1]	RELEASE ME	Engelbert Humperdinck	*Decca*	7
2	[2]	PENNY LANE/STRAWBERRY FIELDS FOREVER	Beatles	*Parlophone*	3
3	3	THIS IS MY SONG	Petula Clark	*Pye*	5
6	4	EDELWEISS	Vince Hill	*Columbia*	5
7	5	ON A CAROUSEL	Hollies	*Parlophone*	4
4	6	HERE COMES MY BABY	Tremeloes	*CBS*	6
5	7	I'M A BELIEVER	Monkees	*RCA Victor*	9
11	8	THERE'S A KIND OF HUSH	Herman's Hermits	*Columbia*	4
8	9	MELLOW YELLOW	Donovan	*Pye*	5
10	10	SNOOPY VS THE RED BARON	Royal Guardsmen	*Stateside*	7
13	11	DETROIT CITY	Tom Jones	*Decca*	4
18	12	GEORGY GIRL	Seekers	*Columbia*	3

In these weeks ■ Cat Stevens never had a number one hit, but for two weeks he enjoys Top Ten hits as both performer, *Matthew And Son*, and writer, *Here Comes My Baby* for the Tremeloes (23.02.67) ■ The Beatles' string of eleven consecutive number ones is broken as, what many consider their best single, *Penny Lane/Strawberry Fields Forever*, fails to get past Engelbert Humperdinck's lush ballad version of *Release Me* (02.03.67)■

March 1967

□ Highest position disc reached ● Act's first ever week on chart

LW	TW	Title	Artist	Label	Wks
9	13	PEEK-A-BOO	New Vaudeville Band	*Fontana*	6
22	14	GIVE IT TO ME	Troggs	*Page One*	3
14	15	I WON'T COME IN WHILE HE'S THERE	Jim Reeves	*RCA Victor*	6
16	[16]	IT TAKES TWO	Marvin Gaye and Kim Weston	*Tamla Motown*	6
31	17	THIS IS MY SONG	Harry Secombe	*Philips*	2
12	18	LET'S SPEND THE NIGHT TOGETHER	Rolling Stones	*Decca*	8
17	19	SINGLE GIRL	Sandy Posey	*MGM*	9
32	20	I'LL TRY ANYTHING	Dusty Springfield	*Philips*	2
37	21	MEMORIES ARE MADE OF THIS	Val Doonican	*Decca*	2
15	22	MATTHEW AND SON	Cat Stevens	*Deram*	9
23	23	LET ME CRY ON YOUR SHOULDER	Ken Dodd	*Columbia*	7
-	24	LOVE IS HERE AND NOW YOU'RE GONE	Supremes	*Tamla Motown*	1
19	25	SUGAR TOWN	Nancy Sinatra	*Reprise*	8
26	[26]	STAY WITH ME BABY	Walker Brothers	*Philips*	4
-	27	AL CAPONE	Prince Buster ●	*Blue Beat*	1
21	28	GREEN GREEN GRASS OF HOME	Tom Jones	*Decca*	18
-	29	I WAS KAISER BILL'S BATMAN	Whistling Jack Smith ●	*Deram*	1
33	30	I'VE PASSED THIS WAY BEFORE	Jimmy Ruffin	*Tamla Motown*	5
20	31	I'VE BEEN A BAD BAD BOY	Paul Jones	*HMV*	8
40	32	THEN YOU CAN TELL ME GOODBYE	Casinos	*President*	2
24	33	INDESCRIBABLY BLUE	Elvis Presley	*RCA Victor*	5
34	34	SO GOOD	Roy Orbison	*London*	2
29	35	BEAT GOES ON	Sonny and Cher	*Atlantic*	4
30	36	LAST TRAIN TO CLARKSVILLE	Monkees	*RCA Victor*	6
35	37	RUN TO THE DOOR	Clinton Ford	*Piccadilly*	5
-	38	SIMON SMITH AND THE AMAZING DANCING BEAR	Alan Price Set	*Decca*	1
38	39	COLD LIGHT OF DAY	Gene Pitney	*Stateside*	2
-	40	KEEP IT OUT OF SIGHT	Paul and Barry Ryan	*Decca*	1

WEEK ENDING 16 MARCH 1967

LW	TW	Title	Artist	Label	Wks
1	[1]	RELEASE ME	Engelbert Humperdinck	*Decca*	8
2	[2]	PENNY LANE/STRAWBERRY FIELDS FOREVER	Beatles	*Parlophone*	4
3	3	THIS IS MY SONG	Petula Clark	*Pye*	6
5	[4]	ON A CAROUSEL	Hollies	*Parlophone*	5
4	5	EDELWEISS	Vince Hill	*Columbia*	6
12	6	GEORGY GIRL	Seekers	*Columbia*	4
8	[7]	THERE'S A KIND OF HUSH	Herman's Hermits	*Columbia*	5
11	[8]	DETROIT CITY	Tom Jones	*Decca*	5
6	9	HERE COMES MY BABY	Tremeloes	*CBS*	7
10	10	SNOOPY VS THE RED BARON	Royal Guardsmen	*Stateside*	8
17	11	THIS IS MY SONG	Harry Secombe	*Philips*	3
14	[12]	GIVE IT TO ME	Troggs	*Page One*	4
20	[13]	I'LL TRY ANYTHING	Dusty Springfield	*Philips*	3
7	14	I'M A BELIEVER	Monkees	*RCA Victor*	10
13	15	PEEK-A-BOO	New Vaudeville Band	*Fontana*	7
21	16	MEMORIES ARE MADE OF THIS	Val Doonican	*Decca*	3
9	17	MELLOW YELLOW	Donovan	*Pye*	6
29	18	I WAS KAISER BILL'S BATMAN	Whistling Jack Smith	*Deram*	2
16	19	IT TAKES TWO	Marvin Gaye and Kim Weston	*Tamla Motown*	7
38	20	SIMON SMITH AND THE AMAZING DANCING BEAR	Alan Price Set	*Decca*	2
15	21	I WON'T COME IN WHILE HE'S THERE	Jim Reeves	*RCA Victor*	7
24	22	LOVE IS HERE AND NOW YOU'RE GONE	Supremes	*Tamla Motown*	2
19	23	SINGLE GIRL	Sandy Posey	*MGM*	10
27	24	AL CAPONE	Prince Buster	*Blue Beat*	2
-	25	TOUCH ME TOUCH ME	Dave Dee, Dozy, Beaky, Mick and Tich	*Fontana*	1
-	[26]	I CAN'T MAKE IT	Small Faces	*Decca*	1
-	27	PUPPET ON A STRING	Sandie Shaw	*Pye*	1
33	28	THEN YOU CAN TELL ME GOODBYE	Casinos	*President*	3
18	29	LET'S SPEND THE NIGHT TOGETHER	Rolling Stones	*Decca*	9
40	[30]	KEEP IT OUT OF SIGHT	Paul and Barry Ryan	*Decca*	2
28	31	GREEN GREEN GRASS OF HOME	Tom Jones	*Decca*	19
34	[32]	SO GOOD	Roy Orbison	*London*	3
37	[33]	RUN TO THE DOOR	Clinton Ford	*Piccadilly*	6
25	34	SUGAR TOWN	Nancy Sinatra	*Reprise*	9
30	35	I'VE PASSED THIS WAY BEFORE	Jimmy Ruffin	*Tamla Motown*	6
-	36	KNOCK ON WOOD	Eddie Floyd ●	*Atlantic*	1
26	37	STAY WITH ME BABY	Walker Brothers	*Philips*	5
23	38	LET ME CRY ON YOUR SHOULDER	Ken Dodd	*Columbia*	8
39	39	COLD LIGHT OF DAY	Gene Pitney	*Stateside*	3
22	40	MATTHEW AND SON	Cat Stevens	*Deram*	10

WEEK ENDING 23 MARCH 1967

LW	TW	Title	Artist	Label	Wks
1	[1]	RELEASE ME	Engelbert Humperdinck	*Decca*	9
5	[2]	EDELWEISS	Vince Hill	*Columbia*	7
6	[3]	GEORGY GIRL	Seekers	*Columbia*	5
3	4	THIS IS MY SONG	Petula Clark	*Pye*	7
2	5	PENNY LANE/STRAWBERRY FIELDS FOREVER	Beatles	*Parlophone*	5
20	6	SIMON SMITH AND THE AMAZING DANCING BEAR	Alan Price Set	*Decca*	3
4	7	ON A CAROUSEL	Hollies	*Parlophone*	6
18	8	I WAS KAISER BILL'S BATMAN	Whistling Jack Smith	*Deram*	3
11	9	THIS IS MY SONG	Harry Secombe	*Philips*	4
7	10	THERE'S A KIND OF HUSH	Herman's Hermits	*Columbia*	6
8	11	DETROIT CITY	Tom Jones	*Decca*	6
16	12	MEMORIES ARE MADE OF THIS	Val Doonican	*Decca*	4
9	13	HERE COMES MY BABY	Tremeloes	*CBS*	8
10	14	SNOOPY VS THE RED BARON	Royal Guardsmen	*Stateside*	9
12	15	GIVE IT TO ME	Troggs	*Page One*	5
27	16	PUPPET ON A STRING	Sandie Shaw	*Pye*	2
14	17	I'M A BELIEVER	Monkees	*RCA Victor*	11
13	18	I'LL TRY ANYTHING	Dusty Springfield	*Philips*	4
22	19	LOVE IS HERE AND NOW YOU'RE GONE	Supremes	*Tamla Motown*	3
15	20	PEEK-A-BOO	New Vaudeville Band	*Fontana*	8
24	21	AL CAPONE	Prince Buster	*Blue Beat*	3
25	22	TOUCH ME TOUCH ME	Dave Dee, Dozy, Beaky, Mick and Tich	*Fontana*	2
21	23	I WON'T COME IN WHILE HE'S THERE	Jim Reeves	*RCA Victor*	8
-	24	IT'S ALL OVER	Cliff Richard	*Columbia*	1
-	25	SOMETHIN' STUPID	Nancy Sinatra and Frank Sinatra ●	*Reprise*	1
19	26	IT TAKES TWO	Marvin Gaye and Kim Weston	*Tamla Motown*	8
17	27	MELLOW YELLOW	Donovan	*Pye*	7
23	28	SINGLE GIRL	Sandy Posey	*MGM*	11
36	29	KNOCK ON WOOD	Eddie Floyd	*Atlantic*	2
28	30	THEN YOU CAN TELL ME GOODBYE	Casinos	*President*	4
30	31	KEEP IT OUT OF SIGHT	Paul and Barry Ryan	*Decca*	3
26	32	I CAN'T MAKE IT	Small Faces	*Decca*	2
32	33	SO GOOD	Roy Orbison	*London*	4
-	34	YOU GOT WHAT IT TAKES	Dave Clark Five	*Columbia*	1
31	35	GREEN GREEN GRASS OF HOME	Tom Jones	*Decca*	20
33	36	RUN TO THE DOOR	Clinton Ford	*Piccadilly*	7
-	37	BECAUSE I LOVE YOU	Georgie Fame	*CBS*	1
29	38	LET'S SPEND THE NIGHT TOGETHER	Rolling Stones	*Decca*	10
-	39	PURPLE HAZE	Jimi Hendrix Experience	*Track*	1
39	40	COLD LIGHT OF DAY	Gene Pitney	*Stateside*	4

WEEK ENDING 30 MARCH 1967

LW	TW	Title	Artist	Label	Wks
1	[1]	RELEASE ME	Engelbert Humperdinck	*Decca*	10
8	[2]	THIS IS MY SONG	Harry Secombe	*Philips*	5
2	3	EDELWEISS	Vince Hill	*Columbia*	8
6	[4]	SIMON SMITH AND THE AMAZING DANCING BEAR	Alan Price Set	*Decca*	4
8	[5]	I WAS KAISER BILL'S BATMAN	Whistling Jack Smith	*Deram*	4
16	6	PUPPET ON A STRING	Sandie Shaw	*Pye*	3
3	7	GEORGY GIRL	Seekers	*Columbia*	6

■With Engelbert Humperdinck, Vince Hill, the Seekers and Petula Clark in the top four positions and Harry Secombe and the Sinatras climbing rapidly, the charts are as ballad-dominated as they have ever been since the days of Eddie Fisher and David Whitfield (23.03.67) ■ But Prince Buster's *Al Capone* gives Jamaican reggae its first British chart outing (09.03.67)■

March 1967

□ Highest position disc reached ● Act's first ever week on chart

LW	TW	Title	Artist	Label	Wks
2	8	THIS IS MY SONG	Petula Clark	*Pye*	8
25	9	SOMETHIN' STUPID	Nancy Sinatra and Frank Sinatra	*Reprise*	2
5	10	PENNY LANE/STRAWBERRY FIELDS FOREVER	Beatles	*Parlophone*	6
12	11	MEMORIES ARE MADE OF THIS	Val Doonican	*Decca*	5
7	12	ON A CAROUSEL	Hollies	*Parlophone*	7
10	13	THERE'S A KIND OF HUSH	Herman's Hermits	*Columbia*	7
24	14	IT'S ALL OVER	Cliff Richard	*Columbia*	2
22	15	TOUCH ME TOUCH ME	Dave Dee, Dozy, Beaky, Mick and Tich	*Fontana*	3
11	16	DETROIT CITY	Tom Jones	*Decca*	7
19	17	LOVE IS HERE AND NOW YOU'RE GONE	Supremes	*Tamla Motown*	4
15	18	GIVE IT TO ME	Troggs	*Page One*	6
18	19	I'LL TRY ANYTHING	Dusty Springfield	*Philips*	5
21	20	AL CAPONE	Prince Buster	*Blue Beat*	4
14	21	SNOOPY VS THE RED BARON	Royal Guardsmen	*Stateside*	10
13	22	HERE COMES MY BABY	Tremeloes	*CBS*	9
29	23	KNOCK ON WOOD	Eddie Floyd	*Atlantic*	3
17	24	I'M A BELIEVER	Monkees	*RCA Victor*	12
20	25	PEEK-A-BOO	New Vaudeville Band	*Fontana*	9
32	26	I CAN'T MAKE IT	Small Faces	*Decca*	3
23	27	I WON'T COME IN WHILE HE'S THERE	Jim Reeves	*RCA Victor*	9
37	28	BECAUSE I LOVE YOU	Georgie Fame	*CBS*	2
34	29	YOU GOT WHAT IT TAKES	Dave Clark Five	*Columbia*	2
31	30	KEEP IT OUT OF SIGHT	Paul and Barry Ryan	*Decca*	4
30	31	THEN YOU CAN TELL ME GOODBYE	Casinos	*President*	5
39	32	PURPLE HAZE	Jimi Hendrix Experience	*Track*	2
-	33	BERNADETTE	Four Tops	*Tamla Motown*	1
26	34	IT TAKES TWO	Marvin Gaye and Kim Weston	*Tamla Motown*	9
27	35	MELLOW YELLOW	Donovan	*Pye*	8
-	36	HAPPY TOGETHER	Turtles ●	*London*	1
28	37	SINGLE GIRL	Sandy Posey	*MGM*	12
35	38	GREEN GREEN GRASS OF HOME	Tom Jones	*Decca*	21
40	39	COLD LIGHT OF DAY	Gene Pitney	*Stateside*	5
-	40	SEVEN DRUNKEN NIGHTS	Dubliners ●	*Major Minor*	1

WEEK ENDING 6 APRIL 1967

LW	TW	Title	Artist	Label	Wks
1	1	RELEASE ME	Engelbert Humperdinck	*Decca*	11
9	2	SOMETHIN' STUPID	Nancy Sinatra and Frank Sinatra	*Reprise*	3
2	3	THIS IS MY SONG	Harry Secombe	*Philips*	6
6	4	PUPPET ON A STRING	Sandie Shaw	*Pye*	4
4	5	SIMON SMITH AND THE AMAZING DANCING BEAR	Alan Price Set	*Decca*	5
5	6	I WAS KAISER BILL'S BATMAN	Whistling Jack Smith	*Deram*	5
3	7	EDELWEISS	Vince Hill	*Columbia*	9
10	8	PENNY LANE/STRAWBERRY FIELDS FOREVER	Beatles	*Parlophone*	7
8	9	THIS IS MY SONG	Petula Clark	*Pye*	9
7	10	GEORGY GIRL	Seekers	*Columbia*	7
14	11	IT'S ALL OVER	Cliff Richard	*Columbia*	3
11	12	MEMORIES ARE MADE OF THIS	Val Doonican	*Decca*	6
15	13	TOUCH ME TOUCH ME	Dave Dee, Dozy, Beaky, Mick and Tich	*Fontana*	4
-	14	A LITTLE BIT ME A LITTLE BIT YOU	Monkees	*RCA Victor*	1
13	15	THERE'S A KIND OF HUSH	Herman's Hermits	*Columbia*	8
12	16	ON A CAROUSEL	Hollies	*Parlophone*	8
-	17	HA! HA! SAID THE CLOWN	Manfred Mann	*Fontana*	1
20	18	AL CAPONE	Prince Buster	*Blue Beat*	5
16	19	DETROIT CITY	Tom Jones	*Decca*	8
17	20	LOVE IS HERE AND NOW YOU'RE GONE	Supremes	*Tamla Motown*	5
23	21	KNOCK ON WOOD	Eddie Floyd	*Atlantic*	4
32	22	PURPLE HAZE	Jimi Hendrix Experience	*Track*	3
28	23	BECAUSE I LOVE YOU	Georgie Fame	*CBS*	3
18	24	GIVE IT TO ME	Troggs	*Page One*	7
33	25	BERNADETTE	Four Tops	*Tamla Motown*	2
19	26	I'LL TRY ANYTHING	Dusty Springfield	*Philips*	6
36	27	HAPPY TOGETHER	Turtles	*London*	2
24	28	I'M A BELIEVER	Monkees	*RCA Victor*	13
29	29	YOU GOT WHAT IT TAKES	Dave Clark Five	*Columbia*	3
26	30	I CAN'T MAKE IT	Small Faces	*Decca*	4
-	31	ARNOLD LAYNE	Pink Floyd ●	*Columbia*	1
21	32	SNOOPY VS THE RED BARON	Royal Guardsmen	*Stateside*	11
40	33	SEVEN DRUNKEN NIGHTS	Dubliners	*Major Minor*	2
-	34	I'M GONNA GET ME A GUN	Cat Stevens	*Deram*	1
22	35	HERE COMES MY BABY	Tremeloes	*CBS*	10
27	36	I WON'T COME IN WHILE HE'S THERE	Jim Reeves	*RCA Victor*	10
30	37	KEEP IT OUT OF SIGHT	Paul and Barry Ryan	*Decca*	5
25	38	PEEK-A-BOO	New Vaudeville Band	*Fontana*	10
-	39	I CAN HEAR THE GRASS GROW	Move	*Deram*	1
-	40	59TH STREET BRIDGE SONG	Harper's Bizarre ●	*Warner Bros*	1

WEEK ENDING 13 APRIL 1967

LW	TW	Title	Artist	Label	Wks
2	1	SOMETHIN' STUPID	Nancy Sinatra and Frank Sinatra	*Reprise*	4
1	2	RELEASE ME	Engelbert Humperdinck	*Decca*	12
4	3	PUPPET ON A STRING	Sandie Shaw	*Pye*	5
14	4	A LITTLE BIT ME A LITTLE BIT YOU	Monkees	*RCA Victor*	2
3	5	THIS IS MY SONG	Harry Secombe	*Philips*	7
17	6	HA! HA! SAID THE CLOWN	Manfred Mann	*Fontana*	2
5	7	SIMON SMITH AND THE AMAZING DANCING BEAR	Alan Price Set	*Decca*	6
6	8	I WAS KAISER BILL'S BATMAN	Whistling Jack Smith	*Deram*	6
11	9	IT'S ALL OVER	Cliff Richard	*Columbia*	4
7	10	EDELWEISS	Vince Hill	*Columbia*	10
22	11	PURPLE HAZE	Jimi Hendrix Experience	*Track*	4
8	12	PENNY LANE/STRAWBERRY FIELDS FOREVER	Beatles	*Parlophone*	8
25	13	BERNADETTE	Four Tops	*Tamla Motown*	3
10	14	GEORGY GIRL	Seekers	*Columbia*	8
23	15	BECAUSE I LOVE YOU	Georgie Fame	*CBS*	4
13	16	TOUCH ME TOUCH ME	Dave Dee, Dozy, Beaky, Mick and Tich	*Fontana*	5
12	16	MEMORIES ARE MADE OF THIS	Val Doonican	*Decca*	7
9	18	THIS IS MY SONG	Petula Clark	*Pye*	10
27	19	HAPPY TOGETHER	Turtles	*London*	3
21	20	KNOCK ON WOOD	Eddie Floyd	*Atlantic*	5
34	21	I'M GONNA GET ME A GUN	Cat Stevens	*Deram*	2
18	22	AL CAPONE	Prince Buster	*Blue Beat*	6
15	23	THERE'S A KIND OF HUSH	Herman's Hermits	*Columbia*	9
20	24	LOVE IS HERE AND NOW YOU'RE GONE	Supremes	*Tamla Motown*	6
33	25	SEVEN DRUNKEN NIGHTS	Dubliners	*Major Minor*	3
31	26	ARNOLD LAYNE	Pink Floyd	*Columbia*	2
16	27	ON A CAROUSEL	Hollies	*Parlophone*	9
29	28	YOU GOT WHAT IT TAKES	Dave Clark Five	*Columbia*	4
24	29	GIVE IT TO ME	Troggs	*Page One*	8
39	30	I CAN HEAR THE GRASS GROW	Move	*Deram*	2
19	31	DETROIT CITY	Tom Jones	*Decca*	9
28	32	I'M A BELIEVER	Monkees	*RCA Victor*	14
26	33	I'LL TRY ANYTHING	Dusty Springfield	*Philips*	7
-	34	JIMMY MACK	Martha and the Vandellas	*Tamla Motown*	1
-	35	DEDICATED TO THE ONE I LOVE	Mamas and the Papas	*RCA Victor*	1
-	36	HI-HO SILVER LINING	Jeff Beck ●	*Columbia*	1
40	37	59TH STREET BRIDGE SONG	Harper's Bizarre	*Warner Bros*	2
30	38	I CAN'T MAKE IT	Small Faces	*Decca*	5
-	39	FUNNY FAMILIAR FORGOTTEN FEELINGS	Tom Jones	*Decca*	1
-	40	RETURN OF THE RED BARON	Royal Guardsmen	*Stateside*	1

WEEK ENDING 20 APRIL 1967

LW	TW	Title	Artist	Label	Wks
1	1	SOMETHIN' STUPID	Nancy Sinatra and Frank Sinatra	*Reprise*	5
3	2	PUPPET ON A STRING	Sandie Shaw	*Pye*	5
4	3	A LITTLE BIT ME A LITTLE BIT YOU	Monkees	*RCA Victor*	3
6	4	HA! HA! SAID THE CLOWN	Manfred Mann	*Fontana*	3
1	5	RELEASE ME	Engelbert Humperdinck	*Decca*	13
11	6	PURPLE HAZE	Jimi Hendrix Experience	*Track*	5

In these weeks ■ Nancy Sinatra and Frank Sinatra become the first people who have already achieved solo number ones to team up and make another. They also consolidate their position as the most successful father and daughter in chart history (13.04.67) ■ Six men in song titles, including two Great War veterans (Kaiser Bill and the Red Baron), a gangster (Al Capone) and three others (Simon Smith, Arnold Layne and Jimmy Mack). There are also two ladies, *Bernadette* and *Georgy Girl* (13.04.67)■

LW	TW	Title	Artist	Label	Wks
5	7	THIS IS MY SONG	Harry Secombe	Philips	8
13	8	BERNADETTE	Four Tops	Tamla Motown	4
9	9	IT'S ALL OVER	Cliff Richard	Columbia	5
21	10	I'M GONNA GET ME A GUN	Cat Stevens	Deram	3
7	11	SIMON SMITH AND THE AMAZING DANCING BEAR	Alan Price Set	Decca	7
19	12	HAPPY TOGETHER	Turtles	London	4
8	13	I WAS KAISER BILL'S BATMAN	Whistling Jack Smith	Deram	7
25	14	SEVEN DRUNKEN NIGHTS	Dubliners	Major Minor	4
15	15	BECAUSE I LOVE YOU	Georgie Fame	CBS	5
30	16	I CAN HEAR THE GRASS GROW	Move	Deram	3
10	17	EDELWEISS	Vince Hill	Columbia	11
35	18	DEDICATED TO THE ONE I LOVE	Mamas and the Papas	RCA Victor	2
20	19	KNOCK ON WOOD	Eddie Floyd	Atlantic	6
26	20	ARNOLD LAYNE	Pink Floyd	Columbia	3
16	21	TOUCH ME TOUCH ME	Dave Dee, Dozy, Beaky, Mick and Tich	Fontana	6
14	22	GEORGY GIRL	Seekers	Columbia	9
12	23	PENNY LANE/STRAWBERRY FIELDS FOREVER	Beatles	Parlophone	9
39	24	FUNNY FAMILIAR FORGOTTEN FEELINGS	Tom Jones	Decca	2
16	25	MEMORIES ARE MADE OF THIS	Val Doonican	Decca	8
34	26	JIMMY MACK	Martha and the Vandellas	Tamla Motown	2
18	27	THIS IS MY SONG	Petula Clark	Pye	11
36	28	HI-HO SILVER LINING	Jeff Beck	Columbia	2
22	29	AL CAPONE	Prince Buster	Blue Beat	7
28	30	YOU GOT WHAT IT TAKES	Dave Clark Five	Columbia	5
24	31	LOVE IS HERE AND NOW YOU'RE GONE	Supremes	Tamla Motown	7
-	32	MAROC 7	Shadows	Columbia	1
-	33	THE BOAT THAT I ROW	Lulu	Columbia	1
37	34	59TH STREET BRIDGE SONG	Harper's Bizarre	Warner Bros	3
23	35	THERE'S A KIND OF HUSH	Herman's Hermits	Columbia	10
-	36	SOOTHE ME	Sam and Dave ●	Stax	1
40	37	RETURN OF THE RED BARON	Royal Guardsmen	Stateside	2
27	38	ON A CAROUSEL	Hollies	Parlophone	10
-	39	OH HOW I MISS YOU	Bachelors	Decca	1
32	40	I'M A BELIEVER	Monkees	RCA Victor	15

WEEK ENDING 27 APRIL 1967

LW	TW	Title	Artist	Label	Wks
2	1	PUPPET ON A STRING	Sandie Shaw	Pye	6
1	2	SOMETHIN' STUPID	Nancy Sinatra and Frank Sinatra	Reprise	6
3	3	A LITTLE BIT ME A LITTLE BIT YOU	Monkees	RCA Victor	4
4	4	HA! HA! SAID THE CLOWN	Manfred Mann	Fontana	4
6	5	PURPLE HAZE	Jimi Hendrix Experience	Track	6
10	6	I'M GONNA GET ME A GUN	Cat Stevens	Deram	4
16	7	I CAN HEAR THE GRASS GROW	Move	Deram	4
5	8	RELEASE ME	Engelbert Humperdinck	Decca	14
18	9	DEDICATED TO THE ONE I LOVE	Mamas and the Papas	RCA Victor	3
8	10	BERNADETTE	Four Tops	Tamla Motown	5
14	11	SEVEN DRUNKEN NIGHTS	Dubliners	Major Minor	5
12	12	HAPPY TOGETHER	Turtles	London	5
24	13	FUNNY FAMILIAR FORGOTTEN FEELINGS	Tom Jones	Decca	3
7	14	THIS IS MY SONG	Harry Secombe	Philips	9
9	15	IT'S ALL OVER	Cliff Richard	Columbia	6
33	16	THE BOAT THAT I ROW	Lulu	Columbia	2
13	17	I WAS KAISER BILL'S BATMAN	Whistling Jack Smith	Deram	8
11	18	SIMON SMITH AND THE AMAZING DANCING BEAR	Alan Price Set	Decca	8
19	19	KNOCK ON WOOD	Eddie Floyd	Atlantic	7
17	20	EDELWEISS	Vince Hill	Columbia	12
15	21	BECAUSE I LOVE YOU	Georgie Fame	CBS	6
26	22	JIMMY MACK	Martha and the Vandellas	Tamla Motown	3
20	23	ARNOLD LAYNE	Pink Floyd	Columbia	4
28	24	HI-HO SILVER LINING	Jeff Beck	Columbia	3
29	25	AL CAPONE	Prince Buster	Blue Beat	8
32	26	MAROC 7	Shadows	Columbia	2
22	27	GEORGY GIRL	Seekers	Columbia	10
25	28	MEMORIES ARE MADE OF THIS	Val Doonican	Decca	9
-	29	SILENCE IS GOLDEN	Tremeloes	CBS	1
39	30	OH HOW I MISS YOU	Bachelors	Decca	2

May 1967

□ Highest position disc reached ● Act's first ever week on chart

LW	TW	Title	Artist	Label	Wks
-	31	PICTURES OF LILY	Who	Track	1
21	32	TOUCH ME TOUCH ME	Dave Dee, Dozy, Beaky, Mick and Tich	Fontana	7
27	33	THIS IS MY SONG	Petula Clark	Pye	12
34	34	59TH STREET BRIDGE SONG	Harper's Bizarre	Warner Bros	4
30	35	YOU GOT WHAT IT TAKES	Dave Clark Five	Columbia	6
23	36	PENNY LANE/STRAWBERRY FIELDS FOREVER	Beatles	Parlophone	10
31	37	LOVE IS HERE AND NOW YOU'RE GONE	Supremes	Tamla Motown	8
-	38	GUNS OF NAVARONE	Skalites ●	Island	1
-	39	IF I WERE A RICH MAN	Topol ●	CBS	1
36	40	SOOTHE ME	Sam and Dave	Stax	2

WEEK ENDING 4 MAY 1967

LW	TW	Title	Artist	Label	Wks
1	1	PUPPET ON A STRING	Sandie Shaw	Pye	7
2	2	SOMETHIN' STUPID	Nancy Sinatra and Frank Sinatra	Reprise	7
5	3	PURPLE HAZE	Jimi Hendrix Experience	Track	7
3	4	A LITTLE BIT ME A LITTLE BIT YOU	Monkees	RCA Victor	5
7	5	I CAN HEAR THE GRASS GROW	Move	Deram	5
9	6	DEDICATED TO THE ONE I LOVE	Mamas and the Papas	RCA Victor	4
4	7	HA! HA! SAID THE CLOWN	Manfred Mann	Fontana	5
6	8	I'M GONNA GET ME A GUN	Cat Stevens	Deram	5
13	9	FUNNY FAMILIAR FORGOTTEN FEELINGS	Tom Jones	Decca	4
16	10	THE BOAT THAT I ROW	Lulu	Columbia	3
8	11	RELEASE ME	Engelbert Humperdinck	Decca	15
10	12	BERNADETTE	Four Tops	Tamla Motown	6
11	13	SEVEN DRUNKEN NIGHTS	Dubliners	Major Minor	6
12	14	HAPPY TOGETHER	Turtles	London	6
29	15	SILENCE IS GOLDEN	Tremeloes	CBS	2
31	16	PICTURES OF LILY	Who	Track	2
24	17	HI-HO SILVER LINING	Jeff Beck	Columbia	4
15	18	IT'S ALL OVER	Cliff Richard	Columbia	7
19	19	KNOCK ON WOOD	Eddie Floyd	Atlantic	8
14	20	THIS IS MY SONG	Harry Secombe	Philips	10
22	21	JIMMY MACK	Martha and the Vandellas	Tamla Motown	4
18	22	SIMON SMITH AND HIS AMAZING DANCING BEAR	Alan Price Set	Decca	9
17	23	I WAS KAISER BILL'S BATMAN	Whistling Jack Smith	Deram	9
26	24	MAROC 7	Shadows	Columbia	3
20	25	EDELWEISS	Vince Hill	Columbia	13
21	26	BECAUSE I LOVE YOU	Georgie Fame	CBS	7
-	27	NEW YORK MINING DISASTER 1941	Bee Gees ●	Polydor	1
23	28	ARNOLD LAYNE	Pink Floyd	Columbia	5
-	29	SWEET SOUL MUSIC	Arthur Conley ●	Atlantic	1
-	30	GONNA GIVE HER ALL THE LOVE I'VE GOT	Jimmy Ruffin	Tamla Motown	1
39	31	IF I WERE A RICH MAN	Topol	CBS	2
30	32	OH HOW I MISS YOU	Bachelors	Decca	3
25	33	AL CAPONE	Prince Buster	Blue Beat	9
-	34	THEN I KISSED HER	Beach Boys	Capitol	1
40	35	SOOTHE ME	Sam and Dave	Stax	3
28	36	MEMORIES ARE MADE OF THIS	Val Doonican	Decca	10
27	37	GEORGY GIRL	Seekers	Columbia	11
38	38	GUNS OF NAVARONE	Skalites	Island	2
34	39	59TH STREET BRIDGE SONG	Harper's Bizarre	Warner Bros	5
35	40	YOU GOT WHAT IT TAKES	Dave Clark Five	Columbia	7

WEEK ENDING 11 MAY 1967

LW	TW	Title	Artist	Label	Wks
1	1	PUPPET ON A STRING	Sandie Shaw	Pye	8
2	2	SOMETHIN' STUPID	Nancy Sinatra and Frank Sinatra	Reprise	8
6	3	DEDICATED TO THE ONE I LOVE	Mamas and the Papas	RCA Victor	5
15	4	SILENCE IS GOLDEN	Tremeloes	CBS	3
16	5	PICTURES OF LILY	Who	Track	3

■Among the performers who have written hits this week are Randy Newman (*Simon Smith And The Amazing Dancing Bear*), Jim Dale (*Georgy Girl*), Neil Diamond (*The Boat That I Row* and *I'm A Believer*) and Paul Simon (*59th Street Bridge Song*) (20.04.67) ■ Sandie Shaw's *Puppet On A String* gives her a third number one and a Eurovision song contest victory. She is the first woman to achieve the former and the first Briton to achieve the latter (27.04.67)■

May 1967

□ Highest position disc reached ● Act's first ever week on chart

LW	TW	Title	Artist	Label	Wks
10	6	THE BOAT THAT I ROW	Lulu	Columbia	4
3	7	PURPLE HAZE	Jimi Hendrix Experience	Track	8
9	8	FUNNY FAMILIAR FORGOTTEN FEELINGS	Tom Jones	Decca	5
5	9	I CAN HEAR THE GRASS GROW	Move	Deram	6
4	10	A LITTLE BIT ME A LITTLE BIT YOU	Monkees	RCA Victor	6
13	11	SEVEN DRUNKEN NIGHTS	Dubliners	Major Minor	7
7	12	HA! HA! SAID THE CLOWN	Manfred Mann	Fontana	6
8	13	I'M GONNA GET ME A GUN	Cat Stevens	Deram	6
17	14	HI-HO SILVER LINING	Jeff Beck	Columbia	5
11	15	RELEASE ME	Engelbert Humperdinck	Decca	16
14	16	HAPPY TOGETHER	Turtles	London	7
27	17	NEW YORK MINING DISASTER 1941	Bee Gees	Polydor	2
12	18	BERNADETTE	Four Tops	Tamla Motown	7
34	19	THEN I KISSED HER	Beach Boys	Capitol	2
19	20	KNOCK ON WOOD	Eddie Floyd	Atlantic	9
29	21	SWEET SOUL MUSIC	Arthur Conley	Atlantic	2
18	22	IT'S ALL OVER	Cliff Richard	Columbia	8
20	23	THIS IS MY SONG	Harry Secombe	Philips	11
21	24	JIMMY MACK	Martha and the Vandellas	Tamla Motown	5
24	25	MAROC 7	Shadows	Columbia	4
30	26	GONNA GIVE HER ALL THE LOVE I'VE GOT	Jimmy Ruffin	Tamla Motown	2
-	27	THE WIND CRIES MARY	Jimi Hendrix Experience	Track	1
31	28	IF I WERE A RICH MAN	Topol	CBS	3
-	29	WATERLOO SUNSET	Kinks	Pye	1
22	30	SIMON SMITH AND HIS AMAZING DANCING BEAR	Alan Price Set	Decca	10
25	31	EDELWEISS	Vince Hill	Columbia	14
23	32	I WAS KAISER BILL'S BATMAN	Whistling Jack Smith	Deram	10
28	33	ARNOLD LAYNE	Pink Floyd	Columbia	6
26	34	BECAUSE I LOVE YOU	Georgie Fame	CBS	8
-	35	CASINO ROYALE	Herb Alpert	A&M	1
38	36	GUNS OF NAVARONE	Skalites	Island	3
-	37	BIRDS AND BEES	Warm Sounds ●	Deram	1
-	38	FIRST CUT IS THE DEEPEST	P P Arnold ●	Immediate	1
32	39	OH HOW I MISS YOU	Bachelors	Decca	4
-	40	MUSIC TO WATCH GIRLS BY	Andy Williams	CBS	1

WEEK ENDING 18 MAY 1967

LW	TW	Title	Artist	Label	Wks
4	1	SILENCE IS GOLDEN	Tremeloes	CBS	4
3	2	DEDICATED TO THE ONE I LOVE	Mamas and the Papas	RCA Victor	6
1	3	PUPPET ON A STRING	Sandie Shaw	Pye	9
5	4	PICTURES OF LILY	Who	Track	4
2	5	SOMETHIN' STUPID	Nancy Sinatra and Frank Sinatra	Reprise	9
6	6	THE BOAT THAT I ROW	Lulu	Columbia	5
8	7	FUNNY FAMILIAR FORGOTTEN FEELINGS	Tom Jones	Decca	6
11	8	SEVEN DRUNKEN NIGHTS	Dubliners	Major Minor	8
29	9	WATERLOO SUNSET	Kinks	Pye	2
7	10	PURPLE HAZE	Jimi Hendrix Experience	Track	9
10	11	A LITTLE BIT ME A LITTLE BIT YOU	Monkees	RCA Victor	7
19	12	THEN I KISSED HER	Beach Boys	Capitol	3
9	13	I CAN HEAR THE GRASS GROW	Move	Deram	7
14	14	HI-HO SILVER LINING	Jeff Beck	Columbia	6
27	15	THE WIND CRIES MARY	Jimi Hendrix Experience	Track	2
17	16	NEW YORK MINING DISASTER 1941	Bee Gees	Polydor	3
21	17	SWEET SOUL MUSIC	Arthur Conley	Atlantic	3
12	18	HA! HA! SAID THE CLOWN	Manfred Mann	Fontana	7
16	19	HAPPY TOGETHER	Turtles	London	8
13	20	I'M GONNA GET ME A GUN	Cat Stevens	Deram	7
15	21	RELEASE ME	Engelbert Humperdinck	Decca	17
20	22	KNOCK ON WOOD	Eddie Floyd	Atlantic	10
-	23	THE HAPPENING	Supremes	Tamla Motown	1
18	24	BERNADETTE	Four Tops	Tamla Motown	8
-	25	FINCHLEY CENTRAL	New Vaudeville Band	Fontana	1
28	26	IF I WERE A RICH MAN	Topol	CBS	4
37	27	BIRDS AND BEES	Warm Sounds	Deram	2
23	28	THIS IS MY SONG	Harry Secombe	Philips	12
25	29	MAROC 7	Shadows	Columbia	5
38	30	FIRST CUT IS THE DEEPEST	P P Arnold	Immediate	2
35	31	CASINO ROYALE	Herb Alpert	A&M	2
24	32	JIMMY MACK	Martha and the Vandellas	Tamla Motown	6
26	33	GONNA GIVE HER ALL THE LOVE I'VE GOT	Jimmy Ruffin	Tamla Motown	3
40	34	MUSIC TO WATCH GIRLS BY	Andy Williams	CBS	2
22	35	IT'S ALL OVER	Cliff Richard	Columbia	9
-	36	ROSES OF PICARDY	Vince Hill	Columbia	1
-	37	WALKING IN THE RAIN	Walker Brothers	Philips	1
31	38	EDELWEISS	Vince Hill	Columbia	15
-	39	YOU GOTTA STOP/LOVE MACHINE	Elvis Presley	RCA	1
39	40	OH HOW I MISS YOU	Bachelors	Decca	5

WEEK ENDING 25 MAY 1967

LW	TW	Title	Artist	Label	Wks
1	1	SILENCE IS GOLDEN	Tremeloes	CBS	5
9	2	WATERLOO SUNSET	Kinks	Pye	3
2	3	DEDICATED TO THE ONE I LOVE	Mamas and the Papas	RCA Victor	7
12	4	THEN I KISSED HER	Beach Boys	Capitol	4
3	5	PUPPET ON A STRING	Sandie Shaw	Pye	10
4	6	PICTURES OF LILY	Who	Track	5
8	7	SEVEN DRUNKEN NIGHTS	Dubliners	Major Minor	9
6	8	THE BOAT THAT I ROW	Lulu	Columbia	6
15	9	THE WIND CRIES MARY	Jimi Hendrix Experience	Track	3
5	10	SOMETHIN' STUPID	Nancy Sinatra and Frank Sinatra	Reprise	10
7	11	FUNNY FAMILIAR FORGOTTEN FEELINGS	Tom Jones	Decca	7
16	12	NEW YORK MINING DISASTER 1941	Bee Gees	Polydor	4
23	13	THE HAPPENING	Supremes	Tamla Motown	2
14	14	HI-HO SILVER LINING	Jeff Beck	Columbia	7
17	15	SWEET SOUL MUSIC	Arthur Conley	Atlantic	4
10	16	PURPLE HAZE	Jimi Hendrix Experience	Track	10
25	17	FINCHLEY CENTRAL	New Vaudeville Band	Fontana	2
11	18	A LITTLE BIT ME A LITTLE BIT YOU	Monkees	RCA Victor	8
21	19	RELEASE ME	Engelbert Humperdinck	Decca	18
13	20	I CAN HEAR THE GRASS GROW	Move	Deram	8
-	21	A WHITER SHADE OF PALE	Procol Harum ●	Deram	1
36	22	ROSES OF PICARDY	Vince Hill	Columbia	2
30	23	FIRST CUT IS THE DEEPEST	P P Arnold	Immediate	3
18	24	HA! HA! SAID THE CLOWN	Manfred Mann	Fontana	8
26	25	IF I WERE A RICH MAN	Topol	CBS	5
19	26	HAPPY TOGETHER	Turtles	London	9
31	27	CASINO ROYALE	Herb Alpert	A&M	3
27	28	BIRDS AND BEES	Warm Sounds	Deram	3
-	29	THERE GOES MY EVERYTHING	Engelbert Humperdinck	Decca	1
20	30	I'M GONNA GET ME A GUN	Cat Stevens	Deram	8
37	31	WALKING IN THE RAIN	Walker Brothers	Philips	2
22	32	KNOCK ON WOOD	Eddie Floyd	Atlantic	11
34	33	MUSIC TO WATCH GIRLS BY	Andy Williams	CBS	3
24	34	BERNADETTE	Four Tops	Tamla Motown	9
28	35	THIS IS MY SONG	Harry Secombe	Philips	13
-	36	OKAY!	Dave Dee, Dozy, Beaky, Mick and Tich	Fontana	1
29	37	MAROC 7	Shadows	Columbia	6
39	38	YOU GOTTA STOP/LOVE MACHINE	Elvis Presley	RCA	2
-	39	I GOT RHYTHM	Happenings ●	Stateside	1
33	40	GONNA GIVE HER ALL THE LOVE I'VE GOT	Jimmy Ruffin	Tamla Motown	4

WEEK ENDING 1 JUNE 1967

LW	TW	Title	Artist	Label	Wks
1	1	SILENCE IS GOLDEN	Tremeloes	CBS	6
2	2	WATERLOO SUNSET	Kinks	Pye	4
3	3	DEDICATED TO THE ONE I LOVE	Mamas and the Papas	RCA Victor	8
21	4	A WHITER SHADE OF PALE	Procol Harum	Deram	2
4	5	THEN I KISSED HER	Beach Boys	Capitol	5
9	6	THE WIND CRIES MARY	Jimi Hendrix Experience	Track	4
29	7	THERE GOES MY EVERYTHING	Engelbert Humperdinck	Decca	2
13	8	THE HAPPENING	Supremes	Tamla Motown	3

In these weeks ■ Elvis Presley's *You Gotta Stop/Love Machine* is his first single ever to miss the Top 30, but worse is to follow. His next single will not even reach the Top 40 (25.05.67) ■ Three of the top four singles are revivals of old songs. Only the Kinks have an original hit (25.05.67)■

June 1967

□ Highest position disc reached ● Act's first ever week on chart

LW	TW	Title	Artist	Label	Wks
6	9	PICTURES OF LILY	Who	*Track*	6
7	10	SEVEN DRUNKEN NIGHTS	Dubliners	*Major Minor*	10
5	11	PUPPET ON A STRING	Sandie Shaw	*Pye*	11
10	12	SOMETHIN' STUPID	Nancy Sinatra and Frank Sinatra	*Reprise*	11
15	13	SWEET SOUL MUSIC	Arthur Conley	*Atlantic*	5
8	14	THE BOAT THAT I ROW	Lulu	*Columbia*	7
12	15	NEW YORK MINING DISASTER 1941	Bee Gees	*Polydor*	5
17	16	FINCHLEY CENTRAL	New Vaudeville Band	*Fontana*	3
11	17	FUNNY FAMILIAR FORGOTTEN FEELINGS	Tom Jones	*Decca*	8
22	18	ROSES OF PICARDY	Vince Hill	*Columbia*	3
14	19	HI-HO SILVER LINING	Jeff Beck	*Columbia*	8
16	20	PURPLE HAZE	Jimi Hendrix Experience	*Track*	11
18	21	A LITTLE BIT ME A LITTLE BIT YOU	Monkees	*RCA Victor*	9
23	22	FIRST CUT IS THE DEEPEST	P P Arnold	*Immediate*	4
19	23	RELEASE ME	Engelbert Humperdinck	*Decca*	19
36	24	OKAY!	Dave Dee, Dozy, Beaky, Mick and Tich	*Fontana*	2
25	25	IF I WERE A RICH MAN	Topol	*CBS*	6
31	26	WALKING IN THE RAIN	Walker Brothers	*Philips*	3
27	27	CASINO ROYALE	Herb Alpert	*A&M*	4
20	28	I CAN HEAR THE GRASS GROW	Move	*Deram*	9
28	29	BIRDS AND BEES	Warm Sounds	*Deram*	4
24	30	HA! HA! SAID THE CLOWN	Manfred Mann	*Fontana*	9
26	31	HAPPY TOGETHER	Turtles	*London*	10
-	32	GIVE ME TIME	Dusty Springfield	*Philips*	1
39	33	I GOT RHYTHM	Happenings	*Stateside*	2
33	34	MUSIC TO WATCH GIRLS BY	Andy Williams	*CBS*	3
32	35	KNOCK ON WOOD	Eddie Floyd	*Atlantic*	12
-	36	GROOVIN'	Young Rascals ●	*Atlantic*	1
-	37	SWEET PEA	Manfred Mann	*Fontana*	1
38	38	YOU GOTTA STOP/LOVE MACHINE	Elvis Presley	*RCA*	3
-	39	NIGHT OF THE LONG GRASS	Troggs	*Page One*	1
34	40	BERNADETTE	Four Tops	*Tamla Motown*	10

LW	TW	*WEEK ENDING* 8 JUNE 1967			Wks
4	1	A WHITER SHADE OF PALE	Procol Harum	*Deram*	3
1	2	SILENCE IS GOLDEN	Tremeloes	*CBS*	7
2	3	WATERLOO SUNSET	Kinks	*Pye*	5
7	4	THERE GOES MY EVERYTHING	Engelbert Humperdinck	*Decca*	3
5	5	THEN I KISSED HER	Beach Boys	*Capitol*	6
8	6	THE HAPPENING	Supremes	*Tamla Motown*	4
3	7	DEDICATED TO THE ONE I LOVE	Mamas and the Papas	*RCA Victor*	9
6	8	THE WIND CRIES MARY	Jimi Hendrix Experience	*Track*	5
13	9	SWEET SOUL MUSIC	Arthur Conley	*Atlantic*	6
9	10	PICTURES OF LILY	Who	*Track*	7
16	11	FINCHLEY CENTRAL	New Vaudeville Band	*Fontana*	4
10	12	SEVEN DRUNKEN NIGHTS	Dubliners	*Major Minor*	11
11	13	PUPPET ON A STRING	Sandie Shaw	*Pye*	12
24	14	OKAY!	Dave Dee, Dozy, Beaky, Mick and Tich	*Fontana*	3
15	15	NEW YORK MINING DISASTER 1941	Bee Gees	*Polydor*	6
18	16	ROSES OF PICARDY	Vince Hill	*Columbia*	4
-	17	CARRIE-ANNE	Hollies	*Parlophone*	1
12	18	SOMETHIN' STUPID	Nancy Sinatra and Frank Sinatra	*Reprise*	12
22	19	FIRST CUT IS THE DEEPEST	P P Arnold	*Immediate*	5
17	20	FUNNY FAMILIAR FORGOTTEN FEELINGS	Tom Jones	*Decca*	9
25	21	IF I WERE A RICH MAN	Topol	*CBS*	7
14	22	THE BOAT THAT I ROW	Lulu	*Columbia*	8
36	23	GROOVIN'	Young Rascals	*Atlantic*	2
32	24	GIVE ME TIME	Dusty Springfield	*Philips*	2
39	25	NIGHT OF THE LONG GRASS	Troggs	*Page One*	2
-	26	PAPER SUN	Traffic ●	*Island*	1
19	27	HI-HO SILVER LINING	Jeff Beck	*Columbia*	9
27	28	CASINO ROYALE	Herb Alpert	*A&M*	5
23	29	RELEASE ME	Engelbert Humperdinck	*Decca*	20
20	30	PURPLE HAZE	Jimi Hendrix Experience	*Track*	12
33	31	I GOT RHYTHM	Happenings	*Stateside*	3
21	32	A LITTLE BIT ME A LITTLE BIT YOU	Monkees	*RCA Victor*	10
26	33	WALKING IN THE RAIN	Walker Brothers	*Philips*	4
-	34	DON'T SLEEP IN THE SUBWAY	Petula Clark	*Pye*	1
29	35	BIRDS AND BEES	Warm Sounds	*Deram*	5
37	36	SWEET PEA	Manfred Mann	*Fontana*	2
-	37	HERE COME THE NICE	Small Faces	*Immediate*	1
34	38	MUSIC TO WATCH GIRLS BY	Andy Williams	*CBS*	4
-	39	TWO STREETS	Val Doonican	*Decca*	1
35	40	KNOCK ON WOOD	Eddie Floyd	*Atlantic*	13

LW	TW	*WEEK ENDING* 15 JUNE 1967			Wks
1	1	A WHITER SHADE OF PALE	Procol Harum	*Deram*	4
4	2	THERE GOES MY EVERYTHING	Engelbert Humperdinck	*Decca*	4
3	3	WATERLOO SUNSET	Kinks	*Pye*	6
2	4	SILENCE IS GOLDEN	Tremeloes	*CBS*	8
17	5	CARRIE-ANNE	Hollies	*Parlophone*	2
6	6	THE HAPPENING	Supremes	*Tamla Motown*	5
9	7	SWEET SOUL MUSIC	Arthur Conley	*Atlantic*	7
5	8	THEN I KISSED HER	Beach Boys	*Capitol*	7
7	9	DEDICATED TO THE ONE I LOVE	Mamas and the Papas	*RCA Victor*	10
14	10	OKAY!	Dave Dee, Dozy, Beaky, Mick and Tich	*Fontana*	4
11	11	FINCHLEY CENTRAL	New Vaudeville Band	*Fontana*	5
26	12	PAPER SUN	Traffic	*Island*	2
16	13	ROSES OF PICARDY	Vince Hill	*Columbia*	5
23	14	GROOVIN'	Young Rascals	*Atlantic*	3
8	15	THE WIND CRIES MARY	Jimi Hendrix Experience	*Track*	6
12	16	SEVEN DRUNKEN NIGHTS	Dubliners	*Major Minor*	12
21	17	IF I WERE A RICH MAN	Topol	*CBS*	8
19	18	FIRST CUT IS THE DEEPEST	P P Arnold	*Immediate*	6
25	19	NIGHT OF THE LONG GRASS	Troggs	*Page One*	3
13	20	PUPPET ON A STRING	Sandie Shaw	*Pye*	13
10	21	PICTURES OF LILY	Who	*Track*	8
34	22	DON'T SLEEP IN THE SUBWAY	Petula Clark	*Pye*	2
20	23	FUNNY FAMILIAR FORGOTTEN FEELINGS	Tom Jones	*Decca*	10
15	24	NEW YORK MINING DISASTER 1941	Bee Gees	*Polydor*	7
18	25	SOMETHIN' STUPID	Nancy Sinatra and Frank Sinatra	*Reprise*	13
37	26	HERE COME THE NICE	Small Faces	*Immediate*	2
24	27	GIVE ME TIME	Dusty Springfield	*Philips*	3
31	28	I GOT RHYTHM	Happenings	*Stateside*	4
22	29	THE BOAT THAT I ROW	Lulu	*Columbia*	9
28	30	CASINO ROYALE	Herb Alpert	*A&M*	6
29	31	RELEASE ME	Engelbert Humperdinck	*Decca*	21
-	32	STRANGE BREW	Cream	*Reaction*	1
-	33	I'LL COME RUNNING	Cliff Richard	*Columbia*	1
-	34	RESPECT	Aretha Franklin ●	*Atlantic*	1
-	35	TAKE ME IN YOUR ARMS AND LOVE ME	Gladys Knight and the Pips ●	*Tamla Motown*	1
-	36	WHAT GOOD AM I	Cilla Black	*Parlophone*	1
27	37	HI-HO SILVER LINING	Jeff Beck	*Columbia*	10
-	38	SEVEN ROOMS OF GLOOM	Four Tops	*Tamla Motown*	1
-	39	IT MUST BE HIM (SEUL SUR SON ETOILE)	Vikki Carr ●	*Liberty*	1
-	40	SHE'D RATHER BE WITH ME	Turtles	*London*	1

LW	TW	*WEEK ENDING* 22 JUNE 1967			Wks
1	1	A WHITER SHADE OF PALE	Procol Harum	*Deram*	5
2	2	THERE GOES MY EVERYTHING	Engelbert Humperdinck	*Decca*	5
5	3	CARRIE-ANNE	Hollies	*Parlophone*	3
4	4	SILENCE IS GOLDEN	Tremeloes	*CBS*	9
3	5	WATERLOO SUNSET	Kinks	*Pye*	7
10	6	OKAY!	Dave Dee, Dozy, Beaky, Mick and Tich	*Fontana*	5
6	7	THE HAPPENING	Supremes	*Tamla Motown*	6
12	8	PAPER SUN	Traffic	*Island*	3
7	9	SWEET SOUL MUSIC	Arthur Conley	*Atlantic*	8
8	10	THEN I KISSED HER	Beach Boys	*Capitol*	8

■Two tube stations in the top eleven, *Waterloo Sunset* and *Finchley Central*. Petula Clark's apt warning *Don't Sleep In The Subway* lies 23 places lower down (08.06.67) ■ Two of the great ladies of soul music, Aretha Franklin and Gladys Knight, make their Top 40 debuts in the same week (15.06.67)■

June 1967

□ Highest position disc reached ● Act's first ever week on chart

LW	TW	Title	Artist	Label	Wks
14	11	GROOVIN'	Young Rascals	Atlantic	4
9	12	DEDICATED TO THE ONE I LOVE	Mamas and the Papas	RCA Victor	11
11	13	FINCHLEY CENTRAL	New Vaudeville Band	Fontana	6
17	14	IF I WERE A RICH MAN	Topol	CBS	9
22	15	DON'T SLEEP IN THE SUBWAY	Petula Clark	Pye	3
26	16	HERE COME THE NICE	Small Faces	Immediate	3
19	17	NIGHT OF THE LONG GRASS	Troggs	Page One	4
13	18	ROSES OF PICARDY	Vince Hill	Columbia	6
40	19	SHE'D RATHER BE WITH ME	Turtles	London	2
18	20	FIRST CUT IS THE DEEPEST	P P Arnold	Immediate	7
38	21	SEVEN ROOMS OF GLOOM	Four Tops	Tamla Motown	2
32	22	STRANGE BREW	Cream	Reaction	2
15	23	WIND CRIES MARY	Jimi Hendrix Experience	Track	7
20	24	PUPPET ON A STRING	Sandie Shaw	Pye	14
16	25	SEVEN DRUNKEN NIGHTS	Dubliners	Major Minor	13
27	26	GIVE ME TIME	Dusty Springfield	Philips	4
34	27	RESPECT	Aretha Franklin	Atlantic	2
36	28	WHAT GOOD AM I	Cilla Black	Parlophone	2
33	29	I'LL COME RUNNING	Cliff Richard	Columbia	2
-	30	ALTERNATE TITLE	Monkees	RCA Victor	1
39	31	IT MUST BE HIM (SEUL SUR SON ETOILE)	Vikki Carr	Liberty	2
28	32	I GOT RHYTHM	Happenings	Stateside	5
25	33	SOMETHIN' STUPID	Nancy Sinatra and Frank Sinatra	Reprise	14
23	34	FUNNY FAMILIAR FORGOTTEN FEELINGS	Tom Jones	Decca	11
21	35	PICTURES OF LILY	Who	Track	9
31	36	RELEASE ME	Engelbert Humperdinck	Decca	22
30	37	CASINO ROYALE	Herb Alpert	A&M	7
35	38	TAKE ME IN YOUR ARMS AND LOVE ME	Gladys Knight and the Pips	Tamla Motown	2
-	39	OLIVE TREE	Judith Durham ●	Columbia	1
-	40	SHAKE	Otis Redding	Stax	1

WEEK ENDING 29 JUNE 1967

LW	TW	Title	Artist	Label	Wks
1	1	A WHITER SHADE OF PALE	Procol Harum	Deram	6
2	2	THERE GOES MY EVERYTHING	Engelbert Humperdinck	Decca	6
3	3	CARRIE-ANNE	Hollies	Parlophone	4
6	4	OKAY!	Dave Dee, Dozy, Beaky, Mick and Tich	Fontana	6
8	5	PAPER SUN	Traffic	Island	4
19	6	SHE'D RATHER BE WITH ME	Turtles	London	3
30	7	ALTERNATE TITLE	Monkees	RCA Victor	2
11	8	GROOVIN'	Young Rascals	Atlantic	5
4	9	SILENCE IS GOLDEN	Tremeloes	CBS	10
7	10	THE HAPPENING	Supremes	Tamla Motown	7
14	11	IF I WERE A RICH MAN	Topol	CBS	10
15	12	DON'T SLEEP IN THE SUBWAY	Petula Clark	Pye	4
9	13	SWEET SOUL MUSIC	Arthur Conley	Atlantic	9
16	14	HERE COME THE NICE	Small Faces	Immediate	4
5	15	WATERLOO SUNSET	Kinks	Pye	8
10	16	THEN I KISSED HER	Beach Boys	Capitol	9
21	17	SEVEN ROOMS OF GLOOM	Four Tops	Tamla Motown	3
13	18	FINCHLEY CENTRAL	New Vaudeville Band	Fontana	7
22	19	STRANGE BREW	Cream	Reaction	3
31	20	IT MUST BE HIM (SEUL SUR SON ETOILE)	Vikki Carr	Liberty	3
17	21	NIGHT OF THE LONG GRASS	Troggs	Page One	5
18	22	ROSES OF PICARDY	Vince Hill	Columbia	7
12	23	DEDICATED TO THE ONE I LOVE	Mamas and the Papas	RCA Victor	12
28	24	WHAT GOOD AM I	Cilla Black	Parlophone	3
27	25	RESPECT	Aretha Franklin	Atlantic	3
29	26	I'LL COME RUNNING	Cliff Richard	Columbia	3
20	27	FIRST CUT IS THE DEEPEST	P P Arnold	Immediate	8
-	28	SEE EMILY PLAY	Pink Floyd	Columbia	1
26	29	GIVE ME TIME	Dusty Springfield	Philips	5
38	30	TAKE ME IN YOUR ARMS AND LOVE ME	Gladys Knight and the Pips	Tamla Motown	3
40	31	SHAKE	Otis Redding	Stax	2
25	32	SEVEN DRUNKEN NIGHTS	Dubliners	Major Minor	14
36	33	RELEASE ME	Engelbert Humperdinck	Decca	23
39	34	OLIVE TREE	Judith Durham	Columbia	2
33	35	SOMETHIN' STUPID	Nancy Sinatra and Frank Sinatra	Reprise	15
32	36	I GOT RHYTHM	Happenings	Stateside	6
24	37	PUPPET ON A STRING	Sandie Shaw	Pye	15
23	38	WIND CRIES MARY	Jimi Hendrix Experience	Track	8
34	39	FUNNY FAMILIAR FORGOTTEN FEELINGS	Tom Jones	Decca	12
-	40	WHEN YOU'RE YOUNG AND IN LOVE	Marvelettes ●	Tamla Motown	1

WEEK ENDING 5 JULY 1967

LW	TW	Title	Artist	Label	Wks
1	1	A WHITER SHADE OF PALE	Procol Harum	Deram	7
2	2	THERE GOES MY EVERYTHING	Engelbert Humperdinck	Decca	7
7	3	ALTERNATE TITLE	Monkees	RCA Victor	3
6	4	SHE'D RATHER BE WITH ME	Turtles	London	4
3	5	CARRIE-ANNE	Hollies	Parlophone	5
20	6	IT MUST BE HIM (SEUL SUR SON ETOILE)	Vikki Carr	Liberty	4
4	7	OKAY!	Dave Dee, Dozy, Beaky, Mick and Tich	Fontana	7
5	8	PAPER SUN	Traffic	Island	5
8	9	GROOVIN'	Young Rascals	Atlantic	6
11	10	IF I WERE A RICH MAN	Topol	CBS	11
25	11	RESPECT	Aretha Franklin	Atlantic	4
14	12	HERE COME THE NICE	Small Faces	Immediate	5
13	13	SWEET SOUL MUSIC	Arthur Conley	Atlantic	10
10	14	THE HAPPENING	Supremes	Tamla Motown	8
17	15	SEVEN ROOMS OF GLOOM	Four Tops	Tamla Motown	4
12	16	DON'T SLEEP IN THE SUBWAY	Petula Clark	Pye	5
28	17	SEE EMILY PLAY	Pink Floyd	Columbia	2
19	18	STRANGE BREW	Cream	Reaction	4
18	19	FINCHLEY CENTRAL	New Vaudeville Band	Fontana	8
9	20	SILENCE IS GOLDEN	Tremeloes	CBS	11
30	21	TAKE ME IN YOUR ARMS AND LOVE ME	Gladys Knight and the Pips	Tamla Motown	4
22	22	ROSES OF PICARDY	Vince Hill	Columbia	8
15	23	WATERLOO SUNSET	Kinks	Pye	9
16	24	THEN I KISSED HER	Beach Boys	Capitol	10
23	25	DEDICATED TO THE ONE I LOVE	Mamas and the Papas	RCA Victor	13
33	26	RELEASE ME	Engelbert Humperdinck	Decca	24
26	27	I'LL COME RUNNING	Cliff Richard	Columbia	4
40	28	WHEN YOU'RE YOUNG AND IN LOVE	Marvelettes	Tamla Motown	2
31	29	SHAKE	Otis Redding	Stax	3
-	30	LET'S PRETEND	Lulu	Columbia	1
24	31	WHAT GOOD AM I	Cilla Black	Parlophone	4
-	32	JUST LOVING YOU	Anita Harris ●	CBS	1
34	33	OLIVE TREE	Judith Durham	Columbia	3
21	34	NIGHT OF THE LONG GRASS	Troggs	Page One	6
-	35	WITH A LITTLE HELP FROM MY FRIENDS	Joe Brown	Pye	1
-	36	YOU ONLY LIVE TWICE	Nancy Sinatra	Reprise	1
32	37	SEVEN DRUNKEN NIGHTS	Dubliners	Major Minor	15
-	38	HERE WE GO AGAIN	Ray Charles	HMV	1
-	39	WITH A LITTLE HELP FROM MY FRIENDS	Young Idea ●	Columbia	1
-	40	MARTA	Bachelors	Decca	1

WEEK ENDING 12 JULY 1967

LW	TW	Title	Artist	Label	Wks
1	1	A WHITER SHADE OF PALE	Procol Harum	Deram	8
-	2	ALL YOU NEED IS LOVE	Beatles	Parlophone	1
3	3	ALTERNATE TITLE	Monkees	RCA Victor	4
2	4	THERE GOES MY EVERYTHING	Engelbert Humperdinck	Decca	8

In these weeks ■ The Monkees' *Alternate Title* was originally to be called *Randy Scouse Git*, but was given its alternate title when the three Americans in the group had the meaning of the title explained to them by their British co-member, Davy Jones (22.06.67) ■ After six months off the chart, the Mike Sammes Singers' *Somewhere My Love* comes back for another long stay (12.07.67)■

July 1967

☐ Highest position disc reached ● Act's first ever week on chart

LW	TW	Title / Artist	Label	Wks
4	5	SHE'D RATHER BE WITH ME Turtles	London	5
6	6	IT MUST BE HIM (SEUL SUR SON ETOILE) Vikki Carr	Liberty	5
5	7	CARRIE-ANNE Hollies	Parlophone	6
17	8	SEE EMILY PLAY Pink Floyd	Columbia	3
10	[9]	IF I WERE A RICH MAN Topol	CBS	12
11	[10]	RESPECT Aretha Franklin	Atlantic	5
9	11	GROOVIN' Young Rascals	Atlantic	7
13	12	SWEET SOUL MUSIC Arthur Conley	Atlantic	11
-	13	SAN FRANCISCO (BE SURE TO WEAR SOME FLOWERS IN YOUR HAIR) Scott McKenzie ●	CBS	1
12	14	HERE COME THE NICE Small Faces	Immediate	6
8	15	PAPER SUN Traffic	Island	6
14	16	THE HAPPENING Supremes	Tamla Motown	9
18	[17]	STRANGE BREW Cream	Reaction	5
15	18	SEVEN ROOMS OF GLOOM Four Tops	Tamla Motown	5
7	19	OKAY! Dave Dee, Dozy, Beaky, Mick and Tich	Fontana	8
16	20	DON'T SLEEP IN THE SUBWAY Petula Clark	Pye	6
28	21	WHEN YOU'RE YOUNG AND IN LOVE Marvelettes	Tamla Motown	3
21	22	TAKE ME IN YOUR ARMS AND LOVE ME Gladys Knight and the Pips	Tamla Motown	5
20	23	SILENCE IS GOLDEN Tremeloes	CBS	12
22	24	ROSES OF PICARDY Vince Hill	Columbia	9
36	25	YOU ONLY LIVE TWICE/JACKSON Nancy Sinatra/Nancy Sinatra and Lee Hazlewood ●	Reprise	2
27	[26]	I'LL COME RUNNING Cliff Richard	Columbia	5
25	27	DEDICATED TO THE ONE I LOVE Mamas and the Papas	RCA Victor	14
29	[28]	SHAKE Otis Redding	Stax	4
39	29	WITH A LITTLE HELP FROM MY FRIENDS Young Idea	Columbia	2
37	30	SEVEN DRUNKEN NIGHTS Dubliners	Major Minor	16
-	31	SOMEWHERE MY LOVE Mike Sammes Singers	HMV	16
30	32	LET'S PRETEND Lulu	Columbia	2
32	33	JUST LOVING YOU Anita Harris	CBS	2
24	34	THEN I KISSED HER Beach Boys	Capitol	11
40	35	MARTA Bachelors	Decca	2
-	36	FUNNY FAMILIAR FORGOTTEN FEELINGS Tom Jones	Decca	13
23	37	WATERLOO SUNSET Kinks	Pye	10
-	38	TONIGHT IN TOKYO Sandie Shaw	Pye	1
-	39	WIND CRIES MARY Jimi Hendrix Experience	Track	9
31	40	WHAT GOOD AM I Cilla Black	Parlophone	5

WEEK ENDING 19 JULY 1967

LW	TW	Title / Artist	Label	Wks
2	[1]	ALL YOU NEED IS LOVE Beatles	Parlophone	2
3	[2]	ALTERNATE TITLE Monkees	RCA Victor	5
6	3	IT MUST BE HIM (SEUL SUR SON ETOILE) Vikki Carr	Liberty	6
1	4	A WHITER SHADE OF PALE Procol Harum	Deram	9
13	5	SAN FRANCISCO (BE SURE TO WEAR SOME FLOWERS IN YOUR HAIR) Scott McKenzie	CBS	2
4	6	THERE GOES MY EVERYTHING Engelbert Humperdinck	Decca	9
5	7	SHE'D RATHER BE WITH ME Turtles	London	6
8	8	SEE EMILY PLAY Pink Floyd	Columbia	4
9	[9]	IF I WERE A RICH MAN Topol	CBS	13
29	[10]	WITH A LITTLE HELP FROM MY FRIENDS Young Idea	Columbia	3
25	[11]	YOU ONLY LIVE TWICE/JACKSON Nancy Sinatra/Nancy Sinatra and Lee Hazlewood	Reprise	3
18	[12]	SEVEN ROOMS OF GLOOM Four Tops	Tamla Motown	6
21	[13]	WHEN YOU'RE YOUNG AND IN LOVE Marvelettes	Tamla Motown	4
31	[14]	SOMEWHERE MY LOVE Mike Sammes Singers	HMV	17
22	15	TAKE ME IN YOUR ARMS AND LOVE ME Gladys Knight and the Pips	Tamla Motown	6
10	16	RESPECT Aretha Franklin	Atlantic	6
14	17	HERE COME THE NICE Small Faces	Immediate	7
17	18	STRANGE BREW Cream	Reaction	6
7	19	CARRIE-ANNE Hollies	Parlophone	7
35	[20]	MARTA Bachelors	Decca	3
38	[21]	TONIGHT IN TOKYO Sandie Shaw	Pye	2
11	22	GROOVIN' Young Rascals	Atlantic	8
-	23	DEATH OF A CLOWN Dave Davies ●	Pye	1
20	24	DON'T SLEEP IN THE SUBWAY Petula Clark	Pye	7
16	25	THE HAPPENING Supremes	Tamla Motown	10
-	26	UP UP AND AWAY Johnny Mann Singers ●	Liberty	1
-	27	007 Desmond Dekker and the Aces ●	Pyramid	1
28	[28]	SHAKE Otis Redding	Stax	5
27	29	DEDICATED TO THE ONE I LOVE Mamas and the Papas	RCA Victor	15
12	30	SWEET SOUL MUSIC Arthur Conley	Atlantic	12
26	31	I'LL COME RUNNING Cliff Richard	Columbia	6
-	[32]	WITH A LITTLE HELP FROM MY FRIENDS Joe Brown	Pye	2
-	33	RELEASE ME Engelbert Humperdinck	Decca	25
30	34	SEVEN DRUNKEN NIGHTS Dubliners	Major Minor	17
32	35	LET'S PRETEND Lulu	Columbia	3
19	36	OKAY! Dave Dee, Dozy, Beaky, Mick and Tich	Fontana	9
15	37	PAPER SUN Traffic	Island	7
23	38	SILENCE IS GOLDEN Tremeloes	CBS	13
33	39	JUST LOVING YOU Anita Harris	CBS	3
-	40	CASINO ROYALE Herb Alpert	A&M	8

WEEK ENDING 26 JULY 1967

LW	TW	Title / Artist	Label	Wks
1	[1]	ALL YOU NEED IS LOVE Beatles	Parlophone	3
3	[2]	IT MUST BE HIM (SEUL SUR SON ETOILE) Vikki Carr	Liberty	7
5	3	SAN FRANCISCO (BE SURE TO WEAR SOME FLOWERS IN YOUR HAIR) Scott McKenzie	CBS	3
2	4	ALTERNATE TITLE Monkees	RCA Victor	6
7	5	SHE'D RATHER BE WITH ME Turtles	London	7
8	[6]	SEE EMILY PLAY Pink Floyd	Columbia	5
4	7	A WHITER SHADE OF PALE Procol Harum	Deram	10
6	8	THERE GOES MY EVERYTHING Engelbert Humperdinck	Decca	10
26	9	UP UP AND AWAY Johnny Mann Singers	Liberty	2
23	10	DEATH OF A CLOWN Dave Davies	Pye	2
35	[11]	LET'S PRETEND Lulu	Columbia	4
16	12	RESPECT Aretha Franklin	Atlantic	7
15	[13]	TAKE ME IN YOUR ARMS AND LOVE ME Gladys Knight and the Pips	Tamla Motown	7
27	[14]	007 Desmond Dekker and the Aces	Pyramid	2
22	15	GROOVIN' Young Rascals	Atlantic	9
19	16	CARRIE-ANNE Hollies	Parlophone	8
11	17	YOU ONLY LIVE TWICE/JACKSON Nancy Sinatra/Nancy Sinatra and Lee Hazlewood	Reprise	4
17	18	HERE COME THE NICE Small Faces	Immediate	8
12	19	SEVEN ROOMS OF GLOOM Four Tops	Tamla Motown	7
39	20	JUST LOVING YOU Anita Harris	CBS	4
-	21	I'LL NEVER FALL IN LOVE AGAIN Tom Jones	Decca	1
21	22	TONIGHT IN TOKYO Sandie Shaw	Pye	3
-	23	I WAS MADE TO LOVE HER Stevie Wonder	Tamla Motown	1
13	24	WHEN YOU'RE YOUNG AND IN LOVE Marvelettes	Tamla Motown	5
-	25	ANNABELLA John Walker ●	Philips	1
-	26	TRAMP Otis Redding and Carla Thomas ●	Stax	1
9	27	IF I WERE A RICH MAN Topol	CBS	14
20	28	MARTA Bachelors	Decca	4
18	29	STRANGE BREW Cream	Reaction	7
24	30	DON'T SLEEP IN THE SUBWAY Petula Clark	Pye	8
14	31	SOMEWHERE MY LOVE Mike Sammes Singers	HMV	18
37	32	PAPER SUN Traffic	Island	8
28	33	SHAKE Otis Redding	Stax	6
10	34	WITH A LITTLE HELP FROM MY FRIENDS Young Idea	Columbia	4
33	35	RELEASE ME Engelbert Humperdinck	Decca	26
25	36	THE HAPPENING Supremes	Tamla Motown	11
30	37	SWEET SOUL MUSIC Arthur Conley	Atlantic	13

■Just after former Seeker Judith Durham's first solo hit drops off the chart, Kink Dave Davies enters the chart on his own, and a week later ex-Walker Brother John Walker makes it three out of three for hit group soloists (26.07.67) ■ After one week listed as *You Only Live Twice*, Nancy Sinatra's Bond song is listed with her B-side duet with producer Lee Hazlewood's, *Jackson* (12.07.67)■

July 1967

□ Highest position disc reached ● Act's first ever week on chart

LW	TW	Title / Artist	Label	Wks
28	38	SILENCE IS GOLDEN Tremeloes	*CBS*	14
-	39	CREEQUE ALLEY Mamas and the Papas	*RCA Victor*	1
27	39	DEDICATED TO THE ONE I LOVE Mamas and the Papas	*RCA Victor*	16

WEEK ENDING 2 AUGUST 1967

LW	TW	Title / Artist	Label	Wks
1	1	ALL YOU NEED IS LOVE Beatles	*Parlophone*	4
3	2	SAN FRANCISCO (BE SURE TO WEAR SOME FLOWERS IN YOUR HAIR) Scott McKenzie	*CBS*	4
10	3	DEATH OF A CLOWN Dave Davies	*Pye*	3
2	4	IT MUST BE HIM (SEUL SUR SON ETOILE) Vikki Carr	*Liberty*	8
4	5	ALTERNATE TITLE Monkees	*RCA Victor*	7
21	6	I'LL NEVER FALL IN LOVE AGAIN Tom Jones	*Decca*	2
5	7	SHE'D RATHER BE WITH ME Turtles	*London*	8
23	8	I WAS MADE TO LOVE HER Stevie Wonder	*Tamla Motown*	2
6	9	SEE EMILY PLAY Pink Floyd	*Columbia*	6
7	10	A WHITER SHADE OF PALE Procol Harum	*Deram*	11
9	11	UP UP AND AWAY Johnny Mann Singers	*Liberty*	3
8	12	THERE GOES MY EVERYTHING Engelbert Humperdinck	*Decca*	11
11	13	LET'S PRETEND Lulu	*Columbia*	5
20	14	JUST LOVING YOU Anita Harris	*CBS*	5
12	15	RESPECT Aretha Franklin	*Atlantic*	8
22	16	GROOVIN' Young Rascals	*Atlantic*	10
39	17	CREEQUE ALLEY Mamas and the Papas	*RCA Victor*	2
13	18	TAKE ME IN YOUR ARMS AND LOVE ME Gladys Knight and the Pips	*Tamla Motown*	8
14	19	007 Desmond Dekker and the Aces	*Pyramid*	3
17	20	YOU ONLY LIVE TWICE/JACKSON Nancy Sinatra/Nancy Sinatra and Lee Hazlewood	*Reprise*	5
26	21	TRAMP Otis Redding and Carla Thomas	*Stax*	2
28	22	MARTA Bachelors	*Decca*	5
22	23	TONIGHT IN TOKYO Sandie Shaw	*Pye*	4
25	24	ANNABELLA John Walker	*Philips*	2
27	25	IF I WERE A RICH MAN Topol	*CBS*	15
16	26	CARRIE-ANNE Hollies	*Parlophone*	9
-	27	GIN HOUSE BLUES Amen Corner ●	*Deram*	1
19	28	SEVEN ROOMS OF GLOOM Four Tops	*Tamla Motown*	8
18	29	HERE COME THE NICE Small Faces	*Immediate*	9
30	30	DON'T SLEEP IN THE SUBWAY Petula Clark	*Pye*	9
31	31	SOMEWHERE MY LOVE Mike Sammes Singers	*HMV*	19
24	32	WHEN YOU'RE YOUNG AND IN LOVE Marvelettes	*Tamla Motown*	6
33	33	SHAKE Otis Redding	*Stax*	7
35	34	RELEASE ME Engelbert Humperdinck	*Decca*	27
29	35	STRANGE BREW Cream	*Reaction*	8
-	36	TRYING TO FORGET Jim Reeves	*RCA Victor*	1
-	37	THE HOUSE THAT JACK BUILT Alan Price Set	*Decca*	1
-	38	EVEN THE BAD TIMES ARE GOOD Tremeloes	*CBS*	1
32	39	PAPER SUN Traffic	*Island*	9
38	40	SILENCE IS GOLDEN Tremeloes	*CBS*	15

WEEK ENDING 9 AUGUST 1967

LW	TW	Title / Artist	Label	Wks
2	1	SAN FRANCISCO (BE SURE TO WEAR SOME FLOWERS IN YOUR HAIR) Scott McKenzie	*CBS*	5
1	2	ALL YOU NEED IS LOVE Beatles	*Parlophone*	5
3	3	DEATH OF A CLOWN Dave Davies	*Pye*	4
6	4	I'LL NEVER FALL IN LOVE AGAIN Tom Jones	*Decca*	3
4	5	IT MUST BE HIM (SEUL SUR SON ETOILE) Vikki Carr	*Liberty*	9
7	6	SHE'D RATHER BE WITH ME Turtles	*London*	9
8	7	I WAS MADE TO LOVE HER Stevie Wonder	*Tamla Motown*	3
11	8	UP UP AND AWAY Johnny Mann Singers	*Liberty*	4
5	9	ALTERNATE TITLE Monkees	*RCA Victor*	8
9	10	SEE EMILY PLAY Pink Floyd	*Columbia*	7
14	11	JUST LOVING YOU Anita Harris	*CBS*	6
17	12	CREEQUE ALLEY Mamas and the Papas	*RCA Victor*	3
12	13	THERE GOES MY EVERYTHING Engelbert Humperdinck	*Decca*	12
13	14	LET'S PRETEND Lulu	*Columbia*	6
38	15	EVEN THE BAD TIMES ARE GOOD Tremeloes	*CBS*	2
20	16	YOU ONLY LIVE TWICE/JACKSON Nancy Sinatra/Nancy Sinatra and Lee Hazlewood	*Reprise*	6
10	17	A WHITER SHADE OF PALE Procol Harum	*Deram*	12
27	18	GIN HOUSE BLUES Amen Corner	*Deram*	2
19	19	007 Desmond Dekker and the Aces	*Pyramid*	4
37	20	THE HOUSE THAT JACK BUILT Alan Price Set	*Decca*	2
18	21	TAKE ME IN YOUR ARMS AND LOVE ME Gladys Knight and the Pips	*Tamla Motown*	9
21	22	TRAMP Otis Redding and Carla Thomas	*Stax*	3
15	23	RESPECT Aretha Franklin	*Atlantic*	9
22	24	MARTA Bachelors	*Decca*	6
24	25	ANNABELLA John Walker	*Philips*	3
-	26	A BAD NIGHT Cat Stevens	*Deram*	1
25	27	IF I WERE A RICH MAN Topol	*CBS*	16
23	28	TONIGHT IN TOKYO Sandie Shaw	*Pye*	5
16	29	GROOVIN' Young Rascals	*Atlantic*	11
-	30	TALLYMAN Jeff Beck	*Columbia*	1
-	31	THINGS GET BETTER Eddie Floyd	*Stax*	1
-	32	YOU KEEP ME HANGING ON Vanilla Fudge ●	*Atlantic*	1
26	33	CARRIE-ANNE Hollies	*Parlophone*	10
28	34	SEVEN ROOMS OF GLOOM Four Tops	*Tamla Motown*	9
29	35	HERE COME THE NICE Small Faces	*Immediate*	10
33	36	SHAKE Otis Redding	*Stax*	8
-	37	TIME SELLER Spencer Davis Group	*Fontana*	1
34	38	RELEASE ME Engelbert Humperdinck	*Decca*	28
36	39	TRYING TO FORGET Jim Reeves	*RCA Victor*	2
-	40	EXCERPT FROM 'A TEENAGE OPERA' Keith West ●	*Parlophone*	1

WEEK ENDING 16 AUGUST 1967

LW	TW	Title / Artist	Label	Wks
1	1	SAN FRANCISCO (BE SURE TO WEAR SOME FLOWERS IN YOUR HAIR) Scott McKenzie	*CBS*	6
2	2	ALL YOU NEED IS LOVE Beatles	*Parlophone*	6
4	3	I'LL NEVER FALL IN LOVE AGAIN Tom Jones	*Decca*	4
3	4	DEATH OF A CLOWN Dave Davies	*Pye*	5
7	5	I WAS MADE TO LOVE HER Stevie Wonder	*Tamla Motown*	4
8	6	UP UP AND AWAY Johnny Mann Singers	*Liberty*	5
11	7	JUST LOVING YOU Anita Harris	*CBS*	7
15	8	EVEN THE BAD TIMES ARE GOOD Tremeloes	*CBS*	3
20	9	THE HOUSE THAT JACK BUILT Alan Price Set	*Decca*	3
5	10	IT MUST BE HIM (SEUL SUR SON ETOILE) Vikki Carr	*Liberty*	10
6	11	SHE'D RATHER BE WITH ME Turtles	*London*	10
12	12	CREEQUE ALLEY Mamas and the Papas	*RCA Victor*	4
10	13	SEE EMILY PLAY Pink Floyd	*Columbia*	8
9	14	ALTERNATE TITLE Monkees	*RCA Victor*	9
16	15	YOU ONLY LIVE TWICE/JACKSON Nancy Sinatra/Nancy Sinatra and Lee Hazlewood	*Reprise*	7
18	16	GIN HOUSE BLUES Amen Corner	*Deram*	3
14	17	LET'S PRETEND Lulu	*Columbia*	7
22	18	TRAMP Otis Redding and Carla Thomas	*Stax*	4
19	19	007 Desmond Dekker and the Aces	*Pyramid*	5
-	20	ITCHYCOO PARK Small Faces	*Immediate*	1
13	21	THERE GOES MY EVERYTHING Engelbert Humperdinck	*Decca*	13
-	22	PLEASANT VALLEY SUNDAY Monkees	*RCA Victor*	1
17	23	A WHITER SHADE OF PALE Procol Harum	*Deram*	13
26	24	A BAD NIGHT Cat Stevens	*Deram*	2
40	25	EXCERPT FROM 'A TEENAGE OPERA' Keith West	*Parlophone*	2
21	26	TAKE ME IN YOUR ARMS AND LOVE ME Gladys Knight and the Pips	*Tamla Motown*	10
-	27	THE DAY I MET MARIE Cliff Richard	*Columbia*	1
32	28	YOU KEEP ME HANGING ON Vanilla Fudge	*Atlantic*	2
25	29	ANNABELLA John Walker	*Philips*	4
37	30	TIME SELLER Spencer Davis Group	*Fontana*	2
23	31	RESPECT Aretha Franklin	*Atlantic*	10

In these weeks ■ Stevie Wonder hits the Top Ten for the first time (02.08.67) ■ Although *San Francisco (Be Sure To Wear Some Flowers In Your Hair)* is the longest title ever at number one, the rest of the chart includes eight one-word titles (09.08.67) ■ Three weeks at number 19 for the most successful chart hit to date with only digits in its title, Desmond Dekker's *007* (16.08.67)■

LW	TW	Title	Artist	Label	Wks
31	32	THINGS GET BETTER	Eddie Floyd	Stax	2
39	[33]	TRYING TO FORGET	Jim Reeves	RCA Victor	2
30	34	TALLYMAN	Jeff Beck	Columbia	2
27	35	IF I WERE A RICH MAN	Topol	CBS	17
24	36	MARTA	Bachelors	Decca	7
-	[37]	GREEN STREET GREEN	New Vaudeville Band	Fontana	1
-	38	MY MAMMY	Happenings	Pye	1
-	39	SOMEWHERE MY LOVE	Mike Sammes Singers	HMV	20
38	40	RELEASE ME	Engelbert Humperdinck	Decca	29

WEEK ENDING 23 AUGUST 1967

LW	TW	Title	Artist	Label	Wks
1	[1]	SAN FRANCISCO (BE SURE TO WEAR SOME FLOWERS IN YOUR HAIR)	Scott McKenzie	CBS	7
3	[2]	I'LL NEVER FALL IN LOVE AGAIN	Tom Jones	Decca	5
2	3	ALL YOU NEED IS LOVE	Beatles	Parlophone	7
8	[4]	EVEN THE BAD TIMES ARE GOOD	Tremeloes	CBS	4
9	5	THE HOUSE THAT JACK BUILT	Alan Price Set	Decca	4
7	[6]	JUST LOVING YOU	Anita Harris	CBS	8
4	7	DEATH OF A CLOWN	Dave Davies	Pye	6
5	8	I WAS MADE TO LOVE HER	Stevie Wonder	Tamla Motown	5
12	[9]	CREEQUE ALLEY	Mamas and the Papas	RCA Victor	5
6	10	UP UP AND AWAY	Johnny Mann Singers	Liberty	6
22	[11]	PLEASANT VALLEY SUNDAY	Monkees	RCA Victor	2
16	[12]	GIN HOUSE BLUES	Amen Corner	Deram	4
10	13	IT MUST BE HIM (SEUL SUR SON ETOILE)	Vikki Carr	Liberty	11
20	14	ITCHYCOO PARK	Small Faces	Immediate	2
11	15	SHE'D RATHER BE WITH ME	Turtles	London	11
21	16	THERE GOES MY EVERYTHING	Engelbert Humperdinck	Decca	14
-	17	WE LOVE YOU/DANDELION	Rolling Stones	Decca	1
25	18	EXCERPT FROM 'A TEENAGE OPERA'	Keith West	Parlophone	3
-	19	THE LAST WALTZ	Engelbert Humperdinck	Decca	1
24	[20]	A BAD NIGHT	Cat Stevens	Deram	3
18	21	TRAMP	Otis Redding and Carla Thomas	Stax	5
14	22	ALTERNATE TITLE	Monkees	RCA Victor	10
15	23	YOU ONLY LIVE TWICE/JACKSON	Nancy Sinatra/Nancy Sinatra and Lee Hazlewood	Reprise	8
27	24	THE DAY I MET MARIE	Cliff Richard	Columbia	2
19	25	007	Desmond Dekker and the Aces	Pyramid	6
-	26	HEROES AND VILLAINS	Beach Boys	Capitol	1
13	27	SEE EMILY PLAY	Pink Floyd	Columbia	9
28	28	YOU KEEP ME HANGING ON	Vanilla Fudge	Atlantic	3
17	29	LET'S PRETEND	Lulu	Columbia	8
23	30	A WHITER SHADE OF PALE	Procol Harum	Deram	14
30	31	TIME SELLER	Spencer Davis Group	Fontana	3
-	32	LET'S GO TO SAN FRANCISCO	Flowerpot Men ●	Deram	1
-	33	THERE MUST BE A WAY	Frankie Vaughan	Columbia	1
38	[34]	MY MAMMY	Happenings	Pye	2
32	35	THINGS GET BETTER	Eddie Floyd	Stax	3
26	36	TAKE ME IN YOUR ARMS AND LOVE ME	Gladys Knight and the Pips	Tamla Motown	11
-	[37]	A GIRL LIKE YOU	Young Rascals	Atlantic	1
-	38	FIVE LITTLE FINGERS	Frankie McBride ●	Emerald	1
35	39	IF I WERE A RICH MAN	Topol	CBS	18
33	40	TRYING TO FORGET	Jim Reeves	RCA Victor	3

September 1967

☐ Highest position disc reached ● Act's first ever week on chart

WEEK ENDING 30 AUGUST 1967

LW	TW	Title	Artist	Label	Wks
1	[1]	SAN FRANCISCO (BE SURE TO WEAR SOME FLOWERS IN YOUR HAIR)	Scott McKenzie	CBS	8
2	[2]	I'LL NEVER FALL IN LOVE AGAIN	Tom Jones	Decca	6
19	3	THE LAST WALTZ	Engelbert Humperdinck	Decca	2
5	[4]	THE HOUSE THAT JACK BUILT	Alan Price Set	Decca	5
4	5	EVEN THE BAD TIMES ARE GOOD	Tremeloes	CBS	5
3	6	ALL YOU NEED IS LOVE	Beatles	Parlophone	8
6	7	JUST LOVING YOU	Anita Harris	CBS	9
8	8	I WAS MADE TO LOVE HER	Stevie Wonder	Tamla Motown	6
7	9	DEATH OF A CLOWN	Dave Davies	Pye	7
17	10	WE LOVE YOU/DANDELION	Rolling Stones	Decca	2
11	[11]	PLEASANT VALLEY SUNDAY	Monkees	RCA Victor	3
18	12	EXCERPT FROM 'A TEENAGE OPERA'	Keith West	Parlophone	4
26	13	HEROES AND VILLAINS	Beach Boys	Capitol	2
10	14	UP UP AND AWAY	Johnny Mann Singers	Liberty	7
9	15	CREEQUE ALLEY	Mamas and the Papas	RCA Victor	6
12	16	GIN HOUSE BLUES	Amen Corner	Deram	5
13	17	IT MUST BE HIM (SEUL SUR SON ETOILE)	Vikki Carr	Liberty	12
14	18	ITCHYCOO PARK	Small Faces	Immediate	3
16	19	THERE GOES MY EVERYTHING	Engelbert Humperdinck	Decca	15
23	20	YOU ONLY LIVE TWICE/JACKSON	Nancy Sinatra/Nancy Sinatra and Lee Hazlewood	Reprise	9
15	21	SHE'D RATHER BE WITH ME	Turtles	London	12
28	22	YOU KEEP ME HANGING ON	Vanilla Fudge	Atlantic	4
24	23	THE DAY I MET MARIE	Cliff Richard	Columbia	3
21	24	TRAMP	Otis Redding and Carla Thomas	Stax	6
32	25	LET'S GO TO SAN FRANCISCO	Flowerpot Men	Deram	2
20	26	A BAD NIGHT	Cat Stevens	Deram	4
22	27	ALTERNATE TITLE	Monkees	RCA Victor	11
27	28	SEE EMILY PLAY	Pink Floyd	Columbia	10
25	29	007	Desmond Dekker and the Aces	Pyramid	7
31	30	TIME SELLER	Spencer Davis Group	Fontana	4
29	31	LET'S PRETEND	Lulu	Columbia	9
-	32	BURNING OF THE MIDNIGHT LAMP	Jimi Hendrix Experience	Track	1
33	33	THERE MUST BE A WAY	Frankie Vaughan	Columbia	2
34	[34]	MY MAMMY	Happenings	Pye	3
30	35	A WHITER SHADE OF PALE	Procol Harum	Deram	15
38	36	FIVE LITTLE FINGERS	Frankie McBride	Emerald	2
-	37	SOUL FINGER	Bar-Kays ●	Stax	1
-	38	SOMEWHERE MY LOVE	Mike Sammes Singers	HMV	21
35	39	THINGS GET BETTER	Eddie Floyd	Stax	4
-	40	WORLD WE KNEW	Frank Sinatra	Reprise	1

WEEK ENDING 6 SEPTEMBER 1967

LW	TW	Title	Artist	Label	Wks
3	[1]	THE LAST WALTZ	Engelbert Humperdinck	Decca	3
2	[2]	I'LL NEVER FALL IN LOVE AGAIN	Tom Jones	Decca	7
1	3	SAN FRANCISCO (BE SURE TO WEAR SOME FLOWERS IN YOUR HAIR)	Scott McKenzie	CBS	9
12	4	EXCERPT FROM 'A TEENAGE OPERA'	Keith West	Parlophone	5
4	5	THE HOUSE THAT JACK BUILT	Alan Price Set	Decca	6
5	6	EVEN THE BAD TIMES ARE GOOD	Tremeloes	CBS	6
7	7	JUST LOVING YOU	Anita Harris	CBS	10
10	[8]	WE LOVE YOU/DANDELION	Rolling Stones	Decca	3
8	9	I WAS MADE TO LOVE HER	Stevie Wonder	Tamla Motown	7
18	10	ITCHYCOO PARK	Small Faces	Immediate	4
11	[11]	PLEASANT VALLEY SUNDAY	Monkees	RCA Victor	4
13	12	HEROES AND VILLAINS	Beach Boys	Capitol	3
6	13	ALL YOU NEED IS LOVE	Beatles	Parlophone	9
23	14	THE DAY I MET MARIE	Cliff Richard	Columbia	4
25	15	LET'S GO TO SAN FRANCISCO	Flowerpot Men	Deram	3
9	16	DEATH OF A CLOWN	Dave Davies	Pye	8
16	17	GIN HOUSE BLUES	Amen Corner	Deram	6
32	[18]	BURNING OF THE MIDNIGHT LAMP	Jimi Hendrix Experience	Track	2
15	19	CREEQUE ALLEY	Mamas and the Papas	RCA Victor	7
14	20	UP UP AND AWAY	Johnny Mann Singers	Liberty	8
17	21	IT MUST BE HIM (SEUL SUR SON ETOILE)	Vikki Carr	Liberty	13
22	22	YOU KEEP ME HANGING ON	Vanilla Fudge	Atlantic	5
-	23	REFLECTIONS	Diana Ross and the Supremes	Tamla Motown	1
19	24	THERE GOES MY EVERYTHING	Engelbert Humperdinck	Decca	16
20	25	YOU ONLY LIVE TWICE/JACKSON	Nancy Sinatra/Nancy Sinatra and Lee Hazlewood	Reprise	10
26	26	A BAD NIGHT	Cat Stevens	Deram	5

■Tom Jones' *I'll Never Fall In Love Again*, the first of three consecutive number 2 hits for the Welsh warbler, is written by 50s great Lonnie Donegan (23.08.67) ■ The Rolling Stones' recorded gratitude to fans for their support during a summer of court cases gives the greatest rock 'n' roll band in the world their only single not to make the top five over a ten year period from 1964 to 1974 (06.09.67) ■ Diana Ross takes lead billing over her fellow Supremes for the first time (06.09.67)■

September 1967

□ Highest position disc reached ● Act's first ever week on chart

LW	TW	Title	Artist	Label	Wks
33	27	THERE MUST BE A WAY	Frankie Vaughan	*Columbia*	3
-	28	BLACK VELVET BAND	Dubliners	*Major Minor*	1
29	29	007	Desmond Dekker and the Aces	*Pyramid*	8
24	30	TRAMP	Otis Redding and Carla Thomas	*Stax*	7
36	31	FIVE LITTLE FINGERS	Frankie McBride	*Emerald*	3
21	32	SHE'D RATHER BE WITH ME	Turtles	*London*	13
37	33	SOUL FINGER	Bar-Kays	*Stax*	2
27	34	ALTERNATE TITLE	Monkees	*RCA Victor*	12
30	35	TIME SELLER	Spencer Davis Group	*Fontana*	5
34	36	MY MAMMY	Happenings	*Pye*	4
-	37	RESPECT	Aretha Franklin	*Atlantic*	11
-	38	YOU'RE MY EVERYTHING	Temptations	*Tamla Motown*	1
-	39	BABY I LOVE YOU	Aretha Franklin	*Atlantic*	1
-	40	FLOWERS IN THE RAIN	Move	*Regal Zonophone*	1

WEEK ENDING 13 SEPTEMBER 1967

LW	TW	Title	Artist	Label	Wks
1	1	THE LAST WALTZ	Engelbert Humperdinck	*Decca*	4
2	2	I'LL NEVER FALL IN LOVE AGAIN	Tom Jones	*Decca*	8
3	3	SAN FRANCISCO (BE SURE TO WEAR SOME FLOWERS IN YOUR HAIR)	Scott McKenzie	*CBS*	10
4	4	EXCERPT FROM 'A TEENAGE OPERA'	Keith West	*Parlophone*	6
15	5	LET'S GO TO SAN FRANCISCO	Flowerpot Men	*Deram*	4
10	6	ITCHYCOO PARK	Small Faces	*Immediate*	5
6	7	EVEN THE BAD TIMES ARE GOOD	Tremeloes	*CBS*	7
12	8	HEROES AND VILLAINS	Beach Boys	*Capitol*	4
7	9	JUST LOVING YOU	Anita Harris	*CBS*	11
8	10	WE LOVE YOU/DANDELION	Rolling Stones	*Decca*	4
9	11	I WAS MADE TO LOVE HER	Stevie Wonder	*Tamla Motown*	8
5	12	THE HOUSE THAT JACK BUILT	Alan Price Set	*Decca*	7
23	13	REFLECTIONS	Diana Ross and the Supremes	*Tamla Motown*	2
14	14	THE DAY I MET MARIE	Cliff Richard	*Columbia*	5
13	15	ALL YOU NEED IS LOVE	Beatles	*Parlophone*	10
27	16	THERE MUST BE A WAY	Frankie Vaughan	*Columbia*	4
11	17	PLEASANT VALLEY SUNDAY	Monkees	*RCA Victor*	5
22	18	YOU KEEP ME HANGING ON	Vanilla Fudge	*Atlantic*	6
18	19	BURNING OF THE MIDNIGHT LAMP	Jimi Hendrix Experience	*Track*	3
40	20	FLOWERS IN THE RAIN	Move	*Regal Zonophone*	2
19	21	CREEQUE ALLEY	Mamas and the Papas	*RCA Victor*	8
28	22	BLACK VELVET BAND	Dubliners	*Major Minor*	2
-	23	HOLE IN MY SHOE	Traffic	*Island*	1
24	24	THERE GOES MY EVERYTHING	Engelbert Humperdinck	*Decca*	17
17	25	GIN HOUSE BLUES	Amen Corner	*Deram*	7
16	26	DEATH OF A CLOWN	Dave Davies	*Pye*	9
25	27	YOU ONLY LIVE TWICE/JACKSON	Nancy Sinatra/Nancy Sinatra and Lee Hazlewood	*Reprise*	11
21	28	IT MUST BE HIM (SEUL SUR SON ETOILE)	Vikki Carr	*Liberty*	14
20	29	UP UP AND AWAY	Johnny Mann Singers	*Liberty*	9
26	30	A BAD NIGHT	Cat Stevens	*Deram*	6
31	31	FIVE LITTLE FINGERS	Frankie McBride	*Emerald*	4
-	32	GOOD TIMES	Eric Burdon and the Animals	*MGM*	1
-	33	WORLD WE KNEW	Frank Sinatra	*Reprise*	2
29	34	007	Desmond Dekker and the Aces	*Pyramid*	9
30	35	TRAMP	Otis Redding and Carla Thomas	*Stax*	8
33	36	SOUL FINGER	Bar-Kays	*Stax*	3
-	37	RELEASE ME	Engelbert Humperdinck	*Decca*	30
32	38	SHE'D RATHER BE WITH ME	Turtles	*London*	14
-	39	SOMEWHERE MY LOVE	Mike Sammes Singers	*HMV*	22
38	40	YOU'RE MY EVERYTHING	Temptations	*Tamla Motown*	2

WEEK ENDING 20 SEPTEMBER 1967

LW	TW	Title	Artist	Label	Wks
1	1	THE LAST WALTZ	Engelbert Humperdinck	*Decca*	5
4	2	EXCERPT FROM 'A TEENAGE OPERA'	Keith West	*Parlophone*	7
6	3	ITCHYCOO PARK	Small Faces	*Immediate*	6
5	4	LET'S GO TO SAN FRANCISCO	Flowerpot Men	*Deram*	5
2	5	I'LL NEVER FALL IN LOVE AGAIN	Tom Jones	*Decca*	9
3	6	SAN FRANCISCO (BE SURE TO WEAR SOME FLOWERS IN YOUR HAIR)	Scott McKenzie	*CBS*	11
13	7	REFLECTIONS	Diana Ross and the Supremes	*Tamla Motown*	3
20	8	FLOWERS IN THE RAIN	Move	*Regal Zonophone*	3
10	9	WE LOVE YOU/DANDELION	Rolling Stones	*Decca*	5
23	10	HOLE IN MY SHOE	Traffic	*Island*	2
7	11	EVEN THE BAD TIMES ARE GOOD	Tremeloes	*CBS*	8
8	12	HEROES AND VILLAINS	Beach Boys	*Capitol*	5
16	13	THERE MUST BE A WAY	Frankie Vaughan	*Columbia*	5
9	14	JUST LOVING YOU	Anita Harris	*CBS*	12
14	15	THE DAY I MET MARIE	Cliff Richard	*Columbia*	6
11	16	I WAS MADE TO LOVE HER	Stevie Wonder	*Tamla Motown*	9
12	17	THE HOUSE THAT JACK BUILT	Alan Price Set	*Decca*	8
22	18	BLACK VELVET BAND	Dubliners	*Major Minor*	3
19	19	BURNING OF THE MIDNIGHT LAMP	Jimi Hendrix Experience	*Track*	4
18	20	YOU KEEP ME HANGING ON	Vanilla Fudge	*Atlantic*	7
15	21	ALL YOU NEED IS LOVE	Beatles	*Parlophone*	11
17	22	PLEASANT VALLEY SUNDAY	Monkees	*RCA Victor*	6
25	23	GIN HOUSE BLUES	Amen Corner	*Deram*	8
-	24	THE LETTER	Box Tops ●	*Stateside*	1
31	25	FIVE LITTLE FINGERS	Frankie McBride	*Emerald*	5
32	26	GOOD TIMES	Eric Burdon and the Animals	*MGM*	2
21	27	CREEQUE ALLEY	Mamas and the Papas	*RCA Victor*	9
-	28	ODE TO BILLY JOE	Bobbie Gentry ●	*Capitol*	1
24	29	THERE GOES MY EVERYTHING	Engelbert Humperdinck	*Decca*	18
-	30	FROM THE UNDERWORLD	Herd ●	*Fontana*	1
-	31	MASSACHUSETTS	Bee Gees	*Polydor*	1
28	32	IT MUST BE HIM (SEUL SUR SON ETOILE)	Vikki Carr	*Liberty*	15
35	33	TRAMP	Otis Redding and Carla Thomas	*Stax*	9
33	34	WORLD WE KNEW	Frank Sinatra	*Reprise*	3
29	35	UP UP AND AWAY	Johnny Mann Singers	*Liberty*	10
40	36	YOU'RE MY EVERYTHING	Temptations	*Tamla Motown*	3
27	37	YOU ONLY LIVE TWICE/JACKSON	Nancy Sinatra/Nancy Sinatra and Lee Hazlewood	*Reprise*	12
26	38	DEATH OF A CLOWN	Dave Davies	*Pye*	10
37	39	RELEASE ME	Engelbert Humperdinck	*Decca*	31
-	40	TRAIN TO SKAVILLE	Ethiopians ●	*Rio*	1

WEEK ENDING 27 SEPTEMBER 1967

LW	TW	Title	Artist	Label	Wks
1	1	THE LAST WALTZ	Engelbert Humperdinck	*Decca*	6
2	2	EXCERPT FROM 'A TEENAGE OPERA'	Keith West	*Parlophone*	8
8	3	FLOWERS IN THE RAIN	Move	*Regal Zonophone*	4
3	4	ITCHYCOO PARK	Small Faces	*Immediate*	7
7	5	REFLECTIONS	Diana Ross and the Supremes	*Tamla Motown*	4
4	6	LET'S GO TO SAN FRANCISCO	Flowerpot Men	*Deram*	6
10	7	HOLE IN MY SHOE	Traffic	*Island*	3
5	8	I'LL NEVER FALL IN LOVE AGAIN	Tom Jones	*Decca*	10
6	9	SAN FRANCISCO (BE SURE TO WEAR SOME FLOWERS IN YOUR HAIR)	Scott McKenzie	*CBS*	12
15	10	THE DAY I MET MARIE	Cliff Richard	*Columbia*	7
13	11	THERE MUST BE A WAY	Frankie Vaughan	*Columbia*	6
11	12	EVEN THE BAD TIMES ARE GOOD	Tremeloes	*CBS*	9
12	13	HEROES AND VILLAINS	Beach Boys	*Capitol*	6
24	14	THE LETTER	Box Tops	*Stateside*	2
9	15	WE LOVE YOU/DANDELION	Rolling Stones	*Decca*	6
14	16	JUST LOVING YOU	Anita Harris	*CBS*	13
31	17	MASSACHUSETTS	Bee Gees	*Polydor*	2
18	18	BLACK VELVET BAND	Dubliners	*Major Minor*	4
16	19	I WAS MADE TO LOVE HER	Stevie Wonder	*Tamla Motown*	10
19	20	BURNING OF THE MIDNIGHT LAMP	Jimi Hendrix Experience	*Track*	5
26	21	GOOD TIMES	Eric Burdon and the Animals	*MGM*	3
30	22	FROM THE UNDERWORLD	Herd	*Fontana*	2
17	23	THE HOUSE THAT JACK BUILT	Alan Price Set	*Decca*	9
28	24	ODE TO BILLY JOE	Bobbie Gentry	*Capitol*	2
20	25	YOU KEEP ME HANGING ON	Vanilla Fudge	*Atlantic*	8
25	26	FIVE LITTLE FINGERS	Frankie McBride	*Emerald*	6

In these weeks ■ After sixteen consecutive weeks of having two Top 40 hits, Engelbert Humperdinck's *Release Me* re-enters to give him three top 40 hits for the next seven weeks (13.09.67) ■ Keith West's *Excerpt From 'A Teenage Opera'* is all about the death of Grocer Jack, but it cannot overtake Engelbert's immovable *Last Waltz*. The full 'Teenage Opera', by Mark Wirtz, was never completed (20.09.67) ■

LW	TW	Title	Artist	Label	Wks
21	27	ALL YOU NEED IS LOVE	Beatles	*Parlophone*	12
22	28	PLEASANT VALLEY SUNDAY	Monkees	*RCA Victor*	7
-	29	WHEN WILL THE GOOD APPLES FALL	Seekers	*Columbia*	1
29	30	THERE GOES MY EVERYTHING	Engelbert Humperdinck	*Decca*	19
36	31	YOU'RE MY EVERYTHING	Temptations	*Tamla Motown*	4
-	32	THINKIN' AIN'T FOR ME	Paul Jones	*HMV*	1
39	33	RELEASE ME	Engelbert Humperdinck	*Decca*	32
23	34	GIN HOUSE BLUES	Amen Corner	*Deram*	9
27	35	CREEQUE ALLEY	Mamas and the Papas	*RCA Victor*	10
34	36	WORLD WE KNEW	Frank Sinatra	*Reprise*	4
-	37	SOMEWHERE MY LOVE	Mike Sammes Singers	*HMV*	23
-	38	TRY MY WORLD	Georgie Fame	*CBS*	1
37	39	YOU ONLY LIVE TWICE/JACKSON	Nancy Sinatra/Nancy Sinatra and Lee Hazlewood	*Reprise*	13
32	40	IT MUST BE HIM (SEUL SUR SON ETOILE)	Vikki Carr	*Liberty*	16

WEEK ENDING 4 OCTOBER 1967

LW	TW	Title	Artist	Label	Wks
1	1	THE LAST WALTZ	Engelbert Humperdinck	*Decca*	7
3	2	FLOWERS IN THE RAIN	Move	*Regal Zonophone*	5
7	3	HOLE IN MY SHOE	Traffic	*Island*	4
2	4	EXCERPT FROM 'A TEENAGE OPERA'	Keith West	*Parlophone*	9
5	5	REFLECTIONS	Diana Ross and the Supremes	*Tamla Motown*	5
17	6	MASSACHUSETTS	Bee Gees	*Polydor*	3
4	7	ITCHYCOO PARK	Small Faces	*Immediate*	8
6	8	LET'S GO TO SAN FRANCISCO	Flowerpot Men	*Deram*	7
14	9	THE LETTER	Box Tops	*Stateside*	3
10	10	THE DAY I MET MARIE	Cliff Richard	*Columbia*	8
11	11	THERE MUST BE A WAY	Frankie Vaughan	*Columbia*	7
16	12	JUST LOVING YOU	Anita Harris	*CBS*	14
8	13	I'LL NEVER FALL IN LOVE AGAIN	Tom Jones	*Decca*	11
9	14	SAN FRANCISCO (BE SURE TO WEAR SOME FLOWERS IN YOUR HAIR)	Scott McKenzie	*CBS*	13
24	15	ODE TO BILLY JOE	Bobbie Gentry	*Capitol*	3
29	16	WHEN WILL THE GOOD APPLES FALL	Seekers	*Columbia*	2
12	17	EVEN THE BAD TIMES ARE GOOD	Tremeloes	*CBS*	10
22	18	FROM THE UNDERWORLD	Herd	*Fontana*	3
18	19	BLACK VELVET BAND	Dubliners	*Major Minor*	5
21	20	GOOD TIMES	Eric Burdon and the Animals	*MGM*	4
13	21	HEROES AND VILLAINS	Beach Boys	*Capitol*	7
-	22	KING MIDAS IN REVERSE	Hollies	*Parlophone*	1
26	23	FIVE LITTLE FINGERS	Frankie McBride	*Emerald*	7
15	24	WE LOVE YOU/DANDELION	Rolling Stones	*Decca*	7
19	25	I WAS MADE TO LOVE HER	Stevie Wonder	*Tamla Motown*	11
30	26	THERE GOES MY EVERYTHING	Engelbert Humperdinck	*Decca*	20
20	27	BURNING OF THE MIDNIGHT LAMP	Jimi Hendrix Experience	*Track*	6
-	28	LOVE LETTERS IN THE SAND	Vince Hill	*Columbia*	1
25	29	YOU KEEP ME HANGING ON	Vanilla Fudge	*Atlantic*	9
31	30	YOU'RE MY EVERYTHING	Temptations	*Tamla Motown*	5
33	31	RELEASE ME	Engelbert Humperdinck	*Decca*	33
39	32	YOU ONLY LIVE TWICE/JACKSON	Nancy Sinatra/Nancy Sinatra and Lee Hazlewood	*Reprise*	14
37	33	SOMEWHERE MY LOVE	Mike Sammes Singers	*HMV*	24
-	34	HOMBURG	Procol Harum	*Regal Zonophone*	1
32	35	THINKIN' AIN'T FOR ME	Paul Jones	*HMV*	2
23	36	THE HOUSE THAT JACK BUILT	Alan Price Set	*Decca*	10
38	37	TRY MY WORLD	Georgie Fame	*CBS*	2
-	38				
-	39	ANYTHING GOES	Harper's Bizarre	*Warner Bros*	1
27	40	ALL YOU NEED IS LOVE	Beatles	*Parlophone*	13

WEEK ENDING 11 OCTOBER 1967

LW	TW	Title	Artist	Label	Wks
6	1	MASSACHUSETTS	Bee Gees	*Polydor*	4
2	2	FLOWERS IN THE RAIN	Move	*Regal Zonophone*	6
1	3	THE LAST WALTZ	Engelbert Humperdinck	*Decca*	8
3	4	HOLE IN MY SHOE	Traffic	*Island*	5
4	5	EXCERPT FROM 'A TEENAGE OPERA'	Keith West	*Parlophone*	10

October 1967

□ Highest position disc reached ● Act's first ever week on chart

LW	TW	Title	Artist	Label	Wks
9	6	THE LETTER	Box Tops	*Stateside*	4
11	7	THERE MUST BE A WAY	Frankie Vaughan	*Columbia*	8
5	8	REFLECTIONS	Diana Ross and the Supremes	*Tamla Motown*	6
34	9	HOMBURG	Procol Harum	*Regal Zonophone*	2
7	10	ITCHYCOO PARK	Small Faces	*Immediate*	9
18	11	FROM THE UNDERWORLD	Herd	*Fontana*	4
8	12	LET'S GO TO SAN FRANCISCO	Flowerpot Men	*Deram*	8
16	13	WHEN WILL THE GOOD APPLES FALL	Seekers	*Columbia*	3
10	14	THE DAY I MET MARIE	Cliff Richard	*Columbia*	9
19	15	BLACK VELVET BAND	Dubliners	*Major Minor*	6
15	16	ODE TO BILLY JOE	Bobbie Gentry	*Capitol*	4
12	17	JUST LOVING YOU	Anita Harris	*CBS*	15
22	18	KING MIDAS IN REVERSE	Hollies	*Parlophone*	2
23	19	FIVE LITTLE FINGERS	Frankie McBride	*Emerald*	8
14	20	SAN FRANCISCO (BE SURE TO WEAR SOME FLOWERS IN YOUR HAIR)	Scott McKenzie	*CBS*	14
38	21	BABY NOW THAT I'VE FOUND YOU	Foundations	*Pye*	2
13	22	I'LL NEVER FALL IN LOVE AGAIN	Tom Jones	*Decca*	12
-	23	YOU'VE NOT CHANGED	Sandie Shaw	*Pye*	1
28	24	LOVE LETTERS IN THE SAND	Vince Hill	*Columbia*	2
20	25	GOOD TIMES	Eric Burdon and the Animals	*MGM*	5
30	26	YOU'RE MY EVERYTHING	Temptations	*Tamla Motown*	6
26	27	THERE GOES MY EVERYTHING	Engelbert Humperdinck	*Decca*	21
21	28	HEROES AND VILLAINS	Beach Boys	*Capitol*	8
17	29	EVEN THE BAD TIMES ARE GOOD	Tremeloes	*CBS*	11
33	30	SOMEWHERE MY LOVE	Mike Sammes Singers	*HMV*	25
27	31	BURNING OF THE MIDNIGHT LAMP	Jimi Hendrix Experience	*Track*	7
31	32	RELEASE ME	Engelbert Humperdinck	*Decca*	34
39	33	ANYTHING GOES	Harper's Bizarre	*Warner Bros*	2
24	34	WE LOVE YOU/DANDELION	Rolling Stones	*Decca*	8
-	35	ZABADAK!	Dave Dee Dozy Beaky Mick and Tich	*Fontana*	1
35	36	THINKIN' AIN'T FOR ME	Paul Jones	*HMV*	3
-	37	WORLD WE KNEW	Frank Sinatra	*Reprise*	5
-	38	YOU KEEP RUNNING AWAY	Four Tops	*Tamla Motown*	1
-	39	BIG SPENDER	Shirley Bassey	*United Artists*	1
32	40	YOU ONLY LIVE TWICE/JACKSON	Nancy Sinatra/Nancy Sinatra and Lee Hazlewood	*Reprise*	15

WEEK ENDING 18 OCTOBER 1967

LW	TW	Title	Artist	Label	Wks
1	1	MASSACHUSETTS	Bee Gees	*Polydor*	5
4	2	HOLE IN MY SHOE	Traffic	*Island*	6
3	3	THE LAST WALTZ	Engelbert Humperdinck	*Decca*	9
2	4	FLOWERS IN THE RAIN	Move	*Regal Zonophone*	7
6	5	THE LETTER	Box Tops	*Stateside*	5
9	6	HOMBURG	Procol Harum	*Regal Zonophone*	3
7	7	THERE MUST BE A WAY	Frankie Vaughan	*Columbia*	9
11	8	FROM THE UNDERWORLD	Herd	*Fontana*	5
5	9	EXCERPT FROM 'A TEENAGE OPERA'	Keith West	*Parlophone*	11
8	10	REFLECTIONS	Diana Ross and the Supremes	*Tamla Motown*	7
13	11	WHEN WILL THE GOOD APPLES FALL	Seekers	*Columbia*	4
10	12	ITCHYCOO PARK	Small Faces	*Immediate*	10
21	13	BABY NOW THAT I'VE FOUND YOU	Foundations	*Pye*	3
35	14	ZABADAK!	Dave Dee Dozy Beaky Mick and Tich	*Fontana*	2
14	15	THE DAY I MET MARIE	Cliff Richard	*Columbia*	10
15	16	BLACK VELVET BAND	Dubliners	*Major Minor*	7
12	17	LET'S GO TO SAN FRANCISCO	Flowerpot Men	*Deram*	9
16	18	ODE TO BILLY JOE	Bobbie Gentry	*Capitol*	5
23	19	YOU'VE NOT CHANGED	Sandie Shaw	*Pye*	2
18	20	KING MIDAS IN REVERSE	Hollies	*Parlophone*	3
17	21	JUST LOVING YOU	Anita Harris	*CBS*	16
22	22	I'LL NEVER FALL IN LOVE AGAIN	Tom Jones	*Decca*	13
24	23	LOVE LETTERS IN THE SAND	Vince Hill	*Columbia*	3
19	24	FIVE LITTLE FINGERS	Frankie McBride	*Emerald*	9
20	25	SAN FRANCISCO (BE SURE TO WEAR SOME FLOWERS IN YOUR HAIR)	Scott McKenzie	*CBS*	15

■Only three American acts in the Top 20 (Box Tops, Diana Ross and the Supremes, Bobbie Gentry), but the Irish Dubliners and the Australian Seekers and some of the Bee Gees ensure the chart is not entirely British (18.10.67) ■ *Massachusetts* is the second American city to top the charts in 1967, but only the third since the charts began. Laramie, in 1955, is the other one (11.10.67)■

October 1967

□ Highest position disc reached ● Act's first ever week on chart

LW	TW	Title	Artist	Label	Wks
26	26	YOU'RE MY EVERYTHING	Temptations	Tamla Motown	7
25	27	GOOD TIMES	Eric Burdon and the Animals	MGM	6
38	28	YOU KEEP RUNNING AWAY	Four Tops	Tamla Motown	2
39	29	BIG SPENDER	Shirley Bassey	United Artists	2
-	30	WORLD OF BROKEN HEARTS	Amen Corner	Deram	1
29	31	EVEN THE BAD TIMES ARE GOOD	Tremeloes	CBS	12
27	32	THERE GOES MY EVERYTHING	Engelbert Humperdinck	Decca	22
32	33	RELEASE ME	Engelbert Humperdinck	Decca	35
28	34	HEROES AND VILLAINS	Beach Boys	Capitol	9
30	35	SOMEWHERE MY LOVE	Mike Sammes Singers	HMV	26
33	36	ANYTHING GOES	Harper's Bizarre	Warner Bros	3
-	37	SAN FRANCISCAN NIGHTS	Eric Burdon	MGM	1
40	38	YOU ONLY LIVE TWICE/JACKSON	Nancy Sinatra/Nancy Sinatra and Lee Hazlewood	Reprise	16
-	39	I WAS MADE TO LOVE HER	Stevie Wonder	Tamla Motown	12
37	40	WORLD WE KNEW	Frank Sinatra	Reprise	6

WEEK ENDING 25 OCTOBER 1967

LW	TW	Title	Artist	Label	Wks
1	1	MASSACHUSETTS	Bee Gees	Polydor	6
3	2	THE LAST WALTZ	Engelbert Humperdinck	Decca	10
2	3	HOLE IN MY SHOE	Traffic	Island	7
13	4	BABY NOW THAT I'VE FOUND YOU	Foundations	Pye	4
4	5	FLOWERS IN THE RAIN	Move	Regal Zonophone	8
5	6	THE LETTER	Box Tops	Stateside	6
14	7	ZABADAK!	Dave Dee Dozy Beaky Mick and Tich	Fontana	3
8	8	FROM THE UNDERWORLD	Herd	Fontana	6
6	9	HOMBURG	Procol Harum	Regal Zonophone	4
7	10	THERE MUST BE A WAY	Frankie Vaughan	Columbia	10
10	11	REFLECTIONS	Diana Ross and the Supremes	Tamla Motown	8
11	12	WHEN WILL THE GOOD APPLES FALL	Seekers	Columbia	5
9	13	EXCERPT FROM 'A TEENAGE OPERA'	Keith West	Parlophone	12
18	14	ODE TO BILLY JOE	Bobbie Gentry	Capitol	6
-	15	AUTUMN ALMANAC	Kinks	Pye	1
12	16	ITCHYCOO PARK	Small Faces	Immediate	11
21	17	JUST LOVING YOU	Anita Harris	CBS	17
15	18	THE DAY I MET MARIE	Cliff Richard	Columbia	11
20	19	KING MIDAS IN REVERSE	Hollies	Parlophone	4
19	20	YOU'VE NOT CHANGED	Sandie Shaw	Pye	3
16	21	BLACK VELVET BAND	Dubliners	Major Minor	8
17	22	LET'S GO TO SAN FRANCISCO	Flowerpot Men	Deram	10
37	23	SAN FRANCISCAN NIGHTS	Eric Burdon	MGM	2
30	24	WORLD OF BROKEN HEARTS	Amen Corner	Deram	2
23	25	LOVE LETTERS IN THE SAND	Vince Hill	Columbia	4
28	26	YOU KEEP RUNNING AWAY	Four Tops	Tamla Motown	3
-	27	IF THE WHOLE WORLD STOPPED LOVING	Val Doonican	Pye	1
-	28	LOVE IS ALL AROUND	Troggs	Page One	1
29	29	BIG SPENDER	Shirley Bassey	United Artists	3
26	30	YOU'RE MY EVERYTHING	Temptations	Tamla Motown	8
24	31	FIVE LITTLE FINGERS	Frankie McBride	Emerald	10
-	32	I CAN SEE FOR MILES	Who	Track	1
22	33	I'LL NEVER FALL IN LOVE AGAIN	Tom Jones	Decca	14
25	34	SAN FRANCISCO (BE SURE TO WEAR SOME FLOWERS IN YOUR HAIR)	Scott McKenzie	CBS	16
27	35	GOOD TIMES	Eric Burdon and the Animals	MGM	7
32	36	THERE GOES MY EVERYTHING	Engelbert Humperdinck	Decca	23
33	37	RELEASE ME	Engelbert Humperdinck	Decca	36
36	38	ANYTHING GOES	Harper's Bizarre	Warner Bros	4
38	39	YOU ONLY LIVE TWICE/JACKSON	Nancy Sinatra/Nancy Sinatra and Lee Hazlewood	Reprise	17
31	40	EVEN THE BAD TIMES ARE GOOD	Tremeloes	CBS	13

WEEK ENDING 1 NOVEMBER 1967

LW	TW	Title	Artist	Label	Wks
1	1	MASSACHUSETTS	Bee Gees	Polydor	7
4	2	BABY NOW THAT I'VE FOUND YOU	Foundations	Pye	5
7	3	ZABADAK!	Dave Dee Dozy Beaky Mick and Tich	Fontana	4
2	4	THE LAST WALTZ	Engelbert Humperdinck	Decca	11
3	5	HOLE IN MY SHOE	Traffic	Island	8
8	6	FROM THE UNDERWORLD	Herd	Fontana	7
9	7	HOMBURG	Procol Harum	Regal Zonophone	5
15	8	AUTUMN ALMANAC	Kinks	Pye	2
5	9	FLOWERS IN THE RAIN	Move	Regal Zonophone	9
6	10	THE LETTER	Box Tops	Stateside	7
10	11	THERE MUST BE A WAY	Frankie Vaughan	Columbia	11
12	12	WHEN WILL THE GOOD APPLES FALL	Seekers	Columbia	6
14	13	ODE TO BILLY JOE	Bobbie Gentry	Capitol	7
13	14	EXCERPT FROM 'A TEENAGE OPERA'	Keith West	Parlophone	13
23	15	SAN FRANCISCAN NIGHTS	Eric Burdon	MGM	3
28	16	LOVE IS ALL AROUND	Troggs	Page One	2
11	17	REFLECTIONS	Diana Ross and the Supremes	Tamla Motown	9
-	18	THERE IS A MOUNTAIN	Donovan	Pye	1
17	19	JUST LOVING YOU	Anita Harris	CBS	18
27	20	IF THE WHOLE WORLD STOPPED LOVING	Val Doonican	Pye	2
32	21	I CAN SEE FOR MILES	Who	Track	2
20	22	YOU'VE NOT CHANGED	Sandie Shaw	Pye	4
21	23	BLACK VELVET BAND	Dubliners	Major Minor	9
18	24	THE DAY I MET MARIE	Cliff Richard	Columbia	12
19	25	KING MIDAS IN REVERSE	Hollies	Parlophone	5
16	26	ITCHYCOO PARK	Small Faces	Immediate	12
26	27	YOU KEEP RUNNING AWAY	Four Tops	Tamla Motown	4
29	28	BIG SPENDER	Shirley Bassey	United Artists	4
24	29	WORLD OF BROKEN HEARTS	Amen Corner	Deram	3
-	30	I'M WONDERING	Stevie Wonder	Tamla Motown	1
30	31	YOU'RE MY EVERYTHING	Temptations	Tamla Motown	9
25	32	LOVE LETTERS IN THE SAND	Vince Hill	Columbia	5
-	33	I FEEL LOVE COMING ON	Felice Taylor ●	President	1
22	34	LET'S GO TO SAN FRANCISCO	Flowerpot Men	Deram	11
-	35	KNOCK ON WOOD	Otis Redding and Carla Thomas	Stax	1
38	36	ANYTHING GOES	Harper's Bizarre	Warner Bros	5
36	37	THERE GOES MY EVERYTHING	Engelbert Humperdinck	Decca	24
33	38	I'LL NEVER FALL IN LOVE AGAIN	Tom Jones	Decca	15
-	39	SOUL MAN	Sam and Dave	Stax	1
31	40	FIVE LITTLE FINGERS	Frankie McBride	Emerald	11

WEEK ENDING 8 NOVEMBER 1967

LW	TW	Title	Artist	Label	Wks
2	1	BABY NOW THAT I'VE FOUND YOU	Foundations	Pye	6
1	2	MASSACHUSETTS	Bee Gees	Polydor	8
3	3	ZABADAK!	Dave Dee Dozy Beaky Mick and Tich	Fontana	5
4	4	THE LAST WALTZ	Engelbert Humperdinck	Decca	12
8	5	AUTUMN ALMANAC	Kinks	Pye	3
6	6	FROM THE UNDERWORLD	Herd	Fontana	8
16	7	LOVE IS ALL AROUND	Troggs	Page One	3
15	8	SAN FRANCISCAN NIGHTS	Eric Burdon	MGM	4
7	9	HOMBURG	Procol Harum	Regal Zonophone	6
11	10	THERE MUST BE A WAY	Frankie Vaughan	Columbia	12
5	11	HOLE IN MY SHOE	Traffic	Island	9
9	12	FLOWERS IN THE RAIN	Move	Regal Zonophone	10
21	13	I CAN SEE FOR MILES	Who	Track	3
18	14	THERE IS A MOUNTAIN	Donovan	Pye	2
10	15	THE LETTER	Box Tops	Stateside	8
20	16	IF THE WHOLE WORLD STOPPED LOVING	Val Doonican	Pye	3
19	17	JUST LOVING YOU	Anita Harris	CBS	19
22	18	YOU'VE NOT CHANGED	Sandie Shaw	Pye	5
12	19	WHEN WILL THE GOOD APPLES FALL	Seekers	Columbia	7
13	20	ODE TO BILLY JOE	Bobbie Gentry	Capitol	8
17	21	REFLECTIONS	Diana Ross and the Supremes	Tamla Motown	10
30	22	I'M WONDERING	Stevie Wonder	Tamla Motown	2
28	23	BIG SPENDER	Shirley Bassey	United Artists	5
23	24	BLACK VELVET BAND	Dubliners	Major Minor	10
33	25	I FEEL LOVE COMING ON	Felice Taylor	President	2
-	26	EVERYBODY KNOWS	Dave Clark Five	Columbia	1
27	27	YOU KEEP RUNNING AWAY	Four Tops	Tamla Motown	5
-	28	CARELESS HANDS	Des O'Connor ●	Columbia	1
14	29	EXCERPT FROM 'A TEENAGE OPERA'	Keith West	Parlophone	14
25	30	KING MIDAS IN REVERSE	Hollies	Parlophone	6
-	31	LET THE HEARTACHES BEGIN	Long John Baldry ●	Pye	1

In these weeks ■ Frankie Vaughan's final week in the top ten comes eleven years less one day after his first (08.11.67) ■ Everybody is joining in with a big schmalzy ballad hit. Soul singer Long John Baldry and Comedian Des O'Connor are the latest two (08.11.67) ■ The Foundations become the first British group with black members to top the charts (08.11.67)■

November 1967

□ Highest position disc reached ● Act's first ever week on chart

LW	TW	Title	Artist	Label	Wks
31	32	YOU'RE MY EVERYTHING	Temptations	*Tamla Motown*	10
37	33	THERE GOES MY EVERYTHING	Engelbert Humperdinck	*Decca*	25
39	34	SOUL MAN	Sam and Dave	*Stax*	2
29	35	WORLD OF BROKEN HEARTS	Amen Corner	*Deram*	4
24	36	THE DAY I MET MARIE	Cliff Richard	*Columbia*	13
-	37	RELEASE ME	Engelbert Humperdinck	*Decca*	37
26	38	ITCHYCOO PARK	Small Faces	*Immediate*	13
-	[39]	BE MINE	Tremeloes	*CBS*	1
35	40	KNOCK ON WOOD	Otis Redding and Carla Thomas	*Stax*	2

WEEK ENDING 15 NOVEMBER 1967

LW	TW	Title	Artist	Label	Wks
1	[1]	BABY NOW THAT I'VE FOUND YOU	Foundations	*Pye*	7
2	2	MASSACHUSETTS	Bee Gees	*Polydor*	9
5	[3]	AUTUMN ALMANAC	Kinks	*Pye*	4
3	4	ZABADAK!	Dave Dee Dozy Beaky Mick and Tich	*Fontana*	6
4	5	THE LAST WALTZ	Engelbert Humperdinck	*Decca*	13
7	6	LOVE IS ALL AROUND	Troggs	*Page One*	4
8	[7]	SAN FRANCISCAN NIGHTS	Eric Burdon	*MGM*	5
14	[8]	THERE IS A MOUNTAIN	Donovan	*Pye*	3
31	9	LET THE HEARTACHES BEGIN	Long John Baldry	*Pye*	2
13	[10]	I CAN SEE FOR MILES	Who	*Track*	4
16	11	IF THE WHOLE WORLD STOPPED LOVING	Val Doonican	*Pye*	4
6	12	FROM THE UNDERWORLD	Herd	*Fontana*	9
26	13	EVERYBODY KNOWS	Dave Clark Five	*Columbia*	2
9	14	HOMBURG	Procol Harum	*Regal Zonophone*	7
10	15	THERE MUST BE A WAY	Frankie Vaughan	*Columbia*	13
11	16	HOLE IN MY SHOE	Traffic	*Island*	10
25	17	I FEEL LOVE COMING ON	Felice Taylor	*President*	3
12	18	FLOWERS IN THE RAIN	Move	*Regal Zonophone*	11
15	19	THE LETTER	Box Tops	*Stateside*	9
18	20	YOU'VE NOT CHANGED	Sandie Shaw	*Pye*	6
19	21	WHEN WILL THE GOOD APPLES FALL	Seekers	*Columbia*	8
17	22	JUST LOVING YOU	Anita Harris	*CBS*	20
22	23	I'M WONDERING	Stevie Wonder	*Tamla Motown*	3
20	24	ODE TO BILLY JOE	Bobbie Gentry	*Capitol*	9
34	25	SOUL MAN	Sam and Dave	*Stax*	3
21	26	REFLECTIONS	Diana Ross and the Supremes	*Tamla Motown*	11
28	27	CARELESS HANDS	Des O'Connor	*Columbia*	2
-	28	ALL MY LOVE	Cliff Richard	*Columbia*	1
23	29	BIG SPENDER	Shirley Bassey	*United Artists*	6
24	30	BLACK VELVET BAND	Dubliners	*Major Minor*	11
27	31	YOU KEEP RUNNING AWAY	Four Tops	*Tamla Motown*	6
32	32	YOU'RE MY EVERYTHING	Temptations	*Tamla Motown*	11
29	33	EXCERPT FROM 'A TEENAGE OPERA'	Keith West	*Parlophone*	15
37	34	RELEASE ME	Engelbert Humperdinck	*Decca*	38
-	35	SO TIRED	Frankie Vaughan	*Columbia*	1
-	36	SOMETHING'S GOTTEN HOLD OF MY HEART	Gene Pitney	*Stateside*	1
35	37	WORLD OF BROKEN HEARTS	Amen Corner	*Deram*	5
-	38	LOVE LETTERS IN THE SAND	Vince Hill	*Columbia*	6
33	39	THERE GOES MY EVERYTHING	Engelbert Humperdinck	*Decca*	26
-	40	LOVE LOVES TO LOVE LOVE	Lulu	*Columbia*	1

WEEK ENDING 22 NOVEMBER 1967

LW	TW	Title	Artist	Label	Wks
9	[1]	LET THE HEARTACHES BEGIN	Long John Baldry	*Pye*	3
1	2	BABY NOW THAT I'VE FOUND YOU	Foundations	*Pye*	8
13	3	EVERYBODY KNOWS	Dave Clark Five	*Columbia*	3
2	4	MASSACHUSETTS	Bee Gees	*Polydor*	10
6	[5]	LOVE IS ALL AROUND	Troggs	*Page One*	5
3	6	AUTUMN ALMANAC	Kinks	*Pye*	5
4	7	ZABADAK!	Dave Dee Dozy Beaky Mick and Tich	*Fontana*	7
5	8	THE LAST WALTZ	Engelbert Humperdinck	*Decca*	14
11	9	IF THE WHOLE WORLD STOPPED LOVING	Val Doonican	*Pye*	5
8	10	THERE IS A MOUNTAIN	Donovan	*Pye*	4
17	[11]	I FEEL LOVE COMING ON	Felice Taylor	*President*	4
10	12	I CAN SEE FOR MILES	Who	*Track*	5
7	13	SAN FRANCISCAN NIGHTS	Eric Burdon	*MGM*	6
15	14	THERE MUST BE A WAY	Frankie Vaughan	*Columbia*	14
27	15	CARELESS HANDS	Des O'Connor	*Columbia*	3
28	16	ALL MY LOVE	Cliff Richard	*Columbia*	2
12	17	FROM THE UNDERWORLD	Herd	*Fontana*	10
36	18	SOMETHING'S GOTTEN HOLD OF MY HEART	Gene Pitney	*Stateside*	2
14	19	HOMBURG	Procol Harum	*Regal Zonophone*	8
16	20	HOLE IN MY SHOE	Traffic	*Island*	11
21	21	WHEN WILL THE GOOD APPLES FALL	Seekers	*Columbia*	9
29	22	BIG SPENDER	Shirley Bassey	*United Artists*	7
20	23	YOU'VE NOT CHANGED	Sandie Shaw	*Pye*	7
25	[24]	SOUL MAN	Sam and Dave	*Stax*	4
-	25	DAYDREAM BELIEVER	Monkees	*RCA Victor*	1
23	26	I'M WONDERING	Stevie Wonder	*Tamla Motown*	4
35	27	SO TIRED	Frankie Vaughan	*Columbia*	2
19	28	THE LETTER	Box Tops	*Stateside*	10
18	29	FLOWERS IN THE RAIN	Move	*Regal Zonophone*	12
-	30	WORLD	Bee Gees	*Polydor*	1
23	31	JUST LOVING YOU	Anita Harris	*CBS*	21
-	32	THANK U VERY MUCH	Scaffold ●	*Parlophone*	1
34	33	RELEASE ME	Engelbert Humperdinck	*Decca*	39
26	34	REFLECTIONS	Diana Ross and the Supremes	*Tamla Motown*	12
-	35	WILD HONEY	Beach Boys	*Capitol*	1
-	36	I'M COMING HOME	Tom Jones	*Decca*	1
-	37	KITES	Simon Dupree and the Big Sound ●	*Parlophone*	1
-	38	TRAIN TOUR TO RAINBOW CITY	Pyramids ●	*President*	1
40	39	LOVE LOVES TO LOVE LOVE	Lulu	*Columbia*	2
24	40	ODE TO BILLY JOE	Bobbie Gentry	*Capitol*	10

WEEK ENDING 29 NOVEMBER 1967

LW	TW	Title	Artist	Label	Wks
1	[1]	LET THE HEARTACHES BEGIN	Long John Baldry	*Pye*	4
3	[2]	EVERYBODY KNOWS	Dave Clark Five	*Columbia*	4
9	[3]	IF THE WHOLE WORLD STOPPED LOVING	Val Doonican	*Pye*	6
2	4	BABY NOW THAT I'VE FOUND YOU	Foundations	*Pye*	9
8	5	THE LAST WALTZ	Engelbert Humperdinck	*Decca*	15
5	6	LOVE IS ALL AROUND	Troggs	*Page One*	6
18	7	SOMETHING'S GOTTEN HOLD OF MY HEART	Gene Pitney	*Stateside*	3
16	8	ALL MY LOVE	Cliff Richard	*Columbia*	3
-	9	HELLO GOODBYE	Beatles	*Parlophone*	1
15	10	CARELESS HANDS	Des O'Connor	*Columbia*	4
7	11	ZABADAK!	Dave Dee Dozy Beaky Mick and Tich	*Fontana*	8
11	12	I FEEL LOVE COMING ON	Felice Taylor	*President*	5
36	13	I'M COMING HOME	Tom Jones	*Decca*	2
10	14	THERE IS A MOUNTAIN	Donovan	*Pye*	5
30	15	WORLD	Bee Gees	*Polydor*	2
4	16	MASSACHUSETTS	Bee Gees	*Polydor*	11
6	17	AUTUMN ALMANAC	Kinks	*Pye*	6
12	18	I CAN SEE FOR MILES	Who	*Track*	6
25	19	DAYDREAM BELIEVER	Monkees	*RCA Victor*	2
13	20	SAN FRANCISCAN NIGHTS	Eric Burdon	*MGM*	7
37	21	KITES	Simon Dupree	*Parlophone*	2
14	22	THERE MUST BE A WAY	Frankie Vaughan	*Columbia*	15
22	23	BIG SPENDER	Shirley Bassey	*United Artists*	8
32	24	THANK U VERY MUCH	Scaffold	*Parlophone*	2
27	25	SO TIRED	Frankie Vaughan	*Columbia*	3
24	26	SOUL MAN	Sam and Dave	*Stax*	5
23	27	YOU'VE NOT CHANGED	Sandie Shaw	*Pye*	8
19	28	HOMBURG	Procol Harum	*Regal Zonophone*	9
35	[29]	WILD HONEY	Beach Boys	*Capitol*	2
17	30	FROM THE UNDERWORLD	Herd	*Fontana*	11
26	31	I'M WONDERING	Stevie Wonder	*Tamla Motown*	5
39	[32]	LOVE LOVES TO LOVE LOVE	Lulu	*Columbia*	3
31	33	JUST LOVING YOU	Anita Harris	*CBS*	22
20	34	HOLE IN MY SHOE	Traffic	*Island*	12
38	[35]	TRAIN TOUR TO RAINBOW CITY	Pyramids	*President*	2
33	36	RELEASE ME	Engelbert Humperdinck	*Decca*	40
-	37	IN AND OUT OF LOVE	Diana Ross and the Supremes	*Tamla Motown*	1

■Dave Clark Five's *Everybody Knows* is a completely different song from their *Everybody Knows* which touched number 37 almost three years earlier (29.11.67) ■ Gene Pitney becomes the first American in the top ten for four weeks (29.11.67) ■ The Scaffold includes Paul McCartney's younger brother Mike McGear, Liverpool poet Roger McGough, and the follically challenged John Gorman. Nobody ever discovers what an 'Aintree iron' is (22.11.67)■

November 1967

□ Highest position disc reached ● Act's first ever week on chart

LW	TW	Title	Artist	Label	Wks
-	38	SAM	Keith West	Parlophone	1
21	39	WHEN WILL THE GOOD APPLES FALL	Seekers	Columbia	10
28	40	THE LETTER	Box Tops	Stateside	11

WEEK ENDING 6 DECEMBER 1967

LW	TW	Title	Artist	Label	Wks
9	1	HELLO GOODBYE	Beatles	Parlophone	2
1	2	LET THE HEARTACHES BEGIN	Long John Baldry	Pye	5
2	3	EVERYBODY KNOWS	Dave Clark Five	Columbia	5
3	4	IF THE WHOLE WORLD STOPPED LOVING	Val Doonican	Pye	7
7	5	SOMETHING'S GOTTEN HOLD OF MY HEART	Gene Pitney	Stateside	4
10	6	CARELESS HANDS	Des O'Connor	Columbia	5
6	7	LOVE IS ALL AROUND	Troggs	Page One	7
4	8	BABY NOW THAT I'VE FOUND YOU	Foundations	Pye	10
15	9	WORLD	Bee Gees	Polydor	3
13	10	I'M COMING HOME	Tom Jones	Decca	3
8	11	ALL MY LOVE	Cliff Richard	Columbia	4
12	12	I FEEL LOVE COMING ON	Felice Taylor	President	6
5	13	THE LAST WALTZ	Engelbert Humperdinck	Decca	16
24	14	THANK U VERY MUCH	Scaffold	Parlophone	3
19	15	DAYDREAM BELIEVER	Monkees	RCA Victor	3
11	16	ZABADAK!	Dave Dee Dozy Beaky Mick and Tich	Fontana	9
21	17	KITES	Simon Dupree	Parlophone	3
37	18	IN AND OUT OF LOVE	Diana Ross and the Supremes	Tamla Motown	2
-	19	HERE WE GO ROUND THE MULBERRY BUSH	Traffic	Island	1
17	20	AUTUMN ALMANAC	Kinks	Pye	7
14	21	THERE IS A MOUNTAIN	Donovan	Pye	6
22	22	THERE MUST BE A WAY	Frankie Vaughan	Columbia	16
18	23	I CAN SEE FOR MILES	Who	Track	7
16	24	MASSACHUSETTS	Bee Gees	Polydor	12
26	25	SOUL MAN	Sam and Dave	Stax	6
25	26	SO TIRED	Frankie Vaughan	Columbia	4
23	27	BIG SPENDER	Shirley Bassey	United Artists	9
20	28	SAN FRANCISCAN NIGHTS	Eric Burdon	MGM	8
29	29	WILD HONEY	Beach Boys	Capitol	3
27	30	YOU'VE NOT CHANGED	Sandie Shaw	Pye	9
33	31	JUST LOVING YOU	Anita Harris	CBS	23
28	32	HOMBURG	Procol Harum	Regal Zonophone	10
36	33	RELEASE ME	Engelbert Humperdinck	Decca	41
32	34	LOVE LOVES TO LOVE LOVE	Lulu	Columbia	4
35	35	TRAIN TOUR TO RAINBOW CITY	Pyramids	President	3
30	36	FROM THE UNDERWORLD	Herd	Fontana	12
-	37	I'LL NEVER FALL IN LOVE AGAIN	Tom Jones	Decca	16
-	38	I HEARD A HEART BREAK LAST NIGHT	Jim Reeves	RCA Victor	1
-	39	FOGGY MOUNTAIN BREAKDOWN	Lester Flatt and Earl Scruggs ●	CBS/Mercury	1
31	40	I'M WONDERING	Stevie Wonder	Tamla Motown	6

WEEK ENDING 13 DECEMBER 1967

LW	TW	Title	Artist	Label	Wks
1	1	HELLO GOODBYE	Beatles	Parlophone	3
3	2	EVERYBODY KNOWS	Dave Clark Five	Columbia	6
2	3	LET THE HEARTACHES BEGIN	Long John Baldry	Pye	6
4	4	IF THE WHOLE WORLD STOPPED LOVING	Val Doonican	Pye	8
10	5	I'M COMING HOME	Tom Jones	Decca	4
5	6	SOMETHING'S GOTTEN HOLD OF MY HEART	Gene Pitney	Stateside	5
6	7	CARELESS HANDS	Des O'Connor	Columbia	6
19	8	HERE WE GO ROUND THE MULBERRY BUSH	Traffic	Island	2
9	9	WORLD	Bee Gees	Polydor	4
14	10	THANK U VERY MUCH	Scaffold	Parlophone	4
11	11	ALL MY LOVE	Cliff Richard	Columbia	5
17	12	KITES	Simon Dupree	Parlophone	4
15	13	DAYDREAM BELIEVER	Monkees	RCA Victor	4
12	14	I FEEL LOVE COMING ON	Felice Taylor	President	7
7	15	LOVE IS ALL AROUND	Troggs	Page One	8
13	16	THE LAST WALTZ	Engelbert Humperdinck	Decca	17
8	17	BABY NOW THAT I'VE FOUND YOU	Foundations	Pye	11
18	18	IN AND OUT OF LOVE	Diana Ross and the Supremes	Tamla Motown	3
22	19	THERE MUST BE A WAY	Frankie Vaughan	Columbia	17
-	20	MAGICAL MYSTERY TOUR (EP)	Beatles	Parlophone	1
27	21	BIG SPENDER	Shirley Bassey	United Artists	10
21	22	THERE IS A MOUNTAIN	Donovan	Pye	7
24	23	MASSACHUSETTS	Bee Gees	Polydor	13
26	24	SO TIRED	Frankie Vaughan	Columbia	5
-	25	WALK AWAY RENEE	Four Tops	Tamla Motown	1
23	26	I CAN SEE FOR MILES	Who	Track	8
31	27	JUST LOVING YOU	Anita Harris	CBS	24
20	28	AUTUMN ALMANAC	Kinks	Pye	8
-	29	TIN SOLDIER	Small Faces	Immediate	1
25	30	SOUL MAN	Sam and Dave	Stax	7
28	31	SAN FRANCISCAN NIGHTS	Eric Burdon	MGM	9
33	32	RELEASE ME	Engelbert Humperdinck	Decca	42
-	33	BALLAD OF BONNIE AND CLYDE	Georgie Fame	CBS	1
-	34	JACKIE	Scott Walker ●	Philips	1
-	35	I ONLY LIVE TO LOVE YOU	Cilla Black	Parlophone	1
16	36	ZABADAK!	Dave Dee Dozy Beaky Mick and Tich	Fontana	10
-	37	SUSANNAH'S STILL ALIVE	Dave Davies	Pye	1
-	38	LA DERNIERE VALSE	Mireille Mathieu ●	Columbia	1
39	39	FOGGY MOUNTAIN BREAKDOWN	Lester Flatt and Earl Scruggs	CBS/Mercury	2
34	40	LOVE LOVES TO LOVE LOVE	Lulu	Columbia	5

WEEK ENDING 20 DECEMBER 1967

LW	TW	Title	Artist	Label	Wks
1	1	HELLO GOODBYE	Beatles	Parlophone	4
5	2	I'M COMING HOME	Tom Jones	Decca	5
20	3	MAGICAL MYSTERY TOUR (EP)	Beatles	Parlophone	2
4	4	IF THE WHOLE WORLD STOPPED LOVING	Val Doonican	Pye	9
6	5	SOMETHING'S GOTTEN HOLD OF MY HEART	Gene Pitney	Stateside	6
3	6	LET THE HEARTACHES BEGIN	Long John Baldry	Pye	7
11	7	ALL MY LOVE	Cliff Richard	Columbia	6
13	8	DAYDREAM BELIEVER	Monkees	RCA Victor	5
10	9	THANK U VERY MUCH	Scaffold	Parlophone	5
8	10	HERE WE GO ROUND THE MULBERRY BUSH	Traffic	Island	3
7	11	CARELESS HANDS	Des O'Connor	Columbia	7
16	12	THE LAST WALTZ	Engelbert Humperdinck	Decca	18
2	13	EVERYBODY KNOWS	Dave Clark Five	Columbia	7
9	14	WORLD	Bee Gees	Polydor	5
12	15	KITES	Simon Dupree	Parlophone	5
25	16	WALK AWAY RENEE	Four Tops	Tamla Motown	2
18	17	IN AND OUT OF LOVE	Diana Ross and the Supremes	Tamla Motown	4
29	18	TIN SOLDIER	Small Faces	Immediate	2
14	19	I FEEL LOVE COMING ON	Felice Taylor	President	8
19	20	THERE MUST BE A WAY	Frankie Vaughan	Columbia	18
24	21	SO TIRED	Frankie Vaughan	Columbia	6
33	22	BALLAD OF BONNIE AND CLYDE	Georgie Fame	CBS	2
17	23	BABY NOW THAT I'VE FOUND YOU	Foundations	Pye	12
21	24	BIG SPENDER	Shirley Bassey	United Artists	11
15	25	LOVE IS ALL AROUND	Troggs	Page One	9
35	26	I ONLY LIVE TO LOVE YOU	Cilla Black	Parlophone	2
37	27	SUSANNAH'S STILL ALIVE	Dave Davies	Pye	2
-	28	THE OTHER MAN'S GRASS	Petula Clark	Pye	1
34	29	JACKIE	Scott Walker	Philips	2
38	30	LA DERNIERE VALSE	Mireille Mathieu	Columbia	2
32	31	RELEASE ME	Engelbert Humperdinck	Decca	43
30	32	SOUL MAN	Sam and Dave	Stax	8
28	33	AUTUMN ALMANAC	Kinks	Pye	9
27	34	JUST LOVING YOU	Anita Harris	CBS	25
-	35	HANDBAGS AND GLADRAGS	Chris Farlowe	Immediate	1
36	36	ZABADAK!	Dave Dee Dozy Beaky Mick and Tich	Fontana	11
22	37	THERE IS A MOUNTAIN	Donovan	Pye	8
26	38	I CAN SEE FOR MILES	Who	Track	9
23	39	MASSACHUSETTS	Bee Gees	Polydor	14
-	40	I'LL NEVER FALL IN LOVE AGAIN	Tom Jones	Decca	17

In these weeks ■ Gene Pitney reaches number five with *Something's Gotten Hold Of My Heart*. When he guests on Marc Almond's version 23 years later, he will enjoy his first and only number one hit (06.12.67) ■ There is nothing unlucky about the Beatles' thirteenth chart-topper. Its seven week run at the top is as long as they ever spend in pole position (06.12.67) ■

December 1967

□ Highest position disc reached ● Act's first ever week on chart

WEEK ENDING 27 DECEMBER 1967

LW	TW	Title / Artist	Label	Wks
1	**1** □	HELLO GOODBYE Beatles	*Parlophone*	5
3	**2** □	MAGICAL MYSTERY TOUR (EP) Beatles	*Parlophone*	3
2	**3**	I'M COMING HOME Tom Jones	*Decca*	6
4	**4**	IF THE WHOLE WORLD STOPPED LOVING Val Doonican	*Pye*	10
5	**5** □	SOMETHING'S GOTTEN HOLD OF MY HEART Gene Pitney	*Stateside*	7
7	**6**	ALL MY LOVE Cliff Richard	*Columbia*	7
8	**7**	DAYDREAM BELIEVER Monkees	*RCA Victor*	6
6	**8**	LET THE HEARTACHES BEGIN Long John Baldry	*Pye*	8
9	**9**	THANK U VERY MUCH Scaffold	*Parlophone*	6
16	**10**	WALK AWAY RENEE Four Tops	*Tamla Motown*	3
11	**11**	CARELESS HANDS Des O'Connor	*Columbia*	8
10	**12**	HERE WE GO ROUND THE MULBERRY BUSH Traffic	*Island*	4
12	**13**	THE LAST WALTZ Engelbert Humperdinck	*Decca*	19
15	**14**	KITES Simon Dupree	*Parlophone*	6
14	**15**	WORLD Bee Gees	*Polydor*	6
13	**16**	EVERYBODY KNOWS Dave Clark Five	*Columbia*	8
17	**17**	IN AND OUT OF LOVE Diana Ross and the Supremes	*Tamla Motown*	5
22	**18**	BALLAD OF BONNIE AND CLYDE Georgie Fame	*CBS*	3
18	**19**	TIN SOLDIER Small Faces	*Immediate*	3
20	**20**	THERE MUST BE A WAY Frankie Vaughan	*Columbia*	19
19	**21**	I FEEL LOVE COMING ON Felice Taylor	*President*	9
24	**22**	BIG SPENDER Shirley Bassey	*United Artists*	12
21	**23**	SO TIRED Frankie Vaughan	*Columbia*	7
28	**24**	THE OTHER MAN'S GRASS Petula Clark	*Pye*	2
23	**25**	BABY NOW THAT I'VE FOUND YOU Foundations	*Pye*	13
30	**26**	LA DERNIERE VALSE Mireille Mathieu	*Columbia*	3
25	**27**	LOVE IS ALL AROUND Troggs	*Page One*	10
29	**28**	JACKIE Scott Walker	*Philips*	3
26	**29**	I ONLY LIVE TO LOVE YOU Cilla Black	*Parlophone*	3
27	**30**	SUSANNAH'S STILL ALIVE Dave Davies	*Pye*	3
31	**31**	RELEASE ME Engelbert Humperdinck	*Decca*	44
32	**32**	SOUL MAN Sam and Dave	*Stax*	9
35	**33**	HANDBAGS AND GLADRAGS Chris Farlowe	*Immediate*	2
34	**34**	JUST LOVING YOU Anita Harris	*CBS*	26
33	**35**	AUTUMN ALMANAC Kinks	*Pye*	10
37	**36**	THERE IS A MOUNTAIN Donovan	*Pye*	9
-	**37**	GIMME LITTLE SIGN Brenton Wood ●	*Liberty*	1
40	**38**	I'LL NEVER FALL IN LOVE AGAIN Tom Jones	*Decca*	18
36	**39**	ZABADAK! Dave Dee Dozy Beaky Mick and Tich	*Fontana*	12
39	**40**	MASSACHUSETTS Bee Gees	*Polydor*	15

■Four weeks at number four for Val Doonican (27.12.67) ■ The Beatles are at number one for the fourth Christmas out of five. This year they are at number two as well (27.12.67) ■ Just to emphasise Engelbert's grip on the music of 1967, French teenager Mireille Mathieu's French version of *The Last Waltz* hits the top 30 (27.12.67)■

1968

..........STATUS QUO have their first two hits en route to becoming one of the ten all-time top chart acts.......the Beatles launch their Apple label with two number ones, their own 'Hey Jude' and Mary Hopkin's 'Those Were The Days'...... Louis Armstrong becomes the oldest artist to reach number one..........

January 1968

□ Highest position disc reached ● Act's first ever week on chart

LW	TW	WEEK ENDING 3 JANUARY 1968	Wks
1	[1]	HELLO GOODBYE Beatles ... *Parlophone*	6
2	[2]	MAGICAL MYSTERY TOUR (EP) Beatles ... *Parlophone*	4
3	3	I'M COMING HOME Tom Jones ... *Decca*	7
9	[4]	THANK U VERY MUCH Scaffold ... *Parlophone*	7
10	5	WALK AWAY RENEE Four Tops ... *Tamla Motown*	4
7	6	DAYDREAM BELIEVER Monkees ... *RCA Victor*	7
5	7	SOMETHING'S GOTTEN HOLD OF MY HEART Gene Pitney ... *Stateside*	8
4	8	IF THE WHOLE WORLD STOPPED LOVING Val Doonican ... *Pye*	11
14	[9]	KITES Simon Dupree and the Big Sound ... *Parlophone*	7
18	10	BALLAD OF BONNIE AND CLYDE Georgie Fame ... *CBS*	4
12	11	HERE WE GO ROUND THE MULBERRY BUSH Traffic ... *Island*	5
15	12	WORLD Bee Gees ... *Polydor*	7
17	13	IN AND OUT OF LOVE Diana Ross and the Supremes ... *Tamla Motown*	6
11	14	CARELESS HANDS Des O'Connor ... *Columbia*	9
8	15	LET THE HEARTACHES BEGIN Long John Baldry ... *Pye*	9
13	16	THE LAST WALTZ Engelbert Humperdinck ... *Decca*	20
16	17	EVERYBODY KNOWS Dave Clark Five ... *Columbia*	9
6	18	ALL MY LOVE Cliff Richard ... *Columbia*	8
19	19	TIN SOLDIER Small Faces ... *Immediate*	4
30	[20]	SUSANNAH'S STILL ALIVE Dave Davies ... *Pye*	4
24	21	THE OTHER MAN'S GRASS Petula Clark ... *Pye*	3
28	[22]	JACKIE Scott Walker ... *Philips*	4
-	23	PARADISE LOST Herd ... *Fontana*	1
22	24	BIG SPENDER Shirley Bassey ... *United Artists*	13
21	25	I FEEL LOVE COMING ON Felice Taylor ... *President*	10
27	26	LOVE IS ALL AROUND Troggs ... *Page One*	11
23	27	SO TIRED Frankie Vaughan ... *Columbia*	8
32	28	SOUL MAN Sam and Dave ... *Stax*	10
29	29	I ONLY LIVE TO LOVE YOU Cilla Black ... *Parlophone*	4
20	30	THERE MUST BE A WAY Frankie Vaughan ... *Columbia*	20
26	31	LA DERNIERE VALSE Mireille Mathieu ... *Columbia*	4
25	32	BABY NOW THAT I'VE FOUND YOU Foundations ... *Pye*	14
31	33	RELEASE ME Engelbert Humperdinck ... *Decca*	45
39	34	ZABADAK! Dave Dee Dozy Beaky Mick and Tich ... *Fontana*	13
-	35	NIGHTS IN WHITE SATIN Moody Blues ... *Deram*	1
-	36	EVERLASTING LOVE Love Affair ● ... *CBS*	1
40	37	MASSACHUSETTS Bee Gees ... *Polydor*	16
-	38	EVERYTHING I AM Plastic Penny ● ... *Page One*	1
-	39	SHE WEARS MY RING Solomon King ● ... *Columbia*	1
37	40	GIMME LITTLE SIGN Brenton Wood ... *Liberty*	2

LW	TW	WEEK ENDING 10 JANUARY 1968	Wks
1	[1]	HELLO GOODBYE Beatles ... *Parlophone*	7
2	[2]	MAGICAL MYSTERY TOUR (EP) Beatles ... *Parlophone*	5
5	[3]	WALK AWAY RENEE Four Tops ... *Tamla Motown*	5
10	4	BALLAD OF BONNIE AND CLYDE Georgie Fame ... *CBS*	5
6	[5]	DAYDREAM BELIEVER Monkees ... *RCA Victor*	8
4	6	THANK U VERY MUCH Scaffold ... *Parlophone*	8
3	7	I'M COMING HOME Tom Jones ... *Decca*	8
8	8	IF THE WHOLE WORLD STOPPED LOVING Val Doonican ... *Pye*	12
9	[9]	KITES Simon Dupree and the Big Sound ... *Parlophone*	8
11	10	HERE WE GO ROUND THE MULBERRY BUSH Traffic ... *Island*	6
7	11	SOMETHING'S GOTTEN HOLD OF MY HEART Gene Pitney ... *Stateside*	9
12	12	WORLD Bee Gees ... *Polydor*	8
14	13	CARELESS HANDS Des O'Connor ... *Columbia*	10
13	14	IN AND OUT OF LOVE Diana Ross and the Supremes ... *Tamla Motown*	7
36	15	EVERLASTING LOVE Love Affair ... *CBS*	2
19	16	TIN SOLDIER Small Faces ... *Immediate*	5
18	17	ALL MY LOVE Cliff Richard ... *Columbia*	9
15	18	LET THE HEARTACHES BEGIN Long John Baldry ... *Pye*	10
16	19	THE LAST WALTZ Engelbert Humperdinck ... *Decca*	21
21	[20]	THE OTHER MAN'S GRASS Petula Clark ... *Pye*	4
23	21	PARADISE LOST Herd ... *Fontana*	2
17	22	EVERYBODY KNOWS Dave Clark Five ... *Columbia*	10
-	23	JUDY IN DISGUISE (WITH GLASSES) John Fred and the Playboy Band ● ... *Pye*	1
22	24	JACKIE Scott Walker ... *Philips*	5
39	25	SHE WEARS MY RING Solomon King ... *Columbia*	2
20	26	SUSANNAH'S STILL ALIVE Dave Davies ... *Pye*	5
38	27	EVERYTHING I AM Plastic Penny ... *Page One*	2
-	28	I SECOND THAT EMOTION Smokey Robinson and the Miracles ● ... *Tamla Motown*	1
29	29	I ONLY LIVE TO LOVE YOU Cilla Black ... *Parlophone*	5
25	30	I FEEL LOVE COMING ON Felice Taylor ... *President*	11
24	31	BIG SPENDER Shirley Bassey ... *United Artists*	14
28	32	SOUL MAN Sam and Dave ... *Stax*	11
-	33	AM I THAT EASY TO FORGET Engelbert Humperdinck ... *Decca*	1
35	34	NIGHTS IN WHITE SATIN Moody Blues ... *Deram*	2
33	35	RELEASE ME Engelbert Humperdinck ... *Decca*	46
30	36	THERE MUST BE A WAY Frankie Vaughan ... *Columbia*	21
27	37	SO TIRED Frankie Vaughan ... *Columbia*	9
26	38	LOVE IS ALL AROUND Troggs ... *Page One*	12
31	39	LA DERNIERE VALSE Mireille Mathieu ... *Columbia*	5
40	40	GIMME LITTLE SIGN Brenton Wood ... *Liberty*	3

LW	TW	WEEK ENDING 17 JANUARY 1968	Wks
1	[1]	HELLO GOODBYE Beatles ... *Parlophone*	8
4	2	BALLAD OF BONNIE AND CLYDE Georgie Fame ... *CBS*	6
15	3	EVERLASTING LOVE Love Affair ... *CBS*	3
2	4	MAGICAL MYSTERY TOUR (EP) Beatles ... *Parlophone*	6
3	5	WALK AWAY RENEE Four Tops ... *Tamla Motown*	6
5	6	DAYDREAM BELIEVER Monkees ... *RCA Victor*	9
7	7	I'M COMING HOME Tom Jones ... *Decca*	9
33	8	AM I THAT EASY TO FORGET Engelbert Humperdinck ... *Decca*	2
8	9	IF THE WHOLE WORLD STOPPED LOVING Val Doonican ... *Pye*	13
6	10	THANK U VERY MUCH Scaffold ... *Parlophone*	9
12	11	WORLD Bee Gees ... *Polydor*	9
9	12	KITES Simon Dupree and the Big Sound ... *Parlophone*	9
23	13	JUDY IN DISGUISE (WITH GLASSES) John Fred and the Playboy Band ... *Pye*	2
16	14	TIN SOLDIER Small Faces ... *Immediate*	6
11	15	SOMETHING'S GOTTEN HOLD OF MY HEART Gene Pitney ... *Stateside*	10
10	16	HERE WE GO ROUND THE MULBERRY BUSH Traffic ... *Island*	7
13	17	CARELESS HANDS Des O'Connor ... *Columbia*	11
25	18	SHE WEARS MY RING Solomon King ... *Columbia*	3
14	19	IN AND OUT OF LOVE Diana Ross and the Supremes ... *Tamla Motown*	8
21	20	PARADISE LOST Herd ... *Fontana*	3
20	21	THE OTHER MAN'S GRASS Petula Clark ... *Pye*	5
27	22	EVERYTHING I AM Plastic Penny ... *Page One*	3
18	23	LET THE HEARTACHES BEGIN Long John Baldry ... *Pye*	11
24	24	JACKIE Scott Walker ... *Philips*	6
17	25	ALL MY LOVE Cliff Richard ... *Columbia*	10
19	26	THE LAST WALTZ Engelbert Humperdinck ... *Decca*	22
34	27	NIGHTS IN WHITE SATIN Moody Blues ... *Deram*	3
22	28	EVERYBODY KNOWS Dave Clark Five ... *Columbia*	11
-	29	THE BEST PART OF BREAKING UP Symbols ● ... *President*	1
40	30	GIMME LITTLE SIGN Brenton Wood ... *Liberty*	4
29	31	I ONLY LIVE TO LOVE YOU Cilla Black ... *Parlophone*	6
-	32	DARLIN' Beach Boys ... *Capitol*	1
-	33	BEND ME SHAPE ME Amen Corner ... *Deram*	1
-	34	I CAN TAKE OR LEAVE YOUR LOVING Herman's Hermits ... *Columbia*	1
-	[35]	MR SECOND CLASS Spencer Davis Group ... *United Artists*	1
26	36	SUSANNAH'S STILL ALIVE Dave Davies ... *Pye*	6
32	37	SOUL MAN Sam and Dave ... *Stax*	12
28	38	I SECOND THAT EMOTION Smokey Robinson and the Miracles ... *Tamla Motown*	2
31	39	BIG SPENDER Shirley Bassey ... *United Artists*	15
-	40	EVERLASTING LOVE Robert Knight ● ... *Monument*	1

In these weeks ■ The Beatles complete three consecutive weeks at number one and number two, while Paul McCartney's brother Mike enjoys his own first Top Ten hit as part of Scaffold (10.01.68) ■ The first week on the chart for *Nights In White Satin* gives the Moody Blues their first Top 40 hit since the departure of lead singer Denny Laine (03.01.68) ■

LW	TW	WEEK ENDING 24 JANUARY 1968		Wks
2	1	BALLAD OF BONNIE AND CLYDE Georgie Fame	*CBS*	7
3	2	EVERLASTING LOVE Love Affair	*CBS*	4
8	3	AM I THAT EASY TO FORGET Engelbert Humperdinck	*Decca*	3
13	4	JUDY IN DISGUISE (WITH GLASSES) John Fred and the Playboy Band	*Pye*	3
4	5	MAGICAL MYSTERY TOUR (EP) Beatles	*Parlophone*	7
6	6	DAYDREAM BELIEVER Monkees	*RCA Victor*	10
5	7	WALK AWAY RENEE Four Tops	*Tamla Motown*	7
1	8	HELLO GOODBYE Beatles	*Parlophone*	9
14	9	TIN SOLDIER Small Faces	*Immediate*	7
22	10	EVERYTHING I AM Plastic Penny	*Page One*	4
33	11	BEND ME SHAPE ME Amen Corner	*Deram*	2
11	12	WORLD Bee Gees	*Polydor*	10
18	13	SHE WEARS MY RING Solomon King	*Columbia*	4
-	14	SUDDENLY YOU LOVE ME Tremeloes	*CBS*	1
20	15	PARADISE LOST Herd	*Fontana*	4
7	16	I'M COMING HOME Tom Jones	*Decca*	10
34	17	I CAN TAKE OR LEAVE YOUR LOVING Herman's Hermits	*Columbia*	2
9	18	IF THE WHOLE WORLD STOPPED LOVING Val Doonican	*Pye*	14
10	19	THANK U VERY MUCH Scaffold	*Parlophone*	10
12	20	KITES Simon Dupree and the Big Sound	*Parlophone*	10
30	21	GIMME LITTLE SIGN Brenton Wood	*Liberty*	5
15	22	SOMETHING'S GOTTEN HOLD OF MY HEART Gene Pitney	*Stateside*	11
16	23	HERE WE GO ROUND THE MULBERRY BUSH Traffic	*Island*	8
27	24	NIGHTS IN WHITE SATIN Moody Blues	*Deram*	4
32	25	DARLIN' Beach Boys	*Capitol*	2
-	26	THE MIGHTY QUINN Manfred Mann	*Fontana*	1
21	27	THE OTHER MAN'S GRASS Petula Clark	*Pye*	6
17	28	CARELESS HANDS Des O'Connor	*Columbia*	12
19	29	IN AND OUT OF LOVE Diana Ross and the Supremes	*Tamla Motown*	9
25	30	ALL MY LOVE Cliff Richard	*Columbia*	11
23	31	LET THE HEARTACHES BEGIN Long John Baldry	*Pye*	12
29	32	THE BEST PART OF BREAKING UP Symbols	*President*	2
31	33	I ONLY LIVE TO LOVE YOU Cilla Black	*Parlophone*	7
26	34	THE LAST WALTZ Engelbert Humperdinck	*Decca*	23
35	35	MR SECOND CLASS Spencer Davis Group	*United Artists*	2
28	36	EVERYBODY KNOWS Dave Clark Five	*Columbia*	12
-	37	SATISFACTION Aretha Franklin	*Atlantic*	1
38	38	I SECOND THAT EMOTION Smokey Robinson and the Miracles	*Tamla Motown*	3
24	39	JACKIE Scott Walker	*Philips*	7
-	40	RELEASE ME Engelbert Humperdinck	*Decca*	47

LW	TW	WEEK ENDING 31 JANUARY 1968		Wks
2	1	EVERLASTING LOVE Love Affair	*CBS*	5
1	2	BALLAD OF BONNIE AND CLYDE Georgie Fame	*CBS*	8
3	3	AM I THAT EASY TO FORGET Engelbert Humperdinck	*Decca*	4
4	4	JUDY IN DISGUISE (WITH GLASSES) John Fred and the Playboy Band	*Pye*	4
11	5	BEND ME SHAPE ME Amen Corner	*Deram*	3
10	6	EVERYTHING I AM Plastic Penny	*Page One*	5
26	7	THE MIGHTY QUINN Manfred Mann	*Fontana*	2
13	8	SHE WEARS MY RING Solomon King	*Columbia*	5
14	9	SUDDENLY YOU LOVE ME Tremeloes	*CBS*	2
9	10	TIN SOLDIER Small Faces	*Immediate*	8
6	11	DAYDREAM BELIEVER Monkees	*RCA Victor*	11
5	12	MAGICAL MYSTERY TOUR (EP) Beatles	*Parlophone*	8
7	13	WALK AWAY RENEE Four Tops	*Tamla Motown*	8
17	14	I CAN TAKE OR LEAVE YOUR LOVING Herman's Hermits	*Columbia*	3
21	15	GIMME LITTLE SIGN Brenton Wood	*Liberty*	6
8	16	HELLO GOODBYE Beatles	*Parlophone*	10
25	17	DARLIN' Beach Boys	*Capitol*	3
12	18	WORLD Bee Gees	*Polydor*	11
15	19	PARADISE LOST Herd	*Fontana*	5
16	20	I'M COMING HOME Tom Jones	*Decca*	11
18	21	IF THE WHOLE WORLD STOPPED LOVING Val Doonican	*Pye*	15
19	22	THANK U VERY MUCH Scaffold	*Parlophone*	11
23	23	HERE WE GO ROUND THE MULBERRY BUSH Traffic	*Island*	9
20	24	KITES Simon Dupree and the Big Sound	*Parlophone*	11
32	25	THE BEST PART OF BREAKING UP Symbols	*President*	3
24	26	NIGHTS IN WHITE SATIN Moody Blues	*Deram*	5
34	27	THE LAST WALTZ Engelbert Humperdinck	*Decca*	24
22	28	SOMETHING'S GOTTEN HOLD OF MY HEART Gene Pitney	*Stateside*	12
29	29	IN AND OUT OF LOVE Diana Ross and the Supremes	*Tamla Motown*	10
-	30	PICTURES OF MATCHSTICK MEN Status Quo ●	*Pye*	1
-	31	SO MUCH LOVE Tony Blackburn ●	*MGM*	1
38	32	I SECOND THAT EMOTION Smokey Robinson and the Miracles	*Tamla Motown*	4
28	33	CARELESS HANDS Des O'Connor	*Columbia*	13
27	34	THE OTHER MAN'S GRASS Petula Clark	*Pye*	7
-	35	ANNIVERSARY WALTZ Anita Harris	*CBS*	1
-	36	HONEY CHILE Martha Reeves and the Vandellas	*Tamla Motown*	1
-	37	DON'T STOP THE CARNIVAL Alan Price Set	*Decca*	1
-	38	BACK ON MY FEET AGAIN Foundations	*Pye*	1
31	39	LET THE HEARTACHES BEGIN Long John Baldry	*Pye*	13
35	40	MR SECOND CLASS Spencer Davis Group	*United Artists*	3

February 1968

☐ Highest position disc reached ● Act's first ever week on chart

LW	TW	WEEK ENDING 7 FEBRUARY 1968		Wks
1	1	EVERLASTING LOVE Love Affair	*CBS*	6
7	2	THE MIGHTY QUINN Manfred Mann	*Fontana*	3
4	3	JUDY IN DISGUISE (WITH GLASSES) John Fred and the Playboy Band	*Pye*	5
3	4	AM I THAT EASY TO FORGET Engelbert Humperdinck	*Decca*	5
5	5	BEND ME SHAPE ME Amen Corner	*Deram*	4
9	6	SUDDENLY YOU LOVE ME Tremeloes	*CBS*	3
2	7	BALLAD OF BONNIE AND CLYDE Georgie Fame	*CBS*	9
15	8	GIMME LITTLE SIGN Brenton Wood	*Liberty*	7
8	9	SHE WEARS MY RING Solomon King	*Columbia*	6
6	10	EVERYTHING I AM Plastic Penny	*Page One*	6
14	11	I CAN TAKE OR LEAVE YOUR LOVING Herman's Hermits	*Columbia*	4
30	12	PICTURES OF MATCHSTICK MEN Status Quo	*Pye*	2
37	13	DON'T STOP THE CARNIVAL Alan Price Set	*Decca*	2
-	14	WORDS Bee Gees	*Capitol*	1
17	15	DARLIN' Beach Boys	*Capitol*	4
11	16	DAYDREAM BELIEVER Monkees	*RCA Victor*	12
10	17	TIN SOLDIER Small Faces	*Immediate*	9
12	18	MAGICAL MYSTERY TOUR (EP) Beatles	*Parlophone*	9
20	19	I'M COMING HOME Tom Jones	*Decca*	12
13	20	WALK AWAY RENEE Four Tops	*Tamla Motown*	9
26	21	NIGHTS IN WHITE SATIN Moody Blues	*Deram*	6
-	22	FIRE BRIGADE Move	*Regal Zonophone*	1
38	23	BACK ON MY FEET AGAIN Foundations	*Pye*	2
19	24	PARADISE LOST Herd	*Fontana*	6
25	25	THE BEST PART OF BREAKING UP Symbols	*President*	4
35	26	ANNIVERSARY WALTZ Anita Harris	*CBS*	2
32	27	I SECOND THAT EMOTION Smokey Robinson and the Miracles	*Tamla Motown*	5
27	28	THE LAST WALTZ Engelbert Humperdinck	*Decca*	25
23	29	HERE WE GO ROUND THE MULBERRY BUSH Traffic	*Island*	10
16	30	HELLO GOODBYE Beatles	*Parlophone*	11
36	31	HONEY CHILE Martha Reeves and the Vandellas	*Tamla Motown*	2
18	32	WORLD Bee Gees	*Polydor*	12
21	33	IF THE WHOLE WORLD STOPPED LOVING Val Doonican	*Pye*	16
22	34	THANK U VERY MUCH Scaffold	*Parlophone*	12
-	35	ROSIE Don Partridge ●	*Columbia*	1
-	36	BEND ME SHAPE ME American Breed ●	*Stateside*	1
31	37	SO MUCH LOVE Tony Blackburn	*MGM*	2

■Georgie Fame's *Ballad Of Bonnie And Clyde*, inspired by but not part of the Warren Beatty/Faye Dunaway film gives him his third number one and the amazing record of never having reached the Top Ten with any single except the three that went all the way (24.01.68) ■ It was revealed that Love Affair did not actually play on their chart-topping hit, but the fans do not seem to mind (31.01.68)■

February 1968

□ Highest position disc reached ● Act's first ever week on chart

LW	TW	Title	Artist	Label	Wks
24	38	KITES	Simon Dupree and the Big Sound	Parlophone	12
29	39	IN AND OUT OF LOVE	Diana Ross and the Supremes	Tamla Motown	11
-	40	GREEN TAMBOURINE	Lemon Pipers ●	Pye	1

WEEK ENDING 14 FEBRUARY 1968

LW	TW	Title	Artist	Label	Wks
2	1	THE MIGHTY QUINN	Manfred Mann	Fontana	4
1	2	EVERLASTING LOVE	Love Affair	CBS	7
5	3	BEND ME SHAPE ME	Amen Corner	Deram	5
4	4	AM I THAT EASY TO FORGET	Engelbert Humperdinck	Decca	6
9	5	SHE WEARS MY RING	Solomon King	Columbia	7
3	6	JUDY IN DISGUISE (WITH GLASSES)	John Fred and the Playboy Band	Pye	6
6	7	SUDDENLY YOU LOVE ME	Tremeloes	CBS	4
8	8	GIMME LITTLE SIGN	Brenton Wood	Liberty	8
12	9	PICTURES OF MATCHSTICK MEN	Status Quo	Pye	3
22	10	FIRE BRIGADE	Move	Regal Zonophone	2
11	11	I CAN TAKE OR LEAVE YOUR LOVING	Herman's Hermits	Columbia	5
15	12	DARLIN'	Beach Boys	Capitol	5
14	13	WORDS	Bee Gees	Capitol	2
7	14	BALLAD OF BONNIE AND CLYDE	Georgie Fame	CBS	10
10	15	EVERYTHING I AM	Plastic Penny	Page One	7
13	16	DON'T STOP THE CARNIVAL	Alan Price Set	Decca	3
16	17	DAYDREAM BELIEVER	Monkees	RCA Victor	13
23	18	BACK ON MY FEET AGAIN	Foundations	Pye	3
21	19	NIGHTS IN WHITE SATIN	Moody Blues	Deram	7
19	20	I'M COMING HOME	Tom Jones	Decca	13
26	21	ANNIVERSARY WALTZ	Anita Harris	CBS	3
35	22	ROSIE	Don Partridge	Columbia	2
40	23	GREEN TAMBOURINE	Lemon Pipers	Pye	2
17	24	TIN SOLDIER	Small Faces	Immediate	10
18	25	MAGICAL MYSTERY TOUR (EP)	Beatles	Parlophone	10
20	26	WALK AWAY RENEE	Four Tops	Tamla Motown	10
25	27	THE BEST PART OF BREAKING UP	Symbols	President	5
36	28	BEND ME SHAPE ME	American Breed	Stateside	2
-	29	TODAY	Sandie Shaw	Pye	1
31	30	HONEY CHILE	Martha Reeves and the Vandellas	Tamla Motown	3
28	31	THE LAST WALTZ	Engelbert Humperdinck	Decca	26
-	32	CINDERELLA ROCKEFELLA	Esther and Abi Ofarim ●	Philips	1
-	33	WHAT A WONDERFUL WORLD/CABARET	Louis Armstrong	HMV	1
24	34	PARADISE LOST	Herd	Fontana	7
-	35	LEGEND OF XANADU	Dave Dee, Dozy, Beaky, Mick and Tich	Fontana	1
27	36	I SECOND THAT EMOTION	Smokey Robinson and the Miracles	Tamla Motown	6
32	37	WORLD	Bee Gees	Polydor	13
29	38	HERE WE GO ROUND THE MULBERRY BUSH	Traffic	Island	11
37	39	SO MUCH LOVE	Tony Blackburn	MGM	3
39	40	IN AND OUT OF LOVE	Diana Ross and the Supremes	Tamla Motown	12

WEEK ENDING 21 FEBRUARY 1968

LW	TW	Title	Artist	Label	Wks
1	1	THE MIGHTY QUINN	Manfred Mann	Fontana	5
32	2	CINDERELLA ROCKEFELLA	Esther and Abi Ofarim	Philips	2
5	3	SHE WEARS MY RING	Solomon King	Columbia	8
2	4	EVERLASTING LOVE	Love Affair	CBS	8
3	5	BEND ME SHAPE ME	Amen Corner	Deram	6
4	6	AM I THAT EASY TO FORGET	Engelbert Humperdinck	Decca	7
9	7	PICTURES OF MATCHSTICK MEN	Status Quo	Pye	4
10	8	FIRE BRIGADE	Move	Regal Zonophone	3
6	9	JUDY IN DISGUISE (WITH GLASSES)	John Fred and the Playboy Band	Pye	7
8	10	GIMME LITTLE SIGN	Brenton Wood	Liberty	9
7	11	SUDDENLY YOU LOVE ME	Tremeloes	CBS	5
13	12	WORDS	Bee Gees	Capitol	3
35	13	LEGEND OF XANADU	Dave Dee, Dozy, Beaky, Mick and Tich	Fontana	2
12	14	DARLIN'	Beach Boys	Capitol	6
16	15	DON'T STOP THE CARNIVAL	Alan Price Set	Decca	4
11	16	I CAN TAKE OR LEAVE YOUR LOVING	Herman's Hermits	Columbia	6
23	17	GREEN TAMBOURINE	Lemon Pipers	Pye	3
18	18	BACK ON MY FEET AGAIN	Foundations	Pye	4
22	19	ROSIE	Don Partridge	Columbia	3
15	20	EVERYTHING I AM	Plastic Penny	Page One	8
14	21	BALLAD OF BONNIE AND CLYDE	Georgie Fame	CBS	11
17	22	DAYDREAM BELIEVER	Monkees	RCA Victor	14
21	23	ANNIVERSARY WALTZ	Anita Harris	CBS	4
28	24	BEND ME SHAPE ME	American Breed	Stateside	3
-	25	DEAR DELILAH	Grapefruit ●	RCA Victor	1
20	26	I'M COMING HOME	Tom Jones	Decca	14
29	27	TODAY	Sandie Shaw	Pye	2
19	28	NIGHTS IN WHITE SATIN	Moody Blues	Deram	8
27	29	THE BEST PART OF BREAKING UP	Symbols	President	6
30	30	HONEY CHILE	Martha Reeves and the Vandellas	Tamla Motown	4
33	31	WHAT A WONDERFUL WORLD/CABARET	Louis Armstrong	HMV	2
26	32	WALK AWAY RENEE	Four Tops	Tamla Motown	11
24	33	TIN SOLDIER	Small Faces	Immediate	11
25	34	MAGICAL MYSTERY TOUR (EP)	Beatles	Parlophone	11
-	35	JENNIFER JUNIPER	Donovan	Pye	1
36	36	I SECOND THAT EMOTION	Smokey Robinson and the Miracles	Tamla Motown	7
-	37	(SITTIN' ON) THE DOCK OF THE BAY	Otis Redding	Stax	1
-	38	LOVE IS BLUE	Paul Mauriat ●	Philips	1
-	39	MY GIRL	Otis Redding	Atlantic	1
-	40	YOU'RE THE ONLY ONE	Val Doonican	Pye	1

WEEK ENDING 28 FEBRUARY 1968

LW	TW	Title	Artist	Label	Wks
2	1	CINDERELLA ROCKEFELLA	Esther and Abi Ofarim	Philips	3
1	2	THE MIGHTY QUINN	Manfred Mann	Fontana	6
13	3	LEGEND OF XANADU	Dave Dee, Dozy, Beaky, Mick and Tich	Fontana	3
5	4	BEND ME SHAPE ME	Amen Corner	Deram	7
3	5	SHE WEARS MY RING	Solomon King	Columbia	9
8	6	FIRE BRIGADE	Move	Regal Zonophone	4
7	7	PICTURES OF MATCHSTICK MEN	Status Quo	Pye	5
12	8	WORDS	Bee Gees	Capitol	4
4	9	EVERLASTING LOVE	Love Affair	CBS	9
11	10	SUDDENLY YOU LOVE ME	Tremeloes	CBS	6
17	11	GREEN TAMBOURINE	Lemon Pipers	Pye	4
10	12	GIMME LITTLE SIGN	Brenton Wood	Liberty	10
6	13	AM I THAT EASY TO FORGET	Engelbert Humperdinck	Decca	8
19	14	ROSIE	Don Partridge	Columbia	4
35	15	JENNIFER JUNIPER	Donovan	Pye	2
14	16	DARLIN'	Beach Boys	Capitol	7
9	17	JUDY IN DISGUISE (WITH GLASSES)	John Fred and the Playboy Band	Pye	8
15	18	DON'T STOP THE CARNIVAL	Alan Price Set	Decca	5
18	19	BACK ON MY FEET AGAIN	Foundations	Pye	5
16	20	I CAN TAKE OR LEAVE YOUR LOVING	Herman's Hermits	Columbia	7
37	21	(SITTIN' ON) THE DOCK OF THE BAY	Otis Redding	Stax	2
25	22	DEAR DELILAH	Grapefruit	RCA Victor	2
23	23	ANNIVERSARY WALTZ	Anita Harris	CBS	5
-	24	GUITAR MAN	Elvis Presley	RCA Victor	1
20	25	EVERYTHING I AM	Plastic Penny	Page One	9
31	26	WHAT A WONDERFUL WORLD/CABARET	Louis Armstrong	HMV	3
21	27	BALLAD OF BONNIE AND CLYDE	Georgie Fame	CBS	12
27	28	TODAY	Sandie Shaw	Pye	3
22	29	DAYDREAM BELIEVER	Monkees	RCA Victor	15
24	30	BEND ME SHAPE ME	American Breed	Stateside	4
38	31	LOVE IS BLUE	Paul Mauriat	Philips	2
29	32	THE BEST PART OF BREAKING UP	Symbols	President	7

In these weeks ■ Manfred Mann become the first group to top the charts with successive lead vocalists. Other groups have used more than one vocalist from within their ranks, but only Manfred Mann replaced their lead singer and duplicated their success with the new vocalist (14.02.68) ■ Esther and Abi Ofarim are the first husband and wife to top the charts since Sonny and Cher, and the first Israelis ever to do so (28.02.68) ■

LW	TW	Title / Artist	Label	Wks
28	33	NIGHTS IN WHITE SATIN Moody Blues	Deram	9
-	34	ME THE PEACEFUL HEART Lulu	Columbia	1
30	35	HONEY CHILE Martha Reeves and the Vandellas	Tamla Motown	5
-	36	DELILAH Tom Jones	Decca	1
39	37	MY GIRL Otis Redding	Atlantic	2
36	38	I SECOND THAT EMOTION Smokey Robinson and the Miracles	Tamla Motown	8
34	39	MAGICAL MYSTERY TOUR (EP) Beatles	Parlophone	12
-	40	SKY PILOT Eric Burdon	MGM	1

WEEK ENDING 6 MARCH 1968

LW	TW	Title / Artist	Label	Wks
1	1	CINDERELLA ROCKEFELLA Esther and Abi Ofarim	Philips	4
3	2	LEGEND OF XANADU Dave Dee, Dozy, Beaky, Mick and Tich	Fontana	4
2	3	THE MIGHTY QUINN Manfred Mann	Fontana	7
6	4	FIRE BRIGADE Move	Regal Zonophone	5
14	5	ROSIE Don Partridge	Columbia	5
15	6	JENNIFER JUNIPER Donovan	Pye	3
7	7	PICTURES OF MATCHSTICK MEN Status Quo	Pye	6
4	8	BEND ME SHAPE ME Amen Corner	Deram	8
5	9	SHE WEARS MY RING Solomon King	Columbia	10
11	10	GREEN TAMBOURINE Lemon Pipers	Pye	5
8	11	WORDS Bee Gees	Capitol	5
36	12	DELILAH Tom Jones	Decca	2
16	13	DARLIN' Beach Boys	Capitol	8
21	14	(SITTIN' ON) THE DOCK OF THE BAY Otis Redding	Stax	3
12	15	GIMME LITTLE SIGN Brenton Wood	Liberty	11
10	16	SUDDENLY YOU LOVE ME Tremeloes	CBS	7
9	17	EVERLASTING LOVE Love Affair	CBS	10
13	18	AM I THAT EASY TO FORGET Engelbert Humperdinck	Decca	9
19	19	BACK ON MY FEET AGAIN Foundations	Pye	6
34	20	ME THE PEACEFUL HEART Lulu	Columbia	2
18	21	DON'T STOP THE CARNIVAL Alan Price Set	Decca	6
22	22	DEAR DELILAH Grapefruit	RCA Victor	3
24	23	GUITAR MAN Elvis Presley	RCA Victor	2
31	24	LOVE IS BLUE Paul Mauriat	Philips	3
17	25	JUDY IN DISGUISE (WITH GLASSES) John Fred and the Playboy Band	Pye	9
26	26	WHAT A WONDERFUL WORLD/CABARET Louis Armstrong	HMV	4
23	27	ANNIVERSARY WALTZ Anita Harris	CBS	6
20	28	I CAN TAKE OR LEAVE YOUR LOVING Herman's Hermits	Columbia	8
-	29	NO ONE CAN BREAK A HEART LIKE YOU Dave Clark Five	Columbia	1
28	30	TODAY Sandie Shaw	Pye	4
-	31	NEVERTHELESS Frankie Vaughan	Columbia	1
30	32	BEND ME SHAPE ME American Breed	Stateside	5
-	33	LOVE IS BLUE Jeff Beck	Columbia	1
29	34	DAYDREAM BELIEVER Monkees	RCA Victor	16
25	35	EVERYTHING I AM Plastic Penny	Page One	10
37	36	MY GIRL Otis Redding	Atlantic	3
-	37	YOU'RE THE ONLY ONE Val Doonican	Pye	2
32	38	THE BEST PART OF BREAKING UP Symbols	President	8
27	39	BALLAD OF BONNIE AND CLYDE Georgie Fame	CBS	13
-	40	NO FACE NO NAME AND NO NUMBER Traffic	Island	1

WEEK ENDING 13 MARCH 1968

LW	TW	Title / Artist	Label	Wks
1	1	CINDERELLA ROCKEFELLA Esther and Abi Ofarim	Philips	5
2	2	LEGEND OF XANADU Dave Dee, Dozy, Beaky, Mick and Tich	Fontana	5
4	3	FIRE BRIGADE Move	Regal Zonophone	6
5	4	ROSIE Don Partridge	Columbia	6
6	5	JENNIFER JUNIPER Donovan	Pye	4
12	6	DELILAH Tom Jones	Decca	3
10	7	GREEN TAMBOURINE Lemon Pipers	Pye	6
3	8	THE MIGHTY QUINN Manfred Mann	Fontana	8
14	9	(SITTIN' ON) THE DOCK OF THE BAY Otis Redding	Stax	4
20	10	ME THE PEACEFUL HEART Lulu	Columbia	3
13	11	DARLIN' Beach Boys	Capitol	9

March 1968

□ Highest position disc reached ● Act's first ever week on chart

LW	TW	Title / Artist	Label	Wks
9	12	SHE WEARS MY RING Solomon King	Columbia	11
7	13	PICTURES OF MATCHSTICK MEN Status Quo	Pye	7
8	14	BEND ME SHAPE ME Amen Corner	Deram	9
11	15	WORDS Bee Gees	Capitol	6
16	16	SUDDENLY YOU LOVE ME Tremeloes	CBS	8
26	17	WHAT A WONDERFUL WORLD/CABARET Louis Armstrong	HMV	5
15	18	GIMME LITTLE SIGN Brenton Wood	Liberty	12
18	19	AM I THAT EASY TO FORGET Engelbert Humperdinck	Decca	10
17	20	EVERLASTING LOVE Love Affair	CBS	11
24	21	LOVE IS BLUE Paul Mauriat	Philips	4
19	22	BACK ON MY FEET AGAIN Foundations	Pye	7
22	23	DEAR DELILAH Grapefruit	RCA Victor	4
23	24	GUITAR MAN Elvis Presley	RCA Victor	3
33	25	LOVE IS BLUE Jeff Beck	Columbia	2
25	26	JUDY IN DISGUISE (WITH GLASSES) John Fred and the Playboy Band	Pye	10
21	27	DON'T STOP THE CARNIVAL Alan Price Set	Decca	7
29	28	NO ONE CAN BREAK A HEART LIKE YOU Dave Clark Five	Columbia	2
31	29	NEVERTHELESS Frankie Vaughan	Columbia	2
-	30	IF I WERE A CARPENTER Four Tops	Tamla Motown	1
-	31	VALLEY OF THE DOLLS Dionne Warwick	Pye	1
-	32	IT'S YOUR DAY TODAY PJ Proby	Liberty	1
30	33	TODAY Sandie Shaw	Pye	5
28	34	I CAN TAKE OR LEAVE YOUR LOVING Herman's Hermits	Columbia	9
-	35	STEP INSIDE LOVE Cilla Black	Parlophone	1
27	36	ANNIVERSARY WALTZ Anita Harris	CBS	7
-	37	LITTLE GIRL Troggs	Page One	1
-	38	AIN'T NOTHIN' BUT A HOUSEPARTY Showstoppers ●	Beacon	1
36	39	MY GIRL Otis Redding	Atlantic	4
-	40	IF I ONLY HAD TIME John Rowles ●	MCA	1

WEEK ENDING 20 MARCH 1968

LW	TW	Title / Artist	Label	Wks
2	1	LEGEND OF XANADU Dave Dee, Dozy, Beaky, Mick and Tich	Fontana	6
1	2	CINDERELLA ROCKEFELLA Esther and Abi Ofarim	Philips	6
6	3	DELILAH Tom Jones	Decca	4
4	4	ROSIE Don Partridge	Columbia	7
9	5	(SITTIN' ON) THE DOCK OF THE BAY Otis Redding	Stax	5
5	6	JENNIFER JUNIPER Donovan	Pye	5
3	7	FIRE BRIGADE Move	Regal Zonophone	7
7	8	GREEN TAMBOURINE Lemon Pipers	Pye	7
10	9	ME THE PEACEFUL HEART Lulu	Columbia	4
17	10	WHAT A WONDERFUL WORLD/CABARET Louis Armstrong	HMV	6
-	11	LADY MADONNA Beatles	Parlophone	1
12	12	SHE WEARS MY RING Solomon King	Columbia	12
30	13	IF I WERE A CARPENTER Four Tops	Tamla Motown	2
11	14	DARLIN' Beach Boys	Capitol	10
8	15	THE MIGHTY QUINN Manfred Mann	Fontana	9
15	16	WORDS Bee Gees	Capitol	7
21	17	LOVE IS BLUE Paul Mauriat	Philips	5
14	18	BEND ME SHAPE ME Amen Corner	Deram	10
13	19	PICTURES OF MATCHSTICK MEN Status Quo	Pye	8
24	20	GUITAR MAN Elvis Presley	RCA Victor	4
23	21	DEAR DELILAH Grapefruit	RCA Victor	5
35	22	STEP INSIDE LOVE Cilla Black	Parlophone	2
25	23	LOVE IS BLUE Jeff Beck	Columbia	3
18	24	GIMME LITTLE SIGN Brenton Wood	Liberty	13
19	25	AM I THAT EASY TO FORGET Engelbert Humperdinck	Decca	11
16	26	SUDDENLY YOU LOVE ME Tremeloes	CBS	9
22	27	BACK ON MY FEET AGAIN Foundations	Pye	8
28	28	NO ONE CAN BREAK A HEART LIKE YOU Dave Clark Five	Columbia	3
38	29	AIN'T NOTHIN' BUT A HOUSEPARTY Showstoppers	Beacon	2
29	30	NEVERTHELESS Frankie Vaughan	Columbia	3

■ Three successive girls' names as song titles at four, five and six. Other girls are at numbers one, 23 and 26 (13.03.68) ■ Three weeks at number seven for the first Top Ten hit by Status Quo (06.03.68) ■ Otis Redding achieves his only UK Top Ten hit three months after his death in a plane crash (13.03.68) ■

March 1968

□ Highest position disc reached ● Act's first ever week on chart

LW	TW	Title	Artist	Label	Wks
20	31	EVERLASTING LOVE	Love Affair	CBS	12
-	32	CONGRATULATIONS	Cliff Richard	Columbia	1
31	33	VALLEY OF THE DOLLS	Dionne Warwick	Pye	2
27	34	DON'T STOP THE CARNIVAL	Alan Price Set	Decca	8
26	35	JUDY IN DISGUISE (WITH GLASSES)	John Fred and the Playboy Band	Pye	11
32	36	IT'S YOUR DAY TODAY	PJ Proby	Liberty	2
-	37	I THANK YOU	Sam and Dave	Stax	1
-	38	CAPTAIN OF YOUR SHIP	Reparata and the Delrons ●	Bell	1
39	39	MY GIRL	Otis Redding	Atlantic	5
40	40	IF I ONLY HAD TIME	John Rowles	MCA	2

WEEK ENDING 27 MARCH 1968

LW	TW	Title	Artist	Label	Wks
11	1	LADY MADONNA	Beatles	Parlophone	2
3	2	DELILAH	Tom Jones	Decca	5
5	3	(SITTIN' ON) THE DOCK OF THE BAY	Otis Redding	Stax	6
2	4	CINDERELLA ROCKEFELLA	Esther and Abi Ofarim	Philips	7
1	5	LEGEND OF XANADU	Dave Dee, Dozy, Beaky, Mick and Tich	Fontana	7
10	6	WHAT A WONDERFUL WORLD/CABARET	Louis Armstrong	HMV	7
4	7	ROSIE	Don Partridge	Columbia	8
32	8	CONGRATULATIONS	Cliff Richard	Columbia	2
6	9	JENNIFER JUNIPER	Donovan	Pye	6
13	10	IF I WERE A CARPENTER	Four Tops	Tamla Motown	3
9	11	ME THE PEACEFUL HEART	Lulu	Columbia	5
22	12	STEP INSIDE LOVE	Cilla Black	Parlophone	3
7	13	FIRE BRIGADE	Move	Regal Zonophone	8
17	14	LOVE IS BLUE	Paul Mauriat	Philips	6
12	15	SHE WEARS MY RING	Solomon King	Columbia	13
8	16	GREEN TAMBOURINE	Lemon Pipers	Pye	8
14	17	DARLIN'	Beach Boys	Capitol	11
40	18	IF I ONLY HAD TIME	John Rowles	MCA	3
20	19	GUITAR MAN	Elvis Presley	RCA Victor	5
29	20	AIN'T NOTHIN' BUT A HOUSEPARTY	Showstoppers	Beacon	3
38	21	CAPTAIN OF YOUR SHIP	Reparata and the Delrons	Bell	2
18	22	BEND ME SHAPE ME	Amen Corner	Deram	11
19	23	PICTURES OF MATCHSTICK MEN	Status Quo	Pye	9
16	24	WORDS	Bee Gees	Capitol	8
15	25	THE MIGHTY QUINN	Manfred Mann	Fontana	10
23	26	LOVE IS BLUE	Jeff Beck	Columbia	4
-	27	CAN'T TAKE MY EYES OFF YOU	Andy Williams	CBS	1
33	28	VALLEY OF THE DOLLS	Dionne Warwick	Pye	3
25	29	AM I THAT EASY TO FORGET	Engelbert Humperdinck	Decca	12
21	30	DEAR DELILAH	Grapefruit	RCA Victor	6
28	31	NO ONE CAN BREAK A HEART LIKE YOU	Dave Clark Five	Columbia	4
24	32	GIMME LITTLE SIGN	Brenton Wood	Liberty	14
-	33	SIMON SAYS	1910 Fruitgum Co ●	Pye	1
37	34	I THANK YOU	Sam and Dave	Stax	2
-	35	SOMETHING HERE IN MY HEART	Paper Dolls ●	Pye	1
39	36	MY GIRL	Otis Redding	Atlantic	6
30	37	NEVERTHELESS	Frankie Vaughan	Columbia	4
26	38	SUDDENLY YOU LOVE ME	Tremeloes	CBS	10
-	39	CRY LIKE A BABY	Box Tops	Bell	1
27	40	BACK ON MY FEET AGAIN	Foundations	Pye	9

WEEK ENDING 3 APRIL 1968

LW	TW	Title	Artist	Label	Wks
1	1	LADY MADONNA	Beatles	Parlophone	3
2	2	DELILAH	Tom Jones	Decca	6
8	3	CONGRATULATIONS	Cliff Richard	Columbia	3
3	4	(SITTIN' ON) THE DOCK OF THE BAY	Otis Redding	Stax	7
6	5	WHAT A WONDERFUL WORLD/CABARET	Louis Armstrong	HMV	8
4	6	CINDERELLA ROCKEFELLA	Esther and Abi Ofarim	Philips	8
10	7	IF I WERE A CARPENTER	Four Tops	Tamla Motown	4
5	8	LEGEND OF XANADU	Dave Dee, Dozy, Beaky, Mick and Tich	Fontana	8
12	9	STEP INSIDE LOVE	Cilla Black	Parlophone	4
7	10	ROSIE	Don Partridge	Columbia	9
18	11	IF I ONLY HAD TIME	John Rowles	MCA	4
14	12	LOVE IS BLUE	Paul Mauriat	Philips	7
9	13	JENNIFER JUNIPER	Donovan	Pye	7
11	14	ME THE PEACEFUL HEART	Lulu	Columbia	6
21	15	CAPTAIN OF YOUR SHIP	Reparata and the Delrons	Bell	3
20	16	AIN'T NOTHIN' BUT A HOUSEPARTY	Showstoppers	Beacon	4
13	17	FIRE BRIGADE	Move	Regal Zonophone	9
33	18	SIMON SAYS	1910 Fruitgum Co	Pye	2
-	19	VALLERI	Monkees	RCA Victor	1
27	20	CAN'T TAKE MY EYES OFF YOU	Andy Williams	CBS	2
15	21	SHE WEARS MY RING	Solomon King	Columbia	14
17	22	DARLIN'	Beach Boys	Capitol	12
-	23	JENNIFER ECCLES	Hollies	Parlophone	1
39	24	CRY LIKE A BABY	Box Tops	Bell	2
16	25	GREEN TAMBOURINE	Lemon Pipers	Pye	9
19	26	GUITAR MAN	Elvis Presley	RCA Victor	6
-	27	I CAN'T LET MAGGIE GO	Honeybus ●	Deram	1
26	28	LOVE IS BLUE	Jeff Beck	Columbia	5
23	29	PICTURES OF MATCHSTICK MEN	Status Quo	Pye	10
28	30	VALLEY OF THE DOLLS	Dionne Warwick	Pye	4
35	31	SOMETHING HERE IN MY HEART	Paper Dolls	Pye	2
-	32	LITTLE GREEN APPLES	Roger Miller	Mercury	1
-	33	JUMBO/THE SINGER SANG HIS SONG	Bee Gees	Polydor	1
22	34	BEND ME SHAPE ME	Amen Corner	Deram	12
-	35	DO YOU REMEMBER	Scaffold	Parlophone	1
-	36	SOMEWHERE IN THE COUNTRY	Gene Pitney	Stateside	1
-	37	I'VE GOT YOU ON MY MIND	Dorian Gray ●	Parlophone	1
24	38	WORDS	Bee Gees	Capitol	9
34	39	I THANK YOU	Sam and Dave	Stax	3
29	40	AM I THAT EASY TO FORGET	Engelbert Humperdinck	Decca	13

WEEK ENDING 10 APRIL 1968

LW	TW	Title	Artist	Label	Wks
3	1	CONGRATULATIONS	Cliff Richard	Columbia	4
2	2	DELILAH	Tom Jones	Decca	7
5	3	WHAT A WONDERFUL WORLD/CABARET	Louis Armstrong	HMV	9
1	4	LADY MADONNA	Beatles	Parlophone	4
11	5	IF I ONLY HAD TIME	John Rowles	MCA	5
4	6	(SITTIN' ON) THE DOCK OF THE BAY	Otis Redding	Stax	8
18	7	SIMON SAYS	1910 Fruitgum Co	Pye	3
9	8	STEP INSIDE LOVE	Cilla Black	Parlophone	5
7	9	IF I WERE A CARPENTER	Four Tops	Tamla Motown	5
23	10	JENNIFER ECCLES	Hollies	Parlophone	2
6	11	CINDERELLA ROCKEFELLA	Esther and Abi Ofarim	Philips	9
19	12	VALLERI	Monkees	RCA Victor	2
15	13	CAPTAIN OF YOUR SHIP	Reparata and the Delrons	Bell	4
27	14	I CAN'T LET MAGGIE GO	Honeybus	Deram	2
10	15	ROSIE	Don Partridge	Columbia	10
16	16	AIN'T NOTHIN' BUT A HOUSEPARTY	Showstoppers	Beacon	5
20	17	CAN'T TAKE MY EYES OFF YOU	Andy Williams	CBS	3
8	18	LEGEND OF XANADU	Dave Dee, Dozy, Beaky, Mick and Tich	Fontana	9
12	19	LOVE IS BLUE	Paul Mauriat	Philips	8
-	20	ROCK AROUND THE CLOCK	Bill Haley and his Comets	MCA	1
14	21	ME THE PEACEFUL HEART	Lulu	Columbia	7
31	22	SOMETHING HERE IN MY HEART	Paper Dolls	Pye	3
24	23	CRY LIKE A BABY	Box Tops	Bell	3
13	24	JENNIFER JUNIPER	Donovan	Pye	8
33	25	JUMBO/THE SINGER SANG HIS SONG	Bee Gees	Polydor	2
17	26	FIRE BRIGADE	Move	Regal Zonophone	10
21	27	SHE WEARS MY RING	Solomon King	Columbia	15
32	28	LITTLE GREEN APPLES	Roger Miller	Mercury	2
22	29	DARLIN'	Beach Boys	Capitol	13
36	30	SOMEWHERE IN THE COUNTRY	Gene Pitney	Stateside	2
25	31	GREEN TAMBOURINE	Lemon Pipers	Pye	10
-	32	PEGGY SUE/RAVE ON	Buddy Holly	MCA	1
-	33	PRETTY BROWN EYES	Jim Reeves	RCA Victor	1
35	34	DO YOU REMEMBER	Scaffold	Parlophone	2
-	35	HELLO HOW ARE YOU	Easybeats	United Artists	1

In these weeks ■ Bubblegum makes its first real chart appearance with the 1910 Fruitgum Co's classic *Simon Says* (27.03.68) ■ Cliff Richard's previous number one, *The Minute You're Gone* had been knocked off the top by the Beatles, so with his Eurovision entry *Congratulations*, he turns the tables (10.03.68)■

LW	TW	Title	Artist	Label	Wks
28	36	LOVE IS BLUE	Jeff Beck	Columbia	6
29	37	PICTURES OF MATCHSTICK MEN	Status Quo	Pye	11
26	38	GUITAR MAN	Elvis Presley	RCA Victor	7
30	39	VALLEY OF THE DOLLS	Dionne Warwick	Pye	5
-	40	FOREVER CAME TODAY	Diana Ross and the Supremes	Tamla Motown	1

WEEK ENDING 17 APRIL 1968

LW	TW	Title	Artist	Label	Wks
1	1	CONGRATULATIONS	Cliff Richard	Columbia	5
3	2	WHAT A WONDERFUL WORLD/CABARET	Louis Armstrong	HMV	10
5	3	IF I ONLY HAD TIME	John Rowles	MCA	6
2	4	DELILAH	Tom Jones	Decca	8
7	5	SIMON SAYS	1910 Fruitgum Co	Pye	4
4	6	LADY MADONNA	Beatles	Parlophone	5
10	7	JENNIFER ECCLES	Hollies	Parlophone	3
6	8	(SITTIN' ON) THE DOCK OF THE BAY	Otis Redding	Stax	9
8	9	STEP INSIDE LOVE	Cilla Black	Parlophone	6
17	10	CAN'T TAKE MY EYES OFF YOU	Andy Williams	CBS	4
9	11	IF I WERE A CARPENTER	Four Tops	Tamla Motown	6
12	12	VALLERI	Monkees	RCA Victor	3
14	13	I CAN'T LET MAGGIE GO	Honeybus	Deram	3
16	14	AIN'T NOTHIN' BUT A HOUSEPARTY	Showstoppers	Beacon	6
13	15	CAPTAIN OF YOUR SHIP	Reparata and the Delrons	Bell	5
11	16	CINDERELLA ROCKEFELLA	Esther and Abi Ofarim	Philips	10
23	17	CRY LIKE A BABY	Box Tops	Bell	4
22	18	SOMETHING HERE IN MY HEART	Paper Dolls	Pye	4
19	19	LOVE IS BLUE	Paul Mauriat	Philips	9
15	20	ROSIE	Don Partridge	Columbia	11
18	21	LEGEND OF XANADU	Dave Dee, Dozy, Beaky, Mick and Tich	Fontana	10
-	22	WHITE HORSES	Jacky ●	Philips	1
28	23	LITTLE GREEN APPLES	Roger Miller	Mercury	3
20	24	ROCK AROUND THE CLOCK	Bill Haley and his Comets	MCA	2
30	25	SOMEWHERE IN THE COUNTRY	Gene Pitney	Stateside	3
35	26	HELLO HOW ARE YOU	Easybeats	United Artists	2
-	27	I DON'T WANT OUR LOVING TO DIE	Herd	Fontana	1
21	28	ME THE PEACEFUL HEART	Lulu	Columbia	8
25	29	JUMBO/THE SINGER SANG HIS SONG	Bee Gees	Polydor	3
27	30	SHE WEARS MY RING	Solomon King	Columbia	16
-	31	LAZY SUNDAY	Small Faces	Immediate	1
26	32	FIRE BRIGADE	Move	Regal Zonophone	11
24	33	JENNIFER JUNIPER	Donovan	Pye	9
34	34	DO YOU REMEMBER	Scaffold	Parlophone	3
32	35	PEGGY SUE/RAVE ON	Buddy Holly	MCA	2
-	36	WONDER BOY	Kinks	Pye	1
-	37	I'VE GOT YOU ON MY MIND	Dorian Gray	Parlophone	2
29	38	DARLIN'	Beach Boys	Capitol	14
40	39	FOREVER CAME TODAY	Diana Ross and the Supremes	Tamla Motown	2
39	40	VALLEY OF THE DOLLS	Dionne Warwick	Pye	6

WEEK ENDING 24 APRIL 1968

LW	TW	Title	Artist	Label	Wks
2	1	WHAT A WONDERFUL WORLD/CABARET	Louis Armstrong	HMV	11
1	2	CONGRATULATIONS	Cliff Richard	Columbia	6
5	3	SIMON SAYS	1910 Fruitgum Co	Pye	5
3	4	IF I ONLY HAD TIME	John Rowles	MCA	7
4	5	DELILAH	Tom Jones	Decca	9
10	6	CAN'T TAKE MY EYES OFF YOU	Andy Williams	CBS	5
7	7	JENNIFER ECCLES	Hollies	Parlophone	4
13	8	I CAN'T LET MAGGIE GO	Honeybus	Deram	4
6	9	LADY MADONNA	Beatles	Parlophone	6
31	10	LAZY SUNDAY	Small Faces	Immediate	2
14	11	AIN'T NOTHIN' BUT A HOUSEPARTY	Showstoppers	Beacon	7
18	12	SOMETHING HERE IN MY HEART	Paper Dolls	Pye	5
15	13	CAPTAIN OF YOUR SHIP	Reparata and the Delrons	Bell	6
9	14	STEP INSIDE LOVE	Cilla Black	Parlophone	7
17	15	CRY LIKE A BABY	Box Tops	Bell	5
12	16	VALLERI	Monkees	RCA Victor	4
11	17	IF I WERE A CARPENTER	Four Tops	Tamla Motown	7

May 1968

□ Highest position disc reached ● Act's first ever week on chart

LW	TW	Title	Artist	Label	Wks
8	18	(SITTIN' ON) THE DOCK OF THE BAY	Otis Redding	Stax	10
22	19	WHITE HORSES	Jacky	Philips	2
26	20	HELLO HOW ARE YOU	Easybeats	United Artists	3
16	21	CINDERELLA ROCKEFELLA	Esther and Abi Ofarim	Philips	11
27	22	I DON'T WANT OUR LOVING TO DIE	Herd	Fontana	2
25	23	SOMEWHERE IN THE COUNTRY	Gene Pitney	Stateside	4
19	24	LOVE IS BLUE	Paul Mauriat	Philips	10
23	25	LITTLE GREEN APPLES	Roger Miller	Mercury	4
-	26	A MAN WITHOUT LOVE	Engelbert Humperdinck	Decca	1
21	27	LEGEND OF XANADU	Dave Dee, Dozy, Beaky, Mick and Tich	Fontana	11
39	28	FOREVER CAME TODAY	Diana Ross and the Supremes	Tamla Motown	3
29	29	JUMBO/THE SINGER SANG HIS SONG	Bee Gees	Polydor	4
20	30	ROSIE	Don Partridge	Columbia	12
-	31	YOUNG GIRL	Union Gap ●	CBS	1
-	32	HONEY	Bobby Goldsboro ●	United Artists	1
24	33	ROCK AROUND THE CLOCK	Bill Haley and his Comets	MCA	3
-	34	THIS WHEEL'S ON FIRE	Julie Driscoll, Brian Auger and the Trinity ●	Marmalade	1
35	35	PEGGY SUE/RAVE ON	Buddy Holly	MCA	3
28	36	ME THE PEACEFUL HEART	Lulu	Columbia	9
-	37	BLACK MAGIC WOMAN	Fleetwood Mac ●	Blue Horizon	1
33	38	JENNIFER JUNIPER	Donovan	Pye	10
-	39	LA LA LA	Massiel ●	Philips	1
36	40	WONDER BOY	Kinks	Pye	2

WEEK ENDING 1 MAY 1968

LW	TW	Title	Artist	Label	Wks
1	1	WHAT A WONDERFUL WORLD/CABARET	Louis Armstrong	HMV	12
3	2	SIMON SAYS	1910 Fruitgum Co	Pye	6
10	3	LAZY SUNDAY	Small Faces	Immediate	3
4	4	IF I ONLY HAD TIME	John Rowles	MCA	8
6	5	CAN'T TAKE MY EYES OFF YOU	Andy Williams	CBS	6
2	6	CONGRATULATIONS	Cliff Richard	Columbia	7
26	7	A MAN WITHOUT LOVE	Engelbert Humperdinck	Decca	2
7	8	JENNIFER ECCLES	Hollies	Parlophone	5
8	9	I CAN'T LET MAGGIE GO	Honeybus	Deram	5
5	10	DELILAH	Tom Jones	Decca	10
12	11	SOMETHING HERE IN MY HEART	Paper Dolls	Pye	6
22	12	I DON'T WANT OUR LOVING TO DIE	Herd	Fontana	3
11	13	AIN'T NOTHIN' BUT A HOUSEPARTY	Showstoppers	Beacon	8
19	14	WHITE HORSES	Jacky	Philips	3
15	15	CRY LIKE A BABY	Box Tops	Bell	6
31	16	YOUNG GIRL	Union Gap	CBS	2
13	17	CAPTAIN OF YOUR SHIP	Reparata and the Delrons	Bell	7
16	18	VALLERI	Monkees	RCA Victor	5
23	19	SOMEWHERE IN THE COUNTRY	Gene Pitney	Stateside	5
32	20	HONEY	Bobby Goldsboro	United Artists	2
18	21	(SITTIN' ON) THE DOCK OF THE BAY	Otis Redding	Stax	11
25	22	LITTLE GREEN APPLES	Roger Miller	Mercury	5
20	23	HELLO HOW ARE YOU	Easybeats	United Artists	4
-	24	RAINBOW VALLEY	Love Affair	CBS	1
17	25	IF I WERE A CARPENTER	Four Tops	Tamla Motown	8
9	26	LADY MADONNA	Beatles	Parlophone	7
14	27	STEP INSIDE LOVE	Cilla Black	Parlophone	8
28	28	FOREVER CAME TODAY	Diana Ross and the Supremes	Tamla Motown	4
21	29	CINDERELLA ROCKEFELLA	Esther and Abi Ofarim	Philips	12
24	30	LOVE IS BLUE	Paul Mauriat	Philips	11
34	31	THIS WHEEL'S ON FIRE	Julie Driscoll, Brian Auger and the Trinity	Marmalade	2
33	32	ROCK AROUND THE CLOCK	Bill Haley and his Comets	MCA	4
29	33	JUMBO/THE SINGER SANG HIS SONG	Bee Gees	Polydor	5
35	34	PEGGY SUE/RAVE ON	Buddy Holly	MCA	4
39	35	LA LA LA	Massiel	Philips	2
-	36	I'VE GOT YOU ON MY MIND	Dorian Gray	Parlophone	3
40	37	WONDER BOY	Kinks	Pye	3

■Louis Armstrong becomes the oldest person ever to top the charts. He will be 67 on 4 July this year (24.04.68) ■ The Eurovision song contest winner, *La La La* by Spain's Massiel, only climbs to number 35 (01.05.68) ■ There are now ten songs in the Top 40 with girl's names in the title (at numbers five, seven, eight, nine, 16, 21, 30, 32, 35 and 38) as well as a *Young Girl* and a *Black Magic Woman*, not to mention *Simon Says* and *Wonder Boy* (24.04.68)■

May 1968

□ Highest position disc reached ● Act's first ever week on chart

LW	TW	Title	Artist	Label	Wks
-	38	JOANNA	Scott Walker	Philips	1
-	39	SUMMERTIME BLUES	Eddie Cochran	Liberty	1
-	40	SLEEPY JOE	Herman's Hermits	Columbia	1

WEEK ENDING 8 MAY 1968

LW	TW	Title	Artist	Label	Wks
1	1	WHAT A WONDERFUL WORLD/CABARET	Louis Armstrong	HMV	13
3	2	LAZY SUNDAY	Small Faces	Immediate	4
2	3	SIMON SAYS	1910 Fruitgum Co	Pye	7
7	4	A MAN WITHOUT LOVE	Engelbert Humperdinck	Decca	3
12	5	I DON'T WANT OUR LOVING TO DIE	Herd	Fontana	4
5	6	CAN'T TAKE MY EYES OFF YOU	Andy Williams	CBS	7
16	7	YOUNG GIRL	Union Gap	CBS	3
4	8	IF I ONLY HAD TIME	John Rowles	MCA	9
20	9	HONEY	Bobby Goldsboro	United Artists	3
8	10	JENNIFER ECCLES	Hollies	Parlophone	6
6	11	CONGRATULATIONS	Cliff Richard	Columbia	8
14	12	WHITE HORSES	Jacky	Philips	4
11	13	SOMETHING HERE IN MY HEART	Paper Dolls	Pye	7
9	14	I CAN'T LET MAGGIE GO	Honeybus	Deram	6
10	15	DELILAH	Tom Jones	Decca	11
13	16	AIN'T NOTHIN' BUT A HOUSEPARTY	Showstoppers	Beacon	9
15	17	CRY LIKE A BABY	Box Tops	Bell	7
24	18	RAINBOW VALLEY	Love Affair	CBS	2
22	19	LITTLE GREEN APPLES	Roger Miller	Mercury	6
19	20	SOMEWHERE IN THE COUNTRY	Gene Pitney	Stateside	6
23	21	HELLO HOW ARE YOU	Easybeats	United Artists	5
40	22	SLEEPY JOE	Herman's Hermits	Columbia	2
38	23	JOANNA	Scott Walker	Philips	2
17	24	CAPTAIN OF YOUR SHIP	Reparata and the Delrons	Bell	8
21	25	(SITTIN' ON) THE DOCK OF THE BAY	Otis Redding	Stax	12
31	26	THIS WHEEL'S ON FIRE	Julie Driscoll, Brian Auger and the Trinity	Marmalade	3
18	27	VALLERI	Monkees	RCA Victor	6
28	28	FOREVER CAME TODAY	Diana Ross and the Supremes	Tamla Motown	5
32	29	ROCK AROUND THE CLOCK	Bill Haley and his Comets	MCA	5
27	30	STEP INSIDE LOVE	Cilla Black	Parlophone	9
-	31	WHEN WE WERE YOUNG	Solomon King	Columbia	1
30	32	LOVE IS BLUE	Paul Mauriat	Philips	12
29	33	CINDERELLA ROCKEFELLA	Esther and Abi Ofarim	Philips	13
25	34	IF I WERE A CARPENTER	Four Tops	Tamla Motown	9
26	35	LADY MADONNA	Beatles	Parlophone	8
34	36	PEGGY SUE/RAVE ON	Buddy Holly	MCA	5
35	37	LA LA LA	Massiel	Philips	3
-	38	FRIENDS	Beach Boys	Capitol	1
39	39	SUMMERTIME BLUES	Eddie Cochran	Liberty	2
37	40	WONDER BOY	Kinks	Pye	4

WEEK ENDING 15 MAY 1968

LW	TW	Title	Artist	Label	Wks
1	1	WHAT A WONDERFUL WORLD/CABARET	Louis Armstrong	HMV	14
4	2	A MAN WITHOUT LOVE	Engelbert Humperdinck	Decca	4
7	3	YOUNG GIRL	Union Gap	CBS	4
2	4	LAZY SUNDAY	Small Faces	Immediate	5
9	5	HONEY	Bobby Goldsboro	United Artists	4
3	6	SIMON SAYS	1910 Fruitgum Co	Pye	8
5	7	I DON'T WANT OUR LOVING TO DIE	Herd	Fontana	5
8	8	IF I ONLY HAD TIME	John Rowles	MCA	10
10	9	CAN'T TAKE MY EYES OFF YOU	Andy Williams	CBS	8
12	10	WHITE HORSES	Jacky	Philips	5
18	11	RAINBOW VALLEY	Love Affair	CBS	3
11	12	CONGRATULATIONS	Cliff Richard	Columbia	9
10	13	JENNIFER ECCLES	Hollies	Parlophone	7
22	14	SLEEPY JOE	Herman's Hermits	Columbia	3
23	15	JOANNA	Scott Walker	Philips	3
16	16	AIN'T NOTHIN' BUT A HOUSEPARTY	Showstoppers	Beacon	10
13	17	SOMETHING HERE IN MY HEART	Paper Dolls	Pye	8
14	18	I CAN'T LET MAGGIE GO	Honeybus	Deram	7
17	19	CRY LIKE A BABY	Box Tops	Bell	8
15	20	DELILAH	Tom Jones	Decca	12
19	21	LITTLE GREEN APPLES	Roger Miller	Mercury	7
20	22	SOMEWHERE IN THE COUNTRY	Gene Pitney	Stateside	7
26	23	THIS WHEEL'S ON FIRE	Julie Driscoll, Brian Auger and the Trinity	Marmalade	4
-	24	HELULE HELULE	Tremeloes	CBS	1
21	25	HELLO HOW ARE YOU	Easybeats	United Artists	6
29	26	ROCK AROUND THE CLOCK	Bill Haley and his Comets	MCA	6
24	27	CAPTAIN OF YOUR SHIP	Reparata and the Delrons	Bell	9
28	28	FOREVER CAME TODAY	Diana Ross and the Supremes	Tamla Motown	6
25	29	(SITTIN' ON) THE DOCK OF THE BAY	Otis Redding	Stax	13
27	30	VALLERI	Monkees	RCA Victor	7
31	31	WHEN WE WERE YOUNG	Solomon King	Columbia	2
-	32	DO YOU KNOW THE WAY TO SAN JOSE	Dionne Warwick	Pye	1
38	33	FRIENDS	Beach Boys	Capitol	2
39	34	SUMMERTIME BLUES	Eddie Cochran	Liberty	3
36	35	PEGGY SUE/RAVE ON	Buddy Holly	MCA	6
-	36	DEBORA	Tyrannosaurus Rex ●	Regal Zonophone	1
40	37	WONDER BOY	Kinks	Pye	5
32	38	LOVE IS BLUE	Paul Mauriat	Philips	13
-	39	BABY COME BACK	Equals ●	President	1
-	40	U.S. MALE	Elvis Presley	RCA Victor	1

WEEK ENDING 22 MAY 1968

LW	TW	Title	Artist	Label	Wks
3	1	YOUNG GIRL	Union Gap	CBS	5
2	2	A MAN WITHOUT LOVE	Engelbert Humperdinck	Decca	5
5	3	HONEY	Bobby Goldsboro	United Artists	5
4	4	LAZY SUNDAY	Small Faces	Immediate	6
1	5	WHAT A WONDERFUL WORLD/CABARET	Louis Armstrong	HMV	15
7	6	I DON'T WANT OUR LOVING TO DIE	Herd	Fontana	6
6	7	SIMON SAYS	1910 Fruitgum Co	Pye	9
9	8	CAN'T TAKE MY EYES OFF YOU	Andy Williams	CBS	9
11	9	RAINBOW VALLEY	Love Affair	CBS	4
10	10	WHITE HORSES	Jacky	Philips	6
8	11	IF I ONLY HAD TIME	John Rowles	MCA	11
14	12	SLEEPY JOE	Herman's Hermits	Columbia	4
15	13	JOANNA	Scott Walker	Philips	4
24	14	HELULE HELULE	Tremeloes	CBS	2
23	15	THIS WHEEL'S ON FIRE	Julie Driscoll, Brian Auger and the Trinity	Marmalade	5
16	16	AIN'T NOTHIN' BUT A HOUSEPARTY	Showstoppers	Beacon	11
12	17	CONGRATULATIONS	Cliff Richard	Columbia	10
40	18	U.S. MALE	Elvis Presley	RCA Victor	2
32	19	DO YOU KNOW THE WAY TO SAN JOSE	Dionne Warwick	Pye	2
21	20	LITTLE GREEN APPLES	Roger Miller	Mercury	8
13	21	JENNIFER ECCLES	Hollies	Parlophone	8
19	22	CRY LIKE A BABY	Box Tops	Bell	9
18	23	I CAN'T LET MAGGIE GO	Honeybus	Deram	8
25	24	HELLO HOW ARE YOU	Easybeats	United Artists	7
17	25	SOMETHING HERE IN MY HEART	Paper Dolls	Pye	9
22	26	SOMEWHERE IN THE COUNTRY	Gene Pitney	Stateside	8
20	27	DELILAH	Tom Jones	Decca	13
31	28	WHEN WE WERE YOUNG	Solomon King	Columbia	3
33	29	FRIENDS	Beach Boys	Capitol	3
26	30	ROCK AROUND THE CLOCK	Bill Haley and his Comets	MCA	7
39	31	BABY COME BACK	Equals	President	2
28	32	FOREVER CAME TODAY	Diana Ross and the Supremes	Tamla Motown	7
-	33	I PRETEND	Des O'Connor	Columbia	1
36	34	DEBORA	Tyrannosaurus Rex	Regal Zonophone	2
-	35	TIME FOR LIVING	Association ●	Warner Bros	1
34	36	SUMMERTIME BLUES	Eddie Cochran	Liberty	4
27	37	CAPTAIN OF YOUR SHIP	Reparata and the Delrons	Bell	10

In these weeks ■ *Debora* by Tyrannosaurus Rex potters around the lower reaches of the chart, to give Marc Bolan his first weeks of chart life (15.05.68) ■ Eddie Cochran's *Summertime Blues* charts again, this time in slightly more seasonal May than its previous appearance in November 1958. There are now three artists in the Top 40 having posthumous hits (01.05.68) ■ Jacky's *White Horses* is the last record to peak at number ten this year (22.05.68)■

LW	TW	Title / Artist	Label	Wks
-	38	THINK Aretha Franklin	Atlantic	1
-	[39]	IT'S MY TIME Everly Brothers	Warner Bros	1
29	40	(SITTIN' ON) THE DOCK OF THE BAY Otis Redding	Stax	13

WEEK ENDING 29 MAY 1968

LW	TW	Title / Artist	Label	Wks
1	[1]	YOUNG GIRL Union Gap	CBS	6
3	[2]	HONEY Bobby Goldsboro	United Artists	6
2	3	A MAN WITHOUT LOVE Engelbert Humperdinck	Decca	6
5	4	WHAT A WONDERFUL WORLD/CABARET Louis Armstrong	HMV	16
4	5	LAZY SUNDAY Small Faces	Immediate	7
6	6	I DON'T WANT OUR LOVING TO DIE Herd	Fontana	7
9	7	RAINBOW VALLEY Love Affair	CBS	5
13	8	JOANNA Scott Walker	Philips	5
19	9	DO YOU KNOW THE WAY TO SAN JOSE Dionne Warwick	Pye	3
15	10	THIS WHEEL'S ON FIRE Julie Driscoll, Brian Auger and the Trinity	Marmalade	6
7	11	SIMON SAYS 1910 Fruitgum Co	Pye	10
12	[12]	SLEEPY JOE Herman's Hermits	Columbia	5
8	13	CAN'T TAKE MY EYES OFF YOU Andy Williams	CBS	10
10	14	WHITE HORSES Jacky	Philips	7
14	15	HELULE HELULE Tremeloes	CBS	3
18	16	U.S. MALE Elvis Presley	RCA Victor	3
11	17	IF I ONLY HAD TIME John Rowles	MCA	12
-	18	JUMPING JACK FLASH Rolling Stones	Decca	1
27	19	DELILAH Tom Jones	Decca	14
31	20	BABY COME BACK Equals	President	3
28	21	WHEN WE WERE YOUNG Solomon King	Columbia	4
33	22	I PRETEND Des O'Connor	Columbia	2
16	23	AIN'T NOTHIN' BUT A HOUSEPARTY Showstoppers	Beacon	12
17	24	CONGRATULATIONS Cliff Richard	Columbia	11
29	[25]	FRIENDS Beach Boys	Capitol	4
35	26	TIME FOR LIVING Association	Warner Bros	2
38	27	THINK Aretha Franklin	Atlantic	2
-	28	HAPPY SONG Otis Redding	Stax	1
21	29	JENNIFER ECCLES Hollies	Parlophone	9
24	30	HELLO HOW ARE YOU Easybeats	United Artists	8
26	31	SOMEWHERE IN THE COUNTRY Gene Pitney	Stateside	9
-	32	BLUE EYES Don Partridge	Columbia	1
-	33	HURDY GURDY MAN Donovan	Pye	1
-	[34]	RAINBOW CHASER Nirvana ●	Island	1
30	35	ROCK AROUND THE CLOCK Bill Haley and his Comets	MCA	8
36	36	SUMMERTIME BLUES Eddie Cochran	Liberty	5
34	37	DEBORA Tyrannosaurus Rex	Regal Zonophone	3
22	38	CRY LIKE A BABY Box Tops	Bell	10
25	39	SOMETHING HERE IN MY HEART Paper Dolls	Pye	10
20	40	LITTLE GREEN APPLES Roger Miller	Mercury	9

WEEK ENDING 5 JUNE 1968

LW	TW	Title / Artist	Label	Wks
1	[1]	YOUNG GIRL Union Gap	CBS	7
3	[2]	A MAN WITHOUT LOVE Engelbert Humperdinck	Decca	7
2	3	HONEY Bobby Goldsboro	United Artists	7
18	4	JUMPING JACK FLASH Rolling Stones	Decca	2
7	[5]	RAINBOW VALLEY Love Affair	CBS	6
6	6	I DON'T WANT OUR LOVING TO DIE Herd	Fontana	8
8	[7]	JOANNA Scott Walker	Philips	6
9	8	DO YOU KNOW THE WAY TO SAN JOSE Dionne Warwick	Pye	4
5	9	LAZY SUNDAY Small Faces	Immediate	8
10	10	THIS WHEEL'S ON FIRE Julie Driscoll, Brian Auger and the Trinity	Marmalade	7
4	11	WHAT A WONDERFUL WORLD/CABARET Louis Armstrong	HMV	17
12	[12]	SLEEPY JOE Herman's Hermits	Columbia	6
11	13	SIMON SAYS 1910 Fruitgum Co	Pye	11
15	14	HELULE HELULE Tremeloes	CBS	4
16	15	U.S. MALE Elvis Presley	RCA Victor	4
14	16	WHITE HORSES Jacky	Philips	8
32	17	BLUE EYES Don Partridge	Columbia	2
17	18	IF I ONLY HAD TIME John Rowles	MCA	13
20	19	BABY COME BACK Equals	President	4
33	20	HURDY GURDY MAN Donovan	Pye	2
13	21	CAN'T TAKE MY EYES OFF YOU Andy Williams	CBS	11
22	22	I PRETEND Des O'Connor	Columbia	3
19	23	DELILAH Tom Jones	Decca	15
21	24	WHEN WE WERE YOUNG Solomon King	Columbia	5
26	25	TIME FOR LIVING Association	Warner Bros	3
27	[26]	THINK Aretha Franklin	Atlantic	3
28	27	HAPPY SONG Otis Redding	Stax	2
24	28	CONGRATULATIONS Cliff Richard	Columbia	12
25	29	FRIENDS Beach Boys	Capitol	5
-	30	SON OF HICKORY HOLLER'S TRAMP OC Smith ●	CBS	1
-	31	LOVIN' THINGS Marmalade ●	CBS	1
23	32	AIN'T NOTHIN' BUT A HOUSEPARTY Showstoppers	Beacon	13
-	33	BOY Lulu	Columbia	1
36	[34]	SUMMERTIME BLUES Eddie Cochran	Liberty	6
-	35	TRIBUTE TO A KING William Bell ●	Stax	1
-	36	QUANDO M'INNAMORO Sandpipers	A&M	1
34	37	RAINBOW CHASER Nirvana	Island	2
37	38	DEBORA Tyrannosaurus Rex	Regal Zonophone	4
29	39	JENNIFER ECCLES Hollies	Parlophone	10
-	40	IT'S MY TIME Everly Brothers	Warner Bros	2

June 1968

□ Highest position disc reached ● Act's first ever week on chart

WEEK ENDING 12 JUNE 1968

LW	TW	Title / Artist	Label	Wks
1	[1]	YOUNG GIRL Union Gap	CBS	8
4	2	JUMPING JACK FLASH Rolling Stones	Decca	3
3	3	HONEY Bobby Goldsboro	United Artists	8
2	4	A MAN WITHOUT LOVE Engelbert Humperdinck	Decca	8
5	[5]	RAINBOW VALLEY Love Affair	CBS	7
10	6	THIS WHEEL'S ON FIRE Julie Driscoll, Brian Auger and the Trinity	Marmalade	8
17	7	BLUE EYES Don Partridge	Columbia	3
20	8	HURDY GURDY MAN Donovan	Pye	3
8	9	DO YOU KNOW THE WAY TO SAN JOSE Dionne Warwick	Pye	5
6	10	I DON'T WANT OUR LOVING TO DIE Herd	Fontana	9
7	11	JOANNA Scott Walker	Philips	7
11	12	WHAT A WONDERFUL WORLD/CABARET Louis Armstrong	HMV	18
22	13	I PRETEND Des O'Connor	Columbia	4
19	14	BABY COME BACK Equals	President	5
14	15	HELULE HELULE Tremeloes	CBS	5
13	16	SIMON SAYS 1910 Fruitgum Co	Pye	12
12	17	SLEEPY JOE Herman's Hermits	Columbia	7
31	18	LOVIN' THINGS Marmalade	CBS	2
16	19	WHITE HORSES Jacky	Philips	9
30	20	SON OF HICKORY HOLLER'S TRAMP OC Smith	CBS	2
9	21	LAZY SUNDAY Small Faces	Immediate	9
15	22	U.S. MALE Elvis Presley	RCA Victor	5
18	23	IF I ONLY HAD TIME John Rowles	MCA	14
24	24	WHEN WE WERE YOUNG Solomon King	Columbia	6
23	25	DELILAH Tom Jones	Decca	16
21	26	CAN'T TAKE MY EYES OFF YOU Andy Williams	CBS	12
26	27	THINK Aretha Franklin	Atlantic	4
25	28	TIME FOR LIVING Association	Warner Bros	4
27	29	HAPPY SONG Otis Redding	Stax	3
33	30	BOY Lulu	Columbia	2
28	31	CONGRATULATIONS Cliff Richard	Columbia	13
35	32	TRIBUTE TO A KING William Bell	Stax	2
36	[33]	QUANDO M'INNAMORO Sandpipers	A&M	2
29	34	FRIENDS Beach Boys	Capitol	6
-	35	YUMMY YUMMY YUMMY Ohio Express ●	Pye	1
32	36	AIN'T NOTHIN' BUT A HOUSEPARTY Showstoppers	Beacon	14
-	37	MONY MONY Tommy James and the Shondells	Major Minor	1
37	38	RAINBOW CHASER Nirvana	Island	3
-	[39]	WHERE IS TOMORROW Cilla Black	Parlophone	1
-	[40]	ANYONE FOR TENNIS Cream	Polydor	1

■Bobby Goldsboro's *Honey* reaches number two. Seven years later, it will be re-issued and duplicate the achievement (29.05.68) ■ A final week of Top 40 success for the most successful chart duo of all time - the Everly Brothers (05.06.68) ■ *Jennifer Eccles* disappears from the chart, but she will reappear on 13 November as the subject of one verse of the Scaffold's number one hit *Lily The Pink* (05.06.68)■

June 1968

□ Highest position disc reached ● Act's first ever week on chart

LW	TW	WEEK ENDING 19 JUNE 1968		Wks
2	[1]	JUMPING JACK FLASH Rolling Stones	*Decca*	4
1	2	YOUNG GIRL Union Gap	*CBS*	9
7	[3]	BLUE EYES Don Partridge	*Columbia*	4
8	[4]	HURDY GURDY MAN Donovan	*Pye*	4
6	[5]	THIS WHEEL'S ON FIRE Julie Driscoll, Brian Auger and the Trinity	*Marmalade*	9
3	6	HONEY Bobby Goldsboro	*United Artists*	9
14	7	BABY COME BACK Equals	*President*	6
9	[8]	DO YOU KNOW THE WAY TO SAN JOSE Dionne Warwick	*Pye*	6
13	9	I PRETEND Des O'Connor	*Columbia*	5
4	10	A MAN WITHOUT LOVE Engelbert Humperdinck	*Decca*	9
5	11	RAINBOW VALLEY Love Affair	*CBS*	8
18	12	LOVIN' THINGS Marmalade	*CBS*	3
20	13	SON OF HICKORY HOLLER'S TRAMP OC Smith	*CBS*	3
10	14	I DON'T WANT OUR LOVING TO DIE Herd	*Fontana*	10
11	15	JOANNA Scott Walker	*Philips*	8
17	16	SLEEPY JOE Herman's Hermits	*Columbia*	8
16	17	SIMON SAYS 1910 Fruitgum Co	*Pye*	13
15	18	HELULE HELULE Tremeloes	*CBS*	6
19	19	WHITE HORSES Jacky	*Philips*	10
12	20	WHAT A WONDERFUL WORLD/CABARET Louis Armstrong	*HMV*	19
-	21	MY NAME IS JACK Manfred Mann	*Fontana*	1
30	22	BOY Lulu	*Columbia*	3
22	23	U.S. MALE Elvis Presley	*RCA Victor*	6
29	[24]	HAPPY SONG Otis Redding	*Stax*	4
35	25	YUMMY YUMMY YUMMY Ohio Express	*Pye*	2
28	26	TIME FOR LIVING Association	*Warner Bros*	5
26	27	CAN'T TAKE MY EYES OFF YOU Andy Williams	*CBS*	13
21	28	LAZY SUNDAY Small Faces	*Immediate*	10
27	29	THINK Aretha Franklin	*Atlantic*	5
23	30	IF I ONLY HAD TIME John Rowles	*MCA*	15
25	31	DELILAH Tom Jones	*Decca*	17
24	32	WHEN WE WERE YOUNG Solomon King	*Columbia*	7
32	33	TRIBUTE TO A KING William Bell	*Stax*	3
37	34	MONY MONY Tommy James and the Shondells	*Major Minor*	2
33	35	QUANDO M'INNAMORO Sandpipers	*A&M*	3
-	36	HUSH NOT A WORD TO MARY John Rowles	*MCA*	1
-	37	YESTERDAY HAS GONE Cupid's Inspiration ●	*Nems*	1
38	38	RAINBOW CHASER Nirvana	*Island*	4
-	39	AIN'T NOTHING LIKE THE REAL THING Marvin Gaye and Tammi Terrell ●	*Tamla Motown*	1
39	40	WHERE IS TOMORROW Cilla Black	*Parlophone*	2

LW	TW	WEEK ENDING 26 JUNE 1968		Wks
1	[1]	JUMPING JACK FLASH Rolling Stones	*Decca*	5
2	2	YOUNG GIRL Union Gap	*CBS*	10
7	3	BABY COME BACK Equals	*President*	7
4	[4]	HURDY GURDY MAN Donovan	*Pye*	5
3	5	BLUE EYES Don Partridge	*Columbia*	5
9	6	I PRETEND Des O'Connor	*Columbia*	6
13	7	SON OF HICKORY HOLLER'S TRAMP OC Smith	*CBS*	4
5	8	THIS WHEEL'S ON FIRE Julie Driscoll, Brian Auger and the Trinity	*Marmalade*	10
12	9	LOVIN' THINGS Marmalade	*CBS*	4
6	10	HONEY Bobby Goldsboro	*United Artists*	10
21	11	MY NAME IS JACK Manfred Mann	*Fontana*	2
25	12	YUMMY YUMMY YUMMY Ohio Express	*Pye*	3
8	13	DO YOU KNOW THE WAY TO SAN JOSE Dionne Warwick	*Pye*	7
10	14	A MAN WITHOUT LOVE Engelbert Humperdinck	*Decca*	10
22	[15]	BOY Lulu	*Columbia*	4
37	16	YESTERDAY HAS GONE Cupid's Inspiration	*Nems*	2
11	17	RAINBOW VALLEY Love Affair	*CBS*	9
36	18	HUSH NOT A WORD TO MARY John Rowles	*MCA*	2
15	19	JOANNA Scott Walker	*Philips*	9
20	20	WHAT A WONDERFUL WORLD/CABARET Louis Armstrong	*HMV*	20
-	21	ONE MORE DANCE Esther and Abi Ofarim	*Philips*	1
14	22	I DON'T WANT OUR LOVING TO DIE Herd	*Fontana*	11
26	23	TIME FOR LIVING Association	*Warner Bros*	6
18	24	HELULE HELULE Tremeloes	*CBS*	7
17	25	SIMON SAYS 1910 Fruitgum Co	*Pye*	14
34	26	MONY MONY Tommy James and the Shondells	*Major Minor*	3
30	27	IF I ONLY HAD TIME John Rowles	*MCA*	16
19	28	WHITE HORSES Jacky	*Philips*	11
29	29	THINK Aretha Franklin	*Atlantic*	6
32	30	WHEN WE WERE YOUNG Solomon King	*Columbia*	8
33	[31]	TRIBUTE TO A KING William Bell	*Stax*	4
16	32	SLEEPY JOE Herman's Hermits	*Columbia*	9
27	33	CAN'T TAKE MY EYES OFF YOU Andy Williams	*CBS*	14
23	34	U.S. MALE Elvis Presley	*RCA Victor*	7
-	35	MACARTHUR PARK Richard Harris ●	*RCA Victor*	1
-	36	GOTTA SEE JANE R Dean Taylor ●	*Tamla Motown*	1
-	37	D.W. WASHBURN Monkees	*RCA Victor*	1
-	38	FIRE Crazy World Of Arthur Brown ●	*Track*	1
-	39	I'LL LOVE YOU FOREVER TODAY Cliff Richard	*Columbia*	1
-	40	DOGS Who	*Track*	1

LW	TW	WEEK ENDING 3 JULY 1968		Wks
3	[1]	BABY COME BACK Equals	*President*	8
7	[2]	SON OF HICKORY HOLLER'S TRAMP OC Smith	*CBS*	5
1	3	JUMPING JACK FLASH Rolling Stones	*Decca*	6
4	[4]	HURDY GURDY MAN Donovan	*Pye*	6
6	5	I PRETEND Des O'Connor	*Columbia*	7
9	[6]	LOVIN' THINGS Marmalade	*CBS*	5
5	7	BLUE EYES Don Partridge	*Columbia*	6
16	8	YESTERDAY HAS GONE Cupid's Inspiration	*Nems*	3
11	9	MY NAME IS JACK Manfred Mann	*Fontana*	3
2	10	YOUNG GIRL Union Gap	*CBS*	11
12	11	YUMMY YUMMY YUMMY Ohio Express	*Pye*	4
18	12	HUSH NOT A WORD TO MARY John Rowles	*MCA*	3
8	13	THIS WHEEL'S ON FIRE Julie Driscoll, Brian Auger and the Trinity	*Marmalade*	11
26	14	MONY MONY Tommy James and the Shondells	*Major Minor*	4
21	15	ONE MORE DANCE Esther and Abi Ofarim	*Philips*	2
10	16	HONEY Bobby Goldsboro	*United Artists*	11
13	17	DO YOU KNOW THE WAY TO SAN JOSE Dionne Warwick	*Pye*	8
15	18	BOY Lulu	*Columbia*	5
35	19	MACARTHUR PARK Richard Harris	*RCA Victor*	2
37	20	D.W. WASHBURN Monkees	*RCA Victor*	2
17	21	RAINBOW VALLEY Love Affair	*CBS*	10
20	22	WHAT A WONDERFUL WORLD/CABARET Louis Armstrong	*HMV*	21
19	23	JOANNA Scott Walker	*Philips*	10
23	24	TIME FOR LIVING Association	*Warner Bros*	7
14	25	A MAN WITHOUT LOVE Engelbert Humperdinck	*Decca*	11
40	26	DOGS Who	*Track*	2
39	[27]	I'LL LOVE YOU FOREVER TODAY Cliff Richard	*Columbia*	2
24	28	HELULE HELULE Tremeloes	*CBS*	8
28	29	WHITE HORSES Jacky	*Philips*	12
38	30	FIRE Crazy World Of Arthur Brown	*Track*	2
36	31	GOTTA SEE JANE R Dean Taylor	*Tamla Motown*	2
-	32	KEEP ON Bruce Channel	*Bell*	1
-	33	WHERE WILL YOU BE Sue Nicholls ●	*Pye*	1
-	[34]	SOME THINGS YOU NEVER GET USED TO Diana Ross and the Supremes	*Tamla Motown*	1
-	35	AIN'T NOTHING LIKE THE REAL THING Marvin Gaye and Tammi Terrell	*Tamla Motown*	2
30	36	WHEN WE WERE YOUNG Solomon King	*Columbia*	9
31	37	TRIBUTE TO A KING William Bell	*Stax*	5
27	38	IF I ONLY HAD TIME John Rowles	*MCA*	17
22	39	I DON'T WANT OUR LOVING TO DIE Herd	*Fontana*	12
-	40	QUANDO M'INNAMORO Sandpipers	*A&M*	4

LW	TW	WEEK ENDING 10 JULY 1968		Wks
1	[1]	BABY COME BACK Equals	*President*	9
2	[2]	SON OF HICKORY HOLLER'S TRAMP OC Smith	*CBS*	6
5	3	I PRETEND Des O'Connor	*Columbia*	8

In these weeks ■ R Dean Taylor is the first white act to chart on the Tamla Motown label (26.06.68) ■ OC Smith becomes the highest placed Smith in chart history, overtaking Muriel Smith's 1953 chart peak of number three and Whistling Jack Smith's more recent 1967 number five placing (03.07.68) ■ Bruce Channel's second hit comes six years after his first. There never is a third hit (03.07.68)■

July 1968

□ Highest position disc reached ● Act's first ever week on chart

LW	TW	Title	Artist	Label	Wks
8	[4]	YESTERDAY HAS GONE	Cupid's Inspiration	Nems	4
3	5	JUMPING JACK FLASH	Rolling Stones	Decca	7
4	6	HURDY GURDY MAN	Donovan	Pye	7
6	7	LOVIN' THINGS	Marmalade	CBS	6
9	[8]	MY NAME IS JACK	Manfred Mann	Fontana	4
11	9	YUMMY YUMMY YUMMY	Ohio Express	Pye	5
7	10	BLUE EYES	Don Partridge	Columbia	7
14	11	MONY MONY	Tommy James and the Shondells	Major Minor	5
19	12	MACARTHUR PARK	Richard Harris	RCA Victor	3
10	13	YOUNG GIRL	Union Gap	CBS	12
12	14	HUSH NOT A WORD TO MARY	John Rowles	MCA	4
15	15	ONE MORE DANCE	Esther and Abi Ofarim	Philips	3
13	16	THIS WHEEL'S ON FIRE	Julie Driscoll, Brian Auger and the Trinity	Marmalade	12
20	[17]	D.W. WASHBURN	Monkees	RCA Victor	3
30	18	FIRE	Crazy World Of Arthur Brown	Track	3
17	19	DO YOU KNOW THE WAY TO SAN JOSE	Dionne Warwick	Pye	9
16	20	HONEY	Bobby Goldsboro	United Artists	12
25	21	A MAN WITHOUT LOVE	Engelbert Humperdinck	Decca	12
32	22	KEEP ON	Bruce Channel	Bell	2
31	23	GOTTA SEE JANE	R Dean Taylor	Tamla Motown	3
33	24	WHERE WILL YOU BE	Sue Nicholls	Pye	2
26	[25]	DOGS	Who	Track	3
18	26	BOY	Lulu	Columbia	6
22	27	WHAT A WONDERFUL WORLD/CABARET	Louis Armstrong	HMV	22
-	28	THIS GUY'S IN LOVE WITH YOU	Herb Alpert	A&M	1
27	29	I'LL LOVE YOU FOREVER TODAY	Cliff Richard	Columbia	3
-	30	LAST NIGHT IN SOHO	Dave Dee, Dozy, Beaky Mick and Tich	Fontana	1
-	31	I CLOSE MY EYES AND COUNT TO TEN	Dusty Springfield	Philips	1
-	[32]	IMPORTANCE OF YOUR LOVE	Vince Hill	Columbia	1
23	33	JOANNA	Scott Walker	Philips	11
35	[34]	AIN'T NOTHING LIKE THE REAL THING	Marvin Gaye and Tammi Terrell	Tamla Motown	3
34	35	SOME THINGS YOU NEVER GET USED TO	Diana Ross and the Supremes	Tamla Motown	2
21	36	RAINBOW VALLEY	Love Affair	CBS	11
-	37	UNIVERSAL	Small Faces	Immediate	1
-	[38]	SMOKEY BLUES AWAY	New Generation ●	Spark	1
-	39	THINK	Aretha Franklin	Atlantic	7
-	40	AMERICA	Nice ●	Immediate	1

WEEK ENDING 17 JULY 1968

LW	TW	Title	Artist	Label	Wks
1	[1]	BABY COME BACK	Equals	President	10
2	[2]	SON OF HICKORY HOLLER'S TRAMP	OC Smith	CBS	7
3	3	I PRETEND	Des O'Connor	Columbia	9
4	[4]	YESTERDAY HAS GONE	Cupid's Inspiration	Nems	5
9	[5]	YUMMY YUMMY YUMMY	Ohio Express	Pye	6
11	6	MONY MONY	Tommy James and the Shondells	Major Minor	6
12	7	MACARTHUR PARK	Richard Harris	RCA Victor	4
18	8	FIRE	Crazy World Of Arthur Brown	Track	4
5	9	JUMPING JACK FLASH	Rolling Stones	Decca	8
8	10	MY NAME IS JACK	Manfred Mann	Fontana	5
10	11	BLUE EYES	Don Partridge	Columbia	8
14	[12]	HUSH NOT A WORD TO MARY	John Rowles	MCA	5
15	[13]	ONE MORE DANCE	Esther and Abi Ofarim	Philips	4
7	14	LOVIN' THINGS	Marmalade	CBS	7
13	15	YOUNG GIRL	Union Gap	CBS	13
28	16	THIS GUY'S IN LOVE WITH YOU	Herb Alpert	A&M	2
-	17	MRS ROBINSON	Simon and Garfunkel	CBS	1
23	18	GOTTA SEE JANE	R Dean Taylor	Tamla Motown	4
24	19	WHERE WILL YOU BE	Sue Nicholls	Pye	3
6	20	HURDY GURDY MAN	Donovan	Pye	8
17	21	D.W. WASHBURN	Monkees	RCA Victor	4
31	22	I CLOSE MY EYES AND COUNT TO TEN	Dusty Springfield	Philips	2
37	23	UNIVERSAL	Small Faces	Immediate	2
30	24	LAST NIGHT IN SOHO	Dave Dee, Dozy, Beaky Mick and Tich	Fontana	2
20	25	HONEY	Bobby Goldsboro	United Artists	13
16	26	THIS WHEEL'S ON FIRE	Julie Driscoll, Brian Auger and the Trinity	Marmalade	13
-	27	DANCE TO THE MUSIC	Sly and the Family Stone ●	Direction	1
-	28	HELP YOURSELF	Tom Jones	Decca	1
22	29	KEEP ON	Bruce Channel	Bell	3
29	30	I'LL LOVE YOU FOREVER TODAY	Cliff Richard	Columbia	4
-	31	HERE COMES THE JUDGE	Pigmeat Markham ●	Chess	1
32	[32]	IMPORTANCE OF YOUR LOVE	Vince Hill	Columbia	2
21	33	A MAN WITHOUT LOVE	Engelbert Humperdinck	Decca	13
27	34	WHAT A WONDERFUL WORLD/CABARET	Louis Armstrong	HMV	23
35	35	SOME THINGS YOU NEVER GET USED TO	Diana Ross and the Supremes	Tamla Motown	3
40	36	AMERICA	Nice	Immediate	2
19	37	DO YOU KNOW THE WAY TO SAN JOSE	Dionne Warwick	Pye	10
-	38	HERE COMES THE JUDGE	Shorty Long ●	Tamla Motown	1
26	39	BOY	Lulu	Columbia	7
25	40	DOGS	Who	Track	4

WEEK ENDING 24 JULY 1968

LW	TW	Title	Artist	Label	Wks
3	[1]	I PRETEND	Des O'Connor	Columbia	10
6	2	MONY MONY	Tommy James and the Shondells	Major Minor	7
1	3	BABY COME BACK	Equals	President	11
7	4	MACARTHUR PARK	Richard Harris	RCA Victor	5
5	[5]	YUMMY YUMMY YUMMY	Ohio Express	Pye	7
2	6	SON OF HICKORY HOLLER'S TRAMP	OC Smith	CBS	8
4	7	YESTERDAY HAS GONE	Cupid's Inspiration	Nems	6
8	8	FIRE	Crazy World Of Arthur Brown	Track	5
16	9	THIS GUY'S IN LOVE WITH YOU	Herb Alpert	A&M	3
17	10	MRS ROBINSON	Simon and Garfunkel	CBS	2
22	11	I CLOSE MY EYES AND COUNT TO TEN	Dusty Springfield	Philips	3
24	12	LAST NIGHT IN SOHO	Dave Dee, Dozy, Beaky Mick and Tich	Fontana	3
10	13	MY NAME IS JACK	Manfred Mann	Fontana	6
12	14	HUSH NOT A WORD TO MARY	John Rowles	MCA	6
13	15	ONE MORE DANCE	Esther and Abi Ofarim	Philips	5
11	16	BLUE EYES	Don Partridge	Columbia	9
19	[17]	WHERE WILL YOU BE	Sue Nicholls	Pye	4
23	18	UNIVERSAL	Small Faces	Immediate	3
9	19	JUMPING JACK FLASH	Rolling Stones	Decca	9
18	20	GOTTA SEE JANE	R Dean Taylor	Tamla Motown	5
29	21	KEEP ON	Bruce Channel	Bell	4
28	22	HELP YOURSELF	Tom Jones	Decca	2
27	23	DANCE TO THE MUSIC	Sly and the Family Stone	Direction	2
20	24	HURDY GURDY MAN	Donovan	Pye	9
15	25	YOUNG GIRL	Union Gap	CBS	14
14	26	LOVIN' THINGS	Marmalade	CBS	8
21	27	D.W. WASHBURN	Monkees	RCA Victor	5
31	28	HERE COMES THE JUDGE	Pigmeat Markham	Chess	2
-	29	SUNSHINE GIRL	Herman's Hermits	Columbia	1
30	30	I'LL LOVE YOU FOREVER TODAY	Cliff Richard	Columbia	5
36	31	AMERICA	Nice	Immediate	3
38	32	HERE COMES THE JUDGE	Shorty Long	Tamla Motown	2
34	33	WHAT A WONDERFUL WORLD/CABARET	Louis Armstrong	HMV	24
-	34	DAYS	Kinks	Pye	1
32	35	IMPORTANCE OF YOUR LOVE	Vince Hill	Columbia	3
35	36	SOME THINGS YOU NEVER GET USED TO	Diana Ross and the Supremes	Tamla Motown	4
-	37	AIN'T NOTHING LIKE THE REAL THING	Marvin Gaye and Tammi Terrell	Tamla Motown	4
25	38	HONEY	Bobby Goldsboro	United Artists	14
26	39	THIS WHEEL'S ON FIRE	Julie Driscoll, Brian Auger and the Trinity	Marmalade	14
-	40	ANGEL OF THE MORNING	PP Arnold	Immediate	1

■ *Dogs* by the Who and *Boy* by Lulu spend two weeks in consecutive positions. They are two of the shortest title and artist combinations (only seven letters each) ever to chart (17.07.68) ■ The song that did more to change film music than possibly any other, *Mrs. Robinson* by Simon and Garfunkel, graduates to the Top Ten (24.07.68) ■

July 1968

□ Highest position disc reached ● Act's first ever week on chart

LW	TW	*WEEK ENDING* 31 JULY 1968			Wks
2	1	MONY MONY	Tommy James and the Shondells	*Major Minor*	8
1	2	I PRETEND	Des O'Connor	*Columbia*	11
8	3	FIRE	Crazy World Of Arthur Brown	*Track*	6
4	4	MACARTHUR PARK	Richard Harris	*RCA Victor*	6
10	5	MRS ROBINSON	Simon and Garfunkel	*CBS*	3
3	6	BABY COME BACK	Equals	*President*	12
11	7	I CLOSE MY EYES AND COUNT TO TEN	Dusty Springfield	*Philips*	4
12	8	LAST NIGHT IN SOHO	Dave Dee, Dozy, Beaky Mick and Tich	*Fontana*	4
6	9	SON OF HICKORY HOLLER'S TRAMP	OC Smith	*CBS*	9
5	10	YUMMY YUMMY YUMMY	Ohio Express	*Pye*	8
9	11	THIS GUY'S IN LOVE WITH YOU	Herb Alpert	*A&M*	4
22	12	HELP YOURSELF	Tom Jones	*Decca*	3
7	13	YESTERDAY HAS GONE	Cupid's Inspiration	*Nems*	7
23	14	DANCE TO THE MUSIC	Sly and the Family Stone	*Direction*	3
29	15	SUNSHINE GIRL	Herman's Hermits	*Columbia*	2
18	16	UNIVERSAL	Small Faces	*Immediate*	4
20	17	GOTTA SEE JANE	R Dean Taylor	*Tamla Motown*	6
21	18	KEEP ON	Bruce Channel	*Bell*	5
34	19	DAYS	Kinks	*Pye*	2
28	20	HERE COMES THE JUDGE	Pigmeat Markham	*Chess*	3
13	21	MY NAME IS JACK	Manfred Mann	*Fontana*	7
17	22	WHERE WILL YOU BE	Sue Nicholls	*Pye*	5
15	23	ONE MORE DANCE	Esther and Abi Ofarim	*Philips*	6
14	24	HUSH NOT A WORD TO MARY	John Rowles	*MCA*	7
16	25	BLUE EYES	Don Partridge	*Columbia*	10
-	26	DO IT AGAIN	Beach Boys	*Capitol*	1
26	27	LOVIN' THINGS	Marmalade	*CBS*	9
19	28	JUMPING JACK FLASH	Rolling Stones	*Decca*	10
25	29	YOUNG GIRL	Union Gap	*CBS*	15
32	30	HERE COMES THE JUDGE	Shorty Long	*Tamla Motown*	3
24	31	HURDY GURDY MAN	Donovan	*Pye*	10
27	32	D.W. WASHBURN	Monkees	*RCA Victor*	6
31	33	AMERICA	Nice	*Immediate*	4
35	34	IMPORTANCE OF YOUR LOVE	Vince Hill	*Columbia*	4
30	35	I'LL LOVE YOU FOREVER TODAY	Cliff Richard	*Columbia*	6
40	36	ANGEL OF THE MORNING	PP Arnold	*Immediate*	2
-	37	ON THE ROAD AGAIN	Canned Heat ●	*Liberty*	1
-	38	BEGGIN'	Time Box ●	*Deram*	1
-	39	WALK ON	Roy Orbison	*London*	1
-	40	YOUR TIME HASN'T COME YET BABY	Elvis Presley	*RCA*	1

LW	TW	*WEEK ENDING* 7 AUGUST 1968			Wks
1	1	MONY MONY	Tommy James and the Shondells	*Major Minor*	9
3	2	FIRE	Crazy World Of Arthur Brown	*Track*	7
2	3	I PRETEND	Des O'Connor	*Columbia*	12
5	4	MRS ROBINSON	Simon and Garfunkel	*CBS*	4
11	5	THIS GUY'S IN LOVE WITH YOU	Herb Alpert	*A&M*	5
7	6	I CLOSE MY EYES AND COUNT TO TEN	Dusty Springfield	*Philips*	5
12	7	HELP YOURSELF	Tom Jones	*Decca*	4
4	8	MACARTHUR PARK	Richard Harris	*RCA Victor*	7
8	9	LAST NIGHT IN SOHO	Dave Dee, Dozy, Beaky Mick and Tich	*Fontana*	5
15	10	SUNSHINE GIRL	Herman's Hermits	*Columbia*	3
6	11	BABY COME BACK	Equals	*President*	13
14	12	DANCE TO THE MUSIC	Sly and the Family Stone	*Direction*	4
10	13	YUMMY YUMMY YUMMY	Ohio Express	*Pye*	9
18	14	KEEP ON	Bruce Channel	*Bell*	6
19	15	DAYS	Kinks	*Pye*	3
9	16	SON OF HICKORY HOLLER'S TRAMP	OC Smith	*CBS*	10
26	17	DO IT AGAIN	Beach Boys	*Capitol*	2
16	18	UNIVERSAL	Small Faces	*Immediate*	5
20	19	HERE COMES THE JUDGE	Pigmeat Markham	*Chess*	4
13	20	YESTERDAY HAS GONE	Cupid's Inspiration	*Nems*	8
17	21	GOTTA SEE JANE	R Dean Taylor	*Tamla Motown*	7
22	22	WHERE WILL YOU BE	Sue Nicholls	*Pye*	6
-	23	HIGH IN THE SKY	Amen Corner	*Deram*	1
24	24	HUSH NOT A WORD TO MARY	John Rowles	*MCA*	8
23	25	ONE MORE DANCE	Esther and Abi Ofarim	*Philips*	7
21	26	MY NAME IS JACK	Manfred Mann	*Fontana*	8
-	27	I'VE GOTTA GET A MESSAGE TO YOU	Bee Gees	*Polydor*	1
40	28	YOUR TIME HASN'T COME YET BABY	Elvis Presley	*RCA*	2
37	29	ON THE ROAD AGAIN	Canned Heat	*Liberty*	2
36	30	ANGEL OF THE MORNING	PP Arnold	*Immediate*	3
-	31	HARD TO HANDLE	Otis Redding	*Atlantic*	1
30	32	HERE COMES THE JUDGE	Shorty Long	*Tamla Motown*	4
29	33	YOUNG GIRL	Union Gap	*CBS*	16
33	34	AMERICA	Nice	*Immediate*	5
27	35	LOVIN' THINGS	Marmalade	*CBS*	10
-	36	ELEANOR RIGBY	Ray Charles	*Stateside*	1
-	37	I SAY A LITTLE PRAYER	Aretha Franklin	*Atlantic*	1
25	38	BLUE EYES	Don Partridge	*Columbia*	11
28	39	JUMPING JACK FLASH	Rolling Stones	*Decca*	11
34	40	IMPORTANCE OF YOUR LOVE	Vince Hill	*Columbia*	5

LW	TW	*WEEK ENDING* 14 AUGUST 1968			Wks
2	1	FIRE	Crazy World Of Arthur Brown	*Track*	8
1	2	MONY MONY	Tommy James and the Shondells	*Major Minor*	10
5	3	THIS GUY'S IN LOVE WITH YOU	Herb Alpert	*A&M*	6
6	4	I CLOSE MY EYES AND COUNT TO TEN	Dusty Springfield	*Philips*	6
3	5	I PRETEND	Des O'Connor	*Columbia*	13
4	6	MRS ROBINSON	Simon and Garfunkel	*CBS*	5
12	7	DANCE TO THE MUSIC	Sly and the Family Stone	*Direction*	5
10	8	SUNSHINE GIRL	Herman's Hermits	*Columbia*	4
7	9	HELP YOURSELF	Tom Jones	*Decca*	5
9	10	LAST NIGHT IN SOHO	Dave Dee, Dozy, Beaky Mick and Tich	*Fontana*	6
17	11	DO IT AGAIN	Beach Boys	*Capitol*	3
15	12	DAYS	Kinks	*Pye*	4
27	13	I'VE GOTTA GET A MESSAGE TO YOU	Bee Gees	*Polydor*	2
14	14	KEEP ON	Bruce Channel	*Bell*	7
8	15	MACARTHUR PARK	Richard Harris	*RCA Victor*	8
11	16	BABY COME BACK	Equals	*President*	14
23	17	HIGH IN THE SKY	Amen Corner	*Deram*	2
13	18	YUMMY YUMMY YUMMY	Ohio Express	*Pye*	10
19	19	HERE COMES THE JUDGE	Pigmeat Markham	*Chess*	5
18	20	UNIVERSAL	Small Faces	*Immediate*	6
16	21	SON OF HICKORY HOLLER'S TRAMP	OC Smith	*CBS*	11
21	22	GOTTA SEE JANE	R Dean Taylor	*Tamla Motown*	8
28	23	YOUR TIME HASN'T COME YET BABY	Elvis Presley	*RCA*	3
31	24	HARD TO HANDLE	Otis Redding	*Atlantic*	2
26	25	MY NAME IS JACK	Manfred Mann	*Fontana*	9
37	26	I SAY A LITTLE PRAYER	Aretha Franklin	*Atlantic*	2
29	27	ON THE ROAD AGAIN	Canned Heat	*Liberty*	3
20	28	YESTERDAY HAS GONE	Cupid's Inspiration	*Nems*	9
30	29	ANGEL OF THE MORNING	PP Arnold	*Immediate*	4
25	30	ONE MORE DANCE	Esther and Abi Ofarim	*Philips*	8
24	31	HUSH NOT A WORD TO MARY	John Rowles	*MCA*	9
32	32	HERE COMES THE JUDGE	Shorty Long	*Tamla Motown*	5
33	33	AMERICA	Nice	*Immediate*	6
-	34	LADY WILLPOWER	Union Gap	*CBS*	1
22	35	WHERE WILL YOU BE	Sue Nicholls	*Pye*	7
-	36	VOICES IN THE SKY	Moody Blues	*Deram*	1
36	37	ELEANOR RIGBY	Ray Charles	*Stateside*	2
-	38	HOLD ME TIGHT	Johnny Nash ●	*Regal Zonophone*	1
-	39	NEED YOUR LOVE SO BAD	Fleetwood Mac	*Blue Horizon*	1
-	40	WALK ON	Roy Orbison	*London*	2

LW	TW	*WEEK ENDING* 21 AUGUST 1968			Wks
2	1	MONY MONY	Tommy James and the Shondells	*Major Minor*	11
1	2	FIRE	Crazy World Of Arthur Brown	*Track*	9
3	3	THIS GUY'S IN LOVE WITH YOU	Herb Alpert	*A&M*	7
11	4	DO IT AGAIN	Beach Boys	*Capitol*	4
9	5	HELP YOURSELF	Tom Jones	*Decca*	6

In these weeks ■ When the Small Faces' *Universal* peaks at number 16, it means at least one record has peaked at every position in the Top 40 during 1968 (31.07.68) ■ *Mony Mony* climbs back to number one, the first record to manage this since *Crying In The Chapel* and *I'm Alive* swapped places at number one for four consecutive weeks in the summer of 1965 (21.08.68)■

September 1968

□ Highest position disc reached ● Act's first ever week on chart

LW	TW	Title	Artist	Label	Wks
4	6	I CLOSE MY EYES AND COUNT TO TEN	Dusty Springfield	Philips	7
13	7	I'VE GOTTA GET A MESSAGE TO YOU	Bee Gees	Polydor	3
8	[8]	SUNSHINE GIRL	Herman's Hermits	Columbia	5
17	9	HIGH IN THE SKY	Amen Corner	Deram	3
7	10	DANCE TO THE MUSIC	Sly and the Family Stone	Direction	6
6	11	MRS ROBINSON	Simon and Garfunkel	CBS	6
5	12	I PRETEND	Des O'Connor	Columbia	14
14	13	KEEP ON	Bruce Channel	Bell	8
12	14	DAYS	Kinks	Pye	5
10	15	LAST NIGHT IN SOHO	Dave Dee, Dozy, Beaky Mick and Tich	Fontana	7
27	16	ON THE ROAD AGAIN	Canned Heat	Liberty	4
26	17	I SAY A LITTLE PRAYER	Aretha Franklin	Atlantic	3
18	18	YUMMY YUMMY YUMMY	Ohio Express	Pye	11
20	19	UNIVERSAL	Small Faces	Immediate	7
38	20	HOLD ME TIGHT	Johnny Nash	Regal Zonophone	2
16	21	BABY COME BACK	Equals	President	15
21	22	SON OF HICKORY HOLLER'S TRAMP	OC Smith	CBS	12
24	23	HARD TO HANDLE	Otis Redding	Atlantic	3
23	24	YOUR TIME HASN'T COME YET BABY	Elvis Presley	RCA	4
22	25	GOTTA SEE JANE	R Dean Taylor	Tamla Motown	9
19	26	HERE COMES THE JUDGE	Pigmeat Markham	Chess	6
15	27	MACARTHUR PARK	Richard Harris	RCA Victor	9
-	28	DREAM A LITTLE DREAM OF ME	Mama Cass ●	RCA	1
36	29	VOICES IN THE SKY	Moody Blues	Deram	2
34	30	LADY WILLPOWER	Union Gap	CBS	2
33	31	AMERICA	Nice	Immediate	7
39	32	NEED YOUR LOVE SO BAD	Fleetwood Mac	Blue Horizon	2
25	33	MY NAME IS JACK	Manfred Mann	Fontana	10
29	34	ANGEL OF THE MORNING	PP Arnold	Immediate	5
32	35	HERE COMES THE JUDGE	Shorty Long	Tamla Motown	6
-	36	DREAM A LITTLE DREAM OF ME	Anita Harris	CBS	1
28	37	YESTERDAY HAS GONE	Cupid's Inspiration	Nems	10
-	38	JESAMINE	Casuals ●	Decca	1
-	39	LAUREL AND HARDY	Equals	President	1
37	40	ELEANOR RIGBY	Ray Charles	Stateside	3

WEEK ENDING 28 AUGUST 1968

LW	TW	Title	Artist	Label	Wks
4	[1]	DO IT AGAIN	Beach Boys	Capitol	5
7	2	I'VE GOTTA GET A MESSAGE TO YOU	Bee Gees	Polydor	4
3	[3]	THIS GUY'S IN LOVE WITH YOU	Herb Alpert	A&M	8
1	4	MONY MONY	Tommy James and the Shondells	Major Minor	12
5	[5]	HELP YOURSELF	Tom Jones	Decca	7
2	6	FIRE	Crazy World Of Arthur Brown	Track	10
9	7	HIGH IN THE SKY	Amen Corner	Deram	4
17	8	I SAY A LITTLE PRAYER	Aretha Franklin	Atlantic	4
8	9	SUNSHINE GIRL	Herman's Hermits	Columbia	6
10	10	DANCE TO THE MUSIC	Sly and the Family Stone	Direction	7
20	11	HOLD ME TIGHT	Johnny Nash	Regal Zonophone	3
13	[12]	KEEP ON	Bruce Channel	Bell	9
6	13	I CLOSE MY EYES AND COUNT TO TEN	Dusty Springfield	Philips	8
12	14	I PRETEND	Des O'Connor	Columbia	15
14	15	DAYS	Kinks	Pye	6
16	16	ON THE ROAD AGAIN	Canned Heat	Liberty	5
11	17	MRS ROBINSON	Simon and Garfunkel	CBS	7
28	18	DREAM A LITTLE DREAM OF ME	Mama Cass	RCA	2
23	19	HARD TO HANDLE	Otis Redding	Atlantic	4
15	20	LAST NIGHT IN SOHO	Dave Dee, Dozy, Beaky Mick and Tich	Fontana	8
30	21	LADY WILLPOWER	Union Gap	CBS	3
24	[22]	YOUR TIME HASN'T COME YET BABY	Elvis Presley	RCA	5
19	23	UNIVERSAL	Small Faces	Immediate	8
38	24	JESAMINE	Casuals	Decca	2
31	25	AMERICA	Nice	Immediate	8
27	26	MACARTHUR PARK	Richard Harris	RCA Victor	10
22	27	SON OF HICKORY HOLLER'S TRAMP	OC Smith	CBS	13
29	28	VOICES IN THE SKY	Moody Blues	Deram	3
21	29	BABY COME BACK	Equals	President	16
26	30	HERE COMES THE JUDGE	Pigmeat Markham	Chess	7
-	31	LITTLE ARROWS	Leapy Lee ●	MCA	1
18	32	YUMMY YUMMY YUMMY	Ohio Express	Pye	12
-	33	ICE IN THE SUN	Status Quo	Pye	1
36	34	DREAM A LITTLE DREAM OF ME	Anita Harris	CBS	2
39	[35]	LAUREL AND HARDY	Equals	President	2
-	36	C'MON MARIANNE	Grapefruit	RCA	1
34	37	ANGEL OF THE MORNING	PP Arnold	Immediate	6
-	38	YESTERDAY'S DREAMS	Four Tops	Tamla Motown	1
25	39	GOTTA SEE JANE	R Dean Taylor	Tamla Motown	10
32	40	NEED YOUR LOVE SO BAD	Fleetwood Mac	Blue Horizon	3

WEEK ENDING 4 SEPTEMBER 1968

LW	TW	Title	Artist	Label	Wks
2	[1]	I'VE GOTTA GET A MESSAGE TO YOU	Bee Gees	Polydor	5
1	2	DO IT AGAIN	Beach Boys	Capitol	6
3	[3]	THIS GUY'S IN LOVE WITH YOU	Herb Alpert	A&M	9
8	[4]	I SAY A LITTLE PRAYER	Aretha Franklin	Atlantic	5
5	[5]	HELP YOURSELF	Tom Jones	Decca	8
7	[6]	HIGH IN THE SKY	Amen Corner	Deram	5
11	7	HOLD ME TIGHT	Johnny Nash	Regal Zonophone	4
6	8	FIRE	Crazy World Of Arthur Brown	Track	11
4	9	MONY MONY	Tommy James and the Shondells	Major Minor	13
16	10	ON THE ROAD AGAIN	Canned Heat	Liberty	6
9	11	SUNSHINE GIRL	Herman's Hermits	Columbia	7
12	[12]	KEEP ON	Bruce Channel	Bell	10
10	13	DANCE TO THE MUSIC	Sly and the Family Stone	Direction	8
18	14	DREAM A LITTLE DREAM OF ME	Mama Cass	RCA	3
21	15	LADY WILLPOWER	Union Gap	CBS	4
14	16	I PRETEND	Des O'Connor	Columbia	16
13	17	I CLOSE MY EYES AND COUNT TO TEN	Dusty Springfield	Philips	9
19	18	HARD TO HANDLE	Otis Redding	Atlantic	5
15	19	DAYS	Kinks	Pye	7
31	20	LITTLE ARROWS	Leapy Lee	MCA	2
-	21	HEY JUDE	Beatles	Apple	1
24	22	JESAMINE	Casuals	Decca	3
17	23	MRS ROBINSON	Simon and Garfunkel	CBS	8
22	24	YOUR TIME HASN'T COME YET BABY	Elvis Presley	RCA	6
20	25	LAST NIGHT IN SOHO	Dave Dee, Dozy, Beaky Mick and Tich	Fontana	9
33	26	ICE IN THE SUN	Status Quo	Pye	2
28	[27]	VOICES IN THE SKY	Moody Blues	Deram	4
25	28	AMERICA	Nice	Immediate	9
38	29	YESTERDAY'S DREAMS	Four Tops	Tamla Motown	2
23	30	UNIVERSAL	Small Faces	Immediate	9
-	31	CLASSICAL GAS	Mason Williams ●	Warner Bros	1
36	32	C'MON MARIANNE	Grapefruit	RCA	2
40	33	NEED YOUR LOVE SO BAD	Fleetwood Mac	Blue Horizon	4
-	34	I LIVE FOR THE SUN	Vanity Fare ●	Page One	1
26	35	MACARTHUR PARK	Richard Harris	RCA Victor	11
27	36	SON OF HICKORY HOLLER'S TRAMP	OC Smith	CBS	14
35	37	LAUREL AND HARDY	Equals	President	3
30	38	HERE COMES THE JUDGE	Pigmeat Markham	Chess	8
29	39	BABY COME BACK	Equals	President	17
-	40	ELEANOR RIGBY	Ray Charles	Stateside	4

WEEK ENDING 11 SEPTEMBER 1968

LW	TW	Title	Artist	Label	Wks
21	[1]	HEY JUDE	Beatles	Apple	2
1	2	I'VE GOTTA GET A MESSAGE TO YOU	Bee Gees	Polydor	6
2	3	DO IT AGAIN	Beach Boys	Capitol	7
4	[4]	I SAY A LITTLE PRAYER	Aretha Franklin	Atlantic	6
7	[5]	HOLD ME TIGHT	Johnny Nash	Regal Zonophone	5
3	6	THIS GUY'S IN LOVE WITH YOU	Herb Alpert	A&M	10
-	7	THOSE WERE THE DAYS	Mary Hopkin ●	Apple	1
5	8	HELP YOURSELF	Tom Jones	Decca	9
6	9	HIGH IN THE SKY	Amen Corner	Deram	6
10	10	ON THE ROAD AGAIN	Canned Heat	Liberty	7
14	[11]	DREAM A LITTLE DREAM OF ME	Mama Cass	RCA	4
22	12	JESAMINE	Casuals	Decca	4

■ Four weeks at number three for Herb Alpert's first vocal hit *This Guy's In Love With You* (04.09.68) ■ In the same week that *Hey Jude* makes what is then the second biggest leap to number one, Mary Hopkin's *These Were The Days* is the highest Top 40 entry of the year, making it a good week for Apple Records (11.09.68) ■

September 1968

□ Highest position disc reached ● Act's first ever week on chart

LW	TW	Title	Artist	Label	Wks
15	13	LADY WILLPOWER	Union Gap	CBS	5
9	14	MONY MONY	Tommy James and the Shondells	Major Minor	14
8	15	FIRE	Crazy World Of Arthur Brown	Track	12
11	16	SUNSHINE GIRL	Herman's Hermits	Columbia	8
20	17	LITTLE ARROWS	Leapy Lee	MCA	3
16	18	I PRETEND	Des O'Connor	Columbia	17
18	19	HARD TO HANDLE	Otis Redding	Atlantic	6
13	20	DANCE TO THE MUSIC	Sly and the Family Stone	Direction	9
12	21	KEEP ON	Bruce Channel	Bell	11
26	22	ICE IN THE SUN	Status Quo	Pye	3
17	23	I CLOSE MY EYES AND COUNT TO TEN	Dusty Springfield	Philips	10
19	24	DAYS	Kinks	Pye	8
31	25	CLASSICAL GAS	Mason Williams	Warner Bros	2
28	26	AMERICA	Nice	Immediate	10
27	[27]	VOICES IN THE SKY	Moody Blues	Deram	5
34	28	I LIVE FOR THE SUN	Vanity Fare	Page One	2
29	29	YESTERDAY'S DREAMS	Four Tops	Tamla Motown	3
23	30	MRS ROBINSON	Simon and Garfunkel	CBS	9
32	31	C'MON MARIANNE	Grapefruit	RCA	3
-	32	HELLO I LOVE YOU	Doors ●	Elektra	1
33	33	NEED YOUR LOVE SO BAD	Fleetwood Mac	Blue Horizon	5
24	34	YOUR TIME HASN'T COME YET BABY	Elvis Presley	RCA	7
25	35	LAST NIGHT IN SOHO	Dave Dee, Dozy, Beaky Mick and Tich	Fontana	10
-	36	DREAM A LITTLE DREAM OF ME	Anita Harris	CBS	3
-	37	WHEN THE SUN COMES SHINING THRU'	Long John Baldry	Pye	1
30	38	UNIVERSAL	Small Faces	Immediate	10
37	39	LAUREL AND HARDY	Equals	President	4
40	40	ELEANOR RIGBY	Ray Charles	Stateside	5

WEEK ENDING 18 SEPTEMBER 1968

LW	TW	Title	Artist	Label	Wks
1	[1]	HEY JUDE	Beatles	Apple	3
7	2	THOSE WERE THE DAYS	Mary Hopkin	Apple	2
2	3	I'VE GOTTA GET A MESSAGE TO YOU	Bee Gees	Polydor	7
4	[4]	I SAY A LITTLE PRAYER	Aretha Franklin	Atlantic	7
3	5	DO IT AGAIN	Beach Boys	Capitol	8
12	6	JESAMINE	Casuals	Decca	5
5	7	HOLD ME TIGHT	Johnny Nash	Regal Zonophone	6
10	[8]	ON THE ROAD AGAIN	Canned Heat	Liberty	8
13	9	LADY WILLPOWER	Union Gap	CBS	6
6	10	THIS GUY'S IN LOVE WITH YOU	Herb Alpert	A&M	11
9	11	HIGH IN THE SKY	Amen Corner	Deram	7
11	12	DREAM A LITTLE DREAM OF ME	Mama Cass	RCA	5
17	13	LITTLE ARROWS	Leapy Lee	MCA	4
8	14	HELP YOURSELF	Tom Jones	Decca	10
19	[15]	HARD TO HANDLE	Otis Redding	Atlantic	7
25	16	CLASSICAL GAS	Mason Williams	Warner Bros	3
22	17	ICE IN THE SUN	Status Quo	Pye	4
18	18	I PRETEND	Des O'Connor	Columbia	18
32	19	HELLO I LOVE YOU	Doors	Elektra	2
16	20	SUNSHINE GIRL	Herman's Hermits	Columbia	9
26	[21]	AMERICA	Nice	Immediate	11
15	22	FIRE	Crazy World Of Arthur Brown	Track	13
20	23	DANCE TO THE MUSIC	Sly and the Family Stone	Direction	10
21	24	KEEP ON	Bruce Channel	Bell	12
14	25	MONY MONY	Tommy James and the Shondells	Major Minor	15
28	26	I LIVE FOR THE SUN	Vanity Fare	Page One	3
29	27	YESTERDAY'S DREAMS	Four Tops	Tamla Motown	4
23	28	I CLOSE MY EYES AND COUNT TO TEN	Dusty Springfield	Philips	11
37	[29]	WHEN THE SUN COMES SHINING THRU'	Long John Baldry	Pye	2
-	30	ONE INCH ROCK	Tyrannosaurus Rex	Regal Zonophone	1
33	[31]	NEED YOUR LOVE SO BAD	Fleetwood Mac	Blue Horizon	6
27	32	VOICES IN THE SKY	Moody Blues	Deram	6
36	33	DREAM A LITTLE DREAM OF ME	Anita Harris	CBS	4
24	34	DAYS	Kinks	Pye	9
-	35	A DAY WITHOUT LOVE	Love Affair	CBS	1
-	36	THE GOOD, THE BAD AND THE UGLY	Hugo Montenegro ●	RCA	1
31	37	C'MON MARIANNE	Grapefruit	RCA	4
-	38	THE WEIGHT	Band ●	Capitol	1
-	39	RED BALLOON	Dave Clark Five	Columbia	1
-	40	I'M A MIDNIGHT MOVER	Wilson Pickett	Atlantic	1

WEEK ENDING 25 SEPTEMBER 1968

LW	TW	Title	Artist	Label	Wks
2	[1]	THOSE WERE THE DAYS	Mary Hopkin	Apple	3
1	2	HEY JUDE	Beatles	Apple	4
6	3	JESAMINE	Casuals	Decca	6
3	4	I'VE GOTTA GET A MESSAGE TO YOU	Bee Gees	Polydor	8
7	[5]	HOLD ME TIGHT	Johnny Nash	Regal Zonophone	7
4	6	I SAY A LITTLE PRAYER	Aretha Franklin	Atlantic	8
5	7	DO IT AGAIN	Beach Boys	Capitol	9
8	[8]	ON THE ROAD AGAIN	Canned Heat	Liberty	9
13	9	LITTLE ARROWS	Leapy Lee	MCA	5
9	10	LADY WILLPOWER	Union Gap	CBS	7
11	11	HIGH IN THE SKY	Amen Corner	Deram	8
16	12	CLASSICAL GAS	Mason Williams	Warner Bros	4
14	13	HELP YOURSELF	Tom Jones	Decca	11
12	14	DREAM A LITTLE DREAM OF ME	Mama Cass	RCA	6
10	15	THIS GUY'S IN LOVE WITH YOU	Herb Alpert	A&M	12
15	16	HARD TO HANDLE	Otis Redding	Atlantic	8
17	17	ICE IN THE SUN	Status Quo	Pye	5
19	18	HELLO I LOVE YOU	Doors	Elektra	3
39	19	RED BALLOON	Dave Clark Five	Columbia	2
26	[20]	I LIVE FOR THE SUN	Vanity Fare	Page One	4
18	21	I PRETEND	Des O'Connor	Columbia	19
35	22	A DAY WITHOUT LOVE	Love Affair	CBS	2
27	[23]	YESTERDAY'S DREAMS	Four Tops	Tamla Motown	5
38	24	THE WEIGHT	Band	Capitol	2
20	25	SUNSHINE GIRL	Herman's Hermits	Columbia	10
21	26	AMERICA	Nice	Immediate	12
-	27	MY LITTLE LADY	Tremeloes	CBS	1
30	[28]	ONE INCH ROCK	Tyrannosaurus Rex	Regal Zonophone	2
24	29	KEEP ON	Bruce Channel	Bell	13
-	30	LIGHT MY FIRE	Jose Feliciano ●	RCA	1
23	31	DANCE TO THE MUSIC	Sly and the Family Stone	Direction	11
25	32	MONY MONY	Tommy James and the Shondells	Major Minor	16
32	33	VOICES IN THE SKY	Moody Blues	Deram	7
28	34	I CLOSE MY EYES AND COUNT TO TEN	Dusty Springfield	Philips	12
22	35	FIRE	Crazy World Of Arthur Brown	Track	14
36	36	THE GOOD, THE BAD AND THE UGLY	Hugo Montenegro	RCA	2
-	37	LES BICYCLETTES DE BELSIZE	Engelbert Humperdinck	Decca	1
31	38	NEED YOUR LOVE SO BAD	Fleetwood Mac	Blue Horizon	7
29	39	WHEN THE SUN COMES SHINING THRU'	Long John Baldry	Pye	3
37	40	C'MON MARIANNE	Grapefruit	RCA	5

WEEK ENDING 2 OCTOBER 1968

LW	TW	Title	Artist	Label	Wks
1	[1]	THOSE WERE THE DAYS	Mary Hopkin	Apple	4
2	2	HEY JUDE	Beatles	Apple	5
3	3	JESAMINE	Casuals	Decca	7
9	4	LITTLE ARROWS	Leapy Lee	MCA	6
5	[5]	HOLD ME TIGHT	Johnny Nash	Regal Zonophone	8
4	6	I'VE GOTTA GET A MESSAGE TO YOU	Bee Gees	Polydor	9
10	7	LADY WILLPOWER	Union Gap	CBS	8
6	8	I SAY A LITTLE PRAYER	Aretha Franklin	Atlantic	9
19	9	RED BALLOON	Dave Clark Five	Columbia	3
11	10	HIGH IN THE SKY	Amen Corner	Deram	9
17	11	ICE IN THE SUN	Status Quo	Pye	6
7	12	DO IT AGAIN	Beach Boys	Capitol	10
12	13	CLASSICAL GAS	Mason Williams	Warner Bros	5
8	14	ON THE ROAD AGAIN	Canned Heat	Liberty	10
14	15	DREAM A LITTLE DREAM OF ME	Mama Cass	RCA	7

In these weeks ■ With *Hello I Love You* at number 18, José Feliciano debuts with his version of another Doors song, *Light My Fire* (25.09.68) ■ Mary Hopkins will be the last British female soloist to top the charts until Tina Charles in 1976 (25.09.68) ■ Lots of *Sun* and *Sky* in the charts, with four *Sun* records and two *Sky* hits, as well as two *Fires* to make it a very hot chart indeed (25.09.68) ■

LW	TW	Title	Artist	Label	Wks
18	16	HELLO I LOVE YOU	Doors	Elektra	4
22	17	A DAY WITHOUT LOVE	Love Affair	CBS	3
27	18	MY LITTLE LADY	Tremeloes	CBS	2
13	19	HELP YOURSELF	Tom Jones	Decca	12
16	20	HARD TO HANDLE	Otis Redding	Atlantic	9
15	21	THIS GUY'S IN LOVE WITH YOU	Herb Alpert	A&M	13
20	22	I LIVE FOR THE SUN	Vanity Fare	Page One	5
30	23	LIGHT MY FIRE	Jose Feliciano	RCA	2
24	24	THE WEIGHT	Band	Capitol	3
26	25	AMERICA	Nice	Immediate	13
21	26	I PRETEND	Des O'Connor	Columbia	20
36	27	THE GOOD, THE BAD AND THE UGLY	Hugo Montenegro	RCA	3
-	28	MARIANNE	Cliff Richard	Columbia	1
23	29	YESTERDAY'S DREAMS	Four Tops	Tamla Motown	6
25	30	SUNSHINE GIRL	Herman's Hermits	Columbia	11
28	31	ONE INCH ROCK	Tyrannosaurus Rex	Regal Zonophone	3
37	32	LES BICYCLETTES DE BELSIZE	Engelbert Humperdinck	Decca	2
-	33	LISTEN TO ME	Hollies	Parlophone	1
-	34	ONLY ONE WOMAN	Marbles ●	Polydor	1
29	35	KEEP ON	Bruce Channel	Bell	14
-	[36]	RED RED WINE	Jimmy James and the Vagabonds ●	Pye	1
31	37	DANCE TO THE MUSIC	Sly and the Family Stone	Direction	12
-	38	I'M A MIDNIGHT MOVER	Wilson Pickett	Atlantic	2
33	39	VOICES IN THE SKY	Moody Blues	Deram	8
-	40	YOU'RE ALL I NEED TO GET BY	Marvin Gaye and Tammi Terrell	Tamla Motown	1

WEEK ENDING 9 OCTOBER 1968

LW	TW	Title	Artist	Label	Wks
1	[1]	THOSE WERE THE DAYS	Mary Hopkin	Apple	5
4	[2]	LITTLE ARROWS	Leapy Lee	MCA	7
3	3	JESAMINE	Casuals	Decca	8
2	4	HEY JUDE	Beatles	Apple	6
7	[5]	LADY WILLPOWER	Union Gap	CBS	9
18	[6]	MY LITTLE LADY	Tremeloes	CBS	2
9	[7]	RED BALLOON	Dave Clark Five	Columbia	4
11	[8]	ICE IN THE SUN	Status Quo	Pye	7
13	[9]	CLASSICAL GAS	Mason Williams	Warner Bros	6
5	10	HOLD ME TIGHT	Johnny Nash	Regal Zonophone	9
17	11	A DAY WITHOUT LOVE	Love Affair	CBS	4
8	12	I SAY A LITTLE PRAYER	Aretha Franklin	Atlantic	10
6	13	I'VE GOTTA GET A MESSAGE TO YOU	Bee Gees	Polydor	10
32	14	LES BICYCLETTES DE BELSIZE	Engelbert Humperdinck	Decca	3
16	[15]	HELLO I LOVE YOU	Doors	Elektra	5
15	16	DREAM A LITTLE DREAM OF ME	Mama Cass	RCA	8
23	17	LIGHT MY FIRE	Jose Feliciano	RCA	3
10	18	HIGH IN THE SKY	Amen Corner	Deram	10
-	19	WRECK OF THE ANTOINETTE	Dave Dee, Dozy, Beaky, Mick and Tich	Fontana	1
12	20	DO IT AGAIN	Beach Boys	Capitol	11
27	21	THE GOOD, THE BAD AND THE UGLY	Hugo Montenegro	RCA	4
19	22	HELP YOURSELF	Tom Jones	Decca	13
33	23	LISTEN TO ME	Hollies	Parlophone	2
22	24	I LIVE FOR THE SUN	Vanity Fare	Page One	6
14	25	ON THE ROAD AGAIN	Canned Heat	Liberty	11
34	26	ONLY ONE WOMAN	Marbles	Polydor	2
28	27	MARIANNE	Cliff Richard	Columbia	2
20	28	HARD TO HANDLE	Otis Redding	Atlantic	10
24	29	THE WEIGHT	Band	Capitol	4
21	30	THIS GUY'S IN LOVE WITH YOU	Herb Alpert	A&M	14
26	31	I PRETEND	Des O'Connor	Columbia	21
29	32	YESTERDAY'S DREAMS	Four Tops	Tamla Motown	7
25	33	AMERICA	Nice	Immediate	14
-	34	M'LADY	Sly and the Family Stone	Direction	1
30	35	SUNSHINE GIRL	Herman's Hermits	Columbia	12
31	36	ONE INCH ROCK	Tyrannosaurus Rex	Regal Zonophone	4
33	37	DANCE TO THE MUSIC	Sly and the Family Stone	Direction	13
-	38	WITH A LITTLE HELP FROM MY FRIENDS	Joe Cocker ●	Regal Zonophone	1
-	39	MY WORLD	Cupid's Inspiration	Nems	1
-	40	SUNSHINE OF YOUR LOVE	Cream	Polydor	1

October 1968

□ Highest position disc reached ● Act's first ever week on chart

WEEK ENDING 16 OCTOBER 1968

LW	TW	Title	Artist	Label	Wks
1	[1]	THOSE WERE THE DAYS	Mary Hopkin	Apple	6
3	[2]	JESAMINE	Casuals	Decca	9
4	3	HEY JUDE	Beatles	Apple	7
2	4	LITTLE ARROWS	Leapy Lee	MCA	8
5	[5]	LADY WILLPOWER	Union Gap	CBS	10
6	[6]	MY LITTLE LADY	Tremeloes	CBS	3
14	7	LES BICYCLETTES DE BELSIZE	Engelbert Humperdinck	Decca	4
7	8	RED BALLOON	Dave Clark Five	Columbia	5
11	9	A DAY WITHOUT LOVE	Love Affair	CBS	5
17	10	LIGHT MY FIRE	Jose Feliciano	RCA	4
9	11	CLASSICAL GAS	Mason Williams	Warner Bros	7
21	12	THE GOOD, THE BAD AND THE UGLY	Hugo Montenegro	RCA	5
23	13	LISTEN TO ME	Hollies	Parlophone	3
8	14	ICE IN THE SUN	Status Quo	Pye	8
10	15	HOLD ME TIGHT	Johnny Nash	Regal Zonophone	10
13	16	I'VE GOTTA GET A MESSAGE TO YOU	Bee Gees	Polydor	11
26	17	ONLY ONE WOMAN	Marbles	Polydor	3
19	18	WRECK OF THE ANTOINETTE	Dave Dee, Dozy, Beaky, Mick and Tich	Fontana	2
15	19	HELLO I LOVE YOU	Doors	Elektra	6
38	20	WITH A LITTLE HELP FROM MY FRIENDS	Joe Cocker	Regal Zonophone	2
12	21	I SAY A LITTLE PRAYER	Aretha Franklin	Atlantic	11
29	22	THE WEIGHT	Band	Capitol	5
20	23	DO IT AGAIN	Beach Boys	Capitol	12
22	24	HELP YOURSELF	Tom Jones	Decca	14
16	25	DREAM A LITTLE DREAM OF ME	Mama Cass	RCA	9
18	26	HIGH IN THE SKY	Amen Corner	Deram	11
24	27	I LIVE FOR THE SUN	Vanity Fare	Page One	7
25	28	ON THE ROAD AGAIN	Canned Heat	Liberty	12
27	29	MARIANNE	Cliff Richard	Columbia	3
-	30	YOU'RE ALL I NEED TO GET BY	Marvin Gaye and Tammi Terrell	Tamla Motown	2
28	31	HARD TO HANDLE	Otis Redding	Atlantic	11
34	[32]	M'LADY	Sly and the Family Stone	Direction	2
40	33	SUNSHINE OF YOUR LOVE	Cream	Polydor	2
31	34	I PRETEND	Des O'Connor	Columbia	22
39	35	MY WORLD	Cupid's Inspiration	Nems	2
32	36	YESTERDAY'S DREAMS	Four Tops	Tamla Motown	8
-	37	I WANT YOU TO BE MY BABY	Billie Davis	Decca	1
-	38	RED RED WINE	Jimmy James and the Vagabonds	Pye	2
33	39	AMERICA	Nice	Immediate	15
-	40	BREAKING DOWN THE WALLS OF HEARTACHE	Bandwagon ●	Direction	1

WEEK ENDING 23 OCTOBER 1968

LW	TW	Title	Artist	Label	Wks
1	[1]	THOSE WERE THE DAYS	Mary Hopkin	Apple	7
3	2	HEY JUDE	Beatles	Apple	8
2	3	JESAMINE	Casuals	Decca	10
4	4	LITTLE ARROWS	Leapy Lee	MCA	9
7	[5]	LES BICYCLETTES DE BELSIZE	Engelbert Humperdinck	Decca	5
9	[6]	A DAY WITHOUT LOVE	Love Affair	CBS	6
12	7	THE GOOD, THE BAD AND THE UGLY	Hugo Montenegro	RCA	6
6	8	MY LITTLE LADY	Tremeloes	CBS	4
5	9	LADY WILLPOWER	Union Gap	CBS	11
10	10	LIGHT MY FIRE	Jose Feliciano	RCA	5
13	[11]	LISTEN TO ME	Hollies	Parlophone	4
17	12	ONLY ONE WOMAN	Marbles	Polydor	4
20	13	WITH A LITTLE HELP FROM MY FRIENDS	Joe Cocker	Regal Zonophone	3
8	14	RED BALLOON	Dave Clark Five	Columbia	6
11	15	CLASSICAL GAS	Mason Williams	Warner Bros	8

■Seven of the Top Ten records are at their chart peak (09.10.68) ■ Jimmy James and the Vagabonds achieve their only hit of the Sixties with a Neil Diamond song that UB40 will take to number one in 1983 (02.10.68) ■ Joe Cocker becomes the third act to hit the Top 40 with the Lennon and McCartney composed *With A Little Help From My Friends*, and will go on to be the first of two to top the charts with the song (09.10.68)■

October 1968

□ Highest position disc reached ● Act's first ever week on chart

LW	TW	Title / Artist	Label	Wks
15	16	HOLD ME TIGHT Johnny Nash	Regal Zonophone	11
18	17	WRECK OF THE ANTOINETTE Dave Dee, Dozy, Beaky, Mick and Tich	Fontana	3
14	18	ICE IN THE SUN Status Quo	Pye	9
19	19	HELLO I LOVE YOU Doors	Elektra	7
16	20	I GOTTA GET A MESSAGE TO YOU Bee Gees	Polydor	12
22	21	THE WEIGHT Band	Capitol	6
29	22	MARIANNE Cliff Richard	Columbia	4
21	23	I SAY A LITTLE PRAYER Aretha Franklin	Atlantic	12
40	24	BREAKING DOWN THE WALLS OF HEARTACHE Bandwagon	Direction	2
33	25	SUNSHINE OF YOUR LOVE Cream	Polydor	3
30	26	YOU'RE ALL I NEED TO GET BY Marvin Gaye and Tammi Terrell	Tamla Motown	3
24	27	HELP YOURSELF Tom Jones	Decca	15
28	28	ON THE ROAD AGAIN Canned Heat	Liberty	13
25	29	DREAM A LITTLE DREAM OF ME Mama Cass	RCA	10
23	30	DO IT AGAIN Beach Boys	Capitol	13
-	31	THIS OLD HEART OF MINE Isley Brothers ●	Tamla Motown	1
-	32	HARPER VALLEY PTA Jeannie C Riley ●	Polydor	1
35	33	MY WORLD Cupid's Inspiration	Nems	3
-	34	ELOISE Barry Ryan ●	MGM	1
32	35	M'LADY Sly and the Family Stone	Direction	3
38	36	RED RED WINE Jimmy James and the Vagabonds	Pye	3
-	37	MEXICO Long John Baldry	Pye	1
-	38	RUDI'S IN LOVE Locomotive ●	Parlophone	1
-	39	WAIT FOR ME MARY-ANNE Marmalade	CBS	1
37	40	I WANT YOU TO BE MY BABY Billie Davis	Decca	2

LW	TW	*WEEK ENDING* 30 OCTOBER 1968		Wks
1	1	THOSE WERE THE DAYS Mary Hopkin	Apple	8
13	2	WITH A LITTLE HELP FROM MY FRIENDS Joe Cocker	Regal Zonophone	4
7	3	THE GOOD, THE BAD AND THE UGLY Hugo Montenegro	RCA	7
4	4	LITTLE ARROWS Leapy Lee	MCA	10
12	5	ONLY ONE WOMAN Marbles	Polydor	5
10	6	LIGHT MY FIRE Jose Feliciano	RCA	6
2	7	HEY JUDE Beatles	Apple	9
3	8	JESAMINE Casuals	Decca	11
5	9	LES BICYCLETTES DE BELSIZE Engelbert Humperdinck	Decca	6
8	10	MY LITTLE LADY Tremeloes	CBS	5
6	11	A DAY WITHOUT LOVE Love Affair	CBS	7
11	12	LISTEN TO ME Hollies	Parlophone	5
14	13	RED BALLOON Dave Clark Five	Columbia	7
17	14	WRECK OF THE ANTOINETTE Dave Dee, Dozy, Beaky, Mick and Tich	Fontana	4
9	15	LADY WILLPOWER Union Gap	CBS	12
34	16	ELOISE Barry Ryan	MGM	2
15	17	CLASSICAL GAS Mason Williams	Warner Bros	9
-	18	ALL ALONG THE WATCHTOWER Jimi Hendrix Experience	Track	1
31	19	THIS OLD HEART OF MINE Isley Brothers	Tamla Motown	2
24	20	BREAKING DOWN THE WALLS OF HEARTACHE Bandwagon	Direction	3
37	21	MEXICO Long John Baldry	Pye	2
16	22	HOLD ME TIGHT Johnny Nash	Regal Zonophone	12
26	23	YOU'RE ALL I NEED TO GET BY Marvin Gaye and Tammi Terrell	Tamla Motown	4
22	24	MARIANNE Cliff Richard	Columbia	5
18	25	ICE IN THE SUN Status Quo	Pye	10
19	26	HELLO I LOVE YOU Doors	Elektra	8
32	27	HARPER VALLEY PTA Jeannie C Riley	Polydor	2
25	28	SUNSHINE OF YOUR LOVE Cream	Polydor	4
-	29	MAGIC BUS Who	Track	1
39	30	WAIT FOR ME MARY-ANNE Marmalade	CBS	2
21	31	THE WEIGHT Band	Capitol	7
23	32	I SAY A LITTLE PRAYER Aretha Franklin	Atlantic	13
38	33	RUDI'S IN LOVE Locomotive	Parlophone	2
-	34	IF I KNEW THEN WHAT I KNOW NOW Val Doonican	Pye	1
-	35	AIN'T GOT NO-I GOT LIFE/DO WHAT YOU GOTTA DO Nina Simone ●	RCA	1
27	36	HELP YOURSELF Tom Jones	Decca	16
-	37	AN OLYMPIC RECORD Barron Knights	Columbia	1
20	38	I GOTTA GET A MESSAGE TO YOU Bee Gees	Polydor	13
40	39	I WANT YOU TO BE MY BABY Billie Davis	Decca	3
35	40	M'LADY Sly and the Family Stone	Direction	4

LW	TW	*WEEK ENDING* 6 NOVEMBER 1968		Wks
2	1	WITH A LITTLE HELP FROM MY FRIENDS Joe Cocker	Regal Zonophone	5
1	2	THOSE WERE THE DAYS Mary Hopkin	Apple	9
3	3	THE GOOD, THE BAD AND THE UGLY Hugo Montenegro	RCA	8
16	4	ELOISE Barry Ryan	MGM	3
19	5	THIS OLD HEART OF MINE Isley Brothers	Tamla Motown	3
5	6	ONLY ONE WOMAN Marbles	Polydor	6
6	7	LIGHT MY FIRE Jose Feliciano	RCA	7
4	8	LITTLE ARROWS Leapy Lee	MCA	11
18	9	ALL ALONG THE WATCHTOWER Jimi Hendrix Experience	Track	2
7	10	HEY JUDE Beatles	Apple	10
8	11	JESAMINE Casuals	Decca	12
9	12	LES BICYCLETTES DE BELSIZE Engelbert Humperdinck	Decca	7
10	13	MY LITTLE LADY Tremeloes	CBS	6
12	14	LISTEN TO ME Hollies	Parlophone	6
11	15	A DAY WITHOUT LOVE Love Affair	CBS	8
20	16	BREAKING DOWN THE WALLS OF HEARTACHE Bandwagon	Direction	4
21	17	MEXICO Long John Baldry	Pye	3
14	18	WRECK OF THE ANTOINETTE Dave Dee, Dozy, Beaky, Mick and Tich	Fontana	5
15	19	LADY WILLPOWER Union Gap	CBS	13
17	20	CLASSICAL GAS Mason Williams	Warner Bros	10
23	21	YOU'RE ALL I NEED TO GET BY Marvin Gaye and Tammi Terrell	Tamla Motown	5
13	22	RED BALLOON Dave Clark Five	Columbia	8
-	23	ELENORE Turtles	London	1
27	24	HARPER VALLEY PTA Jeannie C Riley	Polydor	3
33	25	RUDI'S IN LOVE Locomotive	Parlophone	3
29	26	MAGIC BUS Who	Track	2
34	27	IF I KNEW THEN WHAT I KNOW NOW Val Doonican	Pye	2
35	28	AIN'T GOT NO-I GOT LIFE/DO WHAT YOU GOTTA DO Nina Simone	RCA	2
22	29	HOLD ME TIGHT Johnny Nash	Regal Zonophone	13
28	30	SUNSHINE OF YOUR LOVE Cream	Polydor	5
-	31	MAY I HAVE THE NEXT DREAM WITH YOU Malcolm Roberts ●	Major Minor	1
30	32	WAIT FOR ME MARY-ANNE Marmalade	CBS	3
39	33	I WANT YOU TO BE MY BABY Billie Davis	Decca	4
24	34	MARIANNE Cliff Richard	Columbia	6
37	35	AN OLYMPIC RECORD Barron Knights	Columbia	2
25	36	ICE IN THE SUN Status Quo	Pye	11
-	37	IT'S IN HIS KISS Betty Everett	President	1
-	38	MY WORLD Cupid's Inspiration	Nems	4
36	39	HELP YOURSELF Tom Jones	Decca	17
26	40	HELLO I LOVE YOU Doors	Elektra	9

LW	TW	*WEEK ENDING* 13 NOVEMBER 1968		Wks
3	1	THE GOOD, THE BAD AND THE UGLY Hugo Montenegro	RCA	9
1	2	WITH A LITTLE HELP FROM MY FRIENDS Joe Cocker	Regal Zonophone	6
4	3	ELOISE Barry Ryan	MGM	4
5	4	THIS OLD HEART OF MINE Isley Brothers	Tamla Motown	4
2	5	THOSE WERE THE DAYS Mary Hopkin	Apple	10

In these weeks ■ For three weeks, five of the Top Ten were acts enjoying their only Top Ten hit. Hugo Montenegro, Leapy Lee, Marbles, José Feliciano and the Casuals were the first five acts, and in subsequent weeks Barry Ryan replaces Leapy Lee (30.10.68) ■ The first of two tunes from Clint Eastwood films top the charts. Hugo Montenegro's treatment of the Ennio Morricone title tune from Sergio Leone's third spaghetti Western with Eastwood and Lee Van Cleef, *The Good, The Bad And The Ugly* (13.11.68)■

November 1968

□ Highest position disc reached ● Act's first ever week on chart

LW	TW	Title	Artist	Label	Wks
9	6	ALL ALONG THE WATCHTOWER	Jimi Hendrix Experience	*Track*	3
7	7	LIGHT MY FIRE	Jose Feliciano	*RCA*	8
6	8	ONLY ONE WOMAN	Marbles	*Polydor*	7
16	9	BREAKING DOWN THE WALLS OF HEARTACHE	Bandwagon	*Direction*	5
11	10	JESAMINE	Casuals	*Decca*	13
10	11	HEY JUDE	Beatles	*Apple*	11
12	12	LES BICYCLETTES DE BELSIZE	Engelbert Humperdinck	*Decca*	8
23	13	ELENORE	Turtles	*London*	2
8	14	LITTLE ARROWS	Leapy Lee	*MCA*	12
14	15	LISTEN TO ME	Hollies	*Parlophone*	7
17	16	MEXICO	Long John Baldry	*Pye*	4
13	17	MY LITTLE LADY	Tremeloes	*CBS*	7
28	18	AIN'T GOT NO-I GOT LIFE/DO WHAT YOU GOTTA DO	Nina Simone	*RCA*	3
21	19	YOU'RE ALL I NEED TO GET BY	Marvin Gaye and Tammi Terrell	*Tamla Motown*	6
15	20	A DAY WITHOUT LOVE	Love Affair	*CBS*	9
24	21	HARPER VALLEY PTA	Jeannie C Riley	*Polydor*	4
18	22	WRECK OF THE ANTOINETTE	Dave Dee, Dozy, Beaky, Mick and Tich	*Fontana*	6
-	23	LILY THE PINK	Scaffold	*Parlophone*	1
31	24	MAY I HAVE THE NEXT DREAM WITH YOU	Malcolm Roberts	*Major Minor*	2
25	25	RUDI'S IN LOVE	Locomotive	*Parlophone*	4
27	26	IF I KNEW THEN WHAT I KNOW NOW	Val Doonican	*Pye*	3
22	27	RED BALLOON	Dave Clark Five	*Columbia*	9
26	28	MAGIC BUS	Who	*Track*	3
20	29	CLASSICAL GAS	Mason Williams	*Warner Bros*	11
-	30	I'M A TIGER	Lulu	*Columbia*	1
19	31	LADY WILLPOWER	Union Gap	*CBS*	14
32	32	WAIT FOR ME MARY-ANNE	Marmalade	*CBS*	4
-	33	RAIN AND TEARS	Aphrodite's Child ●	*Mercury*	1
-	34	I'M THE URBAN SPACEMAN	Bonzo Dog Doo-Dah Band ●	*Liberty*	1
29	35	HOLD ME TIGHT	Johnny Nash	*Regal Zonophone*	14
30	36	SUNSHINE OF YOUR LOVE	Cream	*Polydor*	6
37	37	IT'S IN HIS KISS	Betty Everett	*President*	2
35	38	AN OLYMPIC RECORD	Barron Knights	*Columbia*	3
-	39	YESTERDAY'S DREAM	Four Tops	*Tamla Motown*	9
33	40	I WANT YOU TO BE MY BABY	Billie Davis	*Decca*	5

WEEK ENDING 20 NOVEMBER 1968

LW	TW	Title	Artist	Label	Wks
1	1	THE GOOD, THE BAD AND THE UGLY	Hugo Montenegro	*RCA*	10
3	2	ELOISE	Barry Ryan	*MGM*	5
4	3	THIS OLD HEART OF MINE	Isley Brothers	*Tamla Motown*	5
9	4	BREAKING DOWN THE WALLS OF HEARTACHE	Bandwagon	*Direction*	6
2	5	WITH A LITTLE HELP FROM MY FRIENDS	Joe Cocker	*Regal Zonophone*	7
6	6	ALL ALONG THE WATCHTOWER	Jimi Hendrix Experience	*Track*	4
13	7	ELENORE	Turtles	*London*	3
8	8	ONLY ONE WOMAN	Marbles	*Polydor*	8
5	9	THOSE WERE THE DAYS	Mary Hopkin	*Apple*	11
18	10	AIN'T GOT NO-I GOT LIFE/DO WHAT YOU GOTTA DO	Nina Simone	*RCA*	4
7	11	LIGHT MY FIRE	Jose Feliciano	*RCA*	9
23	12	LILY THE PINK	Scaffold	*Parlophone*	2
14	13	LITTLE ARROWS	Leapy Lee	*MCA*	13
26	14	IF I KNEW THEN WHAT I KNOW NOW	Val Doonican	*Pye*	4
16	15	MEXICO	Long John Baldry	*Pye*	5
10	16	JESAMINE	Casuals	*Decca*	14
30	17	I'M A TIGER	Lulu	*Columbia*	2
15	18	LISTEN TO ME	Hollies	*Parlophone*	8
12	19	LES BICYCLETTES DE BELSIZE	Engelbert Humperdinck	*Decca*	9
24	20	MAY I HAVE THE NEXT DREAM WITH YOU	Malcolm Roberts	*Major Minor*	3
19	21	YOU'RE ALL I NEED TO GET BY	Marvin Gaye and Tammi Terrell	*Tamla Motown*	7
21	22	HARPER VALLEY PTA	Jeannie C Riley	*Polydor*	5
17	23	MY LITTLE LADY	Tremeloes	*CBS*	8
11	24	HEY JUDE	Beatles	*Apple*	12
34	25	I'M THE URBAN SPACEMAN	Bonzo Dog Doo-Dah Band	*Liberty*	2
25	26	RUDI'S IN LOVE	Locomotive	*Parlophone*	5
28	27	MAGIC BUS	Who	*Track*	4
22	28	WRECK OF THE ANTOINETTE	Dave Dee, Dozy, Beaky, Mick and Tich	*Fontana*	7
20	29	A DAY WITHOUT LOVE	Love Affair	*CBS*	10
33	30	RAIN AND TEARS	Aphrodite's Child	*Mercury*	2
-	31	1-2-3 O'LEARY	Des O'Connor	*Columbia*	1
-	32	I'M IN A DIFFERENT WORLD	Four Tops	*Tamla Motown*	1
27	33	RED BALLOON	Dave Clark Five	*Columbia*	10
-	34	EENY MEENY	Showstoppers	*MGM*	1
32	35	WAIT FOR ME MARY-ANNE	Marmalade	*CBS*	5
40	36	I WANT YOU TO BE MY BABY	Billie Davis	*Decca*	6
37	37	IT'S IN HIS KISS	Betty Everett	*President*	3
39	38	YESTERDAY'S DREAMS	Four Tops	*Tamla Motown*	10
29	39	CLASSICAL GAS	Mason Williams	*Warner Bros*	12
31	40	LADY WILLPOWER	Union Gap	*CBS*	15

WEEK ENDING 27 NOVEMBER 1968

LW	TW	Title	Artist	Label	Wks
1	1	THE GOOD, THE BAD AND THE UGLY	Hugo Montenegro	*RCA*	11
2	2	ELOISE	Barry Ryan	*MGM*	6
3	3	THIS OLD HEART OF MINE	Isley Brothers	*Tamla Motown*	6
12	4	LILY THE PINK	Scaffold	*Parlophone*	3
6	5	ALL ALONG THE WATCHTOWER	Jimi Hendrix Experience	*Track*	5
4	6	BREAKING DOWN THE WALLS OF HEARTACHE	Bandwagon	*Direction*	7
10	7	AIN'T GOT NO-I GOT LIFE/DO WHAT YOU GOTTA DO	Nina Simone	*RCA*	5
7	8	ELENORE	Turtles	*London*	4
17	9	I'M A TIGER	Lulu	*Columbia*	3
5	10	WITH A LITTLE HELP FROM MY FRIENDS	Joe Cocker	*Regal Zonophone*	8
9	11	THOSE WERE THE DAYS	Mary Hopkin	*Apple*	12
8	12	ONLY ONE WOMAN	Marbles	*Polydor*	9
11	13	LIGHT MY FIRE	Jose Feliciano	*RCA*	10
20	14	MAY I HAVE THE NEXT DREAM WITH YOU	Malcolm Roberts	*Major Minor*	4
22	15	HARPER VALLEY PTA	Jeannie C Riley	*Polydor*	6
31	16	1-2-3 O'LEARY	Des O'Connor	*Columbia*	2
14	17	IF I KNEW THEN WHAT I KNOW NOW	Val Doonican	*Pye*	5
25	18	I'M THE URBAN SPACEMAN	Bonzo Dog Doo-Dah Band	*Liberty*	3
15	19	MEXICO	Long John Baldry	*Pye*	6
13	20	LITTLE ARROWS	Leapy Lee	*MCA*	14
21	21	YOU'RE ALL I NEED TO GET BY	Marvin Gaye and Tammi Terrell	*Tamla Motown*	8
-	22	BUILD ME UP BUTTERCUP	Foundations	*Pye*	1
18	23	LISTEN TO ME	Hollies	*Parlophone*	9
-	24	LOVE CHILD	Diana Ross and the Supremes	*Tamla Motown*	1
24	25	HEY JUDE	Beatles	*Apple*	13
16	26	JESAMINE	Casuals	*Decca*	15
19	27	LES BICYCLETTES DE BELSIZE	Engelbert Humperdinck	*Decca*	10
-	28	RACE WITH THE DEVIL	Gun ●	*CBS*	1
-	29	PRIVATE NUMBER	Judy Clay and William Bell ●	*Stax*	1
26	30	RUDI'S IN LOVE	Locomotive	*Parlophone*	6
30	31	RAIN AND TEARS	Aphrodite's Child	*Mercury*	3
32	32	I'M IN A DIFFERENT WORLD	Four Tops	*Tamla Motown*	2
34	33	EENY MEENY	Showstoppers	*MGM*	2
37	34	IT'S IN HIS KISS	Betty Everett	*President*	4
-	35	SABRE DANCE	Love Sculpture ●	*Parlophone*	1
28	36	WRECK OF THE ANTOINETTE	Dave Dee, Dozy, Beaky, Mick and Tich	*Fontana*	8

■ Vocalist with Aphrodite's Child is future number one hitmaker Demis Roussos. Vangelis is another band member (13.11.68) ■ Lulu's *I'm A Tiger* is written by former hitmaker Marty Wilde (13.11.68) ■ Over four years after its American success, Betty Everett's *It's In His Kiss* makes the British Top 40. The song will resurface some 23 years later, as *The Shoop Shoop Song* and will top the charts, performed by Cher (27.11.68) ■

November 1968

□ Highest position disc reached ● Act's first ever week on chart

LW	TW	Title	Artist	Label	Wks
-	37	QUICK JOEY SMALL	Kasenetz-Katz Singing Orchestral Circus ●	Buddah	1
23	38	MY LITTLE LADY	Tremeloes	CBS	9
27	39	MAGIC BUS	Who	Track	5
29	40	A DAY WITHOUT LOVE	Love Affair	CBS	11

WEEK ENDING 4 DECEMBER 1968

LW	TW	Title	Artist	Label	Wks
1	□ 1	THE GOOD, THE BAD AND THE UGLY	Hugo Montenegro	RCA	12
4	2	LILY THE PINK	Scaffold	Parlophone	4
2	3	ELOISE	Barry Ryan	MGM	7
3	4	THIS OLD HEART OF MINE	Isley Brothers	Tamla Motown	7
6	5	BREAKING DOWN THE WALLS OF HEARTACHE	Bandwagon	Direction	8
16	6	1-2-3 O'LEARY	Des O'Connor	Columbia	3
7	7	AIN'T GOT NO-I GOT LIFE/DO WHAT YOU GOTTA DO	Nina Simone	RCA	6
14	□ 8	MAY I HAVE THE NEXT DREAM WITH YOU	Malcolm Roberts	Major Minor	5
9	□ 9	I'M A TIGER	Lulu	Columbia	4
8	10	ELENORE	Turtles	London	5
5	11	ALL ALONG THE WATCHTOWER	Jimi Hendrix Experience	Track	6
15	12	HARPER VALLEY PTA	Jeannie C Riley	Polydor	7
18	13	I'M THE URBAN SPACEMAN	Bonzo Dog Doo-Dah Band	Liberty	4
22	14	BUILD ME UP BUTTERCUP	Foundations	Pye	2
28	15	RACE WITH THE DEVIL	Gun	CBS	2
11	16	THOSE WERE THE DAYS	Mary Hopkin	Apple	13
12	17	ONLY ONE WOMAN	Marbles	Polydor	10
10	18	WITH A LITTLE HELP FROM MY FRIENDS	Joe Cocker	Regal Zonophone	9
24	19	LOVE CHILD	Diana Ross and the Supremes	Tamla Motown	2
17	20	IF I KNEW THEN WHAT I KNOW NOW	Val Doonican	Pye	6
13	21	LIGHT MY FIRE	Jose Feliciano	RCA	11
35	22	SABRE DANCE	Love Sculpture	Parlophone	2
29	23	PRIVATE NUMBER	Judy Clay and William Bell	Stax	2
20	24	LITTLE ARROWS	Leapy Lee	MCA	15
27	25	LES BICYCLETTES DE BELSIZE	Engelbert Humperdinck	Decca	11
-	26	A MINUTE OF YOUR TIME	Tom Jones	Decca	1
21	27	YOU'RE ALL I NEED TO GET BY	Marvin Gaye and Tammi Terrell	Tamla Motown	9
32	28	I'M IN A DIFFERENT WORLD	Four Tops	Tamla Motown	3
31	□ 29	RAIN AND TEARS	Aphrodite's Child	Mercury	4
25	30	HEY JUDE	Beatles	Apple	14
19	31	MEXICO	Long John Baldry	Pye	7
37	32	QUICK JOEY SMALL	Kasenetz-Katz Singing Orchestral Circus	Buddah	2
23	33	LISTEN TO ME	Hollies	Parlophone	10
-	34	DON'T FORGET TO CATCH ME	Cliff Richard and the Shadows	Columbia	1
33	35	EENY MEENY	Showstoppers	MGM	3
-	36	ALBATROSS	Fleetwood Mac	Blue Horizon	1
-	37	YOURS UNTIL TOMORROW	Gene Pitney	Stateside	1
30	38	RUDI'S IN LOVE	Locomotive	Parlophone	7
-	□ 39	LIVE IN THE SKY	Dave Clark Five	Columbia	1
-	40	TOY	Casuals	Decca	1

WEEK ENDING 11 DECEMBER 1968

LW	TW	Title	Artist	Label	Wks
2	□ 1	LILY THE PINK	Scaffold	Parlophone	5
1	2	THE GOOD, THE BAD AND THE UGLY	Hugo Montenegro	RCA	13
7	3	AIN'T GOT NO-I GOT LIFE	Nina Simone	RCA	7
6	□ 4	1-2-3 O'LEARY	Des O'Connor	Columbia	4
14	5	BUILD ME UP BUTTERCUP	Foundations	Pye	3
13	6	I'M THE URBAN SPACEMAN	Bonzo Dog Doo-Dah Band	Liberty	5
4	7	THIS OLD HEART OF MINE	Isley Brothers	Tamla Motown	8
3	8	ELOISE	Barry Ryan	MGM	8
8	9	MAY I HAVE THE NEXT DREAM WITH YOU	Malcolm Roberts	Major Minor	6
5	10	BREAKING DOWN THE WALLS OF HEARTACHE	Bandwagon	Direction	9
22	11	SABRE DANCE	Love Sculpture	Parlophone	3
9	12	I'M A TIGER	Lulu	Columbia	5
15	13	RACE WITH THE DEVIL	Gun	CBS	3
10	14	ELENORE	Turtles	London	6
12	15	HARPER VALLEY PTA	Jeannie C Riley	Polydor	8
26	16	A MINUTE OF YOUR TIME	Tom Jones	Decca	2
19	17	LOVE CHILD	Diana Ross and the Supremes	Tamla Motown	3
16	18	THOSE WERE THE DAYS	Mary Hopkin	Apple	14
23	19	PRIVATE NUMBER	Judy Clay and William Bell	Stax	3
36	20	ALBATROSS	Fleetwood Mac	Blue Horizon	2
20	21	IF I KNEW THEN WHAT I KNOW NOW	Val Doonican	Pye	7
-	22	OB-LA-DI OB-LA-DA	Marmalade	CBS	1
11	23	ALL ALONG THE WATCHTOWER	Jimi Hendrix Experience	Track	7
-	24	SON OF A PREACHER MAN	Dusty Springfield	Philips	1
18	25	WITH A LITTLE HELP FROM MY FRIENDS	Joe Cocker	Regal Zonophone	10
25	26	LES BICYCLETTES DE BELSIZE	Engelbert Humperdinck	Decca	12
32	27	QUICK JOEY SMALL	Kasenetz-Katz Singing Orchestral Circus	Buddah	3
27	28	YOU'RE ALL I NEED TO GET BY	Marvin Gaye and Tammi Terrell	Tamla Motown	10
34	29	DON'T FORGET TO CATCH ME	Cliff Richard and the Shadows	Columbia	2
17	30	ONLY ONE WOMAN	Marbles	Polydor	11
21	31	LIGHT MY FIRE	Jose Feliciano	RCA	12
28	32	I'M IN A DIFFERENT WORLD	Four Tops	Tamla Motown	4
24	33	LITTLE ARROWS	Leapy Lee	MCA	16
37	□ 34	YOURS UNTIL TOMORROW	Gene Pitney	Stateside	2
29	35	RAIN AND TEARS	Aphrodite's Child	Mercury	5
-	36	STOP HER ON SIGHT (SOS)/HEADLINE NEWS	Edwin Starr	Polydor	1
-	37	ATLANTIS	Donovan	Pye	1
35	38	EENY MEENY	Showstoppers	MGM	4
-	39	HELP YOURSELF	Tom Jones	Decca	18
-	40	I PRETEND	Des O'Connor	Columbia	23

WEEK ENDING 18 DECEMBER 1968

LW	TW	Title	Artist	Label	Wks
1	□ 1	LILY THE PINK	Scaffold	Parlophone	6
3	□ 2	AIN'T GOT NO-I GOT LIFE	Nina Simone	RCA	8
5	3	BUILD ME UP BUTTERCUP	Foundations	Pye	4
4	□ 4	1-2-3 O'LEARY	Des O'Connor	Columbia	5
6	□ 5	I'M THE URBAN SPACEMAN	Bonzo Dog Doo-Dah Band	Liberty	6
2	6	THE GOOD, THE BAD AND THE UGLY	Hugo Montenegro	RCA	14
11	7	SABRE DANCE	Love Sculpture	Parlophone	4
13	□ 8	RACE WITH THE DEVIL	Gun	CBS	4
22	9	OB-LA-DI OB-LA-DA	Marmalade	CBS	2
7	10	THIS OLD HEART OF MINE	Isley Brothers	Tamla Motown	9
10	11	BREAKING DOWN THE WALLS OF HEARTACHE	Bandwagon	Direction	10
12	12	I'M A TIGER	Lulu	Columbia	6
20	13	ALBATROSS	Fleetwood Mac	Blue Horizon	3
19	14	PRIVATE NUMBER	Judy Clay and William Bell	Stax	4
9	15	MAY I HAVE THE NEXT DREAM WITH YOU	Malcolm Roberts	Major Minor	7
16	16	A MINUTE OF YOUR TIME	Tom Jones	Decca	3
15	17	HARPER VALLEY PTA	Jeannie C Riley	Polydor	9
8	18	ELOISE	Barry Ryan	MGM	9
17	19	LOVE CHILD	Diana Ross and the Supremes	Tamla Motown	4
24	20	SON OF A PREACHER MAN	Dusty Springfield	Philips	2
14	21	ELENORE	Turtles	London	7
27	□ 22	QUICK JOEY SMALL	Kasenetz-Katz Singing Orchestral Circus	Buddah	4

In these weeks ■ *Don't Forget To Catch Me* is the final hit by Cliff Richard and the Shadows. It is also Cliff's third consecutive single that misses the Top 20, a lack of success not matched until 1985 (04.12.68) ■ A number of songs from the musical 'Hair' make the charts, but Nina Simone's version of *Ain't Got No - I Got Life* is the first and biggest hit from the show (18.12.68)■

December 1968

□ Highest position disc reached ● Act's first ever week on chart

18 **23** THOSE WERE THE DAYS Mary Hopkin .... *Apple* 15
21 **24** IF I KNEW THEN WHAT I KNOW NOW Val Doonican .... *Pye* 8
36 **25** STOP HER ON SIGHT (SOS)/HEADLINE NEWS Edwin Starr *Polydor* 2
37 **26** ATLANTIS Donovan .... *Pye* 2
32 **27** I'M IN A DIFFERENT WORLD Four Tops .... *Tamla Motown* 5
29 **28** DON'T FORGET TO CATCH ME Cliff Richard and the Shadows .... *Columbia* 3
\- **[29]** I SHALL BE RELEASED Tremeloes .... *CBS* 1
25 **30** WITH A LITTLE HELP FROM MY FRIENDS Joe Cocker .... *Regal Zonophone* 11
23 **31** ALL ALONG THE WATCHTOWER Jimi Hendrix Experience .... *Track* 8
\- **32** FOR ONCE IN MY LIFE Stevie Wonder .... *Tamla Motown* 1
\- **33** SOMETHING'S HAPPENING Herman's Hermits .... *Columbia* 1
\- **34** OB-LA-DI OB-LA-DA Bedrocks ● .... *Columbia* 1
\- **35** TOY Casuals .... *Decca* 1
\- **36** ON MOTHER KELLY'S DOORSTEP Danny La Rue ● ... *Page One* 1
39 **37** HELP YOURSELF Tom Jones .... *Decca* 19
34 **38** YOURS UNTIL TOMORROW Gene Pitney .... *Stateside* 3
\- **[39]** LIVE IN THE SKY Dave Clark Five .... *Columbia* 1
26 **40** LES BICYCLETTES DE BELSIZE Engelbert Humperdinck .... *Decca* 13

LW TW *WEEK ENDING* **25 DECEMBER 1968** **Wks**

1 **[1]** LILY THE PINK Scaffold .... *Parlophone* 7
3 **[2]** BUILD ME UP BUTTERCUP Foundations .... *Pye* 5
2 **3** AIN'T GOT NO-I GOT LIFE Nina Simone .... *RCA* 9
4 **[4]** 1-2-3 O'LEARY Des O'Connor .... *Columbia* 6
7 **[5]** SABRE DANCE Love Sculpture .... *Parlophone* 5
5 **6** I'M THE URBAN SPACEMAN Bonzo Dog Doo-Dah Band .... *Liberty* 7
9 **7** OB-LA-DI OB-LA-DA Marmalade .... *CBS* 3
6 **8** THE GOOD, THE BAD AND THE UGLY Hugo Montenegro .... *RCA* 15
13 **9** ALBATROSS Fleetwood Mac .... *Blue Horizon* 4
8 **10** RACE WITH THE DEVIL Gun .... *CBS* 5
15 **11** MAY I HAVE THE NEXT DREAM WITH YOU Malcolm Roberts .... *Major Minor* 8
11 **12** BREAKING DOWN THE WALLS OF HEARTACHE Bandwagon .... *Direction* 11
12 **13** I'M A TIGER Lulu .... *Columbia* 7
16 **[14]** A MINUTE OF YOUR TIME Tom Jones .... *Decca* 4
21 **15** ELENORE Turtles .... *London* 8
14 **16** PRIVATE NUMBER Judy Clay and William Bell .... *Stax* 5
17 **17** HARPER VALLEY PTA Jeannie C Riley .... *Polydor* 10
18 **18** ELOISE Barry Ryan .... *MGM* 10
10 **19** THIS OLD HEART OF MINE Isley Brothers .... *Tamla Motown* 10
20 **20** SON OF A PREACHER MAN Dusty Springfield .... *Philips* 3
19 **21** LOVE CHILD Diana Ross and the Supremes .... *Tamla Motown* 5
24 **22** IF I KNEW THEN WHAT I KNOW NOW Val Doonican .... *Pye* 9
26 **[23]** ATLANTIS Donovan .... *Pye* 3
23 **24** THOSE WERE THE DAYS Mary Hopkin .... *Apple* 16
22 **25** QUICK JOEY SMALL Kasenetz-Katz Singing Orchestral Circus .... *Buddah* 5
28 **26** DON'T FORGET TO CATCH ME Cliff Richard and the Shadows .... *Columbia* 4
32 **27** FOR ONCE IN MY LIFE Stevie Wonder .... *Tamla Motown* 2
33 **28** SOMETHING'S HAPPENING Herman's Hermits .... *Columbia* 2
29 **[29]** I SHALL BE RELEASED Tremeloes .... *CBS* 2
34 **30** OB-LA-DI OB-LA-DA Bedrocks .... *Columbia* 2
37 **31** HELP YOURSELF Tom Jones .... *Decca* 20
31 **32** ALL ALONG THE WATCHTOWER Jimi Hendrix Experience .... *Track* 9
27 **33** I'M IN A DIFFERENT WORLD Four Tops .... *Tamla Motown* 6
38 **[34]** YOURS UNTIL TOMORROW Gene Pitney .... *Stateside* 4
35 **35** TOY Casuals .... *Decca* 2
\- **36** PLEASE DON'T GO Donald Peers ● .... *Columbia* 1
25 **37** STOP HER ON SIGHT (SOS)/HEADLINE NEWS Edwin Starr *Polydor* 3
\- **38** YOU'RE ALL I NEED TO GET BY Marvin Gaye and Tammi Terrell .... *Tamla Motown* 11
30 **39** WITH A LITTLE HELP FROM MY FRIENDS Joe Cocker .... *Regal Zonophone* 12
\- **40** LITTLE ARROWS Leapy Lee .... *MCA* 17

■Tom Jones' *Help Yourself* becomes the fourth record of the year to complete 20 weeks of chart action (25.12.68) ■ At the age of 60, Donald Peers becomes one of the oldest people ever to make his chart debut (25.12.68) ■ Although the Beatles are not at number one this Christmas, they are nevertheless well represented. Scaffold includes Paul McCartney's brother, *I'm The Urban Spaceman* was produced by Paul McCartney (under the name of Apollo C. Vermouth) and he and John Lennon wrote *Ob-La-Di Ob-La-Da* (25.12.68)■

1969

..........Blues group FLEETWOOD MAC accumulate the most weeks on chart this year and enjoy their only number one, 'Albatross'......the Beatles have their final two number ones ......Jane Birkin and Serge Gainsbourg combine on what is both the first fully foreign language number one and the first number one banned by the BBC, 'Je T'aime...Moi Non Plus'..........

January 1969

□ Highest position disc reached ● Act's first ever week on chart

WEEK ENDING 1 JANUARY 1969

LW	TW	Title	Artist	Label	Wks
7	[1]	OB-LA-DI OB-LA-DA	Marmalade	*CBS*	4
1	2	LILY THE PINK	Scaffold	*Parlophone*	8
2	3	BUILD ME UP BUTTERCUP	Foundations	*Pye*	6
9	4	ALBATROSS	Fleetwood Mac	*Blue Horizon*	5
6	[5]	I'M THE URBAN SPACEMAN	Bonzo Dog Doo-Dah Band	*Liberty*	8
5	6	SABRE DANCE	Love Sculpture	*Parlophone*	6
3	7	AIN'T GOT NO-I GOT LIFE	Nina Simone	*RCA*	10
4	8	1-2-3 O'LEARY	Des O'Connor	*Columbia*	7
20	[9]	SON OF A PREACHER MAN	Dusty Springfield	*Philips*	4
28	10	SOMETHING'S HAPPENING	Herman's Hermits	*Columbia*	3
10	11	RACE WITH THE DEVIL	Gun	*CBS*	6
27	12	FOR ONCE IN MY LIFE	Stevie Wonder	*Tamla Motown*	3
13	13	I'M A TIGER	Lulu	*Columbia*	8
16	14	PRIVATE NUMBER	Judy Clay and William Bell	*Stax*	6
8	15	THE GOOD, THE BAD AND THE UGLY	Hugo Montenegro	*RCA*	16
11	16	MAY I HAVE THE NEXT DREAM WITH YOU	Malcolm Roberts	*Major Minor*	9
14	17	A MINUTE OF YOUR TIME	Tom Jones	*Decca*	5
21	18	LOVE CHILD	Diana Ross and the Supremes	*Tamla Motown*	6
12	19	BREAKING DOWN THE WALLS OF HEARTACHE	Bandwagon	*Direction*	12
30	[20]	OB-LA-DI OB-LA-DA	Bedrocks	*Columbia*	3
26	[21]	DON'T FORGET TO CATCH ME	Cliff Richard and the Shadows	*Columbia*	5
19	22	THIS OLD HEART OF MINE	Isley Brothers	*Tamla Motown*	11
22	23	IF I KNEW THEN WHAT I KNOW NOW	Val Doonican	*Pye*	10
36	24	PLEASE DON'T GO	Donald Peers	*Columbia*	2
15	25	ELENORE	Turtles	*London*	9
17	26	HARPER VALLEY PTA	Jeannie C Riley	*Polydor*	11
25	27	QUICK JOEY SMALL	Kasenetz-Katz Singing Orchestral Circus	*Buddah*	6
23	28	ATLANTIS	Donovan	*Pye*	4
24	29	THOSE WERE THE DAYS	Mary Hopkin	*Apple*	17
35	[30]	TOY	Casuals	*Decca*	3
37	31	STOP HER ON SIGHT (SOS)/HEADLINE NEWS	Edwin Starr	*Polydor*	4
-	32	FOX ON THE RUN	Manfred Mann	*Fontana*	1
-	[33]	ON MOTHER KELLY'S DOORSTEP	Danny La Rue	*Page One*	2
33	34	I'M IN A DIFFERENT WORLD	Four Tops	*Tamla Motown*	7
18	35	ELOISE	Barry Ryan	*MGM*	11
29	36	I SHALL BE RELEASED	Tremeloes	*CBS*	3
31	37	HELP YOURSELF	Tom Jones	*Decca*	21
-	38	SOUL LIMBO	Booker T and the MGs ●	*Stax*	1
-	39	I PRETEND	Des O'Connor	*Columbia*	23
38	40	YOU'RE ALL I NEED TO GET BY	Marvin Gaye and Tammi Terrell	*Tamla Motown*	12

WEEK ENDING 8 JANUARY 1969

LW	TW	Title	Artist	Label	Wks
2	[1]	LILY THE PINK	Scaffold	*Parlophone*	9
3	[2]	BUILD ME UP BUTTERCUP	Foundations	*Pye*	7
1	3	OB-LA-DI OB-LA-DA	Marmalade	*CBS*	5
4	4	ALBATROSS	Fleetwood Mac	*Blue Horizon*	6
5	[5]	I'M THE URBAN SPACEMAN	Bonzo Dog Doo-Dah Band	*Liberty*	9
6	6	SABRE DANCE	Love Sculpture	*Parlophone*	7
7	7	AIN'T GOT NO-I GOT LIFE	Nina Simone	*RCA*	11
10	8	SOMETHING'S HAPPENING	Herman's Hermits	*Columbia*	4
9	[9]	SON OF A PREACHER MAN	Dusty Springfield	*Philips*	5
12	10	FOR ONCE IN MY LIFE	Stevie Wonder	*Tamla Motown*	4
13	11	I'M A TIGER	Lulu	*Columbia*	9
14	12	PRIVATE NUMBER	Judy Clay and William Bell	*Stax*	7
8	13	1-2-3 O'LEARY	Des O'Connor	*Columbia*	8
11	14	RACE WITH THE DEVIL	Gun	*CBS*	7
18	[15]	LOVE CHILD	Diana Ross and the Supremes	*Tamla Motown*	7
15	16	THE GOOD, THE BAD AND THE UGLY	Hugo Montenegro	*RCA*	17
17	17	A MINUTE OF YOUR TIME	Tom Jones	*Decca*	6
16	18	MAY I HAVE THE NEXT DREAM WITH YOU	Malcolm Roberts	*Major Minor*	10
19	19	BREAKING DOWN THE WALLS OF HEARTACHE	Bandwagon	*Direction*	13
22	20	THIS OLD HEART OF MINE	Isley Brothers	*Tamla Motown*	12
26	21	HARPER VALLEY PTA	Jeannie C Riley	*Polydor*	12
31	22	STOP HER ON SIGHT (SOS)/HEADLINE NEWS	Edwin Starr	*Polydor*	5
32	23	FOX ON THE RUN	Manfred Mann	*Fontana*	2
20	24	OB-LA-DI OB-LA-DA	Bedrocks	*Columbia*	4
24	25	PLEASE DON'T GO	Donald Peers	*Columbia*	3
21	26	DON'T FORGET TO CATCH ME	Cliff Richard and the Shadows	*Columbia*	6
23	27	IF I KNEW THEN WHAT I KNOW NOW	Val Doonican	*Pye*	11
25	28	ELENORE	Turtles	*London*	10
-	29	BLACKBERRY WAY	Move	*Regal Zonophone*	1
-	30	GOING UP THE COUNTRY	Canned Heat	*Liberty*	1
-	31	MRS ROBINSON (EP)	Simon and Garfunkel	*CBS*	1
27	32	QUICK JOEY SMALL	Kasenetz-Katz Singing Orchestral Circus	*Buddah*	7
-	[33]	BLUEBIRDS OVER THE MOUNTAIN	Beach Boys	*Capitol*	1
30	34	TOY	Casuals	*Decca*	4
29	35	THOSE WERE THE DAYS	Mary Hopkin	*Apple*	18
33	36	ON MOTHER KELLY'S DOORSTEP	Danny La Rue	*Page One*	3
28	37	ATLANTIS	Donovan	*Pye*	5
38	38	SOUL LIMBO	Booker T and the MGs	*Stax*	2
-	39	YOU GOT SOUL	Johnny Nash	*Major Minor*	1
-	40	LOVE STORY	Jethro Tull ●	*Island*	1

WEEK ENDING 15 JANUARY 1969

LW	TW	Title	Artist	Label	Wks
3	[1]	OB-LA-DI OB-LA-DA	Marmalade	*CBS*	6
4	2	ALBATROSS	Fleetwood Mac	*Blue Horizon*	7
2	3	BUILD ME UP BUTTERCUP	Foundations	*Pye*	8
1	4	LILY THE PINK	Scaffold	*Parlophone*	10
10	5	FOR ONCE IN MY LIFE	Stevie Wonder	*Tamla Motown*	5
8	[6]	SOMETHING'S HAPPENING	Herman's Hermits	*Columbia*	5
5	7	I'M THE URBAN SPACEMAN	Bonzo Dog Doo-Dah Band	*Liberty*	10
6	8	SABRE DANCE	Love Sculpture	*Parlophone*	8
7	9	AIN'T GOT NO-I GOT LIFE	Nina Simone	*RCA*	12
12	10	PRIVATE NUMBER	Judy Clay and William Bell	*Stax*	8
9	11	SON OF A PREACHER MAN	Dusty Springfield	*Philips*	6
23	12	FOX ON THE RUN	Manfred Mann	*Fontana*	3
29	13	BLACKBERRY WAY	Move	*Regal Zonophone*	2
13	14	1-2-3 O'LEARY	Des O'Connor	*Columbia*	9
16	15	THE GOOD, THE BAD AND THE UGLY	Hugo Montenegro	*RCA*	18
22	16	STOP HER ON SIGHT (SOS)/HEADLINE NEWS	Edwin Starr	*Polydor*	6
15	17	LOVE CHILD	Diana Ross and the Supremes	*Tamla Motown*	8
11	18	I'M A TIGER	Lulu	*Columbia*	10
14	19	RACE WITH THE DEVIL	Gun	*CBS*	8
17	20	A MINUTE OF YOUR TIME	Tom Jones	*Decca*	7
18	21	MAY I HAVE THE NEXT DREAM WITH YOU	Malcolm Roberts	*Major Minor*	11
21	22	HARPER VALLEY PTA	Jeannie C Riley	*Polydor*	13
39	23	YOU GOT SOUL	Johnny Nash	*Major Minor*	2
30	24	GOING UP THE COUNTRY	Canned Heat	*Liberty*	2
25	25	PLEASE DON'T GO	Donald Peers	*Columbia*	4
24	26	OB-LA-DI OB-LA-DA	Bedrocks	*Columbia*	5
20	27	THIS OLD HEART OF MINE	Isley Brothers	*Tamla Motown*	13
32	28	QUICK JOEY SMALL	Kasenetz-Katz Singing Orchestral Circus	*Buddah*	8
31	29	MRS ROBINSON (EP)	Simon and Garfunkel	*CBS*	2
38	[30]	SOUL LIMBO	Booker T and the MGs	*Stax*	3
-	31	HEY JUDE	Wilson Pickett	*Atlantic*	1
40	32	LOVE STORY	Jethro Tull	*Island*	2
-	33	YOU'RE ALL I NEED TO GET BY	Marvin Gaye and Tammi Terrell	*Tamla Motown*	13
33	34	BLUEBIRDS OVER THE MOUNTAIN	Beach Boys	*Capitol*	2
-	35	DANCING IN THE STREET	Martha Reeves and the Vandellas	*Tamla Motown*	1
36	36	ON MOTHER KELLY'S DOORSTEP	Danny La Rue	*Page One*	4
34	37	TOY	Casuals	*Decca*	5

In these weeks ■ *Ob-La-Di Ob-La-Da* emulates the achievement of *Lily The Pink* a week earlier by climbing back to number one. With the exception of *Bohemian Rhapsody* at the end of 1991, they are the last records to achieve this feat (15.01.69) ■ Danny La Rue is the first, but by no means the last, female impersonator to have a Top 40 hit (01.01.69)■

LW	TW	Title / Artist	Label	Wks
-	38	TO LOVE SOMEBODY Nina Simone	*RCA*	1
26	39	DON'T FORGET TO CATCH ME Cliff Richard and the Shadows	*Columbia*	7
19	40	BREAKING DOWN THE WALLS OF HEARTACHE Bandwagon	*Direction*	14

LW	TW	*WEEK ENDING* **22 JANUARY 1969**		Wks
1	1	OB-LA-DI OB-LA-DA Marmalade	*CBS*	7
2	2	ALBATROSS Fleetwood Mac	*Blue Horizon*	8
5	3	FOR ONCE IN MY LIFE Stevie Wonder	*Tamla Motown*	6
4	4	LILY THE PINK Scaffold	*Parlophone*	11
13	5	BLACKBERRY WAY Move	*Regal Zonophone*	3
3	6	BUILD ME UP BUTTERCUP Foundations	*Pye*	9
6	7	SOMETHING'S HAPPENING Herman's Hermits	*Columbia*	6
10	8	PRIVATE NUMBER Judy Clay and William Bell	*Stax*	9
7	9	I'M THE URBAN SPACEMAN Bonzo Dog Doo-Dah Band	*Liberty*	11
12	10	FOX ON THE RUN Manfred Mann	*Fontana*	4
8	11	SABRE DANCE Love Sculpture	*Parlophone*	9
16	12	STOP HER ON SIGHT (SOS)/HEADLINE NEWS Edwin Starr	*Polydor*	7
11	13	SON OF A PREACHER MAN Dusty Springfield	*Philips*	7
9	14	AIN'T GOT NO-I GOT LIFE Nina Simone	*RCA*	13
23	15	YOU GOT SOUL Johnny Nash	*Major Minor*	3
17	16	LOVE CHILD Diana Ross and the Supremes	*Tamla Motown*	9
14	17	1-2-3 O'LEARY Des O'Connor	*Columbia*	10
20	18	A MINUTE OF YOUR TIME Tom Jones	*Decca*	8
15	19	THE GOOD, THE BAD AND THE UGLY Hugo Montenegro	*RCA*	19
18	20	I'M A TIGER Lulu	*Columbia*	11
35	21	DANCING IN THE STREET Martha Reeves and the Vandellas	*Tamla Motown*	2
24	22	GOING UP THE COUNTRY Canned Heat	*Liberty*	3
25	23	PLEASE DON'T GO Donald Peers	*Columbia*	5
28	24	QUICK JOEY SMALL Kasenetz-Katz Singing Orchestral Circus	*Buddah*	9
38	25	TO LOVE SOMEBODY Nina Simone	*RCA*	2
19	26	RACE WITH THE DEVIL Gun	*CBS*	9
-	27	I GUESS I'LL ALWAYS LOVE YOU Isley Brothers	*Tamla Motown*	1
21	28	MAY I HAVE THE NEXT DREAM WITH YOU Malcolm Roberts	*Major Minor*	12
31	29	HEY JUDE Wilson Pickett	*Atlantic*	2
29	30	MRS ROBINSON (EP) Simon and Garfunkel	*CBS*	3
-	31	PEOPLE Tymes	*Direction*	1
26	32	OB-LA-DI OB-LA-DA Bedrocks	*Columbia*	6
27	33	THIS OLD HEART OF MINE Isley Brothers	*Tamla Motown*	14
30	34	SOUL LIMBO Booker T and the MGs	*Stax*	4
32	35	LOVE STORY Jethro Tull	*Island*	3
22	36	HARPER VALLEY PTA Jeannie C Riley	*Polydor*	14
-	37	WHITE ROOM Cream	*Polydor*	1
-	38	I PUT A SPELL ON YOU Nina Simone	*Philips*	1
-	39	RING OF FIRE Eric Burdon and the Animals	*MGM*	1
-	40	I'M IN A DIFFERENT WORLD Four Tops	*Tamla Motown*	8

LW	TW	*WEEK ENDING* **29 JANUARY 1969**		Wks
2	1	ALBATROSS Fleetwood Mac	*Blue Horizon*	9
5	2	BLACKBERRY WAY Move	*Regal Zonophone*	4
3	3	FOR ONCE IN MY LIFE Stevie Wonder	*Tamla Motown*	7
1	4	OB-LA-DI OB-LA-DA Marmalade	*CBS*	8
10	5	FOX ON THE RUN Manfred Mann	*Fontana*	5
7	6	SOMETHING'S HAPPENING Herman's Hermits	*Columbia*	7
4	7	LILY THE PINK Scaffold	*Parlophone*	12
8	8	PRIVATE NUMBER Judy Clay and William Bell	*Stax*	10
15	9	YOU GOT SOUL Johnny Nash	*Major Minor*	4
6	10	BUILD ME UP BUTTERCUP Foundations	*Pye*	10
12	11	STOP HER ON SIGHT (SOS)/HEADLINE NEWS Edwin Starr	*Polydor*	8
21	12	DANCING IN THE STREET Martha Reeves and the Vandellas	*Tamla Motown*	3
9	13	I'M THE URBAN SPACEMAN Bonzo Dog Doo-Dah Band	*Liberty*	12
25	14	TO LOVE SOMEBODY Nina Simone	*RCA*	3
11	15	SABRE DANCE Love Sculpture	*Parlophone*	10
23	16	PLEASE DON'T GO Donald Peers	*Columbia*	6
27	17	I GUESS I'LL ALWAYS LOVE YOU Isley Brothers	*Tamla Motown*	2
16	18	LOVE CHILD Diana Ross and the Supremes	*Tamla Motown*	10
24	19	QUICK JOEY SMALL Kasenetz-Katz Singing Orchestral Circus	*Buddah*	10
14	20	AIN'T GOT NO-I GOT LIFE Nina Simone	*RCA*	14
13	21	SON OF A PREACHER MAN Dusty Springfield	*Philips*	8
17	22	1-2-3 O'LEARY Des O'Connor	*Columbia*	11
29	23	HEY JUDE Wilson Pickett	*Atlantic*	3
31	24	PEOPLE Tymes	*Direction*	2
22	25	GOING UP THE COUNTRY Canned Heat	*Liberty*	4
18	26	A MINUTE OF YOUR TIME Tom Jones	*Decca*	9
30	27	MRS ROBINSON (EP) Simon and Garfunkel	*CBS*	4
-	28	I'LL PICK A ROSE FOR MY ROSE Marv Johnson	*Tamla Motown*	1
35	29	LOVE STORY Jethro Tull	*Island*	4
37	30	WHITE ROOM Cream	*Polydor*	2
19	31	THE GOOD, THE BAD AND THE UGLY Hugo Montenegro	*RCA*	20
20	32	I'M A TIGER Lulu	*Columbia*	12
-	33	(IF PARADISE IS) HALF AS NICE Amen Corner	*Immediate*	1
34	34	SOUL LIMBO Booker T and the MGs	*Stax*	5
26	35	RACE WITH THE DEVIL Gun	*CBS*	10
39	36	RING OF FIRE Eric Burdon and the Animals	*MGM*	2
-	37	I'M GONNA MAKE YOU LOVE ME Diana Ross and the Supremes and the Temptations ●	*Tamla Motown*	1
-	38	YOU AIN'T LIVIN' TILL YOU'RE LOVIN' Marvin Gaye and Tammi Terrell	*Tamla Motown*	1
28	39	MAY I HAVE THE NEXT DREAM WITH YOU Malcolm Roberts	*Major Minor*	13
38	40	I PUT A SPELL ON YOU Nina Simone	*Philips*	2

February 1969

☐ Highest position disc reached ● Act's first ever week on chart

LW	TW	*WEEK ENDING* **5 FEBRUARY 1969**		Wks
2	1	BLACKBERRY WAY Move	*Regal Zonophone*	5
1	2	ALBATROSS Fleetwood Mac	*Blue Horizon*	10
3	3	FOR ONCE IN MY LIFE Stevie Wonder	*Tamla Motown*	8
12	4	DANCING IN THE STREET Martha Reeves and the Vandellas	*Tamla Motown*	4
14	5	TO LOVE SOMEBODY Nina Simone	*RCA*	4
9	6	YOU GOT SOUL Johnny Nash	*Major Minor*	5
37	7	I'M GONNA MAKE YOU LOVE ME Diana Ross and the Supremes and the Temptations	*Tamla Motown*	2
16	8	PLEASE DON'T GO Donald Peers	*Columbia*	7
27	9	MRS ROBINSON (EP) Simon and Garfunkel	*CBS*	5
4	10	OB-LA-DI OB-LA-DA Marmalade	*CBS*	9
5	11	FOX ON THE RUN Manfred Mann	*Fontana*	6
17	12	I GUESS I'LL ALWAYS LOVE YOU Isley Brothers	*Tamla Motown*	3
8	13	PRIVATE NUMBER Judy Clay and William Bell	*Stax*	11
6	14	SOMETHING'S HAPPENING Herman's Hermits	*Columbia*	8
11	15	STOP HER ON SIGHT (SOS)/HEADLINE NEWS Edwin Starr	*Polydor*	9
24	16	PEOPLE Tymes	*Direction*	3
28	17	I'LL PICK A ROSE FOR MY ROSE Marv Johnson	*Tamla Motown*	2
-	18	WHERE DO YOU GO TO MY LOVELY Peter Sarstedt ●	*United Artists*	1
33	19	(IF PARADISE IS) HALF AS NICE Amen Corner	*Immediate*	2
-	20	SOUL SISTER BROWN SUGAR Sam and Dave	*Atlantic*	1
23	21	HEY JUDE Wilson Pickett	*Atlantic*	4
38	22	YOU AIN'T LIVIN' TILL YOU'RE LOVIN' Marvin Gaye and Tammi Terrell	*Tamla Motown*	2
18	23	LOVE CHILD Diana Ross and the Supremes	*Tamla Motown*	11
-	24	WICHITA LINEMAN Glen Campbell ●	*Ember*	1
-	25	MOVE IN A LITTLE CLOSER Harmony Grass ●	*RCA*	1
25	26	GOING UP THE COUNTRY Canned Heat	*Liberty*	5
20	27	AIN'T GOT NO-I GOT LIFE Nina Simone	*RCA*	15

■*Dancing In The Street* is far more successful as a re-issue than it was first time round in 1964 (05.02.69) ■ This is the first of four consecutive weeks in which there are three Tamla Motown hits in the Top Ten. There are nine Tamla Motown hits in the Top 40 this week, a record for the label (05.02.69)■

February 1969

☐ Highest position disc reached ● Act's first ever week on chart

LW	TW	Title	Artist	Label	Wks
40	28	I PUT A SPELL ON YOU	Nina Simone	Philips	3
-	29	YOU'RE ALL I NEED TO GET BY	Marvin Gaye and Tammi Terrell	Tamla Motown	14
19	30	QUICK JOEY SMALL	Kasenetz-Katz Singing Orchestral Circus	Buddah	11
30	31	WHITE ROOM	Cream	Polydor	3
-	32	THIS OLD HEART OF MINE	Isley Brothers	Tamla Motown	15
29	33	LOVE STORY	Jethro Tull	Island	5
7	34	LILY THE PINK	Scaffold	Parlophone	13
36	[35]	RING OF FIRE	Eric Burdon and the Animals	MGM	3
10	36	BUILD ME UP BUTTERCUP	Foundations	Pye	11
26	37	A MINUTE OF YOUR TIME	Tom Jones	Decca	10
-	38	IT'S TOO LATE NOW	Long John Baldry	Pye	1
-	39	THE WAY IT USED TO BE	Engelbert Humperdinck	Decca	1
-	40	GENTLE ON MY MIND	Dean Martin	Reprise	1

WEEK ENDING 12 FEBRUARY 1969

LW	TW	Title	Artist	Label	Wks
19	[1]	(IF PARADISE IS) HALF AS NICE	Amen Corner	Immediate	3
2	2	ALBATROSS	Fleetwood Mac	Blue Horizon	11
1	3	BLACKBERRY WAY	Move	Regal Zonophone	6
3	4	FOR ONCE IN MY LIFE	Stevie Wonder	Tamla Motown	9
4	5	DANCING IN THE STREET	Martha Reeves and the Vandellas	Tamla Motown	5
8	6	PLEASE DON'T GO	Donald Peers	Columbia	8
6	7	YOU GOT SOUL	Johnny Nash	Major Minor	6
7	8	I'M GONNA MAKE YOU LOVE ME	Diana Ross and the Supremes and the Temptations	Tamla Motown	3
10	9	OB-LA-DI OB-LA-DA	Marmalade	CBS	10
5	10	TO LOVE SOMEBODY	Nina Simone	RCA	5
12	[11]	I GUESS I'LL ALWAYS LOVE YOU	Isley Brothers	Tamla Motown	4
18	12	WHERE DO YOU GO TO MY LOVELY	Peter Sarstedt	United Artists	2
11	13	FOX ON THE RUN	Manfred Mann	Fontana	7
14	14	SOMETHING'S HAPPENING	Herman's Hermits	Columbia	9
39	15	THE WAY IT USED TO BE	Engelbert Humperdinck	Decca	2
21	[16]	HEY JUDE	Wilson Pickett	Atlantic	5
17	16	I'LL PICK A ROSE FOR MY ROSE	Marv Johnson	Tamla Motown	3
15	18	STOP HER ON SIGHT (SOS)/HEADLINE NEWS	Edwin Starr	Polydor	10
26	19	GOING UP THE COUNTRY	Canned Heat	Liberty	6
34	19	LILY THE PINK	Scaffold	Parlophone	14
16	21	PEOPLE	Tymes	Direction	4
13	22	PRIVATE NUMBER	Judy Clay and William Bell	Stax	12
20	23	SOUL SISTER BROWN SUGAR	Sam and Dave	Atlantic	2
38	24	IT'S TOO LATE NOW	Long John Baldry	Pye	2
30	25	QUICK JOEY SMALL	Kasenetz-Katz Singing Orchestral Circus	Buddah	12
24	26	WICHITA LINEMAN	Glen Campbell	Ember	2
25	27	MOVE IN A LITTLE CLOSER	Harmony Grass	RCA	2
36	28	BUILD ME UP BUTTERCUP	Foundations	Pye	12
22	29	YOU AIN'T LIVIN' TILL YOU'RE LOVIN'	Marvin Gaye and Tammi Terrell	Tamla Motown	3
31	30	WHITE ROOM	Cream	Polydor	4
-	31	MONSIEUR DUPONT	Sandie Shaw	Pye	1
-	31	YOU'VE LOST THAT LOVIN' FEELING	Righteous Brothers	London	1
-	33	THE GOOD, THE BAD AND THE UGLY	Hugo Montenegro	RCA	21
-	[34]	YOU	Bandwagon	Direction	1
37	35	A MINUTE OF YOUR TIME	Tom Jones	Decca	11
-	35	SHE'S NOT THERE	Neil MacArthur ●	Deram	1
40	37	GENTLE ON MY MIND	Dean Martin	Reprise	2
-	38	ALL THE LOVE IN THE WORLD	Consortium ●	Pye	1
-	39	I HEARD IT THROUGH THE GRAPEVINE	Marvin Gaye ●	Tamla Motown	1
-	39	SABRE DANCE	Love Sculpture	Parlophone	11

WEEK ENDING 19 FEBRUARY 1969

LW	TW	Title	Artist	Label	Wks
1	[1]	(IF PARADISE IS) HALF AS NICE	Amen Corner	Immediate	4
12	2	WHERE DO YOU GO TO MY LOVELY	Peter Sarstedt	United Artists	3
8	[3]	I'M GONNA MAKE YOU LOVE ME	Diana Ross and the Supremes and the Temptations	Tamla Motown	4
6	4	PLEASE DON'T GO	Donald Peers	Columbia	9
3	5	BLACKBERRY WAY	Move	Regal Zonophone	7
2	6	ALBATROSS	Fleetwood Mac	Blue Horizon	12
5	7	DANCING IN THE STREET	Martha Reeves and the Vandellas	Tamla Motown	6
7	8	YOU GOT SOUL	Johnny Nash	Major Minor	7
15	9	THE WAY IT USED TO BE	Engelbert Humperdinck	Decca	3
4	10	FOR ONCE IN MY LIFE	Stevie Wonder	Tamla Motown	10
26	11	WICHITA LINEMAN	Glen Campbell	Ember	3
10	12	TO LOVE SOMEBODY	Nina Simone	RCA	6
16	13	I'LL PICK A ROSE FOR MY ROSE	Marv Johnson	Tamla Motown	4
9	14	OB-LA-DI OB-LA-DA	Marmalade	CBS	11
11	15	I GUESS I'LL ALWAYS LOVE YOU	Isley Brothers	Tamla Motown	5
13	16	FOX ON THE RUN	Manfred Mann	Fontana	8
23	17	SOUL SISTER BROWN SUGAR	Sam and Dave	Atlantic	3
21	18	PEOPLE	Tymes	Direction	5
-	18	SURROUND YOURSELF WITH SORROW	Cilla Black	Parlophone	1
14	20	SOMETHING'S HAPPENING	Herman's Hermits	Columbia	10
29	[21]	YOU AIN'T LIVIN' TILL YOU'RE LOVIN'	Marvin Gaye and Tammi Terrell	Tamla Motown	4
19	22	LILY THE PINK	Scaffold	Parlophone	15
31	23	MONSIEUR DUPONT	Sandie Shaw	Pye	2
27	[24]	MOVE IN A LITTLE CLOSER	Harmony Grass	RCA	3
37	25	GENTLE ON MY MIND	Dean Martin	Reprise	3
35	26	A MINUTE OF YOUR TIME	Tom Jones	Decca	12
19	27	GOING UP THE COUNTRY	Canned Heat	Liberty	7
30	[28]	WHITE ROOM	Cream	Polydor	5
22	29	PRIVATE NUMBER	Judy Clay and William Bell	Stax	13
39	30	I HEARD IT THROUGH THE GRAPEVINE	Marvin Gaye	Tamla Motown	2
31	30	YOU'VE LOST THAT LOVIN' FEELING	Righteous Brothers	London	2
16	32	HEY JUDE	Wilson Pickett	Atlantic	6
-	33	FIRST OF MAY	Bee Gees	Polydor	1
35	[34]	SHE'S NOT THERE	Neil MacArthur	Deram	2
24	35	IT'S TOO LATE NOW	Long John Baldry	Pye	3
-	[36]	MOCKINGBIRD	Inez and Charlie Foxx ●	United Artists	1
-	37	LOVE IS LOVE	Barry Ryan	MGM	1
18	38	STOP HER ON SIGHT (SOS)/HEADLINE NEWS	Edwin Starr	Polydor	11
-	39	RIVER DEEP MOUNTAIN HIGH	Ike and Tina Turner	London	1
38	40	ALL THE LOVE IN THE WORLD	Consortium	Pye	2

WEEK ENDING 26 FEBRUARY 1969

LW	TW	Title	Artist	Label	Wks
2	[1]	WHERE DO YOU GO TO MY LOVELY	Peter Sarstedt	United Artists	4
1	2	(IF PARADISE IS) HALF AS NICE	Amen Corner	Immediate	5
3	[3]	I'M GONNA MAKE YOU LOVE ME	Diana Ross and the Supremes and the Temptations	Tamla Motown	5
4	4	PLEASE DON'T GO	Donald Peers	Columbia	10
9	5	THE WAY IT USED TO BE	Engelbert Humperdinck	Decca	4
7	6	DANCING IN THE STREET	Martha Reeves and the Vandellas	Tamla Motown	7
5	7	BLACKBERRY WAY	Move	Regal Zonophone	8
6	8	ALBATROSS	Fleetwood Mac	Blue Horizon	13
11	9	WICHITA LINEMAN	Glen Campbell	Ember	4
13	[10]	I'LL PICK A ROSE FOR MY ROSE	Marv Johnson	Tamla Motown	5
18	11	SURROUND YOURSELF WITH SORROW	Cilla Black	Parlophone	2
8	12	YOU GOT SOUL	Johnny Nash	Major Minor	8
10	13	FOR ONCE IN MY LIFE	Stevie Wonder	Tamla Motown	11
15	14	I GUESS I'LL ALWAYS LOVE YOU	Isley Brothers	Tamla Motown	6

In these weeks ■ Neil MacArthur is really Colin Blunstone, once lead singer of the Zombies, who originally hit the charts with *She's Not There* (12.02.69) ■ The entry of Inez and Charlie Foxx, and Ike and Tina Turner gives the Top 40 four simultaneous male/female duet hits. *River Deep Mountain High* is also the third re-issued hit in the chart (19.02.69)■

LW	TW	Title	Artist	Label	Wks
30	15	YOU'VE LOST THAT LOVIN' FEELING	Righteous Brothers	London	3
12	16	TO LOVE SOMEBODY	Nina Simone	RCA	7
25	17	GENTLE ON MY MIND	Dean Martin	Reprise	4
17	18	SOUL SISTER BROWN SUGAR	Sam and Dave	Atlantic	4
30	19	I HEARD IT THROUGH THE GRAPEVINE	Marvin Gaye	Tamla Motown	3
23	20	MONSIEUR DUPONT	Sandie Shaw	Pye	3
35	[21]	IT'S TOO LATE NOW	Long John Baldry	Pye	4
21	22	YOU AIN'T LIVIN' TILL YOU'RE LOVIN'	Marvin Gaye and Tammi Terrell	Tamla Motown	5
14	23	OB-LA-DI OB-LA-DA	Marmalade	CBS	12
20	24	SOMETHING'S HAPPENING	Herman's Hermits	Columbia	11
37	25	LOVE IS LOVE	Barry Ryan	MGM	2
33	26	FIRST OF MAY	Bee Gees	Polydor	2
16	27	FOX ON THE RUN	Manfred Mann	Fontana	9
22	28	LILY THE PINK	Scaffold	Parlophone	16
18	29	PEOPLE	Tymes	Direction	6
-	30	IF I CAN DREAM	Elvis Presley	RCA	1
27	31	GOING UP THE COUNTRY	Canned Heat	Liberty	8
24	32	MOVE IN A LITTLE CLOSER	Harmony Grass	RCA	4
39	[33]	RIVER DEEP MOUNTAIN HIGH	Ike and Tina Turner	London	2
40	34	ALL THE LOVE IN THE WORLD	Consortium	Pye	3
28	34	WHITE ROOM	Cream	Polydor	6
-	36	GOOD TIMES (BETTER TIMES)	Cliff Richard	Columbia	1
-	36	WINDMILLS OF YOUR MIND	Noel Harrison ●	Reprise	1
-	38	IF YOU LOVE HER	Dick Emery ●	Pye	1
-	39	BREAKFAST ON PLUTO	Don Partridge	Columbia	1
-	40	ONE ROAD	Love Affair	CBS	1

WEEK ENDING 5 MARCH 1969

LW	TW	Title	Artist	Label	Wks
1	[1]	WHERE DO YOU GO TO MY LOVELY	Peter Sarstedt	United Artists	5
2	2	(IF PARADISE IS) HALF AS NICE	Amen Corner	Immediate	6
4	[3]	PLEASE DON'T GO	Donald Peers	Columbia	11
11	4	SURROUND YOURSELF WITH SORROW	Cilla Black	Parlophone	3
19	5	I HEARD IT THROUGH THE GRAPEVINE	Marvin Gaye	Tamla Motown	4
3	6	I'M GONNA MAKE YOU LOVE ME	Diana Ross and the Supremes and the Temptations	Tamla Motown	6
9	[7]	WICHITA LINEMAN	Glen Campbell	Ember	5
20	8	MONSIEUR DUPONT	Sandie Shaw	Pye	4
5	9	THE WAY IT USED TO BE	Engelbert Humperdinck	Decca	5
17	10	GENTLE ON MY MIND	Dean Martin	Reprise	5
26	11	FIRST OF MAY	Bee Gees	Polydor	3
10	12	I'LL PICK A ROSE FOR MY ROSE	Marv Johnson	Tamla Motown	6
15	13	YOU'VE LOST THAT LOVIN' FEELING	Righteous Brothers	London	4
6	14	DANCING IN THE STREET	Martha Reeves and the Vandellas	Tamla Motown	8
18	[15]	SOUL SISTER BROWN SUGAR	Sam and Dave	Atlantic	5
36	16	GOOD TIMES (BETTER TIMES)	Cliff Richard	Columbia	2
30	17	IF I CAN DREAM	Elvis Presley	RCA	2
7	18	BLACKBERRY WAY	Move	Regal Zonophone	9
8	19	ALBATROSS	Fleetwood Mac	Blue Horizon	14
13	20	FOR ONCE IN MY LIFE	Stevie Wonder	Tamla Motown	12
40	21	ONE ROAD	Love Affair	CBS	2
34	[22]	ALL THE LOVE IN THE WORLD	Consortium	Pye	4
23	23	OB-LA-DI OB-LA-DA	Marmalade	CBS	13
29	24	PEOPLE	Tymes	Direction	7
14	25	I GUESS I'LL ALWAYS LOVE YOU	Isley Brothers	Tamla Motown	7
39	26	BREAKFAST ON PLUTO	Don Partridge	Columbia	2
-	26	I CAN HEAR MUSIC	Beach Boys	Capitol	1
12	28	YOU GOT SOUL	Johnny Nash	Major Minor	9
22	28	YOU AIN'T LIVIN' TILL YOU'RE LOVIN'	Marvin Gaye and Tammi Terrell	Tamla Motown	6
-	30	GAMES PEOPLE PLAY	Joe South ●	Capitol	1
28	31	LILY THE PINK	Scaffold	Parlophone	17
25	32	LOVE IS LOVE	Barry Ryan	MGM	3
-	33	SORRY SUZANNE	Hollies	Parlophone	1

March 1969

□ Highest position disc reached ● Act's first ever week on chart

LW	TW	Title	Artist	Label	Wks
36	34	WINDMILLS OF YOUR MIND	Noel Harrison	Reprise	2
32	35	MOVE IN A LITTLE CLOSER	Harmony Grass	RCA	5
-	35	A MINUTE OF YOUR TIME	Tom Jones	Decca	13
-	37	HEY JUDE	Wilson Pickett	Atlantic	7
24	37	SOMETHING'S HAPPENING	Herman's Hermits	Columbia	13
-	39	GET READY	Temptations	Tamla Motown	1
38	40	IF YOU LOVE HER	Dick Emery	Pye	2

WEEK ENDING 12 MARCH 1969

LW	TW	Title	Artist	Label	Wks
1	[1]	WHERE DO YOU GO TO MY LOVELY	Peter Sarstedt	United Artists	6
5	2	I HEARD IT THROUGH THE GRAPEVINE	Marvin Gaye	Tamla Motown	5
9	[3]	THE WAY IT USED TO BE	Engelbert Humperdinck	Decca	6
4	4	SURROUND YOURSELF WITH SORROW	Cilla Black	Parlophone	4
10	5	GENTLE ON MY MIND	Dean Martin	Reprise	6
11	[6]	FIRST OF MAY	Bee Gees	Polydor	4
8	7	MONSIEUR DUPONT	Sandie Shaw	Pye	5
7	8	WICHITA LINEMAN	Glen Campbell	Ember	6
6	9	I'M GONNA MAKE YOU LOVE ME	Diana Ross and the Supremes and the Temptations	Tamla Motown	7
3	10	PLEASE DON'T GO	Donald Peers	Columbia	12
2	11	(IF PARADISE IS) HALF AS NICE	Amen Corner	Immediate	7
13	12	YOU'VE LOST THAT LOVIN' FEELING	Righteous Brothers	London	5
17	13	IF I CAN DREAM	Elvis Presley	RCA	3
33	14	SORRY SUZANNE	Hollies	Parlophone	2
16	15	GOOD TIMES (BETTER TIMES)	Cliff Richard	Columbia	3
12	16	I'LL PICK A ROSE FOR MY ROSE	Marv Johnson	Tamla Motown	7
14	17	DANCING IN THE STREET	Martha Reeves and the Vandellas	Tamla Motown	9
21	18	ONE ROAD	Love Affair	CBS	3
34	19	WINDMILLS OF YOUR MIND	Noel Harrison	Reprise	3
30	20	GAMES PEOPLE PLAY	Joe South	Capitol	2
39	21	GET READY	Temptations	Tamla Motown	2
-	22	BOOM BANG-A-BANG	Lulu	Columbia	1
15	23	SOUL SISTER BROWN SUGAR	Sam and Dave	Atlantic	6
19	24	ALBATROSS	Fleetwood Mac	Blue Horizon	15
24	25	PEOPLE	Tymes	Direction	8
-	26	IN THE BAD BAD OLD DAYS	Foundations	Pye	1
26	27	I CAN HEAR MUSIC	Beach Boys	Capitol	2
28	28	YOU GOT SOUL	Johnny Nash	Major Minor	10
21	29	IT'S TOO LATE NOW	Long John Baldry	Pye	4
32	30	LOVE IS LOVE	Barry Ryan	MGM	4
-	31	DON JUAN	Dave Dee, Dozy, Beaky, Mick and Tich	Fontana	1
28	32	YOU AIN'T LIVIN' TILL YOU'RE LOVIN'	Marvin Gaye and Tammi Terrell	Tamla Motown	7
40	[32]	IF YOU LOVE HER	Dick Emery	Pye	3
22	34	ALL THE LOVE IN THE WORLD	Consortium	Pye	5
-	[34]	YOU'RE MY EVERYTHING	Max Bygraves	Pye	1
-	36	MARIA ELENA	Gene Pitney	Stateside	1
-	37	PASSING STRANGERS	Sarah Vaughan and Billy Eckstine	Mercury	1
26	38	BREAKFAST ON PLUTO	Don Partridge	Columbia	3
31	38	LILY THE PINK	Scaffold	Parlophone	18
23	40	OB-LA-DI OB-LA-DA	Marmalade	CBS	14

WEEK ENDING 19 MARCH 1969

LW	TW	Title	Artist	Label	Wks
1	[1]	WHERE DO YOU GO TO MY LOVELY	Peter Sarstedt	United Artists	7
2	2	I HEARD IT THROUGH THE GRAPEVINE	Marvin Gaye	Tamla Motown	6
3	[3]	THE WAY IT USED TO BE	Engelbert Humperdinck	Decca	7
5	4	GENTLE ON MY MIND	Dean Martin	Reprise	7

■Peter Sarstedt is the brother of Eden Kane, who topped the charts in 1961. Although the McCartney brothers have recently both topped the charts as part of separate groups, the Sarstedts remain the only brothers to have had solo number ones until the Osmonds equal the feat in 1972 (19.03.69)■ *(If Paradise Is) Half As Nice* falls from two to 11. The only positions within the Top Ten that it ever occupied were numbers one and two (12.03.69)■

March 1969

□ Highest position disc reached ● Act's first ever week on chart

LW	TW	Title	Artist	Label	Wks
10	4	PLEASE DON'T GO	Donald Peers	*Columbia*	13
4	6	SURROUND YOURSELF WITH SORROW	Cilla Black	*Parlophone*	5
7	7	MONSIEUR DUPONT	Sandie Shaw	*Pye*	6
8	8	WICHITA LINEMAN	Glen Campbell	*Ember*	7
6	9	FIRST OF MAY	Bee Gees	*Polydor*	5
12	[10]	YOU'VE LOST THAT LOVIN' FEELING	Righteous Brothers	*London*	6
13	[11]	IF I CAN DREAM	Elvis Presley	*RCA*	4
14	12	SORRY SUZANNE	Hollies	*Parlophone*	3
15	13	GOOD TIMES (BETTER TIMES)	Cliff Richard	*Columbia*	4
20	14	GAMES PEOPLE PLAY	Joe South	*Capitol*	3
11	15	(IF PARADISE IS) HALF AS NICE	Amen Corner	*Immediate*	8
18	[16]	ONE ROAD	Love Affair	*CBS*	4
21	17	GET READY	Temptations	*Tamla Motown*	3
26	18	IN THE BAD BAD OLD DAYS	Foundations	*Pye*	2
9	19	I'M GONNA MAKE YOU LOVE ME	Diana Ross and the Supremes and the Temptations	*Tamla Motown*	8
27	20	I CAN HEAR MUSIC	Beach Boys	*Capitol*	3
19	21	WINDMILLS OF YOUR MIND	Noel Harrison	*Reprise*	4
22	22	BOOM BANG-A-BANG	Lulu	*Columbia*	2
31	[23]	DON JUAN	Dave Dee, Dozy, Beaky, Mick and Tich	*Fontana*	2
16	23	I'LL PICK A ROSE FOR MY ROSE	Marv Johnson	*Tamla Motown*	8
36	25	MARIA ELENA	Gene Pitney	*Stateside*	2
-	26	HARLEM SHUFFLE	Bob and Earl ●	*Island*	1
34	27	ALL THE LOVE IN THE WORLD	Consortium	*Pye*	6
40	28	OB-LA-DI OB-LA-DA	Marmalade	*CBS*	15
38	29	BREAKFAST ON PLUTO	Don Partridge	*Columbia*	4
37	30	PASSING STRANGERS	Sarah Vaughan and Billy Eckstine	*Mercury*	2
38	31	LILY THE PINK	Scaffold	*Parlophone*	19
-	32	SOMETHING'S HAPPENING	Herman's Hermits	*Columbia*	14
23	33	SOUL SISTER BROWN SUGAR	Sam and Dave	*Atlantic*	7
17	33	DANCING IN THE STREET	Martha Reeves and the Vandellas	*Tamla Motown*	10
24	35	ALBATROSS	Fleetwood Mac	*Blue Horizon*	16
-	[36]	AFTERGLOW OF YOUR LOVE	Small Faces	*Immediate*	1
-	[36]	EVERYDAY PEOPLE	Sly and the Family Stone	*Direction*	1
-	38	PINBALL WIZARD	Who	*Track*	1
-	38	HELLO WORLD	Tremeloes	*CBS*	1
-	40	THE ISRAELITES	Desmond Dekker and the Aces	*Pyramid*	1
25	40	PEOPLE	Tymes	*Direction*	9

WEEK ENDING 26 MARCH 1969

LW	TW	Title	Artist	Label	Wks
2	[1]	I HEARD IT THROUGH THE GRAPEVINE	Marvin Gaye	*Tamla Motown*	7
1	2	WHERE DO YOU GO TO MY LOVELY	Peter Sarstedt	*United Artists*	8
6	[3]	SURROUND YOURSELF WITH SORROW	Cilla Black	*Parlophone*	6
12	4	SORRY SUZANNE	Hollies	*Parlophone*	4
4	5	GENTLE ON MY MIND	Dean Martin	*Reprise*	8
14	[6]	GAMES PEOPLE PLAY	Joe South	*Capitol*	4
9	7	FIRST OF MAY	Bee Gees	*Polydor*	6
7	8	MONSIEUR DUPONT	Sandie Shaw	*Pye*	7
22	9	BOOM BANG-A-BANG	Lulu	*Columbia*	3
17	[10]	GET READY	Temptations	*Tamla Motown*	4
11	[11]	IF I CAN DREAM	Elvis Presley	*RCA*	5
13	[12]	GOOD TIMES (BETTER TIMES)	Cliff Richard	*Columbia*	5
3	13	THE WAY IT USED TO BE	Engelbert Humperdinck	*Decca*	8
8	14	WICHITA LINEMAN	Glen Campbell	*Ember*	8
18	15	IN THE BAD BAD OLD DAYS	Foundations	*Pye*	3
21	16	WINDMILLS OF YOUR MIND	Noel Harrison	*Reprise*	5
10	17	YOU'VE LOST THAT LOVIN' FEELING	Righteous Brothers	*London*	7
20	18	I CAN HEAR MUSIC	Beach Boys	*Capitol*	4
16	19	ONE ROAD	Love Affair	*CBS*	5
4	20	PLEASE DON'T GO	Donald Peers	*Columbia*	14
40	21	THE ISRAELITES	Desmond Dekker and the Aces	*Pyramid*	1
38	22	HELLO WORLD	Tremeloes	*CBS*	2
26	23	HARLEM SHUFFLE	Bob and Earl	*Island*	2
30	24	PASSING STRANGERS	Sarah Vaughan and Billy Eckstine	*Mercury*	3
38	25	PINBALL WIZARD	Who	*Track*	2
23	26	DON JUAN	Dave Dee, Dozy, Beaky, Mick and Tich	*Fontana*	3
23	27	I'LL PICK A ROSE FOR MY ROSE	Marv Johnson	*Tamla Motown*	9
15	28	(IF PARADISE IS) HALF AS NICE	Amen Corner	*Immediate*	9
-	29	I DON'T KNOW WHY	Stevie Wonder	*Tamla Motown*	1
25	30	MARIA ELENA	Gene Pitney	*Stateside*	3
19	31	I'M GONNA MAKE YOU LOVE ME	Diana Ross and the Supremes and the Temptations	*Tamla Motown*	9
-	31	SANCTUS	Troubadours Du Roi Baudouin ●	*Philips*	1
-	33	MOCKINGBIRD	Inez and Charlie Foxx	*United Artists*	2
31	34	LILY THE PINK	Scaffold	*Parlophone*	20
28	34	OB-LA-DI OB-LA-DA	Marmalade	*CBS*	16
27	36	ALL THE LOVE IN THE WORLD	Consortium	*Pye*	7
29	37	BREAKFAST ON PLUTO	Don Partridge	*Columbia*	5
-	[38]	KUMBAYA	Sandpipers	*A&M*	1
-	[39]	WITH PEN IN HAND	Vikki Carr	*Liberty*	1
-	40	YOU GOT SOUL	Johnny Nash	*Major Minor*	11

WEEK ENDING 2 APRIL 1969

LW	TW	Title	Artist	Label	Wks
1	[1]	I HEARD IT THROUGH THE GRAPEVINE	Marvin Gaye	*Tamla Motown*	8
5	[2]	GENTLE ON MY MIND	Dean Martin	*Reprise*	9
4	[3]	SORRY SUZANNE	Hollies	*Parlophone*	5
9	4	BOOM BANG-A-BANG	Lulu	*Columbia*	4
21	5	THE ISRAELITES	Desmond Dekker and the Aces	*Pyramid*	2
8	[6]	MONSIEUR DUPONT	Sandie Shaw	*Pye*	8
2	7	WHERE DO YOU GO TO MY LOVELY	Peter Sarstedt	*United Artists*	9
6	8	GAMES PEOPLE PLAY	Joe South	*Capitol*	5
15	9	IN THE BAD BAD OLD DAYS	Foundations	*Pye*	4
7	10	FIRST OF MAY	Bee Gees	*Polydor*	7
3	11	SURROUND YOURSELF WITH SORROW	Cilla Black	*Parlophone*	7
12	[12]	GOOD TIMES (BETTER TIMES)	Cliff Richard	*Columbia*	6
10	13	GET READY	Temptations	*Tamla Motown*	5
16	14	WINDMILLS OF YOUR MIND	Noel Harrison	*Reprise*	6
11	15	IF I CAN DREAM	Elvis Presley	*RCA*	6
13	16	THE WAY IT USED TO BE	Engelbert Humperdinck	*Decca*	9
25	17	PINBALL WIZARD	Who	*Track*	3
18	18	I CAN HEAR MUSIC	Beach Boys	*Capitol*	5
14	18	WICHITA LINEMAN	Glen Campbell	*Ember*	9
17	20	YOU'VE LOST THAT LOVIN' FEELING	Righteous Brothers	*London*	8
23	21	HARLEM SHUFFLE	Bob and Earl	*Island*	3
22	22	HELLO WORLD	Tremeloes	*CBS*	3
20	23	PLEASE DON'T GO	Donald Peers	*Columbia*	15
19	24	ONE ROAD	Love Affair	*CBS*	6
-	25	GOODBYE	Mary Hopkin	*Apple*	1
29	26	I DON'T KNOW WHY	Stevie Wonder	*Tamla Motown*	2
24	27	PASSING STRANGERS	Sarah Vaughan and Billy Eckstine	*Mercury*	4
-	28	CUPID	Johnny Nash	*Major Minor*	1
26	28	DON JUAN	Dave Dee, Dozy, Beaky, Mick and Tich	*Fontana*	4
31	30	I'M GONNA MAKE YOU LOVE ME	Diana Ross and the Supremes and the Temptations	*Tamla Motown*	10
30	30	MARIA ELENA	Gene Pitney	*Stateside*	4
34	32	OB-LA-DI OB-LA-DA	Marmalade	*CBS*	17
-	33	MICHAEL AND THE SLIPPER TREE	Equals	*President*	1
31	34	SANCTUS	Troubadours Du Roi Baudouin	*Philips*	2
-	35	ALBATROSS	Fleetwood Mac	*Blue Horizon*	17
-	35	COME BACK AND SHAKE ME	Clodagh Rodgers ●	*RCA*	1
34	35	LILY THE PINK	Scaffold	*Parlophone*	21
28	38	(IF PARADISE IS) HALF AS NICE	Amen Corner	*Immediate*	10
-	39	WALLS FELL DOWN	Marbles	*Polydor*	1
27	40	I'LL PICK A ROSE FOR MY ROSE	Marv Johnson	*Tamla Motown*	10

In these weeks ■ The Righteous Brothers' *You've Lost That Lovin' Feelin'* becomes the first single to be a Top Ten hit in two entirely separate releases. It will go on to complete a hat-trick of Top Ten entries in 1990 (19.03.69) ■ *Sanctus* by Les Troubadours Du Roi Baudouin is an excerpt from the Congolese 'Missa Luba'. It was featured in the hit movie 'If', which explains its chart success (26.03.69)■

April 1969

□ Highest position disc reached ● Act's first ever week on chart

WEEK ENDING 9 APRIL 1969

LW	TW	Title	Artist	Label	Wks
1	[1]	I HEARD IT THROUGH THE GRAPEVINE	Marvin Gaye	Tamla Motown	9
4	[2]	BOOM BANG-A-BANG	Lulu	Columbia	5
5	3	THE ISRAELITES	Desmond Dekker and the Aces	Pyramid	3
2	4	GENTLE ON MY MIND	Dean Martin	Reprise	10
3	5	SORRY SUZANNE	Hollies	Parlophone	6
25	6	GOODBYE	Mary Hopkin	Apple	2
8	7	GAMES PEOPLE PLAY	Joe South	Capitol	6
9	[8]	IN THE BAD BAD OLD DAYS	Foundations	Pye	5
17	9	PINBALL WIZARD	Who	Track	4
18	[10]	I CAN HEAR MUSIC	Beach Boys	Capitol	6
6	11	MONSIEUR DUPONT	Sandie Shaw	Pye	9
11	12	SURROUND YOURSELF WITH SORROW	Cilla Black	Parlophone	8
13	13	GET READY	Temptations	Tamla Motown	6
7	14	WHERE DO YOU GO TO MY LOVELY	Peter Sarstedt	United Artists	10
14	15	WINDMILLS OF YOUR MIND	Noel Harrison	Reprise	7
22	16	HELLO WORLD	Tremeloes	CBS	4
10	17	FIRST OF MAY	Bee Gees	Polydor	8
12	18	GOOD TIMES (BETTER TIMES)	Cliff Richard	Columbia	7
15	19	IF I CAN DREAM	Elvis Presley	RCA	7
21	19	HARLEM SHUFFLE	Bob and Earl	Island	4
16	21	THE WAY IT USED TO BE	Engelbert Humperdinck	Decca	10
26	22	I DON'T KNOW WHY	Stevie Wonder	Tamla Motown	3
20	23	YOU'VE LOST THAT LOVIN' FEELING	Righteous Brothers	London	9
23	24	PLEASE DON'T GO	Donald Peers	Columbia	16
24	25	ONE ROAD	Love Affair	CBS	7
18	26	WICHITA LINEMAN	Glen Campbell	Ember	10
35	27	COME BACK AND SHAKE ME	Clodagh Rodgers	RCA	2
34	[28]	SANCTUS	Troubadours Du Roi Baudouin	Philips	3
28	29	DON JUAN	Dave Dee, Dozy, Beaky, Mick and Tich	Fontana	5
27	30	PASSING STRANGERS	Sarah Vaughan and Billy Eckstine	Mercury	5
33	31	MICHAEL AND THE SLIPPER TREE	Equals	President	2
28	32	CUPID	Johnny Nash	Major Minor	2
39	33	WALLS FELL DOWN	Marbles	Polydor	2
30	34	I'M GONNA MAKE YOU LOVE ME	Diana Ross and the Supremes and the Temptations	Tamla Motown	11
-	35	ROAD RUNNER	Junior Walker and the All Stars	Tamla Motown	1
30	36	MARIA ELENA	Gene Pitney	Stateside	5
-	37	EVERYDAY PEOPLE	Sly and the Family Stone	Direction	2
35	38	LILY THE PINK	Scaffold	Parlophone	22
-	[38]	I'LL BE THERE	Jackie Trent	Pye	1
35	38	ALBATROSS	Fleetwood Mac	Blue Horizon	18

WEEK ENDING 16 APRIL 1969

LW	TW	Title	Artist	Label	Wks
3	[1]	THE ISRAELITES	Desmond Dekker and the Aces	Pyramid	4
6	[2]	GOODBYE	Mary Hopkin	Apple	3
1	3	I HEARD IT THROUGH THE GRAPEVINE	Marvin Gaye	Tamla Motown	10
2	4	BOOM BANG-A-BANG	Lulu	Columbia	6
4	5	GENTLE ON MY MIND	Dean Martin	Reprise	11
9	6	PINBALL WIZARD	Who	Track	5
5	7	SORRY SUZANNE	Hollies	Parlophone	7
9	[8]	IN THE BAD BAD OLD DAYS	Foundations	Pye	6
7	9	GAMES PEOPLE PLAY	Joe South	Capitol	7
15	10	WINDMILLS OF YOUR MIND	Noel Harrison	Reprise	8
10	11	I CAN HEAR MUSIC	Beach Boys	Capitol	7
32	12	CUPID	Johnny Nash	Major Minor	3
11	13	MONSIEUR DUPONT	Sandie Shaw	Pye	10
16	14	HELLO WORLD	Tremeloes	CBS	5
27	15	COME BACK AND SHAKE ME	Clodagh Rodgers	RCA	3
19	16	HARLEM SHUFFLE	Bob and Earl	Island	5
12	17	SURROUND YOURSELF WITH SORROW	Cilla Black	Parlophone	9
22	18	I DON'T KNOW WHY	Stevie Wonder	Tamla Motown	4
18	19	GOOD TIMES (BETTER TIMES)	Cliff Richard	Columbia	8
13	20	GET READY	Temptations	Tamla Motown	7
-	21	MAN OF THE WORLD	Fleetwood Mac	Immediate	1
14	22	WHERE DO YOU GO TO MY LOVELY	Peter Sarstedt	United Artists	11
-	23	MY WAY	Frank Sinatra	Reprise	1
30	23	PASSING STRANGERS	Sarah Vaughan and Billy Eckstine	Mercury	6
31	25	MICHAEL AND THE SLIPPER TREE	Equals	President	3
19	26	IF I CAN DREAM	Elvis Presley	RCA	8
35	26	ROAD RUNNER	Junior Walker and the All Stars	Tamla Motown	2
17	28	FIRST OF MAY	Bee Gees	Polydor	9
33	29	WALLS FELL DOWN	Marbles	Polydor	3
21	30	THE WAY IT USED TO BE	Engelbert Humperdinck	Decca	11
-	[31]	PLASTIC MAN	Kinks	Pye	1
23	32	YOU'VE LOST THAT LOVIN' FEELING	Righteous Brothers	London	10
24	33	PLEASE DON'T GO	Donald Peers	Columbia	17
25	34	ONE ROAD	Love Affair	CBS	8
29	35	DON JUAN	Dave Dee, Dozy, Beaky, Mick and Tich	Fontana	6
-	36	BADGE	Cream	Polydor	1
28	37	SANCTUS	Troubadours Du Roi Baudouin	Philips	4
-	[37]	CROSS TOWN TRAFFIC	Jimi Hendrix	Track	1
26	39	WICHITA LINEMAN	Glen Campbell	Ember	11
-	40	COLOUR OF MY LOVE	Jefferson ●	Pye	1

WEEK ENDING 23 APRIL 1969

LW	TW	Title	Artist	Label	Wks
-	[1]	GET BACK	Beatles with Billy Preston	Apple	1
1	2	THE ISRAELITES	Desmond Dekker and the Aces	Pyramid	5
2	3	GOODBYE	Mary Hopkin	Apple	4
6	[4]	PINBALL WIZARD	Who	Track	6
5	5	GENTLE ON MY MIND	Dean Martin	Reprise	12
3	6	I HEARD IT THROUGH THE GRAPEVINE	Marvin Gaye	Tamla Motown	11
4	7	BOOM BANG-A-BANG	Lulu	Columbia	7
15	8	COME BACK AND SHAKE ME	Clodagh Rodgers	RCA	4
10	9	WINDMILLS OF YOUR MIND	Noel Harrison	Reprise	9
8	10	IN THE BAD BAD OLD DAYS	Foundations	Pye	7
16	11	HARLEM SHUFFLE	Bob and Earl	Island	6
11	12	I CAN HEAR MUSIC	Beach Boys	Capitol	8
12	13	CUPID	Johnny Nash	Major Minor	4
18	14	I DON'T KNOW WHY	Stevie Wonder	Tamla Motown	5
9	15	GAMES PEOPLE PLAY	Joe South	Capitol	8
26	16	ROAD RUNNER	Junior Walker and the All Stars	Tamla Motown	3
23	17	MY WAY	Frank Sinatra	Reprise	2
7	18	SORRY SUZANNE	Hollies	Parlophone	8
14	19	HELLO WORLD	Tremeloes	CBS	6
36	20	BADGE	Cream	Polydor	2
21	21	MAN OF THE WORLD	Fleetwood Mac	Immediate	2
23	22	PASSING STRANGERS	Sarah Vaughan and Billy Eckstine	Mercury	7
13	23	MONSIEUR DUPONT	Sandie Shaw	Pye	11
25	[24]	MICHAEL AND THE SLIPPER TREE	Equals	President	4
19	25	GOOD TIMES (BETTER TIMES)	Cliff Richard	Columbia	9
20	26	GET READY	Temptations	Tamla Motown	8
-	27	MY SENTIMENTAL FRIEND	Herman's Hermits	Columbia	1
29	[28]	WALLS FELL DOWN	Marbles	Polydor	4
-	29	BEHIND A PAINTED SMILE	Isley Brothers	Tamla Motown	1
22	30	WHERE DO YOU GO TO MY LOVELY	Peter Sarstedt	United Artists	12
16	31	IF I CAN DREAM	Elvis Presley	RCA	9
-	32	I'M LIVING IN SHAME	Diana Ross and the Supremes	Tamla Motown	1
28	33	FIRST OF MAY	Bee Gees	Polydor	10
40	34	COLOUR OF MY LOVE	Jefferson	Pye	2
-	35	AQUARIUS/LET THE SUNSHINE IN	Fifth Dimension ●	Liberty	1
32	36	YOU'VE LOST THAT LOVIN' FEELING	Righteous Brothers	London	11
31	37	PLASTIC MAN	Kinks	Pye	2
37	37	CROSS TOWN TRAFFIC	Jimi Hendrix	Track	2
37	39	SANCTUS	Troubadours Du Roi Baudouin	Philips	5
30	39	THE WAY IT USED TO BE	Engelbert Humperdinck	Decca	12

■ *The Israelites* by Desmond Dekker and the Aces becomes Britains first reggae number one, although Marmalade's version of the Beatles' *Ob-La-Di Ob-La-Da* had already introduced the rhythms of reggae to the number one slot (16.04.69) ■ The first week of Top 40 action for the longest-running chart hit of all, Frank Sinatra's *My Way* (16.04.69) ■ The Beatles hit number one in their first chart week for the only time with their record-breaking sixteenth number one (23.04.69) ■

April 1969

□ Highest position disc reached ● Act's first ever week on chart

LW	TW	WEEK ENDING 30 APRIL 1969		Wks
1	1	GET BACK Beatles with Billy Preston	Apple	2
3	2	GOODBYE Mary Hopkin	Apple	5
2	3	THE ISRAELITES Desmond Dekker and the Aces	Pyramid	6
4	4	PINBALL WIZARD Who	Track	7
8	5	COME BACK AND SHAKE ME Clodagh Rodgers	RCA	5
13	6	CUPID Johnny Nash	Major Minor	5
11	7	HARLEM SHUFFLE Bob and Earl	Island	7
9	8	WINDMILLS OF YOUR MIND Noel Harrison	Reprise	10
6	9	I HEARD IT THROUGH THE GRAPEVINE Marvin Gaye	Tamla Motown	12
7	10	BOOM BANG-A-BANG Lulu	Columbia	8
21	11	MAN OF THE WORLD Fleetwood Mac	Immediate	3
5	12	GENTLE ON MY MIND Dean Martin	Reprise	13
16	13	ROAD RUNNER Junior Walker and the All Stars	Tamla Motown	4
10	14	IN THE BAD BAD OLD DAYS Foundations	Pye	8
27	15	MY SENTIMENTAL FRIEND Herman's Hermits	Columbia	2
17	16	MY WAY Frank Sinatra	Reprise	3
14	17	I DON'T KNOW WHY Stevie Wonder	Tamla Motown	6
12	18	I CAN HEAR MUSIC Beach Boys	Capitol	9
15	19	GAMES PEOPLE PLAY Joe South	Capitol	9
29	20	BEHIND A PAINTED SMILE Isley Brothers	Tamla Motown	2
22	21	PASSING STRANGERS Sarah Vaughan and Billy Eckstine	Mercury	8
19	22	HELLO WORLD Tremeloes	CBS	7
34	23	COLOUR OF MY LOVE Jefferson	Pye	3
-	24	DIZZY Tommy Roe	Sateside	1
-	25	THE BOXER Simon and Garfunkel	CBS	1
24	26	MICHAEL AND THE SLIPPER TREE Equals	President	5
18	27	SORRY SUZANNE Hollies	Parlophone	9
20	28	BADGE Cream	Polydor	3
32	29	I'M LIVING IN SHAME Diana Ross and the Supremes	Tamla Motown	2
23	30	MONSIEUR DUPONT Sandie Shaw	Pye	12
25	31	GOOD TIMES (BETTER TIMES) Cliff Richard	Columbia	10
37	32	PLASTIC MAN Kinks	Pye	3
-	33	BLUER THAN BLUE Rolf Harris	Columbia	1
30	33	WHERE DO YOU GO TO MY LOVELY Peter Sarstedt	United Artists	13
35	35	AQUARIUS/LET THE SUNSHINE IN Fifth Dimension	Liberty	2
26	36	GET READY Temptations	Tamla Motown	9
-	36	RAGAMUFFIN MAN Manfred Mann	Fontana	1
28	38	WALLS FELL DOWN Marbles	Polydor	5
-	38	PLEASE DON'T GO Donald Peers	Columbia	18
31	40	IF I CAN DREAM Elvis Presley	RCA	10
-	40	WITH PEN IN HAND Vikki Carr	Liberty	2

LW	TW	WEEK ENDING 7 MAY 1969		Wks
1	1	GET BACK Beatles with Billy Preston	Apple	3
2	2	GOODBYE Mary Hopkin	Apple	6
5	3	COME BACK AND SHAKE ME Clodagh Rodgers	RCA	6
4	4	PINBALL WIZARD Who	Track	8
15	5	MY SENTIMENTAL FRIEND Herman's Hermits	Columbia	3
3	6	THE ISRAELITES Desmond Dekker and the Aces	Pyramid	7
11	7	MAN OF THE WORLD Fleetwood Mac	Immediate	4
20	8	BEHIND A PAINTED SMILE Isley Brothers	Tamla Motown	3
16	9	MY WAY Frank Sinatra	Reprise	4
6	10	CUPID Johnny Nash	Major Minor	6
7	11	HARLEM SHUFFLE Bob and Earl	Island	8
13	12	ROAD RUNNER Junior Walker and the All Stars	Tamla Motown	5
12	13	GENTLE ON MY MIND Dean Martin	Reprise	14
29	14	I'M LIVING IN SHAME Diana Ross and the Supremes	Tamla Motown	3
25	15	THE BOXER Simon and Garfunkel	CBS	2
17	16	I DON'T KNOW WHY Stevie Wonder	Tamla Motown	7
24	17	DIZZY Tommy Roe	Sateside	2
28	18	BADGE Cream	Polydor	4
8	19	WINDMILLS OF YOUR MIND Noel Harrison	Reprise	11
21	20	PASSING STRANGERS Sarah Vaughan and Billy Eckstine	Mercury	9
9	21	I HEARD IT THROUGH THE GRAPEVINE Marvin Gaye	Tamla Motown	13
10	22	BOOM BANG-A-BANG Lulu	Columbia	9
36	23	RAGAMUFFIN MAN Manfred Mann	Fontana	2
19	24	GAMES PEOPLE PLAY Joe South	Capitol	10
35	25	AQUARIUS/LET THE SUNSHINE IN Fifth Dimension	Liberty	3
18	26	I CAN HEAR MUSIC Beach Boys	Capitol	10
27	27	SORRY SUZANNE Hollies	Parlophone	10
23	28	COLOUR OF MY LOVE Jefferson	Pye	4
-	29	GALVESTON Glen Campbell	Ember	1
33	30	BLUER THAN BLUE Rolf Harris	Columbia	2
30	31	MONSIEUR DUPONT Sandie Shaw	Pye	13
26	32	MICHAEL AND THE SLIPPER TREE Equals	President	6
14	33	IN THE BAD BAD OLD DAYS Foundations	Pye	9
31	34	GOOD TIMES (BETTER TIMES) Cliff Richard	Columbia	11
22	35	HELLO WORLD Tremeloes	CBS	8
-	35	MY FRIEND Roy Orbison	London	1
-	37	THE TRACKS OF MY TEARS Smokey Robinson and the Miracles	Tamla Motown	1
-	37	SANCTUS Troubadours Du Roi Baudouin	Philips	6
-	39	TIME IS TIGHT Booker T and the MGs	Stax	1
-	39	I'D RATHER GO BLIND Chicken Shack ●	Blue Horizon	1
-	39	LITTLE GREEN APPLES Roger Miller	Mercury	1

LW	TW	WEEK ENDING 14 MAY 1969		Wks
1	1	GET BACK Beatles with Billy Preston	Apple	4
5	2	MY SENTIMENTAL FRIEND Herman's Hermits	Columbia	4
7	3	MAN OF THE WORLD Fleetwood Mac	Immediate	5
3	4	COME BACK AND SHAKE ME Clodagh Rodgers	RCA	7
2	5	GOODBYE Mary Hopkin	Apple	7
9	6	MY WAY Frank Sinatra	Reprise	5
8	7	BEHIND A PAINTED SMILE Isley Brothers	Tamla Motown	4
6	8	THE ISRAELITES Desmond Dekker and the Aces	Pyramid	8
15	9	THE BOXER Simon and Garfunkel	CBS	3
4	10	PINBALL WIZARD Who	Track	9
17	11	DIZZY Tommy Roe	Sateside	3
12	12	ROAD RUNNER Junior Walker and the All Stars	Tamla Motown	6
11	13	HARLEM SHUFFLE Bob and Earl	Island	9
10	14	CUPID Johnny Nash	Major Minor	7
23	15	RAGAMUFFIN MAN Manfred Mann	Fontana	3
13	16	GENTLE ON MY MIND Dean Martin	Reprise	15
19	17	WINDMILLS OF YOUR MIND Noel Harrison	Reprise	12
22	17	BOOM BANG-A-BANG Lulu	Columbia	10
-	19	LOVE ME TONIGHT Tom Jones	Decca	1
20	20	PASSING STRANGERS Sarah Vaughan and Billy Eckstine	Mercury	10
14	21	I'M LIVING IN SHAME Diana Ross and the Supremes	Tamla Motown	4
28	22	COLOUR OF MY LOVE Jefferson	Pye	5
25	22	AQUARIUS/LET THE SUNSHINE IN Fifth Dimension	Liberty	4
16	24	I DON'T KNOW WHY Stevie Wonder	Tamla Motown	8
18	25	BADGE Cream	Polydor	5
21	26	I HEARD IT THROUGH THE GRAPEVINE Marvin Gaye	Tamla Motown	14
29	27	GALVESTON Glen Campbell	Ember	2
-	28	DICK-A-DUM-DUM Des O'Connor	Columbia	1
24	29	GAMES PEOPLE PLAY Joe South	Capitol	11
37	30	THE TRACKS OF MY TEARS Smokey Robinson and the Miracles	Tamla Motown	2
39	30	TIME IS TIGHT Booker T and the MGs	Stax	2
27	32	SORRY SUZANNE Hollies	Parlophone	11
26	33	I CAN HEAR MUSIC Beach Boys	Capitol	11
30	34	BLUER THAN BLUE Rolf Harris	Columbia	3
-	35	SNAKE IN THE GRASS Dave Dee, Dozy, Beaky, Mick and Tich	Fontana	1
35	36	MY FRIEND Roy Orbison	London	2
-	36	YOU'VE MADE ME SO VERY HAPPY Blood Sweat And Tears ●	CBS	1
-	38	GROOVY BABY Microbe ●	CBS	1

In these weeks ■ Twelve years after the record was first a hit, Sarah Vaughan and Billy Eckstine's *Passing Strangers* improves its best chart position by two places (07.05.69) ■ A sporting look to the charts, with *The Boxer*, *Pinball Wizard*, *Road Runner* and *Games People Play* all in the Top 30 for three consecutive weeks (14.05.69) ■ Jefferson was formerly with the Rockin' Berries. His only chart success comes almost four years after his group's last hit (14.05.69)■

LW	TW	Title	Artist	Label	Wks
-	39	(YOUR LOVE KEEPS LIFTING ME) HIGHER AND HIGHER	Jackie Wilson	MCA	1
37	40	SANCTUS	Troubadours Du Roi Baudouin	Philips	7

WEEK ENDING 21 MAY 1969

LW	TW	Title	Artist	Label	Wks
1	1	GET BACK	Beatles with Billy Preston	Apple	5
2	2	MY SENTIMENTAL FRIEND	Herman's Hermits	Columbia	5
3	3	MAN OF THE WORLD	Fleetwood Mac	Immediate	6
11	4	DIZZY	Tommy Roe	Sateside	4
7	5	BEHIND A PAINTED SMILE	Isley Brothers	Tamla Motown	5
6	6	MY WAY	Frank Sinatra	Reprise	6
4	7	COME BACK AND SHAKE ME	Clodagh Rodgers	RCA	8
5	8	GOODBYE	Mary Hopkin	Apple	8
9	9	THE BOXER	Simon and Garfunkel	CBS	4
15	10	RAGAMUFFIN MAN	Manfred Mann	Fontana	4
10	11	PINBALL WIZARD	Who	Track	10
12	12	ROAD RUNNER	Junior Walker and the All Stars	Tamla Motown	7
22	13	AQUARIUS/LET THE SUNSHINE IN	Fifth Dimension	Liberty	5
19	14	LOVE ME TONIGHT	Tom Jones	Decca	2
21	15	I'M LIVING IN SHAME	Diana Ross and the Supremes	Tamla Motown	5
13	16	HARLEM SHUFFLE	Bob and Earl	Island	10
8	17	THE ISRAELITES	Desmond Dekker and the Aces	Pyramid	9
27	18	GALVESTON	Glen Campbell	Ember	3
14	19	CUPID	Johnny Nash	Major Minor	8
25	20	BADGE	Cream	Polydor	6
20	21	PASSING STRANGERS	Sarah Vaughan and Billy Eckstine	Mercury	11
30	22	THE TRACKS OF MY TEARS	Smokey Robinson and the Miracles	Tamla Motown	3
16	23	GENTLE ON MY MIND	Dean Martin	Reprise	16
28	24	DICK-A-DUM-DUM	Des O'Connor	Columbia	2
17	25	BOOM BANG-A-BANG	Lulu	Columbia	11
-	26	I'D RATHER GO BLIND	Chicken Shack	Blue Horizon	2
30	27	TIME IS TIGHT	Booker T and the MGs	Stax	3
35	28	SNAKE IN THE GRASS	Dave Dee, Dozy, Beaky, Mick and Tich	Fontana	2
24	29	I DON'T KNOW WHY	Stevie Wonder	Tamla Motown	9
22	30	COLOUR OF MY LOVE	Jefferson	Pye	6
-	31	I THREW IT ALL AWAY	Bob Dylan	CBS	1
39	32	(YOUR LOVE KEEPS LIFTING ME) HIGHER AND HIGHER	Jackie Wilson	MCA	2
-	33	HAPPY HEART	Andy Williams	CBS	1
17	34	WINDMILLS OF YOUR MIND	Noel Harrison	Reprise	13
36	35	YOU'VE MADE ME SO VERY HAPPY	Blood Sweat And Tears	CBS	2
-	36	LIVING IN THE PAST	Jethro Tull	Island	1
34	36	BLUER THAN BLUE	Rolf Harris	Columbia	4
38	38	GROOVY BABY	Microbe	CBS	2
-	39	OH HAPPY DAY	Edwin Hawkins Singers ●	Buddah	1
-	40	GIMME GIMME GOOD LOVIN'	Crazy Elephant ●	Major Minor	1
36	40	MY FRIEND	Roy Orbison	London	3

WEEK ENDING 28 MAY 1969

LW	TW	Title	Artist	Label	Wks
1	1	GET BACK	Beatles with Billy Preston	Apple	6
3	2	MAN OF THE WORLD	Fleetwood Mac	Immediate	7
4	3	DIZZY	Tommy Roe	Sateside	5
2	4	MY SENTIMENTAL FRIEND	Herman's Hermits	Columbia	6
6	5	MY WAY	Frank Sinatra	Reprise	7
5	6	BEHIND A PAINTED SMILE	Isley Brothers	Tamla Motown	6
9	7	THE BOXER	Simon and Garfunkel	CBS	5
10	8	RAGAMUFFIN MAN	Manfred Mann	Fontana	5
14	9	LOVE ME TONIGHT	Tom Jones	Decca	3
7	10	COME BACK AND SHAKE ME	Clodagh Rodgers	RCA	9
13	11	AQUARIUS/LET THE SUNSHINE IN	Fifth Dimension	Liberty	6
8	12	GOODBYE	Mary Hopkin	Apple	9
39	13	OH HAPPY DAY	Edwin Hawkins Singers	Buddah	2
24	14	DICK-A-DUM-DUM	Des O'Connor	Columbia	3
27	15	TIME IS TIGHT	Booker T and the MGs	Stax	4
15	16	I'M LIVING IN SHAME	Diana Ross and the Supremes	Tamla Motown	6
12	17	ROAD RUNNER	Junior Walker and the All Stars	Tamla Motown	8
18	18	GALVESTON	Glen Campbell	Ember	4
22	19	THE TRACKS OF MY TEARS	Smokey Robinson and the Miracles	Tamla Motown	4
32	20	(YOUR LOVE KEEPS LIFTING ME) HIGHER AND HIGHER	Jackie Wilson	MCA	3
21	21	PASSING STRANGERS	Sarah Vaughan and Billy Eckstine	Mercury	12
20	22	BADGE	Cream	Polydor	7
28	23	SNAKE IN THE GRASS	Dave Dee, Dozy, Beaky, Mick and Tich	Fontana	3
19	24	CUPID	Johnny Nash	Major Minor	9
23	25	GENTLE ON MY MIND	Dean Martin	Reprise	17
17	25	THE ISRAELITES	Desmond Dekker and the Aces	Pyramid	10
11	27	PINBALL WIZARD	Who	Track	11
16	28	HARLEM SHUFFLE	Bob and Earl	Island	11
26	28	I'D RATHER GO BLIND	Chicken Shack	Blue Horizon	3
38	30	GROOVY BABY	Microbe	CBS	3
30	31	COLOUR OF MY LOVE	Jefferson	Pye	7
40	32	GIMME GIMME GOOD LOVIN'	Crazy Elephant	Major Minor	2
-	32	BIG SHIP	Cliff Richard	Columbia	1
33	34	HAPPY HEART	Andy Williams	CBS	2
36	35	LIVING IN THE PAST	Jethro Tull	Island	2
34	36	WINDMILLS OF YOUR MIND	Noel Harrison	Reprise	14
31	36	I THREW IT ALL AWAY	Bob Dylan	CBS	2
25	38	BOOM BANG-A-BANG	Lulu	Columbia	12
-	39	PROUD MARY	Creedence Clearwater Revival ●	Liberty	1
36	40	BLUER THAN BLUE	Rolf Harris	Columbia	5
-	40	SANCTUS	Troubadours Du Roi Baudouin	Philips	8

June 1969

□ Highest position disc reached ● Act's first ever week on chart

WEEK ENDING 4 JUNE 1969

LW	TW	Title	Artist	Label	Wks
3	1	DIZZY	Tommy Roe	Sateside	6
1	2	GET BACK	Beatles with Billy Preston	Apple	7
2	3	MAN OF THE WORLD	Fleetwood Mac	Immediate	8
-	4	THE BALLAD OF JOHN AND YOKO	Beatles	Apple	1
5	5	MY WAY	Frank Sinatra	Reprise	8
7	6	THE BOXER	Simon and Garfunkel	CBS	6
4	7	MY SENTIMENTAL FRIEND	Herman's Hermits	Columbia	7
6	8	BEHIND A PAINTED SMILE	Isley Brothers	Tamla Motown	7
13	9	OH HAPPY DAY	Edwin Hawkins Singers	Buddah	3
8	10	RAGAMUFFIN MAN	Manfred Mann	Fontana	6
9	11	LOVE ME TONIGHT	Tom Jones	Decca	4
15	11	TIME IS TIGHT	Booker T and the MGs	Stax	5
19	13	THE TRACKS OF MY TEARS	Smokey Robinson and the Miracles	Tamla Motown	5
18	14	GALVESTON	Glen Campbell	Ember	5
20	15	(YOUR LOVE KEEPS LIFTING ME) HIGHER AND HIGHER	Jackie Wilson	MCA	4
11	16	AQUARIUS/LET THE SUNSHINE IN	Fifth Dimension	Liberty	7
28	17	I'D RATHER GO BLIND	Chicken Shack	Blue Horizon	4
14	18	DICK-A-DUM-DUM	Des O'Connor	Columbia	4
10	19	COME BACK AND SHAKE ME	Clodagh Rodgers	RCA	10
12	20	GOODBYE	Mary Hopkin	Apple	10
16	21	I'M LIVING IN SHAME	Diana Ross and the Supremes	Tamla Motown	7
25	22	GENTLE ON MY MIND	Dean Martin	Reprise	18
35	22	LIVING IN THE PAST	Jethro Tull	Island	3
23	24	SNAKE IN THE GRASS	Dave Dee, Dozy, Beaky, Mick and Tich	Fontana	4
32	25	BIG SHIP	Cliff Richard	Columbia	2
-	26	BOOGALOO PARTY	Flamingos ●	Philips	1
32	27	GIMME GIMME GOOD LOVIN'	Crazy Elephant	Major Minor	3
17	28	ROAD RUNNER	Junior Walker and the All Stars	Tamla Motown	9
30	29	GROOVY BABY	Microbe	CBS	4
36	30	I THREW IT ALL AWAY	Bob Dylan	CBS	3
22	31	BADGE	Cream	Polydor	8
27	32	PINBALL WIZARD	Who	Track	12
24	33	CUPID	Johnny Nash	Major Minor	10

■The Beatles almost manage to duplicate their achievement of late 1963 by knocking themselves off the top. Tommy Roe, whose last hit was in the Top Ten with The Beatles *She Loves You*, manages one week at the top, sandwiched between the final two Beatles number ones (04.06.69) ■ Two of the more intelligent titles in British chart history, *Dick-A-Dum-Dum* and *Boom Bang-A-Bang* take consecutive chart positions (21.05.69)■

June 1969

□ Highest position disc reached ● Act's first ever week on chart

LW	TW	Title	Artist	Label	Wks
21	34	PASSING STRANGERS	Sarah Vaughan and Billy Eckstine	Mercury	13
34	35	HAPPY HEART	Andy Williams	CBS	3
39	35	PROUD MARY	Creedence Clearwater Revival	Liberty	2
25	37	THE ISRAELITES	Desmond Dekker and the Aces	Pyramid	11
-	38	WHAT IS A MAN	Four Tops	Tamla Motown	1
28	39	HARLEM SHUFFLE	Bob and Earl	Island	12
40	40	SANCTUS	Troubadours Du Roi Baudouin	Philips	9

WEEK ENDING 11 JUNE 1969

LW	TW	Title	Artist	Label	Wks
4	[1]	THE BALLAD OF JOHN AND YOKO	Beatles	Apple	2
1	2	DIZZY	Tommy Roe	Stateside	7
9	3	OH HAPPY DAY	Edwin Hawkins Singers	Buddah	4
3	4	MAN OF THE WORLD	Fleetwood Mac	Immediate	9
2	5	GET BACK	Beatles with Billy Preston	Apple	8
11	6	TIME IS TIGHT	Booker T and the MGs	Stax	6
5	7	MY WAY	Frank Sinatra	Reprise	9
6	8	THE BOXER	Simon and Garfunkel	CBS	7
13	9	THE TRACKS OF MY TEARS	Smokey Robinson and the Miracles	Tamla Motown	6
10	10	RAGAMUFFIN MAN	Manfred Mann	Fontana	7
15	[11]	(YOUR LOVE KEEPS LIFTING ME) HIGHER AND HIGHER	Jackie Wilson	MCA	5
11	12	LOVE ME TONIGHT	Tom Jones	Decca	5
25	13	BIG SHIP	Cliff Richard	Columbia	3
18	[14]	DICK-A-DUM-DUM	Des O'Connor	Columbia	5
22	15	LIVING IN THE PAST	Jethro Tull	Island	4
16	16	AQUARIUS/LET THE SUNSHINE IN	Fifth Dimension	Liberty	8
14	17	GALVESTON	Glen Campbell	Ember	6
7	18	MY SENTIMENTAL FRIEND	Herman's Hermits	Columbia	8
17	19	I'D RATHER GO BLIND	Chicken Shack	Blue Horizon	5
8	20	BEHIND A PAINTED SMILE	Isley Brothers	Tamla Motown	8
27	21	GIMME GIMME GOOD LOVIN'	Crazy Elephant	Major Minor	4
19	22	COME BACK AND SHAKE ME	Clodagh Rodgers	RCA	11
35	22	PROUD MARY	Creedence Clearwater Revival	Liberty	3
-	24	FROZEN ORANGE JUICE	Peter Sarstedt	United Artists	1
35	25	HAPPY HEART	Andy Williams	CBS	4
20	26	GOODBYE	Mary Hopkin	Apple	11
38	27	WHAT IS A MAN	Four Tops	Tamla Motown	2
21	28	I'M LIVING IN SHAME	Diana Ross and the Supremes	Tamla Motown	8
-	29	BREAKAWAY	Beach Boys	Capitol	1
29	30	GROOVY BABY	Microbe	CBS	5
-	31	TOMORROW TOMORROW	Bee Gees	Polydor	1
24	32	SNAKE IN THE GRASS	Dave Dee, Dozy, Beaky, Mick and Tich	Fontana	5
30	33	I THREW IT ALL AWAY	Bob Dylan	CBS	4
-	34	WAY OF LIFE	Family Dogg ●	Bell	1
28	35	ROAD RUNNER	Junior Walker and the All Stars	Tamla Motown	10
-	36	IN THE GHETTO	Elvis Presley	RCA	1
31	37	BADGE	Cream	Polydor	9
37	38	THE ISRAELITES	Desmond Dekker and the Aces	Pyramid	12
22	39	GENTLE ON MY MIND	Dean Martin	Reprise	19
-	40	BABY MAKE IT SOON	Marmalade	CBS	1

WEEK ENDING 18 JUNE 1969

LW	TW	Title	Artist	Label	Wks
1	[1]	THE BALLAD OF JOHN AND YOKO	Beatles	Apple	3
3	[2]	OH HAPPY DAY	Edwin Hawkins Singers	Buddah	5
2	3	DIZZY	Tommy Roe	Stateside	8
6	[4]	TIME IS TIGHT	Booker T and the MGs	Stax	7
15	5	LIVING IN THE PAST	Jethro Tull	Island	5
5	6	GET BACK	Beatles with Billy Preston	Apple	9
7	7	MY WAY	Frank Sinatra	Reprise	10
13	[8]	BIG SHIP	Cliff Richard	Columbia	4
36	9	IN THE GHETTO	Elvis Presley	RCA	2
8	10	THE BOXER	Simon and Garfunkel	CBS	8
4	11	MAN OF THE WORLD	Fleetwood Mac	Immediate	10
9	12	THE TRACKS OF MY TEARS	Smokey Robinson and the Miracles	Tamla Motown	7
11	13	(YOUR LOVE KEEPS LIFTING ME) HIGHER AND HIGHER	Jackie Wilson	MCA	6
19	[14]	I'D RATHER GO BLIND	Chicken Shack	Blue Horizon	6
10	15	RAGAMUFFIN MAN	Manfred Mann	Fontana	8
17	16	GALVESTON	Glen Campbell	Ember	7
-	17	SOMETHING IN THE AIR	Thunderclap Newman ●	Track	1
34	18	WAY OF LIFE	Family Dogg	Bell	2
12	19	LOVE ME TONIGHT	Tom Jones	Decca	6
22	20	PROUD MARY	Creedence Clearwater Revival	Liberty	4
29	21	BREAKAWAY	Beach Boys	Capitol	2
21	22	GIMME GIMME GOOD LOVIN'	Crazy Elephant	Major Minor	5
14	23	DICK-A-DUM-DUM	Des O'Connor	Columbia	6
24	24	FROZEN ORANGE JUICE	Peter Sarstedt	United Artists	2
-	25	LIGHTS OF CINCINATTI	Scott Walker	Philips	1
20	26	BEHIND A PAINTED SMILE	Isley Brothers	Tamla Motown	9
18	27	MY SENTIMENTAL FRIEND	Herman's Hermits	Columbia	9
40	28	BABY MAKE IT SOON	Marmalade	CBS	2
27	29	WHAT IS A MAN	Four Tops	Tamla Motown	3
26	30	GOODBYE	Mary Hopkin	Apple	12
16	31	AQUARIUS/LET THE SUNSHINE IN	Fifth Dimension	Liberty	9
-	32	WET DREAM	Max Romeo ●	Unity	1
39	33	GENTLE ON MY MIND	Dean Martin	Reprise	20
25	34	HAPPY HEART	Andy Williams	CBS	5
-	35	BORN TO BE WILD	Steppenwolf ●	Stateside	1
-	36	GOOD LOVIN' AIN'T EASY TO COME BY	Marvin Gaye and Tammi Terrell	Tamla Motown	1
22	37	COME BACK AND SHAKE ME	Clodagh Rodgers	RCA	12
31	38	TOMORROW TOMORROW	Bee Gees	Polydor	2
32	39	SNAKE IN THE GRASS	Dave Dee, Dozy, Beaky, Mick and Tich	Fontana	6
30	40	GROOVY BABY	Microbe	CBS	6
33	40	I THREW IT ALL AWAY	Bob Dylan	CBS	5

WEEK ENDING 25 JUNE 1969

LW	TW	Title	Artist	Label	Wks
1	[1]	THE BALLAD OF JOHN AND YOKO	Beatles	Apple	4
2	[2]	OH HAPPY DAY	Edwin Hawkins Singers	Buddah	6
5	[3]	LIVING IN THE PAST	Jethro Tull	Island	6
4	[4]	TIME IS TIGHT	Booker T and the MGs	Stax	8
9	5	IN THE GHETTO	Elvis Presley	RCA	3
3	6	DIZZY	Tommy Roe	Stateside	9
17	7	SOMETHING IN THE AIR	Thunderclap Newman	Track	2
21	8	BREAKAWAY	Beach Boys	Capitol	3
20	9	PROUD MARY	Creedence Clearwater Revival	Liberty	5
12	10	THE TRACKS OF MY TEARS	Smokey Robinson and the Miracles	Tamla Motown	8
8	11	BIG SHIP	Cliff Richard	Columbia	5
24	12	FROZEN ORANGE JUICE	Peter Sarstedt	United Artists	3
13	13	(YOUR LOVE KEEPS LIFTING ME) HIGHER AND HIGHER	Jackie Wilson	MCA	7
22	14	GIMME GIMME GOOD LOVIN'	Crazy Elephant	Major Minor	6
18	15	WAY OF LIFE	Family Dogg	Bell	3
29	[16]	WHAT IS A MAN	Four Tops	Tamla Motown	4
14	17	I'D RATHER GO BLIND	Chicken Shack	Blue Horizon	7
6	18	GET BACK	Beatles with Billy Preston	Apple	10
34	19	HAPPY HEART	Andy Williams	CBS	6
25	20	LIGHTS OF CINCINATTI	Scott Walker	Philips	2
7	21	MY WAY	Frank Sinatra	Reprise	11
11	22	MAN OF THE WORLD	Fleetwood Mac	Immediate	11
10	23	THE BOXER	Simon and Garfunkel	CBS	9
38	[24]	TOMORROW TOMORROW	Bee Gees	Polydor	3
16	25	GALVESTON	Glen Campbell	Ember	8
15	26	RAGAMUFFIN MAN	Manfred Mann	Fontana	9
28	27	BABY MAKE IT SOON	Marmalade	CBS	3
-	28	HELLO SUSIE	Amen Corner	Immediate	1
19	29	LOVE ME TONIGHT	Tom Jones	Decca	7
23	30	DICK-A-DUM-DUM	Des O'Connor	Columbia	7
27	31	MY SENTIMENTAL FRIEND	Herman's Hermits	Columbia	10
32	32	WET DREAM	Max Romeo	Unity	2
31	33	AQUARIUS/LET THE SUNSHINE IN	Fifth Dimension	Liberty	10

In these weeks ■ Chicken Shack's *I'd Rather Go Blind* features vocals by Christine Perfect, who will later in the year marry John McVie, of the band three places higher up the charts, Fleetwood Mac. Before long, she will join her husband's band for its years of greatest success (18.06.69) ■ The Beatles' final week at number one (25.06.69) ■ *Born To Be Wild* is featured in the Peter Fonda/Dennis Hopper film 'Easy Rider' (18.06.69) ■

LW	TW	Title	Artist	Label	Wks
26	34	BEHIND A PAINTED SMILE	Isley Brothers	Tamla Motown	10
30	35	GOODBYE	Mary Hopkin	Apple	13
-	36	LET'S HANG ON	Bandwagon	Direction	1
35	37	BORN TO BE WILD	Steppenwolf	Stateside	2
-	38	MAKE ME AN ISLAND	Joe Dolan ●	Pye	1
36	39	GOOD LOVIN' AIN'T EASY TO COME BY	Marvin Gaye and Tammi Terrell	Tamla Motown	2
-	40	WITHOUT HER	Herb Alpert	A&M	1

WEEK ENDING 2 JULY 1969

LW	TW	Title	Artist	Label	Wks
7	1	SOMETHING IN THE AIR	Thunderclap Newman	Track	3
5	2	IN THE GHETTO	Elvis Presley	RCA	4
1	3	THE BALLAD OF JOHN AND YOKO	Beatles	Apple	5
3	4	LIVING IN THE PAST	Jethro Tull	Island	7
2	5	OH HAPPY DAY	Edwin Hawkins Singers	Buddah	7
4	6	TIME IS TIGHT	Booker T and the MGs	Stax	9
8	7	BREAKAWAY	Beach Boys	Capitol	4
15	8	WAY OF LIFE	Family Dogg	Bell	4
9	9	PROUD MARY	Creedence Clearwater Revival	Liberty	6
12	10	FROZEN ORANGE JUICE	Peter Sarstedt	United Artists	4
11	11	BIG SHIP	Cliff Richard	Columbia	6
14	12	GIMME GIMME GOOD LOVIN'	Crazy Elephant	Major Minor	7
6	13	DIZZY	Tommy Roe	Sateside	10
20	14	LIGHTS OF CINCINATTI	Scott Walker	Philips	3
28	15	HELLO SUSIE	Amen Corner	Immediate	2
10	16	THE TRACKS OF MY TEARS	Smokey Robinson and the Miracles	Tamla Motown	9
13	17	(YOUR LOVE KEEPS LIFTING ME) HIGHER AND HIGHER	Jackie Wilson	MCA	8
17	18	I'D RATHER GO BLIND	Chicken Shack	Blue Horizon	8
27	19	BABY MAKE IT SOON	Marmalade	CBS	4
21	20	MY WAY	Frank Sinatra	Reprise	12
18	21	GET BACK	Beatles with Billy Preston	Apple	11
23	22	THE BOXER	Simon and Garfunkel	CBS	10
22	23	MAN OF THE WORLD	Fleetwood Mac	Immediate	12
16	24	WHAT IS A MAN	Four Tops	Tamla Motown	5
19	25	HAPPY HEART	Andy Williams	CBS	7
25	26	GALVESTON	Glen Campbell	Ember	9
-	27	IT MIEK	Desmond Dekker and the Aces	Pyramid	1
29	28	LOVE ME TONIGHT	Tom Jones	Decca	8
39	29	GOOD LOVIN' AIN'T EASY TO COME BY	Marvin Gaye and Tammi Terrell	Tamla Motown	3
37	30	BORN TO BE WILD	Steppenwolf	Stateside	3
24	31	TOMORROW TOMORROW	Bee Gees	Polydor	4
38	32	MAKE ME AN ISLAND	Joe Dolan	Pye	2
26	33	RAGAMUFFIN MAN	Manfred Mann	Fontana	10
32	34	WET DREAM	Max Romeo	Unity	3
-	35	IT'S YOUR THING	Isley Brothers	Major Minor	1
-	36	SNAKE IN THE GRASS	Dave Dee, Dozy, Beaky, Mick and Tich	Fontana	7
-	37	WHEN TWO WORLDS COLLIDE	Jim Reeves	RCA Victor	1
35	38	GOODBYE	Mary Hopkin	Apple	14
31	39	MY SENTIMENTAL FRIEND	Herman's Hermits	Columbia	11
40	40	WITHOUT HER	Herb Alpert	A&M	2

WEEK ENDING 9 JULY 1969

LW	TW	Title	Artist	Label	Wks
1	1	SOMETHING IN THE AIR	Thunderclap Newman	Track	4
2	2	IN THE GHETTO	Elvis Presley	RCA	5
3	3	THE BALLAD OF JOHN AND YOKO	Beatles	Apple	6
15	4	HELLO SUSIE	Amen Corner	Immediate	3
4	5	LIVING IN THE PAST	Jethro Tull	Island	8
7	6	BREAKAWAY	Beach Boys	Capitol	5
8	7	WAY OF LIFE	Family Dogg	Bell	5
9	8	PROUD MARY	Creedence Clearwater Revival	Liberty	7
-	9	HONKY TONK WOMEN	Rolling Stones	Decca	1
6	10	TIME IS TIGHT	Booker T and the MGs	Stax	10
5	11	OH HAPPY DAY	Edwin Hawkins Singers	Buddah	8
10	12	FROZEN ORANGE JUICE	Peter Sarstedt	United Artists	5
14	13	LIGHTS OF CINCINATTI	Scott Walker	Philips	4
12	14	GIMME GIMME GOOD LOVIN'	Crazy Elephant	Major Minor	8
11	15	BIG SHIP	Cliff Richard	Columbia	7

July 1969

□ Highest position disc reached ● Act's first ever week on chart

LW	TW	Title	Artist	Label	Wks
27	16	IT MIEK	Desmond Dekker and the Aces	Pyramid	2
24	17	WHAT IS A MAN	Four Tops	Tamla Motown	6
19	18	BABY MAKE IT SOON	Marmalade	CBS	5
13	19	DIZZY	Tommy Roe	Sateside	11
-	20	THAT'S THE WAY GOD PLANNED IT	Billy Preston ●	Apple	1
-	21	GIVE PEACE A CHANCE	Plastic Ono Band ●	Apple	1
18	22	I'D RATHER GO BLIND	Chicken Shack	Blue Horizon	9
31	23	TOMORROW TOMORROW	Bee Gees	Polydor	5
16	24	THE TRACKS OF MY TEARS	Smokey Robinson and the Miracles	Tamla Motown	10
-	25	SAVED BY THE BELL	Robin Gibb ●	Polydor	1
21	26	GET BACK	Beatles with Billy Preston	Apple	12
20	27	MY WAY	Frank Sinatra	Reprise	13
17	28	(YOUR LOVE KEEPS LIFTING ME) HIGHER AND HIGHER	Jackie Wilson	MCA	9
32	29	MAKE ME AN ISLAND	Joe Dolan	Pye	3
37	30	WHEN TWO WORLDS COLLIDE	Jim Reeves	RCA Victor	2
-	31	GOODNIGHT MIDNIGHT	Clodagh Rodgers	RCA Victor	1
-	32	CONVERSATIONS	Cilla Black	Parlophone	1
34	33	WET DREAM	Max Romeo	Unity	4
28	34	LOVE ME TONIGHT	Tom Jones	Decca	9
29	35	GOOD LOVIN' AIN'T EASY TO COME BY	Marvin Gaye and Tammi Terrell	Tamla Motown	4
40	36	WITHOUT HER	Herb Alpert	A&M	3
25	37	HAPPY HEART	Andy Williams	CBS	8
26	38	GALVESTON	Glen Campbell	Ember	10
35	39	IT'S YOUR THING	Isley Brothers	Major Minor	2
30	40	BORN TO BE WILD	Steppenwolf	Stateside	4

WEEK ENDING 16 JULY 1969

LW	TW	Title	Artist	Label	Wks
1	1	SOMETHING IN THE AIR	Thunderclap Newman	Track	5
2	2	IN THE GHETTO	Elvis Presley	RCA	6
9	3	HONKY TONK WOMEN	Rolling Stones	Decca	2
21	4	GIVE PEACE A CHANCE	Plastic Ono Band	Apple	2
4	5	HELLO SUSIE	Amen Corner	Immediate	4
7	6	WAY OF LIFE	Family Dogg	Bell	6
16	7	IT MIEK	Desmond Dekker and the Aces	Pyramid	3
6	8	BREAKAWAY	Beach Boys	Capitol	6
18	9	BABY MAKE IT SOON	Marmalade	CBS	6
8	10	PROUD MARY	Creedence Clearwater Revival	Liberty	8
3	11	THE BALLAD OF JOHN AND YOKO	Beatles	Apple	7
5	12	LIVING IN THE PAST	Jethro Tull	Island	9
13	13	LIGHTS OF CINCINATTI	Scott Walker	Philips	5
12	14	FROZEN ORANGE JUICE	Peter Sarstedt	United Artists	6
20	15	THAT'S THE WAY GOD PLANNED IT	Billy Preston	Apple	2
14	16	GIMME GIMME GOOD LOVIN'	Crazy Elephant	Major Minor	9
10	17	TIME IS TIGHT	Booker T and the MGs	Stax	11
25	18	SAVED BY THE BELL	Robin Gibb	Polydor	2
29	19	MAKE ME AN ISLAND	Joe Dolan	Pye	4
11	20	OH HAPPY DAY	Edwin Hawkins Singers	Buddah	9
33	21	WET DREAM	Max Romeo	Unity	5
19	22	DIZZY	Tommy Roe	Sateside	12
31	23	GOODNIGHT MIDNIGHT	Clodagh Rodgers	RCA Victor	2
32	24	CONVERSATIONS	Cilla Black	Parlophone	2
-	25	BARABAJAGAL	Donovan and Jeff Beck ●	Pye	1
35	26	GOOD LOVIN' AIN'T EASY TO COME BY	Marvin Gaye and Tammi Terrell	Tamla Motown	5
26	27	GET BACK	Beatles with Billy Preston	Apple	13
27	28	MY WAY	Frank Sinatra	Reprise	14
-	29	MY CHERIE AMOUR	Stevie Wonder	Tamla Motown	1
39	30	IT'S YOUR THING	Isley Brothers	Major Minor	3
40	31	BORN TO BE WILD	Steppenwolf	Stateside	5
17	32	WHAT IS A MAN	Four Tops	Tamla Motown	7
15	33	BIG SHIP	Cliff Richard	Columbia	8
30	34	WHEN TWO WORLDS COLLIDE	Jim Reeves	RCA Victor	3
22	35	I'D RATHER GO BLIND	Chicken Shack	Blue Horizon	10
37	36	HAPPY HEART	Andy Williams	CBS	9
34	37	LOVE ME TONIGHT	Tom Jones	Decca	10

■ Elvis Presley's first Top Ten hit for three years is kept off the top by the only number one that any member of the Who was ever officially involved in - Thunderclap Newman's *Something In The Air*, produced by Pete Townshend (02.07.69) ■ Stevie Wonder's *My Cherie Amour* is the flip side of *I Don't Know Why*, which finished a nine week chart run on 21 May (16.07.69) ■

July 1969

☐ Highest position disc reached ● Act's first ever week on chart

LW	TW	Title	Artist	Label	Wks
24	38	THE TRACKS OF MY TEARS	Smokey Robinson and the Miracles	Tamla Motown	11
36	39	WITHOUT HER	Herb Alpert	A&M	4
-	40	PEACEFUL	Georgie Fame	CBS	1

WEEK ENDING 23 JULY 1969

LW	TW	Title	Artist	Label	Wks
3	[1]	HONKY TONK WOMEN	Rolling Stones	Decca	3
4	[2]	GIVE PEACE A CHANCE	Plastic Ono Band	Apple	3
1	3	SOMETHING IN THE AIR	Thunderclap Newman	Track	6
2	4	IN THE GHETTO	Elvis Presley	RCA	7
18	5	SAVED BY THE BELL	Robin Gibb	Polydor	3
5	6	HELLO SUSIE	Amen Corner	Immediate	5
7	[7]	IT MIEK	Desmond Dekker and the Aces	Pyramid	4
23	8	GOODNIGHT MIDNIGHT	Clodagh Rodgers	RCA Victor	3
9	[9]	BABY MAKE IT SOON	Marmalade	CBS	7
6	10	WAY OF LIFE	Family Dogg	Bell	7
8	11	BREAKAWAY	Beach Boys	Capitol	7
15	12	THAT'S THE WAY GOD PLANNED IT	Billy Preston	Apple	3
10	13	PROUD MARY	Creedence Clearwater Revival	Liberty	9
13	14	LIGHTS OF CINCINATTI	Scott Walker	Philips	6
11	15	THE BALLAD OF JOHN AND YOKO	Beatles	Apple	8
19	16	MAKE ME AN ISLAND	Joe Dolan	Pye	5
16	17	GIMME GIMME GOOD LOVIN'	Crazy Elephant	Major Minor	10
25	18	BARABAJAGAL	Donovan and Jeff Beck	Pye	2
17	19	TIME IS TIGHT	Booker T and the MGs	Stax	12
24	20	CONVERSATIONS	Cilla Black	Parlophone	3
32	21	WHAT IS A MAN	Four Tops	Tamla Motown	8
29	22	MY CHERIE AMOUR	Stevie Wonder	Tamla Motown	2
12	23	LIVING IN THE PAST	Jethro Tull	Island	10
20	24	OH HAPPY DAY	Edwin Hawkins Singers	Buddah	10
-	25	BRING ON BACK THE GOOD TIMES	Love Affair	CBS	1
22	26	DIZZY	Tommy Roe	Sateside	13
34	27	WHEN TWO WORLDS COLLIDE	Jim Reeves	RCA Victor	4
14	28	FROZEN ORANGE JUICE	Peter Sarstedt	United Artists	7
40	29	PEACEFUL	Georgie Fame	CBS	2
-	30	I CAN SING A RAINBOW-LOVE IS BLUE	Dells ●	Chess	1
28	31	MY WAY	Frank Sinatra	Reprise	15
33	32	BIG SHIP	Cliff Richard	Columbia	9
27	33	GET BACK	Beatles with Billy Preston	Apple	14
-	34	EARLY IN THE MORNING	Vanity Fare	Page One	1
31	35	BORN TO BE WILD	Steppenwolf	Stateside	6
21	36	WET DREAM	Max Romeo	Unity	6
-	[37]	NO MATTER WHAT SIGN YOU ARE	Diana Ross and the Supremes	Tamla Motown	1
-	38	CURLY	Move	Regal Zonophone	1
30	39	IT"S YOUR THING	Isley Brothers	Major Minor	4
-	40	TOO BUSY THINKING ABOUT MY BABY	Marvin Gaye	Tamla Motown	1

WEEK ENDING 30 JULY 1969

LW	TW	Title	Artist	Label	Wks
1	[1]	HONKY TONK WOMEN	Rolling Stones	Decca	4
2	[2]	GIVE PEACE A CHANCE	Plastic Ono Band	Apple	4
5	3	SAVED BY THE BELL	Robin Gibb	Polydor	4
4	4	IN THE GHETTO	Elvis Presley	RCA	8
3	5	SOMETHING IN THE AIR	Thunderclap Newman	Track	7
8	6	GOODNIGHT MIDNIGHT	Clodagh Rodgers	RCA Victor	4
16	7	MAKE ME AN ISLAND	Joe Dolan	Pye	6
7	8	IT MIEK	Desmond Dekker and the Aces	Pyramid	5
9	[9]	BABY MAKE IT SOON	Marmalade	CBS	8
6	10	HELLO SUSIE	Amen Corner	Immediate	6
12	[11]	THAT'S THE WAY GOD PLANNED IT	Billy Preston	Apple	4
18	[12]	BARABAJAGAL	Donovan and Jeff Beck	Pye	3
20	13	CONVERSATIONS	Cilla Black	Parlophone	4
10	14	WAY OF LIFE	Family Dogg	Bell	8
36	15	WET DREAM	Max Romeo	Unity	7
22	16	MY CHERIE AMOUR	Stevie Wonder	Tamla Motown	3
11	17	BREAKAWAY	Beach Boys	Capitol	8
27	18	WHEN TWO WORLDS COLLIDE	Jim Reeves	RCA Victor	5
25	19	BRING ON BACK THE GOOD TIMES	Love Affair	CBS	2
19	20	TIME IS TIGHT	Booker T and the MGs	Stax	13
34	21	EARLY IN THE MORNING	Vanity Fare	Page One	2
15	22	THE BALLAD OF JOHN AND YOKO	Beatles	Apple	9
13	23	PROUD MARY	Creedence Clearwater Revival	Liberty	10
14	24	LIGHTS OF CINCINATTI	Scott Walker	Philips	7
30	25	I CAN SING A RAINBOW-LOVE IS BLUE	Dells	Chess	2
17	26	GIMME GIMME GOOD LOVIN'	Crazy Elephant	Major Minor	11
24	27	OH HAPPY DAY	Edwin Hawkins Singers	Buddah	11
40	28	TOO BUSY THINKING ABOUT MY BABY	Marvin Gaye	Tamla Motown	2
29	29	PEACEFUL	Georgie Fame	CBS	3
28	30	FROZEN ORANGE JUICE	Peter Sarstedt	United Artists	8
-	31	HEATHER HONEY	Tommy Roe	Stateside	1
26	32	DIZZY	Tommy Roe	Sateside	14
23	33	LIVING IN THE PAST	Jethro Tull	Island	11
38	34	CURLY	Move	Regal Zonophone	2
-	35	NEED YOUR LOVE SO BAD	Fleetwood Mac	Blue Horizon	1
33	36	GET BACK	Beatles with Billy Preston	Apple	15
-	37	VIVA BOBBY JOE	Equals	President	1
37	38	NO MATTER WHAT SIGN YOU ARE	Diana Ross and the Supremes	Tamla Motown	2
32	39	BIG SHIP	Cliff Richard	Columbia	10
-	40	THUS SPAKE ZARATHUSTRA	Philharmonia Orchestra, conductor Lorin Maazel ●	Columbia	1

WEEK ENDING 9 AUGUST 1969

LW	TW	Title	Artist	Label	Wks
1	[1]	HONKY TONK WOMEN	Rolling Stones	Decca	5
2	[2]	GIVE PEACE A CHANCE	Plastic Ono Band	Apple	5
5	3	SAVED BY THE BELL	Robin Gibb	Polydor	5
6	[4]	GOODNIGHT MIDNIGHT	Clodagh Rodgers	RCA Victor	5
4	5	IN THE GHETTO	Elvis Presley	RCA	9
16	6	MY CHERIE AMOUR	Stevie Wonder	Tamla Motown	4
7	7	MAKE ME AN ISLAND	Joe Dolan	Pye	7
13	8	CONVERSATIONS	Cilla Black	Parlophone	5
9	[9]	BABY MAKE IT SOON	Marmalade	CBS	9
8	10	IT MIEK	Desmond Dekker and the Aces	Pyramid	6
11	[11]	THAT'S THE WAY GOD PLANNED IT	Billy Preston	Apple	5
5	12	SOMETHING IN THE AIR	Thunderclap Newman	Track	8
19	13	BRING ON BACK THE GOOD TIMES	Love Affair	CBS	3
12	14	BARABAJAGAL	Donovan and Jeff Beck	Pye	4
25	[15]	I CAN SING A RAINBOW-LOVE IS BLUE	Dells	Chess	3
29	16	PEACEFUL	Georgie Fame	CBS	4
21	17	EARLY IN THE MORNING	Vanity Fare	Page One	3
10	18	HELLO SUSIE	Amen Corner	Immediate	7
34	19	CURLY	Move	Regal Zonophone	3
14	20	WAY OF LIFE	Family Dogg	Bell	9
-	21	IN THE YEAR 2525	Zager and Evans ●	RCA	1
17	22	BREAKAWAY	Beach Boys	Capitol	9
18	23	WHEN TWO WORLDS COLLIDE	Jim Reeves	RCA Victor	6
20	24	TIME IS TIGHT	Booker T and the MGs	Stax	14
37	25	VIVA BOBBY JOE	Equals	President	2
31	26	MY WAY	Frank Sinatra	Reprise	15
22	27	THE BALLAD OF JOHN AND YOKO	Beatles	Apple	10
-	28	TEARS WON'T WASH AWAY MY HEARTACHES	Ken Dodd	Columbia	1
26	29	GIMME GIMME GOOD LOVIN'	Crazy Elephant	Major Minor	12
15	30	WET DREAM	Max Romeo	Unity	8
-	31	SI TU DOIS PARTIR	Fairport Convention ●	Island	1
28	32	TOO BUSY THINKING ABOUT MY BABY	Marvin Gaye	Tamla Motown	3
31	33	HEATHER HONEY	Tommy Roe	Stateside	2
32	34	DIZZY	Tommy Roe	Sateside	15
24	35	LIGHTS OF CINCINATTI	Scott Walker	Philips	8
40	36	THUS SPAKE ZARATHUSTRA	Philharmonia Orchestra, conductor Lorin Maazel	Columbia	2
35	37	NEED YOUR LOVE SO BAD	Fleetwood Mac	Blue Horizon	2
23	38	PROUD MARY	Creedence Clearwater Revival	Liberty	11
-	39	I'M A BETTER MAN	Engelbert Humperdinck	Decca	1
38	40	NO MATTER WHAT SIGN YOU ARE	Diana Ross and the Supremes	Tamla Motown	3

In these weeks ■ For a fourth week, there are three hits featuring John Lennon on the chart (30.07.69) ■ For two weeks in a row, Tommy Roe occupies two chart positions in a row (09.08.69) ■ *Thus Spake Zarathustra* is used as the theme to the film '2001: A Space Odyssey', which boosts it into the charts. It is one of two hits concerned with the third millenium (30.07.69)■

A u g u s t 1 9 6 9

□ Highest position disc reached ● Act's first ever week on chart

WEEK ENDING 16 AUGUST 1969

LW	TW	Title	Artist	Label	Wks
1	1	HONKY TONK WOMEN	Rolling Stones	*Decca*	6
3	2	SAVED BY THE BELL	Robin Gibb	*Polydor*	6
7	3	MAKE ME AN ISLAND	Joe Dolan	*Pye*	8
2	4	GIVE PEACE A CHANCE	Plastic Ono Band	*Apple*	6
6	5	MY CHERIE AMOUR	Stevie Wonder	*Tamla Motown*	5
4	6	GOODNIGHT MIDNIGHT	Clodagh Rodgers	*RCA Victor*	6
8	7	CONVERSATIONS	Cilla Black	*Parlophone*	6
17	8	EARLY IN THE MORNING	Vanity Fare	*Page One*	4
13	9	BRING ON BACK THE GOOD TIMES	Love Affair	*CBS*	4
30	10	WET DREAM	Max Romeo	*Unity*	9
5	11	IN THE GHETTO	Elvis Presley	*RCA*	10
32	12	TOO BUSY THINKING ABOUT MY BABY	Marvin Gaye	*Tamla Motown*	4
21	13	IN THE YEAR 2525	Zager and Evans	*RCA*	2
14	14	BARABAJAGAL	Donovan and Jeff Beck	*Pye*	5
15	15	I CAN SING A RAINBOW-LOVE IS BLUE	Dells	*Chess*	4
11	16	THAT'S THE WAY GOD PLANNED IT	Billy Preston	*Apple*	6
23	17	WHEN TWO WORLDS COLLIDE	Jim Reeves	*RCA Victor*	7
9	18	BABY MAKE IT SOON	Marmalade	*CBS*	10
19	19	CURLY	Move	*Regal Zonophone*	4
25	20	VIVA BOBBY JOE	Equals	*President*	3
12	21	SOMETHING IN THE AIR	Thunderclap Newman	*Track*	9
10	22	IT MIEK	Desmond Dekker and the Aces	*Pyramid*	7
18	23	HELLO SUSIE	Amen Corner	*Immediate*	8
20	24	WAY OF LIFE	Family Dogg	*Bell*	10
16	25	PEACEFUL	Georgie Fame	*CBS*	5
28	26	TEARS WON'T WASH AWAY MY HEARTACHES	Ken Dodd	*Columbia*	2
22	27	BREAKAWAY	Beach Boys	*Capitol*	10
39	28	I'M A BETTER MAN	Engelbert Humperdinck	*Decca*	2
31	29	SI TU DOIS PARTIR	Fairport Convention	*Island*	2
33	30	HEATHER HONEY	Tommy Roe	*Stateside*	3
-	31	GOOD MORNING STARSHINE	Oliver ●	*CBS*	1
-	32	JE T'AIME...MOI NON PLUS	Jane Birkin and Serge Gainsbourg ●	*Fontana*	1
36	33	THUS SPAKE ZARATHUSTRA	Philharmonia Orchestra, conductor Lorin Maazel	*Columbia*	3
38	34	PROUD MARY	Creedence Clearwater Revival	*Liberty*	12
37	35	NEED YOUR LOVE SO BAD	Fleetwood Mac	*Blue Horizon*	3
24	36	TIME IS TIGHT	Booker T and the MGs	*Stax*	15
27	37	THE BALLAD OF JOHN AND YOKO	Beatles	*Apple*	11
34	38	DIZZY	Tommy Roe	*Sateside*	16
29	39	GIMME GIMME GOOD LOVIN'	Crazy Elephant	*Major Minor*	13
40	40	NO MATTER WHAT SIGN YOU ARE	Diana Ross and the Supremes	*Tamla Motown*	4

WEEK ENDING 23 AUGUST 1969

LW	TW	Title	Artist	Label	Wks
1	1	HONKY TONK WOMEN	Rolling Stones	*Decca*	7
2	2	SAVED BY THE BELL	Robin Gibb	*Polydor*	7
13	3	IN THE YEAR 2525	Zager and Evans	*RCA*	3
5	4	MY CHERIE AMOUR	Stevie Wonder	*Tamla Motown*	6
3	5	MAKE ME AN ISLAND	Joe Dolan	*Pye*	9
4	6	GIVE PEACE A CHANCE	Plastic Ono Band	*Apple*	7
6	7	GOODNIGHT MIDNIGHT	Clodagh Rodgers	*RCA Victor*	7
12	8	TOO BUSY THINKING ABOUT MY BABY	Marvin Gaye	*Tamla Motown*	5
7	9	CONVERSATIONS	Cilla Black	*Parlophone*	7
8	10	EARLY IN THE MORNING	Vanity Fare	*Page One*	5
9	11	BRING ON BACK THE GOOD TIMES	Love Affair	*CBS*	5
19	12	CURLY	Move	*Regal Zonophone*	5
10	13	WET DREAM	Max Romeo	*Unity*	10
20	14	VIVA BOBBY JOE	Equals	*President*	4
15	15	I CAN SING A RAINBOW-LOVE IS BLUE	Dells	*Chess*	5
11	16	IN THE GHETTO	Elvis Presley	*RCA*	11
32	17	JE T'AIME...MOI NON PLUS	Jane Birkin and Serge Gainsbourg	*Fontana*	2
-	18	DON'T FORGET TO REMEMBER	Bee Gees	*Polydor*	1
28	19	I'M A BETTER MAN	Engelbert Humperdinck	*Decca*	3
-	20	BAD MOON RISING	Creedence Clearwater Revival	*Liberty*	1
29	21	SI TU DOIS PARTIR	Fairport Convention	*Island*	3
18	22	BABY MAKE IT SOON	Marmalade	*CBS*	11
-	23	NATURAL BORN BUGIE	Humble Pie ●	*Immediate*	1
25	24	PEACEFUL	Georgie Fame	*CBS*	6
21	25	SOMETHING IN THE AIR	Thunderclap Newman	*Track*	10
31	26	GOOD MORNING STARSHINE	Oliver	*CBS*	2
26	27	TEARS WON'T WASH AWAY MY HEARTACHES	Ken Dodd	*Columbia*	3
22	28	IT MIEK	Desmond Dekker and the Aces	*Pyramid*	8
17	29	WHEN TWO WORLDS COLLIDE	Jim Reeves	*RCA Victor*	8
23	30	HELLO SUSIE	Amen Corner	*Immediate*	9
24	31	WAY OF LIFE	Family Dogg	*Bell*	11
35	32	NEED YOUR LOVE SO BAD	Fleetwood Mac	*Blue Horizon*	4
14	33	BARABAJAGAL	Donovan and Jeff Beck	*Pye*	6
27	34	BREAKAWAY	Beach Boys	*Capitol*	11
30	35	HEATHER HONEY	Tommy Roe	*Stateside*	4
36	36	TIME IS TIGHT	Booker T and the MGs	*Stax*	16
16	37	THAT'S THE WAY GOD PLANNED IT	Billy Preston	*Apple*	7
37	38	THE BALLAD OF JOHN AND YOKO	Beatles	*Apple*	12
34	39	PROUD MARY	Creedence Clearwater Revival	*Liberty*	13
-	40	SOUL DEEP	Box Tops	*Bell*	1

WEEK ENDING 30 AUGUST 1969

LW	TW	Title	Artist	Label	Wks
3	1	IN THE YEAR 2525	Zager and Evans	*RCA*	4
1	2	HONKY TONK WOMEN	Rolling Stones	*Decca*	8
2	3	SAVED BY THE BELL	Robin Gibb	*Polydor*	8
4	4	MY CHERIE AMOUR	Stevie Wonder	*Tamla Motown*	7
5	5	MAKE ME AN ISLAND	Joe Dolan	*Pye*	10
14	6	VIVA BOBBY JOE	Equals	*President*	5
8	7	TOO BUSY THINKING ABOUT MY BABY	Marvin Gaye	*Tamla Motown*	6
20	8	BAD MOON RISING	Creedence Clearwater Revival	*Liberty*	2
18	9	DON'T FORGET TO REMEMBER	Bee Gees	*Polydor*	2
10	10	EARLY IN THE MORNING	Vanity Fare	*Page One*	6
23	11	NATURAL BORN BUGIE	Humble Pie	*Immediate*	2
11	12	BRING ON BACK THE GOOD TIMES	Love Affair	*CBS*	6
9	13	CONVERSATIONS	Cilla Black	*Parlophone*	8
12	14	CURLY	Move	*Regal Zonophone*	6
6	15	GIVE PEACE A CHANCE	Plastic Ono Band	*Apple*	8
7	16	GOODNIGHT MIDNIGHT	Clodagh Rodgers	*RCA Victor*	8
17	17	JE T'AIME...MOI NON PLUS	Jane Birkin and Serge Gainsbourg	*Fontana*	3
13	18	WET DREAM	Max Romeo	*Unity*	11
26	19	GOOD MORNING STARSHINE	Oliver	*CBS*	3
16	20	IN THE GHETTO	Elvis Presley	*RCA*	12
21	21	SI TU DOIS PARTIR	Fairport Convention	*Island*	4
19	22	I'M A BETTER MAN	Engelbert Humperdinck	*Decca*	4
29	23	WHEN TWO WORLDS COLLIDE	Jim Reeves	*RCA Victor*	9
-	24	CLOUD NINE	Temptations	*Tamla Motown*	1
15	25	I CAN SING A RAINBOW-LOVE IS BLUE	Dells	*Chess*	6
27	26	TEARS WON'T WASH AWAY MY HEARTACHES	Ken Dodd	*Columbia*	4
35	27	HEATHER HONEY	Tommy Roe	*Stateside*	5
22	28	BABY MAKE IT SOON	Marmalade	*CBS*	12
40	29	SOUL DEEP	Box Tops	*Bell*	2
-	30	MARRAKESH EXPRESS	Crosby, Stills and Nash ●	*Atlantic*	1
24	31	PEACEFUL	Georgie Fame	*CBS*	7
28	32	IT MIEK	Desmond Dekker and the Aces	*Pyramid*	9
-	33	MY WAY	Frank Sinatra	*Reprise*	16
-	34	IT'S GETTING BETTER	Mama Cass	*Stateside*	1
-	35	SOUL CLAP '69	Booker T and the MGs	*Stax*	1
31	36	WAY OF LIFE	Family Dogg	*Bell*	12
-	37	I'LL NEVER FALL IN LOVE AGAIN	Bobbie Gentry	*Capitol*	1
-	38	NO MATTER WHAT SIGN YOU ARE	Diana Ross and the Supremes	*Tamla Motown*	5
25	39	SOMETHING IN THE AIR	Thunderclap Newman	*Track*	11
30	40	HELLO SUSIE	Amen Corner	*Immediate*	10

■Nine weeks after the Beatles final week at number one, the Rolling Stones also fall from the top, never to return (30.08.69) ■ The only Bee Gees hit not to feature Robin Gibb hits the Top Ten to join Robin's only solo Top Ten hit (30.08.69) ■ *Si Tu Dois Partir* just fails to become the third French language title in the Top 20 (30.08.69)■

September 1969

□ Highest position disc reached ● Act's first ever week on chart

LW	TW	WEEK ENDING 6 SEPTEMBER 1969		Wks
1	[1]	IN THE YEAR 2525 Zager and Evans	*RCA*	5
8	2	BAD MOON RISING Creedence Clearwater Revival	*Liberty*	3
2	3	HONKY TONK WOMEN Rolling Stones	*Decca*	9
4	[4]	MY CHERIE AMOUR Stevie Wonder	*Tamla Motown*	8
9	5	DON'T FORGET TO REMEMBER Bee Gees	*Polydor*	3
7	6	TOO BUSY THINKING ABOUT MY BABY Marvin Gaye	*Tamla Motown*	7
6	7	VIVA BOBBY JOE Equals	*President*	6
17	8	JE T'AIME...MOI NON PLUS Jane Birkin and Serge Gainsbourg	*Fontana*	4
3	9	SAVED BY THE BELL Robin Gibb	*Polydor*	9
11	10	NATURAL BORN BUGIE Humble Pie	*Immediate*	3
5	11	MAKE ME AN ISLAND Joe Dolan	*Pye*	11
10	12	EARLY IN THE MORNING Vanity Fare	*Page One*	7
14	13	CURLY Move	*Regal Zonophone*	7
19	14	GOOD MORNING STARSHINE Oliver	*CBS*	4
13	15	CONVERSATIONS Cilla Black	*Parlophone*	9
15	16	GIVE PEACE A CHANCE Plastic Ono Band	*Apple*	9
22	17	I'M A BETTER MAN Engelbert Humperdinck	*Decca*	5
12	18	BRING ON BACK THE GOOD TIMES Love Affair	*CBS*	7
16	19	GOODNIGHT MIDNIGHT Clodagh Rodgers	*RCA Victor*	9
18	20	WET DREAM Max Romeo	*Unity*	12
20	21	IN THE GHETTO Elvis Presley	*RCA*	13
26	[22]	TEARS WON'T WASH AWAY MY HEARTACHES Ken Dodd	*Columbia*	5
25	23	I CAN SING A RAINBOW-LOVE IS BLUE Dells	*Chess*	7
27	24	HEATHER HONEY Tommy Roe	*Stateside*	6
21	25	SI TU DOIS PARTIR Fairport Convention	*Island*	5
34	26	IT'S GETTING BETTER Mama Cass	*Stateside*	2
-	27	BIRTH Peddlers ●	*CBS*	1
24	28	CLOUD NINE Temptations	*Tamla Motown*	2
23	29	WHEN TWO WORLDS COLLIDE Jim Reeves	*RCA Victor*	10
30	30	MARRAKESH EXPRESS Crosby, Stills and Nash	*Atlantic*	2
29	31	SOUL DEEP Box Tops	*Bell*	3
37	32	I'LL NEVER FALL IN LOVE AGAIN Bobbie Gentry	*Capitol*	2
-	33	I'VE PASSED THIS WAY BEFORE Jimmy Ruffin	*Tamla Motown*	1
-	34	PUT YOURSELF IN MY PLACE Isley Brothers	*Tamla Motown*	1
-	35	CLEAN UP YOUR OWN BACK YARD Elvis Presley	*RCA*	1
-	36	TEARS IN THE WIND Chicken Shack	*Blue Horizon*	1
32	37	IT MIEK Desmond Dekker and the Aces	*Pyramid*	10
35	38	SOUL CLAP '69 Booker T and the MGs	*Stax*	2
-	39	NOBODY'S CHILD Karen Young ●	*Major Minor*	1
33	40	MY WAY Frank Sinatra	*Reprise*	17

LW	TW	WEEK ENDING 13 SEPTEMBER 1969		Wks
1	[1]	IN THE YEAR 2525 Zager and Evans	*RCA*	6
2	2	BAD MOON RISING Creedence Clearwater Revival	*Liberty*	4
5	3	DON'T FORGET TO REMEMBER Bee Gees	*Polydor*	4
10	[4]	NATURAL BORN BUGIE Humble Pie	*Immediate*	4
6	[5]	TOO BUSY THINKING ABOUT MY BABY Marvin Gaye	*Tamla Motown*	8
8	6	JE T'AIME...MOI NON PLUS Jane Birkin and Serge Gainsbourg	*Fontana*	5
7	7	VIVA BOBBY JOE Equals	*President*	7
4	8	MY CHERIE AMOUR Stevie Wonder	*Tamla Motown*	9
3	9	HONKY TONK WOMEN Rolling Stones	*Decca*	10
9	10	SAVED BY THE BELL Robin Gibb	*Polydor*	10
14	11	GOOD MORNING STARSHINE Oliver	*CBS*	5
11	12	MAKE ME AN ISLAND Joe Dolan	*Pye*	12
13	13	CURLY Move	*Regal Zonophone*	8
12	14	EARLY IN THE MORNING Vanity Fare	*Page One*	8
17	[15]	I'M A BETTER MAN Engelbert Humperdinck	*Decca*	6
28	16	CLOUD NINE Temptations	*Tamla Motown*	3
30	[17]	MARRAKESH EXPRESS Crosby, Stills and Nash	*Atlantic*	3
20	18	WET DREAM Max Romeo	*Unity*	13
32	19	I'LL NEVER FALL IN LOVE AGAIN Bobbie Gentry	*Capitol*	3
19	20	GOODNIGHT MIDNIGHT Clodagh Rodgers	*RCA Victor*	10
15	21	CONVERSATIONS Cilla Black	*Parlophone*	10
16	22	GIVE PEACE A CHANCE Plastic Ono Band	*Apple*	10
34	23	PUT YOURSELF IN MY PLACE Isley Brothers	*Tamla Motown*	2
31	24	SOUL DEEP Box Tops	*Bell*	4
22	25	TEARS WON'T WASH AWAY MY HEARTACHES Ken Dodd	*Columbia*	6
26	26	IT'S GETTING BETTER Mama Cass	*Stateside*	3
27	27	BIRTH Peddlers	*CBS*	2
21	28	IN THE GHETTO Elvis Presley	*RCA*	14
24	29	HEATHER HONEY Tommy Roe	*Stateside*	7
-	30	LAY LADY LAY Bob Dylan	*CBS*	1
29	31	WHEN TWO WORLDS COLLIDE Jim Reeves	*RCA Victor*	11
18	32	BRING ON BACK THE GOOD TIMES Love Affair	*CBS*	8
40	33	MY WAY Frank Sinatra	*Reprise*	18
-	34	THROW DOWN A LINE Cliff and Hank	*Columbia*	1
39	35	NOBODY'S CHILD Karen Young	*Major Minor*	2
35	36	CLEAN UP YOUR OWN BACK YARD Elvis Presley	*RCA*	2
25	37	SI TU DOIS PARTIR Fairport Convention	*Island*	6
36	38	TEARS IN THE WIND Chicken Shack	*Blue Horizon*	2
33	39	I'VE PASSED THIS WAY BEFORE Jimmy Ruffin	*Tamla Motown*	2
38	40	SOUL CLAP '69 Booker T and the MGs	*Stax*	3

LW	TW	WEEK ENDING 20 SEPTEMBER 1969		Wks
2	[1]	BAD MOON RISING Creedence Clearwater Revival	*Liberty*	5
3	[2]	DON'T FORGET TO REMEMBER Bee Gees	*Polydor*	5
1	3	IN THE YEAR 2525 Zager and Evans	*RCA*	7
6	4	JE T'AIME...MOI NON PLUS Jane Birkin and Serge Gainsbourg	*Fontana*	6
4	5	NATURAL BORN BUGIE Humble Pie	*Immediate*	5
5	6	TOO BUSY THINKING ABOUT MY BABY Marvin Gaye	*Tamla Motown*	9
7	7	VIVA BOBBY JOE Equals	*President*	8
11	8	GOOD MORNING STARSHINE Oliver	*CBS*	6
19	9	I'LL NEVER FALL IN LOVE AGAIN Bobbie Gentry	*Capitol*	4
9	10	HONKY TONK WOMEN Rolling Stones	*Decca*	11
8	11	MY CHERIE AMOUR Stevie Wonder	*Tamla Motown*	10
10	12	SAVED BY THE BELL Robin Gibb	*Polydor*	11
12	13	MAKE ME AN ISLAND Joe Dolan	*Pye*	13
34	14	THROW DOWN A LINE Cliff and Hank	*Columbia*	2
-	15	A BOY NAMED SUE Johnny Cash	*CBS*	1
26	16	IT'S GETTING BETTER Mama Cass	*Stateside*	4
27	[17]	BIRTH Peddlers	*CBS*	3
15	18	I'M A BETTER MAN Engelbert Humperdinck	*Decca*	7
-	19	HARE KRISHNA MANTRA Radha Krishna Temple ●	*Apple*	1
13	20	CURLY Move	*Regal Zonophone*	9
14	21	EARLY IN THE MORNING Vanity Fare	*Page One*	9
36	22	CLEAN UP YOUR OWN BACK YARD Elvis Presley	*RCA*	3
24	23	SOUL DEEP Box Tops	*Bell*	5
-	24	LOVE AT FIRST SIGHT Sounds Nice ●	*Parlophone*	1
17	25	MARRAKESH EXPRESS Crosby, Stills and Nash	*Atlantic*	4
18	26	WET DREAM Max Romeo	*Unity*	14
16	27	CLOUD NINE Temptations	*Tamla Motown*	4
23	28	PUT YOURSELF IN MY PLACE Isley Brothers	*Tamla Motown*	3
38	29	TEARS IN THE WIND Chicken Shack	*Blue Horizon*	3
30	30	LAY LADY LAY Bob Dylan	*CBS*	2
35	31	NOBODY'S CHILD Karen Young	*Major Minor*	3
25	32	TEARS WON'T WASH AWAY MY HEARTACHES Ken Dodd	*Columbia*	7
-	33	I SECOND THAT EMOTION Diana Ross and the Supremes and the Temptations	*Tamla Motown*	1
21	34	CONVERSATIONS Cilla Black	*Parlophone*	11
-	35	I'M GONNA MAKE YOU MINE Lou Christie	*Buddah*	1
-	[36]	25 MILES Edwin Starr	*Tamla Motown*	1
29	37	HEATHER HONEY Tommy Roe	*Stateside*	8
33	38	MY WAY Frank Sinatra	*Reprise*	19
-	39	SPACE ODDITY David Bowie ●	*Philips*	1
31	40	WHEN TWO WORLDS COLLIDE Jim Reeves	*RCA Victor*	12

In these weeks ■ Creedence Clearwater Revival, who were to suffer through a record five number two hits in America, enjoy their only taste of number one success on either side of the Atlantic (20.09.69) ■ Anything to do with the Beatles seems to sell. Even the Baker Street mendicant Radha Krishna Temple hit the Top 20 thanks to George Harrison's interest (20.09.69) ■ *Love At First Sight* is the instrumental version of *Je T'Aime ... Moi Non Plus* (20.09.69)■

LW	TW	WEEK ENDING 27 SEPTEMBER 1969			Wks
1	1	BAD MOON RISING	Creedence Clearwater Revival	Liberty	6
4	2	JE T'AIME...MOI NON PLUS	Jane Birkin and Serge Gainsbourg	Fontana	7
2	3	DON'T FORGET TO REMEMBER	Bee Gees	Polydor	6
9	4	I'LL NEVER FALL IN LOVE AGAIN	Bobbie Gentry	Capitol	5
3	5	IN THE YEAR 2525	Zager and Evans	RCA	8
5	6	NATURAL BORN BUGIE	Humble Pie	Immediate	6
8	7	GOOD MORNING STARSHINE	Oliver	CBS	7
6	8	TOO BUSY THINKING ABOUT MY BABY	Marvin Gaye	Tamla Motown	10
7	9	VIVA BOBBY JOE	Equals	President	9
15	10	A BOY NAMED SUE	Johnny Cash	CBS	2
16	11	IT'S GETTING BETTER	Mama Cass	Stateside	5
30	12	LAY LADY LAY	Bob Dylan	CBS	3
28	13	PUT YOURSELF IN MY PLACE	Isley Brothers	Tamla Motown	4
14	14	THROW DOWN A LINE	Cliff and Hank	Columbia	3
27	15	CLOUD NINE	Temptations	Tamla Motown	5
11	16	MY CHERIE AMOUR	Stevie Wonder	Tamla Motown	11
25	17	MARRAKESH EXPRESS	Crosby, Stills and Nash	Atlantic	5
10	18	HONKY TONK WOMEN	Rolling Stones	Decca	12
19	19	HARE KRISHNA MANTRA	Radha Krishna Temple	Apple	2
31	20	NOBODY'S CHILD	Karen Young	Major Minor	4
22	21	CLEAN UP YOUR OWN BACK YARD	Elvis Presley	RCA	4
23	22	SOUL DEEP	Box Tops	Bell	6
12	23	SAVED BY THE BELL	Robin Gibb	Polydor	12
13	24	MAKE ME AN ISLAND	Joe Dolan	Pye	14
39	25	SPACE ODDITY	David Bowie	Philips	2
26	26	WET DREAM	Max Romeo	Unity	15
24	27	LOVE AT FIRST SIGHT	Sounds Nice	Parlophone	2
35	28	I'M GONNA MAKE YOU MINE	Lou Christie	Buddah	2
18	29	I'M A BETTER MAN	Engelbert Humperdinck	Decca	8
21	30	EARLY IN THE MORNING	Vanity Fare	Page One	10
33	31	I SECOND THAT EMOTION	Diana Ross and the Supremes and the Temptations	Tamla Motown	2
20	32	CURLY	Move	Regal Zonophone	10
17	33	BIRTH	Peddlers	CBS	4
32	34	TEARS WON'T WASH AWAY MY HEARTACHES	Ken Dodd	Columbia	8
-	35	FOR ONCE IN MY LIFE	Dorothy Squires	President	1
29	36	TEARS IN THE WIND	Chicken Shack	Blue Horizon	4
36	37	25 MILES	Edwin Starr	Tamla Motown	2
34	38	CONVERSATIONS	Cilla Black	Parlophone	12
38	39	MY WAY	Frank Sinatra	Reprise	20
-	40	PENNY ARCADE	Roy Orbison	London	1

October 1969

□ Highest position disc reached ● Act's first ever week on chart

LW	TW	WEEK ENDING 4 OCTOBER 1969			Wks
1	1	BAD MOON RISING	Creedence Clearwater Revival	Liberty	7
4	2	I'LL NEVER FALL IN LOVE AGAIN	Bobbie Gentry	Capitol	6
-	3	JE T'AIME...MOI NON PLUS	Jane Birkin and Serge Gainsbourg	Major Minor	1
10	4	A BOY NAMED SUE	Johnny Cash	CBS	3
3	5	DON'T FORGET TO REMEMBER	Bee Gees	Polydor	7
7	6	GOOD MORNING STARSHINE	Oliver	CBS	8
14	7	THROW DOWN A LINE	Cliff and Hank	Columbia	4
11	8	IT'S GETTING BETTER	Mama Cass	Stateside	6
12	9	LAY LADY LAY	Bob Dylan	CBS	4
5	10	IN THE YEAR 2525	Zager and Evans	RCA	9
6	11	NATURAL BORN BUGIE	Humble Pie	Immediate	7
19	12	HARE KRISHNA MANTRA	Radha Krishna Temple	Apple	3
9	13	VIVA BOBBY JOE	Equals	President	10
20	14	NOBODY'S CHILD	Karen Young	Major Minor	5
8	15	TOO BUSY THINKING ABOUT MY BABY	Marvin Gaye	Tamla Motown	11
2	16	JE T'AIME...MOI NON PLUS	Jane Birkin and Serge Gainsbourg	Fontana	8
28	17	I'M GONNA MAKE YOU MINE	Lou Christie	Buddah	3
31	18	I SECOND THAT EMOTION	Diana Ross and the Supremes and the Temptations	Tamla Motown	3
27	19	LOVE AT FIRST SIGHT	Sounds Nice	Parlophone	3
25	20	SPACE ODDITY	David Bowie	Philips	3
16	21	MY CHERIE AMOUR	Stevie Wonder	Tamla Motown	12
23	22	SAVED BY THE BELL	Robin Gibb	Polydor	13
33	23	BIRTH	Peddlers	CBS	5
24	24	MAKE ME AN ISLAND	Joe Dolan	Pye	15
13	25	PUT YOURSELF IN MY PLACE	Isley Brothers	Tamla Motown	5
22	26	SOUL DEEP	Box Tops	Bell	7
-	27	DO WHAT YOU GOTTA DO	Four Tops	Tamla Motown	1
29	28	I'M A BETTER MAN	Engelbert Humperdinck	Decca	9
21	29	CLEAN UP YOUR OWN BACK YARD	Elvis Presley	RCA	5
18	30	HONKY TONK WOMEN	Rolling Stones	Decca	13
15	31	CLOUD NINE	Temptations	Tamla Motown	6
-	32	HE AIN'T HEAVY HE'S MY BROTHER	Hollies	Parlophone	1
26	33	WET DREAM	Max Romeo	Unity	16
-	34	OH WELL	Fleetwood Mac	Reprise	1
39	35	MY WAY	Frank Sinatra	Reprise	21
-	36	WHEN TWO WORLDS COLLIDE	Jim Reeves	RCA Victor	13
17	37	MARRAKESH EXPRESS	Crosby, Stills and Nash	Atlantic	6
30	38	EARLY IN THE MORNING	Vanity Fare	Page One	11
-	39	DELTA LADY	Joe Cocker	Regal Zonophone	1
-	40	HUNT	Barry Ryan	Polydor	1

LW	TW	WEEK ENDING 11 OCTOBER 1969			Wks
3	1	JE T'AIME...MOI NON PLUS	Jane Birkin and Serge Gainsbourg	Major Minor	2
2	2	I'LL NEVER FALL IN LOVE AGAIN	Bobbie Gentry	Capitol	7
1	3	BAD MOON RISING	Creedence Clearwater Revival	Liberty	8
4	4	A BOY NAMED SUE	Johnny Cash	CBS	4
9	5	LAY LADY LAY	Bob Dylan	CBS	5
6	6	GOOD MORNING STARSHINE	Oliver	CBS	9
5	7	DON'T FORGET TO REMEMBER	Bee Gees	Polydor	8
7	8	THROW DOWN A LINE	Cliff and Hank	Columbia	5
8	9	IT'S GETTING BETTER	Mama Cass	Stateside	7
14	10	NOBODY'S CHILD	Karen Young	Major Minor	6
17	11	I'M GONNA MAKE YOU MINE	Lou Christie	Buddah	4
12	12	HARE KRISHNA MANTRA	Radha Krishna Temple	Apple	4
20	13	SPACE ODDITY	David Bowie	Philips	4
34	14	OH WELL	Fleetwood Mac	Reprise	2
25	15	PUT YOURSELF IN MY PLACE	Isley Brothers	Tamla Motown	6
32	16	HE AIN'T HEAVY HE'S MY BROTHER	Hollies	Parlophone	2
11	17	NATURAL BORN BUGIE	Humble Pie	Immediate	8
10	18	IN THE YEAR 2525	Zager and Evans	RCA	10
27	19	DO WHAT YOU GOTTA DO	Four Tops	Tamla Motown	2
31	20	CLOUD NINE	Temptations	Tamla Motown	7
15	21	TOO BUSY THINKING ABOUT MY BABY	Marvin Gaye	Tamla Motown	12
19	22	LOVE AT FIRST SIGHT	Sounds Nice	Parlophone	4
13	23	VIVA BOBBY JOE	Equals	President	11
18	24	I SECOND THAT EMOTION	Diana Ross and the Supremes and the Temptations	Tamla Motown	4
22	25	SAVED BY THE BELL	Robin Gibb	Polydor	14
-	26	LOVE'S BEEN GOOD TO ME	Frank Sinatra	Reprise	1
26	27	MY CHERIE AMOUR	Stevie Wonder	Tamla Motown	13
30	28	HONKY TONK WOMEN	Rolling Stones	Decca	14
28	29	I'M A BETTER MAN	Engelbert Humperdinck	Decca	10
33	30	WET DREAM	Max Romeo	Unity	17
26	31	SOUL DEEP	Box Tops	Bell	8
-	32	PENNY ARCADE	Roy Orbison	London	2
16	33	JE T'AIME...MOI NON PLUS	Jane Birkin and Serge Gainsbourg	Fontana	9
40	34	HUNT	Barry Ryan	Polydor	2
23	35	BIRTH	Peddlers	CBS	6
-	36	25 MILES	Edwin Starr	Tamla Motown	3
-	37	RETURN OF DJANGO/DOLLAR IN THE TEETH	Upsetters ●	Upsetter	1
24	38	MAKE ME AN ISLAND	Joe Dolan	Pye	16
39	39	DELTA LADY	Joe Cocker	Regal Zonophone	2
38	40	EARLY IN THE MORNING	Vanity Fare	Page One	12

■For the only time in British chart history, the same recording of the same song holds different chart positions in the same week. The scandalous *Je T'Aime ... Moi Non Plus* is the record in question, as Fontana withdraw their version and Major Minor pick up the licence (04.10.69) ■ Bob Dylan's final Top Ten hit stops one place below Johnny Cash, who wrote the sleeve notes for 'Nashville Skyline', the Dylan album from which *Lay Lady Lay* is taken (11.10.69)■

October 1969

□ Highest position disc reached ● Act's first ever week on chart

LW	TW	WEEK ENDING 18 OCTOBER 1969			Wks
2	1	I'LL NEVER FALL IN LOVE AGAIN	Bobbie Gentry	Capitol	8
1	2	JE T'AIME...MOI NON PLUS	Jane Birkin and Serge Gainsbourg	Major Minor	3
11	3	I'M GONNA MAKE YOU MINE	Lou Christie	Buddah	5
4	4	A BOY NAMED SUE	Johnny Cash	CBS	5
16	5	HE AIN'T HEAVY HE'S MY BROTHER	Hollies	Parlophone	3
10	6	NOBODY'S CHILD	Karen Young	Major Minor	7
5	7	LAY LADY LAY	Bob Dylan	CBS	7
13	8	SPACE ODDITY	David Bowie	Philips	5
14	9	OH WELL	Fleetwood Mac	Reprise	3
6	10	GOOD MORNING STARSHINE	Oliver	CBS	10
-	11	SUGAR SUGAR	Archies ●	RCA	1
3	12	BAD MOON RISING	Creedence Clearwater Revival	Liberty	9
9	13	IT'S GETTING BETTER	Mama Cass	Stateside	8
8	14	THROW DOWN A LINE	Cliff and Hank	Columbia	6
12	15	HARE KRISHNA MANTRA	Radha Krishna Temple	Apple	5
7	16	DON'T FORGET TO REMEMBER	Bee Gees	Polydor	9
19	17	DO WHAT YOU GOTTA DO	Four Tops	Tamla Motown	3
22	18	LOVE AT FIRST SIGHT	Sounds Nice	Parlophone	5
24	19	I SECOND THAT EMOTION	Diana Ross and the Supremes and the Temptations	Tamla Motown	5
37	20	RETURN OF DJANGO/DOLLAR IN THE TEETH	Upsetters	Upsetter	2
26	21	LOVE'S BEEN GOOD TO ME	Frank Sinatra	Reprise	2
15	22	PUT YOURSELF IN MY PLACE	Isley Brothers	Tamla Motown	7
18	23	IN THE YEAR 2525	Zager and Evans	RCA	11
21	24	TOO BUSY THINKING ABOUT MY BABY	Marvin Gaye	Tamla Motown	13
23	25	VIVA BOBBY JOE	Equals	President	12
-	26	FOR ONCE IN MY LIFE	Dorothy Squires	President	2
17	27	NATURAL BORN BUGIE	Humble Pie	Immediate	9
-	28	AND THE SUN WILL SHINE	José Feliciano	RCA	1
25	29	SAVED BY THE BELL	Robin Gibb	Polydor	15
39	30	DELTA LADY	Joe Cocker	Regal Zonophone	3
-	31	EVERYBODY'S TALKING	Nilsson ●	RCA	1
30	32	WET DREAM	Max Romeo	Unity	18
20	33	CLOUD NINE	Temptations	Tamla Motown	8
34	34	HUNT	Barry Ryan	Polydor	3
32	35	PENNY ARCADE	Roy Orbison	London	3
31	36	SOUL DEEP	Box Tops	Bell	9
27	37	MY CHERIE AMOUR	Stevie Wonder	Tamla Motown	14
-	38	MY WAY	Frank Sinatra	Reprise	22
38	39	MAKE ME AN ISLAND	Joe Dolan	Pye	17
28	40	HONKY TONK WOMEN	Rolling Stones	Decca	15

LW	TW	WEEK ENDING 25 OCTOBER 1969			Wks
11	1	SUGAR SUGAR	Archies	RCA	2
1	2	I'LL NEVER FALL IN LOVE AGAIN	Bobbie Gentry	Capitol	9
3	3	I'M GONNA MAKE YOU MINE	Lou Christie	Buddah	6
2	4	JE T'AIME...MOI NON PLUS	Jane Birkin and Serge Gainsbourg	Major Minor	4
5	5	HE AIN'T HEAVY HE'S MY BROTHER	Hollies	Parlophone	4
8	6	SPACE ODDITY	David Bowie	Philips	6
6	7	NOBODY'S CHILD	Karen Young	Major Minor	8
9	8	OH WELL	Fleetwood Mac	Reprise	4
7	9	LAY LADY LAY	Bob Dylan	CBS	8
4	10	A BOY NAMED SUE	Johnny Cash	CBS	6
17	11	DO WHAT YOU GOTTA DO	Four Tops	Tamla Motown	4
10	12	GOOD MORNING STARSHINE	Oliver	CBS	11
21	13	LOVE'S BEEN GOOD TO ME	Frank Sinatra	Reprise	3
13	14	IT'S GETTING BETTER	Mama Cass	Stateside	9
14	15	THROW DOWN A LINE	Cliff and Hank	Columbia	7
16	16	DON'T FORGET TO REMEMBER	Bee Gees	Polydor	10
20	17	RETURN OF DJANGO/DOLLAR IN THE TEETH	Upsetters	Upsetter	3
12	18	BAD MOON RISING	Creedence Clearwater Revival	Liberty	10
18	19	LOVE AT FIRST SIGHT	Sounds Nice	Parlophone	6
30	20	DELTA LADY	Joe Cocker	Regal Zonophone	4
22	21	PUT YOURSELF IN MY PLACE	Isley Brothers	Tamla Motown	8
15	22	HARE KRISHNA MANTRA	Radha Krishna Temple	Apple	6
31	23	EVERYBODY'S TALKING	Nilsson	RCA	2
25	24	VIVA BOBBY JOE	Equals	President	13
23	25	IN THE YEAR 2525	Zager and Evans	RCA	12
26	26	FOR ONCE IN MY LIFE	Dorothy Squires	President	3
24	27	TOO BUSY THINKING ABOUT MY BABY	Marvin Gaye	Tamla Motown	14
19	28	I SECOND THAT EMOTION	Diana Ross and the Supremes and the Temptations	Tamla Motown	6
-	29	WHAT DOES IT TAKE (TO WIN YOUR LOVE)	Junior Walker and the All Stars	Tamla Motown	1
28	30	AND THE SUN WILL SHINE	José Feliciano	RCA	2
38	31	MY WAY	Frank Sinatra	Reprise	23
-	32	LONG SHOT KICK DE BUCKET	Pioneers ●	Trojan	1
33	33	CLOUD NINE	Temptations	Tamla Motown	9
29	34	SAVED BY THE BELL	Robin Gibb	Polydor	16
32	35	WET DREAM	Max Romeo	Unity	19
-	36	THE LIQUIDATOR	Harry J. All Stars ●	Trojan	1
-	37	ROBIN'S RETURN	Neville Dickie ●	Major Minor	1
-	38	GOLDEN SLUMBERS/CARRY THAT WEIGHT	Trash ●	Apple	1
35	39	PENNY ARCADE	Roy Orbison	London	4
27	40	NATURAL BORN BUGIE	Humble Pie	Immediate	10

LW	TW	WEEK ENDING 1 NOVEMBER 1969			Wks
1	1	SUGAR SUGAR	Archies	RCA	3
3	2	I'M GONNA MAKE YOU MINE	Lou Christie	Buddah	7
5	3	HE AIN'T HEAVY HE'S MY BROTHER	Hollies	Parlophone	5
8	4	OH WELL	Fleetwood Mac	Reprise	5
6	5	SPACE ODDITY	David Bowie	Philips	7
2	6	I'LL NEVER FALL IN LOVE AGAIN	Bobbie Gentry	Capitol	10
7	7	NOBODY'S CHILD	Karen Young	Major Minor	9
17	8	RETURN OF DJANGO/DOLLAR IN THE TEETH	Upsetters	Upsetter	4
4	9	JE T'AIME...MOI NON PLUS	Jane Birkin and Serge Gainsbourg	Major Minor	5
10	10	A BOY NAMED SUE	Johnny Cash	CBS	7
9	11	LAY LADY LAY	Bob Dylan	CBS	9
20	12	DELTA LADY	Joe Cocker	Regal Zonophone	5
13	13	LOVE'S BEEN GOOD TO ME	Frank Sinatra	Reprise	4
11	14	DO WHAT YOU GOTTA DO	Four Tops	Tamla Motown	5
14	15	IT'S GETTING BETTER	Mama Cass	Stateside	10
18	16	BAD MOON RISING	Creedence Clearwater Revival	Liberty	11
12	17	GOOD MORNING STARSHINE	Oliver	CBS	12
-	18	WONDERFUL WORLD BEAUTIFUL PEOPLE	Jimmy Cliff ●	Trojan	1
16	19	DON'T FORGET TO REMEMBER	Bee Gees	Polydor	11
-	20	(CALL ME) NUMBER ONE	Tremeloes	CBS	1
19	21	LOVE AT FIRST SIGHT	Sounds Nice	Parlophone	7
29	22	WHAT DOES IT TAKE (TO WIN YOUR LOVE)	Junior Walker and the All Stars	Tamla Motown	2
32	23	LONG SHOT KICK DE BUCKET	Pioneers	Trojan	2
23	24	EVERYBODY'S TALKING	Nilsson	RCA	3
30	25	AND THE SUN WILL SHINE	José Feliciano	RCA	3
21	26	PUT YOURSELF IN MY PLACE	Isley Brothers	Tamla Motown	9
39	27	PENNY ARCADE	Roy Orbison	London	5
15	28	THROW DOWN A LINE	Cliff and Hank	Columbia	8
22	29	HARE KRISHNA MANTRA	Radha Krishna Temple	Apple	7
28	30	I SECOND THAT EMOTION	Diana Ross and the Supremes and the Temptations	Tamla Motown	7
36	31	THE LIQUIDATOR	Harry J. All Stars	Trojan	2
26	32	FOR ONCE IN MY LIFE	Dorothy Squires	President	4
27	33	TOO BUSY THINKING ABOUT MY BABY	Marvin Gaye	Tamla Motown	15
35	34	WET DREAM	Max Romeo	Unity	20
25	35	IN THE YEAR 2525	Zager and Evans	RCA	13
-	36	SWEET DREAM	Jethro Tull	Chrysalis	1
-	37	NO MULE'S FOOL	Family ●	Reprise	1
-	38	COLD TURKEY	Plastic Ono Band	Apple	1
-	39	PUT A LITTLE LOVE IN YOUR HEART	Dave Clark Five	Columbia	1
-	40	HONKY TONK WOMEN	Rolling Stones	Decca	16

In these weeks ■ Two records that will in later years top the charts, reach their peaks first time round in the same week - *Space Oddity* at number five and *He Ain't Heavy He's My Brother* at number three (01.11.69) ■ *Robin's Return* was not a prophetic title. One week after Neville Dickie's debut, Robin Gibb drops out of the 40, never to return as a soloist (25.10.69) ■ Five past, present and future number ones in the Top Ten (01.11.69)■

November 1969

□ Highest position disc reached ● Act's first ever week on chart

WEEK ENDING 8 NOVEMBER 1969

LW	TW	Title / Artist	Label	Wks
1	1	SUGAR SUGAR Archies	RCA	4
4	2	OH WELL Fleetwood Mac	Reprise	6
2	3	I'M GONNA MAKE YOU MINE Lou Christie	Buddah	8
3	4	HE AIN'T HEAVY HE'S MY BROTHER Hollies	Parlophone	6
8	5	RETURN OF DJANGO/DOLLAR IN THE TEETH Upsetters	Upsetter	5
7	6	NOBODY'S CHILD Karen Young	Major Minor	10
5	7	SPACE ODDITY David Bowie	Philips	8
13	8	LOVE'S BEEN GOOD TO ME Frank Sinatra	Reprise	5
6	9	I'LL NEVER FALL IN LOVE AGAIN Bobbie Gentry	Capitol	11
12	10	DELTA LADY Joe Cocker	Regal Zonophone	6
18	11	WONDERFUL WORLD BEAUTIFUL PEOPLE Jimmy Cliff	Trojan	2
10	12	A BOY NAMED SUE Johnny Cash	CBS	8
20	13	(CALL ME) NUMBER ONE Tremeloes	CBS	2
9	14	JE T'AIME...MOI NON PLUS Jane Birkin and Serge Gainsbourg	Major Minor	6
-	15	SOMETHING/COME TOGETHER Beatles	Parlophone	1
14	16	DO WHAT YOU GOTTA DO Four Tops	Tamla Motown	6
22	17	WHAT DOES IT TAKE (TO WIN YOUR LOVE) Junior Walker and the All Stars	Tamla Motown	3
38	18	COLD TURKEY Plastic Ono Band	Apple	2
36	19	SWEET DREAM Jethro Tull	Chrysalis	2
11	20	LAY LADY LAY Bob Dylan	CBS	10
-	21	RUBY DON'T TAKE YOUR LOVE TO TOWN Kenny Rogers and the First Edition ●	Reprise	1
16	22	BAD MOON RISING Creedence Clearwater Revival	Liberty	12
17	23	GOOD MORNING STARSHINE Oliver	CBS	13
31	24	THE LIQUIDATOR Harry J. All Stars	Trojan	3
23	25	LONG SHOT KICK DE BUCKET Pioneers	Trojan	3
24	26	EVERYBODY'S TALKING Nilsson	RCA	4
15	27	IT'S GETTING BETTER Mama Cass	Stateside	11
19	28	DON'T FORGET TO REMEMBER Bee Gees	Polydor	12
-	29	BILJO Clodagh Rodgers	RCA	1
-	30	TERESA Joe Dolan	Pye	1
39	31	PUT A LITTLE LOVE IN YOUR HEART Dave Clark Five	Columbia	2
32	32	FOR ONCE IN MY LIFE Dorothy Squires	President	5
-	33	ROBIN'S RETURN Neville Dickie	Major Minor	2
-	34	I MISS YOU BABY Marv Johnson	Tamla Motown	1
-	35	GOLDEN SLUMBERS/CARRY THAT WEIGHT Trash	Apple	2
25	36	AND THE SUN WILL SHINE José Feliciano	RCA	4
21	37	LOVE AT FIRST SIGHT Sounds Nice	Parlophone	8
37	38	NO MULE'S FOOL Family	Reprise	2
26	39	PUT YOURSELF IN MY PLACE Isley Brothers	Tamla Motown	10
30	40	I SECOND THAT EMOTION Diana Ross and the Supremes and the Temptations	Tamla Motown	8

WEEK ENDING 15 NOVEMBER 1969

LW	TW	Title / Artist	Label	Wks
1	1	SUGAR SUGAR Archies	RCA	5
2	2	OH WELL Fleetwood Mac	Reprise	7
13	3	(CALL ME) NUMBER ONE Tremeloes	CBS	3
4	4	HE AIN'T HEAVY HE'S MY BROTHER Hollies	Parlophone	7
5	5	RETURN OF DJANGO/DOLLAR IN THE TEETH Upsetters	Upsetter	6
15	6	SOMETHING/COME TOGETHER Beatles	Parlophone	2
11	7	WONDERFUL WORLD BEAUTIFUL PEOPLE Jimmy Cliff	Trojan	3
8	8	LOVE'S BEEN GOOD TO ME Frank Sinatra	Reprise	6
6	9	NOBODY'S CHILD Karen Young	Major Minor	11
3	10	I'M GONNA MAKE YOU MINE Lou Christie	Buddah	9
10	11	DELTA LADY Joe Cocker	Regal Zonophone	7
19	12	SWEET DREAM Jethro Tull	Chrysalis	3
17	13	WHAT DOES IT TAKE (TO WIN YOUR LOVE) Junior Walker and the All Stars	Tamla Motown	4
18	14	COLD TURKEY Plastic Ono Band	Apple	3
9	15	I'LL NEVER FALL IN LOVE AGAIN Bobbie Gentry	Capitol	12
7	16	SPACE ODDITY David Bowie	Philips	9
24	17	THE LIQUIDATOR Harry J. All Stars	Trojan	4
12	18	A BOY NAMED SUE Johnny Cash	CBS	9
21	19	RUBY DON'T TAKE YOUR LOVE TO TOWN Kenny Rogers and the First Edition	Reprise	2
14	20	JE T'AIME...MOI NON PLUS Jane Birkin and Serge Gainsbourg	Major Minor	7
25	21	LONG SHOT KICK DE BUCKET Pioneers	Trojan	4
16	22	DO WHAT YOU GOTTA DO Four Tops	Tamla Motown	7
29	23	BILJO Clodagh Rodgers	RCA	2
32	24	FOR ONCE IN MY LIFE Dorothy Squires	President	6
27	25	IT'S GETTING BETTER Mama Cass	Stateside	12
22	26	BAD MOON RISING Creedence Clearwater Revival	Liberty	13
20	27	LAY LADY LAY Bob Dylan	CBS	11
30	28	TERESA Joe Dolan	Pye	2
34	29	I MISS YOU BABY Marv Johnson	Tamla Motown	2
23	30	GOOD MORNING STARSHINE Oliver	CBS	14
-	31	YESTER-ME YESTER-YOU YESTERDAY Stevie Wonder	Tamla Motown	1
38	32	NO MULE'S FOOL Family	Reprise	3
28	33	DON'T FORGET TO REMEMBER Bee Gees	Polydor	13
26	34	EVERYBODY'S TALKING Nilsson	RCA	5
36	35	AND THE SUN WILL SHINE José Feliciano	RCA	5
-	36	THE ONION SONG Marvin Gaye and Tammi Terrell	Tamla Motown	1
31	37	PUT A LITTLE LOVE IN YOUR HEART Dave Clark Five	Columbia	3
-	38	PENNY ARCADE Roy Orbison	London	6
-	39	HERE COMES THE STAR Herman's Hermits	Columbia	1
33	40	ROBIN'S RETURN Neville Dickie	Major Minor	3

WEEK ENDING 22 NOVEMBER 1969

LW	TW	Title / Artist	Label	Wks
1	1	SUGAR SUGAR Archies	RCA	6
3	2	(CALL ME) NUMBER ONE Tremeloes	CBS	4
2	3	OH WELL Fleetwood Mac	Reprise	8
6	4	SOMETHING/COME TOGETHER Beatles	Parlophone	3
5	5	RETURN OF DJANGO/DOLLAR IN THE TEETH Upsetters	Upsetter	7
7	6	WONDERFUL WORLD BEAUTIFUL PEOPLE Jimmy Cliff	Trojan	4
12	7	SWEET DREAM Jethro Tull	Chrysalis	4
9	8	NOBODY'S CHILD Karen Young	Major Minor	12
19	9	RUBY DON'T TAKE YOUR LOVE TO TOWN Kenny Rogers and the First Edition	Reprise	3
31	10	YESTER-ME YESTER-YOU YESTERDAY Stevie Wonder	Tamla Motown	2
4	11	HE AIN'T HEAVY HE'S MY BROTHER Hollies	Parlophone	8
8	12	LOVE'S BEEN GOOD TO ME Frank Sinatra	Reprise	7
13	13	WHAT DOES IT TAKE (TO WIN YOUR LOVE) Junior Walker and the All Stars	Tamla Motown	5
11	14	DELTA LADY Joe Cocker	Regal Zonophone	8
14	15	COLD TURKEY Plastic Ono Band	Apple	4
10	16	I'M GONNA MAKE YOU MINE Lou Christie	Buddah	10
17	17	THE LIQUIDATOR Harry J. All Stars	Trojan	5
16	18	SPACE ODDITY David Bowie	Philips	10
-	19	WINTER WORLD OF LOVE Engelbert Humperdinck	Decca	1
28	20	TERESA Joe Dolan	Pye	3
18	21	A BOY NAMED SUE Johnny Cash	CBS	10
23	22	BILJO Clodagh Rodgers	RCA	3
-	23	GREEN RIVER Creedence Clearwater Revival	Liberty	1
21	24	LONG SHOT KICK DE BUCKET Pioneers	Trojan	5
15	25	I'LL NEVER FALL IN LOVE AGAIN Bobbie Gentry	Capitol	13
29	26	I MISS YOU BABY Marv Johnson	Tamla Motown	3
-	27	MELTING POT Blue Mink ●	Philips	1
-	28	LEAVIN' (DURHAM TOWN) Roger Whittaker ●	Columbia	1
22	29	DO WHAT YOU GOTTA DO Four Tops	Tamla Motown	8
-	30	LOVE IS ALL Malcolm Roberts	Major Minor	1
20	31	JE T'AIME...MOI NON PLUS Jane Birkin and Serge Gainsbourg	Major Minor	8
-	32	TWO LITTLE BOYS Rolf Harris	Columbia	1

■The Beatles miss the Top 3, for the first time since their first single *Love Me Do* seven years earlier (22.11.69) ■ Dorothy Squires is enjoying her first hit since one week of chart fame in 1953. *For Once In My Life* is the first of three hits which will peak at 24, 25 and 25 (15.11.69)■

November 1969

□ Highest position disc reached ● Act's first ever week on chart

LW	TW	Title	Artist	Label	Wks
36	33	THE ONION SONG	Marvin Gaye and Tammi Terrell	Tamla Motown	2
39	34	HERE COMES THE STAR	Herman's Hermits	Columbia	2
32	35	NO MULE'S FOOL	Family	Reprise	4
34	36	EVERYBODY'S TALKING	Nilsson	RCA	6
40	37	ROBIN'S RETURN	Neville Dickie	Major Minor	4
27	38	LAY LADY LAY	Bob Dylan	CBS	12
-	39	THE DEAL	Pat Campbell ●	Major Minor	1
-	40	PROUD MARY	Checkmates Ltd ●	A&M	1

WEEK ENDING 29 NOVEMBER 1969

LW	TW	Title	Artist	Label	Wks
1	1	SUGAR SUGAR	Archies	RCA	7
2	2	(CALL ME) NUMBER ONE	Tremeloes	CBS	5
10	3	YESTER-ME YESTER-YOU YESTERDAY	Stevie Wonder	Tamla Motown	3
3	4	OH WELL	Fleetwood Mac	Reprise	9
9	5	RUBY DON'T TAKE YOUR LOVE TO TOWN	Kenny Rogers and the First Edition	Reprise	4
4	6	SOMETHING/COME TOGETHER	Beatles	Parlophone	4
6	7	WONDERFUL WORLD BEAUTIFUL PEOPLE	Jimmy Cliff	Trojan	5
5	8	RETURN OF DJANGO/DOLLAR IN THE TEETH	Upsetters	Upsetter	8
17	9	THE LIQUIDATOR	Harry J. All Stars	Trojan	6
7	10	SWEET DREAM	Jethro Tull	Chrysalis	5
8	11	NOBODY'S CHILD	Karen Young	Major Minor	13
12	12	LOVE'S BEEN GOOD TO ME	Frank Sinatra	Reprise	8
13	13	WHAT DOES IT TAKE (TO WIN YOUR LOVE)	Junior Walker and the All Stars	Tamla Motown	6
27	14	MELTING POT	Blue Mink	Philips	2
19	15	WINTER WORLD OF LOVE	Engelbert Humperdinck	Decca	2
15	16	COLD TURKEY	Plastic Ono Band	Apple	5
32	17	TWO LITTLE BOYS	Rolf Harris	Columbia	2
11	18	HE AIN'T HEAVY HE'S MY BROTHER	Hollies	Parlophone	9
33	19	THE ONION SONG	Marvin Gaye and Tammi Terrell	Tamla Motown	3
30	20	LOVE IS ALL	Malcolm Roberts	Major Minor	2
23	21	GREEN RIVER	Creedence Clearwater Revival	Liberty	2
16	22	I'M GONNA MAKE YOU MINE	Lou Christie	Buddah	11
14	23	DELTA LADY	Joe Cocker	Regal Zonophone	9
22	24	BILJO	Clodagh Rodgers	RCA	4
26	25	I MISS YOU BABY	Marv Johnson	Tamla Motown	4
28	26	LEAVIN' (DURHAM TOWN)	Roger Whittaker	Columbia	2
24	27	LONG SHOT KICK DE BUCKET	Pioneers	Trojan	6
20	28	TERESA	Joe Dolan	Pye	4
35	29	NO MULE'S FOOL	Family	Reprise	5
40	30	PROUD MARY	Checkmates Ltd	A&M	2
39	31	THE DEAL	Pat Campbell	Major Minor	2
21	32	A BOY NAMED SUE	Johnny Cash	CBS	11
25	33	I'LL NEVER FALL IN LOVE AGAIN	Bobbie Gentry	Capitol	14
18	34	SPACE ODDITY	David Bowie	Philips	11
34	35	HERE COMES THE STAR	Herman's Hermits	Columbia	3
-	36	PENNY ARCADE	Roy Orbison	London	7
-	37	LONELINESS	Des O'Connor	Columbia	1
31	38	JE T'AIME...MOI NON PLUS	Jane Birkin and Serge Gainsbourg	Major Minor	9
-	39	SUSPICIOUS MINDS	Elvis Presley	RCA	1
-	40	TRACY	Cufflinks ●	MCA	1

WEEK ENDING 6 DECEMBER 1969

LW	TW	Title	Artist	Label	Wks
1	1	SUGAR SUGAR	Archies	RCA	8
3	2	YESTER-ME YESTER-YOU YESTERDAY	Stevie Wonder	Tamla Motown	4
5	3	RUBY DON'T TAKE YOUR LOVE TO TOWN	Kenny Rogers and the First Edition	Reprise	5
2	4	(CALL ME) NUMBER ONE	Tremeloes	CBS	6
17	5	TWO LITTLE BOYS	Rolf Harris	Columbia	3
4	6	OH WELL	Fleetwood Mac	Reprise	10
14	7	MELTING POT	Blue Mink	Philips	3
6	8	SOMETHING/COME TOGETHER	Beatles	Parlophone	5
10	9	SWEET DREAM	Jethro Tull	Chrysalis	6
39	10	SUSPICIOUS MINDS	Elvis Presley	RCA	2
7	11	WONDERFUL WORLD BEAUTIFUL PEOPLE	Jimmy Cliff	Trojan	6
15	12	WINTER WORLD OF LOVE	Engelbert Humperdinck	Decca	3
9	13	THE LIQUIDATOR	Harry J. All Stars	Trojan	7
8	14	RETURN OF DJANGO/DOLLAR IN THE TEETH	Upsetters	Upsetter	9
11	15	NOBODY'S CHILD	Karen Young	Major Minor	14
26	16	LEAVIN' (DURHAM TOWN)	Roger Whittaker	Columbia	3
19	17	THE ONION SONG	Marvin Gaye and Tammi Terrell	Tamla Motown	4
12	18	LOVE'S BEEN GOOD TO ME	Frank Sinatra	Reprise	9
16	19	COLD TURKEY	Plastic Ono Band	Apple	6
13	20	WHAT DOES IT TAKE (TO WIN YOUR LOVE)	Junior Walker and the All Stars	Tamla Motown	7
20	21	LOVE IS ALL	Malcolm Roberts	Major Minor	3
24	22	BILJO	Clodagh Rodgers	RCA	5
40	23	TRACY	Cufflinks	MCA	2
21	24	GREEN RIVER	Creedence Clearwater Revival	Liberty	3
18	25	HE AIN'T HEAVY HE'S MY BROTHER	Hollies	Parlophone	10
37	26	LONELINESS	Des O'Connor	Columbia	2
-	27	ALL I HAVE TO DO IS DREAM	Bobbie Gentry and Glen Campbell ●	Capitol	1
25	28	I MISS YOU BABY	Marv Johnson	Tamla Motown	5
22	29	I'M GONNA MAKE YOU MINE	Lou Christie	Buddah	12
-	30	GOOD OLD ROCK'N'ROLL	Dave Clark Five	Columbia	1
33	31	I'LL NEVER FALL IN LOVE AGAIN	Bobbie Gentry	Capitol	15
-	32	HIGHWAY SONG	Nancy Sinatra	Reprise	1
35	33	HERE COMES THE STAR	Herman's Hermits	Columbia	4
28	34	TERESA	Joe Dolan	Pye	5
27	35	LONG SHOT KICK DE BUCKET	Pioneers	Trojan	7
34	36	SPACE ODDITY	David Bowie	Philips	12
23	37	DELTA LADY	Joe Cocker	Regal Zonophone	10
30	38	PROUD MARY	Checkmates Ltd	A&M	3
-	39	GIN GAN GOOLIE	Scaffold	Parlophone	1
29	40	NO MULE'S FOOL	Family	Reprise	6

WEEK ENDING 13 DECEMBER 1969

LW	TW	Title	Artist	Label	Wks
1	1	SUGAR SUGAR	Archies	RCA	9
3	2	RUBY DON'T TAKE YOUR LOVE TO TOWN	Kenny Rogers and the First Edition	Reprise	6
5	3	TWO LITTLE BOYS	Rolf Harris	Columbia	4
2	4	YESTER-ME YESTER-YOU YESTERDAY	Stevie Wonder	Tamla Motown	5
7	5	MELTING POT	Blue Mink	Philips	4
4	6	(CALL ME) NUMBER ONE	Tremeloes	CBS	7
12	7	WINTER WORLD OF LOVE	Engelbert Humperdinck	Decca	4
10	8	SUSPICIOUS MINDS	Elvis Presley	RCA	3
17	9	THE ONION SONG	Marvin Gaye and Tammi Terrell	Tamla Motown	5
11	10	WONDERFUL WORLD BEAUTIFUL PEOPLE	Jimmy Cliff	Trojan	7
8	11	SOMETHING/COME TOGETHER	Beatles	Parlophone	6
21	12	LOVE IS ALL	Malcolm Roberts	Major Minor	4
13	13	THE LIQUIDATOR	Harry J. All Stars	Trojan	8
15	14	NOBODY'S CHILD	Karen Young	Major Minor	15
23	15	TRACY	Cufflinks	MCA	3
9	16	SWEET DREAM	Jethro Tull	Chrysalis	7
27	17	ALL I HAVE TO DO IS DREAM	Bobbie Gentry and Glen Campbell	Capitol	2
6	18	OH WELL	Fleetwood Mac	Reprise	11
16	19	LEAVIN' (DURHAM TOWN)	Roger Whittaker	Columbia	4
24	20	GREEN RIVER	Creedence Clearwater Revival	Liberty	4
-	21	WITHOUT LOVE	Tom Jones	Decca	1
14	22	RETURN OF DJANGO/DOLLAR IN THE TEETH	Upsetters	Upsetter	10
18	23	LOVE'S BEEN GOOD TO ME	Frank Sinatra	Reprise	10
26	24	LONELINESS	Des O'Connor	Columbia	3

In these weeks ■ The Archies complete eight weeks at number one, the longest run at the top by a one-hit wonder (13.12.69) ■ *Yester-Me Yester-You Yester-Day* is the first of four number two hits for Stevie Wonder, before he finally reaches number one in 1984 (06.12.69) ■ The Dave Clark Five's *Good Old Rock 'n' Roll* is a medley of three Chuck Berry hits, two Little Richard songs and one each from Jerry Lee Lewis and Carl Perkins (06.12.69) ■

☐ Highest position disc reached ● Act's first ever week on chart

LW	TW	Title / Artist	Label	Wks
30	25	GOOD OLD ROCK'N'ROLL Dave Clark Five	*Columbia*	2
22	26	BILJO Clodagh Rodgers	*RCA*	6
32	27	HIGHWAY SONG Nancy Sinatra	*Reprise*	2
19	28	COLD TURKEY Plastic Ono Band	*Apple*	7
29	29	I'M GONNA MAKE YOU MINE Lou Christie	*Buddah*	13
20	30	WHAT DOES IT TAKE (TO WIN YOUR LOVE) Junior Walker and the All Stars	*Tamla Motown*	8
25	31	HE AIN'T HEAVY HE'S MY BROTHER Hollies	*Parlophone*	11
38	32	PROUD MARY Checkmates Ltd	*A&M*	4
-	33	A BOY NAMED SUE Johnny Cash	*CBS*	12
-	34	IF I THOUGHT YOU'D CHANGE YOUR MIND Cilla Black	*Parlophone*	1
28	35	I MISS YOU BABY Marv Johnson	*Tamla Motown*	6
-	36	BUT YOU LOVE ME DADDY Jim Reeves	*RCA*	1
-	37	PENNY ARCADE Roy Orbison	*London*	8
34	38	TERESA Joe Dolan	*Pye*	6
-	39	WITH THE EYES OF A CHILD Cliff Richard	*Columbia*	1
31	40	I'LL NEVER FALL IN LOVE AGAIN Bobbie Gentry	*Capitol*	16

WEEK ENDING 20 DECEMBER 1969

LW	TW	Title / Artist	Label	Wks
3	[1]	TWO LITTLE BOYS Rolf Harris	*Columbia*	5
2	[2]	RUBY DON'T TAKE YOUR LOVE TO TOWN Kenny Rogers and the First Edition	*Reprise*	7
1	3	SUGAR SUGAR Archies	*RCA*	10
4	4	YESTER-ME YESTER-YOU YESTERDAY Stevie Wonder	*Tamla Motown*	6
5	5	MELTING POT Blue Mink	*Philips*	5
8	6	SUSPICIOUS MINDS Elvis Presley	*RCA*	4
17	7	ALL I HAVE TO DO IS DREAM Bobbie Gentry and Glen Campbell	*Capitol*	3
7	8	WINTER WORLD OF LOVE Engelbert Humperdinck	*Decca*	5
6	9	(CALL ME) NUMBER ONE Tremeloes	*CBS*	8
15	10	TRACY Cufflinks	*MCA*	4
13	11	THE LIQUIDATOR Harry J. All Stars	*Trojan*	9
21	12	WITHOUT LOVE Tom Jones	*Decca*	2
9	13	THE ONION SONG Marvin Gaye and Tammi Terrell	*Tamla Motown*	6
19	14	LEAVIN' (DURHAM TOWN) Roger Whittaker	*Columbia*	5
12	15	LOVE IS ALL Malcolm Roberts	*Major Minor*	5
25	16	GOOD OLD ROCK'N'ROLL Dave Clark Five	*Columbia*	3
10	17	WONDERFUL WORLD BEAUTIFUL PEOPLE Jimmy Cliff	*Trojan*	8
11	18	SOMETHING/COME TOGETHER Beatles	*Parlophone*	7
24	19	LONELINESS Des O'Connor	*Columbia*	4
39	[20]	WITH THE EYES OF A CHILD Cliff Richard	*Columbia*	2
20	21	GREEN RIVER Creedence Clearwater Revival	*Liberty*	5
36	22	BUT YOU LOVE ME DADDY Jim Reeves	*RCA*	2
27	23	HIGHWAY SONG Nancy Sinatra	*Reprise*	3
14	24	NOBODY'S CHILD Karen Young	*Major Minor*	16
18	25	OH WELL Fleetwood Mac	*Reprise*	12
22	26	RETURN OF DJANGO/DOLLAR IN THE TEETH Upsetters	*Upsetter*	11
16	27	SWEET DREAM Jethro Tull	*Chrysalis*	8
23	28	LOVE'S BEEN GOOD TO ME Frank Sinatra	*Reprise*	11
28	29	COLD TURKEY Plastic Ono Band	*Apple*	8
-	29	SOMEDAY WE'LL BE TOGETHER Diana Ross and the Supremes	*Tamla Motown*	1
29	31	I'M GONNA MAKE YOU MINE Lou Christie	*Buddah*	14
40	32	I'LL NEVER FALL IN LOVE AGAIN Bobbie Gentry	*Capitol*	17
26	33	BILJO Clodagh Rodgers	*RCA*	7
-	34	COMIN' HOME Delaney and Bonnie and Friends ●	*Atlantic*	1
31	35	HE AIN'T HEAVY HE'S MY BROTHER Hollies	*Parlophone*	12
30	36	WHAT DOES IT TAKE (TO WIN YOUR LOVE) Junior Walker and the All Stars	*Tamla Motown*	9
34	37	IF I THOUGHT YOU'D CHANGE YOUR MIND Cilla Black	*Parlophone*	2
-	38	SEVENTH SON Georgie Fame	*CBS*	1
-	39	GIN GAN GOOLIE Scaffold	*Parlophone*	2
-	40	REFLECTIONS OF MY LIFE Marmalade	*Decca*	1

WEEK ENDING 27 DECEMBER 1969

LW	TW	Title / Artist	Label	Wks
1	[1]	TWO LITTLE BOYS Rolf Harris	*Columbia*	6
2	[2]	RUBY DON'T TAKE YOUR LOVE TO TOWN Kenny Rogers and the First Edition	*Reprise*	8
3	3	SUGAR SUGAR Archies	*RCA*	11
6	4	SUSPICIOUS MINDS Elvis Presley	*RCA*	5
5	5	MELTING POT Blue Mink	*Philips*	6
4	6	YESTER-ME YESTER-YOU YESTERDAY Stevie Wonder	*Tamla Motown*	7
7	7	ALL I HAVE TO DO IS DREAM Bobbie Gentry and Glen Campbell	*Capitol*	4
8	8	WINTER WORLD OF LOVE Engelbert Humperdinck	*Decca*	6
10	9	TRACY Cufflinks	*MCA*	5
12	[10]	WITHOUT LOVE Tom Jones	*Decca*	3
13	11	THE ONION SONG Marvin Gaye and Tammi Terrell	*Tamla Motown*	7
16	12	GOOD OLD ROCK'N'ROLL Dave Clark Five	*Columbia*	4
14	13	LEAVIN' (DURHAM TOWN) Roger Whittaker	*Columbia*	6
9	14	(CALL ME) NUMBER ONE Tremeloes	*CBS*	9
15	15	LOVE IS ALL Malcolm Roberts	*Major Minor*	6
11	16	THE LIQUIDATOR Harry J. All Stars	*Trojan*	10
22	17	BUT YOU LOVE ME DADDY Jim Reeves	*RCA*	3
19	[18]	LONELINESS Des O'Connor	*Columbia*	5
21	[19]	GREEN RIVER Creedence Clearwater Revival	*Liberty*	6
24	20	NOBODY'S CHILD Karen Young	*Major Minor*	17
18	21	SOMETHING/COME TOGETHER Beatles	*Parlophone*	8
20	22	WITH THE EYES OF A CHILD Cliff Richard	*Columbia*	3
27	23	SWEET DREAM Jethro Tull	*Chrysalis*	9
17	24	WONDERFUL WORLD BEAUTIFUL PEOPLE Jimmy Cliff	*Trojan*	9
28	25	LOVE'S BEEN GOOD TO ME Frank Sinatra	*Reprise*	12
23	26	HIGHWAY SONG Nancy Sinatra	*Reprise*	4
29	27	SOMEDAY WE'LL BE TOGETHER Diana Ross and the Supremes	*Tamla Motown*	2
26	28	RETURN OF DJANGO/DOLLAR IN THE TEETH Upsetters	*Upsetter*	12
37	29	IF I THOUGHT YOU'D CHANGE YOUR MIND Cilla Black	*Parlophone*	3
40	30	REFLECTIONS OF MY LIFE Marmalade	*Decca*	2
25	31	OH WELL Fleetwood Mac	*Reprise*	13
-	32	SHE SOLD ME MAGIC Lou Christie	*Buddah*	1
33	33	BILJO Clodagh Rodgers	*RCA*	8
31	34	I'M GONNA MAKE YOU MINE Lou Christie	*Buddah*	15
38	35	SEVENTH SON Georgie Fame	*CBS*	2
-	36	A BOY NAMED SUE Johnny Cash	*CBS*	13
-	37	HITCHIN' A RIDE Vanity Fare	*Page One*	1
39	[38]	GIN GAN GOOLIE Scaffold	*Parlophone*	3
-	39	GOOD MORNING STARSHINE Oliver	*CBS*	15
32	40	I'LL NEVER FALL IN LOVE AGAIN Bobbie Gentry	*Capitol*	18

■ No record peaks at number 40 throughout the year. The last record to do so was Cream's *Anyone For Tennis* on 12 June 1968 (27.12.69) ■ Ron Dante sings lead vocals on both *Sugar Sugar* and *Tracy*, giving him two Top Ten hits in the same week (20.12.69) ■ One of Delaney and Bonnie's Friends is Eric Clapton (20.12.69) ■ *Cold Turkey* drops out of the Top 40 two days after Christmas (27.12.69) ■

1970

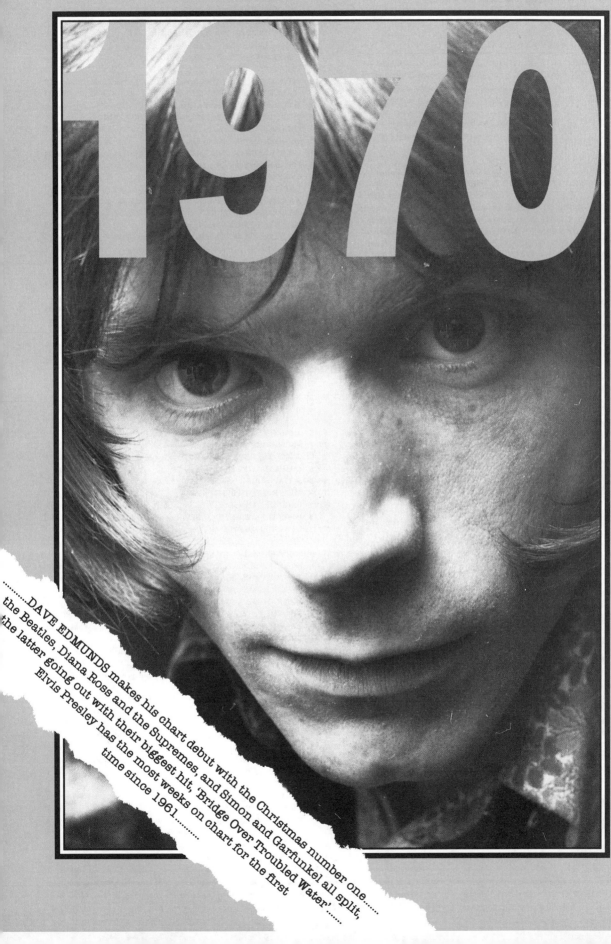

..........DAVE EDMUNDS makes his chart debut with the Christmas number one...... the Beatles, Diana Ross and the Supremes, and Simon and Garfunkel all split, the latter going out with their biggest hit, 'Bridge Over Troubled Water'...... Elvis Presley has the most weeks on chart for the first time since 1961..........

January 1970

□ Highest position disc reached ● Act's first ever week on chart

LW	TW	WEEK ENDING 10 JANUARY 1970			Wks
1	1	TWO LITTLE BOYS	Rolf Harris	Columbia	7
2	2	RUBY DON'T TAKE YOUR LOVE TO TOWN	Kenny Rogers/First Edition	Reprise	9
5	3	MELTING POT	Blue Mink	Philips	7
9	4	TRACY	Cufflinks	MCA	6
7	5	ALL I HAVE TO DO IS DREAM	Bobbie Gentry/Glen Campbell	Capitol	5
3	6	SUGAR, SUGAR	Archies	RCA	12
4	7	SUSPICIOUS MINDS	Elvis Presley	RCA	6
12	8	GOOD OLD ROCK 'N' ROLL	Dave Clark Five	Columbia	5
6	9	YESTER-ME, YESTER-YOU, YESTERDAY	Stevie Wonder	Tamla Motown	8
16	10	THE LIQUIDATOR	Harry J. All Stars	Trojan	11
11	11	THE ONION SONG	Marvin Gaye/Tammi Terrell	Tamla Motown	8
13	12	LEAVIN' (DURHAM TOWN)	Roger Whittaker	Columbia	7
10	13	WITHOUT LOVE	Tom Jones	Decca	4
8	14	WINTER WORLD OF LOVE	Engelbert Humperdinck	Decca	7
14	15	(CALL ME) NUMBER ONE	Tremeloes	CBS	10
30	16	REFLECTIONS OF MY LIFE	Marmalade	Decca	3
17	17	BUT YOU LOVE ME DADDY	Jim Reeves	RCA	4
21	18	SOMETHING/COME TOGETHER	Beatles	Apple	9
47	19	COMIN' HOME	Delaney and Bonnie	Atlantic	2
29	20	IF I THOUGHT YOU'D EVER CHANGE YOUR MIND	Cilla Black	Parlophone	4
26	21	HIGHWAY SONG	Nancy Sinatra	Reprise	5
22	22	WITH THE EYES OF A CHILD	Cliff Richard	Columbia	4
19	23	GREEN RIVER	Creedence Clearwater Revival	Liberty	78
27	24	SOMEDAY WE'LL BE TOGETHER	Diana Ross and Supremes	Tamla Motown	3
35	25	SEVENTH SON	Georgie Fame	CBS	3
15	26	LOVE IS ALL	Malcolm Roberts	Major Minor	7
32	27	SHE SOLD ME MAGIC	Lou Christie	Buddah	2
20	28	NOBODY'S CHILD	Karen Young	Major Minor	18
-	29	GOOD MORNING	Leapy Lee	MCA	1
18	30	LONELINESS	Des O'Connor	Columbia	6
-	31	I'M A MAN	Chicago ●	CBS	1
37	32	HITCHIN' A RIDE	Vanity Fare	Page One	2
-	33	COME AND GET IT	Badfinger ●	Apple	1
31	34	OH WELL	Fleetwood Mac	Reprise	14
24	35	WONDERFUL WORLD BEAUTIFUL PEOPLE	Jimmy Cliff	Trojan	10
-	36	LET IT ALL HANG OUT	Jonathan King	Decca	1
-	37	MY WAY	Frank Sinatra	Reprise	25
23	38	SWEET DREAM	Jethro Tull	Chrysalis	10
25	39	LOVE'S BEEN GOOD TO ME	Frank Sinatra	Reprise	13
-	40	LONG SHOT KICK THE BUCKET	Pioneers	Trojan	8

LW	TW	WEEK ENDING 17 JANUARY 1970			Wks
1	1	TWO LITTLE BOYS	Rolf Harris	Columbia	8
7	2	SUSPICIOUS MINDS	Elvis Presley	RCA	7
5	3	ALL I HAVE TO DO IS DREAM	Bobbie Gentry/Glen Campbell	Capitol	6
2	4	RUBY DON'T TAKE YOUR LOVE TO TOWN	Kenny Rogers/First Edition	Reprise	10
4	5	TRACY	Cufflinks	MCA	7
6	6	SUGAR, SUGAR	Archies	RCA	13
3	7	MELTING POT	Blue Mink	Philips	8
8	8	GOOD OLD ROCK 'N' ROLL	Dave Clark Five	Columbia	6
16	9	REFLECTIONS OF MY LIFE	Marmalade	Decca	4
33	10	COME AND GET IT	Badfinger	Apple	2
13	11	WITHOUT LOVE	Tom Jones	Decca	5
12	12	LEAVIN' (DURHAM TOWN)	Roger Whittaker	Columbia	8
24	13	SOMEDAY WE'LL BE TOGETHER	Diana Ross and Supremes	Tamla Motown	4
9	14	YESTER-ME, YESTER-YOU, YESTERDAY	Stevie Wonder	Tamla Motown	9
17	15	BUT YOU LOVE ME DADDY	Jim Reeves	RCA	5
14	16	WINTER WORLD OF LOVE	Engelbert Humperdinck	Decca	8
10	17	THE LIQUIDATOR	Harry J. All Stars	Trojan	12
-	18	FRIENDS	Arrival ●	Decca	1
11	19	THE ONION SONG	Marvin Gaye/Tammi Terrell	Tamla Motown	9
22	20	WITH THE EYES OF A CHILD	Cliff Richard	Columbia	5
19	21	COMIN' HOME	Delaney and Bonnie	Atlantic	3
23	22	GREEN RIVER	Creedence Clearwater Revival	Liberty	8
31	23	I'M A MAN	Chicago	CBS	2
26	24	LOVE IS ALL	Malcolm Roberts	Major Minor	8
15	25	(CALL ME) NUMBER ONE	Tremeloes	CBS	11
32	26	HITCHIN' A RIDE	Vanity Fare	Page One	3
20	27	IF I THOUGHT YOU'D EVER CHANGE YOUR MIND	Cilla Black	Parlophone	5
21	28	HIGHWAY SONG	Nancy Sinatra	Reprise	6
39	29	LOVE'S BEEN GOOD TO ME	Frank Sinatra	Reprise	14
27	30	SHE SOLD ME MAGIC	Lou Christie	Buddah	3
30	31	LONELINESS	Des O'Connor	Columbia	7
36	32	LET IT ALL HANG OUT	Jonathan King	Decca	2
-	33	VICTORIA	Kinks	Pye	1
-	34	WEDDING BELL BLUES	5th Dimension	Liberty	1
28	35	NOBODY'S CHILD	Karen Young	Major Minor	19
-	36	LEAVIN' ON A JET PLANE	Peter, Paul and Mary	Warner Bros.	1
25	37	SEVENTH SON	Georgie Fame	CBS	4
35	38	WONDERFUL WORLD BEAUTIFUL PEOPLE	Jimmy Cliff	Trojan	12
-	39	I CAN'T GET NEXT TO YOU	Temptations	Tamla Motown	1
18	40	SOMETHING/COME TOGETHER	Beatles	Apple	10

LW	TW	WEEK ENDING 24 JANUARY 1970			Wks
1	1	TWO LITTLE BOYS	Rolf Harris	Columbia	9
4	2	RUBY DON'T TAKE YOUR LOVE TO TOWN	Kenny Rogers/First Edition	Reprise	11
9	3	REFLECTIONS OF MY LIFE	Marmalade	Decca	5
3	4	ALL I HAVE TO IS DREAM	Bobbie Gentry/Glen Campbell	Capitol	7
5	5	TRACY	Cufflinks	MCA	8
2	6	SUSPICIOUS MINDS	Elvis Presley	RCA	8
8	7	GOOD OLD ROCK 'N' ROLL	Dave Clark Five	Columbia	7
10	8	COME AND GET IT	Badfinger	Apple	3
6	9	SUGAR, SUGAR	Archies	RCA	14
7	10	MELTING POT	Blue Mink	Philips	9
18	11	FRIENDS	Arrival	Decca	2
-	12	LOVE GROWS (WHERE MY ROSEMARY GOES)	Edison Lighthouse ●	Bell	1
36	13	LEAVIN' ON A JET PLANE	Peter, Paul and Mary	Warner Bros.	2
13	14	SOMEDAY WE'LL BE TOGETHER	Diana Ross and Supremes	Tamla Motown	5
17	15	THE LIQUIDATOR	Harry J. All Stars	Trojan	13
21	16	COMIN' HOME	Delaney and Bonnie	Atlantic	5
11	17	WITHOUT LOVE	Tom Jones	Decca	6
15	18	BUT YOU LOVE ME DADDY	Jim Reeves	RCA	6
12	19	LEAVIN' (DURHAM TOWN)	Roger Whittaker	Columbia	9
23	20	I'M A MAN	Chicago	CBS	3
27	21	IF I THOUGHT YOU'D EVER CHANGE YOUR MIND	Cilla Black	Parlophone	6
16	22	WINTER WORLD OF LOVE	Engelbert Humperdinck	Decca	9
26	23	HITCHIN' A RIDE	Vanity Fare	Page One	4
14	24	YESTER-ME, YESTER-YOU, YESTERDAY	Stevie Wonder	Tamla Motown	10
30	25	SHE SOLD ME MAGIC	Lou Christie	Buddah	4
39	26	I CAN'T GET NEXT TO YOU	Temptations	Tamla Motown	2
37	27	SEVENTH SON	Georgie Fame	CBS	5
19	28	THE ONION SONG	Marvin Gaye/Tammi Terrell	Tamla Motown	10
-	29	GOOD MORNING	Leapy Lee	MCA	2
-	30	WITCH'S PROMISE	Jethro Tull	Chrysalis	1
32	31	LET IT ALL HANG OUT	Jonathan King	Decca	3
28	32	HIGHWAY SONG	Nancy Sinatra	Reprise	7
34	33	WEDDING BELL BLUES	5th Dimension	Liberty	2
25	34	(CALL ME) NUMBER ONE	Tremeloes	CBS	12
33	35	VICTORIA	Kinks	Pye	2
24	36	LOVE IS ALL	Malcolm Roberts	Major Minor	9
-	37	VENUS	Shocking Blue ●	Penny Farthing	1

In these weeks ■ Elvis Presley's final US number one, *Suspicious Minds*, is kept from the UK top spot by that all time rock classic, *Two Little Boys*, by Rolf Harris (17.01.70) ■ The lead singer on *Tracy* by the Cuff-Links and *Sugar Sugar* by the Archies is the same man, Ron Dante (24.01.70)■

LW	TW	Title	Artist	Label	Wks
22	38	GREEN RIVER	Creedence Clearwater Revival	Liberty	9
-	39	RUB A DUB DUB	Equals	President	4
31	40	LONELINESS	Des O'Connor	Columbia	8

February 1970

□ Highest position disc reached ● Act's first ever week on chart

WEEK ENDING 31 JANUARY 1970

LW	TW	Title	Artist	Label	Wks
12	[1]	LOVE GROWS (WHERE MY ROSEMARY GOES)	Edison Lighthouse	Bell	2
1	2	TWO LITTLE BOYS	Rolf Harris	Columbia	10
3	3	REFLECTIONS OF MY LIFE	Marmalade	Decca	6
8	[4]	COME AND GET IT	Badfinger	Apple	4
4	5	ALL I HAVE TO DO IS DREAM	Bobbie Gentry/Glen Campbell	Capitol	8
6	6	SUSPICIOUS MINDS	Elvis Presley	RCA	9
2	7	RUBY DON'T TAKE YOUR LOVE TO TOWN	Kenny Rogers/First Edition	Reprise	12
11	[8]	FRIENDS	Arrival	Decca	3
13	9	LEAVIN' ON A JET PLANE	Peter, Paul and Mary	Warner Bros.	3
30	10	WITCH'S PROMISE/TEACHER	Jethro Tull	Chrysalis	2
5	11	TRACY	Cufflinks	MCA	9
20	12	I'M A MAN	Chicago	CBS	4
7	13	GOOD OLD ROCK 'N' ROLL	Dave Clark Five	Columbia	8
9	14	SUGAR, SUGAR	Archies	RCA	15
14	15	SOMEDAY WE'LL BE TOGETHER	Diana Ross and Supremes	Tamla Motown	6
10	16	MELTING POT	Blue Mink	Philips	10
15	17	THE LIQUIDATOR	Harry J. All Stars	Trojan	14
19	18	LEAVIN' (DURHAM TOWN)	Roger Whittaker	Columbia	10
18	19	BUT YOU LOVE ME DADDY	Jim Reeves	RCA	7
26	20	I CAN'T GET NEXT TO YOU	Temptations	Tamla Motown	3
16	21	COMIN' HOME	Delaney and Bonnie	Atlantic	6
-	22	TEMMA HARBOUR	Mary Hopkin	Apple	1
23	23	HITCHIN' A RIDE	Vanity Fare	Page One	5
17	24	WITHOUT LOVE	Tom Jones	Decca	7
33	25	WEDDING BELL BLUES	5th Dimension	Liberty	3
31	26	LET IT ALL HANG OUT	Jonathan King	Decca	4
25	27	SHE SOLD ME MAGIC	Lou Christie	Buddah	5
-	28	BOTH SIDES NOW	Judy Collins ●	Elektra	1
-	29	LET'S WORK TOGETHER	Canned Heat	Liberty	1
37	30	VENUS	Shocking Blue	Penny Farthing	3
24	31	YESTER-ME, YESTER-YOU, YESTERDAY	Stevie Wonder	Tamla Motown	11
22	32	WINTER WORLD OF LOVE	Engelbert Humperdinck	Decca	10
29	33	GOOD MORNING	Leapy Lee	MCA	3
39	[34]	RUB A DUB DUB	Equals	President	5
-	35	JUST A LITTLE MISUNDERSTANDING	Contours ●	Tamla Motown	1
-	36	GIRLIE	Peddlers	CBS	1
35	37	VICTORIA	Kinks	Pye	3
21	38	IF I THOUGHT YOU'D EVER CHANGE YOUR MIND	Cilla Black	Parlophone	7
-	39	ELIZABETHAN REGGAE	Boris Gardiner ●	Duke	1
35	40	HIGHWAY SONG	Nancy Sinatra	Reprise	8

WEEK ENDING 7 FEBRUARY 1970

LW	TW	Title	Artist	Label	Wks
1	1	LOVE GROWS (WHERE MY ROSEMARY GOES)	Edison Lighthouse	Bell	3
2	2	TWO LITTLE BOYS	Rolf Harris	Columbia	11
3	3	REFLECTIONS OF MY LIFE	Marmalade	Decca	7
9	4	LEAVIN' ON A JET PLANE	Peter, Paul and Mary	Warner Bros.	4
4	5	COME AND GET IT	Badfinger	Apple	5
10	6	WITCH'S PROMISE/TEACHER	Jethro Tull	Chrysalis	3
7	7	RUBY DON'T TAKE YOUR LOVE TO TOWN	Kenny Rogers/First Edition	Reprise	13
12	[8]	I'M A MAN	Chicago	CBS	5
8	9	FRIENDS	Arrival	Decca	4
22	10	TEMMA HARBOUR	Mary Hopkin	Apple	2
5	11	ALL I HAVE TO DO IS DREAM	Bobbie Gentry/Glen Campbell	Capitol	9
6	12	SUSPICIOUS MINDS	Elvis Presley	RCA	10
20	[13]	I CAN'T GET NEXT TO YOU	Temptations	Tamla Motown	4
11	14	TRACY	Cufflinks	MCA	10
29	15	LET'S WORK TOGETHER	Canned Heat	Liberty	2
23	[16]	HITCHIN' A RIDE	Vanity Fare	Page One	6
15	17	SOMEDAY WE'LL BE TOGETHER	Diana Ross and Supremes	Tamla Motown	7
13	18	GOOD OLD ROCK 'N' ROLL	Dave Clark Five	Columbia	9
14	19	SUGAR, SUGAR	Archies	RCA	16
17	20	THE LIQUIDATOR	Harry J. All Stars	Trojan	15
30	21	VENUS	Shocking Blue	Penny Farthing	4
16	22	MELTING POT	Blue Mink	Philips	11
21	23	COMIN' HOME	Delaney and Bonnie	Atlantic	7
19	24	BUT YOU LOVE ME DADDY	Jim Reeves	RCA	8
28	25	BOTH SIDES NOW	Judy Collins	Elektra	2
18	26	LEAVIN' (DURHAM TOWN)	Roger Whittaker	Columbia	11
26	27	LET IT ALL HANG OUT	Jonathan King	Decca	5
25	28	WEDDING BELL BLUES	5th Dimension	Liberty	4
24	29	WITHOUT LOVE	Tom Jones	Decca	8
-	30	I WANT YOU BACK	Jackson Five ●	Tamla Motown	1
35	[31]	JUST A LITTLE MISUNDERSTANDING	Contours	Tamla Motown	2
-	32	YEARS MAY COME AND YEARS MAY GO	Herman's Hermits	Columbia	1
39	33	ELIZABETHAN REGGAE	Boris Gardiner	Duke	2
36	[34]	GIRLIE	Peddlers	CBS	2
27	35	SHE SOLD ME MAGIC	Lou Christie	Buddah	6
-	36	WAND'RIN' STAR/I TALK TO THE TREES	Lee Marvin/Clint Eastwood ●	Paramount	1
34	37	RUB A DUB DUB	Equals	President	6
32	38	WINTER WORLD OF LOVE	Englebert Humperdinck	Decca	11
31	39	YESTER-ME, YESTER-YOU, YESTERDAY	Stevie Wonder	Tamla Motown	12
33	40	GOOD MORNING	Leapy Lee	MCA	4

WEEK ENDING 14 FEBRUARY 1970

LW	TW	Title	Artist	Label	Wks
1	[1]	LOVE GROWS (WHERE MY ROSEMARY GOES)	Edison Lighthouse	Bell	4
4	[2]	LEAVIN' ON A JET PLANE	Peter, Paul and Mary	Warner Bros.	5
15	3	LET'S WORK TOGETHER	Canned Heat	Liberty	3
6	[4]	WITCH'S PROMISE/TEACHER	Jethro Tull	Chrysalis	4
5	5	COME AND GET IT	Badfinger	Apple	6
3	6	REFLECTIONS OF MY LIFE	Marmalade	Decca	8
2	7	TWO LITTLE BOYS	Rolf Harris	Columbia	12
10	8	TEMMA HARBOUR	Mary Hopkin	Apple	3
8	9	I'M A MAN	Chicago	CBS	6
21	10	VENUS	Shocking Blue	Penny Farthing	5
9	11	FRIENDS	Arrival	Decca	5
30	12	I WANT YOU BACK	Jackson Five	Tamla Motown	2
7	13	RUBY DON'T TAKE YOUR LOVE TO TOWN	K. Rogers/First Edition	Reprise	14
13	14	I CAN'T GET NEXT TO YOU	Temptations	Tamla Motown	5
11	15	ALL I HAVE TO DO IS DREAM	Bobbie Gentry/Glen Campbell	Capitol	10
28	[16]	WEDDING BELL BLUES	5th Dimension	Liberty	5
12	17	SUSPICIOUS MINDS	Elvis Presley	RCA	11
36	18	WAND'RIN' STAR/I TALK TO THE TREES	Lee Marvin/Clint Eastwood	Paramount	2
17	19	SOMEDAY WE'LL BE TOGETHER	Diana Ross and Supremes	Tamla Motown	8
16	20	HITCHIN' A RIDE	Vanity Fare	Page One	7
14	21	TRACY	Cuff-Links	MCA	11
49	22	MY BABY LOVES LOVIN'	White Plains ●	Deram	1
25	23	BOTH SIDES NOW	Judy Collins	Elektra	3
32	24	YEARS MAY COME AND YEARS MAY GO	Herman's Hermits	Columbia	2
20	25	THE LIQUIDATOR	Harry J. All Stars	Trojan	16
19	26	SUGAR, SUGAR	Archies	RCA	17
18	27	GOOD OLD ROCK 'N' ROLL	Dave Clark Five	Columbia	10
22	28	MELTING POT	Blue Mink	Philips	12
27	29	LET IT ALL HANG OUT	Jonathan King	Decca	6
24	30	BUT YOU LOVE ME DADDY	Jim Reeves	RCA	9
26	31	LEAVIN' (DURHAM TOWN)	Roger Whittaker	Columbia	12

■ Edison Lighthouse hit the top in only their second week of chart life, the fastest climb to the top by anybody since the first chart of all (31.01.70) ■ The original copies of Boris Gardiner's *Elizabethan Reggae* had labels showing Bryan Lee and the performer. The record company corrected its error after a few weeks, and the charts showed the correct artist from 28.02.70. We give the correct name from the outset (31.01.70) ■

February 1970

□ Highest position disc reached ● Act's first ever week on chart

LW	TW	Title	Artist	Label	Wks
-	32	RAINDROPS KEEP FALLING ON MY HEAD	Sacha Distel	*Warner Bros.*	1
29	33	WITHOUT LOVE	Tom Jones	*Decca*	9
33	34	ELIZABETHAN REGGAE	Boris Gardiner	*Duke*	3
-	35	NA NA HEY HEY KISS HIM GOODBYE	Steam ●	*Fontana*	1
31	36	JUST A LITTLE MISUNDERSTANDING	Contours	*Tamla Motown*	3
-	37	DOWN ON THE CORNER	Creedence Clearwater Revival	*Liberty*	1
34	38	GIRLIE	Peddlers	*CBS*	3
-	39	SOMETHING'S BURNING	Kenny Rogers/First Edition	*Reprise*	1
-	40	UNITED WE STAND	Brotherhood Of Man ●	*Deram*	1

WEEK ENDING 21 FEBRUARY 1970

LW	TW	Title	Artist	Label	Wks
1	1	LOVE GROWS (WHERE MY ROSEMARY GOES)	Edison Lighthouse	*Bell*	5
3	2	LET'S WORK TOGETHER	Canned Heat	*Liberty*	4
2	3	LEAVIN' ON A JET PLANE	Peter, Paul and Mary	*Warner Bros.*	6
12	4	I WANT YOU BACK	Jackson Five	*Tamla Motown*	3
18	5	WAND'RIN' STAR	Lee Marvin	*Paramount*	3
8	6	TEMMA HARBOUR	Mary Hopkin	*Apple*	4
-	7	INSTANT KARMA	John Lennon and Yoko Ono with the Plastic Ono Band ●	*Apple*	1
4	8	WITCH'S PROMISE/TEACHER	Jethro Tull	*Chrysalis*	5
10	9	VENUS	Shocking Blue	*Penny Farthing*	6
7	10	TWO LITTLE BOYS	Rolf Harris	*Columbia*	13
22	11	MY BABY LOVES LOVIN'	White Plains	*Deram*	2
24	12	YEARS MAY COME AND YEARS MAY GO	Herman's Hermits	*Columbia*	3
5	13	COME AND GET IT	Badfinger	*Apple*	7
9	14	I'M A MAN	Chicago	*CBS*	7
6	15	REFLECTIONS OF MY LIFE	Marmalade	*Decca*	9
20	16	HITCHIN' A RIDE	Vanity Fare	*Page One*	8
14	17	I CAN'T GET NEXT TO YOU	Temptations	*Tamla Motown*	6
13	18	RUBY DON'T TAKE YOUR LOVE TO TOWN	Kenny Rogers/First Edition	*Reprise*	15
40	19	UNITED WE STAND	Brotherhood Of Man	*Deram*	2
23	20	BOTH SIDES NOW	Judy Collins	*Elektra*	4
16	21	WEDDING BELL BLUES	5th Dimension	*Liberty*	6
15	22	ALL I HAVE TO DO IS DREAM	Bobbie Gentry/Glen Campbell	*Capitol*	11
21	23	TRACY	Cufflinks	*MCA*	12
34	24	ELIZABETHAN REGGAE	Boris Gardiner	*Duke*	4
26	25	SUGAR, SUGAR	Archies	*RCA*	18
32	26	RAINDROPS KEEP FALLING ON MY HEAD	Sacha Distel	*Warner Bros.*	2
35	27	NA NA HEY HEY KISS HIM GOODBYE	Steam	*Fontana*	2
11	28	FRIENDS	Arrival	*Decca*	6
19	29	SOMEDAY WE'LL BE TOGETHER	Diana Ross and Supremes	*Tamla Motown*	9
17	30	SUSPICIOUS MINDS	Elvis Presley	*RCA*	12
30	31	BUT YOU LOVE ME DADDY	Jim Reeves	*RCA*	10
39	32	SOMETHING'S BURNING	Kenny Rogers/First Edition	*Reprise*	2
36	33	JUST A LITTLE MISUNDERSTANDING	Contours	*Tamla Motown*	4
29	34	LET IT ALL HANG OUT	Jonathan King	*Decca*	7
25	35	THE LIQUIDATOR	Harry J. All Stars	*Trojan*	17
31	36	LEAVIN' (DURHAM TOWN)	Roger Whittaker	*Columbia*	13
37	37	DOWN ON THE CORNER	Creedence Clearwater Revival	*Liberty*	2
-	38	RAINDROPS KEEP FALLING ON MY HEAD	B.J. Thomas ●	*Warner Bros.*	1
38	39	GIRLIE	Peddlers	*CBS*	4
27	40	GOOD OLD ROCK 'N' ROLL	Dave Clark Five	*Columbia*	11

WEEK ENDING 28 FEBRUARY 1970

LW	TW	Title	Artist	Label	Wks
1	1	LOVE GROWS (WHERE MY ROSEMARY GOES)	Edison Lighthouse	*Bell*	6
5	2	WAND'RIN' STAR	Lee Marvin	*Paramount*	4
2	3	LET'S WORK TOGETHER	Canned Heat	*Liberty*	5
4	4	I WANT YOU BACK	Jackson Five	*Tamla Motown*	4
7	5	INSTANT KARMA	John Lennon and Yoko Ono with the Plastic Ono Band	*Apple*	2
3	6	LEAVIN' ON A JET PLANE	Peter, Paul and Mary	*Warner Bros.*	7
6	7	TEMMA HARBOUR	Mary Hopkin	*Apple*	5
9	8	VENUS	Shocking Blue	*Penny Farthing*	7
11	9	MY BABY LOVES LOVIN'	White Plains	*Deram*	3
19	10	UNITED WE STAND	Brotherhood Of Man	*Deram*	3
12	11	YEARS MAY COME AND YEARS MAY GO	Herman's Hermits	*Columbia*	4
8	12	WITCH'S PROMISE/TEACHER	Jethro Tull	*Chrysalis*	6
-	13	BRIDGE OVER TROUBLED WATER	Simon and Garfunkel	*CBS*	1
20	14	BOTH SIDES NOW	Judy Collins	*Elektra*	5
10	15	TWO LITTLE BOYS	Rolf Harris	*Columbia*	14
26	16	RAINDROPS KEEP FALLING ON MY HEAD	Sacha Distel	*Warner Bros.*	3
17	17	I CAN'T GET NEXT TO YOU	Temptations	*Tamla Motown*	7
14	18	I'M A MAN	Chicago	*CBS*	8
13	19	COME AND GET IT	Badfinger	*Apple*	8
18	20	RUBY DON'T TAKE YOUR LOVE TO TOWN	Kenny Rogers/First Edition	*Reprise*	16
27	21	NA NA HEY HEY KISS HIM GOODBYE	Steam	*Fontana*	3
16	22	HITCHIN' A RIDE	Vanity Fare	*Page One*	9
24	23	ELIZABETHAN REGGAE	Boris Gardiner	*Duke*	5
23	24	TRACY	Cufflinks	*MCA*	13
21	25	WEDDING BELL BLUES	5th Dimension	*Liberty*	7
15	26	REFLECTIONS OF MY LIFE	Marmalade	*Decca*	10
-	27	THAT SAME OLD FEELING	Pickettywitch ●	*Pye*	1
32	28	SOMETHING'S BURNING	Kenny Rogers/First Edition	*Reprise*	3
25	29	SUGAR, SUGAR	Archies	*RCA*	19
-	30	DON'T CRY DADDY	Elvis Presley	*RCA*	1
-	31	TILL	Dorothy Squires	*President*	1
22	32	ALL I HAVE TO DO IS DREAM	Bobbie Gentry/Glen Campbell	*Capitol*	12
-	33	JOY OF LIVING	Cliff and Hank	*Columbia*	1
37	34	DOWN ON THE CORNER	Creedence Clearwater Revival	*Liberty*	3
-	35	SYMPATHY	Rare Bird ●	*Charisma*	1
29	36	SOMEDAY WE'LL BE TOGETHER	Diana Ross and Supremes	*Tamla Motown*	10
-	37	BE YOUNG BE FOOLISH BE HAPPY	Tams ●	*Stateside*	1
-	38	YOU'RE SUCH A GOOD LOOKING WOMAN	Joe Dolan	*Pye*	1
28	39	FRIENDS	Arrival	*Decca*	7
33	40	JUST A LITTLE MISUNDERSTANDING	Contours	*Tamla Motown*	5

WEEK ENDING 7 MARCH 1970

LW	TW	Title	Artist	Label	Wks
2	1	WAND'RIN' STAR	Lee Marvin	*Paramount*	5
4	2	I WANT YOU BACK	Jackson Five	*Tamla Motown*	5
3	3	LET'S WORK TOGETHER	Canned Heat	*Liberty*	6
1	4	LOVE GROWS (WHERE MY ROSEMARY GOES)	Edison Lighthouse	*Bell*	7
5	5	INSTANT KARMA	John Lennon and Yoko Ono with the Plastic Ono Band	*Apple*	3
6	6	LEAVIN' ON A JET PLANE	Peter, Paul and Mary	*Warner Bros.*	8
13	7	BRIDGE OVER TROUBLED WATER	Simon and Garfunkel	*CBS*	2
11	8	YEARS MAY COME AND YEARS MAY GO	Herman's Hermits	*Columbia*	5
9	9	MY BABY LOVES LOVIN'	White Plains	*Deram*	4
7	10	TEMMA HARBOUR	Mary Hopkin	*Apple*	6
10	11	UNITED WE STAND	Brotherhood Of Man	*Deram*	4
8	12	VENUS	Shocking Blue	*Penny Farthing*	8
21	13	NA NA HEY HEY KISS HIM GOODBYE	Steam	*Fontana*	4
23	14	ELIZABETHAN REGGAE	Boris Gardiner	*Duke*	6
16	15	RAINDROPS KEEP FALLING ON MY HEAD	Sacha Distel	*Warner Bros.*	4
28	16	SOMETHING'S BURNING	Kenny Rogers/First Edition	*Reprise*	4

In these weeks ■ After two weeks as a double-sided hit from *Paint Your Wagon*, the charts drop Clint Eastwood's *I Talk To The Trees* and Lee Marvin soars to an unlikely number one (21.02.70) ■ Cliff and Hank are, of course, Cliff Richard and Hank Marvin. *Joy of Living* is Cliff's 50th chart hit (28.02.70)■

LW	TW	Title	Artist	Label	Wks
14	**17**	BOTH SIDES NOW	Judy Collins	*Elektra*	6
30	**18**	DON'T CRY DADDY	Elvis Presley	*RCA*	2
27	**19**	THAT SAME OLD FEELING	Pickettywitch	*Pye*	2
15	**20**	TWO LITTLE BOYS	Rolf Harris	*Columbia*	15
12	**21**	WITCH'S PROMISE/TEACHER	Jethro Tull	*Chrysalis*	7
19	**22**	COME AND GET IT	Badfinger	*Apple*	9
18	**23**	I'M A MAN	Chicago	*CBS*	9
20	**24**	RUBY DON'T TAKE YOUR LOVE TO TOWN	Kenny Rogers/ First Edition	*Reprise*	17
33	**[25]**	JOY OF LIVING	Cliff and Hank	*Columbia*	2
22	**26**	HITCHIN' A RIDE	Vanity Fare	*Page One*	10
32	**27**	ALL I HAVE TO DO IS DREAM	Bobbie Gentry/Glen Campbell	*Capitol*	13
-	**28**	EVERYBODY GET TOGETHER	Dave Clark Five	*Columbia*	1
35	**29**	SYMPATHY	Rare Bird	*Charisma*	2
-	**30**	MY WAY	Frank Sinatra	*Reprise*	16
34	**[31]**	DOWN ON THE CORNER	Creedence Clearwater Revival	*Liberty*	4
-	**32**	FAREWELL IS A LONELY SOUND	Jimmy Ruffin	*Tamla Motown*	1
-	**33**	BUT YOU LOVE ME DADDY	Jim Reeves	*RCA*	4
25	**34**	WEDDING BELL BLUES	5th Dimension	*Liberty*	8
26	**35**	REFLECTIONS OF MY LIFE	Marmalade	*Decca*	11
24	**36**	TRACY	Cufflinks	*MCA*	14
29	**37**	SUGAR, SUGAR	Archies	*RCA*	20
37	**38**	BE YOUNG BE FOOLISH BE HAPPY	Tams	*Stateside*	2
17	**39**	I CAN'T GET NEXT TO YOU	Temptations	*Tamla Motown*	8
-	**40**	RAINDROPS KEEP FALLIN' ON MY HEAD	Bobbie Gentry	*Capitol*	1

WEEK ENDING 14 MARCH 1970

LW	TW	Title	Artist	Label	Wks
1	**[1]**	WAND'RIN' STAR	Lee Marvin	*Paramount*	6
-	**[2]**	LET IT BE	Beatles	*Apple*	1
7	**3**	BRIDGE OVER TROUBLED WATER	Simon and Garfunkel	*CBS*	3
2	**4**	I WANT YOU BACK	Jackson Five	*Tamla Motown*	6
4	**5**	LOVE GROWS (WHERE MY ROSEMARY GOES)	Edison Lighthouse	*Bell*	8
5	**6**	INSTANT KARMA	John Lennon and Yoko Ono with the Plastic Ono Band	*Apple*	4
3	**7**	LET'S WORK TOGETHER	Canned Heat	*Liberty*	7
19	**8**	THAT SAME OLD FEELING	Pickettywitch	*Pye*	3
8	**9**	YEARS MAY COME AND YEARS MAY GO	Herman's Hermits	*Columbia*	6
15	**[10]**	RAINDROPS KEEP FALLING ON MY HEAD	Sacha Distel	*Warner Bros.*	5
18	**11**	DON'T CRY DADDY	Elvis Presley	*RCA*	3
11	**12**	UNITED WE STAND	Brotherhood Of Man	*Deram*	5
13	**13**	NA NA HEY HEY KISS HIM GOODBYE	Steam	*Fontana*	5
9	**14**	MY BABY LOVES LOVIN'	White Plains	*Deram*	5
6	**15**	LEAVIN' ON A JET PLANE	Peter, Paul and Mary	*Warner Bros.*	9
12	**16**	VENUS	Shocking Blue	*Penny Farthing*	9
-	**17**	CAN'T HELP FALLING IN LOVE	Andy Williams	*CBS*	1
16	**18**	SOMETHING'S BURNING	Kenny Rogers/First Edition	*Reprise*	5
10	**19**	TEMMA HARBOUR	Mary Hopkin	*Apple*	7
28	**20**	EVERYBODY GET TOGETHER	Dave Clark Five	*Columbia*	2
20	**21**	TWO LITTLE BOYS	Rolf Harris	*Columbia*	16
-	**22**	YOUNG, GIFTED AND BLACK	Bob and Marcia ●	*Harry*	1
17	**23**	BOTH SIDES NOW	Judy Collins	*Elektra*	7
14	**24**	ELIZABETHAN REGGAE	Boris Gardiner	*Duke*	7
25	**25**	JOY OF LIVING	Cliff and Hank	*Columbia*	3
-	**26**	TILL	Dorothy Squires	*President*	2
29	**27**	SYMPATHY	Rare Bird	*Charisma*	3
-	**28**	YOU'RE SUCH A GOOD LOOKING WOMAN	Joe Dolan	*Pye*	2
32	**29**	FAREWELL IS A LONELY SOUND	Jimmy Ruffin	*Tamla Motown*	2
24	**30**	RUBY DON'T TAKE YOUR LOVE TO TOWN	Kenny Rogers/ First Edition	*Reprise*	18
21	**31**	WITCH'S PROMISE/TEACHER	Jethro Tull	*Chrysalis*	8
30	**32**	MY WAY	Frank Sinatra	*Reprise*	17
23	**33**	I'M A MAN	Chicago	*CBS*	10
33	**34**	BUT YOU LOVE ME DADDY	Jim Reeves	*RCA*	5
31	**35**	DOWN ON THE CORNER	Creedence Clearwater Revival	*Liberty*	5

March 1970

□ Highest position disc reached ● Act's first ever week on chart

LW	TW	Title	Artist	Label	Wks
-	**36**	I'LL GO ON HOPING	Des O'Connor	*Columbia*	1
39	**37**	I CAN'T GET NEXT TO YOU	Temptations	*Tamla Motown*	9
37	**38**	SUGAR, SUGAR	Archies	*RCA*	21
38	**39**	BE YOUNG BE FOOLISH BE HAPPY	Tams	*Stateside*	3
22	**40**	COME AND GET IT	Badfinger	*Apple*	10

WEEK ENDING 21 MARCH 1970

LW	TW	Title	Artist	Label	Wks
1	**[1]**	WAND'RIN' STAR	Lee Marvin	*Paramount*	7
3	**2**	BRIDGE OVER TROUBLED WATER	Simon and Garfunkel	*CBS*	4
2	**3**	LET IT BE	Beatles	*Apple*	2
4	**4**	I WANT YOU BACK	Jackson Five	*Tamla Motown*	7
8	**[5]**	THAT SAME OLD FEELING	Pickettywitch	*Pye*	4
17	**6**	CAN'T HELP FALLING IN LOVE	Andy Williams	*CBS*	2
9	**[7]**	YEARS MAY COME AND YEARS MAY GO	Herman's Hermits	*Columbia*	7
11	**[8]**	DON'T CRY DADDY	Elvis Presley	*RCA*	4
13	**[9]**	NA NA HEY HEY KISS HIM GOODBYE	Steam	*Fontana*	6
6	**10**	INSTANT KARMA	John Lennon and Yoko Ono with the Plastic Ono Band	*Apple*	5
20	**11**	EVERYBODY GET TOGETHER	Dave Clark Five	*Columbia*	3
7	**12**	LET'S WORK TOGETHER	Canned Heat	*Liberty*	8
18	**13**	SOMETHING'S BURNING	Kenny Rogers/First Edition	*Reprise*	6
10	**14**	RAINDROPS KEEP FALLING ON MY HEAD	Sacha Distel	*Warner Bros.*	6
22	**15**	YOUNG, GIFTED AND BLACK	Bob and Marcia	*Harry*	2
12	**16**	UNITED WE STAND	Brotherhood Of Man	*Deram*	6
5	**17**	LOVE GROWS (WHERE MY ROSEMARY GOES)	Edison Lighthouse	*Bell*	9
14	**18**	MY BABY LOVES LOVIN'	White Plains	*Deram*	6
15	**19**	LEAVIN' ON A JET PLANE	Peter, Paul and Mary	*Warner Bros.*	10
21	**20**	TWO LITTLE BOYS	Rolf Harris	*Columbia*	17
24	**21**	ELIZABETHAN REGGAE	Boris Gardiner	*Duke*	8
16	**22**	VENUS	Shocking Blue	*Penny Farthing*	10
29	**23**	FAREWELL IS A LONELY SOUND	Jimmy Ruffin	*Tamla Motown*	3
19	**24**	TEMMA HARBOUR	Mary Hopkin	*Apple*	8
26	**[25]**	TILL	Dorothy Squires	*President*	3
28	**26**	YOU'RE SUCH A GOOD LOOKING WOMAN	Joe Dolan	*Pye*	3
27	**27**	SYMPATHY	Rare Bird	*Charisma*	4
25	**28**	JOY OF LIVING	Cliff and Hank	*Columbia*	4
-	**29**	WHO DO YOU LOVE	Juicy Lucy ●	*Vertigo*	1
32	**30**	MY WAY	Frank Sinatra	*Reprise*	18
23	**31**	BOTH SIDES NOW	Judy Collins	*Elektra*	8
38	**[32]**	BE YOUNG BE FOOLISH BE HAPPY	Tams	*Stateside*	4
-	**33**	NOBODY'S FOOL	Jim Reeves	*RCA*	1
-	**34**	WHEN JULIE COMES AROUND	Cufflinks	*MCA*	1
37	**35**	SUGAR, SUGAR	Archies	*RCA*	22
-	**36**	WHY (MUST WE FALL IN LOVE)	Diana Ross and the Supremes/ Temptations	*Tamla Motown*	1
-	**[37]**	A STREET CALLED HOPE	Gene Pitney	*Stateside*	1
31	**38**	WITCH'S PROMISE/TEACHER	Jethro Tull	*Chrysalis*	9
-	**39**	EVERYBODY'S TALKIN'	Nilsson	*RCA*	1
-	**40**	BY THE WAY	Tremeloes	*CBS*	1

WEEK ENDING 28 MARCH 1970

LW	TW	Title	Artist	Label	Wks
2	**[1]**	BRIDGE OVER TROUBLED WATER	Simon and Garfunkel	*CBS*	5
1	**2**	WAND'RIN' STAR	Lee Marvin	*Paramount*	8
6	**[3]**	CAN'T HELP FALLING IN LOVE	Andy Williams	*CBS*	3
3	**4**	LET IT BE	Beatles	*Apple*	3
5	**[5]**	THAT SAME OLD FEELING	Pickettywitch	*Pye*	5
15	**6**	YOUNG, GIFTED AND BLACK	Bob and Marcia	*Harry*	3
-	**7**	KNOCK KNOCK WHO'S THERE	Mary Hopkin	*Apple*	1
11	**[8]**	EVERYBODY GET TOGETHER	Dave Clark Five	*Columbia*	4

■Andy Williams' version of Elvis Presley's 1962 number one, *Can't Help Falling In Love*, climbs higher than the King's own latest single *Don't Cry Daddy* (21.03.70) ■ Lee Marvin kept both the Beatles and the Jackson Five from hitting number one, but could not keep Simon and Garfunkel out (28.03.70)■

March 1970

□ Highest position disc reached ● Act's first ever week on chart

LW	TW	Title	Artist	Label	Wks
8	**9**	DON'T CRY DADDY	Elvis Presley	*RCA*	5
9	**10**	NA NA HEY HEY KISS HIM GOODBYE	Steam	*Fontana*	7
13	**11**	SOMETHING'S BURNING	Kenny Rogers/First Edition	*Reprise*	7
4	**12**	I WANT YOU BACK	Jackson 5	*Tamla Motown*	8
7	**13**	YEARS MAY COME AND YEARS MAY GO	Herman's Hermits	*Columbia*	8
12	**14**	LET'S WORK TOGETHER	Canned Heat	*Liberty*	9
10	**15**	INSTANT KARMA	John Lennon and Yoko Ono with the Plastic Ono Band	*Apple*	6
14	**16**	RAINDROPS KEEP FALLING ON MY HEAD	Sacha Distel	*Warner Bros.*	7
16	**17**	UNITED WE STAND	Brotherhood Of Man	*Deram*	7
23	**18**	FAREWELL IS A LONELY SOUND	Jimmy Ruffin	*Tamla Motown*	4
17	**19**	LOVE GROWS	Edison Lighthouse	*Bell*	10
26	**20**	YOU'RE SUCH A GOOD LOOKING WOMAN	Joe Dolan	*Pye*	4
18	**21**	MY BABY LOVES LOVIN'	White Plains	*Deram*	7
-	**22**	I CAN'T HELP MYSELF	Four Tops	*Tamla Motown*	1
19	**23**	LEAVIN' ON A JET PLANE	Peter, Paul and Mary	*Warner Bros.*	11
20	**24**	TWO LITTLE BOYS	Rolf Harris	*Columbia*	18
28	**25**	JOY OF LIVING	Cliff and Hank	*Columbia*	5
34	**26**	WHEN JULIE COMES AROUND	Cufflinks	*MCA*	2
27	**27**	SYMPATHY	Rare Bird	*Charisma*	5
21	**28**	ELIZABETHAN REGGAE	Boris Gardiner	*Duke*	9
29	**29**	WHO DO YOU LOVE	Juicy Lucy	*Vertigo*	2
-	**30**	I'LL GO ON HOPING	Des O'Connor	*Columbia*	2
-	**31**	GIMME DAT DING	Pipkins ●	*Columbia*	1
25	**32**	TILL	Dorothy Squires	*President*	4
-	**33**	SPIRIT IN THE SKY	Norman Greenbaum ●	*Reprise*	1
24	**34**	TEMMA HARBOUR	Mary Hopkin	*Apple*	9
33	**35**	NOBODY'S FOOL	Jim Reeves	*RCA*	2
-	**36**	GOOD MORNING FREEDOM	Blue Mink	*Philips*	1
22	**37**	VENUS	Shocking Blue	*Penny Farthing*	11
37	**38**	A STREET CALLED HOPE	Gene Pitney	*Stateside*	2
40	**39**	BY THE WAY	Tremeloes	*CBS*	2
30	**40**	MY WAY	Frank Sinatra	*Reprise*	29

WEEK ENDING 4 APRIL 1970

LW	TW	Title	Artist	Label	Wks
1	**1**	BRIDGE OVER TROUBLED WATER	Simon and Garfunkel	*CBS*	6
7	**2**	KNOCK KNOCK WHO'S THERE	Mary Hopkin	*Apple*	2
3	**3**	CAN'T HELP FALLING IN LOVE	Andy Williams	*CBS*	4
2	**4**	WAND'RIN' STAR	Lee Marvin	*Paramount*	9
6	**5**	YOUNG, GIFTED AND BLACK	Bob and Marcia	*Harry*	4
5	**6**	THAT SAME OLD FEELING	Pickettywitch	*Pye*	6
4	**7**	LET IT BE	Beatles	*Apple*	4
11	**8**	SOMETHING'S BURNING	Kenny Rogers/First Edition	*Reprise*	8
8	**9**	EVERYBODY GET TOGETHER	Dave Clark Five	*Columbia*	5
9	**10**	DON'T CRY DADDY	Elvis Presley	*RCA*	6
10	**11**	NA NA HEY HEY KISS HIM GOODBYE	Steam	*Fontana*	8
12	**12**	I WANT YOU BACK	Jackson 5	*Tamla Motown*	9
-	**13**	ALL KINDS OF EVERYTHING	Dana ●	*Rex*	1
18	**14**	FAREWELL IS A LONELY SOUND	Jimmy Ruffin	*Tamla Motown*	5
33	**15**	SPIRIT IN THE SKY	Norman Greenbaum	*Reprise*	2
13	**16**	YEARS MAY COME AND YEARS MAY GO	Herman's Hermits	*Columbia*	9
22	**17**	I CAN'T HELP MYSELF	Four Tops	*Tamla Motown*	2
20	**18**	YOU'RE SUCH A GOOD LOOKING WOMAN	Joe Dolan	*Pye*	5
29	**19**	WHO DO YOU LOVE	Juicy Lucy	*Vertigo*	3
14	**20**	LET'S WORK TOGETHER	Canned Heat	*Liberty*	10
31	**21**	GIMME DAT DING	Pipkins	*Columbia*	2
26	**22**	WHEN JULIE COMES AROUND	Cufflinks	*MCA*	3
16	**23**	RAINDROPS KEEP FALLING ON MY HEAD	Sacha Distel	*Warner Bros.*	8
15	**24**	INSTANT KARMA	John Lennon and Yoko Ono with the Plastic Ono Band	*Apple*	7
24	**25**	TWO LITTLE BOYS	Rolf Harris	*Columbia*	19
17	**26**	UNITED WE STAND	Brotherhood Of Man	*Deram*	8
19	**27**	LOVE GROWS	Edison Lighthouse	*Bell*	11
28	**28**	ELIZABETHAN REGGAE	Boris Gardiner	*Duke*	10
23	**29**	LEAVIN' ON A JET PLANE	Peter, Paul and Mary	*Warner Bros.*	12
32	**30**	TILL	Dorothy Squires	*President*	5
25	**31**	JOY OF LIVING	Cliff and Hank	*Columbia*	6
35	**32**	NOBODY'S FOOL	Jim Reeves	*RCA*	3
-	**33**	GOVINDA	Radha Krishna Temple	*Apple*	1
21	**34**	MY BABY LOVES LOVIN'	White Plains	*Deram*	9
-	**35**	TRAVELLIN' BAND	Creedence Clearwater Revival	*Liberty*	1
30	**36**	I'LL GO ON HOPING	Des O'Connor	*Columbia*	3
36	**37**	GOOD MORNING FREEDOM	Blue Mink	*Philips*	2
34	**38**	TEMMA HARBOUR	Mary Hopkin	*Apple*	10
-	**39**	NEVER HAD A DREAM COME TRUE	Stevie Wonder	*Tamla Motown*	1
-	**40**	HOUSE OF THE RISING SUN	Frijid Pink ●	*Deram*	1

WEEK ENDING 11 APRIL 1970

LW	TW	Title	Artist	Label	Wks
1	**1**	BRIDGE OVER TROUBLED WATER	Simon and Garfunkel	*CBS*	7
13	**2**	ALL KINDS OF EVERYTHING	Dana	*Rex*	2
3	**3**	CAN'T HELP FALLING IN LOVE	Andy Williams	*CBS*	5
2	**4**	KNOCK KNOCK WHO'S THERE	Mary Hopkin	*Apple*	3
4	**5**	WAND'RIN' STAR	Lee Marvin	*Paramount*	10
15	**6**	SPIRIT IN THE SKY	Norman Greenbaum	*Reprise*	3
6	**7**	THAT SAME OLD FEELING	Pickettywitch	*Pye*	7
5	**8**	YOUNG, GIFTED AND BLACK	Bob and Marcia	*Harry*	5
8	**9**	SOMETHING'S BURNING	Kenny Rogers/First Edition	*Reprise*	9
21	**10**	GIMME DAT DING	Pipkins	*Columbia*	3
7	**11**	LET IT BE	Beatles	*Apple*	5
17	**12**	I CAN'T HELP MYSELF	Four Tops	*Tamla Motown*	3
14	**13**	FAREWELL IS A LONELY SOUND	Jimmy Ruffin	*Tamla Motown*	6
10	**14**	DON'T CRY DADDY	Elvis Presley	*RCA*	7
9	**15**	EVERYBODY GET TOGETHER	Dave Clark Five	*Columbia*	6
22	**16**	WHEN JULIE COMES AROUND	Cufflinks	*MCA*	4
18	**17**	YOU'RE SUCH A GOOD LOOKING WOMAN	Joe Dolan	*Pye*	6
11	**18**	NA NA HEY HEY KISS HIM GOODBYE	Steam	*Fontana*	9
37	**19**	NEVER HAD A DREAM COME TRUE	Stevie Wonder	*Tamla Motown*	2
12	**20**	I WANT YOU BACK	Jackson 5	*Tamla Motown*	10
35	**21**	GOOD MORNING FREEDOM	Blue Mink	*Philips*	3
16	**22**	YEARS MAY COME AND YEARS MAY GO	Herman's Hermits	*Columbia*	10
33	**23**	GOVINDA	Radha Krishna Temple	*Apple*	2
20	**24**	LET'S WORK TOGETHER	Canned Heat	*Liberty*	11
19	**25**	WHO DO YOU LOVE	Juicy Lucy	*Vertigo*	4
23	**26**	RAINDROPS KEEP FALLING ON MY HEAD	Sacha Distel	*Warner Bros.*	9
33	**27**	TRAVELLIN' BAND	Creedence Clearwater Revival	*Liberty*	2
27	**28**	LOVE GROWS	Edison Lighthouse	*Bell*	12
29	**29**	LEAVIN' ON A JET PLANE	Peter, Paul and Mary	*Warner Bros.*	13
25	**30**	TWO LITTLE BOYS	Rolf Harris	*Columbia*	20
34	**31**	MY BABY LOVES LOVIN'	White Plains	*Deram*	10
31	**32**	JOY OF LIVING	Cliff and Hank	*Columbia*	7
-	**33**	RAG MAMA RAG	The Band	*Capitol*	1
-	**34**	WHY (MUST WE FALL IN LOVE)	Diana Ross and the Supremes/ Temptations	*Tamla Motown*	2
-	**35**	BY THE WAY	Tremeloes	*CBS*	2
26	**36**	UNITED WE STAND	Brotherhood Of Man	*Deram*	9
30	**37**	TILL	Dorothy Squires	*President*	6
24	**38**	INSTANT KARMA	John Lennon and Yoko Ono with the Plastic Ono Band	*Apple*	8
38	**39**	HOUSE OF THE RISING SUN	Frijid Pink	*Deram*	2
34	**40**	I'LL GO ON HOPING	Des O'Connor	*Columbia*	4

WEEK ENDING 18 APRIL 1970

LW	TW	Title	Artist	Label	Wks
2	**1**	ALL KINDS OF EVERYTHING	Dana	*Rex*	3
1	**2**	BRIDGE OVER TROUBLED WATER	Simon and Garfunkel	*CBS*	8

In these weeks ■ Mary Hopkin's Eurovision song *Knock Knock Who's There* peaks at number two, but Dana's winner for Ireland goes all the way (18.04.70) ■ The Pipkins and White Plains have the same lead singer - the man who also sang lead on Edison Lighthouse's *Love Grows* and Brotherhood Of Man's *United We Stand*, Tony Burrows (11.04.70)■

LW	TW	Title	Artist	Label	Wks
3	3	CAN'T HELP FALLING IN LOVE	Andy Williams	CBS	6
4	4	KNOCK KNOCK WHO'S THERE	Mary Hopkin	Apple	4
6	5	SPIRIT IN THE SKY	Norman Greenbaum	Reprise	4
10	6	GIMME DAT DING	Pipkins	Columbia	4
8	7	YOUNG, GIFTED AND BLACK	Bob and Marcia	Harry	6
5	8	WAND'RIN' STAR	Lee Marvin	Paramount	11
13	9	FAREWELL IS A LONELY SOUND	Jimmy Ruffin	Tamla Motown	7
12	10	I CAN'T HELP MYSELF	Four Tops	Tamla Motown	4
7	11	THAT SAME OLD FEELING	Pickettywitch	Pye	8
16	12	WHEN JULIE COMES AROUND	Cufflinks	MCA	5
19	13	NEVER HAD A DREAM COME TRUE	Stevie Wonder	Tamla Motown	3
25	14	WHO DO YOU LOVE	Juicy Lucy	Vertigo	5
9	15	SOMETHING'S BURNING	Kenny Rogers/First Edition	Reprise	10
11	16	LET IT BE	Beatles	Apple	6
17	17	YOU'RE SUCH A GOOD LOOKING WOMAN	Joe Dolan	Pye	7
21	18	GOOD MORNING FREEDOM	Blue Mink	Philips	4
27	19	TRAVELLIN' BAND	Creedence Clearwater Revival	Liberty	3
14	20	DON'T CRY DADDY	Elvis Presley	RCA	8
39	21	HOUSE OF THE RISING SUN	Frijid Pink	Deram	3
18	22	NA NA HEY HEY KISS HIM GOODBYE	Steam	Fontana	10
15	23	EVERYBODY GET TOGETHER	Dave Clark Five	Columbia	7
22	24	YEARS MAY COME AND YEARS MAY GO	Herman's Hermits	Columbia	11
33	25	RAG MAMA RAG	The Band	Capitol	2
-	26	BACK HOME	England World Cup Squad ●	Pye	1
-	27	I'VE GOT YOU ON MY MIND	White Plains	Deram	1
-	28	I DON'T BELIEVE IN IF ANYMORE	Roger Whittaker	Columbia	1
23	29	GOVINDA	Radha Krishna Temple	Apple	3
20	30	I WANT YOU BACK	Jackson 5	Tamla Motown	11
34	31	WHY (MUST WE FALL IN LOVE)	Diana Ross and the Supremes/Temptations	Tamla Motown	3
26	32	RAINDROPS KEEP FALLING ON MY HEAD	Sacha Distel	Warner Bros.	10
-	33	DAUGHTER OF DARKNESS	Tom Jones	Decca	1
-	34	ELIZABETHAN REGGAE	Boris Gardiner	Duke	11
-	35	THE SEEKER	Who	Track	1
-	36	DO THE FUNKY CHICKEN	Rufus Thomas ●	Stax	1
30	37	TWO LITTLE BOYS	Rolf Harris	Columbia	21
-	38	NOBODY'S FOOL	Jim Reeves	RCA	4
24	39	LET'S WORK TOGETHER	Canned Heat	Liberty	12
-	40	MY WAY	Frank Sinatra	Reprise	5

WEEK ENDING 25 APRIL 1970

LW	TW	Title	Artist	Label	Wks
1	1	ALL KINDS OF EVERYTHING	Dana	Rex	4
5	2	SPIRIT IN THE SKY	Norman Greenbaum	Reprise	5
2	3	BRIDGE OVER TROUBLED WATER	Simon and Garfunkel	CBS	9
3	4	CAN'T HELP FALLING IN LOVE	Andy Williams	CBS	7
4	5	KNOCK KNOCK WHO'S THERE	Mary Hopkin	Apple	5
6	6	GIMME DAT DING	Pipkins	Columbia	5
7	7	YOUNG, GIFTED AND BLACK	Bob and Marcia	Harry	7
13	8	NEVER HAD A DREAM COME TRUE	Stevie Wonder	Tamla Motown	4
9	9	FAREWELL IS A LONELY SOUND	Jimmy Ruffin	Tamla Motown	8
18	10	GOOD MORNING FREEDOM	Blue Mink	Philips	5
10	11	I CAN'T HELP MYSELF	Four Tops	Tamla Motown	5
12	12	WHEN JULIE COMES AROUND	Cufflinks	MCA	6
8	13	WAND'RIN' STAR	Lee Marvin	Paramount	12
21	14	HOUSE OF THE RISING SUN	Frijid Pink	Deram	4
19	15	TRAVELLIN' BAND	Creedence Clearwater Revival	Liberty	4
25	16	RAG MAMA RAG	The Band	Capitol	3
33	17	DAUGHTER OF DARKNESS	Tom Jones	Decca	2
15	18	SOMETHING'S BURNING	Kenny Rogers/First Edition	Reprise	11
11	19	THAT SAME OLD FEELING	Pickettywitch	Pye	9
14	20	WHO DO YOU LOVE	Juicy Lucy	Vertigo	6
17	21	YOU'RE SUCH A GOOD LOOKING WOMAN	Joe Dolan	Pye	8
28	22	I DON'T BELIEVE IN IF ANYMORE	Roger Whittaker	Columbia	2
26	23	BACK HOME	England World Cup Squad	Pye	2
29	24	GOVINDA	Radha Krishna Temple	Apple	4
20	25	DON'T CRY DADDY	Elvis Presley	RCA	9
16	26	LET IT BE	Beatles	Apple	7
-	27	I CAN'T TELL THE BOTTOM FROM THE TOP	Hollies	Parlaphone	1
35	28	THE SEEKER	Who	Track	2
22	29	NA NA HEY HEY KISS HIM GOODBYE	Steam	Fontana	11
36	30	DO THE FUNKY CHICKEN	Rufus Thomas	Stax	2
-	31	BRONTOSAURUS	Move	Regal Zonophone	1
27	32	I'VE GOT YOU ON MY MIND	White Plains	Deram	2
-	33	IF I COULD (EL CONDOR PASA)	Julie Felix ●	RAK	1
31	34	WHY (MUST WE FALL IN LOVE)	Diana Ross and the Supremes/Temptations	Tamla Motown	4
32	35	RAINDROPS KEEP FALLING ON MY HEAD	Sacha Distel	Warner Bros.	11
23	36	EVERYBODY GET TOGETHER	Dave Clark Five	Columbia	8
37	37	TWO LITTLE BOYS	Rolf Harris	Columbia	22
40	38	MY WAY	Frank Sinatra	Reprise	30
30	39	I WANT YOU BACK	Jackson 5	Tamla Motown	12
34	40	ELIZABETHAN REGGAE	Boris Gardiner	Duke	12

May 1970

□ Highest position disc reached ● Act's first ever week on chart

WEEK ENDING 2 MAY 1970

LW	TW	Title	Artist	Label	Wks
2	1	SPIRIT IN THE SKY	Norman Greenbaum	Reprise	6
1	2	ALL KINDS OF EVERYTHING	Dana	Rex	5
23	3	BACK HOME	England World Cup Squad	Pye	3
3	4	BRIDGE OVER TROUBLED WATER	Simon and Garfunkel	CBS	10
4	5	CAN'T HELP FALLING IN LOVE	Andy Williams	CBS	7
8	6	NEVER HAD A DREAM COME TRUE	Stevie Wonder	Tamla Motown	5
6	7	GIMME DAT DING	Pipkins	Columbia	6
9	8	FAREWELL IS A LONELY SOUND	Jimmy Ruffin	Tamla Motown	9
14	9	HOUSE OF THE RISING SUN	Frijid Pink	Deram	5
12	10	WHEN JULIE COMES AROUND	Cuff Links	MCA	7
15	11	TRAVELLIN' BAND	Creedence Clearwater Revival	Liberty	5
10	12	GOOD MORNING FREEDOM	Blue Mink	Philips	6
7	13	YOUNG, GIFTED AND BLACK	Bob and Marcia	Harry	8
5	14	KNOCK KNOCK WHO'S THERE	Mary Hopkin	Apple	6
17	15	DAUGHTER OF DARKNESS	Tom Jones	Decca	3
16	16	RAG MAMA RAG	The Band	Capitol	4
11	17	I CAN'T HELP MYSELF	Four Tops	Tamla Motown	6
20	18	WHO DO YOU LOVE	Juicy Lucy	Vertigo	7
27	19	I CAN'T TELL THE BOTTOM FROM THE TOP	Hollies	Parlaphone	2
21	20	YOU'RE SUCH A GOOD LOOKING WOMAN	Joe Dolan	Pye	9
13	21	WAND'RIN' STAR	Lee Marvin	Paramount	13
18	22	SOMETHING'S BURNING	Kenny Rogers/First Edition	Reprise	12
22	23	I DON'T BELıEVE IN IF ANYMORE	Roger Whittaker	Columbia	3
32	24	I'VE GOT YOU ON MY MIND	White Plains	Deram	3
19	25	THAT SAME OLD FEELING	Pickettywitch	Pye	10
28	26	THE SEEKER	Who	Track	3
31	27	BRONTOSAURUS	Move	Regal Zonophone	2
33	28	IF I COULD (EL CONDOR PASA)	Julie Felix	RAK	2
30	29	DO THE FUNKY CHICKEN	Rufus Thomas	Stax	3
35	30	RAINDROPS KEEP FALLING ON MY HEAD	Sacha Distel	Warner Bros.	12
25	31	DON'T CRY DADDY	Elvis Presley	RCA	10
-	32	BELFAST BOY	Don Fardon ●	Young Blood	1
38	33	MY WAY	Frank Sinatra	Reprise	31
26	34	LET IT BE	Beatles	Apple	8
-	35	QUESTION	Moody Blues	Threshold	1
29	36	NA NA HEY HEY KISS HIM GOODBYE	Steam	Fontana	12
24	37	GOVINDA	Radha Krishna Temple	Apple	5
34	38	WHY (MUST WE FALL IN LOVE)	Diana Ross and the Supremes/Temptations	Tamla Motown	4

■ England's World Cup Squad have more luck on the charts than on the football field, but that is not the only soccer song in the charts. Don Fardon's *Belfast Boy* is about Manchester United's George Best (02.05.70) ■ Three animals in consecutive chart positions, a Brontosaurus, a Condor and a Chicken at 27, 28 and 29 (02.05.70) ■

May 1970

□ Highest position disc reached ● Act's first ever week on chart

LW	TW	Title	Artist	Label	Wks
-	[39]	OUT DEMONS OUT	Edgar Broughton Band ●	Harvest	1
37	40	TWO LITTLE BOYS	Rolf Harris	Columbia	23

WEEK ENDING 9 MAY 1970

LW	TW	Title	Artist	Label	Wks
1	[1]	SPIRIT IN THE SKY	Norman Greenbaum	Reprise	7
3	2	BACK HOME	England World Cup Squad	Pye	4
2	3	ALL KINDS OF EVERYTHING	Dana	Rex	6
4	4	BRIDGE OVER TROUBLED WATER	Simon and Garfunkel	CBS	11
15	[5]	DAUGHTER OF DARKNESS	Tom Jones	Decca	4
9	6	HOUSE OF THE RISING SUN	Frijid Pink	Deram	6
5	7	CAN'T HELP FALLING IN LOVE	Andy Williams	CBS	8
11	[8]	TRAVELLIN' BAND	Creedence Clearwater Revival	Liberty	6
6	9	NEVER HAD A DREAM COME TRUE	Stevie Wonder	Tamla Motown	6
19	10	I CAN'T TELL THE BOTTOM FROM THE TOP	Hollies	Parlophone	3
7	11	GIMME DAT DING	Pipkins	Columbia	7
10	12	WHEN JULIE COMES AROUND	Cufflinks	MCA	8
12	13	GOOD MORNING FREEDOM	Blue Mink	Philips	7
27	14	BRONTOSAURUS	Move	Regal Zonophone	3
14	15	KNOCK KNOCK WHO'S THERE	Mary Hopkin	Apple	7
8	16	FAREWELL IS A LONELY SOUND	Jimmy Ruffin	Tamla Motown	10
23	17	I DON'T BELIEVE IN IF ANYMORE	Roger Whittaker	Columbia	4
13	18	YOUNG, GIFTED AND BLACK	Bob and Marcia	Harry	9
16	19	RAG MAMA RAG	The Band	Capitol	5
35	20	QUESTION	Moody Blues	Threshold	2
17	21	I CAN'T HELP MYSELF	Four Tops	Tamla Motown	7
24	22	I'VE GOT YOU ON MY MIND	White Plains	Deram	4
21	23	WAND'RIN' STAR	Lee Marvin	Paramount	14
26	24	THE SEEKER	Who	Track	4
28	25	IF I COULD (EL CONDOR PASA)	Julie Felix	RAK	3
29	26	DO THE FUNKY CHICKEN	Rufus Thomas	Stax	4
18	27	WHO DO YOU LOVE	Juicy Lucy	Vertigo	8
-	28	YELLOW RIVER	Christie ●	CBS	1
25	29	THAT SAME OLD FEELING	Pickettywitch	Pye	11
37	30	GOVINDA	Radha Krishna Temple	Apple	6
20	31	YOU'RE SUCH A GOOD LOOKING WOMAN	Joe Dolan	Pye	10
32	[32]	BELFAST BOY	Don Fardon	Young Blood	2
30	33	RAINDROPS KEEP FALLING ON MY HEAD	Sacha Distel	Warner Bros.	13
34	34	LET IT BE	Beatles	Apple	9
-	35	ABRAHAM, MARTIN AND JOHN	Marvin Gaye	Tamla Motown	1
22	36	SOMETHING'S BURNING	Kenny Rogers/First Edition	Reprise	13
-	37	GROOVIN' WITH MR. BLOE	Mr. Bloe ●	DJM	1
-	38	HONEY COME BACK	Glen Campbell	Capitol	1
-	39	UP THE LADDER TO THE ROOF	Supremes	Tamla Motown	1
-	40	DO YOU LOVE ME	Deep Feeling ●	Page One	1

WEEK ENDING 16 MAY 1970

LW	TW	Title	Artist	Label	Wks
2	[1]	BACK HOME	England World Cup Squad	Pye	5
1	2	SPIRIT IN THE SKY	Norman Greenbaum	Reprise	8
20	3	QUESTION	Moody Blues	Threshold	3
6	[4]	HOUSE OF THE RISING SUN	Frijid Pink	Deram	7
3	5	ALL KINDS OF EVERYTHING	Dana	Rex	7
28	6	YELLOW RIVER	Christie	CBS	3
10	[7]	I CAN'T TELL THE BOTTOM FROM THE TOP	Hollies	Parlophone	4
5	8	DAUGHTER OF DARKNESS	Tom Jones	Decca	5
8	9	TRAVELLIN' BAND	Creedence Clearwater Revival	Liberty	7
14	10	BRONTOSAURUS	Move	Regal Zonophone	4
7	11	CAN'T HELP FALLING IN LOVE	Andy Williams	CBS	9
4	12	BRIDGE OVER TROUBLED WATER	Simon and Garfunkel	CBS	12
12	13	WHEN JULIE COMES AROUND	Cufflinks	MCA	9
16	14	FAREWELL IS A LONELY SOUND	Jimmy Ruffin	Tamla Motown	11
17	15	I DON'T BELIEVE IN IF ANYMORE	Roger Whittaker	Columbia	5
9	16	NEVER HAD A DREAM COME TRUE	Stevie Wonder	Tamla Motown	7
19	17	RAG MAMA RAG	The Band	Capitol	6
11	18	GIMME DAT DING	Pipkins	Columbia	8
24	[19]	THE SEEKER	Who	Track	5
22	20	I'VE GOT YOU ON MY MIND	White Plains	Deram	5
13	21	GOOD MORNING FREEDOM	Blue Mink	Philips	8
15	22	KNOCK KNOCK WHO'S THERE	Mary Hopkin	Apple	8
25	23	IF I COULD (EL CONDOR PASA)	Julie Felix	RAK	4
18	24	YOUNG, GIFTED AND BLACK	Bob and Marcia	Harry	10
26	25	DO THE FUNKY CHICKEN	Rufus Thomas	Stax	5
23	26	WAND'RIN' STAR	Lee Marvin	Paramount	15
30	27	GOVINDA	Radha Krishna Temple	Apple	7
38	28	HONEY COME BACK	Glen Campbell	Capitol	2
21	29	I CAN'T HELP MYSELF	Four Tops	Tamla Motown	8
39	30	UP THE LADDER TO THE ROOF	Supremes	Tamla Motown	2
-	31	DON'T YOU KNOW	Butterscotch	RCA	1
27	32	WHO DO YOU LOVE	Juicy Lucy ●	Vertigo	9
35	33	ABRAHAM, MARTIN AND JOHN	Marvin Gaye	Tamla Motown	2
40	[34]	DO YOU LOVE ME	Deep Feeling	Page One	2
31	35	YOU'RE SUCH A GOOD LOOKING WOMAN	Joe Dolan	Pye	11
37	36	GROOVIN' WITH MR. BLOE	Mr. Bloe	DJM	2
-	37	DOWN THE DUSTPIPE	Status Quo	Pye	1
-	38	KENTUCKY RAIN	Elvis Presley	RCA	1
29	39	THAT SAME OLD FEELING	Pickettywitch	Pye	12
-	40	EVERYTHING IS BEAUTIFUL	Ray Stevens ●	CBS	1

WEEK ENDING 23 MAY 1970

LW	TW	Title	Artist	Label	Wks
1	[1]	BACK HOME	England World Cup Squad	Pye	6
2	2	SPIRIT IN THE SKY	Norman Greenbaum	Reprise	9
6	3	YELLOW RIVER	Christie	CBS	4
3	4	QUESTION	Moody Blues	Threshold	4
8	[5]	DAUGHTER OF DARKNESS	Tom Jones	Decca	6
4	6	HOUSE OF THE RISING SUN	Frijid Pink	Deram	8
10	[7]	BRONTOSAURUS	Move	Regal Zonophone	5
15	[8]	I DON'T BELIEVE IN IF ANYMORE	Roger Whittaker	Columbia	6
7	9	I CAN'T TELL THE BOTTOM FROM THE TOP	Hollies	Parlophone	5
5	10	ALL KINDS OF EVERYTHING	Dana	Rex	8
9	11	TRAVELLIN' BAND	Creedence Clearwater Revival	Liberty	8
11	12	CAN'T HELP FALLING IN LOVE	Andy Williams	CBS	10
28	13	HONEY COME BACK	Glen Campbell	Capitol	3
12	14	BRIDGE OVER TROUBLED WATER	Simon and Garfunkel	CBS	13
16	15	NEVER HAD A DREAM COME TRUE	Stevie Wonder	Tamla Motown	8
40	16	EVERYTHING IS BEAUTIFUL	Ray Stevens	CBS	2
20	[17]	I'VE GOT YOU ON MY MIND	White Plains	Deram	6
25	[18]	DO THE FUNKY CHICKEN	Rufus Thomas	Stax	6
23	[19]	IF I COULD (EL CONDOR PASA)	Julie Felix	RAK	5
-	20	ABC	Jackson Five	Tamla Motown	1
36	21	GROOVIN' WITH MR. BLOE	Mr. Bloe	DJM	3
31	22	DON'T YOU KNOW	Butterscotch	RCA	2
14	23	FAREWELL IS A LONELY SOUND	Jimmy Ruffin	Tamla Motown	12
33	24	ABRAHAM, MARTIN AND JOHN	Marvin Gaye	Tamla Motown	3
13	25	WHEN JULIE COMES AROUND	Cufflinks	MCA	10
18	26	GIMME DAT DING	Pipkins	Columbia	9
21	27	GOOD MORNING FREEDOM	Blue Mink	Philips	9
19	28	THE SEEKER	Who	Track	6
22	29	KNOCK KNOCK WHO'S THERE	Mary Hopkin	Apple	9
30	30	UP THE LADDER TO THE ROOF	Supremes	Tamla Motown	3
38	31	KENTUCKY RAIN	Elvis Presley	RCA	2
-	32	COTTONFIELDS	Beach Boys	Capitol	1

In these weeks ■ The charts are full of religion *(Spirit In The Sky, Bridge Over Troubled Water, Govinda)*, politics *(Good Morning Freedom, Young Gifted And Black, Abraham Martin And John)* and sport *(Back Home, Belfast Boy)*. Whatever happened to sex, drugs and rock 'n' roll? (09.05.70)■

LW	TW	Title	Artist	Label	Wks
-	33	WHAT IS TRUTH?	Johnny Cash	CBS	1
17	34	RAG MAMA RAG	The Band	Capitol	7
26	35	WAND'RIN' STAR	Lee Marvin	Paramount	16
-	36	TAKE TO THE MOUNTAINS	Richard Barnes ●	Philips	1
37	37	DOWN THE DUSTPIPE	Status Quo	Pye	2
-	38	SALLY	Gerry Monroe ●	Chapter One	1
-	39	BET YER LIFE I DO	Herman's Hermits	RAK	1
24	40	YOUNG, GIFTED AND BLACK	Bob and Marcia	Harry	11

WEEK ENDING 30 MAY 1970

LW	TW	Title	Artist	Label	Wks
1	[1]	BACK HOME	England World Cup Squad	Pye	7
4	[2]	QUESTION	Moody Blues	Threshold	5
3	3	YELLOW RIVER	Christie	CBS	5
2	4	SPIRIT IN THE SKY	Norman Greenbaum	Reprise	10
13	5	HONEY COME BACK	Glen Campbell	Capitol	4
30	[6]	UP THE LADDER TO THE ROOF	Supremes	Tamla Motown	4
6	7	HOUSE OF THE RISING SUN	Frijid Pink	Deram	9
8	[8]	I DON'T BELIEVE IN IF ANYMORE	Roger Whittaker	Columbia	7
5	9	DAUGHTER OF DARKNESS	Tom Jones	Decca	7
7	10	BRONTOSAURUS	Move	Regal Zonophone	6
20	11	ABC	Jackson Five	Tamla Motown	2
16	12	EVERYTHING IS BEAUTIFUL	Ray Stevens	CBS	3
21	13	GROOVIN' WITH MR. BLOE	Mr. Bloe	DJM	4
32	14	COTTONFIELDS	Beach Boys	Capitol	2
9	15	I CAN'T TELL THE BOTTOM FROM THE TOP	Hollies	Parlophone	6
11	16	TRAVELLIN' BAND	Creedence Clearwater Revival	Liberty	9
17	[17]	I'VE GOT YOU ON MY MIND	White Plains	Deram	7
-	18	THE GREEN MANALISHI	Fleetwood Mac	Reprise	1
22	19	DON'T YOU KNOW	Butterscotch	RCA	3
24	20	ABRAHAM, MARTIN AND JOHN	Marvin Gaye	Tamla Motown	4
10	21	ALL KINDS OF EVERYTHING	Dana	Rex	9
19	22	IF I COULD (EL CONDOR PASA)	Julie Felix	RAK	6
18	23	DO THE FUNKY CHICKEN	Rufus Thomas	Stax	7
28	24	THE SEEKER	Who	Track	7
14	25	BRIDGE OVER TROUBLED WATER	Simon and Garfunkel	CBS	14
31	26	KENTUCKY RAIN	Elvis Presley	RCA	3
25	27	WHEN JULIE COMES AROUND	Cufflinks	MCA	11
12	28	CAN'T HELP FALLING IN LOVE	Andy Williams	CBS	11
39	29	BET YER LIFE I DO	Herman's Hermits	RAK	2
37	30	DOWN THE DUSTPIPE	Status Quo	Pye	3
29	31	KNOCK KNOCK WHO'S THERE	Mary Hopkin	Apple	10
23	32	FAREWELL IS A LONELY SOUND	Jimmy Ruffin	Tamla Motown	13
33	33	WHAT IS TRUTH?	Johnny Cash	CBS	2
-	34	AMERICAN WOMAN	Guess Who	RCA	1
38	35	SALLY	Gerry Monroe	Chapter One	2
15	36	NEVER HAD A DREAM COME TRUE	Stevie Wonder	Tamla Motown	9
-	[37]	KITSCH	Barry Ryan	Polydor	1
35	38	WAND'RIN' STAR	Lee Marvin	Paramount	17
40	39	YOUNG, GIFTED AND BLACK	Bob and Marcia	Harry	12
-	40	IT'S ALL IN THE GAME	Four Tops	Tamla Motown	1

WEEK ENDING 6 JUNE 1970

LW	TW	Title	Artist	Label	Wks
3	[1]	YELLOW RIVER	Christie	CBS	6
1	2	BACK HOME	England World Cup Squad	Pye	8
2	3	QUESTION	Moody Blues	Threshold	6
5	[4]	HONEY COME BACK	Glen Campbell	Capitol	5
9	[5]	DAUGHTER OF DARKNESS	Tom Jones	Decca	8
12	[6]	EVERYTHING IS BEAUTIFUL	Ray Stevens	CBS	4
13	7	GROOVIN' WITH MR. BLOE	Mr. Bloe	DJM	5
11	[8]	ABC	Jackson Five	Tamla Motown	3
4	9	SPIRIT IN THE SKY	Norman Greenbaum	Reprise	11
6	10	UP THE LADDER TO THE ROOF	Supremes	Tamla Motown	5
8	11	I DON'T BELIEVE IN IF ANYMORE	Roger Whittaker	Columbia	8

June 1970

☐ Highest position disc reached ● Act's first ever week on chart

LW	TW	Title	Artist	Label	Wks
14	12	COTTONFIELDS	Beach Boys	Capitol	3
-	13	IN THE SUMMERTIME	Mungo Jerry ●	Dawn	1
20	14	ABRAHAM, MARTIN AND JOHN	Marvin Gaye	Tamla Motown	5
10	15	BRONTOSAURUS	Move	Regal Zonophone	7
7	16	HOUSE OF THE RISING SUN	Frijid Pink	Deram	10
18	17	THE GREEN MANALISHI	Fleetwood Mac	Reprise	2
19	18	DON'T YOU KNOW	Butterscotch	RCA	4
17	19	I'VE GOT YOU ON MY MIND	White Plains	Deram	8
23	20	DO THE FUNKY CHICKEN	Rufus Thomas	Stax	8
33	[21]	WHAT IS TRUTH?	Johnny Cash	CBS	3
26	22	KENTUCKY RAIN	Elvis Presley	RCA	4
22	23	IF I COULD (EL CONDOR PASA)	Julie Felix	RAK	7
29	24	BET YER LIFE I DO	Herman's Hermits	RAK	3
35	25	SALLY	Gerry Monroe	Chapter One	3
15	26	I CAN'T TELL THE BOTTOM FROM THE TOP	Hollies	Parlaphone	7
21	27	ALL KINDS OF EVERYTHING	Dana	Rex	10
25	28	BRIDGE OVER TROUBLED WATER	Simon and Garfunkel	CBS	15
30	29	DOWN THE DUSTPIPE	Status Quo	Pye	4
34	30	AMERICAN WOMAN	Guess Who	RCA	2
40	31	IT'S ALL IN THE GAME	Four Tops	Tamla Motown	2
28	32	CAN'T HELP FALLING IN LOVE	Andy Williams	CBS	12
16	33	TRAVELLIN' BAND	Creedence Clearwater Revival	Liberty	10
-	34	I WILL SURVIVE	Arrival	Decca	1
-	[35]	TAKE TO THE MOUNTAINS	Richard Barnes	Philips	2
-	36	ALL RIGHT NOW	Free ●	Island	1
-	37	GOODBYE SAM HELLO SAMANTHA	Cliff Richard	Columbia	1
-	38	GROUPIE GIRL	Tony Joe White ●	Monument	1
24	39	THE SEEKER	Who	Track	8
31	40	KNOCK KNOCK WHO'S THERE	Mary Hopkin	Apple	11

WEEK ENDING 13 JUNE 1970

LW	TW	Title	Artist	Label	Wks
13	[1]	IN THE SUMMERTIME	Mungo Jerry	Dawn	2
1	2	YELLOW RIVER	Christie	CBS	7
2	3	BACK HOME	England World Cup Squad	Pye	9
7	4	GROOVIN' WITH MR. BLOE	Mr. Bloe	DJM	6
4	5	HONEY COME BACK	Glen Campbell	Capitol	6
3	6	QUESTION	Moody Blues	Threshold	7
12	7	COTTONFIELDS	Beach Boys	Capitol	4
10	8	UP THE LADDER TO THE ROOF	Supremes	Tamla Motown	6
6	9	EVERYTHING IS BEAUTIFUL	Ray Stevens	CBS	5
8	10	ABC	Jackson Five	Tamla Motown	4
25	11	SALLY	Gerry Monroe	Chapter One	4
11	12	I DON'T BELIEVE IN IF ANYMORE	Roger Whittaker	Columbia	9
17	13	THE GREEN MANALISHI	Fleetwood Mac	Reprise	3
14	14	ABRAHAM, MARTIN AND JOHN	Marvin Gaye	Tamla Motown	6
9	15	SPIRIT IN THE SKY	Norman Greenbaum	Reprise	12
5	16	DAUGHTER OF DARKNESS	Tom Jones	Decca	9
18	[17]	DON'T YOU KNOW	Butterscotch ●	RCA	5
15	18	BRONTOSAURUS	Move	Regal Zonophone	8
16	19	HOUSE OF THE RISING SUN	Frijid Pink	Deram	11
37	20	GOODBYE SAM HELLO SAMANTHA	Cliff Richard	Columbia	2
29	21	DOWN THE DUSTPIPE	Status Quo	Pye	5
24	[22]	BET YER LIFE I DO	Herman's Hermits	RAK	4
34	23	I WILL SURVIVE	Arrival	Decca	2
31	24	IT'S ALL IN THE GAME	Four Tops	Tamla Motown	3
19	25	I'VE GOT YOU ON MY MIND	White Plains	Deram	9
22	26	KENTUCKY RAIN	Elvis Presley	RCA	5
36	27	ALL RIGHT NOW	Free	Island	2
30	28	AMERICAN WOMAN	Guess Who	RCA	3
27	29	ALL KINDS OF EVERYTHING	Dana	Rex	11
23	30	IF I COULD (EL CONDOR PASA)	Julie Felix	RAK	8
20	31	DO THE FUNKY CHICKEN	Rufus Thomas	Stax	9
21	32	WHAT IS TRUTH?	Johnny Cash	CBS	4
-	33	VEHICLE	Ides of March ●	Warner Bros.	1
33	34	TRAVELLIN' BAND	Creedence Clearwater Revival	Liberty	11

■The first chart appearance of a song that is to re-appear four times over a period of 21 years *All Right Now* by Free (06.06.70) ■ Having jumped 24 places up the ladder towards the roof, the Supremes then fall four rungs. It is one of the biggest chart climbs ever to be followed by an immediate fall. The next week they climb back up two rungs (06.06.70)■

June 1970

□ Highest position disc reached ● Act's first ever week on chart

LW	TW	Title	Artist	Label	Wks
38	35	GROUPIE GIRL	Tony Joe White	Monument	2
-	36	LOVE OF THE COMMON PEOPLE	Nicky Thomas ●	Trojan	1
35	37	TAKE TO THE MOUNTAINS	Richard Barnes	Philips	3
40	38	KNOCK KNOCK WHO'S THERE	Mary Hopkin	Apple	12
-	39	MY MARIE	Engelbert Humperdinck	Decca	1
26	40	I CAN'T TELL THE BOTTOM FROM THE TOP	Hollies	Parlophone	8

WEEK ENDING 20 JUNE 1970

LW	TW	Title	Artist	Label	Wks
1	1	IN THE SUMMERTIME	Mungo Jerry	Dawn	3
2	2	YELLOW RIVER	Christie	CBS	8
4	3	GROOVIN' WITH MR. BLOE	Mr. Bloe	DJM	7
27	4	ALL RIGHT NOW	Free	Island	3
7	5	COTTONFIELDS	Beach Boys	Capitol	5
5	6	HONEY COME BACK	Glen Campbell	Capitol	7
11	7	SALLY	Gerry Monroe	Chapter One	5
9	8	EVERYTHING IS BEAUTIFUL	Ray Stevens	CBS	6
3	9	BACK HOME	England World Cup Squad	Pye	10
13	10	THE GREEN MANALISHI	Fleetwood Mac	Reprise	4
14	11	ABRAHAM, MARTIN AND JOHN	Marvin Gaye	Tamla Motown	7
6	12	QUESTION	Moody Blues	Threshold	8
8	13	UP THE LADDER TO THE ROOF	Supremes	Tamla Motown	7
10	14	ABC	Jackson Five	Tamla Motown	5
20	15	GOODBYE SAM HELLO SAMANTHA	Cliff Richard	Columbia	3
23	16	I WILL SURVIVE	Arrival	Decca	3
24	17	IT'S ALL IN THE GAME	Four Tops	Tamla Motown	4
21	18	DOWN THE DUSTPIPE	Status Quo	Pye	6
12	19	I DON'T BELIEVE IN IF ANYMORE	Roger Whittaker	Columbia	10
16	20	DAUGHTER OF DARKNESS	Tom Jones	Decca	10
26	21	KENTUCKY RAIN	Elvis Presley	RCA	6
15	22	SPIRIT IN THE SKY	Norman Greenbaum	Reprise	13
32	23	WHAT IS TRUTH?	Johnny Cash	CBS	5
17	24	DON'T YOU KNOW	Butterscotch	RCA	6
28	25	AMERICAN WOMAN	Guess Who	RCA	4
18	26	BRONTOSAURUS	Move	Regal Zonophone	9
22	27	BET YER LIFE I DO	Herman's Hermits	RAK	5
25	28	I'VE GOT YOU ON MY MIND	White Plains	Deram	10
36	29	LOVE OF THE COMMON PEOPLE	Nicky Thomas	Trojan	2
19	30	HOUSE OF THE RISING SUN	Frijid Pink	Deram	12
39	31	MY MARIE	Engelbert Humperdinck	Decca	2
-	32	LOVE LIKE A MAN	Ten Years After ●	Deram	1
-	33	UP AROUND THE BEND	Creedence Clearwater Revival	Liberty	1
35	34	GROUPIE GIRL	Tony Joe White	Monument	3
31	35	DO THE FUNKY CHICKEN	Rufus Thomas	Stax	10
29	36	ALL KINDS OF EVERYTHING	Dana	Rex	12
30	37	IF I COULD (EL CONDOR PASA)	Julie Felix	RAK	9
-	38	BRIDGE OVER TROUBLED WATER	Simon and Garfunkel	CBS	16
-	39	PSYCHEDELIC SHACK	Temptations	Tamla Motown	1
33	40	VEHICLE	Ides of March	Warner Bros.	2

WEEK ENDING 27 JUNE 1970

LW	TW	Title	Artist	Label	Wks
1	1	IN THE SUMMERTIME	Mungo Jerry	Dawn	4
3	2	GROOVIN' WITH MR. BLOE	Mr. Bloe	DJM	8
4	3	ALL RIGHT NOW	Free	Island	4
2	4	YELLOW RIVER	Christie	CBS	9
7	5	SALLY	Gerry Monroe	Chapter One	6
5	6	COTTONFIELDS	Beach Boys	Capitol	6
15	7	GOODBYE SAM HELLO SAMANTHA	Cliff Richard	Columbia	4
6	8	HONEY COME BACK	Glen Campbell	Capitol	8
11	9	ABRAHAM, MARTIN AND JOHN	Marvin Gaye	Tamla Motown	8
10	10	THE GREEN MANALISHI	Fleetwood Mac	Reprise	5
8	11	EVERYTHING IS BEAUTIFUL	Ray Stevens	CBS	7
13	12	UP THE LADDER TO THE ROOF	Supremes	Tamla Motown	8
17	13	IT'S ALL IN THE GAME	Four Tops	Tamla Motown	5
18	14	DOWN THE DUSTPIPE	Status Quo	Pye	7
9	15	BACK HOME	England World Cup Squad	Pye	11
16	16	I WILL SURVIVE	Arrival	Decca	4
12	17	QUESTION	Moody Blues	Threshold	9
33	18	UP AROUND THE BEND	Creedence Clearwater Revival	Liberty	2
19	19	I DON'T BELIEVE IN IF ANYMORE	Roger Whittaker	Columbia	11
24	20	DON'T YOU KNOW	Butterscotch	RCA	7
29	21	LOVE OF THE COMMON PEOPLE	Nicky Thomas	Trojan	3
21	22	KENTUCKY RAIN	Elvis Presley	RCA	7
34	23	GROUPIE GIRL	Tony Joe White	Monument	4
14	24	ABC	Jackson Five	Tamla Motown	6
22	25	SPIRIT IN THE SKY	Norman Greenbaum	Reprise	14
25	26	AMERICAN WOMAN	Guess Who	RCA	5
27	27	BET YER LIFE I DO	Herman's Hermits	RAK	6
20	28	DAUGHTER OF DARKNESS	Tom Jones	Decca	11
30	29	HOUSE OF THE RISING SUN	Frijid Pink	Deram	13
32	30	LOVE LIKE A MAN	Ten Years After	Deram	2
40	31	VEHICLE	Ides of March	Warner Bros.	3
-	32	SOMETHING	Shirley Bassey	United Artists	1
36	33	ALL KINDS OF EVERYTHING	Dana	Rex	13
23	34	WHAT IS TRUTH?	Johnny Cash	CBS	6
26	35	BRONTOSAURUS	Move	Regal Zonophone	10
39	36	PSYCHEDELIC SHACK	Temptations	Tamla Motown	2
-	37	LADY D'ARBANVILLE	Cat Stevens	Island	1
-	38	CAN'T HELP FALLING IN LOVE	Andy Williams	CBS	13
37	39	IF I COULD (EL CONDOR PASA)	Julie Felix	RAK	10
38	40	BRIDGE OVER TROUBLED WATER	Simon and Garfunkel	CBS	17

WEEK ENDING 4 JULY 1970

LW	TW	Title	Artist	Label	Wks
1	1	IN THE SUMMERTIME	Mungo Jerry	Dawn	5
3	2	ALL RIGHT NOW	Free	Island	5
2	3	GROOVIN' WITH MR. BLOE	Mr. Bloe	DJM	9
5	4	SALLY	Gerry Monroe	Chapter One	7
6	5	COTTONFIELDS	Beach Boys	Capitol	7
7	6	GOODBYE SAM HELLO SAMANTHA	Cliff Richard	Columbia	5
4	7	YELLOW RIVER	Christie	CBS	10
13	8	IT'S ALL IN THE GAME	Four Tops	Tamla Motown	6
18	9	UP AROUND THE BEND	Creedence Clearwater Revival	Liberty	3
10	10	THE GREEN MANALISHI	Fleetwood Mac	Reprise	6
8	11	HONEY COME BACK	Glen Campbell	Capitol	9
14	12	DOWN THE DUSTPIPE	Status Quo	Pye	8
9	13	ABRAHAM, MARTIN AND JOHN	Marvin Gaye	Tamla Motown	9
11	14	EVERYTHING IS BEAUTIFUL	Ray Stevens	CBS	8
21	15	LOVE OF THE COMMON PEOPLE	Nicky Thomas	Trojan	4
32	16	SOMETHING	Shirley Bassey	United Artists	2
16	17	I WILL SURVIVE	Arrival	Decca	5
12	18	UP THE LADDER TO THE ROOF	Supremes	Tamla Motown	9
26	19	AMERICAN WOMAN	Guess Who	RCA	6
17	20	QUESTION	Moody Blues	Threshold	10
24	21	ABC	Jackson Five	Tamla Motown	7
-	22	LOLA	Kinks	Pye	1
27	23	BET YER LIFE I DO	Herman's Hermits	RAK	7
15	24	BACK HOME	England World Cup Squad	Pye	12
22	25	KENTUCKY RAIN	Elvis Presley	RCA	8
23	26	GROUPIE GIRL	Tony Joe White	Monument	5
19	27	I DON'T BELIEVE IN IF ANYMORE	Roger Whittaker	Columbia	12
37	28	LADY D'ARBANVILLE	Cat Stevens	Island	2
30	29	LOVE LIKE A MAN	Ten Years After	Deram	3
34	30	WHAT IS TRUTH?	Johnny Cash	CBS	7
-	31	BIG YELLOW TAXI	Joni Mitchell ●	Reprise	1
25	32	SPIRIT IN THE SKY	Norman Greenbaum	Reprise	15
20	33	DON'T YOU KNOW	Butterscotch	RCA	8
36	34	PSYCHEDELIC SHACK	Temptations	Tamla Motown	3
28	35	DAUGHTER OF DARKNESS	Tom Jones	Decca	12
31	36	VEHICLE	Ides of March	Warner Bros.	4
29	37	HOUSE OF THE RISING SUN	Frijid Pink	Deram	14
33	38	ALL KINDS OF EVERYTHING	Dana	Rex	14
-	39	(IT'S LIKE A) SAD OLD KINDA MOVIE	Pickettywitch	Pye	1
-	40	MY MARIE	Engelbert Humperdinck	Decca	3

WEEK ENDING 11 JULY 1970

LW	TW	Title	Artist	Label	Wks
1	1	IN THE SUMMERTIME	Mungo Jerry	Dawn	6

In these weeks ■ Cliff Richard's *Goodbye Sam Hello Samantha* is his 39th top ten hit, but his last for almost three years (04.07.70) ■ Gerry Monroe achieves an unlikely top five placing with his version of Gracie Field's most famous song, *Sally* (04.07.70)■

August 1970

□ Highest position disc reached ● Act's first ever week on chart

LW	TW	Title	Artist	Label	Wks
2	2	ALL RIGHT NOW	Free	Island	6
3	3	GROOVIN' WITH MR. BLOE	Mr. Bloe	DJM	10
9	4	UP AROUND THE BEND	Creedence Clearwater Revival	Liberty	4
8	5	IT'S ALL IN THE GAME	Four Tops	Tamla Motown	7
5	6	COTTONFIELDS	Beach Boys	Capitol	8
4	7	SALLY	Gerry Monroe	Chapter One	8
6	8	GOODBYE SAM HELLO SAMANTHA	Cliff Richard	Columbia	6
15	9	LOVE OF THE COMMON PEOPLE	Nicky Thomas	Trojan	5
10	10	THE GREEN MANALISHI	Fleetwood Mac	Reprise	7
13	11	ABRAHAM, MARTIN AND JOHN	Marvin Gaye	Tamla Motown	10
12	12	DOWN THE DUSTPIPE	Status Quo	Pye	9
16	13	SOMETHING	Shirley Bassey	United Artists	3
11	14	HONEY COME BACK	Glen Campbell	Capitol	10
7	15	YELLOW RIVER	Christie	CBS	11
22	16	LOLA	Kinks	Pye	2
17	17	I WILL SURVIVE	Arrival	Decca	6
14	18	EVERYTHING IS BEAUTIFUL	Ray Stevens	CBS	9
28	19	LADY D'ARBANVILLE	Cat Stevens	Island	3
-	20	THE WONDER OF YOU	Elvis Presley	RCA	1
18	21	UP THE LADDER TO THE ROOF	Supremes	Tamla Motown	10
26	22	GROUPIE GIRL	Tony Joe White	Monument	6
19	23	AMERICAN WOMAN	Guess Who	RCA	7
29	24	LOVE LIKE A MAN	Ten Years After	Deram	4
31	25	BIG YELLOW TAXI	Joni Mitchell	Reprise	2
25	26	KENTUCKY RAIN	Elvis Presley	RCA	9
39	27	(IT'S LIKE A) SAD OLD KINDA MOVIE	Pickettywitch	Pye	2
20	28	QUESTION	Moody Blues	Threshold	11
23	29	BET YER LIFE I DO	Herman's Hermits	RAK	8
-	30	I'LL SAY FOREVER MY LOVE	Jimmy Ruffin	Tamla Motown	1
27	31	I DON'T BELIEVE IN IF ANYMORE	Roger Whittaker	Columbia	13
-	32	NEANDERTHAL MAN	Hotlegs ●	Fontana	1
34	33	PSYCHEDELIC SHACK	Temptations	Tamla Motown	4
40	34	MY MARIE	Engelbert Humperdinck	Decca	4
-	35	WHERE ARE YOU GOING TO MY LOVE	Brotherhood of Man	Deram	1
24	36	BACK HOME	England World Cup Squad	Pye	13
35	37	DAUGHTER OF DARKNESS	Tom Jones	Decca	13
33	38	DON'T YOU KNOW	Butterscotch	RCA	9
-	39	THE LETTER	Joe Cocker	Regal Zonophone	1
37	40	HOUSE OF THE RISING SUN	Frijid Pink	Deram	15

WEEK ENDING 18 JULY 1970

LW	TW	Title	Artist	Label	Wks
1	1	IN THE SUMMERTIME	Mungo Jerry	Dawn	7
2	2	ALL RIGHT NOW	Free	Island	7
4	3	UP AROUND THE BEND	Creedence Clearwater Revival	Liberty	5
16	4	LOLA	Kinks	Pye	3
5	5	IT'S ALL IN THE GAME	Four Tops	Tamla Motown	8
7	6	SALLY	Gerry Monroe	Chapter One	9
6	7	COTTONFIELDS	Beach Boys	Capitol	9
3	8	GROOVIN' WITH MR. BLOE	Mr. Bloe	DJM	11
8	9	GOODBYE SAM HELLO SAMANTHA	Cliff Richard	Columbia	7
13	10	SOMETHING	Shirley Bassey	United Artists	4
9	11	LOVE OF THE COMMON PEOPLE	Nicky Thomas	Trojan	6
19	12	LADY D'ARBANVILLE	Cat Stevens	Island	4
20	13	THE WONDER OF YOU	Elvis Presley	RCA	2
12	14	DOWN THE DUSTPIPE	Status Quo	Pye	10
14	15	HONEY COME BACK	Glen Campbell	Capitol	11
10	16	THE GREEN MANALISHI	Fleetwood Mac	Reprise	8
15	17	YELLOW RIVER	Christie	CBS	12
27	18	(IT'S LIKE A) SAD OLD KINDA MOVIE	Pickettywitch	Pye	3
30	19	I'LL SAY FOREVER MY LOVE	Jimmy Ruffin	Tamla Motown	2
24	20	LOVE LIKE A MAN	Ten Years After	Deram	5
32	21	NEANDERTHAL MAN	Hotlegs	Fontana	2
11	22	ABRAHAM, MARTIN AND JOHN	Marvin Gaye	Tamla Motown	11
23	23	AMERICAN WOMAN	Guess Who	RCA	8
22	24	GROUPIE GIRL	Tony Joe White	Monument	7
18	25	EVERYTHING IS BEAUTIFUL	Ray Stevens	CBS	10
21	26	UP THE LADDER TO THE ROOF	Supremes	Tamla Motown	11
17	27	I WILL SURVIVE	Arrival	Decca	7
25	28	BIG YELLOW TAXI	Joni Mitchell	Reprise	3
-	29	WHAT IS TRUTH?	Johnny Cash	CBS	8
35	30	WHERE ARE YOU GOING TO MY LOVE	Brotherhood of Man	Deram	2
-	31	SIGNED, SEALED, DELIVERED, I'M YOURS	Stevie Wonder	Tamla Motown	1
-	32	NATURAL SINNER	Fair Weather ●	RCA	1
-	33	SONG OF JOY	Miguel Rios ●	A & M	1
-	34	VEHICLE	Ides of March	Warner Bros.	5
36	35	BACK HOME	England World Cup Squad	Pye	14
31	36	I DON'T BELIEVE IN IF ANYMORE	Roger Whittaker	Columbia	14
29	37	BET YER LIFE I DO	Herman's Hermits	RAK	9
28	38	QUESTION	Moody Blues	Threshold	12
-	39	RAINBOW	Marmalade	Decca	1
-	40	SPIRIT IN THE SKY	Norman Greenbaum	Reprise	16

WEEK ENDING 25 JULY 1970

LW	TW	Title	Artist	Label	Wks
1	1	IN THE SUMMERTIME	Mungo Jerry	Dawn	8
2	2	ALL RIGHT NOW	Free	Island	8
13	3	THE WONDER OF YOU	Elvis Presley	RCA	3
4	4	LOLA	Kinks	Pye	4
3	5	UP AROUND THE BEND	Creedence Clearwater Revival	Liberty	6
5	6	IT'S ALL IN THE GAME	Four Tops	Tamla Motown	9
10	7	SOMETHING	Shirley Bassey	United Artists	5
21	8	NEANDERTHAL MAN	Hotlegs	Fontana	3
11	9	LOVE OF THE COMMON PEOPLE	Nicky Thomas	Trojan	7
7	10	COTTONFIELDS	Beach Boys	Capitol	10
12	11	LADY D'ARBANVILLE	Cat Stevens	Island	5
9	12	GOODBYE SAM HELLO SAMANTHA	Cliff Richard	Columbia	8
6	13	SALLY	Gerry Monroe	Chapter One	10
8	14	GROOVIN' WITH MR. BLOE	Mr. Bloe	DJM	12
19	15	I'LL SAY FOREVER MY LOVE	Jimmy Ruffin	Tamla Motown	3
14	16	DOWN THE DUSTPIPE	Status Quo	Pye	11
16	17	THE GREEN MANALISHI	Fleetwood Mac	Reprise	9
17	18	YELLOW RIVER	Christie	CBS	13
15	19	HONEY COME BACK	Glen Campbell	Capitol	12
28	20	BIG YELLOW TAXI	Joni Mitchell	Reprise	4
20	21	LOVE LIKE A MAN	Ten Years After	Deram	6
25	22	EVERYTHING IS BEAUTIFUL	Ray Stevens	CBS	11
18	23	(IT'S LIKE A) SAD OLD KINDA MOVIE	Pickettywitch	Pye	4
31	24	SIGNED, SEALED, DELIVERED, I'M YOURS	Stevie Wonder	Tamla Motown	2
22	25	ABRAHAM, MARTIN AND JOHN	Marvin Gaye	Tamla Motown	12
33	26	SONG OF JOY	Miguel Rios	A & M	2
27	27	I WILL SURVIVE	Arrival	Decca	8
30	28	WHERE ARE YOU GOING TO MY LOVE	Brotherhood of Man	Deram	3
32	29	NATURAL SINNER	Fair Weather	RCA	2
39	30	RAINBOW	Marmalade	Decca	2
23	31	AMERICAN WOMAN	Guess Who	RCA	9
24	32	GROUPIE GIRL	Tony Joe White	Monument	8
36	33	I DON'T BELIEVE IN IF ANYMORE	Roger Whittaker	Columbia	15
29	34	WHAT IS TRUTH?	Johnny Cash	CBS	9
-	35	PSYCHEDELIC SHACK	Temptations	Tamla Motown	5
-	36	REACH OUT AND TOUCH	Diana Ross ●	Tamla Motown	1
37	37	BET YER LIFE I DO	Herman's Hermits	RAK	10
-	38	KENTUCKY RAIN	Elvis Presley	RCA	10
-	39	THE LETTER	Joe Cocker	Regal Zonophone	2
40	40	SPIRIT IN THE SKY	Norman Greenbaum	Reprise	17

WEEK ENDING 1 AUGUST 1970

LW	TW	Title	Artist	Label	Wks
3	1	THE WONDER OF YOU	Elvis Presley	RCA	4
2	2	ALL RIGHT NOW	Free	Island	9
4	3	LOLA	Kinks	Pye	5
1	4	IN THE SUMMERTIME	Mungo Jerry	Dawn	9
7	5	SOMETHING	Shirley Bassey	United Artists	6

■Hotlegs, later to metamorphose into 10 C.C., have their only hit, *Neanderthal Man* (11.07.70) ■ Four weeks at number ten for Fleetwood Mac's *Green Manalishi* (11.07.70) ■ Fair Weather is in reality Andy Fairweather-Low, once lead singer of Amen Corner (18.07.70)■

August 1970

□ Highest position disc reached ● Act's first ever week on chart

LW	TW	Title	Artist	Label	Wks
8	6	NEANDERTHAL MAN	Hotlegs	Fontana	4
6	7	IT'S ALL IN THE GAME	Four Tops	Tamla Motown	10
5	8	UP AROUND THE BEND	Creedence Clearwater Revival	Liberty	7
15	9	I'LL SAY FOREVER MY LOVE	Jimmy Ruffin	Tamla Motown	4
11	10	LADY D'ARBANVILLE	Cat Stevens	Island	6
9	11	LOVE OF THE COMMON PEOPLE	Nicky Thomas	Trojan	8
21	12	LOVE LIKE A MAN	Ten Years After	Deram	7
12	13	GOODBYE SAM HELLO SAMANTHA	Cliff Richard	Columbia	9
10	14	COTTONFIELDS	Beach Boys	Capitol	11
13	15	SALLY	Gerry Monroe	Chapter One	11
23	[16]	(IT'S LIKE A) SAD OLD KINDA MOVIE	Pickettywitch	Pye	5
20	17	BIG YELLOW TAXI	Joni Mitchell	Reprise	5
24	18	SIGNED, SEALED, DELIVERED, I'M YOURS	Stevie Wonder	Tamla Motown	3
14	19	GROOVIN' WITH MR. BLOE	Mr. Bloe	DJM	13
30	20	RAINBOW	Marmalade	Decca	3
19	21	HONEY COME BACK	Glen Campbell	Capitol	13
26	22	SONG OF JOY	Miguel Rios	A & M	3
29	23	NATURAL SINNER	Fair Weather	RCA	3
16	24	DOWN THE DUSTPIPE	Status Quo	Pye	12
18	25	YELLOW RIVER	Christie	CBS	14
28	26	WHERE ARE YOU GOING TO MY LOVE	Brotherhood of Man	Deram	4
17	27	THE GREEN MANALISHI	Fleetwood Mac	Reprise	10
22	28	EVERYTHING IS BEAUTIFUL	Ray Stevens	CBS	12
-	29	TEARS OF A CLOWN	Smokey Robinson and Miracles	Tamla Motown	1
-	30	25 OR 6 TO 4	Chicago	CBS	1
31	31	AMERICAN WOMAN	Guess Who	RCA	10
-	[32]	THE LONG AND WINDING ROAD	Ray Morgan ●	B&C	1
36	33	REACH OUT AND TOUCH	Diana Ross	Tamla Motown	2
-	34	UP THE LADDER TO THE ROOF	Supremes	Tamla Motown	12
-	35	MY WAY	Frank Sinatra	Reprise	23
-	36	SWEET INSPIRATION	Johnny Johnson and Bandwagon	Bell	1
-	37	THE LOVE YOU SAVE	Jackson Five	Tamla Motown	1
25	38	ABRAHAM, MARTIN AND JOHN	Marvin Gaye	Tamla Motown	13
32	39	GROUPIE GIRL	Tony Joe White	Monument	9
27	40	I WILL SURVIVE	Arrival	Decca	9

WEEK ENDING 8 AUGUST 1970

LW	TW	Title	Artist	Label	Wks
1	[1]	THE WONDER OF YOU	Elvis Presley	RCA	5
3	[2]	LOLA	Kinks	Pye	6
6	3	NEANDERTHAL MAN	Hotlegs	Fontana	5
2	4	ALL RIGHT NOW	Free	Island	10
5	5	SOMETHING	Shirley Bassey	United Artists	7
4	6	IN THE SUMMERTIME	Mungo Jerry	Dawn	10
9	[7]	I'LL SAY FOREVER MY LOVE	Jimmy Ruffin	Tamla Motown	5
10	[8]	LADY D'ARBANVILLE	Cat Stevens	Island	7
7	9	IT'S ALL IN THE GAME	Four Tops	Tamla Motown	11
12	[10]	LOVE LIKE A MAN	Ten Years After	Deram	8
8	11	UP AROUND THE BEND	Creedence Clearwater Revival	Liberty	8
17	12	BIG YELLOW TAXI	Joni Mitchell	Reprise	6
11	13	LOVE OF THE COMMON PEOPLE	Nicky Thomas	Trojan	9
20	14	RAINBOW	Marmalade	Decca	4
18	[15]	SIGNED, SEALED, DELIVERED, I'M YOURS	Stevie Wonder	Tamla Motown	4
22	[16]	SONG OF JOY	Miguel Rios	A & M	4
23	17	NATURAL SINNER	Fair Weather	RCA	4
13	18	GOODBYE SAM HELLO SAMANTHA	Cliff Richard	Columbia	10
14	19	COTTONFIELDS	Beach Boys	Capitol	12
15	20	SALLY	Gerry Monroe	Chapter One	12
25	21	YELLOW RIVER	Christie	CBS	15
26	[22]	WHERE ARE YOU GOING TO MY LOVE	Brotherhood of Man	Deram	5
16	23	(IT'S LIKE A) SAD OLD KINDA MOVIE	Pickettywitch	Pye	6
37	24	THE LOVE YOU SAVE	Jackson Five	Tamla Motown	2
29	25	TEARS OF A CLOWN	Smokey Robinson and Miracles	Tamla Motown	2
21	26	HONEY COME BACK	Glen Campbell	Capitol	14
19	27	GROOVIN' WITH MR. BLOE	Mr. Bloe	DJM	14
30	28	25 OR 6 TO 4	Chicago	CBS	2
36	29	SWEET INSPIRATION	Johnny Johnson and Bandwagon	Bell	2
27	30	THE GREEN MANALISHI	Fleetwood Mac	Reprise	11
28	31	EVERYTHING IS BEAUTIFUL	Ray Stevens	CBS	13
24	32	DOWN THE DUSTPIPE	Status Quo	Pye	13
32	33	THE LONG AND WINDING ROAD	Ray Morgan	B&C	2
-	34	MR. PRESIDENT	D,B,M and T ●	Fontana	1
-	35	I DON'T BELIEVE IN IF ANYMORE	Roger Whittaker	Columbia	16
33	36	REACH OUT AND TOUCH	Diana Ross	Tamla Motown	3
-	37	MAKE IT WITH YOU	Bread ●	Elektra	1
40	38	I WILL SURVIVE	Arrival	Decca	10
31	39	AMERICAN WOMAN	Guess Who	RCA	11
-	40	SUMMERTIME BLUES	Who	Track	1

WEEK ENDING 15 AUGUST 1970

LW	TW	Title	Artist	Label	Wks
1	[1]	THE WONDER OF YOU	Elvis Presley	RCA	6
3	[2]	NEANDERTHAL MAN	Hotlegs	Fontana	6
2	3	LOLA	Kinks	Pye	7
5	[4]	SOMETHING	Shirley Bassey	United Artists	8
4	5	ALL RIGHT NOW	Free	Island	11
17	[6]	NATURAL SINNER	Fair Weather	RCA	5
14	7	RAINBOW	Marmalade	Decca	5
6	8	IN THE SUMMERTIME	Mungo Jerry	Dawn	11
7	9	I'LL SAY FOREVER MY LOVE	Jimmy Ruffin	Tamla Motown	6
10	[10]	LOVE LIKE A MAN	Ten Years After	Deram	9
25	11	TEARS OF A CLOWN	Smokey Robinson and Miracles	Tamla Motown	3
8	12	LADY D'ARBANVILLE	Cat Stevens	Island	8
12	13	BIG YELLOW TAXI	Joni Mitchell	Reprise	7
9	14	IT'S ALL IN THE GAME	Four Tops	Tamla Motown	12
15	[15]	SIGNED, SEALED, DELIVERED, I'M YOURS	Stevie Wonder	Tamla Motown	5
28	16	25 OR 6 TO 4	Chicago	CBS	3
24	17	THE LOVE YOU SAVE	Jackson Five	Tamla Motown	3
13	18	LOVE OF THE COMMON PEOPLE	Nicky Thomas	Trojan	10
19	19	COTTONFIELDS	Beach Boys	Capitol	13
18	20	GOODBYE SAM HELLO SAMANTHA	Cliff Richard	Columbia	11
16	21	SONG OF JOY	Miguel Rios	A & M	5
11	22	UP AROUND THE BEND	Creedence Clearwater Revival	Liberty	9
29	23	SWEET INSPIRATION	Johnny Johnson and Bandwagon	Bell	3
23	24	(IT'S LIKE A) SAD OLD KINDA MOVIE	Pickettywitch	Pye	7
21	25	YELLOW RIVER	Christie	CBS	16
22	26	WHERE ARE YOU GOING TO MY LOVE	Brotherhood of Man	Deram	6
20	27	SALLY	Gerry Monroe	Chapter One	13
31	28	EVERYTHING IS BEAUTIFUL	Ray Stevens	CBS	14
27	29	GROOVIN' WITH MR. BLOE	Mr. Bloe	DJM	15
-	30	MAMA TOLD ME NOT TO COME	Three Dog Night ●	Stateside	1
26	31	HONEY COME BACK	Glen Campbell	Capitol	15
32	32	DOWN THE DUSTPIPE	Status Quo	Pye	14
37	33	MAKE IT WITH YOU	Bread	Elektra	2
-	34	IT'S SO EASY	Andy Williams	CBS	1
-	35	WILD WORLD	Jimmy Cliff	Island	1
33	36	THE LONG AND WINDING ROAD	Ray Morgan	B&C	3
-	37	MY WAY	Frank Sinatra	Reprise	24
40	38	SUMMERTIME BLUES	Who	Track	2
-	39	I (WHO HAVE NOTHING)	Tom Jones	Decca	1
-	40	MY WAY	Dorothy Squires	President	1

WEEK ENDING 22 AUGUST 1970

LW	TW	Title	Artist	Label	Wks
1	[1]	THE WONDER OF YOU	Elvis Presley	RCA	7
2	[2]	NEANDERTHAL MAN	Hotlegs	Fontana	7
7	[3]	RAINBOW	Marmalade	Decca	6
3	4	LOLA	Kinks	Pye	8
11	5	TEARS OF A CLOWN	Smokey Robinson and Miracles	Tamla Motown	4
4	6	SOMETHING	Shirley Bassey	United Artists	9
17	7	THE LOVE YOU SAVE	Jackson Five	Tamla Motown	4
6	8	NATURAL SINNER	Fair Weather	RCA	6
8	9	IN THE SUMMERTIME	Mungo Jerry	Dawn	12

In these weeks ■ D, B, M and T are Dozy, Beaky, Mick and Tich enjoying their only hit without their former lead singer Dave Dee (08.08.70) ■ Shirley Bassey's version of George Harrison's *Something* peaks at 4, the same position that the Beatles reached. But her version spent more weeks on the chart than the Beatles (15.08.70)■

LW	TW	Title	Artist	Label	Wks
9	10	I'LL SAY FOREVER MY LOVE	Jimmy Ruffin	*Tamla Motown*	7
13	[11]	BIG YELLOW TAXI	Joni Mitchell	*Reprise*	8
5	12	ALL RIGHT NOW	Free	*Island*	12
10	13	LOVE LIKE A MAN	Ten Years After	*Deram*	10
16	14	25 OR 6 TO 4	Chicago	*CBS*	4
23	15	SWEET INSPIRATION	Johnny Johnson and Bandwagon	*Bell*	4
15	16	SIGNED, SEALED, DELIVERED, I'M YOURS	Stevie Wonder	*Tamla Motown*	6
12	17	LADY D'ARBANVILLE	Cat Stevens	*Island*	9
21	18	SONG OF JOY	Miguel Rios	*A & M*	6
30	19	MAMA TOLD ME NOT TO COME	Three Dog Night	*Stateside*	2
-	20	LOVE IS LIFE	Hot Chocolate ●	*RAK*	1
35	21	WILD WORLD	Jimmy Cliff	*Island*	2
33	22	MAKE IT WITH YOU	Bread	*Elektra*	3
39	23	I (WHO HAVE NOTHING)	Tom Jones	*Decca*	2
24	24	(IT'S LIKE A) SAD OLD KINDA MOVIE	Pickettywitch	*Pye*	8
19	25	COTTONFIELDS	Beach Boys	*Capitol*	14
34	26	IT'S SO EASY	Andy Williams	*CBS*	2
20	27	GOODBYE SAM HELLO SAMANTHA	Cliff Richard	*Columbia*	12
25	28	YELLOW RIVER	Christie	*CBS*	17
18	29	LOVE OF THE COMMON PEOPLE	Nicky Thomas	*Trojan*	11
14	30	IT'S ALL IN THE GAME	Four Tops	*Tamla Motown*	13
22	31	UP AROUND THE BEND	Creedence Clearwater Revival	*Liberty*	10
29	32	GROOVIN' WITH MR. BLOE	Mr. Bloe	*DJM*	16
27	33	SALLY	Gerry Monroe	*Chapter One*	14
-	34	GIVE ME JUST A LITTLE MORE TIME	Chairmen of the Board ●	*Invictus*	1
26	35	WHERE ARE YOU GOING TO MY LOVE	Brotherhood of Man	*Deram*	7
36	36	THE LONG AND WINDING ROAD	Ray Morgan	*B&C*	4
-	37	MR. PRESIDENT	D,B,M and T	*Fontana*	2
28	38	EVERYTHING IS BEAUTIFUL	Ray Stevens	*CBS*	15
31	39	HONEY COME BACK	Glen Campbell	*Capitol*	16
-	40	STRANGE BAND	Family	*Reprise*	1

LW	TW	*WEEK ENDING* **29 AUGUST 1970**			Wks
1	[1]	THE WONDER OF YOU	Elvis Presley	*RCA*	8
5	2	TEARS OF A CLOWN	Smokey Robinson and Miracles	*Tamla Motown*	5
2	3	NEANDERTHAL MAN	Hotlegs	*Fontana*	8
3	4	RAINBOW	Marmalade	*Decca*	7
4	5	LOLA	Kinks	*Pye*	9
8	[6]	NATURAL SINNER	Fair Weather	*RCA*	7
14	[7]	25 OR 6 TO 4	Chicago	*CBS*	5
6	8	SOMETHING	Shirley Bassey	*United Artists*	10
19	9	MAMA TOLD ME NOT TO COME	Three Dog Night	*Stateside*	3
7	10	THE LOVE YOU SAVE	Jackson Five	*Tamla Motown*	5
15	11	SWEET INSPIRATION	Johnny Johnson and Bandwagon	*Bell*	5
13	12	LOVE LIKE A MAN	Ten Years After	*Deram*	11
10	13	I'LL SAY FOREVER MY LOVE	Jimmy Ruffin	*Tamla Motown*	8
12	14	ALL RIGHT NOW	Free	*Island*	13
22	15	MAKE IT WITH YOU	Bread	*Elektra*	4
9	16	IN THE SUMMERTIME	Mungo Jerry	*Dawn*	13
20	17	LOVE IS LIFE	Hot Chocolate	*RAK*	2
16	18	SIGNED, SEALED, DELIVERED, I'M YOURS	Stevie Wonder	*Tamla Motown*	7
34	19	GIVE ME JUST A LITTLE MORE TIME	Chairmen of the Board	*Invictus*	2
17	20	LADY D'ARBANVILLE	Cat Stevens	*Island*	10
11	21	BIG YELLOW TAXI	Joni Mitchell	*Reprise*	9
21	22	WILD WORLD	Jimmy Cliff	*Island*	3
18	23	SONG OF JOY	Miguel Rios	*A & M*	7
26	24	IT'S SO EASY	Andy Williams	*CBS*	3
23	25	I (WHO HAVE NOTHING)	Tom Jones	*Decca*	3
30	26	IT'S ALL IN THE GAME	Four Tops	*Tamla Motown*	14
27	27	GOODBYE SAM HELLO SAMANTHA	Cliff Richard	*Columbia*	13
-	28	WHICH WAY YOU GOIN' BILLY?	Poppy Family ●	*Decca*	1
25	29	COTTONFIELDS	Beach Boys	*Capitol*	15
28	30	YELLOW RIVER	Christie	*CBS*	18
33	31	SALLY	Gerry Monroe	*Chapter One*	15
-	32	DON'T PLAY THAT SONG	Aretha Franklin	*Atlantic*	1
29	33	LOVE OF THE COMMON PEOPLE	Nicky Thomas	*Trojan*	12
37	34	MR. PRESIDENT	D,B,M and T	*Fontana*	3

September 1970

□ Highest position disc reached ● Act's first ever week on chart

LW	TW	Title	Artist	Label	Wks
24	35	(IT'S LIKE A) SAD OLD KINDA MOVIE	Pickettywitch	*Pye*	9
32	36	GROOVIN' WITH MR. BLOE	Mr. Bloe	*DJM*	17
38	37	EVERYTHING IS BEAUTIFUL	Ray Stevens	*CBS*	16
-	[38]	SUMMERTIME BLUES	Who	*Track*	3
-	39	YOU CAN GET IT IF YOU REALLY WANT IT	Desmond Dekker	*Trojan*	1
40	40	STRANGE BAND	Family	*Reprise*	2

LW	TW	*WEEK ENDING* **5 SEPTEMBER 1970**			Wks
1	[1]	THE WONDER OF YOU	Elvis Presley	*RCA*	9
2	2	TEARS OF A CLOWN	Smokey Robinson and Miracles	*Tamla Motown*	6
9	[3]	MAMA TOLD ME NOT TO COME	Three Dog Night	*Stateside*	4
4	4	RAINBOW	Marmalade	*Decca*	8
19	5	GIVE ME JUST A LITTLE MORE TIME	Chairmen of the Board	*Invictus*	3
3	6	NEANDERTHAL MAN	Hotlegs	*Fontana*	9
15	7	MAKE IT WITH YOU	Bread	*Elektra*	5
7	8	25 OR 6 TO 4	Chicago	*CBS*	6
8	9	SOMETHING	Shirley Bassey	*United Artists*	11
11	[10]	SWEET INSPIRATION	Johnny Johnson and Bandwagon	*Bell*	6
6	11	NATURAL SINNER	Fair Weather	*RCA*	8
5	12	LOLA	Kinks	*Pye*	10
22	13	WILD WORLD	Jimmy Cliff	*Island*	4
10	14	THE LOVE YOU SAVE	Jackson Five	*Tamla Motown*	6
17	15	LOVE IS LIFE	Hot Chocolate	*RAK*	3
25	[16]	I (WHO HAVE NOTHING)	Tom Jones	*Decca*	4
24	17	IT'S SO EASY	Andy Williams	*CBS*	4
12	18	LOVE LIKE A MAN	Ten Years After	*Deram*	12
13	19	I'LL SAY FOREVER MY LOVE	Jimmy Ruffin	*Tamla Motown*	9
39	20	YOU CAN GET IT IF YOU REALLY WANT IT	Desmond Dekker	*Trojan*	2
23	21	SONG OF JOY	Miguel Rios	*A & M*	8
16	22	IN THE SUMMERTIME	Mungo Jerry	*Dawn*	14
14	23	ALL RIGHT NOW	Free	*Island*	14
28	24	WHICH WAY YOU GOIN' BILLY?	Poppy Family	*Decca*	2
21	25	BIG YELLOW TAXI	Joni Mitchell	*Reprise*	10
40	26	STRANGE BAND	Family	*Reprise*	3
-	27	JIMMY MACK	Martha and the Vandellas	*Tamla Motown*	1
18	28	SIGNED, SEALED, DELIVERED, I'M YOURS	Stevie Wonder	*Tamla Motown*	8
32	29	DON'T PLAY THAT SONG	Aretha Franklin	*Atlantic*	2
-	30	MONTEGO BAY	Bobby Bloom ●	*Polydor*	1
30	31	YELLOW RIVER	Christie	*CBS*	19
-	32	BLACK NIGHT	Deep Purple ●	*Harvest*	1
34	[33]	MR. PRESIDENT	D,B,M and T	*Fontana*	4
20	34	LADY D'ARBANVILLE	Cat Stevens	*Island*	11
31	35	SALLY	Gerry Monroe	*Chapter One*	16
-	36	BAND OF GOLD	Freda Payne ●	*Invictus*	1
29	37	COTTONFIELDS	Beach Boys	*Capitol*	16
27	38	GOODBYE SAM HELLO SAMANTHA	Cliff Richard	*Columbia*	14
-	39	I AIN'T GOT TIME ANY MORE	Cliff Richard	*Columbia*	1
33	40	LOVE OF THE COMMON PEOPLE	Nicky Thomas	*Trojan*	13

LW	TW	*WEEK ENDING* **12 SEPTEMBER 1970**			Wks
2	[1]	TEARS OF A CLOWN	Smokey Robinson and Miracles	*Tamla Motown*	7
1	2	THE WONDER OF YOU	Elvis Presley	*RCA*	10
3	[3]	MAMA TOLD ME NOT TO COME	Three Dog Night	*Stateside*	5
5	4	GIVE ME JUST A LITTLE MORE TIME	Chairmen of the Board	*Invictus*	4
7	[5]	MAKE IT WITH YOU	Bread	*Elektra*	6
36	6	BAND OF GOLD	Freda Payne	*Invictus*	2
8	[7]	25 OR 6 TO 4	Chicago	*CBS*	7
13	[8]	WILD WORLD	Jimmy Cliff	*Island*	5
4	9	RAINBOW	Marmalade	*Decca*	9
15	10	LOVE IS LIFE	Hot Chocolate	*RAK*	4

■The Poppy Family includes Terry Jacks, who will top the charts as a soloist in 1974 (29.08.70) ■ In America they had eleven top ten hits, including three number ones, but in the UK, *Mama Told Me Not To Come* was Three Dog Nights' only top ten hit (05.09.70)■

September 1970

□ Highest position disc reached ● Act's first ever week on chart

LW	TW	Title	Artist	Label	Wks
24	11	WHICH WAY YOU GOIN' BILLY?	Poppy Family	Decca	2
10	12	SWEET INSPIRATION	Johnny Johnson and Bandwagon	Bell	7
6	13	NEANDERTHAL MAN	Hotlegs	Fontana	10
20	14	YOU CAN GET IT IF YOU REALLY WANT IT	Desmond Dekker	Trojan	3
9	15	SOMETHING	Shirley Bassey	United Artists	12
17	16	IT'S SO EASY	Andy Williams	CBS	5
11	17	NATURAL SINNER	Fair Weather	RCA	9
12	18	LOLA	Kinks	Pye	11
29	19	DON'T PLAY THAT SONG	Aretha Franklin	Atlantic	3
30	20	MONTEGO BAY	Bobby Bloom	Polydor	2
16	21	I (WHO HAVE NOTHING)	Tom Jones	Decca	5
26	22	STRANGE BAND	Family	Reprise	4
27	23	JIMMY MACK	Martha and Vandellas	Tamla Motown	2
39	24	I AIN'T GOT TIME ANY MORE	Cliff Richard	Columbia	2
14	25	THE LOVE YOU SAVE	Jackson 5	Tamla Motown	7
18	26	LOVE LIKE A MAN	Ten Years After	Deram	13
21	27	SONG OF JOY	Miguel Rios	A & M	9
22	28	IN THE SUMMERTIME	Mungo Jerry	Dawn	15
-	29	LONG AS I CAN SEE THE LIGHT	Creedence Clearwater Revival	Liberty	1
23	30	ALL RIGHT NOW	Free	Island	15
19	31	I'LL SAY FOREVER MY LOVE	Jimmy Ruffin	Tamla Motown	10
-	32	AIN'T NO MOUNTAIN HIGH ENOUGH	Diana Ross	Tamla Motown	1
28	33	SIGNED, SEALED, DELIVERED, I'M YOURS	Stevie Wonder	Tamla Motown	9
32	34	BLACK NIGHT	Deep Purple	Harvest	2
31	35	YELLOW RIVER	Christie	CBS	20
25	36	BIG YELLOW TAXI	Joni Mitchell	Reprise	11
-	37	PARANOID	Black Sabbath ●	Vertigo	1
-	38	(THEY LONG TO BE) CLOSE TO YOU	Carpenters ●	A&M	1
-	39	ME AND MY LIFE	Tremeloes	CBS	1
-	40	BLACK PEARL	Horace Faith ●	Trojan	1

WEEK ENDING 19 SEPTEMBER 1970

LW	TW	Title	Artist	Label	Wks
6	[1]	BAND OF GOLD	Freda Payne	Invictus	3
1	2	TEARS OF A CLOWN	Smokey Robinson and Miracles	Tamla Motown	8
4	[3]	GIVE ME JUST A LITTLE MORE TIME	Chairmen of the Board	Invictus	5
2	4	THE WONDER OF YOU	Elvis Presley	RCA	11
3	5	MAMA TOLD ME NOT TO COME	Three Dog Night	Stateside	6
10	[6]	LOVE IS LIFE	Hot Chocolate	RAK	5
5	7	MAKE IT WITH YOU	Bread	Elektra	7
14	8	YOU CAN GET IT IF YOU REALLY WANT IT	Desmond Dekker	Trojan	4
8	9	WILD WORLD	Jimmy Cliff	Island	6
11	10	WHICH WAY YOU GOIN' BILLY?	Poppy Family	Decca	3
9	11	RAINBOW	Marmalade	Decca	10
7	12	25 OR 6 TO 4	Chicago	CBS	8
16	[13]	IT'S SO EASY	Andy Williams	CBS	6
15	14	SOMETHING	Shirley Bassey	United Artists	13
20	15	MONTEGO BAY	Bobby Bloom	Polydor	3
12	16	SWEET INSPIRATION	Johnny Johnson and Bandwagon	Bell	8
19	17	DON'T PLAY THAT SONG	Aretha Franklin	Atlantic	4
22	18	STRANGE BAND	Family	Reprise	5
13	19	NEANDERTHAL MAN	Hotlegs	Fontana	11
34	20	BLACK NIGHT	Deep Purple	Harvest	3
32	21	AIN'T NO MOUNTAIN HIGH ENOUGH	Diana Ross	Tamla Motown	2
23	22	JIMMY MACK	Martha and Vandellas	Tamla Motown	3
21	23	I (WHO HAVE NOTHING)	Tom Jones	Decca	6
17	24	NATURAL SINNER	Fair Weather	RCA	10
18	25	LOLA	Kinks	Pye	12
29	26	LONG AS I CAN SEE THE LIGHT	Creedence Clearwater Revival	Liberty	3
-	27	SWEETHEART	Engelbert Humperdinck	Decca	1
37	28	PARANOID	Black Sabbath	Vertigo	2
25	29	THE LOVE YOU SAVE	Jackson 5	Tamla Motown	8
39	30	ME AND MY LIFE	Tremeloes	CBS	2
38	31	(THEY LONG TO BE) CLOSE TO YOU	Carpenters	A&M	2
24	32	I AIN'T GOT TIME ANY MORE	Cliff Richard	Columbia	3
40	33	BLACK PEARL	Horace Faith	Trojan	2
30	34	ALL RIGHT NOW	Free	Island	16
-	35	OUR WORLD	Blue Mink	Philips	1
31	36	I'LL SAY FOREVER MY LOVE	Jimmy Ruffin	Tamla Motown	11
35	37	YELLOW RIVER	Christie	CBS	21
28	38	IN THE SUMMERTIME	Mungo Jerry	Dawn	16
26	39	LOVE LIKE A MAN	Ten Years After	Deram	14
-	40	BALL OF CONFUSION	Temptations	Tamla Motown	1

WEEK ENDING 26 SEPTEMBER 1970

LW	TW	Title	Artist	Label	Wks
1	[1]	BAND OF GOLD	Freda Payne	Invictus	4
2	2	TEARS OF A CLOWN	Smokey Robinson and Miracles	Tamla Motown	9
3	[3]	GIVE ME JUST A LITTLE MORE TIME	Chairmen of the Board	Invictus	6
8	4	YOU CAN GET IT IF YOU REALLY WANT IT	Desmond Dekker	Trojan	5
4	5	THE WONDER OF YOU	Elvis Presley	RCA	12
5	6	MAMA TOLD ME NOT TO COME	Three Dog Night	Stateside	7
10	[7]	WHICH WAY YOU GOIN' BILLY?	Poppy Family	Decca	4
15	8	MONTEGO BAY	Bobby Bloom	Polydor	4
20	9	BLACK NIGHT	Deep Purple	Harvest	4
7	10	MAKE IT WITH YOU	Bread	Elektra	8
6	11	LOVE IS LIFE	Hot Chocolate	RAK	6
9	12	WILD WORLD	Jimmy Cliff	Island	7
17	[13]	DON'T PLAY THAT SONG	Aretha Franklin	Atlantic	5
18	14	STRANGE BAND	Family	Reprise	6
31	15	(THEY LONG TO BE) CLOSE TO YOU	Carpenters	A&M	3
21	16	AIN'T NO MOUNTAIN HIGH ENOUGH	Diana Ross	Tamla Motown	3
12	17	25 OR 6 TO 4	Chicago	CBS	9
30	18	ME AND MY LIFE	Tremeloes	CBS	3
28	19	PARANOID	Black Sabbath	Vertigo	3
26	[20]	LONG AS I CAN SEE THE LIGHT	Creedence Clearwater Revival	Liberty	4
32	21	I AIN'T GOT TIME ANY MORE	Cliff Richard	Columbia	4
16	22	SWEET INSPIRATION	Johnny Johnson and Bandwagon	Bell	9
13	23	IT'S SO EASY	Andy Williams	CBS	7
22	24	JIMMY MACK	Martha and Vandellas	Tamla Motown	4
11	25	RAINBOW	Marmalade	Decca	11
14	26	SOMETHING	Shirley Bassey	United Artists	14
33	27	BLACK PEARL	Horace Faith	Trojan	3
27	28	SWEETHEART	Engelbert Humperdinck	Decca	2
35	29	OUR WORLD	Blue Mink	Philips	2
40	30	BALL OF CONFUSION	Temptations	Tamla Motown	2
23	31	I (WHO HAVE NOTHING)	Tom Jones	Decca	7
19	32	NEANDERTHAL MAN	Hotlegs	Fontana	12
24	33	NATURAL SINNER	Fair Weather	RCA	11
-	34	MY WAY	Dorothy Squires	President	2
25	35	LOLA	Kinks	Pye	13
-	36	MY WAY	Frank Sinatra	Reprise	34
-	37	HOW CAN I BE SURE	Dusty Springfield	Philips	1
-	[38]	CRY	Gerry Monroe	Chapter One	1
39	39	LOVE LIKE A MAN	Ten Years After	Deram	15
-	40	ANGELS DON'T LIE	Jim Reeves	RCA	1

WEEK ENDING 3 OCTOBER 1970

LW	TW	Title	Artist	Label	Wks
1	[1]	BAND OF GOLD	Freda Payne	Invictus	5
4	[2]	YOU CAN GET IT IF YOU REALLY WANT IT	Desmond Dekker	Trojan	6
8	[3]	MONTEGO BAY	Bobby Bloom	Polydor	5
2	4	TEARS OF A CLOWN	Smokey Robinson and Miracles	Tamla Motown	10
9	5	BLACK NIGHT	Deep Purple	Harvest	5
3	6	GIVE ME JUST A LITTLE MORE TIME	Chairmen of the Board	Invictus	7
7	[7]	WHICH WAY YOU GOIN' BILLY?	Poppy Family	Decca	5
19	8	PARANOID	Black Sabbath	Vertigo	4

In these weeks ■ For two weeks in a row, only one of the top ten records is by a British act, firstly, Hot Chocolate (19.09.70) and then Deep Purple (26.09.70) ■ Chairmen Of The Board's *Give Me Just A Little More Time* climbs to number 3, one place lower than Kylie Minogue will achieve with her version of the same song in 1992 (19.09.70)■

LW	TW	Title	Artist	Label	Wks
5	9	THE WONDER OF YOU	Elvis Presley	RCA	13
11	10	LOVE IS LIFE	Hot Chocolate	RAK	7
14	11	STRANGE BAND	Family	Reprise	7
6	12	MAMA TOLD ME NOT TO COME	Three Dog Night	Stateside	8
16	13	AIN'T NO MOUNTAIN HIGH ENOUGH	Diana Ross	Tamla Motown	4
15	14	(THEY LONG TO BE) CLOSE TO YOU	Carpenters	A&M	4
18	15	ME AND MY LIFE	Tremeloes	CBS	4
10	16	MAKE IT WITH YOU	Bread	Elektra	9
12	17	WILD WORLD	Jimmy Cliff	Island	8
13	18	DON'T PLAY THAT SONG	Aretha Franklin	Atlantic	6
23	19	IT'S SO EASY	Andy Williams	CBS	8
27	20	BLACK PEARL	Horace Faith	Trojan	4
24	21	JIMMY MACK	Martha and Vandellas	Tamla Motown	5
28	22	SWEETHEART	Engelbert Humperdinck	Decca	3
20	23	LONG AS I CAN SEE THE LIGHT	Creedence Clearwater Revival	Liberty	5
29	24	OUR WORLD	Blue Mink	Philips	3
26	25	SOMETHING	Shirley Bassey	United Artists	15
30	26	BALL OF CONFUSION	Temptations	Tamla Motown	3
17	27	25 OR 6 TO 4	Chicago	CBS	10
22	28	SWEET INSPIRATION	Johnny Johnson and Bandwagon	Bell	10
-	29	GASOLINE ALLEY BRED	Hollies	Parlophone	1
36	30	MY WAY	Frank Sinatra	Reprise	35
31	31	I (WHO HAVE NOTHING)	Tom Jones	Decca	8
40	32	ANGELS DON'T LIE	Jim Reeves	RCA	2
21	33	I AIN'T GOT TIME ANY MORE	Cliff Richard	Columbia	5
34	34	MY WAY	Dorothy Squires	President	3
-	35	THE TIPS OF MY FINGERS	Des O'Connor	Columbia	1
-	36	EVERYTHING A MAN COULD EVER NEED	Glen Campbell	Capitol	1
-	37	RUBY TUESDAY	Melanie ●	Buddah	1
32	38	NEANDERTHAL MAN	Hotlegs	Fontana	13
-	39	WOODSTOCK	Matthews Southern Comfort ●	Uni	1
25	40	RAINBOW	Marmalade	Decca	12

WEEK ENDING **10 OCTOBER 1970**

LW	TW	Title	Artist	Label	Wks
1	1	BAND OF GOLD	Freda Payne	Invictus	6
2	2	YOU CAN GET IT IF YOU REALLY WANT IT	Desmond Dekker	Trojan	7
5	3	BLACK NIGHT	Deep Purple	Harvest	6
8	4	PARANOID	Black Sabbath	Vertigo	5
3	5	MONTEGO BAY	Bobby Bloom	Polydor	6
14	6	(THEY LONG TO BE) CLOSE TO YOU	Carpenters	A&M	5
13	7	AIN'T NO MOUNTAIN HIGH ENOUGH	Diana Ross	Tamla Motown	5
15	8	ME AND MY LIFE	Tremeloes	CBS	5
6	9	GIVE ME JUST A LITTLE MORE TIME	Chairmen of the Board	Invictus	8
7	10	WHICH WAY YOU GOIN' BILLY?	Poppy Family	Decca	6
9	11	THE WONDER OF YOU	Elvis Presley	RCA	14
4	12	TEARS OF A CLOWN	Smokey Robinson and Miracles	Tamla Motown	11
18	13	DON'T PLAY THAT SONG	Aretha Franklin	Atlantic	7
20	14	BLACK PEARL	Horace Faith	Trojan	5
11	15	STRANGE BAND	Family	Reprise	8
26	16	BALL OF CONFUSION	Temptations	Tamla Motown	4
10	17	LOVE IS LIFE	Hot Chocolate	RAK	8
12	18	MAMA TOLD ME NOT TO COME	Three Dog Night	Stateside	9
24	19	OUR WORLD	Blue Mink	Philips	4
16	20	MAKE IT WITH YOU	Bread	Elektra	10
23	21	LONG AS I CAN SEE THE LIGHT	Creedence Clearwater Revival	Liberty	6
21	22	JIMMY MACK	Martha and Vandellas	Tamla Motown	6
29	23	GASOLINE ALLEY BRED	Hollies	Parlophone	2
39	24	WOODSTOCK	Matthews Southern Comfort	Uni	2
17	25	WILD WORLD	Jimmy Cliff	Island	9
22	26	SWEETHEART	Engelbert Humperdinck	Decca	4
-	27	STILL WATER	Four Tops	Tamla Motown	1
25	28	SOMETHING	Shirley Bassey	United Artists	16
37	29	RUBY TUESDAY	Melanie	Buddah	2
19	30	IT'S SO EASY	Andy Williams	CBS	9
33	31	I AIN'T GOT TIME ANY MORE	Cliff Richard	Columbia	6

October 1970

□ Highest position disc reached ● Act's first ever week on chart

LW	TW	Title	Artist	Label	Wks
36	32	EVERYTHING A MAN COULD EVER NEED	Glen Campbell	Capitol	2
35	33	THE TIPS OF MY FINGERS	Des O'Connor	Columbia	2
27	34	25 OR 6 TO 4	Chicago	CBS	11
28	35	SWEET INSPIRATION	Johnny Johnson and Bandwagon	Bell	11
-	36	HOW CAN I BE SURE	Dusty Springfield	Philips	2
34	37	MY WAY	Dorothy Squires	President	4
-	38	SHADY LADY	Gene Pitney	Stateside	1
-	39	PATCHES	Clarence Carter ●	Atlantic	1
30	40	MY WAY	Frank Sinatra	Reprise	36

WEEK ENDING **17 OCTOBER 1970**

LW	TW	Title	Artist	Label	Wks
1	1	BAND OF GOLD	Freda Payne	Invictus	7
3	2	BLACK NIGHT	Deep Purple	Harvest	7
2	3	YOU CAN GET IT IF YOU REALLY WANT IT	Desmond Dekker	Trojan	8
8	4	ME AND MY LIFE	Tremeloes	CBS	6
4	5	PARANOID	Black Sabbath	Vertigo	6
7	6	AIN'T NO MOUNTAIN HIGH ENOUGH	Diana Ross	Tamla Motown	6
5	7	MONTEGO BAY	Bobby Bloom	Polydor	7
6	8	(THEY LONG TO BE) CLOSE TO YOU	Carpenters	A&M	6
10	9	WHICH WAY YOU GOIN' BILLY?	Poppy Family	Decca	7
16	10	BALL OF CONFUSION	Temptations	Tamla Motown	5
24	11	WOODSTOCK	Matthews Southern Comfort	Uni	3
15	12	STRANGE BAND	Family	Reprise	9
14	13	BLACK PEARL	Horace Faith	Trojan	6
39	14	PATCHES	Clarence Carter	Atlantic	2
33	15	THE TIPS OF MY FINGERS	Des O'Connor	Columbia	3
12	16	TEARS OF A CLOWN	Smokey Robinson and Miracles	Tamla Motown	12
11	17	THE WONDER OF YOU	Elvis Presley	RCA	15
9	18	GIVE ME JUST A LITTLE MORE TIME	Chairmen of the Board	Invictus	9
23	19	GASOLINE ALLEY BRED	Hollies	Parlophone	3
27	20	STILL WATER	Four Tops	Tamla Motown	2
29	21	RUBY TUESDAY	Melanie	Buddah	3
18	22	MAMA TOLD ME NOT TO COME	Three Dog Night	Stateside	10
21	23	LONG AS I CAN SEE THE LIGHT	Creedence Clearwater Revival	Liberty	7
19	24	OUR WORLD	Blue Mink	Philips	5
-	25	THE WITCH	Rattles ●	Decca	1
20	26	MAKE IT WITH YOU	Bread	Elektra	11
17	27	LOVE IS LIFE	Hot Chocolate	RAK	9
-	28	NEW WORLD IN THE MORNING	Roger Whittaker	Columbia	1
13	29	DON'T PLAY THAT SONG	Aretha Franklin	Atlantic	8
40	30	MY WAY	Frank Sinatra	Reprise	37
25	31	WILD WORLD	Jimmy Cliff	Island	10
22	32	JIMMY MACK	Martha and Vandellas	Tamla Motown	7
26	33	SWEETHEART	Engelbert Humperdinck	Decca	5
32	34	EVERYTHING A MAN COULD EVER NEED	Glen Campbell	Capitol	3
28	35	SOMETHING	Shirley Bassey	United Artists	17
31	36	I AIN'T GOT TIME ANY MORE	Cliff Richard	Columbia	7
30	37	IT'S SO EASY	Andy Williams	CBS	10
-	38	IT'S WONDERFUL	Jimmy Ruffin	Tamla Motown	1
38	39	SHADY LADY	Gene Pitney	Stateside	2
-	40	HEAVEN IS HERE	Julie Felix	RAK	1

WEEK ENDING **24 OCTOBER 1970**

LW	TW	Title	Artist	Label	Wks
1	1	BAND OF GOLD	Freda Payne	Invictus	8
2	2	BLACK NIGHT	Deep Purple	Harvest	8
14	3	PATCHES	Clarence Carter	Atlantic	3
4	4	ME AND MY LIFE	Tremeloes	CBS	7
5	5	PARANOID	Black Sabbath	Vertigo	7
8	6	(THEY LONG TO BE) CLOSE TO YOU	Carpenters	A&M	7

■The titles of the hits betray the uncertainty of the times: *Black Night, Paranoid, Which Way You Goin' Billy?, Strange Band, Ball Of Confusion* and *Wild World*. Only the older generation show any confidence. Andy Williams says *It's So Easy* and Frank Sinatra still does it *My Way* (10.10.70)■

October 1970

□ Highest position disc reached ● Act's first ever week on chart

LW	TW	Title	Artist	Label	Wks
7	7	AIN'T NO MOUNTAIN HIGH ENOUGH	Diana Ross	Tamla Motown	7
3	8	YOU CAN GET IT IF YOU REALLY WANT IT	Desmond Dekker	Trojan	9
10	9	BALL OF CONFUSION	Temptations	Tamla Motown	6
11	10	WOODSTOCK	Matthews Southern Comfort	Uni	4
7	11	MONTEGO BAY	Bobby Bloom	Polydor	8
9	12	WHICH WAY YOU GOIN' BILLY?	Poppy Family	Decca	8
20	13	STILL WATER	Four Tops	Tamla Motown	3
19	[14]	GASOLINE ALLEY BRED	Hollies	Parlophone	4
13	15	BLACK PEARL	Horace Faith	Trojan	7
-	16	WAR	Edwin Starr	Tamla Motown	1
24	[17]	OUR WORLD	Blue Mink	Philips	6
21	18	RUBY TUESDAY	Melanie	Buddah	4
15	19	THE TIPS OF MY FINGERS	Des O'Connor	Columbia	4
17	20	THE WONDER OF YOU	Elvis Presley	RCA	16
18	21	GIVE ME JUST A LITTLE MORE TIME	Chairmen Of The Board	Invictus	10
25	22	THE WITCH	Rattles	Decca	2
12	23	STRANGE BAND	Family	Reprise	10
28	24	NEW WORLD IN THE MORNING	Roger Whittaker	Columbia	2
16	25	TEARS OF A CLOWN	Smokey Robinson and the Miracles	Tamla Motown	13
32	26	JIMMY MACK	Martha and the Vandellas	Tamla Motown	8
38	27	IT'S WONDERFUL	Jimmy Ruffin	Tamla Motown	2
30	28	MY WAY	Frank Sinatra	Reprise	25
23	29	LONG AS I CAN SEE THE LIGHT	Creedence Clearwater Revival	Liberty	8
22	30	MAMA TOLD ME NOT TO COME	Three Dog Night	Stateside	11
26	31	MAKE IT WITH YOU	Bread	Elektra	11
-	32	INDIAN RESERVATION	Don Fardon	Young Blood	1
39	33	SHADY LADY	Gene Pitney	Stateside	3
40	34	HEAVEN IS HERE	Julie Felix	RAK	2
-	35	MY WAY	Dorothy Squires	President	5
29	36	DON'T PLAY THAT SONG	Aretha Franklin	Atlantic	9
27	37	LOVE IS LIFE	Hot Chocolate	RAK	10
35	38	SOMETHING	Shirley Bassey	United Artists	18
-	39	JULIE DO YA LOVE ME?	White Plains	Deram	1
31	40	WILD WORLD	Jimmy Cliff	Island	11

WEEK ENDING 31 OCTOBER 1970

LW	TW	Title	Artist	Label	Wks
10	[1]	WOODSTOCK	Matthews Southern Comfort	Uni	5
3	[2]	PATCHES	Clarence Carter	Atlantic	4
1	3	BAND OF GOLD	Freda Payne	Invictus	9
4	[4]	ME AND MY LIFE	Tremeloes	CBS	8
2	5	BLACK NIGHT	Deep Purple	Harvest	9
5	6	PARANOID	Black Sabbath	Vertigo	8
9	[7]	BALL OF CONFUSION	Temptations	Tamla Motown	7
11	8	MONTEGO BAY	Bobby Bloom	Polydor	9
7	9	AIN'T NO MOUNTAIN HIGH ENOUGH	Diana Ross	Tamla Motown	8
13	[10]	STILL WATER	Four Tops	Tamla Motown	4
6	11	CLOSE TO YOU	Carpenters	A&M	8
8	12	YOU CAN GET IT IF YOU REALLY WANT IT	Desmond Dekker	Trojan	10
18	13	RUBY TUESDAY	Melanie	Buddah	5
22	14	THE WITCH	Rattles	Decca	3
16	15	WAR	Edwin Starr	Tamla Motown	2
14	16	GASOLINE ALLEY BRED	Hollies	Parlophone	5
19	17	THE TIPS OF MY FINGERS	Des O'Connor	Columbia	5
27	18	IT'S WONDERFUL	Jimmy Ruffin	Tamla Motown	3
32	19	INDIAN RESERVATION	Don Fardon	Young Blood	2
24	20	NEW WORLD IN THE MORNING	Roger Whittaker	Columbia	3
15	21	BLACK PEARL	Horace Faith	Trojan	8
12	22	WHICH WAY YOU GOIN' BILLY?	Poppy Family	Decca	9
20	23	THE WONDER OF YOU	Elvis Presley	RCA	17
-	24	SAN BERNADINO	Christie	CBS	1
34	25	HEAVEN IS HERE	Julie Felix	RAK	3
39	26	JULIE DO YA LOVE ME?	White Plains	Deram	2
-	27	SNOWBIRD	Anne Murray ●	Capitol	1
28	28	MY WAY	Frank Sinatra	Reprise	26
26	29	JIMMY MACK	Martha and the Vandellas	Tamla Motown	9
21	30	GIVE ME JUST A LITTLE MORE TIME	Chairmen Of The Board	Invictus	11
23	31	STRANGE BAND	Family	Reprise	11
-	[32]	GET UP I FEEL LIKE BEING A SEX MACHINE	James Brown	Polydor	1
17	33	OUR WORLD	Blue Mink	Philips	7
33	34	SHADY LADY	Gene Pitney	Stateside	4
-	35	WHOLE LOTTA LOVE	C.C.S. ●	RAK	1
35	36	MY WAY	Dorothy Squires	President	6
-	37	RIDE A WHITE SWAN	T. Rex	Fly	1
25	38	TEARS OF A CLOWN	Smokey Robinson and the Miracles	Tamla Motown	14
31	39	MAKE IT WITH YOU	Bread	Elektra	12
29	40	LONG AS I CAN SEE THE LIGHT	Creedence Clearwater Revival	Liberty	9

WEEK ENDING 7 NOVEMBER 1970

LW	TW	Title	Artist	Label	Wks
1	[1]	WOODSTOCK	Matthews Southern Comfort	Uni	6
2	[2]	PATCHES	Clarence Carter	Atlantic	5
5	3	BLACK NIGHT	Deep Purple	Harvest	10
3	4	BAND OF GOLD	Freda Payne	Invictus	10
15	5	WAR	Edwin Starr	Tamla Motown	3
4	6	ME AND MY LIFE	Tremeloes	CBS	9
7	[7]	BALL OF CONFUSION	Temptations	Tamla Motown	8
14	[8]	THE WITCH	Rattles	Decca	4
13	[9]	RUBY TUESDAY	Melanie	Buddah	6
6	10	PARANOID	Black Sabbath	Vertigo	9
10	11	STILL WATER	Four Tops	Tamla Motown	5
19	12	INDIAN RESERVATION	Don Fardon	Young Blood	3
9	13	AIN'T NO MOUNTAIN HIGH ENOUGH	Diana Ross	Tamla Motown	9
11	14	CLOSE TO YOU	Carpenters	A&M	9
-	15	VOODOO CHILE	Jimi Hendrix Experience	Track	1
18	16	IT'S WONDERFUL	Jimmy Ruffin	Tamla Motown	4
16	17	GASOLINE ALLEY BRED	Hollies	Parlophone	6
24	18	SAN BERNADINO	Christie	CBS	2
12	19	YOU CAN GET IT IF YOU REALLY WANT IT	Desmond Dekker	Trojan	11
17	20	THE TIPS OF MY FINGERS	Des O'Connor	Columbia	6
20	21	NEW WORLD IN THE MORNING	Roger Whittaker	Columbia	4
25	[22]	HEAVEN IS HERE	Julie Felix	RAK	4
8	23	MONTEGO BAY	Bobby Bloom	Polydor	10
26	24	JULIE DO YA LOVE ME?	White Plains	Deram	3
-	25	THINK ABOUT YOUR CHILDREN	Mary Hopkin	Apple	1
33	26	OUR WORLD	Blue Mink	Philips	8
27	27	SNOWBIRD	Anne Murray	Capitol	2
21	28	BLACK PEARL	Horace Faith	Trojan	9
34	[29]	SHADY LADY	Gene Pitney	Stateside	5
22	30	WHICH WAY YOU GOIN' BILLY?	Poppy Family	Decca	10
37	31	RIDE A WHITE SWAN	T. Rex	Fly	2
35	32	WHOLE LOTTA LOVE	C.C.S.	RAK	2
23	33	THE WONDER OF YOU	Elvis Presley	RCA	18
28	34	MY WAY	Frank Sinatra	Reprise	27
-	35	MORE GOOD OLD ROCK 'N' ROLL	Dave Clark Five	Columbia	1
29	36	JIMMY MACK	Martha and the Vandellas	Tamla Motown	10
32	37	GET UP I FEEL LIKE BEING A SEX MACHINE	James Brown	Polydor	2
31	38	STRANGE BAND	Family	Reprise	12
-	39	IN MY CHAIR	Status Quo	Pye	1
-	40	CRACKLIN' ROSIE	Neil Diamond ●	Uni	1

WEEK ENDING 14 NOVEMBER 1970

LW	TW	Title	Artist	Label	Wks
1	[1]	WOODSTOCK	Matthews Southern Comfort	Uni	7
2	[2]	PATCHES	Clarence Carter	Atlantic	6
5	[3]	WAR	Edwin Starr	Tamla Motown	4
12	4	INDIAN RESERVATION	Don Fardon	Young Blood	4
15	5	VOODOO CHILE	Jimi Hendrix Experience	Track	2
6	6	ME AND MY LIFE	Tremeloes	CBS	10
18	[7]	SAN BERNADINO	Christie	CBS	3

In these weeks ■ One-hit wonder Matthews' Southern Comfort take Joni Mitchell's *Woodstock* to the top, also giving the Uni label its only chart-topper (31.10.70) ■ The entry of T. Rex's first electric hit *Ride A White Swan* paves the way for the early Seventies' glam rock (31.10.70) ■ Social comment songs doing well include *War, Ball Of Confusion* and *Indian Reservation* (07.11.70)■

December 1970

□ Highest position disc reached ● Act's first ever week on chart

LW	TW	Title	Artist	Label	Wks
8	[8]	THE WITCH	Rattles	Decca	5
9	[9]	RUBY TUESDAY	Melanie	Buddah	7
4	10	BAND OF GOLD	Freda Payne	Invictus	11
3	11	BLACK NIGHT	Deep Purple	Harvest	11
16	12	IT'S WONDERFUL	Jimmy Ruffin	Tamla Motown	5
10	13	PARANOID	Black Sabbath	Vertigo	10
7	14	BALL OF CONFUSION	Temptations	Tamla Motown	9
11	15	STILL WATER	Four Tops	Tamla Motown	6
24	16	JULIE DO YA LOVE ME?	White Plains	Deram	4
21	[17]	NEW WORLD IN THE MORNING	Roger Whittaker	Columbia	5
32	18	WHOLE LOTTA LOVE	C.C.S.	RAK	3
25	[19]	THINK ABOUT YOUR CHILDREN	Mary Hopkin	Apple	2
14	20	CLOSE TO YOU	Carpenters	A&M	10
20	21	THE TIPS OF MY FINGERS	Des O'Connor	Columbia	7
22	[22]	HEAVEN IS HERE	Julie Felix	RAK	5
23	23	MONTEGO BAY	Bobby Bloom	Polydor	11
19	24	YOU CAN GET IT IF YOU REALLY WANT IT	Desmond Dekker	Trojan	12
13	25	AIN'T NO MOUNTAIN HIGH ENOUGH	Diana Ross	Tamla Motown	10
-	26	I'VE LOST YOU	Elvis Presley	RCA	1
17	27	GASOLINE ALLEY BRED	Hollies	Parlophone	7
-	[28]	JULIE DO YA LOVE ME	Bobby Sherman ●	CBS	1
40	29	CRACKLIN' ROSIE	Neil Diamond	Uni	2
31	30	RIDE A WHITE SWAN	T. Rex	Fly	3
27	31	SNOWBIRD	Anne Murray	Capitol	3
-	32	BABY I WON'T LET YOU DOWN	Pickettywitch	Pye	1
39	33	IN MY CHAIR	Status Quo	Pye	2
35	[34]	MORE GOOD OLD ROCK 'N' ROLL	Dave Clark Five	Columbia	2
34	35	MY WAY	Frank Sinatra	Reprise	28
29	36	SHADY LADY	Gene Pitney	Stateside	6
-	37	IT'S A SHAME	Motown Spinners ●	Tamla Motown	1
-	[38]	GO NORTH	Richard Barnes	Philips	1
37	39	GET UP I FEEL LIKE BEING A SEX MACHINE	James Brown	Polydor	3
-	40	YOU'VE GOT ME DANGLING ON A STRING	Chairmen Of The Board	Invictus	1

WEEK ENDING 21 NOVEMBER 1970

LW	TW	Title	Artist	Label	Wks
5	[1]	VOODOO CHILE	Jimi Hendrix Experience	Track	3
1	2	WOODSTOCK	Matthews Southern Comfort	Uni	8
4	[3]	INDIAN RESERVATION	Don Fardon	Young Blood	5
2	4	PATCHES	Clarence Carter	Atlantic	7
3	5	WAR	Edwin Starr	Tamla Motown	5
12	[6]	IT'S WONDERFUL	Jimmy Ruffin	Tamla Motown	6
7	[7]	SAN BERNADINO	Christie	CBS	4
8	[8]	THE WITCH	Rattles	Decca	6
9	[9]	RUBY TUESDAY	Melanie	Buddah	8
29	10	CRACKLIN' ROSIE	Neil Diamond	Uni	3
11	11	BLACK NIGHT	Deep Purple	Harvest	12
6	12	ME AND MY LIFE	Tremeloes	CBS	11
16	13	JULIE DO YA LOVE ME?	White Plains	Deram	5
14	14	BALL OF CONFUSION	Temptations	Tamla Motown	10
30	15	RIDE A WHITE SWAN	T. Rex	Fly	4
-	16	I HEAR YOU KNOCKING	Dave Edmunds ●	MAM	1
10	17	BAND OF GOLD	Freda Payne	Invictus	12
15	18	STILL WATER	Four Tops	Tamla Motown	7
40	19	YOU'VE GOT ME DANGLING ON A STRING	Chairmen Of The Board	Invictus	2
18	20	WHOLE LOTTA LOVE	C.C.S.	RAK	4
17	21	NEW WORLD IN THE MORNING	Roger Whittaker	Columbia	6
19	22	THINK ABOUT YOUR CHILDREN	Mary Hopkin	Apple	3
26	23	I'VE LOST YOU	Elvis Presley	RCA	2
33	24	IN MY CHAIR	Status Quo	Pye	3
37	25	IT'S A SHAME	Motown Spinners	Tamla Motown	2
13	26	PARANOID	Black Sabbath	Vertigo	11
32	[27]	BABY I WON'T LET YOU DOWN	Pickettywitch	Pye	2
22	28	HEAVEN IS HERE	Julie Felix	RAK	6
20	29	CLOSE TO YOU	Carpenters	A&M	11
21	30	THE TIPS OF MY FINGERS	Des O'Connor	Columbia	8
31	31	SNOWBIRD	Anne Murray	Capitol	4
-	[32]	MEMO FROM TURNER	Mick Jagger ●	Decca	1
-	33	MY PRAYER	Gerry Monroe	Chapter One	1
28	34	JULIE DO YA LOVE ME	Bobby Sherman	CBS	2
23	35	MONTEGO BAY	Bobby Bloom	Polydor	12
-	36	I'LL BE THERE	Jackson Five	Tamla Motown	1
24	37	YOU CAN GET IT IF YOU REALLY WANT IT	Desmond Dekker	Trojan	13
-	38	IT'S ONLY MAKE BELIEVE	Glen Campbell	Capitol	1
25	39	AIN'T NO MOUNTAIN HIGH ENOUGH	Diana Ross	Tamla Motown	11
34	40	MORE GOOD OLD ROCK 'N' ROLL	Dave Clark Five	Columbia	3

WEEK ENDING 28 NOVEMBER 1970

LW	TW	Title	Artist	Label	Wks
16	[1]	I HEAR YOU KNOCKING	Dave Edmunds	MAM	2
1	2	VOODOO CHILE	Jimi Hendrix Experience	Track	4
3	[3]	INDIAN RESERVATION	Don Fardon	Young Blood	6
2	4	WOODSTOCK	Matthews Southern Comfort	Uni	9
10	5	CRACKLIN' ROSIE	Neil Diamond	Uni	4
5	6	WAR	Edwin Starr	Tamla Motown	6
15	7	RIDE A WHITE SWAN	T. Rex	Fly	5
4	8	PATCHES	Clarence Carter	Atlantic	8
23	[9]	I'VE LOST YOU	Elvis Presley	RCA	3
13	10	JULIE DO YA LOVE ME?	White Plains	Deram	6
7	11	SAN BERNADINO	Christie	CBS	5
6	12	IT'S WONDERFUL	Jimmy Ruffin	Tamla Motown	7
20	[13]	WHOLE LOTTA LOVE	C.C.S.	RAK	5
9	14	RUBY TUESDAY	Melanie	Buddah	9
8	15	THE WITCH	Rattles	Decca	7
19	16	YOU'VE GOT ME DANGLING ON A STRING	Chairmen Of The Board	Invictus	3
-	17	HOME LOVIN' MAN	Andy Williams	CBS	1
38	18	IT'S ONLY MAKE BELIEVE	Glen Campbell	Capitol	2
22	[19]	THINK ABOUT YOUR CHILDREN	Mary Hopkin	Apple	4
21	20	NEW WORLD IN THE MORNING	Roger Whittaker	Columbia	7
24	[21]	IN MY CHAIR	Status Quo	Pye	4
12	22	ME AND MY LIFE	Tremeloes	CBS	12
33	23	MY PRAYER	Gerry Monroe	Chapter One	2
-	24	WHEN I'M DEAD AND GONE	McGuinness Flint ●	Capitol	1
17	25	BAND OF GOLD	Freda Payne	Invictus	13
36	26	I'LL BE THERE	Jackson Five	Tamla Motown	2
27	[27]	BABY I WON'T LET YOU DOWN	Pickettywitch	Pye	3
11	28	BLACK NIGHT	Deep Purple	Harvest	13
30	29	THE TIPS OF MY FINGERS	Des O'Connor	Columbia	9
26	30	PARANOID	Black Sabbath	Vertigo	12
31	31	SNOWBIRD	Anne Murray	Capitol	5
25	32	IT'S A SHAME	Motown Spinners	Tamla Motown	3
-	33	MY WAY	Frank Sinatra	Reprise	29
-	34	LADY BARBARA	Peter Noone and Herman's Hermits ●	RAK	1
29	35	CLOSE TO YOU	Carpenters	A&M	12
14	36	BALL OF CONFUSION	Temptations	Tamla Motown	11
32	37	MEMO FROM TURNER	Mick Jagger	Decca	2
28	38	HEAVEN IS HERE	Julie Felix	RAK	7
37	39	YOU CAN GET IT IF YOU REALLY WANT IT	Desmond Dekker	Trojan	14
40	40	MORE GOOD OLD ROCK 'N' ROLL	Dave Clark Five	Columbia	4

WEEK ENDING 5 DECEMBER 1970

LW	TW	Title	Artist	Label	Wks
1	[1]	I HERE YOU KNOCKING	Dave Edmunds	MAM	3
2	2	VOODOO CHILE	Jimi Hendrix Experience	Track	5
5	[3]	CRACKLIN' ROSIE	Neil Diamond	Uni	5
3	4	INDIAN RESERVATION	Don Fardon	Young Blood	7
16	[5]	YOU'VE GOT ME DANGLING ON A STRING	Chairmen Of The Board	Invictus	4
24	6	WHEN I'M DEAD AND GONE	McGuinness Flint	Capitol	2
7	7	RIDE A WHITE SWAN	T. Rex	Fly	6
10	[8]	JULIE DO YA LOVE ME?	White Plains	Deram	7
9	[9]	I'VE LOST YOU	Elvis Presley	RCA	4
12	10	IT'S WONDERFUL	Jimmy Ruffin	Tamla Motown	8
4	11	WOODSTOCK	Matthews Southern Comfort	Uni	10
23	12	MY PRAYER	Gerry Monroe	Chapter One	3

■ *Voodoo Chile* gives Jimi Hendrix his only number one, a few months after his death. It is the fourth posthumous chart-topper (21.11.70) ■ Because Led Zeppelin refused to issue any singles in Britain, C.C.S. took a song from Led Zeppelin II unchallenged into the Top 20 (28.11.70)■

December 1970

□ Highest position disc reached ● Act's first ever week on chart

LW	TW	Title	Artist	Label	Wks
6	13	WAR	Edwin Starr	*Tamla Motown*	7
11	14	SAN BERNADINO	Christie	*CBS*	6
26	15	I'LL BE THERE	Jackson Five	*Tamla Motown*	3
8	16	PATCHES	Clarence Carter	*Atlantic*	9
17	17	HOME LOVIN' MAN	Andy Williams	*CBS*	2
18	18	IT'S ONLY MAKE BELIEVE	Glen Campbell	*Capitol*	3
13	19	WHOLE LOTTA LOVE	C.C.S.	*RAK*	6
14	20	RUBY TUESDAY	Melanie	*Buddah*	10
15	21	THE WITCH	Rattles	*Decca*	8
20	22	NEW WORLD IN THE MORNING	Roger Whittaker	*Columbia*	8
21	23	IN MY CHAIR	Status Quo	*Pye*	5
34	24	LADY BARBARA	Peter Noone and Herman's Hermits	*RAK*	2
33	25	MY WAY	Frank Sinatra	*Reprise*	30
32	26	IT'S A SHAME	Motown Spinners	*Tamla Motown*	4
-	27	BLAME IT ON THE PONY EXPRESS	Johnny Johnson and his Bandwagon	*Bell*	1
22	28	ME AND MY LIFE	Tremeloes	*CBS*	13
25	29	BAND OF GOLD	Freda Payne	*Invictus*	14
-	30	NOTHING RHYMED	Gilbert O'Sullivan ●	*MAM*	1
28	31	BLACK NIGHT	Deep Purple	*Harvest*	14
-	32	GRANDAD	Clive Dunn ●	*Columbia*	1
35	33	(THEY LONG TO BE) CLOSE TO YOU	Carpenters	*A&M*	13
29	34	THE TIPS OF MY FINGERS	Des O'Connor	*Columbia*	10
-	35	BROKEN HEARTED	Ken Dodd	*Columbia*	1
19	36	THINK ABOUT YOUR CHILDREN	Mary Hopkin	*Apple*	5
-	37	DEEPER AND DEEPER	Freda Payne	*Invictus*	1
27	38	BABY I WON'T LET YOU DOWN	Pickettywitch	*Pye*	4
31	39	SNOWBIRD	Anne Murray	*Capitol*	6
28	40	HEAVEN HELP US ALL	Stevie Wonder	*Tamla Motown*	1

WEEK ENDING 12 DECEMBER 1970

LW	TW	Title	Artist	Label	Wks
1	1	I HERE YOU KNOCKING	Dave Edmunds	*MAM*	4
6	2	WHEN I'M DEAD AND GONE	McGuiness Flint	*Capitol*	3
3	3	CRACKLIN' ROSIE	Neil Diamond	*Uni*	6
18	4	IT'S ONLY MAKE BELIEVE	Glen Campbell	*Capitol*	4
2	5	VOODOO CHILE	Jimi Hendrix Experience	*Track*	6
7	6	RIDE A WHITE SWAN	T. Rex	*Fly*	7
17	7	HOME LOVIN' MAN	Andy Williams	*CBS*	3
5	8	YOU'VE GOT ME DANGLING ON A STRING	Chairmen Of The Board	*Invictus*	5
4	9	INDIAN RESERVATION	Don Fardon	*Young Blood*	8
9	10	I'VE LOST YOU	Elvis Presley	*RCA*	5
30	11	NOTHING RHYMED	Gilbert O'Sullivan	*MAM*	2
12	12	MY PRAYER	Gerry Monroe	*Chapter One*	4
15	13	I'LL BE THERE	Jackson Five	*Tamla Motown*	4
8	14	JULIE DO YA LOVE ME?	White Plains	*Deram*	8
14	15	SAN BERNADINO	Christie	*CBS*	7
24	16	LADY BARBARA	Peter Noone and Herman's Hermits	*RAK*	3
32	17	GRANDAD	Clive Dunn	*Columbia*	2
19	18	WHOLE LOTTA LOVE	C.C.S.	*RAK*	7
10	19	IT'S WONDERFUL	Jimmy Ruffin	*Tamla Motown*	9
13	20	WAR	Edwin Starr	*Tamla Motown*	8
11	21	WOODSTOCK	Matthews Southern Comfort	*Uni*	11
27	22	BLAME IT ON THE PONY EXPRESS	Johnny Johnson and his Bandwagon	*Bell*	2
16	23	PATCHES	Clarence Carter	*Atlantic*	10
25	24	MY WAY	Frank Sinatra	*Reprise*	31
22	25	NEW WORLD IN THE MORNING	Roger Whittaker	*Columbia*	9
26	26	IT'S A SHAME	Motown Spinners	*Tamla Motown*	5
23	27	IN MY CHAIR	Status Quo	*Pye*	6
39	28	SNOWBIRD	Anne Murray	*Capitol*	7
-	29	YOU'RE READY NOW	Frankie Valli ●	*Philips*	1
35	30	BROKEN HEARTED	Ken Dodd	*Columbia*	2
21	31	THE WITCH	Rattles	*Decca*	9
-	32	APEMAN	Kinks	*Pye*	1
38	33	BABY I WON'T LET YOU DOWN	Pickettywitch	*Pye*	5
29	34	BAND OF GOLD	Freda Payne	*Invictus*	15
20	35	RUBY TUESDAY	Melanie	*Buddah*	11
-	36	HEAVEN HELP US ALL	Stevie Wonder	*Tamla Motown*	2
34	37	THE TIPS OF MY FINGERS	Des O'Connor	*Columbia*	11
36	38	THINK ABOUT YOUR CHILDREN	Mary Hopkin	*Apple*	6
37	39	DEEPER AND DEEPER	Freda Payne	*Invictus*	2
-	40	LONELY DAYS	Bee Gees	*Polydor*	1

WEEK ENDING 19 DECEMBER 1970

LW	TW	Title	Artist	Label	Wks
1	1	I HERE YOU KNOCKING	Dave Edmunds	*MAM*	5
2	2	WHEN I'M DEAD AND GONE	McGuiness Flint	*Capitol*	4
3	3	CRACKLIN' ROSIE	Neil Diamond	*Uni*	7
4	4	IT'S ONLY MAKE BELIEVE	Glen Campbell	*Capitol*	5
13	5	I'LL BE THERE	Jackson Five	*Tamla Motown*	5
17	6	GRANDAD	Clive Dunn	*Columbia*	3
7	7	HOME LOVIN' MAN	Andy Williams	*CBS*	4
11	8	NOTHING RHYMED	Gilbert O'Sullivan	*MAM*	3
12	9	MY PRAYER	Gerry Monroe	*Chapter One*	5
8	10	YOU'VE GOT ME DANGLING ON A STRING	Chairmen Of The Board	*Invictus*	6
5	11	VOODOO CHILE	Jimi Hendrix Experience	*Track*	7
6	12	RIDE A WHITE SWAN	T. Rex	*Fly*	8
9	13	INDIAN RESERVATION	Don Fardon	*Young Blood*	9
10	14	I'VE LOST YOU	Elvis Presley	*RCA*	6
22	15	BLAME IT ON THE PONY EXPRESS	Johnny Johnson and his Bandwagon	*Bell*	3
14	16	JULIE DO YA LOVE ME?	White Plains	*Deram*	9
16	17	LADY BARBARA	Peter Noone and Herman's Hermits	*RAK*	4
30	18	BROKEN HEARTED	Ken Dodd	*Columbia*	3
19	19	IT'S WONDERFUL	Jimmy Ruffin	*Tamla Motown*	10
26	20	IT'S A SHAME	Motown Spinners	*Tamla Motown*	6
21	21	WOODSTOCK	Matthews Southern Comfort	*Uni*	12
18	22	WHOLE LOTTA LOVE	C.C.S.	*RAK*	8
15	23	SAN BERNADINO	Christie	*CBS*	8
25	24	NEW WORLD IN THE MORNING	Roger Whittaker	*Columbia*	10
-	25	MY WAY	Dorothy Squires	*President*	5
24	26	MY WAY	Frank Sinatra	*Reprise*	32
20	27	WAR	Edwin Starr	*Tamla Motown*	9
23	28	PATCHES	Clarence Carter	*Atlantic*	11
28	29	SNOWBIRD	Anne Murray	*Capitol*	8
36	30	HEAVEN HELP US ALL	Stevie Wonder	*Tamla Motown*	3
34	31	BAND OF GOLD	Freda Payne	*Invictus*	16
32	32	APEMAN	Kinks	*Pye*	2
39	33	DEEPER AND DEEPER	Freda Payne	*Invictus*	3
-	34	AMAZING GRACE	Judy Collins ●	*Elektra*	1
-	35	ME AND MY LIFE	Tremeloes	*CBS*	14
40	36	LONELY DAYS	Bee Gees	*Polydor*	2
37	37	THE TIPS OF MY FINGERS	Des O'Connor	*Columbia*	12
-	38	PARANOID	Black Sabbath	*Vertigo*	13
33	39	BABY I WON'T LET YOU DOWN	Pickettywitch	*Pye*	6
35	40	RUBY TUESDAY	Melanie	*Buddah*	12

WEEK ENDING 26 DECEMBER 1970

(no chart compiled: chart for 19 December repeated)

LW	TW	Title	Artist	Label	Wks
1	1	I HERE YOU KNOCKING	Dave Edmunds	*MAM*	6
2	2	WHEN I'M DEAD AND GONE	McGuiness Flint	*Capitol*	5
3	3	CRACKLIN' ROSIE	Neil Diamond	*Uni*	8
4	4	IT'S ONLY MAKE BELIEVE	Glen Campbell	*Capitol*	6
5	5	I'LL BE THERE	Jackson Five	*Tamla Motown*	6
6	6	GRANDAD	Clive Dunn	*Columbia*	4
7	7	HOME LOVIN' MAN	Andy Williams	*CBS*	5
8	8	NOTHING RHYMED	Gilbert O'Sullivan	*MAM*	4
9	9	MY PRAYER	Gerry Monroe	*Chapter One*	6
10	10	YOU'VE GOT ME DANGLING ON A STRING	Chairmen Of The Board	*Invictus*	7
11	11	VOODOO CHILE	Jimi Hendrix Experience	*Track*	8
12	12	RIDE A WHITE SWAN	T. Rex	*Fly*	9
13	13	INDIAN RESERVATION	Don Fardon	*Young Blood*	10
14	14	I'VE LOST YOU	Elvis Presley	*RCA*	7
15	15	BLAME IT ON THE PONY EXPRESS	Johnny Johnson and his Bandwagon	*Bell*	4
16	16	JULIE DO YA LOVE ME?	White Plains	*Deram*	10
17	17	LADY BARBARA	Peter Noone and Herman's Hermits	*RAK*	5
18	18	BROKEN HEARTED	Ken Dodd	*Columbia*	4
19	19	IT'S WONDERFUL	Jimmy Ruffin	*Tamla Motown*	11
20	20	IT'S A SHAME	Motown Spinners	*Tamla Motown*	7

In these weeks ■ For three weeks, the top four records are unchanged and all at their peak positions (12.12.70) ■ Judy Collins' long running vocal version of *Amazing Grace* debuts gently at number 34 (19.12.70) ■ The only record that has spent more weeks on the chart, Frank Sinatra's *My Way* extends its record to 60 weeks (26.12.70) ■ There are no women in the Top 20. The highest placed is Dorothy Squires at no. 25 (26.12.70)■

December 1970

□ Highest position disc reached ● Act's first ever week on chart

21	**21**	WOODSTOCK	Matthews Southern Comfort	*Uni*	13
22	**22**	WHOLE LOTTA LOVE	C.C.S.	*RAK*	9
23	**23**	SAN BERNADINO	Christie	*CBS*	9
24	**24**	NEW WORLD IN THE MORNING	Roger Whittaker	*Columbia*	11
25	**25**	MY WAY	Dorothy Squires	*President*	6
26	**26**	MY WAY	Frank Sinatra	*Reprise*	33
27	**27**	WAR	Edwin Starr	*Tamla Motown*	10
28	**28**	PATCHES	Clarence Carter	*Atlantic*	12
29	**29**	SNOWBIRD	Anne Murray	*Capitol*	9
30	**30**	HEAVEN HELP US ALL	Stevie Wonder	*Tamla Motown*	4
31	**31**	BAND OF GOLD	Freda Payne	*Invictus*	17
32	**32**	APEMAN	Kinks	*Pye*	3
33	**33** □	DEEPER AND DEEPER	Freda Payne	*Invictus*	4
34	**34**	AMAZING GRACE	Judy Collins	*Elektra*	2
35	**35**	ME AND MY LIFE	Tremeloes	*CBS*	15
36	**36**	LONELY DAYS	Bee Gees	*Polydor*	3
37	**37**	THE TIPS OF MY FINGERS	Des O'Connor	*Columbia*	13
38	**38**	PARANOID	Black Sabbath	*Vertigo*	14
39	**39**	BABY I WON'T LET YOU DOWN	Pickettywitch	*Pye*	7
40	**40**	RUBY TUESDAY	Melanie	*Buddah*	13

■Six records occupying the bottom 16 places are by female vocalists, and Pickettywitch also features a female lead singer (26.12.70)■

1971

........MARC BOLAN leads T.Rex to its first two number ones.......George Harrison as the first number one by a former Beatle and Diana Ross gets a solo number one ......Rod Stewart has his first and longest-running number one, 'Maggie May'.........

January 1971

□ Highest position disc reached ● Act's first ever week on chart

LW	TW	*WEEK ENDING* **9 JANUARY 1971**		Wks
6	[1]	GRANDAD Clive Dunn	*Columbia*	5
1	2	I HERE YOU KNOCKING Dave Edmunds	*MAM*	7
2	3	WHEN I'M DEAD AND GONE McGuiness Flint	*Capitol*	6
12	4	RIDE A WHITE SWAN T. Rex	*Fly*	10
5	5	I'LL BE THERE Jackson Five	*Tamla Motown*	7
3	6	CRACKLIN' ROSIE Neil Diamond	*Uni*	9
15	[7]	BLAME IT ON THE PONY EXPRESS Johnny Johnson and his Bandwagon	*Bell*	5
8	8	NOTHING RHYMED Gilbert O'Sullivan	*MAM*	5
4	9	IT'S ONLY MAKE BELIEVE Glen Campbell	*Capitol*	7
7	10	HOME LOVIN' MAN Andy Williams	*CBS*	6
10	11	YOU'VE GOT ME DANGLING ON A STRING Chairmen Of The Board	*Invictus*	8
32	12	APEMAN Kinks	*Pye*	4
17	[13]	LADY BARBARA Peter Noone and Herman's Hermits	*RAK*	6
9	14	MY PRAYER Gerry Munroe	*Chapter One*	7
18	[15]	BROKEN HEARTED Ken Dodd	*Columbia*	5
13	16	INDIAN RESERVATION Don Fardon	*Young Blood*	11
14	17	I'VE LOST YOU Elvis Presley	*RCA*	8
-	18	BLACK SKIN BLUE EYED BOYS Equals	*President*	1
16	19	JULIE DO YA LOVE ME? White Plains	*Deram*	11
11	20	VOODOO CHILE Jimi Hendrix Experience	*Track*	9
34	21	AMAZING GRACE Judy Collins	*Elektra*	3
22	22	WHOLE LOTTA LOVE C.C.S.	*RAK*	10
-	23	YOU DON'T HAVE TO SAY YOU LOVE ME Elvis Presley	*RCA*	1
20	24	IT'S A SHAME Motown Spinners	*Tamla Motown*	8
-	25	YOU'RE READY NOW Frankie Valli ●	*Philips*	2
21	26	WOODSTOCK Matthews Southern Comfort	*Uni*	14
-	27	IN MY CHAIR Status Quo	*Pye*	7
29	28	SNOWBIRD Anne Murray	*Capitol*	10
30	[29]	HEAVEN HELP US ALL Stevie Wonder	*Tamla Motown*	5
25	30	MY WAY Dorothy Squires	*President*	7
26	31	MY WAY Frank Sinatra	*Reprise*	34
23	32	SAN BERNADINO Christie	*CBS*	10
24	33	NEW WORLD IN THE MORNING Roger Whittaker	*Columbia*	12
36	34	LONELY DAYS Bee Gees	*Polydor*	4
-	35	NO MATTER WHAT Badfinger	*Apple*	1
27	36	WAR Edwin Starr	*Tamla Motown*	11
33	37	DEEPER AND DEEPER Freda Payne	*Invictus*	5
31	38	BAND OF GOLD Freda Payne	*Invictus*	18
-	39	RUPERT Jackie Lee	*Pye*	1
19	40	IT'S WONDERFUL Jimmy Ruffin	*Tamla Motown*	12

LW	TW	*WEEK ENDING* **16 JANUARY 1971**		Wks
1	[1]	GRANDAD Clive Dunn	*Columbia*	6
2	2	I HERE YOU KNOCKING Dave Edmunds	*MAM*	8
3	3	WHEN I'M DEAD AND GONE McGuiness Flint	*Capitol*	7
4	4	RIDE A WHITE SWAN T. Rex	*Fly*	11
5	5	I'LL BE THERE Jackson Five	*Tamla Motown*	8
9	6	IT'S ONLY MAKE BELIEVE Glen Campbell	*Capitol*	8
6	7	CRACKLIN' ROSIE Neil Diamond	*Uni*	10
7	8	BLAME IT ON THE PONY EXPRESS Johnny Johnson and his Bandwagon	*Bell*	6
10	9	HOME LOVIN' MAN Andy Williams	*CBS*	7
8	10	NOTHING RHYMED Gilbert O'Sullivan	*MAM*	6
12	11	APEMAN Kinks	*Pye*	5
11	12	YOU'VE GOT ME DANGLING ON A STRING Chairmen Of The Board	*Invictus*	9
25	13	YOU'RE READY NOW Frankie Valli	*Philips*	3
13	14	LADY BARBARA Peter Noone and Herman's Hermits	*RAK*	7
18	15	BLACK SKIN BLUE EYED BOYS Equals	*President*	2
15	16	BROKEN HEARTED Ken Dodd	*Columbia*	6
23	17	YOU DON'T HAVE TO SAY YOU LOVE ME Elvis Presley	*RCA*	2
14	18	MY PRAYER Gerry Munroe	*Chapter One*	8
21	19	AMAZING GRACE Judy Collins	*Elektra*	4
17	20	I'VE LOST YOU Elvis Presley	*RCA*	9
31	21	MY WAY Frank Sinatra	*Reprise*	35
20	22	VOODOO CHILE Jimi Hendrix Experience	*Track*	10
28	[23]	SNOWBIRD Anne Murray	*Capitol*	11
-	24	PUSHBIKE SONG Mixtures ●	*Polydor*	1
24	25	IT'S A SHAME Motown Spinners	*Tamla Motown*	9
16	26	INDIAN RESERVATION Don Fardon	*Young Blood*	12
27	27	IN MY CHAIR Status Quo	*Pye*	8
22	28	WHOLE LOTTA LOVE C.C.S.	*RAK*	11
39	29	RUPERT Jackie Lee	*Pye*	2
-	30	MAN FROM NAZARETH John Paul Joans ●	*RAK*	1
-	[31]	HEAVY MAKES YOU HAPPY Bobby Bloom	*Polydor*	1
19	32	JULIE DO YA LOVE ME? White Plains	*Deram*	12
34	33	LONELY DAYS Bee Gees	*Polydor*	5
35	34	NO MATTER WHAT Badfinger	*Apple*	2
29	35	HEAVEN HELP US ALL Stevie Wonder	*Tamla Motown*	6
26	36	WOODSTOCK Matthews Southern Comfort	*Uni*	15
-	37	WE'VE ONLY JUST BEGUN Carpenters	*A & M*	1
-	38	LAS VEGAS Tony Christie ●	*MCA*	1
-	[39]	WHAT HAVE THEY DONE TO MY SONG MA New Seekers ●	*Buddah*	1
-	40	CANDIDA Dawn ●	*Bell*	1

LW	TW	*WEEK ENDING* **23 JANUARY 1971**		Wks
1	[1]	GRANDAD Clive Dunn	*Columbia*	7
4	[2]	RIDE A WHITE SWAN T. Rex	*Fly*	12
3	3	WHEN I'M DEAD AND GONE McGuiness Flint	*Capitol*	8
5	[4]	I'LL BE THERE Jackson Five	*Tamla Motown*	9
11	[5]	APEMAN Kinks	*Pye*	6
2	6	I HERE YOU KNOCKING Dave Edmunds	*MAM*	9
-	7	MY SWEET LORD George Harrison ●	*Apple*	1
19	8	AMAZING GRACE Judy Collins	*Elektra*	5
17	[9]	YOU DON'T HAVE TO SAY YOU LOVE ME Elvis Presley	*RCA*	3
15	10	BLACK SKIN BLUE EYED BOYS Equals	*President*	3
8	11	BLAME IT ON THE PONY EXPRESS Johnny Johnson and his Bandwagon	*Bell*	7
6	12	IT'S ONLY MAKE BELIEVE Glen Campbell	*Capitol*	9
24	13	PUSHBIKE SONG Mixtures	*Polydor*	2
7	14	CRACKLIN' ROSIE Neil Diamond	*Uni*	11
9	15	HOME LOVIN' MAN Andy Williams	*CBS*	8
34	16	NO MATTER WHAT Badfinger	*Apple*	3
10	17	NOTHING RHYMED Gilbert O'Sullivan	*MAM*	7
13	18	YOU'RE READY NOW Frankie Valli	*Philips*	4
12	19	YOU'VE GOT ME DANGLING ON A STRING Chairmen Of The Board	*Invictus*	10
16	20	BROKEN HEARTED Ken Dodd	*Columbia*	7
-	21	SHE'S A LADY Tom Jones	*Decca*	1
40	22	CANDIDA Dawn	*Bell*	2
21	23	MY WAY Frank Sinatra	*Reprise*	36
-	24	STONED LOVE Supremes	*Tamla Motown*	1
30	[25]	MAN FROM NAZARETH John Paul Joans	*RAK*	2
-	26	RESURRECTION SHUFFLE Ashton, Gardner and Dyke ●	*Capitol*	1
-	27	IT'S THE SAME OLD SONG Weathermen ●	*B & C*	1
23	28	SNOWBIRD Anne Murray	*Capitol*	12
27	29	IN MY CHAIR Status Quo	*Pye*	9
-	30	SUNNY HONEY GIRL Cliff Richard	*Columbia*	1
29	31	RUPERT Jackie Lee	*Pye*	3
14	32	LADY BARBARA Peter Noone and Herman's Hermits	*RAK*	8
38	33	LAS VEGAS Tony Christie	*MCA*	2
18	34	MY PRAYER Gerry Munroe	*Chapter One*	9
33	35	LONELY DAYS Bee Gees	*Polydor*	6
37	36	WE'VE ONLY JUST BEGUN Carpenters	*A & M*	2
-	37	YOUR SONG Elton John ●	*DJM*	1
22	38	VOODOO CHILE Jimi Hendrix Experience	*Track*	11
31	39	HEAVY MAKES YOU HAPPY Bobby Bloom	*Polydor*	2
26	40	INDIAN RESERVATION Don Fardon	*Young Blood*	13

LW	TW	*WEEK ENDING* **30 JANUARY 1971**		Wks
7	[1]	MY SWEET LORD George Harrison	*Apple*	2
1	2	GRANDAD Clive Dunn	*Columbia*	8
13	3	PUSHBIKE SONG Mixtures	*Polydor*	3
2	4	RIDE A WHITE SWAN T. Rex	*Fly*	13

In these weeks ■ Clive Dunn's contribution to rock history, *Grandad* knocks Dave Edmunds off the top and prevents T. Rex from having their first number one (23.01.71) ■ Elton John and George Harrison debut in the same week. Harrison's first hit is much bigger, but Elton John proves longer-lasting (23.01.71) ■ The Weathermen are Jonathan King in disguise (again) (23.01.71)■

LW	TW	Title	Artist	Label	Wks
5	5	APEMAN	Kinks	Pye	7
4	6	I'LL BE THERE	Jackson Five	Tamla Motown	10
6	7	I HERE YOU KNOCKING	Dave Edmunds	MAM	10
8	8	AMAZING GRACE	Judy Collins	Elektra	6
10	9	BLACK SKIN BLUE EYED BOYS	Equals	President	4
14	10	CRACKLIN' ROSIE	Neil Diamond	Uni	12
11	11	BLAME IT ON THE PONY EXPRESS	Johnny Johnson and his Bandwagon	Bell	8
18	12	YOU'RE READY NOW	Frankie Valli	Philips	5
16	13	NO MATTER WHAT	Badfinger	Apple	4
9	14	YOU DON'T HAVE TO SAY YOU LOVE ME	Elvis Presley	RCA	4
26	15	RESURRECTION SHUFFLE	Ashton, Gardner and Dyke	Capitol	2
21	16	SHE'S A LADY	Tom Jones	Decca	2
3	17	WHEN I'M DEAD AND GONE	McGuiness Flint	Capitol	9
12	18	IT'S ONLY MAKE BELIEVE	Glen Campbell	Capitol	10
24	19	STONED LOVE	Supremes	Tamla Motown	2
22	20	CANDIDA	Dawn	Bell	3
17	21	NOTHING RHYMED	Gilbert O'Sullivan	MAM	8
31	22	RUPERT	Jackie Lee	Pye	4
33	23	LAS VEGAS	Tony Christie	MCA	3
23	24	MY WAY	Frank Sinatra	Reprise	37
19	25	YOU'VE GOT ME DANGLING ON A STRING	Chairmen Of The Board	Invictus	11
27	26	IT'S THE SAME OLD SONG	Weathermen	B & C	2
15	27	HOME LOVIN' MAN	Andy Williams	CBS	9
25	28	MAN FROM NAZARETH	John Paul Joans	RAK	3
36	29	WE'VE ONLY JUST BEGUN	Carpenters	A & M	3
37	30	YOUR SONG	Elton John	DJM	2
30	31	SUNNY HONEY GIRL	Cliff Richard	Columbia	2
28	32	SNOWBIRD	Anne Murray	Capitol	13
39	33	HEAVY MAKES YOU HAPPY	Bobby Bloom	Polydor	3
-	34	IT'S IMPOSSIBLE	Perry Como	RCA	1
20	35	BROKEN HEARTED	Ken Dodd	Columbia	8
34	36	MY PRAYER	Gerry Munroe	Chapter One	10
32	37	LADY BARBARA	Peter Noone and Herman's Hermits	RAK	9
-	38	(COME 'ROUND HERE) I'M THE ONE YOU NEED	Smokey Robinson and the Miracles	Tamla Motown	1
40	39	INDIAN RESERVATION	Don Fardon	Young Blood	14
35	40	LONELY DAYS	Bee Gees	Polydor	7

WEEK ENDING 6 FEBRUARY 1971

LW	TW	Title	Artist	Label	Wks
1	1	MY SWEET LORD	George Harrison	Apple	3
3	2	PUSHBIKE SONG	Mixtures	Polydor	4
19	3	STONED LOVE	Supremes	Tamla Motown	3
2	4	GRANDAD	Clive Dunn	Columbia	9
13	5	NO MATTER WHAT	Badfinger	Apple	5
8	6	AMAZING GRACE	Judy Collins	Elektra	7
4	7	RIDE A WHITE SWAN	T. Rex	Fly	14
5	8	APEMAN	Kinks	Pye	8
15	9	RESURRECTION SHUFFLE	Ashton, Gardner and Dyke	Capitol	3
6	10	I'LL BE THERE	Jackson Five	Tamla Motown	11
12	11	YOU'RE READY NOW	Frankie Valli	Philips	6
20	12	CANDIDA	Dawn	Bell	4
30	13	YOUR SONG	Elton John	DJM	3
14	14	YOU DON'T HAVE TO SAY YOU LOVE ME	Elvis Presley	RCA	5
9	15	BLACK SKIN BLUE EYED BOYS	Equals	President	5
17	16	WHEN I'M DEAD AND GONE	McGuiness Flint	Capitol	10
16	17	SHE'S A LADY	Tom Jones	Decca	3
10	18	CRACKLIN' ROSIE	Neil Diamond	Uni	13
7	19	I HERE YOU KNOCKING	Dave Edmunds	MAM	11
11	20	BLAME IT ON THE PONY EXPRESS	Johnny Johnson and his Bandwagon	Bell	9
26	21	IT'S THE SAME OLD SONG	Weathermen	B & C	3
18	22	IT'S ONLY MAKE BELIEVE	Glen Campbell	Capitol	11
31	23	SUNNY HONEY GIRL	Cliff Richard	Columbia	3
27	24	HOME LOVIN' MAN	Andy Williams	CBS	10
28	25	MAN FROM NAZARETH	John Paul Joans	RAK	4
23	26	LAS VEGAS	Tony Christie	MCA	4
21	27	NOTHING RHYMED	Gilbert O'Sullivan	MAM	9
29	28	WE'VE ONLY JUST BEGUN	Carpenters	A & M	4
24	29	MY WAY	Frank Sinatra	Reprise	38
22	30	RUPERT	Jackie Lee	Pye	5
34	31	IT'S IMPOSSIBLE	Perry Como	RCA	2
-	32	BABY JUMP	Mungo Jerry	Dawn	1

February 1971

□ Highest position disc reached ● Act's first ever week on chart

LW	TW	Title	Artist	Label	Wks
33	33	HEAVY MAKES YOU HAPPY	Bobby Bloom	Polydor	4
-	34	TOMORROW NIGHT	Atomic Rooster ●	B & C	1
-	35	IN MY CHAIR	Status Quo	Pye	10
-	36	APACHE DROPOUT	Edgar Broughton Band	Harvest	1
25	37	YOU'VE GOT ME DANGLING ON A STRING	Chairmen of the Board	Invictus	12
32	38	SNOWBIRD	Anne Murray	Capitol	14
38	39	(COME 'ROUND HERE) I'M THE ONE YOU NEED	Smokey Robinson and the Miracles	Tamla Motown	2
-	40	INSIDE LOOKING OUT	Grand Funk Railroad ●	Capitol	1

WEEK ENDING 13 FEBRUARY 1971

LW	TW	Title	Artist	Label	Wks
1	1	MY SWEET LORD	George Harrison	Apple	4
2	2	PUSHBIKE SONG	Mixtures	Polydor	5
3	3	STONED LOVE	Supremes	Tamla Motown	4
9	4	RESURRECTION SHUFFLE	Ashton, Gardner and Dyke	Capitol	4
6	5	AMAZING GRACE	Judy Collins	Elektra	8
5	6	NO MATTER WHAT	Badfinger	Apple	6
13	7	YOUR SONG	Elton John	DJM	4
8	8	APEMAN	Kinks	Pye	9
4	9	GRANDAD	Clive Dunn	Columbia	10
12	10	CANDIDA	Dawn	Bell	5
10	11	I'LL BE THERE	Jackson Five	Tamla Motown	12
11	12	YOU'RE READY NOW	Frankie Valli	Philips	7
31	13	IT'S IMPOSSIBLE	Perry Como	RCA	3
7	14	RIDE A WHITE SWAN	T. Rex	Fly	15
17	15	SHE'S A LADY	Tom Jones	Decca	4
30	16	RUPERT	Jackie Lee	Pye	6
15	17	BLACK SKIN BLUE EYED BOYS	Equals	President	6
14	18	YOU DON'T HAVE TO SAY YOU LOVE ME	Elvis Presley	RCA	6
21	19	IT'S THE SAME OLD SONG	Weathermen	B & C	4
18	20	CRACKLIN' ROSIE	Neil Diamond	Uni	14
26	21	LAS VEGAS	Tony Christie	MCA	5
23	22	SUNNY HONEY GIRL	Cliff Richard	Columbia	4
19	23	I HERE YOU KNOCKING	Dave Edmunds	MAM	12
39	24	(COME 'ROUND HERE) I'M THE ONE YOU NEED	Smokey Robinson and the Miracles	Tamla Motown	3
22	25	IT'S ONLY MAKE BELIEVE	Glen Campbell	Capitol	12
16	26	WHEN I'M DEAD AND GONE	McGuiness Flint	Capitol	11
20	27	BLAME IT ON THE PONY EXPRESS	Johnny Johnson and his Bandwagon	Bell	10
28	28	WE'VE ONLY JUST BEGUN	Carpenters	A & M	5
29	29	MY WAY	Frank Sinatra	Reprise	39
-	30	CHESTNUT MARE	Byrds	CBS	1
-	31	WHO PUT THE LIGHTS OUT	Dana	Rex	1
-	32	FORGET ME NOT	Martha Reeves and the Vandellas	Tamla Motown	1
-	33	AIN'T NOTHING BUT A HOUSEPARTY	Showstoppers	Beacon	1
-	34	I THINK I LOVE YOU	Partridge Family ●	Bell	1
36	35	APACHE DROPOUT	Edgar Broughton Band	Harvest	2
-	36	SONG OF MY LIFE	Petula Clark	Pye	1
34	37	TOMORROW NIGHT	Atomic Rooster	B & C	2
-	38	BROKEN HEARTED	Ken Dodd	Columbia	9
38	39	SNOWBIRD	Anne Murray	Capitol	15
-	40	STONEY END	Barbra Streisand	CBS	1

WEEK ENDING 20 FEBRUARY 1971

LW	TW	Title	Artist	Label	Wks
1	1	MY SWEET LORD	George Harrison	Apple	5
2	2	PUSHBIKE SONG	Mixtures	Polydor	6
4	3	RESURRECTION SHUFFLE	Ashton, Gardner and Dyke	Capitol	5
3	4	STONED LOVE	Supremes	Tamla Motown	5
5	5	AMAZING GRACE	Judy Collins	Elektra	9
6	6	NO MATTER WHAT	Badfinger	Apple	7
13	7	IT'S IMPOSSIBLE	Perry Como	RCA	4
7	8	YOUR SONG	Elton John	DJM	5
9	9	GRANDAD	Clive Dunn	Columbia	11
10	10	CANDIDA	Dawn	Bell	6

■Frank Sinatra's *My Way* clocks up 50 weeks in the Top 40 (30.01.71) ■ The Supremes enjoy their biggest hit without Diana Ross on lead vocals - *Stoned Love* at number three (06.02.71) ■ Heavy metal attacks the charts, with Atomic Rooster and Grand Funk Railroad making their first appearances (06.02.71)■

February 1971

□ Highest position disc reached ● Act's first ever week on chart

LW	TW	Title	Artist	Label	Wks
8	11	APEMAN	Kinks	Pye	10
14	12	RIDE A WHITE SWAN	T. Rex	Fly	16
15	13	SHE'S A LADY	Tom Jones	Decca	5
-	14	BABY JUMP	Mungo Jerry	Dawn	2
12	15	YOU'RE READY NOW	Frankie Valli	Philips	8
16	16	RUPERT	Jackie Lee	Pye	7
24	17	(COME 'ROUND HERE) I'M THE ONE YOU NEED	Smokey Robinson and the Miracles	Tamla Motown	4
18	18	YOU DON'T HAVE TO SAY YOU LOVE ME	Elvis Presley	RCA	7
22	[19]	SUNNY HONEY GIRL	Cliff Richard	Columbia	5
25	20	IT'S ONLY MAKE BELIEVE	Glen Campbell	Capitol	13
11	21	I'LL BE THERE	Jackson Five	Tamla Motown	13
32	22	FORGET ME NOT	Martha Reeves & the Vandellas	Tamla Motown	2
20	23	CRACKLIN' ROSIE	Neil Diamond	Uni	15
17	24	BLACK SKIN BLUE EYED BOYS	Equals	President	7
26	25	WHEN I'M DEAD AND GONE	McGuinness Flint	Capitol	12
-	26	EVERYTHING'S TUESDAY	Chairmen Of The Board	Invictus	1
21	27	LAS VEGAS	Tony Christie	MCA	6
-	28	ROSE GARDEN	Lynn Anderson ●	CBS	1
19	29	IT'S THE SAME OLD SONG	Weathermen	B & C	5
-	30	SWEET CAROLINE	Neil Diamond	Uni	1
29	31	MY WAY	Frank Sinatra	Reprise	40
23	32	I HERE YOU KNOCKING	Dave Edmunds	MAM	13
-	[33]	STOP THE WAR NOW	Edwin Starr	Tamla Motown	1
37	34	TOMORROW NIGHT	Atomic Rooster	B & C	3
34	35	I THINK I LOVE YOU	Partridge Family	Bell	2
36	36	SONG OF MY LIFE	Petula Clark	Pye	2
40	37	STONEY END	Barbra Streisand	CBS	2
30	38	CHESTNUT MARE	Byrds	CBS	2
28	39	WE'VE ONLY JUST BEGUN	Carpenters	A & M	6
31	40	WHO PUT THE LIGHTS OUT	Dana	Rex	2

WEEK ENDING 27 FEBRUARY 1971

LW	TW	Title	Artist	Label	Wks
1	[1]	MY SWEET LORD	George Harrison	Apple	6
2	[2]	PUSHBIKE SONG	Mixtures	Polydor	7
3	[3]	RESURRECTION SHUFFLE	Ashton, Gardner and Dyke	Capitol	6
7	[4]	IT'S IMPOSSIBLE	Perry Como	RCA	5
4	5	STONED LOVE	Supremes	Tamla Motown	6
5	6	AMAZING GRACE	Judy Collins	Elektra	10
14	7	BABY JUMP	Mungo Jerry	Dawn	3
8	8	YOUR SONG	Elton John	DJM	6
10	9	CANDIDA	Dawn	Bell	7
6	10	NO MATTER WHAT	Badfinger	Apple	8
30	11	SWEET CAROLINE	Neil Diamond	Uni	2
9	12	GRANDAD	Clive Dunn	Columbia	12
17	[13]	(COME 'ROUND HERE) I'M THE ONE YOU NEED	Smokey Robinson and the Miracles	Tamla Motown	5
16	[14]	RUPERT	Jackie Lee	Pye	8
22	15	FORGET ME NOT	Martha Reeves & the Vandellas	Tamla Motown	3
13	16	SHE'S A LADY	Tom Jones	Decca	6
11	17	APEMAN	Kinks	Pye	11
35	[18]	I THINK I LOVE YOU	Partridge Family	Bell	3
38	[19]	CHESTNUT MARE	Byrds	CBS	3
26	20	EVERYTHING'S TUESDAY	Chairmen Of The Board	Invictus	2
29	21	IT'S THE SAME OLD SONG	Weathermen	B & C	6
34	22	TOMORROW NIGHT	Atomic Rooster	B & C	4
28	23	ROSE GARDEN	Lynn Anderson	CBS	2
-	24	ANOTHER DAY	Paul McCartney ●	Apple	1
19	25	SUNNY HONEY GIRL	Cliff Richard	Columbia	6
12	26	RIDE A WHITE SWAN	T. Rex	Fly	17
27	27	LAS VEGAS	Tony Christie	MCA	7
40	28	WHO PUT THE LIGHTS OUT	Dana	Rex	3
-	29	ROSE GARDEN	New World ●	RAK	1
21	30	I'LL BE THERE	Jackson Five	Tamla Motown	14
-	31	HOT LOVE	T. Rex	Fly	1
31	32	MY WAY	Frank Sinatra	Reprise	41
37	33	STONEY END	Barbra Streisand	CBS	3
24	34	BLACK SKIN BLUE EYED BOYS	Equals	President	8
15	35	YOU'RE READY NOW	Frankie Valli	Philips	9
-	36	AIN'T NOTHING BUT A HOUSEPARTY	Showstoppers	Beacon	2
-	37	WALKIN'	CCS	Rak	1
36	38	SONG OF MY LIFE	Petula Clark	Pye	3
-	39	STRANGE KIND OF WOMAN	Deep Purple	Harvest	1
23	40	CRACKLIN' ROSIE	Neil Diamond	Uni	16

WEEK ENDING 6 MARCH 1971

LW	TW	Title	Artist	Label	Wks
7	[1]	BABY JUMP	Mungo Jerry	Dawn	4
1	2	MY SWEET LORD	George Harrison	Apple	7
2	3	PUSHBIKE SONG	Mixtures	Polydor	8
24	4	ANOTHER DAY	Paul McCartney	Apple	2
4	5	IT'S IMPOSSIBLE	Perry Como	RCA	6
3	6	RESURRECTION SHUFFLE	Ashton, Gardner and Dyke	Capitol	7
6	7	AMAZING GRACE	Judy Collins	Elektra	11
5	8	STONED LOVE	Supremes	Tamla Motown	7
11	9	SWEET CAROLINE	Neil Diamond	Uni	3
23	10	ROSE GARDEN	Lynn Anderson	CBS	3
15	[11]	FORGET ME NOT	Martha Reeves & the Vandellas	Tamla Motown	4
22	12	TOMORROW NIGHT	Atomic Rooster	B & C	5
8	13	YOUR SONG	Elton John	DJM	7
14	14	RUPERT	Jackie Lee	Pye	9
13	15	(COME 'ROUND HERE) I'M THE ONE YOU NEED	Smokey Robinson and the Miracles	Tamla Motown	6
10	16	NO MATTER WHAT	Badfinger	Apple	9
31	17	HOT LOVE	T. Rex	Fly	2
12	18	GRANDAD	Clive Dunn	Columbia	13
20	19	EVERYTHING'S TUESDAY	Chairmen Of The Board	Invictus	3
9	20	CANDIDA	Dawn	Bell	8
28	21	WHO PUT THE LIGHTS OUT	Dana	Rex	3
19	22	CHESTNUT MARE	Byrds	CBS	4
18	23	I THINK I LOVE YOU	Partridge Family	Bell	4
17	24	APEMAN	Kinks	Pye	12
16	25	SHE'S A LADY	Tom Jones	Decca	7
-	26	I WILL DRINK THE WINE	Frank Sinatra	Reprise	1
29	27	ROSE GARDEN	New World	RAK	2
21	28	IT'S THE SAME OLD SONG	Weathermen	B & C	7
39	29	STRANGE KIND OF WOMAN	Deep Purple	Harvest	2
25	30	SUNNY HONEY GIRL	Cliff Richard	Columbia	7
32	31	MY WAY	Frank Sinatra	Reprise	42
38	[32]	SONG OF MY LIFE	Petula Clark	Pye	4
33	33	STONEY END	Barbra Streisand	CBS	4
30	34	I'LL BE THERE	Jackson Five	Tamla Motown	15
-	35	YOU DON'T HAVE TO SAY YOU LOVE ME	Elvis Presley	RCA	8
-	36	YOU COULD'VE BEEN A LADY	Hot Chocolate	RAK	1
27	37	LAS VEGAS	Tony Christie	MCA	8
26	38	RIDE A WHITE SWAN	T. Rex	Fly	18
37	39	WALKIN'	CCS	Rak	2
35	40	YOU'RE READY NOW	Frankie Valli	Philips	10

WEEK ENDING 13 MARCH 1971

LW	TW	Title	Artist	Label	Wks
1	[1]	BABY JUMP	Mungo Jerry	Dawn	5
4	[2]	ANOTHER DAY	Paul McCartney	Apple	3
2	3	MY SWEET LORD	George Harrison	Apple	8
10	4	ROSE GARDEN	Lynn Anderson	CBS	4
5	5	IT'S IMPOSSIBLE	Perry Como	RCA	7
3	6	PUSHBIKE SONG	Mixtures	Polydor	9
17	7	HOT LOVE	T. Rex	Fly	3
9	[8]	SWEET CAROLINE	Neil Diamond	Uni	4
7	9	AMAZING GRACE	Judy Collins	Elektra	12
8	10	STONED LOVE	Supremes	Tamla Motown	8
6	11	RESURRECTION SHUFFLE	Ashton, Gardner and Dyke	Capitol	8
19	[12]	EVERYTHING'S TUESDAY	Chairmen Of The Board	Invictus	4
12	13	TOMORROW NIGHT	Atomic Rooster	B & C	6
21	[14]	WHO PUT THE LIGHTS OUT	Dana	Rex	4
11	15	FORGET ME NOT	Martha Reeves & the Vandellas	Tamla Motown	5
18	16	GRANDAD	Clive Dunn	Columbia	14
27	17	ROSE GARDEN	New World	RAK	3

In these weeks ■ Another Beatle begins a solo career as Paul McCartney's *Another Day* hits the chart (27.02.71) ■ A very religious Top 10, with *My Sweet Lord* and *Amazing Grace*, not to mention *Resurrection Shuffle* (06.03.71) ■ Frank Sinatra's follow-up to *My Way* was written by British hitmaker Paul Ryan - *I Will Drink The Wine* (06.03.71) ■

LW	TW	Title / Artist	Label	Wks
15	18	(COME 'ROUND HERE) I'M THE ONE YOU NEED Smokey Robinson and the Miracles	*Tamla Motown*	7
16	19	NO MATTER WHAT Badfinger	*Apple*	10
13	20	YOUR SONG Elton John	*DJM*	8
20	21	CANDIDA Dawn	*Bell*	9
29	22	STRANGE KIND OF WOMAN Deep Purple	*Harvest*	3
22	23	CHESTNUT MARE Byrds	*CBS*	5
23	24	I THINK I LOVE YOU Partridge Family	*Bell*	5
26	25	I WILL DRINK THE WINE Frank Sinatra	*Reprise*	2
28	26	IT'S THE SAME OLD SONG Weathermen	*B & C*	8
14	27	RUPERT Jackie Lee	*Pye*	10
31	28	MY WAY Frank Sinatra	*Reprise*	43
24	29	APEMAN Kinks	*Pye*	13
25	30	SHE'S A LADY Tom Jones	*Decca*	8
33	31	STONEY END Barbra Streisand	*CBS*	5
39	32	WALKIN' CCS	*Rak*	3
30	33	SUNNY HONEY GIRL Cliff Richard	*Columbia*	8
-	34	BRIDGET THE MIDGET Ray Stevens	*CBS*	1
-	35	APACHE DROPOUT Edgar Broughton Band	*Harvest*	3
32	36	SONG OF MY LIFE Petula Clark	*Pye*	5
-	37	LOVE THE ONE YOU'RE WITH Stephen Stills ●	*Atlantic*	1
-	38	FUNNY FUNNY Sweet	*RCA*	1
35	39	YOU DON'T HAVE TO SAY YOU LOVE ME Elvis Presley	*RCA*	9
36	40	YOU COULD'VE BEEN A LADY Hot Chocolate	*RAK*	2

LW	TW	*WEEK ENDING* **20 MARCH 1971**		Wks
7	1	HOT LOVE T. Rex	*Fly*	4
1	2	BABY JUMP Mungo Jerry	*Dawn*	6
2	3	ANOTHER DAY Paul McCartney	*Apple*	4
4	4	ROSE GARDEN Lynn Anderson	*CBS*	5
5	5	IT'S IMPOSSIBLE Perry Como	*RCA*	8
3	6	MY SWEET LORD George Harrison	*Apple*	9
6	7	PUSHBIKE SONG Mixtures	*Polydor*	10
22	8	STRANGE KIND OF WOMAN Deep Purple	*Harvest*	4
8	9	SWEET CAROLINE Neil Diamond	*Uni*	5
11	10	RESURRECTION SHUFFLE Ashton, Gardner and Dyke	*Capitol*	9
13	11	TOMORROW NIGHT Atomic Rooster	*B & C*	7
-	12	POWER TO THE PEOPLE John Lennon and the Plastic Ono Band ●	*Apple*	1
9	13	AMAZING GRACE Judy Collins	*Elektra*	13
34	14	BRIDGET THE MIDGET Ray Stevens	*CBS*	2
17	15	ROSE GARDEN New World	*RAK*	4
14	16	WHO PUT THE LIGHTS OUT Dana	*Rex*	5
10	17	STONED LOVE Supremes	*Tamla Motown*	9
12	18	EVERYTHING'S TUESDAY Chairmen Of The Board	*Invictus*	5
25	19	I WILL DRINK THE WINE Frank Sinatra	*Reprise*	3
27	20	RUPERT Jackie Lee	*Pye*	11
32	21	WALKIN' CCS	*Rak*	4
16	22	GRANDAD Clive Dunn	*Columbia*	15
-	23	JACK IN THE BOX Clodagh Rodgers	*RCA*	1
-	24	IF NOT FOR YOU Olivia Newton-John ●	*Pye*	1
15	25	FORGET ME NOT Martha Reeves & the Vandellas	*Tamla Motown*	6
20	26	YOUR SONG Elton John	*DJM*	9
40	27	YOU COULD'VE BEEN A LADY Hot Chocolate	*RAK*	3
23	28	CHESTNUT MARE Byrds	*CBS*	6
-	29	THERE GOES MY EVERYTHING Elvis Presley	*RCA*	1
21	30	CANDIDA Dawn	*Bell*	10
24	31	I THINK I LOVE YOU Partridge Family	*Bell*	6
18	32	(COME 'ROUND HERE) I'M THE ONE YOU NEED Smokey Robinson and the Miracles	*Tamla Motown*	8
38	33	FUNNY FUNNY Sweet	*RCA*	2
36	34	SONG OF MY LIFE Petula Clark	*Pye*	6
19	35	NO MATTER WHAT Badfinger	*Apple*	11
39	36	YOU DON'T HAVE TO SAY YOU LOVE ME Elvis Presley	*RCA*	10
31	37	STONEY END Barbra Streisand	*CBS*	6
37	38	LOVE THE ONE YOU'RE WITH Stephen Stills	*Atlantic*	2
-	39	(WHERE DO I BEGIN) LOVE STORY Andy Williams	*CBS*	1
-	40	HAVE YOU EVER SEEN THE RAIN Creedence Clearwater Revival	*Liberty*	1

April 1971

□ Highest position disc reached ● Act's first ever week on chart

LW	TW	*WEEK ENDING* **27 MARCH 1971**		Wks
1	1	HOT LOVE T. Rex	*Fly*	5
3	2	ANOTHER DAY Paul McCartney	*Apple*	5
4	3	ROSE GARDEN Lynn Anderson	*CBS*	6
2	4	BABY JUMP Mungo Jerry	*Dawn*	7
5	5	IT'S IMPOSSIBLE Perry Como	*RCA*	9
13	6	AMAZING GRACE Judy Collins	*Elektra*	14
6	7	MY SWEET LORD George Harrison	*Apple*	10
9	8	SWEET CAROLINE Neil Diamond	*Uni*	6
14	9	BRIDGET THE MIDGET Ray Stevens	*CBS*	3
23	10	JACK IN THE BOX Clodagh Rodgers	*RCA*	2
7	11	PUSHBIKE SONG Mixtures	*Polydor*	11
12	12	POWER TO THE PEOPLE John Lennon/Plastic Ono Band	*Apple*	2
18	13	EVERYTHING'S TUESDAY Chairmen of the Board	*Invictus*	6
11	14	TOMORROW NIGHT Atomic Rooster	*B & C*	8
15	15	ROSE GARDEN New World	*RAK*	5
10	16	RESURRECTION SHUFFLE Ashton, Gardner and Dyke	*Capitol*	10
16	17	WHO PUT THE LIGHTS OUT Dana	*Rex*	6
8	18	STRANGE KIND OF WOMAN Deep Purple	*Harvest*	5
29	19	THERE GOES MY EVERYTHING Elvis Presley	*RCA*	2
21	20	WALKIN' CCS	*Rak*	5
17	21	STONED LOVE Supremes	*Tamla Motown*	10
24	22	IF NOT FOR YOU Olivia Newton-John	*Pye*	2
19	23	I WILL DRINK THE WINE Frank Sinatra	*Reprise*	4
27	24	YOU COULD'VE BEEN A LADY Hot Chocolate	*RAK*	4
22	25	GRANDAD Clive Dunn	*Columbia*	16
26	26	YOUR SONG Elton John	*DJM*	10
37	27	STONEY END Barbra Streisand	*CBS*	7
39	28	(WHERE DO I BEGIN) LOVE STORY Andy Williams	*CBS*	2
25	29	FORGET ME NOT Martha Reeves and the Vandellas	*Tamla Motown*	7
33	30	FUNNY FUNNY Sweet	*RCA*	3
-	31	SOMETHING OLD SOMETHING NEW Fantastics	*Bell*	1
28	32	CHESTNUT MARE Byrds	*CBS*	7
-	33	APACHE DROPOUT Edgar Broughton Band	*Harvest*	4
34	34	SONG OF MY LIFE Petula Clark	*Pye*	7
31	35	I THINK I LOVE YOU Partridge Family	*Bell*	7
20	36	RUPERT Jackie Lee	*Pye*	12
-	37	MY WAY Frank Sinatra	*Reprise*	44
35	38	NO MATTER WHAT Badfinger	*Apple*	12
-	39	(WHERE DO I BEGIN) LOVE STORY Shirley Bassey	*United Artists*	1
38	40	LOVE THE ONE YOU'RE WITH Stephen Stills	*Atlantic*	3

LW	TW	*WEEK ENDING* **3 APRIL 1971**		Wks
1	1	HOT LOVE T. Rex	*Fly*	6
9	2	BRIDGET THE MIDGET Ray Stevens	*CBS*	4
3	3	ROSE GARDEN Lynn Anderson	*CBS*	7
2	4	ANOTHER DAY Paul McCartney	*Apple*	6
4	5	BABY JUMP Mungo Jerry	*Dawn*	8
10	6	JACK IN THE BOX Clodagh Rodgers	*RCA*	3
12	7	POWER TO THE PEOPLE John Lennon and the Plastic Ono Band	*Apple*	3
19	8	THERE GOES MY EVERYTHING Elvis Presley	*RCA*	3
5	9	IT'S IMPOSSIBLE Perry Como	*RCA*	10
20	10	WALKIN' CCS	*Rak*	6
18	11	STRANGE KIND OF WOMAN Deep Purple	*Harvest*	6
22	12	IF NOT FOR YOU Olivia Newton-John	*Pye*	3
8	13	SWEET CAROLINE Neil Diamond	*Uni*	7
7	14	MY SWEET LORD George Harrison	*Apple*	11
11	15	PUSHBIKE SONG Mixtures	*Polydor*	12
23	16	I WILL DRINK THE WINE Frank Sinatra	*Reprise*	5
15	17	ROSE GARDEN New World	*RAK*	6
14	18	TOMORROW NIGHT Atomic Rooster	*B & C*	9
6	19	AMAZING GRACE Judy Collins	*Elektra*	15
28	20	(WHERE DO I BEGIN) LOVE STORY Andy Williams	*CBS*	3

■Three solo Beatles in the Top 12, but only two in the Top 10. There was never a time when more than two of the Fab Four were in the Top Ten together (20.03.71) ■ Lynn Anderson's only British hit, *Rose Garden*, begins a four week run at number three (27.03.71) ■ A Bob Dylan song already recorded by George Harrison on his 'All Things Must Pass' triple album gives Olivia Newton-John her first hit, *If Not For You* (20.03.71)■

April 1971

☐ Highest position disc reached ● Act's first ever week on chart

LW	TW	Title	Artist	Label	Wks
-	21	DOUBLE BARREL	Dave and Ansil Collins	*Technique*	1
37	22	MY WAY	Frank Sinatra	*Reprise*	58
17	23	WHO PUT THE LIGHTS OUT	Dana	*Rex*	7
24	24	YOU COULD'VE BEEN A LADY	Hot Chocolate	*RAK*	5
25	25	GRANDAD	Clive Dunn	*Columbia*	17
13	26	EVERYTHING'S TUESDAY	Chairmen Of The Board	*Invictus*	7
21	27	STONED LOVE	Supremes	*Tamla Motown*	11
30	28	FUNNY FUNNY	Sweet	*RCA*	4
16	29	RESURRECTION SHUFFLE	Ashton, Gardner and Dyke	*Capitol*	11
31	30	SOMETHING OLD SOMETHING NEW	Fantastics	*Bell*	2
36	31	RUPERT	Jackie Lee	*Pye*	13
32	32	CHESTNUT MARE	Byrds	*CBS*	8
27	33	STONEY END	Barbra Streisand	*CBS*	8
34	34	SONG OF MY LIFE	Petula Clark	*Pye*	8
35	35	I THINK I LOVE YOU	Partridge Family	*Bell*	8
-	[36]	HAVE YOU EVER SEEN THE RAIN	Creedence Clearwater Revival	*Liberty*	2
-	37	MY LITTLE ONE	Marmalade	*Decca*	1
39	38	(WHERE DO I BEGIN) LOVE STORY	Shirley Bassey	*United Artists*	2
-	[39]	DREAM BABY	Glen Campbell	*Capitol*	1
-	[40]	UNDERNEATH THE BLANKET GO	Gilbert O'Sullivan	*MAM*	1

WEEK ENDING 10 APRIL 1971

LW	TW	Title	Artist	Label	Wks
1	[1]	HOT LOVE	T. Rex	*Fly*	7
2	[2]	BRIDGET THE MIDGET	Ray Stevens	*CBS*	5
3	[3]	ROSE GARDEN	Lynn Anderson	*CBS*	8
6	[4]	JACK IN THE BOX	Clodagh Rodgers	*RCA*	4
4	5	ANOTHER DAY	Paul McCartney	*Apple*	7
8	[6]	THERE GOES MY EVERYTHING	Elvis Presley	*RCA*	4
10	[7]	WALKIN'	CCS	*Rak*	7
7	8	POWER TO THE PEOPLE	John Lennon and the Plastic Ono Band	*Apple*	4
9	9	IT'S IMPOSSIBLE	Perry Como	*RCA*	11
5	10	BABY JUMP	Mungo Jerry	*Dawn*	9
11	[11]	STRANGE KIND OF WOMAN	Deep Purple	*Harvest*	7
12	12	IF NOT FOR YOU	Olivia Newton-John	*Pye*	4
20	13	(WHERE DO I BEGIN) LOVE STORY	Andy Williams	*CBS*	4
14	14	MY SWEET LORD	George Harrison	*Apple*	12
13	15	SWEET CAROLINE	Neil Diamond	*Uni*	8
15	16	PUSHBIKE SONG	Mixtures	*Polydor*	13
21	17	DOUBLE BARREL	Dave and Ansil Collins	*Technique*	2
19	18	AMAZING GRACE	Judy Collins	*Elektra*	16
17	19	ROSE GARDEN	New World	*RAK*	7
28	20	FUNNY FUNNY	Sweet	*RCA*	5
30	21	SOMETHING OLD SOMETHING NEW	Fantastics	*Bell*	3
24	22	YOU COULD'VE BEEN A LADY	Hot Chocolate	*RAK*	6
16	23	I WILL DRINK THE WINE	Frank Sinatra	*Reprise*	6
25	24	GRANDAD	Clive Dunn	*Columbia*	18
22	25	MY WAY	Frank Sinatra	*Reprise*	59
-	26	MOZART SYMPHONY NO. 40	Waldo de los Rios ●	*A & M*	1
18	27	TOMORROW NIGHT	Atomic Rooster	*B & C*	10
-	28	REMEMBER ME	Diana Ross	*Tamla Motown*	1
23	29	WHO PUT THE LIGHTS OUT	Dana	*Rex*	8
26	30	EVERYTHING'S TUESDAY	Chairmen Of The Board	*Invictus*	8
37	31	MY LITTLE ONE	Marmalade	*Decca*	2
-	32	KNOCK THREE TIMES	Dawn	*Bell*	1
29	33	RESURRECTION SHUFFLE	Ashton, Gardner and Dyke	*Capitol*	12
38	34	(WHERE DO I BEGIN) LOVE STORY	Shirley Bassey	*United Artists*	3
-	35	MAMA'S PEARL	Jackson Five	*Tamla Motown*	1
-	36	SILVERY RAIN	Cliff Richard	*Columbia*	1
-	37	MOZART 40	Sovereign Collection ●	*Capitol*	1
-	38	INDIANA WANTS ME	R. Dean Taylor	*Tamla Motown*	1
27	39	STONED LOVE	Supremes	*Tamla Motown*	12
36	40	HAVE YOU EVER SEEN THE RAIN	Creedence Clearwater Revival	*Liberty*	3

WEEK ENDING 17 APRIL 1971

LW	TW	Title	Artist	Label	Wks
1	[1]	HOT LOVE	T. Rex	*Fly*	8
2	[2]	BRIDGET THE MIDGET	Ray Stevens	*CBS*	6
3	[3]	ROSE GARDEN	Lynn Anderson	*CBS*	9
17	4	DOUBLE BARREL	Dave and Ansil Collins	*Technique*	3
4	5	JACK IN THE BOX	Clodagh Rodgers	*RCA*	5
13	6	(WHERE DO I BEGIN) LOVE STORY	Andy Williams	*CBS*	5
6	7	THERE GOES MY EVERYTHING	Elvis Presley	*RCA*	5
12	8	IF NOT FOR YOU	Olivia Newton-John	*Pye*	5
7	9	WALKIN'	CCS	*Rak*	8
8	10	POWER TO THE PEOPLE	John Lennon and the Plastic Ono Band	*Apple*	5
5	11	ANOTHER DAY	Paul McCartney	*Apple*	8
9	12	IT'S IMPOSSIBLE	Perry Como	*RCA*	12
10	13	BABY JUMP	Mungo Jerry	*Dawn*	10
26	14	MOZART SYMPHONY NO. 40	Waldo de los Rios	*A & M*	2
20	15	FUNNY FUNNY	Sweet	*RCA*	6
23	16	I WILL DRINK THE WINE	Frank Sinatra	*Reprise*	7
11	17	STRANGE KIND OF WOMAN	Deep Purple	*Harvest*	8
28	18	REMEMBER ME	Diana Ross	*Tamla Motown*	2
16	19	PUSHBIKE SONG	Mixtures	*Polydor*	14
32	20	KNOCK THREE TIMES	Dawn	*Bell*	2
21	21	SOMETHING OLD SOMETHING NEW	Fantastics	*Bell*	4
15	22	SWEET CAROLINE	Neil Diamond	*Uni*	9
18	23	AMAZING GRACE	Judy Collins	*Elektra*	17
31	24	MY LITTLE ONE	Marmalade	*Decca*	3
14	25	MY SWEET LORD	George Harrison	*Apple*	13
25	26	MY WAY	Frank Sinatra	*Reprise*	60
37	[27]	MOZART 40	Sovereign Collection	*Capitol*	2
24	28	GRANDAD	Clive Dunn	*Columbia*	19
-	29	IT DON'T COME EASY	Ringo Starr ●	*Apple*	1
-	30	ROSETTA	Fame and Price Together ●	*CBS*	1
35	31	MAMA'S PEARL	Jackson Five	*Tamla Motown*	2
27	32	TOMORROW NIGHT	Atomic Rooster	*B & C*	11
36	33	SILVERY RAIN	Cliff Richard	*Columbia*	2
34	34	(WHERE DO I BEGIN) LOVE STORY	Shirley Bassey	*United Artists*	4
19	35	ROSE GARDEN	New World	*RAK*	8
-	36	IT'S A SIN TO TELL A LIE	Gerry Monroe	*Chapter One*	1
38	37	INDIANA WANTS ME	R. Dean Taylor	*Tamla Motown*	2
22	38	YOU COULD'VE BEEN A LADY	Hot Chocolate	*RAK*	7
29	39	WHO PUT THE LIGHTS OUT	Dana	*Rex*	9
30	40	EVERYTHING'S TUESDAY	Chairmen Of The Board	*Invictus*	9

WEEK ENDING 24 APRIL 1971

LW	TW	Title	Artist	Label	Wks
1	[1]	HOT LOVE	T. Rex	*Fly*	9
4	2	DOUBLE BARREL	Dave and Ansil Collins	*Technique*	4
2	3	BRIDGET THE MIDGET	Ray Stevens	*CBS*	7
6	4	(WHERE DO I BEGIN) LOVE STORY	Andy Williams	*CBS*	6
3	5	ROSE GARDEN	Lynn Anderson	*CBS*	10
14	6	MOZART SYMPHONY NO. 40	Waldo de los Rios	*A & M*	3
8	[7]	IF NOT FOR YOU	Olivia Newton-John	*Pye*	6
9	8	WALKIN'	CCS	*Rak*	9
21	9	SOMETHING OLD SOMETHING NEW	Fantastics	*Bell*	5
5	10	JACK IN THE BOX	Clodagh Rodgers	*RCA*	6
7	11	THERE GOES MY EVERYTHING	Elvis Presley	*RCA*	6
29	12	IT DON'T COME EASY	Ringo Starr	*Apple*	2
18	13	REMEMBER ME	Diana Ross	*Tamla Motown*	3
15	14	FUNNY FUNNY	Sweet	*RCA*	7
30	15	ROSETTA	Fame and Price Together	*CBS*	2
10	16	POWER TO THE PEOPLE	John Lennon and the Plastic Ono Band	*Apple*	6
11	17	ANOTHER DAY	Paul McCartney	*Apple*	9
20	18	KNOCK THREE TIMES	Dawn	*Bell*	3
17	19	STRANGE KIND OF WOMAN	Deep Purple	*Harvest*	9
12	20	IT'S IMPOSSIBLE	Perry Como	*RCA*	13
-	21	BROWN SUGAR/BITCH/LET IT ROCK	Rolling Stones	*RS*	1
24	22	MY LITTLE ONE	Marmalade	*Decca*	4
26	23	MY WAY	Frank Sinatra	*Reprise*	61

In these weeks ■ The fourth Beatle has his first hit, Ringo Starr with *It Don't Come Easy*. The Beatles are the first group all of whose members have had separate solo hits (17.04.71) ■ 1971's Eurovision song, *Jack In The Box* by Clodagh Rodgers, outcharted both Elvis Presley and John Lennon (10.04.71) ■ Two versions of Mozart's 40th Symphony hit the chart in the same week (10.04.71)■

May 1971

□ Highest position disc reached ● Act's first ever week on chart

LW	TW	Title	Artist	Label	Wks
23	24	AMAZING GRACE	Judy Collins	Elektra	18
31	25	MAMA'S PEARL	Jackson Five	Tamla Motown	3
25	26	MY SWEET LORD	George Harrison	Apple	14
33	27	SILVERY RAIN	Cliff Richard	Columbia	3
27	28	MOZART 40	Sovereign Collection	Capitol	3
36	29	IT'S A SIN TO TELL A LIE	Gerry Monroe	Chapter One	2
37	30	INDIANA WANTS ME	R. Dean Taylor	Tamla Motown	3
16	31	I WILL DRINK THE WINE	Frank Sinatra	Reprise	8
13	32	BABY JUMP	Mungo Jerry	Dawn	11
19	33	PUSHBIKE SONG	Mixtures	Polydor	15
-	34	JIG-A-JIG	East of Eden ●	Deram	1
38	35	YOU COULD'VE BEEN A LADY	Hot Chocolate	RAK	8
28	36	GRANDAD	Clive Dunn	Columbia	20
-	37	SUGAR SUGAR	Sakkarin ●	RCA	1
35	38	ROSE GARDEN	New World	RAK	9
22	39	SWEET CAROLINE	Neil Diamond	Uni	10
34	40	(WHERE DO I BEGIN) LOVE STORY	Shirley Bassey	United Artists	5

WEEK ENDING 1 MAY 1971

LW	TW	Title	Artist	Label	Wks
2	1	DOUBLE BARREL	Dave and Ansil Collins	Technique	5
1	2	HOT LOVE	T. Rex	Fly	10
18	3	KNOCK THREE TIMES	Dawn	Bell	4
21	4	BROWN SUGAR/BITCH/LET IT ROCK	Rolling Stones	RS	2
6	5	MOZART SYMPHONY NO. 40	Waldo de los Rios	A & M	4
3	6	BRIDGET THE MIDGET	Ray Stevens	CBS	8
12	7	IT DON'T COME EASY	Ringo Starr	Apple	3
4	8	(WHERE DO I BEGIN) LOVE STORY	Andy Williams	CBS	7
13	9	REMEMBER ME	Diana Ross	Tamla Motown	4
8	10	WALKIN'	CCS	Rak	10
7	11	IF NOT FOR YOU	Olivia Newton-John	Pye	7
5	12	ROSE GARDEN	Lynn Anderson	CBS	11
11	13	THERE GOES MY EVERYTHING	Elvis Presley	RCA	7
14	14	FUNNY FUNNY	Sweet	RCA	8
15	15	ROSETTA	Fame and Price Together	CBS	3
9	16	SOMETHING OLD SOMETHING NEW	Fantastics	Bell	6
10	17	JACK IN THE BOX	Clodagh Rodgers	RCA	7
22	18	MY LITTLE ONE	Marmalade	Decca	5
17	19	ANOTHER DAY	Paul McCartney	Apple	10
30	20	INDIANA WANTS ME	R. Dean Taylor	Tamla Motown	4
16	21	POWER TO THE PEOPLE	John Lennon and the Plastic Ono Band	Apple	7
34	22	JIG-A-JIG	East of Eden	Deram	2
24	23	AMAZING GRACE	Judy Collins	Elektra	19
20	24	IT'S IMPOSSIBLE	Perry Como	RCA	14
29	25	IT'S A SIN TO TELL A LIE	Gerry Monroe	Chapter One	3
37	26	SUGAR SUGAR	Sakkarin	RCA	2
-	27	DIDN'T I (BLOW YOUR MIND THIS TIME)	Delfonics ●	Bell	1
25	28	MAMA'S PEARL	Jackson Five	Tamla Motown	4
27	29	SILVERY RAIN	Cliff Richard	Columbia	4
19	30	STRANGE KIND OF WOMAN	Deep Purple	Harvest	10
28	31	MOZART 40	Sovereign Collection	Capitol	4
-	32	UN BANC, UN ARBRE, UNE RUE	Severine ●	Philips	1
23	33	MY WAY	Frank Sinatra	Reprise	62
31	34	I WILL DRINK THE WINE	Frank Sinatra	Reprise	9
33	35	PUSHBIKE SONG	Mixtures	Polydor	16
26	36	MY SWEET LORD	George Harrison	Apple	15
32	37	BABY JUMP	Mungo Jerry	Dawn	12
40	38	(WHERE DO I BEGIN) LOVE STORY	Shirley Bassey	United Artists	6
36	39	GRANDAD	Clive Dunn	Columbia	21
-	40	I'LL GIVE YOU THE EARTH	Keith Michell ●	Spark	1

WEEK ENDING 8 MAY 1971

LW	TW	Title	Artist	Label	Wks
1	1	DOUBLE BARREL	Dave and Ansil Collins	Technique	6
3	2	KNOCK THREE TIMES	Dawn	Bell	5
4	3	BROWN SUGAR/BITCH/LET IT ROCK	Rolling Stones	RS	3
7	4	IT DON'T COME EASY	Ringo Starr	Apple	4
5	5	MOZART SYMPHONY NO. 40	Waldo de los Rios	A & M	5
2	6	HOT LOVE	T. Rex	Fly	11
9	7	REMEMBER ME	Diana Ross	Tamla Motown	5
8	8	(WHERE DO I BEGIN) LOVE STORY	Andy Williams	CBS	8
16	9	SOMETHING OLD SOMETHING NEW	Fantastics	Bell	7
6	10	BRIDGET THE MIDGET	Ray Stevens	CBS	9
15	11	ROSETTA	Fame and Price Together	CBS	4
20	12	INDIANA WANTS ME	R. Dean Taylor	Tamla Motown	5
14	13	FUNNY FUNNY	Sweet	RCA	9
11	14	IF NOT FOR YOU	Olivia Newton-John	Pye	8
22	15	JIG-A-JIG	East of Eden	Deram	3
10	16	WALKIN'	CCS	Rak	11
12	17	ROSE GARDEN	Lynn Anderson	CBS	12
25	18	IT'S A SIN TO TELL A LIE	Gerry Monroe	Chapter One	4
26	19	SUGAR SUGAR	Sakkarin	RCA	3
18	20	MY LITTLE ONE	Marmalade	Decca	6
13	21	THERE GOES MY EVERYTHING	Elvis Presley	RCA	8
27	22	DIDN'T I (BLOW YOUR MIND THIS TIME)	Delfonics	Bell	2
-	23	MALT AND BARLEY BLUES	McGuiness Flint	Capitol	1
-	24	MY BROTHER JAKE	Free	Island	1
-	25	HEAVEN MUST HAVE SENT YOU	Elgins ●	Tamla Motown	1
17	26	JACK IN THE BOX	Clodagh Rodgers	RCA	8
28	27	MAMA'S PEARL	Jackson Five	Tamla Motown	5
32	28	UN BANC, UN ARBRE, UNE RUE	Severine	Philips	2
23	29	AMAZING GRACE	Judy Collins	Elektra	20
29	30	SILVERY RAIN	Cliff Richard	Columbia	5
-	31	RAIN	Bruce Ruffin ●	Trojan	1
24	32	IT'S IMPOSSIBLE	Perry Como	RCA	15
-	33	I AM...I SAID	Neil Diamond	Uni	1
31	34	MOZART 40	Sovereign Collection	Capitol	5
35	35	PUSHBIKE SONG	Mixtures	Polydor	17
21	36	POWER TO THE PEOPLE	John Lennon and the Plastic Ono Band	Apple	8
-	37	JUST SEVEN NUMBERS	Four Tops	Tamla Motown	1
33	38	MY WAY	Frank Sinatra	Reprise	63
30	39	STRANGE KIND OF WOMAN	Deep Purple	Harvest	11
34	40	I WILL DRINK THE WINE	Frank Sinatra	Reprise	10

WEEK ENDING 15 MAY 1971

LW	TW	Title	Artist	Label	Wks
2	1	KNOCK THREE TIMES	Dawn	Bell	6
3	2	BROWN SUGAR/BITCH/LET IT ROCK	Rolling Stones	RS	4
1	3	DOUBLE BARREL	Dave and Ansil Collins	Technique	7
4	4	IT DON'T COME EASY	Ringo Starr	Apple	5
5	5	MOZART SYMPHONY NO. 40	Waldo de los Rios	A & M	6
12	6	INDIANA WANTS ME	R. Dean Taylor	Tamla Motown	6
7	7	REMEMBER ME	Diana Ross	Tamla Motown	6
15	8	JIG-A-JIG	East of Eden	Deram	4
6	9	HOT LOVE	T. Rex	Fly	12
8	10	(WHERE DO I BEGIN) LOVE STORY	Andy Williams	CBS	9
28	11	UN BANC, UN ARBRE, UNE RUE	Severine	Philips	3
19	12	SUGAR SUGAR	Sakkarin	RCA	4
13	13	FUNNY FUNNY	Sweet	RCA	10
25	14	HEAVEN MUST HAVE SENT YOU	Elgins	Tamla Motown	2
20	15	MY LITTLE ONE	Marmalade	Decca	7
23	16	MALT AND BARLEY BLUES	McGuiness Flint	Capitol	2
18	17	IT'S A SIN TO TELL A LIE	Gerry Monroe	Chapter One	5
10	18	BRIDGET THE MIDGET	Ray Stevens	CBS	10
11	19	ROSETTA	Fame and Price Together	CBS	5
24	20	MY BROTHER JAKE	Free	Island	2
16	21	WALKIN'	CCS	Rak	12
17	22	ROSE GARDEN	Lynn Anderson	CBS	13
9	23	SOMETHING OLD SOMETHING NEW	Fantastics	Bell	8
-	24	GOOD OLD ARSENAL	Arsenal 1st Team Squad ●	Pye	1
21	25	THERE GOES MY EVERYTHING	Elvis Presley	RCA	9
22	26	DIDN'T I (BLOW YOUR MIND THIS TIME)	Delfonics	Bell	3
31	27	RAIN	Bruce Ruffin	Trojan	2
33	28	I AM...I SAID	Neil Diamond	Uni	2
14	29	IF NOT FOR YOU	Olivia Newton-John	Pye	9
-	30	I'LL GIVE YOU THE EARTH	Keith Michell	Spark	2
38	31	MY WAY	Frank Sinatra	Reprise	64
32	32	IT'S IMPOSSIBLE	Perry Como	RCA	16
-	33	WE CAN WORK IT OUT	Stevie Wonder	Tamla Motown	1

■The strange reggae semi-instrumental *Double Barrel* by Dave and Ansil Collins hits the very top (01.05.71) ■ The Rolling Stones *Brown Sugar/Bitch/Let It Rock* is the first triple-track single to hit the charts, but it just fails to give the Stones a second hat-trick of number one hits (15.05.71) ■ Sakkarin, peaking at number 12, is really Jonathan King (yet again!) (15.05.71)■

May 1971

□ Highest position disc reached ● Act's first ever week on chart

LW	TW	Title	Artist	Label	Wks
-	34	I DID WHAT I DID FOR MARIA	Tony Christie	MCA	1
26	35	JACK IN THE BOX	Clodagh Rodgers	RCA	9
37	36	JUST SEVEN NUMBERS	Four Tops	Tamla Motown	2
29	37	AMAZING GRACE	Judy Collins	Elektra	21
-	38	I THINK OF YOU	Perry Como	RCA	1
27	39	MAMA'S PEARL	Jackson Five	Tamla Motown	6
30	40	SILVERY RAIN	Cliff Richard	Columbia	6

WEEK ENDING 22 MAY 1971

LW	TW	Title	Artist	Label	Wks
1	1	KNOCK THREE TIMES	Dawn	Bell	7
2	2	BROWN SUGAR/BITCH/LET IT ROCK	Rolling Stones	RS	5
6	3	INDIANA WANTS ME	R. Dean Taylor	Tamla Motown	7
4	4	IT DON'T COME EASY	Ringo Starr	Apple	6
3	5	DOUBLE BARREL	Dave and Ansil Collins	Technique	8
5	6	MOZART SYMPHONY NO. 40	Waldo de los Rios	A & M	7
8	7	JIG-A-JIG	East of Eden	Deram	5
14	8	HEAVEN MUST HAVE SENT YOU	Elgins	Tamla Motown	3
16	9	MALT AND BARLEY BLUES	McGuiness Flint	Capitol	3
7	10	REMEMBER ME	Diana Ross	Tamla Motown	7
20	11	MY BROTHER JAKE	Free	Island	3
11	12	UN BANC, UN ARBRE, UNE RUE	Severine	Philips	4
17	13	IT'S A SIN TO TELL A LIE	Gerry Monroe	Chapter One	6
12	14	SUGAR SUGAR	Sakkarin	RCA	5
10	15	(WHERE DO I BEGIN) LOVE STORY	Andy Williams	CBS	10
24	16	GOOD OLD ARSENAL	Arsenal 1st Team Squad	Pye	2
9	17	HOT LOVE	T. Rex	Fly	13
28	18	I AM...I SAID	Neil Diamond	Uni	3
19	19	ROSETTA	Fame and Price Together	CBS	6
27	20	RAIN	Bruce Ruffin	Trojan	3
13	21	FUNNY FUNNY	Sweet	RCA	11
15	22	MY LITTLE ONE	Marmalade	Decca	8
-	23	RAGS TO RICHES	Elvis Presley	RCA	1
34	24	I DID WHAT I DID FOR MARIA	Tony Christie	MCA	2
26	25	DIDN'T I (BLOW YOUR MIND THIS TIME)	Delfonics	Bell	4
23	26	SOMETHING OLD SOMETHING NEW	Fantastics	Bell	9
38	27	I THINK OF YOU	Perry Como	RCA	2
22	28	ROSE GARDEN	Lynn Anderson	CBS	14
18	29	BRIDGET THE MIDGET	Ray Stevens	CBS	11
37	30	AMAZING GRACE	Judy Collins	Elektra	22
33	31	WE CAN WORK IT OUT	Stevie Wonder	Tamla Motown	2
25	32	THERE GOES MY EVERYTHING	Elvis Presley	RCA	10
29	33	IF NOT FOR YOU	Olivia Newton-John	Pye	10
-	34	OH YOU PRETTY THING	Peter Noone ●	RAK	1
-	35	PAY TO THE PIPER	Chairmen Of The Board	Invictus	1
21	36	WALKIN'	CCS	Rak	13
36	37	JUST SEVEN NUMBERS	Four Tops	Tamla Motown	3
32	38	IT'S IMPOSSIBLE	Perry Como	RCA	17
-	39	JUST MY IMAGINATION	Temptations	Tamla Motown	1
30	40	I'LL GIVE YOU THE EARTH	Keith Michell	Spark	3

WEEK ENDING 29 MAY 1971

LW	TW	Title	Artist	Label	Wks
1	1	KNOCK THREE TIMES	Dawn	Bell	8
2	2	BROWN SUGAR/BITCH/LET IT ROCK	Rolling Stones	RS	6
3	3	INDIANA WANTS ME	R. Dean Taylor	Tamla Motown	8
11	4	MY BROTHER JAKE	Free	Island	4
9	5	MALT AND BARLEY BLUES	McGuiness Flint	Capitol	4
8	6	HEAVEN MUST HAVE SENT YOU	Elgins	Tamla Motown	4
7	7	JIG-A-JIG	East of Eden	Deram	6
4	8	IT DON'T COME EASY	Ringo Starr	Apple	7
12	9	UN BANC, UN ARBRE, UNE RUE	Severine	Philips	5
5	10	DOUBLE BARREL	Dave and Ansil Collins	Technique	9
18	11	I AM...I SAID	Neil Diamond	Uni	4
6	12	MOZART SYMPHONY NO. 40	Waldo de los Rios	A & M	8
10	13	REMEMBER ME	Diana Ross	Tamla Motown	8
14	14	SUGAR SUGAR	Sakkarin	RCA	6
13	15	IT'S A SIN TO TELL A LIE	Gerry Monroe	Chapter One	7
23	16	RAGS TO RICHES	Elvis Presley	RCA	2
24	17	I DID WHAT I DID FOR MARIA	Tony Christie	MCA	3
27	18	I THINK OF YOU	Perry Como	RCA	3
20	19	RAIN	Bruce Ruffin	Trojan	4
34	20	OH YOU PRETTY THING	Peter Noone	RAK	2
17	21	HOT LOVE	T. Rex	Fly	14
15	22	(WHERE DO I BEGIN) LOVE STORY	Andy Williams	CBS	11
22	23	MY LITTLE ONE	Marmalade	Decca	9
16	24	GOOD OLD ARSENAL	Arsenal 1st Team Squad	Pye	3
25	25	DIDN'T I (BLOW YOUR MIND THIS TIME)	Delfonics	Bell	5
-	26	I'M GONNA RUN AWAY FROM YOU	Tami Lynn ●	Mojo	1
31	27	WE CAN WORK IT OUT	Stevie Wonder	Tamla Motown	3
26	28	SOMETHING OLD SOMETHING NEW	Fantastics	Bell	10
-	29	HEY WILLY	Hollies	Parlophone	1
-	30	LADY ROSE	Mungo Jerry	Dawn	1
-	31	BANNER MAN	Blue Mink	Regal Zonophone	1
28	32	ROSE GARDEN	Lynn Anderson	CBS	15
39	33	JUST MY IMAGINATION	Temptations	Tamla Motown	2
35	34	PAY TO THE PIPER	Chairmen Of The Board	Invictus	2
38	35	IT'S IMPOSSIBLE	Perry Como	RCA	18
19	36	ROSETTA	Fame and Price Together	CBS	7
21	37	FUNNY FUNNY	Sweet	RCA	12
29	38	BRIDGET THE MIDGET	Ray Stevens	CBS	12
33	39	IF NOT FOR YOU	Olivia Newton-John	Pye	11
40	40	I'LL GIVE YOU THE EARTH	Keith Michell	Spark	4

WEEK ENDING 5 JUNE 1971

LW	TW	Title	Artist	Label	Wks
1	1	KNOCK THREE TIMES	Dawn	Bell	9
3	2	INDIANA WANTS ME	R. Dean Taylor	Tamla Motown	9
6	3	HEAVEN MUST HAVE SENT YOU	Elgins	Tamla Motown	5
4	4	MY BROTHER JAKE	Free	Island	5
2	5	BROWN SUGAR/BITCH/LET IT ROCK	Rolling Stones	RS	7
11	6	I AM...I SAID	Neil Diamond	Uni	5
5	7	MALT AND BARLEY BLUES	McGuiness Flint	Capitol	5
17	8	I DID WHAT I DID FOR MARIA	Tony Christie	MCA	4
16	9	RAGS TO RICHES	Elvis Presley	RCA	3
7	10	JIG-A-JIG	East of Eden	Deram	7
26	11	I'M GONNA RUN AWAY FROM YOU	Tami Lynn	Mojo	2
12	12	MOZART SYMPHONY NO. 40	Waldo de los Rios	A & M	9
30	13	LADY ROSE	Mungo Jerry	Dawn	2
18	14	I THINK OF YOU	Perry Como	RCA	4
8	15	IT DON'T COME EASY	Ringo Starr	Apple	8
31	16	BANNER MAN	Blue Mink	Regal Zonophone	2
10	17	DOUBLE BARREL	Dave and Ansil Collins	Technique	10
15	18	IT'S A SIN TO TELL A LIE	Gerry Monroe	Chapter One	8
20	19	OH YOU PRETTY THING	Peter Noone	RAK	3
9	20	UN BANC, UN ARBRE, UNE RUE	Severine	Philips	6
19	21	RAIN	Bruce Ruffin	Trojan	5
-	22	HE'S GONNA STEP ON YOU AGAIN	John Kongos ●	Fly	1
14	23	SUGAR SUGAR	Sakkarin	RCA	7
13	24	REMEMBER ME	Diana Ross	Tamla Motown	9
29	25	HEY WILLY	Hollies	Parlophone	2
24	26	GOOD OLD ARSENAL	Arsenal 1st Team Squad	Pye	4
33	27	JUST MY IMAGINATION	Temptations	Tamla Motown	3
22	28	(WHERE DO I BEGIN) LOVE STORY	Andy Williams	CBS	12
-	29	LAZY BONES	Jonathan King	Decca	1
32	30	ROSE GARDEN	Lynn Anderson	CBS	16
21	31	HOT LOVE	T. Rex	Fly	15
27	32	WE CAN WORK IT OUT	Stevie Wonder	Tamla Motown	4
25	33	DIDN'T I (BLOW YOUR MIND THIS TIME)	Delfonics	Bell	6
-	34	JOY TO THE WORLD	Three Dog Night	Probe	1
34	35	PAY TO THE PIPER	Chairmen Of The Board	Invictus	3
-	36	CHIRPY CHIRPY CHEEP CHEEP	Middle Of The Road ●	RCA	1
35	37	IT'S IMPOSSIBLE	Perry Como	RCA	19
-	38	AMAZING GRACE	Judy Collins	Elektra	23
-	39	MY WAY	Frank Sinatra	Reprise	65
-	40	I DON'T BLAME YOU AT ALL	Smokey Robinson & Miracles	Tamla Motown	1

WEEK ENDING 12 JUNE 1971

LW	TW	Title	Artist	Label	Wks
1	1	KNOCK THREE TIMES	Dawn	Bell	10
8	2	I DID WHAT I DID FOR MARIA	Tony Christie	MCA	5
2	3	INDIANA WANTS ME	R. Dean Taylor	Tamla Motown	10

In these weeks ■ After 20 hits as the leader of Herman's Hermits, Peter Noone hits the chart with his only solo hit *Oh You Pretty Thing* (22.05.71) ■ A multi-national look to the top of the charts, with hitmakers from UK, America, Canada (R. Dean Taylor), Jamaica (Dave and Ansil Collins), Argentina (Waldo de los Rios) and France (Severine) (29.05.71)■

July 1971

□ Highest position disc reached ● Act's first ever week on chart

LW	TW	Title	Artist	Label	Wks
6	[4]	I AM...I SAID	Neil Diamond	Uni	6
3	5	HEAVEN MUST HAVE SENT YOU	Elgins	*Tamla Motown*	6
4	6	MY BROTHER JAKE	Free	*Island*	6
13	7	LADY ROSE	Mungo Jerry	*Dawn*	3
11	8	I'M GONNA RUN AWAY FROM YOU	Tami Lynn	*Mojo*	3
16	9	BANNER MAN	Blue Mink	*Regal Zonophone*	3
5	10	BROWN SUGAR/BITCH/LET IT ROCK	Rolling Stones	*RS*	8
7	11	MALT AND BARLEY BLUES	McGuiness Flint	*Capitol*	6
19	[12]	OH YOU PRETTY THING	Peter Noone	*RAK*	4
9	13	RAGS TO RICHES	Elvis Presley	*RCA*	4
10	14	JIG-A-JIG	East of Eden	*Deram*	8
22	15	HE'S GONNA STEP ON YOU AGAIN	John Kongos	*Fly*	2
36	16	CHIRPY CHIRPY CHEEP CHEEP	Middle Of The Road	*RCA*	2
14	17	I THINK OF YOU	Perry Como	*RCA*	5
12	18	MOZART SYMPHONY NO. 40	Waldo de los Rios	*A & M*	10
23	19	SUGAR SUGAR	Sakkarin	*RCA*	8
15	20	IT DON'T COME EASY	Ringo Starr	*Apple*	9
21	21	RAIN	Bruce Ruffin	*Trojan*	6
25	[22]	HEY WILLY	Hollies	*Parlophone*	3
20	23	UN BANC, UN ARBRE, UNE RUE	Severine	*Philips*	7
29	24	LAZY BONES	Jonathan King	*Decca*	2
27	25	JUST MY IMAGINATION	Temptations	*Tamla Motown*	4
17	26	DOUBLE BARREL	Dave and Ansil Collins	*Technique*	11
18	27	IT'S A SIN TO TELL A LIE	Gerry Monroe	*Chapter One*	9
24	28	REMEMBER ME	Diana Ross	*Tamla Motown*	10
34	29	JOY TO THE WORLD	Three Dog Night	*Probe*	2
28	30	(WHERE DO I BEGIN) LOVE STORY	Andy Williams	*CBS*	13
32	31	WE CAN WORK IT OUT	Stevie Wonder	*Tamla Motown*	5
40	32	I DON'T BLAME YOU AT ALL	Smokey Robinson & Miracles	*Tamla Motown*	2
-	33	CO-CO	The Sweet	*RCA*	1
31	34	HOT LOVE	T. Rex	*Fly*	16
35	35	PAY TO THE PIPER	Chairmen Of The Board	*Invictus*	4
26	36	GOOD OLD ARSENAL	Arsenal 1st Team Squad	*Pye*	5
30	37	ROSE GARDEN	Lynn Anderson	*CBS*	17
37	38	IT'S IMPOSSIBLE	Perry Como	*RCA*	20
-	39	I'LL GIVE YOU THE EARTH	Keith Michell	*Spark*	5
-	40	BRIDGET THE MIDGET	Ray Stevens	*CBS*	13

WEEK ENDING 19 JUNE 1971

LW	TW	Title	Artist	Label	Wks
16	[1]	CHIRPY CHIRPY CHEEP CHEEP	Middle Of The Road	*RCA*	3
1	2	KNOCK THREE TIMES	Dawn	*Bell*	11
2	3	I DID WHAT I DID FOR MARIA	Tony Christie	*MCA*	6
9	4	BANNER MAN	Blue Mink	*Regal Zonophone*	4
8	5	I'M GONNA RUN AWAY FROM YOU	Tami Lynn	*Mojo*	4
7	6	LADY ROSE	Mungo Jerry	*Dawn*	4
15	7	HE'S GONNA STEP ON YOU AGAIN	John Kongos	*Fly*	3
5	8	HEAVEN MUST HAVE SENT YOU	Elgins	*Tamla Motown*	7
4	9	I AM...I SAID	Neil Diamond	*Uni*	7
3	10	INDIANA WANTS ME	R. Dean Taylor	*Tamla Motown*	11
6	11	MY BROTHER JAKE	Free	*Island*	7
13	12	RAGS TO RICHES	Elvis Presley	*RCA*	5
12	13	OH YOU PRETTY THING	Peter Noone	*RAK*	5
11	14	MALT AND BARLEY BLUES	McGuiness Flint	*Capitol*	7
17	15	I THINK OF YOU	Perry Como	*RCA*	6
10	16	BROWN SUGAR/BITCH/LET IT ROCK	Rolling Stones	*RS*	9
25	17	JUST MY IMAGINATION	Temptations	*Tamla Motown*	5
-	18	DON'T LET IT DIE	Hurricane Smith ●	*Columbia*	1
33	19	CO-CO	The Sweet	*RCA*	2
18	20	MOZART SYMPHONY NO. 40	Waldo de los Rios	*A & M*	11
14	21	JIG-A-JIG	East of Eden	*Deram*	9
32	22	I DON'T BLAME YOU AT ALL	Smokey Robinson & Miracles	*Tamla Motown*	3
24	[23]	LAZY BONES	Jonathan King	*Decca*	3
22	24	HEY WILLY	Hollies	*Parlophone*	4
21	25	RAIN	Bruce Ruffin	*Trojan*	7
29	26	JOY TO THE WORLD	Three Dog Night	*Probe*	3
-	27	PIED PIPER	Bob and Marcia	*Trojan*	1
23	28	UN BANC, UN ARBRE, UNE RUE	Severine	*Philips*	8
27	29	IT'S A SIN TO TELL A LIE	Gerry Monroe	*Chapter One*	10
26	30	DOUBLE BARREL	Dave and Ansil Collins	*Technique*	12
20	31	IT DON'T COME EASY	Ringo Starr	*Apple*	10
-	32	WHEN YOU ARE A KING	White Plains	*Deram*	1
19	33	SUGAR SUGAR	Sakkarin	*RCA*	9
35	34	PAY TO THE PIPER	Chairmen Of The Board	*Invictus*	5
-	35	MY WAY	Frank Sinatra	*Reprise*	66
31	36	WE CAN WORK IT OUT	Stevie Wonder	*Tamla Motown*	6
37	37	ROSE GARDEN	Lynn Anderson	*CBS*	18
-	38	AMAZING GRACE	Judy Collins	*Elektra*	24
28	39	REMEMBER ME	Diana Ross	*Tamla Motown*	11
38	40	IT'S IMPOSSIBLE	Perry Como	*RCA*	21

WEEK ENDING 26 JUNE 1971

LW	TW	Title	Artist	Label	Wks
1	[1]	CHIRPY CHIRPY CHEEP CHEEP	Middle Of The Road	*RCA*	4
3	[2]	I DID WHAT I DID FOR MARIA	Tony Christie	*MCA*	7
4	[3]	BANNER MAN	Blue Mink	*Regal Zonophone*	5
5	[4]	I'M GONNA RUN AWAY FROM YOU	Tami Lynn	*Mojo*	5
6	[5]	LADY ROSE	Mungo Jerry	*Dawn*	5
7	6	HE'S GONNA STEP ON YOU AGAIN	John Kongos	*Fly*	4
2	7	KNOCK THREE TIMES	Dawn	*Bell*	12
18	8	DON'T LET IT DIE	Hurricane Smith	*Columbia*	2
19	9	CO-CO	The Sweet	*RCA*	3
9	10	I AM...I SAID	Neil Diamond	*Uni*	8
8	11	HEAVEN MUST HAVE SENT YOU	Elgins	*Tamla Motown*	8
13	12	OH YOU PRETTY THING	Peter Noone	*RAK*	6
17	13	JUST MY IMAGINATION	Temptations	*Tamla Motown*	6
12	14	RAGS TO RICHES	Elvis Presley	*RCA*	6
10	15	INDIANA WANTS ME	R. Dean Taylor	*Tamla Motown*	12
22	16	I DON'T BLAME YOU AT ALL	Smokey Robinson & Miracles	*Tamla Motown*	4
11	17	MY BROTHER JAKE	Free	*Island*	8
16	18	BROWN SUGAR/BITCH/LET IT ROCK	Rolling Stones	*RS*	10
14	19	MALT AND BARLEY BLUES	McGuiness Flint	*Capitol*	8
15	20	I THINK OF YOU	Perry Como	*RCA*	7
27	21	PIED PIPER	Bob and Marcia	*Trojan*	2
20	22	MOZART SYMPHONY NO. 40	Waldo de los Rios	*A & M*	12
23	[23]	LAZY BONES	Jonathan King	*Decca*	4
26	[24]	JOY TO THE WORLD	Three Dog Night	*Probe*	4
21	25	JIG-A-JIG	East of Eden	*Deram*	10
32	26	WHEN YOU ARE A KING	White Plains	*Deram*	2
30	27	DOUBLE BARREL	Dave and Ansil Collins	*Technique*	13
24	28	HEY WILLY	Hollies	*Parlophone*	5
29	29	IT'S A SIN TO TELL A LIE	Gerry Monroe	*Chapter One*	11
-	30	BLACK AND WHITE	Greyhound ●	*Trojan*	1
-	31	(AND THE) PICTURES IN THE SKY	Medicine Head ●	*Dandelion*	1
-	32	ME AND YOU AND A DOG NAMED BOO	Lobo ●	*Philips*	1
-	33	RIVER DEEP, MOUNTAIN HIGH	Supremes and the Four Tops ●	*Tamla Motown*	1
33	34	SUGAR SUGAR	Sakkarin	*RCA*	10
28	35	UN BANC, UN ARBRE, UNE RUE	Severine	*Philips*	9
35	36	MY WAY	Frank Sinatra	*Reprise*	67
-	37	(WHERE DO I BEGIN) LOVE STORY	Andy Williams	*CBS*	14
37	38	ROSE GARDEN	Lynn Anderson	*CBS*	19
-	39	IF YOU COULD READ MY MIND	Gordon Lightfoot ●	*Reprise*	1
-	40	LEAP UP AND DOWN (WAVE YOUR KNICKERS IN THE AIR)	St Cecilia ●	*Polydor*	1

WEEK ENDING 3 JULY 1971

LW	TW	Title	Artist	Label	Wks
1	[1]	CHIRPY CHIRPY CHEEP CHEEP	Middle Of The Road	*RCA*	5
8	[2]	DON'T LET IT DIE	Hurricane Smith	*Columbia*	3
3	[3]	BANNER MAN	Blue Mink	*Regal Zonophone*	6
6	[4]	HE'S GONNA STEP ON YOU AGAIN	John Kongos	*Fly*	5
9	5	CO-CO	The Sweet	*RCA*	4
2	6	I DID WHAT I DID FOR MARIA	Tony Christie	*MCA*	8
4	7	I'M GONNA RUN AWAY FROM YOU	Tami Lynn	*Mojo*	6
5	8	LADY ROSE	Mungo Jerry	*Dawn*	6
7	9	KNOCK THREE TIMES	Dawn	*Bell*	13
13	10	JUST MY IMAGINATION	Temptations	*Tamla Motown*	7
16	[11]	I DON'T BLAME YOU AT ALL	Smokey Robinson & Miracles	*Tamla Motown*	5

■Norman 'Hurricane' Smith, an EMI engineer with a strange voice and a knack for catchy, simple songs, creates his first and biggest chart hit (19.06.71) ■ *Chirpy Chirpy Cheep Cheep* climbs from 16 to 1, the biggest leap since Dave Edmunds made the same move seven months earlier (19.06.71) ■ Six chart debutants in a week, not a record, but still a large collection of new names (26.06.71)■

July 1971

☐ Highest position disc reached ● Act's first ever week on chart

LW	TW	Title	Artist	Label	Wks
21	12	PIED PIPER	Bob and Marcia	Trojan	3
12	13	OH YOU PRETTY THING	Peter Noone	RAK	7
10	14	I AM...I SAID	Neil Diamond	Uni	9
11	15	HEAVEN MUST HAVE SENT YOU	Elgins	Tamla Motown	9
26	16	WHEN YOU ARE A KING	White Plains	Deram	3
-	17	MONKEY SPANNER	Dave and Ansil Collins	Technique	1
32	18	ME AND YOU AND A DOG NAMED BOO	Lobo	Philips	2
30	19	BLACK AND WHITE	Greyhound	Trojan	2
14	20	RAGS TO RICHES	Elvis Presley	RCA	7
15	21	INDIANA WANTS ME	R. Dean Taylor	Tamla Motown	13
33	22	RIVER DEEP, MOUNTAIN HIGH	Supremes/Four Tops	Tamla Motown	2
31	23	(AND THE) PICTURES IN THE SKY	Medicine Head	Dandelion	2
20	24	I THINK OF YOU	Perry Como	RCA	8
24	25	JOY TO THE WORLD	Three Dog Night	Probe	5
-	26	TOM-TOM TURNAROUND	New World	RAK	1
17	27	MY BROTHER JAKE	Free	Island	9
22	28	MOZART SYMPHONY NO. 40	Waldo de los Rios	A & M	13
40	29	LEAP UP AND DOWN (WAVE YOUR KNICKERS IN THE AIR)	St Cecilia	Polydor	2
23	30	LAZY BONES	Jonathan King	Decca	5
18	31	BROWN SUGAR/BITCH/LET IT ROCK	Rolling Stones	RS	11
-	32	GET DOWN AND GET WITH IT	Slade ●	Polydor	1
28	33	HEY WILLY	Hollies	Parlophone	6
19	34	MALT AND BARLEY BLUES	McGuiness Flint	Capitol	9
25	35	JIG-A-JIG	East of Eden	Deram	11
36	36	MY WAY	Frank Sinatra	Reprise	68
39	37	IF YOU COULD READ MY MIND	Gordon Lightfoot	Reprise	2
34	38	SUGAR SUGAR	Sakkarin	RCA	11
37	39	(WHERE DO I BEGIN) LOVE STORY	Andy Williams	CBS	15
-	40	I LOVE YOU BECAUSE/HE'LL HAVE TO GO/ MOONLIGHT & ROSES	Jim Reeves	RCA	1

WEEK ENDING 10 JULY 1971

LW	TW	Title	Artist	Label	Wks
1	1	CHIRPY CHIRPY CHEEP CHEEP	Middle Of The Road	RCA	6
5	2	CO-CO	Sweet	RCA	5
2	3	DON'T LET IT DIE	Hurricane Smith	Columbia	4
3	4	BANNER MAN	Blue Mink	Regal Zonophone	7
4	5	HE'S GONNA STEP ON YOU AGAIN	John Kongos	Fly	6
7	6	I'M GONNA RUN AWAY FROM YOU	Tami Lynn	Mojo	7
6	7	I DID WHAT I DID FOR MARIA	Tony Christie	MCA	9
10	8	JUST MY IMAGINATION	Temptations	Tamla Motown	8
19	9	BLACK AND WHITE	Greyhound	Trojan	3
8	10	LADY ROSE	Mungo Jerry	Dawn	7
12	11	PIED PIPER	Bob and Marcia	Trojan	4
11	12	I DON'T BLAME YOU AT ALL	Smokey Robinson & Miracles	Tamla Motown	6
16	13	WHEN YOU ARE A KING	White Plains	Deram	4
18	14	ME AND YOU AND A DOG NAMED BOO	Lobo	Philips	3
9	15	KNOCK THREE TIMES	Dawn	Bell	14
22	16	RIVER DEEP, MOUNTAIN HIGH	Supremes/Four Tops	Tamla Motown	3
17	17	MONKEY SPANNER	Dave and Ansil Collins	Technique	2
26	18	TOM-TOM TURNAROUND	New World	RAK	2
14	19	I AM...I SAID	Neil Diamond	Uni	10
15	20	HEAVEN MUST HAVE SENT YOU	Elgins	Tamla Motown	10
-	21	GET IT ON	T. Rex	Fly	1
23	22	(AND THE) PICTURES IN THE SKY	Medicine Head	Dandelion	3
29	23	LEAP UP AND DOWN (WAVE YOUR KNICKERS IN THE AIR)	St Cecilia	Polydor	3
-	24	STREET FIGHTING MAN	Rolling Stones	Decca	1
-	25	TONIGHT	Move	Harvest	1
13	26	OH YOU PRETTY THING	Peter Noone	RAK	8
25	27	JOY TO THE WORLD	Three Dog Night	Probe	6
20	28	RAGS TO RICHES	Elvis Presley	RCA	8
-	29	LA-LA MEANS I LOVE YOU	Delfonics	Bell	1
24	30	I THINK OF YOU	Perry Como	RCA	9
28	31	MOZART SYMPHONY NO. 40	Waldo de los Rios	A & M	14
32	32	GET DOWN AND GET WITH IT	Slade	Polydor	2
37	33	IF YOU COULD READ MY MIND	Gordon Lightfoot	Reprise	3
40	34	I LOVE YOU BECAUSE/HE'LL HAVE TO GO/ MOONLIGHT & ROSES	Jim Reeves	RCA	2
21	35	INDIANA WANTS ME	R. Dean Taylor	Tamla Motown	14
-	36	DEVIL'S ANSWER	Atomic Rooster	B&C	1
30	37	LAZY BONES	Jonathan King	Decca	6
31	38	BROWN SUGAR/BITCH/LET IT ROCK	Rolling Stones	RS	12
36	39	MY WAY	Frank Sinatra	Reprise	69
27	40	MY BROTHER JAKE	Free	Island	10

WEEK ENDING 17 JULY 1971

LW	TW	Title	Artist	Label	Wks
1	1	CHIRPY CHIRPY CHEEP CHEEP	Middle Of The Road	RCA	7
2	2	CO-CO	Sweet	RCA	6
3	3	DON'T LET IT DIE	Hurricane Smith	Columbia	5
21	4	GET IT ON	T. Rex	Fly	2
14	5	ME AND YOU AND A DOG NAMED BOO	Lobo	Philips	4
9	6	BLACK AND WHITE	Greyhound	Trojan	4
17	7	MONKEY SPANNER	Dave and Ansil Collins	Technique	3
4	8	BANNER MAN	Blue Mink	Regal Zonophone	8
5	9	HE'S GONNA STEP ON YOU AGAIN	John Kongos	Fly	7
6	10	I'M GONNA RUN AWAY FROM YOU	Tami Lynn	Mojo	8
8	11	JUST MY IMAGINATION	Temptations	Tamla Motown	9
18	12	TOM-TOM TURNAROUND	New World	RAK	3
11	13	PIED PIPER	Bob and Marcia	Trojan	5
13	14	WHEN YOU ARE A KING	White Plains	Deram	5
12	15	I DON'T BLAME YOU AT ALL	Smokey Robinson & Miracles	Tamla Motown	7
16	16	RIVER DEEP, MOUNTAIN HIGH	Supremes/Four Tops	Tamla Motown	4
10	17	LADY ROSE	Mungo Jerry	Dawn	8
7	18	I DID WHAT I DID FOR MARIA	Tony Christie	MCA	10
25	19	TONIGHT	Move	Harvest	2
23	20	LEAP UP AND DOWN (WAVE YOUR KNICKERS IN THE AIR)	St Cecilia	Polydor	4
15	21	KNOCK THREE TIMES	Dawn	Bell	15
22	22	(AND THE) PICTURES IN THE SKY	Medicine Head	Dandelion	4
24	23	STREET FIGHTING MAN	Rolling Stones	Decca	2
29	24	LA-LA MEANS I LOVE YOU	Delfonics	Bell	2
36	25	DEVIL'S ANSWER	Atomic Rooster	B&C	2
-	26	NEVER ENDING SONG OF LOVE	New Seekers	Philips	1
-	27	WON'T GET FOOLED AGAIN	Who	Track	1
28	28	RAGS TO RICHES	Elvis Presley	RCA	9
32	29	GET DOWN AND GET WITH IT	Slade	Polydor	3
33	30	IF YOU COULD READ MY MIND	Gordon Lightfoot	Reprise	4
20	31	HEAVEN MUST HAVE SENT YOU	Elgins	Tamla Motown	11
-	32	GIRLS ARE OUT TO GET YOU	Fascinations ●	Mojo	1
-	33	HELLO BUDDY	Tremeloes	CBS	1
30	34	I THINK OF YOU	Perry Como	RCA	10
34	35	I LOVE YOU BECAUSE/HE'LL HAVE TO GO/ MOONLIGHT & ROSES	Jim Reeves	RCA	3
-	36	IN MY OWN TIME	Family	Reprise	1
-	37	WATCHING THE RIVER FLOW	Bob Dylan	CBS	1
27	38	JOY TO THE WORLD	Three Dog Night	Probe	7
26	39	OH YOU PRETTY THING	Peter Noone	RAK	9
39	40	MY WAY	Frank Sinatra	Reprise	70

WEEK ENDING 24 JULY 1971

LW	TW	Title	Artist	Label	Wks
4	1	GET IT ON	T. Rex	Fly	3
1	2	CHIRPY CHIRPY CHEEP CHEEP	Middle Of The Road	RCA	8
2	3	CO-CO	Sweet	RCA	7
5	4	ME AND YOU AND A DOG NAMED BOO	Lobo	Philips	5
3	5	DON'T LET IT DIE	Hurricane Smith	Columbia	6
6	6	BLACK AND WHITE	Greyhound	Trojan	5
7	7	MONKEY SPANNER	Dave and Ansil Collins	Technique	4
12	8	TOM-TOM TURNAROUND	New World	RAK	4
8	9	BANNER MAN	Blue Mink	Regal Zonophone	9
11	10	JUST MY IMAGINATION	Temptations	Tamla Motown	10
16	11	RIVER DEEP, MOUNTAIN HIGH	Supremes/Four Tops	Tamla Motown	5
19	12	TONIGHT	Move	Harvest	3
9	13	HE'S GONNA STEP ON YOU AGAIN	John Kongos	Fly	8
7	14	I'M GONNA RUN AWAY FROM YOU	Tami Lynn	Mojo	9

In these weeks ■ Sweet enjoy the first of five number two hits. *Co-Co* was at that time the biggest hit written by Nicky Chinn and Mike Chapman (10.07.71) ■ Skinhead rockers Slade begin one of the most spectacular of all chart careers very quietly (03.03.71) ■ *Get It On* proves to be T. Rex's only big American hit, after it has been renamed *Bang A Gong* (24.07.71)■

26 15 NEVER ENDING SONG OF LOVE New Seekers .... *Philips* 2
14 16 WHEN YOU ARE A KING White Plains .... *Deram* 6
13 17 PIED PIPER Bob and Marcia .... *Trojan* 6
18 18 I DID WHAT I DID FOR MARIA Tony Christie .... *MCA* 11
15 19 I DON'T BLAME YOU AT ALL Smokey Robinson & Miracles .... *Tamla Motown* 8
25 20 DEVIL'S ANSWER Atomic Rooster .... *B&C* 3
23 21 STREET FIGHTING MAN Rolling Stones .... *Decca* 3
27 22 WON'T GET FOOLED AGAIN Who .... *Track* 2
20 23 LEAP UP AND DOWN (WAVE YOUR KNICKERS IN THE AIR) St Cecilia .... *Polydor* 5
24 24 LA-LA MEANS I LOVE YOU Delfonics .... *Bell* 3
29 25 GET DOWN AND GET WITH IT Slade .... *Polydor* 4
21 26 KNOCK THREE TIMES Dawn .... *Bell* 16
22 27 (AND THE) PICTURES IN THE SKY Medicine Head ... *Dandelion* 5
17 28 LADY ROSE Mungo Jerry .... *Dawn* 9
- 29 HEARTBREAK HOTEL/HOUND DOG Elvis Presley .... *RCA* 1
36 30 IN MY OWN TIME Family .... *Reprise* 2
37 31 WATCHING THE RIVER FLOW Bob Dylan .... *CBS* 2
33 32 HELLO BUDDY Tremeloes .... *CBS* 2
32 33 GIRLS ARE OUT TO GET YOU Fascinations .... *Mojo* 2
30 34 IF YOU COULD READ MY MIND Gordon Lightfoot .... *Reprise* 5
35 35 I LOVE YOU BECAUSE/HE'LL HAVE TO GO/ MOONLIGHT & ROSES Jim Reeves .... *RCA* 4
- 36 WHEN LOVE COMES ROUND AGAIN Ken Dodd .... *Columbia* 1
- 37 MOZART SYMPHONY NO. 40 Waldo de los Rios .... *A & M* 15
40 38 MY WAY Frank Sinatra .... *Reprise* 71
- 39 I AM...I SAID Neil Diamond .... *Uni* 11
31 40 HEAVEN MUST HAVE SENT YOU Elgins .... *Tamla Motown* 12

LW TW *WEEK ENDING* **31 JULY 1971** Wks

1 1 GET IT ON T. Rex .... *Fly* 4
2 2 CHIRPY CHIRPY CHEEP CHEEP Middle Of The Road .... *RCA* 9
3 3 CO-CO Sweet .... *RCA* 8
4 4 ME AND YOU AND A DOG NAMED BOO Lobo .... *Philips* 6
15 5 NEVER ENDING SONG OF LOVE New Seekers .... *Philips* 3
8 6 TOM-TOM TURNAROUND New World .... *RAK* 5
7 7 MONKEY SPANNER Dave and Ansil Collins .... *Technique* 5
6 8 BLACK AND WHITE Greyhound .... *Trojan* 6
5 9 DON'T LET IT DIE Hurricane Smith .... *Columbia* 7
20 10 DEVIL'S ANSWER Atomic Rooster .... *B&C* 4
12 11 TONIGHT Move .... *Harvest* 4
23 12 LEAP UP AND DOWN (WAVE YOUR KNICKERS IN THE AIR) St Cecilia .... *Polydor* 6
11 13 RIVER DEEP, MOUNTAIN HIGH Supremes/Four Tops .... *Tamla Motown* 6
9 14 BANNER MAN Blue Mink .... *Regal Zonophone* 10
10 15 JUST MY IMAGINATION Temptations .... *Tamla Motown* 11
- 16 I'M STILL WAITING Diana Ross .... *Tamla Motown* 1
22 17 WON'T GET FOOLED AGAIN Who .... *Track* 3
13 18 HE'S GONNA STEP ON YOU AGAIN John Kongos .... *Fly* 9
16 19 WHEN YOU ARE A KING White Plains .... *Deram* 7
17 20 PIED PIPER Bob and Marcia .... *Trojan* 7
24 21 LA-LA MEANS I LOVE YOU Delfonics .... *Bell* 4
21 22 STREET FIGHTING MAN Rolling Stones .... *Decca* 4
30 23 IN MY OWN TIME Family .... *Reprise* 3
25 24 GET DOWN AND GET WITH IT Slade .... *Polydor* 5
27 25 (AND THE) PICTURES IN THE SKY Medicine Head ... *Dandelion* 6
14 26 I'M GONNA RUN AWAY FROM YOU Tami Lynn .... *Mojo* 10
18 27 I DID WHAT I DID FOR MARIA Tony Christie .... *MCA* 12
26 28 KNOCK THREE TIMES Dawn .... *Bell* 17
29 29 HEARTBREAK HOTEL/HOUND DOG Elvis Presley .... *RCA* 2
31 30 WATCHING THE RIVER FLOW Bob Dylan .... *CBS* 3
28 31 LADY ROSE Mungo Jerry .... *Dawn* 10
- 32 WHAT ARE YOU DOING SUNDAY Dawn .... *Bell* 1
19 33 I DON'T BLAME YOU AT ALL Smokey Robinson & Miracles .... *Tamla Motown* 9
- 34 NEVER CAN SAY GOODBYE Jackson 5 .... *Tamla Motown* 1
- 35 WE WILL Gilbert O'Sullivan .... *MAM* 1
34 36 IF YOU COULD READ MY MIND Gordon Lightfoot .... *Reprise* 6
33 37 GIRLS ARE OUT TO GET YOU Fascinations .... *Mojo* 3
- 38 SWEET HITCH-HIKER Creedence Clearwater Revival .... *United Artists* 1
- 39 SOLDIER BLUE Buffy Sainte-Marie ● .... *RCA* 1

August 1971

□ Highest position disc reached ● Act's first ever week on chart

35 40 I LOVE YOU BECAUSE/HE'LL HAVE TO GO/ MOONLIGHT & ROSES Jim Reeves .... *RCA* 5

LW TW *WEEK ENDING* **7 AUGUST 1971** Wks

1 1 GET IT ON T. Rex .... *Fly* 5
5 2 NEVER ENDING SONG OF LOVE New Seekers .... *Philips* 4
2 3 CHIRPY CHIRPY CHEEP CHEEP Middle Of The Road .... *RCA* 10
10 4 DEVIL'S ANSWER Atomic Rooster .... *B&C* 5
3 5 CO-CO Sweet .... *RCA* 9
4 6 ME AND YOU AND A DOG NAMED BOO Lobo .... *Philips* 7
6 7 TOM-TOM TURNAROUND New World .... *RAK* 6
16 8 I'M STILL WAITING Diana Ross .... *Tamla Motown* 2
7 9 MONKEY SPANNER Dave and Ansil Collins .... *Technique* 6
17 10 WON'T GET FOOLED AGAIN Who .... *Track* 4
23 11 IN MY OWN TIME Family .... *Reprise* 4
8 12 BLACK AND WHITE Greyhound .... *Trojan* 7
29 13 HEARTBREAK HOTEL/HOUND DOG Elvis Presley .... *RCA* 3
11 14 TONIGHT Move .... *Harvest* 5
12 15 LEAP UP AND DOWN (WAVE YOUR KNICKERS IN THE AIR) St Cecilia .... *Polydor* 7
13 16 RIVER DEEP, MOUNTAIN HIGH Supremes and the Four Tops .... *Tamla Motown* 7
24 17 GET DOWN AND GET WITH IT Slade .... *Polydor* 6
9 18 DON'T LET IT DIE Hurricane Smith .... *Columbia* 8
15 19 JUST MY IMAGINATION Temptations .... *Tamla Motown* 12
21 20 LA-LA MEANS I LOVE YOU Delfonics .... *Bell* 5
39 21 SOLDIER BLUE Buffy Sainte-Marie .... *RCA* 2
19 22 WHEN YOU ARE A KING White Plains .... *Deram* 8
14 23 BANNER MAN Blue Mink .... *Regal Zonophone* 11
30 24 WATCHING THE RIVER FLOW Bob Dylan .... *CBS* 4
22 25 STREET FIGHTING MAN Rolling Stones .... *Decca* 5
20 26 PIED PIPER Bob and Marcia .... *Trojan* 8
32 27 WHAT ARE YOU DOING SUNDAY Dawn .... *Bell* 2
- 28 WHEN LOVE COMES ROUND AGAIN Ken Dodd .... *Columbia* 2
18 29 HE'S GONNA STEP ON YOU AGAIN John Kongos .... *Fly* 10
27 30 I DID WHAT I DID FOR MARIA Tony Christie .... *MCA* 13
26 31 I'M GONNA RUN AWAY FROM YOU Tami Lynn .... *Mojo* 11
- 32 MOVE ON UP Curtis Mayfield ● .... *Buddah* 1
34 33 NEVER CAN SAY GOODBYE Jackson 5 .... *Tamla Motown* 2
35 34 WE WILL Gilbert O'Sullivan .... *MAM* 2
25 35 (AND THE) PICTURES IN THE SKY Medicine Head ... *Dandelion* 7
28 36 KNOCK THREE TIMES Dawn .... *Bell* 18
- 37 FLYING MACHINE Cliff Richard .... *Columbia* 1
- 38 BACK STREET LUV Curved Air ● .... *Warner Bros.* 1
- 39 HEY GIRL DON'T BOTHER ME Tams .... *Probe* 1
- 40 THESE THINGS WILL KEEP ME LOVING YOU Velvelettes ● .... *Tamla Motown* 1

LW TW *WEEK ENDING* **14 AUGUST 1971** Wks

1 1 GET IT ON T. Rex .... *Fly* 6
2 2 NEVER ENDING SONG OF LOVE New Seekers .... *Philips* 5
8 3 I'M STILL WAITING Diana Ross .... *Tamla Motown* 3
4 4 DEVIL'S ANSWER Atomic Rooster .... *B&C* 6
11 5 IN MY OWN TIME Family .... *Reprise* 5
6 6 ME AND YOU AND A DOG NAMED BOO Lobo .... *Philips* 8
7 7 TOM-TOM TURNAROUND New World .... *RAK* 7
3 8 CHIRPY CHIRPY CHEEP CHEEP Middle Of The Road .... *RCA* 11
10 9 WON'T GET FOOLED AGAIN Who .... *Track* 5
5 10 CO-CO Sweet .... *RCA* 10
9 11 MONKEY SPANNER Dave and Ansil Collins .... *Technique* 7
15 12 LEAP UP AND DOWN (WAVE YOUR KNICKERS IN THE AIR) St Cecilia .... *Polydor* 8
27 13 WHAT ARE YOU DOING SUNDAY Dawn .... *Bell* 3
13 14 HEARTBREAK HOTEL/HOUND DOG Elvis Presley .... *RCA* 4
12 15 BLACK AND WHITE Greyhound .... *Trojan* 8
14 16 TONIGHT Move .... *Harvest* 6

■Ken Dodd's *When Love Comes Round Again* was the first song to climb to the number 28 position since *I Am ... I Said*, 12 weeks earlier (07.08.71) ■ RCA have learnt how to re-activate back catalogue, with second time around hits for both Jim Reeves and Elvis Presley (24.07.71) ■ St. Cecilia, peaks at number 12, are another Jonathan King creation (14.08.71)■

August 1971

□ Highest position disc reached ● Act's first ever week on chart

LW	TW	Title	Artist	Label	Wks
17	17	GET DOWN AND GET WITH IT	Slade	Polydor	7
21	18	SOLDIER BLUE	Buffy Sainte-Marie	RCA	3
20	[19]	LA-LA MEANS I LOVE YOU	Delfonics	Bell	6
16	20	RIVER DEEP, MOUNTAIN HIGH	Supremes and the Four Tops	Tamla Motown	9
19	21	JUST MY IMAGINATION	Temptations	Tamla Motown	13
32	22	MOVE ON UP	Curtis Mayfield	Buddah	2
18	23	DON'T LET IT DIE	Hurricane Smith	Columbia	9
24	[24]	WATCHING THE RIVER FLOW	Bob Dylan	CBS	5
-	25	LET YOUR YEAH BY YEAH	Pioneers	Trojan	1
39	26	HEY GIRL DON'T BOTHER ME	Tams	Probe	2
-	27	BANGLA DESH	George Harrison	Apple	1
25	28	STREET FIGHTING MAN	Rolling Stones	Decca	6
34	29	WE WILL	Gilbert O'Sullivan	MAM	3
23	30	BANNER MAN	Blue Mink	Regal Zonophone	12
26	31	PIED PIPER	Bob and Marcia	Trojan	9
-	32	IT'S TOO LATE	Carole King	A & M	1
33	[33]	NEVER CAN SAY GOODBYE	Jackson 5	Tamla Motown	3
31	34	I'M GONNA RUN AWAY FROM YOU	Tami Lynn	Mojo	12
22	35	WHEN YOU ARE A KING	White Plains	Deram	9
29	36	HE'S GONNA STEP ON YOU AGAIN	John Kongos	Fly	11
30	37	I DID WHAT I DID FOR MARIA	Tony Christie	MCA	14
28	38	WHEN LOVE COMES ROUND AGAIN	Ken Dodd	Columbia	3
36	39	KNOCK THREE TIMES	Dawn	Bell	19
-	40	SWEET HITCH-HIKER	Creedence Clearwater Revival	United Artists	2

WEEK ENDING 21 AUGUST 1971

LW	TW	Title	Artist	Label	Wks
3	[1]	I'M STILL WAITING	Diana Ross	Tamla Motown	4
2	[2]	NEVER ENDING SONG OF LOVE	New Seekers	Philips	6
1	3	GET IT ON	T. Rex	Fly	7
4	[4]	DEVIL'S ANSWER	Atomic Rooster	B&C	7
5	5	IN MY OWN TIME	Family	Reprise	6
13	6	WHAT ARE YOU DOING SUNDAY	Dawn	Bell	4
7	7	TOM-TOM TURNAROUND	New World	RAK	8
8	8	CHIRPY CHIRPY CHEEP CHEEP	Middle Of The Road	RCA	12
10	9	WON'T GET FOOLED AGAIN	Who	Track	5
14	10	HEARTBREAK HOTEL/HOUND DOG	Elvis Presley	RCA	5
18	11	SOLDIER BLUE	Buffy Sainte-Marie	RCA	4
12	[12]	LEAP UP AND DOWN (WAVE YOUR KNICKERS IN THE AIR)	St Cecilia	Polydor	9
6	13	ME AND YOU AND A DOG NAMED BOO	Lobo	Philips	9
10	14	CO-CO	Sweet	RCA	11
27	15	BANGLA DESH	George Harrison	Apple	2
17	[16]	GET DOWN AND GET WITH IT	Slade	Polydor	8
25	17	LET YOUR YEAH BY YEAH	Pioneers	Trojan	2
11	18	MONKEY SPANNER	Dave and Ansel Collins	Technique	8
26	19	HEY GIRL DON'T BOTHER ME	Tams	Probe	3
15	20	BLACK AND WHITE	Greyhound	Trojan	9
19	21	LA-LA MEANS I LOVE YOU	Delfonics	Bell	7
22	22	MOVE ON UP	Curtis Mayfield	Buddah	3
29	23	WE WILL	Gilbert O'Sullivan	MAM	4
32	24	IT'S TOO LATE	Carole King	A & M	2
16	25	TONIGHT	Move	Harvest	7
24	26	WATCHING THE RIVER FLOW	Bob Dylan	CBS	6
21	27	JUST MY IMAGINATION	Temptations	Tamla Motown	14
38	28	WHEN LOVE COMES ROUND AGAIN	Ken Dodd	Columbia	4
20	29	RIVER DEEP, MOUNTAIN HIGH	Supremes and the Four Tops	Tamla Motown	10
-	30	BACK STREET LUV	Curved Air	Warner Bros.	2
30	31	BANNER MAN	Blue Mink	Regal Zonophone	13
23	32	DON'T LET IT DIE	Hurricane Smith	Columbia	10
33	[33]	NEVER CAN SAY GOODBYE	Jackson 5	Tamla Motown	4
-	[34]	THESE THINGS WILL KEEP ME LOVING YOU	Velvelettes ●	Tamla Motown	2
-	35	FOR ALL WE KNOW	Shirley Bassey	United Artists	1
40	[36]	SWEET HITCH-HIKER	Creedence Clearwater Revival	United Artists	3
-	37	AT THE TOP OF THE STAIRS	Formations	Mojo	1
39	38	KNOCK THREE TIMES	Dawn	Bell	20
-	39	LITTLE DROPS OF SILVER	Gerry Monroe	Chapter One	1
-	40	DID YOU EVER	Nancy and Lee	Reprise	1

WEEK ENDING 28 AUGUST 1971

LW	TW	Title	Artist	Label	Wks
1	[1]	I'M STILL WAITING	Diana Ross	Tamla Motown	5
2	[2]	NEVER ENDING SONG OF LOVE	New Seekers	Philips	7
6	[3]	WHAT ARE YOU DOING SUNDAY	Dawn	Bell	5
3	4	GET IT ON	T. Rex	Fly	8
5	5	IN MY OWN TIME	Family	Reprise	7
17	6	LET YOUR YEAH BY YEAH	Pioneers	Trojan	3
4	7	DEVIL'S ANSWER	Atomic Rooster	B&C	8
11	8	SOLDIER BLUE	Buffy Sainte-Marie	RCA	5
19	9	HEY GIRL DON'T BOTHER ME	Tams	Probe	4
15	[10]	BANGLA DESH	George Harrison	Apple	3
7	11	TOM-TOM TURNAROUND	New World	RAK	9
22	[12]	MOVE ON UP	Curtis Mayfield	Buddah	4
8	13	CHIRPY CHIRPY CHEEP CHEEP	Middle Of The Road	RCA	13
9	14	WON'T GET FOOLED AGAIN	Who	Track	6
24	15	IT'S TOO LATE	Carole King	A & M	3
12	16	LEAP UP AND DOWN (WAVE YOUR KNICKERS IN THE AIR)	St Cecilia	Polydor	10
10	17	HEARTBREAK HOTEL/HOUND DOG	Elvis Presley	RCA	6
16	18	GET DOWN AND GET WITH IT	Slade	Polydor	9
13	19	ME AND YOU AND A DOG NAMED BOO	Lobo	Philips	10
23	20	WE WILL	Gilbert O'Sullivan	MAM	5
30	21	BACK STREET LUV	Curved Air	Warner Bros.	3
14	22	CO-CO	Sweet	RCA	12
21	23	LA-LA MEANS I LOVE YOU	Delfonics	Bell	8
18	24	MONKEY SPANNER	Dave and Ansel Collins	Technique	9
40	25	DID YOU EVER	Nancy and Lee	Reprise	2
-	26	NATHAN JONES	Supremes	Tamla Motown	1
26	27	WATCHING THE RIVER FLOW	Bob Dylan	CBS	7
20	28	BLACK AND WHITE	Greyhound	Trojan	10
28	29	WHEN LOVE COMES ROUND AGAIN	Ken Dodd	Columbia	5
38	30	KNOCK THREE TIMES	Dawn	Bell	21
37	31	AT THE TOP OF THE STAIRS	Formations	Mojo	2
35	32	FOR ALL WE KNOW	Shirley Bassey	United Artists	2
-	33	DADDY DON'T YOU WALK SO FAST	Daniel Boone ●	Penny Farthing	1
34	[34]	THESE THINGS WILL KEEP ME LOVING YOU	Velvelettes	Tamla Motown	3
25	35	TONIGHT	Move	Harvest	8
36	[36]	SWEET HITCH-HIKER	Creedence Clearwater Revival	United Artists	4
29	37	RIVER DEEP, MOUNTAIN HIGH	Supremes and the Four Tops	Tamla Motown	11
27	38	JUST MY IMAGINATION	Temptations	Tamla Motown	15
-	39	YOU'VE GOT A FRIEND	James Taylor	Warner	1
39	40	LITTLE DROPS OF SILVER	Gerry Monroe	Chapter One	2

WEEK ENDING 4 SEPTEMBER 1971

LW	TW	Title	Artist	Label	Wks
1	[1]	I'M STILL WAITING	Diana Ross	Tamla Motown	6
2	[2]	NEVER ENDING SONG OF LOVE	New Seekers	Philips	8
9	3	HEY GIRL DON'T BOTHER ME	Tams	Probe	5
5	[4]	IN MY OWN TIME	Family	Reprise	8
3	5	WHAT ARE YOU DOING SUNDAY	Dawn	Bell	6
6	6	LET YOUR YEAH BY YEAH	Pioneers	Trojan	4
8	[7]	SOLDIER BLUE	Buffy Sainte-Marie	RCA	6
15	8	IT'S TOO LATE	Carole King	A & M	4
7	9	DEVIL'S ANSWER	Atomic Rooster	B&C	9
4	10	GET IT ON	T. Rex	Fly	9
10	11	BANGLA DESH	George Harrison	Apple	4
21	12	BACK STREET LUV	Curved Air	Warner Bros.	4
11	13	TOM-TOM TURNAROUND	New World	RAK	10
12	14	MOVE ON UP	Curtis Mayfield	Buddah	5
14	15	WON'T GET FOOLED AGAIN	Who	Track	7
20	16	WE WILL	Gilbert O'Sullivan	MAM	6
25	17	DID YOU EVER	Nancy and Lee	Reprise	3
17	18	HEARTBREAK HOTEL/HOUND DOG	Elvis Presley	RCA	7
26	19	NATHAN JONES	Supremes	Tamla Motown	2

In these weeks ■ 5 weeks at number two for the New Seekers' *Never Ending Song Of Love* (04.09.71) ■ Diana Ross becomes the first woman to have a number one hit as a part of a group (The Supremes) and then as a soloist (21.08.71) ■ Nancy and Lee were, of course, Sinatra and Hazelwood, enjoying their first hit as a duo for almost four years (21.08.71)■

LW	TW	Title / Artist	Label	Wks
16	20	LEAP UP AND DOWN (WAVE YOUR KNICKERS IN THE AIR) St Cecilia	Polydor	11
18	21	GET DOWN AND GET WITH IT Slade	Polydor	10
13	22	CHIRPY CHIRPY CHEEP CHEEP Middle Of The Road	RCA	14
22	23	CO-CO Sweet	RCA	13
29	24	WHEN LOVE COMES ROUND AGAIN Ken Dodd	Columbia	6
-	25	I BELIEVE (IN LOVE) Hot Chocolate	RAK	1
32	26	FOR ALL WE KNOW Shirley Bassey	United Artists	3
19	27	ME AND YOU AND A DOG NAMED BOO Lobo	Philips	11
33	28	DADDY DON'T YOU WALK SO FAST Daniel Boone	Penny Farthing	2
31	29	AT THE TOP OF THE STAIRS Formations	Mojo	3
24	30	MONKEY SPANNER Dave and Ansel Collins	Technique	10
-	31	REASON TO BELIEVE Rod Stewart ●	Mercury	1
23	32	LA-LA MEANS I LOVE YOU Delfonics	Bell	9
28	33	BLACK AND WHITE Greyhound	Trojan	11
34	[34]	THESE THINGS WILL KEEP ME LOVING YOU Velvelettes	Tamla Motown	4
30	35	KNOCK THREE TIMES Dawn	Bell	22
-	36	YOU'VE GOT A FRIEND James Taylor	Warner	1
-	37	COUSIN NORMAN Marmalade	Decca	1
40	38	LITTLE DROPS OF SILVER Gerry Monroe	Chapter One	3
-	39	TAP TURNS ON THE WATER C.C.S.	RAK	1
38	40	JUST MY IMAGINATION Temptations	Tamla Motown	16

LW	TW	*WEEK ENDING* **11 SEPTEMBER 1971**		Wks
1	[1]	I'M STILL WAITING Diana Ross	Tamla Motown	7
3	2	HEY GIRL DON'T BOTHER ME Tams	Probe	6
5	3	WHAT ARE YOU DOING SUNDAY Dawn	Bell	7
2	4	NEVER ENDING SONG OF LOVE New Seekers	Philips	9
6	[5]	LET YOUR YEAH BY YEAH Pioneers	Trojan	5
17	6	DID YOU EVER Nancy and Lee	Reprise	4
7	[7]	SOLDIER BLUE Buffy Sainte-Marie	RCA	7
19	8	NATHAN JONES Supremes	Tamla Motown	3
12	9	BACK STREET LUV Curved Air	Warner Bros.	5
8	10	IT'S TOO LATE Carole King	A & M	5
4	11	IN MY OWN TIME Family	Reprise	9
11	12	BANGLA DESH George Harrison	Apple	5
10	13	GET IT ON T. Rex	Fly	10
36	14	YOU'VE GOT A FRIEND James Taylor	Warner	2
25	15	I BELIEVE (IN LOVE) Hot Chocolate	RAK	2
14	16	MOVE ON UP Curtis Mayfield	Buddah	6
13	17	TOM-TOM TURNAROUND New World	RAK	11
16	18	WE WILL Gilbert O'Sullivan	MAM	7
31	19	REASON TO BELIEVE Rod Stewart	Mercury	2
37	20	COUSIN NORMAN Marmalade	Decca	2
26	21	FOR ALL WE KNOW Shirley Bassey	United Artists	4
22	22	CHIRPY CHIRPY CHEEP CHEEP Middle Of The Road	RCA	15
-	23	TWEEDLE DEE TWEEDLE DUM Middle Of The Road	RCA	1
28	24	DADDY DON'T YOU WALK SO FAST Daniel Boone	Penny Farthing	3
9	25	DEVIL'S ANSWER Atomic Rooster	B&C	10
39	26	TAP TURNS ON THE WATER C.C.S.	RAK	2
20	27	LEAP UP AND DOWN (WAVE YOUR KNICKERS IN THE AIR) St Cecilia	Polydor	12
24	28	WHEN LOVE COMES ROUND AGAIN Ken Dodd	Columbia	7
18	29	HEARTBREAK HOTEL/HOUND DOG Elvis Presley	RCA	8
29	30	AT THE TOP OF THE STAIRS Formations	Mojo	4
15	31	WON'T GET FOOLED AGAIN Who	Track	8
21	32	GET DOWN AND GET WITH IT Slade	Polydor	11
-	33	MOON SHADOW Cat Stevens	Island	1
27	34	ME AND YOU AND A DOG NAMED BOO Lobo	Philips	12
-	35	ANOTHER TIME, ANOTHER PLACE Engelbert Humperdinck	Decca	1
35	36	KNOCK THREE TIMES Dawn	Bell	23
38	[37]	LITTLE DROPS OF SILVER Gerry Monroe	Chapter One	4
23	38	CO-CO Sweet	RCA	14
-	[39]	BACK SEAT OF MY CAR Paul and Linda McCartney ●	Apple	1
34	40	THESE THINGS WILL KEEP ME LOVING YOU Velvelettes	Tamla Motown	5

September 1971

□ Highest position disc reached ● Act's first ever week on chart

LW	TW	*WEEK ENDING* **18 SEPTEMBER 1971**		Wks
2	[1]	HEY GIRL DON'T BOTHER ME Tams	Probe	8
1	2	I'M STILL WAITING Diana Ross	Tamla Motown	8
6	3	DID YOU EVER Nancy and Lee	Reprise	5
9	[4]	BACK STREET LUV Curved Air	Warner Bros.	6
8	[5]	NATHAN JONES Supremes	Tamla Motown	4
10	[6]	IT'S TOO LATE Carole King	A & M	6
4	7	NEVER ENDING SONG OF LOVE New Seekers	Philips	10
15	[8]	I BELIEVE (IN LOVE) Hot Chocolate	RAK	3
7	9	SOLDIER BLUE Buffy Sainte-Marie	RCA	8
3	10	WHAT ARE YOU DOING SUNDAY Dawn	Bell	8
19	11	MAGGIE MAY Rod Stewart	Mercury	3
14	12	YOU'VE GOT A FRIEND James Taylor	Warner	3
5	13	LET YOUR YEAH BY YEAH Pioneers	Trojan	6
11	14	IN MY OWN TIME Family	Reprise	10
21	15	FOR ALL WE KNOW Shirley Bassey	United Artists	5
23	16	TWEEDLE DEE TWEEDLE DUM Middle Of The Road	RCA	2
20	17	COUSIN NORMAN Marmalade	Decca	3
26	18	TAP TURNS ON THE WATER C.C.S.	RAK	3
28	19	WHEN LOVE COMES ROUND AGAIN Ken Dodd	Columbia	8
18	20	WE WILL Gilbert O'Sullivan	MAM	8
24	21	DADDY DON'T YOU WALK SO FAST Daniel Boone	Penny Farthing	4
12	22	BANGLA DESH George Harrison	Apple	6
25	23	DEVIL'S ANSWER Atomic Rooster	B&C	11
27	24	LEAP UP AND DOWN (WAVE YOUR KNICKERS IN THE AIR) St Cecilia	Polydor	13
-	25	LIFE IS A LONG SONG/UP THE POOL Jethro Tull	Chrysalis	1
29	26	HEARTBREAK HOTEL/HOUND DOG Elvis Presley	RCA	9
17	27	TOM-TOM TURNAROUND New World	RAK	12
13	28	GET IT ON T. Rex	Fly	11
22	29	CHIRPY CHIRPY CHEEP CHEEP Middle Of The Road	RCA	16
16	30	MOVE ON UP Curtis Mayfield	Buddah	7
30	31	AT THE TOP OF THE STAIRS Formations	Mojo	5
-	32	FREEDOM COME, FREEDOM GO Fortunes	Capitol	1
35	33	ANOTHER TIME, ANOTHER PLACE Engelbert Humperdinck	Decca	2
33	34	MOON SHADOW Cat Stevens	Island	2
-	35	(FOR GOD'S SAKE) GIVE MORE POWER TO THE PEOPLE Chi-Lites ●	MCA	1
31	36	WON'T GET FOOLED AGAIN The Who	Track	9
-	37	KEEP ON DANCING Bay City Rollers ●	Bell	1
-	38	REMEMBER Rock Candy ●	MCA	1
37	39	LITTLE DROPS OF SILVER Gerry Monroe	Chapter One	5
36	40	KNOCK THREE TIMES Dawn	Bell	24

LW	TW	*WEEK ENDING* **25 SEPTEMBER 1971**		Wks
1	[1]	HEY GIRL DON'T BOTHER ME Tams	Probe	9
3	[2]	DID YOU EVER Nancy and Lee	Reprise	6
11	3	MAGGIE MAY Rod Stewart	Mercury	4
16	4	TWEEDLE DEE TWEEDLE DUM Middle Of The Road	RCA	3
5	[5]	NATHAN JONES Supremes	Tamla Motown	5
18	6	TAP TURNS ON THE WATER C.C.S.	RAK	4
17	7	COUSIN NORMAN Marmalade	Decca	4
8	[8]	I BELIEVE (IN LOVE) Hot Chocolate	RAK	4
12	9	YOU'VE GOT A FRIEND James Taylor	Warner	4
2	10	I'M STILL WAITING Diana Ross	Tamla Motown	9
4	11	BACK STREET LUV Curved Air	Warner Bros.	7
9	12	SOLDIER BLUE Buffy Sainte-Marie	RCA	9
15	13	FOR ALL WE KNOW Shirley Bassey	United Artists	6
7	14	NEVER ENDING SONG OF LOVE New Seekers	Philips	11
6	15	IT'S TOO LATE Carole King	A & M	7
10	16	WHAT ARE YOU DOING SUNDAY Dawn	Bell	9
21	[17]	DADDY DON'T YOU WALK SO FAST Daniel Boone	Penny Farthing	5
13	18	LET YOUR YEAH BY YEAH Pioneers	Trojan	7
25	19	LIFE IS A LONG SONG/UP THE POOL Jethro Tull	Chrysalis	2
14	20	IN MY OWN TIME Family	Reprise	11
32	21	FREEDOM COME, FREEDOM GO Fortunes	Capitol	2
19	22	WHEN LOVE COMES ROUND AGAIN Ken Dodd	Columbia	9

■The Tams' *Hey Girl Don't Bother Me* takes over from Diana Ross' *I'm Still Waiting* at the top. Neither are new recordings, although both are hits for the first time (18.09.71) ■ Rod Stewart's *Reason To Believe* is abruptly flipped after two weeks of chart life and the B-side, *Maggie May* becomes the first of six number ones for Rod the Mod (18.09.71) ■ The first chart week for the Bay City Rollers, produced by none other than Jonathan King (18.09.71)■

September 1971

□ Highest position disc reached ● Act's first ever week on chart

LW	TW	Title / Artist	Label	Wks
33	**23**	ANOTHER TIME, ANOTHER PLACE Engelbert Humperdinck	*Decca*	3
29	**24**	CHIRPY CHIRPY CHEEP CHEEP Middle Of The Road	*RCA*	17
-	**25**	YOU DON'T HAVE TO BE IN THE ARMY Mungo Jerry	*Dawn*	1
27	**26**	TOM-TOM TURNAROUND New World	*RAK*	13
34	**27**	MOON SHADOW Cat Stevens	*Island*	3
31	**[28]**	AT THE TOP OF THE STAIRS Formations	*Mojo*	6
22	**29**	BANGLA DESH George Harrison	*Apple*	7
-	**30**	BUTTERFLY Danyel Gerard ●	*CBS*	1
30	**31**	MOVE ON UP Curtis Mayfield	*Buddah*	8
35	**[32]**	(FOR GOD'S SAKE) GIVE MORE POWER TO THE PEOPLE Chi-Lites	*MCA*	2
23	**33**	DEVIL'S ANSWER Atomic Rooster	*B&C*	12
24	**34**	LEAP UP AND DOWN (WAVE YOUR KNICKERS IN THE AIR) St Cecilia	*Polydor*	14
20	**35**	WE WILL Gilbert O'Sullivan	*MAM*	9
26	**36**	HEARTBREAK HOTEL/HOUND DOG Elvis Presley	*RCA*	10
39	**[37]**	LITTLE DROPS OF SILVER Gerry Monroe	*Chapter One*	6
28	**38**	GET IT ON T. Rex	*Fly*	12
38	**39**	REMEMBER Rock Candy	*MCA*	2
37	**40**	KEEP ON DANCING Bay City Rollers	*Bell*	2

WEEK ENDING 2 OCTOBER 1971

LW	TW	Title / Artist	Label	Wks
1	**[1]**	HEY GIRL DON'T BOTHER ME Tams	*Probe*	10
3	**2**	MAGGIE MAY Rod Stewart	*Mercury*	5
2	**3**	DID YOU EVER Nancy and Lee	*Reprise*	7
4	**4**	TWEEDLE DEE TWEEDLE DUM Middle Of The Road	*RCA*	4
6	**[5]**	TAP TURNS ON THE WATER C.C.S.	*RAK*	5
7	**[6]**	COUSIN NORMAN Marmalade	*Decca*	5
5	**7**	NATHAN JONES Supremes	*Tamla Motown*	6
9	**8**	YOU'VE GOT A FRIEND James Taylor	*Warner*	5
8	**9**	I BELIEVE (IN LOVE) Hot Chocolate	*RAK*	5
13	**10**	FOR ALL WE KNOW Shirley Bassey	*United Artists*	7
11	**11**	BACK STREET LUV Curved Air	*Warner Bros.*	8
19	**12**	LIFE IS A LONG SONG/UP THE POOL Jethro Tull	*Chrysalis*	3
10	**13**	I'M STILL WAITING Diana Ross	*Tamla Motown*	10
14	**14**	NEVER ENDING SONG OF LOVE New Seekers	*Philips*	12
15	**15**	IT'S TOO LATE Carole King	*A & M*	8
12	**16**	SOLDIER BLUE Buffy Sainte-Marie	*RCA*	10
21	**17**	FREEDOM COME, FREEDOM GO Fortunes	*Capitol*	3
17	**18**	DADDY DON'T YOU WALK SO FAST Daniel Boone	*Penny Farthing*	6
23	**19**	ANOTHER TIME, ANOTHER PLACE Engelbert Humperdinck	*Decca*	4
30	**20**	BUTTERFLY Danyel Gerard	*CBS*	2
25	**21**	YOU DON'T HAVE TO BE IN THE ARMY Mungo Jerry	*Dawn*	2
16	**22**	WHAT ARE YOU DOING SUNDAY Dawn	*Bell*	10
18	**23**	LET YOUR YEAH BY YEAH Pioneers	*Trojan*	8
-	**24**	SIMPLE GAME Four Tops	*Tamla Motown*	1
27	**25**	MOON SHADOW Cat Stevens	*Island*	4
40	**26**	KEEP ON DANCING Bay City Rollers	*Bell*	3
22	**27**	WHEN LOVE COMES ROUND AGAIN Ken Dodd	*Columbia*	10
-	**28**	SULTANA Titanic ●	*CBS*	1
-	**29**	WITCH QUEEN OF NEW ORLEANS Redbone ●	*Epic*	1
24	**30**	CHIRPY CHIRPY CHEEP CHEEP Middle Of The Road	*RCA*	18
-	**31**	SUPERSTAR/FOR ALL WE KNOW Carpenters	*A&M*	1
39	**32**	REMEMBER Rock Candy	*MCA*	3
-	**33**	SPANISH HARLEM Aretha Franklin	*Atlantic*	1
26	**34**	TOM-TOM TURNAROUND New World	*RAK*	14
20	**35**	IN MY OWN TIME Family	*Reprise*	12
-	**36**	I'M LEAVIN' Elvis Presley	*RCA*	1
34	**37**	LEAP UP AND DOWN (WAVE YOUR KNICKERS IN THE AIR) St Cecilia	*Polydor*	15
28	**38**	AT THE TOP OF THE STAIRS Formations	*Mojo*	7
-	**39**	MY WAY Frank Sinatra	*Reprise*	59
38	**40**	GET IT ON T. Rex	*Fly*	13

WEEK ENDING 9 OCTOBER 1971

LW	TW	Title / Artist	Label	Wks
2	**[1]**	MAGGIE MAY Rod Stewart	*Mercury*	6
1	**2**	HEY GIRL DON'T BOTHER ME Tams	*Probe*	11
3	**3**	DID YOU EVER Nancy and Lee	*Reprise*	8
4	**4**	TWEEDLE DEE TWEEDLE DUM Middle Of The Road	*RCA*	5
8	**5**	YOU'VE GOT A FRIEND James Taylor	*Warner*	6
5	**6**	TAP TURNS ON THE WATER C.C.S.	*RAK*	6
10	**7**	FOR ALL WE KNOW Shirley Bassey	*United Artists*	8
6	**8**	COUSIN NORMAN Marmalade	*Decca*	6
17	**9**	FREEDOM COME, FREEDOM GO Fortunes	*Capitol*	4
9	**10**	I BELIEVE (IN LOVE) Hot Chocolate	*RAK*	6
12	**[11]**	LIFE IS A LONG SONG/UP THE POOL Jethro Tull	*Chrysalis*	4
7	**12**	NATHAN JONES Supremes	*Tamla Motown*	7
21	**[13]**	YOU DON'T HAVE TO BE IN THE ARMY Mungo Jerry	*Dawn*	3
29	**14**	WITCH QUEEN OF NEW ORLEANS Redbone	*Epic*	2
11	**15**	BACK STREET LUV Curved Air	*Warner Bros.*	9
13	**16**	I'M STILL WAITING Diana Ross	*Tamla Motown*	11
28	**17**	SULTANA Titanic	*CBS*	2
24	**18**	SIMPLE GAME Four Tops	*Tamla Motown*	2
18	**19**	DADDY DON'T YOU WALK SO FAST Daniel Boone	*Penny Farthing*	7
14	**20**	NEVER ENDING SONG OF LOVE New Seekers	*Philips*	13
19	**21**	ANOTHER TIME, ANOTHER PLACE Engelbert Humperdinck	*Decca*	5
16	**22**	SOLDIER BLUE Buffy Sainte-Marie	*RCA*	11
20	**23**	BUTTERFLY Danyel Gerard	*CBS*	3
25	**24**	MOON SHADOW Cat Stevens	*Island*	5
26	**25**	KEEP ON DANCING Bay City Rollers	*Bell*	4
33	**26**	SPANISH HARLEM Aretha Franklin	*Atlantic*	2
15	**27**	IT'S TOO LATE Carole King	*A & M*	9
31	**28**	SUPERSTAR/FOR ALL WE KNOW Carpenters	*A&M*	2
-	**29**	THE NIGHT THEY DROVE OLD DIXIE DOWN Joan Baez	*Vanguard*	1
22	**30**	WHAT ARE YOU DOING SUNDAY Dawn	*Bell*	11
36	**31**	I'M LEAVIN' Elvis Presley	*RCA*	2
23	**32**	LET YOUR YEAH BY YEAH Pioneers	*Trojan*	9
-	**33**	LOOK AROUND Vince Hill	*Columbia*	1
27	**34**	WHEN LOVE COMES ROUND AGAIN Ken Dodd	*Columbia*	11
30	**35**	CHIRPY CHIRPY CHEEP CHEEP Middle Of The Road	*RCA*	19
-	**36**	MAMMY BLUE Roger Whittaker	*Columbia*	1
-	**37**	TIRED OF BEING ALONE Al Green ●	*London*	1
-	**38**	PUT YOURSELF IN MY PLACE Elgins	*Tamla Motown*	1
39	**39**	MY WAY Frank Sinatra	*Reprise*	60
-	**40**	AMAZING GRACE Judy Collins	*Elektra*	25

WEEK ENDING 16 OCTOBER 1971

LW	TW	Title / Artist	Label	Wks
1	**[1]**	MAGGIE MAY Rod Stewart	*Mercury*	7
4	**[2]**	TWEEDLE DEE TWEEDLE DUM Middle Of The Road	*RCA*	6
2	**3**	HEY GIRL DON'T BOTHER ME Tams	*Probe*	12
5	**[4]**	YOU'VE GOT A FRIEND James Taylor	*Warner*	7
3	**5**	DID YOU EVER Nancy and Lee	*Reprise*	9
7	**[6]**	FOR ALL WE KNOW Shirley Bassey	*United Artists*	9
8	**7**	COUSIN NORMAN Marmalade	*Decca*	7
6	**8**	TAP TURNS ON THE WATER C.C.S.	*RAK*	7
14	**9**	WITCH QUEEN OF NEW ORLEANS Redbone	*Epic*	3
9	**10**	FREEDOM COME, FREEDOM GO Fortunes	*Capitol*	5
11	**[11]**	LIFE IS A LONG SONG/UP THE POOL Jethro Tull	*Chrysalis*	5
18	**12**	SIMPLE GAME Four Tops	*Tamla Motown*	3
23	**13**	BUTTERFLY Danyel Gerard	*CBS*	4
17	**14**	SULTANA Titanic	*CBS*	3
12	**15**	ANOTHER TIME, ANOTHER PLACE Engelbert Humperdinck	*Decca*	6
12	**16**	NATHAN JONES Supremes	*Tamla Motown*	8
10	**17**	I BELIEVE (IN LOVE) Hot Chocolate	*RAK*	7
13	**18**	YOU DON'T HAVE TO BE IN THE ARMY Mungo Jerry	*Dawn*	4
25	**19**	KEEP ON DANCING Bay City Rollers	*Bell*	5
19	**20**	DADDY DON'T YOU WALK SO FAST Daniel Boone	*Penny Farthing*	8
26	**21**	SPANISH HARLEM Aretha Franklin	*Atlantic*	3
24	**[22]**	MOON SHADOW Cat Stevens	*Island*	6
29	**23**	THE NIGHT THEY DROVE OLD DIXIE DOWN Joan Baez	*Vanguard*	2

In these weeks ■ Frank Sinatra's *My Way* enjoys its 73rd and final week in the Top 40 - an all-time record (09.10.71) ■ The full title to Mungo Jerry's *You Don't Have To Be In The Army To Fight In The War* has more words (13) than any hit to date (25.09.71) ■ Two songs from the album *Tapestry* enjoy different fortunes. James Taylor's cover version of *You've Got A Friend* climbs to number 4 while Carole King's original *It's Too Late* drops to number 31 (16.10.71)■

November 1971

□ Highest position disc reached ● Act's first ever week on chart

LW	TW	Title	Artist	Label	Wks
22	24	SOLDIER BLUE	Buffy Sainte-Marie	RCA	12
20	25	NEVER ENDING SONG OF LOVE	New Seekers	Philips	14
28	26	SUPERSTAR/FOR ALL WE KNOW	Carpenters	A&M	3
31	27	I'M LEAVIN'	Elvis Presley	RCA	3
37	28	TIRED OF BEING ALONE	Al Green	London	2
33	29	LOOK AROUND	Vince Hill	Columbia	2
16	30	I'M STILL WAITING	Diana Ross	Tamla Motown	12
27	31	IT'S TOO LATE	Carole King	A & M	10
15	32	BACK STREET LUV	Curved Air	Warner Bros.	10
-	33	BRANDY	Scott English ●	Horse	1
38	34	PUT YOURSELF IN MY PLACE	Elgins	Tamla Motown	2
-	35	MAMMY BLUE	Los Pop Tops ●	A & M	1
36	36	MAMMY BLUE	Roger Whittaker	Columbia	2
34	37	WHEN LOVE COMES ROUND AGAIN	Ken Dodd	Columbia	12
-	38	LADY LOVE BUG	Clodagh Rodgers	RCA	1
35	39	CHIRPY CHIRPY CHEEP CHEEP	Middle Of The Road	RCA	20
30	40	WHAT ARE YOU DOING SUNDAY	Dawn	Bell	12

WEEK ENDING 23 OCTOBER 1971

LW	TW	Title	Artist	Label	Wks
1	[1]	MAGGIE MAY	Rod Stewart	Mercury	8
9	[2]	WITCH QUEEN OF NEW ORLEANS	Redbone	Epic	4
2	3	TWEEDLE DEE TWEEDLE DUM	Middle Of The Road	RCA	7
4	[4]	YOU'VE GOT A FRIEND	James Taylor	Warner	8
12	5	SIMPLE GAME	Four Tops	Tamla Motown	4
10	[6]	FREEDOM COME, FREEDOM GO	Fortunes	Capitol	6
6	7	FOR ALL WE KNOW	Shirley Bassey	United Artists	10
5	8	DID YOU EVER	Nancy and Lee	Reprise	10
3	9	HEY GIRL DON'T BOTHER ME	Tams	Probe	13
14	10	SULTANA	Titanic	CBS	4
8	11	TAP TURNS ON THE WATER	C.C.S.	RAK	8
13	12	BUTTERFLY	Danyel Gerard	CBS	5
15	[13]	ANOTHER TIME, ANOTHER PLACE	Engelbert Humperdinck	Decca	7
21	[14]	SPANISH HARLEM	Aretha Franklin	Atlantic	4
18	15	YOU DON'T HAVE TO BE IN THE ARMY	Mungo Jerry	Dawn	5
11	16	LIFE IS A LONG SONG/UP THE POOL	Jethro Tull	Chrysalis	6
7	17	COUSIN NORMAN	Marmalade	Decca	8
23	18	THE NIGHT THEY DROVE OLD DIXIE DOWN	Joan Baez	Vanguard	3
28	19	TIRED OF BEING ALONE	Al Green	London	3
19	20	KEEP ON DANCING	Bay City Rollers	Bell	6
26	21	SUPERSTAR/FOR ALL WE KNOW	Carpenters	A&M	4
-	22	TILL	Tom Jones	Decca	1
29	23	LOOK AROUND	Vince Hill	Columbia	3
20	24	DADDY DON'T YOU WALK SO FAST	Daniel Boone	Penny Farthing	9
33	25	BRANDY	Scott English	Horse	2
16	26	NATHAN JONES	Supremes	Tamla Motown	9
17	27	I BELIEVE (IN LOVE)	Hot Chocolate	RAK	8
22	28	MOON SHADOW	Cat Stevens	Island	7
27	29	I'M LEAVIN'	Elvis Presley	RCA	4
24	30	SOLDIER BLUE	Buffy Sainte-Marie	RCA	13
25	31	NEVER ENDING SONG OF LOVE	New Seekers	Philips	15
38	32	LADY LOVE BUG	Clodagh Rodgers	RCA	2
34	33	PUT YOURSELF IN MY PLACE	Elgins	Tamla Motown	3
30	34	I'M STILL WAITING	Diana Ross	Tamla Motown	13
35	35	MAMMY BLUE	Los Pop Tops	A & M	2
-	36	CHINA TOWN	Move	Harvest	1
-	37	I WILL RETURN	Springwater ●	Polydor	1
-	38	MY LITTLE GIRL	Autumn ●	Pye	1
-	39	THE LIGHTNING TREE	Settlers ●	York	1
36	40	MAMMY BLUE	Roger Whittaker	Columbia	3

WEEK ENDING 30 OCTOBER 1971

LW	TW	Title	Artist	Label	Wks
1	[1]	MAGGIE MAY	Rod Stewart	Mercury	9
2	[2]	WITCH QUEEN OF NEW ORLEANS	Redbone	Epic	5
3	3	TWEEDLE DEE TWEEDLE DUM	Middle Of The Road	RCA	8
5	4	SIMPLE GAME	Four Tops	Tamla Motown	5
10	[5]	SULTANA	Titanic	CBS	5
7	6	FOR ALL WE KNOW	Shirley Bassey	United Artists	11
6	7	FREEDOM COME, FREEDOM GO	Fortunes	Capitol	7
4	8	YOU'VE GOT A FRIEND	James Taylor	Warner	9
20	9	KEEP ON DANCING	Bay City Rollers	Bell	7
19	10	TIRED OF BEING ALONE	Al Green	London	4
12	[11]	BUTTERFLY	Danyel Gerard	CBS	6
18	12	THE NIGHT THEY DROVE OLD DIXIE DOWN	Joan Baez	Vanguard	4
8	13	DID YOU EVER	Nancy and Lee	Reprise	11
11	14	TAP TURNS ON THE WATER	C.C.S.	RAK	9
9	15	HEY GIRL DON'T BOTHER ME	Tams	Probe	14
13	16	ANOTHER TIME, ANOTHER PLACE	Engelbert Humperdinck	Decca	8
23	17	LOOK AROUND	Vince Hill	Columbia	4
25	18	BRANDY	Scott English	Horse	3
14	19	SPANISH HARLEM	Aretha Franklin	Atlantic	5
22	20	TILL	Tom Jones	Decca	2
17	21	COUSIN NORMAN	Marmalade	Decca	9
21	22	SUPERSTAR/FOR ALL WE KNOW	Carpenters	A&M	5
29	[23]	I'M LEAVIN'	Elvis Presley	RCA	5
37	24	I WILL RETURN	Springwater	Polydor	2
24	25	DADDY DON'T YOU WALK SO FAST	Daniel Boone	Penny Farthing	10
-	26	COZ I LUV YOU	Slade	Polydor	1
16	27	LIFE IS A LONG SONG/UP THE POOL	Jethro Tull	Chrysalis	7
33	[28]	PUT YOURSELF IN MY PLACE	Elgins	Tamla Motown	4
-	29	BANKS OF THE OHIO	Olivia Newton-John	Pye	1
15	30	YOU DON'T HAVE TO BE IN THE ARMY	Mungo Jerry	Dawn	6
36	31	CHINA TOWN	Move	Harvest	2
40	32	MAMMY BLUE	Roger Whittaker	Columbia	4
32	33	LADY LOVE BUG	Clodagh Rodgers	RCA	3
-	34	ALEXANDER GRAHAM BELL	Sweet	RCA	1
27	35	I BELIEVE (IN LOVE)	Hot Chocolate	RAK	9
39	[36]	THE LIGHTNING TREE	Settlers	York	2
38	[37]	MY LITTLE GIRL	Autumn	Pye	2
-	38	RUN BABY RUN/AM I NOT MY BROTHER'S KEEPER	Newbeats	London	1
30	39	SOLDIER BLUE	Buffy Sainte-Marie	RCA	14
26	40	NATHAN JONES	Supremes	Tamla Motown	10

WEEK ENDING 6 NOVEMBER 1971

LW	TW	Title	Artist	Label	Wks
1	[1]	MAGGIE MAY	Rod Stewart	Mercury	10
2	[2]	WITCH QUEEN OF NEW ORLEANS	Redbone	Epic	6
4	[3]	SIMPLE GAME	Four Tops	Tamla Motown	6
10	[4]	TIRED OF BEING ALONE	Al Green	London	5
20	5	TILL	Tom Jones	Decca	3
12	[6]	THE NIGHT THEY DROVE OLD DIXIE DOWN	Joan Baez	Vanguard	5
5	7	SULTANA	Titanic	CBS	6
26	8	COZ I LUV YOU	Slade	Polydor	2
6	9	FOR ALL WE KNOW	Shirley Bassey	United Artists	12
3	10	TWEEDLE DEE TWEEDLE DUM	Middle Of The Road	RCA	9
7	11	FREEDOM COME, FREEDOM GO	Fortunes	Capitol	8
17	[12]	LOOK AROUND	Vince Hill	Columbia	5
18	13	BRANDY	Scott English	Horse	4
19	14	SPANISH HARLEM	Aretha Franklin	Atlantic	6
8	15	YOU'VE GOT A FRIEND	James Taylor	Warner	10
9	16	KEEP ON DANCING	Bay City Rollers	Bell	8
24	17	I WILL RETURN	Springwater	Polydor	3
11	18	BUTTERFLY	Danyel Gerard	CBS	7
-	19	JOHNNY REGGAE	Piglets ●	Bell	1
22	20	SUPERSTAR/FOR ALL WE KNOW	Carpenters	A&M	6
29	21	BANKS OF THE OHIO	Olivia Newton-John	Pye	2
13	22	DID YOU EVER	Nancy and Lee	Reprise	12
14	23	TAP TURNS ON THE WATER	C.C.S.	RAK	10
38	24	RUN BABY RUN/AM I NOT MY BROTHER'S KEEPER	Newbeats	London	2
15	25	HEY GIRL DON'T BOTHER ME	Tams	Probe	15
31	26	CHINA TOWN	Move	Harvest	3
-	27	SURRENDER	Diana Ross	Tamla Motown	1

■Springwater and Autumn debut in the same seasonal week. Edgar Winter and Donna Summer will make their chart debuts later in the decade (23.10.71) ■ Yet more Jonathan King as the The Piglets join in the chart action (06.11.71) ■ Danyel Gerard's hit is not the same *Butterfly* that gave Andy Williams a 1957 number one (30.10.71)■

November 1971

□ Highest position disc reached ● Act's first ever week on chart

LW	TW	Title / Artist	Label	Wks
23	28	I'M LEAVIN' Elvis Presley	RCA	6
16	29	ANOTHER TIME, ANOTHER PLACE Engelbert Humperdinck	Decca	9
-	30	LET'S SEE THE ACTION Who	Track	1
32	[31]	MAMMY BLUE Roger Whittaker	Columbia	5
-	32	GYPSYS TRAMPS AND THIEVES Cher	MCA	1
34	[33]	ALEXANDER GRAHAM BELL Sweet	RCA	2
28	34	PUT YOURSELF IN MY PLACE Elgins	Tamla Motown	5
33	35	LADY LOVE BUG Clodagh Rodgers	RCA	4
36	36	THE LIGHTNING TREE Settlers	York	3
27	37	LIFE IS A LONG SONG/UP THE POOL Jethro Tull	Chrysalis	8
25	38	DADDY DON'T YOU WALK SO FAST Daniel Boone	Penny Farthing	11
21	39	COUSIN NORMAN Marmalade	Decca	10
-	40	RIDERS ON THE STORM Doors	Elektra	1

LW	TW	*WEEK ENDING* **13 NOVEMBER 1971**		Wks
8	[1]	COZ I LUV YOU Slade	Polydor	3
1	2	MAGGIE MAY Rod Stewart	Mercury	11
2	3	WITCH QUEEN OF NEW ORLEANS Redbone	Epic	7
5	4	TILL Tom Jones	Decca	4
3	5	SIMPLE GAME Four Tops	Tamla Motown	7
4	6	TIRED OF BEING ALONE Al Green	London	6
19	7	JOHNNY REGGAE Piglets	Bell	2
17	8	I WILL RETURN Springwater	Polydor	4
6	9	THE NIGHT THEY DROVE OLD DIXIE DOWN Joan Baez	Vanguard	6
7	10	SULTANA Titanic	CBS	7
21	11	BANKS OF THE OHIO Olivia Newton-John	Pye	3
13	[12]	BRANDY Scott English	Horse	5
12	13	LOOK AROUND Vince Hill	Columbia	6
9	14	FOR ALL WE KNOW Shirley Bassey	United Artists	13
10	15	TWEEDLE DEE TWEEDLE DUM Middle Of The Road	RCA	10
32	16	GYPSYS TRAMPS AND THIEVES Cher	MCA	2
16	17	KEEP ON DANCING Bay City Rollers	Bell	9
20	[18]	SUPERSTAR/FOR ALL WE KNOW Carpenters	A&M	7
11	19	FREEDOM COME, FREEDOM GO Fortunes	Capitol	9
24	20	RUN BABY RUN/AM I NOT MY BROTHER'S KEEPER Newbeats	London	3
14	21	SPANISH HARLEM Aretha Franklin	Atlantic	7
27	22	SURRENDER Diana Ross	Tamla Motown	2
15	23	YOU'VE GOT A FRIEND James Taylor	Warner	11
22	24	DID YOU EVER Nancy and Lee	Reprise	13
18	25	BUTTERFLY Danyel Gerard	CBS	8
26	26	CHINA TOWN Move	Harvest	4
30	27	LET'S SEE THE ACTION Who	Track	2
35	[28]	LADY LOVE BUG Clodagh Rodgers	RCA	5
-	29	ERNIE (THE FASTEST MILKMAN IN THE WEST) Benny Hill	Columbia	1
28	30	I'M LEAVIN' Elvis Presley	RCA	7
34	31	PUT YOURSELF IN MY PLACE Elgins	Tamla Motown	6
25	32	HEY GIRL DON'T BOTHER ME Tams	Probe	16
40	33	RIDERS ON THE STORM Doors	Elektra	2
29	34	ANOTHER TIME, ANOTHER PLACE Engelbert Humperdinck	Decca	10
-	[35]	GYPSY EYES/REMEMBER Jimi Hendrix	Track	1
31	36	MAMMY BLUE Roger Whittaker	Columbia	6
-	37	JEEPSTER T. Rex	Fly	1
23	38	TAP TURNS ON THE WATER C.C.S.	RAK	11
33	39	ALEXANDER GRAHAM BELL Sweet	RCA	3
38	40	DADDY DON'T YOU WALK SO FAST Daniel Boone	Penny Farthing	12

LW	TW	*WEEK ENDING* **20 NOVEMBER 1971**		Wks
1	[1]	COZ I LUV YOU Slade	Polydor	4
4	[2]	TILL Tom Jones	Decca	5
7	[3]	JOHNNY REGGAE Piglets	Bell	3
2	4	MAGGIE MAY Rod Stewart	Mercury	12
8	[5]	I WILL RETURN Springwater	Polydor	5
11	[6]	BANKS OF THE OHIO Olivia Newton-John	Pye	4
16	7	GYPSYS TRAMPS AND THIEVES Cher	MCA	3
37	8	JEEPSTER T. Rex	Fly	2
6	9	TIRED OF BEING ALONE Al Green	London	7
9	10	THE NIGHT THEY DROVE OLD DIXIE DOWN Joan Baez	Vanguard	7
3	11	WITCH QUEEN OF NEW ORLEANS Redbone	Epic	8
5	12	SIMPLE GAME Four Tops	Tamla Motown	8
13	13	LOOK AROUND Vince Hill	Columbia	7
20	14	RUN BABY RUN/AM I NOT MY BROTHER'S KEEPER Newbeats	London	4
10	15	SULTANA Titanic	CBS	8
12	16	BRANDY Scott English	Horse	6
29	17	ERNIE (THE FASTEST MILKMAN IN THE WEST) Benny Hill	Columbia	2
22	18	SURRENDER Diana Ross	Tamla Motown	3
18	19	SUPERSTAR/FOR ALL WE KNOW Carpenters	A&M	8
14	20	FOR ALL WE KNOW Shirley Bassey	United Artists	14
17	21	KEEP ON DANCING Bay City Rollers	Bell	10
15	22	TWEEDLE DEE TWEEDLE DUM Middle Of The Road	RCA	11
26	[23]	CHINA TOWN Move	Harvest	5
27	24	LET'S SEE THE ACTION Who	Track	3
19	25	FREEDOM COME, FREEDOM GO Fortunes	Capitol	10
21	26	SPANISH HARLEM Aretha Franklin	Atlantic	8
24	27	DID YOU EVER Nancy and Lee	Reprise	14
-	28	TOKOLOSHE MAN John Kongos	Fly	1
-	29	SING A SONG OF FREEDOM Cliff Richard	Columbia	1
33	30	RIDERS ON THE STORM Doors	Elektra	3
23	31	YOU'VE GOT A FRIEND James Taylor	Warner	12
28	32	LADY LOVE BUG Clodagh Rodgers	RCA	6
25	33	BUTTERFLY Danyel Gerard	CBS	9
30	34	I'M LEAVIN' Elvis Presley	RCA	8
34	35	ANOTHER TIME, ANOTHER PLACE Engelbert Humperdinck	Decca	11
35	36	GYPSY EYES/REMEMBER Jimi Hendrix	Track	2
-	37	BURUNDI BLACK Burundi Steiphenson Black ●	Barclay	1
-	38	FIREBALL Deep Purple	Harvest	1
-	39	SOMETHING TELLS ME (SOMETHING IS GONNA HAPPEN TONIGHT) Cilla Black	Parlophone	1
32	40	HEY GIRL DON'T BOTHER ME Tams	Probe	17

LW	TW	*WEEK ENDING* **27 NOVEMBER 1971**		Wks
1	[1]	COZ I LUV YOU Slade	Polydor	5
8	[2]	JEEPSTER T. Rex	Fly	3
17	3	ERNIE (THE FASTEST MILKMAN IN THE WEST) Benny Hill	Columbia	3
7	[4]	GYPSYS TRAMPS AND THIEVES Cher	MCA	4
3	5	JOHNNY REGGAE Piglets	Bell	4
2	6	TILL Tom Jones	Decca	6
5	7	I WILL RETURN Springwater	Polydor	6
6	8	BANKS OF THE OHIO Olivia Newton-John	Pye	5
4	9	MAGGIE MAY Rod Stewart	Mercury	13
18	[10]	SURRENDER Diana Ross	Tamla Motown	4
9	11	TIRED OF BEING ALONE Al Green	London	8
14	12	RUN BABY RUN/AM I NOT MY BROTHER'S KEEPER Newbeats	London	5
13	13	LOOK AROUND Vince Hill	Columbia	8
28	14	TOKOLOSHE MAN John Kongos	Fly	2
10	15	THE NIGHT THEY DROVE OLD DIXIE DOWN Joan Baez	Vanguard	8
11	16	WITCH QUEEN OF NEW ORLEANS Redbone	Epic	9
16	17	BRANDY Scott English	Horse	7
29	18	SING A SONG OF FREEDOM Cliff Richard	Columbia	2
24	19	LET'S SEE THE ACTION Who	Track	4
12	20	SIMPLE GAME Four Tops	Tamla Motown	9
39	21	SOMETHING TELLS ME (SOMETHING IS GONNA HAPPEN TONIGHT) Cilla Black	Parlophone	2
15	22	SULTANA Titanic	CBS	9
20	23	FOR ALL WE KNOW Shirley Bassey	United Artists	15
19	24	SUPERSTAR/FOR ALL WE KNOW Carpenters	A&M	9
23	25	CHINA TOWN Move	Harvest	6

In these weeks ■ *Brandy* by Scott English stops at number 12. Just over three years later, the same song will give Barry Manilow his first hit, which will hit number 11. He changes the title to *Mandy* (13.11.71) ■ Slade displace Rod Stewart to have the first of their six number ones. They remain joint seventh on the list of all-time number one hitmakers (13.11.71) ■ Burundi Steiphenson Black become the first and only band from Burundi to hit the UK charts (20.11.71)■

LW	TW	Title / Artist	Label	Wks
22	26	TWEEDLE DEE TWEEDLE DUM Middle Of The Road	*RCA*	12
21	27	KEEP ON DANCING Bay City Rollers	*Bell*	11
25	28	FREEDOM COME, FREEDOM GO Fortunes	*Capitol*	11
27	29	DID YOU EVER Nancy and Lee	*Reprise*	15
30	30	RIDERS ON THE STORM Doors	*Elektra*	4
37	31	BURUNDI BLACK Burundi Steiphenson Black	*Barclay*	2
38	32	FIREBALL Deep Purple	*Harvest*	2
32	33	LADY LOVE BUG Clodagh Rodgers	*RCA*	7
-	34	YOU GOTTA HAVE LOVE IN YOUR HEART Supremes and the Four Tops	*Tamla Motown*	1
26	35	SPANISH HARLEM Aretha Franklin	*Atlantic*	9
-	36	HOOKED ON A FEELING Jonathan King	*Decca*	1
-	37	MAMMY BLUE Roger Whittaker	*Columbia*	7
-	38	IS THIS THE WAY TO AMARILLO Tony Christie	*MCA*	1
31	39	YOU'VE GOT A FRIEND James Taylor	*Warner*	13
33	40	BUTTERFLY Danyel Gerard	*CBS*	10

LW	TW	*WEEK ENDING* **4 DECEMBER 1971**		Wks
1	1	COZ I LUV YOU Slade	*Polydor*	6
3	2	ERNIE (THE FASTEST MILKMAN IN THE WEST) Benny Hill	*Columbia*	4
2	3	JEEPSTER T. Rex	*Fly*	4
4	4	GYPSYS TRAMPS AND THIEVES Cher	*MCA*	5
5	5	JOHNNY REGGAE Piglets	*Bell*	5
14	6	TOKOLOSHE MAN John Kongos	*Fly*	3
8	7	BANKS OF THE OHIO Olivia Newton-John	*Pye*	6
6	8	TILL Tom Jones	*Decca*	7
7	9	I WILL RETURN Springwater	*Polydor*	7
12	10	RUN BABY RUN/AM I NOT MY BROTHER'S KEEPER Newbeats	*London*	6
21	11	SOMETHING TELLS ME (SOMETHING IS GONNA HAPPEN TONIGHT) Cilla Black	*Parlophone*	3
10	12	SURRENDER Diana Ross	*Tamla Motown*	5
18	13	SING A SONG OF FREEDOM Cliff Richard	*Columbia*	3
9	14	MAGGIE MAY Rod Stewart	*Mercury*	14
-	15	NO MATTER HOW I TRY Gilbert O'Sullivan	*MAM*	1
-	16	THEME FROM 'SHAFT' Isaac Hayes	*Stax*	1
23	17	FOR ALL WE KNOW Shirley Bassey	*United Artists*	16
15	18	THE NIGHT THEY DROVE OLD DIXIE DOWN Joan Baez	*Vanguard*	9
13	19	LOOK AROUND Vince Hill	*Columbia*	9
19	20	LET'S SEE THE ACTION Who	*Track*	5
32	21	FIREBALL Deep Purple	*Harvest*	3
30	22	RIDERS ON THE STORM Doors	*Elektra*	5
11	23	TIRED OF BEING ALONE Al Green	*London*	9
16	24	WITCH QUEEN OF NEW ORLEANS Redbone	*Epic*	10
38	25	IS THIS THE WAY TO AMARILLO Tony Christie	*MCA*	2
36	26	HOOKED ON A FEELING Jonathan King	*Decca*	2
-	27	IT MUST BE LOVE Labi Siffre ●	*Pye*	1
-	28	SOFTLY WHISPERING I LOVE YOU Congregation ●	*Columbia*	1
34	29	YOU GOTTA HAVE LOVE IN YOUR HEART Supremes and the Four Tops	*Tamla Motown*	2
25	30	CHINA TOWN Move	*Harvest*	7
22	31	SULTANA Titanic	*CBS*	10
17	32	BRANDY Scott English	*Horse*	8
27	33	KEEP ON DANCING Bay City Rollers	*Bell*	12
20	34	SIMPLE GAME Four Tops	*Tamla Motown*	10
29	35	DID YOU EVER Nancy and Lee	*Reprise*	16
24	36	SUPERSTAR/FOR ALL WE KNOW Carpenters	*A&M*	10
28	37	FREEDOM COME, FREEDOM GO Fortunes	*Capitol*	12
26	38	TWEEDLE DEE TWEEDLE DUM Middle Of The Road	*RCA*	13
31	39	BURUNDI BLACK Burundi Steiphenson Black	*Barclay*	3
33	40	LADY LOVE BUG Clodagh Rodgers	*RCA*	8

LW	TW	*WEEK ENDING* **11 DECEMBER 1971**		Wks
2	1	ERNIE (THE FASTEST MILKMAN IN THE WEST) Benny Hill	*Columbia*	5
3	2	JEEPSTER T. Rex	*Fly*	5
1	3	COZ I LUV YOU Slade	*Polydor*	7
6	4	TOKOLOSHE MAN John Kongos	*Fly*	4
4	5	GYPSYS TRAMPS AND THIEVES Cher	*MCA*	6
7	6	BANKS OF THE OHIO Olivia Newton-John	*Pye*	7

December 1971

□ Highest position disc reached ● Act's first ever week on chart

LW	TW	Title / Artist	Label	Wks
16	7	THEME FROM SHAFT Isaac Hayes	*Stax*	2
8	8	TILL Tom Jones	*Decca*	8
15	9	NO MATTER HOW I TRY Gilbert O'Sullivan	*MAM*	2
5	10	JOHNNY REGGAE Piglets	*Bell*	6
10	11	RUN BABY RUN/AM I NOT MY BROTHER'S KEEPER Newbeats	*London*	7
11	12	SOMETHING TELLS ME (SOMETHING IS GONNA HAPPEN TONIGHT) Cilla Black	*Parlophone*	4
9	13	I WILL RETURN Springwater	*Polydor*	8
13	14	SING A SONG OF FREEDOM Cliff Richard	*Columbia*	4
12	15	SURRENDER Diana Ross	*Tamla Motown*	6
20	16	LET'S SEE THE ACTION Who	*Track*	6
27	17	IT MUST BE LOVE Labi Siffre	*Pye*	2
21	18	FIREBALL Deep Purple	*Harvest*	4
14	19	MAGGIE MAY Rod Stewart	*Mercury*	15
28	20	SOFTLY WHISPERING I LOVE YOU Congregation	*Columbia*	2
25	21	IS THIS THE WAY TO AMARILLO Tony Christie	*MCA*	3
-	22	I JUST CAN'T HELP BELIEVING Elvis Presley	*RCA*	1
-	23	SOLEY SOLEY Middle Of The Road	*RCA*	1
19	24	LOOK AROUND Vince Hill	*Columbia*	10
17	25	FOR ALL WE KNOW Shirley Bassey	*United Artists*	17
-	26	MORNING Val Doonican	*Philips*	1
29	27	YOU GOTTA HAVE LOVE IN YOUR HEART Supremes and the Four Tops	*Tamla Motown*	3
26	28	HOOKED ON A FEELING Jonathan King	*Decca*	3
22	29	RIDERS ON THE STORM Doors	*Elektra*	6
23	30	TIRED OF BEING ALONE Al Green	*London*	10
18	31	THE NIGHT THEY DROVE OLD DIXIE DOWN Joan Baez	*Vanguard*	10
-	32	KARA KARA New World	*New World*	1
39	33	BURUNDI BLACK Burundi Steiphenson Black	*Barclay*	4
-	34	WHEN YOU GET RIGHT DOWN TO IT Ronnie Dyson ●	*CBS*	1
24	35	WITCH QUEEN OF NEW ORLEANS Redbone	*Epic*	11
38	36	TWEEDLE DEE TWEEDLE DUM Middle Of The Road	*RCA*	14
35	37	DID YOU EVER Nancy and Lee	*Reprise*	17
-	38	CHIRPY CHIRPY CHEEP CHEEP Middle Of The Road	*RCA*	21
30	39	CHINA TOWN Move	*Harvest*	8
31	40	SULTANA Titanic	*CBS*	11

LW	TW	*WEEK ENDING* **18 DECEMBER 1971**		Wks
1	1	ERNIE (THE FASTEST MILKMAN IN THE WEST) Benny Hill	*Columbia*	6
2	2	JEEPSTER T. Rex	*Fly*	6
3	3	COZ I LUV YOU Slade	*Polydor*	8
7	4	THEME FROM SHAFT Isaac Hayes	*Stax*	3
9	5	NO MATTER HOW I TRY Gilbert O'Sullivan	*MAM*	3
4	6	TOKOLOSHE MAN John Kongos	*Fly*	5
12	7	SOMETHING TELLS ME (SOMETHING IS GONNA HAPPEN TONIGHT) Cilla Black	*Parlophone*	5
5	8	GYPSYS TRAMPS AND THIEVES Cher	*MCA*	7
6	9	BANKS OF THE OHIO Olivia Newton-John	*Pye*	8
8	10	TILL Tom Jones	*Decca*	9
11	11	RUN BABY RUN/AM I NOT MY BROTHER'S KEEPER Newbeats	*London*	8
20	12	SOFTLY WHISPERING I LOVE YOU Congregation	*Columbia*	3
14	13	SING A SONG OF FREEDOM Cliff Richard	*Columbia*	5
10	14	JOHNNY REGGAE Piglets	*Bell*	7
18	15	FIREBALL Deep Purple	*Harvest*	5
17	16	IT MUST BE LOVE Labi Siffre	*Pye*	3
15	17	SURRENDER Diana Ross	*Tamla Motown*	7
23	18	SOLEY SOLEY Middle Of The Road	*RCA*	2
26	19	MORNING Val Doonican	*Philips*	2
21	20	IS THIS THE WAY TO AMARILLO Tony Christie	*MCA*	4
13	21	I WILL RETURN Springwater	*Polydor*	9
22	22	I JUST CAN'T HELP BELIEVING Elvis Presley	*RCA*	2
28	23	HOOKED ON A FEELING Jonathan King	*Decca*	4
24	24	LOOK AROUND Vince Hill	*Columbia*	11
27	25	YOU GOTTA HAVE LOVE IN YOUR HEART Supremes and the Four Tops	*Tamla Motown*	4

■ Labi Siffre brings his own song *It Must Be Love* to the charts. It will later be a hit twice for Madness (04.12.71) ■ Benny Hill's finest hour as he holds T. Rex at bay at the top of the charts (11.12.71) ■ *Jeepster* was not an official T. Rex release. Bolan was changing labels and did not want this LP Track released as a single (11.12.71) ■

□ Highest position disc reached ● Act's first ever week on chart

- **26** SLEEPY SHORES Johnny Pearson Orchestra ● .. *Penny Farthing* 1
25 **27** FOR ALL WE KNOW Shirley Bassey .... *United Artists* 18
32 **28** KARA KARA New World .... *New World* 2
19 **29** MAGGIE MAY Rod Stewart .... *Mercury* 16
16 **30** LET'S SEE THE ACTION Who .... *Track* 7
33 **31** BURUNDI BLACK Burundi Steiphenson Black .... *Barclay* 5
- **32** I'D LIKE TO TEACH THE WORLD TO SING New Seekers .... *Polydor* 1
- **33** THE PERSUADERS John Barry Orchestra .... *CBS* 1
34 **34** WHEN YOU GET RIGHT DOWN TO IT Ronnie Dyson .... *CBS* 2
30 **35** TIRED OF BEING ALONE Al Green .... *London* 11
- **36** THEME FROM 'THE ONEDIN LINE' Vienna Philharmonic Orchestra ● .... *Decca* 1
29 **37** RIDERS ON THE STORM Doors .... *Elektra* 7
- **38** BACK ON THE ROAD Marmalade .... *Decca* 1
38 **39** CHIRPY CHIRPY CHEEP CHEEP Middle Of The Road .... *RCA* 22
- **40** FESTIVAL TIME San Remo Strings ● .... *Tamla Motown* 1

LW	TW	*WEEK ENDING* **25 DECEMBER 1971**	Wks

(no chart published, chart for 18 December repeated)

1 **1** ERNIE (THE FASTEST MILKMAN IN THE WEST) Benny Hill .... *Columbia* 7
2 **2** JEEPSTER T. Rex .... *Fly* 7
3 **3** COZ I LUV YOU Slade .... *Polydor* 9
4 **4** THEME FROM 'SHAFT' Isaac Hayes .... *Stax* 4
5 **5** NO MATTER HOW I TRY Gilbert O'Sullivan .... *MAM* 4
6 **6** TOKOLOSHE MAN John Kongos .... *Fly* 6
7 **7** SOMETHING TELLS ME (SOMETHING IS GONNA HAPPEN TONIGHT) Cilla Black .... *Parlophone* 6
8 **8** GYPSYS TRAMPS AND THIEVES Cher .... *MCA* 8
9 **9** BANKS OF THE OHIO Olivia Newton-John .... *Pye* 9
10 **10** TILL Tom Jones .... *Decca* 10
11 **11** RUN BABY RUN/AM I NOT MY BROTHER'S KEEPER Newbeats .... *London* 9
12 **12** SOFTLY WHISPERING I LOVE YOU Congregation ...... *Columbia* 4
13 **13** SING A SONG OF FREEDOM Cliff Richard .... *Columbia* 6
14 **14** JOHNNY REGGAE Piglets .... *Bell* 8
15 **15** FIREBALL Deep Purple .... *Harvest* 6
16 **16** IT MUST BE LOVE Labi Siffre .... *Pye* 4
17 **17** SURRENDER Diana Ross .... *Tamla Motown* 8
18 **18** SOLEY SOLEY Middle Of The Road .... *RCA* 3
19 **19** MORNING Val Doonican .... *Philips* 3
20 **20** IS THIS THE WAY TO AMARILLO Tony Christie .... *MCA* 5
21 **21** I WILL RETURN Springwater .... *Polydor* 10
22 **22** I JUST CAN'T HELP BELIEVING Elvis Presley .... *RCA* 3
23 **23** HOOKED ON A FEELING Jonathan King .... *Decca* 5
24 **24** LOOK AROUND Vince Hill .... *Columbia* 12
25 **25** YOU GOTTA HAVE LOVE IN YOUR HEART Supremes and the Four Tops .... *Tamla Motown* 5
26 **26** SLEEPY SHORES Johnny Pearson Orchestra ...... *Penny Farthing* 2
27 **27** FOR ALL WE KNOW Shirley Bassey .... *United Artists* 19
28 **28** KARA KARA New World .... *New World* 3
29 **29** MAGGIE MAY Rod Stewart .... *Mercury* 17
30 **30** LET'S SEE THE ACTION Who .... *Track* 8
31 **31** BURUNDI BLACK Burundi Steiphenson Black .... *Barclay* 6
32 **32** I'D LIKE TO TEACH THE WORLD TO SING New Seekers .... *Polydor* 2
33 **33** THE PERSUADERS John Barry Orchestra .... *CBS* 2
34 **34** WHEN YOU GET RIGHT DOWN TO IT Ronnie Dyson .... *CBS* 3
35 **35** TIRED OF BEING ALONE Al Green .... *London* 12
36 **36** THEME FROM 'THE ONEDIN LINE' Vienna Philharmonic Orchestra .... *Decca* 2
37 **37** RIDERS ON THE STORM Doors .... *Elektra* 8
38 **38** BACK ON THE ROAD Marmalade .... *Decca* 2
39 **39** CHIRPY CHIRPY CHEEP CHEEP Middle Of The Road .... *RCA* 23
40 **40** FESTIVAL TIME San Remo Strings .... *Tamla Motown* 2

In these weeks ■ Television theme tunes are successful at Christmas. There is Cilla Black's theme to her own series, *Sleepy Shores* by Johnny Pearson, *The Persuaders* by John Barry, and *Theme From 'The Onedin Lane'* by the Vienna Philharmonic Orchestra (25.12.71)■

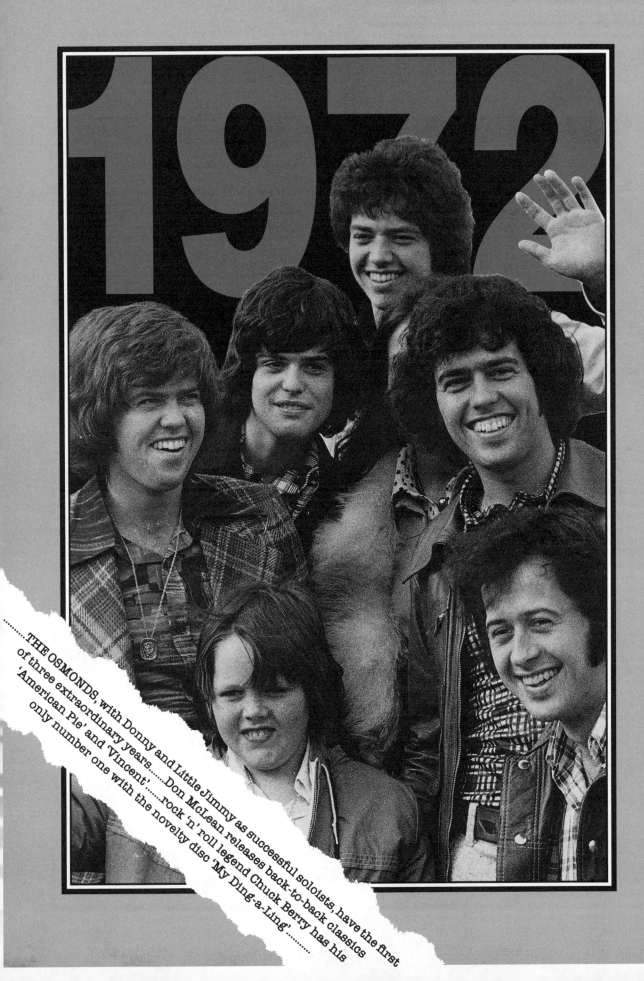

........THE OSMONDS, with Donny and Little Jimmy as successful soloists, have the first of three extraordinary years.......Don McLean releases back-to-back classics 'American Pie' and 'Vincent'.......rock 'n' roll legend Chuck Berry has his only number one with the novelty disc 'My Ding-a-Ling'..........

January 1972

□ Highest position disc reached ● Act's first ever week on chart

WEEK ENDING 1 JANUARY 1972

LW	TW	Title / Artist	Label	Wks
1	1	ERNIE (THE FASTEST MILKMAN IN THE WEST) Benny Hill	Columbia	8
2	2	JEEPSTER T. Rex	Fly	8
7	3	SOMETHING TELLS ME (SOMETHING IS GONNA HAPPEN TONIGHT) Cilla Black	Parlophone	7
32	4	I'D LIKE TO TEACH THE WORLD TO SING New Seekers	Polydor	3
4	5	THEME FROM 'SHAFT' Isaac Hayes	Stax	5
12	6	SOFTLY WHISPERING I LOVE YOU Congregation	Columbia	5
6	7	TOKOLOSHE MAN John Kongos	Fly	7
5	8	NO MATTER HOW I TRY Gilbert O'Sullivan	MAM	5
18	9	SOLEY SOLEY Middle Of The Road	RCA	4
8	10	GYPSIES TRAMPS AND THIEVES Cher	MCA	9
9	11	BANKS OF THE OHIO Olivia Newton-John	Pye	10
19	12	MORNING Val Doonican	Philips	4
26	13	SLEEPY SHORES Johnny Pearson Orchestra	Penny Farthing	3
3	14	COZ I LUV YOU Slade	Polydor	10
16	15	IT MUST BE LOVE Labi Siffre	Pye	5
22	16	I JUST CAN'T HELP BELIEVING Elvis Presley	RCA	4
15	17	FIREBALL Deep Purple	Harvest	7
-	18	MOTHER OF MINE Neil Reid ●	Decca	1
10	19	TILL Tom Jones	Decca	11
20	20	IS THIS THE WAY TO AMARILLO Tony Christie	MCA	6
28	21	KARA KARA New World	New World	4
13	22	SING A SONG OF FREEDOM Cliff Richard	Columbia	7
11	23	RUN BABY RUN/AM I NOT MY BROTHER'S KEEPER Newbeats	London	10
14	24	JOHNNY REGGAE Piglets	Bell	9
36	25	THEME FROM 'THE ONEDIN LINE' Vienna Philharmonic Orchestra	Decca	3
21	26	I WILL RETURN Springwater	Polydor	11
25	27	YOU GOTTA HAVE LOVE IN YOUR HEART Supremes/Four Tops	Tamla Motown	6
24	28	LOOK AROUND Vince Hill	Columbia	13
27	29	FOR ALL WE KNOW Shirley Bassey	United Artists	20
23	30	HOOKED ON A FEELING Jonathan King	Decca	6
30	31	LET'S SEE THE ACTION Who	Track	9
33	32	THE PERSUADERS John Barry Orchestra	CBS	3
17	33	SURRENDER Diana Ross	Tamla Motown	9
-	34	BRAND NEW KEY Melanie	Buddah	1
29	35	MAGGIE MAY Rod Stewart	Mercury	18
-	36	MORNING HAS BROKEN Cat Stevens	Island	1
34	37	WHEN YOU GET RIGHT DOWN TO IT Ronnie Dyson	CBS	4
31	38	BURUNDI BLACK Burundi Steiphenson Black	Barclay	7
38	39	BACK ON THE ROAD Marmalade	Decca	3
35	40	TIRED OF BEING ALONE Al Green	London	13

WEEK ENDING 8 JANUARY 1972

LW	TW	Title / Artist	Label	Wks
4	1	I'D LIKE TO TEACH THE WORLD TO SING New Seekers	Polydor	4
1	2	ERNIE (THE FASTEST MILKMAN IN THE WEST) Benny Hill	Columbia	9
2	3	JEEPSTER T. Rex	Fly	9
6	4	SOFTLY WHISPERING I LOVE YOU Congregation	Columbia	6
9	5	SOLEY SOLEY Middle Of The Road	RCA	5
5	6	THEME FROM 'SHAFT' Isaac Hayes	Stax	6
3	7	SOMETHING TELLS ME (SOMETHING IS GONNA HAPPEN TONIGHT) Cilla Black	Parlophone	8
13	8	SLEEPY SHORES Johnny Pearson Orchestra	Penny Farthing	4
8	9	NO MATTER HOW I TRY Gilbert O'Sullivan	MAM	6
16	10	I JUST CAN'T HELP BELIEVING Elvis Presley	RCA	5
7	11	TOKOLOSHE MAN John Kongos	Fly	8
18	12	MOTHER OF MINE Neil Reid	Decca	2
12	13	MORNING Val Doonican	Philips	5
15	14	IT MUST BE LOVE Labi Siffre	Pye	6
17	15	FIREBALL Deep Purple	Harvest	8
14	16	COZ I LUV YOU Slade	Polydor	11
21	17	KARA KARA New World	New World	5
20	18	IS THIS THE WAY TO AMARILLO Tony Christie	MCA	7
10	19	GYPSIES TRAMPS AND THIEVES Cher	MCA	10
22	20	SING A SONG OF FREEDOM Cliff Richard	Columbia	8
-	21	HORSE WITH NO NAME America ●	Warner Brothers	1
11	22	BANKS OF THE OHIO Olivia Newton-John	Pye	11
-	23	STAY WITH ME Faces	Warner Brothers	1
34	24	BRAND NEW KEY Melanie	Buddah	2
25	25	THEME FROM 'THE ONEDIN LINE' Vienna Philharmonic Orchestra	Decca	4
27	26	YOU GOTTA HAVE LOVE IN YOUR HEART Supremes/Four Tops	Tamla Motown	7
32	27	THE PERSUADERS John Barry Orchestra	CBS	4
24	28	JOHNNY REGGAE Piglets	Bell	10
23	29	RUN BABY RUN/AM I NOT MY BROTHER'S KEEPER Newbeats	London	11
36	30	MORNING HAS BROKEN Cat Stevens	Island	2
30	31	HOOKED ON A FEELING Jonathan King	Decca	7
38	32	BURUNDI BLACK Burundi Steiphenson Black	Barclay	8
33	33	SURRENDER Diana Ross	Tamla Motown	10
37	34	WHEN YOU GET RIGHT DOWN TO IT Ronnie Dyson	CBS	5
39	35	BACK ON THE ROAD Marmalade	Decca	4
26	36	I WILL RETURN Springwater	Polydor	12
19	37	TILL Tom Jones	Decca	12
35	38	MAGGIE MAY Rod Stewart	Mercury	19
-	39	FAMILY AFFAIR Sly and The Family Stone	Epic	1
29	40	FOR ALL WE KNOW Shirley Bassey	United Artists	21

WEEK ENDING 15 JANUARY 1972

LW	TW	Title / Artist	Label	Wks
1	1	I'D LIKE TO TEACH THE WORLD TO SING New Seekers	Polydor	5
12	2	MOTHER OF MINE Neil Reid	Decca	3
2	3	ERNIE (THE FASTEST MILKMAN IN THE WEST) Benny Hill	Columbia	10
4	4	SOFTLY WHISPERING I LOVE YOU Congregation	Columbia	7
5	5	SOLEY SOLEY Middle Of The Road	RCA	6
7	6	SOMETHING TELLS ME (SOMETHING IS GONNA HAPPEN TONIGHT) Cilla Black	Parlophone	9
10	7	I JUST CAN'T HELP BELIEVING Elvis Presley	RCA	6
24	8	BRAND NEW KEY Melanie	Buddah	3
8	9	SLEEPY SHORES Johnny Pearson Orchestra	Penny Farthing	5
3	10	JEEPSTER T. Rex	Fly	10
21	11	HORSE WITH NO NAME America	Warner Brothers	2
9	12	NO MATTER HOW I TRY Gilbert O'Sullivan	MAM	7
30	13	MORNING HAS BROKEN Cat Stevens	Island	3
6	14	THEME FROM 'SHAFT' Isaac Hayes	Stax	7
13	15	MORNING Val Doonican	Philips	6
23	16	STAY WITH ME Faces	Warner Brothers	2
25	17	THEME FROM 'THE ONEDIN LINE' Vienna Philharmonic Orchestra	Decca	5
15	18	FIREBALL Deep Purple	Harvest	9
14	19	IT MUST BE LOVE Labi Siffre	Pye	7
27	20	THE PERSUADERS John Barry Orchestra	CBS	5
18	21	IS THIS THE WAY TO AMARILLO Tony Christie	MCA	8
17	22	KARA KARA New World	New World	6
22	23	BANKS OF THE OHIO Olivia Newton-John	Pye	12
11	24	TOKOLOSHE MAN John Kongos	Fly	9
16	25	COZ I LUV YOU Slade	Polydor	12
20	26	SING A SONG OF FREEDOM Cliff Richard	Columbia	9
19	27	GYPSIES TRAMPS AND THIEVES Cher	MCA	11
-	28	WHERE DID OUR LOVE GO Donnie Elbert ●	London	1
-	29	LET'S STAY TOGETHER Al Green	London	1
39	30	FAMILY AFFAIR Sly and The Family Stone	Epic	2
31	31	HOOKED ON A FEELING Jonathan King	Decca	8
37	32	TILL Tom Jones	Decca	13
-	33	MOON RIVER Greyhound	Trojan	1
-	34	CAN'T LET YOU GO Barry Ryan	Polydor	1
32	35	BURUNDI BLACK Burundi Steiphenson Black	Barclay	9
26	36	YOU GOTTA HAVE LOVE IN YOUR HEART Supremes/Four Tops	Tamla Motown	8
28	37	JOHNNY REGGAE Piglets	Bell	11
-	38	BABY I'M A WANT YOU Bread	Elektra	1

In these weeks ■ The New Seekers' *I'd Like To Teach The World To Sing* becomes the first TV advertisement related song to hit the very top. The original was *I'd Like To Buy The World A Coke* (08.01.72) ■ The first major group produced by George Martin since the Beatles broke up, America, make their chart debut (08.01.72)■

LW	TW	Title	Artist	Label	Wks
-	39	BLESS YOU	Martha Reeves & The Vandellas	Tamla Motown	1
-	40	HAVE YOU SEEN HER	Chi-Lites	MCA	1

February 1972

□ Highest position disc reached ● Act's first ever week on chart

WEEK ENDING 22 JANUARY 1972

LW	TW	Title	Artist	Label	Wks
1	1	I'D LIKE TO TEACH THE WORLD TO SING	New Seekers	Polydor	6
2	2	MOTHER OF MINE	Neil Reid	Decca	4
11	3	HORSE WITH NO NAME	America	Warner Brothers	3
8	4	BRAND NEW KEY	Melanie	Buddah	4
4	5	SOFTLY WHISPERING I LOVE YOU	Congregation	Columbia	8
7	6	I JUST CAN'T HELP BELIEVING	Elvis Presley	RCA	7
5	7	SOLEY SOLEY	Middle Of The Road	RCA	7
16	8	STAY WITH ME	Faces	Warner Brothers	3
9	9	SLEEPY SHORES	Johnny Pearson Orchestra	Penny Farthing	6
13	10	MORNING HAS BROKEN	Cat Stevens	Island	4
12	11	NO MATTER HOW I TRY	Gilbert O'Sullivan	MAM	8
6	12	SOMETHING TELLS ME (SOMETHING IS GONNA HAPPEN TONIGHT)	Cilla Black	Parlophone	10
3	13	ERNIE (THE FASTEST MILKMAN IN THE WEST)	Benny Hill	Columbia	11
14	14	THEME FROM 'SHAFT'	Isaac Hayes	Stax	8
17	15	THEME FROM 'THE ONEDIN LINE'	Vienna Philharmonic Orchestra	Decca	6
28	16	WHERE DID OUR LOVE GO	Donnie Elbert	London	2
29	17	LET'S STAY TOGETHER	Al Green	London	2
10	18	JEEPSTER	T. Rex	Fly	11
15	19	MORNING	Val Doonican	Philips	7
20	20	THE PERSUADERS	John Barry Orchestra	CBS	6
22	21	KARA KARA	New World	New World	7
30	22	FAMILY AFFAIR	Sly and The Family Stone	Epic	3
19	23	IT MUST BE LOVE	Labi Siffre	Pye	8
33	24	MOON RIVER	Greyhound	Trojan	2
21	25	IS THIS THE WAY TO AMARILLO	Tony Christie	MCA	9
18	26	FIREBALL	Deep Purple	Harvest	10
40	27	HAVE YOU SEEN HER	Chi-Lites	MCA	2
38	28	BABY I'M A WANT YOU	Bread	Elektra	2
23	29	BANKS OF THE OHIO	Olivia Newton-John	Pye	13
-	30	ALL I EVER NEED IS YOU	Sonny and Cher	MCA	1
25	31	COZ I LUV YOU	Slade	Polydor	13
24	32	TOKOLOSHE MAN	John Kongos	Fly	10
39	33	BLESS YOU	Martha Reeves & The Vandellas	Tamla Motown	2
34	34	CAN'T LET YOU GO	Barry Ryan	Polydor	2
-	35	GIVE AND TAKE	Pioneers	Trojan	1
26	36	SING A SONG OF FREEDOM	Cliff Richard	Columbia	10
-	37	IF YOU REALLY LOVE ME	Stevie Wonder	Tamla Motown	1
27	38	GYPSIES TRAMPS AND THIEVES	Cher	MCA	12
-	39	FESTIVAL TIME	San Remo Strings	Tamla Motown	1
35	40	BURUNDI BLACK	Burundi Steiphenson Black	Barclay	10

WEEK ENDING 29 JANUARY 1972

LW	TW	Title	Artist	Label	Wks
1	1	I'D LIKE TO TEACH THE WORLD TO SING	New Seekers	Polydor	7
2	2	MOTHER OF MINE	Neil Reid	Decca	5
-	3	TELEGRAM SAM	T. Rex	T. Rex	1
3	4	HORSE WITH NO NAME	America	Warner Brothers	4
4	5	BRAND NEW KEY	Melanie	Buddah	5
6	6	I JUST CAN'T HELP BELIEVING	Elvis Presley	RCA	8
8	7	STAY WITH ME	Faces	Warner Brothers	4
16	8	WHERE DID OUR LOVE GO	Donnie Elbert	London	3
10	9	MORNING HAS BROKEN	Cat Stevens	Island	5
17	10	LET'S STAY TOGETHER	Al Green	London	3
7	11	SOLEY SOLEY	Middle Of The Road	RCA	8
9	12	SLEEPY SHORES	Johnny Pearson Orchestra	Penny Farthing	7
20	13	THE PERSUADERS	John Barry Orchestra	CBS	7
5	14	SOFTLY WHISPERING I LOVE YOU	Congregation	Columbia	9
24	15	MOON RIVER	Greyhound	Trojan	3
15	16	THEME FROM 'THE ONEDIN LINE'	Vienna Philharmonic Orchestra	Decca	7
27	17	HAVE YOU SEEN HER	Chi-Lites	MCA	3
11	18	NO MATTER HOW I TRY	Gilbert O'Sullivan	MAM	9
30	19	ALL I EVER NEED IS YOU	Sonny and Cher	MCA	2
28	20	BABY I'M A WANT YOU	Bread	Elektra	3
13	21	ERNIE (THE FASTEST MILKMAN IN THE WEST)	Benny Hill	Columbia	12
12	22	SOMETHING TELLS ME (SOMETHING IS GONNA HAPPEN TONIGHT)	Cilla Black	Parlophone	11
22	23	FAMILY AFFAIR	Sly and The Family Stone	Epic	4
14	24	THEME FROM 'SHAFT'	Isaac Hayes	Stax	9
37	25	IF YOU REALLY LOVE ME	Stevie Wonder	Tamla Motown	2
21	26	KARA KARA	New World	New World	8
-	27	AMERICAN PIE	Don McLean	United Artists	1
19	28	MORNING	Val Doonican	Philips	8
18	29	JEEPSTER	T. Rex	Fly	12
-	30	SON OF MY FATHER	Chicory Tip	CBS	1
23	31	IT MUST BE LOVE	Labi Siffre	Pye	9
34	32	CAN'T LET YOU GO	Barry Ryan	Polydor	3
26	33	FIREBALL	Deep Purple	Harvest	11
29	34	BANKS OF THE OHIO	Olivia Newton-John	Pye	14
-	35	STORM IN A TEA CUP	Fortunes	Capitol	1
35	36	GIVE AND TAKE	Pioneers	Trojan	2
25	37	IS THIS THE WAY TO AMARILLO	Tony Christie	MCA	10
-	38	MY WORLD	Bee Gees	Polydor	1
40	39	BURUNDI BLACK	Burundi Steiphenson Black	Barclay	11
33	40	BLESS YOU	Martha Reeves & The Vandellas	Tamla Motown	3

WEEK ENDING 5 FEBRUARY 1972

LW	TW	Title	Artist	Label	Wks
3	1	TELEGRAM SAM	T. Rex	T. Rex	2
1	2	I'D LIKE TO TEACH THE WORLD TO SING	New Seekers	Polydor	8
2	3	MOTHER OF MINE	Neil Reid	Decca	6
4	4	HORSE WITH NO NAME	America	Warner Brothers	5
5	5	BRAND NEW KEY	Melanie	Buddah	6
7	6	STAY WITH ME	Faces	Warner Brothers	5
17	7	HAVE YOU SEEN HER	Chi-Lites	MCA	4
8	8	WHERE DID OUR LOVE GO	Donnie Elbert	London	4
10	9	LET'S STAY TOGETHER	Al Green	London	4
6	10	I JUST CAN'T HELP BELIEVING	Elvis Presley	RCA	9
30	11	SON OF MY FATHER	Chicory Tip	CBS	2
15	12	MOON RIVER	Greyhound	Trojan	4
9	13	MORNING HAS BROKEN	Cat Stevens	Island	6
20	14	BABY I'M A WANT YOU	Bread	Elektra	4
23	15	FAMILY AFFAIR	Sly and The Family Stone	Epic	5
19	16	ALL I EVER NEED IS YOU	Sonny and Cher	MCA	3
27	17	AMERICAN PIE	Don McLean	United Artists	2
11	18	SOLEY SOLEY	Middle Of The Road	RCA	9
12	19	SLEEPY SHORES	Johnny Pearson Orchestra	Penny Farthing	8
13	20	THE PERSUADERS	John Barry Orchestra	CBS	8
14	21	SOFTLY WHISPERING I LOVE YOU	Congregation	Columbia	10
25	22	IF YOU REALLY LOVE ME	Stevie Wonder	Tamla Motown	3
35	23	STORM IN A TEA CUP	Fortunes	Capitol	2
18	24	NO MATTER HOW I TRY	Gilbert O'Sullivan	MAM	10
-	25	LOOK WOT YOU DUN	Slade	Polydor	1
38	26	MY WORLD	Bee Gees	Polydor	2
16	27	THEME FROM 'THE ONEDIN LINE'	Vienna Philharmonic Orchestra	Decca	8
-	28	DAY AFTER DAY	Badfinger	Apple	1
24	29	THEME FROM 'SHAFT'	Isaac Hayes	Stax	10
21	30	ERNIE (THE FASTEST MILKMAN IN THE WEST)	Benny Hill	Columbia	13
28	31	MORNING	Val Doonican	Philips	9
26	32	KARA KARA	New World	New World	9
31	33	IT MUST BE LOVE	Labi Siffre	Pye	10
29	34	JEEPSTER	T. Rex	Fly	13
22	35	SOMETHING TELLS ME (SOMETHING IS GONNA HAPPEN TONIGHT)	Cilla Black	Parlophone	12
37	36	IS THIS THE WAY TO AMARILLO	Tony Christie	MCA	11
36	37	GIVE AND TAKE	Pioneers	Trojan	3
34	38	BANKS OF THE OHIO	Olivia Newton-John	Pye	15
-	39	DIAMONDS ARE FOREVER	Shirley Bassey	United Artists	1
32	40	CAN'T LET YOU GO	Barry Ryan	Polydor	4

■For 3 consecutive weeks, the record at no. 26 dropped the next week to no. 36 (8-22.01.72) ■ Melanie's *Brand New Key* peaks at number 4. Four years later a re-written version by the Wurzels (*Combine Harvester (Brand New Key)* will hit the very top (22.01.72) ■ Giorgio Moroder's first chart action is the song that Chicory Tip covered *Son Of My Father* (29.01.72)■

February 1972

□ Highest position disc reached ● Act's first ever week on chart

LW	TW	WEEK ENDING 12 FEBRUARY 1972		Wks
1	[1]	TELEGRAM SAM T. Rex	*T. Rex*	3
11	2	SON OF MY FATHER Chicory Tip	*CBS*	3
3	3	MOTHER OF MINE Neil Reid	*Decca*	7
2	4	I'D LIKE TO TEACH THE WORLD TO SING New Seekers	*Polydor*	9
7	5	HAVE YOU SEEN HER Chi-Lites	*MCA*	5
4	6	HORSE WITH NO NAME America	*Warner Brothers*	6
9	[7]	LET'S STAY TOGETHER Al Green	*London*	5
5	8	BRAND NEW KEY Melanie	*Buddah*	7
25	9	LOOK WOT YOU DUN Slade	*Polydor*	2
16	10	ALL I EVER NEED IS YOU Sonny and Cher	*MCA*	4
6	11	STAY WITH ME Faces	*Warner Brothers*	6
8	12	WHERE DID OUR LOVE GO Donnie Elbert	*London*	5
10	13	I JUST CAN'T HELP BELIEVING Elvis Presley	*RCA*	10
12	14	MOON RIVER Greyhound	*Trojan*	5
17	15	AMERICAN PIE Don McLean	*United Artists*	3
23	16	STORM IN A TEA CUP Fortunes	*Capitol*	3
28	17	DAY AFTER DAY Badfinger	*Apple*	2
14	18	BABY I'M A WANT YOU Bread	*Elektra*	5
15	19	FAMILY AFFAIR Sly and The Family Stone	*Epic*	6
26	20	MY WORLD Bee Gees	*Polydor*	3
20	21	THE PERSUADERS John Barry Orchestra	*CBS*	9
22	22	IF YOU REALLY LOVE ME Stevie Wonder	*Tamla Motown*	4
13	23	MORNING HAS BROKEN Cat Stevens	*Island*	7
19	24	SLEEPY SHORES Johnny Pearson Orchestra	*Penny Farthing*	9
18	25	SOLEY SOLEY Middle Of The Road	*RCA*	10
27	26	THEME FROM 'THE ONEDIN LINE' Vienna Philharmonic Orchestra	*Decca*	9
-	27	WITHOUT YOU Nilsson	*RCA*	1
24	28	NO MATTER HOW I TRY Gilbert O'Sullivan	*MAM*	11
21	29	SOFTLY WHISPERING I LOVE YOU Congregation	*Columbia*	11
-	30	POPPA JOE Sweet	*RCA*	1
-	31	DAY BY DAY Holly Sherwood	*Bell*	1
30	32	ERNIE (THE FASTEST MILKMAN IN THE WEST) Benny Hill	*Columbia*	14
29	33	THEME FROM 'SHAFT' Isaac Hayes	*Stax*	11
32	34	KARA KARA New World	*New World*	10
31	35	MORNING Val Doonican	*Philips*	10
-	36	SUPERSTAR Temptations	*Tamla Motown*	1
-	37	FLIRT Jonathan King	*Decca*	1
39	[38]	DIAMONDS ARE FOREVER Shirley Bassey	*United Artists*	2
-	39	GOT TO BE THERE Michael Jackson ●	*Tamla Motown*	1
33	40	IT MUST BE LOVE Labi Siffre	*Pye*	11

LW	TW	WEEK ENDING 19 FEBRUARY 1972		Wks
2	[1]	SON OF MY FATHER Chicory Tip	*CBS*	4
1	2	TELEGRAM SAM T. Rex	*T. Rex*	4
5	[3]	HAVE YOU SEEN HER Chi-Lites	*MCA*	6
9	[4]	LOOK WOT YOU DUN Slade	*Polydor*	3
3	5	MOTHER OF MINE Neil Reid	*Decca*	8
15	6	AMERICAN PIE Don McLean	*United Artists*	4
4	7	I'D LIKE TO TEACH THE WORLD TO SING New Seekers	*Polydor*	10
10	[8]	ALL I EVER NEED IS YOU Sonny and Cher	*MCA*	5
16	9	STORM IN A TEA CUP Fortunes	*Capitol*	4
7	10	LET'S STAY TOGETHER Al Green	*London*	6
6	11	HORSE WITH NO NAME America	*Warner Brothers*	7
14	12	MOON RIVER Greyhound	*Trojan*	6
17	13	DAY AFTER DAY Badfinger	*Apple*	3
8	14	BRAND NEW KEY Melanie	*Buddah*	8
18	15	BABY I'M A WANT YOU Bread	*Elektra*	6
27	16	WITHOUT YOU Nilsson	*RCA*	2
20	17	MY WORLD Bee Gees	*Polydor*	4
19	18	FAMILY AFFAIR Sly and The Family Stone	*Epic*	7
12	19	WHERE DID OUR LOVE GO Donnie Elbert	*London*	6
22	[20]	IF YOU REALLY LOVE ME Stevie Wonder	*Tamla Motown*	5
11	21	STAY WITH ME Faces	*Warner Brothers*	7
39	22	GOT TO BE THERE Michael Jackson	*Tamla Motown*	2
13	23	I JUST CAN'T HELP BELIEVING Elvis Presley	*RCA*	11
21	24	THE PERSUADERS John Barry Orchestra	*CBS*	10
23	25	MORNING HAS BROKEN Cat Stevens	*Island*	8
30	26	POPPA JOE Sweet	*RCA*	2
24	27	SLEEPY SHORES Johnny Pearson Orchestra	*Penny Farthing*	10
-	28	MOTHER AND CHILD REUNION Paul Simon ●	*CBS*	1
31	[29]	DAY BY DAY Holly Sherwood	*Bell*	2
26	30	THEME FROM 'THE ONEDIN LINE' Vienna Philharmonic Orchestra	*Decca*	10
-	31	SAY YOU DON'T MIND Colin Blunstone ●	*Epic*	1
36	[32]	SUPERSTAR Temptations	*Tamla Motown*	2
25	33	SOLEY SOLEY Middle Of The Road	*RCA*	11
37	34	FLIRT Jonathan King	*Decca*	2
34	35	KARA KARA New World	*New World*	11
33	36	THEME FROM 'SHAFT' Isaac Hayes	*Stax*	12
29	37	SOFTLY WHISPERING I LOVE YOU Congregation	*Columbia*	11
28	38	NO MATTER HOW I TRY Gilbert O'Sullivan	*MAM*	12
-	39	JOHNNY B GOODE Jimi Hendrix	*Polydor*	1
32	40	ERNIE (THE FASTEST MILKMAN IN THE WEST) Benny Hill	*Columbia*	15

LW	TW	WEEK ENDING 26 FEBRUARY 1972		Wks
1	[1]	SON OF MY FATHER Chicory Tip	*CBS*	5
2	2	TELEGRAM SAM T. Rex	*T. Rex*	5
6	3	AMERICAN PIE Don McLean	*United Artists*	5
4	[4]	LOOK WOT YOU DUN Slade	*Polydor*	4
16	5	WITHOUT YOU Nilsson	*RCA*	2
3	6	HAVE YOU SEEN HER Chi-Lites	*MCA*	7
9	[7]	STORM IN A TEA CUP Fortunes	*Capitol*	5
22	8	GOT TO BE THERE Michael Jackson	*Tamla Motown*	3
5	9	MOTHER OF MINE Neil Reid	*Decca*	9
13	[10]	DAY AFTER DAY Badfinger	*Apple*	4
8	11	ALL I EVER NEED IS YOU Sonny and Cher	*MCA*	6
10	12	LET'S STAY TOGETHER Al Green	*London*	7
7	13	I'D LIKE TO TEACH THE WORLD TO SING New Seekers	*Polydor*	11
26	14	POPPA JOE Sweet	*RCA*	3
-	15	BLUE IS THE COLOUR Chelsea Football Team ●	*Penny Farthing*	1
17	[16]	MY WORLD Bee Gees	*Polydor*	5
28	17	MOTHER AND CHILD REUNION Paul Simon	*CBS*	2
14	18	BRAND NEW KEY Melanie	*Buddah*	9
11	19	HORSE WITH NO NAME America	*Warner Brothers*	8
20	[20]	IF YOU REALLY LOVE ME Stevie Wonder	*Tamla Motown*	6
21	21	STAY WITH ME Faces	*Warner Brothers*	8
19	22	WHERE DID OUR LOVE GO Donnie Elbert	*London*	7
12	23	MOON RIVER Greyhound	*Trojan*	7
23	24	I JUST CAN'T HELP BELIEVING Elvis Presley	*RCA*	12
15	25	BABY I'M A WANT YOU Bread	*Elektra*	7
24	26	THE PERSUADERS John Barry Orchestra	*CBS*	11
27	27	SLEEPY SHORES Johnny Pearson Orchestra	*Penny Farthing*	11
31	28	SAY YOU DON'T MIND Colin Blunstone	*Epic*	2
29	[29]	DAY BY DAY Holly Sherwood	*Bell*	3
34	30	FLIRT Jonathan King	*Decca*	3
18	31	FAMILY AFFAIR Sly and The Family Stone	*Epic*	8
25	32	MORNING HAS BROKEN Cat Stevens	*Island*	9
30	33	THEME FROM 'THE ONEDIN LINE' Vienna Philharmonic Orchestra	*Decca*	11
38	34	NO MATTER HOW I TRY Gilbert O'Sullivan	*MAM*	13
39	[35]	JOHNNY B GOODE Jimi Hendrix	*Polydor*	2
-	36	MEET ME ON THE CORNER Lindisfarne ●	*Charisma*	1
37	37	SOFTLY WHISPERING I LOVE YOU Congregation	*Columbia*	12
32	38	SUPERSTAR Temptations	*Tamla Motown*	3
-	39	I CAN'T HELP MYSELF Donnie Elbert	*Avco*	1
-	40	THE BABY Hollies	*Polydor*	1

LW	TW	WEEK ENDING 4 MARCH 1972		Wks
1	[1]	SON OF MY FATHER Chicory Tip	*CBS*	6
3	[2]	AMERICAN PIE Don McLean	*United Artists*	6
5	3	WITHOUT YOU Nilsson	*RCA*	3

In these weeks ■ Sonny and Cher's final hit peaks at number eight, while half of another famous duo, Paul Simon, has his first solo hit (19.02.72) ■ Two boy sopranos in the Top 10 - Michael Jackson and Neil Reid (26.02.72) ■ *Without You* was written by Peter Ham and Tom Evans of Badfinger, who peaked at number ten with their own hit (26.02.72)■

March 1972

□ Highest position disc reached ● Act's first ever week on chart

LW	TW	Title	Artist	Label	Wks
4	4	LOOK WOT YOU DUN	Slade	*Polydor*	5
8	5	GOT TO BE THERE	Michael Jackson	*Tamla Motown*	4
6	6	HAVE YOU SEEN HER	Chi-Lites	*MCA*	8
17	7	MOTHER AND CHILD REUNION	Paul Simon	*CBS*	3
7	8	STORM IN A TEA CUP	Fortunes	*Capitol*	6
15	9	BLUE IS THE COLOUR	Chelsea Football Team	*Penny Farthing*	2
10	10	DAY AFTER DAY	Badfinger	*Apple*	5
14	11	POPPA JOE	Sweet	*RCA*	4
-	12	BEG, STEAL OR BORROW	New Seekers	*Polydor*	1
9	13	MOTHER OF MINE	Neil Reid	*Decca*	10
2	14	TELEGRAM SAM	T. Rex	*T. Rex*	6
13	15	I'D LIKE TO TEACH THE WORLD TO SING	New Seekers	*Polydor*	12
16	16	MY WORLD	Bee Gees	*Polydor*	6
28	17	SAY YOU DON'T MIND	Colin Blunstone	*Epic*	3
11	18	ALL I EVER NEED IS YOU	Sonny and Cher	*MCA*	7
39	19	I CAN'T HELP MYSELF	Donnie Elbert	*Avco*	2
12	20	LET'S STAY TOGETHER	Al Green	*London*	8
-	21	GIVE IRELAND BACK TO THE IRISH	Wings	*Apple*	1
36	22	MEET ME ON THE CORNER	Lindisfarne	*Charisma*	2
-	23	ALONE AGAIN (NATURALLY)	Gilbert O'Sullivan	*MAM*	1
18	24	BRAND NEW KEY	Melanie	*Buddah*	10
26	25	THE PERSUADERS	John Barry Orchestra	*CBS*	12
30	26	FLIRT	Jonathan King	*Decca*	4
23	27	MOON RIVER	Greyhound	*Trojan*	8
19	28	HORSE WITH NO NAME	America	*Warner Brothers*	9
25	29	BABY I'M A WANT YOU	Bread	*Elektra*	8
29	30	DAY BY DAY	Holly Sherwood	*Bell*	4
22	31	WHERE DID OUR LOVE GO	Donnie Elbert	*London*	8
40	32	THE BABY	Hollies	*Polydor*	2
-	33	IT'S ONE OF THOSE NIGHTS	Partridge Family	*Bell*	1
24	34	I JUST CAN'T HELP BELIEVING	Elvis Presley	*RCA*	13
27	35	SLEEPY SHORES	Johnny Pearson Orchestra	*Penny Farthing*	12
-	36	LOVING YOU AIN'T EASY	Pagliaro ●	*Pye*	1
-	37	DESIDERATA	Les Crane ●	*Warner Brothers*	1
21	38	STAY WITH ME	Faces	*Warner Brothers*	9
33	39	THEME FROM 'THE ONEDIN LINE'	Vienna Philharmonic Orchestra	*Decca*	12
-	40	SPIRIT IS WILLING	Peter Straker and the Hands Of Dr Teleny ●	*RCA*	1

LW	TW	*WEEK ENDING* **11 MARCH 1972**			Wks
3	1	WITHOUT YOU	Nilsson	*RCA*	4
2	2	AMERICAN PIE	Don McLean	*United Artists*	7
1	3	SON OF MY FATHER	Chicory Tip	*CBS*	7
12	4	BEG, STEAL OR BORROW	New Seekers	*Polydor*	2
9	5	BLUE IS THE COLOUR	Chelsea Football Team	*Penny Farthing*	3
5	6	GOT TO BE THERE	Michael Jackson	*Tamla Motown*	5
7	7	MOTHER AND CHILD REUNION	Paul Simon	*CBS*	4
4	8	LOOK WOT YOU DUN	Slade	*Polydor*	6
23	9	ALONE AGAIN (NATURALLY)	Gilbert O'Sullivan	*MAM*	2
22	10	MEET ME ON THE CORNER	Lindisfarne	*Charisma*	3
8	11	STORM IN A TEA CUP	Fortunes	*Capitol*	7
11	12	POPPA JOE	Sweet	*RCA*	5
10	13	DAY AFTER DAY	Badfinger	*Apple*	6
6	14	HAVE YOU SEEN HER	Chi-Lites	*MCA*	9
13	15	MOTHER OF MINE	Neil Reid	*Decca*	11
19	16	I CAN'T HELP MYSELF	Donnie Elbert	*Avco*	3
17	17	SAY YOU DON'T MIND	Colin Blunstone	*Epic*	4
14	18	TELEGRAM SAM	T. Rex	*T. Rex*	7
21	19	GIVE IRELAND BACK TO THE IRISH	Wings	*Apple*	2
16	20	MY WORLD	Bee Gees	*Polydor*	7
15	21	I'D LIKE TO TEACH THE WORLD TO SING	New Seekers	*Polydor*	13
26	22	FLIRT	Jonathan King	*Decca*	5
37	23	DESIDERATA	Les Crane	*Warner Brothers*	2
18	24	ALL I EVER NEED IS YOU	Sonny and Cher	*MCA*	8
33	25	IT'S ONE OF THOSE NIGHTS	Partridge Family	*Bell*	2
20	26	LET'S STAY TOGETHER	Al Green	*London*	9
-	27	FLOY JOY	Supremes	*Tamla Motown*	1
35	28	SLEEPY SHORES	Johnny Pearson Orchestra	*Penny Farthing*	13
32	29	THE BABY	Hollies	*Polydor*	3
-	30	HOLD YOUR HEAD UP	Argent ●	*Epic*	1
36	31	LOVING YOU AIN'T EASY	Pagliaro	*Pye*	2
25	32	THE PERSUADERS	John Barry Orchestra	*CBS*	13
24	33	BRAND NEW KEY	Melanie	*Buddah*	11
30	34	DAY BY DAY	Holly Sherwood	*Bell*	5
-	35	JESUS	Cliff Richard	*Columbia*	1
28	36	HORSE WITH NO NAME	America	*Warner Brothers*	10
-	37	TOO BEAUTIFUL TO LAST	Engelbert Humperdinck	*Decca*	1
-	38	BROTHER	CCS	*RAK*	1
29	39	BABY I'M A WANT YOU	Bread	*Elektra*	9
27	40	MOON RIVER	Greyhound	*Trojan*	9

LW	TW	*WEEK ENDING* **18 MARCH 1972**			Wks
1	1	WITHOUT YOU	Nilsson	*RCA*	5
2	2	AMERICAN PIE	Don McLean	*United Artists*	8
4	3	BEG, STEAL OR BORROW	New Seekers	*Polydor*	3
3	4	SON OF MY FATHER	Chicory Tip	*CBS*	8
7	5	MOTHER AND CHILD REUNION	Paul Simon	*CBS*	5
9	6	ALONE AGAIN (NATURALLY)	Gilbert O'Sullivan	*MAM*	3
6	7	GOT TO BE THERE	Michael Jackson	*Tamla Motown*	6
5	8	BLUE IS THE COLOUR	Chelsea Football Team	*Penny Farthing*	4
10	9	MEET ME ON THE CORNER	Lindisfarne	*Charisma*	4
15	10	MOTHER OF MINE	Neil Reid	*Decca*	12
16	11	I CAN'T HELP MYSELF	Donnie Elbert	*Avco*	4
12	12	POPPA JOE	Sweet	*RCA*	6
8	13	LOOK WOT YOU DUN	Slade	*Polydor*	7
11	14	STORM IN A TEA CUP	Fortunes	*Capitol*	8
17	15	SAY YOU DON'T MIND	Colin Blunstone	*Epic*	5
13	16	DAY AFTER DAY	Badfinger	*Apple*	7
19	17	GIVE IRELAND BACK TO THE IRISH	Wings	*Apple*	3
27	18	FLOY JOY	Supremes	*Tamla Motown*	2
25	19	IT'S ONE OF THOSE NIGHTS	Partridge Family	*Bell*	3
23	20	DESIDERATA	Les Crane	*Warner Brothers*	3
30	21	HOLD YOUR HEAD UP	Argent	*Epic*	2
21	22	I'D LIKE TO TEACH THE WORLD TO SING	New Seekers	*Polydor*	14
22	23	FLIRT	Jonathan King	*Decca*	6
14	24	HAVE YOU SEEN HER	Chi-Lites	*MCA*	10
18	25	TELEGRAM SAM	T. Rex	*T. Rex*	8
37	26	TOO BEAUTIFUL TO LAST	Engelbert Humperdinck	*Decca*	2
29	27	THE BABY	Hollies	*Polydor*	4
24	28	ALL I EVER NEED IS YOU	Sonny and Cher	*MCA*	9
20	29	MY WORLD	Bee Gees	*Polydor*	8
28	30	SLEEPY SHORES	Johnny Pearson Orchestra	*Penny Farthing*	14
26	31	LET'S STAY TOGETHER	Al Green	*London*	10
38	32	BROTHER	CCS	*RAK*	2
-	33	HEART OF GOLD	Neil Young ●	*Reprise*	1
-	34	WHAT IS LIFE	Olivia Newton John	*Pye*	1
-	35	THEME FROM 'THE ONEDIN LINE'	Vienna Philharmonic Orchestra	*Decca*	13
31	36	LOVING YOU AIN'T EASY	Pagliaro	*Pye*	3
32	37	THE PERSUADERS	John Barry Orchestra	*CBS*	14
35	38	JESUS	Cliff Richard	*Columbia*	2
34	39	DAY BY DAY	Holly Sherwood	*Bell*	6
36	40	HORSE WITH NO NAME	America	*Warner Brothers*	11

LW	TW	*WEEK ENDING* **25 MARCH 1972**			Wks
1	1	WITHOUT YOU	Nilsson	*RCA*	6
3	2	BEG, STEAL OR BORROW	New Seekers	*Polydor*	4
2	3	AMERICAN PIE	Don McLean	*United Artists*	9
6	4	ALONE AGAIN (NATURALLY)	Gilbert O'Sullivan	*MAM*	4
9	5	MEET ME ON THE CORNER	Lindisfarne	*Charisma*	5
5	6	MOTHER AND CHILD REUNION	Paul Simon	*CBS*	6
21	7	HOLD YOUR HEAD UP	Argent	*Epic*	3
7	8	GOT TO BE THERE	Michael Jackson	*Tamla Motown*	7
20	9	DESIDERATA	Les Crane	*Warner Brothers*	4
18	10	FLOY JOY	Supremes	*Tamla Motown*	3
8	11	BLUE IS THE COLOUR	Chelsea Football Team	*Penny Farthing*	5
4	12	SON OF MY FATHER	Chicory Tip	*CBS*	9

■Top Ten contained three songs about parents - *Son Of My Father, Mother and Child Reunion* and *Mother Of Mine*. *Poppa Joe* was at number 12 (18.03.72) ■ Chelsea became the first football club (as opposed to a national squad) to have a Top 10 hit. *Blue Is The Colour* remains the biggest club hit until 1981 (11.03.72) ■ Paul McCartney's political statement, *Give Ireland Back To The Irish*, was banned by the BBC (04.03.72)■

March 1972

□ Highest position disc reached ● Act's first ever week on chart

LW	TW	Title	Artist	Label	Wks
11	13	I CAN'T HELP MYSELF	Donnie Elbert	Avco	5
19	14	IT'S ONE OF THOSE NIGHTS	Partridge Family	Bell	4
10	15	MOTHER OF MINE	Neil Reid	Decca	13
17	16	GIVE IRELAND BACK TO THE IRISH	Wings	Apple	4
12	17	POPPA JOE	Sweet	RCA	7
13	18	LOOK WOT YOU DUN	Slade	Polydor	8
26	19	TOO BEAUTIFUL TO LAST	Engelbert Humperdinck	Decca	3
22	20	I'D LIKE TO TEACH THE WORLD TO SING	New Seekers	Polydor	15
34	21	WHAT IS LIFE	Olivia Newton John	Pye	2
14	22	STORM IN A TEA CUP	Fortunes	Capitol	9
16	23	DAY AFTER DAY	Badfinger	Apple	8
-	24	SWEET TALKING GUY	Chiffons	London	1
33	25	HEART OF GOLD	Neil Young	Reprise	2
27	26	THE BABY	Hollies	Polydor	5
23	27	FLIRT	Jonathan King	Decca	7
32	28	BROTHER	CCS	RAK	3
24	29	HAVE YOU SEEN HER	Chi-Lites	MCA	11
15	30	SAY YOU DON'T MIND	Colin Blunstone	Epic	6
-	31	BERNADETTE	Four Tops	Tamla Motown	1
-	32	SMOKE GETS IN YOUR EYES	Blue Haze ●	A&M	1
-	33	CRYING, LAUGHING, LOVING, LYING	Labi Siffre	Pye	1
-	34	I'M GONNA BE A COUNTRY GIRL AGAIN	Buffy Sainte-Marie	Vanguard	1
30	35	SLEEPY SHORES	Johnny Pearson Orchestra	Penny Farthing	15
25	36	TELEGRAM SAM	T. Rex	T. Rex	9
38	37	JESUS	Cliff Richard	Columbia	3
29	38	MY WORLD	Bee Gees	Polydor	9
-	39	AT THE CLUB	Drifters	Atlantic	1
36	40	LOVING YOU AIN'T EASY	Pagliaro	Pye	4

WEEK ENDING 1 APRIL 1972

LW	TW	Title	Artist	Label	Wks
1	1	WITHOUT YOU	Nilsson	RCA	7
2	2	BEG, STEAL OR BORROW	New Seekers	Polydor	5
4	3	ALONE AGAIN (NATURALLY)	Gilbert O'Sullivan	MAM	5
3	4	AMERICAN PIE	Don McLean	United Artists	10
7	5	HOLD YOUR HEAD UP	Argent	Epic	4
5	6	MEET ME ON THE CORNER	Lindisfarne	Charisma	6
9	7	DESIDERATA	Les Crane	Warner Brothers	5
6	8	MOTHER AND CHILD REUNION	Paul Simon	CBS	7
10	9	FLOY JOY	Supremes	Tamla Motown	4
8	10	GOT TO BE THERE	Michael Jackson	Tamla Motown	8
14	11	IT'S ONE OF THOSE NIGHTS	Partridge Family	Bell	5
11	12	BLUE IS THE COLOUR	Chelsea Football Team	Penny Farthing	6
13	13	I CAN'T HELP MYSELF	Donnie Elbert	Avco	6
19	14	TOO BEAUTIFUL TO LAST	Engelbert Humperdinck	Decca	4
24	15	SWEET TALKING GUY	Chiffons	London	2
12	16	SON OF MY FATHER	Chicory Tip	CBS	10
25	17	HEART OF GOLD	Neil Young	Reprise	3
-	18	BACK OFF BOOGALOO	Ringo Starr	Apple	1
-	19	YOUNG NEW MEXICAN PUPPETEER	Tom Jones	Decca	1
21	20	WHAT IS LIFE	Olivia Newton John	Pye	3
15	21	MOTHER OF MINE	Neil Reid	Decca	14
17	22	POPPA JOE	Sweet	RCA	8
33	23	CRYING, LAUGHING, LOVING, LYING	Labi Siffre	Pye	2
20	24	I'D LIKE TO TEACH THE WORLD TO SING	New Seekers	Polydor	16
28	25	BROTHER	CCS	RAK	4
-	26	UNTIL IT'S TIME FOR YOU TO GO	Elvis Presley	RCA	1
16	27	GIVE IRELAND BACK TO THE IRISH	Wings	Apple	5
18	28	LOOK WOT YOU DUN	Slade	Polydor	9
-	29	RUN RUN RUN	Jo Jo Gunne	Asylum	1
22	30	STORM IN A TEA CUP	Fortunes	Capitol	10
-	31	AMAZING GRACE	Royal Scots Dragoon Guards Band ●	RCA	1
32	32	SMOKE GETS IN YOUR EYES	Blue Haze	A&M	2
-	33	I AM WHAT I AM	Greyhound	Trojan	1
-	34	WE'LL BE WITH YOU	Potters ●	Pye	1
-	35	NEVER BEFORE	Deep Purple	Purple	1
30	36	SAY YOU DON'T MIND	Colin Blunstone	Epic	7
-	37	TURN YOUR RADIO ON	Ray Stevens	CBS	1
-	38	ALL I EVER NEED IS YOU	Sonny and Cher	MCA	10
34	39	I'M GONNA BE A COUNTRY GIRL AGAIN	Buffy Sainte-Marie	Vanguard	2
31	40	BERNADETTE	Four Tops	Tamla Motown	2

WEEK ENDING 8 APRIL 1972

LW	TW	Title	Artist	Label	Wks
1	1	WITHOUT YOU	Nilsson	RCA	8
2	2	BEG, STEAL OR BORROW	New Seekers	Polydor	6
31	3	AMAZING GRACE	Royal Scots Dragoon Guards Band	RCA	2
3	4	ALONE AGAIN (NATURALLY)	Gilbert O'Sullivan	MAM	6
5	5	HOLD YOUR HEAD UP	Argent	Epic	5
6	6	MEET ME ON THE CORNER	Lindisfarne	Charisma	7
4	7	AMERICAN PIE	Don McLean	United Artists	11
15	8	SWEET TALKING GUY	Chiffons	London	3
7	9	DESIDERATA	Les Crane	Warner Brothers	6
9	10	FLOY JOY	Supremes	Tamla Motown	5
17	11	HEART OF GOLD	Neil Young	Reprise	4
11	12	IT'S ONE OF THOSE NIGHTS	Partridge Family	Bell	6
19	13	YOUNG NEW MEXICAN PUPPETEER	Tom Jones	Decca	2
8	14	MOTHER AND CHILD REUNION	Paul Simon	CBS	8
18	15	BACK OFF BOOGALOO	Ringo Starr	Apple	2
20	16	WHAT IS LIFE	Olivia Newton John	Pye	4
14	17	TOO BEAUTIFUL TO LAST	Engelbert Humperdinck	Decca	5
26	18	UNTIL IT'S TIME FOR YOU TO GO	Elvis Presley	RCA	2
11	19	BLUE IS THE COLOUR	Chelsea Football Team	Penny Farthing	7
23	20	CRYING, LAUGHING, LOVING, LYING	Labi Siffre	Pye	3
29	21	RUN RUN RUN	Jo Jo Gunne	Asylum	2
19	22	GOT TO BE THERE	Michael Jackson	Tamla Motown	10
40	23	BERNADETTE	Four Tops	Tamla Motown	3
21	24	MOTHER OF MINE	Neil Reid	Decca	15
16	25	SON OF MY FATHER	Chicory Tip	CBS	11
25	26	BROTHER	CCS	RAK	5
-	27	DEBORA/ONE INCH ROCK	Tyrannosaurus Rex	Magni Fly	1
22	28	POPPA JOE	Sweet	RCA	9
13	29	I CAN'T HELP MYSELF	Donnie Elbert	Avco	7
-	30	RADANCER	Marmalade	Decca	1
24	31	I'D LIKE TO TEACH THE WORLD TO SING	New Seekers	Polydor	17
32	32	SMOKE GETS IN YOUR EYES	Blue Haze	A&M	3
37	33	TURN YOUR RADIO ON	Ray Stevens	CBS	2
34	34	WE'LL BE WITH YOU	Potters	Pye	2
-	35	COULD IT BE FOREVER	David Cassidy ●	Bell	1
-	36	SACRAMENTO	Middle Of The Road	RCA	1
33	37	I AM WHAT I AM	Greyhound	Trojan	2
28	38	LOOK WOT YOU DUN	Slade	Polydor	10
-	39	COME WHAT MAY	Vicky Leandros ●	Philips	1
-	40	DOWN BY THE LAZY RIVER	Osmonds ●	MGM	1

WEEK ENDING 15 APRIL 1972

LW	TW	Title	Artist	Label	Wks
3	1	AMAZING GRACE	Royal Scots Dragoon Guards Band	RCA	3
1	2	WITHOUT YOU	Nilsson	RCA	9
2	3	BEG, STEAL OR BORROW	New Seekers	Polydor	7
15	4	BACK OFF BOOGALOO	Ringo Starr	Apple	3
8	5	SWEET TALKING GUY	Chiffons	London	4
5	6	HOLD YOUR HEAD UP	Argent	Epic	6
13	7	YOUNG NEW MEXICAN PUPPETEER	Tom Jones	Decca	3
4	8	ALONE AGAIN (NATURALLY)	Gilbert O'Sullivan	MAM	7
9	9	DESIDERATA	Les Crane	Warner Brothers	7
11	10	HEART OF GOLD	Neil Young	Reprise	5
20	11	CRYING, LAUGHING, LOVING, LYING	Labi Siffre	Pye	4
27	12	DEBORA/ONE INCH ROCK	Tyrannosaurus Rex	Magni Fly	2
6	13	MEET ME ON THE CORNER	Lindisfarne	Charisma	8
10	14	FLOY JOY	Supremes	Tamla Motown	6
12	15	IT'S ONE OF THOSE NIGHTS	Partridge Family	Bell	7
7	16	AMERICAN PIE	Don McLean	United Artists	12
21	17	RUN RUN RUN	Jo Jo Gunne	Asylum	3
16	18	WHAT IS LIFE	Olivia Newton John	Pye	5
18	19	UNTIL IT'S TIME FOR YOU TO GO	Elvis Presley	RCA	3
17	20	TOO BEAUTIFUL TO LAST	Engelbert Humperdinck	Decca	6
30	21	RADANCER	Marmalade	Decca	2

In these weeks ■ For the fifth consecutive week, a different record peaks at number 5 (01.04.72) ■ *Desiderata* by Les Crane peaks at number 7. Only Wink Martindale's *Deck Of Cards* has done better as an all-spoken hit single (01.04.72) ■ Teenybop begins officially as David Cassidy and the Osmonds debut in the same week (08.04.72)■

LW	TW	Title	Artist	Label	Wks
14	22	MOTHER AND CHILD REUNION	Paul Simon	*CBS*	9
19	23	BLUE IS THE COLOUR	Chelsea Football Team	*Penny Farthing*	8
-	24	STIR IT UP	Johnny Nash	*CBS*	1
37	25	I AM WHAT I AM	Greyhound	*Trojan*	3
39	26	COME WHAT MAY	Vicky Leandros	*Philips*	2
22	27	GOT TO BE THERE	Michael Jackson	*Tamla Motown*	11
36	28	SACRAMENTO	Middle Of The Road	*RCA*	2
31	29	I'D LIKE TO TEACH THE WORLD TO SING	New Seekers	*Polydor*	18
25	30	SON OF MY FATHER	Chicory Tip	*CBS*	12
29	31	I CAN'T HELP MYSELF	Donnie Elbert	*Avco*	8
26	32	BROTHER	CCS	*RAK*	6
-	33	BEAUTIFUL SUNDAY	Daniel Boone	*Penny Farthing*	1
35	34	COULD IT BE FOREVER	David Cassidy	*Bell*	2
23	35	BERNADETTE	Four Tops	*Tamla Motown*	4
33	36	TURN YOUR RADIO ON	Ray Stevens	*CBS*	3
-	37	A THING CALLED LOVE	Johnny Cash and the Evangel Temple Choir	*CBS*	1
28	38	POPPA JOE	Sweet	*RCA*	10
-	39	TAKE A LOOK AROUND	Temptations	*Tamla Motown*	1
40	40	DOWN BY THE LAZY RIVER	Osmonds	*MGM*	2

WEEK ENDING 22 APRIL 1972

LW	TW	Title	Artist	Label	Wks
1	1	AMAZING GRACE	Royal Scots Dragoon Guards Band	*RCA*	4
2	2	WITHOUT YOU	Nilsson	*RCA*	10
4	3	BACK OFF BOOGALOO	Ringo Starr	*Apple*	4
5	4	SWEET TALKING GUY	Chiffons	*London*	5
19	5	UNTIL IT'S TIME FOR YOU TO GO	Elvis Presley	*RCA*	4
3	6	BEG, STEAL OR BORROW	New Seekers	*Polydor*	8
7	7	YOUNG NEW MEXICAN PUPPETEER	Tom Jones	*Decca*	4
6	8	HOLD YOUR HEAD UP	Argent	*Epic*	7
17	9	RUN RUN RUN	Jo Jo Gunne	*Asylum*	4
8	10	ALONE AGAIN (NATURALLY)	Gilbert O'Sullivan	*MAM*	8
10	11	HEART OF GOLD	Neil Young	*Reprise*	6
9	12	DESIDERATA	Les Crane	*Warner Brothers*	8
11	13	CRYING, LAUGHING, LOVING, LYING	Labi Siffre	*Pye*	5
26	14	COME WHAT MAY	Vicky Leandros	*Philips*	3
12	15	DEBORA/ONE INCH ROCK	Tyrannosaurus Rex	*Magni Fly*	3
14	16	FLOY JOY	Supremes	*Tamla Motown*	7
18	17	WHAT IS LIFE	Olivia Newton John	*Pye*	6
21	18	RADANCER	Marmalade	*Decca*	3
24	19	STIR IT UP	Johnny Nash	*CBS*	2
34	20	COULD IT BE FOREVER	David Cassidy	*Bell*	3
15	21	IT'S ONE OF THOSE NIGHTS	Partridge Family	*Bell*	8
16	22	AMERICAN PIE	Don McLean	*United Artists*	13
28	23	SACRAMENTO	Middle Of The Road	*RCA*	3
13	24	MEET ME ON THE CORNER	Lindisfarne	*Charisma*	9
23	25	BLUE IS THE COLOUR	Chelsea Football Team	*Penny Farthing*	9
39	26	TAKE A LOOK AROUND	Temptations	*Tamla Motown*	2
25	27	I AM WHAT I AM	Greyhound	*Trojan*	4
37	28	A THING CALLED LOVE	Johnny Cash and the Evangel Temple Choir	*CBS*	2
20	29	TOO BEAUTIFUL TO LAST	Engelbert Humperdinck	*Decca*	7
22	30	MOTHER AND CHILD REUNION	Paul Simon	*CBS*	10
-	31	AMAZING GRACE	Judy Collins	*Elektra*	26
30	32	SON OF MY FATHER	Chicory Tip	*CBS*	13
27	33	GOT TO BE THERE	Michael Jackson	*Tamla Motown*	12
29	34	I'D LIKE TO TEACH THE WORLD TO SING	New Seekers	*Polydor*	19
-	35	RUNNIN' AWAY	Sly & The Family Stone	*Epic*	1
33	36	BEAUTIFUL SUNDAY	Daniel Boone	*Penny Farthing*	2
-	37	NEVER BEFORE	Deep Purple	*Purple*	1
31	38	I CAN'T HELP MYSELF	Donnie Elbert	*Avco*	9
35	39	BERNADETTE	Four Tops	*Tamla Motown*	5
-	40	AT THE CLUB/SATURDAY NIGHT AT THE MOVIES	Drifters	*Atlantic*	2

WEEK ENDING 29 APRIL 1972

LW	TW	Title	Artist	Label	Wks
1	1	AMAZING GRACE	Royal Scots Dragoon Guards Band	*RCA*	5
3	2	BACK OFF BOOGALOO	Ringo Starr	*Apple*	5
2	3	WITHOUT YOU	Nilsson	*RCA*	11

May 1972

□ Highest position disc reached ● Act's first ever week on chart

LW	TW	Title	Artist	Label	Wks
4	4	SWEET TALKING GUY	Chiffons	*London*	6
14	5	COME WHAT MAY	Vicky Leandros	*Philips*	4
7	6	YOUNG NEW MEXICAN PUPPETEER	Tom Jones	*Decca*	5
15	7	DEBORA/ONE INCH ROCK	Tyrannosaurus Rex	*Magni Fly*	4
9	8	RUN RUN RUN	Jo Jo Gunne	*Asylum*	5
18	9	RADANCER	Marmalade	*Decca*	4
5	10	UNTIL IT'S TIME FOR YOU TO GO	Elvis Presley	*RCA*	5
20	11	COULD IT BE FOREVER	David Cassidy	*Bell*	4
6	12	BEG, STEAL OR BORROW	New Seekers	*Polydor*	9
19	13	STIR IT UP	Johnny Nash	*CBS*	3
28	14	A THING CALLED LOVE	Johnny Cash and the Evangel Temple Choir	*CBS*	3
13	15	CRYING, LAUGHING, LOVING, LYING	Labi Siffre	*Pye*	6
8	16	HOLD YOUR HEAD UP	Argent	*Epic*	8
11	17	HEART OF GOLD	Neil Young	*Reprise*	7
-	18	TUMBLING DICE	Rolling Stones	*Rolling Stones*	1
12	19	DESIDERATA	Les Crane	*Warner Brothers*	9
27	20	I AM WHAT I AM	Greyhound	*Trojan*	5
10	21	ALONE AGAIN (NATURALLY)	Gilbert O'Sullivan	*MAM*	9
-	22	ROCKET MAN	Elton John	*DJM*	1
26	23	TAKE A LOOK AROUND	Temptations	*Tamla Motown*	3
21	24	IT'S ONE OF THOSE NIGHTS	Partridge Family	*Bell*	9
23	25	SACRAMENTO	Middle Of The Road	*RCA*	4
-	26	OPEN UP	Mungo Jerry	*Dawn*	1
36	27	BEAUTIFUL SUNDAY	Daniel Boone	*Penny Farthing*	3
40	28	AT THE CLUB/SATURDAY NIGHT AT THE MOVIES	Drifters	*Atlantic*	3
35	29	RUNNIN' AWAY	Sly & The Family Stone	*Epic*	2
24	30	MEET ME ON THE CORNER	Lindisfarne	*Charisma*	10
-	31	LEEDS UNITED	Leeds United FC ●	*Chapter One*	1
25	32	BLUE IS THE COLOUR	Chelsea Football Team	*Penny Farthing*	10
-	33	WADE IN THE WATER	Ramsey Lewis ●	*Chess*	1
-	34	ME AND JULIO DOWN BY THE SCHOOL YARD	Paul Simon	*CBS*	1
37	35	NEVER BEFORE	Deep Purple	*Purple*	2
29	36	TOO BEAUTIFUL TO LAST	Engelbert Humperdinck	*Decca*	8
22	37	AMERICAN PIE	Don McLean	*United Artists*	14
-	38	OH BABE WHAT WOULD YOU SAY	Hurricane Smith	*Columbia*	1
-	39	LITTLE PIECE OF LEATHER	Donnie Elbert	*London*	1
-	40	A WHITER SHADE OF PALE	Procol Harum	*Magni Fly*	1

WEEK ENDING 6 MAY 1972

LW	TW	Title	Artist	Label	Wks
1	1	AMAZING GRACE	Royal Scots Dragoon Guards Band	*RCA*	6
2	2	BACK OFF BOOGALOO	Ringo Starr	*Apple*	6
5	3	COME WHAT MAY	Vicky Leandros	*Philips*	5
11	4	COULD IT BE FOREVER	David Cassidy	*Bell*	5
4	5	SWEET TALKING GUY	Chiffons	*London*	7
8	6	RUN RUN RUN	Jo Jo Gunne	*Asylum*	6
14	7	A THING CALLED LOVE	Johnny Cash and the Evangel Temple Choir	*CBS*	4
7	8	DEBORA/ONE INCH ROCK	Tyrannosaurus Rex	*Magni Fly*	5
9	9	RADANCER	Marmalade	*Decca*	5
3	10	WITHOUT YOU	Nilsson	*RCA*	12
6	11	YOUNG NEW MEXICAN PUPPETEER	Tom Jones	*Decca*	6
22	12	ROCKET MAN	Elton John	*DJM*	2
10	13	UNTIL IT'S TIME FOR YOU TO GO	Elvis Presley	*RCA*	6
18	14	TUMBLING DICE	Rolling Stones	*Rolling Stones*	2
13	15	STIR IT UP	Johnny Nash	*CBS*	4
23	16	TAKE A LOOK AROUND	Temptations	*Tamla Motown*	4
16	17	HOLD YOUR HEAD UP	Argent	*Epic*	9
15	18	CRYING, LAUGHING, LOVING, LYING	Labi Siffre	*Pye*	7
29	19	RUNNIN' AWAY	Sly & The Family Stone	*Epic*	3
28	20	AT THE CLUB/SATURDAY NIGHT AT THE MOVIES	Drifters	*Atlantic*	4
27	21	BEAUTIFUL SUNDAY	Daniel Boone	*Penny Farthing*	4
20	22	I AM WHAT I AM	Greyhound	*Trojan*	6
26	23	OPEN UP	Mungo Jerry	*Dawn*	2
-	24	AMAZING GRACE	Judy Collins	*Elektra*	27

■Inspired by the success of the Royal Scots Dragoon Guards' instrumental version, Judy Collins' *Amazing Grace* re-enters the chart (22.04.72) ■ Procol Harum's 1967 number one charts five years on, but is not as successful this time round as the re-issues of Tyrannosaurus Rex's 1968 hit *Debora* and the Drifters' 1965 *At The Club* (29.04.72)■

May 1972

□ Highest position disc reached ● Act's first ever week on chart

LW	TW	Title	Artist	Label	Wks
17	25	HEART OF GOLD	Neil Young	*Reprise*	8
12	26	BEG, STEAL OR BORROW	New Seekers	*Polydor*	10
38	27	OH BABE WHAT WOULD YOU SAY	Hurricane Smith	*Columbia*	2
34	28	ME AND JULIO DOWN BY THE SCHOOL YARD	Paul Simon	*CBS*	2
21	29	ALONE AGAIN (NATURALLY)	Gilbert O'Sullivan	*MAM*	10
19	30	DESIDERATA	Les Crane	*Warner Brothers*	10
33	[31]	WADE IN THE WATER	Ramsey Lewis	*Chess*	2
40	32	A WHITER SHADE OF PALE	Procol Harum	*Magni Fly*	2
25	33	SACRAMENTO	Middle Of The Road	*RCA*	5
-	34	ISN'T LIFE STRANGE	Moody Blues	*Threshold*	1
-	35	EVERYTHING I OWN	Bread	*Elektra*	1
39	36	LITTLE PIECE OF LEATHER	Donnie Elbert	*London*	2
37	37	AMERICAN PIE	Don McLean	*United Artists*	15
24	38	IT'S ONE OF THOSE NIGHTS	Partridge Family	*Bell*	10
30	39	MEET ME ON THE CORNER	Lindisfarne	*Charisma*	11
32	40	BLUE IS THE COLOUR	Chelsea Football Team	*Penny Farthing*	11

WEEK ENDING 13 MAY 1972

LW	TW	Title	Artist	Label	Wks
1	[1]	AMAZING GRACE	Royal Scots Dragoon Guards Band	*RCA*	7
3	[2]	COME WHAT MAY	Vicky Leandros	*Philips*	6
4	3	COULD IT BE FOREVER	David Cassidy	*Bell*	6
7	[4]	A THING CALLED LOVE	Johnny Cash/Evangel Temple Choir	*CBS*	5
14	[5]	TUMBLING DICE	Rolling Stones	*Rolling Stones*	3
9	[6]	RADANCER	Marmalade	*Decca*	6
12	7	ROCKET MAN	Elton John	*DJM*	3
6	8	RUN RUN RUN	Jo Jo Gunne	*Asylum*	7
-	9	METAL GURU	T. Rex	*EMI*	1
5	10	SWEET TALKING GUY	Chiffons	*London*	8
2	11	BACK OFF BOOGALOO	Ringo Starr	*Apple*	7
8	12	DEBORA/ONE INCH ROCK	Tyrannosaurus Rex	*Magni Fly*	6
11	13	YOUNG NEW MEXICAN PUPPETEER	Tom Jones	*Decca*	7
15	14	STIR IT UP	Johnny Nash	*CBS*	5
10	15	WITHOUT YOU	Nilsson	*RCA*	13
13	16	UNTIL IT'S TIME FOR YOU TO GO	Elvis Presley	*RCA*	7
16	17	TAKE A LOOK AROUND	Temptations	*Tamla Motown*	5
27	18	OH BABE WHAT WOULD YOU SAY	Hurricane Smith	*Columbia*	3
20	19	AT THE CLUB/SATURDAY NIGHT AT THE MOVIES	Drifters	*Atlantic*	5
-	20	LEEDS UNITED	Leeds United FC	*Chapter One*	2
19	21	RUNNIN' AWAY	Sly & The Family Stone	*Epic*	4
23	22	OPEN UP	Mungo Jerry	*Dawn*	3
24	23	AMAZING GRACE	Judy Collins	*Elektra*	28
28	24	ME AND JULIO DOWN BY THE SCHOOL YARD	Paul Simon	*CBS*	3
21	25	BEAUTIFUL SUNDAY	Daniel Boone	*Penny Farthing*	5
32	26	A WHITER SHADE OF PALE	Procol Harum	*Magni Fly*	3
22	27	I AM WHAT I AM	Greyhound	*Trojan*	7
26	28	BEG, STEAL OR BORROW	New Seekers	*Polydor*	11
-	29	LADY ELEANOR	Lindisfarne	*Charisma*	1
36	30	LITTLE PIECE OF LEATHER	Donnie Elbert	*London*	3
-	31	SISTER JANE	New World	*RAK*	1
31	32	WADE IN THE WATER	Ramsey Lewis	*Chess*	3
-	[33]	CHANTILLY LACE	Jerry Lee Lewis	*Mercury*	1
-	[34]	THE LION SLEEPS TONIGHT	Dave Newman	*Pye*	1
35	35	EVERYTHING I OWN	Bread	*Elektra*	2
-	36	VINCENT	Don McLean	*United Artists*	1
30	37	DESIDERATA	Les Crane	*Warner Brothers*	11
25	38	HEART OF GOLD	Neil Young	*Reprise*	9
34	39	ISN'T LIFE STRANGE	Moody Blues	*Threshold*	2
29	40	ALONE AGAIN (NATURALLY)	Gilbert O'Sullivan	*MAM*	11

WEEK ENDING 20 MAY 1972

LW	TW	Title	Artist	Label	Wks
9	[1]	METAL GURU	T. Rex	*EMI*	2
1	2	AMAZING GRACE	Royal Scots Dragoon Guards Band	*RCA*	8
3	3	COULD IT BE FOREVER	David Cassidy	*Bell*	7
2	4	COME WHAT MAY	Vicky Leandros	*Philips*	7
7	5	ROCKET MAN	Elton John	*DJM*	4
4	6	A THING CALLED LOVE	Johnny Cash/Evangel Temple Choir	*CBS*	6
5	7	TUMBLING DICE	Rolling Stones	*Rolling Stones*	4
19	8	AT THE CLUB/SATURDAY NIGHT AT THE MOVIES	Drifters	*Atlantic*	6
6	9	RADANCER	Marmalade	*Decca*	7
8	10	RUN RUN RUN	Jo Jo Gunne	*Asylum*	8
10	11	SWEET TALKING GUY	Chiffons	*London*	9
11	12	BACK OFF BOOGALOO	Ringo Starr	*Apple*	8
17	[13]	TAKE A LOOK AROUND	Temptations	*Tamla Motown*	6
20	14	LEEDS UNITED	Leeds United FC	*Chapter One*	3
18	15	OH BABE WHAT WOULD YOU SAY	Hurricane Smith	*Columbia*	4
12	16	DEBORA/ONE INCH ROCK	Tyrannosaurus Rex	*Magni Fly*	7
21	[17]	RUNNIN' AWAY	Sly & The Family Stone	*Epic*	5
14	18	STIR IT UP	Johnny Nash	*CBS*	6
29	19	LADY ELEANOR	Lindisfarne	*Charisma*	2
23	20	AMAZING GRACE	Judy Collins	*Elektra*	29
22	[21]	OPEN UP	Mungo Jerry	*Dawn*	4
26	22	A WHITER SHADE OF PALE	Procol Harum	*Magni Fly*	4
24	23	ME AND JULIO DOWN BY THE SCHOOL YARD	Paul Simon	*CBS*	4
39	24	ISN'T LIFE STRANGE	Moody Blues	*Threshold*	3
13	25	YOUNG NEW MEXICAN PUPPETEER	Tom Jones	*Decca*	8
15	26	WITHOUT YOU	Nilsson	*RCA*	14
31	27	SISTER JANE	New World	*RAK*	2
25	28	BEAUTIFUL SUNDAY	Daniel Boone	*Penny Farthing*	6
36	29	VINCENT	Don McLean	*United Artists*	2
-	30	DOOBEDOOD'NDOOBE DOOBEDOOD'NDOOBE	Diana Ross	*Tamla Motown*	1
30	31	LITTLE PIECE OF LEATHER	Donnie Elbert	*London*	4
35	[32]	EVERYTHING I OWN	Bread	*Elektra*	3
33	[33]	CHANTILLY LACE	Jerry Lee Lewis	*Mercury*	2
-	34	CALIFORNIA MAN	Move	*Harvest*	1
32	35	WADE IN THE WATER	Ramsey Lewis	*Chess*	4
16	36	UNTIL IT'S TIME FOR YOU TO GO	Elvis Presley	*RCA*	8
28	37	BEG, STEAL OR BORROW	New Seekers	*Polydor*	12
-	38	SONG SUNG BLUE	Neil Diamond	*Uni*	1
-	39	WHAT'S YOUR NAME	Chicory Tip	*CBS*	1
-	40	DON'T LET HIM TOUCH YOU	Angelettes ●	*Decca*	1

WEEK ENDING 27 MAY 1972

LW	TW	Title	Artist	Label	Wks
1	[1]	METAL GURU	T. Rex	*EMI*	3
3	[2]	COULD IT BE FOREVER	David Cassidy	*Bell*	8
2	3	AMAZING GRACE	Royal Scots Dragoon Guards Band	*RCA*	9
4	4	COME WHAT MAY	Vicky Leandros	*Philips*	8
5	5	ROCKET MAN	Elton John	*DJM*	5
15	6	OH BABE WHAT WOULD YOU SAY	Hurricane Smith	*Columbia*	5
6	7	A THING CALLED LOVE	Johnny Cash/Evangel Temple Choir	*CBS*	7
8	8	AT THE CLUB/SATURDAY NIGHT AT THE MOVIES	Drifters	*Atlantic*	7
7	9	TUMBLING DICE	Rolling Stones	*Rolling Stones*	5
14	[10]	LEEDS UNITED	Leeds United FC	*Chapter One*	4
29	11	VINCENT	Don McLean	*United Artists*	3
19	12	LADY ELEANOR	Lindisfarne	*Charisma*	3
9	13	RADANCER	Marmalade	*Decca*	8
22	14	A WHITER SHADE OF PALE	Procol Harum	*Magni Fly*	5
23	[15]	ME AND JULIO DOWN BY THE SCHOOL YARD	Paul Simon	*CBS*	5
27	16	SISTER JANE	New World	*RAK*	3
10	17	RUN RUN RUN	Jo Jo Gunne	*Asylum*	9
13	18	TAKE A LOOK AROUND	Temptations	*Tamla Motown*	7
24	19	ISN'T LIFE STRANGE	Moody Blues	*Threshold*	4
34	20	CALIFORNIA MAN	Move	*Harvest*	2
20	21	AMAZING GRACE	Judy Collins	*Elektra*	30
30	22	DOOBEDOOD'NDOOBE DOOBEDOOD'NDOOBE	Diana Ross	*Tamla Motown*	2
17	23	RUNNIN' AWAY	Sly & The Family Stone	*Epic*	6
11	24	SWEET TALKING GUY	Chiffons	*London*	10
18	25	STIR IT UP	Johnny Nash	*CBS*	7

In these weeks ■ Marmalade's *Radancer* is the last record to peak at number six until 1973 (13.05.72) ■ *Everything I Own*, a song later to top the charts in two different versions, peaks at no. 32 in its original version by composer David Gates' own group, Bread (20.05.72) ■ Eurovision winner *Come What May* by Vicky Leandros hits number two, the same position that Britain's entry, *Beg Steal Or Borrow* by the New Seekers, reached six weeks earlier (13.05.72)■

LW	TW	Title	Artist	Label	Wks
39	26	WHAT'S YOUR NAME	Chicory Tip	CBS	2
31	[27]	LITTLE PIECE OF LEATHER	Donnie Elbert	London	5
12	28	BACK OFF BOOGALOO	Ringo Starr	Apple	9
21	29	OPEN UP	Mungo Jerry	Dawn	5
26	30	WITHOUT YOU	Nilsson	RCA	15
38	31	SONG SUNG BLUE	Neil Diamond	Uni	2
28	32	BEAUTIFUL SUNDAY	Daniel Boone	Penny Farthing	7
-	33	ROCKIN' ROBIN	Michael Jackson	Tamla Motown	1
33	34	CHANTILLY LACE	Jerry Lee Lewis	Mercury	3
40	[35]	DON'T LET HIM TOUCH YOU	Angelettes	Decca	2
-	36	MARY HAD A LITTLE LAMB	Wings	Apple	1
25	37	YOUNG NEW MEXICAN PUPPETEER	Tom Jones	Decca	9
-	38	THE FIRST TIME EVER I SAW YOUR FACE	Roberta Flack ●	Atlantic	1
16	39	DEBORA/ONE INCH ROCK	Tyrannosaurus Rex	Magni Fly	8
32	40	EVERYTHING I OWN	Bread	Elektra	4

WEEK ENDING 3 JUNE 1972

LW	TW	Title	Artist	Label	Wks
1	[1]	METAL GURU	T. Rex	EMI	4
5	[2]	ROCKET MAN	Elton John	DJM	6
8	[3]	AT THE CLUB/SATURDAY NIGHT AT THE MOVIES	Drifters	Atlantic	8
6	[4]	OH BABE WHAT WOULD YOU SAY	Hurricane Smith	Columbia	6
11	5	VINCENT	Don McLean	United Artists	4
12	6	LADY ELEANOR	Lindisfarne	Charisma	4
2	7	COULD IT BE FOREVER	David Cassidy	Bell	9
3	8	AMAZING GRACE	Royal Scots Dragoon Guards Band	RCA	10
7	9	A THING CALLED LOVE	Johnny Cash/Evangel Temple Choir	CBS	8
4	10	COME WHAT MAY	Vicky Leandros	Philips	9
20	11	CALIFORNIA MAN	Move	Harvest	3
10	12	LEEDS UNITED	Leeds United FC	Chapter One	5
19	[13]	ISN'T LIFE STRANGE	Moody Blues	Threshold	5
9	14	TUMBLING DICE	Rolling Stones	Rolling Stones	6
14	15	A WHITER SHADE OF PALE	Procol Harum	Magni Fly	6
16	16	SISTER JANE	New World	RAK	4
18	17	TAKE A LOOK AROUND	Temptations	Tamla Motown	8
22	18	DOOBEDOOD'NDOOBE DOOBEDOOD'NDOOBE	Diana Ross	Tamla Motown	3
15	19	ME AND JULIO DOWN BY THE SCHOOL YARD	Paul Simon	CBS	6
36	20	MARY HAD A LITTLE LAMB	Wings	Apple	2
21	21	AMAZING GRACE	Judy Collins	Elektra	31
33	22	ROCKIN' ROBIN	Michael Jackson	Tamla Motown	2
26	23	WHAT'S YOUR NAME	Chicory Tip	CBS	3
23	24	RUNNIN' AWAY	Sly & The Family Stone	Epic	7
-	25	TAKE ME BACK 'OME	Slade	Polydor	1
13	26	RADANCER	Marmalade	Decca	9
27	[27]	LITTLE PIECE OF LEATHER	Donnie Elbert	London	6
24	28	SWEET TALKING GUY	Chiffons	London	11
25	29	STIR IT UP	Johnny Nash	CBS	8
29	30	OPEN UP	Mungo Jerry	Dawn	6
31	31	SONG SUNG BLUE	Neil Diamond	Uni	3
-	32	SUPERSONIC ROCKET SHIP	Kinks	RCA	1
17	33	RUN RUN RUN	Jo Jo Gunne	Asylum	10
38	34	THE FIRST TIME EVER I SAW YOUR FACE	Roberta Flack	Atlantic	2
-	35	LITTLE BIT OF LOVE	Free	Island	1
30	36	WITHOUT YOU	Nilsson	RCA	16
-	37	OH GIRL	Chi-Lites	MCA	1
35	38	DON'T LET HIM TOUCH YOU	Angelettes	Decca	3
34	39	CHANTILLY LACE	Jerry Lee Lewis	Mercury	4
32	40	BEAUTIFUL SUNDAY	Daniel Boone	Penny Farthing	8

WEEK ENDING 10 JUNE 1972

LW	TW	Title	Artist	Label	Wks
1	[1]	METAL GURU	T. Rex	EMI	5
5	2	VINCENT	Don McLean	United Artists	5
6	[3]	LADY ELEANOR	Lindisfarne	Charisma	5
4	[4]	OH BABE WHAT WOULD YOU SAY	Hurricane Smith	Columbia	7
2	5	ROCKET MAN	Elton John	DJM	7
3	6	AT THE CLUB/SATURDAY NIGHT AT THE MOVIES	Drifters	Atlantic	9

June 1972

□ Highest position disc reached ● Act's first ever week on chart

LW	TW	Title	Artist	Label	Wks
7	7	COULD IT BE FOREVER	David Cassidy	Bell	10
11	8	CALIFORNIA MAN	Move	Harvest	4
16	[9]	SISTER JANE	New World	RAK	5
22	10	ROCKIN' ROBIN	Michael Jackson	Tamla Motown	3
8	11	AMAZING GRACE	Royal Scots Dragoon Guards Band	RCA	11
20	12	MARY HAD A LITTLE LAMB	Wings	Apple	3
15	[13]	A WHITER SHADE OF PALE	Procol Harum	Magni Fly	7
25	14	TAKE ME BACK 'OME	Slade	Polydor	2
13	15	ISN'T LIFE STRANGE	Moody Blues	Threshold	6
12	16	LEEDS UNITED	Leeds United FC	Chapter One	6
10	17	COME WHAT MAY	Vicky Leandros	Philips	10
18	18	DOOBEDOOD'NDOOBE DOOBEDOOD'NDOOBE	Diana Ross	Tamla Motown	4
9	19	A THING CALLED LOVE	Johnny Cash/Evangel Temple Choir	CBS	9
19	20	ME AND JULIO DOWN BY THE SCHOOL YARD	Paul Simon	CBS	7
23	21	WHAT'S YOUR NAME	Chicory Tip	CBS	4
21	22	AMAZING GRACE	Judy Collins	Elektra	32
31	23	SONG SUNG BLUE	Neil Diamond	Uni	4
32	24	SUPERSONIC ROCKET SHIP	Kinks	RCA	2
37	25	OH GIRL	Chi-Lites	MCA	2
34	26	THE FIRST TIME EVER I SAW YOUR FACE	Roberta Flack	Atlantic	3
14	27	TUMBLING DICE	Rolling Stones	Rolling Stones	7
35	28	LITTLE BIT OF LOVE	Free	Island	2
-	[29]	JUNGLE FEVER	Chakachas ●	Polydor	1
27	30	LITTLE PIECE OF LEATHER	Donnie Elbert	London	7
26	31	RADANCER	Marmalade	Decca	10
-	32	I'LL TAKE YOU THERE	Staple Singers ●	CBS	1
29	33	STIR IT UP	Johnny Nash	CBS	9
17	34	TAKE A LOOK AROUND	Temptations	Tamla Motown	9
33	35	RUN RUN RUN	Jo Jo Gunne	Asylum	11
-	36	THIRD FINGER LEFT HAND	Pearls ●	Bell	1
-	37	ROCK AND ROLL PART II	Gary Glitter ●	Bell	1
-	38	YOUNG NEW MEXICAN PUPPETEER	Tom Jones	Decca	10
28	39	SWEET TALKING GUY	Chiffons	London	12
40	40	BEAUTIFUL SUNDAY	Daniel Boone	Penny Farthing	9

WEEK ENDING 17 JUNE 1972

LW	TW	Title	Artist	Label	Wks
2	[1]	VINCENT	Don McLean	United Artists	6
1	2	METAL GURU	T. Rex	EMI	6
14	3	TAKE ME BACK 'OME	Slade	Polydor	3
6	4	AT THE CLUB/SATURDAY NIGHT AT THE MOVIES	Drifters	Atlantic	10
10	5	ROCKIN' ROBIN	Michael Jackson	Tamla Motown	4
3	6	LADY ELEANOR	Lindisfarne	Charisma	6
8	[7]	CALIFORNIA MAN	Move	Harvest	5
4	8	OH BABE WHAT WOULD YOU SAY	Hurricane Smith	Columbia	8
9	[9]	SISTER JANE	New World	RAK	6
12	10	MARY HAD A LITTLE LAMB	Wings	Apple	4
5	11	ROCKET MAN	Elton John	DJM	8
18	[12]	DOOBEDOOD'NDOOBE DOOBEDOOD'NDOOBE	Diana Ross	Tamla Motown	5
21	[13]	WHAT'S YOUR NAME	Chicory Tip	CBS	5
7	14	COULD IT BE FOREVER	David Cassidy	Bell	11
15	15	ISN'T LIFE STRANGE	Moody Blues	Threshold	7
23	16	SONG SUNG BLUE	Neil Diamond	Uni	5
24	17	SUPERSONIC ROCKET SHIP	Kinks	RCA	3
11	18	AMAZING GRACE	Royal Scots Dragoon Guards Band	RCA	12
28	19	LITTLE BIT OF LOVE	Free	Island	3
13	20	A WHITER SHADE OF PALE	Procol Harum	Magni Fly	8
37	21	ROCK AND ROLL PART II	Gary Glitter	Bell	2
26	22	THE FIRST TIME EVER I SAW YOUR FACE	Roberta Flack	Atlantic	4
-	23	LITTLE WILLY	Sweet	RCA	1
19	24	A THING CALLED LOVE	Johnny Cash/Evangel Temple Choir	CBS	10

■Don McLean's *Vincent*, about Vincent Van Gogh, becomes the first of two songs about painters to hit number one (17.06.72) ■ Diana Ross just misses the top ten with the second longest nonsense title ever to chart (17.06.72) ■ Roberta Flack's debut hit, from the Clint Eastwood film, *Play Misty For Me*, was written by Kirsty MacColl's father, Ewan MacColl (27.05.72)■

June 1972

□ Highest position disc reached ● Act's first ever week on chart

LW	TW	Title / Artist	Label	Wks
25	25	OH GIRL Chi-Lites	MCA	3
22	26	AMAZING GRACE Judy Collins	Elektra	33
-	27	AMERICAN TRILOGY Elvis Presley	RCA	1
16	28	LEEDS UNITED Leeds United FC	Chapter One	7
17	29	COME WHAT MAY Vicky Leandros	Philips	11
-	30	NUT ROCKER B. Bumble and the Stingers	Stateside	1
36	[31]	THIRD FINGER LEFT HAND Pearls	Bell	2
-	32	CIRCLES New Seekers	Polydor	1
32	33	I'LL TAKE YOU THERE Staple Singers	CBS	2
30	34	LITTLE PIECE OF LEATHER Donnie Elbert	London	8
20	35	ME AND JULIO DOWN BY THE SCHOOL YARD Paul Simon	CBS	8
-	36	PUPPY LOVE Donny Osmond ●	MGM	1
27	37	TUMBLING DICE Rolling Stones	Rolling Stones	8
-	38	I'VE BEEN LONELY FOR SO LONG Frederick Knight ●	Stax	1
29	39	JUNGLE FEVER Chakachas	Polydor	2
-	40	OOH-WAKKA-DOO-WAKKA-DAY Gilbert O'Sullivan	MAM	1

WEEK ENDING 24 JUNE 1972

LW	TW	Title / Artist	Label	Wks
1	[1]	VINCENT Don McLean	United Artists	7
3	2	TAKE ME BACK 'OME Slade	Polydor	4
5	[3]	ROCKIN' ROBIN Michael Jackson	Tamla Motown	5
2	4	METAL GURU T. Rex	EMI	7
4	5	AT THE CLUB/SATURDAY NIGHT AT THE MOVIES Drifters	Atlantic	11
21	6	ROCK AND ROLL PART II Gary Glitter	Bell	3
7	7	CALIFORNIA MAN Move	Harvest	6
23	8	LITTLE WILLY Sweet	RCA	2
10	[9]	MARY HAD A LITTLE LAMB Wings	Apple	5
6	10	LADY ELEANOR Lindisfarne	Charisma	7
9	11	SISTER JANE New World	RAK	7
8	12	OH BABE WHAT WOULD YOU SAY Hurricane Smith	Columbia	9
36	13	PUPPY LOVE Donny Osmond	MGM	2
25	[14]	OH GIRL Chi-Lites	MCA	4
16	15	SONG SUNG BLUE Neil Diamond	Uni	6
17	[16]	SUPERSONIC ROCKET SHIP Kinks	RCA	4
22	17	THE FIRST TIME EVER I SAW YOUR FACE Roberta Flack	Atlantic	5
40	18	OOH-WAKKA-DOO-WAKKA-DAY Gilbert O'Sullivan	MAM	2
11	19	ROCKET MAN Elton John	DJM	9
19	20	LITTLE BIT OF LOVE Free	Island	4
32	21	CIRCLES New Seekers	Polydor	2
15	22	ISN'T LIFE STRANGE Moody Blues	Threshold	8
18	23	AMAZING GRACE Royal Scots Dragoon Guards Band	RCA	13
27	24	AMERICAN TRILOGY Elvis Presley	RCA	2
30	25	NUT ROCKER B. Bumble and the Stingers	Stateside	2
12	26	DOOBEDOOD'NDOOBE DOOBEDOOD'NDOOBE Diana Ross	Tamla Motown	6
13	27	WHAT'S YOUR NAME Chicory Tip	CBS	6
14	28	COULD IT BE FOREVER David Cassidy	Bell	12
20	29	A WHITER SHADE OF PALE Procol Harum	Magni Fly	9
29	30	COME WHAT MAY Vicky Leandros	Philips	12
-	31	WALKIN' IN THE RAIN WITH THE ONE I LOVE Love Unlimited ●	Uni	1
26	32	AMAZING GRACE Judy Collins	Elektra	34
24	33	A THING CALLED LOVE Johnny Cash and the Evangel Temple Choir	CBS	11
38	34	I'VE BEEN LONELY FOR SO LONG Frederick Knight	Stax	2
33	35	I'LL TAKE YOU THERE Staple Singers	CBS	3
-	36	JOIN TOGETHER Who	Track	1
31	37	THIRD FINGER LEFT HAND Pearls	Bell	3
-	38	BETCHA BY GOLLY WOW Stylistics ●	Avco	1
28	39	LEEDS UNITED Leeds United FC	Chapter One	8
39	40	JUNGLE FEVER Chakachas	Polydor	3

WEEK ENDING 1 JULY 1972

LW	TW	Title / Artist	Label	Wks
2	[1]	TAKE ME BACK 'OME Slade	Polydor	5
1	2	VINCENT Don McLean	United Artists	8
13	3	PUPPY LOVE Donny Osmond	MGM	3
8	[4]	LITTLE WILLY Sweet	RCA	3
6	5	ROCK AND ROLL PART II Gary Glitter	Bell	4
3	6	ROCKIN' ROBIN Michael Jackson	Tamla Motown	6
7	7	CALIFORNIA MAN Move	Harvest	7
24	[8]	AMERICAN TRILOGY Elvis Presley	RCA	3
9	9	MARY HAD A LITTLE LAMB Wings	Apple	6
5	10	AT THE CLUB/SATURDAY NIGHT AT THE MOVIES Drifters	Atlantic	12
21	11	CIRCLES New Seekers	Polydor	3
18	12	OOH-WAKKA-DOO-WAKKA-DAY Gilbert O'Sullivan	MAM	3
20	[13]	LITTLE BIT OF LOVE Free	Island	5
15	[14]	SONG SUNG BLUE Neil Diamond	Uni	7
4	15	METAL GURU T. Rex	EMI	8
17	16	THE FIRST TIME EVER I SAW YOUR FACE Roberta Flack	Atlantic	6
11	17	SISTER JANE New World	RAK	8
14	18	OH GIRL Chi-Lites	MCA	5
16	19	SUPERSONIC ROCKET SHIP Kinks	RCA	5
12	20	OH BABE WHAT WOULD YOU SAY Hurricane Smith	Columbia	10
31	21	WALKIN' IN THE RAIN WITH THE ONE I LOVE Love Unlimited	Uni	2
36	22	JOIN TOGETHER Who	Track	2
10	23	LADY ELEANOR Lindisfarne	Charisma	8
25	24	NUT ROCKER B. Bumble and the Stingers	Stateside	3
-	25	I CAN SEE CLEARLY NOW Johnny Nash	CBS	1
23	26	AMAZING GRACE Royal Scots Dragoon Guards Band	RCA	14
34	27	I'VE BEEN LONELY FOR SO LONG Frederick Knight	Stax	3
-	28	SYLVIA'S MOTHER Dr Hook and the Medicine Show ●	CBS	1
32	29	AMAZING GRACE Judy Collins	Elektra	35
35	[30]	I'LL TAKE YOU THERE Staple Singers	CBS	4
27	31	WHAT'S YOUR NAME Chicory Tip	CBS	7
38	32	BETCHA BY GOLLY WOW Stylistics	Avco	2
30	33	COME WHAT MAY Vicky Leandros	Philips	13
26	34	DOOBEDOOD'NDOOBE DOOBEDOOD'NDOOBE Diana Ross	Tamla Motown	7
28	35	COULD IT BE FOREVER David Cassidy	Bell	13
33	36	A THING CALLED LOVE Johnny Cash and the Evangel Temple Choir	CBS	12
22	37	ISN'T LIFE STRANGE Moody Blues	Threshold	9
19	38	ROCKET MAN Elton John	DJM	10
29	39	A WHITER SHADE OF PALE Procol Harum	Magni Fly	10
-	40	TRAGEDY Argent	Epic	1

WEEK ENDING 8 JULY 1972

LW	TW	Title / Artist	Label	Wks
3	[1]	PUPPY LOVE Donny Osmond	MGM	4
5	[2]	ROCK AND ROLL PART II Gary Glitter	Bell	5
1	3	TAKE ME BACK 'OME Slade	Polydor	6
4	[4]	LITTLE WILLY Sweet	RCA	4
2	5	VINCENT Don McLean	United Artists	9
11	6	CIRCLES New Seekers	Polydor	4
6	7	ROCKIN' ROBIN Michael Jackson	Tamla Motown	7
12	[8]	OOH-WAKKA-DOO-WAKKA-DAY Gilbert O'Sullivan	MAM	4
8	9	AMERICAN TRILOGY Elvis Presley	RCA	4
7	10	CALIFORNIA MAN Move	Harvest	8
9	11	MARY HAD A LITTLE LAMB Wings	Apple	7
25	12	I CAN SEE CLEARLY NOW Johnny Nash	CBS	2
28	13	SYLVIA'S MOTHER Dr Hook and the Medicine Show	CBS	2
16	[14]	THE FIRST TIME EVER I SAW YOUR FACE Roberta Flack	Atlantic	7
13	15	LITTLE BIT OF LOVE Free	Island	6
22	16	JOIN TOGETHER Who	Track	3
14	17	SONG SUNG BLUE Neil Diamond	Uni	8
18	18	OH GIRL Chi-Lites	MCA	6
21	19	WALKIN' IN THE RAIN WITH THE ONE I LOVE Love Unlimited	Uni	3
24	20	NUT ROCKER B. Bumble and the Stingers	Stateside	4
19	21	SUPERSONIC ROCKET SHIP Kinks	RCA	6
15	22	METAL GURU T. Rex	EMI	9
10	23	AT THE CLUB/SATURDAY NIGHT AT THE MOVIES Drifters	Atlantic	13

In these weeks ■ Despite the flood of re-issued hits, the only acts in the Top Ten who had been hitmakers since the Sixties were the Move, enjoying their final hit, and the inevitable Elvis Presley (08.07.72) ■ The chart is full of names - Willy, Vincent, Robin, Mary, Sylvia, Jane, Grace (twice) and Eleanor (08.07.72)■

July 1972

□ Highest position disc reached ● Act's first ever week on chart

LW	TW	Title	Artist	Label	Wks
17	24	SISTER JANE	New World	RAK	9
32	25	BETCHA BY GOLLY WOW	Stylistics	Avco	3
27	26	I'VE BEEN LONELY FOR SO LONG	Frederick Knight	Stax	4
20	27	OH BABE WHAT WOULD YOU SAY	Hurricane Smith	Columbia	11
26	28	AMAZING GRACE	Royal Scots Dragoon Guards Band	RCA	15
-	29	STARMAN	David Bowie	RCA	1
-	30	BREAKING UP IS HARD TO DO	Partridge Family	Bell	1
29	31	AMAZING GRACE	Judy Collins	Elektra	36
30	32	I'LL TAKE YOU THERE	Staple Singers	CBS	5
23	33	LADY ELEANOR	Lindisfarne	Charisma	9
40	34	TRAGEDY	Argent	Epic	2
-	35	MAD ABOUT YOU	Bruce Ruffin	Rhino	1
-	36	GIVE ME ONE MORE CHANCE	Donald Peers and the Les Reed Orchestra	Decca	1
33	37	COME WHAT MAY	Vicky Leandros	Philips	14
35	38	COULD IT BE FOREVER	David Cassidy	Bell	14
-	39	JUST WALK IN MY SHOES	Gladys Knight & The Pips	Tamla Motown	1
-	40	SILVER MACHINE	Hawkwind ●	United Artists	1

WEEK ENDING 15 JULY 1972

LW	TW	Title	Artist	Label	Wks
1	1	PUPPY LOVE	Donny Osmond	MGM	5
2	2	ROCK AND ROLL PART II	Gary Glitter	Bell	6
3	3	TAKE ME BACK 'OME	Slade	Polydor	7
13	4	SYLVIA'S MOTHER	Dr Hook and the Medicine Show	CBS	3
6	5	CIRCLES	New Seekers	Polydor	5
4	6	LITTLE WILLY	Sweet	RCA	5
12	7	I CAN SEE CLEARLY NOW	Johnny Nash	CBS	3
5	8	VINCENT	Don McLean	United Artists	10
9	9	AMERICAN TRILOGY	Elvis Presley	RCA	5
7	10	ROCKIN' ROBIN	Michael Jackson	Tamla Motown	8
8	11	OOH-WAKKA-DOO-WAKKA-DAY	Gilbert O'Sullivan	MAM	5
16	12	JOIN TOGETHER	Who	Track	4
30	13	BREAKING UP IS HARD TO DO	Partridge Family	Bell	2
10	14	CALIFORNIA MAN	Move	Harvest	9
11	15	MARY HAD A LITTLE LAMB	Wings	Apple	8
19	16	WALKIN' IN THE RAIN WITH THE ONE I LOVE	Love Unlimited	Uni	4
14	17	THE FIRST TIME EVER I SAW YOUR FACE	Roberta Flack	Atlantic	8
15	18	LITTLE BIT OF LOVE	Free	Island	7
20	19	NUT ROCKER	B. Bumble and the Stingers	Stateside	5
29	20	STARMAN	David Bowie	RCA	2
23	21	AT THE CLUB/SATURDAY NIGHT AT THE MOVIES	Drifters	Atlantic	14
26	22	I'VE BEEN LONELY FOR SO LONG	Frederick Knight	Stax	5
35	23	MAD ABOUT YOU	Bruce Ruffin	Rhino	2
17	24	SONG SUNG BLUE	Neil Diamond	Uni	9
25	25	BETCHA BY GOLLY WOW	Stylistics	Avco	4
24	26	SISTER JANE	New World	RAK	10
27	27	OH BABE WHAT WOULD YOU SAY	Hurricane Smith	Columbia	12
22	28	METAL GURU	T. Rex	EMI	10
-	29	SEASIDE SHUFFLE	Terry Dactyl and the Dinosaurs ●	UK	1
18	30	OH GIRL	Chi-Lites	MCA	7
31	31	AMAZING GRACE	Judy Collins	Elektra	37
28	32	AMAZING GRACE	Royal Scots Dragoon Guards Band	RCA	16
32	33	I'LL TAKE YOU THERE	Staple Singers	CBS	6
34	34	TRAGEDY	Argent	Epic	3
-	35	AUTOMATICALLY SUNSHINE	Supremes	Tamla Motown	1
39	36	JUST WALK IN MY SHOES	Gladys Knight & The Pips	Tamla Motown	2
40	37	SILVER MACHINE	Hawkwind	United Artists	2
-	38	MY GUY	Mary Wells	Tamla Motown	1
21	39	SUPERSONIC ROCKET SHIP	Kinks	RCA	7
37	40	COME WHAT MAY	Vicky Leandros	Philips	15

WEEK ENDING 22 JULY 1972

LW	TW	Title	Artist	Label	Wks
1	1	PUPPY LOVE	Donny Osmond	MGM	6
2	2	ROCK AND ROLL PART II	Gary Glitter	Bell	7
4	3	SYLVIA'S MOTHER	Dr Hook and the Medicine Show	CBS	4
5	4	CIRCLES	New Seekers	Polydor	6
7	5	I CAN SEE CLEARLY NOW	Johnny Nash	CBS	4
6	6	LITTLE WILLY	Sweet	RCA	6
13	7	BREAKING UP IS HARD TO DO	Partridge Family	Bell	3
3	8	TAKE ME BACK 'OME	Slade	Polydor	8
12	9	JOIN TOGETHER	Who	Track	5
9	10	AMERICAN TRILOGY	Elvis Presley	RCA	6
11	11	OOH-WAKKA-DOO-WAKKA-DAY	Gilbert O'Sullivan	MAM	6
29	12	SEASIDE SHUFFLE	Terry Dactyl and the Dinosaurs	UK	2
25	13	BETCHA BY GOLLY WOW	Stylistics	Avco	5
23	14	MAD ABOUT YOU	Bruce Ruffin	Rhino	3
10	15	ROCKIN' ROBIN	Michael Jackson	Tamla Motown	9
16	16	WALKIN' IN THE RAIN WITH THE ONE I LOVE	Love Unlimited	Uni	5
-	17	SCHOOL'S OUT	Alice Cooper ●	Warner Brothers	1
20	18	STARMAN	David Bowie	RCA	3
8	19	VINCENT	Don McLean	United Artists	11
37	20	SILVER MACHINE	Hawkwind	United Artists	3
17	21	THE FIRST TIME EVER I SAW YOUR FACE	Roberta Flack	Atlantic	9
19	22	NUT ROCKER	B. Bumble and the Stingers	Stateside	6
22	23	I'VE BEEN LONELY FOR SO LONG	Frederick Knight	Stax	6
14	24	CALIFORNIA MAN	Move	Harvest	10
35	25	AUTOMATICALLY SUNSHINE	Supremes	Tamla Motown	2
38	26	MY GUY	Mary Wells	Tamla Motown	2
15	27	MARY HAD A LITTLE LAMB	Wings	Apple	9
32	28	AMAZING GRACE	Royal Scots Dragoon Guards Band	RCA	17
24	29	SONG SUNG BLUE	Neil Diamond	Uni	10
18	30	LITTLE BIT OF LOVE	Free	Island	8
21	31	AT THE CLUB/SATURDAY NIGHT AT THE MOVIES	Drifters	Atlantic	15
33	32	I'LL TAKE YOU THERE	Staple Singers	CBS	7
27	33	OH BABE WHAT WOULD YOU SAY	Hurricane Smith	Columbia	13
28	34	METAL GURU	T. Rex	EMI	11
30	35	OH GIRL	Chi-Lites	MCA	8
26	36	SISTER JANE	New World	RAK	11
-	37	WORKING ON A BUILDING OF LOVE	Chairmen Of The Board	Invictus	1
31	38	AMAZING GRACE	Judy Collins	Elektra	38
-	39	IT'S FOUR IN THE MORNING	Faron Young ●	Mercury	1
34	40	TRAGEDY	Argent	Epic	4

WEEK ENDING 29 JULY 1972

LW	TW	Title	Artist	Label	Wks
1	1	PUPPY LOVE	Donny Osmond	MGM	7
3	2	SYLVIA'S MOTHER	Dr Hook and the Medicine Show	CBS	5
2	3	ROCK AND ROLL PART II	Gary Glitter	Bell	8
7	4	BREAKING UP IS HARD TO DO	Partridge Family	Bell	4
12	5	SEASIDE SHUFFLE	Terry Dactyl and the Dinosaurs	UK	3
17	6	SCHOOL'S OUT	Alice Cooper	Warner Brothers	2
5	7	I CAN SEE CLEARLY NOW	Johnny Nash	CBS	5
4	8	CIRCLES	New Seekers	Polydor	7
14	9	MAD ABOUT YOU	Bruce Ruffin	Rhino	4
18	10	STARMAN	David Bowie	RCA	4
6	11	LITTLE WILLY	Sweet	RCA	7
20	12	SILVER MACHINE	Hawkwind	United Artists	4
9	13	JOIN TOGETHER	Who	Track	6
16	14	WALKIN' IN THE RAIN WITH THE ONE I LOVE	Love Unlimited	Uni	6
13	15	BETCHA BY GOLLY WOW	Stylistics	Avco	6
8	16	TAKE ME BACK 'OME	Slade	Polydor	9
25	17	AUTOMATICALLY SUNSHINE	Supremes	Tamla Motown	3
10	18	AMERICAN TRILOGY	Elvis Presley	RCA	7
-	19	POPCORN	Hot Butter ●	Pye	1
26	20	MY GUY	Mary Wells	Tamla Motown	3
11	21	OOH-WAKKA-DOO-WAKKA-DAY	Gilbert O'Sullivan	MAM	7
15	22	ROCKIN' ROBIN	Michael Jackson	Tamla Motown	10

■Terry Dactyl (not his real name!) will later return to chart glory as Jona Lewie. In the meantime his *Seaside Shuffle* is the summer hit of the year (15.07.72) ■ As Elton John's *Rocket Man* falls off the chart, David Bowie's *Starman* takes its place. They both climb higher than the Kinks' *Supersonic Rocket Ship* (08.07.72)■

□ Highest position disc reached ● Act's first ever week on chart

LW	TW	Title	Artist	Label	Wks
23	23	I'VE BEEN LONELY FOR SO LONG	Frederick Knight	Stax	7
22	24	NUT ROCKER	B. Bumble and the Stingers	Stateside	7
24	25	CALIFORNIA MAN	Move	Harvest	11
19	26	VINCENT	Don McLean	United Artists	12
21	27	THE FIRST TIME EVER I SAW YOUR FACE	Roberta Flack	Atlantic	10
37	28	WORKING ON A BUILDING OF LOVE	Chairmen Of The Board	Invictus	2
39	29	IT'S FOUR IN THE MORNING	Faron Young	Mercury	2
28	30	AMAZING GRACE	Royal Scots Dragoon Guards Band	RCA	18
27	31	MARY HAD A LITTLE LAMB	Wings	Apple	10
31	32	AT THE CLUB/SATURDAY NIGHT AT THE MOVIES	Drifters	Atlantic	16
30	33	LITTLE BIT OF LOVE	Free	Island	9
29	34	SONG SUNG BLUE	Neil Diamond	Uni	11
-	[35]	JUST WALK IN MY SHOES	Gladys Knight & The Pips	Tamla Motown	3
-	36	RUN TO ME	Bee Gees	Polydor	1
33	37	OH BABE WHAT WOULD YOU SAY	Hurricane Smith	Columbia	14
-	[38]	MacARTHUR PARK	Richard Harris	Probe	1
36	39	SISTER JANE	New World	RAK	12
38	40	AMAZING GRACE	Judy Collins	Elektra	39

WEEK ENDING 5 AUGUST 1972

LW	TW	Title	Artist	Label	Wks
1	[1]	PUPPY LOVE	Donny Osmond	MGM	8
6	2	SCHOOL'S OUT	Alice Cooper	Warner Brothers	3
2	3	SYLVIA'S MOTHER	Dr Hook and the Medicine Show	CBS	6
5	4	SEASIDE SHUFFLE	Terry Dactyl and the Dinosaurs	UK	4
4	5	BREAKING UP IS HARD TO DO	Partridge Family	Bell	5
3	6	ROCK AND ROLL PART II	Gary Glitter	Bell	9
12	7	SILVER MACHINE	Hawkwind	United Artists	5
7	8	I CAN SEE CLEARLY NOW	Johnny Nash	CBS	6
8	9	CIRCLES	New Seekers	Polydor	8
17	[10]	AUTOMATICALLY SUNSHINE	Supremes	Tamla Motown	4
19	11	POPCORN	Hot Butter	Pye	2
10	12	STARMAN	David Bowie	RCA	5
9	13	MAD ABOUT YOU	Bruce Ruffin	Rhino	5
20	[14]	MY GUY	Mary Wells	Tamla Motown	4
13	15	JOIN TOGETHER	Who	Track	7
15	16	BETCHA BY GOLLY WOW	Stylistics	Avco	7
11	17	LITTLE WILLY	Sweet	RCA	8
16	18	TAKE ME BACK 'OME	Slade	Polydor	10
21	19	OOH-WAKKA-DOO-WAKKA-DAY	Gilbert O'Sullivan	MAM	8
-	20	10538 OVERTURE	Electric Light Orchestra ●	Harvest	1
14	21	WALKIN' IN THE RAIN WITH THE ONE I LOVE	Love Unlimited	Uni	7
18	22	AMERICAN TRILOGY	Elvis Presley	RCA	8
28	23	WORKING ON A BUILDING OF LOVE	Chairmen Of The Board	Invictus	3
29	24	IT'S FOUR IN THE MORNING	Faron Young	Mercury	3
22	25	ROCKIN' ROBIN	Michael Jackson	Tamla Motown	11
36	26	RUN TO ME	Bee Gees	Polydor	2
-	27	THE LOCOMOTION	Little Eva	London	1
24	28	NUT ROCKER	B. Bumble and the Stingers	Stateside	8
26	29	VINCENT	Don McLean	United Artists	13
27	30	THE FIRST TIME EVER I SAW YOUR FACE	Roberta Flack	Atlantic	11
30	31	AMAZING GRACE	Royal Scots Dragoon Guards Band	RCA	19
25	32	CALIFORNIA MAN	Move	Harvest	12
-	33	WATCH ME	Labi Siffre	Pye	1
23	34	I'VE BEEN LONELY FOR SO LONG	Frederick Knight	Stax	8
32	35	AT THE CLUB/SATURDAY NIGHT AT THE MOVIES	Drifters	Atlantic	17
-	36	I GET THE SWEETEST FEELING	Jackie Wilson	MCA	1
40	37	AMAZING GRACE	Judy Collins	Elektra	40
-	38	SAMSON AND DELILAH	Middle Of The Road	RCA	1
31	39	MARY HAD A LITTLE LAMB	Wings	Apple	11
38	40	MacARTHUR PARK	Richard Harris	Probe	2

WEEK ENDING 12 AUGUST 1972

LW	TW	Title	Artist	Label	Wks
2	[1]	SCHOOL'S OUT	Alice Cooper	Warner Brothers	4
4	[2]	SEASIDE SHUFFLE	Terry Dactyl and the Dinosaurs	UK	5
5	[3]	BREAKING UP IS HARD TO DO	Partridge Family	Bell	6
1	4	PUPPY LOVE	Donny Osmond	MGM	9
3	5	SYLVIA'S MOTHER	Dr Hook and the Medicine Show	CBS	7
11	6	POPCORN	Hot Butter	Pye	3
7	7	SILVER MACHINE	Hawkwind	United Artists	6
8	8	I CAN SEE CLEARLY NOW	Johnny Nash	CBS	7
6	9	ROCK AND ROLL PART II	Gary Glitter	Bell	10
9	10	CIRCLES	New Seekers	Polydor	9
12	11	STARMAN	David Bowie	RCA	6
10	12	AUTOMATICALLY SUNSHINE	Supremes	Tamla Motown	5
13	13	MAD ABOUT YOU	Bruce Ruffin	Rhino	6
16	14	BETCHA BY GOLLY WOW	Stylistics	Avco	8
14	15	MY GUY	Mary Wells	Tamla Motown	5
24	16	IT'S FOUR IN THE MORNING	Faron Young	Mercury	4
20	17	10538 OVERTURE	Electric Light Orchestra	Harvest	2
15	18	JOIN TOGETHER	Who	Track	8
26	19	RUN TO ME	Bee Gees	Polydor	3
17	20	LITTLE WILLY	Sweet	RCA	9
27	21	THE LOCOMOTION	Little Eva	London	2
-	22	ALL THE YOUNG DUDES	Mott the Hoople ●	CBS	1
-	23	YOU WEAR IT WELL	Rod Stewart	Mercury	1
23	24	WORKING ON A BUILDING OF LOVE	Chairmen Of The Board	Invictus	4
-	25	LAYLA	Derek & The Dominos ●	Polydor	1
38	[26]	SAMSON AND DELILAH	Middle Of The Road	RCA	2
21	27	WALKIN' IN THE RAIN WITH THE ONE I LOVE	Love Unlimited	Uni	8
18	28	TAKE ME BACK 'OME	Slade	Polydor	11
19	29	OOH-WAKKA-DOO-WAKKA-DAY	Gilbert O'Sullivan	MAM	9
22	30	AMERICAN TRILOGY	Elvis Presley	RCA	9
36	31	I GET THE SWEETEST FEELING	Jackie Wilson	MCA	2
33	32	WATCH ME	Labi Siffre	Pye	2
-	33	TOO BUSY THINKING ABOUT MY BABY	Mardi Gras ●	Bell	1
25	34	ROCKIN' ROBIN	Michael Jackson	Tamla Motown	12
-	35	CONQUISTADOR	Procol Harum	Chrysalis	1
-	36	WHERE IS THE LOVE	Roberta Flack and Donny Hathaway ●	Atlantic	1
31	37	AMAZING GRACE	Royal Scots Dragoon Guards Band	RCA	20
30	38	THE FIRST TIME EVER I SAW YOUR FACE	Roberta Flack	Atlantic	12
-	39	WALK WITH ME TALK WITH ME DARLING	Four Tops	Tamla Motown	1
29	40	VINCENT	Don McLean	United Artists	14

WEEK ENDING 19 AUGUST 1972

LW	TW	Title	Artist	Label	Wks
1	[1]	SCHOOL'S OUT	Alice Cooper	Warner Brothers	5
2	[2]	SEASIDE SHUFFLE	Terry Dactyl and the Dinosaurs	UK	6
7	[3]	SILVER MACHINE	Hawkwind	United Artists	7
4	4	PUPPY LOVE	Donny Osmond	MGM	10
6	[5]	POPCORN	Hot Butter	Pye	4
3	6	BREAKING UP IS HARD TO DO	Partridge Family	Bell	7
23	7	YOU WEAR IT WELL	Rod Stewart	Mercury	2
5	8	SYLVIA'S MOTHER	Dr Hook and the Medicine Show	CBS	8
19	[9]	RUN TO ME	Bee Gees	Polydor	4
16	10	IT'S FOUR IN THE MORNING	Faron Young	Mercury	5
22	11	ALL THE YOUNG DUDES	Mott the Hoople	CBS	2
9	12	ROCK AND ROLL PART II	Gary Glitter	Bell	11
25	13	LAYLA	Derek & The Dominos	Polydor	2
17	14	10538 OVERTURE	Electric Light Orchestra	Harvest	3
21	15	THE LOCOMOTION	Little Eva	London	3
8	16	I CAN SEE CLEARLY NOW	Johnny Nash	CBS	8
12	17	AUTOMATICALLY SUNSHINE	Supremes	Tamla Motown	6
11	18	STARMAN	David Bowie	RCA	7
13	19	MAD ABOUT YOU	Bruce Ruffin	Rhino	7
24	[20]	WORKING ON A BUILDING OF LOVE	Chairmen Of The Board	Invictus	5
10	21	CIRCLES	New Seekers	Polydor	10

In these weeks ■ The Supremes' twelfth and final Top 10 hit is *Automatically Sunshine* (05.08.72) ■ For two weeks, a David Bowie song is at no. 11. First it is his own version of *Starman*, then Mott The Hoople's cover of his *All The Young Dudes* (19.08.72) ■ The top five acts are all enjoying their first chart hits, so are Dr. Hook and all the acts from 10 to 15 (19.08.72)■

LW	TW	Title	Artist	Label	Wks
15	22	MY GUY	Mary Wells	Tamla Motown	6
14	23	BETCHA BY GOLLY WOW	Stylistics	Avco	9
31	24	I GET THE SWEETEST FEELING	Jackie Wilson	MCA	3
-	25	STANDING IN THE ROAD	Blackfoot Sue ●	DJM	1
33	26	TOO BUSY THINKING ABOUT MY BABY	Mardi Gras	Bell	2
35	27	CONQUISTADOR	Procol Harum	Chrysalis	2
20	28	LITTLE WILLY	Sweet	RCA	10
32	[29]	WATCH ME	Labi Siffre	Pye	3
26	30	SAMSON AND DELILAH	Middle Of The Road	RCA	3
29	31	OOH-WAKKA-DOO-WAKKA-DAY	Gilbert O'Sullivan	MAM	10
39	[32]	WALK WITH ME TALK WITH ME DARLING	Four Tops	Tamla Motown	2
36	33	WHERE IS THE LOVE	Roberta Flack and Donny Hathaway	Atlantic	2
30	34	AMERICAN TRILOGY	Elvis Presley	RCA	10
18	35	JOIN TOGETHER	Who	Track	9
-	36	LEAN ON ME	Bill Withers ●	Sussex/A&M	1
-	37	AMAZING GRACE	Judy Collins	Elektra	41
-	38	HEYKENS SERENADE/THE DAY IS OVER	Royal Scots Dragoon Guards Band	RCA	1
38	39	THE FIRST TIME EVER I SAW YOUR FACE	Roberta Flack	Atlantic	13
-	40	JOURNEY	Duncan Browne ●	RAK	1

LW	TW	*WEEK ENDING* **26 AUGUST 1972**			Wks
1	[1]	SCHOOL'S OUT	Alice Cooper	Warner Brothers	6
7	2	YOU WEAR IT WELL	Rod Stewart	Mercury	3
3	[3]	SILVER MACHINE	Hawkwind	United Artists	8
11	4	ALL THE YOUNG DUDES	Mott the Hoople	CBS	3
2	5	SEASIDE SHUFFLE	Terry Dactyl and the Dinosaurs	UK	7
5	6	POPCORN	Hot Butter	Pye	5
13	[7]	LAYLA	Derek & The Dominos	Polydor	3
6	8	BREAKING UP IS HARD TO DO	Partridge Family	Bell	8
14	[9]	10538 OVERTURE	Electric Light Orchestra	Harvest	4
4	10	PUPPY LOVE	Donny Osmond	MGM	11
9	11	RUN TO ME	Bee Gees	Polydor	5
10	12	IT'S FOUR IN THE MORNING	Faron Young	Mercury	6
15	13	THE LOCOMOTION	Little Eva	London	4
25	14	STANDING IN THE ROAD	Blackfoot Sue	DJM	2
16	15	I CAN SEE CLEARLY NOW	Johnny Nash	CBS	9
8	16	SYLVIA'S MOTHER	Dr Hook and the Medicine Show	CBS	9
24	17	I GET THE SWEETEST FEELING	Jackie Wilson	MCA	4
12	18	ROCK AND ROLL PART II	Gary Glitter	Bell	12
21	19	CIRCLES	New Seekers	Polydor	11
-	20	SUGAR ME	Lynsey De Paul ●	MAM	1
19	21	MAD ABOUT YOU	Bruce Ruffin	Rhino	8
26	22	TOO BUSY THINKING ABOUT MY BABY	Mardi Gras	Bell	3
23	23	BETCHA BY GOLLY WOW	Stylistics	Avco	10
27	24	CONQUISTADOR	Procol Harum	Chrysalis	3
20	25	WORKING ON A BUILDING OF LOVE	Chairmen Of The Board	Invictus	6
-	26	VIRGINIA PLAIN	Roxy Music ●	Island	1
36	27	LEAN ON ME	Bill Withers	Sussex/A&M	2
-	28	AIN'T NO SUNSHINE	Michael Jackson	Tamla Motown	1
40	29	JOURNEY	Duncan Browne	RAK	2
17	30	AUTOMATICALLY SUNSHINE	Supremes	Tamla Motown	7
33	31	WHERE IS THE LOVE	Roberta Flack and Donny Hathaway	Atlantic	3
29	32	WATCH ME	Labi Siffre	Pye	4
38	33	HEYKENS SERENADE/THE DAY IS OVER	Royal Scots Dragoon Guards Band	RCA	2
22	34	MY GUY	Mary Wells	Tamla Motown	7
18	35	STARMAN	David Bowie	RCA	8
32	36	WALK WITH ME TALK WITH ME DARLING	Four Tops	Tamla Motown	3
28	37	LITTLE WILLY	Sweet	RCA	11
30	38	SAMSON AND DELILAH	Middle Of The Road	RCA	4
-	39	AMAZING GRACE	Royal Scots Dragoon Guards Band	RCA	21
-	40	WALK IN THE NIGHT	Jnr. Walker and The All Stars	Tamla Motown	1

September 1972

□ Highest position disc reached ● Act's first ever week on chart

LW	TW	*WEEK ENDING* **2 SEPTEMBER 1972**			Wks
2	[1]	YOU WEAR IT WELL	Rod Stewart	Mercury	4
-	2	MAMA WEER ALL CRAZEE NOW	Slade	Polydor	1
1	3	SCHOOL'S OUT	Alice Cooper	Warner Brothers	7
3	4	SILVER MACHINE	Hawkwind	United Artists	9
4	5	ALL THE YOUNG DUDES	Mott the Hoople	CBS	4
12	6	IT'S FOUR IN THE MORNING	Faron Young	Mercury	7
7	[7]	LAYLA	Derek & The Dominos	Polydor	4
6	8	POPCORN	Hot Butter	Pye	6
14	9	STANDING IN THE ROAD	Blackfoot Sue	DJM	3
5	10	SEASIDE SHUFFLE	Terry Dactyl and the Dinosaurs	UK	8
13	[11]	THE LOCOMOTION	Little Eva	London	5
20	12	SUGAR ME	Lynsey De Paul	MAM	2
11	13	RUN TO ME	Bee Gees	Polydor	6
17	14	I GET THE SWEETEST FEELING	Jackie Wilson	MCA	5
9	15	10538 OVERTURE	Electric Light Orchestra	Harvest	5
8	16	BREAKING UP IS HARD TO DO	Partridge Family	Bell	9
10	17	PUPPY LOVE	Donny Osmond	MGM	12
26	18	VIRGINIA PLAIN	Roxy Music	Island	2
15	19	I CAN SEE CLEARLY NOW	Johnny Nash	CBS	10
28	20	AIN'T NO SUNSHINE	Michael Jackson	Tamla Motown	2
22	21	TOO BUSY THINKING ABOUT MY BABY	Mardi Gras	Bell	4
24	[22]	CONQUISTADOR	Procol Harum	Chrysalis	4
18	23	ROCK AND ROLL PART II	Gary Glitter	Bell	13
29	24	JOURNEY	Duncan Browne	RAK	3
27	25	LEAN ON ME	Bill Withers	Sussex/A&M	3
16	26	SYLVIA'S MOTHER	Dr Hook and the Medicine Show	CBS	10
25	27	WORKING ON A BUILDING OF LOVE	Chairmen Of The Board	Invictus	7
19	28	CIRCLES	New Seekers	Polydor	12
31	[29]	WHERE IS THE LOVE	Roberta Flack and Donny Hathaway	Atlantic	4
-	30	LIVING IN HARMONY	Cliff Richard	Columbia	1
33	31	HEYKENS SERENADE/THE DAY IS OVER	Royal Scots Dragoon Guards Band	RCA	3
21	32	MAD ABOUT YOU	Bruce Ruffin	Rhino	9
34	33	MY GUY	Mary Wells	Tamla Motown	8
23	34	BETCHA BY GOLLY WOW	Stylistics	Avco	11
-	[35]	I'M STILL IN LOVE WITH YOU	Al Green	London	1
-	36	COME ON OVER TO MY PLACE	The Drifters	Atlantic	1
30	37	AUTOMATICALLY SUNSHINE	Supremes	Tamla Motown	8
40	38	WALK IN THE NIGHT	Jnr. Walker and The All Stars	Tamla Motown	2
-	39	BIG SIX	Judge Dread ●	Big Shot	1
-	40	LOVE LOVE LOVE	Bobby Hebb	Philips	1

LW	TW	*WEEK ENDING* **9 SEPTEMBER 1972**			Wks
2	[1]	MAMA WEER ALL CRAZEE NOW	Slade	Polydor	2
1	2	YOU WEAR IT WELL	Rod Stewart	Mercury	5
5	[3]	ALL THE YOUNG DUDES	Mott the Hoople	CBS	5
9	[4]	STANDING IN THE ROAD	Blackfoot Sue	DJM	4
6	5	IT'S FOUR IN THE MORNING	Faron Young	Mercury	8
12	6	SUGAR ME	Lynsey De Paul	MAM	3
4	7	SILVER MACHINE	Hawkwind	United Artists	10
18	8	VIRGINIA PLAIN	Roxy Music	Island	3
7	9	LAYLA	Derek & The Dominos	Polydor	5
14	10	I GET THE SWEETEST FEELING	Jackie Wilson	MCA	6
3	11	SCHOOL'S OUT	Alice Cooper	Warner Brothers	5
11	12	THE LOCOMOTION	Little Eva	London	6
13	13	RUN TO ME	Bee Gees	Polydor	7
8	14	POPCORN	Hot Butter	Pye	7
10	15	SEASIDE SHUFFLE	Terry Dactyl and the Dinosaurs	UK	9
20	16	AIN'T NO SUNSHINE	Michael Jackson	Tamla Motown	3
15	17	10538 OVERTURE	Electric Light Orchestra	Harvest	6
25	[18]	LEAN ON ME	Bill Withers	Sussex/A&M	4
17	19	PUPPY LOVE	Donny Osmond	MGM	13
16	20	BREAKING UP IS HARD TO DO	Partridge Family	Bell	10
30	21	LIVING IN HARMONY	Cliff Richard	Columbia	2
19	22	I CAN SEE CLEARLY NOW	Johnny Nash	CBS	11
24	[23]	JOURNEY	Duncan Browne	RAK	4

■Judy Collins' *Amazing Grace* bows out finally after 41 weeks on the chart over more than a year and a half (19.08.72) ■ First time round, *Layla* stops at number 7. Ten years later it will climb to number 4 (26.08.72) ■ Judge Dread begins a chart career which will bring him nine Top 40 hits in five years, without a single play on Radio One (02.09.72)■

September 1972

□ Highest position disc reached ● Act's first ever week on chart

LW	TW	Title	Artist	Label	Wks
21	24	TOO BUSY THINKING ABOUT MY BABY	Mardi Gras	*Bell*	5
38	25	WALK IN THE NIGHT	Jnr. Walker and The All Stars	*Tamla Motown*	3
28	26	CIRCLES	New Seekers	*Polydor*	13
36	27	COME ON OVER TO MY PLACE	The Drifters	*Atlantic*	2
22	28	CONQUISTADOR	Procol Harum	*Chrysalis*	5
39	29	BIG SIX	Judge Dread	*Big Shot*	2
31	30	HEYKENS SERENADE/THE DAY IS OVER	Royal Scots Dragoon Guards Band	*RCA*	4
23	31	ROCK AND ROLL PART II	Gary Glitter	*Bell*	14
40	32	LOVE LOVE LOVE	Bobby Hebb	*Philips*	2
-	33	SUZANNE BEWARE OF THE DEVIL	Dandy Livingstone ●	*Horse*	1
29	34	WHERE IS THE LOVE	Roberta Flack and Donny Hathaway	*Atlantic*	5
26	35	SYLVIA'S MOTHER	Dr Hook and the Medicine Show	*CBS*	11
35	36	I'M STILL IN LOVE WITH YOU	Al Green	*London*	2
32	37	MAD ABOUT YOU	Bruce Ruffin	*Rhino*	10
-	38	WHO WAS IT	Hurricane Smith	*Columbia*	1
-	39	LONG COOL WOMAN IN A BLACK DRESS	Hollies	*Parlophone*	1
-	40	HONKY CAT	Elton John	*DJM*	1

WEEK ENDING 16 SEPTEMBER 1972

LW	TW	Title	Artist	Label	Wks
1	1	MAMA WEER ALL CRAZEE NOW	Slade	*Polydor*	3
2	2	YOU WEAR IT WELL	Rod Stewart	*Mercury*	6
5	3	IT'S FOUR IN THE MORNING	Faron Young	*Mercury*	9
8	4	VIRGINIA PLAIN	Roxy Music	*Island*	4
6	5	SUGAR ME	Lynsey De Paul	*MAM*	4
4	6	STANDING IN THE ROAD	Blackfoot Sue	*DJM*	5
3	7	ALL THE YOUNG DUDES	Mott the Hoople	*CBS*	6
16	8	AIN'T NO SUNSHINE	Michael Jackson	*Tamla Motown*	4
10	9	I GET THE SWEETEST FEELING	Jackie Wilson	*MCA*	7
-	10	HOW CAN I BE SURE	David Cassidy	*Bell*	1
9	11	LAYLA	Derek & The Dominos	*Polydor*	6
21	12	LIVING IN HARMONY	Cliff Richard	*Columbia*	3
7	13	SILVER MACHINE	Hawkwind	*United Artists*	11
-	14	CHILDREN OF THE REVOLUTION	T. Rex	*EMI*	1
12	15	THE LOCOMOTION	Little Eva	*London*	7
11	16	SCHOOL'S OUT	Alice Cooper	*Warner Bros.*	6
14	17	POPCORN	Hot Butter	*Pye*	8
18	18	LEAN ON ME	Bill Withers	*Sussex/A&M*	5
24	19	TOO BUSY THINKING ABOUT MY BABY	Mardi Gras	*Bell*	6
27	20	COME ON OVER TO MY PLACE	The Drifters	*Atlantic*	3
25	21	WALK IN THE NIGHT	Jnr. Walker and The All Stars	*Tamla Motown*	4
-	22	TOO YOUNG	Donny Osmond	*MGM*	1
29	23	BIG SIX	Judge Dread	*Big Shot*	3
20	24	BREAKING UP IS HARD TO DO	Partridge Family	*Bell*	11
-	25	WIG-WAM BAM	Sweet	*RCA*	1
15	26	SEASIDE SHUFFLE	Terry Dactyl and the Dinosaurs	*UK*	10
13	27	RUN TO ME	Bee Gees	*Polydor*	8
33	28	SUZANNE BEWARE OF THE DEVIL	Dandy Livingstone	*Horse*	2
38	29	WHO WAS IT	Hurricane Smith	*Columbia*	2
19	30	PUPPY LOVE	Donny Osmond	*MGM*	14
23	31	JOURNEY	Duncan Browne	*RAK*	5
39	32	LONG COOL WOMAN IN A BLACK DRESS	Hollies	*Parlophone*	2
22	33	I CAN SEE CLEARLY NOW	Johnny Nash	*CBS*	12
40	34	HONKY CAT	Elton John	*DJM*	2
30	35	HEYKENS SERENADE/THE DAY IS OVER	Royal Scots Dragoon Guards Band	*RCA*	5
17	36	10538 OVERTURE	Electric Light Orchestra	*Harvest*	7
26	37	CIRCLES	New Seekers	*Polydor*	14
-	38	MOULDY OLD DOUGH	Lieutenant Pigeon ●	*Decca*	1
36	39	I'M STILL IN LOVE WITH YOU	Al Green	*London*	3
28	40	CONQUISTADOR	Procol Harum	*Chrysalis*	6

WEEK ENDING 23 SEPTEMBER 1972

LW	TW	Title	Artist	Label	Wks
1	1	MAMA WEER ALL CRAZEE NOW	Slade	*Polydor*	4
14	2	CHILDREN OF THE REVOLUTION	T. Rex	*EMI*	2
10	3	HOW CAN I BE SURE	David Cassidy	*Bell*	2
2	4	YOU WEAR IT WELL	Rod Stewart	*Mercury*	7
5	5	SUGAR ME	Lynsey De Paul	*MAM*	5
3	6	IT'S FOUR IN THE MORNING	Faron Young	*Mercury*	10
4	7	VIRGINIA PLAIN	Roxy Music	*Island*	5
8	8	AIN'T NO SUNSHINE	Michael Jackson	*Tamla Motown*	5
22	9	TOO YOUNG	Donny Osmond	*MGM*	2
20	10	COME ON OVER TO MY PLACE	The Drifters	*Atlantic*	4
6	11	STANDING IN THE ROAD	Blackfoot Sue	*DJM*	6
12	12	LIVING IN HARMONY	Cliff Richard	*Columbia*	4
9	13	I GET THE SWEETEST FEELING	Jackie Wilson	*MCA*	8
7	14	ALL THE YOUNG DUDES	Mott the Hoople	*CBS*	7
25	15	WIG-WAM BAM	Sweet	*RCA*	2
21	16	WALK IN THE NIGHT	Jnr. Walker and The All Stars	*Tamla Motown*	5
23	17	BIG SIX	Judge Dread	*Big Shot*	4
28	18	SUZANNE BEWARE OF THE DEVIL	Dandy Livingstone	*Horse*	3
13	19	SILVER MACHINE	Hawkwind	*United Artists*	12
38	20	MOULDY OLD DOUGH	Lieutenant Pigeon	*Decca*	2
18	21	LEAN ON ME	Bill Withers	*Sussex/A&M*	6
11	22	LAYLA	Derek & The Dominos	*Polydor*	7
29	23	WHO WAS IT	Hurricane Smith	*Columbia*	3
15	24	THE LOCOMOTION	Little Eva	*London*	8
17	25	POPCORN	Hot Butter	*Pye*	9
24	26	BREAKING UP IS HARD TO DO	Partridge Family	*Bell*	12
-	27	I DIDN'T KNOW I LOVED YOU (TILL I SAW YOU ROCK 'N' ROLL)	Gary Glitter	*Bell*	1
16	28	SCHOOL'S OUT	Alice Cooper	*Warner Bros.*	7
27	29	RUN TO ME	Bee Gees	*Polydor*	9
-	30	JOHN I'M ONLY DANCING	David Bowie	*RCA*	1
34	31	HONKY CAT	Elton John	*DJM*	3
-	32	MAYBE I KNOW	Seashells ●	*CBS*	1
32	33	LONG COOL WOMAN IN A BLACK DRESS	Hollies	*Parlophone*	3
-	34	LIGHT UP THE FIRE	Parchment ●	*Pye*	1
30	35	PUPPY LOVE	Donny Osmond	*MGM*	15
19	36	TOO BUSY THINKING ABOUT MY BABY	Mardi Gras	*Bell*	7
26	37	SEASIDE SHUFFLE	Terry Dactyl and the Dinosaurs	*UK*	11
33	38	I CAN SEE CLEARLY NOW	Johnny Nash	*CBS*	13
35	39	HEYKENS SERENADE/THE DAY IS OVER	Royal Scots Dragoon Guards Band	*RCA*	6
31	40	JOURNEY	Duncan Browne	*RAK*	6

WEEK ENDING 30 SEPTEMBER 1972

LW	TW	Title	Artist	Label	Wks
3	1	HOW CAN I BE SURE	David Cassidy	*Bell*	3
2	2	CHILDREN OF THE REVOLUTION	T. Rex	*EMI*	3
1	3	MAMA WEER ALL CRAZEE NOW	Slade	*Polydor*	5
20	4	MOULDY OLD DOUGH	Lieutenant Pigeon	*Decca*	3
9	5	TOO YOUNG	Donny Osmond	*MGM*	3
15	6	WIG-WAM BAM	Sweet	*RCA*	3
6	7	IT'S FOUR IN THE MORNING	Faron Young	*Mercury*	11
8	8	AIN'T NO SUNSHINE	Michael Jackson	*Tamla Motown*	6
10	9	COME ON OVER TO MY PLACE	The Drifters	*Atlantic*	5
7	10	VIRGINIA PLAIN	Roxy Music	*Island*	6
4	11	YOU WEAR IT WELL	Rod Stewart	*Mercury*	8
12	12	LIVING IN HARMONY	Cliff Richard	*Columbia*	5
13	13	I GET THE SWEETEST FEELING	Jackie Wilson	*MCA*	9
27	14	I DIDN'T KNOW I LOVED YOU (TILL I SAW YOU ROCK 'N' ROLL)	Gary Glitter	*Bell*	2
5	15	SUGAR ME	Lynsey De Paul	*MAM*	6
18	16	SUZANNE BEWARE OF THE DEVIL	Dandy Livingstone	*Horse*	4
17	17	BIG SIX	Judge Dread	*Big Shot*	5
-	18	YOU'RE A LADY	Peter Skellern ●	*Decca*	1
11	19	STANDING IN THE ROAD	Blackfoot Sue	*DJM*	7
16	20	WALK IN THE NIGHT	Jnr. Walker and The All Stars	*Tamla Motown*	6
-	21	BURNING LOVE	Elvis Presley	*RCA*	1
14	22	ALL THE YOUNG DUDES	Mott the Hoople	*CBS*	8
30	23	JOHN I'M ONLY DANCING	David Bowie	*RCA*	2
23	24	WHO WAS IT	Hurricane Smith	*Columbia*	4
-	25	DONNA	10CC ●	*UK*	1
25	26	POPCORN	Hot Butter	*Pye*	10
24	27	THE LOCOMOTION	Little Eva	*London*	9

In these weeks ■ *Living In Harmony* by Cliff Richard peaks at no. 12, his seventh successive hit to miss the Top 10. In his entire career, this is his worst chart streak (16.09.72) ■ Female stars are very much on the decline. For two weeks Lynsey de Paul is the only woman in the Top 20. Then for two more weeks, there are no women in the Top 20 at all (30.09.72)■

October 1972

□ Highest position disc reached ● Act's first ever week on chart

LW	TW	Title	Artist	Label	Wks
21	28	LEAN ON ME	Bill Withers	Sussex/A&M	7
22	29	LAYLA	Derek & The Dominos	Polydor	8
-	30	BACK STABBERS	O'Jays ●	CBS	1
34	31	LIGHT UP THE FIRE	Parchment	Pye	2
31	32	HONKY CAT	Elton John	DJM	4
35	33	PUPPY LOVE	Donny Osmond	MGM	16
32	34	MAYBE I KNOW	Seashells	CBS	2
-	35	GOODBYE TO LOVE	Carpenters	A&M	1
-	36	YOU CAME, YOU SAW, YOU CONQUERED	Pearls	Bell	1
-	37	BURLESQUE	Family	Reprise	1
26	38	BREAKING UP IS HARD TO DO	Partridge Family	Bell	13
-	39	ALL FALL DOWN	Lindisfarne	Charisma	1
-	40	GUITAR MAN	Bread	Elektra	1

WEEK ENDING 7 OCTOBER 1972

LW	TW	Title	Artist	Label	Wks
1	1	HOW CAN I BE SURE	David Cassidy	Bell	4
2	2	CHILDREN OF THE REVOLUTION	T. Rex	EMI	4
4	3	MOULDY OLD DOUGH	Lieutenant Pigeon	Decca	4
6	4	WIG-WAM BAM	Sweet	RCA	4
5	5	TOO YOUNG	Donny Osmond	MGM	4
18	6	YOU'RE A LADY	Peter Skellern	Decca	2
3	7	MAMA WEER ALL CRAZEE NOW	Slade	Polydor	6
14	8	I DIDN'T KNOW I LOVED YOU (TILL I SAW YOU ROCK 'N' ROLL)	Gary Glitter	Bell	3
7	9	IT'S FOUR IN THE MORNING	Faron Young	Mercury	12
9	10	COME ON OVER TO MY PLACE	The Drifters	Atlantic	6
21	11	BURNING LOVE	Elvis Presley	RCA	2
17	12	BIG SIX	Judge Dread	Big Shot	6
8	13	AIN'T NO SUNSHINE	Michael Jackson	Tamla Motown	7
16	14	SUZANNE BEWARE OF THE DEVIL	Dandy Livingstone	Horse	5
10	15	VIRGINIA PLAIN	Roxy Music	Island	7
12	16	LIVING IN HARMONY	Cliff Richard	Columbia	6
25	17	DONNA	10CC	UK	2
-	18	IN A BROKEN DREAM	Python Lee Jackson ●	Youngblood	1
20	19	WALK IN THE NIGHT	Jnr. Walker and The All Stars	Tamla Motown	7
23	20	JOHN I'M ONLY DANCING	David Bowie	RCA	3
15	21	SUGAR ME	Lynsey De Paul	MAM	7
30	22	BACK STABBERS	O'Jays	CBS	2
11	23	YOU WEAR IT WELL	Rod Stewart	Mercury	9
13	24	I GET THE SWEETEST FEELING	Jackie Wilson	MCA	10
19	25	STANDING IN THE ROAD	Blackfoot Sue	DJM	8
-	26	THERE ARE MORE QUESTIONS THAN ANSWERS	Johnny Nash	CBS	1
35	27	GOODBYE TO LOVE	Carpenters	A&M	2
40	28	GUITAR MAN	Bread	Elektra	2
24	29	WHO WAS IT	Hurricane Smith	Columbia	5
37	30	BURLESQUE	Family	Reprise	2
26	31	POPCORN	Hot Butter	Pye	11
36	32	YOU CAME, YOU SAW, YOU CONQUERED	Pearls	Bell	2
22	33	ALL THE YOUNG DUDES	Mott the Hoople	CBS	9
-	34	ELECTED	Alice Cooper	Warner Brothers	1
-	35	AMERICA	Simon & Garfunkel	CBS	1
32	36	HONKY CAT	Elton John	DJM	5
28	37	LEAN ON ME	Bill Withers	Sussex/A&M	8
33	38	PUPPY LOVE	Donny Osmond	MGM	17
-	39	LONG COOL WOMAN IN A BLACK DRESS	Hollies	Parlophone	4
39	40	ALL FALL DOWN	Lindisfarne	Charisma	2

WEEK ENDING 14 OCTOBER 1972

LW	TW	Title	Artist	Label	Wks
3	1	MOULDY OLD DOUGH	Lieutenant Pigeon	Decca	5
1	2	HOW CAN I BE SURE	David Cassidy	Bell	5
6	3	YOU'RE A LADY	Peter Skellern	Decca	3
8	4	I DIDN'T KNOW I LOVED YOU (TILL I SAW YOU ROCK 'N' ROLL)	Gary Glitter	Bell	4
2	5	CHILDREN OF THE REVOLUTION	T. Rex	EMI	5
4	6	WIG-WAM BAM	Sweet	RCA	5
5	7	TOO YOUNG	Donny Osmond	MGM	5
11	8	BURNING LOVE	Elvis Presley	RCA	3
18	9	IN A BROKEN DREAM	Python Lee Jackson	Youngblood	2
17	10	DONNA	10CC	UK	3
12	11	BIG SIX	Judge Dread	Big Shot	7
20	12	JOHN I'M ONLY DANCING	David Bowie	RCA	4
9	13	IT'S FOUR IN THE MORNING	Faron Young	Mercury	13
14	14	SUZANNE BEWARE OF THE DEVIL	Dandy Livingstone	Horse	6
10	15	COME ON OVER TO MY PLACE	The Drifters	Atlantic	7
7	16	MAMA WEER ALL CRAZEE NOW	Slade	Polydor	7
34	17	ELECTED	Alice Cooper	Warner Brothers	2
22	18	BACK STABBERS	O'Jays	CBS	3
26	19	THERE ARE MORE QUESTIONS THAN ANSWERS	Johnny Nash	CBS	2
19	20	WALK IN THE NIGHT	Jnr. Walker and The All Stars	Tamla Motown	8
28	21	GUITAR MAN	Bread	Elektra	3
27	22	GOODBYE TO LOVE	Carpenters	A&M	3
30	23	BURLESQUE	Family	Reprise	3
15	24	VIRGINIA PLAIN	Roxy Music	Island	8
13	25	AIN'T NO SUNSHINE	Michael Jackson	Tamla Motown	8
-	26	ELMO JAMES	Chairmen Of The Board	Invictus	1
16	27	LIVING IN HARMONY	Cliff Richard	Columbia	7
23	28	YOU WEAR IT WELL	Rod Stewart	Mercury	10
35	29	AMERICA	Simon & Garfunkel	CBS	2
-	30	HOUSE OF THE RISING SUN	Animals	RAK	1
21	31	SUGAR ME	Lynsey De Paul	MAM	8
24	32	I GET THE SWEETEST FEELING	Jackie Wilson	MCA	11
32	33	YOU CAME, YOU SAW, YOU CONQUERED	Pearls	Bell	3
40	34	ALL FALL DOWN	Lindisfarne	Charisma	3
25	35	STANDING IN THE ROAD	Blackfoot Sue	DJM	9
31	36	POPCORN	Hot Butter	Pye	12
-	37	LEADER OF THE PACK	Shangri-Las	Kama Sutra	1
-	38	OH CAROL/BREAKING UP IS HARD TO DO/LITTLE DEVIL	Neil Sedaka	RCA	1
-	39	HALLELUJAH FREEDOM	Junior Campbell ●	Deram	1
-	40	NEW ORLEANS	Harley Quinne ●	Bell	1

WEEK ENDING 21 OCTOBER 1972

LW	TW	Title	Artist	Label	Wks
1	1	MOULDY OLD DOUGH	Lieutenant Pigeon	Decca	6
10	2	DONNA	10CC	UK	4
3	3	YOU'RE A LADY	Peter Skellern	Decca	4
2	4	HOW CAN I BE SURE	David Cassidy	Bell	6
4	5	I DIDN'T KNOW I LOVED YOU (TILL I SAW YOU ROCK 'N' ROLL)	Gary Glitter	Bell	5
9	6	IN A BROKEN DREAM	Python Lee Jackson	Youngblood	3
8	7	BURNING LOVE	Elvis Presley	RCA	4
6	8	WIG-WAM BAM	Sweet	RCA	6
17	9	ELECTED	Alice Cooper	Warner Brothers	3
5	10	CHILDREN OF THE REVOLUTION	T. Rex	EMI	6
11	11	BIG SIX	Judge Dread	Big Shot	8
19	12	THERE ARE MORE QUESTIONS THAN ANSWERS	Johnny Nash	CBS	3
12	13	JOHN I'M ONLY DANCING	David Bowie	RCA	5
7	14	TOO YOUNG	Donny Osmond	MGM	6
-	15	CLAIR	Gilbert O'Sullivan	MAM	1
14	16	SUZANNE BEWARE OF THE DEVIL	Dandy Livingstone	Horse	7
15	17	COME ON OVER TO MY PLACE	The Drifters	Atlantic	8
22	18	GOODBYE TO LOVE	Carpenters	A&M	4
23	19	BURLESQUE	Family	Reprise	4
18	20	BACK STABBERS	O'Jays	CBS	4
26	21	ELMO JAMES	Chairmen Of The Board	Invictus	2
21	22	GUITAR MAN	Bread	Elektra	4
13	23	IT'S FOUR IN THE MORNING	Faron Young	Mercury	14
39	24	HALLELUJAH FREEDOM	Junior Campbell	Deram	2
30	25	HOUSE OF THE RISING SUN	Animals	RAK	2
-	26	LOOP DI LOVE	Shag ●	UK	1
16	27	MAMA WEER ALL CRAZEE NOW	Slade	Polydor	8
24	28	VIRGINIA PLAIN	Roxy Music	Island	9
29	29	AMERICA	Simon & Garfunkel	CBS	3
37	30	LEADER OF THE PACK	Shangri-Las	Kama Sutra	2
20	31	WALK IN THE NIGHT	Jnr. Walker and The All Stars	Tamla Motown	9

■Lieutenant Pigeon's *Mouldy Old Dough* is the only chart-topping single to feature a mother and son combination - Hilda and Rob Woodward (14.10.72) ■ Five old hits return in one week: *House Of The Rising Sun* by the Animals from 1964, *Leader Of The Pack* by the Shangri-Las from 1965 and *Oh Carol/Breaking Up Is Hard To Do/Little Devil* by Neil Sedaka from 1959, 1962 and 1961 respectively (14.10.72)■

October 1972

□ Highest position disc reached ● Act's first ever week on chart

LW	TW	Title	Artist	Label	Wks
40	32	NEW ORLEANS	Harley Quinne	Bell	2
38	33	OH CAROL/BREAKING UP IS HARD TO DO/LITTLE DEVIL	Neil Sedaka	RCA	2
25	34	AIN'T NO SUNSHINE	Michael Jackson	Tamla Motown	9
27	35	LIVING IN HARMONY	Cliff Richard	Columbia	8
-	36	HERE I GO AGAIN	Archie Bell & The Drells ●	Atlantic	1
34	37	ALL FALL DOWN	Lindisfarne	Charisma	4
28	38	YOU WEAR IT WELL	Rod Stewart	Mercury	11
36	39	POPCORN	Hot Butter	Pye	13
-	40	LET'S DANCE	Chris Montez	London	1

WEEK ENDING 28 OCTOBER 1972

LW	TW	Title	Artist	Label	Wks
1	[1]	MOULDY OLD DOUGH	Lieutenant Pigeon	Decca	7
2	[2]	DONNA	10CC	UK	5
6	[3]	IN A BROKEN DREAM	Python Lee Jackson	Youngblood	4
9	[4]	ELECTED	Alice Cooper	Warner Brothers	4
15	5	CLAIR	Gilbert O'Sullivan	MAM	2
5	6	I DIDN'T KNOW I LOVED YOU (TILL I SAW YOU ROCK 'N' ROLL)	Gary Glitter	Bell	6
3	7	YOU'RE A LADY	Peter Skellern	Decca	5
7	8	BURNING LOVE	Elvis Presley	RCA	5
12	[9]	THERE ARE MORE QUESTIONS THAN ANSWERS	Johnny Nash	CBS	4
8	10	WIG-WAM BAM	Sweet	RCA	7
18	11	GOODBYE TO LOVE	Carpenters	A&M	5
4	12	HOW CAN I BE SURE	David Cassidy	Bell	7
13	13	JOHN I'M ONLY DANCING	David Bowie	RCA	6
20	[14]	BACK STABBERS	O'Jays	CBS	5
11	15	BIG SIX	Judge Dread	Big Shot	9
22	[16]	GUITAR MAN	Bread	Elektra	5
10	17	CHILDREN OF THE REVOLUTION	T. Rex	EMI	7
24	18	HALLELUJAH FREEDOM	Junior Campbell	Deram	3
19	19	BURLESQUE	Family	Reprise	5
26	20	LOOP DI LOVE	Shag	UK	2
30	21	LEADER OF THE PACK	Shangri-Las	Kama Sutra	3
14	22	TOO YOUNG	Donny Osmond	MGM	7
21	23	ELMO JAMES	Chairmen Of The Board	Invictus	3
23	24	IT'S FOUR IN THE MORNING	Faron Young	Mercury	15
29	[25]	AMERICA	Simon & Garfunkel	CBS	4
32	26	NEW ORLEANS	Harley Quinne	Bell	3
36	27	HERE I GO AGAIN	Archie Bell & The Drells	Atlantic	2
40	28	LET'S DANCE	Chris Montez	London	2
17	29	COME ON OVER TO MY PLACE	The Drifters	Atlantic	9
25	30	HOUSE OF THE RISING SUN	Animals	RAK	3
33	31	OH CAROL/BREAKING UP IS HARD TO DO/LITTLE DEVIL	Neil Sedaka	RCA	3
16	32	SUZANNE BEWARE OF THE DEVIL	Dandy Livingstone	Horse	8
27	33	MAMA WEER ALL CRAZEE NOW	Slade	Polydor	9
31	34	WALK IN THE NIGHT	Jnr. Walker and The All Stars	Tamla Motown	10
-	35	YOU'LL ALWAYS BE A FRIEND	Hot Chocolate	RAK	1
28	36	VIRGINIA PLAIN	Roxy Music	Island	10
-	37	LAY DOWN	Strawbs ●	A&M	1
-	38	MY DING-A-LING	Chuck Berry	Chess	1
-	39	WHY CAN'T WE BE LOVERS	Holland-Dozier	Invictus	1
34	40	AIN'T NO SUNSHINE	Michael Jackson	Tamla Motown	10

WEEK ENDING 4 NOVEMBER 1972

LW	TW	Title	Artist	Label	Wks
1	[1]	MOULDY OLD DOUGH	Lieutenant Pigeon	Decca	8
5	2	CLAIR	Gilbert O'Sullivan	MAM	3
2	3	DONNA	10CC	UK	6
3	4	IN A BROKEN DREAM	Python Lee Jackson	Youngblood	5
4	5	ELECTED	Alice Cooper	Warner Brothers	5
21	6	LEADER OF THE PACK	Shangri-Las	Kama Sutra	4
20	7	LOOP DI LOVE	Shag	UK	3
7	8	YOU'RE A LADY	Peter Skellern	Decca	6
8	9	BURNING LOVE	Elvis Presley	RCA	6
9	10	THERE ARE MORE QUESTIONS THAN ANSWERS	Johnny Nash	CBS	5
11	11	GOODBYE TO LOVE	Carpenters	A&M	6
6	12	I DIDN'T KNOW I LOVED YOU (TILL I SAW YOU ROCK 'N' ROLL)	Gary Glitter	Bell	7
18	13	HALLELUJAH FREEDOM	Junior Campbell	Deram	4
19	14	BURLESQUE	Family	Reprise	6
15	15	BIG SIX	Judge Dread	Big Shot	10
13	16	JOHN I'M ONLY DANCING	David Bowie	RCA	7
10	17	WIG-WAM BAM	Sweet	RCA	8
12	18	HOW CAN I BE SURE	David Cassidy	Bell	8
28	19	LET'S DANCE	Chris Montez	London	3
16	20	GUITAR MAN	Bread	Elektra	6
26	21	NEW ORLEANS	Harley Quinne	Bell	4
23	22	ELMO JAMES	Chairmen Of The Board	Invictus	4
38	23	MY DING-A-LING	Chuck Berry	Chess	2
27	24	HERE I GO AGAIN	Archie Bell & The Drells	Atlantic	3
22	25	TOO YOUNG	Donny Osmond	MGM	8
31	26	OH CAROL/BREAKING UP IS HARD TO DO/LITTLE DEVIL	Neil Sedaka	RCA	4
25	27	AMERICA	Simon & Garfunkel	CBS	5
24	28	IT'S FOUR IN THE MORNING	Faron Young	Mercury	16
17	29	CHILDREN OF THE REVOLUTION	T. Rex	EMI	8
14	30	BACK STABBERS	O'Jays	CBS	6
-	31	I'M STONE IN LOVE WITH YOU	Stylistics	Avco	1
-	32	HI HO SILVER LINING	Jeff Beck	RAK	1
30	33	HOUSE OF THE RISING SUN	Animals	RAK	4
37	34	LAY DOWN	Strawbs	A&M	2
35	35	YOU'LL ALWAYS BE A FRIEND	Hot Chocolate	RAK	2
29	36	COME ON OVER TO MY PLACE	The Drifters	Atlantic	10
-	[37]	BORSALINO	Bobby Crush ●	Philips	1
39	38	WHY CAN'T WE BE LOVERS	Holland-Dozier	Invictus	2
33	39	MAMA WEER ALL CRAZEE NOW	Slade	Polydor	10
32	40	SUZANNE BEWARE OF THE DEVIL	Dandy Livingstone	Horse	9

WEEK ENDING 11 NOVEMBER 1972

LW	TW	Title	Artist	Label	Wks
2	[1]	CLAIR	Gilbert O'Sullivan	MAM	4
1	2	MOULDY OLD DOUGH	Lieutenant Pigeon	Decca	9
3	3	DONNA	10CC	UK	7
5	[4]	ELECTED	Alice Cooper	Warner Brothers	6
7	5	LOOP DI LOVE	Shag	UK	4
23	6	MY DING-A-LING	Chuck Berry	Chess	3
4	7	IN A BROKEN DREAM	Python Lee Jackson	Youngblood	6
6	8	LEADER OF THE PACK	Shangri-Las	Kama Sutra	5
11	[9]	GOODBYE TO LOVE	Carpenters	A&M	7
13	[10]	HALLELUJAH FREEDOM	Junior Campbell	Deram	5
24	[11]	HERE I GO AGAIN	Archie Bell & The Drells	Atlantic	4
10	12	THERE ARE MORE QUESTIONS THAN ANSWERS	Johnny Nash	CBS	6
14	[13]	BURLESQUE	Family	Reprise	7
9	14	BURNING LOVE	Elvis Presley	RCA	7
19	15	LET'S DANCE	Chris Montez	London	4
8	16	YOU'RE A LADY	Peter Skellern	Decca	7
12	17	I DIDN'T KNOW I LOVED YOU (TILL I SAW YOU ROCK 'N' ROLL)	Gary Glitter	Bell	8
15	18	BIG SIX	Judge Dread	Big Shot	11
31	19	I'M STONE IN LOVE WITH YOU	Stylistics	Avco	2
-	20	CROCODILE ROCK	Elton John	DJM	1
-	21	WHY	Donny Osmond	MGM	1
32	22	HI HO SILVER LINING	Jeff Beck	RAK	2
21	23	NEW ORLEANS	Harley Quinne	Bell	5
20	24	GUITAR MAN	Bread	Elektra	7
17	25	WIG-WAM BAM	Sweet	RCA	9
26	26	OH CAROL/BREAKING UP IS HARD TO DO/LITTLE DEVIL	Neil Sedaka	RCA	5
-	27	CRAZY HORSES	Osmonds	MGM	1
16	28	JOHN I'M ONLY DANCING	David Bowie	RCA	8
38	[29]	WHY CAN'T WE BE LOVERS	Holland-Dozier	Invictus	3
25	30	TOO YOUNG	Donny Osmond	MGM	9
34	31	LAY DOWN	Strawbs	A&M	3
22	32	ELMO JAMES	Chairmen Of The Board	Invictus	5
35	33	YOU'LL ALWAYS BE A FRIEND	Hot Chocolate	RAK	3
27	34	AMERICA	Simon & Garfunkel	CBS	6

In these weeks ■ The charts are full of oldies. The hits by the Shangri-Las, Chris Montez, Neil Sedaka, Jeff Beck, the Animals and the Drifters are all enjoying their second spells of chart success (04.11.72) ■ Holland-Dozier are the first record company executives to have hits on their own label since Herb Alpert on A&M and Frank Sinatra on Reprise (11.11.72)■

LW	TW	Title / Artist	Label	Wks
18	35	HOW CAN I BE SURE David Cassidy	*Bell*	9
30	36	BACK STABBERS O'Jays	*CBS*	7
28	37	IT'S FOUR IN THE MORNING Faron Young	*Mercury*	17
-	38	BABY DON'T GET HOOKED ON ME Mac Davis ●	*CBS*	1
29	39	CHILDREN OF THE REVOLUTION T. Rex	*EMI*	9
-	40	LOOKIN' THROUGH THE WINDOWS Jackson Five	*Tamla Motown*	1

LW	TW	*WEEK ENDING* **18 NOVEMBER 1972**		Wks
1	1	CLAIR Gilbert O'Sullivan	*MAM*	5
6	2	MY DING-A-LING Chuck Berry	*Chess*	4
8	3	LEADER OF THE PACK Shangri-Las	*Kama Sutra*	6
5	4	LOOP DI LOVE Shag	*UK*	5
2	5	MOULDY OLD DOUGH Lieutenant Pigeon	*Decca*	10
21	6	WHY Donny Osmond	*MGM*	2
27	7	CRAZY HORSES Osmonds	*MGM*	2
20	8	CROCODILE ROCK Elton John	*DJM*	2
15	9	LET'S DANCE Chris Montez	*London*	5
19	10	I'M STONE IN LOVE WITH YOU Stylistics	*Avco*	3
4	11	ELECTED Alice Cooper	*Warner Brothers*	7
7	12	IN A BROKEN DREAM Python Lee Jackson	*Youngblood*	7
3	13	DONNA 10CC	*UK*	8
11	14	HERE I GO AGAIN Archie Bell & The Drells	*Atlantic*	5
9	15	GOODBYE TO LOVE Carpenters	*A&M*	8
13	16	BURLESQUE Family	*Reprise*	8
10	17	HALLELUJAH FREEDOM Junior Campbell	*Deram*	6
12	18	THERE ARE MORE QUESTIONS THAN ANSWERS Johnny Nash	*CBS*	7
23	19	NEW ORLEANS Harley Quinne	*Bell*	6
22	20	HI HO SILVER LINING Jeff Beck	*RAK*	3
40	21	LOOKIN' THROUGH THE WINDOWS Jackson Five	*Tamla Motown*	2
18	22	BIG SIX Judge Dread	*Big Shot*	12
-	23	ANGEL/WHAT MADE MILWAUKEE FAMOUS Rod Stewart	*Mercury*	1
26	24	OH CAROL/BREAKING UP IS HARD TO DO/LITTLE DEVIL Neil Sedaka	*RCA*	6
14	25	BURNING LOVE Elvis Presley	*RCA*	8
31	26	LAY DOWN Strawbs	*A&M*	4
-	27	STAY WITH ME Blue Mink	*Regal Zonophone*	1
30	28	TOO YOUNG Donny Osmond	*MGM*	10
33	29	YOU'LL ALWAYS BE A FRIEND Hot Chocolate	*RAK*	4
38	30	BABY DON'T GET HOOKED ON ME Mac Davis	*CBS*	2
24	31	GUITAR MAN Bread	*Elektra*	8
17	32	I DIDN'T KNOW I LOVED YOU (TILL I SAW YOU ROCK 'N' ROLL) Gary Glitter	*Bell*	9
29	33	WHY CAN'T WE BE LOVERS Holland-Dozier	*Invictus*	4
37	34	IT'S FOUR IN THE MORNING Faron Young	*Mercury*	18
16	35	YOU'RE A LADY Peter Skellern	*Decca*	8
25	36	WIG-WAM BAM Sweet	*RCA*	10
-	37	I DON'T BELIEVE IN MIRACLES Colin Blunstone	*Epic*	1
32	38	ELMO JAMES Chairmen Of The Board	*Invictus*	6
28	39	JOHN I'M ONLY DANCING David Bowie	*RCA*	9
-	40	BORSALINO Bobby Crush	*Philips*	2

LW	TW	*WEEK ENDING* **25 NOVEMBER 1972**		Wks
2	1	MY DING-A-LING Chuck Berry	*Chess*	5
7	2	CRAZY HORSES Osmonds	*MGM*	3
1	3	CLAIR Gilbert O'Sullivan	*MAM*	6
6	4	WHY Donny Osmond	*MGM*	3
8	5	CROCODILE ROCK Elton John	*DJM*	3
3	6	LEADER OF THE PACK Shangri-Las	*Kama Sutra*	7
4	7	LOOP DI LOVE Shag	*UK*	6
-	8	GUDBUY T'JANE Slade	*Polydor*	1
10	9	I'M STONE IN LOVE WITH YOU Stylistics	*Avco*	4
23	10	ANGEL/WHAT MADE MILWAUKEE FAMOUS Rod Stewart	*Mercury*	2
9	11	LET'S DANCE Chris Montez	*London*	6
5	12	MOULDY OLD DOUGH Lieutenant Pigeon	*Decca*	11
21	13	LOOKIN' THROUGH THE WINDOWS Jackson Five	*Tamla Motown*	3

December 1972

□ Highest position disc reached ● Act's first ever week on chart

LW	TW	Title / Artist	Label	Wks
14	14	HERE I GO AGAIN Archie Bell & The Drells	*Atlantic*	6
15	15	GOODBYE TO LOVE Carpenters	*A&M*	9
13	16	DONNA 10CC	*UK*	9
11	17	ELECTED Alice Cooper	*Warner Brothers*	8
17	18	HALLELUJAH FREEDOM Junior Campbell	*Deram*	7
20	19	HI HO SILVER LINING Jeff Beck	*RAK*	4
26	20	LAY DOWN Strawbs	*A&M*	5
22	21	BIG SIX Judge Dread	*Big Shot*	13
24	22	OH CAROL/BREAKING UP IS HARD TO DO/LITTLE DEVIL Neil Sedaka	*RCA*	7
29	23	YOU'LL ALWAYS BE A FRIEND Hot Chocolate	*RAK*	5
12	24	IN A BROKEN DREAM Python Lee Jackson	*Youngblood*	8
-	25	BEN Michael Jackson	*Tamla Motown*	1
16	26	BURLESQUE Family	*Reprise*	9
18	27	THERE ARE MORE QUESTIONS THAN ANSWERS Johnny Nash	*CBS*	8
-	28	ROCK ME BABY David Cassidy	*Bell*	1
30	29	BABY DON'T GET HOOKED ON ME Mac Davis	*CBS*	3
-	30	KEEPER OF THE CASTLE Four Tops	*Probe*	1
27	31	STAY WITH ME Blue Mink	*Regal Zonophone*	2
19	32	NEW ORLEANS Harley Quinne	*Bell*	7
37	33	I DON'T BELIEVE IN MIRACLES Colin Blunstone	*Epic*	2
32	34	I DIDN'T KNOW I LOVED YOU (TILL I SAW YOU ROCK 'N' ROLL) Gary Glitter	*Bell*	10
25	35	BURNING LOVE Elvis Presley	*RCA*	9
33	36	WHY CAN'T WE BE LOVERS Holland-Dozier	*Invictus*	5
28	37	TOO YOUNG Donny Osmond	*MGM*	11
36	38	WIG-WAM BAM Sweet	*RCA*	11
-	39	HELP ME MAKE IT THROUGH THE NIGHT Gladys Knight & The Pips	*Tamla Motown*	1
34	40	IT'S FOUR IN THE MORNING Faron Young	*Mercury*	19

LW	TW	*WEEK ENDING* **2 DECEMBER 1972**		Wks
1	1	MY DING-A-LING Chuck Berry	*Chess*	6
2	2	CRAZY HORSES Osmonds	*MGM*	4
4	3	WHY Donny Osmond	*MGM*	4
8	4	GUDBUY T'JANE Slade	*Polydor*	2
5	5	CROCODILE ROCK Elton John	*DJM*	4
10	6	ANGEL/WHAT MADE MILWAUKEE FAMOUS Rod Stewart	*Mercury*	3
3	7	CLAIR Gilbert O'Sullivan	*MAM*	7
6	8	LEADER OF THE PACK Shangri-Las	*Kama Sutra*	8
13	9	LOOKIN' THROUGH THE WINDOWS Jackson Five	*Tamla Motown*	4
9	10	I'M STONE IN LOVE WITH YOU Stylistics	*Avco*	5
11	11	LET'S DANCE Chris Montez	*London*	7
31	12	STAY WITH ME Blue Mink	*Regal Zonophone*	3
20	13	LAY DOWN Strawbs	*A&M*	6
12	14	MOULDY OLD DOUGH Lieutenant Pigeon	*Decca*	12
7	15	LOOP DI LOVE Shag	*UK*	7
25	16	BEN Michael Jackson	*Tamla Motown*	2
19	17	HI HO SILVER LINING Jeff Beck	*RAK*	5
28	18	ROCK ME BABY David Cassidy	*Bell*	2
22	19	OH CAROL/BREAKING UP IS HARD TO DO/LITTLE DEVIL Neil Sedaka	*RCA*	8
16	20	DONNA 10CC	*UK*	10
-	21	SHOTGUN WEDDING Roy C.	*UK*	1
15	22	GOODBYE TO LOVE Carpenters	*A&M*	10
30	23	KEEPER OF THE CASTLE Four Tops	*Probe*	2
23	24	YOU'LL ALWAYS BE A FRIEND Hot Chocolate	*RAK*	6
17	25	ELECTED Alice Cooper	*Warner Brothers*	9
14	26	HERE I GO AGAIN Archie Bell & The Drells	*Atlantic*	7
-	27	LONG HAIRED LOVER FROM LIVERPOOL Little Jimmy Osmond ●	*MGM*	1
39	28	HELP ME MAKE IT THROUGH THE NIGHT Gladys Knight & The Pips	*Tamla Motown*	2
24	29	IN A BROKEN DREAM Python Lee Jackson	*Youngblood*	9
21	30	BIG SIX Judge Dread	*Big Shot*	14

■The top five records are all at their chart peak - for the only time in 1972 (02.12.72) ■ As Python Lee Jackson (guest vocals: Rod Stewart) drop out of the Top 20, Rod Stewart climbs back in (25.11.72) ■ Shag is, needless to say, Jonathan King yet again (18.11.72) ■ Donny Osmond is at no. 3 on his own and at number two with his brothers (02.12.72)■

December 1972

□ Highest position disc reached ● Act's first ever week on chart

LW	TW	Title	Artist	Label	Wks
33	[31]	I DON'T BELIEVE IN MIRACLES	Colin Blunstone	*Epic*	3
29	32	BABY DON'T GET HOOKED ON ME	Mac Davis	*CBS*	4
-	33	NIGHTS IN WHITE SATIN	Moody Blues	*Deram*	1
18	34	HALLELUJAH FREEDOM	Junior Campbell	*Deram*	8
32	35	NEW ORLEANS	Harley Quinne	*Bell*	8
-	36	LITTLE DRUMMER BOY	Royal Scots Dragoon Guards Band	*RCA*	1
26	37	BURLESQUE	Family	*Reprise*	10
27	38	THERE ARE MORE QUESTIONS THAN ANSWERS	Johnny Nash	*CBS*	9
-	39	JUST OUT OF REACH (OF MY TWO EMPTY ARMS)	Ken Dodd	*Columbia*	1
-	[40]	ONLY YOU	Jeff Collins ●	*Polydor*	1

WEEK ENDING 9 DECEMBER 1972

LW	TW	Title	Artist	Label	Wks
1	[1]	MY DING-A-LING	Chuck Berry	*Chess*	7
2	[2]	CRAZY HORSES	Osmonds	*MGM*	5
4	3	GUDBUY T'JANE	Slade	*Polydor*	3
6	[4]	ANGEL/WHAT MADE MILWAUKEE FAMOUS	Rod Stewart	*Mercury*	4
5	[5]	CROCODILE ROCK	Elton John	*DJM*	5
3	6	WHY	Donny Osmond	*MGM*	5
16	[7]	BEN	Michael Jackson	*Tamla Motown*	3
-	8	SOLID GOLD EASY ACTION	T. Rex	*EMI*	1
27	9	LONG HAIRED LOVER FROM LIVERPOOL	Little Jimmy Osmond	*MGM*	2
9	10	LOOKIN' THROUGH THE WINDOWS	Jackson Five	*Tamla Motown*	5
18	[11]	ROCK ME BABY	David Cassidy	*Bell*	3
13	[12]	LAY DOWN	Strawbs	*A&M*	7
12	13	STAY WITH ME	Blue Mink	*Regal Zonophone*	4
7	14	CLAIR	Gilbert O'Sullivan	*MAM*	8
10	15	I'M STONE IN LOVE WITH YOU	Stylistics	*Avco*	6
21	16	SHOTGUN WEDDING	Roy C.	*UK*	2
17	[17]	HI HO SILVER LINING	Jeff Beck	*RAK*	6
28	18	HELP ME MAKE IT THROUGH THE NIGHT	Gladys Knight & The Pips	*Tamla Motown*	3
15	19	LOOP DI LOVE	Shag	*UK*	8
8	20	LEADER OF THE PACK	Shangri-Las	*Kama Sutra*	9
33	21	NIGHTS IN WHITE SATIN	Moody Blues	*Deram*	2
11	22	LET'S DANCE	Chris Montez	*London*	8
-	23	HAPPY XMAS (WAR IS OVER)	John and Yoko/ Plastic Ono Band with The Harlem Community Choir ●	*Apple*	1
14	24	MOULDY OLD DOUGH	Lieutenant Pigeon	*Decca*	13
23	25	KEEPER OF THE CASTLE	Four Tops	*Probe*	3
19	26	OH CAROL/BREAKING UP IS HARD TO DO/LITTLE DEVIL	Neil Sedaka	*RCA*	9
22	27	GOODBYE TO LOVE	Carpenters	*A&M*	11
36	28	LITTLE DRUMMER BOY	Royal Scots Dragoon Guards Band	*RCA*	2
39	[29]	JUST OUT OF REACH (OF MY TWO EMPTY ARMS)	Ken Dodd	*Columbia*	2
-	30	GETTING A DRAG	Lynsey De Paul	*MAM*	1
30	31	BIG SIX	Judge Dread	*Big Shot*	15
-	[32]	DON'T DO THAT	Geordie ●	*Regal Zonophone*	1
-	33	THE JEAN GENIE	David Bowie	*RCA*	1
24	34	YOU'LL ALWAYS BE A FRIEND	Hot Chocolate	*RAK*	7
26	35	HERE I GO AGAIN	Archie Bell & The Drells	*Atlantic*	8
29	36	IN A BROKEN DREAM	Python Lee Jackson	*Youngblood*	10
32	37	BABY DON'T GET HOOKED ON ME	Mac Davis	*CBS*	5
25	38	ELECTED	Alice Cooper	*Warner Brothers*	10
20	39	DONNA	10CC	*UK*	11
-	40	HI HI HI/C.MOON	Wings	*Apple*	1

WEEK ENDING 16 DECEMBER 1972

LW	TW	Title	Artist	Label	Wks
1	[1]	MY DING-A-LING	Chuck Berry	*Chess*	8
3	[2]	GUDBUY T'JANE	Slade	*Polydor*	4
2	3	CRAZY HORSES	Osmonds	*MGM*	6
8	4	SOLID GOLD EASY ACTION	T. Rex	*EMI*	2
9	5	LONG HAIRED LOVER FROM LIVERPOOL	Little Jimmy Osmond	*MGM*	3
6	6	WHY	Donny Osmond	*MGM*	6
5	7	CROCODILE ROCK	Elton John	*DJM*	6
7	8	BEN	Michael Jackson	*Tamla Motown*	4
4	9	ANGEL/WHAT MADE MILWAUKEE FAMOUS	Rod Stewart	*Mercury*	5
16	10	SHOTGUN WEDDING	Roy C.	*UK*	3
13	[11]	STAY WITH ME	Blue Mink	*Regal Zonophone*	5
10	12	LOOKIN' THROUGH THE WINDOWS	Jackson Five	*Tamla Motown*	6
11	13	ROCK ME BABY	David Cassidy	*Bell*	4
12	14	LAY DOWN	Strawbs	*A&M*	8
21	15	NIGHTS IN WHITE SATIN	Moody Blues	*Deram*	3
23	16	HAPPY XMAS (WAR IS OVER)	John and Yoko/ Plastic Ono Band with The Harlem Community Choir	*Apple*	2
17	[17]	HI HO SILVER LINING	Jeff Beck	*RAK*	7
25	[18]	KEEPER OF THE CASTLE	Four Tops	*Probe*	4
18	19	HELP ME MAKE IT THROUGH THE NIGHT	Gladys Knight & The Pips	*Tamla Motown*	4
28	20	LITTLE DRUMMER BOY	Royal Scots Dragoon Guards Band	*RCA*	3
20	21	LEADER OF THE PACK	Shangri-Las	*Kama Sutra*	10
14	22	CLAIR	Gilbert O'Sullivan	*MAM*	9
24	23	MOULDY OLD DOUGH	Lieutenant Pigeon	*Decca*	14
22	24	LET'S DANCE	Chris Montez	*London*	9
26	25	OH CAROL/BREAKING UP IS HARD TO DO/LITTLE DEVIL	Neil Sedaka	*RCA*	10
15	26	I'M STONE IN LOVE WITH YOU	Stylistics	*Avco*	7
40	27	HI HI HI/C.MOON	Wings	*Apple*	2
30	28	GETTING A DRAG	Lynsey De Paul	*MAM*	2
19	29	LOOP DI LOVE	Shag	*UK*	9
29	30	JUST OUT OF REACH (OF MY TWO EMPTY ARMS)	Ken Dodd	*Columbia*	3
33	31	THE JEAN GENIE	David Bowie	*RCA*	2
-	32	BIG SEVEN	Judge Dread	*Big Shot*	1
-	33	ALWAYS ON MY MIND	Elvis Presley	*RCA*	1
-	34	BALL PARK INCIDENT	Wizzard ●	*Harvest*	1
32	35	DON'T DO THAT	Geordie	*Regal Zonophone*	2
-	36	CAN'T KEEP IT IN	Cat Stevens	*Island*	1
-	37	COME SOFTLY TO ME	New Seekers	*Polydor*	1
-	38	I'M ON MY WAY TO A BETTER PLACE	Chairmen Of The Board	*Invictus*	1
-	39	YOU'RE SO VAIN	Carly Simon ●	*Elektra*	1
-	40	DESPERATE DAN	Lieutenant Pigeon	*Decca*	1

WEEK ENDING 23 DECEMBER 1972

LW	TW	Title	Artist	Label	Wks
5	[1]	LONG HAIRED LOVER FROM LIVERPOOL	Little Jimmy Osmond	*MGM*	4
1	2	MY DING-A-LING	Chuck Berry	*Chess*	9
4	3	SOLID GOLD EASY ACTION	T. Rex	*EMI*	3
16	[4]	HAPPY XMAS (WAR IS OVER)	John and Yoko/ Plastic Ono Band with The Harlem Community Choir	*Apple*	3
3	5	CRAZY HORSES	Osmonds	*MGM*	7
2	6	GUDBUY T'JANE	Slade	*Polydor*	5
7	7	CROCODILE ROCK	Elton John	*DJM*	7
8	8	BEN	Michael Jackson	*Tamla Motown*	5
6	9	WHY	Donny Osmond	*MGM*	7
15	10	NIGHTS IN WHITE SATIN	Moody Blues	*Deram*	4
16	11	SHOTGUN WEDDING	Roy C.	*UK*	4
9	12	ANGEL/WHAT MADE MILWAUKEE FAMOUS	Rod Stewart	*Mercury*	6
20	[13]	LITTLE DRUMMER BOY	Royal Scots Dragoon Guards Band	*RCA*	4
19	14	HELP ME MAKE IT THROUGH THE NIGHT	Gladys Knight & The Pips	*Tamla Motown*	5
11	15	STAY WITH ME	Blue Mink	*Regal Zonophone*	6
31	16	THE JEAN GENIE	David Bowie	*RCA*	3

In these weeks ■ Michael Jackson's ode to a rat, *Ben*, is his final solo hit single for almost seven years (09.12.72) ■ The top ten contains three Osmond hits, two featuring Donny on vocals, and two Jackson hits, both featuring Michael on vocals (09.12.72) ■ John Lennon enters the chart with his wife in the same week that Paul McCartney and his wife do, as two thirds of Wings (09.12.72)■

□ Highest position disc reached ● Act's first ever week on chart

LW	TW	Title / Artist	Label	Wks
13	**17**	ROCK ME BABY David Cassidy	*Bell*	5
32	**18**	BIG SEVEN Judge Dread	*Big Shot*	2
28	**19**	GETTING A DRAG Lynsey De Paul	*MAM*	3
12	**20**	LOOKIN' THROUGH THE WINDOWS Jackson Five	*Tamla Motown*	7
14	**21**	LAY DOWN Strawbs	*A&M*	9
27	**22**	HI HI HI/C.MOON Wings	*Apple*	3
18	**23**	KEEPER OF THE CASTLE Four Tops	*Probe*	5
33	**24**	ALWAYS ON MY MIND Elvis Presley	*RCA*	2
22	**25**	CLAIR Gilbert O'Sullivan	*MAM*	10
17	**26**	HI HO SILVER LINING Jeff Beck	*RAK*	8
39	**27**	YOU'RE SO VAIN Carly Simon	*Elektra*	2
21	**28**	LEADER OF THE PACK Shangri-Las	*Kama Sutra*	11
34	**29**	BALL PARK INCIDENT Wizzard	*Harvest*	2
24	**30**	LET'S DANCE Chris Montez	*London*	10
23	**31**	MOULDY OLD DOUGH Lieutenant Pigeon	*Decca*	15
25	**32**	OH CAROL/BREAKING UP IS HARD TO DO/LITTLE DEVIL Neil Sedaka	*RCA*	11
30	**33**	JUST OUT OF REACH (OF MY TWO EMPTY ARMS) Ken Dodd	*Columbia*	4
40	**34**	DESPERATE DAN Lieutenant Pigeon	*Decca*	2
29	**35**	LOOP DI LOVE Shag	*UK*	10
35	**36**	DON'T DO THAT Geordie	*Regal Zonophone*	3
36	**37**	CAN'T KEEP IT IN Cat Stevens	*Island*	2
26	**38**	I'M STONE IN LOVE WITH YOU Stylistics	*Avco*	8
37	**39**	COME SOFTLY TO ME New Seekers	*Polydor*	2
-	**40**	GOODBYE TO LOVE Carpenters	*A&M*	12

LW TW *WEEK ENDING* **30 DECEMBER 1972** Wks

(no chart published, chart for 23rd December repeated)

LW	TW	Title / Artist	Label	Wks
1	**[1]**	LONG HAIRED LOVER FROM LIVERPOOL Little Jimmy Osmond	*MGM*	5
2	**2**	MY DING-A-LING Chuck Berry	*Chess*	10
3	**3**	SOLID GOLD EASY ACTION T. Rex	*EMI*	4
4	**[4]**	HAPPY XMAS (WAR IS OVER) John and Yoko/ Plastic Ono Band with The Harlem Community Choir	*Apple*	4
5	**5**	CRAZY HORSES Osmonds	*MGM*	8
6	**6**	GUDBUY T'JANE Slade	*Polydor*	6
7	**7**	CROCODILE ROCK Elton John	*DJM*	8
8	**8**	BEN Michael Jackson	*Tamla Motown*	6
9	**9**	WHY Donny Osmond	*MGM*	8
10	**10**	NIGHTS IN WHITE SATIN Moody Blues	*Deram*	5
11	**11**	SHOTGUN WEDDING Roy C.	*UK*	5
12	**12**	ANGEL/WHAT MADE MILWAUKEE FAMOUS Rod Stewart	*Mercury*	7
13	**[13]**	LITTLE DRUMMER BOY Royal Scots Dragoon Guards Band	*RCA*	5
14	**14**	HELP ME MAKE IT THROUGH THE NIGHT Gladys Knight & The Pips	*Tamla Motown*	6
15	**15**	STAY WITH ME Blue Mink	*Regal Zonophone*	7
16	**16**	THE JEAN GENIE David Bowie	*RCA*	4
17	**17**	ROCK ME BABY David Cassidy	*Bell*	6
18	**18**	BIG SEVEN Judge Dread	*Big Shot*	3
19	**19**	GETTING A DRAG Lynsey De Paul	*MAM*	4
20	**20**	LOOKIN' THROUGH THE WINDOWS Jackson Five	*Tamla Motown*	8
21	**21**	LAY DOWN Strawbs	*A&M*	10
22	**22**	HI HI HI/C.MOON Wings	*Apple*	4
23	**23**	KEEPER OF THE CASTLE Four Tops	*Probe*	6
24	**24**	ALWAYS ON MY MIND Elvis Presley	*RCA*	3
25	**25**	CLAIR Gilbert O'Sullivan	*MAM*	11
26	**26**	HI HO SILVER LINING Jeff Beck	*RAK*	9
27	**27**	YOU'RE SO VAIN Carly Simon	*Elektra*	3
28	**28**	LEADER OF THE PACK Shangri-Las	*Kama Sutra*	12
29	**29**	BALL PARK INCIDENT Wizzard	*Harvest*	3
30	**30**	LET'S DANCE Chris Montez	*London*	11
31	**31**	MOULDY OLD DOUGH Lieutenant Pigeon	*Decca*	16
32	**32**	OH CAROL/BREAKING UP IS HARD TO DO/LITTLE DEVIL Neil Sedaka	*RCA*	12
33	**33**	JUST OUT OF REACH (OF MY TWO EMPTY ARMS) Ken Dodd	*Columbia*	5
34	**34**	DESPERATE DAN Lieutenant Pigeon	*Decca*	3
35	**35**	LOOP DI LOVE Shag	*UK*	11
36	**36**	DON'T DO THAT Geordie	*Regal Zonophone*	4
37	**37**	CAN'T KEEP IT IN Cat Stevens	*Island*	3
38	**38**	I'M STONE IN LOVE WITH YOU Stylistics	*Avco*	9
39	**39**	COME SOFTLY TO ME New Seekers	*Polydor*	3
40	**40**	GOODBYE TO LOVE Carpenters	*A&M*	13

■Little Jimmy Osmond is the youngest ever solo chart-topper, at 9 years and 245 days old (23.12.72)■

1973

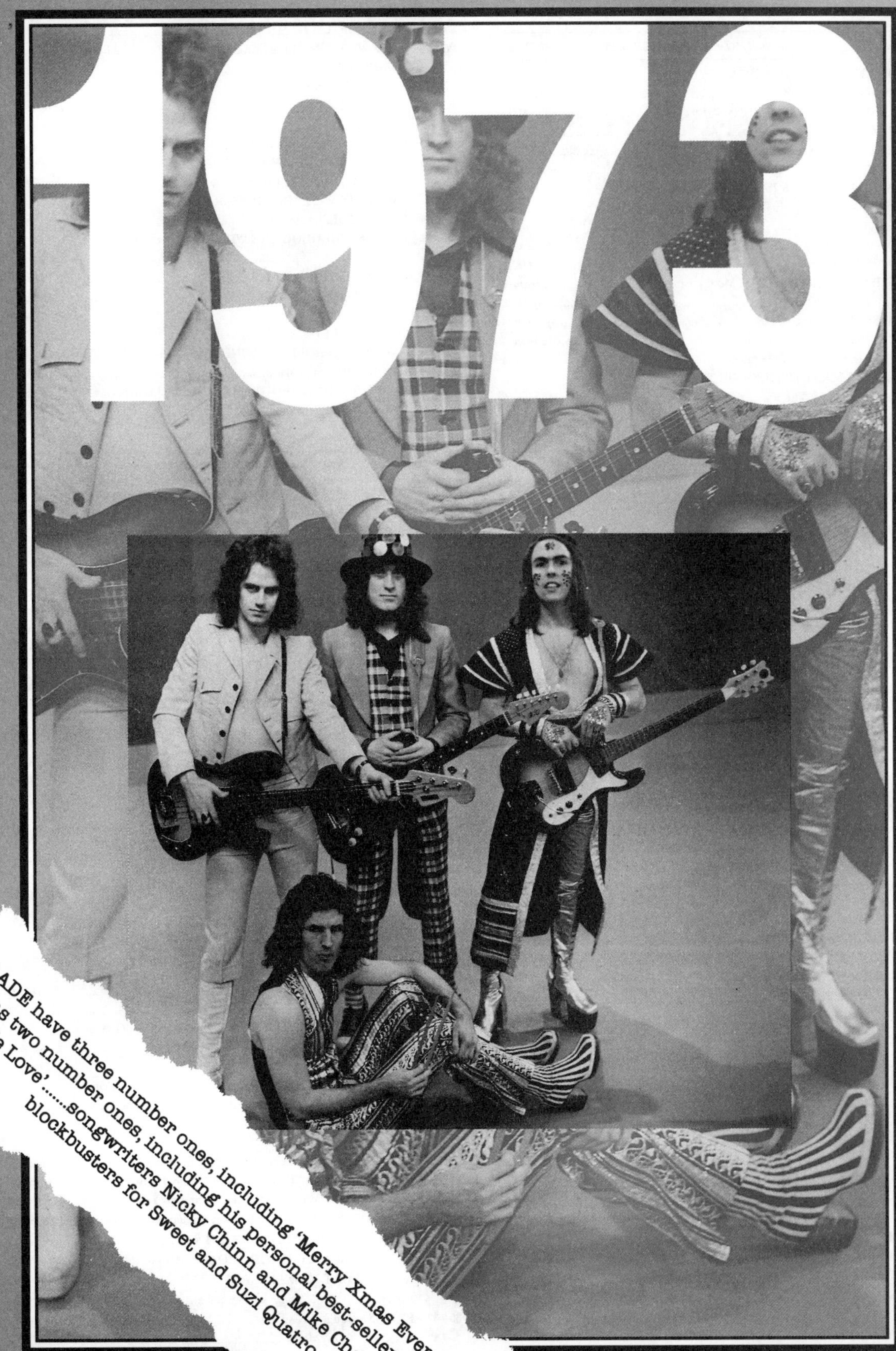

..........SLADE have three number ones, including 'Merry Xmas Everybody'......Gary Glitter has two number ones, including his personal best-seller 'I Love You Love Me Love'......songwriters Nicky Chinn and Mike Chapman pen blockbusters for Sweet and Suzi Quatro..........

January 1973

□ Highest position disc reached ● Act's first ever week on chart

WEEK ENDING 6 JANUARY 1973

LW	TW	Title / Artist	Label	Wks
1	[1]	LONG HAIRED LOVER FROM LIVERPOOL Little Jimmy Osmond	MGM	6
3	[2]	SOLID GOLD EASY ACTION T. Rex	EMI	5
5	3	CRAZY HORSES Osmonds	MGM	9
16	4	THE JEAN GENIE David Bowie	RCA	5
6	5	GUDBUY T'JANE Slade	Polydor	7
4	6	HAPPY XMAS (WAR IS OVER) John and Yoko/ Plastic Ono Band with The Harlem Community Choir	Apple	5
2	7	MY DING-A-LING Chuck Berry	Chess	11
11	[8]	SHOTGUN WEDDING Roy C.	UK	6
10	[9]	NIGHTS IN WHITE SATIN Moody Blues	Deram	6
22	10	HI HI HI/C.MOON Wings	Apple	5
18	11	BIG SEVEN Judge Dread	Big Shot	4
8	12	BEN Michael Jackson	Tamla Motown	7
24	13	ALWAYS ON MY MIND Elvis Presley	RCA	4
14	14	HELP ME MAKE IT THROUGH THE NIGHT Gladys Knight & The Pips	Tamla Motown	7
29	15	BALL PARK INCIDENT Wizzard	Harvest	4
9	16	WHY Donny Osmond	MGM	9
7	17	CROCODILE ROCK Elton John	DJM	9
19	[18]	GETTING A DRAG Lynsey De Paul	MAM	5
13	19	LITTLE DRUMMER BOY Royal Scots Dragoon Guards Band	RCA	6
27	20	YOU'RE SO VAIN Carly Simon	Elektra	4
17	21	ROCK ME BABY David Cassidy	Bell	7
34	22	DESPERATE DAN Lieutenant Pigeon	Decca	4
12	23	ANGEL/WHAT MADE MILWAUKEE FAMOUS Rod Stewart	Mercury	8
20	24	LOOKIN' THROUGH THE WINDOWS Jackson Five	Tamla Motown	9
25	25	CLAIR Gilbert O'Sullivan	MAM	12
15	26	STAY WITH ME Blue Mink	Regal Zonophone	7
39	27	COME SOFTLY TO ME New Seekers	Polydor	4
37	28	CAN'T KEEP IT IN Cat Stevens	Island	4
23	29	KEEPER OF THE CASTLE Four Tops	Probe	7
-	[30]	I'M ON MY WAY TO A BETTER PLACE Chairmen Of The Board	Invictus	2

(Top 30 only this week due to reduced sales information and Christmas postal delays)

WEEK ENDING 13 JANUARY 1973

LW	TW	Title / Artist	Label	Wks
1	[1]	LONG HAIRED LOVER FROM LIVERPOOL Little Jimmy Osmond	MGM	7
4	[2]	THE JEAN GENIE David Bowie	RCA	6
2	3	SOLID GOLD EASY ACTION T. Rex	EMI	6
3	4	CRAZY HORSES Osmonds	MGM	10
10	[5]	HI HI HI/C.MOON Wings	Apple	6
15	[6]	BALL PARK INCIDENT Wizzard	Harvest	5
20	7	YOU'RE SO VAIN Carly Simon	Elektra	5
11	[8]	BIG SEVEN Judge Dread	Big Shot	5
5	9	GUDBUY T'JANE Slade	Polydor	8
13	10	ALWAYS ON MY MIND Elvis Presley	RCA	5
8	11	SHOTGUN WEDDING Roy C.	UK	7
12	12	BEN Michael Jackson	Tamla Motown	8
9	13	NIGHTS IN WHITE SATIN Moody Blues	Deram	7
7	14	MY DING-A-LING Chuck Berry	Chess	12
6	15	HAPPY XMAS (WAR IS OVER) John and Yoko/ Plastic Ono Band with The Harlem Community Choir	Apple	6
-	16	BLOCKBUSTER Sweet	RCA	1
16	17	WHY Donny Osmond	MGM	10
14	18	HELP ME MAKE IT THROUGH THE NIGHT Gladys Knight & The Pips	Tamla Motown	8
22	19	DESPERATE DAN Lieutenant Pigeon	Decca	5
17	20	CROCODILE ROCK Elton John	DJM	10
28	21	CAN'T KEEP IT IN Cat Stevens	Island	5
19	22	LITTLE DRUMMER BOY Royal Scots Dragoon Guards Band	RCA	7
18	23	GETTING A DRAG Lynsey De Paul	MAM	6
27	24	COME SOFTLY TO ME New Seekers	Polydor	5
26	25	STAY WITH ME Blue Mink	Regal Zonophone	8
-	26	WISHING WELL Free	Island	1
25	27	CLAIR Gilbert O'Sullivan	MAM	13
23	28	ANGEL/WHAT MADE MILWAUKEE FAMOUS Rod Stewart	Mercury	9
21	29	ROCK ME BABY David Cassidy	Bell	8
-	30	IF YOU DON'T KNOW ME BY NOW Harold Melvin & The Bluenotes ●	CBS	1
30	31	I'M ON MY WAY TO A BETTER PLACE Chairmen Of The Board	Invictus	3
24	32	LOOKIN' THROUGH THE WINDOWS Jackson Five	Tamla Motown	10
-	33	RELAY The Who	Track	1
29	34	KEEPER OF THE CASTLE Four Tops	Probe	8
-	35	BIG SIX Judge Dread	Big Shot	16
-	[36]	SING DON'T SPEAK Blackfoot Sue	JASM	1
-	37	PAPA WAS A ROLLIN' STONE Temptations	Tamla Motown	1
-	38	LAY DOWN Strawbs	A&M	10
-	39	BIG CITY/THINK ABOUT THAT Dandy Livingstone	Horse	1
-	40	PAPER PLANE Status Quo	Vertigo	1

WEEK ENDING 20 JANUARY 1973

LW	TW	Title / Artist	Label	Wks
1	[1]	LONG HAIRED LOVER FROM LIVERPOOL Little Jimmy Osmond	MGM	8
16	2	BLOCKBUSTER Sweet	RCA	2
2	3	THE JEAN GENIE David Bowie	RCA	7
7	4	YOU'RE SO VAIN Carly Simon	Elektra	6
5	[5]	HI HI HI/C.MOON Wings	Apple	7
6	[6]	BALL PARK INCIDENT Wizzard	Harvest	6
3	7	SOLID GOLD EASY ACTION T. Rex	EMI	7
4	8	CRAZY HORSES Osmonds	MGM	11
10	[9]	ALWAYS ON MY MIND Elvis Presley	RCA	6
8	10	BIG SEVEN Judge Dread	Big Shot	6
18	[11]	HELP ME MAKE IT THROUGH THE NIGHT Gladys Knight & The Pips	Tamla Motown	9
11	12	SHOTGUN WEDDING Roy C.	UK	8
13	13	NIGHTS IN WHITE SATIN Moody Blues	Deram	8
9	14	GUDBUY T'JANE Slade	Polydor	9
26	15	WISHING WELL Free	Island	2
21	16	CAN'T KEEP IT IN Cat Stevens	Island	6
19	[17]	DESPERATE DAN Lieutenant Pigeon	Decca	6
37	18	PAPA WAS A ROLLIN' STONE Temptations	Tamla Motown	2
12	19	BEN Michael Jackson	Tamla Motown	9
24	[20]	COME SOFTLY TO ME New Seekers	Polydor	6
17	21	WHY Donny Osmond	MGM	11
14	22	MY DING-A-LING Chuck Berry	Chess	13
30	23	IF YOU DON'T KNOW ME BY NOW Harold Melvin & The Bluenotes	CBS	2
40	24	PAPER PLANE Status Quo	Vertigo	2
-	25	ME AND MRS JONES Billy Paul ●	Epic	1
22	26	LITTLE DRUMMER BOY Royal Scots Dragoon Guards Band	RCA	8
33	27	RELAY The Who	Track	2
25	28	STAY WITH ME Blue Mink	Regal Zonophone	9
20	29	CROCODILE ROCK Elton John	DJM	11
31	[30]	I'M ON MY WAY TO A BETTER PLACE Chairmen Of The Board	Invictus	4
23	31	GETTING A DRAG Lynsey De Paul	MAM	7
39	32	BIG CITY/THINK ABOUT THAT Dandy Livingstone	Horse	2
15	33	HAPPY XMAS (WAR IS OVER) John and Yoko/ Plastic Ono Band with The Harlem Community Choir	Apple	7
-	34	DO YOU WANNA TOUCH ME (OH YEAH) Gary Glitter	Bell	1
-	35	TAKE ME HOME COUNTRY ROADS Olivia Newton-John	Pye	1
28	36	ANGEL/WHAT MADE MILWAUKEE FAMOUS Rod Stewart	Mercury	10
35	37	BIG SIX Judge Dread	Big Shot	17
-	38	DANIEL Elton John	DJM	1

In these weeks ■ *Paper Plane* is Status Quo's first hit in over two years, and will become their first top ten hit in over four years. It also marks the beginning of a run of hits in every year for the next 20 years (13.01.73) ■ *Happy Xmas (War Is Over)* slips off the chart after a seven week run, but it will return many times to become the second most successful Christmas chart single of all (20.01.73) ■

LW	TW	Title / Artist	Label	Wks
27	39	CLAIR Gilbert O'Sullivan	MAM	14
-	40	HOCUS POCUS Focus ●	Polydor	1

LW	TW	*WEEK ENDING* **27 JANUARY 1973**		Wks
2	[1]	BLOCKBUSTER Sweet	RCA	3
1	2	LONG HAIRED LOVER FROM LIVERPOOL Little Jimmy Osmond	MGM	9
3	3	THE JEAN GENIE David Bowie	RCA	8
4	4	YOU'RE SO VAIN Carly Simon	Elektra	7
34	5	DO YOU WANNA TOUCH ME (OH YEAH) Gary Glitter	Bell	2
6	6	BALL PARK INCIDENT Wizzard	Harvest	7
5	7	HI HI HI/C.MOON Wings	Apple	8
15	8	WISHING WELL Free	Island	3
23	[9]	IF YOU DON'T KNOW ME BY NOW Harold Melvin & The Bluenotes	CBS	3
38	10	DANIEL Elton John	DJM	2
9	11	ALWAYS ON MY MIND Elvis Presley	RCA	7
10	12	BIG SEVEN Judge Dread	Big Shot	7
16	[13]	CAN'T KEEP IT IN Cat Stevens	Island	7
18	[14]	PAPA WAS A ROLLIN' STONE Temptations	Tamla Motown	3
24	15	PAPER PLANE Status Quo	Vertigo	3
25	16	ME AND MRS JONES Billy Paul	Epic	2
7	17	SOLID GOLD EASY ACTION T. Rex	EMI	8
8	18	CRAZY HORSES Osmonds	MGM	12
-	19	PART OF THE UNION Strawbs	A&M	1
17	20	DESPERATE DAN Lieutenant Pigeon	Decca	7
27	[21]	RELAY The Who	Track	3
19	22	BEN Michael Jackson	Tamla Motown	10
11	23	HELP ME MAKE IT THROUGH THE NIGHT Gladys Knight & The Pips	Tamla Motown	10
12	24	SHOTGUN WEDDING Roy C.	UK	9
13	25	NIGHTS IN WHITE SATIN Moody Blues	Deram	9
22	26	MY DING-A-LING Chuck Berry	Chess	14
21	27	WHY Donny Osmond	MGM	12
-	28	ROLL OVER BEETHOVEN Electric Light Orchestra	Harvest	1
32	29	BIG CITY/THINK ABOUT THAT Dandy Livingstone	Horse	3
20	30	COME SOFTLY TO ME New Seekers	Polydor	7
14	31	GUDBUY T'JANE Slade	Polydor	10
30	32	I'M ON MY WAY TO A BETTER PLACE Chairmen Of The Board	Invictus	5
35	33	TAKE ME HOME COUNTRY ROADS Olivia Newton-John	Pye	2
-	34	SYLVIA Focus	Polydor	1
-	35	WHISKY IN THE JAR Thin Lizzy ●	Decca	1
-	36	BABY I LOVE YOU Dave Edmunds	Rockfield	1
-	37	TAKE ME GIRL I'M READY Junior Walker & The Allstars	Tamla Motown	1
28	38	STAY WITH ME Blue Mink	Regal Zonophone	10
40	39	HOCUS POCUS Focus	Polydor	2
37	40	BIG SIX Judge Dread	Big Shot	18

LW	TW	*WEEK ENDING* **3 FEBRUARY 1973**		Wks
1	[1]	BLOCKBUSTER Sweet	RCA	4
5	[2]	DO YOU WANNA TOUCH ME (OH YEAH) Gary Glitter	Bell	3
4	[3]	YOU'RE SO VAIN Carly Simon	Elektra	8
2	4	LONG HAIRED LOVER FROM LIVERPOOL Little Jimmy Osmond	MGM	10
3	5	THE JEAN GENIE David Bowie	RCA	9
10	6	DANIEL Elton John	DJM	3
19	7	PART OF THE UNION Strawbs	A&M	2
8	8	WISHING WELL Free	Island	4
9	[9]	IF YOU DON'T KNOW ME BY NOW Harold Melvin & The Bluenotes	CBS	4
6	10	BALL PARK INCIDENT Wizzard	Harvest	8
15	11	PAPER PLANE Status Quo	Vertigo	4
16	[12]	ME AND MRS JONES Billy Paul	Epic	3
7	13	HI HI HI/C.MOON Wings	Apple	9
11	14	ALWAYS ON MY MIND Elvis Presley	RCA	8
13	15	CAN'T KEEP IT IN Cat Stevens	Island	8
12	16	BIG SEVEN Judge Dread	Big Shot	8
28	17	ROLL OVER BEETHOVEN Electric Light Orchestra	Harvest	2
14	18	PAPA WAS A ROLLIN' STONE Temptations	Tamla Motown	4
18	19	CRAZY HORSES Osmonds	MGM	13

February 1973

□ Highest position disc reached ● Act's first ever week on chart

LW	TW	Title / Artist	Label	Wks
23	20	HELP ME MAKE IT THROUGH THE NIGHT Gladys Knight & The Pips	Tamla Motown	11
34	21	SYLVIA Focus	Polydor	2
21	22	RELAY The Who	Track	4
35	23	WHISKY IN THE JAR Thin Lizzy	Decca	2
-	24	SUPERSTITION Stevie Wonder	Tamla Motown	1
22	25	BEN Michael Jackson	Tamla Motown	11
29	[26]	BIG CITY/THINK ABOUT THAT Dandy Livingstone	Horse	4
33	27	TAKE ME HOME COUNTRY ROADS Olivia Newton-John	Pye	3
17	28	SOLID GOLD EASY ACTION T. Rex	EMI	9
24	29	SHOTGUN WEDDING Roy C.	UK	10
25	30	NIGHTS IN WHITE SATIN Moody Blues	Deram	10
20	31	DESPERATE DAN Lieutenant Pigeon	Decca	8
36	32	BABY I LOVE YOU Dave Edmunds	Rockfield	2
39	33	HOCUS POCUS Focus	Polydor	3
37	34	TAKE ME GIRL I'M READY Junior Walker & The Allstars	Tamla Motown	2
31	35	GUDBUY T'JANE Slade	Polydor	11
27	36	WHY Donny Osmond	MGM	13
30	37	COME SOFTLY TO ME New Seekers	Polydor	8
26	38	MY DING-A-LING Chuck Berry	Chess	15
-	39	REELIN' AND ROCKIN' Chuck Berry	Chess	1
-	[40]	THE LOVE IN YOUR EYES Vicky Leandros	Philips	1

LW	TW	*WEEK ENDING* **10 FEBRUARY 1973**		Wks
1	[1]	BLOCKBUSTER Sweet	RCA	5
2	[2]	DO YOU WANNA TOUCH ME (OH YEAH) Gary Glitter	Bell	4
7	3	PART OF THE UNION Strawbs	A&M	3
3	4	YOU'RE SO VAIN Carly Simon	Elektra	9
6	5	DANIEL Elton John	DJM	4
4	6	LONG HAIRED LOVER FROM LIVERPOOL Little Jimmy Osmond	MGM	11
8	[7]	WISHING WELL Free	Island	5
11	[8]	PAPER PLANE Status Quo	Vertigo	5
21	9	SYLVIA Focus	Polydor	3
17	10	ROLL OVER BEETHOVEN Electric Light Orchestra	Harvest	3
9	11	IF YOU DON'T KNOW ME BY NOW Harold Melvin & The Bluenotes	CBS	5
12	[12]	ME AND MRS JONES Billy Paul	Epic	4
5	13	THE JEAN GENIE David Bowie	RCA	10
15	14	CAN'T KEEP IT IN Cat Stevens	Island	9
18	15	PAPA WAS A ROLLIN' STONE Temptations	Tamla Motown	5
23	16	WHISKY IN THE JAR Thin Lizzy	Decca	3
24	17	SUPERSTITION Stevie Wonder	Tamla Motown	2
27	18	TAKE ME HOME COUNTRY ROADS Olivia Newton-John	Pye	4
10	19	BALL PARK INCIDENT Wizzard	Harvest	9
13	20	HI HI HI/C.MOON Wings	Apple	10
16	21	BIG SEVEN Judge Dread	Big Shot	9
-	22	LOOKING THRU' THE EYES OF LOVE Partridge Family	Bell	1
14	23	ALWAYS ON MY MIND Elvis Presley	RCA	9
20	24	HELP ME MAKE IT THROUGH THE NIGHT Gladys Knight & The Pips	Tamla Motown	12
34	25	TAKE ME GIRL I'M READY Junior Walker & The Allstars	Tamla Motown	3
22	26	RELAY The Who	Track	5
19	27	CRAZY HORSES Osmonds	MGM	14
32	28	BABY I LOVE YOU Dave Edmunds	Rockfield	3
39	29	REELIN' AND ROCKIN' Chuck Berry	Chess	2
33	30	HOCUS POCUS Focus	Polydor	4
26	31	BIG CITY/THINK ABOUT THAT Dandy Livingstone	Horse	5
28	32	SOLID GOLD EASY ACTION T. Rex	EMI	10
25	33	BEN Michael Jackson	Tamla Motown	12
-	34	BIG SIX Judge Dread	Big Shot	20
-	35	IF IT WASN'T FOR THE REASON THAT I LOVE YOU Miki Anthony ●	Bell	1
-	[36]	THERE'S GONNA BE A SHOWDOWN Archie Bell & The Drells	Atlantic	1
36	37	WHY Donny Osmond	MGM	14

■ *Blockbuster* becomes Sweet's only chart-topping single, and the first of five written by Mike Chapman and Nicky Chinn (27.01.73) ■ The usual crop of first names in song titles - Daniel, Dan, Ben, Jane and Sylvia - but also, unusually, two surnames, Mrs. Jones and Beethoven (27.01.73) ■ The writer of *Roll Over Beethoven*, Chuck Berry, enjoys two hit singles of his own at the bottom of the 40 (03.02.73) ■

February 1973

□ Highest position disc reached ● Act's first ever week on chart

LW	TW	Title / Artist	Label	Wks
29	38	SHOTGUN WEDDING Roy C.	UK	11
31	39	DESPERATE DAN Lieutenant Pigeon	Decca	9
38	40	MY DING-A-LING Chuck Berry	Chess	16

LW	TW	*WEEK ENDING* **17 FEBRUARY 1973**		Wks
1	[1]	BLOCKBUSTER Sweet	RCA	6
3	[2]	PART OF THE UNION Strawbs	A&M	4
2	3	DO YOU WANNA TOUCH ME (OH YEAH) Gary Glitter	Bell	5
5	[4]	DANIEL Elton John	DJM	5
9	5	SYLVIA Focus	Polydor	4
10	[6]	ROLL OVER BEETHOVEN Electric Light Orchestra	Harvest	4
16	7	WHISKY IN THE JAR Thin Lizzy	Decca	4
4	8	YOU'RE SO VAIN Carly Simon	Elektra	10
6	9	LONG HAIRED LOVER FROM LIVERPOOL Little Jimmy Osmond	MGM	12
8	10	PAPER PLANE Status Quo	Vertigo	6
17	[11]	SUPERSTITION Stevie Wonder	Tamla Motown	3
28	12	BABY I LOVE YOU Dave Edmunds	Rockfield	4
7	13	WISHING WELL Free	Island	6
22	14	LOOKING THRU' THE EYES OF LOVE Partridge Family	Bell	2
11	15	IF YOU DON'T KNOW ME BY NOW Harold Melvin & The Bluenotes	CBS	6
12	16	ME AND MRS JONES Billy Paul	Epic	5
-	17	CINDY INCIDENTALLY Faces	Warner Bros.	1
18	18	TAKE ME HOME COUNTRY ROADS Olivia Newton-John	Pye	5
-	19	HELLO HURRAY Alice Cooper	Warner Bros.	1
25	20	TAKE ME GIRL I'M READY Junior Walker & The Allstars	Tamla Motown	4
21	21	BIG SEVEN Judge Dread	Big Shot	10
30	22	HOCUS POCUS Focus	Polydor	5
29	23	REELIN' AND ROCKIN' Chuck Berry	Chess	3
23	24	ALWAYS ON MY MIND Elvis Presley	RCA	10
15	25	PAPA WAS A ROLLIN' STONE Temptations	Tamla Motown	6
13	26	THE JEAN GENIE David Bowie	RCA	11
-	27	DOCTOR MY EYES Jackson Five	Tamla Motown	1
24	28	HELP ME MAKE IT THROUGH THE NIGHT Gladys Knight & The Pips	Tamla Motown	13
19	29	BALL PARK INCIDENT Wizzard	Harvest	10
20	30	HI HI HI/C.MOON Wings	Apple	11
-	31	FEEL THE NEED IN ME Detroit Emeralds ●	Janus	1
14	32	CAN'T KEEP IT IN Cat Stevens	Island	10
-	33	STEP INTO A DREAM White Plains	Deram	1
27	34	CRAZY HORSES Osmonds	MGM	15
33	35	BEN Michael Jackson	Tamla Motown	13
-	[36]	I'M JUST A SINGER (IN A ROCK AND ROLL BAND) The Moody Blues	Threshold	1
-	[37]	AVENUES AND ALLEYWAYS Tony Christie	MCA	1
35	38	IF IT WASN'T FOR THE REASON THAT I LOVE YOU Miki Anthony	Bell	2
31	39	BIG CITY/THINK ABOUT THAT Dandy Livingstone	Horse	6
40	40	MY DING-A-LING Chuck Berry	Chess	17

LW	TW	*WEEK ENDING* **24 FEBRUARY 1973**		Wks
1	[1]	BLOCKBUSTER Sweet	RCA	7
2	[2]	PART OF THE UNION Strawbs	A&M	5
3	3	DO YOU WANNA TOUCH ME (OH YEAH) Gary Glitter	Bell	6
5	[4]	SYLVIA Focus	Polydor	5
17	5	CINDY INCIDENTALLY Faces	Warner Bros.	2
7	[6]	WHISKY IN THE JAR Thin Lizzy	Decca	5
4	7	DANIEL Elton John	DJM	6
6	8	ROLL OVER BEETHOVEN Electric Light Orchestra	Harvest	5
14	[9]	LOOKING THRU' THE EYES OF LOVE Partridge Family	Bell	3
12	10	BABY I LOVE YOU Dave Edmunds	Rockfield	5
11	[11]	SUPERSTITION Stevie Wonder	Tamla Motown	4
8	12	YOU'RE SO VAIN Carly Simon	Elektra	11
10	13	PAPER PLANE Status Quo	Vertigo	7
19	14	HELLO HURRAY Alice Cooper	Warner Bros.	2
18	[15]	TAKE ME HOME COUNTRY ROADS Olivia Newton-John	Pye	6
20	[16]	TAKE ME GIRL I'M READY Junior Walker & The Allstars	Tamla Motown	5
9	17	LONG HAIRED LOVER FROM LIVERPOOL Little Jimmy Osmond	MGM	13
23	[18]	REELIN' AND ROCKIN' Chuck Berry	Chess	4
27	19	DOCTOR MY EYES Jackson Five	Tamla Motown	2
22	[20]	HOCUS POCUS Focus	Polydor	6
31	21	FEEL THE NEED IN ME Detroit Emeralds	Janus	2
16	22	ME AND MRS JONES Billy Paul	Epic	6
-	23	KILLING ME SOFTLY WITH HIS SONG Roberta Flack	Atlantic	1
15	24	IF YOU DON'T KNOW ME BY NOW Harold Melvin & The Bluenotes	CBS	7
13	25	WISHING WELL Free	Island	7
21	26	BIG SEVEN Judge Dread	Big Shot	11
-	27	PINBALL WIZARD/SEE ME FEEL ME New Seekers	Polydor	1
26	28	THE JEAN GENIE David Bowie	RCA	12
38	29	IF IT WASN'T FOR THE REASON THAT I LOVE YOU Miki Anthony	Bell	3
33	30	STEP INTO A DREAM White Plains	Deram	2
24	31	ALWAYS ON MY MIND Elvis Presley	RCA	11
28	32	HELP ME MAKE IT THROUGH THE NIGHT Gladys Knight & The Pips	Tamla Motown	14
25	33	PAPA WAS A ROLLIN' STONE Temptations	Tamla Motown	7
30	34	HI HI HI/C.MOON Wings	Apple	12
39	35	BIG CITY/THINK ABOUT THAT Dandy Livingstone	Horse	7
-	36	THAT'S WHEN THE MUSIC TAKES ME Neil Sedaka	RCA	1
-	37	WHY CAN'T WE LIVE TOGETHER Timmy Thomas ●	Mojo	1
32	38	CAN'T KEEP IT IN Cat Stevens	Island	11
36	39	I'M JUST A SINGER (IN A ROCK AND ROLL BAND) The Moody Blues	Threshold	2
34	40	CRAZY HORSES Osmonds	MGM	16

LW	TW	*WEEK ENDING* **3 MARCH 1973**		Wks
-	[1]	CUM ON FEEL THE NOIZE Slade	Polydor	1
2	[2]	PART OF THE UNION Strawbs	A&M	6
1	3	BLOCKBUSTER Sweet	RCA	8
4	[4]	SYLVIA Focus	Polydor	6
5	5	CINDY INCIDENTALLY Faces	Warner Bros.	3
3	6	DO YOU WANNA TOUCH ME (OH YEAH) Gary Glitter	Bell	7
6	7	WHISKY IN THE JAR Thin Lizzy	Decca	6
10	[8]	BABY I LOVE YOU Dave Edmunds	Rockfield	6
9	[9]	LOOKING THRU' THE EYES OF LOVE Partridge Family	Bell	4
21	10	FEEL THE NEED IN ME Detroit Emeralds	Janus	3
7	11	DANIEL Elton John	DJM	7
19	12	DOCTOR MY EYES Jackson Five	Tamla Motown	3
14	13	HELLO HURRAY Alice Cooper	Warner Bros.	3
11	14	SUPERSTITION Stevie Wonder	Tamla Motown	5
8	15	ROLL OVER BEETHOVEN Electric Light Orchestra	Harvest	6
-	16	GONNA MAKE YOU AN OFFER YOU CAN'T REFUSE Jimmy Helms ●	Cube	1
15	17	TAKE ME HOME COUNTRY ROADS Olivia Newton-John	Pye	6
17	18	LONG HAIRED LOVER FROM LIVERPOOL Little Jimmy Osmond	MGM	14
23	19	KILLING ME SOFTLY WITH HIS SONG Roberta Flack	Atlantic	3
18	20	REELIN' AND ROCKIN' Chuck Berry	Chess	5
20	21	HOCUS POCUS Focus	Polydor	7
27	22	PINBALL WIZARD/SEE ME FEEL ME New Seekers	Polydor	2
16	23	TAKE ME GIRL I'M READY Junior Walker & The Allstars	Tamla Motown	6
30	24	STEP INTO A DREAM White Plains	Deram	3
12	25	YOU'RE SO VAIN Carly Simon	Elektra	12
13	26	PAPER PLANE Status Quo	Vertigo	8
29	[27]	IF IT WASN'T FOR THE REASON THAT I LOVE YOU Miki Anthony	Bell	4
36	28	THAT'S WHEN THE MUSIC TAKES ME Neil Sedaka	RCA	2
-	29	NICE ONE CYRIL Cockerel Chorus ●	Young Blood	1
25	30	WISHING WELL Free	Island	8
26	31	BIG SEVEN Judge Dread	Big Shot	12
37	32	WHY CAN'T WE LIVE TOGETHER Timmy Thomas	Mojo	2
22	33	ME AND MRS JONES Billy Paul	Epic	7

In these weeks ■ Tony Christie's *Avenues and Alleyways* is the first record to peak at no. 37 in well over a year (17.02.73) ■ The Jackson Five debut with their version of *Doctor My Eyes*, previously a hit for the writer, Jackson Browne. It is the only example of a hit cover by an act with a surname identical to that of the original hitmaker (17.02.73)■

LW	TW	Title / Artist	Label	Wks
24	34	IF YOU DON'T KNOW ME BY NOW Harold Melvin & The Bluenotes	*CBS*	8
-	35	BY THE DEVIL Blue Mink	*EMI*	1
-	36	HEART OF STONE Kenny ●	*RAK*	1
32	37	HELP ME MAKE IT THROUGH THE NIGHT Gladys Knight & The Pips	*Tamla Motown*	15
-	38	AVENUES AND ALLEYWAYS Tony Christie	*MCA*	2
28	39	THE JEAN GENIE David Bowie	*RCA*	13
31	40	ALWAYS ON MY MIND Elvis Presley	*RCA*	12

WEEK ENDING 10 MARCH 1973

LW	TW	Title / Artist	Label	Wks
1	[1]	CUM ON FEEL THE NOIZE Slade	*Polydor*	2
5	[2]	CINDY INCIDENTALLY Faces	*Warner Bros.*	4
-	[3]	20TH CENTURY BOY T. Rex	*EMI*	1
2	4	PART OF THE UNION Strawbs	*A&M*	7
3	5	BLOCKBUSTER Sweet	*RCA*	9
10	6	FEEL THE NEED IN ME Detroit Emeralds	*Janus*	4
13	7	HELLO HURRAY Alice Cooper	*Warner Bros.*	4
19	8	KILLING ME SOFTLY WITH HIS SONG Roberta Flack	*Atlantic*	4
12	[9]	DOCTOR MY EYES Jackson Five	*Tamla Motown*	4
7	10	WHISKY IN THE JAR Thin Lizzy	*Decca*	7
8	11	BABY I LOVE YOU Dave Edmunds	*Rockfield*	7
4	12	SYLVIA Focus	*Polydor*	7
6	13	DO YOU WANNA TOUCH ME (OH YEAH) Gary Glitter	*Bell*	8
-	14	THE TWELFTH OF NEVER Donny Osmond	*MGM*	1
9	15	LOOKING THRU' THE EYES OF LOVE Partridge Family	*Bell*	5
22	[16]	PINBALL WIZARD/SEE ME FEEL ME New Seekers	*Polydor*	3
16	17	GONNA MAKE YOU AN OFFER YOU CAN'T REFUSE Jimmy Helms	*Cube*	2
14	18	SUPERSTITION Stevie Wonder	*Tamla Motown*	6
29	19	NICE ONE CYRIL Cockerel Chorus	*Young Blood*	2
18	20	LONG HAIRED LOVER FROM LIVERPOOL Little Jimmy Osmond	*MGM*	15
15	21	ROLL OVER BEETHOVEN Electric Light Orchestra	*Harvest*	7
17	22	TAKE ME HOME COUNTRY ROADS Olivia Newton-John	*Pye*	7
20	23	REELIN' AND ROCKIN' Chuck Berry	*Chess*	6
28	24	THAT'S WHEN THE MUSIC TAKES ME Neil Sedaka	*RCA*	3
36	25	HEART OF STONE Kenny	*RAK*	2
21	26	HOCUS POCUS Focus	*Polydor*	8
24	27	STEP INTO A DREAM White Plains	*Deram*	4
32	28	WHY CAN'T WE LIVE TOGETHER Timmy Thomas	*Mojo*	3
23	29	TAKE ME GIRL I'M READY Junior Walker & The Allstars	*Tamla Motown*	7
11	30	DANIEL Elton John	*DJM*	8
-	31	NEVER NEVER NEVER Shirley Bassey	*United Artists*	1
35	32	BY THE DEVIL Blue Mink	*EMI*	2
25	33	YOU'RE SO VAIN Carly Simon	*Elektra*	13
26	34	PAPER PLANE Status Quo	*Vertigo*	9
31	35	BIG SEVEN Judge Dread	*Big Shot*	13
27	36	IF IT WASN'T FOR THE REASON THAT I LOVE YOU Miki Anthony	*Bell*	5
-	[37]	CALIFORNIA SAGA Beach Boys	*Reprise*	1
-	38	TIE A YELLOW RIBBON ROUND THE OLD OAK TREE Dawn	*Bell*	1
-	39	LOOK OF LOVE Gladys Knight & The Pips	*Tamla Motown*	1
-	40	LOVE TRAIN O'Jays	*CBS*	1

WEEK ENDING 17 MARCH 1973

March 1973

□ Highest position disc reached ● Act's first ever week on chart

LW	TW	Title / Artist	Label	Wks
1	[1]	CUM ON FEEL THE NOIZE Slade	*Polydor*	3
14	2	THE TWELFTH OF NEVER Donny Osmond	*MGM*	2
3	[3]	20TH CENTURY BOY T. Rex	*EMI*	2
6	[4]	FEEL THE NEED IN ME Detroit Emeralds	*Janus*	5
2	5	CINDY INCIDENTALLY Faces	*Warner Bros.*	5
7	[6]	HELLO HURRAY Alice Cooper	*Warner Bros.*	5
8	7	KILLING ME SOFTLY WITH HIS SONG Roberta Flack	*Atlantic*	5
17	[8]	GONNA MAKE YOU AN OFFER YOU CAN'T REFUSE Jimmy Helms	*Cube*	3
12	9	SYLVIA Focus	*Polydor*	8
11	10	BABY I LOVE YOU Dave Edmunds	*Rockfield*	8
9	11	DOCTOR MY EYES Jackson Five	*Tamla Motown*	5
4	12	PART OF THE UNION Strawbs	*A&M*	8
-	13	POWER TO ALL OUR FRIENDS Cliff Richard	*EMI*	1
5	14	BLOCKBUSTER Sweet	*RCA*	10
10	15	WHISKY IN THE JAR Thin Lizzy	*Decca*	8
15	16	LOOKING THRU' THE EYES OF LOVE Partridge Family	*Bell*	6
16	17	PINBALL WIZARD/SEE ME FEEL ME New Seekers	*Polydor*	4
19	18	NICE ONE CYRIL Cockerel Chorus	*Young Blood*	3
25	19	HEART OF STONE Kenny	*RAK*	3
31	20	NEVER NEVER NEVER Shirley Bassey	*United Artists*	2
27	[21]	STEP INTO A DREAM White Plains	*Deram*	5
13	22	DO YOU WANNA TOUCH ME (OH YEAH) Gary Glitter	*Bell*	9
28	23	WHY CAN'T WE LIVE TOGETHER Timmy Thomas	*Mojo*	4
24	24	THAT'S WHEN THE MUSIC TAKES ME Neil Sedaka	*RCA*	4
18	25	SUPERSTITION Stevie Wonder	*Tamla Motown*	7
22	26	TAKE ME HOME COUNTRY ROADS Olivia Newton-John	*Pye*	8
39	27	LOOK OF LOVE Gladys Knight & The Pips	*Tamla Motown*	2
40	28	LOVE TRAIN O'Jays	*CBS*	2
20	29	LONG HAIRED LOVER FROM LIVERPOOL Little Jimmy Osmond	*MGM*	16
-	30	GET DOWN Gilbert O'Sullivan	*MAM*	1
-	31	PYJAMARAMA Roxy Music	*Island*	1
38	32	TIE A YELLOW RIBBON ROUND THE OLD OAK TREE Dawn	*Bell*	2
32	33	BY THE DEVIL Blue Mink	*EMI*	3
29	34	TAKE ME GIRL I'M READY Junior Walker & The Allstars	*Tamla Motown*	8
21	35	ROLL OVER BEETHOVEN Electric Light Orchestra	*Harvest*	8
26	36	HOCUS POCUS Focus	*Polydor*	9
-	37	HEAVEN IS MY WOMAN'S LOVE Val Doonican	*Philips*	1
-	38	WHY Donny Osmond	*MGM*	14
-	39	CRAZY Mud ●	*RAK*	1
35	40	BIG SEVEN Judge Dread	*Big Shot*	13

WEEK ENDING 24 MARCH 1973

LW	TW	Title / Artist	Label	Wks
1	[1]	CUM ON FEEL THE NOIZE Slade	*Polydor*	4
2	2	THE TWELFTH OF NEVER Donny Osmond	*MGM*	3
3	[3]	20TH CENTURY BOY T. Rex	*EMI*	3
13	[4]	POWER TO ALL OUR FRIENDS Cliff Richard	*EMI*	2
4	5	FEEL THE NEED IN ME Detroit Emeralds	*Janus*	6
7	[6]	KILLING ME SOFTLY WITH HIS SONG Roberta Flack	*Atlantic*	6
30	7	GET DOWN Gilbert O'Sullivan	*MAM*	2
6	8	HELLO HURRAY Alice Cooper	*Warner Bros.*	6
5	9	CINDY INCIDENTALLY Faces	*Warner Bros.*	6
8	10	GONNA MAKE YOU AN OFFER YOU CAN'T REFUSE Jimmy Helms	*Cube*	4
20	11	NEVER NEVER NEVER Shirley Bassey	*United Artists*	3
19	12	HEART OF STONE Kenny	*RAK*	4
23	13	WHY CAN'T WE LIVE TOGETHER Timmy Thomas	*Mojo*	5
18	[14]	NICE ONE CYRIL Cockerel Chorus	*Young Blood*	4
11	15	DOCTOR MY EYES Jackson Five	*Tamla Motown*	6
32	16	TIE A YELLOW RIBBON ROUND THE OLD OAK TREE Dawn	*Bell*	3
17	17	PINBALL WIZARD/SEE ME FEEL ME New Seekers	*Polydor*	5
24	[18]	THAT'S WHEN THE MUSIC TAKES ME Neil Sedaka	*RCA*	5
28	19	LOVE TRAIN O'Jays	*CBS*	3
12	20	PART OF THE UNION Strawbs	*A&M*	9
14	21	BLOCKBUSTER Sweet	*RCA*	11
10	22	BABY I LOVE YOU Dave Edmunds	*Rockfield*	9
31	23	PYJAMARAMA Roxy Music	*Island*	2
15	24	WHISKY IN THE JAR Thin Lizzy	*Decca*	9
9	25	SYLVIA Focus	*Polydor*	9
27	26	LOOK OF LOVE Gladys Knight & The Pips	*Tamla Motown*	3
16	27	LOOKING THRU' THE EYES OF LOVE Partridge Family	*Bell*	7
29	28	LONG HAIRED LOVER FROM LIVERPOOL Little Jimmy Osmond	*MGM*	17
21	29	STEP INTO A DREAM White Plains	*Deram*	6
22	30	DO YOU WANNA TOUCH ME (OH YEAH) Gary Glitter	*Bell*	10
26	31	TAKE ME HOME COUNTRY ROADS Olivia Newton-John	*Pye*	9
33	32	BY THE DEVIL Blue Mink	*EMI*	4

■Jimmy Helms peaks at number 8 with his only solo hit *Gonna Make You An Offer You Can't Refuse*. Over 17 years later, he will climb to number two as a member of Londonbeat (17.03.73) ■ *Power To All Our Friends* is Cliff Richard's second Eurovision hit. It does not win (24.03.73)■

March 1973

□ Highest position disc reached ● Act's first ever week on chart

LW	TW	Title	Artist	Label	Wks
39	33	CRAZY	Mud	RAK	2
25	34	SUPERSTITION	Stevie Wonder	Tamla Motown	8
-	35	I'M A CLOWN/SOME KIND OF A SUMMER	David Cassidy	Bell	1
37	36	HEAVEN IS MY WOMAN'S LOVE	Val Doonican	Philips	2
-	37	CALIFORNIA SAGA	Beach Boys	Reprise	2
-	38	ALL BECAUSE OF YOU	Geordie	EMI	1
-	39	DANIEL	Elton John	DJM	9
34	40	TAKE ME GIRL I'M READY	Junior Walker & The Allstars	Tamla Motown	9

WEEK ENDING 31 MARCH 1973

LW	TW	Title	Artist	Label	Wks
2	[1]	THE TWELFTH OF NEVER	Donny Osmond	MGM	4
1	2	CUM ON FEEL THE NOIZE	Slade	Polydor	5
7	3	GET DOWN	Gilbert O'Sullivan	MAM	3
4	[4]	POWER TO ALL OUR FRIENDS	Cliff Richard	EMI	3
3	5	20TH CENTURY BOY	T. Rex	EMI	4
5	6	FEEL THE NEED IN ME	Detroit Emeralds	Janus	7
16	7	TIE A YELLOW RIBBON ROUND THE OLD OAK TREE	Dawn	Bell	4
35	8	I'M A CLOWN/SOME KIND OF A SUMMER	David Cassidy	Bell	2
6	9	KILLING ME SOFTLY WITH HIS SONG	Roberta Flack	Atlantic	7
11	10	NEVER NEVER NEVER	Shirley Bassey	United Artists	4
12	[11]	HEART OF STONE	Kenny	RAK	5
13	[12]	WHY CAN'T WE LIVE TOGETHER	Timmy Thomas	Mojo	6
19	13	LOVE TRAIN	O'Jays	CBS	4
10	14	GONNA MAKE YOU AN OFFER YOU CAN'T REFUSE	Jimmy Helms	Cube	5
8	15	HELLO HURRAY	Alice Cooper	Warner Bros.	7
14	16	NICE ONE CYRIL	Cockerel Chorus	Young Blood	5
23	17	PYJAMARAMA	Roxy Music	Island	3
9	18	CINDY INCIDENTALLY	Faces	Warner Bros.	7
17	19	PINBALL WIZARD/SEE ME FEEL ME	New Seekers	Polydor	6
22	20	BABY I LOVE YOU	Dave Edmunds	Rockfield	10
26	[21]	LOOK OF LOVE	Gladys Knight & The Pips	Tamla Motown	4
15	22	DOCTOR MY EYES	Jackson Five	Tamla Motown	7
33	23	CRAZY	Mud	RAK	3
18	24	THAT'S WHEN THE MUSIC TAKES ME	Neil Sedaka	RCA	6
28	25	LONG HAIRED LOVER FROM LIVERPOOL	Little Little Jimmy Osmond	MGM	17
27	26	LOOKING THRU' THE EYES OF LOVE	Partridge Family	Bell	8
38	27	ALL BECAUSE OF YOU	Geordie	EMI	2
32	28	BY THE DEVIL	Blue Mink	EMI	5
29	29	STEP INTO A DREAM	White Plains	Deram	7
-	30	TWEEDLE DEE	Little Jimmy Osmond	MGM	1
21	31	BLOCKBUSTER	Sweet	RCA	12
20	32	PART OF THE UNION	Strawbs	A&M	10
25	33	SYLVIA	Focus	Polydor	10
-	[34]	BREAK UP TO MAKE UP	Stylistics	Avco	1
24	35	WHISKY IN THE JAR	Thin Lizzy	Decca	10
-	36	DUELLING BANJOS	'Deliverance' Soundtrack ●	Warner Bros.	1
31	37	TAKE ME HOME COUNTRY ROADS	Olivia Newton-John	Pye	10
30	38	DO YOU WANNA TOUCH ME (OH YEAH)	Gary Glitter	Bell	11
-	39	AMANDA	Stuart Gillies ●	Philips	1
-	40	GOD GAVE ROCK AND ROLL TO YOU	Argent	Epic	1

WEEK ENDING 7 APRIL 1973

LW	TW	Title	Artist	Label	Wks
3	[1]	GET DOWN	Gilbert O'Sullivan	MAM	4
1	2	THE TWELFTH OF NEVER	Donny Osmond	MGM	5
7	3	TIE A YELLOW RIBBON ROUND THE OLD OAK TREE	Dawn	Bell	5
4	[4]	POWER TO ALL OUR FRIENDS	Cliff Richard	EMI	4
8	5	I'M A CLOWN/SOME KIND OF A SUMMER	David Cassidy	Bell	3
30	6	TWEEDLE DEE	Little Jimmy Osmond	MGM	2
2	7	CUM ON FEEL THE NOIZE	Slade	Polydor	6
10	[8]	NEVER NEVER NEVER	Shirley Bassey	United Artists	5
13	[9]	LOVE TRAIN	O'Jays	CBS	5
9	10	KILLING ME SOFTLY WITH HIS SONG	Roberta Flack	Atlantic	8
6	11	FEEL THE NEED IN ME	Detroit Emeralds	Janus	8
11	12	HEART OF STONE	Kenny	RAK	6
17	13	PYJAMARAMA	Roxy Music	Island	4
12	14	WHY CAN'T WE LIVE TOGETHER	Timmy Thomas	Mojo	7
5	15	20TH CENTURY BOY	T. Rex	EMI	5
16	16	NICE ONE CYRIL	Cockerel Chorus	Young Blood	6
-	17	HELLO HELLO I'M BACK AGAIN	Gary Glitter	Bell	1
23	18	CRAZY	Mud	RAK	4
15	19	HELLO HURRAY	Alice Cooper	Warner Bros.	8
-	20	AMANDA	Stuart Gillies	Philips	1
27	21	ALL BECAUSE OF YOU	Geordie	EMI	3
36	22	DUELLING BANJOS	'Deliverance' Soundtrack	Warner Bros.	2
21	23	LOOK OF LOVE	Gladys Knight & The Pips	Tamla Motown	5
14	24	GONNA MAKE YOU AN OFFER YOU CAN'T REFUSE	Jimmy Helms	Cube	6
24	25	THAT'S WHEN THE MUSIC TAKES ME	Neil Sedaka	RCA	7
25	26	LONG HAIRED LOVER FROM LIVERPOOL	Little Little Jimmy Osmond	MGM	18
28	27	BY THE DEVIL	Blue Mink	EMI	6
40	28	GOD GAVE ROCK AND ROLL TO YOU	Argent	Epic	2
20	29	BABY I LOVE YOU	Dave Edmunds	Rockfield	11
22	30	DOCTOR MY EYES	Jackson Five	Tamla Motown	8
18	31	CINDY INCIDENTALLY	Faces	Warner Bros.	8
-	32	GOOD GRIEF CHRISTINA	Chicory Tip	CBS	1
19	33	PINBALL WIZARD/SEE ME FEEL ME	New Seekers	Polydor	7
-	[34]	HEAVEN IS MY WOMAN'S LOVE	Val Doonican	Philips	3
37	35	TAKE ME HOME COUNTRY ROADS	Olivia Newton-John	Pye	11
34	36	BREAK UP TO MAKE UP	Stylistics	Avco	2
35	37	WHISKY IN THE JAR	Thin Lizzy	Decca	11
-	38	THE RIGHT THING TO DO	Carly Simon	Elektra	1
-	39	I DON'T KNOW WHY	Andy & David Williams ●	MCA	1
-	[40]	SWEET DREAMS	Roy Buchanan ●	Polydor	1

WEEK ENDING 14 APRIL 1973

LW	TW	Title	Artist	Label	Wks
1	[1]	GET DOWN	Gilbert O'Sullivan	MAM	5
3	2	TIE A YELLOW RIBBON ROUND THE OLD OAK TREE	Dawn	Bell	6
5	[3]	I'M A CLOWN/SOME KIND OF A SUMMER	David Cassidy	Bell	4
2	4	THE TWELFTH OF NEVER	Donny Osmond	MGM	6
17	5	HELLO HELLO I'M BACK AGAIN	Gary Glitter	Bell	2
6	6	TWEEDLE DEE	Little Jimmy Osmond	MGM	3
4	7	POWER TO ALL OUR FRIENDS	Cliff Richard	EMI	5
8	[8]	NEVER NEVER NEVER	Shirley Bassey	United Artists	6
9	[9]	LOVE TRAIN	O'Jays	CBS	6
13	[10]	PYJAMARAMA	Roxy Music	Island	5
21	11	ALL BECAUSE OF YOU	Geordie	EMI	4
12	12	HEART OF STONE	Kenny	RAK	7
7	13	CUM ON FEEL THE NOIZE	Slade	Polydor	7
18	14	CRAZY	Mud	RAK	5
14	15	WHY CAN'T WE LIVE TOGETHER	Timmy Thomas	Mojo	8
-	16	DRIVE-IN SATURDAY	David Bowie	RCA	1
15	17	20TH CENTURY BOY	T. Rex	EMI	6
11	18	FEEL THE NEED IN ME	Detroit Emeralds	Janus	9
10	19	KILLING ME SOFTLY WITH HIS SONG	Roberta Flack	Atlantic	9
20	20	AMANDA	Stuart Gillies	Philips	2
22	21	DUELLING BANJOS	'Deliverance' Soundtrack	Warner Bros.	3
16	22	NICE ONE CYRIL	Cockerel Chorus	Young Blood	7
19	23	HELLO HURRAY	Alice Cooper	Warner Bros.	9
32	24	GOOD GRIEF CHRISTINA	Chicory Tip	CBS	2
-	25	MY LOVE	Wings	Apple	1
27	[26]	BY THE DEVIL	Blue Mink	EMI	7
23	27	LOOK OF LOVE	Gladys Knight & The Pips	Tamla Motown	6
24	28	GONNA MAKE YOU AN OFFER YOU CAN'T REFUSE	Jimmy Helms	Cube	7
28	29	GOD GAVE ROCK AND ROLL TO YOU	Argent	Epic	3
38	30	THE RIGHT THING TO DO	Carly Simon	Elektra	2
-	31	GIVING IT ALL AWAY	Roger Daltrey ●	Track	1
-	32	WAM BAM	Handley Family ●	GL	1
-	33	BROTHER LOUIE	Hot Chocolate	RAK	1
-	[34]	NEVERTHELESS (I'M IN LOVE WITH YOU)	Eve Graham/New Seekers	Polydor	1

In these weeks ■ An instrumental from the film 'Deliverance', played by Eric Weissberg and Steve Mandel, actually on guitar and banjo, brings bluegrass music to the charts (31.03.73) ■ Andy and David Williams are the nephews of easy listening superstar Andy Williams (07.04.73) ■ Gilbert O'Sullivan's *Get Down* is the first song admonishing a dog to reach the top (07.05.73)■

LW	TW	Title / Artist	Label	Wks
26	**35**	LONG HAIRED LOVER FROM LIVERPOOL Little Little Jimmy Osmond	*MGM*	19
36	**36**	BREAK UP TO MAKE UP Stylistics	*Avco*	3
39	**[37]**	I DON'T KNOW WHY Andy & David Williams	*MCA*	2
-	**38**	BLOCKBUSTER Sweet	*RCA*	13
25	**39**	THAT'S WHEN THE MUSIC TAKES ME Neil Sedaka	*RCA*	8
40	**40**	SWEET DREAMS Roy Buchanan	*Polydor*	2

WEEK ENDING 21 APRIL 1973

LW	TW	Title / Artist	Label	Wks
2	**[1]**	TIE A YELLOW RIBBON ROUND THE OLD OAK TREE Dawn	*Bell*	7
5	**[2]**	HELLO HELLO I'M BACK AGAIN Gary Glitter	*Bell*	3
1	**3**	GET DOWN Gilbert O'Sullivan	*MAM*	6
6	**[4]**	TWEEDLE DEE Little Jimmy Osmond	*MGM*	4
3	**5**	I'M A CLOWN/SOME KIND OF A SUMMER David Cassidy	*Bell*	5
4	**6**	THE TWELFTH OF NEVER Donny Osmond	*MGM*	7
7	**7**	POWER TO ALL OUR FRIENDS Cliff Richard	*EMI*	6
16	**8**	DRIVE-IN SATURDAY David Bowie	*RCA*	2
8	**9**	NEVER NEVER NEVER Shirley Bassey	*United Artists*	7
10	**[10]**	PYJAMARAMA Roxy Music	*Island*	6
11	**11**	ALL BECAUSE OF YOU Geordie	*EMI*	5
9	**12**	LOVE TRAIN O'Jays	*CBS*	7
20	**[13]**	AMANDA Stuart Gillies	*Philips*	3
14	**14**	CRAZY Mud	*RAK*	6
25	**15**	MY LOVE Wings	*Apple*	2
12	**16**	HEART OF STONE Kenny	*RAK*	8
21	**[17]**	DUELLING BANJOS 'Deliverance' Soundtrack	*Warner Bros.*	4
29	**[18]**	GOD GAVE ROCK AND ROLL TO YOU Argent	*Epic*	4
13	**19**	CUM ON FEEL THE NOIZE Slade	*Polydor*	8
19	**20**	KILLING ME SOFTLY WITH HIS SONG Roberta Flack	*Atlantic*	10
33	**21**	BROTHER LOUIE Hot Chocolate	*RAK*	2
15	**22**	WHY CAN'T WE LIVE TOGETHER Timmy Thomas	*Mojo*	9
18	**23**	FEEL THE NEED IN ME Detroit Emeralds	*Janus*	10
31	**24**	GIVING IT ALL AWAY Roger Daltrey	*Track*	2
24	**25**	GOOD GRIEF CHRISTINA Chicory Tip	*CBS*	3
17	**26**	20TH CENTURY BOY T. Rex	*EMI*	7
-	**27**	SEE MY BABY JIVE Wizzard	*Harvest*	1
22	**28**	NICE ONE CYRIL Cockerel Chorus	*Young Blood*	8
-	**29**	BIG EIGHT Judge Dread	*Big Shot*	1
30	**30**	THE RIGHT THING TO DO Carly Simon	*Elektra*	3
27	**31**	LOOK OF LOVE Gladys Knight & The Pips	*Tamla Motown*	7
-	**32**	NO MORE MR. NICE GUY Alice Cooper	*Warner Bros.*	1
28	**33**	GONNA MAKE YOU AN OFFER YOU CAN'T REFUSE Jimmy Helms	*Cube*	8
23	**34**	HELLO HURRAY Alice Cooper	*Warner Bros.*	10
-	**[35]**	WHATEVER HAPPENED TO YOU Highly Likely ●	*BBC*	1
-	**36**	MEAN GIRL Status Quo	*Pye*	1
-	**37**	COULD IT BE I'M FALLING IN LOVE Detroit Spinners	*Atlantic*	1
-	**38**	HEY MAMA Joe Brown	*Ammo*	1
-	**39**	LETTER TO LUCILLE Tom Jones	*Decca*	1
35	**40**	LONG HAIRED LOVER FROM LIVERPOOL Little Little Jimmy Osmond	*MGM*	20

WEEK ENDING 28 APRIL 1973

LW	TW	Title / Artist	Label	Wks
1	**[1]**	TIE A YELLOW RIBBON ROUND THE OLD OAK TREE Dawn	*Bell*	8
2	**[2]**	HELLO HELLO I'M BACK AGAIN Gary Glitter	*Bell*	4
3	**3**	GET DOWN Gilbert O'Sullivan	*MAM*	7
5	**4**	I'M A CLOWN/SOME KIND OF A SUMMER David Cassidy	*Bell*	6
4	**5**	TWEEDLE DEE Little Jimmy Osmond	*MGM*	5
11	**[6]**	ALL BECAUSE OF YOU Geordie	*EMI*	6
8	**7**	DRIVE-IN SATURDAY David Bowie	*RCA*	3
6	**8**	THE TWELFTH OF NEVER Donny Osmond	*MGM*	8
15	**[9]**	MY LOVE Wings	*Apple*	3
10	**[10]**	PYJAMARAMA Roxy Music	*Island*	7
9	**11**	NEVER NEVER NEVER Shirley Bassey	*United Artists*	8
14	**[12]**	CRAZY Mud	*RAK*	7
12	**13**	LOVE TRAIN O'Jays	*CBS*	8
7	**14**	POWER TO ALL OUR FRIENDS Cliff Richard	*EMI*	7

May 1973

□ Highest position disc reached ● Act's first ever week on chart

LW	TW	Title / Artist	Label	Wks
13	**15**	AMANDA Stuart Gillies	*Philips*	4
27	**16**	SEE MY BABY JIVE Wizzard	*Harvest*	2
24	**17**	GIVING IT ALL AWAY Roger Daltrey	*Track*	3
21	**18**	BROTHER LOUIE Hot Chocolate	*RAK*	3
17	**19**	DUELLING BANJOS 'Deliverance' Soundtrack	*Warner Bros.*	5
29	**20**	BIG EIGHT Judge Dread	*Big Shot*	2
32	**21**	NO MORE MR. NICE GUY Alice Cooper	*Warner Bros.*	2
18	**22**	GOD GAVE ROCK AND ROLL TO YOU Argent	*Epic*	5
25	**23**	GOOD GRIEF CHRISTINA Chicory Tip	*CBS*	4
16	**24**	HEART OF STONE Kenny	*RAK*	9
-	**25**	AND I LOVE YOU SO Perry Como	*RCA*	1
19	**26**	CUM ON FEEL THE NOIZE Slade	*Polydor*	9
30	**27**	THE RIGHT THING TO DO Carly Simon	*Elektra*	4
-	**28**	WONDERFUL DREAM Anne-Marie David ●	*Epic*	1
23	**29**	FEEL THE NEED IN ME Detroit Emeralds	*Janus*	11
-	**[30]**	WAM BAM Handley Family ●	*GL*	2
36	**31**	MEAN GIRL Status Quo	*Pye*	2
20	**32**	KILLING ME SOFTLY WITH HIS SONG Roberta Flack	*Atlantic*	11
22	**33**	WHY CAN'T WE LIVE TOGETHER Timmy Thomas	*Mojo*	10
28	**34**	NICE ONE CYRIL Cockerel Chorus	*Young Blood*	9
26	**35**	20TH CENTURY BOY T. Rex	*EMI*	8
38	**36**	HEY MAMA Joe Brown	*Ammo*	2
39	**37**	LETTER TO LUCILLE Tom Jones	*Decca*	2
-	**[38]**	EVERYDAY Don McLean	*United Artists*	1
37	**39**	COULD IT BE I'M FALLING IN LOVE Detroit Spinners	*Atlantic*	2
40	**40**	LONG HAIRED LOVER FROM LIVERPOOL Little Jimmy Osmond	*MGM*	21

WEEK ENDING 5 MAY 1973

LW	TW	Title / Artist	Label	Wks
1	**[1]**	TIE A YELLOW RIBBON ROUND THE OLD OAK TREE Dawn	*Bell*	9
2	**[2]**	HELLO HELLO I'M BACK AGAIN Gary Glitter	*Bell*	5
7	**[3]**	DRIVE-IN SATURDAY David Bowie	*RCA*	4
-	**4**	HELL RAISER Sweet	*RCA*	1
5	**5**	TWEEDLE DEE Jimmy Osmond	*MGM*	6
16	**6**	SEE MY BABY JIVE Wizzard	*Harvest*	3
6	**7**	ALL BECAUSE OF YOU Geordie	*EMI*	7
3	**8**	GET DOWN Gilbert O'Sullivan	*MAM*	8
18	**9**	BROTHER LOUIE Hot Chocolate	*RAK*	4
4	**10**	I'M A CLOWN/SOME KIND OF A SUMMER David Cassidy	*Bell*	7
17	**11**	GIVING IT ALL AWAY Roger Daltrey	*Track*	4
9	**12**	MY LOVE Wings	*Apple*	4
21	**13**	NO MORE MR. NICE GUY Alice Cooper	*Warner Bros.*	3
10	**14**	PYJAMARAMA Roxy Music	*Island*	8
12	**15**	CRAZY Mud	*RAK*	8
20	**16**	BIG EIGHT Judge Dread	*Big Shot*	3
15	**17**	AMANDA Stuart Gillies	*Philips*	5
8	**18**	THE TWELFTH OF NEVER Donny Osmond	*MGM*	9
23	**19**	GOOD GRIEF CHRISTINA Chicory Tip	*CBS*	5
25	**20**	AND I LOVE YOU SO Perry Como	*RCA*	2
11	**21**	NEVER NEVER NEVER Shirley Bassey	*United Artists*	9
22	**22**	GOD GAVE ROCK AND ROLL TO YOU Argent	*Epic*	6
19	**23**	DUELLING BANJOS 'Deliverance' Soundtrack	*Warner Bros.*	6
13	**24**	LOVE TRAIN O'Jays	*CBS*	9
28	**25**	WONDERFUL DREAM Anne-Marie David	*Epic*	2
14	**26**	POWER TO ALL OUR FRIENDS Cliff Richard	*EMI*	8
31	**27**	MEAN GIRL Status Quo	*Pye*	3
24	**28**	HEART OF STONE Kenny	*RAK*	10
27	**29**	THE RIGHT THING TO DO Carly Simon	*Elektra*	5
39	**30**	COULD IT BE I'M FALLING IN LOVE Detroit Spinners	*Atlantic*	2
37	**[31]**	LETTER TO LUCILLE Tom Jones	*Decca*	3
26	**32**	CUM ON FEEL THE NOIZE Slade	*Polydor*	10
36	**[33]**	HEY MAMA Joe Brown	*Ammo*	3

■Don McLean becomes the only person to chart with the classic Buddy Holly song *Everyday* (28.04.73) ■ Eurovision Winner Anne-Marie David edges one place above Eurovision also-ran Cliff Richard (05.05.73) ■ The most successful female vocalist at the time, Shirley Bassey, drops out of the Top 10 for the last time with her final solo hit, *Never Never Never* (28.04.73)■

May 1973

□ Highest position disc reached ● Act's first ever week on chart

LW	TW	Title / Artist	Label	Wks
-	34	ONE AND ONE IS ONE Medicine Head	Polydor	1
30	35	WAM BAM Handley Family	GL	3
32	36	KILLING ME SOFTLY WITH HIS SONG Roberta Flack	Atlantic	11
-	37	BAD WEATHER Supremes	Tamla Motown	1
29	38	FEEL THE NEED IN ME Detroit Emeralds	Janus	12
35	39	20TH CENTURY BOY T. Rex	EMI	9
-	40	WHATEVER HAPPENED TO YOU Highly Likely	BBC	1

WEEK ENDING 12 MAY 1973

LW	TW	Title / Artist	Label	Wks
1	1	TIE A YELLOW RIBBON ROUND THE OLD OAK TREE Dawn	Bell	10
4	2	HELL RAISER Sweet	RCA	2
2	3	HELLO HELLO I'M BACK AGAIN Gary Glitter	Bell	6
6	4	SEE MY BABY JIVE Wizzard	Harvest	4
11	5	GIVING IT ALL AWAY Roger Daltrey	Track	5
20	6	AND I LOVE YOU SO Perry Como	RCA	3
9	7	BROTHER LOUIE Hot Chocolate	RAK	5
3	8	DRIVE-IN SATURDAY David Bowie	RCA	5
12	9	MY LOVE Wings	Apple	5
13	10	NO MORE MR. NICE GUY Alice Cooper	Warner Bros.	4
7	11	ALL BECAUSE OF YOU Geordie	EMI	8
8	12	GET DOWN Gilbert O'Sullivan	MAM	9
25	13	WONDERFUL DREAM Anne-Marie David	Epic	3
16	14	BIG EIGHT Judge Dread	Big Shot	4
10	15	I'M A CLOWN/SOME KIND OF A SUMMER David Cassidy	Bell	8
5	16	TWEEDLE DEE Little Jimmy Osmond	MGM	7
29	17	THE RIGHT THING TO DO Carly Simon	Elektra	6
21	18	NEVER NEVER NEVER Shirley Bassey	United Artists	10
-	19	ALSO SPRACH ZARATHUSTRA (2001) Deodato ●	Creed Taylor	1
30	20	COULD IT BE I'M FALLING IN LOVE Detroit Spinners	Atlantic	3
19	21	GOOD GRIEF CHRISTINA Chicory Tip	CBS	6
27	22	MEAN GIRL Status Quo	Pye	3
15	23	CRAZY Mud	RAK	9
34	24	ONE AND ONE IS ONE Medicine Head	Polydor	2
14	25	PYJAMARAMA Roxy Music	Island	9
18	26	THE TWELFTH OF NEVER Donny Osmond	MGM	10
-	27	BROKEN DOWN ANGEL Nazareth ●	Mooncrest	1
24	28	LOVE TRAIN O'Jays	CBS	10
26	29	POWER TO ALL OUR FRIENDS Cliff Richard	EMI	10
17	30	AMANDA Stuart Gillies	Philips	6
31	31	LETTER TO LUCILLE Tom Jones	Decca	4
-	32	WALK ON THE WILD SIDE Lou Reed ●	RCA	1
-	33	YOU WANT IT YOU GOT IT Detroit Emeralds	Westbound	1
-	34	24 SYCAMORE Gene Pitney	Pye	1
23	35	DUELLING BANJOS 'Deliverance' Soundtrack	Warner Bros.	7
35	36	WAM BAM Handley Family	GL	4
33	37	HEY MAMA Joe Brown	Ammo	4
-	38	EVERYDAY Don McLean	United Artists	2
38	39	FEEL THE NEED IN ME Detroit Emeralds	Janus	13
-	40	I'VE BEEN DRINKING Jeff Beck and Rod Stewart ●	RAK	1

WEEK ENDING 19 MAY 1973

LW	TW	Title / Artist	Label	Wks
4	1	SEE MY BABY JIVE Wizzard	Harvest	5
2	2	HELL RAISER Sweet	RCA	3
1	3	TIE A YELLOW RIBBON ROUND THE OLD OAK TREE Dawn	Bell	11
3	4	HELLO HELLO I'M BACK AGAIN Gary Glitter	Bell	7
6	5	AND I LOVE YOU SO Perry Como	RCA	4
8	6	DRIVE-IN SATURDAY David Bowie	RCA	6
5	7	GIVING IT ALL AWAY Roger Daltrey	Track	6
7	8	BROTHER LOUIE Hot Chocolate	RAK	6
19	9	ALSO SPRACH ZARATHUSTRA (2001) Deodato	Creed Taylor	2
10	10	NO MORE MR. NICE GUY Alice Cooper	Warner Bros.	5
9	11	MY LOVE Wings	Apple	6
11	12	ALL BECAUSE OF YOU Geordie	EMI	9
13	13	WONDERFUL DREAM Anne-Marie David	Epic	4
24	14	ONE AND ONE IS ONE Medicine Head	Polydor	3
27	15	BROKEN DOWN ANGEL Nazareth	Mooncrest	2
14	16	BIG EIGHT Judge Dread	Big Shot	5
21	17	GOOD GRIEF CHRISTINA Chicory Tip	CBS	7
20	18	COULD IT BE I'M FALLING IN LOVE Detroit Spinners	Atlantic	4
15	19	I'M A CLOWN/SOME KIND OF A SUMMER David Cassidy	Bell	9
16	20	TWEEDLE DEE Little Jimmy Osmond	MGM	8
22	21	MEAN GIRL Status Quo	Pye	4
12	22	GET DOWN Gilbert O'Sullivan	MAM	10
18	23	NEVER NEVER NEVER Shirley Bassey	United Artists	11
32	24	WALK ON THE WILD SIDE Lou Reed	RCA	2
33	25	YOU WANT IT YOU GOT IT Detroit Emeralds	Westbound	2
26	26	THE TWELFTH OF NEVER Donny Osmond	MGM	11
40	27	I'VE BEEN DRINKING Jeff Beck and Rod Stewart	RAK	2
23	28	CRAZY Mud	RAK	10
30	29	AMANDA Stuart Gillies	Philips	7
25	30	PYJAMARAMA Roxy Music	Island	10
-	31	HELP IT ALONG/TOMORROW RISING Cliff Richard	EMI	1
31	32	LETTER TO LUCILLE Tom Jones	Decca	5
17	33	THE RIGHT THING TO DO Carly Simon	Elektra	7
-	34	CAN THE CAN Suzi Quatro ●	RAK	1
-	35	YOU ARE THE SUNSHINE OF MY LIFE Stevie Wonder	Tamla Motown	1
29	36	POWER TO ALL OUR FRIENDS Cliff Richard	EMI	11
28	37	LOVE TRAIN O'Jays	CBS	11
-	38	ALBATROSS Fleetwood Mac	CBS	1
-	39	ARMED AND EXTREMELY DANGEROUS First Choice ●	Bell	1
32	40	CUM ON FEEL THE NOIZE Slade	Polydor	11

WEEK ENDING 26 MAY 1973

LW	TW	Title / Artist	Label	Wks
1	1	SEE MY BABY JIVE Wizzard	Harvest	6
2	2	HELL RAISER Sweet	RCA	4
5	3	AND I LOVE YOU SO Perry Como	RCA	5
3	4	TIE A YELLOW RIBBON ROUND THE OLD OAK TREE Dawn	Bell	12
34	5	CAN THE CAN Suzi Quatro	RAK	2
14	6	ONE AND ONE IS ONE Medicine Head	Polydor	4
9	7	ALSO SPRACH ZARATHUSTRA (2001) Deodato	Creed Taylor	3
4	8	HELLO HELLO I'M BACK AGAIN Gary Glitter	Bell	8
8	9	BROTHER LOUIE Hot Chocolate	RAK	7
7	10	GIVING IT ALL AWAY Roger Daltrey	Track	7
15	11	BROKEN DOWN ANGEL Nazareth	Mooncrest	3
18	12	COULD IT BE I'M FALLING IN LOVE Detroit Spinners	Atlantic	5
13	13	WONDERFUL DREAM Anne-Marie David	Epic	5
11	14	MY LOVE Wings	Apple	7
10	15	NO MORE MR. NICE GUY Alice Cooper	Warner Bros.	6
6	16	DRIVE-IN SATURDAY David Bowie	RCA	7
24	17	WALK ON THE WILD SIDE Lou Reed	RCA	3
35	18	YOU ARE THE SUNSHINE OF MY LIFE Stevie Wonder	Tamla Motown	2
16	19	BIG EIGHT Judge Dread	Big Shot	6
21	20	MEAN GIRL Status Quo	Pye	5
17	21	GOOD GRIEF CHRISTINA Chicory Tip	CBS	8
12	22	ALL BECAUSE OF YOU Geordie	EMI	10
-	23	RUBBER BULLETS 10 C.C.	UK	1
-	24	WALKING IN THE RAIN Partridge Family	Bell	1
25	25	YOU WANT IT YOU GOT IT Detroit Emeralds	Westbound	3
23	26	NEVER NEVER NEVER Shirley Bassey	United Artists	12
20	27	TWEEDLE DEE Little Jimmy Osmond	MGM	9
38	28	ALBATROSS Fleetwood Mac	CBS	2
31	29	HELP IT ALONG/TOMORROW RISING Cliff Richard	EMI	2
27	30	I'VE BEEN DRINKING Jeff Beck and Rod Stewart	RAK	3
22	31	GET DOWN Gilbert O'Sullivan	MAM	11
39	32	ARMED AND EXTREMELY DANGEROUS First Choice	Bell	2
33	33	THE RIGHT THING TO DO Carly Simon	Elektra	8
19	34	I'M A CLOWN/SOME KIND OF A SUMMER David Cassidy	Bell	10
-	35	STUCK IN THE MIDDLE WITH YOU Stealers Wheel ●	AMS	1
-	36	POLK SALAD ANNIE Elvis Presley	RCA	1

In these weeks ■ Three weeks at unlucky 13 for Anne-Marie David, 1973's Eurovision Song Contest winner (26.05.73)■ Deodato's version of the Richard Strauss composition *Also Sprach Zarathustra* becomes one of the biggest classical hits of all time (26.05.73)■

LW	TW	Title	Artist	Label	Wks
-	37	24 SYCAMORE	Gene Pitney	Pye	2
26	38	THE TWELFTH OF NEVER	Donny Osmond	MGM	12
30	39	PYJAMARAMA	Roxy Music	Island	11
-	40	OVER AND OVER	James Boys ●	Penny Farthing	1

WEEK ENDING 2 JUNE 1973

LW	TW	Title	Artist	Label	Wks
1	[1]	SEE MY BABY JIVE	Wizzard	Harvest	7
5	2	CAN THE CAN	Suzi Quatro	RAK	3
3	[3]	AND I LOVE YOU SO	Perry Como	RCA	6
6	4	ONE AND ONE IS ONE	Medicine Head	Polydor	5
2	5	HELL RAISER	Sweet	RCA	5
4	6	TIE A YELLOW RIBBON ROUND THE OLD OAK TREE	Dawn	Bell	13
18	[7]	YOU ARE THE SUNSHINE OF MY LIFE	Stevie Wonder	Tamla Motown	3
7	8	ALSO SPRACH ZARATHUSTRA (2001)	Deodato	Creed Taylor	4
11	[9]	BROKEN DOWN ANGEL	Nazareth	Mooncrest	4
17	[10]	WALK ON THE WILD SIDE	Lou Reed	RCA	4
12	[11]	COULD IT BE I'M FALLING IN LOVE	Detroit Spinners	Atlantic	6
25	[12]	YOU WANT IT YOU GOT IT	Detroit Emeralds	Westbound	4
23	13	RUBBER BULLETS	10 C.C.	UK	2
24	14	WALKING IN THE RAIN	Partridge Family	Bell	2
8	15	HELLO HELLO I'M BACK AGAIN	Gary Glitter	Bell	9
10	16	GIVING IT ALL AWAY	Roger Daltrey	Track	8
28	17	ALBATROSS	Fleetwood Mac	CBS	3
9	18	BROTHER LOUIE	Hot Chocolate	RAK	8
13	19	WONDERFUL DREAM	Anne-Marie David	Epic	6
35	20	STUCK IN THE MIDDLE WITH YOU	Stealers Wheel	AMS	2
16	21	DRIVE-IN SATURDAY	David Bowie	RCA	8
32	22	ARMED AND EXTREMELY DANGEROUS	First Choice	Bell	3
15	23	NO MORE MR. NICE GUY	Alice Cooper	Warner Bros.	7
21	24	GOOD GRIEF CHRISTINA	Chicory Tip	CBS	9
20	25	MEAN GIRL	Status Quo	Pye	6
-	26	WELCOME HOME	Peters & Lee ●	Philips	1
36	27	POLK SALAD ANNIE	Elvis Presley	RCA	2
14	28	MY LOVE	Wings	Apple	8
26	29	NEVER NEVER NEVER	Shirley Bassey	United Artists	13
30	30	I'VE BEEN DRINKING	Jeff Beck and Rod Stewart	RAK	4
-	[31]	NEITHER ONE OF US	Gladys Knight & The Pips	Tamla Motown	1
29	32	HELP IT ALONG/TOMORROW RISING	Cliff Richard	EMI	3
-	33	FRANKENSTEIN	Edgar Winter Group ●	Epic	1
19	34	BIG EIGHT	Judge Dread	Big Shot	7
-	35	SWEET ILLUSION	Junior Campbell	Deram	1
22	36	ALL BECAUSE OF YOU	Geordie	EMI	11
27	37	TWEEDLE DEE	Little Jimmy Osmond	MGM	10
-	38	GIVE ME LOVE (GIVE ME PEACE ON EARTH)	George Harrison	Apple	1
-	39	SNOOPY VERSUS THE RED BARON	Hot Shots ●	Mooncrest	1
31	40	GET DOWN	Gilbert O'Sullivan	MAM	12

June 1973

□ Highest position disc reached ● Act's first ever week on chart

WEEK ENDING 9 JUNE 1973

LW	TW	Title	Artist	Label	Wks
1	[1]	SEE MY BABY JIVE	Wizzard	Harvest	8
2	2	CAN THE CAN	Suzi Quatro	RAK	4
4	[3]	ONE AND ONE IS ONE	Medicine Head	Polydor	6
3	4	AND I LOVE YOU SO	Perry Como	RCA	7
13	5	RUBBER BULLETS	10 C.C.	UK	3
17	6	ALBATROSS	Fleetwood Mac	CBS	4
7	[7]	YOU ARE THE SUNSHINE OF MY LIFE	Stevie Wonder	Tamla Motown	4
5	8	HELL RAISER	Sweet	RCA	6
6	9	TIE A YELLOW RIBBON ROUND THE OLD OAK TREE	Dawn	Bell	14
14	[10]	WALKING IN THE RAIN	Partridge Family	Bell	3
20	11	STUCK IN THE MIDDLE WITH YOU	Stealers Wheel	AMS	3
9	12	BROKEN DOWN ANGEL	Nazareth	Mooncrest	5
10	13	WALK ON THE WILD SIDE	Lou Reed	RCA	5
8	14	ALSO SPRACH ZARATHUSTRA (2001)	Deodato	Creed Taylor	5
12	15	YOU WANT IT YOU GOT IT	Detroit Emeralds	Westbound	5
11	16	COULD IT BE I'M FALLING IN LOVE	Detroit Spinners	Atlantic	7
38	17	GIVE ME LOVE (GIVE ME PEACE ON EARTH)	George Harrison	Apple	2
22	18	ARMED AND EXTREMELY DANGEROUS	First Choice	Bell	4
26	19	WELCOME HOME	Peters & Lee	Philips	2
15	20	HELLO HELLO I'M BACK AGAIN	Gary Glitter	Bell	10
35	21	SWEET ILLUSION	Junior Campbell	Deram	2
33	22	FRANKENSTEIN	Edgar Winter Group	Epic	2
27	[23]	POLK SALAD ANNIE	Elvis Presley	RCA	3
16	24	GIVING IT ALL AWAY	Roger Daltrey	Track	9
39	25	SNOOPY VERSUS THE RED BARON	Hot Shots	Mooncrest	2
19	26	WONDERFUL DREAM	Anne-Marie David	Epic	7
23	27	NO MORE MR. NICE GUY	Alice Cooper	Warner Bros.	8
21	28	DRIVE-IN SATURDAY	David Bowie	RCA	9
25	29	MEAN GIRL	Status Quo	Pye	7
-	30	STANDING ON THE INSIDE	Neil Sedaka	MGM	1
18	31	BROTHER LOUIE	Hot Chocolate	RAK	9
31	32	NEITHER ONE OF US	Gladys Knight & The Pips	Tamla Motown	2
24	33	GOOD GRIEF CHRISTINA	Chicory Tip	CBS	10
29	34	NEVER NEVER NEVER	Shirley Bassey	United Artists	14
28	35	MY LOVE	Wings	Apple	9
-	36	ROCK-A-DOODLE-DOO	Linda Lewis ●	Raft	1
-	37	LIVE AND LET DIE	Wings	Apple	1
30	38	I'VE BEEN DRINKING	Jeff Beck and Rod Stewart	RAK	5
34	39	BIG EIGHT	Judge Dread	Big Shot	8
32	40	HELP IT ALONG/TOMORROW RISING	Cliff Richard	EMI	4

WEEK ENDING 16 JUNE 1973

LW	TW	Title	Artist	Label	Wks
2	[1]	CAN THE CAN	Suzi Quatro	RAK	5
5	2	RUBBER BULLETS	10 C.C.	UK	4
1	3	SEE MY BABY JIVE	Wizzard	Harvest	9
3	4	ONE AND ONE IS ONE	Medicine Head	Polydor	7
6	5	ALBATROSS	Fleetwood Mac	CBS	5
-	6	GROOVER	T. Rex	EMI	1
4	7	AND I LOVE YOU SO	Perry Como	RCA	8
11	[8]	STUCK IN THE MIDDLE WITH YOU	Stealers Wheel	AMS	4
7	9	YOU ARE THE SUNSHINE OF MY LIFE	Stevie Wonder	Tamla Motown	5
10	10	WALKING IN THE RAIN	Partridge Family	Bell	4
17	11	GIVE ME LOVE (GIVE ME PEACE ON EARTH)	George Harrison	Apple	3
25	12	SNOOPY VERSUS THE RED BARON	Hot Shots	Mooncrest	3
13	13	WALK ON THE WILD SIDE	Lou Reed	RCA	6
9	14	TIE A YELLOW RIBBON ROUND THE OLD OAK TREE	Dawn	Bell	15
37	15	LIVE AND LET DIE	Wings	Apple	2
18	[16]	ARMED AND EXTREMELY DANGEROUS	First Choice	Bell	5
12	17	BROKEN DOWN ANGEL	Nazareth	Mooncrest	6
19	18	WELCOME HOME	Peters & Lee	Philips	3
15	19	YOU WANT IT YOU GOT IT	Detroit Emeralds	Westbound	6
21	20	SWEET ILLUSION	Junior Campbell	Deram	3
8	21	HELL RAISER	Sweet	RCA	7
16	22	COULD IT BE I'M FALLING IN LOVE	Detroit Spinners	Atlantic	8
14	23	ALSO SPRACH ZARATHUSTRA (2001)	Deodato	Creed Taylor	6
23	24	POLK SALAD ANNIE	Elvis Presley	RCA	4
22	25	FRANKENSTEIN	Edgar Winter Group	Epic	3
30	[26]	STANDING ON THE INSIDE	Neil Sedaka	MGM	2
-	27	HALLELUJAH DAY	Jackson Five	Tamla Motown	1
-	28	BORN TO BE WITH YOU	Dave Edmunds	Rockfield	1
36	29	ROCK-A-DOODLE-DOO	Linda Lewis	Raft	2
-	30	I'M GONNA LOVE YOU JUST A LITTLE BIT MORE BABY	Barry White ●	Pye	1
-	31	CAN YOU DO IT	Geordie	EMI	1
20	32	HELLO HELLO I'M BACK AGAIN	Gary Glitter	Bell	11
32	33	NEITHER ONE OF US	Gladys Knight & The Pips	Tamla Motown	3
34	34	NEVER NEVER NEVER	Shirley Bassey	United Artists	15

■Perry Como's *And I Love You So* peaks at number 3 over twenty years after his first top ten hit. He is the first person to enjoy a top ten chart career extending over twenty years (02.06.73) ■ Four years after the song had been a top ten hit in America for composer Tony Joe White, Elvis Presley's version of *Polk Salad Annie* stops at number 23 (09.06.73)■

June 1973

☐ Highest position disc reached ● Act's first ever week on chart

LW	TW	Title	Artist	Label	Wks
24	35	GIVING IT ALL AWAY	Roger Daltrey	Track	10
-	36	TAKE ME TO THE MARDI GRAS	Paul Simon	CBS	1
26	37	WONDERFUL DREAM	Anne-Marie David	Epic	8
-	38	HONALOOCHIE BOOGIE	Mott The Hoople	CBS	1
-	[39]	OVER AND OVER	James Boys	Penny Farthing	2
28	40	DRIVE-IN SATURDAY	David Bowie	RCA	10

LW	TW	WEEK ENDING 23 JUNE 1973			Wks
2	[1]	RUBBER BULLETS	10 C.C.	UK	5
5	[2]	ALBATROSS	Fleetwood Mac	CBS	6
1	3	CAN THE CAN	Suzi Quatro	RAK	6
6	[4]	GROOVER	T. Rex	EMI	2
18	5	WELCOME HOME	Peters & Lee	Philips	4
3	6	SEE MY BABY JIVE	Wizzard	Harvest	10
12	7	SNOOPY VERSUS THE RED BARON	Hot Shots	Mooncrest	4
8	8	STUCK IN THE MIDDLE WITH YOU	Stealers Wheel	AMS	5
4	9	ONE AND ONE IS ONE	Medicine Head	Polydor	8
11	10	GIVE ME LOVE (GIVE ME PEACE ON EARTH)	George Harrison	Apple	4
7	11	AND I LOVE YOU SO	Perry Como	RCA	9
10	12	WALKING IN THE RAIN	Partridge Family	Bell	5
14	13	TIE A YELLOW RIBBON ROUND THE OLD OAK TREE	Dawn	Bell	16
15	14	LIVE AND LET DIE	Wings	Apple	3
20	[15]	SWEET ILLUSION	Junior Campbell	Deram	4
16	[16]	ARMED AND EXTREMELY DANGEROUS	First Choice	Bell	6
9	17	YOU ARE THE SUNSHINE OF MY LIFE	Stevie Wonder	Tamla Motown	6
25	[18]	FRANKENSTEIN	Edgar Winter Group	Epic	4
28	19	BORN TO BE WITH YOU	Dave Edmunds	Rockfield	2
31	20	CAN YOU DO IT	Geordie	EMI	2
29	21	ROCK-A-DOODLE-DOO	Linda Lewis	Raft	3
38	22	HONALOOCHIE BOOGIE	Mott The Hoople	CBS	2
30	[23]	I'M GONNA LOVE YOU JUST A LITTLE BIT MORE BABY	Barry White	Pye	2
36	24	TAKE ME TO THE MARDI GRAS	Paul Simon	CBS	2
27	25	HALLELUJAH DAY	Jackson Five	Tamla Motown	2
26	26	STANDING ON THE INSIDE	Neil Sedaka	MGM	3
21	27	HELL RAISER	Sweet	RCA	8
13	28	WALK ON THE WILD SIDE	Lou Reed	RCA	7
17	29	BROKEN DOWN ANGEL	Nazareth	Mooncrest	7
24	30	POLK SALAD ANNIE	Elvis Presley	RCA	5
32	31	HELLO HELLO I'M BACK AGAIN	Gary Glitter	Bell	12
-	32	STEP BY STEP	Joe Simon ●	Mojo	1
23	33	ALSO SPRACH ZARATHUSTRA (2001)	Deodato	Creed Taylor	7
22	34	COULD IT BE I'M FALLING IN LOVE	Detroit Spinners	Atlantic	9
19	35	YOU WANT IT YOU GOT IT	Detroit Emeralds	Westbound	7
-	[36]	GOODBYE IS JUST ANOTHER WORD	New Seekers	Polydor	1
33	37	NEITHER ONE OF US	Gladys Knight & The Pips	Tamla Motown	4
34	38	NEVER NEVER NEVER	Shirley Bassey	United Artists	16
37	39	WONDERFUL DREAM	Anne-Marie David	Epic	9
35	40	GIVING IT ALL AWAY	Roger Daltrey	Track	11

LW	TW	WEEK ENDING 30 JUNE 1973			Wks
-	[1]	SKWEEZE ME PLEEZE ME	Slade	Polydor	1
1	2	RUBBER BULLETS	10 C.C.	UK	6
2	3	ALBATROSS	Fleetwood Mac	CBS	7
5	4	WELCOME HOME	Peters & Lee	Philips	5
4	5	GROOVER	T. Rex	EMI	3
7	6	SNOOPY VERSUS THE RED BARON	Hot Shots	Mooncrest	5
3	7	CAN THE CAN	Suzi Quatro	RAK	7
10	[8]	GIVE ME LOVE (GIVE ME PEACE ON EARTH)	George Harrison	Apple	5
14	[9]	LIVE AND LET DIE	Wings	Apple	4
8	10	STUCK IN THE MIDDLE WITH YOU	Stealers Wheel	AMS	6
19	11	BORN TO BE WITH YOU	Dave Edmunds	Rockfield	3
9	12	ONE AND ONE IS ONE	Medicine Head	Polydor	9
12	13	WALKING IN THE RAIN	Partridge Family	Bell	6
11	14	AND I LOVE YOU SO	Perry Como	RCA	10
6	15	SEE MY BABY JIVE	Wizzard	Harvest	11
13	16	TIE A YELLOW RIBBON ROUND THE OLD OAK TREE	Dawn	Bell	17
24	17	TAKE ME TO THE MARDI GRAS	Paul Simon	CBS	3
20	18	CAN YOU DO IT	Geordie	EMI	3
15	19	SWEET ILLUSION	Junior Campbell	Deram	5
25	[20]	HALLELUJAH DAY	Jackson Five	Tamla Motown	3
-	21	LIFE ON MARS	David Bowie	RCA	1
22	22	HONALOOCHIE BOOGIE	Mott The Hoople	CBS	3
16	23	ARMED AND EXTREMELY DANGEROUS	First Choice	Bell	7
21	24	ROCK-A-DOODLE-DOO	Linda Lewis	Raft	4
23	25	I'M GONNA LOVE YOU JUST A LITTLE BIT MORE BABY	Barry White	Pye	3
26	26	STANDING ON THE INSIDE	Neil Sedaka	MGM	4
17	27	YOU ARE THE SUNSHINE OF MY LIFE	Stevie Wonder	Tamla Motown	7
32	28	STEP BY STEP	Joe Simon	Mojo	2
18	29	FRANKENSTEIN	Edgar Winter Group	Epic	5
28	30	WALK ON THE WILD SIDE	Lou Reed	RCA	8
-	31	RANDY	Blue Mink	EMI	1
-	32	FINDERS KEEPER'S	Chairmen Of The Board	Invictus	1
30	33	POLK SALAD ANNIE	Elvis Presley	RCA	6
29	34	BROKEN DOWN ANGEL	Nazareth	Mooncrest	8
27	35	HELL RAISER	Sweet	RCA	9
36	[36]	GOODBYE IS JUST ANOTHER WORD	New Seekers	Polydor	2
-	37	PILLOW TALK	Sylvia ●	London	1
31	38	HELLO HELLO I'M BACK AGAIN	Gary Glitter	Bell	13
-	39	HYPNOSIS	Mud	RAK	1
37	40	NEITHER ONE OF US	Gladys Knight & The Pips	Tamla Motown	5

LW	TW	WEEK ENDING 7 JULY 1973			Wks
1	[1]	SKWEEZE ME PLEEZE ME	Slade	Polydor	2
4	2	WELCOME HOME	Peters & Lee	Philips	6
2	3	RUBBER BULLETS	10 C.C.	UK	7
21	4	LIFE ON MARS	David Bowie	RCA	2
3	5	ALBATROSS	Fleetwood Mac	CBS	8
6	6	SNOOPY VERSUS THE RED BARON	Hot Shots	Mooncrest	6
11	7	BORN TO BE WITH YOU	Dave Edmunds	Rockfield	4
5	8	GROOVER	T. Rex	EMI	4
17	9	TAKE ME TO THE MARDI GRAS	Paul Simon	CBS	4
8	10	GIVE ME LOVE (GIVE ME PEACE ON EARTH)	George Harrison	Apple	6
9	11	LIVE AND LET DIE	Wings	Apple	5
10	12	STUCK IN THE MIDDLE WITH YOU	Stealers Wheel	AMS	7
18	[13]	CAN YOU DO IT	Geordie	EMI	4
22	14	HONALOOCHIE BOOGIE	Mott The Hoople	CBS	4
24	[15]	ROCK-A-DOODLE-DOO	Linda Lewis	Raft	5
16	16	TIE A YELLOW RIBBON ROUND THE OLD OAK TREE	Dawn	Bell	18
14	17	AND I LOVE YOU SO	Perry Como	RCA	11
19	18	SWEET ILLUSION	Junior Campbell	Deram	6
7	19	CAN THE CAN	Suzi Quatro	RAK	8
20	[20]	HALLELUJAH DAY	Jackson Five	Tamla Motown	4
12	21	ONE AND ONE IS ONE	Medicine Head	Polydor	10
13	22	WALKING IN THE RAIN	Partridge Family	Bell	7
31	23	RANDY	Blue Mink	EMI	2
32	24	FINDERS KEEPER'S	Chairmen Of The Board	Invictus	2
25	25	I'M GONNA LOVE YOU JUST A LITTLE BIT MORE BABY	Barry White	Pye	4
15	26	SEE MY BABY JIVE	Wizzard	Harvest	12
28	27	STEP BY STEP	Joe Simon	Mojo	3
26	28	STANDING ON THE INSIDE	Neil Sedaka	MGM	5
27	29	YOU ARE THE SUNSHINE OF MY LIFE	Stevie Wonder	Tamla Motown	8
37	30	PILLOW TALK	Sylvia	London	2
29	31	FRANKENSTEIN	Edgar Winter Group	Epic	6
-	32	GAYE	Clifford T. Ward ●	Charisma	1
23	33	ARMED AND EXTREMELY DANGEROUS	First Choice	Bell	8

In these weeks ■ Albatross climbs to number two, to that time the most successful reissue of a former number one hit (23.06.73) ■ *Skweeze Me Pleeze Me* is Slade's second consecutive single to enter the charts at no. 1. This achievement remains unequalled (30.06.73) ■ The top four singles are all past, present or future number one hits (30.06.73)■

July 1973

□ Highest position disc reached ● Act's first ever week on chart

LW	TW	Title	Artist	Label	Wks
39	34	HYPNOSIS	Mud	RAK	2
-	35	WAY BACK HOME	Jnr. Walker & The All Stars	Tamla Motown	1
-	36	SATURDAY NIGHT'S ALRIGHT FOR FIGHTING	Elton John	DJM	1
-	37	PEEK-A-BOO	Stylistics	Avco	1
-	38	GIVE IT TO ME NOW	Kenny	RAK	1
34	39	BROKEN DOWN ANGEL	Nazareth	Mooncrest	9
-	40	FREE ELECTRIC BAND	Albert Hammond ●	MUMS	1

WEEK ENDING 14 JULY 1973

LW	TW	Title	Artist	Label	Wks
1	1	SKWEEZE ME PLEEZE ME	Slade	Polydor	3
2	2	WELCOME HOME	Peters & Lee	Philips	7
4	3	LIFE ON MARS	David Bowie	RCA	3
6	4	SNOOPY VERSUS THE RED BARON	Hot Shots	Mooncrest	7
7	5	BORN TO BE WITH YOU	Dave Edmunds	Rockfield	5
3	6	RUBBER BULLETS	10 C.C.	UK	8
9	7	TAKE ME TO THE MARDI GRAS	Paul Simon	CBS	5
5	8	ALBATROSS	Fleetwood Mac	CBS	9
36	9	SATURDAY NIGHT'S ALRIGHT FOR FIGHTING	Elton John	DJM	2
10	10	GIVE ME LOVE (GIVE ME PEACE ON EARTH)	George Harrison	Apple	7
11	11	LIVE AND LET DIE	Wings	Apple	6
14	12	HONALOOCHIE BOOGIE	Mott The Hoople	CBS	5
23	13	RANDY	Blue Mink	EMI	3
27	14	STEP BY STEP	Joe Simon	Mojo	4
13	15	CAN YOU DO IT	Geordie	EMI	5
17	16	AND I LOVE YOU SO	Perry Como	RCA	12
15	17	ROCK-A-DOODLE-DOO	Linda Lewis	Raft	6
-	18	GOING HOME	Osmonds	MGM	1
8	19	GROOVER	T. Rex	EMI	5
16	20	TIE A YELLOW RIBBON ROUND THE OLD OAK TREE	Dawn	Bell	19
20	21	HALLELUJAH DAY	Jackson Five	Tamla Motown	5
30	22	PILLOW TALK	Sylvia	London	3
-	23	ALRIGHT ALRIGHT ALRIGHT	Mungo Jerry	Dawn	1
32	24	GAYE	Clifford T. Ward	Charisma	2
24	25	FINDERS KEEPER'S	Chairmen Of The Board	Invictus	3
12	26	STUCK IN THE MIDDLE WITH YOU	Stealers Wheel	AMS	8
19	27	CAN THE CAN	Suzi Quatro	RAK	9
22	28	WALKING IN THE RAIN	Partridge Family	Bell	8
28	29	STANDING ON THE INSIDE	Neil Sedaka	MGM	6
34	30	HYPNOSIS	Mud	RAK	3
40	31	FREE ELECTRIC BAND	Albert Hammond	MUMS	2
18	32	SWEET ILLUSION	Junior Campbell	Deram	7
21	33	ONE AND ONE IS ONE	Medicine Head	Polydor	11
-	34	YESTERDAY ONCE MORE	Carpenters	A&M	1
25	35	I'M GONNA LOVE YOU JUST A LITTLE BIT MORE BABY	Barry White	Pye	5
-	36	I SAW THE LIGHT	Todd Rundgren ●	Bearsville	1
26	37	SEE MY BABY JIVE	Wizzard	Harvest	13
37	38	PEEK-A-BOO	Stylistics	Avco	2
35	39	WAY BACK HOME	Jnr. Walker & The All Stars	Tamla Motown	2
29	40	YOU ARE THE SUNSHINE OF MY LIFE	Stevie Wonder	Tamla Motown	9

WEEK ENDING 21 JULY 1973

LW	TW	Title	Artist	Label	Wks
2	1	WELCOME HOME	Peters & Lee	Philips	8
-	2	I'M THE LEADER OF THE GANG (I AM)	Gary Glitter	Bell	1
3	3	LIFE ON MARS	David Bowie	RCA	4
1	4	SKWEEZE ME PLEEZE ME	Slade	Polydor	4
23	5	ALRIGHT ALRIGHT ALRIGHT	Mungo Jerry	Dawn	2
18	6	GOING HOME	Osmonds	MGM	2
9	7	SATURDAY NIGHT'S ALRIGHT FOR FIGHTING	Elton John	DJM	3
5	8	BORN TO BE WITH YOU	Dave Edmunds	Rockfield	6
7	9	TAKE ME TO THE MARDI GRAS	Paul Simon	CBS	6
4	10	SNOOPY VERSUS THE RED BARON	Hot Shots	Mooncrest	8
13	11	RANDY	Blue Mink	EMI	4
24	12	GAYE	Clifford T. Ward	Charisma	3
6	13	RUBBER BULLETS	10 C.C.	UK	9
8	14	ALBATROSS	Fleetwood Mac	CBS	10
22	15	PILLOW TALK	Sylvia	London	4
11	16	LIVE AND LET DIE	Wings	Apple	7
17	17	ROCK-A-DOODLE-DOO	Linda Lewis	Raft	7
14	18	STEP BY STEP	Joe Simon	Mojo	5
12	19	HONALOOCHIE BOOGIE	Mott The Hoople	CBS	6
16	20	AND I LOVE YOU SO	Perry Como	RCA	13
25	21	FINDERS KEEPER'S	Chairmen Of The Board	Invictus	4
20	22	TIE A YELLOW RIBBON ROUND THE OLD OAK TREE	Dawn	Bell	20
10	23	GIVE ME LOVE (GIVE ME PEACE ON EARTH)	George Harrison	Apple	8
15	24	CAN YOU DO IT	Geordie	EMI	6
30	25	HYPNOSIS	Mud	RAK	4
34	26	YESTERDAY ONCE MORE	Carpenters	A&M	2
-	27	TOUCH ME IN THE MORNING	Diana Ross	Tamla Motown	1
31	28	FREE ELECTRIC BAND	Albert Hammond	MUMS	3
19	29	GROOVER	T. Rex	EMI	6
21	30	HALLELUJAH DAY	Jackson Five	Tamla Motown	6
-	31	SPANISH EYES	Al Martino	Capitol	1
26	32	STUCK IN THE MIDDLE WITH YOU	Stealers Wheel	AMS	9
27	33	CAN THE CAN	Suzi Quatro	RAK	10
-	34	BAD BAD BOY	Nazareth	Mooncrest	1
38	35	PEEK-A-BOO	Stylistics	Avco	3
28	36	WALKING IN THE RAIN	Partridge Family	Bell	9
36	37	I SAW THE LIGHT	Todd Rundgren	Bearsville	2
32	38	SWEET ILLUSION	Junior Campbell	Deram	8
35	39	I'M GONNA LOVE YOU JUST A LITTLE BIT MORE BABY	Barry White	Pye	6
-	40	ALL RIGHT NOW	Free	Island	1

WEEK ENDING 28 JULY 1973

LW	TW	Title	Artist	Label	Wks
2	1	I'M THE LEADER OF THE GANG (I AM)	Gary Glitter	Bell	2
1	2	WELCOME HOME	Peters & Lee	Philips	9
3	3	LIFE ON MARS	David Bowie	RCA	5
5	4	ALRIGHT ALRIGHT ALRIGHT	Mungo Jerry	Dawn	3
6	5	GOING HOME	Osmonds	MGM	3
4	6	SKWEEZE ME PLEEZE ME	Slade	Polydor	5
7	7	SATURDAY NIGHT'S ALRIGHT FOR FIGHTING	Elton John	DJM	4
12	8	GAYE	Clifford T. Ward	Charisma	4
11	9	RANDY	Blue Mink	EMI	5
8	10	BORN TO BE WITH YOU	Dave Edmunds	Rockfield	7
9	11	TAKE ME TO THE MARDI GRAS	Paul Simon	CBS	7
26	12	YESTERDAY ONCE MORE	Carpenters	A&M	3
10	13	SNOOPY VERSUS THE RED BARON	Hot Shots	Mooncrest	9
15	14	PILLOW TALK	Sylvia	London	5
27	15	TOUCH ME IN THE MORNING	Diana Ross	Tamla Motown	2
31	16	SPANISH EYES	Al Martino	Capitol	2
18	17	STEP BY STEP	Joe Simon	Mojo	6
34	18	BAD BAD BOY	Nazareth	Mooncrest	2
13	19	RUBBER BULLETS	10 C.C.	UK	10
16	20	LIVE AND LET DIE	Wings	Apple	8
25	21	HYPNOSIS	Mud	RAK	5
22	22	TIE A YELLOW RIBBON ROUND THE OLD OAK TREE	Dawn	Bell	21
14	23	ALBATROSS	Fleetwood Mac	CBS	11
20	24	AND I LOVE YOU SO	Perry Como	RCA	14
-	25	YING TONG SONG	The Goons	Decca	1
19	26	HONALOOCHIE BOOGIE	Mott The Hoople	CBS	7
28	27	FREE ELECTRIC BAND	Albert Hammond	MUMS	4
-	28	48 CRASH	Suzi Quatro	RAK	1
40	29	ALL RIGHT NOW	Free	Island	2
21	30	FINDERS KEEPER'S	Chairmen Of The Board	Invictus	5
17	31	ROCK-A-DOODLE-DOO	Linda Lewis	Raft	8
23	32	GIVE ME LOVE (GIVE ME PEACE ON EARTH)	George Harrison	Apple	9
-	33	YOU CAN DO MAGIC	Limmie & The Family Cookin' ●	Avco	1

■Life was difficult for radio DJs, having to play top ten hits titled *Gaye* and *Randy* not to mention *Pillow Talk* (28.07.73) ■ Free's *All Right Now* returns for the first time. It will also chart in 1978, 1982 and 1991 (21.07.73)■

July 1973

☐ Highest position disc reached ● Act's first ever week on chart

LW	TW	Title / Artist	Label	Wks
24	34	CAN YOU DO IT Geordie	*EMI*	7
29	35	GROOVER T. Rex	*EMI*	7
37	36	I SAW THE LIGHT Todd Rundgren	*Bearsville*	3
30	37	HALLELUJAH DAY Jackson Five	*Tamla Motown*	7
32	38	STUCK IN THE MIDDLE WITH YOU Stealers Wheel	*AMS*	10
-	39	I'M DOIN' FINE NOW New York City ●	*RCA*	1
33	40	CAN THE CAN Suzi Quatro	*RAK*	11

WEEK ENDING 4 AUGUST 1973

LW	TW	Title / Artist	Label	Wks
1	[1]	I'M THE LEADER OF THE GANG (I AM) Gary Glitter	*Bell*	3
2	2	WELCOME HOME Peters & Lee	*Philips*	10
4	3	ALRIGHT ALRIGHT ALRIGHT Mungo Jerry	*Dawn*	4
5	[4]	GOING HOME Osmonds	*MGM*	4
3	5	LIFE ON MARS David Bowie	*RCA*	6
28	6	48 CRASH Suzi Quatro	*RAK*	2
12	7	YESTERDAY ONCE MORE Carpenters	*A&M*	4
16	8	SPANISH EYES Al Martino	*Capitol*	3
15	[9]	TOUCH ME IN THE MORNING Diana Ross	*Tamla Motown*	3
9	10	RANDY Blue Mink	*EMI*	6
18	11	BAD BAD BOY Nazareth	*Mooncrest*	3
8	12	GAYE Clifford T. Ward	*Charisma*	5
25	13	YING TONG SONG The Goons	*Decca*	2
7	14	SATURDAY NIGHT'S ALRIGHT FOR FIGHTING Elton John	*DJM*	5
6	15	SKWEEZE ME PLEEZE ME Slade	*Polydor*	6
14	16	PILLOW TALK Sylvia	*London*	6
21	17	HYPNOSIS Mud	*RAK*	6
33	18	YOU CAN DO MAGIC Limmie & The Family Cookin'	*Avco*	2
10	19	BORN TO BE WITH YOU Dave Edmunds	*Rockfield*	8
13	20	SNOOPY VERSUS THE RED BARON Hot Shots	*Mooncrest*	10
29	21	ALL RIGHT NOW Free	*Island*	3
11	22	TAKE ME TO THE MARDI GRAS Paul Simon	*CBS*	8
27	23	FREE ELECTRIC BAND Albert Hammond	*MUMS*	5
19	24	RUBBER BULLETS 10 C.C.	*UK*	11
17	25	STEP BY STEP Joe Simon	*Mojo*	7
23	26	ALBATROSS Fleetwood Mac	*CBS*	12
24	27	AND I LOVE YOU SO Perry Como	*RCA*	15
30	28	FINDERS KEEPER'S Chairmen Of The Board	*Invictus*	6
20	29	LIVE AND LET DIE Wings	*Apple*	9
22	30	TIE A YELLOW RIBBON ROUND THE OLD OAK TREE Dawn	*Bell*	22
39	31	I'M DOIN' FINE NOW New York City	*RCA*	2
-	32	SUMMER (THE FIRST TIME) Bobby Goldsboro	*United Artists*	1
26	33	HONALOOCHIE BOOGIE Mott The Hoople	*CBS*	8
-	34	DANCING ON A SATURDAY NIGHT Barry Blue ●	*Bell*	1
31	35	ROCK-A-DOODLE-DOO Linda Lewis	*Raft*	9
-	36	RISING SUN Medicine Head	*Polydor*	1
-	37	SMARTY PANTS First Choice	*Bell*	1
-	38	PEEK-A-BOO Stylistics	*Avco*	4
-	39	SEE MY BABY JIVE Wizzard	*Harvest*	14
36	40	I SAW THE LIGHT Todd Rundgren	*Bearsville*	4

WEEK ENDING 11 AUGUST 1973

LW	TW	Title / Artist	Label	Wks
1	[1]	I'M THE LEADER OF THE GANG (I AM) Gary Glitter	*Bell*	4
2	2	WELCOME HOME Peters & Lee	*Philips*	11
3	3	ALRIGHT ALRIGHT ALRIGHT Mungo Jerry	*Dawn*	5
6	4	48 CRASH Suzi Quatro	*RAK*	3
7	5	YESTERDAY ONCE MORE Carpenters	*A&M*	5
4	6	GOING HOME Osmonds	*MGM*	5
5	7	LIFE ON MARS David Bowie	*RCA*	7
8	8	SPANISH EYES Al Martino	*Capitol*	4
13	[9]	YING TONG SONG The Goons	*Decca*	3
11	[10]	BAD BAD BOY Nazareth	*Mooncrest*	4
9	11	TOUCH ME IN THE MORNING Diana Ross	*Tamla Motown*	4
18	12	YOU CAN DO MAGIC Limmie & The Family Cookin'	*Avco*	3
12	13	GAYE Clifford T. Ward	*Charisma*	6
10	14	RANDY Blue Mink	*EMI*	7
21	15	ALL RIGHT NOW Free	*Island*	4
17	[16]	HYPNOSIS Mud	*RAK*	7
16	17	PILLOW TALK Sylvia	*London*	7
34	18	DANCING ON A SATURDAY NIGHT Barry Blue	*Bell*	2
23	[19]	FREE ELECTRIC BAND Albert Hammond	*MUMS*	6
14	20	SATURDAY NIGHT'S ALRIGHT FOR FIGHTING Elton John	*DJM*	6
15	21	SKWEEZE ME PLEEZE ME Slade	*Polydor*	7
36	22	RISING SUN Medicine Head	*Polydor*	2
19	23	BORN TO BE WITH YOU Dave Edmunds	*Rockfield*	9
37	24	SMARTY PANTS First Choice	*Bell*	2
31	25	I'M DOIN' FINE NOW New York City	*RCA*	3
32	26	SUMMER (THE FIRST TIME) Bobby Goldsboro	*United Artists*	2
20	27	SNOOPY VERSUS THE RED BARON Hot Shots	*Mooncrest*	11
-	28	LIKE SISTER AND BROTHER Drifters	*Bell*	1
-	29	SAY, HAS ANYBODY SEEN MY SWEET GYPSY ROSE Dawn	*Bell*	1
25	30	STEP BY STEP Joe Simon	*Mojo*	8
22	31	TAKE ME TO THE MARDI GRAS Paul Simon	*CBS*	9
-	32	FOOL Elvis Presley	*RCA*	1
27	33	AND I LOVE YOU SO Perry Como	*RCA*	16
-	34	I'M FREE Roger Daltrey/LSO and Chamber Choir	*Ode*	1
29	35	LIVE AND LET DIE Wings	*Apple*	10
26	36	ALBATROSS Fleetwood Mac	*CBS*	13
24	37	RUBBER BULLETS 10 C.C.	*UK*	12
28	38	FINDERS KEEPER'S Chairmen Of The Board	*Invictus*	7
30	39	TIE A YELLOW RIBBON ROUND THE OLD OAK TREE Dawn	*Bell*	23
-	40	BAND PLAYED THE BOOGIE C.C.S.	*RAK*	1

WEEK ENDING 18 AUGUST 1973

LW	TW	Title / Artist	Label	Wks
1	[1]	I'M THE LEADER OF THE GANG (I AM) Gary Glitter	*Bell*	5
5	[2]	YESTERDAY ONCE MORE Carpenters	*A&M*	6
4	[3]	48 CRASH Suzi Quatro	*RAK*	4
2	4	WELCOME HOME Peters & Lee	*Philips*	12
8	[5]	SPANISH EYES Al Martino	*Capitol*	5
3	6	ALRIGHT ALRIGHT ALRIGHT Mungo Jerry	*Dawn*	6
12	7	YOU CAN DO MAGIC Limmie & The Family Cookin'	*Avco*	4
18	8	DANCING ON A SATURDAY NIGHT Barry Blue	*Bell*	3
9	[9]	YING TONG SONG The Goons	*Decca*	4
6	10	GOING HOME Osmonds	*MGM*	6
11	11	TOUCH ME IN THE MORNING Diana Ross	*Tamla Motown*	5
10	12	BAD BAD BOY Nazareth	*Mooncrest*	5
7	13	LIFE ON MARS David Bowie	*RCA*	8
24	14	SMARTY PANTS First Choice	*Bell*	3
15	15	ALL RIGHT NOW Free	*Island*	5
-	16	YOUNG LOVE Donny Osmond	*MGM*	1
26	17	SUMMER (THE FIRST TIME) Bobby Goldsboro	*United Artists*	3
22	18	RISING SUN Medicine Head	*Polydor*	3
28	19	LIKE SISTER AND BROTHER Drifters	*Bell*	2
13	20	GAYE Clifford T. Ward	*Charisma*	7
16	21	HYPNOSIS Mud	*RAK*	8
14	22	RANDY Blue Mink	*EMI*	8
25	23	I'M DOIN' FINE NOW New York City	*RCA*	4
34	24	I'M FREE Roger Daltrey/LSO and Chamber Choir	*Ode*	2
29	25	SAY, HAS ANYBODY SEEN MY SWEET GYPSY ROSE Dawn	*Bell*	2
17	26	PILLOW TALK Sylvia	*London*	8
19	27	FREE ELECTRIC BAND Albert Hammond	*MUMS*	7
32	28	FOOL Elvis Presley	*RCA*	2
39	29	TIE A YELLOW RIBBON ROUND THE OLD OAK TREE Dawn	*Bell*	24
20	30	SATURDAY NIGHT'S ALRIGHT FOR FIGHTING Elton John	*DJM*	7
33	31	AND I LOVE YOU SO Perry Como	*RCA*	17
21	32	SKWEEZE ME PLEEZE ME Slade	*Polydor*	8
23	33	BORN TO BE WITH YOU Dave Edmunds	*Rockfield*	10
27	34	SNOOPY VERSUS THE RED BARON Hot Shots	*Mooncrest*	12
-	35	I THINK OF YOU Detroit Emeralds	*Westbound*	1
40	[36]	BAND PLAYED THE BOOGIE C.C.S.	*RAK*	2
31	37	TAKE ME TO THE MARDI GRAS Paul Simon	*CBS*	10
-	38	DEAR ELAINE Roy Wood ●	*Harvest*	1

In these weeks ■ Al Martino's *Spanish Eyes* hits the Top Ten 18 years and 293 days after his previous Top Ten hit *The Story Of Tina*. This was a record at the time for the longest gap between Top 10 hits ■ The Goons' *Ying Tong Song* returns to the Top Ten almost seventeen years after it was first a smash. At this time, it was the biggest gap between an original and re-issued top ten hit (11.08.73)■

LW	TW	Title	Artist	Label	Wks
30	39	STEP BY STEP	Joe Simon	*Mojo*	9
35	40	LIVE AND LET DIE	Wings	*Apple*	11

WEEK ENDING 25 AUGUST 1973

LW	TW	Title	Artist	Label	Wks
16	1	YOUNG LOVE	Donny Osmond	*MGM*	2
2	2	YESTERDAY ONCE MORE	Carpenters	*A&M*	7
1	3	I'M THE LEADER OF THE GANG (I AM)	Gary Glitter	*Bell*	6
8	4	DANCING ON A SATURDAY NIGHT	Barry Blue	*Bell*	4
7	5	YOU CAN DO MAGIC	Limmie & The Family Cookin'	*Avco*	5
5	6	SPANISH EYES	Al Martino	*Capitol*	6
3	7	48 CRASH	Suzi Quatro	*RAK*	5
4	8	WELCOME HOME	Peters & Lee	*Philips*	13
14	9	SMARTY PANTS	First Choice	*Bell*	4
6	10	ALRIGHT ALRIGHT ALRIGHT	Mungo Jerry	*Dawn*	7
18	11	RISING SUN	Medicine Head	*Polydor*	4
17	12	SUMMER (THE FIRST TIME)	Bobby Goldsboro	*United Artists*	4
19	13	LIKE SISTER AND BROTHER	Drifters	*Bell*	3
11	14	TOUCH ME IN THE MORNING	Diana Ross	*Tamla Motown*	6
9	15	YING TONG SONG	The Goons	*Decca*	5
24	16	I'M FREE	Roger Daltrey/LSO and Chamber Choir	*Ode*	3
12	17	BAD BAD BOY	Nazareth	*Mooncrest*	6
15	18	ALL RIGHT NOW	Free	*Island*	6
13	19	LIFE ON MARS	David Bowie	*RCA*	9
23	20	I'M DOIN' FINE NOW	New York City	*RCA*	5
10	21	GOING HOME	Osmonds	*MGM*	7
28	22	FOOL	Elvis Presley	*RCA*	3
25	23	SAY, HAS ANYBODY SEEN MY SWEET GYPSY ROSE	Dawn	*Bell*	3
21	24	HYPNOSIS	Mud	*RAK*	9
38	25	DEAR ELAINE	Roy Wood	*Harvest*	2
27	26	FREE ELECTRIC BAND	Albert Hammond	*MUMS*	8
20	27	GAYE	Clifford T. Ward	*Charisma*	8
29	28	TIE A YELLOW RIBBON ROUND THE OLD OAK TREE	Dawn	*Bell*	25
22	29	RANDY	Blue Mink	*EMI*	9
-	30	PICK UP THE PIECES	Hudson Ford ●	*A&M*	1
-	31	ROCK ON	David Essex ●	*CBS*	1
-	32	THE DEAN AND I	10 C.C.	*UK*	1
35	33	I THINK OF YOU	Detroit Emeralds	*Westbound*	2
31	34	AND I LOVE YOU SO	Perry Como	*RCA*	18
-	35	ELECTRIC LADY	Geordie	*EMI*	1
36	36	BAND PLAYED THE BOOGIE	C.C.S.	*RAK*	3
30	37	SATURDAY NIGHT'S ALRIGHT FOR FIGHTING	Elton John	*DJM*	8
-	38	I'VE BEEN HURT	Guy Darrell ●	*Santa Ponsa*	1
-	39	URBAN GUERILLA	Hawkwind	*United Artists*	1
32	40	SKWEEZE ME PLEEZE ME	Slade	*Polydor*	9

September 1973

□ Highest position disc reached ● Act's first ever week on chart

WEEK ENDING 1 SEPTEMBER 1973

LW	TW	Title	Artist	Label	Wks
1	1	YOUNG LOVE	Donny Osmond	*MGM*	3
4	2	DANCING ON A SATURDAY NIGHT	Barry Blue	*Bell*	5
5	3	YOU CAN DO MAGIC	Limmie & The Family Cookin'	*Avco*	6
2	4	YESTERDAY ONCE MORE	Carpenters	*A&M*	8
6	5	SPANISH EYES	Al Martino	*Capitol*	7
3	6	I'M THE LEADER OF THE GANG (I AM)	Gary Glitter	*Bell*	7
13	7	LIKE SISTER AND BROTHER	Drifters	*Bell*	4
8	8	WELCOME HOME	Peters & Lee	*Philips*	14
12	9	SUMMER (THE FIRST TIME)	Bobby Goldsboro	*United Artists*	5
9	10	SMARTY PANTS	First Choice	*Bell*	5
11	11	RISING SUN	Medicine Head	*Polydor*	5
-	12	ANGEL FINGERS	Wizzard	*Harvest*	1
23	13	SAY, HAS ANYBODY SEEN MY SWEET GYPSY ROSE	Dawn	*Bell*	4
7	14	48 CRASH	Suzi Quatro	*RAK*	6
16	15	I'M FREE	Roger Daltrey/LSO and Chamber Choir	*Ode*	4
31	16	ROCK ON	David Essex	*CBS*	2
30	17	PICK UP THE PIECES	Hudson Ford	*A&M*	2
22	18	FOOL	Elvis Presley	*RCA*	4
14	19	TOUCH ME IN THE MORNING	Diana Ross	*Tamla Motown*	7
20	20	I'M DOIN' FINE NOW	New York City	*RCA*	6
15	21	YING TONG SONG	The Goons	*Decca*	6
18	22	ALL RIGHT NOW	Free	*Island*	7
32	23	THE DEAN AND I	10 C.C.	*UK*	2
17	24	BAD BAD BOY	Nazareth	*Mooncrest*	7
19	25	LIFE ON MARS	David Bowie	*RCA*	10
10	26	ALRIGHT ALRIGHT ALRIGHT	Mungo Jerry	*Dawn*	8
-	27	ANGIE	Rolling Stones	*Rolling Stones*	1
25	28	DEAR ELAINE	Roy Wood	*Harvest*	3
21	29	GOING HOME	Osmonds	*MGM*	8
33	30	I THINK OF YOU	Detroit Emeralds	*Westbound*	3
24	31	HYPNOSIS	Mud	*RAK*	10
28	32	TIE A YELLOW RIBBON ROUND THE OLD OAK TREE	Dawn	*Bell*	26
38	33	I'VE BEEN HURT	Guy Darrell	*Santa Ponsa*	2
35	34	ELECTRIC LADY	Geordie	*EMI*	2
26	35	FREE ELECTRIC BAND	Albert Hammond	*MUMS*	9
-	36	FOR THE GOOD TIMES	Perry Como	*RCA*	1
27	37	GAYE	Clifford T. Ward	*Charisma*	9
36	38	BAND PLAYED THE BOOGIE	C.C.S.	*RAK*	4
29	39	RANDY	Blue Mink	*EMI*	10
-	40	NATURAL HIGH	Bloodstone ●	*Decca*	1

WEEK ENDING 8 SEPTEMBER 1973

LW	TW	Title	Artist	Label	Wks
1	1	YOUNG LOVE	Donny Osmond	*MGM*	4
2	2	DANCING ON A SATURDAY NIGHT	Barry Blue	*Bell*	6
12	3	ANGEL FINGERS	Wizzard	*Harvest*	2
4	4	YESTERDAY ONCE MORE	Carpenters	*A&M*	9
5	5	SPANISH EYES	Al Martino	*Capitol*	8
16	6	ROCK ON	David Essex	*CBS*	3
3	7	YOU CAN DO MAGIC	Limmie & The Family Cookin'	*Avco*	7
7	8	LIKE SISTER AND BROTHER	Drifters	*Bell*	5
27	9	ANGIE	Rolling Stones	*Rolling Stones*	2
17	10	PICK UP THE PIECES	Hudson Ford	*A&M*	3
9	11	SUMMER (THE FIRST TIME)	Bobby Goldsboro	*United Artists*	6
13	12	SAY, HAS ANYBODY SEEN MY SWEET GYPSY ROSE	Dawn	*Bell*	5
11	13	RISING SUN	Medicine Head	*Polydor*	6
23	14	THE DEAN AND I	10 C.C.	*UK*	3
8	15	WELCOME HOME	Peters & Lee	*Philips*	15
10	16	SMARTY PANTS	First Choice	*Bell*	6
6	17	I'M THE LEADER OF THE GANG (I AM)	Gary Glitter	*Bell*	8
28	18	DEAR ELAINE	Roy Wood	*Harvest*	4
18	19	FOOL	Elvis Presley	*RCA*	5
15	20	I'M FREE	Roger Daltrey/LSO and Chamber Choir	*Ode*	5
20	21	I'M DOIN' FINE NOW	New York City	*RCA*	7
-	22	OH NO NOT MY BABY	Rod Stewart	*Mercury*	1
14	23	48 CRASH	Suzi Quatro	*RAK*	7
33	24	I'VE BEEN HURT	Guy Darrell	*Santa Ponsa*	3
19	25	TOUCH ME IN THE MORNING	Diana Ross	*Tamla Motown*	8
36	26	FOR THE GOOD TIMES	Perry Como	*RCA*	2
30	27	I THINK OF YOU	Detroit Emeralds	*Westbound*	4
26	28	ALRIGHT ALRIGHT ALRIGHT	Mungo Jerry	*Dawn*	9
25	29	LIFE ON MARS	David Bowie	*RCA*	11
-	30	MONSTER MASH	Bobby Pickett & The Crypt Kickers ●	*London*	1
-	31	OUR LAST SONG TOGETHER	Neil Sedaka	*MGM*	1
34	32	ELECTRIC LADY	Geordie	*EMI*	3
21	33	YING TONG SONG	The Goons	*Decca*	7
-	34	EVERYTHING WILL TURN OUT FINE	Stealers Wheel	*A&M*	1
24	35	BAD BAD BOY	Nazareth	*Mooncrest*	8
29	36	GOING HOME	Osmonds	*MGM*	9
22	37	ALL RIGHT NOW	Free	*Island*	8
-	38	SKYWRITER	Jackson Five	*Tamla Motown*	1
-	39	JOYBRINGER	Manfred Mann's Earthband ●	*Vertigo*	1
-	40	ALL THE WAY FROM MEMPHIS	Mott The Hoople	*CBS*	1

WEEK ENDING 15 SEPTEMBER 1973

LW	TW	Title	Artist	Label	Wks
1	1	YOUNG LOVE	Donny Osmond	*MGM*	5
3	2	ANGEL FINGERS	Wizzard	*Harvest*	3
6	3	ROCK ON	David Essex	*CBS*	4

■Donny Osmond's jump from 16 to 1 is the third time a disc has made that particular leap, but only 4 records had then climbed from a lower position to the top (25.08.73) ■ An American number one in 1962, Bobby 'Boris' Pickett's horror hit *Monster Mash* finally cracks the UK charts (05.09.73)■

September 1973

□ Highest position disc reached ● Act's first ever week on chart

LW	TW	Title	Artist	Label	Wks
2	4	DANCING ON A SATURDAY NIGHT	Barry Blue	*Bell*	7
9	5	ANGIE	Rolling Stones	*Rolling Stones*	3
5	6	SPANISH EYES	Al Martino	*Capitol*	9
22	7	OH NO NOT MY BABY	Rod Stewart	*Mercury*	2
10	[8]	PICK UP THE PIECES	Hudson Ford	*A&M*	4
7	9	YOU CAN DO MAGIC	Limmie & The Family Cookin'	*Avco*	8
14	[10]	THE DEAN AND I	10 C.C.	*UK*	4
8	11	LIKE SISTER AND BROTHER	Drifters	*Bell*	6
12	[12]	SAY, HAS ANYBODY SEEN MY SWEET GYPSY ROSE	Dawn	*Bell*	6
20	[13]	I'M FREE	Roger Daltrey/LSO and Chamber Choir	*Ode*	6
11	14	SUMMER (THE FIRST TIME)	Bobby Goldsboro	*United Artists*	7
19	[15]	FOOL	Elvis Presley	*RCA*	6
4	16	YESTERDAY ONCE MORE	Carpenters	*A&M*	10
15	17	WELCOME HOME	Peters & Lee	*Philips*	16
24	18	I'VE BEEN HURT	Guy Darrell	*Santa Ponsa*	4
16	19	SMARTY PANTS	First Choice	*Bell*	7
13	20	RISING SUN	Medicine Head	*Polydor*	7
30	21	MONSTER MASH	Bobby Pickett & The Crypt Kickers	*London*	2
18	22	DEAR ELAINE	Roy Wood	*Harvest*	5
40	23	ALL THE WAY FROM MEMPHIS	Mott The Hoople	*CBS*	2
26	24	FOR THE GOOD TIMES	Perry Como	*RCA*	3
17	25	I'M THE LEADER OF THE GANG (I AM)	Gary Glitter	*Bell*	9
39	26	JOYBRINGER	Manfred Mann's Earthband	*Vertigo*	2
38	27	SKYWRITER	Jackson Five	*Tamla Motown*	2
-	28	CAROLINE	Status Quo	*Vertigo*	1
21	29	I'M DOIN' FINE NOW	New York City	*RCA*	8
27	30	I THINK OF YOU	Detroit Emeralds	*Westbound*	5
-	31	OOH BABY	Gilbert O'Sullivan	*MAM*	1
-	32	NUTBUSH CITY LIMITS	Ike & Tina Turner	*United Artists*	1
25	33	TOUCH ME IN THE MORNING	Diana Ross	*Tamla Motown*	9
32	34	ELECTRIC LADY	Geordie	*EMI*	4
23	35	48 CRASH	Suzy Quatro	*RAK*	8
34	36	EVERYTHING WILL TURN OUT FINE	Stealers Wheel	*A&M*	2
31	37	OUR LAST SONG TOGETHER	Neil Sedaka	*MGM*	2
29	38	LIFE ON MARS	David Bowie	*RCA*	12
33	39	YING TONG SONG	The Goons	*Decca*	8
28	40	ALRIGHT ALRIGHT ALRIGHT	Mungo Jerry	*Dawn*	10

WEEK ENDING 22 SEPTEMBER 1973

LW	TW	Title	Artist	Label	Wks
2	[1]	ANGEL FINGERS	Wizzard	*Harvest*	4
-	[2]	BALLROOM BLITZ	The Sweet	*RCA*	1
3	[3]	ROCK ON	David Essex	*CBS*	5
21	4	MONSTER MASH	Bobby Pickett & The Crypt Kickers	*London*	3
5	[5]	ANGIE	Rolling Stones	*Rolling Stones*	4
7	[6]	OH NO NOT MY BABY	Rod Stewart	*Mercury*	3
1	7	YOUNG LOVE	Donny Osmond	*MGM*	6
4	8	DANCING ON A SATURDAY NIGHT	Barry Blue	*Bell*	8
6	9	SPANISH EYES	Al Martino	*Capitol*	10
24	10	FOR THE GOOD TIMES	Perry Como	*RCA*	4
10	11	THE DEAN AND I	10 C.C.	*UK*	5
12	[12]	SAY, HAS ANYBODY SEEN MY SWEET GYPSY ROSE	Dawn	*Bell*	7
8	13	PICK UP THE PIECES	Hudson Ford	*A&M*	5
-	14	EYE LEVEL	Simon Park Orchestra	*Columbia*	1
18	15	I'VE BEEN HURT	Guy Darrell	*Santa Ponsa*	5
11	16	LIKE SISTER AND BROTHER	Drifters	*Bell*	7
23	17	ALL THE WAY FROM MEMPHIS	Mott The Hoople	*CBS*	3
32	18	NUTBUSH CITY LIMITS	Ike & Tina Turner	*United Artists*	2
15	19	FOOL	Elvis Presley	*RCA*	7
26	20	JOYBRINGER	Manfred Mann's Earthband	*Vertigo*	3
13	21	I'M FREE	Roger Daltrey/LSO and Chamber Choir	*Ode*	7
16	22	YESTERDAY ONCE MORE	Carpenters	*A&M*	11
28	23	CAROLINE	Status Quo	*Vertigo*	2
9	24	YOU CAN DO MAGIC	Limmie & The Family Cookin'	*Avco*	9
-	25	LAUGHING GNOME	David Bowie	*Deram*	1
31	26	OOH BABY	Gilbert O'Sullivan	*MAM*	2
14	27	SUMMER (THE FIRST TIME)	Bobby Goldsboro	*United Artists*	8
17	28	WELCOME HOME	Peters & Lee	*Philips*	17
27	29	SKYWRITER	Jackson Five	*Tamla Motown*	3
22	30	DEAR ELAINE	Roy Wood	*Harvest*	6
19	31	SMARTY PANTS	First Choice	*Bell*	8
25	32	I'M THE LEADER OF THE GANG (I AM)	Gary Glitter	*Bell*	10
36	[33]	EVERYTHING WILL TURN OUT FINE	Stealers Wheel	*A&M*	3
20	34	RISING SUN	Medicine Head	*Polydor*	8
30	35	I THINK OF YOU	Detroit Emeralds	*Westbound*	6
37	36	OUR LAST SONG TOGETHER	Neil Sedaka	*MGM*	3
-	37	TIE A YELLOW RIBBON ROUND THE OLD OAK TREE	Dawn	*Bell*	27
29	38	I'M DOIN' FINE NOW	New York City	*RCA*	9
33	39	TOUCH ME IN THE MORNING	Diana Ross	*Tamla Motown*	10
-	40	ANGEL	Aretha Franklin	*Atlantic*	1

WEEK ENDING 29 SEPTEMBER 1973

LW	TW	Title	Artist	Label	Wks
14	[1]	EYE LEVEL	Simon Park Orchestra	*Columbia*	2
2	[2]	BALLROOM BLITZ	The Sweet	*RCA*	2
1	3	ANGEL FINGERS	Wizzard	*Harvest*	5
4	4	MONSTER MASH	Bobby Pickett & The Crypt Kickers	*London*	4
3	5	ROCK ON	David Essex	*CBS*	6
6	[6]	OH NO NOT MY BABY	Rod Stewart	*Mercury*	4
5	7	ANGIE	Rolling Stones	*Rolling Stones*	5
18	8	NUTBUSH CITY LIMITS	Ike & Tina Turner	*United Artists*	3
10	9	FOR THE GOOD TIMES	Perry Como	*RCA*	5
17	[10]	ALL THE WAY FROM MEMPHIS	Mott The Hoople	*CBS*	4
20	11	JOYBRINGER	Manfred Mann's Earthband	*Vertigo*	4
15	[12]	I'VE BEEN HURT	Guy Darrell	*Santa Ponsa*	6
9	13	SPANISH EYES	Al Martino	*Capitol*	11
25	14	LAUGHING GNOME	David Bowie	*Deram*	2
7	15	YOUNG LOVE	Donny Osmond	*MGM*	7
11	16	THE DEAN AND I	10 C.C.	*UK*	6
23	17	CAROLINE	Status Quo	*Vertigo*	3
26	[18]	OOH BABY	Gilbert O'Sullivan	*MAM*	3
8	19	DANCING ON A SATURDAY NIGHT	Barry Blue	*Bell*	9
19	20	FOOL	Elvis Presley	*RCA*	8
12	21	SAY, HAS ANYBODY SEEN MY SWEET GYPSY ROSE	Dawn	*Bell*	8
13	22	PICK UP THE PIECES	Hudson Ford	*A&M*	6
16	23	LIKE SISTER AND BROTHER	Drifters	*Bell*	8
21	24	I'M FREE	Roger Daltrey/LSO and Chamber Choir	*Ode*	8
29	[25]	SKYWRITER	Jackson Five	*Tamla Motown*	4
28	26	WELCOME HOME	Peters & Lee	*Philips*	18
22	27	YESTERDAY ONCE MORE	Carpenters	*A&M*	12
27	28	SUMMER (THE FIRST TIME)	Bobby Goldsboro	*United Artists*	9
37	29	TIE A YELLOW RIBBON ROUND THE OLD OAK TREE	Dawn	*Bell*	28
24	30	YOU CAN DO MAGIC	Limmie & The Family Cookin'	*Avco*	10
-	31	THAT LADY	Isley Brothers	*Epic*	1
36	32	OUR LAST SONG TOGETHER	Neil Sedaka	*MGM*	4
31	33	SMARTY PANTS	First Choice	*Bell*	9
32	34	I'M THE LEADER OF THE GANG (I AM)	Gary Glitter	*Bell*	11
-	35	LET'S GET IT ON	Marvin Gaye	*Tamla Motown*	1
-	36	LET THERE BE PEACE ON EARTH (LET IT BEGIN WITH ME)	Michael Ward ●	*Philips*	1
40	[37]	ANGEL	Aretha Franklin	*Atlantic*	2
-	38	GHETTO CHILD	Detroit Spinners	*Atlantic*	1
33	39	EVERYTHING WILL TURN OUT FINE	Stealers Wheel	*A&M*	4
34	40	RISING SUN	Medicine Head	*Polydor*	9

WEEK ENDING 6 OCTOBER 1973

LW	TW	Title	Artist	Label	Wks
1	[1]	EYE LEVEL	Simon Park Orchestra	*Columbia*	3
2	[2]	BALLROOM BLITZ	The Sweet	*RCA*	3
4	[3]	MONSTER MASH	Bobby Pickett & The Crypt Kickers	*London*	5
-	4	MY FREND STAN	Slade	*Polydor*	1
8	5	NUTBUSH CITY LIMITS	Ike & Tina Turner	*United Artists*	4
3	6	ANGEL FINGERS	Wizzard	*Harvest*	6
9	[7]	FOR THE GOOD TIMES	Perry Como	*RCA*	6
14	8	LAUGHING GNOME	David Bowie	*Deram*	3
11	[9]	JOYBRINGER	Manfred Mann's Earthband	*Vertigo*	5
5	10	ROCK ON	David Essex	*CBS*	7
17	11	CAROLINE	Status Quo	*Vertigo*	4

In these weeks ■ Al Martino and Perry Como in the Top 10 together for the first time since 17 September 1954 (22.09.73) ■ Simon Park's *Eye Level* (the theme for the ITV series 'Van der Valk') becomes the last instrumental to top the charts (29.09.73)■

LW	TW	Title	Artist	Label	Wks
6	12	OH NO NOT MY BABY	Rod Stewart	*Mercury*	5
10	13	ALL THE WAY FROM MEMPHIS	Mott The Hoople	*CBS*	5
7	14	ANGIE	Rolling Stones	*Rolling Stones*	6
13	15	SPANISH EYES	Al Martino	*Capitol*	12
-	16	GOODBYE YELLOW BRICK ROAD	Elton John	*DJM*	1
12	17	I'VE BEEN HURT	Guy Darrell	*Santa Ponsa*	7
18	[18]	OOH BABY	Gilbert O'Sullivan	*MAM*	4
19	19	DANCING ON A SATURDAY NIGHT	Barry Blue	*Bell*	10
21	20	SAY, HAS ANYBODY SEEN MY SWEET GYPSY ROSE	Dawn	*Bell*	9
16	21	THE DEAN AND I	10 C.C.	*UK*	7
15	22	YOUNG LOVE	Donny Osmond	*MGM*	8
-	23	A HARD RAIN'S GONNA FALL	Bryan Ferry	*Island*	1
38	24	GHETTO CHILD	Detroit Spinners	*Atlantic*	2
31	25	THAT LADY	Isley Brothers	*Epic*	2
25	26	SKYWRITER	Jackson Five	*Tamla Motown*	5
29	27	TIE A YELLOW RIBBON ROUND THE OLD OAK TREE	Dawn	*Bell*	29
23	28	LIKE SISTER AND BROTHER	Drifters	*Bell*	9
26	29	WELCOME HOME	Peters & Lee	*Philips*	19
27	30	YESTERDAY ONCE MORE	Carpenters	*A&M*	13
35	31	LET'S GET IT ON	Marvin Gaye	*Tamla Motown*	2
22	32	PICK UP THE PIECES	Hudson Ford	*A&M*	7
20	33	FOOL	Elvis Presley	*RCA*	9
-	34	KNOCKIN' ON HEAVEN'S DOOR	Bob Dylan	*CBS*	1
-	35	DECK OF CARDS	Max Bygraves	*Pye*	1
30	36	YOU CAN DO MAGIC	Limmie & The Family Cookin'	*Avco*	11
36	37	LET THERE BE PEACE ON EARTH (LET IT BEGIN WITH ME)	Michael Ward	*Philips*	2
28	38	SUMMER (THE FIRST TIME)	Bobby Goldsboro	*United Artists*	10
-	39	AND I LOVE YOU SO	Perry Como	*RCA*	19
24	40	I'M FREE	Roger Daltrey/LSO and Chamber Choir	*Ode*	9

WEEK ENDING 13 OCTOBER 1973

LW	TW	Title	Artist	Label	Wks
1	[1]	EYE LEVEL	Simon Park Orchestra	*Columbia*	4
4	[2]	MY FREND STAN	Slade	*Polydor*	2
2	3	BALLROOM BLITZ	The Sweet	*RCA*	4
5	[4]	NUTBUSH CITY LIMITS	Ike & Tina Turner	*United Artists*	5
3	5	MONSTER MASH	Bobby Pickett & The Crypt Kickers	*London*	6
8	[6]	LAUGHING GNOME	David Bowie	*Deram*	4
7	[7]	FOR THE GOOD TIMES	Perry Como	*RCA*	7
-	8	DAYDREAMER/PUPPY SONG	David Cassidy	*Bell*	1
11	9	CAROLINE	Status Quo	*Vertigo*	5
9	10	JOYBRINGER	Manfred Mann's Earthband	*Vertigo*	6
6	11	ANGEL FINGERS	Wizzard	*Harvest*	7
16	12	GOODBYE YELLOW BRICK ROAD	Elton John	*DJM*	2
12	13	OH NO NOT MY BABY	Rod Stewart	*Mercury*	6
23	14	A HARD RAIN'S GONNA FALL	Bryan Ferry	*Island*	2
15	15	SPANISH EYES	Al Martino	*Capitol*	13
13	16	ALL THE WAY FROM MEMPHIS	Mott The Hoople	*CBS*	6
10	17	ROCK ON	David Essex	*CBS*	8
17	18	I'VE BEEN HURT	Guy Darrell	*Santa Ponsa*	8
18	19	OOH BABY	Gilbert O'Sullivan	*MAM*	5
24	20	GHETTO CHILD	Detroit Spinners	*Atlantic*	3
14	21	ANGIE	Rolling Stones	*Rolling Stones*	7
25	22	THAT LADY	Isley Brothers	*Epic*	3
20	23	SAY, HAS ANYBODY SEEN MY SWEET GYPSY ROSE	Dawn	*Bell*	10
37	24	LET THERE BE PEACE ON EARTH (LET IT BEGIN WITH ME)	Michael Ward	*Philips*	3
26	[25]	SKYWRITER	Jackson Five	*Tamla Motown*	6
34	26	KNOCKIN' ON HEAVEN'S DOOR	Bob Dylan	*CBS*	2
22	27	YOUNG LOVE	Donny Osmond	*MGM*	9
27	28	TIE A YELLOW RIBBON ROUND THE OLD OAK TREE	Dawn	*Bell*	30
-	29	SHOWDOWN	Electric Light Orchestra	*Harvest*	1
19	30	DANCING ON A SATURDAY NIGHT	Barry Blue	*Bell*	11
21	31	THE DEAN AND I	10 C.C.	*UK*	8
29	32	WELCOME HOME	Peters & Lee	*Philips*	20
28	33	LIKE SISTER AND BROTHER	Drifters	*Bell*	10
-	[34]	SHINE ON SILVER SUN	Strawbs	*A&M*	1
31	35	LET'S GET IT ON	Marvin Gaye	*Tamla Motown*	3
30	36	YESTERDAY ONCE MORE	Carpenters	*A&M*	14
33	37	FOOL	Elvis Presley	*RCA*	10
35	38	DECK OF CARDS	Max Bygraves	*Pye*	2
-	[39]	LOVES ME LIKE A ROCK	Paul Simon	*CBS*	1
-	40	5.15	Who	*Track*	1

WEEK ENDING 20 OCTOBER 1973

LW	TW	Title	Artist	Label	Wks
1	[1]	EYE LEVEL	Simon Park Orchestra	*Columbia*	5
8	2	DAYDREAMER/PUPPY SONG	David Cassidy	*Bell*	2
2	3	MY FREND STAN	Slade	*Polydor*	3
4	[4]	NUTBUSH CITY LIMITS	Ike & Tina Turner	*United Artists*	6
5	5	MONSTER MASH	Bobby Pickett & The Crypt Kickers	*London*	7
6	[6]	LAUGHING GNOME	David Bowie	*Deram*	5
3	7	BALLROOM BLITZ	The Sweet	*RCA*	5
9	8	CAROLINE	Status Quo	*Vertigo*	6
7	9	FOR THE GOOD TIMES	Perry Como	*RCA*	8
12	10	GOODBYE YELLOW BRICK ROAD	Elton John	*DJM*	3
14	11	A HARD RAIN'S GONNA FALL	Bryan Ferry	*Island*	3
20	12	GHETTO CHILD	Detroit Spinners	*Atlantic*	4
10	13	JOYBRINGER	Manfred Mann's Earthband	*Vertigo*	7
29	14	SHOWDOWN	Electric Light Orchestra	*Harvest*	2
11	15	ANGEL FINGERS	Wizzard	*Harvest*	8
-	16	SORROW	David Bowie	*RCA*	1
22	17	THAT LADY	Isley Brothers	*Epic*	4
26	18	KNOCKIN' ON HEAVEN'S DOOR	Bob Dylan	*CBS*	3
15	19	SPANISH EYES	Al Martino	*Capitol*	14
40	[20]	5.15	Who	*Track*	2
18	21	I'VE BEEN HURT	Guy Darrell	*Santa Ponsa*	9
13	22	OH NO NOT MY BABY	Rod Stewart	*Mercury*	7
-	23	THIS FLIGHT TONIGHT	Nazareth	*Mooncrest*	1
24	24	LET THERE BE PEACE ON EARTH (LET IT BEGIN WITH ME)	Michael Ward	*Philips*	4
17	25	ROCK ON	David Essex	*CBS*	9
38	26	DECK OF CARDS	Max Bygraves	*Pye*	3
23	27	SAY, HAS ANYBODY SEEN MY SWEET GYPSY ROSE	Dawn	*Bell*	11
28	28	TIE A YELLOW RIBBON ROUND THE OLD OAK TREE	Dawn	*Bell*	31
16	29	ALL THE WAY FROM MEMPHIS	Mott The Hoople	*CBS*	7
21	30	ANGIE	Rolling Stones	*Rolling Stones*	8
35	31	LET'S GET IT ON	Marvin Gaye	*Tamla Motown*	4
25	32	SKYWRITER	Jackson Five	*Tamla Motown*	7
-	33	HIGHER GROUND	Stevie Wonder	*Tamla Motown*	1
-	34	THE DAY THAT CURLY BILLY SHOT CRAZY SAM McGEE	Hollies	*Polydor*	1
30	35	DANCING ON A SATURDAY NIGHT	Barry Blue	*Bell*	12
-	36	TOP OF THE WORLD	Carpenters	*A&M*	1
32	37	WELCOME HOME	Peters & Lee	*Philips*	21
19	38	OOH BABY	Gilbert O'Sullivan	*MAM*	6
33	39	LIKE SISTER AND BROTHER	Drifters	*Bell*	11
-	40	AND I LOVE YOU SO	Perry Como	*RCA*	20

WEEK ENDING 27 OCTOBER 1973

LW	TW	Title	Artist	Label	Wks
2	[1]	DAYDREAMER/PUPPY SONG	David Cassidy	*Bell*	3
1	2	EYE LEVEL	Simon Park Orchestra	*Columbia*	6
3	3	MY FREND STAN	Slade	*Polydor*	4
16	4	SORROW	David Bowie	*RCA*	2
8	[5]	CAROLINE	Status Quo	*Vertigo*	7
10	[6]	GOODBYE YELLOW BRICK ROAD	Elton John	*DJM*	4
9	7	FOR THE GOOD TIMES	Perry Como	*RCA*	9
6	8	LAUGHING GNOME	David Bowie	*Deram*	6
4	9	NUTBUSH CITY LIMITS	Ike & Tina Turner	*United Artists*	7
11	[10]	A HARD RAIN'S GONNA FALL	Bryan Ferry	*Island*	4
12	11	GHETTO CHILD	Detroit Spinners	*Atlantic*	5
7	12	BALLROOM BLITZ	The Sweet	*RCA*	6
5	13	MONSTER MASH	Bobby Pickett & The Crypt Kickers	*London*	8
17	[14]	THAT LADY	Isley Brothers	*Epic*	5

■Manfred Mann's Earthband hits the Top Ten as Rod Stewart's version of Manfred Mann's 1965 hit *Oh No Not My Baby* drops out (06.10.73) ■ Bryan Ferry's version of Bob Dylan's *A Hard Rain's Gonna Fall* outperforms Dylan's own hit from his film *Pat Garrett And Billy The Kid* (27.10.73)■

October 1973

□ Highest position disc reached ● Act's first ever week on chart

LW	TW	Title / Artist	Label	Wks
24	[15]	LET THERE BE PEACE ON EARTH (LET IT BEGIN WITH ME) Michael Ward	Philips	5
14	16	SHOW DOWN Electric Light Orchestra	Harvest	3
18	17	KNOCKIN' ON HEAVEN'S DOOR Bob Dylan	CBS	4
26	18	DECK OF CARDS Max Bygraves	Pye	4
36	19	TOP OF THE WORLD Carpenters	A&M	2
23	20	THIS FLIGHT TONIGHT Nazareth	Mooncrest	2
20	21	5.15 Who	Track	3
19	22	SPANISH EYES Al Martino	Capitol	15
28	23	TIE A YELLOW RIBBON ROUND THE OLD OAK TREE Dawn	Bell	32
34	[24]	THE DAY THAT CURLY BILLY SHOT CRAZY SAM McGEE Hollies	Polydor	2
27	25	SAY, HAS ANYBODY SEEN MY SWEET GYPSY ROSE Dawn	Bell	12
-	26	PHOTOGRAPH Ringo Starr	Apple	1
13	27	JOYBRINGER Manfred Mann's Earthband	Vertigo	8
-	28	WON'T SOMEBODY DANCE WITH ME Lynsey De Paul	MAM	1
33	[29]	HIGHER GROUND Stevie Wonder	Tamla Motown	2
21	30	I'VE BEEN HURT Guy Darrell	Santa Ponsa	10
25	31	ROCK ON David Essex	CBS	10
-	32	LET ME IN Osmonds	MGM	1
15	33	ANGEL FINGERS Wizzard	Harvest	9
-	34	DYNA-MITE Mud	RAK	1
-	35	DREAMBOAT Limmie & The Family Cookin'	Avco	1
22	36	OH NO NOT MY BABY Rod Stewart	Mercury	8
-	37	DECK OF CARDS Wink Martindale	Dot	1
-	[38]	THE OLD FASHIONED WAY Charles Aznavour ●	Barclay	1
40	39	AND I LOVE YOU SO Perry Como	RCA	21
30	40	ANGIE Rolling Stones	Rolling Stones	9

WEEK ENDING 3 NOVEMBER 1973

LW	TW	Title / Artist	Label	Wks
1	[1]	DAYDREAMER/PUPPY SONG David Cassidy	Bell	4
2	2	EYE LEVEL Simon Park Orchestra	Columbia	7
4	[3]	SORROW David Bowie	RCA	3
32	4	LET ME IN Osmonds	MGM	2
5	5	CAROLINE Status Quo	Vertigo	8
6	[6]	GOODBYE YELLOW BRICK ROAD Elton John	DJM	5
11	[7]	GHETTO CHILD Detroit Spinners	Atlantic	6
3	8	MY FREND STAN Slade	Polydor	5
19	9	TOP OF THE WORLD Carpenters	A&M	3
7	10	FOR THE GOOD TIMES Perry Como	RCA	10
8	11	LAUGHING GNOME David Bowie	Deram	7
16	[12]	SHOW DOWN Electric Light Orchestra	Harvest	4
10	13	A HARD RAIN'S GONNA FALL Bryan Ferry	Island	5
17	[14]	KNOCKIN' ON HEAVEN'S DOOR Bob Dylan	CBS	5
20	15	THIS FLIGHT TONIGHT Nazareth	Mooncrest	3
9	16	NUTBUSH CITY LIMITS Ike & Tina Turner	United Artists	8
18	17	DECK OF CARDS Max Bygraves	Pye	5
15	18	LET THERE BE PEACE ON EARTH (LET IT BEGIN WITH ME) Michael Ward	Philips	6
28	19	WON'T SOMEBODY DANCE WITH ME Lynsey De Paul	MAM	2
34	20	DYNA-MITE Mud	RAK	2
13	21	MONSTER MASH Bobby Pickett & The Crypt Kickers	London	9
21	22	5.15 Who	Track	4
14	23	THAT LADY Isley Brothers	Epic	6
26	24	PHOTOGRAPH Ringo Starr	Apple	2
12	25	THE BALLROOM BLITZ The Sweet	RCA	7
24	26	THE DAY THAT CURLY BILLY SHOT CRAZY SAM McGEE Hollies	Polydor	3
22	27	SPANISH EYES Al Martino	Capitol	16
-	28	DAYTONA DEMON Suzi Quatro	RAK	1
23	29	TIE A YELLOW RIBBON ROUND THE OLD OAK TREE Dawn	Bell	33
37	30	DECK OF CARDS Wink Martindale	Dot	2
-	31	DO YOU WANNA DANCE Barry Blue	Bell	1
35	32	DREAMBOAT Limmie & The Family Cookin'	Avco	2
-	33	HELEN WHEELS Wings	Apple	1
29	34	HIGHER GROUND Stevie Wonder	Tamla Motown	3
-	35	MILLY MOLLY MANDY Glyn Poole ●	York	1
-	36	KEEP ON TRUCKIN' Eddie Kendricks	Tamla Motown	1
39	37	AND I LOVE YOU SO Perry Como	RCA	22
27	38	JOYBRINGER Manfred Mann Earthband	Vertigo	9
-	39	LET'S GET IT ON Marvin Gaye	Tamla Motown	5
38	40	THE OLD FASHIONED WAY Charles Aznavour	Barclay	2

WEEK ENDING 10 NOVEMBER 1973

LW	TW	Title / Artist	Label	Wks
1	[1]	DAYDREAMER/PUPPY SONG David Cassidy	Bell	5
4	[2]	LET ME IN Osmonds	MGM	3
3	[3]	SORROW David Bowie	RCA	4
20	[4]	DYNA-MITE Mud	RAK	3
9	[5]	TOP OF THE WORLD Carpenters	A&M	4
2	6	EYE LEVEL Simon Park Orchestra	Columbia	8
5	7	CAROLINE Status Quo	Vertigo	9
7	8	GHETTO CHILD Detroit Spinners	Atlantic	7
10	9	FOR THE GOOD TIMES Perry Como	RCA	11
6	10	GOODBYE YELLOW BRICK ROAD Elton John	DJM	6
15	[11]	THIS FLIGHT TONIGHT Nazareth	Mooncrest	4
12	[12]	SHOW DOWN Electric Light Orchestra	Harvest	5
24	13	PHOTOGRAPH Ringo Starr	Apple	3
17	14	DECK OF CARDS Max Bygraves	Pye	6
14	15	KNOCKIN' ON HEAVEN'S DOOR Bob Dylan	CBS	6
8	16	MY FREND STAN Slade	Polydor	6
19	17	WON'T SOMEBODY DANCE WITH ME Lynsey De Paul	MAM	3
13	18	A HARD RAIN'S GONNA FALL Bryan Ferry	Island	6
18	19	LET THERE BE PEACE ON EARTH (LET IT BEGIN WITH ME) Michael Ward	Philips	7
31	20	DO YOU WANNA DANCE Barry Blue	Bell	2
11	21	LAUGHING GNOME David Bowie	Deram	8
28	22	DAYTONA DEMON Suzi Quatro	RAK	2
-	23	WHEN I FALL IN LOVE Donny Osmond	MGM	1
23	24	THAT LADY Isley Brothers	Epic	7
22	25	5.15 Who	Track	5
30	26	DECK OF CARDS Wink Martindale	Dot	3
16	27	NUTBUSH CITY LIMITS Ike & Tina Turner	United Artists	9
33	28	HELEN WHEELS Wings	Apple	2
21	29	MONSTER MASH Bobby Pickett & The Crypt Kickers	London	10
26	30	THE DAY THAT CURLY BILLY SHOT CRAZY SAM McGEE Hollies	Polydor	4
32	[31]	DREAMBOAT Limmie & The Family Cookin'	Avco	3
25	32	THE BALLROOM BLITZ The Sweet	RCA	8
29	33	TIE A YELLOW RIBBON ROUND THE OLD OAK TREE Dawn	Bell	34
36	34	KEEP ON TRUCKIN' Eddie Kendricks	Tamla Motown	2
35	[35]	MILLY MOLLY MANDY Glyn Poole	York	2
-	36	MY COO-CA-CHOO Alvin Stardust ●	Magnet	1
27	37	SPANISH EYES Al Martino	Capitol	17
-	38	LAMPLIGHT David Essex	CBS	1
-	[39]	BY YOUR SIDE Peters & Lee	Philips	1
-	40	SWEET UNDERSTANDING LOVE Four Tops	Probe	1

WEEK ENDING 17 NOVEMBER 1973

LW	TW	Title / Artist	Label	Wks
-	[1]	I LOVE YOU LOVE ME LOVE Gary Glitter	Bell	1
2	[2]	LET ME IN Osmonds	MGM	4
1	3	DAYDREAMER/PUPPY SONG David Cassidy	Bell	6
3	4	SORROW David Bowie	RCA	5
4	5	DYNA-MITE Mud	RAK	4
23	6	WHEN I FALL IN LOVE Donny Osmond	MGM	2
5	7	TOP OF THE WORLD Carpenters	A&M	5
13	[8]	PHOTOGRAPH Ringo Starr	Apple	4
20	9	DO YOU WANNA DANCE Barry Blue	Bell	3
8	10	GHETTO CHILD Detroit Spinners	Atlantic	8
11	[11]	THIS FLIGHT TONIGHT Nazareth	Mooncrest	5
9	12	FOR THE GOOD TIMES Perry Como	RCA	12
14	[13]	DECK OF CARDS Max Bygraves	Pye	7
17	[14]	WON'T SOMEBODY DANCE WITH ME Lynsey De Paul	MAM	4
6	15	EYE LEVEL Simon Park Orchestra	Columbia	9

In these weeks ■ Spurred on by the success of Max Bygraves' cover version, Wink Martindale's *Deck Of Cards* re-enters the chart to become one of the very few singles to have been a hit in four different years (1959, 1960, 1963 and 1973) (27.10.73) ■ Final week of chart action for Al Martino, the man who topped the first chart of all (10.11.73) ■ Alvin Stardust, previously a hitmaker as Shane Fenton, makes his chart debut (10.11.73) ■

LW	TW	Title / Artist	Label	Wks
22	**16**	DAYTONA DEMON Suzi Quatro	*RAK*	3
-	**17**	WHY OH WHY OH WHY Gilbert O'Sullivan	*MAM*	1
12	**18**	SHOW DOWN Electric Light Orchestra	*Harvest*	6
10	**19**	GOODBYE YELLOW BRICK ROAD Elton John	*DJM*	7
7	**20**	CAROLINE Status Quo	*Vertigo*	10
15	**21**	KNOCKIN' ON HEAVEN'S DOOR Bob Dylan	*CBS*	7
19	**22**	LET THERE BE PEACE ON EARTH (LET IT BEGIN WITH ME) Michael Ward	*Philips*	8
38	**23**	LAMPLIGHT David Essex	*CBS*	2
-	**24**	PAPER ROSES Marie Osmond	*MGM*	1
26	**25**	DECK OF CARDS Wink Martindale	*Dot*	4
28	**26**	HELEN WHEELS Wings	*Apple*	3
36	**27**	MY COO-CA-CHOO Alvin Stardust	*Magnet*	2
21	**28**	LAUGHING GNOME David Bowie	*Deram*	9
16	**29**	MY FREND STAN Slade	*Polydor*	7
25	**30**	5.15 Who	*Track*	6
18	**31**	A HARD RAIN'S GONNA FALL Bryan Ferry	*Island*	7
27	**32**	NUTBUSH CITY LIMITS Ike & Tina Turner	*United Artists*	10
-	**33**	WILD LOVE Mungo Jerry	*Dawn*	1
40	**34**	SWEET UNDERSTANDING LOVE Four Tops	*Probe*	2
34	**35**	KEEP ON TRUCKIN' Eddie Kendricks	*Tamla Motown*	3
35	**36**	MILLY MOLLY MANDY Glyn Poole	*York*	3
31	**37**	DREAMBOAT Limmie & The Family Cookin'	*Avco*	4
-	**38**	AMOUREUSE Kiki Dee	*Rocket*	1
-	**39**	LONELY DAYS LONELY NIGHTS Don Downing ●	*People*	1
30	**40**	THE DAY THAT CURLY BILLY SHOT CRAZY SAM McGEE Hollies	*Polydor*	4

LW	TW	*WEEK ENDING* **24 NOVEMBER 1973**		Wks
1	**1**	I LOVE YOU LOVE ME LOVE Gary Glitter	*Bell*	2
2	**2**	LET ME IN Osmonds	*MGM*	5
24	**3**	PAPER ROSES Marie Osmond	*MGM*	2
5	**4**	DYNA-MITE Mud	*RAK*	5
4	**5**	SORROW David Bowie	*RCA*	6
6	**6**	WHEN I FALL IN LOVE Donny Osmond	*MGM*	3
9	**7**	DO YOU WANNA DANCE Barry Blue	*Bell*	4
27	**8**	MY COO-CA-CHOO Alvin Stardust	*Magnet*	3
7	**9**	TOP OF THE WORLD Carpenters	*A&M*	6
8	**10**	PHOTOGRAPH Ringo Starr	*Apple*	5
3	**11**	DAYDREAMER/PUPPY SONG David Cassidy	*Bell*	7
17	**12**	WHY OH WHY OH WHY Gilbert O'Sullivan	*MAM*	2
23	**13**	LAMPLIGHT David Essex	*CBS*	3
16	**14**	DAYTONA DEMON Suzi Quatro	*RAK*	4
11	**15**	THIS FLIGHT TONIGHT Nazareth	*Mooncrest*	6
12	**16**	FOR THE GOOD TIMES Perry Como	*RCA*	13
26	**17**	HELEN WHEELS Wings	*Apple*	4
14	**18**	WON'T SOMEBODY DANCE WITH ME Lynsey De Paul	*MAM*	5
13	**19**	DECK OF CARDS Max Bygraves	*Pye*	8
15	**20**	EYE LEVEL Simon Park Orchestra	*Columbia*	10
-	**21**	STREET LIFE Roxy Music	*Island*	1
25	**22**	DECK OF CARDS Wink Martindale	*Dot*	5
18	**23**	SHOW DOWN Electric Light Orchestra	*Harvest*	7
19	**24**	GOODBYE YELLOW BRICK ROAD Elton John	*DJM*	8
38	**25**	AMOUREUSE Kiki Dee	*Rocket*	2
-	**26**	ROLL AWAY THE STONE Mott The Hoople	*CBS*	1
10	**27**	GHETTO CHILD Detroit Spinners	*Atlantic*	9
20	**28**	CAROLINE Status Quo	*Vertigo*	11
21	**29**	KNOCKIN' ON HEAVEN'S DOOR Bob Dylan	*CBS*	8
35	**30**	KEEP ON TRUCKIN' Eddie Kendricks	*Tamla Motown*	4
22	**31**	LET THERE BE PEACE ON EARTH (LET IT BEGIN WITH ME) Michael Ward	*Philips*	9
33	**32**	WILD LOVE Mungo Jerry	*Dawn*	2
34	**33**	SWEET UNDERSTANDING LOVE Four Tops	*Probe*	3
29	**34**	MY FRIEND STAN Slade	*Polydor*	8
-	**35**	YOU WON'T FIND ANOTHER FOOL LIKE ME New Seekers	*Polydor*	1
39	**36**	LONELY DAYS LONELY NIGHTS Don Downing	*People*	2
28	**37**	LAUGHING GNOME David Bowie	*Deram*	10
-	**38**	TRUCK ON (TYKE) T. Rex	*EMI*	1
-	**39**	MIND GAMES John Lennon	*Apple*	1
-	**40**	TIE A YELLOW RIBBON ROUND THE OLD OAK TREE Dawn	*Bell*	35

December 1973

□ Highest position disc reached ● Act's first ever week on chart

LW	TW	*WEEK ENDING* **1 DECEMBER 1973**		Wks
1	**1**	I LOVE YOU LOVE ME LOVE Gary Glitter	*Bell*	3
8	**2**	MY COO-CA-CHOO Alvin Stardust	*Magnet*	4
3	**3**	PAPER ROSES Marie Osmond	*MGM*	3
6	**4**	WHEN I FALL IN LOVE Donny Osmond	*MGM*	4
4	**5**	DYNA-MITE Mud	*RAK*	6
12	**6**	WHY OH WHY OH WHY Gilbert O'Sullivan	*MAM*	3
35	**7**	YOU WON'T FIND ANOTHER FOOL LIKE ME New Seekers	*Polydor*	2
13	**8**	LAMPLIGHT David Essex	*CBS*	4
7	**9**	DO YOU WANNA DANCE Barry Blue	*Bell*	5
2	**10**	LET ME IN Osmonds	*MGM*	6
10	**11**	PHOTOGRAPH Ringo Starr	*Apple*	6
17	**12**	HELEN WHEELS Wings	*Apple*	5
11	**13**	DAYDREAMER/PUPPY SONG David Cassidy	*Bell*	8
9	**14**	TOP OF THE WORLD Carpenters	*A&M*	7
5	**15**	SORROW David Bowie	*RCA*	7
21	**16**	STREET LIFE Roxy Music	*Island*	2
26	**17**	ROLL AWAY THE STONE Mott The Hoople	*CBS*	2
14	**18**	DAYTONA DEMON Suzi Quatro	*RAK*	5
18	**19**	WON'T SOMEBODY DANCE WITH ME Lynsey De Paul	*MAM*	6
38	**20**	TRUCK ON (TYKE) T. Rex	*EMI*	2
16	**21**	FOR THE GOOD TIMES Perry Como	*RCA*	14
19	**22**	DECK OF CARDS Max Bygraves	*Pye*	9
25	**23**	AMOUREUSE Kiki Dee	*Rocket*	3
15	**24**	THIS FLIGHT TONIGHT Nazareth	*Mooncrest*	7
30	**25**	KEEP ON TRUCKIN' Eddie Kendricks	*Tamla Motown*	5
20	**26**	EYE LEVEL Simon Park Orchestra	*Columbia*	11
22	**27**	DECK OF CARDS Wink Martindale	*Dot*	6
-	**28**	LOVE ON A MOUNTAIN TOP Robert Knight	*Monument*	1
24	**29**	GOODBYE YELLOW BRICK ROAD Elton John	*DJM*	9
33	**30**	SWEET UNDERSTANDING LOVE Four Tops	*Probe*	4
39	**31**	MIND GAMES John Lennon	*Apple*	2
36	**32**	LONELY DAYS LONELY NIGHTS Don Downing	*People*	3
27	**33**	GHETTO CHILD Detroit Spinners	*Atlantic*	10
32	**34**	WILD LOVE Mungo Jerry	*Dawn*	3
-	**35**	AND YOU SMILED Matt Monro	*EMI*	1
23	**36**	SHOW DOWN Electric Light Orchestra	*Harvest*	8
-	**37**	RAISED ON ROCK Elvis Presley	*RCA*	1
31	**38**	LET THERE BE PEACE ON EARTH (LET IT BEGIN WITH ME) Michael Ward	*Philips*	10
-	**39**	MILLY MOLLY MANDY Glyn Poole	*York*	4
29	**40**	KNOCKIN' ON HEAVEN'S DOOR Bob Dylan	*CBS*	9

LW	TW	*WEEK ENDING* **8 DECEMBER 1973**		Wks
1	**1**	I LOVE YOU LOVE ME LOVE Gary Glitter	*Bell*	4
3	**2**	PAPER ROSES Marie Osmond	*MGM*	4
7	**3**	YOU WON'T FIND ANOTHER FOOL LIKE ME New Seekers	*Polydor*	3
2	**4**	MY COO-CA-CHOO Alvin Stardust	*Magnet*	5
10	**5**	LET ME IN Osmonds	*MGM*	7
5	**6**	DYNA-MITE Mud	*RAK*	7
8	**7**	LAMPLIGHT David Essex	*CBS*	5
17	**8**	ROLL AWAY THE STONE Mott The Hoople	*CBS*	3
6	**9**	WHY OH WHY OH WHY Gilbert O'Sullivan	*MAM*	4
9	**10**	DO YOU WANNA DANCE Barry Blue	*Bell*	6
16	**11**	STREET LIFE Roxy Music	*Island*	3
4	**12**	WHEN I FALL IN LOVE Donny Osmond	*MGM*	5
20	**13**	TRUCK ON (TYKE) T. Rex	*EMI*	3
11	**14**	PHOTOGRAPH Ringo Starr	*Apple*	7
12	**15**	HELEN WHEELS Wings	*Apple*	6
23	**16**	AMOUREUSE Kiki Dee	*Rocket*	4
14	**17**	TOP OF THE WORLD Carpenters	*A&M*	8
18	**18**	DAYTONA DEMON Suzi Quatro	*RAK*	6
-	**19**	I WISH IT COULD BE CHRISTMAS EVERYDAY Wizzard	*Harvest*	1
15	**20**	SORROW David Bowie	*RCA*	8

■Three Osmond records in the top six (24.11.73) ■ *Goodbye Yellow Brick Road*, the title track from Elton John's latest album, drops out of the chart after reaching number six. It was his fourth consecutive top ten hit, the longest run of top ten hits in his career (01.12.73)■

December 1973

□ Highest position disc reached ● Act's first ever week on chart

LW	TW	Title	Artist	Label	Wks
21	21	FOR THE GOOD TIMES	Perry Como	RCA	15
28	22	LOVE ON A MOUNTAIN TOP	Robert Knight	Monument	2
13	23	DAYDREAMER/PUPPY SONG	David Cassidy	Bell	9
25	24	KEEP ON TRUCKIN'	Eddie Kendricks	Tamla Motown	6
26	25	EYE LEVEL	Simon Park Orchestra	Columbia	12
31	□26	MIND GAMES	John Lennon	Apple	3
24	27	THIS FLIGHT TONIGHT	Nazareth	Mooncrest	8
35	□28	AND YOU SMILED	Matt Monro	EMI	2
30	□29	SWEET UNDERSTANDING LOVE	Four Tops	Probe	5
19	30	WON'T SOMEBODY DANCE WITH ME	Lynsey De Paul	MAM	7
27	31	DECK OF CARDS	Wink Martindale	Dot	7
-	32	FOREVER	Roy Wood	Harvest	1
32	33	LONELY DAYS LONELY NIGHTS	Don Downing	People	4
22	34	DECK OF CARDS	Max Bygraves	Pye	10
-	35	VAYA CON DIOS	Millican & Nesbitt ●	Pye	1
37	□36	RAISED ON ROCK	Elvis Presley	RCA	2
34	37	WILD LOVE	Mungo Jerry	Dawn	4
-	38	POOL HALL RICHARD/I WISH IT WOULD RAIN	Faces	Warner Brothers	1
-	39	VADO VIA	Drupi ●	A&M	1
-	40	TAKE ME HIGH	Cliff Richard	EMI	1

WEEK ENDING 15 DECEMBER 1973

LW	TW	Title	Artist	Label	Wks
-	□1	MERRY XMAS EVERYBODY	Slade	Polydor	1
1	2	I LOVE YOU LOVE ME LOVE	Gary Glitter	Bell	5
4	3	MY COO-CA-CHOO	Alvin Stardust	Magnet	6
3	4	YOU WON'T FIND ANOTHER FOOL LIKE ME	New Seekers	Polydor	4
2	5	PAPER ROSES	Marie Osmond	MGM	5
19	6	I WISH IT COULD BE CHRISTMAS EVERYDAY	Wizzard	Harvest	2
7	□7	LAMPLIGHT	David Essex	CBS	6
8	□8	ROLL AWAY THE STONE	Mott The Hoople	CBS	4
11	□9	STREET LIFE	Roxy Music	Island	4
9	10	WHY OH WHY OH WHY	Gilbert O'Sullivan	MAM	5
6	11	DYNA-MITE	Mud	RAK	8
12	12	WHEN I FALL IN LOVE	Donny Osmond	MGM	6
16	□13	AMOUREUSE	Kiki Dee	Rocket	5
13	14	TRUCK ON (TYKE)	T. Rex	EMI	4
15	15	HELEN WHEELS	Paul McCartney & Wings	Apple	7
5	16	LET ME IN	Osmonds	MGM	8
22	17	LOVE ON A MOUNTAIN TOP	Robert Knight	Monument	3
24	□18	KEEP ON TRUCKIN'	Eddie Kendricks	Tamla Motown	7
10	19	DO YOU WANNA DANCE	Barry Blue	Bell	7
17	20	TOP OF THE WORLD	Carpenters	A&M	9
21	21	FOR THE GOOD TIMES	Perry Como	RCA	16
39	22	VADO VIA	Drupi	A&M	2
35	23	VAYA CON DIOS	Millican & Nesbitt	Pye	2
-	24	THE SHOW MUST GO ON	Leo Sayer ●	Chrysalis	1
-	25	STEP INTO CHRISTMAS	Elton John	DJM	1
38	26	POOL HALL RICHARD/I WISH IT WOULD RAIN	Faces	Warner Brothers	2
-	27	GAUDETE	Steeleye Span ●	Chrysalis	1
20	28	SORROW	David Bowie	RCA	9
25	29	EYE LEVEL	Simon Park Orchestra	Columbia	13
23	30	DAYDREAMER/PUPPY SONG	David Cassidy	Bell	10
32	31	FOREVER	Roy Wood	Harvest	2
28	32	AND YOU SMILED	Matt Monro	EMI	3
26	33	MIND GAMES	John Lennon	Apple	4
29	34	SWEET UNDERSTANDING LOVE	Four Tops	Probe	6
14	35	PHOTOGRAPH	Ringo Starr	Apple	8
33	36	LONELY DAYS LONELY NIGHTS	Don Downing	People	5
-	37	RADAR LOVE	Golden Earring ●	Track	1
-	38	DANCE WITH THE DEVIL	Cozy Powell ●	RAK	1
40	39	TAKE ME HIGH	Cliff Richard	EMI	2
-	40	WALK RIGHT BACK	Perry Como	RCA	1

WEEK ENDING 22 DECEMBER 1973

(Top 30 chart compiled only)

LW	TW	Title	Artist	Label	Wks
1	□1	MERRY XMAS EVERYBODY	Slade	Polydor	2
2	2	I LOVE YOU LOVE ME LOVE	Gary Glitter	Bell	6
4	3	YOU WON'T FIND ANOTHER FOOL LIKE ME	New Seekers	Polydor	5
6	□4	I WISH IT COULD BE CHRISTMAS EVERYDAY	Wizzard	Harvest	3
3	5	MY COO-CA-CHOO	Alvin Stardust	Magnet	7
5	6	PAPER ROSES	Marie Osmond	MGM	6
24	7	THE SHOW MUST GO ON	Leo Sayer	Chrysalis	2
7	8	LAMPLIGHT	David Essex	CBS	7
8	9	ROLL AWAY THE STONE	Mott The Hoople	CBS	5
9	10	STREET LIFE	Roxy Music	Island	5
31	11	FOREVER	Roy Wood	Harvest	3
14	□12	TRUCK ON (TYKE)	T. Rex	EMI	5
10	13	WHY OH WHY OH WHY	Gilbert O'Sullivan	MAM	6
27	□14	GAUDETE	Steeleye Span	Chrysalis	2
12	15	WHEN I FALL IN LOVE	Donny Osmond	MGM	7
17	16	LOVE ON A MOUNTAIN TOP	Robert Knight	Monument	4
38	17	DANCE WITH THE DEVIL	Cozy Powell	RAK	2
13	18	AMOUREUSE	Kiki Dee	Rocket	6
16	19	LET ME IN	Osmonds	MGM	9
26	20	POOL HALL RICHARD/I WISH IT WOULD RAIN	Faces	Warner Brothers	3
22	21	VADO VIA	Drupi	A&M	3
11	22	DYNA-MITE	Mud	RAK	9
23	23	VAYA CON DIOS	Millican & Nesbitt	Pye	3
15	24	HELEN WHEELS	Paul McCartney & Wings	Apple	8
37	25	RADAR LOVE	Golden Earring	Track	2
25	26	STEP INTO CHRISTMAS	Elton John	DJM	2
20	27	TOP OF THE WORLD	Carpenters	A&M	10
19	28	DO YOU WANNA DANCE	Barry Blue	Bell	8
21	29	FOR THE GOOD TIMES	Perry Como	RCA	17
30	30	DAYDREAMER/PUPPY SONG	David Cassidy	Bell	11

WEEK ENDING 29 DECEMBER 1973

(no chart published, chart for 22 December 1973 repeated)

LW	TW	Title	Artist	Label	Wks
1	□1	MERRY XMAS EVERYBODY	Slade	Polydor	3
2	2	I LOVE YOU LOVE ME LOVE	Gary Glitter	Bell	7
3	3	YOU WON'T FIND ANOTHER FOOL LIKE ME	New Seekers	Polydor	6
4	□4	I WISH IT COULD BE CHRISTMAS EVERYDAY	Wizzard	Harvest	4
5	5	MY COO-CA-CHOO	Alvin Stardust	Magnet	8
6	6	PAPER ROSES	Marie Osmond	MGM	7
7	7	THE SHOW MUST GO ON	Leo Sayer	Chrysalis	3
8	8	LAMPLIGHT	David Essex	CBS	8
9	9	ROLL AWAY THE STONE	Mott The Hoople	CBS	6
10	10	STREET LIFE	Roxy Music	Island	6
11	11	FOREVER	Roy Wood	Harvest	4
12	□12	TRUCK ON (TYKE)	T. Rex	EMI	6
13	13	WHY OH WHY OH WHY	Gilbert O'Sullivan	MAM	7
14	□14	GAUDETE	Steeleye Span	Chrysalis	3
15	15	WHEN I FALL IN LOVE	Donny Osmond	MGM	8
16	16	LOVE ON A MOUNTAIN TOP	Robert Knight	Monument	5
17	17	DANCE WITH THE DEVIL	Cozy Powell	RAK	3
18	18	AMOUREUSE	Kiki Dee	Rocket	7
19	19	LET ME IN	Osmonds	MGM	10
20	20	POOL HALL RICHARD/I WISH IT WOULD RAIN	Faces	Warner Brothers	3
21	21	VADO VIA	Drupi	A&M	4
22	22	DYNA-MITE	Mud	RAK	10
23	23	VAYA CON DIOS	Millican & Nesbitt	Pye	4
24	24	HELEN WHEELS	Paul McCartney & Wings	Apple	9
25	25	RADAR LOVE	Golden Earring	Track	3
26	26	STEP INTO CHRISTMAS	Elton John	DJM	3
27	27	TOP OF THE WORLD	Carpenters	A&M	11
28	28	DO YOU WANNA DANCE	Barry Blue	Bell	9
29	29	FOR THE GOOD TIMES	Perry Como	RCA	18
30	30	DAYDREAMER/PUPPY SONG	David Cassidy	Bell	12

In these weeks ■ *And You Smiled* by Matt Monro is the first record to peak at number 28 in over two years (08.12.73) ■ *Merry Xmas Everybody* is the fourth record in 1973 to go straight to number one, a total for one year that was not matched until the 1990s (15.12.73) ■ Four songs with foreign titles in the Top 30 - *Gaudete* (Latin), *Amoureuse* (French), *Vado Via* (Italian) and *Vaya Con Dios* (Spanish) (22.12.73)■

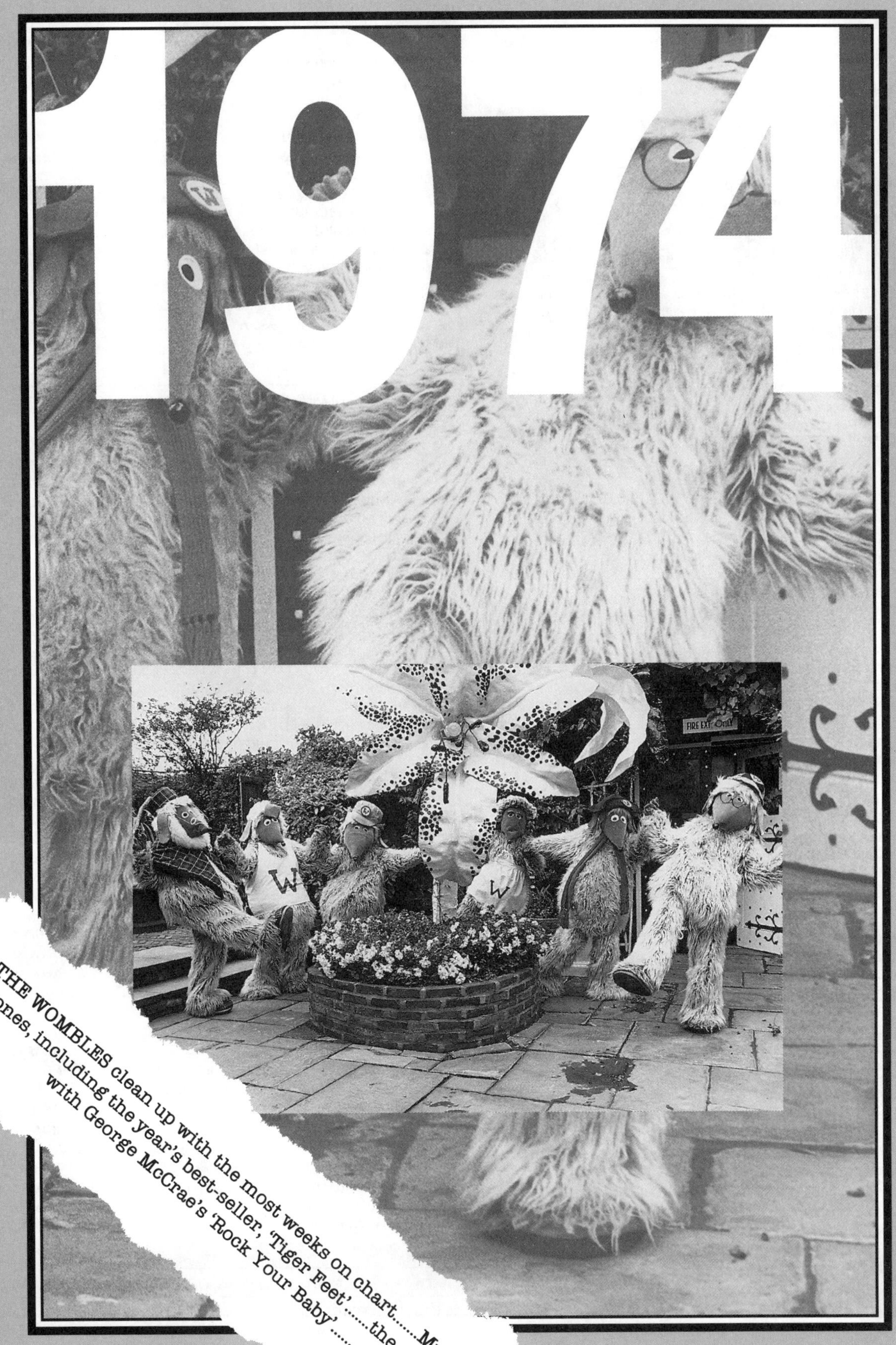

........THE WOMBLES clean up with the most weeks on chart.......Mud have two umber ones, including the year's best-seller, 'Tiger Feet'......the disco era begins with George McCrae's 'Rock Your Baby'.........

January 1974

□ Highest position disc reached ● Act's first ever week on chart

LW	TW	WEEK ENDING 5 JANUARY 1974		Wks
1	[1]	MERRY XMAS EVERYBODY Slade	*Polydor*	4
3	2	YOU WON'T FIND ANOTHER FOOL LIKE ME New Seekers	*Polydor*	7
2	3	I LOVE YOU LOVE ME LOVE Gary Glitter	*Bell*	8
4	[4]	I WISH IT COULD BE CHRISTMAS EVERYDAY Wizzard	*Harvest*	5
5	5	MY COO-CA-CHOO Alvin Stardust	*Magnet*	9
6	6	PAPER ROSES Marie Osmond	*MGM*	8
7	7	THE SHOW MUST GO ON Leo Sayer	*Chrysalis*	4
8	8	LAMPLIGHT David Essex	*CBS*	9
9	9	ROLL AWAY THE STONE Mott The Hoople	*CBS*	7
10	10	STREET LIFE Roxy Music	*Island*	7
11	11	FOREVER Roy Wood	*Harvest*	5
13	12	WHY OH WHY OH WHY Gilbert O'Sullivan	*MAM*	8
16	13	LOVE ON A MOUNTAIN TOP Robert Knight	*Monument*	6
17	14	DANCE WITH THE DEVIL Cozy Powell	*RAK*	4
12	15	TRUCK ON (TYKE) T. Rex	*EMI*	7
20	16	POOL HALL RICHARD/I WISH IT WOULD RAIN Faces	*Warner Brothers*	4
14	17	GAUDETE Steeleye Span	*Chrysalis*	4
15	18	WHEN I FALL IN LOVE Donny Osmond	*MGM*	9
18	19	AMOUREUSE Kiki Dee	*Rocket*	8
23	[20]	VAYA CON DIOS Millican & Nesbitt	*Pye*	5
22	21	DYNA-MITE Mud	*RAK*	11
21	22	VADO VIA Drupi	*A&M*	5
19	23	LET ME IN Osmonds	*MGM*	11
26	[24]	STEP INTO CHRISTMAS Elton John	*DJM*	4
24	25	HELEN WHEELS Wings	*Apple*	10
25	26	RADAR LOVE Golden Earring	*Track*	4
27	27	TOP OF THE WORLD Carpenters	*A&M*	12
28	28	DO YOU WANNA DANCE Barry Blue	*Bell*	10
29	29	FOR THE GOOD TIMES Perry Como	*RCA*	19
30	30	DAYDREAMER/PUPPY SONG David Cassidy	*Bell*	13
-	31	EYE LEVEL Simon Park Orchestra	*Columbia*	16
-	32	KEEP ON TRUCKIN' Eddie Kendricks	*Tamla Motown*	10
-	33	MIND GAMES John Lennon	*Apple*	7
-	34	SORROW David Bowie	*RCA*	12
-	35	PHOTOGRAPH Ringo Starr	*Apple*	11
-	36	SOLITAIRE Andy Williams	*CBS*	1
-	37	TAKE ME HIGH Cliff Richard	*EMI*	5
-	38	SWEET UNDERSTANDING LOVE Four Tops	*Probe*	9
-	39	WALK RIGHT BACK Perry Como	*RCA*	4
-	40	AND YOU SMILED Matt Monro	*EMI*	6

LW	TW	WEEK ENDING 12 JANUARY 1974		Wks
1	[1]	MERRY XMAS EVERYBODY Slade	*Polydor*	5
2	2	YOU WON'T FIND ANOTHER FOOL LIKE ME New Seekers	*Polydor*	8
7	3	THE SHOW MUST GO ON Leo Sayer	*Chrysalis*	5
4	[4]	I WISH IT COULD BE CHRISTMAS EVERYDAY Wizzard	*Harvest*	6
5	5	MY COO-CA-CHOO Alvin Stardust	*Magnet*	10
14	6	DANCE WITH THE DEVIL Cozy Powell	*RAK*	5
3	7	I LOVE YOU LOVE ME LOVE Gary Glitter	*Bell*	9
16	[8]	POOL HALL RICHARD/I WISH IT WOULD RAIN Faces	*Warner Brothers*	5
26	9	RADAR LOVE Golden Earring	*Track*	5
8	10	LAMPLIGHT David Essex	*CBS*	10
13	11	LOVE ON A MOUNTAIN TOP Robert Knight	*Monument*	7
11	12	FOREVER Roy Wood	*Harvest*	6
9	13	ROLL AWAY THE STONE Mott The Hoople	*CBS*	8
6	14	PAPER ROSES Marie Osmond	*MGM*	9
10	15	STREET LIFE Roxy Music	*Island*	8
17	16	GAUDETE Steeleye Span	*Chrysalis*	5
12	17	WHY OH WHY OH WHY Gilbert O'Sullivan	*MAM*	9
15	18	TRUCK ON (TYKE) T. Rex	*EMI*	8
22	19	VADO VIA Drupi	*A&M*	6
18	20	WHEN I FALL IN LOVE Donny Osmond	*MGM*	10
23	21	LET ME IN Osmonds	*MGM*	12
36	22	SOLITAIRE Andy Williams	*CBS*	2
27	23	TOP OF THE WORLD Carpenters	*A&M*	13
28	24	DO YOU WANNA DANCE Barry Blue	*Bell*	11
25	25	HELEN WHEELS Wings	*Apple*	11
24	26	STEP INTO CHRISTMAS Elton John	*DJM*	5
20	27	VAYA CON DIOS Millican & Nesbitt	*Pye*	6
30	28	DAYDREAMER/PUPPY SONG David Cassidy	*Bell*	14
29	29	FOR THE GOOD TIMES Perry Como	*RCA*	20
34	30	SORROW David Bowie	*RCA*	13
21	31	DYNA-MITE Mud	*RAK*	12
19	32	AMOUREUSE Kiki Dee	*Rocket*	9
32	33	KEEP ON TRUCKIN' Eddie Kendricks	*Tamla Motown*	11
37	34	TAKE ME HIGH Cliff Richard	*EMI*	6
31	35	EYE LEVEL Simon Park Orchestra	*Columbia*	17
-	36	GOODBYE YELLOW BRICK ROAD Elton John	*DJM*	10
33	37	MIND GAMES John Lennon	*Apple*	8
-	38	ALL OF MY LIFE Diana Ross	*Tamla Motown*	1
35	39	PHOTOGRAPH Ringo Starr	*Apple*	12
39	40	WALK RIGHT BACK Perry Como	*RCA*	5

LW	TW	WEEK ENDING 19 JANUARY 1974		Wks
2	[1]	YOU WON'T FIND ANOTHER FOOL LIKE ME New Seekers	*Polydor*	9
3	[2]	THE SHOW MUST GO ON Leo Sayer	*Chrysalis*	6
1	3	MERRY XMAS EVERYBODY Slade	*Polydor*	6
6	4	DANCE WITH THE DEVIL Cozy Powell	*RAK*	6
5	5	MY COO-CA-CHOO Alvin Stardust	*Magnet*	11
-	6	TEENAGE RAMPAGE The Sweet	*RCA*	1
9	[7]	RADAR LOVE Golden Earring	*Track*	6
14	8	PAPER ROSES Marie Osmond	*MGM*	10
12	9	FOREVER Roy Wood	*Harvest*	7
-	10	TIGER FEET Mud	*Rak*	1
8	11	POOL HALL RICHARD/I WISH IT WOULD RAIN Faces	*Warner Brothers*	6
11	12	LOVE ON A MOUNTAIN TOP Robert Knight	*Monument*	8
7	13	I LOVE YOU LOVE ME LOVE Gary Glitter	*Bell*	10
22	14	SOLITAIRE Andy Williams	*CBS*	3
10	15	LAMPLIGHT David Essex	*CBS*	11
4	16	I WISH IT COULD BE CHRISTMAS EVERYDAY Wizzard	*Harvest*	7
13	17	ROLL AWAY THE STONE Mott The Hoople	*CBS*	9
17	18	WHY OH WHY OH WHY Gilbert O'Sullivan	*MAM*	10
15	19	STREET LIFE Roxy Music	*Island*	9
38	20	ALL OF MY LIFE Diana Ross	*Tamla Motown*	2
19	21	VADO VIA Drupi	*A&M*	7
18	22	TRUCK ON (TYKE) T. Rex	*EMI*	9
16	23	GAUDETE Steeleye Span	*Chrysalis*	6
27	24	VAYA CON DIOS Millican & Nesbitt	*Pye*	7
-	25	HOW COME Ronnie Lane ●	*GM*	1
29	26	FOR THE GOOD TIMES Perry Como	*RCA*	21
32	27	AMOUREUSE Kiki Dee	*Rocket*	10
34	28	TAKE ME HIGH Cliff Richard	*EMI*	7
-	29	ROCKIN' ROLL BABY The Stylistics	*Avco*	1
-	30	LIVING FOR THE CITY Stevie Wonder	*Tamla Motown*	1
23	31	TOP OF THE WORLD Carpenters	*A&M*	14
-	32	THE LOVE I LOST Harold Melvin & The Bluenotes	*Philadelphia*	1
40	[33]	WALK RIGHT BACK Perry Como	*RCA*	6
30	34	SORROW David Bowie	*RCA*	14
20	35	WHEN I FALL IN LOVE Donny Osmond	*MGM*	11
-	36	THANKS FOR SAVING MY LIFE Billy Paul	*Philadelphia*	1
33	37	KEEP ON TRUCKIN' Eddie Kendricks	*Tamla Motown*	12
-	38	TEENAGE LAMENT '74 Alice Cooper	*Warner Bros.*	1
21	39	LET ME IN Osmonds	*MGM*	13
-	40	AND I LOVE YOU SO Perry Como	*RCA*	23

LW	TW	WEEK ENDING 26 JANUARY 1974		Wks
10	[1]	TIGER FEET Mud	*Rak*	2
6	[2]	TEENAGE RAMPAGE The Sweet	*RCA*	2

In these weeks ■ Faces' guitarist Ronnie Lane has his first solo hit while his band are still in the top twenty with their final top ten hit (19.01.74) ■ A good week for the smoother end of American soul, with new hits by the Stylistics, Harold Melvin and the Bluenotes, Stevie Wonder and Billy Paul all charting at once (19.01.74) ■

LW	TW				Wks
2	3	THE SHOW MUST GO ON	Leo Sayer	*Chrysalis*	7
4	4	DANCE WITH THE DEVIL	Cozy Powell	*RAK*	7
1	5	YOU WON'T FIND ANOTHER FOOL LIKE ME	New Seekers	*Polydor*	10
5	6	MY COO-CA-CHOO	Alvin Stardust	*Magnet*	12
7	[7]	RADAR LOVE	Golden Earring	*Track*	7
9	[8]	FOREVER	Roy Wood	*Harvest*	8
14	9	SOLITAIRE	Andy Williams	*CBS*	4
12	[10]	LOVE ON A MOUNTAIN TOP	Robert Knight	*Monument*	9
11	11	POOL HALL RICHARD/I WISH IT WOULD RAIN	Faces	*Warner Brothers*	7
3	12	MERRY XMAS EVERYBODY	Slade	*Polydor*	7
13	13	I LOVE YOU LOVE ME LOVE	Gary Glitter	*Bell*	11
8	14	PAPER ROSES	Marie Osmond	*MGM*	11
15	15	LAMPLIGHT	David Essex	*CBS*	12
20	16	ALL OF MY LIFE	Diana Ross	*Tamla Motown*	3
21	[17]	VADO VIA	Drupi	*A&M*	8
17	18	ROLL AWAY THE STONE	Mott The Hoople	*CBS*	10
29	19	ROCKIN' ROLL BABY	The Stylistics	*Avco*	2
25	20	HOW COME	Ronnie Lane	*GM*	2
23	21	GAUDETE	Steeleye Span	*Chrysalis*	7
16	22	I WISH IT COULD BE CHRISTMAS EVERYDAY	Wizzard	*Harvest*	8
19	23	STREET LIFE	Roxy Music	*Island*	10
18	24	WHY OH WHY OH WHY	Gilbert O'Sullivan	*MAM*	11
32	25	THE LOVE I LOST	Harold Melvin & The Bluenotes	*Philadelphia*	2
38	26	TEENAGE LAMENT '74	Alice Cooper	*Warner Bros.*	2
-	27	THE MAN WHO SOLD THE WORLD	Lulu	*Polydor*	1
24	28	VAYA CON DIOS	Millican & Nesbitt	*Pye*	8
30	29	LIVING FOR THE CITY	Stevie Wonder	*Tamla Motown*	2
28	30	TAKE ME HIGH	Cliff Richard	*EMI*	8
31	31	TOP OF THE WORLD	Carpenters	*A&M*	15
22	32	TRUCK ON (TYKE)	T. Rex	*EMI*	10
36	[33]	THANKS FOR SAVING MY LIFE	Billy Paul	*Philadelphia*	2
26	34	FOR THE GOOD TIMES	Perry Como	*RCA*	22
-	35	EYE LEVEL	Simon Park Orchestra	*Columbia*	18
-	36	WOMBLING SONG	The Wombles ●	*CBS*	1
27	37	AMOUREUSE	Kiki Dee	*Rocket*	11
33	38	WALK RIGHT BACK	Perry Como	*RCA*	7
-	39	AFTER THE GOLD RUSH	Prelude ●	*Dawn*	1
-	40	HIGHWAY OF MY LIFE	Isley Brothers	*Epic*	1

WEEK ENDING 2 FEBRUARY 1974

LW	TW				Wks
1	[1]	TIGER FEET	Mud	*Rak*	3
2	[2]	TEENAGE RAMPAGE	The Sweet	*RCA*	3
5	3	YOU WON'T FIND ANOTHER FOOL LIKE ME	New Seekers	*Polydor*	11
3	4	THE SHOW MUST GO ON	Leo Sayer	*Chrysalis*	8
4	5	DANCE WITH THE DEVIL	Cozy Powell	*RAK*	8
9	6	SOLITAIRE	Andy Williams	*CBS*	5
7	[7]	RADAR LOVE	Golden Earring	*Track*	8
6	8	MY COO-CA-CHOO	Alvin Stardust	*Magnet*	13
8	9	FOREVER	Roy Wood	*Harvest*	9
10	[10]	LOVE ON A MOUNTAIN TOP	Robert Knight	*Monument*	10
20	[11]	HOW COME	Ronnie Lane	*GM*	3
19	12	ROCKIN' ROLL BABY	The Stylistics	*Avco*	3
27	13	THE MAN WHO SOLD THE WORLD	Lulu	*Polydor*	2
16	14	ALL OF MY LIFE	Diana Ross	*Tamla Motown*	4
11	15	POOL HALL RICHARD/I WISH IT WOULD RAIN	Faces	*Warner Brothers*	8
13	16	I LOVE YOU LOVE ME LOVE	Gary Glitter	*Bell*	12
14	17	PAPER ROSES	Marie Osmond	*MGM*	12
26	18	TEENAGE LAMENT '74	Alice Cooper	*Warner Bros.*	3
15	19	LAMPLIGHT	David Essex	*CBS*	13
29	20	LIVING FOR THE CITY	Stevie Wonder	*Tamla Motown*	3
25	[21]	THE LOVE I LOST	Harold Melvin & The Bluenotes	*Philadelphia*	3
12	22	MERRY XMAS EVERYBODY	Slade	*Polydor*	8
17	23	VADO VIA	Drupi	*A&M*	9
18	24	ROLL AWAY THE STONE	Mott The Hoople	*CBS*	11
40	[25]	HIGHWAY OF MY LIFE	Isley Brothers	*Epic*	2
36	26	WOMBLING SONG	The Wombles	*CBS*	2
30	[27]	TAKE ME HIGH	Cliff Richard	*EMI*	9
34	28	FOR THE GOOD TIMES	Perry Como	*RCA*	23

February 1974

□ Highest position disc reached ● Act's first ever week on chart

LW	TW				Wks
-	[29]	(I CAN'T GET NO) SATISFACTION	Bubble Rock ●	*UK*	1
-	30	STAR	Stealers Wheel	*A&M*	1
-	[31]	GALLOPING HOME	London String Chorale	*Polydor*	1
-	32	NEVER NEVER GONNA GIVE YA UP	Barry White	*Pye*	1
31	33	TOP OF THE WORLD	Carpenters	*A&M*	16
-	34	LOVE'S THEME	Love Unlimited Orchestra ●	*Pye*	1
24	35	WHY OH WHY OH WHY	Gilbert O'Sullivan	*MAM*	12
33	36	THANKS FOR SAVING MY LIFE	Billy Paul	*Philadelphia*	3
39	37	AFTER THE GOLD RUSH	Prelude	*Dawn*	2
21	38	GAUDETE	Steeleye Span	*Chrysalis*	8
28	39	VAYA CON DIOS	Millican & Nesbitt	*Pye*	9
38	40	WALK RIGHT BACK	Perry Como	*RCA*	8

WEEK ENDING 9 FEBRUARY 1974

LW	TW				Wks
1	[1]	TIGER FEET	Mud	*Rak*	4
2	[2]	TEENAGE RAMPAGE	The Sweet	*RCA*	4
5	[3]	DANCE WITH THE DEVIL	Cozy Powell	*RAK*	9
6	[4]	SOLITAIRE	Andy Williams	*CBS*	6
13	5	THE MAN WHO SOLD THE WORLD	Lulu	*Polydor*	3
12	[6]	ROCKIN' ROLL BABY	The Stylistics	*Avco*	4
4	7	THE SHOW MUST GO ON	Leo Sayer	*Chrysalis*	9
3	8	YOU WON'T FIND ANOTHER FOOL LIKE ME	New Seekers	*Polydor*	12
14	[9]	ALL OF MY LIFE	Diana Ross	*Tamla Motown*	5
9	10	FOREVER	Roy Wood	*Harvest*	10
7	11	RADAR LOVE	Golden Earring	*Track*	9
11	12	HOW COME	Ronnie Lane	*GM*	4
10	13	LOVE ON A MOUNTAIN TOP	Robert Knight	*Monument*	11
-	14	DEVIL GATE DRIVE	Suzi Quatro	*RAK*	1
18	15	TEENAGE LAMENT '74	Alice Cooper	*Warner Bros.*	4
8	16	MY COO-CA-CHOO	Alvin Stardust	*Magnet*	14
20	17	LIVING FOR THE CITY	Stevie Wonder	*Tamla Motown*	4
-	18	TEENAGE DREAM	Marc Bolan & T.Rex ●	*EMI*	1
26	19	WOMBLING SONG	The Wombles	*CBS*	3
34	20	LOVE'S THEME	Love Unlimited Orchestra	*Pye*	2
21	[21]	THE LOVE I LOST	Harold Melvin & The Bluenotes	*Philadelphia*	4
17	22	PAPER ROSES	Marie Osmond	*MGM*	13
32	23	NEVER NEVER GONNA GIVE YA UP	Barry White	*Pye*	2
15	24	POOL HALL RICHARD/I WISH IT WOULD RAIN	Faces	*Warner Brothers*	9
30	[25]	STAR	Stealers Wheel	*A&M*	2
16	26	I LOVE YOU LOVE ME LOVE	Gary Glitter	*Bell*	13
25	27	HIGHWAY OF MY LIFE	Isley Brothers	*Epic*	3
37	28	AFTER THE GOLD RUSH	Prelude	*Dawn*	3
29	[29]	(I CAN'T GET NO) SATISFACTION	Bubble Rock	*UK*	2
-	30	MA HE'S MAKING EYES AT ME	Lena Zavaroni ●	*Philips*	1
31	31	GALLOPING HOME	London String Chorale	*Polydor*	2
28	32	FOR THE GOOD TIMES	Perry Como	*RCA*	24
-	33	THE AIR THAT I BREATHE	Hollies	*Polydor*	1
23	34	VADO VIA	Drupi	*A&M*	10
19	35	LAMPLIGHT	David Essex	*CBS*	14
27	36	TAKE ME HIGH	Cliff Richard	*EMI*	10
36	37	THANKS FOR SAVING MY LIFE	Billy Paul	*Philadelphia*	4
24	38	ROLL AWAY THE STONE	Mott The Hoople	*CBS*	12
-	39	BABY WE CAN'T GO WRONG	Cilla Black	*EMI*	1
22	40	MERRY XMAS EVERYBODY	Slade	*Polydor*	9

WEEK ENDING 16 FEBRUARY 1974

LW	TW				Wks
1	[1]	TIGER FEET	Mud	*Rak*	5
14	2	DEVIL GATE DRIVE	Suzi Quatro	*RAK*	2
5	[3]	THE MAN WHO SOLD THE WORLD	Lulu	*Polydor*	4
2	4	TEENAGE RAMPAGE	The Sweet	*RCA*	5
4	5	SOLITAIRE	Andy Williams	*CBS*	7
3	6	DANCE WITH THE DEVIL	Cozy Powell	*RAK*	10
19	7	WOMBLING SONG	The Wombles	*CBS*	4
6	8	ROCKIN' ROLL BABY	The Stylistics	*Avco*	5

■Lulu's first Top 40 hit since her Eurovision hit in 1969 is her version of a David Bowie song. It becomes her biggest hit apart from that Eurovision epic (16.02.74) ■ The most successful chart act of 1974 makes its chart debut at the lonely position of no. 36. The Wombles will go on to score 5 top twenty hits before the year is out (26.01.74)■

February 1974

□ Highest position disc reached ● Act's first ever week on chart

LW	TW	Title / Artist	Label	Wks
9	9	ALL OF MY LIFE Diana Ross	Tamla Motown	6
7	10	THE SHOW MUST GO ON Leo Sayer	Chrysalis	10
12	11	HOW COME Ronnie Lane	GM	5
15	12	TEENAGE LAMENT '74 Alice Cooper	Warner Bros.	5
18	13	TEENAGE DREAM Marc Bolan & T.Rex	EMI	2
13	14	LOVE ON A MOUNTAIN TOP Robert Knight	Monument	12
17	15	LIVING FOR THE CITY Stevie Wonder	Tamla Motown	5
30	16	MA HE'S MAKING EYES AT ME Lena Zavaroni	Philips	2
11	17	RADAR LOVE Golden Earring	Track	10
10	18	FOREVER Roy Wood	Harvest	11
20	19	LOVE'S THEME Love Unlimited Orchestra	Pye	3
8	20	YOU WON'T FIND ANOTHER FOOL LIKE ME New Seekers	Polydor	13
23	21	NEVER NEVER GONNA GIVE YA UP Barry White	Pye	3
-	22	JEALOUS MIND Alvin Stardust	Magnet	1
21	23	THE LOVE I LOST Harold Melvin & The Bluenotes	Philadelphia	5
16	24	MY COO-CA-CHOO Alvin Stardust	Magnet	15
27	25	HIGHWAY OF MY LIFE Isley Brothers	Epic	4
33	26	THE AIR THAT I BREATHE Hollies	Polydor	2
-	27	HAPPINESS IS ME AND YOU Gilbert O'Sullivan	MAM	1
25	28	STAR Stealers Wheel	A&M	3
28	29	AFTER THE GOLD RUSH Prelude	Dawn	4
29	30	(I CAN'T GET NO) SATISFACTION Bubble Rock	UK	3
-	31	SLIP AND SLIDE Medicine Head	Polydor	1
26	32	I LOVE YOU LOVE ME LOVE Gary Glitter	Bell	14
22	33	PAPER ROSES Marie Osmond	MGM	14
31	34	GALLOPING HOME London String Chorale	Polydor	3
-	35	A LITTLE LOVIN' Neil Sedaka	Polydor	1
39	36	BABY WE CAN'T GO WRONG Cilla Black	EMI	2
-	37	SCULLERY Clifford T. Ward	Charisma	1
-	38	REMEMBER (SHA-LA-LA-LA) Bay City Rollers	Bell	1
32	39	FOR THE GOOD TIMES Perry Como	RCA	25
35	40	LAMPLIGHT David Essex	CBS	15

WEEK ENDING 23 FEBRUARY 1974

LW	TW	Title / Artist	Label	Wks
2	1	DEVIL GATE DRIVE Suzi Quatro	RAK	3
1	2	TIGER FEET Mud	Rak	6
22	3	JEALOUS MIND Alvin Stardust	Magnet	2
7	4	WOMBLING SONG The Wombles	CBS	5
3	5	THE MAN WHO SOLD THE WORLD Lulu	Polydor	5
-	6	REBEL REBEL David Bowie	RCA	1
5	7	SOLITAIRE Andy Williams	CBS	8
26	8	THE AIR THAT I BREATHE Hollies	Polydor	3
9	9	ALL OF MY LIFE Diana Ross	Tamla Motown	7
19	10	LOVE'S THEME Love Unlimited Orchestra	Pye	4
4	11	TEENAGE RAMPAGE The Sweet	RCA	6
8	12	ROCKIN' ROLL BABY The Stylistics	Avco	6
16	13	MA HE'S MAKING EYES AT ME Lena Zavaroni	Philips	3
21	14	NEVER NEVER GONNA GIVE YA UP Barry White	Pye	4
-	15	YOU'RE SIXTEEN Ringo Starr	Apple	1
13	16	TEENAGE DREAM Marc Bolan & T.Rex	EMI	3
6	17	DANCE WITH THE DEVIL Cozy Powell	RAK	11
38	18	REMEMBER (SHA-LA-LA-LA) Bay City Rollers	Bell	2
15	19	LIVING FOR THE CITY Stevie Wonder	Tamla Motown	6
-	20	THE MOST BEAUTIFUL GIRL Charlie Rich ●	CBS	1
27	21	HAPPINESS IS ME AND YOU Gilbert O'Sullivan	MAM	2
12	22	TEENAGE LAMENT '74 Alice Cooper	Warner Bros.	6
29	23	AFTER THE GOLD RUSH Prelude	Dawn	5
23	24	THE LOVE I LOST Harold Melvin & The Bluenotes	Philadelphia	6
31	25	SLIP AND SLIDE Medicine Head	Polydor	2
25	26	HIGHWAY OF MY LIFE Isley Brothers	Epic	5
20	27	YOU WON'T FIND ANOTHER FOOL LIKE ME New Seekers	Polydor	14
24	28	MY COO-CA-CHOO Alvin Stardust	Magnet	16
28	29	STAR Stealers Wheel	A&M	4
-	30	BURN BABY BURN Hudson Ford	A&M	1
10	31	THE SHOW MUST GO ON Leo Sayer	Chrysalis	11
11	32	HOW COME Ronnie Lane	GM	6
14	33	LOVE ON A MOUNTAIN TOP Robert Knight	Monument	13
35	34	A LITTLE LOVIN' Neil Sedaka	Polydor	2
34	35	GALLOPING HOME London String Chorale	Polydor	4
17	36	RADAR LOVE Golden Earring	Track	11
36	37	BABY WE CAN'T GO WRONG Cilla Black	EMI	3
-	38	BILLY, DON'T BE A HERO Paper Lace ●	Bus Stop	1
-	39	IT'S YOU Freddie Starr ●	Tiffany	1
-	40	UNTIL YOU COME BACK TO ME Aretha Franklin	Atlantic	1

WEEK ENDING 2 MARCH 1974

LW	TW	Title / Artist	Label	Wks
1	1	DEVIL GATE DRIVE Suzi Quatro	RAK	4
3	2	JEALOUS MIND Alvin Stardust	Magnet	3
8	3	THE AIR THAT I BREATHE Hollies	Polydor	4
4	4	WOMBLING SONG The Wombles	CBS	6
6	5	REBEL REBEL David Bowie	RCA	2
2	6	TIGER FEET Mud	Rak	7
15	7	YOU'RE SIXTEEN Ringo Starr	Apple	2
18	8	REMEMBER (SHA-LA-LA-LA) Bay City Rollers	Bell	3
5	9	THE MAN WHO SOLD THE WORLD Lulu	Polydor	6
13	10	MA HE'S MAKING EYES AT ME Lena Zavaroni	Philips	4
20	11	THE MOST BEAUTIFUL GIRL Charlie Rich	CBS	2
10	12	LOVE'S THEME Love Unlimited Orchestra	Pye	5
7	13	SOLITAIRE Andy Williams	CBS	9
14	14	NEVER NEVER GONNA GIVE YA UP Barry White	Pye	5
38	15	BILLY, DON'T BE A HERO Paper Lace	Bus Stop	2
39	16	IT'S YOU Freddie Starr	Tiffany	2
-	17	JET Paul McCartney & Wings	Apple	1
12	18	ROCKIN' ROLL BABY The Stylistics	Avco	7
21	19	HAPPINESS IS ME AND YOU Gilbert O'Sullivan	MAM	3
30	20	BURN BABY BURN Hudson Ford	A&M	2
16	21	TEENAGE DREAM Marc Bolan & T.Rex	EMI	4
9	22	ALL OF MY LIFE Diana Ross	Tamla Motown	8
17	23	DANCE WITH THE DEVIL Cozy Powell	RAK	12
11	24	TEENAGE RAMPAGE The Sweet	RCA	7
19	25	LIVING FOR THE CITY Stevie Wonder	Tamla Motown	7
25	26	SLIP AND SLIDE Medicine Head	Polydor	3
23	27	AFTER THE GOLD RUSH Prelude	Dawn	6
-	28	CANDLE IN THE WIND Elton John	DJM	1
22	29	TEENAGE LAMENT '74 Alice Cooper	Warner Bros.	7
28	30	MY COO-CA-CHOO Alvin Stardust	Magnet	17
26	31	HIGHWAY OF MY LIFE Isley Brothers	Epic	6
40	32	UNTIL YOU COME BACK TO ME Aretha Franklin	Atlantic	2
27	33	YOU WON'T FIND ANOTHER FOOL LIKE ME New Seekers	Polydor	15
35	34	GALLOPING HOME London String Chorale	Polydor	5
34	35	A LITTLE LOVIN' Neil Sedaka	Polydor	3
-	36	DARK LADY Cher	MCA	1
-	37	WILL YOU STILL LOVE ME TOMORROW Melanie	Neighborhood	1
37	38	BABY WE CAN'T GO WRONG Cilla Black	EMI	4
29	39	STAR Stealers Wheel	A&M	5
32	40	HOW COME Ronnie Lane	GM	7

WEEK ENDING 9 MARCH 1974

LW	TW	Title / Artist	Label	Wks
2	1	JEALOUS MIND Alvin Stardust	Magnet	4
1	2	DEVIL GATE DRIVE Suzi Quatro	RAK	5
3	3	THE AIR THAT I BREATHE Hollies	Polydor	5
7	4	YOU'RE SIXTEEN Ringo Starr	Apple	3
5	5	REBEL REBEL David Bowie	RCA	3
8	6	REMEMBER (SHA-LA-LA-LA) Bay City Rollers	Bell	4
4	7	WOMBLING SONG The Wombles	CBS	7
15	8	BILLY, DON'T BE A HERO Paper Lace	Bus Stop	3
11	9	THE MOST BEAUTIFUL GIRL Charlie Rich	CBS	3
17	10	JET Paul McCartney & Wings	Apple	2
28	11	CANDLE IN THE WIND Elton John	DJM	2
16	12	IT'S YOU Freddie Starr	Tiffany	3
10	13	MA HE'S MAKING EYES AT ME Lena Zavaroni	Philips	5
14	14	NEVER NEVER GONNA GIVE YA UP Barry White	Pye	6
12	15	LOVE'S THEME Love Unlimited Orchestra	Pye	6
6	16	TIGER FEET Mud	Rak	8
9	17	THE MAN WHO SOLD THE WORLD Lulu	Polydor	7

In these weeks ■ The top ten are all British-based acts, although Suzi Quatro at number one is American, and the Bay City Rollers, Lulu and Lena Zavaroni at numbers 8, 9 and 10 are all Scottish (02.03.74) ■ Cilla Black drops off the chart for the final time, but certainly can't go wrong in her subsequent television career (02.03.74)■

LW	TW	Title	Artist	Label	Wks
20	18	BURN BABY BURN	Hudson Ford	A&M	3
19	[19]	HAPPINESS IS ME AND YOU	Gilbert O'Sullivan	MAM	4
13	20	SOLITAIRE	Andy Williams	CBS	10
27	[21]	AFTER THE GOLD RUSH	Prelude	Dawn	7
26	[22]	SLIP AND SLIDE	Medicine Head	Polydor	4
22	23	ALL OF MY LIFE	Diana Ross	Tamla Motown	9
-	24	I GET A LITTLE SENTIMENTAL OVER YOU	New Seekers	Polydor	1
-	25	SCHOOL LOVE	Barry Blue	Bell	1
21	26	TEENAGE DREAM	Marc Bolan & T.Rex	EMI	5
18	27	ROCKIN' ROLL BABY	The Stylistics	Avco	8
-	28	WHO DO YOU THINK YOU ARE	Candlewick Green ●	Decca	1
32	29	UNTIL YOU COME BACK TO ME	Aretha Franklin	Atlantic	3
23	30	DANCE WITH THE DEVIL	Cozy Powell	RAK	13
30	31	MY COO-CA-CHOO	Alvin Stardust	Magnet	18
25	32	LIVING FOR THE CITY	Stevie Wonder	Tamla Motown	8
-	33	SMOKIN' IN THE BOYS ROOM	Brownsville Station ●	Philips	1
24	34	TEENAGE RAMPAGE	The Sweet	RCA	8
-	35	EVERLASTING LOVE	Robert Knight	Monument	1
-	36	FUNKY NASSAU	Beginning Of The End ●	Atlantic	1
-	[37]	WHO'S IN THE STRAWBERRY PATCH WITH SALLY	Tony Orlando and Dawn ●	Bell	1
-	38	JUST MY SOUL RESPONDING	Smokey Robinson ●	Tamla Motown	1
33	39	YOU WON'T FIND ANOTHER FOOL LIKE ME	New Seekers	Polydor	16
-	40	JAMBALAYA	Carpenters	A&M	1

WEEK ENDING 16 MARCH 1974

LW	TW	Title	Artist	Label	Wks
8	[1]	BILLY, DON'T BE A HERO	Paper Lace	Bus Stop	4
1	2	JEALOUS MIND	Alvin Stardust	Magnet	5
3	3	THE AIR THAT I BREATHE	Hollies	Polydor	6
9	4	THE MOST BEAUTIFUL GIRL	Charlie Rich	CBS	4
4	5	YOU'RE SIXTEEN	Ringo Starr	Apple	4
2	6	DEVIL GATE DRIVE	Suzi Quatro	RAK	6
6	7	REMEMBER (SHA-LA-LA-LA)	Bay City Rollers	Bell	5
10	8	JET	Paul McCartney & Wings	Apple	3
12	[9]	IT'S YOU	Freddie Starr	Tiffany	4
7	10	WOMBLING SONG	The Wombles	CBS	8
24	11	I GET A LITTLE SENTIMENTAL OVER YOU	New Seekers	Polydor	2
11	12	CANDLE IN THE WIND	Elton John	DJM	3
5	13	REBEL REBEL	David Bowie	RCA	4
13	14	MA HE'S MAKING EYES AT ME	Lena Zavaroni	Philips	6
18	[15]	BURN BABY BURN	Hudson Ford	A&M	4
14	16	NEVER NEVER GONNA GIVE YA UP	Barry White	Pye	7
25	17	SCHOOL LOVE	Barry Blue	Bell	2
15	18	LOVE'S THEME	Love Unlimited Orchestra	Pye	7
40	19	JAMBALAYA	Carpenters	A&M	2
19	20	HAPPINESS IS ME AND YOU	Gilbert O'Sullivan	MAM	5
28	[21]	WHO DO YOU THINK YOU ARE	Candlewick Green	Decca	2
16	22	TIGER FEET	Mud	Rak	9
20	23	SOLITAIRE	Andy Williams	CBS	11
35	24	EVERLASTING LOVE	Robert Knight	Monument	2
22	25	SLIP AND SLIDE	Medicine Head	Polydor	5
29	[26]	UNTIL YOU COME BACK TO ME	Aretha Franklin	Atlantic	4
33	[27]	SMOKIN' IN THE BOYS ROOM	Brownsville Station	Philips	2
-	28	LONG LIVE LOVE	Olivia Newton-John	Pye	1
21	29	AFTER THE GOLD RUSH	Prelude	Dawn	8
-	30	SEVEN SEAS OF RHYE	Queen ●	EMI	1
36	[31]	FUNKY NASSAU	Beginning Of The End	Atlantic	2
23	32	ALL OF MY LIFE	Diana Ross	Tamla Motown	10
17	33	THE MAN WHO SOLD THE WORLD	Lulu	Polydor	8
-	34	LISTEN TO THE MUSIC	Doobie Brothers ●	Warner Brothers	1
38	[35]	JUST MY SOUL RESPONDING	Smokey Robinson	Tamla Motown	2
-	36	EMMA	Hot Chocolate	RAK	1
-	37	MA-MA-BELLE	Electric Light Orchestra	Warner Brothers	1
-	38	ROCK AROUND THE CLOCK	Bill Haley & The Comets	MCA	1
-	39	WILL YOU STILL LOVE ME TOMORROW	Melanie	Neighborhood	2
-	40	I'VE GOT A THING ABOUT YOU BABY	Elvis Presley	RCA	1

March 1974

□ Highest position disc reached ● Act's first ever week on chart

WEEK ENDING 23 MARCH 1974

LW	TW	Title	Artist	Label	Wks
1	[1]	BILLY, DON'T BE A HERO	Paper Lace	Bus Stop	5
3	[2]	THE AIR THAT I BREATHE	Hollies	Polydor	7
4	3	THE MOST BEAUTIFUL GIRL	Charlie Rich	CBS	5
5	[4]	YOU'RE SIXTEEN	Ringo Starr	Apple	5
2	5	JEALOUS MIND	Alvin Stardust	Magnet	6
11	6	I GET A LITTLE SENTIMENTAL OVER YOU	New Seekers	Polydor	3
8	[7]	JET	Paul McCartney & Wings	Apple	4
7	8	REMEMBER (SHA-LA-LA-LA)	Bay City Rollers	Bell	6
9	[9]	IT'S YOU	Freddie Starr	Tiffany	5
36	10	EMMA	Hot Chocolate	RAK	2
12	[11]	CANDLE IN THE WIND	Elton John	DJM	4
17	12	SCHOOL LOVE	Barry Blue	Bell	3
10	13	WOMBLING SONG	The Wombles	CBS	9
6	14	DEVIL GATE DRIVE	Suzi Quatro	RAK	7
30	15	SEVEN SEAS OF RHYE	Queen	EMI	2
13	16	REBEL REBEL	David Bowie	RCA	5
14	17	MA HE'S MAKING EYES AT ME	Lena Zavaroni	Philips	7
19	18	JAMBALAYA	Carpenters	A&M	3
15	19	BURN BABY BURN	Hudson Ford	A&M	5
-	20	SEASONS IN THE SUN	Terry Jacks ●	Bell	1
28	21	LONG LIVE LOVE	Olivia Newton-John	Pye	2
24	22	EVERLASTING LOVE	Robert Knight	Monument	3
16	23	NEVER NEVER GONNA GIVE YA UP	Barry White	Pye	8
21	24	WHO DO YOU THINK YOU ARE	Candlewick Green	Decca	3
-	25	YOU ARE EVERYTHING	Diana Ross & Marvin Gaye ●	Tamla Motown	1
-	26	ANGEL FACE	Glitter Band ●	Bell	1
26	27	UNTIL YOU COME BACK TO ME	Aretha Franklin	Atlantic	5
37	28	MA-MA-BELLE	Electric Light Orchestra	Warner Brothers	2
27	29	SMOKIN' IN THE BOYS ROOM	Brownsville Station	Philips	3
18	30	LOVE'S THEME	Love Unlimited Orchestra	Pye	8
34	31	LISTEN TO THE MUSIC	Doobie Brothers	Warner Brothers	2
38	32	ROCK AROUND THE CLOCK	Bill Haley & The Comets	MCA	2
23	33	SOLITAIRE	Andy Williams	CBS	12
40	34	I'VE GOT A THING ABOUT YOU BABY	Elvis Presley	RCA	2
22	35	TIGER FEET	Mud	Rak	10
35	36	JUST MY SOUL RESPONDING	Smokey Robinson	Tamla Motown	3
31	37	FUNKY NASSAU	Beginning Of The End	Atlantic	3
-	38	MOCKINGBIRD	Carly Simon and James Taylor ●	Elektra	1
-	[39]	BOOGIE DOWN	Eddie Kendricks	Tamla Motown	1
-	40	WHO'S IN THE STRAWBERRY PATCH WITH SALLY	Tony Orlando and Dawn	Bell	2

WEEK ENDING 30 MARCH 1974

LW	TW	Title	Artist	Label	Wks
1	[1]	BILLY, DON'T BE A HERO	Paper Lace	Bus Stop	6
3	[2]	THE MOST BEAUTIFUL GIRL	Charlie Rich	CBS	6
20	3	SEASONS IN THE SUN	Terry Jacks	Bell	2
2	4	THE AIR THAT I BREATHE	Hollies	Polydor	8
6	[5]	I GET A LITTLE SENTIMENTAL OVER YOU	New Seekers	Polydor	4
10	6	EMMA	Hot Chocolate	RAK	3
4	7	YOU'RE SIXTEEN	Ringo Starr	Apple	6
-	8	REMEMBER ME THIS WAY	Gary Glitter	Bell	1
26	9	ANGEL FACE	Glitter Band	Bell	2
7	10	JET	Paul McCartney & Wings	Apple	5
12	[11]	SCHOOL LOVE	Barry Blue	Bell	4
18	[12]	JAMBALAYA	Carpenters	A&M	4
9	13	IT'S YOU	Freddie Starr	Tiffany	6
11	14	CANDLE IN THE WIND	Elton John	DJM	5
15	15	SEVEN SEAS OF RHYE	Queen	EMI	3
8	16	REMEMBER (SHA-LA-LA-LA)	Bay City Rollers	Bell	7
5	17	JEALOUS MIND	Alvin Stardust	Magnet	7
21	18	LONG LIVE LOVE	Olivia Newton-John	Pye	3
25	19	YOU ARE EVERYTHING	Diana Ross & Marvin Gaye	Tamla Motown	2

■ *Rock Around The Clock* checks in for its eighth and final chart run (16.03.74) ■ Barry White enjoys four weeks with two Top 20 hits, his own and the Love Unlimited hit which he wrote and produced (16.03.74) ■ Paul McCartney's *Jet* is the biggest hit with a dog's name in the title since Lobo's *Me And You And A Dog Named Boo* three years earlier (23.03.74) ■

March 1974

□ Highest position disc reached ● Act's first ever week on chart

LW	TW	Title	Artist	Label	Wks
22	20	EVERLASTING LOVE	Robert Knight	Monument	4
13	21	WOMBLING SONG	The Wombles	CBS	10
24	22	WHO DO YOU THINK YOU ARE	Candlewick Green	Decca	4
19	23	BURN BABY BURN	Hudson Ford	A&M	6
28	24	MA-MA-BELLE	Electric Light Orchestra	Warner Brothers	3
14	25	DEVIL GATE DRIVE	Suzi Quatro	RAK	8
17	26	MA HE'S MAKING EYES AT ME	Lena Zavaroni	Philips	8
32	27	ROCK AROUND THE CLOCK	Bill Haley & The Comets	MCA	3
23	28	NEVER NEVER GONNA GIVE YA UP	Barry White	Pye	9
-	29	GOLDEN AGE OF ROCK & ROLL	Mott The Hoople	CBS	1
31	30	LISTEN TO THE MUSIC	Doobie Brothers	Warner Brothers	3
27	31	UNTIL YOU COME BACK TO ME	Aretha Franklin	Atlantic	6
29	32	SMOKIN' IN THE BOYS ROOM	Brownsville Station	Philips	4
30	33	LOVE THEME	Love Unlimited Orchestra	Pye	9
38	34	MOCKINGBIRD	Carly Simon and James Taylor	Elektra	2
34	35	I'VE GOT A THING ABOUT YOU BABY	Elvis Presley	RCA	3
16	36	REBEL REBEL	David Bowie	RCA	6
-	37	I'M GONNA KNOCK ON YOUR DOOR	Little Jimmy Osmond	MGM	1
33	38	SOLITAIRE	Andy Williams	CBS	13
-	39	THE STING	Ragtimers ●	Pye	1
-	40	HOMELY GIRL	Chi-Lites	Brunswick	1

WEEK ENDING 6 APRIL 1974

LW	TW	Title	Artist	Label	Wks
3	1	SEASONS IN THE SUN	Terry Jacks	Bell	3
1	2	BILLY, DON'T BE A HERO	Paper Lace	Bus Stop	7
6	3	EMMA	Hot Chocolate	RAK	4
8	4	REMEMBER ME THIS WAY	Gary Glitter	Bell	2
9	5	ANGEL FACE	Glitter Band	Bell	3
-	6	EVERYDAY	Slade	Bell	1
5	7	I GET A LITTLE SENTIMENTAL OVER YOU	New Seekers	Polydor	5
2	8	THE MOST BEAUTIFUL GIRL	Charlie Rich	CBS	7
19	9	YOU ARE EVERYTHING	Diana Ross & Marvin Gaye	Tamla Motown	3
4	10	THE AIR THAT I BREATHE	Hollies	Polydor	9
15	11	SEVEN SEAS OF RHYE	Queen	EMI	4
7	12	YOU'RE SIXTEEN	Ringo Starr	Apple	7
11	13	SCHOOL LOVE	Barry Blue	Bell	5
12	14	JAMBALAYA	Carpenters	A&M	5
10	15	JET	Wings	Apple	6
18	16	LONG LIVE LOVE	Olivia Newton-John	Pye	4
14	17	CANDLE IN THE WIND	Elton John	DJM	6
13	18	IT'S YOU	Freddie Starr	Tiffany	7
20	19	EVERLASTING LOVE	Robert Knight	Monument	5
27	20	ROCK AROUND THE CLOCK	Bill Haley & The Comets	MCA	4
29	21	GOLDEN AGE OF ROCK & ROLL	Mott The Hoople	CBS	2
24	22	MA-MA-BELLE	Electric Light Orchestra	Warner Brothers	4
-	23	DOCTOR'S ORDERS	Sunny ●	CBS	1
16	24	REMEMBER (SHA-LA-LA-LA)	Bay City Rollers	Bell	8
37	25	I'M GONNA KNOCK ON YOUR DOOR	Little Jimmy Osmond	MGM	2
21	26	WOMBLING SONG	The Wombles	CBS	11
17	27	JEALOUS MIND	Alvin Stardust	Magnet	8
40	28	HOMELY GIRL	Chi-Lites	Brunswick	2
30	29	LISTEN TO THE MUSIC	Doobie Brothers	Warner Brothers	4
23	30	BURN BABY BURN	Hudson Ford	A&M	7
-	31	THE WAY WE WERE	Barbra Streisand	CBS	1
26	32	MA HE'S MAKING EYES AT ME	Lena Zavaroni	Philips	9
35	33	I'VE GOT A THING ABOUT YOU BABY	Elvis Presley	RCA	4
25	34	DEVIL GATE DRIVE	Suzi Quatro	RAK	9
-	35	THE ENTERTAINER	Marvin Hamlisch ●	MCA	1
-	36	REMEMBER YOU'RE A WOMBLE	The Wombles	CBS	1
34	37	MOCKINGBIRD	Carly Simon and James Taylor	Elektra	3
-	38	A WALKIN' MIRACLE	Limmie & The Family Cookin'	Avco	1
32	39	SMOKIN' IN THE BOYS ROOM	Brownsville Station	Philips	5
22	40	WHO DO YOU THINK YOU ARE	Candlewick Green	Decca	5

WEEK ENDING 13 APRIL 1974

LW	TW	Title	Artist	Label	Wks
1	1	SEASONS IN THE SUN	Terry Jacks	Bell	4
2	2	BILLY, DON'T BE A HERO	Paper Lace	Bus Stop	8
4	3	REMEMBER ME THIS WAY	Gary Glitter	Bell	3
6	4	EVERYDAY	Slade	Bell	2
5	5	ANGEL FACE	Glitter Band	Bell	4
3	6	EMMA	Hot Chocolate	RAK	5
9	7	YOU ARE EVERYTHING	Diana Ross & Marvin Gaye	Tamla Motown	4
-	8	THE CAT CREPT IN	Mud	RAK	1
8	9	THE MOST BEAUTIFUL GIRL	Charlie Rich	CBS	8
11	10	SEVEN SEAS OF RHYE	Queen	EMI	5
16	11	LONG LIVE LOVE	Olivia Newton-John	Pye	5
7	12	I GET A LITTLE SENTIMENTAL OVER YOU	New Seekers	Polydor	6
14	13	JAMBALAYA	Carpenters	A&M	6
23	14	DOCTOR'S ORDERS	Sunny	CBS	2
25	15	I'M GONNA KNOCK ON YOUR DOOR	Little Jimmy Osmond	MGM	3
13	16	SCHOOL LOVE	Barry Blue	Bell	6
20	17	ROCK AROUND THE CLOCK	Bill Haley & The Comets	MCA	5
21	18	GOLDEN AGE OF ROCK & ROLL	Mott The Hoople	CBS	3
17	19	CANDLE IN THE WIND	Elton John	DJM	7
36	20	REMEMBER YOU'RE A WOMBLE	The Wombles	CBS	2
19	21	EVERLASTING LOVE	Robert Knight	Monument	6
28	22	HOMELY GIRL	Chi-Lites	Brunswick	3
38	23	A WALKIN' MIRACLE	Limmie & The Family Cookin'	Avco	2
10	24	THE AIR THAT I BREATHE	Hollies	Polydor	10
12	25	YOU'RE SIXTEEN	Ringo Starr	Apple	8
26	26	WOMBLING SONG	The Wombles	CBS	12
15	27	JET	Wings	Apple	7
18	28	IT'S YOU	Freddie Starr	Tiffany	8
-	29	I KNOW WHAT I LIKE (IN YOUR WARDROBE)	Genesis ●	Charisma	1
22	30	MA-MA-BELLE	Electric Light Orchestra	Warner Brothers	5
-	31	THE STING	Ragtimers	Pye	2
31	32	THE WAY WE WERE	Barbra Streisand	CBS	2
24	33	REMEMBER (SHA-LA-LA-LA)	Bay City Rollers	Bell	9
29	34	LISTEN TO THE MUSIC	Doobie Brothers	Warner Brothers	5
35	35	THE ENTERTAINER	Marvin Hamlisch	MCA	2
-	36	LONG LEGGED WOMAN DRESSED IN BLACK	Mungo Jerry	Dawn	1
27	37	JEALOUS MIND	Alvin Stardust	Magnet	9
32	38	MA HE'S MAKING EYES AT ME	Lena Zavaroni	Philips	10
-	39	YEAR OF DECISION	Three Degrees ●	Philadelphia	1
-	40	HE'S MISSTRA KNOW IT ALL	Stevie Wonder	Tamla Motown	1

WEEK ENDING 20 APRIL 1974

LW	TW	Title	Artist	Label	Wks
1	1	SEASONS IN THE SUN	Terry Jacks	Bell	5
8	2	THE CAT CREPT IN	Mud	RAK	2
4	3	EVERYDAY	Slade	Bell	3
5	4	ANGEL FACE	Glitter Band	Bell	5
7	5	YOU ARE EVERYTHING	Diana Ross & Marvin Gaye	Tamla Motown	5
6	6	EMMA	Hot Chocolate	RAK	6
3	7	REMEMBER ME THIS WAY	Gary Glitter	Bell	4
20	8	REMEMBER YOU'RE A WOMBLE	The Wombles	CBS	3
14	9	DOCTOR'S ORDERS	Sunny	CBS	3
2	10	BILLY, DON'T BE A HERO	Paper Lace	Bus Stop	9
22	11	HOMELY GIRL	Chi-Lites	Brunswick	4
17	12	ROCK AROUND THE CLOCK	Bill Haley & The Comets	MCA	6
15	13	I'M GONNA KNOCK ON YOUR DOOR	Little Jimmy Osmond	MGM	4
10	14	SEVEN SEAS OF RHYE	Queen	EMI	6
23	15	A WALKIN' MIRACLE	Limmie & The Family Cookin'	Avco	3
9	16	THE MOST BEAUTIFUL GIRL	Charlie Rich	CBS	9
-	17	WATERLOO	Abba ●	Epic	1
18	18	GOLDEN AGE OF ROCK & ROLL	Mott The Hoople	CBS	4
11	19	LONG LIVE LOVE	Olivia Newton-John	Pye	6
12	20	I GET A LITTLE SENTIMENTAL OVER YOU	New Seekers	Polydor	7
29	21	I KNOW WHAT I LIKE (IN YOUR WARDROBE)	Genesis	Charisma	2
13	22	JAMBALAYA	Carpenters	A&M	7
26	23	WOMBLING SONG	The Wombles	CBS	13
24	24	THE AIR THAT I BREATHE	Hollies	Polydor	11
36	25	LONG LEGGED WOMAN DRESSED IN BLACK	Mungo Jerry	Dawn	2

In these weeks ■ *The Entertainer* by Marvin Hamlisch, the actual music used in the film 'The Sting', replaces *The Sting* by the Ragtimers in the top 40 (06.04.74) ■ Abba wins the Eurovision song contest with *Waterloo*, and the most successful chart career by any Swedish act is launched (20.04.74)■

LW	TW	Title	Artist	Label	Wks
16	26	SCHOOL LOVE	Barry Blue	*Bell*	7
35	27	THE ENTERTAINER	Marvin Hamlisch	*MCA*	3
-	28	ROCK & ROLL SUICIDE	David Bowie	*RCA*	1
25	29	YOU'RE SIXTEEN	Ringo Starr	*Apple*	9
-	30	BEHIND CLOSED DOORS	Charlie Rich	*Epic*	1
40	31	HE'S MISSTRA KNOW IT ALL	Stevie Wonder	*Tamla Motown*	2
28	32	IT'S YOU	Freddie Starr	*Tiffany*	9
39	33	YEAR OF DECISION	Three Degrees	*Philadelphia*	2
32	34	THE WAY WE WERE	Barbra Streisand	*CBS*	3
31	35	THE STING	Ragtimers	*Pye*	3
27	36	JET	Wings	*Apple*	8
-	37	SATISFACTION GUARANTEED	Harold Melvin & The Bluenotes	*Philadelphia*	1
-	38	DON'T STAY AWAY TOO LONG	Peters & Lee	*Philips*	1
19	39	CANDLE IN THE WIND	Elton John	*DJM*	8
34	40	LISTEN TO THE MUSIC	Doobie Brothers	*Warner Brothers*	6

LW TW *WEEK ENDING* **27 APRIL 1974** Wks

LW	TW	Title	Artist	Label	Wks
1	[1]	SEASONS IN THE SUN	Terry Jacks	*Bell*	6
17	2	WATERLOO	Abba	*Epic*	2
2	3	THE CAT CREPT IN	Mud	*RAK*	3
8	4	REMEMBER YOU'RE A WOMBLE	The Wombles	*CBS*	4
4	5	ANGEL FACE	Glitter Band	*Bell*	6
5	6	YOU ARE EVERYTHING	Diana Ross & Marvin Gaye	*Tamla Motown*	6
3	7	EVERYDAY	Slade	*Bell*	4
9	8	DOCTOR'S ORDERS	Sunny	*CBS*	4
11	9	HOMELY GIRL	Chi-Lites	*Brunswick*	5
15	10	A WALKIN' MIRACLE	Limmie & The Family Cookin'	*Avco*	4
13	[11]	I'M GONNA KNOCK ON YOUR DOOR	Little Jimmy Osmond	*MGM*	5
7	12	REMEMBER ME THIS WAY	Gary Glitter	*Bell*	5
12	13	ROCK AROUND THE CLOCK	Bill Haley & The Comets	*MCA*	7
6	14	EMMA	Hot Chocolate	*RAK*	7
10	15	BILLY, DON'T BE A HERO	Paper Lace	*Bus Stop*	10
18	[16]	GOLDEN AGE OF ROCK & ROLL	Mott The Hoople	*CBS*	5
14	17	SEVEN SEAS OF RHYE	Queen	*EMI*	7
25	18	LONG LEGGED WOMAN DRESSED IN BLACK	Mungo Jerry	*Dawn*	3
38	19	DON'T STAY AWAY TOO LONG	Peters & Lee	*Philips*	2
31	20	HE'S MISSTRA KNOW IT ALL	Stevie Wonder	*Tamla Motown*	3
21	[21]	I KNOW WHAT I LIKE (IN YOUR WARDROBE)	Genesis	*Charisma*	3
19	22	LONG LIVE LOVE	Olivia Newton-John	*Pye*	7
28	23	ROCK & ROLL SUICIDE	David Bowie	*RCA*	2
16	24	THE MOST BEAUTIFUL GIRL	Charlie Rich	*CBS*	10
27	[25]	THE ENTERTAINER	Marvin Hamlisch	*MCA*	4
-	26	ROCK & ROLL WINTER	Wizzard	*Warner Brothers*	1
30	27	BEHIND CLOSED DOORS	Charlie Rich	*Epic*	2
33	28	YEAR OF DECISION	Three Degrees	*Philadelphia*	3
23	29	WOMBLING SONG	The Wombles	*CBS*	14
22	30	JAMBALAYA	Carpenters	*A&M*	8
-	31	I CAN'T STOP	Osmonds	*MCA*	1
24	32	THE AIR THAT I BREATHE	Hollies	*Polydor*	12
20	33	I GET A LITTLE SENTIMENTAL OVER YOU	New Seekers	*Polydor*	8
29	34	YOU'RE SIXTEEN	Ringo Starr	*Apple*	10
-	35	SHANG-A-LANG	Bay City Rollers	*Bell*	1
34	36	THE WAY WE WERE	Barbra Streisand	*CBS*	4
35	37	THE STING	Ragtimers	*Pye*	4
37	38	SATISFACTION GUARANTEED	Harold Melvin & The Bluenotes	*Philadelphia*	2
-	39	I'LL ALWAYS LOVE MY MAMA	Intruders ●	*Philadelphia*	1
36	40	JET	Wings	*Apple*	9

LW TW *WEEK ENDING* **4 MAY 1974** Wks

LW	TW	Title	Artist	Label	Wks
2	[1]	WATERLOO	Abba	*Epic*	3
3	[2]	THE CAT CREPT IN	Mud	*RAK*	4
1	3	SEASONS IN THE SUN	Terry Jacks	*Bell*	7
4	4	REMEMBER YOU'RE A WOMBLE	The Wombles	*CBS*	5
9	[5]	HOMELY GIRL	Chi-Lites	*Brunswick*	6
10	[6]	A WALKIN' MIRACLE	Limmie & The Family Cookin'	*Avco*	5
8	[7]	DOCTOR'S ORDERS	Sunny	*CBS*	5
6	8	YOU ARE EVERYTHING	Diana Ross & Marvin Gaye	*Tamla Motown*	7
26	9	ROCK & ROLL WINTER	Wizzard	*Warner Brothers*	2
5	10	ANGEL FACE	Glitter Band	*Bell*	7
19	11	DON'T STAY AWAY TOO LONG	Peters & Lee	*Philips*	3
35	12	SHANG-A-LANG	Bay City Rollers	*Bell*	2
7	13	EVERYDAY	Slade	*Bell*	5
18	14	LONG LEGGED WOMAN DRESSED IN BLACK	Mungo Jerry	*Dawn*	4
11	15	I'M GONNA KNOCK ON YOUR DOOR	Little Jimmy Osmond	*MGM*	6
28	16	YEAR OF DECISION	Three Degrees	*Philadelphia*	4
20	17	HE'S MISSTRA KNOW IT ALL	Stevie Wonder	*Tamla Motown*	4
14	18	EMMA	Hot Chocolate	*RAK*	8
13	19	ROCK AROUND THE CLOCK	Bill Haley & The Comets	*MCA*	8
12	20	REMEMBER ME THIS WAY	Gary Glitter	*Bell*	6
27	21	BEHIND CLOSED DOORS	Charlie Rich	*Epic*	3
16	22	GOLDEN AGE OF ROCK & ROLL	Mott The Hoople	*CBS*	6
23	23	ROCK & ROLL SUICIDE	David Bowie	*RCA*	3
31	24	I CAN'T STOP	Osmonds	*MCA*	2
25	[25]	THE ENTERTAINER	Marvin Hamlisch	*MCA*	5
21	26	I KNOW WHAT I LIKE (IN YOUR WARDROBE)	Genesis	*Charisma*	4
-	27	SUGAR BABY LOVE	Rubettes ●	*Polydor*	1
-	28	SPIDERS & SNAKES	Jim Stafford ●	*MGM*	1
-	29	THE SOUND OF PHILADELPHIA	MFSB	*Philadelphia*	1
29	30	WOMBLING SONG	The Wombles	*CBS*	15
15	31	BILLY, DON'T BE A HERO	Paper Lace	*Bus Stop*	11
38	[32]	SATISFACTION GUARANTEED	Harold Melvin & The Bluenotes	*Philadelphia*	3
39	33	I'LL ALWAYS LOVE MY MAMA	Intruders	*Philadelphia*	2
24	34	THE MOST BEAUTIFUL GIRL	Charlie Rich	*CBS*	11
30	35	JAMBALAYA	Carpenters	*A&M*	9
17	36	SEVEN SEAS OF RHYE	Queen	*EMI*	8
37	37	THE STING	Ragtimers	*Pye*	5
-	38	BREAK THE RULES	Status Quo	*Vertigo*	1
-	39	THE NIGHT CHICAGO DIED	Paper Lace	*Bus Stop*	1
36	40	THE WAY WE WERE	Barbra Streisand	*CBS*	5

May 1974

□ Highest position disc reached ● Act's first ever week on chart

LW TW *WEEK ENDING* **11 MAY 1974** Wks

LW	TW	Title	Artist	Label	Wks
1	[1]	WATERLOO	Abba	*Epic*	4
27	2	SUGAR BABY LOVE	Rubettes	*Polydor*	2
4	[3]	REMEMBER YOU'RE A WOMBLE	The Wombles	*CBS*	6
11	4	DON'T STAY AWAY TOO LONG	Peters & Lee	*Philips*	4
12	5	SHANG-A-LANG	Bay City Rollers	*Bell*	3
9	[6]	ROCK & ROLL WINTER	Wizzard	*Warner Brothers*	3
5	7	HOMELY GIRL	Chi-Lites	*Brunswick*	7
6	8	A WALKIN' MIRACLE	Limmie & The Family Cookin'	*Avco*	6
3	9	SEASONS IN THE SUN	Terry Jacks	*Bell*	8
17	[10]	HE'S MISSTRA KNOW IT ALL	Stevie Wonder	*Tamla Motown*	5
-	11	RED DRESS	Alvin Stardust	*Magnet*	1
2	12	THE CAT CREPT IN	Mud	*RAK*	5
14	[13]	LONG LEGGED WOMAN DRESSED IN BLACK	Mungo Jerry	*Dawn*	5
39	14	THE NIGHT CHICAGO DIED	Paper Lace	*Bus Stop*	2
8	15	YOU ARE EVERYTHING	Diana Ross & Marvin Gaye	*Tamla Motown*	8
24	16	I CAN'T STOP	Osmonds	*MCA*	3
7	17	DOCTOR'S ORDERS	Sunny	*CBS*	6
28	18	SPIDERS & SNAKES	Jim Stafford	*MGM*	2
10	19	ANGEL FACE	Glitter Band	*Bell*	8
16	20	YEAR OF DECISION	Three Degrees	*Philadelphia*	5
15	21	I'M GONNA KNOCK ON YOUR DOOR	Little Jimmy Osmond	*MGM*	7
23	[22]	ROCK & ROLL SUICIDE	David Bowie	*RCA*	4
21	23	BEHIND CLOSED DOORS	Charlie Rich	*Epic*	4
13	24	EVERYDAY	Slade	*Bell*	6
29	25	THE SOUND OF PHILADELPHIA	MFSB	*Philadelphia*	2
38	26	BREAK THE RULES	Status Quo	*Vertigo*	2
-	27	THIS TOWN AIN'T BIG ENOUGH FOR BOTH OF US	Sparks ●	*Island*	1
25	28	THE ENTERTAINER	Marvin Hamlisch	*MCA*	6
-	29	IF I DIDN'T CARE	David Cassidy	*Bell*	1

■*Rock Around The Clock* slips a place, but *Rock And Roll Winter* and *Rock And Roll Suicide* join Mott The Hoople's *Golden Age Of Rock And Roll* for the most rock-filled chart in ages (27.04.74) ■ Jim Stafford, Charlie Rich and the Carpenters, with their version of Hank Williams' classic *Jambalaya* give the chart a real country flavour (04.05.74)■

May 1974

□ Highest position disc reached ● Act's first ever week on chart

LW	TW	Title / Artist	Label	Wks
30	30	WOMBLING SONG The Wombles	*CBS*	16
19	31	ROCK AROUND THE CLOCK Bill Haley & The Comets	*MCA*	9
33	[32]	I'LL ALWAYS LOVE MY MAMA Intruders	*Philadelphia*	3
26	33	I KNOW WHAT I LIKE (IN YOUR WARDROBE) Genesis	*Charisma*	5
-	34	THERE'S A GHOST IN MY HOUSE R. Dean Taylor	*Tamla Motown*	1
-	[35]	LAST TIME I SAW HIM Diana Ross	*Tamla Motown*	1
32	36	SATISFACTION GUARANTEED Harold Melvin & The Bluenotes	*Philadelphia*	4
-	37	GO Gigliola Cinquetti	*CBS*	1
22	38	GOLDEN AGE OF ROCK & ROLL Mott The Hoople	*CBS*	7
34	39	THE MOST BEAUTIFUL GIRL Charlie Rich	*CBS*	12
31	40	BILLY, DON'T BE A HERO Paper Lace	*Bus Stop*	12

LW	TW	*WEEK ENDING* **18 MAY 1974**		Wks
2	[1]	SUGAR BABY LOVE Rubettes	*Polydor*	4
1	2	WATERLOO Abba	*Epic*	5
4	[3]	DON'T STAY AWAY TOO LONG Peters & Lee	*Philips*	5
5	4	SHANG-A-LANG Bay City Rollers	*Bell*	4
3	5	REMEMBER YOU'RE A WOMBLE The Wombles	*CBS*	7
6	6	ROCK & ROLL WINTER Wizzard	*Warner Brothers*	4
14	7	THE NIGHT CHICAGO DIED Paper Lace	*Bus Stop*	3
7	8	HOMELY GIRL Chi-Lites	*Brunswick*	8
27	9	THIS TOWN AIN'T BIG ENOUGH FOR BOTH OF US Sparks	*Island*	2
11	10	RED DRESS Alvin Stardust	*Magnet*	2
10	11	HE'S MISSTRA KNOW IT ALL Stevie Wonder	*Tamla Motown*	6
8	12	A WALKIN' MIRACLE Limmie & The Family Cookin'	*Avco*	7
20	[13]	YEAR OF DECISION Three Degrees	*Philadelphia*	6
18	[14]	SPIDERS & SNAKES Jim Stafford	*MGM*	3
16	15	I CAN'T STOP Osmonds	*MCA*	4
23	[16]	BEHIND CLOSED DOORS Charlie Rich	*Epic*	5
12	17	THE CAT CREPT IN Mud	*RAK*	6
26	18	BREAK THE RULES Status Quo	*Vertigo*	3
13	19	LONG LEGGED WOMAN DRESSED IN BLACK Mungo Jerry	*Dawn*	6
9	20	SEASONS IN THE SUN Terry Jacks	*Bell*	9
29	21	IF I DIDN'T CARE David Cassidy	*Bell*	2
37	22	GO Gigliola Cinquetti	*CBS*	2
17	23	DOCTOR'S ORDERS Sunny	*CBS*	7
34	24	THERE'S A GHOST IN MY HOUSE R. Dean Taylor	*Tamla Motown*	2
25	25	THE SOUND OF PHILADELPHIA MFSB	*Philadelphia*	3
22	26	ROCK & ROLL SUICIDE David Bowie	*RCA*	5
15	27	YOU ARE EVERYTHING Diana Ross & Marvin Gaye	*Tamla Motown*	9
28	28	THE ENTERTAINER Marvin Hamlisch	*MCA*	7
-	29	I SEE A STAR Mouth & McNeal ●	*Decca*	1
19	30	ANGEL FACE Glitter Band	*Bell*	9
30	31	WOMBLING SONG The Wombles	*CBS*	17
-	[32]	AMERICA David Essex	*CBS*	1
-	33	JUDY TEEN Cockney Rebel ●	*EMI*	1
-	34	(YOU KEEP ME) HANGING ON Cliff Richard	*EMI*	1
31	35	ROCK AROUND THE CLOCK Bill Haley & The Comets	*MCA*	10
21	36	I'M GONNA KNOCK ON YOUR DOOR Little Jimmy Osmond	*MGM*	8
35	37	LAST TIME I SAW HIM Diana Ross	*Tamla Motown*	2
-	[38]	FOR OLD TIMES SAKE Millican and Nesbitt	*Pye*	1
32	39	I'LL ALWAYS LOVE MY MAMA Intruders	*Philadelphia*	4
-	[40]	TOM THE PEEPER Act One ●	*Mercury*	1

LW	TW	*WEEK ENDING* **25 MAY 1974**		Wks
1	[1]	SUGAR BABY LOVE Rubettes	*Polydor*	5
4	[2]	SHANG-A-LANG Bay City Rollers	*Bell*	5
9	3	THIS TOWN AIN'T BIG ENOUGH FOR BOTH OF US Sparks	*Island*	3
3	4	DON'T STAY AWAY TOO LONG Peters & Lee	*Philips*	6
7	5	THE NIGHT CHICAGO DIED Paper Lace	*Bus Stop*	4
2	6	WATERLOO Abba	*Epic*	6
10	[7]	RED DRESS Alvin Stardust	*Magnet*	3
18	[8]	BREAK THE RULES Status Quo	*Vertigo*	4
24	9	THERE'S A GHOST IN MY HOUSE R. Dean Taylor	*Tamla Motown*	3
21	10	IF I DIDN'T CARE David Cassidy	*Bell*	3
6	11	ROCK & ROLL WINTER Wizzard	*Warner Brothers*	5
15	[12]	I CAN'T STOP Osmonds	*MCA*	5
5	13	REMEMBER YOU'RE A WOMBLE The Wombles	*CBS*	8
14	[14]	SPIDERS & SNAKES Jim Stafford	*MGM*	4
8	15	HOMELY GIRL Chi-Lites	*Brunswick*	9
22	16	GO Gigliola Cinquetti	*CBS*	3
11	17	HE'S MISSTRA KNOW IT ALL Stevie Wonder	*Tamla Motown*	7
29	18	I SEE A STAR Mouth & McNeal	*Decca*	2
13	19	YEAR OF DECISION Three Degrees	*Philadelphia*	7
19	20	LONG LEGGED WOMAN DRESSED IN BLACK Mungo Jerry	*Dawn*	7
34	21	(YOU KEEP ME) HANGING ON Cliff Richard	*EMI*	2
25	[22]	THE SOUND OF PHILADELPHIA MFSB	*Philadelphia*	4
-	23	HEY ROCK AND ROLL Showaddywaddy ●	*Bell*	1
20	24	SEASONS IN THE SUN Terry Jacks	*Bell*	10
16	25	BEHIND CLOSED DOORS Charlie Rich	*Epic*	6
-	26	THE 'IN' CROWD Bryan Ferry	*Island*	1
12	27	A WALKIN' MIRACLE Limmie & The Family Cookin'	*Avco*	8
33	28	JUDY TEEN Cockney Rebel	*EMI*	2
26	29	ROCK & ROLL SUICIDE David Bowie	*RCA*	6
17	30	THE CAT CREPT IN Mud	*RAK*	7
28	31	THE ENTERTAINER Marvin Hamlisch	*MCA*	8
23	32	DOCTOR'S ORDERS Sunny	*CBS*	8
27	33	YOU ARE EVERYTHING Diana Ross & Marvin Gaye	*Tamla Motown*	10
32	34	AMERICA David Essex	*CBS*	2
-	35	W.O.L.D. Harry Chapin ●	*Elektra*	1
-	36	I WANT TO GIVE Perry Como	*RCA*	1
-	37	GETTING OVER YOU Andy Williams	*CBS*	1
31	38	WOMBLING SONG The Wombles	*CBS*	18
37	39	LAST TIME I SAW HIM Diana Ross	*Tamla Motown*	3
-	40	THE STREAK Ray Stevens	*Westbound*	1

LW	TW	*WEEK ENDING* **1 JUNE 1974**		Wks
1	[1]	SUGAR BABY LOVE Rubettes	*Polydor*	6
3	[2]	THIS TOWN AIN'T BIG ENOUGH FOR BOTH OF US Sparks	*Island*	4
5	[3]	THE NIGHT CHICAGO DIED Paper Lace	*Bus Stop*	5
9	4	THERE'S A GHOST IN MY HOUSE R. Dean Taylor	*Tamla Motown*	4
4	5	DON'T STAY AWAY TOO LONG Peters & Lee	*Philips*	7
23	6	HEY ROCK AND ROLL Showaddywaddy	*Bell*	2
2	7	SHANG-A-LANG Bay City Rollers	*Bell*	6
16	[8]	GO Gigliola Cinquetti	*CBS*	4
10	[9]	IF I DIDN'T CARE David Cassidy	*Bell*	4
7	10	RED DRESS Alvin Stardust	*Magnet*	4
8	11	BREAK THE RULES Status Quo	*Vertigo*	5
18	12	I SEE A STAR Mouth & McNeal	*Decca*	3
40	13	THE STREAK Ray Stevens	*Westbound*	2
12	14	I CAN'T STOP Osmonds	*MCA*	6
6	15	WATERLOO Abba	*Epic*	7
26	16	THE 'IN' CROWD Bryan Ferry	*Island*	2
28	17	JUDY TEEN Cockney Rebel	*EMI*	3
14	18	SPIDERS & SNAKES Jim Stafford	*MGM*	5
13	19	REMEMBER YOU'RE A WOMBLE The Wombles	*CBS*	9
21	20	(YOU KEEP ME) HANGING ON Cliff Richard	*EMI*	3
11	21	ROCK & ROLL WINTER Wizzard	*Warner Brothers*	6
-	22	A TOUCH TOO MUCH Arrows ●	*Rak*	1
15	23	HOMELY GIRL Chi-Lites	*Brunswick*	10
-	24	JARROW SONG Alan Price	*Warner*	1
19	25	YEAR OF DECISION Three Degrees	*Philadelphia*	8
17	26	HE'S MISSTRA KNOW IT ALL Stevie Wonder	*Tamla Motown*	8
25	27	BEHIND CLOSED DOORS Charlie Rich	*Epic*	7
-	28	SUMMER BREEZE Isley Brothers	*Epic*	1
27	29	A WALKIN' MIRACLE Limmie & The Family Cookin'	*Avco*	9
-	30	DON'T LET THE SUN GO DOWN ON ME Elton John	*DJM*	1

In these weeks ■ R. Dean Taylor, Motown's first white solo act, keeps up his record of having a hit every three years, having previously charted in the summers of 1968 and 1971 (11.05.74) ■ The chart contained five solo hitmakers who previously had charted with groups - David Cassidy, Bryan Ferry, Alan Price, Cozy Powell and Terry Jacks (01.06.74)■

LW	TW	Title	Artist	Label	Wks
-	31	THE MAN IN BLACK	Cozy Powell	Rak	1
36	32	I WANT TO GIVE	Perry Como	RCA	2
22	33	THE SOUND OF PHILADELPHIA	MFSB	Philadelphia	5
35	[34]	W.O.L.D.	Harry Chapin	Elektra	2
20	35	LONG LEGGED WOMAN DRESSED IN BLACK	Mungo Jerry	Dawn	8
-	36	LIVERPOOL LOU	Scaffold	Warner	1
31	37	THE ENTERTAINER	Marvin Hamlisch	MCA	9
24	38	SEASONS IN THE SUN	Terry Jacks	Bell	11
34	39	AMERICA	David Essex	CBS	3
38	40	WOMBLING SONG	The Wombles	CBS	19

WEEK ENDING 8 JUNE 1974

LW	TW	Title	Artist	Label	Wks
1	[1]	SUGAR BABY LOVE	Rubettes	Polydor	7
2	[2]	THIS TOWN AIN'T BIG ENOUGH FOR BOTH OF US	Sparks	Island	5
6	3	HEY ROCK AND ROLL	Showaddywaddy	Bell	3
13	4	THE STREAK	Ray Stevens	Westbound	3
4	5	THERE'S A GHOST IN MY HOUSE	R. Dean Taylor	Tamla Motown	5
3	6	THE NIGHT CHICAGO DIED	Paper Lace	Bus Stop	6
17	7	JUDY TEEN	Cockney Rebel	EMI	4
12	[8]	I SEE A STAR	Mouth & McNeal	Decca	4
9	[9]	IF I DIDN'T CARE	David Cassidy	Bell	5
11	10	BREAK THE RULES	Status Quo	Vertigo	6
5	11	DON'T STAY AWAY TOO LONG	Peters & Lee	Philips	8
8	12	GO	Gigliola Cinquetti	CBS	5
16	[13]	THE 'IN' CROWD	Bryan Ferry	Island	3
7	14	SHANG-A-LANG	Bay City Rollers	Bell	7
20	15	(YOU KEEP ME) HANGING ON	Cliff Richard	EMI	4
22	16	A TOUCH TOO MUCH	Arrows	Rak	2
14	17	I CAN'T STOP	Osmonds	MCA	7
24	18	JARROW SONG	Alan Price	Warner	2
10	19	RED DRESS	Alvin Stardust	Magnet	5
19	20	REMEMBER YOU'RE A WOMBLE	The Wombles	CBS	10
28	21	SUMMER BREEZE	Isley Brothers	Epic	2
36	22	LIVERPOOL LOU	Scaffold	Warner	2
15	23	WATERLOO	Abba	Epic	8
30	24	DON'T LET THE SUN GO DOWN ON ME	Elton John	DJM	2
18	25	SPIDERS & SNAKES	Jim Stafford	MGM	6
31	26	THE MAN IN BLACK	Cozy Powell	Rak	2
-	27	CAN'T GET ENOUGH	Bad Company ●	Island	1
23	28	HOMELY GIRL	Chi-Lites	Brunswick	11
-	29	GUILTY	Pearls	Bell	1
33	30	THE SOUND OF PHILADELPHIA	MFSB	Philadelphia	6
32	[31]	I WANT TO GIVE	Perry Como	RCA	3
25	32	YEAR OF DECISION	Three Degrees	Philadelphia	9
-	[33]	PERSONALITY	Lena Zavaroni	Philips	1
21	34	ROCK & ROLL WINTER	Wizzard	Warner Brothers	7
-	[35]	GETTING OVER YOU	Andy Williams	CBS	2
26	36	HE'S MISSTRA KNOW IT ALL	Stevie Wonder	Tamla Motown	9
-	37	I'D LOVE YOU TO WANT ME	Lobo	UK	1
-	38	OOH I DO	Lynsey De Paul	Warner	1
27	39	BEHIND CLOSED DOORS	Charlie Rich	Epic	8
34	40	W.O.L.D.	Harry Chapin	Elektra	3

WEEK ENDING 15 JUNE 1974

LW	TW	Title	Artist	Label	Wks
4	[1]	THE STREAK	Ray Stevens	Westbound	4
3	[2]	HEY ROCK AND ROLL	Showaddywaddy	Bell	4
5	[3]	THERE'S A GHOST IN MY HOUSE	R. Dean Taylor	Tamla Motown	6
2	4	THIS TOWN AIN'T BIG ENOUGH FOR BOTH OF US	Sparks	Island	6
-	5	ALWAYS YOURS	Gary Glitter	Bell	1
1	6	SUGAR BABY LOVE	Rubettes	Polydor	8
7	7	JUDY TEEN	Cockney Rebel	EMI	5
18	8	JARROW SONG	Alan Price	Warner	3
16	9	A TOUCH TOO MUCH	Arrows	Rak	3
8	10	I SEE A STAR	Mouth & McNeal	Decca	5
12	11	GO	Gigliola Cinquetti	CBS	6
6	12	THE NIGHT CHICAGO DIED	Paper Lace	Bus Stop	7

June 1974

□ Highest position disc reached ● Act's first ever week on chart

LW	TW	Title	Artist	Label	Wks
15	[13]	(YOU KEEP ME) HANGING ON	Cliff Richard	EMI	5
13	14	THE 'IN' CROWD	Bryan Ferry	Island	4
9	15	IF I DIDN'T CARE	David Cassidy	Bell	6
24	[16]	DON'T LET THE SUN GO DOWN ON ME	Elton John	DJM	3
21	17	SUMMER BREEZE	Isley Brothers	Epic	3
22	18	LIVERPOOL LOU	Scaffold	Warner	3
26	19	THE MAN IN BLACK	Cozy Powell	Rak	3
11	20	DON'T STAY AWAY TOO LONG	Peters & Lee	Philips	9
27	21	CAN'T GET ENOUGH	Bad Company	Island	2
29	22	GUILTY	Pearls	Bell	2
14	23	SHANG-A-LANG	Bay City Rollers	Bell	8
37	24	I'D LOVE YOU TO WANT ME	Lobo	UK	2
-	25	ONE MAN BAND	Leo Sayer	Chrysalis	1
20	26	REMEMBER YOU'RE A WOMBLE	The Wombles	CBS	11
10	27	BREAK THE RULES	Status Quo	Vertigo	7
17	28	I CAN'T STOP	Osmonds	MCA	8
19	29	RED DRESS	Alvin Stardust	Magnet	6
38	30	OOH I DO	Lynsey De Paul	Warner	2
31	[31]	I WANT TO GIVE	Perry Como	RCA	4
-	32	I WON'T LAST A DAY WITHOUT YOU	Carpenters	A&M	1
23	33	WATERLOO	Abba	Epic	9
-	34	WALL STREET SHUFFLE	10CC	UK	1
-	35	IF YOU'RE READY (COME GO WITH ME)	Staple Singers	STAX	1
25	36	SPIDERS & SNAKES	Jim Stafford	MGM	7
-	37	GOING DOWN THE ROAD	Roy Wood	Harvest	1
-	38	THE POACHER	Ronnie Lane/Slim Chance	GM	1
-	39	KISSIN' IN THE BACK ROW	Drifters	Bell	1
33	40	PERSONALITY	Lena Zavaroni	Philips	2

WEEK ENDING 22 JUNE 1974

LW	TW	Title	Artist	Label	Wks
5	[1]	ALWAYS YOURS	Gary Glitter	Bell	2
1	2	THE STREAK	Ray Stevens	Westbound	5
2	3	HEY ROCK AND ROLL	Showaddywaddy	Bell	5
3	4	THERE'S A GHOST IN MY HOUSE	R. Dean Taylor	Tamla Motown	7
8	[5]	JUDY TEEN	Cockney Rebel	EMI	6
9	[6]	JARROW SONG	Alan Price	Warner	4
18	[7]	LIVERPOOL LOU	Scaffold	Warner	4
10	[8]	A TOUCH TOO MUCH	Arrows	Rak	4
4	9	THIS TOWN AIN'T BIG ENOUGH FOR BOTH OF US	Sparks	Island	7
24	10	I'D LOVE YOU TO WANT ME	Lobo	UK	3
-	11	SHE	Charles Aznavour	Barclay	1
6	12	SUGAR BABY LOVE	Rubettes	Polydor	9
25	13	ONE MAN BAND	Leo Sayer	Chrysalis	2
39	14	KISSIN' IN THE BACK ROW	Drifters	Bell	2
10	15	I SEE A STAR	Mouth & McNeal	Decca	6
17	[16]	SUMMER BREEZE	Isley Brothers	Epic	4
16	17	DON'T LET THE SUN GO DOWN ON ME	Elton John	DJM	4
22	18	GUILTY	Pearls	Bell	3
14	19	THE 'IN' CROWD	Bryan Ferry	Island	5
19	20	THE MAN IN BLACK	Cozy Powell	Rak	4
37	21	GOING DOWN THE ROAD	Roy Wood	Harvest	2
13	22	(YOU KEEP ME) HANGING ON	Cliff Richard	EMI	6
21	23	CAN'T GET ENOUGH	Bad Company	Island	3
12	24	THE NIGHT CHICAGO DIED	Paper Lace	Bus Stop	8
11	25	GO	Gigliola Cinquetti	CBS	7
30	26	OOH I DO	Lynsey De Paul	Warner	3
20	27	DON'T STAY AWAY TOO LONG	Peters & Lee	Philips	10
34	28	WALL STREET SHUFFLE	10CC	UK	2
15	29	IF I DIDN'T CARE	David Cassidy	Bell	7
-	30	EASY EASY	Scotland World Cup Squad ●	Polydor	1
-	31	BEACH BABY	The First Class ●	UK	1
26	32	REMEMBER YOU'RE A WOMBLE	The Wombles	CBS	12
-	33	YOUNG GIRL	Gary Puckett and the Union Gap	CBS	1
32	34	I WON'T LAST A DAY WITHOUT YOU	Carpenters	A&M	2
35	35	IF YOU'RE READY (COME GO WITH ME)	Staple Singers	STAX	2

■Elton John's *Don't Let The Sun Go Down On Me* peaks at number 16. Seventeen years later, in a duet with George Michael, he will top the charts with the same song (15.06.74) ■ Four towns mentioned in chart titles - Jarrow, Chicago, Liverpool and Waterloo, as well as a street in New York City, Wall St. (15.06.74)■

June 1974

□ Highest position disc reached ● Act's first ever week on chart

LW	TW	Title	Artist	Label	Wks
38	**36**	THE POACHER	Ronnie Lane/Slim Chance	*GM*	2
-	37	DIAMOND DOGS	David Bowie	*RCA*	1
27	38	BREAK THE RULES	Status Quo	*Vertigo*	8
23	39	SHANG-A-LANG	Bay City Rollers	*Bell*	9
31	40	I WANT TO GIVE	Perry Como	*RCA*	5

WEEK ENDING 29 JUNE 1974

LW	TW	Title	Artist	Label	Wks
11	**1**	SHE	Charles Aznavour	*Barclay*	2
1	2	ALWAYS YOURS	Gary Glitter	*Bell*	3
2	3	THE STREAK	Ray Stevens	*Westbound*	6
3	4	HEY ROCK AND ROLL	Showaddywaddy	*Bell*	6
4	5	THERE'S A GHOST IN MY HOUSE	R. Dean Taylor	*Tamla Motown*	8
13	**6**	ONE MAN BAND	Leo Sayer	*Chrysalis*	3
10	7	I'D LOVE YOU TO WANT ME	Lobo	*UK*	4
14	8	KISSIN' IN THE BACK ROW	Drifters	*Bell*	3
8	9	A TOUCH TOO MUCH	Arrows	*Rak*	5
6	10	JARROW SONG	Alan Price	*Warner*	5
7	11	LIVERPOOL LOU	Scaffold	*Warner*	5
5	12	JUDY TEEN	Cockney Rebel	*EMI*	7
18	13	GUILTY	Pearls	*Bell*	4
21	14	GOING DOWN THE ROAD	Roy Wood	*Harvest*	3
23	**15**	CAN'T GET ENOUGH	Bad Company	*Island*	4
17	**16**	DON'T LET THE SUN GO DOWN ON ME	Elton John	*DJM*	5
16	17	SUMMER BREEZE	Isley Brothers	*Epic*	5
20	**18**	THE MAN IN BLACK	Cozy Powell	*Rak*	5
28	19	WALL STREET SHUFFLE	10C.C.	*UK*	3
30	**20**	EASY EASY	Scotland World Cup Squad	*Polydor*	2
33	21	YOUNG GIRL	Gary Puckett and the Union Gap	*CBS*	2
22	22	(YOU KEEP ME) HANGING ON	Cliff Richard	*EMI*	7
31	23	BEACH BABY	The First Class	*UK*	2
-	24	BANANA ROCK	The Wombles	*CBS*	1
26	**25**	OOH I DO	Lynsey De Paul	*Warner*	4
12	26	SUGAR BABY LOVE	Rubettes	*Polydor*	10
-	27	TOO BIG	Suzi Quatro	*RAK*	1
37	28	DIAMOND DOGS	David Bowie	*RCA*	2
15	29	I SEE A STAR	Mouth & McNeal	*Decca*	7
9	30	THIS TOWN AIN'T BIG ENOUGH FOR BOTH OF US	Sparks	*Island*	8
25	31	GO	Gigliola Cinquetti	*CBS*	8
24	32	THE NIGHT CHICAGO DIED	Paper Lace	*Bus Stop*	9
-	**33**	FOXY FOXY	Mott The Hoople	*CBS*	1
35	**34**	IF YOU'RE READY (COME GO WITH ME)	Staple Singers	*STAX*	3
27	35	DON'T STAY AWAY TOO LONG	Peters & Lee	*Philips*	11
36	**36**	THE POACHER	Ronnie Lane/Slim Chance	*GM*	3
-	37	FLOATING IN THE WIND	Hudson Ford	*A&M*	1
-	38	CENTRAL PARK ARREST	Thunderthighs ●	*Philips*	1
34	39	I WON'T LAST A DAY WITHOUT YOU	Carpenters	*A&M*	3
-	40	LAUGHTER IN THE RAIN	Neil Sedaka	*Polydor*	1

WEEK ENDING 6 JULY 1974

LW	TW	Title	Artist	Label	Wks
1	**1**	SHE	Charles Aznavour	*Barclay*	3
8	**2**	KISSIN' IN THE BACK ROW	Drifters	*Bell*	4
2	3	ALWAYS YOURS	Gary Glitter	*Bell*	4
-	4	BANGIN' MAN	Slade	*Polydor*	1
4	5	HEY ROCK AND ROLL	Showaddywaddy	*Bell*	7
7	6	I'D LOVE YOU TO WANT ME	Lobo	*UK*	5
3	7	THE STREAK	Ray Stevens	*Westbound*	7
6	8	ONE MAN BAND	Leo Sayer	*Chrysalis*	4
21	9	YOUNG GIRL	Gary Puckett and the Union Gap	*CBS*	3
13	**10**	GUILTY	Pearls	*Bell*	5
19	11	WALL STREET SHUFFLE	10C.C.	*UK*	4
24	12	BANANA ROCK	The Wombles	*CBS*	2
9	13	A TOUCH TOO MUCH	Arrows	*Rak*	6
11	14	LIVERPOOL LOU	Scaffold	*Warner*	6
-	15	ROCK YOUR BABY	George McCrae ●	*Jayboy*	1
14	16	GOING DOWN THE ROAD	Roy Wood	*Harvest*	4
5	17	THERE'S A GHOST IN MY HOUSE	R. Dean Taylor	*Tamla Motown*	9
16	18	DON'T LET THE SUN GO DOWN ON ME	Elton John	*DJM*	6
12	19	JUDY TEEN	Cockney Rebel	*EMI*	8
10	20	JARROW SONG	Alan Price	*Warner*	6
23	21	BEACH BABY	The First Class	*UK*	3
17	22	SUMMER BREEZE	Isley Brothers	*Epic*	6
18	23	THE MAN IN BLACK	Cozy Powell	*Rak*	6
27	24	TOO BIG	Suzi Quatro	*RAK*	2
40	25	LAUGHTER IN THE RAIN	Neil Sedaka	*Polydor*	2
-	26	IF YOU GO AWAY	Terry Jacks	*Bell*	1
-	27	BAND ON THE RUN	Paul McCartney & Wings	*Apple*	1
28	28	DIAMOND DOGS	David Bowie	*RCA*	3
25	29	OOH I DO	Lynsey De Paul	*Warner*	5
38	**30**	CENTRAL PARK ARREST	Thunderthighs	*Philips*	2
15	31	CAN'T GET ENOUGH	Bad Company	*Island*	5
20	32	EASY EASY	Scotland World Cup Squad	*Polydor*	3
26	33	SUGAR BABY LOVE	Rubettes	*Polydor*	11
33	34	FOXY FOXY	Mott The Hoople	*CBS*	2
37	**35**	FLOATING IN THE WIND	Hudson Ford	*A&M*	2
-	36	MIDNIGHT AT THE OASIS	Maria Muldaur ●	*Reprise*	1
-	37	JUST DON'T WANT TO BE LONELY	Main Ingredient ●	*RCA*	1
35	38	DON'T STAY AWAY TOO LONG	Peters & Lee	*Philips*	12
30	39	THIS TOWN AIN'T BIG ENOUGH FOR BOTH OF US	Sparks	*Island*	9
32	40	THE NIGHT CHICAGO DIED	Paper Lace	*Bus Stop*	10

WEEK ENDING 13 JULY 1974

LW	TW	Title	Artist	Label	Wks
1	**1**	SHE	Charles Aznavour	*Barclay*	4
2	**2**	KISSIN' IN THE BACK ROW	Drifters	*Bell*	5
4	**3**	BANGIN' MAN	Slade	*Polydor*	2
15	4	ROCK YOUR BABY	George McCrae	*Jayboy*	2
6	**5**	I'D LOVE YOU TO WANT ME	Lobo	*UK*	6
8	**6**	ONE MAN BAND	Leo Sayer	*Chrysalis*	5
27	7	BAND ON THE RUN	Paul McCartney & Wings	*Apple*	2
9	8	YOUNG GIRL	Gary Puckett and the Union Gap	*CBS*	4
3	9	ALWAYS YOURS	Gary Glitter	*Bell*	5
11	**10**	WALL STREET SHUFFLE	10C.C.	*UK*	5
5	11	HEY ROCK AND ROLL	Showaddywaddy	*Bell*	8
12	12	BANANA ROCK	The Wombles	*CBS*	3
16	**13**	GOING DOWN THE ROAD	Roy Wood	*Harvest*	5
24	**14**	TOO BIG	Suzi Quatro	*RAK*	3
10	15	GUILTY	Pearls	*Bell*	6
7	16	THE STREAK	Ray Stevens	*Westbound*	8
21	17	BEACH BABY	The First Class	*UK*	4
-	18	THE SIX TEENS	Sweet	*RCA*	1
18	19	DON'T LET THE SUN GO DOWN ON ME	Elton John	*DJM*	7
26	20	IF YOU GO AWAY	Terry Jacks	*Bell*	2
28	**21**	DIAMOND DOGS	David Bowie	*RCA*	4
25	22	LAUGHTER IN THE RAIN	Neil Sedaka	*Polydor*	3
13	23	A TOUCH TOO MUCH	Arrows	*Rak*	7
14	24	LIVERPOOL LOU	Scaffold	*Warner*	7
23	25	THE MAN IN BLACK	Cozy Powell	*Rak*	7
36	26	MIDNIGHT AT THE OASIS	Maria Muldaur	*Reprise*	2
17	27	THERE'S A GHOST IN MY HOUSE	R. Dean Taylor	*Tamla Motown*	10
37	28	JUST DON'T WANT TO BE LONELY	Main Ingredient	*RCA*	2
-	29	SHE'S A WINNER	Intruders	*Philadelphia*	1
30	**30**	CENTRAL PARK ARREST	Thunderthighs	*Philips*	3
-	31	MY GIRL BILL	Jim Stafford	*MGM*	1
20	32	JARROW SONG	Alan Price	*Warner*	7
-	33	WHEN WILL I SEE YOU AGAIN	Three Degrees	*Philadelphia*	1
-	34	LIGHT OF LOVE	T. Rex	*EMI*	1
34	35	FOXY FOXY	Mott The Hoople	*CBS*	3
29	36	OOH I DO	Lynsey De Paul	*Warner*	6
31	37	CAN'T GET ENOUGH	Bad Company	*Island*	6
19	38	JUDY TEEN	Cockney Rebel	*EMI*	9
-	39	BE THANKFUL FOR WHAT YOU'VE GOT	William De Vaughan ●	*Chelsea*	1
-	40	TONIGHT	Rubettes	*Polydor*	1

In these weeks ■ Cliff Richard drops out of the Top 40 and will not return until 1976, the longest absence since his career started almost 16 years earlier (29.06.71) ■ The record that is generally credited with starting the disco boom, George McCrae's *Rock Your Baby* hits the chart (06.07.74)■

LW	TW	*WEEK ENDING* **20 JULY 1974**			Wks
1	[1]	SHE	Charles Aznavour	*Barclay*	5
2	[2]	KISSIN' IN THE BACK ROW	Drifters	*Bell*	6
4	3	ROCK YOUR BABY	George McCrae	*Jayboy*	3
7	4	BAND ON THE RUN	Paul McCartney & Wings	*Apple*	3
3	5	BANGIN' MAN	Slade	*Polydor*	3
8	6	YOUNG GIRL	Gary Puckett and the Union Gap	*CBS*	5
5	7	I'D LOVE YOU TO WANT ME	Lobo	*UK*	7
20	[8]	IF YOU GO AWAY	Terry Jacks	*Bell*	3
12	[9]	BANANA ROCK	The Wombles	*CBS*	4
9	10	ALWAYS YOURS	Gary Glitter	*Bell*	6
18	11	THE SIX TEENS	Sweet	*RCA*	2
10	12	WALL STREET SHUFFLE	10C.C.	*UK*	6
17	[13]	BEACH BABY	The First Class	*UK*	5
-	14	BORN WITH A SMILE ON MY FACE	Stephanie De Sykes/Rain ●	*Bradleys*	1
22	[15]	LAUGHTER IN THE RAIN	Neil Sedaka	*Polydor*	4
11	16	HEY ROCK AND ROLL	Showaddywaddy	*Bell*	9
33	17	WHEN WILL I SEE YOU AGAIN	Three Degrees	*Philadelphia*	2
6	18	ONE MAN BAND	Leo Sayer	*Chrysalis*	6
14	19	TOO BIG	Suzi Quatro	*RAK*	4
29	20	SHE'S A WINNER	Intruders	*Philadelphia*	2
40	21	TONIGHT	Rubettes	*Polydor*	2
34	[22]	LIGHT OF LOVE	T. Rex	*EMI*	2
31	23	MY GIRL BILL	Jim Stafford	*MGM*	2
26	24	MIDNIGHT AT THE OASIS	Maria Muldaur	*Reprise*	3
21	25	DIAMOND DOGS	David Bowie	*RCA*	5
13	26	GOING DOWN THE ROAD	Roy Wood	*Harvest*	6
15	27	GUILTY	Pearls	*Bell*	7
28	28	JUST DON'T WANT TO BE LONELY	Main Ingredient	*RCA*	3
16	29	THE STREAK	Ray Stevens	*Westbound*	9
-	30	YOU MAKE ME FEEL BRAND NEW	Stylistics	*Avco*	1
39	[31]	BE THANKFUL FOR WHAT YOU'VE GOT	William De Vaughan	*Chelsea*	2
30	32	CENTRAL PARK ARREST	Thunderthighs	*Philips*	4
-	33	MIKE OLDFIELD'S SINGLE	Mike Oldfield ●	*Virgin*	1
-	34	RING RING	Abba	*Epic*	1
23	35	A TOUCH TOO MUCH	Arrows	*Rak*	8
24	36	LIVERPOOL LOU	Scaffold	*Warner*	8
35	37	FOXY FOXY	Mott The Hoople	*CBS*	4
27	38	THERE'S A GHOST IN MY HOUSE	R. Dean Taylor	*Tamla Motown*	11
19	39	DON'T LET THE SUN GO DOWN ON ME	Elton John	*DJM*	8
-	[40]	IF YOU TALK IN YOUR SLEEP	Elvis Presley	*RCA*	1

LW	TW	*WEEK ENDING* **27 JULY 1974**			Wks
3	[1]	ROCK YOUR BABY	George McCrae	*Jayboy*	4
1	2	SHE	Charles Aznavour	*Barclay*	6
14	3	BORN WITH A SMILE ON MY FACE	Stephanie De Sykes/Rain	*Bradleys*	2
2	4	KISSIN' IN THE BACK ROW	Drifters	*Bell*	7
4	5	BAND ON THE RUN	Paul McCartney & Wings	*Apple*	4
6	6	YOUNG GIRL	Gary Puckett and the Union Gap	*CBS*	6
17	7	WHEN WILL I SEE YOU AGAIN	Three Degrees	*Philadelphia*	3
5	8	BANGIN' MAN	Slade	*Polydor*	4
11	[9]	THE SIX TEENS	Sweet	*RCA*	3
7	10	I'D LOVE YOU TO WANT ME	Lobo	*UK*	8
8	11	IF YOU GO AWAY	Terry Jacks	*Bell*	4
9	12	BANANA ROCK	The Wombles	*CBS*	5
12	13	WALL STREET SHUFFLE	10C.C.	*UK*	7
30	14	YOU MAKE ME FEEL BRAND NEW	Stylistics	*Avco*	2
21	15	TONIGHT	Rubettes	*Polydor*	3
15	16	LAUGHTER IN THE RAIN	Neil Sedaka	*Polydor*	5
-	17	AMATEUR HOUR	Sparks	*Island*	1
13	18	BEACH BABY	The First Class	*UK*	6
20	19	SHE'S A WINNER	Intruders	*Philadelphia*	3
23	[20]	MY GIRL BILL	Jim Stafford	*MGM*	3
24	[21]	MIDNIGHT AT THE OASIS	Maria Muldaur	*Reprise*	4
16	22	HEY ROCK AND ROLL	Showaddywaddy	*Bell*	10
22	23	LIGHT OF LOVE	T. Rex	*EMI*	3
19	24	TOO BIG	Suzi Quatro	*RAK*	5
18	25	ONE MAN BAND	Leo Sayer	*Chrysalis*	7
-	26	ROCKET	Mud	*RAK*	1
28	[27]	JUST DON'T WANT TO BE LONELY	Main Ingredient	*RCA*	4
10	28	ALWAYS YOURS	Gary Glitter	*Bell*	7
-	29	PLEASE PLEASE ME	David Cassidy	*Bell*	1
25	30	DIAMOND DOGS	David Bowie	*RCA*	6
33	[31]	MIKE OLDFIELD'S SINGLE	Mike Oldfield	*Virgin*	2
34	[32]	RING RING	Abba	*Epic*	2
-	33	STOP LOOK LISTEN	Diana Ross/Marvin Gaye	*Tamla Motown*	1
29	34	THE STREAK	Ray Stevens	*Westbound*	10
26	35	GOING DOWN THE ROAD	Roy Wood	*Harvest*	7
-	36	HONEY HONEY	Sweet Dreams ●	*Bradleys*	1
-	37	YOUR BABY AIN'T YOUR BABY ANYMORE	Paul Da Vinci ●	*Penny Farthing*	1
31	38	BE THANKFUL FOR WHAT YOU'VE GOT	William De Vaughan	*Chelsea*	3
-	39	ROCK THE BOAT	Hues Corporation ●	*RCA*	1
-	40	SUMMERLOVE SENSATION	Bay City Rollers	*Bell*	1

August 1974

□ Highest position disc reached ● Act's first ever week on chart

LW	TW	*WEEK ENDING* **3 AUGUST 1974**			Wks
1	[1]	ROCK YOUR BABY	George McCrae	*Jayboy*	5
3	[2]	BORN WITH A SMILE ON MY FACE	Stephanie De Sykes/Rain	*Bradleys*	3
5	[3]	BAND ON THE RUN	Paul McCartney & Wings	*Apple*	5
7	4	WHEN WILL I SEE YOU AGAIN	Three Degrees	*Philadelphia*	4
2	5	SHE	Charles Aznavour	*Barclay*	7
4	6	KISSIN' IN THE BACK ROW	Drifters	*Bell*	8
6	7	YOUNG GIRL	Gary Puckett and the Union Gap	*CBS*	7
14	8	YOU MAKE ME FEEL BRAND NEW	Stylistics	*Avco*	3
17	9	AMATEUR HOUR	Sparks	*Island*	2
11	10	IF YOU GO AWAY	Terry Jacks	*Bell*	5
9	11	THE SIX TEENS	Sweet	*RCA*	4
15	[12]	TONIGHT	Rubettes	*Polydor*	4
26	13	ROCKET	Mud	*RAK*	2
19	[14]	SHE'S A WINNER	Intruders	*Philadelphia*	4
39	15	ROCK THE BOAT	Hues Corporation	*RCA*	2
12	16	BANANA ROCK	The Wombles	*CBS*	6
40	17	SUMMERLOVE SENSATION	Bay City Rollers	*Bell*	2
16	18	LAUGHTER IN THE RAIN	Neil Sedaka	*Polydor*	6
18	19	BEACH BABY	The First Class	*UK*	7
8	20	BANGIN' MAN	Slade	*Polydor*	5
29	21	PLEASE PLEASE ME	David Cassidy	*Bell*	2
-	22	IT'S ONLY ROCK AND ROLL	Rolling Stones	*Rolling Stones*	1
10	23	I'D LOVE YOU TO WANT ME	Lobo	*UK*	9
23	24	LIGHT OF LOVE	T. Rex	*EMI*	4
-	25	WHAT BECOMES OF THE BROKEN HEARTED	Jimmy Ruffin	*Tamla Motown*	1
20	26	MY GIRL BILL	Jim Stafford	*MGM*	4
33	27	STOP LOOK LISTEN	Diana Ross/Marvin Gaye	*Tamla Motown*	2
13	28	WALL STREET SHUFFLE	10C.C.	*UK*	8
21	29	MIDNIGHT AT THE OASIS	Maria Muldaur	*Reprise*	5
37	30	YOUR BABY AIN'T YOUR BABY ANYMORE	Paul Da Vinci	*Penny Farthing*	2
-	31	I SHOT THE SHERIFF	Eric Clapton ●	*RSO*	1
31	32	MIKE OLDFIELD'S SINGLE	Mike Oldfield	*Virgin*	3
-	33	I'M LEAVING IT ALL UP TO YOU	Donny & Marie Osmond ●	*MGM*	1
22	34	HEY ROCK AND ROLL	Showaddywaddy	*Bell*	11
-	[35]	I FOUND SUNSHINE	Chi-Lites	*Brunswick*	1
36	36	HONEY HONEY	Sweet Dreams	*Bradleys*	2
32	37	RING RING	Abba	*Epic*	3
-	38	IT'S ALL UP TO YOU	Jim Capaldi ●	*Island*	1
28	39	ALWAYS YOURS	Gary Glitter	*Bell*	8
25	40	ONE MAN BAND	Leo Sayer	*Chrysalis*	8

■*Mike Oldfield's Single* was a Theme from his best-selling album *Tubular Bells*, the record that is often credited with establishing the Virgin empire (20.07.74) ■ Paul Da Vinci, who sang lead vocal on the hastily assembled Rubettes number one, *Sugar Baby Love*, enjoys his brief moments of solo chart success (27.07.74)■

August 1974

□ Highest position disc reached ● Act's first ever week on chart

WEEK ENDING 10 AUGUST 1974

LW	TW	Title	Artist	Label	Wks
1	[1]	ROCK YOUR BABY	George McCrae	Jayboy	6
4	2	WHEN WILL I SEE YOU AGAIN	Three Degrees	Philadelphia	5
2	3	BORN WITH A SMILE ON MY FACE	Stephanie De Sykes/Rain	Bradleys	4
8	4	YOU MAKE ME FEEL BRAND NEW	Stylistics	Avco	4
17	5	SUMMERLOVE SENSATION	Bay City Rollers	Bell	3
13	[6]	ROCKET	Mud	RAK	3
9	[7]	AMATEUR HOUR	Sparks	Island	3
3	8	BAND ON THE RUN	Paul McCartney & Wings	Apple	6
6	9	KISSIN' IN THE BACK ROW	Drifters	Bell	9
15	10	ROCK THE BOAT	Hues Corporation	RCA	3
25	11	WHAT BECOMES OF THE BROKEN HEARTED	Jimmy Ruffin	Tamla Motown	2
12	[12]	TONIGHT	Rubettes	Polydor	5
22	13	IT'S ONLY ROCK AND ROLL	Rolling Stones	Rolling Stones	2
7	14	YOUNG GIRL	Gary Puckett and the Union Gap	CBS	8
31	15	I SHOT THE SHERIFF	Eric Clapton	RSO	2
21	[16]	PLEASE PLEASE ME	David Cassidy	Bell	3
5	17	SHE	Charles Aznavour	Barclay	8
14	18	SHE'S A WINNER	Intruders	Philadelphia	5
11	19	THE SIX TEENS	Sweet	RCA	5
26	[20]	MY GIRL BILL	Jim Stafford	MGM	5
33	21	I'M LEAVING IT ALL UP TO YOU	Donny & Marie Osmond	MGM	2
-	22	JUST FOR YOU	Glitter Band	Bell	1
30	23	YOUR BABY AIN'T YOUR BABY ANYMORE	Paul Da Vinci	Penny Farthing	3
10	24	IF YOU GO AWAY	Terry Jacks	Bell	6
16	25	BANANA ROCK	The Wombles	CBS	7
27	26	STOP LOOK LISTEN	Diana Ross/Marvin Gaye	Tamla Motown	3
-	27	HELLO SUMMERTIME	Bobby Goldsboro	United Artists	1
20	28	BANGIN' MAN	Slade	Polydor	6
36	29	HONEY HONEY	Sweet Dreams	Bradleys	3
38	30	IT'S ALL UP TO YOU	Jim Capaldi	Island	2
29	31	MIDNIGHT AT THE OASIS	Maria Muldaur	Reprise	6
-	32	MISS HIT AND RUN	Barry Blue	Bell	1
23	33	I'D LOVE YOU TO WANT ME	Lobo	UK	10
-	34	SUNDOWN	Gordon Lightfoot	Reprise	1
28	35	WALL STREET SHUFFLE	10C.C.	UK	9
19	36	BEACH BABY	The First Class	UK	8
-	37	THIS IS THE STORY OF MY LOVE (BABY)	Wizzard	Warner Bros	1
18	38	LAUGHTER IN THE RAIN	Neil Sedaka	Polydor	7
-	39	MR. SOFT	Cockney Rebel	EMI	1
35	40	I FOUND SUNSHINE	Chi-Lites	Brunswick	2

WEEK ENDING 17 AUGUST 1974

LW	TW	Title	Artist	Label	Wks
2	[1]	WHEN WILL I SEE YOU AGAIN	Three Degrees	Philadelphia	6
1	2	ROCK YOUR BABY	George McCrae	Jayboy	7
4	3	YOU MAKE ME FEEL BRAND NEW	Stylistics	Avco	5
5	4	SUMMERLOVE SENSATION	Bay City Rollers	Bell	4
3	5	BORN WITH A SMILE ON MY FACE	Stephanie De Sykes/Rain	Bradleys	5
10	[6]	ROCK THE BOAT	Hues Corporation	RCA	4
6	7	ROCKET	Mud	RAK	4
11	8	WHAT BECOMES OF THE BROKEN HEARTED	Jimmy Ruffin	Tamla Motown	3
15	[9]	I SHOT THE SHERIFF	Eric Clapton	RSO	3
13	[10]	IT'S ONLY ROCK AND ROLL	Rolling Stones	Rolling Stones	3
7	11	AMATEUR HOUR	Sparks	Island	4
8	12	BAND ON THE RUN	Paul McCartney & Wings	Apple	7
12	13	TONIGHT	Rubettes	Polydor	6
21	14	I'M LEAVING IT ALL UP TO YOU	Donny & Marie Osmond	MGM	3
22	15	JUST FOR YOU	Glitter Band	Bell	2
16	[16]	PLEASE PLEASE ME	David Cassidy	Bell	4
27	17	HELLO SUMMERTIME	Bobby Goldsboro	United Artists	2
18	18	SHE'S A WINNER	Intruders	Philadelphia	6
29	19	HONEY HONEY	Sweet Dreams	Bradleys	4
23	[20]	YOUR BABY AIN'T YOUR BABY ANYMORE	Paul Da Vinci	Penny Farthing	4
9	21	KISSIN' IN THE BACK ROW	Drifters	Bell	10
14	22	YOUNG GIRL	Gary Puckett and the Union Gap	CBS	9
39	23	MR. SOFT	Cockney Rebel	EMI	2
17	24	SHE	Charles Aznavour	Barclay	9
26	[25]	STOP LOOK LISTEN	Diana Ross/Marvin Gaye	Tamla Motown	4
32	[26]	MISS HIT AND RUN	Barry Blue	Bell	2
30	[27]	IT'S ALL UP TO YOU	Jim Capaldi ●	Island	3
-	28	Y VIVA ESPANA	Sylvia	Sonet	1
-	29	NA NA NA	Cozy Powell	RAK	1
20	30	MY GIRL BILL	Jim Stafford	MGM	6
24	31	IF YOU GO AWAY	Terry Jacks	Bell	7
-	32	ROCK 'N' ROLL LADY	Showaddywaddy	Bell	1
34	[33]	SUNDOWN	Gordon Lightfoot	Reprise	2
37	[34]	THIS IS THE STORY OF MY LOVE (BABY)	Wizzard	Warner Bros	2
-	35	RAINBOW	Peters & Lee	Philips	1
19	36	THE SIX TEENS	Sweet	RCA	6
-	37	ANNIE'S SONG	John Denver ●	RCA	1
25	38	BANANA ROCK	The Wombles	CBS	8
40	39	I FOUND SUNSHINE	Chi-Lites	Brunswick	3
28	40	BANGIN' MAN	Slade	Polydor	7

WEEK ENDING 24 AUGUST 1974

LW	TW	Title	Artist	Label	Wks
1	[1]	WHEN WILL I SEE YOU AGAIN	Three Degrees	Philadelphia	7
3	[2]	YOU MAKE ME FEEL BRAND NEW	Stylistics	Avco	6
4	[3]	SUMMERLOVE SENSATION	Bay City Rollers	Bell	5
8	[4]	WHAT BECOMES OF THE BROKEN HEARTED	Jimmy Ruffin	Tamla Motown	4
14	5	I'M LEAVING IT ALL UP TO YOU	Donny & Marie Osmond	MGM	4
2	6	ROCK YOUR BABY	George McCrae	Jayboy	8
6	7	ROCK THE BOAT	Hues Corporation	RCA	5
7	8	ROCKET	Mud	RAK	5
9	[9]	I SHOT THE SHERIFF	Eric Clapton	RSO	4
15	[10]	JUST FOR YOU	Glitter Band	Bell	3
10	11	IT'S ONLY ROCK AND ROLL	Rolling Stones	Rolling Stones	4
23	12	MR. SOFT	Cockney Rebel	EMI	3
19	13	HONEY HONEY	Sweet Dreams	Bradleys	5
5	14	BORN WITH A SMILE ON MY FACE	Stephanie De Sykes/Rain	Bradleys	6
28	15	Y VIVA ESPANA	Sylvia	Sonet	2
11	16	AMATEUR HOUR	Sparks	Island	5
17	17	HELLO SUMMERTIME	Bobby Goldsboro	United Artists	3
13	18	TONIGHT	Rubettes	Polydor	7
-	19	LOVE ME FOR A REASON	Osmonds	MGM	1
29	20	NA NA NA	Cozy Powell	RAK	2
16	21	PLEASE PLEASE ME	David Cassidy	Bell	5
32	22	ROCK 'N' ROLL LADY	Showaddywaddy	Bell	2
18	23	SHE'S A WINNER	Intruders	Philadelphia	7
20	24	YOUR BABY AIN'T YOUR BABY ANYMORE	Paul Da Vinci	Penny Farthing	5
12	25	BAND ON THE RUN	Paul McCartney & Wings	Apple	8
37	26	ANNIE'S SONG	John Denver	RCA	2
35	27	RAINBOW	Peters & Lee	Philips	2
26	28	MISS HIT AND RUN	Barry Blue	Bell	3
-	29	KUNG FU FIGHTING	Carl Douglas ●	Pye	1
21	30	KISSIN' IN THE BACK ROW	Drifters	Bell	11
-	31	CAN'T GET ENOUGH OF YOUR LOVE BABE	Barry White	Pye	1
22	32	YOUNG GIRL	Gary Puckett and the Union Gap	CBS	10
25	33	STOP LOOK LISTEN	Diana Ross/Marvin Gaye	Tamla Motown	5
27	34	IT'S ALL UP TO YOU	Jim Capaldi	Island	4
33	35	SUNDOWN	Gordon Lightfoot	Reprise	3
-	36	HANG ON IN THERE BABY	Johnny Bristol ●	MGM	1
24	37	SHE	Charles Aznavour	Barclay	10
-	38	QUEEN OF CLUBS	K.C. And The Sunshine Band ●	Jayboy	1
30	39	MY GIRL BILL	Jim Stafford	MGM	7
34	40	THIS IS THE STORY OF MY LOVE (BABY)	Wizzard	Warner Bros	3

In these weeks ■ One of the very first Bob Marley compositions to chart, and the first to reach the top 10, was Eric Clapton's version of *I Shot The Sheriff* (17.08.74) ■ Three consecutive 'Rock' discs in the top ten: *Rock Your Baby* at number 6, *Rock The Boat* at number 7 and *Rocket* at number 8 (24.08.74)■

WEEK ENDING 31 AUGUST 1974

LW	TW	Title	Artist	Label	Wks
19	[1]	LOVE ME FOR A REASON	Osmonds	*MGM*	2
1	2	WHEN WILL I SEE YOU AGAIN	Three Degrees	*Philadelphia*	8
2	3	YOU MAKE ME FEEL BRAND NEW	Stylistics	*Avco*	7
5	4	I'M LEAVING IT ALL UP TO YOU	Donny & Marie Osmond	*MGM*	5
3	5	SUMMERLOVE SENSATION	Bay City Rollers	*Bell*	6
4	6	WHAT BECOMES OF THE BROKEN HEARTED	Jimmy Ruffin	*Tamla Motown*	5
15	7	Y VIVA ESPANA	Sylvia	*Sonet*	3
12	[8]	MR. SOFT	Cockney Rebel	*EMI*	4
29	9	KUNG FU FIGHTING	Carl Douglas	*Pye*	2
13	[10]	HONEY HONEY	Sweet Dreams	*Bradleys*	6
7	11	ROCK THE BOAT	Hues Corporation	*RCA*	6
20	12	NA NA NA	Cozy Powell	*RAK*	3
9	13	I SHOT THE SHERIFF	Eric Clapton	*RSO*	5
17	[14]	HELLO SUMMERTIME	Bobby Goldsboro	*United Artists*	4
8	15	ROCKET	Mud	*RAK*	6
6	16	ROCK YOUR BABY	George McCrae	*Jayboy*	9
10	17	JUST FOR YOU	Glitter Band	*Bell*	4
26	18	ANNIE'S SONG	John Denver	*RCA*	3
22	19	ROCK 'N' ROLL LADY	Showaddywaddy	*Bell*	3
11	20	IT'S ONLY ROCK AND ROLL	Rolling Stones	*Rolling Stones*	5
14	21	BORN WITH A SMILE ON MY FACE	Stephanie De Sykes/Rain	*Bradleys*	7
36	22	HANG ON IN THERE BABY	Johnny Bristol	*MGM*	2
24	23	YOUR BABY AIN'T YOUR BABY ANYMORE	Paul Da Vinci	*Penny Farthing*	6
-	24	THE BLACK-EYED BOYS	Paper Lace	*Bus Stop*	1
38	25	QUEEN OF CLUBS	K.C. And The Sunshine Band	*Jayboy*	2
-	26	YOU YOU YOU	Alvin Stardust	*Magnet*	1
18	27	TONIGHT	Rubettes	*Polydor*	8
27	28	RAINBOW	Peters & Lee	*Philips*	3
31	29	CAN'T GET ENOUGH OF YOUR LOVE BABE	Barry White	*Pye*	2
16	30	AMATEUR HOUR	Sparks	*Island*	6
28	31	MISS HIT AND RUN	Barry Blue	*Bell*	4
-	32	BABY LOVE	Diana Ross & The Supremes	*Tamla Motown*	1
25	33	BAND ON THE RUN	Paul McCartney & Wings	*Apple*	9
-	34	ANOTHER SATURDAY NIGHT	Cat Stevens	*Island*	1
-	35	ROCK ME GENTLY	Andy Kim ●	*Capitol*	1
34	36	IT'S ALL UP TO YOU	Jim Capaldi	*Island*	5
30	37	KISSIN' IN THE BACK ROW	Drifters	*Bell*	12
32	38	YOUNG GIRL	Gary Puckett and the Union Gap	*CBS*	11
37	39	SHE	Charles Aznavour	*Barclay*	11
35	40	SUNDOWN	Gordon Lightfoot	*Reprise*	4

WEEK ENDING 7 SEPTEMBER 1974

LW	TW	Title	Artist	Label	Wks
1	[1]	LOVE ME FOR A REASON	Osmonds	*MGM*	3
4	[2]	I'M LEAVING IT ALL UP TO YOU	Donny & Marie Osmond	*MGM*	6
2	3	WHEN WILL I SEE YOU AGAIN	Three Degrees	*Philadelphia*	9
9	4	KUNG FU FIGHTING	Carl Douglas	*Pye*	3
7	5	Y VIVA ESPANA	Sylvia	*Sonet*	4
3	6	YOU MAKE ME FEEL BRAND NEW	Stylistics	*Avco*	8
18	7	ANNIE'S SONG	John Denver	*RCA*	4
6	8	WHAT BECOMES OF THE BROKEN HEARTED	Jimmy Ruffin	*Tamla Motown*	6
8	9	MR. SOFT	Cockney Rebel	*EMI*	5
10	[10]	HONEY HONEY	Sweet Dreams	*Bradleys*	7
22	11	HANG ON IN THERE BABY	Johnny Bristol	*MGM*	3
5	12	SUMMERLOVE SENSATION	Bay City Rollers	*Bell*	7
12	13	NA NA NA	Cozy Powell	*RAK*	4
14	[14]	HELLO SUMMERTIME	Bobby Goldsboro	*United Artists*	5
19	[15]	ROCK 'N' ROLL LADY	Showaddywaddy	*Bell*	4
25	16	QUEEN OF CLUBS	K.C. And The Sunshine Band	*Jayboy*	3
28	[17]	RAINBOW	Peters & Lee	*Philips*	4
17	18	JUST FOR YOU	Glitter Band	*Bell*	5
26	19	YOU YOU YOU	Alvin Stardust	*Magnet*	2
29	20	CAN'T GET ENOUGH OF YOUR LOVE BABE	Barry White	*Pye*	3
11	21	ROCK THE BOAT	Hues Corporation	*RCA*	7
24	22	THE BLACK-EYED BOYS	Paper Lace	*Bus Stop*	2
16	23	ROCK YOUR BABY	George McCrae	*Jayboy*	10
32	24	BABY LOVE	Diana Ross & The Supremes	*Tamla Motown*	2
13	25	I SHOT THE SHERIFF	Eric Clapton	*RSO*	6
15	26	ROCKET	Mud	*RAK*	7
-	27	SMOKE GETS IN YOUR EYES	Bryan Ferry	*Island*	1
34	28	ANOTHER SATURDAY NIGHT	Cat Stevens	*Island*	2
35	29	ROCK ME GENTLY	Andy Kim	*Capitol*	2
21	30	BORN WITH A SMILE ON MY FACE	Stephanie De Sykes/Rain	*Bradleys*	8
20	31	IT'S ONLY ROCK AND ROLL	Rolling Stones	*Rolling Stones*	6
-	32	MACHINE GUN	Commodores ●	*Tamla Motown*	1
31	33	MISS HIT AND RUN	Barry Blue	*Bell*	5
-	[34]	FEEL LIKE MAKING LOVE	Roberta Flack	*Atlantic*	1
30	35	AMATEUR HOUR	Sparks	*Island*	7
33	36	BAND ON THE RUN	Paul McCartney & Wings	*Apple*	10
-	37	WINDOW SHOPPING	R. Dean Taylor	*Polydor*	1
23	38	YOUR BABY AIN'T YOUR BABY ANYMORE	Paul Da Vinci	*Penny Farthing*	7
39	39	SHE	Charles Aznavour	*Barclay*	12
-	40	PINBALL	Brian Protheroe ●	*Chrysalis*	1

September 1974

☐ Highest position disc reached ● Act's first ever week on chart

WEEK ENDING 14 SEPTEMBER 1974

LW	TW	Title	Artist	Label	Wks
1	[1]	LOVE ME FOR A REASON	Osmonds	*MGM*	4
4	2	KUNG FU FIGHTING	Carl Douglas	*Pye*	4
2	3	I'M LEAVING IT ALL UP TO YOU	Donny & Marie Osmond	*MGM*	7
5	[4]	Y VIVA ESPANA	Sylvia	*Sonet*	5
7	5	ANNIE'S SONG	John Denver	*RCA*	5
11	6	HANG ON IN THERE BABY	Johnny Bristol	*MGM*	4
3	7	WHEN WILL I SEE YOU AGAIN	Three Degrees	*Philadelphia*	10
8	8	WHAT BECOMES OF THE BROKEN HEARTED	Jimmy Ruffin	*Tamla Motown*	7
19	9	YOU YOU YOU	Alvin Stardust	*Magnet*	3
13	[10]	NA NA NA	Cozy Powell	*RAK*	5
9	11	MR. SOFT	Cockney Rebel	*EMI*	6
10	12	HONEY HONEY	Sweet Dreams	*Bradleys*	8
6	13	YOU MAKE ME FEEL BRAND NEW	Stylistics	*Avco*	9
24	14	BABY LOVE	Diana Ross & The Supremes	*Tamla Motown*	3
16	15	QUEEN OF CLUBS	K.C. And The Sunshine Band	*Jayboy*	4
22	16	THE BLACK-EYED BOYS	Paper Lace	*Bus Stop*	3
20	17	CAN'T GET ENOUGH OF YOUR LOVE BABE	Barry White	*Pye*	4
15	18	ROCK 'N' ROLL LADY	Showaddywaddy	*Bell*	5
12	19	SUMMERLOVE SENSATION	Bay City Rollers	*Bell*	8
14	20	HELLO SUMMERTIME	Bobby Goldsboro	*United Artists*	6
17	21	RAINBOW	Peters & Lee	*Philips*	5
27	22	SMOKE GETS IN YOUR EYES	Bryan Ferry	*Island*	2
28	23	ANOTHER SATURDAY NIGHT	Cat Stevens	*Island*	3
29	24	ROCK ME GENTLY	Andy Kim	*Capitol*	3
21	25	ROCK THE BOAT	Hues Corporation	*RCA*	8
23	26	ROCK YOUR BABY	George McCrae	*Jayboy*	11
26	27	ROCKET	Mud	*RAK*	8
25	28	I SHOT THE SHERIFF	Eric Clapton	*RSO*	7
32	29	MACHINE GUN	Commodores	*Tamla Motown*	2
-	30	I GOT THE MUSIC IN ME	Kiki Dee Band	*Rocket*	1
18	31	JUST FOR YOU	Glitter Band	*Bell*	6
40	32	PINBALL	Brian Protheroe	*Chrysalis*	2
-	33	IT'S BETTER TO HAVE	Don Covay ●	*Mercury*	1
-	34	THE BITCH IS BACK	Elton John	*DJM*	1
-	35	SILLY LOVE	10C.C.	*UK*	1
-	[36]	SOMETHING 'BOUT YOU BABY I LIKE	Tom Jones	*Decca*	1
37	37	WINDOW SHOPPING	R. Dean Taylor	*Polydor*	2
31	38	IT'S ONLY ROCK AND ROLL	Rolling Stones	*Rolling Stones*	7
34	39	FEEL LIKE MAKING LOVE	Roberta Flack	*Atlantic*	2
30	40	BORN WITH A SMILE ON MY FACE	Stephanie De Sykes/Rain	*Bradleys*	9

WEEK ENDING 21 SEPTEMBER 1974

LW	TW	Title	Artist	Label	Wks
2	[1]	KUNG FU FIGHTING	Carl Douglas	*Pye*	5

■Donny Osmond may have had his last top ten hit as a soloist, but he becomes the only person ever to occupy the top two places on the chart as part of a group and as half of a duo (07.09.74) ■ The Osmonds' chart-topper was written by Johnny Bristol, whose only solo chart hit was also in the top ten (14.09.74)■

September 1974

☐ Highest position disc reached ● Act's first ever week on chart

LW	TW	Title	Artist	Label	Wks
1	2	LOVE ME FOR A REASON	Osmonds	MGM	5
5	3	ANNIE'S SONG	John Denver	RCA	6
6	4	HANG ON IN THERE BABY	Johnny Bristol	MGM	5
3	5	I'M LEAVING IT ALL UP TO YOU	Donny & Marie Osmond	MGM	8
4	6	Y VIVA ESPANA	Sylvia	Sonet	6
9	7	YOU YOU YOU	Alvin Stardust	Magnet	4
17	[8]	CAN'T GET ENOUGH OF YOUR LOVE BABE	Barry White	Pye	5
15	9	QUEEN OF CLUBS	K.C. And The Sunshine Band	Jayboy	5
10	[10]	NA NA NA	Cozy Powell	RAK	6
16	[11]	THE BLACK-EYED BOYS	Paper Lace	Bus Stop	4
8	12	WHAT BECOMES OF THE BROKEN HEARTED	Jimmy Ruffin	Tamla Motown	8
12	13	HONEY HONEY	Sweet Dreams	Bradleys	9
14	14	BABY LOVE	Diana Ross & The Supremes	Tamla Motown	4
7	15	WHEN WILL I SEE YOU AGAIN	Three Degrees	Philadelphia	11
18	16	ROCK 'N' ROLL LADY	Showaddywaddy	Bell	6
13	17	YOU MAKE ME FEEL BRAND NEW	Stylistics	Avco	10
20	18	HELLO SUMMERTIME	Bobby Goldsboro	United Artists	7
21	19	RAINBOW	Peters & Lee	Philips	6
11	20	MR. SOFT	Cockney Rebel	EMI	7
22	21	SMOKE GETS IN YOUR EYES	Bryan Ferry	Island	3
24	22	ROCK ME GENTLY	Andy Kim	Capitol	4
-	23	LONG TALL GLASSES	Leo Sayer	Chrysalis	1
23	24	ANOTHER SATURDAY NIGHT	Cat Stevens	Island	4
34	25	THE BITCH IS BACK	Elton John	DJM	2
29	26	MACHINE GUN	Commodores	Tamla Motown	3
30	27	I GOT THE MUSIC IN ME	Kiki Dee Band	Rocket	2
32	28	PINBALL	Brian Protheroe	Chrysalis	3
33	[29]	IT'S BETTER TO HAVE	Don Covay	Mercury	2
35	30	SILLY LOVE	10C.C.	UK	2
19	31	SUMMERLOVE SENSATION	Bay City Rollers	Bell	9
26	32	ROCK YOUR BABY	George McCrae	Jayboy	12
-	33	GEE BABY	Peter Shelley ●	Magnet	1
-	34	SAD SWEET DREAMER	Sweet Sensation ●	Pye	1
25	35	ROCK THE BOAT	Hues Corporation	RCA	9
37	[36]	WINDOW SHOPPING	R. Dean Taylor	Polydor	3
39	37	FEEL LIKE MAKING LOVE	Roberta Flack	Atlantic	3
28	38	I SHOT THE SHERIFF	Eric Clapton	RSO	8
36	39	SOMETHING 'BOUT YOU BABY I LIKE	Tom Jones	Decca	2
27	40	ROCKET	Mud	RAK	9

WEEK ENDING 28 SEPTEMBER 1974

LW	TW	Title	Artist	Label	Wks
1	[1]	KUNG FU FIGHTING	Carl Douglas	Pye	6
3	2	ANNIE'S SONG	John Denver	RCA	7
4	[3]	HANG ON IN THERE BABY	Johnny Bristol	MGM	6
2	4	LOVE ME FOR A REASON	Osmonds	MGM	6
6	5	Y VIVA ESPANA	Sylvia	Sonet	7
7	[6]	YOU YOU YOU	Alvin Stardust	Magnet	5
9	[7]	QUEEN OF CLUBS	K.C. And The Sunshine Band	Jayboy	6
8	[8]	CAN'T GET ENOUGH OF YOUR LOVE BABE	Barry White	Pye	6
22	9	ROCK ME GENTLY	Andy Kim	Capitol	5
23	10	LONG TALL GLASSES	Leo Sayer	Chrysalis	2
5	11	I'M LEAVING IT ALL UP TO YOU	Donny & Marie Osmond	MGM	9
14	12	BABY LOVE	Diana Ross & The Supremes	Tamla Motown	5
11	13	THE BLACK-EYED BOYS	Paper Lace	Bus Stop	5
10	14	NA NA NA	Cozy Powell	RAK	7
34	15	SAD SWEET DREAMER	Sweet Sensation	Pye	2
33	16	GEE BABY	Peter Shelley	Magnet	2
21	[17]	SMOKE GETS IN YOUR EYES	Bryan Ferry	Island	4
12	18	WHAT BECOMES OF THE BROKEN HEARTED	Jimmy Ruffin	Tamla Motown	9
24	[19]	ANOTHER SATURDAY NIGHT	Cat Stevens	Island	5
-	20	KNOCK ON WOOD	David Bowie	RCA	1
15	21	WHEN WILL I SEE YOU AGAIN	Three Degrees	Philadelphia	12
28	[22]	PINBALL	Brian Protheroe	Chrysalis	4
25	23	THE BITCH IS BACK	Elton John	DJM	3
17	24	YOU MAKE ME FEEL BRAND NEW	Stylistics	Avco	11
26	25	MACHINE GUN	Commodores	Tamla Motown	4
27	26	I GOT THE MUSIC IN ME	Kiki Dee Band	Rocket	3
13	27	HONEY HONEY	Sweet Dreams	Bradleys	10
30	28	SILLY LOVE	10C.C.	UK	3
16	29	ROCK 'N' ROLL LADY	Showaddywaddy	Bell	7
29	30	IT'S BETTER TO HAVE	Don Covay	Mercury	3
-	31	YOU LITTLE TRUST MAKER	Tymes	RCA	1
-	32	REGGAE TUNE	Andy Fairweather Low ●	A&M	1
-	[33]	LIFE IS A ROCK (BUT THE RADIO ROLLED ME)	Reunion ●	RCA	1
20	34	MR. SOFT	Cockney Rebel	EMI	8
-	35	EVERYTHING I OWN	Ken Boothe ●	Trojan	1
18	36	HELLO SUMMERTIME	Bobby Goldsboro	United Artists	8
39	37	SOMETHING 'BOUT YOU BABY I LIKE	Tom Jones	Decca	3
37	38	FEEL LIKE MAKING LOVE	Roberta Flack	Atlantic	4
31	39	SUMMERLOVE SENSATION	Bay City Rollers	Bell	10
19	40	RAINBOW	Peters & Lee	Philips	7

WEEK ENDING 5 OCTOBER 1974

LW	TW	Title	Artist	Label	Wks
1	[1]	KUNG FU FIGHTING	Carl Douglas	Pye	7
2	2	ANNIE'S SONG	John Denver	RCA	8
3	3	HANG ON IN THERE BABY	Johnny Bristol	MGM	7
10	[4]	LONG TALL GLASSES	Leo Sayer	Chrysalis	3
15	5	SAD SWEET DREAMER	Sweet Sensation	Pye	3
16	6	GEE BABY	Peter Shelley	Magnet	3
6	7	YOU YOU YOU	Alvin Stardust	Magnet	6
9	8	ROCK ME GENTLY	Andy Kim	Capitol	6
8	9	CAN'T GET ENOUGH OF YOUR LOVE BABE	Barry White	Pye	7
7	10	QUEEN OF CLUBS	K.C. And The Sunshine Band	Jayboy	7
5	11	Y VIVA ESPANA	Sylvia	Sonet	8
13	12	THE BLACK-EYED BOYS	Paper Lace	Bus Stop	6
35	13	EVERYTHING I OWN	Ken Boothe	Trojan	2
4	14	LOVE ME FOR A REASON	Osmonds	MGM	7
23	[15]	THE BITCH IS BACK	Elton John	DJM	4
11	16	I'M LEAVING IT ALL UP TO YOU	Donny & Marie Osmond	MGM	10
20	17	KNOCK ON WOOD	Bowie	RCA	2
32	18	REGGAE TUNE	Andy Fairweather Low	A&M	2
17	19	SMOKE GETS IN YOUR EYES	Bryan Ferry	Island	5
25	[20]	MACHINE GUN	Commodores	Tamla Motown	5
26	21	I GOT THE MUSIC IN ME	Kiki Dee Band	Rocket	4
12	22	BABY LOVE	Diana Ross & The Supremes	Tamla Motown	6
14	23	NA NA NA	Cozy Powell	RAK	8
28	[24]	SILLY LOVE	10C.C.	UK	4
18	25	WHAT BECOMES OF THE BROKEN HEARTED	Jimmy Ruffin	Tamla Motown	10
22	26	PINBALL	Brian Protheroe	Chrysalis	5
-	27	FAREWELL/BRING IT ON HOME TO ME	Rod Stewart	Mercury	1
31	28	YOU LITTLE TRUST MAKER	Tymes	RCA	2
-	29	(YOU'RE) HAVING MY BABY	Paul Anka	United Artists	1
21	30	WHEN WILL I SEE YOU AGAIN	Three Degrees	Philadelphia	13
-	31	I GET A KICK OUT OF YOU	Gary Shearston ●	Charisma	1
19	32	ANOTHER SATURDAY NIGHT	Cat Stevens	Island	6
-	33	I'M A BELIEVER	Robert Wyatt ●	Virgin	1
33	34	LIFE IS A ROCK (BUT THE RADIO ROLLED ME)	Reunion	RCA	2
30	35	IT'S BETTER TO HAVE	Don Covay	Mercury	4
29	36	ROCK 'N' ROLL LADY	Showaddywaddy	Bell	8
-	37	SAMBA PA TI	Santana	CBS	1
27	38	HONEY HONEY	Sweet Dreams	Bradleys	11
-	39	I CAN'T LEAVE YOU ALONE	George McCrae	Jayboy	1
24	40	YOU MAKE ME FEEL BRAND NEW	Stylistics	Avco	12

WEEK ENDING 12 OCTOBER 1974

LW	TW	Title	Artist	Label	Wks
2	[1]	ANNIE'S SONG	John Denver	RCA	9
8	[2]	ROCK ME GENTLY	Andy Kim	Capitol	7
5	3	SAD SWEET DREAMER	Sweet Sensation	Pye	4
1	4	KUNG FU FIGHTING	Carl Douglas	Pye	8
6	5	GEE BABY	Peter Shelley	Magnet	4
4	6	LONG TALL GLASSES	Leo Sayer	Chrysalis	4

In these weeks ■ John Denver, despite several hit albums and four number ones in America, scores his only UK solo hit with his ode to his wife *Annie's Song* (12.10.74) ■ Ex-Soft Machine vocalist Robert Wyatt achieves something his band never did - a hit single (05.10.74)■

November 1974

□ Highest position disc reached ● Act's first ever week on chart

LW	TW	Title	Artist	Label	Wks
3	7	HANG ON IN THERE BABY	Johnny Bristol	MGM	8
7	8	YOU YOU YOU	Alvin Stardust	Magnet	7
9	9	CAN'T GET ENOUGH OF YOUR LOVE BABE	Barry White	Pye	8
17	10	KNOCK ON WOOD	Bowie	RCA	3
13	11	EVERYTHING I OWN	Ken Boothe	Trojan	3
10	12	QUEEN OF CLUBS	K.C. And The Sunshine Band	Jayboy	8
18	13	REGGAE TUNE	Andy Fairweather Low	A&M	3
31	14	I GET A KICK OUT OF YOU	Gary Shearston	Charisma	2
27	15	FAREWELL/BRING IT ON HOME TO ME	Rod Stewart	Mercury	2
15	16	THE BITCH IS BACK	Elton John	DJM	5
29	17	(YOU'RE) HAVING MY BABY	Paul Anka	United Artists	2
11	18	Y VIVA ESPANA	Sylvia	Sonet	9
21	19	I GOT THE MUSIC IN ME	Kiki Dee Band	Rocket	5
20	20	MACHINE GUN	Commodores	Tamla Motown	6
19	21	SMOKE GETS IN YOUR EYES	Bryan Ferry	Island	6
39	22	I CAN'T LEAVE YOU ALONE	George McCrae	Jayboy	2
28	23	YOU LITTLE TRUST MAKER	Tymes	RCA	3
24	24	SILLY LOVE	10C.C.	UK	5
12	25	THE BLACK-EYED BOYS	Paper Lace	Bus Stop	7
22	26	BABY LOVE	Diana Ross & The Supremes	Tamla Motown	7
37	27	SAMBA PA TI	Santana	CBS	2
14	28	LOVE ME FOR A REASON	Osmonds	MGM	8
33	29	I'M A BELIEVER	Robert Wyatt	Virgin	2
26	30	PINBALL	Brian Protheroe	Chrysalis	6
-	31	ALL OF ME LOVES ALL OF YOU	Bay City Rollers	Bell	1
23	32	NA NA NA	Cozy Powell	RAK	9
-	33	HAPPY ANNIVERSARY	Slim Whitman	United Artists	1
16	34	I'M LEAVING IT ALL UP TO YOU	Donny & Marie Osmond	MGM	11
-	35	I HONESTLY LOVE YOU	Olivia Newton-John	EMI	1
-	36	LEAVE IT	Mike McGear ●	Warner Brothers	1
30	37	WHEN WILL I SEE YOU AGAIN	Three Degrees	Philadelphia	14
-	38	LOVE ME	Diana Ross	Tamla Motown	1
34	39	LIFE IS A ROCK (BUT THE RADIO ROLLED ME)	Reunion	RCA	3
25	40	WHAT BECOMES OF THE BROKEN HEARTED	Jimmy Ruffin	Tamla Motown	11

WEEK ENDING 19 OCTOBER 1974

LW	TW	Title	Artist	Label	Wks
3	1	SAD SWEET DREAMER	Sweet Sensation	Pye	5
11	2	EVERYTHING I OWN	Ken Boothe	Trojan	4
-	3	FAR FAR AWAY	Slade	Polydor	1
5	4	GEE BABY	Peter Shelley	Magnet	5
1	5	ANNIE'S SONG	John Denver	RCA	10
6	6	LONG TALL GLASSES	Leo Sayer	Chrysalis	5
15	7	FAREWELL/BRING IT ON HOME TO ME	Rod Stewart	Mercury	3
2	8	ROCK ME GENTLY	Andy Kim	Capitol	8
14	9	I GET A KICK OUT OF YOU	Gary Shearston	Charisma	3
13	10	REGGAE TUNE	Andy Fairweather Low	A&M	4
31	11	ALL OF ME LOVES ALL OF YOU	Bay City Rollers	Bell	2
17	12	(YOU'RE) HAVING MY BABY	Paul Anka	United Artists	3
22	13	I CAN'T LEAVE YOU ALONE	George McCrae	Jayboy	3
4	14	KUNG FU FIGHTING	Carl Douglas	Pye	9
7	15	HANG ON IN THERE BABY	Johnny Bristol	MGM	9
10	16	KNOCK ON WOOD	Bowie	RCA	4
-	17	ALL I WANT IS YOU	Roxy Music	Island	1
23	18	YOU LITTLE TRUST MAKER	Tymes	RCA	4
-	19	GONNA MAKE YOU A STAR	David Essex	CBS	1
20	20	MACHINE GUN	Commodores	Tamla Motown	7
16	21	THE BITCH IS BACK	Elton John	DJM	6
18	22	Y VIVA ESPANA	Sylvia	Sonet	10
-	23	MINUETTO ALLEGRETTO	The Wombles	CBS	1
8	24	YOU YOU YOU	Alvin Stardust	Magnet	8
-	25	DOWN ON THE BEACH TONIGHT	Drifters	Bell	1
12	26	QUEEN OF CLUBS	K.C. And The Sunshine Band	Jayboy	9
27	27	SAMBA PA TI	Santana	CBS	3
33	28	HAPPY ANNIVERSARY	Slim Whitman	United Artists	2
35	29	I HONESTLY LOVE YOU	Olivia Newton-John	EMI	2
9	30	CAN'T GET ENOUGH OF YOUR LOVE BABE	Barry White	Pye	9
-	31	(HEY THERE) LONELY GIRL	Eddie Holman ●	ABC	1
19	32	I GOT THE MUSIC IN ME	Kiki Dee Band	Rocket	6
-	33	NEVER TURN YOUR BACK ON MOTHER EARTH	Sparks	Island	1
-	34	LET'S PUT IT ALL TOGETHER	Stylistics	Avco	1
25	35	THE BLACK-EYED BOYS	Paper Lace	Bus Stop	8
24	36	SILLY LOVE	10C.C.	UK	6
29	37	I'M A BELIEVER	Robert Wyatt	Virgin	3
-	38	DA DOO RON RON	Crystals	Warner Spector	1
-	39	YOU HAVEN'T DONE NOTHIN'	Stevie Wonder	Tamla Motown	1
36	40	LEAVE IT	Mike McGear	Warner Brothers	2

WEEK ENDING 26 OCTOBER 1974

LW	TW	Title	Artist	Label	Wks
2	1	EVERYTHING I OWN	Ken Boothe	Trojan	5
3	2	FAR FAR AWAY	Slade	Polydor	2
1	3	SAD SWEET DREAMER	Sweet Sensation	Pye	6
11	4	ALL OF ME LOVES ALL OF YOU	Bay City Rollers	Bell	3
4	5	GEE BABY	Peter Shelley	Magnet	6
12	6	(YOU'RE) HAVING MY BABY	Paul Anka	United Artists	4
9	7	I GET A KICK OUT OF YOU	Gary Shearston	Charisma	4
8	8	ROCK ME GENTLY	Andy Kim	Capitol	9
13	9	I CAN'T LEAVE YOU ALONE	George McCrae	Jayboy	4
19	10	GONNA MAKE YOU A STAR	David Essex	CBS	2
7	11	FAREWELL/BRING IT ON HOME TO ME	Rod Stewart	Mercury	4
5	12	ANNIE'S SONG	John Denver	RCA	11
10	13	REGGAE TUNE	Andy Fairweather Low	A&M	5
6	14	LONG TALL GLASSES	Leo Sayer	Chrysalis	6
25	15	DOWN ON THE BEACH TONIGHT	Drifters	Bell	2
17	16	ALL I WANT IS YOU	Roxy Music	Island	2
28	17	HAPPY ANNIVERSARY	Slim Whitman	United Artists	3
31	18	(HEY THERE) LONELY GIRL	Eddie Holman	ABC	2
-	19	LET'S GET TOGETHER AGAIN	Glitter Band	Bell	1
18	20	YOU LITTLE TRUST MAKER	Tymes	RCA	5
33	21	NEVER TURN YOUR BACK ON MOTHER EARTH	Sparks	Island	2
29	22	I HONESTLY LOVE YOU	Olivia Newton-John	EMI	3
-	23	KILLER QUEEN	Queen	EMI	1
23	24	MINUETTO ALLEGRETTO	The Wombles	CBS	2
16	25	KNOCK ON WOOD	Bowie	RCA	5
22	26	Y VIVA ESPANA	Sylvia	Sonet	11
27	27	SAMBA PA TI	Santana	CBS	4
34	28	LET'S PUT IT ALL TOGETHER	Stylistics	Avco	2
20	29	MACHINE GUN	Commodores	Tamla Motown	8
38	30	DA DOO RON RON	Crystals	Warner Spector	2
15	31	HANG ON IN THERE BABY	Johnny Bristol	MGM	10
14	32	KUNG FU FIGHTING	Carl Douglas	Pye	10
-	33	ROCK 'N' SOUL	Hues Corporation	RCA	1
24	34	YOU YOU YOU	Alvin Stardust	Magnet	9
30	35	CAN'T GET ENOUGH OF YOUR LOVE BABE	Barry White	Pye	10
39	36	YOU HAVEN'T DONE NOTHIN'	Stevie Wonder	Tamla Motown	2
26	37	QUEEN OF CLUBS	K.C. And The Sunshine Band	Jayboy	10
-	38	THEN CAME YOU	Dionne Warwicke/Detroit Spinners ●	Atlantic	1
-	39	HOT SHOT	Barry Blue	Bell	1
37	40	I'M A BELIEVER	Robert Wyatt	Virgin	4

WEEK ENDING 2 NOVEMBER 1974

LW	TW	Title	Artist	Label	Wks
1	1	EVERYTHING I OWN	Ken Boothe	Trojan	6
2	2	FAR FAR AWAY	Slade	Polydor	3
10	3	GONNA MAKE YOU A STAR	David Essex	CBS	3
4	4	ALL OF ME LOVES ALL OF YOU	Bay City Rollers	Bell	4
23	5	KILLER QUEEN	Queen	EMI	2
3	6	SAD SWEET DREAMER	Sweet Sensation	Pye	7
6	7	(YOU'RE) HAVING MY BABY	Paul Anka	United Artists	5
15	8	DOWN ON THE BEACH TONIGHT	Drifters	Bell	3
9	9	I CAN'T LEAVE YOU ALONE	George McCrae	Jayboy	5
19	10	LET'S GET TOGETHER AGAIN	Glitter Band	Bell	2
18	11	(HEY THERE) LONELY GIRL	Eddie Holman	ABC	3
7	12	I GET A KICK OUT OF YOU	Gary Shearston	Charisma	5
5	13	GEE BABY	Peter Shelley	Magnet	7
28	14	LET'S PUT IT ALL TOGETHER	Stylistics	Avco	3

■Three consecutive weeks at number 27 for Santana's *Samba Pa Ti* (26.10.74) ■ Paul Anka scores his first top ten hit for 15 years, in uncredited partnership with Odia Coates (26.10.74) ■ *Everything I Own*, a hit two years earlier for writer David Gates' group Bread, tops the chart for the first time, as performed by Jamaican Ken Boothe (26.10.74)■

November 1974

□ Highest position disc reached ● Act's first ever week on chart

LW	TW	Title	Artist	Label	Wks
16	15	ALL I WANT IS YOU	Roxy Music	*Island*	3
21	16	NEVER TURN YOUR BACK ON MOTHER EARTH	Sparks	*Island*	3
24	17	MINUETTO ALLEGRETTO	The Wombles	*CBS*	3
11	18	FAREWELL/BRING IT ON HOME TO ME	Rod Stewart	*Mercury*	5
20	19	YOU LITTLE TRUST MAKER	Tymes	*RCA*	6
13	20	REGGAE TUNE	Andy Fairweather Low	*A&M*	6
17	21	HAPPY ANNIVERSARY	Slim Whitman	*United Artists*	4
22	[22]	I HONESTLY LOVE YOU	Olivia Newton-John	*EMI*	4
30	23	DA DOO RON RON	Crystals	*Warner Spector*	3
12	24	ANNIE'S SONG	John Denver	*RCA*	12
8	25	ROCK ME GENTLY	Andy Kim	*Capitol*	10
-	26	PEPPER BOX	Peppers ●	*Spark*	1
33	27	ROCK 'N' SOUL	Hues Corporation	*RCA*	2
26	28	Y VIVA ESPANA	Sylvia	*Sonet*	12
39	29	HOT SHOT	Barry Blue	*Bell*	2
36	[30]	YOU HAVEN'T DONE NOTHIN'	Stevie Wonder	*Tamla Motown*	3
14	31	LONG TALL GLASSES	Leo Sayer	*Chrysalis*	7
38	32	THEN CAME YOU	Dionne Warwicke/Detroit Spinners	*Atlantic*	2
27	33	SAMBA PA TI	Santana	*CBS*	5
-	34	FAREWELL IS A LONELY SOUND	Jimmy Ruffin	*Tamla Motown*	1
-	35	GET YOUR LOVE BACK	Three Degrees	*Philadelphia*	1
-	[36]	WHATEVER GETS YOU THROUGH THE NIGHT	John Lennon with The Plastic Ono Nuclear Band	*Apple*	1
32	37	KUNG FU FIGHTING	Carl Douglas	*Pye*	11
-	38	YOU'RE THE FIRST, THE LAST, MY EVERYTHING	Barry White	*20th Century*	1
-	39	TOO GOOD TO BE FORGOTTEN	Chi-Lites	*Brunswick*	1
-	40	MAGIC	Pilot ●	*EMI*	1

WEEK ENDING 9 NOVEMBER 1974

LW	TW	Title	Artist	Label	Wks
1	[1]	EVERYTHING I OWN	Ken Boothe	*Trojan*	7
3	2	GONNA MAKE YOU A STAR	David Essex	*CBS*	4
5	3	KILLER QUEEN	Queen	*EMI*	3
4	[4]	ALL OF ME LOVES ALL OF YOU	Bay City Rollers	*Bell*	5
2	5	FAR FAR AWAY	Slade	*Polydor*	4
11	6	(HEY THERE) LONELY GIRL	Eddie Holman	*ABC*	4
8	7	DOWN ON THE BEACH TONIGHT	Drifters	*Bell*	4
10	[8]	LET'S GET TOGETHER AGAIN	Glitter Band	*Bell*	3
7	9	(YOU'RE) HAVING MY BABY	Paul Anka	*United Artists*	6
14	10	LET'S PUT IT ALL TOGETHER	Stylistics	*Avco*	4
9	11	I CAN'T LEAVE YOU ALONE	George McCrae	*Jayboy*	6
15	[12]	ALL I WANT IS YOU	Roxy Music	*Island*	4
12	13	I GET A KICK OUT OF YOU	Gary Shearston	*Charisma*	6
21	[14]	HAPPY ANNIVERSARY	Slim Whitman	*United Artists*	5
16	15	NEVER TURN YOUR BACK ON MOTHER EARTH	Sparks	*Island*	4
17	[16]	MINUETTO ALLEGRETTO	The Wombles	*CBS*	4
26	17	PEPPER BOX	Peppers	*Spark*	2
6	18	SAD SWEET DREAMER	Sweet Sensation	*Pye*	8
23	19	DA DOO RON RON	Crystals	*Warner Spector*	4
38	20	YOU'RE THE FIRST, THE LAST, MY EVERYTHING	Barry White	*20th Century*	2
13	21	GEE BABY	Peter Shelley	*Magnet*	8
-	22	NO HONESTLY	Lynsey De Paul	*Jet*	1
29	[23]	HOT SHOT	Barry Blue	*Bell*	3
27	[24]	ROCK 'N' SOUL	Hues Corporation	*RCA*	3
22	25	I HONESTLY LOVE YOU	Olivia Newton-John	*EMI*	5
18	26	FAREWELL/BRING IT ON HOME TO ME	Rod Stewart	*Mercury*	6
39	27	TOO GOOD TO BE FORGOTTEN	Chi-Lites	*Brunswick*	2
-	28	COSTAFINE TOWN	Splinter ●	*Dark Horse*	1
32	[29]	THEN CAME YOU	Dionne Warwicke/Detroit Spinners	*Atlantic*	3
40	30	MAGIC	Pilot	*EMI*	2
19	31	YOU LITTLE TRUST MAKER	Tymes	*RCA*	7
-	32	JUNIOR'S FARM	Paul McCartney/Wings	*Apple*	1
28	33	Y VIVA ESPANA	Sylvia	*Sonet*	13
35	[34]	GET YOUR LOVE BACK	Three Degrees	*Philadelphia*	2
30	35	YOU HAVEN'T DONE NOTHIN'	Stevie Wonder	*Tamla Motown*	4
25	36	ROCK ME GENTLY	Andy Kim	*Capitol*	11
-	37	THE WILD ONE	Suzi Quatro	*RAK*	1
20	38	REGGAE TUNE	Andy Fairweather Low	*A&M*	7
24	39	ANNIE'S SONG	John Denver	*RCA*	13
34	40	FAREWELL IS A LONELY SOUND	Jimmy Ruffin	*Tamla Motown*	2

WEEK ENDING 16 NOVEMBER 1974

LW	TW	Title	Artist	Label	Wks
2	[1]	GONNA MAKE YOU A STAR	David Essex	*CBS*	5
3	[2]	KILLER QUEEN	Queen	*EMI*	4
1	3	EVERYTHING I OWN	Ken Boothe	*Trojan*	8
6	[4]	(HEY THERE) LONELY GIRL	Eddie Holman	*ABC*	5
20	5	YOU'RE THE FIRST, THE LAST, MY EVERYTHING	Barry White	*20th Century*	3
5	6	FAR FAR AWAY	Slade	*Polydor*	5
4	7	ALL OF ME LOVES ALL OF YOU	Bay City Rollers	*Bell*	6
7	8	DOWN ON THE BEACH TONIGHT	Drifters	*Bell*	5
10	[9]	LET'S PUT IT ALL TOGETHER	Stylistics	*Avco*	5
17	10	PEPPER BOX	Peppers	*Spark*	3
8	11	LET'S GET TOGETHER AGAIN	Glitter Band	*Bell*	4
9	12	(YOU'RE) HAVING MY BABY	Paul Anka	*United Artists*	7
15	[13]	NEVER TURN YOUR BACK ON MOTHER EARTH	Sparks	*Island*	5
12	14	ALL I WANT IS YOU	Roxy Music	*Island*	5
19	15	DA DOO RON RON	Crystals	*Warner Spector*	5
11	16	I CAN'T LEAVE YOU ALONE	George McCrae	*Jayboy*	7
30	17	MAGIC	Pilot	*EMI*	3
37	18	THE WILD ONE	Suzi Quatro	*RAK*	2
16	19	MINUETTO ALLEGRETTO	The Wombles	*CBS*	5
22	20	NO HONESTLY	Lynsey De Paul	*Jet*	2
27	21	TOO GOOD TO BE FORGOTTEN	Chi-Lites	*Brunswick*	3
28	22	COSTAFINE TOWN	Splinter	*Dark Horse*	2
-	23	JUKE BOX JIVE	The Rubettes	*Polydor*	1
14	24	HAPPY ANNIVERSARY	Slim Whitman	*United Artists*	6
32	25	JUNIOR'S FARM	Paul McCartney/Wings	*Apple*	2
23	26	HOT SHOT	Barry Blue	*Bell*	4
-	27	GOODBYE NOTHING TO SAY	Javells/Nosmo King ●	*Pye*	1
-	28	WHERE DID ALL THE GOOD TIMES GO	Donny Osmond	*MGM*	1
24	29	ROCK 'N' SOUL	Hues Corporation	*RCA*	4
40	30	FAREWELL IS A LONELY SOUND	Jimmy Ruffin	*Tamla Motown*	3
13	31	I GET A KICK OUT OF YOU	Gary Shearston	*Charisma*	7
-	32	TELL HIM	Hello ●	*Bell*	1
29	33	THEN CAME YOU	Dionne Warwicke/Detroit Spinners	*Atlantic*	4
-	34	YOU AIN'T SEEN NOTHING YET	Bachman-Turner Overdrive ●	*Mercury*	1
-	35	HOW LONG	Ace ●	*Anchor*	1
33	36	Y VIVA ESPANA	Sylvia	*Sonet*	14
21	37	GEE BABY	Peter Shelley	*Magnet*	9
25	38	I HONESTLY LOVE YOU	Olivia Newton-John	*EMI*	6
34	39	GET YOUR LOVE BACK	Three Degrees	*Philadelphia*	3
-	40	MY BOY	Elvis Presley	*RCA*	1

WEEK ENDING 23 NOVEMBER 1974

LW	TW	Title	Artist	Label	Wks
1	[1]	GONNA MAKE YOU A STAR	David Essex	*CBS*	6
2	[2]	KILLER QUEEN	Queen	*EMI*	5
5	3	YOU'RE THE FIRST, THE LAST, MY EVERYTHING	Barry White	*20th Century*	4
4	[4]	(HEY THERE) LONELY GIRL	Eddie Holman	*ABC*	6
3	5	EVERYTHING I OWN	Ken Boothe	*Trojan*	9
10	[6]	PEPPER BOX	Peppers	*Spark*	4
20	[7]	NO HONESTLY	Lynsey De Paul	*Jet*	3
23	8	JUKE BOX JIVE	The Rubettes	*Polydor*	2
9	[9]	LET'S PUT IT ALL TOGETHER	Stylistics	*Avco*	6
7	10	ALL OF ME LOVES ALL OF YOU	Bay City Rollers	*Bell*	7
8	11	DOWN ON THE BEACH TONIGHT	Drifters	*Bell*	6
11	12	LET'S GET TOGETHER AGAIN	Glitter Band	*Bell*	5
21	13	TOO GOOD TO BE FORGOTTEN	Chi-Lites	*Brunswick*	4
18	14	THE WILD ONE	Suzi Quatro	*RAK*	3
17	15	MAGIC	Pilot	*EMI*	4

In these weeks ■ Slim Whitman's *Happy Anniversary* is his first hit in over 17 years, the biggest gap between hits up to this date (09.11.74) ■ Dionne Warwick added an 'e' to her surname for a few years in the mid-70s for luck, but all that happened was that her chart career stalled, with the one exception of this duet with the Detroit Spinners (09.11.74) ■

December 1974

□ Highest position disc reached ● Act's first ever week on chart

LW	TW	Title	Artist	Label	Wks
-	16	OH YES YOU'RE BEAUTIFUL	Gary Glitter and The Glitter Band	Bell	1
15	17	DA DOO RON RON	Crystals	Warner Spector	6
13	18	NEVER TURN YOUR BACK ON MOTHER EARTH	Sparks	Island	6
14	19	ALL I WANT IS YOU	Roxy Music	Island	6
34	20	YOU AIN'T SEEN NOTHING YET	Bachman-Turner Overdrive	Mercury	2
28	21	WHERE DID ALL THE GOOD TIMES GO	Donny Osmond	MGM	2
22	22	COSTAFINE TOWN	Splinter	Dark Horse	3
32	23	TELL HIM	Hello	Bell	2
25	24	JUNIOR'S FARM	Paul McCartney/Wings	Apple	3
19	25	MINUETTO ALLEGRETTO	The Wombles	CBS	6
35	26	HOW LONG	Ace	Anchor	2
27	27	GOODBYE NOTHING TO SAY	Javells/Nosmo King	Pye	2
40	28	MY BOY	Elvis Presley	RCA	2
-	29	SHA-LA-LA (MAKE ME HAPPY)	Al Green	London	1
6	30	FAR FAR AWAY	Slade	Polydor	6
30	31	FAREWELL IS A LONELY SOUND	Jimmy Ruffin	Tamla Motown	4
24	32	HAPPY ANNIVERSARY	Slim Whitman	United Artists	7
12	33	(YOU'RE) HAVING MY BABY	Paul Anka	United Artists	8
-	34	LUCY IN THE SKY WITH DIAMONDS	Elton John	DJM	1
16	35	I CAN'T LEAVE YOU ALONE	George McCrae	Jayboy	8
26	36	HOT SHOT	Barry Blue	Bell	5
31	37	I GET A KICK OUT OF YOU	Gary Shearston	Charisma	8
-	38	IRE FEELINGS (SKANGA)	Rupie Edwards ●	Cactus	1
-	[39]	TELL ME WHAT YOU WANT	Jimmy Ruffin	Polydor	1
36	40	Y VIVA ESPANA	Sylvia	Sonet	15

WEEK ENDING 30 NOVEMBER 1974

LW	TW	Title	Artist	Label	Wks
1	[1]	GONNA MAKE YOU A STAR	David Essex	CBS	7
3	2	YOU'RE THE FIRST, THE LAST, MY EVERYTHING	Barry White	20th Century	5
16	3	OH YES YOU'RE BEAUTIFUL	Gary Glitter and The Glitter Band	Bell	2
8	4	JUKE BOX JIVE	The Rubettes	Polydor	3
2	5	KILLER QUEEN	Queen	EMI	6
20	6	YOU AIN'T SEEN NOTHING YET	Bachman-Turner Overdrive	Mercury	3
14	[7]	THE WILD ONE	Suzi Quatro	RAK	4
4	8	(HEY THERE) LONELY GIRL	Eddie Holman	ABC	7
6	9	PEPPER BOX	Peppers	Spark	5
13	[10]	TOO GOOD TO BE FORGOTTEN	Chi-Lites	Brunswick	5
15	[11]	MAGIC	Pilot	EMI	5
23	12	TELL HIM	Hello	Bell	3
7	13	NO HONESTLY	Lynsey De Paul	Jet	4
9	14	LET'S PUT IT ALL TOGETHER	Stylistics	Avco	7
28	15	MY BOY	Elvis Presley	RCA	3
5	16	EVERYTHING I OWN	Ken Boothe	Trojan	10
22	[17]	COSTAFINE TOWN	Splinter	Dark Horse	4
34	18	LUCY IN THE SKY WITH DIAMONDS	Elton John	DJM	2
17	19	DA DOO RON RON	Crystals	Warner Spector	7
38	20	IRE FEELINGS (SKANGA)	Rupie Edwards	Cactus	2
24	21	JUNIOR'S FARM	Paul McCartney/Wings	Apple	4
26	22	HOW LONG	Ace	Anchor	3
21	23	WHERE DID ALL THE GOOD TIMES GO	Donny Osmond	MGM	3
29	24	SHA-LA-LA (MAKE ME HAPPY)	Al Green	London	2
18	25	NEVER TURN YOUR BACK ON MOTHER EARTH	Sparks	Island	7
27	[26]	GOODBYE NOTHING TO SAY	Javells/Nosmo King	Pye	3
-	27	TELL ME WHY	Alvin Stardust	Magnet	1
-	28	GET DANCING	Disco Tex and the Sex-O-Lettes ●	Chelsea	1
11	29	DOWN ON THE BEACH TONIGHT	Drifters	Bell	7
10	30	ALL OF ME LOVES ALL OF YOU	Bay City Rollers	Bell	8
-	31	SOUND YOUR FUNKY HORN	K.C. & The Sunshine Band	Jayboy	1
12	32	LET'S GET TOGETHER AGAIN	Glitter Band	Bell	6
-	33	ONLY YOU	Ringo Starr	Apple	1
-	34	LONELY THIS CHRISTMAS	Mud	RAK	1
25	35	MINUETTO ALLEGRETTO	The Wombles	CBS	7
-	36	UNDER MY THUMB	Wayne Gibson ●	Pye	1
-	37	DANCE THE KUNG FU	Carl Douglas	Pye	1
31	38	FAREWELL IS A LONELY SOUND	Jimmy Ruffin	Tamla Motown	5
-	[39]	BLUE ANGEL	Gene Pitney	Bronze	1
32	40	HAPPY ANNIVERSARY	Slim Whitman	United Artists	8

WEEK ENDING 7 DECEMBER 1974

LW	TW	Title	Artist	Label	Wks
2	[1]	YOU'RE THE FIRST, THE LAST, MY EVERYTHING	Barry White	20th Century	6
1	2	GONNA MAKE YOU A STAR	David Essex	CBS	8
4	[3]	JUKE BOX JIVE	The Rubettes	Polydor	4
3	4	OH YES YOU'RE BEAUTIFUL	Gary Glitter and The Glitter Band	Bell	3
6	5	YOU AIN'T SEEN NOTHING YET	Bachman-Turner Overdrive	Mercury	4
12	[6]	TELL HIM	Hello	Bell	4
8	7	(HEY THERE) LONELY GIRL	Eddie Holman	ABC	8
15	8	MY BOY	Elvis Presley	RCA	4
5	9	KILLER QUEEN	Queen	EMI	7
20	10	IRE FEELINGS (SKANGA)	Rupie Edwards	Cactus	3
11	[11]	MAGIC	Pilot	EMI	6
9	12	PEPPER BOX	Peppers	Spark	6
10	13	TOO GOOD TO BE FORGOTTEN	Chi-Lites	Brunswick	6
28	14	GET DANCING	Disco Tex and the Sex-O-Lettes	Chelsea	2
18	15	LUCY IN THE SKY WITH DIAMONDS	Elton John	DJM	3
7	16	THE WILD ONE	Suzi Quatro	RAK	5
13	17	NO HONESTLY	Lynsey De Paul	Jet	5
17	18	COSTAFINE TOWN	Splinter	Dark Horse	5
34	19	LONELY THIS CHRISTMAS	Mud	RAK	2
22	[20]	HOW LONG	Ace	Anchor	4
23	21	WHERE DID ALL THE GOOD TIMES GO	Donny Osmond	MGM	4
24	22	SHA-LA-LA (MAKE ME HAPPY)	Al Green	London	3
21	23	JUNIOR'S FARM	Paul McCartney/Wings	Apple	5
27	24	TELL ME WHY	Alvin Stardust	Magnet	2
31	25	SOUND YOUR FUNKY HORN	K.C. & The Sunshine Band	Jayboy	2
36	26	UNDER MY THUMB	Wayne Gibson	Pye	2
26	27	GOODBYE NOTHING TO SAY	Javells/Nosmo King	Pye	4
-	28	YOU CAN MAKE ME DANCE, SING OR ANYTHING	Faces/Rod Stewart	Warner Bros.	1
-	[29]	ZING WENT THE STRINGS OF MY HEART	Trammps ●	Buddah	1
14	30	LET'S PUT IT ALL TOGETHER	Stylistics	Avco	8
33	31	ONLY YOU	Ringo Starr	Apple	2
-	32	CHERI BABE	Hot Chocolate	RAK	1
-	33	HEY MISTER CHRISTMAS	Showaddywaddy	Bell	1
-	34	DOWN DOWN	Status Quo	Vertigo	1
37	[35]	DANCE THE KUNG FU	Carl Douglas	Pye	2
16	36	EVERYTHING I OWN	Ken Boothe	Trojan	11
-	37	THE BUMP	Kenny ●	RAK	1
30	38	ALL OF ME LOVES ALL OF YOU	Bay City Rollers	Bell	9
-	39	STREETS OF LONDON	Ralph McTell ●	Reprise	1
29	40	DOWN ON THE BEACH TONIGHT	Drifters	Bell	8

WEEK ENDING 14 DECEMBER 1974

LW	TW	Title	Artist	Label	Wks
1	[1]	YOU'RE THE FIRST, THE LAST, MY EVERYTHING	Barry White	20th Century	7
4	[2]	OH YES YOU'RE BEAUTIFUL	Gary Glitter and The Glitter Band	Bell	4
5	3	YOU AIN'T SEEN NOTHING YET	Bachman-Turner Overdrive	Mercury	5
19	4	LONELY THIS CHRISTMAS	Mud	RAK	3
2	5	GONNA MAKE YOU A STAR	David Essex	CBS	9
8	6	MY BOY	Elvis Presley	RCA	5
6	7	TELL HIM	Hello	Bell	5
3	8	JUKE BOX JIVE	The Rubettes	Polydor	5
10	[9]	IRE FEELINGS (SKANGA)	Rupie Edwards	Cactus	4
15	[10]	LUCY IN THE SKY WITH DIAMONDS	Elton John	DJM	4

■Gene Pitney enjoys his final week of solo chart action. His name will not appear on the lists until January 1989, when he duets with Marc Almond on a remake of his 1967 hit *Something's Gotten Hold Of My Heart* (30.11.74) ■ Cover vesions of both a Beatles song (Elton John's *Lucy In The Sky With Diamonds*) and a Stones song (*Under My Thumb* by Wayne Gibson) in the charts (07.12.74)■

December 1974

□ Highest position disc reached ● Act's first ever week on chart

LW	TW	Title / Artist	Label	Wks
14	11	GET DANCING Disco Tex and the Sex-O-Lettes	Chelsea	3
11	12	MAGIC Pilot	EMI	7
13	13	TOO GOOD TO BE FORGOTTEN Chi-Lites	Brunswick	7
39	14	STREETS OF LONDON Ralph McTell	Reprise	2
16	15	THE WILD ONE Suzi Quatro	RAK	6
23	16	JUNIOR'S FARM Paul McCartney/Wings	Apple	6
18	17	COSTAFINE TOWN Splinter	Dark Horse	6
21	18	WHERE DID ALL THE GOOD TIMES GO Donny Osmond	MGM	5
24	19	TELL ME WHY Alvin Stardust	Magnet	3
34	20	DOWN DOWN Status Quo	Vertigo	2
-	21	WOMBLING MERRY CHRISTMAS The Wombles	CBS	1
22	22	SHA-LA-LA (MAKE ME HAPPY) Al Green	London	4
28	23	YOU CAN MAKE ME DANCE, SING OR ANYTHING Faces/Rod Stewart	Warner Bros.	2
20	24	HOW LONG Ace	Anchor	5
26	25	UNDER MY THUMB Wayne Gibson	Pye	3
12	26	PEPPER BOX Peppers	Spark	7
-	27	I CAN HELP Billy Swan ●	Monument	1
-	28	THE IN BETWEENIES/FATHER CHRISTMAS DO NOT TOUCH ME The Goodies	Bradley's	1
9	29	KILLER QUEEN Queen	EMI	8
31	30	ONLY YOU Ringo Starr	Apple	3
33	31	HEY MISTER CHRISTMAS Showaddywaddy	Bell	2
25	32	SOUND YOUR FUNKY HORN K.C. & The Sunshine Band	Jayboy	3
37	33	THE BUMP Kenny	RAK	2
17	34	NO HONESTLY Lynsey De Paul	Jet	6
32	35	CHERI BABE Hot Chocolate	RAK	2
-	36	NEVER CAN SAY GOODBYE Gloria Gaynor	MGM	1
29	37	ZING WENT THE STRINGS OF MY HEART Trammps	Buddah	2
7	38	(HEY THERE) LONELY GIRL Eddie Holman	ABC	9
27	39	GOODBYE NOTHING TO SAY Javells/Nosmo King	Pye	5
-	40	JE T'AIME Moi Non Plus Jane Birkin & Serge Gainsbourg	Antic	1

WEEK ENDING 21 DECEMBER 1974

LW	TW	Title / Artist	Label	Wks
4	1	LONELY THIS CHRISTMAS Mud	RAK	4
3	2	YOU AIN'T SEEN NOTHING YET Bachman-Turner Overdrive	Mercury	6
8	3	JUKE BOX JIVE The Rubettes	Polydor	6
1	4	YOU'RE THE FIRST, THE LAST, MY EVERYTHING Barry White	20th Century	8
21	5	WOMBLING MERRY CHRISTMAS The Wombles	CBS	2
14	6	STREETS OF LONDON Ralph McTell	Reprise	3
6	7	MY BOY Elvis Presley	RCA	6
11	8	GET DANCING Disco Tex and the Sex-O-Lettes	Chelsea	4
2	9	OH YES YOU'RE BEAUTIFUL Gary Glitter and The Glitter Band	Bell	5
7	10	TELL HIM Hello	Bell	6
10	11	LUCY IN THE SKY WITH DIAMONDS Elton John	DJM	5
23	12	YOU CAN MAKE ME DANCE, SING OR ANYTHING Faces/Rod Stewart	Warner Bros.	3
28	13	THE IN BETWEENIES/FATHER CHRISTMAS DO NOT TOUCH ME The Goodies	Bradley's	2
9	14	IRE FEELINGS (SKANGA) Rupie Edwards	Cactus	5
20	15	DOWN DOWN Status Quo	Vertigo	3
19	16	TELL ME WHY Alvin Stardust	Magnet	4
32	17	SOUND YOUR FUNKY HORN K.C. & The Sunshine Band	Jayboy	4
-	18	CHRISTMAS SONG Gilbert O'Sullivan	MAM	1
27	19	I CAN HELP Billy Swan	Monument	2
22	20	SHA-LA-LA (MAKE ME HAPPY) Al Green	London	5
5	21	GONNA MAKE YOU A STAR David Essex	CBS	10
25	22	UNDER MY THUMB Wayne Gibson	Pye	4
31	23	HEY MISTER CHRISTMAS Showaddywaddy	Bell	3
33	24	THE BUMP Kenny	RAK	3
36	25	NEVER CAN SAY GOODBYE Gloria Gaynor	MGM	2
12	26	MAGIC Pilot	EMI	8
-	27	STARDUST David Essex	CBS	1
24	28	HOW LONG Ace	Anchor	6
30	29	ONLY YOU Ringo Starr	Apple	4
37	30	ZING WENT THE STRINGS OF MY HEART Trammps	Buddah	3
35	31	CHERI BABE Hot Chocolate	RAK	3
40	32	JE T'AIME Moi Non Plus Jane Birkin & Serge Gainsbourg	Antic	2
-	33	MS. GRACE Tymes	RCA	1
13	34	TOO GOOD TO BE FORGOTTEN Chi-Lites	Brunswick	8
29	35	KILLER QUEEN Queen	EMI	9
26	36	PEPPER BOX Peppers	Spark	8
-	37	HELP ME MAKE IT THROUGH THE NIGHT John Holt ●	Trojan	1
34	38	NO HONESTLY Lynsey De Paul	Jet	7
38	39	(HEY THERE) LONELY GIRL Eddie Holman	ABC	10
15	40	THE WILD ONE Suzi Quatro	RAK	7

WEEK ENDING 28 DECEMBER 1974

(No chart published, chart for 21st December repeated)

LW	TW	Title / Artist	Label	Wks
1	1	LONELY THIS CHRISTMAS Mud	RAK	5
2	2	YOU AIN'T SEEN NOTHING YET Bachman-Turner Overdrive	Mercury	7
3	3	JUKE BOX JIVE The Rubettes	Polydor	7
4	4	YOU'RE THE FIRST, THE LAST, MY EVERYTHING Barry White	20th Century	9
5	5	WOMBLING MERRY CHRISTMAS The Wombles	CBS	3
6	6	STREETS OF LONDON Ralph McTell	Reprise	4
7	7	MY BOY Elvis Presley	RCA	7
8	8	GET DANCING Disco Tex and the Sex-O-Lettes	Chelsea	5
9	9	OH YES YOU'RE BEAUTIFUL Gary Glitter and The Glitter Band	Bell	6
10	10	TELL HIM Hello	Bell	7
11	11	LUCY IN THE SKY WITH DIAMONDS Elton John	DJM	6
12	12	YOU CAN MAKE ME DANCE, SING OR ANYTHING Faces/Rod Stewart	Warner Bros.	4
13	13	THE IN BETWEENIES/FATHER CHRISTMAS DO NOT TOUCH ME The Goodies	Bradley's	3
14	14	IRE FEELINGS (SKANGA) Rupie Edwards	Cactus	6
15	15	DOWN DOWN Status Quo	Vertigo	4
16	16	TELL ME WHY Alvin Stardust	Magnet	5
17	17	SOUND YOUR FUNKY HORN K.C. & The Sunshine Band	Jayboy	5
18	18	CHRISTMAS SONG Gilbert O'Sullivan	MAM	2
19	19	I CAN HELP Billy Swan	Monument	3
20	20	SHA-LA-LA (MAKE ME HAPPY) Al Green	London	6
21	21	GONNA MAKE YOU A STAR David Essex	CBS	11
22	22	UNDER MY THUMB Wayne Gibson	Pye	5
23	23	HEY MISTER CHRISTMAS Showaddywaddy	Bell	4
24	24	THE BUMP Kenny	RAK	4
25	25	NEVER CAN SAY GOODBYE Gloria Gaynor	MGM	3
26	26	MAGIC Pilot	EMI	9
27	27	STARDUST David Essex	CBS	2
28	28	HOW LONG Ace	Anchor	7
29	29	ONLY YOU Ringo Starr	Apple	5
30	30	ZING WENT THE STRINGS OF MY HEART Trammps	Buddah	4
31	31	CHERI BABE Hot Chocolate	RAK	4
32	32	JE T'AIME Moi Non Plus Jane Birkin & Serge Gainsbourg	Antic	3
33	33	MS. GRACE Tymes	RCA	2
34	34	TOO GOOD TO BE FORGOTTEN Chi-Lites	Brunswick	9
35	35	KILLER QUEEN Queen	EMI	10
36	36	PEPPER BOX Peppers	Spark	9
37	37	HELP ME MAKE IT THROUGH THE NIGHT John Holt	Trojan	2
38	38	NO HONESTLY Lynsey De Paul	Jet	8
39	39	(HEY THERE) LONELY GIRL Eddie Holman	ABC	11
40	40	THE WILD ONE Suzi Quatro	RAK	8

In these weeks ■ Eddie Holman's *Hey There Lonely Girl* drops from 7 to 38, the biggest drop ever recorded from the top ten (14.12.74) ■ For two consecutive weeks, a record plummeted from 12 to 26, as the charts reshuffled themselves for Christmas (21.12.74) ■ *Where Did All The Good Times Go* asked Donny Osmond, as his record peaked at no. 18. Good question. Next week he was out, and did not reappear in the top 40 for almost 14 years (14.12.74)■

1975

........DAVID BOWIE gets his first number one with a re-issue of 'Space Oddity' and egins his Thin White Duke period with 'Golden Years'......the Bay City Rollers are the only act with two number ones this year......Queen begin nine weeks at number one with 'Bohemian Rhapsody'.........

January 1975

□ Highest position disc reached ● Act's first ever week on chart

LW	TW	*WEEK ENDING* **4 JANUARY 1975**	Label	Wks
1	[1]	LONELY THIS CHRISTMAS Mud	*RAK*	6
5	[2]	WOMBLING MERRY CHRISTMAS Wombles	*CBS*	4
3	[3]	JUKE BOX JIVE Rubettes	*Polydor*	8
6	**4**	STREETS OF LONDON Ralph McTell	*Reprise*	5
7	[5]	MY BOY Elvis Presley	*RCA*	8
2	**6**	YOU AIN'T SEEN NOTHING YET Bachman-Turner Overdrive	*Mercury*	8
13	[7]	THE IN BETWEENIES/FATHER CHRISTMAS DO NOT TOUCH ME The Goodies	*Bradley's*	4
4	**8**	YOU'RE THE FIRST, THE LAST, MY EVERYTHING Barry White	*20th Century*	10
9	**9**	OH YES YOU'RE BEAUTIFUL Gary Glitter and The Glitter Band	*Bell*	7
15	**10**	DOWN DOWN Status Quo	*Vertigo*	5
8	**11**	GET DANCING Disco Tex and the Sex-O-Lettes	*Chelsea*	6
18	[12]	CHRISTMAS SONG Gilbert O'Sullivan	*MAM*	3
23	[13]	HEY MISTER CHRISTMAS Showaddywaddy	*Bell*	5
11	**14**	LUCY IN THE SKY WITH DIAMONDS Elton John	*DJM*	7
10	**15**	TELL HIM Hello	*Bell*	8
12	**16**	YOU CAN MAKE ME DANCE, SING OR ANYTHING Faces & Rod Stewart	*Warner Bros.*	5
19	**17**	I CAN HELP Billy Swan	*Monument*	4
14	**18**	IRE FEELINGS (SKANGA) Rupie Edwards	*Cactus*	7
16	**19**	TELL ME WHY Alvin Stardust	*Magnet*	6
21	**20**	GONNA MAKE YOU A STAR David Essex	*CBS*	12
24	**21**	THE BUMP Kenny	*RAK*	5
22	**22**	UNDER MY THUMB Wayne Gibson	*Pye*	6
25	**23**	NEVER CAN SAY GOODBYE Gloria Gaynor	*MGM*	4
17	**24**	SOUND YOUR FUNKY HORN K.C. & The Sunshine Band	*Jayboy*	6
20	**25**	SHA LA LA Al Green	*London*	7
27	**26**	STARDUST David Essex	*CBS*	3
33	**27**	MS. GRACE Tymes	*RCA*	3
-	**28**	ARE YOU READY TO ROCK Wizzard	*Warner Bros.*	1
37	**29**	HELP ME MAKE IT THROUGH THE NIGHT John Holt	*Trojan*	3
26	**30**	MAGIC Pilot	*EMI*	10
32	**31**	JE T'AIME Moi Non Plus Jane Birkin and Serge Gainsbourg	Antic	4
-	**32**	CRYING OVER YOU Ken Boothe	*Trojan*	1
29	**33**	ONLY YOU Ringo Starr	*Apple*	6
30	**34**	ZING WENT THE STRINGS OF MY HEART Trammps	*Buddah*	5
-	**35**	YOU CAN HAVE IT ALL George McCrae	*Jayboy*	1
31	**36**	CHERI BABE Hot Chocolate	*RAK*	5
28	**37**	HOW LONG Ace	*Anchor*	8
34	**38**	TOO GOOD TO BE FORGOTTEN Chi-Lites	*Brunswick*	10
35	**39**	KILLER QUEEN Queen	*EMI*	11
-	**40**	MORNING SIDE OF THE MOUNTAIN Donny & Marie Osmond	*MGM*	1

LW	TW	*WEEK ENDING* **11 JANUARY 1975**	Label	Wks
1	[1]	LONELY THIS CHRISTMAS Mud	*RAK*	7
4	[2]	STREETS OF LONDON Ralph McTell	*Reprise*	6
10	**3**	DOWN DOWN Status Quo	*Vertigo*	6
21	**4**	THE BUMP Kenny	*RAK*	6
2	**5**	WOMBLING MERRY CHRISTMAS Wombles	*CBS*	5
23	**6**	NEVER CAN SAY GOODBYE Gloria Gaynor	*MGM*	5
27	**7**	MS. GRACE Tymes	*RCA*	4
11	**8**	GET DANCING Disco Tex and the Sex-O-Lettes	*Chelsea*	7
17	**9**	I CAN HELP Billy Swan	*Monument*	5
3	**10**	JUKE BOX JIVE Rubettes	*Polydor*	9
7	**11**	THE IN BETWEENIES/FATHER CHRISTMAS DO NOT TOUCH ME The Goodies	*Bradley's*	5
6	**12**	YOU AIN'T SEEN NOTHING YET Bachman-Turner Overdrive	*Mercury*	9
5	**13**	MY BOY Elvis Presley	*RCA*	9
16	**14**	YOU CAN MAKE ME DANCE, SING OR ANYTHING Faces & Rod Stewart	*Warner Bros.*	6
28	**15**	ARE YOU READY TO ROCK Wizzard	*Warner Bros.*	2
26	**16**	STARDUST David Essex	*CBS*	4
14	**17**	LUCY IN THE SKY WITH DIAMONDS Elton John	*DJM*	8
29	**18**	HELP ME MAKE IT THROUGH THE NIGHT John Holt	*Trojan*	4
32	**19**	CRYING OVER YOU Ken Boothe	*Trojan*	2
22	**20**	UNDER MY THUMB Wayne Gibson	*Pye*	7
19	**21**	TELL ME WHY Alvin Stardust	*Magnet*	7
15	**22**	TELL HIM Hello	*Bell*	9
9	**23**	OH YES YOU'RE BEAUTIFUL Gary Glitter and The Glitter Band	*Bell*	8
12	**24**	CHRISTMAS SONG Gilbert O'Sullivan	*MAM*	4
8	**25**	YOU'RE THE FIRST, THE LAST, MY EVERYTHING Barry White	*20th Century*	11
40	**26**	MORNING SIDE OF THE MOUNTAIN Donny & Marie Osmond	*MGM*	2
13	**27**	HEY MISTER CHRISTMAS Showaddywaddy	*Bell*	6
33	**28**	ONLY YOU Ringo Starr	*Apple*	7
18	**29**	IRE FEELINGS (SKANGA) Rupie Edwards	*Cactus*	8
25	**30**	SHA LA LA Al Green	*London*	8
24	**31**	SOUND YOUR FUNKY HORN K.C. & The Sunshine Band	*Jayboy*	7
20	**32**	GONNA MAKE YOU A STAR David Essex	*CBS*	13
35	**33**	YOU CAN HAVE IT ALL George McCrae	*Jayboy*	2
31	**34**	JE T'AIME Moi Non Plus Jane Birkin and Serge Gainsbourg	Antic	5
36	**35**	CHERI BABE Hot Chocolate	*RAK*	6
30	**36**	MAGIC Pilot	*EMI*	11
34	**37**	ZING WENT THE STRINGS OF MY HEART Trammps	*Buddah*	6
-	[38]	DING DONG George Harrison	*Apple*	1
39	**39**	KILLER QUEEN Queen	*EMI*	12
-	**40**	BOOGIE ON REGGAE WOMAN Stevie Wonder	*Tamla Motown*	1

LW	TW	*WEEK ENDING* **18 JANUARY 1975**	Label	Wks
3	[1]	DOWN DOWN Status Quo	*Vertigo*	7
2	[2]	STREETS OF LONDON Ralph McTell	*Reprise*	7
4	[3]	THE BUMP Kenny	*RAK*	7
6	**4**	NEVER CAN SAY GOODBYE Gloria Gaynor	*MGM*	6
7	**5**	MS. GRACE Tymes	*RCA*	5
9	[6]	I CAN HELP Billy Swan	*Monument*	6
16	**7**	STARDUST David Essex	*CBS*	5
1	**8**	LONELY THIS CHRISTMAS Mud	*RAK*	8
8	**9**	GET DANCING Disco Tex and the Sex-O-Lettes	*Chelsea*	8
15	**10**	ARE YOU READY TO ROCK Wizzard	*Warner Bros.*	3
19	[11]	CRYING OVER YOU Ken Boothe	*Trojan*	3
18	**12**	HELP ME MAKE IT THROUGH THE NIGHT John Holt	*Trojan*	5
11	**13**	THE IN BETWEENIES/FATHER CHRISTMAS DO NOT TOUCH ME The Goodies	*Bradley's*	6
13	**14**	MY BOY Elvis Presley	*RCA*	10
26	**15**	MORNING SIDE OF THE MOUNTAIN Donny & Marie Osmond	*MGM*	3
12	**16**	YOU AIN'T SEEN NOTHING YET Bachman-Turner Overdrive	*Mercury*	10
20	[17]	UNDER MY THUMB Wayne Gibson	*Pye*	8
10	**18**	JUKE BOX JIVE Rubettes	*Polydor*	10
17	**19**	LUCY IN THE SKY WITH DIAMONDS Elton John	*DJM*	9
5	**20**	WOMBLING MERRY CHRISTMAS Wombles	*CBS*	6
14	**21**	YOU CAN MAKE ME DANCE, SING OR ANYTHING Faces & Rod Stewart	*Warner Bros.*	7
-	**22**	PROMISED LAND Elvis Presley	*RCA*	1
33	[23]	YOU CAN HAVE IT ALL George McCrae	*Jayboy*	3
40	**24**	BOOGIE ON REGGAE WOMAN Stevie Wonder	*Tamla Motown*	2
25	**25**	YOU'RE THE FIRST, THE LAST, MY EVERYTHING Barry White	*20th Century*	12
23	**26**	OH YES YOU'RE BEAUTIFUL Gary Glitter and The Glitter Band	*Bell*	9
-	**27**	JANUARY Pilot	*EMI*	1
28	**28**	ONLY YOU Ringo Starr	*Apple*	8
-	**29**	ROCK AND ROLL (I GAVE YOU THE BEST YEARS OF MY LIFE) Kevin Johnson ●	*UK*	1
24	**30**	CHRISTMAS SONG Gilbert O'Sullivan	*MAM*	5
32	**31**	GONNA MAKE YOU A STAR David Essex	*CBS*	14
30	**32**	SHA LA LA Al Green	*London*	9
29	**33**	IRE FEELINGS (SKANGA) Rupie Edwards	*Cactus*	9
34	**34**	JE T'AIME Moi Non Plus Jane Birkin and Serge Gainsbourg	Antic	6
-	**35**	Y VIVA ESPANA Sylvia	*Sonet*	16

In these weeks ■ Four songs with the word *Christmas* in their titles among the Top 15 - a very festive chart (04.01.75) ■ Status Quo's only week at the top of the chart out of almost 400 on the charts (18.01.75) ■ In fact the Top 3 acts that week were all enjoying the best chart week of their entire careers (18.01.75) ■ Songs by Chuck Berry, the Rolling Stones and the Beatles provided hits for Elvis Presley, Wayne Gibson and Elton John respectively (18.01.75)■

LW	TW	Title	Artist	Label	Wks
22	36	TELL HIM	Hello	Bell	10
31	37	SOUND YOUR FUNKY HORN	K.C. & The Sunshine Band	Jayboy	8
38	[38]	DING DONG	George Harrison	Apple	2
-	39	PLEASE MR. POSTMAN	Carpenters	A&M	1
35	40	CHERI BABE	Hot Chocolate	RAK	7

WEEK ENDING 25 JANUARY 1975

LW	TW	Title	Artist	Label	Wks
5	[1]	MS. GRACE	Tymes	RCA	6
4	[2]	NEVER CAN SAY GOODBYE	Gloria Gaynor	MGM	7
3	[3]	THE BUMP	Kenny	RAK	8
2	4	STREETS OF LONDON	Ralph McTell	Reprise	8
1	5	DOWN DOWN	Status Quo	Vertigo	8
12	[6]	HELP ME MAKE IT THROUGH THE NIGHT	John Holt	Trojan	6
15	7	MORNING SIDE OF THE MOUNTAIN	Donny & Marie Osmond	MGM	4
10	[8]	ARE YOU READY TO ROCK	Wizzard	Warner Bros.	4
27	9	JANUARY	Pilot	EMI	2
7	10	STARDUST	David Essex	CBS	6
11	[11]	CRYING OVER YOU	Ken Boothe	Trojan	4
6	12	I CAN HELP	Billy Swan	Monument	7
22	13	PROMISED LAND	Elvis Presley	RCA	2
-	14	GOODBYE MY LOVE	The Glitter Band	Bell	1
9	15	GET DANCING	Disco Tex and the Sex-O-Lettes	Chelsea	9
14	16	MY BOY	Elvis Presley	RCA	11
8	17	LONELY THIS CHRISTMAS	Mud	RAK	9
-	18	SOMETHING FOR THE GIRL WITH EVERYTHING	Sparks	Island	1
13	19	THE IN BETWEENIES/FATHER CHRISTMAS DO NOT TOUCH ME	The Goodies	Bradley's	7
-	20	PURELY BY COINCIDENCE	Sweet Sensation	Pye	1
-	21	SUGAR CANDY KISSES	Mac & Katie Kissoon	Polydor	1
24	22	BOOGIE ON REGGAE WOMAN	Stevie Wonder	Tamla Motown	3
29	[23]	ROCK AND ROLL (I GAVE YOU THE BEST YEARS OF MY LIFE)	Kevin Johnson	UK	2
21	24	YOU CAN MAKE ME DANCE, SING OR ANYTHING	Faces & Rod Stewart	Warner Bros.	8
39	25	PLEASE MR. POSTMAN	Carpenters	A&M	2
-	26	FOOTSEE	Wigan's Chosen Few ●	Pye	1
23	27	YOU CAN HAVE IT ALL	George McCrae	Jayboy	4
17	28	UNDER MY THUMB	Wayne Gibson	Pye	9
-	29	BLACK SUPERMAN (MUHAMMAD ALI)	Johnny Wakelin & The Kinshasa Band ●	Pye	1
-	30	ANGIE BABY	Helen Reddy ●	Capitol	1
28	31	ONLY YOU	Ringo Starr	Apple	9
18	32	JUKE BOX JIVE	Rubettes	Polydor	11
16	33	YOU AIN'T SEEN NOTHING YET	Bachman-Turner Overdrive	Mercury	11
-	34	STAR ON A TV SHOW	The Stylistics	Avco	1
-	35	NOW I'M HERE	Queen	EMI	1
-	36	SHOORAH! SHOORAH!	Betty Wright ●	RCA	1
35	37	Y VIVA ESPANA	Sylvia	Sonet	17
-	38	PLEASE TELL HIM THAT I SAID HELLO	Dana	GTO	1
19	39	LUCY IN THE SKY WITH DIAMONDS	Elton John	DJM	10
34	40	JE T'AIME Moi Non Plus	Jane Birkin and Serge Gainsbourg	Antic	7

WEEK ENDING 1 FEBRUARY 1975

LW	TW	Title	Artist	Label	Wks
9	[1]	JANUARY	Pilot	EMI	3
1	2	MS. GRACE	Tymes	RCA	7
3	[3]	THE BUMP	Kenny	RAK	9
2	4	NEVER CAN SAY GOODBYE	Gloria Gaynor	MGM	8
7	[5]	MORNING SIDE OF THE MOUNTAIN	Donny & Marie Osmond	MGM	5
5	6	DOWN DOWN	Status Quo	Vertigo	9
6	7	HELP ME MAKE IT THROUGH THE NIGHT	John Holt	Trojan	7
14	8	GOODBYE MY LOVE	The Glitter Band	Bell	2
13	[9]	PROMISED LAND	Elvis Presley	RCA	3
21	10	SUGAR CANDY KISSES	Mac & Katie Kissoon	Polydor	2
8	11	ARE YOU READY TO ROCK	Wizzard	Warner Bros.	5
22	[12]	BOOGIE ON REGGAE WOMAN	Stevie Wonder	Tamla Motown	4
4	13	STREETS OF LONDON	Ralph McTell	Reprise	9
20	14	PURELY BY COINCIDENCE	Sweet Sensation	Pye	2
25	15	PLEASE MR. POSTMAN	Carpenters	A&M	3

February 1975

□ Highest position disc reached ● Act's first ever week on chart

LW	TW	Title	Artist	Label	Wks
10	16	STARDUST	David Essex	CBS	7
11	17	CRYING OVER YOU	Ken Boothe	Trojan	5
30	18	ANGIE BABY	Helen Reddy	Capitol	2
12	19	I CAN HELP	Billy Swan	Monument	8
35	20	NOW I'M HERE	Queen	EMI	2
29	21	BLACK SUPERMAN (MUHAMMAD ALI)	Johnny Wakelin & The Kinshasa Band	Pye	2
18	22	SOMETHING FOR THE GIRL WITH EVERYTHING	Sparks	Island	2
27	23	YOU CAN HAVE IT ALL	George McCrae	Jayboy	5
34	24	STAR ON A TV SHOW	The Stylistics	Avco	2
26	25	FOOTSEE	Wigan's Chosen Few	Pye	2
23	26	ROCK AND ROLL (I GAVE YOU THE BEST YEARS OF MY LIFE)	Kevin Johnson	UK	3
36	[27]	SHOORAH! SHOORAH!	Betty Wright	RCA	2
-	28	IT MAY BE WINTER OUTSIDE	Love Unlimited	20th Century	1
15	29	GET DANCING	Disco Tex and the Sex-O-Lettes	Chelsea	10
-	30	YOUR KISS IS SWEET	Syreeta ●	Tamla Motown	1
16	31	MY BOY	Elvis Presley	RCA	12
-	32	I'M STONE IN LOVE WITH YOU	Johnny Mathis	CBS	1
32	33	JUKE BOX JIVE	The Rubettes	Polydor	12
19	34	THE IN BETWEENIES/FATHER CHRISTMAS DO NOT TOUCH ME	The Goodies	Bradley's	8
28	35	UNDER MY THUMB	Wayne Gibson	Pye	10
31	36	ONLY YOU	Ringo Starr	Apple	10
38	37	PLEASE TELL HIM THAT I SAID HELLO	Dana	GTO	2
33	38	YOU AIN'T SEEN NOTHING YET	Bachman-Turner Overdrive	Mercury	12
-	39	MY EYES ADORED YOU	Frankie Valli	Private Stock	1
-	40	GOOD LOVE CAN NEVER DIE	Alvin Stardust	Magnet	1

WEEK ENDING 8 FEBRUARY 1975

LW	TW	Title	Artist	Label	Wks
1	[1]	JANUARY	Pilot	EMI	4
8	[2]	GOODBYE MY LOVE	The Glitter Band	Bell	3
10	[3]	SUGAR CANDY KISSES	Mac & Katie Kissoon	Polydor	3
2	4	MS. GRACE	Tymes	RCA	8
4	5	NEVER CAN SAY GOODBYE	Gloria Gaynor	MGM	9
5	6	MORNING SIDE OF THE MOUNTAIN	Donny & Marie Osmond	MGM	6
3	7	THE BUMP	Kenny	RAK	10
15	8	PLEASE MR. POSTMAN	Carpenters	A&M	4
7	9	HELP ME MAKE IT THROUGH THE NIGHT	John Holt	Trojan	8
9	10	PROMISED LAND	Elvis Presley	RCA	4
14	[11]	PURELY BY COINCIDENCE	Sweet Sensation	Pye	3
20	12	NOW I'M HERE	Queen	EMI	3
18	13	ANGIE BABY	Helen Reddy	Capitol	3
21	14	BLACK SUPERMAN (MUHAMMAD ALI)	Johnny Wakelin & The Kinshasa Band	Pye	3
12	15	BOOGIE ON REGGAE WOMAN	Stevie Wonder	Tamla Motown	5
25	16	FOOTSEE	Wigan's Chosen Few	Pye	3
22	[17]	SOMETHING FOR THE GIRL WITH EVERYTHING	Sparks	Island	3
24	18	STAR ON A TV SHOW	The Stylistics	Avco	3
13	19	STREETS OF LONDON	Ralph McTell	Reprise	10
11	20	ARE YOU READY TO ROCK	Wizzard	Warner Bros.	6
16	21	STARDUST	David Essex	CBS	8
40	22	GOOD LOVE CAN NEVER DIE	Alvin Stardust	Magnet	2
17	23	CRYING OVER YOU	Ken Boothe	Trojan	6
28	24	IT MAY BE WINTER OUTSIDE	Love Unlimited	20th Century	2
30	25	YOUR KISS IS SWEET	Syreeta	Tamla Motown	2
6	26	DOWN DOWN	Status Quo	Vertigo	10
27	[27]	SHOORAH! SHOORAH!	Betty Wright	RCA	3
32	28	I'M STONE IN LOVE WITH YOU	Johnny Mathis	CBS	2
37	29	PLEASE TELL HIM THAT I SAID HELLO	Dana	GTO	3
-	30	ROLL ON DOWN THE HIGHWAY	Bachman-Turner Overdrive	Mercury	1
39	31	MY EYES ADORED YOU	Frankie Valli	Private Stock	2

■*January* by Pilot reaches number one with brilliant timing in the week ending 1 February! (01.02.75) ■ It was also the fourth number one in as many weeks - a rate of change at the top very rarely matched (01.02.75) ■ Three brother and sister pairings in the Top 10 - Mac and Katie Kissoon, Donny and Marie Osmond and the Carpenters (08.02.75)■

February 1975

☐ Highest position disc reached ● Act's first ever week on chart

LW	TW	Title / Artist	Label	Wks
26	32	ROCK AND ROLL (I GAVE YOU THE BEST YEARS OF MY LIFE) Kevin Johnson	UK	4
-	33	MAKE ME SMILE (COME UP AND SEE ME) Steve Harley & Cockney Rebel	EMI	1
-	34	MY LAST NIGHT WITH YOU Arrows	RAK	1
19	35	I CAN HELP Billy Swan	Monument	9
-	36	YOUR MAMA WON'T LIKE ME Suzi Quatro	RAK	1
-	[37]	WE LOVE EACH OTHER Charlie Rich	Epic	1
-	38	SHAME SHAME SHAME Shirley & Company ●	All Platinum	1
29	39	GET DANCING Disco Tex and the Sex-O-Lettes	Chelsea	11
-	[40]	SIXTY MINUTE MAN Trammps	Buddah	1

WEEK ENDING 15 FEBRUARY 1975

LW	TW	Title / Artist	Label	Wks
1	[1]	JANUARY Pilot	EMI	5
8	[2]	PLEASE MR. POSTMAN Carpenters	A&M	5
3	[3]	SUGAR CANDY KISSES Mac & Katie Kissoon	Polydor	4
2	4	GOODBYE MY LOVE The Glitter Band	Bell	4
13	[5]	ANGIE BABY Helen Reddy	Capitol	4
7	6	THE BUMP Kenny	RAK	11
14	[7]	BLACK SUPERMAN (MUHAMMAD ALI) Johnny Wakelin & The Kinshasa Band	Pye	4
6	8	MORNING SIDE OF THE MOUNTAIN Donny & Marie Osmond	MGM	7
33	9	MAKE ME SMILE (COME UP AND SEE ME) Steve Harley & Cockney Rebel	EMI	2
16	10	FOOTSEE Wigan's Chosen Few	Pye	4
12	[11]	NOW I'M HERE Queen	EMI	4
18	[12]	STAR ON A TV SHOW The Stylistics	Avco	4
10	13	PROMISED LAND Elvis Presley	RCA	5
25	14	YOUR KISS IS SWEET Syreeta	Tamla Motown	3
38	15	SHAME SHAME SHAME Shirley & Company	All Platinum	2
9	16	HELP ME MAKE IT THROUGH THE NIGHT John Holt	Trojan	9
22	17	GOOD LOVE CAN NEVER DIE Alvin Stardust	Magnet	3
11	18	PURELY BY COINCIDENCE Sweet Sensation	Pye	4
15	19	BOOGIE ON REGGAE WOMAN Stevie Wonder	Tamla Motown	6
24	20	IT MAY BE WINTER OUTSIDE Love Unlimited	20th Century	3
31	21	MY EYES ADORED YOU Frankie Valli	Private Stock	3
30	[22]	ROLL ON DOWN THE HIGHWAY Bachman-Turner Overdrive	Mercury	2
17	23	SOMETHING FOR THE GIRL WITH EVERYTHING Sparks	Island	4
28	24	I'M STONE IN LOVE WITH YOU Johnny Mathis	CBS	3
29	25	PLEASE TELL HIM THAT I SAID HELLO Dana	GTO	4
-	26	THE SECRETS THAT YOU KEEP Mud	RAK	1
5	27	NEVER CAN SAY GOODBYE Gloria Gaynor	MGM	10
4	28	MS. GRACE Tymes	RCA	9
27	29	SHOORAH! SHOORAH! Betty Wright	RCA	4
34	30	MY LAST NIGHT WITH YOU Arrows	RAK	2
36	[31]	YOUR MAMA WON'T LIKE ME Suzi Quatro	RAK	2
-	[32]	LEGO SKANGA Rupie Edwards	Cactus	1
19	33	STREETS OF LONDON Ralph McTell	Reprise	11
-	34	LOVE GAMES Drifters	Bell	1
-	35	SOUTH AFRICAN MAN Hamilton Bohannon ●	Brunswick	1
-	36	NO.9 DREAM John Lennon	Apple	1
20	37	ARE YOU READY TO ROCK Wizzard	Warner Bros.	7
-	38	HOW DOES IT FEEL Slade	Polydor	1
32	39	ROCK AND ROLL (I GAVE YOU THE BEST YEARS OF MY LIFE) Kevin Johnson	UK	5
21	40	STARDUST David Essex	CBS	9

WEEK ENDING 22 FEBRUARY 1975

LW	TW	Title / Artist	Label	Wks
9	[1]	MAKE ME SMILE (COME UP AND SEE ME) Steve Harley & Cockney Rebel	EMI	3
1	2	JANUARY Pilot	EMI	6
2	3	PLEASE MR. POSTMAN Carpenters	A&M	6
3	4	SUGAR CANDY KISSES Mac & Katie Kissoon	Polydor	5
26	5	THE SECRETS THAT YOU KEEP Mud	RAK	2
4	6	GOODBYE MY LOVE The Glitter Band	Bell	5
15	7	SHAME SHAME SHAME Shirley & Company	All Platinum	3
5	8	ANGIE BABY Helen Reddy	Capitol	5
10	[9]	FOOTSEE Wigan's Chosen Few	Pye	5
7	10	BLACK SUPERMAN (MUHAMMAD ALI) Johnny Wakelin & The Kinshasa Band	Pye	5
17	[11]	GOOD LOVE CAN NEVER DIE Alvin Stardust	Magnet	4
21	12	MY EYES ADORED YOU Frankie Valli	Private Stock	4
14	13	YOUR KISS IS SWEET Syreeta	Tamla Motown	4
12	14	STAR ON A TV SHOW The Stylistics	Avco	5
20	15	IT MAY BE WINTER OUTSIDE Love Unlimited	20th Century	4
11	16	NOW I'M HERE Queen	EMI	5
24	17	I'M STONE IN LOVE WITH YOU Johnny Mathis	CBS	4
25	18	PLEASE TELL HIM THAT I SAID HELLO Dana	GTO	5
-	19	ONLY YOU CAN Fox ●	GTO	1
13	20	PROMISED LAND Elvis Presley	RCA	6
6	21	THE BUMP Kenny	RAK	12
18	22	PURELY BY COINCIDENCE Sweet Sensation	Pye	5
-	23	IF Telly Savalas ●	MCA	1
38	24	HOW DOES IT FEEL Slade	Polydor	2
8	25	MORNING SIDE OF THE MOUNTAIN Donny & Marie Osmond	MGM	8
30	26	MY LAST NIGHT WITH YOU Arrows	RAK	3
16	27	HELP ME MAKE IT THROUGH THE NIGHT John Holt	Trojan	10
23	28	SOMETHING FOR THE GIRL WITH EVERYTHING Sparks	Island	5
35	29	SOUTH AFRICAN MAN Hamilton Bohannon	Brunswick	2
22	30	ROLL ON DOWN THE HIGHWAY Bachman-Turner Overdrive	Mercury	3
29	31	SHOORAH! SHOORAH! Betty Wright	RCA	5
-	32	PICK UP THE PIECES Average White Band ●	Atlantic	1
27	33	NEVER CAN SAY GOODBYE Gloria Gaynor	MGM	11
34	34	LOVE GAMES Drifters	Bell	2
36	35	NO.9 DREAM John Lennon	Apple	2
-	36	DREAMER Supertramp ●	A&M	1
19	37	BOOGIE ON REGGAE WOMAN Stevie Wonder	Tamla Motown	7
-	38	MY HEART'S SYMPHONY Gary Lewis & The Playboys ●	United Artists	1
28	39	MS. GRACE Tymes	RCA	10
31	40	YOUR MAMA WON'T LIKE ME Suzi Quatro	RAK	3

WEEK ENDING 1 MARCH 1975

LW	TW	Title / Artist	Label	Wks
1	[1]	MAKE ME SMILE (COME UP AND SEE ME) Steve Harley & Cockney Rebel	EMI	4
23	2	IF Telly Savalas	MCA	2
3	3	PLEASE MR. POSTMAN Carpenters	A&M	7
5	4	THE SECRETS THAT YOU KEEP Mud	RAK	3
19	5	ONLY YOU CAN Fox	GTO	2
7	[6]	SHAME SHAME SHAME Shirley & Company	All Platinum	4
12	7	MY EYES ADORED YOU Frankie Valli	Private Stock	5
4	8	SUGAR CANDY KISSES Mac & Katie Kissoon	Polydor	6
2	9	JANUARY Pilot	EMI	7
9	10	FOOTSEE Wigan's Chosen Few	Pye	6
15	[11]	IT MAY BE WINTER OUTSIDE Love Unlimited	20th Century	5
13	[12]	YOUR KISS IS SWEET Syreeta	Tamla Motown	5
11	13	GOOD LOVE CAN NEVER DIE Alvin Stardust	Magnet	5
8	14	ANGIE BABY Helen Reddy	Capitol	6
10	15	BLACK SUPERMAN (MUHAMMAD ALI) Johnny Wakelin & The Kinshasa Band	Pye	6
6	16	GOODBYE MY LOVE The Glitter Band	Bell	6
18	17	PLEASE TELL HIM THAT I SAID HELLO Dana	GTO	6
14	18	STAR ON A TV SHOW The Stylistics	Avco	6
17	19	I'M STONE IN LOVE WITH YOU Johnny Mathis	CBS	5
16	20	NOW I'M HERE Queen	EMI	6
24	21	HOW DOES IT FEEL Slade	Polydor	3
32	22	PICK UP THE PIECES Average White Band	Atlantic	2
29	23	SOUTH AFRICAN MAN Hamilton Bohannon	Brunswick	3
36	24	DREAMER Supertramp	A&M	2
26	[25]	MY LAST NIGHT WITH YOU Arrows	RAK	4
-	26	MANDY Barry Manilow ●	Arista	1

In these weeks ■ The former number one achieved one of the most spectacular dives from the Top 10 when *Ms. Grace* fell from 4 to 28 (15.02.75) ■ Stevie Wonder and his ex-wife Syreeta enjoy one week of Top 20 togetherness (15.02.75) ■ The son of comic actor Jerry Lewis hits the British Top 40 for the first time with *My Heart's Symphony* (22.02.75) ■ Johnny Mathis returns to the Top 20 for the first time in fourteen years (22.02.75) ■

LW	TW	Title / Artist	Label	Wks
35	27	NO.9 DREAM John Lennon	Apple	3
21	28	THE BUMP Kenny	RAK	13
-	29	YOUNG AMERICANS David Bowie	RCA	1
-	30	SWEET MUSIC Showaddywaddy	Bell	1
31	31	SHOORAH! SHOORAH! Betty Wright	RCA	6
30	32	ROLL ON DOWN THE HIGHWAY Bachman-Turner Overdrive	Mercury	4
34	[33]	LOVE GAMES Drifters	Bell	3
20	34	PROMISED LAND Elvis Presley	RCA	7
27	35	HELP ME MAKE IT THROUGH THE NIGHT John Holt	Trojan	11
38	[36]	MY HEART'S SYMPHONY Gary Lewis & The Playboys	United Artists	2
25	37	MORNING SIDE OF THE MOUNTAIN Donny & Marie Osmond	MGM	9
-	[38]	I'M ON MY WAY Dean Parrish ●	UK	1
40	39	YOUR MAMA WON'T LIKE ME Suzi Quatro	RAK	4
22	40	PURELY BY COINCIDENCE Sweet Sensation	Pye	6

WEEK ENDING 8 MARCH 1975

LW	TW	Title / Artist	Label	Wks
2	[1]	IF Telly Savalas	MCA	3
1	2	MAKE ME SMILE (COME UP AND SEE ME) Steve Harley & Cockney Rebel	EMI	4
4	[3]	THE SECRETS THAT YOU KEEP Mud	RAK	4
5	4	ONLY YOU CAN Fox	GTO	3
7	[5]	MY EYES ADORED YOU Frankie Valli	Private Stock	6
3	6	PLEASE MR. POSTMAN Carpenters	A&M	8
6	7	SHAME SHAME SHAME Shirley & Company	All Platinum	5
-	8	BYE BYE BABY Bay City Rollers	Bell	1
22	9	PICK UP THE PIECES Average White Band	Atlantic	3
10	10	FOOTSEE Wigan's Chosen Few	Pye	7
19	11	I'M STONE IN LOVE WITH YOU Johnny Mathis	CBS	6
17	12	PLEASE TELL HIM THAT I SAID HELLO Dana	GTO	7
24	[13]	DREAMER Supertramp	A&M	3
11	14	IT MAY BE WINTER OUTSIDE Love Unlimited	20th Century	6
21	[15]	HOW DOES IT FEEL Slade	Polydor	4
13	16	GOOD LOVE CAN NEVER DIE Alvin Stardust	Magnet	6
12	17	YOUR KISS IS SWEET Syreeta	Tamla Motown	6
29	[18]	YOUNG AMERICANS David Bowie	RCA	2
30	19	SWEET MUSIC Showaddywaddy	Bell	2
14	20	ANGIE BABY Helen Reddy	Capitol	7
26	21	MANDY Barry Manilow	Arista	2
23	[22]	SOUTH AFRICAN MAN Hamilton Bohannon	Brunswick	4
27	[23]	NO.9 DREAM John Lennon	Apple	4
9	24	JANUARY Pilot	EMI	8
8	25	SUGAR CANDY KISSES Mac & Katie Kissoon	Polydor	7
-	26	THERE'S A WHOLE LOT OF LOVING Guys And Dolls ●	Magnet	1
25	27	MY LAST NIGHT WITH YOU Arrows	RAK	5
15	28	BLACK SUPERMAN (MUHAMMAD ALI) Johnny Wakelin & The Kinshasa Band	Pye	7
-	29	PHILADELPHIA FREEDOM Elton John Band	DJM	1
-	30	WHAT AM I GONNA DO WITH YOU Barry White	20th Century	1
-	31	I CAN DO IT Rubettes	State	1
16	32	GOODBYE MY LOVE The Glitter Band	Bell	7
-	33	HAVING A PARTY The Osmonds	MGM	1
18	34	STAR ON A TV SHOW The Stylistics	Avco	7
-	35	GIRLS Moments And Whatnauts ●	All Platinum	1
-	36	FANCY PANTS Kenny	RAK	1
33	37	LOVE GAMES Drifters	Bell	4
20	38	NOW I'M HERE Queen	EMI	7
36	39	MY HEART'S SYMPHONY Gary Lewis & The Playboys	United Artists	3
28	40	THE BUMP Kenny	RAK	14

WEEK ENDING 15 MARCH 1975

LW	TW	Title / Artist	Label	Wks
1	[1]	IF Telly Savalas	MCA	4
8	2	BYE BYE BABY Bay City Rollers	Bell	2
2	3	MAKE ME SMILE (COME UP AND SEE ME) Steve Harley & Cockney Rebel	EMI	5
4	4	ONLY YOU CAN Fox	GTO	4

March 1975

□ Highest position disc reached ● Act's first ever week on chart

LW	TW	Title / Artist	Label	Wks
3	5	THE SECRETS THAT YOU KEEP Mud	RAK	5
5	6	MY EYES ADORED YOU Frankie Valli	Private Stock	7
9	7	PICK UP THE PIECES Average White Band	Atlantic	4
12	[8]	PLEASE TELL HIM THAT I SAID HELLO Dana	GTO	8
26	9	THERE'S A WHOLE LOT OF LOVING Guys And Dolls	Magnet	2
11	[10]	I'M STONE IN LOVE WITH YOU Johnny Mathis	CBS	7
21	[11]	MANDY Barry Manilow	Arista	3
7	12	SHAME SHAME SHAME Shirley & Company	All Platinum	6
30	13	WHAT AM I GONNA DO WITH YOU Barry White	20th Century	2
6	14	PLEASE MR. POSTMAN Carpenters	A&M	9
13	15	DREAMER Supertramp	A&M	4
15	16	HOW DOES IT FEEL Slade	Polydor	5
35	17	GIRLS Moments And Whatnauts	All Platinum	2
19	18	SWEET MUSIC Showaddywaddy	Bell	3
36	19	FANCY PANTS Kenny	RAK	2
31	20	I CAN DO IT Rubettes	State	2
18	21	YOUNG AMERICANS David Bowie	RCA	3
22	[22]	SOUTH AFRICAN MAN Hamilton Bohannon	Brunswick	5
14	23	IT MAY BE WINTER OUTSIDE Love Unlimited	20th Century	7
29	24	PHILADELPHIA FREEDOM Elton John Band	DJM	2
16	25	GOOD LOVE CAN NEVER DIE Alvin Stardust	Magnet	7
17	26	YOUR KISS IS SWEET Syreeta	Tamla Motown	7
23	27	NO.9 DREAM John Lennon	Apple	5
10	28	FOOTSEE Wigan's Chosen Few	Pye	8
-	29	PLAY ME LIKE YOU PLAY YOUR GUITAR Duane Eddy	GTO	1
33	30	HAVING A PARTY The Osmonds	MGM	2
-	31	REACH OUT I'LL BE THERE Gloria Gaynor	MGM	1
-	32	LET ME BE THE ONE Shadows	EMI	1
25	33	SUGAR CANDY KISSES Mac & Katie Kissoon	Polydor	8
27	34	MY LAST NIGHT WITH YOU Arrows	RAK	6
20	35	ANGIE BABY Helen Reddy	Capitol	8
24	36	JANUARY Pilot	EMI	9
-	37	THE FUNKY GIBBON/SICK MAN BLUES Goodies	Bradley's	1
28	38	BLACK SUPERMAN (MUHAMMAD ALI) Johnny Wakelin & The Kinshasa Band	Pye	8
39	39	MY HEART'S SYMPHONY Gary Lewis & The Playboys	United Artists	4
-	40	LEGO SKANGA Rupie Edwards	Cactus	2

WEEK ENDING 22 MARCH 1975

LW	TW	Title / Artist	Label	Wks
2	[1]	BYE BYE BABY Bay City Rollers	Bell	3
1	2	IF Telly Savalas	MCA	5
4	[3]	ONLY YOU CAN Fox	GTO	5
9	4	THERE'S A WHOLE LOT OF LOVING Guys And Dolls	Magnet	3
13	[5]	WHAT AM I GONNA DO WITH YOU Barry White	20th Century	3
7	[6]	PICK UP THE PIECES Average White Band	Atlantic	5
5	7	THE SECRETS THAT YOU KEEP Mud	RAK	6
19	8	FANCY PANTS Kenny	RAK	3
17	9	GIRLS Moments And Whatnauts	All Platinum	3
20	10	I CAN DO IT Rubettes	State	3
11	[11]	MANDY Barry Manilow	Arista	4
6	12	MY EYES ADORED YOU Frankie Valli	Private Stock	8
3	13	MAKE ME SMILE (COME UP AND SEE ME) Steve Harley & Cockney Rebel	EMI	6
18	[14]	SWEET MUSIC Showaddywaddy	Bell	4
15	15	DREAMER Supertramp	A&M	5
8	16	PLEASE TELL HIM THAT I SAID HELLO Dana	GTO	9
29	17	PLAY ME LIKE YOU PLAY YOUR GUITAR Duane Eddy	GTO	2
10	18	I'M STONE IN LOVE WITH YOU Johnny Mathis	CBS	8
21	19	YOUNG AMERICANS David Bowie	RCA	4
24	20	PHILADELPHIA FREEDOM Elton John Band	DJM	3
-	21	FOX ON THE RUN Sweet	RCA	1
31	22	REACH OUT I'LL BE THERE Gloria Gaynor	MGM	2
37	23	THE FUNKY GIBBON/SICK MAN BLUES Goodies	Bradley's	2
16	24	HOW DOES IT FEEL Slade	Polydor	6
12	25	SHAME SHAME SHAME Shirley & Company	All Platinum	7
-	26	SWING YOUR DADDY Jim Gilstrap ●	Chelsea	1
14	27	PLEASE MR. POSTMAN Carpenters	A&M	10

■The shortest song title ever to hit number one, *If* by Telly Savalas, begins a two-week stay at the top (08.03.75) ■ Duane Eddy returns to the Top 40, after an absence of almost twelve years (15.03.75) ■ Rollermania gets well under way as their *Bye Bye Baby* hits number one in the same week that the man who sang lead vocals on the original version of that song, Frankie Valli, slips out of the Top 10 (22.03.75)■

March 1975

□ Highest position disc reached ● Act's first ever week on chart

LW	TW	Title / Artist	Label	Wks
30	[28]	HAVING A PARTY The Osmonds	MGM	3
-	29	SKIING IN THE SNOW Wigans Ovation ●	Spark	1
27	30	NO.9 DREAM John Lennon	Apple	6
22	31	SOUTH AFRICAN MAN Hamilton Bohannon	Brunswick	6
32	32	LET ME BE THE ONE Shadows	EMI	2
28	33	FOOTSEE Wigan's Chosen Few	Pye	9
-	34	THE UGLY DUCKLING Mike Reid ●	Pye	1
-	35	L.O.V.E. Al Green	London	1
23	36	IT MAYBE WINTER OUTSIDE Love Unlimited	20th Century	8
-	37	LADY MARMALADE Labelle ●	Epic	1
-	38	LOVE ME LOVE MY DOG Peter Shelley	Magnet	1
-	39	WHAT IN THE WORLDS COME OVER YOU Tam White ●	RAK	1
39	40	MY HEART'S SYMPHONY Gary Lewis & The Playboys	United Artists	5

LW	TW	*WEEK ENDING* **29 MARCH 1975**		Wks
1	[1]	BYE BYE BABY Bay City Rollers	Bell	4
4	[2]	THERE'S A WHOLE LOT OF LOVING Guys And Dolls	Magnet	4
9	[3]	GIRLS Moments And Whatnauts	All Platinum	4
2	4	IF Telly Savalas	MCA	6
5	[5]	WHAT AM I GONNA DO WITH YOU Barry White	20th Century	4
8	6	FANCY PANTS Kenny	RAK	4
3	7	ONLY YOU CAN Fox	GTO	6
23	8	THE FUNKY GIBBON/SICK MAN BLUES Goodies	Bradley's	3
10	9	I CAN DO IT Rubettes	State	4
21	10	FOX ON THE RUN Sweet	RCA	2
17	11	PLAY ME LIKE YOU PLAY YOUR GUITAR Duane Eddy	GTO	3
6	12	PICK UP THE PIECES Average White Band	Atlantic	6
11	13	MANDY Barry Manilow	Arista	5
26	14	SWING YOUR DADDY Jim Gilstrap	Chelsea	2
20	15	PHILADELPHIA FREEDOM Elton John Band	DJM	4
14	16	SWEET MUSIC Showaddywaddy	Bell	5
15	17	DREAMER Supertramp	A&M	6
16	18	PLEASE TELL HIM THAT I SAID HELLO Dana	GTO	10
22	19	REACH OUT I'LL BE THERE Gloria Gaynor	MGM	3
18	20	I'M STONE IN LOVE WITH YOU Johnny Mathis	CBS	9
12	21	MY EYES ADORED YOU Frankie Valli	Private Stock	9
34	22	THE UGLY DUCKLING Mike Reid	Pye	2
32	23	LET ME BE THE ONE Shadows	EMI	3
7	24	THE SECRETS THAT YOU KEEP Mud	RAK	7
29	25	SKIING IN THE SNOW Wigans Ovation	Spark	2
38	26	LOVE ME LOVE MY DOG Peter Shelley	Magnet	2
13	27	MAKE ME SMILE (COME UP AND SEE ME) Steve Harley & Cockney Rebel	EMI	7
37	28	LADY MARMALADE Labelle	Epic	2
24	29	HOW DOES IT FEEL Slade	Polydor	7
28	30	HAVING A PARTY The Osmonds	MGM	4
19	31	YOUNG AMERICANS David Bowie	RCA	5
35	32	L.O.V.E. Al Green	London	2
-	33	GOOD LOVIN' GONE BAD Bad Company	Island	1
31	34	SOUTH AFRICAN MAN Hamilton Bohannon	Brunswick	7
25	35	SHAME SHAME SHAME Shirley & Company	All Platinum	8
39	[36]	WHAT IN THE WORLDS COME OVER YOU Tam White	RAK	2
-	37	THE QUEEN OF 1964 Neil Sedaka	Polydor	1
-	[38]	SING A HAPPY SONG George McCrae	Jayboy	1
27	39	PLEASE MR. POSTMAN Carpenters	A&M	11
-	[40]	MY MAN AND ME Lynsey De Paul	Jet	1

LW	TW	*WEEK ENDING* **5 APRIL 1975**		Wks
1	[1]	BYE BYE BABY Bay City Rollers	Bell	5
2	[2]	THERE'S A WHOLE LOT OF LOVING Guys And Dolls	Magnet	5
3	[3]	GIRLS Moments And Whatnauts	All Platinum	5
6	[4]	FANCY PANTS Kenny	RAK	5
10	5	FOX ON THE RUN Sweet	RCA	3
5	6	WHAT AM I GONNA DO WITH YOU Barry White	20th Century	5
9	[7]	I CAN DO IT Rubettes	State	5
14	8	SWING YOUR DADDY Jim Gilstrap	Chelsea	3
11	[9]	PLAY ME LIKE YOU PLAY YOUR GUITAR Duane Eddy	GTO	4
8	10	THE FUNKY GIBBON/SICK MAN BLUES Goodies	Bradley's	4
26	11	LOVE ME LOVE MY DOG Peter Shelley	Magnet	3
23	[12]	LET ME BE THE ONE Shadows	EMI	4
15	13	PHILADELPHIA FREEDOM Elton John Band	DJM	5
19	[14]	REACH OUT I'LL BE THERE Gloria Gaynor	MGM	4
7	15	ONLY YOU CAN Fox	GTO	7
22	16	THE UGLY DUCKLING Mike Reid	Pye	3
4	17	IF Telly Savalas	MCA	7
12	18	PICK UP THE PIECES Average White Band	Atlantic	7
16	19	SWEET MUSIC Showaddywaddy	Bell	6
13	20	MANDY Barry Manilow	Arista	6
25	21	SKIING IN THE SNOW Wigans Ovation	Spark	3
17	22	DREAMER Supertramp	A&M	7
28	23	LADY MARMALADE Labelle	Epic	3
18	24	PLEASE TELL HIM THAT I SAID HELLO Dana	GTO	11
21	25	MY EYES ADORED YOU Frankie Valli	Private Stock	10
32	26	L.O.V.E. Al Green	London	3
20	27	I'M STONE IN LOVE WITH YOU Johnny Mathis	CBS	10
31	28	YOUNG AMERICANS David Bowie	RCA	6
27	29	MAKE ME SMILE (COME UP AND SEE ME) Steve Harley & Cockney Rebel	EMI	8
30	30	HAVING A PARTY The Osmonds	MGM	5
-	31	HONEY Bobby Goldsboro	United Artists	1
24	32	THE SECRETS THAT YOU KEEP Mud	RAK	8
-	33	GET DOWN TONIGHT K.C. And The Sunshine Band	Jayboy	1
33	34	GOOD LOVIN' GONE BAD Bad Company	Island	2
37	[35]	THE QUEEN OF 1964 Neil Sedaka	Polydor	2
-	36	HOLD ON TO LOVE Peter Skellern	Decca	1
-	37	IF Yin And Yan ●	EMI	1
-	38	EXPRESS B.T. Express ●	Pye	1
-	39	A LITTLE LOVE AND UNDERSTANDING Gilbert Becaud ●	Decca	1
36	40	WHAT IN THE WORLDS COME OVER YOU Tam White	RAK	3

LW	TW	*WEEK ENDING* **12 APRIL 1975**		Wks
1	[1]	BYE BYE BABY Bay City Rollers	Bell	6
5	[2]	FOX ON THE RUN Sweet	RCA	4
2	3	THERE'S A WHOLE LOT OF LOVING Guys And Dolls	Magnet	6
10	[4]	THE FUNKY GIBBON/SICK MAN BLUES Goodies	Bradley's	5
4	5	FANCY PANTS Kenny	RAK	6
3	6	GIRLS Moments And Whatnauts	All Platinum	6
8	7	SWING YOUR DADDY Jim Gilstrap	Chelsea	4
11	8	LOVE ME LOVE MY DOG Peter Shelley	Magnet	4
7	9	I CAN DO IT Rubettes	State	6
9	10	PLAY ME LIKE YOU PLAY YOUR GUITAR Duane Eddy	GTO	5
16	11	THE UGLY DUCKLING Mike Reid	Pye	4
13	[12]	PHILADELPHIA FREEDOM Elton John Band	DJM	6
12	13	LET ME BE THE ONE Shadows	EMI	5
14	[14]	REACH OUT I'LL BE THERE Gloria Gaynor	MGM	5
6	15	WHAT AM I GONNA DO WITH YOU Barry White	20th Century	6
21	16	SKIING IN THE SNOW Wigans Ovation	Spark	4
23	[17]	LADY MARMALADE Labelle	Epic	4
17	18	IF Telly Savalas	MCA	8
31	19	HONEY Bobby Goldsboro	United Artists	2
39	20	A LITTLE LOVE AND UNDERSTANDING Gilbert Becaud	Decca	2
36	21	HOLD ON TO LOVE Peter Skellern	Decca	2
15	22	ONLY YOU CAN Fox	GTO	8
-	23	LIFE IS A MINESTRONE 10CC	Mercury	1
26	[24]	L.O.V.E. Al Green	London	4
37	[25]	IF Yin And Yan	EMI	2
-	26	DING-A-DONG Teach-In ●	Polydor	1
19	27	SWEET MUSIC Showaddywaddy	Bell	7
33	28	GET DOWN TONIGHT K.C. And The Sunshine Band	Jayboy	2
-	29	THE TEARS I CRIED Glitter Band	Bell	1
20	30	MANDY Barry Manilow	Arista	7
34	[31]	GOOD LOVIN' GONE BAD Bad Company	Island	3
-	32	SORRY DOESN'T ALWAYS MAKE IT RIGHT Diana Ross	Tamla Motown	1
18	33	PICK UP THE PIECES Average White Band	Atlantic	8
-	34	HURT SO GOOD Susan Cadogan ●	Magnet	1
38	35	EXPRESS B.T. Express	Pye	2

In these weeks ■ The man who went on to become a star of BBC TV's 'Eastenders', Mike Reid, brings cockney comedy to the charts (22.03.75) ■ The Top Five acts are all British (12.04.75) ■ The Shadows' Eurovision entry, *Let Me Be The One* peaks at number 12, four weeks before the contest winner *Ding-A-Dong* by Holland's Teach-In, stops one place lower at number 13 (05.04.75)■

LW	TW	Title	Artist	Label	Wks
35	36	THE QUEEN OF 1964	Neil Sedaka	*Polydor*	3
-	37	THE WAY WE WERE	Gladys Knight And The Pips	*Buddah*	1
24	38	PLEASE TELL HIM THAT I SAID HELLO	Dana	*GTO*	12
25	39	MY EYES ADORED YOU	Frankie Valli	*Private Stock*	11
-	40	TAKE GOOD CARE OF YOURSELF	Three Degrees	*Philadelphia*	1

WEEK ENDING 19 APRIL 1975

LW	TW	Title	Artist	Label	Wks
1	1	BYE BYE BABY	Bay City Rollers	*Bell*	7
2	2	FOX ON THE RUN	Sweet	*RCA*	5
8	3	LOVE ME LOVE MY DOG	Peter Shelley	*Magnet*	5
7	4	SWING YOUR DADDY	Jim Gilstrap	*Chelsea*	5
4	5	THE FUNKY GIBBON/SICK MAN BLUES	Goodies	*Bradley's*	6
3	6	THERE'S A WHOLE LOT OF LOVING	Guys And Dolls	*Magnet*	7
6	7	GIRLS	Moments And Whatnauts	*All Platinum*	7
5	8	FANCY PANTS	Kenny	*RAK*	7
19	9	HONEY	Bobby Goldsboro	*United Artists*	3
11	10	THE UGLY DUCKLING	Mike Reid	*Pye*	5
10	11	PLAY ME LIKE YOU PLAY YOUR GUITAR	Duane Eddy	*GTO*	6
9	12	I CAN DO IT	Rubettes	*State*	7
16	13	SKIING IN THE SNOW	Wigans Ovation	*Spark*	5
23	14	LIFE IS A MINESTRONE	10CC	*Mercury*	2
13	15	LET ME BE THE ONE	Shadows	*EMI*	6
29	16	THE TEARS I CRIED	Glitter Band	*Bell*	2
12	17	PHILADELPHIA FREEDOM	Elton John Band	*DJM*	7
26	18	DING-A-DONG	Teach-In	*Polydor*	2
15	19	WHAT AM I GONNA DO WITH YOU	Barry White	*20th Century*	7
14	20	REACH OUT I'LL BE THERE	Gloria Gaynor	*MGM*	6
20	21	A LITTLE LOVE AND UNDERSTANDING	Gilbert Becaud	*Decca*	3
40	22	TAKE GOOD CARE OF YOURSELF	Three Degrees	*Philadelphia*	2
-	23	LOVING YOU	Minnie Riperton ●	*Epic*	1
21	24	HOLD ON TO LOVE	Peter Skellern	*Decca*	3
34	25	HURT SO GOOD	Susan Cadogan	*Magnet*	2
28	26	GET DOWN TONIGHT	K.C. And The Sunshine Band	*Jayboy*	3
17	27	LADY MARMALADE	Labelle	*Epic*	5
18	28	IF	Telly Savalas	*MCA*	9
24	29	L.O.V.E.	Al Green	*London*	5
32	30	SORRY DOESN'T ALWAYS MAKE IT RIGHT	Diana Ross	*Tamla Motown*	2
-	31	WE'LL FIND OUR DAY	Stephanie de Sykes	*Bradley's*	1
22	32	ONLY YOU CAN	Fox	*GTO*	9
-	33	HOW GLAD I AM	Kiki Dee Band	*Rocket*	1
35	34	EXPRESS	B.T. Express	*Pye*	3
31	35	GOOD LOVIN' GONE BAD	Bad Company	*Island*	4
-	36	NIGHT	Frankie Valli And The Four Seasons	*Mowest*	1
37	37	THE WAY WE WERE	Gladys Knight And The Pips	*Buddah*	2
25	38	IF	Yin And Yan	*EMI*	3
-	39	WHERE IS THE LOVE	Betty Wright	*RCA*	1
-	40	ONLY YESTERDAY	Carpenters	*A&M*	1

WEEK ENDING 26 APRIL 1975

LW	TW	Title	Artist	Label	Wks
1	1	BYE BYE BABY	Bay City Rollers	*Bell*	8
9	2	HONEY	Bobby Goldsboro	*United Artists*	4
2	3	FOX ON THE RUN	Sweet	*RCA*	6
3	4	LOVE ME LOVE MY DOG	Peter Shelley	*Magnet*	6
4	5	SWING YOUR DADDY	Jim Gilstrap	*Chelsea*	6
-	6	OH BOY	Mud	*RAK*	1
23	7	LOVING YOU	Minnie Riperton	*Epic*	2
5	8	THE FUNKY GIBBON/SICK MAN BLUES	Goodies	*Bradley's*	7
14	9	LIFE IS A MINESTRONE	10CC	*Mercury*	3
25	10	HURT SO GOOD	Susan Cadogan	*Magnet*	3
22	11	TAKE GOOD CARE OF YOURSELF	Three Degrees	*Philadelphia*	3
13	12	SKIING IN THE SNOW	Wigans Ovation	*Spark*	6
21	13	A LITTLE LOVE AND UNDERSTANDING	Gilbert Becaud	*Decca*	4
16	14	THE TEARS I CRIED	Glitter Band	*Bell*	3
10	15	THE UGLY DUCKLING	Mike Reid	*Pye*	6
24	16	HOLD ON TO LOVE	Peter Skellern	*Decca*	4

May 1975

□ Highest position disc reached ● Act's first ever week on chart

LW	TW	Title	Artist	Label	Wks
27	17	LADY MARMALADE	Labelle	*Epic*	6
18	18	DING-A-DONG	Teach-In	*Polydor*	3
6	19	THERE'S A WHOLE LOT OF LOVING	Guys And Dolls	*Magnet*	8
17	20	PHILADELPHIA FREEDOM	Elton John Band	*DJM*	8
26	21	GET DOWN TONIGHT	K.C. And The Sunshine Band	*Jayboy*	4
8	22	FANCY PANTS	Kenny	*RAK*	8
7	23	GIRLS	Moments And Whatnauts	*All Platinum*	8
20	24	REACH OUT I'LL BE THERE	Gloria Gaynor	*MGM*	7
11	25	PLAY ME LIKE YOU PLAY YOUR GUITAR	Duane Eddy	*GTO*	7
36	26	NIGHT	Frankie Valli And The Four Seasons	*Mowest*	2
30	27	SORRY DOESN'T ALWAYS MAKE IT RIGHT	Diana Ross	*Tamla Motown*	3
40	28	ONLY YESTERDAY	Carpenters	*A&M*	2
31	29	WE'LL FIND OUR DAY	Stephanie de Sykes	*Bradley's*	2
-	30	LET ME TRY AGAIN	Tammy Jones ●	*Epic*	1
29	31	L.O.V.E.	Al Green	*London*	6
39	32	WHERE IS THE LOVE	Betty Wright	*RCA*	2
33	33	HOW GLAD I AM	Kiki Dee Band	*Rocket*	2
37	34	THE WAY WE WERE	Gladys Knight And The Pips	*Buddah*	3
-	35	SAVE ME	Silver Convention ●	*Magnet*	1
-	36	CALL ME ROUND	Pilot	*EMI*	1
12	37	I CAN DO IT	Rubettes	*State*	8
15	38	LET ME BE THE ONE	Shadows	*EMI*	7
38	39	IF	Yin And Yan	*EMI*	4
-	40	I WANNA DANCE WIT CHOO	Disco Tex And The Sex-O-Lettes	*Chelsea*	1

WEEK ENDING 3 MAY 1975

LW	TW	Title	Artist	Label	Wks
6	1	OH BOY	Mud	*RAK*	2
7	2	LOVING YOU	Minnie Riperton	*Epic*	3
2	3	HONEY	Bobby Goldsboro	*United Artists*	5
10	4	HURT SO GOOD	Susan Cadogan	*Magnet*	4
1	5	BYE BYE BABY	Bay City Rollers	*Bell*	9
4	6	LOVE ME LOVE MY DOG	Peter Shelley	*Magnet*	7
9	7	LIFE IS A MINESTRONE	10CC	*Mercury*	4
14	8	THE TEARS I CRIED	Glitter Band	*Bell*	4
11	9	TAKE GOOD CARE OF YOURSELF	Three Degrees	*Philadelphia*	4
3	10	FOX ON THE RUN	Sweet	*RCA*	7
5	11	SWING YOUR DADDY	Jim Gilstrap	*Chelsea*	7
13	12	A LITTLE LOVE AND UNDERSTANDING	Gilbert Becaud	*Decca*	5
18	13	DING-A-DONG	Teach-In	*Polydor*	4
16	14	HOLD ON TO LOVE	Peter Skellern	*Decca*	5
8	15	THE FUNKY GIBBON/SICK MAN BLUES	Goodies	*Bradley's*	8
26	16	NIGHT	Frankie Valli And The Four Seasons	*Mowest*	3
30	17	LET ME TRY AGAIN	Tammy Jones	*Epic*	2
28	18	ONLY YESTERDAY	Carpenters	*A&M*	3
12	19	SKIING IN THE SNOW	Wigans Ovation	*Spark*	7
29	20	WE'LL FIND OUR DAY	Stephanie de Sykes	*Bradley's*	3
40	21	I WANNA DANCE WIT CHOO	Disco Tex And The Sex-O-Lettes	*Chelsea*	2
15	22	THE UGLY DUCKLING	Mike Reid	*Pye*	7
-	23	STAND BY YOUR MAN	Tammy Wynette ●	*Epic*	1
21	24	GET DOWN TONIGHT	K.C. And The Sunshine Band	*Jayboy*	5
-	25	LOVE LIKE YOU & ME	Gary Glitter	*Bell*	1
17	26	LADY MARMALADE	Labelle	*Epic*	7
27	27	SORRY DOESN'T ALWAYS MAKE IT RIGHT	Diana Ross	*Tamla Motown*	4
32	28	WHERE IS THE LOVE	Betty Wright	*RCA*	3
-	29	PAPA OOH MOW MOW	Sharonettes ●	*Black Magic*	1
35	30	SAVE ME	Silver Convention	*Magnet*	2
-	31	CUT THE CAKE	Average White Band	*Atlantic*	1
34	32	THE WAY WE WERE	Gladys Knight And The Pips	*Buddah*	4
19	33	THERE'S A WHOLE LOT OF LOVING	Guys And Dolls	*Magnet*	9
36	34	CALL ME ROUND	Pilot	*EMI*	2
23	35	GIRLS	Moments And Whatnauts	*All Platinum*	9
22	36	FANCY PANTS	Kenny	*RAK*	9
-	37	TAKE YOUR MAMA FOR A RIDE	Lulu	*Chelsea*	1

■Four animals in the Top Ten - a fox, a dog, a gibbon and a duckling make it a zoological chart week (19.04.75) ■ The next week, food takes over, with honey, minestrone and marmalade all in the Top 20 (26.04.92) ■ *Honey* by Bobby Goldsboro, becomes the first record to hit number two on two entirely different occasions, having been there before in 1968 (26.04.75)■

May 1975

□ Highest position disc reached ● Act's first ever week on chart

LW	TW	Title	Artist	Label	Wks
-	38	HASTA LA VISTA	Sylvia	Sonet	1
25	39	PLAY ME LIKE YOU PLAY YOUR GUITAR	Duane Eddy	GTO	8
20	40	PHILADELPHIA FREEDOM	Elton John Band	DJM	9

WEEK ENDING 10 MAY 1975

LW	TW	Title	Artist	Label	Wks
1	1	OH BOY	Mud	RAK	3
2	2	LOVING YOU	Minnie Riperton	Epic	4
23	3	STAND BY YOUR MAN	Tammy Wynette	Epic	2
4	4	HURT SO GOOD	Susan Cadogan	Magnet	5
3	5	HONEY	Bobby Goldsboro	United Artists	6
17	6	LET ME TRY AGAIN	Tammy Jones	Epic	3
16	7	NIGHT	Frankie Valli And The Four Seasons	Mowest	4
5	8	BYE BYE BABY	Bay City Rollers	Bell	10
9	9	TAKE GOOD CARE OF YOURSELF	Three Degrees	Philadelphia	5
12	10	A LITTLE LOVE AND UNDERSTANDING	Gilbert Becaud	Decca	6
8	11	THE TEARS I CRIED	Glitter Band	Bell	5
21	12	I WANNA DANCE WIT CHOO	Disco Tex And The Sex-O-Lettes	Chelsea	3
25	13	LOVE LIKE YOU & ME	Gary Glitter	Bell	2
18	14	ONLY YESTERDAY	Carpenters	A&M	4
7	15	LIFE IS A MINESTRONE	10CC	Mercury	5
6	16	LOVE ME LOVE MY DOG	Peter Shelley	Magnet	8
20	17	WE'LL FIND OUR DAY	Stephanie de Sykes	Bradley's	4
11	18	SWING YOUR DADDY	Jim Gilstrap	Chelsea	8
13	19	DING-A-DONG	Teach-In	Polydor	5
14	20	HOLD ON TO LOVE	Peter Skellern	Decca	6
10	21	FOX ON THE RUN	Sweet	RCA	8
32	22	THE WAY WE WERE	Gladys Knight And The Pips	Buddah	5
27	23	SORRY DOESN'T ALWAYS MAKE IT RIGHT	Diana Ross	Tamla Motown	5
24	24	GET DOWN TONIGHT	K.C. And The Sunshine Band	Jayboy	6
28	25	WHERE IS THE LOVE	Betty Wright	RCA	4
29	26	PAPA OOH MOW MOW	Sharonettes	Black Magic	2
-	27	DON'T DO IT BABY	Mac And Katie Kissoon	State	1
-	28	ONCE BITTEN TWICE SHY	Ian Hunter	CBS	1
19	29	SKIING IN THE SNOW	Wigans Ovation	Spark	8
30	30	SAVE ME	Silver Convention	Magnet	3
-	31	I'M FOREVER BLOWING BUBBLES	West Ham United 1st Team Squad ●	Pye	1
26	32	LADY MARMALADE	Labelle	Epic	8
-	33	I GET THE SWEETEST FEELING	Jackie Wilson	Brunswick	1
15	34	THE FUNKY GIBBON/SICK MAN BLUES	Goodies	Bradley's	9
-	35	WOMBLING WHITE TIE AND TAILS	Wombles	CBS	1
-	36	SING BABY SING	Stylistics	Avco	1
-	37	STAND BY ME	John Lennon	Apple	1
-	38	AUTOBAHN	Kraftwerk ●	Vertigo	1
38	39	HASTA LA VISTA	Sylvia	Sonet	2
-	40	ISRAELITES	Desmond Dekker	Cactus	1

WEEK ENDING 17 MAY 1975

LW	TW	Title	Artist	Label	Wks
3	1	STAND BY YOUR MAN	Tammy Wynette	Epic	3
1	2	OH BOY	Mud	RAK	4
2	3	LOVING YOU	Minnie Riperton	Epic	5
4	4	HURT SO GOOD	Susan Cadogan	Magnet	6
6	5	LET ME TRY AGAIN	Tammy Jones	Epic	4
12	6	I WANNA DANCE WIT CHOO	Disco Tex And The Sex-O-Lettes	Chelsea	4
14	7	ONLY YESTERDAY	Carpenters	A&M	5
5	8	HONEY	Bobby Goldsboro	United Artists	7
7	9	NIGHT	Frankie Valli And The Four Seasons	Mowest	5
13	10	LOVE LIKE YOU & ME	Gary Glitter	Bell	3
22	11	THE WAY WE WERE	Gladys Knight And The Pips	Buddah	6
36	12	SING BABY SING	Stylistics	Avco	2
10	13	A LITTLE LOVE AND UNDERSTANDING	Gilbert Becaud	Decca	7
-	14	THANKS FOR THE MEMORY	Slade	Polydor	1
9	15	TAKE GOOD CARE OF YOURSELF	Three Degrees	Philadelphia	6
27	16	DON'T DO IT BABY	Mac And Katie Kissoon	State	2
17	17	WE'LL FIND OUR DAY	Stephanie de Sykes	Bradley's	5
11	18	THE TEARS I CRIED	Glitter Band	Bell	6
8	19	BYE BYE BABY	Bay City Rollers	Bell	11
15	20	LIFE IS A MINESTRONE	10CC	Mercury	6
40	21	ISRAELITES	Desmond Dekker	Cactus	2
38	22	AUTOBAHN	Kraftwerk	Vertigo	2
35	23	WOMBLING WHITE TIE AND TAILS	Wombles	CBS	2
19	24	DING-A-DONG	Teach-In	Polydor	6
28	25	ONCE BITTEN TWICE SHY	Ian Hunter	CBS	2
16	26	LOVE ME LOVE MY DOG	Peter Shelley	Magnet	9
20	27	HOLD ON TO LOVE	Peter Skellern	Decca	7
-	28	WHISPERING GRASS	Windsor Davies/Don Estelle ●	EMI	1
33	29	I GET THE SWEETEST FEELING	Jackie Wilson	Brunswick	2
-	30	IMAGINE ME, IMAGINE YOU	Fox	GTO	1
25	31	WHERE IS THE LOVE	Betty Wright	RCA	5
37	32	STAND BY ME	John Lennon	Apple	2
26	33	PAPA OOH MOW MOW	Sharonettes	Black Magic	3
30	34	SAVE ME	Silver Convention	Magnet	4
-	35	SWING LOW SWEET CHARIOT	Eric Clapton	RSO	1
-	36	I'M GONNA RUN AWAY FROM YOU	Tami Lynn	Contempo	1
-	37	ROLL OVER LAY DOWN	Status Quo	Vertigo	1
23	38	SORRY DOESN'T ALWAYS MAKE IT RIGHT	Diana Ross	Tamla Motown	6
-	39	SEND IN THE CLOWNS	Judy Collins	Elektra	1
18	40	SWING YOUR DADDY	Jim Gilstrap	Chelsea	9

WEEK ENDING 24 MAY 1975

LW	TW	Title	Artist	Label	Wks
1	1	STAND BY YOUR MAN	Tammy Wynette	Epic	4
28	2	WHISPERING GRASS	Windsor Davies/Don Estelle	EMI	2
2	3	OH BOY	Mud	RAK	5
3	4	LOVING YOU	Minnie Riperton	Epic	6
11	5	THE WAY WE WERE	Gladys Knight And The Pips	Buddah	7
12	6	SING BABY SING	Stylistics	Avco	3
5	7	LET ME TRY AGAIN	Tammy Jones	Epic	5
4	8	HURT SO GOOD	Susan Cadogan	Magnet	7
16	9	DON'T DO IT BABY	Mac And Katie Kissoon	State	3
7	10	ONLY YESTERDAY	Carpenters	A&M	6
6	11	I WANNA DANCE WIT CHOO	Disco Tex And The Sex-O-Lettes	Chelsea	5
14	12	THANKS FOR THE MEMORY	Slade	Polydor	2
-	13	THREE STEPS TO HEAVEN	Showaddywaddy	Bell	1
39	14	SEND IN THE CLOWNS	Judy Collins	Elektra	2
9	15	NIGHT	Frankie Valli And The Four Seasons	Mowest	6
37	16	ROLL OVER LAY DOWN	Status Quo	Vertigo	2
22	17	AUTOBAHN	Kraftwerk	Vertigo	3
25	18	ONCE BITTEN TWICE SHY	Ian Hunter	CBS	3
21	19	ISRAELITES	Desmond Dekker	Cactus	3
10	20	LOVE LIKE YOU & ME	Gary Glitter	Bell	4
13	21	A LITTLE LOVE AND UNDERSTANDING	Gilbert Becaud	Decca	8
23	22	WOMBLING WHITE TIE AND TAILS	Wombles	CBS	3
30	23	IMAGINE ME, IMAGINE YOU	Fox	GTO	2
8	24	HONEY	Bobby Goldsboro	United Artists	8
29	25	I GET THE SWEETEST FEELING	Jackie Wilson	Brunswick	3
17	26	WE'LL FIND OUR DAY	Stephanie de Sykes	Bradley's	6
15	27	TAKE GOOD CARE OF YOURSELF	Three Degrees	Philadelphia	7
19	28	BYE BYE BABY	Bay City Rollers	Bell	12
35	29	SWING LOW SWEET CHARIOT	Eric Clapton	RSO	2
32	30	STAND BY ME	John Lennon	Apple	3
38	31	SORRY DOESN'T ALWAYS MAKE IT RIGHT	Diana Ross	Tamla Motown	7
-	32	I'LL DO ANYTHING YOU WANT ME TO	Barry White	20th Century	1
-	33	HERE I GO AGAIN	Guys and Dolls	Magnet	1
-	34	THE PROUD ONE	Osmonds	MGM	1
18	35	THE TEARS I CRIED	Glitter Band	Bell	7

In these weeks ■ In the week they won the F.A. Cup, West Ham United score their only chart goal. The team they beat 2-0, Fulham, just failed to make the Top 40 with their sublimely awful *Viva El Fulham* (10.05.75) ■ An old-fashioned look to the top of the chart with Tammy Wynette's seven year old record at number one, and revivals of Eddie Cochran and Buddy Holly hits by Showaddywaddy and Mud (24.05.75)■

June 1975

□ Highest position disc reached ● Act's first ever week on chart

LW	TW	Title	Artist	Label	Wks
36	36	I'M GONNA RUN AWAY FROM YOU	Tami Lynn	Contempo	2
26	37	LOVE ME LOVE MY DOG	Peter Shelley	Magnet	10
33	38	PAPA OOH MOW MOW	Sharonettes	Black Magic	4
31	39	WHERE IS THE LOVE	Betty Wright	RCA	6
-	40	DISCO QUEEN	Hot Chocolate	RAK	1

WEEK ENDING 31 MAY 1975

LW	TW	Title	Artist	Label	Wks
1	1	STAND BY YOUR MAN	Tammy Wynette	Epic	5
2	2	WHISPERING GRASS	Windsor Davies/Don Estelle	EMI	3
6	3	SING BABY SING	Stylistics	Avco	4
5	4	THE WAY WE WERE	Gladys Knight And The Pips	Buddah	8
13	5	THREE STEPS TO HEAVEN	Showaddywaddy	Bell	2
14	6	SEND IN THE CLOWNS	Judy Collins	Elektra	3
12	7	THANKS FOR THE MEMORY	Slade	Polydor	3
11	8	I WANNA DANCE WIT CHOO	Disco Tex And The Sex-O-Lettes	Chelsea	6
7	9	LET ME TRY AGAIN	Tammy Jones	Epic	6
16	10	ROLL OVER LAY DOWN	Status Quo	Vertigo	3
19	11	ISRAELITES	Desmond Dekker	Cactus	4
9	12	DON'T DO IT BABY	Mac And Katie Kissoon	State	4
4	13	LOVING YOU	Minnie Riperton	Epic	7
10	14	ONLY YESTERDAY	Carpenters	A&M	7
3	15	OH BOY	Mud	RAK	6
17	16	AUTOBAHN	Kraftwerk	Vertigo	4
8	17	HURT SO GOOD	Susan Cadogan	Magnet	8
34	18	THE PROUD ONE	Osmonds	MGM	2
15	19	NIGHT	Frankie Valli And The Four Seasons	Mowest	7
18	20	ONCE BITTEN TWICE SHY	Ian Hunter	CBS	4
23	21	IMAGINE ME, IMAGINE YOU	Fox	GTO	3
22	22	WOMBLING WHITE TIE AND TAILS	Wombles	CBS	4
20	23	LOVE LIKE YOU & ME	Gary Glitter	Bell	5
32	24	I'LL DO ANYTHING YOU WANT ME TO	Barry White	20th Century	2
29	25	SWING LOW SWEET CHARIOT	Eric Clapton	RSO	3
25	26	I GET THE SWEETEST FEELING	Jackie Wilson	Brunswick	4
40	27	DISCO QUEEN	Hot Chocolate	RAK	2
26	28	WE'LL FIND OUR DAY	Stephanie de Sykes	Bradley's	7
21	29	A LITTLE LOVE AND UNDERSTANDING	Gilbert Becaud	Decca	9
24	30	HONEY	Bobby Goldsboro	United Artists	9
-	31	TROUBLE	Elvis Presley	RCA	1
30	32	STAND BY ME	John Lennon	Apple	4
-	33	LISTEN TO WHAT THE MAN SAID	Wings	Apple	1
-	34	DISCO STOMP	Hamilton Bohannon	Brunswick	1
28	35	BYE BYE BABY	Bay City Rollers	Bell	13
33	36	HERE I GO AGAIN	Guys and Dolls	Magnet	2
27	37	TAKE GOOD CARE OF YOURSELF	Three Degrees	Philadelphia	8
-	38	SENDING OUT AN S.O.S.	Retta Young ●	All Platinum	1
-	39	THE HUSTLE	Van McCoy ●	Avco	1
36	40	I'M GONNA RUN AWAY FROM YOU	Tami Lynn	Contempo	3

WEEK ENDING 7 JUNE 1975

LW	TW	Title	Artist	Label	Wks
2	1	WHISPERING GRASS	Windsor Davies/Don Estelle	EMI	4
1	2	STAND BY YOUR MAN	Tammy Wynette	Epic	6
5	3	THREE STEPS TO HEAVEN	Showaddywaddy	Bell	3
3	4	SING BABY SING	Stylistics	Avco	5
4	5	THE WAY WE WERE	Gladys Knight And The Pips	Buddah	9
6	6	SEND IN THE CLOWNS	Judy Collins	Elektra	4
18	7	THE PROUD ONE	Osmonds	MGM	3
-	8	I'M NOT IN LOVE	10CC	Mercury	1
10	9	ROLL OVER LAY DOWN	Status Quo	Vertigo	4
11	10	ISRAELITES	Desmond Dekker	Cactus	5
16	11	AUTOBAHN	Kraftwerk	Vertigo	5
7	12	THANKS FOR THE MEMORY	Slade	Polydor	4
8	13	I WANNA DANCE WIT CHOO	Disco Tex And The Sex-O-Lettes	Chelsea	7
20	14	ONCE BITTEN TWICE SHY	Ian Hunter	CBS	5
21	15	IMAGINE ME, IMAGINE YOU	Fox	GTO	4
9	16	LET ME TRY AGAIN	Tammy Jones	Epic	7
12	17	DON'T DO IT BABY	Mac And Katie Kissoon	State	5
33	18	LISTEN TO WHAT THE MAN SAID	Wings	Apple	2
25	19	SWING LOW SWEET CHARIOT	Eric Clapton	RSO	4
27	20	DISCO QUEEN	Hot Chocolate	RAK	3
24	21	I'LL DO ANYTHING YOU WANT ME TO	Barry White	20th Century	3
39	22	THE HUSTLE	Van McCoy	Avco	2
34	23	DISCO STOMP	Hamilton Bohannon	Brunswick	2
15	24	OH BOY	Mud	RAK	7
17	25	HURT SO GOOD	Susan Cadogan	Magnet	9
14	26	ONLY YESTERDAY	Carpenters	A&M	8
22	27	WOMBLING WHITE TIE AND TAILS	Wombles	CBS	5
26	28	I GET THE SWEETEST FEELING	Jackie Wilson	Brunswick	5
13	29	LOVING YOU	Minnie Riperton	Epic	8
-	30	OH WHAT A SHAME	Roy Wood	Jet	1
-	31	WALKING IN RHYTHM	Blackbyrds ●	Fantasy	1
31	32	TROUBLE	Elvis Presley	RCA	2
38	33	SENDING OUT AN S.O.S.	Retta Young	All Platinum	2
32	34	STAND BY ME	John Lennon	Apple	5
19	35	NIGHT	Frankie Valli And The Four Seasons	Mowest	8
-	36	DYNOMITE (PART 1)	Tony Camillo's Bazuka ●	A&M	1
35	37	BYE BYE BABY	Bay City Rollers	Bell	14
29	38	A LITTLE LOVE AND UNDERSTANDING	Gilbert Becaud	Decca	10
23	39	LOVE LIKE YOU & ME	Gary Glitter	Bell	6
-	40	MR. RAFFLES (MAN IT WAS MEAN)	Steve Harley and Cockney Rebel	EMI	1

WEEK ENDING 14 JUNE 1975

LW	TW	Title	Artist	Label	Wks
1	1	WHISPERING GRASS	Windsor Davies/Don Estelle	EMI	5
3	2	THREE STEPS TO HEAVEN	Showaddywaddy	Bell	4
8	3	I'M NOT IN LOVE	10CC	Mercury	2
4	4	SING BABY SING	Stylistics	Avco	6
2	5	STAND BY YOUR MAN	Tammy Wynette	Epic	7
7	6	THE PROUD ONE	Osmonds	MGM	4
5	7	THE WAY WE WERE	Gladys Knight And The Pips	Buddah	10
6	8	SEND IN THE CLOWNS	Judy Collins	Elektra	5
22	9	THE HUSTLE	Van McCoy	Avco	3
18	10	LISTEN TO WHAT THE MAN SAID	Wings	Apple	3
20	11	DISCO QUEEN	Hot Chocolate	RAK	4
11	12	AUTOBAHN	Kraftwerk	Vertigo	6
9	13	ROLL OVER LAY DOWN	Status Quo	Vertigo	5
10	14	ISRAELITES	Desmond Dekker	Cactus	6
30	15	OH WHAT A SHAME	Roy Wood	Jet	2
23	16	DISCO STOMP	Hamilton Bohannon	Brunswick	3
12	17	THANKS FOR THE MEMORY	Slade	Polydor	5
14	18	ONCE BITTEN TWICE SHY	Ian Hunter	CBS	6
15	19	IMAGINE ME, IMAGINE YOU	Fox	GTO	5
21	20	I'LL DO ANYTHING YOU WANT ME TO	Barry White	20th Century	4
19	21	SWING LOW SWEET CHARIOT	Eric Clapton	RSO	5
13	22	I WANNA DANCE WIT CHOO	Disco Tex And The Sex-O-Lettes	Chelsea	8
40	23	MR. RAFFLES (MAN IT WAS MEAN)	Steve Harley and Cockney Rebel	EMI	2
-	24	BABY I LOVE YOU, OK	Kenny	RAK	1
31	25	WALKING IN RHYTHM	Blackbyrds	Fantasy	2
16	26	LET ME TRY AGAIN	Tammy Jones	Epic	8
17	27	DON'T DO IT BABY	Mac And Katie Kissoon	State	6
36	28	DYNOMITE (PART 1)	Tony Camillo's Bazuka	A&M	2
-	29	TEARS ON MY PILLOW	Johnny Nash	CBS	1
33	30	SENDING OUT AN S.O.S.	Retta Young	All Platinum	3
24	31	OH BOY	Mud	RAK	8
-	32	TAKE ME IN YOUR ARMS	Doobie Brothers	Warner Brothers	1
29	33	LOVING YOU	Minnie Riperton	Epic	9
-	34	YOU LAY SO EASY ON MY MIND	Andy Williams	CBS	1
-	35	GET OUT	Harold Melvin And The Bluenotes	Route	1
-	36	MY WHITE BICYCLE	Nazareth	Mooncrest	1
28	37	I GET THE SWEETEST FEELING	Jackie Wilson	Brunswick	6
32	38	TROUBLE	Elvis Presley	RCA	3

■ *Whispering Grass* by the stars of BBC TV's 'It Ain't Half Hot, Mum' becomes one of the oldest songs to top the U.K. charts. It had first been a hit for the Ink Spots in 1940 (07.06.75) ■ *Israelites* by Desmond Dekker returns to the Top 10 six years after it originally reached number one (07.06.75) ■ *Disco Queen* and *Disco Stomp* follow Disco Tex and the Sex-O-Lettes into the Top 20 (14.06.75)■

June 1975

□ Highest position disc reached ● Act's first ever week on chart

LW	TW	Title	Artist	Label	Wks
26	39	ONLY YESTERDAY	Carpenters	*A&M*	9
27	40	WOMBLING WHITE TIE AND TAILS	Wombles	*CBS*	6

WEEK ENDING 21 JUNE 1975

LW	TW	Title	Artist	Label	Wks
1	[1]	WHISPERING GRASS	Windsor Davies/Don Estelle	*EMI*	6
3	2	I'M NOT IN LOVE	10CC	*Mercury*	3
2	3	THREE STEPS TO HEAVEN	Showaddywaddy	*Bell*	5
9	4	THE HUSTLE	Van McCoy	*Avco*	4
6	[5]	THE PROUD ONE	Osmonds	*MGM*	5
10	[6]	LISTEN TO WHAT THE MAN SAID	Wings	*Apple*	4
5	7	STAND BY YOUR MAN	Tammy Wynette	*Epic*	8
4	8	SING BABY SING	Stylistics	*Avco*	7
7	9	THE WAY WE WERE	Gladys Knight And The Pips	*Buddah*	11
16	10	DISCO STOMP	Hamilton Bohannon	*Brunswick*	4
8	11	SEND IN THE CLOWNS	Judy Collins	*Elektra*	6
11	12	DISCO QUEEN	Hot Chocolate	*RAK*	5
15	[13]	OH WHAT A SHAME	Roy Wood	*Jet*	3
29	14	TEARS ON MY PILLOW	Johnny Nash	*CBS*	2
24	15	BABY I LOVE YOU, OK	Kenny	*RAK*	2
12	16	AUTOBAHN	Kraftwerk	*Vertigo*	7
23	17	MR. RAFFLES (MAN IT WAS MEAN)	Steve Harley and Cockney Rebel	*EMI*	3
13	18	ROLL OVER LAY DOWN	Status Quo	*Vertigo*	6
14	19	ISRAELITES	Desmond Dekker	*Cactus*	7
18	20	ONCE BITTEN TWICE SHY	Ian Hunter	*CBS*	7
21	21	SWING LOW SWEET CHARIOT	Eric Clapton	*RSO*	6
-	22	DOING ALRIGHT WITH THE BOYS	Gary Glitter	*Bell*	1
25	[23]	WALKING IN RHYTHM	Blackbyrds	*Fantasy*	3
36	24	MY WHITE BICYCLE	Nazareth	*Mooncrest*	2
-	25	I DON'T LOVE YOU BUT I THINK I LIKE YOU	Gilbert O'Sullivan	*MAM*	1
-	26	MOONSHINE SALLY	Mud	*RAK*	1
19	27	IMAGINE ME, IMAGINE YOU	Fox	*GTO*	6
30	[28]	SENDING OUT AN S.O.S.	Retta Young	*All Platinum*	4
32	[29]	TAKE ME IN YOUR ARMS	Doobie Brothers	*Warner Brothers*	2
17	30	THANKS FOR THE MEMORY	Slade	*Polydor*	6
28	31	DYNOMITE	Tony Camillo's Bazuka	*A&M*	3
34	[32]	YOU LAY SO EASY ON MY MIND	Andy Williams	*CBS*	2
20	33	I'LL DO ANYTHING YOU WANT ME TO	Barry White	*20th Century*	5
26	34	LET ME TRY AGAIN	Tammy Jones	*Epic*	9
-	35	MISTY	Ray Stevens	*Janus*	1
-	36	HAVE YOU SEEN HER/OH GIRL	Chi-Lites	*Brunswick*	1
22	37	I WANNA DANCE WIT CHOO	Disco Tex And The Sex-O-Lettes	*Chelsea*	9
27	38	DON'T DO IT BABY	Mac And Katie Kissoon	*State*	7
-	39	MAKE THE WORLD GO AWAY	Donny And Marie Osmond	*MGM*	1
35	40	GET OUT	Harold Melvin And The Bluenotes	*Route*	2

WEEK ENDING 28 JUNE 1975

LW	TW	Title	Artist	Label	Wks
2	[1]	I'M NOT IN LOVE	10CC	*Mercury*	4
1	2	WHISPERING GRASS	Windsor Davies/Don Estelle	*EMI*	7
3	3	THREE STEPS TO HEAVEN	Showaddywaddy	*Bell*	6
4	4	THE HUSTLE	Van McCoy	*Avco*	5
14	5	TEARS ON MY PILLOW	Johnny Nash	*CBS*	3
22	[6]	DOING ALRIGHT WITH THE BOYS	Gary Glitter	*Bell*	2
5	7	THE PROUD ONE	Osmonds	*MGM*	6
10	8	DISCO STOMP	Hamilton Bohannon	*Brunswick*	5
6	9	LISTEN TO WHAT THE MAN SAID	Wings	*Apple*	5
35	10	MISTY	Ray Stevens	*Janus*	2
26	11	MOONSHINE SALLY	Mud	*RAK*	2
15	[12]	BABY I LOVE YOU, OK	Kenny	*RAK*	3
17	[13]	MR. RAFFLES (MAN IT WAS MEAN)	Steve Harley and Cockney Rebel	*EMI*	4
8	14	SING BABY SING	Stylistics	*Avco*	8
13	15	OH WHAT A SHAME	Roy Wood	*Jet*	4
7	16	STAND BY YOUR MAN	Tammy Wynette	*Epic*	9
12	17	DISCO QUEEN	Hot Chocolate	*RAK*	6
24	18	MY WHITE BICYCLE	Nazareth	*Mooncrest*	3
9	19	THE WAY WE WERE	Gladys Knight And The Pips	*Buddah*	12
25	20	I DON'T LOVE YOU BUT I THINK I LIKE YOU	Gilbert O'Sullivan	*MAM*	2
11	21	SEND IN THE CLOWNS	Judy Collins	*Elektra*	7
36	22	HAVE YOU SEEN HER/OH GIRL	Chi-Lites	*Brunswick*	2
-	23	FOE-DEE-O-DEE	Rubettes	*State*	1
39	24	MAKE THE WORLD GO AWAY	Donny And Marie Osmond	*MGM*	2
23	25	WALKING IN RHYTHM	Blackbyrds	*Fantasy*	4
20	26	ONCE BITTEN TWICE SHY	Ian Hunter	*CBS*	8
21	27	SWING LOW SWEET CHARIOT	Eric Clapton	*RSO*	7
18	28	ROLL OVER LAY DOWN	Status Quo	*Vertigo*	7
16	29	AUTOBAHN	Kraftwerk	*Vertigo*	8
-	30	MAMA NEVER TOLD ME	Sister Sledge ●	*Atlantic*	1
28	31	SENDING OUT AN S.O.S.	Retta Young	*All Platinum*	5
29	32	TAKE ME IN YOUR ARMS	Doobie Brothers	*Warner Brothers*	3
-	33	BLACK PUDDING BERTHA	Goodies	*Bradley's*	1
-	34	SWEARIN' TO GOD	Frankie Valli	*Private Stock*	1
19	35	ISRAELITES	Desmond Dekker	*Cactus*	8
-	36	D.I.V.O.R.C.E.	Tammy Wynette	*Epic*	1
32	37	YOU LAY SO EASY ON MY MIND	Andy Williams	*CBS*	3
27	38	IMAGINE ME, IMAGINE YOU	Fox	*GTO*	7
31	39	DYNOMITE	Tony Camillo's Bazuka	*A&M*	4
30	40	THANKS FOR THE MEMORY	Slade	*Polydor*	7

WEEK ENDING 5 JULY 1975

LW	TW	Title	Artist	Label	Wks
1	[1]	I'M NOT IN LOVE	10CC	*Mercury*	5
5	2	TEARS ON MY PILLOW	Johnny Nash	*CBS*	4
4	[3]	THE HUSTLE	Van McCoy	*Avco*	6
2	4	WHISPERING GRASS	Windsor Davies/Don Estelle	*EMI*	8
10	5	MISTY	Ray Stevens	*Janus*	3
8	[6]	DISCO STOMP	Hamilton Bohannon	*Brunswick*	6
3	7	THREE STEPS TO HEAVEN	Showaddywaddy	*Bell*	7
6	8	DOING ALRIGHT WITH THE BOYS	Gary Glitter	*Bell*	3
22	9	HAVE YOU SEEN HER/OH GIRL	Chi-Lites	*Brunswick*	3
11	[10]	MOONSHINE SALLY	Mud	*RAK*	3
7	11	THE PROUD ONE	Osmonds	*MGM*	7
9	12	LISTEN TO WHAT THE MAN SAID	Wings	*Apple*	6
12	13	BABY I LOVE YOU, OK	Kenny	*RAK*	4
20	[14]	I DON'T LOVE YOU BUT I THINK I LIKE YOU	Gilbert O'Sullivan	*MAM*	3
-	15	EIGHTEEN WITH A BULLET	Pete Wingfield ●	*Island*	1
13	16	MR. RAFFLES (MAN IT WAS MEAN)	Steve Harley and Cockney Rebel	*EMI*	5
18	17	MY WHITE BICYCLE	Nazareth	*Mooncrest*	4
24	[18]	MAKE THE WORLD GO AWAY	Donny And Marie Osmond	*MGM*	3
23	19	FOE-DEE-O-DEE	Rubettes	*State*	2
15	20	OH WHAT A SHAME	Roy Wood	*Jet*	5
30	21	MAMA NEVER TOLD ME	Sister Sledge	*Atlantic*	2
17	22	DISCO QUEEN	Hot Chocolate	*RAK*	7
33	23	BLACK PUDDING BERTHA	Goodies	*Bradley's*	2
19	24	THE WAY WE WERE	Gladys Knight And The Pips	*Buddah*	13
16	25	STAND BY YOUR MAN	Tammy Wynette	*Epic*	10
14	26	SING BABY SING	Stylistics	*Avco*	9
-	27	SOMEONE SAVED MY LIFE TONIGHT	Elton John	*DJM*	1
-	28	JIVE TALKIN'	Bee Gees	*RSO*	1
21	29	SEND IN THE CLOWNS	Judy Collins	*Elektra*	8
36	30	D.I.V.O.R.C.E.	Tammy Wynette	*Epic*	2
34	[31]	SWEARIN' TO GOD	Frankie Valli	*Private Stock*	2
-	32	JE T'AIME	Judge Dread	*Cactus*	1
-	33	SEALED WITH A KISS	Brian Hyland	*ABC*	1
25	34	WALKING IN RHYTHM	Blackbyrds	*Fantasy*	5
27	35	SWING LOW SWEET CHARIOT	Eric Clapton	*RSO*	8
-	36	I WRITE THE SONGS/....FOR LOVE	David Cassidy	*RCA*	1
-	37	BARBADOS	Typically Tropical ●	*Gull*	1
28	38	ROLL OVER LAY DOWN	Status Quo	*Vertigo*	8
32	39	TAKE ME IN YOUR ARMS	Doobie Brothers	*Warner Brothers*	4
29	40	AUTOBAHN	Kraftwerk	*Vertigo*	9

In these weeks ■ The Osmonds and the man on whose television show they first came to fame, Andy Williams, peak in the same week (21.06.75) ■ The Bee Gees return to the chart for the first time in three years, at the start of their period of massive disco success (05.07.75)■

LW	TW	*WEEK ENDING* **12 JULY 1975**		Wks
2	[1]	TEARS ON MY PILLOW Johnny Nash	*CBS*	5
5	[2]	MISTY Ray Stevens	*Janus*	4
3	[3]	THE HUSTLE Van McCoy	*Avco*	7
1	4	I'M NOT IN LOVE 10CC	*Mercury*	6
9	5	HAVE YOU SEEN HER/OH GIRL Chi-Lites	*Brunswick*	4
8	[6]	DOING ALRIGHT WITH THE BOYS Gary Glitter	*Bell*	4
-	7	GIVE A LITTLE LOVE Bay City Rollers	*Bell*	1
6	8	DISCO STOMP Hamilton Bohannon	*Brunswick*	7
4	9	WHISPERING GRASS Windsor Davies/Don Estelle	*EMI*	9
15	10	EIGHTEEN WITH A BULLET Pete Wingfield	*Island*	2
10	11	MOONSHINE SALLY Mud	*RAK*	4
7	12	THREE STEPS TO HEAVEN Showaddywaddy	*Bell*	8
37	13	BARBADOS Typically Tropical	*Gull*	2
17	[14]	MY WHITE BICYCLE Nazareth	*Mooncrest*	5
19	[15]	FOE-DEE-O-DEE Rubettes	*State*	3
13	16	BABY I LOVE YOU, OK Kenny	*RAK*	5
14	17	I DON'T LOVE YOU BUT I THINK I LIKE YOU Gilbert O'Sullivan	*MAM*	4
18	[18]	MAKE THE WORLD GO AWAY Donny And Marie Osmond	*MGM*	4
32	19	JE T'AIME Judge Dread	*Cactus*	2
30	20	D.I.V.O.R.C.E. Tammy Wynette	*Epic*	3
12	21	LISTEN TO WHAT THE MAN SAID Wings	*Apple*	7
23	22	BLACK PUDDING BERTHA Goodies	*Bradley's*	3
28	23	JIVE TALKIN' Bee Gees	*RSO*	2
33	24	SEALED WITH A KISS Brian Hyland	*ABC*	2
16	25	MR. RAFFLES (MAN IT WAS MEAN) Steve Harley and Cockney Rebel	*EMI*	6
-	26	ROLLIN' STONE David Essex	*CBS*	1
21	27	MAMA NEVER TOLD ME Sister Sledge	*Atlantic*	3
27	28	SOMEONE SAVED MY LIFE TONIGHT Elton John	*DJM*	2
-	29	FOOT STOMPIN' MUSIC Hamilton Bohannon	*Brunswick*	1
36	30	I WRITE THE SONGS/....FOR LOVE David Cassidy	*RCA*	2
11	31	THE PROUD ONE Osmonds	*MGM*	8
20	32	OH WHAT A SHAME Roy Wood	*Jet*	6
-	[33]	YOU GO TO MY HEAD Bryan Ferry	*Island*	1
24	34	THE WAY WE WERE Gladys Knight And The Pips	*Buddah*	14
31	35	SWEARIN' TO GOD Frankie Valli	*Private Stock*	3
25	36	STAND BY YOUR MAN Tammy Wynette	*Epic*	11
-	[37]	IT OUGHTA SELL A MILLION Lyn Paul ●	*Polydor*	1
26	38	SING BABY SING Stylistics	*Avco*	10
-	39	NEW YORK CITY T. Rex	*EMI*	1
-	[40]	LONG LOST LOVER Three Degrees	*Philadelphia*	1

LW	TW	*WEEK ENDING* **19 JULY 1975**		Wks
7	[1]	GIVE A LITTLE LOVE Bay City Rollers	*Bell*	2
1	2	TEARS ON MY PILLOW Johnny Nash	*CBS*	6
2	3	MISTY Ray Stevens	*Janus*	5
3	4	THE HUSTLE Van McCoy	*Avco*	8
13	5	BARBADOS Typically Tropical	*Gull*	3
5	6	HAVE YOU SEEN HER/OH GIRL Chi-Lites	*Brunswick*	5
10	[7]	EIGHTEEN WITH A BULLET Pete Wingfield	*Island*	3
4	8	I'M NOT IN LOVE 10CC	*Mercury*	7
8	9	DISCO STOMP Hamilton Bohannon	*Brunswick*	8
19	10	JE T'AIME Judge Dread	*Cactus*	3
26	11	ROLLIN' STONE David Essex	*CBS*	2
23	12	JIVE TALKIN' Bee Gees	*RSO*	3
11	13	MOONSHINE SALLY Mud	*RAK*	5
24	14	SEALED WITH A KISS Brian Hyland	*ABC*	3
9	15	WHISPERING GRASS Windsor Davies/Don Estelle	*EMI*	10
20	16	D.I.V.O.R.C.E. Tammy Wynette	*Epic*	4
14	17	MY WHITE BICYCLE Nazareth	*Mooncrest*	6
6	18	DOING ALRIGHT WITH THE BOYS Gary Glitter	*Bell*	5
22	[19]	BLACK PUDDING BERTHA Goodies	*Bradley's*	4
27	[20]	MAMA NEVER TOLD ME Sister Sledge	*Atlantic*	4
15	21	FOE-DEE-O-DEE Rubettes	*State*	4
28	[22]	SOMEONE SAVED MY LIFE TONIGHT Elton John	*DJM*	3
30	23	I WRITE THE SONGS/....FOR LOVE David Cassidy	*RCA*	3
18	24	MAKE THE WORLD GO AWAY Donny And Marie Osmond	*MGM*	5
12	25	THREE STEPS TO HEAVEN Showaddywaddy	*Bell*	9
17	26	I DON'T LOVE YOU BUT I THINK I LIKE YOU Gilbert O'Sullivan	*MAM*	5
-	27	ACTION Sweet	*RCA*	1
-	28	IT'S IN HIS KISS Linda Lewis	*Arista*	1
29	29	FOOT STOMPIN' MUSIC Hamilton Bohannon	*Brunswick*	2
39	30	NEW YORK CITY T. Rex	*EMI*	2
-	31	BLANKET ON THE GROUND Billie Jo Spears ●	*United Artists*	1
21	32	LISTEN TO WHAT THE MAN SAID Wings	*Apple*	8
33	[33]	YOU GO TO MY HEAD Bryan Ferry	*Island*	2
35	34	SWEARIN' TO GOD Frankie Valli	*Private Stock*	4
-	35	HIGHWIRE Linda Carr And The Love Squad ●	*Chelsea*	1
-	36	HARMOUR LOVE Syreeta	*Tamla Motown*	1
-	[37]	SWEET CHEATIN' RITA Alvin Stardust	*Magnet*	1
-	[38]	PER-SO-NAL-LY Wigan's Ovation	*Spark*	1
16	39	BABY I LOVE YOU, OK Kenny	*RAK*	6
-	40	IF YOU THINK YOU KNOW HOW TO LOVE ME Smokie ●	*RAK*	1

August 1975

□ Highest position disc reached ● Act's first ever week on chart

LW	TW	*WEEK ENDING* **26 JULY 1975**		Wks
1	[1]	GIVE A LITTLE LOVE Bay City Rollers	*Bell*	3
5	2	BARBADOS Typically Tropical	*Gull*	4
2	3	TEARS ON MY PILLOW Johnny Nash	*CBS*	7
3	4	MISTY Ray Stevens	*Janus*	6
11	[5]	ROLLIN' STONE David Essex	*CBS*	3
6	6	HAVE YOU SEEN HER/OH GIRL Chi-Lites	*Brunswick*	6
4	7	THE HUSTLE Van McCoy	*Avco*	9
7	8	EIGHTEEN WITH A BULLET Pete Wingfield	*Island*	4
10	[9]	JE T'AIME Judge Dread	*Cactus*	4
14	10	SEALED WITH A KISS Bryan Hyland	*ABC*	4
12	11	JIVE TALKIN' Bee Gees	*RSO*	4
16	[12]	D.I.V.O.R.C.E. Tammy Wynette	*Epic*	5
28	13	IT'S IN HIS KISS Linda Lewis	*Arista*	2
8	14	I'M NOT IN LOVE 10CC	*Mercury*	8
9	15	DISCO STOMP Hamilton Bohannon	*Brunswick*	9
40	16	IF YOU THINK YOU KNOW HOW TO LOVE ME Smokie	*RAK*	2
27	17	ACTION Sweet	*RCA*	2
23	18	I WRITE THE SONGS/....FOR LOVE David Cassidy	*RCA*	4
21	19	FOE-DEE-O-DEE Rubettes	*State*	5
30	20	NEW YORK CITY T. Rex	*EMI*	3
17	21	MY WHITE BICYCLE Nazareth	*Mooncrest*	7
13	22	MOONSHINE SALLY Mud	*RAK*	6
29	[23]	FOOT STOMPIN' MUSIC Hamilton Bohannon	*Brunswick*	3
19	24	BLACK PUDDING BERTHA Goodies	*Bradley's*	5
-	25	SHERRY Adrian Baker ●	*Magnet*	1
18	26	DOING ALRIGHT WITH THE BOYS Gary Glitter	*Bell*	6
15	27	WHISPERING GRASS Windsor Davies/Don Estelle	*EMI*	11
31	28	BLANKET ON THE GROUND Billie Jo Spears	*United Artists*	2
22	29	SOMEONE SAVED MY LIFE TONIGHT Elton John	*DJM*	4
35	30	HIGHWIRE Linda Carr And The Love Squad	*Chelsea*	2
-	31	DELILAH Sensational Alex Harvey Band ●	*Vertigo*	1
36	[32]	HARMOUR LOVE Syreeta	*Tamla Motown*	2
-	33	7-6-5-4-3-2-1 (BLOW YOUR WHISTLE) Rimshots ●	*All Platinum*	1
-	34	DOLLY MY LOVE Moments ●	*All Platinum*	1
-	35	I CAN'T GIVE YOU ANYTHING (BUT MY LOVE) Stylistics	*Avco*	1
20	36	MAMA NEVER TOLD ME Sister Sledge	*Atlantic*	5
-	37	IT'S BEEN SO LONG George McCrae	*Jay Boy*	1
25	38	THREE STEPS TO HEAVEN Showaddywaddy	*Bell*	10
-	39	LOVE ME BABY Susan Cadogan	*Magnet*	1
24	40	MAKE THE WORLD GO AWAY Donny And Marie Osmond	*MGM*	6

LW	TW	*WEEK ENDING* **2 AUGUST 1975**		Wks
1	[1]	GIVE A LITTLE LOVE Bay City Rollers	*Bell*	4
2	2	BARBADOS Typically Tropical	*Gull*	5
3	3	TEARS ON MY PILLOW Johnny Nash	*CBS*	8
4	4	MISTY Ray Stevens	*Janus*	7

■Johnny Nash's *Tears On My Pillow* is not the same song as the one that Kylie Minogue took to number one sixteen years later (12.07.75) ■ Plenty of lead singers of chart groups having solo hits - David Cassidy of the Partridge Family, Roy Wood of Wizzard, Bryan Ferry of Roxy Music, Frankie Valli of the Four Seasons and Lyn Paul of the New Seekers (12.07.75)■

August 1975

□ Highest position disc reached ● Act's first ever week on chart

LW	TW	Title / Artist	Label	Wks
11	5	JIVE TALKIN' Bee Gees	RSO	5
16	6	IF YOU THINK YOU KNOW HOW TO LOVE ME Smokie	RAK	3
10	7	SEALED WITH A KISS Brian Hyland	ABC	5
13	8	IT'S IN HIS KISS Linda Lewis	Arista	3
7	9	THE HUSTLE Van McCoy	Avco	10
9	10	JE T'AIME Judge Dread	Cactus	5
5	11	ROLLIN' STONE David Essex	CBS	4
35	12	I CAN'T GIVE YOU ANYTHING (BUT MY LOVE) Stylistics	Avco	2
6	13	HAVE YOU SEEN HER/OH GIRL Chi-Lites	Brunswick	7
8	14	EIGHTEEN WITH A BULLET Pete Wingfield	Island	5
17	15	ACTION Sweet	RCA	3
31	16	DELILAH Sensational Alex Harvey Band	Vertigo	2
18	17	I WRITE THE SONGS/....FOR LOVE David Cassidy	RCA	5
12	18	D.I.V.O.R.C.E. Tammy Wynette	Epic	6
20	19	NEW YORK CITY T. Rex	EMI	4
30	20	HIGHWIRE Linda Carr And The Love Squad	Chelsea	3
28	21	BLANKET ON THE GROUND Billie Jo Spears	United Artists	3
25	22	SHERRY Adrian Baker	Magnet	2
34	23	DOLLY MY LOVE Moments	All Platinum	2
14	24	I'M NOT IN LOVE 10CC	Mercury	9
23	25	FOOT STOMPIN' MUSIC Hamilton Bohannon	Brunswick	4
33	26	7-6-5-4-3-2-1 (BLOW YOUR WHISTLE) Rimshots	All Platinum	2
15	27	DISCO STOMP Hamilton Bohannon	Brunswick	10
37	28	IT'S BEEN SO LONG George McCrae	Jay Boy	2
-	29	THE LAST FAREWELL Roger Whittaker	EMI	1
39	30	LOVE ME BABY Susan Cadogan	Magnet	2
-	31	GET IN THE SWING Sparks	Island	1
27	32	WHISPERING GRASS Windsor Davies/Don Estelle	EMI	12
-	33	EL BIMBO Bimbo Jet ●	EMI	1
24	34	BLACK PUDDING BERTHA Goodies	Bradley's	6
21	35	MY WHITE BICYCLE Nazareth	Mooncrest	8
22	36	MOONSHINE SALLY Mud	RAK	7
-	37	SEXY M.F.S.B.	Philadelphia	1
-	38	I DO I DO I DO Abba	Epic	1
26	39	DOING ALRIGHT WITH THE BOYS Gary Glitter	Bell	7
32	40	HARMOUR LOVE Syreeta	Tamla Motown	3

LW	TW	*WEEK ENDING* **9 AUGUST 1975**		Wks
2	1	BARBADOS Typically Tropical	Gull	6
1	2	GIVE A LITTLE LOVE Bay City Rollers	Bell	5
12	3	I CAN'T GIVE YOU ANYTHING (BUT MY LOVE) Stylistics	Avco	3
6	4	IF YOU THINK YOU KNOW HOW TO LOVE ME Smokie	RAK	4
5	5	JIVE TALKIN' Bee Gees	RSO	6
8	6	IT'S IN HIS KISS Linda Lewis	Arista	4
7	7	SEALED WITH A KISS Brian Hyland	ABC	6
16	8	DELILAH Sensational Alex Harvey Band	Vertigo	3
10	9	JE T'AIME Judge Dread	Cactus	6
3	10	TEARS ON MY PILLOW Johnny Nash	CBS	9
17	11	I WRITE THE SONGS/....FOR LOVE David Cassidy	RCA	6
22	12	SHERRY Adrian Baker	Magnet	3
28	13	IT'S BEEN SO LONG George McCrae	Jay Boy	3
29	14	THE LAST FAREWELL Roger Whittaker	EMI	2
19	15	NEW YORK CITY T. Rex	EMI	5
21	16	BLANKET ON THE GROUND Billie Jo Spears	United Artists	4
11	17	ROLLIN' STONE David Essex	CBS	5
23	18	DOLLY MY LOVE Moments	All Platinum	3
15	19	ACTION Sweet	RCA	4
4	20	MISTY Ray Stevens	Janus	8
13	21	HAVE YOU SEEN HER/OH GIRL Chi-Lites	Brunswick	8
18	22	D.I.V.O.R.C.E. Tammy Wynette	Epic	7
9	23	THE HUSTLE Van McCoy	Avco	11
20	24	HIGHWIRE Linda Carr And The Love Squad	Chelsea	4
30	25	LOVE ME BABY Susan Cadogan	Magnet	3
33	26	EL BIMBO Bimbo Jet	EMI	2
26	27	7-6-5-4-3-2-1 (BLOW YOUR WHISTLE) Rimshots	All Platinum	3
31	28	GET IN THE SWING Sparks	Island	2
25	29	FOOT STOMPIN' MUSIC Hamilton Bohannon	Brunswick	5
-	30	BEST THING THAT EVER HAPPENED Gladys Knight And The Pips	Buddah	1
14	31	EIGHTEEN WITH A BULLET Pete Wingfield	Island	6
-	32	ONE NIGHT Mud	RAK	1
-	33	FAME David Bowie	RCA	1
27	34	DISCO STOMP Hamilton Bohannon	Brunswick	11
-	35	SUMMER OF '42 Biddu Orchestra ●	Epic	1
-	36	SUPER WOMBLE Wombles	CBS	1
37	37	SEXY M.F.S.B.	Philadelphia	2
-	38	THAT'S THE WAY (I LIKE IT) K.C. And The Sunshine Band	Jay Boy	1
-	39	LOVE WILL KEEP US TOGETHER The Captain And Tennille ●	A&M	1
24	40	I'M NOT IN LOVE 10CC	Mercury	10

LW	TW	*WEEK ENDING* **16 AUGUST 1975**		Wks
3	1	I CAN'T GIVE YOU ANYTHING (BUT MY LOVE) Stylistics	Avco	5
1	2	BARBADOS Typically Tropical	Gull	7
4	3	IF YOU THINK YOU KNOW HOW TO LOVE ME Smokie	RAK	5
2	4	GIVE A LITTLE LOVE Bay City Rollers	Bell	6
14	5	THE LAST FAREWELL Roger Whittaker	EMI	3
5	6	JIVE TALKIN' Bee Gees	RSO	7
8	7	DELILAH Sensational Alex Harvey Band	Vertigo	4
13	8	IT'S BEEN SO LONG George McCrae	Jay Boy	4
6	9	IT'S IN HIS KISS Linda Lewis	Arista	5
12	10	SHERRY Adrian Baker	Magnet	4
16	11	BLANKET ON THE GROUND Billie Jo Spears	United Artists	5
7	12	SEALED WITH A KISS Brian Hyland	ABC	7
18	13	DOLLY MY LOVE Moments	All Platinum	4
10	14	TEARS ON MY PILLOW Johnny Nash	CBS	10
24	15	HIGHWIRE Linda Carr And The Love Squad	Chelsea	5
9	16	JE T'AIME Judge Dread	Cactus	7
15	17	NEW YORK CITY T. Rex	EMI	6
11	18	I WRITE THE SONGS/....FOR LOVE David Cassidy	RCA	7
26	19	EL BIMBO Bimbo Jet	EMI	3
30	20	BEST THING THAT EVER HAPPENED Gladys Knight And The Pips	Buddah	2
19	21	ACTION Sweet	RCA	5
25	22	LOVE ME BABY Susan Cadogan	Magnet	4
38	23	THAT'S THE WAY (I LIKE IT) K.C. And The Sunshine Band	Jay Boy	2
-	24	SAILING Rod Stewart	Warner Bros.	1
20	25	MISTY Ray Stevens	Janus	9
35	26	SUMMER OF '42 Biddu Orchestra	Epic	2
28	27	GET IN THE SWING Sparks	Island	3
36	28	SUPER WOMBLE Wombles	CBS	2
23	29	THE HUSTLE Van McCoy	Avco	12
33	30	FAME David Bowie	RCA	2
27	31	7-6-5-4-3-2-1 (BLOW YOUR WHISTLE) Rimshots	All Platinum	4
39	32	LOVE WILL KEEP US TOGETHER The Captain And Tennille	A&M	2
32	33	ONE NIGHT Mud	RAK	2
17	34	ROLLIN' STONE David Essex	CBS	6
-	35	DON'T THROW IT ALL AWAY Gary Benson ●	State	1
-	36	ROCHDALE COWBOY Mike Harding ●	Rubber	1
21	37	HAVE YOU SEEN HER/OH GIRL Chi-Lites	Brunswick	9
-	38	ONE OF THESE NIGHTS Eagles ●	Asylum	1
37	39	SEXY M.F.S.B.	Philadelphia	3
-	40	LOVE IN THE SUN Glitter Band	Bell	1

LW	TW	*WEEK ENDING* **23 AUGUST 1975**		Wks
1	1	I CAN'T GIVE YOU ANYTHING (BUT MY LOVE) Stylistics	Avco	6
24	2	SAILING Rod Stewart	Warner Bros.	2
5	3	THE LAST FAREWELL Roger Whittaker	EMI	4
2	4	BARBADOS Typically Tropical	Gull	8
3	5	IF YOU THINK YOU KNOW HOW TO LOVE ME Smokie	RAK	6
8	6	IT'S BEEN SO LONG George McCrae	Jay Boy	5
11	7	BLANKET ON THE GROUND Billie Jo Spears	United Artists	6

In these weeks ■ Thirteen years after it peaked at number three, Brian Hyland's *Sealed With A Kiss* stops at number seven (02.08.75) ■ Four songs with *Love* in the title, as well as another with the word in French, join two *Kiss* songs in the highly romantic Top Ten (09.08.75) ■ *Sailing* by Rod Stewart leaps from 24 to 2. All its weeks in the Top Ten are at number one or two (23.08.75)■

□ Highest position disc reached ● Act's first ever week on chart

LW	TW	Title	Artist	Label	Wks
23	8	THAT'S THE WAY (I LIKE IT)	K.C. And The Sunshine Band	*Jay Boy*	3
6	9	JIVE TALKIN'	Bee Gees	*RSO*	8
13	[10]	DOLLY MY LOVE	Moments	*All Platinum*	5
4	11	GIVE A LITTLE LOVE	Bay City Rollers	*Bell*	7
10	12	SHERRY	Adrian Baker	*Magnet*	5
9	13	IT'S IN HIS KISS	Linda Lewis	*Arista*	6
19	14	EL BIMBO	Bimbo Jet	*EMI*	4
20	15	BEST THING THAT EVER HAPPENED	Gladys Knight And The Pips	*Buddah*	3
12	16	SEALED WITH A KISS	Brian Hyland	*ABC*	8
7	17	DELILAH	Sensational Alex Harvey Band	*Vertigo*	5
26	18	SUMMER OF '42	Biddu Orchestra	*Epic*	3
30	19	FAME	David Bowie	*RCA*	3
28	[20]	SUPER WOMBLE	Wombles	*CBS*	3
17	21	NEW YORK CITY	T. Rex	*EMI*	7
22	[22]	LOVE ME BABY	Susan Cadogan	*Magnet*	5
16	23	JE T'AIME	Judge Dread	*Cactus*	8
15	24	HIGHWIRE	Linda Carr And The Love Squad	*Chelsea*	6
36	25	ROCHDALE COWBOY	Mike Harding	*Rubber*	2
18	26	I WRITE THE SONGS/....FOR LOVE	David Cassidy	*RCA*	8
35	27	DON'T THROW IT ALL AWAY	Gary Benson	*State*	2
-	28	A CHILD'S PRAYER	Hot Chocolate	*RAK*	1
40	29	LOVE IN THE SUN	Glitter Band	*Bell*	2
-	30	BRAZIL	Crispy And Company ●	*Creole*	1
38	31	ONE OF THESE NIGHTS	Eagles	*Asylum*	2
32	[32]	LOVE WILL KEEP US TOGETHER	The Captain And Tennille	*A&M*	3
27	33	GET IN THE SWING	Sparks	*Island*	4
14	34	TEARS ON MY PILLOW	Johnny Nash	*CBS*	11
-	35	JULIE-ANN	Kenny	*RAK*	1
-	36	SUMMERTIME CITY	Mike Batt ●	*Epic*	1
25	37	MISTY	Ray Stevens	*Janus*	10
33	38	ONE NIGHT	Mud	*RAK*	3
-	39	KNOCKIN' ON HEAVEN'S DOOR	Eric Clapton	*RSO*	1
-	40	LOVE WON'T LET ME WAIT	Major Harris	*Atlantic*	1

WEEK ENDING 30 AUGUST 1975

LW	TW	Title	Artist	Label	Wks
1	[1]	I CAN'T GIVE YOU ANYTHING (BUT MY LOVE)	Stylistics	*Avco*	7
2	2	SAILING	Rod Stewart	*Warner Bros.*	3
3	3	THE LAST FAREWELL	Roger Whittaker	*EMI*	5
6	[4]	IT'S BEEN SO LONG	George McCrae	*Jay Boy*	6
8	5	THAT'S THE WAY (I LIKE IT)	K.C. And The Sunshine Band	*Jay Boy*	4
7	[6]	BLANKET ON THE GROUND	Billie Jo Spears	*United Artists*	7
15	[7]	BEST THING THAT EVER HAPPENED	Gladys Knight And The Pips	*Buddah*	4
4	8	BARBADOS	Typically Tropical	*Gull*	9
36	9	SUMMERTIME CITY	Mike Batt	*Epic*	2
5	10	IF YOU THINK YOU KNOW HOW TO LOVE ME	Smokie	*RAK*	7
10	11	DOLLY MY LOVE	Moments	*All Platinum*	6
14	[12]	EL BIMBO	Bimbo Jet	*EMI*	5
-	13	FUNKY MOPED/MAGIC ROUNDABOUT	Jasper Carrott ●	*DJM*	1
18	[14]	SUMMER OF '42	Biddu Orchestra	*Epic*	4
17	15	DELILAH	Sensational Alex Harvey Band	*Vertigo*	6
12	16	SHERRY	Adrian Baker	*Magnet*	6
9	17	JIVE TALKIN'	Bee Gees	*RSO*	9
29	18	LOVE IN THE SUN	Glitter Band	*Bell*	3
35	19	JULIE-ANN	Kenny	*RAK*	2
28	20	A CHILD'S PRAYER	Hot Chocolate	*RAK*	2
19	21	FAME	David Bowie	*RCA*	4
25	[22]	ROCHDALE COWBOY	Mike Harding	*Rubber*	3
27	23	DON'T THROW IT ALL AWAY	Gary Benson	*State*	3
11	24	GIVE A LITTLE LOVE	Bay City Rollers	*Bell*	8
16	25	SEALED WITH A KISS	Brian Hyland	*ABC*	9
20	26	SUPER WOMBLE	Wombles	*CBS*	4
-	27	MOONLIGHTING	Leo Sayer	*Chrysalis*	1
22	28	LOVE ME BABY	Susan Cadogan	*Magnet*	6
31	29	ONE OF THESE NIGHTS	Eagles	*Asylum*	3
30	30	BRAZIL	Crispy And Company	*Creole*	2
23	31	JE T'AIME	Judge Dread	*Cactus*	9
24	32	HIGHWIRE	Linda Carr And The Love Squad	*Chelsea*	7
13	33	IT'S IN HIS KISS	Linda Lewis	*Arista*	7
-	34	FOOL	Al Matthews ●	*CBS*	1
-	35	PANDORA'S BOX	Procol Harum	*Chrysalis*	1
32	36	LOVE WILL KEEP US TOGETHER	The Captain And Tennille	*A&M*	4
40	[37]	LOVE WON'T LET ME WAIT	Major Harris	*Atlantic*	2
39	[38]	KNOCKIN' ON HEAVEN'S DOOR	Eric Clapton	*RSO*	2
-	39	SING A LITTLE SONG	Desmond Dekker	*Cactus*	1
21	40	NEW YORK CITY	T. Rex	*EMI*	8

WEEK ENDING 6 SEPTEMBER 1975

LW	TW	Title	Artist	Label	Wks
2	[1]	SAILING	Rod Stewart	*Warner Bros.*	4
1	2	I CAN'T GIVE YOU ANYTHING (BUT MY LOVE)	Stylistics	*Avco*	8
3	3	THE LAST FAREWELL	Roger Whittaker	*EMI*	6
5	4	THAT'S THE WAY (I LIKE IT)	K.C. And The Sunshine Band	*Jay Boy*	5
4	5	IT'S BEEN SO LONG	George McCrae	*Jay Boy*	7
9	6	SUMMERTIME CITY	Mike Batt	*Epic*	3
6	7	BLANKET ON THE GROUND	Billy Jo Spears	*United Artists*	8
20	8	A CHILD'S PRAYER	Hot Chocolate	*RAK*	3
7	9	BEST THING THAT EVER HAPPENED	Gladys Knight And The Pips	*Buddah*	5
13	10	FUNKY MOPED/MAGIC ROUNDABOUT	Jasper Carrott	*DJM*	2
27	11	MOONLIGHTING	Leo Sayer	*Chrysalis*	2
19	12	JULIE-ANN	Kenny	*RAK*	3
12	13	EL BIMBO	Bimbo Jet	*EMI*	6
11	14	DOLLY MY LOVE	Moments	*All Platinum*	7
14	15	SUMMER OF '42	Biddu Orchestra	*Epic*	5
18	16	LOVE IN THE SUN	Glitter Band	*Bell*	4
21	17	FAME	David Bowie	*RCA*	5
8	18	BARBADOS	Typically Tropical	*Gull*	10
10	19	IF YOU THINK YOU KNOW HOW TO LOVE ME	Smokie	*RAK*	8
26	20	SUPER WOMBLE	Wombles	*CBS*	5
35	21	PANDORA'S BOX	Procol Harum	*Chrysalis*	2
-	22	MOTOR BIKING	Chris Spedding ●	*RAK*	1
29	23	ONE OF THESE NIGHTS	Eagles	*Asylum*	4
39	24	SING A LITTLE SONG	Desmond Dekker	*Cactus*	2
23	25	DON'T THROW IT ALL AWAY	Gary Benson	*State*	4
30	26	BRAZIL	Crispy And Company	*Creole*	3
22	27	ROCHDALE COWBOY	Mike Harding	*Rubber*	4
34	28	FOOL	Al Matthews	*CBS*	2
-	29	HEARTBEAT	Showaddywaddy	*Bell*	1
-	30	I'M ON FIRE	5000 Volts ●	*Phillips*	1
16	31	SHERRY	Adrian Baker	*Magnet*	7
15	32	DELILAH	Sensational Alex Harvey Band	*Vertigo*	7
24	33	GIVE A LITTLE LOVE	Bay City Rollers	*Bell*	9
17	34	JIVE TALKIN'	Bee Gees	*RSO*	10
25	35	SEALED WITH A KISS	Brian Hyland	*ABC*	10
-	36	FEEL LIKE MAKIN' LOVE	Bad Company	*Island*	1
-	37	SOLITAIRE	Carpenters	*A&M*	1
-	38	SCOTCH ON THE ROCKS	Band of the Black Watch ●	*Spark*	1
-	[39]	DO IT AGAIN	Steely Dan ●	*ABC*	1
-	40	LIKE A BUTTERFLY	Mac And Katie Kissoon	*State*	1

WEEK ENDING 13 SEPTEMBER 1975

LW	TW	Title	Artist	Label	Wks
1	[1]	SAILING	Rod Stewart	*Warner Bros.*	5
3	[2]	THE LAST FAREWELL	Roger Whittaker	*EMI*	7
2	3	I CAN'T GIVE YOU ANYTHING (BUT MY LOVE)	Stylistics	*Avco*	9
11	4	MOONLIGHTING	Leo Sayer	*Chrysalis*	3
4	5	THAT'S THE WAY (I LIKE IT)	K.C. And The Sunshine Band	*Jay Boy*	6
6	6	SUMMERTIME CITY	Mike Batt	*Epic*	4
8	7	A CHILD'S PRAYER	Hot Chocolate	*RAK*	4

■Jasper Carrott's double-sided blockbuster joins Mike Harding, Typically Tropical and the Wombles on the funny side of the chart (30.08.75) ■ The Wombles and their musical creator, Mike Batt, enjoy separate Top 20 hits in the same week (06.09.75)■

September 1975

□ Highest position disc reached ● Act's first ever week on chart

LW	TW	Title	Artist	Label	Wks
10	8	FUNKY MOPED/MAGIC ROUNDABOUT	Jasper Carrott	*DJM*	3
9	9	BEST THING THAT EVER HAPPENED	Gladys Knight And The Pips	*Buddah*	6
12	10	JULIE-ANN	Kenny	*RAK*	4
5	11	IT'S BEEN SO LONG	George McCrae	*Jay Boy*	8
30	12	I'M ON FIRE	5000 Volts	*Phillips*	2
29	13	HEARTBEAT	Showaddywaddy	*Bell*	2
7	14	BLANKET ON THE GROUND	Billie Jo Spears	*United Artists*	9
16	15	LOVE IN THE SUN	Glitter Band	*Bell*	5
28	16	FOOL	Al Matthews	*CBS*	3
15	17	SUMMER OF '42	Biddu Orchestra	*Epic*	6
21	18	PANDORA'S BOX	Procol Harum	*Chrysalis*	3
22	19	MOTOR BIKING	Chris Spedding	*RAK*	2
25	20	DON'T THROW IT ALL AWAY	Gary Benson	*State*	5
13	21	EL BIMBO	Bimbo Jet	*EMI*	7
24	22	SING A LITTLE SONG	Desmond Dekker	*Cactus*	3
14	23	DOLLY MY LOVE	Moments	*All Platinum*	8
-	24	UNA PALOMA BLANCA	Jonathan King	*U.K.*	1
23	25	ONE OF THESE NIGHTS	Eagles	*Asylum*	5
-	26	THERE GOES MY FIRST LOVE	Drifters	*Bell*	1
27	27	ROCHDALE COWBOY	Mike Harding	*Rubber*	5
-	28	PALOMA BLANCA	George Baker Selection ●	*Warner Bros.*	1
36	29	FEEL LIKE MAKIN' LOVE	Bad Company	*Island*	2
17	30	FAME	David Bowie	*RCA*	6
40	31	LIKE A BUTTERFLY	Mac And Katie Kissoon	*State*	2
18	32	BARBADOS	Typically Tropical	*Gull*	11
26	33	BRAZIL	Crispy And Company	*Creole*	4
19	34	IF YOU THINK YOU KNOW HOW TO LOVE ME	Smokie	*RAK*	9
38	35	SCOTCH ON THE ROCKS	Band of the Black Watch	*Spark*	2
-	36	FATTIE BUM BUM	Carl Malcolm ●	*UK*	1
37	37	SOLITAIRE	Carpenters	*A&M*	2
-	38	SINGLE GIRL	Sandy Posey	*MGM*	1
20	39	SUPER WOMBLE	Wombles	*CBS*	6
39	40	DO IT AGAIN	Steely Dan	*ABC*	2

WEEK ENDING 20 SEPTEMBER 1975

LW	TW	Title	Artist	Label	Wks
1	[1]	SAILING	Rod Stewart	*Warner Bros.*	6
4	[2]	MOONLIGHTING	Leo Sayer	*Chrysalis*	4
2	3	THE LAST FAREWELL	Roger Whittaker	*EMI*	8
6	[4]	SUMMERTIME CITY	Mike Batt	*Epic*	5
8	[5]	FUNKY MOPED/MAGIC ROUNDABOUT	Jasper Carrott	*DJM*	4
12	6	I'M ON FIRE	5000 Volts	*Phillips*	3
13	[7]	HEARTBEAT	Showaddywaddy	*Bell*	3
7	8	A CHILD'S PRAYER	Hot Chocolate	*RAK*	5
-	9	HOLD ME CLOSE	David Essex	*CBS*	1
5	10	THAT'S THE WAY (I LIKE IT)	K.C. And The Sunshine Band	*Jay Boy*	7
10	11	JULIE-ANN	Kenny	*RAK*	5
3	12	I CAN'T GIVE YOU ANYTHING (BUT MY LOVE)	Stylistics	*Avco*	10
26	13	THERE GOES MY FIRST LOVE	Drifters	*Bell*	2
19	[14]	MOTOR BIKING	Chris Spedding	*RAK*	3
11	15	IT'S BEEN SO LONG	George McCrae	*Jay Boy*	9
18	[16]	PANDORA'S BOX	Procol Harum	*Chrysalis*	4
9	17	BEST THING THAT EVER HAPPENED	Gladys Knight And The Pips	*Buddah*	7
36	18	FATTIE BUM BUM	Carl Malcolm	*UK*	2
24	19	UNA PALOMA BLANCA	Jonathan King	*U.K.*	2
15	20	LOVE IN THE SUN	Glitter Band	*Bell*	6
22	21	SING A LITTLE SONG	Desmond Dekker	*Cactus*	4
16	22	FOOL	Al Matthews	*CBS*	4
14	23	BLANKET ON THE GROUND	Billie Jo Spears	*United Artists*	10
-	24	I ONLY HAVE EYES FOR YOU	Art Garfunkel ●	*CBS*	1
28	25	PALOMA BLANCA	George Baker Selection	*Warner Bros.*	2
20	26	DON'T THROW IT ALL AWAY	Gary Benson	*State*	6
17	27	SUMMER OF '42	Biddu Orchestra	*Epic*	7
29	28	FEEL LIKE MAKIN' LOVE	Bad Company	*Island*	3
35	29	SCOTCH ON THE ROCKS	Band of the Black Watch	*Spark*	3
31	30	LIKE A BUTTERFLY	Mac And Katie Kissoon	*State*	3
21	31	EL BIMBO	Bimbo Jet	*EMI*	8
37	[32]	SOLITAIRE	Carpenters	*A&M*	3
-	33	IT'S TIME FOR LOVE	Chi-Lites	*Brunswick*	1
-	34	FALLIN' IN LOVE	Hamilton Joe Frank and Reynolds ●	*Pye*	1
25	35	ONE OF THESE NIGHTS	Eagles	*Asylum*	6
38	36	SINGLE GIRL	Sandy Posey	*MGM*	2
-	37	FATTIE BUM BUM	Diversions ●	*Gull*	1
27	38	ROCHDALE COWBOY	Mike Harding	*Rubber*	6
30	39	FAME	David Bowie	*RCA*	7
-	[40]	YUM YUM (GIMME SOME)	Fatback Band ●	*Polydor*	1

WEEK ENDING 27 SEPTEMBER 1975

LW	TW	Title	Artist	Label	Wks
1	[1]	SAILING	Rod Stewart	*Warner Bros.*	7
9	2	HOLD ME CLOSE	David Essex	*CBS*	2
2	3	MOONLIGHTING	Leo Sayer	*Chrysalis*	5
6	[4]	I'M ON FIRE	5000 Volts	*Phillips*	4
5	[5]	FUNKY MOPED/MAGIC ROUNDABOUT	Jasper Carrott	*DJM*	5
3	6	THE LAST FAREWELL	Roger Whittaker	*EMI*	9
7	[7]	HEARTBEAT	Showaddywaddy	*Bell*	4
13	8	THERE GOES MY FIRST LOVE	Drifters	*Bell*	3
8	9	A CHILD'S PRAYER	Hot Chocolate	*RAK*	6
24	10	I ONLY HAVE EYES FOR YOU	Art Garfunkel	*CBS*	2
18	11	FATTIE BUM BUM	Carl Malcolm	*UK*	3
19	12	UNA PALOMA BLANCA	Jonathan King	*U.K.*	3
4	13	SUMMERTIME CITY	Mike Batt	*Epic*	6
14	[14]	MOTOR BIKING	Chris Spedding	*RAK*	4
11	15	JULIE-ANN	Kenny	*RAK*	6
21	[16]	SING A LITTLE SONG	Desmond Dekker	*Cactus*	5
22	17	FOOL	Al Matthews	*CBS*	5
16	18	PANDORA'S BOX	Procol Harum	*Chrysalis*	5
10	19	THAT'S THE WAY (I LIKE IT)	K.C. And The Sunshine Band	*Jay Boy*	8
30	20	LIKE A BUTTERFLY	Mac And Katie Kissoon	*State*	4
25	21	PALOMA BLANCA	George Baker Selection	*Warner Bros.*	3
28	22	FEEL LIKE MAKIN' LOVE	Bad Company	*Island*	4
17	23	BEST THING THAT EVER HAPPENED	Gladys Knight And The Pips	*Buddah*	8
12	24	I CAN'T GIVE YOU ANYTHING (BUT MY LOVE)	Stylistics	*Avco*	11
29	25	SCOTCH ON THE ROCKS	Band of the Black Watch	*Spark*	4
33	26	IT'S TIME FOR LOVE	Chi-Lites	*Brunswick*	2
20	27	LOVE IN THE SUN	Glitter Band	*Bell*	7
23	28	BLANKET ON THE GROUND	Billie Jo Spears	*United Artists*	11
15	29	IT'S BEEN SO LONG	George McCrae	*Jay Boy*	10
-	30	WHO LOVES YOU	Four Seasons	*Warner Bros.*	1
-	31	S.O.S.	Abba	*Epic*	1
26	32	DON'T THROW IT ALL AWAY	Gary Benson	*State*	7
34	[33]	FALLIN' IN LOVE	Hamilton Joe Frank and Reynolds	*Pye*	2
37	[34]	FATTIE BUM BUM	Diversions	*Gull*	2
36	[35]	SINGLE GIRL	Sandy Posey	*MGM*	3
-	[36]	CHICK-A-BOOM	53rd And 3rd ●	*UK*	1
-	37	NAPPY LOVE/WILD THING	Goodies	*Bradley's*	1
-	38	FEELINGS	Morris Albert ●	*Decca*	1
31	39	EL BIMBO	Bimbo Jet	*EMI*	9
-	40	NO WOMAN NO CRY	Bob Marley And The Wailers ●	*Island*	1

WEEK ENDING 4 OCTOBER 1975

LW	TW	Title	Artist	Label	Wks
2	[1]	HOLD ME CLOSE	David Essex	*CBS*	3
1	2	SAILING	Rod Stewart	*Warner Bros.*	8
8	[3]	THERE GOES MY FIRST LOVE	Drifters	*Bell*	4
10	4	I ONLY HAVE EYES FOR YOU	Art Garfunkel	*CBS*	3
3	5	MOONLIGHTING	Leo Sayer	*Chrysalis*	6
5	6	FUNKY MOPED/MAGIC ROUNDABOUT	Jasper Carrott	*DJM*	6
7	[7]	HEARTBEAT	Showaddywaddy	*Bell*	5
4	8	I'M ON FIRE	5000 Volts	*Phillips*	5
11	9	FATTIE BUM BUM	Carl Malcolm	*UK*	4
12	10	UNA PALOMA BLANCA	Jonathan King	*U.K.*	4
21	11	PALOMA BLANCA	George Baker	*Warner Bros.*	4
6	12	THE LAST FAREWELL	Roger Whittaker	*EMI*	10
25	13	SCOTCH ON THE ROCKS	Band of the Black Watch	*Spark*	5
30	14	WHO LOVES YOU	Four Seasons	*Warner Bros.*	2

In these weeks ■ The top nine records were by British acts (20.09.75) ■ Sandy Posey's *Single Girl* returns to the Top 40 eight years after its previous chart appearance, but this time round only climbs to number 35 (27.09.75) ■ This is not an era of great lyrics: two versions of *Fattie Bum Bum*, the Goodies' *Nappy Love* and K.C. and the Sunshine Band's *That's The Way (I Like It)* are examples of minimal lyrical skills (27.09.75)■

LW	TW	Title	Artist	Label	Wks
26	15	IT'S TIME FOR LOVE	Chi-Lites	Brunswick	3
31	16	S.O.S.	Abba	Epic	2
14	17	MOTOR BIKING	Chris Spedding	RAK	5
20	[18]	LIKE A BUTTERFLY	Mac And Katie Kissoon	State	5
-	19	BIG TEN	Judge Dread	Cactus	1
16	20	SING A LITTLE SONG	Desmond Dekker	Cactus	6
13	21	SUMMERTIME CITY	Mike Batt	Epic	7
9	22	A CHILD'S PRAYER	Hot Chocolate	RAK	7
38	23	FEELINGS	Morris Albert	Decca	2
18	24	PANDORA'S BOX	Procol Harum	Chrysalis	6
15	25	JULIE-ANN	Kenny	RAK	7
22	26	FEEL LIKE MAKIN' LOVE	Bad Company	Island	5
-	27	L-L-LUCY	Mud	Private Stock	1
19	28	THAT'S THE WAY (I LIKE IT)	K.C. And The Sunshine Band	Jay Boy	9
37	29	NAPPY LOVE/WILD THING	Goodies	Bradley's	2
40	30	NO WOMAN NO CRY	Bob Marley And The Wailers	Island	2
17	31	FOOL	Al Matthews	CBS	6
-	32	JUST A SMILE	Pilot	EMI	1
33	[33]	FALLIN' IN LOVE	Hamilton Joe Frank and Reynolds	Pye	3
-	[34]	INDIAN LOVE CALL	Ray Stevens	Janus	1
28	35	BLANKET ON THE GROUND	Billie Jo Spears	United Artists	12
24	36	I CAN'T GIVE YOU ANYTHING (BUT MY LOVE)	Stylistics	Avco	12
23	37	BEST THING THAT EVER HAPPENED	Gladys Knight And The Pips	Buddah	9
36	38	CHICK-A-BOOM	53rd And 3rd	UK	2
-	39	DO IT ANYWAY YOU WANNA	People's Choice ●	Philadelphia	1
35	40	SINGLE GIRL	Sandy Posey	MGM	4

WEEK ENDING 11 OCTOBER 1975

LW	TW	Title	Artist	Label	Wks
1	[1]	HOLD ME CLOSE	David Essex	CBS	4
4	2	I ONLY HAVE EYES FOR YOU	Art Garfunkel	CBS	4
3	[3]	THERE GOES MY FIRST LOVE	Drifters	Bell	5
8	[4]	I'M ON FIRE	5000 Volts	Phillips	6
10	[5]	UNA PALOMA BLANCA	Jonathan King	U.K.	5
15	6	IT'S TIME FOR LOVE	Chi-Lites	Brunswick	4
6	7	FUNKY MOPED/MAGIC ROUNDABOUT	Jasper Carrott	DJM	7
9	[8]	FATTIE BUM BUM	Carl Malcolm	UK	5
14	9	WHO LOVES YOU	Four Seasons	Warner Bros.	3
11	[10]	PALOMA BLANCA	George Baker	Warner Bros.	5
2	11	SAILING	Rod Stewart	Warner Bros.	9
13	12	SCOTCH ON THE ROCKS	Band of the Black Watch	Spark	6
16	13	S.O.S.	Abba	Epic	3
23	14	FEELINGS	Morris Albert	Decca	3
27	15	L-L-LUCY	Mud	Private Stock	2
7	16	HEARTBEAT	Showaddywaddy	Bell	6
19	17	BIG TEN	Judge Dread	Cactus	2
5	18	MOONLIGHTING	Leo Sayer	Chrysalis	7
18	19	LIKE A BUTTERFLY	Mac And Katie Kissoon	State	6
26	[20]	FEEL LIKE MAKIN' LOVE	Bad Company	Island	6
29	[21]	NAPPY LOVE/WILD THING	Goodies	Bradley's	3
12	22	THE LAST FAREWELL	Roger Whittaker	EMI	11
-	23	SPACE ODDITY	David Bowie	RCA	1
-	24	DON'T PLAY YOUR ROCK AND ROLL TO ME	Smokie	RAK	1
-	25	WHAT A DIFFERENCE A DAY MADE	Esther Phillips ●	Kudu	1
-	26	ISLAND GIRL	Elton John	DJM	1
30	27	NO WOMAN NO CRY	Bob Marley And The Wailers	Island	3
20	28	SING A LITTLE SONG	Desmond Dekker	Cactus	7
17	29	MOTOR BIKING	Chris Spedding	RAK	6
-	30	LOOKS LOOKS LOOKS	Sparks	Island	1
32	[31]	JUST A SMILE	Pilot	EMI	2
-	32	RHINESTONE COWBOY	Glen Campbell	Capitol	1
-	33	REACHING FOR THE BEST	Exciters	20th Century	1
22	34	A CHILD'S PRAYER	Hot Chocolate	RAK	8
34	35	INDIAN LOVE CALL	Ray Stevens	Janus	2
39	[36]	DO IT ANYWAY YOU WANNA	People's Choice	Philadelphia	2
-	37	LOVE IS THE DRUG	Roxy Music	Island	1
31	38	FOOL	Al Matthews	CBS	7
33	39	FALLIN' IN LOVE	Hamilton Joe Frank and Reynolds	Pye	4
38	40	CHICK-A-BOOM	53rd And 3rd	UK	3

October 1975

□ Highest position disc reached ● Act's first ever week on chart

WEEK ENDING 18 OCTOBER 1975

LW	TW	Title	Artist	Label	Wks
1	[1]	HOLD ME CLOSE	David Essex	CBS	5
2	2	I ONLY HAVE EYES FOR YOU	Art Garfunkel	CBS	5
3	[3]	THERE GOES MY FIRST LOVE	Drifters	Bell	6
14	[4]	FEELINGS	Morris Albert	Decca	4
6	[5]	IT'S TIME FOR LOVE	Chi-Lites	Brunswick	5
9	[6]	WHO LOVES YOU	Four Seasons	Warner Bros.	4
13	7	S.O.S.	Abba	Epic	4
12	[8]	SCOTCH ON THE ROCKS	Band of the Black Watch	Spark	7
5	9	UNA PALOMA BLANCA	Jonathan King	U.K.	6
15	[10]	L-L-LUCY	Mud	Private Stock	3
23	11	SPACE ODDITY	David Bowie	RCA	2
24	12	DON'T PLAY YOUR ROCK AND ROLL TO ME	Smokie	RAK	2
8	13	FATTIE BUM BUM	Carl Malcolm	UK	6
17	[14]	BIG TEN	Judge Dread	Cactus	3
10	15	PALOMA BLANCA	George Baker	Warner Bros.	6
7	16	FUNKY MOPED/MAGIC ROUNDABOUT	Jasper Carrott	DJM	8
25	17	WHAT A DIFFERENCE A DAY MADE	Esther Phillips	Kudu	2
19	[18]	LIKE A BUTTERFLY	Mac And Katie Kissoon	State	7
4	19	I'M ON FIRE	5000 Volts	Phillips	7
11	20	SAILING	Rod Stewart	Warner Bros.	10
21	[21]	NAPPY LOVE/WILD THING	Goodies	Bradley's	4
26	22	ISLAND GIRL	Elton John	DJM	2
16	23	HEARTBEAT	Showaddywaddy	Bell	7
27	24	NO WOMAN NO CRY	Bob Marley And The Wailers	Island	4
32	25	RHINESTONE COWBOY	Glen Campbell	Capitol	2
30	[26]	LOOKS LOOKS LOOKS	Sparks	Island	2
37	27	LOVE IS THE DRUG	Roxy Music	Island	2
-	28	HOLD BACK THE NIGHT	Trammps	Buddah	1
20	29	FEEL LIKE MAKIN' LOVE	Bad Company	Island	7
22	30	THE LAST FAREWELL	Roger Whittaker	EMI	12
33	[31]	REACHING FOR THE BEST	Exciters	20th Century	2
18	32	MOONLIGHTING	Leo Sayer	Chrysalis	8
31	33	JUST A SMILE	Pilot	EMI	3
-	34	ROCK ON BROTHER	Chequers ●	Creole	1
-	35	THIS WILL BE	Natalie Cole ●	Capitol	1
-	36	DREAMY LADY	T. Rex Disco Party	EMI	1
-	37	RIDE A WILD HORSE	Dee Clark	Chelsea	1
35	38	INDIAN LOVE CALL	Ray Stevens	Janus	3
-	39	YOU	George Harrison	Apple	1
36	40	DO IT ANYWAY YOU WANNA	People's Choice	Philadelphia	3

WEEK ENDING 25 OCTOBER 1975

LW	TW	Title	Artist	Label	Wks
2	[1]	I ONLY HAVE EYES FOR YOU	Art Garfunkel	CBS	6
1	2	HOLD ME CLOSE	David Essex	CBS	6
3	[3]	THERE GOES MY FIRST LOVE	Drifters	Bell	7
11	4	SPACE ODDITY	David Bowie	RCA	3
4	5	FEELINGS	Morris Albert	Decca	5
7	[6]	S.O.S.	Abba	Epic	5
5	7	IT'S TIME FOR LOVE	Chi-Lites	Brunswick	6
12	[8]	DON'T PLAY YOUR ROCK AND ROLL TO ME	Smokie	RAK	3
6	9	WHO LOVES YOU	Four Seasons	Warner Bros.	5
8	10	SCOTCH ON THE ROCKS	Band of the Black Watch	Spark	8
9	11	UNA PALOMA BLANCA	Jonathan King	U.K.	7
17	12	WHAT A DIFFERENCE A DAY MADE	Esther Phillips	Kudu	3
15	13	PALOMA BLANCA	George Baker	Warner Bros.	7
10	14	L-L-LUCY	Mud	Private Stock	4
14	15	BIG TEN	Judge Dread	Cactus	4
27	16	LOVE IS THE DRUG	Roxy Music	Island	3
25	17	RHINESTONE COWBOY	Glen Campbell	Capitol	3
28	18	HOLD BACK THE NIGHT	Trammps	Buddah	2
16	19	FUNKY MOPED/MAGIC ROUNDABOUT	Jasper Carrott	DJM	9
22	20	ISLAND GIRL	Elton John	DJM	3
13	21	FATTIE BUM BUM	Carl Malcolm	UK	7
24	[22]	NO WOMAN NO CRY	Bob Marley And The Wailers	Island	5
34	23	ROCK ON BROTHER	Chequers	Creole	2
18	24	LIKE A BUTTERFLY	Mac And Katie Kissoon	State	8
-	25	HIGHFLY	John Miles ●	Decca	1

■Two versions of *Paloma Blanca* in the Top 10, one by Jonathan King whose distinctive singing voice can also be heard at the bottom of the chart, on 53rd And 3rd's hit *Chick-A-Boom* (11.10.75) ■ Paul Simon had already had four solo Top 40 hits before his erstwhile partner Art Garfunkel hit the charts, but Garfunkel got to the very top first (25.10.75)■

October 1975

□ Highest position disc reached ● Act's first ever week on chart

LW	TW	Title	Artist	Label	Wks
37	26	RIDE A WILD HORSE	Dee Clark	*Chelsea*	2
19	27	I'M ON FIRE	5000 Volts	*Phillips*	8
21	28	NAPPY LOVE/WILD THING	Goodies	*Bradley's*	5
-	29	I AIN'T LYIN'	George McCrae	*Jayboy*	1
26	30	LOOKS LOOKS LOOKS	Sparks	*Island*	3
-	31	BLUE GUITAR	Justin Hayward/John Lodge ●	*Threshold*	1
35	□32	THIS WILL BE	Natalie Cole	*Capitol*	2
-	33	NEW YORK GROOVE	Hello	*Bell*	1
29	34	FEEL LIKE MAKIN' LOVE	Bad Company	*Island*	8
20	35	SAILING	Rod Stewart	*Warner Bros.*	11
36	36	DREAMY LADY	T. Rex Disco Party	*EMI*	2
30	37	THE LAST FAREWELL	Roger Whittaker	*EMI*	13
31	38	REACHING FOR THE BEST	Exciters	*20th Century*	3
-	□39	CRACKIN' UP	Tommy Hunt ●	*Spark*	1
39	40	YOU	George Harrison	*Apple*	2

WEEK ENDING 1 NOVEMBER 1975

LW	TW	Title	Artist	Label	Wks
1	□1	I ONLY HAVE EYES FOR YOU	Art Garfunkel	*CBS*	7
4	2	SPACE ODDITY	David Bowie	*RCA*	4
3	□3	THERE GOES MY FIRST LOVE	Drifters	*Bell*	8
5	□4	FEELINGS	Morris Albert	*Decca*	6
16	5	LOVE IS THE DRUG	Roxy Music	*Island*	4
6	□6	S.O.S.	Abba	*Epic*	6
2	7	HOLD ME CLOSE	David Essex	*CBS*	7
12	8	WHAT A DIFFERENCE A DAY MADE	Esther Phillips	*Kudu*	4
8	9	DON'T PLAY YOUR ROCK AND ROLL TO ME	Smokie	*RAK*	4
17	10	RHINESTONE COWBOY	Glen Campbell	*Capitol*	4
10	11	SCOTCH ON THE ROCKS	Band of the Black Watch	*Spark*	9
7	12	IT'S TIME FOR LOVE	Chi-Lites	*Brunswick*	7
9	13	WHO LOVES YOU	Four Seasons	*Warner Bros.*	6
20	□14	ISLAND GIRL	Elton John	*DJM*	4
18	15	HOLD BACK THE NIGHT	Trammps	*Buddah*	3
14	16	L-L-LUCY	Mud	*Private Stock*	5
29	17	I AIN'T LYIN'	George McCrae	*Jayboy*	2
25	18	HIGHFLY	John Miles	*Decca*	2
31	19	BLUE GUITAR	Justin Hayward/John Lodge	*Threshold*	2
19	20	FUNKY MOPED/MAGIC ROUNDABOUT	Jasper Carrott	*DJM*	10
23	□21	ROCK ON BROTHER	Chequers	*Creole*	3
15	22	BIG TEN	Judge Dread	*Cactus*	5
33	23	NEW YORK GROOVE	Hello	*Bell*	2
11	24	UNA PALOMA BLANCA	Jonathan King	*U.K.*	8
26	25	RIDE A WILD HORSE	Dee Clark	*Chelsea*	3
-	26	D.I.V.O.R.C.E.	Billy Connolly ●	*Polydor*	1
22	27	NO WOMAN NO CRY	Bob Marley And The Wailers	*Island*	6
-	28	LOVE HURTS	Jim Capaldi	*Island*	1
13	29	PALOMA BLANCA	George Baker	*Warner Bros.*	8
36	□30	DREAMY LADY	T. Rex Disco Party	*EMI*	3
-	31	DARLIN'	David Cassidy	*RCA*	1
32	□32	THIS WILL BE	Natalie Cole	*Capitol*	3
21	33	FATTIE BUM BUM	Carl Malcolm	*UK*	8
28	34	NAPPY LOVE/WILD THING	Goodies	*Bradley's*	6
38	35	REACHING FOR THE BEST	Exciters	*20th Century*	4
-	36	ROCKY	Austin Roberts ●	*Private Stock*	1
27	37	I'M ON FIRE	5000 Volts	*Phillips*	9
40	□38	YOU	George Harrison	*Apple*	3
-	39	SUPERSHIP	George Benson ●	*CTI*	1
-	40	ARE YOU BEING SERVED SIR	John Inman ●	*DJM*	1

WEEK ENDING 8 NOVEMBER 1975

LW	TW	Title	Artist	Label	Wks
2	□1	SPACE ODDITY	David Bowie	*RCA*	5
5	□2	LOVE IS THE DRUG	Roxy Music	*Island*	5
1	3	I ONLY HAVE EYES FOR YOU	Art Garfunkel	*CBS*	8
10	□4	RHINESTONE COWBOY	Glen Campbell	*Capitol*	5
15	□5	HOLD BACK THE NIGHT	Trammps	*Buddah*	4
8	□6	WHAT A DIFFERENCE A DAY MADE	Esther Phillips	*Kudu*	5
6	7	S.O.S.	Abba	*Epic*	7
4	8	FEELINGS	Morris Albert	*Decca*	7
26	9	D.I.V.O.R.C.E.	Billy Connolly	*Polydor*	2
19	10	BLUE GUITAR	Justin Hayward/John Lodge	*Threshold*	3
3	11	THERE GOES MY FIRST LOVE	Drifters	*Bell*	9
9	12	DON'T PLAY YOUR ROCK AND ROLL TO ME	Smokie	*RAK*	5
28	13	LOVE HURTS	Jim Capaldi	*Island*	2
17	14	I AIN'T LYIN'	George McCrae	*Jayboy*	3
23	15	NEW YORK GROOVE	Hello	*Bell*	3
25	□16	RIDE A WILD HORSE	Dee Clark	*Chelsea*	4
18	□17	HIGHFLY	John Miles	*Decca*	3
7	18	HOLD ME CLOSE	David Essex	*CBS*	8
11	19	SCOTCH ON THE ROCKS	Band of the Black Watch	*Spark*	10
14	20	ISLAND GIRL	Elton John	*DJM*	5
12	21	IT'S TIME FOR LOVE	Chi-Lites	*Brunswick*	8
20	22	FUNKY MOPED/MAGIC ROUNDABOUT	Jasper Carrott	*DJM*	11
21	23	ROCK ON BROTHER	Chequers	*Creole*	4
13	24	WHO LOVES YOU	Four Seasons	*Warner Bros.*	7
-	25	IMAGINE	John Lennon	*Apple*	1
-	26	SKY HIGH	Jigsaw ●	*Splash*	1
24	27	UNA PALOMA BLANCA	Jonathan King	*U.K.*	9
16	28	L-L-LUCY	Mud	*Private Stock*	6
27	29	NO WOMAN NO CRY	Bob Marley And The Wailers	*Island*	7
-	30	RIGHT BACK WHERE WE STARTED FROM	Maxine Nightingale	*United Artists*	1
39	31	SUPERSHIP	George Benson	*CTI*	2
22	32	BIG TEN	Judge Dread	*Cactus*	6
31	33	DARLIN'	David Cassidy	*RCA*	2
-	34	LYIN' EYES	Eagles	*Asylum*	1
30	35	DREAMY LADY	T. Rex Disco Party	*EMI*	4
29	36	PALOMA BLANCA	George Baker	*Warner Bros.*	9
32	37	THIS WILL BE	Natalie Cole	*Capitol*	4
-	38	YOU SEXY THING	Hot Chocolate	*RAK*	1
40	□39	ARE YOU BEING SERVED SIR	John Inman	*DJM*	2
-	40	CHANGE WITH THE TIMES	Van McCoy	*Avco*	1

WEEK ENDING 15 NOVEMBER 1975

LW	TW	Title	Artist	Label	Wks
1	□1	SPACE ODDITY	David Bowie	*RCA*	6
9	2	D.I.V.O.R.C.E.	Billy Connolly	*Polydor*	3
2	3	LOVE IS THE DRUG	Roxy Music	*Island*	6
4	□4	RHINESTONE COWBOY	Glen Campbell	*Capitol*	6
13	5	LOVE HURTS	Jim Capaldi	*Island*	3
25	6	IMAGINE	John Lennon	*Apple*	2
5	7	HOLD BACK THE NIGHT	Trammps	*Buddah*	5
10	□8	BLUE GUITAR	Justin Hayward/John Lodge	*Threshold*	4
15	□9	NEW YORK GROOVE	Hello	*Bell*	4
38	10	YOU SEXY THING	Hot Chocolate	*RAK*	2
6	11	WHAT A DIFFERENCE A DAY MADE	Esther Phillips	*Kudu*	6
14	□12	I AIN'T LYIN'	George McCrae	*Jayboy*	4
3	13	I ONLY HAVE EYES FOR YOU	Art Garfunkel	*CBS*	9
26	14	SKY HIGH	Jigsaw	*Splash*	2
8	15	FEELINGS	Morris Albert	*Decca*	8
30	16	RIGHT BACK WHERE WE STARTED FROM	Maxine Nightingale	*United Artists*	2
-	17	BOHEMIAN RHAPSODY	Queen	*Decca*	1
17	18	HIGHFLY	John Miles	*Decca*	4
16	19	RIDE A WILD HORSE	Dee Clark	*Chelsea*	5
19	20	SCOTCH ON THE ROCKS	Band of the Black Watch	*Spark*	11
7	21	S.O.S.	Abba	*Epic*	8
33	22	DARLIN'	David Cassidy	*RCA*	3
34	□23	LYIN' EYES	Eagles	*Asylum*	2
20	24	ISLAND GIRL	Elton John	*DJM*	6
23	25	ROCK ON BROTHER	Chequers	*Creole*	5
11	26	THERE GOES MY FIRST LOVE	Drifters	*Bell*	10
-	27	THIS OLD HEART OF MINE	Rod Stewart	*Riva*	1
-	28	ROCKY	Austin Roberts	*Private Stock*	2
22	29	FUNKY MOPED/MAGIC ROUNDABOUT	Jasper Carrott	*DJM*	12
-	30	WHY DID YOU DO IT	Stretch ●	*Anchor*	1
12	31	DON'T PLAY YOUR ROCK AND ROLL TO ME	Smokie	*RAK*	6
31	32	SUPERSHIP	George Benson	*CTI*	3
-	□33	GOOD-BYE-EE	14/18 ●	*Magnet*	1
21	34	IT'S TIME FOR LOVE	Chi-Lites	*Brunswick*	9
18	35	HOLD ME CLOSE	David Essex	*CBS*	9
40	36	CHANGE WITH THE TIMES	Van McCoy	*Avco*	2

In these weeks ■ Five weeks at number three for the Drifters' *There Goes My First Love* (01.11.75) ■ *Space Oddity* reaches number one six years and 63 days after its chart debut. For over a decade, this is the slowest climb to the top (08.11.75) ■ In the same week, John Lennon's *Imagine* makes its chart debut. Over 5 years later it too will complete a very slow climb to the top (08.11.75)■

LW	TW	Title	Artist	Label	Wks
24	37	WHO LOVES YOU	Four Seasons	*Warner Bros.*	8
-	[38]	PAPA OOM MOW MOW	Gary Glitter	*Bell*	1
39	[39]	ARE YOU BEING SERVED SIR	John Inman	*DJM*	3
27	40	UNA PALOMA BLANCA	Jonathan King	*U.K.*	10

WEEK ENDING 22 NOVEMBER 1975

LW	TW	Title	Artist	Label	Wks
2	[1]	D.I.V.O.R.C.E.	Billy Connolly	*Polydor*	4
1	2	SPACE ODDITY	David Bowie	*RCA*	7
10	3	YOU SEXY THING	Hot Chocolate	*RAK*	3
3	4	LOVE IS THE DRUG	Roxy Music	*Island*	7
5	5	LOVE HURTS	Jim Capaldi	*Island*	4
6	6	IMAGINE	John Lennon	*Apple*	3
4	7	RHINESTONE COWBOY	Glen Campbell	*Capitol*	7
27	8	THIS OLD HEART OF MINE	Rod Stewart	*Riva*	2
17	9	BOHEMIAN RHAPSODY	Queen	*Decca*	2
14	10	SKY HIGH	Jigsaw	*Splash*	3
8	11	BLUE GUITAR	Justin Hayward/John Lodge	*Threshold*	5
9	12	NEW YORK GROOVE	Hello	*Bell*	5
-	13	MONEY HONEY	Bay City Rollers	*Bell*	1
16	14	RIGHT BACK WHERE WE STARTED FROM	Maxine Nightingale	*United Artists*	3
7	15	HOLD BACK THE NIGHT	Trammps	*Buddah*	6
22	[16]	DARLIN'	David Cassidy	*RCA*	4
-	17	ALL AROUND MY HAT	Steeleye Span	*Chrysalis*	1
12	18	I AIN'T LYIN'	George McCrae	*Jayboy*	5
30	19	WHY DID YOU DO IT	Stretch	*Anchor*	2
19	20	RIDE A WILD HORSE	Dee Clark	*Chelsea*	6
11	21	WHAT A DIFFERENCE A DAY MADE	Esther Phillips	*Kudu*	7
28	[22]	ROCKY	Austin Roberts	*Private Stock*	3
23	[23]	LYIN' EYES	Eagles	*Asylum*	3
18	24	HIGHFLY	John Miles	*Decca*	5
-	25	NA NA IS THE SADDEST WORD	Stylistics	*Avco*	1
-	26	LET'S TWIST AGAIN	John Asher ●	*Creole*	1
-	27	IN FOR A PENNY	Slade	*Polydor*	1
20	28	SCOTCH ON THE ROCKS	Band of the Black Watch	*Spark*	12
15	29	FEELINGS	Morris Albert	*Decca*	9
32	[30]	SUPERSHIP	George Benson	*CTI*	4
-	31	FLY ROBIN FLY	Silver Convention	*Magnet*	1
29	32	FUNKY MOPED/MAGIC ROUNDABOUT	Jasper Carrott	*DJM*	13
21	33	S.O.S.	Abba	*Epic*	9
-	[34]	HEAVENLY	Showaddywaddy	*Bell*	1
13	35	I ONLY HAVE EYES FOR YOU	Art Garfunkel	*CBS*	10
-	36	PART TIME LOVE	Gladys Knight & The Pips	*Buddah*	1
24	37	ISLAND GIRL	Elton John	*DJM*	7
38	[38]	PAPA OOM MOW MOW	Gary Glitter	*Bell*	2
26	39	THERE GOES MY FIRST LOVE	Drifters	*Bell*	11
-	40	HOLY ROLLER	Nazareth	*Mountain*	1

WEEK ENDING 29 NOVEMBER 1975

LW	TW	Title	Artist	Label	Wks
9	[1]	BOHEMIAN RHAPSODY	Queen	*Decca*	3
3	[2]	YOU SEXY THING	Hot Chocolate	*RAK*	4
1	3	D.I.V.O.R.C.E.	Billy Connolly	*Polydor*	5
5	[4]	LOVE HURTS	Jim Capaldi	*Island*	5
13	5	MONEY HONEY	Bay City Rollers	*Bell*	2
6	6	IMAGINE	John Lennon	*Apple*	4
8	7	THIS OLD HEART OF MINE	Rod Stewart	*Riva*	3
14	[8]	RIGHT BACK WHERE WE STARTED FROM	Maxine Nightingale	*United Artists*	4
10	[9]	SKY HIGH	Jigsaw	*Splash*	4
2	10	SPACE ODDITY	David Bowie	*RCA*	8
4	11	LOVE IS THE DRUG	Roxy Music	*Island*	8
17	12	ALL AROUND MY HAT	Steeleye Span	*Chrysalis*	2
7	13	RHINESTONE COWBOY	Glen Campbell	*Capitol*	8
12	14	NEW YORK GROOVE	Hello	*Bell*	6
25	15	NA NA IS THE SADDEST WORD	Stylistics	*Avco*	2
26	16	LET'S TWIST AGAIN	John Asher	*Creole*	2
11	17	BLUE GUITAR	Justin Hayward/John Lodge	*Threshold*	6
16	18	DARLIN'	David Cassidy	*RCA*	5
27	19	IN FOR A PENNY	Slade	*Polydor*	2
19	20	WHY DID YOU DO IT	Stretch	*Anchor*	3

December 1975

□ Denotes highest position reached ● Act's first ever week on chart

LW	TW	Title	Artist	Label	Wks
-	21	THE TRAIL OF THE LONESOME PINE	Laurel And Hardy ●	*United Artists*	1
18	22	I AIN'T LYIN'	George McCrae	*Jayboy*	6
23	23	LYIN' EYES	Eagles	*Asylum*	4
22	24	ROCKY	Austin Roberts	*Private Stock*	4
15	25	HOLD BACK THE NIGHT	Trammps	*Buddah*	7
-	26	SHOW ME YOU'RE A WOMAN	Mud	*Private Stock*	1
-	27	HAPPY TO BE ON AN ISLAND IN THE SUN	Demis Roussos ●	*Philips*	1
31	[28]	FLY ROBIN FLY	Silver Convention	*Magnet*	2
-	29	FIRST IMPRESSIONS	Impressions ●	*Curtom*	1
36	[30]	PART TIME LOVE	Gladys Knight & The Pips	*Buddah*	2
28	31	SCOTCH ON THE ROCKS	Band of the Black Watch	*Spark*	13
-	[32]	I'M STILL GONNA NEED YOU	Osmonds	*MGM*	1
30	33	SUPERSHIP	George Benson	*CTI*	5
-	[34]	I'M SO CRAZY	K.C. And The Sunshine Band	*Jayboy*	1
34	35	HEAVENLY	Showaddywaddy	*Bell*	2
40	[36]	HOLY ROLLER	Nazareth	*Mountain*	2
20	37	RIDE A WILD HORSE	Dee Clark	*Chelsea*	7
-	38	LITTLE DARLING	Rubettes	*State*	1
-	39	GOLDEN YEARS	David Bowie	*RCA*	1
29	40	FEELINGS	Morris Albert	*Decca*	10

WEEK ENDING 6 DECEMBER 1975

LW	TW	Title	Artist	Label	Wks
1	[1]	BOHEMIAN RHAPSODY	Queen	*Decca*	4
2	[2]	YOU SEXY THING	Hot Chocolate	*RAK*	5
5	[3]	MONEY HONEY	Bay City Rollers	*Bell*	3
7	[4]	THIS OLD HEART OF MINE	Rod Stewart	*Riva*	4
12	[5]	ALL AROUND MY HAT	Steeleye Span	*Chrysalis*	3
15	6	NA NA IS THE SADDEST WORD	Stylistics	*Avco*	3
3	7	D.I.V.O.R.C.E.	Billy Connolly	*Polydor*	6
4	8	LOVE HURTS	Jim Capaldi	*Island*	6
21	9	THE TRAIL OF THE LONESOME PINE	Laurel And Hardy	*United Artists*	2
6	10	IMAGINE	John Lennon	*Apple*	5
19	11	IN FOR A PENNY	Slade	*Polydor*	3
9	12	SKY HIGH	Jigsaw	*Splash*	5
8	13	RIGHT BACK WHERE WE STARTED FROM	Maxine Nightingale	*United Artists*	5
-	14	LET'S TWIST AGAIN/THE TWIST	Chubby Checker	*London*	1
26	15	SHOW ME YOU'RE A WOMAN	Mud	*Private Stock*	2
20	16	WHY DID YOU DO IT	Stretch	*Anchor*	4
18	17	DARLIN'	David Cassidy	*RCA*	6
16	18	LET'S TWIST AGAIN	John Asher	*Creole*	3
27	19	HAPPY TO BE ON AN ISLAND IN THE SUN	Demis Roussos	*Philips*	2
10	20	SPACE ODDITY	David Bowie	*RCA*	9
13	21	RHINESTONE COWBOY	Glen Campbell	*Capitol*	9
29	22	FIRST IMPRESSIONS	Impressions	*Curtom*	2
14	23	NEW YORK GROOVE	Hello	*Bell*	7
39	24	GOLDEN YEARS	David Bowie	*RCA*	2
24	25	ROCKY	Austin Roberts	*Private Stock*	5
23	26	LYIN' EYES	Eagles	*Asylum*	5
-	27	CAN I TAKE YOU HOME LITTLE GIRL	Drifters	*Bell*	1
28	28	FLY ROBIN FLY	Silver Convention	*Magnet*	3
11	29	LOVE IS THE DRUG	Roxy Music	*Island*	9
38	30	LITTLE DARLING	Rubettes	*State*	2
30	31	PART TIME LOVE	Gladys Knight & The Pips	*Buddah*	3
-	32	ART FOR ART'S SAKE	10.C.C.	*Mercury*	1
-	33	GREEN GREEN GRASS OF HOME	Elvis Presley	*RCA*	1
17	34	BLUE GUITAR	Justin Hayward/John Lodge	*Threshold*	7
35	35	HEAVENLY	Showaddywaddy	*Bell*	3
-	36	RENTA SANTA	Chris Hill ●	*Philips*	1
-	[37]	ALRIGHT BABY	Stevenson's Rocket ●	*Magnet*	1
-	[38]	GAMBLIN' BAR ROOM BLUES	Sensational Alex Harvey Band	*Vertigo*	1
32	39	I'M STILL GONNA NEED YOU	Osmonds	*MGM*	2
-	40	I BELIEVE IN FATHER CHRISTMAS	Greg Lake ●	*Manticore*	1

■Billy Connolly's brief week of glory is ended by Queen's *Bohemian Rhapsody*, which has nine weeks at number one, the longest consecutive run since Paul Anka's *Diana* held the top for nine weeks in 1957 (29.11.75) ■ Gary Glitter's *Papa Oom Mow Mow* is excluded from the BBC playlists and ends a run of eleven consecutive Top 10 hits (22.11.75)■

December 1975

☐ Denotes highest position reached ● Act's first ever week on chart

LW	TW	*WEEK ENDING* **13 DECEMBER 1975**		Wks
1	[1]	BOHEMIAN RHAPSODY Queen	*Decca*	5
2	2	YOU SEXY THING Hot Chocolate	*RAK*	6
9	3	THE TRAIL OF THE LONESOME PINE Laurel And Hardy	*United Artists*	3
3	4	MONEY HONEY Bay City Rollers	*Bell*	4
6	5	NA NA IS THE SADDEST WORD Stylistics	*Avco*	4
5	6	ALL AROUND MY HAT Steeleye Span	*Chrysalis*	4
4	7	THIS OLD HEART OF MINE Rod Stewart	*Riva*	5
15	8	SHOW ME YOU'RE A WOMAN Mud	*Private Stock*	3
14	9	LET'S TWIST AGAIN/THE TWIST Chubby Checker	*London*	2
10	10	IMAGINE John Lennon	*Apple*	6
12	11	SKY HIGH Jigsaw	*Splash*	6
8	12	LOVE HURTS Jim Capaldi	*Island*	7
19	13	HAPPY TO BE ON AN ISLAND IN THE SUN Demis Roussos	*Philips*	3
18	14	LET'S TWIST AGAIN John Asher	*Creole*	4
24	15	GOLDEN YEARS David Bowie	*RCA*	3
40	16	I BELIEVE IN FATHER CHRISTMAS Greg Lake	*Manticore*	2
11	17	IN FOR A PENNY Slade	*Polydor*	4
7	18	D.I.V.O.R.C.E. Billy Connolly	*Polydor*	7
16	19	WHY DID YOU DO IT Stretch	*Anchor*	5
13	20	RIGHT BACK WHERE WE STARTED FROM Maxine Nightingale	*United Artists*	6
27	21	CAN I TAKE YOU HOME LITTLE GIRL Drifters	*Bell*	2
36	22	RENTA SANTA Chris Hill	*Philips*	2
22	23	FIRST IMPRESSIONS Impressions	*Curtom*	3
-	24	CHRISTMAS IN DREADLAND/COME OUTSIDE Judge Dread	*Cactus*	1
-	25	IF I COULD David Essex	*CBS*	1
-	26	WIDE EYED AND LEGLESS Andy Fairweather Low	*A&M*	1
32	27	ART FOR ART'S SAKE 10C.C.	*Mercury*	2
-	28	(THINK OF ME) WHEREVER YOU ARE Ken Dodd	*EMI*	1
33	[29]	GREEN GREEN GRASS OF HOME Elvis Presley	*RCA*	2
17	30	DARLIN' David Cassidy	*RCA*	7
21	31	RHINESTONE COWBOY Glen Campbell	*Capitol*	10
-	32	GLASS OF CHAMPAGNE Sailor ●	*Epic*	1
28	33	FLY ROBIN FLY Silver Convention	*Magnet*	4
-	34	DO THE BUS STOP Fatback Band	*Polydor*	1
30	35	LITTLE DARLING Rubettes	*State*	3
26	36	LYIN' EYES Eagles	*Asylum*	6
23	37	NEW YORK GROOVE Hello	*Bell*	8
20	38	SPACE ODDITY David Bowie	*RCA*	10
31	39	PART TIME LOVE Gladys Knight & The Pips	*Buddah*	4
29	40	LOVE IS THE DRUG Roxy Music	*Island*	10

LW	TW	*WEEK ENDING* **20 DECEMBER 1975**		Wks
1	[1]	BOHEMIAN RHAPSODY Queen	*Decca*	6
3	[2]	THE TRAIL OF THE LONESOME PINE Laurel And Hardy	*United Artists*	4
16	3	I BELIEVE IN FATHER CHRISTMAS Greg Lake	*Manticore*	3
2	4	YOU SEXY THING Hot Chocolate	*RAK*	7
13	5	HAPPY TO BE ON AN ISLAND IN THE SUN Demis Roussos	*Philips*	4
9	6	LET'S TWIST AGAIN/THE TWIST Chubby Checker	*London*	3
5	7	NA NA IS THE SADDEST WORD Stylistics	*Avco*	5
15	8	GOLDEN YEARS David Bowie	*RCA*	4
6	9	ALL AROUND MY HAT Steeleye Span	*Chrysalis*	5
8	10	SHOW ME YOU'RE A WOMAN Mud	*Private Stock*	4
22	11	RENTA SANTA Chris Hill	*Philips*	3
4	12	MONEY HONEY Bay City Rollers	*Bell*	5
21	13	CAN I TAKE YOU HOME LITTLE GIRL Drifters	*Bell*	3
7	14	THIS OLD HEART OF MINE Rod Stewart	*Riva*	6
26	15	WIDE EYED AND LEGLESS Andy Fairweather Low	*A&M*	2
23	16	FIRST IMPRESSIONS Impressions	*Curtom*	4
24	17	CHRISTMAS IN DREADLAND/COME OUTSIDE Judge Dread	*Cactus*	2
-	18	IT'S GONNA BE A COLD COLD CHRISTMAS Dana	*GTO*	1
27	19	ART FOR ART'S SAKE 10C.C.	*Mercury*	3
32	20	GLASS OF CHAMPAGNE Sailor	*Epic*	2
25	21	IF I COULD David Essex	*CBS*	2
11	22	SKY HIGH Jigsaw	*Splash*	7
17	23	IN FOR A PENNY Slade	*Polydor*	5
28	24	(THINK OF ME) WHEREVER YOU ARE Ken Dodd	*EMI*	2
19	25	WHY DID YOU DO IT Stretch	*Anchor*	6
12	26	LOVE HURTS Jim Capaldi	*Island*	8
-	27	MAKE A DAFT NOISE FOR CHRISTMAS Goodies	*Bradley's*	1
-	28	ITCHYCOO PARK Small Faces	*Immediate*	1
34	29	DO THE BUS STOP Fatback Band	*Polydor*	2
29	30	GREEN GREEN GRASS OF HOME Elvis Presley	*RCA*	3
10	31	IMAGINE John Lennon	*Apple*	7
-	32	MAMA MIA Abba ●	*Epic*	1
-	33	KING OF THE COPS Billy Howard ●	*Penny Farthing*	1
33	34	FLY ROBIN FLY Silver Convention	*Magnet*	5
18	35	D.I.V.O.R.C.E. Billy Connolly	*Polydor*	8
20	36	RIGHT BACK WHERE WE STARTED FROM Maxine Nightingale	*United Artists*	7
-	[37]	DANCE OF THE CUCKOOS Band of the Black Watch	*Spark*	1
14	38	LET'S TWIST AGAIN John Asher	*Creole*	5
31	39	RHINESTONE COWBOY Glen Campbell	*Capitol*	11
35	40	LITTLE DARLING Rubettes	*State*	4

LW	TW	*WEEK ENDING* **27 DECEMBER 1975**		Wks
1	[1]	BOHEMIAN RHAPSODY Queen	*Decca*	7
3	[2]	I BELIEVE IN FATHER CHRISTMAS Greg Lake	*Manticore*	4
2	3	THE TRAIL OF THE LONESOME PINE Laurel And Hardy	*United Artists*	5
18	[4]	IT'S GONNA BE A COLD COLD CHRISTMAS Dana	*GTO*	2
6	[5]	LET'S TWIST AGAIN/THE TWIST Chubby Checker	*London*	4
5	6	HAPPY TO BE ON AN ISLAND IN THE SUN Demis Roussos	*Philips*	5
4	7	YOU SEXY THING Hot Chocolate	*RAK*	8
7	8	NA NA IS THE SADDEST WORD Stylistics	*Avco*	6
8	9	GOLDEN YEARS David Bowie	*RCA*	5
11	[10]	RENTA SANTA Chris Hill	*Philips*	4
10	11	SHOW ME YOU'RE A WOMAN Mud	*Private Stock*	5
13	12	CAN I TAKE YOU HOME LITTLE GIRL Drifters	*Bell*	4
15	13	WIDE EYED AND LEGLESS Andy Fairweather Low	*A&M*	3
17	[14]	CHRISTMAS IN DREADLAND/COME OUTSIDE Judge Dread	*Cactus*	3
12	15	MONEY HONEY Bay City Rollers	*Bell*	6
21	16	IF I COULD David Essex	*CBS*	3
19	17	ART FOR ART'S SAKE 10C.C.	*Mercury*	4
20	18	GLASS OF CHAMPAGNE Sailor	*Epic*	3
9	19	ALL AROUND MY HAT Steeleye Span	*Chrysalis*	6
27	[20]	MAKE A DAFT NOISE FOR CHRISTMAS Goodies	*Bradley's*	2
24	[21]	(THINK OF ME) WHEREVER YOU ARE Ken Dodd	*EMI*	3
-	22	IN DULCE JUBILO/ON HORSEBACK Mike Oldfield	*Virgin*	1
28	23	ITCHYCOO PARK Small Faces	*Immediate*	2
14	24	THIS OLD HEART OF MINE Rod Stewart	*Riva*	7
23	25	IN FOR A PENNY Slade	*Polydor*	6
29	26	DO THE BUS STOP Fatback Band	*Polydor*	3
16	27	FIRST IMPRESSIONS Impressions	*Curtom*	5
31	28	IMAGINE John Lennon	*Apple*	8
32	29	MAMA MIA Abba	*Epic*	2
33	29	KING OF THE COPS Billy Howard	*Penny Farthing*	2
22	31	SKY HIGH Jigsaw	*Splash*	8
30	32	GREEN GREEN GRASS OF HOME Elvis Presley	*RCA*	4
26	33	LOVE HURTS Jim Capaldi	*Island*	9
-	[34]	LET'S WOMBLE TO THE PARTY TONIGHT Wombles	*CBS*	1
-	35	GET IT TOGETHER Crispy & Co	*Creole*	1
-	36	I BELIEVE I'M GONNA LOVE YOU Frank Sinatra	*Reprise*	1
-	[37]	SANTA CLAUS IS COMIN' TO TOWN Carpenters	*A&M*	1
25	38	WHY DID YOU DO IT Stretch	*Anchor*	7
35	39	D.I.V.O.R.C.E. Billy Connolly	*Polydor*	9
-	40	BOTH ENDS BURNING Roxy Music	*Island*	1

In these weeks ■ Laurel and Hardy's unlikely hit *Trail of the Lonesome Pine* from the soundtrack of their 1937 film *Way Out West* becomes the oldest recording to hit the charts, but fails to reach the very top (20.12.75) ■ Chubby Checker's *Let's Twist Again/The Twist* dates back scarcely more than ten years, a very new hit in comparison (27.12.75) ■ Two *Christmas* titles in the Top 10 and *Renta Santa* make it a very seasonal chart, despite Demis Roussos (27.12.75)■

1976

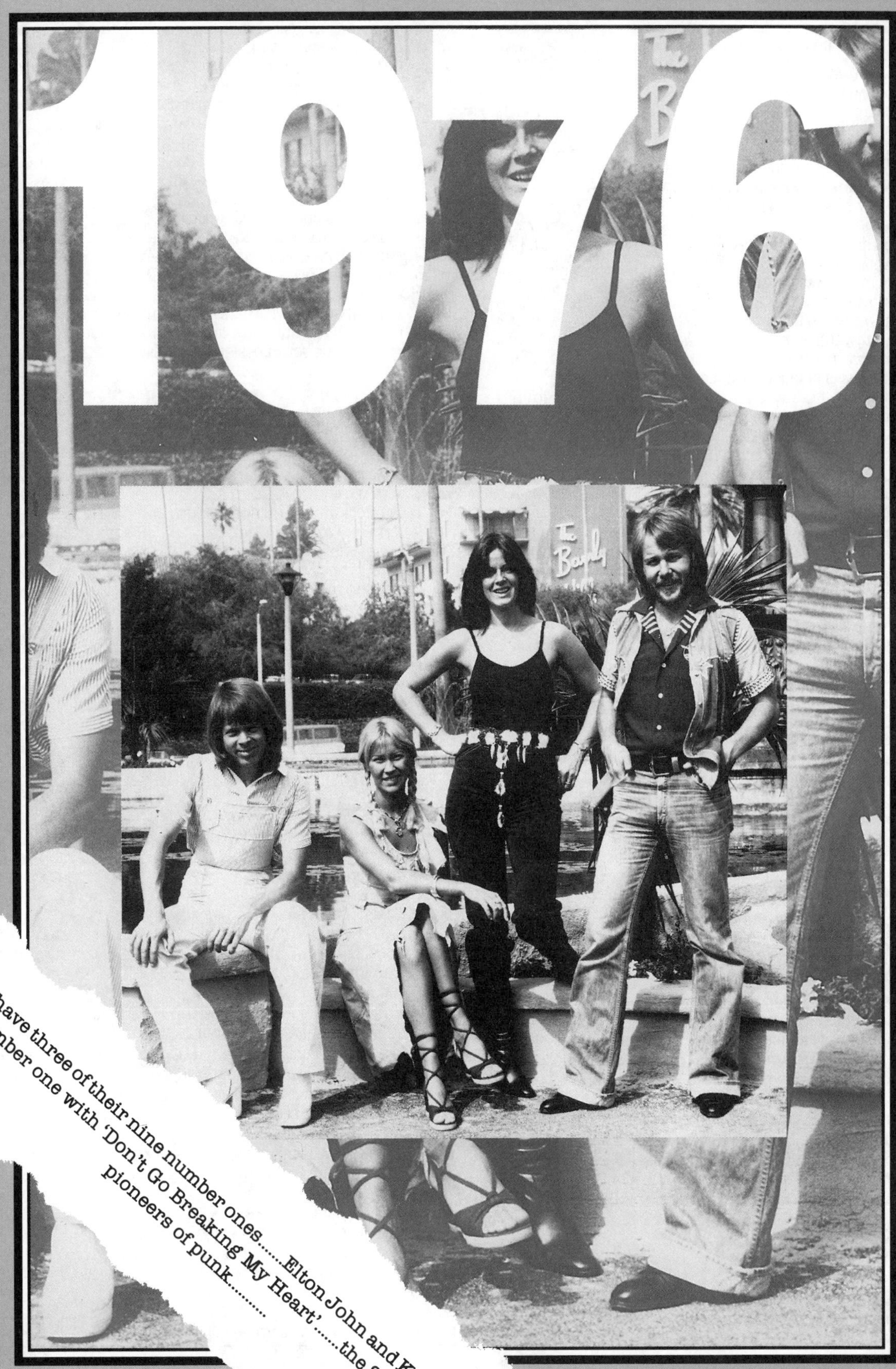

....ABBA have three of their nine number ones.......Elton John and Kiki Dee share six
ks at number one with 'Don't Go Breaking My Heart'.......the Sex Pistols are the
pioneers of punk..........

January 1976

□ Highest position disc reached ● Act's first ever week on chart

LW	TW	*WEEK ENDING* **3 JANUARY 1976**			Wks
(No chart published, chart for 27th December 1975 repeated)					
1	□1	BOHEMIAN RHAPSODY	Queen	*Decca*	8
2	□2	I BELIEVE IN FATHER CHRISTMAS	Greg Lake	*Manticore*	5
3	3	THE TRAIL OF THE LONESOME PINE	Laurel And Hardy	*United Artists*	6
4	□4	IT'S GONNA BE A COLD COLD CHRISTMAS	Dana	*GTO*	3
5	□5	LET'S TWIST AGAIN/THE TWIST	Chubby Checker	*London*	5
6	6	HAPPY TO BE ON AN ISLAND IN THE SUN	Demis Roussos	*Philips*	6
7	7	YOU SEXY THING	Hot Chocolate	*RAK*	9
8	8	NA NA IS THE SADDEST WORD	Stylistics	*Avco*	7
9	9	GOLDEN YEARS	David Bowie	*RCA*	6
10	□10	RENTA SANTA	Chris Hill	*Philips*	5
11	11	SHOW ME YOU'RE A WOMAN	Mud	*Private Stock*	6
12	12	CAN I TAKE YOU HOME LITTLE GIRL	Drifters	*Bell*	5
13	13	WIDE EYED AND LEGLESS	Andy Fairweather Low	*A&M*	4
14	□14	CHRISTMAS IN DREADLAND/COME OUTSIDE	Judge Dread	*Cactus*	4
15	15	MONEY HONEY	Bay City Rollers	*Bell*	7
16	16	IF I COULD	David Essex	*CBS*	4
17	17	ART FOR ART'S SAKE	10.C.C.	*Mercury*	5
18	18	GLASS OF CHAMPAGNE	Sailor	*Epic*	4
19	19	ALL AROUND MY HAT	Steeleye Span	*Chrysalis*	7
20	□20	MAKE A DAFT NOISE FOR CHRISTMAS	Goodies	*Bradley's*	3
21	□21	(THINK OF ME) WHEREVER YOU ARE	Ken Dodd	*EMI*	4
22	22	IN DULCE JUBILO/ON HORSEBACK	Mike Oldfield	*Virgin*	2
23	23	ITCHYCOO PARK	Small Faces	*Immediate*	3
24	24	THIS OLD HEART OF MINE	Rod Stewart	*Riva*	8
25	25	IN FOR A PENNY	Slade	*Polydor*	7
26	26	DO THE BUS STOP	Fatback Band	*Polydor*	4
27	27	FIRST IMPRESSIONS	Impressions	*Curtom*	6
28	28	IMAGINE	John Lennon	*Apple*	9
29	29	MAMMA MIA	Abba	*Epic*	3
29	29	KING OF THE COPS	Billy Howard	*Penny Farthing*	3
31	31	SKY HIGH	Jigsaw	*Splash*	9
32	32	GREEN GREEN GRASS OF HOME	Elvis Presley	*RCA*	5
33	33	LOVE HURTS	Jim Capaldi	*Island*	10
34	□34	LET'S WOMBLE TO THE PARTY TONIGHT	Wombles	*CBS*	2
35	35	GET IT TOGETHER	Crispy & Co	*Creole*	2
36	36	I BELIEVE I'M GONNA LOVE YOU	Frank Sinatra	*Reprise*	2
37	□37	SANTA CLAUS IS COMIN' TO TOWN	Carpenters	*A&M*	2
38	38	WHY DID YOU DO IT	Stretch	*Anchor*	8
39	39	D.I.V.O.R.C.E.	Billy Connolly	*Polydor*	10
40	40	BOTH ENDS BURNING	Roxy Music	*Island*	2

LW	TW	*WEEK ENDING* **10 JANUARY 1976**			Wks
1	□1	BOHEMIAN RHAPSODY	Queen	*Decca*	9
3	□2	THE TRAIL OF THE LONESOME PINE	Laurel And Hardy	*United Artists*	7
2	3	I BELIEVE IN FATHER CHRISTMAS	Greg Lake	*Manticore*	6
18	4	GLASS OF CHAMPAGNE	Sailor	*Epic*	5
5	□5	LET'S TWIST AGAIN/THE TWIST	Chubby Checker	*London*	6
13	□6	WIDE EYED AND LEGLESS	Andy Fairweather Low	*A&M*	5
17	7	ART FOR ART'S SAKE	10.C.C.	*Mercury*	6
9	8	GOLDEN YEARS	David Bowie	*RCA*	7
4	9	IT'S GONNA BE A COLD COLD CHRISTMAS	Dana	*GTO*	4
12	□10	CAN I TAKE YOU HOME LITTLE GIRL	Drifters	*Bell*	6
6	11	HAPPY TO BE ON AN ISLAND IN THE SUN	Demis Roussos	*Philips*	7
29	12	MAMMA MIA	Abba	*Epic*	4
16	□13	IF I COULD	David Essex	*CBS*	5
7	14	YOU SEXY THING	Hot Chocolate	*RAK*	10
15	15	MONEY HONEY	Bay City Rollers	*Bell*	8
14	16	CHRISTMAS IN DREADLAND/COME OUTSIDE	Judge Dread	*Cactus*	5
8	17	NA NA IS THE SADDEST WORD	Stylistics	*Avco*	8
29	18	KING OF THE COPS	Billy Howard	*Penny Farthing*	4
27	19	FIRST IMPRESSIONS	Impressions	*Curtom*	7
11	20	SHOW ME YOU'RE A WOMAN	Mud	*Private Stock*	7
22	21	IN DULCE JUBILO/ON HORSEBACK	Mike Oldfield	*Virgin*	3
10	22	RENTA SANTA	Chris Hill	*Philips*	6
23	23	ITCHYCOO PARK	Small Faces	*Immediate*	4
26	24	DO THE BUS STOP	Fatback Band	*Polydor*	5
35	25	GET IT TOGETHER	Crispy & Co	*Creole*	2
20	26	MAKE A DAFT NOISE FOR CHRISTMAS	Goodies	*Bradley's*	4
21	27	(THINK OF ME) WHEREVER YOU ARE	Ken Dodd	*EMI*	5
-	28	LET THE MUSIC PLAY	Barry White	*20th Century*	1
19	29	ALL AROUND MY HAT	Steeleye Span	*Chrysalis*	8
-	30	MIDNIGHT RIDER	Paul Davidson ●	*Tropical*	1
-	31	MILKY WAY	Sheer Elegance ●	*Pye*	1
40	32	BOTH ENDS BURNING	Roxy Music	*Island*	3
24	33	THIS OLD HEART OF MINE	Rod Stewart	*Riva*	9
36	□34	I BELIEVE I'M GONNA LOVE YOU	Frank Sinatra	*Reprise*	2
28	35	IMAGINE	John Lennon	*Apple*	10
-	□36	DREAMS OF YOU	Ralph McTell	*Warner Brothers*	1
34	37	LET'S WOMBLE TO THE PARTY TONIGHT	Wombles	*CBS*	2
-	38	DANCE OF THE CUCKOOS	Band Of The Black Watch	*Spark*	3
-	39	THE OLD RUGGED CROSS	Ethna Campbell ●	*Philips*	1
31	40	SKY HIGH	Jigsaw	*Splash*	10

LW	TW	*WEEK ENDING* **17 JANUARY 1976**			Wks
1	□1	BOHEMIAN RHAPSODY	Queen	*Decca*	10
4	□2	GLASS OF CHAMPAGNE	Sailor	*Epic*	6
12	3	MAMMA MIA	Abba	*Epic*	5
21	□4	IN DULCE JUBILO/ON HORSEBACK	Mike Oldfield	*Virgin*	4
7	□5	ART FOR ART'S SAKE	10.C.C.	*Mercury*	7
5	6	LET'S TWIST AGAIN/THE TWIST	Chubby Checker	*London*	7
6	7	WIDE EYED AND LEGLESS	Andy Fairweather Low	*A&M*	6
18	8	KING OF THE COPS	Billy Howard	*Penny Farthing*	5
23	9	ITCHYCOO PARK	Small Faces	*Immediate*	5
11	10	HAPPY TO BE ON AN ISLAND IN THE SUN	Demis Roussos	*Philips*	8
2	11	THE TRAIL OF THE LONESOME PINE	Laurel And Hardy	*United Artists*	8
8	12	GOLDEN YEARS	David Bowie	*RCA*	8
13	□13	IF I COULD	David Essex	*CBS*	6
9	14	IT'S GONNA BE A COLD COLD CHRISTMAS	Dana	*GTO*	5
28	15	LET THE MUSIC PLAY	Barry White	*20th Century*	2
-	16	LOVE MACHINE	Miracles ●	*Tamla Motown*	1
-	17	WE DO IT	R & J Stone ●	*RCA*	1
3	18	I BELIEVE IN FATHER CHRISTMAS	Greg Lake	*Manticore*	7
10	19	CAN I TAKE YOU HOME LITTLE GIRL	Drifters	*Bell*	7
24	20	DO THE BUS STOP	Fatback Band	*Polydor*	6
25	□21	GET IT TOGETHER	Crispy & Co	*Creole*	3
31	22	MILKY WAY	Sheer Elegance	*Pye*	2
16	23	CHRISTMAS IN DREADLAND/COME OUTSIDE	Judge Dread	*Cactus*	6
14	24	YOU SEXY THING	Hot Chocolate	*RAK*	11
30	25	MIDNIGHT RIDER	Paul Davidson	*Tropical*	2
19	26	FIRST IMPRESSIONS	Impressions	*Curtom*	8
-	27	EVIL WOMAN	Electric Light Orchestra	*Jet*	1
32	28	BOTH ENDS BURNING	Roxy Music	*Island*	4
20	29	SHOW ME YOU'RE A WOMAN	Mud	*Private Stock*	8
17	30	NA NA IS THE SADDEST WORD	Stylistics	*Avco*	9
15	31	MONEY HONEY	Bay City Rollers	*Bell*	9
22	32	RENTA SANTA	Chris Hill	*Philips*	7
-	33	NO REGRETS	Walker Brothers	*GTO*	1
27	34	(THINK OF ME) WHEREVER YOU ARE	Ken Dodd	*EMI*	6
-	□35	TEARS ON THE TELEPHONE	Claude Francois ●	*Bradley's*	1
26	36	MAKE A DAFT NOISE FOR CHRISTMAS	Goodies	*Bradley's*	5
-	37	LOVE TO LOVE YOU BABY	Donna Summer ●	*GTO*	1
-	38	50 WAYS TO LEAVE YOUR LOVER	Paul Simon	*CBS*	1
-	39	FOREVER AND EVER	Slik ●	*Bell*	1
-	40	DEEP PURPLE	Donny & Marie Osmond	*MGM*	1

LW	TW	*WEEK ENDING* **24 JANUARY 1976**			Wks
1	□1	BOHEMIAN RHAPSODY	Queen	*Decca*	11

In these weeks ■ *Bohemian Rhapsody* becomes the first single since *Diana* in 1957 to spend nine weeks at number one ■ Donna Summer begins the fourth most successful female solo career in chart history (17.01.76) ■ Both *Itchycoo Park* and *Let's Twist Again* are Top 10 hits for the second time (17.01.76)■

LW	TW	Title	Artist	Label	Wks
2	[2]	GLASS OF CHAMPAGNE	Sailor	*Epic*	7
3	3	MAMMA MIA	Abba	*Epic*	6
4	[4]	IN DULCE JUBILO/ON HORSEBACK	Mike Oldfield	*Virgin*	5
16	5	LOVE MACHINE	Miracles	*Tamla Motown*	2
8	[6]	KING OF THE COPS	Billy Howard	*Penny Farthing*	6
17	7	WE DO IT	R & J Stone	*RCA*	2
7	8	WIDE EYED AND LEGLESS	Andy Fairweather Low	*A&M*	7
15	[9]	LET THE MUSIC PLAY	Barry White	*20th Century*	3
25	[10]	MIDNIGHT RIDER	Paul Davidson	*Tropical*	3
5	11	ART FOR ART'S SAKE	10.C.C.	*Mercury*	8
39	12	FOREVER AND EVER	Slik	*Bell*	2
9	13	ITCHYCOO PARK	Small Faces	*Immediate*	6
27	14	EVIL WOMAN	Electric Light Orchestra	*Jet*	2
19	15	CAN I TAKE YOU HOME LITTLE GIRL	Drifters	*Bell*	8
37	16	LOVE TO LOVE YOU BABY	Donna Summer	*GTO*	2
6	17	LET'S TWIST AGAIN/THE TWIST	Chubby Checker	*London*	8
20	[18]	DO THE BUS STOP	Fatback Band	*Polydor*	7
12	19	GOLDEN YEARS	David Bowie	*RCA*	9
22	20	MILKY WAY	Sheer Elegance	*Pye*	3
21	[21]	GET IT TOGETHER	Crispy & Co	*Creole*	4
-	22	ANSWER ME	Barbara Dickson ●	*RSO*	1
-	23	SUNSHINE DAY	Osibisa ●	*Bronze*	1
11	24	THE TRAIL OF THE LONESOME PINE	Laurel And Hardy	*United Artists*	9
28	[25]	BOTH ENDS BURNING	Roxy Music	*Island*	5
33	26	NO REGRETS	Walker Brothers	*GTO*	2
13	27	IF I COULD	David Essex	*CBS*	7
38	28	50 WAYS TO LEAVE YOUR LOVER	Paul Simon	*CBS*	2
-	29	WALK AWAY FROM LOVE	David Ruffin ●	*Tamla Motown*	1
-	30	BABY FACE	Wing And A Prayer Fife And Drum Corps. ●	*Atlantic*	1
10	31	HAPPY TO BE ON AN ISLAND IN THE SUN	Demis Roussos	*Philips*	9
40	32	DEEP PURPLE	Donny & Marie Osmond	*MGM*	2
-	[33]	THE OLD RUGGED CROSS	Ethna Campbell	*Philips*	1
-	34	HOW HIGH THE MOON	Gloria Gaynor	*MGM*	1
-	[35]	DRIVE SAFELY DARLIN'	Tony Christie	*MCA*	1
24	36	YOU SEXY THING	Hot Chocolate	*RAK*	12
26	37	FIRST IMPRESSIONS	Impressions	*Curtom*	9
-	38	LOW RIDER	War ●	*Island*	1
-	39	LIES IN YOUR EYES	Sweet	*RCA*	1
35	40	TEARS ON THE TELEPHONE	Claude Francois	*Bradley's*	2

WEEK ENDING **31 JANUARY 1976**

LW	TW	Title	Artist	Label	Wks
3	[1]	MAMMA MIA	Abba	*Epic*	7
12	2	FOREVER AND EVER	Slik	*Bell*	3
1	3	BOHEMIAN RHAPSODY	Queen	*Decca*	12
5	4	LOVE MACHINE	Miracles	*Tamla Motown*	3
2	5	GLASS OF CHAMPAGNE	Sailor	*Epic*	8
16	6	LOVE TO LOVE YOU BABY	Donna Summer	*GTO*	3
7	7	WE DO IT	R & J Stone	*RCA*	3
4	8	IN DULCE JUBILO/ON HORSEBACK	Mike Oldfield	*Virgin*	6
6	9	KING OF THE COPS	Billy Howard	*Penny Farthing*	7
14	[10]	EVIL WOMAN	Electric Light Orchestra	*Jet*	3
9	11	LET THE MUSIC PLAY	Barry White	*20th Century*	4
10	12	MIDNIGHT RIDER	Paul Davidson	*Tropical*	4
13	13	ITCHYCOO PARK	Small Faces	*Immediate*	7
22	14	ANSWER ME	Barbara Dickson	*RSO*	2
11	15	ART FOR ART'S SAKE	10.C.C.	*Mercury*	9
29	16	WALK AWAY FROM LOVE	David Ruffin	*Tamla Motown*	2
23	[17]	SUNSHINE DAY	Osibisa	*Bronze*	2
20	[18]	MILKY WAY	Sheer Elegance	*Pye*	4
8	19	WIDE EYED AND LEGLESS	Andy Fairweather Low	*A&M*	8
26	20	NO REGRETS	Walker Brothers	*GTO*	3
30	21	BABY FACE	Wing And A Prayer Fife And Drum Corps.	*Atlantic*	2
18	22	DO THE BUS STOP	Fatback Band	*Polydor*	8
28	[23]	50 WAYS TO LEAVE YOUR LOVER	Paul Simon	*CBS*	3
38	24	LOW RIDER	War	*Island*	2
25	[25]	BOTH ENDS BURNING	Roxy Music	*Island*	6
-	26	MOONLIGHT SERENADE/LITTLE BROWN JUG/IN THE MOOD	Glenn Miller	*RCA*	1
32	27	DEEP PURPLE	Donny & Marie Osmond	*MGM*	3
-	28	DECEMBER '63	Four Seasons	*Warner Bros.*	1

February 1976

□ Highest position disc reached ● Act's first ever week on chart

LW	TW	Title	Artist	Label	Wks
21	29	GET IT TOGETHER	Crispy & Co	*Creole*	5
-	30	THE WAY I WANT TO TOUCH YOU	Captain And Tennille	*A&M*	1
-	31	SQUEEZE BOX	Who	*Polydor*	1
17	32	LET'S TWIST AGAIN/THE TWIST	Chubby Checker	*London*	9
34	[33]	HOW HIGH THE MOON	Gloria Gaynor	*MGM*	2
-	34	HONEY I	George McCrae	*Jayboy*	1
39	[35]	LIES IN YOUR EYES	Sweet	*RCA*	2
-	36	IT SHOULD HAVE BEEN ME	Yvonne Fair ●	*Tamla Motown*	1
15	37	CAN I TAKE YOU HOME LITTLE GIRL	Drifters	*Bell*	9
35	38	DRIVE SAFELY DARLIN'	Tony Christie	*MCA*	2
-	39	WEAK SPOT	Evelyn Thomas ●	*20th Century*	1
19	40	GOLDEN YEARS	David Bowie	*RCA*	10

WEEK ENDING **7 FEBRUARY 1976**

LW	TW	Title	Artist	Label	Wks
1	[1]	MAMA MIA	Abba	*Epic*	8
2	2	FOREVER AND EVER	Slik	*Bell*	4
4	3	LOVE MACHINE	Miracles	*Tamla Motown*	4
6	4	LOVE TO LOVE YOU BABY	Donna Summer	*GTO*	4
7	5	WE DO IT	R & J Stone	*RCA*	4
3	6	BOHEMIAN RHAPSODY	Queen	*Decca*	13
5	7	GLASS OF CHAMPAGNE	Sailor	*Epic*	9
28	8	DECEMBER '63	Four Seasons	*Warner Bros.*	2
9	9	KING OF THE COPS	Billy Howard	*Penny Farthing*	8
8	10	IN DULCE JUBILO/ON HORSEBACK	Mike Oldfield	*Virgin*	7
10	11	EVIL WOMAN	Electric Light Orchestra	*Jet*	4
12	12	MIDNIGHT RIDER	Paul Davidson	*Tropical*	5
20	13	NO REGRETS	Walker Brothers	*GTO*	4
13	14	ITCHYCOO PARK	Small Faces	*Immediate*	8
26	15	MOONLIGHT SERENADE/LITTLE BROWN JUG/IN THE MOOD	Glenn Miller	*RCA*	2
11	16	LET THE MUSIC PLAY	Barry White	*20th Century*	5
14	17	ANSWER ME	Barbara Dickson	*RSO*	3
16	18	WALK AWAY FROM LOVE	David Ruffin	*Tamla Motown*	3
18	19	MILKY WAY	Sheer Elegance	*Pye*	5
24	20	LOW RIDER	War	*Island*	3
-	21	RODRIGO'S GUITAR CONCERTO	Manuel And The Music Of The Mountains	*EMI*	2
17	22	SUNSHINE DAY	Osibisa	*Bronze*	3
21	23	BABY FACE	Wing And A Prayer Fife And Drum Corps.	*Atlantic*	3
19	24	WIDE EYED AND LEGLESS	Andy Fairweather Low	*A&M*	9
27	25	DEEP PURPLE	Donny & Marie Osmond	*MGM*	4
31	26	SQUEEZE BOX	Who	*Polydor*	2
23	27	50 WAYS TO LEAVE YOUR LOVER	Paul Simon	*CBS*	4
30	28	THE WAY I WANT TO TOUCH YOU	Captain And Tennille	*A&M*	2
36	29	IT SHOULD HAVE BEEN ME	Yvonne Fair	*Tamla Motown*	2
-	30	SOMETHING'S BEEN MAKING ME BLUE	Smokie	*Rak*	1
-	31	I LOVE MUSIC	The O'Jays	*Philadelphia*	1
39	32	WEAK SPOT	Evelyn Thomas	*20th Century*	2
34	33	HONEY I	George McCrae	*Jayboy*	2
22	34	DO THE BUS STOP	Fatback Band	*Polydor*	9
35	35	LIES IN YOUR EYES	Sweet	*RCA*	3
25	36	BOTH ENDS BURNING	Roxy Music	*Island*	7
-	37	YOUR MAGIC PUT A SPELL ON ME	L.J. Johnson	*Philips*	1
-	[38]	JUST ONE LOOK	Faith, Hope And Charity	*RCA*	1
-	39	TUXEDO JUNCTION	Manhattan Transfer	*Atlantic*	1
-	40	THE OLD RUGGED CROSS	Ethna Campbell	*Philips*	3

WEEK ENDING **14 FEBRUARY 1976**

LW	TW	Title	Artist	Label	Wks
2	[1]	FOREVER AND EVER	Slik	*Bell*	5
1	2	MAMA MIA	Abba	*Epic*	9
8	3	DECEMBER '63	Four Seasons	*Warner Bros.*	3
3	4	LOVE MACHINE	Miracles	*Tamla Motown*	5
4	5	LOVE TO LOVE YOU BABY	Donna Summer	*GTO*	5
5	6	WE DO IT	R & J Stone	*RCA*	5

■ Abba begin their first hat-trick of three consecutive number one releases ■ Glenn Miller achieves the longest gap to date between chart hits, 21 years 312 days (31.07.76) ■ The Miracles have their first and only hit without Smokey Robinson (17.01.76) ■

February 1976

□ Highest position disc reached ● Act's first ever week on chart

LW	TW	Title / Artist	Label	Wks
13	[7]	NO REGRETS Walker Brothers	*GTO*	5
21	8	RODRIGO'S GUITAR CONCERTO Manuel And The Music Of The Mountains	*EMI*	3
17	9	ANSWER ME Barbara Dickson	*RSO*	4
18	10	WALK AWAY FROM LOVE David Ruffin	*Tamla Motown*	4
11	11	EVIL WOMAN Electric Light Orchestra	*Jet*	5
23	12	BABY FACE Wing And A Prayer Fife And Drum Corps.	*Atlantic*	4
12	13	MIDNIGHT RIDER Paul Davidson	*Tropical*	6
14	14	ITCHYCOO PARK Small Faces	*Immediate*	9
20	15	LOW RIDER War	*Island*	4
6	16	BOHEMIAN RHAPSODY Queen	*Decca*	14
15	17	MOONLIGHT SERENADE/LITTLE BROWN JUG/ IN THE MOOD Glenn Miller	*RCA*	3
22	18	SUNSHINE DAY Osibisa	*Bronze*	4
26	19	SQUEEZE BOX Who	*Polydor*	3
9	20	KING OF THE COPS Billy Howard	*Penny Farthing*	9
29	21	IT SHOULD HAVE BEEN ME Yvonne Fair	*Tamla Motown*	3
7	22	GLASS OF CHAMPAGNE Sailor	*Epic*	10
-	23	I LOVE TO LOVE Tina Charles ●	*CBS*	1
10	24	IN DULCE JUBILO/ON HORSEBACK Mike Oldfield	*Virgin*	8
-	25	LET'S CALL IT QUITS Slade	*Polydor*	1
19	26	MILKY WAY Sheer Elegance	*Pye*	6
30	27	SOMETHING'S BEEN MAKING ME BLUE Smokie	*Rak*	2
25	28	DEEP PURPLE Donny & Marie Osmond	*MGM*	5
-	29	DAT Pluto Shervington ●	*Opal*	1
31	30	I LOVE MUSIC The O'Jays	*Philadelphia*	2
39	31	TUXEDO JUNCTION Manhattan Transfer	*Atlantic*	2
32	32	WEAK SPOT Evelyn Thomas	*20th Century*	3
37	33	YOUR MAGIC PUT A SPELL ON ME L.J. Johnson	*Philips*	2
28	34	THE WAY I WANT TO TOUCH YOU Captain And Tennille	*A&M*	3
27	35	50 WAYS TO LEAVE YOUR LOVER Paul Simon	*CBS*	5
-	36	RAIN Status Quo	*Vertigo*	1
33	37	HONEY I George McCrae	*Jayboy*	3
16	38	LET THE MUSIC PLAY Barry White	*20th Century*	6
35	39	LIES IN YOUR EYES Sweet	*RCA*	4
38	40	JUST ONE LOOK Faith, Hope And Charity	*RCA*	2

WEEK ENDING 21 FEBRUARY 1976

LW	TW	Title / Artist	Label	Wks
3	[1]	DECEMBER '63 Four Seasons	*Warner Bros.*	4
1	2	FOREVER AND EVER Slik	*Bell*	6
23	3	I LOVE TO LOVE Tina Charles	*CBS*	2
8	4	RODRIGO'S GUITAR CONCERTO Manuel And The Music Of The Mountains	*EMI*	4
2	5	MAMA MIA Abba	*Epic*	10
5	6	LOVE TO LOVE YOU BABY Donna Summer	*GTO*	6
-	7	CONVOY C.W. McCall	*MGM*	1
4	8	LOVE MACHINE Miracles	*Tamla Motown*	6
6	9	WE DO IT R & J Stone	*RCA*	6
29	10	DAT Pluto Shervington	*Opal*	2
7	11	NO REGRETS Walker Brothers	*GTO*	6
15	12	LOW RIDER War	*Island*	5
17	13	MOONLIGHT SERENADE/LITTLE BROWN JUG/ IN THE MOOD Glenn Miller	*RCA*	4
21	14	IT SHOULD HAVE BEEN ME Yvonne Fair	*Tamla Motown*	4
19	15	SQUEEZE BOX Who	*Polydor*	4
10	16	WALK AWAY FROM LOVE David Ruffin	*Tamla Motown*	5
36	17	RAIN Status Quo	*Vertigo*	2
25	18	LET'S CALL IT QUITS Slade	*Polydor*	2
12	19	BABY FACE Wing And A Prayer Fife And Drum Corps.	*Atlantic*	5
30	20	I LOVE MUSIC The O'Jays	*Philadelphia*	3
27	21	SOMETHING'S BEEN MAKING ME BLUE Smokie	*Rak*	3
-	22	FUNKY WEEKEND Stylistics	*Avco*	1
13	23	MIDNIGHT RIDER Paul Davidson	*Tropical*	7
31	24	TUXEDO JUNCTION Manhattan Transfer	*Atlantic*	3
9	25	ANSWER ME Barbara Dickson	*RSO*	5
32	26	WEAK SPOT Evelyn Thomas	*20th Century*	4
33	[27]	YOUR MAGIC PUT A SPELL ON ME L.J. Johnson	*Philips*	3
11	28	EVIL WOMAN Electric Light Orchestra	*Jet*	6
28	29	DEEP PURPLE Donny & Marie Osmond	*MGM*	6
20	30	KING OF THE COPS Billy Howard	*Penny Farthing*	10
-	31	MISS YOU NIGHTS Cliff Richard	*EMI*	1
16	32	BOHEMIAN RHAPSODY Queen	*Decca*	15
34	33	THE WAY I WANT TO TOUCH YOU Captain And Tennille	*A&M*	4
-	34	LOVE REALLY HURTS WITHOUT YOU Billy Ocean ●	*GTO*	1
26	35	MILKY WAY Sheer Elegance	*Pye*	7
24	36	IN DULCE JUBILO/ON HORSEBACK Mike Oldfield	*Virgin*	9
22	37	GLASS OF CHAMPAGNE Sailor	*Epic*	11
14	38	ITCHYCOO PARK Small Faces	*Immediate*	10
-	39	(DO THE) SPANISH HUSTLE Fatback Band	*Polydor*	1
-	40	CLOUD 99 St. Andrews Chorale ●	*Decca*	1

WEEK ENDING 28 FEBRUARY 1976

LW	TW	Title / Artist	Label	Wks
1	[1]	DECEMBER '63 Four Seasons	*Warner Bros.*	5
3	2	I LOVE TO LOVE Tina Charles	*CBS*	3
4	[3]	RODRIGO'S GUITAR CONCERTO Manuel And The Music Of The Mountains	*EMI*	5
7	4	CONVOY C.W. McCall	*MGM*	2
2	5	FOREVER AND EVER Slik	*Bell*	7
14	6	IT SHOULD HAVE BEEN ME Yvonne Fair	*Tamla Motown*	5
10	7	DAT Pluto Shervington	*Opal*	3
11	8	NO REGRETS Walker Brothers	*GTO*	7
17	9	RAIN Status Quo	*Vertigo*	3
15	10	SQUEEZE BOX Who	*Polydor*	5
18	[11]	LET'S CALL IT QUITS Slade	*Polydor*	3
6	12	LOVE TO LOVE YOU BABY Donna Summer	*GTO*	7
5	13	MAMA MIA Abba	*Epic*	11
8	14	LOVE MACHINE Miracles	*Tamla Motown*	7
13	15	MOONLIGHT SERENADE/LITTLE BROWN JUG/ IN THE MOOD Glenn Miller	*RCA*	5
12	16	LOW RIDER War	*Island*	6
9	17	WE DO IT R & J Stone	*RCA*	7
22	18	FUNKY WEEKEND Stylistics	*Avco*	2
21	19	SOMETHING'S BEEN MAKING ME BLUE Smokie	*Rak*	4
34	20	LOVE REALLY HURTS WITHOUT YOU Billy Ocean	*GTO*	2
19	21	BABY FACE Wing And A Prayer Fife And Drum Corps.	*Atlantic*	6
20	22	I LOVE MUSIC The O'Jays	*Philadelphia*	4
39	23	(DO THE) SPANISH HUSTLE Fatback Band	*Polydor*	2
16	24	WALK AWAY FROM LOVE David Ruffin	*Tamla Motown*	6
31	25	MISS YOU NIGHTS Cliff Richard	*EMI*	2
24	26	TUXEDO JUNCTION Manhattan Transfer	*Atlantic*	4
27	27	YOUR MAGIC PUT A SPELL ON ME L.J. Johnson	*Philips*	4
26	28	WEAK SPOT Evelyn Thomas	*20th Century*	5
-	29	YOU DON'T HAVE TO SAY YOU LOVE ME Guys 'N' Dolls	*Magnet*	1
25	30	ANSWER ME Barbara Dickson	*RSO*	6
40	[31]	CLOUD 99 St. Andrews Chorale	*Decca*	2
28	32	EVIL WOMAN Electric Light Orchestra	*Jet*	7
29	33	DEEP PURPLE Donny & Marie Osmond	*MGM*	7
-	34	IF PARADISE WAS HALF AS NICE Amen Corner	*Immediate*	1
30	35	KING OF THE COPS Billy Howard	*Penny Farthing*	11
32	36	BOHEMIAN RHAPSODY Queen	*Decca*	16
-	37	PEOPLE LIKE YOU PEOPLE LIKE ME Glitter Band	*Bell*	1
23	38	MIDNIGHT RIDER Paul Davidson	*Tropical*	8
-	[39]	INSIDE AMERICA Juggy Jones ●	*Contempo*	1
-	40	LET'S DO THE LATIN HUSTLE M&O Band ●	*Creole*	1

WEEK ENDING 6 MARCH 1976

LW	TW	Title / Artist	Label	Wks
2	1	I LOVE TO LOVE Tina Charles	*CBS*	4
1	2	DECEMBER '63 Four Seasons	*Warner Bros.*	6
4	3	CONVOY C.W. McCall	*MGM*	3
3	4	RODRIGO'S GUITAR CONCERTO Manuel And The Music Of The Mountains	*EMI*	6
6	5	IT SHOULD HAVE BEEN ME Yvonne Fair	*Tamla Motown*	6
7	[6]	DAT Pluto Shervington	*Opal*	4
9	[7]	RAIN Status Quo	*Vertigo*	4
20	8	LOVE REALLY HURTS WITHOUT YOU Billy Ocean	*GTO*	3
5	9	FOREVER AND EVER Slik	*Bell*	8
18	[10]	FUNKY WEEKEND Stylistics	*Avco*	3

In these weeks ■ The Four Seasons achieve their first and only number one 13 years 140 days since their chart debut (21.02.76) ■ *Convoy* by C.W. McCall starts a brief trend in novelties about Citizen's Band radios (21.02.76) ■ Billy Ocean makes his first chart appearance (21.02.76)■

LW	TW	Title / Artist	Label	Wks
10	11	SQUEEZE BOX Who	Polydor	6
29	12	YOU DON'T HAVE TO SAY YOU LOVE ME Guys 'N' Dolls	Magnet	2
22	[13]	I LOVE MUSIC The O'Jays	Philadelphia	5
11	14	LET'S CALL IT QUITS Slade	Polydor	4
23	15	(DO THE) SPANISH HUSTLE Fatback Band	Polydor	3
37	16	PEOPLE LIKE YOU PEOPLE LIKE ME Glitter Band	Bell	2
19	[17]	SOMETHING'S BEEN MAKING ME BLUE Smokie	Rak	5
15	18	MOONLIGHT SERENADE/LITTLE BROWN JUG/ IN THE MOOD Glenn Miller	RCA	6
25	19	MISS YOU NIGHTS Cliff Richard	EMI	3
16	20	LOW RIDER War	Island	7
12	21	LOVE TO LOVE YOU BABY Donna Summer	GTO	8
-	22	I WANNA STAY WITH YOU Gallagher & Lyle ●	A&M	1
8	23	NO REGRETS Walker Brothers	GTO	8
13	24	MAMA MIA Abba	Epic	12
-	25	LET'S DO THE LATIN HUSTLE Eddie Drennon & B.B.S. Unlimited ●	Pye	1
40	26	LET'S DO THE LATIN HUSTLE M&O Band	Creole	2
-	27	FALLING APART AT THE SEAMS Marmalade	Target	1
26	28	TUXEDO JUNCTION Manhattan Transfer	Atlantic	5
27	29	YOUR MAGIC PUT A SPELL ON ME L.J. Johnson	Philips	5
-	30	WAKE UP EVERYBODY Harold Melvin & The Blue Notes	Philadelphia	1
17	31	WE DO IT R & J Stone	RCA	8
14	32	LOVE MACHINE Miracles	Tamla Motown	8
28	33	WEAK SPOT Evelyn Thomas	20th Century	6
31	34	CLOUD 99 St. Andrews Chorale	Decca	3
24	35	WALK AWAY FROM LOVE David Ruffin	Tamla Motown	7
-	36	SHIPS IN THE NIGHT Be-Bop Deluxe ●	Harvest	1
34	37	IF PARADISE WAS HALF AS NICE Amen Corner	Immediate	2
-	38	HEY MISS PAYNE Chequers	Creole	1
21	39	BABY FACE Wing And A Prayer Fife And Drum Corps.	Atlantic	7
-	40	CONCRETE AND CLAY Randy Edelman ●	20th Century	1

LW	TW	*WEEK ENDING* **13 MARCH 1976**		Wks
1	1	I LOVE TO LOVE Tina Charles	CBS	5
2	2	DECEMBER '63 Four Seasons	Warner Bros.	7
3	3	CONVOY C.W. McCall	MGM	4
8	4	LOVE REALLY HURTS WITHOUT YOU Billy Ocean	GTO	4
4	5	RODRIGO'S GUITAR CONCERTO Manuel And The Music Of The Mountains	EMI	7
5	6	IT SHOULD HAVE BEEN ME Yvonne Fair	Tamla Motown	7
16	7	PEOPLE LIKE YOU PEOPLE LIKE ME Glitter Band	Bell	3
7	8	RAIN Status Quo	Vertigo	5
12	9	YOU DON'T HAVE TO SAY YOU LOVE ME Guys 'N' Dolls	Magnet	3
15	[10]	(DO THE) SPANISH HUSTLE Fatback Band	Polydor	4
6	11	DAT Pluto Shervington	Opal	5
22	12	I WANNA STAY WITH YOU Gallagher & Lyle	A&M	2
10	13	FUNKY WEEKEND Stylistics	Avco	4
-	14	SAVE YOUR KISSES FOR ME Brotherhood of Man ●	Pye	1
-	15	YOU SEE THE TROUBLE WITH ME Barry White	20th Century	1
19	16	MISS YOU NIGHTS Cliff Richard	EMI	4
11	17	SQUEEZE BOX Who	Polydor	7
13	18	I LOVE MUSIC The O'Jays	Philadelphia	6
27	19	FALLING APART AT THE SEAMS Marmalade	Target	2
25	[20]	LET'S DO THE LATIN HUSTLE Eddie Drennon & B.B.S. Unlimited	Pye	2
26	21	LET'S DO THE LATIN HUSTLE M&O Band	Creole	3
9	22	FOREVER AND EVER Slik	Bell	9
14	23	LET'S CALL IT QUITS Slade	Polydor	5
17	24	SOMETHING'S BEEN MAKING ME BLUE Smokie	Rak	6
40	25	CONCRETE AND CLAY Randy Edelman	20th Century	2
30	26	WAKE UP EVERYBODY Harold Melvin & The Blue Notes	Philadelphia	2
-	27	TAKE IT TO THE LIMIT Eagles	Asylum	1
21	28	LOVE TO LOVE YOU BABY Donna Summer	GTO	9
-	29	HEY MR. MUSIC MAN Peters And Lee	Philips	1
23	30	NO REGRETS Walker Brothers	GTO	9
-	31	NEVER GONNA FALL IN LOVE AGAIN Dana	GTO	1
36	32	SHIPS IN THE NIGHT Be-Bop Deluxe	Harvest	2
-	[33]	SEAGULL Rainbow Cottage ●	Penny Farthing	1

March 1976

☐ Highest position disc reached ● Act's first ever week on chart

LW	TW	Title / Artist	Label	Wks
29	34	YOUR MAGIC PUT A SPELL ON ME L.J. Johnson	Philips	6
18	35	MOONLIGHT SERENADE/LITTLE BROWN JUG/ IN THE MOOD Glenn Miller	RCA	7
34	36	CLOUD 99 St. Andrews Chorale	Decca	4
38	37	HEY MISS PAYNE Chequers	Creole	2
24	38	MAMA MIA Abba	Epic	13
32	39	LOVE MACHINE Miracles	Tamla Motown	9
-	[40]	LONDON BOYS T.Rex	EMI	1

LW	TW	*WEEK ENDING* **20 MARCH 1976**		Wks
1	1	I LOVE TO LOVE Tina Charles	CBS	6
3	2	CONVOY C.W. McCall	MGM	5
4	[3]	LOVE REALLY HURTS WITHOUT YOU Billy Ocean	GTO	5
14	4	SAVE YOUR KISSES FOR ME Brotherhood of Man	Pye	2
9	[5]	YOU DON'T HAVE TO SAY YOU LOVE ME Guys 'N' Dolls	Magnet	4
15	6	YOU SEE THE TROUBLE WITH ME Barry White	20th Century	2
7	7	PEOPLE LIKE YOU PEOPLE LIKE ME Glitter Band	Bell	4
12	8	I WANNA STAY WITH YOU Gallagher & Lyle	A&M	3
2	9	DECEMBER '63 Four Seasons	Warner Bros.	8
6	10	IT SHOULD HAVE BEEN ME Yvonne Fair	Tamla Motown	8
10	11	(DO THE) SPANISH HUSTLE Fatback Band	Polydor	5
19	12	FALLING APART AT THE SEAMS Marmalade	Target	3
13	13	FUNKY WEEKEND Stylistics	Avco	5
5	14	RODRIGO'S GUITAR CONCERTO Manuel And The Music Of The Mountains	EMI	8
8	15	RAIN Status Quo	Vertigo	6
11	16	DAT Pluto Shervington	Opal	6
-	17	YESTERDAY Beatles	Apple	1
16	18	MISS YOU NIGHTS Cliff Richard	EMI	5
18	19	I LOVE MUSIC The O'Jays	Philadelphia	7
17	20	SQUEEZE BOX Who	Polydor	8
29	21	HEY MR. MUSIC MAN Peters And Lee	Philips	2
25	22	CONCRETE AND CLAY Randy Edelman	20th Century	3
26	[23]	WAKE UP EVERYBODY Harold Melvin & The Blue Notes	Philadelphia	3
21	24	LET'S DO THE LATIN HUSTLE M&O Band	Creole	4
27	25	TAKE IT TO THE LIMIT Eagles	Asylum	2
20	26	LET'S DO THE LATIN HUSTLE Eddie Drennon & B.B.S. Unlimited	Pye	3
24	27	SOMETHING'S BEEN MAKING ME BLUE Smokie	Rak	7
-	28	HELLO HAPPINESS Drifters	Bell	1
32	29	SHIPS IN THE NIGHT Be-Bop Deluxe	Harvest	3
-	[30]	HERE THERE AND EVERYWHERE Emmylou Harris ●	Reprise	1
-	31	I'M MANDY FLY ME 10 C.C.	Mercury	1
37	[32]	HEY MISS PAYNE Chequers	Creole	3
23	33	LET'S CALL IT QUITS Slade	Polydor	6
31	34	NEVER GONNA FALL IN LOVE AGAIN Dana	GTO	2
-	[35]	CAN'T SAY HOW MUCH I LOVE YOU Demis Roussos	Philips	1
-	36	PINBALL WIZARD Elton John	DJM	1
-	37	CITY LIGHTS David Essex	CBS	1
-	[38]	LA BOOGA ROOGA Surprise Sisters ●	Good Earth	1
-	39	WHERE THE HAPPY PEOPLE GO Trammps	Atlantic	1
-	40	JUNGLE ROCK Hank Mizell ●	Charly	1

LW	TW	*WEEK ENDING* **27 MARCH 1976**		Wks
4	1	SAVE YOUR KISSES FOR ME Brotherhood of Man	Pye	3
3	[2]	LOVE REALLY HURTS WITHOUT YOU Billy Ocean	GTO	6
1	3	I LOVE TO LOVE Tina Charles	CBS	7
6	4	YOU SEE THE TROUBLE WITH ME Barry White	20th Century	3
7	[5]	PEOPLE LIKE YOU PEOPLE LIKE ME Glitter Band	Bell	5
5	6	YOU DON'T HAVE TO SAY YOU LOVE ME Guys 'N' Dolls	Magnet	5
8	7	I WANNA STAY WITH YOU Gallagher & Lyle	A&M	4
2	8	CONVOY C.W. McCall	MGM	6
12	[9]	FALLING APART AT THE SEAMS Marmalade	Target	4

■*Save Your Kisses For Me* is the first British song since *Puppet On A String* in 1967 to both win Eurovision and go to number one (27.03.76) ■ *Yesterday* by the Beatles, an American number one in 1965, is finally released as a single in Britain and charts immediately (20.03.76) ■ The same week, *Here There And Everywhere* from the Beatles' 1966 album 'Revolver' becomes a hit single courtesy of Emmylou Harris (20.03.76)■

March 1976

□ Highest position disc reached ● Act's first ever week on chart

LW	TW	Title / Artist	Label	Wks
17	10	YESTERDAY Beatles	*Apple*	2
22	11	CONCRETE AND CLAY Randy Edelman	*20th Century*	4
25	12	TAKE IT TO THE LIMIT Eagles	*Asylum*	3
-	13	MUSIC John Miles	*Decca*	1
11	14	(DO THE) SPANISH HUSTLE Fatback Band	*Polydor*	6
18	15	MISS YOU NIGHTS Cliff Richard	*EMI*	6
24	16	LET'S DO THE LATIN HUSTLE M&O Band	*Creole*	5
9	17	DECEMBER '63 Four Seasons	*Warner Bros.*	9
31	18	I'M MANDY FLY ME 10 C.C.	*Mercury*	2
-	19	HELLO HAPPINESS Drifters	*Bell*	1
26	20	LET'S DO THE LATIN HUSTLE Eddie Drennon & B.B.S. Unlimited	*Pye*	4
36	21	PINBALL WIZARD Elton John	*DJM*	2
21	22	HEY MR. MUSIC MAN Peters and Lee	*Philips*	3
29	23	SHIPS IN THE NIGHT Be-Bop Deluxe	*Harvest*	4
37	24	CITY LIGHTS David Essex	*CBS*	2
14	25	RODRIGO'S GUITAR CONCERTO Manuel And The Music Of The Mountains	*EMI*	9
10	26	IT SHOULD HAVE BEEN ME Yvonne Fair	*Tamla Motown*	9
40	27	JUNGLE ROCK Hank Mizell	*Charly*	2
13	28	FUNKY WEEKEND Stylistics	*Avco*	6
23	29	WAKE UP EVERYBODY Harold Melvin & The Blue Notes	*Philadelphia*	4
-	30	DON'T STOP IT NOW Hot Chocolate	*RAK*	1
15	31	RAIN Status Quo	*Vertigo*	7
30	32	HERE THERE AND EVERYWHERE Emmylou Harris	*Reprise*	2
19	33	I LOVE MUSIC The O'Jays	*Philadelphia*	8
16	34	DAT Pluto Shervington	*Opal*	7
34	35	NEVER GONNA FALL IN LOVE AGAIN Dana	*GTO*	3
-	36	IF YOU LOVE ME Mary Hopkin	*Good Earth*	1
-	37	SPANISH WINE Chris White ●	*Charisma*	1
-	38	SEAGULL Rainbow Cottage	*Penny Farthing*	1
-	39	RIDERS ON THE STORM Doors	*Elektra*	1
-	40	YOU BELONG TO ME Gary Glitter	*Bell*	1

WEEK ENDING 3 APRIL 1976

LW	TW	Title / Artist	Label	Wks
1	1	SAVE YOUR KISSES FOR ME Brotherhood of Man	*Pye*	4
4	2	YOU SEE THE TROUBLE WITH ME Barry White	*20th Century*	4
2	3	LOVE REALLY HURTS WITHOUT YOU Billy Ocean	*GTO*	7
13	4	MUSIC John Miles	*Decca*	2
3	5	I LOVE TO LOVE Tina Charles	*CBS*	8
7	6	I WANNA STAY WITH YOU Gallagher & Lyle	*A&M*	5
21	7	PINBALL WIZARD Elton John	*DJM*	3
10	8	YESTERDAY Beatles	*Apple*	3
9	9	FALLING APART AT THE SEAMS Marmalade	*Target*	5
5	10	PEOPLE LIKE YOU PEOPLE LIKE ME Glitter Band	*Bell*	6
18	11	I'M MANDY FLY ME 10 C.C.	*Mercury*	3
19	12	HELLO HAPPINESS Drifters	*Bell*	2
12	13	TAKE IT TO THE LIMIT Eagles	*Asylum*	4
-	14	FERNANDO Abba	*Epic*	1
6	15	YOU DON'T HAVE TO SAY YOU LOVE ME Guys 'N' Dolls	*Magnet*	6
22	16	HEY MR. MUSIC MAN Peters And Lee	*Philips*	4
11	17	CONCRETE AND CLAY Randy Edelman	*20th Century*	5
27	18	JUNGLE ROCK Hank Mizell	*Charly*	3
8	19	CONVOY C.W. McCall	*MGM*	7
30	20	DON'T STOP IT NOW Hot Chocolate	*RAK*	2
-	21	GIRLS GIRLS GIRLS Sailor	*Epic*	1
-	22	HEY JUDE Beatles	*Apple*	1
29	23	WAKE UP EVERYBODY Harold Melvin & The Blue Notes	*Philadelphia*	5
15	24	MISS YOU NIGHTS Cliff Richard	*EMI*	7
-	25	THEME FROM MAHOGANY (DO YOU KNOW WHERE YOU'RE GOING TO) Diana Ross	*Tamla Motown*	1
23	26	SHIPS IN THE NIGHT Be-Bop Deluxe	*Harvest*	5
-	27	PAPERBACK WRITER Beatles	*Apple*	1
-	28	THERE'S A KIND OF HUSH Carpenters	*A&M*	1
17	29	DECEMBER '63 Four Seasons	*Warner Bros.*	10
24	30	CITY LIGHTS David Essex	*CBS*	3
25	31	RODRIGO'S GUITAR CONCERTO Manuel And The Music Of The Mountains	*EMI*	10
36	32	IF YOU LOVE ME Mary Hopkin	*Good Earth*	2
-	33	DISCO CONNECTION Isaac Hayes	*ABC*	1
39	34	RIDERS ON THE STORM Doors	*Elektra*	2
14	35	(DO THE) SPANISH HUSTLE Fatback Band	*Polydor*	7
26	36	IT SHOULD HAVE BEEN ME Yvonne Fair	*Tamla Motown*	10
37	37	SPANISH WINE Chris White	*Charisma*	2
-	38	MOVIN' Brass Construction ●	*United Artists*	1
-	39	LAZY SUNDAY Small Faces	*Immediate*	1
40	40	YOU BELONG TO ME Gary Glitter	*Bell*	2

WEEK ENDING 10 APRIL 1976

LW	TW	Title / Artist	Label	Wks
1	1	SAVE YOUR KISSES FOR ME Brotherhood of Man	*Pye*	5
2	2	YOU SEE THE TROUBLE WITH ME Barry White	*20th Century*	5
4	3	MUSIC John Miles	*Decca*	3
14	4	FERNANDO Abba	*Epic*	2
3	5	LOVE REALLY HURTS WITHOUT YOU Billy Ocean	*GTO*	8
11	6	I'M MANDY FLY ME 10 C.C.	*Mercury*	4
18	7	JUNGLE ROCK Hank Mizell	*Charly*	4
7	8	PINBALL WIZARD Elton John	*DJM*	4
8	9	YESTERDAY Beatles	*Apple*	4
25	10	THEME FROM MAHOGANY (DO YOU KNOW WHERE YOU'RE GOING TO) Diana Ross	*Tamla Motown*	2
9	11	FALLING APART AT THE SEAMS Marmalade	*Target*	6
12	12	HELLO HAPPINESS Drifters	*Bell*	3
6	13	I WANNA STAY WITH YOU Gallagher & Lyle	*A&M*	6
21	14	GIRLS GIRLS GIRLS Sailor	*Epic*	2
10	15	PEOPLE LIKE YOU PEOPLE LIKE ME Glitter Band	*Bell*	7
17	16	CONCRETE AND CLAY Randy Edelman	*20th Century*	6
13	17	TAKE IT TO THE LIMIT Eagles	*Asylum*	5
22	18	HEY JUDE Beatles	*Apple*	2
20	19	DON'T STOP IT NOW Hot Chocolate	*RAK*	3
-	20	LOVE ME LIKE I LOVE YOU Bay City Rollers	*Bell*	1
15	21	YOU DON'T HAVE TO SAY YOU LOVE ME Guys 'N' Dolls	*Magnet*	7
5	22	I LOVE TO LOVE Tina Charles	*CBS*	9
27	23	PAPERBACK WRITER Beatles	*Apple*	2
28	24	THERE'S A KIND OF HUSH Carpenters	*A&M*	2
33	25	DISCO CONNECTION Isaac Hayes	*ABC*	2
-	26	GET UP AND BOOGIE Silver Convention	*Magnet*	1
24	27	MISS YOU NIGHTS Cliff Richard	*EMI*	8
38	28	MOVIN' Brass Construction	*United Artists*	2
-	29	LIFE IS TOO SHORT GIRL Sheer Elegance	*Pye*	1
-	30	GET BACK Beatles	*Apple*	1
19	31	CONVOY C.W. McCall	*MGM*	8
-	32	STRAWBERRY FIELDS FOREVER Beatles	*Parlophone*	1
34	33	RIDERS ON THE STORM Doors	*Elektra*	3
16	34	HEY MR. MUSIC MAN Peters And Lee	*Philips*	5
26	35	SHIPS IN THE NIGHT Be-Bop Deluxe	*Harvest*	6
30	36	CITY LIGHTS David Essex	*CBS*	4
-	37	ARMS OF MARY Sutherland Brothers/Quiver ●	*CBS*	1
32	38	IF YOU LOVE ME Mary Hopkin	*Good Earth*	3
-	39	YOU SEXY SUGAR PLUM Rodger Collins ●	*Fantasy*	1
-	40	WHERE THE HAPPY PEOPLE GO Trammps	*Atlantic*	1

WEEK ENDING 17 APRIL 1976

LW	TW	Title / Artist	Label	Wks
1	1	SAVE YOUR KISSES FOR ME Brotherhood of Man	*Pye*	6
4	2	FERNANDO Abba	*Epic*	3
3	3	MUSIC John Miles	*Decca*	4
2	4	YOU SEE THE TROUBLE WITH ME Barry White	*20th Century*	6
7	5	JUNGLE ROCK Hank Mizell	*Charly*	5
6	6	I'M MANDY FLY ME 10 C.C.	*Mercury*	5
10	7	THEME FROM MAHOGANY (DO YOU KNOW WHERE YOU'RE GOING TO) Diana Ross	*Tamla Motown*	3
20	8	LOVE ME LIKE I LOVE YOU Bay City Rollers	*Bell*	2
14	9	GIRLS GIRLS GIRLS Sailor	*Epic*	3
8	10	PINBALL WIZARD Elton John	*DJM*	5
19	11	DON'T STOP IT NOW Hot Chocolate	*RAK*	4
18	12	HEY JUDE Beatles	*Apple*	3
9	13	YESTERDAY Beatles	*Apple*	5

In these weeks ■ A re-promotion of the Beatles catalogue gives them five Top 40 re-entries ■ Former Top 10 songs enjoying new hit versions include *Pinball Wizard*, *Concrete And Clay* and *There's A Kind Of Hush* (03.04.76) ■ Hank Mizell has a 70s hit with a record from the 50s (27.03.76)■

LW	TW	Title	Artist	Label	Wks
11	14	FALLING APART AT THE SEAMS	Marmalade	Target	7
13	15	I WANNA STAY WITH YOU	Gallagher & Lyle	A&M	7
12	16	HELLO HAPPINESS	Drifters	Bell	4
25	17	DISCO CONNECTION	Isaac Hayes	ABC	3
-	18	S-S-S- SINGLE BED	Fox	GTO	1
5	19	LOVE REALLY HURTS WITHOUT YOU	Billy Ocean	GTO	9
29	20	LIFE IS TOO SHORT GIRL	Sheer Elegance	Pye	2
26	21	GET UP AND BOOGIE	Silver Convention	Magnet	2
24	[22]	THERE'S A KIND OF HUSH	Carpenters	A&M	3
28	[23]	MOVIN'	Brass Construction	United Artists	3
15	24	PEOPLE LIKE YOU PEOPLE LIKE ME	Glitter Band	Bell	8
-	25	HONKY TONK TRAIN BLUES	Keith Emerson ●	Manticore	1
-	26	ALL BY MYSELF	Eric Carmen ●	Arista	1
23	27	PAPERBACK WRITER	Beatles	Apple	3
30	28	GET BACK	Beatles	Apple	2
22	29	I LOVE TO LOVE	Tina Charles	CBS	10
39	30	YOU SEXY SUGAR PLUM	Rodger Collins	Fantasy	2
37	31	ARMS OF MARY	Sutherland Brothers/Quiver	CBS	2
17	32	TAKE IT TO THE LIMIT	Eagles	Asylum	6
16	33	CONCRETE AND CLAY	Randy Edelman	20th Century	7
32	34	STRAWBERRY FIELDS FOREVER	Beatles	Parlophone	2
40	35	WHERE THE HAPPY PEOPLE GO	Trammps	Atlantic	2
33	36	RIDERS ON THE STORM	Doors	Elektra	4
-	37	HELP	Beatles	Parlophone	1
34	38	HEY MR. MUSIC MAN	Peters And Lee	Philips	6
-	39	FALLEN ANGEL	Frankie Valli	Private Stock	1
31	40	CONVOY	C.W.McCall	MGM	9

WEEK ENDING 24 APRIL 1976

LW	TW	Title	Artist	Label	Wks
1	[1]	SAVE YOUR KISSES FOR ME	Brotherhood of Man	Pye	7
2	2	FERNANDO	Abba	Epic	4
3	3	MUSIC	John Miles	Decca	5
5	4	JUNGLE ROCK	Hank Mizell	Charly	6
7	[5]	THEME FROM MAHOGANY (DO YOU KNOW WHERE YOU'RE GOING TO)	Diana Ross	Tamla Motown	4
6	[6]	I'M MANDY FLY ME	10 C.C.	Mercury	6
9	[7]	GIRLS GIRLS GIRLS	Sailor	Epic	4
8	8	LOVE ME LIKE I LOVE YOU	Bay City Rollers	Bell	3
4	9	YOU SEE THE TROUBLE WITH ME	Barry White	20th Century	7
21	10	GET UP AND BOOGIE	Silver Convention	Magnet	3
18	11	S-S-S- SINGLE BED	Fox	GTO	2
12	12	HEY JUDE	Beatles	Apple	4
11	13	DON'T STOP IT NOW	Hot Chocolate	RAK	5
17	14	DISCO CONNECTION	Isaac Hayes	ABC	4
10	15	PINBALL WIZARD	Elton John	DJM	6
16	16	HELLO HAPPINESS	Drifters	Bell	5
20	17	LIFE IS TOO SHORT GIRL	Sheer Elegance	Pye	3
13	18	YESTERDAY	Beatles	Apple	6
-	19	CONVOY GB	Laurie Lingo And The Dipsticks	State	1
26	20	ALL BY MYSELF	Eric Carmen	Arista	2
39	21	FALLEN ANGEL	Frankie Valli	Private Stock	2
30	[22]	YOU SEXY SUGAR PLUM	Rodger Collins ●	Fantasy	3
22	23	THERE'S A KIND OF HUSH	Carpenters	A&M	4
19	24	LOVE REALLY HURTS WITHOUT YOU	Billy Ocean	GTO	10
25	25	HONKY TONK TRAIN BLUES	Keith Emerson	Manticore	2
23	26	MOVIN'	Brass Construction	United Artists	4
-	27	SILVER STAR	Four Seasons	Warner Brothers	1
14	28	FALLING APART AT THE SEAMS	Marmalade	Target	8
-	29	MORE MORE MORE	Andrea True Connection ●	Buddah	1
15	30	I WANNA STAY WITH YOU	Gallagher & Lyle	A&M	8
31	31	ARMS OF MARY	Sutherland Brothers/Quiver	CBS	3
28	32	GET BACK	Beatles	Apple	3
-	33	LET YOUR LOVE FLOW	Bellamy Brothers ●	Warner Brothers	1
24	34	PEOPLE LIKE YOU PEOPLE LIKE ME	Glitter Band	Bell	9
-	35	MOVIE STAR	Harpo ●	DJM	1
-	36	REGGAE LIKE IT USED TO BE	Paul Nicholas ●	RSO	1
27	37	PAPERBACK WRITER	Beatles	Apple	4
29	38	I LOVE TO LOVE	Tina Charles	CBS	11
-	39	BABY I'M YOURS	Linda Lewis	Arista	1
-	40	CAN'T HELP FALLING IN LOVE	Stylistics	Avco	1

May 1976

□ Highest position disc reached ● Act's first ever week on chart

WEEK ENDING 1 MAY 1976

LW	TW	Title	Artist	Label	Wks
1	[1]	SAVE YOUR KISSES FOR ME	Brotherhood of Man	Pye	8
2	2	FERNANDO	Abba	Epic	5
4	[3]	JUNGLE ROCK	Hank Mizell ●	Charly	7
8	[4]	LOVE ME LIKE I LOVE YOU	Bay City Rollers	Bell	4
11	5	S-S-S- SINGLE BED	Fox	GTO	3
5	6	THEME FROM MAHOGANY (DO YOU KNOW WHERE YOU'RE GOING TO)	Diana Ross	Tamla Motown	5
7	[7]	GIRLS GIRLS GIRLS	Sailor	Epic	5
6	8	I'M MANDY FLY ME	10 C.C.	Mercury	7
10	9	GET UP AND BOOGIE	Silver Convention	Magnet	4
14	[10]	DISCO CONNECTION	Isaac Hayes	ABC	5
3	11	MUSIC	John Miles	Decca	6
17	12	LIFE IS TOO SHORT GIRL	Sheer Elegance	Pye	4
20	13	ALL BY MYSELF	Eric Carmen	Arista	3
19	14	CONVOY GB	Laurie Lingo And The Dipsticks	State	2
13	15	DON'T STOP IT NOW	Hot Chocolate	RAK	6
27	16	SILVER STAR	Four Seasons	Warner Brothers	2
29	17	MORE MORE MORE	Andrea True Connection	Buddah	2
12	18	HEY JUDE	Beatles	Apple	5
31	19	ARMS OF MARY	Sutherland Brothers/Quiver	CBS	4
40	20	CAN'T HELP FALLING IN LOVE	Stylistics	Avco	2
25	[21]	HONKY TONK TRAIN BLUES	Keith Emerson	Manticore	3
21	22	FALLEN ANGEL	Frankie Valli	Private Stock	3
9	23	YOU SEE THE TROUBLE WITH ME	Barry White	20th Century	8
-	24	LOVE HANGOVER	Diana Ross	Tamla Motown	1
-	25	I'LL GO WHERE YOUR MUSIC TAKES ME	Jimmy James And The Vagabonds	Pye	1
22	26	YOU SEXY SUGAR PLUM	Rodger Collins	Fantasy	4
35	27	MOVIE STAR	Harpo	DJM	2
33	28	LET YOUR LOVE FLOW	Bellamy Brothers	Warner Brothers	2
36	29	REGGAE LIKE IT USED TO BE	Paul Nicholas	RSO	2
-	30	DISCO LADY	Johnny Taylor ●	CBS	1
15	31	PINBALL WIZARD	Elton John	DJM	7
-	32	I'M YOUR PUPPET	James And Bobby Purify ●	Mercury	1
39	[33]	BABY I'M YOURS	Linda Lewis	Arista	2
26	34	MOVIN'	Brass Construction	United Artists	5
-	35	NO CHARGE	J.J. Barrie ●	Power Exchange	1
-	36	YOU'RE THE REASON WHY	Rubettes	State	1
23	37	THERE'S A KIND OF HUSH	Carpenters	A&M	5
32	38	GET BACK	Beatles	Apple	4
-	[39]	RAIN FOREST	Biddu Orchestra	Epic	1
28	40	FALLING APART AT THE SEAMS	Marmalade	Target	9

WEEK ENDING 8 MAY 1976

LW	TW	Title	Artist	Label	Wks
2	[1]	FERNANDO	Abba	Epic	6
1	2	SAVE YOUR KISSES FOR ME	Brotherhood of Man	Pye	9
3	3	JUNGLE ROCK	Hank Mizell	Charly	8
14	[4]	CONVOY GB	Laurie Lingo And The Dipsticks	State	3
5	5	S-S-S- SINGLE BED	Fox	GTO	4
16	6	SILVER STAR	Four Seasons	Warner Brothers	3
9	[7]	GET UP AND BOOGIE	Silver Convention	Magnet	5
6	8	THEME FROM MAHOGANY (DO YOU KNOW WHERE YOU'RE GOING TO)	Diana Ross	Tamla Motown	6
12	[9]	LIFE IS TOO SHORT GIRL	Sheer Elegance	Pye	5
10	[10]	DISCO CONNECTION	Isaac Hayes	ABC	6
22	[11]	FALLEN ANGEL	Frankie Valli	Private Stock	4
13	[12]	ALL BY MYSELF	Eric Carmen	Arista	4
7	13	GIRLS GIRLS GIRLS	Sailor	Epic	6
20	14	CAN'T HELP FALLING IN LOVE	Stylistics	Avco	3
11	15	MUSIC	John Miles	Decca	7
19	16	ARMS OF MARY	Sutherland Brothers/Quiver	CBS	5
4	17	LOVE ME LIKE I LOVE YOU	Bay City Rollers	Bell	5
17	18	MORE MORE MORE	Andrea True Connection	Buddah	3
24	19	LOVE HANGOVER	Diana Ross	Tamla Motown	2
28	20	LET YOUR LOVE FLOW	Bellamy Brothers	Warner Brothers	3
8	21	I'M MANDY FLY ME	10 C.C.	Mercury	8
-	22	FOOL TO CRY	Rolling Stones	Rolling Stones	1

■Paul Burnett and Dave Lee Travis become chart stars as Laurie Lingo and the Dipsticks and become the highest charting DJs to date (24.04.76) ■ After Greg Lake's hit at Christmas, Emerson Lake and Palmer colleague Keith Emerson gets his own chart single (17.04.76) ■ James and Bobby Purify's 1966 US Top 10 hit *I'm Your Puppet* succeeds in Britain ten years later as a re-recording (01.05.76)■

May 1976

□ Highest position disc reached ● Act's first ever week on chart

LW	TW	Title	Artist	Label	Wks
29	23	REGGAE LIKE IT USED TO BE	Paul Nicholas	*RSO*	3
27	[24]	MOVIE STAR	Harpo	*DJM*	3
30	[25]	DISCO LADY	Johnny Taylor	*CBS*	2
35	26	NO CHARGE	J.J. Barrie	*Power Exchange*	2
32	27	I'M YOUR PUPPET	James And Bobby Purify	*Mercury*	2
36	[28]	YOU'RE THE REASON WHY	Rubettes	*State*	2
21	29	HONKY TONK TRAIN BLUES	Keith Emerson	*Manticore*	4
25	30	I'LL GO WHERE YOUR MUSIC TAKES ME	Jimmy James And The Vagabonds	*Pye*	2
-	31	LOVE ME LIKE A LOVER	Tina Charles	*CBS*	1
26	32	YOU SEXY SUGAR PLUM	Rodger Collins	*Fantasy*	5
18	33	HEY JUDE	Beatles	*Apple*	6
15	34	DON'T STOP IT NOW	Hot Chocolate	*RAK*	7
23	35	YOU SEE THE TROUBLE WITH ME	Barry White	*20th Century*	9
-	[36]	TOAST OF LOVE	Three Degrees	*Epic*	1
-	[37]	HURT	Elvis Presley	*RCA*	1
33	38	BABY I'M YOURS	Linda Lewis	*Arista*	3
-	39	THE WINKLE MAN	Judge Dread	*Cactus*	1
34	40	MOVIN'	Brass Construction	*United Artists*	6

WEEK ENDING **15 MAY 1976**

LW	TW	Title	Artist	Label	Wks
1	[1]	FERNANDO	Abba	*Epic*	7
2	2	SAVE YOUR KISSES FOR ME	Brotherhood of Man	*Pye*	10
3	[3]	JUNGLE ROCK	Hank Mizell	*Charly*	9
5	[4]	S-S-S- SINGLE BED	Fox	*GTO*	5
18	[5]	MORE MORE MORE	Andrea True Connection	*Buddah*	4
16	6	ARMS OF MARY	Sutherland Brothers/Quiver	*CBS*	6
4	7	CONVOY GB	Laurie Lingo And The Dipsticks	*State*	4
7	8	GET UP AND BOOGIE	Silver Convention	*Magnet*	6
6	9	SILVER STAR	Four Seasons	*Warner Brothers*	4
14	10	CAN'T HELP FALLING IN LOVE	Stylistics	*Avco*	4
26	11	NO CHARGE	J.J. Barrie	*Power Exchange*	3
9	12	LIFE IS TOO SHORT GIRL	Sheer Elegance	*Pye*	6
11	13	FALLEN ANGEL	Frankie Valli	*Private Stock*	5
22	14	FOOL TO CRY	Rolling Stones	*Rolling Stones*	2
19	15	LOVE HANGOVER	Diana Ross	*Tamla Motown*	3
27	16	I'M YOUR PUPPET	James And Bobby Purify	*Mercury*	3
20	17	LET YOUR LOVE FLOW	Bellamy Brothers	*Warner Brothers*	4
10	18	DISCO CONNECTION	Isaac Hayes	*ABC*	7
12	19	ALL BY MYSELF	Eric Carmen	*Arista*	5
23	20	REGGAE LIKE IT USED TO BE	Paul Nicholas	*RSO*	4
17	21	LOVE ME LIKE I LOVE YOU	Bay City Rollers	*Bell*	6
-	22	MY RESISTANCE IS LOW	Robin Sarstedt ●	*Decca*	1
30	[23]	I'LL GO WHERE YOUR MUSIC TAKES ME	Jimmy James And The Vagabonds	*Pye*	3
-	24	DEVIL WOMAN	Cliff Richard	*EMI*	1
24	25	MOVIE STAR	Harpo	*DJM*	4
8	26	DO YOU KNOW WHERE YOU'RE GOING TO	Diana Ross	*Tamla Motown*	7
25	27	DISCO LADY	Johnny Taylor	*CBS*	3
28	[28]	YOU'RE THE REASON WHY	Rubettes	*State*	3
-	29	SILLY LOVE SONGS	Wings	*Parlophone*	1
-	30	MIDNIGHT TRAIN TO GEORGIA	Gladys Knight And The Pips	*Buddah*	1
31	31	LOVE ME LIKE A LOVER	Tina Charles	*CBS*	2
13	32	GIRLS GIRLS GIRLS	Sailor	*Epic*	7
-	33	COMBINE HARVESTER	The Wurzels ●	*EMI*	1
-	34	REQUIEM	Slik	*Bell*	1
39	[35]	THE WINKLE MAN	Judge Dread	*Cactus*	2
15	36	MUSIC	John Miles	*Decca*	8
-	37	SHAKE IT DOWN	Mud	*Private Stock*	1
21	38	I'M MANDY FLY ME	10 C.C.	*Mercury*	9
-	39	SHOW ME THE WAY	Peter Frampton ●	*A&M*	1
-	40	SOUL CITY WALK	Archie Bell And The Drells	*Philadelphia*	1

WEEK ENDING **22 MAY 1976**

LW	TW	Title	Artist	Label	Wks
1	[1]	FERNANDO	Abba	*Epic*	8
11	2	NO CHARGE	J.J. Barrie	*Power Exchange*	4
9	[3]	SILVER STAR	Four Seasons	*Warner Brothers*	5
10	[4]	CAN'T HELP FALLING IN LOVE	Stylistics	*Avco*	5
6	[5]	ARMS OF MARY	Sutherland Brothers/Quiver	*CBS*	7
5	6	MORE MORE MORE	Andrea True Connection	*Buddah*	5
14	7	FOOL TO CRY	Rolling Stones	*Rolling Stones*	3
2	8	SAVE YOUR KISSES FOR ME	Brotherhood of Man	*Pye*	11
3	9	JUNGLE ROCK	Hank Mizell	*Charly*	10
4	10	S-S-S- SINGLE BED	Fox	*GTO*	6
22	11	MY RESISTANCE IS LOW	Robin Sarstedt	*Decca*	2
8	12	GET UP AND BOOGIE	Silver Convention	*Magnet*	7
7	13	CONVOY GB	Laurie Lingo And The Dipsticks	*State*	5
33	14	COMBINE HARVESTER	The Wurzels	*EMI*	2
15	15	LOVE HANGOVER	Diana Ross	*Tamla Motown*	4
29	16	SILLY LOVE SONGS	Wings	*Parlophone*	2
17	17	LET YOUR LOVE FLOW	Bellamy Brothers	*Warner Brothers*	5
13	18	FALLEN ANGEL	Frankie Valli	*Private Stock*	6
16	19	I'M YOUR PUPPET	James And Bobby Purify	*Mercury*	4
12	20	LIFE IS TOO SHORT GIRL	Sheer Elegance	*Pye*	7
24	21	DEVIL WOMAN	Cliff Richard	*EMI*	2
18	22	DISCO CONNECTION	Isaac Hayes	*ABC*	8
19	23	ALL BY MYSELF	Eric Carmen	*Arista*	6
30	24	MIDNIGHT TRAIN TO GEORGIA	Gladys Knight And The Pips	*Buddah*	2
37	25	SHAKE IT DOWN	Mud	*Private Stock*	2
20	26	REGGAE LIKE IT USED TO BE	Paul Nicholas	*RSO*	5
27	27	DISCO LADY	Johnny Taylor	*CBS*	4
21	28	LOVE ME LIKE I LOVE YOU	Bay City Rollers	*Bell*	7
-	29	THIS IS IT	Melba Moore ●	*Buddah*	1
23	30	I'LL GO WHERE YOUR MUSIC TAKES ME	Jimmy James And The Vagabonds	*Pye*	4
40	31	SOUL CITY WALK	Archie Bell And The Drells	*Philadelphia*	2
28	32	YOU'RE THE REASON WHY	Rubettes	*State*	4
39	33	SHOW ME THE WAY	Peter Frampton	*A&M*	2
25	34	MOVIE STAR	Harpo	*DJM*	5
34	35	REQUIEM	Slik	*Bell*	2
35	36	THE WINKLE MAN	Judge Dread	*Cactus*	3
-	37	THE FLASHER	Mistura With Lloyd Michels ●	*Route*	1
-	38	JOLENE	Dolly Parton ●	*RCA*	1
26	39	DO YOU KNOW WHERE YOU'RE GOING TO	Diana Ross	*Tamla Motown*	8
-	40	FOOLED AROUND AND FELL IN LOVE	Elvin Bishop ●	*Capricorn*	1

WEEK ENDING **29 MAY 1976**

LW	TW	Title	Artist	Label	Wks
1	[1]	FERNANDO	Abba	*Epic*	9
2	2	NO CHARGE	J.J. Barrie	*Power Exchange*	5
14	3	COMBINE HARVESTER	The Wurzels	*EMI*	3
11	4	MY RESISTANCE IS LOW	Robin Sarstedt	*Decca*	3
6	[5]	MORE MORE MORE	Andrea True Connection	*Buddah*	6
5	6	ARMS OF MARY	Sutherland Brothers/Quiver	*CBS*	8
16	7	SILLY LOVE SONGS	Wings	*Parlophone*	3
7	8	FOOL TO CRY	Rolling Stones	*Rolling Stones*	4
17	9	LET YOUR LOVE FLOW	Bellamy Brothers	*Warner Brothers*	6
15	[10]	LOVE HANGOVER	Diana Ross	*Tamla Motown*	5
21	11	DEVIL WOMAN	Cliff Richard	*EMI*	3
19	[12]	I'M YOUR PUPPET	James And Bobby Purify	*Mercury*	5
9	13	JUNGLE ROCK	Hank Mizell	*Charly*	11
4	14	CAN'T HELP FALLING IN LOVE	Stylistics	*Avco*	6
10	15	S-S-S- SINGLE BED	Fox	*GTO*	7
8	16	SAVE YOUR KISSES FOR ME	Brotherhood of Man	*Pye*	12
26	[17]	REGGAE LIKE IT USED TO BE	Paul Nicholas	*RSO*	6
24	18	MIDNIGHT TRAIN TO GEORGIA	Gladys Knight And The Pips	*Buddah*	3
12	19	GET UP AND BOOGIE	Silver Convention	*Magnet*	8
29	20	THIS IS IT	Melba Moore	*Buddah*	2
3	21	SILVER STAR	Four Seasons	*Warner Brothers*	6
33	22	SHOW ME THE WAY	Peter Frampton	*A&M*	3
25	23	SHAKE IT DOWN	Mud	*Private Stock*	3
35	[24]	REQUIEM	Slik	*Bell*	3
-	25	HEART ON MY SLEEVE	Gallagher And Lyle	*A&M*	1
30	26	I'LL GO WHERE YOUR MUSIC TAKES ME	Jimmy James And The Vagabonds	*Pye*	5

In these weeks ■ Robin Sarstedt becomes the third of three brothers to reach the Top 10, the first two being Eden Kane and Peter Sarstedt (29.05.76) ■ *Silver Star* by the Four Seasons displays some of the most violent chart behaviour of the 70s (?) ■ Sixties superstars Paul McCartney, the Rolling Stones, Diana Ross and Cliff Richard are reunited in the upper levels of the list (29.05.76)■

LW	TW	Title	Artist	Label	Wks
18	27	FALLEN ANGEL	Frankie Valli	Private Stock	7
38	28	JOLENE	Dolly Parton	RCA	2
37	29	THE FLASHER	Mistura With Lloyd Michels	Route	2
31	30	SOUL CITY WALK	Archie Bell And The Drells	Philadelphia	3
28	31	LOVE ME LIKE I LOVE YOU	Bay City Rollers	Bell	8
20	32	LIFE IS TOO SHORT GIRL	Sheer Elegance	Pye	8
27	33	DISCO LADY	Johnny Taylor	CBS	5
40	[34]	FOOLED AROUND AND FELL IN LOVE	Elvin Bishop	Capricorn	2
-	35	LET'S MAKE A BABY	Billy Paul	Philadelphia	1
22	36	DISCO CONNECTION	Isaac Hayes	ABC	9
-	37	TVC 15	David Bowie	RCA	1
13	38	CONVOY GB	Laurie Lingo And The Dipsticks	State	6
-	39	THE WANDERER	Dion	Philips	1
36	40	THE WINKLE MAN	Judge Dread	Cactus	4

WEEK ENDING 5 JUNE 1976

LW	TW	Title	Artist	Label	Wks
2	[1]	NO CHARGE	J.J. Barrie	Power Exchange	6
3	2	COMBINE HARVESTER	The Wurzels	EMI	4
4	[3]	MY RESISTANCE IS LOW	Robin Sarstedt	Decca	4
1	4	FERNANDO	Abba	Epic	10
7	5	SILLY LOVE SONGS	Wings	Parlophone	4
8	[6]	FOOL TO CRY	Rolling Stones	Rolling Stones	5
9	7	LET YOUR LOVE FLOW	Bellamy Brothers	Warner Brothers	7
6	8	ARMS OF MARY	Sutherland Brothers/Quiver	CBS	9
11	[9]	DEVIL WOMAN	Cliff Richard	EMI	4
18	[10]	MIDNIGHT TRAIN TO GEORGIA	Gladys Knight And The Pips	Buddah	4
10	11	LOVE HANGOVER	Diana Ross	Tamla Motown	6
23	[12]	SHAKE IT DOWN	Mud	Private Stock	4
12	13	I'M YOUR PUPPET	James And Bobby Purify	Mercury	6
5	14	MORE MORE MORE	Andrea True Connection	Buddah	7
22	15	SHOW ME THE WAY	Peter Frampton	A&M	4
21	16	SILVER STAR	Four Seasons	Warner Brothers	7
14	17	CAN'T HELP FALLING IN LOVE	Stylistics	Avco	7
28	18	JOLENE	Dolly Parton	RCA	3
25	19	HEART ON MY SLEEVE	Gallagher And Lyle	A&M	2
16	20	SAVE YOUR KISSES FOR ME	Brotherhood of Man	Pye	13
20	21	THIS IS IT	Melba Moore	Buddah	3
-	22	YOU TO ME ARE EVERYTHING	The Real Thing ●	Pye Int.	1
13	23	JUNGLE ROCK	Hank Mizell	Charly	12
30	24	SOUL CITY WALK	Archie Bell And The Drells	Philadelphia	4
19	25	GET UP AND BOOGIE	Silver Convention	Magnet	9
29	26	THE FLASHER	Mistura With Lloyd Michels	Route	3
15	27	S-S-S- SINGLE BED	Fox	GTO	8
31	28	LOVE ME LIKE I LOVE YOU	Bay City Rollers	Bell	9
-	29	YOU JUST MIGHT SEE ME CRY	Our Kid ●	Polydor	1
35	30	LET'S MAKE A BABY	Billy Paul	Philadelphia	2
39	31	THE WANDERER	Dion	Philips	2
-	[32]	TROCADERO	Showaddywaddy	Bell	1
37	[33]	TVC 15	David Bowie	RCA	2
-	34	YOUNG HEARTS RUN FREE	Candi Staton ●	Warner Bros.	1
24	35	REQUIEM	Slik	Bell	4
26	36	I'LL GO WHERE YOUR MUSIC TAKES ME	Jimmy James And The Vagabonds	Pye	6
-	37	THE BOYS ARE BACK IN TOWN	Thin Lizzy	Vertigo	1
-	38	YOU'RE MY EVERYTHING	Lee Garret ●	Chrysalis	1
17	39	REGGAE LIKE IT USED TO BE	Paul Nicholas	RSO	7
33	40	DISCO LADY	Johnny Taylor	CBS	6

WEEK ENDING 12 JUNE 1976

LW	TW	Title	Artist	Label	Wks
2	[1]	COMBINE HARVESTER	The Wurzels	EMI	5
5	[2]	SILLY LOVE SONGS	Wings	Parlophone	5
1	3	NO CHARGE	J.J. Barrie	Power Exchange	7
4	4	FERNANDO	Abba	Epic	11
22	5	YOU TO ME ARE EVERYTHING	The Real Thing	Pye Int.	2
3	6	MY RESISTANCE IS LOW	Robin Sarstedt	Decca	5
6	7	FOOL TO CRY	Rolling Stones	Rolling Stones	6
7	8	LET YOUR LOVE FLOW	Bellamy Brothers	Warner Brothers	8
21	[9]	THIS IS IT	Melba Moore	Buddah	4
8	10	ARMS OF MARY	Sutherland Brothers/Quiver	CBS	10

June 1976

□ Highest position disc reached ● Act's first ever week on chart

LW	TW	Title	Artist	Label	Wks
10	11	MIDNIGHT TRAIN TO GEORGIA	Gladys Knight And The Pips	Buddah	5
9	12	DEVIL WOMAN	Cliff Richard	EMI	5
-	13	TONIGHT'S THE NIGHT	Rod Stewart	Riva	1
11	14	LOVE HANGOVER	Diana Ross	Tamla Motown	7
29	15	YOU JUST MIGHT SEE ME CRY	Our Kid	Polydor	2
15	16	SHOW ME THE WAY	Peter Frampton	A&M	5
18	17	JOLENE	Dolly Parton	RCA	4
13	18	I'M YOUR PUPPET	James And Bobby Purify	Mercury	7
19	19	HEART ON MY SLEEVE	Gallagher And Lyle	A&M	3
14	20	MORE MORE MORE	Andrea True Connection	Buddah	8
24	21	SOUL CITY WALK	Archie Bell And The Drells	Philadelphia	5
12	22	SHAKE IT DOWN	Mud	Private Stock	5
26	[23]	THE FLASHER	Mistura With Lloyd Michels	Route	4
37	24	THE BOYS ARE BACK IN TOWN	Thin Lizzy	Vertigo	2
20	25	SAVE YOUR KISSES FOR ME	Brotherhood of Man	Pye	14
34	26	YOUNG HEARTS RUN FREE	Candi Staton	Warner Bros.	2
31	27	THE WANDERER	Dion	Philips	3
38	28	YOU'RE MY EVERYTHING	Lee Garret	Chrysalis	2
23	29	JUNGLE ROCK	Hank Mizell	Charly	13
35	30	REQUIEM	Slik	Bell	5
16	31	SILVER STAR	Four Seasons	Warner Brothers	8
-	32	THE CONTINENTAL	Maureen McGovern ●	20th Century	1
25	33	GET UP AND BOOGIE	Silver Convention	Magnet	10
-	34	LET'S STICK TOGETHER	Bryan Ferry	Island	1
33	35	TVC 15	David Bowie	RCA	3
32	36	TROCADERO	Showaddywaddy	Bell	2
-	37	LET'S MAKE A BABY	Billy Paul	Philadelphia	1
27	38	S-S-S- SINGLE BED	Fox	GTO	9
-	39	DAWN	Flintlock ●	Pinnacle	1
36	40	I'LL GO WHERE YOUR MUSIC TAKES ME	Jimmy James And The Vagabonds	Pye	7

WEEK ENDING 19 JUNE 1976

LW	TW	Title	Artist	Label	Wks
1	[1]	COMBINE HARVESTER	The Wurzels	EMI	6
5	2	YOU TO ME ARE EVERYTHING	The Real Thing	Pye Int.	3
2	3	SILLY LOVE SONGS	Wings	Parlophone	6
15	4	YOU JUST MIGHT SEE ME CRY	Our Kid	Polydor	3
3	5	NO CHARGE	J.J. Barrie	Power Exchange	8
19	[6]	HEART ON MY SLEEVE	Gallagher And Lyle	A&M	4
17	[7]	JOLENE	Dolly Parton	RCA	5
13	8	TONIGHT'S THE NIGHT	Rod Stewart	Riva	2
6	9	MY RESISTANCE IS LOW	Robin Sarstedt	Decca	6
16	[10]	SHOW ME THE WAY	Peter Frampton	A&M	6
8	11	LET YOUR LOVE FLOW	Bellamy Brothers	Warner Brothers	9
7	12	FOOL TO CRY	Rolling Stones	Rolling Stones	7
22	13	SHAKE IT DOWN	Mud	Private Stock	6
9	14	THIS IS IT	Melba Moore	Buddah	5
12	15	DEVIL WOMAN	Cliff Richard	EMI	6
11	16	MIDNIGHT TRAIN TO GEORGIA	Gladys Knight And The Pips	Buddah	6
24	17	THE BOYS ARE BACK IN TOWN	Thin Lizzy	Vertigo	3
4	18	FERNANDO	Abba	Epic	12
26	19	YOUNG HEARTS RUN FREE	Candi Staton	Warner Bros.	3
34	20	LET'S STICK TOGETHER	Bryan Ferry	Island	2
-	21	LEADER OF THE PACK	Shangri Las	Contempo	1
21	22	SOUL CITY WALK	Archie Bell And The Drells	Philadelphia	6
28	23	YOU'RE MY EVERYTHING	Lee Garret	Chrysalis	3
32	24	THE CONTINENTAL	Maureen McGovern	20th Century	2
27	25	THE WANDERER	Dion	Philips	4
14	26	LOVE HANGOVER	Diana Ross	Tamla Motown	8
10	27	ARMS OF MARY	Sutherland Brothers/Quiver	CBS	11
23	28	THE FLASHER	Mistura With Lloyd Michels	Route	5
25	29	SAVE YOUR KISSES FOR ME	Brotherhood of Man	Pye	15
39	[30]	DAWN	Flintlock	Pinnacle	2
-	31	WHAT A WONDERFUL WORLD	Johnny Nash	Epic	1
18	32	I'M YOUR PUPPET	James And Bobby Purify	Mercury	8
30	33	REQUIEM	Slik	Bell	6

■J. J. Barrie (Barrie Authors) reaches number one with his country cover, but will never chart again (05.06.76) ■ The Wurzels give new words to Melanie's *Brand New Key* and get a brand new number one (12.06.76) ■ The *Leader Of The Pack* rides and crashes for the third time, following chart drags in 1965 and 1972 (19.06.76)■

June 1976

□ Highest position disc reached ● Act's first ever week on chart

LW	TW	Title	Artist	Label	Wks
-	34	DANCE THE BODY MUSIC	Osibisa	*Bronze*	1
20	35	MORE MORE MORE	Andrea True Connection	*Buddah*	9
-	[36]	SOLD MY SOUL FOR ROCK 'N' ROLL	Linda And The Funky Boys ●	*Spark*	1
-	[37]	I DON'T WANNA PLAY HOUSE	Tammy Wynette	*Epic*	1
37	38	LET'S MAKE A BABY	Billy Paul	*Philadelphia*	2
31	39	SILVER STAR	Four Seasons	*Warner Brothers*	9
-	[40]	COULD IT BE MAGIC	Donna Summer	*GTO*	1

WEEK ENDING 26 JUNE 1976

LW	TW	Title	Artist	Label	Wks
2	[1]	YOU TO ME ARE EVERYTHING	The Real Thing	*Pye Int.*	4
1	2	COMBINE HARVESTER	The Wurzels	*EMI*	7
3	3	SILLY LOVE SONGS	Wings	*Parlophone*	7
4	4	YOU JUST MIGHT SEE ME CRY	Our Kid	*Polydor*	4
8	[5]	TONIGHT'S THE NIGHT	Rod Stewart	*Riva*	3
19	6	YOUNG HEARTS RUN FREE	Candi Staton	*Warner Bros.*	4
20	7	LET'S STICK TOGETHER	Bryan Ferry	*Island*	3
6	8	HEART ON MY SLEEVE	Gallagher And Lyle	*A&M*	5
7	9	JOLENE	Dolly Parton	*RCA*	6
17	10	THE BOYS ARE BACK IN TOWN	Thin Lizzy	*Vertigo*	4
21	11	LEADER OF THE PACK	Shangri Las	*Contempo*	2
10	12	SHOW ME THE WAY	Peter Frampton	*A&M*	7
22	[13]	SOUL CITY WALK	Archie Bell And The Drells	*Philadelphia*	7
5	14	NO CHARGE	J.J. Barrie	*Power Exchange*	9
23	[15]	YOU'RE MY EVERYTHING	Lee Garret	*Chrysalis*	4
25	16	THE WANDERER	Dion	*Philips*	5
14	17	THIS IS IT	Melba Moore	*Buddah*	6
-	18	KISS AND SAY GOODBYE	Manhattans ●	*CBS*	1
11	19	LET YOUR LOVE FLOW	Bellamy Brothers	*Warner Brothers*	10
24	20	THE CONTINENTAL	Maureen McGovern	*20th Century*	3
-	21	THE BOSTON TEA PARTY	Sensational Alex Harvey Band	*Mountain*	1
-	22	I LOVE TO BOOGIE	T. Rex	*EMI*	1
9	23	MY RESISTANCE IS LOW	Robin Sarstedt	*Decca*	7
28	24	THE FLASHER	Mistura With Lloyd Michels	*Route*	6
18	25	FERNANDO	Abba	*Epic*	13
31	26	WHAT A WONDERFUL WORLD	Johnny Nash	*Epic*	2
-	27	THE ROUSSOS PHENOMENON	Demis Roussos	*Philips*	1
16	28	MIDNIGHT TRAIN TO GEORGIA	Gladys Knight And The Pips	*Buddah*	7
13	29	SHAKE IT DOWN	Mud	*Private Stock*	7
12	30	FOOL TO CRY	Rolling Stones	*Rolling Stones*	8
34	[31]	DANCE THE BODY MUSIC	Osibisa	*Bronze*	2
26	32	LOVE HANGOVER	Diana Ross	*Tamla Motown*	9
15	33	DEVIL WOMAN	Cliff Richard	*EMI*	7
-	34	I RECALL A GYPSY WOMAN	Don Williams ●	*ABC*	1
-	35	MISTY BLUE	Dorothy Moore ●	*Contempo*	1
33	36	REQUIEM	Slik	*Bell*	7
29	37	SAVE YOUR KISSES FOR ME	Brotherhood of Man	*Pye*	16
30	38	DAWN	Flintlock	*Pinnacle*	3
32	39	I'M YOUR PUPPET	James And Bobby Purify	*Mercury*	9
37	40	I DON'T WANNA PLAY HOUSE	Tammy Wynette	*Epic*	2

WEEK ENDING 3 JULY 1976

LW	TW	Title	Artist	Label	Wks
1	[1]	YOU TO ME ARE EVERYTHING	The Real Thing	*Pye Int.*	5
4	2	YOU JUST MIGHT SEE ME CRY	Our Kid ●	*Polydor*	5
6	3	YOUNG HEARTS RUN FREE	Candi Staton	*Warner Bros.*	5
7	[4]	LET'S STICK TOGETHER	Bryan Ferry	*Island*	4
5	[5]	TONIGHT'S THE NIGHT	Rod Stewart	*Riva*	4
8	6	HEART ON MY SLEEVE	Gallagher And Lyle	*A&M*	6
11	7	LEADER OF THE PACK	Shangri Las	*Contempo*	3
10	[8]	THE BOYS ARE BACK IN TOWN	Thin Lizzy	*Vertigo*	5
2	9	COMBINE HARVESTER	The Wurzels	*EMI*	8
3	10	SILLY LOVE SONGS	Wings	*Parlophone*	8
18	11	KISS AND SAY GOODBYE	Manhattans	*CBS*	2
27	12	THE ROUSSOS PHENOMENON	Demis Roussos	*Philips*	2
9	13	JOLENE	Dolly Parton	*RCA*	7
-	14	A LITTLE BIT MORE	Dr. Hook	*Capitol*	1
12	15	SHOW ME THE WAY	Peter Frampton	*A&M*	8
20	[16]	THE CONTINENTAL	Maureen McGovern	*20th Century*	4
22	17	I LOVE TO BOOGIE	T. Rex	*EMI*	2
15	18	YOU'RE MY EVERYTHING	Lee Garret	*Chrysalis*	5
35	19	MISTY BLUE	Dorothy Moore	*Contempo*	2
13	20	SOUL CITY WALK	Archie Bell And The Drells	*Philadelphia*	8
-	21	YOU ARE MY LOVE	Liverpool Express ●	*Warner Bros.*	1
16	22	THE WANDERER	Dion	*Philips*	6
21	23	THE BOSTON TEA PARTY	Sensational Alex Harvey Band	*Mountain*	2
-	24	YOU'RE MY BEST FRIEND	Queen	*EMI*	1
26	[25]	WHAT A WONDERFUL WORLD	Johnny Nash	*Epic*	3
-	26	IT ONLY TAKES A MINUTE	100 Ton and a Feather	*UK*	1
34	27	I RECALL A GYPSY WOMAN	Don Williams	*ABC*	2
19	28	LET YOUR LOVE FLOW	Bellamy Brothers	*Warner Brothers*	11
-	29	MAN TO MAN	Hot Chocolate	*RAK*	1
-	[30]	MY SWEET ROSALIE	Brotherhood Of Man	*Pye*	1
14	31	NO CHARGE	J.J. Barrie	*Power Exchange*	10
29	32	SHAKE IT DOWN	Mud	*Private Stock*	8
17	33	THIS IS IT	Melba Moore	*Buddah*	7
-	34	ME AND BABY BROTHER	War	*Island*	1
24	35	THE FLASHER	Mistura With Lloyd Michels	*Route*	7
23	36	MY RESISTANCE IS LOW	Robin Sarstedt	*Decca*	8
31	37	DANCE THE BODY MUSIC	Osibisa	*Bronze*	3
25	38	FERNANDO	Abba	*Epic*	14
28	39	MIDNIGHT TRAIN TO GEORGIA	Gladys Knight And The Pips	*Buddah*	8
30	40	FOOL TO CRY	Rolling Stones	*Rolling Stones*	9

WEEK ENDING 10 JULY 1976

LW	TW	Title	Artist	Label	Wks
1	[1]	YOU TO ME ARE EVERYTHING	The Real Thing	*Pye Int.*	6
3	2	YOUNG HEARTS RUN FREE	Candi Staton	*Warner Bros.*	6
12	3	THE ROUSSOS PHENOMENON	Demis Roussos	*Philips*	3
2	4	YOU JUST MIGHT SEE ME CRY	Our Kid	*Polydor*	6
4	5	LET'S STICK TOGETHER	Bryan Ferry	*Island*	5
11	6	KISS AND SAY GOODBYE	Manhattans	*CBS*	3
14	7	A LITTLE BIT MORE	Dr. Hook	*Capitol*	2
5	8	TONIGHT'S THE NIGHT	Rod Stewart	*Riva*	5
-	9	DON'T GO BREAKING MY HEART	Elton John And Kiki Dee ●	*Rocket*	1
7	10	LEADER OF THE PACK	Shangri Las	*Contempo*	4
10	11	SILLY LOVE SONGS	Wings	*Parlophone*	9
8	12	THE BOYS ARE BACK IN TOWN	Thin Lizzy	*Vertigo*	6
19	13	MISTY BLUE	Dorothy Moore	*Contempo*	3
6	14	HEART ON MY SLEEVE	Gallagher And Lyle	*A&M*	7
24	15	YOU'RE MY BEST FRIEND	Queen	*EMI*	2
23	16	THE BOSTON TEA PARTY	Sensational Alex Harvey Band	*Mountain*	3
13	17	JOLENE	Dolly Parton	*RCA*	8
17	18	I LOVE TO BOOGIE	T. Rex	*EMI*	3
21	19	YOU ARE MY LOVE	Liverpool Express	*Warner Bros.*	2
26	20	IT ONLY TAKES A MINUTE	100 Ton and a Feather	*UK*	2
18	21	YOU'RE MY EVERYTHING	Lee Garret	*Chrysalis*	6
29	22	MAN TO MAN	Hot Chocolate	*RAK*	2
22	23	THE WANDERER	Dion	*Philips*	7
9	24	COMBINE HARVESTER	The Wurzels	*EMI*	9
25	[25]	WHAT A WONDERFUL WORLD	Johnny Nash	*Epic*	4
20	26	SOUL CITY WALK	Archie Bell And The Drells	*Philadelphia*	9
16	27	THE CONTINENTAL	Maureen McGovern	*20th Century*	5
27	28	I RECALL A GYPSY WOMAN	Don Williams	*ABC*	3
15	29	SHOW ME THE WAY	Peter Frampton	*A&M*	9
34	30	ME AND BABY BROTHER	War	*Island*	2
-	31	GOOD VIBRATIONS	Beach Boys	*Capitol*	1
30	32	MY SWEET ROSALIE	Brotherhood Of Man	*Pye*	2
35	33	THE FLASHER	Mistura With Lloyd Michels	*Route*	8
-	34	ONE PIECE AT A TIME	Johnny Cash And The Tennessee Three ●	*CBS*	1
-	35	BACK IN THE U.S.S.R.	The Beatles	*Parlophone*	1
-	[36]	I NEED TO BE IN LOVE	Carpenters	*A&M*	1
-	37	HARVEST FOR THE WORLD	Isley Brothers	*Epic*	1
-	[38]	STRANGE MAGIC	Electric Light Orchestra	*Jet*	1
-	39	HEAVEN MUST BE MISSING AN ANGEL	Tavares ●	*Capitol*	1
37	40	DANCE THE BODY MUSIC	Osibisa	*Bronze*	4

In these weeks ■ The Real Thing have the first and biggest of nine late 70s hits (26.06.76) ■ Hit re-issues include *The Wanderer* by Dion and *Good Vibrations* by the Beach Boys (10.07.76) ■ Rod Stewart's *Tonight's The Night* includes Britt Ekland getting excited at the fades but she will be erased from future album versions after they split (26.06.76) ■

July 1976

□ Highest position disc reached ● Act's first ever week on chart

WEEK ENDING 17 JULY 1976

LW	TW			Wks
3	1	THE ROUSSOS PHENOMENON Demis Roussos	*Philips*	4
9	2	DON'T GO BREAKING MY HEART Elton John And Kiki Dee	*Rocket*	2
7	3	A LITTLE BIT MORE Dr. Hook	*Capitol*	3
2	4	YOUNG HEARTS RUN FREE Candi Staton	*Warner Bros.*	7
6	5	KISS AND SAY GOODBYE Manhattans	*CBS*	4
1	6	YOU TO ME ARE EVERYTHING The Real Thing	*Pye Int.*	7
15	7	YOU'RE MY BEST FRIEND Queen	*EMI*	3
5	8	LET'S STICK TOGETHER Bryan Ferry	*Island*	6
4	9	YOU JUST MIGHT SEE ME CRY Our Kid	*Polydor*	7
13	10	MISTY BLUE Dorothy Moore	*Contempo*	4
10	11	LEADER OF THE PACK Shangri Las	*Contempo*	5
8	12	TONIGHT'S THE NIGHT Rod Stewart	*Riva*	6
18	13	I LOVE TO BOOGIE T. Rex	*EMI*	4
20	14	IT ONLY TAKES A MINUTE 100 Ton and a Feather	*UK*	3
12	15	THE BOYS ARE BACK IN TOWN Thin Lizzy	*Vertigo*	7
19	16	YOU ARE MY LOVE Liverpool Express	*Warner Bros.*	3
22	17	MAN TO MAN Hot Chocolate	*RAK*	3
14	18	HEART ON MY SLEEVE Gallagher And Lyle	*A&M*	8
16	19	THE BOSTON TEA PARTY Sensational Alex Harvey Band	*Mountain*	4
28	20	I RECALL A GYPSY WOMAN Don Williams	*ABC*	4
27	21	THE CONTINENTAL Maureen McGovern	*20th Century*	6
11	22	SILLY LOVE SONGS Wings	*Parlophone*	10
39	23	HEAVEN MUST BE MISSING AN ANGEL Tavares	*Capitol*	2
30	24	ME AND BABY BROTHER War	*Island*	3
25	25	WHAT A WONDERFUL WORLD Johnny Nash	*Epic*	5
24	26	COMBINE HARVESTER The Wurzels	*EMI*	10
37	27	HARVEST FOR THE WORLD Isley Brothers	*Epic*	2
-	28	LOVE ON DELIVERY Billy Ocean	*GTO*	1
35	29	BACK IN THE U.S.S.R. The Beatles	*Parlophone*	2
32	30	MY SWEET ROSALIE Brotherhood Of Man	*Pye*	3
-	31	NO CHANCE (NO CHARGE) Billy Connolly	*Polydor*	1
17	32	JOLENE Dolly Parton	*RCA*	9
34	33	ONE PIECE AT A TIME Johnny Cash And The Tennessee Three	*CBS*	2
-	34	MYSTERY SONG Status Quo	*Vertigo*	1
31	35	GOOD VIBRATIONS Beach Boys	*Capitol*	2
23	36	THE WANDERER Dion	*Philips*	8
36	37	I NEED TO BE IN LOVE Carpenters	*A&M*	2
-	38	A FIFTH OF BEETHOVEN Walter Murphy ●	*Private Stock*	1
-	39	I THOUGHT IT TOOK A LITTLE TIME Diana Ross	*Tamla Motown*	1
29	40	SHOW ME THE WAY Peter Frampton	*A&M*	10

WEEK ENDING 24 JULY 1976

LW	TW			Wks
2	1	DON'T GO BREAKING MY HEART Elton John And Kiki Dee	*Rocket*	3
3	2	A LITTLE BIT MORE Dr. Hook	*Capitol*	4
1	3	THE ROUSSOS PHENOMENON Demis Roussos	*Philips*	5
4	4	YOUNG HEARTS RUN FREE Candi Staton	*Warner Bros.*	8
5	5	KISS AND SAY GOODBYE Manhattans	*CBS*	5
10	6	MISTY BLUE Dorothy Moore	*Contempo*	5
6	7	YOU TO ME ARE EVERYTHING The Real Thing	*Pye Int.*	8
7	8	YOU'RE MY BEST FRIEND Queen	*EMI*	4
14	9	IT ONLY TAKES A MINUTE 100 Ton and a Feather	*UK*	4
8	10	LET'S STICK TOGETHER Bryan Ferry	*Island*	7
16	11	YOU ARE MY LOVE Liverpool Express	*Warner Bros.*	4
23	12	HEAVEN MUST BE MISSING AN ANGEL Tavares	*Capitol*	3
19	13	THE BOSTON TEA PARTY Sensational Alex Harvey Band	*Mountain*	5
9	14	YOU JUST MIGHT SEE ME CRY Our Kid	*Polydor*	8
17	15	MAN TO MAN Hot Chocolate	*RAK*	4
12	16	TONIGHT'S THE NIGHT Rod Stewart	*Riva*	7
11	17	LEADER OF THE PACK Shangri Las	*Contempo*	6
35	18	GOOD VIBRATIONS Beach Boys	*Capitol*	3
29	19	BACK IN THE U.S.S.R. The Beatles	*Parlophone*	3
13	20	I LOVE TO BOOGIE T. Rex	*EMI*	5
-	21	NOW IS THE TIME Jimmy James And The Vagabonds	*Pye*	1
28	22	LOVE ON DELIVERY Billy Ocean	*GTO*	2
27	23	HARVEST FOR THE WORLD Isley Brothers	*Epic*	3
20	24	I RECALL A GYPSY WOMAN Don Williams	*ABC*	5
-	25	JEANS ON David Dundas	*AIR*	1
24	26	ME AND BABY BROTHER War	*Island*	4
34	27	MYSTERY SONG Status Quo	*Vertigo*	2
31	28	NO CHANCE (NO CHARGE) Billy Connolly	*Polydor*	2
15	29	THE BOYS ARE BACK IN TOWN Thin Lizzy	*Vertigo*	8
38	30	A FIFTH OF BEETHOVEN Walter Murphy	*Private Stock*	2
25	31	WHAT A WONDERFUL WORLD Johnny Nash	*Epic*	6
33	32	ONE PIECE AT A TIME Johnny Cash And The Tennessee Three	*CBS*	3
39	33	I THOUGHT IT TOOK A LITTLE TIME Diana Ross	*Tamla Motown*	2
18	34	HEART ON MY SLEEVE Gallagher And Lyle	*A&M*	9
22	35	SILLY LOVE SONGS Wings	*Parlophone*	11
-	36	ROCK & ROLL MUSIC Beach Boys	*Reprise*	1
-	37	(SHAKE, SHAKE, SHAKE) SHAKE YOUR BOOTY KC And The Sunshine Band	*Jayboy*	1
30	38	MY SWEET ROSALIE Brotherhood Of Man	*Pye*	4
-	39	AT THE HOP Danny And The Juniors	*ABC*	1
26	40	COMBINE HARVESTER The Wurzels	*EMI*	11

WEEK ENDING 31 JULY 1976

LW	TW			Wks
1	1	DON'T GO BREAKING MY HEART Elton John And Kiki Dee	*Rocket*	4
2	2	A LITTLE BIT MORE Dr. Hook	*Capitol*	5
3	3	THE ROUSSOS PHENOMENON Demis Roussos	*Philips*	6
5	4	KISS AND SAY GOODBYE Manhattans	*CBS*	6
12	5	HEAVEN MUST BE MISSING AN ANGEL Tavares	*Capitol*	4
4	6	YOUNG HEARTS RUN FREE Candi Staton	*Warner Bros.*	9
6	7	MISTY BLUE Dorothy Moore	*Contempo*	6
25	8	JEANS ON David Dundas	*AIR*	2
9	9	IT ONLY TAKES A MINUTE 100 Ton and a Feather	*UK*	5
8	10	YOU'RE MY BEST FRIEND Queen	*EMI*	5
11	11	YOU ARE MY LOVE Liverpool Express	*Warner Bros.*	5
23	12	HARVEST FOR THE WORLD Isley Brothers	*Epic*	4
24	13	I RECALL A GYPSY WOMAN Don Williams	*ABC*	6
15	14	MAN TO MAN Hot Chocolate	*RAK*	5
21	15	NOW IS THE TIME Jimmy James And The Vagabonds	*Pye*	2
10	16	LET'S STICK TOGETHER Bryan Ferry	*Island*	8
7	17	YOU TO ME ARE EVERYTHING The Real Thing	*Pye Int.*	9
27	18	MYSTERY SONG Status Quo	*Vertigo*	3
19	19	BACK IN THE U.S.S.R. The Beatles	*Parlophone*	4
20	20	I LOVE TO BOOGIE T. Rex	*EMI*	6
26	21	ME AND BABY BROTHER War	*Island*	5
14	22	YOU JUST MIGHT SEE ME CRY Our Kid	*Polydor*	9
22	23	LOVE ON DELIVERY Billy Ocean	*GTO*	3
28	24	NO CHANCE (NO CHARGE) Billy Connolly	*Polydor*	3
17	25	LEADER OF THE PACK Shangri Las	*Contempo*	7
-	26	DR. KISS KISS 5000 Volts	*Philips*	1
37	27	(SHAKE, SHAKE, SHAKE) SHAKE YOUR BOOTY KC And The Sunshine Band	*Jayboy*	2
13	28	THE BOSTON TEA PARTY Sensational Alex Harvey Band	*Mountain*	6
16	29	TONIGHT'S THE NIGHT Rod Stewart	*Riva*	8
-	30	IN ZAIRE Johnny Wakelin	*Pye*	1
30	31	A FIFTH OF BEETHOVEN Walter Murphy	*Private Stock*	3
33	32	I THOUGHT IT TOOK A LITTLE TIME Diana Ross	*Tamla Motown*	3
18	33	GOOD VIBRATIONS Beach Boys	*Capitol*	4
-	34	WHAT I'VE GOT IN MIND Billie Jo Spears	*United Artists*	1
32	35	ONE PIECE AT A TIME Johnny Cash And The Tennessee Three	*CBS*	4
-	36	YOU SHOULD BE DANCING Bee Gees	*RSO*	1
29	37	THE BOYS ARE BACK IN TOWN Thin Lizzy	*Vertigo*	9
38	38	MY SWEET ROSALIE Brotherhood Of Man	*Pye*	5
36	39	ROCK & ROLL MUSIC Beach Boys	*Reprise*	2
39	40	AT THE HOP Danny And The Juniors	*ABC*	2

■ Elton John who has already had five American number one singles, gets his first British chart topper with Kiki Dee, but will have to wait until 1990 for a solo list leader (24.07.76) ■ *The Roussos Phenomenon* is rightly titled. Demis is the first Greek artist to reach number one, and his is the first EP to top the singles chart (17.07.76) ■ Danny and the Juniors are again *At The Hop* (24.07.76) ■

August 1976

□ Highest position disc reached ● Act's first ever week on chart

WEEK ENDING 7 AUGUST 1976

LW	TW	Title	Artist	Label	Wks
1	1	DON'T GO BREAKING MY HEART	Elton John And Kiki Dee	Rocket	5
2	2	A LITTLE BIT MORE	Dr. Hook	Capitol	6
8	3	JEANS ON	David Dundas	AIR	3
3	4	THE ROUSSOS PHENOMENON	Demis Roussos	Philips	7
7	5	MISTY BLUE	Dorothy Moore	Contempo	7
5	6	HEAVEN MUST BE MISSING AN ANGEL	Tavares	Capitol	5
4	7	KISS AND SAY GOODBYE	Manhattans	CBS	7
15	8	NOW IS THE TIME	Jimmy James And The Vagabonds	Pye	3
6	9	YOUNG HEARTS RUN FREE	Candi Staton	Warner Bros.	10
12	10	HARVEST FOR THE WORLD	Isley Brothers	Epic	5
30	11	IN ZAIRE	Johnny Wakelin	Pye	2
26	12	DR. KISS KISS	5000 Volts	Philips	2
9	13	IT ONLY TAKES A MINUTE	100 Ton and a Feather	UK	6
11	14	YOU ARE MY LOVE	Liverpool Express	Warner Bros.	6
18	15	MYSTERY SONG	Status Quo	Vertigo	4
10	16	YOU'RE MY BEST FRIEND	Queen	EMI	6
28	17	THE BOSTON TEA PARTY	Sensational Alex Harvey Band	Mountain	7
14	18	MAN TO MAN	Hot Chocolate	RAK	6
23	19	LOVE ON DELIVERY	Billy Ocean	GTO	4
36	20	YOU SHOULD BE DANCING	Bee Gees	RSO	2
19	21	BACK IN THE U.S.S.R.	The Beatles	Parlophone	5
27	22	(SHAKE, SHAKE, SHAKE) SHAKE YOUR BOOTY	KC And The Sunshine Band	Jayboy	3
34	23	WHAT I'VE GOT IN MIND	Billie Jo Spears	United Artists	2
-	24	HERE COMES THE SUN	Steve Harley And Cockney Rebel	EMI	1
16	25	LET'S STICK TOGETHER	Bryan Ferry	Island	9
20	26	I LOVE TO BOOGIE	T. Rex	EMI	7
24	27	NO CHANCE (NO CHARGE)	Billy Connolly	Polydor	4
-	28	LET 'EM IN	Wings	Parlophone	1
13	29	I RECALL A GYPSY WOMAN	Don Williams	ABC	7
17	30	YOU TO ME ARE EVERYTHING	The Real Thing	Pye Int.	10
31	31	A FIFTH OF BEETHOVEN	Walter Murphy	Private Stock	4
-	32	YOU DON'T HAVE TO GO	Chi-Lites	Brunswick	1
33	33	GOOD VIBRATIONS	Beach Boys	Capitol	5
-	34	YOU'LL NEVER FIND ANOTHER LOVE LIKE MINE	Lou Rawls ●	Philadelphia	1
25	35	LEADER OF THE PACK	Shangri Las	Contempo	8
35	36	ONE PIECE AT A TIME	Johnny Cash And The Tennessee Three	CBS	5
32	37	I THOUGHT IT TOOK A LITTLE TIME	Diana Ross	Tamla Motown	4
21	38	ME AND BABY BROTHER	War	Island	6
22	39	YOU JUST MIGHT SEE ME CRY	Our Kid	Polydor	10
-	40	EXTENDED PLAY	Bryan Ferry	Island	1

WEEK ENDING 14 AUGUST 1976

LW	TW	Title	Artist	Label	Wks
1	1	DON'T GO BREAKING MY HEART	Elton John And Kiki Dee	Rocket	6
2	2	A LITTLE BIT MORE	Dr. Hook	Capitol	7
3	3	JEANS ON	David Dundas	AIR	4
6	4	HEAVEN MUST BE MISSING AN ANGEL	Tavares	Capitol	6
8	5	NOW IS THE TIME	Jimmy James And The Vagabonds	Pye	4
4	6	THE ROUSSOS PHENOMENON	Demis Roussos	Philips	8
11	7	IN ZAIRE	Johnny Wakelin	Pye	3
12	8	DR. KISS KISS	5000 Volts	Philips	3
5	9	MISTY BLUE	Dorothy Moore	Contempo	8
20	10	YOU SHOULD BE DANCING	Bee Gees	RSO	3
15	11	MYSTERY SONG	Status Quo	Vertigo	5
7	12	KISS AND SAY GOODBYE	Manhattans	CBS	8
28	13	LET 'EM IN	Wings	Parlophone	2
10	14	HARVEST FOR THE WORLD	Isley Brothers	Epic	6
40	15	EXTENDED PLAY	Bryan Ferry	Island	2
24	16	HERE COMES THE SUN	Steve Harley And Cockney Rebel	EMI	2
32	17	YOU DON'T HAVE TO GO	Chi-Lites	Brunswick	2
14	18	YOU ARE MY LOVE	Liverpool Express	Warner Bros.	7
9	19	YOUNG HEARTS RUN FREE	Candi Staton	Warner Bros.	11
19	20	LOVE ON DELIVERY	Billy Ocean	GTO	5
34	21	YOU'LL NEVER FIND ANOTHER LOVE LIKE MINE	Lou Rawls	Philadelphia	2
23	22	WHAT I'VE GOT IN MIND	Billie Jo Spears	United Artists	3
21	23	BACK IN THE U.S.S.R.	The Beatles	Parlophone	6
16	24	YOU'RE MY BEST FRIEND	Queen	EMI	7
13	25	IT ONLY TAKES A MINUTE	100 Ton and a Feather	UK	7
22	26	(SHAKE, SHAKE, SHAKE) SHAKE YOUR BOOTY	KC And The Sunshine Band	Jayboy	4
-	27	16 BARS	Stylistics	H&L	1
31	28	A FIFTH OF BEETHOVEN	Walter Murphy	Private Stock	5
29	29	I RECALL A GYPSY WOMAN	Don Williams	ABC	8
17	30	THE BOSTON TEA PARTY	Sensational Alex Harvey Band	Mountain	8
18	31	MAN TO MAN	Hot Chocolate	RAK	7
-	32	MORNING GLORY	James And Bobby Purify	Mercury	1
-	33	AFTERNOON DELIGHT	Starland Vocal Band ●	RCA	1
27	34	NO CHANCE (NO CHARGE)	Billy Connolly	Polydor	5
-	35	NICE AND SLOW	Jesse Green ●	EMI	1
26	36	I LOVE TO BOOGIE	T. Rex	EMI	8
30	37	YOU TO ME ARE EVERYTHING	The Real Thing	Pye Int.	11
35	38	LEADER OF THE PACK	Shangri Las	Contempo	9
-	39	JAILBREAK	Thin Lizzy	Vertigo	1
25	40	LET'S STICK TOGETHER	Bryan Ferry	Island	10

WEEK ENDING 21 AUGUST 1976

LW	TW	Title	Artist	Label	Wks
1	1	DON'T GO BREAKING MY HEART	Elton John And Kiki Dee	Rocket	7
2	2	A LITTLE BIT MORE	Dr. Hook	Capitol	8
3	3	JEANS ON	David Dundas	AIR	5
7	4	IN ZAIRE	Johnny Wakelin	Pye	4
13	5	LET 'EM IN	Wings	Parlophone	3
4	6	HEAVEN MUST BE MISSING AN ANGEL	Tavares	Capitol	7
5	7	NOW IS THE TIME	Jimmy James And The Vagabonds	Pye	5
8	8	DR. KISS KISS	5000 Volts	Philips	4
10	9	YOU SHOULD BE DANCING	Bee Gees	RSO	4
16	10	HERE COMES THE SUN	Steve Harley And Cockney Rebel	EMI	3
22	11	WHAT I'VE GOT IN MIND	Billie Jo Spears	United Artists	4
9	12	MISTY BLUE	Dorothy Moore	Contempo	9
11	13	MYSTERY SONG	Status Quo	Vertigo	6
15	14	EXTENDED PLAY	Bryan Ferry	Island	3
14	15	HARVEST FOR THE WORLD	Isley Brothers	Epic	7
6	16	THE ROUSSOS PHENOMENON	Demis Roussos	Philips	9
17	17	YOU DON'T HAVE TO GO	Chi-Lites	Brunswick	3
21	18	YOU'LL NEVER FIND ANOTHER LOVE LIKE MINE	Lou Rawls	Philadelphia	3
27	19	16 BARS	Stylistics	H&L	2
20	20	LOVE ON DELIVERY	Billy Ocean	GTO	6
12	21	KISS AND SAY GOODBYE	Manhattans	CBS	9
-	22	THE KILLING OF GEORGIE	Rod Stewart	Riva	1
-	23	DANCING QUEEN	Abba	Epic	1
26	24	(SHAKE, SHAKE, SHAKE) SHAKE YOUR BOOTY	KC And The Sunshine Band	Jayboy	5
35	25	NICE AND SLOW	Jesse Green	EMI	2
33	26	AFTERNOON DELIGHT	Starland Vocal Band	RCA	2
19	27	YOUNG HEARTS RUN FREE	Candi Staton	Warner Bros.	12
32	28	MORNING GLORY	James And Bobby Purify	Mercury	2
-	29	BABY WE BETTER TRY AND GET IT TOGETHER	Barry White	20th Century	1
24	30	YOU'RE MY BEST FRIEND	Queen	EMI	8
39	31	JAILBREAK	Thin Lizzy	Vertigo	2
18	32	YOU ARE MY LOVE	Liverpool Express	Warner Bros.	8
28	33	A FIFTH OF BEETHOVEN	Walter Murphy	Private Stock	6
25	34	IT ONLY TAKES A MINUTE	100 Ton and a Feather	UK	8
-	35	IF YOU KNOW WHAT I MEAN	Neil Diamond	CBS	1
-	36	HERE I GO AGAIN	Twiggy ●	Mercury	1
30	37	THE BOSTON TEA PARTY	Sensational Alex Harvey Band	Mountain	9
-	38	NIGHT FEVER	Fatback Band	Spring	1
-	39	LOVING ON THE LOSING SIDE	Tommy Hunt	Spark	1
29	40	I RECALL A GYPSY WOMAN	Don Williams	ABC	9

In these weeks ■ Eight years after its initial appearance on album, *Back In The U.S.S.R.* becomes the final previously unreleased Beatles single to enjoy a Top 40 run; a medley and re-issues will follow (07.08.76) ■ Bryan Ferry's *Extended Play* features *The Price Of Love*, a 1965 Everly Brothers number two (07.08.76) ■ Rod Stewart's *The Killing Of Georgie* concerns the Top 40's first openly gay protagonist (21.08.76)■

September 1976

□ Highest position disc reached ● Act's first ever week on chart

WEEK ENDING 28 AUGUST 1976

LW	TW	Title / Artist	Label	Wks
1	1	DON'T GO BREAKING MY HEART Elton John And Kiki Dee	Rocket	8
5	2	LET 'EM IN Wings	Parlophone	4
2	3	A LITTLE BIT MORE Dr. Hook	Capitol	9
3	4	JEANS ON David Dundas	AIR	6
4	5	IN ZAIRE Johnny Wakelin	Pye	5
9	6	YOU SHOULD BE DANCING Bee Gees	RSO	5
6	7	HEAVEN MUST BE MISSING AN ANGEL Tavares	Capitol	8
8	8	DR. KISS KISS 5000 Volts	Philips	5
17	9	YOU DON'T HAVE TO GO Chi-Lites	Brunswick	4
7	10	NOW IS THE TIME Jimmy James And The Vagabonds	Pye	6
18	11	YOU'LL NEVER FIND ANOTHER LOVE LIKE MINE Lou Rawls	Philadelphia	4
19	12	16 BARS Stylistics	H&L	3
11	13	WHAT I'VE GOT IN MIND Billie Jo Spears	United Artists	5
14	14	EXTENDED PLAY Bryan Ferry	Island	4
10	15	HERE COMES THE SUN Steve Harley And Cockney Rebel	EMI	4
23	16	DANCING QUEEN Abba	Epic	2
13	17	MYSTERY SONG Status Quo	Vertigo	7
22	18	THE KILLING OF GEORGIE Rod Stewart	Riva	2
12	19	MISTY BLUE Dorothy Moore	Contempo	10
16	20	THE ROUSSOS PHENOMENON Demis Roussos	Philips	10
-	21	(LIGHT OT EXPERIENCE) DOINA DE JALE Gheorghe Zamfir ●	Epic	1
25	22	NICE AND SLOW Jesse Green	EMI	3
29	23	BABY WE BETTER TRY AND GET IT TOGETHER Barry White	20th Century	2
36	24	HERE I GO AGAIN Twiggy	Mercury	2
26	25	AFTERNOON DELIGHT Starland Vocal Band	RCA	3
-	26	I CAN'T ASK FOR ANYTHING MORE THAN YOU BABE Cliff Richard	EMI	1
28	27	MORNING GLORY James And Bobby Purify	Mercury	3
15	28	HARVEST FOR THE WORLD Isley Brothers	Epic	8
21	29	KISS AND SAY GOODBYE Manhattans	CBS	10
-	30	Y VIVA SUSPENDERS Judge Dread	Cactus	1
20	31	LOVE ON DELIVERY Billy Ocean	GTO	7
-	32	DANCE LITTLE LADY DANCE Tina Charles	CBS	1
31	33	JAILBREAK Thin Lizzy	Vertigo	3
-	34	ARIA Acker Bilk	Pye	1
-	35	MAKE YOURS A HAPPY HOME Gladys Knight And The Pips	Buddah	1
24	36	(SHAKE, SHAKE, SHAKE) SHAKE YOUR BOOTY KC And The Sunshine Band	Jayboy	6
-	37	HEAVEN IS IN THE BACK SEAT OF MY CADILLAC Hot Chocolate	RAK	1
38	38	NIGHT FEVER Fatback Band	Spring	2
39	39	LOVING ON THE LOSING SIDE Tommy Hunt	Spark	2
33	40	A FIFTH OF BEETHOVEN Walter Murphy	Private Stock	7

WEEK ENDING 4 SEPTEMBER 1976

LW	TW	Title / Artist	Label	Wks
16	1	DANCING QUEEN Abba	Epic	3
2	2	LET 'EM IN Wings	Parlophone	5
1	3	DON'T GO BREAKING MY HEART Elton John And Kiki Dee	Rocket	9
13	4	WHAT I'VE GOT IN MIND Billie Jo Spears	United Artists	6
3	5	A LITTLE BIT MORE Dr. Hook	Capitol	10
5	6	IN ZAIRE Johnny Wakelin	Pye	6
14	7	EXTENDED PLAY Bryan Ferry	Island	5
18	8	THE KILLING OF GEORGIE Rod Stewart	Riva	3
9	9	YOU DON'T HAVE TO GO Chi-Lites	Brunswick	5
4	10	JEANS ON David Dundas	AIR	7
12	11	16 BARS Stylistics	H&L	4
11	12	YOU'LL NEVER FIND ANOTHER LOVE LIKE MINE Lou Rawls	Philadelphia	5
6	13	YOU SHOULD BE DANCING Bee Gees	RSO	6
8	14	DR. KISS KISS 5000 Volts	Philips	6
15	15	HERE COMES THE SUN Steve Harley And Cockney Rebel	EMI	5
21	16	(LIGHT OT EXPERIENCE) DOINA DE JALE Gheorghe Zamfir	Epic	2
22	17	NICE AND SLOW Jesse Green	EMI	4
25	18	AFTERNOON DELIGHT Starland Vocal Band	RCA	4
7	19	HEAVEN MUST BE MISSING AN ANGEL Tavares	Capitol	9
10	20	NOW IS THE TIME Jimmy James And The Vagabonds	Pye	7
23	21	BABY WE BETTER TRY AND GET IT TOGETHER Barry White	20th Century	3
34	22	ARIA Acker Bilk	Pye	2
26	23	I CAN'T ASK FOR ANYTHING MORE THAN YOU BABE Cliff Richard	EMI	2
24	24	HERE I GO AGAIN Twiggy	Mercury	3
37	25	HEAVEN IS IN THE BACK SEAT OF MY CADILLAC Hot Chocolate	RAK	2
-	26	BLINDED BY THE LIGHT Manfred Mann's Earth Band	Bronze	1
32	27	DANCE LITTLE LADY DANCE Tina Charles	CBS	2
17	28	MYSTERY SONG Status Quo	Vertigo	8
-	29	MISSISSIPPI Pussycat ●	Sonet	1
39	30	LOVING ON THE LOSING SIDE Tommy Hunt	Spark	3
20	31	THE ROUSSOS PHENOMENON Demis Roussos	Philips	11
-	32	SHANNON Henry Gross ●	Life Song	1
27	33	MORNING GLORY James And Bobby Purify	Mercury	4
30	34	Y VIVA SUSPENDERS Judge Dread	Cactus	2
-	35	I NEED IT Johnny Guitar Watson ●	DJM	1
19	36	MISTY BLUE Dorothy Moore	Contempo	11
-	37	CAN'T GET BY WITHOUT YOU Real Thing	Pye	1
-	38	WORK ALL DAY Barry Biggs ●	Dynamic	1
35	39	MAKE YOURS A HAPPY HOME Gladys Knight And The Pips	Buddah	2
36	40	(SHAKE, SHAKE, SHAKE) SHAKE YOUR BOOTY KC And The Sunshine Band	Jayboy	7

WEEK ENDING 11 SEPTEMBER 1976

LW	TW	Title / Artist	Label	Wks
1	1	DANCING QUEEN Abba	Epic	4
2	2	LET 'EM IN Wings	Parlophone	6
9	3	YOU DON'T HAVE TO GO Chi-Lites	Brunswick	6
3	4	DON'T GO BREAKING MY HEART Elton John And Kiki Dee	Rocket	10
13	5	YOU SHOULD BE DANCING Bee Gees	RSO	7
8	6	THE KILLING OF GEORGIE Rod Stewart	Riva	4
11	7	16 BARS Stylistics	H&L	5
16	8	(LIGHT OT EXPERIENCE) DOINA DE JALE Gheorghe Zamfir	Epic	3
4	9	WHAT I'VE GOT IN MIND Billie Jo Spears	United Artists	7
12	10	YOU'LL NEVER FIND ANOTHER LOVE LIKE MINE Lou Rawls	Philadelphia	6
7	11	EXTENDED PLAY Bryan Ferry	Island	6
5	12	A LITTLE BIT MORE Dr. Hook	Capitol	11
37	13	CAN'T GET BY WITHOUT YOU Real Thing	Pye	2
26	14	BLINDED BY THE LIGHT Manfred Mann's Earth Band	Bronze	2
21	15	BABY WE BETTER TRY AND GET IT TOGETHER Barry White	20th Century	4
14	16	DR. KISS KISS 5000 Volts	Philips	7
22	17	ARIA Acker Bilk	Pye	3
6	18	IN ZAIRE Johnny Wakelin	Pye	7
24	19	HERE I GO AGAIN Twiggy	Mercury	4
23	20	I CAN'T ASK FOR ANYTHING MORE THAN YOU BABE Cliff Richard	EMI	3
29	21	MISSISSIPPI Pussycat	Sonet	2
27	22	DANCE LITTLE LADY DANCE Tina Charles	CBS	3
-	23	I AM A CIDER DRINKER Wurzels	EMI	1
10	24	JEANS ON David Dundas	AIR	8
-	25	I ONLY WANNA BE WITH YOU Bay City Rollers	Bell	1
19	26	HEAVEN MUST BE MISSING AN ANGEL Tavares	Capitol	10
34	27	Y VIVA SUSPENDERS Judge Dread	Cactus	3
25	28	HEAVEN IS IN THE BACK SEAT OF MY CADILLAC Hot Chocolate	RAK	3
30	29	LOVING ON THE LOSING SIDE Tommy Hunt	Spark	4
15	30	HERE COMES THE SUN Steve Harley And Cockney Rebel	EMI	6
18	31	AFTERNOON DELIGHT Starland Vocal Band	RCA	5
32	32	SHANNON Henry Gross	Life Song	2
17	33	NICE AND SLOW Jesse Green	EMI	5
20	34	NOW IS THE TIME Jimmy James And The Vagabonds	Pye	8

■Gheorghe Zamfir becomes the first Rumanian and the first pan piper to make the Top 10 (11.09.76) ■ Before he gets his own first hit single, Bruce Springsteen scores as a writer with *Blinded By The Light* by Manfred Mann's Earth Band (04.09.76) ■ The Chi-Lites match their career peak position of three established by *Have You Seen Her* (11.09.76)■

September 1976

□ Highest position disc reached ● Act's first ever week on chart

LW	TW	Title	Artist	Label	Wks
-	35	I WANT MORE	Can ●	Virgin	1
-	36	SAILING	Rod Stewart	Warner Bros.	1
33	37	MORNING GLORY	James And Bobby Purify	Mercury	5
-	38	GIRL OF MY BEST FRIEND	Elvis Presley	RCA	1
35	39	I NEED IT	Johnny Guitar Watson	DJM	2
31	40	THE ROUSSOS PHENOMENON	Demis Roussos	Philips	12

WEEK ENDING 18 SEPTEMBER 1976

LW	TW	Title	Artist	Label	Wks
1	[1]	DANCING QUEEN	Abba	Epic	5
6	[2]	THE KILLING OF GEORGIE	Rod Stewart	Riva	5
13	3	CAN'T GET BY WITHOUT YOU	Real Thing	Pye	3
8	[4]	(LIGHT OT EXPERIENCE) DOINA DE JALE	Gheorghe Zamfir	Epic	4
17	[5]	ARIA	Acker Bilk	Pye	4
2	6	LET 'EM IN	Wings	Parlophone	7
7	[7]	16 BARS	Stylistics	H&L	6
3	8	YOU DON'T HAVE TO GO	Chi-Lites	Brunswick	7
23	9	I AM A CIDER DRINKER	Wurzels	EMI	2
25	10	I ONLY WANNA BE WITH YOU	Bay City Rollers	Bell	2
14	11	BLINDED BY THE LIGHT	Manfred Mann's Earth Band	Bronze	3
21	12	MISSISSIPPI	Pussycat	Sonet	3
22	13	DANCE LITTLE LADY DANCE	Tina Charles	CBS	4
4	14	DON'T GO BREAKING MY HEART	Elton John And Kiki Dee	Rocket	11
15	[15]	BABY WE BETTER TRY AND GET IT TOGETHER	Barry White	20th Century	5
9	16	WHAT I'VE GOT IN MIND	Billie Jo Spears	United Artists	8
11	17	EXTENDED PLAY	Bryan Ferry	Island	7
20	18	I CAN'T ASK FOR ANYTHING MORE THAN YOU BABE	Cliff Richard	EMI	4
19	19	HERE I GO AGAIN	Twiggy	Mercury	5
33	20	NICE AND SLOW	Jesse Green	EMI	6
10	21	YOU'LL NEVER FIND ANOTHER LOVE LIKE MINE	Lou Rawls	Philadelphia	7
31	22	AFTERNOON DELIGHT	Starland Vocal Band	RCA	6
36	23	SAILING	Rod Stewart	Warner Bros.	2
12	24	A LITTLE BIT MORE	Dr. Hook	Capitol	12
28	25	HEAVEN IS IN THE BACK SEAT OF MY CADILLAC	Hot Chocolate	RAK	4
-	26	LOVING AND FREE	Kiki Dee	Rocket	1
5	27	YOU SHOULD BE DANCING	Bee Gees	RSO	8
29	[28]	LOVING ON THE LOSING SIDE	Tommy Hunt	Spark	5
38	29	GIRL OF MY BEST FRIEND	Elvis Presley	RCA	2
18	30	IN ZAIRE	Johnny Wakelin	Pye	8
16	31	DR. KISS KISS	5000 Volts	Philips	8
27	32	Y VIVA SUSPENDERS	Judge Dread	Cactus	4
24	33	JEANS ON	David Dundas	AIR	9
-	34	DISCO DUCK	Rick Dees And His Cast Of Idiots ●	RSO	1
-	35	SWEET HOME ALABAMA/DOUBLE TROUBLE	Lynyrd Skynrd	MCA	1
32	36	SHANNON	Henry Gross	Life Song	3
-	37	THE BEST DISCO IN TOWN	Ritchie Family	Polydor	1
-	[38]	WORK ALL DAY	Barry Biggs ●	Dynamic	1
35	39	I WANT MORE	Can	Virgin	2
26	40	HEAVEN MUST BE MISSING AN ANGEL	Tavares	Capitol	11

WEEK ENDING 25 SEPTEMBER 1976

LW	TW	Title	Artist	Label	Wks
1	[1]	DANCING QUEEN	Abba	Epic	6
3	[2]	CAN'T GET BY WITHOUT YOU	Real Thing	Pye	4
9	[3]	I AM A CIDER DRINKER	Wurzels	EMI	3
10	[4]	I ONLY WANNA BE WITH YOU	Bay City Rollers	Bell	3
12	5	MISSISSIPPI	Pussycat	Sonet	4
11	[6]	BLINDED BY THE LIGHT	Manfred Mann's Earth Band	Bronze	4
5	7	ARIA	Acker Bilk	Pye	5
2	8	THE KILLING OF GEORGIE	Rod Stewart	Riva	6
13	9	DANCE LITTLE LADY DANCE	Tina Charles	CBS	5
4	10	(LIGHT OT EXPERIENCE) DOINA DE JALE	Gheorghe Zamfir	Epic	5
23	11	SAILING	Rod Stewart	Warner Bros.	3
8	12	YOU DON'T HAVE TO GO	Chi-Lites	Brunswick	8
6	13	LET 'EM IN	Wings	Parlophone	8
7	14	16 BARS	Stylistics	H&L	7
26	15	LOVING AND FREE	Kiki Dee	Rocket	2
15	16	BABY WE BETTER TRY AND GET IT TOGETHER	Barry White	20th Century	6
18	[17]	I CAN'T ASK FOR ANYTHING MORE THAN YOU BABE	Cliff Richard	EMI	5
19	18	HERE I GO AGAIN	Twiggy	Mercury	6
34	19	DISCO DUCK	Rick Dees And His Cast Of Idiots	RSO	2
27	20	YOU SHOULD BE DANCING	Bee Gees	RSO	9
29	21	GIRL OF MY BEST FRIEND	Elvis Presley	RCA	3
21	22	YOU'LL NEVER FIND ANOTHER LOVE LIKE MINE	Lou Rawls	Philadelphia	8
16	23	WHAT I'VE GOT IN MIND	Billie Jo Spears	United Artists	9
17	24	EXTENDED PLAY	Bryan Ferry	Island	8
37	25	THE BEST DISCO IN TOWN	Ritchie Family	Polydor	2
14	26	DON'T GO BREAKING MY HEART	Elton John And Kiki Dee	Rocket	12
24	27	A LITTLE BIT MORE	Dr. Hook	Capitol	13
25	28	HEAVEN IS IN THE BACK SEAT OF MY CADILLAC	Hot Chocolate	RAK	5
28	29	LOVING ON THE LOSING SIDE	Tommy Hunt	Spark	6
39	30	I WANT MORE	Can	Virgin	3
35	31	SWEET HOME ALABAMA/DOUBLE TROUBLE	Lynyrd Skynrd	MCA	2
20	32	NICE AND SLOW	Jesse Green	EMI	7
-	33	EVERY NITE'S A SATURDAY NIGHT WITH YOU	Drifters	Bell	1
-	34	GET UP OFFA THAT THING	James Brown	Polydor	1
-	[35]	BREAKAWAY	Gallagher And Lyle ●	A&M	1
-	36	DISCO MUSIC (I LIKE IT)	J.A.L.N. Band	Magnet	1
30	37	IN ZAIRE	Johnny Wakelin	Pye	9
-	38	UPTOWN, UPTEMPO WOMAN	Randy Edelman	20th Century	1
22	39	AFTERNOON DELIGHT	Starland Vocal Band	RCA	7
-	40	RUBBER BAND MAN	Detroit Spinners	Atlantic	1

WEEK ENDING 2 OCTOBER 1976

LW	TW	Title	Artist	Label	Wks
1	[1]	DANCING QUEEN	Abba	Epic	7
2	[2]	CAN'T GET BY WITHOUT YOU	Real Thing	Pye	5
5	3	MISSISSIPPI	Pussycat	Sonet	5
3	4	I AM A CIDER DRINKER	Wurzels	EMI	4
4	5	I ONLY WANNA BE WITH YOU	Bay City Rollers	Bell	4
9	[6]	DANCE LITTLE LADY DANCE	Tina Charles	CBS	6
11	7	SAILING	Rod Stewart	Warner Bros.	4
7	8	ARIA	Acker Bilk	Pye	6
6	9	BLINDED BY THE LIGHT	Manfred Mann's Earth Band	Bronze	5
19	10	DISCO DUCK	Rick Dees And His Cast Of Idiots	RSO	3
8	11	THE KILLING OF GEORGIE	Rod Stewart	Riva	7
10	12	(LIGHT OT EXPERIENCE) DOINA DE JALE	Gheorghe Zamfir	Epic	6
21	13	GIRL OF MY BEST FRIEND	Elvis Presley	RCA	4
15	14	LOVING AND FREE	Kiki Dee	Rocket	3
14	15	16 BARS	Stylistics	H&L	8
25	16	THE BEST DISCO IN TOWN	Ritchie Family	Polydor	3
18	[17]	HERE I GO AGAIN	Twiggy	Mercury	7
13	18	LET 'EM IN	Wings	Parlophone	9
16	19	BABY WE BETTER TRY AND GET IT TOGETHER	Barry White	20th Century	7
17	20	I CAN'T ASK FOR ANYTHING MORE THAN YOU BABE	Cliff Richard	EMI	6
12	21	YOU DON'T HAVE TO GO	Chi-Lites	Brunswick	9
-	22	HOWZAT	Sherbet ●	Epic	1
32	23	NICE AND SLOW	Jesse Green	EMI	8
36	24	DISCO MUSIC (I LIKE IT)	J.A.L.N. Band	Magnet	2
34	25	GET UP OFFA THAT THING	James Brown	Polydor	2
39	26	AFTERNOON DELIGHT	Starland Vocal Band	RCA	8
23	27	WHAT I'VE GOT IN MIND	Billie Jo Spears	United Artists	10
29	28	LOVING ON THE LOSING SIDE	Tommy Hunt	Spark	7
30	29	I WANT MORE	Can	Virgin	4

In these weeks ■ Acker Bilk has his first Top 10 single in 14 years (18.09.76) ■ James Brown has his first Top 40 single in six years (25.09.76) ■ American DJ Rick Dees has his first and only hit, *Disco Duck* (18.09.76)■

LW	TW	Title	Artist	Label	Wks
28	30	HEAVEN IS IN THE BACK SEAT OF MY CADILLAC	Hot Chocolate	RAK	6
38	31	UPTOWN, UPTEMPO WOMAN	Randy Edelman	20th Century	2
40	32	RUBBER BAND MAN	Detroit Spinners	Atlantic	2
22	33	YOU'LL NEVER FIND ANOTHER LOVE LIKE MINE	Lou Rawls	Philadelphia	9
31	34	SWEET HOME ALABAMA/DOUBLE TROUBLE	Lynyrd Skynyrd	MCA	3
-	35	WHEN FOREVER HAS GONE	Demis Roussos	Philips	1
-	36	I'LL MEET YOU AT MIDNIGHT	Smokie	RAK	1
24	37	EXTENDED PLAY	Bryan Ferry	Island	9
33	38	EVERY NITE'S A SATURDAY NIGHT WITH YOU	Drifters	Bell	2
26	39	DON'T GO BREAKING MY HEART	Elton John And Kiki Dee	Rocket	13
-	40	HURT	Manhattans	CBS	1

WEEK ENDING 9 OCTOBER 1976

LW	TW	Title	Artist	Label	Wks
1	[1]	DANCING QUEEN	Abba	Epic	8
3	2	MISSISSIPPI	Pussycat	Sonet	6
2	3	CAN'T GET BY WITHOUT YOU	Real Thing	Pye	6
7	4	SAILING	Rod Stewart	Warner Bros.	5
4	5	I AM A CIDER DRINKER	Wurzels	EMI	5
10	[6]	DISCO DUCK	Rick Dees And His Cast Of Idiots	RSO	4
5	7	I ONLY WANNA BE WITH YOU	Bay City Rollers	Bell	5
6	8	DANCE LITTLE LADY DANCE	Tina Charles	CBS	7
9	9	BLINDED BY THE LIGHT	Manfred Mann's Earth Band	Bronze	6
8	10	ARIA	Acker Bilk	Pye	7
13	11	GIRL OF MY BEST FRIEND	Elvis Presley	RCA	5
16	12	THE BEST DISCO IN TOWN	Ritchie Family	Polydor	4
14	[13]	LOVING AND FREE	Kiki Dee	Rocket	4
22	14	HOWZAT	Sherbet	Epic	2
35	15	WHEN FOREVER HAS GONE	Demis Roussos	Philips	2
11	16	THE KILLING OF GEORGIE	Rod Stewart	Riva	8
12	17	(LIGHT OT EXPERIENCE) DOINA DE JALE	Gheorghe Zamfir	Epic	7
36	18	I'LL MEET YOU AT MIDNIGHT	Smokie	RAK	2
17	19	HERE I GO AGAIN	Twiggy	Mercury	8
40	20	HURT	Manhattans	CBS	2
20	21	I CAN'T ASK FOR ANYTHING MORE THAN YOU BABE	Cliff Richard	EMI	7
25	[22]	GET UP OFFA THAT THING	James Brown	Polydor	3
-	23	DON'T TAKE AWAY THE MUSIC	Tavares	Capitol	1
32	24	RUBBER BAND MAN	Detroit Spinners	Atlantic	3
24	25	DISCO MUSIC (I LIKE IT)	J.A.L.N. Band	Magnet	3
29	[26]	I WANT MORE	Can	Virgin	5
21	27	YOU DON'T HAVE TO GO	Chi-Lites	Brunswick	10
31	28	UPTOWN, UPTEMPO WOMAN	Randy Edelman	20th Century	3
38	[29]	EVERY NITE'S A SATURDAY NIGHT WITH YOU	Drifters	Bell	3
-	30	I'D REALLY LOVE TO SEE YOU TONIGHT	England Dan & John Ford Coley ●	Atlantic	1
23	31	NICE AND SLOW	Jesse Green	EMI	9
18	32	LET 'EM IN	Wings	Parlophone	10
28	33	LOVING ON THE LOSING SIDE	Tommy Hunt	Spark	8
-	34	PLAY THAT FUNKY MUSIC	Wild Cherry ●	Epic	1
30	35	HEAVEN IS IN THE BACK SEAT OF MY CADILLAC	Hot Chocolate	RAK	7
27	36	WHAT I'VE GOT IN MIND	Billie Jo Spears	United Artists	10
-	[37]	BENNY AND THE JETS	Elton John	DJM	1
-	38	IF YOU LEAVE ME NOW	Chicago	CBS	1
-	39	SUMMER OF MY LIFE	Simon May ●	Pye	1
-	[40]	UNDER ONE ROOF	Rubettes	State	1

October 1976

□ Highest position disc reached ● Act's first ever week on chart

WEEK ENDING 16 OCTOBER 1976

LW	TW	Title	Artist	Label	Wks
2	[1]	MISSISSIPPI	Pussycat	Sonet	7
1	2	DANCING QUEEN	Abba	Epic	9
4	3	SAILING	Rod Stewart	Warner Bros.	6
14	[4]	HOWZAT	Sherbet	Epic	3
15	5	WHEN FOREVER HAS GONE	Demis Roussos	Philips	3
6	[6]	DISCO DUCK	Rick Dees And His Cast Of Idiots	RSO	5
3	7	CAN'T GET BY WITHOUT YOU	Real Thing	Pye	7
8	8	DANCE LITTLE LADY DANCE	Tina Charles	CBS	8
11	[9]	GIRL OF MY BEST FRIEND	Elvis Presley	RCA	6
12	[10]	THE BEST DISCO IN TOWN	Ritchie Family	Polydor	5
20	11	HURT	Manhattans	CBS	3
7	12	I ONLY WANNA BE WITH YOU	Bay City Rollers	Bell	6
39	13	SUMMER OF MY LIFE	Simon May	Pye	2
38	14	IF YOU LEAVE ME NOW	Chicago	CBS	2
13	15	LOVING AND FREE	Kiki Dee	Rocket	5
5	16	I AM A CIDER DRINKER	Wurzels	EMI	6
10	17	ARIA	Acker Bilk	Pye	8
23	18	DON'T TAKE AWAY THE MUSIC	Tavares	Capitol	2
18	19	I'LL MEET YOU AT MIDNIGHT	Smokie	RAK	3
9	20	BLINDED BY THE LIGHT	Manfred Mann's Earth Band	Bronze	7
25	[21]	DISCO MUSIC (I LIKE IT)	J.A.L.N. Band	Magnet	4
24	22	RUBBER BAND MAN	Detroit Spinners	Atlantic	4
34	23	PLAY THAT FUNKY MUSIC	Wild Cherry	Epic	2
-	24	DANCING WITH THE CAPTAIN	Paul Nicholas	RSO	1
28	[25]	UPTOWN, UPTEMPO WOMAN	Randy Edelman	20th Century	4
30	[26]	I'D REALLY LOVE TO SEE YOU TONIGHT	England Dan & John Ford Coley	Atlantic	2
16	27	THE KILLING OF GEORGIE	Rod Stewart	Riva	9
-	28	COULDN'T GET IT RIGHT	Climax Blues Band ●	BTM	1
26	29	I WANT MORE	Can	Virgin	6
19	30	HERE I GO AGAIN	Twiggy	Mercury	9
22	31	GET UP OFFA THAT THING	James Brown	Polydor	4
-	32	QUEEN OF MY SOUL	Average White Band	Atlantic	1
31	33	NICE AND SLOW	Jesse Green	EMI	10
-	34	SOUL DRACULA	Hot Blood ●	Creole	1
-	35	TEARS OF A CLOWN	Smokey Robinson & the Miracles	Tamla Motown	1
-	36	JAWS	Lalo Schifrin ●	CTI	1
17	37	(LIGHT OT EXPERIENCE) DOINA DE JALE	Gheorghe Zamfir	Epic	8
33	38	LOVING ON THE LOSING SIDE	Tommy Hunt	Spark	9
-	39	LOVE AND AFFECTION	Joan Armatrading ●	A&M	1
29	40	EVERY NITE'S A SATURDAY NIGHT WITH YOU	Drifters	Bell	4

WEEK ENDING 23 OCTOBER 1976

LW	TW	Title	Artist	Label	Wks
1	[1]	MISSISSIPPI	Pussycat	Sonet	8
5	[2]	WHEN FOREVER HAS GONE	Demis Roussos	Philips	4
3	3	SAILING	Rod Stewart	Warner Bros.	7
14	4	IF YOU LEAVE ME NOW	Chicago	CBS	3
11	5	HURT	Manhattans	CBS	4
2	6	DANCING QUEEN	Abba	Epic	10
13	7	SUMMER OF MY LIFE	Simon May	Pye	3
4	8	HOWZAT	Sherbet	Epic	4
18	9	DON'T TAKE AWAY THE MUSIC	Tavares	Capitol	3
6	10	DISCO DUCK	Rick Dees And His Cast Of Idiots	RSO	6
7	11	CAN'T GET BY WITHOUT YOU	Real Thing	Pye	8
19	12	I'LL MEET YOU AT MIDNIGHT	Smokie	RAK	4
9	13	GIRL OF MY BEST FRIEND	Elvis Presley	RCA	7
10	14	THE BEST DISCO IN TOWN	Ritchie Family	Polydor	6
24	15	DANCING WITH THE CAPTAIN	Paul Nicholas	RSO	2
12	16	I ONLY WANNA BE WITH YOU	Bay City Rollers	Bell	7
8	17	DANCE LITTLE LADY DANCE	Tina Charles	CBS	9
15	18	LOVING AND FREE	Kiki Dee	Rocket	6
22	19	RUBBER BAND MAN	Detroit Spinners	Atlantic	5
23	20	PLAY THAT FUNKY MUSIC	Wild Cherry	Epic	3
16	21	I AM A CIDER DRINKER	Wurzels	EMI	7
28	22	COULDN'T GET IT RIGHT	Climax Blues Band	BTM	2
36	23	JAWS	Lalo Schifrin	CTI	2
17	24	ARIA	Acker Bilk	Pye	9
21	25	DISCO MUSIC (I LIKE IT)	J.A.L.N. Band	Magnet	5
39	26	LOVE AND AFFECTION	Joan Armatrading	A&M	2
20	27	BLINDED BY THE LIGHT	Manfred Mann's Earth Band	Bronze	8
26	28	I'D REALLY LOVE TO SEE YOU TONIGHT	England Dan & John Ford Coley	Atlantic	3
32	29	QUEEN OF MY SOUL	Average White Band	Atlantic	2
29	30	I WANT MORE	Can	Virgin	7

■ Pussycat are the first group from Holland to top the chart (16.10.76) ■ After its use as a television theme, *Sailing* by Rod Stewart becomes a Top 3 hit for the second consecutive year (16.10.76) ■ Joan Armatrading makes her first appearance in the singles chart (16.10.76) ■

October 1976

☐ Highest position disc reached ● Act's first ever week on chart

LW	TW	Title	Artist	Label	Wks
25	31	UPTOWN, UPTEMPO WOMAN	Randy Edelman	*20th Century*	5
34	32	SOUL DRACULA	Hot Blood	*Creole*	2
31	33	GET UP OFFA THAT THING	James Brown	*Polydor*	5
-	34	COMING HOME	David Essex	*CBS*	1
35	35	TEARS OF A CLOWN	Smokey Robinson & the Miracles	*Tamla Motown*	2
27	36	THE KILLING OF GEORGIE	Rod Stewart	*Riva*	10
-	37	FAIRY TALE	Dana	*GTO*	1
-	38	FUNNY HOW TIMES SLIP AWAY	Dorothy Moore	*Contempo*	1
40	39	EVERY NITE'S A SATURDAY NIGHT WITH YOU	Drifters	*Bell*	5
-	40	WITHOUT YOU	Nilsson	*RCA*	1

WEEK ENDING 30 OCTOBER 1976

LW	TW	Title	Artist	Label	Wks
1	1	MISSISSIPPI	Pussycat	*Sonet*	9
2	2	WHEN FOREVER HAS GONE	Demis Roussos	*Philips*	5
4	3	IF YOU LEAVE ME NOW	Chicago	*CBS*	4
8	4	HOWZAT	Sherbet	*Epic*	5
5	5	HURT	Manhattans	*CBS*	5
9	6	DON'T TAKE AWAY THE MUSIC	Tavares	*Capitol*	4
7	7	SUMMER OF MY LIFE	Simon May	*Pye*	4
6	8	DANCING QUEEN	Abba	*Epic*	11
15	9	DANCING WITH THE CAPTAIN	Paul Nicholas	*RSO*	3
3	10	SAILING	Rod Stewart	*Warner Bros.*	8
12	11	I'LL MEET YOU AT MIDNIGHT	Smokie	*RAK*	5
13	12	GIRL OF MY BEST FRIEND	Elvis Presley	*RCA*	8
10	13	DISCO DUCK	Rick Dees And His Cast Of Idiots	*RSO*	7
14	14	THE BEST DISCO IN TOWN	Ritchie Family	*Polydor*	7
20	15	PLAY THAT FUNKY MUSIC	Wild Cherry	*Epic*	4
19	16	RUBBER BAND MAN	Detroit Spinners	*Atlantic*	6
22	17	COULDN'T GET IT RIGHT	Climax Blues Band	*BTM*	3
23	18	JAWS	Lalo Schifrin	*CTI*	3
11	19	CAN'T GET BY WITHOUT YOU	Real Thing	*Pye*	9
26	20	LOVE AND AFFECTION	Joan Armatrading	*A&M*	3
17	21	DANCE LITTLE LADY DANCE	Tina Charles	*CBS*	10
25	22	DISCO MUSIC (I LIKE IT)	J.A.L.N. Band	*Magnet*	6
29	23	QUEEN OF MY SOUL	Average White Band	*Atlantic*	3
21	24	I AM A CIDER DRINKER	Wurzels	*EMI*	8
34	25	COMING HOME	David Essex	*CBS*	2
16	26	I ONLY WANNA BE WITH YOU	Bay City Rollers	*Bell*	8
-	27	BEAUTIFUL NOISE	Neil Diamond	*CBS*	1
40	28	WITHOUT YOU	Nilsson	*RCA*	2
28	29	I'D REALLY LOVE TO SEE YOU TONIGHT	England Dan & John Ford Coley	*Atlantic*	4
-	30	YOU MAKE ME FEEL LIKE DANCING	Leo Sayer	*Chrysalis*	1
24	31	ARIA	Acker Bilk	*Pye*	10
18	32	LOVING AND FREE	Kiki Dee	*Rocket*	7
31	33	UPTOWN, UPTEMPO WOMAN	Randy Edelman	*20th Century*	6
35	34	TEARS OF A CLOWN	Smokey Robinson & the Miracles	*Tamla Motown*	3
27	35	BLINDED BY THE LIGHT	Manfred Mann's Earth Band	*Bronze*	9
-	36	SUBSTITUTE	The Who	*Polydor*	1
-	37	REMEMBER YESTERDAY	John Miles	*Decca*	1
32	38	SOUL DRACULA	Hot Blood	*Creole*	3
37	39	FAIRY TALE	Dana	*GTO*	2
30	40	I WANT MORE	Can	*Virgin*	8

WEEK ENDING 6 NOVEMBER 1976

LW	TW	Title	Artist	Label	Wks
1	1	MISSISSIPPI	Pussycat	*Sonet*	10
3	2	IF YOU LEAVE ME NOW	Chicago	*CBS*	5
2	3	WHEN FOREVER HAS GONE	Demis Roussos	*Philips*	6
5	4	HURT	Manhattans	*CBS*	6
6	5	DON'T TAKE AWAY THE MUSIC	Tavares	*Capitol*	5
4	6	HOWZAT	Sherbet	*Epic*	6
7	7	SUMMER OF MY LIFE	Simon May	*Pye*	5
9	8	DANCING WITH THE CAPTAIN	Paul Nicholas	*RSO*	4
10	9	SAILING	Rod Stewart	*Warner Bros.*	9
15	10	PLAY THAT FUNKY MUSIC	Wild Cherry	*Epic*	5
17	11	COULDN'T GET IT RIGHT	Climax Blues Band	*BTM*	4
11	12	I'LL MEET YOU AT MIDNIGHT	Smokie	*RAK*	6
8	13	DANCING QUEEN	Abba	*Epic*	12
18	14	JAWS	Lalo Schifrin	*CTI*	4
36	15	SUBSTITUTE	The Who	*Polydor*	2
30	16	YOU MAKE ME FEEL LIKE DANCING	Leo Sayer	*Chrysalis*	2
12	17	GIRL OF MY BEST FRIEND	Elvis Presley	*RCA*	9
16	18	RUBBER BAND MAN	Detroit Spinners	*Atlantic*	7
20	19	LOVE AND AFFECTION	Joan Armatrading	*A&M*	4
-	20	IF NOT YOU	Dr. Hook	*Capitol*	1
13	21	DISCO DUCK	Rick Dees And His Cast Of Idiots	*RSO*	8
28	22	WITHOUT YOU	Nilsson	*RCA*	3
27	23	BEAUTIFUL NOISE	Neil Diamond	*CBS*	2
25	24	COMING HOME	David Essex	*CBS*	3
14	25	THE BEST DISCO IN TOWN	Ritchie Family	*Polydor*	8
23	26	QUEEN OF MY SOUL	Average White Band	*Atlantic*	4
19	27	CAN'T GET BY WITHOUT YOU	Real Thing	*Pye*	10
-	28	ROCK 'N' ME	Steve Miller Band ●	*Mercury*	1
-	29	LOST IN FRANCE	Bonnie Tyler ●	*RCA*	1
21	30	DANCE LITTLE LADY DANCE	Tina Charles	*CBS*	11
39	31	FAIRY TALE	Dana	*GTO*	3
37	32	REMEMBER YESTERDAY	John Miles	*Decca*	2
-	33	SPINNING ROCK BOOGIE	Hank C. Burnett ●	*Sonet*	1
-	34	LOWDOWN	Boz Scaggs	*CBS*	1
26	35	I ONLY WANNA BE WITH YOU	Bay City Rollers	*Bell*	9
-	36	UNDER THE MOON OF LOVE	Showaddywaddy	*Bell*	1
29	37	I'D REALLY LOVE TO SEE YOU TONIGHT	England Dan & John Ford Coley	*Atlantic*	5
-	38	YOU'RE MY BEST FRIEND	Don Williams	*ABC*	1
24	39	I AM A CIDER DRINKER	Wurzels	*EMI*	9
38	40	SOUL DRACULA	Hot Blood	*Creole*	4

WEEK ENDING 13 NOVEMBER 1976

LW	TW	Title	Artist	Label	Wks
2	1	IF YOU LEAVE ME NOW	Chicago	*CBS*	6
1	2	MISSISSIPPI	Pussycat	*Sonet*	11
16	3	YOU MAKE ME FEEL LIKE DANCING	Leo Sayer	*Chrysalis*	3
5	4	DON'T TAKE AWAY THE MUSIC	Tavares	*Capitol*	6
3	5	WHEN FOREVER HAS GONE	Demis Roussos	*Philips*	7
4	6	HURT	Manhattans	*CBS*	7
10	7	PLAY THAT FUNKY MUSIC	Wild Cherry	*Epic*	6
6	8	HOWZAT	Sherbet	*Epic*	7
7	9	SUMMER OF MY LIFE	Simon May	*Pye*	6
19	10	LOVE AND AFFECTION	Joan Armatrading	*A&M*	5
11	11	COULDN'T GET IT RIGHT	Climax Blues Band	*BTM*	5
8	12	DANCING WITH THE CAPTAIN	Paul Nicholas	*RSO*	5
23	13	BEAUTIFUL NOISE	Neil Diamond	*CBS*	3
20	14	IF NOT YOU	Dr. Hook	*Capitol*	2
14	15	JAWS	Lalo Schifrin	*CTI*	5
15	16	SUBSTITUTE	The Who	*Polydor*	3
18	17	RUBBER BAND MAN	Detroit Spinners	*Atlantic*	8
9	18	SAILING	Rod Stewart	*Warner Bros.*	10
36	19	UNDER THE MOON OF LOVE	Showaddywaddy	*Bell*	2
13	20	DANCING QUEEN	Abba	*Epic*	13
12	21	I'LL MEET YOU AT MIDNIGHT	Smokie	*RAK*	7
29	22	LOST IN FRANCE	Bonnie Tyler	*RCA*	2
22	23	WITHOUT YOU	Nilsson	*RCA*	4
28	24	ROCK 'N' ME	Steve Miller Band	*Mercury*	2
17	25	GIRL OF MY BEST FRIEND	Elvis Presley	*RCA*	10
24	26	COMING HOME	David Essex	*CBS*	4
-	27	LOVE ME	Yvonne Elliman	*RSO*	1
34	28	LOWDOWN	Boz Scaggs	*CBS*	2
33	29	SPINNING ROCK BOOGIE	Hank C. Burnett	*Sonet*	2
26	30	QUEEN OF MY SOUL	Average White Band	*Atlantic*	5
31	31	FAIRY TALE	Dana	*GTO*	4
-	32	SO SAD THE SONG	Gladys Knight & the Pips	*Buddah*	1
21	33	DISCO DUCK	Rick Dees And His Cast Of Idiots	*RSO*	9
32	34	REMEMBER YESTERDAY	John Miles	*Decca*	3
38	35	YOU'RE MY BEST FRIEND	Don Williams	*ABC*	2
-	36	DON'T MAKE ME WAIT TOO LONG	Barry White	*20th Century*	1
-	37	I CAN'T LIVE A DREAM	The Osmonds	*Polydor*	1
-	38	STONEY GROUND	Guys & Dolls	*Magnet*	1
25	39	THE BEST DISCO IN TOWN	Ritchie Family	*Polydor*	9
30	40	DANCE LITTLE LADY DANCE	Tina Charles	*CBS*	12

In these weeks ■ Chicago achieve the only number one of their lengthy career (13.11.76) ■ Bonnie Tyler makes her career debut with *Lost In France* (06.11.76) ■ *Jaws* artist Lalo Schifrin was best known for his theme music for the sixties television series 'Mission: Impossible' (30.10.76) ■

December 1976

□ Highest position disc reached ● Act's first ever week on chart

WEEK ENDING 20 NOVEMBER 1976

LW	TW	Title	Artist	Label	Wks
1	[1]	IF YOU LEAVE ME NOW	Chicago	CBS	7
3	[2]	YOU MAKE ME FEEL LIKE DANCING	Leo Sayer	Chrysalis	4
19	3	UNDER THE MOON OF LOVE	Showaddywaddy	Bell	3
2	4	MISSISSIPPI	Pussycat	Sonet	12
14	[5]	IF NOT YOU	Dr. Hook	Capitol	3
6	6	HURT	Manhattans	CBS	8
16	7	SUBSTITUTE	The Who	Polydor	4
4	8	DON'T TAKE AWAY THE MUSIC	Tavares	Capitol	7
7	9	PLAY THAT FUNKY MUSIC	Wild Cherry	Epic	7
11	[10]	COULDN'T GET IT RIGHT	Climax Blues Band	BTM	6
5	11	WHEN FOREVER HAS GONE	Demis Roussos	Philips	8
10	12	LOVE AND AFFECTION	Joan Armatrading	A&M	6
13	[13]	BEAUTIFUL NOISE	Neil Diamond	CBS	4
12	14	DANCING WITH THE CAPTAIN	Paul Nicholas	RSO	6
22	15	LOST IN FRANCE	Bonnie Tyler	RCA	3
9	16	SUMMER OF MY LIFE	Simon May	Pye	7
15	17	JAWS	Lalo Schifrin	CTI	6
8	18	HOWZAT	Sherbet	Epic	8
24	19	ROCK 'N' ME	Steve Miller Band	Mercury	3
27	20	LOVE ME	Yvonne Elliman	RSO	2
17	21	RUBBER BAND MAN	Detroit Spinners	Atlantic	9
23	22	WITHOUT YOU	Nilsson	RCA	5
-	23	LIVIN' THING	Electric Light Orchestra	Jet	1
29	24	SPINNING ROCK BOOGIE	Hank C. Burnett	Sonet	3
-	25	SORRY SEEMS TO BE THE HARDEST WORD	Elton John	Rocket	1
36	26	DON'T MAKE ME WAIT TOO LONG	Barry White	20th Century	2
18	27	SAILING	Rod Stewart	Warner Bros.	11
31	28	FAIRY TALE	Dana	GTO	5
25	29	GIRL OF MY BEST FRIEND	Elvis Presley	RCA	11
20	30	DANCING QUEEN	Abba	Epic	14
21	31	I'LL MEET YOU AT MIDNIGHT	Smokie	RAK	8
28	32	LOWDOWN	Boz Scaggs	CBS	3
-	33	STOP ME (IF YOU'VE HEARD IT ALL BEFORE)	Billy Ocean	GTO	1
-	34	MONEY MONEY MONEY	Abba	Epic	1
32	35	SO SAD THE SONG	Gladys Knight & the Pips	Buddah	2
-	[36]	HOT VALVES	Be-Bop Deluxe	Harvest	1
-	37	TEENAGE DEPRESSION	Eddie & the Hot Rods	Island	1
26	38	COMING HOME	David Essex	CBS	5
-	[39]	DO YOU FEEL	Peter Frampton	A&M	1
30	40	QUEEN OF MY SOUL	Average White Band	Atlantic	6

WEEK ENDING 27 NOVEMBER 1976

LW	TW	Title	Artist	Label	Wks
1	[1]	IF YOU LEAVE ME NOW	Chicago	CBS	8
3	2	UNDER THE MOON OF LOVE	Showaddywaddy	Bell	4
2	3	YOU MAKE ME FEEL LIKE DANCING	Leo Sayer	Chrysalis	5
-	4	SOMEBODY TO LOVE	Queen	EMI	1
5	[5]	IF NOT YOU	Dr. Hook	Capitol	4
4	6	MISSISSIPPI	Pussycat	Sonet	13
9	[7]	PLAY THAT FUNKY MUSIC	Wild Cherry	Epic	8
20	8	LOVE ME	Yvonne Elliman	RSO	3
15	9	LOST IN FRANCE	Bonnie Tyler	RCA	4
34	10	MONEY MONEY MONEY	Abba	Epic	2
19	[11]	ROCK 'N' ME	Steve Miller Band	Mercury	4
8	12	DON'T TAKE AWAY THE MUSIC	Tavares	Capitol	8
23	13	LIVIN' THING	Electric Light Orchestra	Jet	2
13	14	BEAUTIFUL NOISE	Neil Diamond	CBS	5
-	15	GET BACK	Rod Stewart	Riva	1
12	16	LOVE AND AFFECTION	Joan Armatrading	A&M	7
10	17	COULDN'T GET IT RIGHT	Climax Blues Band	BTM	7
7	18	SUBSTITUTE	The Who	Polydor	5
6	19	HURT	Manhattans	CBS	9
35	[20]	SO SAD THE SONG	Gladys Knight & the Pips	Buddah	3
11	21	WHEN FOREVER HAS GONE	Demis Roussos	Philips	9
25	22	SORRY SEEMS TO BE THE HARDEST WORD	Elton John	Rocket	2
24	23	SPINNING ROCK BOOGIE	Hank C. Burnett	Sonet	4
33	24	STOP ME (IF YOU'VE HEARD IT ALL BEFORE)	Billy Ocean	GTO	2
26	25	DON'T MAKE ME WAIT TOO LONG	Barry White	20th Century	3
14	26	DANCING WITH THE CAPTAIN	Paul Nicholas	RSO	7
28	27	FAIRY TALE	Dana	GTO	6
-	28	WHEN A CHILD IS BORN	Johnny Mathis	CBS	1
27	29	SAILING	Rod Stewart	Warner Bros.	12
22	30	WITHOUT YOU	Nilsson	RCA	6
17	31	JAWS	Lalo Schifrin	CTI	7
18	32	HOWZAT	Sherbet	Epic	9
-	33	LITTLE DOES SHE KNOW	Kursaal Flyers ●	CBS	1
16	34	SUMMER OF MY LIFE	Simon May	Pye	8
37	[35]	TEENAGE DEPRESSION	Eddie & the Hot Rods	Island	2
36	36	HOT VALVES	Be-Bop Deluxe	Harvest	2
30	37	DANCING QUEEN	Abba	Epic	15
-	38	LEAN ON ME	Mud	Private Stock	1
-	39	PORTSMOUTH	Mike Oldfield	Virgin	1
-	[40]	SAY YOU LOVE ME	Fleetwood Mac	Reprise	1

WEEK ENDING 4 DECEMBER 1976

LW	TW	Title	Artist	Label	Wks
2	[1]	UNDER THE MOON OF LOVE	Showaddywaddy	Bell	5
1	2	IF YOU LEAVE ME NOW	Chicago	CBS	9
3	3	YOU MAKE ME FEEL LIKE DANCING	Leo Sayer	Chrysalis	6
4	4	SOMEBODY TO LOVE	Queen	EMI	2
13	5	LIVIN' THING	Electric Light Orchestra	Jet	3
10	6	MONEY MONEY MONEY	Abba	Epic	3
8	7	LOVE ME	Yvonne Elliman	RSO	4
5	8	IF NOT YOU	Dr. Hook	Capitol	5
9	9	LOST IN FRANCE	Bonnie Tyler	RCA	5
6	10	MISSISSIPPI	Pussycat	Sonet	14
22	[11]	SORRY SEEMS TO BE THE HARDEST WORD	Elton John	Rocket	3
15	12	GET BACK	Rod Stewart	Riva	2
11	13	ROCK 'N' ME	Steve Miller Band	Mercury	5
28	14	WHEN A CHILD IS BORN	Johnny Mathis	CBS	2
14	15	BEAUTIFUL NOISE	Neil Diamond	CBS	6
38	16	LEAN ON ME	Mud	Private Stock	2
25	[17]	DON'T MAKE ME WAIT TOO LONG	Barry White	20th Century	4
17	18	COULDN'T GET IT RIGHT	Climax Blues Band	BTM	8
18	19	SUBSTITUTE	The Who	Polydor	6
7	20	PLAY THAT FUNKY MUSIC	Wild Cherry	Epic	9
23	[21]	SPINNING ROCK BOOGIE	Hank C. Burnett	Sonet	5
33	22	LITTLE DOES SHE KNOW	Kursaal Flyers	CBS	2
27	23	FAIRY TALE	Dana	GTO	7
19	24	HURT	Manhattans	CBS	10
24	25	STOP ME (IF YOU'VE HEARD IT ALL BEFORE)	Billy Ocean	GTO	3
39	26	PORTSMOUTH	Mike Oldfield	Virgin	2
20	27	SO SAD THE SONG	Gladys Knight & the Pips	Buddah	4
12	28	DON'T TAKE AWAY THE MUSIC	Tavares	Capitol	9
-	29	YOU'LL NEVER GET TO HEAVEN	Stylistics EP	H&L	1
21	30	WHEN FOREVER HAS GONE	Demis Roussos	Philips	10
16	31	LOVE AND AFFECTION	Joan Armatrading	A&M	8
-	[32]	HANG ON SLOOPY	Sandpipers	Satril	1
26	33	DANCING WITH THE CAPTAIN	Paul Nicholas	RSO	8
-	[34]	WE CAN WORK IT OUT	Four Seasons	Warner Bros	1
-	35	SECRETS	Sutherland Brothers & Quiver	CBS	1
29	36	SAILING	Rod Stewart	Warner Bros.	13
30	37	WITHOUT YOU	Nilsson	RCA	7
-	38	LIVING NEXT DOOR TO ALICE	Smokie	RAK	1
31	39	JAWS	Lalo Schifrin	CTI	8
-	40	HEY MR DREAM MAKER	Cliff Richard	EMI	1

WEEK ENDING 11 DECEMBER 1976

LW	TW	Title	Artist	Label	Wks
1	[1]	UNDER THE MOON OF LOVE	Showaddywaddy	Bell	6
4	[2]	SOMEBODY TO LOVE	Queen	EMI	3
6	3	MONEY MONEY MONEY	Abba	Epic	4
2	4	IF YOU LEAVE ME NOW	Chicago	CBS	10
5	5	LIVIN' THING	Electric Light Orchestra	Jet	4
3	6	YOU MAKE ME FEEL LIKE DANCING	Leo Sayer	Chrysalis	7

■ *Under The Moon Of Love* was the first of two 1961 American hits by Curtis Lee to be covered by Showaddywaddy; the second would be *Pretty Little Angel Eyes* (06.11.76) ■ *Say You Love Me* is the first UK Top 40 hit for the newly-constituted Anglo-American Fleetwood Mac (27.11.76) ■ Rod Stewart and the Four Seasons have successful Beatle covers (04.12.76)■

December 1976

□ Highest position disc reached ● Act's first ever week on chart

LW	TW	Title / Artist	Label	Wks
7	7	LOVE ME Yvonne Elliman	*RSO*	5
14	8	WHEN A CHILD IS BORN Johnny Mathis	*CBS*	3
8	9	IF NOT YOU Dr. Hook	*Capitol*	6
9	10	LOST IN FRANCE Bonnie Tyler	*RCA*	6
12	11	GET BACK Rod Stewart	*Riva*	3
25	12	STOP ME (IF YOU'VE HEARD IT ALL BEFORE) Billy Ocean	*GTO*	4
11	13	SORRY SEEMS TO BE THE HARDEST WORD Elton John	*Rocket*	4
16	14	LEAN ON ME Mud	*Private Stock*	3
13	15	ROCK 'N' ME Steve Miller Band	*Mercury*	6
26	16	PORTSMOUTH Mike Oldfield	*Virgin*	3
17	17	DON'T MAKE ME WAIT TOO LONG Barry White	*20th Century*	5
22	18	LITTLE DOES SHE KNOW Kursaal Flyers	*CBS*	3
23	19	FAIRY TALE Dana	*GTO*	8
10	20	MISSISSIPPI Pussycat	*Sonet*	15
38	21	LIVING NEXT DOOR TO ALICE Smokie	*RAK*	2
21	22	SPINNING ROCK BOOGIE Hank C. Burnett	*Sonet*	6
20	23	PLAY THAT FUNKY MUSIC Wild Cherry	*Epic*	10
-	24	DR. LOVE Tina Charles	*CBS*	1
29	25	YOU'LL NEVER GET TO HEAVEN Stylistics EP	*H&L*	2
27	26	SO SAD THE SONG Gladys Knight & the Pips	*Buddah*	5
-	27	GRANDMA'S PARTY Paul Nicholas	*RSO*	1
-	28	BIONIC SANTA Chris Hill	*Philips*	1
15	29	BEAUTIFUL NOISE Neil Diamond	*CBS*	7
19	30	SUBSTITUTE The Who	*Polydor*	7
40	31	HEY MR DREAM MAKER Cliff Richard	*EMI*	2
-	32	WILD SIDE OF LIFE Status Quo	*Vertigo*	1
24	33	HURT Manhattans	*CBS*	11
34	34	WE CAN WORK IT OUT Four Seasons	*Warner Bros*	2
36	35	SAILING Rod Stewart	*Warner Bros.*	14
31	36	LOVE AND AFFECTION Joan Armatrading	*A&M*	9
-	37	THINGS WE DO FOR LOVE 10 C.C.	*Mercury*	1
28	38	DON'T TAKE AWAY THE MUSIC Tavares	*Capitol*	10
-	39	MAGGIE MAY Rod Stewart	*Mercury*	1
32	40	HANG ON SLOOPY Sandpipers	*Satril*	2

LW	TW	*WEEK ENDING* 18 DECEMBER 1976		Wks
1	1	UNDER THE MOON OF LOVE Showaddywaddy	*Bell*	7
8	2	WHEN A CHILD IS BORN Johnny Mathis	*CBS*	4
2	3	SOMEBODY TO LOVE Queen	*EMI*	4
5	4	LIVIN' THING Electric Light Orchestra	*Jet*	5
3	5	MONEY MONEY MONEY Abba	*Epic*	5
7	6	LOVE ME Yvonne Elliman	*RSO*	6
14	7	LEAN ON ME Mud	*Private Stock*	4
4	8	IF YOU LEAVE ME NOW Chicago	*CBS*	11
16	9	PORTSMOUTH Mike Oldfield	*Virgin*	4
6	10	YOU MAKE ME FEEL LIKE DANCING Leo Sayer	*Chrysalis*	8
28	11	BIONIC SANTA Chris Hill	*Philips*	2
21	12	LIVING NEXT DOOR TO ALICE Smokie	*RAK*	3
11	13	GET BACK Rod Stewart	*Riva*	4
18	14	LITTLE DOES SHE KNOW Kursaal Flyers	*CBS*	4
10	15	LOST IN FRANCE Bonnie Tyler	*RCA*	7
12	16	STOP ME (IF YOU'VE HEARD IT ALL BEFORE) Billy Ocean	*GTO*	5
13	17	SORRY SEEMS TO BE THE HARDEST WORD Elton John	*Rocket*	5
24	18	DR. LOVE Tina Charles	*CBS*	2
32	19	WILD SIDE OF LIFE Status Quo	*Vertigo*	2
27	20	GRANDMA'S PARTY Paul Nicholas	*RSO*	2
17	21	DON'T MAKE ME WAIT TOO LONG Barry White	*20th Century*	6
19	22	FAIRY TALE Dana	*GTO*	9
9	23	IF NOT YOU Dr. Hook	*Capitol*	7
25	24	YOU'LL NEVER GET TO HEAVEN Stylistics EP	*H&L*	3
20	25	MISSISSIPPI Pussycat	*Sonet*	16
-	26	SIDE SHOW Barry Biggs	*Dynamic*	1
37	27	THINGS WE DO FOR LOVE 10 C.C.	*Mercury*	2
22	28	SPINNING ROCK BOOGIE Hank C. Burnett	*Sonet*	7
-	29	I WISH Stevie Wonder	*Motown*	1
26	30	SO SAD THE SONG Gladys Knight & the Pips	*Buddah*	6
39	31	MAGGIE MAY Rod Stewart	*Mercury*	2
15	32	ROCK 'N' ME Steve Miller Band	*Mercury*	7
-	33	HAITIAN DIVORCE Steely Dan	*ABC*	1
31	34	HEY MR DREAM MAKER Cliff Richard	*EMI*	3
23	35	PLAY THAT FUNKY MUSIC Wild Cherry	*Epic*	11
-	36	KEEP IT COMIN' LOVE KC & the Sunshine Band	*Jayboy*	1
-	37	DON'T GIVE UP ON US David Soul ●	*Private Stock*	1
-	38	ANARCHY IN THE UK Sex Pistols ●	*EMI*	1
29	39	BEAUTIFUL NOISE Neil Diamond	*CBS*	8
35	40	SAILING Rod Stewart	*Warner Bros.*	15

LW	TW	*WEEK ENDING* 25 DECEMBER 1976		Wks
2	1	WHEN A CHILD IS BORN Johnny Mathis	*CBS*	5
1	2	UNDER THE MOON OF LOVE Showaddywaddy	*Bell*	8
5	3	MONEY MONEY MONEY Abba	*Epic*	6
3	4	SOMEBODY TO LOVE Queen	*EMI*	5
9	5	PORTSMOUTH Mike Oldfield	*Virgin*	5
4	6	LIVIN' THING Electric Light Orchestra	*Jet*	6
6	7	LOVE ME Yvonne Elliman	*RSO*	7
18	8	DR. LOVE Tina Charles	*CBS*	3
12	9	LIVING NEXT DOOR TO ALICE Smokie	*RAK*	4
11	10	BIONIC SANTA Chris Hill	*Philips*	3
37	11	DON'T GIVE UP ON US David Soul	*Private Stock*	2
7	12	LEAN ON ME Mud	*Private Stock*	5
22	13	FAIRY TALE Dana	*GTO*	10
14	14	LITTLE DOES SHE KNOW Kursaal Flyers	*CBS*	5
20	15	GRANDMA'S PARTY Paul Nicholas	*RSO*	3
8	16	IF YOU LEAVE ME NOW Chicago	*CBS*	12
19	17	WILD SIDE OF LIFE Status Quo	*Vertigo*	3
13	18	GET BACK Rod Stewart	*Riva*	5
27	19	THINGS WE DO FOR LOVE 10 C.C.	*Mercury*	3
16	20	STOP ME (IF YOU'VE HEARD IT ALL BEFORE) Billy Ocean	*GTO*	6
17	21	SORRY SEEMS TO BE THE HARDEST WORD Elton John	*Rocket*	6
29	22	I WISH Stevie Wonder	*Motown*	2
26	23	SIDE SHOW Barry Biggs	*Dynamic*	2
10	24	YOU MAKE ME FEEL LIKE DANCING Leo Sayer	*Chrysalis*	9
33	25	HAITIAN DIVORCE Steely Dan	*ABC*	2
25	26	MISSISSIPPI Pussycat	*Sonet*	17
15	27	LOST IN FRANCE Bonnie Tyler	*RCA*	8
-	28	RING OUT SOLSTICE BELLS Jethro Tull	*Chrysalis*	1
24	29	YOU'LL NEVER GET TO HEAVEN Stylistics EP	*H&L*	4
23	30	IF NOT YOU Dr. Hook	*Capitol*	8
-	31	DADDY COOL Boney M. ●	*Atlantic*	1
-	32	YOU'RE MORE THAN A NUMBER IN MY LITTLE RED BOOK Drifters	*Arista*	1
36	33	KEEP IT COMIN' LOVE KC & the Sunshine Band	*Jayboy*	2
-	34	SING ME AN OLD FASHIONED SONG Billie Jo Spears	*United Artists*	1
-	35	EVERYMAN MUST HAVE A DREAM Liverpool Express	*Warner Bros.*	1
31	36	MAGGIE MAY Rod Stewart	*Mercury*	3
-	37	DON'T CRY FOR ME ARGENTINA Julie Covington ●	*MCA*	1
38	38	ANARCHY IN THE UK Sex Pistols	*EMI*	2
21	39	DON'T MAKE ME WAIT TOO LONG Barry White	*20th Century*	7
30	40	SO SAD THE SONG Gladys Knight & the Pips	*Buddah*	7

In these weeks ■ (25.12.76) Johnny Mathis concludes what is to date the longest period between chart debut and first number one, 18 years and 216 days .... Its two Top 10 Christmas novelties in two successive years for Chris Hill ■ Although Eddie and the Hot Rods have charted in November with *Teenage Depression*, the Sex Pistols have the first proper punk hit, *Anarchy In The UK* (18.12.76)■

1977

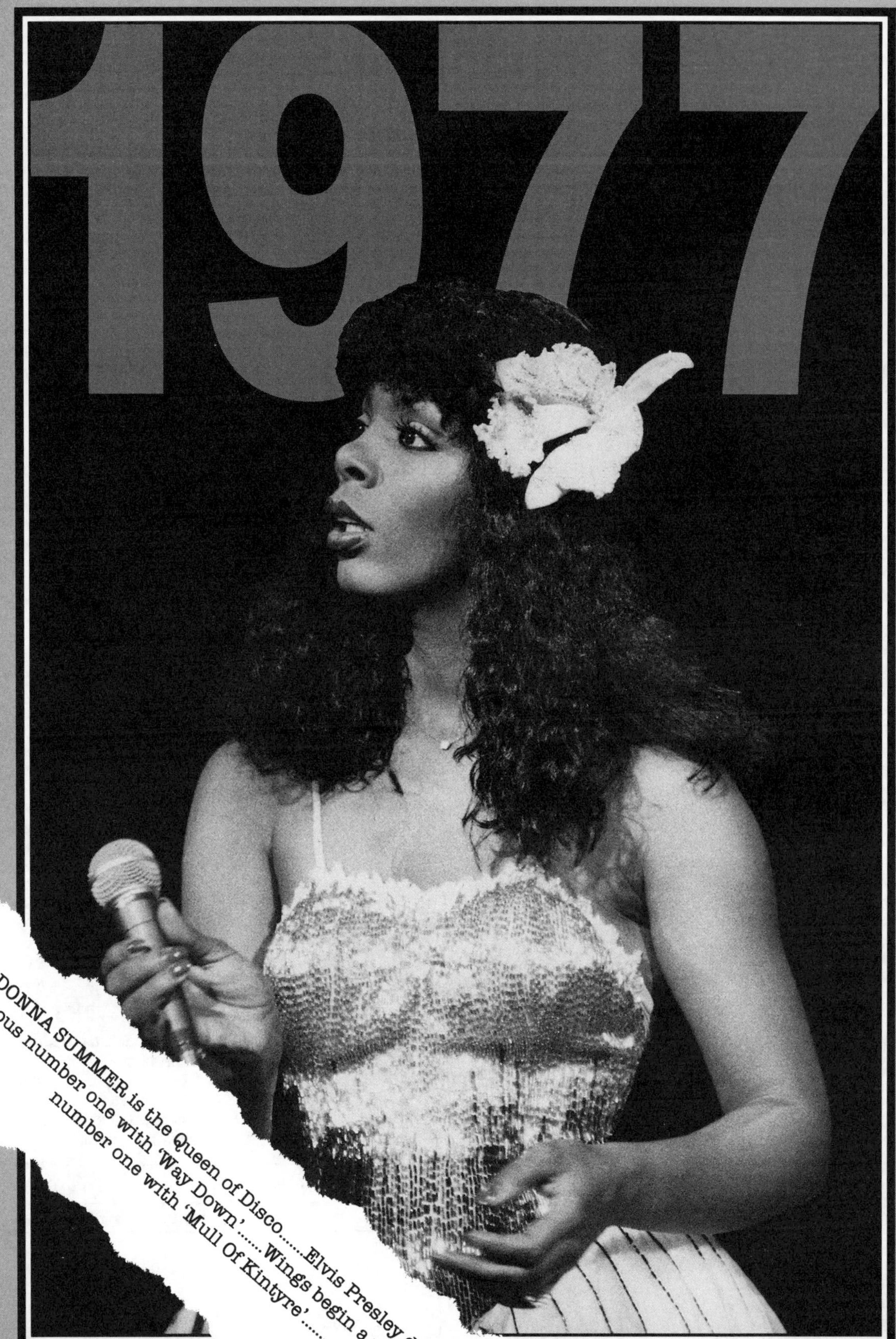

..........DONNA SUMMER is the Queen of Disco.......Elvis Presley dies and has posthumous number one with 'Way Down'.......Wings begin a nine-week stint at number one with 'Mull Of Kintyre'..........

January 1977

□ Highest position disc reached ● Act's first ever week on chart

WEEK ENDING 1 JANUARY 1977

(no chart published, chart for 25th December 1976 repeated)

LW	TW	Title	Artist	Label	Wks
1	[1]	WHEN A CHILD IS BORN	Johnny Mathis	CBS	6
2	2	UNDER THE MOON OF LOVE	Showaddywaddy	Bell	9
3	3	MONEY MONEY MONEY	Abba	Epic	7
4	4	SOMEBODY TO LOVE	Queen	EMI	6
5	5	PORTSMOUTH	Mike Oldfield	Virgin	6
6	6	LIVIN' THING	Electric Light Orchestra	Jet	7
7	7	LOVE ME	Yvonne Elliman	RSO	8
8	8	DR. LOVE	Tina Charles	CBS	4
9	9	LIVING NEXT DOOR TO ALICE	Smokie	RAK	5
10	[10]	BIONIC SANTA	Chris Hill	Philips	4
11	11	DON'T GIVE UP ON US	David Soul	Private Stock	3
12	12	LEAN ON ME	Mud	Private Stock	6
13	[13]	FAIRY TALE	Dana	GTO	11
14	[14]	LITTLE DOES SHE KNOW	Kursaal Flyers	CBS	6
15	15	GRANDMA'S PARTY	Paul Nicholas	RSO	4
16	16	IF YOU LEAVE ME NOW	Chicago	CBS	13
17	17	WILD SIDE OF LIFE	Status Quo	Vertigo	4
18	18	GET BACK	Rod Stewart	Riva	6
19	19	THINGS WE DO FOR LOVE	10 C.C.	Mercury	4
20	20	STOP ME (IF YOU'VE HEARD IT ALL BEFORE)	Billy Ocean	GTO	7
21	21	SORRY SEEMS TO BE THE HARDEST WORD	Elton John	Rocket	7
22	22	I WISH	Stevie Wonder	Motown	3
23	23	SIDE SHOW	Barry Biggs	Dynamic	3
24	24	YOU MAKE ME FEEL LIKE DANCING	Leo Sayer	Chrysalis	10
25	25	HAITIAN DIVORCE	Steely Dan	ABC	3
26	26	MISSISSIPPI	Pussycat	Sonet	18
27	27	LOST IN FRANCE	Bonnie Tyler	RCA	9
28	[28]	RING OUT SOLSTICE BELLS	Jethro Tull	Chrysalis	2
29	29	YOU'LL NEVER GET TO HEAVEN	Stylistics EP	H&L	5
30	30	IF NOT YOU	Dr. Hook	Capitol	9
31	31	DADDY COOL	Boney M.	Atlantic	2
32	32	YOU'RE MORE THAN A NUMBER IN MY LITTLE RED BOOK	Drifters	Arista	2
33	33	KEEP IT COMIN' LOVE	KC & the Sunshine Band	Jayboy	3
34	[34]	SING ME AN OLD FASHIONED SONG	Billie Jo Spears	United Artists	2
35	35	EVERYMAN MUST HAVE A DREAM	Liverpool Express	Warner Bros.	2
36	36	MAGGIE MAY	Rod Stewart	Mercury	4
37	37	DON'T CRY FOR ME ARGENTINA	Julie Covington	MCA	2
38	38	ANARCHY IN THE UK	Sex Pistols	EMI	3
39	39	DON'T MAKE ME WAIT TOO LONG	Barry White	20th Century	8
40	40	SO SAD THE SONG	Gladys Knight & the Pips	Buddah	8

WEEK ENDING 8 JANUARY 1977

(Top 30 chart compiled only)

LW	TW	Title	Artist	Label	Wks
1	[1]	WHEN A CHILD IS BORN	Johnny Mathis	CBS	7
2	2	UNDER THE MOON OF LOVE	Showaddywaddy	Bell	10
5	[3]	PORTSMOUTH	Mike Oldfield	Virgin	7
3	4	MONEY MONEY MONEY	Abba	Epic	8
9	[5]	LIVING NEXT DOOR TO ALICE	Smokie	RAK	6
4	6	SOMEBODY TO LOVE	Queen	EMI	7
8	7	DR. LOVE	Tina Charles	CBS	5
11	8	DON'T GIVE UP ON US	David Soul	Private Stock	4
15	[9]	GRANDMA'S PARTY	Paul Nicholas	RSO	5
12	10	LEAN ON ME	Mud	Private Stock	7
10	11	BIONIC SANTA	Chris Hill	Philips	5
19	12	THINGS WE DO FOR LOVE	10 C.C.	Mercury	5
17	13	WILD SIDE OF LIFE	Status Quo	Vertigo	5
13	14	FAIRY TALE	Dana	GTO	12
6	15	LIVIN' THING	Electric Light Orchestra	Jet	8
14	16	LITTLE DOES SHE KNOW	Kursaal Flyers	CBS	7
22	17	I WISH	Stevie Wonder	Motown	4
7	18	LOVE ME	Yvonne Elliman	RSO	9
24	19	YOU MAKE ME FEEL LIKE DANCING	Leo Sayer	Chrysalis	11
23	20	SIDE SHOW	Barry Biggs	Dynamic	4
20	21	STOP ME (IF YOU'VE HEARD IT ALL BEFORE)	Billy Ocean	GTO	8
32	22	YOU'RE MORE THAN A NUMBER IN MY LITTLE RED BOOK	Drifters	Arista	3
18	23	GET BACK	Rod Stewart	Riva	7
-	[24]	HERE'S TO LOVE	John Christie ●	EMI	1
37	25	DON'T CRY FOR ME ARGENTINA	Julie Covington	MCA	3
25	26	HAITIAN DIVORCE	Steely Dan	ABC	4
-	27	CAR WASH	Rose Royce ●	MCA	1
16	28	IF YOU LEAVE ME NOW	Chicago	CBS	14
35	29	EVERYMAN MUST HAVE A DREAM	Liverpool Express	Warner Bros.	3
29	30	YOU'LL NEVER GET TO HEAVEN	Stylistics EP	H&L	6

WEEK ENDING 15 JANUARY 1977

LW	TW	Title	Artist	Label	Wks
8	[1]	DON'T GIVE UP ON US	David Soul	Private Stock	5
1	2	WHEN A CHILD IS BORN	Johnny Mathis	CBS	8
4	3	MONEY MONEY MONEY	Abba	Epic	9
2	4	UNDER THE MOON OF LOVE	Showaddywaddy	Bell	11
20	5	SIDE SHOW	Barry Biggs	Dynamic	5
12	[6]	THINGS WE DO FOR LOVE	10 C.C.	Mercury	6
25	7	DON'T CRY FOR ME ARGENTINA	Julie Covington	MCA	4
7	8	DR. LOVE	Tina Charles	CBS	6
3	9	PORTSMOUTH	Mike Oldfield	Virgin	8
5	10	LIVING NEXT DOOR TO ALICE	Smokie	RAK	7
13	11	WILD SIDE OF LIFE	Status Quo	Vertigo	6
9	12	GRANDMA'S PARTY	Paul Nicholas	RSO	6
6	13	SOMEBODY TO LOVE	Queen	EMI	8
17	14	I WISH	Stevie Wonder	Motown	5
14	15	FAIRY TALE	Dana	GTO	13
16	16	LITTLE DOES SHE KNOW	Kursaal Flyers	CBS	8
10	17	LEAN ON ME	Mud	Private Stock	8
22	18	YOU'RE MORE THAN A NUMBER IN MY LITTLE RED BOOK	Drifters	Arista	4
15	19	LIVIN' THING	Electric Light Orchestra	Jet	9
11	20	BIONIC SANTA	Chris Hill	Philips	6
27	21	CAR WASH	Rose Royce	MCA	2
18	22	LOVE ME	Yvonne Elliman	RSO	10
-	23	DADDY COOL	Boney M. ●	Atlantic	4
-	24	SUSPICION	Elvis Presley	RCA	1
29	25	EVERYMAN MUST HAVE A DREAM	Liverpool Express	Warner Bros.	4
24	26	HERE'S TO LOVE	John Christie	EMI	2
26	27	HAITIAN DIVORCE	Steely Dan	ABC	5
-	28	LOST WITHOUT YOUR LOVE	Bread	Elektra	1
-	29	WINTER MELODY	Donna Summer	GTO	1
28	30	IF YOU LEAVE ME NOW	Chicago	CBS	15
-	[31]	KEEP IT COMIN' LOVE	KC & the Sunshine Band	Jayboy	5
-	32	SMILE	Pussycat	Sonet	1
-	33	FLIP	Jesse Green	EMI	1
23	34	GET BACK	Rod Stewart	Riva	8
-	35	ISN'T SHE LOVELY	David Parton ●	Pye	1
-	36	SING ME AN OLD FASHIONED SONG	Billie Jo Spears	United Artists	4
21	37	STOP ME (IF YOU'VE HEARD IT ALL BEFORE)	Billy Ocean	GTO	9
-	38	DON'T BELIEVE A WORD	Thin Lizzy	Vertigo	1
-	39	YOU'LL NEVER GET TO HEAVEN (EP)	Stylistics EP	H&L	7
-	40	SORRY SEEMS TO BE THE HARDEST WORD	Elton John	Rocket	9

WEEK ENDING 22 JANUARY 1977

LW	TW	Title	Artist	Label	Wks
1	[1]	DON'T GIVE UP ON US	David Soul	Private Stock	6
7	2	DON'T CRY FOR ME ARGENTINA	Julie Covington	MCA	5
5	[3]	SIDE SHOW	Barry Biggs	Dynamic	6
8	[4]	DR. LOVE	Tina Charles	CBS	7
14	[5]	I WISH	Stevie Wonder	Motown	6
6	[6]	THINGS WE DO FOR LOVE	10 C.C.	Mercury	7

In these weeks ■ Number one album artist Mike Oldfield has his biggest hit single (08.01.77) ■ When Stevie Wonder refuses to edit his LP track *Isn't She Lovely* for release as a single, David Parton has a cover hit (15.01.77) ■ David Soul, Hutch of TV's 'Starsky and Hutch', has a number one, years after he sang as The Covered Man wearing a ski mask on the Merv Griffin USA TV show (15.01.77)■

LW	TW	Title	Artist	Label	Wks
9	7	PORTSMOUTH	Mike Oldfield	Virgin	9
3	8	MONEY MONEY MONEY	Abba	Epic	10
11	[9]	WILD SIDE OF LIFE	Status Quo	Vertigo	7
10	10	LIVING NEXT DOOR TO ALICE	Smokie	RAK	8
18	11	YOU'RE MORE THAN A NUMBER IN MY LITTLE RED BOOK	Drifters	Arista	5
4	12	UNDER THE MOON OF LOVE	Showaddywaddy	Bell	12
2	13	WHEN A CHILD IS BORN	Johnny Mathis	CBS	9
12	14	GRANDMA'S PARTY	Paul Nicholas	RSO	7
35	15	ISN'T SHE LOVELY	David Parton	Pye	2
21	16	CAR WASH	Rose Royce	MCA	3
27	[17]	HAITIAN DIVORCE	Steely Dan	ABC	6
23	18	DADDY COOL	Boney M.	Atlantic	5
15	19	FAIRY TALE	Dana	GTO	14
24	20	SUSPICION	Elvis Presley	RCA	2
38	21	DON'T BELIEVE A WORD	Thin Lizzy	Vertigo	2
19	22	LIVIN' THING	Electric Light Orchestra	Jet	10
22	23	LOVE ME	Yvonne Elliman	RSO	11
25	24	EVERYMAN MUST HAVE A DREAM	Liverpool Express	Warner Bros.	5
-	25	NEW KID IN TOWN	Eagles	Asylum	1
26	26	HERE'S TO LOVE	John Christie	EMI	3
29	[27]	WINTER MELODY	Donna Summer	GTO	2
32	28	SMILE	Pussycat	Sonet	2
28	29	LOST WITHOUT YOUR LOVE	Bread	Elektra	2
33	30	FLIP	Jesse Green	EMI	2
17	31	LEAN ON ME	Mud	Private Stock	9
13	32	SOMEBODY TO LOVE	Queen	EMI	9
31	33	KEEP IT COMIN' LOVE	KC & the Sunshine Band	Jayboy	6
-	[34]	NOBODY BUT YOU	Gladys Knight & the Pips	Buddah	1
16	35	LITTLE DOES SHE KNOW	Kursaal Flyers	CBS	9
-	36	DON'T LEAVE ME THIS WAY	Harold Melvin & the Blue Notes	CBS	1
37	37	STOP ME (IF YOU'VE HEARD IT ALL BEFORE)	Billy Ocean	GTO	10
36	38	SING ME AN OLD FASHIONED SONG	Billie Jo Spears	United Artists	5
30	39	IF YOU LEAVE ME NOW	Chicago	CBS	16
-	40	MISSISSIPPI	Pussycat	Sonet	1

WEEK ENDING 29 JANUARY 1977

LW	TW	Title	Artist	Label	Wks
1	[1]	DON'T GIVE UP ON US	David Soul	Private Stock	7
2	2	DON'T CRY FOR ME ARGENTINA	Julie Covington	MCA	6
3	[3]	SIDE SHOW	Barry Biggs	Dynamic	7
15	[4]	ISN'T SHE LOVELY	David Parton	Pye	3
11	[5]	YOU'RE MORE THAN A NUMBER IN MY LITTLE RED BOOK	Drifters	Arista	6
5	6	I WISH	Stevie Wonder	Motown	7
6	7	THINGS WE DO FOR LOVE	10 C.C.	Mercury	8
18	8	DADDY COOL	Boney M.	Atlantic	6
9	[9]	WILD SIDE OF LIFE	Status Quo	Vertigo	8
16	10	CAR WASH	Rose Royce	MCA	4
12	11	UNDER THE MOON OF LOVE	Showaddywaddy	Bell	13
4	12	DR. LOVE	Tina Charles	CBS	8
20	13	SUSPICION	Elvis Presley	RCA	3
10	14	LIVING NEXT DOOR TO ALICE	Smokie	RAK	9
-	15	WHEN I NEED YOU	Leo Sayer	Chrysalis	1
14	16	GRANDMA'S PARTY	Paul Nicholas	RSO	8
8	17	MONEY MONEY MONEY	Abba	Epic	11
21	18	DON'T BELIEVE A WORD	Thin Lizzy	Vertigo	3
7	19	PORTSMOUTH	Mike Oldfield	Virgin	10
24	20	EVERYMAN MUST HAVE A DREAM	Liverpool Express	Warner Bros.	6
13	21	WHEN A CHILD IS BORN	Johnny Mathis	CBS	10
19	22	FAIRY TALE	Dana	GTO	15
25	23	NEW KID IN TOWN	Eagles	Asylum	2
28	[24]	SMILE	Pussycat	Sonet	3
36	25	DON'T LEAVE ME THIS WAY	Harold Melvin & the Blue Notes	CBS	2
30	[26]	FLIP	Jesse Green	EMI	3
29	[27]	LOST WITHOUT YOUR LOVE	Bread	Elektra	3
-	28	JACK IN THE BOX	Moments	All Platinum	1
-	29	IT TAKES ALL NIGHT LONG	Gary Glitter	Arista	1

February 1977

□ Highest position disc reached ● Act's first ever week on chart

LW	TW	Title	Artist	Label	Wks
-	30	BOOGIE NIGHTS	Heatwave ●	GTO	1
17	31	HAITIAN DIVORCE	Steely Dan	ABC	7
-	32	WHAT CAN I SAY	Boz Scaggs	CBS	1
22	33	LIVIN' THING	Electric Light Orchestra	Jet	11
27	34	WINTER MELODY	Donna Summer	GTO	3
33	35	KEEP IT COMIN' LOVE	KC & the Sunshine Band	Jayboy	7
26	36	HERE'S TO LOVE	John Christie	EMI	4
-	37	MORE THAN A FEELING	Boston ●	Epic	1
-	38	SING ME	The Brothers ●	Bus Stop	1
-	39	EVERY LITTLE TEARDROP	Gallagher & Lyle	A&M	1
-	[40]	THE WRECK OF THE EDMUND FITZGERALD	Gordon Lightfoot	Reprise	1

WEEK ENDING 5 FEBRUARY 1977

LW	TW	Title	Artist	Label	Wks
1	[1]	DON'T GIVE UP ON US	David Soul	Private Stock	8
2	2	DON'T CRY FOR ME ARGENTINA	Julie Covington	MCA	7
3	[3]	SIDE SHOW	Barry Biggs	Dynamic	8
4	[4]	ISN'T SHE LOVELY	David Parton	Pye	4
15	5	WHEN I NEED YOU	Leo Sayer	Chrysalis	2
8	[6]	DADDY COOL	Boney M.	Atlantic	7
5	7	YOU'RE MORE THAN A NUMBER IN MY LITTLE RED BOOK	Drifters	Arista	7
7	8	THINGS WE DO FOR LOVE	10 C.C.	Mercury	9
13	[9]	SUSPICION	Elvis Presley	RCA	4
10	10	CAR WASH	Rose Royce	MCA	5
9	11	WILD SIDE OF LIFE	Status Quo	Vertigo	9
18	[12]	DON'T BELIEVE A WORD	Thin Lizzy	Vertigo	4
6	13	I WISH	Stevie Wonder	Motown	8
25	14	DON'T LEAVE ME THIS WAY	Harold Melvin & the Blue Notes	CBS	3
12	15	DR. LOVE	Tina Charles	CBS	9
28	16	JACK IN THE BOX	Moments	All Platinum	2
16	17	GRANDMA'S PARTY	Paul Nicholas	RSO	9
19	18	PORTSMOUTH	Mike Oldfield	Virgin	11
30	19	BOOGIE NIGHTS	Heatwave	GTO	2
23	[20]	NEW KID IN TOWN	Eagles	Asylum	3
38	21	SING ME	The Brothers	Bus Stop	2
14	22	LIVING NEXT DOOR TO ALICE	Smokie	RAK	10
20	23	EVERYMAN MUST HAVE A DREAM	Liverpool Express	Warner Bros.	7
11	24	UNDER THE MOON OF LOVE	Showaddywaddy	Bell	14
24	25	SMILE	Pussycat	Sonet	4
29	26	IT TAKES ALL NIGHT LONG	Gary Glitter	Arista	2
32	27	WHAT CAN I SAY	Boz Scaggs	CBS	2
-	28	EVERYBODY'S TALKIN' 'BOUT LOVE	Silver Convention	Magnet	1
-	29	MIGHTY POWER OF LOVE	Tavares	Capitol	1
37	30	MORE THAN A FEELING	Boston	Epic	2
26	31	FLIP	Jesse Green	EMI	4
-	32	WAKE UP SUSAN	Detroit Spinners	Atlantic	1
39	33	EVERY LITTLE TEARDROP	Gallagher & Lyle	A&M	2
17	34	MONEY MONEY MONEY	Abba	Epic	12
-	35	YEAR OF THE CAT	Al Stewart ●	RCA	1
27	36	LOST WITHOUT YOUR LOVE	Bread	Elektra	4
-	37	BODY HEAT	James Brown	Polydor	1
-	38	DON'T LEAVE ME THIS WAY	Thelma Houston ●	Motown	1
31	39	HAITIAN DIVORCE	Steely Dan	ABC	8
-	40	CHANSON D'AMOUR	Manhattan Transfer	Atlantic	1

WEEK ENDING 12 FEBRUARY 1977

LW	TW	Title	Artist	Label	Wks
2	[1]	DON'T CRY FOR ME ARGENTINA	Julie Covington	MCA	8
1	2	DON'T GIVE UP ON US	David Soul	Private Stock	9
5	3	WHEN I NEED YOU	Leo Sayer	Chrysalis	3
3	4	SIDE SHOW	Barry Biggs	Dynamic	9
4	5	ISN'T SHE LOVELY	David Parton	Pye	5

■The Drifters, who had their first Top Ten hit in 1960, have their last after many membership changes (29.01.77) ■ *Suspicion* by Elvis Presley is a Top Ten hit fifteen years after it was recorded (05.02.77) ■ *Don't Cry For Me Argentina* by Julie Covington hits the top and will become (until 1985) the best-selling single by a female vocalist (12.02.77)■

February 1977

□ Highest position disc reached ● Act's first ever week on chart

LW	TW	Title / Artist	Label	Wks
14	6	DON'T LEAVE ME THIS WAY Harold Melvin & the Blue Notes	CBS	4
6	7	DADDY COOL Boney M.	Atlantic	8
16	8	JACK IN THE BOX Moments	All Platinum	3
10	[9]	CAR WASH Rose Royce	MCA	6
9	10	SUSPICION Elvis Presley	RCA	5
7	11	YOU'RE MORE THAN A NUMBER IN MY LITTLE RED BOOK Drifters	Arista	8
11	12	WILD SIDE OF LIFE Status Quo	Vertigo	10
12	13	DON'T BELIEVE A WORD Thin Lizzy	Vertigo	5
13	14	I WISH Stevie Wonder	Motown	9
8	15	THINGS WE DO FOR LOVE 10 C.C.	Mercury	10
19	16	BOOGIE NIGHTS Heatwave	GTO	3
23	[17]	EVERYMAN MUST HAVE A DREAM Liverpool Express	Warner Bros.	8
40	18	CHANSON D'AMOUR Manhattan Transfer	Atlantic	2
21	19	SING ME The Brothers	Bus Stop	3
20	[20]	NEW KID IN TOWN Eagles	Asylum	4
-	21	THIS IS TOMORROW Bryan Ferry	Polydor	1
27	22	WHAT CAN I SAY Boz Scaggs	CBS	3
30	23	MORE THAN A FEELING Boston	Epic	3
38	24	DON'T LEAVE ME THIS WAY Thelma Houston	Motown	2
28	[25]	EVERYBODY'S TALKIN' 'BOUT LOVE Silver Convention	Magnet	2
-	25	I WANNA GO BACK New Seekers	CBS	1
29	27	MIGHTY POWER OF LOVE Tavares	Capitol	2
26	28	IT TAKES ALL NIGHT LONG Gary Glitter	Arista	3
32	[29]	WAKE UP SUSAN Detroit Spinners	Atlantic	2
-	30	ROMEO Mr. Big ●	EMI	1
35	[31]	YEAR OF THE CAT Al Stewart	RCA	2
33	[32]	EVERY LITTLE TEARDROP Gallagher & Lyle	A&M	3
-	33	THEY SHOOT HORSES DON'T THEY Racing Cars ●	Chrysalis	1
24	34	UNDER THE MOON OF LOVE Showaddywaddy	Bell	15
22	35	LIVING NEXT DOOR TO ALICE Smokie	RAK	11
37	[36]	BODY HEAT James Brown	Polydor	2
25	37	SMILE Pussycat	Sonet	5
17	38	GRANDMA'S PARTY Paul Nicholas	RSO	10
-	39	DARLIN' DARLIN' BABY O'Jays	Philadelphia	1
-	40	DAZZ Brick ●	Bang	1

LW	TW	*WEEK ENDING* **19 FEBRUARY 1977**		Wks
3	[1]	WHEN I NEED YOU Leo Sayer	Chrysalis	4
1	2	DON'T CRY FOR ME ARGENTINA Julie Covington	MCA	9
2	3	DON'T GIVE UP ON US David Soul	Private Stock	10
4	4	SIDE SHOW Barry Biggs	Dynamic	10
5	5	ISN'T SHE LOVELY David Parton	Pye	6
16	6	BOOGIE NIGHTS Heatwave	GTO	4
6	7	DON'T LEAVE ME THIS WAY Harold Melvin & the Blue Notes	CBS	5
8	8	JACK IN THE BOX Moments	All Platinum	4
7	9	DADDY COOL Boney M.	Atlantic	9
10	10	SUSPICION Elvis Presley	RCA	6
19	11	SING ME The Brothers	Bus Stop	4
18	12	CHANSON D'AMOUR Manhattan Transfer	Atlantic	3
9	13	CAR WASH Rose Royce	MCA	7
11	14	YOU'RE MORE THAN A NUMBER IN MY LITTLE RED BOOK Drifters	Arista	9
13	15	DON'T BELIEVE A WORD Thin Lizzy	Vertigo	6
30	16	ROMEO Mr. Big	EMI	2
21	17	THIS IS TOMORROW Bryan Ferry	Polydor	2
24	18	DON'T LEAVE ME THIS WAY Thelma Houston	Motown	3
22	19	WHAT CAN I SAY Boz Scaggs	CBS	4
17	20	EVERYMAN MUST HAVE A DREAM Liverpool Express	Warner Bros.	9
33	21	THEY SHOOT HORSES DON'T THEY Racing Cars	Chrysalis	2
-	22	BABY I KNOW Rubettes	State	1
12	23	WILD SIDE OF LIFE Status Quo	Vertigo	11
23	24	MORE THAN A FEELING Boston	Epic	4
28	[25]	IT TAKES ALL NIGHT LONG Gary Glitter	Arista	4
20	26	NEW KID IN TOWN Eagles	Asylum	5
27	27	MIGHTY POWER OF LOVE Tavares	Capitol	3
14	28	I WISH Stevie Wonder	Motown	10
-	29	SATURDAY NITE Earth Wind & Fire ●	CBS	1
25	30	EVERYBODY'S TALKIN' 'BOUT LOVE Silver Convention	Magnet	3
-	31	YOU'LL NEVER KNOW WHAT YOU'RE MISSING Real Thing	Pye	1
39	32	DARLIN' DARLIN' BABY O'Jays	Philadelphia	2
15	33	THINGS WE DO FOR LOVE 10 C.C.	Mercury	11
29	34	WAKE UP SUSAN Detroit Spinners	Atlantic	3
25	35	I WANNA GO BACK New Seekers	CBS	2
40	[36]	DAZZ Brick	Bang	2
-	[37]	HA CHA CHA Brass Construction	United Artists	1
-	38	TORN BETWEEN TWO LOVERS Mary MacGregor ●	Ariola	1
31	39	YEAR OF THE CAT Al Stewart	RCA	3
-	40	ROCKARIA Electric Light Orchestra	Jet	1

LW	TW	*WEEK ENDING* **26 FEBRUARY 1977**		Wks
1	[1]	WHEN I NEED YOU Leo Sayer	Chrysalis	5
2	2	DON'T CRY FOR ME ARGENTINA Julie Covington	MCA	10
3	3	DON'T GIVE UP ON US David Soul	Private Stock	11
6	4	BOOGIE NIGHTS Heatwave	GTO	5
7	[5]	DON'T LEAVE ME THIS WAY Harold Melvin & the Blue Notes	CBS	6
12	6	CHANSON D'AMOUR Manhattan Transfer	Atlantic	4
8	[7]	JACK IN THE BOX Moments	All Platinum	5
11	[8]	SING ME The Brothers	Bus Stop	5
4	9	SIDE SHOW Barry Biggs	Dynamic	11
17	10	THIS IS TOMORROW Bryan Ferry	Polydor	3
16	11	ROMEO Mr. Big	EMI	3
19	12	WHAT CAN I SAY Boz Scaggs	CBS	5
9	13	DADDY COOL Boney M.	Atlantic	10
5	14	ISN'T SHE LOVELY David Parton	Pye	7
13	15	CAR WASH Rose Royce	MCA	8
21	16	THEY SHOOT HORSES DON'T THEY Racing Cars	Chrysalis	3
22	17	BABY I KNOW Rubettes	State	2
38	18	TORN BETWEEN TWO LOVERS Mary MacGregor	Ariola	2
10	19	SUSPICION Elvis Presley	RCA	7
-	20	SOUND AND VISION David Bowie	RCA	1
18	21	DON'T LEAVE ME THIS WAY Thelma Houston	Motown	4
24	[22]	MORE THAN A FEELING Boston	Epic	5
14	23	YOU'RE MORE THAN A NUMBER IN MY LITTLE RED BOOK Drifters	Arista	10
32	[24]	DARLIN' DARLIN' BABY O'Jays	Philadelphia	3
27	[25]	MIGHTY POWER OF LOVE Tavares	Capitol	4
29	26	SATURDAY NITE Earth Wind & Fire	CBS	2
20	27	EVERYMAN MUST HAVE A DREAM Liverpool Express	Warner Bros.	10
15	28	DON'T BELIEVE A WORD Thin Lizzy	Vertigo	7
31	29	YOU'LL NEVER KNOW WHAT YOU'RE MISSING Real Thing	Pye	2
40	30	ROCKARIA Electric Light Orchestra	Jet	2
26	31	NEW KID IN TOWN Eagles	Asylum	6
34	32	WAKE UP SUSAN Detroit Spinners	Atlantic	4
-	33	MAYBE I'M AMAZED Wings	Parlophone	1
-	[34]	SOUL CHA CHA Van McCoy	H&L	1
23	35	WILD SIDE OF LIFE Status Quo	Vertigo	12
-	36	FIRST THING IN THE MORNING Kiki Dee	Rocket	1
30	37	EVERYBODY'S TALKIN' 'BOUT LOVE Silver Convention	Magnet	4
25	38	IT TAKES ALL NIGHT LONG Gary Glitter	Arista	5
-	39	ONE DRINK TOO MANY Sailor	Epic	1
-	40	GO YOUR OWN WAY Fleetwood Mac	Warner Brothers	1

LW	TW	*WEEK ENDING* **5 MARCH 1977**		Wks
1	[1]	WHEN I NEED YOU Leo Sayer	Chrysalis	6
4	[2]	BOOGIE NIGHTS Heatwave	GTO	6
6	3	CHANSON D'AMOUR Manhattan Transfer	Atlantic	5
11	[4]	ROMEO Mr. Big	EMI	4
2	5	DON'T CRY FOR ME ARGENTINA Julie Covington	MCA	11

In these weeks ■ After three number twos, Leo Sayer gets a number one (19.02.77) ■ Harold Melvin and the Blue Notes defeat Thelma Houston's cover of *Don't Leave Me This Way*, though Thelma will go to number one in America (26.02.77) ■ Wings have a live hit with a song from the 1970 'McCartney' LP (26.02.77)■

March 1977

□ Highest position disc reached ● Act's first ever week on chart

LW	TW	Title / Artist	Label	Wks
3	6	DON'T GIVE UP ON US David Soul	*Private Stock*	12
5	7	DON'T LEAVE ME THIS WAY Harold Melvin & the Blue Notes	*CBS*	7
8	[8]	SING ME The Brothers	*Bus Stop*	6
7	9	JACK IN THE BOX Moments	*All Platinum*	6
12	[10]	WHAT CAN I SAY Boz Scaggs	*CBS*	6
10	11	THIS IS TOMORROW Bryan Ferry	*Polydor*	4
18	12	TORN BETWEEN TWO LOVERS Mary MacGregor	*Ariola*	3
21	[13]	DON'T LEAVE ME THIS WAY Thelma Houston	*Motown*	5
16	[14]	THEY SHOOT HORSES DON'T THEY Racing Cars	*Chrysalis*	4
20	15	SOUND AND VISION David Bowie	*RCA*	2
9	16	SIDE SHOW Barry Biggs	*Dynamic*	12
17	17	BABY I KNOW Rubettes	*State*	3
-	18	KNOWING ME KNOWING YOU Abba	*Epic*	1
14	19	ISN'T SHE LOVELY David Parton	*Pye*	8
30	20	ROCKARIA Electric Light Orchestra	*Jet*	3
13	21	DADDY COOL Boney M.	*Atlantic*	11
26	22	SATURDAY NITE Earth Wind & Fire	*CBS*	3
19	23	SUSPICION Elvis Presley	*RCA*	8
24	[24]	DARLIN' DARLIN' BABY O'Jays	*Philadelphia*	4
29	25	YOU'LL NEVER KNOW WHAT YOU'RE MISSING Real Thing	*Pye*	3
15	26	CAR WASH Rose Royce	*MCA*	9
22	27	MORE THAN A FEELING Boston	*Epic*	6
33	[28]	MAYBE I'M AMAZED Wings	*Parlophone*	2
23	29	YOU'RE MORE THAN A NUMBER IN MY LITTLE RED BOOK Drifters	*Arista*	11
-	30	ANOTHER SUITCASE IN ANOTHER HALL Barbara Dickson	*MCA*	1
25	31	MIGHTY POWER OF LOVE Tavares	*Capitol*	5
36	[32]	FIRST THING IN THE MORNING Kiki Dee	*Rocket*	2
-	33	CRAZY WATER Elton John	*Rocket*	1
-	34	GROOVY KIND OF LOVE Les Gray ●	*Warner Bros.*	1
39	[35]	ONE DRINK TOO MANY Sailor	*Epic*	2
34	36	SOUL CHA CHA Van McCoy	*H&L*	2
-	37	OH BOY Brotherhood of Man	*Pye*	1
40	[38]	GO YOUR OWN WAY Fleetwood Mac	*Warner Bros.*	2
32	39	WAKE UP SUSAN Detroit Spinners	*Atlantic*	5
-	40	MOODY BLUE Elvis Presley	*RCA*	1

LW	TW	*WEEK ENDING* 12 MARCH 1977		Wks
3	[1]	CHANSON D'AMOUR Manhattan Transfer	*Atlantic*	6
1	2	WHEN I NEED YOU Leo Sayer	*Chrysalis*	7
2	3	BOOGIE NIGHTS Heatwave	*GTO*	7
12	[4]	TORN BETWEEN TWO LOVERS Mary MacGregor	*Ariola*	4
4	5	ROMEO Mr. Big	*EMI*	5
15	6	SOUND AND VISION David Bowie	*RCA*	3
18	7	KNOWING ME KNOWING YOU Abba	*Epic*	2
5	8	DON'T CRY FOR ME ARGENTINA Julie Covington	*MCA*	12
11	[9]	THIS IS TOMORROW Bryan Ferry	*Polydor*	5
7	10	DON'T LEAVE ME THIS WAY Harold Melvin & the Blue Notes	*CBS*	8
17	11	BABY I KNOW Rubettes	*State*	4
10	12	WHAT CAN I SAY Boz Scaggs	*CBS*	7
8	13	SING ME The Brothers	*Bus Stop*	7
6	14	DON'T GIVE UP ON US David Soul	*Private Stock*	13
20	15	ROCKARIA Electric Light Orchestra	*Jet*	4
9	16	JACK IN THE BOX Moments	*All Platinum*	7
13	17	DON'T LEAVE ME THIS WAY Thelma Houston	*Motown*	6
14	18	THEY SHOOT HORSES DON'T THEY Racing Cars	*Chrysalis*	5
-	19	WHEN Showaddywaddy	*Arista*	1
25	20	YOU'LL NEVER KNOW WHAT YOU'RE MISSING Real Thing	*Pye*	4
22	21	SATURDAY NITE Earth Wind & Fire	*CBS*	4
40	22	MOODY BLUE Elvis Presley	*RCA*	2
30	23	ANOTHER SUITCASE IN ANOTHER HALL Barbara Dickson	*MCA*	2
16	24	SIDE SHOW Barry Biggs	*Dynamic*	13
27	25	MORE THAN A FEELING Boston	*Epic*	7
24	26	DARLIN' DARLIN' BABY O'Jays	*Philadelphia*	5
21	27	DADDY COOL Boney M.	*Atlantic*	12
28	[28]	MAYBE I'M AMAZED Wings	*Parlophone*	3
33	29	CRAZY WATER Elton John	*Rocket*	2
37	30	OH BOY Brotherhood of Man	*Pye*	2
-	[31]	IN THE MOOD Ray Stevens	*Warner Brothers*	1
32	[32]	FIRST THING IN THE MORNING Kiki Dee	*Rocket*	3
23	33	SUSPICION Elvis Presley	*RCA*	9
19	34	ISN'T SHE LOVELY David Parton	*Pye*	9
26	35	CAR WASH Rose Royce	*MCA*	10
36	36	SOUL CHA CHA Van McCoy	*H&L*	3
34	37	GROOVY KIND OF LOVE Les Gray	*Warner Brothers*	2
-	38	MY KINDA LIFE Cliff Richard	*EMI*	1
-	39	LOVE IN C MINOR Cerrone ●	*Atlantic*	1
31	40	MIGHTY POWER OF LOVE Tavares	*Capitol*	6

LW	TW	*WEEK ENDING* 19 MARCH 1977		Wks
1	[1]	CHANSON D'AMOUR Manhattan Transfer	*Atlantic*	7
7	2	KNOWING ME KNOWING YOU Abba	*Epic*	3
3	3	BOOGIE NIGHTS Heatwave	*GTO*	8
5	[4]	ROMEO Mr. Big	*EMI*	6
6	5	SOUND AND VISION David Bowie	*RCA*	4
19	6	WHEN Showaddywaddy	*Arista*	2
2	7	WHEN I NEED YOU Leo Sayer	*Chrysalis*	8
4	8	TORN BETWEEN TWO LOVERS Mary MacGregor	*Ariola*	5
15	[9]	ROCKARIA Electric Light Orchestra	*Jet*	5
11	[10]	BABY I KNOW Rubettes	*State*	5
12	11	WHAT CAN I SAY Boz Scaggs	*CBS*	8
8	12	DON'T CRY FOR ME ARGENTINA Julie Covington	*MCA*	13
9	13	THIS IS TOMORROW Bryan Ferry	*Polydor*	6
22	14	MOODY BLUE Elvis Presley	*RCA*	3
17	15	DON'T LEAVE ME THIS WAY Thelma Houston	*Motown*	7
13	16	SING ME The Brothers	*Bus Stop*	8
21	[17]	SATURDAY NITE Earth Wind & Fire	*CBS*	5
18	18	THEY SHOOT HORSES DON'T THEY Racing Cars	*Chrysalis*	6
10	19	DON'T LEAVE ME THIS WAY Harold Melvin & the Blue Notes	*CBS*	9
38	20	MY KINDA LIFE Cliff Richard	*EMI*	2
14	21	DON'T GIVE UP ON US David Soul	*Private Stock*	14
-	22	SUNNY Boney M	*Atlantic*	1
20	23	YOU'LL NEVER KNOW WHAT YOU'RE MISSING Real Thing	*Pye*	5
-	24	LOVE HIT ME Maxine Nightingale	*United Artists*	1
16	25	JACK IN THE BOX Moments	*All Platinum*	8
30	26	OH BOY Brotherhood of Man	*Pye*	3
29	[27]	CRAZY WATER Elton John	*Rocket*	3
23	28	ANOTHER SUITCASE IN ANOTHER HALL Barbara Dickson	*MCA*	3
-	29	I DON'T WANT TO PUT A HOLD ON YOU Berni Flint ●	*EMI*	1
-	30	TEAR ME APART Suzi Quatro	*RAK*	1
39	[31]	LOVE IN C MINOR Cerrone	*Atlantic*	2
37	[32]	GROOVY KIND OF LOVE Les Gray	*Warner Brothers*	3
31	33	IN THE MOOD Ray Stevens	*Warner Brothers*	2
26	34	DARLIN' DARLIN' BABY O'Jays	*Philadelphia*	6
-	35	HOLD BACK THE NIGHT/SWEET ON YOU Graham Parker & Rumour ●	*Vertigo*	1
28	36	MAYBE I'M AMAZED Wings	*Parlophone*	4
-	[37]	I'M QUALIFIED TO SATISFY Barry White	*20th Century*	1
-	38	DOUBLE DUTCH Fatback Band	*Spring*	1
32	39	FIRST THING IN THE MORNING Kiki Dee	*Rocket*	4
24	40	SIDE SHOW Barry Biggs	*Dynamic*	14

LW	TW	*WEEK ENDING* 26 MARCH 1977		Wks
1	[1]	CHANSON D'AMOUR Manhattan Transfer	*Atlantic*	8
2	2	KNOWING ME KNOWING YOU Abba	*Epic*	4

■Manhattan Transfer are number one with a song Art and Dotty Todd took to the American Top Ten in 1958 (12.03.77) ■ David Bowie has his only predominantly instrumental Top Ten hit (12.03.77) ■ Showaddywaddy bring the Kalin Twins' 1958 number one song back to the Top Ten (19.03.77)■

□ Highest position disc reached ● Act's first ever week on chart

LW	TW	Title	Artist	Label	Wks
5	[3]	SOUND AND VISION	David Bowie	RCA	5
6	4	WHEN	Showaddywaddy	Arista	3
-	5	GOING IN WITH MY EYES OPEN	David Soul	Private Stock	1
8	6	TORN BETWEEN TWO LOVERS	Mary MacGregor	Ariola	6
3	7	BOOGIE NIGHTS	Heatwave	GTO	9
14	8	MOODY BLUE	Elvis Presley	RCA	4
4	9	ROMEO	Mr. Big	EMI	7
9	10	ROCKARIA	Electric Light Orchestra	Jet	6
7	11	WHEN I NEED YOU	Leo Sayer	Chrysalis	9
10	12	BABY I KNOW	Rubettes	State	6
26	13	OH BOY	Brotherhood of Man	Pye	4
29	14	I DON'T WANT TO PUT A HOLD ON YOU	Berni Flint	EMI	2
22	15	SUNNY	Boney M	Atlantic	2
23	[16]	YOU'LL NEVER KNOW WHAT YOU'RE MISSING	Real Thing	Pye	6
13	17	THIS IS TOMORROW	Bryan Ferry	Polydor	7
28	[18]	ANOTHER SUITCASE IN ANOTHER HALL	Barbara Dickson	MCA	4
17	19	SATURDAY NITE	Earth Wind & Fire	CBS	6
-	20	RED LIGHT SPELLS DANGER	Billy Ocean	GTO	1
24	21	LOVE HIT ME	Maxine Nightingale	United Artists	2
12	22	DON'T CRY FOR ME ARGENTINA	Julie Covington	MCA	14
20	23	MY KINDA LIFE	Cliff Richard	EMI	3
35	[24]	HOLD BACK THE NIGHT/SWEET ON YOU	Graham Parker & Rumour	Vertigo	2
-	25	LAY BACK IN THE ARMS OF SOMEONE	Smokie	RAK	1
-	26	GIMME SOME	Brendon ●	Magnet	1
-	27	YOU DON'T HAVE TO BE A STAR	Marilyn McCoo/ Billy Davis ●	ABC	1
27	28	CRAZY WATER	Elton John	Rocket	4
30	29	TEAR ME APART	Suzi Quatro	RAK	2
11	30	WHAT CAN I SAY	Boz Scaggs	CBS	9
38	[31]	DOUBLE DUTCH	Fatback Band	Spring	2
16	32	SING ME	The Brothers	Bus Stop	9
21	33	DON'T GIVE UP ON US	David Soul	Private Stock	15
19	34	DON'T LEAVE ME THIS WAY	Harold Melvin & the Blue Notes	CBS	10
31	35	LOVE IN C MINOR	Cerrone	Atlantic	3
15	36	DON'T LEAVE ME THIS WAY	Thelma Houston	Motown	8
-	37	MORE THAN A LOVER	Bonnie Tyler	RCA	1
-	38	TIE YOUR MOTHER DOWN	Queen	EMI	1
33	39	IN THE MOOD	Ray Stevens	Warner Brothers	3
32	40	GROOVY KIND OF LOVE	Les Gray	Warner Brothers	4

WEEK ENDING 2 APRIL 1977

LW	TW	Title	Artist	Label	Wks
2	[1]	KNOWING ME KNOWING YOU	Abba	Epic	5
5	[2]	GOING IN WITH MY EYES OPEN	David Soul	Private Stock	2
1	3	CHANSON D'AMOUR	Manhattan Transfer	Atlantic	9
4	4	WHEN	Showaddywaddy	Arista	4
3	5	SOUND AND VISION	David Bowie	RCA	6
8	[6]	MOODY BLUE	Elvis Presley	RCA	5
15	7	SUNNY	Boney M	Atlantic	3
14	8	I DON'T WANT TO PUT A HOLD ON YOU	Berni Flint	EMI	3
6	9	TORN BETWEEN TWO LOVERS	Mary MacGregor	Ariola	7
7	10	BOOGIE NIGHTS	Heatwave	GTO	10
13	11	OH BOY	Brotherhood of Man	Pye	5
21	12	LOVE HIT ME	Maxine Nightingale	United Artists	3
20	13	RED LIGHT SPELLS DANGER	Billy Ocean	GTO	2
10	14	ROCKARIA	Electric Light Orchestra	Jet	7
9	15	ROMEO	Mr. Big	EMI	8
23	16	MY KINDA LIFE	Cliff Richard	EMI	4
12	17	BABY I KNOW	Rubettes	State	7
25	18	LAY BACK IN THE ARMS OF SOMEONE	Smokie	RAK	2
18	19	ANOTHER SUITCASE IN ANOTHER HALL	Barbara Dickson	MCA	5
19	20	SATURDAY NITE	Earth Wind & Fire	CBS	7
16	21	YOU'LL NEVER KNOW WHAT YOU'RE MISSING	Real Thing	Pye	7
11	22	WHEN I NEED YOU	Leo Sayer	Chrysalis	10
27	23	YOU DON'T HAVE TO BE A STAR	Marilyn McCoo/ Billy Davis	ABC	2
26	24	GIMME SOME	Brendon	Magnet	2
24	25	HOLD BACK THE NIGHT/SWEET ON YOU	Graham Parker & Rumour	Vertigo	3
22	26	DON'T CRY FOR ME ARGENTINA	Julie Covington	MCA	15
29	[27]	TEAR ME APART	Suzi Quatro	RAK	3
37	28	MORE THAN A LOVER	Bonnie Tyler	RCA	2
-	29	ROCKBOTTOM	Lynsey de Paul and Mike Moran ●	Polydor	1
-	30	TOGETHER	O.C. Smith	Caribou	1
38	[31]	TIE YOUR MOTHER DOWN	Queen	EMI	2
17	32	THIS IS TOMORROW	Bryan Ferry	Polydor	8
-	33	SOUTHERN NIGHTS	Glen Campbell	Capitol	1
-	34	HAVE I THE RIGHT	Dead End Kids ●	CBS	1
-	35	FREE	Deniece Williams ●	CBS	1
28	36	CRAZY WATER	Elton John	Rocket	5
33	37	DON'T GIVE UP ON US	David Soul	Private Stock	16
-	38	RIO	Michael Nesmith ●	Island	1
-	[39]	BECAUSE	Demis Roussos	Philips	1
31	40	DOUBLE DUTCH	Fatback Band	Spring	3

WEEK ENDING 9 APRIL 1977

LW	TW	Title	Artist	Label	Wks
1	[1]	KNOWING ME KNOWING YOU	Abba	Epic	6
2	[2]	GOING IN WITH MY EYES OPEN	David Soul	Private Stock	3
4	[3]	WHEN	Showaddywaddy	Arista	5
5	4	SOUND AND VISION	David Bowie	RCA	7
3	5	CHANSON D'AMOUR	Manhattan Transfer	Atlantic	10
8	6	I DON'T WANT TO PUT A HOLD ON YOU	Berni Flint	EMI	4
6	7	MOODY BLUE	Elvis Presley	RCA	6
13	8	RED LIGHT SPELLS DANGER	Billy Ocean	GTO	3
7	9	SUNNY	Boney M	Atlantic	4
11	10	OH BOY	Brotherhood of Man	Pye	6
12	[11]	LOVE HIT ME	Maxine Nightingale	United Artists	4
23	12	YOU DON'T HAVE TO BE A STAR	Marilyn McCoo/ Billy Davis	ABC	3
9	13	TORN BETWEEN TWO LOVERS	Mary MacGregor	Ariola	8
18	14	LAY BACK IN THE ARMS OF SOMEONE	Smokie	RAK	3
16	[15]	MY KINDA LIFE	Cliff Richard	EMI	5
10	16	BOOGIE NIGHTS	Heatwave	GTO	11
17	17	BABY I KNOW	Rubettes	State	8
24	18	GIMME SOME	Brendon	Magnet	3
34	19	HAVE I THE RIGHT	Dead End Kids	CBS	2
35	20	FREE	Deniece Williams	CBS	2
29	21	ROCKBOTTOM	Lynsey de Paul and Mike Moran	Polydor	2
14	22	ROCKARIA	Electric Light Orchestra	Jet	8
21	23	YOU'LL NEVER KNOW WHAT YOU'RE MISSING	Real Thing	Pye	8
-	24	PEARL'S A SINGER	Elkie Brooks ●	A&M	1
19	25	ANOTHER SUITCASE IN ANOTHER HALL	Barbara Dickson	MCA	6
22	26	WHEN I NEED YOU	Leo Sayer	Chrysalis	11
-	27	LONELY BOY	Andrew Gold ●	Asylum	1
25	28	HOLD BACK THE NIGHT/SWEET ON YOU	Graham Parker & Rumour	Vertigo	4
30	29	TOGETHER	O.C. Smith	Caribou	2
-	30	7,000 DOLLARS AND YOU	Stylistics	H&L	1
33	31	SOUTHERN NIGHTS	Glen Campbell	Capitol	2
15	32	ROMEO	Mr. Big	EMI	9
-	33	I WANNA GET NEXT TO YOU	Rose Royce	MCA	1
38	34	RIO	Michael Nesmith	Island	2
-	35	WHODUNIT	Tavares	Capitol	1
28	36	MORE THAN A LOVER	Bonnie Tyler	RCA	3
27	37	TEAR ME APART	Suzi Quatro	RAK	4
-	[38]	WHITE RIOT	The Clash ●	CBS	1
-	39	SIR DUKE	Stevie Wonder	Motown	1
20	40	SATURDAY NITE	Earth Wind & Fire	CBS	8

WEEK ENDING 16 APRIL 1977

LW	TW	Title	Artist	Label	Wks
1	[1]	KNOWING ME KNOWING YOU	Abba	Epic	7
2	[2]	GOING IN WITH MY EYES OPEN	David Soul	Private Stock	4

In these weeks ■ Abba begin their second hat-trick of three consecutive number ones (02.04.77) ■ Elvis Presley has the last Top Ten hit of his lifetime (02.04.77) ■ Elkie Brooks begins her distinguished Top 40 career with *Pearl's A Singer* (09.04.77)■

LW	TW	Title / Artist	Label	Wks
9	[3]	SUNNY Boney M	*Atlantic*	5
3	4	WHEN Showaddywaddy	*Arista*	6
6	5	I DON'T WANT TO PUT A HOLD ON YOU Berni Flint	*EMI*	5
8	6	RED LIGHT SPELLS DANGER Billy Ocean	*GTO*	4
7	7	MOODY BLUE Elvis Presley	*RCA*	7
10	[8]	OH BOY Brotherhood of Man	*Pye*	7
4	9	SOUND AND VISION David Bowie	*RCA*	8
12	10	YOU DON'T HAVE TO BE A STAR Marilyn McCoo/ Billy Davis	*ABC*	4
5	11	CHANSON D'AMOUR Manhattan Transfer	*Atlantic*	11
14	[12]	LAY BACK IN THE ARMS OF SOMEONE Smokie	*RAK*	4
11	13	LOVE HIT ME Maxine Nightingale	*United Artists*	5
18	[14]	GIMME SOME Brendon	*Magnet*	4
20	15	FREE Deniece Williams	*CBS*	3
19	16	HAVE I THE RIGHT Dead End Kids	*CBS*	3
39	17	SIR DUKE Stevie Wonder	*Motown*	2
15	18	MY KINDA LIFE Cliff Richard	*EMI*	6
13	19	TORN BETWEEN TWO LOVERS Mary MacGregor	*Ariola*	9
24	20	PEARL'S A SINGER Elkie Brooks	*A&M*	2
33	21	I WANNA GET NEXT TO YOU Rose Royce	*MCA*	2
27	22	LONELY BOY Andrew Gold	*Asylum*	2
21	23	ROCKBOTTOM Lynsey de Paul and Mike Moran	*Polydor*	3
30	[24]	7,000 DOLLARS AND YOU Stylistics	*H&L*	2
35	25	WHODUNIT Tavares	*Capitol*	2
-	26	HOW MUCH LOVE Leo Sayer	*Chrysalis*	1
36	[27]	MORE THAN A LOVER Bonnie Tyler	*RCA*	4
34	[28]	RIO Michael Nesmith	*Island*	3
-	29	SOLSBURY HILL Peter Gabriel ●	*Charisma*	1
16	30	BOOGIE NIGHTS Heatwave	*GTO*	12
-	[31]	5TH ANNIVERSARY EP Judge Dread	*Cactus*	1
29	32	TOGETHER O.C. Smith	*Caribou*	3
31	33	SOUTHERN NIGHTS Glen Campbell	*Capitol*	3
28	34	HOLD BACK THE NIGHT/SWEET ON YOU Graham Parker & Rumour	*Vertigo*	5
-	35	MARQUEE MOON Television ●	*Elektra*	1
22	36	ROCKARIA Electric Light Orchestra	*Jet*	9
-	37	A STAR IS BORN (EVERGREEN) Barbra Streisand	*CBS*	1
-	38	HOTEL CALIFORNIA Eagles	*Asylum*	1
32	39	ROMEO Mr. Big	*EMI*	10
26	40	WHEN I NEED YOU Leo Sayer	*Chrysalis*	12

LW	TW	*WEEK ENDING* **23 APRIL 1977**		Wks
1	[1]	KNOWING ME KNOWING YOU Abba	*Epic*	8
6	[2]	RED LIGHT SPELLS DANGER Billy Ocean	*GTO*	5
5	[3]	I DON'T WANT TO PUT A HOLD ON YOU Berni Flint	*EMI*	6
15	4	FREE Deniece Williams	*CBS*	4
2	5	GOING IN WITH MY EYES OPEN David Soul	*Private Stock*	5
4	6	WHEN Showaddywaddy	*Arista*	7
16	7	HAVE I THE RIGHT Dead End Kids	*CBS*	4
3	8	SUNNY Boney M	*Atlantic*	6
17	9	SIR DUKE Stevie Wonder	*Motown*	3
10	10	YOU DON'T HAVE TO BE A STAR Marilyn McCoo/ Billy Davis	*ABC*	5
9	11	SOUND AND VISION David Bowie	*RCA*	9
8	12	OH BOY Brotherhood of Man	*Pye*	8
12	13	LAY BACK IN THE ARMS OF SOMEONE Smokie	*RAK*	5
14	[14]	GIMME SOME Brendon	*Magnet*	5
25	15	WHODUNIT Tavares	*Capitol*	3
20	16	PEARL'S A SINGER Elkie Brooks	*A&M*	3
11	17	CHANSON D'AMOUR Manhattan Transfer	*Atlantic*	12
26	18	HOW MUCH LOVE Leo Sayer	*Chrysalis*	2
23	[19]	ROCKBOTTOM Lynsey de Paul and Mike Moran	*Polydor*	4
22	20	LONELY BOY Andrew Gold	*Asylum*	3
7	21	MOODY BLUE Elvis Presley	*RCA*	8
13	22	LOVE HIT ME Maxine Nightingale	*United Artists*	6
29	23	SOLSBURY HILL Peter Gabriel	*Charisma*	2
-	24	THE SHUFFLE Van McCoy	*H&L*	1
32	[25]	TOGETHER O.C. Smith	*Caribou*	4
21	26	I WANNA GET NEXT TO YOU Rose Royce	*MCA*	3
37	27	A STAR IS BORN (EVERGREEN) Barbra Streisand	*CBS*	2
33	[28]	SOUTHERN NIGHTS Glen Campbell	*Capitol*	4
-	[29]	ANOTHER FUNNY HONEYMOON David Dundas	*Air*	1
24	30	7,000 DOLLARS AND YOU Stylistics	*H&L*	3

□ Highest position disc reached ● Act's first ever week on chart

LW	TW	Title / Artist	Label	Wks
-	31	AIN'T GONNA BUMP NO MORE Joe Tex ●	*Epic*	1
38	32	HOTEL CALIFORNIA Eagles	*Asylum*	2
19	33	TORN BETWEEN TWO LOVERS Mary MacGregor	*Ariola*	10
-	34	SMOKE ON THE WATER Deep Purple	*Purple*	1
28	35	RIO Michael Nesmith	*Island*	4
18	36	MY KINDA LIFE Cliff Richard	*EMI*	7
30	37	BOOGIE NIGHTS Heatwave	*GTO*	13
-	38	GOOD MORNING JUDGE 10 C.C.	*Philips*	1
31	39	5TH ANNIVERSARY EP Judge Dread	*Cactus*	2
-	[40]	SAY YOU'LL STAY UNTIL TOMORROW Tom Jones	*EMI*	1

LW	TW	*WEEK ENDING* **30 APRIL 1977**		Wks
1	[1]	KNOWING ME KNOWING YOU Abba	*Epic*	9
2	[2]	RED LIGHT SPELLS DANGER Billy Ocean	*GTO*	6
4	3	FREE Deniece Williams	*CBS*	5
9	4	SIR DUKE Stevie Wonder	*Motown*	4
3	5	I DON'T WANT TO PUT A HOLD ON YOU Berni Flint	*EMI*	7
7	[6]	HAVE I THE RIGHT Dead End Kids	*CBS*	5
10	[7]	YOU DON'T HAVE TO BE A STAR Marilyn McCoo/ Billy Davis	*ABC*	6
5	8	GOING IN WITH MY EYES OPEN David Soul	*Private Stock*	6
16	9	PEARL'S A SINGER Elkie Brooks	*A&M*	4
8	10	SUNNY Boney M	*Atlantic*	7
12	11	OH BOY Brotherhood of Man	*Pye*	9
15	12	WHODUNIT Tavares	*Capitol*	4
-	13	I DON'T WANT TO TALK ABOUT IT/FIRST CUT IS THE DEEPEST Rod Stewart	*Riva*	1
26	[14]	I WANNA GET NEXT TO YOU Rose Royce	*MCA*	4
14	15	GIMME SOME Brendon	*Magnet*	6
13	16	LAY BACK IN THE ARMS OF SOMEONE Smokie	*RAK*	6
23	17	SOLSBURY HILL Peter Gabriel	*Charisma*	3
6	18	WHEN Showaddywaddy	*Arista*	8
20	19	LONELY BOY Andrew Gold	*Asylum*	4
18	20	HOW MUCH LOVE Leo Sayer	*Chrysalis*	3
32	21	HOTEL CALIFORNIA Eagles	*Asylum*	3
24	22	THE SHUFFLE Van McCoy	*H&L*	2
19	23	ROCKBOTTOM Lynsey de Paul and Mike Moran	*Polydor*	5
31	24	AIN'T GONNA BUMP NO MORE Joe Tex	*Epic*	2
27	25	A STAR IS BORN (EVERGREEN) Barbra Streisand	*CBS*	3
11	26	SOUND AND VISION David Bowie	*RCA*	10
34	27	SMOKE ON THE WATER Deep Purple	*Purple*	2
38	28	GOOD MORNING JUDGE 10 C.C.	*Philips*	2
29	[29]	ANOTHER FUNNY HONEYMOON David Dundas	*Air*	2
-	[30]	MARQUEE MOON Television	*Elektra*	1
-	31	WHERE IS THE LOVE Delegation ●	*State*	1
30	32	7,000 DOLLARS AND YOU Stylistics	*H&L*	4
25	33	TOGETHER O.C. Smith	*Caribou*	5
21	34	MOODY BLUE Elvis Presley	*RCA*	9
28	35	SOUTHERN NIGHTS Glen Campbell	*Capitol*	5
-	[36]	YOU'RE MY LIFE Barry Biggs	*Dynamic*	1
22	37	LOVE HIT ME Maxine Nightingale	*United Artists*	7
-	38	MAH NA MAH NA Piero Umiliani ●	*EMI International*	1
35	39	RIO Michael Nesmith	*Island*	5
17	40	CHANSON D'AMOUR Manhattan Transfer	*Atlantic*	13

LW	TW	*WEEK ENDING* **7 MAY 1977**		**Wks**
3	[1]	FREE Deniece Williams	*CBS*	6
4	[2]	SIR DUKE Stevie Wonder	*Motown*	5
2	3	RED LIGHT SPELLS DANGER Billy Ocean	*GTO*	7
13	4	I DON'T WANT TO TALK ABOUT IT/FIRST CUT IS THE DEEPEST Rod Stewart	*Riva*	2
12	[5]	WHODUNIT Tavares	*Capitol*	5
6	[6]	HAVE I THE RIGHT Dead End Kids	*CBS*	6
1	7	KNOWING ME KNOWING YOU Abba	*Epic*	10
9	[8]	PEARL'S A SINGER Elkie Brooks	*A&M*	5
5	9	I DON'T WANT TO PUT A HOLD ON YOU Berni Flint	*EMI*	8
20	[10]	HOW MUCH LOVE Leo Sayer	*Chrysalis*	4

■Peter Gabriel has his first hit since leaving Genesis (16.04.77) ■ Michael Nesmith's *Rio* is the only solo hit by a former Monkee (16.04.77) ■ Stevie Wonder is kept out of number one by a former member of his backing group Wonderlove, Deniece Williams (07.05.77)■

May 1977

□ Highest position disc reached ● Act's first ever week on chart

LW	TW	Title / Artist	Label	Wks
19	11	LONELY BOY Andrew Gold	Asylum	5
24	12	AIN'T GONNA BUMP NO MORE Joe Tex	Epic	3
22	13	THE SHUFFLE Van McCoy	H&L	3
7	14	YOU DON'T HAVE TO BE A STAR Marilyn McCoo/ Billy Davis	ABC	7
21	15	HOTEL CALIFORNIA Eagles	Asylum	4
17	16	SOLSBURY HILL Peter Gabriel	Charisma	4
15	17	GIMME SOME Brendon	Magnet	7
11	18	OH BOY Brotherhood of Man	Pye	10
25	19	A STAR IS BORN (EVERGREEN) Barbra Streisand	CBS	4
16	20	LAY BACK IN THE ARMS OF SOMEONE Smokie	RAK	7
27	21	SMOKE ON THE WATER Deep Purple	Purple	3
-	22	LUCILLE Kenny Rogers	United Artists	1
38	23	MAH NA MAH NA Piero Umiliani	EMI International	2
28	24	GOOD MORNING JUDGE 10 C.C.	Philips	3
8	25	GOING IN WITH MY EYES OPEN David Soul	Private Stock	7
31	26	WHERE IS THE LOVE Delegation	State	2
10	27	SUNNY Boney M	Atlantic	8
14	28	I WANNA GET NEXT TO YOU Rose Royce	MCA	5
23	29	ROCKBOTTOM Lynsey de Paul and Mike Moran	Polydor	6
-	30	LET 'EM IN Billy Paul	Philadelphia	1
18	31	WHEN Showaddywaddy	Arista	9
-	32	GOT TO GIVE IT UP Marvin Gaye	Motown	1
-	33	DON'T STOP Fleetwood Mac	Warner Brothers	1
33	34	TOGETHER O.C. Smith	Caribou	6
-	35	GONNA CAPTURE YOUR HEART Blue ●	Rocket	1
29	36	ANOTHER FUNNY HONEYMOON David Dundas	Air	3
36	37	YOU'RE MY LIFE Barry Biggs	Dynamic	2
-	38	COULD IT BE I'M FALLING IN LOVE (EP) Detroit Spinners	Atlantic	1
-	39	TOO HOT TO HANDLE/SLIP YOUR DISC TO THIS Heatwave	GTO	1
30	40	MARQUEE MOON Television	Elektra	2

WEEK ENDING 14 MAY 1977

LW	TW	Title / Artist	Label	Wks
1	1	FREE Deniece Williams	CBS	7
4	2	I DON'T WANT TO TALK ABOUT IT/FIRST CUT IS THE DEEPEST Rod Stewart	Riva	3
2	3	SIR DUKE Stevie Wonder	Motown	6
12	4	AIN'T GONNA BUMP NO MORE Joe Tex	Epic	4
5	5	WHODUNIT Tavares	Capitol	6
13	6	THE SHUFFLE Van McCoy	H&L	4
6	7	HAVE I THE RIGHT Dead End Kids	CBS	7
15	8	HOTEL CALIFORNIA Eagles	Asylum	5
24	9	GOOD MORNING JUDGE 10 C.C.	Philips	4
8	10	PEARL'S A SINGER Elkie Brooks	A&M	6
19	11	A STAR IS BORN (EVERGREEN) Barbra Streisand	CBS	5
7	12	KNOWING ME KNOWING YOU Abba	Epic	11
3	13	RED LIGHT SPELLS DANGER Billy Ocean	GTO	8
16	14	SOLSBURY HILL Peter Gabriel	Charisma	5
23	15	MAH NA MAH NA Piero Umiliani	EMI International	3
22	16	LUCILLE Kenny Rogers	United Artists	2
10	17	HOW MUCH LOVE Leo Sayer	Chrysalis	5
11	18	LONELY BOY Andrew Gold	Asylum	6
28	19	I WANNA GET NEXT TO YOU Rose Royce	MCA	6
9	20	I DON'T WANT TO PUT A HOLD ON YOU Berni Flint	EMI	9
14	21	YOU DON'T HAVE TO BE A STAR Marilyn McCoo/ Billy Davis	ABC	8
21	22	SMOKE ON THE WATER Deep Purple	Purple	4
26	23	WHERE IS THE LOVE Delegation	State	3
-	24	IT'S A GAME Bay City Rollers	Arista	1
32	25	GOT TO GIVE IT UP Marvin Gaye	Motown	2
30	26	LET 'EM IN Billy Paul	Philadelphia	2
35	27	GONNA CAPTURE YOUR HEART Blue	Rocket	2
25	28	GOING IN WITH MY EYES OPEN David Soul	Private Stock	8
39	29	TOO HOT TO HANDLE/SLIP YOUR DISC TO THIS Heatwave	GTO	2
27	30	SUNNY Boney M	Atlantic	9
17	31	GIMME SOME Brendon	Magnet	8
38	32	COULD IT BE I'M FALLING IN LOVE (EP) Detroit Spinners	Atlantic	2
33	33	DON'T STOP Fleetwood Mac	Warner Brothers	2
-	34	HELLO STRANGER Yvonne Elliman	RSO	1
31	35	WHEN Showaddywaddy	Arista	10
-	36	NAUGHTY NAUGHTY NAUGHTY Joy Sarney ●	Alaska	1
-	37	DISCO INFERNO Trammps	Atlantic	1
18	38	OH BOY Brotherhood of Man	Pye	11
37	39	YOU'RE MY LIFE Barry Biggs	Dynamic	3
20	40	LAY BACK IN THE ARMS OF SOMEONE Smokie	RAK	8

WEEK ENDING 21 MAY 1977

LW	TW	Title / Artist	Label	Wks
2	1	I DON'T WANT TO TALK ABOUT IT/FIRST CUT IS THE DEEPEST Rod Stewart	Riva	4
1	2	FREE Deniece Williams	CBS	8
4	3	AIN'T GONNA BUMP NO MORE Joe Tex	Epic	5
6	4	THE SHUFFLE Van McCoy	H&L	5
16	5	LUCILLE Kenny Rogers	United Artists	3
11	6	A STAR IS BORN (EVERGREEN) Barbra Streisand	CBS	6
5	7	WHODUNIT Tavares	Capitol	7
3	8	SIR DUKE Stevie Wonder	Motown	7
8	9	HOTEL CALIFORNIA Eagles	Asylum	6
9	10	GOOD MORNING JUDGE 10 C.C.	Philips	5
15	11	MAH NA MAH NA Piero Umiliani	EMI International	4
25	12	GOT TO GIVE IT UP Marvin Gaye	Motown	3
14	13	SOLSBURY HILL Peter Gabriel	Charisma	6
7	14	HAVE I THE RIGHT Dead End Kids	CBS	8
18	15	LONELY BOY Andrew Gold	Asylum	7
17	16	HOW MUCH LOVE Leo Sayer	Chrysalis	6
13	17	RED LIGHT SPELLS DANGER Billy Ocean	GTO	9
10	18	PEARL'S A SINGER Elkie Brooks	A&M	7
29	19	TOO HOT TO HANDLE/SLIP YOUR DISC TO THIS Heatwave	GTO	3
-	20	LIDO SHUFFLE Boz Scaggs	CBS	1
24	21	IT'S A GAME Bay City Rollers	Arista	2
23	22	WHERE IS THE LOVE Delegation	State	4
37	23	DISCO INFERNO Trammps	Atlantic	2
27	24	GONNA CAPTURE YOUR HEART Blue	Rocket	3
22	25	SMOKE ON THE WATER Deep Purple	Purple	5
34	26	HELLO STRANGER Yvonne Elliman	RSO	2
36	27	NAUGHTY NAUGHTY NAUGHTY Joy Sarney	Alaska	2
26	28	LET 'EM IN Billy Paul	Philadelphia	3
-	29	TOKYO JOE Bryan Ferry	Polydor	1
12	30	KNOWING ME KNOWING YOU Abba	Epic	12
19	31	I WANNA GET NEXT TO YOU Rose Royce	MCA	7
33	32	DON'T STOP Fleetwood Mac	Warner Brothers	3
32	33	COULD IT BE I'M FALLING IN LOVE (EP) Detroit Spinners	Atlantic	3
-	34	RENDEZVOUS Tina Charles	CBS	1
-	35	SHEENA IS A PUNK ROCKER Ramones ●	Sire	1
-	36	YOU KEEP ME HANGING ON/STOP IN THE NAME OF LOVE Roni Hill ●	Creole	1
-	37	PEACHES The Stranglers ●	United Artists	1
-	38	UPTOWN FESTIVAL Shalamar ●	RCA	1
20	39	I DON'T WANT TO PUT A HOLD ON YOU Berni Flint	EMI	10
-	40	LET YOUR BODY GO DOWN TOWN Martyn Ford Orchestra ●	Mountain	1

WEEK ENDING 28 MAY 1977

LW	TW	Title / Artist	Label	Wks
1	1	I DON'T WANT TO TALK ABOUT IT/FIRST CUT IS THE DEEPEST Rod Stewart	Riva	5
3	2	AIN'T GONNA BUMP NO MORE Joe Tex	Epic	6
6	3	A STAR IS BORN (EVERGREEN) Barbra Streisand	CBS	7
5	4	LUCILLE Kenny Rogers	United Artists	4
10	5	GOOD MORNING JUDGE 10 C.C.	Philips	6
4	6	THE SHUFFLE Van McCoy	H&L	6
2	7	FREE Deniece Williams	CBS	9
11	8	MAH NA MAH NA Piero Umiliani	EMI International	5
12	9	GOT TO GIVE IT UP Marvin Gaye	Motown	4
9	10	HOTEL CALIFORNIA Eagles	Asylum	7

In these weeks ■ Rod Stewart has the first double-sided number one in four years (21.05.77) ■ Shalamar and the Stranglers both begin lengthy Top 40 careers (21.05.77) ■ Joe Tex, who has already had 27 hits in the *Billboard Hot 100*, has his only British success (28.05.77)■

LW	TW	Title	Artist	Label	Wks
8	11	SIR DUKE	Stevie Wonder	*Motown*	8
7	12	WHODUNIT	Tavares	*Capitol*	8
-	13	O.K.	Rock Follies	*Polydor*	1
13	14	SOLSBURY HILL	Peter Gabriel	*Charisma*	7
-	15	WE CAN DO IT	Liverpool Football Team ●	*State*	1
21	16	IT'S A GAME	Bay City Rollers	*Arista*	3
20	17	LIDO SHUFFLE	Boz Scaggs	*CBS*	2
23	18	DISCO INFERNO	Trammps	*Atlantic*	3
24	19	GONNA CAPTURE YOUR HEART	Blue	*Rocket*	4
29	20	TOKYO JOE	Bryan Ferry	*Polydor*	2
18	21	PEARL'S A SINGER	Elkie Brooks	*A&M*	8
35	22	SHEENA IS A PUNK ROCKER	Ramones	*Sire*	2
19	23	TOO HOT TO HANDLE/SLIP YOUR DISC TO THIS	Heatwave	*GTO*	4
-	24	HALFWAY DOWN THE STAIRS	Muppets ●	*Pye*	1
14	25	HAVE I THE RIGHT	Dead End Kids	*CBS*	9
27	26	NAUGHTY NAUGHTY NAUGHTY	Joy Sarney	*Alaska*	3
34	27	RENDEZVOUS	Tina Charles	*CBS*	2
-	28	TELEPHONE LINE	Electric Light Orchestra	*Jet*	1
22	29	WHERE IS THE LOVE	Delegation	*State*	5
38	30	UPTOWN FESTIVAL	Shalamar	*RCA*	2
26	31	HELLO STRANGER	Yvonne Elliman	*RSO*	3
25	32	SMOKE ON THE WATER	Deep Purple	*Purple*	6
-	33	BABY DON'T CHANGE YOUR MIND	Gladys Knight & the Pips	*Buddah*	1
28	34	LET 'EM IN	Billy Paul	*Philadelphia*	4
15	35	LONELY BOY	Andrew Gold	*Asylum*	8
37	36	PEACHES	The Stranglers	*United Artists*	2
-	37	CALENDAR SONG	Trinidad Oil Company ●	*Harvest*	1
40	38	LET YOUR BODY GO DOWN TOWN	Martyn Ford Orchestra	*Mountain*	2
32	39	DON'T STOP	Fleetwood Mac	*Warner Brothers*	4
16	40	HOW MUCH LOVE	Leo Sayer	*Chrysalis*	7

LW	TW	*WEEK ENDING* **4 JUNE 1977**			Wks
1	1	I DON'T WANT TO TALK ABOUT IT/FIRST CUT IS THE DEEPEST	Rod Stewart	*Riva*	6
4	2	LUCILLE	Kenny Rogers	*United Artists*	5
2	3	AIN'T GONNA BUMP NO MORE	Joe Tex	*Epic*	7
3	4	A STAR IS BORN (EVERGREEN)	Barbra Streisand	*CBS*	8
6	5	THE SHUFFLE	Van McCoy	*H&L*	7
5	6	GOOD MORNING JUDGE	10 C.C.	*Philips*	7
9	7	GOT TO GIVE IT UP	Marvin Gaye	*Motown*	5
24	8	HALFWAY DOWN THE STAIRS	Muppets	*Pye*	2
8	9	MAH NA MAH NA	Piero Umiliani	*EMI International*	6
13	10	O.K.	Rock Follies	*Polydor*	2
-	11	GOD SAVE THE QUEEN	Sex Pistols	*Virgin*	1
10	12	HOTEL CALIFORNIA	Eagles	*Asylum*	8
17	13	LIDO SHUFFLE	Boz Scaggs	*CBS*	3
-	14	SPOT THE PIGEON	Genesis	*Charisma*	1
23	15	TOO HOT TO HANDLE/SLIP YOUR DISC TO THIS	Heatwave	*GTO*	5
15	16	WE CAN DO IT	Liverpool Football Team	*State*	2
-	17	YOU'RE MOVING OUT TODAY	Carole Bayer Sager ●	*Elektra*	1
28	18	TELEPHONE LINE	Electric Light Orchestra	*Jet*	2
7	19	FREE	Deniece Williams	*CBS*	10
12	20	WHODUNIT	Tavares	*Capitol*	9
14	21	SOLSBURY HILL	Peter Gabriel	*Charisma*	8
33	22	BABY DON'T CHANGE YOUR MIND	Gladys Knight & the Pips	*Buddah*	2
-	23	SHOW YOU THE WAY TO GO	The Jacksons	*Epic*	1
16	24	IT'S A GAME	Bay City Rollers	*Arista*	4
18	25	DISCO INFERNO	Trammps	*Atlantic*	4
20	26	TOKYO JOE	Bryan Ferry	*Polydor*	3
36	27	PEACHES	The Stranglers	*United Artists*	3
19	28	GONNA CAPTURE YOUR HEART	Blue	*Rocket*	5
22	29	SHEENA IS A PUNK ROCKER	Ramones	*Sire*	3
26	30	NAUGHTY NAUGHTY NAUGHTY	Joy Sarney	*Alaska*	4
-	31	JOIN THE PARTY	Honky ●	*Creole*	1
30	32	UPTOWN FESTIVAL	Shalamar	*RCA*	3
11	33	SIR DUKE	Stevie Wonder	*Motown*	9
37	34	CALENDAR SONG	Trinidad Oil Company	*Harvest*	2
-	35	FEEL LIKE CALLING HOME	Mr. Big	*EMI*	1

June 1977

☐ Highest position disc reached ● Act's first ever week on chart

LW	TW	Title	Artist	Label	Wks
-	36	GOOD OLD FASHIONED LOVERBOY	Queen	*EMI*	1
27	37	RENDEZVOUS	Tina Charles	*CBS*	3
-	38	DON'T LET GO	Manhattan Transfer	*Atlantic*	1
31	39	HELLO STRANGER	Yvonne Elliman	*RSO*	4
-	40	IN THE CITY	The Jam ●	*Polydor*	1

LW	TW	*WEEK ENDING* **11 JUNE 1977**			Wks
1	1	I DON'T WANT TO TALK ABOUT IT/FIRST CUT IS THE DEEPEST	Rod Stewart	*Riva*	7
11	2	GOD SAVE THE QUEEN	Sex Pistols	*Virgin*	2
2	3	LUCILLE	Kenny Rogers	*United Artists*	6
4	4	A STAR IS BORN (EVERGREEN)	Barbra Streisand	*CBS*	9
3	5	AIN'T GONNA BUMP NO MORE	Joe Tex	*Epic*	8
23	6	SHOW YOU THE WAY TO GO	The Jacksons	*Epic*	2
17	7	YOU'RE MOVING OUT TODAY	Carole Bayer Sager	*Elektra*	2
5	8	THE SHUFFLE	Van McCoy	*H&L*	8
6	9	GOOD MORNING JUDGE	10 C.C.	*Philips*	8
8	10	HALFWAY DOWN THE STAIRS	Muppets	*Pye*	3
7	11	GOT TO GIVE IT UP	Marvin Gaye	*Motown*	6
10	12	O.K.	Rock Follies	*Polydor*	3
18	13	TELEPHONE LINE	Electric Light Orchestra	*Jet*	3
13	14	LIDO SHUFFLE	Boz Scaggs	*CBS*	4
26	15	TOKYO JOE	Bryan Ferry	*Polydor*	4
25	16	DISCO INFERNO	Trammps	*Atlantic*	5
15	17	TOO HOT TO HANDLE/SLIP YOUR DISC TO THIS	Heatwave	*GTO*	6
28	18	GONNA CAPTURE YOUR HEART	Blue	*Rocket*	6
16	19	WE CAN DO IT	Liverpool Football Team	*State*	3
9	20	MAH NA MAH NA	Piero Umiliani	*EMI International*	7
22	21	BABY DON'T CHANGE YOUR MIND	Gladys Knight & the Pips	*Buddah*	3
14	22	SPOT THE PIGEON	Genesis	*Charisma*	2
27	23	PEACHES	The Stranglers	*United Artists*	4
12	24	HOTEL CALIFORNIA	Eagles	*Asylum*	9
-	25	FANFARE FOR THE COMMON MAN	Emerson Lake & Palmer ●	*Atlantic*	1
-	26	YOU'RE GONNA GET NEXT TO ME	Bo Kirkland and Ruth Davis ●	*EMI International*	1
-	27	BE GOOD TO YOURSELF	Frankie Miller ●	*Chrysalis*	1
24	28	IT'S A GAME	Bay City Rollers	*Arista*	5
36	29	GOOD OLD FASHIONED LOVERBOY	Queen	*EMI*	2
31	30	JOIN THE PARTY	Honky	*Creole*	2
29	31	SHEENA IS A PUNK ROCKER	Ramones	*Sire*	4
-	32	OH LORI	Alessi ●	*A&M*	1
-	33	SAM	Olivia Newton-John	*EMI*	1
38	34	DON'T LET GO	Manhattan Transfer	*Atlantic*	2
30	35	NAUGHTY NAUGHTY NAUGHTY	Joy Sarney	*Alaska*	5
37	36	RENDEZVOUS	Tina Charles	*CBS*	4
32	37	UPTOWN FESTIVAL	Shalamar	*RCA*	4
-	38	NATURE BOY	George Benson	*Warner Bros.*	1
34	39	CALENDAR SONG	Trinidad Oil Company	*Harvest*	3
20	40	WHODUNIT	Tavares	*Capitol*	10

LW	TW	*WEEK ENDING* **18 JUNE 1977**			Wks
3	1	LUCILLE	Kenny Rogers	*United Artists*	7
1	2	I DON'T WANT TO TALK ABOUT IT/FIRST CUT IS THE DEEPEST	Rod Stewart	*Riva*	8
6	3	SHOW YOU THE WAY TO GO	The Jacksons	*Epic*	3
2	4	GOD SAVE THE QUEEN	Sex Pistols	*Virgin*	3
4	5	A STAR IS BORN (EVERGREEN)	Barbra Streisand	*CBS*	10
7	6	YOU'RE MOVING OUT TODAY	Carole Bayer Sager	*Elektra*	3
10	7	HALFWAY DOWN THE STAIRS	Muppets	*Pye*	4
13	8	TELEPHONE LINE	Electric Light Orchestra	*Jet*	4
5	9	AIN'T GONNA BUMP NO MORE	Joe Tex	*Epic*	9
8	10	THE SHUFFLE	Van McCoy	*H&L*	9
9	11	GOOD MORNING JUDGE	10 C.C.	*Philips*	9

■Marvin Gaye makes his first visit to the Top Ten in seven years with a studio recording from a double live LP (04.06.77) ■ The Sex Pistols just miss being number one for the Silver Jubilee with the punk commentary *God Save The Queen* ■ Kenny Rogers has his first number one eight years after reaching number two with the First Edition (18.06.77)■

June 1977

□ Highest position disc reached ● Act's first ever week on chart

LW	TW	Title / Artist	Label	Wks
11	12	GOT TO GIVE IT UP Marvin Gaye	*Motown*	7
14	[13]	LIDO SHUFFLE Boz Scaggs	*CBS*	5
21	14	BABY DON'T CHANGE YOUR MIND Gladys Knight & the Pips	*Buddah*	4
17	15	TOO HOT TO HANDLE/SLIP YOUR DISC TO THIS Heatwave	*GTO*	7
22	16	SPOT THE PIGEON Genesis	*Charisma*	3
25	17	FANFARE FOR THE COMMON MAN Emerson Lake & Palmer	*Atlantic*	2
12	18	O.K. Rock Follies	*Polydor*	4
23	19	PEACHES The Stranglers	*United Artists*	5
-	20	SO YOU WIN AGAIN Hot Chocolate	*RAK*	1
29	21	GOOD OLD FASHIONED LOVERBOY Queen	*EMI*	3
26	22	YOU'RE GONNA GET NEXT TO ME Bo Kirkland and Ruth Davis	*EMI International*	2
33	23	SAM Olivia Newton-John	*EMI*	2
15	24	TOKYO JOE Bryan Ferry	*Polydor*	5
24	25	HOTEL CALIFORNIA Eagles	*Asylum*	10
16	26	DISCO INFERNO Trammps	*Atlantic*	6
32	27	OH LORI Alessi	*A&M*	2
30	[28]	JOIN THE PARTY Honky	*Creole*	3
27	29	BE GOOD TO YOURSELF Frankie Miller	*Chrysalis*	2
38	30	NATURE BOY George Benson	*Warner Bros.*	2
-	31	I CAN PROVE IT Tony Etoria ●	*GTO*	1
34	[32]	DON'T LET GO Manhattan Transfer	*Atlantic*	3
31	33	SHEENA IS A PUNK ROCKER Ramones	*Sire*	5
18	34	GONNA CAPTURE YOUR HEART Blue	*Rocket*	7
-	35	WE CAN DO IT Liverpool Football Team	*State*	1
20	36	MAH NA MAH NA Piero Umiliani	*EMI International*	8
-	37	BITE YOUR LIP/CHICAGO Elton John/Kiki Dee	*Rocket*	1
-	38	COME WITH ME Jesse Green	*EMI*	1
39	39	CALENDAR SONG Trinidad Oil Company	*Harvest*	4
-	[40]	DREAMIN' Liverpool Express	*Warner Brothers*	1

LW	TW	*WEEK ENDING* 25 JUNE 1977		Wks
3	[1]	SHOW YOU THE WAY TO GO The Jacksons	*Epic*	4
1	2	LUCILLE Kenny Rogers	*United Artists*	8
20	3	SO YOU WIN AGAIN Hot Chocolate	*RAK*	2
5	4	A STAR IS BORN (EVERGREEN) Barbra Streisand	*CBS*	11
2	5	I DON'T WANT TO TALK ABOUT IT/FIRST CUT IS THE DEEPEST Rod Stewart	*Riva*	9
6	[6]	YOU'RE MOVING OUT TODAY Carole Bayer Sager	*Elektra*	4
14	7	BABY DON'T CHANGE YOUR MIND Gladys Knight & the Pips	*Buddah*	5
17	8	FANFARE FOR THE COMMON MAN Emerson Lake & Palmer	*Atlantic*	3
4	9	GOD SAVE THE QUEEN Sex Pistols	*Virgin*	4
8	10	TELEPHONE LINE Electric Light Orchestra	*Jet*	5
7	11	HALFWAY DOWN THE STAIRS Muppets	*Pye*	5
23	12	SAM Olivia Newton-John	*EMI*	3
9	13	AIN'T GONNA BUMP NO MORE Joe Tex	*Epic*	10
12	14	GOT TO GIVE IT UP Marvin Gaye	*Motown*	8
10	15	THE SHUFFLE Van McCoy	*H&L*	10
19	16	PEACHES The Stranglers	*United Artists*	6
13	17	LIDO SHUFFLE Boz Scaggs	*CBS*	6
15	18	TOO HOT TO HANDLE/SLIP YOUR DISC TO THIS Heatwave	*GTO*	8
11	19	GOOD MORNING JUDGE 10 C.C.	*Philips*	10
22	20	YOU'RE GONNA GET NEXT TO ME Bo Kirkland and Ruth Davis	*EMI International*	3
16	21	SPOT THE PIGEON Genesis	*Charisma*	4
27	22	OH LORI Alessi	*A&M*	3
18	23	O.K. Rock Follies	*Polydor*	5
21	24	GOOD OLD FASHIONED LOVERBOY Queen	*EMI*	4
-	25	DO WHAT YOU WANNA DO T Connection ●	*Sunbury Music*	1
30	[26]	NATURE BOY George Benson	*Warner Bros.*	3
29	27	BE GOOD TO YOURSELF Frankie Miller	*Chrysalis*	3
37	[28]	BITE YOUR LIP/CHICAGO Elton John/Kiki Dee	*Rocket*	2
31	29	I CAN PROVE IT Tony Etoria	*GTO*	2
-	30	FEEL THE NEED Detroit Emeralds	*Atlantic*	1
24	31	TOKYO JOE Bryan Ferry	*Polydor*	6
38	32	COME WITH ME Jesse Green	*EMI*	2
-	[33]	KYRILA Demis Roussos	*Philips*	1
32	34	DON'T LET GO Manhattan Transfer	*Atlantic*	4
28	35	JOIN THE PARTY Honky	*Creole*	4
26	36	DISCO INFERNO Trammps	*Atlantic*	7
-	[37]	RHAPSODY Four Seasons	*Warner Bros.*	1
-	38	MA BAKER Boney M	*Atlantic*	1
33	39	SHEENA IS A PUNK ROCKER Ramones	*Sire*	6
-	40	SLOW DOWN John Miles	*Decca*	1

LW	TW	*WEEK ENDING* 2 JULY 1977		Wks
3	[1]	SO YOU WIN AGAIN Hot Chocolate	*RAK*	3
1	2	SHOW YOU THE WAY TO GO The Jacksons	*Epic*	5
8	3	FANFARE FOR THE COMMON MAN Emerson Lake & Palmer	*Atlantic*	4
2	4	LUCILLE Kenny Rogers	*United Artists*	9
7	5	BABY DON'T CHANGE YOUR MIND Gladys Knight & the Pips	*Buddah*	6
6	6	YOU'RE MOVING OUT TODAY Carole Bayer Sager	*Elektra*	5
4	7	A STAR IS BORN (EVERGREEN) Barbra Streisand	*CBS*	12
10	8	TELEPHONE LINE Electric Light Orchestra	*Jet*	6
12	9	SAM Olivia Newton-John	*EMI*	4
16	10	PEACHES The Stranglers	*United Artists*	7
11	11	HALFWAY DOWN THE STAIRS Muppets	*Pye*	6
9	12	GOD SAVE THE QUEEN Sex Pistols	*Virgin*	5
5	13	I DON'T WANT TO TALK ABOUT IT/FIRST CUT IS THE DEEPEST Rod Stewart	*Riva*	10
38	14	MA BAKER Boney M	*Atlantic*	2
17	15	LIDO SHUFFLE Boz Scaggs	*CBS*	7
20	16	YOU'RE GONNA GET NEXT TO ME Bo Kirkland and Ruth Davis	*EMI International*	4
24	[17]	GOOD OLD FASHIONED LOVERBOY Queen	*EMI*	5
18	18	TOO HOT TO HANDLE/SLIP YOUR DISC TO THIS Heatwave	*GTO*	9
21	19	SPOT THE PIGEON Genesis	*Charisma*	5
22	20	OH LORI Alessi	*A&M*	4
25	21	DO WHAT YOU WANNA DO T Connection	*Sunbury Music*	2
30	22	FEEL THE NEED Detroit Emeralds	*Atlantic*	2
14	23	GOT TO GIVE IT UP Marvin Gaye	*Motown*	9
40	24	SLOW DOWN John Miles	*Decca*	2
29	25	I CAN PROVE IT Tony Etoria	*GTO*	3
-	26	EXODUS Bob Marley & the Wailers	*Island*	1
15	27	THE SHUFFLE Van McCoy	*H&L*	11
26	28	NATURE BOY George Benson	*Warner Bros.*	4
32	[29]	COME WITH ME Jesse Green	*EMI*	3
13	30	AIN'T GONNA BUMP NO MORE Joe Tex	*Epic*	11
27	31	BE GOOD TO YOURSELF Frankie Miller	*Chrysalis*	4
19	32	GOOD MORNING JUDGE 10 C.C.	*Philips*	11
28	33	BITE YOUR LIP/CHICAGO Elton John/Kiki Dee	*Rocket*	3
33	34	KYRILA Demis Roussos	*Philips*	2
34	35	DON'T LET GO Manhattan Transfer	*Atlantic*	5
-	[36]	ANYTHING THAT'S ROCK & ROLL Tom Petty & the Heartbreakers ●	*Island*	1
-	37	GIVE A LITTLE BIT Supertramp	*A&M*	1
-	38	WE'RE ALL ALONE Rita Coolidge ●	*A&M*	1
-	39	FARMER BILL'S COWMAN The Wurzels	*EMI*	1
-	40	ONE STEP AWAY Tavares	*Capitol*	1

LW	TW	*WEEK ENDING* 9 JULY 1977		Wks
1	[1]	SO YOU WIN AGAIN Hot Chocolate	*RAK*	4
2	2	SHOW YOU THE WAY TO GO The Jacksons	*Epic*	6
3	3	FANFARE FOR THE COMMON MAN Emerson Lake & Palmer	*Atlantic*	5
5	[4]	BABY DON'T CHANGE YOUR MIND Gladys Knight & the Pips	*Buddah*	7
14	5	MA BAKER Boney M	*Atlantic*	3
9	[6]	SAM Olivia Newton-John	*EMI*	5
4	7	LUCILLE Kenny Rogers	*United Artists*	10

In these weeks ■ Elton John and Kiki Dee, who had a number one duet in 1976, now take different sides of the same single (18.06.77) ■ The Jacksons achieve what the Jackson Five never did, a British number one (25.06.77) ■ After a half dozen Top Ten hits, Hot Chocolate really win with a number one (02.07.77)■

□ Highest position disc reached ● Act's first ever week on chart

LW	TW	Title	Artist	Label	Wks
10	[8]	PEACHES	The Stranglers	United Artists	8
6	9	YOU'RE MOVING OUT TODAY	Carole Bayer Sager	Elektra	6
7	10	A STAR IS BORN (EVERGREEN)	Barbra Streisand	CBS	13
21	[11]	DO WHAT YOU WANNA DO	T Connection	Sunbury Music	3
16	[12]	YOU'RE GONNA GET NEXT TO ME	Bo Kirkland and Ruth Davis	EMI International	5
8	13	TELEPHONE LINE	Electric Light Orchestra	Jet	7
20	14	OH LORI	Alessi	A&M	5
-	15	I FEEL LOVE	Donna Summer	GTO	1
11	16	HALFWAY DOWN THE STAIRS	Muppets	Pye	7
18	17	TOO HOT TO HANDLE/SLIP YOUR DISC TO THIS	Heatwave	GTO	10
24	18	SLOW DOWN	John Miles	Decca	3
12	19	GOD SAVE THE QUEEN	Sex Pistols	Virgin	6
22	20	FEEL THE NEED	Detroit Emeralds	Atlantic	3
25	[21]	I CAN PROVE IT	Tony Etoria	GTO	4
40	22	ONE STEP AWAY	Tavares	Capitol	2
26	23	EXODUS	Bob Marley & the Wailers	Island	2
17	24	GOOD OLD FASHIONED LOVERBOY	Queen	EMI	6
-	25	ANGELO	Brotherhood Of Man	Pye	1
-	[26]	I JUST WANNA BE YOUR EVERYTHING	Andy Gibb ●	RSO	1
13	27	I DON'T WANT TO TALK ABOUT IT/FIRST CUT IS THE DEEPEST	Rod Stewart	Riva	11
-	28	EASY	Commodores	Motown	1
37	[29]	GIVE A LITTLE BIT	Supertramp	A&M	2
38	30	WE'RE ALL ALONE	Rita Coolidge	A&M	2
-	[31]	CENTRE CITY	Fat Larry's Band ●	Atlantic	1
39	[32]	FARMER BILL'S COWMAN	The Wurzels	EMI	2
-	33	I KNEW THE BRIDE	Dave Edmunds	Swan Song	1
28	34	NATURE BOY	George Benson	Warner Bros.	5
15	35	LIDO SHUFFLE	Boz Scaggs	CBS	8
29	36	COME WITH ME	Jesse Green	EMI	4
-	[37]	GOOD GOLLY MISS MOLLY/RIP IT UP	Little Richard	Creole	1
31	38	BE GOOD TO YOURSELF	Frankie Miller	Chrysalis	5
27	39	THE SHUFFLE	Van McCoy	H&L	12
23	40	GOT TO GIVE IT UP	Marvin Gaye	Motown	10

WEEK ENDING 16 JULY 1977

LW	TW	Title	Artist	Label	Wks
1	[1]	SO YOU WIN AGAIN	Hot Chocolate	RAK	5
3	[2]	FANFARE FOR THE COMMON MAN	Emerson Lake & Palmer	Atlantic	6
15	3	I FEEL LOVE	Donna Summer	GTO	2
5	4	MA BAKER	Boney M	Atlantic	4
4	5	BABY DON'T CHANGE YOUR MIND	Gladys Knight & the Pips	Buddah	8
2	6	SHOW YOU THE WAY TO GO	The Jacksons	Epic	7
-	7	PRETTY VACANT	Sex Pistols	Virgin	1
6	8	SAM	Olivia Newton-John	EMI	6
8	9	PEACHES	The Stranglers	United Artists	9
25	10	ANGELO	Brotherhood Of Man	Pye	2
14	11	OH LORI	Alessi	A&M	6
20	[12]	FEEL THE NEED	Detroit Emeralds	Atlantic	4
9	13	YOU'RE MOVING OUT TODAY	Carole Bayer Sager	Elektra	7
12	14	YOU'RE GONNA GET NEXT TO ME	Bo Kirkland and Ruth Davis	EMI International	6
11	15	DO WHAT YOU WANNA DO	T Connection	Sunbury Music	4
10	16	A STAR IS BORN (EVERGREEN)	Barbra Streisand	CBS	14
18	17	SLOW DOWN	John Miles	Decca	4
7	18	LUCILLE	Kenny Rogers	United Artists	11
24	19	GOOD OLD FASHIONED LOVERBOY	Queen	EMI	7
13	20	TELEPHONE LINE	Electric Light Orchestra	Jet	8
28	21	EASY	Commodores	Motown	2
23	22	EXODUS	Bob Marley & the Wailers	Island	3
21	23	I CAN PROVE IT	Tony Etoria	GTO	5
30	24	WE'RE ALL ALONE	Rita Coolidge	A&M	3
22	25	ONE STEP AWAY	Tavares	Capitol	3
26	[26]	I JUST WANNA BE YOUR EVERYTHING	Andy Gibb	RSO	2
19	27	GOD SAVE THE QUEEN	Sex Pistols	Virgin	7
-	28	DREAMS	Fleetwood Mac	Warner Brothers	1
29	[29]	GIVE A LITTLE BIT	Supertramp	A&M	3
33	30	I KNEW THE BRIDE	Dave Edmunds	Swan Song	2
31	[31]	CENTRE CITY	Fat Larry's Band	Atlantic	2
-	32	THE CRUNCH	Rah Band ●	Good Earth	1
-	33	ROADRUNNER	Jonathan Richman ●	Beserkley	1
-	34	THREE RING CIRCUS	Barry Biggs	Dynamic	1
-	[35]	STRAWBERRY LETTER 23	Brothers Johnson ●	A&M	1
36	36	COME WITH ME	Jesse Green	EMI	5
37	[37]	GOOD GOLLY MISS MOLLY/RIP IT UP	Little Richard	Creole	2
27	38	I DON'T WANT TO TALK ABOUT IT/FIRST CUT IS THE DEEPEST	Rod Stewart	Riva	12
16	39	HALFWAY DOWN THE STAIRS	Muppets	Pye	8
-	[40]	HEAVEN ON THE 7TH FLOOR	Paul Nicholas	RSO	1

WEEK ENDING 23 JULY 1977

LW	TW	Title	Artist	Label	Wks
3	[1]	I FEEL LOVE	Donna Summer	GTO	3
1	2	SO YOU WIN AGAIN	Hot Chocolate	RAK	6
4	3	MA BAKER	Boney M	Atlantic	5
2	4	FANFARE FOR THE COMMON MAN	Emerson Lake & Palmer	Atlantic	7
10	5	ANGELO	Brotherhood Of Man	Pye	3
5	6	BABY DON'T CHANGE YOUR MIND	Gladys Knight & the Pips	Buddah	9
7	7	PRETTY VACANT	Sex Pistols	Virgin	2
8	8	SAM	Olivia Newton-John	EMI	7
11	9	OH LORI	Alessi	A&M	7
17	[10]	SLOW DOWN	John Miles	Decca	5
9	11	PEACHES	The Stranglers	United Artists	10
6	12	SHOW YOU THE WAY TO GO	The Jacksons	Epic	8
15	13	DO WHAT YOU WANNA DO	T Connection	Sunbury Music	5
12	14	FEEL THE NEED	Detroit Emeralds	Atlantic	5
14	15	YOU'RE GONNA GET NEXT TO ME	Bo Kirkland and Ruth Davis	EMI International	7
25	[16]	ONE STEP AWAY	Tavares	Capitol	4
19	17	GOOD OLD FASHIONED LOVERBOY	Queen	EMI	8
16	18	A STAR IS BORN (EVERGREEN)	Barbra Streisand	CBS	15
24	19	WE'RE ALL ALONE	Rita Coolidge	A&M	4
21	20	EASY	Commodores	Motown	3
32	21	THE CRUNCH	Rah Band	Good Earth	2
34	[22]	THREE RING CIRCUS	Barry Biggs	Dynamic	2
33	23	ROADRUNNER	Jonathan Richman	Beserkley	2
-	24	IT'S YOUR LIFE	Smokie	RAK	1
28	25	DREAMS	Fleetwood Mac	Warner Brothers	2
26	[26]	I JUST WANNA BE YOUR EVERYTHING	Andy Gibb	RSO	3
22	27	EXODUS	Bob Marley & the Wailers	Island	4
18	28	LUCILLE	Kenny Rogers	United Artists	12
13	29	YOU'RE MOVING OUT TODAY	Carole Bayer Sager	Elektra	8
-	30	ALL AROUND THE WORLD	Jam	Polydor	1
29	31	GIVE A LITTLE BIT	Supertramp	A&M	4
30	32	I KNEW THE BRIDE	Dave Edmunds	Swan Song	3
20	33	TELEPHONE LINE	Electric Light Orchestra	Jet	9
-	[34]	THIS PERFECT DAY	The Saints ●	Harvest	1
27	35	GOD SAVE THE QUEEN	Sex Pistols	Virgin	8
31	36	CENTRE CITY	Fat Larry's Band	Atlantic	3
23	37	I CAN PROVE IT	Tony Etoria	GTO	6
-	38	FLOAT ON	Floaters ●	ABC	1
-	39	NIGHTS ON BROADWAY	Candi Staton	Warner Brothers	1
-	40	A LITTLE BOOGIE WOOGIE IN THE BACK OF MY MIND	Gary Glitter	Arista	1

WEEK ENDING 30 JULY 1977

LW	TW	Title	Artist	Label	Wks
1	[1]	I FEEL LOVE	Donna Summer	GTO	4
3	[2]	MA BAKER	Boney M	Atlantic	6
4	3	FANFARE FOR THE COMMON MAN	Emerson Lake & Palmer	Atlantic	8
5	4	ANGELO	Brotherhood Of Man	Pye	4
2	5	SO YOU WIN AGAIN	Hot Chocolate	RAK	7

■The Detroit Emeralds reach the Top 20 with a re-recording of their Top Five hit of only four years previous (09.07.77) ■ Donna Summer has the first of four Top Ten hits in less than six months (16.07.7) ■ Bee Gee brother Andy Gibb has his first hit, which goes on to become an American number one (23.07.77)■

July 1977

□ Highest position disc reached ● Act's first ever week on chart

LW	TW	Title	Artist	Label	Wks
7	[6]	PRETTY VACANT	Sex Pistols	Virgin	3
6	7	BABY DON'T CHANGE YOUR MIND	Gladys Knight & the Pips	Buddah	10
9	[8]	OH LORI	Alessi	A&M	8
19	9	WE'RE ALL ALONE	Rita Coolidge	A&M	5
20	10	EASY	Commodores	Motown	4
10	11	SLOW DOWN	John Miles	Decca	6
14	12	FEEL THE NEED	Detroit Emeralds	Atlantic	6
8	13	SAM	Olivia Newton-John	EMI	8
27	[14]	EXODUS	Bob Marley & the Wailers	Island	5
-	15	YOU GOT WHAT IT TAKES	Showaddywaddy	Arista	1
38	16	FLOAT ON	Floaters	ABC	2
16	17	ONE STEP AWAY	Tavares	Capitol	5
24	18	IT'S YOUR LIFE	Smokie	RAK	2
11	19	PEACHES	The Stranglers	United Artists	11
21	20	THE CRUNCH	Rah Band	Good Earth	3
23	21	ROADRUNNER	Jonathan Richman	Beserkley	3
30	22	ALL AROUND THE WORLD	Jam	Polydor	2
17	23	GOOD OLD FASHIONED LOVERBOY	Queen	EMI	9
12	24	SHOW YOU THE WAY TO GO	The Jacksons	Epic	9
22	25	THREE RING CIRCUS	Barry Biggs	Dynamic	3
32	[26]	I KNEW THE BRIDE	Dave Edmunds	Swan Song	4
39	27	NIGHTS ON BROADWAY	Candi Staton	Warner Brothers	2
-	28	PROVE IT	Television	Elektra	1
18	29	A STAR IS BORN (EVERGREEN)	Barbra Streisand	CBS	16
25	30	DREAMS	Fleetwood Mac	Warner Brothers	3
13	31	DO WHAT YOU WANNA DO	T Connection	Sunbury Music	6
26	32	I JUST WANNA BE YOUR EVERYTHING	Andy Gibb	RSO	4
15	33	YOU'RE GONNA GET NEXT TO ME	Bo Kirkland and Ruth Davis	EMI International	8
31	34	GIVE A LITTLE BIT	Supertramp	A&M	5
40	35	A LITTLE BOOGIE WOOGIE IN THE BACK OF MY MIND	Gary Glitter	Arista	2
34	36	THIS PERFECT DAY	The Saints	Harvest	2
-	37	SOMETHING BETTER CHANGE	Stranglers	United Artists	1
28	38	LUCILLE	Kenny Rogers	United Artists	13
-	[39]	ROCKY MOUNTAIN WAY	Joe Walsh ●	ABC	1
35	40	GOD SAVE THE QUEEN	Sex Pistols	Virgin	9

WEEK ENDING 6 AUGUST 1977

LW	TW	Title	Artist	Label	Wks
1	[1]	I FEEL LOVE	Donna Summer	GTO	5
4	2	ANGELO	Brotherhood Of Man	Pye	5
3	3	MA BAKER	Boney M	Atlantic	7
5	4	SO YOU WIN AGAIN	Hot Chocolate	RAK	8
3	5	FANFARE FOR THE COMMON MAN	Emerson Lake & Palmer	Atlantic	9
9	[6]	WE'RE ALL ALONE	Rita Coolidge	A&M	6
18	7	IT'S YOUR LIFE	Smokie	RAK	3
6	8	PRETTY VACANT	Sex Pistols	Virgin	4
15	9	YOU GOT WHAT IT TAKES	Showaddywaddy	Arista	2
8	10	OH LORI	Alessi	A&M	9
10	11	EASY	Commodores	Motown	5
11	12	SLOW DOWN	John Miles	Decca	7
20	13	THE CRUNCH	Rah Band	Good Earth	4
16	14	FLOAT ON	Floaters	ABC	3
37	15	SOMETHING BETTER CHANGE	Stranglers	United Artists	2
12	16	FEEL THE NEED	Detroit Emeralds	Atlantic	7
17	17	ONE STEP AWAY	Tavares	Capitol	6
13	18	SAM	Olivia Newton-John	EMI	9
14	19	EXODUS	Bob Marley & the Wailers	Island	6
22	20	ALL AROUND THE WORLD	Jam	Polydor	3
7	21	BABY DON'T CHANGE YOUR MIND	Gladys Knight & the Pips	Buddah	11
23	22	GOOD OLD FASHIONED LOVERBOY	Queen	EMI	10
25	23	THREE RING CIRCUS	Barry Biggs	Dynamic	4
21	24	ROADRUNNER	Jonathan Richman	Beserkley	4
28	[25]	PROVE IT	Television	Elektra	2
27	26	NIGHTS ON BROADWAY	Candi Staton	Warner Brothers	3
30	27	DREAMS	Fleetwood Mac	Warner Brothers	4
19	28	PEACHES	The Stranglers	United Artists	12
26	29	I KNEW THE BRIDE	Dave Edmunds	Swan Song	5
-	30	THAT'S WHAT FRIENDS ARE FOR	Deniece Williams	CBS	1
35	[31]	A LITTLE BOOGIE WOOGIE IN THE BACK OF MY MIND	Gary Glitter	Arista	3
-	32	DANCIN' EASY	Danny Williams	CBS	1
29	33	A STAR IS BORN (EVERGREEN)	Barbra Streisand	CBS	17
-	[34]	YOU MADE ME BELIEVE IN MAGIC	Bay City Rollers	Arista	1
31	35	DO WHAT YOU WANNA DO	T Connection	Sunbury Music	7
-	[36]	SWALLOW MY PRIDE	Ramones	Sire	1
24	37	SHOW YOU THE WAY TO GO	The Jacksons	Epic	10
32	38	I JUST WANNA BE YOUR EVERYTHING	Andy Gibb	RSO	5
-	39	LOVE'S SUCH A WONDERFUL THING	Real Thing	Pye	1
39	40	ROCKY MOUNTAIN WAY	Joe Walsh	ABC	2

WEEK ENDING 13 AUGUST 1977

LW	TW	Title	Artist	Label	Wks
1	[1]	I FEEL LOVE	Donna Summer	GTO	6
2	2	ANGELO	Brotherhood Of Man	Pye	6
9	[3]	YOU GOT WHAT IT TAKES	Showaddywaddy	Arista	3
14	4	FLOAT ON	Floaters	ABC	4
3	5	MA BAKER	Boney M	Atlantic	8
6	[6]	WE'RE ALL ALONE	Rita Coolidge	A&M	7
13	7	THE CRUNCH	Rah Band	Good Earth	5
5	8	FANFARE FOR THE COMMON MAN	Emerson Lake & Palmer	Atlantic	10
11	[9]	EASY	Commodores	Motown	6
7	10	IT'S YOUR LIFE	Smokie	RAK	4
24	[11]	ROADRUNNER	Jonathan Richman	Beserkley	5
8	12	PRETTY VACANT	Sex Pistols	Virgin	5
15	13	SOMETHING BETTER CHANGE	Stranglers	United Artists	3
10	14	OH LORI	Alessi	A&M	10
4	15	SO YOU WIN AGAIN	Hot Chocolate	RAK	9
16	16	FEEL THE NEED	Detroit Emeralds	Atlantic	8
26	17	NIGHTS ON BROADWAY	Candi Staton	Warner Brothers	4
19	18	EXODUS	Bob Marley & the Wailers	Island	7
30	19	THAT'S WHAT FRIENDS ARE FOR	Deniece Williams	CBS	2
12	20	SLOW DOWN	John Miles	Decca	8
-	21	NOBODY DOES IT BETTER	Carly Simon	Elektra	1
23	22	THREE RING CIRCUS	Barry Biggs	Dynamic	5
20	23	ALL AROUND THE WORLD	Jam	Polydor	4
27	[24]	DREAMS	Fleetwood Mac	Warner Brothers	5
21	25	BABY DON'T CHANGE YOUR MIND	Gladys Knight & the Pips	Buddah	12
18	26	SAM	Olivia Newton-John	EMI	10
29	27	I KNEW THE BRIDE	Dave Edmunds	Swan Song	6
-	28	TULANE	Steve Gibbons Band ●	Polydor	1
25	29	PROVE IT	Television	Elektra	3
-	30	DANCIN' IN THE MOONLIGHT	Thin Lizzy	Vertigo	1
-	31	SPANISH STROLL	Mink DeVille	Capitol	1
32	32	DANCIN' EASY	Danny Williams	CBS	2
39	[33]	LOVE'S SUCH A WONDERFUL THING	Real Thing	Pye	2
28	34	PEACHES	The Stranglers	United Artists	13
17	35	ONE STEP AWAY	Tavares	Capitol	7
31	36	A LITTLE BOOGIE WOOGIE IN THE BACK OF MY MIND	Gary Glitter	Arista	4
-	[37]	YOUR SONG	Billy Paul	Philadelphia	1
-	38	IF I HAVE TO GO AWAY	Jigsaw	Splash	1
-	39	DO ANYTHING YOU WANNA DO	Rods	Island	1
33	40	A STAR IS BORN (EVERGREEN)	Barbra Streisand	CBS	18

WEEK ENDING 20 AUGUST 1977

LW	TW	Title	Artist	Label	Wks
2	[1]	ANGELO	Brotherhood Of Man	Pye	7
3	2	YOU GOT WHAT IT TAKES	Showaddywaddy	Arista	4
1	3	I FEEL LOVE	Donna Summer	GTO	7
4	4	FLOAT ON	Floaters	ABC	5

In these weeks ■ Showaddywaddy outdo Marv Johnson's 1960 peak of five with *You Got What It Takes* (13.08.77) ■ The Commodores have their first week in the Top Ten (13.08.77) ■ 'Rumours' will become the longest running LP in British chart history, yet *Dreams*, peaking at 24, is its biggest hit single (13.08.77) ■

LW	TW	Title / Artist	Label	Wks
10	5	IT'S YOUR LIFE Smokie	*RAK*	5
7	6	THE CRUNCH Rah Band	*Good Earth*	6
5	7	MA BAKER Boney M	*Atlantic*	9
6	8	WE'RE ALL ALONE Rita Coolidge	*A&M*	8
13	9	SOMETHING BETTER CHANGE Stranglers	*United Artists*	4
19	10	THAT'S WHAT FRIENDS ARE FOR Deniece Williams	*CBS*	3
9	11	EASY Commodores	*Motown*	7
11	12	ROADRUNNER Jonathan Richman	*Beserkley*	6
23	13	ALL AROUND THE WORLD Jam	*Polydor*	5
21	14	NOBODY DOES IT BETTER Carly Simon	*Elektra*	2
17	15	NIGHTS ON BROADWAY Candi Staton	*Warner Brothers*	5
15	16	SO YOU WIN AGAIN Hot Chocolate	*RAK*	10
14	17	OH LORI Alessi	*A&M*	11
16	18	FEEL THE NEED Detroit Emeralds	*Atlantic*	9
8	19	FANFARE FOR THE COMMON MAN Emerson Lake & Palmer	*Atlantic*	11
18	20	EXODUS Bob Marley & the Wailers	*Island*	8
12	21	PRETTY VACANT Sex Pistols	*Virgin*	6
28	22	TULANE Steve Gibbons Band	*Polydor*	2
30	23	DANCIN' IN THE MOONLIGHT Thin Lizzy	*Vertigo*	2
22	24	THREE RING CIRCUS Barry Biggs	*Dynamic*	6
31	25	SPANISH STROLL Mink DeVille	*Capitol*	2
24	26	DREAMS Fleetwood Mac	*Warner Brothers*	6
-	27	MAGIC FLY Space ●	*Pye*	1
-	28	I THINK I'M GONNA FALL IN LOVE WITH YOU Dooleys ●	*GTO*	1
39	29	DO ANYTHING YOU WANNA DO Rods	*Island*	2
32	30	DANCIN' EASY Danny Williams	*CBS*	3
-	31	I CAN'T GET YOU OUTA MY MIND Yvonne Elliman	*RSO*	1
20	32	SLOW DOWN John Miles	*Decca*	9
-	33	DREAMER Jacksons	*Epic*	1
26	34	SAM Olivia Newton-John	*EMI*	11
27	35	I KNEW THE BRIDE Dave Edmunds	*Swan Song*	7
38	36	IF I HAVE TO GO AWAY Jigsaw	*Splash*	2
-	37	YOU TAKE MY HEART AWAY DeEtta Little and Nelson Pigford ●	*United Artists*	1
37	38	YOUR SONG Billy Paul	*Philadelphia*	2
34	39	PEACHES The Stranglers	*United Artists*	14
29	40	PROVE IT Television	*Elektra*	4

LW	TW	*WEEK ENDING* **27 AUGUST 1977**		Wks
4	[1]	FLOAT ON Floaters	*ABC*	6
1	2	ANGELO Brotherhood Of Man	*Pye*	8
2	3	YOU GOT WHAT IT TAKES Showaddywaddy	*Arista*	5
-	4	WAY DOWN Elvis Presley	*RCA*	1
3	5	I FEEL LOVE Donna Summer	*GTO*	8
6	[6]	THE CRUNCH Rah Band	*Good Earth*	7
8	7	WE'RE ALL ALONE Rita Coolidge	*A&M*	9
10	[8]	THAT'S WHAT FRIENDS ARE FOR Deniece Williams	*CBS*	4
15	9	NIGHTS ON BROADWAY Candi Staton	*Warner Brothers*	6
14	10	NOBODY DOES IT BETTER Carly Simon	*Elektra*	3
7	11	MA BAKER Boney M	*Atlantic*	10
9	12	SOMETHING BETTER CHANGE Stranglers	*United Artists*	5
5	13	IT'S YOUR LIFE Smokie	*RAK*	6
12	14	ROADRUNNER Jonathan Richman	*Beserkley*	7
11	15	EASY Commodores	*Motown*	8
27	16	MAGIC FLY Space	*Pye*	2
22	17	TULANE Steve Gibbons Band	*Polydor*	3
13	18	ALL AROUND THE WORLD Jam	*Polydor*	6
29	19	DO ANYTHING YOU WANNA DO Rods	*Island*	3
18	20	FEEL THE NEED Detroit Emeralds	*Atlantic*	10
-	21	DOWN DEEP INSIDE Donna Summer	*Cassablanca*	1
-	22	OXYGENE Jean Michel Jarre ●	*Polydor*	1
23	23	DANCIN' IN THE MOONLIGHT Thin Lizzy	*Vertigo*	3
25	24	SPANISH STROLL Mink DeVille	*Capitol*	3
26	25	DREAMS Fleetwood Mac	*Warner Brothers*	7
16	26	SO YOU WIN AGAIN Hot Chocolate	*RAK*	11
-	27	GARY GILMOUR'S EYES The Adverts ●	*Anchor*	1
28	28	I THINK I'M GONNA FALL IN LOVE WITH YOU Dooleys	*GTO*	2
-	29	SUNSHINE AFTER THE RAIN Elkie Brooks	*A&M*	1
-	30	SILVER LADY David Soul	*Private Stock*	1
33	31	DREAMER Jacksons	*Epic*	2
30	32	DANCIN' EASY Danny Williams	*CBS*	4
31	33	I CAN'T GET YOU OUTA MY MIND Yvonne Elliman	*RSO*	2
19	34	FANFARE FOR THE COMMON MAN Emerson Lake & Palmer	*Atlantic*	12
21	35	PRETTY VACANT Sex Pistols	*Virgin*	7
37	36	YOU TAKE MY HEART AWAY DeEtta Little and Nelson Pigford	*United Artists*	2
-	37	LET'S CLEAN UP THE GHETTO Philadelphia International All Stars ●	*Philadelphia*	1
24	38	THREE RING CIRCUS Barry Biggs	*Dynamic*	7
36	39	IF I HAVE TO GO AWAY Jigsaw	*Splash*	3
-	[40]	AMERICAN GIRL Tom Petty & the Heartbreakers	*Island*	1

September 1977

□ Highest position disc reached ● Act's first ever week on chart

LW	TW	*WEEK ENDING* **3 SEPTEMBER 1977**		Wks
4	[1]	WAY DOWN Elvis Presley	*RCA*	2
1	2	FLOAT ON Floaters	*ABC*	7
2	3	ANGELO Brotherhood Of Man	*Pye*	9
3	4	YOU GOT WHAT IT TAKES Showaddywaddy	*Arista*	6
16	5	MAGIC FLY Space	*Pye*	2
9	[6]	NIGHTS ON BROADWAY Candi Staton	*Warner Brothers*	7
6	7	THE CRUNCH Rah Band	*Good Earth*	8
8	[8]	THAT'S WHAT FRIENDS ARE FOR Deniece Williams	*CBS*	5
10	9	NOBODY DOES IT BETTER Carly Simon	*Elektra*	4
30	10	SILVER LADY David Soul	*Private Stock*	2
5	11	I FEEL LOVE Donna Summer	*GTO*	9
22	12	OXYGENE PART IV Jean Michel Jarre	*Polydor*	2
17	13	TULANE Steve Gibbons Band	*Polydor*	4
21	14	DOWN DEEP INSIDE Donna Summer	*Cassablanca*	2
23	15	DANCIN' IN THE MOONLIGHT Thin Lizzy	*Vertigo*	4
7	16	WE'RE ALL ALONE Rita Coolidge	*A&M*	10
12	17	SOMETHING BETTER CHANGE Stranglers	*United Artists*	6
18	18	ALL AROUND THE WORLD Jam	*Polydor*	7
11	19	MA BAKER Boney M	*Atlantic*	11
13	20	IT'S YOUR LIFE Smokie	*RAK*	7
24	21	SPANISH STROLL Mink DeVille	*Capitol*	4
14	22	ROADRUNNER ONCE ROADRUNNER TWICE Jonathan Richman	*Beserkley*	8
28	23	I THINK I'M GONNA FALL IN LOVE WITH YOU Dooleys	*GTO*	3
19	24	DO ANYTHING YOU WANNA DO Rods	*Island*	4
29	25	SUNSHINE AFTER THE RAIN Elkie Brooks	*A&M*	2
-	26	TELEPHONE MAN Meri Wilson	*Pye*	1
27	27	GARY GILMOUR'S EYES The Adverts	*Anchor*	2
-	28	LOOKING AFTER NUMBER ONE Boomtown Rats	*Ensign*	1
33	29	I CAN'T GET YOU OUTA MY MIND Yvonne Elliman	*RSO*	3
31	30	DREAMER Jacksons	*Epic*	3
32	31	DANCIN' EASY Danny Williams	*CBS*	5
25	32	DREAMS Fleetwood Mac	*Warner Brothers*	8
15	33	EASY Commodores	*Motown*	9
-	34	DOWN THE HALL Four Seasons	*Warner Brothers*	1
36	[35]	YOU TAKE MY HEART AWAY DeEtta Little and Nelson Pigford	*United Artists*	3
-	36	PIPELINE Bruce Johnston	*CBS*	1
-	37	GIMME DAT BANANA Black Gorilla	*Response*	1
37	38	LET'S CLEAN UP THE GHETTO Philadelphia International All Stars	*Philadelphia*	2
-	39	IT'S NOW OR NEVER Elvis Presley	*RCA*	1
39	40	IF I HAVE TO GO AWAY Jigsaw	*Splash*	4

LW	TW	*WEEK ENDING* **10 SEPTEMBER 1977**		Wks
1	[1]	WAY DOWN Elvis Presley	*RCA*	3
5	[2]	MAGIC FLY Space	*Pye*	3
2	3	FLOAT ON Floaters	*ABC*	8
12	[4]	OXYGENE PART IV Jean Michel Jarre	*Polydor*	3
14	[5]	DOWN DEEP INSIDE Donna Summer	*Cassablanca*	3
3	6	ANGELO Brotherhood Of Man	*Pye*	10

■Candi Staton takes a 1975 American Top Ten Bee Gees song into the UK Top Ten (27.08.77) ■ Two weeks after his death, Elvis Presley has a posthumous number one (03.09.77) ■ In a certain first, two of the top four, *Magic Fly* and *Oxygene Part IV*, are French instrumentals (10.09.77)■

September 1977

☐ Highest position disc reached ● Act's first ever week on chart

LW	TW	Title / Artist	Label	Wks
6	7	NIGHTS ON BROADWAY Candi Staton	Warner Brothers	8
10	8	SILVER LADY David Soul	Private Stock	3
8	9	THAT'S WHAT FRIENDS ARE FOR Deniece Williams	CBS	6
9	10	NOBODY DOES IT BETTER Carly Simon	Elektra	5
24	11	DO ANYTHING YOU WANNA DO Rods	Island	5
4	12	YOU GOT WHAT IT TAKES Showaddywaddy	Arista	7
7	13	THE CRUNCH Rah Band	Good Earth	9
15	☐14	DANCIN' IN THE MOONLIGHT Thin Lizzy	Vertigo	5
13	15	TULANE Steve Gibbons Band	Polydor	5
26	16	TELEPHONE MAN Meri Wilson	Pye	2
28	17	LOOKING AFTER NUMBER ONE Boomtown Rats	Ensign	2
16	18	WE'RE ALL ALONE Rita Coolidge	A&M	11
27	19	GARY GILMOUR'S EYES The Adverts	Anchor	3
21	20	SPANISH STROLL Mink DeVille	Capitol	5
25	21	SUNSHINE AFTER THE RAIN Elkie Brooks	A&M	3
23	22	I THINK I'M GONNA FALL IN LOVE WITH YOU Dooleys	GTO	4
29	23	I CAN'T GET YOU OUTA MY MIND Yvonne Elliman	RSO	4
19	24	MA BAKER Boney M	Atlantic	12
30	25	DREAMER Jacksons	Epic	4
11	26	I FEEL LOVE Donna Summer	GTO	10
-	27	BEST OF MY LOVE Emotions	CBS	1
17	28	SOMETHING BETTER CHANGE Stranglers	United Artists	7
37	29	GIMME DAT BANANA Black Gorilla	Response	2
-	30	BLACK IS BLACK La Belle Epoque	Harvest	1
-	31	ANOTHER STAR Stevie Wonder	Motown	1
22	32	ROADRUNNER ONCE ROADRUNNER TWICE Jonathan Richman	Beserkley	9
36	33	PIPELINE Bruce Johnston	CBS	2
38	☐34	LET'S CLEAN UP THE GHETTO Philadelphia International All Stars	Philadelphia	3
34	35	DOWN THE HALL Four Seasons	Warner Brothers	2
18	36	ALL AROUND THE WORLD Jam	Polydor	8
-	37	BLACK BETTY Ram Jam	Epic	1
20	38	IT'S YOUR LIFE Smokie	RAK	8
-	39	THUNDER IN MY HEART Leo Sayer	Chrysalis	1
-	40	I GOT TO SING J.A.L.N. Band	Magnet	1

LW	TW	*WEEK ENDING* 17 SEPTEMBER 1977		Wks
1	☐1	WAY DOWN Elvis Presley	RCA	4
2	☐2	MAGIC FLY Space	Pye	4
8	3	SILVER LADY David Soul	Private Stock	4
4	☐4	OXYGENE PART IV Jean Michel Jarre	Polydor	4
5	☐5	DOWN DEEP INSIDE Donna Summer	Cassablanca	4
3	6	FLOAT ON Floaters	ABC	9
10	☐7	NOBODY DOES IT BETTER Carly Simon	Elektra	6
7	8	NIGHTS ON BROADWAY Candi Staton	Warner Brothers	9
6	9	ANGELO Brotherhood Of Man	Pye	11
16	10	TELEPHONE MAN Meri Wilson	Pye	3
9	11	THAT'S WHAT FRIENDS ARE FOR Deniece Williams	CBS	7
15	☐12	TULANE Steve Gibbons Band	Polydor	6
17	13	LOOKING AFTER NUMBER ONE Boomtown Rats	Ensign	3
27	14	BEST OF MY LOVE Emotions	CBS	2
14	15	DANCIN' IN THE MOONLIGHT Thin Lizzy	Vertigo	6
12	16	YOU GOT WHAT IT TAKES Showaddywaddy	Arista	8
13	17	THE CRUNCH Rah Band	Good Earth	10
21	18	SUNSHINE AFTER THE RAIN Elkie Brooks	A&M	4
22	19	I THINK I'M GONNA FALL IN LOVE WITH YOU Dooleys	GTO	5
11	20	DO ANYTHING YOU WANNA DO Rods	Island	6
23	21	I CAN'T GET YOU OUTA MY MIND Yvonne Elliman	RSO	5
25	☐22	DREAMER Jacksons	Epic	5
20	23	SPANISH STROLL Mink DeVille	Capitol	6
37	24	BLACK BETTY Ram Jam	Epic	2
19	25	GARY GILMOUR'S EYES The Adverts	Anchor	4
-	26	FROM NEW YORK TO LA Patsy Gallant	EMI	1
30	27	BLACK IS BLACK La Belle Epoque	Harvest	2
39	28	THUNDER IN MY HEART Leo Sayer	Chrysalis	2
31	29	ANOTHER STAR Stevie Wonder	Motown	2
29	30	GIMME DAT BANANA Black Gorilla	Response	3
-	31	WONDROUS STORIES Yes	Atlantic	1
-	32	WAITING IN VAIN Bob Marley and the Wailers	Island	1
26	33	I FEEL LOVE Donna Summer	GTO	11
24	34	MA BAKER Boney M	Atlantic	13
18	35	WE'RE ALL ALONE Rita Coolidge	A&M	12
28	36	SOMETHING BETTER CHANGE Stranglers	United Artists	8
35	37	DOWN THE HALL Four Seasons	Warner Brothers	3
-	38	YOUR GENERATION Generation X	Chrysalis	1
34	39	LET'S CLEAN UP THE GHETTO Philadelphia International All Stars	Philadelphia	4
33	40	PIPELINE Bruce Johnston	CBS	3

LW	TW	*WEEK ENDING* 24 SEPTEMBER 1977		Wks
1	☐1	WAY DOWN Elvis Presley	RCA	5
2	☐2	MAGIC FLY Space	Pye	5
3	3	SILVER LADY David Soul	Private Stock	5
4	☐4	OXYGENE PART IV Jean Michel Jarre	Polydor	5
5	☐5	DOWN DEEP INSIDE Donna Summer	Cassablanca	5
10	6	TELEPHONE MAN Meri Wilson	Pye	4
7	☐7	NOBODY DOES IT BETTER Carly Simon	Elektra	7
14	8	BEST OF MY LOVE Emotions	CBS	3
20	☐9	DO ANYTHING YOU WANNA DO Rods	Island	7
11	10	THAT'S WHAT FRIENDS ARE FOR Deniece Williams	CBS	8
13	11	LOOKING AFTER NUMBER ONE Boomtown Rats	Ensign	4
8	12	NIGHTS ON BROADWAY Candi Staton	Warner Brothers	10
31	13	WONDROUS STORIES Yes	Atlantic	2
27	14	BLACK IS BLACK La Belle Epoque	Harvest	3
6	15	FLOAT ON Floaters	ABC	10
26	16	FROM NEW YORK TO LA Patsy Gallant	EMI	2
15	17	DANCIN' IN THE MOONLIGHT Thin Lizzy	Vertigo	7
25	☐18	GARY GILMOUR'S EYES The Adverts	Anchor	5
9	19	ANGELO Brotherhood Of Man	Pye	12
21	20	I CAN'T GET YOU OUTA MY MIND Yvonne Elliman	RSO	6
18	21	SUNSHINE AFTER THE RAIN Elkie Brooks	A&M	5
24	22	BLACK BETTY Ram Jam	Epic	3
19	23	I THINK I'M GONNA FALL IN LOVE WITH YOU Dooleys	GTO	6
22	24	DREAMER Jacksons	Epic	6
23	25	SPANISH STROLL Mink DeVille	Capitol	7
-	26	I REMEMBER ELVIS PRESLEY Danny Mirror	Sonet	1
28	27	THUNDER IN MY HEART Leo Sayer	Chrysalis	3
32	28	WAITING IN VAIN Bob Marley and the Wailers	Island	2
29	29	ANOTHER STAR Stevie Wonder	Motown	3
30	30	GIMME DAT BANANA Black Gorilla	Response	4
12	31	TULANE Steve Gibbons Band	Polydor	7
-	32	I REMEMBER YESTERDAY Donna Summer	GTO	1
16	33	YOU GOT WHAT IT TAKES Showaddywaddy	Arista	9
-	34	SHE'S A WINDUP Dr. Feelgood	United Artists	1
-	35	COOL OUT TONIGHT David Essex	CBS	1
38	36	YOUR GENERATION Generation X	Chrysalis	2
39	37	LET'S CLEAN UP THE GHETTO Philadelphia International All Stars	Philadelphia	5
17	38	THE CRUNCH Rah Band	Good Earth	11
-	☐39	DAYTIME FRIENDS Kenny Rogers	United Artists	1
-	40	FROM HERE TO ETERNITY Giorgio	Oasis	1

LW	TW	*WEEK ENDING* 1 OCTOBER 1977		Wks
1	☐1	WAY DOWN Elvis Presley	RCA	6
3	2	SILVER LADY David Soul	Private Stock	6
2	3	MAGIC FLY Space	Pye	6
4	4	OXYGENE PART IV Jean Michel Jarre	Polydor	6
5	5	DOWN DEEP INSIDE Donna Summer	Cassablanca	6
6	6	TELEPHONE MAN Meri Wilson	Pye	5
8	7	BEST OF MY LOVE Emotions	CBS	4
14	8	BLACK IS BLACK La Belle Epoque	Harvest	4
16	9	FROM NEW YORK TO LA Patsy Gallant	EMI	3
21	10	SUNSHINE AFTER THE RAIN Elkie Brooks	A&M	6
26	11	I REMEMBER ELVIS PRESLEY Danny Mirror	Sonet	2
7	12	NOBODY DOES IT BETTER Carly Simon	Elektra	8
23	☐13	I THINK I'M GONNA FALL IN LOVE WITH YOU Dooleys	GTO	7
11	14	LOOKING AFTER NUMBER ONE Boomtown Rats	Ensign	5
9	15	DO ANYTHING YOU WANNA DO Rods	Island	8

In these weeks ■ Carly Simon has her only Top Ten hits enter the charts at five year intervals (1972, 1977 and later 1982 and 1987) (17.09.77) ■ Billy Idol makes his chart debut as a member of Generation X (17.09.77) ■ The Boomtown Rats, led by Bob Geldof, just miss the Top Ten with their first hit (24.09.77)■

October 1977

□ Highest position disc reached ● Act's first ever week on chart

LW	TW	Title / Artist	Label	Wks
13	16	WONDROUS STORIES Yes	Atlantic	3
20	17	I CAN'T GET YOU OUTA MY MIND Yvonne Elliman	RSO	7
22	18	BLACK BETTY Ram Jam	Epic	4
12	19	NIGHTS ON BROADWAY Candi Staton	Warner Brothers	11
-	20	NO MORE HEROES Stranglers	United Artists	1
32	21	I REMEMBER YESTERDAY Donna Summer	GTO	2
17	22	DANCIN' IN THE MOONLIGHT Thin Lizzy	Vertigo	8
18	23	GARY GILMOUR'S EYES The Adverts	Anchor	6
-	24	YES SIR I CAN BOOGIE Baccara ●	RCA	1
27	25	THUNDER IN MY HEART Leo Sayer	Chrysalis	4
24	26	DREAMER Jacksons	Epic	7
35	27	COOL OUT TONIGHT David Essex	CBS	2
28	28	WAITING IN VAIN Bob Marley and the Wailers	Island	3
31	29	TULANE Steve Gibbons Band	Polydor	8
40	30	FROM HERE TO ETERNITY Giorgio	Oasis	2
10	31	THAT'S WHAT FRIENDS ARE FOR Deniece Williams	CBS	9
29	32	ANOTHER STAR Stevie Wonder	Motown	4
25	33	SPANISH STROLL Mink DeVille	Capitol	8
-	34	GREATEST LOVE OF ALL George Benson	Arista	1
-	35	DO YOUR DANCE Rose Royce	Warner Brothers	1
15	36	FLOAT ON Floaters	ABC	11
-	37	LOVE HURTS Nazareth	Mountain	1
36	38	YOUR GENERATION Generation X	Chrysalis	3
30	39	GIMME DAT BANANA Black Gorilla	Response	5
-	40	DAYTIME FRIENDS Kenny Rogers	United Artists	1

LW	TW	*WEEK ENDING* **8 OCTOBER 1977**		Wks
2	1	SILVER LADY David Soul	Private Stock	7
1	2	WAY DOWN Elvis Presley	RCA	7
8	3	BLACK IS BLACK La Belle Epoque	Harvest	5
7	4	BEST OF MY LOVE Emotions	CBS	5
3	5	MAGIC FLY Space	Pye	7
9	6	FROM NEW YORK TO LA Patsy Gallant	EMI	4
16	7	WONDROUS STORIES Yes	Atlantic	4
11	8	I REMEMBER ELVIS PRESLEY Danny Mirror	Sonet	3
6	9	TELEPHONE MAN Meri Wilson	Pye	6
5	10	DOWN DEEP INSIDE Donna Summer	Cassablanca	7
4	11	OXYGENE PART IV Jean Michel Jarre	Polydor	7
10	12	SUNSHINE AFTER THE RAIN Elkie Brooks	A&M	7
20	13	NO MORE HEROES Stranglers	United Artists	2
24	14	YES SIR I CAN BOOGIE Baccara	RCA	2
14	15	LOOKING AFTER NUMBER ONE Boomtown Rats	Ensign	6
18	16	BLACK BETTY Ram Jam	Epic	5
21	17	I REMEMBER YESTERDAY Donna Summer	GTO	3
15	18	DO ANYTHING YOU WANNA DO Rods	Island	9
13	19	I THINK I'M GONNA FALL IN LOVE WITH YOU Dooleys	GTO	8
12	20	NOBODY DOES IT BETTER Carly Simon	Elektra	9
17	21	I CAN'T GET YOU OUTA MY MIND Yvonne Elliman	RSO	8
25	22	THUNDER IN MY HEART Leo Sayer	Chrysalis	5
27	23	COOL OUT TONIGHT David Essex	CBS	3
-	24	STAR WARS THEME Meco ●	RCA	1
30	25	FROM HERE TO ETERNITY Giorgio	Oasis	3
23	26	GARY GILMOUR'S EYES The Adverts	Anchor	7
28	27	WAITING IN VAIN Bob Marley and the Wailers	Island	4
-	28	COMPLETE CONTROL Clash	CBS	1
34	29	GREATEST LOVE OF ALL George Benson	Arista	2
35	30	DO YOUR DANCE Rose Royce	Warner Brothers	2
37	31	LOVE HURTS Nazareth	Mountain	2
-	32	ROCKIN' ALL OVER THE WORLD Status Quo	Vertigo	1
32	33	ANOTHER STAR Stevie Wonder	Motown	5
-	34	SHE'S A WINDUP Dr. Feelgood	United Artists	1
-	35	HOME IS WHERE THE HEART IS Gladys Knight & the Pips	Buddah	1
19	36	NIGHTS ON BROADWAY Candi Staton	Warner Brothers	12
26	37	DREAMER Jacksons	Epic	8
-	38	HAPPY DAYS Pratt & McLain ●	Reprise	1
31	39	THAT'S WHAT FRIENDS ARE FOR Deniece Williams	CBS	10
40	40	DAYTIME FRIENDS Kenny Rogers	United Artists	2

LW	TW	*WEEK ENDING* **15 OCTOBER 1977**		Wks
1	1	SILVER LADY David Soul	Private Stock	8
3	2	BLACK IS BLACK La Belle Epoque	Harvest	6
14	3	YES SIR I CAN BOOGIE Baccara	RCA	3
8	4	I REMEMBER ELVIS PRESLEY Danny Mirror	Sonet	4
4	5	BEST OF MY LOVE Emotions	CBS	6
2	6	WAY DOWN Elvis Presley	RCA	8
-	7	YOU'RE IN MY HEART Rod Stewart	Riva	1
6	8	FROM NEW YORK TO LA Patsy Gallant	EMI	5
13	9	NO MORE HEROES Stranglers	United Artists	3
9	10	TELEPHONE MAN Meri Wilson	Pye	7
5	11	MAGIC FLY Space	Pye	8
16	12	BLACK BETTY Ram Jam	Epic	6
24	13	STAR WARS THEME Meco	RCA	2
7	14	WONDROUS STORIES Yes	Atlantic	5
10	15	DOWN DEEP INSIDE Donna Summer	Cassablanca	8
17	16	I REMEMBER YESTERDAY Donna Summer	GTO	4
32	17	ROCKIN' ALL OVER THE WORLD Status Quo	Vertigo	2
11	18	OXYGENE PART IV Jean Michel Jarre	Polydor	8
21	19	I CAN'T GET YOU OUTA MY MIND Yvonne Elliman	RSO	9
12	20	SUNSHINE AFTER THE RAIN Elkie Brooks	A&M	8
25	21	FROM HERE TO ETERNITY Giorgio	Oasis	4
19	22	I THINK I'M GONNA FALL IN LOVE WITH YOU Dooleys	GTO	9
20	23	NOBODY DOES IT BETTER Carly Simon	Elektra	10
22	24	THUNDER IN MY HEART Leo Sayer	Chrysalis	6
23	25	COOL OUT TONIGHT David Essex	CBS	4
-	26	CALLING OCCUPANTS OF INTERPLANETARY CRAFT Carpenters	A&M	1
-	27	HEROES David Bowie	RCA	1
31	28	LOVE HURTS ETC. Nazareth	Mountain	3
29	29	GREATEST LOVE OF ALL George Benson	Arista	3
30	30	DO YOUR DANCE Rose Royce	Warner Brothers	3
38	31	HAPPY DAYS Pratt & McLain	Reprise	2
28	32	COMPLETE CONTROL Clash	CBS	2
27	33	WAITING IN VAIN Bob Marley and the Wailers	Island	5
15	34	LOOKING AFTER NUMBER ONE Boom Town Rats	Ensign	7
-	35	BRICKHOUSE/SWEET LOVE Commodores	Motown	1
18	36	DO ANYTHING YOU WANNA DO Rods	Island	10
-	37	ANGEL OF THE MORNING/ANYWAY YOU WANT ME Mary Mason ●	Epic	1
35	38	HOME IS WHERE THE HEART IS Gladys Knight & the Pips	Buddah	2
34	39	SHE'S A WINDUP Dr. Feelgood	United Artists	2
-	40	LIPSMACKIN' ROCK & ROLLIN' Peter Blake ●	Pepper	1

LW	TW	*WEEK ENDING* **22 OCTOBER 1977**		Wks
1	1	SILVER LADY David Soul	Private Stock	9
2	2	BLACK IS BLACK La Belle Epoque	Harvest	7
3	3	YES SIR I CAN BOOGIE Baccara	RCA	4
7	4	YOU'RE IN MY HEART Rod Stewart	Riva	2
4	5	I REMEMBER ELVIS PRESLEY Danny Mirror	Sonet	5
5	6	BEST OF MY LOVE Emotions	CBS	7
13	7	STAR WARS THFME Meco	RCA	3
9	8	NO MORE HEROES Stranglers	United Artists	4
12	9	BLACK BETTY Ram Jam	Epic	7
6	10	WAY DOWN Elvis Presley	RCA	9
17	11	ROCKIN' ALL OVER THE WORLD Status Quo	Vertigo	3
8	12	FROM NEW YORK TO LA Patsy Gallant	EMI	6
14	13	WONDROUS STORIES Yes	Atlantic	6
16	14	I REMEMBER YESTERDAY Donna Summer	GTO	5
-	15	HOLIDAYS IN THE SUN Sex Pistols	Virgin	1
21	16	FROM HERE TO ETERNITY Giorgio	Oasis	5
10	17	TELEPHONE MAN Meri Wilson	Pye	8
26	18	CALLING OCCUPANTS OF INTERPLANETARY CRAFT Carpenters	A&M	2
19	19	I CAN'T GET YOU OUTA MY MIND Yvonne Elliman	RSO	10
-	20	NAME OF THE GAME Abba	Epic	1
11	21	MAGIC FLY Space	Pye	9
-	22	NEEDLES & PINS Smokie	RAK	1
28	23	LOVE HURTS ETC. Nazareth	Mountain	4

■Yes have nine Top Ten albums in their career but only one week in the Top Ten of the singles chart (08.10.77) ■ A number two for Los Bravos in 1966, *Black Is Black* reaches the same peak for La Belle Epoque in 1977; both acts are continental (15.10.77) ■ Including its subtitle *(The Recognised Anthem Of World Contact Day)*, the new Carpenters hit has the longest title in chart history (15.10.77)■

October 1977

□ Highest position disc reached ● Act's first ever week on chart

LW	TW	Title	Artist	Label	Wks
24	24	THUNDER IN MY HEART	Leo Sayer	*Chrysalis*	7
34	25	LOOKING AFTER NUMBER ONE	Boomtown Rats	*Ensign*	8
27	26	HEROES	David Bowie	*RCA*	2
29	[27]	GREATEST LOVE OF ALL	George Benson	*Arista*	4
37	28	ANGEL OF THE MORNING/ANYWAY YOU WANT ME	Mary Mason	*Epic*	2
-	29	VIRGINIA PLAIN	Roxy Music	*Polydor*	1
-	30	WE ARE THE CHAMPIONS	Queen	*EMI*	1
-	[31]	NEW LIVE AND RARE	Deep Purple	*Purple*	1
30	32	DO YOUR DANCE	Rose Royce	*Warner Brothers*	4
15	33	DOWN DEEP INSIDE	Donna Summer	*Cassablanca*	9
31	34	HAPPY DAYS	Pratt & McLain	*Reprise*	3
18	35	OXYGENE PART IV	Jean Michel Jarre	*Polydor*	9
23	36	NOBODY DOES IT BETTER	Carly Simon	*Elektra*	11
-	37	2.4.6.8.MOTORWAY	Tom Robinson ●	*EMI*	1
-	38	I BELIEVE YOU	Dorothy Moore	*Epic*	1
25	39	COOL OUT TONIGHT	David Essex	*CBS*	5
35	40	BRICKHOUSE/SWEET LOVE	Commodores	*Motown*	2

WEEK ENDING 29 OCTOBER 1977

LW	TW	Title	Artist	Label	Wks
3	[1]	YES SIR I CAN BOOGIE	Baccara	*RCA*	5
2	[2]	BLACK IS BLACK	La Belle Epoque	*Harvest*	8
4	[3]	YOU'RE IN MY HEART	Rod Stewart	*Riva*	3
1	4	SILVER LADY	David Soul	*Private Stock*	10
20	5	NAME OF THE GAME	Abba	*Epic*	2
11	6	ROCKIN' ALL OVER THE WORLD	Status Quo	*Vertigo*	4
9	7	BLACK BETTY	Ram Jam	*Epic*	8
15	[8]	HOLIDAYS IN THE SUN	Sex Pistols	*Virgin*	2
5	9	I REMEMBER ELVIS PRESLEY	Danny Mirror	*Sonet*	6
7	10	STAR WARS THEME	Meco	*RCA*	4
18	11	CALLING OCCUPANTS OF INTERPLANETARY CRAFT	Carpenters	*A&M*	3
8	12	NO MORE HEROES	Stranglers	*United Artists*	5
30	13	WE ARE THE CHAMPIONS	Queen	*EMI*	2
6	14	BEST OF MY LOVE	Emotions	*CBS*	8
37	15	2.4.6.8.MOTORWAY	Tom Robinson	*EMI*	2
14	16	I REMEMBER YESTERDAY	Donna Summer	*GTO*	6
22	17	NEEDLES & PINS	Smokie	*RAK*	2
13	18	WONDROUS STORIES	Yes	*Atlantic*	7
10	19	WAY DOWN	Elvis Presley	*RCA*	10
29	20	VIRGINIA PLAIN	Roxy Music	*Polydor*	2
23	21	LOVE HURTS	Nazareth	*Mountain*	5
19	22	I CAN'T GET YOU OUTA MY MIND	Yvonne Elliman	*RSO*	11
12	23	FROM NEW YORK TO LA	Patsy Gallant	*EMI*	7
16	24	FROM HERE TO ETERNITY	Giorgio	*Oasis*	6
26	25	HEROES	David Bowie	*RCA*	3
38	26	I BELIEVE YOU	Dorothy Moore	*Epic*	2
28	[27]	ANGEL OF THE MORNING/ANYWAY YOU WANT ME	Mary Mason	*Epic*	3
24	28	THUNDER IN MY HEART	Leo Sayer	*Chrysalis*	8
-	29	SHE'S NOT THERE	Santana	*CBS*	1
27	30	GREATEST LOVE OF ALL	George Benson	*Arista*	5
31	[31]	NEW LIVE AND RARE	Deep Purple	*Purple*	2
34	32	HAPPY DAYS	Pratt & McLain	*Reprise*	4
17	33	TELEPHONE MAN	Meri Wilson	*Pye*	9
-	34	LOVE BUG	Tina Charles	*CBS*	1
21	35	MAGIC FLY	Space	*Pye*	10
-	36	HOW DEEP IS YOUR LOVE	Bee Gees	*RSO*	1
-	37	WATER MARGIN	Peter Mac Junior and Godiego	*BBC*	1
40	38	BRICKHOUSE/SWEET LOVE	Commodores	*Motown*	3
32	39	DO YOUR DANCE	Rose Royce	*Warner Brothers*	5
-	[40]	IT'S ECSTASY	Barry White	*20th Century*	1

WEEK ENDING 5 NOVEMBER 1977

LW	TW	Title	Artist	Label	Wks
5	[1]	NAME OF THE GAME	Abba	*Epic*	3
1	2	YES SIR I CAN BOOGIE	Baccara	*RCA*	6
3	[3]	YOU'RE IN MY HEART	Rod Stewart	*Riva*	4
2	4	BLACK IS BLACK	La Belle Epoque	*Harvest*	9
6	5	ROCKIN' ALL OVER THE WORLD	Status Quo	*Vertigo*	5
13	6	WE ARE THE CHAMPIONS	Queen	*EMI*	3
4	7	SILVER LADY	David Soul	*Private Stock*	11
15	8	2.4.6.8.MOTORWAY	Tom Robinson	*EMI*	3
8	9	HOLIDAY IN THE SUN	Sex Pistols	*Virgin*	3
11	10	CALLING OCCUPANTS OF INTERPLANETARY CRAFT	Carpenters	*A&M*	4
7	11	BLACK BETTY	Ram Jam	*Epic*	9
10	12	STAR WARS THEME	Meco	*RCA*	5
17	13	NEEDLES & PINS	Smokie	*RAK*	3
12	14	NO MORE HEROES	Stranglers	*United Artists*	6
20	15	VIRGINIA PLAIN	Roxy Music	*Polydor*	3
9	16	I REMEMBER ELVIS PRESLEY	Danny Mirror	*Sonet*	7
24	17	FROM HERE TO ETERNITY	Giorgio	*Oasis*	7
18	18	WONDROUS STORIES	Yes	*Atlantic*	8
16	19	I REMEMBER YESTERDAY	Donna Summer	*GTO*	7
21	20	LOVE HURTS	Nazareth	*Mountain*	6
26	21	I BELIEVE YOU	Dorothy Moore	*Epic*	3
36	22	HOW DEEP IS YOUR LOVE	Bee Gees	*RSO*	2
-	23	LIVE IN TROUBLE	Barron Knights	*Epic*	1
25	[24]	HEROES	David Bowie	*RCA*	4
29	25	SHE'S NOT THERE	Santana	*CBS*	2
14	26	BEST OF MY LOVE	Emotions	*CBS*	9
-	27	TURN TO STONE	Electric Light Orchestra	*Jet*	1
27	28	ANGEL OF THE MORNING/ANYWAY YOU WANT ME	Mary Mason	*Epic*	4
34	29	LOVE BUG	Tina Charles	*CBS*	2
19	30	WAY DOWN	Elvis Presley	*RCA*	11
23	31	FROM NEW YORK TO LA	Patsy Gallant	*EMI*	8
38	[32]	BRICKHOUSE/SWEET LOVE	Commodores	*Motown*	4
-	33	WATCHIN' THE DETECTIVES	Elvis Costello ●	*Stiff*	1
-	34	BELFAST	Boney M	*Atlantic*	1
-	[35]	THE DANGER OF A STRANGER	Stella Parton ●	*Elektra*	1
32	36	HAPPY DAYS	Pratt & McLain	*Reprise*	5
-	37	DADDY COOL	Darts ●	*Magnet*	1
-	38	MODERN WORLD	Jam	*Polydor*	1
30	39	GREATEST LOVE OF ALL	George Benson	*Arista*	6
-	[40]	BOOGIE ON UP	Rokotto ●	*State*	1

WEEK ENDING 12 NOVEMBER 1977

LW	TW	Title	Artist	Label	Wks
1	[1]	NAME OF THE GAME	Abba	*Epic*	4
2	2	YES SIR I CAN BOOGIE	Baccara	*RCA*	7
3	[3]	YOU'RE IN MY HEART	Rod Stewart	*Riva*	5
5	4	ROCKIN' ALL OVER THE WORLD	Status Quo	*Vertigo*	6
8	[5]	2.4.6.8.MOTORWAY	Tom Robinson	*EMI*	4
6	6	WE ARE THE CHAMPIONS	Queen	*EMI*	4
4	7	BLACK IS BLACK	La Belle Epoque	*Harvest*	10
11	8	BLACK BETTY	Ram Jam	*Epic*	10
10	[9]	CALLING OCCUPANTS OF INTERPLANETARY CRAFT	Carpenters	*A&M*	5
13	[10]	NEEDLES & PINS	Smokie	*RAK*	4
15	[11]	VIRGINIA PLAIN	Roxy Music	*Polydor*	4
22	12	HOW DEEP IS YOUR LOVE	Bee Gees	*RSO*	3
9	13	HOLIDAY IN THE SUN	Sex Pistols	*Virgin*	4
23	14	LIVE IN TROUBLE	Barron Knights	*Epic*	2
7	15	SILVER LADY	David Soul	*Private Stock*	12
20	16	LOVE HURTS	Nazareth	*Mountain*	7
-	17	DANCIN' PARTY	Showaddywaddy	*Arista*	1
25	18	SHE'S NOT THERE	Santana	*CBS*	3
17	19	FROM HERE TO ETERNITY	Giorgio	*Oasis*	8
12	20	STAR WARS THEME	Meco	*RCA*	6
37	21	DADDY COOL	Darts	*Magnet*	2
34	22	BELFAST	Boney M	*Atlantic*	2
21	23	I BELIEVE YOU	Dorothy Moore	*Epic*	4
27	24	TURN TO STONE	Electric Light Orchestra	*Jet*	2
24	25	HEROES	David Bowie	*RCA*	5
29	[26]	LOVE BUG	Tina Charles	*CBS*	3
14	27	NO MORE HEROES	Stranglers	*United Artists*	7
16	28	I REMEMBER ELVIS PRESLEY	Danny Mirror	*Sonet*	8
-	29	I WILL	Ruby Winters ●	*Creole*	1
-	30	GOIN' PLACES	Jacksons	*Epic*	1

In these weeks ■ Tom Robinson becomes the first 'out' gay chart star (22.10.77) ■ A Spanish female duo leads a French female twosome at the top of the chart (29.10.77) ■ Elvis Costello begins his historic chart career (05.12.77)■

LW	TW	Title	Artist	Label	Wks
-	31	EGYPTIAN REGGAE	J. Richman & the Modern Lovers	Beserkley	1
-	32	MY BABY LEFT ME	Slade	Barn	1
33	33	WATCHIN' THE DETECTIVES	Elvis Costello	Stiff	2
28	34	ANGEL OF THE MORNING/ANYWAY YOU WANT ME	Mary Mason	Epic	5
-	35	DON'T IT MAKE MY BROWN EYES BLUE	Crystal Gayle ●	United Artists	1
18	36	WONDROUS STORIES	Yes	Atlantic	9
26	37	BEST OF MY LOVE	Emotions	CBS	10
32	38	BRICKHOUSE/SWEET LOVE	Commodores	Motown	5
-	39	CAPTAIN KREMMEN	Kenny Everett and Mike Vickers ●	DJM	1
-	40	SHOO DOO FU FU OOH	Lenny Williams ●	ABC	1

WEEK ENDING 19 NOVEMBER 1977

LW	TW	Title	Artist	Label	Wks
1	1	NAME OF THE GAME	Abba	Epic	5
6	2	WE ARE THE CHAMPIONS	Queen	EMI	5
4	3	ROCKIN' ALL OVER THE WORLD	Status Quo	Vertigo	7
2	4	YES SIR I CAN BOOGIE	Baccara	RCA	8
5	5	2.4.6.8.MOTORWAY	Tom Robinson	EMI	5
3	6	YOU'RE IN MY HEART	Rod Stewart	Riva	6
14	7	LIVE IN TROUBLE	Barron Knights	Epic	3
17	8	DANCIN' PARTY	Showaddywaddy	Arista	2
12	9	HOW DEEP IS YOUR LOVE	Bee Gees	RSO	4
9	10	CALLING OCCUPANTS OF INTERPLANETARY CRAFT	Carpenters	A&M	6
10	11	NEEDLES & PINS	Smokie	RAK	5
7	12	BLACK IS BLACK	La Belle Epoque	Harvest	11
11	13	VIRGINIA PLAIN	Roxy Music	Polydor	5
21	14	DADDY COOL	Darts	Magnet	3
16	15	LOVE HURTS	Nazareth	Mountain	8
18	16	SHE'S NOT THERE	Santana	CBS	4
13	17	HOLIDAY IN THE SUN	Sex Pistols	Virgin	5
19	18	FROM HERE TO ETERNITY	Giorgio	Oasis	9
8	19	BLACK BETTY	Ram Jam	Epic	11
23	20	I BELIEVE YOU	Dorothy Moore	Epic	5
22	21	BELFAST	Boney M	Atlantic	3
29	22	I WILL	Ruby Winters	Creole	2
31	23	EGYPTIAN REGGAE	J. Richman & the Modern Lovers	Beserkley	2
24	24	TURN TO STONE	Electric Light Orchestra	Jet	3
25	25	HEROES	David Bowie	RCA	6
33	26	WATCHIN' THE DETECTIVES	Elvis Costello	Stiff	3
15	27	SILVER LADY	David Soul	Private Stock	13
30	28	GOIN' PLACES	Jacksons	Epic	2
20	29	STAR WARS THEME	Meco	RCA	7
-	30	FLORAL DANCE	Brighouse & Rastrick Band ●	Transatlantic	1
35	31	DON'T IT MAKE MY BROWN EYES BLUE	Crystal Gayle	United Artists	2
-	32	BABY BABY MY LOVE IS ALL FOR YOU	Deniece Williams	CBS	1
39	33	CAPTAIN KREMMEN	Kenny Everett and Mike Vickers	DJM	2
-	34	LOVE OF MY LIFE	Dooleys	GTO	1
26	35	LOVE BUG	Tina Charles	CBS	4
-	36	MODERN WORLD	Jam	Polydor	1
27	37	NO MORE HEROES	Stranglers	United Artists	8
40	38	SHOO DOO FU FU OOH	Lenny Williams	ABC	2
-	39	GEORGINA BAILEY	Noosha Fox ●	GTO	1
32	40	MY BABY LEFT ME	Slade	Barn	2

WEEK ENDING 26 NOVEMBER 1977

LW	TW	Title	Artist	Label	Wks
1	1	NAME OF THE GAME	Abba	Epic	6
2	2	WE ARE THE CHAMPIONS	Queen	EMI	6
3	3	ROCKIN' ALL OVER THE WORLD	Status Quo	Vertigo	8
8	4	DANCIN' PARTY	Showaddywaddy	Arista	3
-	5	MULL OF KINTYRE/GIRLS SCHOOL	Wings	Parlophone	1
9	6	HOW DEEP IS YOUR LOVE	Bee Gees	RSO	5
14	7	DADDY COOL	Darts	Magnet	4
5	8	2.4.6.8.MOTORWAY	Tom Robinson	EMI	6
4	9	YES SIR I CAN BOOGIE	Baccara	RCA	9
7	10	LIVE IN TROUBLE	Barron Knights	Epic	4

December 1977

□ Highest position disc reached ● Act's first ever week on chart

LW	TW	Title	Artist	Label	Wks
16	11	SHE'S NOT THERE	Santana	CBS	5
6	12	YOU'RE IN MY HEART	Rod Stewart	Riva	7
30	13	FLORAL DANCE	Brighouse & Rastrick Band	Transatlantic	2
22	14	I WILL	Ruby Winters	Creole	3
11	15	NEEDLES & PINS	Smokie	RAK	6
10	16	CALLING OCCUPANTS OF INTERPLANETARY CRAFT	Carpenters	A&M	7
21	17	BELFAST	Boney M	Atlantic	4
23	18	EGYPTIAN REGGAE	J. Richman & the Modern Lovers	Beserkley	3
13	19	VIRGINIA PLAIN	Roxy Music	Polydor	6
15	20	LOVE HURTS	Nazareth	Mountain	9
24	21	TURN TO STONE	Electric Light Orchestra	Jet	4
26	22	WATCHIN' THE DETECTIVES	Elvis Costello	Stiff	4
-	23	MARY OF THE FOURTH FORM	Boomtown Rats	Ensign	1
12	24	BLACK IS BLACK	La Belle Epoque	Harvest	12
34	25	LOVE OF MY LIFE	Dooleys	GTO	2
28	26	GOIN' PLACES	Jacksons	Epic	3
20	27	I BELIEVE YOU	Dorothy Moore	Epic	6
19	28	BLACK BETTY	Ram Jam	Epic	12
-	29	WHITE PUNKS ON DOPE	Tubes ●	A&M	1
31	30	DON'T IT MAKE MY BROWN EYES BLUE	Crystal Gayle	United Artists	3
-	31	GETTIN' READY FOR LOVE	Diana Ross	Motown	1
33	32	CAPTAIN KREMMEN	Kenny Everett and Mike Vickers	DJM	3
32	33	BABY BABY MY LOVE IS ALL FOR YOU	Deniece Williams	CBS	2
25	34	HEROES	David Bowie	RCA	7
39	35	GEORGINA BAILEY	Noosha Fox	GTO	2
17	36	HOLIDAY IN THE SUN	Sex Pistols	Virgin	6
-	37	YOU'RE FABULOUS BABE	Kenny Williams ●	Decca	1
27	38	SILVER LADY	David Soul	Private Stock	14
-	39	ONLY THE STRONG SURVIVE	Billy Paul	Philadelphia	1
29	40	STAR WARS THEME	Meco	RCA	8

WEEK ENDING 3 DECEMBER 1977

LW	TW	Title	Artist	Label	Wks
5	1	MULL OF KINTYRE/GIRLS SCHOOL	Wings	Parlophone	2
2	2	WE ARE THE CHAMPIONS	Queen	EMI	7
3	3	ROCKIN' ALL OVER THE WORLD	Status Quo	Vertigo	9
1	4	NAME OF THE GAME	Abba	Epic	7
6	5	HOW DEEP IS YOUR LOVE	Bee Gees	RSO	6
4	6	DANCIN' PARTY	Showaddywaddy	Arista	4
7	7	DADDY COOL	Darts	Magnet	5
14	8	I WILL	Ruby Winters	Creole	4
13	9	FLORAL DANCE	Brighouse & Rastrick Band	Transatlantic	3
10	10	LIVE IN TROUBLE	Barron Knights	Epic	5
18	11	EGYPTIAN REGGAE	J. Richman & the Modern Lovers	Beserkley	4
8	12	2.4.6.8.MOTORWAY	Tom Robinson	EMI	7
9	13	YES SIR I CAN BOOGIE	Baccara	RCA	10
11	14	SHE'S NOT THERE	Santana	CBS	6
12	15	YOU'RE IN MY HEART	Rod Stewart	Riva	8
15	16	NEEDLES & PINS	Smokie	RAK	7
16	17	CALLING OCCUPANTS OF INTERPLANETARY CRAFT	Carpenters	A&M	8
22	18	WATCHIN' THE DETECTIVES	Elvis Costello	Stiff	5
17	19	BELFAST	Boney M	Atlantic	5
23	20	MARY OF THE FOURTH FORM	Boomtown Rats	Ensign	2
25	21	LOVE OF MY LIFE	Dooleys	GTO	3
21	22	TURN TO STONE	Electric Light Orchestra	Jet	5
-	23	PUT YOUR LOVE IN ME	Hot Chocolate	Rak	1
-	24	GOIN' FOR THE ONE	Yes	Atlantic	1
-	25	DANCE DANCE DANCE	Chic ●	Atlantic	1
26	26	GOIN' PLACES	Jacksons	Epic	4
31	27	GETTIN' READY FOR LOVE	Diana Ross	Motown	2
29	28	WHITE PUNKS ON DOPE	Tubes	A&M	2
30	29	DON'T IT MAKE MY BROWN EYES BLUE	Crystal Gayle	United Artists	4

■The unlisted B-side of Queen's *We Are The Champions*, *We Will Rock You*, also becomes an anthem (19.11.77) ■ The Bee Gees have the first of three top five hits from 'Saturday Night Fever' (03.12.77) ■ Status Quo have three weeks at three with a song by former Creedence Clearwater Revival leader John Fogerty (03.12.77)■

December 1977

□ Highest position disc reached ● Act's first ever week on chart

LW	TW	Title	Artist	Label	Wks
27	30	I BELIEVE YOU	Dorothy Moore	Epic	7
35	[31]	GEORGINA BAILEY	Noosha Fox	GTO	3
-	32	L.A. RUN	Carvells ●	Creole	1
39	[33]	ONLY THE STRONG SURVIVE	Billy Paul	Philadelphia	2
-	34	IT'S A HEARTACHE	Bonnie Tyler	RCA	1
37	[35]	YOU'RE FABULOUS BABE	Kenny Williams	Decca	2
-	36	LOVE'S UNKIND	Donna Summer	GTO	1
20	37	LOVE HURTS ETC.	Nazareth	Mountain	10
24	38	BLACK IS BLACK	La Belle Epoque	Harvest	13
34	39	HEROES	David Bowie	RCA	8
33	40	BABY BABY MY LOVE IS ALL FOR YOU	Deniece Williams	CBS	3

WEEK ENDING 10 DECEMBER 1977

LW	TW	Title	Artist	Label	Wks
1	[1]	MULL OF KINTYRE/GIRLS SCHOOL	Wings	Parlophone	3
9	[2]	FLORAL DANCE	Brighouse & Rastrick Band	Transatlantic	4
5	[3]	HOW DEEP IS YOUR LOVE	Bee Gees	RSO	7
6	[4]	DANCIN' PARTY	Showaddywaddy	Arista	5
8	5	I WILL	Ruby Winters	Creole	5
7	[6]	DADDY COOL	Darts	Magnet	6
2	7	WE ARE THE CHAMPIONS	Queen	EMI	8
3	8	ROCKIN' ALL OVER THE WORLD	Status Quo	Vertigo	10
11	9	EGYPTIAN REGGAE	J. Richman & the Modern Lovers	Beserkley	5
19	10	BELFAST	Boney M	Atlantic	6
4	11	NAME OF THE GAME	Abba	Epic	8
23	12	PUT YOUR LOVE IN ME	Hot Chocolate	Rak	2
21	13	LOVE OF MY LIFE	Dooleys	GTO	4
14	14	SHE'S NOT THERE	Santana	CBS	7
20	[15]	MARY OF THE FOURTH FORM	Boomtown Rats	Ensign	3
36	16	LOVE'S UNKIND	Donna Summer	GTO	2
10	17	LIVE IN TROUBLE	Barron Knights	Epic	6
22	[18]	TURN TO STONE	Electric Light Orchestra	Jet	6
34	19	IT'S A HEARTACHE	Bonnie Tyler	RCA	2
18	20	WATCHIN' THE DETECTIVE	Elvis Costello	Stiff	6
29	21	DON'T IT MAKE MY BROWN EYES BLUE	Crystal Gayle	United Artists	5
25	22	DANCE DANCE DANCE	Chic	Atlantic	2
12	23	2.4.6.8.MOTORWAY	Tom Robinson	EMI	8
13	24	YES SIR I CAN BOOGIE	Baccara	RCA	11
-	25	WHITE CHRISTMAS	Bing Crosby	MCA	1
-	26	MY WAY	Elvis Presley	RCA	1
27	27	GETTIN' READY FOR LOVE	Diana Ross	Motown	3
24	28	GOIN' FOR THE ONE	Yes	Atlantic	2
15	29	YOU'RE IN MY HEART	Rod Stewart	Riva	9
26	30	GOIN' PLACES	Jacksons	Epic	5
32	[31]	L.A. RUN	Carvells	Creole	2
31	32	GEORGINA BAILEY	Noosha Fox	GTO	4
-	33	I LOVE YOU	Donna Summer	Casablanca	1
-	34	ONLY WOMEN BLEED	Julie Covington	Virgin	1
16	35	NEEDLES & PINS	Smokie	RAK	8
33	36	ONLY THE STRONG SURVIVE	Billy Paul	Philadelphia	3
30	37	I BELIEVE YOU	Dorothy Moore	Epic	8
-	38	RUN BACK	Carl Douglas	Pye	1
35	39	YOU'RE FABULOUS BABE	Kenny Williams	Decca	3
-	40	REALLY FREE	John Otway and Wild Willy Barrett ●	Polydor	1

WEEK ENDING 17 DECEMBER 1977

LW	TW	Title	Artist	Label	Wks
1	[1]	MULL OF KINTYRE/GIRLS SCHOOL	Wings	Parlophone	4
2	[2]	FLORAL DANCE	Brighouse & Rastrick Band	Transatlantic	5
3	[3]	HOW DEEP IS YOUR LOVE	Bee Gees	RSO	8
5	[4]	I WILL	Ruby Winters	Creole	6
9	[5]	EGYPTIAN REGGAE	J. Richman & the Modern Lovers	Beserkley	6
6	[6]	DADDY COOL	Darts	Magnet	7
4	7	DANCIN' PARTY	Showaddywaddy	Arista	6
10	[8]	BELFAST	Boney M	Atlantic	7
13	[9]	LOVE OF MY LIFE	Dooleys	GTO	5
7	10	WE ARE THE CHAMPIONS	Queen	EMI	9
8	11	ROCKIN' ALL OVER THE WORLD	Status Quo	Vertigo	11
25	12	WHITE CHRISTMAS	Bing Crosby	MCA	2
16	13	LOVE'S UNKIND	Donna Summer	GTO	3
19	14	IT'S A HEARTACHE	Bonnie Tyler	RCA	3
15	[15]	MARY OF THE FOURTH FORM	Boomtown Rats	Ensign	4
20	16	WATCHIN' THE DETECTIVE	Elvis Costello	Stiff	7
12	17	PUT YOUR LOVE IN ME	Hot Chocolate	Rak	3
11	18	NAME OF THE GAME	Abba	Epic	9
26	19	MY WAY	Elvis Presley	RCA	2
21	20	DON'T IT MAKE MY BROWN EYES BLUE	Crystal Gayle	United Artists	6
18	21	TURN TO STONE	Electric Light Orchestra	Jet	7
22	22	DANCE DANCE DANCE	Chic	Atlantic	3
27	[23]	GETTIN' READY FOR LOVE	Diana Ross	Motown	4
17	24	LIVE IN TROUBLE	Barron Knights	Epic	7
33	25	I LOVE YOU	Donna Summer	Casablanca	2
34	26	ONLY WOMEN BLEED	Julie Covington	Virgin	2
40	[27]	REALLY FREE	John Otway and Wild Willy Barrett	Polydor	2
14	28	SHE'S NOT THERE	Santana	CBS	8
-	29	AS TIME GOES BY	Dooley Wilson ●	United Artists	1
38	30	RUN BACK	Carl Douglas	Pye	2
-	31	LET'S HAVE A QUIET NIGHT IN	David Soul	Private Stock	1
24	32	YES SIR I CAN BOOGIE	Baccara	RCA	12
-	33	JAMMING/PUNKY REGGAE PARTY	Bob Marley & the Wailers	Island	1
-	34	WHO PAYS THE FERRY MAN	Yannis Markopoulos ●	BBC	1
23	35	2.4.6.8.MOTORWAY	Tom Robinson	EMI	9
-	[36]	SLIP SLIDIN' AWAY	Paul Simon	CBS	1
-	37	HOLLYWOOD	Boz Scaggs	Epic	1
36	38	ONLY THE STRONG SURVIVE	Billy Paul	Philadelphia	4
28	39	GOIN' FOR THE ONE	Yes	Atlantic	3
29	40	YOU'RE IN MY HEART	Rod Stewart	Riva	10

WEEK ENDING 24 DECEMBER 1977

LW	TW	Title	Artist	Label	Wks
1	[1]	MULL OF KINTYRE/GIRLS SCHOOL	Wings	Parlophone	5
2	[2]	FLORAL DANCE	Brighouse & Rastrick Band	Transatlantic	6
3	[3]	HOW DEEP IS YOUR LOVE	Bee Gees	RSO	9
4	[4]	I WILL	Ruby Winters	Creole	7
12	[5]	WHITE CHRISTMAS	Bing Crosby	MCA	3
13	6	LOVE'S UNKIND	Donna Summer	GTO	4
14	7	IT'S A HEARTACHE	Bonnie Tyler	RCA	4
6	8	DADDY COOL	Darts	Magnet	8
5	9	EGYPTIAN REGGAE	J. Richman & the Modern Lovers	Beserkley	7
17	[10]	PUT YOUR LOVE IN ME	Hot Chocolate	Rak	4
8	11	BELFAST	Boney M	Atlantic	8
7	12	DANCIN' PARTY	Showaddywaddy	Arista	7
9	13	LOVE OF MY LIFE	Dooleys	GTO	6
19	14	MY WAY	Elvis Presley	RCA	3
16	[15]	WATCHIN' THE DETECTIVE	Elvis Costello	Stiff	8
15	16	MARY OF THE FOURTH FORM	Boomtown Rats	Ensign	5
31	17	LET'S HAVE A QUIET NIGHT IN	David Soul	Private Stock	2
20	18	DON'T IT MAKE MY BROWN EYES BLUE	Crystal Gayle	United Artists	7
22	19	DANCE DANCE DANCE	Chic	Atlantic	4
21	20	TURN TO STONE	Electric Light Orchestra	Jet	8
34	21	WHO PAYS THE FERRY MAN	Yannis Markopoulos	BBC	2
10	22	WE ARE THE CHAMPIONS	Queen	EMI	10
29	23	AS TIME GOES BY	Dooley Wilson	United Artists	2
26	24	ONLY WOMEN BLEED	Julie Covington	Virgin	3
11	25	ROCKIN' ALL OVER THE WORLD	Status Quo	Vertigo	12
25	26	I LOVE YOU	Donna Summer	Casablanca	3
-	27	DON'T DILLY DALLY/WAITING AT THE CHURCH	Muppets	Pye	1
33	28	JAMMING/PUNKY REGGAE PARTY	Bob Marley & the Wailers	Island	2
27	29	REALLY FREE	John Otway and Wild Willy Barrett	Polydor	3
23	30	GETTIN' READY FOR LOVE	Diana Ross	Motown	5
30	31	RUN BACK	Carl Douglas	Pye	3
24	32	LIVE IN TROUBLE	Barron Knights	Epic	8

In these weeks ■ Showaddywaddy improve on Chubby Checker's 1962 peak with *Dancin' Party* (10.12.77) ■ Ruby Winters betters Billy Fury's 1964 performance with *I Will* (10.12.77) ■ Darts take the Rays' 1957 tune *Daddy Cool* into the UK chart for the first time (17.12.77) ■

□ Highest position disc reached ● Act's first ever week on chart

37 [**33**] HOLLYWOOD Boz Scaggs .... *Epic* 2
\- **34** UPTOWN TOP RANKING Althia & Donna ● .... *Lightning* 1
18 **35** NAME OF THE GAME Abba .... *Epic* 10
\- [**36**] LITTLE GIRL The Banned ● .... *Harvest* 1
28 **37** SHE'S NOT THERE Santana .... *CBS* 9
32 **38** YES SIR I CAN BOOGIE Baccara .... *RCA* 13
\- [**39**] DESIREE Neil Diamond .... *CBS* 1
\- [**40**] I DON'T WANT TO LOSE YOUR LOVE Emotions .... *CBS* 1

LW **TW** *WEEK ENDING* **31 DECEMBER 1977** Wks

(no chart published, chart for 24th December repeated)

1 [**1**] MULL OF KINTYRE/GIRLS SCHOOL Wings .... *Parlophone* 6
2 [**2**] FLORAL DANCE Brighouse & Rastrick Band .... *Transatlantic* 7
3 [**3**] HOW DEEP IS YOUR LOVE Bee Gees .... *RSO* 10
4 [**4**] I WILL Ruby Winters .... *Creole* 8
5 [**5**] WHITE CHRISTMAS Bing Crosby .... *MCA* 4
6 **6** LOVE'S UNKIND Donna Summer .... *GTO* 5
7 **7** IT'S A HEARTACHE Bonnie Tyler .... *RCA* 5
8 **8** DADDY COOL Darts .... *Magnet* 9
9 **9** EGYPTIAN REGGAE J. Richman & the Modern Lovers .... *Beserkley* 8
10 [**10**] PUT YOUR LOVE IN ME Hot Chocolate .... *Rak* 5
11 **11** BELFAST Boney M .... *Atlantic* 9
12 **12** DANCIN' PARTY Showaddywaddy .... *Arista* 8
13 **13** LOVE OF MY LIFE Dooleys .... *GTO* 7
14 **14** MY WAY Elvis Presley .... *RCA* 4
15 [**15**] WATCHIN' THE DETECTIVE Elvis Costello .... *Stiff* 9
16 **16** MARY OF THE FOURTH FORM Boomtown Rats .... *Ensign* 6
17 **17** LET'S HAVE A QUIET NIGHT IN David Soul .... *Private Stock* 3
18 **18** DON'T IT MAKE MY BROWN EYES BLUE Crystal Gayle .... *United Artists* 8
19 **19** DANCE DANCE DANCE Chic .... *Atlantic* 5
20 **20** TURN TO STONE Electric Light Orchestra .... *Jet* 9
21 **21** WHO PAYS THE FERRY MAN Yannis Markopoulos .... *BBC* 3
22 **22** WE ARE THE CHAMPIONS Queen .... *EMI* 11
23 **23** AS TIME GOES BY Dooley Wilson .... *United Artists* 3
24 **24** ONLY WOMEN BLEED Julie Covington .... *Virgin* 4
25 **25** ROCKIN' ALL OVER THE WORLD Status Quo .... *Vertigo* 13
26 **26** I LOVE YOU Donna Summer .... *Casablanca* 4
27 **27** DON'T DILLY DALLY/WAITING AT THE CHURCH Muppets .... *Pye* 2
28 **28** JAMMING/PUNKY REGGAE PARTY Bob Marley & the Wailers .... *Island* 3
29 **29** REALLY FREE John Otway and Wild Willy Barrett .... *Polydor* 4
30 **30** GETTIN' READY FOR LOVE Diana Ross .... *Motown* 6
31 **31** RUN BACK Carl Douglas .... *Pye* 4
32 **32** LIVE IN TROUBLE Barron Knights .... *Epic* 9
33 [**33**] HOLLYWOOD Boz Scaggs .... *Epic* 3
34 **34** UPTOWN TOP RANKING Althia & Donna .... *Lightning* 2
35 **35** NAME OF THE GAME Abba .... *Epic* 11
36 [**36**] LITTLE GIRL The Banned .... *Harvest* 2
37 **37** SHE'S NOT THERE Santana .... *CBS* 10
38 **38** YES SIR I CAN BOOGIE Baccara .... *RCA* 14
39 [**39**] DESIREE Neil Diamond .... *CBS* 2
40 [**40**] I DON'T WANT TO LOSE YOUR LOVE Emotions .... *CBS* 2

■ *White Christmas* by Bing Crosby, released years before the British charts began, has its first hit run (31.12.77) ■ *As Time Goes By*, the song Dooley Wilson played again in 'Casablanca', is also a first time chart record (31.12.77) ■ Julie Covington sings Alice Cooper (31.12.77)■

1978

..........BONEY M. have a two-million seller, 'Rivers Of Babylon/Brown Girl In The Ring', and the most weeks on chart this year.......John Travolta and Olivia Newton-John spend a total of sixteen weeks at number one with their two duets from Grease for the best chart performance per release of any act ever....... the Bee Gees have three hits from *Saturday Night Fever*..........

January 1978

□ Highest position disc reached ● Act's first ever week on chart

WEEK ENDING 7 JANUARY 1978

(Top 30 compiled only)

LW	TW	Title	Artist	Label	Wks
1	[1]	MULL OF KINTYRE/GIRLS' SCHOOL	Wings	Parlophone	7
2	[2]	FLORAL DANCE	Brighouse & Rastrick Band	Transatlantic	8
3	[3]	HOW DEEP IS YOUR LOVE	Bee Gees	RSO	11
6	4	LOVE'S UNKIND	Donna Summer	GTO	6
4	5	I WILL	Ruby Winters	Creole	9
7	6	IT'S A HEARTACHE	Bonnie Tyler	RCA	6
8	7	DADDY COOL	Darts	Magnet	10
18	8	DON'T IT MAKE MY BROWN EYES BLUE	Crystal Gayle	United Artists	9
14	[9]	MY WAY	Elvis Presley	RCA	5
19	10	DANCE DANCE DANCE	Chic	Atlantic	6
21	[11]	WHO PAYS THE FERRY MAN	Yannis Markopoulos	BBC	4
11	12	BELFAST	Boney M	Atlantic	10
17	13	LET'S HAVE A QUIET NIGHT IN	David Soul	Private Stock	4
10	14	PUT YOUR LOVE IN ME	Hot Chocolate	Rak	6
12	15	DANCIN' PARTY	Showaddywaddy	Arista	9
5	16	WHITE CHRISTMAS	Bing Crosby	MCA	5
13	17	LOVE OF MY LIFE	Dooleys	GTO	8
34	18	UPTOWN TOP RANKING	Althia & Donna	Lightning	3
24	19	ONLY WOMEN BLEED	Julie Covington	Virgin	5
25	20	ROCKIN' ALL OVER THE WORLD	Status Quo	Vertigo	14
16	21	MARY OF THE FOURTH FORM	Boomtown Rats	Ensign	7
-	22	NATIVE NEW YORKER	Odyssey ●	RCA	1
28	23	JAMMING/PUNKY REGGAE PARTY	Bob Marley & the Wailers	Island	4
9	24	EGYPTIAN REGGAE	J. Richman & the Modern Lovers	Beserkley	9
20	25	TURN TO STONE	Electric Light Orchestra	Jet	10
31	26	RUN BACK	Carl Douglas	Pye	5
29	27	REALLY FREE	John Otway and Wild Willy Barrett	Polydor	5
-	28	FLORAL DANCE	Terry Wogan ●	Philips	1
35	29	NAME OF THE GAME	Abba	Epic	12
26	30	I LOVE YOU	Donna Summer	Casablanca	5

WEEK ENDING 14 JANUARY 1978

LW	TW	Title	Artist	Label	Wks
1	[1]	MULL OF KINTYRE/GIRLS' SCHOOL	Wings	Parlophone	8
2	[2]	FLORAL DANCE	Brighouse & Rastrick Band	Transatlantic	9
4	[3]	LOVE'S UNKIND	Donna Summer	GTO	7
6	[4]	IT'S A HEARTACHE	Bonnie Tyler	RCA	7
8	[5]	DON'T IT MAKE MY BROWN EYES BLUE	Crystal Gayle	United Artists	10
10	[6]	DANCE DANCE DANCE	Chic	Atlantic	7
3	7	HOW DEEP IS YOUR LOVE	Bee Gees	RSO	12
13	[8]	LET'S HAVE A QUIET NIGHT IN	David Soul	Private Stock	5
5	9	I WILL	Ruby Winters	Creole	10
30	[10]	I LOVE YOU	Donna Summer	Casablanca	6
11	[11]	WHO PAYS THE FERRY MAN	Yannis Markopoulos	BBC	5
7	12	DADDY COOL	Darts	Magnet	11
18	13	UPTOWN TOP RANKING	Althia & Donna	Lightning	4
19	14	ONLY WOMEN BLEED	Julie Covington	Virgin	6
-	[15]	AS TIME GOES BY	Dooley Wilson ●	United Artists	4
9	16	MY WAY	Elvis Presley	RCA	6
23	17	JAMMING/PUNKY REGGAE PARTY	Bob Marley & the Wailers	Island	5
14	18	PUT YOUR LOVE IN ME	Hot Chocolate	Rak	7
-	[19]	DON'T DILLY DALLY/WAITING AT THE CHURCH	Muppets	Pye	3
22	20	NATIVE NEW YORKER	Odyssey	RCA	2
12	21	BELFAST	Boney M	Atlantic	11
-	22	ON FIRE	T. Connection	TK	1
17	23	LOVE OF MY LIFE	Dooleys	GTO	9
16	24	WHITE CHRISTMAS	Bing Crosby	MCA	6
26	[25]	RUN BACK	Carl Douglas	Pye	6
15	26	DANCIN' PARTY	Showaddywaddy	Arista	10
24	27	EGYPTIAN REGGAE	J. Richman & the Modern Lovers	Beserkley	10
28	28	FLORAL DANCE	Terry Wogan	Philips	2
25	29	TURN TO STONE	Electric Light Orchestra	Jet	11
-	30	LOVELY DAY	Bill Withers	CBS	1
-	31	IF I HAD WORDS	Scott Fitzgerald and Yvonne Keely ●	Pepper	1
27	32	REALLY FREE	John Otway and Wild Willy Barrett	Polydor	6
-	33	GALAXY	War	MCA	1
-	34	THE GROOVE LINE	Heatwave	GTO	1
-	35	WATCHIN' THE DETECTIVES	Elvis Costello	Stiff	10
21	36	MARY OF THE FOURTH FORM	Boomtown Rats	Ensign	8
20	37	ROCKIN' ALL OVER THE WORLD	Status Quo	Vertigo	15
-	38	WHO'S GONNA LOVE ME	Imperials ●	Power Exchange	1
-	[39]	BENNY'S THEME	Paul Henry and Mayson Glen Orch. ●	Pye	1
-	[40]	I DON'T WANT TO LOSE YOUR LOVE	Emotions	CBS	3

WEEK ENDING 21 JANUARY 1978

LW	TW	Title	Artist	Label	Wks
1	[1]	MULL OF KINTYRE/GIRLS' SCHOOL	Wings	Parlophone	9
13	2	UPTOWN TOP RANKING	Althia & Donna	Lightning	5
3	[3]	LOVE'S UNKIND	Donna Summer	GTO	8
4	[4]	IT'S A HEARTACHE	Bonnie Tyler	RCA	8
2	5	FLORAL DANCE	Brighouse & Rastrick Band	Transatlantic	10
5	6	DON'T IT MAKE MY BROWN EYES BLUE	Crystal Gayle	United Artists	11
7	7	HOW DEEP IS YOUR LOVE	Bee Gees	RSO	13
20	8	NATIVE NEW YORKER	Odyssey	RCA	3
6	9	DANCE DANCE DANCE	Chic	Atlantic	8
8	10	LET'S HAVE A QUIET NIGHT IN	David Soul	Private Stock	6
17	11	JAMMING/PUNKY REGGAE PARTY	Bob Marley & the Wailers	Island	6
14	[12]	ONLY WOMEN BLEED	Julie Covington	Virgin	7
9	13	I WILL	Ruby Winters	Creole	11
-	14	FIGARO	Brotherhood Of Man	Pye	1
11	15	WHO PAYS THE FERRY MAN	Yannis Markopoulos	BBC	6
10	16	I LOVE YOU	Donna Summer	Casablanca	7
30	17	LOVELY DAY	Bill Withers	CBS	2
12	18	DADDY COOL	Darts	Magnet	12
15	19	AS TIME GOES BY	Dooley Wilson	United Artists	5
16	20	MY WAY	Elvis Presley	RCA	7
34	21	THE GROOVE LINE	Heatwave	GTO	2
28	22	FLORAL DANCE	Terry Wogan	Philips	3
18	23	PUT YOUR LOVE IN ME	Hot Chocolate	Rak	8
22	24	ON FIRE	T. Connection	TK	2
19	25	DON'T DILLY DALLY/WAITING AT THE CHURCH	Muppets	Pye	4
33	26	GALAXY	War	MCA	2
31	27	IF I HAD WORDS	Scott Fitzgerald and Yvonne Keely	Pepper	2
27	28	EGYPTIAN REGGAE	J. Richman & the Modern Lovers	Beserkley	11
38	29	WHO'S GONNA LOVE ME	Imperials	Power Exchange	2
21	30	BELFAST	Boney M	Atlantic	12
23	31	LOVE OF MY LIFE	Dooleys	GTO	10
25	32	RUN BACK	Carl Douglas	Pye	7
-	33	SORRY I'M A LADY	Baccara	RCA	1
-	34	WISHING ON A STAR	Rose Royce	Warner Brothers	1
-	35	COCOMOTION	El Coco ●	Pye	1
-	36	HEARTSONG	Gordon Giltrap ●	Electric	1
-	37	MORNING OF OUR LIVES	Modern Lovers ●	Beserkley	1
-	38	HOLLYWOOD	Boz Scaggs	Epic	4
-	[39]	LAY DOWN SALLY	Eric Clapton	RSO	1
-	[40]	JAM JAM JAM	People's Choice	Philadelphia	1

WEEK ENDING 28 JANUARY 1978

LW	TW	Title	Artist	Label	Wks
1	[1]	MULL OF KINTYRE/GIRLS' SCHOOL	Wings	Parlophone	10
2	2	UPTOWN TOP RANKING	Althia & Donna	Lightning	6
3	[3]	LOVE'S UNKIND	Donna Summer	GTO	9
14	4	FIGARO	Brotherhood Of Man	Pye	2
8	[5]	NATIVE NEW YORKER	Odyssey	RCA	4
4	6	IT'S A HEARTACHE	Bonnie Tyler	RCA	9
6	7	DON'T IT MAKE MY BROWN EYES BLUE	Crystal Gayle	United Artists	12
17	8	LOVELY DAY	Bill Withers	CBS	3
9	9	DANCE DANCE DANCE	Chic	Atlantic	9

In these weeks ■ *My Way* is Elvis Presley's first posthumous Top Ten hit since *Way Down* went to number one shortly after his death (07.01.78) ■ Having sung along to the instrumental *Floral Dance* on his radio show to good listener response, Terry Wogan takes his vocal version into the chart (07.01.78) ■ *Mull Of Kintyre/Girl's School* ties *Diana* and *Bohemian Rhapsody* with nine weeks at number one (28.01.78)■

27 10 IF I HAD WORDS Scott Fitzgerald and Yvonne Keely .... *Pepper* 3
11 11 JAMMING/PUNKY REGGAE PARTY Bob Marley & the Wailers .... *Island* 7
5 12 FLORAL DANCE Brighouse & Rastrick Band .... *Transatlantic* 11
10 13 LET'S HAVE A QUIET NIGHT IN David Soul .... *Private Stock* 7
26 14 GALAXY War .... *MCA* 3
12 15 ONLY WOMEN BLEED Julie Covington .... *Virgin* 8
24 16 ON FIRE T. Connection .... *TK* 3
21 17 THE GROOVE LINE Heatwave .... *GTO* 3
16 18 I LOVE YOU Donna Summer .... *Casablanca* 8
15 19 WHO PAYS THE FERRY MAN Yannis Markopoulos .... *BBC* 7
19 20 AS TIME GOES BY Dooley Wilson .... *United Artists* 6
22 21 FLORAL DANCE Terry Wogan .... *Philips* 4
33 22 SORRY I'M A LADY Baccara .... *RCA* 2
29 23 WHO'S GONNA LOVE ME Imperials .... *Power Exchange* 3
7 24 HOW DEEP IS YOUR LOVE Bee Gees .... *RSO* 14
25 25 DON'T DILLY DALLY/WAITING AT THE CHURCH Muppets .... *Pye* 5
13 26 I WILL Ruby Winters .... *Creole* 12
32 27 RUN BACK Carl Douglas .... *Pye* 8
34 28 WISHING ON A STAR Rose Royce .... *Warner Brothers* 2
\- 29 RICH KIDS Rich Kids ● .... *EMI* 1
36 30 HEARTSONG Gordon Giltrap .... *Electric* 2
35 31 COCOMOTION El Coco .... *Pye* 2
18 32 DADDY COOL Darts .... *Magnet* 13
37 33 MORNING OF OUR LIVES Modern Lovers .... *Beserkley* 2
\- 34 DRUMMER MAN Tonight ● .... *TDS* 1
\- 35 HOT LEGS/I WAS ONLY JOKING Rod Stewart .... *Riva* 1
\- 36 QUIT THIS TOWN Eddie & the Hot Rods .... *Island* 1
20 37 MY WAY Elvis Presley .... *RCA* 8
\- 38 FOR A FEW DOLLARS MORE Smokie .... *RAK* 1
\- 39 MR. BLUE SKY Electric Light Orchestra .... *Jet* 1
\- 40 BEAUTY AND THE BEAST David Bowie .... *RCA* 1

LW TW *WEEK ENDING* **4 FEBRUARY 1978** **Wks**

2 1 UPTOWN TOP RANKING Althia & Donna .... *Lightning* 7
1 2 MULL OF KINTYRE/GIRLS' SCHOOL Wings .... *Parlophone* 11
4 3 FIGARO Brotherhood Of Man .... *Pye* 3
10 4 IF I HAD WORDS Scott Fitzgerald and Yvonne Keely .... *Pepper* 4
5 5 NATIVE NEW YORKER Odyssey .... *RCA* 5
3 6 LOVE'S UNKIND Donna Summer .... *GTO* 10
8 7 LOVELY DAY Bill Withers .... *CBS* 4
6 8 IT'S A HEARTACHE Bonnie Tyler .... *RCA* 10
11 9 JAMMING/PUNKY REGGAE PARTY Bob Marley & the Wailers .... *Island* 8
\- 10 TAKE A CHANCE ON ME Abba .... *Epic* 1
9 11 DANCE DANCE DANCE Chic .... *Atlantic* 10
17 12 THE GROOVE LINE Heatwave .... *GTO* 4
22 13 SORRY I'M A LADY Baccara .... *RCA* 3
7 14 DON'T IT MAKE MY BROWN EYES BLUE Crystal Gayle .... *United Artists* 13
14 15 GALAXY War .... *MCA* 4
39 16 MR. BLUE SKY Electric Light Orchestra .... *Jet* 2
23 17 WHO'S GONNA LOVE ME Imperials .... *Power Exchange* 4
35 18 HOT LEGS/I WAS ONLY JOKING Rod Stewart .... *Riva* 2
13 19 LET'S HAVE A QUIET NIGHT IN David Soul .... *Private Stock* 8
\- 20 COME BACK MY LOVE Darts .... *Magnet* 1
\- 21 LOVE IS LIKE OXYGEN Sweet .... *Polydor* 1
15 22 ONLY WOMEN BLEED Julie Covington .... *Virgin* 9
16 23 ON FIRE T. Connection .... *TK* 4
29 24 RICH KIDS Rich Kids .... *EMI* 2
12 25 FLORAL DANCE Brighouse & Rastrick Band .... *Transatlantic* 12
28 26 WISHING ON A STAR Rose Royce .... *Warner Brothers* 3
\- 27 THEME FROM WHICH WAY IS UP Stargard ● .... *MCA* 1
38 28 FOR A FEW DOLLARS MORE Smokie .... *RAK* 2
33 29 MORNING OF OUR LIVES Modern Lovers .... *Beserkley* 3
19 30 WHO PAYS THE FERRY MAN Yannis Markopoulos .... *BBC* 8
24 31 HOW DEEP IS YOUR LOVE Bee Gees .... *RSO* 15
34 32 DRUMMER MAN Tonight .... *TDS* 2
30 33 HEARTSONG Gordon Giltrap .... *Electric* 3
\- 34 STAYIN' ALIVE Bee Gees .... *RSO* 1
\- 35 BLUE BAYOU Linda Ronstadt .... *Asylum* 1
21 36 FLORAL DANCE Terry Wogan .... *Philips* 5

February 1978

□ Highest position disc reached ● Act's first ever week on chart

27 37 RUN BACK Carl Douglas .... *Pye* 9
36 38 QUIT THIS TOWN Eddie & the Hot Rods .... *Island* 2
40 39 BEAUTY AND THE BEAST David Bowie .... *RCA* 2
18 40 I LOVE YOU Donna Summer .... *Casablanca* 9

LW TW *WEEK ENDING* **11 FEBRUARY 1978** **Wks**

3 1 FIGARO Brotherhood Of Man .... *Pye* 4
10 2 TAKE A CHANCE ON ME Abba .... *Epic* 2
1 3 UPTOWN TOP RANKING Althia & Donna .... *Lightning* 8
4 4 IF I HAD WORDS Scott Fitzgerald and Yvonne Keely .... *Pepper* 5
2 5 MULL OF KINTYRE/GIRLS SCHOOL Wings .... *Parlophone* 12
5 6 NATIVE NEW YORKER Odyssey .... *RCA* 6
7 7 LOVELY DAY Bill Withers .... *CBS* 5
13 8 SORRY I'M A LADY Baccara .... *RCA* 4
6 9 LOVE'S UNKIND Donna Summer .... *GTO* 11
9 10 JAMMING/PUNKY REGGAE PARTY Bob Marley & the Wailers .... *Island* 9
26 11 WISHING ON A STAR Rose Royce .... *Warner Brothers* 4
20 12 COME BACK MY LOVE Darts .... *Magnet* 2
12 13 THE GROOVE LINE Heatwave .... *GTO* 5
18 14 HOT LEGS/I WAS ONLY JOKING Rod Stewart .... *Riva* 3
32 15 DRUMMER MAN Tonight .... *TDS* 3
16 16 MR. BLUE SKY Electric Light Orchestra .... *Jet* 3
15 17 GALAXY War .... *MCA* 5
21 18 LOVE IS LIKE OXYGEN Sweet .... *Polydor* 2
11 19 DANCE DANCE DANCE Chic .... *Atlantic* 11
17 20 WHO'S GONNA LOVE ME Imperials .... *Power Exchange* 5
33 21 HEARTSONG Gordon Giltrap .... *Electric* 4
\- 22 FIVE MINUTES Stranglers .... *United Artists* 1
23 23 ON FIRE T. Connection .... *TK* 5
24 24 RICH KIDS Rich Kids .... *EMI* 3
28 25 FOR A FEW DOLLARS MORE Smokie .... *RAK* 3
\- 26 JUST ONE MORE NIGHT Yellow Dog ● .... *Virgin* 1
8 27 IT'S A HEARTACHE Bonnie Tyler .... *RCA* 11
14 28 DON'T IT MAKE MY BROWN EYES BLUE Crystal Gayle .... *United Artists* 14
27 29 THEME FROM WHICH WAY IS UP Stargard .... *MCA* 2
\- 30 JUST THE WAY YOU ARE Billy Joel ● .... *CBS* 1
34 31 STAYIN' ALIVE Bee Gees .... *RSO* 2
\- 32 WORDS Rita Coolidge .... *A&M* 1
\- 33 EMOTIONS Samantha Sang ● .... *Private Stock* 1
22 34 ONLY WOMEN BLEED Julie Covington .... *Virgin* 10
35 35 BLUE BAYOU Linda Ronstadt .... *Asylum* 2
\- 36 CLOSER TO THE HEART Rush ● .... *Mercury* 1
19 37 LET'S HAVE A QUIET NIGHT IN David Soul .... *Private Stock* 9
\- 38 NO TIME TO BE 21 Adverts .... *Bright* 1
29 39 MORNING OF OUR LIVES Modern Lovers .... *Beserkley* 4
\- 40 NERVOUS WRECK Radio Stars ● .... *Chiswick* 1

LW TW *WEEK ENDING* **18 FEBRUARY 1978** **Wks**

2 1 TAKE A CHANCE ON ME Abba .... *Epic* 3
1 2 FIGARO Brotherhood Of Man .... *Pye* 5
4 3 IF I HAD WORDS Scott Fitzgerald and Yvonne Keely .... *Pepper* 6
12 4 COME BACK MY LOVE Darts .... *Magnet* 3
14 5 HOT LEGS/I WAS ONLY JOKING Rod Stewart .... *Riva* 4
11 6 WISHING ON A STAR Rose Royce .... *Warner Brothers* 5
3 7 UPTOWN TOP RANKING Althia & Donna .... *Lightning* 9
16 8 MR. BLUE SKY Electric Light Orchestra .... *Jet* 4
18 9 LOVE IS LIKE OXYGEN Sweet .... *Polydor* 3
8 10 SORRY I'M A LADY Baccara .... *RCA* 5
7 11 LOVELY DAY Bill Withers .... *CBS* 6
5 12 MULL OF KINTYRE/GIRLS SCHOOL Wings .... *Parlophone* 13
6 13 NATIVE NEW YORKER Odyssey .... *RCA* 7
13 14 THE GROOVE LINE Heatwave .... *GTO* 6
15 15 DRUMMER MAN Tonight .... *TDS* 4
26 16 JUST ONE MORE NIGHT Yellow Dog .... *Virgin* 2

■Althia and Donna become the first Jamaican one hit wonders (04.02.78) ■ *Power Pop*, touted as the next trend after punk, fails as the Rich Kids, including former Sex Pistol Glen Matlock and ex-Slik star Midge Ure, peak at 24 with their eponymous debut (11.02.78)■

February 1978

☐ Highest position disc reached ● Act's first ever week on chart

LW	TW	Title	Artist	Label	Wks
25	[17]	FOR A FEW DOLLARS MORE	Smokie	RAK	4
31	18	STAYIN' ALIVE	Bee Gees	RSO	3
29	[19]	THEME FROM WHICH WAY IS UP	Stargard	MCA	3
33	20	EMOTIONS	Samantha Sang	Private Stock	2
22	21	FIVE MINUTES	Stranglers	United Artists	2
10	22	JAMMING/PUNKY REGGAE PARTY	Bob Marley & the Wailers	Island	10
20	23	WHO'S GONNA LOVE ME	Imperials	Power Exchange	6
21	24	HEARTSONG	Gordon Giltrap	Electric	5
-	25	ALL RIGHT NOW	Free	Island	1
30	26	JUST THE WAY YOU ARE	Billy Joel	CBS	2
-	27	WUTHERING HEIGHTS	Kate Bush ●	EMI	1
32	28	WORDS	Rita Coolidge	A&M	2
9	29	LOVE'S UNKIND	Donna Summer	GTO	12
-	30	DON'T TAKE NO FOR AN ANSWER	Tom Robinson Band	EMI	1
-	31	I CAN'T STAND THE RAIN	Eruption ●	Atlantic	1
-	32	FANTASY	Earth Wind & Fire	CBS	1
24	33	RICH KIDS	Rich Kids	EMI	4
38	34	NO TIME TO BE 21	Adverts	Bright	2
17	35	GALAXY	War	MCA	6
27	36	IT'S A HEARTACHE	Bonnie Tyler	RCA	12
35	37	BLUE BAYOU	Linda Ronstadt	Asylum	3
-	38	EVEN THOUGH YOU'RE GONE	Jacksons	Epic	1
40	[39]	NERVOUS WRECK	Radio Stars	Chiswick	2
-	[40]	SWEET SWEET SMILE	Carpenters	A&M	1

WEEK ENDING 25 FEBRUARY 1978

LW	TW	Title	Artist	Label	Wks
1	[1]	TAKE A CHANCE ON ME	Abba	Epic	4
2	2	FIGARO	Brotherhood Of Man	Pye	6
4	3	COME BACK MY LOVE	Darts	Magnet	4
6	4	WISHING ON A STAR	Rose Royce	Warner Brothers	6
3	5	IF I HAD WORDS	Scott Fitzgerald and Yvonne Keely	Pepper	7
8	[6]	MR. BLUE SKY	Electric Light Orchestra	Jet	5
5	7	HOT LEGS/I WAS ONLY JOKING	Rod Stewart	Riva	5
10	[8]	SORRY I'M A LADY	Baccara	RCA	6
16	9	JUST ONE MORE NIGHT	Yellow Dog	Virgin	3
9	10	LOVE IS LIKE OXYGEN	Sweet	Polydor	4
21	[11]	FIVE MINUTES	Stranglers	United Artists	3
18	12	STAYIN' ALIVE	Bee Gees	RSO	4
27	13	WUTHERING HEIGHTS	Kate Bush	EMI	2
15	[14]	DRUMMER MAN	Tonight	TDS	5
11	15	LOVELY DAY	Bill Withers	CBS	7
13	16	NATIVE NEW YORKER	Odyssey	RCA	8
7	17	UPTOWN TOP RANKING	Althia & Donna	Lightning	10
25	18	ALL RIGHT NOW	Free	Island	2
17	19	FOR A FEW DOLLARS MORE	Smokie	RAK	5
14	20	THE GROOVE LINE	Heatwave	GTO	7
19	21	THEME FROM WHICH WAY IS UP	Stargard	MCA	4
20	22	EMOTIONS	Samantha Sang	Private Stock	3
12	23	MULL OF KINTYRE/GIRLS SCHOOL	Wings	Parlophone	14
30	24	DON'T TAKE NO FOR AN ANSWER	Tom Robinson Band	EMI	2
26	25	JUST THE WAY YOU ARE	Billy Joel	CBS	3
32	26	FANTASY	Earth Wind & Fire	CBS	2
24	27	HEARTSONG	Gordon Giltrap	Electric	6
-	28	BAKER STREET	Gerry Rafferty ●	United Artists	1
31	29	I CAN'T STAND THE RAIN	Eruption	Atlantic	2
22	30	JAMMING/PUNKY REGGAE PARTY	Bob Marley & the Wailers	Island	11
38	[31]	EVEN THOUGH YOU'RE GONE	Jacksons	Epic	2
35	32	GALAXY	War	MCA	7
-	33	DENIS	Blondie	Chrysalis	1
33	34	RICH KIDS	Rich Kids	EMI	5
-	35	IS THIS LOVE	Bob Marley & the Wailers	Island	1
28	36	WORDS	Rita Coolidge	A&M	3
-	[37]	WHAT DO I GET?	Buzzcocks ●	United Artists	1
29	38	LOVE'S UNKIND	Donna Summer	GTO	13
-	39	SPREAD YOUR WINGS	Queen	EMI	1
-	40	RUMOUR HAS IT	Donna Summer	Casablanca	1

WEEK ENDING 4 MARCH 1978

LW	TW	Title	Artist	Label	Wks
1	[1]	TAKE A CHANCE ON ME	Abba	Epic	5
3	[2]	COME BACK MY LOVE	Darts	Magnet	5
4	[3]	WISHING ON A STAR	Rose Royce	Warner Brothers	7
12	[4]	STAYIN' ALIVE	Bee Gees	RSO	5
13	5	WUTHERING HEIGHTS	Kate Bush	EMI	3
2	6	FIGARO	Brotherhood Of Man	Pye	7
6	7	MR. BLUE SKY	Electric Light Orchestra	Jet	6
9	[8]	JUST ONE MORE NIGHT	Yellow Dog	Virgin	4
10	[9]	LOVE IS LIKE OXYGEN	Sweet	Polydor	5
5	10	IF I HAD WORDS	Scott Fitzgerald and Yvonne Keely	Pepper	8
33	11	DENIS	Blondie	Chrysalis	2
18	12	ALL RIGHT NOW	Free	Island	3
7	13	HOT LEGS/I WAS ONLY JOKING	Rod Stewart	Riva	6
28	14	BAKER STREET	Gerry Rafferty	United Artists	2
29	15	I CAN'T STAND THE RAIN	Eruption	Atlantic	3
22	16	EMOTIONS	Samantha Sang	Private Stock	4
35	17	IS THIS LOVE	Bob Marley & the Wailers	Island	2
24	[18]	DON'T TAKE NO FOR AN ANSWER	Tom Robinson Band	EMI	3
25	[19]	JUST THE WAY YOU ARE	Billy Joel	CBS	4
8	20	SORRY I'M A LADY	Baccara	RCA	7
26	21	FANTASY	Earth Wind & Fire	CBS	3
14	22	DRUMMER MAN	Tonight	TDS	6
11	23	FIVE MINUTES	Stranglers	United Artists	4
21	24	THEME FROM WHICH WAY IS UP	Stargard	MCA	5
36	[25]	WORDS	Rita Coolidge	A&M	4
19	26	FOR A FEW DOLLARS MORE	Smokie	RAK	6
-	27	LILAC WINE	Elkie Brooks	A&M	1
-	28	WE'VE GOT THE WHOLE WORLD	Nottingham Forest and Paper Lace ●	WB	1
15	29	LOVELY DAY	Bill Withers	CBS	8
40	30	RUMOUR HAS IT	Donna Summer	Casablanca	2
16	31	NATIVE NEW YORKER	Odyssey	RCA	9
-	32	ALLY'S TARTAN ARMY	Andy Cameron ●	Klub	1
23	33	MULL OF KINTYRE/GIRLS SCHOOL	Wings	Parlophone	15
20	34	THE GROOVE LINE	Heatwave	GTO	8
-	[35]	CLASH CITY ROCKERS	Clash	CBS	1
-	36	EVERY 1'S A WINNER	Hot Chocolate	RAK	1
-	37	MATCHSTALK MEN & MATCHSTALK CATS & DOGS	Brian & Michael ●	Pye	1
17	38	UPTOWN TOP RANKING	Althia & Donna	Lightning	11
-	39	BABY COME BACK	Player ●	RSO	1
39	40	SPREAD YOUR WINGS	Queen	EMI	2

WEEK ENDING 11 MARCH 1978

LW	TW	Title	Artist	Label	Wks
5	[1]	WUTHERING HEIGHTS	Kate Bush	EMI	4
1	2	TAKE A CHANCE ON ME	Abba	Epic	6
2	3	COME BACK MY LOVE	Darts	Magnet	6
3	4	WISHING ON A STAR	Rose Royce	Warner Brothers	8
11	5	DENIS	Blondie	Chrysalis	3
4	6	STAYIN' ALIVE	Bee Gees	RSO	6
15	7	I CAN'T STAND THE RAIN	Eruption	Atlantic	4
14	8	BAKER STREET	Gerry Rafferty	United Artists	3
7	9	MR. BLUE SKY	Electric Light Orchestra	Jet	7
8	10	JUST ONE MORE NIGHT	Yellow Dog	Virgin	5
12	[11]	ALL RIGHT NOW	Free	Island	4
17	12	IS THIS LOVE	Bob Marley & the Wailers	Island	3
6	13	FIGARO	Brotherhood Of Man	Pye	8
16	14	EMOTIONS	Samantha Sang	Private Stock	5
21	15	FANTASY	Earth Wind & Fire	CBS	4
9	16	LOVE IS LIKE OXYGEN	Sweet	Polydor	6
10	17	IF I HAD WORDS	Scott Fitzgerald and Yvonne Keely	Pepper	9
37	18	MATCHSTALK MEN & MATCHSTALK CATS & DOGS	Brian & Michael	Pye	2
23	19	FIVE MINUTES	Stranglers	United Artists	5
13	20	HOT LEGS/I WAS ONLY JOKING	Rod Stewart	Riva	7
32	21	ALLY'S TARTAN ARMY	Andy Cameron	Klub	2
27	22	LILAC WINE	Elkie Brooks	A&M	2
22	23	DRUMMER MAN	Tonight	TDS	7
28	[24]	WE'VE GOT THE WHOLE WORLD	Nottingham Forest and Paper Lace	WB	2
19	25	JUST THE WAY YOU ARE	Billy Joel	CBS	5

In these weeks ■ One of the outstanding chart careers of the seventies and eighties begins as Kate Bush debuts with *Wuthering Heights* (18.02.78) ■ *All Right Now* makes its third but not final Top 40 appearance, this time as part of the 'Free' EP (18.02.80) ■ Darts begin their historic and odd feat of three consecutive number twos without ever getting all the way to number one (11.03.78)■

□ Highest position disc reached ● Act's first ever week on chart

LW	TW	Title	Artist	Label	Wks
18	26	DON'T TAKE NO FOR AN ANSWER	Tom Robinson Band	*EMI*	4
36	27	EVERY 1'S A WINNER	Hot Chocolate	*RAK*	2
30	28	RUMOUR HAS IT	Donna Summer	*Casablanca*	3
20	29	SORRY I'M A LADY	Baccara	*RCA*	8
24	30	THEME FROM WHICH WAY IS UP	Stargard	*MCA*	6
-	31	WHENEVER YOU WANT MY LOVE	Real Thing	*Pye*	1
39	32	BABY COME BACK	Player	*RSO*	2
-	33	I LOVE THE SOUND OF BREAKING GLASS	Nick Lowe ●	*Radar*	1
40	34	SPREAD YOUR WINGS	Queen	*EMI*	3
-	35	WALK IN LOVE	Manhattan Transfer	*Atlantic*	1
25	36	WORDS	Rita Coolidge	*A&M*	5
35	37	CLASH CITY ROCKERS	Clash	*CBS*	2
-	38	NEWS OF THE WORLD	Jam	*Polydor*	1
-	39	SOMETIMES WHEN WE TOUCH	Dan Hill ●	*20th Century*	1
33	40	MULL OF KINTYRE/GIRLS SCHOOL	Wings	*Parlophone*	16

WEEK ENDING 18 MARCH 1978

LW	TW	Title	Artist	Label	Wks
1	1	WUTHERING HEIGHTS	Kate Bush	*EMI*	5
2	2	TAKE A CHANCE ON ME	Abba	*Epic*	7
5	3	DENIS	Blondie	*Chrysalis*	4
3	4	COME BACK MY LOVE	Darts	*Magnet*	7
4	5	WISHING ON A STAR	Rose Royce	*Warner Brothers*	9
8	6	BAKER STREET	Gerry Rafferty	*United Artists*	4
7	7	I CAN'T STAND THE RAIN	Eruption	*Atlantic*	5
6	8	STAYIN' ALIVE	Bee Gees	*RSO*	7
9	9	MR. BLUE SKY	Electric Light Orchestra	*Jet*	8
18	10	MATCHSTALK MEN & MATCHSTALK CATS & DOGS	Brian & Michael	*Pye*	3
12	11	IS THIS LOVE	Bob Marley & the Wailers	*Island*	4
14	12	EMOTIONS	Samantha Sang	*Private Stock*	6
21	13	ALLY'S TARTAN ARMY	Andy Cameron	*Klub*	3
15	14	FANTASY	Earth Wind & Fire	*CBS*	5
10	15	JUST ONE MORE NIGHT	Yellow Dog	*Virgin*	6
22	16	LILAC WINE	Elkie Brooks	*A&M*	3
11	17	ALL RIGHT NOW	Free	*Island*	5
13	18	FIGARO	Brotherhood Of Man	*Pye*	9
28	19	RUMOUR HAS IT	Donna Summer	*Casablanca*	4
27	20	EVERY 1'S A WINNER	Hot Chocolate	*RAK*	3
33	21	I LOVE THE SOUND OF BREAKING GLASS	Nick Lowe	*Radar*	2
25	22	JUST THE WAY YOU ARE	Billy Joel	*CBS*	6
16	23	LOVE IS LIKE OXYGEN	Sweet	*Polydor*	7
26	24	DON'T TAKE NO FOR AN ANSWER	Tom Robinson Band	*EMI*	5
17	25	IF I HAD WORDS	Scott Fitzgerald and Yvonne Keely	*Pepper*	10
35	26	WALK IN LOVE	Manhattan Transfer	*Atlantic*	2
19	27	FIVE MINUTES	Stranglers	*United Artists*	6
36	28	WORDS	Rita Coolidge	*A&M*	6
31	29	WHENEVER YOU WANT MY LOVE	Real Thing	*Pye*	2
-	30	FOLLOW YOU FOLLOW ME	Genesis	*Charisma*	1
-	31	(I DON'T WANNA GO TO) CHELSEA	Elvis Costello and Attraction	*Radar*	1
20	32	HOT LEGS/I WAS ONLY JOKING	Rod Stewart	*Riva*	8
32	33	BABY COME BACK	Player	*RSO*	3
-	34	WHAT'S YOUR NAME WHAT'S YOURR NUMBER	Andrea True Connection	*Buddah*	1
38	35	NEWS OF THE WORLD	Jam	*Polydor*	2
24	36	WE'VE GOT THE WHOLE WORLD	Nottingham Forest and Paper Lace	*WB*	3
39	37	SOMETIMES WHEN WE TOUCH	Dan Hill	*20th Century*	2
37	38	CLASH CITY ROCKERS	Clash	*CBS*	3
23	39	DRUMMER MAN	Tonight	*TDS*	8
34	40	SPREAD YOUR WINGS	Queen	*EMI*	4

WEEK ENDING 25 MARCH 1978

LW	TW	Title	Artist	Label	Wks
1	1	WUTHERING HEIGHTS	Kate Bush	*EMI*	6
3	2	DENIS	Blondie	*Chrysalis*	5
10	3	MATCHSTALK MEN & MATCHSTALK CATS & DOGS	Brian & Michael	*Pye*	4
6	4	BAKER STREET	Gerry Rafferty	*United Artists*	5
7	5	I CAN'T STAND THE RAIN	Eruption	*Atlantic*	6
5	6	WISHING ON A STAR	Rose Royce	*Warner Brothers*	10
4	7	COME BACK MY LOVE	Darts	*Magnet*	8
2	8	TAKE A CHANCE ON ME	Abba	*Epic*	8
8	9	STAYIN' ALIVE	Bee Gees	*RSO*	8
21	10	I LOVE THE SOUND OF BREAKING GLASS	Nick Lowe	*Radar*	3
9	11	MR. BLUE SKY	Electric Light Orchestra	*Jet*	9
12	12	EMOTIONS	Samantha Sang	*Private Stock*	7
11	13	IS THIS LOVE	Bob Marley & the Wailers	*Island*	5
20	14	EVERY 1'S A WINNER	Hot Chocolate	*RAK*	4
14	15	FANTASY	Earth Wind & Fire	*CBS*	6
13	16	ALLY'S TARTAN ARMY	Andy Cameron	*Klub*	4
16	17	LILAC WINE	Elkie Brooks	*A&M*	4
29	18	WHENEVER YOU WANT MY LOVE	Real Thing	*Pye*	3
19	19	RUMOUR HAS IT	Donna Summer	*Casablanca*	5
-	20	IF YOU CAN'T GIVE ME LOVE	Suzi Quatro	*RAK*	1
15	21	JUST ONE MORE NIGHT	Yellow Dog	*Virgin*	7
30	22	FOLLOW YOU FOLLOW ME	Genesis	*Charisma*	2
17	23	ALL RIGHT NOW	Free	*Island*	6
26	24	WALK IN LOVE	Manhattan Transfer	*Atlantic*	3
-	25	I WONDER WHY	Showaddywaddy	*Arista*	1
31	26	(I DON'T WANNA GO TO) CHELSEA	Elvis Costello and Attraction	*Radar*	2
35	27	NEWS OF THE WORLD	Jam	*Polydor*	3
22	28	JUST THE WAY YOU ARE	Billy Joel	*CBS*	7
-	28	I'LL GO WHERE YOUR MUSIC TAKES ME	Tina Charles	*CBS*	1
37	30	SOMETIMES WHEN WE TOUCH	Dan Hill	*20th Century*	3
-	31	THE GHOST OF LOVE	Tavares	*Capitol*	1
23	32	LOVE IS LIKE OXYGEN	Sweet	*Polydor*	8
-	33	NEVER LET HER SLIP AWAY	Andrew Gold	*Asylum*	1
-	34	SINGIN' IN THE RAIN	Sheila and B. Devotion ●	*EMI*	1
27	35	FIVE MINUTES	Stranglers	*United Artists*	7
33	36	BABY COME BACK	Player	*RSO*	4
18	37	FIGARO	Brotherhood Of Man	*Pye*	10
-	38	TOO HOT TO TROT/ZOOM	Commodores	*Motown*	1
-	39	TOO MUCH TOO LITTLE TOO LATE	Johnny Mathis and Deniece Williams ●	*CBS*	1
36	40	WE'VE GOT THE WHOLE WORLD	Nottingham Forest and Paper Lace	*WB*	4

WEEK ENDING 1 APRIL 1978

LW	TW	Title	Artist	Label	Wks
1	1	WUTHERING HEIGHTS	Kate Bush	*EMI*	7
2	2	DENIS	Blondie	*Chrysalis*	6
4	3	BAKER STREET	Gerry Rafferty	*United Artists*	6
3	4	MATCHSTALK MEN & MATCHSTALK CATS & DOGS	Brian & Michael	*Pye*	5
5	5	I CAN'T STAND THE RAIN	Eruption	*Atlantic*	7
16	6	ALLY'S TARTAN ARMY	Andy Cameron	*Klub*	5
10	7	I LOVE THE SOUND OF BREAKING GLASS	Nick Lowe	*Radar*	4
7	8	COME BACK MY LOVE	Darts	*Magnet*	9
13	9	IS THIS LOVE	Bob Marley & the Wailers	*Island*	6
20	10	IF YOU CAN'T GIVE ME LOVE	Suzi Quatro	*RAK*	2
12	11	EMOTIONS	Samantha Sang	*Private Stock*	8
6	12	WISHING ON A STAR	Rose Royce	*Warner Brothers*	11
14	13	EVERY 1'S A WINNER	Hot Chocolate	*RAK*	5
25	14	I WONDER WHY	Showaddywaddy	*Arista*	2
8	15	TAKE A CHANCE ON ME	Abba	*Epic*	9
15	16	FANTASY	Earth Wind & Fire	*CBS*	7
26	17	(I DON'T WANNA GO TO) CHELSEA	Elvis Costello and Attraction	*Radar*	3
22	18	FOLLOW YOU FOLLOW ME	Genesis	*Charisma*	3
9	19	STAYIN' ALIVE	Bee Gees	*RSO*	9
24	20	WALK IN LOVE	Manhattan Transfer	*Atlantic*	4
18	21	WHENEVER YOU WANT MY LOVE	Real Thing	*Pye*	4
19	22	RUMOUR HAS IT	Donna Summer	*Casablanca*	6
11	23	MR. BLUE SKY	Electric Light Orchestra	*Jet*	10
17	24	LILAC WINE	Elkie Brooks	*A&M*	5
33	25	NEVER LET HER SLIP AWAY	Andrew Gold	*Asylum*	2
30	26	SOMETIMES WHEN WE TOUCH	Dan Hill	*20th Century*	4
39	27	TOO MUCH TOO LITTLE TOO LATE	Johnny Mathis and Deniece Williams	*CBS*	2
28	28	I'LL GO WHERE YOUR MUSIC TAKES ME	Tina Charles	*CBS*	2
31	29	THE GHOST OF LOVE	Tavares	*Capitol*	2

■Blondie nearly get a number one with their first hit, a gender-change version of Randy and the Rainbows' *Denise* (25.03.78) ■ Kate Bush becomes the first British female vocalist to spend four straight weeks at number one since Mary Hopkin in 1968 (01.04.78) ■ Nick Lowe, one of the multi talented music men of the late seventies and eighties, has his biggest solo hit (01.04.78)■

April 1978

☐ Highest position disc reached ● Act's first ever week on chart

LW	TW	Title / Artist	Label	Wks
-	30	MORE LIKE THE MOVIES Dr. Hook	Capitol	1
21	31	JUST ONE MORE NIGHT Yellow Dog	Virgin	8
34	32	SINGIN' IN THE RAIN Sheila and B. Devotion	EMI	2
23	33	ALL RIGHT NOW Free	Island	7
28	34	JUST THE WAY YOU ARE Billy Joel	CBS	8
-	35	AUTOMATIC LOVER Vibrators ●	Epic	1
36	36	BABY COME BACK Player	RSO	5
40	37	WE'VE GOT THE WHOLE WORLD Nottingham Forest and Paper Lace	WB	5
-	38	EVERYBODY DANCE Chic	Atlantic	1
35	39	FIVE MINUTES Stranglers	United Artists	8
27	40	NEWS OF THE WORLD Jam	Polydor	4

LW	TW	*WEEK ENDING* **8 APRIL 1978**		Wks
4	1	MATCHSTALK MEN & MATCHSTALK CATS & DOGS Brian & Michael	Pye	6
2	2	DENIS Blondie	Chrysalis	7
1	3	WUTHERING HEIGHTS Kate Bush	EMI	8
3	4	BAKER STREET Gerry Rafferty	United Artists	7
14	5	I WONDER WHY Showaddywaddy	Arista	3
10	6	IF YOU CAN'T GIVE ME LOVE Suzi Quatro	RAK	3
5	7	I CAN'T STAND THE RAIN Eruption	Atlantic	8
18	8	FOLLOW YOU FOLLOW ME Genesis	Charisma	4
6	9	ALLY'S TARTAN ARMY Andy Cameron	Klub	6
7	10	I LOVE THE SOUND OF BREAKING GLASS Nick Lowe	Radar	5
25	11	NEVER LET HER SLIP AWAY Andrew Gold	Asylum	3
13	12	EVERY 1'S A WINNER Hot Chocolate	RAK	6
-	13	WITH A LITTLE LUCK Wings	Parlophone	1
9	14	IS THIS LOVE Bob Marley & the Wailers	Island	7
11	15	EMOTIONS Samantha Sang	Private Stock	9
20	16	WALK IN LOVE Manhattan Transfer	Atlantic	5
8	17	COME BACK MY LOVE Darts	Magnet	10
26	18	SOMETIMES WHEN WE TOUCH Dan Hill	20th Century	5
15	19	TAKE A CHANCE ON ME Abba	Epic	10
27	20	TOO MUCH TOO LITTLE TOO LATE Johnny Mathis and Deniece Williams	CBS	3
17	21	(I DON'T WANNA GO TO) CHELSEA Elvis Costello and Attraction	Radar	4
16	22	FANTASY Earth Wind & Fire	CBS	8
30	23	MORE LIKE THE MOVIES Dr. Hook	Capitol	2
22	24	RUMOUR HAS IT Donna Summer	Casablanca	7
19	25	STAYIN' ALIVE Bee Gees	RSO	10
23	26	MR. BLUE SKY Electric Light Orchestra	Jet	11
12	27	WISHING ON A STAR Rose Royce	Warner Brothers	12
28	28	I'LL GO WHERE YOUR MUSIC TAKES ME Tina Charles	CBS	3
21	29	WHENEVER YOU WANT MY LOVE Real Thing	Pye	5
32	30	SINGIN' IN THE RAIN Sheila and B. Devotion	EMI	3
24	31	LILAC WINE Elkie Brooks	A&M	6
29	32	THE GHOST OF LOVE Tavares	Capitol	3
38	33	EVERYBODY DANCE Chic	Atlantic	2
40	34	NEWS OF THE WORLD Jam	Polydor	5
-	35	IT TAKES TWO TO TANGO Richard Myhill ●	Mercury	1
-	36	I LOVE MUSIC O'Jays	Philadelphia	1
34	37	JUST THE WAY YOU ARE Billy Joel	CBS	9
36	38	BABY COME BACK Player	RSO	6
-	39	LONG LIVE ROCK & ROLL Rainbow ●	Polydor	1
35	40	AUTOMATIC LOVER Vibrators	Epic	2

LW	TW	*WEEK ENDING* **15 APRIL 1978**		Wks
1	1	MATCHSTALK MEN & MATCHSTALK CATS & DOGS Brian & Michael	Pye	7
5	2	I WONDER WHY Showaddywaddy	Arista	4
4	3	BAKER STREET Gerry Rafferty	United Artists	8
6	4	IF YOU CAN'T GIVE ME LOVE Suzi Quatro	RAK	4
2	5	DENIS Blondie	Chrysalis	8
11	6	NEVER LET HER SLIP AWAY Andrew Gold	Asylum	4
8	7	FOLLOW YOU FOLLOW ME Genesis	Charisma	5
3	8	WUTHERING HEIGHTS Kate Bush	EMI	9
13	9	WITH A LITTLE LUCK Wings	Parlophone	2
20	10	TOO MUCH TOO LITTLE TOO LATE Johnny Mathis and Deniece Williams	CBS	4
7	11	I CAN'T STAND THE RAIN Eruption	Atlantic	9
10	12	I LOVE THE SOUND OF BREAKING GLASS Nick Lowe	Radar	6
16	13	WALK IN LOVE Manhattan Transfer	Atlantic	6
-	14	NIGHT FEVER Bee Gees	RSO	1
18	15	SOMETIMES WHEN WE TOUCH Dan Hill	20th Century	6
21	16	(I DON'T WANNA GO TO) CHELSEA Elvis Costello and Attraction	Radar	5
23	17	MORE LIKE THE MOVIES Dr. Hook	Capitol	3
9	18	ALLY'S TARTAN ARMY Andy Cameron	Klub	7
12	19	EVERY 1'S A WINNER Hot Chocolate	RAK	7
15	20	EMOTIONS Samantha Sang	Private Stock	10
14	21	IS THIS LOVE Bob Marley & the Wailers	Island	8
30	22	SINGIN' IN THE RAIN Sheila and B. Devotion	EMI	4
-	23	SHE'S SO MODERN Boomtown Rats	Ensign	1
33	24	EVERYBODY DANCE Chic	Atlantic	3
29	25	WHENEVER YOU WANT MY LOVE Real Thing	Pye	6
35	26	IT TAKES TWO TO TANGO Richard Myhill	Mercury	2
28	27	I'LL GO WHERE YOUR MUSIC TAKES ME Tina Charles	CBS	4
25	28	STAYIN' ALIVE Bee Gees	RSO	11
-	29	LET'S ALL CHANT Michael Zager Band ●	Private Stock	1
24	30	RUMOUR HAS IT Donna Summer	Casablanca	8
32	31	THE GHOST OF LOVE Tavares	Capitol	4
-	32	TAKE ME I'M YOURS Squeeze ●	A&M	1
39	33	LONG LIVE ROCK & ROLL Rainbow	Polydor	2
-	34	EGO Elton John	Rocket	1
17	35	COME BACK MY LOVE Darts	Magnet	11
27	36	WISHING ON A STAR Rose Royce	Warner Brothers	13
-	37	THE ONE AND ONLY Gladys Knight & the Pips	Buddah	1
-	38	JACK & JILL Raydio ●	Arista	1
22	39	FANTASY Earth Wind & Fire	CBS	9
-	40	HEY SENORITA War	MCA	1

LW	TW	*WEEK ENDING* **22 APRIL 1978**		Wks
1	1	MATCHSTALK MEN & MATCHSTALK CATS & DOGS Brian & Michael	Pye	8
14	2	NIGHT FEVER Bee Gees	RSO	2
2	3	I WONDER WHY Showaddywaddy	Arista	5
4	4	IF YOU CAN'T GIVE ME LOVE Suzi Quatro	RAK	5
9	5	WITH A LITTLE LUCK Wings	Parlophone	3
6	6	NEVER LET HER SLIP AWAY Andrew Gold	Asylum	5
10	7	TOO MUCH TOO LITTLE TOO LATE Johnny Mathis and Deniece Williams	CBS	5
3	8	BAKER STREET Gerry Rafferty	United Artists	9
7	9	FOLLOW YOU FOLLOW ME Genesis	Charisma	6
5	10	DENIS Blondie	Chrysalis	9
22	11	SINGIN' IN THE RAIN Sheila and B. Devotion	EMI	5
13	12	WALK IN LOVE Manhattan Transfer	Atlantic	7
15	13	SOMETIMES WHEN WE TOUCH Dan Hill	20th Century	7
17	14	MORE LIKE THE MOVIES Dr. Hook	Capitol	4
8	15	WUTHERING HEIGHTS Kate Bush	EMI	10
19	16	EVERY 1'S A WINNER Hot Chocolate	RAK	8
11	17	I CAN'T STAND THE RAIN Eruption	Atlantic	10
24	18	EVERYBODY DANCE Chic	Atlantic	4
23	19	SHE'S SO MODERN Boomtown Rats	Ensign	2
29	20	LET'S ALL CHANT Michael Zager Band	Private Stock	2
26	21	IT TAKES TWO TO TANGO Richard Myhill	Mercury	3
32	22	TAKE ME I'M YOURS Squeeze	A&M	2
16	23	(I DON'T WANNA GO TO) CHELSEA Elvis Costello and Attraction	Radar	6
20	24	EMOTIONS Samantha Sang	Private Stock	11
12	25	I LOVE THE SOUND OF BREAKING GLASS Nick Lowe	Radar	7
18	26	ALLY'S TARTAN ARMY Andy Cameron	Klub	8
-	27	AUTOMATIC LOVER Dee D. Jackson ●	Mercury	1
38	28	JACK & JILL Raydio	Arista	2
25	29	WHENEVER YOU WANT MY LOVE Real Thing	Pye	7
21	30	IS THIS LOVE Bob Marley & the Wailers	Island	9
27	31	I'LL GO WHERE YOUR MUSIC TAKES ME Tina Charles	CBS	5
37	32	THE ONE AND ONLY Gladys Knight & the Pips	Buddah	2
28	33	STAYIN' ALIVE Bee Gees	RSO	12
-	34	DO IT DO IT AGAIN Raffaella Carra ●	Epic	1
34	35	EGO Elton John	Rocket	2

In these weeks ■ Brian and Michael get to number one with their tribute to the painter Lowry six years after Don McLean got there with his homage to Van Gogh (08.04.78) ■ Genesis have their first Top Ten single (08.04.78) ■ Elton John falls short of the top thirty with a new release for the first time since 1972 (15.04.78)■

LW	TW	Title / Artist	Label	Wks
-	[36]	FOXHOLE Television	*Elektra*	1
-	[37]	HAZELL Maggie Bell ●	*Swan Song*	1
33	38	LONG LIVE ROCK & ROLL Rainbow	*Polydor*	3
-	39	BAD OLD DAYS CoCo ●	*Ariola Hansa*	1
-	40	BACK IN LOVE AGAIN Donna Summer	*GTO*	1

WEEK ENDING 29 APRIL 1978

LW	TW	Title / Artist	Label	Wks
2	[1]	NIGHT FEVER Bee Gees	*RSO*	3
1	2	MATCHSTALK MEN & MATCHSTALK CATS & DOGS Brian & Michael	*Pye*	9
3	3	I WONDER WHY Showaddywaddy	*Arista*	6
4	[4]	IF YOU CAN'T GIVE ME LOVE Suzi Quatro	*RAK*	6
7	5	TOO MUCH TOO LITTLE TOO LATE Johnny Mathis and Deniece Williams	*CBS*	6
6	6	NEVER LET HER SLIP AWAY Andrew Gold	*Asylum*	6
9	[7]	FOLLOW YOU FOLLOW ME Genesis	*Charisma*	7
5	8	WITH A LITTLE LUCK Wings	*Parlophone*	4
8	9	BAKER STREET Gerry Rafferty	*United Artists*	10
20	10	LET'S ALL CHANT Michael Zager Band	*Private Stock*	3
11	[11]	SINGIN' IN THE RAIN Sheila and B. Devotion	*EMI*	6
18	12	EVERYBODY DANCE Chic	*Atlantic*	5
27	13	AUTOMATIC LOVER Dee D. Jackson	*Mercury*	2
14	[14]	MORE LIKE THE MOVIES Dr. Hook	*Capitol*	5
19	15	SHE'S SO MODERN Boomtown Rats	*Ensign*	3
39	16	BAD OLD DAYS CoCo	*Ariola Hansa*	2
21	[17]	IT TAKES TWO TO TANGO Richard Myhill	*Mercury*	4
13	18	SOMETIMES WHEN WE TOUCH Dan Hill	*20th Century*	8
12	19	WALK IN LOVE Manhattan Transfer	*Atlantic*	8
10	20	DENIS Blondie	*Chrysalis*	10
-	21	RIVERS OF BABYLON Boney M	*Atlantic*	1
28	22	JACK & JILL Raydio	*Arista*	3
22	23	TAKE ME I'M YOURS Squeeze	*A&M*	3
23	24	(I DON'T WANNA GO TO) CHELSEA Elvis Costello and Attraction	*Radar*	7
34	25	DO IT DO IT AGAIN Raffaella Carra	*Epic*	2
-	26	THEME FROM THE HONG KONG BEAT Richard Denton and Martin Cook ●	*BBC*	1
-	27	BECAUSE THE NIGHT Patti Smith Group ●	*Arista*	1
15	28	WUTHERING HEIGHTS Kate Bush	*EMI*	11
40	29	BACK IN LOVE AGAIN Donna Summer	*GTO*	2
-	30	COME TO ME Ruby Winters	*Creole*	1
17	31	I CAN'T STAND THE RAIN Eruption	*Atlantic*	11
29	32	WHENEVER YOU WANT MY LOVE Real Thing	*Pye*	8
-	[33]	MOVE YOUR BODY Gene Farrow ●	*Magnet*	1
31	34	I'LL GO WHERE YOUR MUSIC TAKES ME Tina Charles	*CBS*	6
35	35	EGO Elton John	*Rocket*	3
25	36	I LOVE THE SOUND OF BREAKING GLASS Nick Lowe	*Radar*	8
16	37	EVERY 1'S A WINNER Hot Chocolate	*RAK*	9
37	38	HAZELL Maggie Bell	*Swan Song*	2
-	[39]	I MUST BE IN LOVE Rutles ●	*Warner Brothers*	1
24	40	EMOTIONS Samantha Sang	*Private Stock*	12

WEEK ENDING 6 MAY 1978

LW	TW	Title / Artist	Label	Wks
1	[1]	NIGHT FEVER Bee Gees	*RSO*	4
21	2	RIVERS OF BABYLON Boney M	*Atlantic*	2
2	3	MATCHSTALK MEN & MATCHSTALK CATS & DOGS Brian & Michael	*Pye*	10
5	4	TOO MUCH TOO LITTLE TOO LATE Johnny Mathis and Deniece Williams	*CBS*	7
6	[5]	NEVER LET HER SLIP AWAY Andrew Gold	*Asylum*	7
13	6	AUTOMATIC LOVER Dee D. Jackson	*Mercury*	3
3	7	I WONDER WHY Showaddywaddy	*Arista*	7
4	8	IF YOU CAN'T GIVE ME LOVE Suzi Quatro	*RAK*	7
8	9	WITH A LITTLE LUCK Wings	*Parlophone*	5
10	10	LET'S ALL CHANT Michael Zager Band	*Private Stock*	4
7	11	FOLLOW YOU FOLLOW ME Genesis	*Charisma*	8
11	12	SINGIN' IN THE RAIN Sheila and B. Devotion	*EMI*	7
16	[13]	BAD OLD DAYS CoCo	*Ariola Hansa*	3
12	14	EVERYBODY DANCE Chic	*Atlantic*	6
15	15	SHE'S SO MODERN Boomtown Rats	*Ensign*	4
22	16	JACK & JILL Raydio	*Arista*	4
9	17	BAKER STREET Gerry Rafferty	*United Artists*	11

□ Highest position disc reached ● Act's first ever week on chart

LW	TW	Title / Artist	Label	Wks
18	18	SOMETIMES WHEN WE TOUCH Dan Hill	*20th Century*	9
23	[19]	TAKE ME I'M YOURS Squeeze	*A&M*	4
14	20	MORE LIKE THE MOVIES Dr. Hook	*Capitol*	6
17	21	IT TAKES TWO TO TANGO Richard Myhill	*Mercury*	5
25	22	DO IT DO IT AGAIN Raffaella Carra	*Epic*	3
27	23	BECAUSE THE NIGHT Patti Smith Group	*Arista*	2
-	24	LOVE IS IN THE AIR John Paul Young ●	*Ariola*	1
26	[25]	THEME FROM THE HONG KONG BEAT Richard Denton and Martin Cook	*BBC*	2
-	26	THE DAY THE WORLD TURNED DAYGLOW X-Ray Spex ●	*EMI*	1
-	27	NICE 'N' SLEAZY Stranglers	*United Artists*	1
30	28	COME TO ME Ruby Winters	*Creole*	2
29	29	BACK IN LOVE AGAIN Donna Summer	*GTO*	3
-	30	BOY FROM NEW YORK CITY Darts	*Magnet*	1
-	31	IT MAKES YOU FEEL LIKE DANCIN' Rose Royce	*Warner Bros.*	1
-	[32]	HEY LORD DON'T ASK ME QUESTIONS Graham Parker	*Vertigo*	1
19	33	WALK IN LOVE Manhattan Transfer	*Atlantic*	9
20	34	DENIS Blondie	*Chrysalis*	11
-	35	(I'M ALWAYS TOUCHED BY YOUR) PRESENCE DEAR Blondie	*Chrysalis*	1
-	36	BOOGIE SHOES K.C. & the Sunshine Band	*TK*	1
-	37	WHAT A WASTE Ian Dury ●	*Stiff*	1
-	38	MORE THAN A WOMAN Tavares	*Capitol*	1
24	39	(I DON'T WANNA GO TO) CHELSEA Elvis Costello and Attraction	*Radar*	8
-	40	FEELS LIKE THE FIRST TIME Foreigner ●	*Atlantic*	1

WEEK ENDING 13 MAY 1978

(From May 13th a Top 75 is compiled and published)

LW	TW	Title / Artist	Label	Wks
2	[1]	RIVERS OF BABYLON Boney M	*Atlantic*	3
1	2	NIGHT FEVER Bee Gees	*RSO*	5
4	[3]	TOO MUCH TOO LITTLE TOO LATE Johnny Mathis and Deniece Williams	*CBS*	7
6	[4]	AUTOMATIC LOVER Dee D. Jackson	*Mercury*	4
5	[5]	NEVER LET HER SLIP AWAY Andrew Gold	*Asylum*	8
3	6	MATCHSTALK MEN & MATCHSTALK CATS & DOGS Brian & Michael	*Pye*	11
23	7	BECAUSE THE NIGHT Patti Smith Group	*Arista*	3
10	[8]	LET'S ALL CHANT Michael Zager Band	*Private Stock*	5
14	[9]	EVERYBODY DANCE Chic	*Atlantic*	7
30	10	BOY FROM NEW YORK CITY Darts	*Magnet*	2
8	11	IF YOU CAN'T GIVE ME LOVE Suzi Quatro	*RAK*	8
15	[12]	SHE'S SO MODERN Boomtown Rats	*Ensign*	5
16	13	JACK & JILL Raydio	*Arista*	5
13	14	BAD OLD DAYS CoCo	*Ariola Hansa*	4
7	15	I WONDER WHY Showaddywaddy	*Arista*	8
12	16	SINGIN' IN THE RAIN Sheila and B. Devotion	*EMI*	8
22	17	DO IT DO IT AGAIN Raffaella Carra	*Epic*	4
11	18	FOLLOW YOU FOLLOW ME Genesis	*Charisma*	9
35	19	(I'M ALWAYS TOUCHED BY YOUR) PRESENCE DEAR Blondie	*Chrysalis*	2
20	20	MORE LIKE THE MOVIES Dr. Hook	*Capitol*	7
-	21	IF I CAN'T HAVE YOU Yvonne Elliman	*RSO*	1
9	22	WITH A LITTLE LUCK Wings	*Parlophone*	6
24	23	LOVE IS IN THE AIR John Paul Young	*Ariola*	2
19	24	TAKE ME I'M YOURS Squeeze	*A&M*	5
21	25	IT TAKES TWO TO TANGO Richard Myhill	*Mercury*	6
26	26	THE DAY THE WORLD TURNED DAYGLOW X-Ray Spex	*EMI*	2
-	27	A BA NI BI Izhar Cohen and Alphabeta ●	*Polydor*	1
38	28	MORE THAN A WOMAN Tavares	*Capitol*	2
27	29	NICE 'N' SLEAZY Stranglers	*United Artists*	2
17	30	BAKER STREET Gerry Rafferty	*United Artists*	12
25	31	THEME FROM THE HONG KONG BEAT Richard Denton and Martin Cook	*BBC*	3
28	32	COME TO ME Ruby Winters	*Creole*	3

■The Bee Gees have their first number one in 9 years 231 days (29.04.78) ■ Chic have the second of five consecutive Top Ten hits (29.04.78) ■ Izhar Cohen and Alphabeta chart with the Eurovision song contest winner from Israel, *A Ba Ni Bi* (13.05.78)■

May 1978

☐ Highest position disc reached ● Act's first ever week on chart

LW	TW	Title / Artist	Label	Wks
-	33	HI TENSION Hi Tension ●	Island	1
29	34	BACK IN LOVE AGAIN Donna Summer	GTO	4
37	35	WHAT A WASTE Ian Dury	Stiff	2
-	36	UP AGAINST THE WALL Tom Robinson Band	EMI	1
31	37	IT MAKES YOU FEEL LIKE DANCIN' Rose Royce	Warner Bros.	2
-	38	WHEN YOU WALK IN THE ROOM Child ●	Ariola	1
40	39	FEELS LIKE THE FIRST TIME Foreigner	Atlantic	2
18	40	SOMETIMES WHEN WE TOUCH Dan Hill	20th Century	10

WEEK ENDING 20 MAY 1978

LW	TW	Title / Artist	Label	Wks
1	1	RIVERS OF BABYLON Boney M	Atlantic	4
2	2	NIGHT FEVER Bee Gees	RSO	6
10	3	BOY FROM NEW YORK CITY Darts	Magnet	3
3	4	TOO MUCH TOO LITTLE TOO LATE Johnny Mathis and Deniece Williams	CBS	8
4	5	AUTOMATIC LOVER Dee D. Jackson	Mercury	5
7	6	BECAUSE THE NIGHT Patti Smith Group	Arista	4
5	7	NEVER LET HER SLIP AWAY Andrew Gold	Asylum	9
23	8	LOVE IS IN THE AIR John Paul Young	Ariola	3
8	9	LET'S ALL CHANT Michael Zager Band	Private Stock	6
21	10	IF I CAN'T HAVE YOU Yvonne Elliman	RSO	2
13	11	JACK & JILL Raydio	Arista	6
17	12	DO IT DO IT AGAIN Raffaella Carra	Epic	5
28	13	MORE THAN A WOMAN Tavares	Capitol	3
12	14	SHE'S SO MODERN Boomtown Rats	Ensign	6
32	15	COME TO ME Ruby Winters	Creole	4
37	16	IT MAKES YOU FEEL LIKE DANCIN' Rose Royce	Warner Bros.	3
6	17	MATCHSTALK MEN & MATCHSTALK CATS & DOGS Brian & Michael	Pye	12
29	18	NICE 'N' SLEAZY Stranglers	United Artists	3
9	19	EVERYBODY DANCE Chic	Atlantic	8
19	20	(I'M ALWAYS TOUCHED BY YOUR) PRESENCE DEAR Blondie	Chrysalis	3
14	21	BAD OLD DAYS CoCo	Ariola Hansa	5
33	22	HI TENSION Hi Tension	Island	2
26	23	THE DAY THE WORLD TURNED DAYGLOW X-Ray Spex	EMI	3
11	24	IF YOU CAN'T GIVE ME LOVE Suzi Quatro	RAK	9
16	25	SINGIN' IN THE RAIN Sheila and B. Devotion	EMI	9
27	26	A BA NI BI Izhar Cohen and Alphabeta	Polydor	2
24	27	TAKE ME I'M YOURS Squeeze	A&M	6
35	28	WHAT A WASTE Ian Dury	Stiff	3
15	29	I WONDER WHY Showaddywaddy	Arista	9
22	30	WITH A LITTLE LUCK Wings	Parlophone	7
34	31	BACK IN LOVE AGAIN Donna Summer	GTO	5
18	32	FOLLOW YOU FOLLOW ME Genesis	Charisma	10
-	33	CA PLANE POUR MOI Plastic Bertrand ●	Sire	1
-	34	BOOGIE SHOES K.C. & the Sunshine Band	TK	1
20	35	MORE LIKE THE MOVIES Dr. Hook	Capitol	8
36	36	UP AGAINST THE WALL Tom Robinson Band	EMI	2
-	37	PUMP IT UP Elvis Costello	Radar	1
-	38	ON A LITTLE STREET IN SINGAPORE Manhattan Transfer	Atlantic	1
-	39	ANGELS WITH DIRTY FACES Sham 69 ●	Polydor	1
-	40	ROSALIE Thin Lizzy	Vertigo	1

WEEK ENDING 27 MAY 1978

LW	TW	Title / Artist	Label	Wks
1	1	RIVERS OF BABYLON Boney M	Atlantic	5
2	2	NIGHT FEVER Bee Gees	RSO	7
3	3	BOY FROM NEW YORK CITY Darts	Magnet	4
10	4	IF I CAN'T HAVE YOU Yvonne Elliman	RSO	3
6	5	BECAUSE THE NIGHT Patti Smith Group	Arista	5
4	6	TOO MUCH TOO LITTLE TOO LATE Johnny Mathis and Deniece Williams	CBS	9
13	7	MORE THAN A WOMAN Tavares	Capitol	4
8	8	LOVE IS IN THE AIR John Paul Young	Ariola	4
12	9	DO IT DO IT AGAIN Raffaella Carra	Epic	6
20	10	(I'M ALWAYS TOUCHED BY YOUR) PRESENCE DEAR Blondie	Chrysalis	4
5	11	AUTOMATIC LOVER Dee D. Jackson	Mercury	6
7	12	NEVER LET HER SLIP AWAY Andrew Gold	Asylum	10
11	13	JACK & JILL Raydio	Arista	7
28	14	WHAT A WASTE Ian Dury	Stiff	4
15	15	COME TO ME Ruby Winters	Creole	5
9	16	LET'S ALL CHANT Michael Zager Band	Private Stock	7
14	17	SHE'S SO MODERN Boomtown Rats	Ensign	7
18	18	NICE 'N' SLEAZY Stranglers	United Artists	4
33	19	CA PLANE POUR MOI Plastic Bertrand	Sire	2
16	20	IT MAKES YOU FEEL LIKE DANCIN' Rose Royce	Warner Bros.	4
26	21	A BA NI BI Izhar Cohen and Alphabeta	Polydor	3
22	22	HI TENSION Hi Tension	Island	3
-	23	YOU'RE THE ONE THAT I WANT John Travolta and Olivia Newton-John ●	RSO	1
39	24	ANGELS WITH DIRTY FACES Sham 69	Polydor	2
-	25	OLE OLA Rod Stewart and the Scottish W.C. Squad	Riva	1
23	26	THE DAY THE WORLD TURNED DAYGLOW X-Ray Spex	EMI	4
19	27	EVERYBODY DANCE Chic	Atlantic	9
17	28	MATCHSTALK MEN & MATCHSTALK CATS & DOGS Brian & Michael	Pye	13
40	29	ROSALIE Thin Lizzy	Vertigo	2
-	30	OH CAROL Smokie	RAK	1
-	31	DAVY'S ON THE ROAD AGAIN Manfred Mann's Earth Band	Bronze	1
21	32	BAD OLD DAYS CoCo	Ariola Hansa	6
36	33	UP AGAINST THE WALL Tom Robinson Band	EMI	3
37	34	PUMP IT UP Elvis Costello	Radar	2
-	35	IT SURE BRINGS OUT THE LOVE IN YOUR EYES David Soul	Private Stock	1
24	36	IF YOU CAN'T GIVE ME LOVE Suzi Quatro	RAK	10
-	37	(DON'T FEAR) THE REAPER Blue Oyster Cult ●	CBS	1
38	38	ON A LITTLE STREET IN SINGAPORE Manhattan Transfer	Atlantic	2
-	39	LOVING YOU HAS MADE ME BANANAS Guy Marks ●	ABC	1
27	40	TAKE ME I'M YOURS Squeeze	A&M	7

WEEK ENDING 3 JUNE 1978

LW	TW	Title / Artist	Label	Wks
1	1	RIVERS OF BABYLON Boney M	Atlantic	6
3	2	BOY FROM NEW YORK CITY Darts	Magnet	5
2	3	NIGHT FEVER Bee Gees	RSO	8
4	4	IF I CAN'T HAVE YOU Yvonne Elliman	RSO	4
8	5	LOVE IS IN THE AIR John Paul Young	Ariola	5
23	6	YOU'RE THE ONE THAT I WANT John Travolta and Olivia Newton-John	RSO	2
5	7	BECAUSE THE NIGHT Patti Smith Group	Arista	6
7	8	MORE THAN A WOMAN Tavares	Capitol	5
14	9	WHAT A WASTE Ian Dury	Stiff	5
19	10	CA PLANE POUR MOI Plastic Bertrand	Sire	3
15	11	COME TO ME Ruby Winters	Creole	6
30	12	OH CAROL Smokie	RAK	2
22	13	HI TENSION Hi Tension	Island	4
13	14	JACK & JILL Raydio	Arista	8
10	15	(I'M ALWAYS TOUCHED BY YOUR) PRESENCE DEAR Blondie	Chrysalis	5
6	16	TOO MUCH TOO LITTLE TOO LATE Johnny Mathis and Deniece Williams	CBS	10
25	17	OLE OLA Rod Stewart and the Scottish W.C. Squad	Riva	2
9	18	DO IT DO IT AGAIN Raffaella Carra	Epic	7
20	19	IT MAKES YOU FEEL LIKE DANCIN' Rose Royce	Warner Bros.	5
21	20	A BA NI BI Izhar Cohen and Alphabeta	Polydor	4
18	21	NICE 'N' SLEAZY Stranglers	United Artists	5
31	22	DAVY'S ON THE ROAD AGAIN Manfred Manns Earth Band	Bronze	2
11	23	AUTOMATIC LOVER Dee D. Jackson	Mercury	7
38	24	ON A LITTLE STREET IN SINGAPORE Manhattan Transfer	Atlantic	3

In these weeks ■ The only Belgian punk hitmaker, Plastic Bertrand, makes his first appearance (20.05.78) ■ Three Bee Gees compositions from 'Saturday Night Fever', *Night Fever*, *If I Can't Have You* and *More Than A Woman*, are in the Top Ten (27.05.78) ■ The top chart performance of the years 1956-90 begins as *You're The One That I Want* debuts (27.05.78) ■

LW	TW	Title	Artist	Label	Wks
26	25	THE DAY THE WORLD TURNED DAYGLOW	X-Ray Spex	EMI	5
34	26	PUMP IT UP	Elvis Costello	Radar	3
-	27	ANNIE'S SONG	James Galway ●	Red Seal	1
35	28	IT SURE BRINGS OUT THE LOVE IN YOUR EYES	David Soul	Private Stock	2
12	29	NEVER LET HER SLIP AWAY	Andrew Gold	Asylum	11
16	30	LET'S ALL CHANT	Michael Zager Band	Private Stock	8
39	31	LOVING YOU HAS MADE ME BANANAS	Guy Marks	ABC	2
-	32	MISS YOU	Rolling Stones	EMI	1
17	33	SHE'S SO MODERN	Boomtown Rats	Ensign	8
37	34	(DON'T FEAR) THE REAPER	Blue Oyster Cult	CBS	2
24	35	ANGELS WITH DIRTY FACES	Sham 69	Polydor	3
-	36	MAKING UP AGAIN	Goldie ●	Bronze	1
-	37	BEAUTIFUL LOVER	Brotherhood Of Man	Pye	1
29	38	ROSALIE	Thin Lizzy	Vertigo	3
28	39	MATCHSTALK MEN & MATCHSTALK CATS & DOGS	Brian & Michael	Pye	14
33	40	UP AGAINST THE WALL	Tom Robinson Band	EMI	4

WEEK ENDING 10 JUNE 1978

LW	TW	Title	Artist	Label	Wks
1	[1]	RIVERS OF BABYLON	Boney M	Atlantic	7
6	2	YOU'RE THE ONE THAT I WANT	John Travolta and Olivia Newton-John	RSO	3
2	3	BOY FROM NEW YORK CITY	Darts	Magnet	6
17	[4]	OLE OLA	Rod Stewart and the Scottish W.C. Squad	Riva	3
4	5	IF I CAN'T HAVE YOU	Yvonne Elliman	RSO	5
3	6	NIGHT FEVER	Bee Gees	RSO	9
8	[7]	MORE THAN A WOMAN	Tavares	Capitol	6
5	8	LOVE IS IN THE AIR	John Paul Young	Ariola	6
7	9	BECAUSE THE NIGHT	Patti Smith Group	Arista	7
10	10	CA PLANE POUR MOI	Plastic Bertrand	Sire	4
9	11	WHAT A WASTE	Ian Dury	Stiff	6
12	12	OH CAROL	Smokie	RAK	3
22	13	DAVY'S ON THE ROAD AGAIN	Manfred Manns Earth Band	Bronze	3
13	14	HI TENSION	Hi Tension	Island	5
27	15	ANNIE'S SONG	James Galway	Red Seal	2
18	16	DO IT DO IT AGAIN	Raffaella Carra	Epic	8
15	17	(I'M ALWAYS TOUCHED BY YOUR) PRESENCE DEAR	Blondie	Chrysalis	6
28	18	IT SURE BRINGS OUT THE LOVE IN YOUR EYES	David Soul	Private Stock	3
35	[19]	ANGELS WITH DIRTY FACES	Sham 69	Polydor	4
11	20	COME TO ME	Ruby Winters	Creole	7
38	21	ROSALIE	Thin Lizzy	Vertigo	4
20	22	A BA NI BI	Izhar Cohen and Alphabeta	Polydor	5
32	23	MISS YOU	Rolling Stones	EMI	2
36	24	MAKING UP AGAIN	Goldie	Bronze	2
-	25	SMURF SONG	Father Abraham and the Smurfs ●	Decca	1
14	26	JACK & JILL	Raydio	Arista	9
37	27	BEAUTIFUL LOVER	Brotherhood Of Man	Pye	2
-	28	NEVER SAY DIE	Black Sabbath	Vertigo	1
21	29	NICE 'N' SLEAZY	Stranglers	United Artists	6
31	30	LOVING YOU HAS MADE ME BANANAS	Guy Marks	ABC	3
26	31	PUMP IT UP	Elvis Costello	Radar	4
16	32	TOO MUCH TOO LITTLE TOO LATE	Johnny Mathis and Deniece Williams	CBS	11
34	33	(DON'T FEAR) THE REAPER	Blue Oyster Cult	CBS	3
19	34	IT MAKES YOU FEEL LIKE DANCIN'	Rose Royce	Warner Bros.	6
-	35	YOU TOOK THE WORDS RIGHT OUT OF MY MOUTH	Meat Loaf	Epic	1
-	36	MIND BLOWING DECISIONS	Heatwave	GTO	1
24	37	ON A LITTLE STREET IN SINGAPORE	Manhattan Transfer	Atlantic	4
29	38	NEVER LET HER SLIP AWAY	Andrew Gold	Asylum	12
33	39	SHE'S SO MODERN	Boomtown Rats	Ensign	9
-	40	DANCIN' IN THE CITY	Marshall Hain ●	Ensign	1

WEEK ENDING 17 JUNE 1978

June 1978

☐ Highest position disc reached ● Act's first ever week on chart

LW	TW	Title	Artist	Label	Wks
2	[1]	YOU'RE THE ONE THAT I WANT	John Travolta and Olivia Newton-John	RSO	4
1	2	RIVERS OF BABYLON	Boney M	Atlantic	8
23	[3]	MISS YOU	Rolling Stones	EMI	3
3	4	BOY FROM NEW YORK CITY	Darts	Magnet	7
12	[5]	OH CAROL	Smokie	RAK	4
13	[6]	DAVY'S ON THE ROAD AGAIN	Manfred Manns Earth Band	Bronze	4
15	7	ANNIE'S SONG	James Galway	Red Seal	3
5	8	IF I CAN'T HAVE YOU	Yvonne Elliman	RSO	6
10	9	CA PLANE POUR MOI	Plastic Bertrand	Sire	5
25	10	SMURF SONG	Father Abraham and the Smurfs	Decca	2
6	11	NIGHT FEVER	Bee Gees	RSO	10
8	12	LOVE IS IN THE AIR	John Paul Young	Ariola	7
4	13	OLE OLA	Rod Stewart and the Scottish W.C. Squad	Riva	4
11	14	WHAT A WASTE	Ian Dury	Stiff	7
7	15	MORE THAN A WOMAN	Tavares	Capitol	7
9	16	BECAUSE THE NIGHT	Patti Smith Group	Arista	8
24	17	MAKING UP AGAIN	Goldie	Bronze	3
14	18	HI TENSION	Hi Tension	Island	6
18	19	IT SURE BRINGS OUT THE LOVE IN YOUR EYES	David Soul	Private Stock	4
37	[20]	ON A LITTLE STREET IN SINGAPORE	Manhattan Transfer	Atlantic	5
27	21	BEAUTIFUL LOVER	Brotherhood Of Man	Pye	3
20	22	COME TO ME	Ruby Winters	Creole	8
40	23	DANCIN' IN THE CITY	Marshall Hain	Ensign	2
31	[24]	PUMP IT UP	Elvis Costello	Radar	5
30	[25]	LOVING YOU HAS MADE ME BANANAS	Guy Marks	ABC	4
36	26	MIND BLOWING DECISIONS	Heatwave	GTO	2
16	27	DO IT DO IT AGAIN	Raffaella Carra	Epic	9
-	28	AIRPORT	Motors ●	Virgin	1
33	29	(DON'T FEAR) THE REAPER	Blue Oyster Cult	CBS	4
-	30	MAN WITH THE CHILD IN HIS EYES	Kate Bush	EMI	1
28	31	NEVER SAY DIE	Black Sabbath	Vertigo	2
21	32	ROSALIE	Thin Lizzy	Vertigo	5
35	[33]	YOU TOOK THE WORDS RIGHT OUT OF MY MOUTH	Meat Loaf ●	Epic	2
17	34	(I'M ALWAYS TOUCHED BY YOUR) PRESENCE DEAR	Blondie	Chrysalis	7
19	35	ANGELS WITH DIRTY FACES	Sham 69	Polydor	5
-	36	JUST LET ME DO MY THING	Sine ●	CBS	1
29	37	NICE 'N' SLEAZY	Stranglers	United Artists	7
-	38	SATISFY MY SOUL	Bob Marley & the Wailers	Island	1
-	[39]	LET'S GO DISCO	Real Thing	Pye	1
22	40	A BI NI BI	Ishar Cohen and Alphabeta	Polydor	6

WEEK ENDING 24 JUNE 1978

LW	TW	Title	Artist	Label	Wks
1	[1]	YOU'RE THE ONE THAT I WANT	John Travolta and Olivia Newton-John	RSO	5
10	[2]	SMURF SONG	Father Abraham and the Smurfs	Decca	3
2	3	RIVERS OF BABYLON	Boney M	Atlantic	9
3	4	MISS YOU	Rolling Stones	EMI	4
7	5	ANNIE'S SONG	James Galway	Red Seal	4
6	[6]	DAVY'S ON THE ROAD AGAIN	Manfred Manns Earth Band	Bronze	5
17	[7]	MAKING UP AGAIN	Goldie	Bronze	4
9	[8]	CA PLANE POUR MOI	Plastic Bertrand	Sire	6
4	9	BOY FROM NEW YORK CITY	Darts	Magnet	8
5	10	OH CAROL	Smokie	RAK	5
28	11	AIRPORT	Motors	Virgin	2
19	[12]	IT SURE BRINGS OUT THE LOVE IN YOUR EYES	David Soul	Private Stock	5
8	13	IF I CAN'T HAVE YOU	Yvonne Elliman	RSO	7
11	14	NIGHT FEVER	Bee Gees	RSO	11
21	[15]	BEAUTIFUL LOVER	Brotherhood Of Man	Pye	4
12	16	LOVE IS IN THE AIR	John Paul Young	Ariola	8
30	17	MAN WITH THE CHILD IN HIS EYES	Kate Bush	EMI	2
15	18	MORE THAN A WOMAN	Tavares	Capitol	8
23	19	DANCIN' IN THE CITY	Marshall Hain	Ensign	3

■Meat Loaf has his first hit single with a slice from what will become the long-time longest running chart album, 'Bat Out Of Hell' (10.06.78) ■ The Rolling Stones have their thirteenth and final top three hit (17.07.78) ■ The Smurfs become the highest charting cartoon characters since the Archies (24.06.78)■

June 1978

□ Highest position disc reached ● Act's first ever week on chart

LW	TW	Title	Artist	Label	Wks
32	20	ROSALIE	Thin Lizzy	Vertigo	6
31	21	NEVER SAY DIE	Black Sabbath	Vertigo	1
26	22	MIND BLOWING DECISIONS	Heatwave	GTO	3
13	23	OLE OLA	Rod Stewart and the Scottish W.C. Squad	Riva	5
35	24	ANGELS WITH DIRTY FACES	Sham 69	Polydor	6
14	25	WHAT A WASTE	Ian Dury	Stiff	8
-	26	LIKE CLOCKWORK	Boomtown Rats	Ensign	1
16	27	BECAUSE THE NIGHT	Patti Smith Group	Arista	9
29	28	(DON'T FEAR) THE REAPER	Blue Oyster Cult	CBS	5
24	29	PUMP IT UP	Elvis Costello	Radar	6
18	30	HI TENSION	Hi Tension	Island	7
-	31	WILD WEST HERO	Electric Light Orchestra	Jet	1
-	32	USE TA BE MY GIRL	O'Jays	Philadelphia	1
-	33	ROCK & ROLL DAMNATION	AC/DC ●	Atlantic	1
20	34	ON A LITTLE STREET IN SINGAPORE	Manhattan Transfer	Atlantic	6
36	35	JUST LET ME DO MY THING	Sine	CBS	2
22	36	COME TO ME	Ruby Winters	Creole	9
38	37	SATISFY MY SOUL	Bob Marley & the Wailers	Island	2
-	38	RUN FOR HOME	Lindisfarne	Mercury	1
33	39	YOU TOOK THE WORDS RIGHT OUT OF MY MOUTH	Meat Loaf	Epic	3
25	40	LOVING YOU HAS MADE ME BANANAS	Guy Marks	ABC	5

WEEK ENDING 1 JULY 1978

LW	TW	Title	Artist	Label	Wks
1	1	YOU'RE THE ONE THAT I WANT	John Travolta and Olivia Newton-John	RSO	6
2	2	SMURF SONG	Father Abraham	Decca	4
5	3	ANNIE'S SONG	James Galway	Red Seal	5
4	4	MISS YOU	Rolling Stones	EMI	5
11	5	AIRPORT	Motors	Virgin	3
3	6	RIVERS OF BABYLON	Boney M	Atlantic	10
17	7	MAN WITH THE CHILD IN HIS EYES	Kate Bush	EMI	3
19	8	DANCIN' IN THE CITY	Marshall Hain	Ensign	4
6	9	DAVY'S ON THE ROAD AGAIN	Manfred Manns Earth Band	Bronze	6
7	10	MAKING UP AGAIN	Goldie	Bronze	5
10	11	OH CAROL	Smokie	RAK	6
22	12	MIND BLOWING DECISIONS	Heatwave	GTO	4
26	13	LIKE CLOCKWORK	Boomtown Rats	Ensign	2
8	14	CA PLANE POUR MOI	Plastic Bertrand	Sire	7
14	15	NIGHT FEVER	Bee Gees	RSO	12
15	16	BEAUTIFUL LOVER	Brotherhood Of Man	Pye	5
9	17	BOY FROM NEW YORK CITY	Darts	Magnet	9
28	18	(DON'T FEAR) THE REAPER	Blue Oyster Cult	CBS	6
12	19	IT SURE BRINGS OUT THE LOVE IN YOUR EYES	David Soul	Private Stock	6
13	20	IF I CAN'T HAVE YOU	Yvonne Elliman	RSO	8
21	21	NEVER SAY DIE	Black Sabbath	Vertigo	2
32	22	USE TA BE MY GIRL	O'Jays	Philadelphia	2
16	23	LOVE IS IN THE AIR	John Paul Young	Ariola	9
-	24	BOOGIE OOGIE OOGIE	A Taste Of Honey ●	Capitol	1
-	25	A LITTLE BIT OF SOAP	Showaddywaddy	Arista	1
-	26	ARGENTINE MELODY	San Jose ●	MCA	1
25	27	WHAT A WASTE	Ian Dury	Stiff	9
33	28	ROCK & ROLL DAMNATION	AC/DC	Atlantic	2
38	29	RUN FOR HOME	Lindisfarne	Mercury	2
37	30	SATISFY MY SOUL	Bob Marley & the Wailers	Island	3
20	31	ROSALIE	Thin Lizzy	Vertigo	7
-	32	(WHITE MAN) IN HAMMERSMITH PALAIS	Clash	CBS	1
35	33	JUST LET ME DO MY THING	Sine	CBS	3
-	34	SUBSTITUTE	Clout ●	Carrere	1
34	35	ON A LITTLE STREET IN SINGAPORE	Manhattan Transfer	Atlantic	7
31	36	WILD WEST HERO	Electric Light Orchestra	Jet	2
18	37	MORE THAN A WOMAN	Tavares	Capitol	9
-	38	FROM EAST TO WEST/SCOTS MACHINE	Voyage ●	GTO	1
30	39	HI TENSION	Hi Tension	Island	8
29	40	PUMP IT UP	Elvis Costello	Radar	7

WEEK ENDING 8 JULY 1978

LW	TW	Title	Artist	Label	Wks
1	1	YOU'RE THE ONE THAT I WANT	John Travolta and Olivia Newton-John	RSO	7
2	2	SMURF SONG	Father Abraham	Decca	5
3	3	ANNIE'S SONG	James Galway	Red Seal	6
5	4	AIRPORT	Motors	Virgin	4
8	5	DANCIN' IN THE CITY	Marshall Hain	Ensign	5
7	6	MAN WITH THE CHILD IN HIS EYES	Kate Bush	EMI	4
4	7	MISS YOU	Rolling Stones	EMI	6
13	8	LIKE CLOCKWORK	Boomtown Rats	Ensign	3
10	9	MAKING UP AGAIN	Goldie	Bronze	6
6	10	RIVERS OF BABYLON	Boney M	Atlantic	11
25	11	A LITTLE BIT OF SOAP	Showaddywaddy	Arista	2
9	12	DAVY'S ON THE ROAD AGAIN	Manfred Manns Earth Band	Bronze	7
12	13	MIND BLOWING DECISIONS	Heatwave	GTO	5
26	14	ARGENTINE MELODY	San Jose	MCA	2
22	15	USE TA BE MY GIRL	O'Jays	Philadelphia	3
11	16	OH CAROL	Smokie	RAK	7
16	17	BEAUTIFUL LOVER	Brotherhood Of Man	Pye	6
-	18	NO-ONE IS INNOCENT/MY WAY	Sex Pistols	Virgin	1
18	19	(DON'T FEAR) THE REAPER	Blue Oyster Cult	CBS	7
14	20	CA PLANE POUR MOI	Plastic Bertrand	Sire	8
19	21	IT SURE BRINGS OUT THE LOVE IN YOUR EYES	David Soul	Private Stock	7
24	22	BOOGIE OOGIE OOGIE	A Taste Of Honey	Capitol	2
29	23	RUN FOR HOME	Lindisfarne	Mercury	3
36	24	WILD WEST HERO	Electric Light Orchestra	Jet	3
34	25	SUBSTITUTE	Clout	Carrere	2
21	26	NEVER SAY DIE	Black Sabbath	Vertigo	3
15	27	NIGHT FEVER	Bee Gees	RSO	13
17	28	BOY FROM NEW YORK CITY	Darts	Magnet	10
30	29	SATISFY MY SOUL	Bob Marley & the Wailers	Island	4
28	30	ROCK & ROLL DAMNATION	AC/DC	Atlantic	3
23	31	LOVE IS IN THE AIR	John Paul Young	Ariola	10
-	32	COME ON DANCE DANCE	Saturday Night Band ●	CBS	1
31	33	ROSALIE	Thin Lizzy	Vertigo	8
38	34	FROM EAST TO WEST/SCOTS MACHINE	Voyage	GTO	2
-	35	MOVIN' OUT (ANTHONY'S SONG)	Billy Joel	CBS	1
33	36	JUST LET ME DO MY THING	Sine	CBS	4
-	37	FLYING HIGH	Commodores	Motown	1
32	38	(WHITE MAN) IN HAMMERSMITH PALAIS	Clash	CBS	2
20	39	IF I CAN'T HAVE YOU	Yvonne Elliman	RSO	9
-	40	DON'T BE CRUEL	Elvis Presley	RCA	1

WEEK ENDING 15 JULY 1978

LW	TW	Title	Artist	Label	Wks
1	1	YOU'RE THE ONE THAT I WANT	John Travolta and Olivia Newton-John	RSO	8
2	2	SMURF SONG	Father Abraham	Decca	6
5	3	DANCIN' IN THE CITY	Marshall Hain	Ensign	6
3	4	ANNIE'S SONG	James Galway	Red Seal	7
4	5	AIRPORT	Motors	Virgin	5
8	6	LIKE CLOCKWORK	Boomtown Rats	Ensign	4
18	7	NO-ONE IS INNOCENT/MY WAY	Sex Pistols	Virgin	2
11	8	A LITTLE BIT OF SOAP	Showaddywaddy	Arista	3
6	9	MAN WITH THE CHILD IN HIS EYES	Kate Bush	EMI	5
7	10	MISS YOU	Rolling Stones	EMI	7
22	11	BOOGIE OOGIE OOGIE	A Taste Of Honey	Capitol	3
23	12	RUN FOR HOME	Lindisfarne	Mercury	4
15	13	USE TA BE MY GIRL	O'Jays	Philadelphia	4
13	14	MIND BLOWING DECISIONS	Heatwave	GTO	6
14	15	ARGENTINE MELODY	San Jose	MCA	3
19	16	(DON'T FEAR) THE REAPER	Blue Oyster Cult	CBS	8
25	17	SUBSTITUTE	Clout	Carrere	3
10	18	RIVERS OF BABYLON	Boney M	Atlantic	12
24	19	WILD WEST HERO	Electric Light Orchestra	Jet	4
9	20	MAKING UP AGAIN	Goldie	Bronze	7
17	21	BEAUTIFUL LOVER	Brotherhood Of Man	Pye	7
12	22	DAVY'S ON THE ROAD AGAIN	Manfred Manns Earth Band	Bronze	8
29	23	SATISFY MY SOUL	Bob Marley & the Wailers	Island	5
30	24	ROCK & ROLL DAMNATION	AC/DC	Atlantic	4

In these weeks ■ James Galway becomes the highest charting solo flautist (01.07.78) ■ Sid Vicious has his way with the Frank Sinatra standard (08.07.78) ■ America's number one chart hit of the rock era, *Don't Be Cruel* by Elvis Presley, makes its British debut twenty two years after its first release (08.07.78)■

LW	TW	Title / Artist	Label	Wks
16	25	OH CAROL Smokie	*RAK*	8
32	26	COME ON DANCE DANCE Saturday Night Band	*CBS*	2
27	27	NIGHT FEVER Bee Gees	*RSO*	14
26	28	NEVER SAY DIE Black Sabbath	*Vertigo*	4
-	29	HOW CAN THIS BE LOVE Andrew Gold	*Asylum*	1
34	30	FROM EAST TO WEST/SCOTS MACHINE Voyage	*GTO*	3
40	31	DON'T BE CRUEL Elvis Presley	*RCA*	2
-	32	STAY Jackson Browne ●	*Asylum*	1
20	33	CA PLANE POUR MOI Plastic Bertrand	*Sire*	9
-	34	COME BACK AND FINISHED WHAT YOU STARTED Gladys Knight & the Pips	*Buddah*	1
21	35	IT SURE BRINGS OUT THE LOVE IN YOUR EYES David Soul	*Private Stock*	8
-	36	5-7-0-5 City Boy ●	*Vertigo*	1
-	37	LIFE'S BEEN GOOD Joe Walsh	*Asylum*	1
38	38	(WHITE MAN) IN HAMMERSMITH PALAIS Clash	*CBS*	3
35	39	MOVIN' OUT (ANTHONY'S SONG) Billy Joel	*CBS*	2
-	40	FOREVER AUTUMN Justin Hayward ●	*CBS*	1

LW	TW	*WEEK ENDING* **22 JULY 1978**		Wks
1	1	YOU'RE THE ONE THAT I WANT John Travolta and Olivia Newton-John	*RSO*	9
2	2	SMURF SONG Father Abraham	*Decca*	7
3	3	DANCIN' IN THE CITY Marshall Hain	*Ensign*	7
17	4	SUBSTITUTE Clout	*Carrere*	4
8	5	A LITTLE BIT OF SOAP Showaddywaddy	*Arista*	4
6	6	LIKE CLOCKWORK Boomtown Rats	*Ensign*	5
19	7	WILD WEST HERO Electric Light Orchestra	*Jet*	5
5	8	AIRPORT Motors	*Virgin*	6
9	9	MAN WITH THE CHILD IN HIS EYES Kate Bush	*EMI*	6
11	10	BOOGIE OOGIE OOGIE A Taste Of Honey	*Capitol*	4
7	11	NO-ONE IS INNOCENT/MY WAY Sex Pistols	*Virgin*	3
13	12	USE TA BE MY GIRL O'Jays	*Philadelphia*	5
4	13	ANNIE'S SONG James Galway	*Red Seal*	8
12	14	RUN FOR HOME Lindisfarne	*Mercury*	5
14	15	MIND BLOWING DECISIONS Heatwave	*GTO*	7
26	16	COME ON DANCE DANCE Saturday Night Band	*CBS*	3
15	17	ARGENTINE MELODY San Jose	*MCA*	4
16	18	(DON'T FEAR) THE REAPER Blue Oyster Cult	*CBS*	9
10	19	MISS YOU Rolling Stones	*EMI*	8
18	20	RIVERS OF BABYLON Boney M	*Atlantic*	13
23	21	SATISFY MY SOUL Bob Marley & the Wailers	*Island*	6
37	22	LIFE'S BEEN GOOD Joe Walsh	*Asylum*	2
36	23	5-7-0-5 City Boy	*Vertigo*	2
20	24	MAKING UP AGAIN Goldie	*Bronze*	8
40	25	FOREVER AUTUMN Justin Hayward	*CBS*	2
24	26	ROCK & ROLL DAMNATION AC/DC	*Atlantic*	5
30	27	FROM EAST TO WEST/SCOTS MACHINE Voyage	*GTO*	4
22	28	DAVY'S ON THE ROAD AGAIN Manfred Manns Earth Band	*Bronze*	9
21	29	BEAUTIFUL LOVER Brotherhood Of Man	*Pye*	8
34	30	COME BACK AND FINISHED WHAT YOU STARTED Gladys Knight & the Pips	*Buddah*	2
32	31	STAY Jackson Browne	*Asylum*	2
25	32	OH CAROL Smokie	*RAK*	9
31	33	DON'T BE CRUEL Elvis Presley	*RCA*	3
-	34	LOVE YOU MORE Buzzcocks	*United Artists*	1
-	35	PRODIGAL SON Steel Pulse	*Island*	1
27	36	NIGHT FEVER Bee Gees	*RSO*	15
29	37	HOW CAN THIS BE LOVE Andrew Gold	*Asylum*	2
-	38	IS THIS A LOVE THING Raydio	*Arista*	1
-	39	SHAME Evelyn 'Champagne' King ●	*RCA*	1
39	40	MOVIN' OUT (ANTHONY'S SONG) Billy Joel	*CBS*	3

LW	TW	*WEEK ENDING* **29 JULY 1978**		Wks
1	1	YOU'RE THE ONE THAT I WANT John Travolta and Olivia Newton-John	*RSO*	10
2	2	SMURF SONG Father Abraham	*Decca*	8
4	3	SUBSTITUTE Clout	*Carrere*	5
3	4	DANCIN' IN THE CITY Marshall Hain	*Ensign*	8
10	5	BOOGIE OOGIE OOGIE A Taste Of Honey	*Capitol*	5
6	6	LIKE CLOCKWORK Boomtown Rats	*Ensign*	6
5	7	A LITTLE BIT OF SOAP Showaddywaddy	*Arista*	5
7	8	WILD WEST HERO Electric Light Orchestra	*Jet*	6
8	9	AIRPORT Motors	*Virgin*	7
14	10	RUN FOR HOME Lindisfarne	*Mercury*	6
11	11	NO-ONE IS INNOCENT/MY WAY Sex Pistols	*Virgin*	4
31	12	STAY Jackson Browne	*Asylum*	3
27	13	FROM EAST TO WEST/SCOTS MACHINE Voyage	*GTO*	5
12	14	USE TA BE MY GIRL O'Jays	*Philadelphia*	6
9	15	MAN WITH THE CHILD IN HIS EYES Kate Bush	*EMI*	7
13	16	ANNIE'S SONG James Galway	*Red Seal*	9
16	17	COME ON DANCE DANCE Saturday Night Band	*CBS*	4
20	18	RIVERS OF BABYLON Boney M	*Atlantic*	14
37	19	HOW CAN THIS BE LOVE Andrew Gold	*Asylum*	3
18	20	(DON'T FEAR) THE REAPER Blue Oyster Cult	*CBS*	10
25	21	FOREVER AUTUMN Justin Hayward	*CBS*	3
23	22	5-7-0-5 City Boy	*Vertigo*	3
22	23	LIFE'S BEEN GOOD Joe Walsh	*Asylum*	3
33	24	DON'T BE CRUEL Elvis Presley	*RCA*	4
19	25	MISS YOU Rolling Stones	*EMI*	9
30	26	COME BACK AND FINISHED WHAT YOU STARTED Gladys Knight & the Pips	*Buddah*	3
21	27	SATISFY MY SOUL Bob Marley & the Wailers	*Island*	7
-	28	NORTHERN LIGHTS Renaissance ●	*Warner Brothers*	1
26	29	ROCK & ROLL DAMNATION AC/DC	*Atlantic*	6
15	30	MIND BLOWING DECISIONS Heatwave	*GTO*	8
-	31	IF THE KIDS ARE UNITED Sham 69	*Polydor*	1
-	32	IDENTITY X-Ray Spex	*EMI International*	1
38	33	IS THIS A LOVE THING Raydio	*Arista*	2
17	34	ARGENTINE MELODY San Jose	*MCA*	5
34	35	LOVE YOU MORE Buzzcocks	*United Artists*	2
28	36	DAVY'S ON THE ROAD AGAIN Manfred Manns Earth Band	*Bronze*	10
35	37	PRODIGAL SON Steel Pulse	*Island*	2
36	38	NIGHT FEVER Bee Gees	*RSO*	16
-	39	WHO ARE YOU Who	*Polydor*	1
-	40	BABY STOP CRYING Bob Dylan	*CBS*	1

August 1978

□ Highest position disc reached ● Act's first ever week on chart

LW	TW	*WEEK ENDING* **5 AUGUST 1978**		Wks
1	1	YOU'RE THE ONE THAT I WANT John Travolta and Olivia Newton-John	*RSO*	11
3	2	SUBSTITUTE Clout	*Carrere*	6
2	3	SMURF SONG Father Abraham	*Decca*	9
4	4	DANCIN' IN THE CITY Marshall Hain	*Ensign*	9
5	5	BOOGIE OOGIE OOGIE A Taste Of Honey	*Capitol*	6
8	6	WILD WEST HERO Electric Light Orchestra	*Jet*	7
7	7	A LITTLE BIT OF SOAP Showaddywaddy	*Arista*	6
6	8	LIKE CLOCKWORK Boomtown Rats	*Ensign*	7
22	9	5-7-0-5 City Boy	*Vertigo*	4
18	10	RIVERS OF BABYLON/BROWN GIRL IN THE RING Boney M	*Atlantic*	15
21	11	FOREVER AUTUMN Justin Hayward	*CBS*	4
10	12	RUN FOR HOME Lindisfarne	*Mercury*	7
31	13	IF THE KIDS ARE UNITED Sham 69	*Polydor*	2
23	14	LIFE'S BEEN GOOD Joe Walsh	*Asylum*	4
12	15	STAY Jackson Browne	*Asylum*	4
14	16	USE TA BE MY GIRL O'Jays	*Philadelphia*	7
26	17	COME BACK AND FINISHED WHAT YOU STARTED Gladys Knight & the Pips	*Buddah*	4
9	18	AIRPORT Motors	*Virgin*	8
13	19	FROM EAST TO WEST/SCOTS MACHINE Voyage	*GTO*	6
11	20	NO-ONE IS INNOCENT/MY WAY Sex Pistols	*Virgin*	5
17	21	COME ON DANCE DANCE Saturday Night Band	*CBS*	5
19	22	HOW CAN THIS BE LOVE Andrew Gold	*Asylum*	4
28	23	NORTHERN LIGHTS Renaissance	*Warner Brothers*	2
15	24	MAN WITH THE CHILD IN HIS EYES Kate Bush	*EMI*	8
32	25	IDENTITY X-Ray Spex	*EMI International*	2
40	26	BABY STOP CRYING Bob Dylan	*CBS*	2

■In one of the strangest chart runs of all time, *Shame* by Evelyn 'Champagne' King spends 23 weeks in the Top 75 but only one in the Top 40 (22.07.78) ■ Bob Dylan has his final Top 40 hit (29.07.78) ■ *Rivers Of Babylon* flows back up the chart due to popularity of the B-side, *Brown Girl In The Ring* (05.08.78)■

August 1978

☐ Highest position disc reached ● Act's first ever week on chart

LW	TW	Title	Artist	Label	Wks
-	27	IT'S ONLY MAKE BELIEVE	Child	Ariola Hansa	1
39	28	WHO ARE YOU	Who	Polydor	2
-	29	ANTHEM	New Seekers	CBS	1
-	30	SUPER NATURE	Cerrone	Atlantic	1
16	31	ANNIE'S SONG	James Galway	Red Seal	10
24	32	DON'T BE CRUEL	Elvis Presley	RCA	5
20	33	(DON'T FEAR) THE REAPER	Blue Oyster Cult	CBS	11
25	34	MISS YOU	Rolling Stones	EMI	10
35	35	LOVE YOU MORE	Buzzcocks	United Artists	3
33	36	IS THIS A LOVE THING	Raydio	Arista	3
29	37	ROCK & ROLL DAMNATION	AC/DC	Atlantic	7
38	38	NIGHT FEVER	Bee Gees	RSO	17
30	39	MIND BLOWING DECISIONS	Heatwave	GTO	9
-	40	STUFF LIKE THAT	Quincy Jones ●	A&M	1

WEEK ENDING 12 AUGUST 1978

LW	TW	Title	Artist	Label	Wks
1	[1]	YOU'RE THE ONE THAT I WANT	John Travolta and Olivia Newton-John	RSO	12
2	[2]	SUBSTITUTE	Clout	Carrere	7
5	[3]	BOOGIE OOGIE OOGIE	A Taste Of Honey	Capitol	7
3	4	SMURF SONG	Father Abraham	Decca	10
-	5	THREE TIMES A LADY	Commodores	Motown	1
10	6	RIVERS OF BABYLON/BROWN GIRL IN THE RING	Boney M	Atlantic	16
11	7	FOREVER AUTUMN	Justin Hayward	CBS	5
4	8	DANCIN' IN THE CITY	Marshall Hain	Ensign	10
13	[9]	IF THE KIDS ARE UNITED	Sham 69	Polydor	3
6	10	WILD WEST HERO	Electric Light Orchestra	Jet	8
23	11	NORTHERN LIGHTS	Renaissance	Warner Brothers	3
9	12	5-7-0-5	City Boy	Vertigo	5
15	13	STAY	Jackson Browne	Asylum	5
7	[14]	A LITTLE BIT OF SOAP	Showaddywaddy	Arista	7
8	15	LIKE CLOCKWORK	Boomtown Rats	Ensign	8
19	16	FROM EAST TO WEST/SCOTS MACHINE	Voyage	GTO	7
12	17	RUN FOR HOME	Lindisfarne	Mercury	8
-	18	IT'S RAINING	Darts	Magnet	1
17	19	COME BACK AND FINISHED WHAT YOU STARTED	Gladys Knight & the Pips	Buddah	5
14	20	LIFE'S BEEN GOOD	Joe Walsh	Asylum	5
26	21	BABY STOP CRYING	Bob Dylan	CBS	3
22	22	HOW CAN THIS BE LOVE	Andrew Gold	Asylum	5
30	23	SUPER NATURE	Cerrone	Atlantic	2
25	[24]	IDENTITY	X-Ray Spex	EMI International	3
16	25	USE TA BE MY GIRL	O'Jays	Philadelphia	8
28	26	WHO ARE YOU	Who	Polydor	3
36	[27]	IS THIS A LOVE THING	Raydio	Arista	4
27	28	IT'S ONLY MAKE BELIEVE	Child	Ariola Hansa	2
18	29	AIRPORT	Motors	Virgin	9
-	30	COLD AS ICE	Foreigner	Atlantic	1
32	31	DON'T BE CRUEL	Elvis Presley	RCA	6
29	32	ANTHEM	New Seekers	CBS	2
20	33	NO-ONE IS INNOCENT/MY WAY	Sex Pistols	Virgin	6
40	[34]	STUFF LIKE THAT	Quincy Jones	A&M	2
24	35	MAN WITH THE CHILD IN HIS EYES	Kate Bush	EMI	9
-	36	WALK ON BY	Stranglers	United Artists	1
-	37	JILTED JOHN	Jilted John ●	EMI International	1
21	38	COME ON DANCE DANCE	Saturday Night Band	CBS	6
-	[39]	SHA LA LA LA LEE	Plastic Bertrand	Vertigo	1
31	40	ANNIE'S SONG	James Galway	Red Seal	11

WEEK ENDING 19 AUGUST 1978

LW	TW	Title	Artist	Label	Wks
5	[1]	THREE TIMES A LADY	Commodores	Motown	2
1	2	YOU'RE THE ONE THAT I WANT	John Travolta and Olivia Newton-John	RSO	13
2	3	SUBSTITUTE	Clout	Carrere	8
18	4	IT'S RAINING	Darts	Magnet	2
6	5	RIVERS OF BABYLON/BROWN GIRL IN THE RING	Boney M	Atlantic	17
7	6	FOREVER AUTUMN	Justin Hayward	CBS	6
3	7	BOOGIE OOGIE OOGIE	A Taste Of Honey	Capitol	8
12	[8]	5-7-0-5	City Boy	Vertigo	6
9	9	IF THE KIDS ARE UNITED	Sham 69	Polydor	4
11	[10]	NORTHERN LIGHTS	Renaissance	Warner Brothers	4
23	11	SUPER NATURE	Cerrone	Atlantic	3
4	12	SMURF SONG	Father Abraham	Decca	11
21	[13]	BABY STOP CRYING	Bob Dylan	CBS	4
28	14	IT'S ONLY MAKE BELIEVE	Child	Ariola Hansa	3
19	[15]	COME BACK AND FINISHED WHAT YOU STARTED	Gladys Knight & the Pips	Buddah	6
8	16	DANCIN' IN THE CITY	Marshall Hain	Ensign	11
20	17	LIFE'S BEEN GOOD	Joe Walsh	Asylum	6
-	18	DREADLOCK HOLIDAY	10 C.C.	Mercury	1
10	19	WILD WEST HERO	Electric Light Orchestra	Jet	9
26	20	WHO ARE YOU	Who	Polydor	4
32	[21]	ANTHEM	New Seekers	CBS	3
13	22	STAY	Jackson Browne	Asylum	6
16	23	FROM EAST TO WEST/SCOTS MACHINE	Voyage	GTO	8
24	[24]	IDENTITY	X-Ray Spex	EMI International	4
37	25	JILTED JOHN	Jilted John	EMI International	2
15	26	LIKE CLOCKWORK	Boomtown Rats	Ensign	9
36	27	WALK ON BY	Stranglers	United Artists	2
14	28	A LITTLE BIT OF SOAP	Showaddywaddy	Arista	8
17	29	RUN FOR HOME	Lindisfarne	Mercury	9
22	30	HOW CAN THIS BE LOVE	Andrew Gold	Asylum	6
-	31	BRITISH HUSTLE	Hi Tension	Island	1
-	32	AN EVERLASTING LOVE	Andy Gibb	RSO	1
33	33	NO-ONE IS INNOCENT/MY WAY	Sex Pistols	Virgin	7
-	34	TOP OF THE POPS	Rezillos ●	Sire	1
25	35	USE TA BE MY GIRL	O'Jays	Philadelphia	9
-	36	OH WHAT A CIRCUS	David Essex	Mercury	1
34	37	STUFF LIKE THAT	Quincy Jones	A&M	3
-	38	YOU MAKE ME FEEL	Sylvester	Fantasy	1
30	39	COLD AS ICE	Foreigner	Atlantic	2
-	40	RAININ' THROUGH MY SUNSHINE	Real Thing	Pye	1

WEEK ENDING 26 AUGUST 1978

LW	TW	Title	Artist	Label	Wks
1	[1]	THREE TIMES A LADY	Commodores	Motown	3
2	2	YOU'RE THE ONE THAT I WANT	John Travolta and Olivia Newton-John	RSO	14
4	3	IT'S RAINING	Darts	Magnet	3
5	4	RIVERS OF BABYLON/BROWN GIRL IN THE RING	Boney M	Atlantic	18
6	[5]	FOREVER AUTUMN	Justin Hayward	CBS	7
18	6	DREADLOCK HOLIDAY	10 C.C.	Mercury	2
3	7	SUBSTITUTE	Clout	Carrere	9
11	[8]	SUPER NATURE	Cerrone	Atlantic	4
7	9	BOOGIE OOGIE OOGIE	A Taste Of Honey	Capitol	9
25	10	JILTED JOHN	Jilted John	EMI International	3
10	11	NORTHERN LIGHTS	Renaissance	Warner Brothers	5
36	12	OH WHAT A CIRCUS	David Essex	Mercury	2
8	13	5-7-0-5	City Boy	Vertigo	7
9	14	IF THE KIDS ARE UNITED	Sham 69	Polydor	5
13	15	BABY STOP CRYING	Bob Dylan	CBS	5
14	16	IT'S ONLY MAKE BELIEVE	Child	Ariola Hansa	4
15	17	COME BACK AND FINISHED WHAT YOU STARTED	Gladys Knight & the Pips	Buddah	7
20	[18]	WHO ARE YOU	Who	Polydor	5
12	19	SMURF SONG	Father Abraham	Decca	12
22	20	STAY	Jackson Browne	Asylum	7
17	21	LIFE'S BEEN GOOD	Joe Walsh	Asylum	7
27	22	WALK ON BY	Stranglers	United Artists	3
21	23	ANTHEM	New Seekers	CBS	4
39	[24]	COLD AS ICE	Foreigner	Atlantic	3
32	25	AN EVERLASTING LOVE	Andy Gibb	RSO	2
34	26	TOP OF THE POPS	Rezillos	Sire	2
31	27	BRITISH HUSTLE	Hi Tension	Island	2
23	28	FROM EAST TO WEST/SCOTS MACHINE	Voyage	GTO	9
16	29	DANCIN' IN THE CITY	Marshall Hain	Ensign	12
24	30	IDENTITY	X-Ray Spex	EMI International	5

In these weeks ■ *Three Times A Lady* by the Commodores is the fastest climbing Motown hit yet (12.08.78) ■ Justin Haywood has the biggest hit by a solo Moody Blue (26.08.78) ■ Graham Fellows makes sure the Top Ten isn't boring as Jilted John (26.08.78) ■

LW	TW	Title	Artist	Label	Wks
-	31	FORGET ABOUT YOU	Motors	*Virgin*	1
-	32	DAVID WATTS/A BOMB IN WARDOUR STREET	Jam	*Polydor*	1
30	33	HOW CAN THIS BE LOVE	Andrew Gold	*Asylum*	7
-	34	I THOUGHT IT WAS YOU	Herbie Hancock ●	*CBS*	1
19	35	WILD WEST HERO	Electric Light Orchestra	*Jet*	10
26	36	LIKE CLOCKWORK	Boomtown Rats	*Ensign*	10
-	37	SIGN OF THE TIMES	Bryan Ferry	*Polydor*	1
29	38	RUN FOR HOME	Lindisfarne	*Mercury*	10
-	39	GALAXY OF LOVE	Crown Heights Affair ●	*Philips*	1
38	40	YOU MAKE ME FEEL	Sylvester	*Fantasy*	2

WEEK ENDING 2 SEPTEMBER 1978

LW	TW	Title	Artist	Label	Wks
1	1	THREE TIMES A LADY	Commodores	*Motown*	4
3	2	IT'S RAINING	Darts	*Magnet*	4
4	3	RIVERS OF BABYLON/BROWN GIRL IN THE RING	Boney M	*Atlantic*	19
6	4	DREADLOCK HOLIDAY	10 C.C.	*Mercury*	3
2	5	YOU'RE THE ONE THAT I WANT	John Travolta and Olivia Newton-John	*RSO*	15
12	6	OH WHAT A CIRCUS	David Essex	*Mercury*	3
10	7	JILTED JOHN	Jilted John	*EMI International*	4
8	8	SUPER NATURE	Cerrone	*Atlantic*	5
5	9	FOREVER AUTUMN	Justin Hayward	*CBS*	8
16	10	IT'S ONLY MAKE BELIEVE	Child	*Ariola Hansa*	5
9	11	BOOGIE OOGIE OOGIE	A Taste Of Honey	*Capitol*	10
7	12	SUBSTITUTE	Clout	*Carrere*	10
15	13	BABY STOP CRYING	Bob Dylan	*CBS*	6
13	14	5-7-0-5	City Boy	*Vertigo*	8
11	15	NORTHERN LIGHTS	Renaissance	*Warner Brothers*	6
14	16	IF THE KIDS ARE UNITED	Sham 69	*Polydor*	6
27	17	BRITISH HUSTLE	Hi Tension	*Island*	3
18	18	WHO ARE YOU	Who	*Polydor*	6
25	19	AN EVERLASTING LOVE	Andy Gibb	*RSO*	3
17	20	COME BACK AND FINISHED WHAT YOU STARTED	Gladys Knight & the Pips	*Buddah*	8
22	21	WALK ON BY	Stranglers	*United Artists*	4
23	22	ANTHEM	New Seekers	*CBS*	5
-	23	PICTURE THIS	Blondie	*Chrysalis*	1
26	24	TOP OF THE POPS	Rezillos	*Sire*	3
-	25	HONG KONG GARDEN	Slouxsie & the Banshees ●	*Polydor*	1
31	26	FORGET ABOUT YOU	Motors	*Virgin*	2
34	27	I THOUGHT IT WAS YOU	Herbie Hancock	*CBS*	2
19	28	SMURF SONG	Father Abraham	*Decca*	13
32	29	DAVID WATTS/A BOMB IN WARDOUR STREET	Jam	*Polydor*	2
21	30	LIFE'S BEEN GOOD	Joe Walsh	*Asylum*	8
-	31	GREASE	Frankie Valli	*RSO*	1
40	32	YOU MAKE ME FEEL	Sylvester	*Fantasy*	3
-	33	KISS YOU ALL OVER	Exile ●	*RAK*	1
39	34	GALAXY OF LOVE	Crown Heights Affair	*Philips*	2
30	35	IDENTITY	X-Ray Spex	*EMI International*	6
-	36	TWO OUT OF THREE AIN'T BAD	Meat Loaf	*Epic*	1
20	37	STAY	Jackson Browne	*Asylum*	8
-	38	HOT SHOT	Karen Young ●	*Atlantic*	1
-	39	AGAIN AND AGAIN	Status Quo	*Vertigo*	1
37	40	SIGN OF THE TIMES	Bryan Ferry	*Polydor*	2

WEEK ENDING 9 SEPTEMBER 1978

LW	TW	Title	Artist	Label	Wks
1	1	THREE TIMES A LADY	Commodores	*Motown*	5
3	2	RIVERS OF BABYLON/BROWN GIRL IN THE RING	Boney M	*Atlantic*	20
2	3	IT'S RAINING	Darts	*Magnet*	5
4	4	DREADLOCK HOLIDAY	10 C.C.	*Mercury*	4
6	5	OH WHAT A CIRCUS	David Essex	*Mercury*	4
7	6	JILTED JOHN	Jilted John	*EMI International*	5
5	7	YOU'RE THE ONE THAT I WANT	John Travolta and Olivia Newton-John	*RSO*	16
8	8	SUPER NATURE	Cerrone	*Atlantic*	6
17	9	BRITISH HUSTLE	Hi Tension	*Island*	4
19	10	AN EVERLASTING LOVE	Andy Gibb	*RSO*	4
10	11	IT'S ONLY MAKE BELIEVE	Child	*Ariola Hansa*	6
9	12	FOREVER AUTUMN	Justin Hayward	*CBS*	9

September 1978

□ Highest position disc reached ● Act's first ever week on chart

LW	TW	Title	Artist	Label	Wks
26	13	FORGET ABOUT YOU	Motors	*Virgin*	3
13	14	BABY STOP CRYING	Bob Dylan	*CBS*	7
25	15	HONG KONG GARDEN	Slouxsie & the Banshees	*Polydor*	2
23	16	PICTURE THIS	Blondie	*Chrysalis*	2
24	17	TOP OF THE POPS	Rezillos	*Sire*	4
12	18	SUBSTITUTE	Clout	*Carrere*	11
33	19	KISS YOU ALL OVER	Exile	*RAK*	2
15	20	NORTHERN LIGHTS	Renaissance	*Warner Brothers*	7
11	21	BOOGIE OOGIE OOGIE	A Taste Of Honey	*Capitol*	11
18	22	WHO ARE YOU	Who	*Polydor*	7
39	23	AGAIN AND AGAIN	Status Quo	*Vertigo*	2
31	24	GREASE	Frankie Valli	*RSO*	2
27	25	I THOUGHT IT WAS YOU	Herbie Hancock	*CBS*	3
29	26	DAVID WATTS/A BOMB IN WARDOUR STREET	Jam	*Polydor*	3
21	27	WALK ON BY	Stranglers	*United Artists*	5
14	28	5-7-0-5	City Boy	*Vertigo*	9
34	29	GALAXY OF LOVE	Crown Heights Affair	*Philips*	3
32	30	YOU MAKE ME FEEL	Sylvester	*Fantasy*	4
16	31	IF THE KIDS ARE UNITED	Sham 69	*Polydor*	7
36	32	TWO OUT OF THREE AIN'T BAD	Meat Loaf	*Epic*	2
20	33	COME BACK AND FINISHED WHAT YOU STARTED	Gladys Knight & the Pips	*Buddah*	9
38	34	HOT SHOT	Karen Young	*Atlantic*	2
28	35	SMURF SONG	Father Abraham	*Decca*	14
-	36	TALKING IN YOUR SLEEP	Crystal Gayle	*United Artists*	1
40	37	SIGN OF THE TIMES	Bryan Ferry	*Polydor*	3
-	38	A ROSE HAS TO DIE	Dooleys	*GTO*	1
-	39	COLD AS ICE	Foreigner	*Warner Bros*	4
-	40	GOT A FEELING	Patrick Juvet ●	*Casablanca*	1

WEEK ENDING 16 SEPTEMBER 1978

LW	TW	Title	Artist	Label	Wks
1	1	THREE TIMES A LADY	Commodores	*Motown*	6
4	2	DREADLOCK HOLIDAY	10 C.C.	*Mercury*	5
2	3	RIVERS OF BABYLON/BROWN GIRL IN THE RING	Boney M	*Atlantic*	21
3	4	IT'S RAINING	Darts	*Magnet*	6
5	5	OH WHAT A CIRCUS	David Essex	*Mercury*	5
6	6	JILTED JOHN	Jilted John	*EMI International*	6
15	7	HONG KONG GARDEN	Slouxsie & the Banshees	*Polydor*	3
9	8	BRITISH HUSTLE	Hi Tension	*Island*	5
8	9	SUPER NATURE	Cerrone	*Atlantic*	7
19	10	KISS YOU ALL OVER	Exile	*RAK*	3
10	11	AN EVERLASTING LOVE	Andy Gibb	*RSO*	5
7	12	YOU'RE THE ONE THAT I WANT	John Travolta and Olivia Newton-John	*RSO*	17
16	13	PICTURE THIS	Blondie	*Chrysalis*	3
23	14	AGAIN AND AGAIN	Status Quo	*Vertigo*	3
25	15	I THOUGHT IT WAS YOU	Herbie Hancock	*CBS*	4
13	16	FORGET ABOUT YOU	Motors	*Virgin*	4
17	17	TOP OF THE POPS	Rezillos	*Sire*	5
11	18	IT'S ONLY MAKE BELIEVE	Child	*Ariola Hansa*	7
24	19	GREASE	Frankie Valli	*RSO*	3
14	20	BABY STOP CRYING	Bob Dylan	*CBS*	8
-	21	SUMMER NIGHT CITY	Abba	*Epic*	1
-	22	YOU'RE THE ONE THAT I WANT	Hylda Baker and Arthur Mullard ●	*Pye*	1
22	23	WHO ARE YOU	Who	*Polydor*	8
29	24	GALAXY OF LOVE	Crown Heights Affair	*Philips*	4
38	25	A ROSE HAS TO DIE	Dooleys	*GTO*	2
30	26	YOU MAKE ME FEEL	Sylvester	*Fantasy*	5
12	27	FOREVER AUTUMN	Justin Hayward	*CBS*	10
26	28	DAVID WATTS/A BOMB IN WARDOUR STREET	Jam	*Polydor*	4
21	29	BOOGIE OOGIE OOGIE	A Taste Of Honey	*Capitol*	12
27	30	WALK ON BY	Stranglers	*United Artists*	6
18	31	SUBSTITUTE	Clout	*Carrere*	12
36	32	TALKING IN YOUR SLEEP	Crystal Gayle	*United Artists*	2
32	33	TWO OUT OF THREE AIN'T BAD	Meat Loaf	*Epic*	3
40	34	GOT A FEELING	Patrick Juvet	*Casablanca*	2

■The Pips finish their Top 20 career; next time there, Gladys Knight will be a soloist (02.09.78) ■ The unlikely chart duo of Hylda Baker and Arthur Mullard debut and peak in the same week (16.09.78) ■ The rudest artist since Judge Dread, Ivor Biggun, creeps into the Top 40 at number 40 (16.09.78)■

September 1978

□ Highest position disc reached ● Act's first ever week on chart

LW	TW	Title / Artist	Label	Wks
20	35	NORTHERN LIGHTS Renaissance	Warner Brothers	8
-	[36]	DON'T KILL THE WHALE Yes	Atlantic	1
28	37	5-7-0-5 City Boy	Vertigo	10
31	38	IF THE KIDS ARE UNITED Sham 69	Polydor	8
34	39	HOT SHOT Karen Young	Atlantic	3
-	40	WINKER'S SONG Ivor Biggun ●	Beggars Banquet	1

WEEK ENDING 23 SEPTEMBER 1978

LW	TW	Title / Artist	Label	Wks
2	[1]	DREADLOCK HOLIDAY 10 C.C.	Mercury	6
1	2	THREE TIMES A LADY Commodores	Motown	7
5	[3]	OH WHAT A CIRCUS David Essex	Mercury	6
6	[4]	JILTED JOHN Jilted John	EMI International	7
3	5	RIVERS OF BABYLON/BROWN GIRL IN THE RING Boney M	Atlantic	22
10	[6]	KISS YOU ALL OVER Exile	RAK	4
21	7	SUMMER NIGHT CITY Abba	Epic	2
4	8	IT'S RAINING Darts	Magnet	7
19	9	GREASE Frankie Valli	RSO	4
7	10	HONG KONG GARDEN Slouxsie & the Banshees	Polydor	4
-	11	SUMMER NIGHTS John Travola and Olivia Newton-John	RSO	1
13	[12]	PICTURE THIS Blondie	Chrysalis	4
14	[13]	AGAIN AND AGAIN Status Quo	Vertigo	4
8	14	BRITISH HUSTLE Hi Tension	Island	6
16	15	FORGET ABOUT YOU Motors	Virgin	5
11	16	AN EVERLASTING LOVE Andy Gibb	RSO	6
-	17	LOVE DON'T LIVE HERE ANYMORE Rose Royce	Whitfield	1
12	18	YOU'RE THE ONE THAT I WANT John Travolta and Olivia Newton-John	RSO	18
15	19	I THOUGHT IT WAS YOU Herbie Hancock	CBS	5
26	20	YOU MAKE ME FEEL Sylvester	Fantasy	6
9	21	SUPER NATURE Cerrone	Atlantic	8
17	22	TOP OF THE POPS Rezillos	Sire	6
22	23	YOU'RE THE ONE THAT I WANT Hylda Baker and Arthur Mullard	Pye	2
18	24	IT'S ONLY MAKE BELIEVE Child	Ariola Hansa	8
28	[25]	DAVID WATTS/A BOMB IN WARDOUR STREET Jam	Polydor	5
24	26	GALAXY OF LOVE Crown Heights Affair	Philips	5
25	27	A ROSE HAS TO DIE Dooleys	GTO	3
32	28	TALKING IN YOUR SLEEP Crystal Gayle	United Artists	3
-	29	I CAN'T STOP LOVIN' YOU Leo Sayer	Chrysalis	1
23	30	WHO ARE YOU Who	Polydor	9
40	31	WINKER'S SONG Ivor Biggun	Beggars Banquet	2
20	32	BABY STOP CRYING Bob Dylan	CBS	9
27	33	FOREVER AUTUMN Justin Hayward	CBS	11
33	34	TWO OUT OF THREE AIN'T BAD Meat Loaf	Epic	4
34	35	GOT A FEELING Patrick Juvet	Casablanca	3
-	36	LUCKY STARS Dean Friedman ●	Lifesong	1
29	37	BOOGIE OOGIE OOGIE A Taste Of Honey	Capitol	13
31	38	SUBSTITUTE Clout	Carrere	13
-	[39]	WHAT YOU WAITING FOR Stargard	MCA	1
-	[40]	WHERE DID OUR LOVE GO/JE VOULAIS TE DIRE Manhatten Transfer	Atlantic	1

WEEK ENDING 30 SEPTEMBER 1978

LW	TW	Title / Artist	Label	Wks
11	[1]	SUMMER NIGHTS John Travola and Olivia Newton-John	RSO	2
1	2	DREADLOCK HOLIDAY 10 C.C.	Mercury	7
9	[3]	GREASE Frankie Valli	RSO	5
17	4	LOVE DON'T LIVE HERE ANYMORE Rose Royce	Whitfield	2
2	5	THREE TIMES A LADY Commodores	Motown	8
3	6	OH WHAT A CIRCUS David Essex	Mercury	7
6	7	KISS YOU ALL OVER Exile	RAK	5
7	8	SUMMER NIGHT CITY Abba	Epic	3
4	9	JILTED JOHN Jilted John	EMI International	8
5	10	RIVERS OF BABYLON/BROWN GIRL IN THE RING Boney M	Atlantic	23
10	11	HONG KONG GARDEN Slouxsie & the Banshees	Polydor	5
12	[12]	PICTURE THIS Blondie	Chrysalis	5
27	13	A ROSE HAS TO DIE Dooleys	GTO	4
13	14	AGAIN AND AGAIN Status Quo	Vertigo	5
14	15	BRITISH HUSTLE Hi Tension	Island	7
20	16	YOU MAKE ME FEEL Sylvester	Fantasy	7
8	17	IT'S RAINING Darts	Magnet	8
15	18	FORGET ABOUT YOU Motors	Virgin	6
29	19	I CAN'T STOP LOVIN' YOU Leo Sayer	Chrysalis	2
16	20	AN EVERLASTING LOVE Andy Gibb	RSO	7
19	21	I THOUGHT IT WAS YOU Herbie Hancock	CBS	6
22	[22]	YOU'RE THE ONE THAT I WANT Hylda Baker and Arthur Mullard	Pye	3
36	23	LUCKY STARS Dean Friedman	Lifesong	2
22	24	TOP OF THE POPS Rezillos	Sire	7
31	25	WINKER'S SONG Ivor Biggun	Beggars Banquet	3
25	26	DAVID WATTS/A BOMB IN WARDOUR STREET Jam	Polydor	6
-	27	NOW THAT WE'VE FOUND LOVE Third World ●	Island	1
-	28	BLAME IT ON THE BOOGIE Jacksons	Epic	1
28	29	TALKING IN YOUR SLEEP Crystal Gayle	United Artists	4
18	30	YOU'RE THE ONE THAT I WANT John Travolta and Olivia Newton-John	RSO	19
26	31	GALAXY OF LOVE Crown Heights Affair	Philips	6
21	32	SUPER NATURE Cerrone	Atlantic	9
-	33	HAVE YOU EVER FALLEN IN LOVE Buzzcocks	United Artists	1
24	34	IT'S ONLY MAKE BELIEVE Child	Ariola Hansa	9
-	[35]	BAMA BOOGIE WOOGIE Cleveland Eton ●	Gull	1
-	[36]	EVE OF THE WAR Jeff Wayne's War Of The Worlds ●	CBS	1
35	37	GOT A FEELING Patrick Juvet	Casablanca	4
-	38	BLAME IT ON THE BOOGIE Mick Jackson ●	Atlantic	1
-	39	RESPECTABLE Rolling Stones	EMI	1
30	40	WHO ARE YOU Who	Polydor	10

WEEK ENDING 7 OCTOBER 1978

LW	TW	Title / Artist	Label	Wks
1	[1]	SUMMER NIGHTS John Travola and Olivia Newton-John	RSO	3
4	[2]	LOVE DON'T LIVE HERE ANYMORE Rose Royce	Whitfield	3
3	[3]	GREASE Frankie Valli	RSO	6
2	4	DREADLOCK HOLIDAY 10 C.C.	Mercury	8
8	[5]	SUMMER NIGHT CITY Abba	Epic	4
23	6	LUCKY STARS Dean Friedman	Lifesong	3
19	7	I CAN'T STOP LOVIN' YOU Leo Sayer	Chrysalis	3
16	8	YOU MAKE ME FEEL Sylvester	Fantasy	8
-	9	RASPUTIN Boney M	Atlantic	1
7	10	KISS YOU ALL OVER Exile	RAK	6
6	11	OH WHAT A CIRCUS David Essex	Mercury	8
5	12	THREE TIMES A LADY Commodores	Motown	9
9	13	JILTED JOHN Jilted John	EMI International	9
12	14	PICTURE THIS Blondie	Chrysalis	6
29	15	TALKING IN YOUR SLEEP Crystal Gayle	United Artists	5
13	16	A ROSE HAS TO DIE Dooleys	GTO	5
-	17	SWEET TALKIN' WOMAN Electric Light Orchestra	Jet	1
27	18	NOW THAT WE'VE FOUND LOVE Third World	Island	2
11	19	HONG KONG GARDEN Slouxsie & the Banshees	Polydor	6
14	20	AGAIN AND AGAIN Status Quo	Vertigo	6
10	21	RIVERS OF BABYLON/BROWN GIRL IN THE RING Boney M	Atlantic	24
25	[22]	WINKER'S SONG Ivor Biggun	Beggars Banquet	4
28	23	BLAME IT ON THE BOOGIE Jacksons	Epic	2
18	24	FORGET ABOUT YOU Motors	Virgin	7
20	25	AN EVERLASTING LOVE Andy Gibb	RSO	8
26	26	DAVID WATTS/A BOMB IN WARDOUR STREET Jam	Polydor	7
-	27	MEXICAN GIRL Smokie	RAK	1
17	28	IT'S RAINING Darts	Magnet	9
15	29	BRITISH HUSTLE Hi Tension	Island	8
33	30	HAVE YOU EVER FALLEN IN LOVE Buzzcocks	United Artists	2
22	31	YOU'RE THE ONE THAT I WANT Hylda Baker and Arthur Mullard	Pye	4
38	32	BLAME IT ON THE BOOGIE Mick Jackson	Atlantic	2
30	33	YOU'RE THE ONE THAT I WANT John Travolta and Olivia Newton-John	RSO	20
39	34	RESPECTABLE Rolling Stones	EMI	2
31	35	GALAXY OF LOVE Crown Heights Affair	Philips	7
-	36	SANDY John Travolta ●	Polydor	1
21	37	I THOUGHT IT WAS YOU Herbie Hancock	CBS	7

In these weeks ■ With two hits averaging eight weeks at number one and no other releases, John Travolta and Olivia Newton-John become and remain the most successful act per release (30.09.78) ■ Peaking at five with *Summer Night City* gives Abba their least successful single in a five year period. Frankie Valli has his biggest solo hit with Barry Gibb's title tune from 'Grease' (07.10.78)■

LW	TW	Title	Artist	Label	Wks
35	38	BAMA BOOGIE WOOGIE	Cleveland Eton	*Gull*	2
-	39	BRANDY	O'Jays	*Philadelphia*	1
-	[40]	L.A. CONNECTION	Rainbow	*Polydor*	1

LW	TW	*WEEK ENDING* 14 OCTOBER 1978			Wks
1	[1]	SUMMER NIGHTS	John Travola and Olivia Newton-John	*RSO*	4
2	[2]	LOVE DON'T LIVE HERE ANYMORE	Rose Royce	*Whitfield*	4
9	3	RASPUTIN	Boney M	*Atlantic*	2
6	4	LUCKY STARS	Dean Friedman	*Lifesong*	4
3	5	GREASE	Frankie Valli	*RSO*	7
7	[6]	I CAN'T STOP LOVIN' YOU	Leo Sayer	*Chrysalis*	4
17	7	SWEET TALKIN' WOMAN	Electric Light Orchestra	*Jet*	2
36	8	SANDY	John Travolta	*Polydor*	2
8	9	YOU MAKE ME FEEL	Sylvester	*Fantasy*	9
18	[10]	NOW THAT WE'VE FOUND LOVE	Third World	*Island*	3
16	[11]	A ROSE HAS TO DIE	Dooleys	*GTO*	6
5	12	SUMMER NIGHT CITY	Abba	*Epic*	5
23	13	BLAME IT ON THE BOOGIE	Jacksons	*Epic*	3
15	14	TALKING IN YOUR SLEEP	Crystal Gayle	*United Artists*	6
4	15	DREADLOCK HOLIDAY	10 C.C.	*Mercury*	9
10	16	KISS YOU ALL OVER	Exile	*RAK*	7
12	17	THREE TIMES A LADY	Commodores	*Motown*	10
14	18	PICTURE THIS	Blondie	*Chrysalis*	7
11	19	OH WHAT A CIRCUS	David Essex	*Mercury*	9
27	20	MEXICAN GIRL	Smokie	*RAK*	2
19	21	HONG KONG GARDEN	Slouxsie & the Banshees	*Polydor*	7
-	22	RAT TRAP	Boomtown Rats	*Ensign*	1
20	23	AGAIN AND AGAIN	Status Quo	*Vertigo*	7
30	24	HAVE YOU EVER FALLEN IN LOVE	Buzzcocks	*United Artists*	3
22	25	WINKER'S SONG	Ivor Biggun	*Beggars Banquet*	5
13	26	JILTED JOHN	Jilted John	*EMI International*	10
-	27	DIPPETY DAY	Father Abraham & the Smurfs	*Decca*	1
21	28	RIVERS OF BABYLON/BROWN GIRL IN THE RING	Boney M	*Atlantic*	25
-	29	MACARTHUR PARK	Donna Summer	*Casablanca*	1
26	30	DAVID WATTS/A BOMB IN WARDOUR STREET	Jam	*Polydor*	8
34	31	RESPECTABLE	Rolling Stones	*EMI*	3
39	32	BRANDY	O'Jays	*Philadelphia*	2
-	33	GIVIN' UP GIVIN' IN	Three Degrees	*Ariola*	1
-	34	DARLIN'	Frankie Miller	*Chrysalis*	1
31	35	YOU'RE THE ONE THAT I WANT	Hylda Baker and Arthur Mullard	*Pye*	5
-	36	ONE FOR YOU ONE FOR ME	Jonathan King	*GTO*	1
-	37	HURRY UP HARRY	Sham 69	*Polydor*	1
32	38	BLAME IT ON THE BOOGIE	Mick Jackson	*Atlantic*	3
-	[39]	DON'T COME CLOSE	Ramones	*Sire*	1
-	40	EVE OF THE WAR	Jeff Wayne's War Of The Worlds	*CBS*	2

LW	TW	*WEEK ENDING* 21 OCTOBER 1978			Wks
1	[1]	SUMMER NIGHTS	John Travola and Olivia Newton-John	*RSO*	5
3	[2]	RASPUTIN	Boney M	*Atlantic*	3
4	[3]	LUCKY STARS	Dean Friedman	*Lifesong*	5
8	4	SANDY	John Travolta	*Polydor*	3
2	5	LOVE DON'T LIVE HERE ANYMORE	Rose Royce	*Whitfield*	5
7	[6]	SWEET TALKIN' WOMAN	Electric Light Orchestra	*Jet*	3
6	7	I CAN'T STOP LOVIN' YOU	Leo Sayer	*Chrysalis*	5
5	8	GREASE	Frankie Valli	*RSO*	8
22	9	RAT TRAP	Boomtown Rats	*Ensign*	2
9	10	YOU MAKE ME FEEL	Sylvester	*Fantasy*	10
10	11	NOW THAT WE'VE FOUND LOVE	Third World	*Island*	4
29	12	MACARTHUR PARK	Donna Summer	*Casablanca*	2
14	13	TALKING IN YOUR SLEEP	Crystal Gayle	*United Artists*	7
13	14	BLAME IT ON THE BOOGIE	Jacksons	*Epic*	4
38	15	BLAME IT ON THE BOOGIE	Mick Jackson	*Atlantic*	4
24	16	HAVE YOU EVER FALLEN IN LOVE	Buzzcocks	*United Artists*	4
37	17	HURRY UP HARRY	Sham 69	*Polydor*	2
11	18	A ROSE HAS TO DIE	Dooleys	*GTO*	7
20	[19]	MEXICAN GIRL	Smokie	*RAK*	3
12	20	SUMMER NIGHT CITY	Abba	*Epic*	6
-	21	PUBLIC IMAGE	Public Image Ltd	*Virgin*	1
16	22	KISS YOU ALL OVER	Exile	*RAK*	8

□ Highest position disc reached ● Act's first ever week on chart

LW	TW	Title	Artist	Label	Wks
15	23	DREADLOCK HOLIDAY	10 C.C.	*Mercury*	10
18	24	PICTURE THIS	Blondie	*Chrysalis*	8
-	25	DOWN IN THE TUBE STATION AT MIDNIGHT	Jam	*Polydor*	1
27	26	DIPPETY DAY	Father Abraham & the Smurfs	*Decca*	2
31	27	RESPECTABLE	Rolling Stones	*EMI*	4
34	28	DARLIN'	Frankie Miller	*Chrysalis*	2
33	29	GIVIN' UP GIVIN' IN	Three Degrees	*Ariola*	2
25	30	WINKER'S SONG	Ivor Biggun	*Beggars Banquet*	6
36	31	ONE FOR YOU ONE FOR ME	Jonathan King	*GTO*	2
17	32	THREE TIMES A LADY	Commodores	*Motown*	11
-	[33]	HARD ROAD	Black Sabbath	*Vertigo*	1
32	34	BRANDY	O'Jays	*Philadelphia*	3
-	35	GOT TO GET YOU INTO MY LIFE	Earth Wind & Fire	*CBS*	1
26	36	JILTED JOHN	Jilted John	*EMI International*	11
28	37	RIVERS OF BABYLON/BROWN GIRL IN THE RING	Boney M	*Atlantic*	26
-	38	GET IT WHILE YOU CAN	Olympic Runners ●	*Polydor*	1
-	[39]	COMING HOME	Marshall Hain	*Harvest*	1
-	40	FOOL (IF YOU THINK IT'S OVER)	Chris Rea ●	*Magnet*	1

LW	TW	*WEEK ENDING* 28 OCTOBER 1978			Wks
1	[1]	SUMMER NIGHTS	John Travola and Olivia Newton-John	*RSO*	6
2	[2]	RASPUTIN	Boney M	*Atlantic*	4
4	3	SANDY	John Travolta	*Polydor*	4
3	4	LUCKY STARS	Dean Friedman	*Lifesong*	6
12	[5]	MACARTHUR PARK	Donna Summer	*Casablanca*	3
6	[6]	SWEET TALKIN' WOMAN	Electric Light Orchestra	*Jet*	4
9	7	RAT TRAP	Boomtown Rats	*Ensign*	3
5	8	LOVE DON'T LIVE HERE ANYMORE	Rose Royce	*Whitfield*	6
14	9	BLAME IT ON THE BOOGIE	Jacksons	*Epic*	5
7	10	I CAN'T STOP LOVIN' YOU	Leo Sayer	*Chrysalis*	6
13	[11]	TALKING IN YOUR SLEEP	Crystal Gayle	*United Artists*	8
11	12	NOW THAT WE'VE FOUND LOVE	Third World	*Island*	5
21	13	PUBLIC IMAGE	Public Image Ltd	*Virgin*	2
16	14	HAVE YOU EVER FALLEN IN LOVE	Buzzcocks	*United Artists*	5
29	15	GIVIN' UP GIVIN' IN	Three Degrees	*Ariola*	3
17	16	HURRY UP HARRY	Sham 69	*Polydor*	3
15	17	BLAME IT ON THE BOOGIE	Mick Jackson	*Atlantic*	5
26	18	DIPPETY DAY	Father Abraham & the Smurfs	*Decca*	3
28	19	DARLIN'	Frankie Miller	*Chrysalis*	3
19	20	MEXICAN GIRL	Smokie	*RAK*	4
10	21	YOU MAKE ME FEEL	Sylvester	*Fantasy*	11
34	22	BRANDY	O'Jays	*Philadelphia*	4
8	23	GREASE	Frankie Valli	*RSO*	9
18	24	A ROSE HAS TO DIE	Dooleys	*GTO*	8
25	25	DOWN IN THE TUBE STATION AT MIDNIGHT	Jam	*Polydor*	2
27	26	RESPECTABLE	Rolling Stones	*EMI*	5
-	27	BICYCLE RACE/FAT BOTTOMED GIRLS	Queen	*Queen*	1
-	28	INSTANT REPLAY	Dan Hartman ●	*Blue Sky*	1
31	[29]	ONE FOR YOU ONE FOR ME	Jonathan King	*GTO*	3
40	[30]	FOOL (IF YOU THINK IT'S OVER)	Chris Rea	*Magnet*	2
22	31	KISS YOU ALL OVER	Exile	*RAK*	9
-	32	PART TIME LOVE	Elton John	*Rocket*	1
35	[33]	GOT TO GET YOU INTO MY LIFE	Earth Wind & Fire	*CBS*	2
20	34	SUMMER NIGHT CITY	Abba	*Epic*	7
38	[35]	GET IT WHILE YOU CAN	Olympic Runners	*Polydor*	2
-	36	SILVER MACHINE	Hawkwind	*United Artists*	1
33	37	HARD ROAD	Black Sabbath	*Vertigo*	2
-	38	TEENAGE KICKS	Undertones ●	*Sir*	1
30	39	WINKER'S SONG	Ivor Biggun	*Beggars Banquet*	7
23	40	DREADLOCK HOLIDAY	10 C.C.	*Mercury*	11

LW	TW	*WEEK ENDING* 4 NOVEMBER 1978			Wks
1	[1]	SUMMER NIGHTS	John Travola and Olivia Newton-John	*RSO*	7
3	[2]	SANDY	John Travolta	*Polydor*	5
7	3	RAT TRAP	Boomtown Rats	*Ensign*	4
2	4	RASPUTIN	Boney M	*Atlantic*	5

■The Electric Light Orchestra complete one of pop's strangest feats: a hat-trick of number sixes (21.10.78) ■ Chris Rea makes his career debut. It will take him eleven more years to reach the Top Ten (21.10.78) ■ John Travolta is at number two as a soloist, kept out of number one only by his duet with Olivia Newton-John. Both songs are from 'Grease' (04.11.78)■

November 1978

□ Highest position disc reached ● Act's first ever week on chart

LW	TW	Title	Artist	Label	Wks
5	5	MACARTHUR PARK	Donna Summer	*Casablanca*	4
6	6	SWEET TALKIN' WOMAN	Electric Light Orchestra	*Jet*	5
4	7	LUCKY STARS	Dean Friedman	*Lifesong*	7
9	8	BLAME IT ON THE BOOGIE	Jacksons	*Epic*	6
13	9	PUBLIC IMAGE	Public Image Ltd	*Virgin*	3
16	10	HURRY UP HARRY	Sham 69	*Polydor*	4
19	11	DARLIN'	Frankie Miller	*Chrysalis*	4
14	12	HAVE YOU EVER FALLEN IN LOVE	Buzzcocks	*United Artists*	6
18	13	DIPPETY DAY	Father Abraham & the Smurfs	*Decca*	4
15	14	GIVIN' UP GIVIN' IN	Three Degrees	*Ariola*	4
25	15	DOWN IN THE TUBE STATION AT MIDNIGHT	Jam	*Polydor*	3
8	16	LOVE DON'T LIVE HERE ANYMORE	Rose Royce	*Whitfield*	7
10	17	I CAN'T STOP LOVIN' YOU	Leo Sayer	*Chrysalis*	7
11	18	TALKING IN YOUR SLEEP	Crystal Gayle	*United Artists*	9
17	19	BLAME IT ON THE BOOGIE	Mick Jackson	*Atlantic*	6
28	20	INSTANT REPLAY	Dan Hartman	*Blue Sky*	2
27	21	BICYCLE RACE/FAT BOTTOMED GIRLS	Queen	*Queen*	2
20	22	MEXICAN GIRL	Smokie	*RAK*	5
26	23	RESPECTABLE	Rolling Stones	*EMI*	6
-	24	HOPELESSLY DEVOTED TO YOU	Olivia Newton-John	*RSO*	1
12	25	NOW THAT WE'VE FOUND LOVE	Third World	*Island*	6
23	26	GREASE	Frankie Valli	*RSO*	10
21	27	YOU MAKE ME FEEL	Sylvester	*Fantasy*	12
-	28	PRETTY LITTLE ANGEL EYES	Showaddywaddy	*Arista*	1
-	29	RADIO RADIO	Elvis Costello	*Radar*	1
32	30	PART TIME LOVE	Elton John	*Rocket*	2
38	31	TEENAGE KICKS	Undertones	*Sir*	2
22	32	BRANDY	O'Jays	*Philadelphia*	5
24	33	A ROSE HAS TO DIE	Dooleys	*GTO*	9
36	34	SILVER MACHINE	Hawkwind	*United Artists*	2
29	35	ONE FOR YOU ONE FOR ME	Jonathan King	*GTO*	4
-	36	ALWAYS AND FOREVER/MIND BLOWING DECISIONS	Heatwave	*GTO*	1
33	37	GOT TO GET YOU INTO MY LIFE	Earth Wind & Fire	*CBS*	3
35	38	GET IT WHILE YOU CAN	Olympic Runners	*Polydor*	3
-	39	PROMISES	Eric Clapton	*RSO*	1
39	40	WINKER'S SONG	Ivor Biggun	*Beggars Banquet*	8

LW	TW	*WEEK ENDING* 11 NOVEMBER 1978			Wks
1	1	SUMMER NIGHTS	John Travola and Olivia Newton-John	*RSO*	8
3	2	RAT TRAP	Boomtown Rats	*Ensign*	5
2	3	SANDY	John Travolta	*Polydor*	6
24	4	HOPELESSLY DEVOTED TO YOU	Olivia Newton-John	*RSO*	2
5	5	MACARTHUR PARK	Donna Summer	*Casablanca*	5
11	6	DARLIN'	Frankie Miller	*Chrysalis*	5
4	7	RASPUTIN	Boney M	*Atlantic*	6
8	8	BLAME IT ON THE BOOGIE	Jacksons	*Epic*	7
6	9	SWEET TALKIN' WOMAN	Electric Light Orchestra	*Jet*	6
-	10	MY BEST FRIEND'S GIRL	Cars ●	*Elektra*	1
9	11	PUBLIC IMAGE	Public Image Ltd	*Virgin*	4
14	12	GIVIN' UP GIVIN' IN	Three Degrees	*Ariola*	5
21	13	BICYCLE RACE/FAT BOTTOMED GIRLS	Queen	*Queen*	3
7	14	LUCKY STARS	Dean Friedman	*Lifesong*	8
13	15	DIPPETY DAY	Father Abraham & the Smurfs	*Decca*	5
28	16	PRETTY LITTLE ANGEL EYES	Showaddywaddy	*Arista*	2
20	17	INSTANT REPLAY	Dan Hartman	*Blue Sky*	3
10	18	HURRY UP HARRY	Sham 69	*Polydor*	5
12	19	HAVE YOU EVER FALLEN IN LOVE	Buzzcocks	*United Artists*	7
15	20	DOWN IN THE TUBE STATION AT MIDNIGHT	Jam	*Polydor*	4
32	21	BRANDY	O'Jays	*Philadelphia*	6
22	22	MEXICAN GIRL	Smokie	*RAK*	6
19	23	BLAME IT ON THE BOOGIE	Mick Jackson	*Atlantic*	7
30	24	PART TIME LOVE	Elton John	*Rocket*	3
23	25	RESPECTABLE	Rolling Stones	*EMI*	7
36	26	ALWAYS AND FOREVER/MIND BLOWING DECISIONS	Heatwave	*GTO*	2
-	27	HANGING ON THE TELEPHONE	Blondie	*Chrysalis*	1
-	28	I LOVE AMERICA	Patrick Juvet	*Casablanca*	1
-	29	TOAST/HOLD ON	Streetband ●	*Logo*	1
17	30	I CAN'T STOP LOVIN' YOU	Leo Sayer	*Chrysalis*	8
26	31	GREASE	Frankie Valli	*RSO*	11
18	32	TALKING IN YOUR SLEEP	Crystal Gayle	*United Artists*	10
29	33	RADIO RADIO	Elvis Costello	*Radar*	2
-	34	GERM FREE ADOLESCENCE	X-Ray Spex	*EMI International*	1
16	35	LOVE DON'T LIVE HERE ANYMORE	Rose Royce	*Whitfield*	8
27	36	YOU MAKE ME FEEL	Sylvester	*Fantasy*	13
25	37	NOW THAT WE'VE FOUND LOVE	Third World	*Island*	7
31	38	TEENAGE KICKS	Undertones	*Sir*	3
-	39	WHAT A NIGHT	City Boy	*Vertigo*	1
37	40	GOT TO GET YOU INTO MY LIFE	Earth Wind & Fire	*CBS*	4

LW	TW	*WEEK ENDING* 18 NOVEMBER 1978			Wks
2	1	RAT TRAP	Boomtown Rats	*Ensign*	6
4	2	HOPELESSLY DEVOTED TO YOU	Olivia Newton-John	*RSO*	3
1	3	SUMMER NIGHTS	John Travola and Olivia Newton-John	*RSO*	9
3	4	SANDY	John Travolta	*Polydor*	7
10	5	MY BEST FRIEND'S GIRL	Cars	*Elektra*	2
6	6	DARLIN'	Frankie Miller	*Chrysalis*	6
16	7	PRETTY LITTLE ANGEL EYES	Showaddywaddy	*Arista*	3
17	8	INSTANT REPLAY	Dan Hartman	*Blue Sky*	4
5	9	MACARTHUR PARK	Donna Summer	*Casablanca*	6
8	10	BLAME IT ON THE BOOGIE	Jacksons	*Epic*	8
7	11	RASPUTIN	Boney M	*Atlantic*	7
12	12	GIVIN' UP GIVIN' IN	Three Degrees	*Ariola*	6
13	13	BICYCLE RACE/FAT BOTTOMED GIRLS	Queen	*Queen*	4
-	14	DO YOU THINK I'M SEXY?	Rod Stewart	*Riva*	1
9	15	SWEET TALKIN' WOMAN	Electric Light Orchestra	*Jet*	7
15	16	DIPPETY DAY	Father Abraham & the Smurfs	*Decca*	6
11	17	PUBLIC IMAGE	Public Image Ltd	*Virgin*	5
27	18	HANGING ON THE TELEPHONE	Blondie	*Chrysalis*	2
18	19	HURRY UP HARRY	Sham 69	*Polydor*	6
19	20	HAVE YOU EVER FALLEN IN LOVE	Buzzcocks	*United Artists*	8
20	21	DOWN IN THE TUBE STATION AT MIDNIGHT	Jam	*Polydor*	5
28	22	I LOVE AMERICA	Patrick Juvet	*Casablanca*	2
26	23	ALWAYS AND FOREVER/MIND BLOWING DECISIONS	Heatwave	*GTO*	3
24	24	PART TIME LOVE	Elton John	*Rocket*	4
29	25	TOAST/HOLD ON	Streetband	*Logo*	2
25	26	RESPECTABLE	Rolling Stones	*EMI*	8
14	27	LUCKY STARS	Dean Friedman	*Lifesong*	9
-	28	DON'T LET IT FADE AWAY	Darts	*Magnet*	1
29	29	RADIO RADIO	Elvis Costello	*Radar*	3
34	30	GERM FREE ADOLESCENCE	X-Ray Spex	*EMI International*	2
-	31	I LOST MY HEART TO A STARSHIP TROOPER	S. Brightman and Hot Gossip ●	*Ariola*	1
23	32	BLAME IT ON THE BOOGIE	Mick Jackson	*Atlantic*	8
-	33	DON'T CRY OUT LOUD	Elkie Brooks	*A&M*	1
-	34	EAST RIVER	Brecker Brothers ●	*Arista*	1
-	35	LAY LOVE ON YOU	Luisa Fernandez ●	*Warner Brothers*	1
-	36	GIVING IT BACK	Phil Hurtt ●	*Fantasy*	1
-	37	PROMISES	Eric Clapton	*RSO*	1
-	38	I LOVE THE NIGHT LIFE	Alicia Bridges ●	*Polydor*	1
-	39	SHOOTING STAR	Dollar ●	*Carrere*	1
-	40	LE FREAK	Chic	*Atlantic*	1

LW	TW	*WEEK ENDING* 25 NOVEMBER 1978			Wks
1	1	RAT TRAP	Boomtown Rats	*Ensign*	7
2	2	HOPELESSLY DEVOTED TO YOU	Olivia Newton-John	*RSO*	4
5	3	MY BEST FRIEND'S GIRL	Cars	*Elektra*	3
14	4	DO YOU THINK I'M SEXY?	Rod Stewart	*Riva*	2
7	5	PRETTY LITTLE ANGEL EYES	Showaddywaddy	*Arista*	4
6	6	DARLIN'	Frankie Miller	*Chrysalis*	7
3	7	SUMMER NIGHTS	John Travola and Olivia Newton-John	*RSO*	10
8	8	INSTANT REPLAY	Dan Hartman	*Blue Sky*	5
18	9	HANGING ON THE TELEPHONE	Blondie	*Chrysalis*	3
4	10	SANDY	John Travolta	*Polydor*	8
13	11	BICYCLE RACE/FAT BOTTOMED GIRLS	Queen	*Queen*	5
22	12	I LOVE AMERICA	Patrick Juvet	*Casablanca*	3
10	13	BLAME IT ON THE BOOGIE	Jacksons	*Epic*	9

In these weeks ■ The Cars enter the Top Ten with the first in what will become an industry craze of picture discs (11.11.78) ■ The Boomtown Rats have the first New Wave number one (18.11.78) ■ It's Olivia Newton-John's turn to peak at two with a solo single from 'Grease' (25.11.78)■

LW	TW	Title / Artist	Label	Wks
23	14	ALWAYS AND FOREVER/MIND BLOWING DECISIONS Heatwave	GTO	4
9	15	MACARTHUR PARK Donna Summer	Casablanca	7
24	16	PART TIME LOVE Elton John	Rocket	5
12	17	GIVIN' UP GIVIN' IN Three Degrees	Ariola	7
25	[18]	TOAST/HOLD ON Streetband	Logo	3
30	[19]	GERM FREE ADOLESCENCE X-Ray Spex	EMI International	3
16	20	DIPPETY DAY Father Abraham & the Smurfs	Decca	7
17	21	PUBLIC IMAGE Public Image Ltd	Virgin	6
11	22	RASPUTIN Boney M	Atlantic	8
40	23	LE FREAK Chic	Atlantic	2
-	24	IN THE BUSH Musique ●	CBS	1
31	25	I LOST MY HEART TO A STARSHIP TROOPER S. Brightman and Hot Gossip	Ariola	2
-	26	TOO MUCH HEAVEN Bee Gees	RSO	1
28	27	DON'T LET IT FADE AWAY Darts	Magnet	2
33	28	DON'T CRY OUT LOUD Elkie Brooks	A&M	2
-	[29]	DANCE (DISCO HEAT) Sylvester	Fantasy	1
39	30	SHOOTING STAR Dollar	Carrere	2
-	[31]	LYDIA Dean Friedman	Lifesong	1
38	[32]	I LOVE THE NIGHT LIFE Alicia Bridges	Polydor	2
35	33	LAY LOVE ON YOU Luisa Fernandez	Warner Brothers	2
15	34	SWEET TALKIN' WOMAN Electric Light Orchestra	Jet	8
29	35	RADIO RADIO Elvis Costello	Radar	4
19	36	HURRY UP HARRY Sham 69	Polydor	7
-	37	PROMISES Buzzcocks	United Artists	1
27	38	LUCKY STARS Dean Friedman	Lifesong	10
21	39	DOWN IN THE TUBE STATION AT MIDNIGHT Jam	Polydor	6
-	[40]	HOMICIDE 999 ●	United Artists	1

LW	TW	*WEEK ENDING* 2 DECEMBER 1978		Wks
4	[1]	DO YOU THINK I'M SEXY? Rod Stewart	Riva	3
1	2	RAT TRAP Boomtown Rats	Ensign	8
2	3	HOPELESSLY DEVOTED TO YOU Olivia Newton-John	RSO	5
3	4	MY BEST FRIEND'S GIRL Cars	Elektra	4
9	[5]	HANGING ON THE TELEPHONE Blondie	Chrysalis	4
5	6	PRETTY LITTLE ANGEL EYES Showaddywaddy	Arista	5
-	7	MARY'S BOY CHILD Boney M	Atlantic	1
8	[8]	INSTANT REPLAY Dan Hartman	Blue Sky	6
25	9	I LOST MY HEART TO A STARSHIP TROOPER S. Brightman and Hot Gossip	Ariola	3
6	10	DARLIN' Frankie Miller	Chrysalis	8
14	11	ALWAYS AND FOREVER/MIND BLOWING DECISIONS Heatwave	GTO	5
28	[12]	DON'T CRY OUT LOUD Elkie Brooks	A&M	3
11	13	BICYCLE RACE/FAT BOTTOMED GIRLS Queen	Queen	6
26	14	TOO MUCH HEAVEN Bee Gees	RSO	2
7	15	SUMMER NIGHTS John Travola and Olivia Newton-John	RSO	11
16	16	PART TIME LOVE Elton John	Rocket	6
12	17	I LOVE AMERICA Patrick Juvet	Casablanca	4
23	18	LE FREAK Chic	Atlantic	3
-	19	A TASTE OF AGGRO Barron Knights	Epic	1
27	20	DON'T LET IT FADE AWAY Darts	Magnet	3
10	21	SANDY John Travolta	Polydor	9
19	22	GERM FREE ADOLESCENCE X-Ray Spex	EMI International	4
17	23	GIVIN' UP GIVIN' IN Three Degrees	Ariola	8
18	24	TOAST/HOLD ON Streetband	Logo	4
-	25	YMCA Village People ●	Mercury	1
24	26	IN THE BUSH Musique	CBS	2
30	27	SHOOTING STAR Dollar	Carrere	3
37	28	PROMISES Buzzcocks	United Artists	2
-	29	TOMMY GUN Clash	CBS	1
-	30	YOU DON'T BRING ME FLOWERS Barbra & Neil ●	CBS	1
33	[31]	LAY LOVE ON YOU Luisa Fernandez	Warner Brothers	3
29	32	DANCE (DISCO HEAT) Sylvester	Fantasy	2
13	33	BLAME IT ON THE BOOGIE Jacksons	Epic	10
15	34	MACARTHUR PARK Donna Summer	Casablanca	8
31	35	LYDIA Dean Friedman	Lifesong	2
-	[36]	ACCIDENT PRONE Status Quo	Vertigo	1
-	37	GREASED LIGHTNING John Travolta	Polydor	1
32	38	I LOVE THE NIGHT LIFE Alicia Bridges	Polydor	3
20	39	DIPPETY DAY Father Abraham & the Smurfs	Decca	8
-	40	LAY YOUR LOVE ON ME Racey ●	RAK	1

December 1978

□ Highest position disc reached ● Act's first ever week on chart

LW	TW	*WEEK ENDING* 9 DECEMBER 1978		Wks
7	[1]	MARY'S BOY CHILD Boney M	Atlantic	2
1	2	DO YOU THINK I'M SEXY? Rod Stewart	Riva	4
14	[3]	TOO MUCH HEAVEN Bee Gees	RSO	3
19	4	A TASTE OF AGGRO Barron Knights	Epic	2
2	5	RAT TRAP Boomtown Rats	Ensign	9
9	[6]	I LOST MY HEART TO A STARSHIP TROOPER S. Brightman and Hot Gossip	Ariola	4
5	7	HANGING ON THE TELEPHONE Blondie	Chrysalis	5
18	8	LE FREAK Chic	Atlantic	4
11	[9]	ALWAYS AND FOREVER/MIND BLOWING DECISIONS Heatwave	GTO	6
3	10	HOPELESSLY DEVOTED TO YOU Olivia Newton-John	RSO	6
4	11	MY BEST FRIEND'S GIRL Cars	Elektra	5
25	12	YMCA Village People	Mercury	2
12	13	DON'T CRY OUT LOUD Elkie Brooks	A&M	4
6	14	PRETTY LITTLE ANGEL EYES Showaddywaddy	Arista	6
8	15	INSTANT REPLAY Dan Hartman	Blue Sky	7
10	16	DARLIN' Frankie Miller	Chrysalis	9
26	17	IN THE BUSH Musique	CBS	3
17	18	I LOVE AMERICA Patrick Juvet	Casablanca	5
20	19	DON'T LET IT FADE AWAY Darts	Magnet	4
16	20	PART TIME LOVE Elton John	Rocket	7
13	21	BICYCLE RACE/FAT BOTTOMED GIRLS Queen	Queen	7
22	22	GERM FREE ADOLESCENCE X-Ray Spex	EMI International	5
37	23	GREASED LIGHTNING John Travolta	Polydor	2
40	24	LAY YOUR LOVE ON ME Racey	RAK	2
30	25	YOU DON'T BRING ME FLOWERS Barbra & Neil	CBS	2
27	26	SHOOTING STAR Dollar	Carrere	4
29	27	TOMMY GUN Clash	CBS	2
-	28	RAINING IN MY HEART Leo Sayer	Chrysalis	1
24	29	TOAST/HOLD ON Streetband	Logo	5
15	30	SUMMER NIGHTS John Travola and Olivia Newton-John	RSO	12
32	31	DANCE (DISCO HEAT) Sylvester	Fantasy	3
-	32	I'M EVERY WOMAN Chaka Khan ●	Warner Brothers	1
21	33	SANDY John Travolta	Polydor	10
-	34	DR. WHO Mankind ●	Pinnacle	1
28	35	PROMISES Buzzcocks	United Artists	3
-	36	I'LL PUT YOU TOGETHER AGAIN Hot Chocolate	RAK	1
38	37	I LOVE THE NIGHT LIFE Alicia Bridges	Polydor	4
35	38	LYDIA Dean Friedman	Lifesong	3
36	39	ACCIDENT PRONE Status Quo	Vertigo	2
-	40	CHRISTMAS IN SMURFLAND Father Abraham	Decca	1

LW	TW	*WEEK ENDING* 16 DECEMBER 1978		Wks
1	[1]	MARY'S BOY CHILD Boney M	Atlantic	3
12	2	YMCA Village People	Mercury	3
2	3	DO YOU THINK I'M SEXY? Rod Stewart	Riva	5
4	4	A TASTE OF AGGRO Barron Knights	Epic	3
3	5	TOO MUCH HEAVEN Bee Gees	RSO	4
6	[6]	I LOST MY HEART TO A STARSHIP TROOPER S. Brightman and Hot Gossip	Ariola	5
8	[7]	LE FREAK Chic	Atlantic	5
25	8	YOU DON'T BRING ME FLOWERS Barbra & Neil	CBS	3
9	[9]	ALWAYS AND FOREVER/MIND BLOWING DECISIONS Heatwave	GTO	7
7	10	HANGING ON THE TELEPHONE Blondie	Chrysalis	6
24	11	LAY YOUR LOVE ON ME Racey	RAK	3
13	[12]	DON'T CRY OUT LOUD Elkie Brooks	A&M	5
5	13	RAT TRAP Boomtown Rats	Ensign	10
14	14	PRETTY LITTLE ANGEL EYES Showaddywaddy	Arista	7
20	[15]	PART TIME LOVE Elton John	Rocket	8
17	[16]	IN THE BUSH Musique	CBS	4
23	17	GREASED LIGHTNING John Travolta	Polydor	3
19	[18]	DON'T LET IT FADE AWAY Darts	Magnet	5
26	19	SHOOTING STAR Dollar	Carrere	5
27	20	TOMMY GUN Clash	CBS	3

■Rod Stewart becomes the third soloist, after Elvis Presley and Cliff Richard, to achieve five number ones (02.12.78) ■ *Mary's Boy Child* is a number one for Boney M twenty one years after if performed similarly for Harry Belafonte (09.12.78) ■ *Song For Guy* is Elton John's only instrumental hit (there is a spoken word passage at the end) (16.12.78)■

December 1978

☐ Highest position disc reached ● Act's first ever week on chart

(Boxed positions are shown as [N].)

LW	TW	Title	Artist	Label	Wks
18	21	I LOVE AMERICA	Patrick Juvet	*Casablanca*	6
-	22	SONG FOR GUY	Elton John	*Rocket*	1
35	23	PROMISES	Buzzcocks	*United Artists*	4
11	24	MY BEST FRIEND'S GIRL	Cars	*Elektra*	6
36	25	I'LL PUT YOU TOGETHER AGAIN	Hot Chocolate	*RAK*	2
10	26	HOPELESSLY DEVOTED TO YOU	Olivia Newton-John	*RSO*	7
34	27	DR. WHO	Mankind	*Pinnacle*	2
-	28	SEPTEMBER	Earth Wind & Fire	*CBS*	1
15	29	INSTANT REPLAY	Dan Hartman	*Blue Sky*	8
-	30	HIT ME WITH YOUR RHYTHM STICK	Ian Dury & the Blockheads	*Stiff*	1
32	31	I'M EVERY WOMAN	Chaka Khan	*Warner Brothers*	2
40	32	CHRISTMAS IN SMURFLAND	Father Abraham	*Decca*	2
16	33	DARLIN'	Frankie Miller	*Chrysalis*	10
-	[34]	ELO EP	Electric Light Orchestra	*Jet*	1
21	35	BICYCLE RACE/FAT BOTTOMED GIRLS	Queen	*Queen*	8
28	36	RAINING IN MY HEART	Leo Sayer	*Chrysalis*	2
22	37	GERM FREE ADOLESCENCE	X-Ray Spex	*EMI International*	6
31	38	DANCE (DISCO HEAT)	Sylvester	*Fantasy*	4
-	39	ONE NATION UNDER A GROOVE	Funkadelic ●	*Warner Brothers*	1
-	40	MY LIFE	Billy Joel	*CBS*	1

WEEK ENDING 23 DECEMBER 1978

LW	TW	Title	Artist	Label	Wks
1	[1]	MARY'S BOY CHILD	Boney M	*Atlantic*	4
2	2	YMCA	Village People	*Mercury*	4
4	[3]	A TASTE OF AGGRO	Barron Knights	*Epic*	4
5	4	TOO MUCH HEAVEN	Bee Gees	*RSO*	5
8	[5]	YOU DON'T BRING ME FLOWERS	Barbra & Neil	*CBS*	4
11	6	LAY YOUR LOVE ON ME	Racey	*RAK*	4
6	7	I LOST MY HEART TO A STARSHIP TROOPER	S. Brightman and Hot Gossip	*Ariola*	6
3	8	DO YOU THINK I'M SEXY?	Rod Stewart	*Riva*	6
7	9	LE FREAK	Chic	*Atlantic*	6
22	10	SONG FOR GUY	Elton John	*Rocket*	2
17	[11]	GREASED LIGHTNING	John Travolta	*Polydor*	4
9	12	ALWAYS AND FOREVER/MIND BLOWING DECISIONS	Heatwave	*GTO*	8
30	13	HIT ME WITH YOUR RHYTHM STICK	Ian Dury & the Blockheads	*Stiff*	2
31	14	I'M EVERY WOMAN	Chaka Khan	*Warner Brothers*	3
12	15	DON'T CRY OUT LOUD	Elkie Brooks	*A&M*	6
16	[16]	IN THE BUSH	Musique	*CBS*	5
10	17	HANGING ON THE TELEPHONE	Blondie	*Chrysalis*	7
19	18	SHOOTING STAR	Dollar	*Carrere*	6
32	[19]	CHRISTMAS IN SMURFLAND	Father Abraham	*Decca*	3
20	20	TOMMY GUN	Clash	*CBS*	4
36	[21]	RAINING IN MY HEART	Leo Sayer	*Chrysalis*	3
18	22	DON'T LET IT FADE AWAY	Darts	*Magnet*	6
25	23	I'LL PUT YOU TOGETHER AGAIN	Hot Chocolate	*RAK*	3
28	24	SEPTEMBER	Earth Wind & Fire	*CBS*	2
27	[25]	DR. WHO	Mankind	*Pinnacle*	3
23	26	PROMISES	Buzzcocks	*United Artists*	5
39	27	ONE NATION UNDER A GROOVE	Funkadelic	*Warner Brothers*	2
13	28	RAT TRAP	Boomtown Rats	*Ensign*	11
14	29	PRETTY LITTLE ANGEL EYES	Showaddywaddy	*Arista*	8
-	30	PLEASE COME HOME FOR CHRISTMAS	Eagles	*Asylum*	1
29	31	INSTANT REPLAY	Dan Hartman	*Blue Sky*	9
-	32	A LITTLE MORE LOVE	Olivia Newton-John	*EMI*	1
38	33	DANCE (DISCO HEAT)	Sylvester	*Fantasy*	5
34	[34]	ELO EP	Electric Light Orchestra	*Jet*	2
-	35	HELLO THIS IS JOANNIE	Paul Evans	*Spring*	1
40	36	MY LIFE	Billy Joel	*CBS*	2
-	37	MIRRORS	Sally Oldfield ●	*Bronze*	1
-	38	JUST THE WAY YOU ARE	Barry White	*20th Century*	1
21	39	I LOVE AMERICA	Patrick Juvet	*Casablanca*	7
-	40	B.A.B.Y.	Rachel Sweet ●	*Stiff*	1

WEEK ENDING 30 DECEMBER 1978

LW	TW	Title	Artist	Label	Wks
1	[1]	MARY'S BOY CHILD	Boney M	*Atlantic*	5
2	2	YMCA	Village People	*Mercury*	5
3	[3]	A TASTE OF AGGRO	Barron Knights	*Epic*	5
4	4	TOO MUCH HEAVEN	Bee Gees	*RSO*	6
5	[5]	YOU DON'T BRING ME FLOWERS	Barbra & Neil	*CBS*	5
6	6	LAY YOUR LOVE ON ME	Racey	*RAK*	5
7	7	I LOST MY HEART TO A STARSHIP TROOPER	S. Brightman and Hot Gossip	*Ariola*	7
8	8	DO YOU THINK I'M SEXY?	Rod Stewart	*Riva*	7
9	9	LE FREAK	Chic	*Atlantic*	7
10	10	SONG FOR GUY	Elton John	*Rocket*	3
11	[11]	GREASED LIGHTNING	John Travolta	*Polydor*	5
12	12	ALWAYS AND FOREVER/MIND BLOWING DECISIONS	Heatwave	*GTO*	9
13	13	HIT ME WITH YOUR RHYTHM STICK	Ian Dury & the Blockheads	*Stiff*	3
14	14	I'M EVERY WOMAN	Chaka Khan	*Warner Brothers*	4
15	15	DON'T CRY OUT LOUD	Elkie Brooks	*A&M*	7
16	[16]	IN THE BUSH	Musique	*CBS*	6
17	17	HANGING ON THE TELEPHONE	Blondie	*Chrysalis*	8
18	18	SHOOTING STAR	Dollar	*Carrere*	7
19	[19]	CHRISTMAS IN SMURFLAND	Father Abraham	*Decca*	4
20	20	TOMMY GUN	Clash	*CBS*	5
21	[21]	RAINING IN MY HEART	Leo Sayer	*Chrysalis*	4
22	22	DON'T LET IT FADE AWAY	Darts	*Magnet*	7
23	23	I'LL PUT YOU TOGETHER AGAIN	Hot Chocolate	*RAK*	4
24	24	SEPTEMBER	Earth Wind & Fire	*CBS*	3
25	[25]	DR. WHO	Mankind	*Pinnacle*	4
26	26	PROMISES	Buzzcocks	*United Artists*	6
27	27	ONE NATION UNDER A GROOVE	Funkadelic	*Warner Brothers*	3
28	28	RAT TRAP	Boomtown Rats	*Ensign*	12
29	29	PRETTY LITTLE ANGEL EYES	Showaddywaddy	*Arista*	9
30	30	PLEASE COME HOME FOR CHRISTMAS	Eagles	*Asylum*	2
31	31	INSTANT REPLAY	Dan Hartman	*Blue Sky*	10
32	32	A LITTLE MORE LOVE	Olivia Newton-John	*EMI*	2
33	33	DANCE (DISCO HEAT)	Sylvester	*Fantasy*	6
34	[34]	ELO EP	Electric Light Orchestra	*Jet*	3
35	35	HELLO THIS IS JOANNIE	Paul Evans	*Spring*	2
36	36	MY LIFE	Billy Joel	*CBS*	3
37	37	MIRRORS	Sally Oldfield	*Bronze*	2
38	38	JUST THE WAY YOU ARE	Barry White	*20th Century*	2
39	39	I LOVE AMERICA	Patrick Juvet	*Casablanca*	8
40	40	B.A.B.Y.	Rachel Sweet	*Stiff*	2

In these weeks ■ Billy Joel climbs the Top 40 with *My Life* as Barry White enters with what will become the biggest UK hit version of his song *Just The Way You Are* (23.12.78) ■ John Travolta's fourth and final hit from 'Grease' is the last chart single of his career, bar a 1990 megamix (23.12.78) ■ The Barron Knights have their biggest chart record since their first hit in 1964 (23.12.78) ■

1979

..........BLONDIE have their first two number ones.......Art Garfunkel has the year's ngest-running number one, 'Bright Eyes'.......Pink Floyd release their first single in twelve years, 'Another Brick In The Wall (Part II)', and it becomes the Christmas number one..........

January 1979

☐ Highest position disc reached ● Act's first ever week on chart

LW	TW	WEEK ENDING 6 JANUARY 1979		Label	Wks
2	1	YMCA	Village People	Mercury	6
1	2	MARY'S BOY CHILD	Boney M	Atlantic	6
6	3	LAY YOUR LOVE ON ME	Racey	RAK	6
3	4	A TASTE OF AGGRO	Barron Knights	Epic	6
10	5	SONG FOR GUY	Elton John	Rocket	4
13	6	HIT ME WITH YOUR RHYTHM STICK	Ian Dury & the Blockheads	Stiff	4
5	7	YOU DON'T BRING ME FLOWERS	Barbra Streisand	CBS	6
4	8	TOO MUCH HEAVEN	Bee Gees	RSO	7
7	9	I LOST MY HEART TO A STARSHIP TROOPER	Sarah Brightman and Hot Gossip	Ariola	8
9	10	LE FREAK	Chic	Atlantic	8
8	11	DO YOU THINK I'M SEXY?	Rod Stewart	Riva	8
12	12	ALWAYS AND FOREVER/MIND BLOWING DECISIONS	Heatwave	GTO	10
11	13	GREASED LIGHTNING	John Travolta	Polydor	6
18	14	SHOOTING STAR	Dollar	Carrere	8
14	15	I'M EVERY WOMAN	Chaka Khan	Warner Brothers	5
23	16	I'LL PUT YOU TOGETHER AGAIN	Hot Chocolate	RAK	5
16	17	IN THE BUSH	Musique	CBS	7
24	18	SEPTEMBER	Earth Wind & Fire	CBS	4
20	19	TOMMY GUN	Clash	CBS	6
26	20	PROMISES	Buzzcocks	United Artists	7
32	21	A LITTLE MORE LOVE	Olivia Newton-John	EMI	3
17	22	HANGING ON THE TELEPHONE	Blondie	Chrysalis	9
21	23	RAINING IN MY HEART	Leo Sayer	Chrysalis	5
35	24	HELLO THIS IS JOANNIE	Paul Evans	Spring	3
22	25	DON'T LET IT FADE AWAY	Darts	Magnet	8
25	26	DR. WHO	Mankind	Pinnacle	5
19	27	CHRISTMAS IN SMURFLAND	Father Abraham	Decca	5
27	28	ONE NATION UNDER A GROOVE	Funkadelic	Warner Brothers	4
38	29	JUST THE WAY YOU ARE	Barry White	20th Century	3
15	30	DON'T CRY OUT LOUD	Elkie Brooks	A&M	8
33	31	DANCE (DISCO HEAT)	Sylvester	Fantasy	7
37	32	MIRRORS	Sally Oldfield	Bronze	3
-	33	YOU NEEDED ME	Anne Murray	Capitol	1
34	34	ELO EP	Electric Light Orchestra	Jet	4
40	35	B.A.B.Y.	Rachel Sweet	Stiff	3
31	36	INSTANT REPLAY	Dan Hartman	Blue Sky	11
28	37	RAT TRAP	Boomtown Rats	Ensign	13
36	38	MY LIFE	Billy Joel	CBS	4
29	39	PRETTY LITTLE ANGEL EYES	Showaddywaddy	Arista	10
-	40	CAR 67	Driver 67 ●	Logo	1

LW	TW	WEEK ENDING 13 JANUARY 1979		Label	Wks
1	1	YMCA	Village People	Mercury	7
6	2	HIT ME WITH YOUR RHYTHM STICK	Ian Dury & the Blockheads	Stiff	5
3	3	LAY YOUR LOVE ON ME	Racey	RAK	7
5	4	SONG FOR GUY	Elton John	Rocket	5
18	5	SEPTEMBER	Earth Wind & Fire	CBS	5
4	6	A TASTE OF AGGRO	Barron Knights	Epic	7
2	7	MARY'S BOY CHILD	Boney M	Atlantic	7
7	8	YOU DON'T BRING ME FLOWERS	Barbra Streisand	CBS	7
10	9	LE FREAK	Chic	Atlantic	9
8	10	TOO MUCH HEAVEN	Bee Gees	RSO	8
9	11	I LOST MY HEART TO A STARSHIP TROOPER	Sarah Brightman and Hot Gossip	Ariola	9
21	12	A LITTLE MORE LOVE	Olivia Newton-John	EMI	4
24	13	HELLO THIS IS JOANNIE	Paul Evans	Spring	4
15	14	I'M EVERY WOMAN	Chaka Khan	Warner Brothers	6
13	15	GREASED LIGHTNING	John Travolta	Polydor	7
16	16	I'LL PUT YOU TOGETHER AGAIN	Hot Chocolate	RAK	6
12	17	ALWAYS AND FOREVER/MIND BLOWING DECISIONS	Heatwave	GTO	11
28	18	ONE NATION UNDER A GROOVE	Funkadelic	Warner Brothers	5
14	19	SHOOTING STAR	Dollar	Carrere	9
11	20	DO YOU THINK I'M SEXY?	Rod Stewart	Riva	9
23	21	RAINING IN MY HEART	Leo Sayer	Chrysalis	6
29	22	JUST THE WAY YOU ARE	Barry White	20th Century	4
19	23	TOMMY GUN	Clash	CBS	7
-	24	RAMA LAMA DING DONG	Rocky Sharpe & the Replays ●	Chiswick	1
26	25	DR. WHO	Mankind	Pinnacle	6
17	26	IN THE BUSH	Musique	CBS	8
40	27	CAR 67	Driver 67	Logo	2
27	28	CHRISTMAS IN SMURFLAND	Father Abraham	Decca	6
38	29	MY LIFE	Billy Joel	CBS	5
32	30	MIRRORS	Sally Oldfield	Bronze	4
-	31	TAKE THAT TO THE BANK	Shalamar	RCA	1
33	32	YOU NEEDED ME	Anne Murray	Capitol	2
-	33	THEME FROM SUPERMAN	Original Soundtrack ●	Warner Bros.	1
-	34	COOL MEDITATION	Third World	Island	1
-	35	DON'T CRY FOR ME ARGENTINA	Shadows	EMI	1
-	36	COULD IT BE MAGIC	Barry Manilow	Arista	1
35	37	B.A.B.Y.	Rachel Sweet	Stiff	4
36	38	INSTANT REPLAY	Dan Hartman	Blue Sky	12
31	39	DANCE (DISCO HEAT)	Sylvester	Fantasy	8
34	40	ELO EP	Electric Light Orchestra	Jet	5

LW	TW	WEEK ENDING 20 JANUARY 1979		Label	Wks
1	1	YMCA	Village People	Mercury	8
2	2	HIT ME WITH YOUR RHYTHM STICK	Ian Dury & the Blockheads	Stiff	6
3	3	LAY YOUR LOVE ON ME	Racey	RAK	8
5	4	SEPTEMBER	Earth Wind & Fire	CBS	6
12	5	A LITTLE MORE LOVE	Olivia Newton-John	EMI	5
13	6	HELLO THIS IS JOANNIE	Paul Evans	Spring	5
9	7	LE FREAK	Chic	Atlantic	10
4	8	SONG FOR GUY	Elton John	Rocket	6
18	9	ONE NATION UNDER A GROOVE	Funkadelic	Warner Brothers	6
27	10	CAR 67	Driver 67	Logo	3
14	11	I'M EVERY WOMAN	Chaka Khan	Warner Brothers	7
8	12	YOU DON'T BRING ME FLOWERS	Barbra Streisand	CBS	8
16	13	I'LL PUT YOU TOGETHER AGAIN	Hot Chocolate	RAK	7
10	14	TOO MUCH HEAVEN	Bee Gees	RSO	9
22	15	JUST THE WAY YOU ARE	Barry White	20th Century	5
11	16	I LOST MY HEART TO A STARSHIP TROOPER	Sarah Brightman and Hot Gossip	Ariola	10
6	17	A TASTE OF AGGRO	Barron Knights	Epic	8
-	18	WOMAN IN LOVE	Three Degrees	Ariola	1
17	19	ALWAYS AND FOREVER/MIND BLOWING DECISIONS	Heatwave	GTO	12
24	20	RAMA LAMA DING DONG	Rocky Sharpe & the Replays	Chiswick	2
30	21	MIRRORS	Sally Oldfield	Bronze	5
19	22	SHOOTING STAR	Dollar	Carrere	10
35	23	DON'T CRY FOR ME ARGENTINA	Shadows	EMI	2
23	24	TOMMY GUN	Clash	CBS	8
25	25	DR. WHO	Mankind	Pinnacle	7
29	26	MY LIFE	Billy Joel	CBS	6
-	27	THIS IS IT	Dan Hartman	Blue Sky	1
32	28	YOU NEEDED ME	Anne Murray	Capitol	3
21	29	RAINING IN MY HEART	Leo Sayer	Chrysalis	7
31	30	TAKE THAT TO THE BANK	Shalamar	RCA	2
36	31	COULD IT BE MAGIC	Barry Manilow	Arista	2
7	32	MARY'S BOY CHILD	Boney M	Atlantic	8
26	33	IN THE BUSH	Musique	CBS	9
34	34	COOL MEDITATION	Third World	Island	2
20	35	DO YOU THINK I'M SEXY?	Rod Stewart	Riva	10
-	36	DESIRE ME	Doll ●	Beggars Banquet	1
39	37	DANCE (DISCO HEAT)	Sylvester	Fantasy	9
-	38	EVERY NIGHT	Phoebe Snow ●	CBS	1
33	39	THEME FROM SUPERMAN	Original Soundtrack	Warner Bros.	2
-	40	DON'T HOLD BACK	Chanson ●	Ariola	1

In these weeks ■ Paul Evans, who first charted in 1959, finally makes the Top Ten in 1979 with a song about the new craze for telephone answering machines (20.01.79) ■ George Clinton has his greatest UK success with Funkadelic (20.01.79) ■ It's a big week for costumed heroes, with Dr. Who and Superman in the chart and the men-in-uniform Village People at number one (20.01.79)■

WEEK ENDING 27 JANUARY 1979

LW	TW		Label	Wks
2	1	HIT ME WITH YOUR RHYTHM STICK Ian Dury & the Blockheads	*Stiff*	7
1	2	YMCA Village People	*Mercury*	9
4	3	SEPTEMBER Earth Wind & Fire	*CBS*	7
5	4	A LITTLE MORE LOVE Olivia Newton-John	*EMI*	6
18	5	WOMAN IN LOVE Three Degrees	*Ariola*	2
-	6	HEART OF GLASS Blondie	*Chrysalis*	1
3	7	LAY YOUR LOVE ON ME Racey	*RAK*	9
6	8	HELLO THIS IS JOANNIE Paul Evans	*Spring*	6
23	9	DON'T CRY FOR ME ARGENTINA Shadows	*EMI*	3
7	10	LE FREAK Chic	*Atlantic*	11
10	11	CAR 67 Driver 67	*Logo*	4
15	12	JUST THE WAY YOU ARE Barry White	*20th Century*	6
9	13	ONE NATION UNDER A GROOVE Funkadelic	*Warner Brothers*	7
8	14	SONG FOR GUY Elton John	*Rocket*	7
26	15	MY LIFE Billy Joel	*CBS*	7
11	16	I'M EVERY WOMAN Chaka Khan	*Warner Brothers*	8
20	17	RAMA LAMA DING DONG Rocky Sharpe & the Replays	*Chiswick*	3
13	18	I'LL PUT YOU TOGETHER AGAIN Hot Chocolate	*RAK*	8
14	19	TOO MUCH HEAVEN Bee Gees	*RSO*	10
30	20	TAKE THAT TO THE BANK Shalamar	*RCA*	3
34	21	COOL MEDITATION Third World	*Island*	3
28	22	YOU NEEDED ME Anne Murray	*Capitol*	4
21	23	MIRRORS Sally Oldfield	*Bronze*	6
27	24	THIS IS IT Dan Hartman	*Blue Sky*	2
-	25	I WAS MADE FOR DANCIN' Leif Garrett ●	*Atlantic*	1
31	26	COULD IT BE MAGIC Barry Manilow	*Arista*	3
-	27	MILK AND ALCOHOL Dr. Feelgood	*United Artists*	1
36	28	DESIRE ME Doll	*Beggars Banquet*	2
12	29	YOU DON'T BRING ME FLOWERS Barbra Streisand	*CBS*	9
16	30	I LOST MY HEART TO A STARSHIP TROOPER Sarah Brightman and Hot Gossip	*Ariola*	11
-	31	KING ROCKER Generation X	*Chrysalis*	1
39	32	THEME FROM SUPERMAN Original Soundtrack	*Warner Bros.*	3
40	33	DON'T HOLD BACK Chanson	*Ariola*	2
29	34	RAINING IN MY HEART Leo Sayer	*Chrysalis*	8
25	35	DR. WHO Mankind	*Pinnacle*	8
17	36	A TASTE OF AGGRO Barron Knights	*Epic*	9
38	37	EVERY NIGHT Phoebe Snow	*CBS*	2
35	38	DO YOU THINK I'M SEXY? Rod Stewart	*Riva*	11
-	39	JE SUIS MUSIC Cerrone	*CBS*	1
33	40	IN THE BUSH Musique	*CBS*	10

February 1979

□ Highest position disc reached ● Act's first ever week on chart

WEEK ENDING 3 FEBRUARY 1979

LW	TW		Label	Wks
6	1	HEART OF GLASS Blondie	*Chrysalis*	2
1	2	HIT ME WITH YOUR RHYTHM STICK Ian Dury & the Blockheads	*Stiff*	8
5	3	WOMAN IN LOVE Three Degrees	*Ariola*	3
2	4	YMCA Village People	*Mercury*	10
3	5	SEPTEMBER Earth Wind & Fire	*CBS*	8
4	6	A LITTLE MORE LOVE Olivia Newton-John	*EMI*	7
11	7	CAR 67 Driver 67	*Logo*	5
-	8	CHIQUITITA Abba	*Epic*	1
7	9	LAY YOUR LOVE ON ME Racey	*RAK*	10
9	10	DON'T CRY FOR ME ARGENTINA Shadows	*EMI*	4
8	11	HELLO THIS IS JOANNIE Paul Evans	*Spring*	7
10	12	LE FREAK Chic	*Atlantic*	12
12	13	JUST THE WAY YOU ARE Barry White	*20th Century*	7
15	14	MY LIFE Billy Joel	*CBS*	8
13	15	ONE NATION UNDER A GROOVE Funkadelic	*Warner Brothers*	8
27	16	MILK AND ALCOHOL Dr. Feelgood	*United Artists*	2
21	17	COOL MEDITATION Third World	*Island*	4
16	18	I'M EVERY WOMAN Chaka Khan	*Warner Brothers*	9
23	19	MIRRORS Sally Oldfield	*Bronze*	7
17	20	RAMA LAMA DING DONG Rocky Sharpe & the Replays	*Chiswick*	4
20	21	TAKE THAT TO THE BANK Shalamar	*RCA*	4
18	22	I'LL PUT YOU TOGETHER AGAIN Hot Chocolate	*RAK*	9
25	23	I WAS MADE FOR DANCIN' Leif Garrett	*Atlantic*	2
22	24	YOU NEEDED ME Anne Murray	*Capitol*	5
24	25	THIS IS IT Dan Hartman	*Blue Sky*	3
14	26	SONG FOR GUY Elton John	*Rocket*	8
-	27	CONTACT Edwin Starr	*20th Century*	1
31	28	KING ROCKER Generation X	*Chrysalis*	2
19	29	TOO MUCH HEAVEN Bee Gees	*RSO*	11
26	30	COULD IT BE MAGIC Barry Manilow	*Arista*	4
-	31	TAKE ON THE WORLD Judas Priest ●	*CBS*	1
28	32	DESIRE ME Doll	*Beggars Banquet*	3
-	33	SHAKE YOUR GROOVE THING Peaches & Herb ●	*Polydor*	1
33	34	DON'T HOLD BACK Chanson	*Ariola*	3
-	35	SIRDANCEALOT Olympic Runners	*Polydor*	1
-	36	(OUR LOVE) DON'T THROW IT ALL AWAY Andy Gibb	*RSO*	1
-	37	SOUND OF THE SUBURBS Members ●	*Virgin*	1
32	38	THEME FROM SUPERMAN Original Soundtrack	*Warner Bros.*	4
-	39	DOCTOR DOCTOR UFO	*Chrysalis*	1
37	40	EVERY NIGHT Phoebe Snow	*CBS*	3

WEEK ENDING 10 FEBRUARY 1979

LW	TW		Label	Wks
1	1	HEART OF GLASS Blondie	*Chrysalis*	3
8	2	CHIQUITITA Abba	*Epic*	2
3	3	WOMAN IN LOVE Three Degrees	*Ariola*	4
2	4	HIT ME WITH YOUR RHYTHM STICK Ian Dury & the Blockheads	*Stiff*	9
10	5	DON'T CRY FOR ME ARGENTINA Shadows	*EMI*	5
4	6	YMCA Village People	*Mercury*	11
23	7	I WAS MADE FOR DANCIN' Leif Garrett	*Atlantic*	3
5	8	SEPTEMBER Earth Wind & Fire	*CBS*	9
7	9	CAR 67 Driver 67	*Logo*	6
6	10	A LITTLE MORE LOVE Olivia Newton-John	*EMI*	8
27	11	CONTACT Edwin Starr	*20th Century*	2
14	12	MY LIFE Billy Joel	*CBS*	9
16	13	MILK AND ALCOHOL Dr. Feelgood	*United Artists*	3
13	14	JUST THE WAY YOU ARE Barry White	*20th Century*	8
11	15	HELLO THIS IS JOANNIE Paul Evans	*Spring*	8
28	16	KING ROCKER Generation X	*Chrysalis*	3
25	17	THIS IS IT Dan Hartman	*Blue Sky*	4
17	18	COOL MEDITATION Third World	*Island*	5
9	19	LAY YOUR LOVE ON ME Racey	*RAK*	11
31	20	TAKE ON THE WORLD Judas Priest	*CBS*	2
-	21	GET DOWN Gene Chandler ●	*20th Century*	1
15	22	ONE NATION UNDER A GROOVE Funkadelic	*Warner Brothers*	9
37	23	SOUND OF THE SUBURBS Members	*Virgin*	2
19	24	MIRRORS Sally Oldfield	*Bronze*	8
30	25	COULD IT BE MAGIC Barry Manilow	*Arista*	5
20	26	RAMA LAMA DING DONG Rocky Sharpe & the Replays	*Chiswick*	5
24	27	YOU NEEDED ME Anne Murray	*Capitol*	6
12	28	LE FREAK Chic	*Atlantic*	13
-	29	AIN'T LOVE A BITCH Rod Stewart	*Riva*	1
18	30	I'M EVERY WOMAN Chaka Khan	*Warner Brothers*	10
21	31	TAKE THAT TO THE BANK Shalamar	*RCA*	5
-	32	I WILL SURVIVE Gloria Gaynor	*Polydor*	1
32	33	DESIRE ME Doll	*Beggars Banquet*	4
33	34	SHAKE YOUR GROOVE THING Peaches & Herb	*Polydor*	2
-	35	BAT OUT OF HELL Meat Loaf	*Epic*	1
-	36	MAY THE SUN SHINE Nazareth	*Mountain*	1
-	37	YOU BET YOUR LOVE Herbie Hancock	*CBS*	1
36	38	(OUR LOVE) DON'T THROW IT ALL AWAY Andy Gibb	*RSO*	2
-	39	DESTINY Jacksons	*Epic*	1
22	40	I'LL PUT YOU TOGETHER AGAIN Hot Chocolate	*RAK*	10

WEEK ENDING 17 FEBRUARY 1979

LW	TW		Label	Wks
1	1	HEART OF GLASS Blondie	*Chrysalis*	4
2	2	CHIQUITITA Abba	*Epic*	3
3	3	WOMAN IN LOVE Three Degrees	*Ariola*	5
7	4	I WAS MADE FOR DANCIN' Leif Garrett	*Atlantic*	4
5	5	DON'T CRY FOR ME ARGENTINA Shadows	*EMI*	6

■Ian Dury and the Blockheads give independent New Wave label Stiff a number one (27.01.79) ■ Blondie achieved the first of their five number ones (03.02.79) ■ Sixties American R&B stars Gene Chandler, Edwin Starr and Peaches and Herb all get a career renaissance thanks to the disco boom (10.02.79)■

February 1979

□ Highest position disc reached ● Act's first ever week on chart

11 6 CONTACT Edwin Starr *20th Century* 3
- 7 TRAGEDY Bee Gees *RSO* 1
4 8 HIT ME WITH YOUR RHYTHM STICK Ian Dury & the Blockheads *Stiff* 10
13 9 MILK AND ALCOHOL Dr. Feelgood *United Artists* 4
9 10 CAR 67 Driver 67 *Logo* 7
16 11 KING ROCKER Generation X *Chrysalis* 4
12 12 MY LIFE Billy Joel *CBS* 10
- 13 OLIVER'S ARMY Elvis Costello & the Attractions *Radar* 1
8 14 SEPTEMBER Earth Wind & Fire *CBS* 10
20 15 TAKE ON THE WORLD Judas Priest *CBS* 3
10 16 A LITTLE MORE LOVE Olivia Newton-John *EMI* 9
18 17 COOL MEDITATION Third World *Island* 6
14 18 JUST THE WAY YOU ARE Barry White *20th Century* 9
29 19 AIN'T LOVE A BITCH Rod Stewart *Riva* 2
17 20 THIS IS IT Dan Hartman *Blue Sky* 5
32 21 I WILL SURVIVE Gloria Gaynor *Polydor* 2
21 22 GET DOWN Gene Chandler *20th Century* 2
6 23 YMCA Village People *Mercury* 12
27 24 YOU NEEDED ME Anne Murray *Capitol* 7
23 25 SOUND OF THE SUBURBS Members *Virgin* 3
24 26 MIRRORS Sally Oldfield *Bronze* 9
- 27 GET IT Darts *Magnet* 1
25 28 COULD IT BE MAGIC Barry Manilow *Arista* 6
31 29 TAKE THAT TO THE BANK Shalamar *RCA* 6
34 30 SHAKE YOUR GROOVE THING Peaches & Herb *Polydor* 3
36 31 MAY THE SUN SHINE Nazareth *Mountain* 2
38 32 (OUR LOVE) DON'T THROW IT ALL AWAY Andy Gibb *RSO* 3
19 33 LAY YOUR LOVE ON ME Racey *RAK* 12
15 34 HELLO THIS IS JOANNIE Paul Evans *Spring* 9
- 35 DOCTOR DOCTOR UFO *Chrysalis* 1
28 36 LE FREAK Chic *Atlantic* 14
35 37 BAT OUT OF HELL Meat Loaf *Epic* 2
- 38 DON'T STOP ME NOW Queen *EMI* 1
- 39 BABY OF MINE/JUST FOR YOU Alan Price *Jet* 1
33 40 DESIRE ME Doll *Beggars Banquet* 5

LW TW *WEEK ENDING* 24 FEBRUARY 1979 Wks

1 1 HEART OF GLASS Blondie *Chrysalis* 5
7 2 TRAGEDY Bee Gees *RSO* 2
2 3 CHIQUITITA Abba *Epic* 4
3 4 WOMAN IN LOVE Three Degrees *Ariola* 6
13 5 OLIVER'S ARMY Elvis Costello & the Attractions *Radar* 2
4 6 I WAS MADE FOR DANCIN' Leif Garrett *Atlantic* 5
21 7 I WILL SURVIVE Gloria Gaynor *Polydor* 3
6 8 CONTACT Edwin Starr *20th Century* 4
5 9 DON'T CRY FOR ME ARGENTINA Shadows *EMI* 7
9 10 MILK AND ALCOHOL Dr. Feelgood *United Artists* 5
19 11 AIN'T LOVE A BITCH Rod Stewart *Riva* 3
22 12 GET DOWN Gene Chandler *20th Century* 3
25 13 SOUND OF THE SUBURBS Members *Virgin* 4
15 14 TAKE ON THE WORLD Judas Priest *CBS* 4
37 15 BAT OUT OF HELL Meat Loaf *Epic* 3
8 16 HIT ME WITH YOUR RHYTHM STICK Ian Dury & the Blockheads *Stiff* 11
11 17 KING ROCKER Generation X *Chrysalis* 5
- 18 CAN YOU FEEL THE FORCE? Real Thing *Pye* 1
17 19 COOL MEDITATION Third World *Island* 7
20 20 THIS IS IT Dan Hartman *Blue Sky* 6
10 21 CAR 67 Driver 67 *Logo* 8
31 22 MAY THE SUN SHINE Nazareth *Mountain* 3
24 23 YOU NEEDED ME Anne Murray *Capitol* 8
- 24 INTO THE VALLEY Skids ● *Virgin* 1
27 25 GET IT Darts *Magnet* 2
30 26 SHAKE YOUR GROOVE THING Peaches & Herb *Polydor* 4
- 27 YOU BET YOUR LOVE Herbie Hancock *Panache/Rondor* 1
- 28 LUCKY NUMBER Lene Lovich ● *Stiff* 1
12 29 MY LIFE Billy Joel *CBS* 11
28 30 COULD IT BE MAGIC Barry Manilow *Arista* 7
38 31 DON'T STOP ME NOW Queen *EMI* 2
39 32 BABY OF MINE/JUST FOR YOU Alan Price *Jet* 2
- 33 HONEY I'M LOST Dooleys *GTO* 1
23 34 YMCA Village People *Mercury* 13
- 35 I WANT YOUR LOVE Chic *Atlantic* 1
- 36 HEAVEN KNOWS Donna Summer *Casablanca* 1
- 37 JUST WHAT I NEEDED Cars *Elektra* 1
- 38 WEEKEND Mick Jackson *Atlantic* 1
14 39 SEPTEMBER Earth Wind & Fire *CBS* 11
32 40 (OUR LOVE) DON'T THROW IT ALL AWAY Andy Gibb *RSO* 4

LW TW *WEEK ENDING* 3 MARCH 1979 Wks

2 1 TRAGEDY Bee Gees *RSO* 3
1 2 HEART OF GLASS Blondie *Chrysalis* 6
5 3 OLIVER'S ARMY Elvis Costello & the Attractions *Radar* 3
7 4 I WILL SURVIVE Gloria Gaynor *Polydor* 4
3 5 CHIQUITITA Abba *Epic* 5
8 6 CONTACT Edwin Starr *20th Century* 5
6 7 I WAS MADE FOR DANCIN' Leif Garrett *Atlantic* 6
28 8 LUCKY NUMBER Lene Lovich *Stiff* 2
4 9 WOMAN IN LOVE Three Degrees *Ariola* 7
25 10 GET IT Darts *Magnet* 3
12 11 GET DOWN Gene Chandler *20th Century* 4
13 12 SOUND OF THE SUBURBS Members *Virgin* 5
11 13 AIN'T LOVE A BITCH Rod Stewart *Riva* 4
18 14 CAN YOU FEEL THE FORCE? Real Thing *Pye* 2
10 15 MILK AND ALCOHOL Dr. Feelgood *United Artists* 6
14 16 TAKE ON THE WORLD Judas Priest *CBS* 5
15 17 BAT OUT OF HELL Meat Loaf *Epic* 4
17 18 KING ROCKER Generation X *Chrysalis* 6
9 19 DON'T CRY FOR ME ARGENTINA Shadows *EMI* 8
24 20 INTO THE VALLEY Skids *Virgin* 2
16 21 HIT ME WITH YOUR RHYTHM STICK Ian Dury & the Blockheads *Stiff* 12
22 22 MAY THE SUN SHINE Nazareth *Mountain* 4
- 23 KEEP ON DANCING Gary's Gang ● *CBS* 1
- 24 SOMETHING ELSE/FRIGGIN' IN THE RIGGIN' Sex Pistols *Virgin* 1
35 25 I WANT YOUR LOVE Chic *Atlantic* 2
- 26 PAINTER MAN Boney M *Atlantic* 1
26 27 SHAKE YOUR GROOVE THING Peaches & Herb *Polydor* 5
31 28 DON'T STOP ME NOW Queen *EMI* 3
37 29 JUST WHAT I NEEDED Cars *Elektra* 2
23 30 YOU NEEDED ME Anne Murray *Capitol* 9
- 31 HOLD THE LINE Toto ● *CBS* 1
33 32 HONEY I'M LOST Dooleys *GTO* 2
27 33 YOU BET YOUR LOVE Herbie Hancock *Panache/Rondor* 2
- 34 STOP YOUR SOBBING Pretenders ● *Real* 1
36 35 HEAVEN KNOWS Donna Summer *Casablanca* 2
- 36 MONEY IN MY POCKET Dennis Brown ● *Atlantic* 1
- 37 WHAT A FOOL BELIEVES Doobie Brothers *Warner Brothers* 1
29 38 MY LIFE Billy Joel *CBS* 12
- 39 ENGLISH CIVIL WAR Clash *CBS* 1
- 40 CLOG DANCE Violinksi ● *Jet* 1

LW TW *WEEK ENDING* 10 MARCH 1979 Wks

1 1 TRAGEDY Bee Gees *RSO* 4
3 2 OLIVER'S ARMY Elvis Costello & the Attractions *Radar* 4
4 3 I WILL SURVIVE Gloria Gaynor *Polydor* 5
8 4 LUCKY NUMBER Lene Lovich *Stiff* 3
14 5 CAN YOU FEEL THE FORCE? Real Thing *Pye* 3
2 6 HEART OF GLASS Blondie *Chrysalis* 7
24 7 SOMETHING ELSE/FRIGGIN' IN THE RIGGIN' Sex Pistols *Virgin* 2
6 8 CONTACT Edwin Starr *20th Century* 6
5 9 CHIQUITITA Abba *Epic* 6
26 10 PAINTER MAN Boney M *Atlantic* 2
11 11 GET DOWN Gene Chandler *20th Century* 5
10 12 GET IT Darts *Magnet* 4
20 13 INTO THE VALLEY Skids *Virgin* 3

In these weeks ■ The Bee Gees have their first number one in 9 years 231 days (03.03.79) ■ The Pretenders make their career debut (03.03.79) ■ New Wave favourites Elvis Costello and Lene Lovich achieve their highest chart positions (10.03.79)■

LW	TW	Title	Artist	Label	Wks
23	14	KEEP ON DANCING	Gary's Gang	*CBS*	2
25	15	I WANT YOUR LOVE	Chic	*Atlantic*	3
12	16	SOUND OF THE SUBURBS	Members	*Virgin*	6
7	17	I WAS MADE FOR DANCIN'	Leif Garrett	*Atlantic*	7
9	18	WOMAN IN LOVE	Three Degrees	*Ariola*	8
33	19	YOU BET YOUR LOVE	Herbie Hancock	*Panache/Rondor*	3
13	20	AIN'T LOVE A BITCH	Rod Stewart	*Riva*	5
17	21	BAT OUT OF HELL	Meat Loaf	*Epic*	5
28	22	DON'T STOP ME NOW	Queen	*EMI*	4
16	23	TAKE ON THE WORLD	Judas Priest	*CBS*	6
15	24	MILK AND ALCOHOL	Dr. Feelgood	*United Artists*	7
-	25	WAITING FOR AN ALIBI	Thin Lizzy	*Vertigo*	1
36	26	MONEY IN MY POCKET	Dennis Brown	*Atlantic*	2
32	27	HONEY I'M LOST	Dooleys	*GTO*	3
39	28	ENGLISH CIVIL WAR	Clash	*CBS*	2
40	29	CLOG DANCE	Violinksi	*Jet*	2
22	30	MAY THE SUN SHINE	Nazareth	*Mountain*	5
37	[31]	WHAT A FOOL BELIEVES	Doobie Brothers	*Warner Brothers*	2
-	[32]	IMPERIAL WIZARD	David Essex	*Mercury*	1
-	33	FOREVER IN BLUE JEANS	Neil Diamond	*CBS*	1
35	[34]	HEAVEN KNOWS	Donna Summer	*Casablanca*	3
31	35	HOLD THE LINE	Toto	*CBS*	2
29	36	JUST WHAT I NEEDED	Cars	*Elektra*	3
34	37	STOP YOUR SOBBING	Pretenders	*Real*	2
19	38	DON'T CRY FOR ME ARGENTINA	Shadows	*EMI*	9
27	39	SHAKE YOUR GROOVE THING	Peaches & Herb	*Polydor*	6
-	[40]	TRASH	Roxy Music	*Polydor*	1

WEEK ENDING 17 MARCH 1979

LW	TW	Title	Artist	Label	Wks
3	[1]	I WILL SURVIVE	Gloria Gaynor	*Polydor*	6
2	[2]	OLIVER'S ARMY	Elvis Costello & the Attractions	*Radar*	5
1	3	TRAGEDY	Bee Gees	*RSO*	5
4	4	LUCKY NUMBER	Lene Lovich	*Stiff*	4
5	[5]	CAN YOU FEEL THE FORCE?	Real Thing	*Pye*	4
7	6	SOMETHING ELSE/FRIGGIN' IN THE RIGGIN'	Sex Pistols	*Virgin*	3
15	7	I WANT YOUR LOVE	Chic	*Atlantic*	4
6	8	HEART OF GLASS	Blondie	*Chrysalis*	8
14	9	KEEP ON DANCING	Gary's Gang	*CBS*	3
8	10	CONTACT	Edwin Starr	*20th Century*	7
10	11	PAINTER MAN	Boney M	*Atlantic*	3
11	12	GET DOWN	Gene Chandler	*20th Century*	6
13	13	INTO THE VALLEY	Skids	*Virgin*	4
12	14	GET IT	Darts	*Magnet*	5
25	15	WAITING FOR AN ALIBI	Thin Lizzy	*Vertigo*	2
16	16	SOUND OF THE SUBURBS	Members	*Virgin*	7
9	17	CHIQUITITA	Abba	*Epic*	7
35	18	HOLD THE LINE	Toto	*CBS*	3
19	19	YOU BET YOUR LOVE	Herbie Hancock	*Panache/Rondor*	4
36	20	JUST WHAT I NEEDED	Cars	*Elektra*	4
26	21	MONEY IN MY POCKET	Dennis Brown	*Atlantic*	3
22	22	DON'T STOP ME NOW	Queen	*EMI*	5
20	23	AIN'T LOVE A BITCH	Rod Stewart	*Riva*	6
27	[24]	HONEY I'M LOST	Dooleys	*GTO*	4
-	25	TURN THE MUSIC UP	Players Association ●	*Vanguard*	1
29	26	CLOG DANCE	Violinksi	*Jet*	3
-	27	IN THE NAVY	Village People	*Mercury*	1
-	28	SULTANS OF SWING	Dire Straits ●	*Vertigo*	1
-	[29]	EVERYBODY'S HAPPY NOWADAYS	Buzzcocks	*United Artists*	1
-	30	STRANGE TOWN	Jam	*Polydor*	1
30	31	MAY THE SUN SHINE	Nazareth	*Mountain*	6
33	32	FOREVER IN BLUE JEANS	Neil Diamond	*CBS*	2
32	33	IMPERIAL WIZARD	David Essex	*Mercury*	2
28	34	ENGLISH CIVIL WAR	Clash	*CBS*	3
31	35	WHAT A FOOL BELIEVES	Doobie Brothers	*Warner Brothers*	3
34	36	HEAVEN KNOWS	Donna Summer	*Casablanca*	4
37	37	STOP YOUR SOBBING	Pretenders	*Real*	3
17	38	I WAS MADE FOR DANCIN'	Leif Garrett	*Atlantic*	8
-	[39]	GIMMIX PLAYLOUD	John Cooper Clark ●	*Epic*	1
18	40	WOMAN IN LOVE	Three Degrees	*Ariola*	9

March 1979

□ Highest position disc reached ● Act's first ever week on chart

WEEK ENDING 24 MARCH 1979

LW	TW	Title	Artist	Label	Wks
1	[1]	I WILL SURVIVE	Gloria Gaynor	*Polydor*	7
2	[2]	OLIVER'S ARMY	Elvis Costello & the Attractions	*Radar*	6
4	[3]	LUCKY NUMBER	Lene Lovich	*Stiff*	5
6	4	SOMETHING ELSE/FRIGGIN' IN THE RIGGIN'	Sex Pistols	*Virgin*	4
5	[5]	CAN YOU FEEL THE FORCE?	Real Thing	*Pye*	5
3	6	TRAGEDY	Bee Gees	*RSO*	6
7	7	I WANT YOUR LOVE	Chic	*Atlantic*	5
9	[8]	KEEP ON DANCING	Gary's Gang	*CBS*	4
15	[9]	WAITING FOR AN ALIBI	Thin Lizzy	*Vertigo*	3
13	[10]	INTO THE VALLEY	Skids	*Virgin*	5
11	11	PAINTER MAN	Boney M	*Atlantic*	4
12	12	GET DOWN	Gene Chandler	*20th Century*	7
22	13	DON'T STOP ME NOW	Queen	*EMI*	6
18	[14]	HOLD THE LINE	Toto	*CBS*	4
21	15	MONEY IN MY POCKET	Dennis Brown	*Atlantic*	4
27	16	IN THE NAVY	Village People	*Mercury*	2
26	[17]	CLOG DANCE	Violinksi	*Jet*	4
19	[18]	YOU BET YOUR LOVE	Herbie Hancock	*Panache/Rondor*	5
14	19	GET IT	Darts	*Magnet*	6
25	20	TURN THE MUSIC UP	Players Association	*Vanguard*	2
20	21	JUST WHAT I NEEDED	Cars	*Elektra*	5
30	22	STRANGE TOWN	Jam	*Polydor*	2
28	23	SULTANS OF SWING	Dire Straits	*Vertigo*	2
8	24	HEART OF GLASS	Blondie	*Chrysalis*	9
34	[25]	ENGLISH CIVIL WAR	Clash	*CBS*	4
10	26	CONTACT	Edwin Starr	*20th Century*	8
-	27	BRIGHT EYES	Art Garfunkel	*20th Century*	1
32	28	FOREVER IN BLUE JEANS	Neil Diamond	*CBS*	3
29	[29]	EVERYBODY'S HAPPY NOWADAYS	Buzzcocks	*United Artists*	2
17	30	CHIQUITITA	Abba	*Epic*	8
24	31	HONEY I'M LOST	Dooleys	*GTO*	5
33	[32]	IMPERIAL WIZARD	David Essex	*Mercury*	3
-	33	COOL FOR CATS	Squeeze	*A&M*	1
16	34	SOUND OF THE SUBURBS	Members	*Virgin*	8
-	35	WOW	Kate Bush	*EMI*	1
35	36	WHAT A FOOL BELIEVES	Doobie Brothers	*Warner Brothers*	4
-	[37]	EVERYTHING IS GREAT	Inner Circle ●	*Island*	1
-	38	HE'S THE GREATEST DANCER	Sister Sledge	*Atlantic*	1
-	[39]	OVERKILL	Motorhead ●	*Bronze*	1
-	[40]	BRISTOL STOMP	Late Show ●	*Decca*	1

WEEK ENDING 31 MARCH 1979

LW	TW	Title	Artist	Label	Wks
1	[1]	I WILL SURVIVE	Gloria Gaynor	*Polydor*	8
16	[2]	IN THE NAVY	Village People	*Mercury*	3
4	[3]	SOMETHING ELSE/FRIGGIN' IN THE RIGGIN'	Sex Pistols	*Virgin*	5
2	4	OLIVER'S ARMY	Elvis Costello & the Attractions	*Radar*	7
3	5	LUCKY NUMBER	Lene Lovich	*Stiff*	6
7	6	I WANT YOUR LOVE	Chic	*Atlantic*	6
5	7	CAN YOU FEEL THE FORCE?	Real Thing	*Pye*	6
20	[8]	TURN THE MUSIC UP	Players Association	*Vanguard*	3
13	[9]	DON'T STOP ME NOW	Queen	*EMI*	7
8	10	KEEP ON DANCING	Gary's Gang	*CBS*	5
6	11	TRAGEDY	Bee Gees	*RSO*	7
9	12	WAITING FOR AN ALIBI	Thin Lizzy	*Vertigo*	4
10	13	INTO THE VALLEY	Skids	*Virgin*	6
15	[14]	MONEY IN MY POCKET	Dennis Brown	*Atlantic*	5
14	15	HOLD THE LINE	Toto	*CBS*	5
33	16	COOL FOR CATS	Squeeze	*A&M*	2
21	[17]	JUST WHAT I NEEDED	Cars	*Elektra*	6
23	18	SULTANS OF SWING	Dire Straits	*Vertigo*	3
27	19	BRIGHT EYES	Art Garfunkel	*20th Century*	2
17	20	CLOG DANCE	Violinksi	*Jet*	5
18	21	YOU BET YOUR LOVE	Herbie Hancock	*Panache/Rondor*	6
11	22	PAINTER MAN	Boney M	*Atlantic*	5
35	23	WOW	Kate Bush	*EMI*	2

■Disco diva Gloria Gaynor reaches number one with the anthemic *I Will Survive* (17.03.79) ■ Dire Straits make their first appearance with *Sultans Of Swing* (17.03.79) ■ The Sex Pistols do better with the Eddie Cochran song *Something Else* than its originator ever did (31.03.79)■

□ Highest position disc reached ● Act's first ever week on chart

LW	TW	Title	Artist	Label	Wks
22	24	STRANGE TOWN	Jam	Polydor	3
38	25	HE'S THE GREATEST DANCER	Sister Sledge	Atlantic	2
-	26	SHAKE YOUR BODY (DOWN TO THE GROUND)	Jacksons	Epic	1
25	27	ENGLISH CIVIL WAR	Clash	CBS	5
28	28	FOREVER IN BLUE JEANS	Neil Diamond	CBS	4
-	29	QUESTIONS AND ANSWERS	Sham 69	Polydor	1
-	30	THE RUNNER	Three Degrees	Ariola	1
26	31	CONTACT	Edwin Starr	20th Century	9
12	32	GET DOWN	Gene Chandler	20th Century	8
-	33	THE STAIRCASE	Siouxsie & the Banshees	Polydor	1
-	34	SOME GIRLS	Racey	RAK	1
29	35	EVERYBODY'S HAPPY NOWADAYS	Buzzcocks	United Artists	3
32	36	IMPERIAL WIZARD	David Essex	Mercury	4
36	37	WHAT A FOOL BELIEVES	Doobie Brothers	Warner Brothers	5
24	38	HEART OF GLASS	Blondie	Chrysalis	10
-	39	FIRE	Pointer Sisters ●	Planet	1
-	40	LET'S FLY AWAY	Voyage	GTO	1

WEEK ENDING 7 APRIL 1979

LW	TW	Title	Artist	Label	Wks
1	1	I WILL SURVIVE	Gloria Gaynor	Polydor	9
2	2	IN THE NAVY	Village People	Mercury	4
19	3	BRIGHT EYES	Art Garfunkel	20th Century	3
6	4	I WANT YOUR LOVE	Chic	Atlantic	7
3	5	SOMETHING ELSE/FRIGGIN' IN THE RIGGIN'	Sex Pistols	Virgin	6
16	6	COOL FOR CATS	Squeeze	A&M	3
5	7	LUCKY NUMBER	Lene Lovich	Stiff	7
18	8	SULTANS OF SWING	Dire Straits	Vertigo	4
8	9	TURN THE MUSIC UP	Players Association	Vanguard	4
4	10	OLIVER'S ARMY	Elvis Costello & the Attractions	Radar	8
34	11	SOME GIRLS	Racey	RAK	2
7	12	CAN YOU FEEL THE FORCE?	Real Thing	Pye	7
9	13	DON'T STOP ME NOW	Queen	EMI	8
14	14	MONEY IN MY POCKET	Dennis Brown	Atlantic	6
10	15	KEEP ON DANCING	Gary's Gang	CBS	6
24	16	STRANGE TOWN	Jam	Polydor	4
12	17	WAITING FOR AN ALIBI	Thin Lizzy	Vertigo	5
25	18	HE'S THE GREATEST DANCER	Sister Sledge	Atlantic	3
13	19	INTO THE VALLEY	Skids	Virgin	7
17	20	JUST WHAT I NEEDED	Cars	Elektra	7
30	21	THE RUNNER	Three Degrees	Ariola	2
15	22	HOLD THE LINE	Toto	CBS	6
26	23	SHAKE YOUR BODY (DOWN TO THE GROUND)	Jacksons	Epic	2
-	24	SILLY THING/WHO KILLED BAMBI	Sex Pistols/Ten Pole Tudor	Virgin	1
20	25	CLOG DANCE	Violinksi	Jet	6
28	26	FOREVER IN BLUE JEANS	Neil Diamond	CBS	5
23	27	WOW	Kate Bush	EMI	3
33	28	THE STAIRCASE	Siouxsie & the Banshees	Polydor	2
21	29	YOU BET YOUR LOVE	Herbie Hancock	Panache/Rondor	7
27	30	ENGLISH CIVIL WAR	Clash	CBS	6
11	31	TRAGEDY	Bee Gees	RSO	8
-	32	I DON'T WANNA LOSE YOU	Kandidate	RAK	1
29	33	QUESTIONS AND ANSWERS	Sham 69	Polydor	2
39	34	FIRE	Pointer Sisters	Planet	2
-	35	REMEMBER THEN	Showaddywaddy	Arista	1
36	36	IMPERIAL WIZARD	David Essex	Mercury	5
-	37	THE LOGICAL SONG	Supertramp	A&M	1
40	38	LET'S FLY AWAY	Voyage	GTO	2
35	39	EVERYBODY'S HAPPY NOWADAYS	Buzzcocks	United Artists	4
-	40	VALLEY OF THE DOLLS	Generation X	Chrysalis	1

WEEK ENDING 14 APRIL 1979

LW	TW	Title	Artist	Label	Wks
3	1	BRIGHT EYES	Art Garfunkel	20th Century	4
6	2	COOL FOR CATS	Squeeze	A&M	4
11	3	SOME GIRLS	Racey	RAK	3
2	4	IN THE NAVY	Village People	Mercury	5
1	5	I WILL SURVIVE	Gloria Gaynor	Polydor	10
18	6	HE'S THE GREATEST DANCER	Sister Sledge	Atlantic	4
24	7	SILLY THING/WHO KILLED BAMBI	Sex Pistols/Ten Pole Tudor	Virgin	2
8	8	SULTANS OF SWING	Dire Straits	Vertigo	5
23	9	SHAKE YOUR BODY (DOWN TO THE GROUND)	Jacksons	Epic	3
21	10	THE RUNNER	Three Degrees	Ariola	3
5	11	SOMETHING ELSE/FRIGGIN' IN THE RIGGIN'	Sex Pistols	Virgin	7
4	12	I WANT YOUR LOVE	Chic	Atlantic	8
9	13	TURN THE MUSIC UP	Players Association	Vanguard	5
27	14	WOW	Kate Bush	EMI	4
16	15	STRANGE TOWN	Jam	Polydor	5
13	16	DON'T STOP ME NOW	Queen	EMI	9
10	17	OLIVER'S ARMY	Elvis Costello & the Attractions	Radar	9
14	18	MONEY IN MY POCKET	Dennis Brown	Atlantic	7
7	19	LUCKY NUMBER	Lene Lovich	Stiff	8
33	20	QUESTIONS AND ANSWERS	Sham 69	Polydor	3
17	21	WAITING FOR AN ALIBI	Thin Lizzy	Vertigo	6
32	22	I DON'T WANNA LOSE YOU	Kandidate	RAK	2
20	23	JUST WHAT I NEEDED	Cars	Elektra	8
37	24	THE LOGICAL SONG	Supertramp	A&M	2
-	25	GOODNIGHT TONIGHT	Wings	Parlophone	1
26	26	FOREVER IN BLUE JEANS	Neil Diamond	CBS	6
35	27	REMEMBER THEN	Showaddywaddy	Arista	2
-	28	POP MUZIK	M ●	MCA	1
40	29	VALLEY OF THE DOLLS	Generation X	Chrysalis	2
28	30	THE STAIRCASE	Siouxsie & the Banshees	Polydor	3
-	31	KNOCK ON WOOD	Amii Stewart ●	Atlantic	1
-	32	HAVEN'T STOPPED DANCING YET	Gonzalez ●	Sidewalk	1
12	33	CAN YOU FEEL THE FORCE?	Real Thing	Pye	8
34	34	FIRE	Pointer Sisters	Planet	3
-	35	HALLELUJAH	Milk & Honey ●	Polydor	1
19	36	INTO THE VALLEY	Skids	Virgin	8
-	37	OFFSHORE BANKING BUSINESS	Members	Virgin	1
15	38	KEEP ON DANCING	Gary's Gang	CBS	7
-	39	IMAGINATION	Rocky Sharpe & the Replays	Chiswick	1
38	40	LET'S FLY AWAY	Voyage	GTO	3

WEEK ENDING 21 APRIL 1979

LW	TW	Title	Artist	Label	Wks
1	1	BRIGHT EYES	Art Garfunkel	20th Century	5
2	2	SOME GIRLS	Racey	RAK	4
2	3	COOL FOR CATS	Squeeze	A&M	5
9	4	SHAKE YOUR BODY (DOWN TO THE GROUND)	Jacksons	Epic	4
35	5	HALLELUJAH	Milk & Honey	Polydor	2
7	6	SILLY THING/WHO KILLED BAMBI	Sex Pistols/Ten Pole Tudor	Virgin	3
6	7	HE'S THE GREATEST DANCER	Sister Sledge	Atlantic	5
4	8	IN THE NAVY	Village People	Mercury	6
5	9	I WILL SURVIVE	Gloria Gaynor	Polydor	11
10	10	THE RUNNER	Three Degrees	Ariola	4
22	11	I DON'T WANNA LOSE YOU	Kandidate	RAK	3
8	12	SULTANS OF SWING	Dire Straits	Vertigo	6
28	13	POP MUZIK	M	MCA	2
14	14	WOW	Kate Bush	EMI	5
12	15	I WANT YOUR LOVE	Chic	Atlantic	9
26	16	FOREVER IN BLUE JEANS	Neil Diamond	CBS	7
27	17	REMEMBER THEN	Showaddywaddy	Arista	3
11	18	SOMETHING ELSE/FRIGGIN' IN THE RIGGIN'	Sex Pistols	Virgin	8
25	19	GOODNIGHT TONIGHT	Wings	Parlophone	2
15	20	STRANGE TOWN	Jam	Polydor	6
13	21	TURN THE MUSIC UP	Players Association	Vanguard	6
20	22	QUESTIONS AND ANSWERS	Sham 69	Polydor	4
24	23	THE LOGICAL SONG	Supertramp	A&M	3
31	24	KNOCK ON WOOD	Amii Stewart	Atlantic	2
30	25	THE STAIRCASE	Siouxsie & the Banshees	Polydor	4
18	26	MONEY IN MY POCKET	Dennis Brown	Atlantic	8
32	27	HAVEN'T STOPPED DANCING YET	Gonzalez	Sidewalk	2

In these weeks ■ Art Garfunkel begins the longest run at number one this year with Mike Batt's song from 'Watership Down'. In an unique occurrence, an Israeli Eurovision Song Contest winner *Hallelujah* hits the Top Ten (21.04.79) ■ Ten Pole Tudor first make the Top Ten on the flip side of a Sex Pistols hit (21.04.79)■

LW	TW	Title	Artist	Label	Wks
-	28	LOVE YOU INSIDE OUT	Bee Gees	*RSO*	1
29	29	VALLEY OF THE DOLLS	Generation X	*Chrysalis*	3
17	30	OLIVER'S ARMY	Elvis Costello & the Attractions	*Radar*	10
37	[31]	OFFSHORE BANKING BUSINESS	Members	*Virgin*	2
16	32	DON'T STOP ME NOW	Queen	*EMI*	10
19	33	LUCKY NUMBER	Lene Lovich	*Stiff*	9
33	34	CAN YOU FEEL THE FORCE?	Real Thing	*Pye*	9
34	35	FIRE	Pointer Sisters	*Planet*	4
36	36	INTO THE VALLEY	Skids	*Virgin*	9
-	[37]	HERE COMES THE NIGHT	Beach Boys	*Caribou*	1
21	38	WAITING FOR AN ALIBI	Thin Lizzy	*Vertigo*	7
-	39	LOVE BALLAD	George Benson	*Warner Brothers*	1
38	40	KEEP ON DANCING	Gary's Gang	*CBS*	8

WEEK ENDING 28 APRIL 1979

LW	TW	Title	Artist	Label	Wks
1	[1]	BRIGHT EYES	Art Garfunkel	*20th Century*	6
3	[2]	SOME GIRLS	Racey	*RAK*	5
3	3	COOL FOR CATS	Squeeze	*A&M*	6
4	[4]	SHAKE YOUR BODY (DOWN TO THE GROUND)	Jacksons	*Epic*	5
13	5	POP MUZIK	M	*MCA*	3
5	6	HALLELUJAH	Milk & Honey	*Polydor*	3
23	[7]	THE LOGICAL SONG	Supertramp	*A&M*	4
6	8	SILLY THING/WHO KILLED BAMBI	Sex Pistols/Ten Pole Tudor	*Virgin*	4
19	9	GOODNIGHT TONIGHT	Wings	*Parlophone*	3
10	[10]	THE RUNNER	Three Degrees	*Ariola*	5
7	11	HE'S THE GREATEST DANCER	Sister Sledge	*Atlantic*	6
11	12	I DON'T WANNA LOSE YOU	Kandidate	*RAK*	4
12	13	SULTANS OF SWING	Dire Straits	*Vertigo*	7
14	[14]	WOW	Kate Bush	*EMI*	6
8	15	IN THE NAVY	Village People	*Mercury*	7
16	[16]	FOREVER IN BLUE JEANS	Neil Diamond	*CBS*	8
17	[17]	REMEMBER THEN	Showaddywaddy	*Arista*	4
22	[18]	QUESTIONS AND ANSWERS	Sham 69	*Polydor*	5
-	19	HOORAY HOORAY IT'S A HOLI HOLIDAY	Boney M	*Atlantic*	1
24	20	KNOCK ON WOOD	Amii Stewart	*Atlantic*	3
28	21	LOVE YOU INSIDE OUT	Bee Gees	*RSO*	2
20	22	STRANGE TOWN	Jam	*Polydor*	7
29	[23]	VALLEY OF THE DOLLS	Generation X	*Chrysalis*	4
25	[24]	THE STAIRCASE	Siouxsie & the Banshees	*Polydor*	5
27	25	HAVEN'T STOPPED DANCING YET	Gonzalez	*Sidewalk*	3
18	26	SOMETHING ELSE/FRIGGIN' IN THE RIGGIN'	Sex Pistols	*Virgin*	9
-	27	BANANA SPLITS	Dickies ●	*A&M*	1
-	28	ONE WAY TICKET	Eruption	*Atlantic*	1
-	29	REUNITED	Peaches & Herb	*Polydor*	1
9	30	I WILL SURVIVE	Gloria Gaynor	*Polydor*	12
15	31	I WANT YOUR LOVE	Chic	*Atlantic*	10
21	32	TURN THE MUSIC UP	Players Association	*Vanguard*	7
39	33	LOVE BALLAD	George Benson	*Warner Brothers*	2
-	34	ONLY YOU	Child	*Ariola*	1
-	35	I'M AN UPSTART	Angelic Upstarts ●	*Warner Brothers*	1
31	36	OFFSHORE BANKING BUSINESS	Members	*Virgin*	3
37	[37]	HERE COMES THE NIGHT	Beach Boys	*Caribou*	2
-	[38]	FEEL THE NEED	Leif Garrett	*Atlantic*	1
-	39	PARISIENNE WALKWAYS	Gary Moore ●	*MCA*	1
-	40	GUILTY	Mike Oldfield	*Virgin*	1

WEEK ENDING 5 MAY 1979

LW	TW	Title	Artist	Label	Wks
1	[1]	BRIGHT EYES	Art Garfunkel	*20th Century*	7
2	[2]	SOME GIRLS	Racey	*RAK*	6
5	3	POP MUZIK	M	*MCA*	4
19	4	HOORAY HOORAY IT'S A HOLI HOLIDAY	Boney M	*Atlantic*	2
9	[5]	GOODNIGHT TONIGHT	Wings	*Parlophone*	4
4	6	SHAKE YOUR BODY (DOWN TO THE GROUND)	Jacksons	*Epic*	6
6	7	HALLELUJAH	Milk & Honey	*Polydor*	4
3	8	COOL FOR CATS	Squeeze	*A&M*	7
7	9	THE LOGICAL SONG	Supertramp	*A&M*	5
20	10	KNOCK ON WOOD	Amii Stewart	*Atlantic*	4

May 1979

□ Highest position disc reached ● Act's first ever week on chart

LW	TW	Title	Artist	Label	Wks
12	[11]	I DON'T WANNA LOSE YOU	Kandidates	*RAK*	5
10	12	THE RUNNER	Three Degrees	*Ariola*	6
21	[13]	LOVE YOU INSIDE OUT	Bee Gees	*RSO*	3
11	14	HE'S THE GREATEST DANCER	Sister Sledge	*Atlantic*	7
25	[15]	HAVEN'T STOPPED DANCING YET	Gonzalez	*Sidewalk*	4
8	16	SILLY THING/WHO KILLED BAMBI	Sex Pistols/Ten Pole Tudor	*Virgin*	5
14	17	WOW	Kate Bush	*EMI*	7
16	18	FOREVER IN BLUE JEANS	Neil Diamond	*CBS*	9
-	19	DOES YOUR MOTHER KNOW	Abba	*Epic*	1
28	20	ONE WAY TICKET	Eruption	*Atlantic*	2
29	21	REUNITED	Peaches & Herb	*Polydor*	2
27	22	BANANA SPLITS	Dickies	*A&M*	2
17	23	REMEMBER THEN	Showaddywaddy	*Arista*	5
24	[24]	THE STAIRCASE	Siouxsie & the Banshees	*Polydor*	6
39	25	PARISIENNE WALKWAYS	Gary Moore	*MCA*	2
23	26	VALLEY OF THE DOLLS	Generation X	*Chrysalis*	5
-	27	ROXANNE	The Police ●	*A&M*	1
-	28	JIMMY JIMMY	Undertones	*Sire*	1
33	[29]	LOVE BALLAD	George Benson	*Warner Brothers*	3
40	30	GUILTY	Mike Oldfield	*Virgin*	2
-	31	BOYS KEEP SWINGIN'	David Bowie	*RCA*	1
-	32	NICE LEGS SHAME ABOUT HER FACE	Monks ●	*Carrere*	1
34	[33]	ONLY YOU	Child	*Ariola*	2
-	34	DANCE AWAY	Roxy Music	*Polydor*	1
35	35	I'M AN UPSTART	Angelic Upstarts	*Warner Brothers*	2
13	36	SULTANS OF SWING	Dire Straits	*Vertigo*	8
26	37	SOMETHING ELSE/FRIGGIN' IN THE RIGGIN'	Sex Pistols	*Virgin*	10
18	38	QUESTIONS AND ANSWERS	Sham 69	*Polydor*	6
38	39	FEEL THE NEED	Leif Garrett	*Atlantic*	2
-	40	THE NUMBER ONE SONG IN HEAVEN	Sparks	*Virgin*	1

WEEK ENDING 12 MAY 1979

LW	TW	Title	Artist	Label	Wks
1	[1]	BRIGHT EYES	Art Garfunkel	*20th Century*	8
3	[2]	POP MUZIK	M	*MCA*	5
4	[3]	HOORAY HOORAY IT'S A HOLI HOLIDAY	Boney M	*Atlantic*	3
19	[4]	DOES YOUR MOTHER KNOW	Abba	*Epic*	2
2	5	SOME GIRLS	Racey	*RAK*	7
21	6	REUNITED	Peaches & Herb	*Polydor*	3
22	[7]	BANANA SPLITS	Dickies	*A&M*	3
5	8	GOODNIGHT TONIGHT	Wings	*Parlophone*	5
10	9	KNOCK ON WOOD	Amii Stewart	*Atlantic*	5
9	10	THE LOGICAL SONG	Supertramp	*A&M*	6
20	11	ONE WAY TICKET	Eruption	*Atlantic*	3
6	12	SHAKE YOUR BODY (DOWN TO THE GROUND)	Jacksons	*Epic*	7
13	[13]	LOVE YOU INSIDE OUT	Bee Gees	*RSO*	4
7	14	HALLELUJAH	Milk & Honey	*Polydor*	5
31	15	BOYS KEEP SWINGIN'	David Bowie	*RCA*	2
8	16	COOL FOR CATS	Squeeze	*A&M*	8
11	17	I DON'T WANNA LOSE YOU	Kandidates	*RAK*	6
27	18	ROXANNE	The Police	*A&M*	2
15	19	HAVEN'T STOPPED DANCING YET	Gonzalez	*Sidewalk*	5
34	20	DANCE AWAY	Roxy Music	*Polydor*	2
25	21	PARISIENNE WALKWAYS	Gary Moore	*MCA*	3
30	[22]	GUILTY	Mike Oldfield	*Virgin*	3
18	23	FOREVER IN BLUE JEANS	Neil Diamond	*CBS*	10
28	24	JIMMY JIMMY	Undertones	*Sire*	2
32	25	NICE LEGS SHAME ABOUT HER FACE	Monks	*Carrere*	2
-	26	LOVE SONG	The Damned ●	*Chiswick*	1
12	27	THE RUNNER	Three Degrees	*Ariola*	7
24	28	THE STAIRCASE	Siouxsie & the Banshees	*Polydor*	7
26	29	VALLEY OF THE DOLLS	Generation X	*Chrysalis*	6
-	30	BOOGIE WONDERLAND	Earth Wind & Fire	*CBS*	1
35	[31]	I'M AN UPSTART	Angelic Upstarts	*Warner Brothers*	3
23	32	REMEMBER THEN	Showaddywaddy	*Arista*	6
16	33	SILLY THING/WHO KILLED BAMBI	Sex Pistols/Ten Pole Tudor	*Virgin*	6

■Police reach the Top 40 for the first time with *Roxanne* (05.05.79) ■ Boney M have their ninth consecutive and final Top Ten hit (05.05.79) ■ Abba have their only Top Ten hit with a male lead vocal (12.05.79)■

May 1979

□ Highest position disc reached ● Act's first ever week on chart

LW	TW	Title / Artist	Label	Wks
40	34	THE NUMBER ONE SONG IN HEAVEN Sparks	Virgin	2
29	35	LOVE BALLAD George Benson	Warner Brothers	4
-	36	BRIDGE OVER TROUBLED WATER Linda Clifford ●	RSO	1
14	37	HE'S THE GREATEST DANCER Sister Sledge	Atlantic	8
33	38	ONLY YOU Child	Ariola	3
-	39	I WANT YOU TO WANT ME Cheap Trick ●	Epic	1
-	40	AS LONG AS THE PRICE IS RIGHT Dr. Feelgood	United Artists	1

LW	TW	*WEEK ENDING* 19 MAY 1979		Wks
1	1	BRIGHT EYES Art Garfunkel	20th Century	9
2	2	POP MUZIK M	MCA	6
3	3	HOORAY HOORAY IT'S A HOLI HOLIDAY Boney M	Atlantic	4
4	4	DOES YOUR MOTHER KNOW Abba	Epic	3
6	5	REUNITED Peaches & Herb	Polydor	4
9	6	KNOCK ON WOOD Amii Stewart	Atlantic	6
20	7	DANCE AWAY Roxy Music	Polydor	3
21	8	PARISIENNE WALKWAYS Gary Moore	MCA	4
11	9	ONE WAY TICKET Eruption	Atlantic	4
-	10	SUNDAY GIRL Blondie	Chrysalis	1
7	11	BANANA SPLITS Dickies	A&M	4
18	12	ROXANNE The Police	A&M	3
10	13	THE LOGICAL SONG Supertramp	A&M	7
8	14	GOODNIGHT TONIGHT Wings	Parlophone	6
5	15	SOME GIRLS Racey	RAK	8
13	16	LOVE YOU INSIDE OUT Bee Gees	RSO	5
24	17	JIMMY JIMMY Undertones	Sire	3
12	18	SHAKE YOUR BODY (DOWN TO THE GROUND) Jacksons	Epic	8
15	19	BOYS KEEP SWINGIN' David Bowie	RCA	3
17	20	I DON'T WANNA LOSE YOU Kandidates	RAK	7
19	21	HAVEN'T STOPPED DANCING YET Gonzalez	Sidewalk	6
14	22	HALLELUJAH Milk & Honey	Polydor	6
25	23	NICE LEGS SHAME ABOUT HER FACE Monks	Carrere	3
30	24	BOOGIE WONDERLAND Earth Wind & Fire	CBS	2
34	25	THE NUMBER ONE SONG IN HEAVEN Sparks	Virgin	3
-	26	THEME FROM DEER HUNTER Shadows	EMI	1
26	27	LOVE SONG The Damned	Chiswick	2
22	28	GUILTY Mike Oldfield	Virgin	4
-	29	HOT STUFF Donna Summer	Casablanca	1
36	30	BRIDGE OVER TROUBLED WATER Linda Clifford	RSO	2
28	31	THE STAIRCASE Siouxsie & the Banshees	Polydor	8
16	32	COOL FOR CATS Squeeze	A&M	9
-	33	SHINE A LITTLE LOVE Electric Light Orchestra	Jet	1
31	34	I'M AN UPSTART Angelic Upstarts	Warner Brothers	4
-	35	I FOUGHT THE LAW Clash	CBS	1
38	36	ONLY YOU Child	Ariola	4
-	37	SAY WHEN Lene Lovich	Stiff	1
35	38	LOVE BALLAD George Benson	Warner Brothers	5
39	39	I WANT YOU TO WANT ME Cheap Trick	Epic	2
27	40	THE RUNNER Three Degrees	Ariola	8

LW	TW	*WEEK ENDING* 26 MAY 1979		Wks
10	1	SUNDAY GIRL Blondie	Chrysalis	2
7	2	DANCE AWAY Roxy Music	Polydor	4
2	3	POP MUZIK M	MCA	7
4	4	DOES YOUR MOTHER KNOW Abba	Epic	4
5	5	REUNITED Peaches & Herb	Polydor	5
1	6	BRIGHT EYES Art Garfunkel	20th Century	10
3	7	HOORAY HOORAY IT'S A HOLI HOLIDAY Boney M	Atlantic	5
24	8	BOOGIE WONDERLAND Earth Wind & Fire	CBS	3
19	9	BOYS KEEP SWINGIN' David Bowie	RCA	4
9	10	ONE WAY TICKET Eruption	Atlantic	5
6	11	KNOCK ON WOOD Amii Stewart	Atlantic	7
8	12	PARISIENNE WALKWAYS Gary Moore	MCA	5
12	13	ROXANNE The Police	A&M	4
33	14	SHINE A LITTLE LOVE Electric Light Orchestra	Jet	2
11	15	BANANA SPLITS Dickies	A&M	5
17	16	JIMMY JIMMY Undertones	Sire	4
13	17	THE LOGICAL SONG Supertramp	A&M	8
25	18	THE NUMBER ONE SONG IN HEAVEN Sparks	Virgin	4
23	19	NICE LEGS SHAME ABOUT HER FACE Monks	Carrere	4
27	20	LOVE SONG The Damned	Chiswick	3
26	21	THEME FROM DEER HUNTER Shadows	EMI	2
16	22	LOVE YOU INSIDE OUT Bee Gees	RSO	6
35	23	I FOUGHT THE LAW Clash	CBS	2
29	24	HOT STUFF Donna Summer	Casablanca	2
-	25	AIN'T NO STOPPIN' US NOW McFadden & Whitehead ●	Philadelphia	1
15	26	SOME GIRLS Racey	RAK	9
28	27	GUILTY Mike Oldfield	Virgin	5
30	28	BRIDGE OVER TROUBLED WATER Linda Clifford	RSO	3
-	29	MASQUERADE Skids	Virgin	1
39	30	I WANT YOU TO WANT ME Cheap Trick	Epic	3
14	31	GOODNIGHT TONIGHT Wings	Parlophone	7
37	32	SAY WHEN Lene Lovich	Stiff	2
-	33	WHO WERE YOU WITH IN THE MOONLIGHT Dollar	Carrere	1
-	34	ACCIDENTS WILL HAPPEN Elvis Costello	Radar	1
-	35	PRIME TIME Tubes	A&M	1
-	36	H.A.P.P.Y. RADIO Edwin Starr	RCA	1
-	37	GET DANCIN' Bombers ●	Magnet Flamingo	1
18	38	SHAKE YOUR BODY (DOWN TO THE GROUND) Jacksons	Epic	9
20	39	I DON'T WANNA LOSE YOU Kandidates	RAK	8
21	40	HAVEN'T STOPPED DANCING YET Gonzalez	Sidewalk	7

LW	TW	*WEEK ENDING* 2 JUNE 1979		Wks
1	1	SUNDAY GIRL Blondie	Chrysalis	3
2	2	DANCE AWAY Roxy Music	Polydor	5
3	3	POP MUZIK M	MCA	8
5	4	REUNITED Peaches & Herb	Polydor	6
8	5	BOOGIE WONDERLAND Earth Wind & Fire	CBS	4
4	6	DOES YOUR MOTHER KNOW Abba	Epic	5
9	7	BOYS KEEP SWINGIN' David Bowie	RCA	5
6	8	BRIGHT EYES Art Garfunkel	20th Century	11
21	9	THEME FROM DEER HUNTER Shadows	EMI	3
12	10	PARISIENNE WALKWAYS Gary Moore	MCA	6
24	11	HOT STUFF Donna Summer	Casablanca	3
13	12	ROXANNE The Police	A&M	5
10	13	ONE WAY TICKET Eruption	Atlantic	6
11	14	KNOCK ON WOOD Amii Stewart	Atlantic	8
25	15	AIN'T NO STOPPIN' US NOW McFadden & Whitehead	Philadelphia	2
14	16	SHINE A LITTLE LOVE Electric Light Orchestra	Jet	3
7	17	HOORAY HOORAY IT'S A HOLI HOLIDAY Boney M	Atlantic	6
18	18	THE NUMBER ONE SONG IN HEAVEN Sparks	Virgin	5
-	19	RING MY BELL Anita Ward ●	TK	1
16	20	JIMMY JIMMY Undertones	Sire	5
29	21	MASQUERADE Skids	Virgin	2
20	22	LOVE SONG The Damned	Chiswick	4
19	23	NICE LEGS SHAME ABOUT HER FACE Monks	Carrere	5
36	24	H.A.P.P.Y. RADIO Edwin Starr	RCA	2
-	25	ARE FRIENDS ELECTRIC Tubeway Army ●	Beggers Banquet	1
27	26	GUILTY Mike Oldfield	Virgin	6
15	27	BANANA SPLITS Dickies	A&M	6
28	28	BRIDGE OVER TROUBLED WATER Linda Clifford	RSO	4
30	29	I WANT YOU TO WANT ME Cheap Trick	Epic	4
33	30	WHO WERE YOU WITH IN THE MOONLIGHT Dollar	Carrere	2
32	31	SAY WHEN Lene Lovich	Stiff	3
23	32	I FOUGHT THE LAW Clash	CBS	3
-	33	WE ARE FAMILY Sister Sledge	Atlantic	1
35	34	PRIME TIME Tubes	A&M	2
17	35	THE LOGICAL SONG Supertramp	A&M	9
34	36	ACCIDENTS WILL HAPPEN Elvis Costello	Radar	2
-	37	NIGHT OWL Gerry Rafferty	United Artists	1
-	38	CAVATINA (ORIGINAL SOUNDTRACK FROM DEER HUNTER) John Williams ●	Cube	1
-	39	IS THERE ANYBODY THERE/ANOTHER PIECE OF MEAT Scorpions ●	Harvest	1
31	40	GOODNIGHT TONIGHT Wings	Parlophone	8

In these weeks ■ Robin Scott reaches number two as M and will go on to top the American Hot 100 (19.05.79) ■ Amii Stewart outperforms originator Eddie Floyd with *Knock On Wood* and the Clash improve on the Bobby Fuller Four placing on *I Fought The Law* (26.05.79) ■ Gary Numan debuts under the group name Tubeway Army (02.06.79)■

June 1979

□ Highest position disc reached ● Act's first ever week on chart

WEEK ENDING 9 JUNE 1979

LW	TW	Title / Artist	Label	Wks
1	[1]	SUNDAY GIRL Blondie	*Chrysalis*	4
2	[2]	DANCE AWAY Roxy Music	*Polydor*	6
19	3	RING MY BELL Anita Ward	*TK*	2
5	[4]	BOOGIE WONDERLAND Earth Wind & Fire	*CBS*	5
4	5	REUNITED Peaches & Herb	*Polydor*	7
16	[6]	SHINE A LITTLE LOVE Electric Light Orchestra	*Jet*	4
3	7	POP MUZIK M	*MCA*	9
15	8	AIN'T NO STOPPIN' US NOW McFadden & Whitehead	*Philadelphia*	3
7	9	BOYS KEEP SWINGIN' David Bowie	*RCA*	6
9	10	THEME FROM DEER HUNTER Shadows	*EMI*	4
11	[11]	HOT STUFF Donna Summer	*Casablanca*	4
6	12	DOES YOUR MOTHER KNOW Abba	*Epic*	6
10	13	PARISIENNE WALKWAYS Gary Moore	*MCA*	7
18	[14]	THE NUMBER ONE SONG IN HEAVEN Sparks	*Virgin*	6
13	15	ONE WAY TICKET Eruption	*Atlantic*	7
12	16	ROXANNE The Police	*A&M*	6
21	17	MASQUERADE Skids	*Virgin*	3
8	18	BRIGHT EYES Art Garfunkel	*20th Century*	12
20	19	JIMMY JIMMY Undertones	*Sire*	6
25	20	ARE FRIENDS ELECTRIC Tubeway Army	*Beggers Banquet*	2
33	21	WE ARE FAMILY Sister Sledge	*Atlantic*	2
24	22	H.A.P.P.Y. RADIO Edwin Starr	*RCA*	3
14	23	KNOCK ON WOOD Amii Stewart	*Atlantic*	9
32	24	I FOUGHT THE LAW Clash	*CBS*	4
-	25	UP THE JUNCTION Squeeze	*A&M*	1
22	26	LOVE SONG The Damned	*Chiswick*	5
23	27	NICE LEGS SHAME ABOUT HER FACE Monks	*Carrere*	6
30	28	WHO WERE YOU WITH IN THE MOONLIGHT Dollar	*Carrere*	3
17	29	HOORAY HOORAY IT'S A HOLI HOLIDAY Boney M	*Atlantic*	7
36	30	ACCIDENTS WILL HAPPEN Elvis Costello	*Radar*	3
29	31	I WANT YOU TO WANT ME Cheap Trick	*Epic*	5
38	32	CAVATINA (ORIGINAL SOUNDTRACK FROM DEER HUNTER) John Williams	*Cube*	2
-	33	THE LONE RANGER Quantum Jump ●	*Electric*	1
37	34	NIGHT OWL Gerry Rafferty	*United Artists*	2
34	35	PRIME TIME Tubes	*A&M*	3
26	36	GUILTY Mike Oldfield	*Virgin*	7
31	37	SAY WHEN Lene Lovich	*Stiff*	4
-	38	GERTCHA Chas & Dave ●	*EMI*	1
28	39	BRIDGE OVER TROUBLED WATER Linda Clifford	*RSO*	5
27	40	BANANA SPLITS Dickies	*A&M*	7

WEEK ENDING 16 JUNE 1979

LW	TW	Title / Artist	Label	Wks
3	[1]	RING MY BELL Anita Ward	*TK*	3
1	2	SUNDAY GIRL Blondie	*Chrysalis*	5
2	3	DANCE AWAY Roxy Music	*Polydor*	7
4	[4]	BOOGIE WONDERLAND Earth Wind & Fire	*CBS*	6
8	[5]	AIN'T NO STOPPIN' US NOW McFadden & Whitehead	*Philadelphia*	4
6	[6]	SHINE A LITTLE LOVE Electric Light Orchestra	*Jet*	5
20	7	ARE FRIENDS ELECTRIC Tubeway Army	*Beggers Banquet*	3
21	[8]	WE ARE FAMILY Sister Sledge	*Atlantic*	3
10	[9]	THEME FROM DEER HUNTER Shadows	*EMI*	5
22	10	H.A.P.P.Y. RADIO Edwin Starr	*RCA*	4
5	11	REUNITED Peaches & Herb	*Polydor*	8
11	12	HOT STUFF Donna Summer	*Casablanca*	5
25	13	UP THE JUNCTION Squeeze	*A&M*	2
17	[14]	MASQUERADE Skids	*Virgin*	4
9	15	BOYS KEEP SWINGIN' David Bowie	*RCA*	7
33	16	THE LONE RANGER Quantum Jump	*Electric*	2
14	17	THE NUMBER ONE SONG IN HEAVEN Sparks	*Virgin*	7
28	18	WHO WERE YOU WITH IN THE MOONLIGHT Dollar	*Carrere*	4
7	19	POP MUZIK M	*MCA*	10
13	20	PARISIENNE WALKWAYS Gary Moore	*MCA*	8
19	21	JIMMY JIMMY Undertones	*Sire*	7
18	22	BRIGHT EYES Art Garfunkel	*20th Century*	13
24	23	I FOUGHT THE LAW Clash	*CBS*	5
37	24	SAY WHEN Lene Lovich	*Stiff*	5
12	25	DOES YOUR MOTHER KNOW Abba	*Epic*	7
34	26	NIGHT OWL Gerry Rafferty	*United Artists*	3
38	27	GERTCHA Chas & Dave	*EMI*	2
30	[28]	ACCIDENTS WILL HAPPEN Elvis Costello	*Radar*	4
-	29	LIVING ON THE FRONT LINE Eddy Grant ●	*Ice Ensign*	1
32	30	CAVATINA (ORIGINAL SOUNDTRACK FROM DEER HUNTER) John Williams	*Cube*	3
15	31	ONE WAY TICKET Eruption	*Atlantic*	8
16	32	ROXANNE The Police	*A&M*	7
31	33	I WANT YOU TO WANT ME Cheap Trick	*Epic*	6
35	[34]	PRIME TIME Tubes	*A&M*	4
23	35	KNOCK ON WOOD Amii Stewart	*Atlantic*	10
-	36	HEAD OVER HEELS IN LOVE Kevin Keegan ●	*RAK*	1
-	37	MAYBE Thom Pace ●	*RSO*	1
-	38	CRACKIN' UP Nick Lowe	*Radar*	1
-	39	GO WEST Village People	*Mercury*	1
-	[40]	I'D BE SURPRISINGLY GOOD FOR YOU Linda Lewis	*Ariola*	1

WEEK ENDING 23 JUNE 1979

LW	TW	Title / Artist	Label	Wks
1	[1]	RING MY BELL Anita Ward	*TK*	4
7	2	ARE FRIENDS ELECTRIC Tubeway Army	*Beggers Banquet*	4
3	3	DANCE AWAY Roxy Music	*Polydor*	8
2	4	SUNDAY GIRL Blondie	*Chrysalis*	6
4	5	BOOGIE WONDERLAND Earth Wind & Fire	*CBS*	7
13	6	UP THE JUNCTION Squeeze	*A&M*	3
5	7	AIN'T NO STOPPIN' US NOW McFadden & Whitehead	*Philadelphia*	5
16	8	THE LONE RANGER Quantum Jump	*Electric*	3
8	9	WE ARE FAMILY Sister Sledge	*Atlantic*	4
9	10	THEME FROM DEER HUNTER Shadows	*EMI*	6
6	11	SHINE A LITTLE LOVE Electric Light Orchestra	*Jet*	6
10	12	H.A.P.P.Y. RADIO Edwin Starr	*RCA*	5
26	13	NIGHT OWL Gerry Rafferty	*United Artists*	4
30	14	CAVATINA (ORIGINAL SOUNDTRACK FROM DEER HUNTER) John Williams	*Cube*	4
14	15	MASQUERADE Skids	*Virgin*	5
18	16	WHO WERE YOU WITH IN THE MOONLIGHT Dollar	*Carrere*	5
12	17	HOT STUFF Donna Summer	*Casablanca*	6
17	18	THE NUMBER ONE SONG IN HEAVEN Sparks	*Virgin*	8
24	[19]	SAY WHEN Lene Lovich	*Stiff*	6
11	20	REUNITED Peaches & Herb	*Polydor*	9
29	21	LIVING ON THE FRONT LINE Eddy Grant	*Ice Ensign*	2
23	[22]	I FOUGHT THE LAW Clash	*CBS*	6
19	23	POP MUZIK M	*MCA*	11
-	24	LIGHT MY FIRE/137 DISCO HEAVEN Amii Stewart	*Atlantic*	1
39	25	GO WEST Village People	*Mercury*	2
15	26	BOYS KEEP SWINGIN' David Bowie	*RCA*	8
27	27	GERTCHA Chas & Dave	*EMI*	3
-	28	SILLY GAMES Janet Kay ●	*Scope*	1
37	29	MAYBE Thom Pace	*RSO*	2
22	30	BRIGHT EYES Art Garfunkel	*20th Century*	14
36	[31]	HEAD OVER HEELS IN LOVE Kevin Keegan	*RAK*	2
-	32	LADY LYNDA Beach Boys	*Caribou*	1
-	[33]	HALF WAY HOTEL Voyager ●	*Mountain*	1
38	[34]	CRACKIN' UP Nick Lowe	*Radar*	2
-	35	DO ANYTHING YOU WANT TO Thin Lizzy	*Vertigo*	1
-	36	OLD SIAM SIR Wings	*Parlophone*	1
-	37	BABYLON'S BURNING Ruts ●	*Virgin*	1
20	38	PARISIENNE WALKWAYS Gary Moore	*MCA*	9
-	39	SPACE BASS Slick ●	*Fantasy*	1
-	40	DANCE WITH ME Carrie Lucas ●	*Solar*	1

WEEK ENDING 30 JUNE 1979

LW	TW	Title / Artist	Label	Wks
2	[1]	ARE FRIENDS ELECTRIC Tubeway Army	*Beggers Banquet*	5
1	2	RING MY BELL Anita Ward	*TK*	5
6	3	UP THE JUNCTION Squeeze	*A&M*	4
5	[4]	BOOGIE WONDERLAND Earth Wind & Fire	*CBS*	8
8	[5]	THE LONE RANGER Quantum Jump	*Electric*	4

■Former chart artist Frederick Knight scores as writer and producer of Anita Ward's number one *Ring My Bell*, originally with Stacy Lattisaw in mind (16.06.79) ■ Linda Lewis charts with the fourth Top 40 tune from 'Evita'. Amii Stewart has the second Top 40 version of *Light My Fire*, neither were by the originators The Doors (23.06.79)■

June 1979

☐ Highest position disc reached ● Act's first ever week on chart

LW	TW	Title	Artist	Label	Wks
3	6	DANCE AWAY	Roxy Music	Polydor	9
4	7	SUNDAY GIRL	Blondie	Chrysalis	7
7	8	AIN'T NO STOPPIN' US NOW	McFadden & Whitehead	Philadelphia	6
12	[9]	H.A.P.P.Y. RADIO	Edwin Starr	RCA	6
13	10	NIGHT OWL	Gerry Rafferty	United Artists	5
9	11	WE ARE FAMILY	Sister Sledge	Atlantic	5
10	12	THEME FROM DEER HUNTER	Shadows	EMI	7
14	[13]	CAVATINA (ORIGINAL SOUNDTRACK FROM DEER HUNTER)	John Williams	Cube	5
16	[14]	WHO WERE YOU WITH IN THE MOONLIGHT	Dollar	Carrere	6
21	15	LIVING ON THE FRONT LINE	Eddy Grant	Ice Ensign	3
15	16	MASQUERADE	Skids	Virgin	6
11	17	SHINE A LITTLE LOVE	Electric Light Orchestra	Jet	7
24	18	LIGHT MY FIRE/137 DISCO HEAVEN	Amii Stewart	Atlantic	2
19	[19]	SAY WHEN	Lene Lovich	Stiff	7
27	[20]	GERTCHA	Chas & Dave	EMI	4
25	21	GO WEST	Village People	Mercury	3
37	22	BABYLON'S BURNING	Ruts	Virgin	2
28	23	SILLY GAMES	Janet Kay	Scope	2
-	24	C'MON EVERYBODY	Sex Pistols	Virgin	1
22	25	I FOUGHT THE LAW	Clash	CBS	7
29	26	MAYBE	Thom Pace	RSO	3
32	27	LADY LYNDA	Beach Boys	Caribou	2
17	28	HOT STUFF	Donna Summer	Casablanca	7
35	29	DO ANYTHING YOU WANT TO	Thin Lizzy	Vertigo	2
39	30	SPACE BASS	Slick	Fantasy	2
-	31	WANTED	Dooleys	GTO	1
20	32	REUNITED	Peaches & Herb	Polydor	10
31	33	HEAD OVER HEELS IN LOVE	Kevin Keegan	RAK	3
-	34	BORN TO BE ALIVE	Patrick Hernandez ●	GEM	1
36	[35]	OLD SIAM SIR	Wings	Parlophone	2
-	36	MARRIED MEN	Bonnie Tyler	RCA	1
-	37	STRANGLEHOLD	UK Subs ●	GEM	1
18	38	THE NUMBER ONE SONG IN HEAVEN	Sparks	Virgin	9
33	39	HALF WAY HOTEL	Voyager	Mountain	2
-	[40]	ONE RULE FOR YOU	After The Fire ●	CBS	1

WEEK ENDING 7 JULY 1979

LW	TW	Title	Artist	Label	Wks
1	[1]	ARE FRIENDS ELECTRIC	Tubeway Army	Beggers Banquet	6
3	[2]	UP THE JUNCTION	Squeeze	A&M	5
23	3	SILLY GAMES	Janet Kay	Scope	3
2	4	RING MY BELL	Anita Ward	TK	6
10	[5]	NIGHT OWL	Gerry Rafferty	United Artists	6
18	6	LIGHT MY FIRE/137 DISCO HEAVEN	Amii Stewart	Atlantic	3
5	7	THE LONE RANGER	Quantum Jump	Electric	5
4	8	BOOGIE WONDERLAND	Earth Wind & Fire	CBS	9
24	9	C'MON EVERYBODY	Sex Pistols	Virgin	2
6	10	DANCE AWAY	Roxy Music	Polydor	10
7	11	SUNDAY GIRL	Blondie	Chrysalis	8
15	12	LIVING ON THE FRONT LINE	Eddy Grant	Ice Ensign	4
8	13	AIN'T NO STOPPIN' US NOW	McFadden & Whitehead	Philadelphia	7
14	[14]	WHO WERE YOU WITH IN THE MOONLIGHT	Dollar	Carrere	7
9	15	H.A.P.P.Y. RADIO	Edwin Starr	RCA	7
13	16	CAVATINA (ORIGINAL SOUNDTRACK FROM DEER HUNTER)	John Williams	Cube	6
11	17	WE ARE FAMILY	Sister Sledge	Atlantic	6
21	18	GO WEST	Village People	Mercury	4
12	19	THEME FROM DEER HUNTER	Shadows	EMI	8
26	20	MAYBE	Thom Pace	RSO	4
22	21	BABYLON BURNING	Ruts	Virgin	3
-	22	GOOD TIMES	Chic	Atlantic	1
19	23	SAY WHEN	Lene Lovich	Stiff	8
20	24	GERTCHA	Chas & Dave	EMI	5
16	25	MASQUERADE	Skids	Virgin	7
29	26	DO ANYTHING YOU WANT TO	Thin Lizzy	Vertigo	3
31	27	WANTED	Dooleys	GTO	2
27	28	LADY LYNDA	Beach Boys	Caribou	3
-	29	GIRLS TALK	Dave Edmunds	Swan Song	1
34	30	BORN TO BE ALIVE	Patrick Hernandez	GEM	2
30	31	SPACE BASS	Slick	Fantasy	3
-	32	BREAKFAST IN AMERICA	Supertramp	A&M	1
37	33	STRANGLE HOLD	UK Subs	GEM	2
-	34	DEATH DISCO	Public Image Ltd	Virgin	1
36	[35]	MARRIED MEN	Bonnie Tyler	RCA	2
-	36	CHUCK E'S IN LOVE	Rickie Lee Jones ●	Warner Bros.	1
17	37	SHINE A LITTLE LOVE	Electric Light Orchestra	Jet	8
35	38	OLD SIAM SIR	Wings	Parlophone	3
-	39	BAD GIRLS	Donna Summer	Casablanca	1
33	40	HEAD OVER HEELS IN LOVE	Kevin Keegan	RAK	4

WEEK ENDING 14 JULY 1979

LW	TW	Title	Artist	Label	Wks
1	[1]	ARE FRIENDS ELECTRIC	Tubeway Army	Beggers Banquet	7
3	[2]	SILLY GAMES	Janet Kay	Scope	4
9	[3]	C'MON EVERYBODY	Sex Pistols	Virgin	3
2	4	UP THE JUNCTION	Squeeze	A&M	6
6	[5]	LIGHT MY FIRE/137 DISCO HEAVEN	Amii Stewart	Atlantic	4
5	6	NIGHT OWL	Gerry Rafferty	United Artists	7
21	[7]	BABYLON BURNING	Ruts	Virgin	4
28	8	LADY LYNDA	Beach Boys	Caribou	4
7	9	THE LONE RANGER	Quantum Jump	Electric	6
4	10	RING MY BELL	Anita Ward	TK	7
12	[11]	LIVING ON THE FRONT LINE	Eddy Grant	Ice Ensign	5
22	12	GOOD TIMES	Chic	Atlantic	2
27	13	WANTED	Dooleys	GTO	3
26	[14]	DO ANYTHING YOU WANT TO	Thin Lizzy	Vertigo	4
18	[15]	GO WEST	Village People	Mercury	5
31	[16]	SPACE BASS	Slick	Fantasy	4
20	17	MAYBE	Thom Pace	RSO	5
15	18	H.A.P.P.Y. RADIO	Edwin Starr	RCA	8
16	19	CAVATINA (ORIGINAL SOUNDTRACK FROM DEER HUNTER)	John Williams	Cube	7
14	20	WHO WERE YOU WITH IN THE MOONLIGHT	Dollar	Carrere	8
29	21	GIRLS TALK	Dave Edmunds	Swan Song	2
39	22	BAD GIRLS	Donna Summer	Casablanca	2
8	23	BOOGIE WONDERLAND	Earth Wind & Fire	CBS	10
-	24	MY SHARONA	Knack ●	Capitol	1
30	25	BORN TO BE ALIVE	Patrick Hernandez	GEM	3
32	26	BREAKFAST IN AMERICA	Supertramp	A&M	2
23	27	SAY WHEN	Lene Lovich	Stiff	9
24	28	GERTCHA	Chas & Dave	EMI	6
10	29	DANCE AWAY	Roxy Music	Polydor	11
36	30	CHUCK E'S IN LOVE	Rickie Lee Jones	Warner Bros.	2
11	31	SUNDAY GIRL	Blondie	Chrysalis	9
34	32	DEATH DISCO	Public Image Ltd	Virgin	2
-	33	PLAYGROUND TWIST	Siouxsie & the Banshees	Polydor	1
-	34	IF I HAD YOU	Korgis ●	Rialto	1
17	35	WE ARE FAMILY	Sister Sledge	Atlantic	7
35	36	MARRIED MEN	Bonnie Tyler	RCA	3
19	37	THEME FROM DEER HUNTER	Shadows	EMI	9
-	38	CAN'T STAND LOSING YOU	Police	A&M	1
13	39	AIN'T NO STOPPIN' US NOW	McFadden & Whitehead	Philadelphia	8
25	40	MASQUERADE	Skids	Virgin	8

WEEK ENDING 21 JULY 1979

LW	TW	Title	Artist	Label	Wks
1	[1]	ARE FRIENDS ELECTRIC	Tubeway Army	Beggers Banquet	8
2	[2]	SILLY GAMES	Janet Kay	Scope	5
3	[3]	C'MON EVERYBODY	Sex Pistols	Virgin	4
21	[4]	GIRLS TALK	Dave Edmunds	Swan Song	3
12	[5]	GOOD TIMES	Chic	Atlantic	3
8	[6]	LADY LYNDA	Beach Boys	Caribou	5
6	7	NIGHT OWL	Gerry Rafferty	United Artists	8
5	8	LIGHT MY FIRE/137 DISCO HEAVEN	Amii Stewart	Atlantic	5
4	9	UP THE JUNCTION	Squeeze	A&M	7
13	10	WANTED	Dooleys	GTO	4
7	11	BABYLON BURNING	Ruts	Virgin	5
26	12	BREAKFAST IN AMERICA	Supertramp	A&M	3

In these weeks ■ Squeeze have their second consecutive number two, but will never reach the very top (07.07.79) ■ The Sex Pistols have their seventh straight Top Ten hit, their last (07.07.79) ■ In a case of unusual chart movement, *Lady Lynda* slips one place (07.07.79) then climbs twenty for the Beach Boys' first Top Ten in nine years (14.07.79)■

LW	TW	Title	Artist	Label	Wks
25	13	BORN TO BE ALIVE	Patrick Hernandez	GEM	4
17	[14]	MAYBE	Thom Pace	RSO	6
-	15	DON'T LIKE MONDAYS	Boomtown Rats	Ensign	1
14	16	DO ANYTHING YOU WANT TO	Thin Lizzy	Vertigo	5
15	17	GO WEST	Village People	Mercury	6
11	18	LIVING ON THE FRONT LINE	Eddy Grant	Ice Ensign	6
38	19	CAN'T STAND LOSING YOU	Police	A&M	2
32	[20]	DEATH DISCO	Public Image Ltd	Virgin	3
16	21	SPACE BASS	Slick	Fantasy	5
22	22	BAD GIRLS	Donna Summer	Casablanca	3
-	23	ANGEL EYES/VOULEZ VOUS	Abba	Epic	1
24	24	MY SHARONA	Knack	Capitol	2
34	25	IF I HAD YOU	Korgis	Rialto	2
-	[26]	STRANGLE HOLD	UK Subs	GEM	3
9	27	THE LONE RANGER	Quantum Jump	Electric	7
33	[28]	PLAYGROUND TWIST	Siouxsie & the Banshees	Polydor	2
-	[29]	D.J.	David Bowie	RCA	1
23	30	BOOGIE WONDERLAND	Earth Wind & Fire	CBS	11
30	31	CHUCK E'S IN LOVE	Rickie Lee Jones	Warner Bros.	3
10	32	RING MY BELL	Anita Ward	TK	8
-	33	STAY WITH ME TILL DAWN	Judie Tzuke ●	Rocket	1
20	34	WHO WERE YOU WITH IN THE MOONLIGHT	Dollar	Carrere	9
-	35	WE DON'T TALK ANYMORE	Cliff Richard	EMI	1
31	35	SUNDAY GIRL	Blondie	Chrysalis	10
35	37	WE ARE FAMILY	Sister Sledge	Atlantic	8
-	38	KID	The Pretenders	Real	1
36	39	MARRIED MEN	Bonnie Tyler	RCA	4
18	40	H.A.P.P.Y. RADIO	Edwin Starr	RCA	9

LW	TW	*WEEK ENDING* **28 JULY 1979**			Wks
15	[1]	DON'T LIKE MONDAYS	Boomtown Rats	Ensign	2
1	2	ARE FRIENDS ELECTRIC	Tubeway Army	Beggers Banquet	9
2	3	SILLY GAMES	Janet Kay	Scope	6
4	[4]	GIRLS TALK	Dave Edmunds	Swan Song	4
10	5	WANTED	Dooleys	GTO	5
24	[6]	MY SHARONA	Knack	Capitol	3
5	7	GOOD TIMES	Chic	Atlantic	4
3	8	C'MON EVERYBODY	Sex Pistols	Virgin	5
6	9	LADY LYNDA	Beach Boys	Caribou	6
12	10	BREAKFAST IN AMERICA	Supertramp	A&M	4
8	11	LIGHT MY FIRE/137 DISCO HEAVEN	Amii Stewart	Atlantic	6
23	12	ANGEL EYES/VOULEZ VOUS	Abba	Epic	2
13	13	BORN TO BE ALIVE	Patrick Hernandez	GEM	5
22	[14]	BAD GIRLS	Donna Summer	Casablanca	4
19	15	CAN'T STAND LOSING YOU	Police	A&M	3
14	16	MAYBE	Thom Pace	RSO	7
11	17	BABYLON BURNING	Ruts	Virgin	6
31	[18]	CHUCK E'S IN LOVE	Rickie Lee Jones	Warner Bros.	4
16	19	DO ANYTHING YOU WANT TO	Thin Lizzy	Vertigo	6
25	20	IF I HAD YOU	Korgis	Rialto	3
-	21	BEAT THE CLOCK	Sparks	Virgin	1
17	22	GO WEST	Village People	Mercury	7
35	23	WE DON'T TALK ANYMORE	Cliff Richard	EMI	2
18	24	LIVING ON THE FRONT LINE	Eddy Grant	Ice Ensign	7
21	25	SPACE BASS	Slick	Fantasy	6
20	26	DEATH DISCO	Public Image Ltd	Virgin	4
-	27	THE DIARY OF HORACE WIMP	Electric Light Orchestra	Jet	1
7	28	NIGHT OWL	Gerry Rafferty	United Artists	9
9	29	UP THE JUNCTION	Squeeze	A&M	8
33	30	STAY WITH ME TILL DAWN	Judie Tzuke	Rocket	2
29	31	D.J.	David Bowie	RCA	2
-	32	DUKE OF EARL	Darts	Magnet	1
-	[33]	BOOGIE DOWN	Real Thing	Pye	1
26	34	STRANGLE HOLD	UK Subs	GEM	4
-	35	HARMONY IN MY HEAD	Buzzcocks	United Artists	1
38	36	KID	The Pretenders	Real	2
-	37	OOH WHAT A LIFE	Gibson Brothers	Island	1
-	[38]	SINCE I DON'T HAVE YOU	Art Garfunkel	CBS	1
-	39	HERE COMES THE SUMMER	Undertones	Sire	1
27	40	THE LONE RANGER	Quantum Jump	Electric	8

August 1979

□ Highest position disc reached ● Act's first ever week on chart

LW	TW	*WEEK ENDING* **4 AUGUST 1979**			Wks
1	[1]	DON'T LIKE MONDAYS	Boomtown Rats	Ensign	3
15	[2]	CAN'T STAND LOSING YOU	Police	A&M	4
5	3	WANTED	Dooleys	GTO	6
4	[4]	GIRLS TALK	Dave Edmunds	Swan Song	5
12	5	ANGEL EYES/VOULEZ VOUS	Abba	Epic	3
3	6	SILLY GAMES	Janet Kay	Scope	7
2	7	ARE FRIENDS ELECTRIC	Tubeway Army	Beggers Banquet	10
6	8	MY SHARONA	Knack	Capitol	4
10	[9]	BREAKFAST IN AMERICA	Supertramp	A&M	5
21	[10]	BEAT THE CLOCK	Sparks	Virgin	2
13	11	BORN TO BE ALIVE	Patrick Hernandez	GEM	6
7	12	GOOD TIMES	Chic	Atlantic	5
20	[13]	IF I HAD YOU	Korgis	Rialto	4
23	14	WE DON'T TALK ANYMORE	Cliff Richard	EMI	3
14	15	BAD GIRLS	Donna Summer	Casablanca	5
8	16	C'MON EVERYBODY	Sex Pistols	Virgin	6
27	17	THE DIARY OF HORACE WIMP	Electric Light Orchestra	Jet	2
9	18	LADY LYNDA	Beach Boys	Caribou	7
17	19	BABYLON BURNING	Ruts	Virgin	7
18	20	CHUCK E'S IN LOVE	Rickie Lee Jones	Warner Bros.	5
16	21	MAYBE	Thom Pace	RSO	8
32	22	DUKE OF EARL	Darts	Magnet	2
-	23	HERSHAM BOYS	Sham 69	Polydor	1
19	24	DO ANYTHING YOU WANT TO	Thin Lizzy	Vertigo	7
11	25	LIGHT MY FIRE/137 DISCO HEAVEN	Amii Stewart	Atlantic	7
-	26	AFTER THE LOVE HAS GONE	Earth Wind & Fire	CBS	1
30	27	STAY WITH ME TILL DAWN	Judie Tzuke	Rocket	3
26	28	DEATH DISCO	Public Image Ltd	Virgin	5
-	29	MORNING DANCE	Spyro Gyra ●	Infinity	1
37	30	OOH WHAT A LIFE	Gibson Brothers	Island	2
-	31	SWEET LITTLE ROCK 'N' ROLLER	Showaddywaddy	Arista	1
35	[32]	HARMONY IN MY HEAD	Buzzcocks	United Artists	2
36	[33]	KID	The Pretenders	Real	3
39	[34]	HERE COMES THE SUMMER	Undertones	Sire	2
33	35	BOOGIE DOWN	Real Thing	Pye	2
31	36	D.J.	David Bowie	RCA	3
-	[37]	THE BITCH	Olympic Runners	Polydor	1
28	38	NIGHT OWL	Gerry Rafferty	United Artists	10
-	39	ROCK AROUND THE CLOCK	Telex ●	Sire	1
-	[40]	THE BOSS	Diana Ross	Motown	1

LW	TW	*WEEK ENDING* **11 AUGUST 1979**			Wks
1	[1]	DON'T LIKE MONDAYS	Boomtown Rats	Ensign	4
14	2	WE DON'T TALK ANYMORE	Cliff Richard	EMI	4
5	[3]	ANGEL EYES/VOULEZ VOUS	Abba	Epic	4
2	4	CAN'T STAND LOSING YOU	Police	A&M	5
3	5	WANTED	Dooleys	GTO	7
-	6	REASONS TO BE CHEERFUL	Ian Dury & the Blockheads	Stiff	1
23	7	HERSHAM BOYS	Sham 69	Polydor	2
17	[8]	THE DIARY OF HORACE WIMP	Electric Light Orchestra	Jet	3
4	9	GIRLS TALK	Dave Edmunds	Swan Song	6
11	[10]	BORN TO BE ALIVE	Patrick Hernandez	GEM	7
10	11	BEAT THE CLOCK	Sparks	Virgin	3
8	12	MY SHARONA	Knack	Capitol	5
9	13	BREAKFAST IN AMERICA	Supertramp	A&M	6
26	14	AFTER THE LOVE HAS GONE	Earth Wind & Fire	CBS	2
12	15	GOOD TIMES	Chic	Atlantic	6
13	16	IF I HAD YOU	Korgis	Rialto	5
22	17	DUKE OF EARL	Darts	Magnet	3
27	18	STAY WITH ME TILL DAWN	Judie Tzuke	Rocket	4
7	19	ARE FRIENDS ELECTRIC	Tubeway Army	Beggers Banquet	11
6	20	SILLY GAMES	Janet Kay	Scope	8
15	21	BAD GIRLS	Donna Summer	Casablanca	6
18	22	LADY LYNDA	Beach Boys	Caribou	8
29	23	MORNING DANCE	Spyro Gyra	Infinity	2
-	24	GANGSTERS	Specials ●	2 Tons	1

■The Boomtown Rats have their second consecutive and longest running number one (28.07.79) ■ The Police visit the Top Ten for the first time (04.08.79) ■ America's number one single of the year, *My Sharona* by the Knack, spends two weeks in the British Top Ten (28.07.79 - 04.08.79)■

August 1979

□ Highest position disc reached ● Act's first ever week on chart

LW	TW	Title	Artist	Label	Wks
30	25	OOH WHAT A LIFE	Gibson Brothers	Island	3
16	26	C'MON EVERYBODY	Sex Pistols	Virgin	7
-	27	BANG BANG	B.A. Robertson ●	Asylum	1
20	28	CHUCK E'S IN LOVE	Rickie Lee Jones	Warner Bros.	6
31	29	SWEET LITTLE ROCK 'N' ROLLER	Showaddywaddy	Arista	2
-	30	IS SHE REALLY GOING OUT WITH HIM	Joe Jackson ●	A&M	1
-	31	JUST WHEN I NEEDED YOU MOST	Randy Vanwarmer ●	Island	1
-	32	ANGEL EYES	Roxy Music	Polydor	1
32	33	HARMONY IN MY HEAD	Buzzcocks	United Artists	3
39	□34	ROCK AROUND THE CLOCK	Telex	Sire	2
33	35	KID	The Pretenders	Real	4
25	36	LIGHT MY FIRE/137 DISCO HEAVEN	Amii Stewart	Atlantic	8
35	37	BOOGIE DOWN	Real Thing	Pye	3
37	38	THE BITCH	Olympic Runners	Polydor	2
-	39	GOTTA GO HOME	Boney M	Atlantic	1
21	40	MAYBE	Thom Pace	RSO	9

WEEK ENDING 18 AUGUST 1979

LW	TW	Title	Artist	Label	Wks
1	□1	DON'T LIKE MONDAYS	Boomtown Rats	Ensign	5
2	2	WE DON'T TALK ANYMORE	Cliff Richard	EMI	5
6	□3	REASONS TO BE CHEERFUL	Ian Dury & the Blockheads	Stiff	2
14	□4	AFTER THE LOVE HAS GONE	Earth Wind & Fire	CBS	3
3	5	ANGEL EYES/VOULEZ VOUS	Abba	Epic	5
7	□6	HERSHAM BOYS	Sham 69	Polydor	3
4	7	CAN'T STAND LOSING YOU	Police	A&M	6
5	8	WANTED	Dooleys	GTO	8
17	9	DUKE OF EARL	Darts	Magnet	4
8	10	THE DIARY OF HORACE WIMP	Electric Light Orchestra	Jet	4
27	11	BANG BANG	B.A. Robertson	Asylum	2
11	12	BEAT THE CLOCK	Sparks	Virgin	4
32	13	ANGEL EYES	Roxy Music	Polydor	1
24	14	GANGSTERS	Specials	2 Tons	2
9	15	GIRLS TALK	Dave Edmunds	Swan Song	7
18	□16	STAY WITH ME TILL DAWN	Judie Tzuke	Rocket	5
29	17	SWEET LITTLE ROCK 'N' ROLLER	Showaddywaddy	Arista	3
10	18	BORN TO BE ALIVE	Patrick Hernandez	GEM	8
25	19	OOH WHAT A LIFE	Gibson Brothers	Island	4
23	20	MORNING DANCE	Spyro Gyra	Infinity	3
16	21	IF I HAD YOU	Korgis	Rialto	6
39	22	GOTTA GO HOME	Boney M	Atlantic	2
30	23	IS SHE REALLY GOING OUT WITH HIM	Joe Jackson	A&M	2
13	24	BREAKFAST IN AMERICA	Supertramp	A&M	7
12	25	MY SHARONA	Knack	Capitol	6
15	26	GOOD TIMES	Chic	Atlantic	7
31	27	JUST WHEN I NEEDED YOU MOST	Randy Vanwarmer	Island	2
21	28	BAD GIRLS	Donna Summer	Casablanca	7
-	□29	TEENAGE WARNING	Angelic Upstarts	Warner Brothers	1
-	30	MONEY	Flying Lizards ●	Virgin	1
20	31	SILLY GAMES	Janet Kay	Scope	9
-	32	LOST IN MUSIC	Sister Sledge	Atlantic	1
-	33	IF I SAID YOU HAD A BEAUTIFUL BODY WOULD YOU HOLD IT AGAINST ME	Bellamy Brothers	Warner Brothers	1
-	□34	GIRLS GIRLS GIRLS	Kandidate	RAK	1
-	35	GONE GONE GONE	Johnny Mathis	CBS	1
-	36	YOU NEVER KNOW WHAT YOU'VE GOT	Me & You ●	Laser	1
-	□37	ROCK LOBSTER	B52's ●	Island	1
19	38	ARE FRIENDS ELECTRIC	Tubeway Army	Beggers Banquet	12
34	39	ROCK AROUND THE CLOCK	Telex	Sire	3
-	□40	YOU NEED WHEELS	Merton Parkas ●	Beggars Banquet	1

WEEK ENDING 25 AUGUST 1979

LW	TW	Title	Artist	Label	Wks
2	□1	WE DON'T TALK ANYMORE	Cliff Richard	EMI	6
1	2	DON'T LIKE MONDAYS	Boomtown Rats	Ensign	6
11	3	BANG BANG	B.A. Robertson	Asylum	3
3	4	REASONS TO BE CHEERFUL	Ian Dury & the Blockheads	Stiff	3
4	5	AFTER THE LOVE HAS GONE	Earth Wind & Fire	CBS	4
9	□6	DUKE OF EARL	Darts	Magnet	5
6	7	HERSHAM BOYS	Sham 69	Polydor	4
14	8	GANGSTERS	Specials	2 Tons	3
5	9	ANGEL EYES/VOULEZ VOUS	Abba	Epic	6
10	10	THE DIARY OF HORACE WIMP	Electric Light Orchestra	Jet	5
19	11	OOH WHAT A LIFE	Gibson Brothers	Island	5
13	12	ANGEL EYES	Roxy Music	Polydor	2
23	□13	IS SHE REALLY GOING OUT WITH HIM	Joe Jackson	A&M	3
12	14	BEAT THE CLOCK	Sparks	Virgin	5
17	□15	SWEET LITTLE ROCK 'N' ROLLER	Showaddywaddy	Arista	4
8	16	WANTED	Dooleys	GTO	9
20	□17	MORNING DANCE	Spyro Gyra	Infinity	4
30	18	MONEY	Flying Lizards	Virgin	2
7	19	CAN'T STAND LOSING YOU	Police	A&M	7
16	20	STAY WITH ME TILL DAWN	Judie Tzuke	Rocket	6
18	21	BORN TO BE ALIVE	Patrick Hernandez	GEM	9
22	22	GOTTA GO HOME	Boney M	Atlantic	3
-	23	STREET LIFE	Crusaders ●	MCA	1
21	24	IF I HAD YOU	Korgis	Rialto	7
-	25	WHEN YOU ARE YOUNG	Jam	Polydor	1
-	26	DUCHESS	Stranglers	United Artists	1
27	27	JUST WHEN I NEEDED YOU MOST	Randy Vanwarmer	Island	3
15	28	GIRLS TALK	Dave Edmunds	Swan Song	8
35	29	GONE GONE GONE	Johnny Mathis	CBS	2
32	30	LOST IN MUSIC	Sister Sledge	Atlantic	2
29	31	TEENAGE WARNING	Angelic Upstarts	Warner Brothers	2
36	32	YOU NEVER KNOW WHAT YOU'VE GOT	Me & You	Laser	2
33	33	IF I SAID YOU HAD A BEAUTIFUL BODY WOULD YOU HOLD IT AGAINST ME	Bellamy Brothers	Warner Brothers	2
34	34	GIRLS GIRLS GIRLS	Kandidate	RAK	2
-	35	REGGAE FOR IT NOW	Billy Lovelady ●	Charisma	1
-	36	GET IT RIGHT NEXT TIME	Gerry Rafferty	United Artists	1
37	□37	ROCK LOBSTER	B52's	Island	2
24	38	BREAKFAST IN AMERICA	Supertramp	A&M	8
-	39	STRUT YOUR FUNKY STUFF	Frantique ●	Philadelphia	1
26	40	GOOD TIMES	Chic	Atlantic	8

WEEK ENDING 1 SEPTEMBER 1979

LW	TW	Title	Artist	Label	Wks
1	□1	WE DON'T TALK ANYMORE	Cliff Richard	EMI	7
2	2	DON'T LIKE MONDAYS	Boomtown Rats	Ensign	7
3	3	BANG BANG	B.A. Robertson	Asylum	4
12	□4	ANGEL EYES	Roxy Music	Polydor	3
5	5	AFTER THE LOVE HAS GONE	Earth Wind & Fire	CBS	5
8	□6	GANGSTERS	Specials	2 Tons	4
6	7	DUKE OF EARL	Darts	Magnet	6
18	8	MONEY	Flying Lizards	Virgin	3
4	9	REASONS TO BE CHEERFUL	Ian Dury & the Blockheads	Stiff	4
11	□10	OOH WHAT A LIFE	Gibson Brothers	Island	6
27	11	JUST WHEN I NEEDED YOU MOST	Randy Vanwarmer	Island	4
7	12	HERSHAM BOYS	Sham 69	Polydor	5
13	□13	IS SHE REALLY GOING OUT WITH HIM	Joe Jackson	A&M	4
9	14	ANGEL EYES/VOULEZ VOUS	Abba	Epic	7
22	15	GOTTA GO HOME	Boney M	Atlantic	4
23	16	STREET LIFE	Crusaders	MCA	2
15	17	SWEET LITTLE ROCK 'N' ROLLER	Showaddywaddy	Arista	5
25	18	WHEN YOU ARE YOUNG	Jam	Polydor	2
10	19	THE DIARY OF HORACE WIMP	Electric Light Orchestra	Jet	6
-	20	CARS	Gary Numan	Beggars Banquet	1
17	21	MORNING DANCE	Spyro Gyra	Infinity	5
33	22	IF I SAID YOU HAD A BEAUTIFUL BODY WOULD YOU HOLD IT AGAINST ME	Bellamy Brothers	Warner Brothers	3
-	23	LOVE'S GOTTA HOLD ON ME	Dollar	Carrere	1
30	24	LOST IN MUSIC	Sister Sledge	Atlantic	3
26	25	DUCHESS	Stranglers	United Artists	2
16	26	WANTED	Dooleys	GTO	10
20	27	STAY WITH ME TILL DAWN	Judie Tzuke	Rocket	7
29	28	GONE GONE GONE	Johnny Mathis	CBS	3
31	□29	TEENAGE WARNING	Angelic Upstarts	Warner Brothers	3
35	30	REGGAE FOR IT NOW	Billy Lovelady	Charisma	2
32	□31	YOU NEVER KNOW WHAT YOU'VE GOT	Me & You	Laser	3
14	32	BEAT THE CLOCK	Sparks	Virgin	6
28	33	GIRLS TALK	Dave Edmunds	Swan Song	9

In these weeks ■ The Bellamy Brothers *If I Said You Have A Beautiful Body Would You Hold It Against Me* has more words in its title (14) than any other British hit single (18.08.79) ■ Cliff Richard has his first number one in 11 years 124 days, giving him at least one chart topper in the 50s, 60s and 70s (25.08.79) ■ Randy Crawford debuts as guest vocalist on the Crusaders' *Street Life* (25.06.79)■

September 1979

□ Highest position disc reached ● Act's first ever week on chart

Boxed (highest position reached) numbers are shown as [n].

LW	TW	Title	Artist	Label	Wks
-	34	BOY OH BOY	Racey	RAK	1
39	35	STRUT YOUR FUNKY STUFF	Frantique	Philadelphia	2
-	36	SPIRAL SCRATCH	Buzzcocks	New Hormones	1
-	37	LINES	Planets ●	Rialto	1
-	38	DON'T BRING ME DOWN	Electric Light Orchestra	Jet	1
19	39	CAN'T STAND LOSING YOU	Police	A&M	8
36	40	GET IT RIGHT NEXT TIME	Gerry Rafferty	United Artists	2

WEEK ENDING 8 SEPTEMBER 1979

LW	TW	Title	Artist	Label	Wks
1	[1]	WE DON'T TALK ANYMORE	Cliff Richard	EMI	8
3	[2]	BANG BANG	B.A. Robertson	Asylum	5
20	3	CARS	Gary Numan	Beggars Banquet	2
4	[4]	ANGEL EYES	Roxy Music	Polydor	4
8	[5]	MONEY	Flying Lizards	Virgin	4
6	[6]	GANGSTERS	Specials	2 Tons	5
16	7	STREET LIFE	Crusaders	MCA	3
2	8	DON'T LIKE MONDAYS	Boomtown Rats	Ensign	8
11	9	JUST WHEN I NEEDED YOU MOST	Randy Vanwarmer	Island	5
5	10	AFTER THE LOVE HAS GONE	Earth Wind & Fire	CBS	6
38	11	DON'T BRING ME DOWN	Electric Light Orchestra	Jet	2
10	12	OOH WHAT A LIFE	Gibson Brothers	Island	7
15	13	GOTTA GO HOME	Boney M	Atlantic	5
25	[14]	DUCHESS	Stranglers	United Artists	3
13	15	IS SHE REALLY GOING OUT WITH HIM	Joe Jackson	A&M	5
23	16	LOVE'S GOTTA HOLD ON ME	Dollar	Carrere	2
18	[17]	WHEN YOU ARE YOUNG	Jam	Polydor	3
7	18	DUKE OF EARL	Darts	Magnet	7
22	19	IF I SAID YOU HAD A BEAUTIFUL BODY WOULD YOU HOLD IT AGAINST ME	Bellamy Brothers	Warner Brothers	4
9	20	REASONS TO BE CHEERFUL	Ian Dury & the Blockheads	Stiff	5
17	21	SWEET LITTLE ROCK 'N' ROLLER	Showaddywaddy	Arista	6
12	22	HERSHAM BOYS	Sham 69	Polydor	6
21	23	MORNING DANCE	Spyro Gyra	Infinity	6
24	24	LOST IN MUSIC	Sister Sledge	Atlantic	4
28	25	GONE GONE GONE	Johnny Mathis	CBS	4
35	26	STRUT YOUR FUNKY STUFF	Frantique	Philadelphia	3
30	27	REGGAE FOR IT NOW	Billy Lovelady	Charisma	3
34	28	BOY OH BOY	Racey	RAK	2
14	29	ANGEL EYES/VOULEZ VOUS	Abba	Epic	8
29	30	TEENAGE WARNING	Angelic Upstarts	Warner Brothers	4
19	31	THE DIARY OF HORACE WIMP	Electric Light Orchestra	Jet	7
-	32	CRUEL TO BE KIND	Nick Lowe	Radar	1
40	33	GET IT RIGHT NEXT TIME	Gerry Rafferty	United Artists	3
-	34	SAIL ON	Commodores	Motown	1
31	35	YOU NEVER KNOW WHAT YOU'VE GOT	Me & You	Laser	4
37	[36]	LINES	Planets	Rialto	2
36	37	SPIRAL SCRATCH	Buzzcocks	New Hormones	2
-	[38]	IN THE BROWNIES	Billy Connolly	Polydor	1
26	39	WANTED	Dooleys	GTO	11
-	40	TIME FOR ACTION	Secret Affair ●	I-Spy	1

WEEK ENDING 15 SEPTEMBER 1979

LW	TW	Title	Artist	Label	Wks
1	[1]	WE DON'T TALK ANYMORE	Cliff Richard	EMI	9
3	2	CARS	Gary Numan	Beggars Banquet	3
2	3	BANG BANG	B.A. Robertson	Asylum	6
11	4	DON'T BRING ME DOWN	Electric Light Orchestra	Jet	3
7	[5]	STREET LIFE	Crusaders	MCA	4
4	6	ANGEL EYES	Roxy Music	Polydor	5
19	7	IF I SAID YOU HAD A BEAUTIFUL BODY WOULD YOU HOLD IT AGAINST ME	Bellamy Brothers	Warner Brothers	5
9	[8]	JUST WHEN I NEEDED YOU MOST	Randy Vanwarmer	Island	6
16	9	LOVE'S GOTTA HOLD ON ME	Dollar	Carrere	3
5	10	MONEY	Flying Lizards	Virgin	5
6	11	GANGSTERS	Specials	2 Tons	6
13	[12]	GOTTA GO HOME	Boney M	Atlantic	6
12	13	OOH WHAT A LIFE	Gibson Brothers	Island	8
14	[14]	DUCHESS	Stranglers	United Artists	4
10	15	AFTER THE LOVE HAS GONE	Earth Wind & Fire	CBS	7
8	16	DON'T LIKE MONDAYS	Boomtown Rats	Ensign	9
24	[17]	LOST IN MUSIC	Sister Sledge	Atlantic	5
27	18	REGGAE FOR IT NOW	Billy Lovelady	Charisma	4
18	19	DUKE OF EARL	Darts	Magnet	8
15	20	IS SHE REALLY GOING OUT WITH HIM	Joe Jackson	A&M	6
25	21	GONE GONE GONE	Johnny Mathis	CBS	5
17	22	WHEN YOU ARE YOUNG	Jam	Polydor	4
26	23	STRUT YOUR FUNKY STUFF	Frantique	Philadelphia	4
34	24	SAIL ON	Commodores	Motown	2
28	25	BOY OH BOY	Racey	RAK	3
32	26	CRUEL TO BE KIND	Nick Lowe	Radar	2
40	27	TIME FOR ACTION	Secret Affair	I-Spy	2
-	[28]	TOMORROWS GIRLS	U.K. Subs	Gems	1
-	[29]	SOMETHING THAT I SAID	Ruts	Virgin	1
33	[30]	GET IT RIGHT NEXT TIME	Gerry Rafferty	United Artists	4
37	[31]	SPIRAL SCRATCH	Buzzcocks	New Hormones	3
-	32	SLAP AND TICKLE	Squeeze	A&M	1
-	33	SINCE YOU'VE BEEN GONE	Rainbow	Polydor	1
22	34	HERSHAM BOYS	Sham 69	Polydor	7
-	35	KATE BUSH LIVE ON STAGE	Kate Bush	EMI	1
21	36	SWEET LITTLE ROCK 'N' ROLLER	Showaddywaddy	Arista	7
-	37	THE PRINCE	Madness ●	2 Tone	1
38	[38]	IN THE BROWNIES	Billy Connolly	Polydor	2
20	39	REASONS TO BE CHEERFUL	Ian Dury & the Blockheads	Stiff	6
29	40	ANGEL EYES/VOULEZ VOUS	Abba	Epic	9

WEEK ENDING 22 SEPTEMBER 1979

LW	TW	Title	Artist	Label	Wks
2	[1]	CARS	Gary Numan	Beggars Banquet	4
1	2	WE DON'T TALK ANYMORE	Cliff Richard	EMI	10
4	[3]	DON'T BRING ME DOWN	Electric Light Orchestra	Jet	4
7	4	IF I SAID YOU HAD A BEAUTIFUL BODY WOULD YOU HOLD IT AGAINST ME	Bellamy Brothers	Warner Brothers	6
9	5	LOVE'S GOTTA HOLD ON ME	Dollar	Carrere	4
5	6	STREET LIFE	Crusaders	MCA	5
3	7	BANG BANG	B.A. Robertson	Asylum	7
-	8	MESSAGE IN A BOTTLE	Police	A&M	1
8	9	JUST WHEN I NEEDED YOU MOST	Randy Vanwarmer	Island	7
6	10	ANGEL EYES	Roxy Music	Polydor	6
23	11	STRUT YOUR FUNKY STUFF	Frantique	Philadelphia	5
18	[12]	REGGAE FOR IT NOW	Billy Lovelady	Charisma	5
12	13	GOTTA GO HOME	Boney M	Atlantic	7
24	14	SAIL ON	Commodores	Motown	3
21	[15]	GONE GONE GONE	Johnny Mathis	CBS	6
26	16	CRUEL TO BE KIND	Nick Lowe	Radar	3
10	17	MONEY	Flying Lizards	Virgin	6
14	18	DUCHESS	Stranglers	United Artists	5
11	19	GANGSTERS	Specials	2 Tons	7
17	20	LOST IN MUSIC	Sister Sledge	Atlantic	6
27	21	TIME FOR ACTION	Secret Affair	I-Spy	3
25	[22]	BOY OH BOY	Racey	RAK	4
37	23	THE PRINCE	Madness	2 Tone	2
16	24	DON'T LIKE MONDAYS	Boomtown Rats	Ensign	10
32	25	SLAP AND TICKLE	Squeeze	A&M	2
33	26	SINCE YOU'VE BEEN GONE	Rainbow	Polydor	2
35	27	KATE BUSH LIVE ON STAGE	Kate Bush	EMI	2
28	[28]	TOMORROWS GIRLS	U.K. Subs	Gems	2
-	29	DON'T STOP 'TIL YOU GET ENOUGH	Michael Jackson	Epic	1
30	[30]	GET IT RIGHT NEXT TIME	Gerry Rafferty	United Artists	5
13	31	OOH WHAT A LIFE	Gibson Brothers	Island	9
22	32	WHEN YOU ARE YOUNG	Jam	Polydor	5
29	33	SOMETHING THAT I SAID	Ruts	Virgin	2
-	34	BACK OF MY HAND	Jags ●	Island	1
-	35	WHAT EVER YOU WANT	Status Quo	Vertigo	1
-	36	YOU CAN DO IT	Al Hudson & the Soul Partners ●	MCA	1
15	37	AFTER THE LOVE HAS GONE	Earth Wind & Fire	CBS	8
-	38	DIM ALL THE LIGHTS	Donna Summer	Casablanca	1
20	39	IS SHE REALLY GOING OUT WITH HIM	Joe Jackson	A&M	7
-	40	NIGHTS IN WHITE SATIN	Dickies	A&M	1

■*Angel Eyes* by Roxy Music replaces *Angel Eyes* by Abba, a completely different song, in the Top Ten (01.09.79) ■ Two American rock 'n' roll standards that never charted in Britain *Money* and *Duke Of Earl*; finally make it in new versions (08.09.79) ■ Gary Numan is the only act to have two number ones under two different billings with the first two hits (22.09.79)■

September 1979

□ Highest position disc reached ● Act's first ever week on chart

LW	TW	WEEK ENDING 29 SEPTEMBER 1979		Wks
8	[1]	MESSAGE IN A BOTTLE Police	*A&M*	2
1	2	CARS Gary Numan	*Beggars Banquet*	5
4	[3]	IF I SAID YOU HAD A BEAUTIFUL BODY WOULD YOU HOLD IT AGAINST ME Bellamy Brothers	*Warner Brothers*	7
5	[4]	LOVE'S GOTTA HOLD ON ME Dollar	*Carrere*	5
3	5	DON'T BRING ME DOWN Electric Light Orchestra	*Jet*	5
2	6	WE DON'T TALK ANYMORE Cliff Richard	*EMI*	11
-	7	DREAMING Blondie	*Chrysalis*	1
14	[8]	SAIL ON Commodores	*Motown*	4
6	9	STREET LIFE Crusaders	*MCA*	6
11	[10]	STRUT YOUR FUNKY STUFF Frantique	*Philadelphia*	6
26	11	SINCE YOU'VE BEEN GONE Rainbow	*Polydor*	3
35	12	WHAT EVER YOU WANT Status Quo	*Vertigo*	2
21	[13]	TIME FOR ACTION Secret Affair	*I-Spy*	4
16	14	CRUEL TO BE KIND Nick Lowe	*Radar*	4
12	15	REGGAE FOR IT NOW Billy Lovelady	*Charisma*	6
29	16	DON'T STOP 'TIL YOU GET ENOUGH Michael Jackson	*Epic*	2
9	17	JUST WHEN I NEEDED YOU MOST Randy Vanwarmer	*Island*	8
15	18	GONE GONE GONE Johnny Mathis	*CBS*	7
7	19	BANG BANG B.A. Robertson	*Asylum*	8
10	20	ANGEL EYES Roxy Music	*Polydor*	7
23	21	THE PRINCE Madness	*2 Tone*	3
-	22	GOTTA GO HOME/EL LUTE Boney M	*Atlantic*	1
27	23	KATE BUSH LIVE ON STAGE Kate Bush	*EMI*	3
-	24	VIDEO KILLED THE RADIO STAR Buggles ●	*Island*	1
18	25	DUCHESS Stranglers	*United Artists*	6
22	26	BOY OH BOY Racey	*RAK*	5
20	27	LOST IN MUSIC Sister Sledge	*Atlantic*	7
25	28	SLAP AND TICKLE Squeeze	*A&M*	3
36	29	YOU CAN DO IT Al Hudson & the Soul Partners	*MCA*	2
34	30	BACK OF MY HAND Jags	*Island*	2
-	31	QUEEN OF HEARTS Dave Edmunds	*Swan Song*	1
38	32	DIM ALL THE LIGHTS Donna Summer	*Casablanca*	2
17	33	MONEY Flying Lizards	*Virgin*	7
-	34	EVERY DAY HURTS Sad Cafe ●	*RCA*	1
32	35	WHEN YOU ARE YOUNG Jam	*Polydor*	6
19	36	GANGSTERS Specials	*2 Tons*	8
30	37	GET IT RIGHT NEXT TIME Gerry Rafferty	*United Artists*	6
28	38	TOMORROWS GIRLS U.K. Subs	*Gems*	3
40	[39]	NIGHTS IN WHITE SATIN Dickies	*A&M*	2
-	40	THE LONELIEST MAN IN THE WORLD Tourists ●	*Logo*	1

LW	TW	WEEK ENDING 6 OCTOBER 1979		Wks
1	[1]	MESSAGE IN A BOTTLE Police	*A&M*	3
7	[2]	DREAMING Blondie	*Chrysalis*	2
2	3	CARS Gary Numan	*Beggars Banquet*	6
12	[4]	WHAT EVER YOU WANT Status Quo	*Vertigo*	3
3	5	IF I SAID YOU HAD A BEAUTIFUL BODY WOULD YOU HOLD IT AGAINST ME Bellamy Brothers	*Warner Brothers*	8
24	6	VIDEO KILLED THE RADIO STAR Buggles	*Island*	2
16	7	DON'T STOP 'TIL YOU GET ENOUGH Michael Jackson	*Epic*	3
11	8	SINCE YOU'VE BEEN GONE Rainbow	*Polydor*	4
4	9	LOVE'S GOTTA HOLD ON ME Dollar	*Carrere*	6
5	10	DON'T BRING ME DOWN Electric Light Orchestra	*Jet*	6
23	11	KATE BUSH LIVE ON STAGE Kate Bush	*EMI*	4
14	[12]	CRUEL TO BE KIND Nick Lowe	*Radar*	5
8	13	SAIL ON Commodores	*Motown*	5
10	14	STRUT YOUR FUNKY STUFF Frantique	*Philadelphia*	7
13	15	TIME FOR ACTION Secret Affair	*I-Spy*	5
21	[16]	THE PRINCE Madness	*2 Tone*	4
6	17	WE DON'T TALK ANYMORE Cliff Richard	*EMI*	12
9	18	STREET LIFE Crusaders	*MCA*	7
15	19	REGGAE FOR IT NOW Billy Lovelady	*Charisma*	7
31	20	QUEEN OF HEARTS Dave Edmunds	*Swan Song*	2
34	21	EVERY DAY HURTS Sad Cafe	*RCA*	2
29	22	YOU CAN DO IT Al Hudson & the Soul Partners	*MCA*	3
18	23	GONE GONE GONE Johnny Mathis	*CBS*	8
28	[24]	SLAP AND TICKLE Squeeze	*A&M*	4
22	25	GOTTA GO HOME/EL LUTE Boney M	*Atlantic*	2
17	26	JUST WHEN I NEEDED YOU MOST Randy Vanwarmer	*Island*	9
30	27	BACK OF MY HAND Jags	*Island*	3
-	28	ONE DAY AT A TIME Lena Martell ●	*Pye*	1
26	29	BOY OH BOY Racey	*RAK*	6
-	30	CHOSEN FEW Dooleys	*GTO*	1
27	31	LOST IN MUSIC Sister Sledge	*Atlantic*	8
32	32	DIM ALL THE LIGHTS Donna Summer	*Casablanca*	3
-	33	CHARADE Skids	*Virgin*	1
-	34	O.K. FRED Erroll Dunkley ●	*Scope*	1
40	35	THE LONELIEST MAN IN THE WORLD Tourists	*Logo*	2
20	36	ANGEL EYES Roxy Music	*Polydor*	8
19	37	BANG BANG B.A. Robertson	*Asylum*	9
-	38	THE DEVIL WENT DOWN TO GEORGIA Charlie Daniels ●	*Epic*	1
-	39	DON'T BE A DUMMY John Du Cann ●	*Vertigo*	1
-	40	WHEN YOU'RE IN LOVE WITH A BEAUTIFUL WOMAN Dr Hook	*Capitol*	1

LW	TW	WEEK ENDING 13 OCTOBER 1979		Wks
1	[1]	MESSAGE IN A BOTTLE Police	*A&M*	4
6	2	VIDEO KILLED THE RADIO STAR Buggles	*Island*	3
2	3	DREAMING Blondie	*Chrysalis*	3
7	4	DON'T STOP 'TIL YOU GET ENOUGH Michael Jackson	*Epic*	4
4	5	WHAT EVER YOU WANT Status Quo	*Vertigo*	4
8	[6]	SINCE YOU'VE BEEN GONE Rainbow	*Polydor*	5
3	7	CARS Gary Numan	*Beggars Banquet*	7
5	8	IF I SAID YOU HAD A BEAUTIFUL BODY WOULD YOU HOLD IT AGAINST ME Bellamy Brothers	*Warner Brothers*	9
28	9	ONE DAY AT A TIME Lena Martell	*Pye*	2
11	[10]	KATE BUSH LIVE ON STAGE Kate Bush	*EMI*	5
21	11	EVERY DAY HURTS Sad Cafe	*RCA*	3
9	12	LOVE'S GOTTA HOLD ON ME Dollar	*Carrere*	7
13	13	SAIL ON Commodores	*Motown*	6
12	14	CRUEL TO BE KIND Nick Lowe	*Radar*	6
22	[15]	YOU CAN DO IT Al Hudson & the Soul Partners	*MCA*	4
30	16	CHOSEN FEW Dooleys	*GTO*	2
14	17	STRUT YOUR FUNKY STUFF Frantique	*Philadelphia*	8
20	18	QUEEN OF HEARTS Dave Edmunds	*Swan Song*	3
16	19	THE PRINCE Madness	*2 Tone*	5
10	20	DON'T BRING ME DOWN Electric Light Orchestra	*Jet*	7
15	21	TIME FOR ACTION Secret Affair	*I-Spy*	6
17	22	WE DON'T TALK ANYMORE Cliff Richard	*EMI*	13
34	23	O.K. FRED Erroll Dunkley	*Scope*	2
18	24	STREET LIFE Crusaders	*MCA*	8
24	25	SLAP AND TICKLE Squeeze	*A&M*	5
40	26	WHEN YOU'RE IN LOVE WITH A BEAUTIFUL WOMAN Dr Hook	*Capitol*	2
38	27	THE DEVIL WENT DOWN TO GEORGIA Charlie Daniels	*Epic*	2
27	28	BACK OF MY HAND Jags	*Island*	4
32	[29]	DIM ALL THE LIGHTS Donna Summer	*Casablanca*	4
-	30	TUSK Fleetwood Mac	*Warner Bros.*	1
19	31	REGGAE FOR IT NOW Billy Lovelady	*Charisma*	8
35	[32]	THE LONELIEST MAN IN THE WORLD Tourists	*Logo*	3
39	[33]	DON'T BE A DUMMY John Du Cann	*Vertigo*	2
-	34	STAR Earth Wind & Fire	*CBS*	1
-	[35]	POINT OF VIEW Matumbi ●	*Matumbi*	1
-	36	THE GREAT ROCK 'N' ROLL SWINDLE/ROCK AROUND Sex Pistols	*Virgin*	1
-	37	MAKING PLANS FOR NIGEL XTC ●	*Virgin*	1
25	38	GOTTA GO HOME/EL LUTE Boney M	*Atlantic*	3
-	[39]	SING A HAPPY SONG O'Jays	*Philadelphia*	1
-	40	SPIRIT BODY & SOUL Nolan Sisters ●	*Epic*	1

LW	TW	WEEK ENDING 20 OCTOBER 1979		Wks
2	[1]	VIDEO KILLED THE RADIO STAR Buggles	*Island*	4
1	2	MESSAGE IN A BOTTLE Police	*A&M*	5
4	[3]	DON'T STOP 'TIL YOU GET ENOUGH Michael Jackson	*Epic*	5
3	4	DREAMING Blondie	*Chrysalis*	4
9	5	ONE DAY AT A TIME Lena Martell	*Pye*	3

In these weeks ■ The Police begin a hat-trick of three consecutive number ones with three straight official releases. Annie Lennox and Dave Stewart make their Top 40 debuts as members of the Tourists (29.09.79) ■ After a 21 year chart career, Johnny Mathis really is gone gone gone from the Top 40 for good (13.10.79)■

LW	TW	Title / Artist	Label	Wks
11	6	EVERY DAY HURTS Sad Cafe	*RCA*	4
6	7	SINCE YOU'VE BEEN GONE Rainbow	*Polydor*	6
5	8	WHAT EVER YOU WANT Status Quo	*Vertigo*	5
26	9	WHEN YOU'RE IN LOVE WITH A BEAUTIFUL WOMAN Dr Hook	*Capitol*	3
16	10	CHOSEN FEW Dooleys	*GTO*	3
18	[11]	QUEEN OF HEARTS Dave Edmunds	*Swan Song*	4
23	12	O.K. FRED Erroll Dunkley	*Scope*	3
10	13	KATE BUSH LIVE ON STAGE Kate Bush	*EMI*	6
7	14	CARS Gary Numan	*Beggars Banquet*	8
15	[15]	YOU CAN DO IT Al Hudson & the Soul Partners	*MCA*	5
8	16	IF I SAID YOU HAD A BEAUTIFUL BODY WOULD YOU HOLD IT AGAINST ME Bellamy Brothers	*Warner Brothers*	10
28	[17]	BACK OF MY HAND Jags	*Island*	5
30	18	TUSK Fleetwood Mac	*Warner Bros.*	2
14	19	CRUEL TO BE KIND Nick Lowe	*Radar*	7
27	20	THE DEVIL WENT DOWN TO GEORGIA Charlie Daniels	*Epic*	3
36	[21]	THE GREAT ROCK 'N' ROLL SWINDLE/ROCK AROUND Sex Pistols	*Virgin*	2
19	22	THE PRINCE Madness	*2 Tone*	6
-	23	MY FORBIDDEN LOVER Chic	*Atlantic*	1
21	24	TIME FOR ACTION Secret Affair	*I-Spy*	7
34	25	STAR Earth Wind & Fire	*CBS*	2
12	26	LOVE'S GOTTA HOLD ON ME Dollar	*Carrere*	8
-	27	GONNA GET ALONG WITHOUT YOU NOW Viola Wills ●	*Ariola*	1
37	28	MAKING PLANS FOR NIGEL XTC	*Virgin*	1
-	29	LUTON AIRPORT Cats UK ●	*WEA*	1
-	30	GIMME GIMME GIMME Abba	*Epic*	1
-	[31]	CHARADE Skids	*Virgin*	2
25	32	SLAP AND TICKLE Squeeze	*A&M*	6
-	33	CRAZY LITTLE THING CALLED LOVE Queen	*EMI*	1
17	34	STRUT YOUR FUNKY STUFF Frantique	*Philadelphia*	9
40	35	SPIRIT BODY & SOUL Nolan Sisters	*Epic*	2
20	36	DON'T BRING ME DOWN Electric Light Orchestra	*Jet*	8
-	37	LET ME KNOW (I HAVE A RIGHT) Gloria Gaynor	*Polydor*	1
13	38	SAIL ON Commodores	*Motown*	7
39	[39]	SING A HAPPY SONG O'Jays	*Philadelphia*	2
-	40	NUCLEAR DEVICE (WIZARD OF AUS) Stranglers	*United Artists*	1

November 1979

□ Highest position disc reached ● Act's first ever week on chart

LW	TW	*WEEK ENDING* **27 OCTOBER 1979**		Wks
5	1	ONE DAY AT A TIME Lena Martell	*Pye*	4
1	2	VIDEO KILLED THE RADIO STAR Buggles	*Island*	5
9	3	WHEN YOU'RE IN LOVE WITH A BEAUTIFUL WOMAN Dr Hook	*Capitol*	4
3	4	DON'T STOP 'TIL YOU GET ENOUGH Michael Jackson	*Epic*	6
6	5	EVERY DAY HURTS Sad Cafe	*RCA*	5
30	6	GIMME GIMME GIMME Abba	*Epic*	2
10	[7]	CHOSEN FEW Dooleys	*GTO*	4
2	8	MESSAGE IN A BOTTLE Police	*A&M*	6
18	9	TUSK Fleetwood Mac	*Warner Bros.*	3
4	10	DREAMING Blondie	*Chrysalis*	5
12	[11]	O.K. FRED Erroll Dunkley	*Scope*	4
7	12	SINCE YOU'VE BEEN GONE Rainbow	*Polydor*	7
8	13	WHAT EVER YOU WANT Status Quo	*Vertigo*	6
11	14	QUEEN OF HEARTS Dave Edmunds	*Swan Song*	5
20	15	THE DEVIL WENT DOWN TO GEORGIA Charlie Daniels	*Epic*	4
27	16	GONNA GET ALONG WITHOUT YOU NOW Viola Wills	*Ariola*	2
28	[17]	MAKING PLANS FOR NIGEL XTC	*Virgin*	2
23	18	MY FORBIDDEN LOVER Chic	*Atlantic*	2
15	19	YOU CAN DO IT Al Hudson & the Soul Partners	*MCA*	6
17	20	BACK OF MY HAND Jags	*Island*	6
33	21	CRAZY LITTLE THING CALLED LOVE Queen	*EMI*	2
-	22	SHE'S IN LOVE WITH YOU Suzi Quatro	*RAK*	1
21	23	THE GREAT ROCK 'N' ROLL SWINDLE/ROCK AROUND Sex Pistols	*Virgin*	3
29	24	LUTON AIRPORT Cats UK	*WEA*	2
13	25	KATE BUSH LIVE ON STAGE Kate Bush	*EMI*	7
-	26	ON MY RADIO Selecter ●	*2 Tone*	1
25	27	STAR Earth Wind & Fire	*CBS*	3
22	28	THE PRINCE Madness	*2 Tone*	7
-	29	THE SPARROW Ramblers ●	*Decca*	1
16	30	IF I SAID YOU HAD A BEAUTIFUL BODY WOULD YOU HOLD IT AGAINST ME Bellamy Brothers	*Warner Brothers*	11
19	31	CRUEL TO BE KIND Nick Lowe	*Radar*	8
37	[32]	LET ME KNOW (I HAVE A RIGHT) Gloria Gaynor	*Polydor*	2
-	33	RISE Herb Alpert	*A&M*	1
35	[34]	SPIRIT BODY & SOUL Nolan Sisters	*Epic*	3
-	[35]	SMASH IT UP Damned	*Chiswick*	1
40	[36]	NUCLEAR DEVICE (WIZARD OF AUS) Stranglers	*United Artists*	2
14	37	CARS Gary Numan	*Beggars Banquet*	9
26	38	LOVE'S GOTTA HOLD ON ME Dollar	*Carrere*	9
-	39	YOU'VE GOT MY NUMBER Undertones	*Sire*	1
-	[40]	HEARTACHE TONIGHT Eagles	*Asylum*	1

LW	TW	*WEEK ENDING* **3 NOVEMBER 1979**		Wks
1	[1]	ONE DAY AT A TIME Lena Martell	*Pye*	5
3	2	WHEN YOU'RE IN LOVE WITH A BEAUTIFUL WOMAN Dr Hook	*Capitol*	5
5	[3]	EVERY DAY HURTS Sad Cafe	*RCA*	6
6	4	GIMME GIMME GIMME Abba	*Epic*	3
2	5	VIDEO KILLED THE RADIO STAR Buggles	*Island*	6
4	6	DON'T STOP 'TIL YOU GET ENOUGH Michael Jackson	*Epic*	7
7	[7]	CHOSEN FEW Dooleys	*GTO*	5
9	8	TUSK Fleetwood Mac	*Warner Bros.*	4
16	9	GONNA GET ALONG WITHOUT YOU NOW Viola Wills	*Ariola*	3
21	10	CRAZY LITTLE THING CALLED LOVE Queen	*EMI*	3
11	[11]	O.K. FRED Erroll Dunkley	*Scope*	5
8	12	MESSAGE IN A BOTTLE Police	*A&M*	7
10	13	DREAMING Blondie	*Chrysalis*	6
15	[14]	THE DEVIL WENT DOWN TO GEORGIA Charlie Daniels	*Epic*	5
18	[15]	MY FORBIDDEN LOVER Chic	*Atlantic*	3
27	[16]	STAR Earth Wind & Fire	*CBS*	4
14	17	QUEEN OF HEARTS Dave Edmunds	*Swan Song*	6
12	18	SINCE YOU'VE BEEN GONE Rainbow	*Polydor*	8
13	19	WHAT EVER YOU WANT Status Quo	*Vertigo*	7
22	20	SHE'S IN LOVE WITH YOU Suzi Quatro	*RAK*	2
26	21	ON MY RADIO Selecter	*2 Tone*	2
23	22	THE GREAT ROCK 'N' ROLL SWINDLE/ROCK AROUND Sex Pistols	*Virgin*	4
17	23	MAKING PLANS FOR NIGEL XTC	*Virgin*	3
20	24	BACK OF MY HAND Jags	*Island*	7
19	25	YOU CAN DO IT Al Hudson & the Soul Partners	*MCA*	7
29	26	THE SPARROW Ramblers	*Decca*	2
24	27	LUTON AIRPORT Cats UK	*WEA*	3
-	28	MESSAGE TO YOU RUDY/NITE KLUB Specials/Rico	*2 Tone*	1
-	29	ETON RIFLES Jam	*Polydor*	1
-	30	HE WAS BEAUTIFUL (CAVATINA) Iris Williams	*Columbia*	1
33	31	RISE Herb Alpert	*A&M*	2
-	32	STILL Commodores	*Motown*	1
-	33	LADIES NIGHT Kool & the Gang ●	*Mercury*	1
39	34	YOU'VE GOT MY NUMBER Undertones	*Sire*	2
-	35	I DON'T WANT TO BE A FREAK Dynasty ●	*Solar*	1
34	36	SPIRIT BODY & SOUL Nolan Sisters	*Epic*	4
32	37	LET ME KNOW (I HAVE A RIGHT) Gloria Gaynor	*Polydor*	3
-	38	SAD EYES Robert John ●	*EMI*	1
36	39	NUCLEAR DEVICE (WIZARD OF AUS) Stranglers	*United Artists*	3
30	40	IF I SAID YOU HAD A BEAUTIFUL BODY WOULD YOU HOLD IT AGAINST ME Bellamy Brothers	*Warner Brothers*	12

LW	TW	*WEEK ENDING* **10 NOVEMBER 1979**		Wks
2	[1]	WHEN YOU'RE IN LOVE WITH A BEAUTIFUL WOMAN Dr Hook	*Capitol*	6
1	2	ONE DAY AT A TIME Lena Martell	*Pye*	6
4	[3]	GIMME GIMME GIMME Abba	*Epic*	4
3	4	EVERY DAY HURTS Sad Cafe	*RCA*	7

■Michael Jackson enjoys the first in his string of hits produced by Quincy Jones (20.10.79) ■ The lead track on the Kate Bush EP is *Them Heavy People* (20.10.79) ■ The 2 Tone label is in its heyday with hits by Madness and Selecter (27.10.79), then the Specials featuring Rico + (03.11.79)■

November 1979

□ Highest position disc reached ● Act's first ever week on chart

LW	TW	Title / Artist	Label	Wks
10	5	CRAZY LITTLE THING CALLED LOVE Queen	EMI	4
8	6	TUSK Fleetwood Mac	Warner Bros.	5
29	7	ETON RIFLES Jam	Polydor	2
9	8	GONNA GET ALONG WITHOUT YOU NOW Viola Wills	Ariola	4
21	9	ON MY RADIO Selecter	Two Tone	3
32	10	STILL Commodores	Motown	2
20	11	SHE'S IN LOVE WITH YOU Suzi Quatro	RAK	3
5	12	VIDEO KILLED THE RADIO STAR Buggles	Island	7
11	13	O.K. FRED Erroll Dunkley	Scope	6
7	14	CHOSEN FEW Dooleys	GTO	6
26	15	THE SPARROW Ramblers	Decca	3
6	16	DON'T STOP 'TIL YOU GET ENOUGH Michael Jackson	Epic	8
23	17	MAKING PLANS FOR NIGEL XTC	Virgin	4
16	18	STAR Earth Wind & Fire	CBS	5
28	19	MESSAGE TO YOU RUDY/NITE KLUB Specials/Rico	2 Tone	2
15	20	MY FORBIDDEN LOVER Chic	Atlantic	4
33	21	LADIES NIGHT Kool & the Gang	Mercury	2
27	22	LUTON AIRPORT Cats UK	WEA	4
12	23	MESSAGE IN A BOTTLE Police	A&M	8
14	24	THE DEVIL WENT DOWN TO GEORGIA Charlie Daniels	Epic	6
-	25	KNOCKED IT OFF B.A. Robertson	Asylum	1
31	26	RISE Herb Alpert	A&M	3
-	27	NO MORE TEARS (ENOUGH IS ENOUGH) Donna Summer/ Barbra Streisand ●	Casablanca	1
22	28	THE GREAT ROCK 'N' ROLL SWINDLE/ROCK AROUND Sex Pistols	Virgin	5
30	29	HE WAS BEAUTIFUL (CAVATINA) Iris Williams	Columbia	2
35	30	I DON'T WANT TO BE A FREAK Dynasty	Solar	2
18	31	SINCE YOU'VE BEEN GONE Rainbow	Polydor	9
34	32	YOU'VE GOT MY NUMBER Undertones	Sire	3
25	33	YOU CAN DO IT Al Hudson & the Soul Partners	MCA	8
38	34	SAD EYES Robert John	EMI	2
13	35	DREAMING Blondie	Chrysalis	7
17	36	QUEEN OF HEARTS Dave Edmunds	Swan Song	7
-	37	SARAH Thin Lizzy	Vertigo	1
19	38	WHAT EVER YOU WANT Status Quo	Vertigo	8
-	39	BIRD SONG Lene Lovich	Stiff	1
-	40	IT'S A DISCO NIGHT (ROCK DON'T STOP) Isley Brothers	Epic	1

WEEK ENDING 17 NOVEMBER 1979

LW	TW	Title / Artist	Label	Wks
1	1	WHEN YOU'RE IN LOVE WITH A BEAUTIFUL WOMAN Dr Hook	Capitol	7
2	2	ONE DAY AT A TIME Lena Martell	Pye	7
5	3	CRAZY LITTLE THING CALLED LOVE Queen	EMI	5
7	4	ETON RIFLES Jam	Polydor	3
10	5	STILL Commodores	Motown	3
3	6	GIMME GIMME GIMME Abba	Epic	5
4	7	EVERY DAY HURTS Sad Cafe	RCA	8
9	8	ON MY RADIO Selecter	Two Tone	4
6	9	TUSK Fleetwood Mac	Warner Bros.	6
19	10	MESSAGE TO YOU RUDY/NITE KLUB Specials/Rico	2 Tone	3
11	11	SHE'S IN LOVE WITH YOU Suzi Quatro	RAK	4
8	12	GONNA GET ALONG WITHOUT YOU NOW Viola Wills	Ariola	5
15	13	THE SPARROW Ramblers	Decca	4
27	14	NO MORE TEARS (ENOUGH IS ENOUGH) Donna Summer/ Barbra Streisand	Casablanca	2
25	15	KNOCKED IT OFF B.A. Robertson	Asylum	2
21	16	LADIES NIGHT Kool & the Gang	Mercury	3
26	17	RISE Herb Alpert	A&M	4
29	18	HE WAS BEAUTIFUL (CAVATINA) Iris Williams	Columbia	3
13	19	O.K. FRED Erroll Dunkley	Scope	7
17	20	MAKING PLANS FOR NIGEL XTC	Virgin	5
18	21	STAR Earth Wind & Fire	CBS	6
-	22	ONE STEP BEYOND Madness	Stiff	1
20	23	MY FORBIDDEN LOVER Chic	Atlantic	5
40	24	IT'S A DISCO NIGHT (ROCK DON'T STOP) Isley Brothers	Epic	2
12	25	VIDEO KILLED THE RADIO STAR Buggles	Island	8
30	26	I DON'T WANT TO BE A FREAK Dynasty	Solar	3
37	27	SARAH Thin Lizzy	Vertigo	2
14	28	CHOSEN FEW Dooleys	GTO	7
22	29	LUTON AIRPORT Cats UK	WEA	5
24	30	THE DEVIL WENT DOWN TO GEORGIA Charlie Daniels	Epic	7
16	31	DON'T STOP 'TIL YOU GET ENOUGH Michael Jackson	Epic	9
-	32	ROCKABILLY REBEL Matchbox ●	Magnet	1
-	33	CONFUSION/LAST TRAIN TO LONDON Electric Light Orchestra	Jet	1
-	34	QUE SERA MI VIDA Gibson Brothers	Island	1
-	35	DIAMOND SMILES Boomtown Rats	Ensign	1
-	36	MONKEY CHOP Dan-I ●	Island	1
34	37	SAD EYES Robert John	EMI	3
-	38	LET YOUR HEART DANCE Secret Affair	I-Spy	1
39	39	BIRD SONG Lene Lovich	Stiff	2
28	40	THE GREAT ROCK 'N' ROLL SWINDLE/ROCK AROUND Sex Pistols	Virgin	6

WEEK ENDING 24 NOVEMBER 1979

LW	TW	Title / Artist	Label	Wks
1	1	WHEN YOU'RE IN LOVE WITH A BEAUTIFUL WOMAN Dr Hook	Capitol	8
3	2	CRAZY LITTLE THING CALLED LOVE Queen	EMI	6
4	3	ETON RIFLES Jam	Polydor	4
5	4	STILL Commodores	Motown	4
2	5	ONE DAY AT A TIME Lena Martell	Pye	8
14	6	NO MORE TEARS (ENOUGH IS ENOUGH) Donna Summer/ Barbra Streisand	Casablanca	3
6	7	GIMME GIMME GIMME Abba	Epic	6
15	8	KNOCKED IT OFF B.A. Robertson	Asylum	3
16	9	LADIES NIGHT Kool & the Gang	Mercury	4
22	10	ONE STEP BEYOND Madness	Stiff	2
13	11	THE SPARROW Ramblers	Decca	5
10	12	MESSAGE TO YOU RUDY/NITE KLUB Specials/Rico	2 Tone	4
17	13	RISE Herb Alpert	A&M	5
11	14	SHE'S IN LOVE WITH YOU Suzi Quatro	RAK	5
-	15	COMPLEX Gary Numan	Beggars Banquet	1
8	16	ON MY RADIO Selecter	Two Tone	5
33	17	CONFUSION/LAST TRAIN TO LONDON Electric Light Orchestra	Jet	2
34	18	QUE SERA MI VIDA Gibson Brothers	Island	2
12	19	GONNA GET ALONG WITHOUT YOU NOW Viola Wills	Ariola	6
26	20	I DON'T WANT TO BE A FREAK Dynasty	Solar	4
24	21	IT'S A DISCO NIGHT (ROCK DON'T STOP) Isley Brothers	Epic	3
18	22	HE WAS BEAUTIFUL (CAVATINA) Iris Williams	Columbia	4
35	23	DIAMOND SMILES Boomtown Rats	Ensign	2
7	24	EVERY DAY HURTS Sad Cafe	RCA	9
9	25	TUSK Fleetwood Mac	Warner Bros.	7
32	26	ROCKABILLY REBEL Matchbox	Magnet	2
-	27	NIGHTS IN WHITE SATIN Moody Blues	Deram	1
-	28	I ONLY WANT TO BE WITH YOU Tourists	Logo	1
27	29	SARAH Thin Lizzy	Vertigo	3
36	30	MONKEY CHOP Dan-I	Island	2
37	31	SAD EYES Robert John	EMI	4
38	32	LET YOUR HEART DANCE Secret Affair	I-Spy	2
20	33	MAKING PLANS FOR NIGEL XTC	Virgin	6
-	34	WORKING FOR THE YANKEE DOLLAR Skids	Virgin	1
-	35	UNION CITY BLUE Blondie	Chrysalis	1
-	36	IS IT LOVE YOU'RE AFTER Rose Royce	Whitfield	1
19	37	O.K. FRED Erroll Dunkley	Scope	8
29	38	LUTON AIRPORT Cats UK	WEA	6
-	39	A NIGHT AT DADDY GEE'S Showaddywaddy	Arista	1
28	40	CHOSEN FEW Dooleys	GTO	8

WEEK ENDING 1 DECEMBER 1979

LW	TW	Title / Artist	Label	Wks
1	1	WHEN YOU'RE IN LOVE WITH A BEAUTIFUL WOMAN Dr Hook	Capitol	9
2	2	CRAZY LITTLE THING CALLED LOVE Queen	EMI	7
6	3	NO MORE TEARS (ENOUGH IS ENOUGH) Donna Summer/ Barbra Streisand	Casablanca	4
4	4	STILL Commodores	Motown	5
-	5	WALKING ON THE MOON Police	A&M	1
15	6	COMPLEX Gary Numan	Beggars Banquet	2
10	7	ONE STEP BEYOND Madness	Stiff	3

In these weeks ■ Dr Hook have the biggest hit of their career, *When You're In Love With A Beautiful Woman* (17.11.79) ■ Herb Alpert has his first Top 20 hit in eleven years (17.11.79) ■ Having enjoyed a Top 5 hit with Neil Diamond the previous year, Barbra Streisand now performs the feat with Donna Summer (01.12.79)■

December 1979

□ Highest position disc reached ● Act's first ever week on chart

LW	TW	Title	Artist	Label	Wks
17	[8]	CONFUSION/LAST TRAIN TO LONDON	Electric Light Orchestra	*Jet*	3
3	9	ETON RIFLES	Jam	*Polydor*	5
8	10	KNOCKED IT OFF	B.A. Robertson	*Asylum*	4
9	11	LADIES NIGHT	Kool & the Gang	*Mercury*	5
18	12	QUE SERA MI VIDA	Gibson Brothers	*Island*	3
23	[13]	DIAMOND SMILES	Boomtown Rats	*Ensign*	3
21	[14]	IT'S A DISCO NIGHT (ROCK DON'T STOP)	Isley Brothers	*Epic*	4
11	15	THE SPARROW	Ramblers	*Decca*	6
5	16	ONE DAY AT A TIME	Lena Martell	*Pye*	9
12	17	MESSAGE TO YOU RUDY/NITE KLUB	Specials/Rico	*2 Tone*	5
26	[18]	ROCKABILLY REBEL	Matchbox	*Magnet*	3
7	19	GIMME GIMME GIMME	Abba	*Epic*	7
13	20	RISE	Herb Albert	*A&M*	6
35	21	UNION CITY BLUE	Blondie	*Chrysalis*	2
28	22	I ONLY WANT TO BE WITH YOU	Tourists	*Logo*	2
27	23	NIGHTS IN WHITE SATIN	Moody Blues	*Deram*	2
29	[24]	SARAH	Thin Lizzy	*Vertigo*	4
-	25	OFF THE WALL	Michael Jackson	*Epic*	1
-	26	ANOTHER BRICK IN A WALL	Pink Floyd	*Harvest*	1
14	27	SHE'S IN LOVE WITH YOU	Suzi Quatro	*RAK*	6
16	28	ON MY RADIO	Selecter	*Two Tone*	6
22	29	HE WAS BEAUTIFUL (CAVATINA)	Iris Williams	*Columbia*	5
30	[30]	MONKEY CHOP	Dan-I	*Island*	3
-	31	MY SIMPLE HEART	Three Degrees	*Ariola*	1
34	32	WORKING FOR THE YANKEE DOLLAR	Skids	*Virgin*	2
20	33	I DON'T WANT TO BE A FREAK	Dynasty	*Solar*	5
36	34	IS IT LOVE YOU'RE AFTER	Rose Royce	*Whitfield*	2
19	35	GONNA GET ALONG WITHOUT YOU NOW	Viola Wills	*Ariola*	7
-	36	LIVING ON AN ISLAND	Status Quo	*Vertigo*	1
24	37	EVERY DAY HURTS	Sad Cafe	*RCA*	10
-	38	RAPPER'S DELIGHT	Sugarhill Gang ●	*Sugarhill*	1
32	39	LET YOUR HEART DANCE	Secret Affair	*I-Spy*	3
31	40	SAD EYES	Robert John	*EMI*	5

WEEK ENDING 8 DECEMBER 1979

LW	TW	Title	Artist	Label	Wks
5	[1]	WALKING ON THE MOON	Police	*A&M*	2
26	2	ANOTHER BRICK IN A WALL	Pink Floyd	*Harvest*	2
3	[3]	NO MORE TEARS (ENOUGH IS ENOUGH)	Donna Summer/Barbra Streisand	*Casablanca*	5
1	4	WHEN YOU'RE IN LOVE WITH A BEAUTIFUL WOMAN	Dr Hook	*Capitol*	10
12	[5]	QUE SERA MI VIDA	Gibson Brothers	*Island*	4
22	6	I ONLY WANT TO BE WITH YOU	Tourists	*Logo*	3
2	7	CRAZY LITTLE THING CALLED LOVE	Queen	*EMI*	8
6	8	COMPLEX	Gary Numan	*Beggars Banquet*	3
8	9	CONFUSION/LAST TRAIN TO LONDON	Electric Light Orchestra	*Jet*	4
7	10	ONE STEP BEYOND	Madness	*Stiff*	4
4	11	STILL	Commodores	*Motown*	6
38	12	RAPPER'S DELIGHT	Sugarhill Gang	*Sugarhill*	2
9	13	ETON RIFLES	Jam	*Polydor*	6
23	14	NIGHTS IN WHITE SATIN	Moody Blues	*Deram*	3
13	15	DIAMOND SMILES	Boomtown Rats	*Ensign*	4
21	16	UNION CITY BLUE	Blondie	*Chrysalis*	3
14	17	IT'S A DISCO NIGHT (ROCK DON'T STOP)	Isley Brothers	*Epic*	5
11	18	LADIES NIGHT	Kool & the Gang	*Mercury*	6
15	19	THE SPARROW	Ramblers	*Decca*	7
10	20	KNOCKED IT OFF	B.A. Robertson	*Asylum*	5
18	21	ROCKABILLY REBEL	Matchbox	*Magnet*	4
25	22	OFF THE WALL	Michael Jackson	*Epic*	2
20	23	RISE	Herb Albert	*A&M*	7
24	[24]	SARAH	Thin Lizzy	*Vertigo*	5
33	25	I DON'T WANT TO BE A FREAK	Dynasty	*Solar*	6
31	26	MY SIMPLE HEART	Three Degrees	*Ariola*	2
16	27	ONE DAY AT A TIME	Lena Martell	*Pye*	10
32	28	WORKING FOR THE YANKEE DOLLAR	Skids	*Virgin*	3
34	29	IS IT LOVE YOU'RE AFTER	Rose Royce	*Whitfield*	3
36	30	LIVING ON AN ISLAND	Status Quo	*Vertigo*	2
-	31	WONDERFUL CHRISTMAS TIME	Paul McCartney	*Parlophone*	1
17	32	MESSAGE TO YOU RUDY/NITE KLUB	Specials/Rico	*2 Tone*	6
-	33	BRASS IN POCKET	Pretenders	*Real*	1
19	34	GIMME GIMME GIMME	Abba	*Epic*	8
-	35	SPACER	Sheila and B. Devotion	*Carrere*	1
-	[36]	SHE'S NOT THERE/KICKS EP	UK Subs	*Gem*	1
-	[37]	MELLOW MELLOW RIGHT ON	Lowrell ●	*Avi*	1
30	38	MONKEY CHOP	Dan-I	*Island*	4
27	39	SHE'S IN LOVE WITH YOU	Suzi Quatro	*RAK*	7
-	40	IT'S MY HOUSE	Diana Ross	*Motown*	1

WEEK ENDING 15 DECEMBER 1979

LW	TW	Title	Artist	Label	Wks
2	[1]	ANOTHER BRICK IN A WALL	Pink Floyd	*Harvest*	3
1	2	WALKING ON THE MOON	Police	*A&M*	3
12	[3]	RAPPER'S DELIGHT	Sugarhill Gang	*Sugarhill*	3
6	[4]	I ONLY WANT TO BE WITH YOU	Tourists	*Logo*	4
3	5	NO MORE TEARS (ENOUGH IS ENOUGH)	Donna Summer/Barbra Streisand	*Casablanca*	6
5	6	QUE SERA MI VIDA	Gibson Brothers	*Island*	5
22	[7]	OFF THE WALL	Michael Jackson	*Epic*	3
4	8	WHEN YOU'RE IN LOVE WITH A BEAUTIFUL WOMAN	Dr Hook	*Capitol*	11
10	9	ONE STEP BEYOND	Madness	*Stiff*	5
26	10	MY SIMPLE HEART	Three Degrees	*Ariola*	3
9	11	CONFUSION/LAST TRAIN TO LONDON	Electric Light Orchestra	*Jet*	5
7	12	CRAZY LITTLE THING CALLED LOVE	Queen	*EMI*	9
16	[13]	UNION CITY BLUE	Blondie	*Chrysalis*	4
14	14	NIGHTS IN WHITE SATIN	Moody Blues	*Deram*	4
8	15	COMPLEX	Gary Numan	*Beggars Banquet*	4
15	16	DIAMOND SMILES	Boomtown Rats	*Ensign*	5
11	17	STILL	Commodores	*Motown*	7
30	18	LIVING ON AN ISLAND	Status Quo	*Vertigo*	3
21	19	ROCKABILLY REBEL	Matchbox	*Magnet*	5
31	20	WONDERFUL CHRISTMAS TIME	Paul McCartney	*Parlophone*	2
-	21	I HAVE A DREAM	Abba	*Epic*	1
17	22	IT'S A DISCO NIGHT (ROCK DON'T STOP)	Isley Brothers	*Epic*	6
-	23	JOHN I'M ONLY DANCING (AGAIN)	David Bowie	*RCA*	1
29	24	IS IT LOVE YOU'RE AFTER	Rose Royce	*Whitfield*	4
24	25	SARAH	Thin Lizzy	*Vertigo*	6
-	26	DAY TRIP TO BANGOR	Fiddler's Dream ●	*Dingles*	1
28	27	WORKING FOR THE YANKEE DOLLAR	Skids	*Virgin*	4
19	28	THE SPARROW	Ramblers	*Decca*	8
-	29	MY FEET KEEP DANCING	Chic	*Atlantic*	1
33	30	BRASS IN POCKET	Pretenders	*Real*	2
-	31	TEARS OF A CLOWN/RANKING FULL STOP	Beat ●	*2 Tone*	1
27	32	ONE DAY AT A TIME	Lena Martell	*Pye*	11
18	33	LADIES NIGHT	Kool & the Gang	*Mercury*	7
-	[34]	BOMBER	Motorhead	*Bronze*	1
-	35	PLEASE DON'T GO	K.C. & the Sunshine Band	*T.K.*	1
-	[36]	IT'S MY HOUSE	Storm ●	*Scope*	1
35	37	SPACER	Sheila and B. Devotion	*Carrere*	2
36	38	SHE'S NOT THERE/KICKS EP	UK Subs	*Gem*	2
40	39	IT'S MY HOUSE	Diana Ross	*Motown*	3
-	40	BLUE PETER	Mike Oldfield	*Virgin*	1

WEEK ENDING 22 DECEMBER 1979

LW	TW	Title	Artist	Label	Wks
1	[1]	ANOTHER BRICK IN A WALL	Pink Floyd	*Harvest*	4
21	[2]	I HAVE A DREAM	Abba	*Epic*	2
2	3	WALKING ON THE MOON	Police	*A&M*	4
26	4	DAY TRIP TO BANGOR	Fiddler's Dream	*Dingles*	2
4	5	I ONLY WANT TO BE WITH YOU	Tourists	*Logo*	5
3	6	RAPPER'S DELIGHT	Sugarhill Gang	*Sugarhill*	4
20	7	WONDERFUL CHRISTMAS TIME	Paul McCartney	*Parlophone*	3
6	8	QUE SERA MI VIDA	Gibson Brothers	*Island*	6
10	[9]	MY SIMPLE HEART	Three Degrees	*Ariola*	4
30	10	BRASS IN POCKET	Pretenders	*Real*	3
5	11	NO MORE TEARS (ENOUGH IS ENOUGH)	Donna Summer/Barbra Streisand	*Casablanca*	7
7	12	OFF THE WALL	Michael Jackson	*Epic*	4

■The Sugarhill Gang begin one of the chart trends of the eighties a month early with *Rapper's Delight* (01.12.79) ■ Pink Floyd score their first number one with their first single since *See Emily Play* in 1967 (15.12.79) ■ Three months after the Dickies touched the Top 40 with their adrenalinized version of *Nights In White Satin*, the Moody Blues' original is back in the Top 20 (15.12.79)■

December 1979

□ Highest position disc reached ● Act's first ever week on chart

23 **13** JOHN I'M ONLY DANCING (AGAIN) David Bowie .... *RCA* 2
13 **14** UNION CITY BLUE Blondie .... *Chrysalis* 5
11 **15** CONFUSION/LAST TRAIN TO LONDON Electric Light Orchestra .... *Jet* 6
18 **16** LIVING ON AN ISLAND Status Quo .... *Vertigo* 4
24 **17** IS IT LOVE YOU'RE AFTER Rose Royce .... *Whitfield* 5
14 **18** NIGHTS IN WHITE SATIN Moody Blues .... *Deram* 5
9 **19** ONE STEP BEYOND Madness .... *Stiff* 6
31 **20** TEARS OF A CLOWN/RANKING FULL STOP Beat .... *2 Tone* 2
8 **21** WHEN YOU'RE IN LOVE WITH A BEAUTIFUL WOMAN Dr Hook .... *Capitol* 12
19 **22** ROCKABILLY REBEL Matchbox .... *Magnet* 6
15 **23** COMPLEX Gary Numan .... *Beggars Banquet* 5
27 **24** WORKING FOR THE YANKEE DOLLAR Skids .... *Virgin* 5
\- **25** IT WON'T SEEM LIKE CHRISTMAS WITHOUT YOU Elvis Presley .... *RCA* 1
12 **26** CRAZY LITTLE THING CALLED LOVE Queen .... *EMI* 10
16 **27** DIAMOND SMILES Boomtown Rats .... *Ensign* 6
35 **28** PLEASE DON'T GO K.C. & the Sunshine Band .... *T.K.* 2
\- **29** LONDON CALLING Clash .... *CBS* 1
40 **30** BLUE PETER Mike Oldfield .... *Virgin* 2
28 **31** THE SPARROW Ramblers .... *Decca* 9
29 **32** MY FEET KEEP DANCING Chic .... *Atlantic* 2
37 **33** SPACER Sheila and B. Devotion .... *Carrere* 3
39 **34** IT'S MY HOUSE Diana Ross .... *Motown* 4
\- **35** MOONLIGHT & MUZAK M .... *MCA* 1
\- **36** CHRISTMAS WRAPPIN' Kurtis Blow ● .... *Mercury* 1
36 **37** IT'S MY HOUSE Storm .... *Scope* 2
\- **38** I'M BORN AGAIN Boney M .... *Atlantic* 1
\- **39** I WANNA HOLD YOUR HAND Dollar .... *Carrere* 1
32 **40** ONE DAY AT A TIME Lena Martell .... *Pye* 12

LW TW *WEEK ENDING* **29 DECEMBER 1979** Wks

(no chart published, chart for 22 December repeated)

1 **1** ANOTHER BRICK IN A WALL Pink Floyd .... *Harvest* 5
2 **2** I HAVE A DREAM Abba .... *Epic* 3
3 **3** WALKING ON THE MOON Police .... *A&M* 5
4 **4** DAY TRIP TO BANGOR Fiddler's Dream .... *Dingles* 3
5 **5** I ONLY WANT TO BE WITH YOU Tourists .... *Logo* 6
6 **6** RAPPER'S DELIGHT Sugarhill Gang .... *Sugarhill* 5
7 **7** WONDERFUL CHRISTMAS TIME Paul McCartney ... *Parlophone* 4
8 **8** QUE SERA MI VIDA Gibson Brothers .... *Island* 7
9 **9** MY SIMPLE HEART Three Degrees .... *Ariola* 5
10 **10** BRASS IN POCKET Pretenders .... *Real* 4
11 **11** NO MORE TEARS (ENOUGH IS ENOUGH) Donna Summer/ Barbra Streisand .... *Casablanca* 8
12 **12** OFF THE WALL Michael Jackson .... *Epic* 5
13 **13** JOHN I'M ONLY DANCING (AGAIN) David Bowie .... *RCA* 3
14 **14** UNION CITY BLUE Blondie .... *Chrysalis* 6
15 **15** CONFUSION/LAST TRAIN TO LONDON Electric Light Orchestra .... *Jet* 7
16 **16** LIVING ON AN ISLAND Status Quo .... *Vertigo* 5
17 **17** IS IT LOVE YOU'RE AFTER Rose Royce .... *Whitfield* 6
18 **18** NIGHTS IN WHITE SATIN Moody Blues .... *Deram* 6
19 **19** ONE STEP BEYOND Madness .... *Stiff* 7
20 **20** TEARS OF A CLOWN/RANKING FULL STOP Beat .... *2 Tone* 3
21 **21** WHEN YOU'RE IN LOVE WITH A BEAUTIFUL WOMAN Dr Hook .... *Capitol* 13
22 **22** ROCKABILLY REBEL Matchbox .... *Magnet* 7
23 **23** COMPLEX Gary Numan .... *Beggars Banquet* 6
24 **24** WORKING FOR THE YANKEE DOLLAR Skids .... *Virgin* 6
25 **25** IT WON'T SEEM LIKE CHRISTMAS WITHOUT YOU Elvis Presley .... *RCA* 2
26 **26** CRAZY LITTLE THING CALLED LOVE Queen .... *EMI* 11
27 **27** DIAMOND SMILES Boomtown Rats .... *Ensign* 7
28 **28** PLEASE DON'T GO K.C. & the Sunshine Band .... *T.K.* 3
29 **29** LONDON CALLING Clash .... *CBS* 2
30 **30** BLUE PETER Mike Oldfield .... *Virgin* 3
31 **31** THE SPARROW Ramblers .... *Decca* 10
32 **32** MY FEET KEEP DANCING Chic .... *Atlantic* 3
33 **33** SPACER Sheila and B. Devotion .... *Carrere* 4
34 **34** IT'S MY HOUSE Diana Ross .... *Motown* 5
35 **35** MOONLIGHT & MUZAK M .... *MCA* 2
36 **36** CHRISTMAS WRAPPIN' Kurtis Blow .... *Mercury* 2
37 **37** IT'S MY HOUSE Storm .... *Scope* 3
38 **38** I'M BORN AGAIN Boney M .... *Atlantic* 2
39 **39** I WANNA HOLD YOUR HAND Dollar .... *Carrere* 2
40 **40** ONE DAY AT A TIME Lena Martell .... *Pye* 13

In these weeks ■ Abba had singles peak at every position between one and seven, including the number two *I Have A Dream* (22-29.12.79) ■ He has been dead for two years, but Elvis Presley who first had a Christmas hit in 1957, has another one (22-29.12.79) ■ K.C. and the Sunshine Band succeed with the original of a 1992 number one, *Please Don't Go* (22-29.12.79)■

1980

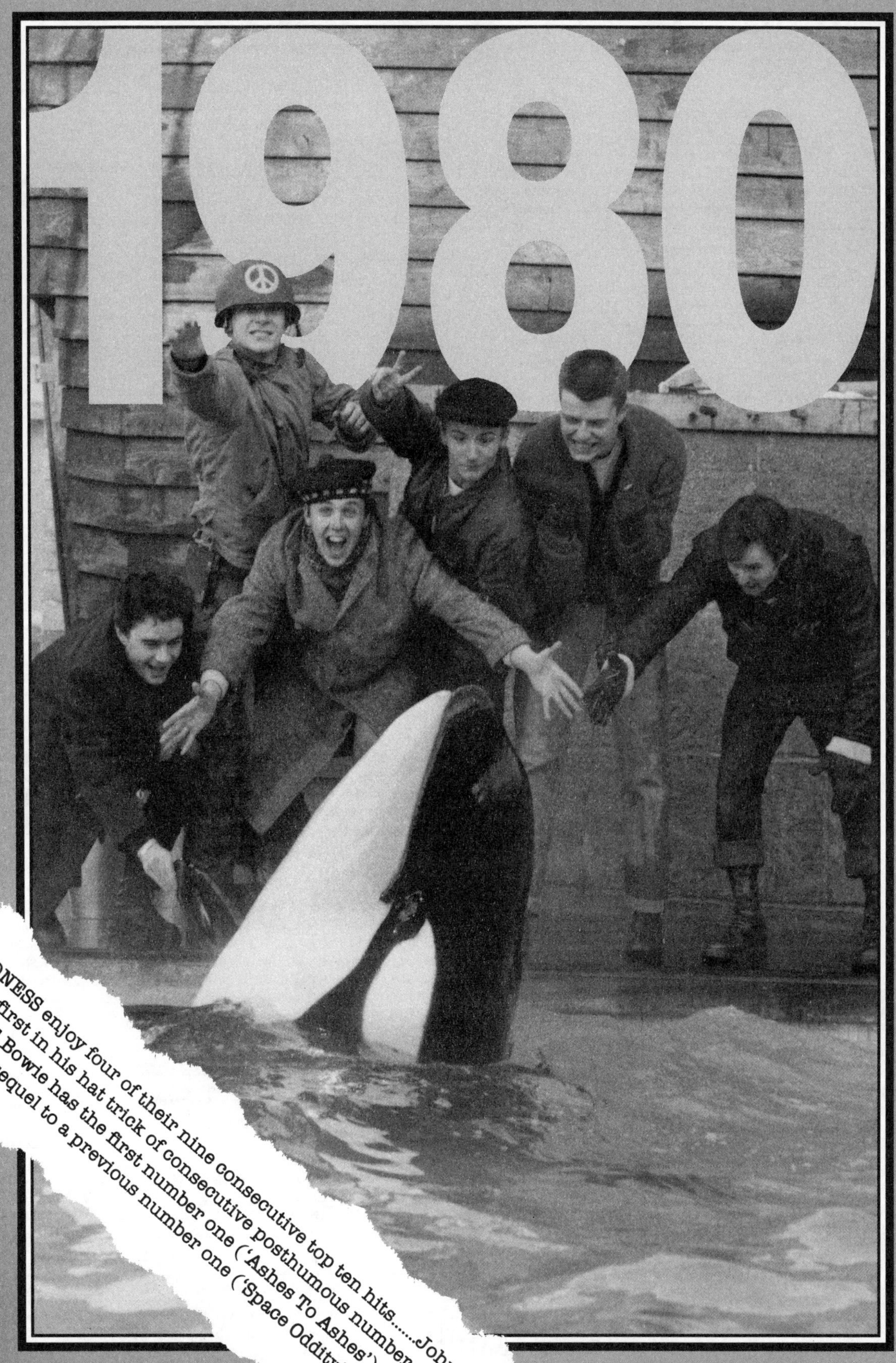

......MADNESS enjoy four of their nine consecutive top ten hits......John Lennon has the first in his hat trick of consecutive posthumous number ones...... David Bowie has the first number one ('Ashes To Ashes') that is the sequel to a previous number one ('Space Oddity').........

January 1980

□ Highest position disc reached ● Act's first ever week on chart

LW	TW	WEEK ENDING 5 JANUARY 1980		Wks
1	[1]	ANOTHER BRICK IN THE WALL Pink Floyd	*Harvest*	6
2	[2]	I HAVE A DREAM Abba	*Epic*	4
4	[3]	DAY TRIP TO BANGOR Fiddler's Dram	*Dingles*	4
5	[4]	I ONLY WANT TO BE WITH YOU Tourists	*Logo*	7
10	5	BRASS IN POCKET Pretenders	*Real*	5
7	[6]	WONDERFUL CHRISTMASTIME Paul McCartney	*Parlophone*	5
6	7	RAPPER'S DELIGHT Sugarhill Gang	*Sugarhill*	6
3	8	WALKING ON THE MOON Police	*A&M*	6
8	9	QUE SERA MI VIDA Gibson Brothers	*Island*	8
9	10	MY SIMPLE HEART Three Degrees	*Ariola*	6
12	11	OFF THE WALL Michael Jackson	*Epic*	6
13	[12]	JOHN I'M ONLY DANCING (AGAIN) David Bowie	*RCA*	4
25	[13]	IT WON'T SEEM LIKE CHRISTMAS WITHOUT YOU Elvis Presley	*RCA*	3
14	14	NO MORE TEARS (ENOUGH IS ENOUGH) Donna Summer and Barbra Streisand	*CBS/Casablanca*	9
17	15	IS IT LOVE YOU'RE AFTER Rose Royce	*Whitfield*	7
14	16	UNION CITY BLUE Blondie	*Chrysalis*	7
20	17	TEARS OF A CLOWN/RANKING FULL STOP Beat	*2 Tone*	4
16	18	LIVING ON AN ISLAND Status Quo	*Vertigo*	6
18	19	NIGHTS IN WHITE SATIN Moody Blues	*Deram*	7
28	20	PLEASE DON'T GO KC and the Sunshine Band	*TK*	4
32	[21]	MY FEET KEEP DANCING Chic	*Atlantic*	4
19	22	ONE STEP BEYOND Madness	*Stiff*	8
24	23	WORKING FOR THE YANKEE DOLLAR Skids	*Virgin*	7
-	24	WITH YOU I'M BORN AGAIN Billy Preston and Syreeta	*Motown*	1
22	25	ROCKABILLY REBEL Matchbox	*Magnet*	8
15	26	CONFUSION/LAST TRAIN TO LONDON Electric Light Orchestra	*Jet*	8
30	27	BLUE PETER Mike Oldfield	*Virgin*	4
-	[28]	A MERRY JINGLE Greedies ●	*Vertigo*	1
29	29	LONDON CALLING Clash	*CBS*	3
36	[30]	CHRISTMAS RAPPIN' Kurtis Blow	*Mercury*	2
21	31	WHEN YOU'RE IN LOVE WITH A BEAUTIFUL WOMAN Dr. Hook	*Capitol*	14
26	32	CRAZY LITTLE THING CALLED LOVE Queen	*EMI*	12
33	33	SPACER Sheila and B. Devotion	*Carrere*	5
35	34	MOONLIGHT AND MUZAK M	*MCA*	3
40	35	ONE DAY AT A TIME Lena Martell	*Pye*	14
38	36	I'M BORN AGAIN Boney M	*Atlantic/Hansa*	3
31	37	THE SPARROW Ramblers	*Decca*	11
34	38	IT'S MY HOUSE Diana Ross	*Motown*	5
-	39	GREEN ONIONS Booker T. and the MG's	*Atlantic*	1
-	40	I'M IN THE MOOD FOR DANCING Nolans	*Epic*	1

LW	TW	WEEK ENDING 12 JANUARY 1980		Wks
1	[1]	ANOTHER BRICK IN THE WALL Pink Floyd	*Harvest*	7
2	[2]	I HAVE A DREAM Abba	*Epic*	5
5	3	BRASS IN POCKET Pretenders	*Real*	6
3	4	DAY TRIP TO BANGOR Fiddler's Dram	*Dingles*	5
4	5	I ONLY WANT TO BE WITH YOU Tourists	*Logo*	8
17	[6]	TEARS OF A CLOWN/RANKING FULL STOP Beat	*2 Tone*	5
20	7	PLEASE DON'T GO KC and the Sunshine Band	*TK*	5
7	8	RAPPER'S DELIGHT Sugarhill Gang	*Sugarhill*	7
8	9	WALKING ON THE MOON Police	*A&M*	7
10	10	MY SIMPLE HEART Three Degrees	*Ariola*	7
24	11	WITH YOU I'M BORN AGAIN Billy Preston and Syreeta	*Motown*	2
12	[12]	JOHN I'M ONLY DANCING (AGAIN) David Bowie	*RCA*	5
15	[13]	IS IT LOVE YOU'RE AFTER Rose Royce	*Whitfield*	8
-	14	MY GIRL Madness	*Stiff*	1
29	15	LONDON CALLING Clash	*CBS*	4
9	16	QUE SERA MI VIDA Gibson Brothers	*Island*	9
18	17	LIVING ON AN ISLAND Status Quo	*Vertigo*	7
6	18	WONDERFUL CHRISTMASTIME Paul McCartney	*Parlophone*	6
27	[19]	BLUE PETER Mike Oldfield	*Virgin*	5
40	20	I'M IN THE MOOD FOR DANCING Nolans	*Epic*	2
23	21	WORKING FOR THE YANKEE DOLLAR Skids	*Virgin*	8
21	22	MY FEET KEEP DANCING Chic	*Atlantic*	5
16	23	UNION CITY BLUE Blondie	*Chrysalis*	8
13	24	IT WON'T SEEM LIKE CHRISTMAS WITHOUT YOU Elvis Presley	*RCA*	4
11	25	OFF THE WALL Michael Jackson	*Epic*	7
39	26	GREEN ONIONS Booker T. and the MG's	*Atlantic*	2
22	27	ONE STEP BEYOND Madness	*Stiff*	9
33	28	SPACER Sheila and B. Devotion	*Carrere*	6
14	29	NO MORE TEARS (ENOUGH IS ENOUGH) Donna Summer and Barbra Streisand	*CBS/Casablanca*	10
-	30	I WANNA HOLD YOUR HAND Dollar	*Carrere*	1
-	31	BETTER LOVE NEXT TIME Dr. Hook	*Capitol*	1
38	[32]	IT'S MY HOUSE Diana Ross	*Motown*	6
34	[33]	MOONLIGHT AND MUZAK M	*MCA*	4
-	34	WE GOT THE FUNK Positive Force	*Sugarhill*	1
36	[35]	I'M BORN AGAIN Boney M	*Atlantic/Hansa*	4
-	[36]	THE WALK Inmates ●	*Radar*	1
-	37	BABE Styx	*A&M*	1
-	38	SPIRITS (HAVING FLOWN) Bee Gees	*RSO*	1
19	39	NIGHTS IN WHITE SATIN Moody Blues	*Deram*	8
25	40	ROCKABILLY REBEL Matchbox	*Magnet*	9

LW	TW	WEEK ENDING 19 JANUARY 1980		Wks
3	[1]	BRASS IN POCKET Pretenders	*Real*	7
11	[2]	WITH YOU I'M BORN AGAIN Billy Preston and Syreeta	*Motown*	3
7	[3]	PLEASE DON'T GO KC and the Sunshine Band	*TK*	6
14	4	MY GIRL Madness	*Stiff*	2
1	5	ANOTHER BRICK IN THE WALL Pink Floyd	*Harvest*	8
20	6	I'M IN THE MOOD FOR DANCING Nolans	*Epic*	3
2	7	I HAVE A DREAM Abba	*Epic*	6
6	8	TEARS OF A CLOWN/RANKING FULL STOP Beat	*2 Tone*	6
4	9	DAY TRIP TO BANGOR Fiddler's Dram	*Dingles*	6
5	10	I ONLY WANT TO BE WITH YOU Tourists	*Logo*	9
15	[11]	LONDON CALLING Clash	*CBS*	5
26	12	GREEN ONIONS Booker T. and the MG's	*Atlantic*	3
13	[13]	IS IT LOVE YOU'RE AFTER Rose Royce	*Whitfield*	9
31	14	BETTER LOVE NEXT TIME Dr. Hook	*Capitol*	2
8	15	RAPPER'S DELIGHT Sugarhill Gang	*Sugarhill*	7
10	16	MY SIMPLE HEART Three Degrees	*Ariola*	8
37	17	BABE Styx	*A&M*	2
12	18	JOHN I'M ONLY DANCING (AGAIN) David Bowie	*RCA*	6
30	19	I WANNA HOLD YOU'RE HAND Dollar	*Carrere*	2
21	[20]	WORKING FOR THE YANKEE DOLLAR Skids	*Virgin*	9
22	[21]	MY FEET KEEP DANCING Chic	*Atlantic*	6
28	22	SPACER Sheila and B. Devotion	*Carrere*	7
16	23	QUE SERA MI VIDA Gibson Brothers	*Island*	10
19	24	BLUE PETER Mike Oldfield	*Virgin*	6
-	25	I HEAR YOU NOW Jon and Vangelis ●	*Polydor*	1
38	26	SPIRITS (HAVING FLOWN) Bee Gees	*RSO*	2
-	27	IT'S DIFFERENT FOR GIRLS Joe Jackson	*A&M*	1
17	28	LIVING ON AN ISLAND Status Quo	*Vertigo*	8
25	29	OFF THE WALL Michael Jackson	*Epic*	8
-	30	JAZZ CARNIVAL Azymuth ●	*Milestone*	1
-	31	7TEEN Regents ●	*Rialto*	1
34	32	WE GOT THE FUNK Positive Force	*Sugarhill*	2
9	33	WALKING ON THE MOON Police	*A&M*	8
27	34	ONE STEP BEYOND Madness	*Stiff*	10
23	35	UNION CITY BLUE Blondie	*Chrysalis*	9
-	[36]	YOUNG BLOOD UFO	*Chrysalis*	1
-	[37]	SARAH Fleetwood Mac	*Warner Bros*	1
-	38	ESCAPE (THE PINA COLADA SONG) Rupert Holmes ●	*Infinity*	1
33	39	MOONLIGHT AND MUZAK M	*MCA*	5
36	40	THE WALK Inmates	*Radar*	2

LW	TW	WEEK ENDING 26 JANUARY 1980		Wks
1	[1]	BRASS IN POCKET Pretenders	*Real*	8
2	[2]	WITH YOU I'M BORN AGAIN Billy Preston and Syreeta	*Motown*	4

In these weeks ■ The Tourists' version of *I Only Want To Be With You* peaks at four, as did Dusty Springfield's and The Bay City Roller's versions (05.01.80) ■ Pink Floyd, Rose Royce, *Blue Peter*, *Union City Blue*, *Green Onions* and *Nights In White Satin* are all charting (12.01.80) ■ Brass In Pocket becomes the first new number one in the 80s (19.01.80)■

□ Highest position disc reached ● Act's first ever week on chart

LW	TW	Title	Artist	Label	Wks
4	[3]	MY GIRL	Madness	Stiff	3
6	4	I'M IN THE MOOD FOR DANCING	Nolans	Epic	4
3	5	PLEASE DON'T GO	KC and the Sunshine Band	TK	7
17	[6]	BABE	Styx	A&M	3
12	[7]	GREEN ONIONS	Booker T. and the MG's	Atlantic	4
14	[8]	BETTER LOVE NEXT TIME	Dr. Hook	Capitol	3
19	[9]	I WANNA HOLD YOUR HAND	Dollar	Carrere	3
5	10	ANOTHER BRICK IN THE WALL	Pink Floyd	Harvest	9
8	11	TEARS OF A CLOWN/RANKING FULL STOP	Beat	2 Tone	7
27	12	IT'S DIFFERENT FOR GIRLS	Joe Jackson	A&M	2
7	13	I HAVE A DREAM	Abba	Epic	7
11	14	LONDON CALLING	Clash	CBS	6
-	15	TOO MUCH TOO YOUNG (EP)	Special AKA	2 Tone	1
26	[16]	SPIRITS (HAVING FLOWN)	Bee Gees	RSO	3
25	17	I HEAR YOU NOW	Jon and Vangelis	Polydor	2
32	[18]	WE GOT THE FUNK	Positive Force	Sugarhill	3
13	19	IS IT LOVE YOU'RE AFTER	Rose Royce	Whitfield	10
22	20	SPACER	Sheila and B. Devotion	Carrere	8
30	21	JAZZ CARNIVAL	Azymuth	Milestone	2
31	22	7TEEN	Regents	Rialto	2
15	23	RAPPER'S DELIGHT	Sugarhill Gang	Sugarhill	8
9	24	DAY TRIP TO BANGOR	Fiddler's Dram	Dingles	7
10	25	I ONLY WANT TO BE WITH YOU	Tourists	Logo	10
-	26	LIVING BY NUMBERS	New Musik	GTO	1
38	27	ESCAPE (THE PINA COLADA SONG)	Rupert Holmes	Infinity	2
20	28	WORKING FOR THE YANKEE DOLLAR	Skids	Virgin	10
-	29	TOO HOT	Kool and the Gang	Mercury	1
-	30	BUZZ BUZZ A DIDDLE IT	Matchbox	Magnet	1
21	31	MY FEET KEEP DANCING	Chic	Atlantic	7
24	32	BLUE PETER	Mike Oldfield	Virgin	7
-	33	COWARD OF THE COUNTY	Kenny Rogers	United Artists	1
-	[34]	I'VE GOT TO LOVE SOMEBODY	Sister Sledge	Atlantic	1
-	35	STRANGE LITTLE GIRL	Sad Cafe	RCA	1
36	[36]	YOUNG BLOOD	UFO	Chrysalis	2
37	[37]	SARAH	Fleetwood Mac	Warner Bros	2
16	38	MY SIMPLE HEART	Three Degrees	Ariola	9
-	[39]	PARADISE BIRD/THE LETTER	Amii Stewart	Atlantic/Hansa	1
-	[40]	WONDERLAND	Commodores	Motown	1

WEEK ENDING 2 FEBRUARY 1980

LW	TW	Title	Artist	Label	Wks
15	[1]	TOO MUCH TOO YOUNG (EP)	Special AKA	2 Tone	2
1	2	BRASS IN POCKET	Pretenders	Real	9
3	[3]	MY GIRL	Madness	Stiff	4
4	4	I'M IN THE MOOD FOR DANCING	Nolans	Epic	5
12	[5]	IT'S DIFFERENT FOR GIRLS	Joe Jackson	A&M	3
2	6	WITH YOU I'M BORN AGAIN	Billy Preston and Syreeta	Motown	5
6	7	BABE	Styx	A&M	4
5	8	PLEASE DON'T GO	KC and the Sunshine Band	TK	8
7	9	GREEN ONIONS	Booker T. and the MG's	Atlantic	5
33	10	COWARD OF THE COUNTY	Kenny Rogers	United Artists	2
9	11	I WANNA HOLD YOUR HAND	Dollar	Carrere	4
22	12	7TEEN	Regents	Rialto	3
8	13	BETTER LOVE NEXT TIME	Dr. Hook	Capitol	4
-	14	SOMEONE'S LOOKING AT YOU	Boomtown Rats	Ensign	1
17	15	I HEAR YOU NOW	Jon and Vangelis	Polydor	3
14	16	LONDON CALLING	Clash	CBS	7
11	17	TEARS OF A CLOWN/RANKING FULL STOP	Beat	2 Tone	8
20	[18]	SPACER	Sheila and B. Devotion	Carrere	9
21	[19]	JAZZ CARNIVAL	Azymuth	Milestone	3
26	20	LIVING BY NUMBERS	New Musik	GTO	2
16	21	SPIRITS (HAVING FLOWN)	Bee Gees	RSO	4
30	[22]	BUZZ BUZZ A DIDDLE IT	Matchbox	Magnet	2
29	[23]	TOO HOT	Kool and the Gang	Mercury	2
10	24	ANOTHER BRICK IN THE WALL	Pink Floyd	Harvest	10
18	25	WE GOT THE FUNK	Positive Force	Sugarhill	4
13	26	I HAVE A DREAM	Abba	Epic	8
27	27	ESCAPE (THE PINA COLADA SONG)	Rupert Holmes	Infinity	3
19	28	IS IT LOVE YOU'RE AFTER	Rose Royce	Whitfield	11
-	29	THREE MINUTE HERO	Selecter	2 Tone	1
-	30	SAVE ME	Queen	EMI	1
-	31	JANE	Jefferson Starship	Solar	1
35	[32]	STRANGE LITTLE GIRL	Sad Cafe	RCA	2
23	33	RAPPER'S DELIGHT	Sugarhill Gang	Sugarhill	9
-	[34]	MAMA'S BOY	Suzi Quatro	RAK	1
-	35	LIVING IN THE PLASTIC AGE	Buggles	Island	1
-	36	BABY I LOVE YOU	Ramones	Sire	1
-	37	AND THE BEAT GOES ON	Whispers	Solar	1
25	38	I ONLY WANT TO BE WITH YOU	Tourists	Logo	11
34	39	I'VE GOT TO LOVE SOMEBODY	Sister Sledge	Atlantic	2
-	40	CAPTAIN BEAKY	Keith Michell	Polydor	1

WEEK ENDING 9 FEBRUARY 1980

LW	TW	Title	Artist	Label	Wks
1	[1]	TOO MUCH TOO YOUNG (EP)	Special AKA	2 Tone	3
10	2	COWARD OF THE COUNTY	Kenny Rogers	United Artists	3
4	[3]	I'M IN THE MOOD FOR DANCING	Nolans	Epic	6
3	4	MY GIRL	Madness	Stiff	5
5	[5]	IT'S DIFFERENT FOR GIRLS	Joe Jackson	A&M	4
7	[6]	BABE	Styx	A&M	5
2	7	BRASS IN POCKET	Pretenders	Real	10
14	8	SOMEONE'S LOOKING AT YOU	Boomtown Rats	Ensign	2
6	9	WITH YOU I'M BORN AGAIN	Billy Preston and Syreeta	Motown	6
9	10	GREEN ONIONS	Booker T. and the MG's	Atlantic	6
12	[11]	7TEEN	Regents	Rialto	4
15	12	I HEAR YOU NOW	Jon and Vangelis	Polydor	4
20	[13]	LIVING BY NUMBERS	New Musik	GTO	3
8	14	PLEASE DON'T GO	KC and the Sunshine Band	TK	9
40	15	CAPTAIN BEAKY	Keith Michell	Polydor	2
11	16	I WANNA HOLD YOUR HAND	Dollar	Carrere	5
13	17	BETTER LOVE NEXT TIME	Dr. Hook	Capitol	5
37	18	AND THE BEAT GOES ON	Whispers	Solar	2
18	19	SPACER	Sheila and B. Devotion	Carrere	10
30	20	SAVE ME	Queen	EMI	2
29	21	THREE MINUTE HERO	Selecter	2 Tone	2
19	22	JAZZ CARNIVAL	Azymuth	Milestone	4
27	[23]	ESCAPE (THE PINA COLADA SONG)	Rupert Holmes	Infinity	4
22	24	BUZZ BUZZ A DIDDLE IT	Matchbox	Magnet	3
36	25	BABY I LOVE YOU	Ramones	Sire	2
-	26	RIDERS IN THE SKY	Shadows	EMI	1
-	27	CARRIE	Cliff Richard	EMI	1
35	28	LIVING IN THE PLASTIC AGE	Buggles	Island	2
23	29	TOO HOT	Kool and the Gang	Mercury	3
31	30	JANE	Jefferson Starship	Solar	2
21	31	SPIRITS (HAVING FLOWN)	Bee Gees	RSO	5
25	32	WE GOT THE FUNK	Positive Force	Sugarhill Gang	5
-	33	UNDERPASS	John Foxx	Virgin	1
16	34	LONDON CALLING	Clash	CBS	8
-	35	ROCK WITH YOU	Michael Jackson	Epic	1
32	36	STRANGE LITTLE GIRL	Sad Cafe	RCA	3
17	37	TEARS OF A CLOWN/RANKING FULL STOP	Beat	2 Tone	9
34	38	MAMA'S BOY	Suzi Quatro	RAK	2
-	[39]	MUSIC MAKES YOU FEEL LIKE DANCING	Brass Construction	United Artists	1
-	[40]	DANCE STANCE	Dexy's Midnight Runners ●	Oddball	1

WEEK ENDING 16 FEBRUARY 1980

LW	TW	Title	Artist	Label	Wks
2	[1]	COWARD OF THE COUNTY	Kenny Rogers	United Artists	4
1	2	TOO MUCH TOO YOUNG (EP)	Special AKA	2 Tone	4
3	[3]	I'M IN THE MOOD FOR DANCING	Nolans	Epic	7
8	[4]	SOMEONE'S LOOKING AT YOU	Boomtown Rats	Ensign	3
15	[5]	CAPTAIN BEAKY	Keith Michell	Polydor	3
18	6	AND THE BEAT GOES ON	Whispers	Solar	3
5	7	IT'S DIFFERENT FOR GIRLS	Joe Jackson	A&M	5
12	[8]	I HEAR YOU NOW	Jon and Vangelis	Polydor	5
6	9	BABE	Styx	A&M	6
4	10	MY GIRL	Madness	Stiff	6
20	[11]	SAVE ME	Queen	EMI	3
35	12	ROCK WITH YOU	Michael Jackson	Epic	2

■The Specials leap 14 places to number one, two other Ska bands on their 2 Tone label are charting and former 2 Tone outfit Madness are at three (02.02.80) ■ Ska, Country and Pop make it a musically diverse top three (09.02.80)■

February 1980

☐ Highest position disc reached ● Act's first ever week on chart

LW	TW	Title	Artist	Label	Wks
27	13	CARRIE	Cliff Richard	EMI	2
13	14	LIVING BY NUMBERS	New Musik	GTO	4
11	15	7TEEN	Regents	Rialto	5
21	[16]	THREE MINUTE HERO	Selecter	2 Tone	3
-	17	I CANT STAND UP FOR FALLING DOWN	Elvis Costello	F Beat	1
-	18	SO GOOD TO BE BACK HOME AGAIN	Tourists	Logo	1
7	19	BRASS IN POCKET	Pretenders	Real	11
25	20	BABY I LOVE YOU	Ramones	Sire	3
26	21	RIDERS IN THE SKY	Shadows	EMI	2
24	[22]	BUZZ BUZZ A DIDDLE IT	Matchbox	Magnet	4
29	[23]	TOO HOT	Kool and the Gang	Mercury	4
17	24	BETTER LOVE NEXT TIME	Dr. Hook	Capitol	6
10	25	GREEN ONIONS	Booker T. and the MG's	Atlantic	7
31	26	JANE	Jefferson Starship	Solar	3
28	27	LIVING IN THE PLASTIC AGE	Buggles	Island	3
23	28	ESCAPE (THE PINA COLADA SONG)	Rupert Holmes	Infinity	5
22	29	JAZZ CARNIVAL	Azymuth	Milestone	5
19	30	SPACER	Sheila and B. Devotion	Carrere	11
33	[31]	UNDERPASS	John Foxx	Virgin	2
9	32	WITH YOU I'M BORN AGAIN	Billy Preston and Syreeta	Motown	7
14	33	PLEASE DON'T GO	KC and the Sunshine Band	TK	10
-	34	TOUCH TOO MUCH	AC/DC	Atlantic	1
16	35	I WANNA HOLD YOUR HAND	Dollar	Carrere	6
31	36	SPIRITS (HAVING FLOWN)	Bee Gees	RSO	6
-	37	ALL NIGHT LONG	Rainbow	Polydor	1
-	38	GAMES WITHOUT FRONTIERS	Peter Gabriel	Charisma	1
-	39	SINGING THE BLUES	Dave Edmunds	Swansong	1
-	[40]	MAYBE TOMORROW	Chords ●	Polydor	1

WEEK ENDING 23 FEBRUARY 1980

LW	TW	Title	Artist	Label	Wks
1	[1]	COWARD OF THE COUNTY	Kenny Rogers	United Artists	5
6	[2]	AND THE BEAT GOES ON	Whispers	Solar	4
-	3	ATOMIC	Blondie	Chrysalis	1
2	4	TOO MUCH TOO YOUNG (EP)	Special AKA	2 Tone	5
5	[5]	CAPTAIN BEAKY	Keith Michell	Polydor	4
13	6	CARRIE	Cliff Richard	EMI	3
4	7	SOMEONE'S LOOKING AT YOU	Boomtown Rats	Ensign	4
20	[8]	BABY I LOVE YOU	Ramones	Sire	4
17	9	I CAN'T STAND UP FOR FALLING DOWN	Elvis Costello	F Beat	2
18	10	SO GOOD TO BE BACK HOME AGAIN	Tourists	Logo	2
3	11	I'M IN THE MOOD FOR DANCING	Nolans	Epic	8
12	12	ROCK WITH YOU	Michael Jackson	Epic	3
8	13	I HEAR YOU NOW	Jon and Vangelis	Polydor	6
-	14	TAKE THAT LOOK OFF YOUR FACE	Marti Webb ●	Polydor	1
15	15	7TEEN	Regents	Rialto	6
21	16	RIDERS IN THE SKY	Shadows	EMI	3
9	17	BABE	Styx	A&M	7
27	18	LIVING IN THE PLASTIC AGE	Buggles	Island	4
7	19	IT'S DIFFERENT FOR GIRLS	Joe Jackson	A&M	6
11	20	SAVE ME	Queen	EMI	4
16	21	THREE MINUTE HERO	Selecter	2 Tone	4
14	22	LIVING BY NUMBERS	New Musik	GTO	5
-	23	TOGETHER WE ARE BEAUTIFUL	Fern Kinney ●	WEA	1
23	24	TOO HOT	Kool and the Gang	Mercury	5
38	25	GAMES WITHOUT FRONTIERS	Peter Gabriel	Charisma	2
22	26	BUZZ BUZZ A DIDDLE IT	Matchbox	Magnet	5
26	27	JANE	Jefferson Starship	Solar	4
-	28	AT THE EDGE	Stiff Little Fingers ●	Chrysalis	1
10	29	MY GIRL	Madness	Stiff	7
37	30	ALL NIGHT LONG	Rainbow	Polydor	2
39	31	SINGING THE BLUES	Dave Edmunds	Swansong	2
-	[32]	ON THE RADIO	Donna Summer	Casablanca	1
31	33	UNDERPASS	John Foxx	Virgin	3
34	34	TOUCH TOO MUCH	AC/DC	Atlantic	2
28	35	ESCAPE (THE PINA COLADA SONG)	Rupert Holmes	Infinity	6
25	36	GREEN ONIONS	Booker T. and the MG's	Atlantic	8
-	37	I'VE DONE EVERYTHING FOR YOU	Sammy Hagar ●	Capitol	1
-	38	SO LONELY	Police	A&M	1
-	39	DO THAT TO ME ONE MORE TIME	Captain and Tennille	Casablanca	1
-	40	HOT DOG	Shakin' Stevens ●	Epic	1

WEEK ENDING 1 MARCH 1980

LW	TW	Title	Artist	Label	Wks
3	[1]	ATOMIC	Blondie	Chrysalis	2
1	2	COWARD OF THE COUNTY	Kenny Rogers	United Artists	6
2	3	AND THE BEAT GOES ON	Whispers	Solar	5
6	[4]	CARRIE	Cliff Richard	EMI	4
9	5	I CAN'T STAND UP FOR FALLING DOWN	Elvis Costello	F Beat	3
14	6	TAKE THAT LOOK OFF YOU FACE	Marti Webb	Polydor	2
12	[7]	ROCK WITH YOU	Michael Jackson	Epic	4
10	[8]	SO GOOD TO BE BACK HOME AGAIN	Tourists	Logo	3
23	9	TOGETHER WE ARE BEAUTIFUL	Fern Kinney	WEA	2
5	10	CAPTAIN BEAKY	Keith Michell	Polydor	5
8	11	BABY I LOVE YOU	Ramones	Sire	5
16	[12]	RIDERS IN THE SKY	Shadows	EMI	4
4	13	TOO MUCH TOO YOUNG (EP)	Special AKA	2 Tone	6
7	14	SOMEONE'S LOOKING AT YOU	Boomtown Rats	Ensign	5
11	15	I'M IN THE MOOD FOR DANCING	Nolans	Epic	9
18	[16]	LIVING IN THE PLASTIC AGE	Buggles	Island	5
25	17	GAMES WITHOUT FRONTIERS	Peter Gabriel	Charisma	3
13	18	I HEAR YOU NOW	Jon and Vangelis	Polydor	7
38	19	SO LONELY	Police	A&M	2
-	20	HANDS OFF SHE'S MINE	Beat	Go Feet	1
27	[21]	JANE	Jefferson Starship	Solar	5
30	22	ALL NIGHT LONG	Rainbow	Polydor	3
-	[23]	ALABAMA SONG	David Bowie	RCA	1
20	24	SAVE ME	Queen	EMI	5
28	25	AT THE EDGE	Stiff Little Fingers	Chrysalis	2
22	26	LIVING BY NUMBERS	New Musik	GTO	6
21	27	THREE MINUTE HERO	Selecter	2 Tone	5
31	[28]	SINGING THE BLUES	Dave Edmunds	Swansong	3
34	[29]	TOUCH TOO MUCH	AC/DC	Atlantic	3
39	30	DO THAT TO ME ONE MORE TIME	Captain and Tennille	Casablanca	2
24	31	TOO HOT	Kool and the Gang	Mercury	6
26	32	BUZZ BUZZ A DIDDLE IT	Matchbox	Magnet	6
15	33	7TEEN	Regents	Rialto	7
-	34	TURNING JAPANESE	Vapors ●	United Artists	1
32	35	ON THE RADIO	Donna Summer	Casablanca	2
37	[36]	I'VE DONE EVERYTHING FOR YOU	Sammy Hagar	Capitol	2
17	37	BABE	Styx	A&M	8
-	38	RUNNING FREE	Iron Maiden ●	EMI	1
33	39	UNDERPASS	John Foxx	Virgin	4
-	40	CUBA/BETTER DO IT SALSA	Gibson Brothers	Island	1

WEEK ENDING 8 MARCH 1980

LW	TW	Title	Artist	Label	Wks
1	[1]	ATOMIC	Blondie	Chrysalis	3
9	2	TOGETHER WE ARE BEAUTIFUL	Fern Kinney	WEA	3
6	[3]	TAKE THAT LOOK OFF YOUR FACE	Marti Webb	Polydor	3
5	[4]	I CAN'T STAND UP FOR FALLING DOWN	Elvis Costello	F Beat	4
3	5	AND THE BEAT GOES ON	Whispers	Solar	6
2	6	COWARD OF THE COUNTY	Kenny Rogers	United Artists	7
4	7	CARRIE	Cliff Richard	EMI	5
17	8	GAMES WITHOUT FRONTIERS	Peter Gabriel	Charisma	4
7	9	ROCK WITH YOU	Michael Jackson	Epic	5
22	10	ALL NIGHT LONG	Rainbow	Polydor	4
8	11	SO GOOD TO BE BACK HOME AGAIN	Tourists	Logo	4
19	12	SO LONELY	Police	A&M	3
12	13	RIDERS IN THE SKY	Shadows	EMI	5
11	14	BABY I LOVE YOU	Ramones	Sire	6
25	[15]	AT THE EDGE	Stiff Little Fingers	Chrysalis	3
20	16	HANDS OFF SHE'S MINE	Beat	Go Feet	2
10	17	CAPTAIN BEAKY	Keith Michell	Polydor	6
34	18	TURNING JAPANESE	Vapors	United Artists	2

In these weeks ■ Shakin' Stevens makes his Top 40 debut (23.02.80) ■ Making their first appearance, Iron Maiden join five other heavy rock acts in the Top 40 (01.03.80) ■ Cliff Richard peaks at four, The Shadows at number 12 (01.03.80)■

LW	TW	Title	Artist	Label	Wks
40	19	CUBA/BETTER DO IT SALSA	Gibson Brothers	*Island*	2
16	20	LIVING IN THE PLASTIC AGE	Buggles	*Island*	6
13	21	TOO MUCH TOO YOUNG (EP)	Special AKA	*2 Tone*	7
14	22	SOMEONE'S LOOKING AT YOU	Boomtown Rats	*Ensign*	6
-	23	DANCE YOURSELF DIZZY	Liquid Gold ●	*Polo*	1
21	24	JANE	Jefferson Starship	*Solar*	6
30	25	DO THAT TO ME ONE MORE TIME	Captain and Tennille	*Casablanca*	3
23	26	ALABAMA SONG	David Bowie	*RCA*	2
15	27	I'M IN THE MOOD FOR DANCING	Nolans	*Epic*	10
28	28	SINGING THE BLUES	Dave Edmunds	*Swansong*	4
29	29	TOUCH TOO MUCH	AC/DC	*Atlantic*	4
-	30	HOT DOG	Shakin' Stevens	*Epic*	2
-	31	WORKING MY WAY BACK TO YOU-FORGIVE ME GIRL	Detroit Spinners	*Atlantic*	1
-	32	STOMP	Brothers Johnson	*A&M*	1
27	33	THREE MINUTE HERO	Selecter	*2 Tone*	6
38	34	RUNNING FREE	Iron Maiden	*EMI*	2
-	35	WORZEL'S SONG	Jon Pertwee ●	*Decca*	1
18	36	I HEAR YOU NOW	Jon and Vangelis	*Polydor*	8
35	37	ON THE RADIO	Donna Summer	*Casablanca*	3
-	38	TONIGHT I'M ALRIGHT	Narada Michael Walden ●	*Atlantic*	1
-	39	ECHO BEACH	Martha and the Muffins ●	*Dindisc*	1
-	40	ANOTHER NAIL IN MY HEART	Squeeze	*A&M*	1

WEEK ENDING 15 MARCH 1980

LW	TW	Title	Artist	Label	Wks
2	1	TOGETHER WE ARE BEAUTIFUL	Fern Kinney	*WEA*	4
1	2	ATOMIC	Blondie	*Chrysalis*	4
3	3	TAKE THAT LOOK OFF YOUR FACE	Marti Webb	*Polydor*	4
8	4	GAMES WITHOUT FRONTIERS	Peter Gabriel	*Charisma*	5
10	5	ALL NIGHT LONG	Rainbow	*Polydor*	5
12	6	SO LONELY	Police	*A&M*	4
25	7	DO THAT TO ME ONE MORE TIME	Captain and Tennille	*Casablanca*	4
18	8	TURNING JAPANESE	Vapors	*United Artists*	3
16	9	HANDS OFF SHE'S MINE	Beat	*Go Feet*	3
5	10	AND THE BEAT GOES ON	Whispers	*Solar*	7
7	11	CARRIE	Cliff Richard	*EMI*	6
4	12	I CAN'T STAND UP FOR FALLING DOWN	Elvis Costello	*F Beat*	5
9	13	ROCK WITH YOU	Michael Jackson	*Epic*	6
23	14	DANCE YOURSELF DIZZY	Liquid Gold	*Polo*	2
6	15	COWARD OF THE COUNTY	Kenny Rogers	*United Artists*	8
19	16	CUBA/BETTER DO IT SALSA	Gibson Brothers	*Island*	3
13	17	RIDERS IN THE SKY	Shadows	*EMI*	6
15	18	AT THE EDGE	Stiff Little Fingers	*Chrysalis*	4
11	19	SO GOOD TO BE BACK HOME AGAIN	Tourists	*Logo*	5
31	20	WORKING MY WAY BACK TO YOU-FORGIVE ME GIRL	Detroit Spinners	*Atlantic*	2
39	21	ECHO BEACH	Martha and the Muffins	*Dindisc*	2
14	22	BABY I LOVE YOU	Ramones	*Sire*	7
-	23	SPIRIT OF RADIO	Rush	*Mercury*	1
26	24	ALABAMA SONG	David Bowie	*RCA*	3
32	25	STOMP	Brothers Johnson	*A&M*	2
24	26	JANE	Jefferson Starship	*Solar*	7
40	27	ANOTHER NAIL IN MY HEART	Squeeze	*A&M*	3
-	28	POISON IVY	Lambrettas ●	*Rocket*	1
17	29	CAPTAIN BEAKY	Keith Michell	*Polydor*	7
-	30	WARHEAD	UK Subs	*Gem*	1
30	31	HOT DOG	Shakin' Stevens	*Epic*	3
20	32	LIVING IN THE PLASTIC AGE	Buggles	*Island*	7
35	33	WORZEL'S SONG	Jon Pertwee	*Decca*	2
-	34	HOLDIN' ON	Tony Rallo and the Midnight Band ●	*Calibre*	1
-	35	TURN IT ON AGAIN	Genesis	*Charisma*	1
-	36	HAPPY HOUSE	Siouxsie and the Banshees	*Polydor*	1
38	37	TONIGHT I'M ALRIGHT	Narada Michael Walden	*Atlantic*	2
28	38	SINGING THE BLUES	Dave Edmunds	*Swansong*	5
-	39	LOVE PATROL	Dooleys	*GTO*	1
-	40	MY WORLD	Secret Affair	*I-Spy*	1

March 1980

□ Highest position disc reached ● Act's first ever week on chart

WEEK ENDING 22 MARCH 1980

LW	TW	Title	Artist	Label	Wks
-	1	GOING UNDERGROUND/DREAMS OF CHILDREN	Jam	*Polydor*	1
1	2	TOGETHER WE ARE BEAUTIFUL	Fern Kinney	*WEA*	5
3	3	TAKE THAT LOOK OFF YOUR FACE	Marti Webb	*Polydor*	5
8	4	TURNING JAPANESE	Vapors	*United Artists*	4
14	5	DANCE YOURSELF DIZZY	Liquid Gold	*Polo*	3
4	6	GAMES WITHOUT FRONTIERS	Peter Gabriel	*Charisma*	6
2	7	ATOMIC	Blondie	*Chrysalis*	5
20	8	WORKING MY WAY BACK TO YOU-FORGIVE ME GIRL	Detroit Spinners	*Atlantic*	3
5	9	ALL NIGHT LONG	Rainbow	*Polydor*	6
7	10	DO THAT TO ME ONE MORE TIME	Captain and Tennille	*Casablanca*	5
6	11	SO LONELY	Police	*A&M*	5
16	12	CUBA/BETTER DO IT SALSA	Gibson Brothers	*Island*	4
9	13	HANDS OFF SHE'S MINE	Beat	*Go Feet*	4
25	14	STOMP	Brothers Johnson	*A&M*	3
21	15	ECHO BEACH	Martha and the Muffins	*Dindisc*	3
23	16	SPIRIT OF RADIO	Rush	*Mercury*	2
10	17	AND THE BEAT GOES ON	Whispers	*Solar*	8
15	18	COWARD OF THE COUNTY	Kenny Rogers	*United Artists*	9
11	19	CARRIE	Cliff Richard	*EMI*	7
18	20	AT THE EDGE	Stiff Little Fingers	*Chrysalis*	5
13	21	ROCK WITH YOU	Michael Jackson	*Epic*	7
12	22	I CAN'T STAND UP FOR FALLING DOWN	Elvis Costello	*F Beat*	6
36	23	HAPPY HOUSE	Siouxsie and the Banshees	*Polydor*	2
31	24	HOT DOG	Shakin' Stevens	*Epic*	4
35	25	TURN IT ON AGAIN	Genesis	*Charisma*	2
27	26	ANOTHER NAIL IN MY HEART	Squeeze	*A&M*	4
28	27	POISON IVY	Lambrettas	*Rocket*	2
40	28	MY WORLD	Secret Affair	*I-Spy*	2
-	29	JANUARY FEBRUARY	Barbara Dickson	*Epic*	1
39	30	LOVE PATROL	Dooleys	*GTO*	2
-	31	LET'S DO ROCK STEADY	Bodysnatchers ●	*2 Tone*	1
17	32	RIDERS IN THE SKY	Shadows	*EMI*	7
24	33	ALABAMA SONG	David Bowie	*RCA*	4
37	34	TONIGHT I'M ALRIGHT	Narada Michael Walden	*Atlantic*	3
-	35	DON'T PUSH IT DON'T FORCE IT	Leon Haywood ●	*20th Century*	1
26	36	JANE	Jefferson Starship	*Solar*	8
19	37	SO GOOD TO BE BACK HOME AGAIN	Tourists	*Logo*	6
30	38	WARHEAD	UK Subs	*Gem*	2
33	39	WORZEL'S SONG	Jon Pertwee	*Decca*	3
-	40	KING/FOOD FOR THOUGHT	UB40 ●	*Graduate*	1

WEEK ENDING 29 MARCH 1980

LW	TW	Title	Artist	Label	Wks
1	1	GOING UNDERGOUND/DREAMS OF CHILDREN	Jam	*Polydor*	2
2	2	TOGETHER WE ARE BEAUTIFUL	Fern Kinney	*WEA*	6
4	3	TURNING JAPANESE	Vapors	*United Artists*	5
5	4	DANCE YOURSELF DIZZY	Liquid Gold	*Polo*	4
8	5	WORKING MY WAY BACK TO YOU-FORGIVE ME GIRL	Detroit Spinners	*Atlantic*	4
3	6	TAKE THAT LOOK OFF YOUR FACE	Marti Webb	*Polydor*	6
9	7	ALL NIGHT LONG	Rainbow	*Polydor*	7
10	8	DO THAT TO ME ONE MORE TIME	Captain and Tennille	*Casablanca*	6
6	9	GAMES WITHOUT FRONTIERS	Peter Gabriel	*Charisma*	7
15	10	ECHO BEACH	Martha and the Muffins	*Dindisc*	4
14	11	STOMP	Brothers Johnson	*A&M*	4
27	12	POISON IVY	Lambrettas	*Rocket*	3
16	13	SPIRIT OF RADIO	Rush	*Mercury*	3
12	14	CUBA/BETTER DO IT SALSA	Gibson Brothers	*Island*	5
13	15	HANDS OFF SHE'S MINE	Beat	*Go Feet*	5
11	16	SO LONELY	Police	*A&M*	6

■Debbie Harry (Blondie), Graham Bonnet (Rainbow), Annie Lennox (Tourists), Sting (Police) and Bob Geldof (Boomtown Rats) will all go on to solo Top 40 success (08.03.80) ■ *Going Underground* is only the tenth hit to go straight in at number one, The Jam only the seventh act, and the first since Slade on 15.12.73 to do so (22.03.80)■

March 1980

□ Highest position disc reached ● Act's first ever week on chart

LW	TW	Title	Artist	Label	Wks
26	17	ANOTHER NAIL IN MY HEART	Squeeze	A&M	5
7	18	ATOMIC	Blondie	Chrysalis	6
29	19	JANUARY FEBRUARY	Barbara Dickson	Epic	2
40	20	KING/FOOD FOR THOUGHT	UB40	Graduate	2
23	21	HAPPY HOUSE	Siouxsie and the Banshees	Polydor	3
18	22	AT THE EDGE	Stiff Little Fingers	Chrysalis	6
25	23	TURN IT ON AGAIN	Genesis	Polydor	3
31	24	LET'S DO ROCK STEADY	Bodysnatchers	2 Tone	2
-	25	LIVING AFTER MIDNIGHT	Judas Priest	CBS	1
24	26	HOT DOG	Shakin' Stevens	Epic	5
28	27	MY WORLD	Secret Affair	I-Spy	3
-	28	KOOL IN THE KAFTAN	BA Robertson	Asylum	1
30	29	LOVE PATROL	Dooleys	GTO	3
35	30	DON'T PUSH IT DON'T FORCE IT	Leon Haywood	20th Century	2
-	31	MY OH MY	Sad Cafe	RCA	1
-	32	NO ONE DRIVING	John Foxx	Metal Beat	1
17	33	AND THE BEAT GOES ON	Whispers	Solar	9
-	34	NE-NE-NA-NA-NA-NA-NU-NU	Bad Manners ●	Magnet	1
-	35	THE MONKEES (EP)	Monkees	Arista	1
-	36	BEAR CAGE	Stranglers	United Artists	1
34	37	TONIGHT I'M ALRIGHT	Narada Michael Walden	Atlantic	4
-	38	SEXY EYES	Dr. Hook	Capitol	1
18	39	COWARD OF THE COUNTY	Kenny Rogers	United Artists	10
-	40	GENO	Dexy's Midnight Runners	Parlophone	1

WEEK ENDING 5 APRIL 1980

LW	TW	Title	Artist	Label	Wks
1	1	GOING UNDERGROUND/DREAMS OF CHILDREN	Jam	Polydor	3
4	2	DANCE YOURSELF DIZZY	Liquid Gold	Polo	5
5	3	WORKING MY WAY BACK TO YOU-FORGIVE ME GIRL	Detroit Spinners	Atlantic	5
3	4	TURNING JAPANESE	Vapors	United Artists	6
2	5	TOGETHER WE ARE BEAUTIFUL	Fern Kinney	WEA	7
11	6	STOMP	Brothers Johnson	A&M	5
12	7	POISON IVY	Lambrettas	Rocket	4
23	8	TURN IT ON AGAIN	Genesis	Charisma	4
38	9	SEXY EYES	Dr. Hook	Capitol	2
20	10	KING/FOOD FOR THOUGHT	UB40	Graduate	3
10	11	ECHO BEACH	Martha and the Muffins	Dindisc	5
19	12	JANUARY FEBRUARY	Barbara Dickson	Epic	3
7	13	ALL NIGHT LONG	Rainbow	Polydor	8
-	14	WORK REST AND PLAY (EP)	Madness	Stiff	1
25	15	LIVING AFTER MIDNIGHT	Judas Priest	CBS	2
8	16	DO THAT TO ME ONE MORE TIME	Captain and Tennille	Casablanca	7
27	17	MY WORLD	Secret Affair	I-Spy	4
17	18	ANOTHER NAIL IN MY HEART	Squeeze	A&M	6
30	19	DON'T PUSH IT DON'T FORCE IT	Leon Haywood	20th Century	3
21	20	HAPPY HOUSE	Siouxsie and the Banshees	Polydor	4
6	21	TAKE THAT LOOK OFF YOUR FACE	Marti Webb	Polydor	7
9	22	GAMES WITHOUT FRONTIERS	Peter Gabriel	Charisma	8
13	23	SPIRIT OF RADIO	Rush	Mercury	4
14	24	CUBA/BETTER DO IT SALSA	Gibson Brothers	Island	6
28	25	KOOL IN THE KAFTAN	BA Robertson	Asylum	2
-	26	TALK OF THE TOWN	Pretenders	Real	1
24	27	LET'S DO ROCK STEADY	Bodysnatchers	2 Tone	3
15	28	HANDS OFF SHE'S MINE	Beat	Go Feet	6
29	29	LOVE PATROL	Dooleys	GTO	4
16	30	SO LONELY	Police	A&M	7
31	31	MY OH MY	Sad Cafe	RCA	2
32	32	NO ONE DRIVING	John Foxx	Metal Beat	2
26	33	HOT DOG	Shakin' Stevens	Epic	6
-	34	MISSING WORDS	Selecter	2 Tone	1
18	35	ATOMIC	Blondie	Chrysalis	7
-	36	HIM	Rupert Holmes	MCA	1
40	37	GENO	Dexy's Midnight Runners	Parlophone	2
35	38	THE MONKEES (EP)	Monkees	Arista	2
34	39	NE-NE-NA-NA-NA-NA-NU-NU	Bad Manners	Magnet	2
-	40	SILVER DREAM MACHINE	David Essex	Mercury	1

WEEK ENDING 12 APRIL 1980

LW	TW	Title	Artist	Label	Wks
3	1	WORKING MY WAY BACK TO YOU-FORGIVE ME GIRL	Detroit Spinners	Atlantic	6
2	2	DANCE YOURSELF DIZZY	Liquid Gold	Polo	6
1	3	GOING UNDERGROUND/DREAMS OF CHILDREN	Jam	Polydor	4
9	4	SEXY EYES	Dr. Hook	Capitol	3
10	5	KING/FOOD FOR THOUGHT	UB40	Graduate	4
14	6	WORK REST AND PLAY (EP)	Madness	Stiff	2
4	7	TURNING JAPANESE	Vapors	United Artists	7
7	8	POISON IVY	Lambrettas	Rocket	5
6	9	STOMP	Brothers Johnson	A&M	6
8	10	TURN IT ON AGAIN	Genesis	Charisma	5
12	11	JANUARY FEBRUARY	Barbara Dickson	Epic	4
15	12	LIVING AFTER MIDNIGHT	Judas Priest	CBS	3
26	13	TALK OF THE TOWN	Pretenders	Real	2
5	14	TOGETHER WE ARE BEAUTIFUL	Fern Kinney	WEA	8
11	15	ECHO BEACH	Martha and the Muffins	Dindisc	6
17	16	MY WORLD	Secret Affair	I-Spy	5
20	17	HAPPY HOUSE	Siouxsie and the Banshees	Polydor	5
19	18	DON'T PUSH IT DON'T FORCE IT	Leon Haywood	20th Century	4
40	19	SILVER DREAM MACHINE	David Essex	Mercury	2
13	20	ALL NIGHT LONG	Rainbow	Polydor	9
-	21	CALL ME	Blondie	Chrysalis	1
27	22	LET'S DO ROCK STEADY	Bodysnatchers	2 Tone	4
18	23	ANOTHER NAIL IN MY HEART	Squeeze	A&M	7
31	24	MY OH MY	Sad Cafe	RCA	3
25	25	KOOL IN THE KAFTAN	BA Robertson	Asylum	3
21	26	TAKE THAT LOOK OFF YOUR FACE	Marti Webb	Polydor	8
16	27	DO THAT TO ME ONE MORE TIME	Captain and Tennille	Casablanca	8
23	28	SPIRIT OF RADIO	Rush	Mercury	5
37	29	GENO	Dexy's Midnight Runners	Parlophone	3
34	30	MISSING WORDS	Selecter	2 Tone	2
29	31	LOVE PATROL	Dooleys	GTO	5
36	32	HIM	Rupert Holmes	MCA	2
22	33	GAMES WITHOUT FRONTIERS	Peter Gabriel	Charisma	9
38	34	THE MONKEES (EP)	The Monkees	Arista	3
32	35	NO ONE DRIVING	John Foxx	Metal Beat	3
24	36	CUBA/BETTER DO IT SALSA	Gibson Brothers	Island	7
-	37	WHEELS OF STEEL	Saxon ●	Carrere	1
39	38	NE-NE-NA-NA-NA-NA-NU-NU	Bad Manners	Magnet	3
28	39	HANDS OFF SHE'S MINE	Beat	Go Feet	7
-	40	CHECK OUT THE GROOVE	Bobby Thurston ●	Epic	1

WEEK ENDING 19 APRIL 1980

LW	TW	Title	Artist	Label	Wks
1	1	WORKING MY WAY BACK TO YOU-FORGIVE ME GIRL	Detroit Spinners	Atlantic	7
21	2	CALL ME	Blondie	Chrysalis	2
2	3	DANCE YOURSELF DIZZY	Liquid Gold	Polo	7
5	4	KING/FOOD FOR THOUGHT	UB40	Graduate	5
4	5	SEXY EYES	Dr. Hook	Capitol	4
3	6	GOING UNDERGROUND/DREAMS OF CHILDREN	Jam	Polydor	5
6	7	WORK REST AND PLAY (EP)	Madness	Stiff	3
13	8	TALK OF THE TOWN	Pretenders	Real	3
19	9	SILVER DREAM MACHINE	David Essex	Mercury	3
8	10	POISON IVY	Lambrettas	Rocket	6
11	11	JANUARY FEBRUARY	Barbara Dickson	Epic	5
29	12	GENO	Dexy's Midnight Runners	Parlophone	4
10	13	TURN IT ON AGAIN	Genesis	Charisma	6
18	14	DON'T PUSH IT DON"T FORCE IT	Leon Haywood	20th Century	5
9	15	STOMP	Brothers Johnson	A&M	7
12	16	LIVING AFTER MIDNIGHT	Judas Priest	CBS	4
7	17	TURNING JAPANESE	Vapors	United Artists	8
16	18	MY WORLD	Secret Affair	I-Spy	6
25	19	KOOL IN THE KAFTAN	BA Robertson	Asylum	4
17	20	HAPPY HOUSE	Siouxsie and the Banshees	Polydor	6
15	21	ECHO BEACH	Martha and the Muffins	Dindisc	7
22	22	LET'S DO ROCK STEADY	Bodysnatchers	2 Tone	5
24	23	MY OH MY	Sad Cafe	RCA	4
-	24	TOCCATA	Sky ●	Arista	1

In these weeks ■ The Monkees are back in the Top 40 for the first time in nearly 12 years (29.03.80) ■ Three double A-sides, two EPs and one medley mean the Top 40 contains 50 songs (12.04.80)■

LW	TW	Title	Artist	Label	Wks
37	25	WHEELS OF STEEL	Saxon	*Carrere*	2
30	26	MISSING WORDS	Selecter	*2 Tone*	3
23	27	ANOTHER NAIL IN MY HEART	Squeeze	*A &M*	8
14	28	TOGETHER WE ARE BEAUTIFUL	Fern Kinney	*WEA*	9
-	29	MY PERFECT COUSIN	Undertones	*Sire*	1
40	30	CHECK OUT THE GROOVE	Bobby Thurston	*Epic*	2
32	[31]	HIM	Rupert Holmes	*MCA*	3
-	32	HI FIDELITY	Elvis Costello and the Attractions	*F Beat*	1
34	[33]	THE MONKEES (EP)	Monkees	*Arista*	4
-	34	DON'T MAKE WAVES	Nolans	*Epic*	1
20	35	ALL NIGHT LONG	Rainbow	*Polydor*	10
38	36	NE-NE-NA-NA-NA-NA-NU-NU	Bad Manners	*Magnet*	4
-	37	DEAR MISS LONELY HEARTS	Phil Lynott ●	*Vertigo*	1
-	[38]	CLEAN CLEAN	Buggles	*Island*	1
28	39	SPIRIT OF RADIO	Rush	*Mercury*	6
26	40	TAKE THAT LOOK OFF YOUR FACE	Marti Webb	*Polydor*	9

WEEK ENDING 26 APRIL 1980

LW	TW	Title	Artist	Label	Wks
2	[1]	CALL ME	Blondie	*Chrysalis*	3
12	2	GENO	Dexy's Midnight Runners	*Parlophone*	5
1	3	WORKING MY WAY BACK TO YOU-FORGIVE ME GIRL	Detroit Spinners	*Atlantic*	8
4	[4]	KING/FOOD FOR THOUGHT	UB40	*Graduate*	6
5	5	SEXY EYES	Dr. Hook	*Capitol*	5
9	6	SILVER DREAM MACHINE	David Essex	*Mercury*	4
-	7	COMING UP	Paul McCartney	*Parlophone*	1
3	8	DANCE YOURSELF DIZZY	Liquid Gold	*Polo*	8
8	9	TALK OF THE TOWN	Pretenders	*Real*	4
7	10	WORK REST AND PLAY (EP)	Madness	*Stiff*	4
24	11	TOCCATA	Sky	*Ariola*	2
14	[12]	DON'T PUSH IT DON'T FORCE IT	Leon Haywood	*20th Century*	6
11	13	JANUARY FEBRUARY	Barbara Dickson	*Epic*	6
23	[14]	MY OH MY	Sad Cafe	*RCA*	5
10	15	POISON IVY	Lambrettas	*Rocket*	7
13	16	TURN IT ON AGAIN	Genesis	*Charisma*	7
19	[17]	KOOL IN THE KAFTAN	BA Robertson	*Asylum*	5
16	18	LIVING AFTER MIDNIGHT	Judas Priest	*CBS*	5
18	19	MY WORLD	Secret Affair	*I-Spy*	7
6	20	GOING UNDERGROUND/DREAMS OF CHILDREN	Jam	*Polydor*	6
29	21	MY PERFECT COUSIN	Undertones	*Sire*	2
20	22	HAPPY HOUSE	Siouxsie and the Banshees	*Polydor*	7
26	[23]	MISSING WORDS	Selecter	*2 Tone*	4
22	24	LET'S DO ROCK STEADY	Bodysnatchers	*2 Tone*	6
34	25	DON'T MAKE WAVES	Nolans	*Epic*	2
30	26	CHECK OUT THE GROOVE	Bobby Thurston	*Epic*	3
-	27	THE GROOVE	Rodney Franklin ●	*CBS*	1
25	28	WHEELS OF STEEL	Saxon	*Carrere*	3
15	29	STOMP	Brothers Johnson	*A&M*	8
32	[30]	HI FIDELITY	Elvis Costello and the Attractions	*F Beat*	2
-	31	STARING AT THE RUDE BOYS	Ruts	*Virgin*	1
37	[32]	DEAR MISS LONELY HEARTS	Phil Lynott	*Vertigo*	2
31	33	HIM	Rupert Holmes	*MCA*	4
17	34	TURNING JAPANESE	Vapors	*United Artists*	9
-	35	I SHOULDA LOVED YA	Narada Michael Walden	*Atlantic*	1
36	36	NE-NE-NA-NA-NA-NA-NU-NU	Bad Manners	*Magnet*	5
33	37	THE MONKEES (EP)	Monkees	*Arista*	5
38	[38]	CLEAN CLEAN	Buggles	*Island*	2
-	[39]	ROUGH BOYS	Pete Townshend ●	*Atco*	1
-	[40]	ALL FOR LEYNA	Billy Joel	*CBS*	1

WEEK ENDING 3 MAY 1980

LW	TW	Title	Artist	Label	Wks
2	[1]	GENO	Dexy's Midnight Runners	*Parlophone*	6
7	[2]	COMING UP	Paul McCartney	*Parlophone*	2
1	3	CALL ME	Blondie	*Chrysalis*	4
6	[4]	SILVER DREAM MACHINE	David Essex	*Mercury*	5
11	[5]	TOCCATA	Sky	*Ariola*	3
4	6	KING/FOOD FOR THOUGHT	UB40	*Graduate*	7
3	7	WORKING MY WAY BACK TO YOU-FORGIVE ME GIRL	Detroit Spinners	*Atlantic*	9
5	8	SEXY EYES	Dr. Hook	*Capitol*	6
9	9	TALK OF THE TOWN	Pretenders	*Real*	5

May 1980

□ Highest position disc reached ● Act's first ever week on chart

LW	TW	Title	Artist	Label	Wks
26	[10]	CHECK OUT THE GROOVE	Bobby Thurston	*Epic*	4
21	11	MY PERFECT COUSIN	Undertones	*Sire*	3
12	[12]	DON'T PUSH IT DON'T FORCE IT	Leon Haywood	*20th Century*	7
27	13	THE GROOVE	Rodney Franklin	*CBS*	2
10	14	WORK REST AND PLAY (EP)	Madness	*Stiff*	5
-	15	WHAT'S ANOTHER YEAR	Johnny Logan ●	*Epic*	1
14	16	MY OH MY	Sad Cafe	*RCA*	6
8	17	DANCE YOURSELF DIZZY	Liquid Gold	*Polo*	9
13	18	JANUARY FEBRUARY	Barbara Dickson	*Epic*	7
35	19	I SHOULDA LOVED YA	Narada Michael Walden	*Atlantic*	2
28	[20]	WHEELS OF STEEL	Saxon	*Carrere*	4
15	21	POISON IVY	Lambrettas	*Rocket*	8
17	22	KOOL IN THE KAFTAN	BA Robertson	*Asylum*	6
-	23	GOLDEN YEARS (EP)	Motorhead	*Bronze*	1
23	24	MISSING WORDS	Selecter	*2 Tone*	5
25	25	DON'T MAKE WAVES	Nolans	*Epic*	3
24	26	LET'S DO ROCK STEADY	Bodysnatchers	*2 Tone*	7
-	27	THE GREATEST COCKNEY RIP OFF	Cockney Rejects ●	*Zonophone*	1
36	[28]	NE-NE-NA-NA-NA-NA-NU-NU	Bad Manners	*Magnet*	6
-	29	BREATHING	Kate Bush	*EMI*	1
-	30	FOOL FOR YOUR LOVING	Whitesnake ●	*United Artists*	1
-	31	NO DOUBT ABOUT IT	Hot Chocolate	*RAK*	1
31	32	STARING AT THE RUDE BOYS	Ruts	*Virgin*	2
20	33	GOING UNDERGROUND/DREAMS OF CHILDREN	Jam	*Polydor*	7
-	[34]	TAKE GOOD CARE OF MY BABY	Smokie	*RAK*	1
-	35	A FOREST	Cure ●	*Fiction*	1
-	36	HOLD ON TO MY LOVE	Jimmy Ruffin	*RSO*	1
32	37	DEAR MISS LONELY HEARTS	Phil Lynott	*Vertigo*	3
-	38	THIS WORLD OF WATER	New Musik	*GTO*	1
-	39	LET'S GO ROUND AGAIN	Average White Band	*RCA*	1
-	[40]	IN THE CITY	Jam	*Polydor*	1

WEEK ENDING 10 MAY 1980

LW	TW	Title	Artist	Label	Wks
1	[1]	GENO	Dexy's Midnight Runners	*Parlophone*	7
15	2	WHAT'S ANOTHER YEAR	Johnny Logan	*Epic*	2
2	3	COMING UP	Paul McCartney	*Parlophone*	3
3	4	CALL ME	Blondie	*Chrysalis*	5
4	5	SILVER DREAM MACHINE	David Essex	*Mercury*	6
5	6	TOCCATA	Sky	*Ariola*	4
13	[7]	THE GROOVE	Rodney Franklin	*CBS*	3
23	[8]	GOLDEN YEARS (EP)	Motorhead	*Bronze*	2
31	9	NO DOUBT ABOUT IT	Hot Chocolate	*RAK*	2
11	10	MY PERFECT COUSIN	Undertones	*Sire*	4
19	11	I SHOULDA LOVED YA	Narada Michael Walden	*Atlantic*	3
10	12	CHECK OUT THE GROOVE	Bobby Thurston	*Epic*	5
8	13	KING/FOOD FOR THOUGHT	UB40	*Graduate*	8
36	14	HOLD ON TO MY LOVE	Jimmy Ruffin	*RSO*	2
25	15	DON'T MAKE WAVES	Nolans	*Epic*	4
8	16	SEXY EYES	Dr. Hook	*Capitol*	7
-	17	MIRROR IN THE BATHROOM	Beat	*Go Feet*	1
7	18	WORKING MY WAY BACK TO YOU-FORGIVE ME GIRL	Detroit Spinners	*Atlantic*	10
12	19	DON'T PUSH IT DON'T FORCE IT	Leon Haywood	*20th Century*	8
20	[20]	WHEELS OF STEEL	Saxon	*Carrere*	5
30	21	FOOL FOR YOUR LOVING	Whitesnake	*United Artists*	2
9	22	TALK OF THE TOWN	Pretenders	*Real*	6
27	23	THE GREATEST COCKNEY RIP OFF	Cockney Rejects	*Zonophone*	2
16	24	MY OH MY	Sad Cafe	*RCA*	7
-	25	SHE'S OUT OF MY LIFE	Michael Jackson	*Epic*	1
29	26	BREATHING	Kate Bush	*EMI*	2
32	27	STARING AT THE RUDE BOYS	Ruts	*Virgin*	3
39	28	LET'S GO ROUND AGAIN	Average White Band	*RCA*	2
14	29	WORK REST AND PLAY (EP)	Madness	*Stiff*	6
-	30	JUST CAN'T GIVE YOU UP	Mystic Merlin ●	*Capitol*	1
38	[31]	THIS WORLD OF WATER	New Musik	*GTO*	2

■Paul McCartney's aptly named *Coming Up* has just leapt 55 places from 62 to seven (26.04.80) ■ Trevor Horn (Buggles) and Narada Michael Walden will both go on to greater production success (26.04.80)■

May 1980

□ Highest position disc reached ● Act's first ever week on chart

LW	TW	Title	Artist	Label	Wks
35	32	A FOREST	Cure	Fiction	2
28	33	NE-NE-NA-NA-NA-NA-NU-NU	Bad Manners	Magnet	7
34	34	TAKE GOOD CARE OF MY BABY	Smokie	RAK	2
-	35	YOU GAVE ME LOVE	Crown Heights Affair	Mercury	1
-	36	THE BUCKET OF WATER SONG	Four Bucketeers ●	CBS	1
24	37	MISSING WORDS	Selecter	2 Tone	6
22	38	KOOL IN THE KAFTAN	BA Robertson	Asylum	7
-	39	POLICE AND THIEVES	Junior Murvin ●	Island	1
17	40	DANCE YOURSELF DIZZY	Liquid Gold	Polo	10

WEEK ENDING 17 MAY 1980

LW	TW	Title	Artist	Label	Wks
2	1	WHAT'S ANOTHER YEAR	Johnny Logan	Epic	3
1	2	GENO	Dexy's Midnight Runners	Parlophone	8
3	3	COMING UP	Paul McCartney	Parlophone	4
17	4	MIRROR IN THE BATHROOM	Beat	Go Feet	2
25	5	SHE'S OUT OF MY LIFE	Michael Jackson	Epic	2
9	6	NO DOUBT ABOUT IT	Hot Chocolate	RAK	3
14	7	HOLD ONTO MY LOVE	Jimmy Ruffin	RSO	3
11	8	I SHOULDA LOVED YA	Narada Michael Walden	Atlantic	4
10	9	MY PERFECT COUSIN	Undertones	Sire	5
5	10	SILVER DREAM MACHINE	David Essex	Mercury	7
7	11	THE GROOVE	Rodney Franklin	CBS	4
8	12	GOLDEN YEARS (EP)	Motorhead	Bronze	3
15	13	DON'T MAKE WAVES	Nolans	Epic	5
4	14	CALL ME	Blondie	Chrysalis	6
6	15	TOCCATA	Sky	Ariola	5
12	16	CHECK OUT THE GROOVE	Bobby Thurston	Epic	6
28	17	LET'S GO ROUND AGAIN	Average White Band	RCA	3
-	18	OVER YOU	Roxy Music	Polydor	1
26	19	BREATHING	Kate Bush	EMI	3
21	20	FOOL FOR YOUR LOVING	Whitesnake	United Artists	3
23	21	THE GREATEST COCKNEY RIP OFF	Cockney Rejects	Zonophone	3
27	22	STARING AT THE RUDE BOYS	Ruts	Virgin	4
-	23	THEME FROM MASH (SUICIDE IS PAINLESS)	Mash ●	CBS	1
30	24	JUST CAN'T GIVE YOU UP	Mystic Merlin	Capitol	2
35	25	YOU GAVE ME LOVE	Crown Heights Affair	Mercury	2
36	26	THE BUCKET OF WATER SONG	Four Bucketeers	CBS	2
20	27	WHEELS OF STEEL	Saxon	Carrere	6
19	28	DON'T PUSH IT DON'T FORCE IT	Leon Hawood	20th Century	9
33	29	NE-NE-NA-NA-NA-NA-NU-NU	Bad Manners	Magnet	8
-	30	YOU'LL ALWAYS FIND ME IN THE KITCHEN AT PARTIES	Jona Lewie ●	Stiff	1
32	31	A FOREST	Cure	Fiction	3
31	32	THIS WORLD OF WATER	New Musik	GTO	3
-	33	MIDNITE DYNAMOS	Matchbox	Magnet	1
16	34	SEXY EYES	Dr. Hook	Capitol	8
13	35	KING/FOOD FOR THOUGHT	UB40	Graduate	9
22	36	TALK OF THE TOWN	Pretenders	Real	7
-	37	LET'S GET SERIOUS	Jermaine Jackson ●	Motown	1
39	38	POLICE AND THIEVES	Junior Murvin	Island	2
-	39	TEENAGE	UK Subs	Gem	1
-	40	CRYING	Don McLean	EMI	1

WEEK ENDING 24 MAY 1980

LW	TW	Title	Artist	Label	Wks
1	1	WHAT'S ANOTHER YEAR	Johnny Logan	Epic	4
6	2	NO DOUBT ABOUT IT	Hot Chocolate	RAK	4
5	3	SHE'S OUT OF MY LIFE	Michael Jackson	Epic	3
4	4	MIRROR IN THE BATHROOM	Beat	Go Feet	3
2	5	GENO	Dexy's Midnight Runners	Parlophone	9
23	6	THEME FROM MASH (SUICIDE IS PAINLESS)	Mash	CBS	2
18	7	OVER YOU	Roxy Music	Polydor	2
7	8	HOLD ONTO MY LOVE	Jimmy Ruffin	RSO	4
8	9	I SHOULDA LOVED YA	Narada Michael Walden	Atlantic	5
-	10	WE ARE GLASS	Gary Numan	Beggars Banquet	1
3	11	COMING UP	Paul McCartney	Parlophone	5
13	12	DON'T MAKE WAVES	Nolans	Epic	6
20	13	FOOL FOR YOUR LOVING	Whitesnake	United Artists	4
11	14	THE GROOVE	Rodney Franklin	CBS	5
10	15	SILVER DREAM MACHINE	David Essex	Mercury	8
19	16	BREATHING	Kate Bush	EMI	4
17	17	LET'S GO ROUND AGAIN	Average White Band	RCA	4
-	18	RAT RACE/RUDE BOYS OUTA JAIL	Specials	2 Tone	1
25	19	YOU GAVE ME LOVE	Crown Heights Affair	Mercury	3
12	20	GOLDEN YEARS (EP)	Motorhead	Bronze	4
15	21	TOCCATA	Sky	Ariola	6
16	22	CHECK OUT THE GROOVE	Bobby Thurston	Epic	7
37	23	LET'S GET SERIOUS	Jermaine Jackson	Motown	2
24	24	JUST CAN'T GIVE YOU UP	Mystic Merlin	Capitol	3
-	25	FUNKY TOWN	Lipps Inc ●	Casablanca	1
33	26	MIDNITE DYNAMOS	Matchbox	Magnet	2
30	27	YOU'LL ALWAYS FIND ME IN THE KITCHEN AT PARTIES	Jona Lewie	Stiff	2
40	28	CRYING	Don McLean	EMI	2
9	29	MY PERFECT COUSIN	Undertones	Sire	6
21	30	THE GREATEST COCKNEY RIP OFF	Cockney Rejects	Zonophone	4
22	31	STARING AT THE RUDE BOYS	Ruts	Virgin	5
39	32	TEENAGE	UK Subs	Gem	2
29	33	NE-NE-NA-NA-NA-NA-NU-NU	Bad Manners	Magnet	9
-	34	BACK TOGETHER AGAIN	Roberta Flack and Donny Hathaway	Atlantic	1
38	35	POLICE AND THIEVES	Junior Murvin	Island	3
26	36	THE BUCKET OF WATER SONG	Four Bucketeers	CBS	3
14	37	CALL ME	Blondie	Chrysalis	7
27	38	WHEELS OF STEEL	Saxon	Carrere	7
-	39	MESSAGES	Orchestral Manoeuvres In The Dark ●	Dindisc	1
32	40	THIS WORLD OF WATER	New Musik	GTO	4

WEEK ENDING 31 MAY 1980

LW	TW	Title	Artist	Label	Wks
6	1	THEME FROM MASH (SUICIDE IS PAINLESS)	Mash	CBS	3
2	2	NO DOUBT ABOUT IT	Hot Chocolate	RAK	5
1	3	WHAT'S ANOTHER YEAR	Johnny Logan	Epic	5
3	4	SHE'S OUT OF MY LIFE	Michael Jackson	Epic	4
10	5	WE ARE GLASS	Gary Numan	Beggars Banquet	2
7	6	OVER YOU	Roxy Music	Polydor	3
4	7	MIRROR IN THE BATHROOM	Beat	Go Feet	4
18	8	RAT RACE/RUDE BOYS OUTA JAIL	Specials	2 Tone	2
25	9	FUNKY TOWN	Lipps Inc	Casablanca	2
5	10	GENO	Dexy's Midnight Runners	Parlophone	10
8	11	HOLD ON TO MY LOVE	Jimmy Ruffin	RSO	5
17	12	LET'S GO ROUND AGAIN	Average White Band	RCA	5
28	13	CRYING	Don McLean	EMI	3
13	14	FOOL FOR YOUR LOVING	Whitesnake	United Artists	5
12	15	DON'T MAKE WAVES	Nolans	Epic	7
9	16	I SHOULDA LOVED YA	Narada Michael Walden	Atlantic	6
19	17	YOU GAVE ME LOVE	Crown Heights Affair	Mercury	4
26	18	MIDNITE DYNAMOS	Matchbox	Magnet	3
27	19	YOU'LL ALWAYS FIND ME IN THE KITCHEN AT PARTIES	Jona Lewie	Stiff	3
-	20	D-A-A-ANCE	Lambrettas	Rocket	1
23	21	LET'S GET SERIOUS	Jermaine Jackson	Motown	3
34	22	BACK TOGETHER AGAIN	Roberta Flack and Donny Hathaway	Atlantic	2
24	23	JUST CAN'"T GIVE YOU UP	Mystic Merlin	Capitol	4
11	24	COMING UP	Paul McCartney	Parlophone	6
-	25	I'M ALIVE	Electric Light Orchestra	Jet	1
39	26	MESSAGES	Orchestral Manoeuvres In The Dark	Dindisc	2
35	27	POLICE AND THIEVES	Junior Murvin	Island	4
20	28	GOLDEN YEARS (EP)	Motorhead	Bronze	5
-	29	TWILIGHT ZONE-TWILIGHT TONE	Manhattan Transfer	Atlantic	1
16	30	BREATHING	Kate Bush	EMI	5
-	31	EVERYBODY'S GOT TO LEARN SOMETIME	Korgis	Rialto	1
32	32	TEENAGE	UK Subs	Gem	3
-	33	NO SELF CONTROL	Peter Gabriel	Charisma	1
15	34	SILVER DREAM MACHINE	David Essex	Mercury	9
-	35	I'M FOREVER BLOWING BUBBLES	Cockney Rejects	Zonophone	1

In these weeks ■ Johnny Logan becomes only the third foreign Eurovision Winner, after Dana and Abba, to score a number one (17.05.80) ■ Michael Jackson lands his fourth straight Top Ten hit from 'Off The Wall' - that's nothing, he'll take five from 'Thriller' and six from 'Bad' (17.05.80) ■ *Ne-Ne-Na-Na-Na-Na-Nu-Nu* has spent ten weeks in the Top 40 without climbing higher than 28 (31.05.80)■

LW	TW	Title / Artist	Label	Wks
-	[36]	NOBODY'S HERO/TIN SOLDIERS Stiff Little Fingers	*Chrysalis*	1
-	37	CHINATOWN Thin Lizzy	*Vertigo*	1
40	38	THIS WORLD OF WATER New Musik	*GTO*	5
33	39	NE-NE-NA-NA-NA-NU-NU Bad Manners	*Magnet*	10
-	[40]	BODY LANGUAGE Detroit Spinners	*Atlantic*	1

LW	TW	*WEEK ENDING* **7 JUNE 1980**		Wks
1	[1]	THEME FROM MASH (SUICIDE IS PAINLESS) Mash	*CBS*	4
2	[2]	NO DOUBT ABOUT IT Hot Chocolate	*RAK*	6
9	3	FUNKY TOWN Lipps Inc	*Casablanca*	3
13	4	CRYING Don McLean	*EMI*	4
8	[5]	RAT RACE/RUDE BOYS OUTA JAIL Specials	*2 Tone*	3
6	6	OVER YOU Roxy Music	*Polydor*	4
5	7	WE ARE GLASS Gary Numan	*Beggars Banquet*	3
4	8	SHE'S OUT OF MY LIFE Michael Jackson	*Epic*	5
21	9	LET'S GET SERIOUS Jermaine Jackson	*Motown*	4
3	10	WHAT'S ANOTHER YEAR Johnny Logan	*Epic*	6
7	11	MIRROR IN THE BATHROOM Beat	*Go Feet*	5
17	12	YOU GAVE ME LOVE Crown Heights Affair	*Mercury*	4
12	13	LET'S GO ROUND AGAIN Average White Band	*RCA*	6
22	14	BACK TOGETHER AGAIN Roberta Flack and Donny Hathaway	*Atlantic*	3
11	15	HOLD ON TO MY LOVE Jimmy Ruffin	*RSO*	6
18	16	MIDNITE DYNAMOS Matchbox	*Magnet*	4
10	17	GENO Dexy's Midnight Runners	*Parlophone*	11
14	18	FOOL FOR YOUR LOVING Whitesnake	*United Artists*	6
19	19	YOU'LL ALWAYS FIND ME IN THE KITCHEN AT PARTIES Jona Lewie	*Stiff*	4
23	[20]	JUST CAN'T GIVE YOU UP Mystic Merlin	*Capitol*	5
20	21	D-A-A-ANCE Lambrettas	*Rocket*	2
25	22	I'M ALIVE Electric Light Orchestra	*Jet*	2
-	23	BREAKING THE LAW Judas Priest	*CBS*	1
15	24	DON'T MAKE WAVES Nolans	*Epic*	8
16	25	I SHOULDA LOVED YA Narada Michael Walden	*Atlantic*	7
26	26	MESSAGES Orchestral Manoeuvres In The Dark	*Dindisc*	3
31	27	EVERYBODY'S GOT TO LEARN SOMETIME Korgis	*Rialto*	2
27	28	POLICE AND THIEVES Junior Murvin	*Island*	5
-	29	BEHIND THE GROOVE Teena Marie ●	*Motown*	1
37	30	CHINATOWN Thin Lizzy	*Vertigo*	2
29	31	TWILIGHT ZONE-TWILIGHT TONE Manhattan Transfer	*Atlantic*	2
-	32	SUBSTITUTE Liquid Gold	*Polo*	1
-	[33]	LITTLE JEANNIE Elton John	*Rocket*	1
-	34	SANCTUARY Iron Maiden	*EMI*	1
-	35	CHRISTINE Siouxsie and the Banshees	*Polydor*	1
36	[36]	NOBODY'S HERO/TIN SOLDIERS Stiff Little Fingers	*Chrysalis*	2
30	37	BREATHING Kate Bush	*EMI*	6
-	38	THE SCRATCH Surface Noise ●	*WEA*	1
34	39	SILVER DREAM MACHINE David Essex	*Mercury*	10
-	40	IF LOVING YOU IS WRONG (I DON'T WANT TO BE RIGHT) Rod Stewart	*Mercury*	1

LW	TW	*WEEK ENDING* **14 JUNE 1980**		Wks
1	[1]	THEME FROM MASH (SUICIDE IS PAINLESS) Mash	*CBS*	5
4	2	CRYING Don McLean	*EMI*	5
3	3	FUNKY TOWN Lipps Inc	*Casablanca*	4
2	4	NO DOUBT ABOUT IT Hot Chocolate	*RAK*	7
6	[5]	OVER YOU Roxy Music	*Polydor*	5
14	6	BACK TOGETHER AGAIN Roberta Flack and Donny Hathaway	*Atlantic*	4
5	7	RAT RACE/RUDE BOYS OUTA JAIL Specials	*2 Tone*	4
9	[8]	LET'S GET SERIOUS Jermaine Jackson	*Motown*	5
7	9	WE ARE GLASS Gary Numan	*Beggars Banquet*	4
12	[10]	YOU GAVE ME LOVE Crown Heights Affair	*Mercury*	6
8	11	SHE'S OUT OF MY LIFE Michael Jackson	*Epic*	6
21	[12]	D-A-A-ANCE Lambrettas	*Rocket*	3
12	13	LET'S GO ROUND AGAIN Average White Band	*RCA*	7
26	14	MESSAGES Orchestral Manoeuvres In The Dark	*Dindisc*	4
16	15	MIDNITE DYNAMOS Matchbox	*Magnet*	5
19	[16]	YOU'LL ALWAYS FIND ME IN THE KITCHEN AT PARTIES Jona Lewie	*Stiff*	5

June 1980

□ Highest position disc reached ● Act's first ever week on chart

LW	TW	Title / Artist	Label	Wks
29	17	BEHIND THE GROOVE Teena Marie	*Motown*	2
23	18	BREAKING THE LAW Judas Priest	*CBS*	2
27	19	EVERYBODY'S GOT TO LEARN SOMETIME Korgis	*Rialto*	3
22	[20]	I'M ALIVE Electric Light Orchestra	*Jet*	3
32	21	SUBSTITUTE Liquid Gold	*Polo*	2
35	[22]	CHRISTINE Siouxsie and the Banshees	*Polydor*	2
28	[23]	POLICE AND THIEVES Junior Murvin	*Island*	6
20	24	JUST CAN'T GIVE YOU UP Mystic Merlin	*Capitol*	6
31	[25]	TWILIGHT ZONE-TWILIGHT TONE Manhattan Transfer	*Atlantic*	3
11	26	MIRROR IN THE BATHROOM Beat	*Go Feet*	6
40	27	IF LOVING YOU IS WRONG (I DON'T WANT TO BE RIGHT) Rod Stewart	*Mercury*	2
38	28	THE SCRATCH Surface Noise	*WEA*	2
34	[29]	SANCTUARY Iron Maiden	*EMI*	2
30	30	CHINATOWN Thin Lizzy	*Vertigo*	3
-	31	SIX PACK Police	*A&M*	1
10	32	WHAT'S ANOTHER YEAR Johnny Logan	*Epic*	7
15	33	HOLD ON TO MY LOVE Jimmy Ruffin	*RSO*	7
-	34	PLAY THE GAME Queen	*EMI*	1
17	35	GENO Dexy's Midnight Runners	*Parlophone*	12
-	[36]	NEW AMSTERDAM Elvis Costello	*F Beat*	1
33	37	LITTLE JEANNIE Elton John	*Rocket*	2
18	38	FOOL FOR YOUR LOVING Whitesnake	*United Artists*	7
-	[39]	WHO WANTS THE WORLD Stranglers	*United Artists*	1
-	40	TO BE OR NOT TO BE BA Robertson	*Asylum*	1

LW	TW	*WEEK ENDING* **21 JUNE 1980**		Wks
2	[1]	CRYING Don McLean	*EMI*	6
1	2	THEME FROM MASH (SUICIDE IS PAINLESS) Mash	*CBS*	6
3	3	FUNKY TOWN Lipps Inc	*Casablanca*	5
6	4	BACK TOGETHER AGAIN Roberta Flack and Donny Hathaway	*Atlantic*	5
4	5	NO DOUBT ABOUT IT Hot Chocolate	*RAK*	8
19	6	EVERYBODY'S GOT TO LEARN SOMETIME Korgis	*Rialto*	4
17	7	BEHIND THE GROOVE Teena Marie	*Motown*	3
8	[8]	LET'S GET SERIOUS Jermaine Jackson	*Motown*	6
5	9	OVER YOU Roxy Music	*Polydor*	6
10	[10]	YOU GAVE ME LOVE Crown Heights Affair	*Mercury*	7
7	11	RAT RACE/RUDE BOYS OUTA JAIL Specials	*2 Tone*	5
18	12	BREAKING THE LAW Judas Priest	*CBS*	3
14	[13]	MESSAGES Orchestral Manoeuvres In The Dark	*Dindisc*	5
15	[14]	MIDNITE DYNAMOS Matchbox	*Magnet*	6
12	15	D-A-A-ANCE Lambrettas	*Rocket*	4
21	16	SUBSTITUTE Liquid Gold	*Polo*	3
31	[17]	SIX PACK Police	*A&M*	2
34	18	PLAY THE GAME Queen	*EMI*	2
9	19	WE ARE GLASS Gary Numan	*Beggars Banquet*	5
20	[20]	I'M ALIVE Electric Light Orchestra	*Jet*	4
16	21	YOU'LL ALWAYS FIND ME IN THE KITCHEN AT PARTIES Jona Lewie	*Stiff*	6
-	22	SIMON TEMPLAR/TWO PINTS OF LAGER AND A PACKET OF CRISPS PLEASE Splodgenessabounds ●	*Deram*	1
30	23	CHINATOWN Thin Lizzy	*Vertigo*	4
27	24	IF LOVING YOU IS WRONG (I DON'T WANT TO BE RIGHT) Rod Stewart	*Mercury*	3
25	[25]	TWILIGHT ZONE-TWILIGHT TONE Manhattan Transfer	*Atlantic*	4
28	[26]	THE SCRATCH Surface Noise	*WEA*	3
22	27	CHRISTINE Siouxsie and the Banshees	*Polydor*	3
40	28	TO BE OR NOT TO BE BA Robertson	*Asylum*	2
-	29	MY WAY OF THINKING/I THINK IT'S GOING TO RAIN UB40	*Graduate*	1
23	30	POLICE AND THIEVES Junior Murvin	*Island*	7
-	31	JUMP TO THE BEAT Stacy Lattisaw ●	*Atlantic*	1
11	32	SHE'S OUT OF MY LIFE Michael Jackson	*Epic*	7
24	33	JUST CAN'T GIVE YOU UP Mystic Merlin	*Capitol*	7
13	34	LET'S GO ROUND AGAIN Average White Band	*RCA*	8

■The Jackson brothers appear side by side at eight and nine (07.06.80) ■ The Police chart with a pack of six separate singles but when Gallup take over the collating of the chart this will be classed as an album (14.06.80)■

June 1980

☐ Highest position disc reached ● Act's first ever week on chart

LW	TW	Title / Artist	Label	Wks
-	35	(I'M NOT YOUR) STEPPING STONE Sex Pistols	Virgin	1
29	36	SANCTUARY Iron Maiden	EMI	3
-	37	LET'S HANG ON Darts	Magnet	1
37	38	LITTLE JEANNIE Elton John	Rocket	3
-	39	XANADU Olivia Newton John and the Electric Light Orchestra ●	Jet	1
-	40	747 (STRANGERS IN THE NIGHT) Saxon	Carrere	1

LW	TW	*WEEK ENDING* **28 JUNE 1980**		Wks
1	[1]	CRYING Don McLean	EMI	7
3	[2]	FUNKY TOWN Lipps Inc	Casablanca	6
4	[3]	BACK TOGETHER AGAIN Roberta Flack and Donny Hathaway	Atlantic	6
2	4	THEME FROM MASH (SUICIDE IS PAINLESS) Mash	CBS	7
6	[5]	EVERYBODY'S GOT TO LEARN SOMETIME Korgis	Rialto	5
7	[6]	BEHIND THE GROOVE Teena Marie	Motown	4
22	[7]	SIMON TEMPLAR/TWO PINTS OF LAGER AND A PACKET OF CRISPS PLEASE Splodgenessabounds	Deram	2
16	[8]	SUBSTITUTE Liquid Gold	Polo	4
8	9	LET'S GET SERIOUS Jermaine Jackson	Motown	7
11	10	RAT RACE/RUDE BOYS OUTA JAIL Specials	2 Tone	6
31	11	JUMP TO THE BEAT Stacy Lattisaw	Atlantic	2
10	12	YOU GAVE ME LOVE Crown Heights Affair	Mercury	8
13	[13]	MESSAGES Orchestral Manoeuvres In The Dark	Dindisc	6
39	14	XANADU Olivia Newton-John and the Electric Light Orchestra	Jet	2
5	15	NO DOUBT ABOUT IT Hot Chocolate	RAK	9
18	16	PLAY THE GAME Queen	EMI	3
9	17	OVER YOU Roxy Music	Polydor	7
12	18	BREAKING THE LAW Judas Priest	CBS	4
29	19	MY WAY OF THINKING/I THINK IT'S GOING TO RAIN UB40	Graduate	2
-	20	WATERFALLS Paul McCartney	Parlophone	1
14	21	MIDNITE DYNAMOS Matchbox	Magnet	7
15	22	D-A-A-ANCE Lambrettas	Rocket	5
23	23	CHINATOWN Thin Lizzy	Vertigo	5
27	24	CHRISTINE Siouxsie and the Banshees	Polydor	4
28	25	TO BE OR NOT TO BE BA Robertson	Asylum	3
20	26	I'M ALIVE Electric Light Orchestra	Jet	5
40	27	747 (STRANGERS IN THE NIGHT) Saxon	Carrere	2
21	28	YOU'LL ALWAYS FIND ME IN THE KITCHEN AT PARTIES Jona Lewie	Stiff	7
35	29	(I'M NOT YOUR) STEPPING STONE Sex Pistols	Virgin	2
-	30	USE IT UP AND WEAR IT OUT Odyssey	RCA	1
24	31	IF LOVING YOU IS WRONG (I DON'T WANT TO BE RIGHT) Rod Stewart	Mercury	4
-	32	COULD YOU BE LOVED Bob Marley and the Wailers	Island	1
25	33	TWILIGHT ZONE-TWILIGHT TONE Manhattan Transfer	Atlantic	5
17	34	SIX PACK Police	A&M	3
26	35	THE SCRATCH Surface Noise	WEA	4
37	36	LET'S HANG ON Darts	Magnet	2
30	37	POLICE AND THIEVES Junior Murvin	Island	8
19	38	WE ARE GLASS Gary Numan	Beggars Banquet	6
-	39	NEW AMSTERDAM Elvis Costello	F Beat	2
-	40	THEME FROM THE INVADERS Yellow Magic Orchestra ●	A&M	1

LW	TW	*WEEK ENDING* **5 JULY 1980**		Wks
1	[1]	CRYING Don McLean	EMI	8
2	[2]	FUNKY TOWN Lipps Inc	Casablanca	7
14	3	XANADU Olivia Newton-John and the Electric Light Orchestra	Jet	3
3	4	BACK TOGETHER AGAIN Roberta Flack and Donny Hathaway	Atlantic	7
5	[5]	EVERYBODY'S GOT TO LEARN SOMETIME Korgis	Rialto	6
11	6	JUMP TO THE BEAT Stacy Lattisaw	Atlantic	3
7	[7]	SIMON TEMPLAR/TWO PINTS OF LAGER AND A PACKET OF CRISPS PLEASE Splodgenessabounds	Deram	3
19	8	MY WAY OF THINKING/I THINK IT'S GOING TO RAIN UB40	Graduate	3
25	[9]	TO BE OR NOT TO BE BA Robertson	Asylum	4
6	10	BEHIND THE GROOVE Teena Marie	Motown	5
20	11	WATERFALLS Paul McCartney	Parlophone	2
30	12	USE IT UP AND WEAR IT OUT Odyssey	RCA	2
8	13	SUBSTITUTE Liquid Gold	Polo	5
16	[14]	PLAY THE GAME Queen	EMI	4
4	15	THEME FROM MASH (SUICIDE IS PAINLESS) Mash	CBS	8
-	16	CUPID-I'VE LOVED YOU FOR A LONG TIME Detroit Spinners	Atlantic	1
21	17	MIDNITE DYNAMOS Matchbox	Magnet	8
9	18	LET'S GET SERIOUS Jermaine Jackson	Motown	8
27	19	747 (STRANGERS IN THE NIGHT) Saxon	Carrere	3
13	20	MESSAGES Orchestral Manoeuvres In The Dark	Dindisc	7
32	21	COULD YOU BE LOVED Bob Marley and the Wailers	Island	2
23	22	CHINATOWN Thin Lizzy	Vertigo	6
31	[23]	IF LOVING YOU IS WRONG (I DON'T WANNA BE RIGHT) Rod Stewart	Mercury	5
24	24	CHRISTINE Siouxsie and the Banshees	Polydor	5
22	25	D-A-A-ANCE Lambrettas	Rocket	6
26	26	I'M ALIVE Electric Light Orchestra	Jet	6
12	27	YOU GAVE ME LOVE Crown Heights Affair	Mercury	9
18	28	BREAKING THE LAW Judas Priest	CBS	5
36	29	LET'S HANG ON Darts	Magnet	3
-	30	LOVE WILL TEAR US APART Joy Division ●	Factory	1
17	31	OVER YOU Roxy Music	Polydor	8
15	32	NO DOUBT ABOUT IT Hot Chocolate	RAK	10
10	33	RAT RACE/RUDE BOYS OUTA JAIL Specials	2 Tone	7
29	34	(I'M NOT YOUR) STEPPING STONE Sex Pistols	Virgin	3
-	35	A LOVER'S HOLIDAY/GLOW OF LOVE Change ●	WEA	1
40	36	THEME FROM THE INVADERS Yellow Magic Orchestra	A&M	2
-	37	LIP UP FATTY Bad Manners	Magnet	1
-	38	WHOLE LOTTA ROSIE AC/DC	Atlantic	1
-	39	ME MYSELF I Joan Armatrading	A&M	1
26	40	THE SCRATCH Surface Noise	WEA	5

LW	TW	*WEEK ENDING* **12 JULY 1980**		Wks
3	[1]	XANADU Olivia Newton-John and the Electric Light Orchestra	Jet	4
12	2	USE IT UP AND WEAR IT OUT Odyssey	RCA	3
6	[3]	JUMP TO THE BEAT Stacy Lattisaw	Atlantic	4
1	4	CRYING Don McLean	EMI	9
16	5	CUPID-I'VE LOVED YOU FOR A LONG TIME Detroit Spinners	Atlantic	2
2	6	FUNKY TOWN Lipps Inc	Casablanca	8
8	7	MY WAY OF THINKING/I THINK IT'S GOING TO RAIN UB40	Graduate	4
5	8	EVERYBODY'S GOT TO LEARN SOMETIME Korgis	Rialto	7
21	9	COULD YOU BE LOVED Bob Marley and the Wailers	Island	3
7	10	SIMON TEMPLAR/TWO PINTS OF LAGER AND A PACKET OF CRISPS PLEASE Splodgenessabounds	Deram	4
11	11	WATERFALLS Paul McCartney	Parlophone	3
9	12	TO BE OR NOT TO BE BA Robertson	Asylum	5
4	13	BACK TOGETHER AGAIN Roberta Flack and Donny Hathaway	Atlantic	8
19	14	747 (STRANGERS IN THE NIGHT) Saxon	Carrere	4
10	15	BEHIND THE GROOVE Teena Marie	Motown	6
-	16	BABOOSHKA Kate Bush	EMI	1
14	17	PLAY THE GAME Queen	EMI	5
30	18	LOVE WILL TEAR US APART Joy Division	Factory	2
13	19	SUBSTITUTE Liquid Gold	Polo	6
-	20	EMOTIONAL RESCUE Rolling Stones	Rolling Stones	1
22	[21]	CHINATOWN Thin Lizzy	Vertigo	7
-	22	MORE THAN I CAN SAY Leo Sayer	Chrysalis	1
23	[23]	IF LOVING YOU IS WRONG (I DON'T WANT TO BE RIGHT) Rod Stewart	Mercury	6
29	24	LET'S HANG ON Darts	Magnet	4
36	25	THEME FROM THE INVADERS Yellow Magic Orchestra	A&M	3
24	26	CHRISTINE Siouxsie and the Banshees	Polydor	6

In these weeks ■ There are four double A-sides currently charting (05.07.80) ■ Cult indie band Joy Division chart after lead singer Ian Curtis' suicide on 18.05.80 (05.07.80) ■ Stacy Lattisaw hits the top three aged 13 (12.07.80)■

August 1980

□ Highest position disc reached ● Act's first ever week on chart

LW	TW	Title	Artist	Label	Wks
17	27	MIDNITE DYNAMOS	Matchbox	*Magnet*	9
34	28	(I'M NOT YOUR) STEPPING STONE	Sex Pistols	*Virgin*	4
35	29	A LOVER'S HOLIDAY/GLOW OF LOVE	Change	*WEA*	2
-	30	WEDNESDAY WEEK	Undertones	*Sire*	1
39	31	ME MYSELF I	Joan Armatrading	*A&M*	2
15	32	THEME FROM MASH (SUICIDE IS PAINLESS)	Mash	*CBS*	9
37	33	LIP UP FATTY	Bad Manners	*Magnet*	2
-	34	NEON KNIGHTS	Black Sabbath	*Vertigo*	1
-	□35	KING'S CALL	Phil Lynott	*Vertigo*	1
27	36	YOU GAVE ME LOVE	Crown Heights Affair	*Mercury*	10
38	37	WHOLE LOTTA ROSIE	AC/DC	*Atlantic*	2
18	38	LET'S GET SERIOUS	Jermaine Jackson	*Motown*	9
20	39	MESSAGES	Orchestral Manoeuvres In The Dark	*Dindisc*	8
-	40	FANTASY	Gerard Kenny ●	*RCA*	1

WEEK ENDING **19 JULY 1980**

LW	TW	Title	Artist	Label	Wks
1	□1	XANADU	Olivia Newton-John and the Electric Light Orchestra	*Jet*	5
2	2	USE IT UP AND WEAR IT OUT	Odyssey	*RCA*	4
3	□3	JUMP TO THE BEAT	Stacy Lattisaw	*Atlantic*	5
5	□4	CUPID-I'VE LOVED YOU FOR A LONG TIME	Detroit Spinners	*Atlantic*	3
9	□5	COULD YOU BE LOVED	Bob Marley and the Wailers	*Island*	4
7	□6	MY WAY OF THINKING/I THINK IT'S GOING TO RAIN	UB40	*Graduate*	5
16	7	BABOOSHKA	Kate Bush	*EMI*	2
4	8	CRYING	Don McLean	*EMI*	10
11	□9	WATERFALLS	Paul McCartney	*Parlophone*	4
22	10	MORE THAN I CAN SAY	Leo Sayer	*Chrysalis*	2
12	11	TO BE OR NOT TO BE	BA Robertson	*Asylum*	6
6	12	FUNKY TOWN	Lipps Inc	*Casablanca*	9
14	□13	747 (STRANGERS IN THE NIGHT)	Saxon	*Carrere*	5
8	14	EVERYBODY'S GOT TO LEARN SOMETIME	Korgis	*Rialto*	8
10	15	SIMON TEMPLAR/TWO PINTS OF LAGER AND A PACKET OF CRISPS PLEASE	Splodgenessabounds	*Deram*	5
24	16	LET'S HANG ON	Darts	*Magnet*	5
18	17	LOVE WILL TEAR US APART	Joy Division	*Factory*	3
13	18	BACK TOGETHER AGAIN	Roberta Flack and Donny Hathaway	*Atlantic*	9
20	19	EMOTIONAL RESCUE	Rolling Stones	*Rolling Stones*	2
-	20	THERE THERE MY DEAR	Dexy's Midnight Runners	*Parlophone*	1
28	□21	(I'M NOT YOUR) STEPPING STONE	Sex Pistols	*Virgin*	5
17	22	PLAY THE GAME	Queen	*EMI*	6
29	23	A LOVER'S HOLIDAY/GLOW OF LOVE	Change	*WEA*	3
26	24	CHRISTINE	Siouxsie and the Banshees	*Polydor*	7
34	25	NEON KNIGHTS	Black Sabbath	*Vertigo*	2
25	26	THEME FROM THE INVADERS	Yellow Magic Orchestra	*A&M*	4
31	27	ME MYSELF I	Joan Armatrading	*A&M*	3
33	28	LIP UP FATTY	Bad Manners	*Magnet*	3
21	29	CHINATOWN	Thin Lizzy	*Vertigo*	8
15	30	BEHIND THE GROOVE	Teena Marie	*Motown*	7
-	31	UPSIDE DOWN	Diana Ross	*Motown*	1
30	32	WEDNESDAY WEEK	Undertones	*Sire*	2
23	33	IF LOVING YOU IS WRONG (I DON'T WANNA BE RIGHT)	Rod Stewart	*Mercury*	7
40	□34	FANTASY	Gerard Kenny	*RCA*	2
-	35	MY GIRL	Whispers	*Solar*	1
37	□36	WHOLE LOTTA ROSIE	AC/DC	*Atlantic*	3
19	37	SUBSTITUTE	Liquid Gold	*Polo*	7
-	38	OOPS UPSIDE YOU HEAD	Gap Band ●	*Mercury*	1
-	39	DOES SHE HAVE A FRIEND	Gene Chandler	*Mercury*	1
-	40	MARIANA	Gibson Brothers	*Island*	1

WEEK ENDING **26 JULY 1980**

LW	TW	Title	Artist	Label	Wks
2	□1	USE IT UP AND WEAR IT OUT	Odyssey	*RCA*	5
1	2	XANADU	Olivia Newton-John and the Electric Light Orchestra	*Jet*	6
10	3	MORE THAN I CAN SAY	Leo Sayer	*Chrysalis*	3
3	4	JUMP TO THE BEAT	Stacy Lattisaw	*Atlantic*	6
5	□5	COULD YOU BE LOVED	Bob Marley and the Wailers	*Island*	5
4	6	CUPID-I'VE LOVED YOU FOR A LONG TIME	Detroit Spinners	*Atlantic*	4
7	7	BABOOSHKA	Kate Bush	*EMI*	3
31	8	UPSIDE DOWN	Diana Ross	*Motown*	2
19	□9	EMOTIONAL RESCUE	Rolling Stones	*Rolling Stones*	3
6	10	MY WAY OF THINKING/I THINK IT'S GOING TO RAIN	UB40	*Graduate*	6
16	□11	LET'S HANG ON	Darts	*Magnet*	6
20	12	THERE THERE MY DEAR	Dexy's Midnight Runners	*Parlophone*	2
17	□13	LOVE WILL TEAR US APART	Joy Division	*Factory*	4
23	□14	A LOVER'S HOLIDAY/GLOW OF LOVE	Change	*WEA*	4
13	15	747 (STRANGERS IN THE NIGHT)	Saxon	*Carrere*	6
9	16	WATERFALLS	Paul McCartney	*Parlophone*	5
26	□17	THEME FROM THE INVADERS	Yellow Magic Orchestra	*A&M*	5
8	18	CRYING	Don McLean	*EMI*	11
38	19	OOPS UPSIDE YOUR HEAD	Gap Band	*Mercury*	2
32	20	WEDNESDAY WEEK	Undertones	*Sire*	3
28	21	LIP UP FATTY	Bad Manners	*Magnet*	4
25	□22	NEON KNIGHTS	Black Sabbath	*Vertigo*	3
40	23	MARIANA	Gibson Brothers	*Island*	2
12	24	FUNKY TOWN	Lipps Inc	*Casablanca*	10
-	25	ARE YOU GETTING ENOUGH OF WHAT MAKES YOU HAPPY	Hot Chocolate	*RAK*	1
35	□26	MY GIRL	Whispers	*Solar*	2
11	27	TO BE OR NOT TO BE	BA Robertson	*Asylum*	7
27	28	ME MYSELF I	Joan Armatrading	*A&M*	4
-	29	9 TO 5	Sheena Easton ●	*EMI*	1
22	30	PLAY THE GAME	Queen	*EMI*	7
-	□31	SANCTUARY	New Musik	*GTO*	1
39	32	DOES SHE HAVE A FRIEND	Gene Chandler	*20th Century*	2
-	33	FUNKIN' FOR JAMAICA (N.Y.)	Tom Browne ●	*Arista*	1
21	34	(I'M NOT YOUR) STEPPING STONE	Sex Pistols	*Virgin*	6
14	35	EVERYBODY'S GOT TO LEARN SOMETIME	Korgis	*Rialto*	9
-	□36	BRAZILIAN LOVE AFFAIR	George Duke ●	*Epic*	1
34	37	FANTASY	Gerard Kenny	*RCA*	3
-	38	BURNING CAR	John Foxx	*Metal Beat*	1
-	39	SLEEP WALK	Ultravox ●	*Chrysalis*	1
15	40	SIMON TEMPLAR/TWO PINTS OF LAGER AND A PACKET OF CRISPS PLEASE	Splodgenessabounds	*Deram*	6

WEEK ENDING **2 AUGUST 1980**

LW	TW	Title	Artist	Label	Wks
1	□1	USE IT UP AND WEAR IT OUT	Odyssey	*RCA*	6
3	□2	MORE THAN I CAN SAY	Leo Sayer	*Chrysalis*	4
8	3	UPSIDE DOWN	Diana Ross	*Motown*	3
2	4	XANADU	Olivia Newton-John and the Electric Light Orchestra	*Jet*	7
7	□5	BABOOSHKA	Kate Bush	*EMI*	4
5	6	COULD YOU BE LOVED	Bob Marley and the Wailers	*Island*	6
12	□7	THERE THERE MY DEAR	Dexy's Midnight Runners	*Parlophone*	3
4	8	JUMP TO THE BEAT	Stacy Lattisaw	*Atlantic*	7
-	9	WINNER TAKES IT ALL	Abba	*Epic*	1
6	10	CUPID-I'VE LOVED YOU FOR A LONG TIME	Detroit Spinners	*Atlantic*	5
20	□11	WEDNESDAY WEEK	Undertones	*Sire*	4
9	12	EMOTIONAL RESCUE	Rolling Stones	*Rolling Stones*	4
11	13	LET'S HANG ON	Darts	*Magnet*	7
10	14	MY WAY OF THINKING/I THINK IT'S GOING TO RAIN	UB40	*Graduate*	7
21	□15	LIP UP FATTY	Bad Manners	*Magnet*	5
13	16	LOVE WILL TEAR US APART	Joy Division	*Factory*	5
14	17	A LOVER'S HOLIDAY/GLOW OF LOVE	Change	*WEA*	5
19	18	OOPS UPSIDE YOUR HEAD	Gap Band	*Mercury*	3
17	19	THEME FROM THE INVADERS	Yellow Magic Orchestra	*A&M*	6
29	20	9 TO 5	Sheena Easton	*EMI*	2
28	□21	ME MYSELF I	Joan Armatrading	*A&M*	5
-	22	GIVE ME THE NIGHT	George Benson	*Warner Brothers*	1

■John Foxx enters at 38 while his old band, now led by Midge Ure, debuts one place lower (26.07.80) ■ *Upside Down* becomes Diana Ross' biggest hit since *I'm Still Waiting* exactly nine years ago (02.08.80)■

August 1980

□ Highest position disc reached ● Act's first ever week on chart

LW	TW	Title / Artist	Label	Wks
23	23	MARIANA Gibson Brothers	*Island*	3
33	24	FUNKIN' FOR JAMAICA (N.Y.) Tom Browne	*Arista*	2
16	25	WATERFALLS Paul McCartney	*Parlophone*	6
22	26	NEON KNIGHTS Black Sabbath	*Vertigo*	4
25	27	ARE YOU GETTING ENOUGH OF WHAT MAKES YOU HAPPY Hot Chocolate	*RAK*	2
32	[28]	DOES SHE HAVE A FRIEND Gene Chandler	*20th Century*	3
26	29	MY GIRL Whispers	*Solar*	3
-	30	OH YEAH (ON THE RADIO) Roxy Music	*Polydor*	1
-	31	PRIVATE LIFE Grace Jones ●	*Island*	1
-	[32]	BURNIN' HOT Jermaine Jackson	*Motown*	1
31	33	SANCTUARY New Musik	*GTO*	2
39	34	SLEEP WALK Ultravox	*Chrysalis*	2
15	35	747 (STRANGERS IN THE NIGHT) Saxon	*Carrere*	7
38	36	BURNING CAR John Foxx	*Metal Beat*	2
27	37	TO BE OR NOT TO BE BA Robertson	*Asylum*	8
36	38	BRAZILIAN LOVE AFFAIR George Duke	*Epic*	2
-	[39]	MY GUY-MY GIRL Amii Stewart and Johnny Bristol ●	*Atlantic*	1
24	40	FUNKY TOWN Lipps Inc	*Casablanca*	11

WEEK ENDING 9 AUGUST 1980

LW	TW	Title / Artist	Label	Wks
9	[1]	WINNER TAKES IT ALL Abba	*Epic*	2
3	[2]	UPSIDE DOWN Diana Ross	*Motown*	4
1	3	USE IT UP AND WEAR IT OUT Odyssey	*RCA*	7
2	4	MORE THAN I CAN SAY Leo Sayer	*Chrysalis*	5
20	5	9 TO 5 Sheena Easton	*EMI*	3
5	6	BABOOSHKA Kate Bush	*EMI*	5
18	7	OOPS UPSIDE YOUR HEAD Gap Band	*Mercury*	4
6	8	COULD YOU BE LOVED Bob Marley and the Wailers	*Island*	7
30	9	OH YEAH (ON THE RADIO) Roxy Music	*Polydor*	2
22	10	GIVE ME THE NIGHT George Benson	*Warner Brothers*	2
7	11	THERE THERE MY DEAR Dexy's Midnight Runners	*Parlophone*	4
11	12	WEDNESDAY WEEK Undertones	*Sire*	5
4	13	XANADU Olivia Newton-John and the Electric Light Orchestra	*Jet*	8
23	14	MARIANA Gibson Brothers	*Island*	4
15	[15]	LIP UP FATTY Bad Manners	*Magnet*	6
24	16	FUNKIN' FOR JAMAICA (N.Y.) Tom Browne	*Arista*	3
8	17	JUMP TO THE BEAT Stacy Lattisaw	*Atlantic*	8
13	18	LET'S HANG ON Darts	*Magnet*	8
12	19	EMOTIONAL RESCUE Rolling Stones	*Rolling Stones*	5
10	20	CUPID-I'VE LOVED YOU FOR A LONG TIME Detroit Spinners	*Atlantic*	6
27	21	ARE YOU GETTING ENOUGH OF WHAT MAKES YOU HAPPY Hot Chocolate	*RAK*	3
16	22	LOVE WILL TEAR US APART Joy Division	*Factory*	6
17	23	A LOVER'S HOLIDAY/GLOW OF LOVE Change	*WEA*	6
-	24	ALL OVER THE WORLD Electric Light Orchestra	*Jet*	1
31	25	PRIVATE LIFE Grace Jones	*Island*	2
-	26	TOM HARK Piranhas ●	*Sire*	1
19	27	THEME FROM THE INVADERS Yellow Magic Orchestra	*A&M*	7
21	28	ME MYSELF I Joan Armatrading	*A&M*	6
-	29	FEELS LIKE I'M IN LOVE Kelly Marie ●	*Calibre*	1
28	30	DOES SHE HAVE A FRIEND Gene Chandler	*20th Century*	4
33	[31]	SANCTUARY New Musik	*GTO*	3
32	[32]	BURNIN' HOT Jermaine Jackson	*Motown*	2
34	33	SLEEP WALK Ultravox	*Chrysalis*	3
14	34	MY WAY OF THINKING/I THINK IT'S GOING TO RAIN UB40	*Graduate*	8
36	35	BURNING CAR John Foxx	*Metal Beat*	3
26	36	NEON KNIGHTS Black Sabbath	*Vertigo*	5
-	37	THE SUNSHINE OF YOUR SMILE Mike Berry	*Polydor*	1
29	38	MY GIRL Whispers	*Solar*	4
-	[39]	FREE ME Roger Daltrey	*Polydor*	1
-	40	YOU GOTTA BE A HUSTLER IF YOU WANT TO GET ON Sue Wilkinson ●	*Cheapskate*	1

WEEK ENDING 16 AUGUST 1980

LW	TW	Title / Artist	Label	Wks
1	[1]	WINNER TAKES IT ALL Abba	*Epic*	3
2	[2]	UPSIDE DOWN Diana Ross	*Motown*	5
5	[3]	9 TO 5 Sheena Easton	*EMI*	4
-	4	ASHES TO ASHES David Bowie	*RCA*	1
9	[5]	OH YEAH (ON THE RADIO) Roxy Music	*Polydor*	3
7	[6]	OOPS UPSIDE YOUR HEAD Gap Band	*Mercury*	5
10	[7]	GIVE ME THE NIGHT George Benson	*Warner Brothers*	3
4	8	MORE THAN I CAN SAY Leo Sayer	*Chrysalis*	6
3	9	USE IT UP AND WEAR IT OUT Odyssey	*RCA*	8
16	[10]	FUNKIN' FOR JAMAICA (N.Y.) Tom Browne	*Arista*	4
14	[11]	MARIANA Gibson Brothers	*Island*	5
6	12	BABOOSHKA Kate Bush	*EMI*	6
26	13	TOM HARK Piranhas	*Sire*	2
8	14	COULD YOU BE LOVED Bob Marley and the Wailers	*Island*	8
15	[15]	LIP UP FATTY Bad Manners	*Magnet*	7
29	16	FEELS LIKE I'M IN LOVE Kelly Marie	*Calibre*	2
21	[17]	ARE YOU GETTING ENOUGH OF WHAT MAKES YOU HAPPY Hot Chocolate	*RAK*	4
24	18	ALL OVER THE WORLD Electric Light Orchestra	*Jet*	2
11	19	THERE THERE MY DEAR Dexy's Midnight Runners	*Parlophone*	5
13	20	XANADU Olivia Newton-John and the Electric Light Orchestra	*Jet*	9
18	21	LET'S HANG ON Darts	*Magnet*	9
37	22	SUNSHINE OF YOUR SMILE Mike Berry	*Polydor*	2
12	23	WEDNESDAY WEEK Undertones	*Sire*	6
25	24	PRIVATE LIFE Grace Jones	*Island*	3
28	25	ME MYSELF I Joan Armatrading	*A&M*	7
36	26	NEON KNIGHTS Black Sabbath	*Vertigo*	6
-	27	CAN'T STOP THE MUSIC Village People	*Mercury*	1
27	28	THEME FROM THE INVADERS Yellow Magic Orchestra	*A&M*	8
33	[29]	SLEEP WALK Ultravox	*Chrysalis*	4
40	30	YOU GOTTA BE A HUSTLER IF YOU WANT TO GET ON Sue Wilkinson	*Cheapskate*	2
-	31	BANK ROBBER Clash	*CBS*	1
17	32	JUMP TO THE BEAT Stacy Lattisaw	*Atlantic*	9
-	33	IT'S STILL ROCK 'N' ROLL TO ME Billy Joel	*CBS*	1
-	[34]	C30 C60 C90 GO Bow Wow Wow ●	*EMI*	1
-	35	MODERN GIRL Sheena Easton	*EMI*	1
30	36	DOES SHE HAVE A FRIEND Gene Chandler	*20th Century*	5
20	37	CUPID-I'VE LOVED YOU FOR A LONG TIME Detroit Spinners	*Atlantic*	7
31	38	SANCTUARY New Musik	*GTO*	4
39	[39]	FREE ME Roger Daltrey	*Polydor*	2
-	40	A WALK IN THE PARK Nick Straker Band ●	*Polydor*	1

WEEK ENDING 23 AUGUST 1980

LW	TW	Title / Artist	Label	Wks
4	[1]	ASHES TO ASHES David Bowie	*RCA*	2
1	2	WINNER TAKES IT ALL Abba	*Epic*	4
-	3	START Jam	*Polydor*	1
3	4	9 TO 5 Sheena Easton	*EMI*	5
2	5	UPSIDE DOWN Diana Ross	*Motown*	6
5	6	OH YEAH (ON THE RADIO) Roxy Music	*Polydor*	4
6	7	OOPS UPSIDE YOUR HEAD Gap Band	*Mercury*	6
16	8	FEELS LIKE I'M IN LOVE Kelly Marie	*Calibre*	3
13	9	TOM HARK Piranhas	*Sire*	3
7	10	GIVE ME THE NIGHT George Benson	*Warner Brothers*	4
18	[11]	ALL OVER THE WORLD Electric Light Orchestra	*Jet*	3
10	12	FUNKIN' FOR JAMAICA (N.Y.) Tom Browne	*Arista*	5
22	13	SUNSHINE OF YOUR SMILE Mike Berry	*Polydor*	3
8	14	MORE THAN I CAN SAY Leo Sayer	*Chrysalis*	7
11	15	MARIANA Gibson Brothers	*Island*	6
19	16	THERE THERE MY DEAR Dexy's Midnight Runners	*Parlophone*	6
24	[17]	PRIVATE LIFE Grace Jones	*Island*	4
9	18	USE IT UP AND WEAR IT OUT Odyssey	*RCA*	9
15	19	LIP UP FATTY Bad Manners	*Magnet*	8
-	20	DREAMIN' Cliff Richard	*EMI*	1
27	21	CAN'T STOP THE MUSIC Village People	*Mercury*	2
12	22	BABOOSHKA Kate Bush	*EMI*	7
14	23	COULD YOU BE LOVED Bob Marley and the Wailers	*Island*	9

In these weeks ■ Abba return to pole position after a run of six Top 5 near misses (09.08.80) ■ Only four weeks after her Top 40 debut, Sheena Easton holds down two chart positions in the same week (16.08.80) ■ Exactly ten years after its first chart run, Black Sabbath's *Paranoid* re-enters at number 37 (23.08.80) ■

LW	TW	Title	Artist	Label	Wks
31	24	BANK ROBBER	Clash	*CBS*	2
35	25	MODERN GIRL	Sheena Easton	*EMI*	2
30	26	YOU GOTTA BE A HUSTLER IF YOU WANT TO GET ON	Sue Wilkinson	*Cheapskate*	3
-	27	EIGHTH DAY	Hazel O'Connor ●	*A&M*	1
40	28	A WALK IN THE PARK	Nick Straker Band	*Polydor*	2
17	29	ARE YOU GETTING ENOUGH OF WHAT MAKES YOU HAPPY	Hot Chocolate	*RAK*	5
33	30	IT'S STILL ROCK 'N' ROLL TO ME	Billy Joel	*CBS*	2
29	31	SLEEP WALK	Ultravox	*Chrysalis*	5
-	32	MARIE MARIE	Shakin' Stevens	*Epic*	1
-	33	BEST FRIEND-STAND DOWN MARGARET	Beat	*Go Feet*	1
23	34	WEDNESDAY WEEK	Undertones	*Sire*	7
20	35	XANADU	Olivia Newton-John and the Electric Light Orchestra	*Jet*	10
34	36	C30 C60 C90 GO	Bow Wow Wow	*EMI*	2
-	37	PARANOID	Black Sabbath	*Nems*	1
-	[38]	BIKO	Peter Gabriel	*Charisma*	1
-	39	CIRCUS GAMES	Skids	*Virgin*	1
-	40	SUMMER FUN	Barracudas ●	*Zonophone*	1

WEEK ENDING 30 AUGUST 1980

LW	TW	Title	Artist	Label	Wks
1	[1]	ASHES TO ASHES	David Bowie	*RCA*	3
3	2	START	Jam	*Polydor*	2
4	[3]	9 TO 5	Sheena Easton	*EMI*	6
2	4	WINNER TAKES IT ALL	Abba	*Epic*	5
8	5	FEELS LIKE I'M IN LOVE	Kelly Marie	*Calibre*	4
9	[6]	TOM HARK	Piranhas	*Sire*	4
5	7	UPSIDE DOWN	Diana Ross	*Motown*	7
-	8	I DIE: YOU DIE	Gary Numan	*Beggars Banquet*	1
7	9	OOPS UPSIDE YOUR HEAD	Gap Band	*Mercury*	7
13	10	SUNSHINE OF YOUR SMILE	Mike Berry	*Polydor*	4
6	11	OH YEAH (ON THE RADIO)	Roxy Music	*Polydor*	5
10	12	GIVE ME THE NIGHT	George Benson	*Warner Brothers*	5
27	13	EIGHTH DAY	Hazel O'Connor	*A&M*	2
20	14	DREAMIN'	Cliff Richard	*EMI*	2
11	15	ALL OVER THE WORLD	Electric Light Orchestra	*Jet*	4
12	16	FUNKIN' FOR JAMAICA (N.Y.)	Tom Browne	*Arista*	6
21	17	CAN'T STOP THE MUSIC	Village People	*Mercury*	3
25	18	MODERN GIRL	Sheena Easton	*EMI*	3
24	19	BANK ROBBER	Clash	*CBS*	3
30	20	IT'S STILL ROCK 'N' ROLL TO ME	Billy Joel	*CBS*	3
15	21	MARIANA	Gibson Brothers	*Island*	7
32	22	MARIE MARIE	Shakin' Stevens	*Epic*	2
14	23	MORE THAN I CAN SAY	Leo Sayer	*Chrysalis*	8
17	24	PRIVATE LIFE	Grace Jones	*Island*	5
26	[25]	YOU GOTTA BE A HUSTLER IF YOU WANT TO GET ON	Sue Wilkinson	*Cheapskate*	4
19	26	LIP UP FATTY	Bad Manners	*Magnet*	9
37	27	PARANOID	Black Sabbath	*Nems*	2
28	28	A WALK IN THE PARK	Nick Straker Band	*Polydor*	3
31	[29]	SLEEP WALK	Ultravox	*Chrysalis*	6
33	30	BEST FRIEND-STAND DOWN MARGARET	Beat	*Go Feet*	2
18	31	USE IT UP AND WEAR IT OUT	Odyssey	*RCA*	10
-	[32]	MAGIC	Olivia Newton-John	*Jet*	1
39	33	CIRCUS GAMES	Skids	*Virgin*	2
-	34	IT'S ONLY LOVE/BEYOND THE REEF	Elvis Presley	*RCA*	1
23	35	COULD YOU BE LOVED	Bob Marley and the Wailers	*Island*	10
29	36	ARE YOU GETTING ENOUGH OF WHAT MAKES YOU HAPPY	Hot Chocolate	*RAK*	6
40	[37]	SUMMER FUN	Barracudas	*Zonophone*	2
-	38	I GOT YOU	Split Enz ●	*A&M*	1
-	39	I WANT TO BE STRAIGHT	Ian Dury and the Blockheads	*Stiff*	1
38	40	BIKO	Peter Gabriel	*Charisma*	2

September 1980

□ Highest position disc reached ● Act's first ever week on chart

WEEK ENDING 6 SEPTEMBER 1980

LW	TW	Title	Artist	Label	Wks
2	[1]	START	Jam	*Polydor*	3
1	2	ASHES TO ASHES	David Bowie	*RCA*	4
5	3	FEELS LIKE I'M IN LOVE	Kelly Marie	*Calibre*	5
3	4	9 TO 5	Sheena Easton	*EMI*	7
13	[5]	EIGHTH DAY	Hazel O'Connor	*A&M*	3
8	[6]	I DIE: YOU DIE	Gary Numan	*Beggars Banquet*	2
6	7	TOM HARK	Piranhas	*Sire*	5
4	8	WINNER TAKES IT ALL	Abba	*Epic*	6
10	[9]	SUNSHINE OF YOUR SMILE	Mike Berry	*Polydor*	5
14	10	DREAMIN'	Cliff Richard	*EMI*	3
17	[11]	CAN'T STOP THE MUSIC	Village People	*Mercury*	4
19	[12]	BANK ROBBER	Clash	*CBS*	4
18	13	MODERN GIRL	Sheena Easton	*EMI*	4
7	14	UPSIDE DOWN	Diana Ross	*Motown*	8
9	15	OOPS UPSIDE YOUR HEAD	Gap Band	*Mercury*	8
12	16	GIVE ME THE NIGHT	George Benson	*Warner Brothers*	6
34	17	IT'S ONLY LOVE/BEYOND THE REEF	Elvis Presley	*RCA*	2
15	18	ALL OVER THE WORLD	Electric Light Orchestra	*Jet*	5
11	19	OH YEAH (ON THE RADIO)	Roxy Music	*Polydor*	6
20	20	IT'S STILL ROCK 'N' ROLL TO ME	Billy Joel	*CBS*	4
22	21	MARIE MARIE	Shakin' Stevens	*Epic*	3
28	22	A WALK IN THE PARK	Nick Straker Band	*Polydor*	4
16	23	FUNKIN' FOR JAMAICA (N.Y.)	Tom Browne	*Arista*	7
27	24	PARANOID	Black Sabbath	*Nems*	3
39	25	I WANT TO BE STRAIGHT	Ian Dury and the Blockheads	*Stiff*	2
-	26	ONE DAY I'LL FLY AWAY	Randy Crawford ●	*Warner Brothers*	1
30	27	BEST FRIEND-STAND DOWN MARGARET	Beat	*Go Feet*	3
24	28	PRIVATE LIFE	Grace Jones	*Island*	6
25	29	YOU GOTTA BE A HUSTLER IF YOU WANT TO GET ON	Sue Wilkinson	*Cheapskate*	5
29	30	SLEEP WALK	Ultravox	*Chrysalis*	7
-	31	UNITED	Judas Priest	*CBS*	1
-	32	I OWE YOU ONE	Shalamar	*Solar*	1
33	33	CIRCUS GAMES	Skids	*Virgin*	3
32	34	MAGIC	Olivia Newton-John	*Jet*	2
38	35	I GOT YOU	Split Enz	*A&M*	2
-	[36]	THE WHISPER	Selecter	*Chrysalis*	1
37	[37]	SUMMER FUN	Barracudas	*Zonophone*	3
21	38	MARIANA	Gibson Brothers	*Island*	8
26	39	LIP UP FATTY	Bad Manners	*Magnet*	10
23	40	MORE THAN I CAN SAY	Leo Sayer	*Chrysalis*	9

WEEK ENDING 13 SEPTEMBER 1980

LW	TW	Title	Artist	Label	Wks
3	[1]	FEELS LIKE I'M IN LOVE	Kelly Marie	*Calibre*	6
1	2	START	Jam	*Polydor*	4
2	3	ASHES TO ASHES	David Bowie	*RCA*	5
26	4	ONE DAY I'LL FLY AWAY	Randy Crawford	*Warner Brothers*	2
5	[5]	EIGHTH DAY	Hazel O'Connor	*A&M*	4
4	6	9 TO 5	Sheena Easton	*EMI*	8
17	7	IT'S ONLY LOVE/BEYOND THE REEF	Elvis Presley	*RCA*	3
10	[8]	DREAMIN'	Cliff Richard	*EMI*	4
7	9	TOM HARK	Piranhas	*Sire*	6
13	10	MODERN GIRL	Sheena Easton	*EMI*	5
9	11	SUNSHINE OF YOUR SMILE	Mike Berry	*Polydor*	6
6	12	I DIE: YOU DIE	Gary Numan	*Beggars Banquet*	3
12	13	BANK ROBBER	Clash	*CBS*	5
11	14	CAN'T STOP THE MUSIC	Village People	*Mercury*	5
20	15	IT'S STILL ROCK 'N' ROLL TO ME	Billy Joel	*CBS*	5
8	16	WINNER TAKES IT ALL	Abba	*Epic*	7
24	17	PARANOID	Black Sabbath	*Nems*	4
-	18	ANOTHER ONE BITES THE DUST	Queen	*EMI*	1
15	19	OOPS UPSIDE YOUR HEAD	Gap Band	*Mercury*	9
22	[20]	A WALK IN THE PARK	Nick Straker Band	*Polydor*	5
21	21	MARIE MARIE	Shakin' Stevens	*Epic*	4
27	[22]	BEST FRIEND-STAND DOWN MARGARET	Beat	*Go Feet*	4
14	23	UPSIDE DOWN	Diana Ross	*Motown*	9
32	24	I OWE YOU ONE	Shalamar	*Solar*	2
25	25	I WANT TO BE STRAIGHT	Ian Dury and the Blockheads	*Stiff*	3
31	[26]	UNITED	Judas Priest	*CBS*	2
35	27	I GOT YOU	Split Enz	*A&M*	3
16	28	GIVE ME THE NIGHT	George Benson	*Warner Brothers*	7
18	29	ALL OVER THE WORLD	Electric Light Orchestra	*Jet*	6
-	30	MASTERBLASTER (JAMMIN')	Stevie Wonder	*Motown*	1

■Nineteen acts in the Top 40 have had or will have a number one hit (30.08.80) ■ The last time Elvis and Cliff were resident in the Top Ten together was 21.06.69, Elvis with *In The Ghetto* and Cliff with *Big Ship* (13.09.80) ■ Nine weeks ago she was unknown, now Sheena Easton places two discs inside the Top Ten (13.09.80)■

September 1980

□ Highest position disc reached ● Act's first ever week on chart

LW	TW	Title	Artist	Label	Wks
23	31	FUNKIN' FOR JAMAICA (N.Y.)	Tom Browne	*Arista*	8
33	[32]	CIRCUS GAMES	Skids	*Virgin*	4
19	33	OH YEAH (ON THE RADIO)	Roxy Music	*Polydor*	7
34	34	MAGIC	Olivia Newton-John	*Jet*	3
-	[35]	TASTE OF BITTER LOVE	Gladys Knight and the Pips	*CBS*	1
-	36	BAGGY TROUSERS	Madness	*Stiff*	1
29	37	YOU GOTTA BE A HUSTLER IF YOU WANT TO GET ON	Sue Wilkinson	*Cheapskate*	6
-	38	SEARCHING	Change	*WEA*	1
-	39	GENERALS AND MAJORS/DON'T LOSE YOUR TEMPER	XTC	*Virgin*	1
-	40	TWO LITTLE BOYS/HORSE	Splodgenessabounds	*Deram*	1

WEEK ENDING 20 SEPTEMBER 1980

LW	TW	Title	Artist	Label	Wks
1	[1]	FEELS LIKE I'M IN LOVE	Kelly Marie	*Calibre*	7
4	[2]	ONE DAY I'LL FLY AWAY	Randy Crawford	*Warner Brothers*	3
7	[3]	IT'S ONLY LOVE/BEYOND THE REEF	Elvis Presley	*RCA*	4
30	4	MASTERBLASTER (JAMMIN')	Stevie Wonder	*Motown*	2
2	5	START	Jam	*Polydor*	5
5	6	EIGHTH DAY	Hazel O'Connor	*A&M*	5
3	7	ASHES TO ASHES	David Bowie	*RCA*	6
10	[8]	MODERN GIRL	Sheena Easton	*EMI*	6
8	9	DREAMIN'	Cliff Richard	*EMI*	5
18	10	ANOTHER ONE BITES THE DUST	Queen	*EMI*	2
6	11	9 TO 5	Sheena Easton	*EMI*	9
11	12	SUNSHINE OF YOUR SMILE	Mike Berry	*Polydor*	7
14	13	CAN'T STOP THE MUSIC	Village People	*Mercury*	6
17	[14]	PARANOID	Black Sabbath	*Nems*	5
15	15	IT'S STILL ROCK 'N' ROLL TO ME	Billy Joel	*CBS*	6
13	16	BANK ROBBER	Clash	*CBS*	6
9	17	TOM HARK	Piranhas	*Sire*	7
12	18	I DIE: YOU DIE	Gary Numan	*Beggars Banquet*	4
21	[19]	MARIE MARIE	Shakin' Stevens	*Epic*	5
20	[20]	A WALK IN THE PARK	Nick Straker Band	*Polydor*	6
36	21	BAGGY TROUSERS	Madness	*Stiff*	2
25	[22]	I WANT TO BE STRAIGHT	Ian Dury and the Blockheads	*Stiff*	4
24	23	I OWE YOU ONE	Shalamar	*Solar*	3
22	24	BEST FRIEND-STAND DOWN MARGARET	Beat	*Go Feet*	5
27	25	I GOT YOU	Split Enz	*A&M*	4
40	[26]	TWO LITTLE BOYS/HORSE	Splodgenessabounds	*Deram*	2
38	27	SEARCHING	Change	*WEA*	2
-	28	D.I.S.C.O.	Ottawan ●	*Carrere*	1
26	29	UNITED	Judas Priest	*CBS*	3
16	30	WINNER TAKES IT ALL	Abba	*Epic*	8
19	31	OOPS UPSIDE YOUR HEAD	Gap Band	*Mercury*	10
39	[32]	GENERALS AND MAJORS/DON'T LOSE YOUR TEMPER	XTC	*Virgin*	2
23	33	UPSIDE DOWN	Diana Ross	*Motown*	10
-	34	IF YOU'RE LOOKIN' FOR A WAY OUT	Odyssey	*RCA*	1
-	35	THREE LITTLE BIRDS	Bob Marley and the Wailers	*Island*	1
-	36	MY OLD PIANO	Diana Ross	*Motown*	1
35	37	TASTE OF BITTER LOVE	Gladys Knight and the Pips	*CBS*	2
28	38	GIVE ME THE NIGHT	George Benson	*Warner Brothers*	8
-	39	YOU SHOOK ME ALL NIGHT LONG	AC/DC	*Atlantic*	1
32	40	CIRCUS GAMES	Skids	*Virgin*	5

WEEK ENDING 27 SEPTEMBER 1980

LW	TW	Title	Artist	Label	Wks
-	[1]	DON'T STAND SO CLOSE TO ME	Police	*A&M*	1
2	[2]	ONE DAY I'LL FLY AWAY	Randy Crawford	*Warner Brothers*	4
4	3	MASTERBLASTER (JAMMIN')	Stevie Wonder	*Motown*	3
1	4	FEELS LIKE I'M IN LOVE	Kelly Marie	*Calibre*	8
21	5	BAGGY TROUSERS	Madness	*Stiff*	3
3	6	IT'S ONLY LOVE/BEYOND THE REEF	Elvis Presley	*RCA*	5
10	[7]	ANOTHER ONE BITES THE DUST	Queen	*EMI*	3
28	8	D.I.S.C.O.	Ottawan	*Carrere*	2
8	9	MODERN GIRL	Sheena Easton	*EMI*	7
6	10	EIGHTH DAY	Hazel O'Connor	*A&M*	6
5	11	START	Jam	*Polydor*	6
9	12	DREAMIN'	Cliff Richard	*EMI*	6
36	13	MY OLD PIANO	Diana Ross	*Motown*	2
15	[14]	IT'S STILL ROCK 'N' ROLL TO ME	Billy Joel	*CBS*	7
7	15	ASHES TO ASHES	David Bowie	*RCA*	7
23	16	I OWE YOU ONE	Shalamar	*Solar*	4
11	17	9 TO 5	Sheena Easton	*EMI*	10
12	18	SUNSHINE OF YOUR SMILE	Mike Berry	*Polydor*	8
14	19	PARANOID	Black Sabbath	*Nems*	6
20	[20]	A WALK IN THE PARK	Nick Straker Band	*Polydor*	7
19	21	MARIE MARIE	Shakin' Stevens	*Epic*	6
25	22	I GOT YOU	Split Enz	*A&M*	5
13	23	CAN'T STOP THE MUSIC	Village People	*Mercury*	7
27	24	SEARCHING	Change	*WEA*	3
35	25	THREE LITTLE BIRDS	Bob Marley and the Wailers	*Island*	2
16	26	BANK ROBBER	Clash	*CBS*	7
26	27	TWO LITTLE BOYS/HORSE	Splodgenessabounds	*Deram*	3
22	28	I WANT TO BE STRAIGHT	Ian Dury and the Blockheads	*Stiff*	5
34	29	IF YOU'RE LOOKIN' FOR A WAY OUT	Odyssey	*RCA*	2
24	30	BEST FRIEND-STAND DOWN MARGARET	Beat	*Go Feet*	6
-	31	STEREOTYPE/INTERNATIONAL JET SET	Specials	*2 Tone*	1
17	32	TOM HARK	Piranhas	*Sire*	8
32	33	GENERALS AND MAJORS/DON'T LOSE YOUR TEMPER	XTC	*Virgin*	3
18	34	I DIE: YOU DIE	Gary Numan	*Beggars Banquet*	5
-	35	AMIGO	Black Slate ●	*Ensign*	1
31	36	OOPS UPSIDE YOUR HEAD	Gap Band	*Mercury*	11
-	37	KILLER ON THE LOOSE	Thin Lizzy	*Vertigo*	1
39	[38]	YOU SHOOK ME ALL NIGHT LONG	AC/DC	*Atlantic*	2
29	39	UNITED	Judas Priest	*CBS*	4
-	40	GOTTA PULL MYSELF TOGETHER	Nolans	*Epic*	1

WEEK ENDING 4 OCTOBER 1980

LW	TW	Title	Artist	Label	Wks
1	[1]	DON'T STAND SO CLOSE TO ME	Police	*A&M*	2
3	[2]	MASTERBLASTER (JAMMIN')	Stevie Wonder	*Motown*	4
8	3	D.I.S.C.O.	Ottawan	*Carrere*	3
5	4	BAGGY TROUSERS	Madness	*Stiff*	4
2	5	ONE DAY I'LL FLY AWAY	Randy Crawford	*Warner Brothers*	5
13	6	MY OLD PIANO	Diana Ross	*Motown*	3
4	7	FEELS LIKE I'M IN LOVE	Kelly Marie	*Calibre*	9
7	8	ANOTHER ONE BITES THE DUST	Queen	*EMI*	4
6	9	IT'S ONLY LOVE/BEYOND THE REEF	Elvis Presley	*RCA*	6
35	10	AMIGO	Black Slate	*Ensign*	2
24	[11]	SEARCHING	Change	*WEA*	4
22	[12]	I GOT YOU	Split Enz	*A&M*	6
16	[13]	I OWE YOU ONE	Shalamar	*Solar*	5
10	14	EIGHTH DAY	Hazel O'Connor	*A&M*	7
9	15	MODERN GIRL	Sheena Easton	*EMI*	8
14	16	IT'S STILL ROCK 'N' ROLL TO ME	Billy Joel	*CBS*	8
25	[17]	THREE LITTLE BIRDS	Bob Marley and the Wailers	*Island*	3
37	18	KILLER ON THE LOOSE	Thin Lizzy	*Vertigo*	2
19	19	PARANOID	Black Sabbath	*Nems*	7
29	20	IF YOU'RE LOOKIN' FOR A WAY OUT	Odyssey	*RCA*	3
12	21	DREAMIN'	Cliff Richard	*EMI*	7
-	22	TROUBLE	Gillan ●	*Virgin*	1
-	23	YOU'RE LYING	Linx ●	*Chrysalis*	1
20	24	A WALK IN THE PARK	Nick Straker Band	*Polydor*	8
31	25	STEREOTYPE/INTERNATIONAL JET SET	Specials	*2 Tone*	2
21	26	MARIE MARIE	Shakin' Stevens	*Epic*	7
27	27	TWO LITTLE BOYS/HORSE	Splodgenessabounds	*Deram*	4
40	28	GOTTA PULL MYSELF TOGETHER	Nolans	*Epic*	2
-	29	CASANOVA	Coffee ●	*De-Lite*	1
18	30	SUNSHINE OF YOUR SMILE	Mike Berry	*Polydor*	9
17	31	9 TO 5	Sheena Easton	*EMI*	11
11	32	START	Jam	*Polydor*	7
32	33	TOM HARK	Piranhas	*Sire*	9
30	34	BEST FRIEND-STAND DOWN MARGARET	Beat	*Go Feet*	7
28	35	I WANT TO BE STRAIGHT	Ian Dury and the Blockheads	*Stiff*	6
15	36	ASHES TO ASHES	David Bowie	*RCA*	8
33	37	GENERALS AND MAJORS/DON'T LOSE YOUR TEMPER	XTC	*Virgin*	4
-	38	WHEN YOU ASK ABOUT LOVE	Matchbox	*Magnet*	1

In these weeks ■ Seven acts who made their chart debut in the 50s or 60s are represented: Elvis (1956), Mike Berry (1961), Diana Ross (1964), Stevie Wonder (1966), Gladys Knight (1967) and David Bowie (1969) (20.09.80) ■ The Police become the second group to score an instant number one this year (27.09.80) ■ Stevie Wonder has his third number two in nearly 15 years, without, as yet a number one (04.10.80)■

LW	TW	Title	Artist	Label	Wks
23	39	CAN'T STOP THE MUSIC	Village People	Mercury	8
-	40	WHAT'S IN A KISS	Gilbert O'Sullivan	CBS	1

October 1980

□ Highest position disc reached ● Act's first ever week on chart

WEEK ENDING 11 OCTOBER 1980

LW	TW	Title	Artist	Label	Wks
1	□1	DON'T STAND SO CLOSE TO ME	Police	A&M	3
3	□2	D.I.S.C.O.	Ottawan	Carrere	4
4	□3	BAGGY TROUSERS	Madness	Stiff	5
2	4	MASTERBLASTER (JAMMIN')	Stevie Wonder	Motown	5
6	□5	MY OLD PIANO	Diana Ross	Motown	4
25	□6	STEREOTYPE/INTERNATIONAL JET SET	Specials	2 Tone	3
20	7	IF YOU'RE LOOKIN' FOR A WAY OUT	Odyssey	RCA	4
5	8	ONE DAY I'LL FLY AWAY	Randy Crawford	Warner Brothers	6
10	□9	AMIGO	Black Slate	Ensign	3
18	□10	KILLER ON THE LOOSE	Thin Lizzy	Vertigo	3
-	11	ET LES OISEAUX CHANTAIENT (AND THE BIRDS WERE SINGING)	Sweet People ●	Polydor	1
7	12	FEELS LIKE I'M IN LOVE	Kelly Marie	Calibre	10
11	13	SEARCHING	Change	WEA	5
22	□14	TROUBLE	Gillan	Virgin	2
38	15	WHEN YOU ASK ABOUT LOVE	Matchbox	Magnet	2
8	16	ANOTHER ONE BITES THE DUST	Queen	EMI	5
17	□17	THREE LITTLE BIRDS	Bob Marley and the Wailers	Island	4
12	18	I GOT YOU	Split Enz	A&M	7
29	19	CASANOVA	Coffee	De-Lite	2
9	20	IT'S ONLY LOVE/BEYOND THE REEF	Elvis Presley	RCA	7
13	21	I OWE YOU ONE	Shalamar	Solar	6
-	22	WOMAN IN LOVE	Barbra Streisand	CBS	1
23	23	YOU'RE LYING	Linx	Chrysalis	2
14	24	EIGHTH DAY	Hazel O'Connor	A&M	8
28	25	GOTTA PULL MYSELF TOGETHER	Nolans	Epic	3
-	26	LOVE X LOVE	George Benson	Warner Brothers	1
-	27	WHAT YOU'RE PROPOSING	Status Quo	Vertigo	1
16	28	IT'S STILL ROCK 'N' ROLL TO ME	Billy Joel	CBS	9
15	29	MODERN GIRL	Sheena Easton	EMI	9
19	30	PARANOID	Black Sabbath	Nems	8
-	31	ALL OUT OF LOVE	Air Supply ●	Arista	1
21	32	DREAMIN'	Cliff Richard	EMI	8
-	33	ARMY DREAMERS	Kate Bush	EMI	1
-	34	PARTY LIGHTS	Gap Band	Mercury	1
-	35	ENOLA GAY	Orchestral Manoeuvres In The Dark	Dindisc	1
40	36	WHAT'S IN A KISS	Gilbert O'Sullivan	CBS	2
24	37	A WALK IN THE PARK	Nick Straker Band	Polydor	9
-	38	SPECIAL BREW	Bad Manners	Magnet	1
27	39	TWO LITTLE BOYS/HORSE	Splodgenessabounds	Deram	5
31	40	9 TO 5	Sheena Easton	EMI	12

WEEK ENDING 18 OCTOBER 1980

LW	TW	Title	Artist	Label	Wks
1	□1	DON'T STAND SO CLOSE TO ME	Police	A&M	4
2	□2	D.I.S.C.O.	Ottawan	Carrere	5
3	□3	BAGGY TROUSERS	Madness	Stiff	6
11	□4	ET LES OISEAUX CHANTAIENT (AND THE BIRDS WERE SINGING)	Sweet People	Polydor	2
27	5	WHAT YOU'RE PROPOSING	Status Quo	Vertigo	2
4	6	MASTERBLASTER (JAMMIN')	Stevie Wonder	Motown	6
7	7	IF YOU'RE LOOKIN' FOR A WAY OUT	Odyssey	RCA	5
5	8	MY OLD PIANO	Diana Ross	Motown	5
22	9	WOMAN IN LOVE	Barbra Streisand	CBS	2
15	10	WHEN YOU ASK ABOUT LOVE	Matchbox	Magnet	3
9	11	AMIGO	Black Slate	Ensign	4
10	12	KILLER ON THE LOOSE	Thin Lizzy	Vertigo	4
19	□13	CASANOVA	Coffee	De-Lite	3
25	14	GOTTA PULL MYSELF TOGETHER	Nolans	Epic	4
23	□15	YOU'RE LYING	Linx	Chrysalis	3
13	16	SEARCHING	Change	WEA	6
17	□17	THREE LITTLE BIRDS	Bob Marley and the Wailers	Island	5
35	18	ENOLA GAY	Orchestral Manoeuvres In The Dark	Dindisc	2
8	19	ONE DAY I'LL FLY AWAY	Randy Crawford	Warner Brothers	7
14	20	TROUBLE	Gillan	Virgin	3
26	21	LOVE X LOVE	George Benson	Warner Brothers	2
6	22	STEREOTYPE/INTERNATIONAL JET SET	Specials	2 Tone	4
16	23	ANOTHER ONE BITES THE DUST	Queen	EMI	6
31	24	ALL OUT OF LOVE	Air Supply	Arista	2
38	25	SPECIAL BREW	Bad Manners	Magnet	2
33	26	ARMY DREAMERS	Kate Bush	EMI	2
12	27	FEELS LIKE I'M IN LOVE	Kelly Marie	Calibre	11
18	28	I GOT YOU	Split Enz	A&M	8
36	29	WHAT'S IN A KISS	Gilbert O'Sullivan	CBS	3
21	30	I OWE YOU ONE	Shalamar	Solar	7
20	31	IT'S ONLY LOVE/BEYOND THE REEF	Elvis Presley	RCA	8
34	32	PARTY LIGHTS	Gap Band	Mercury	2
-	□33	SHE'S SO COLD	Rolling Stones	Rolling Stones	1
-	34	I NEED YOUR LOVIN'	Teena Marie	Motown	1
-	35	LET ME TALK	Earth Wind And Fire	CBS	1
-	36	WHY DO LOVERS BREAK EACH OTHERS HEARTS	Showaddywaddy	Arista	1
-	37	DOG EAT DOG	Adam and the Ants ●	CBS	1
29	38	MODERN GIRL	Sheena Easton	EMI	10
30	39	PARANOID	Black Sabbath	Nems	9
24	40	EIGHTH DAY	Hazel O'Connor	A&M	9

WEEK ENDING 25 OCTOBER 1980

LW	TW	Title	Artist	Label	Wks
9	□1	WOMAN IN LOVE	Barbra Streisand	CBS	3
2	□2	D.I.S.C.O.	Ottawan	Carrere	6
1	3	DON'T STAND SO CLOSE TO ME	Police	A&M	5
5	4	WHAT YOU'RE PROPOSING	Status Quo	Vertigo	3
3	5	BAGGY TROUSERS	Madness	Stiff	7
10	6	WHEN YOU ASK ABOUT LOVE	Matchbox	Magnet	4
7	7	IF YOU'RE LOOKIN' FOR A WAY OUT	Odyssey	RCA	6
4	8	ET LES OISEAUX CHANTAIENT (AND THE BIRDS WERE SINGING)	Sweet People	Polydor	3
14	□9	GOTTA PULL MYSELF TOGETHER	Nolans	Epic	5
21	□10	LOVE X LOVE	George Benson	Warner Brothers	3
8	11	MY OLD PIANO	Diana Ross	Motown	6
18	12	ENOLA GAY	Orchestral Manoeuvres In The Dark	Dindisc	3
13	□13	CASANOVA	Coffee	De-Lite	4
6	14	MASTERBLASTER (JAMMIN')	Stevie Wonder	Motown	7
25	15	SPECIAL BREW	Bad Manners	Magnet	3
11	16	AMIGO	Black Slate	Ensign	5
15	17	YOU'RE LYING	Linx	Chrysalis	4
12	18	KILLER ON THE LOOSE	Thin Lizzy	Vertigo	5
37	19	DOG EAT DOG	Adam and the Ants	CBS	2
24	20	ALL OUT OF LOVE	Air Supply	Arista	3
16	21	SEARCHING	Change	WEA	7
17	22	THREE LITTLE BIRDS	Bob Marley and the Wailers	Island	6
22	23	STEREOTYPE/INTERNATIONAL JET SET	Specials	2 Tone	5
36	24	WHY DO LOVERS BREAK EACH OTHERS HEARTS	Showaddywaddy	Arista	2
20	25	TROUBLE	Gillan	Virgin	4
26	26	ARMY DREAMERS	Kate Bush	EMI	3
29	27	WHAT'S IN A KISS	Gilbert O'Sullivan	CBS	4
34	□28	I NEED YOUR LOVIN'	Teena Marie	Motown	2
35	□29	LET ME TALK	Earth Wind And Fire	CBS	2
19	30	ONE DAY I'LL FLY AWAY	Randy Crawford	Warner Brothers	8
-	□31	TOWERS OF LONDON	XTC	Virgin	1
32	32	PARTY LIGHTS	Gap Band	Mercury	3
-	33	NEVER KNEW LOVE LIKE THIS BEFORE	Stephanie Mills ●	20th Century	1
27	34	FEELS LIKE I'M IN LOVE	Kelly Marie	Calibre	12
33	35	SHE'S SO COLD	Rolling Stones	Rolling Stones	2
23	36	ANOTHER ONE BITES THE DUST	Queen	EMI	7
-	37	LOVING JUST FOR FUN	Kelly Marie	Calibre	1
-	38	ONE MAN WOMAN	Sheena Easton	EMI	1
30	39	I OWE YOU ONE	Shalamar	Solar	8
-	□40	DON'T SAY I TOLD YOU SO	Tourists	RCA	1

■Gilbert O'Sullivan returns to the chart after a five year hiatus (04.10.80) ■ Adam and the Ants debut inauspiciously at number 37 (18.10.80) ■ Barbra Streisand leads the pack with the biggest hit of her 15 year career. There are eight other female soloists behind her (25.10.80)■

November 1980

□ Highest position disc reached ● Act's first ever week on chart

LW	TW	*WEEK ENDING* 1 NOVEMBER 1980		Wks
1	1	WOMAN IN LOVE Barbra Streisand	*CBS*	4
4	2	WHAT YOU'RE PROPOSING Status Quo	*Vertigo*	4
2	3	D.I.S.C.O. Ottawan	*Carrere*	7
6	4	WHEN YOU ASK ABOUT LOVE Matchbox	*Magnet*	5
15	5	SPECIAL BREW Bad Manners	*Magnet*	4
7	6	IF YOU'RE LOOKIN' FOR A WAY OUT Odyssey	*RCA*	7
5	7	BAGGY TROUSERS Madness	*Stiff*	8
12	8	ENOLA GAY Orchestral Manoeuvres In The Dark	*Dindisc*	4
9	9	GOTTA PULL MYSELF TOGETHER Nolans	*Epic*	6
3	10	DON'T STAND SO CLOSE TO ME Police	*A&M*	6
20	11	ALL OUT OF LOVE Air Supply	*Arista*	4
10	12	LOVE X LOVE George Benson	*Warner Brothers*	4
19	13	DOG EAT DOG Adam and the Ants	*CBS*	3
8	14	ET LES OISEAUX CHANTAIENT (AND THE BIRDS WERE SINGING) Sweet People	*Polydor*	4
13	15	CASANOVA Coffee	*De-Lite*	5
26	16	ARMY DREAMERS Kate Bush	*EMI*	4
38	17	ONE MAN WOMAN Sheena Easton	*EMI*	2
17	18	YOU'RE LYING Linx	*Chrysalis*	5
27	19	WHAT'S IN A KISS Gilbert O'Sullivan	*CBS*	5
-	20	FASHION David Bowie	*RCA*	1
37	21	LOVING JUST FOR FUN Kelly Marie	*Calibre*	2
24	22	WHY DO LOVERS BREAK EACH OTHER'S HEARTS Showaddywaddy	*Arista*	3
16	23	AMIGO Black Slate	*Ensign*	6
14	24	MASTERBLASTER (JAMMIN') Stevie Wonder	*Motown*	8
-	25	SUDDENLY Olivia Newton-John and Cliff Richard ●	*Jet*	1
33	26	NEVER KNEW LOVE LIKE THIS BEFORE Stephanie Mills	*20th Century*	2
18	27	KILLER ON THE LOOSE Thin Lizzy	*Vertigo*	6
11	28	MY OLD PIANO Diana Ross	*Motown*	7
-	29	LOVELY ONE Jacksons	*Epic*	1
32	30	PARTY LIGHTS Gap Band	*Mercury*	4
-	31	I COULD BE SO GOOD FOR YOU Dennis Waterman ●	*EMI*	1
28	32	I NEED YOUR LOVIN' Teena Marie	*Motown*	3
31	33	TOWERS OF LONDON XTC	*Virgin*	2
-	34	THE EARTH DIES SCREAMING/DREAM A LIE UB40	*Graduate*	1
29	35	LET ME TALK Earth Wind And Fire	*CBS*	3
21	36	SEARCHING Change	*WEA*	8
-	37	PARTY IN PARIS UK Subs	*Gem*	1
-	38	ACE OF SPADES Motorhead	*Bronze*	1
22	39	THREE LITTLE BIRDS Bob Marley and the Wailers	*Island*	7
25	40	TROUBLE Gillan	*Virgin*	5

LW	TW	*WEEK ENDING* 8 NOVEMBER 1980		Wks
1	1	WOMAN IN LOVE Barbra Streisand	*CBS*	5
2	2	WHAT YOU'RE PROPOSING Status Quo	*Vertigo*	5
5	3	SPECIAL BREW Bad Manners	*Magnet*	5
13	4	DOG EAT DOG Adam and the Ants	*CBS*	4
-	5	THE TIDE IS HIGH Blondie	*Chrysalis*	1
4	6	WHEN YOU ASK ABOUT LOVE Matchbox	*Magnet*	6
6	7	IF YOU'RE LOOKIN' FOR A WAY OUT Odyssey	*RCA*	8
20	8	FASHION David Bowie	*RCA*	2
8	9	ENOLA GAY Orchestral Manoeuvres In The Dark	*Dindisc*	5
3	10	D.I.S.C.O. Ottawan	*Carrere*	8
9	11	GOTTA PULL MYSELF TOGETHER Nolans	*Epic*	7
11	12	ALL OUT OF LOVE Air Supply	*Arista*	5
7	13	BAGGY TROUSERS Madness	*Stiff*	9
17	14	ONE MAN WOMAN Sheena Easton	*EMI*	3
25	15	SUDDENLY Olivia Newton-John and Cliff Richard	*Jet*	2
10	16	DON'T STAND SO CLOSE TO ME Police	*A&M*	7
16	17	ARMY DREAMERS Kate Bush	*EMI*	5
26	18	NEVER KNEW LOVE LIKE THIS BEFORE Stephanie Mills	*20th Century*	3
31	19	I COULD BE SO GOOD FOR YOU Dennis Waterman	*EMI*	2
12	20	LOVE X LOVE George Benson	*Warner Brothers*	5
38	21	ACE OF SPADES Motorhead	*Bronze*	2
21	22	LOVING JUST FOR FUN Kelly Marie	*Calibre*	3
22	23	WHY DO LOVERS BREAK EACH OTHER'S HEARTS Showaddywaddy	*Arista*	4
15	24	CASANOVA Coffee	*De-Lite*	6
34	25	THE EARTH DIES SCREAMING/DREAM A LIE UB40	*Graduate*	2
19	26	WHAT'S IN A KISS Gilbert O'Sullivan	*CBS*	6
14	27	ET LES OISEAUX CHANTAIENT (AND THE BIRDS WERE SINGING) Sweet People	*Polydor*	5
18	28	YOU'RE LYING Linx	*Chrysalis*	6
-	29	SAME OLD SCENE Roxy Music	*Polydor*	1
-	30	(JUST LIKE) STARTING OVER John Lennon	*Geffen*	1
29	31	LOVELY ONE Jacksons	*Epic*	2
23	32	AMIGO Black Slate	*Ensign*	7
-	33	CELEBRATION Kool and the Gang	*De-Lite*	1
24	34	MASTERBLASTER (JAMMIN') Stevie Wonder	*Motown*	9
30	35	PARTY LIGHTS Gap Band	*Mercury*	5
32	36	I NEED YOUR LOVIN' Teena Marie	*Motown*	4
-	37	PASSION Rod Stewart	*Riva*	1
-	38	THE NIGHT THE WINE AND THE ROSES Liquid Gold	*Polo*	1
-	39	I LIKE (WHAT YOU'RE DOING TO ME) Young & Co. ●	*Excalibur*	1
37	40	PARTY IN PARIS UK Subs	*Gem*	2

LW	TW	*WEEK ENDING* 15 NOVEMBER 1980		Wks
5	1	THE TIDE IS HIGH Blondie	*Chrysalis*	2
1	2	WOMAN IN LOVE Barbra Streisand	*CBS*	6
3	3	SPECIAL BREW Bad Manners	*Magnet*	6
19	4	I COULD BE SO GOOD FOR YOU Dennis Waterman	*EMI*	3
2	5	WHAT YOU'RE PROPOSING Status Quo	*Vertigo*	6
8	6	FASHION David Bowie	*RCA*	3
4	7	DOG EAT DOG Adam and the Ants	*CBS*	5
9	8	ENOLA GAY Orchestral Manoeuvres In The Dark	*Dindisc*	6
18	9	NEVER KNEW LOVE LIKE THIS BEFORE Stephanie Mills	*20th Century*	4
7	10	IF YOU'RE LOOKIN' FOR A WAY OUT Odyssey	*RCA*	9
6	11	WHEN YOU ASK ABOUT LOVE Matchbox	*Magnet*	7
29	12	SAME OLD SCENE Roxy Music	*Polydor*	2
-	13	SUPER TROUPER Abba	*Epic*	1
25	14	THE EARTH DIES SCREAMING/DREAM A LIE UB40	*Graduate*	3
21	15	ACE OF SPADES Motorhead	*Bronze*	3
11	16	GOTTA PULL MYSELF TOGETHER Nolans	*Epic*	8
15	17	SUDDENLY Olivia Newton-John and Cliff Richard	*Jet*	3
14	18	ONE MAN WOMAN Sheena Easton	*EMI*	4
12	19	ALL OUT OF LOVE Air Supply	*Arista*	6
30	20	(JUST LIKE) STARTING OVER John Lennon	*Geffen*	2
10	21	D.I.S.C.O. Ottawan	*Carrere*	9
33	22	CELEBRATION Kool and the Gang	*De-Lite*	2
13	23	BAGGY TROUSERS Madness	*Stiff*	10
22	24	LOVING JUST FOR FUN Kelly Marie	*Calibre*	4
17	25	ARMY DREAMERS Kate Bush	*EMI*	6
37	26	PASSION Rod Stewart	*Riva*	2
20	27	LOVE X LOVE George Benson	*Warner Brothers*	6
23	28	WHY DO LOVERS BREAK EACH OTHER'S HEARTS Showaddywaddy	*Arista*	5
26	29	WHAT'S IN A KISS Gilbert O'Sullivan	*CBS*	7
39	30	I LIKE (WHAT YOU'RE DOING TO ME) Young & Co.	*Excalibur*	2
16	31	DON'T STAND SO CLOSE TO ME Police	*A&M*	8
38	32	THE NIGHT THE WINE AND THE ROSES Liquid Gold	*Polo*	2
-	33	BOURGIE BOURGIE Gladys Knight and the Pips	*CBS*	1
-	34	I'M COMING OUT Diana Ross	*Motown*	1
-	35	WOMEN IN UNIFORM Iron Maiden	*EMI*	1
31	36	LOVELY ONE Jacksons	*Epic*	3
-	37	FALCON Rah Band	*DJM*	1
24	38	CASANOVA Coffee	*De-Lite*	7
-	39	INHERIT THE WIND Wilton Felder ●	*MCA*	1
-	40	LONELY TOGETHER Barry Manilow	*Arista*	1

In these weeks ■ Olivia Newton-John has enjoyed solo hits, hits with two different men and a whole group of them ... (01.11.80) ■ After five years John Lennon makes a welcome return to the charts (08.11.80) ■ Blondie score their fifth chart-topper and their third within a year (15.11.80)■

December 1980

□ Highest position disc reached ● Act's first ever week on chart

WEEK ENDING 22 NOVEMBER 1980

LW	TW	Title	Artist	Label	Wks
1	1	THE TIDE IS HIGH	Blondie	*Chrysalis*	3
13	2	SUPER TROUPER	Abba	*Epic*	2
2	3	WOMAN IN LOVE	Barbra Streisand	*CBS*	7
4	4	I COULD BE SO GOOD FOR YOU	Dennis Waterman	*EMI*	4
6	5	FASHION	David Bowie	*RCA*	4
9	6	NEVER KNEW LOVE LIKE THIS BEFORE	Stephanie Mills	*20th Century*	5
3	7	SPECIAL BREW	Bad Manners	*Magnet*	7
7	8	DOG EAT DOG	Adam and the Ants	*CBS*	6
8	9	ENOLA GAY	Orchestral Manoeuvres In The Dark	*Dindisc*	7
5	10	WHAT YOU'RE PROPOSING	Status Quo	*Vertigo*	7
14	11	THE EARTH DIES SCREAMING/DREAM A LIE	UB40	*Graduate*	4
22	12	CELEBRATION	Kool and the Gang	*De-Lite*	3
20	13	(JUST LIKE) STARTING OVER	John Lennon	*Geffen*	3
12	14	SAME OLD SCENE	Roxy Music	*Polydor*	3
15	15	ACE OF SPADES	Motorhead	*Bronze*	4
10	16	IF YOU'RE LOOKIN' FOR A WAY OUT	Odyssey	*RCA*	10
11	17	WHEN YOU ASK ABOUT LOVE	Matchbox	*Magnet*	8
34	18	I'M COMING OUT	Diana Ross	*Motown*	2
-	19	TO CUT A LONG STORY SHORT	Spandau Ballet ●	*Reformation*	1
17	20	SUDDENLY	Olivia Newton-John and Cliff Richard	*Jet*	4
19	21	ALL OUT OF LOVE	Air Supply	*Arista*	7
26	22	PASSION	Rod Stewart	*Riva*	3
-	23	BANANA REPUBLIC	Boomtown Rats	*Ensign*	1
16	24	GOTTA PULL MYSELF TOGETHER	Nolans	*Epic*	9
18	25	ONE MAN WOMAN	Sheena Easton	*EMI*	5
30	26	I LIKE (WHAT YOU'RE DOING TO ME)	Young & Co.	*Excalibur*	3
21	27	D.I.S.C.O.	Ottawan	*Carrere*	10
24	28	LOVING JUST FOR FUN	Kelly Marie	*Calibre*	5
25	29	ARMY DREAMERS	Kate Bush	*EMI*	7
-	30	DO YOU FEEL MY LOVE	Eddy Grant	*Ensign*	1
-	31	EMBARRASSMENT	Madness	*Stiff*	1
33	32	BOURGIE BOURGIE	Gladys Knight and the Pips	*CBS*	2
32	33	THE NIGHT THE WINE AND THE ROSES	Liquid Gold	*Polo*	3
-	34	LADY	Kenny Rogers	*United Artists*	1
37	35	FALCON	Rah Band	*DJM*	2
40	36	LONELY TOGETHER	Barry Manilow	*Arista*	2
28	37	WHY DO LOVERS BREAK EACH OTHER'S HEARTS	Showaddywaddy	*Arista*	6
23	38	BAGGY TROUSERS	Madness	*Stiff*	11
35	39	WOMEN IN UNIFORM	Iron Maiden	*EMI*	2
-	40	DON'T WALK AWAY	Electric Light Orchestra	*Jet*	1

WEEK ENDING 29 NOVEMBER 1980

LW	TW	Title	Artist	Label	Wks
2	1	SUPER TROUPER	Abba	*Epic*	3
1	2	THE TIDE IS HIGH	Blondie	*Chrysalis*	4
4	3	I COULD BE SO GOOD FOR YOU	Dennis Waterman	*EMI*	5
6	4	NEVER KNEW LOVE LIKE THIS BEFORE	Stephanie Mills	*20th Century*	6
5	5	FASHION	David Bowie	*RCA*	5
3	6	WOMAN IN LOVE	Barbra Streisand	*CBS*	8
12	7	CELEBRATION	Kool and the Gang	*De-Lite*	4
13	8	(JUST LIKE) STARTING OVER	John Lennon	*Geffen*	4
23	9	BANANA REPUBLIC	Boomtown Rats	*Ensign*	2
11	10	THE EARTH DIES SCREAMING/DREAM A LIE	UB40	*Graduate*	5
19	11	TO CUT A LONG STORY SHORT	Spandau Ballet	*Reformation*	2
31	12	EMBARRASSMENT	Madness	*Stiff*	2
9	13	ENOLA GAY	Orchestral Manoeuvres In The Dark	*Dindisc*	8
7	14	SPECIAL BREW	Bad Manners	*Magnet*	8
30	15	DO YOU FEEL MY LOVE	Eddy Grant	*Ensign*	2
14	16	SAME OLD SCENE	Roxy Music	*Polydor*	4
22	17	PASSION	Rod Stewart	*Riva*	4
18	18	I'M COMING OUT	Diana Ross	*Motown*	3
8	19	DOG EAT DOG	Adam and the Ants	*CBS*	7
26	20	I LIKE (WHAT YOU'RE DOING TO ME)	Young & Co.	*Excalibur*	4
10	21	WHAT YOU'RE PROPOSING	Status Quo	*Vertigo*	8
15	22	ACE OF SPADES	Motorhead	*Bronze*	5
-	23	ROCK 'N' ROLL AIN'T NOISE POLLUTION	AC/DC	*Atlantic*	1
16	24	IF YOU'RE LOOKIN' FOR A WAY OUT	Odyssey	*RCA*	11
34	25	LADY	Kenny Rogers	*United Artists*	2
40	26	DON'T WALK AWAY	Electric Light Orchestra	*Jet*	2
20	27	SUDDENLY	Olivia Newton-John and Cliff Richard	*Jet*	5
17	28	WHEN YOU ASK ABOUT LOVE	Matchbox	*Magnet*	9
36	29	LONELY TOGETHER	Barry Manilow	*Arista*	3
25	30	ONE MAN WOMAN	Sheena Easton	*EMI*	6
-	31	LOVE ON THE ROCKS	Neil Diamond	*Capitol*	1
28	32	LOVING JUST FOR FUN	Kelly Marie	*Calibre*	6
-	33	KISS ON MY LIST	Daryl Hall and John Oates ●	*RCA*	1
27	34	D.I.S.C.O.	Ottawan	*Carrere*	11
-	35	THERE'S NO ONE QUITE LIKE GRANDMA	St Winifred's School Choir ●	*MFP*	1
32	36	BOURGIE BOURGIE	Gladys Knight and the Pips	*CBS*	3
21	37	ALL OUT OF LOVE	Air Supply	*Arista*	8
35	38	FALCON	Rah Band	*DJM*	3
33	39	THE NIGHT THE WINE AND THE ROSES	Liquid Gold	*Polo*	4
-	40	GIRLS CAN GET IT	Dr. Hook	*Mercury*	1

WEEK ENDING 6 DECEMBER 1980

LW	TW	Title	Artist	Label	Wks
1	1	SUPER TROUPER	Abba	*Epic*	4
2	2	THE TIDE IS HIGH	Blondie	*Chrysalis*	5
9	3	BANANA REPUBLIC	Boomtown Rats	*Ensign*	3
12	4	EMBARRASSMENT	Madness	*Stiff*	3
11	5	TO CUT A LONG STORY SHORT	Spandau Ballet	*Reformation*	3
3	6	I COULD BE SO GOOD FOR YOU	Dennis Waterman	*EMI*	6
4	7	NEVER KNEW LOVE LIKE THIS BEFORE	Stephanie Mills	*20th Century*	7
7	8	CELEBRATION	Kool and the Gang	*De-Lite*	5
15	9	DO YOU FEEL MY LOVE	Eddy Grant	*Ensign*	3
8	10	(JUST LIKE) STARTING OVER	John Lennon	*Geffen*	5
10	11	THE EARTH DIES SCREAMING/DREAM A LIE	UB40	*Graduate*	6
5	12	FASHION	David Bowie	*RCA*	6
18	13	I'M COMING OUT	Diana Ross	*Motown*	4
6	14	WOMAN IN LOVE	Barbra Streisand	*CBS*	9
-	15	STOP THE CAVALRY	Jona Lewie	*Stiff*	1
35	16	THERE'S NO ONE QUITE LIKE GRANDMA	St Winifred's School Choir	*MFP*	2
23	17	ROCK 'N' ROLL AIN'T NOISE POLLUTION	AC/DC	*Atlantic*	2
22	18	ACE OF SPADES	Motorhead	*Bronze*	6
17	19	PASSION	Rod Stewart	*Riva*	5
20	20	I LIKE (WHAT YOU'RE DOING TO ME)	Young & Co.	*Excalibur*	5
26	21	DON'T WALK AWAY	Electric Light Orchestra	*Jet*	3
25	22	LADY	Kenny Rogers	*United Artists*	3
-	23	RUNAWAY BOYS	Stray Cats ●	*Arista*	1
16	24	SAME OLD SCLNE	Roxy Music	*Polydor*	5
14	25	SPECIAL BREW	Bad Manners	*Magnet*	9
13	26	ENOLA GAY	Orchestral Manoeuvres In The Dark	*Dindisc*	9
31	27	LOVE ON THE ROCKS	Neil Diamond	*Capitol*	2
19	28	DOG EAT DOG	Adam and the Ants	*CBS*	8
29	29	LONELY TOGETHER	Barry Manilow	*Arista*	4
-	30	FLASH	Queen	*EMI*	1
-	31	ANTMUSIC	Adam and the Ants	*CBS*	1
21	32	WHAT YOU'RE PROPOSING	Status Quo	*Vertigo*	9
-	33	LOOKING FOR CLUES	Robert Palmer ●	*Island*	1
-	34	LIES	Status Quo	*Vertigo*	1
-	35	BLUE MOON	Showaddywaddy	*Arista*	1
33	36	KISS ON MY LIST	Daryl Hall and John Oates	*RCA*	2
24	37	IF YOU'RE LOOKIN' FOR A WAY OUT	Odyssey	*RCA*	12
-	38	OVER THE RAINBOW/YOU BELONG TO ME	Matchbox	*Magnet*	1
-	39	DECEMBER WILL BE MAGIC AGAIN	Kate Bush	*EMI*	1
-	40	THE CALL UP	Clash	*CBS*	1

■A golden year for Madness: five hits, (two in the same chart this week), four top tens and 33 weeks on the chart (22.11.80) ■ Abba claim their ninth and final number one surpassing the Rolling Stones in this category. Only the Beatles, Elvis and Cliff can better their total (29.11.80)■

December 1980

[n] Highest position disc reached ● Act's first ever week on chart

WEEK ENDING 13 DECEMBER 1980

LW	TW	Title	Artist	Label	Wks
1	[1]	SUPER TROUPER	Abba	Epic	5
16	2	THERE'S NO ONE QUITE LIKE GRANDMA	St Winifred's School Choir	MFP	3
15	[3]	STOP THE CAVALRY	Jona Lewie	Stiff	2
4	[4]	EMBARRASSMENT	Madness	Stiff	4
3	5	BANANA REPUBLIC	Boomtown Rats	Ensign	4
5	6	TO CUT A LONG STORY SHORT	Spandau Ballet	Reformation	4
2	7	THE TIDE IS HIGH	Blondie	Chrysalis	6
9	[8]	DO YOU FEEL MY LOVE	Eddy Grant	Ensign	4
-	9	DE DO DO DO DE DA DA DA	Police	A&M	1
23	10	RUNAWAY BOYS	Stray Cats	Arista	2
8	11	CELEBRATION	Kool and the Gang	De-Lite	6
22	[12]	LADY	Kenny Rogers	United Artists	4
7	13	NEVER KNEW LOVE LIKE THIS BEFORE	Stephanie Mills	20th Century	8
6	14	I COULD BE SO GOOD FOR YOU	Dennis Waterman	EMI	7
17	[15]	ROCK 'N' ROLL AIN'T NOISE POLLUTION	AC/DC	Atlantic	3
31	16	ANTMUSIC	Adam and the Ants	CBS	2
34	17	LIES	Status Quo	Vertigo	2
11	18	THE EARTH DIES SCREAMING/DREAM A LIE	UB40	Graduate	7
13	19	I'M COMING OUT	Diana Ross	Motown	5
30	20	FLASH	Queen	EMI	2
10	21	(JUST LIKE) STARTING OVER	John Lennon	Geffen	6
27	22	LOVE ON THE ROCKS	Neil Diamond	Capitol	3
21	23	DON'T WALK AWAY	Electric Light Orchestra	Jet	4
12	24	FASHION	David Bowie	RCA	7
29	25	LONELY TOGETHER	Barry Manilow	Arista	5
20	26	I LIKE (WHAT YOU'RE DOING TO ME)	Young & Co.	Excalibur	6
14	27	WOMAN IN LOVE	Barbra Streisand	CBS	10
19	28	PASSION	Rod Stewart	Riva	6
39	[29]	DECEMBER WILL BE MAGIC AGAIN	Kate Bush	EMI	2
18	30	ACE OF SPADES	Motorhead	Bronze	7
38	31	OVER THE RAINBOW/YOU BELONG TO ME	Matchbox	Magnet	2
35	[32]	BLUE MOON	Showaddywaddy	Arista	2
33	[33]	LOOKING FOR CLUES	Robert Palmer	Island	2
-	34	RABBIT	Chas and Dave	Rockney	1
24	35	SAME OLD SCENE	Roxy Music	Polydor	6
-	36	NEVER MIND THE PRESENTS	Barron Knights	Epic	1
-	37	LORRAINE	Bad Manners	Magnet	1
36	38	KISS ON MY LIST	Daryl Hall and John Oates	RCA	3
26	39	ENOLA GAY	Orchestral Manoeuvres In The Dark	Dindisc	10
-	40	WHO'S GONNA ROCK YOU	Nolans	Epic	1

WEEK ENDING 20 DECEMBER 1980

LW	TW	Title	Artist	Label	Wks
21	[1]	(JUST LIKE) STARTING OVER	John Lennon	Geffen	7
2	2	THERE'S NO ONE QUITE LIKE GRANDMA	St Winifred's School Choir	MFP	4
3	[3]	STOP THE CAVALRY	Jona Lewie	Stiff	3
1	4	SUPER TROUPER	Abba	Epic	6
9	[5]	DE DO DO DO DE DA DA DA	Police	A&M	2
4	6	EMBARRASSMENT	Madness	Stiff	5
5	7	BANANA REPUBLIC	Boomtown Rats	Ensign	5
6	8	TO CUT A LONG STORY SHORT	Spandau Ballet	Reformation	5
10	[9]	RUNAWAY BOYS	Stray Cats	Arista	3
16	10	ANTMUSIC	Adam and the Ants	CBS	3
8	11	DO YOU FEEL MY LOVE	Eddy Grant	Ensign	5
20	12	FLASH	Queen	EMI	3
12	13	LADY	Kenny Rogers	United Artists	5
7	14	THE TIDE IS HIGH	Blondie	Chrysalis	7
17	15	LIES/DON'T DRIVE MY CAR	Status Quo	Vertigo	3
11	16	CELEBRATION	Kool and the Gang	De-Lite	7
15	17	ROCK 'N' ROLL AIN'T NOISE POLLUTION	AC/DC	Atlantic	4
34	18	RABBIT	Chas and Dave	Rockney	2
22	19	LOVE ON THE ROCKS	Neil Diamond	Capitol	4
13	20	NEVER KNEW LOVE LIKE THIS BEFORE	Stephanie Mills	20th Century	9
19	21	I'M COMING OUT	Diana Ross	Motown	6
18	22	THE EARTH DIES SCREAMING/DREAM A LIE	UB40	Graduate	8
23	23	DON'T WALK AWAY	Electric Light Orchestra	Jet	5
31	24	OVER THE RAINBOW/YOU BELONG TO ME	Matchbox	Magnet	3
25	25	LONELY TOGETHER	Barry Manilow	Arista	6
14	26	I COULD BE SO GOOD FOR YOU	Dennis Waterman	EMI	8
36	27	NEVER MIND THE PRESENTS	Barron Knights	Epic	2
26	28	I LIKE (WHAT YOU'RE DOING TO ME)	Young & Co.	Excalibur	7
28	29	PASSION	Rod Stewart	Riva	7
29	30	DECEMBER WILL BE MAGIC AGAIN	Kate Bush	EMI	3
-	31	TOO NICE TO TALK TO	Beat	Go Feet	1
32	[32]	BLUE MOON	Showaddywaddy	Arista	3
33	[33]	LOOKING FOR CLUES	Robert Palmer	Island	3
-	34	DO NOTHING	Specials	2 Tone	1
-	35	THIS WRECKAGE	Gary Numan	Beggars Banquet	1
-	36	IT'S HARD TO BE HUMBLE	Mac Davis	Casablanca	1
30	37	ACE OF SPADES	Motorhead	Bronze	8
37	38	LORRAINE	Bad Manners	Magnet	2
40	39	WHO'S GONNA ROCK YOU	Nolans	Epic	2
-	40	IF I COULD ONLY MAKE YOU CARE	Mike Berry	Polydor	1

WEEK ENDING 27 DECEMBER 1980

LW	TW	Title	Artist	Label	Wks
2	[1]	THERE'S NO ONE QUITE LIKE GRANDMA	St Winifred's School Choir	MFP	5
1	2	(JUST LIKE) STARTING OVER	John Lennon	Geffen	8
3	[3]	STOP THE CAVALRY	Jona Lewie	Stiff	4
-	4	HAPPY CHRISTMAS (WAR IS OVER)	John Lennon	Apple	1
4	5	SUPER TROUPER	Abba	Epic	7
5	6	DE DO DO DO DE DA DA DA	Police	A&M	3
10	7	ANTMUSIC	Adam and the Ants	CBS	4
6	8	EMBARRASSMENT	Madness	Stiff	6
-	9	IMAGINE	John Lennon	Parlophone	1
9	10	RUNAWAY BOYS	Stray Cats	Arista	4
7	11	BANANA REPUBLIC	Boomtown Rats	Ensign	6
15	12	LIES/DON'T DRIVE MY CAR	Status Quo	Vertigo	4
18	13	RABBIT	Chas and Dave	Rockney	3
13	14	LADY	Kenny Rogers	United Artists	6
12	15	FLASH	Queen	EMI	4
8	16	TO CUT A LONG STORY SHORT	Spandau Ballet	Reformation	6
27	[17]	NEVER MIND THE PRESENTS	Barron Knights	Epic	3
19	18	LOVE ON THE ROCKS	Neil Diamond	Capitol	5
24	19	OVER THE RAINBOW/YOU BELONG TO ME	Matchbox	Magnet	4
14	20	THE TIDE IS HIGH	Blondie	Chrysalis	8
11	21	DO YOU FEEL MY LOVE	Eddy Grant	Ensign	6
25	22	LONELY TOGETHER	Barry Manilow	Arista	7
31	23	TOO NICE TO TALK TO	Beat	Go Feet	2
34	24	DO NOTHING	Specials	2 Tone	2
16	25	CELEBRATION	Kool and the Gang	De-Lite	8
23	26	DON'T WALK AWAY	Electric Light Orchestra	Jet	6
17	27	ROCK 'N' ROLL AIN'T NOISE POLLUTION	AC/DC	Atlantic	5
35	28	THIS WRECKAGE	Gary Numan	Beggars Banquet	2
36	29	IT'S HARD TO BE HUMBLE	Mac Davis	Casablanca	2
26	30	I COULD BE SO GOOD FOR YOU	Dennis Waterman	EMI	9
39	31	WHO'S GONNA ROCK YOU	Nolans	Epic	3
30	32	DECEMBER WILL BE MAGIC AGAIN	Kate Bush	EMI	4
33	[33]	LOOKING FOR CLUES	Robert Palmer	Island	4
32	34	BLUE MOON	Showaddywaddy	Arista	4
21	35	I'M COMING OUT	Diana Ross	Motown	7
38	36	LORRAINE	Bad Manners	Magnet	3
40	37	IF I COULD ONLY MAKE YOU CARE	Mike Berry	Polydor	2
22	38	THE EARTH DIES SCREAMING/DREAM A LIE	UB40	Graduate	9
20	39	NEVER KNEW LOVE LIKE THIS BEFORE	Stephanie Mills	20th Century	10
-	40	RUNAROUND SUE	Racey	RAK	1

In these weeks ■ After John Lennon's tragic death *Just Like Starting Over* rebounds 20 places to number one. Only *Hey Jude* and Elvis' *Surrender* have made similar dramatic moves (20.12.80) ■ Lennon becomes the first artist since Ruby Murray on 25.03.55 to place three discs in the Top Ten (27.12.80)■

1981

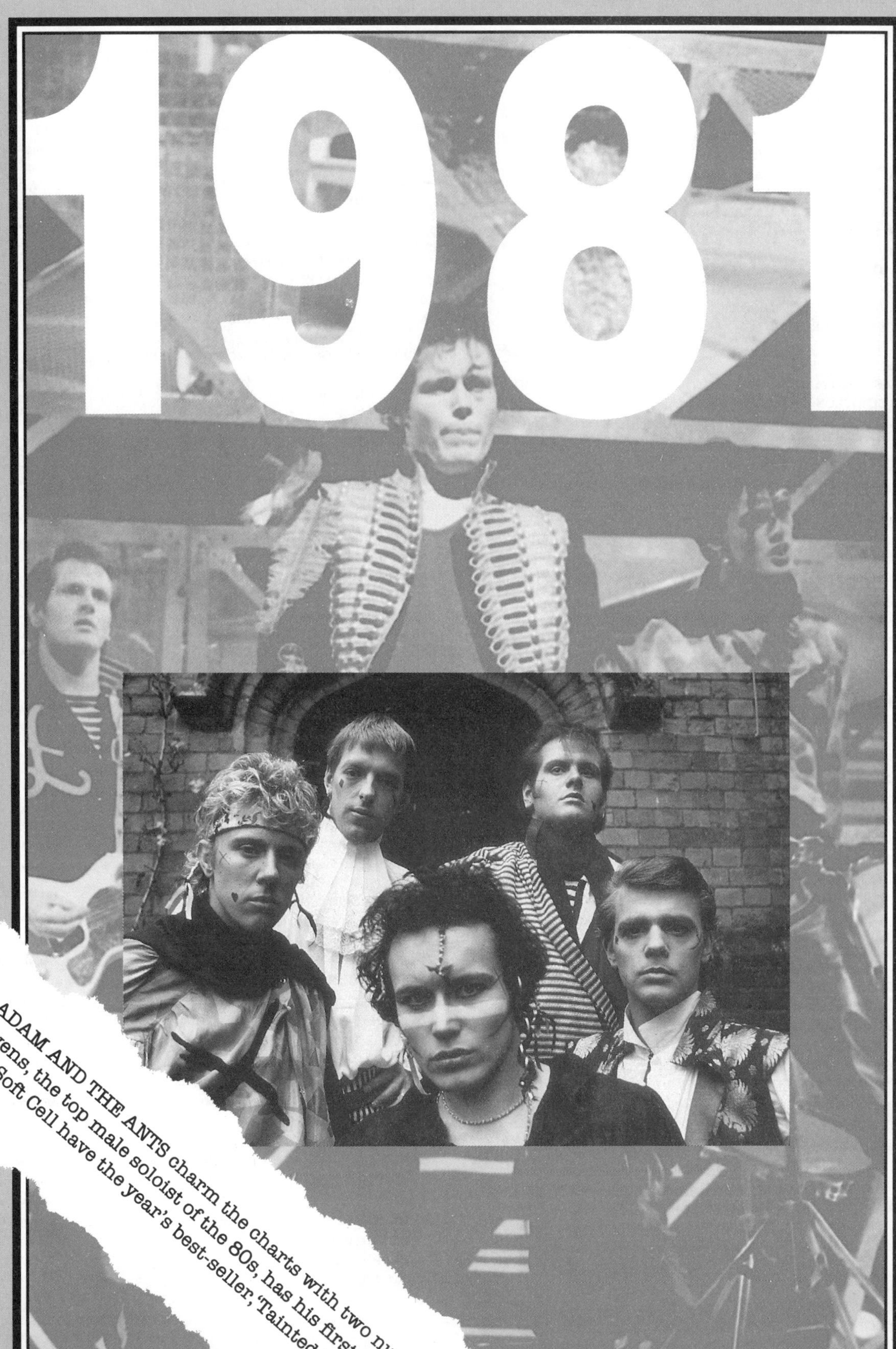

.........ADAM AND THE ANTS charm the charts with two number ones.......
akin' Stevens, the top male soloist of the 80s, has his first two number ones.......
Soft Cell have the year's best-seller, 'Tainted Love'.........

January 1981

□ Highest position disc reached ● Act's first ever week on chart

WEEK ENDING 3 JANUARY 1981

(no chart compiled: chart of 27 December 1980 repeated)

LW	TW	Title	Artist	Label	Wks
1	[1]	THERE'S NO ONE QUITE LIKE GRANDMA	St Winifred's School Choir	MFP	6
2	2	(JUST LIKE) STARTING OVER	John Lennon	Geffen	9
3	[3]	STOP THE CAVALRY	Jona Lewie	Stiff	5
4	4	HAPPY CHRISTMAS (WAR IS OVER)	John Lennon	Apple	2
5	5	SUPER TROUPER	Abba	Epic	8
6	6	DE DO DO DO DE DA DA DA	Police	A&M	4
7	7	ANTMUSIC	Adam and the Ants	CBS	5
8	8	EMBARRASSMENT	Madness	Stiff	7
9	9	IMAGINE	John Lennon	Parlophone	2
10	10	RUNAWAY BOYS	Stray Cats	Arista	5
11	11	BANANA REPUBLIC	Boomtown Rats	Ensign	7
12	12	LIES/DON'T DRIVE MY CAR	Status Quo	Vertigo	5
13	13	RABBIT	Chas and Dave	Rockney	4
14	14	LADY	Kenny Rogers	United Artists	7
15	15	FLASH	Queen	EMI	5
16	16	TO CUT A LONG STORY SHORT	Spandau Ballet	Reformation	7
17	[17]	NEVER MIND THE PRESENTS	Barron Knights	Epic	4
18	18	LOVE ON THE ROCKS	Neil Diamond	Capitol	6
19	19	OVER THE RAINBOW/YOU BELONG TO ME	Matchbox	Magnet	5
20	20	THE TIDE IS HIGH	Blondie	Chrysalis	9
21	21	DO YOU FEEL MY LOVE	Eddy Grant	Ensign	7
22	22	LONELY TOGETHER	Barry Manilow	Arista	8
23	23	TOO NICE TO TALK TO	Beat	Go Feet	3
24	24	DO NOTHING	Specials	2 Tone	3
25	25	CELEBRATION	Kool and the Gang	De-Lite	9
26	26	DON'T WALK AWAY	Electric Light Orchestra	Jet	7
27	27	ROCK 'N' ROLL AIN'T NOISE POLLUTION	AC/DC	Atlantic	6
28	28	THIS WRECKAGE	Gary Numan	Beggars Banquet	3
29	29	IT'S HARD TO BE HUMBLE	Mac Davis	Casablanca	3
30	30	I COULD BE SO GOOD FOR YOU	Dennis Waterman	EMI	10
31	31	WHO'S GONNA ROCK YOU	Nolans	Epic	4
32	32	DECEMBER WILL BE MAGIC AGAIN	Kate Bush	EMI	5
33	[33]	LOOKING FOR CLUES	Robert Palmer	Island	5
34	34	BLUE MOON	Showaddywaddy	Arista	5
35	35	I'M COMING OUT	Diana Ross	Motown	8
36	36	LORRAINE	Bad Manners	Magnet	4
37	37	IF I COULD ONLY MAKE YOU CARE	Mike Berry	Polydor	3
38	38	THE EARTH DIES SCREAMING/DREAM A LIE	UB40	Graduate	10
39	39	NEVER KNEW LOVE LIKE THIS BEFORE	Stephanie Mills	20th Century	11
40	40	RUNAROUND SUE	Racey	RAK	2

WEEK ENDING 10 JANUARY 1981

LW	TW	Title	Artist	Label	Wks
9	[1]	IMAGINE	John Lennon	Parlophone	3
4	[2]	HAPPY CHRISTMAS (WAR IS OVER)	John Lennon	Apple	3
3	[3]	STOP THE CAVALRY	Jona Lewie	Stiff	6
7	4	ANTMUSIC	Adam and the Ants	CBS	6
2	5	(JUST LIKE) STARTING OVER	John Lennon	Geffen	10
1	6	THERE'S NO ONE QUITE LIKE GRANDMA	St Winifred's School Choir	MFP	7
6	7	DE DO DO DO DE DA DA DA	Police	A&M	5
5	8	SUPER TROUPER	Abba	Epic	9
8	9	EMBARRASSMENT	Madness	Stiff	8
15	[10]	FLASH	Queen	EMI	6
13	11	RABBIT	Chas and Dave	Rockney	5
10	12	RUNAWAY BOYS	Stray Cats	Arista	6
11	13	BANANA REPUBLIC	Boomtown Rats	Ensign	8
12	14	LIES/DON'T DRIVE MY CAR	Status Quo	Vertigo	6
24	15	DO NOTHING/MAGGIE'S FARM	Specials	2 Tone	4
16	16	TO CUT A LONG STORY SHORT	Spandau Ballet	Reformation	8
18	[17]	LOVE ON THE ROCKS	Neil Diamond	Capitol	7
19	18	OVER THE RAINBOW/YOU BELONG TO ME	Matchbox	Magnet	6
14	19	LADY	Kenny Rogers	United Artists	8
23	20	TOO NICE TO TALK TO	Beat	Go Feet	4
22	[21]	LONELY TOGETHER	Barry Manilow	Arista	9
17	22	NEVER MIND THE PRESENTS	Barron Knights	Epic	5
21	23	DO YOU FEEL MY LOVE	Eddy Grant	Ensign	8
31	24	WHO'S GONNA ROCK YOU	Nolans	Epic	5
26	25	DON'T WALK AWAY	Electric Light Orchestra	Jet	8
25	26	CELEBRATION	Kool and the Gang	De-Lite	10
28	27	THIS WRECKAGE	Gary Numan	Beggars Banquet	4
20	28	THE TIDE IS HIGH	Blondie	Chrysalis	10
40	29	RUNAROUND SUE	Racey	RAK	3
-	30	I AM THE BEAT	Look ●	MCA	1
-	31	I AIN'T GONNA STAND FOR IT	Stevie Wonder	Motown	1
34	[32]	BLUE MOON	Showaddywaddy	Arista	6
36	33	LORRAINE	Bad Manners	Magnet	5
29	34	IT'S HARD TO BE HUMBLE	Mac Davis	Casablanca	4
-	35	DON'T STOP THE MUSIC	Yarborough and Peoples ●	EMI	1
32	36	DECEMBER WILL BE MAGIC AGAIN	Kate Bush	EMI	6
-	37	MY GIRL	Rod Stewart	Riva	1
37	38	IF I COULD ONLY MAKE YOU CARE	Mike Berry	Polydor	4
-	39	YOUNG PARISIANS	Adam and the Ants	Decca	1
33	[40]	LOOKING FOR CLUES	Robert Palmer	Island	6

WEEK ENDING 17 JANUARY 1981

LW	TW	Title	Artist	Label	Wks
1	[1]	IMAGINE	John Lennon	Parlophone	4
4	[2]	ANTMUSIC	Adam and the Ants	CBS	7
2	3	HAPPY CHRISTMAS (WAR IS OVER)	John Lennon	Apple	4
15	[4]	DO NOTHING/MAGGIE'S FARM	Specials	2 Tone	5
5	5	(JUST LIKE) STARTING OVER	John Lennon	Geffen	11
3	6	STOP THE CAVALRY	Jona Lewie	Stiff	7
20	[7]	TOO NICE TO TALK TO	Beat	Go Feet	5
11	[8]	RABBIT	Chas and Dave	Rockney	6
7	9	DE DO DO DO DE DA DA DA	Police	A&M	6
10	[10]	FLASH	Queen	EMI	7
14	[11]	LIES/DON'T DRIVE MY CAR	Status Quo	Vertigo	7
24	[12]	WHO'S GONNA ROCK YOU	Nolans	Epic	6
9	13	EMBARRASSMENT	Madness	Stiff	9
30	14	I AM THE BEAT	Look	MCA	2
18	[15]	OVER THE RAINBOW/YOU BELONG TO ME	Matchbox	Magnet	7
12	16	RUNAWAY BOYS	Stray Cats	Arista	7
31	17	I AIN'T GONNA STAND FOR IT	Stevie Wonder	Motown	2
29	18	RUNAROUND SUE	Racey	RAK	4
35	19	DON'T STOP THE MUSIC	Yarborough and Peoples	EMI	2
27	[20]	THIS WRECKAGE	Gary Numan	Beggars Banquet	5
17	21	LOVE ON THE ROCKS	Neil Diamond	Capitol	8
6	22	THERE'S NO ONE QUITE LIKE GRANDMA	St Winifred's School Choir	MFP	8
39	23	YOUNG PARISIANS	Adam and the Ants	Decca	2
21	24	LONELY TOGETHER	Barry Manilow	Arista	10
-	25	SCARY MONSTERS (AND SUPER CREEPS)	David Bowie	RCA	1
19	26	LADY	Kenny Rogers	United Artists	9
34	[27]	IT'S HARD TO BE HUMBLE	Mac Davis	Casablanca	5
8	28	SUPER TROUPER	Abba	Epic	10
33	29	LORRAINE	Bad Manners	Magnet	6
13	30	BANANA REPUBLIC	Boomtown Rats	Ensign	9
-	31	BURN RUBBER ON ME	Gap Band	Mercury	1
37	[32]	MY GIRL	Rod Stewart	Riva	2
-	33	FADE TO GREY	Visage ●	Polydor	1
-	[34]	GUILTY	Barbra Streisand and Barry Gibb ●	CBS	1
16	35	TO CUT A LONG STORY SHORT	Spandau Ballet	Reformation	9
-	36	IN THE AIR TONIGHT	Phil Collins ●	Virgin	1
22	37	NEVER MIND THE PRESENTS	Barron Knights	Epic	6
23	38	DO YOU FEEL MY LOVE	Eddy Grant	Ensign	9
-	[39]	RAPP PAYBACK	James Brown	RCA	1
-	[40]	I'M IN LOVE AGAIN	Sad Cafe	RCA	1

WEEK ENDING 24 JANUARY 1981

LW	TW	Title	Artist	Label	Wks
1	[1]	IMAGINE	John Lennon	Parlophone	5

In these weeks ■ In the aftermath of his death, John Lennon continues to dominate the chart, with three hits in the Top Five for two consecutive weeks (17.01.81) ■ James Brown's *Rapp Payback* is his first Top 40 hit for 4 years, and his last for another five years (17.01.81)■

February 1981

□ Highest position disc reached ● Act's first ever week on chart

LW	TW	Title	Artist	Label	Wks
2	[2]	ANTMUSIC	Adam and the Ants	CBS	8
-	3	WOMAN	John Lennon	Geffen	1
36	4	IN THE AIR TONIGHT	Phil Collins	Virgin	2
4	5	DO NOTHING/MAGGIE'S FARM	Specials	2 Tone	6
14	[6]	I AM THE BEAT	Look	MCA	3
7	[7]	TOO NICE TO TALK TO	Beat	Go Feet	6
19	8	DON'T STOP THE MUSIC	Yarborough and Peoples	EMI	3
3	9	HAPPY CHRISTMAS (WAR IS OVER)	John Lennon	Apple	5
10	[10]	FLASH	Queen	EMI	8
23	11	YOUNG PARISIANS	Adam and the Ants	Decca	3
17	12	I AIN'T GONNA STAND FOR IT	Stevie Wonder	Motown	3
18	[13]	RUNAROUND SUE	Racey	RAK	5
-	14	RAPTURE	Blondie	Chrysalis	1
5	15	(JUST LIKE) STARTING OVER	John Lennon	Geffen	12
-	16	VIENNA	Ultravox	Chrysalis	1
12	17	WHO'S GONNA ROCK YOU	Nolans	Epic	7
8	18	RABBIT	Chas and Dave	Rockney	7
6	19	STOP THE CAVALRY	Jona Lewie	Stiff	8
25	[20]	SCARY MONSTERS (AND SUPER CREEPS)	David Bowie	RCA	2
15	21	OVER THE RAINBOW/YOU BELONG TO ME	Matchbox	Magnet	8
29	22	LORRAINE	Bad Manners	Magnet	7
33	23	FADE TO GREY	Visage	Polydor	2
9	24	DE DO DO DO DE DA DA DA	Police	A&M	7
-	25	ROMEO AND JULIET	Dire Straits	Vertigo	1
11	26	LIES/DON'T DRIVE MY CAR	Status Quo	Vertigo	8
-	27	IT'S MY TURN	Diana Ross	Motown	1
13	28	EMBARRASSMENT	Madness	Stiff	10
-	29	GANGSTERS OF THE GROOVE	Heatwave	GTO	1
31	30	BURN RUBBER ON ME	Gap Band	Mercury	2
20	31	THIS WRECKAGE	Gary Numan	Beggars Banquet	6
24	32	LONELY TOGETHER	Barry Manilow	Arista	11
-	33	A LITTLE IN LOVE	Cliff Richard	EMI	1
27	34	IT'S HARD TO BE HUMBLE	Mac Davis	Casablanca	6
16	35	RUNAWAY BOYS	Stray Cats	Arista	8
-	36	TWILIGHT CAFE	Susan Fassbender ●	CBS	1
21	37	LOVE ON THE ROCKS	Neil Diamond	Capitol	9
-	38	THE RETURN OF THE LOS PALMAS SEVEN	Madness	Stiff	1
39	[39]	RAPP PAYBACK	James Brown	RCA	2
-	[40]	I SHOT THE SHERIFF	Light Of The World ●	Ensign	1

WEEK ENDING 31 JANUARY 1981

LW	TW	Title	Artist	Label	Wks
1	[1]	IMAGINE	John Lennon	Parlophone	6
3	2	WOMAN	John Lennon	Geffen	2
4	3	IN THE AIR TONIGHT	Phil Collins	Virgin	3
2	4	ANTMUSIC	Adam and the Ants	CBS	9
14	[5]	RAPTURE	Blondie	Chrysalis	2
16	6	VIENNA	Ultravox	Chrysalis	2
8	[7]	DON'T STOP THE MUSIC	Yarborough and Peoples	EMI	4
6	8	I AM THE BEAT	Look	MCA	4
11	[9]	YOUNG PARISIANS	Adam and the Ants	Decca	4
12	[10]	I AIN'T GONNA STAND FOR IT	Stevie Wonder	Motown	4
5	11	DO NOTHING/MAGGIE'S FARM	Specials	2 Tone	7
23	12	FADE TO GREY	Visage	Polydor	3
7	13	TOO NICE TO TALK TO	Beat	Go Feet	7
10	14	FLASH	Queen	EMI	9
13	15	RUNAROUND SUE	Racey	RAK	6
25	16	ROMEO AND JULIET	Dire Straits	Vertigo	2
33	17	A LITTLE IN LOVE	Cliff Richard	EMI	2
38	18	THE RETURN OF THE LOS PALMAS SEVEN	Madness	Stiff	2
29	[19]	GANGSTERS OF THE GROOVE	Heatwave	GTO	2
20	[20]	SCARY MONSTERS (AND SUPER CREEPS)	David Bowie	RCA	3
22	[21]	LORRAINE	Bad Manners	Magnet	8
15	22	(JUST LIKE) STARTING OVER	John Lennon	Geffen	13
9	23	HAPPY CHRISTMAS (WAR IS OVER)	John Lennon	Apple	6
-	24	THE FREEZE	Spandau Ballet	Reformation	1
27	25	IT'S MY TURN	Diana Ross	Motown	2
30	26	BURN RUBBER ON ME	Gap Band	Mercury	3
17	27	WHO'S GONNA ROCK YOU	Nolans	Epic	8
-	28	I SURRENDER	Rainbow	Polydor	1
36	29	TWILIGHT CAFE	Susan Fassbender	CBS	2
18	30	RABBIT	Chas and Dave	Rockney	8
21	31	OVER THE RAINBOW/YOU BELONG TO ME	Matchbox	Magnet	9
19	32	STOP THE CAVALRY	Jona Lewie	Stiff	9
34	33	IT'S HARD TO BE HUMBLE	Mac Davis	Casablanca	7
-	34	SGT. ROCK (IS GOING TO HELP ME)	XTC	Virgin	1
-	35	GIVE PEACE A CHANCE	Plastic Ono Band	Apple	1
26	36	LIES/DON'T DRIVE MY CAR	Status Quo	Vertigo	9
-	[37]	TURN ME ON TURN ME OFF	Honey Bane ●	Zonophone	1
28	38	EMBARRASSMENT	Madness	Stiff	11
-	39	HANG TOGETHER	Odyssey	RCA	1
-	40	THE ELEPHANT'S GRAVEYARD (GUILTY)	Boomtown Rats	Ensign	1

WEEK ENDING 7 FEBRUARY 1981

LW	TW	Title	Artist	Label	Wks
2	[1]	WOMAN	John Lennon	Geffen	3
3	[2]	IN THE AIR TONIGHT	Phil Collins	Virgin	4
6	3	VIENNA	Ultravox	Chrysalis	3
1	4	IMAGINE	John Lennon	Parlophone	7
5	[5]	RAPTURE	Blondie	Chrysalis	3
4	6	ANTMUSIC	Adam and the Ants	CBS	10
7	[7]	DON'T STOP THE MUSIC	Yarborough and Peoples	EMI	5
12	[8]	FADE TO GREY	Visage	Polydor	4
9	[9]	YOUNG PARISIANS	Adam and the Ants	Decca	5
8	10	I AM THE BEAT	Look	MCA	5
16	11	ROMEO AND JULIET	Dire Straits	Vertigo	3
28	12	I SURRENDER	Rainbow	Polydor	2
10	13	I AIN'T GONNA STAND FOR IT	Stevie Wonder	Motown	5
18	14	THE RETURN OF THE LOS PALMAS SEVEN	Madness	Stiff	3
17	[15]	A LITTLE IN LOVE	Cliff Richard	EMI	3
25	[16]	IT'S MY TURN	Diana Ross	Motown	3
24	[17]	THE FREEZE	Spandau Ballet	Reformation	2
11	18	DO NOTHING/MAGGIE'S FARM	Specials	2 Tone	8
-	19	THE OLDEST SWINGER IN TOWN	Fred Wedlock ●	Rocket	1
19	20	GANGSTERS OF THE GROOVE	Heatwave	GTO	3
29	[21]	TWILIGHT CAFE	Susan Fassbender	CBS	3
26	[22]	BURN RUBBER ON ME	Gap Band	Mercury	4
13	23	TOO NICE TO TALK TO	Beat	Go Feet	8
14	24	FLASH	Queen	EMI	10
21	25	LORRAINE	Bad Manners	Magnet	9
40	[26]	THE ELEPHANT'S GRAVEYARD (GUILTY)	Boomtown Rats	Ensign	2
15	27	RUNAROUND SUE	Racey	RAK	7
34	28	SGT. ROCK (IS GOING TO HELP ME)	XTC	Virgin	2
20	29	SCARY MONSTERS (AND SUPER CREEPS)	David Bowie	RCA	4
-	30	SHADDAP YOU FACE	Joe Dolce Music Theatre ●	Epic	1
-	31	WE'LL BRING THE HOUSE DOWN	Slade	Cheapskate	1
27	32	WHO'S GONNA ROCK YOU	Nolans	Epic	9
35	[33]	GIVE PEACE A CHANCE	Plastic Ono Band	Apple	2
-	34	I'M IN LOVE WITH A GERMAN FILM STAR	Passions ●	Polydor	1
-	35	ROCK THIS TOWN	Stray Cats	Arista	1
39	[36]	HANG TOGETHER	Odyssey	RCA	2
37	[37]	TURN ME ON TURN ME OFF	Honey Bane	Zonophone	2
-	38	THE BED"S TOO BIG WITHOUT YOU	Sheila Hylton ●	Island	1
-	39	JUST WHEN I NEEDED YOU MOST	Barbara Jones ●	Sonet	1
-	40	CAR TROUBLE	Adam and the Ants	Do It	1

WEEK ENDING 14 FEBRUARY 1981

LW	TW	Title	Artist	Label	Wks
1	[1]	WOMAN	John Lennon	Geffen	4
3	[2]	VIENNA	Ultravox	Chrysalis	4
30	3	SHADDAP YOU FACE	Joe Dolce Music Theatre	Epic	2
2	4	IN THE AIR TONIGHT	Phil Collins	Virgin	5
12	5	I SURRENDER	Rainbow	Polydor	3
4	6	IMAGINE	John Lennon	Parlophone	8
19	7	THE OLDEST SWINGER IN TOWN	Fred Wedlock	Rocket	2
5	8	RAPTURE	Blondie	Chrysalis	4

■ John Lennon equals the record originally set by Frankie Laine in having the top two singles of the week (31.01.81) ■ John Lennon knocks himself off number one, not only achieving a hat-trick of number ones within the space of seven weeks, but also equalling the record of the Beatles, who deposed themselves on 12 December 1964 (07.02.81) ■ Two Midge Ure records in the Top 10, by Visage and by Ultravox (07.02.81) ■

February 1981

☐ Highest position disc reached ● Act's first ever week on chart

LW	TW	Title	Artist	Label	Wks
6	9	ANTMUSIC	Adam and the Ants	*CBS*	11
14	10	THE RETURN OF THE LOS PALMAS SEVEN	Madness	*Stiff*	4
7	11	DON'T STOP THE MUSIC	Yarborough and Peoples	*EMI*	6
11	12	ROMEO AND JULIET	Dire Straits	*Vertigo*	4
8	13	FADE TO GREY	Visage	*Polydor*	5
35	14	ROCK THIS TOWN	Stray Cats	*Arista*	2
9	15	YOUNG PARISIANS	Adam and the Ants	*Decca*	6
15	16	A LITTLE IN LOVE	Cliff Richard	*EMI*	4
31	17	WE'LL BRING THE HOUSE DOWN	Slade	*Cheapskate*	2
17	18	THE FREEZE	Spandau Ballet	*Reformation*	3
28	19	SGT. ROCK (IS GOING TO HELP ME)	XTC	*Virgin*	3
10	20	I AM THE BEAT	Look	*MCA*	6
21	[21]	TWILIGHT CAFE	Susan Fassbender	*CBS*	4
16	22	IT'S MY TURN	Diana Ross	*Motown*	4
20	23	GANGSTERS OF THE GROOVE	Heatwave	*GTO*	4
22	24	BURN RUBBER ON ME	Gap Band	*Mercury*	5
13	25	I AIN'T GONNA STAND FOR IT	Stevie Wonder	*Motown*	6
34	26	I'M IN LOVE WITH A GERMAN FILM STAR	Passions	*Polydor*	2
26	27	THE ELEPHANT'S GRAVEYARD (GUILTY)	Boomtown Rats	*Ensign*	3
-	28	MESSAGE OF LOVE	Pretenders	*Real*	1
-	29	THAT'S ENTERTAINMENT	Jam	*Metronome*	1
18	30	DO NOTHING/MAGGIE'S FARM	Specials	*2 Tone*	9
39	[31]	JUST WHEN I NEEDED YOU MOST	Barbara Jones	*Sonet*	2
-	[32]	MUTUALLY ASSURED DESTRUCTION	Gillan	*Virgin*	1
40	[33]	CAR TROUBLE	Adam and the Ants	*Do It*	2
-	34	SOUTHERN FREEEZ	Freeez ●	*Beggars Banquet*	1
38	[35]	THE BED'S TOO BIG WITHOUT YOU	Sheila Hylton	*Island*	2
25	36	LORRAINE	Bad Manners	*Magnet*	10
36	37	HANG TOGETHER	Odyssey	*RCA*	3
-	38	ONCE IN A LIFETIME	Talking Heads ●	*Sire*	1
-	39	(DO) THE HUCKLEBUCK	Coast To Coast ●	*Polydor*	1
-	40	I MADE IT THROUGH THE RAIN	Barry Manilow	*Arista*	1

WEEK ENDING 21 FEBRUARY 1981

LW	TW	Title	Artist	Label	Wks
3	[1]	SHADDAP YOU FACE	Joe Dolce Music Theatre	*Epic*	3
2	[2]	VIENNA	Ultravox	*Chrysalis*	5
1	3	WOMAN	John Lennon	*Geffen*	5
5	4	I SURRENDER	Rainbow	*Polydor*	4
4	5	IN THE AIR TONIGHT	Phil Collins	*Virgin*	6
7	[6]	THE OLDEST SWINGER IN TOWN	Fred Wedlock	*Rocket*	3
10	[7]	THE RETURN OF THE LOS PALMAS SEVEN	Madness	*Stiff*	5
12	[8]	ROMEO AND JULIET	Dire Straits	*Vertigo*	5
14	[9]	ROCK THIS TOWN	Stray Cats	*Arista*	3
17	[10]	WE'LL BRING THE HOUSE DOWN	Slade	*Cheapskate*	3
28	[11]	MESSAGE OF LOVE	Pretenders	*Real*	2
13	12	FADE TO GREY	Visage	*Polydor*	6
8	13	RAPTURE	Blondie	*Chrysalis*	5
39	14	(DO) THE HUCKLEBUCK	Coast To Coast	*Polydor*	2
-	15	ST. VALENTINE'S DAY MASSACRE (EP)	Motorhead/Girlschool ●	*Bronze*	1
19	[16]	SGT. ROCK (IS GOING TO HELP ME)	XTC	*Virgin*	4
6	17	IMAGINE	John Lennon	*Parlophone*	9
9	18	ANTMUSIC	Adam and the Ants	*CBS*	12
11	19	DON'T STOP THE MUSIC	Yarborough and Peoples	*EMI*	7
16	20	A LITTLE IN LOVE	Cliff Richard	*EMI*	5
-	21	JEALOUS GUY	Roxy Music	*Polydor*	1
15	22	YOUNG PARISIANS	Adam and the Ants	*Decca*	7
34	23	SOUTHERN FREEEZ	Freeez	*Beggars Banquet*	2
18	24	THE FREEZE	Spandau Ballet	*Reformation*	4
21	25	TWILIGHT CAFE	Susan Fassbender	*CBS*	5
29	26	THAT'S ENTERTAINMENT	Jam	*Metronome*	2
23	27	GANGSTERS OF THE GROOVE	Heatwave	*GTO*	5
26	28	I'M IN LOVE WITH A GERMAN FILM STAR	Passions	*Polydor*	3
24	29	BURN RUBBER ON ME	Gap Band	*Mercury*	6
22	30	IT'S MY TURN	Diana Ross	*Motown*	5
20	31	I AM THE BEAT	Look	*MCA*	7
27	32	THE ELEPHANT'S GRAVEYARD (GUILTY)	Boomtown Rats	*Ensign*	4
32	33	MUTUALLY ASSURED DESTRUCTION	Gillan	*Virgin*	2
-	34	SOMEBODY (HELP ME OUT)	Beggar and Co. ●	*Ensign*	1
38	35	ONCE IN A LIFETIME	Talking Heads	*Sire*	2
31	36	JUST WHEN I NEEDED YOU MOST	Barbara Jones	*Sonet*	3
40	[37]	I MADE IT THROUGH THE RAIN	Barry Manilow	*Arista*	2
-	38	HOT LOVE	Kelly Marie	*Calibre*	1
-	39	KINGS OF THE WILD FRONTIER	Adam and the Ants	*CBS*	1
33	40	CAR TROUBLE	Adam and the Ants	*Do It*	3

WEEK ENDING 28 FEBRUARY 1981

LW	TW	Title	Artist	Label	Wks
1	[1]	SHADDAP YOU FACE	Joe Dolce Music Theatre	*Epic*	4
2	[2]	VIENNA	Ultravox	*Chrysalis*	6
4	[3]	I SURRENDER	Rainbow	*Polydor*	5
3	4	WOMAN	John Lennon	*Geffen*	6
15	[5]	ST. VALENTINE'S DAY MASSACRE (EP)	Motorhead/Girlschool	*Bronze*	2
21	6	JEALOUS GUY	Roxy Music	*Polydor*	2
7	[7]	THE RETURN OF THE LOS PALMAS SEVEN	Madness	*Stiff*	6
14	8	(DO) THE HUCKLEBUCK	Coast To Coast	*Polydor*	3
23	9	SOUTHERN FREEEZ	Freeez	*Beggars Banquet*	3
6	10	THE OLDEST SWINGER IN TOWN	Fred Wedlock	*Rocket*	4
9	11	ROCK THIS TOWN	Stray Cats	*Arista*	4
5	12	IN THE AIR TONIGHT	Phil Collins	*Virgin*	7
10	13	WE'LL BRING THE HOUSE DOWN	Slade	*Cheapskate*	4
8	14	ROMEO AND JULIET	Dire Straits	*Vertigo*	6
11	15	MESSAGE OF LOVE	Pretenders	*Real*	3
12	16	FADE TO GREY	Visage	*Polydor*	7
39	17	KINGS OF THE WILD FRONTIER	Adam and the Ants	*CBS*	2
16	18	SGT. ROCK (IS GOING TO HELP ME)	XTC	*Virgin*	5
-	19	SOMETHING 'BOUT YOU BABY I LIKE	Status Quo	*Vertigo*	1
18	20	ANTMUSIC	Adam and the Ants	*CBS*	13
26	[21]	THAT'S ENTERTAINMENT	Jam	*Metronome*	3
34	22	SOMEBODY (HELP ME OUT)	Beggar and Co.	*Ensign*	2
17	23	IMAGINE	John Lennon	*Parlophone*	10
35	24	ONCE IN A LIFETIME	Talking Heads	*Sire*	3
28	[25]	I'M IN LOVE WITH A GERMAN FILM STAR	Passions	*Polydor*	4
-	26	FOUR FROM TOYAH (EP)	Toyah ●	*Safari*	1
13	27	RAPTURE	Blondie	*Chrysalis*	6
20	28	A LITTLE IN LOVE	Cliff Richard	*EMI*	6
-	29	REWARD	Teardrop Explodes ●	*Mercury*	1
24	30	THE FREEZE	Spandau Ballet	*Reformation*	5
38	31	HOT LOVE	Kelly Marie	*Calibre*	2
22	32	YOUNG PARISIANS	Adam and the Ants	*Decca*	8
19	33	DON'T STOP THE MUSIC	Yarborough and Peoples	*EMI*	8
25	34	TWILIGHT CAFE	Susan Fassbender	*CBS*	6
27	35	GANGSTERS OF THE GROOVE	Heatwave	*GTO*	6
29	36	BURN RUBBER ON ME	Gap Band	*Mercury*	7
33	37	MUTUALLY ASSURED DESTRUCTION	Gillan	*Virgin*	3
40	38	CAR TROUBLE	Adam and the Ants	*Do It*	4
-	39	JONES VS JONES/SUMMER MADNESS/FUNKY STUFF	Kool and the Gang	*De-Lite*	1
-	40	STAR	Kiki Dee	*Ariola*	1

WEEK ENDING 7 MARCH 1981

LW	TW	Title	Artist	Label	Wks
1	[1]	SHADDAP YOU FACE	Joe Dolce Music Theatre	*Epic*	5
2	[2]	VIENNA	Ultravox	*Chrysalis*	7
6	3	JEALOUS GUY	Roxy Music	*Polydor*	3
3	4	I SURRENDER	Rainbow	*Polydor*	6
5	[5]	ST. VALENTINE'S DAY MASSACRE (EP)	Motorhead/Girlschool	*Bronze*	3
17	6	KINGS OF THE WILD FRONTIER	Adam and the Ants	*CBS*	3
8	7	(DO) THE HUCKLEBUCK	Coast To Coast	*Polydor*	4
9	[8]	SOUTHERN FREEEZ	Freeez	*Beggars Banquet*	4
19	[9]	SOMETHING 'BOUT YOU BABY I LIKE	Status Quo	*Vertigo*	2
7	10	THE RETURN OF THE LOS PALMAS SEVEN	Madness	*Stiff*	7
4	11	WOMAN	John Lennon	*Geffen*	7
11	12	ROCK THIS TOWN	Stray Cats	*Arista*	5
10	13	THE OLDEST SWINGER IN TOWN	Fred Wedlock	*Rocket*	5

In these weeks ■ Two heavy metal bands, Motorhead and Girlschool, combined to achieve the highest chart position of either of their careers. The lead song on their hit EP was their version of Johnny Kidd's *Please Don't Touch* (28.02.81) ■ Toyah became one of the first acts to debut with an EP, the lead track of which was *It's A Mystery* (28.02.81)■

LW	TW	Title / Artist	Label	Wks
24	14	ONCE IN A LIFETIME Talking Heads	*Sire*	4
22	15	SOMEBODY (HELP ME OUT) Beggar and Co.	*Ensign*	3
26	16	FOUR FROM TOYAH (EP) Toyah	*Safari*	2
14	17	ROMEO AND JULIET Dire Straits	*Vertigo*	7
-	18	KIDS IN AMERICA Kim Wilde ●	*RAK*	1
15	19	MESSAGE OF LOVE Pretenders	*Real*	4
13	20	WE'LL BRING THE HOUSE DOWN Slade	*Cheapskate*	5
12	21	IN THE AIR TONIGHT Phil Collins	*Virgin*	8
21	22	THAT'S ENTERTAINMENT Jam	*Metronome*	4
18	23	SGT. ROCK (IS GOING TO HELP ME) XTC	*Virgin*	6
31	24	HOT LOVE Kelly Marie	*Calibre*	3
29	25	REWARD Teardrop Explodes	*Mercury*	2
16	26	FADE TO GREY Visage	*Polydor*	8
40	27	STAR Kiki Dee	*Ariola*	2
20	28	ANTMUSIC Adam and the Ants	*CBS*	14
-	29	THIS OLE HOUSE Shakin' Stevens	*Epic*	1
25	30	I'M IN LOVE WITH A GERMAN FILM STAR Passions	*Polydor*	5
39	31	JONES VS JONES/SUMMER MADNESS/FUNKY STUFF Kool and the Gang	*De-Lite*	2
23	32	IMAGINE John Lennon	*Parlophone*	11
30	33	THE FREEZE Spandau Ballet	*Reformation*	6
-	34	CAN YOU FEEL IT Jacksons	*Epic*	1
-	35	YOU BETTER YOU BET Who	*Polydor*	1
27	36	RAPTURE Blondie	*Chrysalis*	7
-	37	WALKING ON THIN ICE Yoko Ono ●	*Geffen*	1
38	38	CAR TROUBLE Adam and the Ants	*Do It*	5
28	39	A LITTLE IN LOVE Cliff Richard	*EMI*	7
32	40	YOUNG PARISIANS Adam and the Ants	*Decca*	9

WEEK ENDING **14 MARCH 1981**

LW	TW	Title / Artist	Label	Wks
3	1	JEALOUS GUY Roxy Music	*Polydor*	4
6	2	KINGS OF THE WILD FRONTIER Adam and the Ants	*CBS*	4
1	3	SHADDAP YOU FACE Joe Dolce Music Theatre	*Epic*	6
2	4	VIENNA Ultravox	*Chrysalis*	8
7	5	(DO) THE HUCKLEBUCK Coast To Coast	*Polydor*	5
18	6	KIDS IN AMERICA Kim Wilde	*RAK*	2
29	7	THIS OLE HOUSE Shakin' Stevens	*Epic*	2
8	8	SOUTHERN FREEEZ Freeez	*Beggars Banquet*	5
9	9	SOMETHING 'BOUT YOU BABY I LIKE Status Quo	*Vertigo*	3
5	10	ST. VALENTINE'S DAY MASSACRE (EP) Motorhead/Girlschool	*Bronze*	4
16	11	FOUR FROM TOYAH (EP) Toyah	*Safari*	3
4	12	I SURRENDER Rainbow	*Polydor*	7
25	13	REWARD Teardrop Explodes	*Mercury*	3
14	14	ONCE IN A LIFETIME Talking Heads	*Sire*	5
15	15	SOMEBODY (HELP ME OUT) Beggar and Co.	*Ensign*	4
35	16	YOU BETTER YOU BET Who	*Polydor*	2
27	17	STAR Kiki Dee	*Ariola*	3
10	18	THE RETURN OF THE LOS PALMAS SEVEN Madness	*Stiff*	8
12	19	ROCK THIS TOWN Stray Cats	*Arista*	6
-	20	I MISSED AGAIN Phil Collins	*Virgin*	1
31	21	JONES VS JONES/SUMMER MADNESS/FUNKY STUFF Kool and the Gang	*De-Lite*	3
24	22	HOT LOVE Kelly Marie	*Calibre*	4
11	23	WOMAN John Lennon	*Geffen*	8
13	24	THE OLDEST SWINGER IN TOWN Fred Wedlock	*Rocket*	6
22	25	THAT'S ENTERTAINMENT Jam	*Metronome*	5
-	26	PLANET EARTH Duran Duran ●	*EMI*	1
-	27	LATELY Stevie Wonder	*Motown*	1
28	28	ANTMUSIC Adam and the Ants	*CBS*	15
19	29	MESSAGE OF LOVE Pretenders	*Real*	5
20	30	WE'LL BRING THE HOUSE DOWN Slade	*Cheapskate*	6
34	31	CAN YOU FEEL IT Jacksons	*Epic*	2
-	32	MIND OF A TOY Visage	*Polydor*	1
17	33	ROMEO AND JULIET Dire Straits	*Vertigo*	8
30	34	I'M IN LOVE WITH A GERMAN FILM STAR Passions	*Polydor*	6
37	35	WALKING ON THIN ICE Yoko Ono	*Geffen*	2
23	36	SGT. ROCK (IS GOING TO HELP ME) XTC	*Virgin*	7
-	37	CAN YOU HANDLE IT Sharon Redd ●	*Epic*	1
-	38	EINSTEIN A GO-GO Landscape ●	*RCA*	1
-	39	CEREMONY New Order ●	*Factory*	1
26	40	FADE TO GREY Visage	*Polydor*	9

March 1981

□ Highest position disc reached ● Act's first ever week on chart

WEEK ENDING **21 MARCH 1981**

LW	TW	Title / Artist	Label	Wks
1	1	JEALOUS GUY Roxy Music	*Polydor*	5
7	2	THIS OLE HOUSE Shakin' Stevens	*Epic*	3
6	3	KIDS IN AMERICA Kim Wilde	*RAK*	3
2	4	KINGS OF THE WILD FRONTIER Adam and the Ants	*CBS*	5
5	5	(DO) THE HUCKLEBUCK Coast To Coast	*Polydor*	6
13	6	REWARD Teardrop Explodes	*Mercury*	4
4	7	VIENNA Ultravox	*Chrysalis*	9
11	8	FOUR FROM TOYAH (EP) Toyah	*Safari*	4
16	9	YOU BETTER YOU BET Who	*Polydor*	3
3	10	SHADDAP YOU FACE Joe Dolce Music Theatre	*Epic*	7
8	11	SOUTHERN FREEEZ Freeez	*Beggars Banquet*	6
9	12	SOMETHING 'BOUT YOU BABY I LIKE Status Quo	*Vertigo*	4
17	13	STAR Kiki Dee	*Ariola*	4
20	14	I MISSED AGAIN Phil Collins	*Virgin*	2
10	15	ST. VALENTINE'S DAY MASSACRE (EP) Motorhead/Girlschool	*Bronze*	5
14	16	ONCE IN A LIFETIME Talking Heads	*Sire*	6
21	17	JONES VS JONES/SUMMER MADNESS/FUNKY STUFF Kool and the Gang	*De-Lite*	4
27	18	LATELY Stevie Wonder	*Motown*	2
15	19	SOMEBODY (HELP ME OUT) Beggar and Co.	*Ensign*	5
26	20	PLANET EARTH Duran Duran	*EMI*	2
38	21	EINSTEIN A GO-GO Landscape	*RCA*	2
12	22	I SURRENDER Rainbow	*Polydor*	8
22	23	HOT LOVE Kelly Marie	*Calibre*	5
32	24	MIND OF A TOY Visage	*Polydor*	2
-	25	INTUITION Linx	*Chrysalis*	1
-	26	IT'S A LOVE THING Whispers	*Solar*	1
18	27	THE RETURN OF THE LOS PALMAS SEVEN Madness	*Stiff*	9
31	28	CAN YOU FEEL IT Jacksons	*Epic*	3
19	29	ROCK THIS TOWN Stray Cats	*Arista*	7
-	30	WHAT BECOMES OF THE BROKEN HEARTED Dave Stewart and Colin Blunstone ●	*Stiff*	1
-	31	TWILIGHT ZONE/WRATHCHILD Iron Maiden	*EMI*	1
23	32	WOMAN John Lennon	*Geffen*	9
37	33	CAN YOU HANDLE IT Sharon Redd	*Epic*	2
39	34	CEREMONY New Order	*Factory*	2
-	35	ATTENTION TO ME Nolans	*Epic*	1
25	36	THAT'S ENTERTAINMENT Jam	*Metronome*	6
28	37	ANTMUSIC Adam and the Ants	*CBS*	16
24	38	THE OLDEST SWINGER IN TOWN Fred Wedlock	*Rocket*	7
-	39	JOHN I'M ONLY DANCING/BIG GREEN CAR Polecats ●	*Mercury*	1
35	40	WALKING ON THIN ICE Yoko Ono	*Geffen*	3

WEEK ENDING **28 MARCH 1981**

LW	TW	Title / Artist	Label	Wks
2	1	THIS OLE HOUSE Shakin' Stevens	*Epic*	4
3	2	KIDS IN AMERICA Kim Wilde	*RAK*	4
1	3	JEALOUS GUY Roxy Music	*Polydor*	6
8	4	FOUR FROM TOYAH (EP) Toyah	*Safari*	5
4	5	KINGS OF THE WILD FRONTIER Adam and the Ants	*CBS*	6
18	6	LATELY Stevie Wonder	*Motown*	3
5	7	(DO) THE HUCKLEBUCK Coast To Coast	*Polydor*	7
6	8	REWARD Teardrop Explodes	*Mercury*	5
9	9	YOU BETTER YOU BET Who	*Polydor*	4
-	10	CAPSTICK COMES HOME/THE SHEFFIELD GRINDER Tony Capstick and the Carlton Main Frickley Colliery Band ●	*Dingles*	1
21	11	EINSTEIN A GO-GO Landscape	*RCA*	3
20	12	PLANET EARTH Duran Duran	*EMI*	3
25	13	INTUITION Linx	*Chrysalis*	2
24	14	MIND OF A TOY Visage	*Polydor*	3
13	15	STAR Kiki Dee	*Ariola*	5
7	16	VIENNA Ultravox	*Chrysalis*	10
14	17	I MISSED AGAIN Phil Collins	*Virgin*	3

■ Kim Wilde's *Kids In America* reaches number two, the same position that her father Marty reached with his biggest hit *A Teenager In Love* 24 years earlier. Only the Sinatras, Frank and Nancy, have been a more successful father and daughter in British chart history (28.03.81) ■ Another geographical chart, with hits about America, Sheffield, the planet Earth, Vienna and New Orleans (28.03.81) ■

March 1981

□ Highest position disc reached ● Act's first ever week on chart

LW	TW	Title / Artist	Label	Wks
17	18	JONES VS JONES/SUMMER MADNESS/FUNKY STUFF Kool and the Gang	*De-Lite*	5
30	19	WHAT BECOMES OF THE BROKEN HEARTED Dave Stewart and Colin Blunstone	*Stiff*	2
26	20	IT'S A LOVE THING Whispers	*Solar*	2
11	21	SOUTHERN FREEEZ Freeez	*Beggars Banquet*	7
12	22	SOMETHING 'BOUT YOU BABY I LIKE Status Quo	*Vertigo*	5
-	23	D-DAYS Hazel O'Connor	*Albion*	1
-	24	MAKING YOUR MIND UP Bucks Fizz ●	*RCA*	1
10	25	SHADDAP YOU FACE Joe Dolce Music Theatre	*Epic*	8
28	26	CAN YOU FEEL IT Jacksons	*Epic*	4
16	27	ONCE IN A LIFETIME Talking Heads	*Sire*	7
23	28	HOT LOVE Kelly Marie	*Calibre*	6
35	29	ATTENTION TO ME Nolans	*Epic*	2
19	30	SOMEBODY (HELP ME OUT) Beggar and Co.	*Ensign*	6
33	[31]	CAN YOU HANDLE IT Sharon Redd	*Epic*	3
31	32	TWILIGHT ZONE/WRATHCHILD Iron Maiden	*EMI*	2
15	33	ST. VALENTINE'S DAY MASSACRE (EP) Motorhead/Girlschool	*Bronze*	6
-	[34]	JITTERBUGGIN' Heatwave	*GTO*	1
-	35	SLOW MOTION Ultravox	*Island*	1
39	36	JOHN I'M ONLY DANCING/BIG GREEN CAR Polecats	*Mercury*	2
-	37	NEW ORLEANS Gillan	*Virgin*	1
22	38	I SURRENDER Rainbow	*Polydor*	9
34	39	CEREMONY New Order	*Factory*	3
-	[40]	I SAW HER STANDING THERE Elton John Band featuring John Lennon and the Muscle Shoals Horns ●	*DJM*	1

LW	TW	*WEEK ENDING* **4 APRIL 1981**		Wks
1	[1]	THIS OLE HOUSE Shakin' Stevens	*Epic*	5
2	[2]	KIDS IN AMERICA Kim Wilde	*RAK*	5
10	[3]	CAPSTICK COMES HOME/THE SHEFFIELD GRINDER Tony Capstick and the Carlton Main Frickley Colliery Band	*Dingles*	2
6	4	LATELY Stevie Wonder	*Motown*	4
24	5	MAKING YOUR MIND UP Bucks Fizz	*RCA*	2
4	6	FOUR FROM TOYAH (EP) Toyah	*Safari*	6
3	7	JEALOUS GUY Roxy Music	*Polydor*	7
11	8	EINSTEIN A GO-GO Landscape	*RCA*	4
7	9	(DO) THE HUCKLEBUCK Coast To Coast	*Polydor*	8
13	10	INTUITION Linx	*Chrysalis*	3
20	11	IT'S A LOVE THING Whispers	*Solar*	3
23	12	D-DAYS Hazel O'Connor	*Albion*	2
14	[13]	MIND OF A TOY Visage	*Polydor*	4
9	14	YOU BETTER YOU BET Who	*Polydor*	5
8	15	REWARD Teardrop Explodes	*Mercury*	6
12	16	PLANET EARTH Duran Duran	*EMI*	4
19	17	WHAT BECOMES OF THE BROKEN HEARTED Dave Stewart and Colin Blunstone	*Stiff*	3
5	18	KINGS OF THE WILD FRONTIER Adam and the Ants	*CBS*	7
15	19	STAR Kiki Dee	*Ariola*	6
18	20	JONES VS JONES/SUMMER MADNESS/FUNKY STUFF Kool and the Gang	*De-Lite*	6
29	21	ATTENTION TO ME Nolans	*Epic*	3
16	22	VIENNA Ultravox	*Chrysalis*	11
26	23	CAN YOU FEEL IT Jacksons	*Epic*	5
17	24	I MISSED AGAIN Phil Collins	*Virgin*	4
37	25	NEW ORLEANS Gillan	*Virgin*	2
-	26	NIGHT GAMES Graham Bonnet ●	*Vertigo*	1
-	[27]	MY MUM IS ONE IN A MILLION The Children Of Tansley School ●	*EMI*	1
22	28	SOMETHING 'BOUT YOU BABY I LIKE Status Quo	*Vertigo*	6
-	29	JUST A FEELING Bad Manners	*Magnet*	1
21	30	SOUTHERN FREEEZ Freeez	*Beggars Banquet*	8
-	31	GOOD THING GOING Sugar Minott ●	*RCA*	1
-	[32]	UP THE HILL BACKWARDS David Bowie	*RCA*	1
35	[33]	SLOW MOTION Ultravox	*Island*	2
25	34	SHADDAP YOU FACE Joe Dolce Music Theatre	*Epic*	9
34	35	JITTERBUGGIN' Heatwave	*GTO*	2
36	36	JOHN I'M ONLY DANCING/BIG GREEN CAR Polecats	*Mercury*	3
27	37	ONCE IN A LIFETIME Talking Heads	*Sire*	8
31	38	CAN YOU HANDLE IT Sharon Redd	*Epic*	4
28	39	HOT LOVE Kelly Marie	*Calibre*	7
40	[40]	I SAW HER STANDING THERE Elton John Band featuring John Lennon and the Muscle Shoals Horns	*DJM*	2

LW	TW	*WEEK ENDING* **11 APRIL 1981**		Wks
1	[1]	THIS OLE HOUSE Shakin' Stevens	*Epic*	6
5	2	MAKING YOUR MIND UP Bucks Fizz	*RCA*	3
4	[3]	LATELY Stevie Wonder	*Motown*	5
2	4	KIDS IN AMERICA Kim Wilde	*RAK*	6
8	[5]	EINSTEIN A GO-GO Landscape	*RCA*	5
3	6	CAPSTICK COMES HOME/THE SHEFFIELD GRINDER Tony Capstick and the Carlton Main Frickley Colliery Band	*Dingles*	3
10	[7]	INTUITION Linx	*Chrysalis*	4
6	8	FOUR FROM TOYAH (EP) Toyah	*Safari*	7
11	[9]	IT'S A LOVE THING Whispers	*Solar*	4
12	[10]	D-DAYS Hazel O'Connor	*Albion*	3
23	11	CAN YOU FEEL IT Jacksons	*Epic*	6
26	12	NIGHT GAMES Graham Bonnet	*Vertigo*	2
17	[13]	WHAT BECOMES OF THE BROKEN HEARTED Dave Stewart and Colin Blunstone	*Stiff*	4
31	14	GOOD THING GOING Sugar Minott	*RCA*	2
21	15	ATTENTION TO ME Nolans	*Epic*	4
13	16	MIND OF A TOY Visage	*Polydor*	5
9	17	(DO) THE HUCKLEBUCK Coast To Coast	*Polydor*	9
7	18	JEALOUS GUY Roxy Music	*Polydor*	8
-	19	CHI MAI (THEME FROM THE LIFE AND TIMES OF DAVID LLOYD GEORGE) Ennio Morricone ●	*BBC*	1
29	20	JUST A FEELING Bad Manners	*Magnet*	2
15	21	REWARD Teardrop Explodes	*Mercury*	7
16	22	PLANET EARTH Duran Duran	*EMI*	5
14	23	YOU BETTER YOU BET Who	*Polydor*	6
25	24	NEW ORLEANS Gillan	*Virgin*	3
20	25	JONES VS JONES/SUMMER MADNESS/FUNKY STUFF Kool and the Gang	*De-Lite*	7
18	26	KINGS OF THE WILD FRONTIER Adam and the Ants	*CBS*	8
-	27	AND THE BANDS PLAYED ON Saxon	*Carrere*	1
19	28	STAR Kiki Dee	*Ariola*	7
-	29	MUSCLEBOUND/GLOW Spandau Ballet	*Reformation*	1
24	30	I MISSED AGAIN Phil Collins	*Virgin*	5
-	31	FLOWERS OF ROMANCE Public Image Ltd	*Virgin*	1
32	[32]	UP THE HILL BACKWARDS David Bowie	*RCA*	2
-	33	WATCHING THE WHEELS John Lennon	*Geffen*	1
35	[34]	JITTERBUGGIN' Heatwave	*GTO*	3
36	[35]	JOHN I'M ONLY DANCING/BIG GREEN CAR Polecats	*Mercury*	4
-	36	MAKE THAT MOVE Shalamar	*Solar*	1
-	[37]	SKATEAWAY Dire Straits	*Vertigo*	1
-	38	I'M SO HAPPY/TIME Light Of The World	*Mercury*	1
-	39	ONLY CRYING Keith Marshall ●	*Arrival*	1
33	40	SLOW MOTION Ultravox	*Island*	3

LW	TW	*WEEK ENDING* **18 APRIL 1981**		Wks
2	[1]	MAKING YOUR MIND UP Bucks Fizz	*RCA*	4
1	2	THIS OLE HOUSE Shakin' Stevens	*Epic*	7
3	[3]	LATELY Stevie Wonder	*Motown*	6
19	4	CHI MAI (THEME FROM THE LIFE AND TIMES OF DAVID LLOYD GEORGE) Ennio Morricone	*BBC*	2
5	[5]	EINSTEIN A GO-GO Landscape	*RCA*	6
12	[6]	NIGHT GAMES Graham Bonnet	*Vertigo*	3
14	7	GOOD THING GOING Sugar Minott	*RCA*	3
11	8	CAN YOU FEEL IT Jacksons	*Epic*	7
9	[9]	IT'S A LOVE THING Whispers	*Solar*	5
7	10	INTUITION Linx	*Chrysalis*	5
4	11	KIDS IN AMERICA Kim Wilde	*RAK*	7
10	12	D-DAYS Hazel O'Connor	*Albion*	4

In these weeks ■ *This Ole House*, Shaky's first number one, is the sixth song to be number one in two different versions. It was over 26 years since Rosemary Clooney topped the charts with the same song, which is at this time the biggest gap between different versions of the same song at number one (04.04.81)■

□ Highest position disc reached ● Act's first ever week on chart

LW	TW	Title / Artist	Label	Wks
13	[13]	WHAT BECOMES OF THE BROKEN HEARTED Dave Stewart and Colin Blunstone	*Stiff*	5
15	**14**	ATTENTION TO ME Nolans	*Epic*	5
20	**15**	JUST A FEELING Bad Manners	*Magnet*	3
8	**16**	FOUR FROM TOYAH (EP) Toyah	*Safari*	8
6	**17**	CAPSTICK COMES HOME/THE SHEFFIELD GRINDER Tony Capstick and the Carlton Main Frickley Colliery Band	*Dingles*	4
29	**18**	MUSCLEBOUND/GLOW Spandau Ballet	*Reformation*	2
27	**19**	AND THE BANDS PLAYED ON Saxon	*Carrere*	2
24	**20**	NEW ORLEANS Gillan	*Virgin*	4
16	**21**	MIND OF A TOY Visage	*Polydor*	6
17	**22**	(DO) THE HUCKLEBUCK Coast To Coast	*Polydor*	10
22	**23**	PLANET EARTH Duran Duran	*EMI*	6
31	[24]	FLOWERS OF ROMANCE Public Image Ltd	*Virgin*	2
39	**25**	ONLY CRYING Keith Marshall	*Arrival*	2
-	**26**	BERMUDA TRIANGLE Barry Manilow	*Arista*	1
25	**27**	JONES VS JONES/SUMMER MADNESS/FUNKY STUFF Kool and the Gang	*De-Lite*	8
-	**28**	CAN'T GET ENOUGH OF YOU Eddy Grant	*Ice*	1
-	**29**	DON'T BREAK MY HEART AGAIN Whitesnake	*Liberty*	1
33	[30]	WATCHING THE WHEELS John Lennon	*Geffen*	2
26	**31**	KINGS OF THE WILD FRONTIER Adam and the Ants	*CBS*	9
36	**32**	MAKE THAT MOVE Shalamar	*Solar*	2
-	**33**	HIT AND RUN Girlschool ●	*Bronze*	1
18	**34**	JEALOUS GUY Roxy Music	*Polydor*	9
38	[35]	I'M SO HAPPY/TIME Light Of The World	*Mercury*	2
32	**36**	UP THE HILL BACKWARDS David Bowie	*RCA*	3
-	[37]	CROCODILES Echo and the Bunnymen ●	*Korova*	1
37	**38**	SKATEAWAY Dire Straits	*Vertigo*	2
-	**39**	AI NO CORRIDA (I-NO-KO-REE-DA) Quincy Jones	*A&M*	1
-	**40**	IS VIC THERE Department S ●	*Demon*	1

WEEK ENDING 25 APRIL 1981

LW	TW	Title / Artist	Label	Wks
1	[1]	MAKING YOUR MIND UP Bucks Fizz	*RCA*	5
4	[2]	CHI MAI (THEME FROM THE LIFE AND TIMES OF DAVID LLOYD GEORGE) Ennio Morricone	*BBC*	3
2	**3**	THIS OLE HOUSE Shakin' Stevens	*Epic*	8
7	[4]	GOOD THING GOING Sugar Minott	*RCA*	4
3	**5**	LATELY Stevie Wonder	*Motown*	7
5	**6**	EINSTEIN A GO-GO Landscape	*RCA*	7
8	**7**	CAN YOU FEEL IT Jacksons	*Epic*	8
6	**8**	NIGHT GAMES Graham Bonnet	*Vertigo*	4
9	[9]	IT'S A LOVE THING Whispers	*Solar*	6
14	**10**	ATTENTION TO ME Nolans	*Epic*	6
10	**11**	INTUITION Linx	*Chrysalis*	6
19	[12]	AND THE BANDS PLAYED ON Saxon	*Carrere*	3
15	[13]	JUST A FEELING Bad Manners	*Magnet*	4
11	**14**	KIDS IN AMERICA Kim Wilde	*RAK*	8
18	**15**	MUSCLEBOUND/GLOW Spandau Ballet	*Reformation*	3
12	**16**	D-DAYS Hazel O'Connor	*Albion*	5
-	**17**	STARS ON 45 Starsound ●	*CBS*	1
20	**18**	NEW ORLEANS Gillan	*Virgin*	5
13	**19**	WHAT BECOMES OF THE BROKEN HEARTED Dave Stewart and Colin Blunstone	*Stiff*	6
-	**20**	GREY DAY Madness	*Stiff*	1
25	**21**	ONLY CRYING Keith Marshall	*Arrival*	3
28	**22**	CAN'T GET ENOUGH OF YOU Eddy Grant	*Ice*	2
26	**23**	BERMUDA TRIANGLE Barry Manilow	*Arista*	2
17	**24**	CAPSTICK COMES HOME/THE SHEFFIELD GRINDER Tony Capstick and the Carlton Main Frickley Colliery Band	*Dingles*	5
29	**25**	DON'T BREAK MY HEART AGAIN Whitesnake	*Liberty*	2
24	**26**	FLOWERS OF ROMANCE Public Image Ltd	*Virgin*	3
16	**27**	FOUR FROM TOYAH (EP) Toyah	*Safari*	9
-	**28**	DROWNING/ALL OUT TO GET YOU Beat	*Go Feet*	1
39	**29**	AI NO CORRIDA (I-NO-KO-REE-DA) Quincy Jones	*A&M*	2
40	**30**	IS VIC THERE Department S	*Demon*	2
22	**31**	(DO) THE HUCKLEBUCK Coast To Coast	*Polydor*	11
21	**32**	MIND OF A TOY Visage	*Polydor*	7
32	**33**	MAKE THAT MOVE Shalamar	*Solar*	3
30	**34**	WATCHING THE WHEELS John Lennon	*Geffen*	3
33	**35**	HIT AND RUN Girlschool	*Bronze*	2
-	[36]	HUMPIN' Gap Band	*Mercury*	1
37	[37]	CROCODILES Echo and the Bunnymen	*Korova*	2
31	**38**	KINGS OF THE WILD FRONTIER Adam and the Ants	*CBS*	10
-	**39**	KEEP ON LOVING YOU REO Speedwagon ●	*Epic*	1
23	**40**	PLANET EARTH Duran Duran	*EMI*	7

WEEK ENDING 2 MAY 1981

LW	TW	Title / Artist	Label	Wks
1	[1]	MAKING YOUR MIND UP Bucks Fizz	*RCA*	6
2	[2]	CHI MAI (THEME FROM THE LIFE AND TIMES OF DAVID LLOYD GEORGE) Ennio Morricone	*BBC*	4
17	**3**	STARS ON 45 Starsound	*CBS*	2
4	[4]	GOOD THING GOING Sugar Minott	*RCA*	5
20	**5**	GREY DAY Madness	*Stiff*	2
7	[6]	CAN YOU FEEL IT Jacksons	*Epic*	9
3	**7**	THIS OLE HOUSE Shakin' Stevens	*Epic*	9
8	**8**	NIGHT GAMES Graham Bonnet	*Vertigo*	5
6	**9**	EINSTEIN A GO-GO Landscape	*RCA*	8
5	**10**	LATELY Stevie Wonder	*Motown*	8
9	**11**	IT'S A LOVE THING Whispers	*Solar*	7
10	**12**	ATTENTION TO ME Nolans	*Epic*	7
15	**13**	MUSCLEBOUND/GLOW Spandau Ballet	*Reformation*	4
21	**14**	ONLY CRYING Keith Marshall	*Arrival*	4
12	**15**	AND THE BANDS PLAYED ON Saxon	*Carrere*	4
13	**16**	JUST A FEELING Bad Manners	*Magnet*	5
18	[17]	NEW ORLEANS Gillan	*Virgin*	6
22	**18**	CAN'T GET ENOUGH OF YOU Eddy Grant	*Ice*	3
11	**19**	INTUITION Linx	*Chrysalis*	7
16	**20**	D-DAYS Hazel O'Connor	*Albion*	6
19	**21**	WHAT BECOMES OF THE BROKEN HEARTED Dave Stewart and Colin Blunstone	*Stiff*	7
28	[22]	DROWNING/ALL OUT TO GET YOU Beat	*Go Feet*	2
14	**23**	KIDS IN AMERICA Kim Wilde	*RAK*	9
26	[24]	FLOWERS OF ROMANCE Public Image Ltd	*Virgin*	4
25	**25**	DON'T BREAK MY HEART AGAIN Whitesnake	*Liberty*	3
23	**26**	BERMUDA TRIANGLE Barry Manilow	*Arista*	3
29	**27**	AI NO CORRIDA (I-NO-KO-REE-DA) Quincy Jones	*A&M*	3
30	**28**	IS VIC THERE Department S	*Demon*	3
39	**29**	KEEP ON LOVING YOU REO Speedwagon	*Epic*	2
33	[30]	MAKE THAT MOVE Shalamar	*Solar*	4
-	**31**	STRAY CAT STRUT Stray Cats	*Arista*	1
35	[32]	HIT AND RUN Girlschool	*Bronze*	3
27	**33**	FOUR FROM TOYAH (EP) Toyah	*Safari*	10
-	[34]	THE MAGNIFICENT SEVEN Clash	*CBS*	1
-	[35]	FLYING HIGH Freeez	*Beggars Banquet*	1
36	[36]	HUMPIN' Gap Band	*Mercury*	2
-	**37**	SWORDS OF A THOUSAND MEN Ten Pole Tudor ●	*Stiff*	1
-	[38]	LOVE GAMES Level 42 ●	*Polydor*	1
-	**39**	YOU DRIVE ME CRAZY Shakin' Stevens	*Epic*	1
38	**40**	KINGS OF THE WILD FRONTIER Adam and the Ants	*CBS*	11

WEEK ENDING 9 MAY 1981

LW	TW	Title / Artist	Label	Wks
-	[1]	STAND AND DELIVER Adam and the Ants	*CBS*	1
3	[2]	STARS ON 45 Starsound	*CBS*	3
2	**3**	CHI MAI (THEME FROM THE LIFE AND TIMES OF DAVID LLOYD GEORGE) Ennio Morricone	*BBC*	5
1	**4**	MAKING YOUR MIND UP Bucks Fizz	*RCA*	7
39	**5**	YOU DRIVE ME CRAZY Shakin' Stevens	*Epic*	2
5	**6**	GREY DAY Madness	*Stiff*	3
4	**7**	GOOD THING GOING Sugar Minott	*RCA*	6
6	**8**	CAN YOU FEEL IT Jacksons	*Epic*	10
12	[9]	ATTENTION TO ME Nolans	*Epic*	8
13	[10]	MUSCLEBOUND/GLOW Spandau Ballet	*Reformation*	5
8	**11**	NIGHT GAMES Graham Bonnet	*Vertigo*	6
14	[12]	ONLY CRYING Keith Marshall	*Arrival*	5
18	[13]	CAN'T GET ENOUGH OF YOU Eddy Grant	*Ice*	4
11	**14**	IT'S A LOVE THING Whispers	*Solar*	8

■Quincy Jones' *Ai No Corrida* is the first Japanese language title to hit the charts since Kyu Sakamoto's *Sukiyaki* in 1963 (18.04.81) ■ *Stand And Deliver* becomes the 11th single since the first ever chart week to crash in at number one (09.05.81)■

May 1981

□ Highest position disc reached ● Act's first ever week on chart

LW	TW	Title	Artist	Label	Wks
26	[15]	BERMUDA TRIANGLE	Barry Manilow	Arista	4
15	16	AND THE BANDS PLAYED ON	Saxon	Carrere	5
25	[17]	DON'T BREAK MY HEART AGAIN	Whitesnake	Liberty	4
16	18	JUST A FEELING	Bad Manners	Magnet	6
7	19	THIS OLE HOUSE	Shakin' Stevens	Epic	10
9	20	EINSTEIN A GO-GO	Landscape	RCA	9
29	21	KEEP ON LOVING YOU	REO Speedwagon	Epic	3
37	22	SWORDS OF A THOUSAND MEN	Ten Pole Tudor	Stiff	2
17	23	NEW ORLEANS	Gillan	Virgin	7
27	24	AI NO CORRIDA (I-NO-KO-REE-DA)	Quincy Jones	A&M	4
10	25	LATELY	Stevie Wonder	Motown	9
31	26	STRAY CAT STRUT	Stray Cats	Arista	2
-	27	WHEN HE SHINES	Sheena Easton	EMI	1
-	28	KILLERS LIVE (EP)	Thin Lizzy	Vertigo	1
28	29	IS VIC THERE	Department S	Demon	4
-	30	TREASON (IT'S JUST A STORY)	Teardrop Explodes	Mercury	1
22	31	DROWNING/ALL OUT TO GET YOU	Beat	Go Feet	3
-	32	CHEQUERED LOVE	Kim Wilde	RAK	1
20	33	D-DAYS	Hazel O'Connor	Albion	7
-	34	THE SOUND OF THE CROWD	Human League ●	Virgin	1
24	35	FLOWERS OF ROMANCE	Public Image Ltd	Virgin	5
-	36	IT'S GOING TO HAPPEN	Undertones	Ardeck	1
30	37	MAKE THAT MOVE	Shalamar	Solar	5
34	38	THE MAGNIFICENT SEVEN	Clash	CBS	2
38	39	LOVE GAMES	Level 42	Polydor	2
19	40	INTUITION	Linx	Chrysalis	8

WEEK ENDING 16 MAY 1981

LW	TW	Title	Artist	Label	Wks
1	[1]	STAND AND DELIVER	Adam and the Ants	CBS	2
5	[2]	YOU DRIVE ME CRAZY	Shakin' Stevens	Epic	3
2	3	STARS ON 45	Starsound	CBS	4
6	[4]	GREY DAY	Madness	Stiff	4
3	5	CHI MAI (THEME FROM THE LIFE AND TIMES OF DAVID LLOYD GEORGE)	Ennio Morricone	BBC	6
4	6	MAKING YOUR MIND UP	Bucks Fizz	RCA	8
21	[7]	KEEP ON LOVING YOU	REO Speedwagon	Epic	4
-	8	OSSIE'S DREAM	Tottenham Hotspur FA Cup Final Squad ●	Shelf	1
32	9	CHEQUERED LOVE	Kim Wilde	RAK	2
22	10	SWORDS OF A THOUSAND MEN	Ten Pole Tudor	Stiff	3
8	11	CAN YOU FEEL IT	Jacksons	Epic	11
9	12	ATTENTION TO ME	Nolans	Epic	9
7	13	GOOD THING GOING	Sugar Minott	RCA	7
26	14	STRAY CAT STRUT	Stray Cats	Arista	3
10	15	MUSCLEBOUND/GLOW	Spandau Ballet	Reformation	6
24	16	AI NO CORRIDA (I-NO-KO-REE-DA)	Quincy Jones	A&M	5
12	17	ONLY CRYING	Keith Marshall	Arrival	6
13	18	CAN'T GET ENOUGH OF YOU	Eddy Grant	Ice	5
15	19	BERMUDA TRIANGLE	Barry Manilow	Arista	5
-	20	BETTE DAVIS EYES	Kim Carnes ●	EMI America	1
17	21	DON'T BREAK MY HEART AGAIN	Whitesnake	Liberty	5
29	[22]	IS VIC THERE	Department S	Demon	5
27	23	WHEN HE SHINES	Sheena Easton	EMI	2
28	24	KILLERS LIVE (EP)	Thin Lizzy	Vertigo	2
30	25	TREASON (IT'S JUST A STORY)	Teardrop Explodes	Mercury	2
31	26	DROWNING/ALL OUT TO GET YOU	Beat	Go Feet	4
34	27	THE SOUND OF THE CROWD	Human League	Virgin	2
19	28	THIS OLE HOUSE	Shakin' Stevens	Epic	11
36	29	IT'S GOING TO HAPPEN	Undertones	Ardeck	2
16	30	AND THE BANDS PLAYED ON	Saxon	Carrere	6
11	31	NIGHT GAMES	Graham Bonnet	Vertigo	7
18	32	JUST A FEELING	Bad Manners	Magnet	7
23	33	NEW ORLEANS	Gillan	Virgin	8
20	34	EINSTEIN A GO-GO	Landscape	RCA	10
25	35	LATELY	Stevie Wonder	Motown	10
14	36	IT'S A LOVE THING	Whispers	Solar	9
-	37	I WANT TO BE FREE	Toyah	Safari	1
-	38	CARELESS MEMORIES	Duran Duran	EMI	1
-	39	BEING WITH YOU	Smokey Robinson	Motown	1
35	40	FLOWERS OF ROMANCE	Public Image Ltd	Virgin	6

WEEK ENDING 23 MAY 1981

LW	TW	Title	Artist	Label	Wks
1	[1]	STAND AND DELIVER	Adam and the Ants	CBS	3
2	[2]	YOU DRIVE ME CRAZY	Shakin' Stevens	Epic	4
3	3	STARS ON 45	Starsound	CBS	5
9	[4]	CHEQUERED LOVE	Kim Wilde	RAK	3
8	[5]	OSSIE'S DREAM	Tottenham Hotspur FA Cup Final Squad	Shelf	2
10	[6]	SWORDS OF A THOUSAND MEN	Ten Pole Tudor	Stiff	4
7	[7]	KEEP ON LOVING YOU	REO Speedwagon	Epic	5
4	8	GREY DAY	Madness	Stiff	5
5	9	CHI MAI (THEME FROM THE LIFE AND TIMES OF DAVID LLOYD GEORGE)	Ennio Morricone	BBC	7
20	[10]	BETTE DAVIS EYES	Kim Carnes	EMI America	2
14	[11]	STRAY CAT STRUT	Stray Cats	Arista	4
23	[12]	WHEN HE SHINES	Sheena Easton	EMI	3
37	13	I WANT TO BE FREE	Toyah	Safari	2
16	[14]	AI NO CORRIDA (I-NO-KO-REE-DA)	Quincy Jones	A&M	6
27	15	THE SOUND OF THE CROWD	Human League	Virgin	3
6	16	MAKING YOUR MIND UP	Bucks Fizz	RCA	9
17	17	ONLY CRYING	Keith Marshall	Arrival	7
25	[18]	TREASON (IT'S JUST A STORY)	Teardrop Explodes	Mercury	3
24	[19]	KILLERS LIVE (EP)	Thin Lizzy	Vertigo	3
12	20	ATTENTION TO ME	Nolans	Epic	10
29	21	IT'S GOING TO HAPPEN	Undertones	Ardeck	3
15	22	MUSCLEBOUND/GLOW	Spandau Ballet	Reformation	7
39	23	BEING WITH YOU	Smokey Robinson	Motown	2
18	24	CAN'T GET ENOUGH OF YOU	Eddy Grant	Ice	6
26	25	DROWNING/ALL OUT TO GET YOU	Beat	Go Feet	5
22	26	IS VIC THERE	Department S	Demon	6
11	27	CAN YOU FEEL IT	Jacksons	Epic	12
-	28	HOW 'BOUT US	Champaign ●	CBS	1
13	29	GOOD THING GOING	Sugar Minott	RCA	8
19	30	BERMUDA TRIANGLE	Barry Manilow	Arista	6
21	31	DON'T BREAK MY HEART AGAIN	Whitesnake	Liberty	6
-	32	AIN'T NO STOPPING	Enigma ●	Creole	1
31	33	NIGHT GAMES	Graham Bonnet	Vertigo	8
-	34	CHARIOTS OF FIRE	Vangelis ●	Polydor	1
-	35	DON'T LET IT PASS YOU BY/DON'T SLOW DOWN	UB40	DEP International	1
-	[36]	HI-DE-HI	Paul Shane and the Yellowcoats ●	EMI	1
38	[37]	CARELESS MEMORIES	Duran Duran	EMI	2
-	38	ROCKABILLY GUY	Polecats	Mercury	1
-	[39]	POCKET CALCULATOR	Kraftwerk	EMI	1
-	40	IS THAT LOVE	Squeeze	A&M	1

WEEK ENDING 30 MAY 1981

LW	TW	Title	Artist	Label	Wks
1	[1]	STAND AND DELIVER	Adam and the Ants	CBS	4
2	[2]	YOU DRIVE ME CRAZY	Shakin' Stevens	Epic	5
3	3	STARS ON 45	Starsound	CBS	6
4	[4]	CHEQUERED LOVE	Kim Wilde	RAK	4
5	[5]	OSSIE'S DREAM	Tottenham Hotspur FA Cup Final Squad	Shelf	3
6	[6]	SWORDS OF A THOUSAND MEN	Ten Pole Tudor	Stiff	5
23	7	BEING WITH YOU	Smokey Robinson	Motown	3
7	8	KEEP ON LOVING YOU	REO Speedwagon	Epic	6
13	9	I WANT TO BE FREE	Toyah	Safari	3
10	[10]	BETTE DAVIS EYES	Kim Carnes	EMI America	3
28	11	HOW 'BOUT US	Champaign	CBS	2
15	[12]	THE SOUND OF THE CROWD	Human League	Virgin	4
-	[13]	ALL THOSE YEARS AGO	George Harrison	Dark Horse	1
11	14	STRAY CAT STRUT	Stray Cats	Arista	5
8	15	GREY DAY	Madness	Stiff	6
35	[16]	DON'T LET IT PASS YOU BY/DON'T SLOW DOWN	UB40	DEP International	2
32	17	AIN'T NO STOPPING	Enigma	Creole	2
21	[18]	IT'S GOING TO HAPPEN	Undertones	Ardeck	4
12	19	WHEN HE SHINES	Sheena Easton	EMI	4
9	20	CHI MAI (THEME FROM THE LIFE AND TIMES OF DAVID LLOYD GEORGE)	Ennio Morricone	BBC	8
18	21	TREASON (IT'S JUST A STORY)	Teardrop Explodes	Mercury	4

In these weeks ■ For four weeks, the top two are unchanged, for three of those weeks the top three are unchanged, and for one week the top six are unchanged (30.05.81) ■ George Harrison's tribute to John Lennon, *All Those Years Ago*, is his first hit on his own Dark Horse label (30.05.81)■

June 1981

□ Highest position disc reached ● Act's first ever week on chart

LW	TW	Title / Artist	Label	Wks
14	22	AI NO CORRIDA (I-NO-KO-REE-DA) Quincy Jones	A&M	7
-	23	WILL YOU Hazel O'Connor	A&M	1
-	24	ONE DAY IN YOUR LIFE Michael Jackson	Motown	1
34	25	CHARIOTS OF FIRE Vangelis	Polydor	2
16	26	MAKING YOUR MIND UP Bucks Fizz	RCA	10
19	27	KILLERS LIVE (EP) Thin Lizzy	Vertigo	4
-	28	MORE THAN IN LOVE Kate Robbins ●	RCA	1
17	29	ONLY CRYING Keith Marshall	Arrival	8
-	30	LET'S JUMP THE BROOMSTICK Coast To Coast	Polydor	1
25	31	DROWNING/ALL OUT TO GET YOU Beat	Go Feet	6
-	32	SPELLBOUND Siouxsie and the Banshees	Polydor	1
26	33	IS VIC THERE Department S	Demon	7
-	[34]	JUST THE TWO OF US Grover Washington Jr ●	Elektra	1
24	35	CAN'T GET ENOUGH OF YOU Eddy Grant	Ice	7
38	36	ROCKABILLY GUY Polecats	Mercury	2
37	[37]	CARELESS MEMORIES Duran Duran	EMI	3
36	38	HI-DE-HI Paul Shane and the Yellowcoats	EMI	2
27	39	CAN YOU FEEL IT Jacksons	Epic	13
29	40	GOOD THING GOING Sugar Minott	RCA	9

WEEK ENDING 6 JUNE 1981

LW	TW	Title / Artist	Label	Wks
1	[1]	STAND AND DELIVER Adam and the Ants	CBS	5
2	[2]	YOU DRIVE ME CRAZY Shakin' Stevens	Epic	6
7	3	BEING WITH YOU Smokey Robinson	Motown	4
-	[4]	FUNERAL PYRE Jam	Polydor	1
4	5	CHEQUERED LOVE Kim Wilde	RAK	5
11	6	HOW 'BOUT US Champaign	CBS	3
3	7	STARS ON 45 Starsound	CBS	7
9	[8]	I WANT TO BE FREE Toyah	Safari	4
6	9	SWORDS OF A THOUSAND MEN Ten Pole Tudor	Stiff	6
23	10	WILL YOU Hazel O'Connor	A&M	2
10	11	BETTE DAVIS EYES Kim Carnes	EMI America	4
24	12	ONE DAY IN YOUR LIFE Michael Jackson	Motown	2
28	13	MORE THAN IN LOVE Kate Robbins	RCA	2
8	14	KEEP ON LOVING YOU REO Speedwagon	Epic	7
13	15	ALL THOSE YEARS AGO George Harrison	Dark Horse	2
17	16	AIN'T NO STOPPING Enigma	Creole	3
5	17	OSSIE'S DREAM Tottenham Hotspur FA Cup Final Squad	Shelf	4
12	18	THE SOUND OF THE CROWD Human League	Virgin	5
25	19	CHARIOTS OF FIRE Vangelis	Polydor	3
14	20	STRAY CAT STRUT Stray Cats	Arista	6
16	21	DON'T LET IT PASS YOU BY/DON'T SLOW DOWN UB40	DEP International	3
18	22	IT'S GOING TO HAPPEN Undertones	Ardeck	5
-	23	GOING BACK TO MY ROOTS Odyssey	RCA	1
19	24	WHEN HE SHINES Sheena Easton	EMI	5
21	25	TREASON (IT'S JUST A STORY) Teardrop Explodes	Mercury	5
22	26	AI NO CORRIDA (I-NO-KO-REE-DA) Quincy Jones	A&M	8
15	27	GREY DAY Madness	Stiff	7
20	28	CHI MAI (THEME FROM THE LIFE AND TIMES OF DAVID LLOYD GEORGE) Ennio Morricone	BBC	9
32	29	SPELLBOUND Siouxsie and the Banshees	Polydor	2
30	30	LET'S JUMP THE BROOMSTICK Coast To Coast	Polydor	2
27	31	KILLERS LIVE (EP) Thin Lizzy	Vertigo	5
31	32	DROWNING/ALL OUT TO GET YOU Beat	Go Feet	7
-	33	TAKE IT TO THE TOP Kool and the Gang	De-Lite	1
34	[34]	JUST THE TWO OF US Grover Washington Jr	Elektra	2
36	[35]	ROCKABILLY GUY Polecats	Mercury	3
29	36	ONLY CRYING Keith Marshall	Arrival	9
26	37	MAKING YOUR MIND UP Bucks Fizz	RCA	11
37	38	CARELESS MEMORIES Duran Duran	EMI	4
33	39	IS VIC THERE Department S	Demon	8
-	40	IS THAT LOVE Squeeze	A&M	2

WEEK ENDING 13 JUNE 1981

LW	TW	Title / Artist	Label	Wks
3	[1]	BEING WITH YOU Smokey Robinson	Motown	5
13	[2]	MORE THAN IN LOVE Kate Robbins	RCA	3
12	3	ONE DAY IN YOUR LIFE Michael Jackson	Motown	3
4	[4]	FUNERAL PYRE Jam	Polydor	2
1	5	STAND AND DELIVER Adam and the Ants	CBS	6
6	6	HOW 'BOUT US Champaign	CBS	4
2	7	YOU DRIVE ME CRAZY Shakin' Stevens	Epic	7
23	8	GOING BACK TO MY ROOTS Odyssey	RCA	2
10	9	WILL YOU Hazel O'Connor	A&M	3
8	10	I WANT TO BE FREE Toyah	Safari	5
16	[11]	AIN'T NO STOPPING Enigma	Creole	4
19	[12]	CHARIOTS OF FIRE Vangelis	Polydor	4
7	13	STARS ON 45 Starsound	CBS	8
11	14	BETTE DAVIS EYES Kim Carnes	EMI America	5
15	15	ALL THOSE YEARS AGO George Harrison	Dark Horse	3
9	16	SWORDS OF A THOUSAND MEN Ten Pole Tudor	Stiff	7
-	17	ALL STOOD STILL Ultravox	Chrysalis	1
5	18	CHEQUERED LOVE Kim Wilde	RAK	6
21	19	DON'T LET IT PASS YOU BY/DON'T SLOW DOWN UB40	DEP International	4
14	20	KEEP ON LOVING YOU REO Speedwagon	Epic	8
18	21	THE SOUND OF THE CROWD Human League	Virgin	6
-	22	TEDDY BEAR Red Sovine ●	Starday	1
29	23	SPELLBOUND Siouxsie and the Banshees	Polydor	3
33	24	TAKE IT TO THE TOP Kool and the Gang	De-Lite	2
-	25	PIECE OF THE ACTION Bucks Fizz	RCA	1
17	26	OSSIE'S DREAM Tottenham Hotspur FA Cup Final Squad	Shelf	5
20	27	STRAY CAT STRUT Stray Cats	Arista	7
30	[28]	LET'S JUMP THE BROOMSTICK Coast To Coast	Polydor	3
-	29	IF LEAVING ME IS EASY Phil Collins	Virgin	1
25	30	TREASON (IT'S JUST A STORY) Teardrop Explodes	Mercury	6
-	31	BODY TALK Imagination ●	R&B	1
22	32	IT'S GOING TO HAPPEN Undertones	Ardeck	6
24	33	WHEN HE SHINES Sheena Easton	EMI	6
-	34	MEMORY Elaine Paige ●	Polydor	1
40	[35]	IS THAT LOVE Squeeze	A&M	3
-	[36]	TOO DRUNK TO FUCK Dead Kennedys ●	Cherry Red	1
-	[37]	WOULD I LIE TO YOU Whitesnake	Liberty	1
-	38	DANCING ON THE FLOOR (HOOKED ON LOVE) Third World	CBS	1
28	39	CHI MAI (THEME FROM THE LIFE AND TIMES OF DAVID LLOYD GEORGE) Ennio Morricone	BBC	10
34	40	JUST THE TWO OF US Grover Washington Jr	Elektra	3

WEEK ENDING 20 JUNE 1981

LW	TW	Title / Artist	Label	Wks
1	[1]	BEING WITH YOU Smokey Robinson	Motown	6
3	2	ONE DAY IN YOUR LIFE Michael Jackson	Motown	4
2	3	MORE THAN IN LOVE Kate Robbins	RCA	4
22	[4]	TEDDY BEAR Red Sovine	Starday	2
6	[5]	HOW 'BOUT US Champaign	CBS	5
8	6	GOING BACK TO MY ROOTS Odyssey	RCA	3
5	7	STAND AND DELIVER Adam and the Ants	CBS	7
9	[8]	WILL YOU Hazel O'Connor	A&M	4
17	9	ALL STOOD STILL Ultravox	Chrysalis	2
7	10	YOU DRIVE ME CRAZY Shakin' Stevens	Epic	8
10	11	I WANT TO BE FREE Toyah	Safari	6
4	12	FUNERAL PYRE Jam	Polydor	3
11	13	AIN'T NO STOPPING Enigma	Creole	5
12	14	CHARIOTS OF FIRE Vangelis	Polydor	5
34	15	MEMORY Elaine Paige	Polydor	2
16	16	SWORDS OF A THOUSAND MEN Ten Pole Tudor	Stiff	8
25	17	PIECE OF THE ACTION Bucks Fizz	RCA	2
19	18	DON'T LET IT PASS YOU BY/DON'T SLOW DOWN UB40	DEP International	5
31	19	BODY TALK Imagination	R&B	2
15	20	ALL THOSE YEARS AGO George Harrison	Dark Horse	4
-	21	GHOST TOWN Specials	2 Tone	1
24	22	TAKE IT TO THE TOP Kool and the Gang	De-Lite	3
23	23	SPELLBOUND Siouxsie and the Banshees	Polydor	4
13	24	STARS ON 45 Starsound	CBS	9
14	25	BETTE DAVIS EYES Kim Carnes	EMI America	6
18	26	CHEQUERED LOVE Kim Wilde	RAK	7
29	27	IF LEAVING ME IS EASY Phil Collins	Virgin	2
28	[28]	LET'S JUMP THE BROOMSTICK Coast To Coast	Polydor	4

■Red Sovine's maudlin tale of warm-hearted C.B. truckers, *Teddy Bear*, climbs to number four just over a year after the country superstar's death (20.06.81) ■ The Enigma that reaches a career best position of 11 with *Ain't No Stopping* is not the same Enigma that will top the charts in 1991 with *Sadness* (13.06.81)■

June 1981

□ Highest position disc reached ● Act's first ever week on chart

LW	TW	Title	Artist	Label	Wks
20	29	KEEP ON LOVING YOU	REO Speedwagon	*Epic*	9
21	30	THE SOUND OF THE CROWD	Human League	*Virgin*	7
38	31	DANCING ON THE FLOOR (HOOKED ON LOVE)	Third World	*CBS*	2
-	32	THROW AWAY THE KEY	Linx	*Chrysalis*	1
-	33	NO LAUGHING IN HEAVEN	Gillan	*Virgin*	1
-	34	YOU MIGHT NEED SOMEBODY	Randy Crawford	*Warner Brothers*	1
-	35	WIKKA WRAP	Evasions ●	*Groove*	1
35	36	IS THAT LOVE	Squeeze	*A&M*	4
37	[37]	WOULD I LIE TO YOU	Whitesnake	*Liberty*	2
-	38	NO WOMAN NO CRY	Bob Marley and the Wailers	*Island*	1
-	[39]	MULTIPLICATION	Showaddywaddy	*Arista*	1
-	[40]	NORMAN BATES	Landscape	*RCA*	1

WEEK ENDING 27 JUNE 1981

LW	TW	Title	Artist	Label	Wks
2	[1]	ONE DAY IN YOUR LIFE	Michael Jackson	*Motown*	5
1	2	BEING WITH YOU	Smokey Robinson	*Motown*	7
3	3	MORE THAN IN LOVE	Kate Robbins and Beyond	*RCA*	5
4	[4]	TEDDY BEAR	Red Sovine	*Starday*	3
6	5	GOING BACK TO MY ROOTS	Odyssey	*RCA*	4
21	6	GHOST TOWN	Specials	*2 Tone*	2
5	7	HOW 'BOUT US	Champaign	*CBS*	6
9	[8]	ALL STOOD STILL	Ultravox	*Chrysalis*	3
15	9	MEMORY	Elaine Paige	*Polydor*	3
8	10	WILL YOU	Hazel O'Connor	*A&M*	5
19	11	BODY TALK	Imagination	*R&B*	3
17	[12]	PIECE OF THE ACTION	Bucks Fizz	*RCA*	3
7	13	STAND AND DELIVER	Adam and the Ants	*CBS*	8
11	14	I WANT TO BE FREE	Toyah	*Safari*	7
22	[15]	TAKE IT TO THE TOP	Kool and the Gang	*De-Lite*	4
10	16	YOU DRIVE ME CRAZY	Shakin' Stevens	*Epic*	9
27	[17]	IF LEAVING ME IS EASY	Phil Collins	*Virgin*	3
-	18	CAN CAN	Bad Manners	*Magnet*	1
13	19	AIN'T NO STOPPING	Enigma	*Creole*	6
38	20	NO WOMAN NO CRY	Bob Marley and the Wailers	*Island*	2
14	21	CHARIOTS OF FIRE	Vangelis	*Polydor*	6
23	[22]	SPELLBOUND	Siouxsie and the Banshees	*Polydor*	5
32	23	THROW AWAY THE KEY	Linx	*Chrysalis*	2
12	24	FUNERAL PYRE	Jam	*Polydor*	4
18	25	DON'T LET IT PASS YOU BY/DON'T SLOW DOWN	UB40	*DEP International*	6
-	26	RAZZAMATAZZ	Quincy Jones	*A&M*	1
31	27	DANCING ON THE FLOOR (HOOKED ON LOVE)	Third World	*CBS*	3
34	28	YOU MIGHT NEED SOMEBODY	Randy Crawford	*Warner Brothers*	2
-	29	CAN'T HAPPEN HERE	Rainbow	*Polydor*	1
-	30	WORDY RAPPINGHOOD	Tom Tom Club ●	*Island*	1
35	31	WIKKA WRAP	Evasions	*Groove*	2
33	32	NO LAUGHING IN HEAVEN	Gillan	*Virgin*	2
-	[33]	DOORS OF YOUR HEART	Beat	*Go Feet*	1
-	[34]	THE RACE IS ON	Dave Edmunds and the Stray Cats ●	*Swansong*	1
-	[35]	THE RIVER	Bruce Springsteen ●	*CBS*	1
24	36	STARS ON 45	Starsound	*CBS*	10
20	37	ALL THOSE YEARS AGO	George Harrison	*Dark Horse*	5
16	38	SWORDS OF A THOUSAND MEN	Ten Pole Tudor	*Stiff*	9
28	39	LET'S JUMP THE BROOMSTICK	Coast To Coast	*Polydor*	5
-	40	THERE'S A GUY WORKS DOWN THE CHIP SHOP SWEARS HE'S ELVIS	Kirsty MacColl ●	*Polydor*	1

WEEK ENDING 4 JULY 1981

LW	TW	Title	Artist	Label	Wks
1	[1]	ONE DAY IN YOUR LIFE	Michael Jackson	*Motown*	6
6	2	GHOST TOWN	Specials	*2 Tone*	3
18	[3]	CAN CAN	Bad Manners	*Magnet*	2
5	[4]	GOING BACK TO MY ROOTS	Odyssey	*RCA*	5
2	5	BEING WITH YOU	Smokey Robinson	*Motown*	8
9	[6]	MEMORY	Elaine Paige	*Polydor*	4
11	7	BODY TALK	Imagination	*R&B*	4
3	8	MORE THAN IN LOVE	Kate Robbins and Beyond	*RCA*	6
4	9	TEDDY BEAR	Red Sovine	*Starday*	4
7	10	HOW 'BOUT US	Champaign	*CBS*	7
8	11	ALL STOOD STILL	Ultravox	*Chrysalis*	4
20	12	NO WOMAN NO CRY	Bob Marley and the Wailers	*Island*	3
12	13	PIECE OF THE ACTION	Bucks Fizz	*RCA*	4
30	14	WORDY RAPPINGHOOD	Tom Tom Club	*Island*	2
-	15	STARS ON 45 (VOLUME 2)	Starsound	*CBS*	1
26	16	RAZZAMATAZZ	Quincy Jones	*A&M*	2
28	17	YOU MIGHT NEED SOMEBODY	Randy Crawford	*Warner Brothers*	3
15	18	TAKE IT TO THE TOP	Kool and the Gang	*De-Lite*	5
10	19	WILL YOU	Hazel O'Connor	*A&M*	6
31	[20]	WIKKA WRAP	Evasions	*Groove*	3
23	[21]	THROW AWAY THE KEY	Linx	*Chrysalis*	3
40	22	THERE'S A GUY WORKS DOWN THE CHIP SHOP SWEARS HE'S ELVIS	Kirsty MacColl	*Polydor*	2
17	23	IF LEAVING ME IS EASY	Phil Collins	*Virgin*	4
14	24	I WANT TO BE FREE	Toyah	*Safari*	8
27	25	DANCING ON THE FLOOR (HOOKED ON LOVE)	Third World	*CBS*	4
13	26	STAND AND DELIVER	Adam and the Ants	*CBS*	9
-	27	NEW LIFE	Depeche Mode ●	*Mute*	1
16	28	YOU DRIVE ME CRAZY	Shakin' Stevens	*Epic*	10
29	29	CAN'T HAPPEN HERE	Rainbow	*Polydor*	2
21	30	CHARIOTS OF FIRE	Vangelis	*Polydor*	7
32	[31]	NO LAUGHING IN HEAVEN	Gillan	*Virgin*	3
22	32	SPELLBOUND	Siouxsie and the Banshees	*Polydor*	6
33	[33]	DOORS OF YOUR HEART	Beat	*Go Feet*	2
-	34	FOR YOUR EYES ONLY	Sheena Easton	*EMI*	1
35	[35]	THE RIVER	Bruce Springsteen	*CBS*	2
25	36	DON'T LET IT PASS YOU BY/DON'T SLOW DOWN	UB40	*DEP International*	7
19	37	AIN'T NO STOPPING	Enigma	*Creole*	7
24	38	FUNERAL PYRE	Jam	*Polydor*	5
34	39	THE RACE IS ON	Dave Edmunds and the Stray Cats	*Swansong*	2
-	40	ME NO POP I	Kid Creole and the Coconuts present Coati Mundi ●	*Ze*	1

WEEK ENDING 11 JULY 1981

LW	TW	Title	Artist	Label	Wks
2	[1]	GHOST TOWN	Specials	*2 Tone*	4
1	2	ONE DAY IN YOUR LIFE	Michael Jackson	*Motown*	7
3	[3]	CAN CAN	Bad Manners	*Magnet*	3
15	4	STARS ON 45 (VOLUME 2)	Starsound	*CBS*	2
4	5	GOING BACK TO MY ROOTS	Odyssey	*RCA*	6
7	6	BODY TALK	Imagination	*R&B*	5
6	7	MEMORY	Elaine Paige	*Polydor*	5
5	8	BEING WITH YOU	Smokey Robinson	*Motown*	9
12	9	NO WOMAN NO CRY	Bob Marley and the Wailers	*Island*	4
14	10	WORDY RAPPINGHOOD	Tom Tom Club	*Island*	3
16	[11]	RAZZAMATAZZ	Quincy Jones	*A&M*	3
17	12	YOU MIGHT NEED SOMEBODY	Randy Crawford	*Warner Brothers*	4
25	13	DANCING ON THE FLOOR (HOOKED ON LOVE)	Third World	*CBS*	5
-	14	MOTORHEAD LIVE	Motorhead	*Bronze*	1
13	15	PIECE OF THE ACTION	Bucks Fizz	*RCA*	5
22	16	THERE'S A GUY WORKS DOWN THE CHIP SHOP SWEARS HE'S ELVIS	Kirsty MacColl	*Polydor*	3
8	17	MORE THAN IN LOVE	Kate Robbins and Beyond	*RCA*	7
10	18	HOW 'BOUT US	Champaign	*CBS*	8
9	19	TEDDY BEAR	Red Sovine	*Starday*	5
11	20	ALL STOOD STILL	Ultravox	*Chrysalis*	5
27	21	NEW LIFE	Depeche Mode	*Mute*	2
21	22	THROW AWAY THE KEY	Linx	*Chrysalis*	4
20	23	WIKKA WRAP	Evasions	*Groove*	4
29	24	CAN'T HAPPEN HERE	Rainbow	*Polydor*	3
18	25	TAKE IT TO THE TOP	Kool and the Gang	*De-Lite*	6
-	26	SAT IN YOUR LAP	Kate Bush	*EMI*	1
34	27	FOR YOUR EYES ONLY	Sheena Easton	*EMI*	2

In these weeks ■ Motown displaces Motown at number one, the only time the influential label is ever to achieve this feat (27.06.81) ■ *Memory* by Elaine Paige, from Andrew Lloyd Webber's musical extravaganza 'Cats', is the biggest hit single from a London show by the artist who created the song in the show. It will retain that title until Jason Donovan tops the charts in 1991 with *Any Dream Will Do*, another Lloyd Webber song (04.07.81)■

LW	TW	Title	Artist	Label	Wks
26	28	STAND AND DELIVER	Adam and the Ants	*CBS*	10
19	29	WILL YOU	Hazel O'Connor	*A&M*	7
24	30	I WANT TO BE FREE	Toyah	*Safari*	9
23	31	IF LEAVING ME IS EASY	Phil Collins	*Virgin*	5
40	[32]	ME NO POP I	Kid Creole and the Coconuts present Coati Mundi	*Ze*	2
33	[33]	DOORS OF YOUR HEART	Beat	*Go Feet*	3
31	34	NO LAUGHING IN HEAVEN	Gillan	*Virgin*	4
39	35	THE RACE IS ON	Dave Edmunds and the Stray Cats	*Swansong*	3
-	36	TAKE IT ON THE RUN	REO Speedwagon	*Epic*	1
32	37	SPELLBOUND	Siouxsie and the Banshees	*Polydor*	7
-	38	I'M IN LOVE	Evelyn King	*RCA*	1
-	39	VISAGE	Visage	*Polydor*	1
28	40	YOU DRIVE ME CRAZY	Shakin' Stevens	*Epic*	11

WEEK ENDING 18 JULY 1981

LW	TW	Title	Artist	Label	Wks
1	[1]	GHOST TOWN	Specials	*2 Tone*	5
4	[2]	STARS ON 45 (VOLUME 2)	Starsound	*CBS*	3
3	[3]	CAN CAN	Bad Manners	*Magnet*	4
6	[4]	BODY TALK	Imagination	*R&B*	6
2	5	ONE DAY IN YOUR LIFE	Michael Jackson	*Motown*	8
14	[6]	MOTORHEAD LIVE	Motorhead	*Bronze*	2
10	[7]	WORDY RAPPINGHOOD	Tom Tom Club	*Island*	4
9	[8]	NO WOMAN NO CRY	Bob Marley and the Wailers	*Island*	5
5	9	GOING BACK TO MY ROOTS	Odyssey	*RCA*	7
7	10	MEMORY	Elaine Paige	*Polydor*	6
12	[11]	YOU MIGHT NEED SOMEBODY	Randy Crawford	*Warner Brothers*	5
13	12	DANCING ON THE FLOOR (HOOKED ON LOVE)	Third World	*CBS*	6
11	13	RAZZAMATAZZ	Quincy Jones	*A&M*	4
16	[14]	THERE'S A GUY WORKS DOWN THE CHIP SHOP SWEARS HE'S ELVIS	Kirsty MacColl	*Polydor*	4
26	15	SAT IN YOUR LAP	Kate Bush	*EMI*	2
15	16	PIECE OF THE ACTION	Bucks Fizz	*RCA*	6
-	17	LAY ALL YOUR LOVE ON ME	Abba	*Epic*	1
-	18	CHANT NO. 1 (I DON'T NEED THIS PRESSURE ON)	Spandau Ballet	*Reformation*	1
21	19	NEW LIFE	Depeche Mode	*Mute*	3
24	[20]	CAN'T HAPPEN HERE	Rainbow	*Polydor*	4
27	21	FOR YOUR EYES ONLY	Sheena Easton	*EMI*	3
22	22	THROW AWAY THE KEY	Linx	*Chrysalis*	5
23	23	WIKKA WRAP	Evasions	*Groove*	5
20	24	ALL STOOD STILL	Ultravox	*Chrysalis*	6
39	25	VISAGE	Visage	*Polydor*	2
-	26	NEVER SURRENDER	Saxon	*Carrere*	1
8	27	BEING WITH YOU	Smokey Robinson	*Motown*	10
18	28	HOW 'BOUT US	Champaign	*CBS*	9
17	29	MORE THAN IN LOVE	Kate Robbins and Beyond	*RCA*	8
-	30	WALK RIGHT NOW	Jacksons	*Epic*	1
25	31	TAKE IT TO THE TOP	Kool and the Gang	*De-Lite*	7
38	32	I'M IN LOVE	Evelyn King	*RCA*	2
-	33	SHOW ME	Dexy's Midnight Runners	*Mercury*	1
36	34	TAKE IT ON THE RUN	REO Speedwagon	*Epic*	2
19	35	TEDDY BEAR	Red Sovine	*Starday*	6
31	36	IF LEAVING ME IS EASY	Phil Collins	*Virgin*	6
-	37	BEACH BOY GOLD	Gidea Park ●	*Sonet*	1
32	38	ME NO POP I	Kid Creole and the Coconuts present Coati Mundi	*Ze*	3
-	39	COMPUTER LOVE/THE MODEL	Kraftwerk	*EMI*	1
28	40	STAND AND DELIVER	Adam and the Ants	*CBS*	11

WEEK ENDING 25 JULY 1981

LW	TW	Title	Artist	Label	Wks
1	[1]	GHOST TOWN	Specials	*2 Tone*	6
2	[2]	STARS ON 45 (VOLUME 2)	Starsound	*CBS*	4
3	[3]	CAN CAN	Bad Manners	*Magnet*	5
18	4	CHANT NO. 1 (I DON'T NEED THIS PRESSURE ON)	Spandau Ballet	*Reformation*	2
4	5	BODY TALK	Imagination	*R&B*	7
6	[6]	MOTORHEAD LIVE	Motorhead	*Bronze*	3
17	[7]	LAY ALL YOUR LOVE ON ME	Abba	*Epic*	2
7	8	WORDY RAPPINGHOOD	Tom Tom Club	*Island*	5

August 1981

□ Highest position disc reached ● Act's first ever week on chart

LW	TW	Title	Artist	Label	Wks
-	9	HAPPY BIRTHDAY	Stevie Wonder	*Motown*	1
12	[10]	DANCING ON THE FLOOR (HOOKED ON LOVE)	Third World	*CBS*	7
15	[11]	SAT IN YOUR LAP	Kate Bush	*EMI*	3
8	12	NO WOMAN NO CRY	Bob Marley and the Wailers	*Island*	6
5	13	ONE DAY IN YOUR LIFE	Michael Jackson	*Motown*	9
11	14	YOU MIGHT NEED SOMEBODY	Randy Crawford	*Warner Brothers*	6
19	15	NEW LIFE	Depeche Mode	*Mute*	4
21	16	FOR YOUR EYES ONLY	Sheena Easton	*EMI*	4
9	17	GOING BACK TO MY ROOTS	Odyssey	*RCA*	8
26	[18]	NEVER SURRENDER	Saxon	*Carrere*	2
10	19	MEMORY	Elaine Paige	*Polydor*	7
30	20	WALK RIGHT NOW	Jacksons	*Epic*	2
13	21	RAZZAMATAZZ	Quincy Jones	*A&M*	5
-	22	GREEN DOOR	Shakin' Stevens	*Epic*	1
33	23	SHOW ME	Dexy's Midnight Runners	*Mercury*	2
14	24	THERE'S A GUY WORKS DOWN THE CHIP SHOP SWEARS HE'S ELVIS	Kirsty MacColl	*Polydor*	5
25	25	VISAGE	Visage	*Polydor*	3
20	26	CAN'T HAPPEN HERE	Rainbow	*Polydor*	5
32	[27]	I'M IN LOVE	Evelyn King	*RCA*	3
34	28	TAKE IT ON THE RUN	REO Speedwagon	*Epic*	3
-	29	GIRLS ON FILM	Duran Duran	*EMI*	1
-	30	BACK TO THE SIXTIES	Tight Fit ●	*Jive*	1
22	31	THROW AWAY THE KEY	Linx	*Chrysalis*	6
23	32	WIKKA WRAP	Evasions	*Groove*	6
-	33	HOOKED ON CLASSICS	Royal Philharmonic Orchestra ●	*RCA*	1
16	34	PIECE OF THE ACTION	Bucks Fizz	*RCA*	7
37	35	BEACH BOY GOLD	Gidea Park	*Sonet*	2
39	36	COMPUTER LOVE/THE MODEL	Kraftwerk	*EMI*	2
24	37	ALL STOOD STILL	Ultravox	*Chrysalis*	7
-	38	SHE'S A BAD MAMA JAMA (SHE'S BUILT SHE'S STACKED)	Carl Carlton ●	*20th Century*	1
27	39	BEING WITH YOU	Smokey Robinson	*Motown*	11
29	40	MORE THAN IN LOVE	Kate Robbins and Beyond	*RCA*	9

WEEK ENDING 1 AUGUST 1981

LW	TW	Title	Artist	Label	Wks
22	[1]	GREEN DOOR	Shakin' Stevens	*Epic*	2
1	2	GHOST TOWN	Specials	*2 Tone*	7
4	[3]	CHANT NO. 1 (I DON'T NEED THIS PRESSURE ON)	Spandau Ballet	*Reformation*	3
9	4	HAPPY BIRTHDAY	Stevie Wonder	*Motown*	2
2	5	STARS ON 45 (VOLUME 2)	Starsound	*CBS*	5
3	6	CAN CAN	Bad Manners	*Magnet*	6
33	7	HOOKED ON CLASSICS	Royal Philharmonic Orchestra	*RCA*	2
5	8	BODY TALK	Imagination	*R&B*	8
7	9	LAY ALL YOUR LOVE ON ME	Abba	*Epic*	3
10	[10]	DANCING ON THE FLOOR (HOOKED ON LOVE)	Third World	*CBS*	8
16	11	FOR YOUR EYES ONLY	Sheena Easton	*EMI*	5
15	12	NEW LIFE	Depeche Mode	*Mute*	5
11	13	SAT IN YOUR LAP	Kate Bush	*EMI*	4
30	14	BACK TO THE SIXTIES	Tight Fit	*Jive*	2
20	15	WALK RIGHT NOW	Jacksons	*Epic*	3
8	16	WORDY RAPPINGHOOD	Tom Tom Club	*Island*	6
14	17	YOU MIGHT NEED SOMEBODY	Randy Crawford	*Warner Brothers*	7
12	18	NO WOMAN NO CRY	Bob Marley and the Wailers	*Island*	7
6	19	MOTORHEAD LIVE	Motorhead	*Bronze*	4
18	20	NEVER SURRENDER	Saxon	*Carrere*	3
25	[21]	VISAGE	Visage	*Polydor*	4
13	22	ONE DAY IN YOUR LIFE	Michael Jackson	*Motown*	10
29	23	GIRLS ON FILM	Duran Duran	*EMI*	2
23	24	SHOW ME	Dexy's Midnight Runners	*Mercury*	3
35	25	BEACH BOY GOLD	Gidea Park	*Sonet*	3
28	26	TAKE IT ON THE RUN	REO Speedwagon	*Epic*	4
17	27	GOING BACK TO MY ROOTS	Odyssey	*RCA*	9

■The death of Bob Marley on 11 May pushes his *No Woman No Cry* into the Top 10, to end up 14 places higher than on its original chart outing six years earlier (18.07.81)■ Shakin' Stevens leaps from 22 to one with his revival of the 1956 hit *Green Door*. It is the second biggest leap to the top so far recorded (01.08.81)■

August 1981

□ Highest position disc reached ● Act's first ever week on chart

LW	TW	Title	Artist	Label	Wks
19	28	MEMORY	Elaine Paige	Polydor	8
21	29	RAZZAMATAZZ	Quincy Jones	A&M	6
27	30	I'M IN LOVE	Evelyn King	RCA	4
26	31	CAN'T HAPPEN HERE	Rainbow	Polydor	6
24	32	THERE'S A GUY WORKS DOWN THE CHIP SHOP SWEARS HE'S ELVIS	Kirsty MacColl	Polydor	6
-	33	THE CARIBBEAN DISCO SHOW	Lobo ●	Polydor	1
38	[34]	SHE'S A BAD MAMA JAMA (SHE'S BUILT SHE'S STACKED)	Carl Carlton	20th Century	2
-	35	WATER ON GLASS/BOYS	Kim Wilde	RAK	1
-	36	SI SI JE SUIS UN ROCK STAR	Bill Wyman ●	A&M	1
-	[37]	I LOVE YOU YES I LOVE YOU	Eddy Grant	Ice	1
31	38	THROW AWAY THE KEY	Linx	Chrysalis	7
-	[39]	DANCING THE NIGHT AWAY	Voggue ●	Mercury	1
-	40	HOLD ON TIGHT	Electric Light Orchestra	Jet	1

WEEK ENDING 8 AUGUST 1981

LW	TW	Title	Artist	Label	Wks
1	[1]	GREEN DOOR	Shakin' Stevens	Epic	3
4	[2]	HAPPY BIRTHDAY	Stevie Wonder	Motown	3
7	3	HOOKED ON CLASSICS	Royal Philharmonic Orchestra	RCA	3
3	4	CHANT NO. 1 (I DON'T NEED THIS PRESSURE ON)	Spandau Ballet	Reformation	4
2	5	GHOST TOWN	Specials	2 Tone	8
6	6	CAN CAN	Bad Manners	Magnet	7
15	[7]	WALK RIGHT NOW	Jacksons	Epic	4
11	[8]	FOR YOUR EYES ONLY	Sheena Easton	EMI	6
5	9	STARS ON 45 (VOLUME 2)	Starsound	CBS	6
14	10	BACK TO THE SIXTIES	Tight Fit	Jive	3
12	[11]	NEW LIFE	Depeche Mode	Mute	6
10	12	DANCING ON THE FLOOR (HOOKED ON LOVE)	Third World	CBS	9
8	13	BODY TALK	Imagination	R&B	9
9	14	LAY ALL YOUR LOVE ON ME	Abba	Epic	4
23	15	GIRLS ON FILM	Duran Duran	EMI	3
24	[16]	SHOW ME	Dexy's Midnight Runners	Mercury	4
35	17	WATER ON GLASS/BOYS	Kim Wilde	RAK	2
13	18	SAT IN YOUR LAP	Kate Bush	EMI	5
40	19	HOLD ON TIGHT	Electric Light Orchestra	Jet	2
25	20	BEACH BOY GOLD	Gidea Park	Sonet	4
21	[21]	VISAGE	Visage	Polydor	5
16	22	WORDY RAPPINGHOOD	Tom Tom Club	Island	7
18	23	NO WOMAN NO CRY	Bob Marley and the Wailers	Island	8
17	24	YOU MIGHT NEED SOMEBODY	Randy Crawford	Warner Brothers	8
26	25	TAKE IT ON THE RUN	REO Speedwagon	Epic	5
20	26	NEVER SURRENDER	Saxon	Carrere	4
33	27	THE CARIBBEAN DISCO SHOW	Lobo	Polydor	2
36	28	SI SI JE SUIS UN ROCK STAR	Bill Wyman	A&M	2
-	29	LOVE ACTION (I BELIEVE IN LOVE)	Human League	Virgin	1
30	30	I'M IN LOVE	Evelyn King	RCA	5
22	31	ONE DAY IN YOUR LIFE	Michael Jackson	Motown	11
-	[32]	BACKFIRED	Debbie Harry ●	Chrysalis	1
19	33	MOTORHEAD LIVE	Motorhead	Bronze	5
-	34	STARTRAX CLUB DISCO	Startrax ●	Picksy	1
34	35	SHE'S A BAD MAMA JAMA (SHE'S BUILT SHE'S STACKED)	Carl Carlton	20th Century	3
-	36	WUNDERBAR	Tenpole Tudor	Stiff	1
-	37	ARABIAN NIGHTS	Siouxsie and the Banshees	Polydor	1
28	38	MEMORY	Elaine Paige	Polydor	9
-	39	FIRE	U2 ●	Island	1
37	40	I LOVE YOU YES I LOVE YOU	Eddy Grant	Ice	2

WEEK ENDING 15 AUGUST 1981

LW	TW	Title	Artist	Label	Wks
1	[1]	GREEN DOOR	Shakin' Stevens	Epic	4
3	[2]	HOOKED ON CLASSICS	Royal Philharmonic Orchestra	RCA	4
2	3	HAPPY BIRTHDAY	Stevie Wonder	Motown	4
10	[4]	BACK TO THE SIXTIES	Tight Fit	Jive	4
4	5	CHANT NO. 1 (I DON'T NEED THIS PRESSURE ON)	Spandau Ballet	Reformation	5
15	6	GIRLS ON FILM	Duran Duran	EMI	4
29	7	LOVE ACTION (I BELIEVE IN LOVE)	Human League	Virgin	2
7	8	WALK RIGHT NOW	Jacksons	Epic	5
19	9	HOLD ON TIGHT	Electric Light Orchestra	Jet	3
8	10	FOR YOUR EYES ONLY	Sheena Easton	EMI	7
20	[11]	BEACH BOY GOLD	Gidea Park	Sonet	5
5	12	GHOST TOWN	Specials	2 Tone	9
17	13	WATER ON GLASS/BOYS	Kim Wilde	RAK	3
27	14	THE CARIBBEAN DISCO SHOW	Lobo	Polydor	3
11	15	NEW LIFE	Depeche Mode	Mute	7
6	16	CAN CAN	Bad Manners	Magnet	8
12	17	DANCING ON THE FLOOR (HOOKED ON LOVE)	Third World	CBS	10
16	18	SHOW ME	Dexy's Midnight Runners	Mercury	5
-	19	JAPANESE BOY	Aneka ●	Hansa	1
13	20	BODY TALK	Imagination	R&B	10
36	21	WUNDERBAR	Tenpole Tudor	Stiff	2
28	22	SI SI JE SUIS UN ROCK STAR	Bill Wyman	A&M	3
-	23	ONE IN TEN	UB40	DEP International	1
14	24	LAY ALL YOUR LOVE ON ME	Abba	Epic	5
25	25	TAKE IT ON THE RUN	REO Speedwagon	Epic	6
-	26	TAINTED LOVE	Soft Cell ●	Some Bizzare	1
9	27	STARS ON 45 (VOLUME 2)	Starsound	CBS	7
34	27	STARTRAX CLUB DISCO	Startrax	Picksy	2
18	29	SAT IN YOUR LAP	Kate Bush	EMI	6
21	30	VISAGE	Visage	Polydor	6
-	31	I LOVE MUSIC	Enigma	Creole	1
24	32	YOU MIGHT NEED SOMEBODY	Randy Crawford	Warner Brothers	9
30	33	I'M IN LOVE	Evelyn King	RCA	6
37	34	ARABIAN NIGHTS	Siouxsie and the Banshees	Polydor	2
35	35	SHE'S A BAD MAMA JAMA (SHE'S BUILT SHE'S STACKED)	Carl Carlton	20th Century	4
32	36	BACKFIRED	Debbie Harry	Chrysalis	2
26	37	NEVER SURRENDER	Saxon	Carrere	5
22	38	WORDY RAPPINGHOOD	Tom Tom Club	Island	8
39	39	FIRE	U2	Island	2
-	40	RAINY NIGHT IN GEORGIA	Randy Crawford	Warner Brothers	1

WEEK ENDING 22 AUGUST 1981

LW	TW	Title	Artist	Label	Wks
1	[1]	GREEN DOOR	Shakin' Stevens	Epic	5
2	[2]	HOOKED ON CLASSICS	Royal Philharmonic Orchestra	RCA	5
7	[3]	LOVE ACTION (I BELIEVE IN LOVE)	Human League	Virgin	3
19	4	JAPANESE BOY	Aneka	Hansa	2
6	[5]	GIRLS ON FILM	Duran Duran	EMI	5
9	6	HOLD ON TIGHT	Electric Light Orchestra	Jet	4
3	7	HAPPY BIRTHDAY	Stevie Wonder	Motown	5
4	8	BACK TO THE SIXTIES	Tight Fit	Jive	5
26	9	TAINTED LOVE	Soft Cell	Some Bizzare	2
14	10	THE CARIBBEAN DISCO SHOW	Lobo	Polydor	4
13	[11]	WATER ON GLASS/BOYS	Kim Wilde	RAK	4
5	12	CHANT NO. 1 (I DON'T NEED THIS PRESSURE ON)	Spandau Ballet	Reformation	6
11	13	BEACH BOY GOLD	Gidea Park	Sonet	6
22	[14]	SI SI JE SUIS UN ROCK STAR	Bill Wyman	A&M	4
10	15	FOR YOUR EYES ONLY	Sheena Easton	EMI	8
23	16	ONE IN TEN	UB40	DEP International	2
8	17	WALK RIGHT NOW	Jacksons	Epic	6
15	18	NEW LIFE	Depeche Mode	Mute	8
25	[19]	TAKE IT ON THE RUN	REO Speedwagon	Epic	7
21	20	WUNDERBAR	Tenpole Tudor	Stiff	3
27	21	STARTRAX CLUB DISCO	Startrax	Picksy	3
12	22	GHOST TOWN	Specials	2 Tone	10
18	23	SHOW ME	Dexy's Midnight Runners	Mercury	6
17	24	DANCING ON THE FLOOR (HOOKED ON LOVE)	Third World	CBS	11
31	[25]	I LOVE MUSIC	Enigma	Creole	2
16	26	CAN CAN	Bad Manners	Magnet	9
-	27	ABACAB	Genesis	Charisma	1
24	28	LAY ALL YOUR LOVE ON ME	Abba	Epic	6

In these weeks ■ The medley craze goes wild. The RPO are at number two with a collection of classic tunes to a disco beat, while Tight Fit, Gidea Park, Lobo, Starsound and Startrax are all in the charts with medley discs (15.08.81) ■ The Rolling Stones have never been particularly successful as solo acts. Bill Wyman's *Si Si Je Suis Un Rock Star* is the biggest hit single by any solo Stone (22.08.81) ■

LW	TW	Title	Artist	Label	Wks
-	29	CHEMISTRY	Nolans	Epic	1
40	30	RAINY NIGHT IN GEORGIA	Randy Crawford	Warner Brothers	2
27	31	STARS ON 45 (VOLUME 2)	Starsound	CBS	8
34	[32]	ARABIAN NIGHTS	Siouxsie and the Banshees	Polydor	3
30	33	VISAGE	Visage	Polydor	7
20	34	BODY TALK	Imagination	R&B	11
29	35	SAT IN YOUR LAP	Kate Bush	EMI	7
39	36	FIRE	U2	Island	3
-	37	THE THIN WALL	Ultravox	Chrysalis	1
-	38	EVERYBODY SALSA	Modern Romance ●	WEA	1
35	39	SHE'S A BAD MAMA JAMA (SHE'S BUILT SHE'S STACKED)	Carl Carlton	20th Century	5
36	40	BACKFIRED	Debbie Harry	Chrysalis	3

WEEK ENDING 29 AUGUST 1981

LW	TW	Title	Artist	Label	Wks
4	[1]	JAPANESE BOY	Aneka	Hansa	3
9	2	TAINTED LOVE	Soft Cell	Some Bizzare	3
2	3	HOOKED ON CLASSICS	Royal Philharmonic Orchestra	RCA	6
1	4	GREEN DOOR	Shakin' Stevens	Epic	6
6	5	HOLD ON TIGHT	Electric Light Orchestra	Jet	5
3	6	LOVE ACTION (I BELIEVE IN LOVE)	Human League	Virgin	4
5	7	GIRLS ON FILM	Duran Duran	EMI	6
10	[8]	THE CARIBBEAN DISCO SHOW	Lobo	Polydor	5
8	9	BACK TO THE SIXTIES	Tight Fit	Jive	6
16	10	ONE IN TEN	UB40	DEP International	3
7	11	HAPPY BIRTHDAY	Stevie Wonder	Motown	6
27	12	ABACAB	Genesis	Charisma	2
11	13	WATER ON GLASS/BOYS	Kim Wilde	RAK	5
13	14	BEACH BOY GOLD	Gidea Park	Sonet	7
-	15	SHE'S GOT CLAWS	Gary Numan	Beggars Banquet	1
20	[16]	WUNDERBAR	Tenpole Tudor	Stiff	4
14	17	SI SI JE SUIS UN ROCK STAR	Bill Wyman	A&M	5
21	[18]	STARTRAX CLUB DISCO	Startrax	Picksy	4
37	19	THE THIN WALL	Ultravox	Chrysalis	2
12	20	CHANT NO. 1 (I DON'T NEED THIS PRESSURE ON)	Spandau Ballet	Reformation	7
19	21	TAKE IT ON THE RUN	REO Speedwagon	Epic	8
30	22	RAINY NIGHT IN GEORGIA	Randy Crawford	Warner Brothers	3
15	23	FOR YOUR EYES ONLY	Sheena Easton	EMI	9
17	24	WALK RIGHT NOW	Jacksons	Epic	7
25	[25]	I LOVE MUSIC	Enigma	Creole	3
29	26	CHEMISTRY	Nolans	Epic	2
-	27	WIRED FOR SOUND	Cliff Richard	EMI	1
-	28	START ME UP	Rolling Stones	EMI	1
38	29	EVERYBODY SALSA	Modern Romance	WEA	2
22	30	GHOST TOWN	Specials	2 Tone	11
18	31	NEW LIFE	Depeche Mode	Mute	9
-	32	HAND HELD IN BLACK AND WHITE	Dollar	WEA	1
-	33	ONE OF THOSE NIGHTS	Bucks Fizz	RCA	1
32	34	ARABIAN NIGHTS	Siouxsie and the Banshees	Polydor	4
36	[35]	FIRE	U2	Island	4
26	36	CAN CAN	Bad Manners	Magnet	10
-	37	SLOW HAND	Pointer Sisters	Planet	1
24	38	DANCING ON THE FLOOR (HOOKED ON LOVE)	Third World	CBS	12
23	39	SHOW ME	Dexy's Midnight Runners	Mercury	7
-	40	YOU'LL NEVER KNOW	Hi Gloss ●	Epic	1

WEEK ENDING 5 SEPTEMBER 1981

LW	TW	Title	Artist	Label	Wks
2	[1]	TAINTED LOVE	Soft Cell	Some Bizzare	4
1	2	JAPANESE BOY	Aneka	Hansa	4
6	[3]	LOVE ACTION (I BELIEVE IN LOVE)	Human League	Virgin	5
5	[4]	HOLD ON TIGHT	Electric Light Orchestra	Jet	6
3	5	HOOKED ON CLASSICS	Royal Philharmonic Orchestra	RCA	7
15	[6]	SHE'S GOT CLAWS	Gary Numan	Beggars Banquet	2
10	[7]	ONE IN TEN	UB40	DEP International	4
4	8	GREEN DOOR	Shakin' Stevens	Epic	7
12	[9]	ABACAB	Genesis	Charisma	3
8	10	THE CARIBBEAN DISCO SHOW	Lobo	Polydor	6
27	11	WIRED FOR SOUND	Cliff Richard	EMI	2
7	12	GIRLS ON FILM	Duran Duran	EMI	7

September 1981

□ Highest position disc reached ● Act's first ever week on chart

(Boxed positions are shown here as [n].)

LW	TW	Title	Artist	Label	Wks
28	13	START ME UP	Rolling Stones	EMI	2
19	[14]	THE THIN WALL	Ultravox	Chrysalis	3
26	[15]	CHEMISTRY	Nolans	Epic	3
19	16	EVERYBODY SALSA	Modern Romance	WEA	3
16	17	WUNDERBAR	Tenpole Tudor	Stiff	5
9	18	BACK TO THE SIXTIES	Tight Fit	Jive	7
11	19	HAPPY BIRTHDAY	Stevie Wonder	Motown	7
22	20	RAINY NIGHT IN GEORGIA	Randy Crawford	Warner Brothers	4
17	21	SI SI JE SUIS UN ROCK STAR	Bill Wyman	A&M	6
13	22	WATER ON GLASS/BOYS	Kim Wilde	RAK	6
-	23	SOUVENIR	Orchestral Manoeuvres In The Dark	Dindisc	1
18	24	STARTRAX CLUB DISCO	Startrax	Picksy	5
21	25	TAKE IT ON THE RUN	REO Speedwagon	Epic	9
14	26	BEACH BOY GOLD	Gidea Park	Sonet	8
25	27	I LOVE MUSIC	Enigma	Creole	4
-	28	HANDS UP (GIVE ME YOUR HEART)	Ottawan	Carrere	1
37	29	SLOW HAND	Pointer Sisters	Planet	2
40	30	YOU'LL NEVER KNOW	Hi Gloss	Epic	2
32	31	HAND HELD IN BLACK AND WHITE	Dollar	WEA	2
33	32	ONE OF THOSE NIGHTS	Bucks Fizz	RCA	2
-	33	PASSIONATE FRIEND	Teardrop Explodes	Zoo	1
23	34	FOR YOUR EYES ONLY	Sheena Easton	EMI	10
20	35	CHANT NO. 1 (I DON'T NEED THIS PRESSURE ON)	Spandau Ballet	Reformation	8
-	36	HOLLIEDAZE	Hollies	EMI	1
34	37	ARABIAN NIGHTS	Siouxsie and the Banshees	Polydor	5
-	38	EVERLASTING LOVE	Rex Smith and Rachel Sweet ●	CBS	1
35	39	FIRE	U2	Island	5
-	[40]	EUROPE (AFTER THE RAIN)	John Foxx	Virgin	1

WEEK ENDING 12 SEPTEMBER 1981

LW	TW	Title	Artist	Label	Wks
1	[1]	TAINTED LOVE	Soft Cell	Some Bizzare	5
-	2	PRINCE CHARMING	Adam and the Ants	CBS	1
2	3	JAPANESE BOY	Aneka	Hansa	5
11	[4]	WIRED FOR SOUND	Cliff Richard	EMI	3
4	5	HOLD ON TIGHT	Electric Light Orchestra	Jet	7
3	6	LOVE ACTION (I BELIEVE IN LOVE)	Human League	Virgin	6
13	[7]	START ME UP	Rolling Stones	EMI	3
23	8	SOUVENIR	Orchestral Manoeuvres In The Dark	Dindisc	2
7	9	ONE IN TEN	UB40	DEP International	5
6	10	SHE'S GOT CLAWS	Gary Numan	Beggars Banquet	3
28	11	HANDS UP (GIVE ME YOUR HEART)	Ottawan	Carrere	2
16	[12]	EVERYBODY SALSA	Modern Romance	WEA	4
9	13	ABACAB	Genesis	Charisma	4
14	[14]	THE THIN WALL	Ultravox	Chrysalis	4
5	15	HOOKED ON CLASSICS	Royal Philharmonic Orchestra	RCA	8
29	16	SLOW HAND	Pointer Sisters	Planet	3
10	17	THE CARIBBEAN DISCO SHOW	Lobo	Polydor	7
20	[18]	RAINY NIGHT IN GEORGIA	Randy Crawford	Warner Brothers	5
12	19	GIRLS ON FILM	Duran Duran	EMI	8
15	20	CHEMISTRY	Nolans	Epic	4
8	21	GREEN DOOR	Shakin' Stevens	Epic	8
32	22	ONE OF THOSE NIGHTS	Bucks Fizz	RCA	3
30	23	YOU'LL NEVER KNOW	Hi Gloss	Epic	3
31	24	HAND HELD IN BLACK AND WHITE	Dollar	WEA	3
18	25	BACK TO THE SIXTIES	Tight Fit	Jive	8
-	26	PRETEND	Alvin Stardust	Stiff	1
17	27	WUNDERBAR	Tenpole Tudor	Stiff	6
25	28	TAKE IT ON THE RUN	REO Speedwagon	Epic	10
24	29	STARTRAX CLUB DISCO	Startrax	Picksy	6
19	30	HAPPY BIRTHDAY	Stevie Wonder	Motown	8
-	31	IN AND OUT OF LOVE	Imagination	R&B	1
33	32	PASSIONATE FRIEND	Teardrop Explodes	Zoo	2
-	33	SO THIS IS ROMANCE	Linx	Chrysalis	1
27	34	I LOVE MUSIC	Enigma	Creole	5
38	[35]	EVERLASTING LOVE	Rex Smith and Rachel Sweet	CBS	2
36	36	HOLLIEDAZE	Hollies	EMI	2
21	37	SI SI JE SUIS UN ROCK STAR	Bill Wyman	A&M	7

■U2's first chart hit, *Fire*, spends five weeks in the Top 40 without climbing higher than number 35 (29.08.81) ■ The Hollies, absent from the charts for over seven years, come back for their final newly-recorded hit, which is needless to say a medley of many of their old hits (05.09.81)■

September 1981

□ Highest position disc reached ● Act's first ever week on chart

LW	TW	Title	Artist	Label	Wks
22	38	WATER ON GLASS/BOYS	Kim Wilde	RAK	7
-	39	ENDLESS LOVE	Diana Ross and Lionel Richie ●	Motown	1
26	40	BEACH BOY GOLD	Gidea Park	Sonet	9

WEEK ENDING 19 SEPTEMBER 1981

LW	TW	Title	Artist	Label	Wks
2	1	PRINCE CHARMING	Adam and the Ants	CBS	2
1	2	TAINTED LOVE	Soft Cell	Some Bizzare	6
8	3	SOUVENIR	Orchestral Manoeuvres In The Dark	Dindisc	3
11	4	HANDS UP (GIVE ME YOUR HEART)	Ottawan	Carrere	3
4	5	WIRED FOR SOUND	Cliff Richard	EMI	4
3	6	JAPANESE BOY	Aneka	Hansa	6
5	7	HOLD ON TIGHT	Electric Light Orchestra	Jet	8
26	8	PRETEND	Alvin Stardust	Stiff	2
7	9	START ME UP	Rolling Stones	EMI	4
6	10	LOVE ACTION (I BELIEVE IN LOVE)	Human League	Virgin	7
16	11	SLOW HAND	Pointer Sisters	Planet	4
9	12	ONE IN TEN	UB40	DEP International	6
39	13	ENDLESS LOVE	Diana Ross and Lionel Richie	Motown	2
12	14	EVERYBODY SALSA	Modern Romance	WEA	5
14	15	THE THIN WALL	Ultravox	Chrysalis	5
10	16	SHE'S GOT CLAWS	Gary Numan	Beggars Banquet	4
23	17	YOU'LL NEVER KNOW	Hi Gloss	Epic	4
13	18	ABACAB	Genesis	Charisma	5
33	19	SO THIS IS ROMANCE	Linx	Chrysalis	2
22	20	ONE OF THOSE NIGHTS	Bucks Fizz	RCA	4
18	21	RAINY NIGHT IN GEORGIA	Randy Crawford	Warner Brothers	6
31	22	IN AND OUT OF LOVE	Imagination	R&B	2
17	23	THE CARIBBEAN DISCO SHOW	Lobo	Polydor	8
24	24	HAND HELD IN BLACK AND WHITE	Dollar	WEA	4
-	25	BIRDIE SONG	Tweets ●	PRT	1
20	26	CHEMISTRY	Nolans	Epic	5
19	27	GIRLS ON FILM	Duran Duran	EMI	9
36	28	HOLLIEDAZE	Hollies	EMI	3
32	29	PASSIONATE FRIEND	Teardrop Explodes	Zoo	3
-	30	UNDER YOUR THUMB	Godley and Creme ●	Polydor	1
15	31	HOOKED ON CLASSICS	Royal Philharmonic Orchestra	RCA	9
21	32	GREEN DOOR	Shakin' Stevens	Epic	9
-	33	STARS ON 45 (VOLUME 3)	Starsound	CBS	1
30	34	HAPPY BIRTHDAY	Stevie Wonder	Motown	9
-	35	SEASONS OF GOLD	Gidea Park	Polo	1
27	36	WUNDERBAR	Tenpole Tudor	Stiff	7
35	37	EVERLASTING LOVE	Rex Smith and Rachel Sweet	CBS	3
-	38	CLASSICAL MUDDLEY	Portsmouth Sinfonia ●	Springtime	1
25	39	BACK TO THE SIXTIES	Tight Fit	Jive	9
34	40	I LOVE MUSIC	Enigma	Creole	6

WEEK ENDING 26 SEPTEMBER 1981

LW	TW	Title	Artist	Label	Wks
1	1	PRINCE CHARMING	Adam and the Ants	CBS	3
2	2	TAINTED LOVE	Soft Cell	Some Bizzare	7
4	3	HANDS UP (GIVE ME YOUR HEART)	Ottawan	Carrere	4
3	4	SOUVENIR	Orchestral Manoeuvres In The Dark	Dindisc	4
8	5	PRETEND	Alvin Stardust	Stiff	3
5	6	WIRED FOR SOUND	Cliff Richard	EMI	5
13	7	ENDLESS LOVE	Diana Ross and Lionel Richie	Motown	3
25	8	BIRDIE SONG	Tweets	PRT	2
-	9	INVISIBLE SUN	Police	A&M	1
11	10	SLOW HAND	Pointer Sisters	Planet	5
30	11	UNDER YOUR THUMB	Godley and Creme	Polydor	2
17	12	YOU'LL NEVER KNOW	Hi Gloss	Epic	5
6	13	JAPANESE BOY	Aneka	Hansa	7
7	14	HOLD ON TIGHT	Electric Light Orchestra	Jet	9
10	15	LOVE ACTION (I BELIEVE IN LOVE)	Human League	Virgin	8
9	16	START ME UP	Rolling Stones	EMI	5
33	17	STARS ON 45 (VOLUME 3)	Starsound	CBS	2
19	18	SO THIS IS ROMANCE	Linx	Chrysalis	3
24	19	HAND HELD IN BLACK AND WHITE	Dollar	WEA	5
20	20	ONE OF THOSE NIGHTS	Bucks Fizz	RCA	5
22	21	IN AND OUT OF LOVE	Imagination	R&B	3
-	22	SHUT UP	Madness	Stiff	1
14	23	EVERYBODY SALSA	Modern Romance	WEA	6
-	24	JUST CAN'T GET ENOUGH	Depeche Mode	Mute	1
15	25	THE THIN WALL	Ultravox	Chrysalis	6
12	26	ONE IN TEN	UB40	DEP International	7
29	27	PASSIONATE FRIEND	Teardrop Explodes	Zoo	4
18	28	ABACAB	Genesis	Charisma	6
-	29	THE ORIGINAL BIRD DANCE	Electronicas ●	Polydor	1
35	30	SEASONS OF GOLD	Gidea Park	Polo	2
21	31	RAINY NIGHT IN GEORGIA	Randy Crawford	Warner Brothers	7
28	32	HOLLIEDAZE	Hollies	EMI	4
16	33	SHE'S GOT CLAWS	Gary Numan	Beggars Banquet	5
26	34	CHEMISTRY	Nolans	Epic	6
23	35	THE CARIBBEAN DISCO SHOW	Lobo	Polydor	9
-	36	IT'S MY PARTY	Dave Stewart and Barbara Gaskin ●	Broken	1
-	37	MULE (CHANT NO. 2)	Beggar and Co.	RCA	1
37	38	EVERLASTING LOVE	Rex Smith and Rachel Sweet	CBS	4
-	39	QUIET LIFE	Japan ●	Hansa	1
-	40	JUST ANOTHER BROKEN HEART	Sheena Easton	EMI	1

WEEK ENDING 3 OCTOBER 1981

LW	TW	Title	Artist	Label	Wks
1	1	PRINCE CHARMING	Adam and the Ants	CBS	4
9	2	INVISIBLE SUN	Police	A&M	2
3	3	HANDS UP (GIVE ME YOUR HEART)	Ottawan	Carrere	5
5	4	PRETEND	Alvin Stardust	Stiff	4
4	5	SOUVENIR	Orchestral Manoeuvres In The Dark	Dindisc	5
11	6	UNDER YOUR THUMB	Godley and Creme	Polydor	3
8	7	BIRDIE SONG	Tweets	PRT	3
2	8	TAINTED LOVE	Soft Cell	Some Bizzare	8
7	9	ENDLESS LOVE	Diana Ross and Lionel Richie	Motown	4
22	10	SHUT UP	Madness	Stiff	2
10	11	SLOW HAND	Pointer Sisters	Planet	6
24	12	JUST CAN'T GET ENOUGH	Depeche Mode	Mute	2
12	13	YOU'LL NEVER KNOW	Hi Gloss	Epic	6
6	14	WIRED FOR SOUND	Cliff Richard	EMI	6
18	15	SO THIS IS ROMANCE	Linx	Chrysalis	4
21	16	IN AND OUT OF LOVE	Imagination	R&B	4
36	17	IT'S MY PARTY	Dave Stewart and Barbara Gaskin	Broken	2
17	18	STARS ON 45 (VOLUME 3)	Starsound	CBS	3
19	19	HAND HELD IN BLACK AND WHITE	Dollar	WEA	6
14	20	HOLD ON TIGHT	Electric Light Orchestra	Jet	10
13	21	JAPANESE BOY	Aneka	Hansa	8
29	22	THE ORIGINAL BIRD DANCE	Electronicas	Polydor	2
16	23	START ME UP	Rolling Stones	EMI	6
20	24	ONE OF THOSE NIGHTS	Bucks Fizz	RCA	6
27	25	PASSIONATE FRIEND	Teardrop Explodes	Zoo	5
39	26	QUIET LIFE	Japan	Hansa	2
23	27	EVERYBODY SALSA	Modern Romance	WEA	7
30	28	SEASONS OF GOLD	Gidea Park	Polo	3
15	29	LOVE ACTION (I BELIEVE IN LOVE)	Human League	Virgin	9
-	30	WALKIN' IN THE SUNSHINE	Bad Manners	Magnet	1
-	31	LOCK UP YOUR DAUGHTERS	Slade	RCA	1
-	32	THUNDER IN THE MOUNTAINS	Toyah	Safari	1
26	33	ONE IN TEN	UB40	DEP International	8
-	34	MAD EYED SCREAMER	Creatures ●	Polydor	1
-	35	LET'S HANG ON	Barry Manilow	Arista	1
31	36	RAINY NIGHT IN GEORGIA	Randy Crawford	Warner Brothers	8
40	37	JUST ANOTHER BROKEN HEART	Sheena Easton	EMI	2
-	38	BACK TO THE SIXTIES PART 2	Tight Fit	Jive	1
33	39	SHE'S GOT CLAWS	Gary Numan	Beggars Banquet	6
25	40	THE THIN WALL	Ultravox	Chrysalis	7

WEEK ENDING 10 OCTOBER 1981

LW	TW	Title	Artist	Label	Wks
1	1	PRINCE CHARMING	Adam and the Ants	CBS	5
7	2	BIRDIE SONG	Tweets	PRT	4
2	3	INVISIBLE SUN	Police	A&M	3
6	4	UNDER YOUR THUMB	Godley and Creme	Polydor	4
3	5	HANDS UP (GIVE ME YOUR HEART)	Ottawan	Carrere	6
4	6	PRETEND	Alvin Stardust	Stiff	5

In these weeks ■ Three weeks after Spandau Ballet's *Chant Number One (I Don't Need This Pressure On)* slips from the Top 40, Beggar and Co. slip in with *Chant Number One* (26.09.81) ■ Five consecutive titles consist of only two words, from number seven to number eleven (03.10.81)■

LW	TW	Title	Artist	Label	Wks
10	[7]	SHUT UP	Madness	*Stiff*	3
17	8	IT'S MY PARTY	Dave Stewart and Barbara Gaskin	*Broken*	3
9	9	ENDLESS LOVE	Diana Ross and Lionel Richie	*Motown*	5
5	10	SOUVENIR	Orchestral Manoeuvres In The Dark	*Dindisc*	6
12	11	JUST CAN'T GET ENOUGH	Depeche Mode	*Mute*	3
8	12	TAINTED LOVE	Soft Cell	*Some Bizzare*	9
32	13	THUNDER IN THE MOUNTAINS	Toyah	*Safari*	2
11	14	SLOW HAND	Pointer Sisters	*Planet*	7
13	15	YOU'LL NEVER KNOW	Hi Gloss	*Epic*	7
30	16	WALKIN' IN THE SUNSHINE	Bad Manners	*Magnet*	2
15	17	SO THIS IS ROMANCE	Linx	*Chrysalis*	5
16	18	IN AND OUT OF LOVE	Imagination	*R&B*	5
26	[19]	QUIET LIFE	Japan	*Hansa*	3
14	20	WIRED FOR SOUND	Cliff Richard	*EMI*	7
-	21	OPEN YOUR HEART	Human League	*Virgin*	1
22	[22]	THE ORIGINAL BIRD DANCE	Electronicas	*Polydor*	3
-	23	GOOD YEAR FOR THE ROSES	Elvis Costello	*F Beat*	1
19	24	HAND HELD IN BLACK AND WHITE	Dollar	*WEA*	7
34	25	MAD EYED SCREAMER	Creatures	*Polydor*	2
18	26	STARS ON 45 (VOLUME 3)	Starsound	*CBS*	4
25	27	PASSIONATE FRIEND	Teardrop Explodes	*Zoo*	6
-	28	HAPPY BIRTHDAY	Altered Images ●	*Epic*	1
31	[29]	LOCK UP YOUR DAUGHTERS	Slade	*RCA*	2
35	30	LET'S HANG ON	Barry Manilow	*Arista*	2
24	31	ONE OF THOSE NIGHTS	Bucks Fizz	*RCA*	7
28	32	SEASONS OF GOLD	Gidea Park	*Polo*	4
38	[33]	BACK TO THE SIXTIES PART 2	Tight Fit	*Jive*	2
21	34	JAPANESE BOY	Aneka	*Hansa*	9
29	35	LOVE ACTION (I BELIEVE IN LOVE)	Human League	*Virgin*	10
37	36	JUST ANOTHER BROKEN HEART	Sheena Easton	*EMI*	3
23	37	START ME UP	Rolling Stones	*EMI*	7
20	38	HOLD ON TIGHT	Electric Light Orchestra	*Jet*	11
-	39	PROCESSION/EVERYTHING'S GONE GREEN	New Order	*Factory*	1
-	40	IT'S RAINING	Shakin' Stevens	*Epic*	1

Week Ending 17 October 1981

LW	TW	Title	Artist	Label	Wks
8	[1]	IT'S MY PARTY	Dave Stewart and Barbara Gaskin	*Broken*	4
2	[2]	BIRDIE SONG	Tweets	*PRT*	5
4	[3]	UNDER YOUR THUMB	Godley and Creme	*Polydor*	5
1	4	PRINCE CHARMING	Adam and the Ants	*CBS*	6
13	5	THUNDER IN THE MOUNTAINS	Toyah	*Safari*	3
21	[6]	OPEN YOUR HEART	Human League	*Virgin*	2
5	7	HANDS UP (GIVE ME YOUR HEART)	Ottawan	*Carrere*	7
11	[8]	JUST CAN'T GET ENOUGH	Depeche Mode	*Mute*	4
3	9	INVISIBLE SUN	Police	*A&M*	4
16	[10]	WALKIN' IN THE SUNSHINE	Bad Manners	*Magnet*	3
40	11	IT'S RAINING	Shakin' Stevens	*Epic*	2
7	12	SHUT UP	Madness	*Stiff*	4
9	13	ENDLESS LOVE	Diana Ross and Lionel Richie	*Motown*	6
23	14	GOOD YEAR FOR THE ROSES	Elvis Costello	*F Beat*	2
6	15	PRETEND	Alvin Stardust	*Stiff*	6
28	16	HAPPY BIRTHDAY	Altered Images	*Epic*	2
10	17	SOUVENIR	Orchestral Manoeuvres In The Dark	*Dindisc*	7
-	18	O SUPERMAN	Laurie Anderson ●	*Warner Brothers*	1
19	[19]	QUIET LIFE	Japan	*Hansa*	4
12	20	TAINTED LOVE	Soft Cell	*Some Bizzare*	10
30	21	LET'S HANG ON	Barry Manilow	*Arista*	3
14	22	SLOW HAND	Pointer Sisters	*Planet*	8
15	23	YOU'LL NEVER KNOW	Hi Gloss	*Epic*	8
22	24	THE ORIGINAL BIRD DANCE	Electronicas	*Polydor*	4
25	25	MAD EYED SCREAMER	Creatures	*Polydor*	3
18	26	IN AND OUT OF LOVE	Imagination	*R&B*	6
17	27	SO THIS IS ROMANCE	Linx	*Chrysalis*	6
24	28	HAND HELD IN BLACK AND WHITE	Dollar	*WEA*	8
29	[29]	LOCK UP YOUR DAUGHTERS	Slade	*RCA*	3
27	30	PASSIONATE FRIEND	Teardrop Explodes	*Zoo*	7
-	31	LABELLED WITH LOVE	Squeeze	*A&M*	1
26	32	STARS ON 45 (VOLUME 3)	Starsound	*CBS*	5
36	[33]	JUST ANOTHER BROKEN HEART	Sheena Easton	*EMI*	4
-	34	WHEN YOU WERE SWEET SIXTEEN	Fureys and Davey Arthur ●	*Ritz*	1
33	35	BACK TO THE SIXTIES PART 2	Tight Fit	*Jive*	3

October 1981

□ Highest position disc reached ● Act's first ever week on chart

LW	TW	Title	Artist	Label	Wks
-	36	HOLD ME	BA Robertson and Maggie Bell ●	*Swansong*	1
20	37	WIRED FOR SOUND	Cliff Richard	*EMI*	8
39	[38]	PROCESSION/EVERYTHING'S GONE GREEN	New Order	*Factory*	2
-	39	NIGHTMARE	Gillan	*Virgin*	1
35	40	LOVE ACTION (I BELIEVE IN LOVE)	Human League	*Virgin*	11

Week Ending 24 October 1981

LW	TW	Title	Artist	Label	Wks
1	[1]	IT'S MY PARTY	Dave Stewart and Barbara Gaskin	*Broken*	5
18	[2]	O SUPERMAN	Laurie Anderson	*Warner Brothers*	2
2	3	BIRDIE SONG	Tweets	*PRT*	6
5	[4]	THUNDER IN THE MOUNTAINS	Toyah	*Safari*	4
16	5	HAPPY BIRTHDAY	Altered Images	*Epic*	3
6	[6]	OPEN YOUR HEART	Human League	*Virgin*	3
-	7	ABSOLUTE BEGINNERS	Jam	*Polydor*	1
3	8	UNDER YOUR THUMB	Godley and Creme	*Polydor*	6
14	9	GOOD YEAR FOR THE ROSES	Elvis Costello	*F Beat*	3
11	[10]	IT'S RAINING	Shakin' Stevens	*Epic*	3
10	11	WALKIN' IN THE SUNSHINE	Bad Manners	*Magnet*	4
8	12	JUST CAN'T GET ENOUGH	Depeche Mode	*Mute*	5
7	13	HANDS UP (GIVE ME YOUR HEART)	Ottawan	*Carrere*	8
4	14	PRINCE CHARMING	Adam and the Ants	*CBS*	7
12	15	SHUT UP	Madness	*Stiff*	5
21	16	LET'S HANG ON	Barry Manilow	*Arista*	4
13	17	ENDLESS LOVE	Diana Ross and Lionel Richie	*Motown*	7
36	18	HOLD ME	BA Robertson and Maggie Bell	*Swansong*	2
31	19	LABELLED WITH LOVE	Squeeze	*A&M*	2
15	20	PRETEND	Alvin Stardust	*Stiff*	7
19	21	QUIET LIFE	Japan	*Hansa*	5
20	22	TAINTED LOVE	Soft Cell	*Some Bizzare*	11
9	23	INVISIBLE SUN	Police	*A&M*	5
25	[24]	MAD EYED SCREAMER	Creatures	*Polydor*	4
17	25	SOUVENIR	Orchestral Manoeuvres In The Dark	*Dindisc*	8
34	26	WHEN YOU WERE SWEET SIXTEEN	Fureys and Davey Arthur	*Ritz*	2
-	27	EVERY LITTLE THING SHE DOES IS MAGIC	Police	*A&M*	1
-	28	TONIGHT I'M YOURS (DON'T HURT ME)	Rod Stewart	*Riva*	1
-	29	WHEN SHE WAS MY GIRL	Four Tops	*Casablanca*	1
26	30	IN AND OUT OF LOVE	Imagination	*R&B*	7
29	31	LOCK UP YOUR DAUGHTERS	Slade	*RCA*	4
-	32	DEAD CITIES	Exploited ●	*Secret*	1
22	33	SLOW HAND	Pointer Sisters	*Planet*	9
23	34	YOU'LL NEVER KNOW	Hi Gloss	*Epic*	9
27	35	SO THIS IS ROMANCE	Linx	*Chrysalis*	7
-	36	JOAN OF ARC	Orchestral Manoeuvres In The Dark	*Dindisc*	1
39	37	NIGHTMARE	Gillan	*Virgin*	2
24	38	THE ORIGINAL BIRD DANCE	Electronicas	*Polydor*	5
-	39	AND THEN SHE KISSED ME	Gary Glitter	*Bell*	1
-	40	PHYSICAL	Olivia Newton-John	*EMI*	1

Week Ending 31 October 1981

LW	TW	Title	Artist	Label	Wks
1	[1]	IT'S MY PARTY	Dave Stewart and Barbara Gaskin	*Broken*	6
5	[2]	HAPPY BIRTHDAY	Altered Images	*Epic*	4
2	3	O SUPERMAN	Laurie Anderson	*Warner Brothers*	3
7	[4]	ABSOLUTE BEGINNERS	Jam	*Polydor*	2
3	5	BIRDIE SONG	Tweets	*PRT*	7
27	6	EVERY LITTLE THING SHE DOES IS MAGIC	Police	*A&M*	2
4	7	THUNDER IN THE MOUNTAINS	Toyah	*Safari*	5
9	8	GOOD YEAR FOR THE ROSES	Elvis Costello	*F Beat*	4
19	9	LABELLED WITH LOVE	Squeeze	*A&M*	3
10	[10]	IT'S RAINING	Shakin' Stevens	*Epic*	4
6	11	OPEN YOUR HEART	Human League	*Virgin*	4
16	[12]	LET'S HANG ON	Barry Manilow	*Arista*	5
18	13	HOLD ME	BA Robertson and Maggie Bell	*Swansong*	3
29	14	WHEN SHE WAS MY GIRL	Four Tops	*Casablanca*	2
8	15	UNDER YOUR THUMB	Godley and Creme	*Polydor*	7

■The weatherman is busy at the top of the charts, with *Thunder In The Mountains*, *Invisible Sun*, *Walkin' In The Sunshine* and *It's Raining* among the top eleven singles (17.10.81) ■ Two of the Top 10 are songs with titles that have been Top 10 hits before - but different songs, *Happy Birthday* and *It's Raining*. Two more are song titles that will be used for different Top 10 hits in 1986, *Absolute Beginners* and *Open Your Heart* (24.10.81)■

October 1981

□ Highest position disc reached ● Act's first ever week on chart

LW	TW	Title	Artist	Label	Wks
11	16	WALKIN' IN THE SUNSHINE	Bad Manners	Magnet	5
12	17	JUST CAN'T GET ENOUGH	Depeche Mode	Mute	6
28	18	TONIGHT I'M YOURS (DON'T HURT ME)	Rod Stewart	Riva	2
15	19	SHUT UP	Madness	Stiff	6
13	20	HANDS UP (GIVE ME YOUR HEART)	Ottawan	Carrere	9
36	21	JOAN OF ARC	Orchestral Manoeuvres In The Dark	Dindisc	2
26	22	WHEN YOU WERE SWEET SIXTEEN	Fureys and Davey Arthur	Ritz	3
14	23	PRINCE CHARMING	Adam and the Ants	CBS	8
21	24	QUIET LIFE	Japan	Hansa	6
17	25	ENDLESS LOVE	Diana Ross and Lionel Richie	Motown	8
23	26	INVISIBLE SUN	Police	A&M	6
24	27	MAD EYED SCREAMER	Creatures	Polydor	5
22	28	TAINTED LOVE	Soft Cell	Some Bizzare	12
40	29	PHYSICAL	Olivia Newton-John	EMI	2
20	30	PRETEND	Alvin Stardust	Stiff	8
32	31	DEAD CITIES	Exploited	Secret	2
25	32	SOUVENIR	Orchestral Manoeuvres In The Dark	Dindisc	9
-	33	BEGIN THE BEGUINE (VOLVER A EMPEZAR)	Julio Iglesias ●	CBS	1
-	34	TOM SAWYER	Rush	Exit	1
31	35	LOCK UP YOUR DAUGHTERS	Slade	RCA	5
37	36	NIGHTMARE	Gillan	Virgin	3
-	37	TWILIGHT	Electric Light Orchestra	Jet	1
-	38	LOVE ME TONIGHT	Trevor Walters ●	Magnet	1
39	39	AND THEN SHE KISSED ME	Gary Glitter	Bell	2
-	40	FAVOURITE SHIRTS (BOY MEETS GIRL)	Haircut 100 ●	Arista	1

WEEK ENDING 7 NOVEMBER 1981

LW	TW	Title	Artist	Label	Wks
1	1	IT'S MY PARTY	Dave Stewart and Barbara Gaskin	Broken	7
2	2	HAPPY BIRTHDAY	Altered Images	Epic	5
6	3	EVERY LITTLE THING SHE DOES IS MAGIC	Police	A&M	3
9	4	LABELLED WITH LOVE	Squeeze	A&M	4
14	5	WHEN SHE WAS MY GIRL	Four Tops	Casablanca	3
8	6	GOOD YEAR FOR THE ROSES	Elvis Costello	F Beat	5
21	7	JOAN OF ARC	Orchestral Manoeuvres In The Dark	Dindisc	3
4	8	ABSOLUTE BEGINNERS	Jam	Polydor	3
5	9	BIRDIE SONG	Tweets	PRT	8
11	10	OPEN YOUR HEART	Human League	Virgin	5
13	11	HOLD ME	BA Robertson and Maggie Bell	Swansong	4
12	12	LET'S HANG ON	Barry Manilow	Arista	6
18	13	TONIGHT I'M YOURS (DON'T HURT ME)	Rod Stewart	Riva	3
10	14	IT'S RAINING	Shakin' Stevens	Epic	5
3	15	O SUPERMAN	Laurie Anderson	Warner Brothers	4
7	16	THUNDER IN THE MOUNTAINS	Toyah	Safari	6
22	17	WHEN YOU WERE SWEET SIXTEEN	Fureys and Davey Arthur	Ritz	4
29	18	PHYSICAL	Olivia Newton-John	EMI	3
40	19	FAVOURITE SHIRTS (BOY MEETS GIRL)	Haircut 100	Arista	2
16	20	WALKIN' IN THE SUNSHINE	Bad Manners	Magnet	6
33	21	BEGIN THE BEGUINE (VOLVER A EMPEZAR)	Julio Iglesias	CBS	2
17	22	JUST CAN'T GET ENOUGH	Depeche Mode	Mute	7
20	23	HANDS UP (GIVE ME YOUR HEART)	Ottawan	Carrere	10
15	24	UNDER YOUR THUMB	Godley and Creme	Polydor	8
23	25	PRINCE CHARMING	Adam and the Ants	CBS	9
34	26	TOM SAWYER	Rush	Exit	2
19	27	SHUT UP	Madness	Stiff	7
25	28	ENDLESS LOVE	Diana Ross and Lionel Richie	Motown	9
24	29	QUIET LIFE	Japan	Hansa	7
37	30	TWILIGHT	Electric Light Orchestra	Jet	2
38	31	LOVE ME TONIGHT	Trevor Walters	Magnet	2
-	32	STEPPIN' OUT	Kool and the Gang	De-Lite	1
-	33	KEEP IT DARK	Genesis	Charisma	1
31	34	DEAD CITIES	Exploited	Secret	3
27	35	MAD EYED SCREAMER	Creatures	Polydor	6
28	36	TAINTED LOVE	Soft Cell	Some Bizzare	13
-	37	LET'S GROOVE	Earth Wind and Fire	CBS	1
-	38	YOU GOT THE FLOOR	Arthur Adams ●	RCA	1
36	39	NIGHTMARE	Gillan	Virgin	4
-	40	WHY DO FOOLS FALL IN LOVE	Diana Ross	Capitol	1

WEEK ENDING 14 NOVEMBER 1981

LW	TW	Title	Artist	Label	Wks
3	1	EVERY LITTLE THING SHE DOES IS MAGIC	Police	A&M	4
2	2	HAPPY BIRTHDAY	Altered Images	Epic	6
5	3	WHEN SHE WAS MY GIRL	Four Tops	Casablanca	4
4	4	LABELLED WITH LOVE	Squeeze	A&M	5
7	5	JOAN OF ARC	Orchestral Manoeuvres In The Dark	Dindisc	4
1	6	IT'S MY PARTY	Dave Stewart and Barbara Gaskin	Broken	8
21	7	BEGIN THE BEGUINE (VOLVER A EMPEZAR)	Julio Iglesias	CBS	3
-	8	UNDER PRESSURE	Queen and David Bowie ●	EMI	1
19	9	FAVOURITE SHIRTS (BOY MEETS GIRL)	Haircut 100	Arista	3
13	10	TONIGHT I'M YOURS (DON'T HURT ME)	Rod Stewart	Riva	4
18	11	PHYSICAL	Olivia Newton-John	EMI	4
6	12	GOOD YEAR FOR THE ROSES	Elvis Costello	F Beat	6
11	13	HOLD ME	BA Robertson and Maggie Bell	Swansong	5
17	14	WHEN YOU WERE SWEET SIXTEEN	Fureys and Davey Arthur	Ritz	5
10	15	OPEN YOUR HEART	Human League	Virgin	6
9	16	BIRDIE SONG	Tweets	PRT	9
12	17	LET'S HANG ON	Barry Manilow	Arista	7
14	18	IT'S RAINING	Shakin' Stevens	Epic	6
8	19	ABSOLUTE BEGINNERS	Jam	Polydor	4
37	20	LET'S GROOVE	Earth Wind and Fire	CBS	2
16	21	THUNDER IN THE MOUNTAINS	Toyah	Safari	7
40	22	WHY DO FOOLS FALL IN LOVE	Diana Ross	Capitol	2
-	23	AY AY AY AY MOOSEY	Modern Romance	WEA	1
15	24	O SUPERMAN	Laurie Anderson	Warner Brothers	5
32	25	STEPPIN' OUT	Kool and the Gang	De-Lite	2
26	26	TOM SAWYER	Rush	Exit	3
-	27	THE VOICE	Ultravox	Chrysalis	1
-	28	BEDSITTER	Soft Cell	Some Bizzare	1
-	29	I GO TO SLEEP	Pretenders	Real	1
30	30	TWILIGHT	Electric Light Orchestra	Jet	3
31	31	LOVE ME TONIGHT	Trevor Walters	Magnet	3
-	32	VISIONS OF CHINA	Japan	Virgin	1
22	33	JUST CAN'T GET ENOUGH	Depeche Mode	Mute	8
20	34	WALKIN' IN THE SUNSHINE	Bad Manners	Magnet	7
-	35	YES TONIGHT JOSEPHINE	Jets ●	EMI	1
23	36	HANDS UP (GIVE ME YOUR HEART)	Ottawan	Carrere	11
-	37	THE LUNATICS (HAVE TAKEN OVER THE ASYLUM)	Fun Boy Three ●	Chrysalis	1
33	38	KEEP IT DARK	Genesis	Charisma	2
-	39	TEARS ARE NOT ENOUGH	ABC ●	Neutron	1
24	40	UNDER YOUR THUMB	Godley and Creme	Polydor	9

WEEK ENDING 21 NOVEMBER 1981

LW	TW	Title	Artist	Label	Wks
8	1	UNDER PRESSURE	Queen and David Bowie	EMI	2
1	2	EVERY LITTLE THING SHE DOES IS MAGIC	Police	A&M	5
7	3	BEGIN THE BEGUINE (VOLVER A EMPEZAR)	Julio Iglesias	CBS	4
9	4	FAVOURITE SHIRTS (BOY MEETS GIRL)	Haircut 100	Arista	4
5	5	JOAN OF ARC	Orchestral Manoeuvres In The Dark	Dindisc	5
3	6	WHEN SHE WAS MY GIRL	Four Tops	Casablanca	5
11	7	PHYSICAL	Olivia Newton-John	EMI	5
10	8	TONIGHT I'M YOURS (DON'T HURT ME)	Rod Stewart	Riva	5
20	9	LET'S GROOVE	Earth Wind and Fire	CBS	3
4	10	LABELLED WITH LOVE	Squeeze	A&M	6
2	11	HAPPY BIRTHDAY	Altered Images	Epic	7
29	12	I GO TO SLEEP	Pretenders	Real	2
28	13	BEDSITTER	Soft Cell	Some Bizzare	2
14	14	WHEN YOU WERE SWEET SIXTEEN	Fureys and Davey Arthur	Ritz	6
6	15	IT'S MY PARTY	Dave Stewart and Barbara Gaskin	Broken	9
12	16	GOOD YEAR FOR THE ROSES	Elvis Costello	F Beat	7
23	17	AY AY AY AY MOOSEY	Modern Romance	WEA	2
25	18	STEPPIN' OUT	Kool and the Gang	De-Lite	3

In these weeks ■ Queen and David Bowie combine to give only the second instance (after Frank and Nancy Sinatra) of two number one hit makers getting together to create another chart-topper (21.11.81) ■ Olivia Newton-John's *Physical* enjoyed a ten-week run at no. 1 in the States, to make it the biggest chart hit of the decade there, but in Britain it manages just one week at number seven (21.11.81) ■ The Four Tops' tenth Top 10 hit *When She Was My Girl*, comes ten years after their ninth (14.11.81)■

LW	TW	Title / Artist	Label	Wks
22	19	WHY DO FOOLS FALL IN LOVE Diana Ross	Capitol	3
13	20	HOLD ME BA Robertson and Maggie Bell	Swansong	6
15	21	OPEN YOUR HEART Human League	Virgin	7
16	22	BIRDIE SONG Tweets	PRT	10
27	23	THE VOICE Ultravox	Chrysalis	2
17	24	LET'S HANG ON Barry Manilow	Arista	8
26	25	TOM SAWYER Rush	Exit	4
39	26	TEARS ARE NOT ENOUGH ABC	Neutron	2
19	27	ABSOLUTE BEGINNERS Jam	Polydor	5
18	28	IT'S RAINING Shakin' Stevens	Epic	7
31	29	LOVE ME TONIGHT Trevor Walters	Magnet	4
37	30	THE LUNATICS (HAVE TAKEN OVER THE ASYLUM) Fun Boy Three	Chrysalis	2
35	31	YES TONIGHT JOSEPHINE Jets	EMI	2
-	32	CAMBODIA Kim Wilde	RAK	1
32	33	VISIONS OF CHINA Japan	Virgin	2
30	34	TWILIGHT Electric Light Orchestra	Jet	4
-	35	PAINT ME DOWN Spandau Ballet	Reformation	1
-	36	TURN YOUR LOVE AROUND George Benson	Warner Brothers	1
-	37	DADDY'S HOME Cliff Richard	EMI	1
-	38	FLASHBACK Imagination	R&B	1
21	39	THUNDER IN THE MOUNTAINS Toyah	Safari	8
-	40	ME AND MR SANCHEZ Blue Rondo a la Turk ●	Virgin	1

WEEK ENDING 28 NOVEMBER 1981

LW	TW	Title / Artist	Label	Wks
1	1	UNDER PRESSURE Queen and David Bowie	EMI	3
3	2	BEGIN THE BEGUINE (VOLVER A EMPEZAR) Julio Iglesias	CBS	5
9	3	LET'S GROOVE Earth Wind and Fire	CBS	4
4	4	FAVOURITE SHIRTS (BOY MEETS GIRL) Haircut 100	Arista	5
13	5	BEDSITTER Soft Cell	Some Bizzare	3
5	6	JOAN OF ARC Orchestral Manoeuvres In The Dark	Dindisc	6
19	7	WHY DO FOOLS FALL IN LOVE Diana Ross	Capitol	4
7	8	PHYSICAL Olivia Newton-John	EMI	6
2	9	EVERY LITTLE THING SHE DOES IS MAGIC Police	A&M	6
12	10	I GO TO SLEEP Pretenders	Real	3
8	11	TONIGHT I'M YOURS (DON'T HURT ME) Rod Stewart	Riva	6
17	12	AY AY AY AY MOOSEY Modern Romance	WEA	3
6	13	WHEN SHE WAS MY GIRL Four Tops	Casablanca	6
18	14	STEPPIN' OUT Kool and the Gang	De-Lite	4
37	15	DADDY'S HOME Cliff Richard	EMI	2
11	16	HAPPY BIRTHDAY Altered Images	Epic	8
10	17	LABELLED WITH LOVE Squeeze	A&M	7
23	18	THE VOICE Ultravox	Chrysalis	3
26	19	TEARS ARE NOT ENOUGH ABC	Neutron	3
14	20	WHEN YOU WERE SWEET SIXTEEN Fureys and Davey Arthur	Ritz	7
30	21	THE LUNATICS (HAVE TAKEN OVER THE ASYLUM) Fun Boy Three	Chrysalis	3
22	22	BIRDIE SONG Tweets	PRT	11
-	23	FOUR MORE FROM TOYAH Toyah	Safari	1
32	24	CAMBODIA Kim Wilde	RAK	2
31	25	YES TONIGHT JOSEPHINE Jets	EMI	3
-	26	WEDDING BELLS Godley and Creme	Polydor	1
29	27	LOVE ME TONIGHT Trevor Walters	Magnet	5
38	28	FLASHBACK Imagination	R&B	2
15	29	IT'S MY PARTY Dave Stewart and Barbara Gaskin	Broken	10
35	30	PAINT ME DOWN Spandau Ballet	Reformation	2
36	31	TURN YOUR LOVE AROUND George Benson	Warner Brothers	2
33	32	VISIONS OF CHINA Japan	Virgin	3
25	33	TOM SAWYER Rush	Exit	5
16	34	GOOD YEAR FOR THE ROSES Elvis Costello	F Beat	8
20	35	HOLD ME BA Robertson and Maggie Bell	Swansong	7
-	36	BUONA SERA (DON'T BE ANGRY) Bad Manners	Magnet	1
-	37	MY OWN WAY Duran Duran	EMI	1
24	38	LET'S HANG ON Barry Manilow	Arista	9
-	39	WE KILL THE WORLD (DON'T KILL THE WORLD) Boney M	Atlantic	1
21	40	OPEN YOUR HEART Human League	Virgin	8

WEEK ENDING 5 DECEMBER 1981

December 1981

□ Highest position disc reached ● Act's first ever week on chart

LW	TW	Title / Artist	Label	Wks
2	1	BEGIN THE BEGUINE (VOLVER A EMPEZAR) Julio Iglesias	CBS	6
1	2	UNDER PRESSURE Queen and David Bowie	EMI	4
3	3	LET'S GROOVE Earth Wind and Fire	CBS	5
5	4	BEDSITTER Soft Cell	Some Bizzare	4
7	5	WHY DO FOOLS FALL IN LOVE Diana Ross	Capitol	5
15	6	DADDY'S HOME Cliff Richard	EMI	3
10	7	I GO TO SLEEP Pretenders	Real	4
4	8	FAVOURITE SHIRTS (BOY MEETS GIRL) Haircut 100	Arista	6
-	9	DON'T YOU WANT ME Human League	Virgin	1
12	10	AY AY AY AY MOOSEY Modern Romance	WEA	4
8	11	PHYSICAL Olivia Newton-John	EMI	7
14	12	STEPPIN' OUT Kool and the Gang	De-Lite	5
6	13	JOAN OF ARC Orchestral Manoeuvres In The Dark	Dindisc	7
23	14	FOUR MORE FROM TOYAH Toyah	Safari	2
11	15	TONIGHT I'M YOURS (DON'T HURT ME) Rod Stewart	Riva	7
18	16	THE VOICE Ultravox	Chrysalis	4
9	17	EVERY LITTLE THING SHE DOES IS MAGIC Police	A&M	7
24	18	CAMBODIA Kim Wilde	RAK	3
19	19	TEARS ARE NOT ENOUGH ABC	Neutron	4
21	20	THE LUNATICS (HAVE TAKEN OVER THE ASYLUM) Fun Boy Three	Chrysalis	4
26	21	WEDDING BELLS Godley and Creme	Polydor	2
13	22	WHEN SHE WAS MY GIRL Four Tops	Casablanca	7
28	23	FLASHBACK Imagination	R&B	3
-	24	IT MUST BE LOVE Madness	Stiff	1
25	25	YES TONIGHT JOSEPHINE Jets	EMI	4
37	26	MY OWN WAY Duran Duran	EMI	2
-	27	ROCK 'N' ROLL Status Quo	Vertigo	1
-	28	WILD IS THE WIND David Bowie	RCA	1
31	29	TURN YOUR LOVE AROUND George Benson	Warner Brothers	3
27	30	LOVE ME TONIGHT Trevor Walters	Magnet	6
22	31	BIRDIE SONG Tweets	PRT	12
20	32	WHEN YOU WERE SWEET SIXTEEN Fureys and Davey Arthur	Ritz	8
-	33	LOVE NEEDS NO DISGUISE Gary Numan and Dramatis	Beggars Banquet	1
36	34	BUONA SERA (DON'T BE ANGRY) Bad Manners	Magnet	2
-	35	THE LAND OF MAKE BELIEVE Bucks Fizz	RCA	1
-	36	DEAD RINGER FOR LOVE Meat Loaf	Epic	1
-	37	MIRROR MIRROR Dollar	WEA	1
-	38	FOOTSTEPS Showaddywaddy	Bell	1
39	39	WE KILL THE WORLD (DON'T KILL THE WORLD) Boney M	Atlantic	2
16	40	HAPPY BIRTHDAY Altered Images	Epic	9

WEEK ENDING 12 DECEMBER 1981

LW	TW	Title / Artist	Label	Wks
9	1	DON'T YOU WANT ME Human League	Virgin	2
6	2	DADDY'S HOME Cliff Richard	EMI	4
1	3	BEGIN THE BEGUINE (VOLVER A EMPEZAR) Julio Iglesias	CBS	7
5	4	WHY DO FOOLS FALL IN LOVE Diana Ross	Capitol	6
3	5	LET'S GROOVE Earth Wind and Fire	CBS	6
4	6	BEDSITTER Soft Cell	Some Bizzare	5
24	7	IT MUST BE LOVE Madness	Stiff	2
2	8	UNDER PRESSURE Queen and David Bowie	EMI	5
-	9	ANT RAP Adam and the Ants	CBS	1
21	10	WEDDING BELLS Godley and Creme	Polydor	3
-	11	ONE OF US Abba	Epic	1
18	12	CAMBODIA Kim Wilde	RAK	4
7	13	I GO TO SLEEP Pretenders	Real	5
14	14	FOUR MORE FROM TOYAH Toyah	Safari	3
10	15	AY AY AY AY MOOSEY Modern Romance	WEA	5
23	16	FLASHBACK Imagination	R&B	4
27	17	ROCK 'N' ROLL Status Quo	Vertigo	2
12	18	STEPPIN' OUT Kool and the Gang	De-Lite	6
11	19	PHYSICAL Olivia Newton-John	EMI	8
20	20	THE LUNATICS (HAVE TAKEN OVER THE ASYLUM) Fun Boy Three	Chrysalis	5
8	21	FAVOURITE SHIRTS (BOY MEETS GIRL) Haircut 100	Arista	7

■ *Begin The Beguine (Volver A Empezar)* becomes the first Spanish language single to top the charts and Julio Iglesias is the only ex-Real Madrid goalkeeper to hit the top (though not the only goalkeeper, of course. Gordon Banks has been there too) (05.12.81) ■ Meat Loaf's *Dead Ringer For Love* features the uncredited vocal talents of Cher, enjoying her first Top 40 acting for almost eight years (05.12.81) ■

December 1981

□ Highest position disc reached ● Act's first ever week on chart

LW	TW	Title	Artist	Label	Wks
26	22	MY OWN WAY	Duran Duran	*EMI*	3
16	23	THE VOICE	Ultravox	*Chrysalis*	5
35	24	THE LAND OF MAKE BELIEVE	Bucks Fizz	*RCA*	2
28	25	WILD IS THE WIND	David Bowie	*RCA*	2
37	26	MIRROR MIRROR	Dollar	*WEA*	2
25	27	YES TONIGHT JOSEPHINE	Jets	*EMI*	5
-	28	SPIRITS IN THE MATERIAL WORLD	Police	*A&M*	1
31	29	BIRDIE SONG	Tweets	*PRT*	13
19	30	TEARS ARE NOT ENOUGH	ABC	*Neutron*	5
29	31	TURN YOUR LOVE AROUND	George Benson	*Warner Brothers*	4
13	32	JOAN OF ARC	Orchestral Manoeuvres In The Dark	*Dindisc*	8
33	[33]	LOVE NEEDS NO DISGUISE	Gary Numan and Dramatis	*Beggars Banquet*	2
36	[34]	BUONA SERA (DON'T BE ANGRY)	Bad Manners	*Magnet*	3
38	35	FOOTSTEPS	Showaddywaddy	*Bell*	2
36	36	DEAD RINGER FOR LOVE	Meat Loaf	*Epic*	2
15	37	TONIGHT I'M YOURS (DON'T HURT ME)	Rod Stewart	*Riva*	8
17	38	EVERY LITTLE THING SHE DOES IS MAGIC	Police	*A&M*	8
-	39	PAINT ME DOWN	Spandau Ballet	*Reformation*	3
39	40	WE KILL THE WORLD (DON'T KILL THE WORLD)	Boney M	*Atlantic*	3

WEEK ENDING 19 DECEMBER 1981

LW	TW	Title	Artist	Label	Wks
1	[1]	DON'T YOU WANT ME	Human League	*Virgin*	3
2	[2]	DADDY'S HOME	Cliff Richard	*EMI*	5
11	[3]	ONE OF US	Abba	*Epic*	2
9	4	ANT RAP	Adam and the Ants	*CBS*	2
7	[5]	IT MUST BE LOVE	Madness	*Stiff*	3
3	6	BEGIN THE BEGUINE (VOLVER A EMPEZAR)	Julio Iglesias	*CBS*	8
4	7	WHY DO FOOLS FALL IN LOVE	Diana Ross	*Capitol*	7
10	8	WEDDING BELLS	Godley and Creme	*Polydor*	4
6	9	BEDSITTER	Soft Cell	*Some Bizzare*	6
24	10	THE LAND OF MAKE BELIEVE	Bucks Fizz	*RCA*	3
5	11	LET'S GROOVE	Earth Wind and Fire	*CBS*	7
17	12	ROCK 'N' ROLL	Status Quo	*Vertigo*	3
28	13	SPIRITS IN THE MATERIAL WORLD	Police	*A&M*	2
22	[14]	MY OWN WAY	Duran Duran	*EMI*	4
12	15	CAMBODIA	Kim Wilde	*RAK*	5
8	16	UNDER PRESSURE	Queen and David Bowie	*EMI*	6
13	17	I GO TO SLEEP	Pretenders	*Real*	6
16	18	FLASHBACK	Imagination	*R&B*	5
26	19	MIRROR MIRROR	Dollar	*WEA*	3
20	[20]	THE LUNATICS (HAVE TAKEN OVER THE ASYLUM)	Fun Boy Three	*Chrysalis*	6
15	21	AY AY AY AY MOOSEY	Modern Romance	*WEA*	6
14	22	FOUR MORE FROM TOYAH	Toyah	*Safari*	4
-	23	YOUNG TURKS	Rod Stewart	*Riva*	1
18	24	STEPPIN' OUT	Kool and the Gang	*De-Lite*	7
23	25	THE VOICE	Ultravox	*Chrysalis*	6
-	26	I'LL FIND MY WAY HOME	Jon and Vangelis	*Polydor*	1
25	27	WILD IS THE WIND	David Bowie	*RCA*	3
29	28	BIRDIE SONG	Tweets	*PRT*	14
-	29	I COULD BE HAPPY	Altered Images	*Epic*	1
-	30	WAITING FOR A GIRL LIKE YOU	Foreigner	*Atlantic*	1
36	31	DEAD RINGER FOR LOVE	Meat Loaf	*Epic*	3
30	32	TEARS ARE NOT ENOUGH	ABC	*Neutron*	6
27	33	YES TONIGHT JOSEPHINE	Jets	*EMI*	6
34	[34]	BUONA SERA (DON'T BE ANGRY)	Bad Manners	*Magnet*	4
19	35	PHYSICAL	Olivia Newton-John	*EMI*	9
-	36	STARS OVER 45	Chas and Dave	*Rockney*	1
31	37	TURN YOUR LOVE AROUND	George Benson	*Warner Brothers*	5
35	38	FOOTSTEPS	Showaddywaddy	*Bell*	3
21	39	FAVOURITE SHIRTS (BOY MEETS GIRL)	Haircut 100	*Arista*	8
-	40	HOKEY COKEY	Snowmen ●	*Stiff*	1

WEEK ENDING 26 DECEMBER 1981

LW	TW	Title	Artist	Label	Wks
1	[1]	DON'T YOU WANT ME	Human League	*Virgin*	4
2	[2]	DADDY'S HOME	Cliff Richard	*EMI*	6
3	[3]	ONE OF US	Abba	*Epic*	3
4	4	ANT RAP	Adam and the Ants	*CBS*	3
10	5	THE LAND OF MAKE BELIEVE	Bucks Fizz	*RCA*	4
5	6	IT MUST BE LOVE	Madness	*Stiff*	4
8	[7]	WEDDING BELLS	Godley and Creme	*Polydor*	5
12	[8]	ROCK 'N' ROLL	Status Quo	*Vertigo*	4
19	9	MIRROR MIRROR	Dollar	*WEA*	4
26	10	I'LL FIND MY WAY HOME	Jon and Vangelis	*Polydor*	2
23	[11]	YOUNG TURKS	Rod Stewart	*Riva*	2
13	[12]	SPIRITS IN THE MATERIAL WORLD	Police	*A&M*	3
7	13	WHY DO FOOLS FALL IN LOVE	Diana Ross	*Capitol*	8
6	14	BEGIN THE BEGUINE (VOLVER A EMPEZAR)	Julio Iglesias	*CBS*	9
14	15	MY OWN WAY	Duran Duran	*EMI*	5
9	16	BEDSITTER	Soft Cell	*Some Bizzare*	7
15	17	CAMBODIA	Kim Wilde	*RAK*	6
40	[18]	HOKEY COKEY	Snowmen	*Stiff*	2
30	19	WAITING FOR A GIRL LIKE YOU	Foreigner	*Atlantic*	2
29	20	I COULD BE HAPPY	Altered Images	*Epic*	2
36	[21]	STARS OVER 45	Chas and Dave	*Rockney*	2
28	22	BIRDIE SONG	Tweets	*PRT*	15
18	23	FLASHBACK	Imagination	*R&B*	6
27	[24]	WILD IS THE WIND	David Bowie	*RCA*	4
11	25	LET'S GROOVE	Earth Wind and Fire	*CBS*	8
-	26	GET DOWN ON IT	Kool and the Gang	*De-Lite*	1
20	27	THE LUNATICS (HAVE TAKEN OVER THE ASYLUM)	Fun Boy Three	*Chrysalis*	7
-	28	HAPPY CHRISTMAS (WAR IS OVER)	John Lennon	*Parlophone*	1
22	29	FOUR MORE FROM TOYAH	Toyah	*Safari*	5
31	30	DEAD RINGER FOR LOVE	Meat Loaf	*Epic*	4
38	[31]	FOOTSTEPS	Showaddywaddy	*Bell*	4
-	[32]	MERRY XMAS EVERYBODY	Slade	*Polydor*	1
-	33	I WANNA BE A WINNER	Brown Sauce ●	*BBC*	1
17	34	I GO TO SLEEP	Pretenders	*Real*	7
27	35	UNDER PRESSURE	Queen and David Bowie	*EMI*	7
35	36	PHYSICAL	Olivia Newton-John	*EMI*	10
-	37	DON'T WALK AWAY	Four Tops	*Casablanca*	1
21	38	AY AY AY AY MOOSEY	Modern Romance	*WEA*	7
34	39	BUONA SERA (DON'T BE ANGRY)	Bad Manners	*Magnet*	5
-	[40]	CHRISTMAS ON 45	Holly and the Ivys ●	*Decca*	1

In these weeks ■ Apart from four past, present or future number ones in the Top 40, there are also new versions of two previous chart-toppers, *Why Do Fools Fall In Love* and *Yes Tonight Josephine*, and snippets of other number ones on Chas and Dave's singalong medley *Stars Over 45* (19.12.81)■

1982

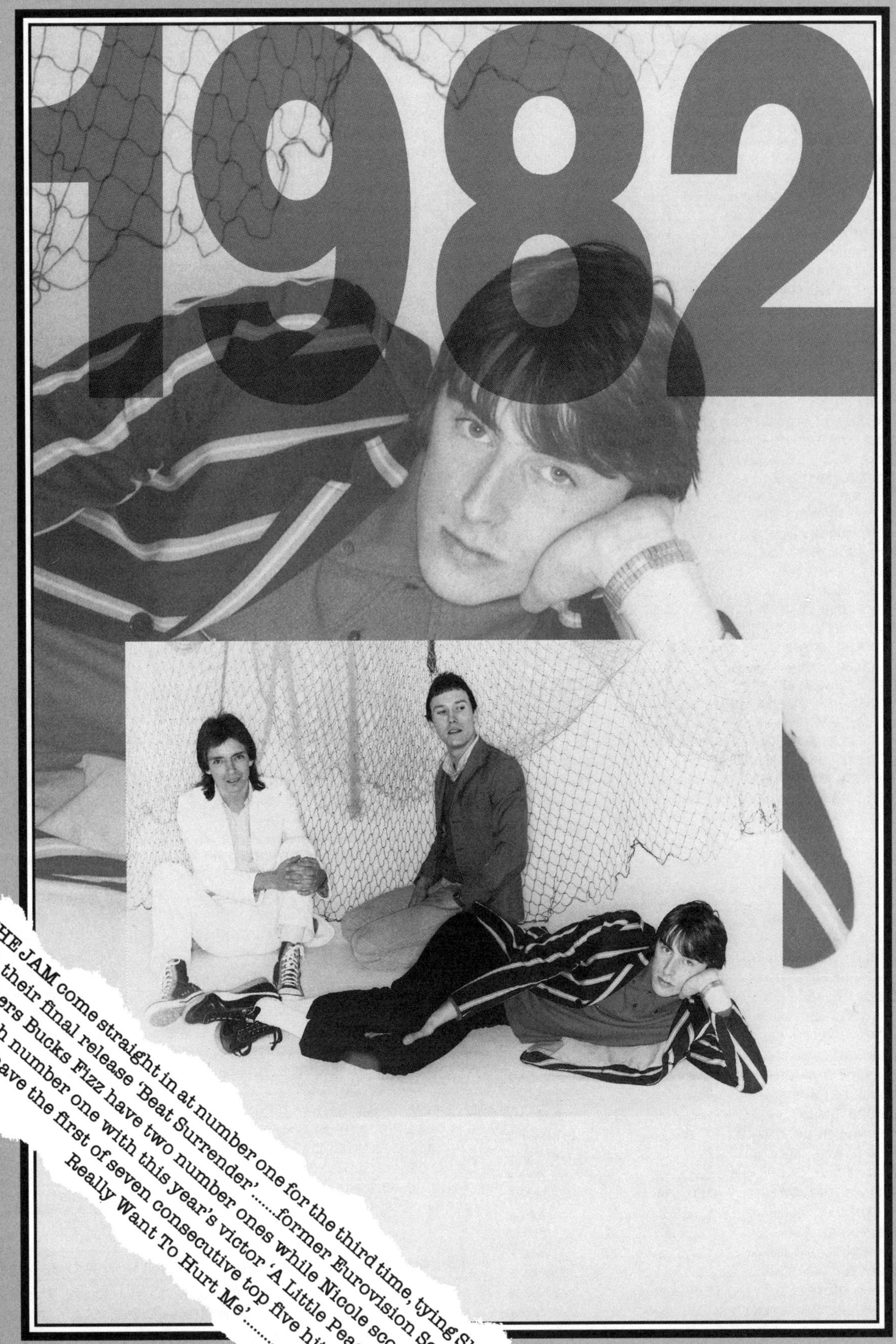

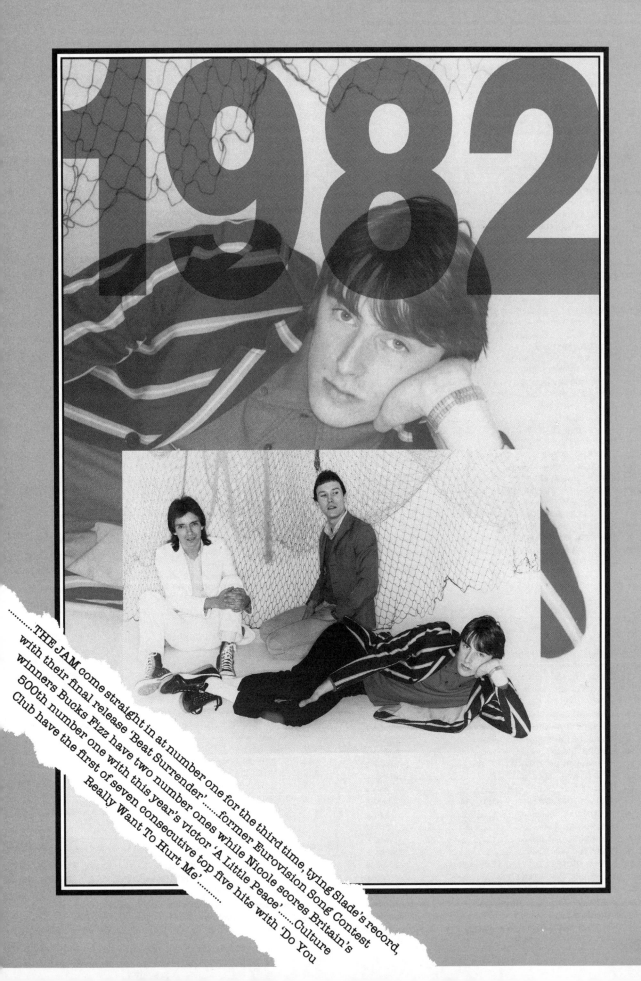

........**THE JAM** come straight in at number one for the third time, tying Slade's record, with their final release 'Beat Surrender'......former Eurovision Song Contest winners Bucks Fizz have two number ones while Nicole scores Britain's 500th number one with this year's victor 'A Little Peace'......Culture Club have the first of seven consecutive top five hits with 'Do You Really Want To Hurt Me'.........

January 1982

□ Highest position disc reached ● Act's first ever week on chart

LW	TW	WEEK ENDING 2 JANUARY 1982		Wks
(no chart published, chart for 26 December 1981 repeated)				
1	[1]	DON'T YOU WANT ME Human League	Virgin	5
2	[2]	DADDY'S HOME Cliff Richard	EMI	7
3	[3]	ONE OF US Abba	Epic	4
4	4	ANT RAP Adam and the Ants	CBS	4
5	5	THE LAND OF MAKE BELIEVE Bucks Fizz	RCA	5
6	6	IT MUST BE LOVE Madness	Stiff	5
7	[7]	WEDDING BELLS Godley and Creme	Polydor	6
8	[8]	ROCK 'N' ROLL Status Quo	Vertigo	5
9	9	MIRROR MIRROR Dollar	WEA	5
10	10	I'LL FIND MY WAY HOME Jon and Vangelis	Polydor	3
11	[11]	YOUNG TURKS Rod Stewart	Riva	3
12	[12]	SPIRITS IN THE MATERIAL WORLD Police	A&M	4
13	13	WHY DO FOOLS FALL IN LOVE Diana Ross	Capitol	9
14	14	BEGIN THE BEGUINE (VOLVER A EMPEZAR) Julio Iglesias	CBS	10
15	15	MY OWN WAY Duran Duran	EMI	6
16	16	BEDSITTER Soft Cell	Some Bizzare	8
17	17	CAMBODIA Kim Wilde	RAK	7
18	[18]	HOKEY COKEY Snowmen	Stiff	3
19	19	WAITING FOR A GIRL LIKE YOU Foreigner	Atlantic	3
20	20	I COULD BE HAPPY Altered Images	Epic	3
21	[21]	STARS OVER 45 Chas and Dave	Rockney	3
22	22	BIRDIE SONG Tweets	PRT	16
23	23	FLASHBACK Imagination	R&B	7
24	[24]	WILD IS THE WIND David Bowie	RCA	5
25	25	LET'S GROOVE Earth Wind and Fire	CBS	9
26	26	GET DOWN ON IT Kool and the Gang	De-Lite	2
27	27	THE LUNATICS (HAVE TAKEN OVER THE ASYLUM) Fun Boy Three	Chrysalis	8
28	28	HAPPY CHRISTMAS (WAR IS OVER) John Lennon	Parlophone	2
29	29	FOUR MORE FROM TOYAH Toyah	Safari	6
30	30	DEAD RINGER FOR LOVE Meat Loaf	Epic	5
31	[31]	FOOTSTEPS Showaddywaddy	Bell	5
32	[32]	MERRY XMAS EVERYBODY Slade	Polydor	2
33	33	I WANNA BE A WINNER Brown Sauce	BBC	2
34	34	I GO TO SLEEP Pretenders	Real	8
35	35	UNDER PRESSURE Queen and David Bowie	EMI	8
36	36	PHYSICAL Olivia Newton-John	EMI	11
37	37	DON'T WALK AWAY Four Tops	Casablanca	2
38	38	AY AY AY AY MOOSEY Modern Romance	WEA	8
39	39	BUONA SERA (DON'T BE ANGRY) Bad Manners	Magnet	6
40	[40]	CHRISTMAS ON 45 Holly and the Ivys	Decca	2

LW	TW	WEEK ENDING 9 JANUARY 1982		Wks
1	[1]	DON'T YOU WANT ME Human League	Virgin	6
5	2	THE LAND OF MAKE BELIEVE Bucks Fizz	RCA	6
4	[3]	ANT RAP Adam and the Ants	CBS	5
6	[4]	IT MUST BE LOVE Madness	Stiff	6
3	5	ONE OF US Abba	Epic	5
2	6	DADDY'S HOME Cliff Richard	EMI	8
26	7	GET DOWN ON IT Kool and the Gang	De-Lite	3
9	8	MIRROR MIRROR Dollar	WEA	6
10	9	I'LL FIND MY WAY HOME Jon and Vangelis	Polydor	4
20	10	I COULD BE HAPPY Altered Images	Epic	4
7	11	WEDDING BELLS Godley and Creme	Polydor	7
19	12	WAITING FOR A GIRL LIKE YOU Foreigner	Atlantic	4
8	13	ROCK 'N' ROLL Status Quo	Vertigo	6
11	14	YOUNG TURKS Rod Stewart	Riva	4
12	15	SPIRITS IN THE MATERIAL WORLD Police	A&M	5
15	16	MY OWN WAY Duran Duran	EMI	7
22	17	BIRDIE SONG Tweets	PRT	17
23	18	FLASHBACK Imagination	R&B	8
17	19	CAMBODIA Kim Wilde	RAK	8
13	20	WHY DO FOOLS FALL IN LOVE Diana Ross	Capitol	10
-	21	THE MODEL/COMPUTER LOVE Kraftwerk	EMI	1
16	22	BEDSITTER Soft Cell	Some Bizzare	9
18	23	HOKEY COKEY Snowmen	Stiff	4
29	24	FOUR MORE FROM TOYAH Toyah	Safari	7
-	25	YELLOW PEARL Phil Lynott	Vertigo	1
37	26	DON'T WALK AWAY Four Tops	Casablanca	3
21	27	STARS OVER 45 Chas and Dave	Rockney	4
24	28	WILD IS THE WIND David Bowie	RCA	6
27	29	THE LUNATICS (HAVE TAKEN OVER THE ASYLUM) Fun Boy Three	Chrysalis	9
30	30	DEAD RINGER FOR LOVE Meat Loaf	Epic	6
33	31	I WANNA BE A WINNER Brown Sauce	BBC	3
25	32	LET'S GROOVE Earth Wind and Fire	CBS	10
36	33	PHYSICAL Olivia Newton-John	EMI	12
14	34	BEGIN THE BEGUINE (VOLVER A EMPEZAR) Julio Iglesias	CBS	11
31	35	FOOTSTEPS Showaddywaddy	Bell	6
28	36	HAPPY CHRISTMAS (WAR IS OVER) John Lennon	Parlophone	3
39	37	BUONA SERA (DON'T BE ANGRY) Bad Manners	Magnet	7
35	38	UNDER PRESSURE Queen and David Bowie	EMI	9
38	39	AY AY AY AY MOOSEY Modern Romance	WEA	9
40	[40]	CHRISTMAS ON 45 Holly and the Ivys	Decca	3

LW	TW	WEEK ENDING 16 JANUARY 1982		Wks
2	[1]	THE LAND OF MAKE BELIEVE Bucks Fizz	RCA	7
1	2	DON'T YOU WANT ME Human League	Virgin	7
7	[3]	GET DOWN ON IT Kool and the Gang	De-Lite	4
8	[4]	MIRROR MIRROR Dollar	WEA	7
3	5	ANT RAP Adam and the Ants	CBS	6
5	6	ONE OF US Abba	Epic	6
10	[7]	I COULD BE HAPPY Altered Images	Epic	5
9	8	I'LL FIND MY WAY HOME Jon and Vangelis	Polydor	5
4	9	IT MUST BE LOVE Madness	Stiff	7
21	10	THE MODEL/COMPUTER LOVE Kraftwerk	EMI	2
12	11	WAITING FOR A GIRL LIKE YOU Foreigner	Atlantic	5
6	12	DADDY'S HOME Cliff Richard	EMI	9
-	13	OH JULIE Shakin' Stevens	Epic	1
14	14	YOUNG TURKS Rod Stewart	Riva	5
13	15	ROCK 'N' ROLL Status Quo	Vertigo	7
16	16	MY OWN WAY Duran Duran	EMI	8
11	17	WEDDING BELLS Godley and Creme	Polydor	8
15	18	SPIRITS IN THE MATERIAL WORLD Police	A&M	6
-	19	BEING BOILED Human League	Fast Product	1
31	20	I WANNA BE A WINNER Brown Sauce	BBC	4
17	21	BIRDIE SONG Tweets	PRT	18
25	22	YELLOW PEARL Phil Lynott	Vertigo	2
26	23	DON'T WALK AWAY Four Tops	Casablanca	4
27	24	STARS OVER 45 Chas and Dave	Rockney	5
-	25	GOLDEN BROWN Stranglers	Liberty	1
30	26	DEAD RINGER FOR LOVE Meat Loaf	Epic	7
-	27	ARTHUR'S THEME (BEST THAT YOU CAN DO) Christopher Cross ●	Warner Bros	1
23	28	HOKEY COKEY Snowmen	Stiff	5
28	29	WILD IS THE WIND David Bowie	RCA	7
-	30	DROWNING IN BERLIN Mobiles ●	Rialto	1
18	31	FLASHBACK Imagination	R&B	9
22	32	BEDSITTER Soft Cell	Some Bizzare	10
-	33	I JUST WANNA (SPEND SOME TIME WITH YOU) Alton Edwards ●	Streetwave	1
20	34	WHY DO FOOLS FALL IN LOVE Diana Ross	Capitol	11
34	35	BEGIN THE BEGUINE (VOLVER A EMPEZAR) Julio Iglesias	CBS	12
-	36	EASIER SAID THAN DONE Shakatak ●	Polydor	1
32	37	LET'S GROOVE Earth Wind and Fire	CBS	11
-	38	HERE IS THE NEWS/TICKET TO THE MOON Electric Light Orchestra	Jet	1
19	39	CAMBODIA Kim Wilde	RAK	9
24	40	FOUR MORE FROM TOYAH Toyah	Safari	8

LW	TW	WEEK ENDING 23 JANUARY 1982		Wks
1	[1]	THE LAND OF MAKE BELIEVE Bucks Fizz	RCA	8
10	2	THE MODEL/COMPUTER LOVE Kraftwerk	EMI	3
13	3	OH JULIE Shakin' Stevens	Epic	2

In these weeks ■ Brackets are beginning to get more common in titles. Christopher Cross and Alton Edwards set the scene for later entries by OMD, Daryl Hall and John Oates and many more throughout the year (16.01.82) ■ Abba's final week in the top 10 was with their eighteenth consecutive top 10 hit (16.01.82)■

February 1982

□ Highest position disc reached ● Act's first ever week on chart

LW	TW	Title / Artist	Label	Wks
3	4	GET DOWN ON IT Kool and the Gang	*De-Lite*	5
2	5	DON'T YOU WANT ME Human League	*Virgin*	8
8	[6]	I'LL FIND MY WAY HOME Jon and Vangelis	*Polydor*	6
26	7	DEAD RINGER FOR LOVE Meat Loaf	*Epic*	8
11	[8]	WAITING FOR A GIRL LIKE YOU Foreigner	*Atlantic*	6
19	9	BEING BOILED Human League	*Fast Product*	2
7	10	I COULD BE HAPPY Altered Images	*Epic*	6
4	11	MIRROR MIRROR Dollar	*WEA*	8
9	12	IT MUST BE LOVE Madness	*Stiff*	8
30	13	DROWNING IN BERLIN Mobiles	*Rialto*	2
22	[14]	YELLOW PEARL Phil Lynott	*Vertigo*	3
5	15	ANT RAP Adam and the Ants	*CBS*	7
25	16	GOLDEN BROWN Stranglers	*Liberty*	2
6	17	ONE OF US Abba	*Epic*	7
27	18	ARTHUR'S THEME (BEST THAT YOU CAN DO) Christopher Cross	*Warner Bros*	2
23	19	DON'T WALK AWAY Four Tops	*Casablanca*	5
33	[20]	I JUST WANNA (SPEND SOME TIME WITH YOU) Alton Edwards	*Streetwave*	2
14	21	YOUNG TURKS Rod Stewart	*Riva*	6
36	22	EASIER SAID THAN DONE Shakatak	*Polydor*	2
20	23	I WANNA BE A WINNER Brown Sauce	*BBC*	5
12	24	DADDY'S HOME Cliff Richard	*EMI*	10
15	25	ROCK 'N' ROLL Status Quo	*Vertigo*	8
38	26	HERE IS THE NEWS/TICKET TO THE MOON Electric Light Orchestra	*Jet*	2
16	27	MY OWN WAY Duran Duran	*EMI*	9
31	28	FLASHBACK Imagination	*R&B*	10
21	29	BIRDIE SONG Tweets	*PRT*	19
17	30	WEDDING BELLS Godley and Creme	*Polydor*	9
-	31	MAID OF ORLEANS (THE WALTZ JOAN OF ARC) Orchestral Manoeuvres In The Dark	*Dindisc*	1
29	32	WILD IS THE WIND David Bowie	*RCA*	8
28	33	HOKEY COKEY Snowmen	*Stiff*	6
24	34	STARS OVER 45 Chas and Dave	*Rockney*	6
-	35	LANDSLIDE Olivia Newton-John	*EMI*	1
-	36	RESTLESS Gillan	*Virgin*	1
-	37	NEVER GIVE UP ON A GOOD THING George Benson	*Warner Bros*	1
18	38	SPIRITS IN THE MATERIAL WORLD Police	*A&M*	7
-	39	LISTEN Stiff Little Fingers	*Chrysalis*	1
32	40	BEDSITTER Soft Cell	*Some Bizzare*	11

WEEK ENDING 30 JANUARY 1982

LW	TW	Title / Artist	Label	Wks
3	[1]	OH JULIE Shakin' Stevens	*Epic*	3
1	2	THE LAND OF MAKE BELIEVE Bucks Fizz	*RCA*	9
2	3	THE MODEL/COMPUTER LOVE Kraftwerk	*EMI*	4
16	4	GOLDEN BROWN Stranglers	*Liberty*	3
4	5	GET DOWN ON IT Kool and the Gang	*De-Lite*	6
9	[6]	BEING BOILED Human League	*Fast Product*	3
6	7	I'LL FIND MY WAY HOME Jon and Vangelis	*Polydor*	7
11	8	MIRROR MIRROR Dollar	*WEA*	9
7	9	DEAD RINGER FOR LOVE Meat Loaf	*Epic*	9
18	10	ARTHUR'S THEME (BEST THAT YOU CAN DO) Christopher Cross	*Warner Bros*	3
8	11	WAITING FOR A GIRL LIKE YOU Foreigner	*Atlantic*	7
5	12	DON'T YOU WANT ME Human League	*Virgin*	9
10	13	I COULD BE HAPPY Altered Images	*Epic*	7
13	14	DROWNING IN BERLIN Mobiles	*Rialto*	3
23	[15]	I WANNA BE A WINNER Brown Sauce	*BBC*	6
19	[16]	DON'T WALK AWAY Four Tops	*Casablanca*	6
31	17	MAID OF ORLEANS (THE WALTZ JOAN OF ARC) Orchestral Manoeuvres In The Dark	*Dindisc*	2
12	18	IT MUST BE LOVE Madness	*Stiff*	9
22	19	EASIER SAID THAN DONE Shakatak	*Polydor*	3
20	[20]	I JUST WANNA (SPEND SOME TIME WITH YOU) Alton Edwards	*Streetwave*	3
14	21	YELLOW PEARL Phil Lynott	*Vertigo*	4
17	22	ONE OF US Abba	*Epic*	8
15	23	ANT RAP Adam and the Ants	*CBS*	8
26	[24]	HERE IS THE NEWS/TICKET TO THE MOON Electric Light Orchestra	*Jet*	3
21	25	YOUNG TURKS Rod Stewart	*Riva*	7
37	26	NEVER GIVE UP ON A GOOD THING George Benson	*Warner Bros*	2
25	27	ROCK 'N' ROLL Status Quo	*Vertigo*	9
24	28	DADDY'S HOME Cliff Richard	*EMI*	11
35	29	LANDSLIDE Olivia Newton-John	*EMI*	2
-	30	FOOL IF YOU THINK IT'S OVER Elkie Brooks	*A&M*	1
-	[31]	TROUBLE Lindsey Buckingham ●	*Mercury*	1
-	32	SENSES WORKING OVERTIME XTC	*Virgin*	1
-	33	EUROPEAN SON Japan	*Hansa*	1
39	34	LISTEN Stiff Little Fingers	*Chrysalis*	2
29	35	BIRDIE SONG Tweets	*PRT*	20
-	36	LOVE PLUS ONE Haircut 100	*Arista*	1
-	37	MIRROR MIRROR Diana Ross	*Capitol*	1
-	38	THE BOILER Rhoda with the Specials AKA ●	*2 Tone*	1
-	39	THEME FROM 'HILL STREET BLUES' Mike Post and Larry Carlton ●	*Elektra*	1
-	40	I CAN'T GO FOR THAT (NO CAN DO) Daryl Hall and John Oates	*RCA*	1

WEEK ENDING 6 FEBRUARY 1982

LW	TW	Title / Artist	Label	Wks
3	[1]	THE MODEL/COMPUTER LOVE Kraftwerk	*EMI*	5
1	2	OH JULIE Shakin' Stevens	*Epic*	4
4	3	GOLDEN BROWN Stranglers	*Liberty*	4
2	4	THE LAND OF MAKE BELIEVE Bucks Fizz	*RCA*	10
9	[5]	DEAD RINGER FOR LOVE Meat Loaf	*Epic*	10
17	6	MAID OF ORLEANS (THE WALTZ JOAN OF ARC) Orchestral Manoeuvres In The Dark	*Dindisc*	3
10	[7]	ARTHUR'S THEME (BEST THAT YOU CAN DO) Christopher Cross	*Warner Bros*	4
5	8	GET DOWN ON IT Kool and the Gang	*De-Lite*	7
14	[9]	DROWNING IN BERLIN Mobiles	*Rialto*	4
6	10	BEING BOILED Human League	*Fast Product*	4
7	11	I'LL FIND MY WAY HOME Jon and Vangelis	*Polydor*	8
19	[12]	EASIER SAID THAN DONE Shakatak	*Polydor*	4
11	13	WAITING FOR A GIRL LIKE YOU Foreigner	*Atlantic*	8
-	14	LET'S GET IT UP AC/DC	*Atlantic*	1
32	15	SENSES WORKING OVERTIME XTC	*Virgin*	2
8	16	MIRROR MIRROR Dollar	*WEA*	10
13	17	I COULD BE HAPPY Altered Images	*Epic*	8
16	18	DON'T WALK AWAY Four Tops	*Casablanca*	7
15	19	I WANNA BE A WINNER Brown Sauce	*BBC*	7
-	20	SAY HELLO WAVE GOODBYE Soft Cell	*Some Bizzare*	1
26	21	NEVER GIVE UP ON A GOOD THING George Benson	*Warner Bros*	3
12	22	DON'T YOU WANT ME Human League	*Virgin*	10
20	23	I JUST WANNA (SPEND SOME TIME WITH YOU) Alton Edwards	*Streetwave*	4
21	24	YELLOW PEARL Phil Lynott	*Vertigo*	5
-	[25]	RESTLESS Gillan	*Virgin*	2
24	26	HERE IS THE NEWS/TICKET TO THE MOON Electric Light Orchestra	*Jet*	4
40	27	I CAN'T GO FOR THAT (NO CAN DO) Daryl Hall and John Oates	*RCA*	2
18	28	IT MUST BE LOVE Madness	*Stiff*	10
-	29	THE LION SLEEPS TONIGHT Tight Fit	*Jive*	1
22	30	ONE OF US Abba	*Epic*	9
33	[31]	EUROPEAN SON Japan	*Ariola*	2
23	32	ANT RAP Adam and the Ants	*CBS*	9
34	[33]	LISTEN Stiff Little Fingers	*Chrysalis*	3
39	34	THEME FROM 'HILL STREET BLUES' Mike Post and Larry Carlton	*Elektra*	2
38	35	THE BOILER Rhoda with the Specials AKA	*2 Tone*	2
36	36	LOVE PLUS ONE Haircut 100	*Arista*	2
31	37	TROUBLE Lindsey Buckingham	*Mercury*	2
25	38	YOUNG TURKS Rod Stewart	*Riva*	8
-	[39]	THAT GIRL Stevie Wonder	*Motown*	1
-	[40]	DO YOU BELIEVE IN THE WESTWORLD Theatre Of Hate ●	*Burning Rome*	1

■ Kraftwerk's *The Model/Computer Love* slips from 2 to 3 before jumping to number 1, the last time a record has dipped on the chart before going back to the very top (30.01.82) ■ Brown Sauce were Noel Edmonds, John Craven, Keith Chegwin and Maggie Philbin from BBC TV's 'Multicoloured Swap Shop' (30.01.82) ■

February 1982

□ Highest position disc reached ● Act's first ever week on chart

LW	TW	WEEK ENDING 13 FEBRUARY 1982		Wks
-	[1]	TOWN CALLED MALICE/PRECIOUS Jam	*Polydor*	1
3	[2]	GOLDEN BROWN Stranglers	*Liberty*	5
2	3	OH JULIE Shakin' Stevens	*Epic*	5
1	4	THE MODEL/COMPUTER LOVE Kraftwerk	*EMI*	6
5	[5]	DEAD RINGER FOR LOVE Meat Loaf	*Epic*	11
6	6	MAID OF ORLEANS (THE WALTZ JOAN OF ARC) Orchestral Manoeuvres In The Dark	*Dindisc*	4
7	[7]	ARTHUR'S THEME (BEST THAT YOU CAN DO) Christopher Cross	*Warner Bros*	5
29	8	THE LION SLEEPS TONIGHT Tight Fit	*Jive*	2
4	9	THE LAND OF MAKE BELIEVE Bucks Fizz	*RCA*	11
9	10	DROWNING IN BERLIN Mobiles	*Rialto*	5
27	11	I CAN'T GO FOR THAT (NO CAN DO) Daryl Hall and John Oates	*RCA*	3
36	12	LOVE PLUS ONE Haircut 100	*Arista*	3
12	13	EASIER SAID THAN DONE Shakatak	*Polydor*	5
8	14	GET DOWN ON IT Kool and the Gang	*De-Lite*	8
13	15	WAITING FOR A GIRL LIKE YOU Foreigner	*Atlantic*	9
10	16	BEING BOILED Human League	*Fast Product*	5
15	17	SENSES WORKING OVERTIME XTC	*Virgin*	3
20	18	SAY HELLO WAVE GOODBYE Soft Cell	*Some Bizzare*	2
11	19	I'LL FIND MY WAY HOME Jon and Vangelis	*Polydor*	9
23	[20]	I JUST WANNA (SPEND SOME TIME WITH YOU) Alton Edwards	*Streetwave*	5
18	21	DON'T WALK AWAY Four Tops	*Casablanca*	8
14	22	LET'S GET IT UP AC/DC	*Atlantic*	2
21	23	NEVER GIVE UP ON A GOOD THING George Benson	*Warner Bros*	4
16	24	MIRROR MIRROR Dollar	*WEA*	11
19	25	I WANNA BE A WINNER Brown Sauce	*BBC*	8
-	26	CENTREFOLD J Geils Band ●	*EMI America*	1
17	27	I COULD BE HAPPY Altered Images	*Epic*	9
22	28	DON'T YOU WANT ME Human League	*Virgin*	11
-	29	FOOL IF YOU THINK IT'S OVER Elkie Brooks	*A&M*	2
34	30	THEME FROM 'HILL STREET BLUES' Mike Post and Larry Carlton	*Elektra*	3
26	31	HERE IS THE NEWS/TICKET TO THE MOON Electric Light Orchestra	*Jet*	5
-	32	LANDSLIDE Olivia Newton-John	*EMI*	2
33	[33]	LISTEN Stiff Little Fingers	*Chrysalis*	4
24	34	YELLOW PEARL Phil Lynott	*Vertigo*	6
37	35	TROUBLE Lindsey Buckingham	*Mercury*	3
-	[36]	MIRROR MIRROR Diana Ross	*Capitol*	2
-	[37]	TURN UP THE NIGHT Black Sabbath	*Vertigo*	1
31	38	EUROPEAN SON Japan	*Ariola*	3
-	39	MICKEY Toni Basil ●	*Radialchoice*	1
-	40	SEE YOU Depeche Mode	*Mute*	1

LW	TW	WEEK ENDING 20 FEBRUARY 1982		Wks
1	[1]	TOWN CALLED MALICE/PRECIOUS Jam	*Polydor*	2
2	[2]	GOLDEN BROWN Stranglers	*Liberty*	6
18	[3]	SAY HELLO WAVE GOODBYE Soft Cell	*Some Bizzare*	3
6	[4]	MAID OF ORLEANS (THE WALTZ JOAN OF ARC) Orchestral Manoeuvres In The Dark	*Dindisc*	5
4	5	THE MODEL/COMPUTER LOVE Kraftwerk	*EMI*	7
8	6	THE LION SLEEPS TONIGHT Tight Fit	*Jive*	3
3	7	OH JULIE Shakin' Stevens	*Epic*	6
7	8	ARTHUR'S THEME (BEST THAT YOU CAN DO) Christopher Cross	*Warner Bros*	6
5	9	DEAD RINGER FOR LOVE Meat Loaf	*Epic*	12
17	[10]	SENSES WORKING OVERTIME XTC	*Virgin*	4
12	11	LOVE PLUS ONE Haircut 100	*Arista*	4
11	12	I CAN'T GO FOR THAT (NO CAN DO) Daryl Hall and John Oates	*RCA*	4
22	[13]	LET'S GET IT UP AC/DC	*Atlantic*	3
23	[14]	NEVER GIVE UP ON A GOOD THING George Benson	*Warner Bros*	5
13	15	EASIER SAID THAN DONE Shakatak	*Polydor*	6
10	16	DROWNING IN BERLIN Mobiles	*Rialto*	6
26	17	CENTREFOLD J Geils Band	*EMI America*	2
32	[18]	LANDSLIDE Olivia Newton-John	*EMI*	3
9	19	THE LAND OF MAKE BELIEVE Bucks Fizz	*RCA*	12
14	20	GET DOWN ON IT Kool and the Gang	*De-Lite*	9
29	21	FOOL IF YOU THINK IT'S OVER Elkie Brooks	*A&M*	3
20	22	I JUST WANNA (SPEND SOME TIME WITH YOU) Alton Edwards	*Streetwave*	6
16	23	BEING BOILED Human League	*Fast Product*	6
39	24	MICKEY Toni Basil	*Radialchoice*	2
19	25	I'LL FIND MY WAY HOME Jon and Vangelis	*Polydor*	10
-	26	CARDIAC ARREST Madness	*Stiff*	1
21	27	DON'T WALK AWAY Four Tops	*Casablanca*	9
-	28	LOVE MAKES THE WORLD GO ROUND Jets	*EMI*	1
-	[29]	I'VE HAD ENOUGH Earth Wind and Fire	*CBS*	1
-	[30]	YOU'RE THE ONE FOR ME D-Train ●	*Epic*	1
40	31	SEE YOU Depeche Mode	*Mute*	2
30	32	THEME FROM 'HILL STREET BLUES' Mike Post and Larry Carlton	*Elektra*	4
-	33	RUN TO THE HILLS Iron Maiden	*EMI*	1
25	34	I WANNA BE A WINNER Brown Sauce	*BBC*	9
-	35	SHOWROOM DUMMIES Kraftwerk	*EMI*	1
-	36	IT AIN'T WHAT YOU DO IT'S THE WAY THAT YOU DO IT Fun Boy Three and Bananarama ●	*Chrysalis*	1
27	37	I COULD BE HAPPY Altered Images	*Epic*	10
24	38	MIRROR MIRROR Dollar	*WEA*	12
15	39	WAITING FOR A GIRL LIKE YOU Foreigner	*Atlantic*	10
-	[40]	DO YOU BELIEVE IN THE WESTWORLD Theatre Of Hate	*Burning Rome*	2

LW	TW	WEEK ENDING 27 FEBRUARY 1982		Wks
1	[1]	TOWN CALLED MALICE/PRECIOUS Jam	*Polydor*	3
6	2	THE LION SLEEPS TONIGHT Tight Fit	*Jive*	4
17	[3]	CENTREFOLD J Geils Band	*EMI America*	3
11	4	LOVE PLUS ONE Haircut 100	*Arista*	5
3	5	SAY HELLO WAVE GOODBYE Soft Cell	*Some Bizzare*	4
2	6	GOLDEN BROWN Stranglers	*Liberty*	7
4	7	MAID OF ORLEANS (THE WALTZ JOAN OF ARC) Orchestral Manoeuvres In The Dark	*Dindisc*	6
11	[8]	I CAN'T GO FOR THAT (NO CAN DO) Daryl Hall and John Oates	*RCA*	5
36	9	IT AIN'T WHAT YOU DO IT'S THE WAY THAT YOU DO IT Fun Boy Three and Bananarama	*Chrysalis*	2
31	10	SEE YOU Depeche Mode	*Mute*	3
24	11	MICKEY Toni Basil	*Radialchoice*	3
8	12	ARTHUR'S THEME (BEST THAT YOU CAN DO) Christopher Cross	*Warner Bros*	7
5	13	THE MODEL/COMPUTER LOVE Kraftwerk	*EMI*	8
7	14	OH JULIE Shakin' Stevens	*Epic*	7
9	15	DEAD RINGER FOR LOVE Meat Loaf	*Epic*	13
10	16	SENSES WORKING OVERTIME XTC	*Virgin*	5
21	[17]	FOOL IF YOU THINK IT'S OVER Elkie Brooks	*A&M*	4
14	18	NEVER GIVE UP ON A GOOD THING George Benson	*Warner Bros*	6
33	19	RUN TO THE HILLS Iron Maiden	*EMI*	2
-	20	DEUTSCHER GIRLS Adam and the Ants	*EG*	1
13	21	LET'S GET IT UP AC/DC	*Atlantic*	4
-	22	CLASSIC Adrian Gurvitz ●	*RAK*	1
-	23	GO WILD IN THE COUNTRY Bow Wow Wow	*RCA*	1
16	24	DROWNING IN BERLIN Mobiles	*Rialto*	7
32	[25]	THEME FROM 'HILL STREET BLUES' Mike Post and Larry Carlton	*Elektra*	5
15	26	EASIER SAID THAN DONE Shakatak	*Polydor*	7
18	27	LANDSLIDE Olivia Newton-John	*EMI*	4
26	28	CARDIAC ARREST Madness	*Stiff*	2
-	29	STARS ON STEVIE Starsound	*CBS*	1
-	30	SOME GUYS HAVE ALL THE LUCK Robert Palmer	*Island*	1
19	31	THE LAND OF MAKE BELIEVE Bucks Fizz	*RCA*	13
20	32	GET DOWN ON IT Kool and the Gang	*De-Lite*	10
-	33	I WON'T CLOSE MY EYES UB40	*DEP International*	1
-	34	HEAD OVER HEELS Abba	*Epic*	1
35	35	SHOWROOM DUMMIES Kraftwerk	*EMI*	2

In these weeks ■ After moving only slightly from 20 to 18, Soft Cell's *Say Hello Wave Goodbye* suddenly leapt to number 3, before falling back to 5 one week later (29.02.82) ■ Elkie Brooks version of Chris Rea's *Fool If You Think It's Over* brought Rea's name back into the public eye. Since 1982 he has never had a year out of the top 75 (27.02.82)■

LW	TW	Title	Artist	Label	Wks
30	36	YOU'RE THE ONE FOR ME	D-Train	*Epic*	2
-	[37]	QUEEN OF THE RAPPING SCENE (NOTHING EVER GOES THE WAY YOU PLAN)	Modern Romance	*WEA*	1
23	38	BEING BOILED	Human League	*Fast Product*	7
-	39	TURN UP THE NIGHT	Black Sabbath	*Vertigo*	2
-	40	RESTLESS	Gillan	*Virgin*	3

March 1982

□ Highest position disc reached ● Act's first ever week on chart

WEEK ENDING 6 MARCH 1982

LW	TW	Title	Artist	Label	Wks
2	[1]	THE LION SLEEPS TONIGHT	Tight Fit	*Jive*	5
11	[2]	MICKEY	Toni Basil	*Radialchoice*	4
1	3	TOWN CALLED MALICE/PRECIOUS	Jam	*Polydor*	4
4	4	LOVE PLUS ONE	Haircut 100	*Arista*	6
3	5	CENTREFOLD	J Geils Band	*EMI America*	4
9	6	IT AIN'T WHAT YOU DO IT'S THE WAY THAT YOU DO IT	Fun Boy Three and Bananarama	*Chrysalis*	3
5	7	SAY HELLO WAVE GOODBYE	Soft Cell	*Some Bizzare*	5
10	8	SEE YOU	Depeche Mode	*Mute*	4
6	9	GOLDEN BROWN	Stranglers	*Liberty*	8
7	10	MAID OF ORLEANS (THE WALTZ JOAN OF ARC)	Orchestral Manoeuvres In The Dark	*Dindisc*	7
19	11	RUN TO THE HILLS	Iron Maiden	*EMI*	3
8	12	I CAN'T GO FOR THAT (NO CAN DO)	Daryl Hall and John Oates	*RCA*	6
20	[13]	DEUTSCHER GIRLS	Adam and the Ants	*EG*	2
28	[14]	CARDIAC ARREST	Madness	*Stiff*	3
-	15	POISON ARROW	ABC	*Neutron*	1
23	16	GO WILD IN THE COUNTRY	Bow Wow Wow	*RCA*	2
18	17	NEVER GIVE UP ON A GOOD THING	George Benson	*Warner Bros*	7
22	18	CLASSIC	Adrian Gurvitz	*RAK*	2
16	19	SENSES WORKING OVERTIME	XTC	*Virgin*	6
29	20	STARS ON STEVIE	Starsound	*CBS*	2
15	21	DEAD RINGER FOR LOVE	Meat Loaf	*Epic*	14
12	22	ARTHUR'S THEME (BEST THAT YOU CAN DO)	Christopher Cross	*Warner Bros*	8
30	23	SOME GUYS HAVE ALL THE LUCK	Robert Palmer	*Island*	2
17	24	FOOL IF YOU THINK IT'S OVER	Elkie Brooks	*A&M*	5
35	[25]	SHOWROOM DUMMIES	Kraftwerk	*EMI*	3
-	26	LOVE MAKES THE WORLD GO ROUND	Jets	*EMI*	2
13	27	THE MODEL/COMPUTER LOVE	Kraftwerk	*EMI*	9
25	28	THEME FROM 'HILL STREET BLUES'	Mike Post and Larry Carlton	*Elektra*	6
14	29	OH JULIE	Shakin' Stevens	*Epic*	8
34	30	HEAD OVER HEELS	Abba	*Epic*	2
36	31	YOU'RE THE ONE FOR ME	D-Train	*Epic*	3
33	[32]	I WON'T CLOSE MY EYES	UB40	*DEP International*	2
27	33	LANDSLIDE	Olivia Newton-John	*EMI*	5
21	34	LET'S GET IT UP	AC/DC	*Atlantic*	5
-	35	MUSIC FOR CHAMELEONS	Gary Numan	*Beggars Banquet*	1
24	36	DROWNING IN BERLIN	Mobiles	*Rialto*	8
26	37	EASIER SAID THAN DONE	Shakatak	*Polydor*	8
-	38	PARTY FEARS TWO	Associates ●	*Associates*	1
-	39	SEVEN TEARS	Goombay Dance Band ●	*Epic*	1
-	40	JUST AN ILLUSION	Imagination	*R&B*	1

WEEK ENDING 13 MARCH 1982

LW	TW	Title	Artist	Label	Wks
1	[1]	THE LION SLEEPS TONIGHT	Tight Fit	*Jive*	6
2	[2]	MICKEY	Toni Basil	*Radialchoice*	5
4	[3]	LOVE PLUS ONE	Haircut 100	*Arista*	7
6	[4]	IT AIN'T WHAT YOU DO IT'S THE WAY THAT YOU DO IT	Fun Boy Three and Bananarama	*Chrysalis*	4
5	5	CENTREFOLD	J Geils Band	*EMI America*	5
8	[6]	SEE YOU	Depeche Mode	*Mute*	5
11	[7]	RUN TO THE HILLS	Iron Maiden	*EMI*	4
39	8	SEVEN TEARS	Goombay Dance Band	*Epic*	2
16	9	GO WILD IN THE COUNTRY	Bow Wow Wow	*RCA*	3
15	10	POISON ARROW	ABC	*Neutron*	2
3	11	TOWN CALLED MALICE/PRECIOUS	Jam	*Polydor*	5
18	12	CLASSIC	Adrian Gurvitz	*RAK*	3
13	[13]	DEUTSCHER GIRLS	Adam and the Ants	*EG*	3
20	[14]	STARS ON STEVIE	Starsound	*CBS*	3
14	15	CARDIAC ARREST	Madness	*Stiff*	4
23	[16]	SOME GUYS HAVE ALL THE LUCK	Robert Palmer	*Island*	3
7	17	SAY HELLO WAVE GOODBYE	Soft Cell	*Some Bizzare*	6
40	18	JUST AN ILLUSION	Imagination	*R&B*	2
10	19	MAID OF ORLEANS (THE WALTZ JOAN OF ARC)	Orchestral Manoeuvres In The Dark	*Dindisc*	8
12	20	I CAN'T GO FOR THAT (NO CAN DO)	Daryl Hall and John Oates	*RCA*	7
26	[21]	LOVE MAKES THE WORLD GO ROUND	Jets	*EMI*	3
35	22	MUSIC FOR CHAMELEONS	Gary Numan	*Beggars Banquet*	2
9	23	GOLDEN BROWN	Stranglers	*Liberty*	9
-	24	QUIEREME MUCHO (YOURS)	Julio Iglesias	*CBS*	1
38	25	PARTY FEARS TWO	Associates	*Associates*	2
30	26	HEAD OVER HEELS	Abba	*Epic*	3
28	27	THEME FROM 'HILL STREET BLUES'	Mike Post and Larry Carlton	*Elektra*	7
24	28	FOOL IF YOU THINK IT'S OVER	Elkie Brooks	*A&M*	6
-	[29]	BAAL'S HYMN (EP)	David Bowie	*RCA*	1
-	30	LAYLA	Derek and the Dominoes	*RSO*	1
17	31	NEVER GIVE UP ON A GOOD THING	George Benson	*Warner Bros*	8
-	32	TAKE MY HEART (YOU CAN HAVE IT IF YOU WANT IT)	Kool and the Gang	*De-Lite*	1
-	33	DAMNED DON'T CRY	Visage	*Polydor*	1
25	34	SHOWROOM DUMMIES	Kraftwerk	*EMI*	4
31	35	YOU'RE THE ONE FOR ME	D-Train	*Epic*	4
-	36	YOUR HONOUR	Pluto	*KR*	1
-	37	A BUNCH OF THYME	Foster and Allen ●	*Ritz*	1
-	38	DON'T LOVE ME TOO HARD	Nolans	*Epic*	1
29	39	OH JULIE	Shakin' Stevens	*Epic*	9
32	40	I WON'T CLOSE MY EYES	UB40	*DEP International*	3

WEEK ENDING 20 MARCH 1982

LW	TW	Title	Artist	Label	Wks
1	[1]	THE LION SLEEPS TONIGHT	Tight Fit	*Jive*	7
8	2	SEVEN TEARS	Goombay Dance Band	*Epic*	3
2	3	MICKEY	Toni Basil	*Radialchoice*	6
3	4	LOVE PLUS ONE	Haircut 100	*Arista*	8
4	5	IT AIN'T WHAT YOU DO IT'S THE WAY THAT YOU DO IT	Fun Boy Three and Bananarama	*Chrysalis*	5
10	[6]	POISON ARROW	ABC	*Neutron*	3
9	[7]	GO WILD IN THE COUNTRY	Bow Wow Wow	*RCA*	4
18	8	JUST AN ILLUSION	Imagination	*R&B*	3
5	9	CENTREFOLD	J Geils Band	*EMI America*	6
12	10	CLASSIC	Adrian Gurvitz	*RAK*	4
6	11	SEE YOU	Depeche Mode	*Mute*	6
24	12	QUIEREME MUCHO (YOURS)	Julio Iglesias	*CBS*	2
7	13	RUN TO THE HILLS	Iron Maiden	*EMI*	5
15	[14]	CARDIAC ARREST	Madness	*Stiff*	5
25	15	PARTY FEARS TWO	Associates	*Associates*	3
30	16	LAYLA	Derek and the Dominoes	*RSO*	2
14	17	STARS ON STLVIE	Starsound	*CBS*	4
16	18	SOME GUYS HAVE ALL THE LUCK	Robert Palmer	*Island*	4
13	19	DEUTSCHER GIRLS	Adam and the Ants	EG	4
11	20	TOWN CALLED MALICE/PRECIOUS	Jam	*Polydor*	6
22	21	MUSIC FOR CHAMELEONS	Gary Numan	*Beggars Banquet*	3
21	22	LOVE MAKES THE WORLD GO ROUND	Jets	*EMI*	4
33	23	DAMNED DON'T CRY	Visage	*Polydor*	2
17	24	SAY HELLO WAVE GOODBYE	Soft Cell	*Some Bizzare*	7
26	[25]	HEAD OVER HEELS	Abba	*Epic*	4
36	26	YOUR HONOUR	Pluto	*KR*	2
19	27	MAID OF ORLEANS (THE WALTZ JOAN OF ARC)	Orchestral Manoeuvres In The Dark	*Dindisc*	9
20	28	I CAN'T GO FOR THAT (NO CAN DO)	Daryl Hall and John Oates	*RCA*	8
38	29	DON'T LOVE ME TOO HARD	Nolans	*Epic*	2
32	30	TAKE MY HEART (YOU CAN HAVE IT IF YOU WANT IT)	Kool and the Gang	*De-Lite*	2
-	31	AIN'T NO PLEASING YOU	Chas and Dave	*Rockney*	1

■Medley champs Tight Fit score their only chart-topper with a non-Medley record of *The Lion Sleeps Tonight.* It has nine credited writers, the most for any number one hit (06.03.82) ■ The top four records were all at their peak positions by acts having their biggest ever chart hits (13.03.82)■

March 1982

□ Highest position disc reached ● Act's first ever week on chart

LW	TW	Title	Artist	Label	Wks
37	32	A BUNCH OF THYME	Foster and Allen	Ritz	2
29	33	BAAL'S HYMN (EP)	David Bowie	RCA	2
27	34	THEME FROM 'HILL STREET BLUES'	Mike Post and Larry Carlton	Elektra	8
-	35	HAVE YOU EVER BEEN IN LOVE	Leo Sayer	Chrysalis	1
-	36	IS IT A DREAM	Classix Nouveaux ●	Liberty	1
-	37	ARE YOU LONESOME TONIGHT	Elvis Presley	RCA	1
35	38	YOU'RE THE ONE FOR ME	D-Train	Epic	5
23	39	GOLDEN BROWN	Stranglers	Liberty	10
28	40	FOOL IF YOU THINK IT'S OVER	Elkie Brooks	A&M	7

WEEK ENDING 27 MARCH

LW	TW	Title	Artist	Label	Wks
2	1	SEVEN TEARS	Goombay Dance Band	Epic	4
1	2	THE LION SLEEPS TONIGHT	Tight Fit	Jive	8
12	3	QUIEREME MUCHO (YOURS)	Julio Iglesias	CBS	3
8	4	JUST AN ILLUSION	Imagination	R&B	4
3	5	MICKEY	Toni Basil	Radialchoice	7
6	6	POISON ARROW	ABC	Neutron	4
16	7	LAYLA	Derek and the Dominoes	RSO	3
10	8	CLASSIC	Adrian Gurvitz	RAK	5
15	9	PARTY FEARS TWO	Associates	Associates	4
4	10	LOVE PLUS ONE	Haircut 100	Arista	9
7	11	GO WILD IN THE COUNTRY	Bow Wow Wow	RCA	5
5	12	IT AIN'T WHAT YOU DO IT'S THE WAY THAT YOU DO IT	Fun Boy Three and Bananarama	Chrysalis	6
11	13	SEE YOU	Depeche Mode	Mute	7
31	14	AIN'T NO PLEASING YOU	Chas and Dave	Rockney	2
13	15	RUN TO THE HILLS	Iron Maiden	EMI	6
-	16	GHOSTS	Japan	Virgin	1
9	17	CENTREFOLD	J Geils Band	EMI America	7
23	18	DAMNED DON'T CRY	Visage	Polydor	3
21	19	MUSIC FOR CHAMELEONS	Gary Numan	Beggars Banquet	4
14	20	CARDIAC ARREST	Madness	Stiff	6
35	21	HAVE YOU EVER BEEN IN LOVE	Leo Sayer	Chrysalis	2
26	22	YOUR HONOUR	Pluto	KR	3
36	23	IS IT A DREAM	Classix Nouveaux	Liberty	2
17	24	STARS ON STEVIE	Starsound	CBS	5
18	25	SOME GUYS HAVE ALL THE LUCK	Robert Palmer	Island	5
29	26	DON'T LOVE ME TOO HARD	Nolans	Epic	3
37	27	ARE YOU LONESOME TONIGHT	Elvis Presley	RCA	2
32	28	A BUNCH OF THYME	Foster and Allen	Ritz	3
30	29	TAKE MY HEART (YOU CAN HAVE IT IF YOU WANT IT)	Kool and the Gang	De-Lite	3
19	30	DEUTSCHE GIRLS	Adam and the Ants	EG	5
33	31	BAAL'S HYMN (EP)	David Bowie	RCA	3
25	32	HEAD OVER HEELS	Abba	Epic	5
-	33	MY CAMERA NEVER LIES	Bucks Fizz	RCA	1
22	34	LOVE MAKES THE WORLD GO ROUND	Jets	EMI	5
-	35	GIVE ME BACK MY HEART	Dollar	WEA	1
-	36	DEAR JOHN	Status Quo	Vertigo	1
-	37	A NEW FASHION	Bill Wyman	A&M	1
-	38	MEMORY	Barbra Streisand	CBS	1
20	39	TOWN CALLED MALICE/PRECIOUS	Jam	Polydor	7
24	40	SAY HELLO WAVE GOODBYE	Soft Cell	Some Bizzare	8

WEEK ENDING 3 APRIL 1982

LW	TW	Title	Artist	Label	Wks
1	1	SEVEN TEARS	Goombay Dance Band	Epic	5
4	2	JUST AN ILLUSION	Imagination	R&B	5
3	3	QUIEREME MUCHO (YOURS)	Julio Iglesias	CBS	4
7	4	LAYLA	Derek and the Dominoes	RSO	4
33	5	MY CAMERA NEVER LIES	Bucks Fizz	RCA	2
2	6	THE LION SLEEPS TONIGHT	Tight Fit	Jive	9
14	7	AIN'T NO PLEASING YOU	Chas and Dave	Rockney	3
6	8	POISON ARROW	ABC	Neutron	5
16	9	GHOSTS	Japan	Virgin	2
9	10	PARTY FEARS TWO	Associates	Associates	5
18	11	DAMNED DON'T CRY	Visage	Polydor	4
8	12	CLASSIC	Adrian Gurvitz	RAK	6
5	13	MICKEY	Toni Basil	Radialchoice	8
21	14	HAVE YOU EVER BEEN IN LOVE	Leo Sayer	Chrysalis	3
35	15	GIVE ME BACK MY HEART	Dollar	WEA	2
23	16	IS IT A DREAM	Classix Nouveaux	Liberty	3
-	17	SEE THOSE EYES	Altered Images	Epic	1
-	18	MORE THAN THIS	Roxy Music	EG	1
22	19	YOUR HONOUR	Pluto	KR	4
11	20	GO WILD IN THE COUNTRY	Bow Wow Wow	RCA	6
14	21	DON'T LOVE ME TOO HARD	Nolans	Epic	4
12	22	IT AIN'T WHAT YOU DO IT'S THE WAY THAT YOU DO IT	Fun Boy Three and Bananarama	Chrysalis	7
10	23	LOVE PLUS ONE	Haircut 100	Arista	10
28	24	A BUNCH OF THYME	Foster and Allen	Ritz	4
36	25	DEAR JOHN	Status Quo	Vertigo	2
19	26	MUSIC FOR CHAMELEONS	Gary Numan	Beggars Banquet	5
13	27	SEE YOU	Depeche Mode	Mute	8
27	28	ARE YOU LONESOME TONIGHT	Elvis Presley	RCA	3
20	29	CARDIAC ARREST	Madness	Stiff	7
-	30	HOUSE ON FIRE	Boomtown Rats	Mercury	1
-	31	BLUE EYES	Elton John	Rocket	1
15	32	RUN TO THE HILLS	Iron Maiden	EMI	7
-	33	IRON FIST	Motorhead	Bronze	1
38	34	MEMORY	Barbra Streisand	CBS	2
-	35	I CAN MAKE YOU FEEL GOOD	Shalamar	Solar	1
24	36	STARS ON STEVIE	Starsound	CBS	6
-	37	NIGHT BIRDS	Shakatak	Polydor	1
29	38	TAKE MY HEART (YOU CAN HAVE IT IF YOU WANT IT)	Kool and the Gang	De-Lite	4
25	39	SOME GUYS HAVE ALL THE LUCK	Robert Palmer	Island	6
17	40	CENTREFOLD	J Geils Band	EMI America	8

WEEK ENDING 10 APRIL 1982

LW	TW	Title	Artist	Label	Wks
1	1	SEVEN TEARS	Goombay Dance Band	Epic	6
5	2	MY CAMERA NEVER LIES	Bucks Fizz	RCA	3
2	3	JUST AN ILLUSION	Imagination	R&B	6
7	4	AIN'T NO PLEASING YOU	Chas and Dave	Rockney	4
9	5	GHOSTS	Japan	Virgin	3
18	6	MORE THAN THIS	Roxy Music	EG	2
15	7	GIVE ME BACK MY HEART	Dollar	WEA	3
4	8	LAYLA	Derek and the Dominoes	RSO	5
3	9	QUIEREME MUCHO (YOURS)	Julio Iglesias	CBS	5
14	10	HAVE YOU EVER BEEN IN LOVE	Leo Sayer	Chrysalis	4
16	11	IS IT A DREAM	Classix Nouveaux	Liberty	4
11	12	DAMNED DON'T CRY	Visage	Polydor	5
25	13	DEAR JOHN	Status Quo	Vertigo	3
21	14	DON'T LOVE ME TOO HARD	Nolans	Epic	5
8	15	POISON ARROW	ABC	Neutron	6
37	16	NIGHT BIRDS	Shakatak	Polydor	2
17	17	SEE THOSE EYES	Altered Images	Epic	2
24	18	A BUNCH OF THYME	Foster and Allen	Ritz	5
-	19	EBONY AND IVORY	Paul McCartney with Stevie Wonder ●	Parlophone	1
6	20	THE LION SLEEPS TONIGHT	Tight Fit	Jive	10
12	21	CLASSIC	Adrian Gurvitz	RAK	7
10	22	PARTY FEARS TWO	Associates	Associates	6
31	23	BLUE EYES	Elton John	Rocket	2
30	24	HOUSE ON FIRE	Boomtown Rats	Mercury	2
28	25	ARE YOU LONESOME TONIGHT	Elvis Presley	RCA	4
13	26	MICKEY	Toni Basil	Radialchoice	9
35	27	I CAN MAKE YOU FEEL GOOD	Shalamar	Solar	2
19	28	YOUR HONOUR	Pluto	KR	5
33	29	IRON FIST	Motorhead	Bronze	2
-	30	PAPA'S GOT A BRAND NEW PIGBAG	Pigbag ●	Y Records	1
26	31	MUSIC FOR CHAMELEONS	Gary Numan	Beggars Banquet	6
-	32	FANTASTIC DAY	Haircut 100	Arista	1
20	33	GO WILD IN THE COUNTRY	Bow Wow Wow	RCA	7
-	34	STONE COLD	Rainbow	Polydor	1
-	35	THIS TIME (WE'LL GET IT RIGHT)	England World Cup Squad	England	1
34	36	MEMORY	Barbra Streisand	CBS	3

In these weeks ■ Almost ten years after its original release, *Layla* by Derek & the Dominoes surpasses its peak position in 1972 and climbs three places higher to number 4 (03.04.82) ■ The 1982 hit version of *Are You Lonesome Tonight* is a live Las Vegas recording in which Elvis Presley forgets the words of the spoken section (10.04.82)■

LW	TW	Title	Artist	Label	Wks
-	37	REALLY SAYING SOMETHING	Bananarama with Funboy Three ●	*Deram*	1
32	38	RUN TO THE HILLS	Iron Maiden	*EMI*	8
-	39	EVER SO LONELY	Monsoon ●	*Mobile Suit*	1
23	40	LOVE PLUS ONE	Haircut 100	*Arista*	11

WEEK ENDING 17 APRIL 1982

LW	TW	Title	Artist	Label	Wks
2	1	MY CAMERA NEVER LIES	Bucks Fizz	*RCA*	4
4	2	AIN'T NO PLEASING YOU	Chas and Dave	*Rockney*	5
19	3	EBONY AND IVORY	Paul McCartney with Stevie Wonder	*Parlophone*	2
1	4	SEVEN TEARS	Goombay Dance Band	*Epic*	7
7	5	GIVE ME BACK MY HEART	Dollar	*WEA*	4
6	6	MORE THAN THIS	Roxy Music	*EG*	3
5	7	GHOSTS	Japan	*Virgin*	4
3	8	JUST AN ILLUSION	Imagination	*R&B*	7
30	9	PAPA'S GOT A BRAND NEW PIGBAG	Pigbag	*Y Records*	2
13	10	DEAR JOHN	Status Quo	*Vertigo*	4
17	11	SEE THOSE EYES	Altered Images	*Epic*	3
11	12	IS IT A DREAM	Classix Nouveaux	*Liberty*	5
10	13	HAVE YOU EVER BEEN IN LOVE	Leo Sayer	*Chrysalis*	5
14	14	DON'T LOVE ME TOO HARD	Nolans	*Epic*	6
16	15	NIGHT BIRDS	Shakatak	*Polydor*	3
-	16	ONE STEP FURTHER	Bardo ●	*Epic*	1
23	17	BLUE EYES	Elton John	*Rocket*	3
8	18	LAYLA	Derek and the Dominoes	*RSO*	6
32	19	FANTASTIC DAY	Haircut 100	*Arista*	2
27	20	I CAN MAKE YOU FEEL GOOD	Shalamar	*Solar*	3
18	21	A BUNCH OF THYME	Foster and Allen	*Ritz*	6
12	22	DAMNED DON'T CRY	Visage	*Polydor*	6
9	23	QUIEREME MUCHO (YOURS)	Julio Iglesias	*CBS*	6
37	24	REALLY SAYING SOMETHING	Bananarama & Funboy Three	*Deram*	2
35	25	THIS TIME (WE'LL GET IT RIGHT)	England World Cup Squad	*England*	2
24	26	HOUSE ON FIRE	Boomtown Rats	*Mercury*	3
15	27	POISON ARROW	ABC	*Neutron*	7
39	28	EVER SO LONELY	Monsoon	*Mobile Suit*	2
25	29	ARE YOU LONESOME TONIGHT	Elvis Presley	*RCA*	5
29	30	IRON FIST	Motorhead	*Bronze*	3
20	31	THE LION SLEEPS TONIGHT	Tight Fit	*Jive*	11
-	32	CAT PEOPLE (PUTTING OUT FIRE)	David Bowie	*MCA*	1
22	33	PARTY FEARS TWO	Associates	*Associates*	7
-	34	FREEZE-FRAME	J Geils Band	*EMI America*	1
26	35	MICKEY	Toni Basil	*Radialchoice*	10
28	36	YOUR HONOUR	Pluto	*KR*	6
34	37	STONE COLD	Rainbow	*Polydor*	2
33	38	GO WILD IN THE COUNTRY	Bow Wow Wow	*RCA*	8
36	39	MEMORY	Barbra Streisand	*CBS*	4
-	40	PROMISED YOU A MIRACLE	Simple Minds ●	*Virgin*	1

WEEK ENDING 24 APRIL 1982

LW	TW	Title	Artist	Label	Wks
2	1	EBONY AND IVORY	Paul McCartney with Stevie Wonder	*Parlophone*	3
1	2	MY CAMERA NEVER LIES	Bucks Fizz	*RCA*	5
9	3	PAPA'S GOT A BRAND NEW PIGBAG	Pigbag	*Y Records*	3
5	4	GIVE ME BACK MY HEART	Dollar	*WEA*	5
2	5	AIN'T NO PLEASING YOU	Chas and Dave	*Rockney*	6
16	6	ONE STEP FURTHER	Bardo	*Epic*	2
6	7	MORE THAN THIS	Roxy Music	*EG*	4
17	8	BLUE EYES	Elton John	*Rocket*	4
15	9	NIGHT BIRDS	Shakatak	*Polydor*	4
20	10	I CAN MAKE YOU FEEL GOOD	Shalamar	*Solar*	4
25	11	THIS TIME (WE'LL GET IT RIGHT)	England World Cup Squad	*England*	3
19	12	FANTASTIC DAY	Haircut 100	*Arista*	3
4	13	SEVEN TEARS	Goombay Dance Band	*Epic*	8
7	14	GHOSTS	Japan	*Virgin*	5
8	15	JUST AN ILLUSION	Imagination	*R&B*	8
10	16	DEAR JOHN	Status Quo	*Vertigo*	5

May 1982

□ Highest position disc reached ● Act's first ever week on chart

LW	TW	Title	Artist	Label	Wks
24	17	REALLY SAYING SOMETHING	Bananarama & Funboy Three	*Deram*	3
28	18	EVER SO LONELY	Monsoon	*Mobile Suit*	3
11	19	SEE THOSE EYES	Altered Images	*Epic*	4
14	20	DON'T LOVE ME TOO HARD	Nolans	*Epic*	7
12	21	IS IT A DREAM	Classix Nouveaux	*Liberty*	6
-	22	SHIRLEY	Shakin' Stevens	*Epic*	1
13	23	HAVE YOU EVER BEEN IN LOVE	Leo Sayer	*Chrysalis*	6
18	24	LAYLA	Derek and the Dominoes	*RSO*	7
22	25	DAMNED DON'T CRY	Visage	*Polydor*	7
32	26	CAT PEOPLE (PUTTING OUT FIRE)	David Bowie	*MCA*	2
34	27	FREEZE-FRAME	J Geils Band	*EMI America*	2
40	28	PROMISED YOU A MIRACLE	Simple Minds	*Virgin*	2
26	29	HOUSE ON FIRE	Boomtown Rats	*Mercury*	4
-	30	VIEW FROM A BRIDGE	Kim Wilde	*RAK*	1
-	31	INSTINCTION	Spandau Ballet	*Chrysalis*	1
21	32	A BUNCH OF THYME	Foster and Allen	*Ritz*	7
23	33	QUIEREME MUCHO (YOURS)	Julio Iglesias	*CBS*	7
-	34	I WON'T LET YOU DOWN	PhD ●	*WEA*	1
-	35	GIRL CRAZY	Hot Chocolate	*RAK*	1
-	36	PRIVATE EYES	Daryl Hall and John Oates	*RCA*	1
29	37	ARE YOU LONESOME TONIGHT	Elvis Presley	*RCA*	6
30	38	IRON FIST	Motorhead	*Bronze*	4
-	39	I LOVE ROCK 'N' ROLL	Joan Jett and the Blackhearts ●	*Epic*	1
27	40	POISON ARROW	ABC	*Neutron*	8

WEEK ENDING 1 MAY 1982

LW	TW	Title	Artist	Label	Wks
1	1	EBONY AND IVORY	Paul McCartney with Stevie Wonder	*Parlophone*	4
6	2	ONE STEP FURTHER	Bardo	*Epic*	3
3	3	PAPA'S GOT A BRAND NEW PIGBAG	Pigbag	*Y Records*	4
11	4	THIS TIME (WE'LL GET IT RIGHT)	England World Cup Squad	*England*	4
17	5	REALLY SAYING SOMETHING	Bananarama & Funboy Three	*Deram*	4
22	6	SHIRLEY	Shakin' Stevens	*Epic*	2
10	7	I CAN MAKE YOU FEEL GOOD	Shalamar	*Solar*	5
4	8	GIVE ME BACK MY HEART	Dollar	*WEA*	6
12	9	FANTASTIC DAY	Haircut 100	*Arista*	4
8	10	BLUE EYES	Elton John	*Rocket*	5
2	11	MY CAMERA NEVER LIES	Bucks Fizz	*RCA*	6
5	12	AIN'T NO PLEASING YOU	Chas and Dave	*Rockney*	7
34	13	I WON'T LET YOU DOWN	PhD	*WEA*	2
7	14	MORE THAN THIS	Roxy Music	*EG*	5
9	15	NIGHT BIRDS	Shakatak	*Polydor*	5
18	16	EVER SO LONELY	Monsoon	*Mobile Suit*	4
39	17	I LOVE ROCK 'N' ROLL	Joan Jett and the Blackhearts	*Epic*	2
30	18	VIEW FROM A BRIDGE	Kim Wilde	*RAK*	2
28	19	PROMISED YOU A MIRACLE	Simple Minds	*Virgin*	3
16	20	DEAR JOHN	Status Quo	*Vertigo*	6
15	21	JUST AN ILLUSION	Imagination	*R&B*	9
31	22	INSTINCTION	Spandau Ballet	*Chrysalis*	2
13	23	SEVEN TEARS	Goombay Dance Band	*Epic*	9
-	24	WE HAVE A DREAM	Scotland World Cup Squad	*WEA*	1
14	25	GHOSTS	Japan	*Virgin*	6
35	26	GIRL CRAZY	Hot Chocolate	*RAK*	2
19	27	SEE THOSE EYES	Altered Images	*Epic*	5
26	28	CAT PEOPLE (PUTTING OUT FIRE)	David Bowie	*MCA*	3
27	29	FREEZE-FRAME	J Geils Band	*EMI America*	3
20	30	DON'T LOVE ME TOO HARD	Nolans	*Epic*	8
-	31	ONLY YOU	Yazoo ●	*Mute*	1
36	32	PRIVATE EYES	Daryl Hall and John Oates	*RCA*	2
-	33	BODY LANGUAGE	Queen	*EMI*	1
-	34	SHOUT SHOUT (KNOCK YOURSELF OUT)	Rocky Sharpe and the Replays	*Chiswick*	1
-	35	STAY	Barry Manilow	*Arista*	1

■Stevie Wonder finally has a number one, in duet with Paul McCartney, who has by now had number ones as part of a quintet (Beatles and Billy Preston), a quartet (Beatles), a trio (Wings) and a duo. Both men will have solo number ones before the decade is much older (24.04.82) ■ Britian's Eurovision entry fails to go that one step further to top the charts (01.05.82)■

May 1982

□ Highest position disc reached ● Act's first ever week on chart

LW	TW	Title / Artist	Label	Wks
-	[36]	THE SONG THAT I SING (THEME FROM 'WE'LL MEET AGAIN') Stutz Bearcats and the Denis King Orchestra ●	Multi Media Tapes	1
-	37	FORGET ME NOTS Patrice Rushen ●	Elektra	1
-	[38]	I SPECIALISE IN LOVE Sharon Brown ●	Virgin	1
32	39	A BUNCH OF THYME Foster and Allen	Ritz	8
21	40	IS IT A DREAM Classix Nouveaux	Liberty	7

WEEK ENDING 8 MAY 1982

LW	TW	Title / Artist	Label	Wks
1	[1]	EBONY AND IVORY Paul McCartney with Stevie Wonder	Parlophone	5
4	[2]	THIS TIME (WE'LL GET IT RIGHT) England World Cup Squad	England	5
13	[3]	I WON'T LET YOU DOWN PhD	WEA	3
17	[4]	I LOVE ROCK 'N' ROLL Joan Jett and the Blackhearts	Epic	3
5	[5]	REALLY SAYING SOMETHING Bananarama & Funboy Three	Deram	5
2	6	ONE STEP FURTHER Bardo	Epic	4
3	7	PAPA'S GOT A BRAND NEW PIGBAG Pigbag	Y Records	5
-	8	A LITTLE PEACE Nicole ●	CBS	1
7	9	I CAN MAKE YOU FEEL GOOD Shalamar	Solar	6
9	10	FANTASTIC DAY Haircut 100	Arista	5
6	11	SHIRLEY Shakin' Stevens	Epic	3
16	[12]	EVER SO LONELY Monsoon	Mobile Suit	5
24	13	WE HAVE A DREAM Scotland World Cup Squad	WEA	2
31	14	ONLY YOU Yazoo	Mute	2
19	15	PROMISED YOU A MIRACLE Simple Minds	Virgin	4
18	[16]	VIEW FROM A BRIDGE Kim Wilde	RAK	3
22	17	INSTINCTION Spandau Ballet	Chrysalis	3
26	18	GIRL CRAZY Hot Chocolate	RAK	3
10	19	BLUE EYES Elton John	Rocket	6
8	20	GIVE ME BACK MY HEART Dollar	WEA	7
34	21	SHOUT SHOUT (KNOCK YOURSELF OUT) Rocky Sharpe and the Replays	Chiswick	2
12	22	AIN'T NO PLEASING YOU Chas and Dave	Rockney	8
35	[23]	STAY Barry Manilow	Arista	2
15	24	NIGHT BIRDS Shakatak	Polydor	6
33	[25]	BODY LANGUAGE Queen	EMI	2
11	26	MY CAMERA NEVER LIES Bucks Fizz	RCA	7
37	27	FORGET ME NOTS Patrice Rushen	Elektra	2
14	28	MORE THAN THIS Roxy Music	EG	6
28	29	CAT PEOPLE (PUTTING OUT FIRE) David Bowie	MCA	4
-	30	TOTTENHAM TOTTENHAM Tottenham Hotspur FA Cup Final Squad	Rockney	1
-	31	MAMA USED TO SAY Junior ●	Mercury	1
-	32	FANTASY ISLAND Tight Fit	Jive	1
29	33	FREEZE-FRAME J Geils Band	EMI America	4
-	34	THE MEANING OF LOVE Depeche Mode	Mute	1
-	35	CLUB COUNTRY Associates	Associates	1
36	[36]	THE SONG THAT I SING (THEME FROM 'WE'LL MEET AGAIN') Stutz Bearcats and the Denis King Orchestra	Multi Media Tapes	2
32	37	PRIVATE EYES Daryl Hall and John Oates	RCA	3
20	38	DEAR JOHN Status Quo	Vertigo	7
-	39	ISLAND OF LOST SOULS Blondie	Chrysalis	1
38	40	I SPECIALISE IN LOVE Sharon Brown	Virgin	2

WEEK ENDING 15 MAY 1982

LW	TW	Title / Artist	Label	Wks
8	[1]	A LITTLE PEACE Nicole	CBS	2
1	2	EBONY AND IVORY Paul McCartney with Stevie Wonder	Parlophone	6
3	[3]	I WON'T LET YOU DOWN PhD	WEA	4
4	[4]	I LOVE ROCK 'N' ROLL Joan Jett and the Blackhearts	Epic	4
13	[5]	WE HAVE A DREAM Scotland World Cup Squad	WEA	3
5	6	REALLY SAYING SOMETHING Bananarama & Funboy Three	Deram	6
14	7	ONLY YOU Yazoo	Mute	3
2	8	THIS TIME (WE'LL GET IT RIGHT) England World Cup Squad	England	6
18	9	GIRL CRAZY Hot Chocolate	RAK	4
17	[10]	INSTINCTION Spandau Ballet	Chrysalis	4
27	11	FORGET ME NOTS Patrice Rushen	Elektra	3
34	[12]	THE MEANING OF LOVE Depeche Mode	Mute	2
15	[13]	PROMISED YOU A MIRACLE Simple Minds	Virgin	5
10	14	FANTASTIC DAY Haircut 100	Arista	6
32	15	FANTASY ISLAND Tight Fit	Jive	2
9	16	I CAN MAKE YOU FEEL GOOD Shalamar	Solar	7
7	17	PAPA'S GOT A BRAND NEW PIGBAG Pigbag	Y Records	6
31	18	MAMA USED TO SAY Junior	Mercury	2
30	[19]	TOTTENHAM TOTTENHAM Tottenham Hotspur FA Cup Final Squad	Rockney	2
12	20	EVER SO LONELY Monsoon	Mobile Suit	6
6	21	ONE STEP FURTHER Bardo	Epic	5
18	22	SHOUT SHOUT (KNOCK YOURSELF OUT) Rocky Sharpe and the Replays	Chiswick	3
11	23	SHIRLEY Shakin' Stevens	Epic	4
39	24	ISLAND OF LOST SOULS Blondie	Chrysalis	2
16	25	VIEW FROM A BRIDGE Kim Wilde	RAK	4
-	26	THE LOOK OF LOVE ABC	Neutron	1
23	27	STAY Barry Manilow	Arista	3
19	28	BLUE EYES Elton John	Rocket	7
20	29	GIVE ME BACK MY HEART Dollar	WEA	8
35	30	CLUB COUNTRY Associates	Associates	2
25	31	BODY LANGUAGE Queen	EMI	3
24	32	NIGHT BIRDS Shakatak	Polydor	7
-	33	THE NUMBER OF THE BEAST Iron Maiden	EMI	1
33	34	FREEZE-FRAME J Geils Band	EMI America	5
-	35	HUNGRY LIKE THE WOLF Duran Duran	EMI	1
22	36	AIN'T NO PLEASING YOU Chas and Dave	Rockney	9
29	37	CAT PEOPLE (PUTTING OUT FIRE) David Bowie	MCA	5
-	38	SUSPICIOUS MINDS Candi Staton	Sugarhill	1
40	39	I SPECIALISE IN LOVE Sharon Brown	Virgin	3
-	40	THE TELEPHONE ALWAYS RINGS Fun Boy Three	Chrysalis	1

WEEK ENDING 22 MAY 1982

LW	TW	Title / Artist	Label	Wks
1	[1]	A LITTLE PEACE Nicole	CBS	3
7	[2]	ONLY YOU Yazoo	Mute	4
3	[3]	I WON'T LET YOU DOWN PhD	WEA	5
4	[4]	I LOVE ROCK 'N' ROLL Joan Jett and the Blackhearts	Epic	5
-	5	GOODY TWO SHOES Adam Ant	CBS	1
5	6	WE HAVE A DREAM Scotland World Cup Squad	WEA	4
9	[7]	GIRL CRAZY Hot Chocolate	RAK	5
-	8	HOUSE OF FUN Madness	Stiff	1
2	9	EBONY AND IVORY Paul McCartney with Stevie Wonder	Parlophone	7
11	10	FORGET ME NOTS Patrice Rushen	Elektra	4
15	11	FANTASY ISLAND Tight Fit	Jive	3
6	12	REALLY SAYING SOMETHING Bananarama & Funboy Three	Deram	7
26	13	THE LOOK OF LOVE ABC	Neutron	2
18	14	MAMA USED TO SAY Junior	Mercury	3
8	15	THIS TIME (WE'LL GET IT RIGHT) England World Cup Squad	England	7
10	16	INSTINCTION Spandau Ballet	Chrysalis	5
12	17	THE MEANING OF LOVE Depeche Mode	Mute	3
13	18	PROMISED YOU A MIRACLE Simple Minds	Virgin	6
22	[19]	SHOUT SHOUT (KNOCK YOURSELF OUT) Rocky Sharpe and the Replays	Chiswick	4
35	20	HUNGRY LIKE THE WOLF Duran Duran	EMI	2
24	21	ISLAND OF LOST SOULS Blondie	Chrysalis	3
30	22	CLUB COUNTRY Associates	Associates	3
14	23	FANTASTIC DAY Haircut 100	Arista	7
19	24	TOTTENHAM TOTTENHAM Tottenham Hotspur FA Cup Final Squad	Rockney	3
16	25	I CAN MAKE YOU FEEL GOOD Shalamar	Solar	8
33	26	THE NUMBER OF THE BEAST Iron Maiden	EMI	2
17	27	PAPA'S GOT A BRAND NEW PIGBAG Pigbag	Y Records	7
-	28	CANTONESE BOY Japan	Virgin	1
20	29	EVER SO LONELY Monsoon	Mobile Suit	7
-	30	3x3 (EP) Genesis	Charisma	1

In these weeks ■ The German teenager Nicole's Eurovision winner *A Little Peace* becomes the 500th number one hit in almost 30 years (15.05.82) ■ Two football teams in the top 10, and another at no. 19 (15.05.82) ■

LW	TW	Title	Artist	Label	Wks
40	31	THE TELEPHONE ALWAYS RINGS	Fun Boy Three	*Chrysalis*	2
25	32	VIEW FROM A BRIDGE	Kim Wilde	*RAK*	5
21	33	ONE STEP FURTHER	Bardo	*Epic*	6
-	34	LOVE IS ALL IS ALL RIGHT	UB40	*DEP International*	1
38	35	SUSPICIOUS MINDS	Candi Staton	*Sugarhill*	2
23	36	SHIRLEY	Shakin' Stevens	*Epic*	5
27	37	STAY	Barry Manilow	*Arista*	4
28	38	BLUE EYES	Elton John	*Rocket*	8
-	39	TEMPTATION	New Order	*Factory*	1
-	40	I'VE NEVER BEEN TO ME	Charlene ●	*Motown*	1

WEEK ENDING 29 MAY 1982

LW	TW	Title	Artist	Label	Wks
8	[1]	HOUSE OF FUN	Madness	*Stiff*	2
5	2	GOODY TWO SHOES	Adam Ant	*CBS*	2
2	3	ONLY YOU	Yazoo	*Mute*	5
1	4	A LITTLE PEACE	Nicole	*CBS*	4
11	[5]	FANTASY ISLAND	Tight Fit	*Jive*	4
13	6	THE LOOK OF LOVE	ABC	*Neutron*	3
3	7	I WON'T LET YOU DOWN	PhD	*WEA*	6
10	[8]	FORGET ME NOTS	Patrice Rushen	*Elektra*	5
14	9	MAMA USED TO SAY	Junior	*Mercury*	4
4	10	I LOVE ROCK 'N' ROLL	Joan Jett and the Blackhearts	*Epic*	6
7	11	GIRL CRAZY	Hot Chocolate	*RAK*	6
20	12	HUNGRY LIKE THE WOLF	Duran Duran	*EMI*	3
6	13	WE HAVE A DREAM	Scotland World Cup Squad	*WEA*	5
21	14	ISLAND OF LOST SOULS	Blondie	*Chrysalis*	4
17	15	THE MEANING OF LOVE	Depeche Mode	*Mute*	4
-	16	TORCH	Soft Cell	*Some Bizzare*	1
22	17	CLUB COUNTRY	Associates	*Associates*	4
16	18	INSTINCTION	Spandau Ballet	*Chrysalis*	6
26	19	THE NUMBER OF THE BEAST	Iron Maiden	*EMI*	3
19	20	SHOUT SHOUT (KNOCK YOURSELF OUT)	Rocky Sharpe and the Replays	*Chiswick*	5
30	21	3x3 (EP)	Genesis	*Charisma*	2
18	22	PROMISED YOU A MIRACLE	Simple Minds	*Virgin*	7
12	23	REALLY SAYING SOMETHING	Bananarama & Funboy Three	*Deram*	8
28	[24]	CANTONESE BOY	Japan	*Virgin*	2
9	25	EBONY AND IVORY	Paul McCartney with Stevie Wonder	*Parlophone*	8
15	26	THIS TIME (WE'LL GET IT RIGHT)	England World Cup Squad	*England*	8
24	27	TOTTENHAM TOTTENHAM	Tottenham Hotspur FA Cup Final Squad	*Rockney*	4
31	28	THE TELEPHONE ALWAYS RINGS	Fun Boy Three	*Chrysalis*	3
34	[29]	LOVE IS ALL IS ALL RIGHT	UB40	*DEP International*	2
40	30	I'VE NEVER BEEN TO ME	Charlene	*Motown*	2
35	[31]	SUSPICIOUS MINDS	Candi Staton	*Sugarhill*	3
-	32	THE BACK OF LOVE	Echo and the Bunnymen	*Korova*	1
-	33	BRAVE NEW WORLD	Toyah	*Safari*	1
39	34	TEMPTATION	New Order	*Factory*	2
-	35	I'M A WONDERFUL THING (BABY)	Kid Creole and the Coconuts	*Ze*	1
-	36	PINKY BLUE	Altered Images	*Epic*	1
-	37	FIREWORKS	Siouxsie and the Banshees	*Polydor*	1
29	38	EVER SO LONELY	Monsoon	*Mobile Suit*	8
-	39	AFTER THE GOLDRUSH	Prelude	*After Hours*	1
27	40	PAPA'S GOT A BRAND NEW PIGBAG	Pigbag	*Y Records*	8

WEEK ENDING 5 JUNE 1982

June 1982

□ Highest position disc reached ● Act's first ever week on chart

LW	TW	Title	Artist	Label	Wks
1	[1]	HOUSE OF FUN	Madness	*Stiff*	3
2	2	GOODY TWO SHOES	Adam Ant	*CBS*	3
16	3	TORCH	Soft Cell	*Some Bizzare*	2
3	4	ONLY YOU	Yazoo	*Mute*	6
6	5	THE LOOK OF LOVE	ABC	*Neutron*	4
5	6	FANTASY ISLAND	Tight Fit	*Jive*	5
9	[7]	MAMA USED TO SAY	Junior	*Mercury*	5
12	8	HUNGRY LIKE THE WOLF	Duran Duran	*EMI*	4
7	9	I WON'T LET YOU DOWN	PhD	*WEA*	7
4	10	A LITTLE PEACE	Nicole	*CBS*	5
8	11	FORGET ME NOTS	Patrice Rushen	*Elektra*	6
14	12	ISLAND OF LOST SOULS	Blondie	*Chrysalis*	5
11	13	GIRL CRAZY	Hot Chocolate	*RAK*	7
17	14	CLUB COUNTRY	Associates	*Associates*	5
30	15	I'VE NEVER BEEN TO ME	Charlene	*Motown*	3
10	16	I LOVE ROCK 'N' ROLL	Joan Jett and the Blackhearts	*Epic*	7
15	17	THE MEANING OF LOVE	Depeche Mode	*Mute*	5
13	18	WE HAVE A DREAM	Scotland World Cup Squad	*WEA*	6
21	19	3x3 (EP)	Genesis	*Charisma*	3
19	20	THE NUMBER OF THE BEAST	Iron Maiden	*EMI*	4
28	21	THE TELEPHONE ALWAYS RINGS	Fun Boy Three	*Chrysalis*	4
37	[22]	FIREWORKS	Siouxsie and the Banshees	*Polydor*	2
18	23	INSTINCTION	Spandau Ballet	*Chrysalis*	7
35	24	I'M A WONDERFUL THING (BABY)	Kid Creole and the Coconuts	*Ze*	2
24	25	CANTONESE BOY	Japan	*Virgin*	3
20	26	SHOUT SHOUT (KNOCK YOURSELF OUT)	Rocky Sharpe and the Replays	*Chiswick*	6
32	27	THE BACK OF LOVE	Echo and the Bunnymen	*Korova*	2
33	28	BRAVE NEW WORLD	Toyah	*Safari*	2
-	29	WORK THAT BODY	Diana Ross	*Capitol*	1
22	30	PROMISED YOU A MIRACLE	Simple Minds	*Virgin*	8
29	31	LOVE IS ALL IS ALL RIGHT	UB40	*DEP International*	3
27	32	TOTTENHAM TOTTENHAM	Tottenham Hotspur FA Cup Final Squad	*Rockney*	5
39	33	AFTER THE GOLDRUSH	Prelude	*After Hours*	2
34	34	TEMPTATION	New Order	*Factory*	3
31	35	SUSPICIOUS MINDS	Candi Staton	*Sugarhill*	4
36	36	PINKY BLUE	Altered Images	*Epic*	2
26	37	THIS TIME (WE'LL GET IT RIGHT)	England World Cup Squad	*England*	9
-	38	I WANT CANDY	Bow Wow Wow	*RCA*	1
23	39	REALLY SAYING SOMETHING	Bananarama & Funboy Three	*Deram*	9
25	40	EBONY AND IVORY	Paul McCartney with Stevie Wonder	*Parlophone*	9

WEEK ENDING 12 JUNE 1982

LW	TW	Title	Artist	Label	Wks
2	[1]	GOODY TWO SHOES	Adam Ant	*CBS*	4
1	2	HOUSE OF FUN	Madness	*Stiff*	4
3	3	TORCH	Soft Cell	*Some Bizzare*	3
5	[4]	THE LOOK OF LOVE	ABC	*Neutron*	5
6	[5]	FANTASY ISLAND	Tight Fit	*Jive*	6
8	6	HUNGRY LIKE THE WOLF	Duran Duran	*EMI*	5
7	[7]	MAMA USED TO SAY	Junior	*Mercury*	6
4	8	ONLY YOU	Yazoo	*Mute*	7
15	9	I'VE NEVER BEEN TO ME	Charlene	*Motown*	4
19	[10]	3x3 (EP)	Genesis	*Charisma*	4
12	[11]	ISLAND OF LOST SOULS	Blondie	*Chrysalis*	6
11	12	FORGET ME NOTS	Patrice Rushen	*Elektra*	7
14	[13]	CLUB COUNTRY	Associates	*Associates*	6
38	14	I WANT CANDY	Bow Wow Wow	*RCA*	2
9	15	I WON'T LET YOU DOWN	PhD	*WEA*	8
10	16	A LITTLE PEACE	Nicole	*CBS*	6
24	17	I'M A WONDERFUL THING (BABY)	Kid Creole and the Coconuts	*Ze*	3
20	[18]	THE NUMBER OF THE BEAST	Iron Maiden	*EMI*	5
13	19	GIRL CRAZY	Hot Chocolate	*RAK*	8
21	20	THE TELEPHONE ALWAYS RINGS	Fun Boy Three	*Chrysalis*	5
17	21	THE MEANING OF LOVE	Depeche Mode	*Mute*	6
29	22	WORK THAT BODY	Diana Ross	*Capitol*	2
28	23	BRAVE NEW WORLD	Toyah	*Safari*	3
27	24	THE BACK OF LOVE	Echo and the Bunnymen	*Korova*	3
22	25	FIREWORKS	Siouxsie and the Banshees	*Polydor*	3
23	26	INSTINCTION	Spandau Ballet	*Chrysalis*	8
-	27	DO I DO	Stevie Wonder	*Motown*	1
33	[28]	AFTER THE GOLDRUSH	Prelude	*After Hours*	3
34	[29]	TEMPTATION	New Order	*Factory*	4
31	30	LOVE IS ALL IS ALL RIGHT	UB40	*DEP International*	4

■The lead track on Genesis' *3 x 3* EP was the strangely titled *Paperlate* (12.06.82) ■ No Americans in the top 10: only the German Nicole is not British (05.06.82)■

June 1982

□ Highest position disc reached ● Act's first ever week on chart

LW	TW	Title	Artist	Label	Wks
26	31	SHOUT SHOUT (KNOCK YOURSELF OUT)	Rocky Sharpe and the Replays	*Chiswick*	7
25	32	CANTONESE BOY	Japan	*Virgin*	4
16	33	I LOVE ROCK 'N' ROLL	Joan Jett and the Blackhearts	*Epic*	8
-	34	BEATLES MOVIE MEDLEY	Beatles	*Parlophone*	1
36	[35]	PINKY BLUE	Altered Images	*Epic*	3
18	36	WE HAVE A DREAM	Scotland World Cup Squad	*WEA*	7
-	[37]	SINCE YOU'RE GONE	Cars	*Elektra*	1
-	38	IKO IKO	Natasha ●	*Towerbell*	1
35	39	SUSPICIOUS MINDS	Candi Staton	*Sugarhill*	5
30	40	PROMISED YOU A MIRACLE	Simple Minds	*Virgin*	9

WEEK ENDING 19 JUNE 1982

LW	TW	Title	Artist	Label	Wks
1	[1]	GOODY TWO SHOES	Adam Ant	*CBS*	5
3	[2]	TORCH	Soft Cell	*Some Bizzare*	4
9	3	I'VE NEVER BEEN TO ME	Charlene	*Motown*	5
4	[4]	THE LOOK OF LOVE	ABC	*Neutron*	6
2	5	HOUSE OF FUN	Madness	*Stiff*	5
6	6	HUNGRY LIKE THE WOLF	Duran Duran	*EMI*	6
17	7	I'M A WONDERFUL THING (BABY)	Kid Creole and the Coconuts	*Ze*	4
5	8	FANTASY ISLAND	Tight Fit	*Jive*	7
-	[9]	WE TAKE MYSTERY (TO BED)	Gary Numan	*Beggars Banquet*	1
22	10	WORK THAT BODY	Diana Ross	*Capitol*	3
10	11	3x3 (EP)	Genesis	*Charisma*	5
7	12	MAMA USED TO SAY	Junior	*Mercury*	7
8	13	ONLY YOU	Yazoo	*Mute*	8
14	14	I WANT CANDY	Bow Wow Wow	*RCA*	3
27	15	DO I DO	Stevie Wonder	*Motown*	2
13	16	CLUB COUNTRY	Associates	*Associates*	7
20	[17]	THE TELEPHONE ALWAYS RINGS	Fun Boy Three	*Chrysalis*	6
-	18	INSIDE OUT	Odyssey	*RCA*	1
24	[19]	THE BACK OF LOVE	Echo and the Bunnymen	*Korova*	4
11	20	ISLAND OF LOST SOULS	Blondie	*Chrysalis*	7
23	[21]	BRAVE NEW WORLD	Toyah	*Safari*	4
12	22	FORGET ME NOTS	Patrice Rushen	*Elektra*	8
25	23	FIREWORKS	Siouxsie and the Banshees	*Polydor*	4
38	24	IKO IKO	Natasha	*Towerbell*	2
34	25	BEATLES MOVIE MEDLEY	Beatles	*Parlophone*	2
18	26	THE NUMBER OF THE BEAST	Iron Maiden	*EMI*	6
-	27	NO REGRETS	Midge Ure ●	*Chrysalis*	1
-	28	GOING TO A GO GO	Rolling Stones	*Rolling Stones*	1
28	29	AFTER THE GOLDRUSH	Prelude	*After Hours*	4
-	30	A NIGHT TO REMEMBER	Shalamar	*Solar*	1
29	31	TEMPTATION	New Order	*Factory*	5
-	32	LAS PALABRAS DE AMOR	Queen	*EMI*	1
-	33	AVALON	Roxy Music	*EG*	1
15	34	I WON'T LET YOU DOWN	PhD	*WEA*	9
-	[35]	IKO IKO	Belle Stars ●	*Stiff*	1
-	36	SPACE AGE LOVE SONG	A Flock Of Seagulls ●	*Jive*	1
-	37	SHE DON'T FOOL ME	Status Quo	*Vertigo*	1
-	38	ABRACADABRA	Steve Miller Band	*Mercury*	1
-	39	MURPHY'S LAW	Cheri ●	*Polydor*	1
19	40	GIRL CRAZY	Hot Chocolate	*RAK*	9

WEEK ENDING 26 JUNE 1982

LW	TW	Title	Artist	Label	Wks
3	[1]	I'VE NEVER BEEN TO ME	Charlene	*Motown*	6
1	2	GOODY TWO SHOES	Adam Ant	*CBS*	6
2	3	TORCH	Soft Cell	*Some Bizzare*	5
7	[4]	I'M A WONDERFUL THING (BABY)	Kid Creole and the Coconuts	*Ze*	5
6	[5]	HUNGRY LIKE THE WOLF	Duran Duran	*EMI*	7
4	6	THE LOOK OF LOVE	ABC	*Neutron*	7
18	7	INSIDE OUT	Odyssey	*RCA*	2
10	8	WORK THAT BODY	Diana Ross	*Capitol*	4
14	[9]	I WANT CANDY	Bow Wow Wow	*RCA*	4
15	[10]	DO I DO	Stevie Wonder	*Motown*	3
9	11	WE TAKE MYSTERY (TO BED)	Gary Numan	*Beggars Banquet*	2
38	12	ABRACADABRA	Steve Miller Band	*Mercury*	2
33	[13]	AVALON	Roxy Music	*EG*	2
5	14	HOUSE OF FUN	Madness	*Stiff*	6
8	15	FANTASY ISLAND	Tight Fit	*Jive*	8
24	16	IKO IKO	Natasha	*Towerbell*	3
12	17	MAMA USED TO SAY	Junior	*Mercury*	8
25	18	BEATLES MOVIE MEDLEY	Beatles	*Parlophone*	3
27	19	NO REGRETS	Midge Ure	*Chrysalis*	2
11	20	3x3 (EP)	Genesis	*Charisma*	6
13	21	ONLY YOU	Yazoo	*Mute*	9
32	22	LAS PALABRAS DE AMOR	Queen	*EMI*	2
19	23	THE BACK OF LOVE	Echo and the Bunnymen	*Korova*	5
21	24	BRAVE NEW WORLD	Toyah	*Safari*	5
30	25	A NIGHT TO REMEMBER	Shalamar	*Solar*	2
28	[26]	GOING TO A GO GO	Rolling Stones	*Rolling Stones*	2
17	27	THE TELEPHONE ALWAYS RINGS	Fun Boy Three	*Chrysalis*	7
39	28	MURPHY'S LAW	Cheri	*Polydor*	2
16	29	CLUB COUNTRY	Associates	*Associates*	8
20	30	ISLAND OF LOST SOULS	Blondie	*Chrysalis*	8
-	31	MUSIC AND LIGHTS	Imagination	*R&B*	1
23	32	FIREWORKS	Siouxsie and the Banshees	*Polydor*	5
-	33	HAPPY TALK	Captain Sensible ●	*A&M*	1
36	[34]	SPACE AGE LOVE SONG	A Flock Of Seagulls	*Jive*	2
29	35	AFTER THE GOLDRUSH	Prelude	*After Hours*	5
37	[36]	SHE DON'T FOOL ME	Status Quo	*Vertigo*	2
-	37	NOW THOSE DAYS ARE GONE	Bucks Fizz	*RCA*	1
-	38	HEART (STOP BEATING IN TIME)	Leo Sayer	*Chrysalis*	1
-	39	VIDEOTHEQUE	Dollar	*WEA*	1
-	40	STREETWALKIN'	Shakatak	*Polydor*	1

WEEK ENDING 3 JULY 1982

LW	TW	Title	Artist	Label	Wks
33	[1]	HAPPY TALK	Captain Sensible	*A&M*	2
1	2	I'VE NEVER BEEN TO ME	Charlene	*Motown*	7
7	[3]	INSIDE OUT	Odyssey	*RCA*	3
12	4	ABRACADABRA	Steve Miller Band	*Mercury*	3
31	[5]	MUSIC AND LIGHTS	Imagination	*R&B*	2
4	6	I'M A WONDERFUL THING (BABY)	Kid Creole and the Coconuts	*Ze*	6
8	[7]	WORK THAT BODY	Diana Ross	*Capitol*	5
5	8	HUNGRY LIKE THE WOLF	Duran Duran	*EMI*	8
2	9	GOODY TWO SHOES	Adam Ant	*CBS*	7
18	[10]	BEATLES MOVIE MEDLEY	Beatles	*Parlophone*	4
19	11	NO REGRETS	Midge Ure	*Chrysalis*	3
3	12	TORCH	Soft Cell	*Some Bizzare*	6
-	13	JUST WHO IS THE 5 O'CLOCK HERO	Jam	*Polydor*	1
16	14	IKO IKO	Natasha	*Towerbell*	4
9	15	I WANT CANDY	Bow Wow Wow	*RCA*	5
13	16	AVALON	Roxy Music	*EG*	3
25	17	A NIGHT TO REMEMBER	Shalamar	*Solar*	3
6	18	THE LOOK OF LOVE	ABC	*Neutron*	8
10	19	DO I DO	Stevie Wonder	*Motown*	4
37	20	NOW THOSE DAYS ARE GONE	Bucks Fizz	*RCA*	2
28	21	MURPHY'S LAW	Cheri	*Polydor*	3
22	22	LAS PALABRAS DE AMOR	Queen	*EMI*	3
11	23	WE TAKE MYSTERY (TO BED)	Gary Numan	*Beggars Banquet*	3
14	24	HOUSE OF FUN	Madness	*Stiff*	7
-	25	FOR THOSE ABOUT TO ROCK (WE SALUTE YOU)	AC/DC	*Atlantic*	1
38	26	HEART (STOP BEATING IN TIME)	Leo Sayer	*Chrysalis*	2
15	27	FANTASY ISLAND	Tight Fit	*Jive*	9
-	28	FREEBIRD	Lynyrd Skynyrd	*MCA*	1
20	29	3x3 (EP)	Genesis	*Charisma*	7
39	30	VIDEOTHEQUE	Dollar	*WEA*	2
23	31	THE BACK OF LOVE	Echo and the Bunnymen	*Korova*	6
26	32	GOING TO A GO GO	Rolling Stones	*Rolling Stones*	3
24	33	BRAVE NEW WORLD	Toyah	*Safari*	6
-	34	NIGHT TRAIN	Visage	*Polydor*	1
27	35	THE TELEPHONE ALWAYS RINGS	Fun Boy Three	*Chrysalis*	8
17	36	MAMA USED TO SAY	Junior	*Mercury*	9
21	37	ONLY YOU	Yazoo	*Mute*	10
40	[38]	STREETWALKIN'	Shakatak	*Polydor*	2

In these weeks ■ Captain Sensible's version of the *South Pacific* tune *Happy Talk* leapt from 33 to 1, the biggest jump to the top ever recorded (05.07.82) ■ Charlene becomes the only white act to have a British number one on the Motown label - several years after the track was originally recorded (26.06.82)■

LW	TW	Title	Artist	Label	Wks
29	39	CLUB COUNTRY	Associates	Associates	9
36	40	SHE DON'T FOOL ME	Status Quo	Vertigo	3

July 1982

□ Highest position disc reached ● Act's first ever week on chart

WEEK ENDING **10 JULY 1982**

LW	TW	Title	Artist	Label	Wks
1	1	HAPPY TALK	Captain Sensible	A&M	3
4	2	ABRACADABRA	Steve Miller Band	Mercury	4
3	3	INSIDE OUT	Odyssey	RCA	4
-	4	FAME	Irene Cara ●	RSO	1
5	5	MUSIC AND LIGHTS	Imagination	R&B	3
17	6	A NIGHT TO REMEMBER	Shalamar	Solar	4
2	7	I'VE NEVER BEEN TO ME	Charlene	Motown	8
13	8	JUST WHO IS THE 5 O'CLOCK HERO	Jam	Polydor	2
11	9	NO REGRETS	Midge Ure	Chrysalis	4
7	10	WORK THAT BODY	Diana Ross	Capitol	6
10	11	BEATLES MOVIE MEDLEY	Beatles	Parlophone	5
14	12	IKO IKO	Natasha	Towerbell	5
20	13	NOW THOSE DAYS ARE GONE	Bucks Fizz	RCA	3
6	14	I'M A WONDERFUL THING (BABY)	Kid Creole and the Coconuts	Ze	7
25	15	FOR THOSE ABOUT TO ROCK (WE SALUTE YOU)	AC/DC	Atlantic	2
8	16	HUNGRY LIKE THE WOLF	Duran Duran	EMI	9
22	17	LAS PALABRAS DE AMOR	Queen	EMI	4
21	18	MURPHY'S LAW	Cheri	Polydor	4
16	19	AVALON	Roxy Music	EG	4
-	20	SHY BOY	Bananarama	London	1
34	21	NIGHT TRAIN	Visage	Polydor	2
28	22	FREEBIRD	Lynyrd Skynyrd	MCA	2
18	23	THE LOOK OF LOVE	ABC	Neutron	9
15	24	I WANT CANDY	Bow Wow Wow	RCA	6
12	25	TORCH	Soft Cell	Some Bizzare	7
19	26	DO I DO	Stevie Wonder	Motown	5
26	27	HEART (STOP BEATING IN TIME)	Leo Sayer	Chrysalis	3
9	28	GOODY TWO SHOES	Adam Ant	CBS	8
30	29	VIDEOTHEQUE	Dollar	WEA	3
-	30	DA DA DA	Trio ●	Mobile Suit	1
-	31	I SECOND THAT EMOTION	Japan	Hansa	1
-	32	ME AND MY GIRL (NIGHT-CLUBBING)	David Essex	Mercury	1
-	33	TAKE IT AWAY	Paul McCartney	Parlophone	1
27	34	FANTASY ISLAND	Tight Fit	Jive	10
23	35	WE TAKE MYSTERY (TO BED)	Gary Numan	Beggars Banquet	4
-	36	IT STARTED WITH A KISS	Hot Chocolate	RAK	1
32	37	GOING TO A GO GO	Rolling Stones	Rolling Stones	4
-	38	ROCK THE CASBAH	Clash	CBS	1
38	39	STREETWALKIN'	Shakatak	Polydor	3
33	40	BRAVE NEW WORLD	Toyah	Safari	7

WEEK ENDING **17 JULY 1982**

LW	TW	Title	Artist	Label	Wks
4	1	FAME	Irene Cara	RSO	2
2	2	ABRACADABRA	Steve Miller Band	Mercury	5
1	3	HAPPY TALK	Captain Sensible	A&M	4
3	4	INSIDE OUT	Odyssey	RCA	5
6	5	A NIGHT TO REMEMBER	Shalamar	Solar	5
5	6	MUSIC AND LIGHTS	Imagination	R&B	4
30	7	DA DA DA	Trio	Mobile Suit	2
13	8	NOW THOSE DAYS ARE GONE	Bucks Fizz	RCA	4
20	9	SHY BOY	Bananarama	London	2
12	10	IKO IKO	Natasha	Towerbell	6
9	11	NO REGRETS	Midge Ure	Chrysalis	5
36	12	IT STARTED WITH A KISS	Hot Chocolate	RAK	2
18	13	MURPHY'S LAW	Cheri	Polydor	5
21	14	NIGHT TRAIN	Visage	Polydor	3
15	15	FOR THOSE ABOUT TO ROCK (WE SALUTE YOU)	AC/DC	Atlantic	3
8	16	JUST WHO IS THE 5 O'CLOCK HERO	Jam	Polydor	3
10	17	WORK THAT BODY	Diana Ross	Capitol	7
11	18	BEATLES MOVIE MEDLEY	Beatles	Parlophone	6
17	19	LAS PALABRAS DE AMOR	Queen	EMI	5
31	20	I SECOND THAT EMOTION	Japan	Hansa	2
22	21	FREEBIRD	Lynyrd Skynyrd	MCA	3
7	22	I'VE NEVER BEEN TO ME	Charlene	Motown	9
27	23	HEART (STOP BEATING IN TIME)	Leo Sayer	Chrysalis	4
-	24	DON'T GO	Yazoo	Mute	1
14	25	I'M A WONDERFUL THING (BABY)	Kid Creole and the Coconuts	Ze	8
29	26	VIDEOTHEQUE	Dollar	WEA	4
16	27	HUNGRY LIKE THE WOLF	Duran Duran	EMI	10
32	28	ME AND MY GIRL (NIGHT-CLUBBING)	David Essex	Mercury	2
19	29	AVALON	Roxy Music	EG	5
33	30	TAKE IT AWAY	Paul McCartney	Parlophone	2
-	31	COME ON EILEEN	Dexy's Midnight Runners with the Emerald Express	Mercury	1
26	32	DO I DO	Stevie Wonder	Motown	6
38	33	ROCK THE CASBAH	Clash	CBS	2
24	34	I WANT CANDY	Bow Wow Wow	RCA	7
-	35	THE ONLY WAY OUT	Cliff Richard	EMI	1
-	36	CHALK DUST-THE UMPIRE STRIKES BACK	Brat ●	Hansa	1
-	37	TOO LATE	Junior	Mercury	1
-	38	LOVE IS IN CONTROL (FINGER ON THE TRIGGER)	Donna Summer	Warner Bros	1
-	39	I WAS TIRED OF BEING ALONE	Patrice Rushen	Elektra	1
-	40	THE BIG BEAN	Pigbag	Y Records	1

WEEK ENDING **24 JULY 1982**

LW	TW	Title	Artist	Label	Wks
1	1	FAME	Irene Cara	RSO	3
7	2	DA DA DA	Trio	Mobile Suit	3
2	3	ABRACADABRA	Steve Miller Band	Mercury	6
9	4	SHY BOY	Bananarama	London	3
24	5	DON'T GO	Yazoo	Mute	2
-	6	DRIVING IN MY CAR	Madness	Stiff	1
5	7	A NIGHT TO REMEMBER	Shalamar	Solar	6
12	8	IT STARTED WITH A KISS	Hot Chocolate	RAK	3
31	9	COME ON EILEEN	Dexy's Midnight Runners with the Emerald Express	Mercury	2
4	10	INSIDE OUT	Odyssey	RCA	6
8	11	NOW THOSE DAYS ARE GONE	Bucks Fizz	RCA	5
6	12	MUSIC AND LIGHTS	Imagination	R&B	5
14	13	NIGHT TRAIN	Visage	Polydor	4
20	14	I SECOND THAT EMOTION	Japan	Hansa	3
10	15	IKO IKO	Natasha	Towerbell	7
3	16	HAPPY TALK	Captain Sensible	A&M	5
35	17	THE ONLY WAY OUT	Cliff Richard	EMI	2
13	18	MURPHY'S LAW	Cheri	Polydor	6
11	19	NO REGRETS	Midge Ure	Chrysalis	6
28	20	ME AND MY GIRL (NIGHT-CLUBBING)	David Essex	Mercury	3
26	21	VIDEOTHEQUE	Dollar	WEA	5
23	22	HEART (STOP BEATING IN TIME)	Leo Sayer	Chrysalis	5
21	23	FREEBIRD	Lynyrd Skynyrd	MCA	4
15	24	FOR THOSE ABOUT TO ROCK (WE SALUTE YOU)	AC/DC	Atlantic	4
30	25	TAKE IT AWAY	Paul McCartney	Parlophone	3
-	26	STOOL PIGEON	Kid Creole and the Coconuts	Ze	1
18	27	BEATLES MOVIE MEDLEY	Beatles	Parlophone	7
37	28	TOO LATE	Junior	Mercury	2
19	29	LAS PALABRAS DE AMOR	Queen	EMI	6
36	30	CHALK DUST-THE UMPIRE STRIKES BACK	Brat	Hansa	2
33	31	ROCK THE CASBAH	Clash	CBS	3
38	32	LOVE IS IN CONTROL (FINGER ON THE TRIGGER)	Donna Summer	Warner Bros	2
16	33	JUST WHO IS THE 5 O'CLOCK HERO	Jam	Polydor	4
22	34	I'VE NEVER BEEN TO ME	Charlene	Motown	10
-	35	STRANGE LITTLE GIRL	Stranglers	Liberty	1
-	36	THE CLAPPING SONG	Belle Stars	Stiff	1
17	37	WORK THAT BODY	Diana Ross	Capitol	8
-	38	NIGHTS IN WHITE SATIN	Elkie Brooks	A&M	1
-	39	ARTHUR DALEY (E'S ALRIGHT)	Firm ●	Bark	1
39	40	I WAS TIRED OF BEING ALONE	Patrice Rushen	Elektra	2

■Six years after it originally hit the charts, Lynyrd Skynyrd's *Freebird* EP climbs to its highest ever chart position - no. 21 (17.07.82) ■ *Happy Talk* drops almost as fast as it climbs, to become the only number one never to occupy a chart position between 3 and 16 (24.07.82)■

July 1982

□ Highest position disc reached ● Act's first ever week on chart

LW	TW	WEEK ENDING 31 JULY 1982		Wks
1	1	FAME Irene Cara	*RSO*	4
9	2	COME ON EILEEN Dexy's Midnight Runners with the Emerald Express	*Mercury*	3
5	3	DON'T GO Yazoo	*Mute*	3
6	4	DRIVING IN MY CAR Madness	*Stiff*	2
2	5	DA DA DA Trio	*Mobile Suit*	4
4	6	SHY BOY Bananarama	*London*	4
8	7	IT STARTED WITH A KISS Hot Chocolate	*RAK*	4
3	8	ABRACADABRA Steve Miller Band	*Mercury*	7
14	9	I SECOND THAT EMOTION Japan	*Hansa*	4
7	10	A NIGHT TO REMEMBER Shalamar	*Solar*	7
26	11	STOOL PIGEON Kid Creole and the Coconuts	*Ze*	2
13	12	NIGHT TRAIN Visage	*Polydor*	5
10	13	INSIDE OUT Odyssey	*RCA*	7
17	14	THE ONLY WAY OUT Cliff Richard	*EMI*	3
20	15	ME AND MY GIRL (NIGHT-CLUBBING) David Essex	*Mercury*	4
11	16	NOW THOSE DAYS ARE GONE Bucks Fizz	*RCA*	6
21	17	VIDEOTHEQUE Dollar	*WEA*	6
12	18	MUSIC AND LIGHTS Imagination	*R&B*	6
35	19	STRANGE LITTLE GIRL Stranglers	*Liberty*	2
25	20	TAKE IT AWAY Paul McCartney	*Parlophone*	4
15	21	IKO IKO Natasha	*Towerbell*	8
18	22	MURPHY'S LAW Cheri	*Polydor*	7
36	23	THE CLAPPING SONG Belle Stars	*Stiff*	2
30	24	CHALK DUST-THE UMPIRE STRIKES BACK Brat	*Hansa*	3
28	25	TOO LATE Junior	*Mercury*	3
19	26	NO REGRETS Midge Ure	*Chrysalis*	7
32	27	LOVE IS IN CONTROL (FINGER ON THE TRIGGER) Donna Summer	*Warner Bros*	3
39	28	ARTHUR DALEY (E'S ALRIGHT) Firm	*Bark*	2
23	29	FREEBIRD Lynyrd Skynyrd	*MCA*	5
16	30	HAPPY TALK Captain Sensible	*A&M*	6
24	31	FOR THOSE ABOUT TO ROCK (WE SALUTE YOU) AC/DC	*Atlantic*	5
31	32	ROCK THE CASBAH Clash	*CBS*	4
38	33	NIGHTS IN WHITE SATIN Elkie Brooks	*A&M*	2
-	34	THE HANGING GARDEN Cure	*Fiction*	1
22	35	HEART (STOP BEATING IN TIME) Leo Sayer	*Chrysalis*	6
29	36	LAS PALABRAS DE AMOR Queen	*EMI*	7
-	37	TODAY Talk Talk ●	*EMI*	1
-	38	HURRY HOME Wavelength ●	*Ariola*	1
-	39	WAR CHILD Blondie	*Chrysalis*	1
33	40	JUST WHO IS THE 5 O'CLOCK HERO Jam	*Polydor*	5

LW	TW	WEEK ENDING 7 AUGUST 1982		Wks
2	1	COME ON EILEEN Dexy's Midnight Runners with the Emerald Express	*Mercury*	4
1	2	FAME Irene Cara	*RSO*	5
3	3	DON'T GO Yazoo	*Mute*	4
4	4	DRIVING IN MY CAR Madness	*Stiff*	3
7	5	IT STARTED WITH A KISS Hot Chocolate	*RAK*	5
5	6	DA DA DA Trio	*Mobile Suit*	5
6	7	SHY BOY Bananarama	*London*	5
11	8	STOOL PIGEON Kid Creole and the Coconuts	*Ze*	3
9	9	I SECOND THAT EMOTION Japan	*Hansa*	5
14	10	THE ONLY WAY OUT Cliff Richard	*EMI*	4
19	11	STRANGE LITTLE GIRL Stranglers	*Liberty*	3
8	12	ABRACADABRA Steve Miller Band	*Mercury*	8
15	13	ME AND MY GIRL (NIGHT-CLUBBING) David Essex	*Mercury*	5
10	14	A NIGHT TO REMEMBER Shalamar	*Solar*	8
20	15	TAKE IT AWAY Paul McCartney	*Parlophone*	5
12	16	NIGHT TRAIN Visage	*Polydor*	6
28	17	ARTHUR DALEY (E'S ALRIGHT) Firm	*Bark*	3
17	18	VIDEOTHEQUE Dollar	*WEA*	7
23	19	THE CLAPPING SONG Belle Stars	*Stiff*	3
24	20	CHALK DUST-THE UMPIRE STRIKES BACK Brat	*Hansa*	4
-	21	MY GIRL LOLLIPOP (MY BOY LOLLIPOP) Bad Manners	*Magnet*	1
27	22	LOVE IS IN CONTROL (FINGER ON THE TRIGGER) Donna Summer	*Warner Bros*	4
13	23	INSIDE OUT Odyssey	*RCA*	8
16	24	NOW THOSE DAYS ARE GONE Bucks Fizz	*RCA*	7
25	25	TOO LATE Junior	*Mercury*	4
-	26	JOHN WAYNE IS BIG LEGGY Haysi Fantayzee ●	*Regard*	1
38	27	HURRY HOME Wavelength	*Ariola*	2
35	28	HEART (STOP BEATING IN TIME) Leo Sayer	*Chrysalis*	7
-	29	EYE OF THE TIGER Survivor ●	*Scotti Brothers*	1
32	30	ROCK THE CASBAH Clash	*CBS*	5
-	31	SUMMERTIME Fun Boy Three	*Chrysalis*	1
21	32	IKO IKO Natasha	*Towerbell*	9
33	33	NIGHTS IN WHITE SATIN Elkie Brooks	*A&M*	3
-	34	18 CARAT LOVE AFFAIR/LOVE HANGOVER Associates	*Associates*	1
37	35	TODAY Talk Talk	*EMI*	2
22	36	MURPHY'S LAW Cheri	*Polydor*	8
18	37	MUSIC AND LIGHTS Imagination	*R&B*	7
-	38	MACHINERY Sheena Easton	*EMI*	1
-	39	CAN'T TAKE MY EYES OFF YOU Boystown Gang ●	*ERC*	1
-	40	BAMBOO HOUSES/BAMBOO MUSIC Sylvian Sakamoto ●	*Virgin*	1

LW	TW	WEEK ENDING 14 AUGUST 1982		Wks
1	1	COME ON EILEEN Dexy's Midnight Runners with the Emerald Express	*Mercury*	5
2	2	FAME Irene Cara	*RSO*	6
3	3	DON'T GO Yazoo	*Mute*	5
4	4	DRIVING IN MY CAR Madness	*Stiff*	4
5	5	IT STARTED WITH A KISS Hot Chocolate	*RAK*	6
29	6	EYE OF THE TIGER Survivor	*Scotti Brothers*	2
8	7	STOOL PIGEON Kid Creole and the Coconuts	*Ze*	4
11	8	STRANGE LITTLE GIRL Stranglers	*Liberty*	4
21	9	MY GIRL LOLLIPOP (MY BOY LOLLIPOP) Bad Manners	*Magnet*	2
7	10	SHY BOY Bananarama	*London*	6
9	11	I SECOND THAT EMOTION Japan	*Hansa*	6
19	12	THE CLAPPING SONG Belle Stars	*Stiff*	4
6	13	DA DA DA Trio	*Mobile Suit*	6
10	14	THE ONLY WAY OUT Cliff Richard	*EMI*	5
15	15	TAKE IT AWAY Paul McCartney	*Parlophone*	6
17	16	ARTHUR DALEY (E'S ALRIGHT) Firm	*Bark*	4
13	17	ME AND MY GIRL (NIGHT-CLUBBING) David Essex	*Mercury*	6
22	18	LOVE IS IN CONTROL (FINGER ON THE TRIGGER) Donna Summer	*Warner Bros*	5
20	19	CHALK DUST-THE UMPIRE STRIKES BACK Brat	*Hansa*	5
25	20	TOO LATE Junior	*Mercury*	5
39	21	CAN'T TAKE MY EYES OFF YOU Boystown Gang	*ERC*	2
26	22	JOHN WAYNE IS BIG LEGGY Haysi Fantayzee	*Regard*	2
-	23	BIG FUN Kool and the Gang	*De-Lite*	1
16	24	NIGHT TRAIN Visage	*Polydor*	7
34	25	18 CARAT LOVE AFFAIR/LOVE HANGOVER Associates	*Associates*	2
31	26	SUMMERTIME Fun Boy Three	*Chrysalis*	2
27	27	HURRY HOME Wavelength	*Ariola*	3
12	28	ABRACADABRA Steve Miller Band	*Mercury*	9
18	29	VIDEOTHEQUE Dollar	*WEA*	8
40	30	BAMBOO HOUSES/BAMBOO MUSIC Sylvian Sakamoto	*Virgin*	2
14	31	A NIGHT TO REMEMBER Shalamar	*Solar*	9
30	32	ROCK THE CASBAH Clash	*CBS*	6
28	33	HEART (STOP BEATING IN TIME) Leo Sayer	*Chrysalis*	8
-	34	I EAT CANNIBALS PART 1 Toto Coelo ●	*Radialchoice*	1
24	35	NOW THOSE DAYS ARE GONE Bucks Fizz	*RCA*	8
35	36	TODAY Talk Talk	*EMI*	3
23	37	INSIDE OUT Odyssey	*RCA*	9
38	38	MACHINERY Sheena Easton	*EMI*	2
-	39	WHEN THE TIGERS BROKE FREE Pink Floyd	*Harvest*	1
-	40	UNDER THE BOARDWALK Tom Tom Club	*Island*	1

In these weeks ■ Almost three years after their number one hit, Pink Floyd release a follow-up single, *When The Tigers Broke Free.* It is less successful (14.08.82) ■ David Sylvian from Japan and Riuichi Sakamoto from the Japanese Yellow Magic Orchestra combine for a double-sided Oriental top 30 hit (14.08.82)■

September 1982

□ Highest position disc reached ● Act's first ever week on chart

WEEK ENDING 21 AUGUST 1982

LW	TW	Title / Artist	Label	Wks
1	1	COME ON EILEEN Dexy's Midnight Runners with the Emerald Express	*Mercury*	6
6	2	EYE OF THE TIGER Survivor	*Scotti Brothers*	3
2	3	FAME Irene Cara	*RSO*	7
3	4	DON'T GO Yazoo	*Mute*	6
5	5	IT STARTED WITH A KISS Hot Chocolate	*RAK*	7
21	6	CAN'T TAKE MY EYES OFF YOU Boystown Gang	*ERC*	3
8	7	STRANGE LITTLE GIRL Stranglers	*Liberty*	5
4	8	DRIVING IN MY CAR Madness	*Stiff*	5
7	9	STOOL PIGEON Kid Creole and the Coconuts	*Ze*	5
9	10	MY GIRL LOLLIPOP (MY BOY LOLLIPOP) Bad Manners	*Magnet*	3
12	11	THE CLAPPING SONG Belle Stars	*Stiff*	5
34	12	I EAT CANNIBALS PART 1 Toto Coelo	*Radialchoice*	2
-	13	WHAT Soft Cell	*Some Bizzare*	1
16	14	ARTHUR DALEY (E'S ALRIGHT) Firm	*Bark*	5
23	15	BIG FUN Kool and the Gang	*De-Lite*	2
22	16	JOHN WAYNE IS BIG LEGGY Haysi Fantayzee	*Regard*	3
27	17	HURRY HOME Wavelength	*Ariola*	4
26	18	SUMMERTIME Fun Boy Three	*Chrysalis*	3
10	19	SHY BOY Bananarama	*London*	7
11	20	I SECOND THAT EMOTION Japan	*Hansa*	7
25	21	18 CARAT LOVE AFFAIR/LOVE HANGOVER Associates	*Associates*	3
13	22	DA DA DA Trio	*Mobile Suit*	7
15	23	TAKE IT AWAY Paul McCartney	*Parlophone*	7
18	24	LOVE IS IN CONTROL (FINGER ON THE TRIGGER) Donna Summer	*Warner Bros*	6
14	25	THE ONLY WAY OUT Cliff Richard	*EMI*	6
-	26	HI-FIDELITY Kids From 'Fame' featuring Valerie Landsburg ●	*RCA*	1
-	27	SAVE A PRAYER Duran Duran	*EMI*	1
36	28	TODAY Talk Talk	*EMI*	4
20	29	TOO LATE Junior	*Mercury*	6
19	30	CHALK DUST-THE UMPIRE STRIKES BACK Brat	*Hansa*	6
-	31	SPREAD A LITTLE HAPPINESS Sting ●	*A&M*	1
17	32	ME AND MY GIRL (NIGHT-CLUBBING) David Essex	*Mercury*	7
-	33	NOBODY'S FOOL Haircut 100	*Arista*	1
-	34	CHERRY PINK AND APPLE BLOSSOM WHITE Modern Romance featuring John Du Prez	*WEA*	1
40	35	UNDER THE BOARDWALK Tom Tom Club	*Island*	2
-	36	WOT Captain Sensible	*A&M*	1
-	37	WALKING ON SUNSHINE Rocker's Revenge featuring Donnie Calvin ●	*London*	1
30	38	BAMBOO HOUSES/BAMBOO MUSIC Sylvian Sakamoto	*Virgin*	3
38	39	MACHINERY Sheena Easton	*EMI*	3
32	40	ROCK THE CASBAH Clash	*CBS*	7

WEEK ENDING 28 AUGUST 1982

LW	TW	Title / Artist	Label	Wks
1	1	COME ON EILEEN Dexy's Midnight Runners with the Emerald Express	*Mercury*	7
2	2	EYE OF THE TIGER Survivor	*Scotti Brothers*	4
13	3	WHAT Soft Cell	*Some Bizzare*	2
6	4	CAN'T TAKE MY EYES OFF YOU Boystown Gang	*ERC*	4
27	5	SAVE A PRAYER Duran Duran	*EMI*	2
3	6	FAME Irene Cara	*RSO*	8
26	7	HI-FIDELITY Kids From 'Fame' featuring Valerie Landsburg	*RCA*	2
4	8	DON'T GO Yazoo	*Mute*	7
12	9	I EAT CANNIBALS PART 1 Toto Coelo	*Radialchoice*	3
33	10	NOBODY'S FOOL Haircut 100	*Arista*	2
16	11	JOHN WAYNE IS BIG LEGGY Haysi Fantayzee	*Regard*	4
5	12	IT STARTED WITH A KISS Hot Chocolate	*RAK*	8
7	13	STRANGE LITTLE GIRL Stranglers	*Liberty*	6
15	14	BIG FUN Kool and the Gang	*De-Lite*	3
10	15	MY GIRL LOLLIPOP (MY BOY LOLLIPOP) Bad Manners	*Magnet*	4
11	16	THE CLAPPING SONG Belle Stars	*Stiff*	6
9	17	STOOL PIGEON Kid Creole and the Coconuts	*Ze*	6
8	18	DRIVING IN MY CAR Madness	*Stiff*	6
37	19	WALKING ON SUNSHINE Rocker's Revenge featuring Donnie Calvin	*London*	2
-	20	WHITE BOYS AND HEROES Gary Numan	*Beggars Banquet*	1
17	21	HURRY HOME Wavelength	*Ariola*	5
34	22	CHERRY PINK AND APPLE BLOSSOM WHITE Modern Romance featuring John Du Prez	*WEA*	2
24	23	LOVE IS IN CONTROL (FINGER ON THE TRIGGER) Donna Summer	*Warner Bros*	7
18	24	SUMMERTIME Fun Boy Three	*Chrysalis*	4
14	25	ARTHUR DALEY (E'S ALRIGHT) Firm	*Bark*	6
28	26	TODAY Talk Talk	*EMI*	5
21	27	18 CARAT LOVE AFFAIR/LOVE HANGOVER Associates	*Associates*	4
-	28	GIVE ME YOUR HEART TONIGHT Shakin' Stevens	*Epic*	1
35	29	UNDER THE BOARDWALK Tom Tom Club	*Island*	3
31	30	SPREAD A LITTLE HAPPINESS Sting	*A&M*	2
36	31	WOT Captain Sensible	*A&M*	2
-	32	THE MESSAGE Grandmaster Flash and the Furious Five ●	*Sugarhill*	1
23	33	TAKE IT AWAY Paul McCartney	*Parlophone*	8
25	34	THE ONLY WAY OUT Cliff Richard	*EMI*	7
29	35	TOO LATE Junior	*Mercury*	7
32	36	ME AND MY GIRL (NIGHT-CLUBBING) David Essex	*Mercury*	8
30	37	CHALK DUST-THE UMPIRE STRIKES BACK Brat	*Hansa*	7
20	38	I SECOND THAT EMOTION Japan	*Hansa*	8
19	39	SHY BOY Bananarama	*London*	8
-	40	BACKCHAT Queen	*EMI*	1

WEEK ENDING 4 SEPTEMBER 1982

LW	TW	Title / Artist	Label	Wks
2	1	EYE OF THE TIGER Survivor	*Scotti Brothers*	5
1	2	COME ON EILEEN Dexy's Midnight Runners with the Emerald Express	*Mercury*	8
5	3	SAVE A PRAYER Duran Duran	*EMI*	3
3	4	WHAT Soft Cell	*Some Bizzare*	3
7	5	HI-FIDELITY Kids From 'Fame' featuring Valerie Landsburg	*RCA*	3
4	6	CAN'T TAKE MY EYES OFF YOU Boystown Gang	*ERC*	5
19	7	WALKING ON SUNSHINE Rocker's Revenge featuring Donnie Calvin	*London*	3
9	8	I EAT CANNIBALS PART 1 Toto Coelo	*Radialchoice*	4
10	9	NOBODY'S FOOL Haircut 100	*Arista*	3
6	10	FAME Irene Cara	*RSO*	9
11	11	JOHN WAYNE IS BIG LEGGY Haysi Fantayzee	*Regard*	5
28	12	GIVE ME YOUR HEART TONIGHT Shakin' Stevens	*Epic*	2
-	13	PRIVATE INVESTIGATIONS Dire Straits	*Vertigo*	1
14	14	BIG FUN Kool and the Gang	*De-Lite*	4
26	15	TODAY Talk Talk	*EMI*	6
22	16	CHERRY PINK AND APPLE BLOSSOM WHITE Modern Romance featuring John Du Prez	*WEA*	3
12	17	IT STARTED WITH A KISS Hot Chocolate	*RAK*	9
30	18	SPREAD A LITTLE HAPPINESS Sting	*A&M*	3
32	19	THE MESSAGE Grandmaster Flash and the Furious Five	*Sugarhill*	2
20	20	WHITE BOYS AND HEROES Gary Numan	*Beggars Banquet*	2
21	21	HURRY HOME Wavelength	*Ariola*	6
8	22	DON'T GO Yazoo	*Mute*	8
13	23	STRANGE LITTLE GIRL Stranglers	*Liberty*	7
27	24	LOVE HANGOVER Associates	*Associates*	5
29	25	UNDER THE BOARDWALK Tom Tom Club	*Island*	4
24	26	SUMMERTIME Fun Boy Three	*Chrysalis*	5
16	27	THE CLAPPING SONG Belle Stars	*Stiff*	7
-	28	ALL OF MY HEART ABC	*Neutron*	1
31	29	WOT Captain Sensible	*A&M*	3
23	30	LOVE IS IN CONTROL (FINGER ON THE TRIGGER) Donna Summer	*Warner Bros*	8
15	31	MY GIRL LOLLIPOP (MY BOY LOLLIPOP) Bad Manners	*Magnet*	5
-	32	SADDLE UP David Christie ●	*KR*	1

■With film themes at number 2 and number 3, television hits back with the Firm's 'Minder' hit and the first of several hits for the television kids from 'Fame' (21.08.82) ■ Sting's debut hit is also from a film, but Haysi Fantayzee's *John Wayne Is Big Leggy* is not (21.08.82)■

September 1982

□ Highest position disc reached ● Act's first ever week on chart

LW	TW	Title	Artist	Label	Wks
-	33	LEAVE IN SILENCE	Depeche Mode	Mute	1
-	34	THERE IT IS	Shalamar	Solar	1
25	35	ARTHUR DALEY (E'S ALRIGHT)	Firm	Bark	7
-	36	SO HERE I AM	UB40	DEP International	1
-	37	WINDPOWER	Thomas Dolby ●	Venice In Peril	1
17	38	STOOL PIGEON	Kid Creole and the Coconuts	Ze	7
-	39	LOVE COME DOWN	Evelyn King	RCA	1
-	40	WHY	Carly Simon	WEA	1

LW	TW	WEEK ENDING 11 SEPTEMBER 1982			Wks
1	1	EYE OF THE TIGER	Survivor	Scotti Brothers	6
3	2	SAVE A PRAYER	Duran Duran	EMI	4
2	3	COME ON EILEEN	Dexy's Midnight Runners with the Emerald Express	Mercury	9
13	4	PRIVATE INVESTIGATIONS	Dire Straits	Vertigo	2
7	5	WALKING ON SUNSHINE	Rocker's Revenge featuring Donnie Calvin	London	4
5	6	HI-FIDELITY	Kids From 'Fame' featuring Valerie Landsburg	RCA	4
4	7	WHAT	Soft Cell	Some Bizzare	4
28	8	ALL OF MY HEART	ABC	Neutron	2
8	9	I EAT CANNIBALS PART 1	Toto Coelo	Radialchoice	5
6	10	CAN'T TAKE MY EYES OFF YOU	Boystown Gang	ERC	6
12	11	GIVE ME YOUR HEART TONIGHT	Shakin' Stevens	Epic	3
9	12	NOBODY'S FOOL	Haircut 100	Arista	4
19	13	THE MESSAGE	Grandmaster Flash and the Furious Five	Sugarhill	3
15	14	TODAY	Talk Talk	EMI	7
16	15	CHERRY PINK AND APPLE BLOSSOM WHITE	Modern Romance featuring John Du Prez	WEA	4
18	16	SPREAD A LITTLE HAPPINESS	Sting	A&M	4
34	17	THERE IT IS	Shalamar	Solar	2
11	18	JOHN WAYNE IS BIG LEGGY	Haysi Fantayzee	Regard	6
32	19	SADDLE UP	David Christie	KR	2
10	20	FAME	Irene Cara	RSO	10
33	21	LEAVE IN SILENCE	Depeche Mode	Mute	2
25	22	UNDER THE BOARDWALK	Tom Tom Club	Island	5
14	23	BIG FUN	Kool and the Gang	De-Lite	5
40	24	WHY	Carly Simon	WEA	2
20	25	WHITE BOYS AND HEROES	Gary Numan	Beggars Banquet	3
29	26	WOT	Captain Sensible	A&M	4
36	27	SO HERE I AM	UB40	DEP International	2
-	28	INVITATIONS	Shakatak	Polydor	1
39	29	LOVE COME DOWN	Evelyn King	RCA	2
22	30	DON'T GO	Yazoo	Mute	9
37	31	WINDPOWER	Thomas Dolby	Venice In Peril	2
21	32	HURRY HOME	Wavelength	Ariola	7
24	33	LOVE HANGOVER	Associates	Associates	6
26	34	SUMMERTIME	Fun Boy Three	Chrysalis	6
17	35	IT STARTED WITH A KISS	Hot Chocolate	RAK	10
30	36	LOVE IS IN CONTROL (FINGER ON THE TRIGGER)	Donna Summer	Warner Bros	9
-	37	WHO PUT THE BOMP (IN THE BOMP-A-BOMP-A-BOMP)	Showaddywaddy	RCA	1
-	38	GLITTERING PRIZE	Simple Minds	Virgin	1
23	39	STRANGE LITTLE GIRL	Stranglers	Liberty	8
-	40	RUFF MIX	Wonder Dogs ●	Flip	1

LW	TW	WEEK ENDING 18 SEPTEMBER 1982			Wks
1	1	EYE OF THE TIGER	Survivor	Scotti Brothers	7
4	2	PRIVATE INVESTIGATIONS	Dire Straits	Vertigo	3
2	3	SAVE A PRAYER	Duran Duran	EMI	5
5	4	WALKING ON SUNSHINE	Rocker's Revenge featuring Donnie Calvin	London	5
-	5	THE BITTEREST PILL (I EVER HAD TO SWALLOW)	Jam	Polydor	1
8	6	ALL OF MY HEART	ABC	Neutron	3
6	7	HI-FIDELITY	Kids From 'Fame' featuring Valerie Landsburg	RCA	5
13	8	THE MESSAGE	Grandmaster Flash and the Furious Five	Sugarhill	4
3	9	COME ON EILEEN	Dexy's Midnight Runners with the Emerald Express	Mercury	10
17	10	THERE IT IS	Shalamar	Solar	3
11	11	GIVE ME YOUR HEART TONIGHT	Shakin' Stevens	Epic	4
19	12	SADDLE UP	David Christie	KR	3
9	13	I EAT CANNIBALS PART 1	Toto Coelo	Radialchoice	6
14	14	TODAY	Talk Talk	EMI	8
7	15	WHAT	Soft Cell	Some Bizzare	5
12	16	NOBODY'S FOOL	Haircut 100	Arista	5
24	17	WHY	Carly Simon	WEA	3
29	18	LOVE COME DOWN	Evelyn King	RCA	3
10	19	CAN'T TAKE MY EYES OFF YOU	Boystown Gang	ERC	7
15	20	CHERRY PINK AND APPLE BLOSSOM WHITE	Modern Romance featuring John Du Prez	WEA	5
16	21	SPREAD A LITTLE HAPPINESS	Sting	A&M	5
-	22	FRIEND OR FOE	Adam Ant	CBS	1
21	23	LEAVE IN SILENCE	Depeche Mode	Mute	3
28	24	INVITATIONS	Shakatak	Polydor	2
22	25	UNDER THE BOARDWALK	Tom Tom Club	Island	6
18	26	JOHN WAYNE IS BIG LEGGY	Haysi Fantayzee	Regard	7
27	27	SO HERE I AM	UB40	DEP International	3
38	28	GLITTERING PRIZE	Simple Minds	Virgin	2
20	29	FAME	Irene Cara	RSO	11
23	30	BIG FUN	Kool and the Gang	De-Lite	6
40	31	RUFF MIX	Wonder Dogs	Flip	2
31	32	WINDPOWER	Thomas Dolby	Venice In Peril	3
-	33	HARD TO SAY I'M SORRY	Chicago	Full Moon	1
-	34	AND I'M TELLING YOU I'M NOT GOING	Jennifer Holliday ●	Geffen	1
33	35	LOVE HANGOVER	Associates	Associates	7
-	36	JUST WHAT I ALWAYS WANTED	Mari Wilson ●	Compact	1
25	37	WHITE BOYS AND HEROES	Gary Numan	Beggars Banquet	4
37	38	WHO PUT THE BOMP (IN THE BOMP-A-BOMP-A-BOMP)	Showaddywaddy	RCA	2
32	39	HURRY HOME	Wavelength	Ariola	8
-	40	ZOOM	Fat Larry's Band	WMOT	1

LW	TW	WEEK ENDING 25 SEPTEMBER 1982			Wks
1	1	EYE OF THE TIGER	Survivor	Scotti Brothers	8
5	2	THE BITTEREST PILL (I EVER HAD TO SWALLOW)	Jam	Polydor	2
2	3	PRIVATE INVESTIGATIONS	Dire Straits	Vertigo	4
4	4	WALKING ON SUNSHINE	Rocker's Revenge featuring Donnie Calvin	London	6
6	5	ALL OF MY HEART	ABC	Neutron	4
10	6	THERE IT IS	Shalamar	Solar	4
3	7	SAVE A PRAYER	Duran Duran	EMI	6
8	8	THE MESSAGE	Grandmaster Flash and the Furious Five	Sugarhill	5
12	9	SADDLE UP	David Christie	KR	4
22	10	FRIEND OR FOE	Adam Ant	CBS	2
11	11	GIVE ME YOUR HEART TONIGHT	Shakin' Stevens	Epic	5
17	12	WHY	Carly Simon	WEA	4
7	13	HI-FIDELITY	Kids From 'Fame' featuring Valerie Landsburg	RCA	6
9	14	COME ON EILEEN	Dexy's Midnight Runners with the Emerald Express	Mercury	11
18	15	LOVE COME DOWN	Evelyn King	RCA	4
14	16	TODAY	Talk Talk	EMI	9
40	17	ZOOM	Fat Larry's Band	WMOT	2
23	18	LEAVE IN SILENCE	Depeche Mode	Mute	4
36	19	JUST WHAT I ALWAYS WANTED	Mari Wilson	Compact	2
19	20	CAN'T TAKE MY EYES OFF YOU	Boystown Gang	ERC	8
13	21	I EAT CANNIBALS PART 1	Toto Coelo	Radialchoice	7
33	22	HARD TO SAY I'M SORRY	Chicago	Full Moon	2
15	23	WHAT	Soft Cell	Some Bizzare	6
16	24	NOBODY'S FOOL	Haircut 100	Arista	6
28	25	GLITTERING PRIZE	Simple Minds	Virgin	3

In these weeks ■ It was a number one hit in two different versions in 1955, but the 1982 versions of *Cherry Pink And Apple Blossom White* by Modern Romance only reached number 15 (11.09.82) ■ The Wonder Dogs were a computer-generated pack of hounds barking their way alongside a disco beat - the 1982 version of the Danish Singing Dogs of 1955 (11.09.82)■

October 1982

□ Highest position disc reached ● Act's first ever week on chart

LW	TW	Title / Artist	Label	Wks
-	26	PASS THE DUTCHIE Musical Youth ●	MCA	1
25	27	UNDER THE BOARDWALK Tom Tom Club	Island	7
20	28	CHERRY PINK AND APPLE BLOSSOM WHITE Modern Romance featuring John Du Prez	WEA	6
21	29	SPREAD A LITTLE HAPPINESS Sting	A&M	6
24	30	INVITATIONS Shakatak	Polydor	3
27	31	SO HERE I AM UB40	DEP International	4
34	32	AND I'M TELLING YOU I'M NOT GOING Jennifer Holliday	Geffen	2
31	33	RUFF MIX Wonder Dogs	Flip	3
-	34	TAKE A CHANCE WITH ME Roxy Music	EG	1
-	35	DO YA WANNA FUNK Sylvester with Patrick Cowley ●	London	1
-	36	GIVE ME SOME KINDA MAGIC Dollar	WEA	1
29	37	FAME Irene Cara	RSO	12
-	38	DO YOU REALLY WANT TO HURT ME Culture Club ●	Virgin	1
32	39	WINDPOWER Thomas Dolby	Venice In Peril	4
-	40	THE HOUSE OF THE RISING SUN Animals	RAK	1

WEEK ENDING 2 OCTOBER 1982

LW	TW	Title / Artist	Label	Wks
26	1	PASS THE DUTCHIE Musical Youth	MCA	2
2	2	THE BITTEREST PILL (I EVER HAD TO SWALLOW) Jam	Polydor	3
17	3	ZOOM Fat Larry's Band	WMOT	3
1	4	EYE OF THE TIGER Survivor	Scotti Brothers	9
6	5	THERE IT IS Shalamar	Solar	5
4	6	WALKING ON SUNSHINE Rocker's Revenge featuring Donnie Calvin	London	7
15	7	LOVE COME DOWN Evelyn King	RCA	5
3	8	PRIVATE INVESTIGATIONS Dire Straits	Vertigo	5
10	9	FRIEND OR FOE Adam Ant	CBS	3
12	10	WHY Carly Simon	WEA	5
22	11	HARD TO SAY I'M SORRY Chicago	Full Moon	3
5	12	ALL OF MY HEART ABC	Neutron	5
9	13	SADDLE UP David Christie	KR	5
19	14	JUST WHAT I ALWAYS WANTED Mari Wilson	Compact	3
38	15	DO YOU REALLY WANT TO HURT ME Culture Club	Virgin	2
8	16	THE MESSAGE Grandmaster Flash and the Furious Five	Sugarhill	6
25	17	GLITTERING PRIZE Simple Minds	Virgin	4
7	18	SAVE A PRAYER Duran Duran	EMI	7
18	19	LEAVE IN SILENCE Depeche Mode	Mute	5
14	20	COME ON EILEEN Dexy's Midnight Runners with the Emerald Express	Mercury	12
13	21	HI-FIDELITY Kids From 'Fame' featuring Valerie Landsburg	RCA	7
11	22	GIVE ME YOUR HEART TONIGHT Shakin' Stevens	Epic	6
16	23	TODAY Talk Talk	EMI	10
30	24	INVITATIONS Shakatak	Polydor	4
31	25	SO HERE I AM UB40	DEP International	5
-	26	JACKIE WILSON SAID Kevin Rowland and Dexy's Midnight Runners	Mercury	1
34	27	TAKE A CHANCE WITH ME Roxy Music	EG	2
40	28	THE HOUSE OF THE RISING SUN Animals	RAK	2
-	29	REAP THE WILD WIND Ultravox	Chrysalis	1
-	30	DANGER GAMES Pinkees ●	Creole	1
-	31	IN THE HEAT OF THE NIGHT Imagination	R&B	1
35	32	DO YA WANNA FUNK Sylvester with Patrick Cowley	London	2
-	33	SHOULD I STAY OR SHOULD I GO/STRAIGHT TO HELL Clash	CBS	1
36	34	GIVE ME SOME KINDA MAGIC Dollar	WEA	2
21	35	I EAT CANNIBALS PART 1 Toto Coelo	Radialchoice	8
32	36	AND I'M TELLING YOU I'M NOT GOING Jennifer Holliday	Geffen	3
23	37	WHAT Soft Cell	Some Bizzare	7
-	38	STARMAKER Kids From 'Fame'	RCA	1
-	39	CHANCES Hot Chocolate	RAK	1
37	40	FAME Irene Cara	RSO	13

WEEK ENDING 9 OCTOBER 1982

LW	TW	Title / Artist	Label	Wks
1	1	PASS THE DUTCHIE Musical Youth	MCA	3
3	2	ZOOM Fat Larry's Band	WMOT	4
15	3	DO YOU REALLY WANT TO HURT ME Culture Club	Virgin	3
11	4	HARD TO SAY I'M SORRY Chicago	Full Moon	4
26	5	JACKIE WILSON SAID Kevin Rowland and Dexy's Midnight Runners	Mercury	2
5	6	THERE IT IS Shalamar	Solar	6
7	7	LOVE COME DOWN Evelyn King	RCA	6
14	8	JUST WHAT I ALWAYS WANTED Mari Wilson	Compact	4
9	9	FRIEND OR FOE Adam Ant	CBS	4
2	10	THE BITTEREST PILL (I EVER HAD TO SWALLOW) Jam	Polydor	4
4	11	EYE OF THE TIGER Survivor	Scotti Brothers	10
6	12	WALKING ON SUNSHINE Rocker's Revenge featuring Donnie Calvin	London	8
10	13	WHY Carly Simon	WEA	6
38	14	STARMAKER Kids From 'Fame'	RCA	2
13	15	SADDLE UP David Christie	KR	6
17	16	GLITTERING PRIZE Simple Minds	Virgin	5
12	17	ALL OF MY HEART ABC	Neutron	6
8	18	PRIVATE INVESTIGATIONS Dire Straits	Vertigo	6
28	19	THE HOUSE OF THE RISING SUN Animals	RAK	3
16	20	THE MESSAGE Grandmaster Flash and the Furious Five	Sugarhill	7
29	21	REAP THE WILD WIND Ultravox	Chrysalis	2
19	22	LEAVE IN SILENCE Depeche Mode	Mute	6
22	23	GIVE ME YOUR HEART TONIGHT Shakin' Stevens	Epic	7
33	24	SHOULD I STAY OR SHOULD I GO/STRAIGHT TO HELL Clash	CBS	2
31	25	IN THE HEAT OF THE NIGHT Imagination	R&B	2
27	26	TAKE A CHANCE WITH ME Roxy Music	EG	3
25	27	SO HERE I AM UB40	DEP International	6
-	28	LIFELINE Spandau Ballet	Reformation	1
24	29	INVITATIONS Shakatak	Polydor	5
30	30	DANGER GAMES Pinkees	Creole	2
23	31	TODAY Talk Talk	EMI	11
39	32	CHANCES Hot Chocolate	RAK	2
-	33	BACK ON THE CHAIN GANG Pretenders	Real	1
18	34	SAVE A PRAYER Duran Duran	EMI	8
32	35	DO YA WANNA FUNK Sylvester with Patrick Cowley	London	3
20	36	COME ON EILEEN Dexy's Midnight Runners with the Emerald Express	Mercury	13
-	37	NEVER GIVE YOU UP Sharon Redd	Prelude	1
34	38	GIVE ME SOME KINDA MAGIC Dollar	WEA	3
-	39	ANNIE, I'M NOT YOUR DADDY Kid Creole and the Coconuts	Ze	1
-	40	ATHENA Who	Polydor	1

WEEK ENDING 16 OCTOBER 1982

LW	TW	Title / Artist	Label	Wks
1	1	PASS THE DUTCHIE Musical Youth	MCA	4
3	2	DO YOU REALLY WANT TO HURT ME Culture Club	Virgin	4
2	3	ZOOM Fat Larry's Band	WMOT	5
14	4	STARMAKER Kids From 'Fame'	RCA	3
4	5	HARD TO SAY I'M SORRY Chicago	Full Moon	5
5	6	JACKIE WILSON SAID Kevin Rowland and Dexy's Midnight Runners	Mercury	3
7	7	LOVE COME DOWN Evelyn King	RCA	7
8	8	JUST WHAT I ALWAYS WANTED Mari Wilson	Compact	5
6	9	THERE IT IS Shalamar	Solar	7
28	10	LIFELINE Spandau Ballet	Reformation	2
9	11	FRIEND OR FOE Adam Ant	CBS	5
13	12	WHY Carly Simon	WEA	7
19	13	THE HOUSE OF THE RISING SUN Animals	RAK	4
-	14	LOVE ME DO Beatles	Parlophone	1
39	15	ANNIE, I'M NOT YOUR DADDY Kid Creole and the Coconuts	Ze	2
10	16	THE BITTEREST PILL (I EVER HAD TO SWALLOW) Jam	Polydor	5
12	17	WALKING ON SUNSHINE Rocker's Revenge featuring Donnie Calvin	London	9

■For three consecutive weeks a different record peaked at number 32 (09.10.82) ■ Musical Youth's leap of 25 places to the very top was not even the biggest jump of 1982, but it remains the third biggest jump to number one ever (02.10.82)■

October 1982

□ Highest position disc reached ● Act's first ever week on chart

LW	TW	Title	Artist	Label	Wks
16	18	GLITTERING PRIZE	Simple Minds	Virgin	6
11	19	EYE OF THE TIGER	Survivor	Scotti Brothers	11
21	20	REAP THE WILD WIND	Ultravox	Chrysalis	3
15	21	SADDLE UP	David Christie	KR	7
-	22	ZIGGY STARDUST	Bauhaus ●	Beggars Banquet	1
17	23	ALL OF MY HEART	ABC	Neutron	7
24	24	SHOULD I STAY OR SHOULD I GO/STRAIGHT TO HELL	Clash	CBS	3
22	25	LEAVE IN SILENCE	Depeche Mode	Mute	7
18	26	PRIVATE INVESTIGATIONS	Dire Straits	Vertigo	7
30	27	DANGER GAMES	Pinkees	Creole	3
25	28	IN THE HEAT OF THE NIGHT	Imagination	R&B	3
27	29	SO HERE I AM	UB40	DEP International	7
33	30	BACK ON THE CHAIN GANG	Pretenders	Real	2
29	31	INVITATIONS	Shakatak	Polydor	6
37	32	NEVER GIVE YOU UP	Sharon Redd	Prelude	2
26	33	TAKE A CHANCE WITH ME	Roxy Music	EG	4
-	34	LIFE IN TOKYO	Japan	Hansa	1
31	35	TODAY	Talk Talk	EMI	12
-	36	I WANNA DO IT WITH YOU	Barry Manilow	Arista	1
-	37	LOVE'S COMIN' AT YA	Melba Moore	EMI America	1
-	38	MAD WORLD	Tears For Fears ●	Mercury	1
-	39	BE LOUD BE PROUD BE HEARD	Toyah	Safari	1
-	40	AMOR	Julio Iglesias	CBS	1

WEEK ENDING 23 OCTOBER 1982

LW	TW	Title	Artist	Label	Wks
2	[1]	DO YOU REALLY WANT TO HURT ME	Culture Club	Virgin	5
1	2	PASS THE DUTCHIE	Musical Youth	MCA	5
4	[3]	STARMAKER	Kids From 'Fame'	RCA	4
3	4	ZOOM	Fat Larry's Band	WMOT	6
14	5	LOVE ME DO	Beatles	Parlophone	2
5	6	HARD TO SAY I'M SORRY	Chicago	Full Moon	6
10	[7]	LIFELINE	Spandau Ballet	Reformation	3
27	[8]	DANGER GAMES	Pinkees	Creole	4
15	9	ANNIE, I'M NOT YOUR DADDY	Kid Creole and the Coconuts	Ze	3
6	10	JACKIE WILSON SAID	Kevin Rowland and Dexy's Midnight Runners	Mercury	4
13	[11]	THE HOUSE OF THE RISING SUN	Animals	RAK	5
20	12	REAP THE WILD WIND	Ultravox	Chrysalis	4
36	13	I WANNA DO IT WITH YOU	Barry Manilow	Arista	2
8	14	JUST WHAT I ALWAYS WANTED	Mari Wilson	Compact	6
7	15	LOVE COME DOWN	Evelyn King	RCA	8
38	16	MAD WORLD	Tears For Fears	Mercury	2
24	[17]	SHOULD I STAY OR SHOULD I GO/STRAIGHT TO HELL	Clash	CBS	4
22	18	ZIGGY STARDUST	Bauhaus	Beggars Banquet	2
9	19	THERE IT IS	Shalamar	Solar	8
-	20	I'LL BE SATISFIED	Shakin' Stevens	Epic	1
11	21	FRIEND OR FOE	Adam Ant	CBS	6
30	22	BACK ON THE CHAIN GANG	Pretenders	Real	3
12	23	WHY	Carly Simon	WEA	8
28	24	IN THE HEAT OF THE NIGHT	Imagination	R&B	4
18	25	GLITTERING PRIZE	Simple Minds	Virgin	7
37	26	LOVE'S COMIN' AT YA	Melba Moore	EMI America	2
32	27	NEVER GIVE YOU UP	Sharon Redd	Prelude	3
34	[28]	LIFE IN TOKYO	Japan	Hansa	2
33	29	TAKE A CHANCE WITH ME	Roxy Music	EG	5
-	30	I DON'T WANNA DANCE	Eddy Grant	Ice	1
-	31	OOH LA LA LA (LET'S GO DANCIN')	Kool and the Gang	De-Lite	1
19	32	EYE OF THE TIGER	Survivor	Scotti Brothers	12
40	33	AMOR	Julio Iglesias	CBS	2
17	34	WALKING ON SUNSHINE	Rocker's Revenge featuring Donnie Calvin	London	10
39	35	BE LOUD BE PROUD BE HEARD	Toyah	Safari	2
29	36	SO HERE I AM	UB40	DEP International	8
-	37	ZAMBEZI	Piranhas featuring Boring Bob Grover	Dakota	1
-	38	DO IT TO THE MUSIC	Raw Silk ●	KR	1
-	39	CRY BOY CRY	Blue Zoo ●	Magnet	1
16	40	THE BITTEREST PILL (I EVER HAD TO SWALLOW)	Jam	Polydor	6

WEEK ENDING 30 OCTOBER 1982

LW	TW	Title	Artist	Label	Wks
1	[1]	DO YOU REALLY WANT TO HURT ME	Culture Club	Virgin	6
9	[2]	ANNIE, I'M NOT YOUR DADDY	Kid Creole and the Coconuts	Ze	4
3	[3]	STARMAKER	Kids From 'Fame'	RCA	5
5	[4]	LOVE ME DO	Beatles	Parlophone	3
2	5	PASS THE DUTCHIE	Musical Youth	MCA	6
16	6	MAD WORLD	Tears For Fears	Mercury	3
7	[7]	LIFELINE	Spandau Ballet	Reformation	4
4	8	ZOOM	Fat Larry's Band	WMOT	7
6	9	HARD TO SAY I'M SORRY	Chicago	Full Moon	7
13	10	I WANNA DO IT WITH YOU	Barry Manilow	Arista	3
30	11	I DON'T WANNA DANCE	Eddy Grant	Ice	2
8	12	DANGER GAMES	Pinkees	Creole	5
12	13	REAP THE WILD WIND	Ultravox	Chrysalis	5
11	14	THE HOUSE OF THE RISING SUN	Animals	RAK	6
18	15	ZIGGY STARDUST	Bauhaus	Beggars Banquet	3
31	16	OOH LA LA LA (LET'S GO DANCIN')	Kool and the Gang	De-Lite	2
10	17	JACKIE WILSON SAID	Kevin Rowland and Dexy's Midnight Runners	Mercury	5
17	18	SHOULD I STAY OR SHOULD I GO/STRAIGHT TO HELL	Clash	CBS	5
20	19	I'LL BE SATISFIED	Shakin' Stevens	Epic	2
15	20	LOVE COME DOWN	Evelyn King	RCA	9
26	21	LOVE'S COMIN' AT YA	Melba Moore	EMI America	3
24	[22]	IN THE HEAT OF THE NIGHT	Imagination	R&B	5
14	23	JUST WHAT I ALWAYS WANTED	Mari Wilson	Compact	7
22	24	BACK ON THE CHAIN GANG	Pretenders	Real	4
27	25	NEVER GIVE YOU UP	Sharon Redd	Prelude	4
23	26	WHY	Carly Simon	WEA	9
37	27	ZAMBEZI	Piranhas featuring Boring Bob Grover	Dakota	2
21	28	FRIEND OR FOE	Adam Ant	CBS	7
-	29	HEARTBREAKER	Dionne Warwick	Arista	1
35	[30]	BE LOUD BE PROUD BE HEARD	Toyah	Safari	3
25	31	GLITTERING PRIZE	Simple Minds	Virgin	8
-	[32]	THE DAY BEFORE YOU CAME	Abba	Epic	1
38	33	DO IT TO THE MUSIC	Raw Silk	KR	2
33	34	AMOR	Julio Iglesias	CBS	3
39	35	CRY BOY CRY	Blue Zoo	Magnet	2
-	36	MUSCLES	Diana Ross	Capitol	1
28	37	LIFE IN TOKYO	Japan	Hansa	3
-	38	CAROLINE (LIVE AT THE NEC)	Status Quo	Vertigo	1
-	39	JACK AND DIANE	John Cougar ●	Riva	1
-	40	MANEATER	Daryl Hall and John Oates	RCA	1

WEEK ENDING 6 NOVEMBER 1982

LW	TW	Title	Artist	Label	Wks
1	[1]	DO YOU REALLY WANT TO HURT ME	Culture Club	Virgin	7
11	2	I DON'T WANNA DANCE	Eddy Grant	Ice	3
6	[3]	MAD WORLD	Tears For Fears	Mercury	4
3	4	STARMAKER	Kids From 'Fame'	RCA	6
29	5	HEARTBREAKER	Dionne Warwick	Arista	2
2	6	ANNIE, I'M NOT YOUR DADDY	Kid Creole and the Coconuts	Ze	5
4	7	LOVE ME DO	Beatles	Parlophone	4
10	[8]	I WANNA DO IT WITH YOU	Barry Manilow	Arista	4
7	9	LIFELINE	Spandau Ballet	Reformation	5
19	[10]	I'LL BE SATISFIED	Shakin' Stevens	Epic	3
16	11	OOH LA LA LA (LET'S GO DANCIN')	Kool and the Gang	De-Lite	3
9	12	HARD TO SAY I'M SORRY	Chicago	Full Moon	8
38	[13]	CAROLINE (LIVE AT THE NEC)	Status Quo	Vertigo	2
5	14	PASS THE DUTCHIE	Musical Youth	MCA	7
21	[15]	LOVE'S COMIN' AT YA	Melba Moore	EMI America	4
8	16	ZOOM	Fat Larry's Band	WMOT	8
24	17	BACK ON THE CHAIN GANG	Pretenders	Real	5

In these weeks ■ *Should I Stay Or Should I Go* by the Clash peaks at number 17. Almost 9 years later its use in a jeans commercial will take it to number one (23.10.82) ■ In the same week a number one of sixteen years earlier, the Animals' *House Of The Rising Sun* peaks on re-issue at number eleven (23.10.82) ■ And 20 years on, the Beatles' *Love Me Do* becomes a top 10 hit at last (23.10.82) ■

LW	TW	Title / Artist	Label	Wks
-	18	(SEXUAL) HEALING Marvin Gaye	CBS	1
15	19	ZIGGY STARDUST Bauhaus	Beggars Banquet	4
40	20	MANEATER Daryl Hall and John Oates	RCA	2
13	21	REAP THE WILD WIND Ultravox	Chrysalis	6
27	22	ZAMBEZI Piranhas featuring Boring Bob Grover	Dakota	3
14	23	THE HOUSE OF THE RISING SUN Animals	RAK	7
25	24	NEVER GIVE YOU UP Sharon Redd	Prelude	5
18	25	SHOULD I STAY OR SHOULD I GO/STRAIGHT TO HELL Clash	CBS	6
17	26	JACKIE WILSON SAID Kevin Rowland and Dexy's Midnight Runners	Mercury	6
33	27	DO IT TO THE MUSIC Raw Silk	KR	3
36	28	MUSCLES Diana Ross	Capitol	2
12	29	DANGER GAMES Pinkees	Creole	6
39	30	JACK AND DIANE John Cougar	Riva	2
22	31	IN THE HEAT OF THE NIGHT Imagination	R&B	6
34	32	AMOR Julio Iglesias	CBS	4
-	33	THE GIRL IS MINE Michael Jackson and Paul McCartney ●	Epic	1
35	34	CRY BOY CRY Blue Zoo	Magnet	3
32	35	THE DAY BEFORE YOU CAME Abba	Epic	2
30	36	BE LOUD BE PROUD BE HEARD Toyah	Safari	4
-	37	LIVING ON THE CEILING Blancmange ●	London	1
-	38	IT'S RAINING AGAIN Supertramp	Rondor	1
20	39	LOVE COME DOWN Evelyn King	RCA	10
23	40	JUST WHAT I ALWAYS WANTED Mari Wilson	Compact	8

LW	TW	*WEEK ENDING* **13 NOVEMBER 1982**		Wks
2	[1]	I DON'T WANNA DANCE Eddy Grant	Ice	4
5	[2]	HEARTBREAKER Dionne Warwick	Arista	3
3	[3]	MAD WORLD Tears For Fears	Mercury	5
1	4	DO YOU REALLY WANT TO HURT ME Culture Club	Virgin	8
18	5	(SEXUAL) HEALING Marvin Gaye	CBS	2
11	[6]	OOH LA LA LA (LET'S GO DANCIN') Kool and the Gang	De-Lite	4
4	7	STARMAKER Kids From 'Fame'	RCA	7
8	[8]	I WANNA DO IT WITH YOU Barry Manilow	Arista	5
33	9	THE GIRL IS MINE Michael Jackson and Paul McCartney	Epic	2
20	10	MANEATER Daryl Hall and John Oates	RCA	3
-	11	THEME FROM 'HARRY'S GAME' Clannad ●	RCA	1
6	12	ANNIE, I'M NOT YOUR DADDY Kid Creole and the Coconuts	Ze	6
10	13	I'LL BE SATISFIED Shakin' Stevens	Epic	4
13	14	CAROLINE (LIVE AT THE NEC) Status Quo	Vertigo	3
7	15	LOVE ME DO Beatles	Parlophone	5
15	16	LOVE'S COMIN' AT YA Melba Moore	EMI America	5
22	[17]	ZAMBEZI Piranhas featuring Boring Bob Grover	Dakota	4
9	18	LIFELINE Spandau Ballet	Reformation	6
37	19	LIVING ON THE CEILING Blancmange	London	2
24	20	NEVER GIVE YOU UP Sharon Redd	Prelude	6
34	21	CRY BOY CRY Blue Zoo	Magnet	4
17	22	BACK ON THE CHAIN GANG Pretenders	Real	6
28	23	MUSCLES Diana Ross	Capitol	3
-	24	YOUNG GUNS (GO FOR IT) Wham! ●	Innervision	1
30	25	JACK AND DIANE John Cougar	Riva	3
19	26	ZIGGY STARDUST Bauhaus	Beggars Banquet	5
27	27	DO IT TO THE MUSIC Raw Silk	KR	4
21	28	REAP THE WILD WIND Ultravox	Chrysalis	7
-	29	STATE OF INDEPENDENCE Donna Summer	Warner Brothers	1
12	30	HARD TO SAY I'M SORRY Chicago	Full Moon	9
23	31	THE HOUSE OF THE RISING SUN Animals	RAK	8
-	32	RIO Duran Duran	EMI	1
38	33	IT'S RAINING AGAIN Supertramp	Rondor	2
14	34	PASS THE DUTCHIE Musical Youth	MCA	8
35	35	THE DAY BEFORE YOU CAME Abba	Epic	3
31	36	IN THE HEAT OF THE NIGHT Imagination	R&B	7
25	37	SHOULD I STAY OR SHOULD I GO/STRAIGHT TO HELL Clash	CBS	7
-	38	SAVE YOUR LOVE Renee and Renato ●	Hollywood	1
16	39	ZOOM Fat Larry's Band	WMOT	9
32	40	AMOR Julio Iglesias	CBS	5

November 1982

□ Highest position disc reached ● Act's first ever week on chart

LW	TW	*WEEK ENDING* **20 NOVEMBER 1982**		Wks
1	[1]	I DON'T WANNA DANCE Eddy Grant	Ice	5
2	[2]	HEARTBREAKER Dionne Warwick	Arista	4
3	[3]	MAD WORLD Tears For Fears	Mercury	6
5	[4]	(SEXUAL) HEALING Marvin Gaye	CBS	3
11	[5]	THEME FROM 'HARRY'S GAME' Clannad	RCA	2
10	[6]	MANEATER Daryl Hall and John Oates	RCA	4
4	7	DO YOU REALLY WANT TO HURT ME Culture Club	Virgin	9
9	[8]	THE GIRL IS MINE Michael Jackson and Paul McCartney	Epic	3
-	9	MIRROR MAN Human League	Virgin	1
24	10	YOUNG GUNS (GO FOR IT) Wham!	Innervision	2
6	11	OOH LA LA LA (LET'S GO DANCIN') Kool and the Gang	De-Lite	5
19	12	LIVING ON THE CEILING Blancmange	London	3
32	13	RIO Duran Duran	EMI	2
29	[14]	STATE OF INDEPENDENCE Donna Summer	Warner Brothers	2
23	[15]	MUSCLES Diana Ross	Capitol	4
8	16	I WANNA DO IT WITH YOU Barry Manilow	Arista	6
14	17	CAROLINE (LIVE AT THE NEC) Status Quo	Vertigo	4
27	[18]	DO IT TO THE MUSIC Raw Silk	KR	5
7	19	STARMAKER Kids From 'Fame'	RCA	8
17	20	ZAMBEZI Piranhas featuring Boring Bob Grover	Dakota	5
21	21	CRY BOY CRY Blue Zoo	Magnet	5
13	22	I'LL BE SATISFIED Shakin' Stevens	Epic	5
12	23	ANNIE, I'M NOT YOUR DADDY Kid Creole and the Coconuts	Ze	8
38	24	SAVE YOUR LOVE Renee and Renato	Hollywood	2
20	25	NEVER GIVE YOU UP Sharon Redd	Prelude	7
16	26	LOVE'S COMIN' AT YA Melba Moore	EMI America	6
25	27	JACK AND DIANE John Cougar	Riva	4
-	28	WISHING (IF I HAD A PHOTOGRAPH OF YOU) A Flock Of Seagulls	Jive	1
15	29	LOVE ME DO Beatles	Parlophone	6
22	30	BACK ON THE CHAIN GANG Pretenders	Real	7
-	31	YOUTH OF TODAY Musical Youth	MCA	1
-	32	BEST YEARS OF OUR LIVES Modern Romance	WEA	1
33	33	IT'S RAINING AGAIN Supertramp	Rondor	3
-	34	THE OTHER SIDE OF LOVE Yazoo	Mute	1
-	35	TRULY Lionel Richie ●	Motown	1
-	36	SOMEONE SOMEWHERE (IN SUMMERTIME) Simple Minds	Virgin	1
35	37	THE DAY BEFORE YOU CAME Abba	Epic	4
30	38	HARD TO SAY I'M SORRY Chicago	Full Moon	10
-	39	TALK TALK Talk Talk	EMI	1
-	40	HERE I GO AGAIN/BLOODY LUXURY Whitesnake	Liberty	1

LW	TW	*WEEK ENDING* **27 NOVEMBER 1982**		Wks
1	[1]	I DON'T WANNA DANCE Eddy Grant	Ice	6
9	[2]	MIRROR MAN Human League	Virgin	2
2	3	HEARTBREAKER Dionne Warwick	Arista	5
10	4	YOUNG GUNS (GO FOR IT) Wham!	Innervision	3
4	5	(SEXUAL) HEALING Marvin Gaye	CBS	4
3	6	MAD WORLD Tears For Fears	Mercury	7
12	[7]	LIVING ON THE CEILING Blancmange	London	4
5	8	THEME FROM 'HARRY'S GAME' Clannad	RCA	3
24	9	SAVE YOUR LOVE Renee and Renato	Hollywood	3
6	10	MANEATER Daryl Hall and John Oates	RCA	5
13	11	RIO Duran Duran	EMI	3
8	12	THE GIRL IS MINE Michael Jackson and Paul McCartney	Epic	4
21	[13]	CRY BOY CRY Blue Zoo	Magnet	6
28	14	WISHING (IF I HAD A PHOTOGRAPH OF YOU) Flock Of Seagulls	Jive	2
14	15	STATE OF INDEPENDENCE Donna Summer	Warner Brothers	3
31	16	YOUTH OF TODAY Musical Youth	MCA	2
35	17	TRULY Lionel Richie	Motown	2

■The top six records are all at their peak, and only one record in the top 10 is falling (20.11.82) ■ As Abba's *The Day Before You Came* slips out of the 40, the band who two years later will take that song a little higher up the chart enjoy the peak chart position of their entire career - Blancmange at no. 7 with *Living On The Ceiling* (27.11.82)■

November 1982

□ Highest position disc reached ● Act's first ever week on chart

LW	TW	Title / Artist	Label	Wks
7	18	DO YOU REALLY WANT TO HURT ME Culture Club	*Virgin*	10
15	19	MUSCLES Diana Ross	*Capitol*	5
34	20	THE OTHER SIDE OF LOVE Yazoo	*Mute*	2
32	21	BEST YEARS OF OUR LIVES Modern Romance	*WEA*	2
11	22	OOH LA LA LA (LET'S GO DANCIN') Kool and the Gang	*De-Lite*	6
16	23	I WANNA DO IT WITH YOU Barry Manilow	*Arista*	7
18	24	DO IT TO THE MUSIC Raw Silk	*KR*	6
17	25	CAROLINE (LIVE AT THE NEC) Status Quo	*Vertigo*	5
39	26	TALK TALK Talk Talk	*EMI*	2
20	27	ZAMBEZI Piranhas featuring Boring Bob Grover	*Dakota*	6
-	28	HYMN Ultravox	*Chrysalis*	1
33	29	IT'S RAINING AGAIN Supertramp	*Rondor*	4
22	30	I'LL BE SATISFIED Shakin' Stevens	*Epic*	6
25	31	NEVER GIVE YOU UP Sharon Redd	*Prelude*	8
-	32	OUR HOUSE Madness	*Stiff*	1
26	33	LOVE'S COMIN' AT YA Melba Moore	*EMI America*	7
-	34	TIME (CLOCK OF THE HEART) Culture Club	*Virgin*	1
-	35	NIGHTPORTER Japan	*Virgin*	1
19	36	STARMAKER Kids From 'Fame'	*RCA*	9
27	37	JACK AND DIANE John Cougar	*Riva*	5
40	38	HERE I GO AGAIN/BLOODY LUXURY Whitesnake	*Liberty*	2
30	39	BACK ON THE CHAIN GANG Pretenders	*Real*	8
-	□40	BACK TO LOVE Evelyn King	*RCA*	1

LW	TW	*WEEK ENDING* 4 DECEMBER 1982		Wks
-	□1	BEAT SURRENDER Jam	*Polydor*	1
2	□2	MIRROR MAN Human League	*Virgin*	3
4	□3	YOUNG GUNS (GO FOR IT) Wham!	*Innervision*	4
1	4	I DON'T WANNA DANCE Eddy Grant	*Ice*	7
9	5	SAVE YOUR LOVE Renee and Renato	*Hollywood*	4
17	□6	TRULY Lionel Richie	*Motown*	3
7	□7	LIVING ON THE CEILING Blancmange	*London*	5
3	8	HEARTBREAKER Dionne Warwick	*Arista*	6
34	9	TIME (CLOCK OF THE HEART) Culture Club	*Virgin*	2
11	10	RIO Duran Duran	*EMI*	4
14	11	WISHING (IF I HAD A PHOTOGRAPH OF YOU) A Flock Of Seagulls	*Jive*	3
5	12	(SEXUAL) HEALING Marvin Gaye	*CBS*	5
16	□13	YOUTH OF TODAY Musical Youth	*MCA*	3
20	14	THE OTHER SIDE OF LOVE Yazoo	*Mute*	3
6	15	MAD WORLD Tears For Fears	*Mercury*	8
28	16	HYMN Ultravox	*Chrysalis*	2
32	17	OUR HOUSE Madness	*Stiff*	2
21	18	BEST YEARS OF OUR LIVES Modern Romance	*WEA*	3
15	19	STATE OF INDEPENDENCE Donna Summer	*Warner Brothers*	4
8	20	THEME FROM 'HARRY'S GAME' Clannad	*RCA*	4
10	21	MANEATER Daryl Hall and John Oates	*RCA*	6
13	22	CRY BOY CRY Blue Zoo	*Magnet*	7
26	□23	TALK TALK Talk Talk	*EMI*	3
12	24	THE GIRL IS MINE Michael Jackson and Paul McCartney	*Epic*	5
-	25	FRIENDS Shalamar	*Solar*	1
19	26	MUSCLES Diana Ross	*Capitol*	6
29	27	IT'S RAINING AGAIN Supertramp	*Rondor*	5
22	28	OOH LA LA LA (LET'S GO DANCIN') Kool and the Gang	*De-Lite*	7
35	29	NIGHTPORTER Japan	*Virgin*	2
18	30	DO YOU REALLY WANT TO HURT ME Culture Club	*Virgin*	11
24	31	DO IT TO THE MUSIC Raw Silk	*KR*	7
-	32	WHERE THE HEART IS Soft Cell	*Some Bizzare*	1
-	□33	DESPERATE BUT NOT SERIOUS Adam Ant	*CBS*	1
38	□34	HERE I GO AGAIN/BLOODY LUXURY Whitesnake	*Liberty*	3
-	35	LET'S GET THIS STRAIGHT (FROM THE START)/OLD Dexy's Midnight Runners	*Mercury*	1
27	36	ZAMBEZI Piranhas featuring Boring Bob Grover	*Dakota*	7
-	37	IF YOU CAN'T STAND THE HEAT Bucks Fizz	*RCA*	1
-	38	BUFFALO GALS Malcolm McLaren and the World's Famous Supreme Team ●	*Charisma*	1
-	39	PEACE ON EARTH-LITTLE DRUMMER BOY David Bowie and Bing Crosby ●	*RCA*	1
-	□40	I'M ALRIGHT Young Steve and the Afternoon Boys ●	*RCA*	1

LW	TW	*WEEK ENDING* 11 DECEMBER 1982		Wks
1	□1	BEAT SURRENDER Jam	*Polydor*	2
2	□2	MIRROR MAN Human League	*Virgin*	4
5	3	SAVE YOUR LOVE Renee and Renato	*Hollywood*	5
3	4	YOUNG GUNS (GO FOR IT) Wham!	*Innervision*	5
9	5	TIME (CLOCK OF THE HEART) Culture Club	*Virgin*	3
6	□6	TRULY Lionel Richie	*Motown*	4
7	□7	LIVING ON THE CEILING Blancmange	*London*	6
4	8	I DON'T WANNA DANCE Eddy Grant	*Ice*	8
10	□9	RIO Duran Duran	*EMI*	5
11	□10	WISHING (IF I HAD A PHOTOGRAPH OF YOU) A Flock Of Seagulls	*Jive*	4
18	11	BEST YEARS OF OUR LIVES Modern Romance	*WEA*	4
17	12	OUR HOUSE Madness	*Stiff*	3
14	□13	THE OTHER SIDE OF LOVE Yazoo	*Mute*	4
16	14	HYMN Ultravox	*Chrysalis*	3
8	15	HEARTBREAKER Dionne Warwick	*Arista*	7
13	16	YOUTH OF TODAY Musical Youth	*MCA*	4
12	17	(SEXUAL) HEALING Marvin Gaye	*CBS*	6
35	18	LET'S GET THIS STRAIGHT (FROM THE START)/OLD Dexy's Midnight Runners	*Mercury*	2
25	19	FRIENDS Shalamar	*Solar*	2
19	20	STATE OF INDEPENDENCE Donna Summer	*Warner Brothers*	5
32	21	WHERE THE HEART IS Soft Cell	*Some Bizzare*	2
39	22	PEACE ON EARTH-LITTLE DRUMMER BOY David Bowie and Bing Crosby	*RCA*	2
15	23	MAD WORLD Tears For Fears	*Mercury*	9
38	24	BUFFALO GALS Malcolm McLaren and the World's Famous Supreme Team	*Charisma*	2
20	25	THEME FROM 'HARRY'S GAME' Clannad	*RCA*	5
21	26	MANEATER Daryl Hall and John Oates	*RCA*	7
-	27	YOU CAN'T HURRY LOVE Phil Collins	*Virgin*	1
27	28	IT'S RAINING AGAIN Supertramp	*Rondor*	6
37	29	IF YOU CAN'T STAND THE HEAT Bucks Fizz	*RCA*	2
22	30	CRY BOY CRY Blue Zoo	*Magnet*	8
23	31	TALK TALK Talk Talk	*EMI*	4
24	32	THE GIRL IS MINE Michael Jackson and Paul McCartney	*Epic*	6
-	33	I FEEL LOVE Donna Summer	*Casablanca*	1
26	34	MUSCLES Diana Ross	*Capitol*	7
-	35	THE SHAKIN' STEVENS EP Shakin' Stevens	*Epic*	1
34	36	HERE I GO AGAIN/BLOODY LUXURY Whitesnake	*Liberty*	4
-	37	HI DE HI-HI DE HO Kool and the Gang	*De-Lite*	1
-	38	LITTLE TOWN Cliff Richard	*EMI*	1
29	39	NIGHTPORTER Japan	*Virgin*	3
31	40	DO IT TO THE MUSIC Raw Silk	*KR*	8

LW	TW	*WEEK ENDING* 18 DECEMBER 1982		Wks
3	□1	SAVE YOUR LOVE Renee and Renato	*Hollywood*	6
1	2	BEAT SURRENDER Jam	*Polydor*	3
5	□3	TIME (CLOCK OF THE HEART) Culture Club	*Virgin*	4
35	4	THE SHAKIN' STEVENS EP Shakin' Stevens	*Epic*	2
12	□5	OUR HOUSE Madness	*Stiff*	4
6	□6	TRULY Lionel Richie	*Motown*	5
2	7	MIRROR MAN Human League	*Virgin*	5
4	8	YOUNG GUNS (GO FOR IT) Wham!	*Innervision*	6
11	9	BEST YEARS OF OUR LIVES Modern Romance	*WEA*	5
22	10	PEACE ON EARTH-LITTLE DRUMMER BOY David Bowie and Bing Crosby	*RCA*	3
7	11	LIVING ON THE CEILING Blancmange	*London*	7
19	□12	FRIENDS Shalamar	*Solar*	3
14	13	HYMN Ultravox	*Chrysalis*	4
9	14	RIO Duran Duran	*EMI*	6
10	15	WISHING (IF I HAD A PHOTOGRAPH OF YOU) A Flock Of Seagulls	*Jive*	5
13	16	THE OTHER SIDE OF LOVE Yazoo	*Mute*	5

In these weeks ■ Jam's final release gives them their third to go straight to the top, equalling Slade's record, set in 1973 (04.12.82) ■ After nine consecutive top 10 hits with official releases, Adam Ant's latest stalls at number 33. His situation appeared to be *Desparate But Not Serious* (04.12.82)■

December 1982

□ Highest position disc reached ● Act's first ever week on chart

LW	TW	Title / Artist	Label	Wks
27	**17**	YOU CAN'T HURRY LOVE Phil Collins	*Virgin*	2
18	**18**	LET'S GET THIS STRAIGHT (FROM THE START)/OLD Dexy's Midnight Runners	*Mercury*	3
24	**19**	BUFFALO GALS Malcolm McLaren and the World's Famous Supreme Team	*Charisma*	3
29	**20**	IF YOU CAN'T STAND THE HEAT Bucks Fizz	*RCA*	3
38	**21**	LITTLE TOWN Cliff Richard	*EMI*	2
33	**22**	I FEEL LOVE Donna Summer	*Casablanca*	2
16	**23**	YOUTH OF TODAY Musical Youth	*MCA*	5
21	**24**	WHERE THE HEART IS Soft Cell	*Some Bizzare*	3
8	**25**	I DON'T WANNA DANCE Eddy Grant	*Ice*	9
28	**26**	IT'S RAINING AGAIN Supertramp	*Rondor*	7
-	**27**	ALL THE LOVE IN THE WORLD Dionne Warwick	*Arista*	1
-	**28**	SINGALONG-A-SANTA Santa Claus and the Christmas Trees ●	*Polydor*	1
37	**[29]**	HI DE HI-HI DE HO Kool and the Gang	*De-Lite*	2
-	**30**	A WINTER'S TALE David Essex	*Mercury*	1
-	**31**	UNDER ATTACK Abba	*Epic*	1
31	**32**	TALK TALK Talk Talk	*EMI*	5
17	**33**	(SEXUAL) HEALING Marvin Gaye	*CBS*	7
-	**34**	DEAR ADDY Kid Creole and the Coconuts	*Ze*	1
39	**35**	NIGHTPORTER Japan	*Virgin*	4
20	**36**	STATE OF INDEPENDENCE Donna Summer	*Warner Brothers*	6
15	**37**	HEARTBREAKER Dionne Warwick	*Arista*	8
23	**38**	MAD WORLD Tears For Fears	*Mercury*	10
-	**39**	CACHARPAYA (ANDES PUMPSA DESI) Incantation ●	*Beggars Banquet*	1
-	**40**	I'M GONNA SIT RIGHT DOWN AND WRITE MYSELF A LETTER Barry Manilow	*Arista*	1

WEEK ENDING 25 DECEMBER 1982

LW	TW	Title / Artist	Label	Wks
1	**[1]**	SAVE YOUR LOVE Renee and Renato	*Hollywood*	7
4	**[2]**	THE SHAKIN' STEVENS EP Shakin' Stevens	*Epic*	3
10	**[3]**	PEACE ON EARTH-LITTLE DRUMMER BOY David Bowie and Bing Crosby	*RCA*	4
3	**4**	TIME (CLOCK OF THE HEART) Culture Club	*Virgin*	5
5	**[5]**	OUR HOUSE Madness	*Stiff*	5
17	**6**	YOU CAN'T HURRY LOVE Phil Collins	*Virgin*	3
30	**7**	A WINTER'S TALE David Essex	*Mercury*	2
9	**8**	BEST YEARS OF OUR LIVES Modern Romance	*WEA*	6
6	**9**	TRULY Lionel Richie	*Motown*	6
2	**10**	BEAT SURRENDER Jam	*Polydor*	4
21	**[11]**	LITTLE TOWN Cliff Richard	*EMI*	3
7	**12**	MIRROR MAN Human League	*Virgin*	6
8	**13**	YOUNG GUNS (GO FOR IT) Wham!	*Innervision*	7
27	**14**	ALL THE LOVE IN THE WORLD Dionne Warwick	*Arista*	2
12	**15**	FRIENDS Shalamar	*Solar*	4
13	**16**	HYMN Ultravox	*Chrysalis*	5
18	**[17]**	LET'S GET THIS STRAIGHT (FROM THE START)/OLD Dexy's Midnight Runners	*Mercury*	4
19	**18**	BUFFALO GALS Malcolm McLaren & the World's Famous Supreme Team	*Charisma*	4
28	**[19]**	SINGALONG-A-SANTA Santa Claus and the Christmas Trees	*Polydor*	2
20	**20**	IF YOU CAN'T STAND THE HEAT Bucks Fizz	*RCA*	4
14	**21**	RIO Duran Duran	*EMI*	7
11	**22**	LIVING ON THE CEILING Blancmange	*London*	8
22	**23**	I FEEL LOVE Donna Summer	*Casablanca*	3
15	**24**	WISHING (IF I HAD A PHOTOGRAPH OF YOU) A Flock Of Seagulls	*Jive*	6
16	**25**	THE OTHER SIDE OF LOVE Yazoo	*Mute*	6
31	**[26]**	UNDER ATTACK Abba	*Epic*	2
24	**27**	WHERE THE HEART IS Soft Cell	*Some Bizzare*	4
39	**28**	CACHARPAYA (ANDES PUMPSA DESI) Incantation	*Beggars Banquet*	2
34	**29**	DEAR ADDY Kid Creole and the Coconuts	*Ze*	2
25	**30**	I DON'T WANNA DANCE Eddy Grant	*Ice*	10
26	**31**	IT'S RAINING AGAIN Supertramp	*Rondor*	8
29	**32**	HI DE HI-HI DE HO Kool and the Gang	*De-Lite*	3
-	**33**	ORVILLE'S SONG Keith Harris and Orville ●	*BBC*	1
-	**34**	THEME FROM 'ET (THE EXTRA TERRESTRIAL)' John Williams ●	*MCA*	1
32	**35**	TALK TALK Talk Talk	*EMI*	6
40	**[36]**	I'M GONNA SIT RIGHT DOWN AND WRITE MYSELF A LETTER Barry Manilow	*Arista*	2
33	**37**	(SEXUAL) HEALING Marvin Gaye	*CBS*	8
23	**38**	YOUTH OF TODAY Musical Youth	*MCA*	6
-	**39**	HEARTACHE AVENUE Maisonettes ●	*Ready Steady Go*	1
35	**40**	NIGHTPORTER Japan	*Virgin*	5

■The lead track on *The Shakin' Stevens EP* was his cover of Elvis Presley's *Blue Christmas*. Presley's version only reached number 11, in 1964 (25.12.82) ■ 20 of the top 40 records are by acts who have topped the charts, or who would soon do so, a very high proportion (25.12.82)■

1983

.........MICHAEL JACKSON has his second through fourth top ten hits from *Thriller*........
Phil Collins has his first number one and the Police their last of five........
long-awaited number ones are enjoyed by Bonnie Tyler, Duran Duran,
Spandau Ballet, KC and the Sunshine Band,
UB40 and Billy Joel..........

January 1983

□ Highest position disc reached ● Act's first ever week on chart

WEEK ENDING 1 JANUARY 1983

LW	TW	Title / Artist	Label	Wks
1	[1]	SAVE YOUR LOVE Renee and Renato	*Hollywood*	8
2	[2]	THE SHAKIN' STEVENS EP Shakin' Stevens	*Epic*	4
3	[3]	PEACE ON EARTH-LITTLE DRUMMER BOY David Bowie and Bing Crosby	*RCA*	5
4	4	TIME (CLOCK OF THE HEART) Culture Club	*Virgin*	6
5	[5]	OUR HOUSE Madness	*Stiff*	6
6	6	YOU CAN'T HURRY LOVE Phil Collins	*Virgin*	4
7	7	A WINTER'S TALE David Essex	*Mercury*	3
8	8	BEST YEARS OF OUR LIVES Modern Romance	*WEA*	7
9	9	TRULY Lionel Richie	*Motown*	7
10	10	BEAT SURRENDER Jam	*Polydor*	5
11	[11]	LITTLE TOWN Cliff Richard	*EMI*	4
12	12	MIRROR MAN Human League	*Virgin*	7
13	13	YOUNG GUNS (GO FOR IT) Wham!	*Innervision*	8
14	14	ALL THE LOVE IN THE WORLD Dionne Warwick	*Arista*	3
15	15	FRIENDS Shalamar	*Solar*	5
16	16	HYMN Ultravox	*Chrysalis*	6
17	[17]	LET'S GET THIS STRAIGHT (FROM THE START)/OLD Dexy's Midnight Runners	*Mercury*	5
18	18	BUFFALO GALS Malcolm McLaren & the World's Famous Supreme Team	*Charisma*	5
19	[19]	SINGALONG-A-SANTA Santa Claus and the Christmas Trees	*Polydor*	3
20	20	IF YOU CAN'T STAND THE HEAT Bucks Fizz	*RCA*	5
21	21	RIO Duran Duran	*EMI*	8
22	22	LIVING ON THE CEILING Blancmange	*London*	9
23	23	I FEEL LOVE Donna Summer	*Casablanca*	4
24	24	WISHING (IF I HAD A PHOTOGRAPH OF YOU) A Flock Of Seagulls	*Jive*	7
25	25	THE OTHER SIDE OF LOVE Yazoo	*Mute*	7
26	[26]	UNDER ATTACK Abba	*Epic*	3
27	27	WHERE THE HEART IS Soft Cell	*Some Bizzare*	5
28	28	CACHARPAYA (ANDES PUMPSA DESI) Incantation	*Beggars Banquet*	3
29	29	DEAR ADDY Kid Creole and the Coconuts	*Ze*	3
30	30	I DON'T WANNA DANCE Eddy Grant	*Ice*	11
31	31	IT'S RAINING AGAIN Supertramp	*Rondor*	9
32	32	HI DE HI-HI DE HO Kool and the Gang	*De-Lite*	4
33	33	ORVILLE'S SONG Keith Harris and Orville	*BBC*	2
34	34	THEME FROM 'ET (THE EXTRA TERRESTRIAL)' John Williams	*MCA*	2
35	35	TALK TALK Talk Talk	*EMI*	7
36	[36]	I'M GONNA SIT RIGHT DOWN AND WRITE MYSELF A LETTER Barry Manilow	*Arista*	3
37	37	(SEXUAL) HEALING Marvin Gaye	*CBS*	9
38	38	YOUTH OF TODAY Musical Youth	*MCA*	7
39	39	HEARTACHE AVENUE Maisonettes	*Ready Steady Go*	2
40	40	NIGHTPORTER Japan	*Virgin*	6

WEEK ENDING 8 JANUARY 1983

LW	TW	Title / Artist	Label	Wks
1	[1]	SAVE YOUR LOVE Renee and Renato	*Hollywood*	9
6	2	YOU CAN'T HURRY LOVE Phil Collins	*Virgin*	5
7	3	A WINTER'S TALE David Essex	*Mercury*	4
8	[4]	BEST YEARS OF OUR LIVES Modern Romance	*WEA*	8
5	[5]	OUR HOUSE Madness	*Stiff*	7
4	6	TIME (CLOCK OF THE HEART) Culture Club	*Virgin*	7
2	7	THE SHAKIN' STEVENS EP Shakin' Stevens	*Epic*	5
33	8	ORVILLE'S SONG Keith Harris and Orville	*BBC*	3
3	9	PEACE ON EARTH-LITTLE DRUMMER BOY David Bowie and Bing Crosby	*RCA*	6
14	[10]	ALL THE LOVE IN THE WORLD Dionne Warwick	*Arista*	4
18	11	BUFFALO GALS Malcolm McLaren & the World's Famous Supreme Team	*Charisma*	6
16	12	HYMN Ultravox	*Chrysalis*	7
20	13	IF YOU CAN'T STAND THE HEAT Bucks Fizz	*RCA*	6
13	14	YOUNG GUNS (GO FOR IT) Wham!	*Innervision*	9
10	15	BEAT SURRENDER Jam	*Polydor*	6
28	16	CACHARPAYA (ANDES PUMPSA DESI) Incantation	*Beggars Banquet*	4
9	17	TRULY Lionel Richie	*Motown*	8
11	18	LITTLE TOWN Cliff Richard	*EMI*	5
15	19	FRIENDS Shalamar	*Solar*	6
12	20	MIRROR MAN Human League	*Virgin*	8
17	21	LET'S GET THIS STRAIGHT (FROM THE START)/OLD Dexy's Midnight Runners	*Mercury*	6
23	22	I FEEL LOVE Donna Summer	*Casablanca*	5
21	23	RIO Duran Duran	*EMI*	9
34	24	THEME FROM 'ET (THE EXTRA TERRESTRIAL)' John Williams	*MCA*	3
24	25	WISHING (IF I HAD A PHOTOGRAPH OF YOU) A Flock Of Seagulls	*Jive*	8
26	[26]	UNDER ATTACK Abba	*Epic*	4
22	27	LIVING ON THE CEILING Blancmange	*London*	10
25	28	THE OTHER SIDE OF LOVE Yazoo	*Mute*	8
39	29	HEARTACHE AVENUE Maisonettes	*Ready Steady Go*	3
19	30	SINGALONG-A-SANTA Santa Claus and the Christmas Trees	*Polydor*	4
29	31	DEAR ADDY Kid Creole and the Coconuts	*Ze*	4
38	32	YOUTH OF TODAY Musical Youth	*MCA*	8
30	33	I DON'T WANNA DANCE Eddy Grant	*Ice*	12
-	34	THE STORY OF THE BLUES Wah! ●	*Eternal*	1
32	35	HI DE HI - HI DE HO Kool and the Gang	*De-Lite*	5
27	36	WHERE THE HEART IS Soft Cell	*Some Bizzare*	6
37	37	(SEXUAL) HEALING Marvin Gaye	*CBS*	10
-	38	DOWN UNDER Men At Work ●	*Epic*	1
-	39	CHANGES Imagination	*R&B*	1
-	40	EUROPEAN FEMALE Stranglers	*Epic*	1

WEEK ENDING 15 JANUARY 1983

LW	TW	Title / Artist	Label	Wks
2	[1]	YOU CAN'T HURRY LOVE Phil Collins	*Virgin*	6
3	[2]	A WINTER'S TALE David Essex	*Mercury*	5
1	3	SAVE YOUR LOVE Renee and Renato	*Hollywood*	10
8	[4]	ORVILLE'S SONG Keith Harris and Orville	*BBC*	4
4	5	BEST YEARS OF OUR LIVES Modern Romance	*WEA*	9
34	6	THE STORY OF THE BLUES Wah!	*Eternal*	2
38	7	DOWN UNDER Men At Work	*Epic*	2
6	8	TIME (CLOCK OF THE HEART) Culture Club	*Virgin*	8
11	[9]	BUFFALO GALS Malcolm McLaren & the World's Famous Supreme Team	*Charisma*	7
13	[10]	IF YOU CAN'T STAND THE HEAT Bucks Fizz	*RCA*	7
12	[11]	HYMN Ultravox	*Chrysalis*	8
10	12	ALL THE LOVE IN THE WORLD Dionne Warwick	*Arista*	5
5	13	OUR HOUSE Madness	*Stiff*	8
16	14	CACHARPAYA (ANDES PUMPSA DESI) Incantation	*Beggars Banquet*	5
29	15	HEARTACHE AVENUE Maisonettes	*Ready Steady Go*	4
40	16	EUROPEAN FEMALE Stranglers	*Epic*	2
24	[17]	THEME FROM 'ET (THE EXTRA TERRESTRIAL)' John Williams	*MCA*	4
14	18	YOUNG GUNS (GO FOR IT) Wham!	*Innervision*	10
-	19	STEPPIN' OUT Joe Jackson	*A&M*	1
19	20	FRIENDS Shalamar	*Solar*	7
22	[21]	I FEEL LOVE Donna Summer	*Casablanca*	6
-	22	ELECTRIC AVENUE Eddy Grant	*Ice*	1
21	23	LET'S GET THIS STRAIGHT (FROM THE START)/OLD Dexy's Midnight Runners	*Mercury*	7
15	24	BEAT SURRENDER Jam	*Polydor*	7
7	25	THE SHAKIN' STEVENS EP Shakin' Stevens	*Epic*	6
26	[26]	UNDER ATTACK Abba	*Epic*	5
17	27	TRULY Lionel Richie	*Motown*	9
27	28	LIVING ON THE CEILING Blancmange	*London*	11
20	29	MIRROR MAN Human League	*Virgin*	9
25	30	WISHING (IF I HAD A PHOTOGRAPH OF YOU) A Flock Of Seagulls	*Jive*	9
39	[31]	CHANGES Imagination	*R&B*	2
-	32	GLORIA Laura Branigan ●	*Atlantic*	1
23	33	RIO Duran Duran	*EMI*	10
28	34	THE OTHER SIDE OF LOVE Yazoo	*Mute*	9
-	35	MY LOVE IS WAITING Marvin Gaye	*CBS*	1

In these weeks ■ Keith Harris becomes the first ventriloquist to have a top ten hit, and Orville is the first dummy in the top five (15.01.83) ■ Four weeks at no. 26 for Abba's *Under Attack* (15.01.83) ■ David Bowie and Bing Crosby's *Peace On Earth - Little Drummer Boy* medley duet falls from number 9 out of the top 40 (15.01.83)■

LW	TW	Title / Artist	Label	Wks
-	36	MIND UP TONIGHT Melba Moore	*Capitol*	1
-	37	OH DIANE Fleetwood Mac	*Warner Brothers*	1
-	38	HOLD ME TIGHTER IN THE RAIN Billy Griffin ●	*CBS*	1
31	39	DEAR ADDY Kid Creole and the Coconuts	*Ze*	5
37	40	(SEXUAL) HEALING Marvin Gaye	*CBS*	11

WEEK ENDING 22 JANUARY 1983

LW	TW	Title / Artist	Label	Wks
1	[1]	YOU CAN'T HURRY LOVE Phil Collins	*Virgin*	7
7	2	DOWN UNDER Men At Work	*Epic*	3
6	[3]	THE STORY OF THE BLUES Wah!	*Eternal*	3
22	4	ELECTRIC AVENUE Eddy Grant	*Ice*	2
4	5	ORVILLE'S SONG Keith Harris and Orville	*BBC*	5
2	6	A WINTER'S TALE David Essex	*Mercury*	6
15	[7]	HEARTACHE AVENUE Maisonettes	*Ready Steady Go*	5
19	8	STEPPIN' OUT Joe Jackson	*A&M*	2
16	[9]	EUROPEAN FEMALE Stranglers	*Epic*	3
13	10	OUR HOUSE Madness	*Stiff*	9
9	11	BUFFALO GALS Malcolm McLaren & the World's Famous Supreme Team	*Charisma*	8
14	[12]	CACHARPAYA (ANDES PUMPSA DESI) Incantation	*Beggars Banquet*	6
3	13	SAVE YOUR LOVE Renee and Renato	*Hollywood*	11
5	14	BEST YEARS OF OUR LIVES Modern Romance	*WEA*	10
12	15	ALL THE LOVE IN THE WORLD Dionne Warwick	*Arista*	6
10	16	IF YOU CAN'T STAND THE HEAT Bucks Fizz	*RCA*	8
8	17	TIME (CLOCK OF THE HEART) Culture Club	*Virgin*	9
11	18	HYMN Ultravox	*Chrysalis*	9
-	19	SIGN OF THE TIMES Belle Stars	*Stiff*	1
32	20	GLORIA Laura Branigan	*Atlantic*	2
17	21	THEME FROM 'ET (THE EXTRA TERRESTRIAL)' John Williams	*MCA*	5
21	22	I FEEL LOVE Donna Summer	*Casablanca*	7
-	23	NEW YEAR'S DAY U2	*Island*	1
-	24	TWISTING BY THE POOL Dire Straits	*Vertigo*	1
36	25	MIND UP TONIGHT Melba Moore	*Capitol*	2
37	26	OH DIANE Fleetwood Mac	*Warner Brothers*	2
-	27	THE CUTTER Echo and the Bunnymen	*Korova*	1
38	28	HOLD ME TIGHTER IN THE RAIN Billy Griffin	*CBS*	2
18	29	YOUNG GUNS (GO FOR IT) Wham!	*Innervision*	11
20	30	FRIENDS Shalamar	*Solar*	8
-	31	UP WHERE WE BELONG Joe Cocker and Jennifer Warnes ●	*Island*	1
-	32	PLEASE PLEASE ME Beatles	*Parlophone*	1
-	33	TOO SHY Kajagoogoo ●	*EMI*	1
35	[34]	MY LOVE IS WAITING Marvin Gaye	*CBS*	2
-	35	THE CHINESE WAY Level 42	*Polydor*	1
23	36	LET'S GET THIS STRAIGHT (FROM THE START)/OLD Dexy's Midnight Runners	*Mercury*	8
28	37	LIVING ON THE CEILING Blancmange	*London*	12
-	38	IN THE NAME OF LOVE Sharon Redd	*Prelude*	1
27	39	TRULY Lionel Richie	*Motown*	10
31	40	CHANGES Imagination	*R&B*	3

WEEK ENDING 29 JANUARY 1983

LW	TW	Title / Artist	Label	Wks
2	[1]	DOWN UNDER Men At Work	*Epic*	4
1	2	YOU CAN'T HURRY LOVE Phil Collins	*Virgin*	8
4	3	ELECTRIC AVENUE Eddy Grant	*Ice*	3
3	4	THE STORY OF THE BLUES Wah!	*Eternal*	4
19	5	SIGN OF THE TIMES Belle Stars	*Stiff*	2
8	[6]	STEPPIN' OUT Joe Jackson	*A&M*	3
7	[7]	HEARTACHE AVENUE Maisonettes	*Ready Steady Go*	6
20	8	GLORIA Laura Branigan	*Atlantic*	3
5	9	ORVILLE'S SONG Keith Harris and Orville	*BBC*	6
33	10	TOO SHY Kajagoogoo	*EMI*	2
27	11	THE CUTTER Echo and the Bunnymen	*Korova*	2
23	12	NEW YEAR'S DAY U2	*Island*	2
9	13	EUROPEAN FEMALE Stranglers	*Epic*	4
12	14	CACHARPAYA (ANDES PUMPSA DESI) Incantation	*Beggars Banquet*	7
6	15	A WINTER'S TALE David Essex	*Mercury*	7
11	16	BUFFALO GALS Malcolm McLaren & the World's Famous Supreme Team	*Charisma*	9
24	17	TWISTING BY THE POOL Dire Straits	*Vertigo*	2
26	18	OH DIANE Fleetwood Mac	*Warner Brothers*	3
28	19	HOLD ME TIGHTER IN THE RAIN Billy Griffin	*CBS*	3
13	20	SAVE YOUR LOVE Renee and Renato	*Hollywood*	12
10	21	OUR HOUSE Madness	*Stiff*	10
25	[22]	MIND UP TONIGHT Melba Moore	*Capitol*	3
15	23	ALL THE LOVE IN THE WORLD Dionne Warwick	*Arista*	7
-	24	LAST NIGHT A DJ SAVED MY LIFE Indeep ●	*Sound Of New York*	1
31	25	UP WHERE WE BELONG Joe Cocker and Jennifer Warnes	*Island*	2
17	26	TIME (CLOCK OF THE HEART) Culture Club	*Virgin*	10
18	27	HYMN Ultravox	*Chrysalis*	10
14	28	BEST YEARS OF OUR LIVES Modern Romance	*WEA*	11
32	[29]	PLEASE PLEASE ME Beatles	*Parlophone*	2
21	30	THEME FROM 'ET (THE EXTRA TERRESTRIAL)' John Williams	*MCA*	6
38	[31]	IN THE NAME OF LOVE Sharon Redd	*Prelude*	2
16	32	IF YOU CAN'T STAND THE HEAT Bucks Fizz	*RCA*	9
22	33	I FEEL LOVE Donna Summer	*Casablanca*	8
-	34	WHAM RAP (ENJOY WHAT YOU DO) Wham!	*Innervision*	1
35	35	THE CHINESE WAY Level 42	*Polydor*	2
-	36	DOWN IN THE TUBE STATION AT MIDNIGHT Jam	*Polydor*	1
-	37	GOING UNDERGROUND/DREAMS OF CHILDREN Jam	*Polydor*	1
-	38	ALL AROUND THE WORLD Jam	*Polydor*	1
-	39	NEWS OF THE WORLD Jam	*Polydor*	1
-	40	NATURE BOY Central Line ●	*Mercury*	1

February 1983

□ Highest position disc reached ● Act's first ever week on chart

WEEK ENDING 5 FEBRUARY 1983

LW	TW	Title / Artist	Label	Wks
2	[1]	DOWN UNDER Men At Work	*Epic*	5
3	[2]	ELECTRIC AVENUE Eddy Grant	*Ice*	4
2	3	YOU CAN'T HURRY LOVE Phil Collins	*Virgin*	9
5	4	SIGN OF THE TIMES Belle Stars	*Stiff*	3
10	5	TOO SHY Kajagoogoo	*EMI*	3
8	[6]	GLORIA Laura Branigan	*Atlantic*	4
4	7	THE STORY OF THE BLUES Wah!	*Eternal*	5
11	[8]	THE CUTTER Echo and the Bunnymen	*Korova*	3
6	9	STEPPIN' OUT Joe Jackson	*A&M*	4
12	[10]	NEW YEAR'S DAY U2	*Island*	3
34	11	WHAM RAP (ENJOY WHAT YOU DO) Wham!	*Innervision*	2
25	12	UP WHERE WE BELONG Joe Cocker and Jennifer Warnes	*Island*	3
7	13	HEARTACHE AVENUE Maisonettes	*Ready Steady Go*	7
17	[14]	TWISTING BY THE POOL Dire Straits	*Vertigo*	3
24	15	LAST NIGHT A DJ SAVED MY LIFE Indeep	*Sound Of New York*	2
18	16	OH DIANE Fleetwood Mac	*Warner Brothers*	4
19	[17]	HOLD ME TIGHTER IN THE RAIN Billy Griffin	*CBS*	4
9	18	ORVILLE'S SONG Keith Harris and Orville	*BBC*	7
-	19	CHANGE Tears For Fears	*Mercury*	1
-	20	BILLIE JEAN Michael Jackson	*Epic*	1
37	[21]	GOING UNDERGROUND/DREAMS OF CHILDREN Jam	*Polydor*	2
-	22	CHRISTIAN China Crisis ●	*Virgin*	1
16	23	BUFFALO GALS Malcolm McLaren & the World's Famous Supreme Team	*Charisma*	10
22	24	MIND UP TONIGHT Melba Moore	*Capitol*	4
35	25	THE CHINESE WAY Level 42	*Polydor*	3
14	26	CACHARPAYA (ANDES PUMPSA DESI) Incantation	*Beggars Banquet*	8
40	27	NATURE BOY Central Line	*Mercury*	2
13	28	EUROPEAN FEMALE Stranglers	*Epic*	5
15	29	A WINTER'S TALE David Essex	*Mercury*	8
36	[30]	DOWN IN THE TUBE STATION AT MIDNIGHT Jam	*Polydor*	2
29	31	PLEASE PLEASE ME Beatles	*Parlophone*	3

■Two 'Avenues' and a 'House' in the Top Ten (22.01.83) ■ Jam announce their split, Polydor re-release practically all their singles, and four of them take consecutive positions from 36 to 39 (29.01.83) ■ *Please Please Me* is less successful twenty years on than it had been in 1963, and also unlike 1963, less successful than *Love Me Do* (29.01.83)■

February 1983

□ Highest position disc reached ● Act's first ever week on chart

LW	TW	Title / Artist	Label	Wks
-	32	THE HARDER THEY COME Rockers Revenge featuring Donnie Calvin	London	1
-	33	1999 Prince ●	Warner Brothers	1
23	34	ALL THE LOVE IN THE WORLD Dionne Warwick	Arista	8
21	35	OUR HOUSE Madness	Stiff	11
-	36	SHINY SHINY Haysi Fantayzee	Regard	1
31	37	IN THE NAME OF LOVE Sharon Redd	Prelude	3
-	38	LOVE ON YOUR SIDE Thompson Twins ●	Arista	1
-	39	AFRICA Toto	CBS	1
20	40	SAVE YOUR LOVE Renee and Renato	Hollywood	13

WEEK ENDING 12 FEBRUARY 1983

LW	TW	Title / Artist	Label	Wks
1	[1]	DOWN UNDER Men At Work	Epic	6
5	2	TOO SHY Kajagoogoo	EMI	4
2	3	ELECTRIC AVENUE Eddy Grant	Ice	5
4	4	SIGN OF THE TIMES Belle Stars	Stiff	4
19	5	CHANGE Tears For Fears	Mercury	2
6	[6]	GLORIA Laura Branigan	Atlantic	5
12	[7]	UP WHERE WE BELONG Joe Cocker and Jennifer Warnes	Island	4
3	8	YOU CAN'T HURRY LOVE Phil Collins	Virgin	10
11	9	WHAM RAP (ENJOY WHAT YOU DO) Wham!	Innervision	3
16	10	OH DIANE Fleetwood Mac	Warner Brothers	5
8	11	THE CUTTER Echo and the Bunnymen	Korova	4
7	12	THE STORY OF THE BLUES Wah!	Eternal	6
10	13	NEW YEAR'S DAY U2	Island	4
15	14	LAST NIGHT A DJ SAVED MY LIFE Indeep	Sound Of New York	3
14	15	TWISTING BY THE POOL Dire Straits	Vertigo	4
9	16	STEPPIN' OUT Joe Jackson	A&M	5
20	17	BILLIE JEAN Michael Jackson	Epic	2
22	18	CHRISTIAN China Crisis	Virgin	2
39	19	AFRICA Toto	CBS	2
17	20	HOLD ME TIGHTER IN THE RAIN Billy Griffin	CBS	5
27	[21]	NATURE BOY Central Line	Mercury	3
21	22	GOING UNDERGROUND/DREAMS OF CHILDREN Jam	Polydor	3
13	23	HEARTACHE AVENUE Maisonettes	Ready Steady Go	8
25	[24]	THE CHINESE WAY Level 42	Polydor	4
33	[25]	1999 Prince	Warner Brothers	2
-	26	THE TUNNEL OF LOVE Fun Boy Three	Chrysalis	1
38	27	LOVE ON YOUR SIDE Thompson Twins	Arista	2
36	28	SHINY SHINY Haysi Fantayzee	Regard	2
-	29	JAILHOUSE ROCK Elvis Presley	RCA	1
32	[30]	THE HARDER THEY COME Rockers Revenge featuring Donnie Calvin	London	2
18	31	ORVILLE'S SONG Keith Harris and Orville	BBC	8
-	32	GET THE BALANCE RIGHT Depeche Mode	Mute	1
-	33	COLD SWEAT Thin Lizzy	Vertigo	1
30	34	DOWN IN THE TUBE STATION AT MIDNIGHT Jam	Polydor	3
-	[35]	HE KNOWS YOU KNOW Marillion ●	EMI	1
24	36	MIND UP TONIGHT Melba Moore	Capitol	5
23	37	BUFFALO GALS Malcolm McLaren & the World's Famous Supreme Team	Charisma	11
-	38	BABY COME TO ME Patti Austin and James Ingram ●	Qwest	1
-	39	HEY LITTLE GIRL Icehouse ●	Chrysalis	1
-	40	NEVER GONNA GIVE YOU UP Musical Youth	MCA	1

WEEK ENDING 19 FEBRUARY 1983

LW	TW	Title / Artist	Label	Wks
2	[1]	TOO SHY Kajagoogoo	EMI	5
1	2	DOWN UNDER Men At Work	Epic	7
4	[3]	SIGN OF THE TIMES Belle Stars	Stiff	5
5	[4]	CHANGE Tears For Fears	Mercury	3
17	5	BILLIE JEAN Michael Jackson	Epic	3
19	6	AFRICA Toto	CBS	3
7	[7]	UP WHERE WE BELONG Joe Cocker and Jennifer Warnes	Island	5
9	[8]	WHAM RAP (ENJOY WHAT YOU DO) Wham!	Innervision	4
10	[9]	OH DIANE Fleetwood Mac	Warner Brothers	6
3	10	ELECTRIC AVENUE Eddy Grant	Ice	6
6	11	GLORIA Laura Branigan	Atlantic	6
18	[12]	CHRISTIAN China Crisis	Virgin	3
14	[13]	LAST NIGHT A DJ SAVED MY LIFE Indeep	Sound Of New York	4
26	14	THE TUNNEL OF LOVE Fun Boy Three	Chrysalis	2
27	15	LOVE ON YOUR SIDE Thompson Twins	Arista	3
40	16	NEVER GONNA GIVE YOU UP Musical Youth	MCA	2
8	17	YOU CAN'T HURRY LOVE Phil Collins	Virgin	11
11	18	THE CUTTER Echo and the Bunnymen	Korova	5
15	19	TWISTING BY THE POOL Dire Straits	Vertigo	5
12	20	THE STORY OF THE BLUES Wah!	Eternal	7
13	21	NEW YEAR'S DAY U2	Island	5
32	22	GET THE BALANCE RIGHT Depeche Mode	Mute	2
28	23	SHINY SHINY Haysi Fantayzee	Regard	3
-	24	TOMORROW'S (JUST ANOTHER DAY)/MADNESS IS ALL IN THE MIND Madness	Stiff	1
21	25	NATURE BOY Central Line	Mercury	4
25	26	1999 Prince	Warner Brothers	3
29	[27]	JAILHOUSE ROCK Elvis Presley	RCA	2
33	28	COLD SWEAT Thin Lizzy	Vertigo	2
24	29	THE CHINESE WAY Level 42	Polydor	5
16	30	STEPPIN' OUT Joe Jackson	A&M	6
20	31	HOLD ME TIGHTER IN THE RAIN Billy Griffin	CBS	6
30	32	THE HARDER THEY COME Rockers Revenge featuring Donnie Calvin	London	3
-	33	COMMUNICATION Spandau Ballet	Reformation	1
39	34	HEY LITTLE GIRL Icehouse	Chrysalis	2
38	35	BABY COME TO ME Patti Austin and James Ingram	Qwest	2
22	36	GOING UNDERGROUND/DREAMS OF CHILDREN Jam	Polydor	4
-	37	GENETIC ENGINEERING Orchestral Manoeuvres In The Dark	Telegraph	1
-	38	SWEET DREAMS (ARE MADE OF THIS) Eurythmics ●	RCA	1
35	39	HE KNOWS YOU KNOW Marillion	EMI	2
-	40	SHE MEANS NOTHING TO ME Phil Everly and Cliff Richard ●	Capitol	1

WEEK ENDING 26 FEBRUARY 1983

LW	TW	Title / Artist	Label	Wks
1	[1]	TOO SHY Kajagoogoo	EMI	6
5	2	BILLIE JEAN Michael Jackson	Epic	4
6	[3]	AFRICA Toto	CBS	4
4	[4]	CHANGE Tears For Fears	Mercury	4
3	5	SIGN OF THE TIMES Belle Stars	Stiff	6
2	6	DOWN UNDER Men At Work	Epic	8
7	[7]	UP WHERE WE BELONG Joe Cocker and Jennifer Warnes	Island	6
16	8	NEVER GONNA GIVE YOU UP Musical Youth	MCA	3
24	9	TOMORROW'S (JUST ANOTHER DAY)/MADNESS IS ALL IN THE MIND Madness	Stiff	2
8	10	WHAM RAP (ENJOY WHAT YOU DO) Wham!	Innervision	5
14	11	THE TUNNEL OF LOVE Fun Boy Three	Chrysalis	3
15	12	LOVE ON YOUR SIDE Thompson Twins	Arista	4
9	13	OH DIANE Fleetwood Mac	Warner Brothers	7
-	14	TOTAL ECLIPSE OF THE HEART Bonnie Tyler	CBS	1
12	15	CHRISTIAN China Crisis	Virgin	4
23	[16]	SHINY SHINY Haysi Fantayzee	Regard	4
34	[17]	HEY LITTLE GIRL Icehouse	Chrysalis	3
13	18	LAST NIGHT A DJ SAVED MY LIFE Indeep	Sound Of New York	5
35	19	BABY COME TO ME Patti Austin and James Ingram	Qwest	3
11	20	GLORIA Laura Branigan	Atlantic	7
38	21	SWEET DREAMS (ARE MADE OF THIS) Eurythmics	RCA	2
22	22	GET THE BALANCE RIGHT Depeche Mode	Mute	3
10	23	ELECTRIC AVENUE Eddy Grant	Ice	7
33	24	COMMUNICATION Spandau Ballet	Reformation	2
37	25	GENETIC ENGINEERING Orchestral Manoeuvres In The Dark	Telegraph	2
17	26	YOU CAN'T HURRY LOVE Phil Collins	Virgin	12

In these weeks ■ One of the most prolific and influential acts of the 1980s, Prince, makes his chart debut (05.02.83) ■ His *1999* peaks at number 25, but one year later it will become his biggest chart hit, reaching number 2 (12.02.83)■

LW	TW	Title	Artist	Label	Wks
28	27	COLD SWEAT	Thin Lizzy	Vertigo	3
20	28	THE STORY OF THE BLUES	Wah!	Eternal	8
40	29	SHE MEANS NOTHING TO ME	Phil Everly and Cliff Richard	Capitol	2
-	30	WAVES	Blancmange	London	1
25	31	NATURE BOY	Central Line	Mercury	5
18	32	THE CUTTER	Echo and the Bunnymen	Korova	6
32	33	THE HARDER THEY COME	Rockers Revenge featuring Donnie Calvin	London	4
26	34	1999	Prince	Warner Brothers	4
-	35	ROCK THE BOAT	Forrest ●	CBS	1
21	36	NEW YEAR'S DAY	U2	Island	6
27	37	JAILHOUSE ROCK	Elvis Presley	RCA	3
19	38	TWISTING BY THE POOL	Dire Straits	Vertigo	6
29	39	THE CHINESE WAY	Level 42	Polydor	6
-	40	NA NA HEY HEY KISS HIM GOODBYE	Bananarama	London	1

WEEK ENDING 5 MARCH 1983

LW	TW	Title	Artist	Label	Wks
2	1	BILLIE JEAN	Michael Jackson	Epic	5
14	2	TOTAL ECLIPSE OF THE HEART	Bonnie Tyler	CBS	2
1	3	TOO SHY	Kajagoogoo	EMI	7
6	4	AFRICA	Toto	CBS	5
21	5	SWEET DREAMS (ARE MADE OF THIS)	Eurythmics	RCA	3
8	6	NEVER GONNA GIVE YOU UP	Musical Youth	MCA	4
4	7	CHANGE	Tears For Fears	Mercury	5
9	8	TOMORROW'S (JUST ANOTHER DAY)/MADNESS IS ALL IN THE MIND	Madness	Stiff	3
12	9	LOVE ON YOUR SIDE	Thompson Twins	Arista	5
11	10	THE TUNNEL OF LOVE	Fun Boy Three	Chrysalis	4
7	11	UP WHERE WE BELONG	Joe Cocker and Jennifer Warnes	Island	7
35	12	ROCK THE BOAT	Forrest	CBS	2
22	13	GET THE BALANCE RIGHT	Depeche Mode	Mute	4
10	14	WHAM RAP (ENJOY WHAT YOU DO)	Wham!	Innervision	6
24	15	COMMUNICATION	Spandau Ballet	Reformation	3
5	16	SIGN OF THE TIMES	Belle Stars	Stiff	7
17	17	HEY LITTLE GIRL	Icehouse	Chrysalis	4
19	18	BABY COME TO ME	Patti Austin and James Ingram	Qwest	4
29	19	SHE MEANS NOTHING TO ME	Phil Everly and Cliff Richard	Capitol	3
16	20	SHINY SHINY	Haysi Fantayzee	Regard	5
40	21	NA NA HEY HEY KISS HIM GOODBYE	Bananarama	London	2
6	22	DOWN UNDER	Men At Work	Epic	9
13	23	OH DIANE	Fleetwood Mac	Warner Brothers	8
15	24	CHRISTIAN	China Crisis	Virgin	5
25	25	GENETIC ENGINEERING	Orchestral Manoeuvres In The Dark	Telegraph	3
30	26	WAVES	Blancmange	London	2
18	27	LAST NIGHT A DJ SAVED MY LIFE	Indeep	Sound Of New York	6
-	28	HIGH LIFE	Modern Romance	WEA	1
20	29	GLORIA	Laura Branigan	Atlantic	8
-	30	YOU CAN'T HIDE (YOUR LOVE FROM ME)	David Joseph ●	Island	1
-	31	RIP IT UP	Orange Juice ●	Polydor	1
-	32	SOWETO	Malcolm McLaren	Charisma	1
27	33	COLD SWEAT	Thin Lizzy	Vertigo	4
-	34	WE'VE GOT TONIGHT	Kenny Rogers and Sheena Easton ●	Liberty	1
34	35	1999	Prince	Warner Brothers	5
23	36	ELECTRIC AVENUE	Eddy Grant	Ice	8
26	37	YOU CAN'T HURRY LOVE	Phil Collins	Virgin	13
-	38	MIDNIGHT SUMMER DREAM	Stranglers	Epic	1
-	39	DROP THE PILOT	Joan Armatrading	A&M	1
-	40	NUMBERS/BARRIERS	Soft Cell	Some Bizzare	1

WEEK ENDING 12 MARCH 1983

March 1983

□ Highest position disc reached ● Act's first ever week on chart

LW	TW	Title	Artist	Label	Wks
2	1	TOTAL ECLIPSE OF THE HEART	Bonnie Tyler	CBS	3
1	2	BILLIE JEAN	Michael Jackson	Epic	6
5	3	SWEET DREAMS (ARE MADE OF THIS)	Eurythmics	RCA	4
12	4	ROCK THE BOAT	Forrest	CBS	3
4	5	AFRICA	Toto	CBS	6
3	6	TOO SHY	Kajagoogoo	EMI	8
21	7	NA NA HEY HEY KISS HIM GOODBYE	Bananarama	London	3
8	8	TOMORROW'S (JUST ANOTHER DAY)/MADNESS IS ALL IN THE MIND	Madness	Stiff	4
9	9	LOVE ON YOUR SIDE	Thompson Twins	Arista	6
6	10	NEVER GONNA GIVE YOU UP	Musical Youth	MCA	5
18	11	BABY COME TO ME	Patti Austin and James Ingram	Qwest	5
15	12	COMMUNICATION	Spandau Ballet	Reformation	4
10	13	THE TUNNEL OF LOVE	Fun Boy Three	Chrysalis	5
19	14	SHE MEANS NOTHING TO ME	Phil Everly and Cliff Richard	Capitol	4
13	15	GET THE BALANCE RIGHT	Depeche Mode	Mute	5
7	16	CHANGE	Tears For Fears	Mercury	6
17	17	HEY LITTLE GIRL	Icehouse	Chrysalis	5
28	18	HIGH LIFE	Modern Romance	WEA	2
11	19	UP WHERE WE BELONG	Joe Cocker and Jennifer Warnes	Island	8
25	20	GENETIC ENGINEERING	Orchestral Manoeuvres In The Dark	Telegraph	4
26	21	WAVES	Blancmange	London	3
31	22	RIP IT UP	Orange Juice	Polydor	2
14	23	WHAM RAP (ENJOY WHAT YOU DO)	Wham!	Innervision	7
30	24	YOU CAN'T HIDE (YOUR LOVE FROM ME)	David Joseph	Island	2
40	25	NUMBERS/BARRIERS	Soft Cell	Some Bizzare	2
20	26	SHINY SHINY	Haysi Fantayzee	Regard	6
16	27	SIGN OF THE TIMES	Belle Stars	Stiff	8
34	28	WE'VE GOT TONIGHT	Kenny Rogers and Sheena Easton	Liberty	2
39	29	DROP THE PILOT	Joan Armatrading	A&M	2
23	30	OH DIANE	Fleetwood Mac	Warner Brothers	9
-	31	RUN FOR YOUR LIFE	Bucks Fizz	RCA	1
22	32	DOWN UNDER	Men At Work	Epic	10
32	33	SOWETO	Malcolm McLaren	Charisma	2
24	34	CHRISTIAN	China Crisis	Virgin	6
38	35	MIDNIGHT SUMMER DREAM	Stranglers	Epic	2
27	36	LAST NIGHT A DJ SAVED MY LIFE	Indeep	Sound Of New York	10
-	37	FIELDS OF FIRE (400 MILES)	Big Country ●	Mercury	1
-	38	JOY	Band AKA ●	Epic	1
-	39	MAGGIE	Foster and Allen	Ritz	1
-	40	GARDEN PARTY	Mezzoforte ●	Steinar	1

WEEK ENDING 19 MARCH 1983

LW	TW	Title	Artist	Label	Wks
1	1	TOTAL ECLIPSE OF THE HEART	Bonnie Tyler	CBS	4
3	2	SWEET DREAMS (ARE MADE OF THIS)	Eurythmics	RCA	5
2	3	BILLIE JEAN	Michael Jackson	Epic	7
4	4	ROCK THE BOAT	Forrest	CBS	4
7	5	NA NA HEY HEY KISS HIM GOODBYE	Bananarama	London	4
-	6	SPEAK LIKE A CHILD	Style Council ●	Polydor	1
5	7	AFRICA	Toto	CBS	7
18	8	HIGH LIFE	Modern Romance	WEA	3
14	9	SHE MEANS NOTHING TO ME	Phil Everly and Cliff Richard	Capitol	5
22	10	RIP IT UP	Orange Juice	Polydor	3
11	11	BABY COME TO ME	Patti Austin and James Ingram	Qwest	6
9	12	LOVE ON YOUR SIDE	Thompson Twins	Arista	7
12	13	COMMUNICATION	Spandau Ballet	Reformation	5
6	14	TOO SHY	Kajagoogoo	EMI	9
8	15	TOMORROW'S (JUST ANOTHER DAY)/MADNESS IS ALL IN THE MIND	Madness	Stiff	5
24	16	YOU CAN'T HIDE (YOUR LOVE FROM ME)	David Joseph	Island	3
10	17	NEVER GONNA GIVE YOU UP	Musical Youth	MCA	6
13	18	THE TUNNEL OF LOVE	Fun Boy Three	Chrysalis	6
21	19	WAVES	Blancmange	London	4
17	20	HEY LITTLE GIRL	Icehouse	Chrysalis	6

■Icehouse's *Hey Little Girl* is not the same song as Del Shannon's 1962 hit, Orange Juice's *Rip It Up* is not the Elvis Presley/Little Richard classic and Laura Branigan's *Gloria* is not the Them hit. However, *Rock The Boat* is a remake of the Hues Corporation hit, Phil Collins' *You Can't Hurry Love* and the Supremes' song and Bananarama's hit is a new version of the Steam classic (05.03.83)■

March 1983

☐ Highest position disc reached ● Act's first ever week on chart

LW	TW	Title	Artist	Label	Wks
31	21	RUN FOR YOUR LIFE	Bucks Fizz	RCA	2
20	22	GENETIC ENGINEERING	Orchestral Manoeuvres In The Dark	Telegraph	5
19	23	UP WHERE WE BELONG	Joe Cocker and Jennifer Warnes	Island	9
38	[24]	JOY	Band AKA	Epic	2
16	25	CHANGE	Tears For Fears	Mercury	7
15	26	GET THE BALANCE RIGHT	Depeche Mode	Mute	6
39	[27]	MAGGIE	Foster and Allen	Ritz	2
29	28	DROP THE PILOT	Joan Armatrading	A&M	3
40	29	GARDEN PARTY	Mezzoforte	Steinar	2
-	30	VISIONS IN BLUE	Ultravox	Chrysalis	1
25	31	NUMBERS/BARRIERS	Soft Cell	Some Bizzare	3
-	32	BOXERBEAT	JoBoxers ●	RCA	1
28	33	WE'VE GOT TONIGHT	Kenny Rogers and Sheena Easton	Liberty	3
37	34	FIELDS OF FIRE (400 MILES)	Big Country	Mercury	2
-	35	ORCHARD ROAD	Leo Sayer	Chrysalis	1
-	36	DON'T TALK TO ME ABOUT LOVE	Altered Images	Epic	1
-	37	BLUE MONDAY	New Order	Factory	1
-	[38]	ALL TOMORROW'S PARTIES	Japan	Hansa	1
23	39	WHAM RAP (ENJOY WHAT YOU DO)	Wham!	Innervision	8
33	40	SOWETO	Malcolm McLaren	Charisma	3

WEEK ENDING 26 MARCH 1983

LW	TW	Title	Artist	Label	Wks
-	[1]	IS THERE SOMETHING I SHOULD KNOW	Duran Duran	EMI	1
1	2	TOTAL ECLIPSE OF THE HEART	Bonnie Tyler	CBS	5
2	3	SWEET DREAMS (ARE MADE OF THIS)	Eurythmics	RCA	6
6	[4]	SPEAK LIKE A CHILD	Style Council	Polydor	2
-	5	LET'S DANCE	David Bowie	EMI America	1
4	6	ROCK THE BOAT	Forrest	CBS	5
5	7	NA NA HEY HEY KISS HIM GOODBYE	Bananarama	London	5
3	8	BILLIE JEAN	Michael Jackson	Epic	8
10	9	RIP IT UP	Orange Juice	Polydor	4
8	10	HIGH LIFE	Modern Romance	WEA	4
28	[11]	DROP THE PILOT	Joan Armatrading	A&M	4
36	12	DON'T TALK TO ME ABOUT LOVE	Altered Images	Epic	2
16	[13]	YOU CAN'T HIDE (YOUR LOVE FROM ME)	David Joseph	Island	4
21	[14]	RUN FOR YOUR LIFE	Bucks Fizz	RCA	3
30	[15]	VISIONS IN BLUE	Ultravox	Chrysalis	2
9	16	SHE MEANS NOTHING TO ME	Phil Everly and Cliff Richard	Capitol	6
29	[17]	GARDEN PARTY	Mezzoforte	Steinar	3
11	18	BABY COME TO ME	Patti Austin and James Ingram	Qwest	7
19	[19]	WAVES	Blancmange	London	5
13	20	COMMUNICATION	Spandau Ballet	Reformation	6
32	21	BOXERBEAT	JoBoxers	RCA	2
12	22	LOVE ON YOUR SIDE	Thompson Twins	Arista	8
7	23	AFRICA	Toto	CBS	8
37	24	BLUE MONDAY	New Order	Factory	2
24	25	JOY	Band AKA	Epic	3
-	26	WHISTLE DOWN THE WIND	Nick Heyward ●	Arista	1
35	27	ORCHARD ROAD	Leo Sayer	Chrysalis	2
27	28	MAGGIE	Foster and Allen	Ritz	3
14	29	TOO SHY	Kajagoogoo	EMI	10
15	30	TOMORROW'S (JUST ANOTHER DAY)/MADNESS IS ALL IN THE MIND	Madness	Stiff	6
34	31	FIELDS OF FIRE (400 MILES)	Big Country	Mercury	3
22	32	GENETIC ENGINEERING	Orchestral Manoeuvres In The Dark	Telegraph	6
20	33	HEY LITTLE GIRL	Icehouse	Chrysalis	7
18	34	THE TUNNEL OF LOVE	Fun Boy Three	Chrysalis	7
17	35	NEVER GONNA GIVE YOU UP	Musical Youth	MCA	7
-	36	CRY ME A RIVER	Mari Wilson	Compact	1
23	37	UP WHERE WE BELONG	Joe Cocker and Jennifer Warnes	Island	10
-	38	BREAKAWAY	Tracey Ullman ●	Stiff	1
-	39	HOPE (I WISH YOU'D BELIEVE ME)	Wah!	WEA	1
26	40	GET THE BALANCE RIGHT	Depeche Mode	Mute	7

WEEK ENDING 2 APRIL 1983

LW	TW	Title	Artist	Label	Wks
1	[1]	IS THERE SOMETHING I SHOULD KNOW	Duran Duran	EMI	2
5	2	LET'S DANCE	David Bowie	EMI America	2
2	3	TOTAL ECLIPSE OF THE HEART	Bonnie Tyler	CBS	6
4	[4]	SPEAK LIKE A CHILD	Style Council	Polydor	3
3	5	SWEET DREAMS (ARE MADE OF THIS)	Eurythmics	RCA	7
21	6	BOXERBEAT	JoBoxers	RCA	3
12	[7]	DON'T TALK TO ME ABOUT LOVE	Altered Images	Epic	3
9	8	RIP IT UP	Orange Juice	Polydor	5
7	9	NA NA HEY HEY KISS HIM GOODBYE	Bananarama	London	6
6	10	ROCK THE BOAT	Forrest	CBS	6
8	11	BILLIE JEAN	Michael Jackson	Epic	9
11	12	DROP THE PILOT	Joan Armatrading	A&M	5
31	13	FIELDS OF FIRE (400 MILES)	Big Country	Mercury	4
13	14	YOU CAN'T HIDE (YOUR LOVE FROM ME)	David Joseph	Island	5
26	15	WHISTLE DOWN THE WIND	Nick Heyward	Arista	2
27	[16]	ORCHARD ROAD	Leo Sayer	Chrysalis	3
24	17	BLUE MONDAY	New Order	Factory	3
38	18	BREAKAWAY	Tracey Ullman	Stiff	2
17	19	GARDEN PARTY	Mezzoforte	Steinar	4
-	20	OOH TO BE AH	Kajagoogoo	EMI	1
14	21	RUN FOR YOUR LIFE	Bucks Fizz	RCA	4
15	22	VISIONS IN BLUE	Ultravox	Chrysalis	3
10	23	HIGH LIFE	Modern Romance	WEA	5
-	24	TWO HEARTS BEAT AS ONE	U2	Island	1
19	25	WAVES	Blancmange	London	6
25	26	JOY	Band AKA	Epic	4
-	27	SNOT RAP	Kenny Everett ●	RCA	1
18	28	BABY COME TO ME	Patti Austin and James Ingram	Qwest	8
20	29	COMMUNICATION	Spandau Ballet	Reformation	7
36	30	CRY ME A RIVER	Mari Wilson	Compact	2
16	31	SHE MEANS NOTHING TO ME	Phil Everly and Cliff Richard	Capitol	7
-	32	I AM (I'M ME)	Twisted Sister ●	Atlantic	1
28	33	MAGGIE	Foster and Allen	Ritz	4
22	34	LOVE ON YOUR SIDE	Thompson Twins	Arista	9
23	35	AFRICA	Toto	CBS	9
-	36	THE CELTIC SOUL BROTHERS	Kevin Rowland and Dexy's Midnight Runners	Mercury	1
39	[37]	HOPE (I WISH YOU'D BELIEVE ME)	Wah!	WEA	2
-	38	THE HOUSE THAT JACK BUILT	Tracie ●	Respond	1
-	39	WORDS	FR David ●	Carrere	1
-	40	YOUNG FREE AND SINGLE	Sunfire ●	Warner Brothers	1

WEEK ENDING 9 APRIL 1983

LW	TW	Title	Artist	Label	Wks
2	[1]	LET'S DANCE	David Bowie	EMI America	3
1	2	IS THERE SOMETHING I SHOULD KNOW	Duran Duran	EMI	3
6	3	BOXERBEAT	JoBoxers	RCA	4
4	[4]	SPEAK LIKE A CHILD	Style Council	Polydor	4
5	5	SWEET DREAMS (ARE MADE OF THIS)	Eurythmics	RCA	8
18	6	BREAKAWAY	Tracey Ullman	Stiff	3
20	[7]	OOH TO BE AH	Kajagoogoo	EMI	2
3	8	TOTAL ECLIPSE OF THE HEART	Bonnie Tyler	CBS	7
-	9	CHURCH OF THE POISON MIND	Culture Club	Virgin	1
27	10	SNOT RAP	Kenny Everett	RCA	2
7	11	DON'T TALK TO ME ABOUT LOVE	Altered Images	Epic	4
8	12	RIP IT UP	Orange Juice	Polydor	6
13	13	FIELDS OF FIRE (400 MILES)	Big Country	Mercury	5
17	14	BLUE MONDAY	New Order	Factory	4
15	15	WHISTLE DOWN THE WIND	Nick Heyward	Arista	3
9	16	NA NA HEY HEY KISS HIM GOODBYE	Bananarama	London	7
10	17	ROCK THE BOAT	Forrest	CBS	7
24	[18]	TWO HEARTS BEAT AS ONE	U2	Island	2
16	19	ORCHARD ROAD	Leo Sayer	Chrysalis	4
11	20	BILLIE JEAN	Michael Jackson	Epic	10
39	21	WORDS	FR David	Carrere	2
12	22	DROP THE PILOT	Joan Armatrading	A&M	6

In these weeks ■ Duran Duran emulate Jam by coming straight in at number one with their first chart-topping hit (26.03.83) ■ Mezzoforte are the first act from Iceland to hit the UK charts (26.03.83) ■

LW	TW	Title	Artist	Label	Wks
38	23	THE HOUSE THAT JACK BUILT	Tracie	Respond	2
36	24	THE CELTIC SOUL BROTHERS	Kevin Rowland and Dexy's Midnight Runners	Mercury	2
14	25	YOU CAN'T HIDE (YOUR LOVE FROM ME)	David Joseph	Island	6
19	26	GARDEN PARTY	Mezzoforte	Steinar	5
30	27	CRY ME A RIVER	Mari Wilson	Compact	3
21	28	RUN FOR YOUR LIFE	Bucks Fizz	RCA	5
32	29	I AM (I'M ME)	Twisted Sister	Atlantic	2
-	30	BEAT IT	Michael Jackson	Epic	1
22	31	VISIONS IN BLUE	Ultravox	Chrysalis	4
25	32	WAVES	Blancmange	London	7
23	33	HIGH LIFE	Modern Romance	WEA	6
40	34	YOUNG FREE AND SINGLE	Sunfire	Warner Brothers	2
29	35	COMMUNICATION	Spandau Ballet	Reformation	8
26	36	JOY	Band AKA	Epic	5
28	37	BABY COME TO ME	Patti Austin and James Ingram	Qwest	9
33	38	MAGGIE	Foster and Allen	Ritz	5
-	39	LAST FILM	Kissing The Pink ●	Magnet	1
34	40	LOVE ON YOUR SIDE	Thompson Twins	Arista	10

WEEK ENDING **16 APRIL 1983**

LW	TW	Title	Artist	Label	Wks
1	1	LET'S DANCE	David Bowie	EMI America	4
9	2	CHURCH OF THE POISON MIND	Culture Club	Virgin	2
2	3	IS THERE SOMETHING I SHOULD KNOW	Duran Duran	EMI	4
6	4	BREAKAWAY	Tracey Ullman	Stiff	4
30	5	BEAT IT	Michael Jackson	Epic	2
3	6	BOXERBEAT	JoBoxers	RCA	5
7	7	OOH TO BE AH	Kajagoogoo	EMI	3
21	8	WORDS	FR David	Carrere	3
10	9	SNOT RAP	Kenny Everett	RCA	3
13	10	FIELDS OF FIRE (400 MILES)	Big Country	Mercury	6
4	11	SPEAK LIKE A CHILD	Style Council	Polydor	5
23	12	THE HOUSE THAT JACK BUILT	Tracie	Respond	3
15	13	WHISTLE DOWN THE WIND	Nick Heyward	Arista	4
14	14	BLUE MONDAY	New Order	Factory	5
5	15	SWEET DREAMS (ARE MADE OF THIS)	Eurythmics	RCA	9
8	16	TOTAL ECLIPSE OF THE HEART	Bonnie Tyler	CBS	8
11	17	DON'T TALK TO ME ABOUT LOVE	Altered Images	Epic	5
12	18	RIP IT UP	Orange Juice	Polydor	7
29	19	I AM (I'M ME)	Twisted Sister	Atlantic	3
24	20	THE CELTIC SOUL BROTHERS	Kevin Rowland and Dexy's Midnight Runners	Mercury	3
16	21	NA NA HEY HEY KISS HIM GOODBYE	Bananarama	London	8
18	22	TWO HEARTS BEAT AS ONE	U2	Island	3
-	23	LOVE IS A STRANGER	Eurythmics	RCA	1
17	24	ROCK THE BOAT	Forrest	CBS	8
20	25	BILLIE JEAN	Michael Jackson	Epic	11
19	26	ORCHARD ROAD	Leo Sayer	Chrysalis	5
27	27	CRY ME A RIVER	Mari Wilson	Compact	4
34	28	YOUNG FREE AND SINGLE	Sunfire	Warner Brothers	3
22	29	DROP THE PILOT	Joan Armatrading	A&M	7
26	30	GARDEN PARTY	Mezzoforte	Steinar	6
25	31	YOU CAN'T HIDE (YOUR LOVE FROM ME)	David Joseph	Island	7
39	32	LAST FILM	Kissing The Pink	Magnet	2
28	33	RUN FOR YOUR LIFE	Bucks Fizz	RCA	6
-	34	OVERKILL	Men At Work	Epic	1
-	35	SHE'S IN PARTIES	Bauhaus	Beggars Banquet	1
-	36	ROSANNA	Toto	CBS	1
-	37	TRUE LOVE WAYS	Cliff Richard and the London Philharmonic Orchestra	EMI	1
-	38	FRIDAY NIGHT (LIVE)	Kids From Fame	RCA	1
-	39	TWIST (ROUND AND ROUND)	Chill Fac-Torr ●	Philly World	1
-	40	WE ARE DETECTIVE	Thompson Twins	Arista	1

WEEK ENDING **23 APRIL 1983**

April 1983

□ Highest position disc reached ● Act's first ever week on chart

LW	TW	Title	Artist	Label	Wks
1	1	LET'S DANCE	David Bowie	EMI America	5
2	2	CHURCH OF THE POISON MIND	Culture Club	Virgin	3
5	3	BEAT IT	Michael Jackson	Epic	3
8	4	WORDS	FR David	Carrere	4
4	5	BREAKAWAY	Tracey Ullman	Stiff	5
23	6	LOVE IS A STRANGER	Eurythmics	RCA	2
6	7	BOXERBEAT	JoBoxers	RCA	6
7	8	OOH TO BE AH	Kajagoogoo	EMI	4
12	9	THE HOUSE THAT JACK BUILT	Tracie	Respond	4
-	10	TRUE	Spandau Ballet	Reformation	1
3	11	IS THERE SOMETHING I SHOULD KNOW	Duran Duran	EMI	5
14	12	BLUE MONDAY	New Order	Factory	6
9	13	SNOT RAP	Kenny Everett	RCA	4
37	14	TRUE LOVE WAYS	Cliff Richard and the London Philharmonic Orchestra	EMI	2
10	15	FIELDS OF FIRE (400 MILES)	Big Country	Mercury	7
-	16	(KEEP FEELING) FASCINATION	Human League	Virgin	1
13	17	WHISTLE DOWN THE WIND	Nick Heyward	Arista	5
19	18	I AM (I'M ME)	Twisted Sister	Atlantic	4
36	19	ROSANNA	Toto	CBS	2
28	20	YOUNG FREE AND SINGLE	Sunfire	Warner Brothers	4
40	21	WE ARE DETECTIVE	Thompson Twins	Arista	2
20	22	THE CELTIC SOUL BROTHERS	Kevin Rowland and Dexy's Midnight Runners	Mercury	4
11	23	SPEAK LIKE A CHILD	Style Council	Polydor	6
38	24	FRIDAY NIGHT (LIVE)	Kids From Fame	RCA	2
15	25	SWEET DREAMS (ARE MADE OF THIS)	Eurythmics	RCA	10
35	26	SHE'S IN PARTIES	Bauhaus	Beggars Banquet	2
16	27	TOTAL ECLIPSE OF THE HEART	Bonnie Tyler	CBS	9
-	28	FLIGHT OF ICARUS	Iron Maiden	EMI	1
32	29	LAST FILM	Kissing The Pink	Magnet	3
34	30	OVERKILL	Men At Work	Epic	2
-	31	TEMPTATION	Heaven 17 ●	Virgin	1
18	32	RIP IT UP	Orange Juice	Polydor	8
17	33	DON'T TALK TO ME ABOUT LOVE	Altered Images	Epic	6
-	34	I'M NEVER GIVING UP	Sweet Dreams ●	Ariola	1
26	35	ORCHARD ROAD	Leo Sayer	Chrysalis	6
25	36	BILLIE JEAN	Michael Jackson	Epic	12
39	37	TWIST (ROUND AND ROUND)	Chill Fac-Torr	Philly World	2
27	38	CRY ME A RIVER	Mari Wilson	Compact	5
-	39	DANCING TIGHT	Galaxy featuring Phil Fearon ●	Ensign	1
21	40	NA NA HEY HEY KISS HIM GOODBYE	Bananarama	London	9

WEEK ENDING **30 APRIL 1983**

LW	TW	Title	Artist	Label	Wks
10	1	TRUE	Spandau Ballet	Reformation	2
4	2	WORDS	FR David	Carrere	5
3	3	BEAT IT	Michael Jackson	Epic	4
16	4	(KEEP FEELING) FASCINATION	Human League	Virgin	2
2	5	CHURCH OF THE POISON MIND	Culture Club	Virgin	4
1	6	LET'S DANCE	David Bowie	EMI America	6
6	7	LOVE IS A STRANGER	Eurythmics	RCA	3
14	8	TRUE LOVE WAYS	Cliff Richard and the London Philharmonic Orchestra	EMI	3
21	9	WE ARE DETECTIVE	Thompson Twins	Arista	3
5	10	BREAKAWAY	Tracey Ullman	Stiff	6
28	11	FLIGHT OF ICARUS	Iron Maiden	EMI	2
19	12	ROSANNA	Toto	CBS	3
12	13	BLUE MONDAY	New Order	Factory	7
31	14	TEMPTATION	Heaven 17	Virgin	2
9	15	THE HOUSE THAT JACK BUILT	Tracie	Respond	5
8	16	OOH TO BE AH	Kajagoogoo	EMI	5
24	17	FRIDAY NIGHT (LIVE)	Kids From Fame	RCA	3
18	18	I AM (I'M ME)	Twisted Sister	Atlantic	5
7	19	BOXERBEAT	JoBoxers	RCA	7
39	20	DANCING TIGHT	Galaxy featuring Phil Fearon	Ensign	2
20	21	YOUNG FREE AND SINGLE	Sunfire	Warner Brothers	5
-	22	PALE SHELTER	Tears For Fears	Mercury	1
34	23	I'M NEVER GIVING UP	Sweet Dreams	Ariola	2
29	24	LAST FILM	Kissing The Pink	Magnet	4
30	25	OVERKILL	Men At Work	Epic	3
13	26	SNOT RAP	Kenny Everett	RCA	5
11	27	IS THERE SOMETHING I SHOULD KNOW	Duran Duran	EMI	6

■On the back of the success of *Sweet Dreams (Are Made Of This)*, the Eurythmics' previous single *Love Is A Stranger* makes a chart comeback (16.04.83) ■ The group Sweet Dreams become the first act to have the same name as a simultaneous hit single by another act (23.04.83)■

April 1983

□ Highest position disc reached ● Act's first ever week on chart

LW	TW	Title / Artist	Label	Wks
26	28	SHE'S IN PARTIES Bauhaus	Beggars Banquet	3
15	29	FIELDS OF FIRE (400 MILES) Big Country	Mercury	8
17	30	WHISTLE DOWN THE WIND Nick Heyward	Arista	6
-	31	OUR LIPS ARE SEALED Fun Boy Three	Chrysalis	1
22	32	THE CELTIC SOUL BROTHERS Kevin Rowland and Dexy's Midnight Runners	Mercury	5
25	33	SWEET DREAMS (ARE MADE OF THIS) Eurythmics	RCA	11
27	34	TOTAL ECLIPSE OF THE HEART Bonnie Tyler	CBS	10
-	35	HEY! Julio Iglesias	CBS	1
23	36	SPEAK LIKE A CHILD Style Council	Polydor	7
-	37	MISS THE GIRL Creatures	Wonderland	1
-	38	POWER AND THE GLORY Saxon	Carrere	1
37	39	TWIST (ROUND AND ROUND) Chill Fac-Torr	Philly World	3
-	[40]	FROM ME TO YOU Beatles	Parlophone	1

LW	TW	*WEEK ENDING* 7 MAY 1983		Wks
1	[1]	TRUE Spandau Ballet	Reformation	3
2	[2]	WORDS FR David	Carrere	6
4	3	(KEEP FEELING) FASCINATION Human League	Virgin	3
3	4	BEAT IT Michael Jackson	Epic	5
22	[5]	PALE SHELTER Tears For Fears	Mercury	2
20	6	DANCING TIGHT Galaxy featuring Phil Fearon	Ensign	3
9	[7]	WE ARE DETECTIVE Thompson Twins	Arista	4
14	8	TEMPTATION Heaven 17	Virgin	3
6	9	LET'S DANCE David Bowie	EMI America	7
5	10	CHURCH OF THE POISON MIND Culture Club	Virgin	5
8	11	TRUE LOVE WAYS Cliff Richard and the London Philharmonic Orchestra	EMI	4
7	12	LOVE IS A STRANGER Eurythmics	RCA	4
17	13	FRIDAY NIGHT (LIVE) Kids From Fame	RCA	4
11	14	FLIGHT OF ICARUS Iron Maiden	EMI	3
12	15	ROSANNA Toto	CBS	4
31	16	OUR LIPS ARE SEALED Fun Boy Three	Chrysalis	2
13	17	BLUE MONDAY New Order	Factory	8
10	18	BREAKAWAY Tracey Ullman	Stiff	7
24	[19]	LAST FILM Kissing The Pink	Magnet	5
18	20	I AM (I'M ME) Twisted Sister	Atlantic	6
23	[21]	I'M NEVER GIVING UP Sweet Dreams	Ariola	3
15	22	THE HOUSE THAT JACK BUILT Tracie	Respond	6
21	23	YOUNG FREE AND SINGLE Sunfire	Warner Brothers	6
25	24	OVERKILL Men At Work	Epic	4
19	25	BOXERBEAT JoBoxers	RCA	8
37	26	MISS THE GIRL Creatures	Wonderland	2
16	27	OOH TO BE AH Kajagoogoo	EMI	6
-	28	BLIND VISION Blancmange	London	1
-	29	CAN'T GET USED TO LOSING YOU Beat	Go Feet	1
-	30	CANDY GIRL New Edition ●	London	1
35	[31]	HEY! Julio Iglesias	CBS	2
38	[32]	POWER AND THE GLORY Saxon	Carrere	2
-	33	NOT NOW JOHN Pink Floyd	Harvest	1
27	34	IS THERE SOMETHING I SHOULD KNOW Duran Duran	EMI	7
-	35	FAMILY MAN Daryl Hall and John Oates	RCA	1
-	36	CREATURES OF THE NIGHT Kiss ●	Casablanca	1
39	37	TWIST (ROUND AND ROUND) Chill Fac-Torr	Philly World	4
28	38	SHE'S IN PARTIES Bauhaus	Beggars Banquet	4
-	[39]	THUNDER AND LIGHTNING Thin Lizzy	Vertigo	1
-	40	SWEET MEMORY Belle Stars	Stiff	1

LW	TW	*WEEK ENDING* 14 MAY 1983		Wks
1	[1]	TRUE Spandau Ballet	Reformation	4
3	[2]	(KEEP FEELING) FASCINATION Human League	Virgin	4
8	3	TEMPTATION Heaven 17	Virgin	4
2	4	WORDS FR David	Carrere	7
6	5	DANCING TIGHT Galaxy featuring Phil Fearon	Ensign	4
5	6	PALE SHELTER Tears For Fears	Mercury	3
30	7	CANDY GIRL New Edition	London	2
7	8	WE ARE DETECTIVE Thompson Twins	Arista	5
16	9	OUR LIPS ARE SEALED Fun Boy Three	Chrysalis	3
29	10	CAN'T GET USED TO LOSING YOU Beat	Go Feet	2
4	11	BEAT IT Michael Jackson	Epic	6
28	12	BLIND VISION Blancmange	London	2
9	13	LET'S DANCE David Bowie	EMI America	8
11	14	TRUE LOVE WAYS Cliff Richard and the London Philharmonic Orchestra	EMI	5
13	15	FRIDAY NIGHT (LIVE) Kids From Fame	RCA	5
10	16	CHURCH OF THE POISON MIND Culture Club	Virgin	6
12	17	LOVE IS A STRANGER Eurythmics	RCA	5
17	18	BLUE MONDAY New Order	Factory	9
19	[19]	LAST FILM Kissing The Pink	Magnet	6
15	20	ROSANNA Toto	CBS	5
26	[21]	MISS THE GIRL Creatures	Wonderland	3
24	22	OVERKILL Men At Work	Epic	5
14	23	FLIGHT OF ICARUS Iron Maiden	EMI	4
35	24	FAMILY MAN Daryl Hall and John Oates	RCA	2
18	25	BREAKAWAY Tracey Ullman	Stiff	8
-	26	DON'T STOP THAT CRAZY RHYTHM Modern Romance	WEA	1
25	27	BOXERBEAT JoBoxers	RCA	9
21	28	I'M NEVER GIVING UP Sweet Dreams	Ariola	4
40	29	SWEET MEMORY Belle Stars	Stiff	2
33	[30]	NOT NOW JOHN Pink Floyd	Harvest	2
20	31	I AM (I'M ME) Twisted Sister	Atlantic	7
-	32	MUSIC (PART 1) D Train	Prelude	1
-	33	BUFFALO SOLDIER Bob Marley and the Wailers	Island	1
36	[34]	CREATURES OF THE NIGHT Kiss	Casablanca	2
-	35	WHAT KINDA BOY YOU LOOKING FOR (GIRL) Hot Chocolate	RAK	1
-	36	STOP AND GO David Grant ●	Chrysalis	1
-	37	BAD BOYS Wham!	Innervision	1
23	38	YOUNG FREE AND SINGLE Sunfire	Warner Brothers	7
22	39	THE HOUSE THAT JACK BUILT Tracie	Respond	7
27	40	OOH TO BE AH Kajagoogoo	EMI	7

LW	TW	*WEEK ENDING* 21 MAY 1983		Wks
1	[1]	TRUE Spandau Ballet	Reformation	5
3	[2]	TEMPTATION Heaven 17	Virgin	5
7	3	CANDY GIRL New Edition	London	3
5	[4]	DANCING TIGHT Galaxy featuring Phil Fearon	Ensign	5
10	5	CAN'T GET USED TO LOSING YOU Beat	Go Feet	3
2	6	(KEEP FEELING) FASCINATION Human League	Virgin	5
9	[7]	OUR LIPS ARE SEALED Fun Boy Three	Chrysalis	4
6	8	PALE SHELTER Tears For Fears	Mercury	4
4	9	WORDS FR David	Carrere	8
12	[10]	BLIND VISION Blancmange	London	3
8	11	WE ARE DETECTIVE Thompson Twins	Arista	6
37	12	BAD BOYS Wham!	Innervision	2
35	13	WHAT KINDA BOY YOU LOOKING FOR (GIRL) Hot Chocolate	RAK	2
26	[14]	DON'T STOP THAT CRAZY RHYTHM Modern Romance	WEA	2
24	15	FAMILY MAN Daryl Hall and John Oates	RCA	3
11	16	BEAT IT Michael Jackson	Epic	7
33	17	BUFFALO SOLDIER Bob Marley and the Wailers	Island	2
15	18	FRIDAY NIGHT (LIVE) Kids From Fame	RCA	6
19	[19]	LAST FILM Kissing The Pink	Magnet	7
-	20	NOBODY'S DIARY Yazoo	Mute	1
22	[21]	OVERKILL Men At Work	Epic	6
29	[22]	SWEET MEMORY Belle Stars	Stiff	3
21	23	MISS THE GIRL Creatures	Wonderland	4
13	24	LET'S DANCE David Bowie	EMI America	9
14	25	TRUE LOVE WAYS Cliff Richard and the London Philharmonic Orchestra	EMI	6
18	26	BLUE MONDAY New Order	Factory	10
32	27	MUSIC (PART 1) D Train	Prelude	2
-	28	FEEL THE NEED IN ME Forrest	CBS	1
16	29	CHURCH OF THE POISON MIND Culture Club	Virgin	7
20	30	ROSANNA Toto	CBS	6
17	31	LOVE IS A STRANGER Eurythmics	RCA	6
30	32	NOT NOW JOHN Pink Floyd	Harvest	3
-	33	MORNIN' Al Jarreau ●	Warner Brothers	1
36	34	STOP AND GO David Grant	Chrysalis	2

In these weeks ■ Pink Floyd's fifth and final top 40 hit, over a period of 16 years, spends it final week on the chart. Their success as an albums act was never reflected in their deliberately restricted singles sales (21.05.83)■

LW	TW	Title / Artist	Label	Wks
-	35	GLORY GLORY MAN. UTD Manchester United FC ●	EMI	1
-	36	COUNTDOWN/NEW WORLD MAN Rush	Mercury	1
-	37	SHIPBUILDING Robert Wyatt	Rough Trade	1
-	38	JUST GOT LUCKY JoBoxers	RCA	1
25	39	BREAKAWAY Tracey Ullman	Stiff	9
23	40	FLIGHT OF ICARUS Iron Maiden	EMI	5

WEEK ENDING 28 MAY 1983

LW	TW	Title / Artist	Label	Wks
3	1	CANDY GIRL New Edition	London	4
1	2	TRUE Spandau Ballet	Reformation	6
5	3	CAN'T GET USED TO LOSING YOU Beat	Go Feet	4
2	4	TEMPTATION Heaven 17	Virgin	6
12	5	BAD BOYS Wham!	Innervision	3
4	6	DANCING TIGHT Galaxy featuring Phil Fearon	Ensign	6
-	7	EVERY BREATH YOU TAKE Police	A&M	1
20	8	NOBODY'S DIARY Yazoo	Mute	2
7	9	OUR LIPS ARE SEALED Fun Boy Three	Chrysalis	5
13	10	WHAT KINDA BOY YOU LOOKING FOR (GIRL) Hot Chocolate	RAK	3
17	11	BUFFALO SOLDIER Bob Marley and the Wailers	Island	3
-	12	MONEY GO ROUND (PART 1) Style Council	Polydor	1
35	13	GLORY GLORY MAN. UTD Manchester United FC	EMI	2
10	14	BLIND VISION Blancmange	London	4
6	15	(KEEP FEELING) FASCINATION Human League	Virgin	6
38	16	JUST GOT LUCKY JoBoxers	RCA	2
9	17	WORDS FR David	Carrere	9
8	18	PALE SHELTER Tears For Fears	Mercury	5
-	19	LOVE TOWN Booker Newberry III ●	Polydor	1
28	20	FEEL THE NEED IN ME Forrest	CBS	2
14	21	DON'T STOP THAT CRAZY RHYTHM Modern Romance	WEA	3
15	22	FAMILY MAN Daryl Hall and John Oates	RCA	4
27	23	MUSIC (PART 1) D Train	Prelude	3
11	24	WE ARE DETECTIVE Thompson Twins	Arista	7
-	25	LADY LOVE ME (ONE MORE TIME) George Benson	Warner Bros	1
16	26	BEAT IT Michael Jackson	Epic	8
34	27	STOP AND GO David Grant	Chrysalis	3
33	28	MORNIN' Al Jarreau	Warner Brothers	2
22	29	SWEET MEMORY Belle Stars	Stiff	4
21	30	OVERKILL Men At Work	Epic	7
18	31	FRIDAY NIGHT (LIVE) Kids From Fame	RCA	7
26	32	BLUE MONDAY New Order	Factory	11
-	33	WAITING FOR A TRAIN Flash and the Pan ●	Easy Beat	1
-	34	IN A BIG COUNTRY Big Country	Mercury	1
37	35	SHIPBUILDING Robert Wyatt	Rough Trade	2
19	36	LAST FILM Kissing The Pink	Magnet	8
24	37	LET'S DANCE David Bowie	EMI America	10
36	38	COUNTDOWN/NEW WORLD MAN Rush	Mercury	2
25	39	TRUE LOVE WAYS Cliff Richard and the London Philharmonic Orchestra	EMI	7
-	40	JUICY FRUIT Mtume ●	Epic	1

June 1983

□ Highest position disc reached ● Act's first ever week on chart

WEEK ENDING 4 JUNE 1983

LW	TW	Title / Artist	Label	Wks
7	1	EVERY BREATH YOU TAKE Police	A&M	2
5	2	BAD BOYS Wham!	Innervision	4
1	3	CANDY GIRL New Edition	London	5
8	4	NOBODY'S DIARY Yazoo	Mute	3
3	5	CAN'T GET USED TO LOSING YOU Beat	Go Feet	5
11	6	BUFFALO SOLDIER Bob Marley and the Wailers	Island	4
16	7	JUST GOT LUCKY JoBoxers	RCA	3
19	8	LOVE TOWN Booker Newberry III	Polydor	2
4	9	TEMPTATION Heaven 17	Virgin	7
2	10	TRUE Spandau Ballet	Reformation	7
12	11	MONEY GO ROUND (PART 1) Style Council	Polydor	2
10	12	WHAT KINDA BOY YOU LOOKING FOR (GIRL) Hot Chocolate	RAK	4
13	13	GLORY GLORY MAN. UTD Manchester United FC	EMI	3
9	14	OUR LIPS ARE SEALED Fun Boy Three	Chrysalis	6
25	15	LADY LOVE ME (ONE MORE TIME) George Benson	Warner Bros	2
6	16	DANCING TIGHT Galaxy featuring Phil Fearon	Ensign	7
20	17	FEEL THE NEED IN ME Forrest	CBS	3
34	18	IN A BIG COUNTRY Big Country	Mercury	2
27	19	STOP AND GO David Grant	Chrysalis	4
14	20	BLIND VISION Blancmange	London	5
33	21	WAITING FOR A TRAIN Flash and the Pan	Easy Beat	2
17	22	WORDS FR David	Carrere	10
15	23	(KEEP FEELING) FASCINATION Human League	Virgin	7
23	24	MUSIC (PART 1) D Train	Prelude	4
18	25	PALE SHELTER Tears For Fears	Mercury	6
-	26	LET'S LIVE IT UP (NITE PEOPLE) David Joseph	Island	1
-	27	I GUESS THAT'S WHY THEY CALL IT THE BLUES Elton John	Rocket	1
28	28	MORNIN' Al Jarreau	Warner Brothers	3
-	29	BRING ME CLOSER Altered Images	Epic	1
-	30	FLASHDANCE...WHAT A FEELING Irene Cara	Casablanca	1
22	31	FAMILY MAN Daryl Hall and John Oates	RCA	5
-	32	WE CAME TO DANCE Ultravox	Chrysalis	1
21	33	DON'T STOP THAT CRAZY RHYTHM Modern Romance	WEA	4
40	34	JUICY FRUIT Mtume	Epic	2
-	35	THE HEAT IS ON Agnetha Faltskog ●	Epic	1
-	36	THE KIDS ARE BACK Twisted Sister	Atlantic	1
-	37	BABY JANE Rod Stewart	Warner Brothers	1
26	38	BEAT IT Michael Jackson	Epic	9
-	39	HANG ON NOW Kajagoogoo	EMI	1
-	40	DREAM TO SLEEP H_20 ●	RCA	1

WEEK ENDING 11 JUNE 1983

LW	TW	Title / Artist	Label	Wks
1	1	EVERY BREATH YOU TAKE Police	A&M	3
2	2	BAD BOYS Wham!	Innervision	5
4	3	NOBODY'S DIARY Yazoo	Mute	4
6	4	BUFFALO SOLDIER Bob Marley and the Wailers	Island	5
3	5	CANDY GIRL New Edition	London	6
8	6	LOVE TOWN Booker Newberry III	Polydor	3
7	7	JUST GOT LUCKY JoBoxers	RCA	4
-	8	CHINA GIRL David Bowie	EMI America	1
30	9	FLASHDANCE...WHAT A FEELING Irene Cara	Casablanca	2
5	10	CAN'T GET USED TO LOSING YOU Beat	Go Feet	6
15	11	LADY LOVE ME (ONE MORE TIME) George Benson	Warner Bros	3
21	12	WAITING FOR A TRAIN Flash and the Pan	Easy Beat	3
11	13	MONEY GO ROUND (PART 1) Style Council	Polydor	3
9	14	TEMPTATION Heaven 17	Virgin	8
39	15	HANG ON NOW Kajagoogoo	EMI	2
10	16	TRUE Spandau Ballet	Reformation	8
18	17	IN A BIG COUNTRY Big Country	Mercury	3
27	18	I GUESS THAT'S WHY THEY CALL IT THE BLUES Elton John	Rocket	2
37	19	BABY JANE Rod Stewart	Warner Brothers	2
12	20	WHAT KINDA BOY YOU LOOKING FOR (GIRL) Hot Chocolate	RAK	5
17	21	FEEL THE NEED IN ME Forrest	CBS	4
16	22	DANCING TIGHT Galaxy featuring Phil Fearon	Ensign	8
14	23	OUR LIPS ARE SEALED Fun Boy Three	Chrysalis	7
32	24	WE CAME TO DANCE Ultravox	Chrysalis	2
13	25	GLORY GLORY MAN. UTD Manchester United FC	EMI	4
19	26	STOP AND GO David Grant	Chrysalis	5
40	27	DREAM TO SLEEP H_20	RCA	2
26	28	LET'S LIVE IT UP (NITE PEOPLE) David Joseph	Island	2
-	29	PILLS AND SOAP Imposter ●	Imp	1
-	30	DARK IS THE NIGHT Shakatak	Polydor	1
29	31	BRING ME CLOSER Altered Images	Epic	2
36	32	THE KIDS ARE BACK Twisted Sister	Atlantic	2
-	33	DEAD GIVEAWAY Shalamar	Solar	1
-	34	LOOKING AT MIDNIGHT Imagination	R&B	1
20	35	BLIND VISION Blancmange	London	6
34	36	JUICY FRUIT Mtume	Epic	3
35	37	THE HEAT IS ON Agnetha Faltskog	Epic	2
-	38	WANNA BE STARTIN' SOMETHING Michael Jackson	Epic	1

■ Booker Newberry III joins George Hamilton IV and Napoleon XIV as the only solo acts in chart history with Roman numerals after their names (28.05.83) ■ The Imposter, who enters the chart with *Pills And Soap* is really Elvis Costello who is really Declan McManus (11.06.83) ■ *Can't Get Used To Losing You* by the Beat peaks at no. 3, one place lower than the best achieved by Andy Williams' original version, 20 years earlier (28.05.83) ■

June 1983

□ Highest position disc reached ● Act's first ever week on chart

LW	TW	Title	Artist	Label	Wks
22	39	WORDS	FR David	Carrere	11
28	40	MORNIN'	Al Jarreau	Warner Brothers	4

WEEK ENDING 18 JUNE 1983

LW	TW	Title	Artist	Label	Wks
1	[1]	EVERY BREATH YOU TAKE	Police	A&M	4
8	[2]	CHINA GIRL	David Bowie	EMI America	2
2	3	BAD BOYS	Wham!	Innervision	6
9	4	FLASHDANCE...WHAT A FEELING	Irene Cara	Casablanca	3
3	5	NOBODY'S DIARY	Yazoo	Mute	5
19	6	BABY JANE	Rod Stewart	Warner Brothers	3
4	7	BUFFALO SOLDIER	Bob Marley and the Wailers	Island	6
6	8	LOVE TOWN	Booker Newberry III	Polydor	4
18	9	I GUESS THAT'S WHY THEY CALL IT THE BLUES	Elton John	Rocket	3
12	10	WAITING FOR A TRAIN	Flash and the Pan	Easy Beat	4
11	[11]	LADY LOVE ME (ONE MORE TIME)	George Benson	Warner Bros	4
7	12	JUST GOT LUCKY	JoBoxers	RCA	5
15	[13]	HANG ON NOW	Kajagoogoo	EMI	3
38	14	WANNA BE STARTIN' SOMETHING	Michael Jackson	Epic	2
30	[15]	DARK IS THE NIGHT	Shakatak	Polydor	2
29	[16]	PILLS AND SOAP	Imposter	Imp	2
5	17	CANDY GIRL	New Edition	London	7
24	[18]	WE CAME TO DANCE	Ultravox	Chrysalis	3
27	19	DREAM TO SLEEP	H_2O	RCA	3
33	20	DEAD GIVEAWAY	Shalamar	Solar	2
17	21	IN A BIG COUNTRY	Big Country	Mercury	4
10	22	CAN'T GET USED TO LOSING YOU	Beat	Go Feet	7
-	23	WHEN WE WERE YOUNG	Bucks Fizz	RCA	1
-	24	GARDEN PARTY	Marillion	EMI	1
14	25	TEMPTATION	Heaven 17	Virgin	9
13	26	MONEY GO ROUND (PART 1)	Style Council	Polydor	4
-	27	MOONLIGHT SHADOW	Mike Oldfield	Virgin	1
20	28	WHAT KINDA BOY YOU LOOKING FOR (GIRL)	Hot Chocolate	RAK	6
16	29	TRUE	Spandau Ballet	Reformation	9
21	30	FEEL THE NEED IN ME	Forrest	CBS	5
22	31	DANCING TIGHT	Galaxy featuring Phil Fearon	Ensign	9
34	32	LOOKING AT MIDNIGHT	Imagination	R&B	2
31	33	BRING ME CLOSER	Altered Images	Epic	3
23	34	OUR LIPS ARE SEALED	Fun Boy Three	Chrysalis	8
26	35	STOP AND GO	David Grant	Chrysalis	6
37	36	THE HEAT IS ON	Agnetha Faltskog	Epic	3
32	37	THE KIDS ARE BACK	Twisted Sister	Atlantic	3
36	38	JUICY FRUIT	Mtume	Epic	4
28	39	LET'S LIVE IT UP (NITE PEOPLE)	David Joseph	Island	3
-	40	TAKE THAT SITUATION	Nick Heyward	Arista	1

WEEK ENDING 25 JUNE 1983

LW	TW	Title	Artist	Label	Wks
1	[1]	EVERY BREATH YOU TAKE	Police	A&M	5
6	2	BABY JANE	Rod Stewart	Warner Brothers	4
2	3	CHINA GIRL	David Bowie	EMI America	3
4	4	FLASHDANCE...WHAT A FEELING	Irene Cara	Casablanca	4
3	5	BAD BOYS	Wham!	Innervision	7
9	6	I GUESS THAT'S WHY THEY CALL IT THE BLUES	Elton John	Rocket	4
10	[7]	WAITING FOR A TRAIN	Flash and the Pan	Easy Beat	5
14	[8]	WANNA BE STARTIN' SOMETHING	Michael Jackson	Epic	3
5	9	NOBODY'S DIARY	Yazoo	Mute	6
23	[10]	WHEN WE WERE YOUNG	Bucks Fizz	RCA	2
11	[11]	LADY LOVE ME (ONE MORE TIME)	George Benson	Warner Bros	5
20	12	DEAD GIVEAWAY	Shalamar	Solar	3
8	13	LOVE TOWN	Booker Newberry III	Polydor	5
7	14	BUFFALO SOLDIER	Bob Marley and the Wailers	Island	7
15	[15]	DARK IS THE NIGHT	Shakatak	Polydor	3
24	[16]	GARDEN PARTY	Marillion	EMI	2
19	[17]	DREAM TO SLEEP	H_2O	RCA	4
13	18	HANG ON NOW	Kajagoogoo	EMI	4
27	19	MOONLIGHT SHADOW	Mike Oldfield	Virgin	2
18	20	WE CAME TO DANCE	Ultravox	Chrysalis	4
40	21	TAKE THAT SITUATION	Nick Heyward	Arista	2
12	22	JUST GOT LUCKY	JoBoxers	RCA	6
-	23	IOU	Freeez	Beggars Banquet	1
-	24	CONFUSION (HITS US EVERY TIME)	Truth ●	Formation	1
-	25	ROCK 'N' ROLL IS KING	Electric Light Orchestra	Jet	1
21	26	IN A BIG COUNTRY	Big Country	Mercury	5
16	27	PILLS AND SOAP	Imposter	Imp	3
22	28	CAN'T GET USED TO LOSING YOU	Beat	Go Feet	8
32	29	LOOKING AT MIDNIGHT	Imagination	R&B	3
-	30	WHEREVER I LAY MY HAT (THAT'S MY HOME)	Paul Young ●	CBS	1
17	31	CANDY GIRL	New Edition	London	8
25	32	TEMPTATION	Heaven 17	Virgin	10
-	33	COME LIVE WITH ME	Heaven 17	Virgin	1
-	34	IT'S OVER	Funk Masters ●	Master Funk	1
29	35	TRUE	Spandau Ballet	Reformation	10
-	36	SHE WORKS HARD FOR THE MONEY	Donna Summer	Mercury	1
-	[37]	I WON'T HOLD YOU BACK	Toto	CBS	1
28	38	WHAT KINDA BOY YOU LOOKING FOR (GIRL)	Hot Chocolate	RAK	7
-	39	WAR BABY	Tom Robinson	Panic	1
38	40	JUICY FRUIT	Mtume	Epic	5

WEEK ENDING 2 JULY 1983

LW	TW	Title	Artist	Label	Wks
2	[1]	BABY JANE	Rod Stewart	Warner Brothers	5
1	2	EVERY BREATH YOU TAKE	Police	A&M	6
4	3	FLASHDANCE...WHAT A FEELING	Irene Cara	Casablanca	5
19	[4]	MOONLIGHT SHADOW	Mike Oldfield	Virgin	3
9	[5]	I GUESS THAT'S WHY THEY CALL IT THE BLUES	Elton John	Rocket	5
3	6	CHINA GIRL	David Bowie	EMI America	4
23	7	IOU	Freeez	Beggars Banquet	2
12	[8]	DEAD GIVEAWAY	Shalamar	Solar	4
5	9	BAD BOYS	Wham!	Innervision	8
10	[10]	WHEN WE WERE YOUNG	Bucks Fizz	RCA	3
7	11	WAITING FOR A TRAIN	Flash and the Pan	Easy Beat	6
30	12	WHEREVER I LAY MY HAT (THAT'S MY HOME)	Paul Young	CBS	2
8	13	WANNA BE STARTIN' SOMETHING	Michael Jackson	Epic	4
21	14	TAKE THAT SITUATION	Nick Heyward	Arista	3
25	15	ROCK 'N' ROLL IS KING	Electric Light Orchestra	Jet	2
33	16	COME LIVE WITH ME	Heaven 17	Virgin	2
39	17	WAR BABY	Tom Robinson	Panic	2
17	18	DREAM TO SLEEP	H_2O	RCA	5
11	19	LADY LOVE ME (ONE MORE TIME)	George Benson	Warner Brothers	6
9	20	NOBODY'S DIARY	Yazoo	Mute	7
15	21	DARK IS THE NIGHT	Shakatak	Polydor	4
24	[22]	CONFUSION (HITS US EVERY TIME)	Truth	Formation	2
16	23	GARDEN PARTY	Marillion	EMI	3
14	24	BUFFALO SOLDIER	Bob Marley and the Wailers	Island	8
13	25	LOVE TOWN	Booker Newberry III	Polydor	6
-	26	THE TROOPER	Iron Maiden	EMI	1
18	27	HANG ON NOW	Kajagoogoo	EMI	5
-	28	FORBIDDEN COLOURS	David Sylvian and Riuichi Sakamoto	Virgin	1
34	29	IT'S OVER	Funk Masters	Master Funk	2
20	30	WE CAME TO DANCE	Ultravox	Chrysalis	5
-	31	ALL NIGHT LONG	Mary Jane Girls ●	Gordy	1
29	32	LOOKING AT MIDNIGHT	Imagination	R&B	4
36	33	SHE WORKS HARD FOR THE MONEY	Donna Summer	Mercury	2
22	34	JUST GOT LUCKY	JoBoxers	RCA	7
-	35	TANTALISE (WO WO EE YEH YEH)	Jimmy The Hoover ●	Innervision	1
28	36	CAN'T GET USED TO LOSING YOU	Beat	Go Feet	9
26	37	IN A BIG COUNTRY	Big Country	Mercury	6

In these weeks ■ Rod Stewart's sixth and so far final chart-topper takes over from Police's fifth and so far final chart-topper (02.07.83) ■ Flash and the Pan consisted of George Young (brother of the AC/DC Youngs) and Harry Vanda, both survivors of the 60s group, the Easybeats (25.06.83) ■

LW	TW	Title / Artist	Label	Wks
37	**38**	I WON'T HOLD YOU BACK Toto	*CBS*	2
31	**39**	CANDY GIRL New Edition	*London*	9
-	**40**	DON'T TRY TO STOP IT Roman Holiday ●	*Jive*	1

July 1983

□ Highest position disc reached ● Act's first ever week on chart

WEEK ENDING 9 JULY 1983

LW	TW	Title / Artist	Label	Wks
1	[1]	BABY JANE Rod Stewart	*Warner Brothers*	6
3	[2]	FLASHDANCE...WHAT A FEELING Irene Cara	*Casablanca*	6
12	**3**	WHEREVER I LAY MY HAT (THAT'S MY HOME) Paul Young	*CBS*	3
4	[4]	MOONLIGHT SHADOW Mike Oldfield	*Virgin*	4
7	**5**	IOU Freeez	*Beggars Banquet*	3
17	[6]	WAR BABY Tom Robinson	*Panic*	3
16	**7**	COME LIVE WITH ME Heaven 17	*Virgin*	3
8	[8]	DEAD GIVEAWAY Shalamar	*Solar*	5
2	**9**	EVERY BREATH YOU TAKE Police	*A&M*	7
5	**10**	I GUESS THAT'S WHY THEY CALL IT THE BLUES Elton John	*Rocket*	6
14	[11]	TAKE THAT SITUATION Nick Heyward	*Arista*	4
26	[12]	THE TROOPER Iron Maiden	*EMI*	2
10	**13**	WHEN WE WERE YOUNG Bucks Fizz	*RCA*	4
15	**14**	ROCK 'N' ROLL IS KING Electric Light Orchestra	*Jet*	3
29	**15**	IT'S OVER Funk Masters	*Master Funk*	3
9	**16**	BAD BOYS Wham!	*Innervision*	9
6	**17**	CHINA GIRL David Bowie	*EMI America*	5
11	**18**	WAITING FOR A TRAIN Flash and the Pan	*Easy Beat*	7
-	**19**	DOUBLE DUTCH Malcolm McLaren	*Charisma*	1
28	**20**	FORBIDDEN COLOURS David Sylvian and Riuichi Sakamoto	*Virgin*	2
13	**21**	WANNA BE STARTIN' SOMETHING Michael Jackson	*Epic*	5
18	**22**	DREAM TO SLEEP $H_2 0$	*RCA*	6
22	**23**	CONFUSION (HITS US EVERY TIME) Truth	*Formation*	3
31	**24**	ALL NIGHT LONG Mary Jane Girls	*Gordy*	2
19	**25**	LADY LOVE ME (ONE MORE TIME) George Benson	*Warner Brothers*	7
35	**26**	TANTALISE (WO WO EE YEH YEH) Jimmy The Hoover	*Innervision*	2
21	**27**	DARK IS THE NIGHT Shakatak	*Polydor*	5
20	**28**	NOBODY'S DIARY Yazoo	*Mute*	8
-	**29**	WHO'S THAT GIRL Eurythmics	*RCA*	1
33	**30**	SHE WORKS HARD FOR THE MONEY Donna Summer	*Mercury*	3
24	**31**	BUFFALO SOLDIER Bob Marley and the Wailers	*Island*	9
40	**32**	DON'T TRY TO STOP IT Roman Holiday	*Jive*	2
23	**33**	GARDEN PARTY Marillion	*EMI*	4
-	**34**	THE WALK Cure	*Fiction*	1
25	**35**	LOVE TOWN Booker Newberry III	*Polydor*	7
-	**36**	CRUEL SUMMER Bananarama	*London*	1
-	**37**	IT'S A MISTAKE Men At Work	*Epic*	1
-	[38]	TRANSFER AFFECTION A Flock Of Seagulls	*Jive*	1
27	**39**	HANG ON NOW Kajagoogoo	*EMI*	6
-	**40**	EVERYDAY I WRITE THE BOOK Elvis Costello and the Attractions	*F Beat*	1

WEEK ENDING 16 JULY 1983

LW	TW	Title / Artist	Label	Wks
1	[1]	BABY JANE Rod Stewart	*Warner Brothers*	7
3	**2**	WHEREVER I LAY MY HAT (THAT'S MY HOME) Paul Young	*CBS*	4
5	**3**	IOU Freeez	*Beggars Banquet*	4
4	[4]	MOONLIGHT SHADOW Mike Oldfield	*Virgin*	5
2	**5**	FLASHDANCE...WHAT A FEELING Irene Cara	*Casablanca*	7
7	**6**	COME LIVE WITH ME Heaven 17	*Virgin*	4
6	**7**	WAR BABY Tom Robinson	*Panic*	4
15	[8]	IT'S OVER Funk Masters	*Master Funk*	4
29	**9**	WHO'S THAT GIRL Eurythmics	*RCA*	2
19	**10**	DOUBLE DUTCH Malcolm McLaren	*Charisma*	2
8	**11**	DEAD GIVEAWAY Shalamar	*Solar*	6
12	[12]	THE TROOPER Iron Maiden	*EMI*	3
14	[13]	ROCK 'N' ROLL IS KING Electric Light Orchestra	*Jet*	4
11	**14**	TAKE THAT SITUATION Nick Heyward	*Arista*	5
10	**15**	I GUESS THAT'S WHY THEY CALL IT THE BLUES Elton John	*Rocket*	7
24	**16**	ALL NIGHT LONG Mary Jane Girls	*Gordy*	3
34	**17**	THE WALK Cure	*Fiction*	2
20	**18**	FORBIDDEN COLOURS David Sylvian and Riuichi Sakamoto	*Virgin*	3
26	**19**	TANTALISE (WO WO EE YEH YEH) Jimmy The Hoover	*Innervision*	3
9	**20**	EVERY BREATH YOU TAKE Police	*A&M*	8
36	**21**	CRUEL SUMMER Bananarama	*London*	2
13	**22**	WHEN WE WERE YOUNG Bucks Fizz	*RCA*	5
32	**23**	DON'T TRY TO STOP IT Roman Holiday	*Jive*	3
16	**24**	BAD BOYS Wham!	*Innervision*	10
18	**25**	WAITING FOR A TRAIN Flash and the Pan	*Easy Beat*	8
23	**26**	CONFUSION (HITS US EVERY TIME) Truth	*Formation*	4
17	**27**	CHINA GIRL David Bowie	*EMI America*	6
21	**28**	WANNA BE STARTIN' SOMETHING Michael Jackson	*Epic*	6
30	**29**	SHE WORKS HARD FOR THE MONEY Donna Summer	*Mercury*	4
-	**30**	NEVER STOP Echo and the Bunnymen	*Korova*	1
22	**31**	DREAM TO SLEEP H20	*RCA*	7
40	**32**	EVERYDAY I WRITE THE BOOK Elvis Costello and the Attractions	*F Beat*	2
37	**33**	IT'S A MISTAKE Men At Work	*Epic*	2
-	**34**	TELL ME WHY Musical Youth	*MCA*	1
28	**35**	NOBODY'S DIARY Yazoo	*Mute*	9
-	**36**	THE FIRST PICTURE OF YOU Lotus Eaters ●	*Sylvan*	1
25	**37**	LADY LOVE ME (ONE MORE TIME) George Benson	*Warner Brothers*	8
-	[38]	GET DOWN SATURDAY NIGHT Oliver Cheatham ●	*MCA*	1
-	[39]	AFTER A FASHION Midge Ure and Mick Karn ●	*Musicfest*	1
27	**40**	DARK IS THE NIGHT Shakatak	*Polydor*	6

WEEK ENDING 23 JULY 1983

LW	TW	Title / Artist	Label	Wks
2	[1]	WHEREVER I LAY MY HAT (THAT'S MY HOME) Paul Young	*CBS*	5
3	[2]	IOU Freeez	*Beggars Banquet*	5
1	**3**	BABY JANE Rod Stewart	*Warner Brothers*	8
9	**4**	WHO'S THAT GIRL Eurythmics	*RCA*	3
4	**5**	MOONLIGHT SHADOW Mike Oldfield	*Virgin*	6
6	**6**	COME LIVE WITH ME Heaven 17	*Virgin*	5
10	**7**	DOUBLE DUTCH Malcolm McLaren	*Charisma*	3
5	**8**	FLASHDANCE...WHAT A FEELING Irene Cara	*Casablanca*	8
7	**9**	WAR BABY Tom Robinson	*Panic*	5
8	**10**	IT'S OVER Funk Masters	*Master Funk*	5
21	**11**	CRUEL SUMMER Bananarama	*London*	3
17	[12]	THE WALK Cure	*Fiction*	3
16	[13]	ALL NIGHT LONG Mary Jane Girls	*Gordy*	4
-	**14**	WRAPPED AROUND YOUR FINGER Police	*A&M*	1
30	[15]	NEVER STOP Echo and the Bunnymen	*Korova*	2
18	[16]	FORBIDDEN COLOURS David Sylvian and Riuichi Sakamoto	*Virgin*	4
13	**17**	ROCK 'N' ROLL IS KING Electric Light Orchestra	*Jet*	5
19	[18]	TANTALISE (WO WO EE YEH YEH) Jimmy The Hoover	*Innervision*	4
12	**19**	THE TROOPER Iron Maiden	*EMI*	4
23	**20**	DON'T TRY TO STOP IT Roman Holiday	*Jive*	4
-	**21**	THE CROWN Gary Byrd and the GB Experience ●	*Motown*	1
11	**22**	DEAD GIVEAWAY Shalamar	*Solar*	7
-	**23**	IT'S LATE Shakin' Stevens	*Epic*	1
14	**24**	TAKE THAT SITUATION Nick Heyward	*Arista*	6
29	[25]	SHE WORKS HARD FOR THE MONEY Donna Summer	*Mercury*	5
15	**26**	I GUESS THAT'S WHY THEY CALL IT THE BLUES Elton John	*Rocket*	8
36	**27**	THE FIRST PICTURE OF YOU Lotus Eaters	*Sylvan*	2
20	**28**	EVERY BREATH YOU TAKE Police	*A&M*	9
-	**29**	DO IT AGAIN-BILLIE JEAN Clubhouse ●	*Island*	1
-	**30**	GIVE IT UP KC and the Sunshine Band	*Epic*	1
-	**31**	FEEL LIKE MAKIN' LOVE George Benson	*Warner Brothers*	1

■Mike Oldfield's *Moonlight Shadow* spends three weeks at its peak position of number 4. The vocals are by Maggie Reilly (16.07.83) ■ Two different members of Japan have simultaneous hits as halves of a duo: David Sylvian with Riuichi Sakamoto and Mick Karn with Midge Ure (16.07.83)■

July 1983

□ Highest position disc reached ● Act's first ever week on chart

LW	TW	Title	Artist	Label	Wks
-	32	RIGHT NOW	Creatures	*Wonderland*	1
34	[33]	TELL ME WHY	Musical Youth	*MCA*	2
32	34	EVERYDAY I WRITE THE BOOK	Elvis Costello and the Attractions	*F Beat*	3
-	35	WATCHING	Thompson Twins	*Arista*	1
24	36	BAD BOYS	Wham!	*Innervision*	11
25	37	WAITING FOR A TRAIN	Flash and the Pan	*Easy Beat*	9
-	38	TROUBLE IN PARADISE	Al Jarreau	*WEA International*	1
39	[39]	AFTER A FASHION	Midge Ure and Mick Karn	*Musicfest*	2
-	40	GIVE IT SOME EMOTION	Tracie	*Respond*	1

WEEK ENDING 30 JULY 1983

LW	TW	Title	Artist	Label	Wks
1	[1]	WHEREVER I LAY MY HAT (THAT'S MY HOME)	Paul Young	*CBS*	6
2	[2]	IOU	Freeez	*Beggars Banquet*	6
4	3	WHO'S THAT GIRL	Eurythmics	*RCA*	4
7	4	DOUBLE DUTCH	Malcolm McLaren	*Charisma*	4
6	[5]	COME LIVE WITH ME	Heaven 17	*Virgin*	6
21	[6]	THE CROWN	Gary Byrd and the GB Experience	*Motown*	2
5	7	MOONLIGHT SHADOW	Mike Oldfield	*Virgin*	7
14	8	WRAPPED AROUND YOUR FINGER	Police	*A&M*	2
3	9	BABY JANE	Rod Stewart	*Warner Brothers*	9
11	10	CRUEL SUMMER	Bananarama	*London*	4
29	[11]	DO IT AGAIN-BILLIE JEAN	Clubhouse	*Island*	2
23	12	IT'S LATE	Shakin' Stevens	*Epic*	2
8	13	FLASHDANCE...WHAT A FEELING	Irene Cara	*Casablanca*	9
10	14	IT'S OVER	Funk Masters	*Master Funk*	6
20	15	DON'T TRY TO STOP IT	Roman Holiday	*Jive*	5
12	16	THE WALK	Cure	*Fiction*	4
15	17	NEVER STOP	Echo and the Bunnymen	*Korova*	3
9	18	WAR BABY	Tom Robinson	*Panic*	6
30	19	GIVE IT UP	KC and the Sunshine Band	*Epic*	2
16	20	FORBIDDEN COLOURS	David Sylvian and Riuichi Sakamoto	*Virgin*	5
13	21	ALL NIGHT LONG	Mary Jane Girls	*Gordy*	5
18	22	TANTALISE (WO WO EE YEH YEH)	Jimmy The Hoover	*Innervision*	5
17	23	ROCK 'N' ROLL IS KING	Electric Light Orchestra	*Jet*	6
19	24	THE TROOPER	Iron Maiden	*EMI*	5
27	25	THE FIRST PICTURE OF YOU	Lotus Eaters	*Sylvan*	3
-	26	EVERYTHING COUNTS	Depeche Mode	*Mute*	1
-	27	CLUB TROPICANA	Wham!	*Innervision*	1
31	[28]	FEEL LIKE MAKIN' LOVE	George Benson	*Warner Brothers*	2
32	29	RIGHT NOW	Creatures	*Wonderland*	2
34	30	EVERYDAY I WRITE THE BOOK	Elvis Costello and the Attractions	*F Beat*	4
-	31	BIG LOG	Robert Plant ●	*WEA*	1
22	32	DEAD GIVEAWAY	Shalamar	*Solar*	8
35	33	WATCHING	Thompson Twins	*Arista*	2
-	34	FREAK	Bruce Foxton ●	*Arista*	1
25	35	SHE WORKS HARD FOR THE MONEY	Donna Summer	*Mercury*	6
38	[36]	TROUBLE IN PARADISE	Al Jarreau	*WEA International*	2
33	37	TELL ME WHY	Musical Youth	*MCA*	3
40	38	GIVE IT SOME EMOTION	Tracie	*Respond*	2
26	39	I GUESS THAT'S WHY THEY CALL IT THE BLUES	Elton John	*Rocket*	9
28	40	EVERY BREATH YOU TAKE	Police	*A&M*	10

WEEK ENDING 6 AUGUST 1983

LW	TW	Title	Artist	Label	Wks
1	[1]	WHEREVER I LAY MY HAT (THAT'S MY HOME)	Paul Young	*CBS*	7
2	[2]	IOU	Freeez	*Beggars Banquet*	7
4	[3]	DOUBLE DUTCH	Malcolm McLaren	*Charisma*	5
3	4	WHO'S THAT GIRL	Eurythmics	*RCA*	5
19	5	GIVE IT UP	KC and the Sunshine Band	*Epic*	3
6	[6]	THE CROWN	Gary Byrd and the GB Experience	*Motown*	3
8	7	WRAPPED AROUND YOUR FINGER	Police	*A&M*	3
10	[8]	CRUEL SUMMER	Bananarama	*London*	5
5	9	COME LIVE WITH ME	Heaven 17	*Virgin*	7
27	10	CLUB TROPICANA	Wham!	*Innervision*	2
12	[11]	IT'S LATE	Shakin' Stevens	*Epic*	3
7	12	MOONLIGHT SHADOW	Mike Oldfield	*Virgin*	8
11	13	DO IT AGAIN-BILLIE JEAN	Clubhouse	*Island*	3
15	[14]	DON'T TRY TO STOP IT	Roman Holiday	*Jive*	6
31	15	BIG LOG	Robert Plant	*WEA*	2
26	16	EVERYTHING COUNTS	Depeche Mode	*Mute*	2
13	17	FLASHDANCE...WHAT A FEELING	Irene Cara	*Casablanca*	10
16	18	THE WALK	Cure	*Fiction*	5
9	19	BABY JANE	Rod Stewart	*Warner Brothers*	10
29	20	RIGHT NOW	Creatures	*Wonderland*	3
14	21	IT'S OVER	Funk Masters	*Master Funk*	7
17	22	NEVER STOP	Echo and the Bunnymen	*Korova*	4
25	23	THE FIRST PICTURE OF YOU	Lotus Eaters	*Sylvan*	4
-	24	I'M STILL STANDING	Elton John	*Rocket*	1
-	25	ROCKIT	Herbie Hancock	*CBS*	1
18	26	WAR BABY	Tom Robinson	*Panic*	7
34	27	FREAK	Bruce Foxton	*Arista*	2
30	[28]	EVERYDAY I WRITE THE BOOK	Elvis Costello and the Attractions	*F Beat*	5
28	29	FEEL LIKE MAKIN' LOVE	George Benson	*Warner Brothers*	3
20	30	FORBIDDEN COLOURS	David Sylvian and Riuichi Sakamoto	*Virgin*	6
21	31	ALL NIGHT LONG	Mary Jane Girls	*Gordy*	6
22	32	TANTALISE (WO WO EE YEH YEH)	Jimmy The Hoover	*Innervision*	6
38	33	GIVE IT SOME EMOTION	Tracie	*Respond*	3
-	34	LOVE BLONDE	Kim Wilde	*RAK*	1
33	35	WATCHING	Thompson Twins	*Arista*	3
23	36	ROCK 'N' ROLL IS KING	Electric Light Orchestra	*Jet*	7
-	37	WAIT UNTIL TONIGHT (MY LOVE)	Galaxy featuring Phil Fearon	*Ensign*	1
-	38	THE SUN GOES DOWN (LIVING IT UP)	Level 42	*Polydor*	1
24	39	THE TROOPER	Iron Maiden	*EMI*	6
-	40	WATCHING YOU WATCHING ME	David Grant	*Chrysalis*	1

WEEK ENDING 13 AUGUST 1983

LW	TW	Title	Artist	Label	Wks
5	[1]	GIVE IT UP	KC and the Sunshine Band	*Epic*	4
1	2	WHEREVER I LAY MY HAT (THAT'S MY HOME)	Paul Young	*CBS*	8
2	3	IOU	Freeez	*Beggars Banquet*	8
3	4	DOUBLE DUTCH	Malcolm McLaren	*Charisma*	6
10	5	CLUB TROPICANA	Wham!	*Innervision*	3
6	[6]	THE CROWN	Gary Byrd and the GB Experience	*Motown*	4
4	7	WHO'S THAT GIRL	Eurythmics	*RCA*	6
-	8	LONG HOT SUMMER	Style Council	*Polydor*	1
24	9	I'M STILL STANDING	Elton John	*Rocket*	2
16	10	EVERYTHING COUNTS	Depeche Mode	*Mute*	3
15	[11]	BIG LOG	Robert Plant	*WEA*	3
-	12	GOLD	Spandau Ballet	*Reformation*	1
8	13	CRUEL SUMMER	Bananarama	*London*	6
11	14	IT'S LATE	Shakin' Stevens	*Epic*	4
25	15	ROCKIT	Herbie Hancock	*CBS*	2
12	16	MOONLIGHT SHADOW	Mike Oldfield	*Virgin*	9
20	17	RIGHT NOW	Creatures	*Wonderland*	4
7	18	WRAPPED AROUND YOUR FINGER	Police	*A&M*	4
9	19	COME LIVE WITH ME	Heaven 17	*Virgin*	8
14	20	DON'T TRY TO STOP IT	Roman Holiday	*Jive*	7
23	21	THE FIRST PICTURE OF YOU	Lotus Eaters	*Sylvan*	5
13	22	DO IT AGAIN-BILLIE JEAN	Clubhouse	*Island*	4
27	[23]	FREAK	Bruce Foxton	*Arista*	3
34	24	LOVE BLONDE	Kim Wilde	*RAK*	2
17	25	FLASHDANCE...WHAT A FEELING	Irene Cara	*Casablanca*	11
37	26	WAIT UNTIL TONIGHT (MY LOVE)	Galaxy featuring Phil Fearon	*Ensign*	2
19	27	BABY JANE	Rod Stewart	*Warner Brothers*	11
33	28	GIVE IT SOME EMOTION	Tracie	*Respond*	4
21	29	IT'S OVER	Funk Masters	*Master Funk*	8
18	30	THE WALK	Cure	*Fiction*	6

In these weeks ■ Two members of major chart groups enjoy their first solo hits in the same week - Robert Plant of Led Zeppelin and Bruce Foxton of Jam (30.07.83) ■ Nine years to the week after their chart debut, KC and the Sunshine Band enjoy their first and so far only number one (13.08.83) ■

LW	TW	Title / Artist	Label	Wks
-	31	TOUR DE FRANCE Kraftwerk	EMI	1
29	32	FEEL LIKE MAKIN' LOVE George Benson	Warner Brothers	4
38	33	THE SUN GOES DOWN (LIVING IT UP) Level 42	Polydor	2
40	34	WATCHING YOU WATCHING ME David Grant	Chrysalis	2
22	35	NEVER STOP Echo and the Bunnymen	Korova	5
28	36	EVERYDAY I WRITE THE BOOK Elvis Costello and the Attractions	F Beat	6
-	37	GUILTY OF LOVE Whitesnake	Liberty	1
26	38	WAR BABY Tom Robinson	Panic	8
-	39	WALKING IN THE RAIN Modern Romance	WEA	1
30	40	FORBIDDEN COLOURS David Sylvian and Riuichi Sakamoto	Virgin	7

LW	TW	*WEEK ENDING* **20 AUGUST 1983**		Wks
1	[1]	GIVE IT UP KC and the Sunshine Band	Epic	5
12	[2]	GOLD Spandau Ballet	Reformation	2
8	[3]	LONG HOT SUMMER Style Council	Polydor	2
5	[4]	CLUB TROPICANA Wham!	Innervision	4
9	5	I'M STILL STANDING Elton John	Rocket	3
10	[6]	EVERYTHING COUNTS Depeche Mode	Mute	4
4	7	DOUBLE DUTCH Malcolm McLaren	Charisma	7
15	[8]	ROCKIT Herbie Hancock	CBS	3
2	9	WHEREVER I LAY MY HAT (THAT'S MY HOME) Paul Young	CBS	9
3	10	IOU Freeez	Beggars Banquet	9
6	11	THE CROWN Gary Byrd and the GB Experience	Motown	5
11	12	BIG LOG Robert Plant	WEA	4
7	13	WHO'S THAT GIRL Eurythmics	RCA	7
17	[14]	RIGHT NOW Creatures	Wonderland	5
21	[15]	THE FIRST PICTURE OF YOU Lotus Eaters	Sylvan	6
13	16	CRUEL SUMMER Bananarama	London	7
34	17	WATCHING YOU WATCHING ME David Grant	Chrysalis	3
16	18	MOONLIGHT SHADOW Mike Oldfield	Virgin	10
-	19	WINGS OF A DOVE Madness	Stiff	1
26	[20]	WAIT UNTIL TONIGHT (MY LOVE) Galaxy featuring Phil Fearon	Ensign	3
33	21	THE SUN GOES DOWN (LIVING IT UP) Level 42	Polydor	3
14	22	IT'S LATE Shakin' Stevens	Epic	5
24	[23]	LOVE BLONDE Kim Wilde	RAK	3
28	[24]	GIVE IT SOME EMOTION Tracie	Respond	5
23	25	FREAK Bruce Foxton	Arista	4
18	26	WRAPPED AROUND YOUR FINGER Police	A&M	5
19	27	COME LIVE WITH ME Heaven 17	Virgin	9
31	28	TOUR DE FRANCE Kraftwerk	EMI	2
-	29	COME DANCING Kinks	Arista	1
39	30	WALKING IN THE RAIN Modern Romance	WEA	2
37	[31]	GUILTY OF LOVE Whitesnake	Liberty	2
20	32	DON'T TRY TO STOP IT Roman Holiday	Jive	8
-	33	DISAPPEARING ACT Shalamar	Solar	1
25	34	FLASHDANCE...WHAT A FEELING Irene Cara	Casablanca	12
-	35	BAD DAY Carmel ●	London	1
-	36	RED RED WINE UB40	DEP International	1
-	37	DON'T CRY Asia ●	Geffen	1
22	38	DO IT AGAIN-BILLIE JEAN Clubhouse	Island	5
29	39	IT'S OVER Funk Masters	Master Funk	9
27	40	BABY JANE Rod Stewart	Warner Brothers	12

LW	TW	*WEEK ENDING* **27 AUGUST 1983**		Wks
1	[1]	GIVE IT UP KC and the Sunshine Band	Epic	6
2	[2]	GOLD Spandau Ballet	Reformation	3
3	[3]	LONG HOT SUMMER Style Council	Polydor	3
5	[4]	I'M STILL STANDING Elton John	Rocket	4
4	5	CLUB TROPICANA Wham!	Innervision	5
19	6	WINGS OF A DOVE Madness	Stiff	2
6	7	EVERYTHING COUNTS Depeche Mode	Mute	5
8	[8]	ROCKIT Herbie Hancock	CBS	4
36	9	RED RED WINE UB40	DEP International	2
17	[10]	WATCHING YOU WATCHING ME David Grant	Chrysalis	4
7	11	DOUBLE DUTCH Malcolm McLaren	Charisma	8
29	[12]	COME DANCING Kinks	Arista	2
30	13	WALKING IN THE RAIN Modern Romance	WEA	3

September 1983

□ Highest position disc reached ● Act's first ever week on chart

LW	TW	Title / Artist	Label	Wks
21	14	THE SUN GOES DOWN (LIVING IT UP) Level 42	Polydor	4
15	[15]	THE FIRST PICTURE OF YOU Lotus Eaters	Sylvan	7
10	16	IOU Freeez	Beggars Banquet	10
12	17	BIG LOG Robert Plant	WEA	5
11	18	THE CROWN Gary Byrd and the GB Experience	Motown	6
14	19	RIGHT NOW Creatures	Wonderland	6
9	20	WHEREVER I LAY MY HAT (THAT'S MY HOME) Paul Young	CBS	10
20	21	WAIT UNTIL TONIGHT (MY LOVE) Galaxy featuring Phil Fearon	Ensign	4
28	[22]	TOUR DE FRANCE Kraftwerk	EMI	3
23	[23]	LOVE BLONDE Kim Wilde	RAK	4
13	24	WHO'S THAT GIRL Eurythmics	RCA	8
24	25	GIVE IT SOME EMOTION Tracie	Respond	6
35	26	BAD DAY Carmel	London	2
-	27	WHAT AM I GONNA DO Rod Stewart	Warner Brothers	1
33	28	DISAPPEARING ACT Shalamar	Solar	2
18	29	MOONLIGHT SHADOW Mike Oldfield	Virgin	11
16	30	CRUEL SUMMER Bananarama	London	8
31	[31]	GUILTY OF LOVE Whitesnake	Liberty	3
22	32	IT'S LATE Shakin' Stevens	Epic	6
37	[33]	DON'T CRY Asia	Geffen	2
27	34	COME LIVE WITH ME Heaven 17	Virgin	10
-	[35]	BLUE WORLD Moody Blues	Threshold	1
-	36	TONIGHT I CELEBRATE MY LOVE Peabo Bryson and Roberta Flack ●	Capitol	1
-	37	(SHE'S) SEXY AND 17 Stray Cats	Arista	1
-	[38]	JUST OUTSIDE OF HEAVEN H20	RCA	1
26	39	WRAPPED AROUND YOUR FINGER Police	A&M	6
25	40	FREAK Bruce Foxton	Arista	5

LW	TW	*WEEK ENDING* **3 SEPTEMBER 1983**		Wks
9	[1]	RED RED WINE UB40	DEP International	3
1	2	GIVE IT UP KC and the Sunshine Band	Epic	7
2	3	GOLD Spandau Ballet	Reformation	4
6	4	WINGS OF A DOVE Madness	Stiff	3
4	5	I'M STILL STANDING Elton John	Rocket	5
5	6	CLUB TROPICANA Wham!	Innervision	6
3	7	LONG HOT SUMMER/PARIS MATCH Style Council	Polydor	4
27	8	WHAT AM I GONNA DO Rod Stewart	Warner Brothers	2
13	9	WALKING IN THE RAIN Modern Romance	WEA	4
10	[10]	WATCHING YOU WATCHING ME David Grant	Chrysalis	5
14	11	THE SUN GOES DOWN (LIVING IT UP) Level 42	Polydor	5
8	12	ROCKIT Herbie Hancock	CBS	5
12	13	COME DANCING Kinks	Arista	3
7	14	EVERYTHING COUNTS Depeche Mode	Mute	6
26	[15]	BAD DAY Carmel	London	3
36	16	TONIGHT I CELEBRATE MY LOVE Peabo Bryson and Roberta Flack	Capitol	2
-	17	CONFUSION New Order	Factory	1
28	[18]	DISAPPEARING ACT Shalamar	Solar	3
11	19	DOUBLE DUTCH Malcolm McLaren	Charisma	9
-	20	MAMA Genesis	Virgin	1
15	21	THE FIRST PICTURE OF YOU Lotus Eaters	Sylvan	8
-	22	CHANCE Big Country	Mercury	1
22	23	TOUR DE FRANCE Kraftwerk	EMI	4
17	24	BIG LOG Robert Plant	WEA	6
16	25	IOU Freeez	Beggars Banquet	11
18	26	THE CROWN Gary Byrd and the GB Experience	Motown	7
23	27	LOVE BLONDE Kim Wilde	RAK	5
19	28	RIGHT NOW Creatures	Wonderland	7
21	29	WAIT UNTIL TONIGHT (MY LOVE) Galaxy featuring Phil Fearon	Ensign	5
-	30	WARRIORS Gary Numan	Beggars Banquet	1
20	31	WHEREVER I LAY MY HAT (THAT'S MY HOME) Paul Young	CBS	11
37	32	(SHE'S) SEXY AND 17 Stray Cats	Arista	2
25	33	GIVE IT SOME EMOTION Tracie	Respond	7

■ *Don't Cry* by Asia is the first record to peak at number 33 for 55 weeks (27.08.83) ■ Jam's *Paris Match* receives equal chart billing with *The Long Hot Summer* to become the first French journal to hit the top 10 since Brotherhood Of Man's *Figaro* over five years earlier (03.09.83) ■

September 1983

□ Highest position disc reached ● Act's first ever week on chart

LW	TW	Title	Artist	Label	Wks
24	34	WHO'S THAT GIRL	Eurythmics	RCA	9
29	35	MOONLIGHT SHADOW	Mike Oldfield	Virgin	12
-	36	NEVER SAY DIE (GIVE A LITTLE BIT MORE)	Cliff Richard	EMI	1
-	37	JOHNNY FRIENDLY	JoBoxers	RCA	1
38	38	JUST OUTSIDE OF HEAVEN	H20	RCA	2
35	39	BLUE WORLD	Moody Blues	Threshold	2
-	40	RIDERS ON THE STORM	Annabel Lamb ●	A&M	1

WEEK ENDING 10 SEPTEMBER 1983

LW	TW	Title	Artist	Label	Wks
1	1	RED RED WINE	UB40	DEP International	4
4	2	WINGS OF A DOVE	Madness	Stiff	4
8	3	WHAT AM I GONNA DO	Rod Stewart	Warner Brothers	3
2	4	GIVE IT UP	KC and the Sunshine Band	Epic	8
20	5	MAMA	Genesis	Virgin	2
3	6	GOLD	Spandau Ballet	Reformation	5
16	7	TONIGHT I CELEBRATE MY LOVE	Peabo Bryson and Roberta Flack	Capitol	3
5	8	I'M STILL STANDING	Elton John	Rocket	6
9	9	WALKING IN THE RAIN	Modern Romance	WEA	5
11	10	THE SUN GOES DOWN (LIVING IT UP)	Level 42	Polydor	6
6	11	CLUB TROPICANA	Wham!	Innervision	7
17	12	CONFUSION	New Order	Factory	2
7	13	LONG HOT SUMMER/PARIS MATCH	Style Council	Polydor	5
10	14	WATCHING YOU WATCHING ME	David Grant	Chrysalis	6
22	15	CHANCE	Big Country	Mercury	2
15	16	BAD DAY	Carmel	London	4
12	17	ROCKIT	Herbie Hancock	CBS	6
13	18	COME DANCING	Kinks	Arista	4
18	19	DISAPPEARING ACT	Shalamar	Solar	4
30	20	WARRIORS	Gary Numan	Beggars Banquet	2
-	21	DOLCE VITA	Ryan Paris ●	Carrere	1
14	22	EVERYTHING COUNTS	Depeche Mode	Mute	7
36	23	NEVER SAY DIE (GIVE A LITTLE BIT MORE)	Cliff Richard	EMI	2
-	24	OL' RAG BLUES	Status Quo	Vertigo	1
23	25	TOUR DE FRANCE	Kraftwerk	EMI	5
25	26	IOU	Freeez	Beggars Banquet	12
-	27	COME BACK AND STAY	Paul Young	CBS	1
-	28	CRUSHED BY THE WHEELS OF INDUSTRY	Heaven 17	Virgin	1
32	29	(SHE'S) SEXY AND 17	Stray Cats	Arista	3
19	30	DOUBLE DUTCH	Malcolm McLaren	Charisma	10
21	31	THE FIRST PICTURE OF YOU	Lotus Eaters	Sylvan	9
24	32	BIG LOG	Robert Plant	WEA	7
26	33	THE CROWN	Gary Byrd and the GB Experience	Motown	8
40	34	RIDERS ON THE STORM	Annabel Lamb	A&M	2
37	35	JOHNNY FRIENDLY	JoBoxers	RCA	2
31	36	WHEREVER I LAY MY HAT (THAT'S MY HOME)	Paul Young	CBS	12
-	37	A STEP IN THE RIGHT DIRECTION	Truth	Formation	1
27	38	LOVE BLONDE	Kim Wilde	RAK	6
35	39	MOONLIGHT SHADOW	Mike Oldfield	Virgin	13
29	40	WAIT UNTIL TONIGHT (MY LOVE)	Galaxy featuring Phil Fearon	Ensign	6

WEEK ENDING 17 SEPTEMBER 1983

LW	TW	Title	Artist	Label	Wks
1	1	RED RED WINE	UB40	DEP International	5
7	2	TONIGHT I CELEBRATE MY LOVE	Peabo Bryson and Roberta Flack	Capitol	4
-	3	KARMA CHAMELEON	Culture Club	Virgin	1
5	4	MAMA	Genesis	Virgin	3
21	5	DOLCE VITA	Ryan Paris	Carrere	2
27	6	COME BACK AND STAY	Paul Young	CBS	2
3	7	WHAT AM I GONNA DO	Rod Stewart	Warner Brothers	4
2	8	WINGS OF A DOVE	Madness	Stiff	5
9	9	WALKING IN THE RAIN	Modern Romance	WEA	6
10	10	THE SUN GOES DOWN (LIVING IT UP)	Level 42	Polydor	7
24	11	OL' RAG BLUES	Status Quo	Vertigo	2
15	12	CHANCE	Big Country	Mercury	3
4	13	GIVE IT UP	KC and the Sunshine Band	Epic	9
12	14	CONFUSION	New Order	Factory	3
8	15	I'M STILL STANDING	Elton John	Rocket	7
6	16	GOLD	Spandau Ballet	Reformation	6
28	17	CRUSHED BY THE WHEELS OF INDUSTRY	Heaven 17	Virgin	2
11	18	CLUB TROPICANA	Wham!	Innervision	8
14	19	WATCHING YOU WATCHING ME	David Grant	Chrysalis	7
23	20	NEVER SAY DIE (GIVE A LITTLE BIT MORE)	Cliff Richard	EMI	3
20	21	WARRIORS	Gary Numan	Beggars Banquet	3
19	22	DISAPPEARING ACT	Shalamar	Solar	5
17	23	ROCKIT	Herbie Hancock	CBS	7
13	24	LONG HOT SUMMER/PARIS MATCH	Style Council	Polydor	6
18	25	COME DANCING	Kinks	Arista	5
16	26	BAD DAY	Carmel	London	5
34	27	RIDERS ON THE STORM	Annabel Lamb	A&M	3
22	28	EVERYTHING COUNTS	Depeche Mode	Mute	8
29	29	(SHE'S) SEXY AND 17	Stray Cats	Arista	4
-	30	GO DEH YAKA (GO TO THE TOP)	Monyaka ●	Polydor	1
35	31	JOHNNY FRIENDLY	JoBoxers	RCA	3
37	32	A STEP IN THE RIGHT DIRECTION	Truth	Formation	2
-	33	BIG APPLE	Kajagoogoo	EMI	1
-	34	TAHITI	David Essex	Mercury	1
-	35	THERE'S SOMETHING WRONG IN PARADISE	Kid Creole and the Coconuts	Island	1
25	36	TOUR DE FRANCE	Kraftwerk	EMI	6
-	37	BLUE MONDAY	New Order	Factory	1
-	38	BODY WORK	Hot Streak ●	Polydor	1
-	39	DR HECKYLL AND MR JIVE	Men At Work	Epic	1
-	40	WHAT I GOT IS WHAT YOU NEED	Unique ●	Prelude	1

WEEK ENDING 24 SEPTEMBER 1983

LW	TW	Title	Artist	Label	Wks
3	1	KARMA CHAMELEON	Culture Club	Virgin	2
1	2	RED RED WINE	UB40	DEP International	6
2	3	TONIGHT I CELEBRATE MY LOVE	Peabo Bryson and Roberta Flack	Capitol	5
6	4	COME BACK AND STAY	Paul Young	CBS	3
4	5	MAMA	Genesis	Virgin	4
5	6	DOLCE VITA	Ryan Paris	Carrere	3
9	7	WALKING IN THE RAIN	Modern Romance	WEA	7
-	8	MODERN LOVE	David Bowie	EMI America	1
11	9	OL' RAG BLUES	Status Quo	Vertigo	3
7	10	WHAT AM I GONNA DO	Rod Stewart	Warner Brothers	5
12	11	CHANCE	Big Country	Mercury	4
33	12	BIG APPLE	Kajagoogoo	EMI	2
8	13	WINGS OF A DOVE	Madness	Stiff	6
10	14	THE SUN GOES DOWN (LIVING IT UP)	Level 42	Polydor	8
20	15	NEVER SAY DIE (GIVE A LITTLE BIT MORE)	Cliff Richard	EMI	4
30	16	GO DEH YAKA (GO TO THE TOP)	Monyaka	Polydor	2
17	17	CRUSHED BY THE WHEELS OF INDUSTRY	Heaven 17	Virgin	3
13	18	GIVE IT UP	KC and the Sunshine Band	Epic	10
34	19	TAHITI	David Essex	Mercury	2
37	20	BLUE MONDAY	New Order	Factory	2
-	21	SOUL INSIDE	Soft Cell	Some Bizzare	1
14	22	CONFUSION	New Order	Factory	4
15	23	I'M STILL STANDING	Elton John	Rocket	8
16	24	GOLD	Spandau Ballet	Reformation	7
18	25	CLUB TROPICANA	Wham!	Innervision	9
38	26	BODY WORK	Hot Streak	Polydor	2
19	27	WATCHING YOU WATCHING ME	David Grant	Chrysalis	8
27	28	RIDERS ON THE STORM	Annabel Lamb	A&M	4
-	29	REBEL RUN	Toyah	Safari	1
40	30	WHAT I GOT IS WHAT YOU NEED	Unique	Prelude	2
39	31	DR HECKYLL AND MR JIVE	Men At Work	Epic	2
25	32	COME DANCING	Kinks	Arista	6
32	33	A STEP IN THE RIGHT DIRECTION	Truth	Formation	3
23	34	ROCKIT	Herbie Hancock	CBS	8
22	35	DISAPPEARING ACT	Shalamar	Solar	6

In these weeks ■ The Kinks enjoy their final week in the top 40 with their 20th hit single, but the first in over eleven years (24.09.83) ■ Cliff Richard's *Never Say Die (Give A Little More)* is his 77th top 40 hit, but only the 4th with brackets in the title. Only one of those, *Wind Me Up (Let Me Go)* hit the top 10 (24.09.83)■

LW	TW	Title / Artist	Label	Wks
35	36	THERE'S SOMETHING WRONG IN PARADISE Kid Creole and the Coconuts	*Island*	2
21	37	WARRIORS Gary Numan	*Beggars Banquet*	4
24	38	LONG HOT SUMMER/PARIS MATCH Style Council	*Polydor*	7
-	39	THIS IS NOT A LOVE SONG Public Image Ltd	*Virgin*	1
26	40	BAD DAY Carmel	*London*	6

WEEK ENDING 1 OCTOBER 1983

LW	TW	Title / Artist	Label	Wks
1	1	KARMA CHAMELEON Culture Club	*Virgin*	3
2	2	RED RED WINE UB40	*DEP International*	7
8	3	MODERN LOVE David Bowie	*EMI America*	2
3	4	TONIGHT I CELEBRATE MY LOVE Peabo Bryson and Roberta Flack	*Capitol*	6
4	5	COME BACK AND STAY Paul Young	*CBS*	4
5	6	MAMA Genesis	*Virgin*	5
6	7	DOLCE VITA Ryan Paris	*Carrere*	4
12	8	BIG APPLE Kajagoogoo	*EMI*	3
11	9	CHANCE Big Country	*Mercury*	5
9	10	OL' RAG BLUES Status Quo	*Vertigo*	4
7	11	WALKING IN THE RAIN Modern Romance	*WEA*	8
20	12	BLUE MONDAY New Order	*Factory*	3
19	13	TAHITI David Essex	*Mercury*	3
16	14	GO DEH YAKA (GO TO THE TOP) Monyaka	*Polydor*	3
39	15	THIS IS NOT A LOVE SONG Public Image Ltd	*Virgin*	2
21	16	SOUL INSIDE Soft Cell	*Some Bizzare*	2
-	17	DEAR PRUDENCE Siouxsie and the Banshees	*Wonderland*	1
17	18	CRUSHED BY THE WHEELS OF INDUSTRY Heaven 17	*Virgin*	4
26	19	BODY WORK Hot Streak	*Polydor*	3
10	20	WHAT AM I GONNA DO Rod Stewart	*Warner Brothers*	6
15	21	NEVER SAY DIE (GIVE A LITTLE BIT MORE) Cliff Richard	*EMI*	5
-	22	NEW SONG Howard Jones ●	*WEA*	1
-	23	68 GUNS Alarm ●	*IRS*	1
29	24	REBEL RUN Toyah	*Safari*	2
14	25	THE SUN GOES DOWN (LIVING IT UP) Level 42	*Polydor*	9
13	26	WINGS OF A DOVE Madness	*Stiff*	7
30	27	WHAT I GOT IS WHAT YOU NEED Unique	*Prelude*	3
-	28	BLUE HAT FOR A BLUE DAY Nick Heyward	*Arista*	1
-	29	SUPERMAN (GIOCA JOUER) Black Lace ●	*Flair*	1
-	30	IN YOUR EYES George Benson	*Warner Brothers*	1
-	31	THEY DON'T KNOW Tracey Ullman	*Stiff*	1
-	32	MIDNIGHT AT THE LOST AND FOUND Meat Loaf	*Cleveland International*	1
31	33	DR HECKYLL AND MR JIVE Men At Work	*Epic*	3
18	34	GIVE IT UP KC and the Sunshine Band	*Epic*	11
-	35	LOVE IN ITSELF.2 Depeche Mode	*Mute*	1
22	36	CONFUSION New Order	*Factory*	5
36	37	THERE'S SOMETHING WRONG IN PARADISE Kid Creole and the Coconuts	*Island*	3
23	38	I'M STILL STANDING Elton John	*Rocket*	9
-	39	TEARS ON THE TELEPHONE Hot Chocolate	*RAK*	1
24	40	GOLD Spandau Ballet	*Reformation*	8

WEEK ENDING 8 OCTOBER 1983

LW	TW	Title / Artist	Label	Wks
1	1	KARMA CHAMELEON Culture Club	*Virgin*	4
3	2	MODERN LOVE David Bowie	*EMI America*	3
2	3	RED RED WINE UB40	*DEP International*	8
17	4	DEAR PRUDENCE Siouxsie and the Banshees	*Wonderland*	2
15	5	THIS IS NOT A LOVE SONG Public Image Ltd	*Virgin*	3
5	6	COME BACK AND STAY Paul Young	*CBS*	5
4	7	TONIGHT I CELEBRATE MY LOVE Peabo Bryson and Roberta Flack	*Capitol*	7
13	8	TAHITI David Essex	*Mercury*	4
31	9	THEY DON'T KNOW Tracey Ullman	*Stiff*	2
12	10	BLUE MONDAY New Order	*Factory*	4
6	11	MAMA Genesis	*Virgin*	6
8	12	BIG APPLE Kajagoogoo	*EMI*	4
22	13	NEW SONG Howard Jones	*WEA*	2
9	14	CHANCE Big Country	*Mercury*	6
30	15	IN YOUR EYES George Benson	*Warner Brothers*	2
29	16	SUPERMAN (GIOCA JOUER) Black Lace	*Flair*	2

October 1983

□ Highest position disc reached ● Act's first ever week on chart

LW	TW	Title / Artist	Label	Wks
7	17	DOLCE VITA Ryan Paris	*Carrere*	5
14	18	GO DEH YAKA (GO TO THE TOP) Monyaka	*Polydor*	4
23	19	68 GUNS Alarm	*IRS*	2
10	20	OL' RAG BLUES Status Quo	*Vertigo*	5
19	21	BODY WORK Hot Streak	*Polydor*	4
11	22	WALKING IN THE RAIN Modern Romance	*WEA*	9
18	23	CRUSHED BY THE WHEELS OF INDUSTRY Heaven 17	*Virgin*	5
28	24	BLUE HAT FOR A BLUE DAY Nick Heyward	*Arista*	2
16	25	SOUL INSIDE Soft Cell	*Some Bizzare*	3
35	26	LOVE IN ITSELF.2 Depeche Mode	*Mute*	2
27	27	WHAT I GOT IS WHAT YOU NEED Unique	*Prelude*	4
32	28	MIDNIGHT AT THE LOST AND FOUND Meat Loaf	*Cleveland International*	2
-	29	(HEY YOU) THE ROCKSTEADY CREW Rocksteady Crew ●	*Charisma*	1
21	30	NEVER SAY DIE (GIVE A LITTLE BIT MORE) Cliff Richard	*EMI*	6
-	31	ALL NIGHT LONG (ALL NIGHT) Lionel Richie	*Motown*	1
24	32	REBEL RUN Toyah	*Safari*	3
-	33	POP GOES MY LOVE Freeez	*Beggars Banquet*	1
20	34	WHAT AM I GONNA DO Rod Stewart	*Warner Brothers*	7
25	35	THE SUN GOES DOWN (LIVING IT UP) Level 42	*Polydor*	10
26	36	WINGS OF A DOVE Madness	*Stiff*	8
39	37	TEARS ON THE TELEPHONE Hot Chocolate	*RAK*	2
-	38	LOVE WILL FIND A WAY David Grant	*Chrysalis*	1
-	39	LONDON TOWN Bucks Fizz	*RCA*	1
-	40	SUPERSTAR Lydia Murdock ●	*Korova*	1

WEEK ENDING 15 OCTOBER 1983

LW	TW	Title / Artist	Label	Wks
1	1	KARMA CHAMELEON Culture Club	*Virgin*	5
9	2	THEY DON'T KNOW Tracey Ullman	*Stiff*	3
4	3	DEAR PRUDENCE Siouxsie and the Banshees	*Wonderland*	3
2	4	MODERN LOVE David Bowie	*EMI America*	4
13	5	NEW SONG Howard Jones	*WEA*	3
5	6	THIS IS NOT A LOVE SONG Public Image Ltd	*Virgin*	4
15	7	IN YOUR EYES George Benson	*Warner Brothers*	3
3	8	RED RED WINE UB40	*DEP International*	9
10	9	BLUE MONDAY New Order	*Factory*	5
8	10	TAHITI David Essex	*Mercury*	5
29	11	(HEY YOU) THE ROCKSTEADY CREW Rocksteady Crew	*Charisma*	2
16	12	SUPERMAN (GIOCA JOUER) Black Lace	*Flair*	3
6	13	COME BACK AND STAY Paul Young	*CBS*	6
7	14	TONIGHT I CELEBRATE MY LOVE Peabo Bryson and Roberta Flack	*Capitol*	8
24	15	BLUE HAT FOR A BLUE DAY Nick Heyward	*Arista*	3
31	16	ALL NIGHT LONG (ALL NIGHT) Lionel Richie	*Motown*	2
19	17	68 GUNS Alarm	*IRS*	3
12	18	BIG APPLE Kajagoogoo	*EMI*	5
11	19	MAMA Genesis	*Virgin*	7
17	20	DOLCE VITA Ryan Paris	*Carrere*	6
28	21	MIDNIGHT AT THE LOST AND FOUND Meat Loaf	*Cleveland International*	3
14	22	CHANCE Big Country	*Mercury*	7
18	23	GO DEH YAKA (GO TO THE TOP) Monyaka	*Polydor*	5
26	24	LOVE IN ITSELF.2 Depeche Mode	*Mute*	3
-	25	SAY SAY SAY Paul McCartney and Michael Jackson	*Parlophone*	1
38	26	LOVE WILL FIND A WAY David Grant	*Chrysalis*	2
21	27	BODY WORK Hot Streak	*Polydor*	5
33	28	POP GOES MY LOVE Freeez	*Beggars Banquet*	2
20	29	OL' RAG BLUES Status Quo	*Vertigo*	6
40	30	SUPERSTAR Lydia Murdock	*Korova*	2
22	31	WALKING IN THE RAIN Modern Romance	*WEA*	10
27	32	WHAT I GOT IS WHAT YOU NEED Unique	*Prelude*	5
-	33	AUTODRIVE Herbie Hancock	*CBS*	1
23	34	CRUSHED BY THE WHEELS OF INDUSTRY Heaven 17	*Virgin*	6
-	35	KISSING WITH CONFIDENCE Will Powers ●	*Island*	1

■The third song from the Beatles' white album to hit the charts is Siouxsie and the Banshees' *Dear Prudence*. By reaching no. 3 it outperforms the Beatles' own version of *Back In The USSR* in 1976, but does not match Marmalade's no. 1 hit in 1968 with *Ob-La-Di Ob-La-Da* (15.10.83)■

October 1983

□ Highest position disc reached ● Act's first ever week on chart

LW	TW	Title	Artist	Label	Wks
-	36	THE SAFETY DANCE	Men Without Hats ●	Statik	1
39	37	LONDON TOWN	Bucks Fizz	RCA	2
-	38	PLEASE DON'T MAKE ME CRY	UB40	DEP International	1
25	39	SOUL INSIDE	Soft Cell	Some Bizzare	4
-	40	KISS THE BRIDE	Elton John	Rocket	1

WEEK ENDING 22 OCTOBER 1983

LW	TW	Title	Artist	Label	Wks
1	1	KARMA CHAMELEON	Culture Club	Virgin	6
2	2	THEY DON'T KNOW	Tracey Ullman	Stiff	4
5	3	NEW SONG	Howard Jones	WEA	4
16	4	ALL NIGHT LONG (ALL NIGHT)	Lionel Richie	Motown	3
3	5	DEAR PRUDENCE	Siouxsie and the Banshees	Wonderland	4
11	6	(HEY YOU) THE ROCKSTEADY CREW	Rocksteady Crew	Charisma	3
7	7	IN YOUR EYES	George Benson	Warner Brothers	4
4	8	MODERN LOVE	David Bowie	EMI America	5
12	9	SUPERMAN (GIOCA JOUER)	Black Lace	Flair	4
25	10	SAY SAY SAY	Paul McCartney and Michael Jackson	Parlophone	2
6	11	THIS IS NOT A LOVE SONG	Public Image Ltd	Virgin	5
9	12	BLUE MONDAY	New Order	Factory	6
36	13	THE SAFETY DANCE	Men Without Hats	Statik	2
15	14	BLUE HAT FOR A BLUE DAY	Nick Heyward	Arista	4
38	15	PLEASE DON'T MAKE ME CRY	UB40	DEP International	2
8	16	RED RED WINE	UB40	DEP International	10
21	17	MIDNIGHT AT THE LOST AND FOUND	Meat Loaf	Cleveland International	4
30	18	SUPERSTAR	Lydia Murdock	Korova	3
10	19	TAHITI	David Essex	Mercury	6
17	20	68 GUNS	Alarm	IRS	4
24	21	LOVE IN ITSELF.2	Depeche Mode	Mute	4
14	22	TONIGHT I CELEBRATE MY LOVE	Peabo Bryson and Roberta Flack	Capitol	9
13	23	COME BACK AND STAY	Paul Young	CBS	7
26	24	LOVE WILL FIND A WAY	David Grant	Chrysalis	3
-	25	UPTOWN GIRL	Billy Joel	CBS	1
28	26	POP GOES MY LOVE	Freeez	Beggars Banquet	3
18	27	BIG APPLE	Kajagoogoo	EMI	6
19	28	MAMA	Genesis	Virgin	8
20	29	DOLCE VITA	Ryan Paris	Carrere	7
40	30	KISS THE BRIDE	Elton John	Rocket	2
23	31	GO DEH YAKA (GO TO THE TOP)	Monyaka	Polydor	6
35	32	KISSING WITH CONFIDENCE	Will Powers	Island	2
-	33	OVER AND OVER	Shalamar	Solar	1
37	34	LONDON TOWN	Bucks Fizz	RCA	3
22	35	CHANCE	Big Country	Mercury	8
-	36	SISTER SURPRISE	Gary Numan	Beggars Banquet	1
-	37	REILLY	Olympic Orchestra ●	Red Bus	1
27	38	BODY WORK	Hot Streak	Polydor	6
-	39	UNCONDITIONAL LOVE	Donna Summer	Mercury	1
-	40	MOTOR MANIA	Roman Holiday	Jive	1

WEEK ENDING 29 OCTOBER 1983

LW	TW	Title	Artist	Label	Wks
1	1	KARMA CHAMELEON	Culture Club	Virgin	7
4	2	ALL NIGHT LONG (ALL NIGHT)	Lionel Richie	Motown	4
2	3	THEY DON'T KNOW	Tracey Ullman	Stiff	5
-	4	UNION OF THE SNAKE	Duran Duran	EMI	1
3	5	NEW SONG	Howard Jones	WEA	5
6	6	(HEY YOU) THE ROCKSTEADY CREW	Rocksteady Crew	Charisma	4
25	7	UPTOWN GIRL	Billy Joel	CBS	2
13	8	THE SAFETY DANCE	Men Without Hats	Statik	3
7	9	IN YOUR EYES	George Benson	Warner Brothers	5
9	10	SUPERMAN (GIOCA JOUER)	Black Lace	Flair	5
5	11	DEAR PRUDENCE	Siouxsie and the Banshees	Wonderland	5
15	12	PLEASE DON'T MAKE ME CRY	UB40	DEP International	3
10	13	SAY SAY SAY	Paul McCartney and Michael Jackson	Parlophone	3
18	14	SUPERSTAR	Lydia Murdock	Korova	4
12	15	BLUE MONDAY	New Order	Factory	7
8	16	MODERN LOVE	David Bowie	EMI America	6
17	17	MIDNIGHT AT THE LOST AND FOUND	Meat Loaf	Cleveland International	5
11	18	THIS IS NOT A LOVE SONG	Public Image Ltd	Virgin	6
14	19	BLUE HAT FOR A BLUE DAY	Nick Heyward	Arista	5
16	20	RED RED WINE	UB40	DEP International	11
-	21	PUSS 'N BOOTS	Adam Ant	CBS	1
21	22	LOVE IN ITSELF.2	Depeche Mode	Mute	5
30	23	KISS THE BRIDE	Elton John	Rocket	3
-	24	THE LOVE CATS	Cure	Fiction	1
24	25	LOVE WILL FIND A WAY	David Grant	Chrysalis	4
33	26	OVER AND OVER	Shalamar	Solar	2
32	27	KISSING WITH CONFIDENCE	Will Powers	Island	3
39	28	UNCONDITIONAL LOVE	Donna Summer	Mercury	2
19	29	TAHITI	David Essex	Mercury	7
22	30	TONIGHT I CELEBRATE MY LOVE	Peabo Bryson and Roberta Flack	Capitol	10
26	31	POP GOES MY LOVE	Freeez	Beggars Banquet	4
36	32	SISTER SURPRISE	Gary Numan	Beggars Banquet	2
20	33	68 GUNS	Alarm	IRS	5
37	34	REILLY	Olympic Orchestra	Red Bus	2
23	35	COME BACK AND STAY	Paul Young	CBS	8
34	36	LONDON TOWN	Bucks Fizz	RCA	4
-	37	MICRO KID	Level 42	Polydor	1
28	38	MAMA	Genesis	Virgin	9
-	39	LOVE HOW YOU FEEL	Sharon Redd	Prelude	1
-	40	DESTINATION ZULULAND	King Kurt ●	Stiff	1

WEEK ENDING 5 NOVEMBER 1983

LW	TW	Title	Artist	Label	Wks
7	1	UPTOWN GIRL	Billy Joel	CBS	3
2	2	ALL NIGHT LONG (ALL NIGHT)	Lionel Richie	Motown	5
4	3	UNION OF THE SNAKE	Duran Duran	EMI	2
1	4	KARMA CHAMELEON	Culture Club	Virgin	8
3	5	THEY DON'T KNOW	Tracey Ullman	Stiff	6
8	6	THE SAFETY DANCE	Men Without Hats	Statik	4
5	7	NEW SONG	Howard Jones	WEA	6
6	8	(HEY YOU) THE ROCKSTEADY CREW	Rocksteady Crew	Charisma	5
21	9	PUSS 'N BOOTS	Adam Ant	CBS	2
12	10	PLEASE DON'T MAKE ME CRY	UB40	DEP International	4
10	11	SUPERMAN (GIOCA JOUER)	Black Lace	Flair	6
24	12	THE LOVE CATS	Cure	Fiction	2
9	13	IN YOUR EYES	George Benson	Warner Brothers	6
13	14	SAY SAY SAY	Paul McCartney and Michael Jackson	Parlophone	4
11	15	DEAR PRUDENCE	Siouxsie and the Banshees	Wonderland	6
14	16	SUPERSTAR	Lydia Murdock	Korova	5
27	17	KISSING WITH CONFIDENCE	Will Powers	Island	4
15	18	BLUE MONDAY	New Order	Factory	8
-	19	CRY JUST A LITTLE BIT	Shakin' Stevens	Epic	1
23	20	KISS THE BRIDE	Elton John	Rocket	4
-	21	THE SUN AND THE RAIN	Madness	Stiff	1
28	22	UNCONDITIONAL LOVE	Donna Summer	Mercury	3
26	23	OVER AND OVER	Shalamar	Solar	3
-	24	A MESS OF BLUES	Status Quo	Vertigo	1
-	25	THAT WAS THEN BUT THIS IS NOW	ABC	Neutron	1
-	26	SYNCHRONICITY II	Police	A&M	1
19	27	BLUE HAT FOR A BLUE DAY	Nick Heyward	Arista	6
16	28	MODERN LOVE	David Bowie	EMI America	7
20	29	RED RED WINE	UB40	DEP International	12
18	30	THIS IS NOT A LOVE SONG	Public Image Ltd	Virgin	7
17	31	MIDNIGHT AT THE LOST AND FOUND	Meat Loaf	Cleveland International	6
-	32	007	Musical Youth	MCA	1
-	33	LICK IT UP	Kiss	Vertigo	1
-	34	ONLY FOR LOVE	Limahl ●	EMI	1
22	35	LOVE IN ITSELF.2	Depeche Mode	Mute	6
40	36	DESTINATION ZULULAND	King Kurt	Stiff	2
-	37	GUNS FOR HIRE	AC/DC	Atlantic	1

In these weeks ■ Culture Club's *Karma Chameleon* becomes the first record to spend six weeks at number one since Art Garfunkel's *Bright Eyes* on 19 May 1979 (29.10.83) ■ Former lead singers of Haircut 100 and Kajagoogoo, Nick Heyward and Limahl respectively, enjoy solo hits (05.11.83)■

□ Highest position disc reached ● Act's first ever week on chart

LW	TW	Title	Artist	Label	Wks
25	38	LOVE WILL FIND A WAY	David Grant	*Chrysalis*	5
39	[39]	LOVE HOW YOU FEEL	Sharon Redd	*Prelude*	2
34	40	REILLY	Olympic Orchestra	*Red Bus*	3

WEEK ENDING 12 NOVEMBER 1983

LW	TW	Title	Artist	Label	Wks
1	[1]	UPTOWN GIRL	Billy Joel	*CBS*	4
2	[2]	ALL NIGHT LONG (ALL NIGHT)	Lionel Richie	*Motown*	6
14	3	SAY SAY SAY	Paul McCartney and Michael Jackson	*Parlophone*	5
19	4	CRY JUST A LITTLE BIT	Shakin' Stevens	*Epic*	2
9	[5]	PUSS 'N BOOTS	Adam Ant	*CBS*	3
3	6	UNION OF THE SNAKE	Duran Duran	*EMI*	3
6	7	THE SAFETY DANCE	Men Without Hats	*Statik*	5
4	8	KARMA CHAMELEON	Culture Club	*Virgin*	9
21	9	THE SUN AND THE RAIN	Madness	*Stiff*	2
12	10	THE LOVE CATS	Cure	*Fiction*	3
10	11	PLEASE DON'T MAKE ME CRY	UB40	*DEP International*	5
8	12	(HEY YOU) THE ROCKSTEADY CREW	Rocksteady Crew	*Charisma*	6
5	13	THEY DON'T KNOW	Tracey Ullman	*Stiff*	7
7	14	NEW SONG	Howard Jones	*WEA*	7
24	[15]	A MESS OF BLUES	Status Quo	*Vertigo*	2
22	16	UNCONDITIONAL LOVE	Donna Summer	*Mercury*	4
26	[17]	SYNCHRONICITY II	Police	*A&M*	2
25	[18]	THAT WAS THEN BUT THIS IS NOW	ABC	*Neutron*	2
13	19	IN YOUR EYES	George Benson	*Warner Brothers*	7
34	20	ONLY FOR LOVE	Limahl	*EMI*	2
-	21	UNDERCOVER OF THE NIGHT	Rolling Stones	*Rolling Stones*	1
17	22	KISSING WITH CONFIDENCE	Will Powers	*Island*	5
11	23	SUPERMAN (GIOCA JOUER)	Black Lace	*Flair*	7
20	24	KISS THE BRIDE	Elton John	*Rocket*	5
18	25	BLUE MONDAY	New Order	*Factory*	9
32	[26]	007	Musical Youth	*MCA*	2
-	27	RIGHT BY YOUR SIDE	Eurythmics	*RCA*	1
16	28	SUPERSTAR	Lydia Murdock	*Korova*	6
40	29	REILLY	Olympic Orchestra	*Red Bus*	4
-	30	LOVE WILL TEAR US APART	Joy Division	*Factory*	1
33	[31]	LICK IT UP	Kiss	*Vertigo*	2
-	32	CALLING YOUR NAME	Marilyn ●	*Mercury*	1
23	33	OVER AND OVER	Shalamar	*Solar*	4
15	34	DEAR PRUDENCE	Siouxsie and the Banshees	*Wonderland*	7
-	35	OBLIVIOUS	Aztec Camera ●	*WEA*	1
-	36	NEVER NEVER	Assembly ●	*Mute*	1
30	37	THIS IS NOT A LOVE SONG	Public Image Ltd	*Virgin*	8
37	38	GUNS FOR HIRE	AC/DC	*Atlantic*	2
29	39	RED RED WINE	UB40	*DEP International*	13
36	40	DESTINATION ZULULAND	King Kurt	*Stiff*	3

WEEK ENDING 19 NOVEMBER 1983

LW	TW	Title	Artist	Label	Wks
1	[1]	UPTOWN GIRL	Billy Joel	*CBS*	5
3	[2]	SAY SAY SAY	Paul McCartney and Michael Jackson	*Parlophone*	6
4	[3]	CRY JUST A LITTLE BIT	Shakin' Stevens	*Epic*	3
2	4	ALL NIGHT LONG (ALL NIGHT)	Lionel Richie	*Motown*	7
9	[5]	THE SUN AND THE RAIN	Madness	*Stiff*	3
5	6	PUSS 'N BOOTS	Adam Ant	*CBS*	4
10	[7]	THE LOVE CATS	Cure	*Fiction*	4
7	8	THE SAFETY DANCE	Men Without Hats	*Statik*	6
8	9	KARMA CHAMELEON	Culture Club	*Virgin*	10
36	10	NEVER NEVER	Assembly	*Mute*	2
21	[11]	UNDERCOVER OF THE NIGHT	Rolling Stones	*Rolling Stones*	2
-	12	A SOLID BOND IN YOUR HEART	Style Council	*Polydor*	1
6	13	UNION OF THE SNAKE	Duran Duran	*EMI*	4
16	[14]	UNCONDITIONAL LOVE	Donna Summer	*Mercury*	5
11	15	PLEASE DON'T MAKE ME CRY	UB40	*DEP International*	6
20	[16]	ONLY FOR LOVE	Limahl	*EMI*	3
-	17	LOVE OF THE COMMON PEOPLE	Paul Young	*CBS*	1
12	18	(HEY YOU) THE ROCKSTEADY CREW	Rocksteady Crew	*Charisma*	7
30	[19]	LOVE WILL TEAR US APART	Joy Division	*Factory*	2
15	20	A MESS OF BLUES	Status Quo	*Vertigo*	3
32	21	CALLING YOUR NAME	Marilyn	*Mercury*	2
18	22	THAT WAS THEN BUT THIS IS NOW	ABC	*Neutron*	3
27	23	RIGHT BY YOUR SIDE	Eurythmics	*RCA*	2
-	24	THRILLER	Michael Jackson	*Epic*	1
17	25	SYNCHRONICITY II	Police	*A&M*	3
14	26	NEW SONG	Howard Jones	*WEA*	8
13	27	THEY DON'T KNOW	Tracey Ullman	*Stiff*	8
-	28	THAT'S ALL	Genesis	*Charisma*	1
35	29	OBLIVIOUS	Aztec Camera	*WEA*	2
26	30	007	Musical Youth	*MCA*	3
-	31	HOLD ME NOW	Thompson Twins	*Arista*	1
-	32	THIS CHARMING MAN	Smiths ●	*Rough Trade*	1
19	33	IN YOUR EYES	George Benson	*Warner Brothers*	8
23	34	SUPERMAN (GIOCA JOUER)	Black Lace	*Flair*	8
29	35	REILLY	Olympic Orchestra	*Red Bus*	5
-	36	LET'S STAY TOGETHER	Tina Turner ●	*Capitol*	1
-	37	OWNER OF A LONELY HEART	Yes	*Atco*	1
25	38	BLUE MONDAY	New Order	*Factory*	10
24	39	KISS THE BRIDE	Elton John	*Rocket*	6
22	40	KISSING WITH CONFIDENCE	Will Powers	*Island*	6

WEEK ENDING 26 NOVEMBER 1983

LW	TW	Title	Artist	Label	Wks
1	[1]	UPTOWN GIRL	Billy Joel	*CBS*	6
2	[2]	SAY SAY SAY	Paul McCartney and Michael Jackson	*Parlophone*	7
3	[3]	CRY JUST A LITTLE BIT	Shakin' Stevens	*Epic*	4
10	[4]	NEVER NEVER	Assembly	*Mute*	3
17	5	LOVE OF THE COMMON PEOPLE	Paul Young	*CBS*	2
4	6	ALL NIGHT LONG (ALL NIGHT)	Lionel Richie	*Motown*	8
5	7	THE SUN AND THE RAIN	Madness	*Stiff*	4
7	8	THE LOVE CATS	Cure	*Fiction*	5
21	9	CALLING YOUR NAME	Marilyn	*Mercury*	3
24	[10]	THRILLER	Michael Jackson	*Epic*	2
12	[11]	A SOLID BOND IN YOUR HEART	Style Council	*Polydor*	2
6	12	PUSS 'N BOOTS	Adam Ant	*CBS*	5
11	13	UNDERCOVER OF THE NIGHT	Rolling Stones	*Rolling Stones*	3
31	14	HOLD ME NOW	Thompson Twins	*Arista*	2
23	15	RIGHT BY YOUR SIDE	Eurythmics	*RCA*	3
36	16	LET'S STAY TOGETHER	Tina Turner	*Capitol*	2
16	17	ONLY FOR LOVE	Limahl	*EMI*	4
9	18	KARMA CHAMELEON	Culture Club	*Virgin*	11
8	19	THE SAFETY DANCE	Men Without Hats	*Statik*	7
29	20	OBLIVIOUS	Aztec Camera	*WEA*	3
19	21	LOVE WILL TEAR US APART	Joy Division	*Factory*	3
14	22	UNCONDITIONAL LOVE	Donna Summer	*Mercury*	6
28	23	THAT'S ALL	Genesis	*Charisma*	2
20	24	A MESS OF BLUES	Status Quo	*Vertigo*	4
-	25	WATERFRONT	Simple Minds	*Virgin*	1
35	[26]	REILLY	Olympic Orchestra	*Red Bus*	6
18	27	(HEY YOU) THE ROCKSTEADY CREW	Rocksteady Crew	*Charisma*	8
13	28	UNION OF THE SNAKE	Duran Duran	*EMI*	5
37	29	OWNER OF A LONELY HEART	Yes	*Atco*	2
32	30	THIS CHARMING MAN	Smiths	*Rough Trade*	2
15	31	PLEASE DON'T MAKE ME CRY	UB40	*DEP International*	7
-	32	BARK AT THE MOON	Ozzy Osbourne ●	*Epic*	1
-	[33]	THANK YOU FOR THE MUSIC	Abba	*Epic*	1
-	34	PLEASE DON'T FALL IN LOVE	Cliff Richard	*EMI*	1
-	35	ISLANDS IN THE STREAM	Kenny Rogers and Dolly Parton ●	*RCA*	1
-	36	MY OH MY	Slade	*RCA*	1
-	37	RAT RAPPING (BRILLIANT ISN'T IT)	Roland Rat Superstar ●	*Rodent*	1
26	38	NEW SONG	Howard Jones	*WEA*	9
27	39	THEY DON'T KNOW	Tracey Ullman	*Stiff*	9
-	40	LISTEN TO THE RADIO: ATMOSPHERICS	Tom Robinson and Crew	*Panic*	1

■After slipping from 10 to 13 to 14, Paul McCartney and Michael Jackson's *Say Say Say* suddenly leaps to number three. However it cannot get past Billy Joel's *Uptown Girl* and becomes the ninth single featuring Paul McCartney to stop at number 2 (19.11.83) ■ Four animals in the top 10 - *Puss 'n' Boots, Union Of The Snake, Karma Chameleon* and *The Love Cats* (12.11.83)■

December 1983

□ Highest position disc reached ● Act's first ever week on chart

LW	TW	WEEK ENDING 3 DECEMBER 1983			Wks
1	[1]	UPTOWN GIRL	Billy Joel	CBS	7
5	[2]	LOVE OF THE COMMON PEOPLE	Paul Young	CBS	3
2	3	SAY SAY SAY	Paul McCartney and Michael Jackson	Parlophone	8
9	[4]	CALLING YOUR NAME	Marilyn	Mercury	4
14	5	HOLD ME NOW	Thompson Twins	Arista	3
4	6	NEVER NEVER	Assembly	Mute	4
16	7	LET'S STAY TOGETHER	Tina Turner	Capitol	3
3	8	CRY JUST A LITTLE BIT	Shakin' Stevens	Epic	5
-	9	ONLY YOU	Flying Pickets ●	10	1
15	[10]	RIGHT BY YOUR SIDE	Eurythmics	RCA	4
10	11	THRILLER	Michael Jackson	Epic	3
11	12	A SOLID BOND IN YOUR HEART	Style Council	Polydor	3
25	[13]	WATERFRONT	Simple Minds	Virgin	2
8	14	THE LOVE CATS	Cure	Fiction	6
36	15	MY OH MY	Slade	RCA	2
6	16	ALL NIGHT LONG (ALL NIGHT)	Lionel Richie	Motown	9
7	17	THE SUN AND THE RAIN	Madness	Stiff	5
20	[18]	OBLIVIOUS	Aztec Camera	WEA	4
13	19	UNDERCOVER OF THE NIGHT	Rolling Stones	Rolling Stones	4
34	20	PLEASE DON'T FALL IN LOVE	Cliff Richard	EMI	2
-	21	MOVE OVER DARLING	Tracey Ullman	Stiff	1
12	22	PUSS 'N BOOTS	Adam Ant	CBS	6
23	23	THAT'S ALL	Genesis	Charisma	3
32	24	BARK AT THE MOON	Ozzy Osbourne	Epic	2
30	[25]	THIS CHARMING MAN	Smiths	Rough Trade	3
35	26	ISLANDS IN THE STREAM	Kenny Rogers and Dolly Parton	RCA	2
17	27	ONLY FOR LOVE	Limahl	EMI	5
29	28	OWNER OF A LONELY HEART	Yes	Atco	3
18	29	KARMA CHAMELEON	Culture Club	Virgin	12
-	30	CLUB FANTASTIC MEGAMIX	Wham!	Innervision	1
-	31	WHAT IS LOVE	Howard Jones	WEA	1
19	32	THE SAFETY DANCE	Men Without Hats	Statik	8
37	33	RAT RAPPING (BRILLIANT ISN'T IT)	Roland Rat Superstar	Rodent	2
33	34	THANK YOU FOR THE MUSIC	Abba	Epic	2
21	35	LOVE WILL TEAR US APART	Joy Division	Factory	4
26	36	REILLY	Olympic Orchestra	Red Bus	7
22	37	UNCONDITIONAL LOVE	Donna Summer	Mercury	7
-	38	THAT'S LOVE THAT IT IS	Blancmange	London	1
40	[39]	LISTEN TO THE RADIO: ATMOSPHERICS	Tom Robinson and Crew	Panic	2
-	40	THE WAY YOU ARE	Tears For Fears	Mercury	1

LW	TW	WEEK ENDING 10 DECEMBER 1983			Wks
9	[1]	ONLY YOU	Flying Pickets	10	2
2	[2]	LOVE OF THE COMMON PEOPLE	Paul Young	CBS	4
1	3	UPTOWN GIRL	Billy Joel	CBS	8
5	[4]	HOLD ME NOW	Thompson Twins	Arista	4
15	5	MY OH MY	Slade	RCA	3
7	[6]	LET'S STAY TOGETHER	Tina Turner	Capitol	4
4	7	CALLING YOUR NAME	Marilyn	Mercury	5
21	[8]	MOVE OVER DARLING	Tracey Ullman	Stiff	2
20	9	PLEASE DON'T FALL IN LOVE	Cliff Richard	EMI	3
6	10	NEVER NEVER	Assembly	Mute	5
-	11	VICTIMS	Culture Club	Virgin	1
3	12	SAY SAY SAY	Paul McCartney and Michael Jackson	Parlophone	9
8	13	CRY JUST A LITTLE BIT	Shakin' Stevens	Epic	6
10	14	RIGHT BY YOUR SIDE	Eurythmics	RCA	5
26	15	ISLANDS IN THE STREAM	Kenny Rogers and Dolly Parton	RCA	3
11	16	THRILLER	Michael Jackson	Epic	4
13	17	WATERFRONT	Simple Minds	Virgin	3
30	18	CLUB FANTASTIC MEGAMIX	Wham!	Innervision	2
23	19	THAT'S ALL	Genesis	Charisma	4
18	20	OBLIVIOUS	Aztec Camera	WEA	5
24	[21]	BARK AT THE MOON	Ozzy Osbourne	Epic	3
-	22	TELL HER ABOUT IT	Billy Joel	CBS	1
31	23	WHAT IS LOVE	Howard Jones	WEA	2
16	24	ALL NIGHT LONG (ALL NIGHT)	Lionel Richie	Motown	10
12	25	A SOLID BOND IN YOUR HEART	Style Council	Polydor	4
14	26	THE LOVE CATS	Cure	Fiction	7
17	27	THE SUN AND THE RAIN	Madness	Stiff	6
29	28	KARMA CHAMELEON	Culture Club	Virgin	13
25	29	THIS CHARMING MAN	Smiths	Rough Trade	4
28	30	OWNER OF A LONELY HEART	Yes	Atco	4
40	31	THE WAY YOU ARE	Tears For Fears	Mercury	2
19	32	UNDERCOVER OF THE NIGHT	Rolling Stones	Rolling Stones	5
38	[33]	THAT'S LOVE THAT IT IS	Blancmange	London	2
33	34	RAT RAPPING (BRILLIANT ISN'T IT)	Roland Rat Superstar	Rodent	3
-	35	2000 MILES	Pretenders	Real	1
-	36	MARGUERITA TIME	Status Quo	Vertigo	1
22	37	PUSS 'N BOOTS	Adam Ant	CBS	7
-	38	MANY RIVERS TO CROSS	UB40	DEP International	1
36	39	REILLY	Olympic Orchestra	Red Bus	8
-	40	READ 'EM AND WEEP	Barry Manilow	Arista	1

LW	TW	WEEK ENDING 17 DECEMBER 1983			Wks
1	[1]	ONLY YOU	Flying Pickets	10	3
2	[2]	LOVE OF THE COMMON PEOPLE	Paul Young	CBS	5
5	3	MY OH MY	Slade	RCA	4
11	4	VICTIMS	Culture Club	Virgin	2
4	5	HOLD ME NOW	Thompson Twins	Arista	5
6	[6]	LET'S STAY TOGETHER	Tina Turner	Capitol	5
9	[7]	PLEASE DON'T FALL IN LOVE	Cliff Richard	EMI	4
22	8	TELL HER ABOUT IT	Billy Joel	CBS	2
8	9	MOVE OVER DARLING	Tracey Ullman	Stiff	3
3	10	UPTOWN GIRL	Billy Joel	CBS	9
15	11	ISLANDS IN THE STREAM	Kenny Rogers and Dolly Parton	RCA	4
16	12	THRILLER	Michael Jackson	Epic	5
7	13	CALLING YOUR NAME	Marilyn	Mercury	6
23	14	WHAT IS LOVE	Howard Jones	WEA	3
18	[15]	CLUB FANTASTIC MEGAMIX	Wham!	Innervision	3
19	[16]	THAT'S ALL	Genesis	Charisma	5
13	17	CRY JUST A LITTLE BIT	Shakin' Stevens	Epic	7
12	18	SAY SAY SAY	Paul McCartney and Michael Jackson	Parlophone	10
14	19	RIGHT BY YOUR SIDE	Eurythmics	RCA	6
40	20	READ 'EM AND WEEP	Barry Manilow	Arista	2
17	21	WATERFRONT	Simple Minds	Virgin	4
10	22	NEVER NEVER	Assembly	Mute	6
35	23	2000 MILES	Pretenders	Real	2
38	24	MANY RIVERS TO CROSS	UB40	DEP International	2
36	25	MARGUERITA TIME	Status Quo	Vertigo	2
21	26	BARK AT THE MOON	Ozzy Osbourne	Epic	4
20	27	OBLIVIOUS	Aztec Camera	WEA	6
34	28	RAT RAPPING (BRILLIANT ISN'T IT)	Roland Rat Superstar	Rodent	4
31	29	THE WAY YOU ARE	Tears For Fears	Mercury	3
-	30	STRAIGHT AHEAD	Kool and the Gang	De-Lite	1
26	31	THE LOVE CATS	Cure	Fiction	8
28	32	KARMA CHAMELEON	Culture Club	Virgin	14
29	33	THIS CHARMING MAN	Smiths	Rough Trade	5
24	34	ALL NIGHT LONG (ALL NIGHT)	Lionel Richie	Motown	11
-	35	MERRY XMAS EVERYBODY	Slade	Polydor	1
27	36	THE SUN AND THE RAIN	Madness	Stiff	7
-	37	COLD AS CHRISTMAS	Elton John	Rocket	1
30	38	OWNER OF A LONELY HEART	Yes	Atco	5
25	39	A SOLID BOND IN YOUR HEART	Style Council	Polydor	5
33	40	THAT'S LOVE THAT IT IS	Blancmange	London	3

LW	TW	WEEK ENDING 24 DECEMBER 1983			Wks
1	[1]	ONLY YOU	Flying Pickets	10	4
3	[2]	MY OH MY	Slade	RCA	5

In these weeks ■ Abba's final week in the top 40 is with their 25th hit, aptly titled *Thank You For The Music* (03.12.83) ■ *Only You* by the Flying Picketts is the first *a capella* chart-topper (10.12.83)■

LW	TW	Title / Artist	Label	Wks
4	3	VICTIMS Culture Club	*Virgin*	3
2	4	LOVE OF THE COMMON PEOPLE Paul Young	*CBS*	6
25	5	MARGUERITA TIME Status Quo	*Vertigo*	3
5	6	HOLD ME NOW Thompson Twins	*Arista*	6
8	7	TELL HER ABOUT IT Billy Joel	*CBS*	3
11	8	ISLANDS IN THE STREAM Kenny Rogers and Dolly Parton	*RCA*	5
6	9	LET'S STAY TOGETHER Tina Turner	*Capitol*	6
7	10	PLEASE DON'T FALL IN LOVE Cliff Richard	*EMI*	5
14	11	WHAT IS LOVE Howard Jones	*WEA*	4
9	12	MOVE OVER DARLING Tracey Ullman	*Stiff*	4
12	13	THRILLER Michael Jackson	*Epic*	6
10	14	UPTOWN GIRL Billy Joel	*CBS*	10
23	15	2000 MILES Pretenders	*Real*	3
24	16	MANY RIVERS TO CROSS UB40	*DEP International*	3
20	17	READ 'EM AND WEEP Barry Manilow	*Arista*	3
16	18	THAT'S ALL Genesis	*Charisma*	6
30	19	STRAIGHT AHEAD Kool and the Gang	*De-Lite*	2
35	20	MERRY XMAS EVERYBODY Slade	*Polydor*	2
15	21	CLUB FANTASTIC MEGAMIX Wham!	*Innervision*	4
-	22	PIPES OF PEACE Paul McCartney	*Parlophone*	1
13	23	CALLING YOUR NAME Marilyn	*Mercury*	7
17	24	CRY JUST A LITTLE BIT Shakin' Stevens	*Epic*	8
18	25	SAY SAY SAY Paul McCartney and Michael Jackson	*Parlophone*	11
-	26	WHAT ARE WE GONNA GET 'ER INDOORS Dennis Waterman and George Cole ●	*EMI*	1
28	27	RAT RAPPING (BRILLIANT ISN'T IT) Roland Rat Superstar	*Rodent*	5
19	28	RIGHT BY YOUR SIDE Eurythmics	*RCA*	7
29	29	THE WAY YOU ARE Tears For Fears	*Mercury*	4
22	30	NEVER NEVER Assembly	*Mute*	7
21	31	WATERFRONT Simple Minds	*Virgin*	5
-	32	SWEET SURRENDER Rod Stewart	*Warner Brothers*	1
37	33	COLD AS CHRISTMAS Elton John	*Rocket*	2
-	34	CHRISTMAS COUNTDOWN Frank Kelly ●	*Ritz*	1
32	35	KARMA CHAMELEON Culture Club	*Virgin*	15
-	36	I CAN HELP Elvis Presley	*RCA*	1
-	37	CHRISTMAS SPECTRE Jingle Belles ●	*Passion*	1
26	38	BARK AT THE MOON Ozzy Osbourne	*Epic*	5
-	39	SINGALONG-A-SANTA AGAIN Santa Claus and the Christmas Trees	*Polydor*	1
27	40	OBLIVIOUS Aztec Camera	*WEA*	7

LW	TW	*WEEK ENDING* **31 DECEMBER 1983**		Wks
		(no chart published, chart for 24 December repeated)		
1	1	ONLY YOU Flying Pickets	*10*	5
2	2	MY OH MY Slade	*RCA*	6

□ Highest position disc reached ● Act's first ever week on chart

LW	TW	Title / Artist	Label	Wks
3	3	VICTIMS Culture Club	*Virgin*	4
4	4	LOVE OF THE COMMON PEOPLE Paul Young	*CBS*	7
5	5	MARGUERITA TIME Status Quo	*Vertigo*	4
6	6	HOLD ME NOW Thompson Twins	*Arista*	7
7	7	TELL HER ABOUT IT Billy Joel	*CBS*	4
8	8	ISLANDS IN THE STREAM Kenny Rogers and Dolly Parton	*RCA*	6
9	9	LET'S STAY TOGETHER Tina Turner	*Capitol*	7
10	10	PLEASE DON'T FALL IN LOVE Cliff Richard	*EMI*	6
11	11	WHAT IS LOVE Howard Jones	*WEA*	5
12	12	MOVE OVER DARLING Tracey Ullman	*Stiff*	5
13	13	THRILLER Michael Jackson	*Epic*	7
14	14	UPTOWN GIRL Billy Joel	*CBS*	11
15	15	2000 MILES Pretenders	*Real*	4
16	16	MANY RIVERS TO CROSS UB40	*DEP International*	4
17	17	READ 'EM AND WEEP Barry Manilow	*Arista*	4
18	18	THAT'S ALL Genesis	*Charisma*	7
19	19	STRAIGHT AHEAD Kool and the Gang	*De-Lite*	3
20	20	MERRY XMAS EVERYBODY Slade	*Polydor*	3
21	21	CLUB FANTASTIC MEGAMIX Wham!	*Innervision*	5
22	22	PIPES OF PEACE Paul McCartney	*Parlophone*	2
23	23	CALLING YOUR NAME Marilyn	*Mercury*	8
24	24	CRY JUST A LITTLE BIT Shakin' Stevens	*Epic*	9
25	25	SAY SAY SAY Paul McCartney and Michael Jackson	*Parlophone*	12
26	26	WHAT ARE WE GONNA GET 'ER INDOORS Dennis Waterman and George Cole	*EMI*	2
27	27	RAT RAPPING (BRILLIANT ISN'T IT) Roland Rat Superstar	*Rodent*	6
28	28	RIGHT BY YOUR SIDE Eurythmics	*RCA*	8
29	29	THE WAY YOU ARE Tears For Fears	*Mercury*	5
30	30	NEVER NEVER Assembly	*Mute*	8
31	31	WATERFRONT Simple Minds	*Virgin*	6
32	32	SWEET SURRENDER Rod Stewart	*Warner Brothers*	2
33	33	COLD AS CHRISTMAS Elton John	*Rocket*	3
34	34	CHRISTMAS COUNTDOWN Frank Kelly	*Ritz*	2
35	35	KARMA CHAMELEON Culture Club	*Virgin*	16
36	36	I CAN HELP Elvis Presley	*RCA*	2
37	37	CHRISTMAS SPECTRE Jingle Belles	*Passion*	2
38	38	BARK AT THE MOON Ozzy Osbourne	*Epic*	6
39	39	SINGALONG-A-SANTA AGAIN Santa Claus and the Christmas Trees	*Polydor*	2
40	40	OBLIVIOUS Aztec Camera	*WEA*	8

■Slade's biggest hit for nine years peaks at number 2 and brings their classic *Merry Xmas Everybody* back to the top 20 for the first time for 10 years (24.12.83)■

1984

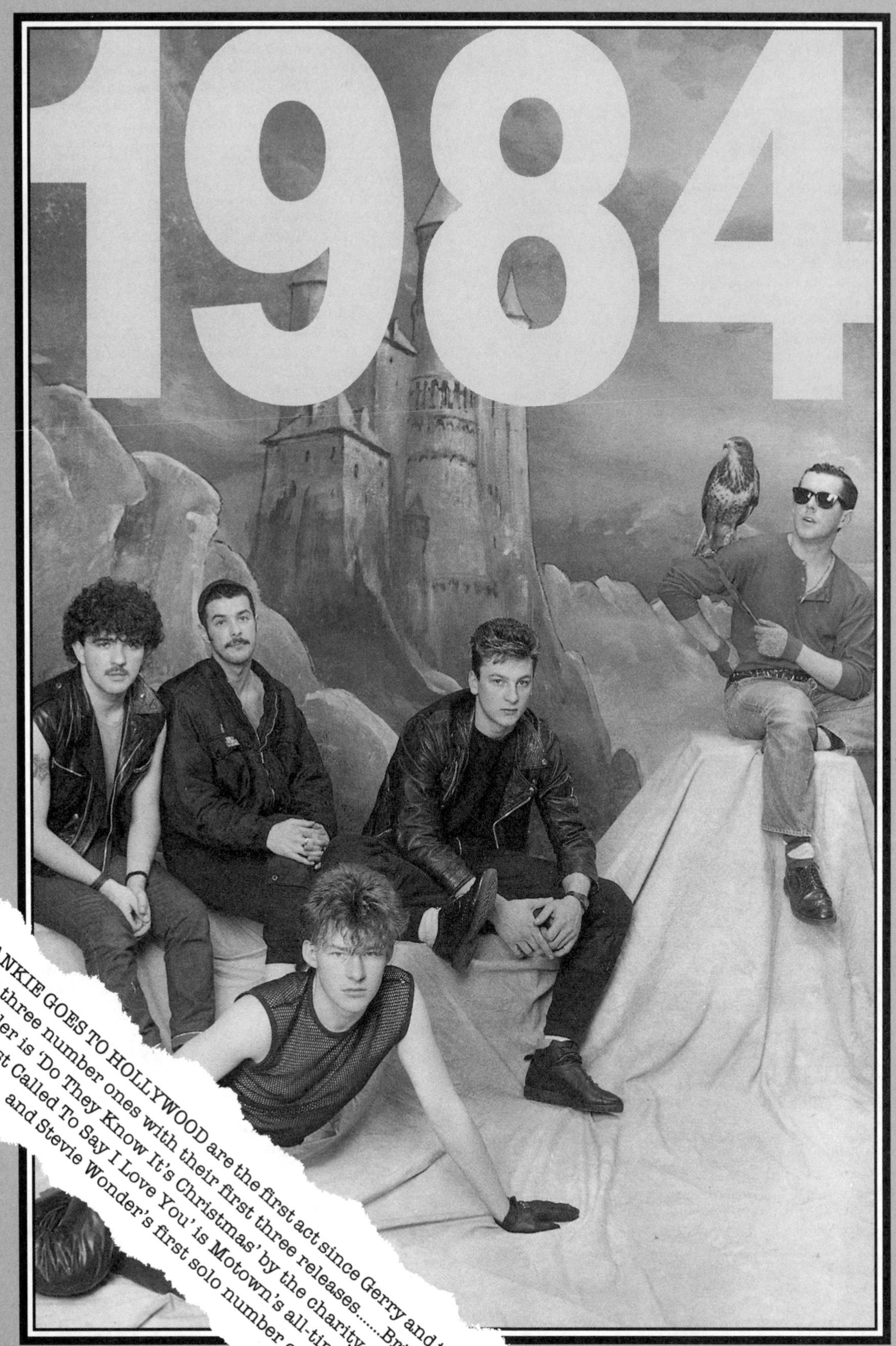

........FRANKIE GOES TO HOLLYWOOD are the first act since Gerry and the Pacemakers to have three number ones with their first three releases.......Britain's all-time best-seller is 'Do They Know It's Christmas' by the charity group Band Aid ...... 'I Just Called To Say I Love You' is Motown's all-time UK best-seller and Stevie Wonder's first solo number one..........

January 1984

□ Highest position disc reached ● Act's first ever week on chart

LW	TW	WEEK ENDING 7 JANUARY 1984	Wks
1	1	ONLY YOU Flying Pickets *10*	6
2	2	MY OH MY Slade .... *RCA*	7
4	3	LOVE OF THE COMMON PEOPLE Paul Young .... *CBS*	8
3	4	VICTIMS Culture Club .... *Virgin*	5
5	5	MARGUERITA TIME Status Quo .... *Vertigo*	5
7	6	TELL HER ABOUT IT Billy Joel .... *CBS*	5
8	7	ISLANDS IN THE STREAM Kenny Rogers and Dolly Parton .... *RCA*	7
6	8	HOLD ME NOW Thompson Twins .... *Arista*	8
22	9	PIPES OF PEACE Paul McCartney .... *Parlophone*	3
11	10	WHAT IS LOVE Howard Jones .... *WEA*	6
13	11	THRILLER Michael Jackson .... *Epic*	8
9	12	LET'S STAY TOGETHER Tina Turner .... *Capitol*	8
10	13	PLEASE DON'T FALL IN LOVE Cliff Richard .... *EMI*	7
14	14	UPTOWN GIRL Billy Joel .... *CBS*	12
12	15	MOVE OVER DARLING Tracey Ullman .... *Stiff*	6
15	16	2000 MILES Pretenders .... *Real*	5
16	17	MANY RIVERS TO CROSS UB40 .... *DEP International*	5
27	18	RAT RAPPING (BRILLIANT ISN'T IT) Roland Rat Superstar .... *Rodent*	7
19	19	STRAIGHT AHEAD Kool and the Gang .... *De-Lite*	4
20	20	MERRY XMAS EVERYBODY Slade .... *Polydor*	4
26	21	WHAT ARE WE GONNA GET 'ER INDOORS .... Dennis Waterman and George Cole .... *EMI*	3
24	22	CRY JUST A LITTLE BIT Shakin' Stevens .... *Epic*	10
17	23	READ 'EM AND WEEP Barry Manilow .... *Arista*	5
23	24	CALLING YOUR NAME Marilyn .... *Mercury*	9
21	25	CLUB FANTASTIC MEGAMIX Wham! .... *Innervision*	6
34	26	CHRISTMAS COUNTDOWN Frank Kelly .... *Ritz*	3
18	27	THAT'S ALL Genesis .... *Charisma*	8
29	28	THE WAY YOU ARE Tears For Fears .... *Mercury*	6
25	29	SAY SAY SAY Paul McCartney and Michael Jackson .... *Parlophone*	13
35	30	KARMA CHAMELEON Culture Club .... *Virgin*	17
28	31	RIGHT BY YOUR SIDE Eurythmics .... *RCA*	9
32	32	SWEET SURRENDER Rod Stewart .... *Warner Brothers*	3
36	33	I CAN HELP Elvis Presley .... *RCA*	3
31	34	WATERFRONT Simple Minds .... *Virgin*	7
-	35	RELAX Frankie Goes To Hollywood ● .... *ZTT*	1
-	36	RUNNING WITH THE NIGHT Lionel Richie .... *Motown*	1
-	37	SUPERMAN (GIOCA JOUER) Black Lace .... *Flair*	1
37	38	CHRISTMAS SPECTRE Jingle Belles .... *Passion*	3
-	39	ALL NIGHT LONG (ALL NIGHT) Lionel Richie .... *Motown*	1
-	40	BIRD OF PARADISE Snowy White ● .... *Towerbell*	1

LW	TW	WEEK ENDING 14 JANUARY 1984	Wks
9	1	PIPES OF PEACE Paul McCartney .... *Parlophone*	4
10	2	WHAT IS LOVE Howard Jones .... *WEA*	7
5	3	MARGUERITA TIME Status Quo .... *Vertigo*	6
6	4	TELL HER ABOUT IT Billy Joel .... *CBS*	6
3	5	LOVE OF THE COMMON PEOPLE Paul Young .... *CBS*	9
35	6	RELAX Frankie Goes To Hollywood .... *ZTT*	2
4	7	VICTIMS Culture Club .... *Virgin*	6
7	8	ISLANDS IN THE STREAM Kenny Rogers and Dolly Parton .... *RCA*	8
8	9	HOLD ME NOW Thompson Twins .... *Arista*	9
1	10	ONLY YOU Flying Pickets *10*	7
2	11	MY OH MY Slade .... *RCA*	8
11	12	THRILLER Michael Jackson .... *Epic*	9
-	13	A ROCKIN' GOOD WAY Shaky and Bonnie ● .... *Epic*	1
18	14	RAT RAPPING (BRILLIANT ISN'T IT) Roland Rat Superstar .... *Rodent*	8
19	15	STRAIGHT AHEAD Kool and the Gang .... *De-Lite*	5
14	16	UPTOWN GIRL Billy Joel .... *CBS*	13
12	17	LET'S STAY TOGETHER Tina Turner .... *Capitol*	9
-	18	THAT'S LIVING ALRIGHT (FROM 'AUF WIEDERSEHEN PET') Joe Fagin ● .... *Towerbell*	1
40	19	BIRD OF PARADISE Snowy White .... *Towerbell*	2
17	20	MANY RIVERS TO CROSS UB40 .... *DEP International*	6
15	21	MOVE OVER DARLING Tracey Ullman .... *Stiff*	7
36	22	RUNNING WITH THE NIGHT Lionel Richie .... *Motown*	2
32	23	SWEET SURRENDER Rod Stewart .... *Warner Brothers*	4
28	24	THE WAY YOU ARE Tears For Fears .... *Mercury*	7
16	25	2000 MILES Pretenders .... *Real*	6
13	26	PLEASE DON'T FALL IN LOVE Cliff Richard .... *EMI*	8
25	27	CLUB FANTASTIC MEGAMIX Wham! .... *Innervision*	7
-	28	LOVE IS A WONDERFUL COLOUR Icicle Works ● .... *Beggars Banquet*	1
22	29	CRY JUST A LITTLE BIT Shakin' Stevens .... *Epic*	11
33	30	I CAN HELP Elvis Presley .... *RCA*	4
24	31	CALLING YOUR NAME Marilyn .... *Mercury*	10
-	32	KING OF PAIN Police .... *A&M*	1
29	33	SAY SAY SAY Paul McCartney and Michael Jackson .... *Parlophone*	14
23	34	READ 'EM AND WEEP Barry Manilow .... *Arista*	6
30	35	KARMA CHAMELEON Culture Club .... *Virgin*	18
-	36	WISHFUL THINKING China Crisis .... *Virgin*	1
27	37	THAT'S ALL Genesis .... *Charisma*	9
-	38	I AM WHAT I AM Gloria Gaynor .... *Chrysalis*	1
-	39	WHERE IS MY MAN Eartha Kitt .... *Record Shack*	1
-	40	GIVE ME MORE TIME Whitesnake .... *Liberty*	1

LW	TW	WEEK ENDING 21 JANUARY 1984	Wks
1	1	PIPES OF PEACE Paul McCartney .... *Parlophone*	5
6	2	RELAX Frankie Goes To Hollywood .... *ZTT*	3
2	3	WHAT IS LOVE Howard Jones .... *WEA*	8
18	4	THAT'S LIVING ALRIGHT (FROM 'AUF WIEDERSEHEN PET') Joe Fagin .... *Towerbell*	2
13	5	A ROCKIN' GOOD WAY Shaky and Bonnie .... *Epic*	2
19	6	BIRD OF PARADISE Snowy White .... *Towerbell*	3
3	7	MARGUERITA TIME Status Quo .... *Vertigo*	7
4	8	TELL HER ABOUT IT Billy Joel .... *CBS*	7
22	9	RUNNING WITH THE NIGHT Lionel Richie .... *Motown*	3
8	10	ISLANDS IN THE STREAM Kenny Rogers and Dolly Parton .... *RCA*	9
-	11	NOBODY TOLD ME John Lennon .... *Polydor*	1
9	12	HOLD ME NOW Thompson Twins .... *Arista*	10
-	13	WONDERLAND Big Country .... *Mercury*	1
5	14	LOVE OF THE COMMON PEOPLE Paul Young .... *CBS*	10
28	15	LOVE IS A WONDERFUL COLOUR Icicle Works .... *Beggars Banquet*	2
36	16	WISHFUL THINKING China Crisis .... *Virgin*	2
32	17	KING OF PAIN Police .... *A&M*	2
12	18	THRILLER Michael Jackson .... *Epic*	10
15	19	STRAIGHT AHEAD Kool and the Gang .... *De-Lite*	6
-	20	HERE COMES THE RAIN AGAIN Eurythmics .... *RCA*	1
14	21	RAT RAPPING (BRILLIANT ISN'T IT) Roland Rat Superstar .... *Rodent*	9
7	22	VICTIMS Culture Club .... *Virgin*	7
-	23	GIRLS JUST WANT TO HAVE FUN Cyndi Lauper ● .... *Portrait*	1
38	24	I AM WHAT I AM Gloria Gaynor .... *Chrysalis*	2
10	25	ONLY YOU Flying Pickets *10*	8
23	26	SWEET SURRENDER Rod Stewart .... *Warner Brothers*	5
17	27	LET'S STAY TOGETHER Tina Turner .... *Capitol*	10
-	28	(FEELS LIKE) HEAVEN Fiction Factory ● .... *CBS*	1
40	29	GIVE ME MORE TIME Whitesnake .... *Liberty*	2
11	30	MY OH MY Slade .... *RCA*	9
-	31	BREAK MY STRIDE Matthew Wilder ● .... *Epic*	1
20	32	MANY RIVERS TO CROSS UB40 .... *DEP International*	7
16	33	UPTOWN GIRL Billy Joel .... *CBS*	14
-	34	WHERE WERE YOU HIDING WHEN THE STORM BROKE Alarm .... *IRS*	1
-	35	SIXTEEN Musical Youth .... *MCA*	1
21	36	MOVE OVER DARLING Tracey Ullman .... *Stiff*	8
39	37	WHERE IS MY MAN Eartha Kitt .... *Record Shack*	2
30	38	I CAN HELP Elvis Presley .... *RCA*	5
-	39	HUMAN TOUCH Rick Springfield ● .... *RCA*	1
-	40	HOLIDAY Madonna ● .... *Sire*	1

In these weeks ■ By falling from number 1 to number 10, Flying Pickets *Only You* makes the second biggest fall from the top ever recorded, 26 years and 4 days after the biggest ever fall (14.01.84) ■ Eartha Kitt makes her chart comeback over 28½ years after her previous chart entry. This is the only instance of an act waiting over 20 years between newly-recorded chart hits (14.01.84) ■ Elvis Presley's final week in the Top 40 is also Madonna's first (21.01.84)■

February 1984

□ Highest position disc reached ● Act's first ever week on chart

WEEK ENDING 28 JANUARY 1984

LW	TW	Title	Artist	Label	Wks
2	1	RELAX	Frankie Goes To Hollywood	ZTT	4
1	2	PIPES OF PEACE	Paul McCartney	Parlophone	6
4	3	THAT'S LIVING ALRIGHT (FROM 'AUF WIEDERSEHEN PET')	Joe Fagin	Towerbell	3
3	4	WHAT IS LOVE	Howard Jones	WEA	9
5	5	A ROCKIN' GOOD WAY	Shaky and Bonnie	Epic	3
11	6	NOBODY TOLD ME	John Lennon	Polydor	2
6	7	BIRD OF PARADISE	Snowy White	Towerbell	4
13	8	WONDERLAND	Big Country	Mercury	2
16	9	WISHFUL THINKING	China Crisis	Virgin	3
23	10	GIRLS JUST WANT TO HAVE FUN	Cyndi Lauper	Portrait	2
20	11	HERE COMES THE RAIN AGAIN	Eurythmics	RCA	2
28	12	(FEELS LIKE) HEAVEN	Fiction Factory	CBS	2
24	13	I AM WHAT I AM	Gloria Gaynor	Chrysalis	3
31	14	BREAK MY STRIDE	Matthew Wilder	Epic	2
7	15	MARGUERITA TIME	Status Quo	Vertigo	8
9	16	RUNNING WITH THE NIGHT	Lionel Richie	Motown	4
-	17	THE KILLING MOON	Echo and the Bunnymen	Korova	1
8	18	TELL HER ABOUT IT	Billy Joel	CBS	8
15	19	LOVE IS A WONDERFUL COLOUR	Icicle Works	Beggars Banquet	3
-	20	SPEED YOUR LOVE TO ME	Simple Minds	Virgin	1
17	21	KING OF PAIN	Police	A&M	3
34	22	WHERE WERE YOU HIDING WHEN THE STORM BROKE	Alarm	IRS	2
19	23	STRAIGHT AHEAD	Kool and the Gang	De-Lite	7
10	24	ISLANDS IN THE STREAM	Kenny Rogers and Dolly Parton	RCA	10
12	25	HOLD ME NOW	Thompson Twins	Arista	11
-	26	WHAT DIFFERENCE DOES IT MAKE	Smiths	Rough Trade	1
18	27	THRILLER	Michael Jackson	Epic	11
14	28	LOVE OF THE COMMON PEOPLE	Paul Young	CBS	11
40	29	HOLIDAY	Madonna	Sire	2
29	30	GIVE ME MORE TIME	Whitesnake	Liberty	3
39	31	HUMAN TOUCH	Rick Springfield	RCA	2
21	32	RAT RAPPING (BRILLIANT ISN'T IT)	Roland Rat Superstar	Rodent	10
-	33	SPICE OF LIFE	Manhattan Transfer	Atlantic	1
35	34	SIXTEEN	Musical Youth	MCA	2
-	35	HYPERACTIVE!	Thomas Dolby	Parlophone	1
37	36	WHERE IS MY MAN	Eartha Kitt	Record Shack	3
27	37	LET'S STAY TOGETHER	Tina Turner	Capitol	11
22	38	VICTIMS	Culture Club	Virgin	8
-	39	SOS	ABC	Neutron	1
-	40	A NIGHT IN NEW YORK	Elbow Bones and the Racketeers ●	EMI America	1

WEEK ENDING 4 FEBRUARY 1984

LW	TW	Title	Artist	Label	Wks
1	1	RELAX	Frankie Goes To Hollywood	ZTT	5
10	2	GIRLS JUST WANT TO HAVE FUN	Cyndi Lauper	Portrait	3
3	3	THAT'S LIVING ALRIGHT (FROM 'AUF WIEDERSEHEN PET')	Joe Fagin	Towerbell	4
-	4	RADIO GA GA	Queen	EMI	1
14	5	BREAK MY STRIDE	Matthew Wilder	Epic	3
12	6	(FEELS LIKE) HEAVEN	Fiction Factory	CBS	3
2	7	PIPES OF PEACE	Paul McCartney	Parlophone	7
11	8	HERE COMES THE RAIN AGAIN	Eurythmics	RCA	3
17	9	THE KILLING MOON	Echo and the Bunnymen	Korova	2
8	10	WONDERLAND	Big Country	Mercury	3
5	11	A ROCKIN' GOOD WAY	Shaky and Bonnie	Epic	4
-	12	NEW MOON ON MONDAY	Duran Duran	EMI	1
29	13	HOLIDAY	Madonna	Sire	3
6	14	NOBODY TOLD ME	John Lennon	Polydor	3
9	15	WISHFUL THINKING	China Crisis	Virgin	4
4	16	WHAT IS LOVE	Howard Jones	WEA	10
13	17	I AM WHAT I AM	Gloria Gaynor	Chrysalis	4
-	18	DOCTOR! DOCTOR!	Thompson Twins	Arista	1
7	19	BIRD OF PARADISE	Snowy White	Towerbell	5
26	20	WHAT DIFFERENCE DOES IT MAKE	Smiths	Rough Trade	2
20	21	SPEED YOUR LOVE TO ME	Simple Minds	Virgin	2
22	22	WHERE WERE YOU HIDING WHEN THE STORM BROKE	Alarm	IRS	3
31	23	HUMAN TOUCH	Rick Springfield	RCA	3
16	24	RUNNING WITH THE NIGHT	Lionel Richie	Motown	5
-	25	LOVE THEME FROM 'THE THORN BIRDS'	Juan Martin ●	WEA	1
33	26	SPICE OF LIFE	Manhattan Transfer	Atlantic	2
34	27	SIXTEEN	Musical Youth	MCA	3
15	28	MARGUERITA TIME	Status Quo	Vertigo	9
35	29	HYPERACTIVE!	Thomas Dolby	Parlophone	2
25	30	HOLD ME NOW	Thompson Twins	Arista	12
19	31	LOVE IS A WONDERFUL COLOUR	Icicle Works	Beggars Banquet	4
24	32	ISLANDS IN THE STREAM	Kenny Rogers and Dolly Parton	RCA	11
40	33	A NIGHT IN NEW YORK	Elbow Bones and the Racketeers	EMI America	2
18	34	TELL HER ABOUT IT	Billy Joel	CBS	9
-	35	LET THE MUSIC PLAY	Shannon ●	Club	1
23	36	STRAIGHT AHEAD	Kool and the Gang	De-Lite	8
27	37	THRILLER	Michael Jackson	Epic	12
-	38	WOULDN'T IT BE GOOD	Nik Kershaw ●	MCA	1
36	39	WHERE IS MY MAN	Eartha Kitt	Record Shack	4
39	40	SOS	ABC	Neutron	2

WEEK ENDING 11 FEBRUARY 1984

LW	TW	Title	Artist	Label	Wks
1	1	RELAX	Frankie Goes To Hollywood	ZTT	6
4	2	RADIO GA GA	Queen	EMI	2
2	3	GIRLS JUST WANT TO HAVE FUN	Cyndi Lauper	Portrait	4
5	4	BREAK MY STRIDE	Matthew Wilder	Epic	4
18	5	DOCTOR! DOCTOR!	Thompson Twins	Arista	2
3	6	THAT'S LIVING ALRIGHT (FROM 'AUF WIEDERSEHEN PET')	Joe Fagin	Towerbell	5
13	7	HOLIDAY	Madonna	Sire	4
6	8	(FEELS LIKE) HEAVEN	Fiction Factory	CBS	4
12	9	NEW MOON ON MONDAY	Duran Duran	EMI	2
8	10	HERE COMES THE RAIN AGAIN	Eurythmics	RCA	4
9	11	THE KILLING MOON	Echo and the Bunnymen	Korova	3
25	12	LOVE THEME FROM 'THE THORN BIRDS'	Juan Martin	WEA	2
20	13	WHAT DIFFERENCE DOES IT MAKE	Smiths	Rough Trade	3
10	14	WONDERLAND	Big Country	Mercury	4
17	15	I AM WHAT I AM	Gloria Gaynor	Chrysalis	5
11	16	A ROCKIN' GOOD WAY	Shaky and Bonnie	Epic	5
15	17	WISHFUL THINKING	China Crisis	Virgin	5
7	18	PIPES OF PEACE	Paul McCartney	Parlophone	8
26	19	SPICE OF LIFE	Manhattan Transfer	Atlantic	3
29	20	HYPERACTIVE!	Thomas Dolby	Parlophone	3
14	21	NOBODY TOLD ME	John Lennon	Polydor	4
19	22	BIRD OF PARADISE	Snowy White	Towerbell	6
27	23	SIXTEEN	Musical Youth	MCA	4
23	24	HUMAN TOUCH/SOULS	Rick Springfield	RCA	4
16	25	WHAT IS LOVE	Howard Jones	WEA	11
-	26	MICHAEL CAINE	Madness	Stiff	1
35	27	LET THE MUSIC PLAY	Shannon	Club	2
22	28	WHERE WERE YOU HIDING WHEN THE STORM BROKE	Alarm	IRS	4
-	29	PUNCH AND JUDY	Marillion	EMI	1
-	30	SOMEBODY'S WATCHING ME	Rockwell ●	Motown	1
-	31	99 RED BALLOONS	Nena ●	Epic	1
38	32	WOULDN'T IT BE GOOD	Nik Kershaw	MCA	2
33	33	A NIGHT IN NEW YORK	Elbow Bones and the Racketeers	EMI America	3
-	34	SOUL TRAIN	Swans Way ●	Exit	1
21	35	SPEED YOUR LOVE TO ME	Simple Minds	Virgin	3
-	36	STREET DANCE	Break Machine ●	Record Shack	1
-	37	ONE SMALL DAY	Ultravox	Chrysalis	1
30	38	HOLD ME NOW	Thompson Twins	Arista	13
24	39	RUNNING WITH THE NIGHT	Lionel Richie	Motown	6
-	40	RUN RUNAWAY	Slade	RCA	1

■Despite being banned by Radio One, Frankie Goes To Hollywood's *Relax* knocks Paul McCartney's first solo chart-topper from number one (28.01.84) ■ For the first six weeks of 1984, there is a different record at no. 2 each week (11.02.84) ■ Rockwell is the son of Motown founder Benny Gordy, but not in the end one of Motown's most successful acts (11.02.84)■

February 1984

□ Highest position disc reached ● Act's first ever week on chart

WEEK ENDING 18 FEBRUARY

LW	TW	Title / Artist	Label	Wks
1	1	RELAX Frankie Goes To Hollywood	ZTT	7
2	2	RADIO GA GA Queen	EMI	3
5	3	DOCTOR! DOCTOR! Thompson Twins	Arista	3
3	4	GIRLS JUST WANT TO HAVE FUN Cyndi Lauper	Portrait	5
4	5	BREAK MY STRIDE Matthew Wilder	Epic	5
7	6	HOLIDAY Madonna	Sire	5
6	7	THAT'S LIVING ALRIGHT (FROM 'AUF WIEDERSEHEN PET') Joe Fagin	Towerbell	6
-	8	MY EVER CHANGING MOODS Style Council	Polydor	1
9	9	NEW MOON ON MONDAY Duran Duran	EMI	3
12	10	LOVE THEME FROM 'THE THORN BIRDS' Juan Martin	WEA	3
31	11	99 RED BALLOONS Nena	Epic	2
13	12	WHAT DIFFERENCE DOES IT MAKE Smiths	Rough Trade	4
26	13	MICHAEL CAINE Madness	Stiff	2
32	14	WOULDN'T IT BE GOOD Nik Kershaw	MCA	3
30	15	SOMEBODY'S WATCHING ME Rockwell	Motown	2
8	16	(FEELS LIKE) HEAVEN Fiction Factory	CBS	5
20	17	HYPERACTIVE! Thomas Dolby	Parlophone	4
10	18	HERE COMES THE RAIN AGAIN Eurythmics	RCA	5
27	19	LET THE MUSIC PLAY Shannon	Club	3
34	20	SOUL TRAIN Swans Way	Exit	2
14	21	WONDERLAND Big Country	Mercury	5
19	22	SPICE OF LIFE Manhattan Transfer	Atlantic	4
15	23	I AM WHAT I AM Gloria Gaynor	Chrysalis	6
-	24	HIDE AND SEEK Howard Jones	WEA	1
11	25	THE KILLING MOON Echo and the Bunnymen	Korova	4
-	26	JOANNA/TONIGHT Kool and the Gang	De-Lite	1
36	27	STREET DANCE Break Machine	Record Shack	2
-	28	AN INNOCENT MAN Billy Joel	CBS	1
37	29	ONE SMALL DAY Ultravox	Chrysalis	2
23	30	SIXTEEN Musical Youth	MCA	5
-	31	MAIN THEME FROM 'THE THORN BIRDS' Henry Mancini and his Orchestra	Warner Brothers	1
29	32	PUNCH AND JUDY Marillion	EMI	2
33	33	A NIGHT IN NEW YORK Elbow Bones and the Racketeers	EMI America	4
40	34	RUN RUNAWAY Slade	RCA	2
16	35	A ROCKIN' GOOD WAY Shaky and Bonnie	Epic	6
-	36	GET OUT OF YOUR LAZY BED Matt Bianco ●	WEA	1
17	37	WISHFUL THINKING China Crisis	Virgin	6
-	38	I GAVE YOU MY HEART (DIDN'T I) Hot Chocolate	RAK	1
22	39	BIRD OF PARADISE Snowy White	Towerbell	7
24	40	HUMAN TOUCH/SOULS Rick Springfield	RCA	5

WEEK ENDING 25 FEBRUARY 1984

LW	TW	Title / Artist	Label	Wks
1	1	RELAX Frankie Goes To Hollywood	ZTT	8
11	2	99 RED BALLOONS Nena	Epic	3
3	3	DOCTOR! DOCTOR! Thompson Twins	Arista	4
2	4	RADIO GA GA Queen	EMI	4
8	5	MY EVER CHANGING MOODS Style Council	Polydor	2
5	6	BREAK MY STRIDE Matthew Wilder	Epic	6
15	7	SOMEBODY'S WATCHING ME Rockwell	Motown	3
4	8	GIRLS JUST WANT TO HAVE FUN Cyndi Lauper	Portrait	6
14	9	WOULDN'T IT BE GOOD Nik Kershaw	MCA	4
26	10	JOANNA/TONIGHT Kool and the Gang	De-Lite	2
13	11	MICHAEL CAINE Madness	Stiff	3
28	12	AN INNOCENT MAN Billy Joel	CBS	2
6	13	HOLIDAY Madonna	Sire	6
19	14	LET THE MUSIC PLAY Shannon	Club	4
24	15	HIDE AND SEEK Howard Jones	WEA	2
27	16	STREET DANCE Break Machine	Record Shack	3
7	17	THAT'S LIVING ALRIGHT (FROM 'AUF WIEDERSEHEN PET') Joe Fagin	Towerbell	7
12	18	WHAT DIFFERENCE DOES IT MAKE Smiths	Rough Trade	5
34	19	RUN RUNAWAY Slade	RCA	3
9	20	NEW MOON ON MONDAY Duran Duran	EMI	4
36	21	GET OUT OF YOUR LAZY BED Matt Bianco	WEA	2
17	22	HYPERACTIVE! Thomas Dolby	Parlophone	5
20	23	SOUL TRAIN Swans Way	Exit	3
10	24	LOVE THEME FROM 'THE THORN BIRDS' Juan Martin	WEA	4
31	25	MAIN THEME FROM 'THE THORN BIRDS' Henry Mancini and his Orchestra	Warner Brothers	2
16	26	(FEELS LIKE) HEAVEN Fiction Factory	CBS	6
29	27	ONE SMALL DAY Ultravox	Chrysalis	3
38	28	I GAVE YOU MY HEART (DIDN'T I) Hot Chocolate	RAK	2
18	29	HERE COMES THE RAIN AGAIN Eurythmics	RCA	6
22	30	SPICE OF LIFE Manhattan Transfer	Atlantic	5
-	31	JUMP Van Halen ●	Warner Brothers	1
23	32	I AM WHAT I AM Gloria Gaynor	Chrysalis	7
33	33	A NIGHT IN NEW YORK Elbow Bones and the Racketeers	EMI America	5
-	34	THE POLITICS OF DANCING Re-Flex ●	EMI	1
-	35	MORE MORE MORE Carmel	London	1
32	36	PUNCH AND JUDY Marillion	EMI	3
21	37	WONDERLAND Big Country	Mercury	6
-	38	DOWN IN THE SUBWAY Soft Cell	Some Bizzare	1
-	39	CRY AND BE FREE Marilyn	Love	1
25	40	THE KILLING MOON Echo and the Bunnymen	Korova	5

WEEK ENDING 3 MARCH 1984

LW	TW	Title / Artist	Label	Wks
2	1	99 RED BALLOONS Nena	Epic	4
1	2	RELAX Frankie Goes To Hollywood	ZTT	9
10	3	JOANNA/TONIGHT Kool and the Gang	De-Lite	3
9	4	WOULDN'T IT BE GOOD Nik Kershaw	MCA	5
3	5	DOCTOR! DOCTOR! Thompson Twins	Arista	5
7	6	SOMEBODY'S WATCHING ME Rockwell	Motown	4
4	7	RADIO GA GA Queen	EMI	5
12	8	AN INNOCENT MAN Billy Joel	CBS	3
5	9	MY EVER CHANGING MOODS Style Council	Polydor	3
19	10	RUN RUNAWAY Slade	RCA	4
16	11	STREET DANCE Break Machine	Record Shack	4
6	12	BREAK MY STRIDE Matthew Wilder	Epic	7
8	13	GIRLS JUST WANT TO HAVE FUN Cyndi Lauper	Portrait	7
15	14	HIDE AND SEEK Howard Jones	WEA	3
14	15	LET THE MUSIC PLAY Shannon	Club	5
11	16	MICHAEL CAINE Madness	Stiff	4
21	17	GET OUT OF YOUR LAZY BED Matt Bianco	WEA	3
13	18	HOLIDAY Madonna	Sire	7
28	19	I GAVE YOU MY HEART (DIDN'T I) Hot Chocolate	RAK	3
31	20	JUMP Van Halen	Warner Brothers	2
18	21	WHAT DIFFERENCE DOES IT MAKE Smiths	Rough Trade	6
20	22	NEW MOON ON MONDAY Duran Duran	EMI	5
25	23	MAIN THEME FROM 'THE THORN BIRDS' Henry Mancini and his Orchestra	Warner Brothers	3
17	24	THAT'S LIVING ALRIGHT (FROM 'AUF WIEDERSEHEN PET') Joe Fagin	Towerbell	8
35	25	MORE MORE MORE Carmel	London	2
-	26	THE MUSIC OF TORVILL AND DEAN (EP) Richard Hartley and the Michael Reed Orchestra ●	Safari	1
23	27	SOUL TRAIN Swans Way	Exit	4
34	28	THE POLITICS OF DANCING Re-Flex	EMI	2
22	29	HYPERACTIVE! Thomas Dolby	Parlophone	6
38	30	DOWN IN THE SUBWAY Soft Cell	Some Bizzare	2
39	31	CRY AND BE FREE Marilyn	Love	2
24	32	LOVE THEME FROM 'THE THORN BIRDS' Juan Martin	WEA	5
27	33	ONE SMALL DAY Ultravox	Chrysalis	4
26	34	(FEELS LIKE) HEAVEN Fiction Factory	CBS	7
-	35	'ULLO JOHN ! GOTTA NEW MOTOR? Alexei Sayle ●	Springtime	1
30	36	SPICE OF LIFE Manhattan Transfer	Atlantic	6
-	37	FRAGGLE ROCK THEME Fraggles ●	RCA	1
-	38	BREAKIN' DOWN (SUGAR SAMBA) Julia and Company ●	London	1
-	39	TO BE OR NOT TO BE (THE HITLER RAP) Mel Brooks ●	Island	1
29	40	HERE COMES THE RAIN AGAIN Eurythmics	RCA	7

In these weeks ■ Henry Mancini's first top 40 hit for almost 20 years provides the first ever instance of two different themes from one television programme hitting the charts (18.02.84) ■ *The Music of Torvill and Dean* is the only instance of Olympic gold medal-winning music becoming a hit. The main theme is Ravel's *Bolero* (03.03.84)■

March 1984

□ Highest position disc reached ● Act's first ever week on chart

WEEK ENDING 10 MARCH 1984

LW	TW	Title / Artist	Label	Wks
1	[1]	99 RED BALLOONS Nena	*Epic*	5
3	[2]	JOANNA/TONIGHT Kool and the Gang	*De-Lite*	4
2	3	RELAX Frankie Goes To Hollywood	*ZTT*	10
4	[4]	WOULDN'T IT BE GOOD Nik Kershaw	*MCA*	6
11	5	STREET DANCE Break Machine	*Record Shack*	5
6	[6]	SOMEBODY'S WATCHING ME Rockwell	*Motown*	5
10	[7]	RUN RUNAWAY Slade	*RCA*	5
8	[8]	AN INNOCENT MAN Billy Joel	*CBS*	4
5	9	DOCTOR! DOCTOR! Thompson Twins	*Arista*	6
20	10	JUMP Van Halen	*Warner Brothers*	3
26	11	THE MUSIC OF TORVILL AND DEAN (EP) Richard Hartley and the Michael Reed Orchestra	*Safari*	2
14	[12]	HIDE AND SEEK Howard Jones	*WEA*	4
19	[13]	I GAVE YOU MY HEART (DIDN'T I) Hot Chocolate	*RAK*	4
15	[14]	LET THE MUSIC PLAY Shannon	*Club*	6
17	[15]	GET OUT OF YOUR LAZY BED Matt Bianco	*WEA*	4
7	16	RADIO GA GA Queen	*EMI*	6
9	17	MY EVER CHANGING MOODS Style Council	*Polydor*	4
12	18	BREAK MY STRIDE Matthew Wilder	*Epic*	8
38	19	BREAKIN' DOWN (SUGAR SAMBA) Julia and Company	*London*	2
13	20	GIRLS JUST WANT TO HAVE FUN Cyndi Lauper	*Portrait*	8
35	21	'ULLO JOHN ! GOTTA NEW MOTOR? Alexei Sayle	*Springtime*	2
16	22	MICHAEL CAINE Madness	*Stiff*	5
25	[23]	MORE MORE MORE Carmel	*London*	3
30	[24]	DOWN IN THE SUBWAY Soft Cell	*Some Bizzare*	3
-	25	HELLO Lionel Richie	*Motown*	1
18	26	HOLIDAY Madonna	*Sire*	8
-	27	WHAT DO I DO Phil Fearon and Galaxy	*Ensign*	1
28	[28]	THE POLITICS OF DANCING Re-Flex	*EMI*	3
23	29	MAIN THEME FROM 'THE THORN BIRDS' Henry Mancini and his Orchestra	*Warner Brothers*	4
21	30	WHAT DIFFERENCE DOES IT MAKE Smiths	*Rough Trade*	7
39	31	TO BE OR NOT TO BE (THE HITLER RAP) Mel Brooks	*Island*	2
-	32	MY GUY Tracey Ullman	*Stiff*	1
37	[33]	FRAGGLE ROCK THEME Fraggles	*RCA*	2
-	34	DANCE HALL DAYS Wang Chung ●	*Geffen*	1
31	35	CRY AND BE FREE Marilyn	*Love*	3
-	36	IT'S RAINING MEN Weather Girls ●	*CBS*	1
-	37	YOUR LOVE IS KING Sade ●	*Epic*	1
-	38	ROBERT DE NIRO'S WAITING Bananarama	*London*	1
-	39	RENEGADES OF FUNK Afrika Bambaataa and the Soul Sonic Force ●	*Tommy Boy*	1
-	[40]	HELP Tina Turner	*Capitol*	1

WEEK ENDING 17 MARCH 1984

LW	TW	Title / Artist	Label	Wks
1	[1]	99 RED BALLOONS Nena	*Epic*	6
2	[2]	JOANNA/TONIGHT Kool and the Gang	*De-Lite*	5
5	[3]	STREET DANCE Break Machine	*Record Shack*	6
4	[4]	WOULDN'T IT BE GOOD Nik Kershaw	*MCA*	7
25	5	HELLO Lionel Richie	*Motown*	2
3	6	RELAX Frankie Goes To Hollywood	*ZTT*	11
10	[7]	JUMP Van Halen	*Warner Brothers*	4
8	[8]	AN INNOCENT MAN Billy Joel	*CBS*	5
6	9	SOMEBODY'S WATCHING ME Rockwell	*Motown*	6
11	10	THE MUSIC OF TORVILL AND DEAN (EP) Richard Hartley and the Michael Reed Orchestra	*Safari*	3
36	11	IT'S RAINING MEN Weather Girls	*CBS*	2
12	[12]	HIDE AND SEEK Howard Jones	*WEA*	5
27	13	WHAT DO I DO Phil Fearon and Galaxy	*Ensign*	2
7	14	RUN RUNAWAY Slade	*RCA*	6
19	[15]	BREAKIN' DOWN (SUGAR SAMBA) Julia and Company	*London*	3
13	16	I GAVE YOU MY HEART (DIDN'T I) Hot Chocolate	*RAK*	5
31	17	TO BE OR NOT TO BE (THE HITLER RAP) Mel Brooks	*Island*	3
21	18	'ULLO JOHN ! GOTTA NEW MOTOR? Alexei Sayle	*Springtime*	3
9	19	DOCTOR! DOCTOR! Thompson Twins	*Arista*	7
37	20	YOUR LOVE IS KING Sade	*Epic*	2
14	21	LET THE MUSIC PLAY Shannon	*Club*	7
38	22	ROBERT DE NIRO'S WAITING Bananarama	*London*	2
15	23	GET OUT OF YOUR LAZY BED Matt Bianco	*WEA*	5
32	24	MY GUY Tracey Ullman	*Stiff*	2
18	25	BREAK MY STRIDE Matthew Wilder	*Epic*	9
34	26	DANCE HALL DAYS Wang Chung	*Geffen*	2
17	27	MY EVER CHANGING MOODS Style Council	*Polydor*	5
16	28	RADIO GA GA Queen	*EMI*	7
24	29	DOWN IN THE SUBWAY Soft Cell	*Some Bizzare*	4
39	[30]	RENEGADES OF FUNK Afrika Bambaataa and the Soul Sonic Force	*Tommy Boy*	2
23	31	MORE MORE MORE Carmel	*London*	4
20	32	GIRLS JUST WANT TO HAVE FUN Cyndi Lauper	*Portrait*	9
22	33	MICHAEL CAINE Madness	*Stiff*	6
28	34	THE POLITICS OF DANCING Re-Flex	*EMI*	4
26	35	HOLIDAY Madonna	*Sire*	9
33	36	FRAGGLE ROCK THEME Fraggles	*RCA*	3
-	37	THE LION'S MOUTH Kajagoogoo	*EMI*	1
29	38	MAIN THEME FROM 'THE THORN BIRDS' Henry Mancini and his Orchestra	*Warner Brothers*	5
30	39	WHAT DIFFERENCE DOES IT MAKE Smiths	*Rough Trade*	8
40	[40]	HELP Tina Turner	*Capitol*	2

WEEK ENDING 24 MARCH 1984

LW	TW	Title / Artist	Label	Wks
5	[1]	HELLO Lionel Richie	*Motown*	3
1	2	99 RED BALLOONS Nena	*Epic*	7
3	[3]	STREET DANCE Break Machine	*Record Shack*	7
2	4	JOANNA/TONIGHT Kool and the Gang	*De-Lite*	6
11	5	IT'S RAINING MEN Weather Girls	*CBS*	3
4	6	WOULDN'T IT BE GOOD Nik Kershaw	*MCA*	8
13	7	WHAT DO I DO Phil Fearon and Galaxy	*Ensign*	3
22	8	ROBERT DE NIRO'S WAITING Bananarama	*London*	3
20	9	YOUR LOVE IS KING Sade	*Epic*	3
7	10	JUMP Van Halen	*Warner Brothers*	5
8	11	AN INNOCENT MAN Billy Joel	*CBS*	6
17	[12]	TO BE OR NOT TO BE (THE HITLER RAP) Mel Brooks	*Island*	4
10	13	THE MUSIC OF TORVILL AND DEAN (EP) Richard Hartley and the Michael Reed Orchestra	*Safari*	4
-	14	IT'S A MIRACLE Culture Club	*Virgin*	1
18	[15]	'ULLO JOHN ! GOTTA NEW MOTOR? Alexei Sayle	*Springtime*	4
6	16	RELAX Frankie Goes To Hollywood	*ZTT*	12
9	17	SOMEBODY'S WATCHING ME Rockwell	*Motown*	7
12	18	HIDE AND SEEK Howard Jones	*WEA*	6
15	19	BREAKIN' DOWN (SUGAR SAMBA) Julia and Company	*London*	4
14	20	RUN RUNAWAY Slade	*RCA*	7
26	[21]	DANCE HALL DAYS Wang Chung	*Geffen*	3
-	22	A LOVE WORTH WAITING FOR Shakin' Stevens	*Epic*	1
24	[23]	MY GUY Tracey Ullman	*Stiff*	3
16	24	I GAVE YOU MY HEART (DIDN'T I) Hot Chocolate	*RAK*	6
37	[25]	THE LION'S MOUTH Kajagoogoo	*EMI*	2
19	26	DOCTOR! DOCTOR! Thompson Twins	*Arista*	8
21	27	LET THE MUSIC PLAY Shannon	*Club*	8
-	28	CHERRY OH BABY UB40	*DEP International*	1
-	29	PEOPLE ARE PEOPLE Depeche Mode	*Mute*	1
-	30	LUCKY STAR Madonna	*Sire*	1
23	31	GET OUT OF YOUR LAZY BED Matt Bianco	*WEA*	6
30	32	RENEGADES OF FUNK Afrika Bambaataa and the Soul Sonic Force	*Tommy Boy*	3
-	33	SWIMMING HORSES Siouxsie and the Banshees	*Wonderland*	1
25	34	BREAK MY STRIDE Matthew Wilder	*Epic*	10
27	35	MY EVER CHANGING MOODS Style Council	*Polydor*	6
-	36	UP ON THE CATWALK Simple Minds	*Virgin*	1
28	37	RADIO GA GA Queen	*EMI*	8
-	38	NELSON MANDELA Special AKA	*2 Tone*	1
-	39	BORROWED TIME John Lennon	*Polydor*	1
40	[40]	HELP Tina Turner	*Capitol*	3

WEEK ENDING 31 MARCH 1984

LW	TW	Title / Artist	Label	Wks
1	[1]	HELLO Lionel Richie	*Motown*	4

■Two songs with film stars in their title in the charts at the same time *Michael Caine* by Madness and *Robert de Niro's Waiting* by Bananarama. These are the first hits with a film star in the title since Kim Carnes' *Bette Davis Eyes* in 1981 (10.03.84) ■ Three weeks at no. 40 for Tina Turner's version of the Beatles' *Help* (24.03.84)■

□ Denotes highest position reached ● Act's first ever week on chart

LW	TW	Title / Artist	Label	Wks
5	[2]	IT'S RAINING MEN Weather Girls	CBS	4
8	[3]	ROBERT DE NIRO'S WAITING Bananarama	London	4
14	[4]	IT'S A MIRACLE Culture Club	Virgin	2
7	[5]	WHAT DO I DO Phil Fearon and Galaxy	Ensign	4
9	[6]	YOUR LOVE IS KING Sade	Epic	4
22	7	A LOVE WORTH WAITING FOR Shakin' Stevens	Epic	2
3	8	STREET DANCE Break Machine	Record Shack	8
29	9	PEOPLE ARE PEOPLE Depeche Mode	Mute	2
4	10	JOANNA/TONIGHT Kool and the Gang	De-Lite	7
2	11	99 RED BALLOONS Nena	Epic	8
6	12	WOULDN'T IT BE GOOD Nik Kershaw	MCA	9
-	13	YOU TAKE ME UP Thompson Twins	Arista	1
13	14	THE MUSIC OF TORVILL AND DEAN (EP) Richard Hartley and the Michael Reed Orchestra	Safari	5
28	15	CHERRY OH BABY UB40	DEP International	2
10	16	JUMP Van Halen	Warner Brothers	6
11	17	AN INNOCENT MAN Billy Joel	CBS	7
12	18	TO BE OR NOT TO BE (THE HITLER RAP) Mel Brooks	Island	5
15	19	'ULLO JOHN ! GOTTA NEW MOTOR? Alexei Sayle	Springtime	5
-	20	PYT (PRETTY YOUNG THING) Michael Jackson	Epic	1
16	21	RELAX Frankie Goes To Hollywood	ZTT	13
21	22	DANCE HALL DAYS Wang Chung	Geffen	4
18	23	HIDE AND SEEK Howard Jones	WEA	7
19	24	BREAKIN' DOWN (SUGAR SAMBA) Julia and Company	London	5
25	[25]	THE LION'S MOUTH Kajagoogoo	EMI	3
17	26	SOMEBODY'S WATCHING ME Rockwell	Motown	8
30	27	LUCKY STAR Madonna	Sire	2
33	[28]	SWIMMING HORSES Siouxsie and the Banshees	Wonderland	2
38	29	NELSON MANDELA Special AKA	2 Tone	2
36	30	UP ON THE CATWALK Simple Minds	Virgin	2
27	31	LET THE MUSIC PLAY Shannon	Club	9
20	32	RUN RUNAWAY Slade	RCA	8
39	33	BORROWED TIME John Lennon	Polydor	2
23	34	MY GUY Tracey Ullman	Stiff	4
24	35	I GAVE YOU MY HEART (DIDN'T I) Hot Chocolate	RAK	7
-	36	GLAD IT'S ALL OVER/DAMNED ON 45 Captain Sensible	A&M	1
-	37	AIN'T NOBODY Rufus and Chaka Khan ●	Warner Brothers	1
-	38	WOOD BEEZ (PRAY LIKE ARETHA FRANKLIN) Scritti Politti ●	Virgin	1
26	39	DOCTOR! DOCTOR! Thompson Twins	Arista	9
-	40	THAT'S THE WAY (I LIKE IT) Dead Or Alive ●	Epic	1

WEEK ENDING 7 APRIL 1984

LW	TW	Title / Artist	Label	Wks
1	[1]	HELLO Lionel Richie	Motown	5
7	[2]	A LOVE WORTH WAITING FOR Shakin' Stevens	Epic	3
3	[3]	ROBERT DE NIRO'S WAITING Bananarama	London	5
13	4	YOU TAKE ME UP Thompson Twins	Arista	2
9	5	PEOPLE ARE PEOPLE Depeche Mode	Mute	3
2	6	IT'S RAINING MEN Weather Girls	CBS	5
4	7	IT'S A MIRACLE Culture Club	Virgin	3
5	8	WHAT DO I DO Phil Fearon and Galaxy	Ensign	5
14	[9]	THE MUSIC OF TORVILL AND DEAN (EP) Richard Hartley and the Michael Reed Orchestra	Safari	6
6	10	YOUR LOVE IS KING Sade	Epic	5
20	[11]	PYT (PRETTY YOUNG THING) Michael Jackson	Epic	2
15	[12]	CHERRY OH BABY UB40	DEP International	3
8	13	STREET DANCE Break Machine	Record Shack	9
29	14	NELSON MANDELA Special AKA	2 Tone	3
36	15	GLAD IT'S ALL OVER/DAMNED ON 45 Captain Sensible	A&M	2
27	16	LUCKY STAR Madonna	Sire	3
10	17	JOANNA/TONIGHT Kool and the Gang	De-Lite	8
37	18	AIN'T NOBODY Rufus and Chaka Khan	Warner Brothers	2
17	19	AN INNOCENT MAN Billy Joel	CBS	8
11	20	99 RED BALLOONS Nena	Epic	9
12	21	WOULDN'T IT BE GOOD Nik Kershaw	MCA	10
16	22	JUMP Van Halen	Warner Brothers	7
21	23	RELAX Frankie Goes To Hollywood	ZTT	14
18	24	TO BE OR NOT TO BE (THE HITLER RAP) Mel Brooks	Island	6
38	25	WOOD BEEZ (PRAY LIKE ARETHA FRANKLIN) Scritti Politti	Virgin	2
-	26	AGAINST ALL ODDS (TAKE A LOOK AT ME NOW) Phil Collins	Virgin	1
30	[27]	UP ON THE CATWALK Simple Minds	Virgin	3
22	28	DANCE HALL DAYS Wang Chung	Geffen	5
19	29	'ULLO JOHN ! GOTTA NEW MOTOR? Alexei Sayle	Springtime	6
40	30	THAT'S THE WAY (I LIKE IT) Dead Or Alive	Epic	2
-	31	THE CATERPILLAR Cure	Fiction	1
33	[32]	BORROWED TIME John Lennon	Polydor	3
28	33	SWIMMING HORSES Siouxsie and the Banshees	Wonderland	3
-	34	BABY YOU'RE DYNAMITE Cliff Richard	EMI	1
24	35	BREAKIN' DOWN (SUGAR SAMBA) Julia and Company	London	6
26	36	SOMEBODY'S WATCHING ME Rockwell	Motown	9
-	[37]	SHE'S STRANGE Cameo ●	Club	1
25	38	THE LION'S MOUTH Kajagoogoo	EMI	4
-	39	HEAVEN Psychedelic Furs ●	CBS	1
-	40	SOMEDAY Gap Band	Total Experience	1

WEEK ENDING 14 APRIL 1984

LW	TW	Title / Artist	Label	Wks
1	[1]	HELLO Lionel Richie	Motown	6
2	[2]	A LOVE WORTH WAITING FOR Shakin' Stevens	Epic	4
4	3	YOU TAKE ME UP Thompson Twins	Arista	3
5	[4]	PEOPLE ARE PEOPLE Depeche Mode	Mute	4
3	5	ROBERT DE NIRO'S WAITING Bananarama	London	6
15	[6]	GLAD IT'S ALL OVER/DAMNED ON 45 Captain Sensible	A&M	3
7	7	IT'S A MIRACLE Culture Club	Virgin	4
6	8	IT'S RAINING MEN Weather Girls	CBS	6
14	[9]	NELSON MANDELA Special AKA	2 Tone	4
26	10	AGAINST ALL ODDS (TAKE A LOOK AT ME NOW) Phil Collins	Virgin	2
8	11	WHAT DO I DO Phil Fearon and Galaxy	Ensign	6
11	12	PYT (PRETTY YOUNG THING) Michael Jackson	Epic	3
18	13	AIN'T NOBODY Rufus and Chaka Khan	Warner Brothers	3
16	[14]	LUCKY STAR Madonna	Sire	4
10	15	YOUR LOVE IS KING Sade	Epic	6
12	16	CHERRY OH BABY UB40	DEP International	4
25	17	WOOD BEEZ (PRAY LIKE ARETHA FRANKLIN) Scritti Politti	Virgin	3
-	18	I WANT TO BREAK FREE Queen	EMI	1
13	19	STREET DANCE Break Machine	Record Shack	10
31	20	THE CATERPILLAR Cure	Fiction	2
23	21	RELAX Frankie Goes To Hollywood	ZTT	15
40	22	SOMEDAY Gap Band	Total Experience	2
9	23	THE MUSIC OF TORVILL AND DEAN (EP) Richard Hartley and the Michael Reed Orchestra	Safari	7
-	[24]	GIVE ME TONIGHT Shannon	Club	1
30	25	THAT'S THE WAY (I LIKE IT) Dead Or Alive	Epic	3
-	26	JUST BE GOOD TO ME SOS Band ●	Tabu	1
34	[27]	BABY YOU'RE DYNAMITE Cliff Richard	EMI	2
-	28	LOCOMOTION Orchestral Manoeuvres In The Dark	Virgin	1
39	[29]	HEAVEN Psychedelic Furs	CBS	2
-	30	WHEN YOU SAY YOU LOVE SOMEBODY (IN THE HEART) Kool and the Gang	De-Lite	1
27	31	UP ON THE CATWALK Simple Minds	Virgin	4
-	32	DON'T TELL ME Blancmange	London	1
17	33	JOANNA/TONIGHT Kool and the Gang	De-Lite	9
-	34	DR MABUSE Propaganda ●	ZTT	1
-	35	DANCING GIRLS Nik Kershaw	MCA	1
-	36	I'M FALLING Bluebells ●	London	1
22	37	JUMP Van Halen	Warner Brothers	8
21	38	WOULDN'T IT BE GOOD Nik Kershaw	MCA	11
20	39	99 RED BALLOONS Nena	Epic	10
19	40	AN INNOCENT MAN Billy Joel	CBS	9

WEEK ENDING 21 APRIL 1984

LW	TW	Title / Artist	Label	Wks
1	[1]	HELLO Lionel Richie	Motown	7
3	[2]	YOU TAKE ME UP Thompson Twins	Arista	4
2	3	A LOVE WORTH WAITING FOR Shakin' Stevens	Epic	5

In these weeks ■ The only one of Madonna's singles never to hit the Top 10, *Lucky Star* peaks at no. 14 (14.04.84) ■ Six real people mentioned in the titles of singles in the top 25 - Robert de Niro, Jayne Torvill and Christopher Dean, Nelson Mandela, Adolf Hitler and Aretha Franklin (07.04.84)■

May 1984

□ Denotes highest position reached ● Act's first ever week on chart

LW	TW	Title	Artist	Label	Wks
10	4	AGAINST ALL ODDS (TAKE A LOOK AT ME NOW)	Phil Collins	*Virgin*	3
18	5	I WANT TO BREAK FREE	Queen	*EMI*	2
4	6	PEOPLE ARE PEOPLE	Depeche Mode	*Mute*	5
6	7	GLAD IT'S ALL OVER/DAMNED ON 45	Captain Sensible	*A&M*	4
13	8	AIN'T NOBODY	Rufus and Chaka Khan	*Warner Brothers*	4
9	9	NELSON MANDELA	Special AKA	*2 Tone*	5
17	10	WOOD BEEZ (PRAY LIKE ARETHA FRANKLIN)	Scritti Politti	*Virgin*	4
30	11	WHEN YOU SAY YOU LOVE SOMEBODY (IN THE HEART)	Kool and the Gang	*De-Lite*	2
5	12	ROBERT DE NIRO'S WAITING	Bananarama	*London*	7
26	13	JUST BE GOOD TO ME	SOS Band	*Tabu*	2
20	14	THE CATERPILLAR	Cure	*Fiction*	3
32	15	DON'T TELL ME	Blancmange	*London*	2
7	16	IT'S A MIRACLE	Culture Club	*Virgin*	5
22	17	SOMEDAY	Gap Band	*Total Experience*	3
8	18	IT'S RAINING MEN	Weather Girls	*CBS*	7
28	19	LOCOMOTION	Orchestral Manoeuvres In The Dark	*Virgin*	2
14	20	LUCKY STAR	Madonna	*Sire*	5
12	21	PYT (PRETTY YOUNG THING)	Michael Jackson	*Epic*	4
25	22	THAT'S THE WAY (I LIKE IT)	Dead Or Alive	*Epic*	4
11	23	WHAT DO I DO	Phil Fearon and Galaxy	*Ensign*	7
24	24	GIVE ME TONIGHT	Shannon	*Club*	2
35	25	DANCING GIRLS	Nik Kershaw	*MCA*	2
36	26	I'M FALLING	Bluebells	*London*	2
34	27	DR MABUSE	Propaganda	*ZTT*	2
16	28	CHERRY OH BABY	UB40	*DEP International*	5
21	29	RELAX	Frankie Goes To Hollywood	*ZTT*	16
15	30	YOUR LOVE IS KING	Sade	*Epic*	7
27	31	BABY YOU'RE DYNAMITE	Cliff Richard	*EMI*	3
-	32	SILVER	Echo and the Bunnymen	*Korova*	1
29	33	HEAVEN	Psychedelic Furs	*CBS*	3
19	34	STREET DANCE	Break Machine	*Record Shack*	11
-	35	ONE LOVE-PEOPLE GET READY	Bob Marley and the Wailers	*Island*	1
-	36	TO ALL THE GIRLS I'VE LOVED BEFORE	Julio Iglesias and Willie Nelson ●	*CBS*	1
-	37	WHEN YOU'RE YOUNG AND IN LOVE	Flying Pickets	*10*	1
-	38	AUTOMATIC	Pointer Sisters	*Planet*	1
23	39	THE MUSIC OF TORVILL AND DEAN (EP)	Richard Hartley and the Michael Reed Orchestra	*Safari*	8
-	40	SOMEBODY ELSE'S GUY	Jocelyn Brown ●	*Fourth & Broadway*	1

LW	TW	*WEEK ENDING* **28 APRIL 1984**			Wks
1	1	HELLO	Lionel Richie	*Motown*	8
4	2	AGAINST ALL ODDS (TAKE A LOOK AT ME NOW)	Phil Collins	*Virgin*	4
5	3	I WANT TO BREAK FREE	Queen	*EMI*	3
2	4	YOU TAKE ME UP	Thompson Twins	*Arista*	5
-	5	THE REFLEX	Duran Duran	*EMI*	1
3	6	A LOVE WORTH WAITING FOR	Shakin' Stevens	*Epic*	6
11	7	WHEN YOU SAY YOU LOVE SOMEBODY (IN THE HEART)	Kool and the Gang	*De-Lite*	3
7	8	GLAD IT'S ALL OVER/DAMNED ON 45	Captain Sensible	*A&M*	5
6	9	PEOPLE ARE PEOPLE	Depeche Mode	*Mute*	6
19	10	LOCOMOTION	Orchestral Manoeuvres In The Dark	*Virgin*	3
15	11	DON'T TELL ME	Blancmange	*London*	3
8	12	AIN'T NOBODY	Rufus and Chaka Khan	*Warner Brothers*	5
37	13	WHEN YOU'RE YOUNG AND IN LOVE	Flying Pickets	*10*	2
10	14	WOOD BEEZ (PRAY LIKE ARETHA FRANKLIN)	Scritti Politti	*Virgin*	5
26	15	I'M FALLING	Bluebells	*London*	3
9	16	NELSON MANDELA	Special AKA	*2 Tone*	6
13	17	JUST BE GOOD TO ME	SOS Band	*Tabu*	3
25	18	DANCING GIRLS	Nik Kershaw	*MCA*	3
14	19	THE CATERPILLAR	Cure	*Fiction*	4
38	20	AUTOMATIC	Pointer Sisters	*Planet*	2
-	21	THIEVES LIKE US	New Order	*Factory*	1
35	22	ONE LOVE-PEOPLE GET READY	Bob Marley and the Wailers	*Island*	2
12	23	ROBERT DE NIRO'S WAITING	Bananarama	*London*	8
22	24	THAT'S THE WAY (I LIKE IT)	Dead Or Alive	*Epic*	5
17	25	SOMEDAY	Gap Band	*Total Experience*	4
24	26	GIVE ME TONIGHT	Shannon	*Club*	3
18	27	IT'S RAINING MEN	Weather Girls	*CBS*	8
16	28	IT'S A MIRACLE	Culture Club	*Virgin*	6
29	29	RELAX	Frankie Goes To Hollywood	*ZTT*	17
32	30	SILVER	Echo and the Bunnymen	*Korova*	2
40	31	SOMEBODY ELSE'S GUY	Jocelyn Brown	*Fourth & Broadway*	2
21	32	PYT (PRETTY YOUNG THING)	Michael Jackson	*Epic*	5
27	33	DR MABUSE	Propaganda	*ZTT*	3
20	34	LUCKY STAR	Madonna	*Sire*	6
36	35	TO ALL THE GIRLS I'VE LOVED BEFORE	Julio Iglesias and Willie Nelson	*CBS*	2
-	36	HAND IN GLOVE	Sandie Shaw	*Rough Trade*	1
23	37	WHAT DO I DO	Phil Fearon and Galaxy	*Ensign*	8
-	38	PEARLY DEWDROPS DROPS	Cocteau Twins ●	*4AD*	1
-	39	LOVE GAMES	Belle and the Devotions ●	*CBS*	1
-	40	EAT IT	Weird Al Yankovic ●	*Scotti Brothers*	1

LW	TW	*WEEK ENDING* **5 MAY 1984**			Wks
5	1	THE REFLEX	Duran Duran	*EMI*	2
2	2	AGAINST ALL ODDS (TAKE A LOOK AT ME NOW)	Phil Collins	*Virgin*	5
3	3	I WANT TO BREAK FREE	Queen	*EMI*	4
1	4	HELLO	Lionel Richie	*Motown*	9
20	5	AUTOMATIC	Pointer Sisters	*Planet*	3
10	6	LOCOMOTION	Orchestral Manoeuvres In The Dark	*Virgin*	4
13	7	WHEN YOU'RE YOUNG AND IN LOVE	Flying Pickets	*10*	3
11	8	DON'T TELL ME	Blancmange	*London*	4
22	9	ONE LOVE-PEOPLE GET READY	Bob Marley and the Wailers	*Island*	3
4	10	YOU TAKE ME UP	Thompson Twins	*Arista*	6
15	11	I'M FALLING	Bluebells	*London*	4
7	12	WHEN YOU SAY YOU LOVE SOMEBODY (IN THE HEART)	Kool and the Gang	*De-Lite*	4
12	13	AIN'T NOBODY	Rufus and Chaka Khan	*Warner Brothers*	6
18	14	DANCING GIRLS	Nik Kershaw	*MCA*	4
6	15	A LOVE WORTH WAITING FOR	Shakin' Stevens	*Epic*	7
8	16	GLAD IT'S ALL OVER/DAMNED ON 45	Captain Sensible	*A&M*	6
17	17	JUST BE GOOD TO ME	SOS Band	*Tabu*	4
21	18	THIEVES LIKE US	New Order	*Factory*	2
-	19	THE LEBANON	Human League	*Virgin*	1
9	20	PEOPLE ARE PEOPLE	Depeche Mode	*Mute*	7
39	21	LOVE GAMES	Belle and the Devotions	*CBS*	2
16	22	NELSON MANDELA	Special AKA	*2 Tone*	7
14	23	WOOD BEEZ (PRAY LIKE ARETHA FRANKLIN)	Scritti Politti	*Virgin*	6
35	24	TO ALL THE GIRLS I'VE LOVED BEFORE	Julio Iglesias and Willie Nelson	*CBS*	3
31	25	SOMEBODY ELSE'S GUY	Jocelyn Brown	*Fourth & Broadway*	3
19	26	THE CATERPILLAR	Cure	*Fiction*	5
36	27	HAND IN GLOVE	Sandie Shaw	*Rough Trade*	2
-	28	FOOTLOOSE	Kenny Loggins ●	*CBS*	1
38	29	PEARLY DEWDROPS DROPS	Cocteau Twins	*4AD*	2
30	30	SILVER	Echo and the Bunnymen	*Korova*	3
29	31	RELAX	Frankie Goes To Hollywood	*ZTT*	18
26	32	GIVE ME TONIGHT	Shannon	*Club*	4
-	33	THE LONGEST TIME	Billy Joel	*CBS*	1
25	34	SOMEDAY	Gap Band	*Total Experience*	5
24	35	THAT'S THE WAY (I LIKE IT)	Dead Or Alive	*Epic*	6
40	36	EAT IT	Weird Al Yankovic	*Scotti Brothers*	2
34	37	LUCKY STAR	Madonna	*Sire*	7
-	38	STAY WITH ME TONIGHT	Jeffrey Osborne ●	*A&M*	1
23	39	ROBERT DE NIRO'S WAITING	Bananarama	*London*	9
32	40	PYT (PRETTY YOUNG THING)	Michael Jackson	*Epic*	6

■Two sets of twins in the charts, neither of which are twins or even duos - the Thompson Twins and the Cocteau Twins (28.04.84) ■ After 18 weeks of top 40 life, *Relax* reaches its lowest point before starting to climb the charts again (05.05.84)■

May 1984

□ Highest position disc reached ● Act's first ever week on chart

WEEK ENDING 12 MAY 1984

LW	TW	Title	Artist	Label	Wks
1	[1]	THE REFLEX	Duran Duran	*EMI*	3
2	[2]	AGAINST ALL ODDS (TAKE A LOOK AT ME NOW)	Phil Collins	*Virgin*	6
3	[3]	I WANT TO BREAK FREE	Queen	*EMI*	5
5	4	AUTOMATIC	Pointer Sisters	*Planet*	4
6	[5]	LOCOMOTION	Orchestral Manoeuvres In The Dark	*Virgin*	5
9	6	ONE LOVE-PEOPLE GET READY	Bob Marley and the Wailers	*Island*	4
7	[7]	WHEN YOU'RE YOUNG AND IN LOVE	Flying Pickets	*10*	4
8	[8]	DON'T TELL ME	Blancmange	*London*	5
28	9	FOOTLOOSE	Kenny Loggins	*CBS*	2
4	10	HELLO	Lionel Richie	*Motown*	10
19	[11]	THE LEBANON	Human League	*Virgin*	2
21	12	LOVE GAMES	Belle and the Devotions	*CBS*	3
14	[13]	DANCING GIRLS	Nik Kershaw	*MCA*	5
11	14	I'M FALLING	Bluebells	*London*	5
12	15	WHEN YOU SAY YOU LOVE SOMEBODY (IN THE HEART)	Kool and the Gang	*De-Lite*	5
25	16	SOMEBODY ELSE'S GUY	Jocelyn Brown	*Fourth & Broadway*	4
24	[17]	TO ALL THE GIRLS I'VE LOVED BEFORE	Julio Iglesias and Willie Nelson	*CBS*	4
-	18	LET'S HEAR IT FOR THE BOY	Deniece Williams	*CBS*	1
13	19	AIN'T NOBODY	Rufus and Chaka Khan	*Warner Brothers*	7
17	20	JUST BE GOOD TO ME	SOS Band	*Tabu*	5
10	21	YOU TAKE ME UP	Thompson Twins	*Arista*	7
18	22	THIEVES LIKE US	New Order	*Factory*	3
-	23	ASSASSING	Marillion	*EMI*	1
38	24	STAY WITH ME TONIGHT	Jeffrey Osborne	*A&M*	2
33	[25]	THE LONGEST TIME	Billy Joel	*CBS*	2
31	26	RELAX	Frankie Goes To Hollywood	*ZTT*	19
15	27	A LOVE WORTH WAITING FOR	Shakin' Stevens	*Epic*	8
-	28	I'LL BE AROUND	Terri Wells ●	*Philly World*	1
16	29	GLAD IT'S ALL OVER/DAMNED ON 45	Captain Sensible	*A&M*	7
29	30	PEARLY DEWDROPS DROPS	Cocteau Twins	*4AD*	3
27	31	HAND IN GLOVE	Sandie Shaw	*Rough Trade*	3
-	32	BREAK DANCE PARTY	Break Machine	*Record Shack*	1
23	33	WOOD BEEZ (PRAY LIKE ARETHA FRANKLIN)	Scritti Politti	*Virgin*	7
22	34	NELSON MANDELA	Special AKA	*2 Tone*	8
-	35	LOVE WARS	Womack and Womack ●	*Elektra*	1
20	36	PEOPLE ARE PEOPLE	Depeche Mode	*Mute*	8
26	37	THE CATERPILLAR	Cure	*Fiction*	6
-	38	LOVE ME TENDER	Roland Rat Superstar	*Rodent*	1
30	39	SILVER	Echo and the Bunnymen	*Korova*	4
-	40	SEARCHIN' (I GOTTA FIND A MAN)	Hazell Dean ●	*Proto*	1

WEEK ENDING 19 MAY 1984

LW	TW	Title	Artist	Label	Wks
1	[1]	THE REFLEX	Duran Duran	*EMI*	4
4	[2]	AUTOMATIC	Pointer Sisters	*Planet*	5
2	3	AGAINST ALL ODDS (TAKE A LOOK AT ME NOW)	Phil Collins	*Virgin*	7
3	4	I WANT TO BREAK FREE	Queen	*EMI*	6
6	[5]	ONE LOVE-PEOPLE GET READY	Bob Marley and the Wailers	*Island*	5
9	[6]	FOOTLOOSE	Kenny Loggins	*CBS*	3
5	7	LOCOMOTION	Orchestral Manoeuvres In The Dark	*Virgin*	6
18	8	LET'S HEAR IT FOR THE BOY	Deniece Williams	*CBS*	2
8	9	DON'T TELL ME	Blancmange	*London*	6
7	10	WHEN YOU'RE YOUNG AND IN LOVE	Flying Pickets	*10*	5
12	[11]	LOVE GAMES	Belle and the Devotions	*CBS*	4
11	12	THE LEBANON	Human League	*Virgin*	3
16	[13]	SOMEBODY ELSE'S GUY	Jocelyn Brown	*Fourth & Broadway*	5
13	14	DANCING GIRLS	Nik Kershaw	*MCA*	6
10	15	HELLO	Lionel Richie	*Motown*	11
32	16	BREAK DANCE PARTY	Break Machine	*Record Shack*	2
28	[17]	I'LL BE AROUND	Terri Wells	*Philly World*	2
24	[18]	STAY WITH ME TONIGHT	Jeffrey Osborne	*A&M*	3
14	19	I'M FALLING	Bluebells	*London*	6
20	20	JUST BE GOOD TO ME	SOS Band	*Tabu*	6
17	21	TO ALL THE GIRLS I'VE LOVED BEFORE	Julio Iglesias and Willie Nelson	*CBS*	5
23	[22]	ASSASSING	Marillion	*EMI*	2
15	23	WHEN YOU SAY YOU LOVE SOMEBODY (IN THE HEART)	Kool and the Gang	*De-Lite*	6
26	24	RELAX	Frankie Goes To Hollywood	*ZTT*	20
35	25	LOVE WARS	Womack and Womack	*Elektra*	2
19	26	AIN'T NOBODY	Rufus and Chaka Khan	*Warner Brothers*	8
25	27	THE LONGEST TIME	Billy Joel	*CBS*	3
40	28	SEARCHIN' (I GOTTA FIND A MAN)	Hazell Dean	*Proto*	2
-	29	DANCING WITH TEARS IN MY EYES	Ultravox	*Chrysalis*	1
-	30	GOING DOWN TOWN TONIGHT	Status Quo	*Vertigo*	1
-	31	I FEEL LIKE BUDDY HOLLY	Alvin Stardust	*Chrysalis*	1
38	[32]	LOVE ME TENDER	Roland Rat Superstar	*Rodent*	2
-	33	EACH AND EVERY ONE	Everything But The Girl ●	*blanco y negro*	1
21	34	YOU TAKE ME UP	Thompson Twins	*Arista*	8
30	35	PEARLY DEWDROPS DROPS	Cocteau Twins	*4AD*	4
-	36	HIGH ENERGY	Evelyn Thomas	*Record Shack*	1
29	37	GLAD IT'S ALL OVER/DAMNED ON 45	Captain Sensible	*A&M*	8
22	38	THIEVES LIKE US	New Order	*Factory*	4
27	39	A LOVE WORTH WAITING FOR	Shakin' Stevens	*Epic*	9
-	[40]	YOU DON'T LOVE ME	Marilyn	*Love*	1

WEEK ENDING 26 MAY 1984

LW	TW	Title	Artist	Label	Wks
1	[1]	THE REFLEX	Duran Duran	*EMI*	5
2	[2]	AUTOMATIC	Pointer Sisters	*Planet*	6
8	3	LET'S HEAR IT FOR THE BOY	Deniece Williams	*CBS*	3
-	4	WAKE ME UP BEFORE YOU GO GO	Wham!	*Epic*	1
4	5	I WANT TO BREAK FREE	Queen	*EMI*	7
5	6	ONE LOVE-PEOPLE GET READY	Bob Marley and the Wailers	*Island*	6
6	7	FOOTLOOSE	Kenny Loggins	*CBS*	4
3	8	AGAINST ALL ODDS (TAKE A LOOK AT ME NOW)	Phil Collins	*Virgin*	8
16	[9]	BREAK DANCE PARTY	Break Machine	*Record Shack*	3
29	10	DANCING WITH TEARS IN MY EYES	Ultravox	*Chrysalis*	2
-	11	GROOVIN' (YOU'RE THE BEST THING)/BIG BOSS GROOVE	Style Council	*Polydor*	1
7	12	LOCOMOTION	Orchestral Manoeuvres In The Dark	*Virgin*	7
28	13	SEARCHIN' (I GOTTA FIND A MAN)	Hazell Dean	*Proto*	3
25	[14]	LOVE WARS	Womack and Womack	*Elektra*	3
9	15	DON'T TELL ME	Blancmange	*London*	7
10	16	WHEN YOU'RE YOUNG AND IN LOVE	Flying Pickets	*10*	6
31	17	I FEEL LIKE BUDDY HOLLY	Alvin Stardust	*Chrysalis*	2
17	18	I'LL BE AROUND	Terri Wells	*Philly World*	3
18	19	STAY WITH ME TONIGHT	Jeffrey Osborne	*A&M*	4
13	20	SOMEBODY ELSE'S GUY	Jocelyn Brown	*Fourth & Broadway*	6
24	21	RELAX	Frankie Goes To Hollywood	*ZTT*	21
12	22	THE LEBANON	Human League	*Virgin*	4
30	23	GOING DOWN TOWN TONIGHT	Status Quo	*Vertigo*	2
11	24	LOVE GAMES	Belle and the Devotions	*CBS*	5
-	25	PEARL IN THE SHELL	Howard Jones	*WEA*	1
36	26	HIGH ENERGY	Evelyn Thomas	*Record Shack*	2
14	27	DANCING GIRLS	Nik Kershaw	*MCA*	7
33	[28]	EACH AND EVERY ONE	Everything But The Girl	*blanco y negro*	2
15	29	HELLO	Lionel Richie	*Motown*	12
20	30	JUST BE GOOD TO ME	SOS Band	*Tabu*	7
21	31	TO ALL THE GIRLS I'VE LOVED BEFORE	Julio Iglesias and Willie Nelson	*CBS*	6
22	32	ASSASSING	Marillion	*EMI*	3
19	33	I'M FALLING	Bluebells	*London*	7
-	34	DANCING IN THE DARK	Bruce Springsteen	*CBS*	1
27	35	THE LONGEST TIME	Billy Joel	*CBS*	4
32	36	LOVE ME TENDER	Roland Rat Superstar	*Rodent*	3
23	37	WHEN YOU SAY YOU LOVE SOMEBODY (IN THE HEART)	Kool and the Gang	*De-Lite*	7
26	38	AIN'T NOBODY	Rufus and Chaka Khan	*Warner Brothers*	9

In these weeks ■ One of the less convincing covers of Elvis Presley's hits was Roland Rat Superstar's version of *Love Me Tender* (19.05.84) ■ Three film songs in the top ten, two from the same film, *Footloose'*. They are *Footloose* and *Let's Here It For The Boy*, and Phil Collins' *Against All Odds* from the film of the same name (19.05.84)■

LW	TW	Title	Artist	Label	Wks
-	39	LOVE LIES LOST	Helen Terry ●	Virgin	1
40	[40]	YOU DON'T LOVE ME	Marilyn	Love	2

WEEK ENDING 2 JUNE 1984

LW	TW	Title	Artist	Label	Wks
4	[1]	WAKE ME UP BEFORE YOU GO GO	Wham!	Epic	2
3	[2]	LET'S HEAR IT FOR THE BOY	Deniece Williams	CBS	4
1	3	THE REFLEX	Duran Duran	EMI	6
2	4	AUTOMATIC	Pointer Sisters	Planet	7
11	[5]	GROOVIN' (YOU'RE THE BEST THING)/BIG BOSS GROOVE	Style Council	Polydor	2
10	6	DANCING WITH TEARS IN MY EYES	Ultravox	Chrysalis	3
17	[7]	I FEEL LIKE BUDDY HOLLY	Alvin Stardust	Chrysalis	3
13	8	SEARCHIN' (I GOTTA FIND A MAN)	Hazell Dean	Proto	4
5	9	I WANT TO BREAK FREE	Queen	EMI	8
8	10	AGAINST ALL ODDS (TAKE A LOOK AT ME NOW)	Phil Collins	Virgin	9
26	11	HIGH ENERGY	Evelyn Thomas	Record Shack	3
6	12	ONE LOVE-PEOPLE GET READY	Bob Marley and the Wailers	Island	7
9	13	BREAK DANCE PARTY	Break Machine	Record Shack	4
7	14	FOOTLOOSE	Kenny Loggins	CBS	5
25	15	PEARL IN THE SHELL	Howard Jones	WEA	2
14	16	LOVE WARS	Womack and Womack	Elektra	4
21	17	RELAX	Frankie Goes To Hollywood	ZTT	22
12	18	LOCOMOTION	Orchestral Manoeuvres In The Dark	Virgin	8
-	19	HEAVEN KNOWS I'M MISERABLE NOW	Smiths	Rough Trade	1
23	[20]	GOING DOWN TOWN TONIGHT	Status Quo	Vertigo	3
-	21	RED GUITAR	David Sylvian ●	Virgin	1
-	22	SAD SONGS (SAY SO MUCH)	Elton John	Rocket	1
-	23	THINKING OF YOU	Sister Sledge	Cotillion	1
18	24	I'LL BE AROUND	Terri Wells	Philly World	4
19	25	STAY WITH ME TONIGHT	Jeffrey Osborne	A&M	5
15	26	DON'T TELL ME	Blancmange	London	8
20	27	SOMEBODY ELSE'S GUY	Jocelyn Brown	Fourth & Broadway	7
34	[28]	DANCING IN THE DARK	Bruce Springsteen	CBS	2
-	29	SO TIRED	Ozzy Osbourne	Epic	1
-	30	ONE BETTER DAY	Madness	Stiff	1
28	31	EACH AND EVERY ONE	Everything But The Girl	blanco y negro	3
16	32	WHEN YOU'RE YOUNG AND IN LOVE	Flying Pickets	10	7
20	33	JUST BE GOOD TO ME	SOS Band	Tabu	8
39	[34]	LOVE LIES LOST	Helen Terry	Virgin	2
-	35	SMALLTOWN BOY	Bronski Beat ●	Forbidden Fruit	1
22	36	THE LEBANON	Human League	Virgin	5
27	37	DANCING GIRLS	Nik Kershaw	MCA	8
-	38	DAZZLE	Siouxsie and the Banshees	Wonderland	1
29	39	HELLO	Lionel Richie	Motown	13
-	40	WHEN AM I GOING TO MAKE A LIVING	Sade	Epic	1

WEEK ENDING 9 JUNE 1984

LW	TW	Title	Artist	Label	Wks
1	[1]	WAKE ME UP BEFORE YOU GO GO	Wham!	Epic	3
2	[2]	LET'S HEAR IT FOR THE BOY	Deniece Williams	CBS	5
6	[3]	DANCING WITH TEARS IN MY EYES	Ultravox	Chrysalis	4
3	4	THE REFLEX	Duran Duran	EMI	7
-	5	ONLY WHEN YOU LEAVE	Spandau Ballet	Reformation	1
8	[6]	SEARCHIN' (I GOTTA FIND A MAN)	Hazell Dean	Proto	5
5	7	GROOVIN' (YOU'RE THE BEST THING)/BIG BOSS GROOVE	Style Council	Polydor	3
15	8	PEARL IN THE SHELL	Howard Jones	WEA	3
11	9	HIGH ENERGY	Evelyn Thomas	Record Shack	4
19	[10]	HEAVEN KNOWS I'M MISERABLE NOW	Smiths	Rough Trade	2
7	11	I FEEL LIKE BUDDY HOLLY	Alvin Stardust	Chrysalis	4
22	12	SAD SONGS (SAY SO MUCH)	Elton John	Rocket	2
35	13	SMALLTOWN BOY	Bronski Beat	Forbidden Fruit	2
4	14	AUTOMATIC	Pointer Sisters	Planet	8
9	15	I WANT TO BREAK FREE	Queen	EMI	9
17	16	RELAX	Frankie Goes To Hollywood	ZTT	23
21	[17]	RED GUITAR	David Sylvian	Virgin	2
30	18	ONE BETTER DAY	Madness	Stiff	2

June 1984

□ Highest position disc reached ● Act's first ever week on chart

LW	TW	Title	Artist	Label	Wks
23	19	THINKING OF YOU	Sister Sledge	Cotillion	2
13	20	BREAK DANCE PARTY	Break Machine	Record Shack	5
14	21	FOOTLOOSE	Kenny Loggins	CBS	6
10	22	AGAINST ALL ODDS (TAKE A LOOK AT ME NOW)	Phil Collins	Virgin	10
16	23	LOVE WARS	Womack and Womack	Elektra	5
12	24	ONE LOVE-PEOPLE GET READY	Bob Marley and the Wailers	Island	8
29	25	SO TIRED	Ozzy Osbourne	Epic	2
-	26	FAREWELL MY SUMMER LOVE	Michael Jackson	Motown	1
20	27	GOING DOWN TOWN TONIGHT	Status Quo	Vertigo	4
18	28	LOCOMOTION	Orchestral Manoeuvres In The Dark	Virgin	9
-	29	ROUGH JUSTICE	Bananarama	London	1
-	30	INFATUATION	Rod Stewart	Warner Brothers	1
-	31	SUSANNA	Art Company ●	Epic	1
31	32	EACH AND EVERY ONE	Everything But The Girl	blanco y negro	4
38	[33]	DAZZLE	Siouxsie and the Banshees	Wonderland	2
28	34	DANCING IN THE DARK	Bruce Springsteen	CBS	3
24	35	I'LL BE AROUND	Terri Wells	Philly World	5
40	[36]	WHEN AM I GOING TO MAKE A LIVING	Sade	Epic	2
-	37	LOVE ALL DAY	Nick Heyward	Arista	1
25	38	STAY WITH ME TONIGHT	Jeffrey Osborne	A&M	6
-	39	CHANGE OF HEART	Change	WEA	1
26	40	DON'T TELL ME	Blancmange	London	9

WEEK ENDING 16 JUNE 1984

LW	TW	Title	Artist	Label	Wks
-	[1]	TWO TRIBES	Frankie Goes To Hollywood	ZTT	1
1	2	WAKE ME UP BEFORE YOU GO GO	Wham!	Epic	4
5	[3]	ONLY WHEN YOU LEAVE	Spandau Ballet	Reformation	2
13	4	SMALLTOWN BOY	Bronski Beat	Forbidden Fruit	3
9	[5]	HIGH ENERGY	Evelyn Thomas	Record Shack	5
3	6	DANCING WITH TEARS IN MY EYES	Ultravox	Chrysalis	5
8	[7]	PEARL IN THE SHELL	Howard Jones	WEA	4
12	8	SAD SONGS (SAY SO MUCH)	Elton John	Rocket	3
2	9	LET'S HEAR IT FOR THE BOY	Deniece Williams	CBS	6
10	[10]	HEAVEN KNOWS I'M MISERABLE NOW	Smiths	Rough Trade	3
16	11	RELAX	Frankie Goes To Hollywood	ZTT	24
6	12	SEARCHIN' (I GOTTA FIND A MAN)	Hazell Dean	Proto	6
7	13	GROOVIN' (YOU'RE THE BEST THING)/BIG BOSS GROOVE	Style Council	Polydor	4
19	14	THINKING OF YOU	Sister Sledge	Cotillion	3
26	15	FAREWELL MY SUMMER LOVE	Michael Jackson	Motown	2
11	16	I FEEL LIKE BUDDY HOLLY	Alvin Stardust	Chrysalis	5
18	[17]	ONE BETTER DAY	Madness	Stiff	3
-	18	I WON'T LET THE SUN GO DOWN ON ME	Nik Kershaw	MCA	1
4	19	THE REFLEX	Duran Duran	EMI	8
31	20	SUSANNA	Art Company	Epic	2
25	21	SO TIRED	Ozzy Osbourne	Epic	3
15	22	I WANT TO BREAK FREE	Queen	EMI	10
29	[23]	ROUGH JUSTICE	Bananarama	London	2
14	24	AUTOMATIC	Pointer Sisters	Planet	9
17	25	RED GUITAR	David Sylvian	Virgin	3
39	26	CHANGE OF HEART	Change	WEA	2
30	[27]	INFATUATION	Rod Stewart	Warner Brothers	2
22	28	AGAINST ALL ODDS (TAKE A LOOK AT ME NOW)	Phil Collins	Virgin	11
23	29	LOVE WARS	Womack and Womack	Elektra	6
20	30	BREAK DANCE PARTY	Break Machine	Record Shack	6
37	[31]	LOVE ALL DAY	Nick Heyward	Arista	2
21	32	FOOTLOOSE	Kenny Loggins	CBS	7
-	33	ABSOLUTE	Scritti Politti	Virgin	1
24	34	ONE LOVE-PEOPLE GET READY	Bob Marley and the Wailers	Island	9
27	35	GOING DOWN TOWN TONIGHT	Status Quo	Vertigo	5
-	36	WHITE LINES (DON'T DON'T DO IT)	Grandmaster Flash and Melle Mel	Sugarhill	1

■George Michael's first of eight number ones either as a soloist or as half of a duo is *Wake Me Up Before You Go Go* (02.06.84) ■ While *Relax* enjoys its 24th week of chart success, another long-running hit makes it debut, *White Lines (Don't Don't Do It)* by Grandmaster Flash and Melle Mel (16.06.84)■

June 1984

□ Highest position disc reached ● Act's first ever week on chart

LW	TW	Title / Artist	Label	Wks
34	37	DANCING IN THE DARK Bruce Springsteen	*CBS*	4
36	38	WHEN AM I GOING TO MAKE A LIVING Sade	*Epic*	3
-	39	TALKING LOUD AND CLEAR Orchestral Manoeuvres In The Dark	*Virgin*	1
-	40	I WANNA BE LOVED Elvis Costello and the Attractions	*F Beat*	1

WEEK ENDING 23 JUNE 1984

LW	TW	Title / Artist	Label	Wks
1	[1]	TWO TRIBES Frankie Goes To Hollywood	*ZTT*	2
2	2	WAKE ME UP BEFORE YOU GO GO Wham!	*Epic*	5
4	[3]	SMALLTOWN BOY Bronski Beat	*Forbidden Fruit*	4
18	4	I WON'T LET THE SUN GO DOWN ON ME Nik Kershaw	*MCA*	2
11	5	RELAX Frankie Goes To Hollywood	*ZTT*	25
3	6	ONLY WHEN YOU LEAVE Spandau Ballet	*Reformation*	3
8	[7]	SAD SONGS (SAY SO MUCH) Elton John	*Rocket*	4
15	8	FAREWELL MY SUMMER LOVE Michael Jackson	*Motown*	3
5	9	HIGH ENERGY Evelyn Thomas	*Record Shack*	6
7	10	PEARL IN THE SHELL Howard Jones	*WEA*	5
14	[11]	THINKING OF YOU Sister Sledge	*Cotillion*	4
20	[12]	SUSANNA Art Company	*Epic*	3
10	13	HEAVEN KNOWS I'M MISERABLE NOW Smiths	*Rough Trade*	4
6	14	DANCING WITH TEARS IN MY EYES Ultravox	*Chrysalis*	6
12	15	SEARCHIN' (I GOTTA FIND A MAN) Hazell Dean	*Proto*	7
9	16	LET'S HEAR IT FOR THE BOY Deniece Williams	*CBS*	7
13	17	GROOVIN' (YOU'RE THE BEST THING)/BIG BOSS GROOVE Style Council	*Polydor*	5
16	18	I FEEL LIKE BUDDY HOLLY Alvin Stardust	*Chrysalis*	6
26	19	CHANGE OF HEART Change	*WEA*	3
21	[20]	SO TIRED Ozzy Osbourne	*Epic*	4
36	21	WHITE LINES (DON'T DON'T DO IT) Grandmaster Flash and Melle Mel	*Sugarhill*	2
33	22	ABSOLUTE Scritti Politti	*Virgin*	2
39	23	TALKING LOUD AND CLEAR Orchestral Manoeuvres In The Dark	*Virgin*	2
-	24	JUMP (FOR MY LOVE) Pointer Sisters	*Planet*	1
17	25	ONE BETTER DAY Madness	*Stiff*	4
23	26	ROUGH JUSTICE Bananarama	*London*	3
19	27	THE REFLEX Duran Duran	*EMI*	9
22	28	I WANT TO BREAK FREE Queen	*EMI*	11
40	29	I WANNA BE LOVED/TURNING THE TOWN RED Elvis Costello and the Attractions	*F Beat*	2
27	30	INFATUATION Rod Stewart	*Warner Brothers*	3
31	[31]	LOVE ALL DAY Nick Heyward	*Arista*	3
24	32	AUTOMATIC Pointer Sisters	*Planet*	10
25	33	RED GUITAR David Sylvian	*Virgin*	4
-	34	STUCK ON YOU Lionel Richie	*Motown*	1
-	35	BREAKIN'...THERE'S NO STOPPING US Ollie and Jerry ●	*Polydor*	1
-	36	TIME AFTER TIME Cyndi Lauper	*Portrait*	1
30	37	BREAK DANCE PARTY Break Machine	*Record Shack*	7
37	38	DANCING IN THE DARK Bruce Springsteen	*CBS*	5
28	39	AGAINST ALL ODDS (TAKE A LOOK AT ME NOW) Phil Collins	*Virgin*	12
-	40	PERFECT SKIN Lloyd Cole and the Commotions ●	*Polydor*	1

WEEK ENDING 30 JUNE 1984

LW	TW	Title / Artist	Label	Wks
1	[1]	TWO TRIBES Frankie Goes To Hollywood	*ZTT*	3
4	[2]	I WON'T LET THE SUN GO DOWN ON ME Nik Kershaw	*MCA*	3
5	3	RELAX Frankie Goes To Hollywood	*ZTT*	26
3	4	SMALLTOWN BOY Bronski Beat	*Forbidden Fruit*	5
2	5	WAKE ME UP BEFORE YOU GO GO Wham!	*Epic*	6
24	[6]	JUMP (FOR MY LOVE) Pointer Sisters	*Planet*	2
8	[7]	FAREWELL MY SUMMER LOVE Michael Jackson	*Motown*	4
35	8	BREAKIN'...THERE'S NO STOPPING US Ollie and Jerry	*Polydor*	2
7	9	SAD SONGS (SAY SO MUCH) Elton John	*Rocket*	5
36	10	TIME AFTER TIME Cyndi Lauper	*Portrait*	2
11	[11]	THINKING OF YOU Sister Sledge	*Cotillion*	5
21	12	WHITE LINES (DON'T DON'T DO IT) Grandmaster Flash and Melle Mel	*Sugarhill*	3
12	13	SUSANNA Art Company	*Epic*	4
9	14	HIGH ENERGY Evelyn Thomas	*Record Shack*	7
23	15	TALKING LOUD AND CLEAR Orchestral Manoeuvres In The Dark	*Virgin*	3
6	16	ONLY WHEN YOU LEAVE Spandau Ballet	*Reformation*	4
19	[17]	CHANGE OF HEART Change	*WEA*	4
34	18	STUCK ON YOU Lionel Richie	*Motown*	2
22	19	ABSOLUTE Scritti Politti	*Virgin*	3
13	20	HEAVEN KNOWS I'M MISERABLE NOW Smiths	*Rough Trade*	5
20	21	SO TIRED Ozzy Osbourne	*Epic*	5
10	22	PEARL IN THE SHELL Howard Jones	*WEA*	6
14	23	DANCING WITH TEARS IN MY EYES Ultravox	*Chrysalis*	7
15	24	SEARCHIN' (I GOTTA FIND A MAN) Hazell Dean	*Proto*	8
29	[25]	I WANNA BE LOVED/TURNING THE TOWN RED Elvis Costello and the Attractions	*F Beat*	3
16	26	LET'S HEAR IT FOR THE BOY Deniece Williams	*CBS*	8
-	27	DANCE ME UP Gary Glitter	*Arista*	1
-	28	LOVE RESURRECTION Alison Moyet ●	*CBS*	1
-	29	LIFE ON YOUR OWN Human League	*Virgin*	1
40	30	PERFECT SKIN Lloyd Cole and the Commotions	*Polydor*	2
-	31	GOODNIGHT SAIGON/LEAVE A TENDER MOMENT ALONE Billy Joel	*CBS*	1
17	32	GROOVIN' (YOU'RE THE BEST THING)/BIG BOSS GROOVE Style Council	*Polydor*	6
-	33	WAITING IN VAIN Bob Marley and the Wailers	*Island*	1
18	34	I FEEL LIKE BUDDY HOLLY Alvin Stardust	*Chrysalis*	7
27	35	THE REFLEX Duran Duran	*EMI*	10
-	36	YOUNG AT HEART Bluebells	*London*	1
31	37	LOVE ALL DAY Nick Heyward	*Arista*	4
25	38	ONE BETTER DAY Madness	*Stiff*	5
30	39	INFATUATION Rod Stewart	*Warner Brothers*	4
-	40	WHAT'S LOVE GOT TO DO WITH IT Tina Turner	*Capitol*	1

WEEK ENDING 7 JULY 1984

LW	TW	Title / Artist	Label	Wks
1	[1]	TWO TRIBES Frankie Goes To Hollywood	*ZTT*	4
3	2	RELAX Frankie Goes To Hollywood	*ZTT*	27
2	3	I WON'T LET THE SUN GO DOWN ON ME Nik Kershaw	*MCA*	4
10	4	TIME AFTER TIME Cyndi Lauper	*Portrait*	3
8	[5]	BREAKIN'...THERE'S NO STOPPING US Ollie and Jerry	*Polydor*	3
6	[6]	JUMP (FOR MY LOVE) Pointer Sisters	*Planet*	3
4	7	SMALLTOWN BOY Bronski Beat	*Forbidden Fruit*	6
7	8	FAREWELL MY SUMMER LOVE Michael Jackson	*Motown*	5
5	9	WAKE ME UP BEFORE YOU GO GO Wham!	*Epic*	7
12	10	WHITE LINES (DON'T DON'T DO IT) Grandmaster Flash and Melle Mel	*Sugarhill*	4
15	[11]	TALKING LOUD AND CLEAR Orchestral Manoeuvres In The Dark	*Virgin*	4
18	[12]	STUCK ON YOU Lionel Richie	*Motown*	3
11	13	THINKING OF YOU Sister Sledge	*Cotillion*	6
28	14	LOVE RESURRECTION Alison Moyet	*CBS*	2
9	15	SAD SONGS (SAY SO MUCH) Elton John	*Rocket*	6
29	[16]	LIFE ON YOUR OWN Human League	*Virgin*	2
19	[17]	ABSOLUTE Scritti Politti	*Virgin*	4
40	18	WHAT'S LOVE GOT TO DO WITH IT Tina Turner	*Capitol*	2
17	19	CHANGE OF HEART Change	*WEA*	5
36	20	YOUNG AT HEART Bluebells	*London*	2
-	21	WHEN DOVES CRY Prince	*Warner Brothers*	1
13	22	SUSANNA Art Company	*Epic*	5
14	23	HIGH ENERGY Evelyn Thomas	*Record Shack*	8
16	24	ONLY WHEN YOU LEAVE Spandau Ballet	*Reformation*	5
27	[25]	DANCE ME UP Gary Glitter	*Arista*	2
30	[26]	PERFECT SKIN Lloyd Cole and the Commotions	*Polydor*	3
25	27	I WANNA BE LOVED/TURNING THE TOWN RED Elvis Costello and the Attractions	*F Beat*	4
-	28	SISTER OF MERCY Thompson Twins	*Arista*	1
31	[29]	GOODNIGHT SAIGON/LEAVE A TENDER MOMENT ALONE Billy Joel	*CBS*	2
21	30	SO TIRED Ozzy Osbourne	*Epic*	6
33	[31]	WAITING IN VAIN Bob Marley and the Wailers	*Island*	2

In these weeks ■ Frankie Goes To Hollywood occupy the top two positions for the first time since John Lennon three and half years earlier (07.07.84) ■ Alison Moyet's debut solo hit is the second chart record to include the word *Resurrection* in the title, after Ashton, Gardner and Dyke's *Resurrection Shuffle*. Both made the top ten (30.06.84)■

LW	TW	Title	Artist	Label	Wks
-	32	LAMENT	Ultravox	*Chrysalis*	1
22	33	PEARL IN THE SHELL	Howard Jones	*WEA*	7
24	34	SEARCHIN' (I GOTTA FIND A MAN)	Hazell Dean	*Proto*	9
20	35	HEAVEN KNOWS I'M MISERABLE NOW	Smiths	*Rough Trade*	6
-	36	SWEET SOMEBODY	Shannon	*Club*	1
-	37	STATE OF SHOCK	Jacksons with Mick Jagger	*Epic*	1
26	38	LET'S HEAR IT FOR THE BOY	Deniece Williams	*CBS*	9
23	39	DANCING WITH TEARS IN MY EYES	Ultravox	*Chrysalis*	8
35	40	THE REFLEX	Duran Duran	*EMI*	11

WEEK ENDING 14 JULY 1984

LW	TW	Title	Artist	Label	Wks
1	[1]	TWO TRIBES	Frankie Goes To Hollywood	*ZTT*	5
2	2	RELAX	Frankie Goes To Hollywood	*ZTT*	28
4	[3]	TIME AFTER TIME	Cyndi Lauper	*Portrait*	4
3	4	I WON'T LET THE SUN GO DOWN ON ME	Nik Kershaw	*MCA*	5
-	5	HOLE IN MY SHOE	neil ●	*WEA*	1
5	6	BREAKIN'...THERE'S NO STOPPING US	Ollie and Jerry	*Polydor*	4
6	7	JUMP (FOR MY LOVE)	Pointer Sisters	*Planet*	4
21	8	WHEN DOVES CRY	Prince	*Warner Brothers*	2
10	9	WHITE LINES (DON'T DON'T DO IT)	Grandmaster Flash and Melle Mel	*Sugarhill*	5
18	10	WHAT'S LOVE GOT TO DO WITH IT	Tina Turner	*Capitol*	3
28	[11]	SISTER OF MERCY	Thompson Twins	*Arista*	2
7	12	SMALLTOWN BOY	Bronski Beat	*Forbidden Fruit*	7
14	13	LOVE RESURRECTION	Alison Moyet	*CBS*	3
20	14	YOUNG AT HEART	Bluebells	*London*	3
11	15	TALKING LOUD AND CLEAR	Orchestral Manoeuvres In The Dark	*Virgin*	5
8	16	FAREWELL MY SUMMER LOVE	Michael Jackson	*Motown*	6
12	17	STUCK ON YOU	Lionel Richie	*Motown*	4
9	18	WAKE ME UP BEFORE YOU GO GO	Wham!	*Epic*	8
13	19	THINKING OF YOU	Sister Sledge	*Cotillion*	7
37	20	STATE OF SHOCK	Jacksons with Mick Jagger	*Epic*	2
16	21	LIFE ON YOUR OWN	Human League	*Virgin*	3
32	[22]	LAMENT	Ultravox	*Chrysalis*	2
15	23	SAD SONGS (SAY SO MUCH)	Elton John	*Rocket*	7
17	24	ABSOLUTE	Scritti Politti	*Virgin*	5
23	25	HIGH ENERGY	Evelyn Thomas	*Record Shack*	9
-	26	SEVEN SEAS	Echo and the Bunnymen	*Korova*	1
19	27	CHANGE OF HEART	Change	*WEA*	6
-	28	EVERYBODY'S LAUGHING	Phil Fearon and Galaxy	*Ensign*	1
36	29	SWEET SOMEBODY	Shannon	*Club*	2
22	30	SUSANNA	Art Company	*Epic*	6
29	31	GOODNIGHT SAIGON/LEAVE A TENDER MOMENT ALONE	Billy Joel	*CBS*	3
26	32	PERFECT SKIN	Lloyd Cole and the Commotions	*Polydor*	4
-	33	DOWN ON THE STREET	Shakatak	*Polydor*	1
31	34	WAITING IN VAIN	Bob Marley and the Wailers	*Island*	3
24	35	ONLY WHEN YOU LEAVE	Spandau Ballet	*Reformation*	6
25	36	DANCE ME UP	Gary Glitter	*Arista*	3
27	37	I WANNA BE LOVED/TURNING THE TOWN RED	Elvis Costello and the Attractions	*F Beat*	5
-	38	YOU THINK YOU'RE A MAN	Divine ●	*Proto*	1
30	39	SO TIRED	Ozzy Osbourne	*Epic*	7
-	40	COME BACK	Mighty Wah!	*Eternal*	1

WEEK ENDING 21 JULY 1984

LW	TW	Title	Artist	Label	Wks
1	[1]	TWO TRIBES	Frankie Goes To Hollywood	*ZTT*	6
5	[2]	HOLE IN MY SHOE	neil	*WEA*	2
2	3	RELAX	Frankie Goes To Hollywood	*ZTT*	29
3	4	TIME AFTER TIME	Cyndi Lauper	*Portrait*	5
8	5	WHEN DOVES CRY	Prince	*Warner Brothers*	3
10	6	WHAT'S LOVE GOT TO DO WITH IT	Tina Turner	*Capitol*	4
4	7	I WON'T LET THE SUN GO DOWN ON ME	Nik Kershaw	*MCA*	6
9	8	WHITE LINES (DON'T DON'T DO IT)	Grandmaster Flash and Melle Mel	*Sugarhill*	6
7	9	JUMP (FOR MY LOVE)	Pointer Sisters	*Planet*	5
14	10	YOUNG AT HEART	Bluebells	*London*	4
11	[11]	SISTER OF MERCY	Thompson Twins	*Arista*	3
13	12	LOVE RESURRECTION	Alison Moyet	*CBS*	4

July 1984

□ Highest position disc reached ● Act's first ever week on chart

LW	TW	Title	Artist	Label	Wks
6	13	BREAKIN'...THERE'S NO STOPPING US	Ollie and Jerry	*Polydor*	5
20	[14]	STATE OF SHOCK	Jacksons with Mick Jagger	*Epic*	3
28	15	EVERYBODY'S LAUGHING	Phil Fearon and Galaxy	*Ensign*	2
15	16	TALKING LOUD AND CLEAR	Orchestral Manoeuvres In The Dark	*Virgin*	6
26	17	SEVEN SEAS	Echo and the Bunnymen	*Korova*	2
17	18	STUCK ON YOU	Lionel Richie	*Motown*	5
12	19	SMALLTOWN BOY	Bronski Beat	*Forbidden Fruit*	8
16	20	FAREWELL MY SUMMER LOVE	Michael Jackson	*Motown*	7
33	21	DOWN ON THE STREET	Shakatak	*Polydor*	2
18	22	WAKE ME UP BEFORE YOU GO GO	Wham!	*Epic*	9
22	23	LAMENT	Ultravox	*Chrysalis*	3
19	24	THINKING OF YOU	Sister Sledge	*Cotillion*	8
29	[25]	SWEET SOMEBODY	Shannon	*Club*	3
38	26	YOU THINK YOU'RE A MAN	Divine	*Proto*	2
23	27	SAD SONGS (SAY SO MUCH)	Elton John	*Rocket*	8
40	28	COME BACK	Mighty Wah!	*Eternal*	2
21	29	LIFE ON YOUR OWN	Human League	*Virgin*	4
-	30	CLOSEST THING TO HEAVEN	Kane Gang ●	*Kitchenware*	1
27	31	CHANGE OF HEART	Change	*WEA*	7
24	32	ABSOLUTE	Scritti Politti	*Virgin*	6
-	33	EYES WITHOUT A FACE	Billy Idol ●	*Chrysalis*	1
-	34	TOSSING AND TURNING	Windjammer ●	*MCA*	1
30	35	SUSANNA	Art Company	*Epic*	7
31	36	GOODNIGHT SAIGON/LEAVE A TENDER MOMENT ALONE	Billy Joel	*CBS*	4
25	37	HIGH ENERGY	Evelyn Thomas	*Record Shack*	10
-	38	ON THE WINGS OF LOVE	Jeffrey Osborne	*A&M*	1
-	39	THE DAY BEFORE YOU CAME	Blancmange	*London*	1
34	40	WAITING IN VAIN	Bob Marley and the Wailers	*Island*	4

WEEK ENDING 28 JULY 1984

LW	TW	Title	Artist	Label	Wks
1	[1]	TWO TRIBES	Frankie Goes To Hollywood	*ZTT*	7
2	[2]	HOLE IN MY SHOE	neil	*WEA*	3
3	3	RELAX	Frankie Goes To Hollywood	*ZTT*	30
5	[4]	WHEN DOVES CRY	Prince	*Warner Brothers*	4
6	5	WHAT'S LOVE GOT TO DO WITH IT	Tina Turner	*Capitol*	5
4	6	TIME AFTER TIME	Cyndi Lauper	*Portrait*	6
8	[7]	WHITE LINES (DON'T DON'T DO IT)	Grandmaster Flash and Melle Mel	*Sugarhill*	7
10	[8]	YOUNG AT HEART	Bluebells	*London*	5
7	9	I WON'T LET THE SUN GO DOWN ON ME	Nik Kershaw	*MCA*	7
12	[10]	LOVE RESURRECTION	Alison Moyet	*CBS*	5
9	11	JUMP (FOR MY LOVE)	Pointer Sisters	*Planet*	6
15	12	EVERYBODY'S LAUGHING	Phil Fearon and Galaxy	*Ensign*	3
11	13	SISTER OF MERCY	Thompson Twins	*Arista*	4
13	14	BREAKIN'...THERE'S NO STOPPING US	Ollie and Jerry	*Polydor*	6
21	15	DOWN ON THE STREET	Shakatak	*Polydor*	3
17	[16]	SEVEN SEAS	Echo and the Bunnymen	*Korova*	3
26	17	YOU THINK YOU'RE A MAN	Divine	*Proto*	3
30	18	CLOSEST THING TO HEAVEN	Kane Gang	*Kitchenware*	2
14	19	STATE OF SHOCK	Jacksons with Mick Jagger	*Epic*	4
28	[20]	COME BACK	Mighty Wah!	*Eternal*	3
33	21	EYES WITHOUT A FACE	Billy Idol	*Chrysalis*	2
39	[22]	THE DAY BEFORE YOU CAME	Blancmange	*London*	2
-	23	IT'S A HARD LIFE	Queen	*EMI*	1
16	24	TALKING LOUD AND CLEAR	Orchestral Manoeuvres In The Dark	*Virgin*	7
25	[25]	SWEET SOMEBODY	Shannon	*Club*	4
19	26	SMALLTOWN BOY	Bronski Beat	*Forbidden Fruit*	9
18	27	STUCK ON YOU	Lionel Richie	*Motown*	6
22	28	WAKE ME UP BEFORE YOU GO GO	Wham!	*Epic*	10
20	29	FAREWELL MY SUMMER LOVE	Michael Jackson	*Motown*	8
24	30	THINKING OF YOU	Sister Sledge	*Cotillion*	9
38	31	ON THE WINGS OF LOVE	Jeffrey Osborne	*A&M*	2
23	32	LAMENT	Ultravox	*Chrysalis*	4

■neil (Nigel Planer as 'The Young Ones' TV hippy) makes the highest chart debut for 30 years with his cover of Traffic's *Hole In My Shoe*. Both versions of the song peaked at number 2 (14.07.84) ■ For five consecutive weeks, the record at no. 11 is at its peak position (21.07.84)■

July 1984

☐ Highest position disc reached ● Act's first ever week on chart

LW	TW	Title	Artist	Label	Wks
34	33	TOSSING AND TURNING	Windjammer	*MCA*	2
-	34	SELF CONTROL	Laura Branigan	*Atlantic*	1
-	35	WHATEVER I DO (WHEREVER I GO)	Hazell Dean	*Proto*	1
27	36	SAD SONGS (SAY SO MUCH)	Elton John	*Rocket*	9
29	37	LIFE ON YOUR OWN	Human League	*Virgin*	5
-	38	AGADOO	Black Lace	*Flair*	1
32	39	ABSOLUTE	Scritti Politti	*Virgin*	7
37	40	HIGH ENERGY	Evelyn Thomas	*Record Shack*	11

WEEK ENDING 4 AUGUST 1984

LW	TW	Title	Artist	Label	Wks
1	1	TWO TRIBES	Frankie Goes To Hollywood	*ZTT*	8
2	2	HOLE IN MY SHOE	neil	*WEA*	4
3	3	RELAX	Frankie Goes To Hollywood	*ZTT*	31
4	4	WHEN DOVES CRY	Prince	*Warner Brothers*	5
5	5	WHAT'S LOVE GOT TO DO WITH IT	Tina Turner	*Capitol*	6
23	6	IT'S A HARD LIFE	Queen	*EMI*	2
7	7	WHITE LINES (DON'T DON'T DO IT)	Grandmaster Flash and Melle Mel	*Sugarhill*	8
6	8	TIME AFTER TIME	Cyndi Lauper	*Portrait*	7
15	9	DOWN ON THE STREET	Shakatak	*Polydor*	4
12	10	EVERYBODY'S LAUGHING	Phil Fearon and Galaxy	*Ensign*	4
8	11	YOUNG AT HEART	Bluebells	*London*	6
-	12	CARELESS WHISPER	George Michael ●	*Epic*	1
35	13	WHATEVER I DO (WHEREVER I GO)	Hazell Dean	*Proto*	2
10	14	LOVE RESURRECTION	Alison Moyet	*CBS*	6
18	15	CLOSEST THING TO HEAVEN	Kane Gang	*Kitchenware*	3
17	16	YOU THINK YOU'RE A MAN	Divine	*Proto*	4
9	17	I WON'T LET THE SUN GO DOWN ON ME	Nik Kershaw	*MCA*	8
21	18	EYES WITHOUT A FACE	Billy Idol	*Chrysalis*	3
38	19	AGADOO	Black Lace	*Flair*	2
31	20	ON THE WINGS OF LOVE	Jeffrey Osborne	*A&M*	3
33	21	TOSSING AND TURNING	Windjammer	*MCA*	3
22	22	THE DAY BEFORE YOU CAME	Blancmange	*London*	3
11	23	JUMP (FOR MY LOVE)	Pointer Sisters	*Planet*	7
20	24	COME BACK	Mighty Wah!	*Eternal*	4
34	25	SELF CONTROL	Laura Branigan	*Atlantic*	2
16	26	SEVEN SEAS	Echo and the Bunnymen	*Korova*	4
13	27	SISTER OF MERCY	Thompson Twins	*Arista*	5
14	28	BREAKIN'...THERE'S NO STOPPING US	Ollie and Jerry	*Polydor*	7
19	29	STATE OF SHOCK	Jacksons with Mick Jagger	*Epic*	5
28	30	WAKE ME UP BEFORE YOU GO GO	Wham!	*Epic*	11
26	31	SMALLTOWN BOY	Bronski Beat	*Forbidden Fruit*	10
-	32	SOME GUYS HAVE ALL THE LUCK	Rod Stewart	*Warner Brothers*	1
27	33	STUCK ON YOU	Lionel Richie	*Motown*	7
24	34	TALKING LOUD AND CLEAR	Orchestral Manoeuvres In The Dark	*Virgin*	8
25	35	SWEET SOMEBODY	Shannon	*Club*	5
-	36	SUNGLASSES	Tracey Ullman	*Stiff*	1
29	37	FAREWELL MY SUMMER LOVE	Michael Jackson	*Motown*	9
30	38	THINKING OF YOU	Sister Sledge	*Cotillion*	10
-	39	LOVE SONGS ARE BACK AGAIN (MEDLEY)	Band Of Gold ●	*RCA*	1
32	40	LAMENT	Ultravox	*Chrysalis*	5

WEEK ENDING 11 AUGUST 1984

LW	TW	Title	Artist	Label	Wks
1	1	TWO TRIBES	Frankie Goes To Hollywood	*ZTT*	9
12	2	CARELESS WHISPER	George Michael	*Epic*	2
5	3	WHAT'S LOVE GOT TO DO WITH IT	Tina Turner	*Capitol*	7
19	4	AGADOO	Black Lace	*Flair*	3
4	5	WHEN DOVES CRY	Prince	*Warner Brothers*	6
3	6	RELAX	Frankie Goes To Hollywood	*ZTT*	32
2	7	HOLE IN MY SHOE	neil	*WEA*	5
13	8	WHATEVER I DO (WHEREVER I GO)	Hazell Dean	*Proto*	3
6	9	IT'S A HARD LIFE	Queen	*EMI*	3
7	10	WHITE LINES (DON'T DON'T DO IT)	Grandmaster Flash and Melle Mel	*Sugarhill*	9
10	11	EVERYBODY'S LAUGHING	Phil Fearon and Galaxy	*Ensign*	5
15	12	CLOSEST THING TO HEAVEN	Kane Gang	*Kitchenware*	4
25	13	SELF CONTROL	Laura Branigan	*Atlantic*	3
9	14	DOWN ON THE STREET	Shakatak	*Polydor*	5
20	15	ON THE WINGS OF LOVE	Jeffrey Osborne	*A&M*	4
8	16	TIME AFTER TIME	Cyndi Lauper	*Portrait*	8
11	17	YOUNG AT HEART	Bluebells	*London*	7
16	18	YOU THINK YOU'RE A MAN	Divine	*Proto*	5
18	19	EYES WITHOUT A FACE	Billy Idol	*Chrysalis*	4
21	20	TOSSING AND TURNING	Windjammer	*MCA*	4
14	21	LOVE RESURRECTION	Alison Moyet	*CBS*	7
22	22	THE DAY BEFORE YOU CAME	Blancmange	*London*	4
-	23	STUCK ON YOU	Trevor Walters	*I&S*	1
23	24	JUMP (FOR MY LOVE)	Pointer Sisters	*Planet*	8
32	25	SOME GUYS HAVE ALL THE LUCK	Rod Stewart	*Warner Brothers*	2
36	26	SUNGLASSES	Tracey Ullman	*Stiff*	2
17	27	I WON'T LET THE SUN GO DOWN ON ME	Nik Kershaw	*MCA*	9
27	28	SISTER OF MERCY	Thompson Twin	*Arista*	6
24	29	COME BACK	Mighty Wah!	*Eternal*	5
39	30	LOVE SONGS ARE BACK AGAIN (MEDLEY)	Band Of Gold	*RCA*	2
26	31	SEVEN SEAS	Echo and the Bunnymen	*Korova*	5
28	32	BREAKIN'...THERE'S NO STOPPING US	Ollie and Jerry	*Polydor*	8
-	33	LIKE TO GET TO KNOW YOU WELL	Howard Jones	*WEA*	1
33	34	STUCK ON YOU	Lionel Richie	*Motown*	8
-	35	NERVOUS SHAKEDOWN	AC/DC	*Atlantic*	1
30	36	WAKE ME UP BEFORE YOU GO GO	Wham!	*Epic*	12
-	37	JUST THE WAY YOU LIKE IT	SOS Band	*Tabu*	1
31	38	SMALLTOWN BOY	Bronski Beat	*Forbidden Fruit*	11
29	39	STATE OF SHOCK	Jacksons with Mick Jagger	*Epic*	6
-	40	THE MORE YOU LIVE THE MORE YOU LOVE	A Flock Of Seagulls	*Jive*	1

WEEK ENDING 18 AUGUST 1984

LW	TW	Title	Artist	Label	Wks
2	1	CARELESS WHISPER	George Michael	*Epic*	3
4	2	AGADOO	Black Lace	*Flair*	4
1	3	TWO TRIBES	Frankie Goes To Hollywood	*ZTT*	10
8	4	WHATEVER I DO (WHEREVER I GO)	Hazell Dean	*Proto*	4
3	5	WHAT'S LOVE GOT TO DO WITH IT	Tina Turner	*Capitol*	8
13	6	SELF CONTROL	Laura Branigan	*Atlantic*	4
6	7	RELAX	Frankie Goes To Hollywood	*ZTT*	33
5	8	WHEN DOVES CRY	Prince	*Warner Brothers*	7
10	9	WHITE LINES (DON'T DON'T DO IT)	Grandmaster Flash and Melle Mel	*Sugarhill*	10
33	10	LIKE TO GET TO KNOW YOU WELL	Howard Jones	*WEA*	2
15	11	ON THE WINGS OF LOVE	Jeffrey Osborne	*A&M*	5
9	12	IT'S A HARD LIFE	Queen	*EMI*	4
7	13	HOLE IN MY SHOE	neil	*WEA*	6
12	14	CLOSEST THING TO HEAVEN	Kane Gang	*Kitchenware*	5
23	15	STUCK ON YOU	Trevor Walters	*I&S*	2
11	16	EVERYBODY'S LAUGHING	Phil Fearon and Galaxy	*Ensign*	6
14	17	DOWN ON THE STREET	Shakatak	*Polydor*	6
20	18	TOSSING AND TURNING	Windjammer	*MCA*	5
26	19	SUNGLASSES	Tracey Ullman	*Stiff*	3
25	20	SOME GUYS HAVE ALL THE LUCK	Rod Stewart	*Warner Brothers*	3
16	21	TIME AFTER TIME	Cyndi Lauper	*Portrait*	9
18	22	YOU THINK YOU'RE A MAN	Divine	*Proto*	6
17	23	YOUNG AT HEART	Bluebells	*London*	8
30	24	LOVE SONGS ARE BACK AGAIN (MEDLEY)	Band Of Gold	*RCA*	3
19	25	EYES WITHOUT A FACE	Billy Idol	*Chrysalis*	5
22	26	THE DAY BEFORE YOU CAME	Blancmange	*London*	5
-	27	2 MINUTES TO MIDNIGHT	Iron Maiden	*EMI*	1
-	28	DR BEAT	Miami Sound Machine ●	*Epic*	1
40	29	THE MORE YOU LIVE THE MORE YOU LOVE	A Flock Of Seagulls	*Jive*	2
-	30	PASSENGERS	Elton John	*Rocket*	1
21	31	LOVE RESURRECTION	Alison Moyet	*CBS*	8

In these weeks ■ *Two Tribes* becomes the first record to spend 9 weeks at number one since *You're The One That I Want* in 1978 (11.08.84) ■ Three consecutive weeks at no. 22 for Blancmange's version of Abba's *The Day Before You Came*. Abba's version only reached no. 32, making Blancmange the only act ever to outperform Abba on the British charts■

LW	TW	Title	Artist	Label	Wks
37	32	JUST THE WAY YOU LIKE IT	SOS Band	*Tabu*	2
27	33	I WON'T LET THE SUN GO DOWN ON ME	Nik Kershaw	*MCA*	10
-	34	I NEED YOU	Pointer Sisters	*Planet*	1
35	35	NERVOUS SHAKEDOWN	AC/DC	*Atlantic*	2
29	36	COME BACK	Mighty Wah!	*Eternal*	6
-	37	THE INK IN THE WELL	David Sylvian	*Virgin*	1
-	38	MOTHERS TALK	Tears For Fears	*Mercury*	1
34	39	STUCK ON YOU	Lionel Richie	*Motown*	9
24	40	JUMP (FOR MY LOVE)	Pointer Sisters	*Planet*	9

LW	TW	*WEEK ENDING* **25 AUGUST 1984**			Wks
1	1	CARELESS WHISPER	George Michael	*Epic*	4
2	2	AGADOO	Black Lace	*Flair*	5
-	3	I JUST CALLED TO SAY I LOVE YOU	Stevie Wonder	*Motown*	1
10	4	LIKE TO GET TO KNOW YOU WELL	Howard Jones	*WEA*	3
3	5	TWO TRIBES	Frankie Goes To Hollywood	*ZTT*	11
6	6	SELF CONTROL	Laura Branigan	*Atlantic*	5
4	7	WHATEVER I DO (WHEREVER I GO)	Hazell Dean	*Proto*	5
5	8	WHAT'S LOVE GOT TO DO WITH IT	Tina Turner	*Capitol*	9
15	9	STUCK ON YOU	Trevor Walters	*I&S*	3
9	10	WHITE LINES (DON'T DON'T DO IT)	Grandmaster Flash and Melle Mel	*Sugarhill*	11
27	11	2 MINUTES TO MIDNIGHT	Iron Maiden	*EMI*	2
7	12	RELAX	Frankie Goes To Hollywood	*ZTT*	34
11	13	ON THE WINGS OF LOVE	Jeffrey Osborne	*A&M*	6
8	14	WHEN DOVES CRY	Prince	*Warner Brothers*	8
30	15	PASSENGERS	Elton John	*Rocket*	2
28	16	DR BEAT	Miami Sound Machine	*Epic*	2
12	17	IT'S A HARD LIFE	Queen	*EMI*	5
19	18	SUNGLASSES	Tracey Ullman	*Stiff*	4
20	19	SOME GUYS HAVE ALL THE LUCK	Rod Stewart	*Warner Brothers*	4
14	20	CLOSEST THING TO HEAVEN	Kane Gang	*Kitchenware*	6
18	21	TOSSING AND TURNING	Windjammer	*MCA*	6
38	22	MOTHERS TALK	Tears For Fears	*Mercury*	2
-	23	I'LL FLY FOR YOU	Spandau Ballet	*Reformation*	1
17	24	DOWN ON THE STREET	Shakatak	*Polydor*	7
13	25	HOLE IN MY SHOE	neil	*WEA*	7
16	26	EVERYBODY'S LAUGHING	Phil Fearon and Galaxy	*Ensign*	7
24	27	LOVE SONGS ARE BACK AGAIN (MEDLEY)	Band Of Gold	*RCA*	4
29	28	THE MORE YOU LIVE THE MORE YOU LOVE	A Flock Of Seagulls	*Jive*	3
34	29	I NEED YOU	Pointer Sisters	*Planet*	2
21	30	TIME AFTER TIME	Cyndi Lauper	*Portrait*	10
22	31	YOU THINK YOU'RE A MAN	Divine	*Proto*	7
23	32	YOUNG AT HEART	Bluebells	*London*	9
26	33	THE DAY BEFORE YOU CAME	Blancmange	*London*	6
25	34	EYES WITHOUT A FACE	Billy Idol	*Chrysalis*	6
39	35	STUCK ON YOU	Lionel Richie	*Motown*	10
37	36	THE INK IN THE WELL	David Sylvian	*Virgin*	2
32	37	JUST THE WAY YOU LIKE IT	SOS Band	*Tabu*	3
33	38	I WON'T LET THE SUN GO DOWN ON ME	Nik Kershaw	*MCA*	11
35	39	NERVOUS SHAKEDOWN	AC/DC	*Atlantic*	3
-	40	ARE YOU READY	Break Machine	*Record Shack*	1

September 1984

□ Highest position disc reached ● Act's first ever week on chart

LW	TW	*WEEK ENDING* **1 SEPTEMBER 1984**			Wks
1	1	CARELESS WHISPER	George Michael	*Epic*	5
3	2	I JUST CALLED TO SAY I LOVE YOU	Stevie Wonder	*Motown*	2
2	3	AGADOO	Black Lace	*Flair*	6
4	4	LIKE TO GET TO KNOW YOU WELL	Howard Jones	*WEA*	4
6	5	SELF CONTROL	Laura Branigan	*Atlantic*	6
15	6	PASSENGERS	Elton John	*Rocket*	3
16	7	DR BEAT	Miami Sound Machine	*Epic*	3
7	8	WHATEVER I DO (WHEREVER I GO)	Hazell Dean	*Proto*	6
5	9	TWO TRIBES	Frankie Goes To Hollywood	*ZTT*	12
9	10	STUCK ON YOU	Trevor Walters	*I&S*	4
23	11	I'LL FLY FOR YOU	Spandau Ballet	*Reformation*	2
8	12	WHAT'S LOVE GOT TO DO WITH IT	Tina Turner	*Capitol*	10
10	13	WHITE LINES (DON'T DON'T DO IT)	Grandmaster Flash and Melle Mel	*Sugarhill*	12
11	14	2 MINUTES TO MIDNIGHT	Iron Maiden	*EMI*	3
19	15	SOME GUYS HAVE ALL THE LUCK	Rod Stewart	*Warner Brothers*	5
13	16	ON THE WINGS OF LOVE	Jeffrey Osborne	*A&M*	7
22	17	MOTHERS TALK	Tears For Fears	*Mercury*	3
-	18	GHOSTBUSTERS	Ray Parker Jr ●	*Arista*	1
14	19	WHEN DOVES CRY	Prince	*Warner Brothers*	9
12	20	RELAX	Frankie Goes To Hollywood	*ZTT*	35
18	21	SUNGLASSES	Tracey Ullman	*Stiff*	5
-	22	BIG IN JAPAN	Alphaville ●	*WEA*	1
-	23	WILLIAM IT WAS REALLY NOTHING	Smiths	*Rough Trade*	1
-	24	MASTER AND SERVANT	Depeche Mode	*Mute*	1
29	25	I NEED YOU	Pointer Sisters	*Planet*	3
28	26	THE MORE YOU LIVE THE MORE YOU LOVE	A Flock Of Seagulls	*Jive*	4
27	27	LOVE SONGS ARE BACK AGAIN (MEDLEY)	Band Of Gold	*RCA*	5
17	28	IT'S A HARD LIFE	Queen	*EMI*	6
40	29	ARE YOU READY	Break Machine	*Record Shack*	2
20	30	CLOSEST THING TO HEAVEN	Kane Gang	*Kitchenware*	7
26	31	EVERYBODY'S LAUGHING	Phil Fearon and Galaxy	*Ensign*	8
-	32	MADAM BUTTERFLY (UN BEL DI VEDREMO)	Malcolm McLaren	*Charisma*	1
21	33	TOSSING AND TURNING	Windjammer	*MCA*	7
-	34	TALKING IN YOUR SLEEP	Bucks Fizz	*RCA*	1
25	35	HOLE IN MY SHOE	neil	*WEA*	8
24	36	DOWN ON THE STREET	Shakatak	*Polydor*	8
-	37	HOT WATER	Level 42	*Polydor*	1
31	38	YOU THINK YOU'RE A MAN	Divine	*Proto*	8
-	39	SUNSET NOW	Heaven 17	*Virgin*	1
-	40	GIRL YOU'RE SO TOGETHER	Michael Jackson	*Motown*	1

LW	TW	*WEEK ENDING* **8 SEPTEMBER 1984**			Wks
2	1	I JUST CALLED TO SAY I LOVE YOU	Stevie Wonder	*Motown*	3
1	2	CARELESS WHISPER	George Michael	*Epic*	6
3	3	AGADOO	Black Lace	*Flair*	7
4	4	LIKE TO GET TO KNOW YOU WELL	Howard Jones	*WEA*	5
6	5	PASSENGERS	Elton John	*Rocket*	4
18	6	GHOSTBUSTERS	Ray Parker Jr	*Arista*	2
7	7	DR BEAT	Miami Sound Machine	*Epic*	4
5	8	SELF CONTROL	Laura Branigan	*Atlantic*	7
11	9	I'LL FLY FOR YOU	Spandau Ballet	*Reformation*	3
8	10	WHATEVER I DO (WHEREVER I GO)	Hazell Dean	*Proto*	7
22	11	BIG IN JAPAN	Alphaville	*WEA*	2
24	12	MASTER AND SERVANT	Depeche Mode	*Mute*	2
9	13	TWO TRIBES	Frankie Goes To Hollywood	*ZTT*	13
17	14	MOTHERS TALK	Tears For Fears	*Mercury*	4
32	15	MADAM BUTTERFLY (UN BEL DI VEDREMO)	Malcolm McLaren	*Charisma*	2
10	16	STUCK ON YOU	Trevor Walters	*I&S*	5
23	17	WILLIAM IT WAS REALLY NOTHING	Smiths	*Rough Trade*	2
13	18	WHITE LINES (DON'T DON'T DO IT)	Grandmaster Flash and Melle Mel	*Sugarhill*	13
12	19	WHAT'S LOVE GOT TO DO WITH IT	Tina Turner	*Capitol*	11
15	20	SOME GUYS HAVE ALL THE LUCK	Rod Stewart	*Warner Brothers*	6
34	21	TALKING IN YOUR SLEEP	Bucks Fizz	*RCA*	2
20	22	RELAX	Frankie Goes To Hollywood	*ZTT*	36
16	23	ON THE WINGS OF LOVE	Jeffrey Osborne	*A&M*	8
19	24	WHEN DOVES CRY	Prince	*Warner Brothers*	10
14	25	2 MINUTES TO MIDNIGHT	Iron Maiden	*EMI*	4
37	26	HOT WATER	Level 42	*Polydor*	2
29	27	ARE YOU READY	Break Machine	*Record Shack*	3
39	28	SUNSET NOW	Heaven 17	*Virgin*	2
25	29	I NEED YOU	Pointer Sisters	*Planet*	4
21	30	SUNGLASSES	Tracey Ullman	*Stiff*	6

■ 18 years and 218 days after his chart debut, and in his 301st week of chart success, Stevie Wonder finally achieves a solo number one hit (08.09.84) ■ Miami Sound Machine have Gloria Estefan as their lead singer, but she does not get top billing on this first hit (08.09.84) ■

September 1984

□ Highest position disc reached ● Act's first ever week on chart

LW	TW	Title	Artist	Label	Wks
26	31	THE MORE YOU LIVE THE MORE YOU LOVE	A Flock Of Seagulls	*Jive*	5
-	32	LOST IN MUSIC	Sister Sledge	*Cotillion*	1
40	[33]	GIRL YOU'RE SO TOGETHER	Michael Jackson	*Motown*	2
28	34	IT'S A HARD LIFE	Queen	*EMI*	7
27	35	LOVE SONGS ARE BACK AGAIN (MEDLEY)	Band Of Gold	*RCA*	6
30	36	CLOSEST THING TO HEAVEN	Kane Gang	*Kitchenware*	8
-	37	TOUR DE FRANCE	Kraftwerk	*EMI*	1
-	38	TORTURE	Jacksons	*Epic*	1
-	39	ALL I NEED IS EVERYTHING	Aztec Camera	*WEA*	1
31	40	EVERYBODY'S LAUGHING	Phil Fearon and Galaxy	*Ensign*	9

WEEK ENDING 15 SEPTEMBER 1984

LW	TW	Title	Artist	Label	Wks
1	[1]	I JUST CALLED TO SAY I LOVE YOU	Stevie Wonder	*Motown*	4
2	2	CARELESS WHISPER	George Michael	*Epic*	7
6	3	GHOSTBUSTERS	Ray Parker Jr	*Arista*	3
3	4	AGADOO	Black Lace	*Flair*	8
4	5	LIKE TO GET TO KNOW YOU WELL	Howard Jones	*WEA*	6
5	6	PASSENGERS	Elton John	*Rocket*	5
7	7	DR BEAT	Miami Sound Machine	*Epic*	5
-	8	PRIDE (IN THE NAME OF LOVE)	U2	*Island*	1
11	9	BIG IN JAPAN	Alphaville	*WEA*	3
8	10	SELF CONTROL	Laura Branigan	*Atlantic*	8
12	11	MASTER AND SERVANT	Depeche Mode	*Mute*	3
9	12	I'LL FLY FOR YOU	Spandau Ballet	*Reformation*	4
15	[13]	MADAM BUTTERFLY (UN BEL DI VEDREMO)	Malcolm McLaren	*Charisma*	3
32	14	LOST IN MUSIC	Sister Sledge	*Cotillion*	2
21	[15]	TALKING IN YOUR SLEEP	Bucks Fizz	*RCA*	3
10	16	WHATEVER I DO (WHEREVER I GO)	Hazell Dean	*Proto*	8
13	17	TWO TRIBES	Frankie Goes To Hollywood	*ZTT*	14
14	18	MOTHERS TALK	Tears For Fears	*Mercury*	5
26	19	HOT WATER	Level 42	*Polydor*	3
18	20	WHITE LINES (DON'T DON'T DO IT)	Grandmaster Flash and Melle Mel	*Sugarhill*	14
17	21	WILLIAM IT WAS REALLY NOTHING	Smiths	*Rough Trade*	3
16	22	STUCK ON YOU	Trevor Walters	*I&S*	6
-	23	A LETTER TO YOU	Shakin' Stevens	*Epic*	1
28	[24]	SUNSET NOW	Heaven 17	*Virgin*	3
20	25	SOME GUYS HAVE ALL THE LUCK	Rod Stewart	*Warner Brothers*	7
38	[26]	TORTURE	Jacksons	*Epic*	2
19	27	WHAT'S LOVE GOT TO DO WITH IT	Tina Turner	*Capitol*	12
37	28	TOUR DE FRANCE	Kraftwerk	*EMI*	2
22	29	RELAX	Frankie Goes To Hollywood	*ZTT*	37
29	30	I NEED YOU	Pointer Sisters	*Planet*	5
27	31	ARE YOU READY	Break Machine	*Record Shack*	4
24	32	WHEN DOVES CRY	Prince	*Warner Brothers*	11
-	33	TESLA GIRLS	Orchestral Manoeuvres In The Dark	*Virgin*	1
39	[34]	ALL I NEED IS EVERYTHING	Aztec Camera	*WEA*	2
23	35	ON THE WINGS OF LOVE	Jeffrey Osborne	*A&M*	9
31	36	THE MORE YOU LIVE THE MORE YOU LOVE	A Flock Of Seagulls	*Jive*	6
33	37	GIRL YOU'RE SO TOGETHER	Michael Jackson	*Motown*	3
-	38	HUMAN RACING	Nik Kershaw	*MCA*	1
25	39	2 MINUTES TO MIDNIGHT	Iron Maiden	*EMI*	5
-	40	MR SOLITAIRE	Animal Nightlife ●	*Island*	1

WEEK ENDING 22 SEPTEMBER 1984

LW	TW	Title	Artist	Label	Wks
1	[1]	I JUST CALLED TO SAY I LOVE YOU	Stevie Wonder	*Motown*	5
3	[2]	GHOSTBUSTERS	Ray Parker Jr	*Arista*	4
2	3	CARELESS WHISPER	George Michael	*Epic*	8
8	4	PRIDE (IN THE NAME OF LOVE)	U2	*Island*	2
4	5	AGADOO	Black Lace	*Flair*	9
7	[6]	DR BEAT	Miami Sound Machine	*Epic*	6
14	7	LOST IN MUSIC	Sister Sledge	*Cotillion*	3
9	[8]	BIG IN JAPAN	Alphaville	*WEA*	4
11	[9]	MASTER AND SERVANT	Depeche Mode	*Mute*	4
6	10	PASSENGERS	Elton John	*Rocket*	6
23	11	A LETTER TO YOU	Shakin' Stevens	*Epic*	2
5	12	LIKE TO GET TO KNOW YOU WELL	Howard Jones	*WEA*	7
13	[13]	MADAM BUTTERFLY (UN BEL DI VEDREMO)	Malcolm McLaren	*Charisma*	4
10	14	SELF CONTROL	Laura Branigan	*Atlantic*	9
12	15	I'LL FLY FOR YOU	Spandau Ballet	*Reformation*	5
15	16	TALKING IN YOUR SLEEP	Bucks Fizz	*RCA*	4
-	17	BLUE JEAN	David Bowie	*EMI America*	1
19	[18]	HOT WATER	Level 42	*Polydor*	4
-	19	HAMMER TO FALL	Queen	*EMI*	1
38	20	HUMAN RACING	Nik Kershaw	*MCA*	2
33	[21]	TESLA GIRLS	Orchestral Manoeuvres In The Dark	*Virgin*	2
-	22	WHY	Bronski Beat	*Forbidden Fruit*	1
20	23	WHITE LINES (DON'T DON'T DO IT)	Grandmaster Flash and Melle Mel	*Sugarhill*	15
28	[24]	TOUR DE FRANCE	Kraftwerk	*EMI*	3
-	25	PURPLE RAIN	Prince and the Revolution	*Warner Brothers*	1
26	[26]	TORTURE	Jacksons	*Epic*	3
-	27	LOVE KILLS	Freddie Mercury ●	*CBS*	1
-	28	APOLLO 9	Adam Ant	*CBS*	1
17	29	TWO TRIBES	Frankie Goes To Hollywood	*ZTT*	15
18	30	MOTHERS TALK	Tears For Fears	*Mercury*	6
24	31	SUNSET NOW	Heaven 17	*Virgin*	4
16	32	WHATEVER I DO (WHEREVER I GO)	Hazell Dean	*Proto*	9
-	33	IF IT HAPPENS AGAIN	UB40	*DEP International*	1
-	34	SMOOTH OPERATOR	Sade	*Epic*	1
22	35	STUCK ON YOU	Trevor Walters	*I&S*	7
40	36	MR SOLITAIRE	Animal Nightlife	*Island*	2
34	37	ALL I NEED IS EVERYTHING/JUMP	Aztec Camera	*WEA*	3
21	38	WILLIAM IT WAS REALLY NOTHING	Smiths	*Rough Trade*	4
-	39	THE MEDICINE SONG	Stephanie Mills	*Club*	1
27	40	WHAT'S LOVE GOT TO DO WITH IT	Tina Turner	*Capitol*	13

WEEK ENDING 29 SEPTEMBER 1984

LW	TW	Title	Artist	Label	Wks
1	[1]	I JUST CALLED TO SAY I LOVE YOU	Stevie Wonder	*Motown*	6
2	[2]	GHOSTBUSTERS	Ray Parker Jr	*Arista*	5
4	[3]	PRIDE (IN THE NAME OF LOVE)	U2	*Island*	3
7	[4]	LOST IN MUSIC	Sister Sledge	*Cotillion*	4
3	5	CARELESS WHISPER	George Michael	*Epic*	9
17	[6]	BLUE JEAN	David Bowie	*EMI America*	2
22	7	WHY	Bronski Beat	*Forbidden Fruit*	2
5	8	AGADOO	Black Lace	*Flair*	10
8	9	BIG IN JAPAN	Alphaville	*WEA*	5
11	[10]	A LETTER TO YOU	Shakin' Stevens	*Epic*	3
6	11	DR BEAT	Miami Sound Machine	*Epic*	7
27	12	LOVE KILLS	Freddie Mercury	*CBS*	2
19	[13]	HAMMER TO FALL	Queen	*EMI*	2
9	14	MASTER AND SERVANT	Depeche Mode	*Mute*	5
28	15	APOLLO 9	Adam Ant	*CBS*	2
25	16	PURPLE RAIN	Prince and the Revolution	*Warner Brothers*	2
33	17	IF IT HAPPENS AGAIN	UB40	*DEP International*	2
13	18	MADAM BUTTERFLY (UN BEL DI VEDREMO)	Malcolm McLaren	*Charisma*	5
20	[19]	HUMAN RACING	Nik Kershaw	*MCA*	3
12	20	LIKE TO GET TO KNOW YOU WELL	Howard Jones	*WEA*	8
18	21	HOT WATER	Level 42	*Polydor*	5
10	22	PASSENGERS	Elton John	*Rocket*	7
16	23	TALKING IN YOUR SLEEP	Bucks Fizz	*RCA*	5
14	24	SELF CONTROL	Laura Branigan	*Atlantic*	10
21	25	TESLA GIRLS	Orchestral Manoeuvres In The Dark	*Virgin*	3
15	26	I'LL FLY FOR YOU	Spandau Ballet	*Reformation*	6
-	27	EAST OF EDEN	Big Country	*Mercury*	1
24	28	TOUR DE FRANCE	Kraftwerk	*EMI*	4
34	29	SMOOTH OPERATOR	Sade	*Epic*	2
26	30	TORTURE	Jacksons	*Epic*	4
23	31	WHITE LINES (DON'T DON'T DO IT)	Grandmaster Flash and Melle Mel	*Sugarhill*	16
36	32	MR SOLITAIRE	Animal Nightlife	*Island*	3
39	33	THE MEDICINE SONG	Stephanie Mills	*Club*	2

In these weeks ■ After 37 weeks in the Top 40, *Relax* drops out of sight, but it goes on to clock up a full 52 weeks in the Top 75 (15.09.84) ■ Three other records which spent over 30 weeks in the Top 75 are on the chart this week, *Ghostbusters* at no. 3, *Agadoo* at no. 4 and *White Lines (Don't Don't Do It)* at no. 20 (15.09.84)■

October 1984

☐ Highest position disc reached ● Act's first ever week on chart

LW	TW	Title / Artist	Label	Wks
29	34	TWO TRIBES Frankie Goes To Hollywood	ZTT	16
32	35	WHATEVER I DO (WHEREVER I GO) Hazell Dean	Proto	10
-	36	MYSTERY Dio ●	Vertigo	1
-	37	DRIVE Cars	Elektra	1
-	[38]	CATH/WILL SHE ALWAYS BE WAITING Bluebells	London	1
-	39	TOGETHER IN ELECTRIC DREAMS Giorgio Moroder and Philip Oakey ●	Virgin	1
30	40	MOTHERS TALK Tears For Fears	Mercury	7

WEEK ENDING 6 OCTOBER 1984

LW	TW	Title / Artist	Label	Wks
1	[1]	I JUST CALLED TO SAY I LOVE YOU Stevie Wonder	Motown	7
2	[2]	GHOSTBUSTERS Ray Parker Jr	Arista	6
-	3	THE WAR SONG Culture Club	Virgin	1
3	4	PRIDE (IN THE NAME OF LOVE) U2	Island	4
4	5	LOST IN MUSIC Sister Sledge	Cotillion	5
7	[6]	WHY Bronski Beat	Forbidden Fruit	3
6	7	BLUE JEAN David Bowie	EMI America	3
16	[8]	PURPLE RAIN Prince and the Revolution	Warner Brothers	3
17	[9]	IF IT HAPPENS AGAIN UB40	DEP International	3
12	[10]	LOVE KILLS Freddie Mercury	CBS	3
5	11	CARELESS WHISPER George Michael	Epic	10
10	12	A LETTER TO YOU Shakin' Stevens	Epic	4
15	[13]	APOLLO 9 Adam Ant	CBS	3
9	14	BIG IN JAPAN Alphaville	WEA	6
37	15	DRIVE Cars	Elektra	2
8	16	AGADOO Black Lace	Flair	11
27	[17]	EAST OF EDEN Big Country	Mercury	2
11	18	DR BEAT Miami Sound Machine	Epic	8
13	19	HAMMER TO FALL Queen	EMI	3
19	20	HUMAN RACING Nik Kershaw	MCA	4
39	21	TOGETHER IN ELECTRIC DREAMS Giorgio Moroder and Philip Oakey	Virgin	2
29	22	SMOOTH OPERATOR Sade	Epic	3
18	23	MADAM BUTTERFLY (UN BEL DI VEDREMO) Malcolm McLaren	Charisma	6
14	24	MASTER AND SERVANT Depeche Mode	Mute	6
32	[25]	MR SOLITAIRE Animal Nightlife	Island	4
25	26	TESLA GIRLS Orchestral Manoeuvres In The Dark	Virgin	4
21	27	HOT WATER Level 42	Polydor	6
-	28	NO MORE LONELY NIGHTS (BALLAD) Paul McCartney	Parlophone	1
33	[29]	THE MEDICINE SONG Stephanie Mills	Club	3
22	30	PASSENGERS Elton John	Rocket	8
20	31	LIKE TO GET TO KNOW YOU WELL Howard Jones	WEA	9
-	32	SKIN DEEP Stranglers	Epic	1
24	33	SELF CONTROL Laura Branigan	Atlantic	11
36	[34]	MYSTERY Dio	Vertigo	2
23	35	TALKING IN YOUR SLEEP Bucks Fizz	RCA	6
26	36	I'LL FLY FOR YOU Spandau Ballet	Reformation	7
28	37	TOUR DE FRANCE Kraftwerk	EMI	5
-	38	MISSING YOU John Waite ●	EMI America	1
31	39	WHITE LINES (DON'T DON'T DO IT) Grandmaster Flash and Melle Mel	Sugarhill	17
38	40	CATH/WILL SHE ALWAYS BE WAITING Bluebells	London	2

WEEK ENDING 13 OCTOBER 1984

LW	TW	Title / Artist	Label	Wks
1	[1]	I JUST CALLED TO SAY I LOVE YOU Stevie Wonder	Motown	8
3	[2]	THE WAR SONG Culture Club	Virgin	2
-	3	FREEDOM Wham!	Epic	1
2	4	GHOSTBUSTERS Ray Parker Jr	Arista	7
15	[5]	DRIVE Cars	Elektra	3
28	6	NO MORE LONELY NIGHTS (BALLAD) Paul McCartney	Parlophone	2
6	7	WHY Bronski Beat	Forbidden Fruit	4
4	8	PRIDE (IN THE NAME OF LOVE) U2	Island	5
21	9	TOGETHER IN ELECTRIC DREAMS Giorgio Moroder and Philip Oakey	Virgin	3
8	10	PURPLE RAIN Prince and the Revolution	Warner Brothers	4
5	11	LOST IN MUSIC Sister Sledge	Cotillion	6
9	12	IF IT HAPPENS AGAIN UB40	DEP International	4
-	13	SHOUT TO THE TOP Style Council	Polydor	1
10	14	LOVE KILLS Freddie Mercury	CBS	4
13	15	APOLLO 9 Adam Ant	CBS	4
38	16	MISSING YOU John Waite	EMI America	2
7	17	BLUE JEAN David Bowie	EMI America	4
11	18	CARELESS WHISPER George Michael	Epic	11
12	19	A LETTER TO YOU Shakin' Stevens	Epic	5
-	20	I'M GONNA TEAR YOUR PLAYHOUSE DOWN Paul Young	CBS	1
32	21	SKIN DEEP Stranglers	Epic	2
22	22	SMOOTH OPERATOR Sade	Epic	4
14	23	BIG IN JAPAN Alphaville	WEA	7
17	24	EAST OF EDEN Big Country	Mercury	3
16	25	AGADOO Black Lace	Flair	12
18	26	DR BEAT Miami Sound Machine	Epic	9
25	27	MR SOLITAIRE Animal Nightlife	Island	5
19	28	HAMMER TO FALL Queen	EMI	4
29	[29]	THE MEDICINE SONG Stephanie Mills	Club	4
20	30	HUMAN RACING Nik Kershaw	MCA	5
23	31	MADAM BUTTERFLY (UN BEL DI VEDREMO) Malcolm McLaren	Charisma	7
27	32	HOT WATER Level 42	Polydor	7
24	33	MASTER AND SERVANT Depeche Mode	Mute	7
-	34	MODERN GIRL Meat Loaf	Arista	1
-	35	ALL CRIED OUT Alison Moyet	CBS	1
26	36	TESLA GIRLS Orchestral Manoeuvres In The Dark	Virgin	5
33	37	SELF CONTROL Laura Branigan	Atlantic	12
-	[38]	COVER ME Bruce Springsteen	CBS	1
30	39	PASSENGERS Elton John	Rocket	9
31	40	LIKE TO GET TO KNOW YOU WELL Howard Jones	WEA	10

WEEK ENDING 20 OCTOBER 1984

LW	TW	Title / Artist	Label	Wks
3	[1]	FREEDOM Wham!	Epic	2
1	2	I JUST CALLED TO SAY I LOVE YOU Stevie Wonder	Motown	9
2	3	THE WAR SONG Culture Club	Virgin	3
6	4	NO MORE LONELY NIGHTS (BALLAD) Paul McCartney	Parlophone	3
9	5	TOGETHER IN ELECTRIC DREAMS Giorgio Moroder and Philip Oakey	Virgin	4
5	6	DRIVE Cars	Elektra	4
13	[7]	SHOUT TO THE TOP Style Council	Polydor	2
4	8	GHOSTBUSTERS Ray Parker Jr	Arista	8
20	[9]	I'M GONNA TEAR YOUR PLAYHOUSE DOWN Paul Young	CBS	2
16	10	MISSING YOU John Waite	EMI America	3
7	11	WHY Bronski Beat	Forbidden Fruit	5
35	12	ALL CRIED OUT Alison Moyet	CBS	2
8	13	PRIDE (IN THE NAME OF LOVE) U2	Island	6
10	14	PURPLE RAIN Prince and the Revolution	Warner Brothers	5
21	[15]	SKIN DEEP Stranglers	Epic	3
12	16	IF IT HAPPENS AGAIN UB40	DEP International	5
11	17	LOST IN MUSIC Sister Sledge	Cotillion	7
14	18	LOVE KILLS Freddie Mercury	CBS	5
22	[19]	SMOOTH OPERATOR Sade	Epic	5
18	20	CARELESS WHISPER George Michael	Epic	12
15	21	APOLLO 9 Adam Ant	CBS	5
-	22	I FEEL FOR YOU Chaka Khan	Warner Brothers	1
-	23	LOVE'S GREAT ADVENTURE Ultravox	Chrysalis	1
25	24	AGADOO Black Lace	Flair	13
-	25	HIGHLY STRUNG Spandau Ballet	Reformation	1
34	26	MODERN GIRL Meat Loaf	Arista	2
17	27	BLUE JEAN David Bowie	EMI America	5
19	28	A LETTER TO YOU Shakin' Stevens	Epic	6
29	[29]	THE MEDICINE SONG Stephanie Mills	Club	5
-	30	TOO LATE FOR GOODBYES Julian Lennon ●	Charisma	1
23	31	BIG IN JAPAN Alphaville	WEA	8
27	32	MR SOLITAIRE Animal Nightlife	Island	6
-	33	THE SECOND TIME Kim Wilde	MCA	1
24	34	EAST OF EDEN Big Country	Mercury	4

■Alison Moyet's *All Cried Out* is the first record to climb from the number 35 position since Ollie and Jerry's only top 40 hit, *Breakin' ... There's No Stopping Us* leapt from 35 to 8 seventeen weeks earlier (20.10.84) ■ Three weeks at no. 29 for Stephanie Mills' *Medicine Song* (13.10.84)■

October 1984

□ Highest position disc reached ● Act's first ever week on chart

LW	TW	Title	Artist	Label	Wks
26	35	DR BEAT	Miami Sound Machine	Epic	10
-	36	PENNY LOVER	Lionel Richie	Motown	1
28	37	HAMMER TO FALL	Queen	EMI	5
38	38	COVER ME	Bruce Springsteen	CBS	2
-	39	GOTTA GET YOU HOME TONIGHT	Eugene Wilde ●	Fourth & Broadway	1
-	40	LISTEN TO YOUR FATHER	Feargal Sharkey ●	Zarjazz	1

WEEK ENDING 27 OCTOBER 1984

LW	TW	Title	Artist	Label	Wks
1	1	FREEDOM	Wham!	Epic	3
4	2	NO MORE LONELY NIGHTS (BALLAD)	Paul McCartney	Parlophone	4
5	3	TOGETHER IN ELECTRIC DREAMS	Giorgio Moroder and Philip Oakey	Virgin	5
2	4	I JUST CALLED TO SAY I LOVE YOU	Stevie Wonder	Motown	10
22	5	I FEEL FOR YOU	Chaka Khan	Warner Brothers	2
3	6	THE WAR SONG	Culture Club	Virgin	4
6	7	DRIVE	Cars	Elektra	5
12	8	ALL CRIED OUT	Alison Moyet	CBS	3
10	9	MISSING YOU	John Waite	EMI America	4
7	10	SHOUT TO THE TOP	Style Council	Polydor	3
9	11	I'M GONNA TEAR YOUR PLAYHOUSE DOWN	Paul Young	CBS	3
30	12	TOO LATE FOR GOODBYES	Julian Lennon	Charisma	2
23	13	LOVE'S GREAT ADVENTURE	Ultravox	Chrysalis	2
8	14	GHOSTBUSTERS	Ray Parker Jr	Arista	9
25	15	HIGHLY STRUNG	Spandau Ballet	Reformation	2
11	16	WHY	Bronski Beat	Forbidden Fruit	6
26	17	MODERN GIRL	Meat Loaf	Arista	3
15	18	SKIN DEEP	Stranglers	Epic	4
13	19	PRIDE (IN THE NAME OF LOVE)	U2	Island	7
19	20	SMOOTH OPERATOR	Sade	Epic	6
14	21	PURPLE RAIN	Prince and the Revolution	Warner Brothers	6
36	22	PENNY LOVER	Lionel Richie	Motown	2
-	23	THE WANDERER	Status Quo	Vertigo	1
17	24	LOST IN MUSIC	Sister Sledge	Cotillion	8
-	25	CARIBBEAN QUEEN (NO MORE LOVE ON THE RUN)	Billy Ocean	Jive	1
20	26	CARELESS WHISPER	George Michael	Epic	13
16	27	IF IT HAPPENS AGAIN	UB40	DEP International	6
18	28	LOVE KILLS	Freddie Mercury	CBS	6
33	29	THE SECOND TIME	Kim Wilde	MCA	2
40	30	LISTEN TO YOUR FATHER	Feargal Sharkey	Zarjazz	2
24	31	AGADOO	Black Lace	Flair	14
39	32	GOTTA GET YOU HOME TONIGHT	Eugene Wilde	Fourth & Broadway	2
21	33	APOLLO 9	Adam Ant	CBS	6
-	34	GIMME ALL YOUR LOVIN'	ZZ Top ●	Warner Brothers	1
29	35	THE MEDICINE SONG	Stephanie Mills	Club	6
32	36	MR SOLITAIRE	Animal Nightlife	Island	7
28	37	A LETTER TO YOU	Shakin' Stevens	Epic	7
31	38	BIG IN JAPAN	Alphaville	WEA	9
27	39	BLUE JEAN	David Bowie	EMI America	6
-	40	NEVER ENDING STORY	Limahl	EMI	1

WEEK ENDING 3 NOVEMBER 1984

LW	TW	Title	Artist	Label	Wks
1	1	FREEDOM	Wham!	Epic	4
5	2	I FEEL FOR YOU	Chaka Khan	Warner Brothers	3
2	3	NO MORE LONELY NIGHTS (BALLAD)	Paul McCartney	Parlophone	5
3	4	TOGETHER IN ELECTRIC DREAMS	Giorgio Moroder and Philip Oakey	Virgin	6
-	5	THE WILD BOYS	Duran Duran	Parlophone	1
12	6	TOO LATE FOR GOODBYES	Julian Lennon	Charisma	3
23	7	THE WANDERER	Status Quo	Vertigo	2
8	8	ALL CRIED OUT	Alison Moyet	CBS	4
4	9	I JUST CALLED TO SAY I LOVE YOU	Stevie Wonder	Motown	11
9	10	MISSING YOU	John Waite	EMI America	5
7	11	DRIVE	Cars	Elektra	6
25	12	CARIBBEAN QUEEN (NO MORE LOVE ON THE RUN)	Billy Ocean	Jive	2
13	13	LOVE'S GREAT ADVENTURE	Ultravox	Chrysalis	3
6	14	THE WAR SONG	Culture Club	Virgin	5
34	15	GIMME ALL YOUR LOVIN'	ZZ Top	Warner Brothers	2
10	16	SHOUT TO THE TOP	Style Council	Polydor	4
17	17	MODERN GIRL	Meat Loaf	Arista	4
22	18	PENNY LOVER	Lionel Richie	Motown	3
14	19	GHOSTBUSTERS	Ray Parker Jr	Arista	10
40	20	NEVER ENDING STORY	Limahl	EMI	2
15	21	HIGHLY STRUNG	Spandau Ballet	Reformation	3
11	22	I'M GONNA TEAR YOUR PLAYHOUSE DOWN	Paul Young	CBS	4
30	23	LISTEN TO YOUR FATHER	Feargal Sharkey	Zarjazz	3
32	24	GOTTA GET YOU HOME TONIGHT	Eugene Wilde	Fourth & Broadway	3
19	25	PRIDE (IN THE NAME OF LOVE)	U2	Island	8
18	26	SKIN DEEP	Stranglers	Epic	5
16	27	WHY	Bronski Beat	Forbidden Fruit	7
-	28	I'M SO EXCITED	Pointer Sisters	Planet	1
29	29	THE SECOND TIME	Kim Wilde	MCA	3
20	30	SMOOTH OPERATOR	Sade	Epic	7
24	31	LOST IN MUSIC	Sister Sledge	Cotillion	9
-	32	ACES HIGH	Iron Maiden	EMI	1
21	33	PURPLE RAIN	Prince and the Revolution	Warner Brothers	7
26	34	CARELESS WHISPER	George Michael	Epic	14
31	35	AGADOO	Black Lace	Flair	15
-	36	THIS IS MINE	Heaven 17	Virgin	1
27	37	IF IT HAPPENS AGAIN	UB40	DEP International	7
-	38	BERSERKER	Gary Numan	Numa	1
-	39	HARD HABIT TO BREAK	Chicago	Full Moon	1
-	40	I SHOULD HAVE KNOWN BETTER	Jim Diamond ●	A&M	1

WEEK ENDING 10 NOVEMBER 1984

LW	TW	Title	Artist	Label	Wks
2	1	I FEEL FOR YOU	Chaka Khan	Warner Brothers	4
1	2	FREEDOM	Wham!	Epic	5
5	3	THE WILD BOYS	Duran Duran	Parlophone	2
3	4	NO MORE LONELY NIGHTS (BALLAD)	Paul McCartney	Parlophone	6
4	5	TOGETHER IN ELECTRIC DREAMS	Giorgio Moroder and Philip Oakey	Virgin	7
6	6	TOO LATE FOR GOODBYES	Julian Lennon	Charisma	4
7	7	THE WANDERER	Status Quo	Vertigo	3
8	8	ALL CRIED OUT	Alison Moyet	CBS	5
12	9	CARIBBEAN QUEEN (NO MORE LOVE ON THE RUN)	Billy Ocean	Jive	3
20	10	NEVER ENDING STORY	Limahl	EMI	3
15	11	GIMME ALL YOUR LOVIN'	ZZ Top	Warner Brothers	3
13	12	LOVE'S GREAT ADVENTURE	Ultravox	Chrysalis	4
40	13	I SHOULD HAVE KNOWN BETTER	Jim Diamond	A&M	2
9	14	I JUST CALLED TO SAY I LOVE YOU	Stevie Wonder	Motown	12
10	15	MISSING YOU	John Waite	EMI America	6
28	16	I'M SO EXCITED	Pointer Sisters	Planet	2
11	17	DRIVE	Cars	Elektra	7
18	18	PENNY LOVER	Lionel Richie	Motown	4
17	19	MODERN GIRL	Meat Loaf	Arista	5
32	20	ACES HIGH	Iron Maiden	EMI	2
39	21	HARD HABIT TO BREAK	Chicago	Full Moon	2
24	22	GOTTA GET YOU HOME TONIGHT	Eugene Wilde	Fourth & Broadway	4
22	23	I'M GONNA TEAR YOUR PLAYHOUSE DOWN	Paul Young	CBS	5
23	24	LISTEN TO YOUR FATHER	Feargal Sharkey	Zarjazz	4
14	25	THE WAR SONG	Culture Club	Virgin	6
16	26	SHOUT TO THE TOP	Style Council	Polydor	5
19	27	GHOSTBUSTERS	Ray Parker Jr	Arista	11
36	28	THIS IS MINE	Heaven 17	Virgin	2
-	29	SOMEBODY/BLASPHEMOUS RUMOURS	Depeche Mode	Mute	1
21	30	HIGHLY STRUNG	Spandau Ballet	Reformation	4
27	31	WHY	Bronski Beat	Forbidden Fruit	8

In these weeks ■ Ex-group members enjoying solo hits include Chaka Khan (from Rufus), Paul McCartney (Beatles), Philip Oakey (Human League), Alison Moyet (Yazoo), John Waite (Babys), Lionel Richie (Commodores), Ray Parker Jr. (Raydio), Limahl (Kajagoogoo), Feargal Sharkey (Undertones), George Michael (Wham!) and Jim Diamond (PhD) (03.11.84)■

LW	TW	Title / Artist	Label	Wks
38	[32]	BERSERKER Gary Numan	*Numa*	2
35	33	AGADOO Black Lace	*Flair*	16
25	34	PRIDE (IN THE NAME OF LOVE) U2	*Island*	9
-	35	LET IT ALL BLOW Dazz Band ●	*Motown*	1
31	36	LOST IN MUSIC Sister Sledge	*Cotillion*	10
29	37	THE SECOND TIME Kim Wilde	*MCA*	4
34	38	CARELESS WHISPER George Michael	*Epic*	15
26	39	SKIN DEEP Stranglers	*Epic*	6
30	40	SMOOTH OPERATOR Sade	*Epic*	8

WEEK ENDING 17 NOVEMBER 1984

LW	TW	Title / Artist	Label	Wks
1	[1]	I FEEL FOR YOU Chaka Khan	*Warner Brothers*	5
3	[2]	THE WILD BOYS Duran Duran	*Parlophone*	3
13	3	I SHOULD HAVE KNOWN BETTER Jim Diamond	*A&M*	3
2	4	FREEDOM Wham!	*Epic*	6
10	5	NEVER ENDING STORY Limahl	*EMI*	4
9	[6]	CARIBBEAN QUEEN (NO MORE LOVE ON THE RUN) Billy Ocean	*Jive*	4
7	[7]	THE WANDERER Status Quo	*Vertigo*	4
8	[8]	ALL CRIED OUT Alison Moyet	*CBS*	6
6	9	TOO LATE FOR GOODBYES Julian Lennon	*Charisma*	5
11	[10]	GIMME ALL YOUR LOVIN' ZZ Top	*Warner Brothers*	4
21	11	HARD HABIT TO BREAK Chicago	*Full Moon*	3
12	[12]	LOVE'S GREAT ADVENTURE Ultravox	*Chrysalis*	5
4	13	NO MORE LONELY NIGHTS (BALLAD) Paul McCartney	*Parlophone*	7
16	14	I'M SO EXCITED Pointer Sisters	*Planet*	3
5	15	TOGETHER IN ELECTRIC DREAMS *Giorgio Moroder and* Philip Oakey	*Virgin*	8
29	[16]	SOMEBODY/BLASPHEMOUS RUMOURS Depeche Mode	*Mute*	2
-	17	THE RIDDLE Nik Kershaw	*MCA*	1
22	[18]	GOTTA GET YOU HOME TONIGHT Eugene Wilde	*Fourth & Broadway*	5
14	19	I JUST CALLED TO SAY I LOVE YOU Stevie Wonder	*Motown*	13
15	20	MISSING YOU John Waite	*EMI America*	7
19	21	MODERN GIRL Meat Loaf	*Arista*	6
18	22	PENNY LOVER Lionel Richie	*Motown*	5
28	[23]	THIS IS MINE Heaven 17	*Virgin*	3
-	24	SEXCRIME (NINETEEN EIGHTY FOUR) Eurythmics	*Virgin*	1
20	25	ACES HIGH Iron Maiden	*EMI*	3
-	26	TREAT HER LIKE A LADY Temptations	*Motown*	1
17	27	DRIVE Cars	*Elektra*	8
35	28	LET IT ALL BLOW Dazz Band	*Motown*	2
24	29	LISTEN TO YOUR FATHER Feargal Sharkey	*Zarjazz*	5
25	30	THE WAR SONG Culture Club	*Virgin*	7
-	31	I WON'T RUN AWAY Alvin Stardust	*Chrysalis*	1
27	32	GHOSTBUSTERS Ray Parker Jr	*Arista*	12
26	33	SHOUT TO THE TOP Style Council	*Polydor*	6
-	34	HALF A MINUTE Matt Bianco	*WEA*	1
23	35	I'M GONNA TEAR YOUR PLAYHOUSE DOWN Paul Young	*CBS*	6
-	36	LOUISE Human League	*Virgin*	1
32	37	BERSERKER Gary Numan	*Numa*	3
-	38	ALL JOIN HANDS Slade	*RCA*	1
-	39	ONE NIGHT IN BANGKOK Murray Head ●	*RCA*	1
-	40	IF THIS IS IT Huey Lewis and the News ●	*Chrysalis*	1

WEEK ENDING 24 NOVEMBER 1984

LW	TW	Title / Artist	Label	Wks
1	[1]	I FEEL FOR YOU Chaka Khan	*Warner Brothers*	6
3	2	I SHOULD HAVE KNOWN BETTER Jim Diamond	*A&M*	4
2	3	THE WILD BOYS Duran Duran	*Parlophone*	4
5	[4]	NEVER ENDING STORY Limahl	*EMI*	5
17	5	THE RIDDLE Nik Kershaw	*MCA*	2
6	[6]	CARIBBEAN QUEEN (NO MORE LOVE ON THE RUN) Billy Ocean	*Jive*	5
24	7	SEXCRIME (NINETEEN EIGHTY FOUR) Eurythmics	*Virgin*	2
11	[8]	HARD HABIT TO BREAK Chicago	*Full Moon*	4
4	9	FREEDOM Wham!	*Epic*	7
7	10	THE WANDERER Status Quo	*Vertigo*	5
14	[11]	I'M SO EXCITED Pointer Sisters	*Planet*	4
26	[12]	TREAT HER LIKE A LADY Temptations	*Motown*	2
8	13	ALL CRIED OUT Alison Moyet	*CBS*	7
28	14	LET IT ALL BLOW Dazz Band	*Motown*	3
10	15	GIMME ALL YOUR LOVIN' ZZ Top	*Warner Brothers*	5
12	16	LOVE'S GREAT ADVENTURE Ultravox	*Chrysalis*	6
16	17	SOMEBODY/BLASPHEMOUS RUMOURS Depeche Mode	*Mute*	3
31	18	I WON'T RUN AWAY Alvin Stardust	*Chrysalis*	2
9	19	TOO LATE FOR GOODBYES Julian Lennon	*Charisma*	6
38	20	ALL JOIN HANDS Slade	*RCA*	2
15	21	TOGETHER IN ELECTRIC DREAMS Giorgio Moroder and Philip Oakey	*Virgin*	9
13	22	NO MORE LONELY NIGHTS (BALLAD) Paul McCartney	*Parlophone*	8
18	23	GOTTA GET YOU HOME TONIGHT Eugene Wilde	*Fourth & Broadway*	6
-	24	TEARDROPS Shakin' Stevens	*Epic*	1
19	25	I JUST CALLED TO SAY I LOVE YOU Stevie Wonder	*Motown*	14
36	26	LOUISE Human League	*Virgin*	2
39	27	ONE NIGHT IN BANGKOK Murray Head	*RCA*	2
34	28	HALF A MINUTE Matt Bianco	*WEA*	2
23	29	THIS IS MINE Heaven 17	*Virgin*	4
22	30	PENNY LOVER Lionel Richie	*Motown*	6
20	31	MISSING YOU John Waite	*EMI America*	8
-	32	PRIVATE DANCER Tina Turner	*Capitol*	1
-	[33]	WE ARE FAMILY Sister Sledge	*Cotillion*	1
-	34	WARNING SIGN Nick Heyward	*Arista*	1
-	35	FRESH Kool and the Gang	*De-Lite*	1
-	36	LIKE A VIRGIN Madonna	*Sire*	1
21	37	MODERN GIRL Meat Loaf	*Arista*	7
-	38	RESPECT YOURSELF Kane Gang	*Kitchenware*	1
40	[39]	IF THIS IS IT Huey Lewis and the News	*Chrysalis*	2
27	40	DRIVE Cars	*Elektra*	9

December 1984

□ Highest position disc reached ● Act's first ever week on chart

WEEK ENDING 1 DECEMBER 1984

LW	TW	Title / Artist	Label	Wks
2	[1]	I SHOULD HAVE KNOWN BETTER Jim Diamond	*A&M*	5
1	2	I FEEL FOR YOU Chaka Khan	*Warner Brothers*	7
-	3	THE POWER OF LOVE Frankie Goes To Hollywood	*ZTT*	1
5	4	THE RIDDLE Nik Kershaw	*MCA*	3
4	5	NEVER ENDING STORY Limahl	*EMI*	6
7	6	SEXCRIME (NINETEEN EIGHTY FOUR) Eurythmics	*Virgin*	3
24	7	TEARDROPS Shakin' Stevens	*Epic*	2
8	[8]	HARD HABIT TO BREAK Chicago	*Full Moon*	5
3	9	THE WILD BOYS Duran Duran	*Parlophone*	5
6	10	CARIBBEAN QUEEN (NO MORE LOVE ON THE RUN) Billy Ocean	*Jive*	6
18	11	I WON'T RUN AWAY Alvin Stardust	*Chrysalis*	3
14	[12]	LET IT ALL BLOW Dazz Band	*Motown*	4
12	13	TREAT HER LIKE A LADY Temptations	*Motown*	3
26	14	LOUISE Human League	*Virgin*	3
20	[15]	ALL JOIN HANDS Slade	*RCA*	3
11	16	I'M SO EXCITED Pointer Sisters	*Planet*	5
27	17	ONE NIGHT IN BANGKOK Murray Head	*RCA*	3
10	18	THE WANDERER Status Quo	*Vertigo*	6
35	19	FRESH Kool and the Gang	*De-Lite*	2
9	20	FREEDOM Wham!	*Epic*	8
15	21	GIMME ALL YOUR LOVIN' ZZ Top	*Warner Brothers*	6
13	22	ALL CRIED OUT Alison Moyet	*CBS*	8
28	[23]	HALF A MINUTE Matt Bianco	*WEA*	3
38	24	RESPECT YOURSELF Kane Gang	*Kitchenware*	2
34	[25]	WARNING SIGN Nick Heyward	*Arista*	2
-	26	DO THE CONGA Black Lace	*Flair*	1
36	27	LIKE A VIRGIN Madonna	*Sire*	2
25	28	I JUST CALLED TO SAY I LOVE YOU Stevie Wonder	*Motown*	15
22	29	NO MORE LONELY NIGHTS (BALLAD) Paul McCartney	*Parlophone*	9
16	30	LOVE'S GREAT ADVENTURE Ultravox	*Chrysalis*	7
32	31	PRIVATE DANCER Tina Turner	*Capitol*	2
17	32	SOMEBODY/BLASPHEMOUS RUMOURS Depeche Mode	*Mute*	4
21	33	TOGETHER IN ELECTRIC DREAMS Giorgio Moroder and Philip Oakey	*Virgin*	10

■Duran Duran's *The Wild Boys* is accompanied by the most expensive rock video thus far produced. Michael Jackson went on to break this particular record (17.11.84) ■ For two weeks in a row, a record jumps from 24 to 7, but neither of them reach number one (01.12.84)■

December 1984

□ Highest position disc reached ● Act's first ever week on chart

LW	TW	Title	Artist	Label	Wks
19	34	TOO LATE FOR GOODBYES	Julian Lennon	Charisma	7
-	35	WHERE THE ROSE IS SOWN	Big Country	Mercury	1
23	36	GOTTA GET YOU HOME TONIGHT	Eugene Wilde	Fourth & Broadway	7
-	37	THE MEDAL SONG	Culture Club	Virgin	1
33	38	WE ARE FAMILY	Sister Sledge	Cotillion	2
-	39	WE ALL STAND TOGETHER	Paul McCartney & the Frog Chorus	Parlophone	1
-	40	INVISIBLE	Alison Moyet	CBS	1

WEEK ENDING 8 DECEMBER 1984

LW	TW	Title	Artist	Label	Wks
3	[1]	THE POWER OF LOVE	Frankie Goes To Hollywood	ZTT	2
1	2	I SHOULD HAVE KNOWN BETTER	Jim Diamond	A&M	6
4	[3]	THE RIDDLE	Nik Kershaw	MCA	4
6	[4]	SEXCRIME (NINETEEN EIGHTY FOUR)	Eurythmics	Virgin	4
7	[5]	TEARDROPS	Shakin' Stevens	Epic	3
2	6	I FEEL FOR YOU	Chaka Khan	Warner Brothers	8
11	[7]	I WON'T RUN AWAY	Alvin Stardust	Chrysalis	4
27	8	LIKE A VIRGIN	Madonna	Sire	3
39	9	WE ALL STAND TOGETHER	Paul McCartney & the Frog Chorus	Parlophone	2
5	10	NEVER ENDING STORY	Limahl	EMI	7
8	11	HARD HABIT TO BREAK	Chicago	Full Moon	6
19	12	FRESH	Kool and the Gang	De-Lite	3
14	[13]	LOUISE	Human League	Virgin	4
12	14	LET IT ALL BLOW	Dazz Band	Motown	5
26	15	DO THE CONGA	Black Lace	Flair	2
17	16	ONE NIGHT IN BANGKOK	Murray Head	RCA	4
10	17	CARIBBEAN QUEEN (NO MORE LOVE ON THE RUN)	Billy Ocean	Jive	7
13	18	TREAT HER LIKE A LADY	Temptations	Motown	4
9	19	THE WILD BOYS	Duran Duran	Parlophone	6
15	20	ALL JOIN HANDS	Slade	RCA	4
24	[21]	RESPECT YOURSELF	Kane Gang	Kitchenware	3
16	22	I'M SO EXCITED	Pointer Sisters	Planet	6
-	23	ROUND AND ROUND	Spandau Ballet	Reformation	1
40	24	INVISIBLE	Alison Moyet	CBS	2
20	25	FREEDOM	Wham!	Epic	9
31	[26]	PRIVATE DANCER	Tina Turner	Capitol	3
25	27	WARNING SIGN	Nick Heyward	Arista	3
29	28	NO MORE LONELY NIGHTS (BALLAD)	Paul McCartney	Parlophone	10
35	[29]	WHERE THE ROSE IS SOWN	Big Country	Mercury	2
-	30	LAY YOUR HANDS ON ME	Thompson Twins	Arista	1
18	31	THE WANDERER	Status Quo	Vertigo	7
37	[32]	THE MEDAL SONG	Culture Club	Virgin	2
23	33	HALF A MINUTE	Matt Bianco	WEA	4
28	34	I JUST CALLED TO SAY I LOVE YOU	Stevie Wonder	Motown	16
-	35	SHOUT	Tears For Fears	Mercury	1
-	36	THANK GOD IT'S CHRISTMAS	Queen	EMI	1
22	37	ALL CRIED OUT	Alison Moyet	CBS	9
21	38	GIMME ALL YOUR LOVIN'	ZZ Top	Warner Brothers	7
-	39	EVERYTHING MUST CHANGE	Paul Young	CBS	1
-	40	NO MERCY	Stranglers	Epic	1

WEEK ENDING 15 DECEMBER 1984

LW	TW	Title	Artist	Label	Wks
-	[1]	DO THEY KNOW IT'S CHRISTMAS	Band Aid ●	Mercury	1
-	[2]	LAST CHRISTMAS/EVERYTHING SHE WANTS	Wham!	Epic	1
1	3	THE POWER OF LOVE	Frankie Goes To Hollywood	ZTT	3
9	4	WE ALL STAND TOGETHER	Paul McCartney & the Frog Chorus	Parlophone	3
8	5	LIKE A VIRGIN	Madonna	Sire	4
2	6	I SHOULD HAVE KNOWN BETTER	Jim Diamond	A&M	7
5	7	TEARDROPS	Shakin' Stevens	Epic	4
3	8	THE RIDDLE	Nik Kershaw	MCA	5
4	9	SEXCRIME (NINETEEN EIGHTY FOUR)	Eurythmics	Virgin	5
7	10	I WON'T RUN AWAY	Alvin Stardust	Chrysalis	5
12	[11]	FRESH	Kool and the Gang	De-Lite	4
16	[12]	ONE NIGHT IN BANGKOK	Murray Head	RCA	5
15	13	DO THE CONGA	Black Lace	Flair	3
6	14	I FEEL FOR YOU	Chaka Khan	Warner Brothers	9
13	15	LOUISE	Human League	Virgin	5
-	16	NELLIE THE ELEPHANT	Toy Dolls ●	Volume	1
39	17	EVERYTHING MUST CHANGE	Paul Young	CBS	2
10	18	NEVER ENDING STORY	Limahl	EMI	8
23	19	ROUND AND ROUND	Spandau Ballet	Reformation	2
30	20	LAY YOUR HANDS ON ME	Thompson Twins	Arista	2
36	[21]	THANK GOD IT'S CHRISTMAS	Queen	EMI	2
-	22	ANOTHER ROCK AND ROLL CHRISTMAS	Gary Glitter	MLM	1
20	23	ALL JOIN HANDS	Slade	RCA	5
11	24	HARD HABIT TO BREAK	Chicago	Full Moon	7
24	25	INVISIBLE	Alison Moyet	CBS	3
21	26	RESPECT YOURSELF	Kane Gang	Kitchenware	4
14	27	LET IT ALL BLOW	Dazz Band	Motown	6
18	28	TREAT HER LIKE A LADY	Temptations	Motown	5
19	29	THE WILD BOYS	Duran Duran	Parlophone	7
26	30	PRIVATE DANCER	Tina Turner	Capitol	4
17	31	CARIBBEAN QUEEN (NO MORE LOVE ON THE RUN)	Billy Ocean	Jive	8
35	32	SHOUT	Tears For Fears	Mercury	2
-	33	GHOSTBUSTERS	Ray Parker Jr	Arista	13
29	34	WHERE THE ROSE IS SOWN	Big Country	Mercury	3
34	35	I JUST CALLED TO SAY I LOVE YOU	Stevie Wonder	Motown	17
25	36	FREEDOM	Wham!	Epic	10
40	[37]	NO MERCY	Stranglers	Epic	2
28	38	NO MORE LONELY NIGHTS (BALLAD)	Paul McCartney	Parlophone	11
22	39	I'M SO EXCITED	Pointer Sisters	Planet	7
-	40	IT AIN'T NECESSARILY SO	Bronski Beat	Forbidden Fruit	1

WEEK ENDING 22 DECEMBER 1984

LW	TW	Title	Artist	Label	Wks
1	[1]	DO THEY KNOW IT'S CHRISTMAS	Band Aid	Mercury	2
2	[2]	LAST CHRISTMAS/EVERYTHING SHE WANTS	Wham!	Epic	2
4	[3]	WE ALL STAND TOGETHER	Paul McCartney & the Frog Chorus	Parlophone	4
5	4	LIKE A VIRGIN	Madonna	Sire	5
3	5	THE POWER OF LOVE	Frankie Goes To Hollywood	ZTT	4
16	6	NELLIE THE ELEPHANT	Toy Dolls	Volume	2
22	[7]	ANOTHER ROCK AND ROLL CHRISTMAS	Gary Glitter	MLM	2
8	8	THE RIDDLE	Nik Kershaw	MCA	6
17	[9]	EVERYTHING MUST CHANGE	Paul Young	CBS	3
13	[10]	DO THE CONGA	Black Lace	Flair	4
7	11	TEARDROPS	Shakin' Stevens	Epic	5
11	12	FRESH	Kool and the Gang	De-Lite	5
32	13	SHOUT	Tears For Fears	Mercury	3
12	14	ONE NIGHT IN BANGKOK	Murray Head	RCA	6
33	15	GHOSTBUSTERS	Ray Parker Jr	Arista	14
10	16	I WON'T RUN AWAY	Alvin Stardust	Chrysalis	6
9	17	SEXCRIME (NINETEEN EIGHTY FOUR)	Eurythmics	Virgin	6
6	18	I SHOULD HAVE KNOWN BETTER	Jim Diamond	A&M	8
19	19	ROUND AND ROUND	Spandau Ballet	Reformation	3
20	20	LAY YOUR HANDS ON ME	Thompson Twins	Arista	3
14	21	I FEEL FOR YOU	Chaka Khan	Warner Brothers	10
21	22	THANK GOD IT'S CHRISTMAS	Queen	EMI	3
25	23	INVISIBLE	Alison Moyet	CBS	4
15	24	LOUISE	Human League	Virgin	6
23	25	ALL JOIN HANDS	Slade	RCA	6
-	26	I WANT TO KNOW WHAT LOVE IS	Foreigner	Atlantic	1
18	27	NEVER ENDING STORY	Limahl	EMI	9
26	28	RESPECT YOURSELF	Kane Gang	Kitchenware	5
24	29	HARD HABIT TO BREAK	Chicago	Full Moon	8
27	30	LET IT ALL BLOW	Dazz Band	Motown	7
28	31	TREAT HER LIKE A LADY	Temptations	Motown	6
29	32	THE WILD BOYS	Duran Duran	Parlophone	8
40	33	IT AIN'T NECESSARILY SO	Bronski Beat	Forbidden Fruit	2
35	34	I JUST CALLED TO SAY I LOVE YOU	Stevie Wonder	Motown	18
30	35	PRIVATE DANCER	Tina Turner	Capitol	5
-	36	I WISH IT COULD BE CHRISTMAS EVERYDAY	Wizzard	Harvest	1

In these weeks ■ For eleven consecutive weeks there is a different song at number two. The sequence is broken by Wham!'s million-selling *Last Christmas/Everything She Wants* which cannot climb past the biggest selling single in British chart history, Band Aid's *Do They Know It's Christmas* (22.12.84) ■ Frankie Goes To Hollywood equals Gerry and the Pacemakers' record of achieving three number ones with each of their first three releases (08.12.84) ■

December 1984

□ Highest position disc reached ● Act's first ever week on chart

LW	TW	Title / Artist	Label	Wks
-	37	SOUL DEEP (PART 1) Council Collective ●	Polydor	1
21	38	CARIBBEAN QUEEN (NO MORE LOVE ON THE RUN) Billy Ocean	Jive	9
-	39	SO NEAR TO CHRISTMAS Alvin Stardust	Chrysalis	1
34	40	WHERE THE ROSE IS SOWN Big Country	Mercury	4

WEEK ENDING 29 DECEMBER 1984

LW	TW	Title / Artist	Label	Wks
1	□1	DO THEY KNOW IT'S CHRISTMAS Band Aid	Mercury	3
2	□2	LAST CHRISTMAS/EVERYTHING SHE WANTS Wham!	Epic	3
3	□3	WE ALL STAND TOGETHER Paul McCartney & the Frog Chorus	Parlophone	5
6	□4	NELLIE THE ELEPHANT Toy Dolls	Volume	3
4	5	LIKE A VIRGIN Madonna	Sire	6
5	6	THE POWER OF LOVE Frankie Goes To Hollywood	ZTT	5
15	7	GHOSTBUSTERS Ray Parker Jr	Arista	15
7	8	ANOTHER ROCK AND ROLL CHRISTMAS Gary Glitter	MLM	3
9	□9	EVERYTHING MUST CHANGE Paul Young	CBS	4
13	10	SHOUT Tears For Fears	Mercury	4
26	11	I WANT TO KNOW WHAT LOVE IS Foreigner	Atlantic	2
8	12	THE RIDDLE Nik Kershaw	MCA	7
12	13	FRESH Kool and the Gang	De-Lite	6
10	14	DO THE CONGA Black Lace	Flair	5
14	15	ONE NIGHT IN BANGKOK Murray Head	RCA	7
11	16	TEARDROPS Shakin' Stevens	Epic	6
17	17	SEXCRIME (NINETEEN EIGHTY FOUR) Eurythmics	Virgin	7
16	18	I WON'T RUN AWAY Alvin Stardust	Chrysalis	7
20	19	LAY YOUR HANDS ON ME Thompson Twins	Arista	4
18	20	I SHOULD HAVE KNOWN BETTER Jim Diamond	A&M	9
34	21	I JUST CALLED TO SAY I LOVE YOU Stevie Wonder	Motown	19
19	22	ROUND AND ROUND Spandau Ballet	Reformation	4
36	□23	I WISH IT COULD BE CHRISTMAS EVERYDAY Wizzard	Harvest	2
37	□24	SOUL DEEP (PART 1) Council Collective	Polydor	2
21	25	I FEEL FOR YOU Chaka Khan	Warner Brothers	11
23	26	INVISIBLE Alison Moyet	CBS	5
25	27	ALL JOIN HANDS Slade	RCA	7
24	28	LOUISE Human League	Virgin	7
39	□29	SO NEAR TO CHRISTMAS Alvin Stardust	Chrysalis	2
33	30	IT AIN'T NECESSARILY SO Bronski Beat	Forbidden Fruit	3
32	31	THE WILD BOYS Duran Duran	Parlophone	9
22	32	THANK GOD IT'S CHRISTMAS Queen	EMI	4
27	33	NEVER ENDING STORY Limahl	EMI	10
29	34	HARD HABIT TO BREAK Chicago	Full Moon	9
-	35	STEP OFF (PART 1) Grandmaster Melle Mel and the Furious Five	Sugarhill	1
30	36	LET IT ALL BLOW Dazz Band	Motown	8
35	37	PRIVATE DANCER Tina Turner	Capitol	6
28	38	RESPECT YOURSELF Kane Gang	Kitchenware	6
-	39	FREEDOM Wham!	Epic	1
-	40	POLICE OFFICER Smiley Culture ●	Fashion	1

■Gary Glitter's final hit gives him his twelfth top ten hit, and his first for over 9 years (22.12.84) ■ Six of the top 40 have the word *Christmas* in their title, while several others are clearly festive offerings (29.12.84)■

1985

……..MADONNA gets into the groove with six fresh top five hits, including her first number one……in the wake of Band Aid, three one-off charity groups go to number one……Jennifer Rush has the year's best seller, 'The Power Of Love'………

January 1985

☐ Highest position disc reached ● Act's first ever week on chart

WEEK ENDING 5 JANUARY 1985

LW	TW	Title	Artist	Label	Wks
1	[1]	DO THEY KNOW IT'S CHRISTMAS	Band Aid	*Mercury*	4
2	[2]	EVERYTHING SHE WANTS/LAST CHRISTMAS	Wham!	*Epic*	4
3	[3]	WE ALL STAND TOGETHER	Paul McCartney and the Frog Chorus	*Parlophone*	6
5	4	LIKE A VIRGIN	Madonna	*Sire*	7
4	5	NELLIE THE ELEPHANT	Toy Dolls	*Volume*	4
7	[6]	GHOSTBUSTERS	Ray Parker Jr	*Arista*	16
6	7	THE POWER OF LOVE	Frankie Goes To Hollywood	*ZTT*	6
10	8	SHOUT	Tears For Fears	*Mercury*	5
9	[9]	EVERYTHING MUST CHANGE	Paul Young	*CBS*	5
11	10	I WANT TO KNOW WHAT LOVE IS	Foreigner	*Atlantic*	3
12	11	THE RIDDLE	Nik Kershaw	*MCA*	8
8	12	ANOTHER ROCK AND ROLL CHRISTMAS	Gary Glitter	*Arista*	4
14	13	DO THE CONGA	Black Lace	*Flair*	6
13	14	FRESH	Kool and the Gang	*De-Lite*	7
15	15	ONE NIGHT IN BANGKOK	Murray Head	*RCA*	8
19	16	LAY YOUR HANDS ON ME	Thompson Twins	*Arista*	5
17	17	SEXCRIME (NINETEEN EIGHTY FOUR)	Eurythmics	*Virgin*	8
22	[18]	ROUND AND ROUND	Spandau Ballet	*Reformation*	5
20	19	I SHOULD HAVE KNOWN BETTER	Jim Diamond	*A&M*	10
16	20	TEARDROPS	Shakin' Stevens	*Epic*	7
25	21	I FEEL FOR YOU	Chaka Khan	*Warner Brothers*	12
18	22	I WON'T RUN AWAY	Alvin Stardust	*Chrysalis*	8
21	23	I JUST CALLED TO SAY I LOVE YOU	Stevie Wonder	*Motown*	20
30	24	IT AIN'T NECESSARILY SO	Bronski Beat	*Forbidden Fruit*	4
26	25	INVISIBLE	Alison Moyet	*CBS*	6
31	26	THE WILD BOYS	Duran Duran	*Parlophone*	10
28	27	LOUISE	Human League	*Virgin*	8
24	28	SOUL DEEP (PART 1)	Council Collective	*Polydor*	3
27	29	ALL JOIN HANDS	Slade	*RCA*	8
35	30	STEP OFF (PART 1)	Grandmaster Melle Mel and the Furious Five	*Sugarhill*	2
38	31	RESPECT YOURSELF	Kane Gang	*Kitchenware*	7
-	32	AGADOO	Black Lace	*Flair*	17
-	[33]	TREAT HER LIKE A LADY	Temptations	*Motown*	7
40	34	POLICE OFFICER	Smiley Culture	*Fashion*	2
39	[35]	FREEDOM	Wham!	*Epic*	2
23	36	I WISH IT COULD BE CHRISTMAS EVERYDAY	Wizzard	*Harvest*	3
-	37	SAN DAMIANO (HEART AND SOUL)	Sal Solo ●	*MCA*	1
36	38	LET IT ALL BLOW	Dazz Band	*Motown*	9
34	39	HARD HABIT TO BREAK	Chicago	*Full Moon*	10
29	40	SO NEAR TO CHRISTMAS	Alvin Stardust	*Chrysalis*	3

WEEK ENDING 12 JANUARY 1985

LW	TW	Title	Artist	Label	Wks
1	[1]	DO THEY KNOW IT'S CHRISTMAS	Band Aid	*Mercury*	5
2	[2]	EVERYTHING SHE WANTS/LAST CHRISTMAS	Wham!	*Epic*	5
4	[3]	LIKE A VIRGIN	Madonna	*Sire*	8
10	4	I WANT TO KNOW WHAT LOVE IS	Foreigner	*Atlantic*	4
3	5	WE ALL STAND TOGETHER	Paul McCartney and the Frog Chorus	*Parlophone*	7
5	6	NELLIE THE ELEPHANT	Toy Dolls	*Volume*	5
8	7	SHOUT	Tears For Fears	*Mercury*	6
6	8	GHOSTBUSTERS	Ray Parker Jr	*Arista*	17
9	[9]	EVERYTHING MUST CHANGE	Paul Young	*CBS*	6
7	10	THE POWER OF LOVE	Frankie Goes To Hollywood	*ZTT*	7
30	11	STEP OFF (PART 1)	Grandmaster Melle Mel and the Furious Five	*Sugarhill*	3
14	12	FRESH	Kool and the Gang	*De-Lite*	8
16	[13]	LAY YOUR HANDS ON ME	Thompson Twins	*Arista*	6
11	14	THE RIDDLE	Nik Kershaw	*MCA*	9
34	15	POLICE OFFICER	Smiley Culture	*Fashion*	3
15	16	ONE NIGHT IN BANGKOK	Murray Head	*RCA*	9
37	17	SAN DAMIANO (HEART AND SOUL)	Sal Solo	*MCA*	2
13	18	DO THE CONGA	Black Lace	*Flair*	7
24	19	IT AIN'T NECESSARILY SO	Bronski Beat	*Forbidden Fruit*	5
18	20	ROUND AND ROUND	Spandau Ballet	*Reformation*	6
25	[21]	INVISIBLE	Alison Moyet	*CBS*	7
17	22	SEXCRIME (NINETEEN EIGHTY FOUR)	Eurythmics	*Virgin*	9
26	23	THE WILD BOYS	Duran Duran	*Parlophone*	11
23	24	I JUST CALLED TO SAY I LOVE YOU	Stevie Wonder	*Motown*	21
21	25	I FEEL FOR YOU	Chaka Khan	*Warner Brothers*	13
28	26	SOUL DEEP (PART 1)	Council Collective	*Polydor*	4
20	27	TEARDROPS	Shakin' Stevens	*Epic*	8
19	28	I SHOULD HAVE KNOWN BETTER	Jim Diamond	*A&M*	11
32	29	AGADOO	Black Lace	*Flair*	18
22	30	I WON'T RUN AWAY	Alvin Stardust	*Chrysalis*	9
12	31	ANOTHER ROCK AND ROLL CHRISTMAS	Gary Glitter	*Arista*	5
-	32	SINCE YESTERDAY	Strawberry Switchblade ●	*Korova*	1
-	33	SHARP DRESSED MAN	ZZ Top	*Warner Brothers*	1
-	34	I KNOW HIM SO WELL	Elaine Paige and Barbara Dickson ●	*RCA*	1
-	35	THANK YOU MY LOVE	Imagination	*R&B*	1
27	36	LOUISE	Human League	*Virgin*	9
-	37	SAY YEAH	Limit ●	*Portrait*	1
38	38	LET IT ALL BLOW	Dazz Band	*Motown*	10
-	39	FRIENDS	Amii Stewart	*RCA*	1
-	40	ATMOSPHERE	Russ Abbot ●	*Spirit*	1

WEEK ENDING 19 JANUARY 1985

LW	TW	Title	Artist	Label	Wks
4	[1]	I WANT TO KNOW WHAT LOVE IS	Foreigner	*Atlantic*	5
1	2	DO THEY KNOW IT'S CHRISTMAS	Band Aid	*Mercury*	6
2	3	EVERYTHING SHE WANTS/LAST CHRISTMAS	Wham!	*Epic*	6
3	4	LIKE A VIRGIN	Madonna	*Sire*	9
7	5	SHOUT	Tears For Fears	*Mercury*	7
34	6	I KNOW HIM SO WELL	Elaine Paige and Barbara Dickson	*RCA*	2
8	7	GHOSTBUSTERS	Ray Parker Jr	*Arista*	18
11	[8]	STEP OFF (PART 1)	Grandmaster Melle Mel and the Furious Five	*Sugarhill*	4
9	[9]	EVERYTHING MUST CHANGE	Paul Young	*CBS*	7
32	10	SINCE YESTERDAY	Strawberry Switchblade	*Korova*	2
5	11	WE ALL STAND TOGETHER	Paul McCartney and the Frog Chorus	*Parlophone*	8
15	[12]	POLICE OFFICER	Smiley Culture	*Fashion*	4
-	13	1999/LITTLE RED CORVETTE	Prince	*Warner Brothers*	1
6	14	NELLIE THE ELEPHANT	Toy Dolls	*Volume*	6
17	[15]	SAN DAMIANO (HEART AND SOUL)	Sal Solo	*MCA*	3
19	[16]	IT AIN'T NECESSARILY SO	Bronski Beat	*Forbidden Fruit*	6
39	17	FRIENDS	Amii Stewart	*RCA*	2
40	18	ATMOSPHERE	Russ Abbot	*Spirit*	2
37	19	SAY YEAH	Limit	*Portrait*	2
10	20	THE POWER OF LOVE	Frankie Goes To Hollywood	*ZTT*	8
-	21	LOVE AND PRIDE	King ●	*CBS*	1
33	[22]	SHARP DRESSED MAN	ZZ Top	*Warner Brothers*	2
13	23	LAY YOUR HANDS ON ME	Thompson Twins	*Arista*	7
12	24	FRESH	Kool and the Gang	*De-Lite*	9
21	25	INVISIBLE	Alison Moyet	*CBS*	8
35	26	THANK YOU MY LOVE	Imagination	*R&B*	2
-	27	SOLID	Ashford and Simpson ●	*Capitol*	1
-	28	THIS IS MY NIGHT	Chaka Khan	*Warner Brothers*	1
-	29	YAH MO B THERE	James Ingram with Michael McDonald ●	*Qwest*	1
16	30	ONE NIGHT IN BANGKOK	Murray Head	*RCA*	10
-	[31]	NEUTRON DANCE	Pointer Sisters	*Planet*	1
14	32	THE RIDDLE	Nik Kershaw	*MCA*	10
20	33	ROUND AND ROUND	Spandau Ballet	*Reformation*	7
-	[34]	I HEAR TALK	Bucks Fizz	*RCA*	1
-	35	JUST A SHADOW	Big Country	*Mercury*	1
-	36	DANCING IN THE DARK	Bruce Springsteen	*CBS*	1
-	37	LOVERBOY	Billy Ocean	*Jive*	1
-	38	CLOSE (TO THE EDIT)	Art Of Noise ●	*ZTT*	1
23	39	THE WILD BOYS	Duran Duran	*Parlophone*	12
-	40	CAN I	Cashmere ●	*Fourth & Broadway*	1

WEEK ENDING 26 JANUARY 1985

LW	TW	Title	Artist	Label	Wks
1	[1]	I WANT TO KNOW WHAT LOVE IS	Foreigner	*Atlantic*	6
13	[2]	1999/LITTLE RED CORVETTE	Prince	*Warner Brothers*	2

In these weeks ■ *Ghostbusters* peaks at number six second time around after the film is released in the UK (05.01.85) ■ *I Just Called To Say I Love You* bows out after 21 consecutive weeks (12.01.85) ■ Prince and Bruce Springsteen both re-enter with songs that underperformed last year (19.01.85) ■ Prince at two, King at six (26.01.85)■

LW	TW	Title / Artist	Label	Wks
6	3	I KNOW HIM SO WELL Elaine Paige and Barbara Dickson	RCA	3
5	[4]	SHOUT Tears For Fears	Mercury	8
10	[5]	SINCE YESTERDAY Strawberry Switchblade	Korova	3
21	6	LOVE AND PRIDE King	CBS	2
4	7	LIKE A VIRGIN Madonna	Sire	10
3	8	EVERYTHING SHE WANTS/LAST CHRISTMAS Wham!	Epic	7
2	9	DO THEY KNOW IT'S CHRISTMAS Band Aid	Mercury	7
18	10	ATMOSPHERE Russ Abbot	Spirit	3
8	11	STEP OFF (PART 1) Grandmaster Melle Mel and the Furious Five	Sugarhill	5
17	[12]	FRIENDS Amii Stewart	RCA	3
27	13	SOLID Ashford and Simpson	Capitol	2
9	14	EVERYTHING MUST CHANGE Paul Young	CBS	8
12	15	POLICE OFFICER Smiley Culture	Fashion	5
7	16	GHOSTBUSTERS Ray Parker Jr	Arista	19
19	[17]	SAY YEAH Limit	Portrait	3
28	18	THIS IS MY NIGHT Chaka Khan	Warner Brothers	2
15	19	SAN DAMIANO (HEART AND SOUL) Sal Solo	MCA	4
36	20	DANCING IN THE DARK Bruce Springsteen	CBS	2
29	21	YAH MO B THERE James Ingram with Michael McDonald	Qwest	2
26	[22]	THANK YOU MY LOVE Imagination	R&B	3
16	23	IT AIN'T NECESSARILY SO Bronski Beat	Forbidden Fruit	7
37	24	LOVERBOY Billy Ocean	Jive	2
22	25	SHARP DRESSED MAN ZZ Top	Warner Brothers	3
35	[26]	JUST A SHADOW Big Country	Mercury	2
11	27	WE ALL STAND TOGETHER Paul McCartney and the Frog Chorus	Parlophone	9
-	28	RUN TO YOU Bryan Adams ●	A&M	1
40	[29]	CAN I Cashmere	Fourth & Broadway	2
38	30	CLOSE (TO THE EDIT) Art Of Noise	ZTT	2
-	31	WE BELONG Pat Benatar ●	Chrysalis	1
14	32	NELLIE THE ELEPHANT Toy Dolls	Volume	7
31	33	NEUTRON DANCE Pointer Sisters	Planet	2
34	[34]	I HEAR TALK Bucks Fizz	RCA	2
20	35	THE POWER OF LOVE Frankie Goes To Hollywood	ZTT	9
-	36	SUSSUDIO Phil Collins	Virgin	1
25	37	INVISIBLE Alison Moyet	CBS	9
-	38	A NEW ENGLAND Kirsty MacColl	Stiff	1
24	39	FRESH Kool and the Gang	De-Lite	10
-	40	20/20 George Benson	Warner Brothers	1

February 1985

□ Highest position disc reached ● Act's first ever week on chart

WEEK ENDING 2 FEBRUARY 1985

LW	TW	Title / Artist	Label	Wks
1	[1]	I WANT TO KNOW WHAT LOVE IS Foreigner	Atlantic	7
3	2	I KNOW HIM SO WELL Elaine Paige and Barbara Dickson	RCA	4
2	3	1999/LITTLE RED CORVETTE Prince	Warner Brothers	3
6	4	LOVE AND PRIDE King	CBS	3
4	5	SHOUT Tears For Fears	Mercury	9
13	6	SOLID Ashford and Simpson	Capitol	3
5	7	SINCE YESTERDAY Strawberry Switchblade	Korova	4
10	8	ATMOSPHERE Russ Abbot	Spirit	4
7	9	LIKE A VIRGIN Madonna	Sire	11
20	10	DANCING IN THE DARK Bruce Springsteen	CBS	3
8	11	EVERYTHING SHE WANTS/LAST CHRISTMAS Wham!	Epic	8
21	[12]	YAH MO B THERE James Ingram with Michael McDonald	Qwest	3
12	13	FRIENDS Amii Stewart	RCA	4
18	[14]	THIS IS MY NIGHT Chaka Khan	Warner Brothers	3
11	15	STEP OFF (PART 1) Grandmaster Melle Mel and the Furious Five	Sugarhill	6
24	16	LOVERBOY Billy Ocean	Jive	3
9	17	DO THEY KNOW IT'S CHRISTMAS Band Aid	Mercury	8
28	18	RUN TO YOU Bryan Adams	A&M	2
36	19	SUSSUDIO Phil Collins	Virgin	2
16	20	GHOSTBUSTERS Ray Parker Jr	Arista	20
30	21	CLOSE (TO THE EDIT) Art Of Noise	ZTT	3
38	22	A NEW ENGLAND Kirsty MacColl	Stiff	2
17	23	SAY YEAH Limit	Portrait	4
22	24	THANK YOU MY LOVE Imagination	R&B	4
31	25	WE BELONG Pat Benatar	Chrysalis	2
14	26	EVERYTHING MUST CHANGE Paul Young	CBS	9
15	27	POLICE OFFICER Smiley Culture	Fashion	6
19	28	SAN DAMIANO (HEART AND SOUL) Sal Solo	MCA	5
26	29	JUST A SHADOW Big Country	Mercury	3
29	30	CAN I Cashmere	Fourth & Broadway	3
-	31	THINKING OF YOU Colourfield ●	Chrysalis	1
-	32	NIGHTSHIFT Commodores	Motown	1
27	33	WE ALL STAND TOGETHER Paul McCartney and the Frog Chorus	Parlophone	10
34	[34]	I HEAR TALK Bucks Fizz	RCA	3
23	35	IT AIN'T NECESSARILY SO Bronski Beat	Forbidden Fruit	8
-	36	THIS HOUSE (IS WHERE YOUR LOVE STANDS) Big Sound Authority ●	Source	1
25	37	SHARP DRESSED MAN ZZ Top	Warner Brothers	4
33	38	NEUTRON DANCE Pointer Sisters	Planet	3
32	39	NELLIE THE ELEPHANT Toy Dolls	Volume	8
40	40	20/20 George Benson	Warner Brothers	2

WEEK ENDING 9 FEBRUARY 1985

LW	TW	Title / Artist	Label	Wks
2	[1]	I KNOW HIM SO WELL Elaine Paige and Barbara Dickson	RCA	5
4	[2]	LOVE AND PRIDE King	CBS	4
1	3	I WANT TO KNOW WHAT LOVE IS Foreigner	Atlantic	8
6	4	SOLID Ashford and Simpson	Capitol	4
3	5	1999/LITTLE RED CORVETTE Prince	Warner Brothers	4
10	6	DANCING IN THE DARK Bruce Springsteen	CBS	4
8	[7]	ATMOSPHERE Russ Abbot	Spirit	5
5	8	SHOUT Tears For Fears	Mercury	10
7	9	SINCE YESTERDAY Strawberry Switchblade	Korova	5
21	10	CLOSE (TO THE EDIT) Art Of Noise	ZTT	4
18	[11]	RUN TO YOU Bryan Adams	A&M	3
19	[12]	SUSSUDIO Phil Collins	Virgin	3
22	13	A NEW ENGLAND Kirsty MacColl	Stiff	3
12	14	YAH MO B THERE James Ingram with Michael McDonald	Qwest	4
9	15	LIKE A VIRGIN Madonna	Sire	12
16	16	LOVERBOY Billy Ocean	Jive	4
31	17	THINKING OF YOU Colourfield	Chrysalis	2
-	18	THINGS CAN ONLY GET BETTER Howard Jones	WEA	1
32	19	NIGHTSHIFT Commodores	Motown	2
13	20	FRIENDS Amii Stewart	RCA	5
11	21	EVERYTHING SHE WANTS/LAST CHRISTMAS Wham!	Epic	9
-	22	THIS IS NOT AMERICA David Bowie and the Pat Metheny Group ●	EMI America	1
25	23	WE BELONG Pat Benatar	Chrysalis	3
14	24	THIS IS MY NIGHT Chaka Khan	Warner Brothers	4
36	25	THIS HOUSE (IS WHERE YOUR LOVE STANDS) Big Sound Authority	Source	2
20	26	GHOSTBUSTERS Ray Parker Jr	Arista	21
24	27	THANK YOU MY LOVE Imagination	R&B	5
15	28	STEP OFF (PART 1) Grandmaster Melle Mel and the Furious Five	Sugarhill	7
30	[29]	CAN I Cashmere	Fourth & Broadway	4
17	30	DO THEY KNOW IT'S CHRISTMAS Band Aid	Mercury	9
23	31	SAY YEAH Limit	Portrait	5
-	32	LOVE LIKE BLOOD Killing Joke ●	EG	1
28	33	SAN DAMIANO (HEART AND SOUL) Sal Solo	MCA	6
-	34	YOU'RE THE INSPIRATION Chicago	Full Moon	1
-	35	HOW SOON IS NOW Smiths	Rough Trade	1
27	36	POLICE OFFICER Smiley Culture	Fashion	7
34	37	I HEAR TALK Bucks Fizz	RCA	4
-	38	PERSONALITY/LET HER FEEL IT Eugene Wilde/Simplicious ●	Fourth & Broadway	1
40	39	20/20 George Benson	Warner Brothers	3
-	40	YOU SPIN ME ROUND (LIKE A RECORD) Dead Or Alive	Epic	1

■ Only four records are peaking as everything slides down the chart (02.02.85) ■ The Commodores are back in the chart for the first time since 26 July 1980 (02.02.85) ■ *You Spin Me Round (Like A Record)* finally makes the Top 40 after ten weeks bubbling under (09.02.85) ■

February 1985

□ Highest position disc reached ● Act's first ever week on chart

LW	TW	*WEEK ENDING* **16 FEBRUARY 1985**		Wks
1	1	I KNOW HIM SO WELL Elaine Paige and Barbara Dickson	*RCA*	6
2	2	LOVE AND PRIDE King	*CBS*	5
4	3	SOLID Ashford and Simpson	*Capitol*	5
6	4	DANCING IN THE DARK Bruce Springsteen	*CBS*	5
3	5	I WANT TO KNOW WHAT LOVE IS Foreigner	*Atlantic*	9
5	6	1999/LITTLE RED CORVETTE Prince	*Warner Brothers*	5
18	7	THINGS CAN ONLY GET BETTER Howard Jones	*WEA*	2
7	8	ATMOSPHERE Russ Abbot	*Spirit*	6
10	9	CLOSE (TO THE EDIT) Art Of Noise	*ZTT*	5
13	10	A NEW ENGLAND Kirsty MacColl	*Stiff*	4
11	11	RUN TO YOU Bryan Adams	*A&M*	4
12	12	SUSSUDIO Phil Collins	*Virgin*	4
17	13	THINKING OF YOU Colourfield	*Chrysalis*	3
22	14	THIS IS NOT AMERICA David Bowie and the Pat Metheny Group	*EMI America*	2
16	15	LOVERBOY Billy Ocean	*Jive*	5
8	16	SHOUT Tears For Fears	*Mercury*	11
19	17	NIGHTSHIFT Commodores	*Motown*	3
9	18	SINCE YESTERDAY Strawberry Switchblade	*Korova*	6
40	19	YOU SPIN ME ROUND (LIKE A RECORD) Dead Or Alive	*Epic*	2
34	20	YOU'RE THE INSPIRATION Chicago	*Full Moon*	2
25	21	THIS HOUSE (IS WHERE YOUR LOVE STANDS) Big Sound Authority	*Source*	3
23	22	WE BELONG Pat Benatar	*Chrysalis*	4
15	23	LIKE A VIRGIN Madonna	*Sire*	13
32	24	LOVE LIKE BLOOD Killing Joke	*EG*	2
14	25	YAH MO B THERE James Ingram with Michael McDonald	*Qwest*	5
35	26	HOW SOON IS NOW Smiths	*Rough Trade*	2
20	27	FRIENDS Amii Stewart	*RCA*	6
-	28	CHANGE YOUR MIND Sharpe and Numan ●	*Polydor*	1
27	29	THANK YOU MY LOVE Imagination	*R&B*	6
29	30	CAN I Cashmere	*Fourth & Broadway*	5
39	31	20/20 George Benson	*Warner Brothers*	4
26	32	GHOSTBUSTERS Ray Parker Jr	*Arista*	22
21	33	EVERYTHING SHE WANTS/LAST CHRISTMAS Wham!	*Epic*	10
38	34	PERSONALITY/LET HER FEEL IT Eugene Wilde/Simplicious	*Fourth & Broadway*	2
24	35	THIS IS MY NIGHT Chaka Khan	*Warner Brothers*	5
-	36	MISLED Kool and the Gang	*De-Lite*	1
28	37	STEP OFF (PART 1) Grandmaster Melle Mel and the Furious Five	*Sugarhill*	8
30	38	DO THEY KNOW IT'S CHRISTMAS Band Aid	*Mercury*	10
-	39	THE BOYS OF SUMMER Don Henley ●	*Geffen*	1
31	40	SAY YEAH Limit	*Portrait*	6

LW	TW	*WEEK ENDING* **23 FEBRUARY 1985**		Wks
1	1	I KNOW HIM SO WELL Elaine Paige and Barbara Dickson	*RCA*	7
2	2	LOVE AND PRIDE King	*CBS*	6
3	3	SOLID Ashford and Simpson	*Capitol*	6
4	4	DANCING IN THE DARK Bruce Springsteen	*CBS*	6
19	5	YOU SPIN ME ROUND (LIKE A RECORD) Dead Or Alive	*Epic*	3
7	6	THINGS CAN ONLY GET BETTER Howard Jones	*WEA*	3
10	7	A NEW ENGLAND Kirsty MacColl	*Stiff*	5
9	8	CLOSE (TO THE EDIT) Art Of Noise	*ZTT*	6
17	9	NIGHTSHIFT Commodores	*Motown*	4
6	10	1999/LITTLE RED CORVETTE Prince	*Warner Brothers*	6
11	11	RUN TO YOU Bryan Adams	*A&M*	5
10	12	I WANT TO KNOW WHAT LOVE IS Foreigner	*Atlantic*	10
13	13	THINKING OF YOU Colourfield	*Chrysalis*	4
20	14	YOU'RE THE INSPIRATION Chicago	*Full Moon*	3
8	15	ATMOSPHERE Russ Abbot	*Spirit*	7
15	16	LOVERBOY Billy Ocean	*Jive*	6
14	17	THIS IS NOT AMERICA David Bowie and the Pat Metheny Group	*EMI America*	3
12	18	SUSSUDIO Phil Collins	*Virgin*	5
24	19	LOVE LIKE BLOOD Killing Joke	*EG*	3
28	20	CHANGE YOUR MIND Sharpe and Numan	*Polydor*	2
21	21	THIS HOUSE (IS WHERE YOUR LOVE STANDS) Big Sound Authority	*Source*	4
39	22	THE BOYS OF SUMMER Don Henley	*Geffen*	2
16	23	SHOUT Tears For Fears	*Mercury*	12
26	24	HOW SOON IS NOW Smiths	*Rough Trade*	3
18	25	SINCE YESTERDAY Strawberry Switchblade	*Korova*	7
22	26	WE BELONG Pat Benatar	*Chrysalis*	5
-	27	LET'S GO CRAZY/TAKE ME WITH U Prince and the Revolution	*Paisley Park*	1
36	28	MISLED Kool and the Gang	*De-Lite*	2
31	29	20/20 George Benson	*Warner Brothers*	5
-	30	THEME FROM SHAFT Eddy and the Soul Band ●	*Club*	1
23	31	LIKE A VIRGIN Madonna	*Sire*	14
30	32	CAN I Cashmere	*Fourth & Broadway*	6
25	33	YAH MO B THERE James Ingram with Michael McDonald	*Qwest*	6
34	34	PERSONALITY/LET HER FEEL IT Eugene Wilde/Simplicious	*Fourth & Broadway*	3
32	35	GHOSTBUSTERS Ray Parker Jr	*Arista*	23
27	36	FRIENDS Amii Stewart	*RCA*	7
38	37	DO THEY KNOW IT'S CHRISTMAS Band Aid	*Mercury*	11
33	38	EVERYTHING SHE WANTS/LAST CHRISTMAS Wham!	*Epic*	11
-	39	JUST ANOTHER NIGHT Mick Jagger	*CBS*	1
29	40	THANK YOU MY LOVE Imagination	*R&B*	7

LW	TW	*WEEK ENDING* **2 MARCH 1985**		Wks
1	1	I KNOW HIM SO WELL Elaine Paige and Barbara Dickson	*RCA*	8
5	2	YOU SPIN ME ROUND (LIKE A RECORD) Dead Or Alive	*Epic*	4
2	3	LOVE AND PRIDE King	*CBS*	7
3	4	SOLID Ashford and Simpson	*Capitol*	7
4	5	DANCING IN THE DARK Bruce Springsteen	*CBS*	7
9	6	NIGHTSHIFT Commodores	*Motown*	5
6	7	THINGS CAN ONLY GET BETTER Howard Jones	*WEA*	4
7	8	A NEW ENGLAND Kirsty MacColl	*Stiff*	6
27	9	LET'S GO CRAZY/TAKE ME WITH U Prince and the Revolution	*Paisley Park*	2
8	10	CLOSE (TO THE EDIT) Art Of Noise	*ZTT*	7
11	11	RUN TO YOU Bryan Adams	*A&M*	6
13	12	THINKING OF YOU Colourfield	*Chrysalis*	5
22	13	THE BOYS OF SUMMER Don Henley	*Geffen*	3
14	14	YOU'RE THE INSPIRATION Chicago	*Full Moon*	4
10	15	1999/LITTLE RED CORVETTE Prince	*Warner Brothers*	7
19	16	LOVE LIKE BLOOD Killing Joke	*EG*	4
20	17	CHANGE YOUR MIND Sharpe and Numan	*Polydor*	3
16	18	LOVERBOY Billy Ocean	*Jive*	7
30	19	THEME FROM SHAFT Eddy and the Soul Band	*Club*	2
15	20	ATMOSPHERE Russ Abbot	*Spirit*	8
12	21	I WANT TO KNOW WHAT LOVE IS Foreigner	*Atlantic*	11
-	22	KISS ME Stephen 'Tin Tin' Duffy ●	*10*	1
17	23	THIS IS NOT AMERICA David Bowie and the Pat Metheny Group	*EMI America*	4
-	24	MATERIAL GIRL Madonna	*Sire*	1
18	25	SUSSUDIO Phil Collins	*Virgin*	6
-	26	LEGS ZZ Top	*Warner Brothers*	1
21	27	THIS HOUSE (IS WHERE YOUR LOVE STANDS) Big Sound Authority	*Source*	5
24	28	HOW SOON IS NOW Smiths	*Rough Trade*	4
23	29	SHOUT Tears For Fears	*Mercury*	13
-	30	BREAKING UP MY HEART Shakin' Stevens	*Epic*	1
35	31	GHOSTBUSTERS Ray Parker Jr	*Arista*	24
28	32	MISLED Kool and the Gang	*De-Lite*	3
-	33	METHOD OF MODERN LOVE Daryl Hall and John Oates	*RCA*	1
-	34	THE LAST KISS David Cassidy	*Arista*	1
39	35	JUST ANOTHER NIGHT Mick Jagger	*CBS*	2
-	36	WHO COMES TO BOOGIE Little Benny and the Masters ●	*Bluebird*	1
26	37	WE BELONG Pat Benatar	*Chrysalis*	6
31	38	LIKE A VIRGIN Madonna	*Sire*	15
-	39	DO WHAT YOU DO Jermaine Jackson	*Arista*	1
25	40	SINCE YESTERDAY Strawberry Switchblade	*Korova*	8

In these weeks ■ There are no less than eight duos in the chart (16.02.85) ■ There is a log jam as seven of the top ten records are at their highest position (23.02.85) ■ Madonna and Prince both have two records in the Top 40 (02.03.85)■

March 1985

□ Highest position disc reached ● Act's first ever week on chart

WEEK ENDING 9 MARCH 1985

LW	TW	Title	Artist	Label	Wks
2	1	YOU SPIN ME ROUND (LIKE A RECORD)	Dead Or Alive	Epic	5
1	2	I KNOW HIM SO WELL	Elaine Paige and Barbara Dickson	RCA	9
6	3	NIGHTSHIFT	Commodores	Motown	6
22	4	KISS ME	Stephen 'Tin Tin' Duffy	10	2
24	5	MATERIAL GIRL	Madonna	Sire	2
4	6	SOLID	Ashford and Simpson	Capitol	8
9	7	LET'S GO CRAZY/TAKE ME WITH U	Prince and the Revolution	Paisley Park	3
3	8	LOVE AND PRIDE	King	CBS	8
5	9	DANCING IN THE DARK	Bruce Springsteen	CBS	8
7	10	THINGS CAN ONLY GET BETTER	Howard Jones	WEA	5
34	11	THE LAST KISS	David Cassidy	Arista	2
13	12	THE BOYS OF SUMMER	Don Henley	Geffen	4
19	13	THEME FROM SHAFT	Eddy and the Soul Band	Club	3
8	14	A NEW ENGLAND	Kirsty MacColl	Stiff	7
30	15	BREAKING UP MY HEART	Shakin' Stevens	Epic	2
26	16	LEGS	ZZ Top	Warner Brothers	2
11	17	RUN TO YOU	Bryan Adams	A&M	7
39	18	DO WHAT YOU DO	Jermaine Jackson	Arista	2
16	19	LOVE LIKE BLOOD	Killing Joke	EG	5
-	20	EASY LOVER	Philip Bailey (duet with Phil Collins) ●	CBS/Virgin	1
10	21	CLOSE (TO THE EDIT)	Art Of Noise	ZTT	8
12	22	THINKING OF YOU	Colourfield	Chrysalis	6
14	23	YOU'RE THE INSPIRATION	Chicago	Full Moon	5
17	24	CHANGE YOUR MIND	Sharpe and Numan	Polydor	4
33	25	METHOD OF MODERN LOVE	Daryl Hall and John Oates	RCA	2
-	26	EVERY TIME YOU GO AWAY	Paul Young	CBS	1
18	27	LOVERBOY	Billy Ocean	Jive	8
15	28	1999/LITTLE RED CORVETTE	Prince	Warner Brothers	8
23	29	THIS IS NOT AMERICA	David Bowie and the Pat Metheny Group	EMI America	5
21	30	I WANT TO KNOW WHAT LOVE IS	Foreigner	Atlantic	12
-	31	WE CLOSE OUR EYES	Go West ●	Chrysalis	1
35	32	JUST ANOTHER NIGHT	Mick Jagger	CBS	3
36	33	WHO COMES TO BOOGIE	Little Benny and the Masters	Bluebird	2
25	34	SUSSUDIO	Phil Collins	Virgin	7
20	35	ATMOSPHERE	Russ Abbot	Spirit	9
27	36	THIS HOUSE (IS WHERE YOUR LOVE STANDS)	Big Sound Authority	Source	6
-	37	HANGIN' ON A STRING (CONTEMPLATING)	Loose Ends ●	Virgin	1
-	38	FALLING ANGELS RIDING	David Essex	Mercury	1
-	39	THE BELLE OF ST MARK	Sheila E ●	Warner Brothers	1
-	40	MR TELEPHONE MAN	New Edition	MCA	1

WEEK ENDING 16 MARCH 1985

LW	TW	Title	Artist	Label	Wks
2	1	YOU SPIN ME ROUND (LIKE A RECORD)	Dead Or Alive	Epic	6
20	2	EASY LOVER	Philip Bailey (duet with Phil Collins)	CBS/Virgin	2
5	3	MATERIAL GIRL	Madonna	Sire	3
4	4	KISS ME	Stephen 'Tin Tin' Duffy	10	3
3	5	NIGHTSHIFT	Commodores	Motown	7
11	6	THE LAST KISS	David Cassidy	Arista	3
18	7	DO WHAT YOU DO	Jermaine Jackson	Arista	3
2	8	I KNOW HIM SO WELL	Elaine Paige and Barbara Dickson	RCA	10
26	9	EVERY TIME YOU GO AWAY	Paul Young	CBS	2
7	10	LET'S GO CRAZY/TAKE ME WITH U	Prince and the Revolution	Paisley Park	4
-	11	THAT OLE DEVIL CALLED LOVE	Alison Moyet	CBS	1
6	12	SOLID	Ashford and Simpson	Capitol	9
9	13	DANCING IN THE DARK	Bruce Springsteen	CBS	9
15	14	BREAKING UP MY HEART	Shakin' Stevens	Epic	3
-	15	WIDE BOY	Nik Kershaw	MCA	1
31	16	WE CLOSE OUR EYES	Go West	Chrysalis	2
8	17	LOVE AND PRIDE	King	CBS	9
16	18	LEGS	ZZ Top	Warner Brothers	3
10	19	THINGS CAN ONLY GET BETTER	Howard Jones	WEA	6
12	20	THE BOYS OF SUMMER	Don Henley	Geffen	5
25	21	METHOD OF MODERN LOVE	Daryl Hall and John Oates	RCA	3
37	22	HANGIN' ON A STRING (CONTEMPLATING)	Loose Ends	Virgin	2
13	23	THEME FROM SHAFT	Eddy and the Soul Band	Club	4
39	24	THE BELLE OF ST MARK	Sheila E	Warner Brothers	2
14	25	A NEW ENGLAND	Kirsty MacColl	Stiff	8
40	26	MR TELEPHONE MAN	New Edition	MCA	2
17	27	RUN TO YOU	Bryan Adams	A&M	8
19	28	LOVE LIKE BLOOD	Killing Joke	EG	6
38	29	FALLING ANGELS RIDING	David Essex	Mercury	2
22	30	THINKING OF YOU	Colourfield	Chrysalis	7
23	31	YOU'RE THE INSPIRATION	Chicago	Full Moon	6
24	32	CHANGE YOUR MIND	Sharpe and Numan	Polydor	5
-	33	BETWEEN THE WARS (EP)	Billy Bragg ●	Go! Discs	1
21	34	CLOSE (TO THE EDIT)	Art Of Noise	ZTT	9
27	35	LOVERBOY	Billy Ocean	Jive	9
-	36	STARVATION/TAM TAM POUR L'ETHIOPIE	Starvation ●	Zarjazz	1
-	37	SOME LIKE IT HOT	Power Station ●	Parlophone	1
32	38	JUST ANOTHER NIGHT	Mick Jagger	CBS	4
28	39	1999/LITTLE RED CORVETTE	Prince	Warner Brothers	9
-	40	ABSOLUTE REALITY	Alarm	IRS	1

WEEK ENDING 23 MARCH 1985

LW	TW	Title	Artist	Label	Wks
2	1	EASY LOVER	Philip Bailey (duet with Phil Collins)	CBS/Virgin	3
11	2	THAT OLE DEVIL CALLED LOVE	Alison Moyet	CBS	2
3	3	MATERIAL GIRL	Madonna	Sire	4
9	4	EVERY TIME YOU GO AWAY	Paul Young	CBS	3
4	5	KISS ME	Stephen 'Tin Tin' Duffy	10	4
1	6	YOU SPIN ME ROUND (LIKE A RECORD)	Dead Or Alive	Epic	7
7	7	DO WHAT YOU DO	Jermaine Jackson	Arista	4
6	8	THE LAST KISS	David Cassidy	Arista	4
16	9	WE CLOSE OUR EYES	Go West	Chrysalis	3
8	10	I KNOW HIM SO WELL	Elaine Paige and Barbara Dickson	RCA	11
5	11	NIGHTSHIFT	Commodores	Motown	8
15	12	WIDE BOY	Nik Kershaw	MCA	2
13	13	DANCING IN THE DARK	Bruce Springsteen	CBS	10
-	14	PIE JESU	Sarah Brightman and Paul Miles-Kingston ●	HMV	1
33	15	BETWEEN THE WARS (EP)	Billy Bragg	Go! Discs	2
10	16	LET'S GO CRAZY/TAKE ME WITH U	Prince and the Revolution	Paisley Park	5
37	17	SOME LIKE IT HOT	Power Station	Parlophone	2
24	18	THE BELLE OF ST MARK	Sheila E	Warner Brothers	3
26	19	MR TELEPHONE MAN	New Edition	MCA	3
22	20	HANGIN' ON A STRING (CONTEMPLATING)	Loose Ends	Virgin	3
12	21	SOLID	Ashford and Simpson	Capitol	10
14	22	BREAKING UP MY HEART	Shakin' Stevens	Epic	4
20	23	THE BOYS OF SUMMER	Don Henley	Geffen	6
17	24	LOVE AND PRIDE	King	CBS	10
-	25	DANCING IN THE DARK (EP)	Big Daddy ●	Making Waves	1
21	26	METHOD OF MODERN LOVE	Daryl Hall and John Oates	RCA	4
23	27	THEME FROM SHAFT	Eddy and the Soul Band	Club	5
-	28	MOVE CLOSER	Phyllis Nelson ●	Carrere	1
18	29	LEGS	ZZ Top	Warner Brothers	4
19	30	THINGS CAN ONLY GET BETTER	Howard Jones	WEA	7
29	31	FALLING ANGELS RIDING	David Essex	Mercury	3
-	32	COVER ME	Bruce Springsteen	CBS	1
36	33	STARVATION/TAM TAM POUR L'ETHIOPIE	Starvation	Zarjazz	2
-	34	THE HEAT IS ON	Glenn Frey ●	MCA	1
40	35	ABSOLUTE REALITY	Alarm	IRS	2
27	36	RUN TO YOU	Bryan Adams	A&M	9
-	37	NOW THAT WE'VE FOUND LOVE	Third World	Island	1
-	38	WON'T YOU HOLD MY HAND NOW	King	CBS	1

■Sheila E plays drums on Prince's hit at seven and enters with her own solo hit at 39 (09.03.85) ■ David Cassidy's first week in the Top Ten since 11 May 74 (16.03.85) ■ Two versions of Springsteen's *Dancing In The Dark* are charting. 'The Boss' also has *Cover Me* from the 'Born In The USA' album entering at 32 (23.03.85)■

March 1985

□ Highest position disc reached ● Act's first ever week on chart

LW	TW	Title / Artist	Label	Wks
-	39	COULD IT BE I'M FALLING IN LOVE David Grant and Jaki Graham ●	Chrysalis	1
-	40	SPEND THE NIGHT Cool Notes ●	Abstract Dance	1

WEEK ENDING 30 MARCH 1985

LW	TW	Title / Artist	Label	Wks
1	1	EASY LOVER Philip Bailey (duet with Phil Collins)	CBS/Virgin	4
2	2	THAT OLE DEVIL CALLED LOVE Alison Moyet	CBS	3
14	3	PIE JESU Sarah Brightman and Paul Miles-Kingston	HMV	2
4	4	EVERY TIME YOU GO AWAY Paul Young	CBS	4
-	5	WELCOME TO THE PLEASURE DOME Frankie Goes To Hollywood	ZTT	1
7	6	DO WHAT YOU DO Jermaine Jackson	Arista	5
3	7	MATERIAL GIRL Madonna	Sire	5
9	8	WE CLOSE OUR EYES Go West	Chrysalis	4
5	9	KISS ME Stephen 'Tin Tin' Duffy	10	5
12	10	WIDE BOY Nik Kershaw	MCA	3
8	11	THE LAST KISS David Cassidy	Arista	5
6	12	YOU SPIN ME ROUND (LIKE A RECORD) Dead Or Alive	Epic	8
20	13	HANGIN' ON A STRING (CONTEMPLATING) Loose Ends	Virgin	4
17	14	SOME LIKE IT HOT Power Station	Parlophone	3
15	15	BETWEEN THE WARS (EP) Billy Bragg	Go! Discs	3
-	16	EVERYBODY WANTS TO RULE THE WORLD Tears For Fears	Mercury	1
11	17	NIGHTSHIFT Commodores	Motown	9
32	18	COVER ME Bruce Springsteen	CBS	2
28	19	MOVE CLOSER Phyllis Nelson	Carrere	2
19	20	MR TELEPHONE MAN New Edition	MCA	4
25	21	DANCING IN THE DARK (EP) Big Daddy	Making Waves	2
18	22	THE BELLE OF ST MARK Sheila E	Warner Brothers	4
34	23	THE HEAT IS ON Glenn Frey	MCA	2
39	24	COULD IT BE I'M FALLING IN LOVE David Grant and Jaki Graham	Chrysalis	2
37	25	NOW THAT WE'VE FOUND LOVE Third World	Island	2
38	26	WON'T YOU HOLD MY HAND NOW King	CBS	2
13	27	DANCING IN THE DARK Bruce Springsteen	CBS	11
10	28	I KNOW HIM SO WELL Elaine Paige and Barbara Dickson	RCA	12
-	29	SHAKESPEARE'S SISTER Smiths	Rough Trade	1
16	30	LET'S GO CRAZY/TAKE ME WITH U Prince and the Revolution	Paisley Park	6
40	31	SPEND THE NIGHT Cool Notes	Abstract Dance	2
21	32	SOLID Ashford and Simpson	Capitol	11
-	33	GRIMLY FIENDISH Damned	MCA	1
-	34	LOVE IS A BATTLEFIELD Pat Benatar	Chrysalis	1
22	35	BREAKING UP MY HEART Shakin' Stevens	Epic	5
33	36	STARVATION/TAM TAM POUR L'ETHIOPIE Starvation	Zarjazz	3
23	37	THE BOYS OF SUMMER Don Henley	Geffen	7
-	38	CAN'T FIGHT THIS FEELING REO Speedwagon	Epic	1
-	39	SOMEBODY Bryan Adams	A&M	1
-	40	LET'S GO TOGETHER Change	Cooltempo	1

WEEK ENDING 6 APRIL 1985

LW	TW	Title / Artist	Label	Wks
1	1	EASY LOVER Philip Bailey (duet with Phil Collins)	CBS/Virgin	5
5	2	WELCOME TO THE PLEASURE DOME Frankie Goes To Hollywood	ZTT	2
3	3	PIE JESU Sarah Brightman and Paul Miles-Kingston	HMV	3
2	4	THAT OLE DEVIL CALLED LOVE Alison Moyet	CBS	4
16	5	EVERYBODY WANTS TO RULE THE WORLD Tears For Fears	Mercury	2
8	6	WE CLOSE OUR EYES Go West	Chrysalis	5
4	7	EVERY TIME YOU GO AWAY Paul Young	CBS	5
6	8	DO WHAT YOU DO Jermaine Jackson	Arista	6
10	9	WIDE BOY Nik Kershaw	MCA	4
9	10	KISS ME Stephen 'Tin Tin' Duffy	10	6
7	11	MATERIAL GIRL Madonna	Sire	6
24	12	COULD IT BE I'M FALLING IN LOVE David Grant and Jaki Graham	Chrysalis	3
13	13	HANGIN' ON A STRING (CONTEMPLATING) Loose Ends	Virgin	5
19	14	MOVE CLOSER Phyllis Nelson	Carrere	3
14	15	SOME LIKE IT HOT Power Station	Parlophone	4
18	16	COVER ME Bruce Springsteen	CBS	3
23	17	THE HEAT IS ON Glenn Frey	MCA	3
31	18	SPEND THE NIGHT Cool Notes	Abstract Dance	3
11	19	THE LAST KISS David Cassidy	Arista	6
12	20	YOU SPIN ME ROUND (LIKE A RECORD) Dead Or Alive	Epic	9
33	21	GRIMLY FIENDISH Damned	MCA	2
25	22	NOW THAT WE'VE FOUND LOVE Third World	Island	3
21	23	DANCING IN THE DARK (EP) Big Daddy	Making Waves	3
26	24	WON'T YOU HOLD MY HAND NOW King	CBS	3
15	25	BETWEEN THE WARS (EP) Billy Bragg	Go! Discs	4
29	26	SHAKESPEARE'S SISTER Smiths	Rough Trade	2
-	27	CLOUDS ACROSS THE MOON Rah Band	RCA	1
38	28	CAN'T FIGHT THIS FEELING REO Speedwagon	Epic	2
34	29	LOVE IS A BATTLEFIELD Pat Benatar	Chrysalis	2
17	30	NIGHTSHIFT Commodores	Motown	10
22	31	THE BELLE OF ST MARK Sheila E	Warner Brothers	5
20	32	MR TELEPHONE MAN New Edition	MCA	5
27	33	DANCING IN THE DARK Bruce Springsteen	CBS	12
28	34	I KNOW HIM SO WELL Elaine Paige and Barbara Dickson	RCA	13
39	35	SOMEBODY Bryan Adams	A&M	2
-	36	BE NEAR ME ABC	Neutron	1
40	37	LET'S GO TOGETHER Change	Cooltempo	2
-	38	LIFE IN A NORTHERN TOWN Dream Academy ●	blanco y negro	1
-	39	SUPER GRAN Billy Connolly	Stiff	1
-	40	BLACK MAN RAY China Crisis	Virgin	1

WEEK ENDING 13 APRIL 1985

LW	TW	Title / Artist	Label	Wks
1	1	EASY LOVER Philip Bailey (duet with Phil Collins)	CBS/Virgin	6
2	2	WELCOME TO THE PLEASURE DOME Frankie Goes To Hollywood	ZTT	3
5	3	EVERYBODY WANTS TO RULE THE WORLD Tears For Fears	Mercury	3
3	4	PIE JESU Sarah Brightman and Paul Miles-Kingston	HMV	4
6	5	WE CLOSE OUR EYES Go West	Chrysalis	6
4	6	THAT OLE DEVIL CALLED LOVE Alison Moyet	CBS	5
-	7	WE ARE THE WORLD USA For Africa ●	CBS	1
14	8	MOVE CLOSER Phyllis Nelson	Carrere	4
7	9	EVERY TIME YOU GO AWAY Paul Young	CBS	6
12	10	COULD IT BE I'M FALLING IN LOVE David Grant and Jaki Graham	Chrysalis	4
9	11	WIDE BOY Nik Kershaw	MCA	5
8	12	DO WHAT YOU DO Jermaine Jackson	Arista	7
18	13	SPEND THE NIGHT Cool Notes	Abstract Dance	4
17	14	THE HEAT IS ON Glenn Frey	MCA	4
10	15	KISS ME Stephen 'Tin Tin' Duffy	10	7
11	16	MATERIAL GIRL Madonna	Sire	7
13	17	HANGIN' ON A STRING (CONTEMPLATING) Loose Ends	Virgin	6
27	18	CLOUDS ACROSS THE MOON Rah Band	RCA	2
28	19	CAN'T FIGHT THIS FEELING REO Speedwagon	Epic	3
16	20	COVER ME Bruce Springsteen	CBS	4
15	21	SOME LIKE IT HOT Power Station	Parlophone	5
21	22	GRIMLY FIENDISH Damned	MCA	3
29	23	LOVE IS A BATTLEFIELD Pat Benatar	Chrysalis	3
24	24	WON'T YOU HOLD MY HAND NOW King	CBS	4
38	25	LIFE IN A NORTHERN TOWN Dream Academy	blanco y negro	2
36	26	BE NEAR ME ABC	Neutron	2
-	27	ONE MORE NIGHT Phil Collins	Virgin	1
25	28	BETWEEN THE WARS (EP) Billy Bragg	Go! Discs	5
23	29	DANCING IN THE DARK (EP) Big Daddy	Making Waves	4

In these weeks ■ The Smiths chart with a title that will later be put to good use by Siobhan Fahey (30.03.85) ■ After their first three hits made number one, Frankie Goes To Hollywood fail to make the quartet but only by one position (06.04.85) ■ Band Aid American style - USA For Africa crash in at seven (13.04.85)■

LW	TW	Title / Artist	Label	Wks
20	30	YOU SPIN ME ROUND (LIKE A RECORD) Dead Or Alive	*Epic*	10
22	31	NOW THAT WE'VE FOUND LOVE Third World	*Island*	4
40	32	BLACK MAN RAY China Crisis	*Virgin*	2
19	33	THE LAST KISS David Cassidy	*Arista*	7
39	34	SUPER GRAN Billy Connolly	*Stiff*	2
30	35	NIGHTSHIFT Commodores	*Motown*	11
35	36	SOMEBODY Bryan Adams	*A&M*	3
33	37	DANCING IN THE DARK Bruce Springsteen	*CBS*	13
26	38	SHAKESPEARE'S SISTER Smiths	*Rough Trade*	3
-	39	THAT WAS YESTERDAY Foreigner	*Atlantic*	1
37	40	LET'S GO TOGETHER Change	*Cooltempo*	3

LW	TW	*WEEK ENDING* **20 APRIL 1985**		Wks
7	[1]	WE ARE THE WORLD USA For Africa	*CBS*	2
3	[2]	EVERYBODY WANTS TO RULE THE WORLD Tears For Fears	*Mercury*	4
1	3	EASY LOVER Philip Bailey (duet with Phil Collins)	*CBS/Virgin*	7
8	4	MOVE CLOSER Phyllis Nelson	*Carrere*	5
2	5	WELCOME TO THE PLEASURE DOME Frankie Goes To Hollywood	*ZTT*	4
5	6	WE CLOSE OUR EYES Go West	*Chrysalis*	7
10	7	COULD IT BE I'M FALLING IN LOVE David Grant and Jaki Graham	*Chrysalis*	5
27	8	ONE MORE NIGHT Phil Collins	*Virgin*	2
18	9	CLOUDS ACROSS THE MOON Rah Band	*RCA*	3
4	10	PIE JESU Sarah Brightman and Paul Miles-Kingston	*HMV*	5
13	[11]	SPEND THE NIGHT Cool Notes	*Abstract Dance*	5
14	[12]	THE HEAT IS ON Glenn Frey	*MCA*	5
9	13	EVERY TIME YOU GO AWAY Paul Young	*CBS*	7
6	14	THAT OLE DEVIL CALLED LOVE Alison Moyet	*CBS*	6
25	[15]	LIFE IN A NORTHERN TOWN Dream Academy	*blanco y negro*	3
19	[16]	CAN'T FIGHT THIS FEELING REO Speedwagon	*Epic*	4
23	[17]	LOVE IS A BATTLEFIELD Pat Benatar	*Chrysalis*	4
11	18	WIDE BOY Nik Kershaw	*MCA*	6
32	19	BLACK MAN RAY China Crisis	*Virgin*	3
-	20	LOOK MAMA Howard Jones	*WEA*	1
12	21	DO WHAT YOU DO Jermaine Jackson	*Arista*	8
-	22	DON'T YOU (FORGET ABOUT ME) Simple Minds	*Virgin*	1
-	23	LOVER COME BACK TO ME Dead Or Alive	*Epic*	1
-	24	I FEEL LOVE (MEDLEY) Bronski Beat and Marc Almond ●	*Forbidden Fruit*	1
24	25	WON'T YOU HOLD MY HAND NOW King	*CBS*	5
22	26	GRIMLY FIENDISH Damned	*MCA*	4
15	27	KISS ME Stephen 'Tin Tin' Duffy	*10*	8
21	28	SOME LIKE IT HOT Power Station	*Parlophone*	6
17	29	HANGIN' ON A STRING (CONTEMPLATING) Loose Ends	*Virgin*	7
39	30	THAT WAS YESTERDAY Foreigner	*Atlantic*	2
16	31	MATERIAL GIRL Madonna	*Sire*	8
34	[32]	SUPER GRAN Billy Connolly	*Stiff*	3
26	33	BE NEAR ME ABC	*Neutron*	3
20	34	COVER ME Bruce Springsteen	*CBS*	5
31	35	NOW THAT WE'VE FOUND LOVE Third World	*Island*	5
30	36	YOU SPIN ME ROUND (LIKE A RECORD) Dead Or Alive	*Epic*	11
36	37	SOMEBODY Bryan Adams	*A&M*	4
-	38	SO FAR AWAY Dire Straits	*Vertigo*	1
-	39	STAINSBY GIRLS Chris Rea	*Magnet*	1
-	40	EYE TO EYE Chaka Khan	*Warner Brothers*	1

LW	TW	*WEEK ENDING* **27 APRIL 1985**		Wks
1	[1]	WE ARE THE WORLD USA For Africa	*CBS*	3
2	[2]	EVERYBODY WANTS TO RULE THE WORLD Tears For Fears	*Mercury*	5
4	3	MOVE CLOSER Phyllis Nelson	*Carrere*	6
8	[4]	ONE MORE NIGHT Phil Collins	*Virgin*	3
7	[5]	COULD IT BE I'M FALLING IN LOVE David Grant and Jaki Graham	*Chrysalis*	6
9	[6]	CLOUDS ACROSS THE MOON Rah Band	*RCA*	4
24	7	I FEEL LOVE (MEDLEY) Bronski Beat and Marc Almond	*Forbidden Fruit*	2
22	8	DON'T YOU (FORGET ABOUT ME) Simple Minds	*Virgin*	2
6	9	WE CLOSE OUR EYES Go West	*Chrysalis*	8
20	[10]	LOOK MAMA Howard Jones	*WEA*	2
23	[11]	LOVER COME BACK TO ME Dead Or Alive	*Epic*	2
5	12	WELCOME TO THE PLEASURE DOME Frankie Goes To Hollywood	*ZTT*	5
3	13	EASY LOVER Philip Bailey (duet with Phil Collins)	*CBS/Virgin*	8
19	[14]	BLACK MAN RAY China Crisis	*Virgin*	4
15	[15]	LIFE IN A NORTHERN TOWN Dream Academy	*blanco y negro*	4
11	16	SPEND THE NIGHT Cool Notes	*Abstract Dance*	6
17	[17]	LOVE IS A BATTLEFIELD Pat Benatar	*Chrysalis*	5
12	18	THE HEAT IS ON Glenn Frey	*MCA*	6
40	19	EYE TO EYE Chaka Khan	*Warner Brothers*	2
-	20	FEEL SO REAL Steve Arrington ●	*Atlantic*	1
16	21	CAN'T FIGHT THIS FEELING REO Speedwagon	*Epic*	5
38	22	SO FAR AWAY Dire Straits	*Vertigo*	2
-	23	I WAS BORN TO LOVE YOU Freddie Mercury	*CBS*	1
14	24	THAT OLE DEVIL CALLED LOVE Alison Moyet	*CBS*	7
13	25	EVERY TIME YOU GO AWAY Paul Young	*CBS*	8
10	26	PIE JESU Sarah Brightman and Paul Miles-Kingston	*HMV*	6
39	27	STAINSBY GIRLS Chris Rea	*Magnet*	2
30	[28]	THAT WAS YESTERDAY Foreigner	*Atlantic*	3
18	29	WIDE BOY Nik Kershaw	*MCA*	7
26	30	GRIMLY FIENDISH Damned	*MCA*	5
-	31	WOULD I LIE TO YOU Eurythmics	*RCA*	1
29	32	HANGIN' ON A STRING (CONTEMPLATING) Loose Ends	*Virgin*	8
25	33	WON'T YOU HOLD MY HAND NOW King	*CBS*	6
-	34	RHYTHM OF THE NIGHT DeBarge ●	*Gordy*	1
32	35	SUPER GRAN Billy Connolly	*Stiff*	4
-	36	NO REST New Model Army ●	*EMI*	1
-	37	CRY Godley and Creme	*Polydor*	1
21	38	DO WHAT YOU DO Jermaine Jackson	*Arista*	9
-	39	I WANT YOUR LOVIN' (JUST A LITTLE BIT) Curtis Hairston ●	*London*	1
27	40	KISS ME Stephen 'Tin Tin' Duffy	*10*	9

M a y   1 9 8 5

☐ Highest position disc reached ● Act's first ever week on chart

LW	TW	*WEEK ENDING* **4 MAY 1985**		Wks
3	[1]	MOVE CLOSER Phyllis Nelson	*Carrere*	7
1	2	WE ARE THE WORLD USA For Africa	*CBS*	4
2	3	EVERYBODY WANTS TO RULE THE WORLD Tears For Fears	*Mercury*	6
-	4	19 Paul Hardcastle ●	*Chrysalis*	1
7	5	I FEEL LOVE (MEDLEY) Bronski Beat and Marc Almond	*Forbidden Fruit*	3
4	6	ONE MORE NIGHT Phil Collins	*Virgin*	4
8	[7]	DON'T YOU (FORGET ABOUT ME) Simple Minds	*Virgin*	3
-	8	THE UNFORGETTABLE FIRE U2	*Island*	1
6	9	CLOUDS ACROSS THE MOON Rah Band	*RCA*	5
5	10	COULD IT BE I'M FALLING IN LOVE David Grant and Jaki Graham	*Chrysalis*	7
20	11	FEEL SO REAL Steve Arrington	*Atlantic*	2
11	12	LOVER COME BACK TO ME Dead Or Alive	*Epic*	3
10	13	LOOK MAMA Howard Jones	*WEA*	3
23	14	I WAS BORN TO LOVE YOU Freddie Mercury	*CBS*	2
14	15	BLACK MAN RAY China Crisis	*Virgin*	5
19	[16]	EYE TO EYE Chaka Khan	*Warner Brothers*	3
34	17	RHYTHM OF THE NIGHT DeBarge	*Gordy*	2
9	18	WE CLOSE OUR EYES Go West	*Chrysalis*	9
13	19	EASY LOVER Philip Bailey (duet with Phil Collins)	*CBS/Virgin*	9
22	[20]	SO FAR AWAY Dire Straits	*Vertigo*	3
16	21	SPEND THE NIGHT Cool Notes	*Abstract Dance*	7
39	22	I WANT YOUR LOVIN' (JUST A LITTLE BIT) Curtis Hairston	*London*	2

■Duran Duran spin-off, The Power Station, sit next to former Duran Duran vocalist, Stephen 'Tin Tin' Duffy (20.04.85) ■ King are joined in the chart by Queen vocalist Freddie Mercury (27.04.85) ■ Paul Hardcastle's first week in the Top 40 is with a Top Five position (04.05.85)■

May 1985

□ Highest position disc reached ● Act's first ever week on chart

LW	TW	Title	Artist	Label	Wks
17	23	LOVE IS A BATTLEFIELD	Pat Benatar	*Chrysalis*	5
12	24	WELCOME TO THE PLEASURE DOME	Frankie Goes To Hollywood	*ZTT*	6
31	25	WOULD I LIE TO YOU	Eurythmics	*RCA*	2
15	26	LIFE IN A NORTHERN TOWN	Dream Academy	*blanco y negro*	5
27	27	STAINSBY GIRLS	Chris Rea	*Magnet*	3
18	28	THE HEAT IS ON	Glenn Frey	*MCA*	7
37	29	CRY	Godley and Creme	*Polydor*	2
36	30	NO REST	New Model Army	*EMI*	2
21	31	CAN'T FIGHT THIS FEELING	REO Speedwagon	*Epic*	6
-	32	DON'T FALL IN LOVE (I SAID)	Toyah	*Portrait*	1
-	33	WALK LIKE A MAN	Divine	*Proto*	1
28	34	THAT WAS YESTERDAY	Foreigner	*Atlantic*	4
24	35	THAT OLE DEVIL CALLED LOVE	Alison Moyet	*CBS*	8
25	36	EVERY TIME YOU GO AWAY	Paul Young	*CBS*	9
26	37	PIE JESU	Sarah Brightman and Paul Miles-Kingston	*HMV*	7
-	38	RAGE TO LOVE	Kim Wilde	*MCA*	1
-	39	LOVE DON'T LIVE HERE ANYMORE	Jimmy Nail ●	*Virgin*	1
-	40	FREE YOURSELF	Untouchables ●	*Stiff*	1

WEEK ENDING 11 MAY 1985

LW	TW	Title	Artist	Label	Wks
4	[1]	19	Paul Hardcastle	*Chrysalis*	2
1	2	MOVE CLOSER	Phyllis Nelson	*Carrere*	8
5	[3]	I FEEL LOVE (MEDLEY)	Bronski Beat and Marc Almond	*Forbidden Fruit*	4
3	4	EVERYBODY WANTS TO RULE THE WORLD	Tears For Fears	*Mercury*	7
2	5	WE ARE THE WORLD	USA For Africa	*CBS*	5
8	[6]	THE UNFORGETTABLE FIRE	U2	*Island*	2
11	7	FEEL SO REAL	Steve Arrington	*Atlantic*	3
7	8	DON'T YOU (FORGET ABOUT ME)	Simple Minds	*Virgin*	4
17	9	RHYTHM OF THE NIGHT	DeBarge	*Gordy*	3
6	10	ONE MORE NIGHT	Phil Collins	*Virgin*	5
14	[11]	I WAS BORN TO LOVE YOU	Freddie Mercury	*CBS*	3
9	12	CLOUDS ACROSS THE MOON	Rah Band	*RCA*	6
-	13	WALLS COME TUMBLING DOWN	Style Council	*Polydor*	1
12	14	LOVER COME BACK TO ME	Dead Or Alive	*Epic*	4
10	15	COULD IT BE I'M FALLING IN LOVE	David Grant and Jaki Graham	*Chrysalis*	8
22	16	I WANT YOUR LOVIN' (JUST A LITTLE BIT)	Curtis Hairston	*London*	3
25	[17]	WOULD I LIE TO YOU	Eurythmics	*RCA*	3
13	18	LOOK MAMA	Howard Jones	*WEA*	4
29	[19]	CRY	Godley and Creme	*Polydor*	3
39	20	LOVE DON'T LIVE HERE ANYMORE	Jimmy Nail	*Virgin*	2
16	21	EYE TO EYE	Chaka Khan	*Warner Brothers*	4
32	[22]	DON'T FALL IN LOVE (I SAID)	Toyah	*Portrait*	2
20	23	SO FAR AWAY	Dire Straits	*Vertigo*	4
15	24	BLACK MAN RAY	China Crisis	*Virgin*	6
33	25	WALK LIKE A MAN	Divine	*Proto*	2
27	[26]	STAINSBY GIRLS	Chris Rea	*Magnet*	4
18	27	WE CLOSE OUR EYES	Go West	*Chrysalis*	10
30	[28]	NO REST	New Model Army	*EMI*	3
38	29	RAGE TO LOVE	Kim Wilde	*MCA*	2
-	30	SLAVE TO LOVE	Bryan Ferry	*EG*	1
40	31	FREE YOURSELF	Untouchables	*Stiff*	2
-	32	SHAKE THE DISEASE	Depeche Mode	*Mute*	1
-	33	MAGIC TOUCH	Loose Ends	*Virgin*	1
19	34	EASY LOVER	Philip Bailey (duet with Phil Collins)	*CBS/Virgin*	10
21	35	SPEND THE NIGHT	Cool Notes	*Abstract Dance*	8
-	36	CALL ME	Go West	*Chrysalis*	1
23	37	LOVE IS A BATTLEFIELD	Pat Benatar	*Chrysalis*	6
-	38	ALL FALL DOWN	Five Star ●	*Tent*	1
24	39	WELCOME TO THE PLEASURE DOME	Frankie Goes To Hollywood	*ZTT*	7
26	40	LIFE IN A NORTHERN TOWN	Dream Academy	*blanco y negro*	6

WEEK ENDING 18 MAY 1985

LW	TW	Title	Artist	Label	Wks
1	[1]	19	Paul Hardcastle	*Chrysalis*	3
2	2	MOVE CLOSER	Phyllis Nelson	*Carrere*	9
3	[3]	I FEEL LOVE (MEDLEY)	Bronski Beat and Marc Almond	*Forbidden Fruit*	5
9	[4]	RHYTHM OF THE NIGHT	DeBarge	*Gordy*	4
7	[5]	FEEL SO REAL	Steve Arrington	*Atlantic*	4
13	[6]	WALLS COME TUMBLING DOWN	Style Council	*Polydor*	2
-	7	A VIEW TO A KILL	Duran Duran	*Parlophone*	1
20	8	LOVE DON'T LIVE HERE ANYMORE	Jimmy Nail	*Virgin*	3
4	9	EVERYBODY WANTS TO RULE THE WORLD	Tears For Fears	*Mercury*	8
8	10	DON'T YOU (FORGET ABOUT ME)	Simple Minds	*Virgin*	5
11	[11]	I WAS BORN TO LOVE YOU	Freddie Mercury	*CBS*	4
6	12	THE UNFORGETTABLE FIRE	U2	*Island*	3
16	[13]	I WANT YOUR LOVIN' (JUST A LITTLE BIT)	Curtis Hairston	*London*	4
30	14	SLAVE TO LOVE	Bryan Ferry	*EG*	2
-	15	KAYLEIGH	Marillion	*EMI*	1
10	16	ONE MORE NIGHT	Phil Collins	*Virgin*	6
5	17	WE ARE THE WORLD	USA For Africa	*CBS*	6
17	18	WOULD I LIE TO YOU	Eurythmics	*RCA*	4
19	[19]	CRY	Godley and Creme	*Polydor*	4
33	20	MAGIC TOUCH	Loose Ends	*Virgin*	2
12	21	CLOUDS ACROSS THE MOON	Rah Band	*RCA*	7
29	22	RAGE TO LOVE	Kim Wilde	*MCA*	3
25	[23]	WALK LIKE A MAN	Divine	*Proto*	3
36	24	CALL ME	Go West	*Chrysalis*	2
32	25	SHAKE THE DISEASE	Depeche Mode	*Mute*	2
31	26	FREE YOURSELF	Untouchables	*Stiff*	3
14	27	LOVER COME BACK TO ME	Dead Or Alive	*Epic*	5
38	28	ALL FALL DOWN	Five Star	*Tent*	2
18	29	LOOK MAMA	Howard Jones	*WEA*	5
15	30	COULD IT BE I'M FALLING IN LOVE	David Grant and Jaki Graham	*Chrysalis*	9
-	31	OUT IN THE FIELDS	Gary Moore and Phil Lynott ●	*10*	1
-	32	HERE WE GO	Everton 1985 ●	*Columbia*	1
-	33	GET IT ON	Power Station	*Parlophone*	1
22	34	DON'T FALL IN LOVE (I SAID)	Toyah	*Portrait*	3
-	35	WE ALL FOLLOW MAN UTD	Manchester Utd Football Team	*Columbia*	1
26	36	STAINSBY GIRLS	Chris Rea	*Magnet*	5
21	37	EYE TO EYE	Chaka Khan	*Warner Brothers*	5
-	38	OBSESSION	Animotion ●	*Mercury*	1
-	39	WALKING ON SUNSHINE	Katrina and the Waves ●	*Capitol*	1
-	40	THE WORD GIRL	Scritti Politti	*Virgin*	1

WEEK ENDING 25 MAY 1985

LW	TW	Title	Artist	Label	Wks
1	[1]	19	Paul Hardcastle	*Chrysalis*	4
7	[2]	A VIEW TO A KILL	Duran Duran	*Parlophone*	2
8	[3]	LOVE DON'T LIVE HERE ANYMORE	Jimmy Nail	*Virgin*	4
2	4	MOVE CLOSER	Phyllis Nelson	*Carrere*	10
3	5	I FEEL LOVE (MEDLEY)	Bronski Beat and Marc Almond	*Forbidden Fruit*	6
4	6	RHYTHM OF THE NIGHT	DeBarge	*Gordy*	5
15	7	KAYLEIGH	Marillion	*EMI*	2
5	8	FEEL SO REAL	Steve Arrington	*Atlantic*	5
6	9	WALLS COME TUMBLING DOWN	Style Council	*Polydor*	3
35	[10]	WE ALL FOLLOW MAN UTD	Manchester Utd Football Team	*Columbia*	2
14	11	SLAVE TO LOVE	Bryan Ferry	*EG*	3
11	12	I WAS BORN TO LOVE YOU	Freddie Mercury	*CBS*	5
10	13	DON'T YOU (FORGET ABOUT ME)	Simple Minds	*Virgin*	6
32	[14]	HERE WE GO	Everton 1985	*Columbia*	2
9	15	EVERYBODY WANTS TO RULE THE WORLD	Tears For Fears	*Mercury*	9
20	[16]	MAGIC TOUCH	Loose Ends	*Virgin*	3
24	17	CALL ME	Go West	*Chrysalis*	3
31	18	OUT IN THE FIELDS	Gary Moore and Phil Lynott	*10*	2
22	19	RAGE TO LOVE	Kim Wilde	*MCA*	4
39	20	WALKING ON SUNSHINE	Katrina and the Waves	*Capitol*	2
25	21	SHAKE THE DISEASE	Depeche Mode	*Mute*	3

In these weeks ■ New entries for Divine, Jimmy Nail and Toyah - all at various times perhaps better known for their acting abilities (04.05.85) ■ Everton take an early lead in the football chart wars but Manchester United will eventually triumph, finishing four places higher in this 'league table' (18.05.85) ■ Duran Duran are back in at seven, the Power Station can only manage 33 (18.05.85)■

13	**22**	I WANT YOUR LOVIN' (JUST A LITTLE BIT)	Curtis Hairston	*London*	5
19	**23**	CRY	Godley and Creme	*Polydor*	5
33	**24**	GET IT ON	Power Station	*Parlophone*	2
18	**25**	WOULD I LIE TO YOU	Eurythmics	*RCA*	5
12	**26**	THE UNFORGETTABLE FIRE	U2	*Island*	4
36	**27**	FREE YOURSELF	Untouchables	*Stiff*	4
38	**28**	OBSESSION	Animotion	*Mercury*	2
40	**29**	THE WORD GIRL	Scritti Politti	*Virgin*	2
23	**30**	WALK LIKE A MAN	Divine	*Proto*	4
28	**31**	ALL FALL DOWN	Five Star	*Tent*	3
27	**32**	LOVER COME BACK TO ME	Dead Or Alive	*Epic*	6
17	**33**	WE ARE THE WORLD	USA For Africa	*CBS*	7
16	**34**	ONE MORE NIGHT	Phil Collins	*Virgin*	7
-	**35**	ICING ON THE CAKE	Stephen 'Tin Tin' Duffy	*10*	1
-	**36**	THINKING ABOUT YOUR LOVE	Skipworth and Turner ●	*Fourth & Broadway*	1
-	**37**	SUDDENLY	Billy Ocean	*Jive*	1
-	**38**	SO IN LOVE	Orchestral Manoeuvres In The Dark	*Virgin*	1
34	**39**	DON'T FALL IN LOVE (I SAID)	Toyah	*Portrait*	4
-	**40**	THE LIVE EP	Gary Numan	*Numa*	1

WEEK ENDING **1 JUNE 1985**

LW	TW	Title	Artist	Label	Wks
1	**1**	19	Paul Hardcastle	*Chrysalis*	5
2	**2**	A VIEW TO A KILL	Duran Duran	*Parlophone*	3
3	**3**	LOVE DON'T LIVE HERE ANYMORE	Jimmy Nail	*Virgin*	5
7	**4**	KAYLEIGH	Marillion	*EMI*	3
6	**5**	RHYTHM OF THE NIGHT	DeBarge	*Gordy*	6
4	**6**	MOVE CLOSER	Phyllis Nelson	*Carrere*	11
5	**7**	I FEEL LOVE (MEDLEY)	Bronski Beat and Marc Almond	*Forbidden Fruit*	7
18	**8**	OUT IN THE FIELDS	Gary Moore and Phil Lynott	*10*	3
20	**9**	WALKING ON SUNSHINE	Katrina and the Waves	*Capitol*	3
11	**10**	SLAVE TO LOVE	Bryan Ferry	*EG*	4
8	**11**	FEEL SO REAL	Steve Arrington	*Atlantic*	6
28	**12**	OBSESSION	Animotion	*Mercury*	3
17	**13**	CALL ME	Go West	*Chrysalis*	4
10	**14**	WE ALL FOLLOW MAN UTD	Manchester Utd Football Team	*Columbia*	3
29	**15**	THE WORD GIRL	Scritti Politti	*Virgin*	3
9	**16**	WALLS COME TUMBLING DOWN	Style Council	*Polydor*	4
16	**17**	MAGIC TOUCH	Loose Ends	*Virgin*	4
12	**18**	I WAS BORN TO LOVE YOU	Freddie Mercury	*CBS*	6
37	**19**	SUDDENLY	Billy Ocean	*Jive*	2
35	**20**	ICING ON THE CAKE	Stephen 'Tin Tin' Duffy	*10*	2
21	**21**	SHAKE THE DISEASE	Depeche Mode	*Mute*	4
24	**22**	GET IT ON	Power Station	*Parlophone*	3
13	**23**	DON'T YOU (FORGET ABOUT ME)	Simple Minds	*Virgin*	7
36	**24**	THINKING ABOUT YOUR LOVE	Skipworth and Turner	*Fourth & Broadway*	2
15	**25**	EVERYBODY WANTS TO RULE THE WORLD	Tears For Fears	*Mercury*	10
19	**26**	RAGE TO LOVE	Kim Wilde	*MCA*	5
40	**27**	THE LIVE EP	Gary Numan	*Numa*	2
38	**28**	SO IN LOVE	Orchestral Manoeuvres In The Dark	*Virgin*	2
23	**29**	CRY	Godley and Creme	*Polydor*	6
31	**30**	ALL FALL DOWN	Five Star	*Tent*	4
27	**31**	FREE YOURSELF	Untouchables	*Stiff*	5
-	**32**	HISTORY	Mai Tai ●	*Hot Melt*	1
14	**33**	HERE WE GO	Everton 1985	*Columbia*	3
22	**34**	I WANT YOUR LOVIN' (JUST A LITTLE BIT)	Curtis Hairston	*London*	6
30	**35**	WALK LIKE A MAN	Divine	*Proto*	5
-	**36**	DUEL	Propaganda	*ZTT*	1
-	**37**	CHERISH	Kool and the Gang	*De-Lite*	1
-	**38**	HEAVEN	Bryan Adams	*A&M*	1
-	**39**	WALKING ON THE CHINESE WALL	Philip Bailey	*CBS*	1
26	**40**	THE UNFORGETTABLE FIRE	U2	*Island*	5

June 1985

□ Highest position disc reached ● Act's first ever week on chart

WEEK ENDING **8 JUNE 1985**

LW	TW	Title	Artist	Label	Wks
1	**1**	19	Paul Hardcastle	*Chrysalis*	6
2	**2**	A VIEW TO A KILL	Duran Duran	*Parlophone*	4
4	**3**	KAYLEIGH	Marillion	*EMI*	4
-	**4**	YOU'LL NEVER WALK ALONE	Crowd ●	*Spartan*	1
8	**5**	OUT IN THE FIELDS	Gary Moore and Phil Lynott	*10*	4
12	**6**	OBSESSION	Animotion	*Mercury*	4
3	**7**	LOVE DON'T LIVE HERE ANYMORE	Jimmy Nail	*Virgin*	6
9	**8**	WALKING ON SUNSHINE	Katrina and the Waves	*Capitol*	4
19	**9**	SUDDENLY	Billy Ocean	*Jive*	3
15	**10**	THE WORD GIRL	Scritti Politti	*Virgin*	4
5	**11**	RHYTHM OF THE NIGHT	DeBarge	*Gordy*	7
13	**12**	CALL ME	Go West	*Chrysalis*	5
10	**13**	SLAVE TO LOVE	Bryan Ferry	*EG*	5
20	**14**	ICING ON THE CAKE	Stephen 'Tin Tin' Duffy	*10*	3
7	**15**	I FEEL LOVE (MEDLEY)	Bronski Beat and Marc Almond	*Forbidden Fruit*	8
32	**16**	HISTORY	Mai Tai	*Hot Melt*	2
6	**17**	MOVE CLOSER	Phyllis Nelson	*Carrere*	12
21	**18**	SHAKE THE DISEASE	Depeche Mode	*Mute*	5
30	**19**	ALL FALL DOWN	Five Star	*Tent*	5
11	**20**	FEEL SO REAL	Steve Arrington	*Atlantic*	7
36	**21**	DUEL	Propaganda	*ZTT*	2
37	**22**	CHERISH	Kool and the Gang	*De-Lite*	2
-	**23**	LOVING THE ALIEN	David Bowie	*EMI America*	1
24	**24**	THINKING ABOUT YOUR LOVE	Skipworth and Turner	*Fourth & Broadway*	3
-	**25**	CRAZY FOR YOU	Madonna	*Geffen*	1
17	**26**	MAGIC TOUCH	Loose Ends	*Virgin*	5
28	**27**	SO IN LOVE	Orchestral Manoeuvres In The Dark	*Virgin*	3
16	**28**	WALLS COME TUMBLING DOWN	Style Council	*Polydor*	5
-	**29**	FRANKIE	Sister Sledge	*Atlantic*	1
22	**30**	GET IT ON	Power Station	*Parlophone*	4
18	**31**	I WAS BORN TO LOVE YOU	Freddie Mercury	*CBS*	7
23	**32**	DON'T YOU (FORGET ABOUT ME)	Simple Minds	*Virgin*	8
14	**33**	WE ALL FOLLOW MAN UTD	Manchester Utd Football Team	*Columbia*	4
27	**34**	THE LIVE EP	Gary Numan	*Numa*	3
-	**35**	JOHNNY COME HOME	Fine Young Cannibals ●	*London*	1
25	**36**	EVERYBODY WANTS TO RULE THE WORLD	Tears For Fears	*Mercury*	11
-	**37**	PAISLEY PARK	Prince and the Revolution	*Warner Brothers*	1
38	**38**	HEAVEN	Bryan Adams	*A&M*	2
31	**39**	FREE YOURSELF	Untouchables	*Stiff*	6
39	**40**	WALKING ON THE CHINESE WALL	Philip Bailey	*CBS*	2

WEEK ENDING **15 JUNE 1985**

LW	TW	Title	Artist	Label	Wks
4	**1**	YOU'LL NEVER WALK ALONE	Crowd	*Spartan*	2
3	**2**	KAYLEIGH	Marillion	*EMI*	5
1	**3**	19	Paul Hardcastle	*Chrysalis*	7
9	**4**	SUDDENLY	Billy Ocean	*Jive*	4
6	**5**	OBSESSION	Animotion	*Mercury*	5
2	**6**	A VIEW TO A KILL	Duran Duran	*Parlophone*	5
5	**7**	OUT IN THE FIELDS	Gary Moore and Phil Lynott	*10*	5
10	**8**	THE WORD GIRL	Scritti Politti	*Virgin*	5
25	**9**	CRAZY FOR YOU	Madonna	*Geffen*	2
16	**10**	HISTORY	Mai Tai	*Hot Melt*	3
29	**11**	FRANKIE	Sister Sledge	*Atlantic*	2
8	**12**	WALKING ON SUNSHINE	Katrina and the Waves	*Capitol*	5
22	**13**	CHERISH	Kool and the Gang	*De-Lite*	3
14	**14**	ICING ON THE CAKE	Stephen 'Tin Tin' Duffy	*10*	4
19	**15**	ALL FALL DOWN	Five Star	*Tent*	6
35	**16**	JOHNNY COME HOME	Fine Young Cannibals	*London*	2
12	**17**	CALL ME	Go West	*Chrysalis*	6
7	**18**	LOVE DON'T LIVE HERE ANYMORE	Jimmy Nail	*Virgin*	7
23	**19**	LOVING THE ALIEN	David Bowie	*EMI America*	2
-	**20**	BEN	Marti Webb	*Starblend*	1
21	**21**	DUEL	Propaganda	*ZTT*	3
11	**22**	RHYTHM OF THE NIGHT	DeBarge	*Gordy*	8
-	**23**	I'M ON FIRE/BORN IN THE USA	Bruce Springsteen	*CBS*	1

■The last of Bryan Ferry's five solo and ten Roxy Music Top Ten hits reaches its peak (01.06.85) ■ Gerry Marsden's Crowd charity disc spends its first week in the Top Five (08.06.85)■

June 1985

□ Highest position disc reached ● Act's first ever week on chart

LW	TW	Title	Artist	Label	Wks
37	24	PAISLEY PARK	Prince and the Revolution	*Warner Brothers*	2
17	25	MOVE CLOSER	Phyllis Nelson	*Carrere*	13
13	26	SLAVE TO LOVE	Bryan Ferry	*EG*	6
15	27	I FEEL LOVE (MEDLEY)	Bronski Beat and Marc Almond	*Forbidden Fruit*	9
27	28	SO IN LOVE	Orchestral Manoeuvres In The Dark	*Virgin*	4
18	29	SHAKE THE DISEASE	Depeche Mode	*Mute*	6
-	30	AXEL F	Harold Faltermeyer ●	*MCA*	1
24	31	THINKING ABOUT YOUR LOVE	Skipworth and Turner	*Fourth & Broadway*	4
-	32	IF YOU LOVE SOMEBODY SET THEM FREE	Sting	*A&M*	1
20	33	FEEL SO REAL	Steve Arrington	*Atlantic*	8
40	[34]	WALKING ON THE CHINESE WALL	Philip Bailey	*CBS*	3
26	35	MAGIC TOUCH	Loose Ends	*Virgin*	6
31	36	I WAS BORN TO LOVE YOU	Freddie Mercury	*CBS*	8
-	37	KING IN A CATHOLIC STYLE (WAKE UP)	China Crisis	*Virgin*	1
32	38	DON'T YOU (FORGET ABOUT ME)	Simple Minds	*Virgin*	9
34	39	THE LIVE EP	Gary Numan	*Numa*	4
30	40	GET IT ON	Power Station	*Parlophone*	5

WEEK ENDING 22 JUNE 1985

LW	TW	Title	Artist	Label	Wks
1	[1]	YOU'LL NEVER WALK ALONE	Crowd	*Spartan*	3
11	2	FRANKIE	Sister Sledge	*Atlantic*	3
9	3	CRAZY FOR YOU	Madonna	*Geffen*	3
2	4	KAYLEIGH	Marillion	*EMI*	6
4	5	SUDDENLY	Billy Ocean	*Jive*	5
8	[6]	THE WORD GIRL	Scritti Politti	*Virgin*	6
13	7	CHERISH	Kool and the Gang	*De-Lite*	4
5	8	OBSESSION	Animotion	*Mercury*	6
10	9	HISTORY	Mai Tai	*Hot Melt*	4
30	10	AXEL F	Harold Faltermeyer	*MCA*	2
6	11	A VIEW TO A KILL	Duran Duran	*Parlophone*	6
20	12	BEN	Marti Webb	*Starblend*	2
23	13	I'M ON FIRE/BORN IN THE USA	Bruce Springsteen	*CBS*	2
3	14	19	Paul Hardcastle	*Chrysalis*	8
16	15	JOHNNY COME HOME	Fine Young Cannibals	*London*	3
7	16	OUT IN THE FIELDS	Gary Moore and Phil Lynott	*10*	6
12	17	WALKING ON SUNSHINE	Katrina and the Waves	*Capitol*	6
15	18	ALL FALL DOWN	Five Star	*Tent*	7
19	[19]	LOVING THE ALIEN	David Bowie	*EMI America*	3
14	20	ICING ON THE CAKE	Stephen 'Tin Tin' Duffy	*10*	5
21	[21]	DUEL	Propaganda	*ZTT*	4
24	22	PAISLEY PARK	Prince and the Revolution	*Warner Brothers*	3
17	23	CALL ME	Go West	*Chrysalis*	7
-	24	HEAD OVER HEELS	Tears For Fears	*Mercury*	1
18	25	LOVE DON'T LIVE HERE ANYMORE	Jimmy Nail	*Virgin*	8
37	26	KING IN A CATHOLIC STYLE (WAKE UP)	China Crisis	*Virgin*	2
22	27	RHYTHM OF THE NIGHT	DeBarge	*Gordy*	9
32	28	IF YOU LOVE SOMEBODY SET THEM FREE	Sting	*A&M*	2
25	29	MOVE CLOSER	Phyllis Nelson	*Carrere*	14
-	30	TOMB OF MEMORIES	Paul Young	*CBS*	1
29	31	SHAKE THE DISEASE	Depeche Mode	*Mute*	7
-	[32]	ACT OF WAR	Elton John and Millie Jackson ●	*Rocket*	1
28	33	SO IN LOVE	Orchestral Manoeuvres In The Dark	*Virgin*	5
26	34	SLAVE TO LOVE	Bryan Ferry	*EG*	7
27	35	I FEEL LOVE (MEDLEY)	Bronski Beat and Marc Almond	*Forbidden Fruit*	10
34	36	WALKING ON THE CHINESE WALL	Philip Bailey	*CBS*	4
-	37	THE SHADOW OF LOVE	Damned	*MCA*	1
-	38	(BURN IT UP) BRING IT DOWN! (THIS INSANE THING)	Redskins ●	*Decca*	1
-	39	TURN IT UP	Conway Brothers ●	*10*	1
31	40	THINKING ABOUT YOUR LOVE	Skipworth and Turner	*Fourth & Broadway*	5

WEEK ENDING 29 JUNE 1985

LW	TW	Title	Artist	Label	Wks
2	[1]	FRANKIE	Sister Sledge	*Atlantic*	4
3	[2]	CRAZY FOR YOU	Madonna	*Geffen*	4
1	3	YOU'LL NEVER WALK ALONE	Crowd	*Spartan*	4
10	4	AXEL F	Harold Faltermeyer	*MCA*	3
7	5	CHERISH	Kool and the Gang	*De-Lite*	5
5	6	SUDDENLY	Billy Ocean	*Jive*	6
4	7	KAYLEIGH	Marillion	*EMI*	7
9	[8]	HISTORY	Mai Tai	*Hot Melt*	5
12	9	BEN	Marti Webb	*Starblend*	3
6	10	THE WORD GIRL	Scritti Politti	*Virgin*	7
13	11	I'M ON FIRE/BORN IN THE USA	Bruce Springsteen	*CBS*	3
15	12	JOHNNY COME HOME	Fine Young Cannibals	*London*	4
8	13	OBSESSION	Animotion	*Mercury*	7
24	14	HEAD OVER HEELS	Tears For Fears	*Mercury*	2
11	15	A VIEW TO A KILL	Duran Duran	*Parlophone*	7
14	16	19	Paul Hardcastle	*Chrysalis*	9
30	17	TOMB OF MEMORIES	Paul Young	*CBS*	2
22	[18]	PAISLEY PARK	Prince and the Revolution	*Warner Brothers*	4
26	[19]	KING IN A CATHOLIC STYLE (WAKE UP)	China Crisis	*Virgin*	3
16	20	OUT IN THE FIELDS	Gary Moore and Phil Lynott	*10*	7
18	21	ALL FALL DOWN	Five Star	*Tent*	8
-	22	LIFE IN ONE DAY	Howard Jones	*WEA*	1
-	23	N-N-NINETEEN NOT OUT	Commentators ●	*Oval*	1
17	24	WALKING ON SUNSHINE	Katrina and the Waves	*Capitol*	7
21	25	DUEL	Propaganda	*ZTT*	5
28	[26]	IF YOU LOVE SOMEBODY SET THEM FREE	Sting	*A&M*	3
20	27	ICING ON THE CAKE	Stephen 'Tin Tin' Duffy	*10*	6
19	28	LOVING THE ALIEN	David Bowie	*EMI America*	4
37	29	THE SHADOW OF LOVE	Damned	*MCA*	2
39	30	TURN IT UP	Conway Brothers	*10*	2
23	31	CALL ME	Go West	*Chrysalis*	8
32	[32]	ACT OF WAR	Elton John and Millie Jackson	*Rocket*	2
38	[33]	(BURN IT UP) BRING IT DOWN! (THIS INSANE THING)	Redskins	*Decca*	2
-	34	IN TOO DEEP	Dead Or Alive	*Epic*	1
-	35	SHE SELLS SANCTUARY	Cult ●	*Beggars Banquet*	1
-	36	MY TOOT TOOT	Denise LaSalle ●	*Epic*	1
-	37	LIVE IS LIFE	Opus ●	*Polydor*	1
-	38	SMUGGLER'S BLUES	Glenn Frey	*BBC*	1
29	39	MOVE CLOSER	Phyllis Nelson	*Carrere*	15
27	40	RHYTHM OF THE NIGHT	DeBarge	*Gordy*	10

WEEK ENDING 6 JULY 1985

LW	TW	Title	Artist	Label	Wks
1	[1]	FRANKIE	Sister Sledge	*Atlantic*	5
4	[2]	AXEL F	Harold Faltermeyer	*MCA*	4
2	3	CRAZY FOR YOU	Madonna	*Geffen*	5
5	[4]	CHERISH	Kool and the Gang	*De-Lite*	6
9	[5]	BEN	Marti Webb	*Starblend*	4
3	6	YOU'LL NEVER WALK ALONE	Crowd	*Spartan*	5
6	7	SUDDENLY	Billy Ocean	*Jive*	7
11	8	I'M ON FIRE/BORN IN THE USA	Bruce Springsteen	*CBS*	4
8	9	HISTORY	Mai Tai	*Hot Melt*	6
7	10	KAYLEIGH	Marillion	*EMI*	8
12	11	JOHNNY COME HOME	Fine Young Cannibals	*London*	5
14	[12]	HEAD OVER HEELS	Tears For Fears	*Mercury*	3
23	[13]	N-N-NINETEEN NOT OUT	Commentators	*Oval*	2
22	14	LIFE IN ONE DAY	Howard Jones	*WEA*	2
10	15	THE WORD GIRL	Scritti Politti	*Virgin*	8
17	[16]	TOMB OF MEMORIES	Paul Young	*CBS*	3
36	17	MY TOOT TOOT	Denise LaSalle	*Epic*	2
13	18	OBSESSION	Animotion	*Mercury*	8
34	19	IN TOO DEEP	Dead Or Alive	*Epic*	2
19	20	KING IN A CATHOLIC STYLE (WAKE UP)	China Crisis	*Virgin*	4
18	21	PAISLEY PARK	Prince and the Revolution	*Warner Brothers*	5
30	22	TURN IT UP	Conway Brothers	*10*	3
15	23	A VIEW TO A KILL	Duran Duran	*Parlophone*	8
16	24	19	Paul Hardcastle	*Chrysalis*	10
29	[25]	THE SHADOW OF LOVE	Damned	*MCA*	3
37	26	LIVE IS LIFE	Opus	*Polydor*	2
-	27	COME TO MILTON KEYNES	Style Council	*Polydor*	1

In these weeks ■ *Frankie, Ben, Johnny* and *Axel* all appear in the Top Fifteen (22.06.85) ■ Sister Sledge are the first all female group, not including St. Winifred's School Choir, to hit number one since the Three Degrees in 1974 (29.06.85) ■ This is Simply Red's first week of chart action (06.06.85)■

LW	TW	Title / Artist	Label	Wks
38	28	SMUGGLER'S BLUES Glenn Frey	*BBC*	2
25	29	DUEL Propaganda	*ZTT*	6
35	30	SHE SELLS SANCTUARY Cult	*Beggars Banquet*	2
26	31	IF YOU LOVE SOMEBODY SET THEM FREE Sting	*A&M*	4
21	32	ALL FALL DOWN Five Star	*Tent*	9
-	33	MONEY'S TOO TIGHT TO MENTION Simply Red ●	*Elektra*	1
33	34	(BURN IT UP) BRING IT DOWN! (THIS INSANE THING) Redskins	*Decca*	3
20	35	OUT IN THE FIELDS Gary Moore and Phil Lynott	*10*	8
24	36	WALKING ON SUNSHINE Katrina and the Waves	*Capitol*	8
-	37	THERE MUST BE AN ANGEL (PLAYING WITH MY HEART) Eurythmics	*RCA*	1
32	38	ACT OF WAR Elton John and Millie Jackson	*Rocket*	3
-	39	ROUND AND AROUND Jaki Graham ●	*EMI*	1
27	40	ICING ON THE CAKE Stephen 'Tin Tin' Duffy	*10*	7

LW	TW	*WEEK ENDING* **13 JULY 1985**		Wks
1	1	FRANKIE Sister Sledge	*Atlantic*	6
2	2	AXEL F Harold Faltermeyer	*MCA*	5
3	3	CRAZY FOR YOU Madonna	*Geffen*	6
4	4	CHERISH Kool and the Gang	*De-Lite*	7
8	5	I'M ON FIRE/BORN IN THE USA Bruce Springsteen	*CBS*	5
5	6	BEN Marti Webb	*Starblend*	5
17	7	MY TOOT TOOT Denise LaSalle	*Epic*	3
11	8	JOHNNY COME HOME Fine Young Cannibals	*London*	6
9	9	HISTORY Mai Tai	*Hot Melt*	7
37	10	THERE MUST BE AN ANGEL (PLAYING WITH MY HEART) Eurythmics	*RCA*	2
7	11	SUDDENLY Billy Ocean	*Jive*	8
12	12	HEAD OVER HEELS Tears For Fears	*Mercury*	4
10	13	KAYLEIGH Marillion	*EMI*	9
19	14	IN TOO DEEP Dead Or Alive	*Epic*	3
26	15	LIVE IS LIFE Opus	*Polydor*	3
13	16	N-N-NINETEEN NOT OUT Commentators	*Oval*	3
14	17	LIFE IN ONE DAY Howard Jones	*WEA*	3
22	18	TURN IT UP Conway Brothers	*10*	4
6	19	YOU'LL NEVER WALK ALONE Crowd	*Spartan*	6
16	20	TOMB OF MEMORIES Paul Young	*CBS*	4
33	21	MONEY'S TOO TIGHT TO MENTION Simply Red	*Elektra*	2
28	22	SMUGGLER'S BLUES Glenn Frey	*BBC*	3
27	23	COME TO MILTON KEYNES Style Council	*Polydor*	2
15	24	THE WORD GIRL Scritti Politti	*Virgin*	9
25	25	THE SHADOW OF LOVE Damned	*MCA*	4
30	26	SHE SELLS SANCTUARY Cult	*Beggars Banquet*	3
39	27	ROUND AND AROUND Jaki Graham	*EMI*	2
18	28	OBSESSION Animotion	*Mercury*	9
23	29	A VIEW TO A KILL Duran Duran	*Parlophone*	9
20	30	KING IN A CATHOLIC STYLE (WAKE UP) China Crisis	*Virgin*	5
24	31	19 Paul Hardcastle	*Chrysalis*	11
21	32	PAISLEY PARK Prince and the Revolution	*Warner Brothers*	6
-	33	IN YOUR CAR Cool Notes	*Abstract Dance*	1
-	34	DANCIN' IN THE KEY OF LIFE Steve Arrington	*Atlantic*	1
-	35	ALL NIGHT HOLIDAY Russ Abbott	*Spirit*	1
-	36	LOVING YOU Feargal Sharkey	*Virgin*	1
-	37	LOVE IS JUST THE GREAT PRETENDER Animal Nightlife	*Island*	1
32	38	ALL FALL DOWN Five Star	*Tent*	10
-	39	LIVING ON VIDEO Trans-X ●	*Boiling Point*	1
-	40	GENIE Brooklyn Bronx and Queens ●	*Cooltempo*	1

July 1985

□ Highest position disc reached ● Act's first ever week on chart

LW	TW	*WEEK ENDING* **20 JULY 1985**		Wks
1	1	FRANKIE Sister Sledge	*Atlantic*	7
2	2	AXEL F Harold Faltermeyer	*MCA*	6
10	3	THERE MUST BE AN ANGEL (PLAYING WITH MY HEART) Eurythmics	*RCA*	3
4	4	CHERISH Kool and the Gang	*De-Lite*	8
3	5	CRAZY FOR YOU Madonna	*Geffen*	7
7	6	MY TOOT TOOT Denise LaSalle	*Epic*	4
5	7	I'M ON FIRE/BORN IN THE USA Bruce Springsteen	*CBS*	6
15	8	LIVE IS LIFE Opus	*Polydor*	4
8	9	JOHNNY COME HOME Fine Young Cannibals	*London*	7
6	10	BEN Marti Webb	*Starblend*	6
18	11	TURN IT UP Conway Brothers	*10*	5
27	12	ROUND AND AROUND Jaki Graham	*EMI*	3
21	13	MONEY'S TOO TIGHT TO MENTION Simply Red	*Elektra*	3
12	14	HEAD OVER HEELS Tears For Fears	*Mercury*	5
33	15	IN YOUR CAR Cool Notes	*Abstract Dance*	2
14	16	IN TOO DEEP Dead Or Alive	*Epic*	4
9	17	HISTORY Mai Tai	*Hot Melt*	8
39	18	LIVING ON VIDEO Trans-X	*Boiling Point*	2
26	19	SHE SELLS SANCTUARY Cult	*Beggars Banquet*	4
11	20	SUDDENLY Billy Ocean	*Jive*	9
13	21	KAYLEIGH Marillion	*EMI*	10
17	22	LIFE IN ONE DAY Howard Jones	*WEA*	4
34	23	DANCIN' IN THE KEY OF LIFE Steve Arrington	*Atlantic*	2
16	24	N-N-NINETEEN NOT OUT Commentators	*Oval*	4
35	25	ALL NIGHT HOLIDAY Russ Abbott	*Spirit*	2
22	26	SMUGGLER'S BLUES Glenn Frey	*BBC*	4
25	27	THE SHADOW OF LOVE Damned	*MCA*	5
37	28	LOVE IS JUST THE GREAT PRETENDER Animal Nightlife	*Island*	2
23	29	COME TO MILTON KEYNES Style Council	*Polydor*	3
19	30	YOU'LL NEVER WALK ALONE Crowd	*Spartan*	7
36	31	LOVING YOU Feargal Sharkey	*Virgin*	2
20	32	TOMB OF MEMORIES Paul Young	*CBS*	5
29	33	A VIEW TO A KILL Duran Duran	*Parlophone*	10
-	34	WHITE WEDDING Billy Idol	*Chrysalis*	1
28	35	OBSESSION Animotion	*Mercury*	10
31	36	19 Paul Hardcastle	*Chrysalis*	12
-	37	WE DON'T NEED ANOTHER HERO (THUNDERDOME) Tina Turner	*Capitol*	1
-	38	DARE ME Pointer Sisters	*Planet*	1
-	39	MONEY FOR NOTHING Dire Straits	*Vertigo*	1
-	40	LET ME BE THE ONE Five Star	*Tent*	1

LW	TW	*WEEK ENDING* **27 JULY 1985**		Wks
3	1	THERE MUST BE AN ANGEL (PLAYING WITH MY HEART) Eurythmics	*RCA*	4
1	2	FRANKIE Sister Sledge	*Atlantic*	8
2	3	AXEL F Harold Faltermeyer	*MCA*	7
-	4	INTO THE GROOVE Madonna	*Sire*	1
4	5	CHERISH Kool and the Gang	*De-Lite*	9
5	6	CRAZY FOR YOU Madonna	*Geffen*	8
8	7	LIVE IS LIFE Opus	*Polydor*	5
6	8	MY TOOT TOOT Denise LaSalle	*Epic*	5
12	9	ROUND AND AROUND Jaki Graham	*EMI*	4
18	10	LIVING ON VIDEO Trans-X	*Boiling Point*	3
37	11	WE DON'T NEED ANOTHER HERO (THUNDERDOME) Tina Turner	*Capitol*	2
7	12	I'M ON FIRE/BORN IN THE USA Bruce Springsteen	*CBS*	7
15	13	IN YOUR CAR Cool Notes	*Abstract Dance*	3
13	14	MONEY'S TOO TIGHT TO MENTION Simply Red	*Elektra*	4
39	15	MONEY FOR NOTHING Dire Straits	*Vertigo*	2
9	16	JOHNNY COME HOME Fine Young Cannibals	*London*	8
11	17	TURN IT UP Conway Brothers	*10*	6
34	18	WHITE WEDDING Billy Idol	*Chrysalis*	2
19	19	SHE SELLS SANCTUARY Cult	*Beggars Banquet*	5
25	20	ALL NIGHT HOLIDAY Russ Abbott	*Spirit*	3
23	21	DANCIN' IN THE KEY OF LIFE Steve Arrington	*Atlantic*	3
40	22	LET ME BE THE ONE Five Star	*Tent*	2
38	23	DARE ME Pointer Sisters	*Planet*	2
14	24	HEAD OVER HEELS Tears For Fears	*Mercury*	6
10	25	BEN Marti Webb	*Starblend*	7
16	26	IN TOO DEEP Dead Or Alive	*Epic*	5
22	27	LIFE IN ONE DAY Howard Jones	*WEA*	5
21	28	KAYLEIGH Marillion	*EMI*	11
17	29	HISTORY Mai Tai	*Hot Melt*	9
31	30	LOVING YOU Feargal Sharkey	*Virgin*	3

■No UK acts in the Top Five for the first time since 15 October 1977 (13.07.85) ■ Three weeks at two for *Axel F*, the nearest an instrumental has come to hitting the top since *Eye Level* in 1973 (20.07.85) ■ Madonna has two singles in the Top Ten but on separate record labels (27.07.85)■

☐ Highest position disc reached ● Act's first ever week on chart

LW	TW	Title	Artist	Label	Wks
20	31	SUDDENLY	Billy Ocean	Jive	10
28	32	LOVE IS JUST THE GREAT PRETENDER	Animal Nightlife	Island	3
26	33	SMUGGLER'S BLUES	Glenn Frey	BBC	5
33	34	A VIEW TO A KILL	Duran Duran	Parlophone	11
-	35	IN BETWEEN DAYS	Cure	Fiction	1
-	36	LONG TIME	Arrow ●	London	1
-	37	TOO MANY GAMES	Maze featuring Frankie Beverly ●	Capitol	1
-	38	EMPTY ROOMS	Gary Moore	10	1
27	39	THE SHADOW OF LOVE	Damned	MCA	6
-	40	SECRET	Orchestral Manoeuvres In The Dark	Virgin	1

WEEK ENDING 3 AUGUST 1985

LW	TW	Title	Artist	Label	Wks
4	1	INTO THE GROOVE	Madonna	Sire	2
1	2	THERE MUST BE AN ANGEL (PLAYING WITH MY HEART)	Eurythmics	RCA	5
11	3	WE DON'T NEED ANOTHER HERO (THUNDERDOME)	Tina Turner	Capitol	3
2	4	FRANKIE	Sister Sledge	Atlantic	9
3	5	AXEL F	Harold Faltermeyer	MCA	8
7	6	LIVE IS LIFE	Opus	Polydor	6
5	7	CHERISH	Kool and the Gang	De-Lite	10
15	8	MONEY FOR NOTHING	Dire Straits	Vertigo	3
10	9	LIVING ON VIDEO	Trans-X	Boiling Point	4
9	10	ROUND AND AROUND	Jaki Graham	EMI	5
18	11	WHITE WEDDING	Billy Idol	Chrysalis	3
6	12	CRAZY FOR YOU	Madonna	Geffen	9
8	13	MY TOOT TOOT	Denise LaSalle	Epic	6
13	14	IN YOUR CAR	Cool Notes	Abstract Dance	4
19	15	SHE SELLS SANCTUARY	Cult	Beggars Banquet	6
14	16	MONEY'S TOO TIGHT TO MENTION	Simply Red	Elektra	5
23	17	DARE ME	Pointer Sisters	Planet	3
22	18	LET ME BE THE ONE	Five Star	Tent	3
12	19	I'M ON FIRE/BORN IN THE USA	Bruce Springsteen	CBS	8
35	20	IN BETWEEN DAYS	Cure	Fiction	2
-	21	GLORY DAYS	Bruce Springsteen	CBS	1
-	22	I GOT YOU BABE	UB40 guest vocals by Chrissie Hynde	DEP International	1
-	23	DON QUIXOTE	Nik Kershaw	MCA	1
16	24	JOHNNY COME HOME	Fine Young Cannibals	London	9
20	25	ALL NIGHT HOLIDAY	Russ Abbott	Spirit	4
21	26	DANCIN' IN THE KEY OF LIFE	Steve Arrington	Atlantic	4
30	27	LOVING YOU	Feargal Sharkey	Virgin	4
17	28	TURN IT UP	Conway Brothers	10	7
38	29	EMPTY ROOMS	Gary Moore	10	2
36	30	LONG TIME	Arrow	London	2
24	31	HEAD OVER HEELS	Tears For Fears	Mercury	7
-	32	HOLIDAY	Madonna	Sire	1
-	33	RASPBERRY BERET	Prince and the Revolution	Paisley Park	1
40	34	SECRET	Orchestral Manoeuvres In The Dark	Virgin	2
-	35	EXCITABLE	Amazulu ●	Island	1
37	36	TOO MANY GAMES	Maze featuring Frankie Beverly	Capitol	2
25	37	BEN	Marti Webb	Starblend	8
-	38	TAKE ME HOME	Phil Collins	Virgin	1
-	39	GOODBYE GIRL	Go West	Chrysalis	1
26	40	IN TOO DEEP	Dead Or Alive	Epic	6

WEEK ENDING 10 AUGUST 1985

LW	TW	Title	Artist	Label	Wks
1	1	INTO THE GROOVE	Madonna	Sire	3
2	2	THERE MUST BE AN ANGEL (PLAYING WITH MY HEART)	Eurythmics	RCA	6
3	3	WE DON'T NEED ANOTHER HERO (THUNDERDOME)	Tina Turner	Capitol	4
8	4	MONEY FOR NOTHING	Dire Straits	Vertigo	4
32	5	HOLIDAY	Madonna	Sire	2
11	6	WHITE WEDDING	Billy Idol	Chrysalis	4
22	7	I GOT YOU BABE	UB40 guest vocals by Chrissie Hynde	DEP International	2
7	8	CHERISH	Kool and the Gang	De-Lite	11
6	9	LIVE IS LIFE	Opus	Polydor	7
4	10	FRANKIE	Sister Sledge	Atlantic	10
23	11	DON QUIXOTE	Nik Kershaw	MCA	2
5	12	AXEL F	Harold Faltermeyer	MCA	9
9	13	LIVING ON VIDEO	Trans-X	Boiling Point	5
10	14	ROUND AND AROUND	Jaki Graham	EMI	6
12	15	CRAZY FOR YOU	Madonna	Geffen	10
20	16	IN BETWEEN DAYS	Cure	Fiction	3
21	17	GLORY DAYS	Bruce Springsteen	CBS	2
13	18	MY TOOT TOOT	Denise LaSalle	Epic	7
15	19	SHE SELLS SANCTUARY	Cult	Beggars Banquet	7
14	20	IN YOUR CAR	Cool Notes	Abstract Dance	5
18	21	LET ME BE THE ONE	Five Star	Tent	4
17	22	DARE ME	Pointer Sisters	Planet	4
29	23	EMPTY ROOMS	Gary Moore	10	3
16	24	MONEY'S TOO TIGHT TO MENTION	Simply Red	Elektra	6
35	25	EXCITABLE	Amazulu	Island	2
27	26	LOVING YOU	Feargal Sharkey	Virgin	5
33	27	RASPBERRY BERET	Prince and the Revolution	Paisley Park	2
38	28	TAKE ME HOME	Phil Collins	Virgin	2
19	29	I'M ON FIRE/BORN IN THE USA	Bruce Springsteen	CBS	9
39	30	GOODBYE GIRL	Go West	Chrysalis	2
-	31	SAY I'M YOUR NUMBER ONE	Princess ●	Supreme	1
-	32	DRIVE	Cars	Elektra	1
24	33	JOHNNY COME HOME	Fine Young Cannibals	London	10
26	34	DANCIN' IN THE KEY OF LIFE	Steve Arrington	Atlantic	5
30	35	LONG TIME	Arrow	London	3
36	36	TOO MANY GAMES	Maze featuring Frankie Beverly	Capitol	3
34	37	SECRET	Orchestral Manoeuvres In The Dark	Virgin	3
25	38	ALL NIGHT HOLIDAY	Russ Abbott	Spirit	5
-	39	I WONDER IF I TAKE YOU HOME	Lisa Lisa and Cult Jam with Full Force ●	CBS	1
-	40	YOU'RE THE ONE FOR ME	D-Train	Prelude	1

WEEK ENDING 17 AUGUST 1985

LW	TW	Title	Artist	Label	Wks
1	1	INTO THE GROOVE	Madonna	Sire	4
5	2	HOLIDAY	Madonna	Sire	3
7	3	I GOT YOU BABE	UB40 guest vocals by Chrissie Hynde	DEP International	3
3	4	WE DON'T NEED ANOTHER HERO (THUNDERDOME)	Tina Turner	Capitol	5
4	5	MONEY FOR NOTHING	Dire Straits	Vertigo	5
2	6	THERE MUST BE AN ANGEL (PLAYING WITH MY HEART)	Eurythmics	RCA	7
6	7	WHITE WEDDING	Billy Idol	Chrysalis	5
32	8	DRIVE	Cars	Elektra	2
-	9	RUNNING UP THAT HILL	Kate Bush	EMI	1
11	10	DON QUIXOTE	Nik Kershaw	MCA	3
31	11	SAY I'M YOUR NUMBER ONE	Princess	Supreme	2
9	12	LIVE IS LIFE	Opus	Polydor	8
25	13	EXCITABLE	Amazulu	Island	3
8	14	CHERISH	Kool and the Gang	De-Lite	12
16	15	IN BETWEEN DAYS	Cure	Fiction	4
12	16	AXEL F	Harold Faltermeyer	MCA	10
10	17	FRANKIE	Sister Sledge	Atlantic	11
13	18	LIVING ON VIDEO	Trans-X	Boiling Point	6
15	19	CRAZY FOR YOU	Madonna	Geffen	11
17	20	GLORY DAYS	Bruce Springsteen	CBS	3
14	21	ROUND AND AROUND	Jaki Graham	EMI	7
21	22	LET ME BE THE ONE	Five Star	Tent	5
23	23	EMPTY ROOMS	Gary Moore	10	4
19	24	SHE SELLS SANCTUARY	Cult	Beggars Banquet	8
27	25	RASPBERRY BERET	Prince and the Revolution	Paisley Park	3
39	26	I WONDER IF I TAKE YOU HOME	Lisa Lisa and Cult Jam with Full Force	CBS	2
40	27	YOU'RE THE ONE FOR ME	D-Train	Prelude	2
28	28	TAKE ME HOME	Phil Collins	Virgin	3
30	29	GOODBYE GIRL	Go West	Chrysalis	3
18	30	MY TOOT TOOT	Denise LaSalle	Epic	8
22	31	DARE ME	Pointer Sisters	Planet	5
20	32	IN YOUR CAR	Cool Notes	Abstract Dance	6
-	33	TARZAN BOY	Baltimora ●	Columbia	1

In these weeks ■ Madonna lands her first number one while *Holiday* re-enters at 32 (03.08.85) ■ The Cars *'Drive'* re-enters after accompanying moving footage of a starving child at the Live Aid concert (10.08.85) ■ With the top two records Madonna equals Frankie Goes To Hollywood's achievement of 07.07.84 - she also has another hit at 19 (17.05.85)■

LW	TW	Title	Artist	Label	Wks
26	34	LOVING YOU	Feargal Sharkey	*Virgin*	6
37	35	SECRET	Orchestral Manoeuvres In The Dark	*Virgin*	4
29	36	I'M ON FIRE/BORN IN THE USA	Bruce Springsteen	*CBS*	10
24	37	MONEY'S TOO TIGHT TO MENTION	Simply Red	*Elektra*	7
-	38	ROCK 'N' ROLL CHILDREN	Dio	*Vertigo*	1
-	39	ALONE WITHOUT YOU	King	*CBS*	1
-	40	TAKES A LITTLE TIME	Total Contrast ●	*London*	1

WEEK ENDING 24 AUGUST 1985

LW	TW	Title	Artist	Label	Wks
1	□ 1	INTO THE GROOVE	Madonna	*Sire*	5
3	2	I GOT YOU BABE	UB40 guest vocals by Chrissie Hynde	*DEP International*	4
2	3	HOLIDAY	Madonna	*Sire*	4
9	4	RUNNING UP THAT HILL	Kate Bush	*EMI*	2
8	5	DRIVE	Cars	*Elektra*	3
5	6	MONEY FOR NOTHING	Dire Straits	*Vertigo*	6
4	7	WE DON'T NEED ANOTHER HERO (THUNDERDOME)	Tina Turner	*Capitol*	6
7	8	WHITE WEDDING	Billy Idol	*Chrysalis*	6
6	9	THERE MUST BE AN ANGEL (PLAYING WITH MY HEART)	Eurythmics	*RCA*	8
11	10	SAY I'M YOUR NUMBER ONE	Princess	*Supreme*	3
33	11	TARZAN BOY	Baltimora	*Columbia*	2
13	□ 12	EXCITABLE	Amazulu	*Island*	4
39	13	ALONE WITHOUT YOU	King	*CBS*	2
10	14	DON QUIXOTE	Nik Kershaw	*MCA*	4
26	15	I WONDER IF I TAKE YOU HOME	Lisa Lisa and Cult Jam with Full Force	*CBS*	3
12	16	LIVE IS LIFE	Opus	*Polydor*	9
27	17	YOU'RE THE ONE FOR ME	D-Train	*Prelude*	3
14	18	CHERISH	Kool and the Gang	*De-Lite*	13
28	19	TAKE ME HOME	Phil Collins	*Virgin*	4
15	20	IN BETWEEN DAYS	Cure	*Fiction*	5
17	21	FRANKIE	Sister Sledge	*Atlantic*	12
40	22	TAKES A LITTLE TIME	Total Contrast	*London*	2
16	23	AXEL F	Harold Faltermeyer	*MCA*	11
19	24	CRAZY FOR YOU	Madonna	*Geffen*	12
29	□ 25	GOODBYE GIRL	Go West	*Chrysalis*	4
25	26	RASPBERRY BERET	Prince and the Revolution	*Paisley Park*	4
22	27	LET ME BE THE ONE	Five Star	*Tent*	6
18	28	LIVING ON VIDEO	Trans-X	*Boiling Point*	7
23	29	EMPTY ROOMS	Gary Moore	*10*	5
21	30	ROUND AND AROUND	Jaki Graham	*EMI*	8
24	31	SHE SELLS SANCTUARY	Cult	*Beggars Banquet*	9
38	32	ROCK 'N' ROLL CHILDREN	Dio	*Vertigo*	2
20	33	GLORY DAYS	Bruce Springsteen	*CBS*	4
-	34	STORIES OF JOHNNY	Marc Almond ●	*Some Bizzare*	1
32	35	IN YOUR CAR	Cool Notes	*Abstract Dance*	7
-	36	BODY AND SOUL	Mai Tai	*Hot Melt*	1
30	37	MY TOOT TOOT	Denise LaSalle	*Epic*	9
31	38	DARE ME	Pointer Sisters	*Planet*	6
35	39	SECRET	Orchestral Manoeuvres In The Dark	*Virgin*	5
-	40	I CAN DREAM ABOUT YOU	Dan Hartman	*MCA*	1

WEEK ENDING 31 AUGUST 1985

September 1985

□ Highest position disc reached ● Act's first ever week on chart

LW	TW	Title	Artist	Label	Wks
2	□ 1	I GOT YOU BABE	UB40 guest vocals by Chrissie Hynde	*DEP International*	5
1	2	INTO THE GROOVE	Madonna	*Sire*	6
4	□ 3	RUNNING UP THAT HILL	Kate Bush	*EMI*	3
5	□ 4	DRIVE	Cars	*Elektra*	4
11	5	TARZAN BOY	Baltimora	*Columbia*	3
3	6	HOLIDAY	Madonna	*Sire*	5
10	□ 7	SAY I'M YOUR NUMBER ONE	Princess	*Supreme*	4
6	8	MONEY FOR NOTHING	Dire Straits	*Vertigo*	7
13	9	ALONE WITHOUT YOU	King	*CBS*	3
7	10	WE DON'T NEED ANOTHER HERO (THUNDERDOME)	Tina Turner	*Capitol*	7
8	11	WHITE WEDDING	Billy Idol	*Chrysalis*	7
15	□ 12	I WONDER IF I TAKE YOU HOME	Lisa Lisa and Cult Jam with Full Force	*CBS*	4
12	13	EXCITABLE	Amazulu	*Island*	5
9	14	THERE MUST BE AN ANGEL (PLAYING WITH MY HEART)	Eurythmics	*RCA*	9
17	□ 15	YOU'RE THE ONE FOR ME	D-Train	*Prelude*	4
40	16	I CAN DREAM ABOUT YOU	Dan Hartman	*MCA*	2
22	□ 17	TAKES A LITTLE TIME	Total Contrast	*London*	3
36	18	BODY AND SOUL	Mai Tai	*Hot Melt*	2
19	□ 19	TAKE ME HOME	Phil Collins	*Virgin*	5
18	20	CHERISH	Kool and the Gang	*De-Lite*	14
14	21	DON QUIXOTE	Nik Kershaw	*MCA*	5
-	22	DON'T MESS WITH DR DREAM	Thompson Twins	*Arista*	1
34	□ 23	STORIES OF JOHNNY	Marc Almond	*Some Bizzare*	2
16	24	LIVE IS LIFE	Opus	*Polydor*	10
23	25	AXEL F	Harold Faltermeyer	*MCA*	12
32	26	ROCK 'N' ROLL CHILDREN	Dio	*Vertigo*	3
25	27	GOODBYE GIRL	Go West	*Chrysalis*	5
20	28	IN BETWEEN DAYS	Cure	*Fiction*	6
27	29	LET ME BE THE ONE	Five Star	*Tent*	7
-	30	YESTERDAY'S MEN	Madness	*Zarjazz*	1
24	31	CRAZY FOR YOU	Madonna	*Geffen*	13
21	32	FRANKIE	Sister Sledge	*Atlantic*	13
-	33	KNOCK ON WOOD/LIGHT MY FIRE	Amii Stewart	*Sedition*	1
-	34	HOLDING OUT FOR A HERO	Bonnie Tyler	*CBS*	1
30	35	ROUND AND AROUND	Jaki Graham	*EMI*	9
26	36	RASPBERRY BERET	Prince and the Revolution	*Paisley Park*	5
-	37	THE SHOW	Rebecca Storm ●	*Towerbell*	1
29	38	EMPTY ROOMS	Gary Moore	*10*	6
-	39	DON'T STOP THE DANCE	Bryan Ferry	*EG*	1
-	40	DO NOT DISTURB	Bananarama	*London*	1

WEEK ENDING 7 SEPTEMBER 1985

LW	TW	Title	Artist	Label	Wks
-	□ 1	DANCING IN THE STREET	David Bowie and Mick Jagger ●	*EMI America*	1
1	2	I GOT YOU BABE	UB40 guest vocals by Chrissie Hynde	*DEP International*	6
5	□ 3	TARZAN BOY	Baltimora	*Columbia*	4
2	4	INTO THE GROOVE	Madonna	*Sire*	7
3	5	RUNNING UP THAT HILL	Kate Bush	*EMI*	4
4	6	DRIVE	Cars	*Elektra*	5
7	□ 7	SAY I'M YOUR NUMBER ONE	Princess	*Supreme*	5
9	□ 8	ALONE WITHOUT YOU	King	*CBS*	4
8	9	MONEY FOR NOTHING	Dire Straits	*Vertigo*	8
34	10	HOLDING OUT FOR A HERO	Bonnie Tyler	*CBS*	2
18	11	BODY AND SOUL	Mai Tai	*Hot Melt*	3
16	□ 12	I CAN DREAM ABOUT YOU	Dan Hartman	*MCA*	3
12	13	I WONDER IF I TAKE YOU HOME	Lisa Lisa and Cult Jam with Full Force	*CBS*	5
6	14	HOLIDAY	Madonna	*Sire*	6
22	□ 15	DON'T MESS WITH DR DREAM	Thompson Twins	*Arista*	2
33	16	KNOCK ON WOOD/LIGHT MY FIRE	Amii Stewart	*Sedition*	2
11	17	WHITE WEDDING	Billy Idol	*Chrysalis*	8
10	18	WE DON'T NEED ANOTHER HERO (THUNDERDOME)	Tina Turner	*Capitol*	8
15	19	YOU'RE THE ONE FOR ME	D-Train	*Prelude*	5
-	20	PART TIME LOVER	Stevie Wonder	*Motown*	1
30	21	YESTERDAY'S MEN	Madness	*Zarjazz*	2
13	22	EXCITABLE	Amazulu	*Island*	6
-	23	LAVENDER	Marillion	*EMI*	1
17	24	TAKES A LITTLE TIME	Total Contrast	*London*	4
14	25	THERE MUST BE AN ANGEL (PLAYING WITH MY HEART)	Eurythmics	*RCA*	10
39	26	DON'T STOP THE DANCE	Bryan Ferry	*EG*	2
23	27	STORIES OF JOHNNY	Marc Almond	*Some Bizzare*	3
37	28	THE SHOW	Rebecca Storm	*Towerbell*	2
19	29	TAKE ME HOME	Phil Collins	*Virgin*	6
20	30	CHERISH	Kool and the Gang	*De-Lite*	15
-	31	THE POWER OF LOVE	Huey Lewis and the News	*Chrysalis*	1
21	32	DON QUIXOTE	Nik Kershaw	*MCA*	6
24	33	LIVE IS LIFE	Opus	*Polydor*	11

■Ten female soloists, four all female groups and five groups with a female vocalist dominate the Top 40 (31.08.85) ■ *I Got You Babe* is the number one record exactly 20 years after it first hit the top (31.08.85) ■ A charity record makes number one for the fourth time this year - Bowie and Jaggers Live Aid jaunt bounds in at number one (07.09.85)■

September 1985

□ Highest position disc reached ● Act's first ever week on chart

LW	TW	Title / Artist	Label	Wks
40	34	DO NOT DISTURB Bananarama	London	2
26	35	ROCK 'N' ROLL CHILDREN Dio	Vertigo	4
25	36	AXEL F Harold Faltermeyer	MCA	13
27	37	GOODBYE GIRL Go West	Chrysalis	6
-	38	BODY ROCK Maria Vidal ●	EMI America	1
28	39	IN BETWEEN DAYS Cure	Fiction	7
29	40	LET ME BE THE ONE Five Star	Tent	8

LW	TW	*WEEK ENDING* **14 SEPTEMBER 1985**		Wks
1	1	DANCING IN THE STREET David Bowie and Mick Jagger	EMI America	2
10	2	HOLDING OUT FOR A HERO Bonnie Tyler	CBS	3
2	3	I GOT YOU BABE UB40 guest vocals by Chrissie Hynde	DEP International	7
3	4	TARZAN BOY Baltimora	Columbia	5
20	5	PART TIME LOVER Stevie Wonder	Motown	2
6	6	DRIVE Cars	Elektra	6
4	7	INTO THE GROOVE Madonna	Sire	8
5	8	RUNNING UP THAT HILL Kate Bush	EMI	5
7	9	SAY I'M YOUR NUMBER ONE Princess	Supreme	6
11	10	BODY AND SOUL Mai Tai	Hot Melt	4
8	11	ALONE WITHOUT YOU King	CBS	5
16	12	KNOCK ON WOOD/LIGHT MY FIRE Amii Stewart	Sedition	3
23	13	LAVENDER Marillion	EMI	2
9	14	MONEY FOR NOTHING Dire Straits	Vertigo	9
12	15	I CAN DREAM ABOUT YOU Dan Hartman	MCA	4
15	16	DON'T MESS WITH DR DREAM Thompson Twins	Arista	3
13	17	I WONDER IF I TAKE YOU HOME Lisa Lisa and Cult Jam with Full Force	CBS	6
21	18	YESTERDAY'S MEN Madness	Zarjazz	3
31	19	THE POWER OF LOVE Huey Lewis and the News	Chrysalis	2
17	20	WHITE WEDDING Billy Idol	Chrysalis	9
26	21	DON'T STOP THE DANCE Bryan Ferry	EG	3
28	22	THE SHOW Rebecca Storm	Towerbell	3
14	23	HOLIDAY Madonna	Sire	7
19	24	YOU'RE THE ONE FOR ME D-Train	Prelude	6
18	25	WE DON'T NEED ANOTHER HERO (THUNDERDOME) Tina Turner	Capitol	9
38	26	BODY ROCK Maria Vidal	EMI America	2
22	27	EXCITABLE Amazulu	Island	7
24	28	TAKES A LITTLE TIME Total Contrast	London	5
-	29	IF I WAS Midge Ure	Chrysalis	1
-	30	LEAN ON ME (AH-LI-AYO) Red Box ●	Sire	1
34	31	DO NOT DISTURB Bananarama	London	3
25	32	THERE MUST BE AN ANGEL (PLAYING WITH MY HEART) Eurythmics	RCA	11
-	33	SHE'S SO BEAUTIFUL Cliff Richard	EMI	1
-	34	TRAPPED Colonel Abrams ●	MCA	1
27	35	STORIES OF JOHNNY Marc Almond	Some Bizzare	4
-	36	BRAND NEW FRIEND Lloyd Cole and the Commotions	Polydor	1
-	37	I'LL BE GOOD Rene and Angela ●	Club	1
-	38	REBEL YELL Billy Idol	Chrysalis	1
30	39	CHERISH Kool and the Gang	De-Lite	16
-	40	WHAT'S YOUR PROBLEM Blancmange	London	1

LW	TW	*WEEK ENDING* **21 SEPTEMBER 1985**		Wks
1	1	DANCING IN THE STREET David Bowie and Mick Jagger	EMI America	3
2	2	HOLDING OUT FOR A HERO Bonnie Tyler	CBS	4
5	3	PART TIME LOVER Stevie Wonder	Motown	3
4	4	TARZAN BOY Baltimora	Columbia	6
13	5	LAVENDER Marillion	EMI	3
3	6	I GOT YOU BABE UB40 guest vocals by Chrissie Hynde	DEP International	8
12	7	KNOCK ON WOOD/LIGHT MY FIRE Amii Stewart	Sedition	4
29	8	IF I WAS Midge Ure	Chrysalis	2
10	9	BODY AND SOUL Mai Tai	Hot Melt	5
-	10	ANGEL Madonna	Sire	1
19	11	THE POWER OF LOVE Huey Lewis and the News	Chrysalis	3
7	12	INTO THE GROOVE Madonna	Sire	9
6	13	DRIVE Cars	Elektra	7
9	14	SAY I'M YOUR NUMBER ONE Princess	Supreme	7
8	15	RUNNING UP THAT HILL Kate Bush	EMI	6
26	16	BODY ROCK Maria Vidal	EMI America	3
33	17	SHE'S SO BEAUTIFUL Cliff Richard	EMI	2
30	18	LEAN ON ME (AH-LI-AYO) Red Box	Sire	2
11	19	ALONE WITHOUT YOU King	CBS	6
18	20	YESTERDAY'S MEN Madness	Zarjazz	4
14	21	MONEY FOR NOTHING Dire Straits	Vertigo	10
15	22	I CAN DREAM ABOUT YOU Dan Hartman	MCA	5
21	23	DON'T STOP THE DANCE Bryan Ferry	EG	4
17	24	I WONDER IF I TAKE YOU HOME Lisa Lisa and Cult Jam with Full Force	CBS	7
38	25	REBEL YELL Billy Idol	Chrysalis	2
16	26	DON'T MESS WITH DR DREAM Thompson Twins	Arista	4
36	27	BRAND NEW FRIEND Lloyd Cole and the Commotions	Polydor	2
34	28	TRAPPED Colonel Abrams	MCA	2
22	29	THE SHOW Rebecca Storm	Towerbell	4
20	30	WHITE WEDDING Billy Idol	Chrysalis	10
37	31	I'LL BE GOOD Rene and Angela	Club	2
25	32	WE DON'T NEED ANOTHER HERO (THUNDERDOME) Tina Turner	Capitol	10
23	33	HOLIDAY Madonna	Sire	8
24	34	YOU'RE THE ONE FOR ME D-Train	Prelude	7
-	35	SINGLE LIFE Cameo	Club	1
-	36	THE POWER OF LOVE Jennifer Rush ●	CBS	1
28	37	TAKES A LITTLE TIME Total Contrast	London	6
-	38	LOVE TAKE OVER Five Star	Tent	1
-	39	IS IT A DREAM Damned	MCA	1
40	40	WHAT'S YOUR PROBLEM Blancmange	London	2

LW	TW	*WEEK ENDING* **28 SEPTEMBER 1985**		Wks
1	1	DANCING IN THE STREET David Bowie and Mick Jagger	EMI America	4
2	2	HOLDING OUT FOR A HERO Bonnie Tyler	CBS	5
3	3	PART TIME LOVER Stevie Wonder	Motown	4
8	4	IF I WAS Midge Ure	Chrysalis	3
10	5	ANGEL Madonna	Sire	2
18	6	LEAN ON ME (AH-LI-AYO) Red Box	Sire	3
5	7	LAVENDER Marillion	EMI	4
7	8	KNOCK ON WOOD/LIGHT MY FIRE Amii Stewart	Sedition	5
4	9	TARZAN BOY Baltimora	Columbia	7
9	10	BODY AND SOUL Mai Tai	Hot Melt	6
16	11	BODY ROCK Maria Vidal	EMI America	4
11	12	THE POWER OF LOVE Huey Lewis and the News	Chrysalis	4
25	13	REBEL YELL Billy Idol	Chrysalis	3
6	14	I GOT YOU BABE UB40 guest vocals by Chrissie Hynde	DEP International	9
36	15	THE POWER OF LOVE Jennifer Rush	CBS	2
28	16	TRAPPED Colonel Abrams	MCA	3
-	17	THE LODGERS Style Council	Polydor	1
17	18	SHE'S SO BEAUTIFUL Cliff Richard	EMI	3
13	19	DRIVE Cars	Elektra	8
12	20	INTO THE GROOVE Madonna	Sire	10
-	21	IT'S CALLED A HEART Depeche Mode	Mute	1
27	22	BRAND NEW FRIEND Lloyd Cole and the Commotions	Polydor	3
15	23	RUNNING UP THAT HILL Kate Bush	EMI	7
31	24	I'LL BE GOOD Rene and Angela	Club	3
35	25	SINGLE LIFE Cameo	Club	2
14	26	SAY I'M YOUR NUMBER ONE Princess	Supreme	8
21	27	MONEY FOR NOTHING Dire Straits	Vertigo	11
20	28	YESTERDAY'S MEN Madness	Zarjazz	5
19	29	ALONE WITHOUT YOU King	CBS	7
24	30	I WONDER IF I TAKE YOU HOME Lisa Lisa and Cult Jam with Full Force	CBS	8
-	31	MY HEART GOES BANG (GET ME TO THE DOCTOR) Dead Or Alive	Epic	1
23	32	DON'T STOP THE DANCE Bryan Ferry	EG	5
22	33	I CAN DREAM ABOUT YOU Dan Hartman	MCA	6

In these weeks ■ *Into The Groove, The Power Of Love, We Don't Need Another Hero* and *Body Rock* are all film themes whilst *The Show* is a TV theme (14.09.85) ■ Different songs - same title, Huey Lewis and Jennifer Rush take Frankie Goes To Hollywood's lead and have a hit with *The Power Of Love* (21.05.85)■

October 1985

□ Highest position disc reached ● Act's first ever week on chart

LW	TW	Title	Artist	Label	Wks
39	[34]	IS IT A DREAM	Damned	MCA	2
38	35	LOVE TAKE OVER	Five Star	Tent	2
-	36	CLOSE TO ME	Cure	Fiction	1
26	37	DON'T MESS WITH DR DREAM	Thompson Twins	Arista	5
-	38	ST ELMO'S FIRE (MAN IN MOTION)	John Parr ●	London	1
30	39	WHITE WEDDING	Billy Idol	Chrysalis	11
29	40	THE SHOW	Rebecca Storm	Towerbell	5

WEEK ENDING 5 OCTOBER 1985

LW	TW	Title	Artist	Label	Wks
4	[1]	IF I WAS	Midge Ure	Chrysalis	4
15	2	THE POWER OF LOVE	Jennifer Rush	CBS	3
1	3	DANCING IN THE STREET	David Bowie and Mick Jagger	EMI America	5
6	4	LEAN ON ME (AH-LI-AYO)	Red Box	Sire	4
3	5	PART TIME LOVER	Stevie Wonder	Motown	5
5	6	ANGEL	Madonna	Sire	3
2	7	HOLDING OUT FOR A HERO	Bonnie Tyler	CBS	6
13	8	REBEL YELL	Billy Idol	Chrysalis	4
7	9	LAVENDER	Marillion	EMI	5
16	10	TRAPPED	Colonel Abrams	MCA	4
12	[11]	THE POWER OF LOVE	Huey Lewis and the News	Chrysalis	5
11	12	BODY ROCK	Maria Vidal	EMI America	5
17	[13]	THE LODGERS	Style Council	Polydor	2
8	14	KNOCK ON WOOD/LIGHT MY FIRE	Amii Stewart	Sedition	6
10	15	BODY AND SOUL	Mai Tai	Hot Melt	7
9	16	TARZAN BOY	Baltimora	Columbia	8
18	17	SHE'S SO BEAUTIFUL	Cliff Richard	EMI	4
21	[18]	IT'S CALLED A HEART	Depeche Mode	Mute	2
22	[19]	BRAND NEW FRIEND	Lloyd Cole and the Commotions	Polydor	4
-	20	RUNNING FREE	Iron Maiden	EMI	1
25	21	SINGLE LIFE	Cameo	Club	3
24	[22]	I'LL BE GOOD	Rene and Angela	Club	4
31	[23]	MY HEART GOES BANG (GET ME TO THE DOCTOR)	Dead Or Alive	Epic	2
36	[24]	CLOSE TO ME	Cure	Fiction	2
14	25	I GOT YOU BABE	UB40 guest vocals by Chrissie Hynde	DEP International	10
-	26	THE BOY WITH THE THORN IN HIS SIDE	Smiths	Rough Trade	1
38	27	ST ELMO'S FIRE (MAN IN MOTION)	John Parr	London	2
35	28	LOVE TAKE OVER	Five Star	Tent	3
20	29	INTO THE GROOVE	Madonna	Sire	11
19	30	DRIVE	Cars	Elektra	9
-	31	RAIN	Cult	Beggars Banquet	1
26	32	SAY I'M YOUR NUMBER ONE	Princess	Supreme	9
23	33	RUNNING UP THAT HILL	Kate Bush	EMI	8
27	34	MONEY FOR NOTHING	Dire Straits	Vertigo	12
34	35	IS IT A DREAM	Damned	MCA	3
-	36	TAKE ON ME	A-Ha ●	Warner Brothers	1
30	37	I WONDER IF I TAKE YOU HOME	Lisa Lisa and Cult Jam with Full Force	CBS	9
29	38	ALONE WITHOUT YOU	King	CBS	8
-	39	SOMETHING ABOUT YOU	Level 42	Polydor	1
-	[40]	STRENGTH	Alarm	IRS	1

WEEK ENDING 12 OCTOBER 1985

LW	TW	Title	Artist	Label	Wks
2	[1]	THE POWER OF LOVE	Jennifer Rush	CBS	4
1	2	IF I WAS	Midge Ure	Chrysalis	5
4	[3]	LEAN ON ME (AH-LI-AYO)	Red Box	Sire	5
10	4	TRAPPED	Colonel Abrams	MCA	5
5	5	PART TIME LOVER	Stevie Wonder	Motown	6
8	[6]	REBEL YELL	Billy Idol	Chrysalis	5
3	7	DANCING IN THE STREET	David Bowie and Mick Jagger	EMI America	6
6	8	ANGEL	Madonna	Sire	4
7	9	HOLDING OUT FOR A HERO	Bonnie Tyler	CBS	7
27	10	ST ELMO'S FIRE (MAN IN MOTION)	John Parr	London	3
12	[11]	BODY ROCK	Maria Vidal	EMI America	6
-	12	ALIVE AND KICKING	Simple Minds	Virgin	1
9	13	LAVENDER	Marillion	EMI	6
36	14	TAKE ON ME	A-Ha	Warner Brothers	2
11	15	THE POWER OF LOVE	Huey Lewis and the News	Chrysalis	6
21	16	SINGLE LIFE	Cameo	Club	4
17	[17]	SHE'S SO BEAUTIFUL	Cliff Richard	EMI	5
13	18	THE LODGERS	Style Council	Polydor	3
20	[19]	RUNNING FREE	Iron Maiden	EMI	2
-	20	GAMBLER	Madonna	Geffen	1
14	21	KNOCK ON WOOD/LIGHT MY FIRE	Amii Stewart	Sedition	7
22	[22]	I'LL BE GOOD	Rene and Angela	Club	5
26	[23]	THE BOY WITH THE THORN IN HIS SIDE	Smiths	Rough Trade	2
24	[24]	CLOSE TO ME	Cure	Fiction	3
28	[25]	LOVE TAKE OVER	Five Star	Tent	4
31	26	RAIN	Cult	Beggars Banquet	2
15	27	BODY AND SOUL	Mai Tai	Hot Melt	8
16	28	TARZAN BOY	Baltimora	Columbia	9
19	29	BRAND NEW FRIEND	Lloyd Cole and the Commotions	Polydor	5
-	30	MIAMI VICE THEME	Jan Hammer ●	MCA	1
39	31	SOMETHING ABOUT YOU	Level 42	Polydor	2
23	32	MY HEART GOES BANG (GET ME TO THE DOCTOR)	Dead Or Alive	Epic	3
-	33	SLAVE TO THE RHYTHM	Grace Jones	ZTT	1
-	34	THIS IS ENGLAND	Clash	CBS	1
25	35	I GOT YOU BABE	UB40 guest vocals by Chrissie Hynde	DEP International	11
18	36	IT'S CALLED A HEART	Depeche Mode	Mute	3
29	37	INTO THE GROOVE	Madonna	Sire	12
-	38	I BELIEVE (A SOULFUL RE-RECORDING)	Tears For Fears	Mercury	1
-	39	LIPSTICK POWDER AND PAINT	Shakin' Stevens	Epic	1
-	40	YEH YEH	Matt Bianco	WEA	1

WEEK ENDING 19 OCTOBER 1985

LW	TW	Title	Artist	Label	Wks
1	[1]	THE POWER OF LOVE	Jennifer Rush	CBS	5
2	2	IF I WAS	Midge Ure	Chrysalis	6
4	[3]	TRAPPED	Colonel Abrams	MCA	6
3	4	LEAN ON ME (AH-LI-AYO)	Red Box	Sire	6
14	5	TAKE ON ME	A-Ha	Warner Brothers	3
10	[6]	ST ELMO'S FIRE (MAN IN MOTION)	John Parr	London	4
20	7	GAMBLER	Madonna	Geffen	2
12	8	ALIVE AND KICKING	Simple Minds	Virgin	2
6	9	REBEL YELL	Billy Idol	Chrysalis	6
30	10	MIAMI VICE THEME	Jan Hammer	MCA	2
5	11	PART TIME LOVER	Stevie Wonder	Motown	7
9	12	HOLDING OUT FOR A HERO	Bonnie Tyler	CBS	8
7	13	DANCING IN THE STREET	David Bowie and Mick Jagger	EMI America	7
33	14	SLAVE TO THE RHYTHM	Grace Jones	ZTT	2
16	[15]	SINGLE LIFE	Cameo	Club	5
8	16	ANGEL	Madonna	Sire	5
26	[17]	RAIN	Cult	Beggars Banquet	3
39	18	LIPSTICK POWDER AND PAINT	Shakin' Stevens	Epic	2
-	19	NIKITA	Elton John	Rocket	1
11	20	BODY ROCK	Maria Vidal	EMI America	7
31	21	SOMETHING ABOUT YOU	Level 42	Polydor	3
17	22	SHE'S SO BEAUTIFUL	Cliff Richard	EMI	6
38	[23]	I BELIEVE (A SOULFUL RE-RECORDING)	Tears For Fears	Mercury	2
34	[24]	THIS IS ENGLAND	Clash	CBS	2
25	[25]	LOVE TAKE OVER	Five Star	Tent	5
15	26	THE POWER OF LOVE	Huey Lewis and the News	Chrysalis	7
19	27	RUNNING FREE	Iron Maiden	EMI	3
23	28	THE BOY WITH THE THORN IN HIS SIDE	Smiths	Rough Trade	3
22	29	I'LL BE GOOD	Rene and Angela	Club	6
24	30	CLOSE TO ME	Cure	Fiction	4
40	31	YEH YEH	Matt Bianco	WEA	2
13	32	LAVENDER	Marillion	EMI	7
-	33	BRING ON THE DANCING HORSES	Echo and the Bunnymen	Korova	1

■Midge Ure accomplishes something Ultravox never did - a number one record (05.10.85) ■ Jennifer Rush creeps slowly to number one, after two weeks at number two. The record will become the biggest selling disc by a female artist and the last million seller until Bryan Adams in 1991 (12.10.85)■

October 1985

□ Highest position disc reached ● Act's first ever week on chart

LW	TW	Title	Artist	Label	Wks
18	34	THE LODGERS	Style Council	*Polydor*	4
21	35	KNOCK ON WOOD/LIGHT MY FIRE	Amii Stewart	*Sedition*	8
-	36	THE SWEETEST TABOO	Sade	*Epic*	1
-	37	THE TASTE OF YOUR TEARS	King	*CBS*	1
29	38	BRAND NEW FRIEND	Lloyd Cole and the Commotions	*Polydor*	6
-	39	SLEEPING BAG	ZZ Top	*Warner Brothers*	1
-	40	KING FOR A DAY	Thompson Twins	*Arista*	1

WEEK ENDING 26 OCTOBER 1985

LW	TW	Title	Artist	Label	Wks
1	[1]	THE POWER OF LOVE	Jennifer Rush	*CBS*	6
5	[2]	TAKE ON ME	A-Ha	*Warner Brothers*	4
3	[3]	TRAPPED	Colonel Abrams	*MCA*	7
7	[4]	GAMBLER	Madonna	*Geffen*	3
10	[5]	MIAMI VICE THEME	Jan Hammer	*MCA*	3
6	[6]	ST ELMO'S FIRE (MAN IN MOTION)	John Parr	*London*	5
8	[7]	ALIVE AND KICKING	Simple Minds	*Virgin*	3
2	8	IF I WAS	Midge Ure	*Chrysalis*	7
19	9	NIKITA	Elton John	*Rocket*	2
4	10	LEAN ON ME (AH-LI-AYO)	Red Box	*Sire*	7
9	11	REBEL YELL	Billy Idol	*Chrysalis*	7
14	[12]	SLAVE TO THE RHYTHM	Grace Jones	*ZTT*	3
21	13	SOMETHING ABOUT YOU	Level 42	*Polydor*	4
-	14	ELECTION DAY	Arcadia ●	*Parlophone*	1
18	15	LIPSTICK POWDER AND PAINT	Shakin' Stevens	*Epic*	3
11	16	PART TIME LOVER	Stevie Wonder	*Motown*	8
17	[17]	RAIN	Cult	*Beggars Banquet*	4
12	18	HOLDING OUT FOR A HERO	Bonnie Tyler	*CBS*	9
15	19	SINGLE LIFE	Cameo	*Club*	6
37	20	THE TASTE OF YOUR TEARS	King	*CBS*	2
13	21	DANCING IN THE STREET	David Bowie and Mick Jagger	*EMI America*	8
20	22	BODY ROCK	Maria Vidal	*EMI America*	8
33	23	BRING ON THE DANCING HORSES	Echo and the Bunnymen	*Korova*	2
31	24	YEH YEH	Matt Bianco	*WEA*	3
22	25	SHE'S SO BEAUTIFUL	Cliff Richard	*EMI*	7
-	26	CLOUDBUSTING	Kate Bush	*EMI*	1
39	[27]	SLEEPING BAG	ZZ Top	*Warner Brothers*	2
24	28	THIS IS ENGLAND	Clash	*CBS*	3
40	29	KING FOR A DAY	Thompson Twins	*Arista*	2
16	30	ANGEL	Madonna	*Sire*	6
36	[31]	THE SWEETEST TABOO	Sade	*Epic*	2
-	32	A GOOD HEART	Feargal Sharkey	*Virgin*	1
23	33	I BELIEVE (A SOULFUL RE-RECORDING)	Tears For Fears	*Mercury*	3
25	34	LOVE TAKE OVER	Five Star	*Tent*	6
-	35	DON'T BREAK MY HEART	UB40	*DEP International*	1
-	36	CITIES IN DUST	Siouxsie and the Bansheees	*Wonderland*	1
30	37	CLOSE TO ME	Cure	*Fiction*	5
29	38	I'LL BE GOOD	Rene and Angela	*Club*	7
28	39	THE BOY WITH THE THORN IN HIS SIDE	Smiths	*Rough Trade*	4
26	40	THE POWER OF LOVE	Huey Lewis and the News	*Chrysalis*	8

WEEK ENDING 2 NOVEMBER 1985

LW	TW	Title	Artist	Label	Wks
1	[1]	THE POWER OF LOVE	Jennifer Rush	*CBS*	7
2	[2]	TAKE ON ME	A-Ha	*Warner Brothers*	5
3	[3]	TRAPPED	Colonel Abrams	*MCA*	8
9	4	NIKITA	Elton John	*Rocket*	3
4	5	GAMBLER	Madonna	*Geffen*	4
6	[6]	ST ELMO'S FIRE (MAN IN MOTION)	John Parr	*London*	6
14	[7]	ELECTION DAY	Arcadia	*Parlophone*	2
5	8	MIAMI VICE THEME	Jan Hammer	*MCA*	4
13	9	SOMETHING ABOUT YOU	Level 42	*Polydor*	5
7	10	ALIVE AND KICKING	Simple Minds	*Virgin*	4
15	[11]	LIPSTICK POWDER AND PAINT	Shakin' Stevens	*Epic*	4
32	12	A GOOD HEART	Feargal Sharkey	*Virgin*	2
12	13	SLAVE TO THE RHYTHM	Grace Jones	*ZTT*	4
10	14	LEAN ON ME (AH-LI-AYO)	Red Box	*Sire*	8
20	15	THE TASTE OF YOUR TEARS	King	*CBS*	3
8	16	IF I WAS	Midge Ure	*Chrysalis*	8
24	17	YEH YEH	Matt Bianco	*WEA*	4
11	18	REBEL YELL	Billy Idol	*Chrysalis*	8
35	19	DON'T BREAK MY HEART	UB40	*DEP International*	2
26	[20]	CLOUDBUSTING	Kate Bush	*EMI*	2
23	[21]	BRING ON THE DANCING HORSES	Echo and the Bunnymen	*Korova*	3
29	[22]	KING FOR A DAY	Thompson Twins	*Arista*	3
36	23	CITIES IN DUST	Siouxsie and the Bansheees	*Wonderland*	2
16	24	PART TIME LOVER	Stevie Wonder	*Motown*	9
17	25	RAIN	Cult	*Beggars Banquet*	5
-	26	ROAD TO NOWHERE	Talking Heads	*EMI*	1
27	[27]	SLEEPING BAG	ZZ Top	*Warner Brothers*	3
18	28	HOLDING OUT FOR A HERO	Bonnie Tyler	*CBS*	10
-	29	STAIRWAY TO HEAVEN	Far Corporation ●	*Arista*	1
21	30	DANCING IN THE STREET	David Bowie and Mick Jagger	*EMI America*	9
-	31	HOWARDS' WAY THEME	Simon May Orchestra ●	*BBC*	1
22	32	BODY ROCK	Maria Vidal	*EMI America*	9
19	33	SINGLE LIFE	Cameo	*Club*	7
-	34	UNCLE SAM	Madness	*Zarjazz*	1
31	35	THE SWEETEST TABOO	Sade	*Epic*	3
30	36	ANGEL	Madonna	*Sire*	7
25	37	SHE'S SO BEAUTIFUL	Cliff Richard	*EMI*	8
-	38	SISTERS ARE DOIN' IT FOR THEMSELVES	Eurythmics and Aretha Franklin ●	*RCA*	1
-	39	BROTHERS IN ARMS	Dire Straits	*Vertigo*	1
-	40	YOU ARE MY WORLD	Communards ●	*London*	1

WEEK ENDING 9 NOVEMBER 1985

LW	TW	Title	Artist	Label	Wks
1	[1]	THE POWER OF LOVE	Jennifer Rush	*CBS*	8
2	[2]	TAKE ON ME	A-Ha	*Warner Brothers*	6
4	[3]	NIKITA	Elton John	*Rocket*	4
12	4	A GOOD HEART	Feargal Sharkey	*Virgin*	3
3	5	TRAPPED	Colonel Abrams	*MCA*	9
9	[6]	SOMETHING ABOUT YOU	Level 42	*Polydor*	6
19	7	DON'T BREAK MY HEART	UB40	*DEP International*	3
5	8	GAMBLER	Madonna	*Geffen*	5
6	9	ST ELMO'S FIRE (MAN IN MOTION)	John Parr	*London*	7
7	10	ELECTION DAY	Arcadia	*Parlophone*	3
10	11	ALIVE AND KICKING	Simple Minds	*Virgin*	5
15	12	THE TASTE OF YOUR TEARS	King	*CBS*	4
17	[13]	YEH YEH	Matt Bianco	*WEA*	5
8	14	MIAMI VICE THEME	Jan Hammer	*MCA*	5
11	15	LIPSTICK POWDER AND PAINT	Shakin' Stevens	*Epic*	5
29	16	STAIRWAY TO HEAVEN	Far Corporation	*Arista*	2
26	17	ROAD TO NOWHERE	Talking Heads	*EMI*	2
38	18	SISTERS ARE DOIN' IT FOR THEMSELVES	Eurythmics and Aretha Franklin	*RCA*	2
13	19	SLAVE TO THE RHYTHM	Grace Jones	*ZTT*	5
20	[20]	CLOUDBUSTING	Kate Bush	*EMI*	3
23	21	CITIES IN DUST	Siouxsie and the Bansheees	*Wonderland*	3
31	22	HOWARDS' WAY THEME	Simon May Orchestra	*BBC*	2
39	23	BROTHERS IN ARMS	Dire Straits	*Vertigo*	2
16	24	IF I WAS	Midge Ure	*Chrysalis*	9
14	25	LEAN ON ME (AH-LI-AYO)	Red Box	*Sire*	9
18	26	REBEL YELL	Billy Idol	*Chrysalis*	9
21	27	BRING ON THE DANCING HORSES	Echo and the Bunnymen	*Korova*	4
34	28	UNCLE SAM	Madness	*Zarjazz*	2
22	29	KING FOR A DAY	Thompson Twins	*Arista*	4
40	[30]	YOU ARE MY WORLD	Communards	*London*	2
-	31	JUST FOR MONEY	Paul Hardcastle	*Chrysalis*	1
-	32	THE SHOW	Doug E Fresh and the Get Fresh Crew ●	*Cooltempo*	1
24	33	PART TIME LOVER	Stevie Wonder	*Motown*	10
27	34	SLEEPING BAG	ZZ Top	*Warner Brothers*	4
28	35	HOLDING OUT FOR A HERO	Bonnie Tyler	*CBS*	11
-	36	IT'S ONLY LOVE	Bryan Adams and Tina Turner ●	*A&M*	1
-	37	LOST WEEKEND	Lloyd Cole and the Commotions	*Polydor*	1

In these weeks ■ The Top Seven records are all at their peak (26.10.85) ■ Madonna has had at least two hits in the Top 40 every week for fifteen weeks (02.11.85) ■ Elton John has his first solo week in the Top Three since 3 June 1972 (09.11.85)■

November 1985

□ Highest position disc reached ● Act's first ever week on chart

LW	TW	Title / Artist	Label	Wks
25	38	RAIN Cult	*Beggars Banquet*	6
-	39	THE WHOLE OF THE MOON Waterboys ●	*Ensign*	1
32	40	BODY ROCK Maria Vidal	*EMI America*	10

LW	TW	*WEEK ENDING* 16 NOVEMBER 1985		Wks
4	[1]	A GOOD HEART Feargal Sharkey	*Virgin*	4
1	2	THE POWER OF LOVE Jennifer Rush	*CBS*	9
2	3	TAKE ON ME A-Ha	*Warner Brothers*	7
3	4	NIKITA Elton John	*Rocket*	5
7	5	DON'T BREAK MY HEART UB40	*DEP International*	4
6	[6]	SOMETHING ABOUT YOU Level 42	*Polydor*	7
5	7	TRAPPED Colonel Abrams	*MCA*	10
16	[8]	STAIRWAY TO HEAVEN Far Corporation	*Arista*	3
-	9	ONE VISION Queen	*EMI*	1
18	10	SISTERS ARE DOIN' IT FOR THEMSELVES Eurythmics and Aretha Franklin	*RCA*	3
12	[11]	THE TASTE OF YOUR TEARS King	*CBS*	5
17	12	ROAD TO NOWHERE Talking Heads	*EMI*	3
32	13	THE SHOW Doug E Fresh and the Get Fresh Crew	*Cooltempo*	2
8	14	GAMBLER Madonna	*Geffen*	6
13	15	YEH YEH Matt Bianco	*WEA*	6
10	16	ELECTION DAY Arcadia	*Parlophone*	4
9	17	ST ELMO'S FIRE (MAN IN MOTION) John Parr	*London*	8
11	18	ALIVE AND KICKING Simple Minds	*Virgin*	6
31	[19]	JUST FOR MONEY Paul Hardcastle	*Chrysalis*	2
15	20	LIPSTICK POWDER AND PAINT Shakin' Stevens	*Epic*	6
22	[21]	HOWARDS' WAY THEME Simon May Orchestra	*BBC*	3
23	22	BROTHERS IN ARMS Dire Straits	*Vertigo*	3
14	23	MIAMI VICE THEME Jan Hammer	*MCA*	6
37	24	LOST WEEKEND Lloyd Cole and the Commotions	*Polydor*	2
28	25	UNCLE SAM Madness	*Zarjazz*	3
19	26	SLAVE TO THE RHYTHM Grace Jones	*ZTT*	6
20	27	CLOUDBUSTING Kate Bush	*EMI*	4
21	28	CITIES IN DUST Siouxsie and the Banshees	*Wonderland*	4
39	29	THE WHOLE OF THE MOON Waterboys	*Ensign*	2
30	[30]	YOU ARE MY WORLD Communards	*London*	3
36	31	IT'S ONLY LOVE Bryan Adams and Tina Turner	*A&M*	2
27	32	BRING ON THE DANCING HORSES Echo and the Bunnymen	*Korova*	5
-	33	THAT'S WHAT FRIENDS ARE FOR Dionne Warwick and Friends ●	*Arista*	1
-	34	SAY YOU SAY ME Lionel Richie	*Motown*	1
26	35	REBEL YELL Billy Idol	*Chrysalis*	10
25	36	LEAN ON ME (AH-LI-AYO) Red Box	*Sire*	10
24	37	IF I WAS Midge Ure	*Chrysalis*	10
-	38	SEE THE DAY Dee C Lee ●	*CBS*	1
-	39	THAT CERTAIN SMILE Midge Ure	*Chrysalis*	1
-	40	YOUR PERSONAL TOUCH Evelyn 'Champagne' King	*RCA*	1

LW	TW	*WEEK ENDING* 23 NOVEMBER 1985		Wks
1	[1]	A GOOD HEART Feargal Sharkey	*Virgin*	5
-	2	I'M YOUR MAN Wham!	*Epic*	1
5	[3]	DON'T BREAK MY HEART UB40	*DEP International*	5
2	4	THE POWER OF LOVE Jennifer Rush	*CBS*	10
3	5	TAKE ON ME A-Ha	*Warner Brothers*	8
4	6	NIKITA Elton John	*Rocket*	6
9	[7]	ONE VISION Queen	*EMI*	2
6	8	SOMETHING ABOUT YOU Level 42	*Polydor*	8
10	[9]	SISTERS ARE DOIN' IT FOR THEMSELVES Eurythmics and Aretha Franklin	*RCA*	4
12	10	ROAD TO NOWHERE Talking Heads	*EMI*	4
8	11	STAIRWAY TO HEAVEN Far Corporation	*Arista*	4
13	12	THE SHOW Doug E Fresh and the Get Fresh Crew	*Cooltempo*	3
7	13	TRAPPED Colonel Abrams	*MCA*	11
34	14	SAY YOU SAY ME Lionel Richie	*Motown*	2
11	15	THE TASTE OF YOUR TEARS King	*CBS*	6
22	[16]	BROTHERS IN ARMS Dire Straits	*Vertigo*	4
24	[17]	LOST WEEKEND Lloyd Cole and the Commotions	*Polydor*	3
38	18	SEE THE DAY Dee C Lee	*CBS*	2
33	19	THAT'S WHAT FRIENDS ARE FOR Dionne Warwick and Friends	*Arista*	2
19	20	JUST FOR MONEY Paul Hardcastle	*Chrysalis*	3
21	[21]	HOWARDS' WAY THEME Simon May Orchestra	*BBC*	4
14	22	GAMBLER Madonna	*Geffen*	7
-	23	SAVING ALL MY LOVE FOR YOU Whitney Houston ●	*Arista*	1
25	24	UNCLE SAM Madness	*Zarjazz*	4
-	25	SEPARATE LIVES Phil Collins and Marilyn Martin ●	*Virgin*	1
29	[26]	THE WHOLE OF THE MOON Waterboys	*Ensign*	3
17	27	ST ELMO'S FIRE (MAN IN MOTION) John Parr	*London*	9
39	[28]	THAT CERTAIN SMILE Midge Ure	*Chrysalis*	2
31	[29]	IT'S ONLY LOVE Bryan Adams and Tina Turner	*A&M*	3
15	30	YEH YEH Matt Bianco	*WEA*	7
23	31	MIAMI VICE THEME Jan Hammer	*MCA*	7
16	32	ELECTION DAY Arcadia	*Parlophone*	5
30	33	YOU ARE MY WORLD Communards	*London*	4
18	34	ALIVE AND KICKING Simple Minds	*Virgin*	7
20	35	LIPSTICK POWDER AND PAINT Shakin' Stevens	*Epic*	7
-	36	MATED David Grant and Jaki Graham	*EMI*	1
40	[37]	YOUR PERSONAL TOUCH Evelyn 'Champagne' King	*RCA*	2
26	38	SLAVE TO THE RHYTHM Grace Jones	*ZTT*	7
28	39	CITIES IN DUST Siouxsie and the Banshees	*Wonderland*	5
-	40	WHEN LOVE BREAKS DOWN Prefab Sprout ●	*Kitchenware*	1

LW	TW	*WEEK ENDING* 30 NOVEMBER 1985		Wks
2	[1]	I'M YOUR MAN Wham!	*Epic*	2
1	2	A GOOD HEART Feargal Sharkey	*Virgin*	6
3	[3]	DON'T BREAK MY HEART UB40	*DEP International*	6
18	4	SEE THE DAY Dee C Lee	*CBS*	3
4	5	THE POWER OF LOVE Jennifer Rush	*CBS*	11
10	[6]	ROAD TO NOWHERE Talking Heads	*EMI*	5
12	[7]	THE SHOW Doug E Fresh and the Get Fresh Crew	*Cooltempo*	4
7	8	ONE VISION Queen	*EMI*	3
23	9	SAVING ALL MY LOVE FOR YOU Whitney Houston	*Arista*	2
25	10	SEPARATE LIVES Phil Collins and Marilyn Martin	*Virgin*	2
14	11	SAY YOU SAY ME Lionel Richie	*Motown*	3
5	12	TAKE ON ME A-Ha	*Warner Brothers*	9
8	13	SOMETHING ABOUT YOU Level 42	*Polydor*	9
9	14	SISTERS ARE DOIN' IT FOR THEMSELVES Eurythmics and Aretha Franklin	*RCA*	5
6	15	NIKITA Elton John	*Rocket*	7
19	[16]	THAT'S WHAT FRIENDS ARE FOR Dionne Warwick and Friends	*Arista*	3
11	17	STAIRWAY TO HEAVEN Far Corporation	*Arista*	5
16	18	BROTHERS IN ARMS Dire Straits	*Vertigo*	5
17	19	LOST WEEKEND Lloyd Cole and the Commotions	*Polydor*	4
13	20	TRAPPED Colonel Abrams	*MCA*	12
24	[21]	UNCLE SAM Madness	*Zarjazz*	5
36	22	MATED David Grant and Jaki Graham	*EMI*	2
15	23	THE TASTE OF YOUR TEARS King	*CBS*	7
-	24	DON'T LOOK DOWN-THE SEQUEL Go West	*Chrysalis*	1
40	[25]	WHEN LOVE BREAKS DOWN Prefab Sprout	*Kitchenware*	2
-	26	SPIES LIKE US Paul McCartney	*Parlophone*	1
21	27	HOWARDS' WAY THEME Simon May Orchestra	*BBC*	5
26	28	THE WHOLE OF THE MOON Waterboys	*Ensign*	4
-	29	SUN CITY Artists United Against Apartheid ●	*Manhattan*	1
-	[30]	REVOLUTION Cult	*Beggars Banquet*	1
-	31	HEART OF LOTHIAN Marillion	*EMI*	1
29	32	IT'S ONLY LOVE Bryan Adams and Tina Turner	*A&M*	4
-	33	WHEN A HEART BEATS Nik Kershaw	*MCA*	1
28	34	THAT CERTAIN SMILE Midge Ure	*Chrysalis*	3
-	35	WE BUILT THIS CITY Starship ●	*RCA*	1
20	36	JUST FOR MONEY Paul Hardcastle	*Chrysalis*	4
-	37	AFTER THE LOVE HAS GONE Princess	*Supreme*	1
22	38	GAMBLER Madonna	*Geffen*	8
-	39	DON'T YOU JUST KNOW IT Amazulu	*Island*	1
-	40	WEST END GIRLS Pet Shop Boys ●	*Parlophone*	1

■A proliferation of pairings: Eurythmics and Aretha Franklin, Dionne Warwick and Friends, Phil Collins and Marilyn Martin, Bryan Adams and Tina Turner, David Grant and Jaki Graham (23.11.85) ■ King, Queen, Princess and Prince share eleven Top 40 hits between them this year (30.11.85) ■ The Pet Shop Boys make their Top 40 debut (30.11.85)■

December 1985

□ Highest position disc reached ● Act's first ever week on chart

LW	TW	*WEEK ENDING* **7 DECEMBER 1985**			Wks
2	1	I'M YOUR MAN	Wham!	*Epic*	3
9	2	SAVING ALL MY LOVE FOR YOU	Whitney Houston	*Arista*	3
4	3	SEE THE DAY	Dee C Lee	*CBS*	4
2	4	A GOOD HEART	Feargal Sharkey	*Virgin*	7
10	5	SEPARATE LIVES	Phil Collins and Marilyn Martin	*Virgin*	3
3	6	DON'T BREAK MY HEART	UB40	*DEP International*	7
7	7	THE SHOW	Doug E Fresh and the Get Fresh Crew	*Cooltempo*	5
6	8	ROAD TO NOWHERE	Talking Heads	*EMI*	6
11	9	SAY YOU SAY ME	Lionel Richie	*Motown*	4
5	10	THE POWER OF LOVE	Jennifer Rush	*CBS*	12
15	11	NIKITA	Elton John	*Rocket*	8
-	12	DRESS YOU UP	Madonna	*Sire*	1
24	13	DON'T LOOK DOWN-THE SEQUEL	Go West	*Chrysalis*	2
12	14	TAKE ON ME	A-Ha	*Warner Brothers*	10
8	15	ONE VISION	Queen	*EMI*	4
16	16	THAT'S WHAT FRIENDS ARE FOR	Dionne Warwick and Friends	*Arista*	4
26	17	SPIES LIKE US	Paul McCartney	*Parlophone*	2
14	18	SISTERS ARE DOIN' IT FOR THEMSELVES	Eurythmics and Aretha Franklin	*RCA*	6
35	19	WE BUILT THIS CITY	Starship	*RCA*	2
22	20	MATED	David Grant and Jaki Graham	*EMI*	3
29	21	SUN CITY	Artists United Against Apartheid	*Manhattan*	2
13	22	SOMETHING ABOUT YOU	Level 42	*Polydor*	10
40	23	WEST END GIRLS	Pet Shop Boys	*Parlophone*	2
-	24	DO THEY KNOW IT'S CHRISTMAS	Band Aid	*Mercury*	1
25	25	WHEN LOVE BREAKS DOWN	Prefab Sprout	*Kitchenware*	3
21	26	UNCLE SAM	Madness	*Zarjazz*	6
33	27	WHEN A HEART BEATS	Nik Kershaw	*MCA*	2
18	28	BROTHERS IN ARMS	Dire Straits	*Vertigo*	6
31	29	HEART OF LOTHIAN	Marillion	*EMI*	2
30	30	REVOLUTION	Cult	*Beggars Banquet*	2
37	31	AFTER THE LOVE HAS GONE	Princess	*Supreme*	2
17	32	STAIRWAY TO HEAVEN	Far Corporation	*Arista*	6
39	33	DON'T YOU JUST KNOW IT	Amazulu	*Island*	2
19	34	LOST WEEKEND	Lloyd Cole and the Commotions	*Polydor*	5
-	35	SHE'S STRANGE	Cameo	*Club*	1
20	36	TRAPPED	Colonel Abrams	*MCA*	13
27	37	HOWARDS' WAY THEME	Simon May Orchestra	*BBC*	6
-	38	MERRY CHRISTMAS EVERYONE	Shakin' Stevens	*Epic*	1
-	39	HIT THAT PERFECT BEAT	Bronski Beat	*Forbidden Fruit*	1
28	40	THE WHOLE OF THE MOON	Waterboys	*Ensign*	5

LW	TW	*WEEK ENDING* **14 DECEMBER 1985**			Wks
2	1	SAVING ALL MY LOVE FOR YOU	Whitney Houston	*Arista*	4
1	2	I'M YOUR MAN	Wham!	*Epic*	4
3	3	SEE THE DAY	Dee C Lee	*CBS*	5
5	4	SEPARATE LIVES	Phil Collins and Marilyn Martin	*Virgin*	4
12	5	DRESS YOU UP	Madonna	*Sire*	2
24	6	DO THEY KNOW IT'S CHRISTMAS	Band Aid	*Mercury*	2
4	7	A GOOD HEART	Feargal Sharkey	*Virgin*	8
9	8	SAY YOU SAY ME	Lionel Richie	*Motown*	5
23	9	WEST END GIRLS	Pet Shop Boys	*Parlophone*	3
38	10	MERRY CHRISTMAS EVERYONE	Shakin' Stevens	*Epic*	2
7	11	THE SHOW	Doug E Fresh and the Get Fresh Crew	*Cooltempo*	6
6	12	DON'T BREAK MY HEART	UB40	*DEP International*	8
13	13	DON'T LOOK DOWN-THE SEQUEL	Go West	*Chrysalis*	3
19	14	WE BUILT THIS CITY	Starship	*RCA*	3
8	15	ROAD TO NOWHERE	Talking Heads	*EMI*	7
17	16	SPIES LIKE US	Paul McCartney	*Parlophone*	3
-	17	SANTA CLAUS IS COMIN' TO TOWN/MY HOMETOWN	Bruce Springsteen	*CBS*	1
11	18	NIKITA	Elton John	*Rocket*	9
33	19	DON'T YOU JUST KNOW IT	Amazulu	*Island*	3
20	20	MATED	David Grant and Jaki Graham	*EMI*	4
16	21	THAT'S WHAT FRIENDS ARE FOR	Dionne Warwick and Friends	*Arista*	5
21	22	SUN CITY	Artists United Against Apartheid	*Manhattan*	3
14	23	TAKE ON ME	A-Ha	*Warner Brothers*	11
35	24	SHE'S STRANGE	Cameo	*Club*	2
15	25	ONE VISION	Queen	*EMI*	5
39	26	HIT THAT PERFECT BEAT	Bronski Beat	*Forbidden Fruit*	2
10	27	THE POWER OF LOVE	Jennifer Rush	*CBS*	13
25	28	WHEN LOVE BREAKS DOWN	Prefab Sprout	*Kitchenware*	4
18	29	SISTERS ARE DOIN' IT FOR THEMSELVES	Eurythmics and Aretha Franklin	*RCA*	7
27	30	WHEN A HEART BEATS	Nik Kershaw	*MCA*	3
31	31	AFTER THE LOVE HAS GONE	Princess	*Supreme*	3
-	32	LAST CHRISTMAS	Wham!	*Epic*	1
-	33	RUN TO THE HILLS (LIVE)	Iron Maiden	*EMI*	1
-	34	WRAP HER UP	Elton John	*Rocket*	1
-	35	LEAVING ME NOW	Level 42	*Polydor*	1
22	36	SOMETHING ABOUT YOU	Level 42	*Polydor*	11
-	37	WALKING IN THE AIR	Aled Jones ●	*EMI*	1
28	38	BROTHERS IN ARMS	Dire Straits	*Vertigo*	7
-	39	GIRLIE GIRLIE	Sophia George ●	*Winner*	1
-	40	MR DJ	Concept ●	*Fourth & Broadway*	1

LW	TW	*WEEK ENDING* **21 DECEMBER 1985**			Wks
1	1	SAVING ALL MY LOVE FOR YOU	Whitney Houston	*Arista*	5
10	2	MERRY CHRISTMAS EVERYONE	Shakin' Stevens	*Epic*	3
6	3	DO THEY KNOW IT'S CHRISTMAS	Band Aid	*Mercury*	3
2	4	I'M YOUR MAN	Wham!	*Epic*	5
9	5	WEST END GIRLS	Pet Shop Boys	*Parlophone*	4
3	6	SEE THE DAY	Dee C Lee	*CBS*	6
4	7	SEPARATE LIVES	Phil Collins and Marilyn Martin	*Virgin*	5
5	8	DRESS YOU UP	Madonna	*Sire*	3
17	9	SANTA CLAUS IS COMIN' TO TOWN/MY HOMETOWN	Bruce Springsteen	*CBS*	2
32	10	LAST CHRISTMAS	Wham!	*Epic*	2
8	11	SAY YOU SAY ME	Lionel Richie	*Motown*	6
14	12	WE BUILT THIS CITY	Starship	*RCA*	4
7	13	A GOOD HEART	Feargal Sharkey	*Virgin*	9
37	14	WALKING IN THE AIR	Aled Jones	*EMI*	2
13	15	DON'T LOOK DOWN-THE SEQUEL	Go West	*Chrysalis*	4
16	16	SPIES LIKE US	Paul McCartney	*Parlophone*	4
26	17	HIT THAT PERFECT BEAT	Bronski Beat	*Forbidden Fruit*	3
11	18	THE SHOW	Doug E Fresh and the Get Fresh Crew	*Cooltempo*	7
19	19	DON'T YOU JUST KNOW IT	Amazulu	*Island*	4
12	20	DON'T BREAK MY HEART	UB40	*DEP International*	9
27	21	THE POWER OF LOVE	Jennifer Rush	*CBS*	14
24	22	SHE'S STRANGE	Cameo	*Club*	3
34	23	WRAP HER UP	Elton John	*Rocket*	2
15	24	ROAD TO NOWHERE	Talking Heads	*EMI*	8
39	25	GIRLIE GIRLIE	Sophia George	*Winner*	2
33	26	RUN TO THE HILLS (LIVE)	Iron Maiden	*EMI*	2
40	27	MR DJ	Concept	*Fourth & Broadway*	2
35	28	LEAVING ME NOW	Level 42	*Polydor*	2
31	29	AFTER THE LOVE HAS GONE	Princess	*Supreme*	4
20	30	MATED	David Grant and Jaki Graham	*EMI*	5
21	31	THAT'S WHAT FRIENDS ARE FOR	Dionne Warwick and Friends	*Arista*	6
-	32	RUSSIANS	Sting	*A&M*	1
18	33	NIKITA	Elton John	*Rocket*	10
23	34	TAKE ON ME	A-Ha	*Warner Brothers*	12
22	35	SUN CITY	Artists United Against Apartheid	*Manhattan*	4
-	36	RING OF ICE	Jennifer Rush	*CBS*	1
29	37	SISTERS ARE DOIN' IT FOR THEMSELVES	Eurythmics and Aretha Franklin	*RCA*	8
25	38	ONE VISION	Queen	*EMI*	6
-	39	THE HOKEY-COKEY	Black Lace	*Flair*	1
30	40	WHEN A HEART BEATS	Nik Kershaw	*MCA*	4

LW	TW	*WEEK ENDING* **28 DECEMBER 1985**			Wks
2	1	MERRY CHRISTMAS EVERYONE	Shakin' Stevens	*Epic*	4
1	2	SAVING ALL MY LOVE FOR YOU	Whitney Houston	*Arista*	6
3	3	DO THEY KNOW IT'S CHRISTMAS	Band Aid	*Mercury*	4
5	4	WEST END GIRLS	Pet Shop Boys	*Parlophone*	5

In these weeks ■ Another hit for Madonna, her 8th in 1985. She has managed 69 weeks in the Top 40 with at least one record on the charts since 8 June 85 (07.12.85) ■ Bruce Springsteen notches up a creditable 5th hit this year (14.12.85) ■ Band Aid makes its second visit to the Top Three only 47 weeks after its first entry (21.12.85)■

□ Highest position disc reached ● Act's first ever week on chart

14	**5**	WALKING IN THE AIR Aled Jones	*EMI*	3
10	**6**	LAST CHRISTMAS Wham!	*Epic*	3
7	**7**	SEPARATE LIVES Phil Collins and Marilyn Martin	*Virgin*	6
4	**8**	I'M YOUR MAN Wham!	*Epic*	6
8	**9**	DRESS YOU UP Madonna	*Sire*	4
6	**10**	SEE THE DAY Dee C Lee	*CBS*	7
9	**11**	SANTA CLAUS IS COMIN' TO TOWN/MY HOMETOWN Bruce Springsteen	*CBS*	3
12	**12**	WE BUILT THIS CITY Starship	*RCA*	5
17	**13**	HIT THAT PERFECT BEAT Bronski Beat	*Forbidden Fruit*	4
11	**14**	SAY YOU SAY ME Lionel Richie	*Motown*	7
25	**15**	GIRLIE GIRLIE Sophia George	*Winner*	3
16	**16**	SPIES LIKE US Paul McCartney	*Parlophone*	5
19	**17**	DON'T YOU JUST KNOW IT Amazulu	*Island*	5
13	**18**	A GOOD HEART Feargal Sharkey	*Virgin*	10
15	**19**	DON'T LOOK DOWN-THE SEQUEL Go West	*Chrysalis*	5
23	**20**	WRAP HER UP Elton John	*Rocket*	3
-	**21**	SATURDAY LOVE Cherelle with Alexander O'Neal ●	*Tabu*	1
21	**22**	THE POWER OF LOVE Jennifer Rush	*CBS*	15
28	**23**	LEAVING ME NOW Level 42	*Polydor*	3
18	**24**	THE SHOW Doug E Fresh and the Get Fresh Crew	*Cooltempo*	8
22	**25**	SHE'S STRANGE Cameo	*Club*	4
32	**26**	RUSSIANS Sting	*A&M*	2
20	**27**	DON'T BREAK MY HEART UB40	*DEP International*	10
29	**28**	AFTER THE LOVE HAS GONE Princess	*Supreme*	5
24	**29**	ROAD TO NOWHERE Talking Heads	*EMI*	9
26	**30**	RUN TO THE HILLS (LIVE) Iron Maiden	*EMI*	3
39	**31**	THE HOKEY-COKEY Black Lace	*Flair*	2
27	**32**	MR DJ Concept	*Fourth & Broadway*	3
36	**33**	RING OF ICE Jennifer Rush	*CBS*	2
-	**34**	WE ALL STAND TOGETHER Paul McCartney and the Frog Chorus	*Parlophone*	1
31	**35**	THAT'S WHAT FRIENDS ARE FOR Dionne Warwick and Friends	*Arista*	7
-	**36**	ABIDE WITH ME Inspirational Choir with the Royal Choral Society ●	*Portrait*	1
34	**37**	TAKE ON ME A-Ha	*Warner Brothers*	13
-	**38**	ALICE I WANT YOU JUST FOR ME Full Force ●	*CBS*	1
-	**39**	THE SUN ALWAYS SHINES ON TV A-Ha	*Warner Bros*	1
-	**40**	BECAUSE Julian Lennon	*EMI*	1

■Shaky grabs his 4th chart topper with the 1985 Christmas number one (28.12.85)■ The 'Cup Final' hymn *Abide With Me* makes a second consecutive Christmas visit to the Top 40 (28.12.85)

1986

......MADONNA dominates the year with five top five hits, including two number ones ...Wham! break up after their fourth and final number one......Jackie Wilson hits the top posthumously with 'Reet Petite' 29 years and 42 days after making his chart debut with the same song setting new records for Slowest Number One by both artist and recording.........

January 1986

□ Highest position disc reached ● Act's first ever week on chart

LW	TW	*WEEK ENDING* 4 JANUARY 1986	Wks
1	[1]	MERRY CHRISTMAS EVERYONE Shakin' Stevens .... *Epic*	5
2	2	SAVING ALL MY LOVE FOR YOU Whitney Houston .... *Arista*	7
4	3	WEST END GIRLS Pet Shop Boys .... *Parlophone*	6
3	4	DO THEY KNOW IT'S CHRISTMAS Band Aid .... *Mercury*	5
5	[5]	WALKING IN THE AIR Aled Jones .... *EMI*	4
6	[6]	LAST CHRISTMAS Wham! .... *Epic*	4
9	7	DRESS YOU UP Madonna .... *Sire*	5
8	8	I'M YOUR MAN Wham! .... *Epic*	7
7	9	SEPARATE LIVES Phil Collins and Marilyn Martin .... *Virgin*	7
10	10	SEE THE DAY Dee C Lee .... *CBS*	8
13	11	HIT THAT PERFECT BEAT Bronski Beat .... *Forbidden Fruit*	5
12	[12]	WE BUILT THIS CITY Starship .... *RCA*	6
16	[13]	SPIES LIKE US Paul McCartney .... *Parlophone*	6
15	14	GIRLIE GIRLIE Sophia George .... *Winner*	4
17	[15]	DON'T YOU JUST KNOW IT Amazulu .... *Island*	6
14	16	SAY YOU SAY ME Lionel Richie .... *Motown*	8
18	17	A GOOD HEART Feargal Sharkey .... *Virgin*	11
19	18	DON'T LOOK DOWN-THE SEQUEL Go West .... *Chrysalis*	6
20	19	WRAP HER UP Elton John .... *Rocket*	4
11	20	SANTA CLAUS IS COMIN' TO TOWN/MY HOMETOWN Bruce Sprongsteen .... *CBS*	4
21	21	SATURDAY LOVE Cherelle with Alexander O'Neal .... *Tabu*	2
24	22	THE SHOW Doug E Fresh and the Get Fresh Crew .... *Cooltempo*	9
23	23	LEAVING ME NOW Level 42 .... *Polydor*	4
27	24	DON'T BREAK MY HEART UB40 .... *DEP International*	11
26	25	RUSSIANS Sting .... *A&M*	3
25	26	SHE'S STRANGE Cameo .... *Club*	5
39	27	THE SUN ALWAYS SHINES ON TV A-Ha .... *Warner Bros*	2
28	[28]	AFTER THE LOVE HAS GONE Princess .... *Supreme*	6
33	29	RING OF ICE Jennifer Rush .... *CBS*	3
30	30	RUN TO THE HILLS (LIVE) Iron Maiden .... *EMI*	4
29	31	ROAD TO NOWHERE Talking Heads .... *EMI*	10
34	[32]	WE ALL STAND TOGETHER Paul McCartney and the Frog Chorus .... *Parlophone*	2
37	33	TAKE ON ME A-Ha .... *Warner Brothers*	14
31	34	THE HOKEY-COKEY Black Lace .... *Flair*	3
22	35	THE POWER OF LOVE Jennifer Rush .... *CBS*	16
38	[36]	ALICE I WANT YOU JUST FOR ME Full Force .... *CBS*	2
re	37	MATED David Grant and Jaki Graham .... *EMI*	1
-	38	WHO'S ZOOMIN' WHO Aretha Franklin .... *Arista*	1
32	39	MR DJ Concept .... *Fourth & Broadway*	4
-	[40]	WHITE CHRISTMAS Keith Harris and Orville .... *Columbia*	1

LW	TW	*WEEK ENDING* 11 JANUARY 1986	Wks
3	[1]	WEST END GIRLS Pet Shop Boys .... *Parlophone*	7
2	2	SAVING ALL MY LOVE FOR YOU Whitney Houston .... *Arista*	8
1	3	MERRY CHRISTMAS EVERYONE Shakin' Stevens .... *Epic*	6
11	4	HIT THAT PERFECT BEAT Bronski Beat .... *Forbidden Fruit*	6
27	5	THE SUN ALWAYS SHINES ON TV A-Ha .... *Warner Bros*	3
7	6	DRESS YOU UP Madonna .... *Sire*	6
14	[7]	GIRLIE GIRLIE Sophia George .... *Winner*	5
5	8	WALKING IN THE AIR Aled Jones .... *EMI*	5
8	9	I'M YOUR MAN Wham! .... *Epic*	8
21	10	SATURDAY LOVE Cherelle with Alexander O'Neal .... *Tabu*	3
9	11	SEPARATE LIVES Phil Collins and Marilyn Martin .... *Virgin*	8
19	[12]	WRAP HER UP Elton John .... *Rocket*	5
4	13	DO THEY KNOW IT'S CHRISTMAS Band Aid .... *Mercury*	6
6	14	LAST CHRISTMAS Wham! .... *Epic*	5
12	15	WE BUILT THIS CITY Starship .... *RCA*	7
10	16	SEE THE DAY Dee C Lee .... *CBS*	9
15	17	DON'T YOU JUST KNOW IT Amazulu .... *Island*	7
13	18	SPIES LIKE US Paul McCartney .... *Parlophone*	7
18	19	DON'T LOOK DOWN-THE SEQUEL Go West .... *Chrysalis*	7
25	20	RUSSIANS Sting .... *A&M*	4
23	21	LEAVING ME NOW Level 42 .... *Polydor*	5
16	22	SAY YOU SAY ME Lionel Richie .... *Motown*	9
29	23	RING OF ICE Jennifer Rush .... *CBS*	4
17	24	A GOOD HEART Feargal Sharkey .... *Virgin*	12
38	25	WHO'S ZOOMIN' WHO Aretha Franklin .... *Arista*	2
-	26	YOU LITTLE THIEF Feargal Sharkey .... *Virgin*	1
36	27	ALICE I WANT YOU JUST FOR ME Full Force .... *CBS*	3
26	28	SHE'S STRANGE Cameo .... *Club*	6
28	29	AFTER THE LOVE HAS GONE Princess .... *Supreme*	7
-	30	WALK OF LIFE Dire Straits .... *Vertigo*	1
-	31	BROKEN WINGS Mr Mister ● .... *RCA*	1
33	32	TAKE ON ME A-Ha .... *Warner Brothers*	15
35	33	THE POWER OF LOVE Jennifer Rush .... *CBS*	17
-	34	TORTURE King .... *CBS*	1
-	35	SUSPICIOUS MINDS Fine Young Cannibals .... *London*	1
39	36	MR DJ Concept .... *Fourth & Broadway*	5
31	37	ROAD TO NOWHERE Talking Heads .... *EMI*	11
22	38	THE SHOW Doug E Fresh and the Get Fresh Crew .... *Cooltempo*	10
-	39	IT'S ALRIGHT (BABY'S COMING BACK) Eurythmics .... *RCA*	1
24	40	DON'T BREAK MY HEART UB40 .... *DEP International*	12

LW	TW	*WEEK ENDING* 18 JANUARY 1986	Wks
1	[1]	WEST END GIRLS Pet Shop Boys .... *Parlophone*	8
5	2	THE SUN ALWAYS SHINES ON TV A-Ha .... *Warner Bros*	4
4	[3]	HIT THAT PERFECT BEAT Bronski Beat .... *Forbidden Fruit*	7
30	4	WALK OF LIFE Dire Straits .... *Vertigo*	2
26	[5]	YOU LITTLE THIEF Feargal Sharkey .... *Virgin*	2
10	[6]	SATURDAY LOVE Cherelle with Alexander O'Neal .... *Tabu*	4
7	[7]	GIRLIE GIRLIE Sophia George .... *Winner*	6
31	8	BROKEN WINGS Mr Mister .... *RCA*	2
2	9	SAVING ALL MY LOVE FOR YOU Whitney Houston .... *Arista*	9
27	10	ALICE I WANT YOU JUST FOR ME Full Force .... *CBS*	4
25	[11]	WHO'S ZOOMIN' WHO Aretha Franklin .... *Arista*	3
20	[12]	RUSSIANS Sting .... *A&M*	5
39	13	IT'S ALRIGHT (BABY'S COMING BACK) Eurythmics .... *RCA*	2
23	[14]	RING OF ICE Jennifer Rush .... *CBS*	5
21	[15]	LEAVING ME NOW Level 42 .... *Polydor*	6
12	16	WRAP HER UP Elton John .... *Rocket*	6
35	17	SUSPICIOUS MINDS Fine Young Cannibals .... *London*	2
8	18	WALKING IN THE AIR Aled Jones .... *EMI*	6
11	19	SEPARATE LIVES Phil Collins and Marilyn Martin .... *Virgin*	9
3	20	MERRY CHRISTMAS EVERYONE Shakin' Stevens .... *Epic*	7
6	21	DRESS YOU UP Madonna .... *Sire*	7
-	22	SYSTEM ADDICT Five Star .... *Tent*	1
34	[23]	TORTURE King .... *CBS*	2
15	24	WE BUILT THIS CITY Starship .... *RCA*	8
-	25	ONLY LOVE Nana Mouskouri ● .... *Carrere*	1
18	26	SPIES LIKE US Paul McCartney .... *Parlophone*	8
9	27	I'M YOUR MAN Wham! .... *Epic*	9
17	28	DON'T YOU JUST KNOW IT Amazulu .... *Island*	8
-	29	SPIRIT OF 76 Alarm .... *IRS*	1
29	30	AFTER THE LOVE HAS GONE Princess .... *Supreme*	8
19	31	DON'T LOOK DOWN-THE SEQUEL Go West .... *Chrysalis*	8
-	32	THE PHANTOM OF THE OPERA Sarah Brightman and Steve Harley ● .... *Polydor*	1
16	33	SEE THE DAY Dee C Lee .... *CBS*	10
-	34	SHAKE YOUR FOUNDATIONS AC/DC .... *Atlantic*	1
33	35	THE POWER OF LOVE Jennifer Rush .... *CBS*	18
14	36	LAST CHRISTMAS Wham! .... *Epic*	6
22	37	SAY YOU SAY ME Lionel Richie .... *Motown*	10
32	38	TAKE ON ME A-Ha .... *Warner Brothers*	16
24	39	A GOOD HEART Feargal Sharkey .... *Virgin*	13
-	40	PULL UP TO THE BUMPER Grace Jones .... *Island*	1

LW	TW	*WEEK ENDING* 25 JANUARY 1985	Wks
2	[1]	THE SUN ALWAYS SHINES ON TV A-Ha .... *Warner Bros*	5
4	[2]	WALK OF LIFE Dire Straits .... *Vertigo*	3
1	3	WEST END GIRLS Pet Shop Boys .... *Parlophone*	9
8	[4]	BROKEN WINGS Mr Mister .... *RCA*	3
5	[5]	YOU LITTLE THIEF Feargal Sharkey .... *Virgin*	3
6	[6]	SATURDAY LOVE Cherelle with Alexander O'Neal .... *Tabu*	5
3	7	HIT THAT PERFECT BEAT Bronski Beat .... *Forbidden Fruit*	8
25	8	ONLY LOVE Nana Mouskouri .... *Carrere/Philips*	2

In these weeks ■ Six Christmas records are charting (04.01.86) ■ George Michael appears on four Top 40 singles; two by Wham!, Band Aid and he also features on the Elton John record (11.01.86) ■ *Who's Zooming Who* is Aretha Franklin's highest charting single since *I Say A Little Prayer* in 1968 (18.01.86)■

LW	TW	Title	Artist	Label	Wks
10	[9]	ALICE I WANT YOU JUST FOR ME	Full Force	*CBS*	5
17	10	SUSPICIOUS MINDS	Fine Young Cannibals	*London*	3
11	[11]	WHO'S ZOOMIN' WHO	Aretha Franklin	*Arista*	4
13	[12]	IT'S ALRIGHT (BABY'S COMING BACK)	Eurythmics	*RCA*	3
22	13	SYSTEM ADDICT	Five Star	*Tent*	2
12	14	RUSSIANS	Sting	*A&M*	6
-	15	BORDERLINE	Madonna	*Sire*	1
7	16	GIRLIE GIRLIE	Sophia George	*Winner*	7
15	17	LEAVING ME NOW	Level 42	*Polydor*	7
14	18	RING OF ICE	Jennifer Rush	*CBS*	6
9	19	SAVING ALL MY LOVE FOR YOU	Whitney Houston	*Arista*	10
40	20	PULL UP TO THE BUMPER	Grace Jones	*Island*	2
32	21	THE PHANTOM OF THE OPERA	Sarah Brightman and Steve Harley	*Polydor*	2
29	[22]	SPIRIT OF 76	Alarm	*IRS*	2
-	23	LIFE'S WHAT YOU MAKE IT	Talk Talk	*EMI*	1
34	24	SHAKE YOUR FOUNDATIONS	AC/DC	*Atlantic*	2
16	25	WRAP HER UP	Elton John	*Rocket*	7
19	26	SEPARATE LIVES	Phil Collins and Marilyn Martin	*Virgin*	10
23	27	TORTURE	King	*CBS*	3
-	28	WHEN THE GOING GETS TOUGH THE TOUGH GET GOING	Billy Ocean	*Jive*	1
-	29	IN A LIFETIME	Clannad additional vocals: Bono	*RCA*	1
18	30	WALKING IN THE AIR	Aled Jones	*EMI*	7
-	31	LIVING IN AMERICA	James Brown	*Scotti Brothers*	1
21	32	DRESS YOU UP	Madonna	*Sire*	8
27	33	I'M YOUR MAN	Wham!	*Epic*	10
-	34	IMAGINATION	Belouis Some ●	*Parlophone*	1
24	35	WE BUILT THIS CITY	Starship	*RCA*	9
-	36	HOW WILL I KNOW	Whitney Houston	*Arista*	1
-	37	IF I RULED THE WORLD	Kurtis Blow	*Club*	1
-	[38]	CUT ME DOWN	Lloyd Cole and the Commotions	*Polydor*	1
28	39	DON'T YOU JUST KNOW IT	Amazulu	*Island*	9
30	40	AFTER THE LOVE HAS GONE	Princess	*Supreme*	9

WEEK ENDING 1 FEBRUARY 1986

LW	TW	Title	Artist	Label	Wks
1	[1]	THE SUN ALWAYS SHINES ON TV	A-Ha	*Warner Bros*	6
8	[2]	ONLY LOVE	Nana Mouskouri	*Carrere/Philips*	3
2	3	WALK OF LIFE	Dire Straits	*Vertigo*	4
15	4	BORDERLINE	Madonna	*Sire*	2
4	5	BROKEN WINGS	Mr Mister	*RCA*	4
28	6	WHEN THE GOING GETS TOUGH THE TOUGH GET GOING	Billy Ocean	*Jive*	2
3	7	WEST END GIRLS	Pet Shop Boys	*Parlophone*	10
10	[8]	SUSPICIOUS MINDS	Fine Young Cannibals	*London*	4
6	9	SATURDAY LOVE	Cherelle with Alexander O'Neal	*Tabu*	6
13	10	SYSTEM ADDICT	Five Star	*Tent*	3
5	11	YOU LITTLE THIEF	Feargal Sharkey	*Virgin*	4
21	12	THE PHANTOM OF THE OPERA	Sarah Brightman and Steve Harley	*Polydor*	3
9	13	ALICE I WANT YOU JUST FOR ME	Full Force	*CBS*	6
12	14	IT'S ALRIGHT (BABY'S COMING BACK)	Eurythmics	*RCA*	6
20	15	PULL UP TO THE BUMPER/LA VIE EN ROSE	Grace Jones	*Island*	3
7	16	HIT THAT PERFECT BEAT	Bronski Beat	*Forbidden Fruit*	9
-	17	SANCTIFY YOURSELF	Simple Minds	*Virgin*	1
11	18	WHO'S ZOOMIN' WHO	Aretha Franklin	*Arista*	5
31	19	LIVING IN AMERICA	James Brown	*Scotti Brothers*	2
29	[20]	IN A LIFETIME	Clannad additional vocals: Bono	*RCA*	2
14	21	RUSSIANS	Sting	*A&M*	7
23	22	LIFE'S WHAT YOU MAKE IT	Talk Talk	*EMI*	2
36	23	HOW WILL I KNOW	Whitney Houston	*Arista*	2
16	24	GIRLIE GIRLIE	Sophia George	*Winner*	8
34	25	IMAGINATION	Belouis Some	*Parlophone*	2
17	26	LEAVING ME NOW	Level 42	*Polydor*	8
22	27	SPIRIT OF 76	Alarm	*IRS*	3
19	28	SAVING ALL MY LOVE FOR YOU	Whitney Houston	*Arista*	11
-	29	SHOT IN THE DARK	Ozzy Osbourne	*Epic*	1
37	30	IF I RULED THE WORLD	Kurtis Blow	*Club*	2
18	31	RING OF ICE	Jennifer Rush	*CBS*	7
-	32	MY MAGIC MAN	Rochelle ●	*Warner Bros*	1
24	33	SHAKE YOUR FOUNDATIONS	AC/DC	*Atlantic*	3
-	34	THE CAPTAIN OF HER HEART	Double ●	*Polydor*	1

February 1986

□ Highest position disc reached ● Act's first ever week on chart

LW	TW	Title	Artist	Label	Wks
-	35	IF YOU'RE READY (COME GO WITH ME)	Ruby Turner featuring Jonathan Butler ●	*Jive*	1
26	36	SEPARATE LIVES	Phil Collins and Marilyn Martin	*Virgin*	11
-	37	RISE	Public Image Ltd	*Virgin*	1
38	[38]	CUT ME DOWN	Lloyd Cole and the Commotions	*Polydor*	2
-	39	DON'T LET ME BE MISUNDERSTOOD	Costello Show	*F-Beat*	1
-	40	THE PROMISE	Arcadia	*Parlophone*	1

WEEK ENDING 8 FEBRUARY 1986

LW	TW	Title	Artist	Label	Wks
6	[1]	WHEN THE GOING GETS TOUGH THE TOUGH GET GOING	Billy Ocean	*Jive*	3
1	2	THE SUN ALWAYS SHINES ON TV	A-Ha	*Warner Bros*	7
4	3	BORDERLINE	Madonna	*Sire*	3
2	4	ONLY LOVE	Nana Mouskouri	*Carrere/Philips*	4
3	5	WALK OF LIFE	Dire Straits	*Vertigo*	5
10	6	SYSTEM ADDICT	Five Star	*Tent*	4
12	[7]	THE PHANTOM OF THE OPERA	Sarah Brightman and Steve Harley	*Polydor*	4
19	8	LIVING IN AMERICA	James Brown	*Scotti Brothers*	3
8	9	SUSPICIOUS MINDS	Fine Young Cannibals	*London*	5
17	[10]	SANCTIFY YOURSELF	Simple Minds	*Virgin*	2
5	11	BROKEN WINGS	Mr Mister	*RCA*	5
15	[12]	PULL UP TO THE BUMPER/LA VIE EN ROSE	Grace Jones	*Island*	4
9	13	SATURDAY LOVE	Cherelle with Alexander O'Neal	*Tabu*	7
34	14	THE CAPTAIN OF HER HEART	Double	*Polydor*	2
11	15	YOU LITTLE THIEF	Feargal Sharkey	*Virgin*	5
22	[16]	LIFE'S WHAT YOU MAKE IT	Talk Talk	*EMI*	3
14	17	IT'S ALRIGHT (BABY'S COMING BACK)	Eurythmics	*RCA*	7
-	18	ELOISE	Damned	*MCA*	1
23	19	HOW WILL I KNOW	Whitney Houston	*Arista*	3
37	20	RISE	Public Image Ltd	*Virgin*	2
29	21	SHOT IN THE DARK	Ozzy Osbourne	*Epic*	2
13	22	ALICE I WANT YOU JUST FOR ME	Full Force	*CBS*	7
7	23	WEST END GIRLS	Pet Shop Boys	*Parlophone*	11
30	[24]	IF I RULED THE WORLD	Kurtis Blow	*Club*	3
25	25	IMAGINATION	Belouis Some	*Parlophone*	3
20	26	IN A LIFETIME	Clannad additional vocals: Bono	*RCA*	3
32	[27]	MY MAGIC MAN	Rochelle	*Warner Bros*	2
16	28	HIT THAT PERFECT BEAT	Bronski Beat	*Forbidden Fruit*	10
18	29	WHO'S ZOOMIN' WHO	Aretha Franklin	*Arista*	6
-	30	BURNING HEART	Survivor	*Scotti Brothers*	1
-	31	CHAIN REACTION	Diana Ross	*Capitol*	1
35	32	IF YOU'RE READY (COME GO WITH ME)	Ruby Turner featuring Jonathan Butler	*Jive*	2
39	[33]	DON'T LET ME BE MISUNDERSTOOD	Costello Show	*F-Beat*	2
-	34	STARTING TOGETHER	Su Pollard ●	*Rainbow*	1
-	35	DON'T WASTE MY TIME	Paul Hardcastle	*Chrysalis*	1
-	36	RADIO AFRICA	Latin Quarter ●	*Rockin' Horse*	1
40	[37]	THE PROMISE	Arcadia	*Parlophone*	2
26	38	LEAVING ME NOW	Level 42	*Polydor*	9
-	39	TURNING AWAY	Shakin' Stevens	*Epic*	1
21	40	RUSSIANS	Sting	*A&M*	8

WEEK ENDING 15 FEBRUARY 1986

LW	TW	Title	Artist	Label	Wks
1	[1]	WHEN THE GOING GETS TOUGH THE TOUGH GET GOING	Billy Ocean	*Jive*	4
3	[2]	BORDERLINE	Madonna	*Sire*	4
6	[3]	SYSTEM ADDICT	Five Star	*Tent*	5
18	4	ELOISE	Damned	*MCA*	2
8	[5]	LIVING IN AMERICA	James Brown	*Scotti Brothers*	4
2	6	THE SUN ALWAYS SHINES ON TV	A-Ha	*Warner Bros*	8
4	7	ONLY LOVE	Nana Mouskouri	*Carrere/Philips*	5
14	[8]	THE CAPTAIN OF HER HEART	Double	*Polydor*	3
34	9	STARTING TOGETHER	Su Pollard	*Rainbow*	2

■First number one ever by a wholly Norwegian act (25.01.86) ■ Nana Mouskouri emulates Vicky Leandros as the highest charting Greek female singer. The sales of two versions of her hit are being combined (08.02.86) ■ James Brown's first week in the Top 40 was 23.09.65, this is his first week in the Top Ten (08.02.86)■

February 1986

□ Highest position disc reached ● Act's first ever week on chart

LW	TW	Title	Artist	Label	Wks
19	10	HOW WILL I KNOW	Whitney Houston	*Arista*	4
7	11	THE PHANTOM OF THE OPERA	Sarah Brightman and Steve Harley	*Polydor*	5
20	12	RISE	Public Image Ltd	*Virgin*	3
5	13	WALK OF LIFE	Dire Straits	*Vertigo*	6
31	14	CHAIN REACTION	Diana Ross	*Capitol*	2
30	15	BURNING HEART	Survivor	*Scotti Brothers*	2
12	16	PULL UP TO THE BUMPER/LA VIE EN ROSE	Grace Jones	*Island*	5
9	17	SUSPICIOUS MINDS	Fine Young Cannibals	*London*	6
10	18	SANCTIFY YOURSELF	Simple Minds	*Virgin*	3
16	19	LIFE'S WHAT YOU MAKE IT	Talk Talk	*EMI*	4
21	□20	SHOT IN THE DARK	Ozzy Osbourne	*Epic*	3
11	21	BROKEN WINGS	Mr Mister	*RCA*	6
25	22	IMAGINATION	Belouis Some	*Parlophone*	4
39	23	TURNING AWAY	Shakin' Stevens	*Epic*	2
36	24	RADIO AFRICA	Latin Quarter	*Rockin' Horse*	2
35	25	DON'T WASTE MY TIME	Paul Hardcastle	*Chrysalis*	2
24	26	IF I RULED THE WORLD	Kurtis Blow	*Club*	4
13	27	SATURDAY LOVE	Cherelle with Alexander O'Neal	*Tabu*	8
27	28	MY MAGIC MAN	Rochelle	*Warner Bros*	3
15	29	YOU LITTLE THIEF	Feargal Sharkey	*Virgin*	6
32	□30	IF YOU'RE READY (COME GO WITH ME)	Ruby Turner featuring Jonathan Butler	*Jive*	3
26	31	IN A LIFETIME	Clannad additional vocals: Bono	*RCA*	4
-	32	AND SHE WAS	Talking Heads	*EMI*	1
17	33	IT'S ALRIGHT (BABY'S COMING BACK)	Eurythmics	*RCA*	8
33	34	DON'T LET ME BE MISUNDERSTOOD	Costello Show	*F-Beat*	3
22	35	ALICE I WANT YOU JUST FOR ME	Full Force	*CBS*	8
29	36	WHO'S ZOOMIN' WHO	Aretha Franklin	*Arista*	7
28	37	HIT THAT PERFECT BEAT	Bronski Beat	*Forbidden Fruit*	11
23	38	WEST END GIRLS	Pet Shop Boys	*Parlophone*	12
-	39	ONE DANCE WON'T DO	Audrey Hall ●	*Germain*	1
-	40	I'M NOT GOING TO LET YOU	Colonel Abrams	*MCA*	1

WEEK ENDING 22 FEBRUARY 1986

LW	TW	Title	Artist	Label	Wks
1	□1	WHEN THE GOING GETS TOUGH THE TOUGH GET GOING	Billy Ocean	*Jive*	5
9	□2	STARTING TOGETHER	Su Pollard	*Rainbow*	3
4	□3	ELOISE	Damned	*MCA*	3
14	4	CHAIN REACTION	Diana Ross	*Capitol*	3
10	□5	HOW WILL I KNOW	Whitney Houston	*Arista*	5
2	6	BORDERLINE	Madonna	*Sire*	5
3	7	SYSTEM ADDICT	Five Star	*Tent*	6
15	8	BURNING HEART	Survivor	*Scotti Brothers*	3
5	9	LIVING IN AMERICA	James Brown	*Scotti Brothers*	5
8	10	THE CAPTAIN OF HER HEART	Double	*Polydor*	4
12	□11	RISE	Public Image Ltd	*Virgin*	4
7	12	ONLY LOVE	Nana Mouskouri	*Carrere/Philips*	6
25	13	DON'T WASTE MY TIME	Paul Hardcastle	*Chrysalis*	3
13	14	WALK OF LIFE	Dire Straits	*Vertigo*	7
23	□15	TURNING AWAY	Shakin' Stevens	*Epic*	3
6	16	THE SUN ALWAYS SHINES ON TV	A-Ha	*Warner Bros*	9
22	□17	IMAGINATION	Belouis Some	*Parlophone*	5
11	18	THE PHANTOM OF THE OPERA	Sarah Brightman and Steve Harley	*Polydor*	6
24	□19	RADIO AFRICA	Latin Quarter	*Rockin' Horse*	3
32	20	AND SHE WAS	Talking Heads	*EMI*	2
16	21	PULL UP TO THE BUMPER/LA VIE EN ROSE	Grace Jones	*Island*	6
19	22	LIFE'S WHAT YOU MAKE IT	Talk Talk	*EMI*	5
-	23	STRIPPED	Depeche Mode	*Mute*	1
-	24	MANIC MONDAY	Bangles ●	*CBS*	1
18	25	SANCTIFY YOURSELF	Simple Minds	*Virgin*	4
17	26	SUSPICIOUS MINDS	Fine Young Cannibals	*London*	7
39	27	ONE DANCE WON'T DO	Audrey Hall	*Germain*	2
20	28	SHOT IN THE DARK	Ozzy Osbourne	*Epic*	4
21	29	BROKEN WINGS	Mr Mister	*RCA*	7
40	30	I'M NOT GOING TO LET YOU	Colonel Abrams	*MCA*	2
30	31	IF YOU'RE READY (COME GO WITH ME)	Ruby Turner featuring Jonathan Butler	*Jive*	4
26	32	IF I RULED THE WORLD	Kurtis Blow	*Club*	5
28	33	MY MAGIC MAN	Rochelle	*Warner Bros*	4
-	34	IF YOU WERE HERE TONIGHT	Alexander O'Neal ●	*Tabu*	1
-	□35	SWEETEST GIRL	Madness	*Zarjazz*	1
-	36	POWER OF LOVE/DO YOU BELIEVE IN LOVE	Huey Lewis and the News	*Chrysalis*	1
27	37	SATURDAY LOVE	Cherelle with Alexander O'Neal	*Tabu*	9
29	38	YOU LITTLE THIEF	Feargal Sharkey	*Virgin*	7
-	39	HEAVEN MUST BE MISSING AN ANGEL	Tavares	*Capitol*	1
33	40	IT'S ALRIGHT (BABY'S COMING BACK)	Eurythmics	*RCA*	9

WEEK ENDING 1 MARCH 1986

LW	TW	Title	Artist	Label	Wks
1	□1	WHEN THE GOING GETS TOUGH THE TOUGH GET GOING	Billy Ocean	*Jive*	6
4	2	CHAIN REACTION	Diana Ross	*Capitol*	4
2	3	STARTING TOGETHER	Su Pollard	*Rainbow*	4
3	4	ELOISE	Damned	*MCA*	4
8	5	BURNING HEART	Survivor	*Scotti Brothers*	4
5	6	HOW WILL I KNOW	Whitney Houston	*Arista*	6
-	7	LOVE MISSILE F1-11	Sigue Sigue Sputnik ●	*Parlophone*	1
13	□8	DON'T WASTE MY TIME	Paul Hardcastle	*Chrysalis*	4
7	9	SYSTEM ADDICT	Five Star	*Tent*	7
24	10	MANIC MONDAY	Bangles	*CBS*	2
6	11	BORDERLINE	Madonna	*Sire*	6
11	12	RISE	Public Image Ltd	*Virgin*	5
9	13	LIVING IN AMERICA	James Brown	*Scotti Brothers*	6
12	14	ONLY LOVE	Nana Mouskouri	*Carrere/Philips*	7
23	□15	STRIPPED	Depeche Mode	*Mute*	2
15	16	TURNING AWAY	Shakin' Stevens	*Epic*	4
10	17	THE CAPTAIN OF HER HEART	Double	*Polydor*	5
36	18	POWER OF LOVE/DO YOU BELIEVE IN LOVE	Huey Lewis and the News	*Chrysalis*	2
20	19	AND SHE WAS	Talking Heads	*EMI*	3
17	20	IMAGINATION	Belouis Some	*Parlophone*	6
19	21	RADIO AFRICA	Latin Quarter	*Rockin' Horse*	4
16	22	THE SUN ALWAYS SHINES ON TV	A-Ha	*Warner Bros*	10
14	23	WALK OF LIFE	Dire Straits	*Vertigo*	8
34	24	IF YOU WERE HERE TONIGHT	Alexander O'Neal	*Tabu*	2
39	25	HEAVEN MUST BE MISSING AN ANGEL	Tavares	*Capitol*	2
-	26	HOUNDS OF LOVE	Kate Bush	*EMI*	1
27	27	ONE DANCE WON'T DO	Audrey Hall	*Germain*	3
-	28	THEME FROM NEW YORK NEW YORK	Frank Sinatra	*Reprise*	1
30	29	I'M NOT GOING TO LET YOU	Colonel Abrams	*MCA*	3
18	30	THE PHANTOM OF THE OPERA	Sarah Brightman and Steve Harley	*Polydor*	7
25	31	SANCTIFY YOURSELF	Simple Minds	*Virgin*	5
21	32	PULL UP TO THE BUMPER/LA VIE EN ROSE	Grace Jones	*Island*	7
22	33	LIFE'S WHAT YOU MAKE IT	Talk Talk	*EMI*	6
-	34	(NOTHING SERIOUS) JUST BUGGIN'	Whistle ●	*Champion*	1
35	□35	SWEETEST GIRL	Madness	*Zarjazz*	2
29	36	BROKEN WINGS	Mr Mister	*RCA*	8
-	37	HI HO SILVER	Jim Diamond	*A&M*	1
28	38	SHOT IN THE DARK	Ozzy Osbourne	*Epic*	5
-	39	SILENT RUNNING (ON DANGEROUS GROUND)	Mike + the Mechanics ●	*WEA*	1
33	40	MY MAGIC MAN	Rochelle	*Warner Bros*	5

WEEK ENDING 8 MARCH 1986

LW	TW	Title	Artist	Label	Wks
2	□1	CHAIN REACTION	Diana Ross	*Capitol*	5
1	2	WHEN THE GOING GETS TOUGH THE TOUGH GET GOING	Billy Ocean	*Jive*	7
7	□3	LOVE MISSILE F1-11	Sigue Sigue Sputnik	*Parlophone*	2
10	4	MANIC MONDAY	Bangles	*CBS*	3
3	5	STARTING TOGETHER	Su Pollard	*Rainbow*	5
5	6	BURNING HEART	Survivor	*Scotti Brothers*	5
6	7	HOW WILL I KNOW	Whitney Houston	*Arista*	7
4	8	ELOISE	Damned	*MCA*	5

In these weeks ■ Cosmopolitan Top Ten as Swiss duo Double join a Greek soloist and a Norwegian trio. Jamaica and Ireland are also represented at 39 and 31 (15.02.86) ■ Early 80s Kings Madness peak at a dissapointing 35. Their lowest charting single to date is a cover of a Scritti Politti track (22.02.86) ■ Let's hear it for the over-forties: Sinatra (70), Brown (57), Mouskouri (49), Ross (41), Shaky, Ozzy, Huey and Billy are no spring chickens either! (22.02.86)■

☐ Highest position disc reached ● Act's first ever week on chart

LW	TW	Title / Artist	Label	Wks
8	9	DON'T WASTE MY TIME Paul Hardcastle	*Chrysalis*	5
28	10	THEME FROM NEW YORK NEW YORK Frank Sinatra	*Reprise*	2
18	11	POWER OF LOVE/DO YOU BELIEVE IN LOVE Huey Lewis and the News	*Chrysalis*	3
25	12	HEAVEN MUST BE MISSING AN ANGEL Tavares	*Capitol*	3
24	13	IF YOU WERE HERE TONIGHT Alexander O'Neal	*Tabu*	3
34	14	(NOTHING SERIOUS) JUST BUGGIN' Whistle	*Champion*	2
12	15	RISE Public Image Ltd	*Virgin*	6
37	16	HI HO SILVER Jim Diamond	*A&M*	2
19	17	AND SHE WAS Talking Heads	*EMI*	4
26	18	HOUNDS OF LOVE Kate Bush	*EMI*	2
13	19	LIVING IN AMERICA James Brown	*Scotti Brothers*	7
27	20	ONE DANCE WON'T DO Audrey Hall	*Germain*	4
9	21	SYSTEM ADDICT Five Star	*Tent*	8
15	22	STRIPPED Depeche Mode	*Mute*	3
11	23	BORDERLINE Madonna	*Sire*	7
29	24	I'M NOT GOING TO LET YOU Colonel Abrams	*MCA*	4
39	25	SILENT RUNNING (ON DANGEROUS GROUND) Mike + the Mechanics	*WEA*	2
17	26	THE CAPTAIN OF HER HEART Double	*Polydor*	6
-	27	KISS Prince	*Paisley Park*	1
16	28	TURNING AWAY Shakin' Stevens	*Epic*	5
-	29	KYRIE Mr Mister	*RCA*	1
20	30	IMAGINATION Belouis Some	*Parlophone*	7
-	31	THE HONEYTHIEF Hipsway ●	*Mercury*	1
-	32	DIGGING YOUR SCENE Blow Monkeys ●	*RCA*	1
23	33	WALK OF LIFE Dire Straits	*Vertigo*	9
14	34	ONLY LOVE Nana Mouskouri	*Carrere/Philips*	8
-	35	LOVE IS THE DRUG Grace Jones	*Island*	1
-	36	ROCK ME TONIGHT (FOR OLD TIME'S SAKE) Freddie Jackson ●	*Capitol*	1
21	37	RADIO AFRICA Latin Quarter	*Rockin' Horse*	5
-	38	POGUETRY IN MOTION Pogues ●	*Stiff*	1
-	39	CALLING AMERICA Electric Light Orchestra	*Epic*	1
-	40	CANDYMAN Siouxsie and the Banshees	*Wonderland*	1

WEEK ENDING 15 MARCH 1986

LW	TW	Title / Artist	Label	Wks
1	1	CHAIN REACTION Diana Ross	*Capitol*	6
4	2	MANIC MONDAY Bangles	*CBS*	4
3	3	LOVE MISSILE F1-11 Sigue Sigue Sputnik	*Parlophone*	3
10	4	THEME FROM NEW YORK NEW YORK Frank Sinatra	*Reprise*	3
2	5	WHEN THE GOING GETS TOUGH THE TOUGH GET GOING Billy Ocean	*Jive*	8
16	6	HI HO SILVER Jim Diamond	*A&M*	3
14	7	(NOTHING SERIOUS) JUST BUGGIN' Whistle	*Champion*	3
-	8	ABSOLUTE BEGINNERS David Bowie	*Virgin*	1
11	9	POWER OF LOVE/DO YOU BELIEVE IN LOVE Huey Lewis and the News	*Chrysalis*	4
6	10	BURNING HEART Survivor	*Scotti Brothers*	6
5	11	STARTING TOGETHER Su Pollard	*Rainbow*	6
7	12	HOW WILL I KNOW Whitney Houston	*Arista*	8
27	13	KISS Prince	*Paisley Park*	2
13	14	IF YOU WERE HERE TONIGHT Alexander O'Neal	*Tabu*	4
9	15	DON'T WASTE MY TIME Paul Hardcastle	*Chrysalis*	6
12	16	HEAVEN MUST BE MISSING AN ANGEL Tavares	*Capitol*	4
-	17	MOVE AWAY Culture Club	*Virgin*	1
29	18	KYRIE Mr Mister	*RCA*	2
8	19	ELOISE Damned	*MCA*	6
32	20	DIGGING YOUR SCENE Blow Monkeys	*RCA*	2
25	21	SILENT RUNNING (ON DANGEROUS GROUND) Mike + the Mechanics	*WEA*	3
31	22	THE HONEYTHIEF Hipsway	*Mercury*	2
-	23	NO ONE IS TO BLAME Howard Jones	*WEA*	1
18	24	HOUNDS OF LOVE Kate Bush	*EMI*	3
20	25	ONE DANCE WON'T DO Audrey Hall	*Germain*	5
36	26	ROCK ME TONIGHT (FOR OLD TIME'S SAKE) Freddie Jackson	*Capitol*	2
-	27	HARLEM SHUFFLE Rolling Stones	*Rolling Stones*	1
39	28	CALLING AMERICA Electric Light Orchestra	*Epic*	2
38	29	POGUETRY IN MOTION Pogues	*Stiff*	2
17	30	AND SHE WAS Talking Heads	*EMI*	5
-	31	LOVE COMES QUICKLY Pet Shop Boys	*Parlophone*	1
34	32	ONLY LOVE Nana Mouskouri	*Carrere/Philips*	9
24	33	I'M NOT GOING TO LET YOU Colonel Abrams	*MCA*	5
40	34	CANDYMAN Siouxsie and the Banshees	*Wonderland*	2
19	35	LIVING IN AMERICA James Brown	*Scotti Brothers*	8
15	36	RISE Public Image Ltd	*Virgin*	7
21	37	SYSTEM ADDICT Five Star	*Tent*	9
-	38	YOU TO ME ARE EVERYTHING Real Thing	*PRT*	1
35	39	LOVE IS THE DRUG Grace Jones	*Island*	2
22	40	STRIPPED Depeche Mode	*Mute*	4

WEEK ENDING 22 MARCH 1986

LW	TW	Title / Artist	Label	Wks
1	1	CHAIN REACTION Diana Ross	*Capitol*	7
8	2	ABSOLUTE BEGINNERS David Bowie	*Virgin*	2
2	3	MANIC MONDAY Bangles	*CBS*	5
-	4	LIVING DOLL Cliff Richard and the Young Ones ●	*WEA*	1
6	5	HI HO SILVER Jim Diamond	*A&M*	4
13	6	KISS Prince	*Paisley Park*	3
17	7	MOVE AWAY Culture Club	*Virgin*	2
7	8	(NOTHING SERIOUS) JUST BUGGIN' Whistle	*Champion*	4
4	9	THEME FROM NEW YORK NEW YORK Frank Sinatra	*Reprise*	4
3	10	LOVE MISSILE F1-11 Sigue Sigue Sputnik	*Parlophone*	4
9	11	POWER OF LOVE/DO YOU BELIEVE IN LOVE Huey Lewis and the News	*Chrysalis*	5
20	12	DIGGING YOUR SCENE Blow Monkeys	*RCA*	3
27	13	HARLEM SHUFFLE Rolling Stones	*Rolling Stones*	2
5	14	WHEN THE GOING GETS TOUGH THE TOUGH GET GOING Billy Ocean	*Jive*	9
18	15	KYRIE Mr Mister	*RCA*	3
23	16	NO ONE IS TO BLAME Howard Jones	*WEA*	2
22	17	THE HONEYTHIEF Hipsway	*Mercury*	3
26	18	ROCK ME TONIGHT (FOR OLD TIME'S SAKE) Freddie Jackson	*Capitol*	3
38	19	YOU TO ME ARE EVERYTHING Real Thing	*PRT*	2
14	20	IF YOU WERE HERE TONIGHT Alexander O'Neal	*Tabu*	5
31	21	LOVE COMES QUICKLY Pet Shop Boys	*Parlophone*	2
-	22	TOUCH ME (I WANT YOUR BODY) Samantha Fox ●	*Jive*	1
10	23	BURNING HEART Survivor	*Scotti Brothers*	7
12	24	HOW WILL I KNOW Whitney Houston	*Arista*	9
16	25	HEAVEN MUST BE MISSING AN ANGEL Tavares	*Capitol*	5
-	26	PETER GUNN Art Of Noise featuring Duane Eddy	*China*	1
15	27	DON'T WASTE MY TIME Paul Hardcastle	*Chrysalis*	7
21	28	SILENT RUNNING (ON DANGEROUS GROUND) Mike + the Mechanics	*WEA*	4
11	29	STARTING TOGETHER Su Pollard	*Rainbow*	7
-	30	WONDERFUL WORLD Sam Cooke	*RCA*	1
28	31	CALLING AMERICA Electric Light Orchestra	*Epic*	3
29	32	POGUETRY IN MOTION Pogues	*Stiff*	3
19	33	ELOISE Damned	*MCA*	7
34	34	CANDYMAN Siouxsie and the Banshees	*Wonderland*	3
25	35	ONE DANCE WON'T DO Audrey Hall	*Germain*	6
-	36	OVERJOYED Stevie Wonder	*Motown*	1
-	37	SECRET LOVERS Atlantic Starr ●	*A&M*	1
24	38	HOUNDS OF LOVE Kate Bush	*EMI*	4
30	39	AND SHE WAS Talking Heads	*EMI*	6
-	40	DARE TO DREAM/BOTH SIDES NOW Viola Wills	*Streetwave*	1

WEEK ENDING 29 MARCH 1986

LW	TW	Title / Artist	Label	Wks
4	1	LIVING DOLL Cliff Richard and the Young Ones	*WEA*	2
1	2	CHAIN REACTION Diana Ross	*Capitol*	8
2	3	ABSOLUTE BEGINNERS David Bowie	*Virgin*	3
22	4	TOUCH ME (I WANT YOUR BODY) Samantha Fox	*Jive*	2
30	5	WONDERFUL WORLD Sam Cooke	*RCA*	2
19	6	YOU TO ME ARE EVERYTHING Real Thing	*PRT*	3
5	7	HI HO SILVER Jim Diamond	*A&M*	5
3	8	MANIC MONDAY Bangles	*CBS*	6
6	9	KISS Prince	*Paisley Park*	4
7	10	MOVE AWAY Culture Club	*Virgin*	3

■This is the first Madonna-less chart since 08.06.85 (15.03.86) ■ Diana Ross last occupied the top slot on 11.09.71. This gap of 14 years 192 days is the longest to date (15.03.86) ■ Frank Sinatra is the oldest act ever to have a Top Ten single (15.03.86) ■ Cliff Richard, Frank Sinatra, Huey Lewis, Real Thing, Tavares, Duane Eddy and Sam Cooke are all charting with re-makes/re-issues of their old hits (22.03.86)■

March 1986

□ Highest position disc reached ● Act's first ever week on chart

LW	TW	Title / Artist	Label	Wks
15	[11]	KYRIE Mr Mister	RCA	4
26	12	PETER GUNN Art Of Noise featuring Duane Eddy	China	2
12	13	DIGGING YOUR SCENE Blow Monkeys	RCA	4
13	14	HARLEM SHUFFLE Rolling Stones	Rolling Stones	3
8	15	(NOTHING SERIOUS) JUST BUGGIN' Whistle	Champion	5
-	16	A KIND OF MAGIC Queen	EMI	1
10	17	LOVE MISSILE F1-11 Sigue Sigue Sputnik	Parlophone	5
11	18	POWER OF LOVE/DO YOU BELIEVE IN LOVE Huey Lewis and the News	Chrysalis	6
21	[19]	LOVE COMES QUICKLY Pet Shop Boys	Parlophone	3
16	20	NO ONE IS TO BLAME Howard Jones	WEA	3
17	21	THE HONEYTHIEF Hipsway	Mercury	4
9	22	THEME FROM NEW YORK NEW YORK Frank Sinatra	Reprise	5
14	23	WHEN THE GOING GETS TOUGH THE TOUGH GET GOING Billy Ocean	Jive	10
37	24	SECRET LOVERS Atlantic Starr	A&M	2
36	25	OVERJOYED Stevie Wonder	Motown	2
18	26	ROCK ME TONIGHT (FOR OLD TIME'S SAKE) Freddie Jackson	Capitol	4
-	27	ROCK ME AMADEUS Falco ●	A&M	1
20	28	IF YOU WERE HERE TONIGHT Alexander O'Neal	Tabu	6
25	29	HEAVEN MUST BE MISSING AN ANGEL Tavares	Capitol	6
-	30	SHELLSHOCK New Order	Factory	1
24	31	HOW WILL I KNOW Whitney Houston	Arista	10
31	32	CALLING AMERICA Electric Light Orchestra	Epic	4
-	33	HELLO DARLING Tippa Irie ●	UK Bubblers	1
-	34	E=MC2 Big Audio Dynamite ●	CBS	1
40	[35]	DARE TO DREAM/BOTH SIDES NOW Viola Wills	Streetwave	2
27	36	DON'T WASTE MY TIME Paul Hardcastle	Chrysalis	8
28	37	SILENT RUNNING (ON DANGEROUS GROUND) Mike + the Mechanics	WEA	5
23	38	BURNING HEART Survivor	Scotti Brothers	8
32	39	POGUETRY IN MOTION Pogues	Stiff	4
-	40	C'MON! C'MON Bronski Beat	Forbidden Fruit	1

WEEK ENDING 5 APRIL 1986

LW	TW	Title / Artist	Label	Wks
1	[1]	LIVING DOLL Cliff Richard and the Young Ones	WEA	3
5	[2]	WONDERFUL WORLD Sam Cooke	RCA	3
4	[3]	TOUCH ME (I WANT YOUR BODY) Samantha Fox	Jive	3
-	4	A DIFFERENT CORNER George Michael	Epic	1
6	[5]	YOU TO ME ARE EVERYTHING Real Thing	PRT	4
2	6	CHAIN REACTION Diana Ross	Capitol	9
16	7	A KIND OF MAGIC Queen	EMI	2
3	8	ABSOLUTE BEGINNERS David Bowie	Virgin	4
12	9	PETER GUNN Art Of Noise featuring Duane Eddy	China	3
27	10	ROCK ME AMADEUS Falco	A&M	2
7	11	HI HO SILVER Jim Diamond	A&M	6
8	12	MANIC MONDAY Bangles	CBS	7
11	13	KYRIE Mr Mister	RCA	5
24	14	SECRET LOVERS Atlantic Starr	A&M	3
9	15	KISS Prince	Paisley Park	5
10	16	MOVE AWAY Culture Club	Virgin	4
25	[17]	OVERJOYED Stevie Wonder	Motown	3
13	18	DIGGING YOUR SCENE Blow Monkeys	RCA	5
19	[19]	LOVE COMES QUICKLY Pet Shop Boys	Parlophone	4
34	20	E=MC2 Big Audio Dynamite	CBS	2
18	21	POWER OF LOVE/DO YOU BELIEVE IN LOVE Huey Lewis and the News	Chrysalis	7
14	22	HARLEM SHUFFLE Rolling Stones	Rolling Stones	4
-	23	TRAIN OF THOUGHT A-Ha	Warner Bros	1
33	24	HELLO DARLING Tippa Irie	UK Bubblers	2
15	25	(NOTHING SERIOUS) JUST BUGGIN' Whistle	Champion	6
20	26	NO ONE IS TO BLAME Howard Jones	WEA	4
-	27	HAVE YOU EVER HAD IT BLUE Style Council	Polydor	1
30	[28]	SHELLSHOCK New Order	Factory	2
40	29	C'MON! C'MON Bronski Beat	Forbidden Fruit	2
23	30	WHEN THE GOING GETS TOUGH THE TOUGH GET GOING Billy Ocean	Jive	11
17	31	LOVE MISSILE F1-11 Sigue Sigue Sputnik	Parlophone	6
21	32	THE HONEYTHIEF Hipsway	Mercury	5
26	33	ROCK ME TONIGHT (FOR OLD TIME'S SAKE) Freddie Jackson	Capitol	5
22	34	THEME FROM NEW YORK NEW YORK Frank Sinatra	Reprise	6
-	35	THE FINEST SOS Band	Tabu	1
-	36	IS YOUR LOVE STRONG ENOUGH Bryan Ferry	EG	1
28	37	IF YOU WERE HERE TONIGHT Alexander O'Neal	Tabu	7
32	38	CALLING AMERICA Electric Light Orchestra	Epic	5
31	39	HOW WILL I KNOW Whitney Houston	Arista	11
35	40	DARE TO DREAM/BOTH SIDES NOW Viola Wills	Streetwave	3

WEEK ENDING 12 APRIL 1986

LW	TW	Title / Artist	Label	Wks
1	[1]	LIVING DOLL Cliff Richard and the Young Ones	WEA	4
4	2	A DIFFERENT CORNER George Michael	Epic	2
2	3	WONDERFUL WORLD Sam Cooke	RCA	4
3	4	TOUCH ME (I WANT YOUR BODY) Samantha Fox	Jive	4
10	5	ROCK ME AMADEUS Falco	A&M	3
5	6	YOU TO ME ARE EVERYTHING Real Thing	PRT	5
7	7	A KIND OF MAGIC Queen	EMI	3
9	[8]	PETER GUNN Art Of Noise featuring Duane Eddy	China	4
23	9	TRAIN OF THOUGHT A-Ha	Warner Bros	2
14	[10]	SECRET LOVERS Atlantic Starr	A&M	4
20	[11]	E=MC2 Big Audio Dynamite	CBS	3
6	12	CHAIN REACTION Diana Ross	Capitol	10
8	13	ABSOLUTE BEGINNERS David Bowie	Virgin	5
27	[14]	HAVE YOU EVER HAD IT BLUE Style Council	Polydor	2
-	15	ALL THE THINGS SHE SAID Simple Minds	Virgin	1
13	16	KYRIE Mr Mister	RCA	6
11	17	HI HO SILVER Jim Diamond	A&M	7
-	18	LOOK AWAY Big Country	Mercury	1
17	19	OVERJOYED Stevie Wonder	Motown	4
12	20	MANIC MONDAY Bangles	CBS	8
19	21	LOVE COMES QUICKLY Pet Shop Boys	Parlophone	5
24	[22]	HELLO DARLING Tippa Irie	UK Bubblers	3
35	23	THE FINEST SOS Band	Tabu	2
18	24	DIGGING YOUR SCENE Blow Monkeys	RCA	6
29	25	C'MON! C'MON Bronski Beat	Forbidden Fruit	3
15	26	KISS Prince	Paisley Park	6
16	27	MOVE AWAY Culture Club	Virgin	5
21	28	POWER OF LOVE/DO YOU BELIEVE IN LOVE Huey Lewis and the News	Chrysalis	8
36	29	IS YOUR LOVE STRONG ENOUGH Bryan Ferry	EG	2
28	30	SHELLSHOCK New Order	Factory	3
25	31	(NOTHING SERIOUS) JUST BUGGIN' Whistle	Champion	7
22	32	HARLEM SHUFFLE Rolling Stones	Rolling Stones	5
26	33	NO ONE IS TO BLAME Howard Jones	WEA	5
32	34	THE HONEYTHIEF Hipsway	Mercury	6
33	35	ROCK ME TONIGHT (FOR OLD TIME'S SAKE) Freddie Jackson	Capitol	6
-	36	CAN'T WAIT ANOTHER MINUTE Five Star	Tent	1
-	37	WHAT HAVE YOU DONE FOR ME LATELY Janet Jackson ●	A&M	1
30	38	WHEN THE GOING GETS TOUGH THE TOUGH GET GOING Billy Ocean	Jive	12
34	39	THEME FROM NEW YORK NEW YORK Frank Sinatra	Reprise	7
-	40	MARLENE ON THE WALL Suzanne Vega ●	A&M	1

WEEK ENDING 19 APRIL 1986

LW	TW	Title / Artist	Label	Wks
2	[1]	A DIFFERENT CORNER George Michael	Epic	3
1	2	LIVING DOLL Cliff Richard and the Young Ones	WEA	5
5	3	ROCK ME AMADEUS Falco	A&M	4
7	4	A KIND OF MAGIC Queen	EMI	4
4	5	TOUCH ME (I WANT YOUR BODY) Samantha Fox	Jive	5
3	6	WONDERFUL WORLD Sam Cooke	RCA	5
6	7	YOU TO ME ARE EVERYTHING Real Thing	PRT	6
9	[8]	TRAIN OF THOUGHT A-Ha	Warner Bros	3
15	[9]	ALL THE THINGS SHE SAID Simple Minds	Virgin	2
18	10	LOOK AWAY Big Country	Mercury	2
10	11	SECRET LOVERS Atlantic Starr	A&M	5
8	12	PETER GUNN Art Of Noise featuring Duane Eddy	China	5

In these weeks ■ Cliff Richard (45) replaces Diana Ross (41) for his first number one since 15.09.79 (29.03.86) ■ Sophia George, Audrey Hall and now Tippa Irie make it a golden year for reggae (29.03.86) ■ Two singles from films are in the Top Ten, *A Kind Of Magic*, 'Highlander' and *Absolute Beginners*, 'Absolute Beginners' (05.04.86)■

LW	TW	Title / Artist	Label	Wks
11	13	E=MC2 Big Audio Dynamite	*CBS*	4
36	14	CAN'T WAIT ANOTHER MINUTE Five Star	*Tent*	2
14	15	HAVE YOU EVER HAD IT BLUE Style Council	*Polydor*	3
37	16	WHAT HAVE YOU DONE FOR ME LATELY Janet Jackson	*A&M*	2
23	[17]	THE FINEST SOS Band	*Tabu*	3
12	18	CHAIN REACTION Diana Ross	*Capitol*	11
17	19	HI HO SILVER Jim Diamond	*A&M*	8
25	[20]	C'MON! C'MON Bronski Beat	*Forbidden Fruit*	4
13	21	ABSOLUTE BEGINNERS David Bowie	*Virgin*	6
29	[22]	IS YOUR LOVE STRONG ENOUGH Bryan Ferry	*EG*	3
22	23	HELLO DARLING Tippa Irie	*UK Bubblers*	4
19	24	OVERJOYED Stevie Wonder	*Motown*	5
16	25	KYRIE Mr Mister	*RCA*	7
-	26	JUST SAY NO Grange Hill Cast ●	*BBC*	1
40	27	MARLENE ON THE WALL Suzanne Vega	*A&M*	2
-	28	DRIVING AWAY FROM HOME (JIM'S TUNE) It's Immaterial ●	*Siren*	1
24	29	DIGGING YOUR SCENE Blow Monkeys	*RCA*	7
21	30	LOVE COMES QUICKLY Pet Shop Boys	*Parlophone*	6
20	31	MANIC MONDAY Bangles	*CBS*	9
26	32	KISS Prince	*Paisley Park*	7
-	33	THE GREATEST LOVE OF ALL Whitney Houston	*Arista*	1
-	34	THIS IS LOVE Gary Numan	*Numa*	1
28	35	POWER OF LOVE/DO YOU BELIEVE IN LOVE Huey Lewis and the News	*Chrysalis*	9
-	36	STROLLIN' ON Maxi Priest ●	*10*	1
-	37	I'LL KEEP ON LOVING YOU Princess	*Supreme*	1
-	38	SOME PEOPLE Belouis Some	*Parlophone*	1
-	39	YOU AND ME TONIGHT Aurra ●	*10*	1
27	40	MOVE AWAY Culture Club	*Virgin*	6

WEEK ENDING **26 APRIL 1986**

LW	TW	Title / Artist	Label	Wks
1	[1]	A DIFFERENT CORNER George Michael	*Epic*	4
3	2	ROCK ME AMADEUS Falco	*A&M*	5
4	[3]	A KIND OF MAGIC Queen	*EMI*	5
2	4	LIVING DOLL Cliff Richard and the Young Ones	*WEA*	6
26	[5]	JUST SAY NO Grange Hill Cast	*BBC*	2
16	6	WHAT HAVE YOU DONE FOR ME LATELY Janet Jackson	*A&M*	3
10	[7]	LOOK AWAY Big Country	*Mercury*	3
14	8	CAN'T WAIT ANOTHER MINUTE Five Star	*Tent*	3
5	9	TOUCH ME (I WANT YOUR BODY) Samantha Fox	*Jive*	6
-	10	LIVE TO TELL Madonna	*Sire*	1
9	11	ALL THE THINGS SHE SAID Simple Minds	*Virgin*	3
6	12	WONDERFUL WORLD Sam Cooke	*RCA*	6
8	13	TRAIN OF THOUGHT A-Ha	*Warner Bros*	4
7	14	YOU TO ME ARE EVERYTHING Real Thing	*PRT*	7
11	15	SECRET LOVERS Atlantic Starr	*A&M*	6
33	16	THE GREATEST LOVE OF ALL Whitney Houston	*Arista*	2
17	[17]	THE FINEST SOS Band	*Tabu*	4
28	[18]	DRIVING AWAY FROM HOME (JIM'S TUNE) It's Immaterial	*Siren*	2
13	19	E=MC2 Big Audio Dynamite	*CBS*	5
39	20	YOU AND ME TONIGHT Aurra	*10*	2
27	[21]	MARLENE ON THE WALL Suzanne Vega	*A&M*	3
12	22	PETER GUNN Art Of Noise featuring Duane Eddy	*China*	6
-	23	LESSONS IN LOVE Level 42	*Polydor*	1
20	24	C'MON! C'MON Bronski Beat	*Forbidden Fruit*	5
15	25	HAVE YOU EVER HAD IT BLUE Style Council	*Polydor*	4
37	26	I'LL KEEP ON LOVING YOU Princess	*Supreme*	2
-	27	I HEARD IT THROUGH THE GRAPEVINE Marvin Gaye	*Motown*	1
34	28	THIS IS LOVE Gary Numan	*Numa*	2
-	29	A QUESTION OF LUST Depeche Mode	*Mute*	1
22	30	IS YOUR LOVE STRONG ENOUGH Bryan Ferry	*EG*	4
-	31	STARS Hear 'n' Aid ●	*Vertigo*	1
36	[32]	STROLLIN' ON Maxi Priest	*10*	2
19	33	HI HO SILVER Jim Diamond	*A&M*	9
21	34	ABSOLUTE BEGINNERS David Bowie	*Virgin*	7
18	35	CHAIN REACTION Diana Ross	*Capitol*	12
38	36	SOME PEOPLE Belouis Some	*Parlophone*	2
-	37	THERE'LL BE SAD SONGS TO MAKE YOU CRY Billy Ocean	*Jive*	1

May 1986

□ Highest position disc reached ● Act's first ever week on chart

LW	TW	Title / Artist	Label	Wks
-	38	ALL AND ALL Joyce Sims ●	*London*	1
23	39	HELLO DARLING Tippa Irie	*UK Bubblers*	5
-	40	WHY CAN'T THIS BE LOVE Van Halen	*Warner Bros*	1

WEEK ENDING **3 MAY 1986**

LW	TW	Title / Artist	Label	Wks
1	[1]	A DIFFERENT CORNER George Michael	*Epic*	5
2	2	ROCK ME AMADEUS Falco	*A&M*	6
6	[3]	WHAT HAVE YOU DONE FOR ME LATELY Janet Jackson	*A&M*	4
10	4	LIVE TO TELL Madonna	*Sire*	2
5	[5]	JUST SAY NO Grange Hill Cast	*BBC*	3
3	6	A KIND OF MAGIC Queen	*EMI*	6
8	[7]	CAN'T WAIT ANOTHER MINUTE Five Star	*Tent*	4
7	8	LOOK AWAY Big Country	*Mercury*	4
23	9	LESSONS IN LOVE Level 42	*Polydor*	2
16	10	THE GREATEST LOVE OF ALL Whitney Houston	*Arista*	3
27	11	I HEARD IT THROUGH THE GRAPEVINE Marvin Gaye	*Motown*	2
20	[12]	YOU AND ME TONIGHT Aurra	*10*	3
4	13	LIVING DOLL Cliff Richard and the Young Ones	*WEA*	7
9	14	TOUCH ME (I WANT YOUR BODY) Samantha Fox	*Jive*	7
11	15	ALL THE THINGS SHE SAID Simple Minds	*Virgin*	4
15	16	SECRET LOVERS Atlantic Starr	*A&M*	7
17	[17]	THE FINEST SOS Band	*Tabu*	5
12	18	WONDERFUL WORLD Sam Cooke	*RCA*	7
-	19	ON MY OWN Patti LaBelle and Michael McDonald ●	*MCA*	1
14	20	YOU TO ME ARE EVERYTHING Real Thing	*PRT*	8
13	21	TRAIN OF THOUGHT A-Ha	*Warner Bros*	5
18	22	DRIVING AWAY FROM HOME (JIM'S TUNE) It's Immaterial	*Siren*	3
21	23	MARLENE ON THE WALL Suzanne Vega	*A&M*	4
26	24	I'LL KEEP ON LOVING YOU Princess	*Supreme*	3
38	25	ALL AND ALL Joyce Sims	*London*	2
31	26	STARS Hear 'n' Aid	*Vertigo*	2
19	27	E=MC2 Big Audio Dynamite	*CBS*	6
29	[28]	A QUESTION OF LUST Depeche Mode	*Mute*	2
37	29	THERE'LL BE SAD SONGS TO MAKE YOU CRY Billy Ocean	*Jive*	2
-	30	SLEDGEHAMMER Peter Gabriel	*Charisma*	1
40	31	WHY CAN'T THIS BE LOVE Van Halen	*Warner Bros*	2
32	[32]	STROLLIN' ON Maxi Priest	*10*	3
36	[33]	SOME PEOPLE Belouis Some	*Parlophone*	3
22	34	PETER GUNN Art Of Noise featuring Duane Eddy	*China*	7
-	35	BOYS DON'T CRY Cure	*Fiction*	1
24	36	C'MON! C'MON Bronski Beat	*Forbidden Fruit*	6
-	37	TENDER LOVE Force MD's ●	*Tommy Boy*	1
25	38	HAVE YOU EVER HAD IT BLUE Style Council	*Polydor*	5
-	39	YOUR LATEST TRICK Dire Straits	*Vertigo*	1
-	40	THE QUEEN'S BIRTHDAY St John's College School Choir and the Band of the Grenadier Guards ●	*Columbia*	1

WEEK ENDING **10 MAY 1986**

LW	TW	Title / Artist	Label	Wks
2	[1]	ROCK ME AMADEUS Falco	*A&M*	7
4	[2]	LIVE TO TELL Madonna	*Sire*	3
9	[3]	LESSONS IN LOVE Level 42	*Polydor*	3
19	4	ON MY OWN Patti LaBelle and Michael McDonald	*MCA*	2
3	5	WHAT HAVE YOU DONE FOR ME LATELY Janet Jackson	*A&M*	5
1	6	A DIFFERENT CORNER George Michael	*Epic*	6
7	[7]	CAN'T WAIT ANOTHER MINUTE Five Star	*Tent*	5
11	[8]	I HEARD IT THROUGH THE GRAPEVINE Marvin Gaye	*Motown*	3
6	9	A KIND OF MAGIC Queen	*EMI*	7
10	10	THE GREATEST LOVE OF ALL Whitney Houston	*Arista*	4
-	11	THE CHICKEN SONG Spitting Image ●	*Virgin*	1
5	12	JUST SAY NO Grange Hill Cast	*BBC*	4
12	13	YOU AND ME TONIGHT Aurra	*10*	4

■Marvin Gaye and Sam Cooke owe their current success to Levi jeans TV Commercials, Jim Diamond's hit is a TV theme and the cast of TV's Grange Hill peak at five (26.04.86) ■ Falco becomes the first Austrian to top the UK charts (10.05.86) ■ More TV - Spitting Image debut at 11 (10.05.86)■

May 1986

□ Highest position disc reached ● Act's first ever week on chart

LW	TW	Title	Artist	Label	Wks
8	14	LOOK AWAY	Big Country	Mercury	5
30	15	SLEDGEHAMMER	Peter Gabriel	Charisma	2
24	[16]	I'LL KEEP ON LOVING YOU	Princess	Supreme	4
16	17	SECRET LOVERS	Atlantic Starr	A&M	8
25	18	ALL AND ALL	Joyce Sims	London	3
17	19	THE FINEST	SOS Band	Tabu	6
15	20	ALL THE THINGS SHE SAID	Simple Minds	Virgin	5
13	21	LIVING DOLL	Cliff Richard and the Young Ones	WEA	8
31	22	WHY CAN'T THIS BE LOVE	Van Halen	Warner Bros	3
35	23	BOYS DON'T CRY	Cure	Fiction	2
14	24	TOUCH ME (I WANT YOUR BODY)	Samantha Fox	Jive	8
18	25	WONDERFUL WORLD	Sam Cooke	RCA	8
39	[26]	YOUR LATEST TRICK	Dire Straits	Vertigo	2
29	27	THERE'LL BE SAD SONGS TO MAKE YOU CRY	Billy Ocean	Jive	3
20	28	YOU TO ME ARE EVERYTHING	Real Thing	PRT	9
26	29	STARS	Hear 'n' Aid	Vertigo	3
28	30	A QUESTION OF LUST	Depeche Mode	Mute	3
23	31	MARLENE ON THE WALL	Suzanne Vega	A&M	5
22	32	DRIVING AWAY FROM HOME (JIM'S TUNE)	It's Immaterial	Siren	4
32	33	STROLLIN' ON	Maxi Priest	10	4
37	34	TENDER LOVE	Force MD's	Tommy Boy	2
-	35	ROCK LOBSTER	B-52's	Island	1
21	36	TRAIN OF THOUGHT	A-Ha	Warner Bros	6
-	37	SNOOKER LOOPY	Matchroom Mob with Chas and Dave ●	Rockney	1
-	38	ROUGH BOY	ZZ Top	Warner Bros	1
-	39	THE BIG SKY	Kate Bush	EMI	1
-	40	SPIRIT IN THE SKY	Dr and the Medics ●	IRS	1

WEEK ENDING 17 MAY 1986

LW	TW	Title	Artist	Label	Wks
11	[1]	THE CHICKEN SONG	Spitting Image	Virgin	2
4	[2]	ON MY OWN	Patti LaBelle and Michael McDonald	MCA	3
3	[3]	LESSONS IN LOVE	Level 42	Polydor	4
1	4	ROCK ME AMADEUS	Falco	A&M	8
2	5	LIVE TO TELL	Madonna	Sire	4
5	6	WHAT HAVE YOU DONE FOR ME LATELY	Janet Jackson	A&M	6
15	7	SLEDGEHAMMER	Peter Gabriel	Charisma	3
10	[8]	THE GREATEST LOVE OF ALL	Whitney Houston	Arista	5
8	9	I HEARD IT THROUGH THE GRAPEVINE	Marvin Gaye	Motown	4
7	10	CAN'T WAIT ANOTHER MINUTE	Five Star	Tent	6
37	11	SNOOKER LOOPY	Matchroom Mob with Chas and Dave	Rockney	2
6	12	A DIFFERENT CORNER	George Michael	Epic	7
22	13	WHY CAN'T THIS BE LOVE	Van Halen	Warner Bros	4
27	14	THERE'LL BE SAD SONGS TO MAKE YOU CRY	Billy Ocean	Jive	4
9	15	A KIND OF MAGIC	Queen	EMI	8
18	[16]	ALL AND ALL	Joyce Sims	London	4
40	17	SPIRIT IN THE SKY	Dr and the Medics	IRS	2
13	18	YOU AND ME TONIGHT	Aurra	10	5
16	19	I'LL KEEP ON LOVING YOU	Princess	Supreme	5
35	20	ROCK LOBSTER/PLANET CLAIRE	B-52's	Island	2
14	21	LOOK AWAY	Big Country	Mercury	6
23	[22]	BOYS DON'T CRY	Cure	Fiction	3
34	[23]	TENDER LOVE	Force MD's	Tommy Boy	3
17	24	SECRET LOVERS	Atlantic Starr	A&M	9
-	25	ROLLIN' HOME	Status Quo	Vertigo	1
26	[26]	YOUR LATEST TRICK	Dire Straits	Vertigo	3
12	27	JUST SAY NO	Grange Hill Cast	BBC	5
19	28	THE FINEST	SOS Band	Tabu	7
38	29	ROUGH BOY	ZZ Top	Warner Bros	2
20	30	ALL THE THINGS SHE SAID	Simple Minds	Virgin	6
21	31	LIVING DOLL	Cliff Richard and the Young Ones	WEA	9
25	32	WONDERFUL WORLD	Sam Cooke	RCA	9
24	33	TOUCH ME (I WANT YOUR BODY)	Samantha Fox	Jive	9
-	34	ADDICTED TO LOVE	Robert Palmer	Island	1
-	35	SET ME FREE	Jaki Graham	EMI	1
-	36	IF SHE KNEW WHAT SHE WANTS	Bangles	CBS	1
39	[37]	THE BIG SKY	Kate Bush	EMI	2
29	38	STARS	Hear 'n' Aid	Vertigo	4
-	39	SINFUL	Pete Wylie ●	MDM	1
32	40	DRIVING AWAY FROM HOME (JIM'S TUNE)	It's Immaterial	Siren	5

WEEK ENDING 24 MAY 1986

LW	TW	Title	Artist	Label	Wks
1	[1]	THE CHICKEN SONG	Spitting Image	Virgin	3
2	[2]	ON MY OWN	Patti LaBelle and Michael McDonald	MCA	4
3	[3]	LESSONS IN LOVE	Level 42	Polydor	5
7	[4]	SLEDGEHAMMER	Peter Gabriel	Charisma	4
17	5	SPIRIT IN THE SKY	Dr and the Medics	IRS	3
11	[6]	SNOOKER LOOPY	Matchroom Mob with Chas and Dave	Rockney	3
4	7	ROCK ME AMADEUS	Falco	A&M	9
13	[8]	WHY CAN'T THIS BE LOVE	Van Halen	Warner Bros	5
25	[9]	ROLLIN' HOME	Status Quo	Vertigo	2
5	10	LIVE TO TELL	Madonna	Sire	5
8	11	THE GREATEST LOVE OF ALL	Whitney Houston	Arista	6
20	[12]	ROCK LOBSTER/PLANET CLAIRE	B-52's	Island	3
14	13	THERE'LL BE SAD SONGS TO MAKE YOU CRY	Billy Ocean	Jive	5
10	14	CAN'T WAIT ANOTHER MINUTE	Five Star	Tent	7
6	15	WHAT HAVE YOU DONE FOR ME LATELY	Janet Jackson	A&M	7
34	16	ADDICTED TO LOVE	Robert Palmer	Island	2
16	17	ALL AND ALL	Joyce Sims	London	5
9	18	I HEARD IT THROUGH THE GRAPEVINE	Marvin Gaye	Motown	5
-	19	HOLDING BACK THE YEARS	Simply Red	WEA	1
35	20	SET ME FREE	Jaki Graham	EMI	2
12	21	A DIFFERENT CORNER	George Michael	Epic	8
18	22	YOU AND ME TONIGHT	Aurra	10	6
29	[23]	ROUGH BOY	ZZ Top	Warner Bros	3
19	24	I'LL KEEP ON LOVING YOU	Princess	Supreme	6
22	25	BOYS DON'T CRY	Cure	Fiction	4
15	26	A KIND OF MAGIC	Queen	EMI	9
-	27	WHO MADE WHO	AC/DC	Atlantic	1
39	28	SINFUL	Pete Wylie	MDM	2
23	29	TENDER LOVE	Force MD's	Tommy Boy	4
-	30	MINE ALL MINE/PARTY FREAK	Cashflow ●	Club	1
36	[31]	IF SHE KNEW WHAT SHE WANTS	Bangles	CBS	2
26	32	YOUR LATEST TRICK	Dire Straits	Vertigo	4
21	33	LOOK AWAY	Big Country	Mercury	7
-	34	LOVE TOUCH	Rod Stewart	Warner Bros	1
-	35	I CAN'T WAIT	Nu Shooz ●	Atlantic	1
24	36	SECRET LOVERS	Atlantic Starr	A&M	10
-	37	CAN'T GET BY WITHOUT YOU	Real Thing	PRT	1
-	38	BAD BOY	Miami Sound Machine	Epic	1
-	39	TIME	Freddie Mercury	EMI	1
-	40	BASSLINE	Mantronix ●	10	1

WEEK ENDING 31 MAY 1986

LW	TW	Title	Artist	Label	Wks
1	[1]	THE CHICKEN SONG	Spitting Image	Virgin	4
2	[2]	ON MY OWN	Patti LaBelle and Michael McDonald	MCA	5
5	3	SPIRIT IN THE SKY	Dr and the Medics	IRS	4
4	[4]	SLEDGEHAMMER	Peter Gabriel	Charisma	5
3	5	LESSONS IN LOVE	Level 42	Polydor	6
19	6	HOLDING BACK THE YEARS	Simply Red	WEA	2
6	7	SNOOKER LOOPY	Matchroom Mob with Chas and Dave	Rockney	4
8	[8]	WHY CAN'T THIS BE LOVE	Van Halen	Warner Bros	6
20	9	SET ME FREE	Jaki Graham	EMI	3
16	10	ADDICTED TO LOVE	Robert Palmer	Island	3
9	11	ROLLIN' HOME	Status Quo	Vertigo	3
13	[12]	THERE'LL BE SAD SONGS TO MAKE YOU CRY	Billy Ocean	Jive	6
-	13	EVERYBODY WANTS TO RUN THE WORLD	Tears For Fears	Mercury	1

In these weeks ■ Only five previous acts have celebrated a number one after only two weeks on the chart (17.05.86) ■ Phil Collins of Genesis and Mike Rutherford (Mike + The Mechanics) have both charted so far this year but it is former Genesis frontman Peter Gabriel who has the biggest smash with *Sledgehammer* (24.05.86)■

June 1986

□ Highest position disc reached ● Act's first ever week on chart

LW	TW	Title	Artist	Label	Wks
12	14	ROCK LOBSTER/PLANET CLAIRE	B-52's	*Island*	4
7	15	ROCK ME AMADEUS	Falco	*A&M*	10
27	16	WHO MADE WHO	AC/DC	*Atlantic*	2
10	17	LIVE TO TELL	Madonna	*Sire*	6
30	18	MINE ALL MINE/PARTY FREAK	Cashflow	*Club*	2
14	19	CAN'T WAIT ANOTHER MINUTE	Five Star	*Tent*	8
28	20	SINFUL	Pete Wylie	*MDM*	3
35	21	I CAN'T WAIT	Nu Shooz	*Atlantic*	2
37	22	CAN'T GET BY WITHOUT YOU	Real Thing	*PRT*	2
17	23	ALL AND ALL	Joyce Sims	*London*	6
11	24	THE GREATEST LOVE OF ALL	Whitney Houston	*Arista*	7
-	25	INVISIBLE TOUCH	Genesis	*Virgin*	1
38	26	BAD BOY	Miami Sound Machine	*Epic*	2
34	27 □	LOVE TOUCH	Rod Stewart	*Warner Bros*	2
-	28	BIG MOUTH STRIKES AGAIN	Smiths	*Rough Trade*	1
-	29	OPPORTUNITIES (LET'S MAKE LOTS OF MONEY)	Pet Shop Boys	*Parlophone*	1
23	30	ROUGH BOY	ZZ Top	*Warner Bros*	4
15	31	WHAT HAVE YOU DONE FOR ME LATELY	Janet Jackson	*A&M*	8
18	32	I HEARD IT THROUGH THE GRAPEVINE	Marvin Gaye	*Motown*	6
39	33	TIME	Freddie Mercury	*EMI*	2
40	34 □	BASSLINE	Mantronix	*10*	2
-	35	VIENNA CALLING	Falco	*A&M*	1
21	36	A DIFFERENT CORNER	George Michael	*Epic*	9
25	37	BOYS DON'T CRY	Cure	*Fiction*	5
-	38	DISENCHANTED	Communards	*London*	1
24	39	I'LL KEEP ON LOVING YOU	Princess	*Supreme*	7
22	40	YOU AND ME TONIGHT	Aurra	*10*	7

WEEK ENDING 7 JUNE 1986

LW	TW	Title	Artist	Label	Wks
3	1 □	SPIRIT IN THE SKY	Dr and the Medics	*IRS*	5
6	2 □	HOLDING BACK THE YEARS	Simply Red	*WEA*	3
1	3	THE CHICKEN SONG	Spitting Image	*Virgin*	5
4	4 □	SLEDGEHAMMER	Peter Gabriel	*Charisma*	6
13	5 □	EVERYBODY WANTS TO RUN THE WORLD	Tears For Fears	*Mercury*	2
2	6	ON MY OWN	Patti LaBelle and Michael McDonald	*MCA*	6
5	7	LESSONS IN LOVE	Level 42	*Polydor*	7
10	8	ADDICTED TO LOVE	Robert Palmer	*Island*	4
9	9	SET ME FREE	Jaki Graham	*EMI*	4
21	10	I CAN'T WAIT	Nu Shooz	*Atlantic*	3
22	11	CAN'T GET BY WITHOUT YOU	Real Thing	*PRT*	3
7	12	SNOOKER LOOPY	Matchroom Mob with Chas and Dave	*Rockney*	5
20	13 □	SINFUL	Pete Wylie	*MDM*	4
8	14	WHY CAN'T THIS BE LOVE	Van Halen	*Warner Bros*	7
18	15 □	MINE ALL MINE/PARTY FREAK	Cashflow	*Club*	3
25	16	INVISIBLE TOUCH	Genesis	*Virgin*	2
29	17	OPPORTUNITIES (LET'S MAKE LOTS OF MONEY)	Pet Shop Boys	*Parlophone*	2
12	18	THERE'LL BE SAD SONGS TO MAKE YOU CRY	Billy Ocean	*Jive*	7
35	19	VIENNA CALLING	Falco	*A&M*	2
11	20	ROLLIN' HOME	Status Quo	*Vertigo*	4
26	21	BAD BOY	Miami Sound Machine	*Epic*	3
-	22	21ST CENTURY BOY	Sigue Sigue Sputnik	*EMI*	1
17	23	LIVE TO TELL	Madonna	*Sire*	7
16	24	WHO MADE WHO	AC/DC	*Atlantic*	3
14	25	ROCK LOBSTER/PLANET CLAIRE	B-52's	*Island*	5
28	26 □	BIG MOUTH STRIKES AGAIN	Smiths	*Rough Trade*	2
15	27	ROCK ME AMADEUS	Falco	*A&M*	11
19	28	CAN'T WAIT ANOTHER MINUTE	Five Star	*Tent*	9
38	29 □	DISENCHANTED	Communards	*London*	2
-	30	NASTY	Janet Jackson	*A&M*	1
27	31	LOVE TOUCH	Rod Stewart	*Warner Bros*	3
33	32 □	TIME	Freddie Mercury	*EMI*	3
-	33	TOO GOOD TO BE FORGOTTEN	Amazulu	*Island*	1
31	34	WHAT HAVE YOU DONE FOR ME LATELY	Janet Jackson	*A&M*	9
23	35	ALL AND ALL	Joyce Sims	*London*	7
-	36	VENUS	Bananarama	*London*	1
-	37	AMITYVILLE (THE HOUSE ON THE HILL)	Lovebug Starski ●	*Epic*	1
-	38	GOD THANK YOU WOMAN	Culture Club	*Virgin*	1
34	39	BASSLINE	Mantronix	*10*	3
-	40	MEDICINE SHOW	Big Audio Dynamite	*CBS*	1

WEEK ENDING 14 JUNE 1986

LW	TW	Title	Artist	Label	Wks
1	1 □	SPIRIT IN THE SKY	Dr and the Medics	*IRS*	6
2	2 □	HOLDING BACK THE YEARS	Simply Red	*WEA*	4
10	3	I CAN'T WAIT	Nu Shooz	*Atlantic*	4
4	4 □	SLEDGEHAMMER	Peter Gabriel	*Charisma*	7
8	5 □	ADDICTED TO LOVE	Robert Palmer	*Island*	5
11	6 □	CAN'T GET BY WITHOUT YOU	Real Thing	*PRT*	4
9	7 □	SET ME FREE	Jaki Graham	*EMI*	5
5	8	EVERYBODY WANTS TO RUN THE WORLD	Tears For Fears	*Mercury*	3
6	9	ON MY OWN	Patti LaBelle and Michael McDonald	*MCA*	7
19	10 □	VIENNA CALLING	Falco	*A&M*	3
17	11 □	OPPORTUNITIES (LET'S MAKE LOTS OF MONEY)	Pet Shop Boys	*Parlophone*	3
3	12	THE CHICKEN SONG	Spitting Image	*Virgin*	6
7	13	LESSONS IN LOVE	Level 42	*Polydor*	8
13	14	SINFUL	Pete Wylie	*MDM*	5
16	15 □	INVISIBLE TOUCH	Genesis	*Virgin*	3
-	16	HUNTING HIGH AND LOW	A-Ha	*Warner Bros*	1
15	17	MINE ALL MINE/PARTY FREAK	Cashflow	*Club*	4
21	18	BAD BOY	Miami Sound Machine	*Epic*	4
37	19	AMITYVILLE (THE HOUSE ON THE HILL)	Lovebug Starski	*Epic*	2
22	20 □	21ST CENTURY BOY	Sigue Sigue Sputnik	*EMI*	2
33	21	TOO GOOD TO BE FORGOTTEN	Amazulu	*Island*	2
30	22	NASTY	Janet Jackson	*A&M*	2
14	23	WHY CAN'T THIS BE LOVE	Van Halen	*Warner Bros*	8
-	24	NEW BEGINNING (MAMBA SEYRA)	Bucks Fizz	*Polydor*	1
-	25	MY FAVOURITE WASTE OF TIME	Owen Paul ●	*Epic*	1
36	26	VENUS	Bananarama	*London*	2
18	27	THERE'LL BE SAD SONGS TO MAKE YOU CRY	Billy Ocean	*Jive*	8
12	28	SNOOKER LOOPY	Matchroom Mob with Chas and Dave	*Rockney*	6
40	29 □	MEDICINE SHOW	Big Audio Dynamite	*CBS*	2
-	30	HAPPY HOUR	Housemartins ●	*Go! Discs*	1
38	31 □	GOD THANK YOU WOMAN	Culture Club	*Virgin*	2
29	32	DISENCHANTED	Communards	*London*	3
20	33	ROLLIN' HOME	Status Quo	*Vertigo*	5
26	34	BIG MOUTH STRIKES AGAIN	Smiths	*Rough Trade*	3
-	35	JUMP BACK (SET ME FREE)	Dhar Braxton ●	*Fourth & Broadway*	1
-	36	CALL OF THE WILD	Midge Ure	*Chrysalis*	1
24	37	WHO MADE WHO	AC/DC	*Atlantic*	4
-	38	WHEN TOMORROW COMES	Eurythmics	*RCA*	1
32	39	TIME	Freddie Mercury	*EMI*	4
23	40	LIVE TO TELL	Madonna	*Sire*	8

WEEK ENDING 21 JUNE 1986

LW	TW	Title	Artist	Label	Wks
1	1 □	SPIRIT IN THE SKY	Dr and the Medics	*IRS*	7
-	2	THE EDGE OF HEAVEN	Wham!	*Epic*	1
3	3	I CAN'T WAIT	Nu Shooz	*Atlantic*	5
2	4	HOLDING BACK THE YEARS	Simply Red	*WEA*	5
16	5 □	HUNTING HIGH AND LOW	A-Ha	*Warner Bros*	2
5	6	ADDICTED TO LOVE	Robert Palmer	*Island*	6
6	7	CAN'T GET BY WITHOUT YOU	Real Thing	*PRT*	5
4	8	SLEDGEHAMMER	Peter Gabriel	*Charisma*	8
21	9	TOO GOOD TO BE FORGOTTEN	Amazulu	*Island*	3
10	10 □	VIENNA CALLING	Falco	*A&M*	4
24	11	NEW BEGINNING (MAMBA SEYRA)	Bucks Fizz	*Polydor*	2

■Genesis themselves enter at 25 with the title track of their new album, the first of five singles to be taken from it (31.05.86) ■ For the second time this year a cover of a former number one has turned the trick again (07.06.86)■

June 1986

□ Highest position disc reached ● Act's first ever week on chart

LW	TW	Title	Artist	Label	Wks
30	12	HAPPY HOUR	Housemartins	Go! Discs	2
19	13	AMITYVILLE (THE HOUSE ON THE HILL)	Lovebug Starski	Epic	3
25	14	MY FAVOURITE WASTE OF TIME	Owen Paul	Epic	2
11	15	OPPORTUNITIES (LET'S MAKE LOTS OF MONEY)	Pet Shop Boys	Parlophone	4
7	16	SET ME FREE	Jaki Graham	EMI	6
15	17	INVISIBLE TOUCH	Genesis	Virgin	4
18	18	BAD BOY	Miami Sound Machine	Epic	5
22	19	NASTY	Janet Jackson	A&M	3
9	20	ON MY OWN	Patti LaBelle and Michael McDonald	MCA	8
-	21	FRIENDS WILL BE FRIENDS	Queen	EMI	1
26	22	VENUS	Bananarama	London	3
13	23	LESSONS IN LOVE	Level 42	Polydor	9
14	24	SINFUL	Pete Wylie	MDM	6
12	25	THE CHICKEN SONG	Spitting Image	Virgin	7
-	26	UNDERGROUND	David Bowie	EMI America	1
8	27	EVERYBODY WANTS TO RUN THE WORLD	Tears For Fears	Mercury	4
17	28	MINE ALL MINE/PARTY FREAK	Cashflow	Club	5
36	29	CALL OF THE WILD	Midge Ure	Chrysalis	2
38	30	WHEN TOMORROW COMES	Eurythmics	RCA	2
20	31	21ST CENTURY BOY	Sigue Sigue Sputnik	EMI	3
35	32	JUMP BACK (SET ME FREE)	Dhar Braxton	Fourth & Broadway	2
28	33	SNOOKER LOOPY	Matchroom Mob with Chas and Dave	Rockney	7
-	34	THE TEACHER	Big Country	Mercury	1
31	35	GOD THANK YOU WOMAN	Culture Club	Virgin	3
29	36	MEDICINE SHOW	Big Audio Dynamite	CBS	3
23	37	WHY CAN'T THIS BE LOVE	Van Halen	Warner Bros	9
-	38	IT'S 'ORRIBLE BEING IN LOVE (WHEN YOU'RE 8½)	Claire and Friends ●	BBC	1
-	39	LET'S GO ALL THE WAY	Sly Fox ●	Capitol	1
27	40	THERE'LL BE SAD SONGS TO MAKE YOU CRY	Billy Ocean	Jive	9

WEEK ENDING 28 JUNE 1986

LW	TW	Title	Artist	Label	Wks
2	1	THE EDGE OF HEAVEN	Wham!	Epic	2
3	2	I CAN'T WAIT	Nu Shooz	Atlantic	6
12	3	HAPPY HOUR	Housemartins	Go! Discs	3
1	4	SPIRIT IN THE SKY	Dr and the Medics	IRS	8
9	5	TOO GOOD TO BE FORGOTTEN	Amazulu	Island	4
5	6	HUNTING HIGH AND LOW	A-Ha	Warner Bros	3
14	7	MY FAVOURITE WASTE OF TIME	Owen Paul	Epic	3
11	8	NEW BEGINNING (MAMBA SEYRA)	Bucks Fizz	Polydor	3
4	9	HOLDING BACK THE YEARS	Simply Red	WEA	6
6	10	ADDICTED TO LOVE	Robert Palmer	Island	7
7	11	CAN'T GET BY WITHOUT YOU	Real Thing	PRT	6
13	12	AMITYVILLE (THE HOUSE ON THE HILL)	Lovebug Starski	Epic	4
-	13	PAPA DON'T PREACH	Madonna	Sire	1
21	14	FRIENDS WILL BE FRIENDS	Queen	EMI	2
22	15	VENUS	Bananarama	London	4
18	16	BAD BOY	Miami Sound Machine	Epic	6
10	17	VIENNA CALLING	Falco	A&M	5
8	18	SLEDGEHAMMER	Peter Gabriel	Charisma	9
19	19	NASTY	Janet Jackson	A&M	4
15	20	OPPORTUNITIES (LET'S MAKE LOTS OF MONEY)	Pet Shop Boys	Parlophone	5
26	21	UNDERGROUND	David Bowie	EMI America	2
16	22	SET ME FREE	Jaki Graham	EMI	7
17	23	INVISIBLE TOUCH	Genesis	Virgin	5
-	24	DO YA DO YA (WANNA PLEASE ME)	Samantha Fox	Jive	1
20	25	ON MY OWN	Patti LaBelle and Michael McDonald	MCA	9
38	26	IT'S 'ORRIBLE BEING IN LOVE (WHEN YOU'RE 8½)	Claire and Friends	BBC	2
29	27	CALL OF THE WILD	Midge Ure	Chrysalis	3
34	28	THE TEACHER	Big Country	Mercury	2
-	29	HEADLINES	Midnight Star ●	Solar	1
39	30	LET'S GO ALL THE WAY	Sly Fox	Capitol	2
-	31	(BANG ZOOM) LET'S GO	Real Roxanne with Hitman Howie Tee ●	Cooltempo	1
-	32	I CAN'T STOP	Gary Numan	Numa	1
23	33	LESSONS IN LOVE	Level 42	Polydor	10
32	34	JUMP BACK (SET ME FREE)	Dhar Braxton	Fourth & Broadway	3
30	35	WHEN TOMORROW COMES	Eurythmics	RCA	3
25	36	THE CHICKEN SONG	Spitting Image	Virgin	8
-	37	BRILLIANT MIND	Furniture ●	Stiff	1
-	38	PARANOIMIA	Art Of Noise with Max Headroom	China	1
28	39	MINE ALL MINE/PARTY FREAK	Cashflow	Club	6
24	40	SINFUL	Pete Wylie	MDM	7

WEEK ENDING 5 JULY 1986

LW	TW	Title	Artist	Label	Wks
1	1	THE EDGE OF HEAVEN	Wham!	Epic	3
13	2	PAPA DON'T PREACH	Madonna	Sire	2
3	3	HAPPY HOUR	Housemartins	Go! Discs	4
7	4	MY FAVOURITE WASTE OF TIME	Owen Paul	Epic	4
2	5	I CAN'T WAIT	Nu Shooz	Atlantic	7
5	6	TOO GOOD TO BE FORGOTTEN	Amazulu	Island	5
6	7	HUNTING HIGH AND LOW	A-Ha	Warner Bros	4
8	8	NEW BEGINNING (MAMBA SEYRA)	Bucks Fizz	Polydor	4
15	9	VENUS	Bananarama	London	5
4	10	SPIRIT IN THE SKY	Dr and the Medics	IRS	9
11	11	CAN'T GET BY WITHOUT YOU	Real Thing	PRT	7
24	12	DO YA DO YA (WANNA PLEASE ME)	Samantha Fox	Jive	2
12	13	AMITYVILLE (THE HOUSE ON THE HILL)	Lovebug Starski	Epic	5
14	14	FRIENDS WILL BE FRIENDS	Queen	EMI	3
9	15	HOLDING BACK THE YEARS	Simply Red	WEA	7
10	16	ADDICTED TO LOVE	Robert Palmer	Island	8
29	17	HEADLINES	Midnight Star	Solar	2
31	18	(BANG ZOOM) LET'S GO	Real Roxanne with Hitman Howie Tee	Cooltempo	2
26	19	IT'S 'ORRIBLE BEING IN LOVE (WHEN YOU'RE 8½)	Claire and Friends	BBC	3
16	20	BAD BOY	Miami Sound Machine	Epic	7
19	21	NASTY	Janet Jackson	A&M	5
18	22	SLEDGEHAMMER	Peter Gabriel	Charisma	10
30	23	LET'S GO ALL THE WAY	Sly Fox	Capitol	3
17	24	VIENNA CALLING	Falco	A&M	6
21	25	UNDERGROUND	David Bowie	EMI America	3
38	26	PARANOIMIA	Art Of Noise with Max Headroom	China	2
32	27	I CAN'T STOP	Gary Numan	Numa	2
27	28	CALL OF THE WILD	Midge Ure	Chrysalis	4
37	29	BRILLIANT MIND	Furniture	Stiff	2
20	30	OPPORTUNITIES (LET'S MAKE LOTS OF MONEY)	Pet Shop Boys	Parlophone	6
23	31	INVISIBLE TOUCH	Genesis	Virgin	6
25	32	ON MY OWN	Patti LaBelle and Michael McDonald	MCA	10
22	33	SET ME FREE	Jaki Graham	EMI	8
28	34	THE TEACHER	Big Country	Mercury	3
-	35	LEFT OF CENTRE	Suzanne Vega	A&M	1
34	36	JUMP BACK (SET ME FREE)	Dhar Braxton	Fourth & Broadway	4
-	37	LEVI STUBBS TEARS (EP)	Billy Bragg	Go! Discs	1
-	38	HIGHER LOVE	Steve Winwood ●	Island	1
-	39	THE PROMISE YOU MADE	Cock Robin ●	CBS	1
-	40	ROSES	Haywoode ●	CBS	1

WEEK ENDING 12 JULY 1986

LW	TW	Title	Artist	Label	Wks
2	1	PAPA DON'T PREACH	Madonna	Sire	3
1	2	THE EDGE OF HEAVEN	Wham!	Epic	4
4	3	MY FAVOURITE WASTE OF TIME	Owen Paul	Epic	5
3	4	HAPPY HOUR	Housemartins	Go! Discs	5
6	5	TOO GOOD TO BE FORGOTTEN	Amazulu	Island	6
23	6	LET'S GO ALL THE WAY	Sly Fox	Capitol	4
5	7	I CAN'T WAIT	Nu Shooz	Atlantic	8

In these weeks ■ Wham! grab their fifth and final number one (28.06.86) ■ Bucks Fizz enjoy their biggest success for four years (28.06.86) ■ The last time Steve Winwood graced the Top 40 was with the Spencer Davis group in January 1968 (05.07.86) ■

□ Highest position disc reached ● Act's first ever week on chart

LW	TW	Title / Artist	Label	Wks
9	[8]	VENUS Bananarama	London	6
8	9	NEW BEGINNING (MAMBA SEYRA) Bucks Fizz	Polydor	5
12	[10]	DO YA DO YA (WANNA PLEASE ME) Samantha Fox	Jive	3
7	11	HUNTING HIGH AND LOW A-Ha	Warner Bros	5
18	12	(BANG ZOOM) LET'S GO Real Roxanne with Hitman Howie Tee	Cooltempo	3
19	[13]	IT'S 'ORRIBLE BEING IN LOVE (WHEN YOU'RE 8½) Claire and Friends	BBC	4
26	14	PARANOIMIA Art Of Noise with Max Headroom	China	3
10	15	SPIRIT IN THE SKY Dr and the Medics	IRS	10
17	[16]	HEADLINES Midnight Star	Solar	3
-	17	EVERY BEAT OF MY HEART Rod Stewart	Warner Bros	1
11	18	CAN'T GET BY WITHOUT YOU Real Thing	PRT	8
15	19	HOLDING BACK THE YEARS Simply Red	WEA	8
14	20	FRIENDS WILL BE FRIENDS Queen	EMI	4
16	21	ADDICTED TO LOVE Robert Palmer	Island	9
-	22	SING OUR OWN SONG UB40	DEP International	1
13	23	AMITYVILLE (THE HOUSE ON THE HILL) Lovebug Starski	Epic	6
38	24	HIGHER LOVE Steve Winwood	Island	2
40	25	ROSES Haywoode	CBS	2
29	26	BRILLIANT MIND Furniture	Stiff	3
28	[27]	CALL OF THE WILD Midge Ure	Chrysalis	5
27	28	I CAN'T STOP Gary Numan	Numa	3
37	[29]	LEVI STUBBS TEARS (EP) Billy Bragg	Go! Discs	2
20	30	BAD BOY Miami Sound Machine	Epic	8
25	31	UNDERGROUND David Bowie	EMI America	4
35	[32]	LEFT OF CENTRE Suzanne Vega	A&M	2
22	33	SLEDGEHAMMER Peter Gabriel	Charisma	11
39	34	THE PROMISE YOU MADE Cock Robin	CBS	2
21	35	NASTY Janet Jackson	A&M	6
-	36	TELL ME TOMORROW Princess	Supreme	1
-	37	SMILE Audrey Hall	Germain	1
-	38	CAMOUFLAGE Stan Ridgeway ●	IRS	1
32	39	ON MY OWN Patti LaBelle and Michael McDonald	MCA	11
-	40	THE LADY IN RED Chris De Burgh ●	A&M	1

WEEK ENDING 19 JULY 1986

LW	TW	Title / Artist	Label	Wks
1	[1]	PAPA DON'T PREACH Madonna	Sire	4
17	[2]	EVERY BEAT OF MY HEART Rod Stewart	Warner Bros	2
6	[3]	LET'S GO ALL THE WAY Sly Fox	Capitol	5
3	4	MY FAVOURITE WASTE OF TIME Owen Paul	Epic	6
2	5	THE EDGE OF HEAVEN Wham!	Epic	5
22	6	SING OUR OWN SONG UB40	DEP International	2
4	7	HAPPY HOUR Housemartins	Go! Discs	6
8	[8]	VENUS Bananarama	London	7
5	9	TOO GOOD TO BE FORGOTTEN Amazulu	Island	7
40	10	THE LADY IN RED Chris De Burgh	A&M	2
12	[11]	(BANG ZOOM) LET'S GO Real Roxanne with Hitman Howie Tee	Cooltempo	4
14	[12]	PARANOIMIA Art Of Noise with Max Headroom	China	4
7	13	I CAN'T WAIT Nu Shooz	Atlantic	9
24	14	HIGHER LOVE Steve Winwood	Island	3
13	15	IT'S 'ORRIBLE BEING IN LOVE (WHEN YOU'RE 8½) Claire and Friends	BBC	5
10	16	DO YA DO YA (WANNA PLEASE ME) Samantha Fox	Jive	4
38	17	CAMOUFLAGE Stan Ridgeway	IRS	2
9	18	NEW BEGINNING (MAMBA SEYRA) Bucks Fizz	Polydor	6
25	19	ROSES Haywoode	CBS	3
16	20	HEADLINES Midnight Star	Solar	4
26	[21]	BRILLIANT MIND Furniture	Stiff	4
11	22	HUNTING HIGH AND LOW A-Ha	Warner Bros	6
37	23	SMILE Audrey Hall	Germain	2
-	24	WHAT'S THE COLOUR OF MONEY Hollywood Beyond ●	WEA	1
18	25	CAN'T GET BY WITHOUT YOU Real Thing	PRT	9
15	26	SPIRIT IN THE SKY Dr and the Medics	IRS	11
20	27	FRIENDS WILL BE FRIENDS Queen	EMI	5
19	28	HOLDING BACK THE YEARS Simply Red	WEA	9
21	29	ADDICTED TO LOVE Robert Palmer	Island	10
-	30	I DIDN'T MEAN TO TURN YOU ON Robert Palmer	Island	1
34	31	THE PROMISE YOU MADE Cock Robin	CBS	3
29	32	LEVI STUBBS TEARS (EP) Billy Bragg	Go! Discs	3
-	33	SO MACHO/CRUISING Sinitta ●	Fanfare	1
36	[34]	TELL ME TOMORROW Princess	Supreme	2
32	35	LEFT OF CENTRE Suzanne Vega	A&M	3
23	36	AMITYVILLE (THE HOUSE ON THE HILL) Lovebug Starski	Epic	7
27	37	CALL OF THE WILD Midge Ure	Chrysalis	6
33	38	SLEDGEHAMMER Peter Gabriel	Charisma	12
-	39	AIN'T NOTHIN' GOIN' ON BUT THE RENT Gwen Guthrie ●	Boiling Point	1
-	40	SUN STREET Katrina and the Waves	Capitol	1

WEEK ENDING 26 JULY 1986

LW	TW	Title / Artist	Label	Wks
1	[1]	PAPA DON'T PREACH Madonna	Sire	5
10	2	THE LADY IN RED Chris De Burgh	A&M	3
2	3	EVERY BEAT OF MY HEART Rod Stewart	Warner Bros	3
3	4	LET'S GO ALL THE WAY Sly Fox	Capitol	6
6	[5]	SING OUR OWN SONG UB40	DEP International	3
4	6	MY FAVOURITE WASTE OF TIME Owen Paul	Epic	7
17	7	CAMOUFLAGE Stan Ridgeway	IRS	3
24	8	WHAT'S THE COLOUR OF MONEY Hollywood Beyond	WEA	2
8	9	VENUS Bananarama	London	8
7	10	HAPPY HOUR Housemartins	Go! Discs	7
30	11	I DIDN'T MEAN TO TURN YOU ON Robert Palmer	Island	2
5	12	THE EDGE OF HEAVEN Wham!	Epic	6
14	[13]	HIGHER LOVE Steve Winwood	Island	4
19	14	ROSES Haywoode	CBS	4
11	15	(BANG ZOOM) LET'S GO Real Roxanne with Hitman Howie Tee	Cooltempo	5
33	16	SO MACHO/CRUISING Sinitta	Fanfare	2
12	17	PARANOIMIA Art Of Noise with Max Headroom	China	5
9	18	TOO GOOD TO BE FORGOTTEN Amazulu	Island	8
23	19	SMILE Audrey Hall	Germain	3
-	20	SOME CANDY TALKING Jesus and Mary Chain ●	blanco y negro	1
39	21	AIN'T NOTHIN' GOIN' ON BUT THE RENT Gwen Guthrie	Boiling Point	2
13	22	I CAN'T WAIT Nu Shooz	Atlantic	10
21	23	BRILLIANT MIND Furniture	Stiff	5
15	24	IT'S 'ORRIBLE BEING IN LOVE (WHEN YOU'RE 8½) Claire and Friends	BBC	6
-	25	FIND THE TIME Five Star	Tent	1
16	26	DO YA DO YA (WANNA PLEASE ME) Samantha Fox	Jive	5
20	27	HEADLINES Midnight Star	Solar	5
31	[28]	THE PROMISE YOU MADE Cock Robin	CBS	4
18	29	NEW BEGINNING (MAMBA SEYRA) Bucks Fizz	Polydor	7
-	30	FIGHT FOR OURSELVES Spandau Ballet	Reformation	1
22	31	HUNTING HIGH AND LOW A-Ha	Warner Bros	7
-	32	PRESS Paul McCartney	MPL	1
40	33	SUN STREET Katrina and the Waves	Capitol	2
26	34	SPIRIT IN THE SKY Dr and the Medics	IRS	12
28	35	HOLDING BACK THE YEARS Simply Red	WEA	10
25	36	CAN'T GET BY WITHOUT YOU Real Thing	PRT	10
-	37	DANCING ON THE CEILING Lionel Richie	Motown	1
-	38	RED SKY Status Quo	Vertigo	1
27	39	FRIENDS WILL BE FRIENDS Queen	EMI	6
29	40	ADDICTED TO LOVE Robert Palmer	Island	11

WEEK ENDING 2 AUGUST 1986

LW	TW	Title / Artist	Label	Wks
2	[1]	THE LADY IN RED Chris De Burgh	A&M	4
1	2	PAPA DON'T PREACH Madonna	Sire	6
4	[3]	LET'S GO ALL THE WAY Sly Fox	Capitol	7
3	4	EVERY BEAT OF MY HEART Rod Stewart	Warner Bros	4
16	5	SO MACHO/CRUISING Sinitta	Fanfare	3
7	6	CAMOUFLAGE Stan Ridgeway	IRS	4
8	[7]	WHAT'S THE COLOUR OF MONEY Hollywood Beyond	WEA	3
5	8	SING OUR OWN SONG UB40	DEP International	4
11	[9]	I DIDN'T MEAN TO TURN YOU ON Robert Palmer	Island	3

■The chart is home to both the Housemartins and Cock Robin, Sly and Samantha Fox (12.07.86) ■ Sinitta finally makes it into the Top 40 after 15 weeks of trying (19.07.86) ■ Paul McCartney notches up his 31st post-Beatles Top 40 hit, Status Quo go one better with 32 (26.07.86)■

August 1986

□ Highest position disc reached ● Act's first ever week on chart

LW	TW	Title / Artist	Label	Wks
25	10	FIND THE TIME Five Star	Tent	2
14	11	ROSES Haywoode	CBS	5
6	12	MY FAVOURITE WASTE OF TIME Owen Paul	Epic	8
20	13	SOME CANDY TALKING Jesus and Mary Chain	blanco y negro	2
19	14	SMILE Audrey Hall	Germain	4
30	15	FIGHT FOR OURSELVES Spandau Ballet	Reformation	2
9	16	VENUS Bananarama	London	9
21	17	AIN'T NOTHIN' GOIN' ON BUT THE RENT Gwen Guthrie	Boiling Point	3
-	18	PANIC Smiths	Rough Trade	1
13	19	HIGHER LOVE Steve Winwood	Island	5
10	20	HAPPY HOUR Housemartins	Go! Discs	8
38	21	RED SKY Status Quo	Vertigo	2
15	22	(BANG ZOOM) LET'S GO Real Roxanne with Hitman Howie Tee	Cooltempo	6
33	23	SUN STREET Katrina and the Waves	Capitol	3
37	24	DANCING ON THE CEILING Lionel Richie	Motown	2
18	25	TOO GOOD TO BE FORGOTTEN Amazulu	Island	9
-	26	SHOUT Lulu	Decca/London	1
-	27	I WANT TO WAKE UP WITH YOU Boris Gardiner	Revue	1
12	28	THE EDGE OF HEAVEN Wham!	Epic	7
17	29	PARANOIMIA Art Of Noise with Max Headroom	China	6
28	30	THE PROMISE YOU MADE Cock Robin	CBS	5
32	31	PRESS Paul McCartney	MPL	2
24	32	IT'S 'ORRIBLE BEING IN LOVE (WHEN YOU'RE 8½) Claire and Friends	BBC	7
23	33	BRILLIANT MIND Furniture	Stiff	6
22	34	I CAN'T WAIT Nu Shooz	Atlantic	11
27	35	HEADLINES Midnight Star	Solar	6
-	36	CALLING ALL THE HEROES It Bites ●	Virgin	1
29	37	NEW BEGINNING (MAMBA SEYRA) Bucks Fizz	Polydor	8
31	38	HUNTING HIGH AND LOW A-Ha	Warner Bros	8
40	39	ADDICTED TO LOVE Robert Palmer	Island	12
34	40	SPIRIT IN THE SKY Dr and the Medics	IRS	13

WEEK ENDING 9 AUGUST 1986

LW	TW	Title / Artist	Label	Wks
1	1	THE LADY IN RED Chris De Burgh	A&M	5
5	2	SO MACHO/CRUISING Sinitta	Fanfare	4
2	3	PAPA DON'T PREACH Madonna	Sire	7
6	4	CAMOUFLAGE Stan Ridgeway	IRS	5
27	5	I WANT TO WAKE UP WITH YOU Boris Gardiner	Revue	2
3	6	LET'S GO ALL THE WAY Sly Fox	Capitol	8
10	7	FIND THE TIME Five Star	Tent	3
7	8	WHAT'S THE COLOUR OF MONEY Hollywood Beyond	WEA	4
4	9	EVERY BEAT OF MY HEART Rod Stewart	Warner Bros	5
9	10	I DIDN'T MEAN TO TURN YOU ON Robert Palmer	Island	4
18	11	PANIC Smiths	Rough Trade	2
17	12	AIN'T NOTHIN' GOIN' ON BUT THE RENT Gwen Guthrie	Boiling Point	4
8	13	SING OUR OWN SONG UB40	DEP International	5
11	14	ROSES Haywoode	CBS	6
15	15	FIGHT FOR OURSELVES Spandau Ballet	Reformation	3
26	16	SHOUT Lulu	Decca/London	2
36	17	CALLING ALL THE HEROES It Bites	Virgin	2
14	18	SMILE Audrey Hall	Germain	5
21	19	RED SKY Status Quo	Vertigo	3
13	20	SOME CANDY TALKING Jesus and Mary Chain	blanco y negro	3
12	21	MY FAVOURITE WASTE OF TIME Owen Paul	Epic	9
23	22	SUN STREET Katrina and the Waves	Capitol	4
24	23	DANCING ON THE CEILING Lionel Richie	Motown	3
19	24	HIGHER LOVE Steve Winwood	Island	6
16	25	VENUS Bananarama	London	10
31	26	PRESS Paul McCartney	MPL	3
20	27	HAPPY HOUR Housemartins	Go! Discs	9
-	28	ANYONE CAN FALL IN LOVE Anita Dobson ●	BBC	1
25	29	TOO GOOD TO BE FORGOTTEN Amazulu	Island	10
22	30	(BANG ZOOM) LET'S GO Real Roxanne with Hitman Howie Tee	Cooltempo	7
-	31	I CAN PROVE IT Phil Fearon	Ensign	1
29	32	PARANOIMIA Art Of Noise with Max Headroom	China	7
28	33	THE EDGE OF HEAVEN Wham!	Epic	8
-	34	OH PEOPLE Patti LaBelle ●	MCA	1
-	35	THE WAY IT IS Bruce Hornsby and the Range ●	RCA	1
30	36	THE PROMISE YOU MADE Cock Robin	CBS	6
-	37	CAN YOU FEEL THE FORCE Real Thing	PRT	1
-	38	BREAKING AWAY Jaki Graham	EMI	1
-	39	BURN Doctor and the Medics	IRS	1
33	40	BRILLIANT MIND Furniture	Stiff	7

WEEK ENDING 16 AUGUST 1986

LW	TW	Title / Artist	Label	Wks
1	1	THE LADY IN RED Chris De Burgh	A&M	6
5	2	I WANT TO WAKE UP WITH YOU Boris Gardiner	Revue	3
2	3	SO MACHO/CRUISING Sinitta	Fanfare	5
28	4	ANYONE CAN FALL IN LOVE Anita Dobson	BBC	2
12	5	AIN'T NOTHIN' GOIN' ON BUT THE RENT Gwen Guthrie	Boiling Point	5
4	6	CAMOUFLAGE Stan Ridgeway	IRS	6
3	7	PAPA DON'T PREACH Madonna	Sire	8
16	8	SHOUT Lulu	Decca/London	3
7	9	FIND THE TIME Five Star	Tent	4
17	10	CALLING ALL THE HEROES It Bites	Virgin	3
11	11	PANIC Smiths	Rough Trade	3
6	12	LET'S GO ALL THE WAY Sly Fox	Capitol	9
8	13	WHAT'S THE COLOUR OF MONEY Hollywood Beyond	WEA	5
9	14	EVERY BEAT OF MY HEART Rod Stewart	Warner Bros	6
10	15	I DIDN'T MEAN TO TURN YOU ON Robert Palmer	Island	5
15	16	FIGHT FOR OURSELVES Spandau Ballet	Reformation	4
31	17	I CAN PROVE IT Phil Fearon	Ensign	2
23	18	DANCING ON THE CEILING Lionel Richie	Motown	4
19	19	RED SKY Status Quo	Vertigo	4
14	20	ROSES Haywoode	CBS	7
13	21	SING OUR OWN SONG UB40	DEP International	6
38	22	BREAKING AWAY Jaki Graham	EMI	2
18	23	SMILE Audrey Hall	Germain	6
37	24	CAN YOU FEEL THE FORCE Real Thing	PRT	2
26	25	PRESS Paul McCartney	MPL	4
34	26	OH PEOPLE Patti LaBelle	MCA	2
-	27	GIRLS AND BOYS Prince and the Revolution	Paisley Park	1
35	28	THE WAY IT IS Bruce Hornsby and the Range	RCA	2
39	29	BURN Doctor and the Medics	IRS	2
-	30	WHEN I THINK OF YOU Janet Jackson	A&M	1
22	31	SUN STREET Katrina and the Waves	Capitol	5
21	32	MY FAVOURITE WASTE OF TIME Owen Paul	Epic	10
-	33	WE DON'T HAVE TO... Jermaine Stewart ●	10	1
24	34	HIGHER LOVE Steve Winwood	Island	7
20	35	SOME CANDY TALKING Jesus and Mary Chain	blanco y negro	4
27	36	HAPPY HOUR Housemartins	Go! Discs	10
-	37	BROTHER LOUIE Modern Talking ●	RCA	1
-	38	GLORY OF LOVE Peter Cetera ●	Full Moon	1
-	39	DREAMTIME Daryl Hall ●	RCA	1
25	40	VENUS Bananarama	London	11

WEEK ENDING 23 AUGUST 1986

LW	TW	Title / Artist	Label	Wks
2	1	I WANT TO WAKE UP WITH YOU Boris Gardiner	Revue	4
1	2	THE LADY IN RED Chris De Burgh	A&M	7
3	3	SO MACHO/CRUISING Sinitta	Fanfare	6
4	4	ANYONE CAN FALL IN LOVE Anita Dobson	BBC	3
5	5	AIN'T NOTHIN' GOIN' ON BUT THE RENT Gwen Guthrie	Boiling Point	6
10	6	CALLING ALL THE HEROES It Bites	Virgin	4
18	7	DANCING ON THE CEILING Lionel Richie	Motown	5
17	8	I CAN PROVE IT Phil Fearon	Ensign	3
6	9	CAMOUFLAGE Stan Ridgeway	IRS	7
8	10	SHOUT Lulu	Decca/London	4
27	11	GIRLS AND BOYS Prince and the Revolution	Paisley Park	2
37	12	BROTHER LOUIE Modern Talking	RCA	2
7	13	PAPA DON'T PREACH Madonna	Sire	9
11	14	PANIC Smiths	Rough Trade	4
33	15	WE DON'T HAVE TO... Jermaine Stewart	10	2

In these weeks ■ Chris De Burgh has the first number one by an Irish act since the Boomtown Rats - Feargal Sharkey was from Derry and Johnny Logan from Australia (02.08.86) ■ Anita Dobson is the first of a flurry of Eastenders hits (09.08.86) ■ Lulu is back in the Top Ten for the first time since 02.03.74 with the re-recording of her first hit on London and the original on Decca (16.08.86)■

LW	TW	Title	Artist	Label	Wks
9	16	FIND THE TIME	Five Star	Tent	5
22	17	BREAKING AWAY	Jaki Graham	EMI	3
38	18	GLORY OF LOVE	Peter Cetera	Full Moon	2
-	19	HUMAN	Human League	Virgin	1
13	20	WHAT'S THE COLOUR OF MONEY	Hollywood Beyond	WEA	6
30	21	WHEN I THINK OF YOU	Janet Jackson	A&M	2
12	22	LET'S GO ALL THE WAY	Sly Fox	Capitol	10
28	23	THE WAY IT IS	Bruce Hornsby and the Range	RCA	3
15	24	I DIDN'T MEAN TO TURN YOU ON	Robert Palmer	Island	6
-	25	A QUESTION OF TIME	Depeche Mode	Mute	1
14	26	EVERY BEAT OF MY HEART	Rod Stewart	Warner Bros	7
19	27	RED SKY	Status Quo	Vertigo	5
-	28	DON'T LEAVE ME THIS WAY	Communards	London	1
26	29	OH PEOPLE	Patti LaBelle	MCA	3
16	30	FIGHT FOR OURSELVES	Spandau Ballet	Reformation	5
24	31	CAN YOU FEEL THE FORCE	Real Thing	PRT	3
29	32	BURN	Doctor and the Medics	IRS	3
39	33	DREAMTIME	Daryl Hall	RCA	2
25	34	PRESS	Paul McCartney	MPL	5
20	35	ROSES	Haywoode	CBS	8
-	36	LOVE CAN'T TURN AROUND	Farley 'Jackmaster' Funk ●	Chicago	1
21	37	SING OUR OWN SONG	UB40	DEP International	7
-	38	YOU GIVE LOVE A BAD NAME	Bon Jovi ●	Vertigo	1
23	39	SMILE	Audrey Hall	Germain	7
-	40	NICE IN NICE	Stranglers	Epic	1

WEEK ENDING 30 AUGUST 1986

LW	TW	Title	Artist	Label	Wks
1	1	I WANT TO WAKE UP WITH YOU	Boris Gardiner	Revue	5
3	2	SO MACHO/CRUISING	Sinitta	Fanfare	7
2	3	THE LADY IN RED	Chris De Burgh	A&M	8
12	4	BROTHER LOUIE	Modern Talking	RCA	3
28	5	DON'T LEAVE ME THIS WAY	Communards	London	2
15	6	WE DON'T HAVE TO...	Jermaine Stewart	10	3
4	7	ANYONE CAN FALL IN LOVE	Anita Dobson	BBC	4
5	8	AIN'T NOTHIN' GOIN' ON BUT THE RENT	Gwen Guthrie	Boiling Point	7
18	9	GLORY OF LOVE	Peter Cetera	Full Moon	3
19	10	HUMAN	Human League	Virgin	2
7	11	DANCING ON THE CEILING	Lionel Richie	Motown	6
11	12	GIRLS AND BOYS	Prince and the Revolution	Paisley Park	3
6	13	CALLING ALL THE HEROES	It Bites	Virgin	5
8	14	I CAN PROVE IT	Phil Fearon	Ensign	4
21	15	WHEN I THINK OF YOU	Janet Jackson	A&M	3
17	16	BREAKING AWAY	Jaki Graham	EMI	4
25	17	A QUESTION OF TIME	Depeche Mode	Mute	2
23	18	THE WAY IT IS	Bruce Hornsby and the Range	RCA	4
10	19	SHOUT	Lulu	Decca/London	5
36	20	LOVE CAN'T TURN AROUND	Farley 'Jackmaster' Funk	Chicago	2
9	21	CAMOUFLAGE	Stan Ridgeway	IRS	8
13	22	PAPA DON'T PREACH	Madonna	Sire	10
14	23	PANIC	Smiths	Rough Trade	5
16	24	FIND THE TIME	Five Star	Tent	6
38	25	YOU GIVE LOVE A BAD NAME	Bon Jovi	Vertigo	2
-	26	(I JUST) DIED IN YOUR ARMS	Cutting Crew ●	Siren	1
22	27	LET'S GO ALL THE WAY	Sly Fox	Capitol	11
33	28	DREAMTIME	Daryl Hall	RCA	3
20	29	WHAT'S THE COLOUR OF MONEY	Hollywood Beyond	WEA	7
32	30	BURN	Doctor and the Medics	IRS	4
29	31	OH PEOPLE	Patti LaBelle	MCA	4
40	32	NICE IN NICE	Stranglers	Epic	2
-	33	IN TOO DEEP	Genesis	Charisma	1
-	34	TYPICAL MALE	Tina Turner	Capitol	1
-	35	STUCK WITH YOU	Huey Lewis and the News	Chrysalis	1
31	36	CAN YOU FEEL THE FORCE	Real Thing	PRT	4
27	37	RED SKY	Status Quo	Vertigo	6
26	38	EVERY BEAT OF MY HEART	Rod Stewart	Warner Bros	8
-	39	HEARTLAND	The The ●	Some Bizzare	1
24	40	I DIDN'T MEAN TO TURN YOU ON	Robert Palmer	Island	7

September 1986

□ Highest position disc reached ● Act's first ever week on chart

WEEK ENDING 6 SEPTEMBER 1986

LW	TW	Title	Artist	Label	Wks
1	1	I WANT TO WAKE UP WITH YOU	Boris Gardiner	Revue	6
5	2	DON'T LEAVE ME THIS WAY	Communards	London	3
6	3	WE DON'T HAVE TO...	Jermaine Stewart	10	4
4	4	BROTHER LOUIE	Modern Talking	RCA	4
9	5	GLORY OF LOVE	Peter Cetera	Full Moon	4
-	6	RAGE HARD	Frankie Goes To Hollywood	ZTT	1
2	7	SO MACHO/CRUISING	Sinitta	Fanfare	8
10	8	HUMAN	Human League	Virgin	3
3	9	THE LADY IN RED	Chris De Burgh	A&M	9
15	10	WHEN I THINK OF YOU	Janet Jackson	A&M	4
8	11	AIN'T NOTHIN' GOIN' ON BUT THE RENT	Gwen Guthrie	Boiling Point	8
11	12	DANCING ON THE CEILING	Lionel Richie	Motown	7
12	13	GIRLS AND BOYS	Prince and the Revolution	Paisley Park	4
26	14	(I JUST) DIED IN YOUR ARMS	Cutting Crew	Siren	2
18	15	THE WAY IT IS	Bruce Hornsby and the Range	RCA	5
20	16	LOVE CAN'T TURN AROUND	Farley 'Jackmaster' Funk	Chicago	3
7	17	ANYONE CAN FALL IN LOVE	Anita Dobson	BBC	5
13	18	CALLING ALL THE HEROES	It Bites	Virgin	6
14	19	I CAN PROVE IT	Phil Fearon	Ensign	5
17	20	A QUESTION OF TIME	Depeche Mode	Mute	3
16	21	BREAKING AWAY	Jaki Graham	EMI	5
25	22	YOU GIVE LOVE A BAD NAME	Bon Jovi	Vertigo	3
-	23	HOLIDAY RAP	MC Miker G and DJ Sven ●	Debut	1
-	24	WASTED YEARS	Iron Maiden	EMI	1
33	25	IN TOO DEEP	Genesis	Charisma	2
35	26	STUCK WITH YOU	Huey Lewis and the News	Chrysalis	2
24	27	FIND THE TIME	Five Star	Tent	7
-	28	WORD UP	Cameo	Club	1
-	29	THORN IN MY SIDE	Eurythmics	RCA	1
32	30	NICE IN NICE	Stranglers	Epic	3
19	31	SHOUT	Lulu	Decca/London	6
28	32	DREAMTIME	Daryl Hall	RCA	4
34	33	TYPICAL MALE	Tina Turner	Capitol	2
39	34	HEARTLAND	The The	Some Bizzare	2
23	35	PANIC	Smiths	Rough Trade	6
21	36	CAMOUFLAGE	Stan Ridgeway	IRS	9
-	37	WALK THIS WAY	Run DMC ●	London	1
-	38	PRETTY IN PINK	Psychedelic Furs	CBS	1
-	39	HOLD ON TIGHT	Samantha Fox	Jive	1
22	40	PAPA DON'T PREACH	Madonna	Sire	11

WEEK ENDING 13 SEPTEMBER 1986

LW	TW	Title	Artist	Label	Wks
2	1	DON'T LEAVE ME THIS WAY	Communards	London	4
1	2	I WANT TO WAKE UP WITH YOU	Boris Gardiner	Revue	7
3	3	WE DON'T HAVE TO...	Jermaine Stewart	10	5
6	4	RAGE HARD	Frankie Goes To Hollywood	ZTT	2
5	5	GLORY OF LOVE	Peter Cetera	Full Moon	5
23	6	HOLIDAY RAP	MC Miker G and DJ Sven	Debut	2
4	7	BROTHER LOUIE	Modern Talking	RCA	5
14	8	(I JUST) DIED IN YOUR ARMS	Cutting Crew	Siren	3
7	9	SO MACHO/CRUISING	Sinitta	Fanfare	9
8	10	HUMAN	Human League	Virgin	4
16	11	LOVE CAN'T TURN AROUND	Farley 'Jackmaster' Funk	Chicago	4
10	12	WHEN I THINK OF YOU	Janet Jackson	A&M	5
28	13	WORD UP	Cameo	Club	2
22	14	YOU GIVE LOVE A BAD NAME	Bon Jovi	Vertigo	4
37	15	WALK THIS WAY	Run DMC	London	2
29	16	THORN IN MY SIDE	Eurythmics	RCA	2
15	17	THE WAY IT IS	Bruce Hornsby and the Range	RCA	6
24	18	WASTED YEARS	Iron Maiden	EMI	2
9	19	THE LADY IN RED	Chris De Burgh	A&M	10

■ *Love Can't Turn Around* is the first House record to chart (23.08.86) ■ High Energy takes a hold of the Top Ten with the Communards, Modern Talking and Sinitta (13.09.86) ■

September 1986

□ Highest position disc reached ● Act's first ever week on chart

LW	TW	Title	Artist	Label	Wks
11	20	AIN'T NOTHIN' GOIN' ON BUT THE RENT	Gwen Guthrie	Boiling Point	9
12	21	DANCING ON THE CEILING	Lionel Richie	Motown	8
13	22	GIRLS AND BOYS	Prince and the Revolution	Paisley Park	5
25	23	IN TOO DEEP	Genesis	Charisma	3
26	24	STUCK WITH YOU	Huey Lewis and the News	Chrysalis	3
38	25	PRETTY IN PINK	Psychedelic Furs	CBS	2
39	26	HOLD ON TIGHT	Samantha Fox	Jive	2
-	27	SWEET FREEDOM	Michael McDonald ●	MCA	1
18	28	CALLING ALL THE HEROES	It Bites	Virgin	7
21	29	BREAKING AWAY	Jaki Graham	EMI	6
17	30	ANYONE CAN FALL IN LOVE	Anita Dobson	BBC	6
-	31	RAIN OR SHINE	Five Star	Tent	1
19	32	I CAN PROVE IT	Phil Fearon	Ensign	6
20	33	A QUESTION OF TIME	Depeche Mode	Mute	4
-	34	RUMORS	Timex Social Club ●	Cooltempo	1
34	35	HEARTLAND	The The	Some Bizzare	3
33	36	TYPICAL MALE	Tina Turner	Capitol	3
30	37	NICE IN NICE	Stranglers	Epic	4
-	38	(FOREVER) LIVE AND DIE	Orchestral Manoeuvres In The Dark	Virgin	1
-	39	ROCK 'N' ROLL MERCENARIES	Meat Loaf with John Parr	Arista	1
32	40	DREAMTIME	Daryl Hall	RCA	5

WEEK ENDING 20 SEPTEMBER 1986

LW	TW	Title	Artist	Label	Wks
1	1	DON'T LEAVE ME THIS WAY	Communards	London	5
3	2	WE DON'T HAVE TO...	Jermaine Stewart	10	6
5	3	GLORY OF LOVE	Peter Cetera	Full Moon	6
8	4	(I JUST) DIED IN YOUR ARMS	Cutting Crew	Siren	4
2	5	I WANT TO WAKE UP WITH YOU	Boris Gardiner	Revue	8
13	6	WORD UP	Cameo	Club	3
4	7	RAGE HARD	Frankie Goes To Hollywood	ZTT	3
6	8	HOLIDAY RAP	MC Miker G and DJ Sven	Debut	3
15	9	WALK THIS WAY	Run DMC	London	3
16	10	THORN IN MY SIDE	Eurythmics	RCA	3
11	11	LOVE CAN'T TURN AROUND	Farley 'Jackmaster' Funk	Chicago	5
7	12	BROTHER LOUIE	Modern Talking	RCA	6
31	13	RAIN OR SHINE	Five Star	Tent	2
9	14	SO MACHO/CRUISING	Sinitta	Fanfare	10
14	15	YOU GIVE LOVE A BAD NAME	Bon Jovi	Vertigo	5
10	16	HUMAN	Human League	Virgin	5
27	17	SWEET FREEDOM	Michael McDonald	MCA	2
25	18	PRETTY IN PINK	Psychedelic Furs	CBS	3
12	19	WHEN I THINK OF YOU	Janet Jackson	A&M	6
34	20	RUMORS	Timex Social Club	Cooltempo	2
24	21	STUCK WITH YOU	Huey Lewis and the News	Chrysalis	4
23	22	IN TOO DEEP	Genesis	Charisma	4
17	23	THE WAY IT IS	Bruce Hornsby and the Range	RCA	7
38	24	(FOREVER) LIVE AND DIE	Orchestral Manoeuvres In The Dark	Virgin	2
19	25	THE LADY IN RED	Chris De Burgh	A&M	11
26	26	HOLD ON TIGHT	Samantha Fox	Jive	3
-	27	ONE GREAT THING	Big Country	Mercury	1
18	28	WASTED YEARS	Iron Maiden	EMI	3
35	29	HEARTLAND	The The	Some Bizzare	4
20	30	AIN'T NOTHIN' GOIN' ON BUT THE RENT	Gwen Guthrie	Boiling Point	10
39	31	ROCK 'N' ROLL MERCENARIES	Meat Loaf with John Parr	Arista	2
21	32	DANCING ON THE CEILING	Lionel Richie	Motown	9
-	33	MONTEGO BAY	Amazulu	Island	1
22	34	GIRLS AND BOYS	Prince and the Revolution	Paisley Park	6
-	35	SLOW DOWN	Loose Ends	Virgin	1
-	36	ALWAYS THERE	Marti Webb and the Simon May Orchestra	BBC	1
-	37	DREAMER	BB+Q	Cooltempo	1
-	38	BRAND NEW LOVER	Dead Or Alive	Epic	1
36	39	TYPICAL MALE	Tina Turner	Capitol	4
30	40	ANYONE CAN FALL IN LOVE	Anita Dobson	BBC	7

WEEK ENDING 27 SEPTEMBER 1986

LW	TW	Title	Artist	Label	Wks
1	1	DON'T LEAVE ME THIS WAY	Communards	London	6
2	2	WE DON'T HAVE TO...	Jermaine Stewart	10	7
6	3	WORD UP	Cameo	Club	4
13	4	RAIN OR SHINE	Five Star	Tent	3
4	5	(I JUST) DIED IN YOUR ARMS	Cutting Crew	Siren	5
3	6	GLORY OF LOVE	Peter Cetera	Full Moon	7
10	7	THORN IN MY SIDE	Eurythmics	RCA	4
9	8	WALK THIS WAY	Run DMC	London	4
5	9	I WANT TO WAKE UP WITH YOU	Boris Gardiner	Revue	9
11	10	LOVE CAN'T TURN AROUND	Farley 'Jackmaster' Funk	Chicago	6
8	11	HOLIDAY RAP	MC Miker G and DJ Sven	Debut	4
17	12	SWEET FREEDOM	Michael McDonald	MCA	3
20	13	RUMORS	Timex Social Club	Cooltempo	3
24	14	(FOREVER) LIVE AND DIE	Orchestral Manoeuvres In The Dark	Virgin	3
21	15	STUCK WITH YOU	Huey Lewis and the News	Chrysalis	5
7	16	RAGE HARD	Frankie Goes To Hollywood	ZTT	4
12	17	BROTHER LOUIE	Modern Talking	RCA	7
18	18	PRETTY IN PINK	Psychedelic Furs	CBS	4
27	19	ONE GREAT THING	Big Country	Mercury	2
15	20	YOU GIVE LOVE A BAD NAME	Bon Jovi	Vertigo	6
14	21	SO MACHO/CRUISING	Sinitta	Fanfare	11
22	22	IN TOO DEEP	Genesis	Charisma	5
33	23	MONTEGO BAY	Amazulu	Island	2
36	24	ALWAYS THERE	Marti Webb and the Simon May Orchestra	BBC	2
16	25	HUMAN	Human League	Virgin	6
-	26	YOU CAN CALL ME AL	Paul Simon	Warner Bros	1
19	27	WHEN I THINK OF YOU	Janet Jackson	A&M	7
-	28	WHO WANTS TO LIVE FOREVER	Queen	EMI	1
35	29	SLOW DOWN	Loose Ends	Virgin	2
-	30	STATE OF THE NATION	New Order	Factory	1
38	31	BRAND NEW LOVER	Dead Or Alive	Epic	2
29	32	HEARTLAND	The The	Some Bizzare	5
-	33	SAME OLD STORY	Ultravox	Chrysalis	1
-	34	TRUE COLORS	Cyndi Lauper	Portrait	1
37	35	DREAMER	BB+Q	Cooltempo	2
26	36	HOLD ON TIGHT	Samantha Fox	Jive	4
31	37	ROCK 'N' ROLL MERCENARIES	Meat Loaf with John Parr	Arista	3
25	38	THE LADY IN RED	Chris De Burgh	A&M	12
23	39	THE WAY IT IS	Bruce Hornsby and the Range	RCA	8
30	40	AIN'T NOTHIN' GOIN' ON BUT THE RENT	Gwen Guthrie	Boiling Point	11

WEEK ENDING 4 OCTOBER 1986

LW	TW	Title	Artist	Label	Wks
1	1	DON'T LEAVE ME THIS WAY	Communards	London	7
4	2	RAIN OR SHINE	Five Star	Tent	4
-	3	TRUE BLUE	Madonna	Sire	1
3	4	WORD UP	Cameo	Club	5
7	5	THORN IN MY SIDE	Eurythmics	RCA	5
2	6	WE DON'T HAVE TO...	Jermaine Stewart	10	8
5	7	(I JUST) DIED IN YOUR ARMS	Cutting Crew	Siren	6
8	8	WALK THIS WAY	Run DMC	London	5
26	9	YOU CAN CALL ME AL	Paul Simon	Warner Bros	2
6	10	GLORY OF LOVE	Peter Cetera	Full Moon	8
14	11	(FOREVER) LIVE AND DIE	Orchestral Manoeuvres In The Dark	Virgin	4
15	12	STUCK WITH YOU	Huey Lewis and the News	Chrysalis	6
10	13	LOVE CAN'T TURN AROUND	Farley 'Jackmaster' Funk	Chicago	7
-	14	I'VE BEEN LOSING YOU	A-Ha	Warner Bros	1
24	15	ALWAYS THERE	Marti Webb and the Simon May Orchestra	BBC	3

In these weeks ■ Frankie Goes To Hollywood complete the best start in chart history: 1-1-1-2-4 (13.09.86) ■ Timex Social Club and Cyndi Lauper chart with American spelt hits (27.09.86) ■ Madonna's highest debut yet, in at three with her 12th Top Five hit (04.10.86)■

LW	TW	Title	Artist	Label	Wks
13	16	RUMORS	Timex Social Club	*Cooltempo*	4
12	17	SWEET FREEDOM	Michael McDonald	*MCA*	4
23	18	MONTEGO BAY	Amazulu	*Island*	3
22	[19]	IN TOO DEEP	Genesis	*Charisma*	6
9	20	I WANT TO WAKE UP WITH YOU	Boris Gardiner	*Revue*	10
34	21	TRUE COLORS	Cyndi Lauper	*Portrait*	2
19	22	ONE GREAT THING	Big Country	*Mercury*	3
-	23	SUBURBIA	Pet Shop Boys	*Parlophone*	1
28	[24]	WHO WANTS TO LIVE FOREVER	Queen	*EMI*	2
18	25	PRETTY IN PINK	Psychedelic Furs	*CBS*	5
-	26	WALK LIKE AN EGYPTIAN	Bangles	*CBS*	1
29	[27]	SLOW DOWN	Loose Ends	*Virgin*	3
11	28	HOLIDAY RAP	MC Miker G and DJ Sven	*Debut*	5
-	29	IN THE ARMY NOW	Status Quo	*Vertigo*	1
-	30	WONDERLAND	Paul Young	*CBS*	1
33	[31]	SAME OLD STORY	Ultravox	*Chrysalis*	3
21	32	SO MACHO/CRUISING	Sinitta	*Fanfare*	12
31	33	BRAND NEW LOVER	Dead Or Alive	*Epic*	3
-	34	WORLD SHUT YOUR MOUTH	Julian Cope ●	*Island*	1
17	35	BROTHER LOUIE	Modern Talking	*RCA*	8
16	36	RAGE HARD	Frankie Goes To Hollywood	*ZTT*	5
-	37	MIDAS TOUCH	Midnight Star	*Solar*	1
-	38	ALL I WANT	Howard Jones	*WEA*	1
20	39	YOU GIVE LOVE A BAD NAME	Bon Jovi	*Vertigo*	7
30	40	STATE OF THE NATION	New Order	*Factory*	2

WEEK ENDING 11 OCTOBER 1986

LW	TW	Title	Artist	Label	Wks
3	[1]	TRUE BLUE	Madonna	*Sire*	2
2	[2]	RAIN OR SHINE	Five Star	*Tent*	5
1	3	DON'T LEAVE ME THIS WAY	Communards	*London*	8
-	4	EVERY LOSER WINS	Nick Berry ●	*BBC*	1
9	5	YOU CAN CALL ME AL	Paul Simon	*Warner Bros*	3
4	6	WORD UP	Cameo	*Club*	6
5	7	THORN IN MY SIDE	Eurythmics	*RCA*	6
14	[8]	I'VE BEEN LOSING YOU	A-Ha	*Warner Bros*	2
29	9	IN THE ARMY NOW	Status Quo	*Vertigo*	2
23	10	SUBURBIA	Pet Shop Boys	*Parlophone*	2
6	11	WE DON'T HAVE TO...	Jermaine Stewart	*10*	9
11	12	(FOREVER) LIVE AND DIE	Orchestral Manoeuvres In The Dark	*Virgin*	5
8	13	WALK THIS WAY	Run DMC	*London*	6
7	14	(I JUST) DIED IN YOUR ARMS	Cutting Crew	*Siren*	7
12	15	STUCK WITH YOU	Huey Lewis and the News	*Chrysalis*	7
18	[16]	MONTEGO BAY	Amazulu	*Island*	4
15	17	ALWAYS THERE	Marti Webb and the Simon May Orchestra	*BBC*	4
21	18	TRUE COLORS	Cyndi Lauper	*Portrait*	3
-	19	ALL I ASK OF YOU	Cliff Richard and Sarah Brightman ●	*Polydor*	1
26	20	WALK LIKE AN EGYPTIAN	Bangles	*CBS*	2
13	21	LOVE CAN'T TURN AROUND	Farley 'Jackmaster' Funk	*Chicago*	8
16	22	RUMORS	Timex Social Club	*Cooltempo*	5
10	23	GLORY OF LOVE	Peter Cetera	*Full Moon*	9
30	[24]	WONDERLAND	Paul Young	*CBS*	2
19	25	IN TOO DEEP	Genesis	*Charisma*	7
17	26	SWEET FREEDOM	Michael McDonald	*MCA*	5
37	27	MIDAS TOUCH	Midnight Star	*Solar*	2
34	28	WORLD SHUT YOUR MOUTH	Julian Cope	*Island*	2
27	29	SLOW DOWN	Loose Ends	*Virgin*	4
20	30	I WANT TO WAKE UP WITH YOU	Boris Gardiner	*Revue*	11
24	31	WHO WANTS TO LIVE FOREVER	Queen	*EMI*	3
-	32	DON'T STAND SO CLOSE TO ME 86	Police	*A&M*	1
22	33	ONE GREAT THING	Big Country	*Mercury*	4
-	34	THE WIZARD	Paul Hardcastle	*Chrysalis*	1
38	[35]	ALL I WANT	Howard Jones	*WEA*	2
32	36	SO MACHO/CRUISING	Sinitta	*Fanfare*	13
-	37	TO BE A LOVER	Billy Idol	*Chrysalis*	1
-	38	YOU'RE EVERYTHING TO ME	Boris Gardiner	*Revue*	1
-	39	THINK FOR A MINUTE	Housemartins	*Go! Discs*	1
25	40	PRETTY IN PINK	Psychedelic Furs	*CBS*	6

October 1986

□ Highest position disc reached ● Act's first ever week on chart

WEEK ENDING 18 OCTOBER 1986

LW	TW	Title	Artist	Label	Wks
4	[1]	EVERY LOSER WINS	Nick Berry	*BBC*	2
1	2	TRUE BLUE	Madonna	*Sire*	3
2	3	RAIN OR SHINE	Five Star	*Tent*	6
5	[4]	YOU CAN CALL ME AL	Paul Simon	*Warner Bros*	4
9	5	IN THE ARMY NOW	Status Quo	*Vertigo*	3
3	6	DON'T LEAVE ME THIS WAY	Communards	*London*	9
19	7	ALL I ASK OF YOU	Cliff Richard and Sarah Brightman	*Polydor*	2
10	[8]	SUBURBIA	Pet Shop Boys	*Parlophone*	3
20	9	WALK LIKE AN EGYPTIAN	Bangles	*CBS*	3
8	10	I'VE BEEN LOSING YOU	A-Ha	*Warner Bros*	3
7	11	THORN IN MY SIDE	Eurythmics	*RCA*	7
6	12	WORD UP	Cameo	*Club*	7
18	13	TRUE COLORS	Cyndi Lauper	*Portrait*	4
17	14	ALWAYS THERE	Marti Webb and the Simon May Orchestra	*BBC*	5
12	15	(FOREVER) LIVE AND DIE	Orchestral Manoeuvres In The Dark	*Virgin*	6
16	[16]	MONTEGO BAY	Amazulu	*Island*	5
15	17	STUCK WITH YOU	Huey Lewis and the News	*Chrysalis*	8
11	18	WE DON'T HAVE TO...	Jermaine Stewart	*10*	10
13	19	WALK THIS WAY	Run DMC	*London*	7
28	20	WORLD SHUT YOUR MOUTH	Julian Cope	*Island*	3
14	21	(I JUST) DIED IN YOUR ARMS	Cutting Crew	*Siren*	8
27	22	MIDAS TOUCH	Midnight Star	*Solar*	3
34	23	THE WIZARD	Paul Hardcastle	*Chrysalis*	2
32	[24]	DON'T STAND SO CLOSE TO ME 86		*A&M*	2
38	25	YOU'RE EVERYTHING TO ME	Boris Gardiner	*Revue*	2
24	26	WONDERLAND	Paul Young	*CBS*	3
22	27	RUMORS	Timex Social Club	*Cooltempo*	6
39	28	THINK FOR A MINUTE	Housemartins	*Go! Discs*	2
37	29	TO BE A LOVER	Billy Idol	*Chrysalis*	2
21	30	LOVE CAN'T TURN AROUND	Farley 'Jackmaster' Funk	*Chicago*	9
23	31	GLORY OF LOVE	Peter Cetera	*Full Moon*	10
-	32	DON'T GET ME WRONG	Pretenders	*Real*	1
26	33	SWEET FREEDOM	Michael McDonald	*MCA*	6
30	34	I WANT TO WAKE UP WITH YOU	Boris Gardiner	*Revue*	12
29	35	SLOW DOWN	Loose Ends	*Virgin*	5
25	36	IN TOO DEEP	Genesis	*Charisma*	8
-	37	GIRLS AIN'T NOTHING BUT TROUBLE	DJ Jazzy Jeff and Fresh Prince ●	*Champion*	1
31	38	WHO WANTS TO LIVE FOREVER	Queen	*EMI*	4
-	39	(THEY LONG TO BE) CLOSE TO YOU	Gwen Guthrie	*Boiling Point*	1
-	40	STAY WITH ME	Mission ●	*Mercury*	1

WEEK ENDING 25 OCTOBER 1986

LW	TW	Title	Artist	Label	Wks
1	[1]	EVERY LOSER WINS	Nick Berry	*BBC*	3
2	2	TRUE BLUE	Madonna	*Sire*	4
7	[3]	ALL I ASK OF YOU	Cliff Richard and Sarah Brightman	*Polydor*	3
5	4	IN THE ARMY NOW	Status Quo	*Vertigo*	4
4	5	YOU CAN CALL ME AL	Paul Simon	*Warner Bros*	5
9	6	WALK LIKE AN EGYPTIAN	Bangles	*CBS*	4
3	7	RAIN OR SHINE	Five Star	*Tent*	7
8	[8]	SUBURBIA	Pet Shop Boys	*Parlophone*	4
6	9	DON'T LEAVE ME THIS WAY	Communards	*London*	10
22	10	MIDAS TOUCH	Midnight Star	*Solar*	4
25	[11]	YOU'RE EVERYTHING TO ME	Boris Gardiner	*Revue*	3
13	[12]	TRUE COLORS	Cyndi Lauper	*Portrait*	5
14	[13]	ALWAYS THERE	Marti Webb and the Simon May Orchestra	*BBC*	6
32	14	DON'T GET ME WRONG	Pretenders	*Real*	2
23	[15]	THE WIZARD	Paul Hardcastle	*Chrysalis*	3
10	16	I'VE BEEN LOSING YOU	A-Ha	*Warner Bros*	4
11	17	THORN IN MY SIDE	Eurythmics	*RCA*	8

■TV Times: Thursday 7.30pm - Top Of The Pops finishes with Paul Hardcastle's 'The Wizard' theme tune and on comes Nick Berry in 'Eastenders', while 'Howard's Way' (theme tune at 17) is 7.15pm on Sunday (11.10.86) ■ Paul Simon secures his biggest solo hit (18.10.86)■

□ Highest position disc reached ● Act's first ever week on chart

LW	TW	Title / Artist	Label	Wks
12	18	WORD UP Cameo	*Club*	8
20	[19]	WORLD SHUT YOUR MOUTH Julian Cope	*Island*	4
15	20	(FOREVER) LIVE AND DIE Orchestral Manoeuvres In The Dark	*Virgin*	7
37	[21]	GIRLS AIN'T NOTHING BUT TROUBLE DJ Jazzy Jeff and Fresh Prince	*Champion*	2
28	22	THINK FOR A MINUTE Housemartins	*Go! Discs*	3
16	23	MONTEGO BAY Amazulu	*Island*	6
17	24	STUCK WITH YOU Huey Lewis and the News	*Chrysalis*	9
24	25	DON'T STAND SO CLOSE TO ME 86	*A&M*	3
-	26	TO HAVE AND TO HOLD Catherine Stock ●	*Sierra*	1
29	27	TO BE A LOVER Billy Idol	*Chrysalis*	3
18	28	WE DON'T HAVE TO... Jermaine Stewart	*10*	11
39	29	(THEY LONG TO BE) CLOSE TO YOU Gwen Guthrie	*Boiling Point*	2
40	[30]	STAY WITH ME Mission	*Mercury*	2
27	31	RUMORS Timex Social Club	*Cooltempo*	7
19	32	WALK THIS WAY Run DMC	*London*	8
21	33	(I JUST) DIED IN YOUR ARMS Cutting Crew	*Siren*	9
-	34	ALWAYS THE SUN Stranglers	*Epic*	1
30	35	LOVE CAN'T TURN AROUND Farley 'Jackmaster' Funk	*Chicago*	10
-	36	YOU KEEP ME HANGIN' ON Kim Wilde	*MCA*	1
-	37	TAKE MY BREATH AWAY (LOVE THEME FROM 'TOP GUN') Berlin ●	*CBS*	1
-	38	SHOWING OUT (GET FRESH AT THE WEEKEND) Mel and Kim ●	*Supreme*	1
26	39	WONDERLAND Paul Young	*CBS*	4
-	40	LIVIN' ON A PRAYER Bon Jovi	*Vertigo*	1

LW	TW	*WEEK ENDING* **1 NOVEMBER 1986**		Wks
1	[1]	EVERY LOSER WINS Nick Berry	*BBC*	4
4	[2]	IN THE ARMY NOW Status Quo	*Vertigo*	5
3	[3]	ALL I ASK OF YOU Cliff Richard and Sarah Brightman	*Polydor*	4
6	4	WALK LIKE AN EGYPTIAN Bangles	*CBS*	5
2	5	TRUE BLUE Madonna	*Sire*	5
5	6	YOU CAN CALL ME AL Paul Simon	*Warner Bros*	6
37	7	TAKE MY BREATH AWAY (LOVE THEME FROM 'TOP GUN') Berlin	*CBS*	2
10	[8]	MIDAS TOUCH Midnight Star	*Solar*	5
8	9	SUBURBIA Pet Shop Boys	*Parlophone*	5
14	[10]	DON'T GET ME WRONG Pretenders	*Real*	3
11	[11]	YOU'RE EVERYTHING TO ME Boris Gardiner	*Revue*	4
12	[12]	TRUE COLORS Cyndi Lauper	*Portrait*	6
7	13	RAIN OR SHINE Five Star	*Tent*	8
-	14	NOTORIOUS Duran Duran	*EMI*	1
36	15	YOU KEEP ME HANGIN' ON Kim Wilde	*MCA*	2
-	16	ASK Smiths	*Rough Trade*	1
26	[17]	TO HAVE AND TO HOLD Catherine Stock	*Sierra*	2
22	[18]	THINK FOR A MINUTE Housemartins	*Go! Discs*	4
15	19	THE WIZARD Paul Hardcastle	*Chrysalis*	4
13	20	ALWAYS THERE Marti Webb and the Simon May Orchestra	*BBC*	7
9	21	DON'T LEAVE ME THIS WAY Communards	*London*	11
27	[22]	TO BE A LOVER Billy Idol	*Chrysalis*	4
21	23	GIRLS AIN'T NOTHING BUT TROUBLE DJ Jazzy Jeff and Fresh Prince	*Champion*	3
38	24	SHOWING OUT (GET FRESH AT THE WEEKEND) Mel and Kim	*Supreme*	2
29	25	(THEY LONG TO BE) CLOSE TO YOU Gwen Guthrie	*Boiling Point*	3
-	26	SOMETHING OUTA NOTHING Letitia Dean and Paul Medford ●	*BBC*	1
40	27	LIVIN' ON A PRAYER Bon Jovi	*Vertigo*	2
19	28	WORLD SHUT YOUR MOUTH Julian Cope	*Island*	5
16	29	I'VE BEEN LOSING YOU A-Ha	*Warner Bros*	5
34	[30]	ALWAYS THE SUN Stranglers	*Epic*	2
-	31	DON'T GIVE UP Peter Gabriel and Kate Bush ●	*Virgin*	1
17	32	THORN IN MY SIDE Eurythmics	*RCA*	9
-	33	FOR AMERICA Red Box	*Sire*	1
-	34	THIS IS THE WORLD CALLING Bob Geldof ●	*Mercury*	1
18	35	WORD UP Cameo	*Club*	9
-	36	BREAKOUT Swing Out Sister ●	*Mercury*	1
24	37	STUCK WITH YOU Huey Lewis and the News	*Chrysalis*	10
30	38	STAY WITH ME Mission	*Mercury*	3
-	39	BECAUSE I LOVE YOU Shakin' Stevens	*Epic*	1
-	40	ANOTHERLOVERHOLENYOHEAD Prince and the Revolution	*Paisley Park*	1

LW	TW	*WEEK ENDING* **8 NOVEMBER 1986**		Wks
7	[1]	TAKE MY BREATH AWAY (LOVE THEME FROM 'TOP GUN') Berlin	*CBS*	3
1	2	EVERY LOSER WINS Nick Berry	*BBC*	5
2	3	IN THE ARMY NOW Status Quo	*Vertigo*	6
4	4	WALK LIKE AN EGYPTIAN Bangles	*CBS*	6
3	5	ALL I ASK OF YOU Cliff Richard and Sarah Brightman	*Polydor*	5
15	6	YOU KEEP ME HANGIN' ON Kim Wilde	*MCA*	3
14	[7]	NOTORIOUS Duran Duran	*EMI*	2
24	8	SHOWING OUT (GET FRESH AT THE WEEKEND) Mel and Kim	*Supreme*	3
8	9	MIDAS TOUCH Midnight Star	*Solar*	6
10	[10]	DON'T GET ME WRONG Pretenders	*Real*	4
5	11	TRUE BLUE Madonna	*Sire*	6
26	[12]	SOMETHING OUTA NOTHING Letitia Dean and Paul Medford	*BBC*	2
6	13	YOU CAN CALL ME AL Paul Simon	*Warner Bros*	7
16	[14]	ASK Smiths	*Rough Trade*	2
27	15	LIVIN' ON A PRAYER Bon Jovi	*Vertigo*	3
31	16	DON'T GIVE UP Peter Gabriel and Kate Bush	*Virgin*	2
36	17	BREAKOUT Swing Out Sister	*Mercury*	2
9	18	SUBURBIA Pet Shop Boys	*Parlophone*	6
12	19	TRUE COLORS Cyndi Lauper	*Portrait*	7
-	20	THROUGH THE BARRICADES Spandau Ballet	*Reformation*	1
11	21	YOU'RE EVERYTHING TO ME Boris Gardiner	*Revue*	5
33	22	FOR AMERICA Red Box	*Sire*	2
22	23	TO BE A LOVER Billy Idol	*Chrysalis*	5
39	24	BECAUSE I LOVE YOU Shakin' Stevens	*Epic*	2
34	[25]	THIS IS THE WORLD CALLING Bob Geldof	*Mercury*	2
25	26	(THEY LONG TO BE) CLOSE TO YOU Gwen Guthrie	*Boiling Point*	4
13	27	RAIN OR SHINE Five Star	*Tent*	9
18	28	THINK FOR A MINUTE Housemartins	*Go! Discs*	5
17	29	TO HAVE AND TO HOLD Catherine Stock	*Sierra*	3
23	30	GIRLS AIN'T NOTHING BUT TROUBLE DJ Jazzy Jeff and Fresh Prince	*Champion*	4
21	31	DON'T LEAVE ME THIS WAY Communards	*London*	12
19	32	THE WIZARD Paul Hardcastle	*Chrysalis*	5
-	33	(WAITING FOR) THE GHOST TRAIN Madness	*Zarjazz*	1
20	34	ALWAYS THERE Marti Webb and the Simon May Orchestra	*BBC*	8
-	35	THE FINAL COUNTDOWN Europe ●	*Epic*	1
40	[36]	ANOTHERLOVERHOLENYOHEAD Prince and the Revolution	*Paisley Park*	2
30	37	ALWAYS THE SUN Stranglers	*Epic*	3
-	38	DON'T FORGET ME (WHEN I'M GONE) Glass Tiger ●	*Manhattan*	1
35	39	WORD UP Cameo	*Club*	10
-	40	EXPERIMENT IV Kate Bush	*EMI*	1

LW	TW	*WEEK ENDING* **15 NOVEMBER 1986**		Wks
1	[1]	TAKE MY BREATH AWAY (LOVE THEME FROM 'TOP GUN') Berlin	*CBS*	4
6	[2]	YOU KEEP ME HANGIN' ON Kim Wilde	*MCA*	4
4	[3]	WALK LIKE AN EGYPTIAN Bangles	*CBS*	7
8	4	SHOWING OUT (GET FRESH AT THE WEEKEND) Mel and Kim	*Supreme*	4
17	5	BREAKOUT Swing Out Sister	*Mercury*	3
3	6	IN THE ARMY NOW Status Quo	*Vertigo*	7
2	7	EVERY LOSER WINS Nick Berry	*BBC*	6

In these weeks ■ Kate Bush has previously guested on Peter Gabriel's *Games Without Frontiers* in 1980; this time she receives full artist credit (01.11.86) ■ A plethora of parenthesis as brackets begin or end five Top 40 titles (08.11.86)■

LW	TW	Title / Artist	Label	Wks
20	8	THROUGH THE BARRICADES Spandau Ballet	*Reformation*	2
16	9	DON'T GIVE UP Peter Gabriel and Kate Bush	*Virgin*	3
5	10	ALL I ASK OF YOU Cliff Richard and Sarah Brightman	*Polydor*	6
15	11	LIVIN' ON A PRAYER Bon Jovi	*Vertigo*	4
7	12	NOTORIOUS Duran Duran	*EMI*	3
22	13	FOR AMERICA Red Box	*Sire*	3
35	14	THE FINAL COUNTDOWN Europe	*Epic*	2
10	15	DON'T GET ME WRONG Pretenders	*Real*	5
12	16	SOMETHING OUTA NOTHING Letitia Dean and Paul Medford	*BBC*	3
9	17	MIDAS TOUCH Midnight Star	*Solar*	7
24	18	BECAUSE I LOVE YOU Shakin' Stevens	*Epic*	3
11	19	TRUE BLUE Madonna	*Sire*	7
33	20	(WAITING FOR) THE GHOST TRAIN Madness	*Zarjazz*	2
14	21	ASK Smiths	*Rough Trade*	3
-	22	GHOSTDANCING Simple Minds	*Virgin*	1
40	23	EXPERIMENT IV Kate Bush	*EMI*	2
13	24	YOU CAN CALL ME AL Paul Simon	*Warner Bros*	8
25	25	THIS IS THE WORLD CALLING Bob Geldof	*Mercury*	3
-	26	EACH TIME YOU BREAK MY HEART Nick Kamen ●	*WEA*	1
-	27	FRENCH KISSIN' IN THE USA Debbie Harry	*Chrysalis*	1
26	28	(THEY LONG TO BE) CLOSE TO YOU Gwen Guthrie	*Boiling Point*	5
18	29	SUBURBIA Pet Shop Boys	*Parlophone*	7
19	30	TRUE COLORS Cyndi Lauper	*Portrait*	8
38	31	DON'T FORGET ME (WHEN I'M GONE) Glass Tiger	*Manhattan*	2
23	32	TO BE A LOVER Billy Idol	*Chrysalis*	6
-	33	SOMETIMES Erasure ●	*Mute*	1
28	34	THINK FOR A MINUTE Housemartins	*Go! Discs*	6
21	35	YOU'RE EVERYTHING TO ME Boris Gardiner	*Revue*	6
-	36	SWEET LOVE Anita Baker ●	*Elektra*	1
27	37	RAIN OR SHINE Five Star	*Tent*	10
-	38	LOVE IS THE SLUG We've Got A Fuzzbox And We're Gonna Use It ●	*Vindaloo*	1
34	39	ALWAYS THERE Marti Webb and the Simon May Orchestra	*BBC*	9
29	40	TO HAVE AND TO HOLD Catherine Stock	*Sierra*	4

LW	TW	*WEEK ENDING* **22 NOVEMBER 1986**		Wks
1	1	TAKE MY BREATH AWAY (LOVE THEME FROM 'TOP GUN') Berlin	*CBS*	5
2	2	YOU KEEP ME HANGIN' ON Kim Wilde	*MCA*	5
4	3	SHOWING OUT (GET FRESH AT THE WEEKEND) Mel and Kim	*Supreme*	5
5	4	BREAKOUT Swing Out Sister	*Mercury*	4
14	5	THE FINAL COUNTDOWN Europe	*Epic*	3
8	6	THROUGH THE BARRICADES Spandau Ballet	*Reformation*	3
11	7	LIVIN' ON A PRAYER Bon Jovi	*Vertigo*	5
3	8	WALK LIKE AN EGYPTIAN Bangles	*CBS*	8
9	9	DON'T GIVE UP Peter Gabriel and Kate Bush	*Virgin*	4
13	10	FOR AMERICA Red Box	*Sire*	4
27	11	FRENCH KISSIN' IN THE USA Debbie Harry	*Chrysalis*	2
26	12	EACH TIME YOU BREAK MY HEART Nick Kamen	*WEA*	2
22	13	GHOSTDANCING Simple Minds	*Virgin*	2
18	14	BECAUSE I LOVE YOU Shakin' Stevens	*Epic*	4
10	15	ALL I ASK OF YOU Cliff Richard and Sarah Brightman	*Polydor*	7
33	16	SOMETIMES Erasure	*Mute*	2
6	17	IN THE ARMY NOW Status Quo	*Vertigo*	8
20	18	(WAITING FOR) THE GHOST TRAIN Madness	*Zarjazz*	3
36	19	SWEET LOVE Anita Baker	*Elektra*	2
12	20	NOTORIOUS Duran Duran	*EMI*	4
7	21	EVERY LOSER WINS Nick Berry	*BBC*	7
-	22	THE SKYE BOAT SONG Roger Whittaker and Des O'Connor ●	*Tembo*	1
-	23	IF I SAY YES Five Star	*Tent*	1
-	24	WARRIORS (OF THE WASTELAND) Frankie Goes To Hollywood	*ZTT*	1
15	25	DON'T GET ME WRONG Pretenders	*Real*	6
-	26	STRANGER IN A STRANGE LAND Iron Maiden	*EMI*	1
17	27	MIDAS TOUCH Midnight Star	*Solar*	8
-	28	LAND OF CONFUSION Genesis	*Virgin*	1
31	29	DON'T FORGET ME (WHEN I'M GONE) Glass Tiger	*Manhattan*	3
19	30	TRUE BLUE Madonna	*Sire*	8

December 1986

☐ Highest position disc reached ● Act's first ever week on chart

LW	TW	Title / Artist	Label	Wks
38	31	LOVE IS THE SLUG We've Got A Fuzzbox And We're Gonna Use It	*Vindaloo*	2
16	32	SOMETHING OUTA NOTHING Letitia Dean and Paul Medford	*BBC*	4
21	33	ASK Smiths	*Rough Trade*	4
-	34	ANYTHING Damned	*MCA*	1
23	35	EXPERIMENT IV Kate Bush	*EMI*	3
25	36	THIS IS THE WORLD CALLING Bob Geldof	*Mercury*	4
-	37	I'VE BEEN IN LOVE BEFORE Cutting Crew	*Siren*	1
24	38	YOU CAN CALL ME AL Paul Simon	*Warner Bros*	9
30	39	TRUE COLORS Cyndi Lauper	*Portrait*	9
-	40	ALL FALL DOWN Ultravox	*Chrysalis*	1

LW	TW	*WEEK ENDING* **29 NOVEMBER 1986**		Wks
1	1	TAKE MY BREATH AWAY (LOVE THEME FROM 'TOP GUN') Berlin	*CBS*	6
5	2	THE FINAL COUNTDOWN Europe	*Epic*	4
2	3	YOU KEEP ME HANGIN' ON Kim Wilde	*MCA*	6
3	4	SHOWING OUT (GET FRESH AT THE WEEKEND) Mel and Kim	*Supreme*	6
4	5	BREAKOUT Swing Out Sister	*Mercury*	5
7	6	LIVIN' ON A PRAYER Bon Jovi	*Vertigo*	6
16	7	SOMETIMES Erasure	*Mute*	3
12	8	EACH TIME YOU BREAK MY HEART Nick Kamen	*WEA*	3
11	9	FRENCH KISSIN' IN THE USA Debbie Harry	*Chrysalis*	3
10	10	FOR AMERICA Red Box	*Sire*	5
6	11	THROUGH THE BARRICADES Spandau Ballet	*Reformation*	4
9	12	DON'T GIVE UP Peter Gabriel and Kate Bush	*Virgin*	5
19	13	SWEET LOVE Anita Baker	*Elektra*	3
8	14	WALK LIKE AN EGYPTIAN Bangles	*CBS*	9
23	15	IF I SAY YES Five Star	*Tent*	2
13	16	GHOSTDANCING Simple Minds	*Virgin*	3
22	17	THE SKYE BOAT SONG Roger Whittaker and Des O'Connor	*Tembo*	2
14	18	BECAUSE I LOVE YOU Shakin' Stevens	*Epic*	5
24	19	WARRIORS (OF THE WASTELAND) Frankie Goes To Hollywood	*ZTT*	2
15	20	ALL I ASK OF YOU Cliff Richard and Sarah Brightman	*Polydor*	8
28	21	LAND OF CONFUSION Genesis	*Virgin*	2
26	22	STRANGER IN A STRANGE LAND Iron Maiden	*EMI*	2
18	23	(WAITING FOR) THE GHOST TRAIN Madness	*Zarjazz*	4
17	24	IN THE ARMY NOW Status Quo	*Vertigo*	9
-	25	THE RAIN Oran 'Juice' Jones ●	*Def Jam*	1
-	26	SO COLD THE NIGHT Communards	*London*	1
-	27	WAR Bruce Springsteen	*CBS*	1
21	28	EVERY LOSER WINS Nick Berry	*BBC*	8
29	29	DON'T FORGET ME (WHEN I'M GONE) Glass Tiger	*Manhattan*	4
40	30	ALL FALL DOWN Ultravox	*Chrysalis*	2
37	31	I'VE BEEN IN LOVE BEFORE Cutting Crew	*Siren*	2
34	32	ANYTHING Damned	*MCA*	2
-	33	SHAKE YOU DOWN Gregory Abbott ●	*CBS*	1
-	34	SHIVER George Benson	*Warner Bros*	1
-	35	STEP RIGHT UP Jaki Graham	*EMI*	1
20	36	NOTORIOUS Duran Duran	*EMI*	5
25	37	DON'T GET ME WRONG Pretenders	*Real*	7
-	38	THE MIRACLE OF LOVE Eurythmics	*RCA*	1
-	39	CANDY Cameo	*Club*	1
30	40	TRUE BLUE Madonna	*Sire*	9

LW	TW	*WEEK ENDING* **6 DECEMBER 1986**		Wks
2	1	THE FINAL COUNTDOWN Europe	*Epic*	5
1	2	TAKE MY BREATH AWAY (LOVE THEME FROM 'TOP GUN') Berlin	*CBS*	7
7	3	SOMETIMES Erasure	*Mute*	4
6	4	LIVIN' ON A PRAYER Bon Jovi	*Vertigo*	7
8	5	EACH TIME YOU BREAK MY HEART Nick Kamen	*WEA*	4

■With a combined age of 105, Roger Whittaker and Des O'Connor are the oldest charting duo (22.11.86) ■ Land of confusion - This weeks chart contains references to Europe, America, France, Egypt, Berlin and Skye (29.11.86)■

December 1986

□ Highest position disc reached ● Act's first ever week on chart

LW	TW	Title	Artist	Label	Wks
5	6	BREAKOUT	Swing Out Sister	Mercury	6
3	7	YOU KEEP ME HANGIN' ON	Kim Wilde	MCA	7
9	[8]	FRENCH KISSIN' IN THE USA	Debbie Harry	Chrysalis	4
4	9	SHOWING OUT (GET FRESH AT THE WEEKEND)	Mel and Kim	Supreme	7
17	[10]	THE SKYE BOAT SONG	Roger Whittaker and Des O'Connor	Tembo	3
10	11	FOR AMERICA	Red Box	Sire	6
25	12	THE RAIN	Oran 'Juice' Jones	Def Jam	2
13	[13]	SWEET LOVE	Anita Baker	Elektra	4
26	14	SO COLD THE NIGHT	Communards	London	2
33	15	SHAKE YOU DOWN	Gregory Abbott	CBS	2
15	16	IF I SAY YES	Five Star	Tent	3
11	17	THROUGH THE BARRICADES	Spandau Ballet	Reformation	5
27	[18]	WAR	Bruce Springsteen	CBS	2
19	[19]	WARRIORS (OF THE WASTELAND)	Frankie Goes To Hollywood	ZTT	3
21	20	LAND OF CONFUSION	Genesis	Virgin	3
34	21	SHIVER	George Benson	Warner Bros	2
14	22	WALK LIKE AN EGYPTIAN	Bangles	CBS	10
-	23	CARAVAN OF LOVE	Housemartins	Go! Discs	1
12	24	DON'T GIVE UP	Peter Gabriel and Kate Bush	Virgin	6
18	25	BECAUSE I LOVE YOU	Shakin' Stevens	Epic	6
35	26	STEP RIGHT UP	Jaki Graham	EMI	2
39	[27]	CANDY	Cameo	Club	2
-	28	CRY WOLF	A-Ha	Warner Bros	1
38	29	THE MIRACLE OF LOVE	Eurythmics	RCA	2
23	30	(WAITING FOR) THE GHOST TRAIN	Madness	Zarjazz	5
20	31	ALL I ASK OF YOU	Cliff Richard and Sarah Brightman	Polydor	9
-	32	IS THIS LOVE	Alison Moyet	CBS	1
22	33	STRANGER IN A STRANGE LAND	Iron Maiden	EMI	3
16	34	GHOSTDANCING	Simple Minds	Virgin	4
31	35	I'VE BEEN IN LOVE BEFORE	Cutting Crew	Siren	3
24	36	IN THE ARMY NOW	Status Quo	Vertigo	10
30	37	ALL FALL DOWN	Ultravox	Chrysalis	3
29	38	DON'T FORGET ME (WHEN I'M GONE)	Glass Tiger	Manhattan	5
-	39	BECAUSE OF YOU	Dexy's Midnight Runners	Mercury	1
-	40	REET PETITE	Jackie Wilson	SMP	1

WEEK ENDING 13 DECEMBER 1986

LW	TW	Title	Artist	Label	Wks
1	[1]	THE FINAL COUNTDOWN	Europe	Epic	6
3	[2]	SOMETIMES	Erasure	Mute	5
23	3	CARAVAN OF LOVE	Housemartins	Go! Discs	2
12	[4]	THE RAIN	Oran 'Juice' Jones	Def Jam	3
2	5	TAKE MY BREATH AWAY (LOVE THEME FROM 'TOP GUN')	Berlin	CBS	8
15	[6]	SHAKE YOU DOWN	Gregory Abbott	CBS	3
4	7	LIVIN' ON A PRAYER	Bon Jovi	Vertigo	8
-	8	OPEN YOUR HEART	Madonna	Sire	1
5	9	EACH TIME YOU BREAK MY HEART	Nick Kamen	WEA	5
14	10	SO COLD THE NIGHT	Communards	London	3
8	11	FRENCH KISSIN' IN THE USA	Debbie Harry	Chrysalis	5
6	12	BREAKOUT	Swing Out Sister	Mercury	7
10	13	THE SKYE BOAT SONG	Roger Whittaker and Des O'Connor	Tembo	4
40	14	REET PETITE	Jackie Wilson	SMP	2
7	15	YOU KEEP ME HANGIN' ON	Kim Wilde	MCA	8
28	16	CRY WOLF	A-Ha	Warner Bros	2
20	17	LAND OF CONFUSION	Genesis	Virgin	4
9	18	SHOWING OUT (GET FRESH AT THE WEEKEND)	Mel and Kim	Supreme	8
21	[19]	SHIVER	George Benson	Warner Bros	3
11	20	FOR AMERICA	Red Box	Sire	7
26	21	STEP RIGHT UP	Jaki Graham	EMI	3
13	22	SWEET LOVE	Anita Baker	Elektra	5
18	23	WAR	Bruce Springsteen	CBS	3
32	24	IS THIS LOVE	Alison Moyet	CBS	2
39	25	BECAUSE OF YOU	Dexy's Midnight Runners	Mercury	2
16	26	IF I SAY YES	Five Star	Tent	4
27	[27]	CANDY	Cameo	Club	3
17	28	THROUGH THE BARRICADES	Spandau Ballet	Reformation	6
29	29	THE MIRACLE OF LOVE	Eurythmics	RCA	3
-	30	BIG FUN	Gap Band	Total Experience	1
22	31	WALK LIKE AN EGYPTIAN	Bangles	CBS	11
19	32	WARRIORS (OF THE WASTELAND)	Frankie Goes To Hollywood	ZTT	4
31	33	ALL I ASK OF YOU	Cliff Richard and Sarah Brightman	Polydor	10
-	34	DREAMIN'	Status Quo	Vertigo	1
-	35	O' MY FATHER HAD A RABBIT	Ray Moore ●	Play	1
24	36	DON'T GIVE UP	Peter Gabriel and Kate Bush	Virgin	7
25	37	BECAUSE I LOVE YOU	Shakin' Stevens	Epic	7
-	38	NO MORE THE FOOL	Elkie Brooks	Legend	1
-	39	ONLY LOVE REMAINS	Paul McCartney	Parlophone	1
36	40	IN THE ARMY NOW	Status Quo	Vertigo	11

WEEK ENDING 20 DECEMBER 1986

LW	TW	Title	Artist	Label	Wks
3	[1]	CARAVAN OF LOVE	Housemartins	Go! Discs	3
14	2	REET PETITE	Jackie Wilson	SMP	3
1	3	THE FINAL COUNTDOWN	Europe	Epic	7
8	[4]	OPEN YOUR HEART	Madonna	Sire	2
2	5	SOMETIMES	Erasure	Mute	6
4	6	THE RAIN	Oran 'Juice' Jones	Def Jam	4
6	7	SHAKE YOU DOWN	Gregory Abbott	CBS	4
10	[8]	SO COLD THE NIGHT	Communards	London	4
7	9	LIVIN' ON A PRAYER	Bon Jovi	Vertigo	9
16	10	CRY WOLF	A-Ha	Warner Bros	3
5	11	TAKE MY BREATH AWAY (LOVE THEME FROM 'TOP GUN')	Berlin	CBS	9
24	12	IS THIS LOVE	Alison Moyet	CBS	3
9	13	EACH TIME YOU BREAK MY HEART	Nick Kamen	WEA	6
11	14	FRENCH KISSIN' IN THE USA	Debbie Harry	Chrysalis	6
30	15	BIG FUN	Gap Band	Total Experience	2
17	16	LAND OF CONFUSION	Genesis	Virgin	5
21	17	STEP RIGHT UP	Jaki Graham	EMI	4
13	18	THE SKYE BOAT SONG	Roger Whittaker and Des O'Connor	Tembo	5
12	19	BREAKOUT	Swing Out Sister	Mercury	8
25	20	BECAUSE OF YOU	Dexy's Midnight Runners	Mercury	3
19	21	SHIVER	George Benson	Warner Bros	4
15	22	YOU KEEP ME HANGIN' ON	Kim Wilde	MCA	9
22	23	SWEET LOVE	Anita Baker	Elektra	6
18	24	SHOWING OUT (GET FRESH AT THE WEEKEND)	Mel and Kim	Supreme	9
34	25	DREAMIN'	Status Quo	Vertigo	2
20	26	FOR AMERICA	Red Box	Sire	8
35	27	O' MY FATHER HAD A RABBIT	Ray Moore	Play	2
29	28	THE MIRACLE OF LOVE	Eurythmics	RCA	4
27	29	CANDY	Cameo	Club	4
38	30	NO MORE THE FOOL	Elkie Brooks	Legend	2
26	31	IF I SAY YES	Five Star	Tent	5
23	32	WAR	Bruce Springsteen	CBS	4
33	33	ALL I ASK OF YOU	Cliff Richard and Sarah Brightman	Polydor	11
39	[34]	ONLY LOVE REMAINS	Paul McCartney	Parlophone	2
28	35	THROUGH THE BARRICADES	Spandau Ballet	Reformation	7
-	36	HYMN TO HER	Pretenders	Real	1
-	37	OVER THE HILLS AND FAR AWAY	Gary Moore	10	1
-	38	SANTA CLAUS IS ON THE DOLE/FIRST ATHEIST TABERNACLE CHOIR	Spitting Image	Virgin	1
31	39	WALK LIKE AN EGYPTIAN	Bangles	CBS	12
-	40	THE BOY IN THE BUBBLE	Paul Simon	Warner Bros	1

WEEK ENDING 27 DECEMBER 1986

LW	TW	Title	Artist	Label	Wks
2	[1]	REET PETITE	Jackie Wilson	SMP	4
1	2	CARAVAN OF LOVE	Housemartins	Go! Discs	4
3	3	THE FINAL COUNTDOWN	Europe	Epic	8
4	[4]	OPEN YOUR HEART	Madonna	Sire	3
5	5	SOMETIMES	Erasure	Mute	7

In these weeks ■ Alison Moyet and Vince Clarke both formerly of Yazoo are charting - Vince with Erasure (06.12.86) ■ In at 39 are Dexy's Midnight Runners whose last Top Ten hit was *Jackie Wilson Said*. Remarkably, the man himself enters the chart himself at number 40 (06.12.86)■

6 **6** THE RAIN Oran 'Juice' Jones .... *Def Jam* 5
10 **7** CRY WOLF A-Ha .... *Warner Bros* 4
12 **8** IS THIS LOVE Alison Moyet .... *CBS* 4
7 **9** SHAKE YOU DOWN Gregory Abbott .... *CBS* 5
9 **10** LIVIN' ON A PRAYER Bon Jovi .... *Vertigo* 10
8 **11** SO COLD THE NIGHT Communards .... *London* 5
15 **12** BIG FUN Gap Band .... *Total Experience* 3
20 **13** BECAUSE OF YOU Dexy's Midnight Runners .... *Mercury* 4
11 **14** TAKE MY BREATH AWAY (LOVE THEME FROM 'TOP GUN') Berlin .... *CBS* 10
17 **15** STEP RIGHT UP Jaki Graham .... *EMI* 5
16 **16** LAND OF CONFUSION Genesis .... *Virgin* 6
25 **17** DREAMIN' Status Quo .... *Vertigo* 3
30 **18** NO MORE THE FOOL Elkie Brooks .... *Legend* 3
14 **19** FRENCH KISSIN' IN THE USA Debbie Harry .... *Chrysalis* 7
18 **20** THE SKYE BOAT SONG Roger Whittaker and Des O'Connor .... *Tembo* 6
13 **21** EACH TIME YOU BREAK MY HEART Nick Kamen .... *WEA* 7
38 **22** SANTA CLAUS IS ON THE DOLE/FIRST ATHEIST TABERNACLE CHOIR Spitting Image .... *Virgin* 2
19 **23** BREAKOUT Swing Out Sister .... *Mercury* 9
27 **24** O' MY FATHER HAD A RABBIT Ray Moore .... *Play* 3
28 **25** THE MIRACLE OF LOVE Eurythmics .... *RCA* 5

□ Highest position disc reached ● Act's first ever week on chart

21 **26** SHIVER George Benson .... *Warner Bros* 5
36 **27** HYMN TO HER Pretenders .... *Real* 2
22 **28** YOU KEEP ME HANGIN' ON Kim Wilde .... *MCA* 10
33 **29** ALL I ASK OF YOU Cliff Richard and Sarah Brightman .... *Polydor* 12
24 **30** SHOWING OUT (GET FRESH AT THE WEEKEND) Mel and Kim .... *Supreme* 10
37 **31** OVER THE HILLS AND FAR AWAY Gary Moore *10* 2
29 **32** CANDY Cameo .... *Club* 5
40 **33** THE BOY IN THE BUBBLE Paul Simon .... *Warner Bros* 2
- **34** BALLERINA GIRL Lionel Richie .... *Motown* 1
34 **35** ONLY LOVE REMAINS Paul McCartney .... *Parlophone* 3
26 **36** FOR AMERICA Red Box .... *Sire* 9
39 **37** WALK LIKE AN EGYPTIAN Bangles .... *CBS* 13
23 **38** SWEET LOVE Anita Baker .... *Elektra* 7
31 **39** IF I SAY YES Five Star .... *Tent* 6
35 **40** THROUGH THE BARRICADES Spandau Ballet .... *Reformation* 8

■29 years 42 days after his chart debut, Jackie Wilson finally lands a number one breaking Stevie Wonder's existing record for patience by over ten years (27.12.86)■

1987

..........THE PET SHOP BOYS spend the most weeks at number one this year with two titles, including the Christmas number one 'Always On My Mind'......Madonna has the most weeks on chart for the third consecutive year, a record for consistent success, and overtakes Sandie Shaw with the most number ones by a female soloist......'Jack Your Body' by Steve 'Silk' Hurley begins the house era..........

January 1987

□ Highest position disc reached ● Act's first ever week on chart

LW	TW	*WEEK ENDING* 3 JANUARY 1987			Wks
1	1	REET PETITE	Jackie Wilson	*SMP*	5
2	2	CARAVAN OF LOVE	Housemartins	*Go! Discs*	5
3	3	THE FINAL COUNTDOWN	Europe	*Epic*	9
4	4	OPEN YOUR HEART	Madonna	*Sire*	4
7	5	CRY WOLF	A-Ha	*Warner Bros*	5
6	6	THE RAIN	Oran 'Juice' Jones	*Def Jam*	6
5	7	SOMETIMES	Erasure	*Mute*	8
8	8	IS THIS LOVE	Alison Moyet	*CBS*	5
9	9	SHAKE YOU DOWN	Gregory Abbott	*CBS*	6
10	10	LIVIN' ON A PRAYER	Bon Jovi	*Vertigo*	11
11	11	SO COLD THE NIGHT	Communards	*London*	6
12	12	BIG FUN	Gap Band	*Total Experience*	4
14	13	TAKE MY BREATH AWAY (LOVE THEME FROM 'TOP GUN')	Berlin	*CBS*	11
16	14	LAND OF CONFUSION	Genesis	*Virgin*	7
17	15	DREAMIN'	Status Quo	*Vertigo*	4
13	16	BECAUSE OF YOU	Dexy's Midnight Runners	*Mercury*	5
15	17	STEP RIGHT UP	Jaki Graham	*EMI*	6
18	18	NO MORE THE FOOL	Elkie Brooks	*Legend*	4
19	19	FRENCH KISSIN' IN THE USA	Debbie Harry	*Chrysalis*	8
21	20	EACH TIME YOU BREAK MY HEART	Nick Kamen	*WEA*	8
23	21	BREAKOUT	Swing Out Sister	*Mercury*	10
22	22	SANTA CLAUS IS ON THE DOLE/FIRST ATHEIST TABERNACLE CHOIR	Spitting Image	*Virgin*	3
25	23	THE MIRACLE OF LOVE	Eurythmics	*RCA*	6
20	24	THE SKYE BOAT SONG	Roger Whittaker and Des O'Connor	*Tembo*	7
27	25	HYMN TO HER	Pretenders	*Real*	3
28	26	YOU KEEP ME HANGIN' ON	Kim Wilde	*MCA*	11
30	27	SHOWING OUT (GET FRESH AT THE WEEKEND)	Mel and Kim	*Supreme*	11
26	28	SHIVER	George Benson	*Warner Bros*	6
24	29	O' MY FATHER HAD A RABBIT	Ray Moore	*Play*	4
29	30	ALL I ASK OF YOU	Cliff Richard and Sarah Brightman	*Polydor*	13
31	31	OVER THE HILLS AND FAR AWAY	Gary Moore	*10*	3
33	32	THE BOY IN THE BUBBLE	Paul Simon	*Warner Bros*	3
34	33	BALLERINA GIRL	Lionel Richie	*Motown*	2
39	34	IF I SAY YES	Five Star	*Tent*	7
32	35	CANDY	Cameo	*Club*	6
38	36	SWEET LOVE	Anita Baker	*Elektra*	8
26	37	FOR AMERICA	Red Box	*Sire*	10
37	38	WALK LIKE AN EGYPTIAN	Bangles	*CBS*	14
35	39	ONLY LOVE REMAINS	Paul McCartney	*Parlophone*	4
-	40	A SPACEMAN CAME TRAVELLING/THE BALLROOM OF ROMANCE	Chris De Burgh	*A&M*	1

LW	TW	*WEEK ENDING* 10 JANUARY 1987			Wks
1	1	REET PETITE	Jackie Wilson	*SMP*	6
2	2	CARAVAN OF LOVE	Housemartins	*Go! Discs*	6
8	3	IS THIS LOVE	Alison Moyet	*CBS*	6
3	4	THE FINAL COUNTDOWN	Europe	*Epic*	10
5	5	CRY WOLF	A-Ha	*Warner Bros*	6
4	6	OPEN YOUR HEART	Madonna	*Sire*	5
7	7	SOMETIMES	Erasure	*Mute*	9
6	8	THE RAIN	Oran 'Juice' Jones	*Def Jam*	7
12	9	BIG FUN	Gap Band	*Total Experience*	5
9	10	SHAKE YOU DOWN	Gregory Abbott	*CBS*	7
18	11	NO MORE THE FOOL	Elkie Brooks	*Legend*	5
11	12	SO COLD THE NIGHT	Communards	*London*	7
10	13	LIVIN' ON A PRAYER	Bon Jovi	*Vertigo*	12
14	14	LAND OF CONFUSION	Genesis	*Virgin*	8
17	15	STEP RIGHT UP	Jaki Graham	*EMI*	7
13	16	TAKE MY BREATH AWAY (LOVE THEME FROM 'TOP GUN')	Berlin	*CBS*	12
15	17	DREAMIN'	Status Quo	*Vertigo*	5
-	18	JACK YOUR BODY	Steve 'Silk' Hurley ●	*London*	1
25	19	HYMN TO HER	Pretenders	*Real*	4
31	20	OVER THE HILLS AND FAR AWAY	Gary Moore	*10*	4
20	21	EACH TIME YOU BREAK MY HEART	Nick Kamen	*WEA*	9
19	22	FRENCH KISSIN' IN THE USA	Debbie Harry	*Chrysalis*	9
21	23	BREAKOUT	Swing Out Sister	*Mercury*	11
33	24	BALLERINA GIRL	Lionel Richie	*Motown*	3
23	25	THE MIRACLE OF LOVE	Eurythmics	*RCA*	7
26	26	YOU KEEP ME HANGIN' ON	Kim Wilde	*MCA*	12
16	27	BECAUSE OF YOU	Dexy's Midnight Runners	*Mercury*	6
27	28	SHOWING OUT (GET FRESH AT THE WEEKEND)	Mel and Kim	*Supreme*	12
34	29	IF I SAY YES	Five Star	*Tent*	8
28	30	SHIVER	George Benson	*Warner Bros*	7
32	31	THE BOY IN THE BUBBLE	Paul Simon	*Warner Bros*	4
-	32	C'EST LA VIE	Robbie Nevil ●	*Manhattan*	1
22	33	SANTA CLAUS IS ON THE DOLE/FIRST ATHEIST TABERNACLE CHOIR	Spitting Image	*Virgin*	4
35	34	CANDY	Cameo	*Club*	7
38	35	WALK LIKE AN EGYPTIAN	Bangles	*CBS*	15
-	36	REAL WILD CHILD (WILD ONE)	Iggy Pop ●	*A&M*	1
30	37	ALL I ASK OF YOU	Cliff Richard and Sarah Brightman	*Polydor*	14
-	38	SURRENDER	Swing Out Sister	*Mercury*	1
36	39	SWEET LOVE	Anita Baker	*Elektra*	9
37	40	FOR AMERICA	Red Box	*Sire*	11

LW	TW	*WEEK ENDING* 17 JANUARY 1987			Wks
1	1	REET PETITE	Jackie Wilson	*SMP*	7
18	2	JACK YOUR BODY	Steve 'Silk' Hurley	*London*	2
3	3	IS THIS LOVE	Alison Moyet	*CBS*	7
9	4	BIG FUN	Gap Band	*Total Experience*	6
11	5	NO MORE THE FOOL	Elkie Brooks	*Legend*	6
32	6	C'EST LA VIE	Robbie Nevil	*Manhattan*	2
2	7	CARAVAN OF LOVE	Housemartins	*Go! Discs*	7
19	8	HYMN TO HER	Pretenders	*Real*	5
7	9	SOMETIMES	Erasure	*Mute*	10
38	10	SURRENDER	Swing Out Sister	*Mercury*	2
8	11	THE RAIN	Oran 'Juice' Jones	*Def Jam*	8
6	12	OPEN YOUR HEART	Madonna	*Sire*	6
5	13	CRY WOLF	A-Ha	*Warner Bros*	7
4	14	THE FINAL COUNTDOWN	Europe	*Epic*	11
-	15	IT DIDN'T MATTER	Style Council	*Polydor*	1
14	16	LAND OF CONFUSION	Genesis	*Virgin*	9
24	17	BALLERINA GIRL/DEEP RIVER WOMAN	Lionel Richie	*Motown*	4
36	18	REAL WILD CHILD (WILD ONE)	Iggy Pop	*A&M*	2
10	19	SHAKE YOU DOWN	Gregory Abbott	*CBS*	8
20	20	OVER THE HILLS AND FAR AWAY	Gary Moore	*10*	5
12	21	SO COLD THE NIGHT	Communards	*London*	8
13	22	LIVIN' ON A PRAYER	Bon Jovi	*Vertigo*	13
15	23	STEP RIGHT UP	Jaki Graham	*EMI*	8
-	24	WASTELAND	Mission	*Mercury*	1
16	25	TAKE MY BREATH AWAY (LOVE THEME FROM 'TOP GUN')	Berlin	*CBS*	13
31	26	THE BOY IN THE BUBBLE	Paul Simon	*Warner Bros*	5
17	27	DREAMIN'	Status Quo	*Vertigo*	6
-	28	WALKING DOWN YOUR STREET	Bangles	*CBS*	1
-	29	SOMETHING IN MY HOUSE	Dead Or Alive	*Epic*	1
-	30	THIS WHEEL'S ON FIRE	Siouxsie and the Banshees	*Wonderland*	1
-	31	RAT IN MI KITCHEN	UB40	*DEP International*	1
-	32	DOWN TO EARTH	Curiosity Killed The Cat ●	*Mercury*	1
-	33	TRAMPOLENE	Julian Cope	*Island*	1
-	34	ONCE BITTEN TWICE SHY	Vesta Williams ●	*A&M*	1
-	35	ALMAZ	Randy Crawford	*Warner Bros*	1
-	36	I LOVE MY RADIO	Taffy ●	*Transglobal*	1
-	37	I.O.U.	Freeez	*Citybeat*	1
23	38	BREAKOUT	Swing Out Sister	*Mercury*	12
-	39	VICTORY	Kool and the Gang	*Club*	1
-	40	JACK THE GROOVE	Raze ●	*Champion*	1

In these weeks ■ After two quiet weeks at the beginning of the year, there are fourteen new entries in the Top 40, including four by brand new acts (17.01.87) ■ Jackie Wilson's *Reet Petite* finally dropped from the top, 29 years and 10 weeks after it first hit the charts. This is, by over three years, the longest ever period between initial chart entry of a record and its final fall from the top (17.01.87)■

□ Highest position disc reached ● Act's first ever week on chart

WEEK ENDING 24 JANUARY 1987

LW	TW	Title / Artist	Label	Wks
2	[1]	JACK YOUR BODY Steve 'Silk' Hurley	London	3
1	2	REET PETITE Jackie Wilson	SMP	8
3	[3]	IS THIS LOVE Alison Moyet	CBS	8
6	4	C'EST LA VIE Robbie Nevil	Manhattan	3
5	[5]	NO MORE THE FOOL Elkie Brooks	Legend	7
4	6	BIG FUN Gap Band	Total Experience	7
10	[7]	SURRENDER Swing Out Sister	Mercury	3
8	[8]	HYMN TO HER Pretenders	Real	6
15	[9]	IT DIDN'T MATTER Style Council	Polydor	2
18	[10]	REAL WILD CHILD (WILD ONE) Iggy Pop	A&M	3
24	[11]	WASTELAND Mission	Mercury	2
29	[12]	SOMETHING IN MY HOUSE Dead Or Alive	Epic	2
31	13	RAT IN MI KITCHEN UB40	DEP International	2
30	[14]	THIS WHEEL'S ON FIRE Siouxsie and the Banshees	Wonderland	2
32	15	DOWN TO EARTH Curiosity Killed The Cat	Mercury	2
28	[16]	WALKING DOWN YOUR STREET Bangles	CBS	2
9	17	SOMETIMES Erasure	Mute	11
11	18	THE RAIN Oran 'Juice' Jones	Def Jam	9
17	19	BALLERINA GIRL/DEEP RIVER WOMAN Lionel Richie	Motown	5
35	20	ALMAZ Randy Crawford	Warner Bros	2
40	21	JACK THE GROOVE Raze	Champion	2
-	22	HEARTACHE Pepsi and Shirlie ●	Polydor	1
37	[23]	I.O.U. Freeez	Citybeat	2
36	24	I LOVE MY RADIO Taffy	Transglobal	2
7	25	CARAVAN OF LOVE Housemartins	Go! Discs	8
34	26	ONCE BITTEN TWICE SHY Vesta Williams	A&M	2
16	27	LAND OF CONFUSION Genesis	Virgin	10
19	28	SHAKE YOU DOWN Gregory Abbott	CBS	9
20	29	OVER THE HILLS AND FAR AWAY Gary Moore	10	6
13	30	CRY WOLF A-Ha	Warner Bros	8
12	31	OPEN YOUR HEART Madonna	Sire	7
14	32	THE FINAL COUNTDOWN Europe	Epic	12
33	33	TRAMPOLENE Julian Cope	Island	2
39	34	VICTORY Kool and the Gang	Club	2
-	35	YOU SEXY THING Hot Chocolate	EMI	1
26	36	THE BOY IN THE BUBBLE Paul Simon	Warner Bros	6
22	37	LIVIN' ON A PRAYER Bon Jovi	Vertigo	14
21	38	SO COLD THE NIGHT Communards	London	9
-	39	BEHIND THE MASK Eric Clapton	Duck	1
-	40	LOVE IS FOREVER Billy Ocean	Jive	1

WEEK ENDING 31 JANUARY 1987

LW	TW	Title / Artist	Label	Wks
1	[1]	JACK YOUR BODY Steve 'Silk' Hurley	London	4
-	2	I KNEW YOU WERE WAITING (FOR ME) Aretha Franklin and George Michael ●	Epic	1
4	[3]	C'EST LA VIE Robbie Nevil	Manhattan	4
3	4	IS THIS LOVE Alison Moyet	CBS	9
5	[5]	NO MORE THE FOOL Elkie Brooks	Legend	8
2	6	REET PETITE Jackie Wilson	SMP	9
22	7	HEARTACHE Pepsi and Shirlie	Polydor	2
15	8	DOWN TO EARTH Curiosity Killed The Cat	Mercury	3
7	9	SURRENDER Swing Out Sister	Mercury	4
20	10	ALMAZ Randy Crawford	Warner Bros	3
6	11	BIG FUN Gap Band	Total Experience	8
13	[12]	RAT IN MI KITCHEN UB40	DEP International	3
11	13	WASTELAND Mission	Mercury	3
12	14	SOMETHING IN MY HOUSE Dead Or Alive	Epic	3
24	15	I LOVE MY RADIO Taffy	Transglobal	3
8	16	HYMN TO HER Pretenders	Real	7
10	17	REAL WILD CHILD (WILD ONE) Iggy Pop	A&M	4
14	18	THIS WHEEL'S ON FIRE Siouxsie and the Banshees	Wonderland	3
9	19	IT DIDN'T MATTER Style Council	Polydor	3
21	[20]	JACK THE GROOVE Raze	Champion	3
35	21	YOU SEXY THING Hot Chocolate	EMI	2
16	22	WALKING DOWN YOUR STREET Bangles	CBS	3
23	[23]	I.O.U. Freeez	Citybeat	3
-	24	THE MUSIC OF THE NIGHT/WISHING YOU WERE SOMEHOW HERE Michael Crawford ●/Sarah Brightman	Polydor	1
26	25	ONCE BITTEN TWICE SHY Vesta Williams	A&M	3
19	26	BALLERINA GIRL/DEEP RIVER WOMAN Lionel Richie	Motown	6
-	27	IT DOESN'T HAVE TO BE THIS WAY Blow Monkeys	RCA	1
39	28	BEHIND THE MASK Eric Clapton	Duck	2
-	29	MAGIC SMILE Rosie Vela ●	A&M	1
34	[30]	VICTORY Kool and the Gang	Club	3
17	31	SOMETIMES Erasure	Mute	12
18	32	THE RAIN Oran 'Juice' Jones	Def Jam	10
33	33	TRAMPOLENE Julian Cope	Island	3
40	[34]	LOVE IS FOREVER Billy Ocean	Jive	2
-	35	CROSS THAT BRIDGE Ward Brothers ●	Siren	1
-	[36]	BEST KEPT SECRET China Crisis	Virgin	1
28	37	SHAKE YOU DOWN Gregory Abbott	CBS	10
25	38	CARAVAN OF LOVE Housemartins	Go! Discs	9
-	[39]	YOU DON'T KNOW Berlin	Mercury	1
31	40	OPEN YOUR HEART Madonna	Sire	8

WEEK ENDING 7 FEBRUARY 1987

LW	TW	Title / Artist	Label	Wks
2	[1]	I KNEW YOU WERE WAITING (FOR ME) Aretha Franklin and George Michael	Epic	2
7	[2]	HEARTACHE Pepsi and Shirlie	Polydor	3
1	3	JACK YOUR BODY Steve 'Silk' Hurley	London	5
10	[4]	ALMAZ Randy Crawford	Warner Bros	4
8	5	DOWN TO EARTH Curiosity Killed The Cat	Mercury	4
3	6	C'EST LA VIE Robbie Nevil	Manhattan	5
15	7	I LOVE MY RADIO Taffy	Transglobal	4
5	8	NO MORE THE FOOL Elkie Brooks	Legend	9
9	9	SURRENDER Swing Out Sister	Mercury	5
4	10	IS THIS LOVE Alison Moyet	CBS	10
27	11	IT DOESN'T HAVE TO BE THIS WAY Blow Monkeys	RCA	2
-	[12]	SHOPLIFTERS OF THE WORLD UNITE Smiths	Rough Trade	1
6	13	REET PETITE Jackie Wilson	SMP	10
21	14	YOU SEXY THING Hot Chocolate	EMI	3
12	15	RAT IN MI KITCHEN UB40	DEP International	4
25	16	ONCE BITTEN TWICE SHY Vesta Williams	A&M	4
11	17	BIG FUN Gap Band	Total Experience	9
16	18	HYMN TO HER Pretenders	Real	8
24	19	THE MUSIC OF THE NIGHT/WISHING YOU WERE SOMEHOW HERE Michael Crawford/Sarah Brightman	Polydor	2
20	[20]	JACK THE GROOVE Raze	Champion	4
14	21	SOMETHING IN MY HOUSE Dead Or Alive	Epic	4
13	22	WASTELAND Mission	Mercury	4
28	23	BEHIND THE MASK Eric Clapton	Duck	3
-	24	STAY OUT OF MY LIFE Five Star	Tent	1
-	25	MALE STRIPPER Man 2 Man meets Man Parrish ●	Bolts	1
17	26	REAL WILD CHILD (WILD ONE) Iggy Pop	A&M	5
29	[27]	MAGIC SMILE Rosie Vela	A&M	2
-	28	ROCK THE NIGHT Europe	Epic	1
18	29	THIS WHEEL'S ON FIRE Siouxsie and the Banshees	Wonderland	4
23	30	I.O.U. Freeez	Citybeat	4
33	[31]	TRAMPOLENE Julian Cope	Island	4
35	[32]	CROSS THAT BRIDGE Ward Brothers	Siren	2
-	33	THE FUTURE'S SO BRIGHT I GOTTA WEAR SHADES Timbuk 3 ●	IRS	1
19	34	IT DIDN'T MATTER Style Council	Polydor	4
30	35	VICTORY Kool and the Gang	Club	4
-	36	GIGOLO Damned	MCA	1
34	[37]	LOVE IS FOREVER Billy Ocean	Jive	3
-	38	COMING AROUND AGAIN Carly Simon	Arista	1
36	39	BEST KEPT SECRET China Crisis	Virgin	2
39	40	YOU DON'T KNOW Berlin	Mercury	2

■Eleven of the top 16 records in the chart were at their peak, and three of the other five were still climbing (24.01.87) ■ Legendary American rocker Iggy Pop enjoyed his only Top 40 hit, years after his greatest live successes, with his version of a song written by Australian chart star Johnny O'Keefe and first recorded in America by 'Ivan', who was really Jerry Allison of the Crickets (24.01.87)■

February 1987

□ Highest position disc reached ● Act's first ever week on chart

WEEK ENDING 14 FEBRUARY 1987

LW	TW	Title / Artist	Label	Wks
1	1	I KNEW YOU WERE WAITING (FOR ME) Aretha Franklin and George Michael	*Epic*	3
2	2	HEARTACHE Pepsi and Shirlie	*Polydor*	4
5	3	DOWN TO EARTH Curiosity Killed The Cat	*Mercury*	5
4	4	ALMAZ Randy Crawford	*Warner Bros*	5
11	5	IT DOESN'T HAVE TO BE THIS WAY Blow Monkeys	*RCA*	3
7	6	I LOVE MY RADIO Taffy	*Transglobal*	5
19	7	THE MUSIC OF THE NIGHT/WISHING YOU WERE SOMEHOW HERE Michael Crawford/Sarah Brightman	*Polydor*	3
3	8	JACK YOUR BODY Steve 'Silk' Hurley	*London*	6
25	9	MALE STRIPPER Man 2 Man meets Man Parrish	*Bolts*	2
14	10	YOU SEXY THING Hot Chocolate	*EMI*	4
24	11	STAY OUT OF MY LIFE Five Star	*Tent*	2
12	12	SHOPLIFTERS OF THE WORLD UNITE Smiths	*Rough Trade*	2
8	13	NO MORE THE FOOL Elkie Brooks	*Legend*	10
16	14	ONCE BITTEN TWICE SHY Vesta Williams	*A&M*	5
10	15	IS THIS LOVE Alison Moyet	*CBS*	11
6	16	C'EST LA VIE Robbie Nevil	*Manhattan*	6
23	17	BEHIND THE MASK Eric Clapton	*Duck*	4
-	18	RUNNING IN THE FAMILY Level 42	*Polydor*	1
-	19	STAND BY ME Ben E King	*Atlantic*	1
28	20	ROCK THE NIGHT Europe	*Epic*	2
9	21	SURRENDER Swing Out Sister	*Mercury*	6
38	22	COMING AROUND AGAIN Carly Simon	*Arista*	2
13	23	REET PETITE Jackie Wilson	*SMP*	11
15	24	RAT IN MI KITCHEN UB40	*DEP International*	5
33	25	THE FUTURE'S SO BRIGHT I GOTTA WEAR SHADES Timbuk 3	*IRS*	2
17	26	BIG FUN Gap Band	*Total Experience*	10
27	27	MAGIC SMILE Rosie Vela	*A&M*	3
-	28	WHEN A MAN LOVES A WOMAN Percy Sledge	*Atlantic*	1
36	29	GIGOLO Damned	*MCA*	2
-	30	CRUSH ON YOU Jets ●	*MCA*	1
21	31	SOMETHING IN MY HOUSE Dead Or Alive	*Epic*	5
18	32	HYMN TO HER Pretenders	*Real*	9
22	33	WASTELAND Mission	*Mercury*	5
32	34	CROSS THAT BRIDGE Ward Brothers	*Siren*	3
-	35	FORGOTTEN TOWN Christians ●	*Island*	1
20	36	JACK THE GROOVE Raze	*Champion*	5
37	37	LOVE IS FOREVER Billy Ocean	*Jive*	4
30	38	I.O.U. Freeez	*Citybeat*	5
-	39	LIVE IT UP Mental As Anything ●	*Epic*	1
29	40	THIS WHEEL'S ON FIRE Siouxsie and the Banshees	*Wonderland*	5

WEEK ENDING 21 FEBRUARY 1987

LW	TW	Title / Artist	Label	Wks
19	1	STAND BY ME Ben E King	*Atlantic*	2
1	2	I KNEW YOU WERE WAITING (FOR ME) Aretha Franklin and George Michael	*Epic*	4
5	3	DOWN TO EARTH Curiosity Killed The Cat	*Mercury*	6
2	4	HEARTACHE Pepsi and Shirlie	*Polydor*	5
28	5	WHEN A MAN LOVES A WOMAN Percy Sledge	*Atlantic*	2
9	6	MALE STRIPPER Man 2 Man meets Man Parrish	*Bolts*	3
4	7	ALMAZ Randy Crawford	*Warner Bros*	6
5	8	IT DOESN'T HAVE TO BE THIS WAY Blow Monkeys	*RCA*	4
11	9	STAY OUT OF MY LIFE Five Star	*Tent*	3
18	10	RUNNING IN THE FAMILY Level 42	*Polydor*	2
7	11	THE MUSIC OF THE NIGHT/WISHING YOU WERE SOMEHOW HERE Michael Crawford/Sarah Brightman	*Polydor*	4
6	12	I LOVE MY RADIO Taffy	*Transglobal*	6
10	13	YOU SEXY THING Hot Chocolate	*EMI*	5
22	14	COMING AROUND AGAIN Carly Simon	*Arista*	3
17	15	BEHIND THE MASK Eric Clapton	*Duck*	5
14	16	ONCE BITTEN TWICE SHY Vesta Williams	*A&M*	6
20	17	ROCK THE NIGHT Europe	*Epic*	3
30	18	CRUSH ON YOU Jets	*MCA*	2
39	19	LIVE IT UP Mental As Anything	*Epic*	2
8	20	JACK YOUR BODY Steve 'Silk' Hurley	*London*	7
25	21	THE FUTURE'S SO BRIGHT I GOTTA WEAR SHADES Timbuk 3	*IRS*	3
-	22	SONIC BOOM BOY Westworld ●	*RCA*	1
-	23	THE RIGHT THING Simply Red	*WEA*	1
12	24	SHOPLIFTERS OF THE WORLD UNITE Smiths	*Rough Trade*	3
-	25	SKIN TRADE Duran Duran	*EMI*	1
-	26	YOU ARE MY WORLD ('87) Communards	*London*	1
13	27	NO MORE THE FOOL Elkie Brooks	*Legend*	11
15	28	IS THIS LOVE Alison Moyet	*CBS*	12
35	29	FORGOTTEN TOWN Christians	*Island*	2
16	30	C'EST LA VIE Robbie Nevil	*Manhattan*	7
21	31	SURRENDER Swing Out Sister	*Mercury*	7
27	32	MAGIC SMILE Rosie Vela	*A&M*	4
23	33	REET PETITE Jackie Wilson	*SMP*	12
24	34	RAT IN MI KITCHEN UB40	*DEP International*	6
-	35	HOW MANY LIES Spandau Ballet	*Reformation*	1
-	36	HAVE YOU EVER LOVED SOMEBODY Freddie Jackson	*Capitol*	1
-	37	GOOD TO GO LOVER/OUTSIDE IN THE RAIN Gwen Guthrie	*Boiling Point*	1
-	38	SOUL MAN Sam Moore and Lou Reed ●	*A&M*	1
26	39	BIG FUN Gap Band	*Total Experience*	11
-	40	TRICK OF THE NIGHT Bananarama	*London*	1

WEEK ENDING 28 FEBRUARY 1987

LW	TW	Title / Artist	Label	Wks
1	1	STAND BY ME Ben E King	*Atlantic*	3
5	2	WHEN A MAN LOVES A WOMAN Percy Sledge	*Atlantic*	3
3	3	DOWN TO EARTH Curiosity Killed The Cat	*Mercury*	7
6	4	MALE STRIPPER Man 2 Man meets Man Parrish	*Bolts*	4
2	5	I KNEW YOU WERE WAITING (FOR ME) Aretha Franklin and George Michael	*Epic*	5
4	6	HEARTACHE Pepsi and Shirlie	*Polydor*	6
10	7	RUNNING IN THE FAMILY Level 42	*Polydor*	3
19	8	LIVE IT UP Mental As Anything	*Epic*	3
18	9	CRUSH ON YOU Jets	*MCA*	3
14	10	COMING AROUND AGAIN Carly Simon	*Arista*	4
22	11	SONIC BOOM BOY Westworld	*RCA*	2
17	12	ROCK THE NIGHT Europe	*Epic*	4
9	13	STAY OUT OF MY LIFE Five Star	*Tent*	4
8	14	IT DOESN'T HAVE TO BE THIS WAY Blow Monkeys	*RCA*	5
23	15	THE RIGHT THING Simply Red	*WEA*	2
15	16	BEHIND THE MASK Eric Clapton	*Duck*	6
-	17	MANHATTAN SKYLINE A-Ha	*Warner Bros*	1
-	18	LOVE REMOVAL MACHINE Cult	*Beggars Banquet*	1
11	19	THE MUSIC OF THE NIGHT/WISHING YOU WERE SOMEHOW HERE Michael Crawford/Sarah Brightman	*Polydor*	5
13	20	YOU SEXY THING Hot Chocolate	*EMI*	6
26	21	YOU ARE MY WORLD ('87) Communards	*London*	2
7	22	ALMAZ Randy Crawford	*Warner Bros*	7
-	23	I GET THE SWEETEST FEELING Jackie Wilson	*SMP*	1
25	24	SKIN TRADE Duran Duran	*EMI*	2
12	25	I LOVE MY RADIO Taffy	*Transglobal*	7
16	26	ONCE BITTEN TWICE SHY Vesta Williams	*A&M*	7
29	27	FORGOTTEN TOWN Christians	*Island*	3
-	28	IT DOESN'T HAVE TO BE Erasure	*Mute*	1
21	29	THE FUTURE'S SO BRIGHT I GOTTA WEAR SHADES Timbuk 3	*IRS*	4
38	30	SOUL MAN Sam Moore and Lou Reed	*A&M*	2
-	31	MISSIONARY MAN Eurythmics	*RCA*	1
40	32	TRICK OF THE NIGHT Bananarama	*London*	2
36	33	HAVE YOU EVER LOVED SOMEBODY Freddie Jackson	*Capitol*	2
35	34	HOW MANY LIES Spandau Ballet	*Reformation*	2
20	35	JACK YOUR BODY Steve 'Silk' Hurley	*London*	8
-	36	(YOU GOTTA) FIGHT FOR YOUR RIGHT (TO PARTY) Beastie Boys ●	*Def Jam*	1
-	37	I AM THE LAW Anthrax ●	*Island*	1
33	38	REET PETITE Jackie Wilson	*SMP*	13
37	39	GOOD TO GO LOVER/OUTSIDE IN THE RAIN Gwen Guthrie	*Boiling Point*	2
-	40	WHO IS IT Mantronix	*10*	1

In these weeks ■ The top 7 records were all at their peak, a chart record (14.02.87) ■ Only four weeks after Jackie Wilson's 1957 hit drops from the top spot, Ben E. King's 1961 classic *Stand By Me* makes the 7th biggest jump ever to number one from number 19 (21.02.87)■

March 1987

□ Highest position disc reached ● Act's first ever week on chart

LW	TW	WEEK ENDING 7 MARCH 1987		Wks
1	[1]	STAND BY ME Ben E King	Atlantic	4
2	[2]	WHEN A MAN LOVES A WOMAN Percy Sledge	Atlantic	4
8	[3]	LIVE IT UP Mental As Anything	Epic	4
4	[4]	MALE STRIPPER Man 2 Man meets Man Parrish	Bolts	5
9	[5]	CRUSH ON YOU Jets	MCA	4
7	[6]	RUNNING IN THE FAMILY Level 42	Polydor	4
-	7	EVERYTHING I OWN Boy George ●	Virgin	1
3	8	DOWN TO EARTH Curiosity Killed The Cat	Mercury	8
-	9	THE GREAT PRETENDER Freddie Mercury	Parlophone	1
23	10	I GET THE SWEETEST FEELING Jackie Wilson	SMP	2
15	[11]	THE RIGHT THING Simply Red	WEA	3
10	12	COMING AROUND AGAIN Carly Simon	Arista	5
17	[13]	MANHATTAN SKYLINE A-Ha	Warner Bros	2
11	14	SONIC BOOM BOY Westworld	RCA	3
6	15	HEARTACHE Pepsi and Shirlie	Polydor	7
12	16	ROCK THE NIGHT Europe	Epic	5
5	17	I KNEW YOU WERE WAITING (FOR ME) Aretha Franklin and George Michael	Epic	6
18	[18]	LOVE REMOVAL MACHINE Cult	Beggars Banquet	2
13	19	STAY OUT OF MY LIFE Five Star	Tent	5
28	20	IT DOESN'T HAVE TO BE Erasure	Mute	2
16	21	BEHIND THE MASK Eric Clapton	Duck	7
24	[22]	SKIN TRADE Duran Duran	EMI	3
21	23	YOU ARE MY WORLD ('87) Communards	London	3
14	24	IT DOESN'T HAVE TO BE THIS WAY Blow Monkeys	RCA	6
-	25	RESPECTABLE Mel and Kim	Supreme	1
36	26	(YOU GOTTA) FIGHT FOR YOUR RIGHT (TO PARTY) Beastie Boys	Def Jam	2
27	27	FORGOTTEN TOWN Christians	Island	4
19	28	THE MUSIC OF THE NIGHT/WISHING YOU WERE SOMEHOW HERE Michael Crawford/Sarah Brightman	Polydor	6
-	29	'MOONLIGHTING' THEME Al Jarreau	WEA	1
-	30	WEAK IN THE PRESENCE OF BEAUTY Alison Moyet	CBS	1
31	[31]	MISSIONARY MAN Eurythmics	RCA	2
37	[32]	I AM THE LAW Anthrax	Island	2
20	33	YOU SEXY THING Hot Chocolate	EMI	7
22	34	ALMAZ Randy Crawford	Warner Bros	8
30	35	SOUL MAN Sam Moore and Lou Reed	A&M	3
25	36	I LOVE MY RADIO Taffy	Transglobal	8
-	37	WATCHING THE WILDLIFE Frankie Goes To Hollywood	ZTT	1
-	38	WILD FRONTIER Gary Moore	10	1
-	39	LOVING YOU IS SWEETER THAN EVER Nick Kamen	WEA	1
32	40	TRICK OF THE NIGHT Bananarama	London	3

LW	TW	WEEK ENDING 14 MARCH 1987		Wks
7	[1]	EVERYTHING I OWN Boy George	Virgin	2
1	2	STAND BY ME Ben E King	Atlantic	5
10	[3]	I GET THE SWEETEST FEELING Jackie Wilson	SMP	3
9	[4]	THE GREAT PRETENDER Freddie Mercury	Parlophone	2
3	5	LIVE IT UP Mental As Anything	Epic	5
2	6	WHEN A MAN LOVES A WOMAN Percy Sledge	Atlantic	5
25	7	RESPECTABLE Mel and Kim	Supreme	2
5	8	CRUSH ON YOU Jets	MCA	5
4	9	MALE STRIPPER Man 2 Man meets Man Parrish	Bolts	6
6	10	RUNNING IN THE FAMILY Level 42	Polydor	5
29	11	'MOONLIGHTING' THEME Al Jarreau	WEA	2
11	12	THE RIGHT THING Simply Red	WEA	4
12	13	COMING AROUND AGAIN Carly Simon	Arista	6
13	14	MANHATTAN SKYLINE A-Ha	Warner Bros	3
8	15	DOWN TO EARTH Curiosity Killed The Cat	Mercury	9
30	16	WEAK IN THE PRESENCE OF BEAUTY Alison Moyet	CBS	2
20	17	IT DOESN'T HAVE TO BE Erasure	Mute	3
14	18	SONIC BOOM BOY Westworld	RCA	4
18	19	LOVE REMOVAL MACHINE Cult	Beggars Banquet	3
-	20	SIGN 'O' THE TIMES Prince	Paisley Park	1
26	21	(YOU GOTTA) FIGHT FOR YOUR RIGHT (TO PARTY) Beastie Boys	Def Jam	3
27	[22]	FORGOTTEN TOWN Christians	Island	5
16	23	ROCK THE NIGHT Europe	Epic	6
-	24	TONIGHT TONIGHT TONIGHT Genesis	Virgin	1
39	25	LOVING YOU IS SWEETER THAN EVER Nick Kamen	WEA	2
22	26	SKIN TRADE Duran Duran	EMI	4
15	27	HEARTACHE Pepsi and Shirlie	Polydor	8
17	28	I KNEW YOU WERE WAITING (FOR ME) Aretha Franklin and George Michael	Epic	7
23	29	YOU ARE MY WORLD ('87) Communards	London	4
19	30	STAY OUT OF MY LIFE Five Star	Tent	6
-	31	RESPECT YOURSELF Bruce Willis ●	Motown	1
-	32	SEVERINA Mission	Mercury	1
37	33	WATCHING THE WILDLIFE Frankie Goes To Hollywood	ZTT	2
32	34	I AM THE LAW Anthrax	Island	3
38	[35]	WILD FRONTIER Gary Moore	10	2
21	36	BEHIND THE MASK Eric Clapton	Duck	8
24	37	IT DOESN'T HAVE TO BE THIS WAY Blow Monkeys	RCA	7
-	38	DON'T NEED A GUN Billy Idol	Chrysalis	1
35	39	SOUL MAN Sam Moore and Lou Reed	A&M	4
31	40	MISSIONARY MAN Eurythmics	RCA	3

LW	TW	WEEK ENDING 21 MARCH 1987		Wks
1	[1]	EVERYTHING I OWN Boy George	Virgin	3
7	2	RESPECTABLE Mel and Kim	Supreme	3
3	[3]	I GET THE SWEETEST FEELING Jackie Wilson	SMP	4
4	[4]	THE GREAT PRETENDER Freddie Mercury	Parlophone	3
5	5	LIVE IT UP Mental As Anything	Epic	6
2	6	STAND BY ME Ben E King	Atlantic	6
16	7	WEAK IN THE PRESENCE OF BEAUTY Alison Moyet	CBS	3
11	[8]	'MOONLIGHTING' THEME Al Jarreau	WEA	3
6	9	WHEN A MAN LOVES A WOMAN Percy Sledge	Atlantic	6
8	10	CRUSH ON YOU Jets	MCA	6
31	11	RESPECT YOURSELF Bruce Willis	Motown	2
10	12	RUNNING IN THE FAMILY Level 42	Polydor	6
9	13	MALE STRIPPER Man 2 Man meets Man Parrish	Bolts	7
21	14	(YOU GOTTA) FIGHT FOR YOUR RIGHT (TO PARTY) Beastie Boys	Def Jam	4
17	15	IT DOESN'T HAVE TO BE Erasure	Mute	4
20	16	SIGN 'O' THE TIMES Prince	Paisley Park	2
25	17	LOVING YOU IS SWEETER THAN EVER Nick Kamen	WEA	3
12	18	THE RIGHT THING Simply Red	WEA	5
24	19	TONIGHT TONIGHT TONIGHT Genesis	Virgin	2
13	20	COMING AROUND AGAIN Carly Simon	Arista	7
14	21	MANHATTAN SKYLINE A-Ha	Warner Bros	4
22	[22]	FORGOTTEN TOWN Christians	Island	6
15	23	DOWN TO EARTH Curiosity Killed The Cat	Mercury	10
18	24	SONIC BOOM BOY Westworld	RCA	5
32	[25]	SEVERINA Mission	Mercury	2
38	[26]	DON'T NEED A GUN Billy Idol	Chrysalis	2
27	27	HEARTACHE Pepsi and Shirlie	Polydor	9
33	[28]	WATCHING THE WILDLIFE Frankie Goes To Hollywood	ZTT	3
19	29	LOVE REMOVAL MACHINE Cult	Beggars Banquet	4
23	30	ROCK THE NIGHT Europe	Epic	7
-	31	LET'S WAIT AWHILE Janet Jackson	Breakout	1
29	32	YOU ARE MY WORLD ('87) Communards	London	5
-	33	I'D RATHER GO BLIND Ruby Turner	Jive	1
26	34	SKIN TRADE Duran Duran	EMI	5
28	35	I KNEW YOU WERE WAITING (FOR ME) Aretha Franklin and George Michael	Epic	8
-	36	SEXY GIRL Lillo Thomas ●	Capitol	1
-	37	WHAT YOU GET IS WHAT YOU SEE Tina Turner	Capitol	1
-	38	IF YOU LET ME STAY Terence Trent D'Arby ●	CBS	1
30	39	STAY OUT OF MY LIFE Five Star	Tent	7
35	40	WILD FRONTIER Gary Moore	10	3

LW	TW	WEEK ENDING 28 MARCH 1987		Wks
2	[1]	RESPECTABLE Mel and Kim	Supreme	4
1	2	EVERYTHING I OWN Boy George	Virgin	4
3	[3]	I GET THE SWEETEST FEELING Jackie Wilson	SMP	5
-	[4]	WITH OR WITHOUT YOU U2	Island	1

■Of the top six singles, three were singles re-issued from over fifteen years before, two were remakes of post hits and only one was a new recording of a new song *Live It Up* by Mental As Anything (14.03.87) ■ *Everything I Own* becomes the eleventh song to hit number one in two different versions (14.03.87)■

March 1987

□ Highest position disc reached ● Act's first ever week on chart

LW	TW	Title	Artist	Label	Wks
4	5	THE GREAT PRETENDER	Freddie Mercury	Parlophone	4
7	6	WEAK IN THE PRESENCE OF BEAUTY	Alison Moyet	CBS	4
11	7	RESPECT YOURSELF	Bruce Willis	Motown	3
5	8	LIVE IT UP	Mental As Anything	Epic	7
31	9	LET'S WAIT AWHILE	Janet Jackson	Breakout	2
16	10	SIGN 'O' THE TIMES	Prince	Paisley Park	3
14	11	(YOU GOTTA) FIGHT FOR YOUR RIGHT (TO PARTY)	Beastie Boys	Def Jam	5
15	12	IT DOESN'T HAVE TO BE	Erasure	Mute	5
8	13	'MOONLIGHTING' THEME	Al Jarreau	WEA	4
6	14	STAND BY ME	Ben E King	Atlantic	7
-	15	BIG TIME	Peter Gabriel	Virgin	1
17	16	LOVING YOU IS SWEETER THAN EVER	Nick Kamen	WEA	4
10	17	CRUSH ON YOU	Jets	MCA	7
19	18	TONIGHT TONIGHT TONIGHT	Genesis	Virgin	3
9	19	WHEN A MAN LOVES A WOMAN	Percy Sledge	Atlantic	7
13	20	MALE STRIPPER	Man 2 Man meets Man Parrish	Bolts	8
12	21	RUNNING IN THE FAMILY	Level 42	Polydor	7
38	22	IF YOU LET ME STAY	Terence Trent D'Arby	CBS	2
36	23	SEXY GIRL	Lillo Thomas	Capitol	2
-	24	LEAN ON ME	Club Nouveau ●	King Jay	1
-	25	EVER FALLEN IN LOVE	Fine Young Cannibals	London	1
25	26	SEVERINA	Mission	Mercury	3
33	27	I'D RATHER GO BLIND	Ruby Turner	Jive	2
18	28	THE RIGHT THING	Simply Red	WEA	6
22	29	FORGOTTEN TOWN	Christians	Island	7
37	30	WHAT YOU GET IS WHAT YOU SEE	Tina Turner	Capitol	2
20	31	COMING AROUND AGAIN	Carly Simon	Arista	8
26	32	DON'T NEED A GUN	Billy Idol	Chrysalis	3
28	33	WATCHING THE WILDLIFE	Frankie Goes To Hollywood	ZTT	4
-	34	THE IRISH ROVER	Pogues and the Dubliners ●	Stiff	1
24	35	SONIC BOOM BOY	Westworld	RCA	6
21	36	MANHATTAN SKYLINE	A-Ha	Warner Bros	5
23	37	DOWN TO EARTH	Curiosity Killed The Cat	Mercury	11
-	38	LET MY PEOPLE GO GO	Rainmakers ●	Mercury	1
-	39	STILL OF THE NIGHT	Whitesnake	EMI	1
-	40	KEEP YOUR EYE ON ME	Herb Alpert	Breakout	1

WEEK ENDING 4 APRIL 1987

LW	TW	Title	Artist	Label	Wks
-	1	LET IT BE	Ferry Aid ●	Sun	1
1	2	RESPECTABLE	Mel and Kim	Supreme	5
9	3	LET'S WAIT AWHILE	Janet Jackson	Breakout	3
4	4	WITH OR WITHOUT YOU	U2	Island	2
-	5	LA ISLA BONITA	Madonna	Sire	1
2	6	EVERYTHING I OWN	Boy George	Virgin	5
24	7	LEAN ON ME	Club Nouveau	King Jay	2
6	8	WEAK IN THE PRESENCE OF BEAUTY	Alison Moyet	CBS	5
3	9	I GET THE SWEETEST FEELING	Jackie Wilson	SMP	6
5	10	THE GREAT PRETENDER	Freddie Mercury	Parlophone	5
7	11	RESPECT YOURSELF	Bruce Willis	Motown	4
10	12	SIGN 'O' THE TIMES	Prince	Paisley Park	4
15	13	BIG TIME	Peter Gabriel	Virgin	2
8	14	LIVE IT UP	Mental As Anything	Epic	8
22	15	IF YOU LET ME STAY	Terence Trent D'Arby	CBS	3
11	16	(YOU GOTTA) FIGHT FOR YOUR RIGHT (TO PARTY)	Beastie Boys	Def Jam	6
25	17	EVER FALLEN IN LOVE	Fine Young Cannibals	London	2
16	18	LOVING YOU IS SWEETER THAN EVER	Nick Kamen	WEA	5
12	19	IT DOESN'T HAVE TO BE	Erasure	Mute	6
13	20	'MOONLIGHTING' THEME	Al Jarreau	WEA	5
34	21	THE IRISH ROVER	Pogues and the Dubliners	Stiff	2
-	22	ORDINARY DAY	Curiosity Killed The Cat	Mercury	1
14	23	STAND BY ME	Ben E King	Atlantic	8
27	24	I'D RATHER GO BLIND	Ruby Turner	Jive	3
18	25	TONIGHT TONIGHT TONIGHT	Genesis	Virgin	4
23	26	SEXY GIRL	Lillo Thomas	Capitol	3
39	27	STILL OF THE NIGHT	Whitesnake	EMI	2
20	28	MALE STRIPPER	Man 2 Man meets Man Parrish	Bolts	9
19	29	WHEN A MAN LOVES A WOMAN	Percy Sledge	Atlantic	8
-	30	DAY IN DAY OUT	David Bowie	EMI America	1
17	31	CRUSH ON YOU	Jets	MCA	8
30	32	WHAT YOU GET IS WHAT YOU SEE	Tina Turner	Capitol	3
40	33	KEEP YOUR EYE ON ME	Herb Alpert	Breakout	2
38	34	LET MY PEOPLE GO GO	Rainmakers	Mercury	2
29	35	FORGOTTEN TOWN	Christians	Island	8
21	36	RUNNING IN THE FAMILY	Level 42	Polydor	8
-	37	CAN'T BE WITH YOU TONIGHT	Judy Boucher ●	Orbitone	1
-	38	OUT WITH HER	Blow Monkeys	RCA	1
26	39	SEVERINA	Mission	Mercury	4
28	40	THE RIGHT THING	Simply Red	WEA	7

WEEK ENDING 11 APRIL 1987

LW	TW	Title	Artist	Label	Wks
1	1	LET IT BE	Ferry Aid	Sun	2
2	2	RESPECTABLE	Mel and Kim	Supreme	6
5	3	LA ISLA BONITA	Madonna	Sire	2
3	4	LET'S WAIT AWHILE	Janet Jackson	Breakout	4
4	5	WITH OR WITHOUT YOU	U2	Island	3
7	6	LEAN ON ME	Club Nouveau	King Jay	3
15	7	IF YOU LET ME STAY	Terence Trent D'Arby	CBS	4
21	8	THE IRISH ROVER	Pogues and the Dubliners	Stiff	3
8	9	WEAK IN THE PRESENCE OF BEAUTY	Alison Moyet	CBS	6
17	10	EVER FALLEN IN LOVE	Fine Young Cannibals	London	3
22	11	ORDINARY DAY	Curiosity Killed The Cat	Mercury	2
9	12	I GET THE SWEETEST FEELING	Jackie Wilson	SMP	7
6	13	EVERYTHING I OWN	Boy George	Virgin	6
37	14	CAN'T BE WITH YOU TONIGHT	Judy Boucher	Orbitone	2
12	15	SIGN 'O' THE TIMES	Prince	Paisley Park	5
13	16	BIG TIME	Peter Gabriel	Virgin	3
-	17	WANTED DEAD OR ALIVE	Bon Jovi	Vertigo	1
11	18	RESPECT YOURSELF	Bruce Willis	Motown	5
30	19	DAY IN DAY OUT	David Bowie	EMI America	2
10	20	THE GREAT PRETENDER	Freddie Mercury	Parlophone	6
14	21	LIVE IT UP	Mental As Anything	Epic	9
27	22	STILL OF THE NIGHT	Whitesnake	EMI	3
-	23	LIVING IN A BOX	Living In A Box ●	Chrysalis	1
24	24	I'D RATHER GO BLIND	Ruby Turner	Jive	4
16	25	(YOU GOTTA) FIGHT FOR YOUR RIGHT (TO PARTY)	Beastie Boys	Def Jam	7
33	26	KEEP YOUR EYE ON ME	Herb Alpert	Breakout	3
18	27	LOVING YOU IS SWEETER THAN EVER	Nick Kamen	WEA	6
34	28	LET MY PEOPLE GO GO	Rainmakers	Mercury	3
19	29	IT DOESN'T HAVE TO BE	Erasure	Mute	7
38	30	OUT WITH HER	Blow Monkeys	RCA	2
26	31	SEXY GIRL	Lillo Thomas	Capitol	4
-	32	ANOTHER STEP (CLOSER TO YOU)	Kim Wilde and Junior ●	MCA	1
28	33	MALE STRIPPER	Man 2 Man meets Man Parrish	Bolts	10
20	34	'MOONLIGHTING' THEME	Al Jarreau	WEA	6
25	35	TONIGHT TONIGHT TONIGHT	Genesis	Virgin	5
-	36	RADIO HEART	Radio Heart featuring Gary Numan ●	GFM	1
23	37	STAND BY ME	Ben E King	Atlantic	9
32	38	WHAT YOU GET IS WHAT YOU SEE	Tina Turner	Capitol	4
31	39	CRUSH ON YOU	Jets	MCA	9
29	40	WHEN A MAN LOVES A WOMAN	Percy Sledge	Atlantic	9

WEEK ENDING 18 APRIL 1987

LW	TW	Title	Artist	Label	Wks
1	1	LET IT BE	Ferry Aid	Sun	3
3	2	LA ISLA BONITA	Madonna	Sire	3
6	3	LEAN ON ME	Club Nouveau	King Jay	4
14	4	CAN'T BE WITH YOU TONIGHT	Judy Boucher	Orbitone	3
4	5	LET'S WAIT AWHILE	Janet Jackson	Breakout	5
2	6	RESPECTABLE	Mel and Kim	Supreme	7
7	7	IF YOU LET ME STAY	Terence Trent D'Arby	CBS	5
5	8	WITH OR WITHOUT YOU	U2	Island	4
10	9	EVER FALLEN IN LOVE	Fine Young Cannibals	London	4
23	10	LIVING IN A BOX	Living In A Box	Chrysalis	2
8	11	THE IRISH ROVER	Pogues and the Dubliners	Stiff	4
11	12	ORDINARY DAY	Curiosity Killed The Cat	Mercury	3
17	13	WANTED DEAD OR ALIVE	Bon Jovi	Vertigo	2

In these weeks ■ As the *'Moonlighting' Theme* drops out of the Top 10, one of the stars of 'Moonlighting', Bruce Willis, moves up to number 7 (28.03.87) ■ Ferry Aid's version of *Let It Be* becomes the first cover version of a Beatles single to do better than the Beatles' original, which only got to number two (04.04.87) ■ Less than three years after their record-breaking period of chart glory, Frankie Goes To Hollywood slips out of the top 40 forever (04.04.87)■

LW	TW	Title	Artist	Label	Wks
-	14	THE SLIGHTEST TOUCH	Five Star	*Tent*	1
9	15	WEAK IN THE PRESENCE OF BEAUTY	Alison Moyet	*CBS*	7
22	[16]	STILL OF THE NIGHT	Whitesnake	*EMI*	4
19	[17]	DAY IN DAY OUT	David Bowie	*EMI America*	3
28	[18]	LET MY PEOPLE GO GO	Rainmakers	*Mercury*	4
26	[19]	KEEP YOUR EYE ON ME	Herb Alpert	*Breakout*	4
32	20	ANOTHER STEP (CLOSER TO YOU)	Kim Wilde and Junior	*MCA*	2
15	21	SIGN 'O' THE TIMES	Prince	*Paisley Park*	6
18	22	RESPECT YOURSELF	Bruce Willis	*Motown*	6
-	23	WHY CAN'T I BE YOU	Cure	*Fiction*	1
12	24	I GET THE SWEETEST FEELING	Jackie Wilson	*SMP*	8
16	25	BIG TIME	Peter Gabriel	*Virgin*	4
24	26	I'D RATHER GO BLIND	Ruby Turner	*Jive*	5
20	27	THE GREAT PRETENDER	Freddie Mercury	*Parlophone*	7
13	28	EVERYTHING I OWN	Boy George	*Virgin*	7
-	29	NOTHING'S GONNA STOP US NOW	Starship	*Grunt*	1
-	30	DIAMOND LIGHTS	Glenn and Chris ●	*Record Shack*	1
-	31	(SOMETHING INSIDE) SO STRONG	Labi Siffre	*China*	1
-	32	A BOY FROM NOWHERE	Tom Jones	*Epic*	1
21	33	LIVE IT UP	Mental As Anything	*Epic*	10
25	34	(YOU GOTTA) FIGHT FOR YOUR RIGHT (TO PARTY)	Beastie Boys	*Def Jam*	8
36	[35]	RADIO HEART	Radio Heart featuring Gary Numan	*GFM*	2
30	36	OUT WITH HER	Blow Monkeys	*RCA*	3
-	37	BIG LOVE	Fleetwood Mac	*Warner Bros*	1
27	38	LOVING YOU IS SWEETER THAN EVER	Nick Kamen	*WEA*	7
-	39	NEVER TAKE ME ALIVE	Spear Of Destiny ●	*10*	1
-	40	BOOPS (HERE TO GO)	Sly and Robbie ●	*Fourth + Broadway*	1

WEEK ENDING 25 APRIL 1987

LW	TW	Title	Artist	Label	Wks
2	[1]	LA ISLA BONITA	Madonna	*Sire*	4
4	[2]	CAN'T BE WITH YOU TONIGHT	Judy Boucher	*Orbitone*	4
3	[3]	LEAN ON ME	Club Nouveau	*King Jay*	5
1	4	LET IT BE	Ferry Aid	*Sun*	4
6	5	RESPECTABLE	Mel and Kim	*Supreme*	8
10	6	LIVING IN A BOX	Living In A Box	*Chrysalis*	3
7	[7]	IF YOU LET ME STAY	Terence Trent D'Arby	*CBS*	6
14	8	THE SLIGHTEST TOUCH	Five Star	*Tent*	2
5	9	LET'S WAIT AWHILE	Janet Jackson	*Breakout*	6
9	10	EVER FALLEN IN LOVE	Fine Young Cannibals	*London*	5
8	11	WITH OR WITHOUT YOU	U2	*Island*	5
32	12	A BOY FROM NOWHERE	Tom Jones	*Epic*	2
-	13	SHEILA TAKE A BOW	Smiths	*Rough Trade*	1
20	14	ANOTHER STEP (CLOSER TO YOU)	Kim Wilde and Junior	*MCA*	3
29	15	NOTHING'S GONNA STOP US NOW	Starship	*Grunt*	2
13	16	WANTED DEAD OR ALIVE	Bon Jovi	*Vertigo*	3
30	17	DIAMOND LIGHTS	Glenn and Chris	*Record Shack*	2
31	18	(SOMETHING INSIDE) SO STRONG	Labi Siffre	*China*	2
12	19	ORDINARY DAY	Curiosity Killed The Cat	*Mercury*	4
11	20	THE IRISH ROVER	Pogues and the Dubliners	*Stiff*	5
23	[21]	WHY CAN'T I BE YOU	Cure	*Fiction*	2
18	22	LET MY PEOPLE GO GO	Rainmakers	*Mercury*	5
16	23	STILL OF THE NIGHT	Whitesnake	*EMI*	5
-	24	TO BE WITH YOU AGAIN	Level 42	*Polydor*	1
39	25	NEVER TAKE ME ALIVE	Spear Of Destiny	*10*	2
19	26	KEEP YOUR EYE ON ME	Herb Alpert	*Breakout*	5
37	27	BIG LOVE	Fleetwood Mac	*Warner Bros*	2
17	28	DAY IN DAY OUT	David Bowie	*EMI America*	4
-	29	ALONE AGAIN OR	Damned	*MCA*	1
15	30	WEAK IN THE PRESENCE OF BEAUTY	Alison Moyet	*CBS*	8
-	31	MEET EL PRESIDENTE	Duran Duran	*EMI*	1
22	32	RESPECT YOURSELF	Bruce Willis	*Motown*	7
40	33	BOOPS (HERE TO GO)	Sly and Robbie	*Fourth + Broadway*	2
21	34	SIGN 'O' THE TIMES	Prince	*Paisley Park*	7
-	35	CARRIE	Europe	*Epic*	1
26	36	I'D RATHER GO BLIND	Ruby Turner	*Jive*	6
24	37	I GET THE SWEETEST FEELING	Jackie Wilson	*SMP*	9
28	38	EVERYTHING I OWN	Boy George	*Virgin*	8
34	39	(YOU GOTTA) FIGHT FOR YOUR RIGHT (TO PARTY)	Beastie Boys	*Def Jam*	9
27	40	THE GREAT PRETENDER	Freddie Mercury	*Parlophone*	8

May 1987

□ Highest position disc reached ● Act's first ever week on chart

WEEK ENDING 2 MAY 1987

LW	TW	Title	Artist	Label	Wks
1	[1]	LA ISLA BONITA	Madonna	*Sire*	5
2	[2]	CAN'T BE WITH YOU TONIGHT	Judy Boucher	*Orbitone*	5
15	3	NOTHING'S GONNA STOP US NOW	Starship	*Grunt*	3
8	[4]	THE SLIGHTEST TOUCH	Five Star	*Tent*	3
3	5	LEAN ON ME	Club Nouveau	*King Jay*	6
6	6	LIVING IN A BOX	Living In A Box	*Chrysalis*	4
12	7	A BOY FROM NOWHERE	Tom Jones	*Epic*	3
7	8	IF YOU LET ME STAY	Terence Trent D'Arby	*CBS*	7
14	9	ANOTHER STEP (CLOSER TO YOU)	Kim Wilde and Junior	*MCA*	4
13	[10]	SHEILA TAKE A BOW	Smiths	*Rough Trade*	2
5	11	RESPECTABLE	Mel and Kim	*Supreme*	9
17	[12]	DIAMOND LIGHTS	Glenn and Chris	*Record Shack*	3
10	13	EVER FALLEN IN LOVE	Fine Young Cannibals	*London*	6
24	14	TO BE WITH YOU AGAIN	Level 42	*Polydor*	2
9	15	LET'S WAIT AWHILE	Janet Jackson	*Breakout*	7
18	16	(SOMETHING INSIDE) SO STRONG	Labi Siffre	*China*	3
4	17	LET IT BE	Ferry Aid	*Sun*	5
11	18	WITH OR WITHOUT YOU	U2	*Island*	6
-	19	APRIL SKIES	Jesus and Mary Chain	*blanco y negro*	1
16	20	WANTED DEAD OR ALIVE	Bon Jovi	*Vertigo*	4
27	21	BIG LOVE	Fleetwood Mac	*Warner Bros*	3
19	22	ORDINARY DAY	Curiosity Killed The Cat	*Mercury*	5
25	23	NEVER TAKE ME ALIVE	Spear Of Destiny	*10*	3
31	[24]	MEET EL PRESIDENTE	Duran Duran	*EMI*	2
26	25	KEEP YOUR EYE ON ME	Herb Alpert	*Breakout*	6
21	26	WHY CAN'T I BE YOU	Cure	*Fiction*	3
35	27	CARRIE	Europe	*Epic*	2
29	28	ALONE AGAIN OR	Damned	*MCA*	2
33	29	BOOPS (HERE TO GO)	Sly and Robbie	*Fourth + Broadway*	3
-	30	BACK AND FORTH	Cameo	*Club*	1
22	31	LET MY PEOPLE GO GO	Rainmakers	*Mercury*	6
-	32	LIL' DEVIL	Cult	*Beggars Banquet*	1
20	33	THE IRISH ROVER	Pogues and the Dubliners	*Stiff*	6
23	34	STILL OF THE NIGHT	Whitesnake	*EMI*	6
32	35	RESPECT YOURSELF	Bruce Willis	*Motown*	8
-	36	TWILIGHT WORLD	Swing Out Sister	*Mercury*	1
-	37	REAL FASHION REGGAE STYLE	Carey Johnson ●	*Oval*	1
-	38	LET YOURSELF GO	Sybil ●	*Champion*	1
-	39	WISHING I WAS LUCKY	Wet Wet Wet ●	*Precious*	1
-	40	SHATTERED DREAMS	Johnny Hates Jazz ●	*Virgin*	1

WEEK ENDING 9 MAY 1987

LW	TW	Title	Artist	Label	Wks
3	[1]	NOTHING'S GONNA STOP US NOW	Starship	*Grunt*	4
2	[2]	CAN'T BE WITH YOU TONIGHT	Judy Boucher	*Orbitone*	6
1	3	LA ISLA BONITA	Madonna	*Sire*	6
7	4	A BOY FROM NOWHERE	Tom Jones	*Epic*	4
4	5	THE SLIGHTEST TOUCH	Five Star	*Tent*	4
6	6	LIVING IN A BOX	Living In A Box	*Chrysalis*	5
16	7	(SOMETHING INSIDE) SO STRONG	Labi Siffre	*China*	4
19	[8]	APRIL SKIES	Jesus and Mary Chain	*blanco y negro*	2
9	9	ANOTHER STEP (CLOSER TO YOU)	Kim Wilde and Junior	*MCA*	5
14	[10]	TO BE WITH YOU AGAIN	Level 42	*Polydor*	3
5	11	LEAN ON ME	Club Nouveau	*King Jay*	7
8	12	IF YOU LET ME STAY	Terence Trent D'Arby	*CBS*	8
21	13	BIG LOVE	Fleetwood Mac	*Warner Bros*	4
12	14	DIAMOND LIGHTS	Glenn and Chris	*Record Shack*	4
10	15	SHEILA TAKE A BOW	Smiths	*Rough Trade*	3
30	16	BACK AND FORTH	Cameo	*Club*	2
32	17	LIL' DEVIL	Cult	*Beggars Banquet*	2
11	18	RESPECTABLE	Mel and Kim	*Supreme*	10
23	19	NEVER TAKE ME ALIVE	Spear Of Destiny	*10*	4
13	20	EVER FALLEN IN LOVE	Fine Young Cannibals	*London*	7
15	21	LET'S WAIT AWHILE	Janet Jackson	*Breakout*	8
29	22	BOOPS (HERE TO GO)	Sly and Robbie	*Fourth + Broadway*	4

■Grace Slick, lead vocalist on Starship's *Nothing's Gonna Stop Us Now*, becomes the oldest woman to top the charts at the age of 47 years and 232 days (09.05.87) ■ Spurs' footballers Hoddle and Waddle take their *Diamond Lights* to number 12 at that time the best chart showing by professional sportsmen not performing a sport-related song (02.05.87)■

May 1987

□ Highest position disc reached ● Act's first ever week on chart

LW	TW	Title	Artist	Label	Wks
-	23	STRANGELOVE	Depeche Mode	Mute	1
18	24	WITH OR WITHOUT YOU	U2	Island	7
37	25	REAL FASHION REGGAE STYLE	Carey Johnson	Oval	2
24	26	MEET EL PRESIDENTE	Duran Duran	EMI	3
27	27	CARRIE	Europe	Epic	3
28	28	ALONE AGAIN OR	Damned	MCA	3
39	29	WISHING I WAS LUCKY	Wet Wet Wet	Precious	2
40	30	SHATTERED DREAMS	Johnny Hates Jazz	Virgin	2
26	31	WHY CAN'T I BE YOU	Cure	Fiction	4
36	32	TWILIGHT WORLD	Swing Out Sister	Mercury	2
20	33	WANTED DEAD OR ALIVE	Bon Jovi	Vertigo	5
17	34	LET IT BE	Ferry Aid	Sun	6
38	35	LET YOURSELF GO	Sybil	Champion	2
25	36	KEEP YOUR EYE ON ME	Herb Alpert	Breakout	7
-	37	BA-NA-NA-BAM-BOO	Westworld	RCA	1
22	38	ORDINARY DAY	Curiosity Killed The Cat	Mercury	6
-	39	DOMINOES	Robbie Nevil	Manhattan	1
-	40	PRIME MOVER	Zodiac Mindwarp and the Love Reaction ●	Mercury	1

WEEK ENDING 16 MAY 1987

LW	TW	Title	Artist	Label	Wks
1	1	NOTHING'S GONNA STOP US NOW	Starship	Grunt	5
2	2	CAN'T BE WITH YOU TONIGHT	Judy Boucher	Orbitone	7
4	3	A BOY FROM NOWHERE	Tom Jones	Epic	5
7	4	(SOMETHING INSIDE) SO STRONG	Labi Siffre	China	5
6	5	LIVING IN A BOX	Living In A Box	Chrysalis	6
9	6	ANOTHER STEP (CLOSER TO YOU)	Kim Wilde and Junior	MCA	6
3	7	LA ISLA BONITA	Madonna	Sire	7
5	8	THE SLIGHTEST TOUCH	Five Star	Tent	5
13	9	BIG LOVE	Fleetwood Mac	Warner Bros	5
8	10	APRIL SKIES	Jesus and Mary Chain	blanco y negro	3
17	11	LIL' DEVIL	Cult	Beggars Banquet	3
22	12	BOOPS (HERE TO GO)	Sly and Robbie	Fourth + Broadway	5
16	13	BACK AND FORTH	Cameo	Club	3
19	14	NEVER TAKE ME ALIVE	Spear Of Destiny	10	5
10	15	TO BE WITH YOU AGAIN	Level 42	Polydor	4
23	16	STRANGELOVE	Depeche Mode	Mute	2
11	17	LEAN ON ME	Club Nouveau	King Jay	8
30	18	SHATTERED DREAMS	Johnny Hates Jazz	Virgin	3
25	19	REAL FASHION REGGAE STYLE	Carey Johnson	Oval	3
12	20	IF YOU LET ME STAY	Terence Trent D'Arby	CBS	9
29	21	WISHING I WAS LUCKY	Wet Wet Wet	Precious	3
27	22	CARRIE	Europe	Epic	4
14	23	DIAMOND LIGHTS	Glenn and Chris	Record Shack	5
40	24	PRIME MOVER	Zodiac Mindwarp and the Love Reaction	Mercury	2
18	25	RESPECTABLE	Mel and Kim	Supreme	11
39	26	DOMINOES	Robbie Nevil	Manhattan	2
28	27	ALONE AGAIN OR	Damned	MCA	4
24	28	WITH OR WITHOUT YOU	U2	Island	8
15	29	SHEILA TAKE A BOW	Smiths	Rough Trade	4
-	30	THERE'S A GHOST IN MY HOUSE	Fall ●	Beggars Banquet	1
20	31	EVER FALLEN IN LOVE	Fine Young Cannibals	London	8
35	32	LET YOURSELF GO	Sybil	Champion	3
-	33	SERIOUS	Donna Allen ●	Portrait	1
32	34	TWILIGHT WORLD	Swing Out Sister	Mercury	3
-	35	HOT SHOT TOTTENHAM!	Tottenham Hotspur FC/Chas & Dave	Rainbow	1
21	36	LET'S WAIT AWHILE	Janet Jackson	Breakout	9
37	37	BA-NA-NA-BAM-BOO	Westworld	RCA	2
-	38	JACK MIX II	Mirage ●	Debut	1
-	39	YOU'RE THE VOICE	John Farnham ●	Wheatley	1
-	40	WATCHDOGS	UB40	DEP International	1

WEEK ENDING 23 MAY 1987

LW	TW	Title	Artist	Label	Wks
1	1	NOTHING'S GONNA STOP US NOW	Starship	Grunt	6
3	2	A BOY FROM NOWHERE	Tom Jones	Epic	6
2	3	CAN'T BE WITH YOU TONIGHT	Judy Boucher	Orbitone	8
4	4	(SOMETHING INSIDE) SO STRONG	Labi Siffre	China	6
18	5	SHATTERED DREAMS	Johnny Hates Jazz	Virgin	4
-	6	INCOMMUNICADO	Marillion	EMI	1
5	7	LIVING IN A BOX	Living In A Box	Chrysalis	7
6	8	ANOTHER STEP (CLOSER TO YOU)	Kim Wilde and Junior	MCA	7
9	9	BIG LOVE	Fleetwood Mac	Warner Bros	6
-	10	I WANNA DANCE WITH SOMEBODY (WHO LOVES ME)	Whitney Houston	Arista	1
13	11	BACK AND FORTH	Cameo	Club	4
12	12	BOOPS (HERE TO GO)	Sly and Robbie	Fourth + Broadway	6
11	13	LIL' DEVIL	Cult	Beggars Banquet	4
21	14	WISHING I WAS LUCKY	Wet Wet Wet	Precious	4
8	15	THE SLIGHTEST TOUCH	Five Star	Tent	6
14	16	NEVER TAKE ME ALIVE	Spear Of Destiny	10	6
7	17	LA ISLA BONITA	Madonna	Sire	8
35	18	HOT SHOT TOTTENHAM!	Tottenham Hotspur FC/Chas & Dave	Rainbow	2
24	19	PRIME MOVER	Zodiac Mindwarp and the Love Reaction	Mercury	3
16	20	STRANGELOVE	Depeche Mode	Mute	3
38	21	JACK MIX II	Mirage	Debut	2
19	22	REAL FASHION REGGAE STYLE	Carey Johnson	Oval	4
-	23	BORN TO RUN	Bruce Springsteen	CBS	1
10	24	APRIL SKIES	Jesus and Mary Chain	blanco y negro	4
-	25	HOLD ME NOW	Johnny Logan	Epic	1
33	26	SERIOUS	Donna Allen	Portrait	2
22	27	CARRIE	Europe	Epic	5
-	28	FIVE GET OVER EXCITED	Housemartins	Go! Discs	1
15	29	TO BE WITH YOU AGAIN	Level 42	Polydor	5
26	30	DOMINOES	Robbie Nevil	Manhattan	3
30	31	THERE'S A GHOST IN MY HOUSE	Fall	Beggars Banquet	2
39	32	YOU'RE THE VOICE	John Farnham	Wheatley	2
20	33	IF YOU LET ME STAY	Terence Trent D'Arby	CBS	10
17	34	LEAN ON ME	Club Nouveau	King Jay	9
-	35	FRIDAY ON MY MIND	Gary Moore	10	1
32	36	LET YOURSELF GO	Sybil	Champion	4
27	37	ALONE AGAIN OR	Damned	MCA	5
23	38	DIAMOND LIGHTS	Glenn and Chris	Record Shack	6
40	39	WATCHDOGS	UB40	DEP International	2
25	40	RESPECTABLE	Mel and Kim	Supreme	12

WEEK ENDING 30 MAY 1987

LW	TW	Title	Artist	Label	Wks
1	1	NOTHING'S GONNA STOP US NOW	Starship	Grunt	7
10	2	I WANNA DANCE WITH SOMEBODY (WHO LOVES ME)	Whitney Houston	Arista	2
25	3	HOLD ME NOW	Johnny Logan	Epic	2
2	4	A BOY FROM NOWHERE	Tom Jones	Epic	7
5	5	SHATTERED DREAMS	Johnny Hates Jazz	Virgin	5
6	6	INCOMMUNICADO	Marillion	EMI	2
21	7	JACK MIX II	Mirage	Debut	3
3	8	CAN'T BE WITH YOU TONIGHT	Judy Boucher	Orbitone	9
4	9	(SOMETHING INSIDE) SO STRONG	Labi Siffre	China	7
14	10	WISHING I WAS LUCKY	Wet Wet Wet	Precious	5
11	11	BACK AND FORTH	Cameo	Club	5
9	12	BIG LOVE	Fleetwood Mac	Warner Bros	7
28	13	FIVE GET OVER EXCITED	Housemartins	Go! Discs	2
7	14	LIVING IN A BOX	Living In A Box	Chrysalis	8
26	15	SERIOUS	Donna Allen	Portrait	3
23	16	BORN TO RUN	Bruce Springsteen	CBS	2
8	17	ANOTHER STEP (CLOSER TO YOU)	Kim Wilde and Junior	MCA	8
19	18	PRIME MOVER	Zodiac Mindwarp and the Love Reaction	Mercury	4
12	19	BOOPS (HERE TO GO)	Sly and Robbie	Fourth + Broadway	7
13	20	LIL' DEVIL	Cult	Beggars Banquet	5
16	21	NEVER TAKE ME ALIVE	Spear Of Destiny	10	7
15	22	THE SLIGHTEST TOUCH	Five Star	Tent	7
-	23	VICTIM OF LOVE	Erasure	Mute	1
17	24	LA ISLA BONITA	Madonna	Sire	9
22	25	REAL FASHION REGGAE STYLE	Carey Johnson	Oval	5

In these weeks ■ Johnny Logan, a one-hit wonder from 1980 when he won the Eurovision Song Contest, becomes the first performer ever to win the contest twice, and thus rubs his name off the list of one-hit wonders (23.05.87) ■ Tom Jones' first hit for 10 years, and his first Top 10 hit for 15 years, becomes his fifth hit to peak at number two (23.05.87)■

June 1987

☐ Highest position disc reached ● Act's first ever week on chart

LW	TW	Title	Artist	Label	Wks
35	[26]	FRIDAY ON MY MIND	Gary Moore	10	2
-	27	GOODBYE STRANGER	Pepsi and Shirlie	Polydor	1
32	28	YOU'RE THE VOICE	John Farnham	Wheatley	3
27	29	CARRIE	Europe	Epic	6
20	30	STRANGELOVE	Depeche Mode	Mute	4
-	31	LOOKING FOR A NEW LOVE	Jody Watley ●	MCA	1
18	32	HOT SHOT TOTTENHAM!	Tottenham Hotspur FC/Chas & Dave	Rainbow	3
-	33	LUKA	Suzanne Vega	A&M	1
-	34	INFIDELITY	Simply Red	WEA	1
-	35	NO SLEEP TILL BROOKLYN	Beastie Boys	Def Jam	1
24	36	APRIL SKIES	Jesus and Mary Chain	blanco y negro	5
-	37	NOTHING'S GONNA STOP ME NOW	Samantha Fox	Jive	1
29	38	TO BE WITH YOU AGAIN	Level 42	Polydor	6
30	39	DOMINOES	Robbie Nevil	Manhattan	4
40	40	RESPECTABLE	Mel and Kim	Supreme	13

WEEK ENDING 6 JUNE 1987

LW	TW	Title	Artist	Label	Wks
2	[1]	I WANNA DANCE WITH SOMEBODY (WHO LOVES ME)	Whitney Houston	Arista	3
1	2	NOTHING'S GONNA STOP US NOW	Starship	Grunt	8
3	3	HOLD ME NOW	Johnny Logan	Epic	3
7	[4]	JACK MIX II	Mirage	Debut	4
5	[5]	SHATTERED DREAMS	Johnny Hates Jazz	Virgin	6
10	[6]	WISHING I WAS LUCKY	Wet Wet Wet	Precious	6
23	[7]	VICTIM OF LOVE	Erasure	Mute	2
15	[8]	SERIOUS	Donna Allen	Portrait	4
4	9	A BOY FROM NOWHERE	Tom Jones	Epic	8
27	10	GOODBYE STRANGER	Pepsi and Shirlie	Polydor	2
13	[11]	FIVE GET OVER EXCITED	Housemartins	Go! Discs	3
6	12	INCOMMUNICADO	Marillion	EMI	3
-	13	I STILL HAVEN'T FOUND WHAT I'M LOOKING FOR	U2	Island	1
8	14	CAN'T BE WITH YOU TONIGHT	Judy Boucher	Orbitone	10
9	15	(SOMETHING INSIDE) SO STRONG	Labi Siffre	China	8
35	16	NO SLEEP TILL BROOKLYN	Beastie Boys	Def Jam	2
11	17	BACK AND FORTH	Cameo	Club	6
37	18	NOTHING'S GONNA STOP ME NOW	Samantha Fox	Jive	2
12	19	BIG LOVE	Fleetwood Mac	Warner Bros	8
14	20	LIVING IN A BOX	Living In A Box	Chrysalis	9
16	21	BORN TO RUN	Bruce Springsteen	CBS	3
28	22	YOU'RE THE VOICE	John Farnham	Wheatley	4
33	[23]	LUKA	Suzanne Vega	A&M	2
31	24	LOOKING FOR A NEW LOVE	Jody Watley	MCA	2
22	25	THE SLIGHTEST TOUCH	Five Star	Tent	8
17	26	ANOTHER STEP (CLOSER TO YOU)	Kim Wilde and Junior	MCA	9
-	27	IT'S TRICKY	Run-DMC	London	1
19	28	BOOPS (HERE TO GO)	Sly and Robbie	Fourth + Broadway	8
26	29	FRIDAY ON MY MIND	Gary Moore	10	3
-	30	IS THIS LOVE	Whitesnake	EMI	1
34	31	INFIDELITY	Simply Red	WEA	2
20	32	LIL' DEVIL	Cult	Beggars Banquet	6
18	33	PRIME MOVER	Zodiac Mindwarp and the Love Reaction	Mercury	5
-	34	IT'S NOT UNUSUAL	Tom Jones	Decca	1
24	35	LA ISLA BONITA	Madonna	Sire	10
-	36	UNDER THE BOARDWALK	Bruce Willis	Motown	1
-	37	WHEN SMOKEY SINGS	ABC	Neutron	1
21	38	NEVER TAKE ME ALIVE	Spear Of Destiny	10	8
-	39	LET'S DANCE	Chris Rea	Magnet	1
-	40	KEEP ME IN MIND	Boy George	Virgin	1

WEEK ENDING 13 JUNE 1987

LW	TW	Title	Artist	Label	Wks
1	[1]	I WANNA DANCE WITH SOMEBODY (WHO LOVES ME)	Whitney Houston	Arista	4
3	[2]	HOLD ME NOW	Johnny Logan	Epic	4
2	3	NOTHING'S GONNA STOP US NOW	Starship	Grunt	9
-	4	I WANT YOUR SEX	George Michael	Epic	1
4	5	JACK MIX II	Mirage	Debut	5
13	[6]	I STILL HAVEN'T FOUND WHAT I'M LOOKING FOR	U2	Island	2
5	7	SHATTERED DREAMS	Johnny Hates Jazz	Virgin	7
7	8	VICTIM OF LOVE	Erasure	Mute	3
10	[9]	GOODBYE STRANGER	Pepsi and Shirlie	Polydor	3
6	10	WISHING I WAS LUCKY	Wet Wet Wet	Precious	7
18	11	NOTHING'S GONNA STOP ME NOW	Samantha Fox	Jive	3
8	12	SERIOUS	Donna Allen	Portrait	5
-	13	STAR TREKKIN'	Firm	Bark	1
16	[14]	NO SLEEP TILL BROOKLYN	Beastie Boys	Def Jam	3
22	15	YOU'RE THE VOICE	John Farnham	Wheatley	5
27	[16]	IT'S TRICKY	Run-DMC	London	2
36	17	UNDER THE BOARDWALK	Bruce Willis	Motown	2
24	18	LOOKING FOR A NEW LOVE	Jody Watley	MCA	3
11	19	FIVE GET OVER EXCITED	Housemartins	Go! Discs	4
9	20	A BOY FROM NOWHERE	Tom Jones	Epic	9
37	21	WHEN SMOKEY SINGS	ABC	Neutron	2
30	22	IS THIS LOVE	Whitesnake	EMI	2
34	23	IT'S NOT UNUSUAL	Tom Jones	Decca	2
14	24	CAN'T BE WITH YOU TONIGHT	Judy Boucher	Orbitone	11
23	25	LUKA	Suzanne Vega	A&M	3
15	26	(SOMETHING INSIDE) SO STRONG	Labi Siffre	China	9
39	27	LET'S DANCE	Chris Rea	Magnet	2
-	[28]	THE GAME	Echo and the Bunnymen	WEA	1
40	29	KEEP ME IN MIND	Boy George	Virgin	2
12	30	INCOMMUNICADO	Marillion	EMI	4
19	31	BIG LOVE	Fleetwood Mac	Warner Bros	9
17	32	BACK AND FORTH	Cameo	Club	7
20	33	LIVING IN A BOX	Living In A Box	Chrysalis	10
-	34	DON'T DREAM IT'S OVER	Crowded House ●	Capitol	1
-	35	DIAMONDS	Herb Alpert	Breakout	1
-	36	FAKE	Alexander O'Neal	Tabu	1
31	37	INFIDELITY	Simply Red	WEA	3
-	[38]	ROCK STEADY	Whispers	Solar	1
-	39	PLEASURE PRINCIPLE	Janet Jackson	Breakout	1
-	40	COMIN' ON STRONG	Broken English ●	EMI	1

WEEK ENDING 20 JUNE 1987

LW	TW	Title	Artist	Label	Wks
13	[1]	STAR TREKKIN'	Firm	Bark	2
1	2	I WANNA DANCE WITH SOMEBODY (WHO LOVES ME)	Whitney Houston	Arista	5
4	[3]	I WANT YOUR SEX	George Michael	Epic	2
2	4	HOLD ME NOW	Johnny Logan	Epic	5
3	5	NOTHING'S GONNA STOP US NOW	Starship	Grunt	10
17	6	UNDER THE BOARDWALK	Bruce Willis	Motown	3
6	7	I STILL HAVEN'T FOUND WHAT I'M LOOKING FOR	U2	Island	3
11	[8]	NOTHING'S GONNA STOP ME NOW	Samantha Fox	Jive	4
15	9	YOU'RE THE VOICE	John Farnham	Wheatley	6
8	10	VICTIM OF LOVE	Erasure	Mute	4
5	11	JACK MIX II	Mirage	Debut	6
9	12	GOODBYE STRANGER	Pepsi and Shirlie	Polydor	4
18	[13]	LOOKING FOR A NEW LOVE	Jody Watley	MCA	4
21	14	WHEN SMOKEY SINGS	ABC	Neutron	3
10	15	WISHING I WAS LUCKY	Wet Wet Wet	Precious	8
22	16	IS THIS LOVE	Whitesnake	EMI	3
16	17	IT'S TRICKY	Run-DMC	London	3
7	18	SHATTERED DREAMS	Johnny Hates Jazz	Virgin	8
14	19	NO SLEEP TILL BROOKLYN	Beastie Boys	Def Jam	4
23	20	IT'S NOT UNUSUAL	Tom Jones	Decca	3
-	21	MISFIT	Curiosity Killed The Cat	Mercury	1
12	22	SERIOUS	Donna Allen	Portrait	6
25	[23]	LUKA	Suzanne Vega	A&M	4
39	[24]	PLEASURE PRINCIPLE	Janet Jackson	Breakout	2
27	25	LET'S DANCE	Chris Rea	Magnet	3
40	26	COMIN' ON STRONG	Broken English	EMI	2
35	[27]	DIAMONDS	Herb Alpert	Breakout	2
28	[28]	THE GAME	Echo and the Bunnymen	WEA	2
34	29	DON'T DREAM IT'S OVER	Crowded House	Capitol	2
-	30	PROMISED YOU A MIRACLE (LIVE)	Simple Minds	Virgin	1

■George Michael misses a hat-trick of number ones when the controversial *I Want Your Sex* stops at no. 3 (20.06.87) ■ Two very similar titles in the Top 10, but they are completely different songs: *Nothing's Gonna Stop Us Now* and *Nothing's Gonna Stop Me Now* (20.06.87) ■ The Firm's *Star Trekking* is the first number one hit featuring only a male lead vocalist since Boy George's *Everything I Own* six number ones ago (20.06.87)■

June 1987

□ Highest position disc reached ● Act's first ever week on chart

LW	TW	Title	Artist	Label	Wks
-	31	WISHING WELL	Terence Trent D'Arby	*CBS*	1
-	32	IF I WAS YOUR GIRLFRIEND	Prince	*Paisley Park*	1
36	33	FAKE	Alexander O'Neal	*Tabu*	2
-	34	SCALES OF JUSTICE	Living In A Box	*Chrysalis*	1
24	35	CAN'T BE WITH YOU TONIGHT	Judy Boucher	*Orbitone*	12
20	36	A BOY FROM NOWHERE	Tom Jones	*Epic*	10
-	37	LIFETIME LOVE	Joyce Sims	*London*	1
29	38	KEEP ME IN MIND	Boy George	*Virgin*	3
-	39	ALWAYS	Atlantic Starr	*Warner Bros*	1
19	40	FIVE GET OVER EXCITED	Housemartins	*Go! Discs*	5

WEEK ENDING **27 JUNE 1987**

LW	TW	Title	Artist	Label	Wks
1	1	STAR TREKKIN'	Firm	*Bark*	3
2	2	I WANNA DANCE WITH SOMEBODY (WHO LOVES ME)	Whitney Houston	*Arista*	6
6	3	UNDER THE BOARDWALK	Bruce Willis	*Motown*	4
3	4	I WANT YOUR SEX	George Michael	*Epic*	3
-	5	IT'S A SIN	Pet Shop Boys	*Parlophone*	1
4	6	HOLD ME NOW	Johnny Logan	*Epic*	6
9	7	YOU'RE THE VOICE	John Farnham	*Wheatley*	7
8	8	NOTHING'S GONNA STOP ME NOW	Samantha Fox	*Jive*	5
21	9	MISFIT	Curiosity Killed The Cat	*Mercury*	2
5	10	NOTHING'S GONNA STOP US NOW	Starship	*Grunt*	11
16	11	IS THIS LOVE	Whitesnake	*EMI*	4
14	12	WHEN SMOKEY SINGS	ABC	*Neutron*	4
7	13	I STILL HAVEN'T FOUND WHAT I'M LOOKING FOR	U2	*Island*	4
31	14	WISHING WELL	Terence Trent D'Arby	*CBS*	2
10	15	VICTIM OF LOVE	Erasure	*Mute*	5
13	16	LOOKING FOR A NEW LOVE	Jody Watley	*MCA*	5
20	17	IT'S NOT UNUSUAL	Tom Jones	*Decca*	4
25	18	LET'S DANCE	Chris Rea	*Magnet*	4
12	19	GOODBYE STRANGER	Pepsi and Shirlie	*Polydor*	5
11	20	JACK MIX II	Mirage	*Debut*	7
26	21	COMIN' ON STRONG	Broken English	*EMI*	3
30	22	PROMISED YOU A MIRACLE (LIVE)	Simple Minds	*Virgin*	2
32	23	IF I WAS YOUR GIRLFRIEND	Prince	*Paisley Park*	2
17	24	IT'S TRICKY	Run-DMC	*London*	4
39	25	ALWAYS	Atlantic Starr	*Warner Bros*	2
-	26	MY PRETTY ONE	Cliff Richard	*EMI*	1
29	27	DON'T DREAM IT'S OVER	Crowded House	*Capitol*	3
24	28	PLEASURE PRINCIPLE	Janet Jackson	*Breakout*	3
19	29	NO SLEEP TILL BROOKLYN	Beastie Boys	*Def Jam*	5
34	30	SCALES OF JUSTICE	Living In A Box	*Chrysalis*	2
18	31	SHATTERED DREAMS	Johnny Hates Jazz	*Virgin*	9
27	32	DIAMONDS	Herb Alpert	*Breakout*	3
15	33	WISHING I WAS LUCKY	Wet Wet Wet	*Precious*	9
37	34	LIFETIME LOVE	Joyce Sims	*London*	2
-	35	SWEET SIXTEEN	Billy Idol	*Chrysalis*	1
23	36	LUKA	Suzanne Vega	*A&M*	5
-	37	THROWING IT ALL AWAY	Genesis	*Virgin*	1
28	38	THE GAME	Echo and the Bunnymen	*WEA*	3
22	39	SERIOUS	Donna Allen	*Portrait*	7
-	40	TIME WILL CRAWL	David Bowie	*EMI America*	1

WEEK ENDING **4 JULY 1987**

LW	TW	Title	Artist	Label	Wks
5	1	IT'S A SIN	Pet Shop Boys	*Parlophone*	2
1	2	STAR TREKKIN'	Firm	*Bark*	4
3	3	UNDER THE BOARDWALK	Bruce Willis	*Motown*	5
2	4	I WANNA DANCE WITH SOMEBODY (WHO LOVES ME)	Whitney Houston	*Arista*	7
14	5	WISHING WELL	Terence Trent D'Arby	*CBS*	3
7	6	YOU'RE THE VOICE	John Farnham	*Wheatley*	8
9	7	MISFIT	Curiosity Killed The Cat	*Mercury*	3
4	8	I WANT YOUR SEX	George Michael	*Epic*	4
11	9	IS THIS LOVE	Whitesnake	*EMI*	5
26	10	MY PRETTY ONE	Cliff Richard	*EMI*	2
12	11	WHEN SMOKEY SINGS	ABC	*Neutron*	5
18	12	LET'S DANCE	Chris Rea	*Magnet*	5
6	13	HOLD ME NOW	Johnny Logan	*Epic*	7
8	14	NOTHING'S GONNA STOP ME NOW	Samantha Fox	*Jive*	6
10	15	NOTHING'S GONNA STOP US NOW	Starship	*Grunt*	12
25	16	ALWAYS	Atlantic Starr	*Warner Bros*	3
-	17	THE LIVING DAYLIGHTS	A-Ha	*Warner Bros*	1
21	18	COMIN' ON STRONG	Broken English	*EMI*	4
22	19	PROMISED YOU A MIRACLE (LIVE)	Simple Minds	*Virgin*	3
23	20	IF I WAS YOUR GIRLFRIEND	Prince	*Paisley Park*	3
13	21	I STILL HAVEN'T FOUND WHAT I'M LOOKING FOR	U2	*Island*	5
15	22	VICTIM OF LOVE	Erasure	*Mute*	6
35	23	SWEET SIXTEEN	Billy Idol	*Chrysalis*	2
16	24	LOOKING FOR A NEW LOVE	Jody Watley	*MCA*	6
17	25	IT'S NOT UNUSUAL	Tom Jones	*Decca*	5
-	26	SWEETEST SMILE	Black ●	*A&M*	1
27	27	DON'T DREAM IT'S OVER	Crowded House	*Capitol*	4
-	28	ALONE	Heart ●	*Capitol*	1
19	29	GOODBYE STRANGER	Pepsi and Shirlie	*Polydor*	6
20	30	JACK MIX II	Mirage	*Debut*	8
30	31	SCALES OF JUSTICE	Living In A Box	*Chrysalis*	3
37	32	THROWING IT ALL AWAY	Genesis	*Virgin*	2
40	33	TIME WILL CRAWL	David Bowie	*EMI America*	2
24	34	IT'S TRICKY	Run-DMC	*London*	5
28	35	PLEASURE PRINCIPLE	Janet Jackson	*Breakout*	4
32	36	DIAMONDS	Herb Alpert	*Breakout*	4
34	37	LIFETIME LOVE	Joyce Sims	*London*	3
-	38	HOOVERVILLE (AND THEY PROMISED US THE WORLD)	Christians	*Island*	1
-	39	(YOUR LOVE KEEPS LIFTING ME) HIGHER AND HIGHER	Jackie Wilson	*SMP*	1
33	40	WISHING I WAS LUCKY	Wet Wet Wet	*Precious*	10

WEEK ENDING **11 JULY 1987**

LW	TW	Title	Artist	Label	Wks
1	1	IT'S A SIN	Pet Shop Boys	*Parlophone*	3
3	2	UNDER THE BOARDWALK	Bruce Willis	*Motown*	6
2	3	STAR TREKKIN'	Firm	*Bark*	5
5	4	WISHING WELL	Terence Trent D'Arby	*CBS*	4
17	5	THE LIVING DAYLIGHTS	A-Ha	*Warner Bros*	2
10	6	MY PRETTY ONE	Cliff Richard	*EMI*	3
16	7	ALWAYS	Atlantic Starr	*Warner Bros*	4
4	8	I WANNA DANCE WITH SOMEBODY (WHO LOVES ME)	Whitney Houston	*Arista*	8
6	9	YOU'RE THE VOICE	John Farnham	*Wheatley*	9
7	10	MISFIT	Curiosity Killed The Cat	*Mercury*	4
9	11	IS THIS LOVE	Whitesnake	*EMI*	6
26	12	SWEETEST SMILE	Black	*A&M*	2
12	13	LET'S DANCE	Chris Rea	*Magnet*	6
11	14	WHEN SMOKEY SINGS	ABC	*Neutron*	6
28	15	ALONE	Heart	*Capitol*	2
-	16	F.L.M.	Mel and Kim	*Supreme*	1
23	17	SWEET SIXTEEN	Billy Idol	*Chrysalis*	3
18	18	COMIN' ON STRONG	Broken English	*EMI*	5
8	19	I WANT YOUR SEX	George Michael	*Epic*	5
13	20	HOLD ME NOW	Johnny Logan	*Epic*	8
39	21	(YOUR LOVE KEEPS LIFTING ME) HIGHER AND HIGHER	Jackie Wilson	*SMP*	2
32	22	THROWING IT ALL AWAY	Genesis	*Virgin*	3
14	23	NOTHING'S GONNA STOP ME NOW	Samantha Fox	*Jive*	7
20	24	IF I WAS YOUR GIRLFRIEND	Prince	*Paisley Park*	4
19	25	PROMISED YOU A MIRACLE (LIVE)	Simple Minds	*Virgin*	4
-	26	A LITTLE BOOGIE WOOGIE (IN THE BACK OF MY MIND)	Shakin' Stevens	*Epic*	1
38	27	HOOVERVILLE (AND THEY PROMISED US THE WORLD)	Christians	*Island*	2
15	28	NOTHING'S GONNA STOP US NOW	Starship	*Grunt*	13
21	29	I STILL HAVEN'T FOUND WHAT I'M LOOKING FOR	U2	*Island*	6
-	30	CATCH	Cure	*Fiction*	1
-	31	JIVE TALKIN'	Boogie Box High ●	*Hardback*	1
-	32	SONGBIRD	Kenny G ●	*Arista*	1
27	33	DON'T DREAM IT'S OVER	Crowded House	*Capitol*	5

In these weeks ■ Cliff Richard returns to the Top 40 after a gap of almost two years (27.06.87) ■ *When Smokey Sings* and *Promised You A Miracle* both peak in the same week, although the voices of Smokey Robinson and the Miracles have not been heard in the charts for six years (04.07.87)■

LW	TW	Title	Artist	Label	Wks
22	34	VICTIM OF LOVE	Erasure	*Mute*	7
34	35	LOOKING FOR A NEW LOVE	Jody Watley	*MCA*	7
31	36	SCALES OF JUSTICE	Living In A Box	*Chrysalis*	4
-	37	JUST DON'T WANT TO BE LONELY	Freddie McGregor ●	*Germain*	1
37	38	LIFETIME LOVE	Joyce Sims	*London*	4
25	39	IT'S NOT UNUSUAL	Tom Jones	*Decca*	6
30	40	JACK MIX II	Mirage	*Debut*	9

WEEK ENDING 18 JULY 1987

LW	TW	Title	Artist	Label	Wks
1	1	IT'S A SIN	Pet Shop Boys	*Parlophone*	4
2	2	UNDER THE BOARDWALK	Bruce Willis	*Motown*	7
-	3	WHO'S THAT GIRL	Madonna	*Sire*	1
4	4	WISHING WELL	Terence Trent D'Arby	*CBS*	5
7	5	ALWAYS	Atlantic Starr	*Warner Bros*	5
5	6	THE LIVING DAYLIGHTS	A-Ha	*Warner Bros*	3
16	7	F.L.M.	Mel and Kim	*Supreme*	2
12	8	SWEETEST SMILE	Black	*A&M*	3
15	9	ALONE	Heart	*Capitol*	3
3	10	STAR TREKKIN'	Firm	*Bark*	6
6	11	MY PRETTY ONE	Cliff Richard	*EMI*	4
8	12	I WANNA DANCE WITH SOMEBODY (WHO LOVES ME)	Whitney Houston	*Arista*	9
26	13	A LITTLE BOOGIE WOOGIE (IN THE BACK OF MY MIND)	Shakin' Stevens	*Epic*	2
31	14	JIVE TALKIN'	Boogie Box High	*Hardback*	2
21	15	(YOUR LOVE KEEPS LIFTING ME) HIGHER AND HIGHER	Jackie Wilson	SMP	3
10	16	MISFIT	Curiosity Killed The Cat	*Mercury*	5
9	17	YOU'RE THE VOICE	John Farnham	*Wheatley*	10
17	18	SWEET SIXTEEN	Billy Idol	*Chrysalis*	4
11	19	IS THIS LOVE	Whitesnake	*EMI*	7
13	20	LET'S DANCE	Chris Rea	*Magnet*	7
27	21	HOOVERVILLE (AND THEY PROMISED US THE WORLD)	Christians	*Island*	3
14	22	WHEN SMOKEY SINGS	ABC	*Neutron*	7
37	23	JUST DON'T WANT TO BE LONELY	Freddie McGregor	*Germain*	2
22	24	THROWING IT ALL AWAY	Genesis	*Virgin*	4
32	25	SONGBIRD	Kenny G	*Arista*	2
18	26	COMIN' ON STRONG	Broken English	*EMI*	6
30	27	CATCH	Cure	*Fiction*	2
-	28	I HEARD A RUMOUR	Bananarama	*London*	1
19	29	I WANT YOUR SEX	George Michael	*Epic*	6
28	30	NOTHING'S GONNA STOP US NOW	Starship	*Grunt*	14
24	31	IF I WAS YOUR GIRLFRIEND	Prince	*Paisley Park*	5
-	32	LA BAMBA	Los Lobos ●	*Slash*	1
20	33	HOLD ME NOW	Johnny Logan	*Epic*	9
-	34	LABOUR OF LOVE	Hue And Cry ●	*Circa*	1
-	35	I REALLY DIDN'T MEAN IT	Luther Vandross ●	*Epic*	1
25	36	PROMISED YOU A MIRACLE (LIVE)	Simple Minds	*Virgin*	5
-	37	OOPS UPSIDE YOUR HEAD	Gap Band	*Club*	1
-	38	SOLD	Boy George	*Virgin*	1
29	39	I STILL HAVEN'T FOUND WHAT I'M LOOKING FOR	U2	*Island*	7
23	40	NOTHING'S GONNA STOP ME NOW	Samantha Fox	*Jive*	8

WEEK ENDING 25 JULY 1987

LW	TW	Title	Artist	Label	Wks
3	1	WHO'S THAT GIRL	Madonna	*Sire*	2
1	2	IT'S A SIN	Pet Shop Boys	*Parlophone*	5
5	3	ALWAYS	Atlantic Starr	*Warner Bros*	6
2	4	UNDER THE BOARDWALK	Bruce Willis	*Motown*	8
32	5	LA BAMBA	Los Lobos	*Slash*	2
9	6	ALONE	Heart	*Capitol*	4
7	7	F.L.M.	Mel and Kim	*Supreme*	3
4	8	WISHING WELL	Terence Trent D'Arby	*CBS*	6
8	9	SWEETEST SMILE	Black	*A&M*	4
14	10	JIVE TALKIN'	Boogie Box High	*Hardback*	3
6	11	THE LIVING DAYLIGHTS	A-Ha	*Warner Bros*	4
23	12	JUST DON'T WANT TO BE LONELY	Freddie McGregor	*Germain*	3

August 1987

□ Highest position disc reached ● Act's first ever week on chart

LW	TW	Title	Artist	Label	Wks
13	13	A LITTLE BOOGIE WOOGIE (IN THE BACK OF MY MIND)	Shakin' Stevens	*Epic*	3
10	14	STAR TREKKIN'	Firm	*Bark*	7
28	15	I HEARD A RUMOUR	Bananarama	*London*	2
11	16	MY PRETTY ONE	Cliff Richard	*EMI*	5
34	17	LABOUR OF LOVE	Hue And Cry	*Circa*	2
12	18	I WANNA DANCE WITH SOMEBODY (WHO LOVES ME)	Whitney Houston	*Arista*	10
15	19	(YOUR LOVE KEEPS LIFTING ME) HIGHER AND HIGHER	Jackie Wilson	SMP	4
-	20	SHE'S ON IT	Beastie Boys	*Def Jam*	1
21	21	HOOVERVILLE (AND THEY PROMISED US THE WORLD)	Christians	*Island*	4
25	22	SONGBIRD	Kenny G	*Arista*	3
18	23	SWEET SIXTEEN	Billy Idol	*Chrysalis*	5
19	24	IS THIS LOVE	Whitesnake	*EMI*	8
37	25	OOPS UPSIDE YOUR HEAD	Gap Band	*Club*	2
38	26	SOLD	Boy George	*Virgin*	2
17	27	YOU'RE THE VOICE	John Farnham	*Wheatley*	11
16	28	MISFIT	Curiosity Killed The Cat	*Mercury*	6
35	29	I REALLY DIDN'T MEAN IT	Luther Vandross	*Epic*	2
20	30	LET'S DANCE	Chris Rea	*Magnet*	8
22	31	WHEN SMOKEY SINGS	ABC	*Neutron*	8
27	32	CATCH	Cure	*Fiction*	3
-	33	SUGAR MICE	Marillion	*EMI*	1
-	34	I SURRENDER (TO THE SPIRIT OF THE NIGHT)	Samantha Fox	*Jive*	1
-	35	YOU CAUGHT MY EYE	Judy Boucher	*Orbitone*	1
24	36	THROWING IT ALL AWAY	Genesis	*Virgin*	5
-	37	PERSONAL TOUCH	Errol Brown ●	*WEA*	1
30	38	NOTHING'S GONNA STOP US NOW	Starship	*Grunt*	15
26	39	COMIN' ON STRONG	Broken English	*EMI*	7
29	40	I WANT YOUR SEX	George Michael	*Epic*	7

WEEK ENDING 1 AUGUST 1987

LW	TW	Title	Artist	Label	Wks
5	1	LA BAMBA	Los Lobos	*Slash*	3
1	2	WHO'S THAT GIRL	Madonna	*Sire*	3
3	3	ALWAYS	Atlantic Starr	*Warner Bros*	7
2	4	IT'S A SIN	Pet Shop Boys	*Parlophone*	6
6	5	ALONE	Heart	*Capitol*	5
4	6	UNDER THE BOARDWALK	Bruce Willis	*Motown*	9
10	7	JIVE TALKIN'	Boogie Box High	*Hardback*	4
7	8	F.L.M.	Mel and Kim	*Supreme*	4
12	9	JUST DON'T WANT TO BE LONELY	Freddie McGregor	*Germain*	4
20	10	SHE'S ON IT	Beastie Boys	*Def Jam*	2
8	11	WISHING WELL	Terence Trent D'Arby	*CBS*	7
13	12	A LITTLE BOOGIE WOOGIE (IN THE BACK OF MY MIND)	Shakin' Stevens	*Epic*	4
17	13	LABOUR OF LOVE	Hue And Cry	*Circa*	3
15	14	I HEARD A RUMOUR	Bananarama	*London*	3
9	15	SWEETEST SMILE	Black	*A&M*	5
29	16	I REALLY DIDN'T MEAN IT	Luther Vandross	*Epic*	3
11	17	THE LIVING DAYLIGHTS	A-Ha	*Warner Bros*	5
35	18	YOU CAUGHT MY EYE	Judy Boucher	*Orbitone*	2
-	19	TRUE FAITH	New Order	*Factory*	1
25	20	OOPS UPSIDE YOUR HEAD	Gap Band	*Club*	3
18	21	I WANNA DANCE WITH SOMEBODY (WHO LOVES ME)	Whitney Houston	*Arista*	11
33	22	SUGAR MICE	Marillion	*EMI*	2
22	23	SONGBIRD	Kenny G	*Arista*	4
26	24	SOLD	Boy George	*Virgin*	3
37	25	PERSONAL TOUCH	Errol Brown	*WEA*	2
16	26	MY PRETTY ONE	Cliff Richard	*EMI*	6
21	27	HOOVERVILLE (AND THEY PROMISED US THE WORLD)	Christians	*Island*	5
-	28	CALL ME	Spagna ●	*CBS*	1
14	29	STAR TREKKIN'	Firm	*Bark*	8

■*A Little Boogie Woogie (In The Back Of My Mind)* was the last of 15 consecutive Top 40 hits for Gary Glitter. Ten years later it was the last of 21 consecutive Top 20 hits for Shakin' Stevens (01.08.87) ■ *La Bamba* hits number one, written by Ritchie Valens. The other two stars who died in the 1959 plane crash, Buddy Holly and the Big Bopper, had already written number ones (*That'll Be The Day* and *Oh Boy* by Buddy Holly, *Running Bear* by the Big Bopper), so this hit completes the tragic coincidence (01.08.87)■

August 1987

□ Highest position disc reached ● Act's first ever week on chart

LW	TW	Title	Artist	Label	Wks
-	30	ROADBLOCK	Stock Aitken Waterman ●	*Breakout*	1
34	31	I SURRENDER (TO THE SPIRIT OF THE NIGHT)	Samantha Fox	*Jive*	2
19	32	(YOUR LOVE KEEPS LIFTING ME) HIGHER AND HIGHER	Jackie Wilson	SMP	5
-	33	TOY BOY	Sinitta	*Fanfare*	1
-	34	ANIMAL	Def Leppard ●	*Bludgeon Riffola*	1
-	35	GIRLS GIRLS GIRLS	Motley Crue ●	*Elektra*	1
23	36	SWEET SIXTEEN	Billy Idol	*Chrysalis*	6
24	37	IS THIS LOVE	Whitesnake	*EMI*	9
-	38	SOMEWHERE OUT THERE	Linda Ronstadt and James Ingram ●	*MCA*	1
28	39	MISFIT	Curiosity Killed The Cat	*Mercury*	7
27	40	YOU'RE THE VOICE	John Farnham	*Wheatley*	12

WEEK ENDING 8 AUGUST 1987

LW	TW	Title	Artist	Label	Wks
1	[1]	LA BAMBA	Los Lobos	*Slash*	4
2	2	WHO'S THAT GIRL	Madonna	*Sire*	4
5	[3]	ALONE	Heart	*Capitol*	6
3	4	ALWAYS	Atlantic Starr	*Warner Bros*	8
-	5	I JUST CAN'T STOP LOVING YOU	Michael Jackson with Siedah Garrett	*Epic*	1
13	[6]	LABOUR OF LOVE	Hue And Cry	*Circa*	4
19	7	TRUE FAITH	New Order	*Factory*	2
28	8	CALL ME	Spagna	*CBS*	2
7	9	JIVE TALKIN'	Boogie Box High	*Hardback*	5
10	[10]	SHE'S ON IT	Beastie Boys	*Def Jam*	3
4	11	IT'S A SIN	Pet Shop Boys	*Parlophone*	7
9	12	JUST DON'T WANT TO BE LONELY	Freddie McGregor	*Germain*	5
6	13	UNDER THE BOARDWALK	Bruce Willis	*Motown*	10
8	14	F.L.M.	Mel and Kim	*Supreme*	5
14	15	I HEARD A RUMOUR	Bananarama	*London*	4
34	16	ANIMAL	Def Leppard	*Bludgeon Riffola*	2
30	17	ROADBLOCK	Stock Aitken Waterman	*Breakout*	2
16	18	I REALLY DIDN'T MEAN IT	Luther Vandross	*Epic*	4
12	19	A LITTLE BOOGIE WOOGIE (IN THE BACK OF MY MIND)	Shakin' Stevens	*Epic*	5
18	20	YOU CAUGHT MY EYE	Judy Boucher	*Orbitone*	3
11	21	WISHING WELL	Terence Trent D'Arby	*CBS*	8
33	22	TOY BOY	Sinitta	*Fanfare*	2
38	23	SOMEWHERE OUT THERE	Linda Ronstadt and James Ingram	*MCA*	2
22	24	SUGAR MICE	Marillion	*EMI*	3
20	25	OOPS UPSIDE YOUR HEAD	Gap Band	*Club*	4
25	26	PERSONAL TOUCH	Errol Brown	*WEA*	3
15	27	SWEETEST SMILE	Black	*A&M*	6
35	28	GIRLS GIRLS GIRLS	Motley Crue	*Elektra*	2
31	29	I SURRENDER (TO THE SPIRIT OF THE NIGHT)	Samantha Fox	*Jive*	3
17	30	THE LIVING DAYLIGHTS	A-Ha	*Warner Bros*	6
-	31	SWEET LITTLE MYSTERY	Wet Wet Wet	*Precious*	1
-	32	NEVER GONNA GIVE YOU UP	Rick Astley ●	*RCA*	1
21	33	I WANNA DANCE WITH SOMEBODY (WHO LOVES ME)	Whitney Houston	*Arista*	12
24	34	SOLD	Boy George	*Virgin*	4
29	35	STAR TREKKIN'	Firm	*Bark*	9
-	36	FUNKY TOWN	Pseudo Echo ●	*RCA*	1
-	37	LIPS LIKE SUGAR	Echo and the Bunnymen	*WEA*	1
23	38	SONGBIRD	Kenny G	*Arista*	5
-	39	JUST CALL	Sherrick ●	*Warner Bros*	1
26	40	MY PRETTY ONE	Cliff Richard	*EMI*	7

WEEK ENDING 15 AUGUST 1987

LW	TW	Title	Artist	Label	Wks
5	[1]	I JUST CAN'T STOP LOVING YOU	Michael Jackson with Siedah Garrett	*Epic*	2
1	2	LA BAMBA	Los Lobos	*Slash*	5
8	3	CALL ME	Spagna	*CBS*	3
7	[4]	TRUE FAITH	New Order	*Factory*	3
3	5	ALONE	Heart	*Capitol*	7
6	[6]	LABOUR OF LOVE	Hue And Cry	*Circa*	5
4	7	ALWAYS	Atlantic Starr	*Warner Bros*	9
2	8	WHO'S THAT GIRL	Madonna	*Sire*	5
16	9	ANIMAL	Def Leppard	*Bludgeon Riffola*	3
22	10	TOY BOY	Sinitta	*Fanfare*	3
23	11	SOMEWHERE OUT THERE	Linda Ronstadt and James Ingram	*MCA*	3
31	12	SWEET LITTLE MYSTERY	Wet Wet Wet	*Precious*	2
17	[13]	ROADBLOCK	Stock Aitken Waterman	*Breakout*	3
32	14	NEVER GONNA GIVE YOU UP	Rick Astley	*RCA*	2
12	15	JUST DON'T WANT TO BE LONELY	Freddie McGregor	*Germain*	6
15	16	I HEARD A RUMOUR	Bananarama	*London*	5
9	17	JIVE TALKIN'	Boogie Box High	*Hardback*	6
10	18	SHE'S ON IT	Beastie Boys	*Def Jam*	4
11	19	IT'S A SIN	Pet Shop Boys	*Parlophone*	8
13	20	UNDER THE BOARDWALK	Bruce Willis	*Motown*	11
18	21	I REALLY DIDN'T MEAN IT	Luther Vandross	*Epic*	5
20	22	YOU CAUGHT MY EYE	Judy Boucher	*Orbitone*	4
14	23	F.L.M.	Mel and Kim	*Supreme*	6
36	24	FUNKY TOWN	Pseudo Echo	*RCA*	2
29	[25]	I SURRENDER (TO THE SPIRIT OF THE NIGHT)	Samantha Fox	*Jive*	4
28	[26]	GIRLS GIRLS GIRLS	Motley Crue	*Elektra*	3
21	27	WISHING WELL	Terence Trent D'Arby	*CBS*	9
19	28	A LITTLE BOOGIE WOOGIE (IN THE BACK OF MY MIND)	Shakin' Stevens	*Epic*	6
-	29	NEVER SAY GOODBYE	Bon Jovi	*Vertigo*	1
-	30	HAPPY WHEN IT RAINS	Jesus And Mary Chain	*blanco y negro*	1
39	31	JUST CALL	Sherrick	*Warner Bros*	2
25	32	OOPS UPSIDE YOUR HEAD	Gap Band	*Club*	5
-	33	SAY YOU REALLY WANT ME	Kim Wilde	*MCA*	1
-	34	BRIDGE TO YOUR HEART	Wax ●	*RCA*	1
26	35	PERSONAL TOUCH	Errol Brown	*WEA*	4
37	[36]	LIPS LIKE SUGAR	Echo and the Bunnymen	*WEA*	2
24	37	SUGAR MICE	Marillion	*EMI*	4
-	38	U GOT THE LOOK	Prince	*Paisley Park*	1
27	39	SWEETEST SMILE	Black	*A&M*	7
30	40	THE LIVING DAYLIGHTS	A-Ha	*Warner Bros*	7

WEEK ENDING 22 AUGUST 1987

LW	TW	Title	Artist	Label	Wks
1	[1]	I JUST CAN'T STOP LOVING YOU	Michael Jackson with Siedah Garrett	*Epic*	3
3	[2]	CALL ME	Spagna	*CBS*	4
14	3	NEVER GONNA GIVE YOU UP	Rick Astley	*RCA*	3
10	[4]	TOY BOY	Sinitta	*Fanfare*	4
4	5	TRUE FAITH	New Order	*Factory*	4
9	[6]	ANIMAL	Def Leppard	*Bludgeon Riffola*	4
2	7	LA BAMBA	Los Lobos	*Slash*	6
11	[8]	SOMEWHERE OUT THERE	Linda Ronstadt and James Ingram	*MCA*	4
12	9	SWEET LITTLE MYSTERY	Wet Wet Wet	*Precious*	3
-	10	WHAT HAVE I DONE TO DESERVE THIS	Pet Shop Boys and Dusty Springfield ●	*Parlophone*	1
24	11	FUNKY TOWN	Pseudo Echo	*RCA*	3
6	12	LABOUR OF LOVE	Hue And Cry	*Circa*	6
-	[13]	GIRLFRIEND IN A COMA	Smiths	*Rough Trade*	1
5	14	ALONE	Heart	*Capitol*	8
8	15	WHO'S THAT GIRL	Madonna	*Sire*	6
13	16	ROADBLOCK	Stock Aitken Waterman	*Breakout*	4
7	17	ALWAYS	Atlantic Starr	*Warner Bros*	10
-	18	WHENEVER YOU'RE READY	Five Star	*Tent*	1
38	19	U GOT THE LOOK	Prince	*Paisley Park*	2
34	20	BRIDGE TO YOUR HEART	Wax	*RCA*	2
29	[21]	NEVER SAY GOODBYE	Bon Jovi	*Vertigo*	2
-	22	DIDN'T WE ALMOST HAVE IT ALL	Whitney Houston	*Arista*	1
31	23	JUST CALL	Sherrick	*Warner Bros*	3
-	[24]	WILD FLOWER	Cult	*Beggars Banquet*	1
30	[25]	HAPPY WHEN IT RAINS	Jesus And Mary Chain	*blanco y negro*	2

In these weeks ■ For the seventh consecutive week, the record at number 40 has fallen, and for the sixth consecutive week it has fallen at least 10 places (15.08.87) ■ Stock Aitken Waterman discovery Rick Astley makes his solo chart debut, having already appeared on Ferry Aid's number one hit *Let It Be* (08.08.87)■

September 1987

□ Highest position disc reached ● Act's first ever week on chart

LW	TW	Title	Artist	Label	Wks
17	26	JIVE TALKIN'	Boogie Box High	Hardback	7
-	27	THE $5.98 EP-GARAGE DAYS REVISITED	Metallica ●	Vertigo	1
16	28	I HEARD A RUMOUR	Bananarama	London	6
33	29	SAY YOU REALLY WANT ME	Kim Wilde	MCA	2
26	30	GIRLS GIRLS GIRLS	Motley Crue	Elektra	4
21	31	I REALLY DIDN'T MEAN IT	Luther Vandross	Epic	6
15	32	JUST DON'T WANT TO BE LONELY	Freddie McGregor	Germain	7
-	33	WONDERFUL LIFE	Black	A&M	1
25	34	I SURRENDER (TO THE SPIRIT OF THE NIGHT)	Samantha Fox	Jive	5
-	35	THE MOTIVE	Then Jerico ●	London	1
20	36	UNDER THE BOARDWALK	Bruce Willis	Motown	12
23	37	F.L.M.	Mel and Kim	Supreme	7
19	38	IT'S A SIN	Pet Shop Boys	Parlophone	9
18	39	SHE'S ON IT	Beastie Boys	Def Jam	5
-	40	PAPA WAS A ROLLIN' STONE	Temptations	Motown	1

WEEK ENDING 29 AUGUST 1987

LW	TW	Title	Artist	Label	Wks
3	1	NEVER GONNA GIVE YOU UP	Rick Astley	RCA	4
10	2	WHAT HAVE I DONE TO DESERVE THIS	Pet Shop Boys and Dusty Springfield	Parlophone	2
1	3	I JUST CAN'T STOP LOVING YOU	Michael Jackson with Siedah Garrett	Epic	4
4	4	TOY BOY	Sinitta	Fanfare	5
2	5	CALL ME	Spagna	CBS	5
9	6	SWEET LITTLE MYSTERY	Wet Wet Wet	Precious	4
5	7	TRUE FAITH	New Order	Factory	5
11	8	FUNKY TOWN	Pseudo Echo	RCA	4
6	9	ANIMAL	Def Leppard	Bludgeon Riffola	5
8	10	SOMEWHERE OUT THERE	Linda Ronstadt and James Ingram	MCA	5
18	11	WHENEVER YOU'RE READY	Five Star	Tent	2
20	12	BRIDGE TO YOUR HEART	Wax	RCA	3
19	13	U GOT THE LOOK	Prince	Paisley Park	3
22	14	DIDN'T WE ALMOST HAVE IT ALL	Whitney Houston	Arista	2
7	15	LA BAMBA	Los Lobos	Slash	7
13	16	GIRLFRIEND IN A COMA	Smiths	Rough Trade	2
12	17	LABOUR OF LOVE	Hue And Cry	Circa	7
33	18	WONDERFUL LIFE	Black	A&M	2
-	19	WIPEOUT	Fat Boys and the Beach Boys ●	Urban	1
15	20	WHO'S THAT GIRL	Madonna	Sire	7
16	21	ROADBLOCK	Stock Aitken Waterman	Breakout	5
-	22	SOME PEOPLE	Cliff Richard	EMI	1
35	23	THE MOTIVE	Then Jerico	London	2
14	24	ALONE	Heart	Capitol	9
23	25	JUST CALL	Sherrick	Warner Bros	4
21	26	NEVER SAY GOODBYE	Bon Jovi	Vertigo	3
17	27	ALWAYS	Atlantic Starr	Warner Bros	11
-	28	HEART AND SOUL	T'Pau ●	Siren	1
27	29	THE $5.98 EP-GARAGE DAYS REVISITED	Metallica	Vertigo	2
-	30	WILD FLOWER	Cult	Beggars Banquet	1
40	31	PAPA WAS A ROLLIN' STONE	Temptations	Motown	2
29	32	SAY YOU REALLY WANT ME	Kim Wilde	MCA	3
25	33	HAPPY WHEN IT RAINS	Jesus And Mary Chain	blanco y negro	3
-	34	CASANOVA	Levert ●	Atlantic	1
-	35	HOURGLASS	Squeeze	A&M	1
26	36	JIVE TALKIN'	Boogie Box High	Hardback	8
28	37	I HEARD A RUMOUR	Bananarama	London	7
31	38	I REALLY DIDN'T MEAN IT	Luther Vandross	Epic	7
30	39	GIRLS GIRLS GIRLS	Motley Crue	Elektra	5
36	40	UNDER THE BOARDWALK	Bruce Willis	Motown	13

WEEK ENDING 5 SEPTEMBER 1987

LW	TW	Title	Artist	Label	Wks
1	1	NEVER GONNA GIVE YOU UP	Rick Astley	RCA	5
2	2	WHAT HAVE I DONE TO DESERVE THIS	Pet Shop Boys and Dusty Springfield	Parlophone	3
19	3	WIPEOUT	Fat Boys and the Beach Boys	Urban	2
4	4	TOY BOY	Sinitta	Fanfare	6
6	5	SWEET LITTLE MYSTERY	Wet Wet Wet	Precious	5
5	6	CALL ME	Spagna	CBS	6
3	7	I JUST CAN'T STOP LOVING YOU	Michael Jackson with Siedah Garrett	Epic	5
18	8	WONDERFUL LIFE	Black	A&M	3
28	9	HEART AND SOUL	T'Pau	Siren	2
8	10	FUNKY TOWN	Pseudo Echo	RCA	5
13	11	U GOT THE LOOK	Prince	Paisley Park	4
12	12	BRIDGE TO YOUR HEART	Wax	RCA	4
11	13	WHENEVER YOU'RE READY	Five Star	Tent	3
14	14	DIDN'T WE ALMOST HAVE IT ALL	Whitney Houston	Arista	3
22	15	SOME PEOPLE	Cliff Richard	EMI	2
10	16	SOMEWHERE OUT THERE	Linda Ronstadt and James Ingram	MCA	6
9	17	ANIMAL	Def Leppard	Bludgeon Riffola	6
23	18	THE MOTIVE	Then Jerico	London	3
7	19	TRUE FAITH	New Order	Factory	6
34	20	CASANOVA	Levert	Atlantic	2
35	21	HOURGLASS	Squeeze	A&M	2
-	22	NEVER LET ME DOWN AGAIN	Depeche Mode	Mute	1
15	23	LA BAMBA	Los Lobos	Slash	8
17	24	LABOUR OF LOVE	Hue And Cry	Circa	8
16	25	GIRLFRIEND IN A COMA	Smiths	Rough Trade	3
20	26	WHO'S THAT GIRL	Madonna	Sire	8
-	27	ME AND THE FARMER	Housemartins	Go! Discs	1
25	28	JUST CALL	Sherrick	Warner Bros	5
26	29	NEVER SAY GOODBYE	Bon Jovi	Vertigo	4
30	30	WILD FLOWER	Cult	Beggars Banquet	2
24	31	ALONE	Heart	Capitol	10
31	32	PAPA WAS A ROLLIN' STONE	Temptations	Motown	3
21	33	ROADBLOCK	Stock Aitken Waterman	Breakout	6
-	34	I DON'T WANT TO BE A HERO	Johnny Hates Jazz	Virgin	1
-	35	PUMP UP THE VOLUME/ANITINA (THE FIRST TIME I SEE SHE DANCE)	M/A/R/R/S ●	4AD	1
27	36	ALWAYS	Atlantic Starr	Warner Bros	12
33	37	HAPPY WHEN IT RAINS	Jesus And Mary Chain	blanco y negro	4
-	38	LIES	Jonathan Butler ●	Jive	1
29	39	THE $5.98 EP - GARAGE DAYS REVISITED	Metallica	Vertigo	3
-	40	SCREAM UNTIL YOU LIKE IT	W.A.S.P. ●	Capitol	1

WEEK ENDING 12 SEPTEMBER 1987

LW	TW	Title	Artist	Label	Wks
1	1	NEVER GONNA GIVE YOU UP	Rick Astley	RCA	6
3	2	WIPEOUT	Fat Boys and the Beach Boys	Urban	3
2	3	WHAT HAVE I DONE TO DESERVE THIS	Pet Shop Boys and Dusty Springfield	Parlophone	4
-	4	WHERE THE STREETS HAVE NO NAME	U2	Island	1
9	5	HEART AND SOUL	T'Pau	Siren	3
4	6	TOY BOY	Sinitta	Fanfare	7
15	7	SOME PEOPLE	Cliff Richard	EMI	3
5	8	SWEET LITTLE MYSTERY	Wet Wet Wet	Precious	6
8	9	WONDERFUL LIFE	Black	A&M	4
20	10	CASANOVA	Levert	Atlantic	3
35	11	PUMP UP THE VOLUME/ANITINA (THE FIRST TIME I SEE SHE DANCE)	M/A/R/R/S	4AD	2
12	12	BRIDGE TO YOUR HEART	Wax	RCA	5
11	13	U GOT THE LOOK	Prince	Paisley Park	5
6	14	CALL ME	Spagna	CBS	7
27	15	ME AND THE FARMER	Housemartins	Go! Discs	2
21	16	HOURGLASS	Squeeze	A&M	3
7	17	I JUST CAN'T STOP LOVING YOU	Michael Jackson with Siedah Garrett	Epic	6
18	18	THE MOTIVE	Then Jerico	London	4
34	19	I DON'T WANT TO BE A HERO	Johnny Hates Jazz	Virgin	2
10	20	FUNKY TOWN	Pseudo Echo	RCA	6
14	21	DIDN'T WE ALMOST HAVE IT ALL	Whitney Houston	Arista	4
16	22	SOMEWHERE OUT THERE	Linda Ronstadt and James Ingram	MCA	7
13	23	WHENEVER YOU'RE READY	Five Star	Tent	4
-	24	IT'S OVER	Level 42	Polydor	1
17	25	ANIMAL	Def Leppard	Bludgeon Riffola	7

■M/A/R/R/S hit is listed as a double-sided hit even though only one side, *Pump Up The Volume* was ever played or requested in the shops. It still got to number one (05.09.87) ■ *Wipeout*, originally an instrumental hit by the Surfaris in 1963, becomes one of the few songs to hit the Top 10 in both vocal and instrumental versions. Others include *Amazing Grace*, *Don't Cry For Me Argentina* and *Oh Mein Papa* (05.09.87)■

September 1987

□ Highest position disc reached ● Act's first ever week on chart

LW	TW	Title / Artist	Label	Wks
22	26	NEVER LET ME DOWN AGAIN Depeche Mode	Mute	2
19	27	TRUE FAITH New Order	Factory	7
-	28	HOUSE NATION House Master Boyz and the Rude Boy Of House ●	Magnetic Dance	1
38	29	LIES Jonathan Butler	Jive	2
24	30	LABOUR OF LOVE Hue And Cry	Circa	9
23	31	LA BAMBA Los Lobos	Slash	9
40	32	SCREAM UNTIL YOU LIKE IT W.A.S.P.	Capitol	2
-	33	STOP TO LOVE Luther Vandross	Epic	1
26	34	WHO'S THAT GIRL Madonna	Sire	9
-	35	TOMORROW Communards	London	1
-	36	HEY MATTHEW Karel Fialka ●	IRS	1
-	37	NEVER LET ME DOWN David Bowie	EMI America	1
33	38	ROADBLOCK Stock Aitken Waterman	Breakout	7
25	39	GIRLFRIEND IN A COMA Smiths	Rough Trade	4
28	40	JUST CALL Sherrick	Warner Bros	6

WEEK ENDING 19 SEPTEMBER 1987

LW	TW	Title / Artist	Label	Wks
1	1	NEVER GONNA GIVE YOU UP Rick Astley	RCA	7
11	2	PUMP UP THE VOLUME/ANITINA (THE FIRST TIME I SEE SHE DANCE) M/A/R/R/S	4AD	3
2	3	WIPEOUT Fat Boys and the Beach Boys	Urban	4
5	4	HEART AND SOUL T'Pau	Siren	4
4	5	WHERE THE STREETS HAVE NO NAME U2	Island	2
7	6	SOME PEOPLE Cliff Richard	EMI	4
-	7	CAUSING A COMMOTION Madonna	Sire	1
3	8	WHAT HAVE I DONE TO DESERVE THIS Pet Shop Boys and Dusty Springfield	Parlophone	5
10	9	CASANOVA Levert	Atlantic	4
6	10	TOY BOY Sinitta	Fanfare	8
24	11	IT'S OVER Level 42	Polydor	2
28	12	HOUSE NATION House Master Boyz and the Rude Boy Of House	Magnetic Dance	2
9	13	WONDERFUL LIFE Black	A&M	5
8	14	SWEET LITTLE MYSTERY Wet Wet Wet	Precious	7
19	15	I DON'T WANT TO BE A HERO Johnny Hates Jazz	Virgin	3
12	16	BRIDGE TO YOUR HEART Wax	RCA	6
15	17	ME AND THE FARMER Housemartins	Go! Discs	3
29	18	LIES Jonathan Butler	Jive	3
16	19	HOURGLASS Squeeze	A&M	4
36	20	HEY MATTHEW Karel Fialka	IRS	2
14	21	CALL ME Spagna	CBS	8
18	22	THE MOTIVE Then Jerico	London	5
13	23	U GOT THE LOOK Prince	Paisley Park	6
33	24	STOP TO LOVE Luther Vandross	Epic	2
35	25	TOMORROW Communards	London	2
-	26	I NEED LOVE LL Cool J ●	Def Jam	1
20	27	FUNKY TOWN Pseudo Echo	RCA	7
21	28	DIDN'T WE ALMOST HAVE IT ALL Whitney Houston	Arista	5
26	29	NEVER LET ME DOWN AGAIN Depeche Mode	Mute	3
17	30	I JUST CAN'T STOP LOVING YOU Michael Jackson with Siedah Garrett	Epic	7
-	31	POUR SOME SUGAR ON ME Def Leppard	Bludgeon Riffola	1
22	32	SOMEWHERE OUT THERE Linda Ronstadt and James Ingram	MCA	8
-	33	JACK LE FREAK Chic	Atlantic	1
37	34	NEVER LET ME DOWN David Bowie	EMI America	2
-	35	CARS ('E' REG MODEL) Gary Numan	Beggars Banquet	1
-	36	CROCKETT'S THEME Jan Hammer	MCA	1
23	37	WHENEVER YOU'RE READY Five Star	Tent	5
27	38	TRUE FAITH New Order	Factory	8
-	39	NIGHT YOU MURDERED LOVE ABC	Neutron	1
25	40	ANIMAL Def Leppard	Bludgeon Riffola	8

WEEK ENDING 26 SEPTEMBER 1987

LW	TW	Title / Artist	Label	Wks
1	1	NEVER GONNA GIVE YOU UP Rick Astley	RCA	8
2	2	PUMP UP THE VOLUME/ANITINA (THE FIRST TIME I SEE SHE DANCE) M/A/R/R/S	4AD	4
6	3	SOME PEOPLE Cliff Richard	EMI	5
7	4	CAUSING A COMMOTION Madonna	Sire	2
-	5	BAD Michael Jackson	Epic	1
4	6	HEART AND SOUL T'Pau	Siren	5
3	7	WIPEOUT Fat Boys and the Beach Boys	Urban	5
12	8	HOUSE NATION House Master Boyz and the Rude Boy Of House	Magnetic Dance	3
20	9	HEY MATTHEW Karel Fialka	IRS	3
11	10	IT'S OVER Level 42	Polydor	3
15	11	I DON'T WANT TO BE A HERO Johnny Hates Jazz	Virgin	4
9	12	CASANOVA Levert	Atlantic	5
5	13	WHERE THE STREETS HAVE NO NAME U2	Island	3
10	14	TOY BOY Sinitta	Fanfare	9
8	15	WHAT HAVE I DONE TO DESERVE THIS Pet Shop Boys and Dusty Springfield	Parlophone	6
26	16	I NEED LOVE LL Cool J	Def Jam	2
13	17	WONDERFUL LIFE Black	A&M	6
18	18	LIES Jonathan Butler	Jive	4
36	19	CROCKETT'S THEME Jan Hammer	MCA	2
31	20	POUR SOME SUGAR ON ME Def Leppard	Bludgeon Riffola	2
14	21	SWEET LITTLE MYSTERY Wet Wet Wet	Precious	8
33	22	JACK LE FREAK Chic	Atlantic	2
25	23	TOMORROW Communards	London	3
16	24	BRIDGE TO YOUR HEART Wax	RCA	7
24	25	STOP TO LOVE Luther Vandross	Epic	3
35	26	CARS ('E' REG MODEL) Gary Numan	Beggars Banquet	2
19	27	HOURGLASS Squeeze	A&M	5
17	28	ME AND THE FARMER Housemartins	Go! Discs	4
21	29	CALL ME Spagna	CBS	9
23	30	U GOT THE LOOK Prince	Paisley Park	7
39	31	NIGHT YOU MURDERED LOVE ABC	Neutron	2
22	32	THE MOTIVE Then Jerico	London	6
-	33	FULL METAL JACKET (I WANNA BE YOUR DRILL INSTRUCTOR) Abigail Mead and Nigel Goulding ●	Warner Bros	1
-	34	COME SEE ABOUT ME Shakin' Stevens	Epic	1
34	35	NEVER LET ME DOWN David Bowie	EMI America	3
28	36	DIDN'T WE ALMOST HAVE IT ALL Whitney Houston	Arista	6
30	37	I JUST CAN'T STOP LOVING YOU Michael Jackson with Siedah Garrett	Epic	8
27	38	FUNKY TOWN Pseudo Echo	RCA	8
-	39	WHO WILL YOU RUN TO Heart	Capitol	1
32	40	SOMEWHERE OUT THERE Linda Ronstadt and James Ingram	MCA	9

WEEK ENDING 3 OCTOBER 1987

LW	TW	Title / Artist	Label	Wks
2	1	PUMP UP THE VOLUME/ANITINA (THE FIRST TIME I SEE SHE DANCE) M/A/R/R/S	4AD	5
1	2	NEVER GONNA GIVE YOU UP Rick Astley	RCA	9
5	3	BAD Michael Jackson	Epic	2
3	4	SOME PEOPLE Cliff Richard	EMI	6
4	5	CAUSING A COMMOTION Madonna	Sire	3
19	6	CROCKETT'S THEME Jan Hammer	MCA	3
33	7	FULL METAL JACKET (I WANNA BE YOUR DRILL INSTRUCTOR) Abigail Mead and Nigel Goulding	Warner Bros	2
8	8	HOUSE NATION House Master Boyz and the Rude Boy Of House	Magnetic Dance	4
16	9	I NEED LOVE LL Cool J	Def Jam	3
9	10	HEY MATTHEW Karel Fialka	IRS	4
6	11	HEART AND SOUL T'Pau	Siren	6
7	12	WIPEOUT Fat Boys and the Beach Boys	Urban	6
-	13	THIS CORROSION Sisters Of Mercy ●	Merciful Release	1
11	14	I DON'T WANT TO BE A HERO Johnny Hates Jazz	Virgin	5
10	15	IT'S OVER Level 42	Polydor	4
26	16	CARS ('E' REG MODEL) Gary Numan	Beggars Banquet	3
12	17	CASANOVA Levert	Atlantic	6
20	18	POUR SOME SUGAR ON ME Def Leppard	Bludgeon Riffola	3
22	19	JACK LE FREAK Chic	Atlantic	3
14	20	TOY BOY Sinitta	Fanfare	10
-	21	BRILLIANT DISGUISE Bruce Springsteen	CBS	1
-	22	YOU WIN AGAIN Bee Gees	Warner Bros	1

In these weeks ■ For the sixth consecutive week, the record at number 4 is at its peak (26.09.87) ■ Jan Hammer follows the Kids From 'Fame' in scoring two Top 10 hits from the same television show, in his case 'Miami Vice' (03.10.87)■

October 1987

□ Highest position disc reached ● Act's first ever week on chart

LW	TW	Title / Artist	Label	Wks
23	23	TOMORROW Communards	London	4
18	24	LIES Jonathan Butler	Jive	5
15	25	WHAT HAVE I DONE TO DESERVE THIS Pet Shop Boys and Dusty Springfield	Parlophone	7
17	26	WONDERFUL LIFE Black	A&M	7
34	27	COME SEE ABOUT ME Shakin' Stevens	Epic	2
25	28	STOP TO LOVE Luther Vandross	Epic	4
13	29	WHERE THE STREETS HAVE NO NAME U2	Island	4
39	30	WHO WILL YOU RUN TO Heart	Capitol	2
31	31	NIGHT YOU MURDERED LOVE ABC	Neutron	3
-	32	CRAZY CRAZY NIGHTS Kiss	Vertigo	1
-	33	LET'S WORK Mick Jagger	CBS	1
-	34	I FOUND LOVIN' Fatback Band	Master Mix	1
24	35	BRIDGE TO YOUR HEART Wax	RCA	8
-	36	VALERIE Steve Winwood	Island	1
21	37	SWEET LITTLE MYSTERY Wet Wet Wet	Precious	9
-	38	THE CIRCUS Erasure	Mute	1
-	39	I FOUND LOVIN' Steve Walsh ●	A1	1
-	40	THE REAL THING Jellybean featuring Steven Dante ●	Chrysalis	1

LW	TW	*WEEK ENDING* **10 OCTOBER 1987**		Wks
1	1	PUMP UP THE VOLUME/ANITINA (THE FIRST TIME I SEE SHE DANCE) M/A/R/R/S	4AD	6
7	2	FULL METAL JACKET (I WANNA BE YOUR DRILL INSTRUCTOR) Abigail Mead and Nigel Goulding	Warner Bros	3
3	3	BAD Michael Jackson	Epic	3
2	4	NEVER GONNA GIVE YOU UP Rick Astley	RCA	10
6	5	CROCKETT'S THEME Jan Hammer	MCA	4
22	6	YOU WIN AGAIN Bee Gees	Warner Bros	2
13	7	THIS CORROSION Sisters Of Mercy	Merciful Release	2
4	8	SOME PEOPLE Cliff Richard	EMI	7
9	9	I NEED LOVE LL Cool J	Def Jam	4
5	10	CAUSING A COMMOTION Madonna	Sire	4
8	11	HOUSE NATION House Master Boyz and the Rude Boy Of House	Magnetic Dance	5
32	12	CRAZY CRAZY NIGHTS Kiss	Vertigo	2
14	13	I DON'T WANT TO BE A HERO Johnny Hates Jazz	Virgin	6
10	14	HEY MATTHEW Karel Fialka	IRS	5
34	15	I FOUND LOVIN' Fatback Band	Master Mix	2
16	16	CARS ('E' REG MODEL) Gary Numan	Beggars Banquet	4
11	17	HEART AND SOUL T'Pau	Siren	7
12	18	WIPEOUT Fat Boys and the Beach Boys	Urban	7
15	19	IT'S OVER Level 42	Polydor	5
21	20	BRILLIANT DISGUISE Bruce Springsteen	CBS	2
38	21	THE CIRCUS Erasure	Mute	2
39	22	I FOUND LOVIN' Steve Walsh	A1	2
36	23	VALERIE Steve Winwood	Island	2
27	24	COME SEE ABOUT ME Shakin' Stevens	Epic	3
19	25	JACK LE FREAK Chic	Atlantic	4
17	26	CASANOVA Levert	Atlantic	7
23	27	TOMORROW Communards	London	5
18	28	POUR SOME SUGAR ON ME Def Leppard	Bludgeon Riffola	4
40	29	THE REAL THING Jellybean featuring Steven Dante	Chrysalis	2
30	30	WHO WILL YOU RUN TO Heart	Capitol	3
33	31	LET'S WORK Mick Jagger	CBS	2
20	32	TOY BOY Sinitta	Fanfare	11
24	33	LIES Jonathan Butler	Jive	6
-	34	STRONG AS STEEL Five Star	Tent	1
-	35	MONY MONY Billy Idol	Chrysalis	1
31	36	NIGHT YOU MURDERED LOVE ABC	Neutron	4
-	37	COME ON LET'S GO Los Lobos	Slash	1
-	38	WALK THE DINOSAUR Was Not Was ●	Fontana	1
-	39	LITTLE LIES Fleetwood Mac	Warner Bros	1
-	40	GIRLS/SHE'S CRAFTY Beastie Boys	Def Jam	1

LW	TW	*WEEK ENDING* **17 OCTOBER 1987**		Wks
6	1	YOU WIN AGAIN Bee Gees	Warner Bros	3
2	2	FULL METAL JACKET (I WANNA BE YOUR DRILL INSTRUCTOR) Abigail Mead and Nigel Goulding	Warner Bros	4
1	3	PUMP UP THE VOLUME/ANITINA (THE FIRST TIME I SEE SHE DANCE) M/A/R/R/S	4AD	7
5	4	CROCKETT'S THEME Jan Hammer	MCA	5
12	5	CRAZY CRAZY NIGHTS Kiss	Vertigo	3
3	6	BAD Michael Jackson	Epic	4
15	7	I FOUND LOVIN' Fatback Band	Master Mix	3
9	8	I NEED LOVE LL Cool J	Def Jam	5
22	9	I FOUND LOVIN' Steve Walsh	A1	3
4	10	NEVER GONNA GIVE YOU UP Rick Astley	RCA	11
7	11	THIS CORROSION Sisters Of Mercy	Merciful Release	3
21	12	THE CIRCUS Erasure	Mute	3
29	13	THE REAL THING Jellybean featuring Steven Dante	Chrysalis	3
8	14	SOME PEOPLE Cliff Richard	EMI	8
10	15	CAUSING A COMMOTION Madonna	Sire	5
34	16	STRONG AS STEEL Five Star	Tent	2
35	17	MONY MONY Billy Idol	Chrysalis	2
38	18	WALK THE DINOSAUR Was Not Was	Fontana	2
23	19	VALERIE Steve Winwood	Island	3
-	20	RAIN IN THE SUMMERTIME Alarm	IRS	1
39	21	LITTLE LIES Fleetwood Mac	Warner Bros	2
-	22	LOVE IN THE FIRST DEGREE Bananarama	London	1
16	23	CARS ('E' REG MODEL) Gary Numan	Beggars Banquet	5
11	24	HOUSE NATION House Master Boyz and the Rude Boy Of House	Magnetic Dance	6
13	25	I DON'T WANT TO BE A HERO Johnny Hates Jazz	Virgin	7
37	26	COME ON LET'S GO Los Lobos	Slash	2
19	27	IT'S OVER Level 42	Polydor	6
14	28	HEY MATTHEW Karel Fialka	IRS	6
-	29	MAYBE TOMORROW UB40	DEP International	1
-	30	DANCE LITTLE SISTER Terence Trent D'Arby	CBS	1
17	31	HEART AND SOUL T'Pau	Siren	8
18	32	WIPEOUT Fat Boys and the Beach Boys	Urban	8
24	33	COME SEE ABOUT ME Shakin' Stevens	Epic	4
40	34	GIRLS/SHE'S CRAFTY Beastie Boys	Def Jam	2
-	35	JUST LIKE HEAVEN Cure	Fiction	1
-	36	I DON'T THINK THAT MAN SHOULD SLEEP ALONE Ray Parker Jr	Geffen	1
30	37	WHO WILL YOU RUN TO Heart	Capitol	4
20	38	BRILLIANT DISGUISE Bruce Springsteen	CBS	3
26	39	CASANOVA Levert	Atlantic	8
25	40	JACK LE FREAK Chic	Atlantic	5

LW	TW	*WEEK ENDING* **24 OCTOBER 1987**		Wks
1	1	YOU WIN AGAIN Bee Gees	Warner Bros	4
4	2	CROCKETT'S THEME Jan Hammer	MCA	6
2	3	FULL METAL JACKET (I WANNA BE YOUR DRILL INSTRUCTOR) Abigail Mead and Nigel Goulding	Warner Bros	5
5	4	CRAZY CRAZY NIGHTS Kiss	Vertigo	4
22	5	LOVE IN THE FIRST DEGREE/MR SLEAZE Bananarama/Stock Aitken Waterman	London	2
3	6	PUMP UP THE VOLUME/ANITINA (THE FIRST TIME I SEE SHE DANCE) M/A/R/R/S	4AD	8
12	7	THE CIRCUS Erasure	Mute	4
17	8	MONY MONY Billy Idol	Chrysalis	3
7	9	I FOUND LOVIN' Fatback Band	Master Mix	4
-	10	FAITH George Michael	Epic	1
21	11	LITTLE LIES Fleetwood Mac	Warner Bros	3
18	12	WALK THE DINOSAUR Was Not Was	Fontana	3
13	13	THE REAL THING Jellybean featuring Steven Dante	Chrysalis	4
9	14	I FOUND LOVIN' Steve Walsh	A1	4
29	15	MAYBE TOMORROW UB40	DEP International	2
8	16	I NEED LOVE LL Cool J	Def Jam	6
-	17	RENT Pet Shop Boys	Parlophone	1
20	18	RAIN IN THE SUMMERTIME Alarm	IRS	2
16	19	STRONG AS STEEL Five Star	Tent	3
6	20	BAD Michael Jackson	Epic	5
26	21	COME ON LET'S GO Los Lobos	Slash	3
10	22	NEVER GONNA GIVE YOU UP Rick Astley	RCA	12

■For seven consecutive weeks, the record at number 14 is falling down the charts (24.10.87) ■ The Bee Gees equal Elvis Presley and Cliff Richard's achievement of having number one hits in three decades, but Cliff will soon extend his record to four and then five decades (17.10.87)■

October 1987

□ Highest position disc reached ● Act's first ever week on chart

LW	TW	Title / Artist	Label	Wks
30	23	DANCE LITTLE SISTER Terence Trent D'Arby	*CBS*	2
36	24	I DON'T THINK THAT MAN SHOULD SLEEP ALONE Ray Parker Jr	*Geffen*	2
19	25	VALERIE Steve Winwood	*Island*	4
11	26	THIS CORROSION Sisters Of Mercy	*Merciful Release*	4
14	27	SOME PEOPLE Cliff Richard	*EMI*	9
15	28	CAUSING A COMMOTION Madonna	*Sire*	6
35	[29]	JUST LIKE HEAVEN Cure	*Fiction*	2
-	30	BEETHOVEN (I LOVE TO LISTEN TO) Eurythmics	*RCA*	1
-	31	NO MEMORY Scarlet Fantastic ●	*Arista*	1
25	32	I DON'T WANT TO BE A HERO Johnny Hates Jazz	*Virgin*	8
27	33	IT'S OVER Level 42	*Polydor*	7
-	[34]	WHEN THE FINGERS POINT Christians	*Island*	1
-	[35]	SHE'S MINE Cameo	*Club*	1
24	36	HOUSE NATION House Master Boyz and the Rude Boy Of House	*Magnetic Dance*	7
-	37	SO THE STORY GOES Living In A Box featuring Bobby Womack	*Chrysalis*	1
-	[38]	MONY MONY Amazulu	*EMI*	1
31	39	HEART AND SOUL T'Pau	*Siren*	9
23	40	CARS ('E' REG MODEL) Gary Numan	*Beggars Banquet*	6

WEEK ENDING 31 OCTOBER 1987

LW	TW	Title / Artist	Label	Wks
1	[1]	YOU WIN AGAIN Bee Gees	*Warner Bros*	5
10	[2]	FAITH George Michael	*Epic*	2
5	[3]	LOVE IN THE FIRST DEGREE/MR SLEAZE Bananarama/Stock Aitken Waterman	*London*	3
2	4	CROCKETT'S THEME Jan Hammer	*MCA*	7
11	[5]	LITTLE LIES Fleetwood Mac	*Warner Bros*	4
7	[6]	THE CIRCUS Erasure	*Mute*	5
8	[7]	MONY MONY Billy Idol	*Chrysalis*	4
17	[8]	RENT Pet Shop Boys	*Parlophone*	2
4	9	CRAZY CRAZY NIGHTS Kiss	*Vertigo*	5
12	[10]	WALK THE DINOSAUR Was Not Was	*Fontana*	4
-	11	WHENEVER YOU NEED SOMEBODY Rick Astley	*RCA*	1
3	12	FULL METAL JACKET (I WANNA BE YOUR DRILL INSTRUCTOR) Abigail Mead and Nigel Goulding	*Warner Bros*	6
13	[13]	THE REAL THING Jellybean featuring Steven Dante	*Chrysalis*	5
15	[14]	MAYBE TOMORROW UB40	*DEP International*	3
24	15	I DON'T THINK THAT MAN SHOULD SLEEP ALONE Ray Parker Jr	*Geffen*	3
6	16	PUMP UP THE VOLUME/ANITINA (THE FIRST TIME I SEE SHE DANCE) M/A/R/R/S	*4AD*	9
9	17	I FOUND LOVIN' Fatback Band	*Master Mix*	5
21	[18]	COME ON LET'S GO Los Lobos	*Slash*	4
-	19	CHINA IN YOUR HAND T'Pau	*Siren*	1
23	[20]	DANCE LITTLE SISTER Terence Trent D'Arby	*CBS*	3
14	21	I FOUND LOVIN' Steve Walsh	*A1*	5
-	22	GOT MY MIND SET ON YOU George Harrison	*Dark Horse*	1
19	23	STRONG AS STEEL Five Star	*Tent*	4
18	24	RAIN IN THE SUMMERTIME Alarm	*IRS*	3
30	[25]	BEETHOVEN (I LOVE TO LISTEN TO) Eurythmics	*RCA*	2
-	26	WANTED Style Council	*Polydor*	1
20	27	BAD Michael Jackson	*Epic*	6
22	28	NEVER GONNA GIVE YOU UP Rick Astley	*RCA*	13
16	29	I NEED LOVE LL Cool J	*Def Jam*	7
31	30	NO MEMORY Scarlet Fantastic	*Arista*	2
29	31	JUST LIKE HEAVEN Cure	*Fiction*	3
-	[32]	TEARS FROM HEAVEN Heartbeat ●	*Priority*	1
25	33	VALERIE Steve Winwood	*Island*	5
37	[34]	SO THE STORY GOES Living In A Box featuring Bobby Womack	*Chrysalis*	2
28	35	CAUSING A COMMOTION Madonna	*Sire*	7
34	36	WHEN THE FINGERS POINT Christians	*Island*	2
-	[37]	THE RIGHT STUFF Bryan Ferry	*Virgin*	1
-	38	HERE I GO AGAIN Whitesnake	*EMI*	1
-	39	REMEMBER ME Cliff Richard	*EMI*	1
38	40	MONY MONY Amazulu	*EMI*	2

WEEK ENDING 7 NOVEMBER 1987

LW	TW	Title / Artist	Label	Wks
1	[1]	YOU WIN AGAIN Bee Gees	*Warner Bros*	6
2	[2]	FAITH George Michael	*Epic*	3
11	[3]	WHENEVER YOU NEED SOMEBODY Rick Astley	*RCA*	2
3	4	LOVE IN THE FIRST DEGREE/MR SLEAZE Bananarama/Stock Aitken Waterman	*London*	4
19	5	CHINA IN YOUR HAND T'Pau	*Siren*	2
5	6	LITTLE LIES Fleetwood Mac	*Warner Bros*	5
22	7	GOT MY MIND SET ON YOU George Harrison	*Dark Horse*	2
7	8	MONY MONY Billy Idol	*Chrysalis*	5
4	9	CROCKETT'S THEME Jan Hammer	*MCA*	8
10	[10]	WALK THE DINOSAUR Was Not Was	*Fontana*	5
6	11	THE CIRCUS Erasure	*Mute*	6
-	12	BARCELONA Freddie Mercury and Montserrat Caballe ●	*Polydor*	1
15	[13]	I DON'T THINK THAT MAN SHOULD SLEEP ALONE Ray Parker Jr	*Geffen*	4
8	14	RENT Pet Shop Boys	*Parlophone*	3
-	15	NEVER CAN SAY GOODBYE Communards	*London*	1
9	16	CRAZY CRAZY NIGHTS Kiss	*Vertigo*	6
38	17	HERE I GO AGAIN Whitesnake	*EMI*	2
12	18	FULL METAL JACKET (I WANNA BE YOUR DRILL INSTRUCTOR) Abigail Mead and Nigel Goulding	*Warner Bros*	7
13	19	THE REAL THING Jellybean featuring Steven Dante	*Chrysalis*	6
26	[20]	WANTED Style Council	*Polydor*	2
14	21	MAYBE TOMORROW UB40	*DEP International*	4
20	22	DANCE LITTLE SISTER Terence Trent D'Arby	*CBS*	4
18	23	COME ON LET'S GO Los Lobos	*Slash*	5
-	24	(I'VE HAD) THE TIME OF MY LIFE Bill Medley and Jennifer Warnes ●	*RCA*	1
16	25	PUMP UP THE VOLUME/ANITINA (THE FIRST TIME I SEE SHE DANCE) M/A/R/R/S	*4AD*	10
-	26	MY BABY JUST CARES FOR ME Nina Simone	*Charly*	1
30	27	NO MEMORY Scarlet Fantastic	*Arista*	3
-	28	PAID IN FULL Eric B and Rakim ●	*Fourth + Broadway*	1
-	29	JACK MIX IV Mirage	*Debut*	1
17	30	I FOUND LOVIN' Fatback Band	*Master Mix*	6
25	31	BEETHOVEN (I LOVE TO LISTEN TO) Eurythmics	*RCA*	3
32	[32]	TEARS FROM HEAVEN Heartbeat	*Priority*	2
23	33	STRONG AS STEEL Five Star	*Tent*	5
27	34	BAD Michael Jackson	*Epic*	7
39	[35]	REMEMBER ME Cliff Richard	*EMI*	2
-	36	DARKLANDS Jesus And Mary Chain	*blanco y negro*	1
28	37	NEVER GONNA GIVE YOU UP Rick Astley	*RCA*	14
21	38	I FOUND LOVIN' Steve Walsh	*A1*	6
-	39	DINNER WITH GERSHWIN Donna Summer	*Warner Bros*	1
-	40	WARM WET CIRCLES Marillion	*EMI*	1

WEEK ENDING 14 NOVEMBER 1987

LW	TW	Title / Artist	Label	Wks
5	[1]	CHINA IN YOUR HAND T'Pau	*Siren*	3
7	[2]	GOT MY MIND SET ON YOU George Harrison	*Dark Horse*	3
1	3	YOU WIN AGAIN Bee Gees	*Warner Bros*	7
3	4	WHENEVER YOU NEED SOMEBODY Rick Astley	*RCA*	3
2	5	FAITH George Michael	*Epic*	4
15	6	NEVER CAN SAY GOODBYE Communards	*London*	2
4	7	LOVE IN THE FIRST DEGREE/MR SLEAZE Bananarama/Stock Aitken Waterman	*London*	5
12	[8]	BARCELONA Freddie Mercury and Montserrat Caballe	*Polydor*	2
6	9	LITTLE LIES Fleetwood Mac	*Warner Bros*	6
24	10	(I'VE HAD) THE TIME OF MY LIFE Bill Medley and Jennifer Warnes	*RCA*	2
26	11	MY BABY JUST CARES FOR ME Nina Simone	*Charly*	2
17	12	HERE I GO AGAIN Whitesnake	*EMI*	3
29	13	JACK MIX IV Mirage	*Debut*	2
8	14	MONY MONY Billy Idol	*Chrysalis*	6
28	[15]	PAID IN FULL Eric B and Rakim	*Fourth + Broadway*	2
13	16	I DON'T THINK THAT MAN SHOULD SLEEP ALONE Ray Parker Jr	*Geffen*	5
9	17	CROCKETT'S THEME Jan Hammer	*MCA*	9
10	18	WALK THE DINOSAUR Was Not Was	*Fontana*	6
11	19	THE CIRCUS Erasure	*Mute*	7

In these weeks ■ *China In Your Hand* by T'Pau becomes the 600th single to top the charts (14.11.87) ■ Freddie Mercury hits the Top 10 as half of a duo. He has already been there as a soloist, as a member of a quartet (Queen) and a quintet (Queen and David Bowie). He never made it as part of a trio (14.11.87) ■

LW	TW	Title / Artist	Label	Wks
-	20	SO EMOTIONAL Whitney Houston	Arista	1
14	21	RENT Pet Shop Boys	Parlophone	4
40	22	WARM WET CIRCLES Marillion	EMI	2
39	23	DINNER WITH GERSHWIN Donna Summer	Warner Bros	2
27	24	NO MEMORY Scarlet Fantastic	Arista	4
20	25	WANTED Style Council	Polydor	3
16	26	CRAZY CRAZY NIGHTS Kiss	Vertigo	7
19	27	THE REAL THING Jellybean featuring Steven Dante	Chrysalis	7
-	28	CRITICIZE Alexander O'Neal	Tabu	1
-	29	I STARTED SOMETHING I COULDN'T FINISH Smiths	Rough Trade	1
18	30	FULL METAL JACKET (I WANNA BE YOUR DRILL INSTRUCTOR) Abigail Mead and Nigel Goulding	Warner Bros	8
21	31	MAYBE TOMORROW UB40	DEP International	5
-	32	SOME GUYS HAVE ALL THE LUCK Maxi Priest	10	1
36	33	DARKLANDS Jesus And Mary Chain	blanco y negro	2
22	34	DANCE LITTLE SISTER Terence Trent D'Arby	CBS	5
25	35	PUMP UP THE VOLUME/ANITINA (THE FIRST TIME I SEE SHE DANCE) M/A/R/R/S	4AD	11
-	36	I DON'T NEED NO DOCTOR W.A.S.P.	Capitol	1
23	37	COME ON LET'S GO Los Lobos	Slash	6
-	38	SHO' YOU RIGHT Barry White	Breakout	1
35	39	REMEMBER ME Cliff Richard	EMI	3
30	40	I FOUND LOVIN' Fatback Band	Master Mix	7

WEEK ENDING 21 NOVEMBER 1987

LW	TW	Title / Artist	Label	Wks
1	1	CHINA IN YOUR HAND T'Pau	Siren	4
2	2	GOT MY MIND SET ON YOU George Harrison	Dark Horse	4
4	3	WHENEVER YOU NEED SOMEBODY Rick Astley	RCA	4
6	4	NEVER CAN SAY GOODBYE Communards	London	3
11	5	MY BABY JUST CARES FOR ME Nina Simone	Charly	3
10	6	(I'VE HAD) THE TIME OF MY LIFE Bill Medley and Jennifer Warnes	RCA	3
3	7	YOU WIN AGAIN Bee Gees	Warner Bros	8
13	8	JACK MIX IV Mirage	Debut	3
20	9	SO EMOTIONAL Whitney Houston	Arista	2
8	10	BARCELONA Freddie Mercury and Montserrat Caballe	Polydor	3
12	11	HERE I GO AGAIN Whitesnake	EMI	4
5	12	FAITH George Michael	Epic	5
7	13	LOVE IN THE FIRST DEGREE/MR SLEAZE Bananarama/Stock Aitken Waterman	London	6
28	14	CRITICIZE Alexander O'Neal	Tabu	2
9	15	LITTLE LIES Fleetwood Mac	Warner Bros	7
15	16	PAID IN FULL Eric B and Rakim	Fourth + Broadway	3
23	17	DINNER WITH GERSHWIN Donna Summer	Warner Bros	3
32	18	SOME GUYS HAVE ALL THE LUCK Maxi Priest	10	2
14	19	MONY MONY Billy Idol	Chrysalis	7
38	20	SHO' YOU RIGHT Barry White	Breakout	2
18	21	WALK THE DINOSAUR Was Not Was	Fontana	7
17	22	CROCKETT'S THEME Jan Hammer	MCA	10
29	23	I STARTED SOMETHING I COULDN'T FINISH Smiths	Rough Trade	2
16	24	I DON'T THINK THAT MAN SHOULD SLEEP ALONE Ray Parker Jr	Geffen	6
-	25	LETTER FROM AMERICA Proclaimers ●	Chrysalis	1
-	26	TO BE REBORN Boy George	Virgin	1
22	27	WARM WET CIRCLES Marillion	EMI	3
24	28	NO MEMORY Scarlet Fantastic	Arista	5
19	29	THE CIRCUS Erasure	Mute	8
-	30	BUILD Housemartins	Go! Discs	1
36	31	I DON'T NEED NO DOCTOR W.A.S.P.	Capitol	2
21	32	RENT Pet Shop Boys	Parlophone	5
-	33	I WANT TO BE YOUR PROPERTY Blue Mercedes ●	MCA	1
33	34	DARKLANDS Jesus And Mary Chain	blanco y negro	3
27	35	THE REAL THING Jellybean featuring Steven Dante	Chrysalis	8
26	36	CRAZY CRAZY NIGHTS Kiss	Vertigo	8
35	37	PUMP UP THE VOLUME/ANITINA (THE FIRST TIME I SEE SHE DANCE) M/A/R/R/S	4AD	12
30	38	FULL METAL JACKET (I WANNA BE YOUR DRILL INSTRUCTOR) Abigail Mead and Nigel Goulding	Warner Bros	9
-	39	SO AMAZING Luther Vandross	Epic	1
-	40	NEVER GONNA GIVE YOU UP Rick Astley	RCA	15

December 1987

□ Highest position disc reached ● Act's first ever week on chart

WEEK ENDING 28 NOVEMBER 1987

LW	TW	Title / Artist	Label	Wks
1	1	CHINA IN YOUR HAND T'Pau	Siren	5
2	2	GOT MY MIND SET ON YOU George Harrison	Dark Horse	5
3	3	WHENEVER YOU NEED SOMEBODY Rick Astley	RCA	5
4	4	NEVER CAN SAY GOODBYE Communards	London	4
9	5	SO EMOTIONAL Whitney Houston	Arista	3
6	6	(I'VE HAD) THE TIME OF MY LIFE Bill Medley and Jennifer Warnes	RCA	4
5	7	MY BABY JUST CARES FOR ME Nina Simone	Charly	4
14	8	CRITICIZE Alexander O'Neal	Tabu	3
11	9	HERE I GO AGAIN Whitesnake	EMI	5
25	10	LETTER FROM AMERICA Proclaimers	Chrysalis	2
8	11	JACK MIX IV Mirage	Debut	4
18	12	SOME GUYS HAVE ALL THE LUCK Maxi Priest	10	3
17	13	DINNER WITH GERSHWIN Donna Summer	Warner Bros	4
20	14	SHO' YOU RIGHT Barry White	Breakout	3
7	15	YOU WIN AGAIN Bee Gees	Warner Bros	9
13	16	LOVE IN THE FIRST DEGREE/MR SLEAZE Bananarama/Stock Aitken Waterman	London	7
10	17	BARCELONA Freddie Mercury and Montserrat Caballe	Polydor	4
26	18	TO BE REBORN Boy George	Virgin	2
30	19	BUILD Housemartins	Go! Discs	2
16	20	PAID IN FULL Eric B and Rakim	Fourth + Broadway	4
12	21	FAITH George Michael	Epic	6
15	22	LITTLE LIES Fleetwood Mac	Warner Bros	8
-	23	ONCE UPON A LONG AGO Paul McCartney	Parlophone	1
33	24	I WANT TO BE YOUR PROPERTY Blue Mercedes	MCA	2
23	25	I STARTED SOMETHING I COULDN'T FINISH Smiths	Rough Trade	3
-	26	THERE AIN'T NOTHING LIKE SHAGGIN' Tams	Virgin	1
-	27	WHAT DO YOU WANT TO MAKE THOSE EYES AT ME FOR Shakin' Stevens	Epic	1
-	28	SATELLITE Hooters ●	CBS	1
-	29	WHO FOUND WHO Jellybean featuring Elisa Fiorillo	Chrysalis	1
-	30	I'VE BEEN IN LOVE BEFORE Cutting Crew	Siren	1
-	31	HYSTERIA Def Leppard	Bludgeon Riffola	1
19	32	MONY MONY Billy Idol	Chrysalis	8
39	33	SO AMAZING Luther Vandross	Epic	2
-	34	I WON'T CRY Glen Goldsmith ●	Reproduction	1
-	35	TURN BACK THE CLOCK Johnny Hates Jazz	Virgin	1
-	36	I COULD NEVER TAKE THE PLACE OF YOUR MAN Prince	Paisley Park	1
22	37	CROCKETT'S THEME Jan Hammer	MCA	11
21	38	WALK THE DINOSAUR Was Not Was	Fontana	8
28	39	NO MEMORY Scarlet Fantastic	Arista	6
-	40	REBEL WITHOUT A PAUSE Public Enemy ●	Def Jam	1

WEEK ENDING 5 DECEMBER 1987

LW	TW	Title / Artist	Label	Wks
1	1	CHINA IN YOUR HAND T'Pau	Siren	6
2	2	GOT MY MIND SET ON YOU George Harrison	Dark Horse	6
10	3	LETTER FROM AMERICA Proclaimers	Chrysalis	3
8	4	CRITICIZE Alexander O'Neal	Tabu	4
4	5	NEVER CAN SAY GOODBYE Communards	London	5
5	6	SO EMOTIONAL Whitney Houston	Arista	4
27	7	WHAT DO YOU WANT TO MAKE THOSE EYES AT ME FOR Shakin' Stevens	Epic	2
3	8	WHENEVER YOU NEED SOMEBODY Rick Astley	RCA	6
6	9	(I'VE HAD) THE TIME OF MY LIFE Bill Medley and Jennifer Warnes	RCA	5
9	10	HERE I GO AGAIN Whitesnake	EMI	6
7	11	MY BABY JUST CARES FOR ME Nina Simone	Charly	5
12	12	SOME GUYS HAVE ALL THE LUCK Maxi Priest	10	4
18	13	TO BE REBORN Boy George	Virgin	3
23	14	ONCE UPON A LONG AGO Paul McCartney	Parlophone	2
19	15	BUILD Housemartins	Go! Discs	3
-	16	THE WAY YOU MAKE ME FEEL Michael Jackson	Epic	1

■George Harrison's biggest hit since 1970 spends 4 weeks at number two, but cannot displace T'Pau at the top (05.12.87) ■ The Tams belatedly follow up their number one hit, over sixteen years after *Hey Girl Don't Bother Me* dropped off the charts (28.11.87)■

December 1987

□ Highest position disc reached ● Act's first ever week on chart

LW	TW	Title / Artist	Label	Wks
14	17	SHO' YOU RIGHT Barry White	Breakout	4
29	18	WHO FOUND WHO Jellybean featuring Elisa Fiorillo	Chrysalis	2
11	19	JACK MIX IV Mirage	Debut	5
13	20	DINNER WITH GERSHWIN Donna Summer	Warner Bros	5
26	21	THERE AIN'T NOTHING LIKE SHAGGIN' Tams	Virgin	2
28	22	SATELLITE Hooters	CBS	2
24	23	I WANT TO BE YOUR PROPERTY Blue Mercedes	MCA	3
30	24	I'VE BEEN IN LOVE BEFORE Cutting Crew	Siren	2
16	25	LOVE IN THE FIRST DEGREE/MR SLEAZE Bananarama/Stock Aitken Waterman	London	8
31	26	HYSTERIA Def Leppard	Bludgeon Riffola	2
35	27	TURN BACK THE CLOCK Johnny Hates Jazz	Virgin	2
15	28	YOU WIN AGAIN Bee Gees	Warner Bros	10
36	29	I COULD NEVER TAKE THE PLACE OF YOUR MAN Prince	Paisley Park	2
-	30	LOVE LETTERS Alison Moyet	CBS	1
21	31	FAITH George Michael	Epic	7
17	32	BARCELONA Freddie Mercury and Montserrat Caballe	Polydor	5
20	33	PAID IN FULL Eric B and Rakim	4th & Broadway	5
34	34	I WON'T CRY Glen Goldsmith	Reproduction	2
-	35	I'M THE MAN Anthrax	Island	1
-	36	SOMEWHERE SOMEBODY Five Star	Tent	1
40	37	REBEL WITHOUT A PAUSE Public Enemy	Def Jam	2
22	38	LITTLE LIES Fleetwood Mac	Warner Bros	9
-	39	ROCKIN' AROUND THE CHRISTMAS TREE Kim Wilde and Mel Smith ●	10	1
-	40	FAIRYTALE OF NEW YORK Pogues featuring Kirsty MacColl	Pogue Mahone	1

LW	TW	*WEEK ENDING* **12 DECEMBER 1987**		Wks
1	1	CHINA IN YOUR HAND T'Pau	Siren	7
-	2	WHEN I FALL IN LOVE Rick Astley	RCA	1
16	3	THE WAY YOU MAKE ME FEEL Michael Jackson	Epic	2
-	4	ALWAYS ON MY MIND Pet Shop Boys	Parlophone	1
7	5	WHAT DO YOU WANT TO MAKE THOSE EYES AT ME FOR Shakin' Stevens	Epic	3
3	6	LETTER FROM AMERICA Proclaimers	Chrysalis	4
2	7	GOT MY MIND SET ON YOU George Harrison	Dark Horse	7
4	8	CRITICIZE Alexander O'Neal	Tabu	5
30	9	LOVE LETTERS Alison Moyet	CBS	2
14	10	ONCE UPON A LONG AGO Paul McCartney	Parlophone	3
18	11	WHO FOUND WHO Jellybean featuring Elisa Fiorillo	Chrysalis	3
6	12	SO EMOTIONAL Whitney Houston	Arista	5
39	13	ROCKIN' AROUND THE CHRISTMAS TREE Kim Wilde and Mel Smith	10	2
5	14	NEVER CAN SAY GOODBYE Communards	London	6
-	15	THE LOOK OF LOVE Madonna	Sire	1
12	16	SOME GUYS HAVE ALL THE LUCK Maxi Priest	10	5
15	17	BUILD Housemartins	Go! Discs	4
13	18	TO BE REBORN Boy George	Virgin	4
40	19	FAIRYTALE OF NEW YORK Pogues featuring Kirsty MacColl	Pogue Mahone	2
35	20	I'M THE MAN Anthrax	Island	2
9	21	(I'VE HAD) THE TIME OF MY LIFE Bill Medley and Jennifer Warnes	RCA	6
22	22	SATELLITE Hooters	CBS	3
36	23	SOMEWHERE SOMEBODY Five Star	Tent	2
8	24	WHENEVER YOU NEED SOMEBODY Rick Astley	RCA	7
24	25	I'VE BEEN IN LOVE BEFORE Cutting Crew	Siren	3
10	26	HERE I GO AGAIN Whitesnake	EMI	7
27	27	TURN BACK THE CLOCK Johnny Hates Jazz	Virgin	3
11	28	MY BABY JUST CARES FOR ME Nina Simone	Charly	6
21	29	THERE AIN'T NOTHING LIKE SHAGGIN' Tams	Virgin	3
29	30	I COULD NEVER TAKE THE PLACE OF YOUR MAN Prince	Paisley Park	3
23	31	I WANT TO BE YOUR PROPERTY Blue Mercedes	MCA	4
-	32	ANGEL EYES (HOME AND AWAY) Wet Wet Wet	Precious	1
-	33	EV'RY TIME WE SAY GOODBYE Simply Red	WEA	1
20	34	DINNER WITH GERSHWIN Donna Summer	Warner Bros	6
19	35	JACK MIX IV Mirage	Debut	6
-	36	CHILDREN SAY Level 42	Polydor	1
17	37	SHO' YOU RIGHT Barry White	Breakout	5
26	38	HYSTERIA Def Leppard	Bludgeon Riffola	3
25	39	LOVE IN THE FIRST DEGREE/MR SLEAZE Bananarama/Stock Aitken Waterman	London	9
34	40	I WON'T CRY Glen Goldsmith	Reproduction	3

LW	TW	*WEEK ENDING* **19 DECEMBER 1987**		Wks
4	1	ALWAYS ON MY MIND Pet Shop Boys	Parlophone	2
2	2	WHEN I FALL IN LOVE Rick Astley	RCA	2
3	3	THE WAY YOU MAKE ME FEEL Michael Jackson	Epic	3
9	4	LOVE LETTERS Alison Moyet	CBS	3
1	5	CHINA IN YOUR HAND T'Pau	Siren	8
13	6	ROCKIN' AROUND THE CHRISTMAS TREE Kim Wilde and Mel Smith	10	3
5	7	WHAT DO YOU WANT TO MAKE THOSE EYES AT ME FOR Shakin' Stevens	Epic	4
19	8	FAIRYTALE OF NEW YORK Pogues featuring Kirsty MacColl	Pogue Mahone	3
15	9	THE LOOK OF LOVE Madonna	Sire	2
11	10	WHO FOUND WHO Jellybean featuring Elisa Fiorillo	Chrysalis	4
8	11	CRITICIZE Alexander O'Neal	Tabu	6
6	12	LETTER FROM AMERICA Proclaimers	Chrysalis	5
7	13	GOT MY MIND SET ON YOU George Harrison	Dark Horse	8
10	14	ONCE UPON A LONG AGO Paul McCartney	Parlophone	4
27	15	TURN BACK THE CLOCK Johnny Hates Jazz	Virgin	4
12	16	SO EMOTIONAL Whitney Houston	Arista	6
33	17	EV'RY TIME WE SAY GOODBYE Simply Red	WEA	2
14	18	NEVER CAN SAY GOODBYE Communards	London	7
-	19	HEAVEN IS A PLACE ON EARTH Belinda Carlisle ●	Virgin	1
-	20	WHEN I FALL IN LOVE Nat 'King' Cole	Capitol	1
32	21	ANGEL EYES (HOME AND AWAY) Wet Wet Wet	Precious	2
36	22	CHILDREN SAY Level 42	Polydor	2
20	23	I'M THE MAN Anthrax	Island	3
22	24	SATELLITE Hooters	CBS	4
-	25	TOUCHED BY THE HAND OF GOD New Order	Factory	1
23	26	SOMEWHERE SOMEBODY Five Star	Tent	3
16	27	SOME GUYS HAVE ALL THE LUCK Maxi Priest	10	6
25	28	I'VE BEEN IN LOVE BEFORE Cutting Crew	Siren	4
21	29	(I'VE HAD) THE TIME OF MY LIFE Bill Medley and Jennifer Warnes	RCA	7
-	30	JINGO Jellybean	Chrysalis	1
17	31	BUILD Housemartins	Go! Discs	5
26	32	HERE I GO AGAIN Whitesnake	EMI	8
28	33	MY BABY JUST CARES FOR ME Nina Simone	Charly	7
-	34	LAST NIGHT I DREAMT I DREAMT THAT SOMEBODY LOVED ME Smiths	Rough Trade	1
24	35	WHENEVER YOU NEED SOMEBODY Rick Astley	RCA	8
-	36	TIGHTEN UP (I JUST CAN'T STOP DANCIN') Wally Jump Jr and the Criminal Element ●	Breakout	1
-	37	G.T.O. Sinitta	Fanfare	1
18	38	TO BE REBORN Boy George	Virgin	5
-	39	IDEAL WORLD Christians	Island	1
-	40	REASON TO LIVE Kiss	Vertigo	1

LW	TW	*WEEK ENDING* **26 DECEMBER 1987**		Wks
1	1	ALWAYS ON MY MIND Pet Shop Boys	Parlophone	3
8	2	FAIRYTALE OF NEW YORK Pogues featuring Kirsty MacColl	Pogue Mahone	4
6	3	ROCKIN' AROUND THE CHRISTMAS TREE Kim Wilde and Mel Smith	10	4
2	4	WHEN I FALL IN LOVE Rick Astley	RCA	3
4	5	LOVE LETTERS Alison Moyet	CBS	4
3	6	THE WAY YOU MAKE ME FEEL Michael Jackson	Epic	4
20	7	WHEN I FALL IN LOVE Nat 'King' Cole	Capitol	2
19	8	HEAVEN IS A PLACE ON EARTH Belinda Carlisle	Virgin	2
5	9	CHINA IN YOUR HAND T'Pau	Siren	9

In these weeks ■ George Harrison and Paul McCartney, who first hit the top ten as Beatles just under twenty five years earlier, both drop out of the Top 10 for the last time in the same week (19.12.87) ■ As is traditional at Christmas, most of the biggest hits are old songs, including *Always On My Mind*, *When I Fall In Love* (in two versions), *Rockin' Around The Christmas Tree*, *Love Letters* and *What Do You Want To Make Those Eyes At Me For* (26.12.87)■

7	**10**	WHAT DO YOU WANT TO MAKE THOSE EYES AT ME FOR Shakin' Stevens	*Epic*	5
17	**[11]**	EV'RY TIME WE SAY GOODBYE Simply Red	*WEA*	3
10	**12**	WHO FOUND WHO Jellybean featuring Elisa Fiorillo	*Chrysalis*	5
21	**13**	ANGEL EYES (HOME AND AWAY) Wet Wet Wet	*Precious*	3
9	**14**	THE LOOK OF LOVE Madonna	*Sire*	3
15	**15**	TURN BACK THE CLOCK Johnny Hates Jazz	*Virgin*	5
12	**16**	LETTER FROM AMERICA Proclaimers	*Chrysalis*	6
11	**17**	CRITICIZE Alexander O'Neal	*Tabu*	7
13	**18**	GOT MY MIND SET ON YOU George Harrison	*Dark Horse*	9
30	**19**	JINGO Jellybean	*Chrysalis*	2
25	**[20]**	TOUCHED BY THE HAND OF GOD New Order	*Factory*	2
14	**21**	ONCE UPON A LONG AGO Paul McCartney	*Parlophone*	5
16	**22**	SO EMOTIONAL Whitney Houston	*Arista*	7
22	**23**	CHILDREN SAY Level 42	*Polydor*	3
36	**[24]**	TIGHTEN UP (I JUST CAN'T STOP DANCIN') Wally Jump Jr and the Criminal Element	*Breakout*	2
39	**25**	IDEAL WORLD Christians	*Island*	2
18	**26**	NEVER CAN SAY GOODBYE Communards	*London*	8
37	**27**	G.T.O. Sinitta	*Fanfare*	2

December 1987

□ Highest position disc reached ● Act's first ever week on chart

-	**28**	HOUSE ARREST Krush ●	*Club*	1
33	**29**	MY BABY JUST CARES FOR ME Nina Simone	*Charly*	8
34	**[30]**	LAST NIGHT I DREAMT I DREAMT THAT SOMEBODY LOVED ME Smiths	*Rough Trade*	2
-	**31**	I FOUND SOMEONE Cher	*Geffen*	1
24	**32**	SATELLITE Hooters	*CBS*	5
40	**[33]**	REASON TO LIVE Kiss	*Vertigo*	2
27	**34**	SOME GUYS HAVE ALL THE LUCK Maxi Priest	*10*	7
28	**35**	I'VE BEEN IN LOVE BEFORE Cutting Crew	*Siren*	5
29	**36**	(I'VE HAD) THE TIME OF MY LIFE Bill Medley and Jennifer Warnes	*RCA*	8
-	**37**	RISE TO THE OCCASION Climie Fisher ●	*EMI*	1
23	**38**	I'M THE MAN Anthrax	*Island*	4
26	**39**	SOMEWHERE SOMEBODY Five Star	*Tent*	4
-	**40**	THERE'S THE GIRL Heart	*Capitol*	1

■This is the final Christmas of the first 40 years of the charts without Cliff Richard somewhere in the top 10 (26.12.87) ■ Ace producer Jelly Bean is enjoying two Top 20 hits (26.12.87) ■ Sixties hitmakers still in the charts include Paul McCartney, George Harrison, Nat 'King' Cole, Cher, Bill Medley and Nina Simone (26.12.87)■

1988

..........A soap opera star at the beginning of the year, KYLIE MINOGUE winds up the year's chart champ...... Yazz and the Plastic Population have the year's best seller, 'The Only Way Is Up'......Cliff Richard is number one at Christmas for the first time in twenty-eight years..........

January 1988

□ Highest position disc reached ● Act's first ever week on chart

LW	TW	*WEEK ENDING* **2 JANUARY 1988**		Wks
1	[1]	ALWAYS ON MY MIND Pet Shop Boys	*Parlophone*	4
2	[2]	FAIRYTALE OF NEW YORK Pogues featuring Kirsty MacColl	*Pogue Mahone*	5
3	[3]	ROCKIN' AROUND THE CHRISTMAS TREE Kim Wilde and Mel Smith	*10*	5
7	[4]	WHEN I FALL IN LOVE Nat 'King' Cole	*Capitol*	3
8	5	HEAVEN IS A PLACE ON EARTH Belinda Carlisle	*Virgin*	3
5	6	LOVE LETTERS Alison Moyet	*CBS*	5
4	7	WHEN I FALL IN LOVE Rick Astley	*RCA*	4
6	8	THE WAY YOU MAKE ME FEEL Michael Jackson	*Epic*	5
9	9	CHINA IN YOUR HAND T'Pau	*Siren*	10
13	10	ANGEL EYES (HOME AND AWAY) Wet Wet Wet	*Precious*	4
11	[11]	EV'RY TIME WE SAY GOODBYE Simply Red	*WEA*	4
10	12	WHAT DO YOU WANT TO MAKE THOSE EYES AT ME FOR Shakin' Stevens	*Epic*	6
15	13	TURN BACK THE CLOCK Johnny Hates Jazz	*Virgin*	6
12	14	WHO FOUND WHO Jellybean featuring Elisa Fiorillo	*Chrysalis*	6
16	15	LETTER FROM AMERICA Proclaimers	*Chrysalis*	7
14	16	THE LOOK OF LOVE Madonna	*Sire*	4
17	17	CRITICIZE Alexander O'Neal	*Tabu*	8
18	18	GOT MY MIND SET ON YOU George Harrison	*Dark Horse*	10
19	19	JINGO Jellybean	*Chrysalis*	3
28	20	HOUSE ARREST Krush	*Club*	2
31	21	I FOUND SOMEONE Cher	*Geffen*	2
20	22	TOUCHED BY THE HAND OF GOD New Order	*Factory*	3
-	23	STUTTER RAP (NO SLEEP TIL BEDTIME) Morris Minor and the Majors ●	*10*	1
29	24	MY BABY JUST CARES FOR ME Nina Simone	*Charly*	9
22	25	SO EMOTIONAL Whitney Houston	*Arista*	8
25	26	IDEAL WORLD Christians	*Island*	3
24	27	TIGHTEN UP (I JUST CAN'T STOP DANCIN') Wally Jump Jr and the Criminal Element	*Breakout*	3
21	28	ONCE UPON A LONG AGO Paul McCartney	*Parlophone*	6
23	29	CHILDREN SAY Level 42	*Polydor*	4
27	30	G.T.O. Sinitta	*Fanfare*	3
37	31	RISE TO THE OCCASION Climie Fisher	*EMI*	2
26	32	NEVER CAN SAY GOODBYE Communards	*London*	9
33	[33]	REASON TO LIVE Kiss	*Vertigo*	3
40	[34]	THERE'S THE GIRL Heart	*Capitol*	2
-	35	THE WISHING WELL G.O.S.H. ●	*MBS*	1
32	36	SATELLITE Hooters	*CBS*	6
-	[37]	WALKING IN THE AIR Peter Auty and the Sinfonia Of London ●	*CBS*	1
36	38	(I'VE HAD) THE TIME OF MY LIFE Bill Medley and Jennifer Warnes	*RCA*	9
-	[39]	SONGS FOR CHRISTMAS '87 (EP) Mini Pops ●	*Bright*	1
34	40	SOME GUYS HAVE ALL THE LUCK Maxi Priest	*10*	8

LW	TW	*WEEK ENDING* **9 JANUARY 1988**		Wks
1	[1]	ALWAYS ON MY MIND Pet Shop Boys	*Parlophone*	5
5	2	HEAVEN IS A PLACE ON EARTH Belinda Carlisle	*Virgin*	4
8	[3]	THE WAY YOU MAKE ME FEEL Michael Jackson	*Epic*	6
2	4	FAIRYTALE OF NEW YORK Pogues featuring Kirsty MacColl	*Pogue Mahone*	6
10	[5]	ANGEL EYES (HOME AND AWAY) Wet Wet Wet	*Precious*	5
6	6	LOVE LETTERS Alison Moyet	*CBS*	6
20	7	HOUSE ARREST Krush	*Club*	3
23	8	STUTTER RAP (NO SLEEP TIL BEDTIME) Morris Minor and the Majors	*10*	2
21	9	I FOUND SOMEONE Cher	*Geffen*	3
3	10	ROCKIN' AROUND THE CHRISTMAS TREE Kim Wilde and Mel Smith	*10*	6
7	11	MY ARMS KEEP MISSING YOU Rick Astley	*RCA*	5
13	[12]	TURN BACK THE CLOCK Johnny Hates Jazz	*Virgin*	7
9	13	CHINA IN YOUR HAND T'Pau	*Siren*	11
4	14	WHEN I FALL IN LOVE Nat 'King' Cole	*Capitol*	4
16	15	THE LOOK OF LOVE Madonna	*Sire*	5
14	16	WHO FOUND WHO Jellybean featuring Elisa Fiorillo	*Chrysalis*	7
19	17	JINGO Jellybean	*Chrysalis*	4
17	18	CRITICIZE Alexander O'Neal	*Tabu*	9
-	19	ALL DAY AND ALL OF THE NIGHT Stranglers	*Epic*	1
30	20	G.T.O. Sinitta	*Fanfare*	4
-	21	COME INTO MY LIFE Joyce Sims	*Sleeping Bag*	1
12	22	WHAT DO YOU WANT TO MAKE THOSE EYES AT ME FOR Shakin' Stevens	*Epic*	7
31	23	RISE TO THE OCCASION Climie Fisher	*EMI*	3
11	24	EV'RY TIME WE SAY GOODBYE Simply Red	*WEA*	5
25	25	SO EMOTIONAL Whitney Houston	*Arista*	9
22	26	TOUCHED BY THE HAND OF GOD New Order	*Factory*	4
26	27	IDEAL WORLD Christians	*Island*	4
18	28	GOT MY MIND SET ON YOU George Harrison	*Dark Horse*	11
-	29	SIGN YOUR NAME Terence Trent D'Arby	*CBS*	1
15	30	LETTER FROM AMERICA Proclaimers	*Chrysalis*	8
27	31	TIGHTEN UP (I JUST CAN'T STOP DANCIN') Wally Jump Jr and the Criminal Element	*Breakout*	4
-	32	BEHIND THE WHEEL Depeche Mode	*Mute*	1
29	33	CHILDREN SAY Level 42	*Polydor*	5
35	34	THE WISHING WELL G.O.S.H.	*MBS*	2
-	35	FATHER FIGURE George Michael	*Epic*	1
33	36	REASON TO LIVE Kiss	*Vertigo*	4
34	37	THERE'S THE GIRL Heart	*Capitol*	3
28	38	ONCE UPON A LONG AGO Paul McCartney	*Parlophone*	7
32	39	NEVER CAN SAY GOODBYE Communards	*London*	10
36	40	SATELLITE Hooters	*CBS*	7

LW	TW	*WEEK ENDING* **16 JANUARY 1988**		Wks
2	[1]	HEAVEN IS A PLACE ON EARTH Belinda Carlisle	*Virgin*	5
1	2	ALWAYS ON MY MIND Pet Shop Boys	*Parlophone*	6
7	[3]	HOUSE ARREST Krush	*Club*	4
8	[4]	STUTTER RAP (NO SLEEP TIL BEDTIME) Morris Minor and the Majors	*10*	3
9	[5]	I FOUND SOMEONE Cher	*Geffen*	4
5	6	ANGEL EYES (HOME AND AWAY) Wet Wet Wet	*Precious*	6
19	[7]	ALL DAY AND ALL OF THE NIGHT Stranglers	*Epic*	2
29	8	SIGN YOUR NAME Terence Trent D'Arby	*CBS*	2
21	9	COME INTO MY LIFE Joyce Sims	*Sleeping Bag*	2
23	[10]	RISE TO THE OCCASION Climie Fisher	*EMI*	4
35	[11]	FATHER FIGURE George Michael	*Epic*	2
17	[12]	JINGO Jellybean	*Chrysalis*	5
-	13	I THINK WE'RE ALONE NOW Tiffany ●	*MCA*	1
11	14	MY ARMS KEEP MISSING YOU Rick Astley	*RCA*	6
20	[15]	G.T.O. Sinitta	*Fanfare*	5
3	16	THE WAY YOU MAKE ME FEEL Michael Jackson	*Epic*	7
-	17	HEATSEEKER AC/DC	*Atlantic*	1
6	18	LOVE LETTERS Alison Moyet	*CBS*	7
4	19	FAIRYTALE OF NEW YORK Pogues featuring Kirsty MacColl	*Pogue Mahone*	7
12	20	TURN BACK THE CLOCK Johnny Hates Jazz	*Virgin*	8
32	[21]	BEHIND THE WHEEL Depeche Mode	*Mute*	2
27	22	IDEAL WORLD Christians	*Island*	5
-	23	I CAN'T HELP IT Bananarama	*London*	1
34	24	THE WISHING WELL G.O.S.H.	*MBS*	3
16	25	WHO FOUND WHO Jellybean featuring Elisa Fiorillo	*Chrysalis*	8
-	26	ROK DA HOUSE Beatmasters featuring the Cookie Crew ●	*Rhythm King*	1
14	27	WHEN I FALL IN LOVE Nat 'King' Cole	*Capitol*	5
13	28	CHINA IN YOUR HAND T'Pau	*Siren*	12
26	29	TOUCHED BY THE HAND OF GOD New Order	*Factory*	5
18	30	CRITICIZE Alexander O'Neal	*Tabu*	10
10	31	ROCKIN' AROUND THE CHRISTMAS TREE Kim Wilde and Mel Smith	*10*	7
-	[32]	BRING THE NOISE Public Enemy	*Def Jam*	1
-	33	O L'AMOUR Dollar	*London*	1
31	34	TIGHTEN UP (I JUST CAN'T STOP DANCIN') Wally Jump Jr and the Criminal Element	*Breakout*	5
-	35	NEW SENSATION INXS ●	*Mercury*	1
15	36	THE LOOK OF LOVE Madonna	*Sire*	6
-	37	JENNIFER SHE SAID Lloyd Cole and the Commotions	*Polydor*	1

In these weeks ■ This was the last week in the first forty years of the charts in which two versionsof the same song appeared together in the Top ten (02.01.88) ■ *Rockin' Around The Christmas Tree* falls 21 places. The original version, by Brenda Lee, fell 24 places within the Top 40 exactly twenty five years earlier (16.01.88) ■ Rick Astley's *When I Fall In Love* is officially flipped, so *My Arms Keep Missing You* becomes the charted side (09.01.88)■

LW	TW	Title / Artist	Label	Wks
-	38	YOU'RE ALL I NEED Motley Crue	*Elektra*	1
-	39	WHEN WILL I BE FAMOUS Bros ●	*CBS*	1
24	40	EV'RY TIME WE SAY GOODBYE Simply Red	*WEA*	6

LW	TW	*WEEK ENDING* **23 JANUARY 1988**		Wks
1	1	HEAVEN IS A PLACE ON EARTH Belinda Carlisle	*Virgin*	6
8	2	SIGN YOUR NAME Terence Trent D'Arby	*CBS*	3
13	3	I THINK WE'RE ALONE NOW Tiffany	*MCA*	2
3	4	HOUSE ARREST Krush	*Club*	5
4	5	STUTTER RAP (NO SLEEP TIL BEDTIME) Morris Minor and the Majors	*10*	4
5	6	I FOUND SOMEONE Cher	*Geffen*	5
7	7	ALL DAY AND ALL OF THE NIGHT Stranglers	*Epic*	3
9	8	COME INTO MY LIFE Joyce Sims	*Sleeping Bag*	3
6	9	ANGEL EYES (HOME AND AWAY) Wet Wet Wet	*Precious*	7
10	10	RISE TO THE OCCASION Climie Fisher	*EMI*	5
2	11	ALWAYS ON MY MIND Pet Shop Boys	*Parlophone*	7
17	12	HEATSEEKER AC/DC	*Atlantic*	2
11	13	FATHER FIGURE George Michael	*Epic*	3
26	14	ROK DA HOUSE Beatmasters featuring the Cookie Crew	*Rhythm King*	2
22	15	IDEAL WORLD Christians	*Island*	6
39	16	WHEN WILL I BE FAMOUS Bros	*CBS*	2
12	17	JINGO Jellybean	*Chrysalis*	6
33	18	O L'AMOUR Dollar	*London*	2
15	19	G.T.O. Sinitta	*Fanfare*	6
23	20	I CAN'T HELP IT Bananarama	*London*	2
14	21	MY ARMS KEEP MISSING YOU Rick Astley	*RCA*	7
24	22	THE WISHING WELL G.O.S.H.	*MBS*	4
38	23	YOU'RE ALL I NEED Motley Crue	*Elektra*	2
21	24	BEHIND THE WHEEL Depeche Mode	*Mute*	3
35	25	NEW SENSATION INXS	*Mercury*	2
16	26	THE WAY YOU MAKE ME FEEL Michael Jackson	*Epic*	8
-	27	HOT IN THE CITY Billy Idol	*Chrysalis*	1
20	28	TURN BACK THE CLOCK Johnny Hates Jazz	*Virgin*	9
-	29	TIRED OF GETTING PUSHED AROUND 2 Men A Drum Machine and a Trumpet ●	*ffrr*	1
-	30	CANDLE IN THE WIND (LIVE) Elton John	*Rocket*	1
37	31	JENNIFER SHE SAID Lloyd Cole and the Commotions	*Polydor*	2
18	32	LOVE LETTERS Alison Moyet	*CBS*	8
-	33	THE JACK THAT HOUSE BUILT Jack 'n' Chill ●	*Oval*	1
32	34	BRING THE NOISE Public Enemy	*Def Jam*	2
-	35	SHAKE YOUR LOVE Debbie Gibson ●	*Atlantic*	1
-	36	WILD HEARTED WOMAN All About Eve ●	*Mercury*	1
-	37	SAY IT AGAIN Jermaine Stewart	*10*	1
-	38	PARADISE Black	*A&M*	1
19	39	FAIRYTALE OF NEW YORK Pogues featuring Kirsty MacColl	*Pogue Mahone*	8
28	40	CHINA IN YOUR HAND T'Pau	*Siren*	13

LW	TW	*WEEK ENDING* **30 JANUARY 1988**		Wks
3	1	I THINK WE'RE ALONE NOW Tiffany	*MCA*	3
1	2	HEAVEN IS A PLACE ON EARTH Belinda Carlisle	*Virgin*	7
2	3	SIGN YOUR NAME Terence Trent D'Arby	*CBS*	4
4	4	HOUSE ARREST Krush	*Club*	6
5	5	STUTTER RAP (NO SLEEP TIL BEDTIME) Morris Minor and the Majors	*10*	5
16	6	WHEN WILL I BE FAMOUS Bros	*CBS*	3
8	7	COME INTO MY LIFE Joyce Sims	*Sleeping Bag*	4
14	8	ROK DA HOUSE Beatmasters featuring the Cookie Crew	*Rhythm King*	3
18	9	O L'AMOUR Dollar	*London*	3
10	10	RISE TO THE OCCASION Climie Fisher	*EMI*	6
6	11	I FOUND SOMEONE Cher	*Geffen*	6
12	12	HEATSEEKER AC/DC	*Atlantic*	3
7	13	ALL DAY AND ALL OF THE NIGHT Stranglers	*Epic*	4
15	14	IDEAL WORLD Christians	*Island*	7
9	15	ANGEL EYES (HOME AND AWAY) Wet Wet Wet	*Precious*	8
30	16	CANDLE IN THE WIND (LIVE) Elton John	*Rocket*	2

February 1988

□ Highest position disc reached ● Act's first ever week on chart

LW	TW	Title / Artist	Label	Wks
35	17	SHAKE YOUR LOVE Debbie Gibson	*Atlantic*	2
27	18	HOT IN THE CITY Billy Idol	*Chrysalis*	2
33	19	THE JACK THAT HOUSE BUILT Jack 'n' Chill	*Oval*	2
11	20	ALWAYS ON MY MIND Pet Shop Boys	*Parlophone*	8
29	21	TIRED OF GETTING PUSHED AROUND 2 Men A Drum Machine and a Trumpet	*ffrr*	2
20	22	I CAN'T HELP IT Bananarama	*London*	3
13	23	FATHER FIGURE George Michael	*Epic*	4
-	24	TELL IT TO MY HEART Taylor Dayne ●	*Arista*	1
37	25	SAY IT AGAIN Jermaine Stewart	*10*	2
23	26	YOU'RE ALL I NEED Motley Crue	*Elektra*	3
25	27	NEW SENSATION INXS	*Mercury*	3
17	28	JINGO Jellybean	*Chrysalis*	7
21	29	MY ARMS KEEP MISSING YOU Rick Astley	*RCA*	8
22	30	THE WISHING WELL G.O.S.H.	*MBS*	5
-	31	I SHOULD BE SO LUCKY Kylie Minogue ●	*PWL*	1
-	32	GIVE ME THE REASON Luther Vandross	*Epic*	1
-	33	VALENTINE T'Pau	*Siren*	1
36	34	WILD HEARTED WOMAN All About Eve	*Mercury*	2
-	35	NO MORE LIES Sharpe and Numan	*Polydor*	1
-	36	I WANNA BE A FLINSTONE Screaming Blue Messiahs ●	*WEA*	1
19	37	G.T.O. Sinitta	*Fanfare*	7
-	38	MANDINKA Sinead O'Connor ●	*Ensign*	1
-	39	I GOT DA FEELIN'/IT'S LIKE THAT Y'ALL Sweet Tee ●	*Cooltempo*	1
38	40	PARADISE Black	*A&M*	2

LW	TW	*WEEK ENDING* **6 FEBRUARY 1988**		Wks
1	1	I THINK WE'RE ALONE NOW Tiffany	*MCA*	4
6	2	WHEN WILL I BE FAMOUS Bros	*CBS*	4
2	3	HEAVEN IS A PLACE ON EARTH Belinda Carlisle	*Virgin*	8
3	4	SIGN YOUR NAME Terence Trent D'Arby	*CBS*	5
8	5	ROK DA HOUSE Beatmasters featuring the Cookie Crew	*Rhythm King*	4
4	6	HOUSE ARREST Krush	*Club*	7
9	7	O L'AMOUR Dollar	*London*	4
24	8	TELL IT TO MY HEART Taylor Dayne	*Arista*	2
17	9	SHAKE YOUR LOVE Debbie Gibson	*Atlantic*	3
16	10	CANDLE IN THE WIND (LIVE) Elton John	*Rocket*	3
7	11	COME INTO MY LIFE Joyce Sims	*Sleeping Bag*	5
19	12	THE JACK THAT HOUSE BUILT Jack 'n' Chill	*Oval*	3
18	13	HOT IN THE CITY Billy Idol	*Chrysalis*	3
5	14	STUTTER RAP (NO SLEEP TIL BEDTIME) Morris Minor and the Majors	*10*	6
14	15	IDEAL WORLD Christians	*Island*	8
31	16	I SHOULD BE SO LUCKY Kylie Minogue	*PWL*	2
25	17	SAY IT AGAIN Jermaine Stewart	*10*	3
21	18	TIRED OF GETTING PUSHED AROUND 2 Men A Drum Machine and a Trumpet	*ffrr*	3
10	19	RISE TO THE OCCASION Climie Fisher	*EMI*	7
33	20	VALENTINE T'Pau	*Siren*	2
12	21	HEATSEEKER AC/DC	*Atlantic*	4
11	22	I FOUND SOMEONE Cher	*Geffen*	7
13	23	ALL DAY AND ALL OF THE NIGHT Stranglers	*Epic*	5
15	24	ANGEL EYES (HOME AND AWAY) Wet Wet Wet	*Precious*	9
-	25	GIVE ME ALL YOUR LOVE Whitesnake	*EMI*	1
32	26	GIVE ME THE REASON Luther Vandross	*Epic*	2
-	27	GET OUTTA MY DREAMS GET INTO MY CAR Billy Ocean	*Jive*	1
36	28	I WANNA BE A FLINSTONE Screaming Blue Messiahs	*WEA*	2
38	29	MANDINKA Sinead O'Connor	*Ensign*	2
20	30	ALWAYS ON MY MIND Pet Shop Boys	*Parlophone*	9
39	31	I GOT DA FEELIN'/IT'S LIKE THAT Y'ALL Sweet Tee	*Cooltempo*	2
27	32	NEW SENSATION INXS	*Mercury*	4
34	33	WILD HEARTED WOMAN All About Eve	*Mercury*	3
35	34	NO MORE LIES Sharpe and Numan	*Polydor*	2

■AC/DC achieve their highest ever chart placing with this, their twelfth Top 40 hit to miss the Top ten (23.01.88) ■ Enter the first of the Neighbours' cast, and by far the most successful in chart terms - Kylie Minogue (30.01.88)■

February 1988

□ Highest position disc reached ● Act's first ever week on chart

LW	TW	Title	Artist	Label	Wks
-	[35]	VICTORIA	Fall	Beggars Banquet	1
-	36	GIMME HOPE JO'ANNA	Eddy Grant	Ice	1
22	37	I CAN'T HELP IT	Bananarama	London	4
-	38	SPY IN THE HOUSE OF LOVE	Was Not Was	Fontana	1
-	39	LET'S GET BRUTAL	Nitro Deluxe ●	Cooltempo	1
28	40	JINGO	Jellybean	Chrysalis	8

WEEK ENDING 13 FEBRUARY 1988

LW	TW	Title	Artist	Label	Wks
1	[1]	I THINK WE'RE ALONE NOW	Tiffany	MCA	5
16	2	I SHOULD BE SO LUCKY	Kylie Minogue	PWL	3
2	3	WHEN WILL I BE FAMOUS	Bros	CBS	5
8	4	TELL IT TO MY HEART	Taylor Dayne	Arista	3
10	[5]	CANDLE IN THE WIND (LIVE)	Elton John	Rocket	4
12	[6]	THE JACK THAT HOUSE BUILT	Jack 'n' Chill	Oval	4
9	[7]	SHAKE YOUR LOVE	Debbie Gibson	Atlantic	4
27	8	GET OUTTA MY DREAMS GET INTO MY CAR	Billy Ocean	Jive	2
5	9	ROK DA HOUSE	Beatmasters featuring the Cookie Crew	Rhythm King	5
17	10	SAY IT AGAIN	Jermaine Stewart	10	4
7	11	O L'AMOUR	Dollar	London	5
4	12	SIGN YOUR NAME	Terence Trent D'Arby	CBS	6
3	13	HEAVEN IS A PLACE ON EARTH	Belinda Carlisle	Virgin	9
13	14	HOT IN THE CITY	Billy Idol	Chrysalis	4
20	15	VALENTINE	T'Pau	Siren	3
6	16	HOUSE ARREST	Krush	Club	8
11	17	COME INTO MY LIFE	Joyce Sims	Sleeping Bag	6
25	[18]	GIVE ME ALL YOUR LOVE	Whitesnake	EMI	2
18	19	TIRED OF GETTING PUSHED AROUND	2 Men A Drum Machine and a Trumpet	ffrr	4
-	20	TOWER OF STRENGTH	Mission	Mercury	1
15	21	IDEAL WORLD	Christians	Island	9
29	22	MANDINKA	Sinead O'Connor	Ensign	3
14	23	STUTTER RAP (NO SLEEP TIL BEDTIME)	Morris Minor and the Majors	10	7
39	[24]	LET'S GET BRUTAL	Nitro Deluxe	Cooltempo	2
36	25	GIMME HOPE JO'ANNA	Eddy Grant	Ice	2
38	26	SPY IN THE HOUSE OF LOVE	Was Not Was	Fontana	2
19	27	RISE TO THE OCCASION	Climie Fisher	EMI	8
26	28	GIVE ME THE REASON	Luther Vandross	Epic	3
28	29	I WANNA BE A FLINSTONE	Screaming Blue Messiahs	WEA	3
22	30	I FOUND SOMEONE	Cher	Geffen	8
21	31	HEATSEEKER	AC/DC	Atlantic	5
-	32	DIGNITY	Deacon Blue ●	CBS	1
-	[33]	HEAVEN KNOWS	Robert Plant	Esparanza	1
-	34	NEVER KNEW LOVE LIKE THIS	Alexander O'Neal featuring Cherelle	Tabu	1
24	35	ANGEL EYES (HOME AND AWAY)	Wet Wet Wet	Precious	10
33	36	WILD HEARTED WOMAN	All About Eve	Mercury	4
31	37	I GOT DA FEELIN'/IT'S LIKE THAT Y'ALL	Sweet Tee	Cooltempo	3
34	38	NO MORE LIES	Sharpe and Numan	Polydor	3
23	39	ALL DAY AND ALL OF THE NIGHT	Stranglers	Epic	6
35	40	VICTORIA	Fall	Beggars Banquet	2

WEEK ENDING 20 FEBRUARY

LW	TW	Title	Artist	Label	Wks
2	[1]	I SHOULD BE SO LUCKY	Kylie Minogue	PWL	4
1	2	I THINK WE'RE ALONE NOW	Tiffany	MCA	6
4	[3]	TELL IT TO MY HEART	Taylor Dayne	Arista	4
8	4	GET OUTTA MY DREAMS GET INTO MY CAR	Billy Ocean	Jive	3
-	5	BEAT DIS	Bomb The Bass ●	Mister-Ron	1
3	6	WHEN WILL I BE FAMOUS	Bros	CBS	6
5	7	CANDLE IN THE WIND (LIVE)	Elton John	Rocket	5
10	8	SAY IT AGAIN	Jermaine Stewart	10	5
15	[9]	VALENTINE	T'Pau	Siren	4
7	10	SHAKE YOUR LOVE	Debbie Gibson	Atlantic	5
6	11	THE JACK THAT HOUSE BUILT	Jack 'n' Chill	Oval	5
25	12	GIMME HOPE JO'ANNA	Eddy Grant	Ice	3
20	13	TOWER OF STRENGTH	Mission	Mercury	2
9	14	ROK DA HOUSE	Beatmasters featuring the Cookie Crew	Rhythm King	6
12	15	SIGN YOUR NAME	Terence Trent D'Arby	CBS	7
14	16	HOT IN THE CITY	Billy Idol	Chrysalis	5
22	[17]	MANDINKA	Sinead O'Connor	Ensign	4
18	[18]	GIVE ME ALL YOUR LOVE	Whitesnake	EMI	3
11	19	O L'AMOUR	Dollar	London	6
13	20	HEAVEN IS A PLACE ON EARTH	Belinda Carlisle	Virgin	10
26	[21]	SPY IN THE HOUSE OF LOVE	Was Not Was	Fontana	3
16	22	HOUSE ARREST	Krush	Club	9
17	23	COME INTO MY LIFE	Joyce Sims	Sleeping Bag	7
24	[24]	LET'S GET BRUTAL	Nitro Deluxe	Cooltempo	3
-	25	DOCTORIN' THE HOUSE	Coldcut featuring Yazz and the Plastic Population ●	Ahead Of Our Time	1
34	[26]	NEVER KNEW LOVE LIKE THIS	Alexander O'Neal featuring Cherelle	Tabu	2
-	27	MAN IN THE MIRROR	Michael Jackson	Epic	1
19	28	TIRED OF GETTING PUSHED AROUND	2 Men A Drum Machine and a Trumpet	ffrr	5
-	29	JOE LE TAXI	Vanessa Paradis ●	FA Productions	1
-	30	HAZY SHADE OF WINTER	Bangles	Def Jam	1
32	[31]	DIGNITY	Deacon Blue	CBS	2
-	32	C'MON EVERYBODY	Eddie Cochran	Liberty	1
-	33	WHEN WE WAS FAB	George Harrison	Dark Horse	1
-	[34]	TWO HEARTS	Cliff Richard	EMI	1
28	35	GIVE ME THE REASON	Luther Vandross	Epic	4
33	36	HEAVEN KNOWS	Robert Plant	Esparanza	2
-	37	I DON'T MIND AT ALL	Bourgeois Tagg ●	Island	1
21	38	IDEAL WORLD	Christians	Island	10
-	39	GOING BACK TO CALI/JACK THE RIPPER	LL Cool J	Def Jam	1
23	40	STUTTER RAP (NO SLEEP TIL BEDTIME)	Morris Minor and the Majors	10	8

WEEK ENDING 27 FEBRUARY 1988

LW	TW	Title	Artist	Label	Wks
1	[1]	I SHOULD BE SO LUCKY	Kylie Minogue	PWL	5
5	[2]	BEAT DIS	Bomb The Bass	Mister-Ron	2
4	[3]	GET OUTTA MY DREAMS GET INTO MY CAR	Billy Ocean	Jive	4
3	4	TELL IT TO MY HEART	Taylor Dayne	Arista	5
2	5	I THINK WE'RE ALONE NOW	Tiffany	MCA	7
-	6	SUEDEHEAD	Morrissey ●	HMV	1
8	[7]	SAY IT AGAIN	Jermaine Stewart	10	6
12	8	GIMME HOPE JO'ANNA	Eddy Grant	Ice	4
-	9	TOGETHER FOREVER	Rick Astley	RCA	1
25	10	DOCTORIN' THE HOUSE	Coldcut featuring Yazz and the Plastic Population	Ahead Of Our Time	2
6	11	WHEN WILL I BE FAMOUS	Bros	CBS	7
13	[12]	TOWER OF STRENGTH	Mission	Mercury	3
10	13	SHAKE YOUR LOVE	Debbie Gibson	Atlantic	6
29	14	JOE LE TAXI	Vanessa Paradis	FA Productions	2
9	15	VALENTINE	T'Pau	Siren	5
7	16	CANDLE IN THE WIND (LIVE)	Elton John	Rocket	6
-	17	DOMINION	Sisters Of Mercy	Merciful Release	1
11	18	THE JACK THAT HOUSE BUILT	Jack 'n' Chill	Oval	6
32	19	C'MON EVERYBODY	Eddie Cochran	Liberty	2
30	20	HAZY SHADE OF WINTER	Bangles	Def Jam	2
27	[21]	MAN IN THE MIRROR	Michael Jackson	Epic	2
21	22	SPY IN THE HOUSE OF LOVE	Was Not Was	Fontana	4
17	23	MANDINKA	Sinead O'Connor	Ensign	5
-	24	THAT'S THE WAY IT IS	Mel and Kim	Supreme	1
33	[25]	WHEN WE WAS FAB	George Harrison	Dark Horse	2
26	[26]	NEVER KNEW LOVE LIKE THIS	Alexander O'Neal featuring Cherelle	Tabu	3
14	27	ROK DA HOUSE	Beatmasters featuring the Cookie Crew	Rhythm King	7
16	28	HOT IN THE CITY	Billy Idol	Chrysalis	6
-	29	CRASH	Primitives ●	RCA	1
15	30	SIGN YOUR NAME	Terence Trent D'Arby	CBS	8
24	31	LET'S GET BRUTAL	Nitro Deluxe	Cooltempo	4

In these weeks ■ For two weeks running, a new act makes its chart debut within the Top ten, the first time this has happened since the chart became a Top 40. Neither Bomb The Bass nor Morrisey ever achieve a number one, however (27.02.88) ■ Four songs with *House* in the title betrays the musical fashion (20.02.88) ■ Kylie Minogue is the third consecutive female solo vocalist at number one - the first time this has ever happened (20.02.88) ■

LW	TW	Title	Artist	Label	Wks
31	32	DIGNITY	Deacon Blue	CBS	3
-	33	PEOPLE ARE STRANGE	Echo and the Bunnymen	WEA	1
-	34	GOODGROOVE	Derek B ●	Music Of Life	1
37	35	I DON'T MIND AT ALL	Bourgeois Tagg	Island	2
20	36	HEAVEN IS A PLACE ON EARTH	Belinda Carlisle	Virgin	11
39	37	GOING BACK TO CALI/JACK THE RIPPER	LL Cool J	Def Jam	2
18	38	GIVE ME ALL YOUR LOVE	Whitesnake	EMI	4
-	39	I GET WEAK	Belinda Carlisle	Virgin	1
22	40	HOUSE ARREST	Krush	Club	10

WEEK ENDING 5 MARCH 1988

LW	TW	Title	Artist	Label	Wks
1	1	I SHOULD BE SO LUCKY	Kylie Minogue	PWL	6
2	2	BEAT DIS	Bomb The Bass	Mister-Ron	3
3	3	GET OUTTA MY DREAMS GET INTO MY CAR	Billy Ocean	Jive	5
9	4	TOGETHER FOREVER	Rick Astley	RCA	2
6	5	SUEDEHEAD	Morrissey	HMV	2
4	6	TELL IT TO MY HEART	Taylor Dayne	Arista	6
14	7	JOE LE TAXI	Vanessa Paradis	FA Productions	3
8	8	GIMME HOPE JO'ANNA	Eddy Grant	Ice	5
10	9	DOCTORIN' THE HOUSE	Coldcut featuring Yazz and the Plastic Population	Ahead Of Our Time	3
5	10	I THINK WE'RE ALONE NOW	Tiffany	MCA	8
7	11	SAY IT AGAIN	Jermaine Stewart	10	7
20	12	HAZY SHADE OF WINTER	Bangles	Def Jam	3
17	13	DOMINION	Sisters Of Mercy	Merciful Release	2
19	14	C'MON EVERYBODY	Eddie Cochran	Liberty	3
29	15	CRASH	Primitives	RCA	2
24	16	THAT'S THE WAY IT IS	Mel and Kim	Supreme	2
39	17	I GET WEAK	Belinda Carlisle	Virgin	2
12	18	TOWER OF STRENGTH	Mission	Mercury	4
34	19	GOODGROOVE	Derek B	Music Of Life	2
-	20	SHIP OF FOOLS	Erasure	Mute	1
11	21	WHEN WILL I BE FAMOUS	Bros	CBS	8
22	22	SPY IN THE HOUSE OF LOVE	Was Not Was	Fontana	5
16	23	CANDLE IN THE WIND (LIVE)	Elton John	Rocket	7
15	24	VALENTINE	T'Pau	Siren	6
21	25	MAN IN THE MIRROR	Michael Jackson	Epic	3
13	26	SHAKE YOUR LOVE	Debbie Gibson	Atlantic	7
18	27	THE JACK THAT HOUSE BUILT	Jack 'n' Chill	Oval	7
-	28	LOVE IS CONTAGIOUS	Taja Sevelle ●	Paisley Park	1
33	29	PEOPLE ARE STRANGE	Echo and the Bunnymen	WEA	2
25	30	WHEN WE WAS FAB	George Harrison	Dark Horse	3
26	31	NEVER KNEW LOVE LIKE THIS	Alexander O'Neal featuring Cherelle	Tabu	4
-	32	HEART OF GOLD	Johnny Hates Jazz	Virgin	1
-	33	HOW MEN ARE	Aztec Camera	WEA	1
23	34	MANDINKA	Sinead O'Connor	Ensign	6
-	35	NEVER/THESE DREAMS	Heart	Capitol	1
-	36	FOR A FRIEND	Communards	London	1
-	37	DON'T TURN AROUND	Aswad ●	Mango	1
-	38	I'M NOT SCARED	Eighth Wonder ●	CBS	1
32	39	DIGNITY	Deacon Blue	CBS	4
-	40	RECKLESS	Afrika Bambaataa and UB40 ●	EMI	1

WEEK ENDING 12 MARCH 1988

LW	TW	Title	Artist	Label	Wks
1	1	I SHOULD BE SO LUCKY	Kylie Minogue	PWL	7
4	2	TOGETHER FOREVER	Rick Astley	RCA	3
2	3	BEAT DIS	Bomb The Bass	Mister-Ron	4
7	4	JOE LE TAXI	Vanessa Paradis	FA Productions	4
3	5	GET OUTTA MY DREAMS GET INTO MY CAR	Billy Ocean	Jive	6
9	6	DOCTORIN' THE HOUSE	Coldcut featuring Yazz and the Plastic Population	Ahead Of Our Time	4
8	7	GIMME HOPE JO'ANNA	Eddy Grant	Ice	6
5	8	SUEDEHEAD	Morrissey	HMV	3
15	9	CRASH	Primitives	RCA	3
16	10	THAT'S THE WAY IT IS	Mel and Kim	Supreme	3
12	11	HAZY SHADE OF WINTER	Bangles	Def Jam	4
20	12	SHIP OF FOOLS	Erasure	Mute	2
17	13	I GET WEAK	Belinda Carlisle	Virgin	3
6	14	TELL IT TO MY HEART	Taylor Dayne	Arista	7
13	15	DOMINION	Sisters Of Mercy	Merciful Release	3
19	16	GOODGROOVE	Derek B	Music Of Life	3
28	17	LOVE IS CONTAGIOUS	Taja Sevelle	Paisley Park	2
14	18	C'MON EVERYBODY	Eddie Cochran	Liberty	4
10	19	I THINK WE'RE ALONE NOW	Tiffany	MCA	9
35	20	NEVER/THESE DREAMS	Heart	Capitol	2
-	21	I KNOW YOU GOT SOUL	Eric B and Rakim	Cooltempo	1
37	22	DON'T TURN AROUND	Aswad	Mango	2
32	23	HEART OF GOLD	Johnny Hates Jazz	Virgin	2
11	24	SAY IT AGAIN	Jermaine Stewart	10	8
33	25	HOW MEN ARE	Aztec Camera	WEA	2
38	26	I'M NOT SCARED	Eighth Wonder	CBS	2
40	27	RECKLESS	Afrika Bambaataa and UB40	EMI	2
36	28	FOR A FRIEND	Communards	London	2
18	29	TOWER OF STRENGTH	Mission	Mercury	5
-	30	WHERE DO BROKEN HEARTS GO	Whitney Houston	Arista	1
29	31	PEOPLE ARE STRANGE	Echo and the Bunnymen	WEA	3
22	32	SPY IN THE HOUSE OF LOVE	Was Not Was	Fontana	6
25	33	MAN IN THE MIRROR	Michael Jackson	Epic	4
-	34	I WANT HER	Keith Sweat ●	Vintertainment	1
-	35	JUST LIKE PARADISE	David Lee Roth ●	Warner Bros	1
21	36	WHEN WILL I BE FAMOUS	Bros	CBS	9
31	37	NEVER KNEW LOVE LIKE THIS	Alexander O'Neal featuring Cherelle	Tabu	5
-	38	CRAZY	Icehouse	Chrysalis	1
23	39	CANDLE IN THE WIND (LIVE)	Elton John	Rocket	8
24	40	VALENTINE	T'Pau	Siren	7

March 1988

□ Highest position disc reached ● Act's first ever week on chart

WEEK ENDING 19 MARCH 1988

LW	TW	Title	Artist	Label	Wks
1	1	I SHOULD BE SO LUCKY	Kylie Minogue	PWL	8
2	2	TOGETHER FOREVER	Rick Astley	RCA	4
4	3	JOE LE TAXI	Vanessa Paradis	FA Productions	5
22	4	DON'T TURN AROUND	Aswad	Mango	3
9	5	CRASH	Primitives	RCA	4
12	6	SHIP OF FOOLS	Erasure	Mute	3
17	7	LOVE IS CONTAGIOUS	Taja Sevelle	Paisley Park	3
3	8	BEAT DIS	Bomb The Bass	Mister-Ron	5
6	9	DOCTORIN' THE HOUSE	Coldcut featuring Yazz and the Plastic Population	Ahead Of Our Time	5
5	10	GET OUTTA MY DREAMS GET INTO MY CAR	Billy Ocean	Jive	7
13	11	I GET WEAK	Belinda Carlisle	Virgin	4
20	12	NEVER/THESE DREAMS	Heart	Capitol	3
21	13	I KNOW YOU GOT SOUL	Eric B and Rakim	Cooltempo	2
7	14	GIMME HOPE JO'ANNA	Eddy Grant	Ice	7
10	15	THAT'S THE WAY IT IS	Mel and Kim	Supreme	4
30	16	WHERE DO BROKEN HEARTS GO	Whitney Houston	Arista	2
-	17	DROP THE BOY	Bros	CBS	1
27	18	RECKLESS	Afrika Bambaataa and UB40	EMI	3
23	19	HEART OF GOLD	Johnny Hates Jazz	Virgin	3
26	20	I'M NOT SCARED	Eighth Wonder	CBS	3
11	21	HAZY SHADE OF WINTER	Bangles	Def Jam	5
-	22	COULD'VE BEEN	Tiffany	MCA	1
14	23	TELL IT TO MY HEART	Taylor Dayne	Arista	8
16	24	GOODGROOVE	Derek B	Music Of Life	4
15	25	DOMINION	Sisters Of Mercy	Merciful Release	4
25	26	HOW MEN ARE	Aztec Camera	WEA	3
35	27	JUST LIKE PARADISE	David Lee Roth	Warner Bros	2
8	28	SUEDEHEAD	Morrissey	HMV	4
-	29	BASS (HOW LOW CAN YOU GO)	Simon Harris ●	ffrr	1
-	30	CROSS MY BROKEN HEART	Sinitta	Fanfare	1
34	31	I WANT HER	Keith Sweat	Vintertainment	2
-	32	DAYS OF NO TRUST	Magnum ●	Polydor	1
19	33	I THINK WE'RE ALONE NOW	Tiffany	MCA	10
18	34	C'MON EVERYBODY	Eddie Cochran	Liberty	5
28	35	FOR A FRIEND	Communards	London	3
-	36	TEMPTATION	Wet Wet Wet	Precious	1

■ *Reckless* becomes the first record to enter the chart at no. 40 for 10 weeks (05.03.88) ■ *Joe Le Taxi* is only the second French language record to hit the top 3, after the famous *Je T'Aime ... Moi Mon Plus*, which topped the charts in 1969 (19.03.88) ■

March 1988

□ Highest position disc reached ● Act's first ever week on chart

LW	TW	Title	Artist	Label	Wks
-	**37**	ONLY IN MY DREAMS	Debbie Gibson	*Atlantic*	1
-	**38**	LOVE CHANGES (EVERYTHING)	Climie Fisher	*EMI*	1
24	**39**	SAY IT AGAIN	Jermaine Stewart	*10*	9
-	**40**	I FOUGHT THE LAW	Clash	*CBS*	1

WEEK ENDING 26 MARCH 1988

LW	TW	Title	Artist	Label	Wks
4	**1**	DON'T TURN AROUND	Aswad	*Mango*	4
17	**2**	DROP THE BOY	Bros	*CBS*	2
1	**3**	I SHOULD BE SO LUCKY	Kylie Minogue	*PWL*	9
-	**4**	CAN I PLAY WITH MADNESS	Iron Maiden	*EMI*	1
22	**5**	COULD'VE BEEN	Tiffany	*MCA*	2
3	**6**	JOE LE TAXI	Vanessa Paradis	*FA Productions*	6
5	**7**	CRASH	Primitives	*RCA*	5
12	**8**	NEVER/THESE DREAMS	Heart	*Capitol*	4
6	**9**	SHIP OF FOOLS	Erasure	*Mute*	4
11	**10**	I GET WEAK	Belinda Carlisle	*Virgin*	5
2	**11**	TOGETHER FOREVER	Rick Astley	*RCA*	5
7	**12**	LOVE IS CONTAGIOUS	Taja Sevelle	*Paisley Park*	4
20	**13**	I'M NOT SCARED	Eighth Wonder	*CBS*	4
30	**14**	CROSS MY BROKEN HEART	Sinitta	*Fanfare*	2
16	**15**	WHERE DO BROKEN HEARTS GO	Whitney Houston	*Arista*	3
29	**16**	BASS (HOW LOW CAN YOU GO)	Simon Harris	*ffrr*	2
18	**17**	RECKLESS	Afrika Bambaataa and UB40	*EMI*	4
-	**18**	STAY ON THESE ROADS	A-Ha	*Warner Bros*	1
13	**19**	I KNOW YOU GOT SOUL	Eric B and Rakim	*Cooltempo*	3
9	**20**	DOCTORIN' THE HOUSE	Coldcut featuring Yazz and the Plastic Population	*Ahead Of Our Time*	6
10	**21**	GET OUTTA MY DREAMS GET INTO MY CAR	Billy Ocean	*Jive*	8
37	**22**	ONLY IN MY DREAMS	Debbie Gibson	*Atlantic*	2
8	**23**	BEAT DIS	Bomb The Bass	*Mister-Ron*	6
19	**24**	HEART OF GOLD	Johnny Hates Jazz	*Virgin*	4
36	**25**	TEMPTATION	Wet Wet Wet	*Precious*	2
38	**26**	LOVE CHANGES (EVERYTHING)	Climie Fisher	*EMI*	2
31	**27**	I WANT HER	Keith Sweat	*Vintertainment*	3
15	**28**	THAT'S THE WAY IT IS	Mel and Kim	*Supreme*	5
40	**29**	I FOUGHT THE LAW	Clash	*CBS*	2
14	**30**	GIMME HOPE JO'ANNA	Eddy Grant	*Ice*	8
27	**31**	JUST LIKE PARADISE	David Lee Roth	*Warner Bros*	3
32	**32**	DAYS OF NO TRUST	Magnum	*Polydor*	2
-	**33**	DREAMING	Glen Goldsmith	*Reproduction*	1
-	**34**	PROVE YOUR LOVE	Taylor Dayne	*Arista*	1
26	**35**	HOW MEN ARE	Aztec Camera	*WEA*	4
23	**36**	TELL IT TO MY HEART	Taylor Dayne	*Arista*	9
-	**37**	AIN'T COMPLAINING	Status Quo	*Vertigo*	1
21	**38**	HAZY SHADE OF WINTER	Bangles	*Def Jam*	6
24	**39**	GOODGROOVE	Derek B	*Music Of Life*	5
-	**40**	JUST A MIRAGE	Jellybean featuring Adele Bertei	*Chrysalis*	1

WEEK ENDING 2 APRIL 1988

LW	TW	Title	Artist	Label	Wks
1	**1**	DON'T TURN AROUND	Aswad	*Mango*	5
2	**2**	DROP THE BOY	Bros	*CBS*	3
4	**3**	CAN I PLAY WITH MADNESS	Iron Maiden	*EMI*	2
5	**4**	COULD'VE BEEN	Tiffany	*MCA*	3
18	**5**	STAY ON THESE ROADS	A-Ha	*Warner Bros*	2
14	**6**	CROSS MY BROKEN HEART	Sinitta	*Fanfare*	3
-	**7**	HEART	Pet Shop Boys	*Parlophone*	1
3	**8**	I SHOULD BE SO LUCKY	Kylie Minogue	*PWL*	10
8	**9**	NEVER/THESE DREAMS	Heart	*Capitol*	5
13	**10**	I'M NOT SCARED	Eighth Wonder	*CBS*	5
26	**11**	LOVE CHANGES (EVERYTHING)	Climie Fisher	*EMI*	3
16	**12**	BASS (HOW LOW CAN YOU GO)	Simon Harris	*ffrr*	3
22	**13**	ONLY IN MY DREAMS	Debbie Gibson	*Atlantic*	3
15	**14**	WHERE DO BROKEN HEARTS GO	Whitney Houston	*Arista*	4
7	**15**	CRASH	Primitives	*RCA*	6
10	**16**	I GET WEAK	Belinda Carlisle	*Virgin*	6
25	**17**	TEMPTATION	Wet Wet Wet	*Precious*	3
9	**18**	SHIP OF FOOLS	Erasure	*Mute*	5
17	**19**	RECKLESS	Afrika Bambaataa and UB40	*EMI*	5
6	**20**	JOE LE TAXI	Vanessa Paradis	*FA Productions*	7
12	**21**	LOVE IS CONTAGIOUS	Taja Sevelle	*Paisley Park*	5
37	**22**	AIN'T COMPLAINING	Status Quo	*Vertigo*	2
11	**23**	TOGETHER FOREVER	Rick Astley	*RCA*	6
33	**24**	DREAMING	Glen Goldsmith	*Reproduction*	2
34	**25**	PROVE YOUR LOVE	Taylor Dayne	*Arista*	2
27	**26**	I WANT HER	Keith Sweat	*Vintertainment*	4
21	**27**	GET OUTTA MY DREAMS GET INTO MY CAR	Billy Ocean	*Jive*	9
40	**28**	JUST A MIRAGE	Jellybean featuring Adele Bertei	*Chrysalis*	2
-	**29**	EVERYWHERE	Fleetwood Mac	*Warner Bros*	1
19	**30**	I KNOW YOU GOT SOUL	Eric B and Rakim	*Cooltempo*	4
-	**31**	GIRLFRIEND	Pebbles ●	*MCA*	1
20	**32**	DOCTORIN' THE HOUSE	Coldcut featuring Yazz and the Plastic Population	*Ahead Of Our Time*	7
-	**33**	THAT'S THE WAY I WANNA ROCK 'N' ROLL	AC/DC	*Atlantic*	1
-	**34**	PINK CADILLAC	Natalie Cole	*Manhattan*	1
29	**35**	I FOUGHT THE LAW	Clash	*CBS*	3
-	**36**	SEX TALK (LIVE)	T'Pau	*Siren*	1
-	**37**	WHO'S LEAVING WHO	Hazell Dean	*EMI*	1
31	**38**	JUST LIKE PARADISE	David Lee Roth	*Warner Bros*	4
23	**39**	BEAT DIS	Bomb The Bass	*Mister-Ron*	7
-	**40**	PIANO IN THE DARK	Brenda Russell ●	*Breakout*	1

WEEK ENDING 9 APRIL 1988

LW	TW	Title	Artist	Label	Wks
7	**1**	HEART	Pet Shop Boys	*Parlophone*	2
2	**2**	DROP THE BOY	Bros	*CBS*	4
1	**3**	DON'T TURN AROUND	Aswad	*Mango*	6
4	**4**	COULD'VE BEEN	Tiffany	*MCA*	4
3	**5**	CAN I PLAY WITH MADNESS	Iron Maiden	*EMI*	3
6	**6**	CROSS MY BROKEN HEART	Sinitta	*Fanfare*	4
11	**7**	LOVE CHANGES (EVERYTHING)	Climie Fisher	*EMI*	4
5	**8**	STAY ON THESE ROADS	A-Ha	*Warner Bros*	3
10	**9**	I'M NOT SCARED	Eighth Wonder	*CBS*	6
8	**10**	I SHOULD BE SO LUCKY	Kylie Minogue	*PWL*	11
13	**11**	ONLY IN MY DREAMS	Debbie Gibson	*Atlantic*	4
17	**12**	TEMPTATION	Wet Wet Wet	*Precious*	4
29	**13**	EVERYWHERE	Fleetwood Mac	*Warner Bros*	2
9	**14**	NEVER/THESE DREAMS	Heart	*Capitol*	6
25	**15**	PROVE YOUR LOVE	Taylor Dayne	*Arista*	3
24	**16**	DREAMING	Glen Goldsmith	*Reproduction*	3
14	**17**	WHERE DO BROKEN HEARTS GO	Whitney Houston	*Arista*	5
12	**18**	BASS (HOW LOW CAN YOU GO)	Simon Harris	*ffrr*	4
22	**19**	AIN'T COMPLAINING	Status Quo	*Vertigo*	3
37	**20**	WHO'S LEAVING WHO	Hazell Dean	*EMI*	2
28	**21**	JUST A MIRAGE	Jellybean featuring Adele Bertei	*Chrysalis*	3
33	**22**	THAT'S THE WAY I WANNA ROCK 'N' ROLL	AC/DC	*Atlantic*	2
31	**23**	GIRLFRIEND	Pebbles	*MCA*	2
34	**24**	PINK CADILLAC	Natalie Cole	*Manhattan*	2
36	**25**	SEX TALK (LIVE)	T'Pau	*Siren*	2
16	**26**	I GET WEAK	Belinda Carlisle	*Virgin*	7
15	**27**	CRASH	Primitives	*RCA*	7
-	**28**	ARMAGEDDON IT	Def Leppard	*Bludgeon Riffola*	1
40	**29**	PIANO IN THE DARK	Brenda Russell	*Breakout*	2
19	**30**	RECKLESS	Afrika Bambaataa and UB40	*EMI*	6
-	**31**	I NEED A MAN	Eurythmics	*RCA*	1
-	**32**	SIDEWALKING	Jesus And Mary Chain	*blanco y negro*	1
18	**33**	SHIP OF FOOLS	Erasure	*Mute*	6
26	**34**	I WANT HER	Keith Sweat	*Vintertainment*	5
20	**35**	JOE LE TAXI	Vanessa Paradis	*FA Productions*	8
-	**36**	I WANT YOU BACK	Bananarama	*London*	1
23	**37**	TOGETHER FOREVER	Rick Astley	*RCA*	7
27	**38**	GET OUTTA MY DREAMS GET INTO MY CAR	Billy Ocean	*Jive*	10
21	**39**	LOVE IS CONTAGIOUS	Taja Sevelle	*Paisley Park*	6
-	**40**	GET LUCKY	Jermaine Stewart	*Siren*	1

WEEK ENDING 16 APRIL 1988

LW	TW	Title	Artist	Label	Wks
1	**1**	HEART	Pet Shop Boys	*Parlophone*	3

In these weeks ■ Wet Wet Wet's song *Temptation* just fails to match the Top ten achievements of the Everly Brothers and Heaven 17 with different songs of the same title, so *The Power Of Love* remains the only title used by three completely different top ten hits (09.04.88)■

LW	TW	Title	Artist	Label	Wks
2	[2]	DROP THE BOY	Bros	*CBS*	5
7	3	LOVE CHANGES (EVERYTHING)	Climie Fisher	*EMI*	5
4	[4]	COULD'VE BEEN	Tiffany	*MCA*	5
13	5	EVERYWHERE	Fleetwood Mac	*Warner Bros*	3
6	[6]	CROSS MY BROKEN HEART	Sinitta	*Fanfare*	5
9	[7]	I'M NOT SCARED	Eighth Wonder	*CBS*	7
15	[8]	PROVE YOUR LOVE	Taylor Dayne	*Arista*	4
20	9	WHO'S LEAVING WHO	Hazell Dean	*EMI*	3
3	10	DON'T TURN AROUND	Aswad	*Mango*	7
24	11	PINK CADILLAC	Natalie Cole	*Manhattan*	3
16	[12]	DREAMING	Glen Goldsmith	*Reproduction*	4
23	13	GIRLFRIEND	Pebbles	*MCA*	3
36	14	I WANT YOU BACK	Bananarama	*London*	2
21	15	JUST A MIRAGE	Jellybean featuring Adele Bertei	*Chrysalis*	4
11	16	ONLY IN MY DREAMS	Debbie Gibson	*Atlantic*	5
8	17	STAY ON THESE ROADS	A-Ha	*Warner Bros*	4
5	18	CAN I PLAY WITH MADNESS	Iron Maiden	*EMI*	4
12	19	TEMPTATION	Wet Wet Wet	*Precious*	5
28	[20]	ARMAGEDDON IT	Def Leppard	*Bludgeon Riffola*	2
10	21	I SHOULD BE SO LUCKY	Kylie Minogue	*PWL*	12
40	22	GET LUCKY	Jermaine Stewart	*Siren*	2
25	[23]	SEX TALK (LIVE)	T'Pau	*Siren*	3
19	24	AIN'T COMPLAINING	Status Quo	*Vertigo*	4
-	25	THEME FROM S EXPRESS	S Express ●	*Rhythm King*	1
31	[26]	I NEED A MAN	Eurythmics	*RCA*	2
22	27	THAT'S THE WAY I WANNA ROCK 'N' ROLL	AC/DC	*Atlantic*	3
29	28	PIANO IN THE DARK	Brenda Russell	*Breakout*	3
-	29	LET'S ALL CHANT	Mick and Pat ●	*PWL*	1
32	[30]	SIDEWALKING	Jesus And Mary Chain	*blanco y negro*	2
-	31	I WANT YOU BACK '88	Michael Jackson and the Jackson Five	*Motown*	1
14	32	NEVER/THESE DREAMS	Heart	*Capitol*	7
17	33	WHERE DO BROKEN HEARTS GO	Whitney Houston	*Arista*	6
-	34	A LOVE SUPREME	Will Downing ●	*Fourth + Broadway*	1
-	35	MARY'S PRAYER	Danny Wilson ●	*Virgin*	1
18	36	BASS (HOW LOW CAN YOU GO)	Simon Harris	*ffrr*	5
34	37	I WANT HER	Keith Sweat	*Vintertainment*	6
27	38	CRASH	Primitives	*RCA*	8
-	39	SHE'S LIKE THE WIND	Patrick Swayze featuring Wendy Fraser ●	*RCA*	1
-	40	EVERY ANGEL	All About Eve	*Eden*	1

WEEK ENDING 23 APRIL 1988

LW	TW	Title	Artist	Label	Wks
1	[1]	HEART	Pet Shop Boys	*Parlophone*	4
3	[2]	LOVE CHANGES (EVERYTHING)	Climie Fisher	*EMI*	6
25	3	THEME FROM S EXPRESS	S Express	*Rhythm King*	2
5	[4]	EVERYWHERE	Fleetwood Mac	*Warner Bros*	4
11	[5]	PINK CADILLAC	Natalie Cole	*Manhattan*	4
9	6	WHO'S LEAVING WHO	Hazell Dean	*EMI*	4
14	7	I WANT YOU BACK	Bananarama	*London*	3
13	[8]	GIRLFRIEND	Pebbles	*MCA*	4
2	9	DROP THE BOY	Bros	*CBS*	6
31	10	I WANT YOU BACK '88	Michael Jackson and the Jackson Five	*Motown*	2
8	11	PROVE YOUR LOVE	Taylor Dayne	*Arista*	5
4	12	COULD'VE BEEN	Tiffany	*MCA*	6
15	[13]	JUST A MIRAGE	Jellybean featuring Adele Bertei	*Chrysalis*	5
-	14	ONE MORE TRY	George Michael	*Epic*	1
35	15	MARY'S PRAYER	Danny Wilson	*Virgin*	2
12	16	DREAMING	Glen Goldsmith	*Reproduction*	5
22	17	GET LUCKY	Jermaine Stewart	*Siren*	3
7	18	I'M NOT SCARED	Eighth Wonder	*CBS*	8
29	19	LET'S ALL CHANT	Mick and Pat	*PWL*	2
6	20	CROSS MY BROKEN HEART	Sinitta	*Fanfare*	6
34	21	A LOVE SUPREME	Will Downing	*Fourth + Broadway*	2
10	22	DON'T TURN AROUND	Aswad	*Mango*	8
20	23	ARMAGEDDON IT	Def Leppard	*Bludgeon Riffola*	3
39	24	SHE'S LIKE THE WIND	Patrick Swayze featuring Wendy Fraser	*RCA*	2
-	25	THE PAYBACK MIX PART ONE	James Brown	*Urban*	1
28	[26]	PIANO IN THE DARK	Brenda Russell	*Breakout*	4
16	27	ONLY IN MY DREAMS	Debbie Gibson	*Atlantic*	6
26	28	I NEED A MAN	Eurythmics	*RCA*	3

May 1988

□ Highest position disc reached ● Act's first ever week on chart

LW	TW	Title	Artist	Label	Wks
23	29	SEX TALK (LIVE)	T'Pau	*Siren*	4
40	[30]	EVERY ANGEL	All About Eve	*Eden*	2
19	31	TEMPTATION	Wet Wet Wet	*Precious*	6
17	32	STAY ON THESE ROADS	A-Ha	*Warner Bros*	5
-	33	I GAVE IT UP (WHEN I FELL IN LOVE)	Luther Vandross	*Epic*	1
18	34	CAN I PLAY WITH MADNESS	Iron Maiden	*EMI*	5
-	35	PERFECT	Fairground Attraction ●	*RCA*	1
-	36	BEYOND THE PALE	Mission	*Mercury*	1
21	37	I SHOULD BE SO LUCKY	Kylie Minogue	*PWL*	13
-	38	WHEN WILL YOU MAKE MY TELEPHONE RING	Deacon Blue	*CBS*	1
-	39	IT TAKES TWO	Rob Base and DJ E-Z Rock ●	*Citybeat*	1
27	40	THAT'S THE WAY I WANNA ROCK 'N' ROLL	AC/DC	*Atlantic*	4

WEEK ENDING 30 APRIL 1988

LW	TW	Title	Artist	Label	Wks
3	[1]	THEME FROM S EXPRESS	S Express	*Rhythm King*	3
1	2	HEART	Pet Shop Boys	*Parlophone*	5
15	[3]	MARY'S PRAYER	Danny Wilson	*Virgin*	3
6	[4]	WHO'S LEAVING WHO	Hazell Dean	*EMI*	5
7	[5]	I WANT YOU BACK	Bananarama	*London*	4
5	6	PINK CADILLAC	Natalie Cole	*Manhattan*	5
2	7	LOVE CHANGES (EVERYTHING)	Climie Fisher	*EMI*	7
14	[8]	ONE MORE TRY	George Michael	*Epic*	2
10	9	I WANT YOU BACK '88	Michael Jackson and the Jackson Five	*Motown*	3
4	10	EVERYWHERE	Fleetwood Mac	*Warner Bros*	5
8	11	GIRLFRIEND	Pebbles	*MCA*	5
35	12	PERFECT	Fairground Attraction	*RCA*	2
17	[13]	GET LUCKY	Jermaine Stewart	*Siren*	4
25	14	THE PAYBACK MIX PART ONE	James Brown	*Urban*	2
19	15	LET'S ALL CHANT	Mick and Pat	*PWL*	3
21	16	A LOVE SUPREME	Will Downing	*Fourth + Broadway*	3
24	[17]	SHE'S LIKE THE WIND	Patrick Swayze featuring Wendy Fraser	*RCA*	3
13	18	JUST A MIRAGE	Jellybean featuring Adele Bertei	*Chrysalis*	6
11	19	PROVE YOUR LOVE	Taylor Dayne	*Arista*	6
9	20	DROP THE BOY	Bros	*CBS*	7
12	21	COULD'VE BEEN	Tiffany	*MCA*	7
16	22	DREAMING	Glen Goldsmith	*Reproduction*	6
26	[23]	PIANO IN THE DARK	Brenda Russell	*Breakout*	4
39	[24]	IT TAKES TWO	Rob Base and DJ E-Z Rock	*Citybeat*	2
18	25	I'M NOT SCARED	Eighth Wonder	*CBS*	9
-	26	OUT OF REACH	Primitives	*Lazy*	1
20	27	CROSS MY BROKEN HEART	Sinitta	*Fanfare*	7
33	[28]	I GAVE IT UP (WHEN I FELL IN LOVE)	Luther Vandross	*Epic*	2
-	29	WALK AWAY	Joyce Sims	*ffrr*	1
-	30	DIVINE EMOTIONS	Narada	*Reprise*	1
22	31	DON'T TURN AROUND	Aswad	*Mango*	9
36	[32]	BEYOND THE PALE	Mission	*Mercury*	2
-	33	BORN AGAIN	Christians	*Island*	1
38	[34]	WHEN WILL YOU MAKE MY TELEPHONE RING	Deacon Blue	*CBS*	2
-	35	BROKEN LAND	Adventures ●	*Elektra*	1
-	36	THERE IS ALWAYS SOMETHING THERE TO REMIND ME	Housemartins	Go! Discs	1
23	37	ARMAGEDDON IT	Def Leppard	*Bludgeon Riffola*	4
29	38	SEX TALK (LIVE)	T'Pau	*Siren*	5
-	39	PUMP UP THE BITTER	Star Turn On 45 (Pints) ●	*Pacific*	1
30	40	EVERY ANGEL	All About Eve	*Eden*	3

WEEK ENDING 7 MAY 1988

LW	TW	Title	Artist	Label	Wks
1	[1]	THEME FROM S EXPRESS	S Express	*Rhythm King*	4
12	2	PERFECT	Fairground Attraction	*RCA*	3
3	[3]	MARY'S PRAYER	Danny Wilson	*Virgin*	4
4	[4]	WHO'S LEAVING WHO	Hazell Dean	*EMI*	6
5	[5]	I WANT YOU BACK	Bananarama	*London*	5

■Eight consecutive weeks in which a record peaks at no. 2. Four different records during this period just miss out on a number one (23.04.88) ■ The Bananarama *I Want You Back* is not the same song as the Jackson Five *I Want You Back*, although they both are at their peak in the same week (07.05.88)■

May 1988

□ Highest position disc reached ● Act's first ever week on chart

LW	TW	Title / Artist	Label	Wks
6	6	PINK CADILLAC Natalie Cole	*Manhattan*	6
2	7	HEART Pet Shop Boys	*Parlophone*	6
9	8	I WANT YOU BACK '88 Michael Jackson and the Jackson Five	*Motown*	4
8	9	ONE MORE TRY George Michael	*Epic*	3
-	10	BLUE MONDAY 1988 New Order	*Factory*	1
15	11	LET'S ALL CHANT Mick and Pat	*PWL*	4
14	12	THE PAYBACK MIX PART ONE James Brown	*Urban*	3
7	13	LOVE CHANGES (EVERYTHING) Climie Fisher	*EMI*	8
16	14	A LOVE SUPREME Will Downing	*Fourth + Broadway*	4
39	15	PUMP UP THE BITTER Star Turn On 45 (Pints)	*Pacific*	2
10	16	EVERYWHERE Fleetwood Mac	*Warner Bros*	6
-	17	LOADSAMONEY (DOIN' UP THE HOUSE) Harry Enfield ●	*Mercury*	1
-	18	ALPHABET STREET Prince	*Paisley Park*	1
13	19	GET LUCKY Jermaine Stewart	*Siren*	5
17	20	SHE'S LIKE THE WIND Patrick Swayze featuring Wendy Fraser	*RCA*	4
11	21	GIRLFRIEND Pebbles	*MCA*	6
30	22	DIVINE EMOTIONS Narada	*Reprise*	2
23	23	PIANO IN THE DARK Brenda Russell	*Breakout*	5
29	24	WALK AWAY Joyce Sims	*ffrr*	2
26	25	OUT OF REACH Primitives	*Lazy*	2
33	26	BORN AGAIN Christians	*Island*	2
24	27	IT TAKES TWO Rob Base and DJ E-Z Rock	*Citybeat*	3
18	28	JUST A MIRAGE Jellybean featuring Adele Bertei	*Chrysalis*	7
-	29	START TALKING LOVE Magnum	*Polydor*	1
35	30	BROKEN LAND Adventures	*Elektra*	2
20	31	DROP THE BOY Bros	*CBS*	8
28	32	I GAVE IT UP (WHEN I FELL IN LOVE) Luther Vandross	*Epic*	3
19	33	PROVE YOUR LOVE Taylor Dayne	*Arista*	7
22	34	DREAMING Glen Goldsmith	*Reproduction*	7
36	35	THERE IS ALWAYS SOMETHING THERE TO REMIND ME Housemartins	Go! Discs	2
-	36	BAD YOUNG BROTHER Derek B	*Tuff Audio*	1
34	37	WHEN WILL YOU MAKE MY TELEPHONE RING Deacon Blue	*CBS*	3
21	38	COULD'VE BEEN Tiffany	*MCA*	8
-	39	THE KING OF ROCK 'N' ROLL Prefab Sprout	*Kitchenware*	1
32	40	BEYOND THE PALE Mission	*Mercury*	3

LW	TW	*WEEK ENDING* 14 MAY 1988		Wks
2	1	PERFECT Fairground Attraction	*RCA*	4
1	2	THEME FROM S EXPRESS S Express	*Rhythm King*	5
10	3	BLUE MONDAY 1988 New Order	*Factory*	2
17	4	LOADSAMONEY (DOIN' UP THE HOUSE) Harry Enfield	*Mercury*	2
-	5	WITH A LITTLE HELP FROM MY FRIENDS/SHE'S LEAVING HOME Wet Wet Wet/Billy Bragg with Cara Tivey	*Childline*	1
5	6	I WANT YOU BACK Bananarama	*London*	6
3	7	MARY'S PRAYER Danny Wilson	*Virgin*	5
4	8	WHO'S LEAVING WHO Hazell Dean	*EMI*	7
18	9	ALPHABET STREET Prince	*Paisley Park*	2
8	10	I WANT YOU BACK '88 Michael Jackson and the Jackson Five	*Motown*	5
6	11	PINK CADILLAC Natalie Cole	*Manhattan*	7
15	12	PUMP UP THE BITTER Star Turn On 45 (Pints)	*Pacific*	3
-	13	ANFIELD RAP (RED MACHINE IN FULL EFFECT) Liverpool FC	*Virgin*	1
11	14	LET'S ALL CHANT Mick and Pat	*PWL*	5
-	15	GOT TO BE CERTAIN Kylie Minogue	*PWL*	1
22	16	DIVINE EMOTIONS Narada	*Reprise*	3
14	17	A LOVE SUPREME Will Downing	*Fourth + Broadway*	5
7	18	HEART Pet Shop Boys	*Parlophone*	7
9	19	ONE MORE TRY George Michael	*Epic*	4
12	20	THE PAYBACK MIX PART ONE James Brown	*Urban*	4
16	21	EVERYWHERE Fleetwood Mac	*Warner Bros*	7
29	22	START TALKING LOVE Magnum	*Polydor*	2
30	23	BROKEN LAND Adventures	*Elektra*	3
20	24	SHE'S LIKE THE WIND Patrick Swayze featuring Wendy Fraser	*RCA*	5
26	25	BORN AGAIN Christians	*Island*	3
36	26	BAD YOUNG BROTHER Derek B	*Tuff Audio*	2
24	27	WALK AWAY Joyce Sims	*ffrr*	3
39	28	THE KING OF ROCK 'N' ROLL Prefab Sprout	*Kitchenware*	2
13	29	LOVE CHANGES (EVERYTHING) Climie Fisher	*EMI*	9
19	30	GET LUCKY Jermaine Stewart	*Siren*	6
-	31	CIRCLE IN THE SAND Belinda Carlisle	*Virgin*	1
23	32	PIANO IN THE DARK Brenda Russell	*Breakout*	6
-	33	SOMEWHERE IN MY HEART Aztec Camera	*WEA*	1
21	34	GIRLFRIEND Pebbles	*MCA*	7
-	35	NOTHIN' BUT A GOOD TIME Poison ●	*Capitol*	1
25	36	OUT OF REACH Primitives	*Lazy*	3
-	37	OUT OF THE BLUE Debbie Gibson	*Atlantic*	1
-	38	IM NIN'ALU Ofra Haza ●	*WEA*	1
-	39	CALYPSO CRAZY Billy Ocean	*Jive*	1
-	40	WHAT ABOUT LOVE Heart	*Capitol*	1

LW	TW	*WEEK ENDING* 21 MAY 1988		Wks
5	1	WITH A LITTLE HELP FROM MY FRIENDS/SHE'S LEAVING HOME Wet Wet Wet/Billy Bragg with Cara Tivey	*Childline*	2
1	2	PERFECT Fairground Attraction	*RCA*	5
13	3	ANFIELD RAP (RED MACHINE IN FULL EFFECT) Liverpool FC	*Virgin*	2
15	4	GOT TO BE CERTAIN Kylie Minogue	*PWL*	2
3	5	BLUE MONDAY 1988 New Order	*Factory*	3
4	6	LOADSAMONEY (DOIN' UP THE HOUSE) Harry Enfield	*Mercury*	3
2	7	THEME FROM S EXPRESS S Express	*Rhythm King*	6
16	8	DIVINE EMOTIONS Narada	*Reprise*	4
6	9	I WANT YOU BACK Bananarama	*London*	7
7	10	MARY'S PRAYER Danny Wilson	*Virgin*	6
9	11	ALPHABET STREET Prince	*Paisley Park*	3
31	12	CIRCLE IN THE SAND Belinda Carlisle	*Virgin*	2
8	13	WHO'S LEAVING WHO Hazell Dean	*EMI*	8
28	14	THE KING OF ROCK 'N' ROLL Prefab Sprout	*Kitchenware*	3
11	15	PINK CADILLAC Natalie Cole	*Manhattan*	8
26	16	BAD YOUNG BROTHER Derek B	*Tuff Audio*	3
33	17	SOMEWHERE IN MY HEART Aztec Camera	*WEA*	2
10	18	I WANT YOU BACK '88 Michael Jackson and the Jackson Five	*Motown*	6
40	19	WHAT ABOUT LOVE Heart	*Capitol*	2
23	20	BROKEN LAND Adventures	*Elektra*	4
12	21	PUMP UP THE BITTER Star Turn On 45 (Pints)	*Pacific*	4
-	22	DON'T GO Hothouse Flowers ●	*ffrr*	1
14	23	LET'S ALL CHANT Mick and Pat	*PWL*	6
17	24	A LOVE SUPREME Will Downing	*Fourth + Broadway*	6
38	25	IM NIN'ALU Ofra Haza	*WEA*	2
19	26	ONE MORE TRY George Michael	*Epic*	5
37	27	OUT OF THE BLUE Debbie Gibson	*Atlantic*	2
18	28	HEART Pet Shop Boys	*Parlophone*	8
24	29	SHE'S LIKE THE WIND Patrick Swayze featuring Wendy Fraser	*RCA*	6
-	30	MY ONE TEMPTATION Mica Paris ●	*Fourth + Broadway*	1
-	31	OH PATTI (DON'T FEEL SORRY FOR LOVERBOY) Scritti Politti	*Virgin*	1
21	32	EVERYWHERE Fleetwood Mac	*Warner Bros*	8
22	33	START TALKING LOVE Magnum	*Polydor*	3
-	34	CHECK THIS OUT LA Mix ●	*Breakout*	1
39	35	CALYPSO CRAZY Billy Ocean	*Jive*	2
25	36	BORN AGAIN Christians	*Island*	4
-	37	THIS IS ME Climie Fisher	*EMI*	1
-	38	HEY MR HEARTACHE Kim Wilde	*MCA*	1
27	39	WALK AWAY Joyce Sims	*ffrr*	4
20	40	THE PAYBACK MIX PART ONE James Brown	*Urban*	5

In these weeks ■ Two 1988 remixes of past hits in the top ten together for two weeks - *Blue Monday* and *I Want You Back* (14.05.88) ■ Ofra Haza is by no means the first Israeli in our charts, but she is the first to sing entirely in Hebrew (14.05.88)■

LW	TW	WEEK ENDING 28 MAY 1988		Wks
1	[1]	WITH A LITTLE HELP FROM MY FRIENDS/SHE'S LEAVING HOME Wet Wet Wet/Billy Bragg with Cara Tivey	*Childline*	3
4	[2]	GOT TO BE CERTAIN Kylie Minogue	*PWL*	3
2	3	PERFECT Fairground Attraction	*RCA*	6
3	4	ANFIELD RAP (RED MACHINE IN FULL EFFECT) Liverpool FC	*Virgin*	3
5	5	BLUE MONDAY 1988 New Order	*Factory*	4
12	6	CIRCLE IN THE SAND Belinda Carlisle	*Virgin*	3
14	[7]	THE KING OF ROCK 'N' ROLL Prefab Sprout	*Kitchenware*	4
17	8	SOMEWHERE IN MY HEART Aztec Camera	*WEA*	3
8	9	DIVINE EMOTIONS Narada	*Reprise*	5
7	10	THEME FROM S EXPRESS S Express	*Rhythm King*	7
22	[11]	DON'T GO Hothouse Flowers	*ffrr*	2
6	12	LOADSAMONEY (DOIN' UP THE HOUSE) Harry Enfield	*Mercury*	4
34	13	CHECK THIS OUT LA Mix	*Breakout*	2
19	[14]	WHAT ABOUT LOVE Heart	*Capitol*	3
25	[15]	IM NIN'ALU Ofra Haza	*WEA*	3
16	[16]	BAD YOUNG BROTHER Derek B	*Tuff Audio*	4
30	17	MY ONE TEMPTATION Mica Paris	*Fourth + Broadway*	2
31	18	OH PATTI (DON'T FEEL SORRY FOR LOVERBOY) Scritti Politti	*Virgin*	2
27	[19]	OUT OF THE BLUE Debbie Gibson	*Atlantic*	3
10	20	MARY'S PRAYER Danny Wilson	*Virgin*	7
9	21	I WANT YOU BACK Bananarama	*London*	8
37	[22]	THIS IS ME Climie Fisher	*EMI*	2
20	23	BROKEN LAND Adventures	*Elektra*	5
15	24	PINK CADILLAC Natalie Cole	*Manhattan*	9
-	25	GIVE A LITTLE LOVE Aswad	*Mango*	1
13	26	WHO'S LEAVING WHO Hazell Dean	*EMI*	9
-	27	LOVE WILL SAVE THE DAY Whitney Houston	*Arista*	1
-	[28]	LIFE AT A TOP PEOPLE'S HEALTH FARM Style Council	*Polydor*	1
11	29	ALPHABET STREET Prince	*Paisley Park*	4
-	30	LOST IN YOU Rod Stewart	*Warner Bros*	1
38	[31]	HEY MR HEARTACHE Kim Wilde	*MCA*	2
18	32	I WANT YOU BACK '88 Michael Jackson and the Jackson Five	*Motown*	7
-	33	NAUGHTY GIRLS (NEED LOVE TOO) Samantha Fox	*Jive*	1
-	[34]	WHO GETS THE LOVE Status Quo	*Vertigo*	1
-	35	VOYAGE VOYAGE Desireless ●	*CBS*	1
-	36	DON'T CALL ME BABY Voice Of The Beehive ●	*ffrr*	1
-	[37]	RUN'S HOUSE Run DMC	*London*	1
-	38	THE LOVERS Alexander O'Neal	*Tabu*	1
23	39	LET'S ALL CHANT Mick and Pat	*PWL*	7
-	40	MOVIN' 1988 Brass Construction	*Syncopate*	1

June 1988

□ Highest position disc reached ● Act's first ever week on chart

LW	TW	WEEK ENDING 4 JUNE 1988		Wks
1	[1]	WITH A LITTLE HELP FROM MY FRIENDS/SHE'S LEAVING HOME Wet Wet Wet/Billy Bragg with Cara Tivey	*Childline*	4
2	[2]	GOT TO BE CERTAIN Kylie Minogue	*PWL*	4
3	3	PERFECT Fairground Attraction	*RCA*	7
6	[4]	CIRCLE IN THE SAND Belinda Carlisle	*Virgin*	4
8	5	SOMEWHERE IN MY HEART Aztec Camera	*WEA*	4
13	6	CHECK THIS OUT LA Mix	*Breakout*	3
7	[7]	THE KING OF ROCK 'N' ROLL Prefab Sprout	*Kitchenware*	5
17	8	MY ONE TEMPTATION Mica Paris	*Fourth + Broadway*	3
5	9	BLUE MONDAY 1988 New Order	*Factory*	5
27	[10]	LOVE WILL SAVE THE DAY Whitney Houston	*Arista*	2
11	[11]	DON'T GO Hothouse Flowers	*ffrr*	3
4	12	ANFIELD RAP (RED MACHINE IN FULL EFFECT) Liverpool FC	*Virgin*	4
18	[13]	OH PATTI (DON'T FEEL SORRY FOR LOVERBOY) Scritti Politti	*Virgin*	3
35	14	VOYAGE VOYAGE Desireless	*CBS*	2
14	15	WHAT ABOUT LOVE Heart	*Capitol*	4
15	16	IM NIN'ALU Ofra Haza	*WEA*	4
10	17	THEME FROM S EXPRESS S Express	*Rhythm King*	8
25	18	GIVE A LITTLE LOVE Aswad	*Mango*	2
19	[19]	OUT OF THE BLUE Debbie Gibson	*Atlantic*	4
9	20	DIVINE EMOTIONS Narada	*Reprise*	6
30	[21]	LOST IN YOU Rod Stewart	*Warner Bros*	2
-	22	DOCTORIN' THE TARDIS Timelords ●	*KLF Communications*	1
-	23	I SAW HIM STANDING THERE Tiffany	*MCA*	1
40	[24]	MOVIN' 1988 Brass Construction	*Syncopate*	2
-	25	ANOTHER WEEKEND Five Star	*Tent*	1
22	26	THIS IS ME Climie Fisher	*EMI*	3
36	27	DON'T CALL ME BABY Voice Of The Beehive	*ffrr*	2
38	[28]	THE LOVERS Alexander O'Neal	*Tabu*	2
28	29	LIFE AT A TOP PEOPLE'S HEALTH FARM Style Council	*Polydor*	2
12	30	LOADSAMONEY (DOIN' UP THE HOUSE) Harry Enfield	*Mercury*	5
33	[31]	NAUGHTY GIRLS (NEED LOVE TOO) Samantha Fox	*Jive*	2
-	32	WILD WORLD Maxi Priest	*10*	1
16	33	BAD YOUNG BROTHER Derek B	*Tuff Audio*	5
34	[34]	WHO GETS THE LOVE Status Quo	*Vertigo*	2
20	35	MARY'S PRAYER Danny Wilson	*Virgin*	8
-	36	MOONCHILD Fields Of The Nephilim ●	*Situation Two*	1
-	[37]	GET IT Stevie Wonder and Michael Jackson ●	*Motown*	1
31	38	HEY MR HEARTACHE Kim Wilde	*MCA*	3
-	39	I'M REAL James Brown	*Scotti Brothers*	1
21	40	I WANT YOU BACK Bananarama	*London*	9

LW	TW	WEEK ENDING 11 JUNE 1988		Wks
1	[1]	WITH A LITTLE HELP FROM MY FRIENDS/SHE'S LEAVING HOME Wet Wet Wet/Billy Bragg with Cara Tivey	*Childline*	5
2	[2]	GOT TO BE CERTAIN Kylie Minogue	*PWL*	5
5	[3]	SOMEWHERE IN MY HEART Aztec Camera	*WEA*	5
22	4	DOCTORIN' THE TARDIS Timelords	*KLF Communications*	2
14	[5]	VOYAGE VOYAGE Desireless	*CBS*	3
4	6	CIRCLE IN THE SAND Belinda Carlisle	*Virgin*	5
8	[7]	MY ONE TEMPTATION Mica Paris	*Fourth + Broadway*	4
23	[8]	I SAW HIM STANDING THERE Tiffany	*MCA*	2
6	9	CHECK THIS OUT LA Mix	*Breakout*	4
3	10	PERFECT Fairground Attraction	*RCA*	8
18	[11]	GIVE A LITTLE LOVE Aswad	*Mango*	3
-	12	EVERY DAY IS LIKE SUNDAY Morrissey	*HMV*	1
7	13	THE KING OF ROCK 'N' ROLL Prefab Sprout	*Kitchenware*	6
13	14	OH PATTI (DON'T FEEL SORRY FOR LOVERBOY) Scritti Politti	*Virgin*	4
32	15	WILD WORLD Maxi Priest	*10*	2
10	16	LOVE WILL SAVE THE DAY Whitney Houston	*Arista*	3
11	17	DON'T GO Hothouse Flowers	*ffrr*	4
25	[18]	ANOTHER WEEKEND Five Star	*Tent*	2
-	19	CHAINS OF LOVE (REMIX) Erasure	*Mute*	1
9	20	BLUE MONDAY 1988 New Order	*Factory*	6
12	21	ANFIELD RAP (RED MACHINE IN FULL EFFECT) Liverpool FC	*Virgin*	5
21	22	LOST IN YOU Rod Stewart	*Warner Bros*	3
27	23	DON'T CALL ME BABY Voice Of The Beehive	*ffrr*	3
-	24	BOYS (SUMMERTIME LOVE) Sabrina ●	*Ibiza*	1
19	25	OUT OF THE BLUE Debbie Gibson	*Atlantic*	5
15	26	WHAT ABOUT LOVE Heart	*Capitol*	5
17	27	THEME FROM S EXPRESS S Express	*Rhythm King*	9
36	[28]	MOONCHILD Fields Of The Nephilim	*Situation Two*	2
16	29	IM NIN'ALU Ofra Haza	*WEA*	5
28	30	THE LOVERS Alexander O'Neal	*Tabu*	3
39	[31]	I'M REAL James Brown	*Scotti Brothers*	2
24	32	MOVIN' 1988 Brass Construction	*Syncopate*	3
-	33	TRIBUTE (RIGHT ON) Pasadenas ●	*CBS*	1
20	34	DIVINE EMOTIONS Narada	*Reprise*	7
-	35	PARADISE (REMIX) Sade	*Epic*	1
-	36	DON'T BLAME IT ON THAT GIRL/WAP-BAM-BOOGIE Matt Bianco	*WEA*	1

■Two people who have both had hit singles with Paul McCartney and with Diana Ross combine for their own hit duet, but Stevie Wonder and Michael Jackson have done much better alone than together (04.06.88) ■ Their record label gives the game away. The Timelords will reappear on the charts in years to come as the KLF, although without the help of Gary Glitter who performs on *Doctorin' The Tardis* (04.06.88)■

June 1988

□ Highest position disc reached ● Act's first ever week on chart

LW	TW	Title	Artist	Label	Wks
-	37	YOU HAVE PLACED A CHILL IN MY HEART	Eurythmics	RCA	1
30	38	LOADSAMONEY (DOIN' UP THE HOUSE)	Harry Enfield	Mercury	6
37	39	GET IT	Stevie Wonder and Michael Jackson	Motown	2
-	[40]	TELL ME	Nick Kamen	WEA	1

WEEK ENDING 18 JUNE 1988

LW	TW	Title	Artist	Label	Wks
4	[1]	DOCTORIN' THE TARDIS	Timelords	KLF Communications	3
-	2	I OWE YOU NOTHING	Bros	CBS	1
1	3	WITH A LITTLE HELP FROM MY FRIENDS/SHE'S LEAVING HOME	Wet Wet Wet/Billy Bragg with Cara Tivey	Childline	6
24	4	BOYS (SUMMERTIME LOVE)	Sabrina	Ibiza	2
5	[5]	VOYAGE VOYAGE	Desireless	CBS	4
2	6	GOT TO BE CERTAIN	Kylie Minogue	PWL	6
15	7	WILD WORLD	Maxi Priest	10	3
3	8	SOMEWHERE IN MY HEART	Aztec Camera	WEA	6
12	[9]	EVERY DAY IS LIKE SUNDAY	Morrissey	HMV	2
8	10	I SAW HIM STANDING THERE	Tiffany	MCA	3
19	[11]	CHAINS OF LOVE (REMIX)	Erasure	Mute	2
7	12	MY ONE TEMPTATION	Mica Paris	Fourth + Broadway	5
6	13	CIRCLE IN THE SAND	Belinda Carlisle	Virgin	6
11	14	GIVE A LITTLE LOVE	Aswad	Mango	4
23	[15]	DON'T CALL ME BABY	Voice Of The Beehive	ffrr	4
33	16	TRIBUTE (RIGHT ON)	Pasadenas	CBS	2
10	17	PERFECT	Fairground Attraction	RCA	9
9	18	CHECK THIS OUT	LA Mix	Breakout	5
-	19	THE TWIST (YO, TWIST)	Fat Boys with Chubby Checker	Tin Pan Apple	1
-	[20]	LUCRETIA MY REFLECTION	Sisters Of Mercy	Merciful Release	1
36	21	DON'T BLAME IT ON THAT GIRL/WAP-BAM-BOOGIE	Matt Bianco	WEA	2
18	22	ANOTHER WEEKEND	Five Star	Tent	3
13	23	THE KING OF ROCK 'N' ROLL	Prefab Sprout	Kitchenware	7
14	24	OH PATTI (DON'T FEEL SORRY FOR LOVERBOY)	Scritti Politti	Virgin	5
37	25	YOU HAVE PLACED A CHILL IN MY HEART	Eurythmics	RCA	2
-	26	BLOOD THAT MOVES THE BODY	A-Ha	Warner Brothers	1
17	27	DON'T GO	Hothouse Flowers	ffrr	5
-	28	CAR WASH/IS IT LOVE YOU'RE AFTER	Rose Royce	MCA	1
35	[29]	PARADISE (REMIX)	Sade	Epic	2
-	30	BREAKFAST IN BED	UB40 with Chrissie Hynde Hynde	DEP International	1
16	31	LOVE WILL SAVE THE DAY	Whitney Houston	Arista	4
-	32	THERE'S MORE TO LOVE	Communards	London	1
22	33	LOST IN YOU	Rod Stewart	Warner Bros	4
20	34	BLUE MONDAY 1988	New Order	Factory	7
-	35	IN THE AIR TONIGHT	Phil Collins	Virgin	1
27	36	THEME FROM S EXPRESS	S Express	Rhythm King	10
-	37	WHAT YOU SEE IS WHAT YOU GET	Glen Goldsmith	Reproduction	1
-	38	TOUGHER THAN THE REST	Bruce Springsteen	CBS	1
31	39	I'M REAL	James Brown	Scotti Brothers	3
40	[40]	TELL ME	Nick Kamen	WEA	2

WEEK ENDING 25 JUNE 1988

LW	TW	Title	Artist	Label	Wks
2	[1]	I OWE YOU NOTHING	Bros	CBS	2
1	2	DOCTORIN' THE TARDIS	Timelords	KLF Communications	4
4	[3]	BOYS (SUMMERTIME LOVE)	Sabrina	Ibiza	3
19	4	THE TWIST (YO, TWIST)	Fat Boys with Chubby Checker	Tin Pan Apple	2
7	[5]	WILD WORLD	Maxi Priest	10	4
16	6	TRIBUTE (RIGHT ON)	Pasadenas	CBS	3
5	7	VOYAGE VOYAGE	Desireless	CBS	5
35	8	IN THE AIR TONIGHT	Phil Collins	Virgin	2
30	9	BREAKFAST IN BED	UB40 with Chrissie Hynde Hynde	DEP International	2
3	10	WITH A LITTLE HELP FROM MY FRIENDS/SHE'S LEAVING HOME	Wet Wet Wet/Billy Bragg with Cara Tivey	Childline	7
11	[11]	CHAINS OF LOVE (REMIX)	Erasure	Mute	3
6	12	GOT TO BE CERTAIN	Kylie Minogue	PWL	7
9	13	EVERY DAY IS LIKE SUNDAY	Morrissey	HMV	3
8	14	SOMEWHERE IN MY HEART	Aztec Camera	WEA	7
10	15	I SAW HIM STANDING THERE	Tiffany	MCA	4
15	16	DON'T CALL ME BABY	Voice Of The Beehive	ffrr	5
21	17	DON'T BLAME IT ON THAT GIRL/WAP-BAM-BOOGIE	Matt Bianco	WEA	3
25	18	YOU HAVE PLACED A CHILL IN MY HEART	Eurythmics	RCA	3
12	19	MY ONE TEMPTATION	Mica Paris	Fourth + Broadway	6
28	[20]	CAR WASH/IS IT LOVE YOU'RE AFTER	Rose Royce	MCA	2
38	21	TOUGHER THAN THE REST	Bruce Springsteen	CBS	2
20	22	LUCRETIA MY REFLECTION	Sisters Of Mercy	Merciful Release	2
13	23	CIRCLE IN THE SAND	Belinda Carlisle	Virgin	7
-	24	PUSH IT/TRAMP	Salt-N-Pepa ●	Champion/ffrr	1
26	[25]	BLOOD THAT MOVES THE BODY	A-Ha	Warner Brothers	2
-	26	FAST CAR	Tracy Chapman ●	Elektra	1
32	27	THERE'S MORE TO LOVE	Communards	London	2
14	28	GIVE A LITTLE LOVE	Aswad	Mango	5
29	[29]	PARADISE (REMIX)	Sade	Epic	3
17	30	PERFECT	Fairground Attraction	RCA	10
-	31	I WILL BE WITH YOU	T'Pau	Siren	1
-	32	MAYBE (WE SHOULD CALL IT A DAY)	Hazell Dean	EMI	1
37	[33]	WHAT YOU SEE IS WHAT YOU GET	Glen Goldsmith	Reproduction	2
-	[34]	ATMOSPHERE	Joy Division	Factory	1
-	35	I DON'T WANNA GO ON WITH YOU LIKE THAT	Elton John	Rocket	1
-	36	NOTHING'S GONNA CHANGE MY LOVE FOR YOU	Glenn Medeiros ●	London	1
24	37	OH PATTI (DON'T FEEL SORRY FOR LOVERBOY)	Scritti Politti	Virgin	6
18	38	CHECK THIS OUT	LA Mix	Breakout	6
-	39	EVERLASTING	Natalie Cole	Manhattan	1
-	40	NEVER TEAR US APART	INXS	Mercury	1

WEEK ENDING 2 JULY 1988

LW	TW	Title	Artist	Label	Wks
1	[1]	I OWE YOU NOTHING	Bros	CBS	3
4	[2]	THE TWIST (YO TWIST)	Fat Boys and Chubby Checker	Tin Pan Apple	3
3	[3]	BOYS (SUMMERTIME LOVE)	Sabrina	Ibiza	4
8	[4]	IN THE AIR TONIGHT	Phil Collins	Virgin	3
6	[5]	TRIBUTE (RIGHT ON)	Pasadenas	CBS	4
9	[6]	BREAKFAST IN BED	UB40 and Chrissie Hynde	DEP International	3
24	7	PUSH IT/TRAMP	Salt-N-Pepa	Champion/ffrr	2
2	8	DOCTORIN' THE TARDIS	Timelords	KLF Communications	5
5	9	WILD WORLD	Maxi Priest	10	5
26	10	FAST CAR	Tracy Chapman	Elektra	2
36	11	NOTHING'S GONNA CHANGE MY LOVE FOR YOU	Glenn Medeiros	London	2
7	12	VOYAGE VOYAGE	Desireless	CBS	6
11	13	CHAINS OF LOVE	Erasure	Mute	4
17	14	WAP BAM BOOGIE/DON'T BLAME IT ON THE GIRL	Matt Bianco	WEA	4
21	15	TOUGHER THAN THE REST	Bruce Springsteen	CBS	3
18	[16]	YOU HAVE PLACED A CHILL IN MY HEART	Eurythmics	RCA	4
31	17	I WILL BE WITH YOU	T'Pau	Siren	2
32	18	MAYBE (WE SHOULD CALL IT DAY)	Hazell Dean	EMI	2
12	19	GOT TO BE CERTAIN	Kylie Minogue	PWL	8
20	[20]	CAR WASH/IS IT LOVE YOU'RE AFTER	Rose Royce	MCA	3
27	21	THERE'S MORE TO LOVE	Communards	London	3

In these weeks ■ For two weeks there are three Lennon/McCartney titles in the top ten: the Childline charity disc covering two 'Sergeant Pepper' tracks and Tiffany's version of a song from the first Beatles' album, *I Saw Him Standing There* (18.06.88) ■ *The Twist* easily out performs the original Chubby checker version of 1960, 1962 and 1975, but like *Let's Twist Again*, cannot quite get to number one (02.07.88)■

July 1988

□ Highest position disc reached ● Act's first ever week on chart

LW	TW	Title	Artist	Label	Wks
10	22	WITH A LITTLE HELP FROM MY FRIENDS/SHE'S LEAVING HOME	Wet Wet Wet/Billy Bragg and Cara Tivey	*Childline*	8
-	23	DON'T BELIEVE THE HYPE	Public Enemy	*Def Jam*	1
14	24	SOMEWHERE IN MY HEART	Aztec Camera	*WEA*	8
16	25	DON'T CALL ME BABY	Voice Of The Beehive	*ffrr*	6
13	26	EVERYDAY IS LIKE SUNDAY	Morrissey	*HMV*	4
40	27	NEVER TEAR US APART	INXS	*Mercury*	2
15	28	I SAW HIM STANDING THERE	Tiffany	*MCA*	5
39	29	EVERLASTING	Natalie Cole	*Manhattan*	2
35	[30]	I DON'T WANNA GO ON WITH YOU LIKE THAT	Elton John	*Rocket*	2
29	31	PARADISE	Sade	*Epic*	4
-	32	ROSES ARE RED	Mac Band featuring the McCampbell Brothers ●	*MCA*	1
19	33	MY ONE TEMPTATION	Mica Paris	Fourth + Broadway	7
-	34	FOLLOW THE LEADER	Eric B and Rakim	*MCA*	1
34	35	ATMOSPHERE	Joy Division	*Factory*	2
-	36	CROSS MY HEART	Eighth Wonder	*CBS*	1
23	37	CIRCLE IN THE SAND	Belinda Carlisle	*Virgin*	8
33	38	WHAT YOU SEE IS WHAT YOU GET	Glen Goldsmith	*Reproduction*	3
28	39	GIVE A LITTLE LOVE	Aswad	*Mango*	6
-	40	IT MUST HAVE BEEN LOVE	Magnum	*Polydor*	1

WEEK ENDING 9 JULY 1988

LW	TW	Title	Artist	Label	Wks
11	[1]	NOTHING'S GONNA CHANGE MY LOVE FOR YOU	Glenn Medeiros	*London*	3
2	[2]	THE TWIST (YO TWIST)	Fat Boys and Chubby Checker	*Tin Pan Apple*	4
7	3	PUSH IT/TRAMP	Salt-N-Pepa	*Champion/ffrr*	3
1	4	I OWE YOU NOTHING	Bros	*CBS*	4
4	5	IN THE AIR TONIGHT	Phil Collins	*Virgin*	4
3	6	BOYS (SUMMERTIME LOVE)	Sabrina	*Ibiza*	5
10	7	FAST CAR	Tracy Chapman	*Elektra*	3
6	8	BREAKFAST IN BED	UB40 and Chrissie Hynde Hynde	*DEP International*	4
5	9	TRIBUTE (RIGHT ON)	Pasadenas	*CBS*	5
9	10	WILD WORLD	Maxi Priest	*10*	6
14	[11]	WAP BAM BOOGIE/DON'T BLAME IT ON THE GIRL	Matt Bianco	*WEA*	5
8	12	DOCTORIN' THE TARDIS	Timelords	*KLF Communications*	6
15	[13]	TOUGHER THAN THE REST	Bruce Springsteen	*CBS*	4
17	[14]	I WILL BE WITH YOU	T'Pau	*Siren*	3
18	15	MAYBE (WE SHOULD CALL IT DAY)	Hazell Dean	*EMI*	3
32	16	ROSES ARE RED	Mac Band featuring the McCampbell Brothers	*MCA*	2
12	17	VOYAGE VOYAGE	Desireless	*CBS*	7
23	[18]	DON'T BELIEVE THE HYPE	Public Enemy	*Def Jam*	2
16	19	YOU HAVE PLACED A CHILL IN MY HEART	Eurythmics	*RCA*	5
21	[20]	THERE'S MORE TO LOVE	Communards	*London*	4
34	[21]	FOLLOW THE LEADER	Eric B and Rakim	*MCA*	2
36	22	CROSS MY HEART	Eighth Wonder	*CBS*	2
-	23	I DON'T WANT TO TALK ABOUT IT	Everything But The Girl	*blanco y negro*	1
27	[24]	NEVER TEAR US APART	INXS	*Mercury*	3
20	25	CAR WASH/IS IT LOVE YOU'RE AFTER	Rose Royce	*MCA*	4
13	26	CHAINS OF LOVE	Erasure	*Mute*	5
19	27	GOT TO BE CERTAIN	Kylie Minogue	*PWL*	9
29	[28]	EVERLASTING	Natalie Cole	*Manhattan*	3
24	29	SOMEWHERE IN MY HEART	Aztec Camera	*WEA*	9
30	[30]	I DON'T WANNA GO ON WITH YOU LIKE THAT	Elton John	*Rocket*	3
22	31	WITH A LITTLE HELP FROM MY FRIENDS/SHE'S LEAVING HOME	Wet Wet Wet/Billy Bragg and Cara Tivey	*Childline*	9
-	32	I WANT YOUR LOVE	Transvision Vamp ●	*MCA*	1
40	[33]	IT MUST HAVE BEEN LOVE	Magnum	*Polydor*	2
-	34	FOOLISH BEAT	Debbie Gibson	*Atlantic*	1
-	35	ALL FIRED UP	Pat Benatar	*Chrysalis*	1
25	36	DON'T CALL ME BABY	Voice Of The Beehive	*ffrr*	7
-	37	TOMORROW PEOPLE	Ziggy Marley and the Melody Makers ●	*Virgin*	1
-	38	IN MY DREAMS	Will Downing	*4th + Broadway*	1
-	39	HEAT IT UP	Wee Papa Girl Rappers ●	*Jive*	1
26	40	EVERYDAY IS LIKE SUNDAY	Morrissey	*HMV*	5

WEEK ENDING 16 JULY 1988

LW	TW	Title	Artist	Label	Wks
1	[1]	NOTHING'S GONNA CHANGE MY LOVE FOR YOU	Glenn Medeiros	*London*	4
3	[2]	PUSH IT/TRAMP	Salt-N-Pepa	*Champion/ffrr*	4
2	3	THE TWIST (YO TWIST)	Fat Boys and Chubby Checker	*Tin Pan Apple*	5
4	4	I OWE YOU NOTHING	Bros	*CBS*	5
7	[5]	FAST CAR	Tracy Chapman	*Elektra*	4
23	6	I DON'T WANT TO TALK ABOUT IT	Everything But The Girl	*blanco y negro*	2
8	7	BREAKFAST IN BED	UB40 and Chrissie Hynde Hynde	*DEP International*	5
6	8	BOYS (SUMMERTIME LOVE)	Sabrina	*Ibiza*	6
16	9	ROSES ARE RED	Mac Band featuring the McCampbell Brothers	*MCA*	3
5	10	IN THE AIR TONIGHT	Phil Collins	*Virgin*	5
9	11	TRIBUTE (RIGHT ON)	Pasadenas	*CBS*	6
11	12	WAP BAM BOOGIE/DON'T BLAME IT ON THE GIRL	Matt Bianco	*WEA*	6
22	[13]	CROSS MY HEART	Eighth Wonder	*CBS*	3
-	14	DIRTY DIANA	Michael Jackson	*Epic*	1
32	15	I WANT YOUR LOVE	Transvision Vamp	*MCA*	2
13	16	TOUGHER THAN THE REST	Bruce Springsteen	*CBS*	5
10	17	WILD WORLD	Maxi Priest	*10*	7
34	18	FOOLISH BEAT	Debbie Gibson	*Atlantic*	2
-	19	MONKEY	George Michael	*Epic*	1
-	20	LOVE BITES	Def Leppard	*Bludgeon Riffola*	1
14	21	I WILL BE WITH YOU	T'Pau	*Siren*	4
15	22	MAYBE (WE SHOULD CALL IT DAY)	Hazell Dean	*EMI*	4
20	23	THERE'S MORE TO LOVE	Communards	*London*	5
24	[24]	NEVER TEAR US APART	INXS	*Mercury*	4
21	25	FOLLOW THE LEADER	Eric B and Rakim	*MCA*	3
17	26	VOYAGE VOYAGE	Desireless	*CBS*	8
12	27	DOCTORIN' THE TARDIS	Timelords	*KLF Communications*	7
37	28	TOMORROW PEOPLE	Ziggy Marley and the Melody Makers	*Virgin*	2
39	29	HEAT IT UP	Wee Papa Girl Rappers	*Jive*	2
35	30	ALL FIRED UP	Pat Benatar	*Chrysalis*	2
18	31	DON'T BELIEVE THE HYPE	Public Enemy	*Def Jam*	3
28	32	EVERLASTING	Natalie Cole	*Manhattan*	4
19	33	YOU HAVE PLACED A CHILL IN MY HEART	Eurythmics	*RCA*	6
38	[34]	IN MY DREAMS	Will Downing	*Fourth + Broadway*	2
31	35	WITH A LITTLE HELP FROM MY FRIENDS/SHE'S LEAVING HOME	Wet Wet Wet/Billy Bragg and Cara Tivey	*Childline*	10
-	36	FIESTA	Pogues	*Pogue Mahone*	1
27	37	GOT TO BE CERTAIN	Kylie Minogue	*PWL*	10
-	38	YOU CAME	Kim Wilde	*MCA*	1
26	39	CHAINS OF LOVE	Erasure	*Mute*	6
25	40	CAR WASH/IS IT LOVE YOU'RE AFTER	Rose Royce	*MCA*	5

WEEK ENDING 23 JULY 1988

LW	TW	Title	Artist	Label	Wks
1	[1]	NOTHING'S GONNA CHANGE MY LOVE FOR YOU	Glenn Medeiros	*London*	5
2	[2]	PUSH IT/TRAMP	Salt-N-Pepa	*Champion/ffrr*	5
6	[3]	I DON'T WANT TO TALK ABOUT IT	Everything But The Girl	*blanco y negro*	3
14	[4]	DIRTY DIANA	Michael Jackson	*Epic*	2
15	[5]	I WANT YOUR LOVE	Transvision Vamp	*MCA*	3
3	6	THE TWIST (YO TWIST)	Fat Boys and Chubby Checker	*Tin Pan Apple*	6
5	7	FAST CAR	Tracy Chapman	*Elektra*	5

■Two consecutive chart toppers with the word *Nothing* in the title (09.07.88) ■ Three second generation hitmakers in the chart together - Ziggy Marley, son of Bob; Natalie Cole, daughter of Nat; and Kim Wilde, daughter of Marty (16.07.88)■

July 1988

□ Highest position disc reached ● Act's first ever week on chart

LW	TW	Title / Artist	Label	Wks
9	[8]	ROSES ARE RED Mac Band featuring the McCampbell Brothers	MCA	4
18	[9]	FOOLISH BEAT Debbie Gibson	Atlantic	3
7	10	BREAKFAST IN BED UB40 and Chrissie Hynde	DEP International	6
4	11	I OWE YOU NOTHING Bros	CBS	6
20	12	LOVE BITES Def Leppard	Bludgeon Riffola	2
19	[13]	MONKEY George Michael	Epic	2
13	14	CROSS MY HEART Eighth Wonder	CBS	4
8	15	BOYS (SUMMERTIME LOVE) Sabrina	Ibiza	7
38	16	YOU CAME Kim Wilde	MCA	2
12	17	WAP BAM BOOGIE/DON'T BLAME IT ON THE GIRL Matt Bianco	WEA	7
11	18	TRIBUTE (RIGHT ON) Pasadenas	CBS	7
10	19	IN THE AIR TONIGHT Phil Collins	Virgin	6
-	20	SUPERFLY GUY S Express	Rhythm King	1
29	[21]	HEAT IT UP Wee Papa Girl Rappers	Jive	3
28	[22]	TOMORROW PEOPLE Ziggy Marley and the Melody Makers	Virgin	3
16	23	TOUGHER THAN THE REST Bruce Springsteen	CBS	6
36	[24]	FIESTA Pogues	Pogue Mahone	2
30	25	ALL FIRED UP Pat Benatar	Chrysalis	3
24	26	NEVER TEAR US APART INXS	Mercury	5
17	27	WILD WORLD Maxi Priest	10	8
-	28	THE ONLY WAY IS UP Yazz and the Plastic Population ●	Big Life	1
-	[29]	GLAM SLAM Prince	Paisley Park	1
21	30	I WILL BE WITH YOU T'Pau	Siren	5
26	31	VOYAGE VOYAGE Desireless	CBS	9
22	32	MAYBE (WE SHOULD CALL IT DAY) Hazell Dean	EMI	5
23	33	THERE'S MORE TO LOVE Communards	London	6
34	[34]	IN MY DREAMS Will Downing	Fourth + Broadway	3
27	35	DOCTORIN' THE TARDIS Timelords	KLF Communications	8
-	36	REACH OUT I'LL BE THERE Four Tops	Motown	1
25	37	FOLLOW THE LEADER Eric B and Rakim	MCA	4
-	38	(WHAT CAN I SAY) TO MAKE YOU LOVE ME Alexander O'Neal	Tabu	1
-	39	FEEL THE NEED IN ME Shakin' Stevens	Epic	1
-	40	I'M TOO SCARED Steven Dante ●	Cooltempo	1

WEEK ENDING 30 JULY 1988

LW	TW	Title / Artist	Label	Wks
1	[1]	NOTHING'S GONNA CHANGE MY LOVE FOR YOU Glenn Medeiros	London	6
2	[2]	PUSH IT/TRAMP Salt-N-Pepa	Champion/ffrr	6
3	[3]	I DON'T WANT TO TALK ABOUT IT Everything But The Girl	blanco y negro	4
4	[4]	DIRTY DIANA Michael Jackson	Epic	3
5	[5]	I WANT YOUR LOVE Transvision Vamp	MCA	4
16	6	YOU CAME Kim Wilde	MCA	3
20	7	SUPERFLY GUY S Express	Rhythm King	2
8	[8]	ROSES ARE RED Mac Band featuring the McCampbell Brothers	MCA	5
9	[9]	FOOLISH BEAT Debbie Gibson	Atlantic	4
28	10	THE ONLY WAY IS UP Yazz and the Plastic Population	Big Life	2
12	[11]	LOVE BITES Def Leppard	Bludgeon Riffola	3
7	12	FAST CAR Tracy Chapman	Elektra	6
6	13	THE TWIST (YO TWIST) Fat Boys and Chubby Checker	Tin Pan Apple	7
13	14	MONKEY George Michael	Epic	3
36	15	REACH OUT I'LL BE THERE Four Tops	Motown	2
11	16	I OWE YOU NOTHING Bros	CBS	7
10	17	BREAKFAST IN BED UB40 and Chrissie Hynde	DEP International	7
17	18	WAP BAM BOOGIE/DON'T BLAME IT ON THE GIRL Matt Bianco	WEA	8
14	19	CROSS MY HEART Eighth Wonder	CBS	5
18	20	TRIBUTE (RIGHT ON) Pasadenas	CBS	8
21	[21]	HEAT IT UP Wee Papa Girl Rappers	Jive	4
-	22	I NEED YOU B.V.S.M.P. ●	Debut	1
25	23	ALL FIRED UP Pat Benatar	Chrysalis	4
22	24	TOMORROW PEOPLE Ziggy Marley and the Melody Makers	Virgin	4
15	25	BOYS (SUMMERTIME LOVE) Sabrina	Ibiza	8
39	[26]	FEEL THE NEED IN ME Shakin' Stevens	Epic	2
38	[27]	(WHAT CAN I SAY) TO MAKE YOU LOVE ME Alexander O'Neal	Tabu	2
24	28	FIESTA Pogues	Pogue Mahone	3
29	[29]	GLAM SLAM Prince	Paisley Park	2
-	30	PEEK A BOO Siouxsie and the Banshees	Wonderland	1
19	31	IN THE AIR TONIGHT Phil Collins	Virgin	7
-	32	FIND MY LOVE Fairground Attraction	RCA	1
23	33	TOUGHER THAN THE REST Bruce Springsteen	CBS	7
40	[34]	I'M TOO SCARED Steven Dante	Cooltempo	2
-	35	HUSTLE! (TO THE MUSIC...) Funky Worm ●	Fon	1
-	36	MARTHA'S HARBOUR All About Eve	Mercury	1
-	37	I SAY NOTHING Voice Of The Beehive	London	1
26	38	NEVER TEAR US APART INXS	Mercury	6
-	39	HAPPY EVER AFTER Julia Fordham ●	Circa	1
-	40	LIKE DREAMERS DO Mica Paris featuring Courtney Pine	Fourth + Broadway	1

WEEK ENDING 6 AUGUST 1988

LW	TW	Title / Artist	Label	Wks
10	[1]	THE ONLY WAY IS UP Yazz and the Plastic Population	Big Life	3
-	[2]	THE LOCO-MOTION Kylie Minogue	PWL	1
1	3	NOTHING'S GONNA CHANGE MY LOVE FOR YOU Glenn Medeiros	London	7
6	4	YOU CAME Kim Wilde	MCA	4
2	5	PUSH IT/TRAMP Salt-N-Pepa	Champion/ffrr	7
7	6	SUPERFLY GUY S Express	Rhythm King	3
22	7	I NEED YOU B.V.S.M.P.	Debut	2
3	8	I DON'T WANT TO TALK ABOUT IT Everything But The Girl	blanco y negro	5
5	9	I WANT YOUR LOVE Transvision Vamp	MCA	5
4	10	DIRTY DIANA Michael Jackson	Epic	4
8	11	ROSES ARE RED Mac Band featuring the McCampbell Brothers	MCA	6
15	12	REACH OUT I'LL BE THERE Four Tops	Motown	3
9	13	FOOLISH BEAT Debbie Gibson	Atlantic	5
32	14	FIND MY LOVE Fairground Attraction	RCA	2
11	15	LOVE BITES Def Leppard	Bludgeon Riffola	4
30	[16]	PEEK A BOO Siouxsie and the Banshees	Wonderland	2
35	17	HUSTLE! (TO THE MUSIC...) Funky Worm	Fon	2
12	18	FAST CAR Tracy Chapman	Elektra	7
23	[19]	ALL FIRED UP Pat Benatar	Chrysalis	5
14	20	MONKEY George Michael	Epic	4
13	21	THE TWIST (YO TWIST) Fat Boys and Chubby Checker	Tin Pan Apple	8
36	22	MARTHA'S HARBOUR All About Eve	Mercury	2
16	23	I OWE YOU NOTHING Bros	CBS	8
18	24	WAP BAM BOOGIE/DON'T BLAME IT ON THE GIRL Matt Bianco	WEA	9
37	25	I SAY NOTHING Voice Of The Beehive	London	2
17	26	BREAKFAST IN BED UB40 and Chrissie Hynde	DEP International	8
26	27	FEEL THE NEED IN ME Shakin' Stevens	Epic	3
27	28	(WHAT CAN I SAY) TO MAKE YOU LOVE ME Alexander O'Neal	Tabu	3
40	29	LIKE DREAMERS DO Mica Paris featuring Courtney Pine	Fourth + Broadway	2
39	30	HAPPY EVER AFTER Julia Fordham	Circa	2
20	31	TRIBUTE (RIGHT ON) Pasadenas	CBS	9
21	32	HEAT IT UP Wee Papa Girl Rappers	Jive	5
19	33	CROSS MY HEART Eighth Wonder	CBS	6
-	34	THE HARDER I TRY Brother Beyond ●	Parlophone	1
34	35	I'M TOO SCARED Steven Dante	Cooltempo	3
25	36	BOYS (SUMMERTIME LOVE) Sabrina	Ibiza	9
-	37	HANDS TO HEAVEN Breathe ●	Siren	1
24	38	TOMORROW PEOPLE Ziggy Marley and the Melody Makers	Virgin	5

In these weeks ■ Kylie Minogue's version of *The Loco-Motion* exactly matches the chart success of Little Eva's original 26 years earlier (06.08.88) ■ Everthing But The Girl cannot quite match Rod Stewart's achievement in topping the charts with *I Don't Want To Talk About It* eleven years earlier (06.08.88)■

LW	TW	Title	Artist	Label	Wks
-	39	GOOD TRADITION	Tanita Tikaram ●	WEA	1
-	40	ROCK MY WORLD	Five Star	Tent	1

LW	TW	*WEEK ENDING* **13 AUGUST 1988**			Wks
1	1	THE ONLY WAY IS UP	Yazz and the Plastic Population	*Big Life*	4
2	2	THE LOCO-MOTION	Kylie Minogue	*PWL*	2
4	3	YOU CAME	Kim Wilde	*MCA*	5
7	4	I NEED YOU	B.V.S.M.P.	*Debut*	3
6	5	SUPERFLY GUY	S Express	*Rhythm King*	4
-	6	THE EVIL THAT MEN DO	Iron Maiden	*EMI*	1
3	7	NOTHING'S GONNA CHANGE MY LOVE FOR YOU	Glenn Medeiros	*London*	8
14	8	FIND MY LOVE	Fairground Attraction	*RCA*	3
5	9	PUSH IT/TRAMP	Salt-N-Pepa	*Champion/ffrr*	8
9	10	I WANT YOUR LOVE	Transvision Vamp	*MCA*	6
12	11	REACH OUT I'LL BE THERE	Four Tops	*Motown*	4
8	12	I DON'T WANT TO TALK ABOUT IT	Everything But The Girl	*blanco y negro*	6
17	13	HUSTLE! (TO THE MUSIC...)	Funky Worm	*Fon*	3
11	14	ROSES ARE RED	Mac Band featuring the McCampbell Brothers	*MCA*	7
22	15	MARTHA'S HARBOUR	All About Eve	*Mercury*	3
10	16	DIRTY DIANA	Michael Jackson	*Epic*	5
37	17	HANDS TO HEAVEN	Breathe	*Siren*	2
16	18	PEEK A BOO	Siouxsie and the Banshees	*Wonderland*	3
13	19	FOOLISH BEAT	Debbie Gibson	*Atlantic*	6
19	20	ALL FIRED UP	Pat Benatar	*Chrysalis*	6
15	21	LOVE BITES	Def Leppard	*Bludgeon Riffola*	5
25	22	I SAY NOTHING	Voice Of The Beehive	*London*	3
39	23	GOOD TRADITION	Tanita Tikaram	*WEA*	2
34	24	THE HARDER I TRY	Brother Beyond	*Parlophone*	2
24	25	WAP BAM BOOGIE/DON'T BLAME IT ON THE GIRL	Matt Bianco	*WEA*	10
29	26	LIKE DREAMERS DO	Mica Paris featuring Courtney Pine	*Fourth + Broadway*	3
30	27	HAPPY EVER AFTER	Julia Fordham	*Circa*	3
40	28	ROCK MY WORLD	Five Star	*Tent*	2
21	29	THE TWIST (YO TWIST)	Fat Boys and Chubby Checker	*Tin Pan Apple*	9
18	30	FAST CAR	Tracy Chapman	*Elektra*	8
23	31	I OWE YOU NOTHING	Bros	*CBS*	9
20	32	MONKEY	George Michael	*Epic*	5
-	33	MY LOVE	Julio Iglesias	*CBS*	1
-	34	WORKING IN A GOLDMINE	Aztec Camera	*WEA*	1
-	35	SOMEWHERE DOWN THE CRAZY RIVER	Robbie Robertson ●	*Geffen*	1
-	36	ON THE BEACH	Chris Rea	*WEA*	1
26	37	BREAKFAST IN BED	UB40 and Chrissie Hynde	*DEP International*	9
-	38	WHEN IT'S LOVE	Van Halen	*Warner Bros*	1
27	39	FEEL THE NEED IN ME	Shakin' Stevens	*Epic*	4
28	40	(WHAT CAN I SAY) TO MAKE YOU LOVE ME	Alexander O'Neal	*Tabu*	4

LW	TW	*WEEK ENDING* **20 AUGUST 1988**			Wks
1	1	THE ONLY WAY IS UP	Yazz and the Plastic Population	*Big Life*	5
2	2	THE LOCO-MOTION	Kylie Minogue	*PWL*	3
4	3	I NEED YOU	B.V.S.M.P.	*Debut*	4
3	4	YOU CAME	Kim Wilde	*MCA*	6
6	5	THE EVIL THAT MEN DO	Iron Maiden	*EMI*	2
17	6	HANDS TO HEAVEN	Breathe	*Siren*	3
8	7	FIND MY LOVE	Fairground Attraction	*RCA*	4
24	8	THE HARDER I TRY	Brother Beyond	*Parlophone*	3
5	9	SUPERFLY GUY	S Express	*Rhythm King*	5
15	10	MARTHA'S HARBOUR	All About Eve	*Mercury*	4
11	11	REACH OUT I'LL BE THERE	Four Tops	*Motown*	5
7	12	NOTHING'S GONNA CHANGE MY LOVE FOR YOU	Glenn Medeiros	*London*	9
13	13	HUSTLE! (TO THE MUSIC...)	Funky Worm	*Fon*	4

□ Highest position disc reached ● Act's first ever week on chart

LW	TW	Title	Artist	Label	Wks
10	14	I WANT YOUR LOVE	Transvision Vamp	*MCA*	7
23	15	GOOD TRADITION	Tanita Tikaram	*WEA*	3
9	16	PUSH IT/TRAMP	Salt-N-Pepa	*Champion/ffrr*	9
3	17	MY LOVE	Julio Iglesias	*CBS*	2
14	18	ROSES ARE RED	Mac Band featuring the McCampbell Brothers	*MCA*	8
36	19	ON THE BEACH	Chris Rea	*WEA*	2
12	20	I DON'T WANT TO TALK ABOUT IT	Everything But The Girl	*blanco y negro*	7
19	21	FOOLISH BEAT	Debbie Gibson	*Atlantic*	7
35	22	SOMEWHERE DOWN THE CRAZY RIVER	Robbie Robertson	*Geffen*	2
22	23	I SAY NOTHING	Voice Of The Beehive	*London*	4
-	24	KING OF EMOTION	Big Country	*Mercury*	1
18	25	PEEK A BOO	Siouxsie and the Banshees	*Wonderland*	4
20	26	ALL FIRED UP	Pat Benatar	*Chrysalis*	7
16	27	DIRTY DIANA	Michael Jackson	*Epic*	6
38	28	WHEN IT'S LOVE	Van Halen	*Warner Bros*	2
26	29	LIKE DREAMERS DO	Mica Paris featuring Courtney Pine	*Fourth + Broadway*	4
-	30	RUNNING ALL OVER THE WORLD	Status Quo	*Vertigo*	1
34	31	WORKING IN A GOLDMINE	Aztec Camera	*WEA*	2
27	32	HAPPY EVER AFTER	Julia Fordham	*Circa*	4
21	33	LOVE BITES	Def Leppard	*Bludgeon Riffola*	6
-	34	ANYTHING FOR YOU	Gloria Estefan and Miami Sound Machine	*Epic*	1
-	35	SWEET CHILD O' MINE	Guns N' Roses ●	*Geffen*	1
25	36	WAP BAM BOOGIE/DON'T BLAME IT ON THE GIRL	Matt Bianco	*WEA*	11
-	37	TEARDROPS	Womack and Womack	*Fourth + Broadway*	1
-	38	RUSH HOUR	Jane Wiedlin ●	*Manhattan*	1
-	39	YE KE YE KE	Mory Kante ●	*London*	1
28	40	ROCK MY WORLD	Five Star	*Tent*	3

LW	TW	*WEEK ENDING* **27 AUGUST 1988**			Wks
1	1	THE ONLY WAY IS UP	Yazz and the Plastic Population	*Big Life*	6
2	2	THE LOCO-MOTION	Kylie Minogue	*PWL*	4
8	3	THE HARDER I TRY	Brother Beyond	*Parlophone*	4
6	4	HANDS TO HEAVEN	Breathe	*Siren*	4
3	5	I NEED YOU	B.V.S.M.P.	*Debut*	5
17	6	MY LOVE	Julio Iglesias	*CBS*	3
7	7	FIND MY LOVE	Fairground Attraction	*RCA*	5
4	8	YOU CAME	Kim Wilde	*MCA*	7
5	9	THE EVIL THAT MEN DO	Iron Maiden	*EMI*	3
15	10	GOOD TRADITION	Tanita Tikaram	*WEA*	4
9	11	SUPERFLY GUY	S Express	*Rhythm King*	6
19	12	ON THE BEACH	Chris Rea	*WEA*	3
11	13	REACH OUT I'LL BE THERE	Four Tops	*Motown*	6
10	14	MARTHA'S HARBOUR	All About Eve	*Mercury*	5
22	15	SOMEWHERE DOWN THE CRAZY RIVER	Robbie Robertson	*Geffen*	3
24	16	KING OF EMOTION	Big Country	*Mercury*	2
30	17	RUNNING ALL OVER THE WORLD	Status Quo	*Vertigo*	2
37	18	TEARDROPS	Womack and Womack	*Fourth + Broadway*	2
13	19	HUSTLE! (TO THE MUSIC...)	Funky Worm	*Fon*	5
-	20	MEGABLAST/DON'T MAKE ME WAIT	Bomb The Bass	*Mister-ron*	1
38	21	RUSH HOUR	Jane Wiedlin	*Manhattan*	2
16	22	PUSH IT/TRAMP	Salt-N-Pepa	*Champion/ffrr*	10
14	23	I WANT YOUR LOVE	Transvision Vamp	*MCA*	8
35	24	SWEET CHILD O' MINE	Guns N' Roses	*Geffen*	2
34	25	ANYTHING FOR YOU	Gloria Estefan and Miami Sound Machine	*Epic*	2
-	26	TOUCHY!	A-Ha	*Warner Bros*	1
12	27	NOTHING'S GONNA CHANGE MY LOVE FOR YOU	Glenn Medeiros	*London*	10
28	28	WHEN IT'S LOVE	Van Halen	*Warner Bros*	3

■*My Love* by Julio Iglesias features Stevie Wonder. It is his second top ten collaboration, after his 1982 number one with Paul McCartney. It is Iglesias' third collaborative hit single, and by some way his most successful (27.08.88) ■ To tie in with the Comic Relief 1988 charity run, Status Quo re-record *Rocking All Over The World* as *Running All Over The World* (20.08.88)■

August 1988

□ Highest position disc reached ● Act's first ever week on chart

LW	TW	Title	Artist	Label	Wks
39	29	YE KE YE KE	Mory Kante	London	2
18	30	ROSES ARE RED	Mac Band featuring the McCampbell Brothers	MCA	9
-	31	THE RACE	Yello ●	Mercury	1
20	32	I DON'T WANT TO TALK ABOUT IT	Everything But The Girl	blanco y negro	8
-	33	SOLDIER OF LOVE	Donny Osmond	Virgin	1
-	34	SUPERSTITIOUS	Europe	Epic	1
-	35	I WON'T BLEED FOR YOU	Climie Fisher	EMI	1
-	36	WHERE DID I GO WRONG	UB40	DEP International	1
-	37	EVERY GIRL AND BOY	Spagna	CBS	1
21	38	FOOLISH BEAT	Debbie Gibson	Atlantic	8
-	39	JUMP START	Natalie Cole	Manhattan	1
31	40	WORKING IN A GOLDMINE	Aztec Camera	WEA	3

WEEK ENDING 3 SEPTEMBER 1988

LW	TW	Title	Artist	Label	Wks
1	1	THE ONLY WAY IS UP	Yazz and the Plastic Population	Big Life	7
3	2	THE HARDER I TRY	Brother Beyond	Parlophone	5
2	3	THE LOCO-MOTION	Kylie Minogue	PWL	5
4	4	HANDS TO HEAVEN	Breathe	Siren	5
6	5	MY LOVE	Julio Iglesias	CBS	4
20	6	MEGABLAST/DON'T MAKE ME WAIT	Bomb The Bass	Mister-ron	2
18	7	TEARDROPS	Womack and Womack	Fourth + Broadway	3
5	8	I NEED YOU	B.V.S.M.P.	Debut	6
-	9	GROOVY KIND OF LOVE	Phil Collins	Virgin	1
7	10	FIND MY LOVE	Fairground Attraction	RCA	6
10	11	GOOD TRADITION	Tanita Tikaram	WEA	5
26	12	TOUCHY!	A-Ha	Warner Bros	2
8	13	YOU CAME	Kim Wilde	MCA	8
31	14	THE RACE	Yello	Mercury	2
21	15	RUSH HOUR	Jane Wiedlin	Manhattan	3
15	16	SOMEWHERE DOWN THE CRAZY RIVER	Robbie Robertson	Geffen	4
17	17	RUNNING ALL OVER THE WORLD	Status Quo	Vertigo	3
-	18	HEAVEN IN MY HANDS	Level 42	Polydor	1
25	19	ANYTHING FOR YOU	Gloria Estefan and Miami Sound Machine	Epic	3
-	20	HARVESTER OF SORROW	Metallica	Vertigo	1
16	21	KING OF EMOTION	Big Country	Mercury	3
12	22	ON THE BEACH	Chris Rea	WEA	4
9	23	THE EVIL THAT MEN DO	Iron Maiden	EMI	4
24	24	SWEET CHILD O' MINE	Guns N' Roses	Geffen	3
37	25	EVERY GIRL AND BOY	Spagna	CBS	2
36	26	WHERE DID I GO WRONG	UB40	DEP International	2
11	27	SUPERFLY GUY	S Express	Rhythm King	7
-	28	HE AIN'T HEAVY HE'S MY BROTHER	Hollies	EMI	1
33	29	SOLDIER OF LOVE	Donny Osmond	Virgin	2
29	30	YE KE YE KE	Mory Kante	London	3
13	31	REACH OUT I'LL BE THERE	Four Tops	Motown	7
-	32	HE AIN'T HEAVY HE'S MY BROTHER	Bill Medley ●	Scotti Bros	1
-	33	TEARS RUN RINGS	Marc Almond	Parlophone	1
-	34	I'M GONNA BE	Proclaimers	Chrysalis	1
34	35	SUPERSTITIOUS	Europe	Epic	2
39	36	JUMP START	Natalie Cole	Manhattan	2
19	37	HUSTLE! (TO THE MUSIC...)	Funky Worm	Fon	6
14	38	MARTHA'S HARBOUR	All About Eve	Mercury	6
-	39	WAY BEHIND ME	Primitives	Lazy	1
-	40	EASY	Commodores	Motown	1

WEEK ENDING 10 SEPTEMBER 1988

LW	TW	Title	Artist	Label	Wks
9	1	GROOVY KIND OF LOVE	Phil Collins	Virgin	2
2	2	THE HARDER I TRY	Brother Beyond	Parlophone	6
1	3	THE ONLY WAY IS UP	Yazz and the Plastic Population	Big Life	8
7	4	TEARDROPS	Womack and Womack	Fourth + Broadway	4
28	5	HE AIN'T HEAVY HE'S MY BROTHER	Hollies	EMI	2
6	6	MEGABLAST/DON'T MAKE ME WAIT	Bomb The Bass	Mister-ron	3
5	7	MY LOVE	Julio Iglesias	CBS	5
14	8	THE RACE	Yello	Mercury	3
3	9	THE LOCO-MOTION	Kylie Minogue	PWL	6
4	10	HANDS TO HEAVEN	Breathe	Siren	6
12	11	TOUCHY!	A-Ha	Warner Bros	3
18	12	HEAVEN IN MY HANDS	Level 42	Polydor	2
15	13	RUSH HOUR	Jane Wiedlin	Manhattan	4
8	14	I NEED YOU	B.V.S.M.P.	Debut	7
19	15	ANYTHING FOR YOU	Gloria Estefan and Miami Sound Machine	Epic	4
-	16	ANOTHER PART OF ME	Michael Jackson	Epic	1
11	17	GOOD TRADITION	Tanita Tikaram	WEA	6
10	18	FIND MY LOVE	Fairground Attraction	RCA	7
34	19	I'M GONNA BE	Proclaimers	Chrysalis	2
40	20	EASY	Commodores	Motown	2
-	21	LOVELY DAY	Bill Withers	CBS	1
13	22	YOU CAME	Kim Wilde	MCA	9
25	23	EVERY GIRL AND BOY	Spagna	CBS	3
24	24	SWEET CHILD O' MINE	Guns N' Roses	Geffen	4
32	25	HE AIN'T HEAVY HE'S MY BROTHER	Bill Medley	Scotti Bros	2
-	26	MAKE ME LAUGH	Anthrax	Island	1
26	27	WHERE DID I GO WRONG	UB40	DEP International	3
33	28	TEARS RUN RINGS	Marc Almond	Parlophone	2
16	29	SOMEWHERE DOWN THE CRAZY RIVER	Robbie Robertson	Geffen	5
17	30	RUNNING ALL OVER THE WORLD	Status Quo	Vertigo	4
-	31	BIG FUN	Inner City featuring Kevin Saunderson ●	10	1
20	32	HARVESTER OF SORROW	Metallica	Vertigo	2
-	33	STOP THIS CRAZY THING	Coldcut featuring Junior Reid	Ahead Of Our Time	1
21	34	KING OF EMOTION	Big Country	Mercury	4
27	35	SUPERFLY GUY	S Express	Rhythm King	8
-	36	SHAKE YOUR THANG (IT'S YOUR THING)	Salt-N-Pepa featuring EU	ffrr	1
-	37	NOTHING CAN DIVIDE US	Jason Donovan ●	PWL	1
36	38	JUMP START	Natalie Cole	Manhattan	3
29	39	SOLDIER OF LOVE	Donny Osmond	Virgin	3
22	40	ON THE BEACH	Chris Rea	WEA	5

WEEK ENDING 17 SEPTEMBER 1988

LW	TW	Title	Artist	Label	Wks
1	1	GROOVY KIND OF LOVE	Phil Collins	Virgin	3
5	2	HE AIN'T HEAVY HE'S MY BROTHER	Hollies	EMI	3
4	3	TEARDROPS	Womack and Womack	Fourth + Broadway	5
-	4	I QUIT	Bros	CBS	1
2	5	THE HARDER I TRY	Brother Beyond	Parlophone	7
21	6	LOVELY DAY	Bill Withers	CBS	2
3	7	THE ONLY WAY IS UP	Yazz and the Plastic Population	Big Life	9
8	8	THE RACE	Yello	Mercury	4
6	9	MEGABLAST/DON'T MAKE ME WAIT	Bomb The Bass	Mister-ron	4
15	10	ANYTHING FOR YOU	Gloria Estefan and Miami Sound Machine	Epic	5
7	11	MY LOVE	Julio Iglesias	CBS	6
13	12	RUSH HOUR	Jane Wiedlin	Manhattan	5
37	13	NOTHING CAN DIVIDE US	Jason Donovan	PWL	2
19	14	I'M GONNA BE	Proclaimers	Chrysalis	3
16	15	ANOTHER PART OF ME	Michael Jackson	Epic	2
10	16	HANDS TO HEAVEN	Breathe	Siren	7
20	17	EASY	Commodores	Motown	3
9	18	THE LOCO-MOTION	Kylie Minogue	PWL	7
11	19	TOUCHY!	A-Ha	Warner Bros	4
31	20	BIG FUN	Inner City featuring Kevin Saunderson	10	2
12	21	HEAVEN IN MY HANDS	Level 42	Polydor	3
36	22	SHAKE YOUR THANG (IT'S YOUR THING)	Salt-N-Pepa featuring EU	ffrr	2
23	23	EVERY GIRL AND BOY	Spagna	CBS	4
14	24	I NEED YOU	B.V.S.M.P.	Debut	8

In these weeks ■ *Rush Hour* by Jane Wiedlin becomes the first record to go up from no. 13 since *Check This Out* by LA Mix 15 weeks earlier (17.09.88) ■ Glenn Medeiros leapt from 11 to one, Yazz jumped from ten to one and next Phil Collins leaps from nine to one. The Hollies will break the mathematically pleasing sequence in two weeks time (10.09.88) ■

LW	TW	Title	Artist	Label	Wks
33	25	STOP THIS CRAZY THING	Coldcut featuring Junior Reid	Ahead Of Our Time	2
28	[26]	TEARS RUN RINGS	Marc Almond	Parlophone	3
25	27	HE AIN'T HEAVY HE'S MY BROTHER	Bill Medley	Scotti Bros	3
26	28	MAKE ME LAUGH	Anthrax	Island	2
-	29	RIDING ON A TRAIN	Pasadenas	CBS	1
24	30	SWEET CHILD O' MINE	Guns N' Roses	Geffen	5
18	31	FIND MY LOVE	Fairground Attraction	RCA	8
17	32	GOOD TRADITION	Tanita Tikaram	WEA	7
27	33	WHERE DID I GO WRONG	UB40	DEP International	4
22	34	YOU CAME	Kim Wilde	MCA	10
30	35	RUNNING ALL OVER THE WORLD	Status Quo	Vertigo	5
-	[36]	WAY BEHIND ME	Primitives	Lazy	2
-	37	REVOLUTION BABY	Transvision Vamp	MCA	1
29	38	SOMEWHERE DOWN THE CRAZY RIVER	Robbie Robertson	Geffen	6
-	39	WORLD WITHOUT YOU	Belinda Carlisle	Virgin	1
-	[40]	STALEMATE	Mac Band	MCA	1

WEEK ENDING 24 SEPTEMBER 1988

LW	TW	Title	Artist	Label	Wks
2	[1]	HE AIN'T HEAVY HE'S MY BROTHER	Hollies	EMI	4
1	2	GROOVY KIND OF LOVE	Phil Collins	Virgin	4
3	[3]	TEARDROPS	Womack and Womack	Fourth + Broadway	6
6	[4]	LOVELY DAY	Bill Withers	CBS	3
13	[5]	NOTHING CAN DIVIDE US	Jason Donovan	PWL	3
4	6	I QUIT	Bros	CBS	2
8	[7]	THE RACE	Yello	Mercury	5
20	8	BIG FUN	Inner City featuring Kevin Saunderson	10	3
-	9	DOMINO DANCING	Pet Shop Boys	Parlophone	1
7	10	THE ONLY WAY IS UP	Yazz and the Plastic Population	Big Life	10
10	11	ANYTHING FOR YOU	Gloria Estefan and Miami Sound Machine	Epic	6
14	12	I'M GONNA BE	Proclaimers	Chrysalis	4
5	13	THE HARDER I TRY	Brother Beyond	Parlophone	8
9	14	MEGABLAST/DON'T MAKE ME WAIT	Bomb The Bass	Mister-ron	5
17	[15]	EASY	Commodores	Motown	4
-	16	SHE WANTS TO DANCE WITH ME	Rick Astley	RCA	1
12	17	RUSH HOUR	Jane Wiedlin	Manhattan	6
-	18	BAD MEDICINE	Bon Jovi	Vertigo	1
15	19	ANOTHER PART OF ME	Michael Jackson	Epic	3
29	20	RIDING ON A TRAIN	Pasadenas	CBS	2
25	[21]	STOP THIS CRAZY THING	Coldcut featuring Junior Reid	Ahead Of Our Time	3
22	[22]	SHAKE YOUR THANG (IT'S YOUR THING)	Salt-N-Pepa featuring EU	ffrr	3
11	23	MY LOVE	Julio Iglesias	CBS	7
-	24	ONE MOMENT IN TIME	Whitney Houston	Arista	1
16	25	HANDS TO HEAVEN	Breathe	Siren	8
18	26	THE LOCO-MOTION	Kylie Minogue	PWL	8
19	27	TOUCHY!	A-Ha	Warner Bros	5
26	28	TEARS RUN RINGS	Marc Almond	Parlophone	4
23	29	EVERY GIRL AND BOY	Spagna	CBS	5
37	[30]	REVOLUTION BABY	Transvision Vamp	MCA	2
-	31	LOVE TRUTH AND HONESTY	Bananarama	London	1
-	[32]	SPARE PARTS	Bruce Springsteen	CBS	1
-	33	TURN IT INTO LOVE	Hazell Dean	EMI	1
39	[34]	WORLD WITHOUT YOU	Belinda Carlisle	Virgin	2
24	35	I NEED YOU	B.V.S.M.P.	Debut	9
21	36	HEAVEN IN MY HANDS	Level 42	Polydor	4
-	37	FAKE 88	Alexander O'Neal	Tabu	1
27	38	HE AIN'T HEAVY HE'S MY BROTHER	Bill Medley	Scotti Bros	4
30	39	SWEET CHILD O' MINE	Guns N' Roses	Geffen	6
-	[40]	IT'S YER MONEY I'M AFTER BABY	Wonder Stuff ●	Polydor	1

October 1988

□ Highest position disc reached ● Act's first ever week on chart

WEEK ENDING 1 OCTOBER 1988

LW	TW	Title	Artist	Label	Wks
1	[1]	HE AIN'T HEAVY HE'S MY BROTHER	Hollies	EMI	5
2	2	GROOVY KIND OF LOVE	Phil Collins	Virgin	5
-	3	DESIRE	U2	Island	1
3	4	TEARDROPS	Womack and Womack	Fourth + Broadway	7
4	5	LOVELY DAY	Bill Withers	CBS	4
5	6	NOTHING CAN DIVIDE US	Jason Donovan	PWL	4
9	[7]	DOMINO DANCING	Pet Shop Boys	Parlophone	2
24	8	ONE MOMENT IN TIME	Whitney Houston	Arista	2
8	9	BIG FUN	Inner City featuring Kevin Saunderson	10	4
16	10	SHE WANTS TO DANCE WITH ME	Rick Astley	RCA	2
12	[11]	I'M GONNA BE	Proclaimers	Chrysalis	5
7	12	THE RACE	Yello	Mercury	6
20	[13]	RIDING ON A TRAIN	Pasadenas	CBS	3
6	14	I QUIT	Bros	CBS	3
11	15	ANYTHING FOR YOU	Gloria Estefan and Miami Sound Machine	Epic	7
10	16	THE ONLY WAY IS UP	Yazz and the Plastic Population	Big Life	11
18	[17]	BAD MEDICINE	Bon Jovi	Vertigo	2
15	18	EASY	Commodores	Motown	5
-	19	A LITTLE RESPECT	Erasure	Mute	1
-	20	I DON"T WANT YOUR LOVE	Duran Duran	EMI	1
14	21	MEGABLAST/DON'T MAKE ME WAIT	Bomb The Bass	Mister-ron	6
22	[22]	SHAKE YOUR THANG (IT'S YOUR THING)	Salt-N-Pepa featuring EU	ffrr	4
13	23	THE HARDER I TRY	Brother Beyond	Parlophone	9
37	24	FAKE 88	Alexander O'Neal	Tabu	2
-	25	DON'T WORRY BE HAPPY	Bobby McFerrin ●	Manhattan	1
17	26	RUSH HOUR	Jane Wiedlin	Manhattan	7
21	27	STOP THIS CRAZY THING	Coldcut featuring Junior Reid	Ahead Of Our Time	4
31	28	LOVE TRUTH AND HONESTY	Bananarama	London	2
33	29	TURN IT INTO LOVE	Hazell Dean	EMI	2
30	[30]	REVOLUTION BABY	Transvision Vamp	MCA	3
19	31	ANOTHER PART OF ME	Michael Jackson	Epic	4
32	[32]	SPARE PARTS	Bruce Springsteen	CBS	2
23	33	MY LOVE	Julio Iglesias	CBS	8
-	34	WEE RULE	Wee Papa Girl Rappers	Jive	1
34	35	WORLD WITHOUT YOU	Belinda Carlisle	Virgin	3
28	36	TEARS RUN RINGS	Marc Almond	Parlophone	5
-	37	SECRET GARDEN	T'Pau	Siren	1
-	38	I DON'T BELIEVE IN MIRACLES	Sinitta	Fanfare	1
25	39	HANDS TO HEAVEN	Breathe	Siren	9
26	40	THE LOCO-MOTION	Kylie Minogue	PWL	9

WEEK ENDING 8 OCTOBER 1988

LW	TW	Title	Artist	Label	Wks
3	[1]	DESIRE	U2	Island	2
1	2	HE AIN'T HEAVY HE'S MY BROTHER	Hollies	EMI	6
8	3	ONE MOMENT IN TIME	Whitney Houston	Arista	3
4	4	TEARDROPS	Womack and Womack	Fourth + Broadway	8
2	5	GROOVY KIND OF LOVE	Phil Collins	Virgin	6
6	6	NOTHING CAN DIVIDE US	Jason Donovan	PWL	5
10	7	SHE WANTS TO DANCE WITH ME	Rick Astley	RCA	3
5	8	LOVELY DAY	Bill Withers	CBS	5
7	9	DOMINO DANCING	Pet Shop Boys	Parlophone	3
9	10	BIG FUN	Inner City featuring Kevin Saunderson	10	5
25	11	DON'T WORRY BE HAPPY	Bobby McFerrin	Manhattan	2
19	12	A LITTLE RESPECT	Erasure	Mute	2
13	[13]	RIDING ON A TRAIN	Pasadenas	CBS	4
20	[14]	I DON"T WANT YOUR LOVE	Duran Duran	EMI	2
11	15	I'M GONNA BE	Proclaimers	Chrysalis	6
24	[16]	FAKE 88	Alexander O'Neal	Tabu	3
34	17	WEE RULE	Wee Papa Girl Rappers	Jive	2
12	18	THE RACE	Yello	Mercury	7
17	19	BAD MEDICINE	Bon Jovi	Vertigo	3
15	20	ANYTHING FOR YOU	Gloria Estefan and Miami Sound Machine	Epic	8
29	[21]	TURN IT INTO LOVE	Hazell Dean	EMI	3
37	22	SECRET GARDEN	T'Pau	Siren	2

■The Hollies' re-issued hit tops the chart over 23 years after their only other number one - to that time by far the biggest gap between number ones (24.09.88) ■ Bobby McFerrin achieves the first big a cappella hit since the Housemartins' *Caravan Of Love* (01.10.88)■

October 1988

□ Highest position disc reached ● Act's first ever week on chart

LW	TW	Title	Artist	Label	Wks
16	23	THE ONLY WAY IS UP	Yazz and the Plastic Population	Big Life	12
14	24	I QUIT	Bros	CBS	4
28	25	LOVE TRUTH AND HONESTY	Bananarama	London	3
18	26	EASY	Commodores	Motown	6
38	27	I DON'T BELIEVE IN MIRACLES	Sinitta	Fanfare	2
22	28	SHAKE YOUR THANG (IT'S YOUR THING)	Salt-N-Pepa featuring EU	ffrr	5
21	29	MEGABLAST/DON'T MAKE ME WAIT	Bomb The Bass	Mister-ron	7
26	30	THE HARDER I TRY	Brother Beyond	Parlophone	10
26	31	RUSH HOUR	Jane Wiedlin	Manhattan	8
-	32	NEVER TRUST A STRANGER	Kim Wilde	MCA	1
30	33	REVOLUTION BABY	Transvision Vamp	MCA	4
27	34	STOP THIS CRAZY THING	Coldcut featuring Junior Reid	Ahead Of Our Time	5
-	35	BURN IT UP	Beatmasters with PP Arnold	Rhythm King	1
-	□36	SO IN LOVE WITH YOU	Spear Of Destiny	Virgin	1
-	37	CHARLOTTE ANNE	Julian Cope	Island	1
-	38	ALL OF ME	Sabrina	PWL	1
36	39	TEARS RUN RINGS	Marc Almond	Parlophone	6
31	40	ANOTHER PART OF ME	Michael Jackson	Epic	5

WEEK ENDING 15 OCTOBER 1988

LW	TW	Title	Artist	Label	Wks
3	□1	ONE MOMENT IN TIME	Whitney Houston	Arista	4
1	2	DESIRE	U2	Island	3
11	3	DON'T WORRY BE HAPPY	Bobby McFerrin	Manhattan	3
4	4	TEARDROPS	Womack and Womack	Fourth + Broadway	9
2	5	HE AIN'T HEAVY HE'S MY BROTHER	Hollies	EMI	7
7	6	SHE WANTS TO DANCE WITH ME	Rick Astley	RCA	4
12	7	A LITTLE RESPECT	Erasure	Mute	3
17	8	WEE RULE	Wee Papa Girl Rappers	Jive	3
6	9	NOTHING CAN DIVIDE US	Jason Donovan	PWL	6
5	10	GROOVY KIND OF LOVE	Phil Collins	Virgin	7
10	11	BIG FUN	Inner City featuring Kevin Saunderson	10	6
9	12	DOMINO DANCING	Pet Shop Boys	Parlophone	4
13	□13	RIDING ON A TRAIN	Pasadenas	CBS	5
8	14	LOVELY DAY	Bill Withers	CBS	6
32	15	NEVER TRUST A STRANGER	Kim Wilde	MCA	2
35	16	BURN IT UP	Beatmasters with PP Arnold	Rhythm King	2
16	17	FAKE 88	Alexander O'Neal	Tabu	4
14	18	I DON"T WANT YOUR LOVE	Duran Duran	EMI	3
22	19	SECRET GARDEN	T'Pau	Siren	3
-	20	WE CALL IT ACIEED	D.Mob (featuring Gary Haisman) ●	ffrr	1
-	21	HARVEST FOR THE WORLD	Christians	Island	1
21	22	TURN IT INTO LOVE	Hazell Dean	EMI	4
25	□23	LOVE TRUTH AND HONESTY	Bananarama	London	4
15	24	I'M GONNA BE	Proclaimers	Chrysalis	7
27	25	I DON'T BELIEVE IN MIRACLES	Sinitta	Fanfare	3
18	26	THE RACE	Yello	Mercury	8
19	27	BAD MEDICINE	Bon Jovi	Vertigo	4
20	28	ANYTHING FOR YOU	Gloria Estefan and Miami Sound Machine	Epic	9
-	29	ORINOCO FLOW	Enya ●	WEA	1
23	30	THE ONLY WAY IS UP	Yazz and the Plastic Population	Big Life	13
38	31	ALL OF ME	Sabrina	PWL	2
28	32	SHAKE YOUR THANG (IT'S YOUR THING)	Salt-N-Pepa featuring EU	ffrr	6
24	33	I QUIT	Bros	CBS	5
29	34	MEGABLAST/DON'T MAKE ME WAIT	Bomb The Bass	Mister-ron	8
37	□35	CHARLOTTE ANNE	Julian Cope	Island	2
-	36	ANY LOVE	Luther Vandross	Epic	1
36	37	SO IN LOVE WITH YOU	Spear Of Destiny	Virgin	2
26	38	EASY	Commodores	Motown	7
30	39	THE HARDER I TRY	Brother Beyond	Parlophone	11
-	40	GIRL YOU KNOW IT'S TRUE	Milli Vanilli ●	Cooltempo	1

WEEK ENDING 22 OCTOBER 1988

LW	TW	Title	Artist	Label	Wks
1	□1	ONE MOMENT IN TIME	Whitney Houston	Arista	5
3	□2	DON'T WORRY BE HAPPY	Bobby McFerrin	Manhattan	4
20	□3	WE CALL IT ACIEED	D.Mob (featuring Gary Haisman)	ffrr	2
7	□4	A LITTLE RESPECT	Erasure	Mute	4
29	5	ORINOCO FLOW	Enya	WEA	2
8	□6	WEE RULE	Wee Papa Girl Rappers	Jive	4
15	□7	NEVER TRUST A STRANGER	Kim Wilde	MCA	3
6	8	SHE WANTS TO DANCE WITH ME	Rick Astley	RCA	5
21	9	HARVEST FOR THE WORLD	Christians	Island	2
4	10	TEARDROPS	Womack and Womack	Fourth + Broadway	10
-	11	JE SAIS NE PAS POURQUOI	Kylie Minogue	PWL	1
9	12	NOTHING CAN DIVIDE US	Jason Donovan	PWL	7
10	13	GROOVY KIND OF LOVE	Phil Collins	Virgin	8
5	14	HE AIN'T HEAVY HE'S MY BROTHER	Hollies	EMI	8
16	15	BURN IT UP	Beatmasters with PP Arnold	Rhythm King	3
11	16	BIG FUN	Inner City featuring Kevin Saunderson	10	7
2	17	DESIRE	U2	Island	4
19	□18	SECRET GARDEN	T'Pau	Siren	4
13	19	RIDING ON A TRAIN	Pasadenas	CBS	6
40	20	GIRL YOU KNOW IT'S TRUE	Milli Vanilli	Cooltempo	2
12	21	DOMINO DANCING	Pet Shop Boys	Parlophone	5
25	□22	I DON'T BELIEVE IN MIRACLES	Sinitta	Fanfare	4
23	□23	LOVE TRUTH AND HONESTY	Bananarama	London	5
14	24	LOVELY DAY	Bill Withers	CBS	7
31	□25	ALL OF ME	Sabrina	PWL	3
17	26	FAKE 88	Alexander O'Neal	Tabu	5
22	27	TURN IT INTO LOVE	Hazell Dean	EMI	5
18	28	I DON"T WANT YOUR LOVE	Duran Duran	EMI	4
-	29	REAL GONE KID	Deacon Blue	CBS	1
-	30	CAN YOU PARTY	Royal House ●	Champion	1
36	□31	ANY LOVE	Luther Vandross	Epic	2
-	32	I'LL HOUSE YOU	Richie Rich meets the Jungle Brothers ●	Gee Street	1
24	33	I'M GONNA BE	Proclaimers	Chrysalis	8
26	34	THE RACE	Yello	Mercury	9
35	□35	CHARLOTTE ANNE	Julian Cope	Island	3
-	36	TWIST IN MY SOBRIETY	Tanita Tikaram	WEA	1
-	37	ACID MAN	Jolly Roger ●	10	1
-	38	SHE MAKES MY DAY	Robert Palmer	EMI	1
28	39	ANYTHING FOR YOU	Gloria Estefan and Miami Sound Machine	Epic	10
27	40	BAD MEDICINE	Bon Jovi	Vertigo	5

WEEK ENDING 29 OCTOBER 1988

LW	TW	Title	Artist	Label	Wks
5	□1	ORINOCO FLOW	Enya	WEA	3
11	□2	JE SAIS NE PAS POURQUOI	Kylie Minogue	PWL	2
1	3	ONE MOMENT IN TIME	Whitney Houston	Arista	6
3	4	WE CALL IT ACIEED	D.Mob (featuring Gary Haisman)	ffrr	3
4	5	A LITTLE RESPECT	Erasure	Mute	5
2	6	DON'T WORRY BE HAPPY	Bobby McFerrin	Manhattan	5
6	7	WEE RULE	Wee Papa Girl Rappers	Jive	5
9	□8	HARVEST FOR THE WORLD	Christians	Island	3
7	9	NEVER TRUST A STRANGER	Kim Wilde	MCA	4
20	10	GIRL YOU KNOW IT'S TRUE	Milli Vanilli	Cooltempo	3
-	11	STAND UP FOR YOUR LOVE RIGHTS	Yazz	Big Life	1
10	12	TEARDROPS	Womack and Womack	Fourth + Broadway	11
8	13	SHE WANTS TO DANCE WITH ME	Rick Astley	RCA	6
15	□14	BURN IT UP	Beatmasters with PP Arnold	Rhythm King	4
16	15	BIG FUN	Inner City featuring Kevin Saunderson	10	8
13	16	GROOVY KIND OF LOVE	Phil Collins	Virgin	9
30	17	CAN YOU PARTY	Royal House	Champion	2
38	18	SHE MAKES MY DAY	Robert Palmer	EMI	2
-	19	KISS	Art Of Noise featuring Tom Jones	China	1
12	20	NOTHING CAN DIVIDE US	Jason Donovan	PWL	8
29	21	REAL GONE KID	Deacon Blue	CBS	2
32	□22	I'LL HOUSE YOU	Richie Rich meets the Jungle Brothers	Gee Street	2
18	23	SECRET GARDEN	T'Pau	Siren	5
19	24	RIDING ON A TRAIN	Pasadenas	CBS	7
22	25	I DON'T BELIEVE IN MIRACLES	Sinitta	Fanfare	5
14	26	HE AIN'T HEAVY HE'S MY BROTHER	Hollies	EMI	9

In these weeks ■ *Girl You Know It's True* sang Milli Vanilli. It wasn't true. The two people who toured as Milli Vanilli were not the people who performed on the records (15.10.88) ■ Kylie Minogue becomes the first woman to achieve a hat-trick of number two hits (29.10.88)■

LW	TW	Title / Artist	Label	Wks
25	27	ALL OF ME Sabrina	PWL	4
37	28	ACID MAN Jolly Roger	10	2
36	29	TWIST IN MY SOBRIETY Tanita Tikaram	WEA	2
17	30	DESIRE U2	Island	5
-	31	WELCOME TO THE JUNGLE/NIGHTRAIN Guns N' Roses	Geffen	1
23	32	LOVE TRUTH AND HONESTY Bananarama	London	6
21	33	DOMINO DANCING Pet Shop Boys	Parlophone	6
-	34	TAKE A LOOK Level 42	Polydor	1
-	35	THE PARTY Kraze ●	Big Beat	1
-	36	1-2-3 Gloria Estefan and Miami Sound Machine	Epic	1
24	37	LOVELY DAY Bill Withers	CBS	8
-	38	NOTHIN' AT ALL Heart	Capitol	1
-	39	THE FIRST TIME Robin Beck ●	Mercury	1
27	40	TURN IT INTO LOVE Hazell Dean	EMI	6

November 1988

□ Highest position disc reached ● Act's first ever week on chart

WEEK ENDING 5 NOVEMBER 1988

LW	TW	Title / Artist	Label	Wks
1	1	ORINOCO FLOW Enya	WEA	4
2	2	JE SAIS NE PAS POURQUOI Kylie Minogue	PWL	3
10	3	GIRL YOU KNOW IT'S TRUE Milli Vanilli	Cooltempo	4
11	4	STAND UP FOR YOUR LOVE RIGHTS Yazz	Big Life	2
19	5	KISS Art Of Noise featuring Tom Jones	China	2
3	6	ONE MOMENT IN TIME Whitney Houston	Arista	7
4	7	WE CALL IT ACIEED D.Mob (featuring Gary Haisman)	ffrr	4
18	8	SHE MAKES MY DAY Robert Palmer	EMI	3
7	9	WEE RULE Wee Papa Girl Rappers	Jive	6
5	10	A LITTLE RESPECT Erasure	Mute	6
8	11	HARVEST FOR THE WORLD Christians	Island	4
6	12	DON'T WORRY BE HAPPY Bobby McFerrin	Manhattan	6
9	13	NEVER TRUST A STRANGER Kim Wilde	MCA	5
17	14	CAN YOU PARTY Royal House	Champion	3
21	15	REAL GONE KID Deacon Blue	CBS	3
14	16	BURN IT UP Beatmasters with PP Arnold	Rhythm King	5
39	17	THE FIRST TIME Robin Beck	Mercury	2
16	18	GROOVY KIND OF LOVE Phil Collins	Virgin	10
12	19	TEARDROPS Womack and Womack	Fourth + Broadway	12
13	20	SHE WANTS TO DANCE WITH ME Rick Astley	RCA	7
20	21	NOTHING CAN DIVIDE US Jason Donovan	PWL	9
15	22	BIG FUN Inner City featuring Kevin Saunderson	10	9
28	23	ACID MAN Jolly Roger	10	3
36	24	1-2-3 Gloria Estefan and Miami Sound Machine	Epic	2
31	25	WELCOME TO THE JUNGLE/NIGHTRAIN Guns N' Roses	Geffen	2
29	26	TWIST IN MY SOBRIETY Tanita Tikaram	WEA	3
22	27	I'LL HOUSE YOU Richie Rich meets the Jungle Brothers	Gee Street	3
-	28	LET'S STICK TOGETHER '88 Bryan Ferry	EG	1
35	29	THE PARTY Kraze	Big Beat	2
-	30	HE AIN'T NO COMPETITION Brother Beyond	Parlophone	1
-	31	I WISH U HEAVEN Prince	Paisley Park	1
34	32	TAKE A LOOK Level 42	Polydor	2
25	33	I DON'T BELIEVE IN MIRACLES Sinitta	Fanfare	6
24	34	RIDING ON A TRAIN Pasadenas	CBS	8
23	35	SECRET GARDEN T'Pau	Siren	6
26	36	HE AIN'T HEAVY HE'S MY BROTHER Hollies	EMI	10
30	37	DESIRE U2	Island	6
27	38	ALL OF ME Sabrina	PWL	5
-	39	MISSING YOU Chris De Burgh	A&M	1
-	40	HERE COMES THAT SOUND Simon Harris	ffrr	1

WEEK ENDING 12 NOVEMBER 1988

LW	TW	Title / Artist	Label	Wks
1	1	ORINOCO FLOW Enya	WEA	5
2	2	JE SAIS NE PAS POURQUOI Kylie Minogue	PWL	4
4	3	STAND UP FOR YOUR LOVE RIGHTS Yazz	Big Life	3
3	4	GIRL YOU KNOW IT'S TRUE Milli Vanilli	Cooltempo	5
17	5	THE FIRST TIME Robin Beck	Mercury	3
8	6	SHE MAKES MY DAY Robert Palmer	EMI	4
5	7	KISS Art Of Noise featuring Tom Jones	China	3
30	8	HE AIN'T NO COMPETITION Brother Beyond	Parlophone	2
24	9	1-2-3 Gloria Estefan and Miami Sound Machine	Epic	3
15	10	REAL GONE KID Deacon Blue	CBS	4
7	11	WE CALL IT ACIEED D.Mob (featuring Gary Haisman)	ffrr	5
28	12	LET'S STICK TOGETHER '88 Bryan Ferry	EG	2
6	13	ONE MOMENT IN TIME Whitney Houston	Arista	8
10	14	A LITTLE RESPECT Erasure	Mute	7
39	15	MISSING YOU Chris De Burgh	A&M	2
11	16	HARVEST FOR THE WORLD Christians	Island	5
14	17	CAN YOU PARTY Royal House	Champion	4
-	18	NEED YOU TONIGHT INXS	Mercury	1
9	19	WEE RULE Wee Papa Girl Rappers	Jive	7
13	20	NEVER TRUST A STRANGER Kim Wilde	MCA	6
12	21	DON'T WORRY BE HAPPY Bobby McFerrin	Manhattan	7
-	22	TWIST AND SHOUT Salt-N-Pepa	ffrr	1
26	23	TWIST IN MY SOBRIETY Tanita Tikaram	WEA	4
25	24	WELCOME TO THE JUNGLE/NIGHTRAIN Guns N' Roses	Geffen	3
23	25	ACID MAN Jolly Roger	10	4
31	26	I WISH U HEAVEN Prince	Paisley Park	2
16	27	BURN IT UP Beatmasters with PP Arnold	Rhythm King	6
18	28	GROOVY KIND OF LOVE Phil Collins	Virgin	11
22	29	BIG FUN Inner City featuring Kevin Saunderson	10	10
20	30	SHE WANTS TO DANCE WITH ME Rick Astley	RCA	8
19	31	TEARDROPS Womack and Womack	Fourth + Broadway	13
-	32	TIL I LOVED YOU Barbra Streisand and Don Johnson ●	CBS	1
29	33	THE PARTY Kraze	Big Beat	3
-	34	WHAT KIND OF FOOL All About Eve	Mercury	1
32	35	TAKE A LOOK Level 42	Polydor	3
-	36	BREATHE LIFE INTO ME Mica Paris	Fourth + Broadway	1
-	37	HANDLE WITH CARE Traveling Wilburys ●	Wilbury	1
40	38	HERE COMES THAT SOUND Simon Harris	ffrr	2
21	39	NOTHING CAN DIVIDE US Jason Donovan	PWL	10
-	40	BITTER SWEET Marc Almond	Some Bizzare	1

WEEK ENDING 19 NOVEMBER 1988

LW	TW	Title / Artist	Label	Wks
5	1	THE FIRST TIME Robin Beck	Mercury	4
3	2	STAND UP FOR YOUR LOVE RIGHTS Yazz	Big Life	4
2	3	JE SAIS NE PAS POURQUOI Kylie Minogue	PWL	5
18	4	NEED YOU TONIGHT INXS	Mercury	2
1	5	ORINOCO FLOW Enya	WEA	6
8	6	HE AIN'T NO COMPETITION Brother Beyond	Parlophone	3
4	7	GIRL YOU KNOW IT'S TRUE Milli Vanilli	Cooltempo	6
15	8	MISSING YOU Chris De Burgh	A&M	3
6	9	SHE MAKES MY DAY Robert Palmer	EMI	5
10	10	REAL GONE KID Deacon Blue	CBS	5
9	11	1-2-3 Gloria Estefan and Miami Sound Machine	Epic	4
22	12	TWIST AND SHOUT Salt-N-Pepa	ffrr	2
-	13	THE CLAIRVOYANT Iron Maiden	EMI	1
12	14	LET'S STICK TOGETHER '88 Bryan Ferry	EG	3
7	15	KISS Art Of Noise featuring Tom Jones	China	4
32	16	TIL I LOVED YOU Barbra Streisand and Don Johnson	CBS	2
11	17	WE CALL IT ACIEED D.Mob (featuring Gary Haisman)	ffrr	6
17	18	CAN YOU PARTY Royal House	Champion	5
13	19	ONE MOMENT IN TIME Whitney Houston	Arista	9
14	20	A LITTLE RESPECT Erasure	Mute	8
37	21	HANDLE WITH CARE Traveling Wilburys	Wilbury	2
23	22	TWIST IN MY SOBRIETY Tanita Tikaram	WEA	5
20	23	NEVER TRUST A STRANGER Kim Wilde	MCA	7
26	24	I WISH U HEAVEN Prince	Paisley Park	3
21	25	DON'T WORRY BE HAPPY Bobby McFerrin	Manhattan	8
16	26	HARVEST FOR THE WORLD Christians	Island	6
19	27	WEE RULE Wee Papa Girl Rappers	Jive	8
36	28	BREATHE LIFE INTO ME Mica Paris	Fourth + Broadway	2
34	29	WHAT KIND OF FOOL All About Eve	Mercury	2
-	30	NATHAN JONES Bananarama	London	1
-	31	SUCCESS Sigue Sigue Sputnik	Parlophone	1
-	32	RADIO ROMANCE Tiffany	MCA	1
-	33	LIFE'S JUST A BALLGAME Womack and Womack	Fourth + Broadway	1
24	34	WELCOME TO THE JUNGLE/NIGHTRAIN Guns N' Roses	Geffen	4

■ *Bitter Sweet* is the last record to peak at no. 40 until Belinda Carlisle's *Runaway Horses* in March 1990 (12.11.88) ■ For the second time in 1988, and for the second time ever, three solo ladies top the charts consecutively - Coca-Cola star Robin Beck is the third (19.11.88) ■

November 1988

□ Highest position disc reached ● Act's first ever week on chart

LW	TW	Title	Artist	Label	Wks
25	35	ACID MAN	Jolly Roger	*10*	5
29	36	BIG FUN	Inner City featuring Kevin Saunderson	*10*	11
28	37	GROOVY KIND OF LOVE	Phil Collins	*Virgin*	12
-	38	JACK TO THE SOUND OF THE UNDERGROUND	Hithouse ●	*Supreme*	1
-	39	IN YOUR ROOM	Bangles	*CBS*	1
31	40	TEARDROPS	Womack and Womack	*Fourth + Broadway*	14

WEEK ENDING 26 NOVEMBER 1988

LW	TW	Title	Artist	Label	Wks
1	1	THE FIRST TIME	Robin Beck	*Mercury*	5
4	2	NEED YOU TONIGHT	INXS	*Mercury*	3
8	3	MISSING YOU	Chris De Burgh	*A&M*	4
12	4	TWIST AND SHOUT	Salt-N-Pepa	*ffrr*	3
2	5	STAND UP FOR YOUR LOVE RIGHTS	Yazz	*Big Life*	5
13	6	THE CLAIRVOYANT	Iron Maiden	*EMI*	2
-	7	LEFT TO MY OWN DEVICES	Pet Shop Boys	*Parlophone*	1
10	8	REAL GONE KID	Deacon Blue	*CBS*	6
6	9	HE AIN'T NO COMPETITION	Brother Beyond	*Parlophone*	4
3	10	JE SAIS NE PAS POURQUOI	Kylie Minogue	*PWL*	6
7	11	GIRL YOU KNOW IT'S TRUE	Milli Vanilli	*Cooltempo*	7
-	12	SMOOTH CRIMINAL	Michael Jackson	*Epic*	1
5	13	ORINOCO FLOW	Enya	*WEA*	7
11	14	1-2-3	Gloria Estefan and Miami Sound Machine	*Epic*	5
9	15	SHE MAKES MY DAY	Robert Palmer	*EMI*	6
-	16	TWO HEARTS	Phil Collins	*Virgin*	1
16	17	TIL I LOVED YOU	Barbra Streisand and Don Johnson	*CBS*	3
-	18	TAKE ME TO YOUR HEART	Rick Astley	*RCA*	1
-	19	SAY A LITTLE PRAYER	Bomb The Bass featuring Maureen	*Rhythm King*	1
30	20	NATHAN JONES	Bananarama	*London*	2
32	21	RADIO ROMANCE	Tiffany	*MCA*	2
14	22	LET'S STICK TOGETHER '88	Bryan Ferry	*EG*	4
21	23	HANDLE WITH CARE	Traveling Wilburys	*Wilbury*	3
-	24	FREAKS (LIVE)	Marillion	*EMI*	1
38	25	JACK TO THE SOUND OF THE UNDERGROUND	Hithouse	*Supreme*	2
15	26	KISS	Art Of Noise featuring Tom Jones	*China*	5
28	27	BREATHE LIFE INTO ME	Mica Paris	*Fourth + Broadway*	3
17	28	WE CALL IT ACIEED	D.Mob (featuring Gary Haisman)	*ffrr*	7
22	29	TWIST IN MY SOBRIETY	Tanita Tikaram	*WEA*	6
-	30	STAKKER HUMANOID	Humanoid ●	*Westside*	1
31	31	SUCCESS	Sigue Sigue Sputnik	*Parlophone*	2
33	32	LIFE'S JUST A BALLGAME	Womack and Womack	*Fourth + Broadway*	2
-	33	SUDDENLY	Angry Anderson ●	*Food For Thought*	1
18	34	CAN YOU PARTY	Royal House	*Champion*	6
39	35	IN YOUR ROOM	Bangles	*CBS*	2
20	36	A LITTLE RESPECT	Erasure	*Mute*	9
24	37	I WISH U HEAVEN	Prince	*Paisley Park*	4
19	38	ONE MOMENT IN TIME	Whitney Houston	*Arista*	10
-	39	LOVE HOUSE	Samantha Fox	*Jive*	1
29	40	WHAT KIND OF FOOL	All About Eve	*Mercury*	3

WEEK ENDING 3 DECEMBER 1988

LW	TW	Title	Artist	Label	Wks
1	1	THE FIRST TIME	Robin Beck	*Mercury*	6
-	2	CAT AMONG THE PIGEONS/SILENT NIGHT	Bros	*CBS*	1
3	3	MISSING YOU	Chris De Burgh	*A&M*	5
7	4	LEFT TO MY OWN DEVICES	Pet Shop Boys	*Parlophone*	2
2	5	NEED YOU TONIGHT	INXS	*Mercury*	4
16	6	TWO HEARTS	Phil Collins	*Virgin*	2
-	7	MISTLETOE AND WINE	Cliff Richard	*EMI*	1
12	8	SMOOTH CRIMINAL	Michael Jackson	*Epic*	2
4	9	TWIST AND SHOUT	Salt-N-Pepa	*ffrr*	4
19	10	SAY A LITTLE PRAYER	Bomb The Bass featuring Maureen	*Rhythm King*	2
8	11	REAL GONE KID	Deacon Blue	*CBS*	7
18	12	TAKE ME TO YOUR HEART	Rick Astley	*RCA*	2
21	13	RADIO ROMANCE	Tiffany	*MCA*	3
25	14	JACK TO THE SOUND OF THE UNDERGROUND	Hithouse	*Supreme*	3
9	15	HE AIN'T NO COMPETITION	Brother Beyond	*Parlophone*	5
33	16	SUDDENLY	Angry Anderson	*Food For Thought*	2
5	17	STAND UP FOR YOUR LOVE RIGHTS	Yazz	*Big Life*	6
30	18	STAKKER HUMANOID	Humanoid	*Westside*	2
20	19	NATHAN JONES	Bananarama	*London*	3
6	20	THE CLAIRVOYANT	Iron Maiden	*EMI*	3
10	21	JE SAIS NE PAS POURQUOI	Kylie Minogue	*PWL*	7
11	22	GIRL YOU KNOW IT'S TRUE	Milli Vanilli	*Cooltempo*	8
15	23	SHE MAKES MY DAY	Robert Palmer	*EMI*	7
-	24	KISSING A FOOL	George Michael	*Epic*	1
14	25	1-2-3	Gloria Estefan and Miami Sound Machine	*Epic*	6
27	26	BREATHE LIFE INTO ME	Mica Paris	*Fourth + Broadway*	4
13	27	ORINOCO FLOW	Enya	*WEA*	8
17	28	TIL I LOVED YOU	Barbra Streisand and Don Johnson	*CBS*	4
24	29	FREAKS (LIVE)	Marillion	*EMI*	2
23	30	HANDLE WITH CARE	Traveling Wilburys	*Wilbury*	4
-	31	ENCHANTED LADY	Pasadenas	*CBS*	1
39	32	LOVE HOUSE	Samantha Fox	*Jive*	2
-	33	KOKOMO	Beach Boys	*Elektra*	1
-	34	BURNING BRIDGES (ON AND OFF AND ON AGAIN)	Status Quo	*Vertigo*	1
32	35	LIFE'S JUST A BALLGAME	Womack and Womack	*Fourth + Broadway*	3
35	36	IN YOUR ROOM	Bangles	*CBS*	3
-	37	DOWNTOWN '88	Petula Clark	*PRT*	1
22	38	LET'S STICK TOGETHER '88	Bryan Ferry	*EG*	5
29	39	TWIST IN MY SOBRIETY	Tanita Tikaram	*WEA*	7
28	40	WE CALL IT ACIEED	D.Mob (featuring Gary Haisman)	*ffrr*	8

WEEK ENDING 10 DECEMBER 1988

LW	TW	Title	Artist	Label	Wks
7	1	MISTLETOE AND WINE	Cliff Richard	*EMI*	2
-	2	ESPECIALLY FOR YOU	Kylie Minogue and Jason Donovan ●	*PWL*	1
16	3	SUDDENLY	Angry Anderson	*Food For Thought*	3
2	4	CAT AMONG THE PIGEONS/SILENT NIGHT	Bros	*CBS*	2
1	5	THE FIRST TIME	Robin Beck	*Mercury*	7
6	6	TWO HEARTS	Phil Collins	*Virgin*	3
-	7	CRACKERS INTERNATIONAL (EP)	Erasure	*Mute*	1
12	8	TAKE ME TO YOUR HEART	Rick Astley	*RCA*	3
8	9	SMOOTH CRIMINAL	Michael Jackson	*Epic*	3
3	10	MISSING YOU	Chris De Burgh	*A&M*	6
4	11	LEFT TO MY OWN DEVICES	Pet Shop Boys	*Parlophone*	3
10	12	SAY A LITTLE PRAYER	Bomb The Bass featuring Maureen	*Rhythm King*	3
5	13	NEED YOU TONIGHT	INXS	*Mercury*	5
13	14	RADIO ROMANCE	Tiffany	*MCA*	4
19	15	NATHAN JONES	Bananarama	*London*	4
14	16	JACK TO THE SOUND OF THE UNDERGROUND	Hithouse	*Supreme*	4
18	17	STAKKER HUMANOID	Humanoid	*Westside*	3
24	18	KISSING A FOOL	George Michael	*Epic*	2
9	19	TWIST AND SHOUT	Salt-N-Pepa	*ffrr*	5
34	20	BURNING BRIDGES (ON AND OFF AND ON AGAIN)	Status Quo	*Vertigo*	2
11	21	REAL GONE KID	Deacon Blue	*CBS*	8
-	22	GOOD LIFE	Inner City	*10*	1
-	23	FINE TIME	New Order	*Factory*	1
37	24	DOWNTOWN '88	Petula Clark	*PRT*	2
33	25	KOKOMO	Beach Boys	*Elektra*	2
15	26	HE AIN'T NO COMPETITION	Brother Beyond	*Parlophone*	6
21	27	JE SAIS NE PAS POURQUOI	Kylie Minogue	*PWL*	8
-	28	YOU ARE THE ONE	A-Ha	*Warner Bros*	1
17	29	STAND UP FOR YOUR LOVE RIGHTS	Yazz	*Big Life*	7
-	30	LOCO IN ACAPULCO	Four Tops	*Arista*	1
-	31	BORN TO BE MY BABY	Bon Jovi	*Vertigo*	1
31	32	ENCHANTED LADY	Pasadenas	*CBS*	2
22	33	GIRL YOU KNOW IT'S TRUE	Milli Vanilli	*Cooltempo*	9
-	34	FOUR LETTER WORD	Kim Wilde	*MCA*	1
26	35	BREATHE LIFE INTO ME	Mica Paris	*Fourth + Broadway*	5

In these weeks ■ Cliff Richard becomes the first and only act to have number one hits in each of 4 decades (10.12.88) ■ Angry Anderson's *Suddenly* is the song of the wedding of Charlene and Scott in 'Neighbours'. They are played by Kylie Minogue and Jason Donovan, whose one-off duet keeps Angry unhappy at number three (10.12.88)■

LW	TW	Title / Artist	Label	Wks
23	36	SHE MAKES MY DAY Robert Palmer	EMI	8
32	37	LOVE HOUSE Samantha Fox	Jive	3
-	38	9AM (THE COMFORT ZONE) Londonbeat ●	Anxious	1
20	39	THE CLAIRVOYANT Iron Maiden	EMI	4
-	40	CHRISTMAS SONG/THANK YOU FOR A GOOD YEAR Alexander O'Neal	Tabu	1

LW	TW	*WEEK ENDING* **17 DECEMBER 1988**		Wks
1	[1]	MISTLETOE AND WINE Cliff Richard	EMI	3
2	2	ESPECIALLY FOR YOU Kylie Minogue and Jason Donovan	PWL	2
3	[3]	SUDDENLY Angry Anderson	Food For Thought	4
7	4	CRACKERS INTERNATIONAL (EP) Erasure	Mute	2
4	5	CAT AMONG THE PIGEONS/SILENT NIGHT Bros	CBS	3
22	6	GOOD LIFE Inner City	10	2
6	7	TWO HEARTS Phil Collins	Virgin	4
8	[8]	TAKE ME TO YOUR HEART Rick Astley	RCA	4
20	9	BURNING BRIDGES (ON AND OFF AND ON AGAIN) Status Quo	Vertigo	3
-	10	ANGEL OF HARLEM U2	Island	1
9	11	SMOOTH CRIMINAL Michael Jackson	Epic	4
5	12	THE FIRST TIME Robin Beck	Mercury	8
24	13	DOWNTOWN '88 Petula Clark	PRT	3
12	14	SAY A LITTLE PRAYER Bomb The Bass featuring Maureen	Rhythm King	4
23	15	FINE TIME New Order	Factory	2
15	16	NATHAN JONES Bananarama	London	5
10	17	MISSING YOU Chris De Burgh	A&M	7
14	18	RADIO ROMANCE Tiffany	MCA	5
11	19	LEFT TO MY OWN DEVICES Pet Shop Boys	Parlophone	4
17	20	STAKKER HUMANOID Humanoid	Westside	4
13	21	NEED YOU TONIGHT INXS	Mercury	6
31	22	BORN TO BE MY BABY Bon Jovi	Vertigo	2
30	23	LOCO IN ACAPULCO Four Tops	Arista	2
16	24	JACK TO THE SOUND OF THE UNDERGROUND Hithouse	Supreme	5
28	25	YOU ARE THE ONE A-Ha	Warner Bros	2
18	26	KISSING A FOOL George Michael	Epic	3
25	27	KOKOMO Beach Boys	Elektra	3
34	28	FOUR LETTER WORD Kim Wilde	MCA	2
38	29	9AM (THE COMFORT ZONE) Londonbeat	Anxious	2
40	[30]	CHRISTMAS SONG/THANK YOU FOR A GOOD YEAR Alexander O'Neal	Tabu	2
-	31	BUFFALO STANCE Neneh Cherry ●	Circa	1
21	32	REAL GONE KID Deacon Blue	CBS	9
19	33	TWIST AND SHOUT Salt-N-Pepa	ffrr	6
-	34	HANDLE WITH CARE Traveling Wilburys	Wilbury	5
27	35	JE SAIS NE PAS POURQUOI Kylie Minogue	PWL	9
-	36	TRUE LOVE Shakin' Stevens	Epic	1
29	37	STAND UP FOR YOUR LOVE RIGHTS Yazz	Big Life	8
-	38	PUT A LITTLE LOVE IN YOUR HEART Annie Lennox and Al Green ●	A&M	1
32	39	ENCHANTED LADY Pasadenas	CBS	3
-	40	MINNIE THE MOOCHER Reggae Philharmonic Orchestra ●	Mango	1

LW	TW	*WEEK ENDING* **24 DECEMBER 1988**		Wks
1	[1]	MISTLETOE AND WINE Cliff Richard	EMI	4
2	2	ESPECIALLY FOR YOU Kylie Minogue and Jason Donovan	PWL	3
4	3	CRACKERS INTERNATIONAL (EP) Erasure	Mute	3
3	4	SUDDENLY Angry Anderson	Food For Thought	5
6	5	GOOD LIFE Inner City	10	3
5	6	CAT AMONG THE PIGEONS/SILENT NIGHT Bros	CBS	4
9	7	BURNING BRIDGES (ON AND OFF AND ON AGAIN) Status Quo	Vertigo	4
7	8	TWO HEARTS Phil Collins	Virgin	5
10	[9]	ANGEL OF HARLEM U2	Island	2
13	[10]	DOWNTOWN '88 Petula Clark	PRT	4
15	[11]	FINE TIME New Order	Factory	3
8	12	TAKE ME TO YOUR HEART Rick Astley	RCA	5

December 1988

□ Highest position disc reached ● Act's first ever week on chart

LW	TW	Title / Artist	Label	Wks
31	13	BUFFALO STANCE Neneh Cherry	Circa	2
11	14	SMOOTH CRIMINAL Michael Jackson	Epic	5
23	15	LOCO IN ACAPULCO Four Tops	Arista	3
16	16	NATHAN JONES Bananarama	London	6
14	17	SAY A LITTLE PRAYER Bomb The Bass featuring Maureen	Rhythm King	5
12	18	THE FIRST TIME Robin Beck	Mercury	9
28	19	FOUR LETTER WORD Kim Wilde	MCA	3
25	20	YOU ARE THE ONE A-Ha	Warner Bros	3
29	21	9AM (THE COMFORT ZONE) Londonbeat	Anxious	3
17	22	MISSING YOU Chris De Burgh	A&M	8
22	23	BORN TO BE MY BABY Bon Jovi	Vertigo	3
18	24	RADIO ROMANCE Tiffany	MCA	6
21	25	NEED YOU TONIGHT INXS	Mercury	7
19	26	LEFT TO MY OWN DEVICES Pet Shop Boys	Parlophone	5
-	27	KEEPING THE DREAM ALIVE Freiheit ●	CBS	1
36	28	TRUE LOVE Shakin' Stevens	Epic	2
24	29	JACK TO THE SOUND OF THE UNDERGROUND Hithouse	Supreme	6
30	[30]	CHRISTMAS SONG/THANK YOU FOR A GOOD YEAR Alexander O'Neal	Tabu	3
20	31	STAKKER HUMANOID Humanoid	Westside	5
38	32	PUT A LITTLE LOVE IN YOUR HEART Annie Lennox and Al Green	A&M	2
34	33	HANDLE WITH CARE Traveling Wilburys	Wilbury	6
27	34	KOKOMO Beach Boys	Elektra	4
40	[35]	MINNIE THE MOOCHER Reggae Philharmonic Orchestra	Mango	2
-	36	EVENING FALLS... Enya	WEA	1
26	37	KISSING A FOOL George Michael	Epic	4
-	38	RHYTHM IS GONNA GET YOU Gloria Estefan and Miami Sound Machine	Epic	1
-	39	JOHN KETTLEY (IS A WEATHERMAN) A Tribe Of Toffs ●	Completely Different	1
-	40	I LIVE FOR YOUR LOVE Natalie Cole	EMI Manhattan	1

LW	TW	*WEEK ENDING* **31 DECEMBER 1988**		Wks
1	[1]	MISTLETOE AND WINE Cliff Richard	EMI	5
2	2	ESPECIALLY FOR YOU Kylie Minogue and Jason Donovan	PWL	4
3	3	CRACKERS INTERNATIONAL (EP) Erasure	Mute	4
4	4	SUDDENLY Angry Anderson	Food For Thought	6
7	[5]	BURNING BRIDGES (ON AND OFF AND ON AGAIN) Status Quo	Vertigo	5
5	6	GOOD LIFE Inner City	10	4
13	7	BUFFALO STANCE Neneh Cherry	Circa	3
6	8	CAT AMONG THE PIGEONS/SILENT NIGHT Bros	CBS	5
15	9	LOCO IN ACAPULCO Four Tops	Arista	4
8	10	TWO HEARTS Phil Collins	Virgin	6
10	11	DOWNTOWN '88 Petula Clark	PRT	5
9	12	ANGEL OF HARLEM U2	Island	3
14	13	SMOOTH CRIMINAL Michael Jackson	Epic	6
19	14	FOUR LETTER WORD Kim Wilde	MCA	4
27	15	KEEPING THE DREAM ALIVE Freiheit	CBS	2
12	16	TAKE ME TO YOUR HEART Rick Astley	RCA	6
11	17	FINE TIME New Order	Factory	4
20	18	YOU ARE THE ONE A-Ha	Warner Bros	4
21	[19]	9AM (THE COMFORT ZONE) Londonbeat	Anxious	4
36	[20]	EVENING FALLS... Enya	WEA	2
19	21	JOHN KETTLEY (IS A WEATHERMAN) A Tribe Of Toffs	Completely Different	2
18	22	THE FIRST TIME Robin Beck	Mercury	10
28	[23]	TRUE LOVE Shakin' Stevens	Epic	3
16	24	NATHAN JONES Bananarama	London	7
25	25	NEED YOU TONIGHT INXS	Mercury	8
17	26	SAY A LITTLE PRAYER Bomb The Bass featuring Maureen	Rhythm King	6
24	27	RADIO ROMANCE Tiffany	MCA	7

■The lead track on Erasure's *Crackers International EP* was *Stop!* (24.12.88) ■ Bros' version of *Silent Night* brought the carol back into the Top ten after a gap of 36 years. Bing Crosby was in the Top ten with his version at Christmas 1952 (24.12.88)■

December 1988

□ Highest position disc reached ● Act's first ever week on chart

Last week	This week	Title / Artist	Label	Weeks
32	[28]	PUT A LITTLE LOVE IN YOUR HEART Annie Lennox and Al Green	*A&M*	3
23	**29**	BORN TO BE MY BABY Bon Jovi	*Vertigo*	4
22	**30**	MISSING YOU Chris De Burgh	*A&M*	9
33	**31**	HANDLE WITH CARE Traveling Wilburys	*Wilbury*	7
38	**32**	RHYTHM IS GONNA GET YOU Gloria Estefan and Miami Sound Machine	*Epic*	2
26	**33**	LEFT TO MY OWN DEVICES Pet Shop Boys	*Parlophone*	6
40	[34]	I LIVE FOR YOUR LOVE Natalie Cole	*EMI Manhattan*	2
30	**35**	CHRISTMAS SONG/THANK YOU FOR A GOOD YEAR Alexander O'Neal	*Tabu*	4
29	**36**	JACK TO THE SOUND OF THE UNDERGROUND Hithouse	*Supreme*	7
34	**37**	KOKOMO Beach Boys	*Elektra*	5
31	**38**	STAKKER HUMANOID Humanoid	*Westside*	6
-	**39**	WAITING FOR A STAR TO FALL Boy Meets Girl ●	*RCA*	1
35	**40**	MINNIE THE MOOCHER Reggae Philharmonic Orchestra	*Mango*	3

In these weeks ■ The Beach Boys and the Travelling Wilburys are probably the oldest five piece band, along with the Rolling Stones, ever to chart. The average age of the Wilburys is probably a little higher than the Beach Boys (31.12.88) ■ Only one new entry in the Top 40, the fewest of the year (31.12.88)■

1989

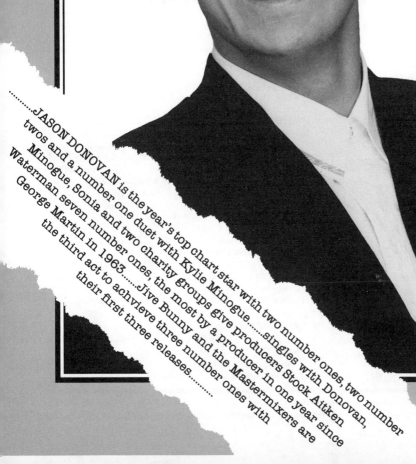

..........**JASON DONOVAN** is the year's top chart star with two number ones, two number twos and a number one duet with **Kylie Minogue**......singles with Donovan, Minogue, **Sonia** and two charity groups give producers **Stock Aitken Waterman** seven number ones, the most by a producer in one year since **George Martin** in 1963.......**Jive Bunny and the Mastermixers** are the third act to achvieve three number ones with their first three releases..........

January 1989

□ Highest position disc reached ● Act's first ever week on chart

LW	TW	WEEK ENDING 7 JANUARY 1989		Wks
2	[1]	ESPECIALLY FOR YOU Kylie Minogue and Jason Donovan	PWL	5
3	[2]	CRACKERS INTERNATIONAL (EP) Erasure	Mute	5
4	[3]	SUDDENLY Angry Anderson	Food For Thought	7
6	[4]	GOOD LIFE Inner City	10	5
1	5	MISTLETOE AND WINE Cliff Richard	EMI	6
7	6	BUFFALO STANCE Neneh Cherry	Circa	4
9	[7]	LOCO IN ACAPULCO Four Tops	Arista	5
5	8	BURNING BRIDGES (ON AND OFF AND ON AGAIN) Status Quo	Vertigo	6
14	9	FOUR LETTER WORD Kim Wilde	MCA	5
8	10	CAT AMONG THE PIGEONS/SILENT NIGHT Bros	CBS	6
10	11	TWO HEARTS Phil Collins	Virgin	7
13	12	SMOOTH CRIMINAL Michael Jackson	Epic	7
11	13	DOWNTOWN '88 Petula Clark	PRT	6
16	14	TAKE ME TO YOUR HEART Rick Astley	RCA	7
18	15	YOU ARE THE ONE A-Ha	Warner Bros	5
15	16	KEEPING THE DREAM ALIVE Freiheit	CBS	3
12	17	ANGEL OF HARLEM U2	Island	4
22	18	THE FIRST TIME Robin Beck	Mercury	11
17	19	FINE TIME New Order	Factory	5
27	20	RADIO ROMANCE Tiffany	MCA	8
25	21	NEED YOU TONIGHT INXS	Mercury	9
29	22	9AM (THE COMFORT ZONE) Londonbeat	Anxious	5
24	23	NATHAN JONES Bananarama	London	8
26	24	SAY A LITTLE PRAYER Bomb The Bass featuring Maureen	Rhythm King	7
-	25	ALL SHE WANTS IS Duranduran	EMI	1
21	26	JOHN KETTLEY (IS A WEATHERMAN) A Tribe Of Toffs	Completely Different	3
33	27	LEFT TO MY OWN DEVICES Pet Shop Boys	Parlophone	7
32	28	RHYTHM IS GONNA GET YOU Gloria Estefan and Miami Sound Machine	Epic	3
-	29	SHE DRIVES ME CRAZY Fine Young Cannibals	London	1
36	30	JACK TO THE SOUND OF THE UNDERGROUND Hithouse	Supreme	8
39	31	WAITING FOR A STAR TO FALL Boy Meets Girl	RCA	2
20	32	EVENING FALLS... Enya	WEA	3
29	33	BORN TO BE MY BABY Bon Jovi	Vertigo	5
-	34	STAND UP FOR YOUR LOVE RIGHTS Yazz	Big Life	1
28	35	PUT A LITTLE LOVE IN YOUR HEART Annie Lennox and Al Green	A&M	4
23	36	TRUE LOVE Shakin' Stevens	Epic	4
-	37	LOVE LIKE A RIVER Climie Fisher	EMI	1
38	38	STAKKER HUMANOID Humanoid	Westside	7
-	39	BABY I LOVE YOUR WAY-FREEBIRD Will To Power ●	Epic	1
34	40	I LIVE FOR YOUR LOVE Natalie Cole	EMI Manhattan	3

LW	TW	WEEK ENDING 14 JANUARY 1989		Wks
1	[1]	ESPECIALLY FOR YOU Kylie Minogue and Jason Donovan	PWL	6
2	[2]	CRACKERS INTERNATIONAL (EP) Erasure	Mute	6
6	[3]	BUFFALO STANCE Neneh Cherry	Circa	5
4	[4]	GOOD LIFE Inner City	10	6
3	5	SUDDENLY Angry Anderson	Food For Thought	8
9	[6]	FOUR LETTER WORD Kim Wilde	MCA	6
7	[7]	LOCO IN ACAPULCO Four Tops	Arista	6
29	8	SHE DRIVES ME CRAZY Fine Young Cannibals	London	2
25	[9]	ALL SHE WANTS IS Duranduran	EMI	2
39	10	BABY I LOVE YOUR WAY-FREEBIRD Will To Power	Epic	2
8	11	BURNING BRIDGES (ON AND OFF AND ON AGAIN) Status Quo	Vertigo	7
31	12	WAITING FOR A STAR TO FALL Boy Meets Girl	RCA	3
15	[13]	YOU ARE THE ONE A-Ha	Warner Bros	6
16	[14]	KEEPING THE DREAM ALIVE Freiheit	CBS	4
11	15	TWO HEARTS Phil Collins	Virgin	8
28	[16]	RHYTHM IS GONNA GET YOU Gloria Estefan and Miami Sound Machine	Epic	4
-	17	THE LIVING YEARS Mike and the Mechanics	WEA	1
5	18	MISTLETOE AND WINE Cliff Richard	EMI	7
-	19	SOMETHING'S GOTTEN HOLD OF MY HEART Marc Almond featuring Gene Pitney	Parlophone	1
12	20	SMOOTH CRIMINAL Michael Jackson	Epic	8
10	21	CAT AMONG THE PIGEONS/SILENT NIGHT Bros	CBS	7
37	[22]	LOVE LIKE A RIVER Climie Fisher	EMI	2
14	23	TAKE ME TO YOUR HEART Rick Astley	RCA	8
-	24	YOU GOT IT Roy Orbison	Virgin	1
13	25	DOWNTOWN '88 Petula Clark	PRT	7
22	26	9AM (THE COMFORT ZONE) Londonbeat	Anxious	6
20	27	RADIO ROMANCE Tiffany	MCA	9
19	28	FINE TIME New Order	Factory	6
-	29	BORN THIS WAY (LET'S DANCE) Cookie Crew ●	ffrr	1
-	30	GET ON THE DANCE FLOOR Rob Base and DJ E-Z Rock	Supreme	1
-	31	CUDDLY TOY Roachford ●	CBS	1
-	32	BABY DON'T FORGET MY NUMBER Milli Vanilli	Cooltempo	1
-	33	HIT THE GROUND Darling Buds ●	CBS	1
40	34	I LIVE FOR YOUR LOVE Natalie Cole	EMI Manhattan	4
17	35	ANGEL OF HARLEM U2	Island	5
21	36	NEED YOU TONIGHT INXS	Mercury	10
24	37	SAY A LITTLE PRAYER Bomb The Bass featuring Maureen	Rhythm King	8
-	38	WAIT Robert Howard and Kym Mazelle ●	RCA	1
-	39	YEAH! BUDDY Royal House	Champion	1
-	40	RESPECT Adeva ●	Cooltempo	1

LW	TW	WEEK ENDING 21 JANUARY 1989		Wks
1	[1]	ESPECIALLY FOR YOU Kylie Minogue and Jason Donovan	PWL	7
2	[2]	CRACKERS INTERNATIONAL (EP) Erasure	Mute	7
3	[3]	BUFFALO STANCE Neneh Cherry	Circa	6
17	4	THE LIVING YEARS Mike and the Mechanics	WEA	2
8	[5]	SHE DRIVES ME CRAZY Fine Young Cannibals	London	3
10	[6]	BABY I LOVE YOUR WAY-FREEBIRD Will To Power	Epic	3
24	7	YOU GOT IT Roy Orbison	Virgin	2
4	8	GOOD LIFE Inner City	10	7
12	[9]	WAITING FOR A STAR TO FALL Boy Meets Girl	RCA	4
19	10	SOMETHING'S GOTTEN HOLD OF MY HEART Marc Almond featuring Gene Pitney	Parlophone	2
31	11	CUDDLY TOY Roachford	CBS	2
6	12	FOUR LETTER WORD Kim Wilde	MCA	7
9	13	ALL SHE WANTS IS Duranduran	EMI	3
7	14	LOCO IN ACAPULCO Four Tops	Arista	7
5	15	SUDDENLY Angry Anderson	Food For Thought	9
14	16	KEEPING THE DREAM ALIVE Freiheit	CBS	5
30	17	GET ON THE DANCE FLOOR Rob Base and DJ E-Z Rock	Supreme	2
16	18	RHYTHM IS GONNA GET YOU Gloria Estefan and Miami Sound Machine	Epic	5
32	19	BABY DON'T FORGET MY NUMBER Milli Vanilli	Cooltempo	2
13	20	YOU ARE THE ONE A-Ha	Warner Bros	7
-	21	LOVE TRAIN Holly Johnson ●	MCA	1
38	22	WAIT Robert Howard and Kym Mazelle	RCA	2
29	[23]	BORN THIS WAY (LET'S DANCE) Cookie Crew	ffrr	2
40	24	RESPECT Adeva	Cooltempo	2
22	25	LOVE LIKE A RIVER Climie Fisher	EMI	3
11	26	BURNING BRIDGES (ON AND OFF AND ON AGAIN) Status Quo	Vertigo	8
33	[27]	HIT THE GROUND Darling Buds	CBS	2
-	28	WHERE IS THE LOVE Will Downing and Mica Paris ●	Fourth + Broadway	1
-	29	BE MY TWIN Brother Beyond	Parlophone	1
34	30	I LIVE FOR YOUR LOVE Natalie Cole	EMI Manhattan	5
-	[31]	STUPID QUESTION New Model Army	EMI	1
15	32	TWO HEARTS Phil Collins	Virgin	9
-	33	THAT'S THE WAY LOVE IS Ten City ●	Atlantic	1
-	34	TRACIE Level 42	Polydor	1
39	[35]	YEAH! BUDDY Royal House	Champion	2
20	36	SMOOTH CRIMINAL Michael Jackson	Epic	9

In these weeks ■ Gene Pitney and Roy Orbison return to the charts in the same week, Orbison after over 19 years and Pitney after almost fifteen years' absence (14.01.89) ■ Two members of Genesis in the Top 20 together and separately - Phil Collins at 15 and Mike Rutherford at 17 (14.01.89) ■

February 1989

[ ] Highest position disc reached ● Act's first ever week on chart

LW	TW	Title	Artist	Label	Wks
-	37	BREAK 4 LOVE	Raze	Champion	1
-	38	MY PREROGATIVE	Bobby Brown ●	MCA	1
25	39	DOWNTOWN '88	Petula Clark	PRT	8
-	40	AFTER THE WAR	Gary Moore	Virgin	1

WEEK ENDING 28 JANUARY 1989

LW	TW	Title	Artist	Label	Wks
10	[1]	SOMETHING'S GOTTEN HOLD OF MY HEART	Marc Almond featuring Gene Pitney	Parlophone	3
4	[2]	THE LIVING YEARS	Mike and the Mechanics	WEA	3
1	3	ESPECIALLY FOR YOU	Kylie Minogue and Jason Donovan	PWL	8
7	4	YOU GOT IT	Roy Orbison	Virgin	3
5	[5]	SHE DRIVES ME CRAZY	Fine Young Cannibals	London	4
2	6	CRACKERS INTERNATIONAL (EP)	Erasure	Mute	8
11	7	CUDDLY TOY	Roachford	CBS	3
3	8	BUFFALO STANCE	Neneh Cherry	Circa	7
6	9	BABY I LOVE YOUR WAY-FREEBIRD	Will To Power	Epic	4
21	10	LOVE TRAIN	Holly Johnson	MCA	2
9	11	WAITING FOR A STAR TO FALL	Boy Meets Girl	RCA	5
8	12	GOOD LIFE	Inner City	10	8
22	13	WAIT	Robert Howard and Kym Mazelle	RCA	3
17	[14]	GET ON THE DANCE FLOOR	Rob Base and DJ E-Z Rock	Supreme	3
29	15	BE MY TWIN	Brother Beyond	Parlophone	2
19	[16]	BABY DON'T FORGET MY NUMBER	Milli Vanilli	Cooltempo	3
33	17	THAT'S THE WAY LOVE IS	Ten City	Atlantic	2
12	18	FOUR LETTER WORD	Kim Wilde	MCA	8
28	[19]	WHERE IS THE LOVE	Will Downing and Mica Paris	Fourth + Broadway	2
24	20	RESPECT	Adeva	Cooltempo	3
-	21	BIG AREA	Then Jerico	London	1
14	22	LOCO IN ACAPULCO	Four Tops	Arista	8
30	[23]	I LIVE FOR YOUR LOVE	Natalie Cole	EMI Manhattan	6
16	24	KEEPING THE DREAM ALIVE	Freiheit	CBS	6
15	25	SUDDENLY	Angry Anderson	Food For Thought	10
13	26	ALL SHE WANTS IS	Duranduran	EMI	4
38	27	MY PREROGATIVE	Bobby Brown	MCA	2
34	28	TRACIE	Level 42	Polydor	2
18	29	RHYTHM IS GONNA GET YOU	Gloria Estefan and Miami Sound Machine	Epic	6
37	30	BREAK 4 LOVE	Raze	Champion	2
31	[31]	STUPID QUESTION	New Model Army	EMI	2
20	32	YOU ARE THE ONE	A-Ha	Warner Bros	8
23	33	BORN THIS WAY (LET'S DANCE)	Cookie Crew	ffrr	3
-	34	THE LOVER IN ME	Sheena Easton	MCA	1
-	35	GRIP '89 (GET A) GRIP (ON YOURSELF)	Stranglers	EMI	1
27	36	HIT THE GROUND	Darling Buds	CBS	3
40	[37]	AFTER THE WAR	Gary Moore	Virgin	2
-	38	IT'S ONLY LOVE	Simply Red	Elektra	1
-	39	I ONLY WANNA BE WITH YOU	Samantha Fox	Jive	1
-	40	FISHERMAN'S BLUES	Waterboys	Ensign	1

WEEK ENDING 4 FEBRUARY 1989

LW	TW	Title	Artist	Label	Wks
1	[1]	SOMETHING'S GOTTEN HOLD OF MY HEART	Marc Almond featuring Gene Pitney	Parlophone	4
2	[2]	THE LIVING YEARS	Mike and the Mechanics	WEA	4
4	[3]	YOU GOT IT	Roy Orbison	Virgin	4
7	[4]	CUDDLY TOY	Roachford	CBS	4
10	5	LOVE TRAIN	Holly Johnson	MCA	3
5	6	SHE DRIVES ME CRAZY	Fine Young Cannibals	London	5
3	7	ESPECIALLY FOR YOU	Kylie Minogue and Jason Donovan	PWL	9
17	[8]	THAT'S THE WAY LOVE IS	Ten City	Atlantic	3
6	9	CRACKERS INTERNATIONAL (EP)	Erasure	Mute	9
13	10	WAIT	Robert Howard and Kym Mazelle	RCA	4
9	11	BABY I LOVE YOUR WAY-FREEBIRD	Will To Power	Epic	5
8	12	BUFFALO STANCE	Neneh Cherry	Circa	8
21	[13]	BIG AREA	Then Jerico	London	2
15	[14]	BE MY TWIN	Brother Beyond	Parlophone	3
11	15	WAITING FOR A STAR TO FALL	Boy Meets Girl	RCA	6
16	[16]	BABY DON'T FORGET MY NUMBER	Milli Vanilli	Cooltempo	4
20	[17]	RESPECT	Adeva	Cooltempo	4
27	18	MY PREROGATIVE	Bobby Brown	MCA	3
12	19	GOOD LIFE	Inner City	10	9
14	20	GET ON THE DANCE FLOOR	Rob Base and DJ E-Z Rock	Supreme	4
19	21	WHERE IS THE LOVE	Will Downing and Mica Paris	Fourth + Broadway	3
38	22	IT'S ONLY LOVE	Simply Red	Elektra	2
34	23	THE LOVER IN ME	Sheena Easton	MCA	2
-	24	LOVE CHANGES EVERYTHING	Michael Ball ●	Really Useful	1
28	[25]	TRACIE	Level 42	Polydor	3
23	26	I LIVE FOR YOUR LOVE	Natalie Cole	EMI Manhattan	7
-	27	FINE TIME	Yazz	Big Life	1
30	[28]	BREAK 4 LOVE	Raze	Champion	3
39	29	I ONLY WANNA BE WITH YOU	Samantha Fox	Jive	2
18	30	FOUR LETTER WORD	Kim Wilde	MCA	9
-	31	LOOKING FOR LINDA	Hue And Cry	Circa	1
40	[32]	FISHERMAN'S BLUES	Waterboys	Ensign	2
35	[33]	GRIP '89 (GET A) GRIP (ON YOURSELF)	Stranglers	EMI	2
22	34	LOCO IN ACAPULCO	Four Tops	Arista	9
25	35	SUDDENLY	Angry Anderson	Food For Thought	11
-	36	SHE WON'T TALK TO ME	Luther Vandross	Epic	1
-	[37]	I CAN DO THIS	Monie Love ●	Cooltempo	1
-	38	LOST IN YOUR EYES	Debbie Gibson	Atlantic	1
-	[39]	PEACE IN OUR TIME	Big Country	Mercury	1
24	40	KEEPING THE DREAM ALIVE	Freiheit	CBS	7

WEEK ENDING 11 FEBRUARY

LW	TW	Title	Artist	Label	Wks
1	[1]	SOMETHING'S GOTTEN HOLD OF MY HEART	Marc Almond featuring Gene Pitney	Parlophone	5
2	[2]	THE LIVING YEARS	Mike and the Mechanics	WEA	5
3	[3]	YOU GOT IT	Roy Orbison	Virgin	5
5	[4]	LOVE TRAIN	Holly Johnson	MCA	4
4	5	CUDDLY TOY	Roachford	CBS	5
-	[6]	THE LAST OF THE FAMOUS INTERNATIONAL PLAYBOYS	Morrissey	HMV	1
10	[7]	WAIT	Robert Howard and Kym Mazelle	RCA	5
8	[8]	THAT'S THE WAY LOVE IS	Ten City	Atlantic	4
18	9	MY PREROGATIVE	Bobby Brown	MCA	4
6	10	SHE DRIVES ME CRAZY	Fine Young Cannibals	London	6
27	11	FINE TIME	Yazz	Big Life	2
24	12	LOVE CHANGES EVERYTHING	Michael Ball	Really Useful	2
22	[13]	IT'S ONLY LOVE	Simply Red	Elektra	3
13	14	BIG AREA	Then Jerico	London	3
23	[15]	THE LOVER IN ME	Sheena Easton	MCA	3
7	16	ESPECIALLY FOR YOU	Kylie Minogue and Jason Donovan	PWL	10
9	17	CRACKERS INTERNATIONAL (EP)	Erasure	Mute	10
17	18	RESPECT	Adeva	Cooltempo	5
11	19	BABY I LOVE YOUR WAY-FREEBIRD	Will To Power	Epic	6
29	20	I ONLY WANNA BE WITH YOU	Samantha Fox	Jive	3
14	21	BE MY TWIN	Brother Beyond	Parlophone	4
16	22	BABY DON'T FORGET MY NUMBER	Milli Vanilli	Cooltempo	5
31	23	LOOKING FOR LINDA	Hue And Cry	Circa	2
12	24	BUFFALO STANCE	Neneh Cherry	Circa	9
21	25	WHERE IS THE LOVE	Will Downing and Mica Paris	Fourth + Broadway	4
-	26	HOLD ME IN YOUR ARMS	Rick Astley	RCA	1
15	27	WAITING FOR A STAR TO FALL	Boy Meets Girl	RCA	7
28	[28]	BREAK 4 LOVE	Raze	Champion	4
20	29	GET ON THE DANCE FLOOR	Rob Base and DJ E-Z Rock	Supreme	5
19	30	GOOD LIFE	Inner City	10	10
-	31	ROCKET	Def Leppard	Bludgeon Riffola	1
-	32	I DON"T WANT A LOVER	Texas ●	Mercury	1
-	33	EVERY ROSE HAS ITS THORN	Poison	Enigma	1
36	[34]	SHE WON'T TALK TO ME	Luther Vandross	Epic	2
26	35	I LIVE FOR YOUR LOVE	Natalie Cole	EMI Manhattan	8

■Six of the top ten singles are by people who have been there before as part of other bands - Marc Almond of Soft Cell, Mike Rutherford of Genesis, Holly Johnson of Frankie Goes To Hollywood, Morrissey of the Smiths, Robert Howard of the Blow Monkeys and Bobby Brown of New Edition (11.02.89)■

February 1989

□ Highest position disc reached ● Act's first ever week on chart

LW	TW	Title	Artist	Label	Wks
38	36	LOST IN YOUR EYES	Debbie Gibson	Atlantic	2
-	37	STOP	Sam Brown ●	A&M	1
25	38	TRACIE	Level 42	Polydor	4
39	[39]	PEACE IN OUR TIME	Big Country	Mercury	2
37	40	I CAN DO THIS	Monie Love	Cooltempo	2

WEEK ENDING 18 FEBRUARY 1989

LW	TW	Title	Artist	Label	Wks
1	[1]	SOMETHING'S GOTTEN HOLD OF MY HEART	Marc Almond featuring Gene Pitney	Parlophone	6
-	2	BELFAST CHILD	Simple Minds	Virgin	1
12	3	LOVE CHANGES EVERYTHING	Michael Ball	Really Useful	3
2	4	THE LIVING YEARS	Mike and the Mechanics	WEA	6
4	5	LOVE TRAIN	Holly Johnson	MCA	5
9	[6]	MY PREROGATIVE	Bobby Brown	MCA	5
3	7	YOU GOT IT	Roy Orbison	Virgin	6
6	8	THE LAST OF THE FAMOUS INTERNATIONAL PLAYBOYS	Morrissey	HMV	2
11	[9]	FINE TIME	Yazz	Big Life	3
7	10	WAIT	Robert Howard and Kym Mazelle	RCA	6
26	11	HOLD ME IN YOUR ARMS	Rick Astley	RCA	2
5	12	CUDDLY TOY	Roachford	CBS	6
8	13	THAT'S THE WAY LOVE IS	Ten City	Atlantic	5
13	14	IT'S ONLY LOVE	Simply Red	Elektra	4
15	[15]	THE LOVER IN ME	Sheena Easton	MCA	4
20	[16]	I ONLY WANNA BE WITH YOU	Samantha Fox	Jive	4
37	17	STOP	Sam Brown	A&M	2
23	18	LOOKING FOR LINDA	Hue And Cry	Circa	3
10	19	SHE DRIVES ME CRAZY	Fine Young Cannibals	London	7
31	20	ROCKET	Def Leppard	Bludgeon Riffola	2
32	21	I DON"T WANT A LOVER	Texas	Mercury	2
14	22	BIG AREA	Then Jerico	London	4
16	23	ESPECIALLY FOR YOU	Kylie Minogue and Jason Donovan	PWL	11
33	24	EVERY ROSE HAS ITS THORN	Poison	Enigma	2
18	25	RESPECT	Adeva	Cooltempo	6
17	26	CRACKERS INTERNATIONAL (EP)	Erasure	Mute	11
19	27	BABY I LOVE YOUR WAY-FREEBIRD	Will To Power	Epic	7
24	28	BUFFALO STANCE	Neneh Cherry	Circa	10
-	29	HEY MUSIC LOVER	S Express	Rhythm King	1
21	30	BE MY TWIN	Brother Beyond	Parlophone	5
28	31	BREAK 4 LOVE	Raze	Champion	5
-	32	PROMISED LAND	Style Council	Polydor	1
-	33	CAN'T STAY AWAY FROM YOU	Gloria Estefan and Miami Sound Machine	Epic	1
36	34	LOST IN YOUR EYES	Debbie Gibson	Atlantic	3
22	35	BABY DON'T FORGET MY NUMBER	Milli Vanilli	Cooltempo	6
27	36	WAITING FOR A STAR TO FALL	Boy Meets Girl	RCA	8
-	37	WHAT I AM	Edie Brickell and the New Bohemians ●	Geffen	1
-	[38]	CAN U DIG IT	Pop Will Eat Itself ●	RCA	1
30	39	GOOD LIFE	Inner City	10	11
-	40	WILD THING/LOC'ED AFTER DARK	Tone Loc ●	Fourth + Broadway	1

WEEK ENDING 25 FEBRUARY 1989

LW	TW	Title	Artist	Label	Wks
2	[1]	BELFAST CHILD	Simple Minds	Virgin	2
3	[2]	LOVE CHANGES EVERYTHING	Michael Ball	Really Useful	4
1	3	SOMETHING'S GOTTEN HOLD OF MY HEART	Marc Almond featuring Gene Pitney	Parlophone	7
-	4	LEAVE ME ALONE	Michael Jackson	Epic	1
17	5	STOP	Sam Brown	A&M	3
6	[6]	MY PREROGATIVE	Bobby Brown	MCA	6
4	7	THE LIVING YEARS	Mike and the Mechanics	WEA	7
5	8	LOVE TRAIN	Holly Johnson	MCA	6
9	[9]	FINE TIME	Yazz	Big Life	4
11	[10]	HOLD ME IN YOUR ARMS	Rick Astley	RCA	3
7	11	YOU GOT IT	Roy Orbison	Virgin	7
-	12	HELP!	Bananarama/La Na Nee Nee Noo Noo ●	London	1
21	13	I DON"T WANT A LOVER	Texas	Mercury	3
29	14	HEY MUSIC LOVER	S Express	Rhythm King	2
20	[15]	ROCKET	Def Leppard	Bludgeon Riffola	3
18	[16]	LOOKING FOR LINDA	Hue And Cry	Circa	4
10	17	WAIT	Robert Howard and Kym Mazelle	RCA	7
16	18	I ONLY WANNA BE WITH YOU	Samantha Fox	Jive	5
13	19	THAT'S THE WAY LOVE IS	Ten City	Atlantic	6
24	20	EVERY ROSE HAS ITS THORN	Poison	Enigma	3
8	21	THE LAST OF THE FAMOUS INTERNATIONAL PLAYBOYS	Morrissey	HMV	3
19	22	SHE DRIVES ME CRAZY	Fine Young Cannibals	London	8
33	23	CAN'T STAY AWAY FROM YOU	Gloria Estefan and Miami Sound Machine	Epic	2
14	24	IT'S ONLY LOVE	Simply Red	Elektra	5
15	25	THE LOVER IN ME	Sheena Easton	MCA	5
12	26	CUDDLY TOY	Roachford	CBS	7
32	[27]	PROMISED LAND	Style Council	Polydor	2
-	28	NOTHING HAS BEEN PROVED	Dusty Springfield	Parlophone	1
23	29	ESPECIALLY FOR YOU	Kylie Minogue and Jason Donovan	PWL	12
40	30	WILD THING/LOC'ED AFTER DARK	Tone Loc	Fourth + Broadway	2
-	31	BLOW THE HOUSE DOWN	Living In A Box	Chrysalis	1
37	32	WHAT I AM	Edie Brickell and the New Bohemians	Geffen	2
-	33	TURN UP THE BASS	Tyree featuring Rock Steady ●	ffrr	1
-	34	EVERYTHING COUNTS	Depeche Mode	Mute	1
34	35	LOST IN YOUR EYES	Debbie Gibson	Atlantic	4
26	36	CRACKERS INTERNATIONAL (EP)	Erasure	Mute	12
22	37	BIG AREA	Then Jerico	London	5
25	38	RESPECT	Adeva	Cooltempo	7
38	39	CAN U DIG IT	Pop Will Eat Itself	RCA	2
27	40	BABY I LOVE YOUR WAY-FREEBIRD	Will To Power	Epic	8

WEEK ENDING 4 MARCH 1989

LW	TW	Title	Artist	Label	Wks
1	[1]	BELFAST CHILD	Simple Minds	Virgin	3
4	[2]	LEAVE ME ALONE	Michael Jackson	Epic	2
2	3	LOVE CHANGES EVERYTHING	Michael Ball	Really Useful	5
5	[4]	STOP	Sam Brown	A&M	4
12	5	HELP!	Bananarama/La Na Nee Nee Noo Noo	London	2
14	[6]	HEY MUSIC LOVER	S Express	Rhythm King	3
6	7	MY PREROGATIVE	Bobby Brown	MCA	7
13	[8]	I DON"T WANT A LOVER	Texas	Mercury	4
-	9	TOO MANY BROKEN HEARTS	Jason Donovan	PWL	1
23	10	CAN'T STAY AWAY FROM YOU	Gloria Estefan and Miami Sound Machine	Epic	3
10	11	HOLD ME IN YOUR ARMS	Rick Astley	RCA	4
3	12	SOMETHING'S GOTTEN HOLD OF MY HEART	Marc Almond featuring Gene Pitney	Parlophone	8
8	13	LOVE TRAIN	Holly Johnson	MCA	7
20	14	EVERY ROSE HAS ITS THORN	Poison	Enigma	4
16	15	LOOKING FOR LINDA	Hue And Cry	Circa	5
33	16	TURN UP THE BASS	Tyree featuring Rock Steady	ffrr	2
31	17	BLOW THE HOUSE DOWN	Living In A Box	Chrysalis	2
9	18	FINE TIME	Yazz	Big Life	5
15	19	ROCKET	Def Leppard	Bludgeon Riffola	4
28	20	NOTHING HAS BEEN PROVED	Dusty Springfield	Parlophone	2
30	[21]	WILD THING/LOC'ED AFTER DARK	Tone Loc	Fourth + Broadway	3
7	22	THE LIVING YEARS	Mike and the Mechanics	WEA	8
34	23	EVERYTHING COUNTS	Depeche Mode	Mute	2
17	24	WAIT	Robert Howard and Kym Mazelle	RCA	8
19	25	THAT'S THE WAY LOVE IS	Ten City	Atlantic	7
-	26	WAGES DAY	Deacon Blue	CBS	1
11	27	YOU GOT IT	Roy Orbison	Virgin	8
-	28	MEAN MAN	W.A.S.P.	Capitol	1
27	29	PROMISED LAND	Style Council	Polydor	3
-	30	THIS TIME I KNOW IT'S FOR REAL	Donna Summer	Warner Bros	1
32	[31]	WHAT I AM	Edie Brickell and the New Bohemians	Geffen	3
-	32	I'D RATHER JACK	Reynolds Girls ●	PWL	1

In these weeks ■ Gene Pitney celebrates his 48th birthday at number one, but tumbles a couple of days later (18.02.89) ■ La Na Nee Nee Noo Noo are Dawn French, Jennifer Saunders and Kathy Burke, working with Bananarama for Comic Relief (25.02.89)■

LW	TW	Title	Artist	Label	Wks
-	33	CELEBRATE THE WORLD	Womack and Womack	*Fourth + Broadway*	1
-	34	STRAIGHT UP	Paula Abdul ●	*Siren*	1
18	35	I ONLY WANNA BE WITH YOU	Samantha Fox	*Jive*	6
24	36	IT'S ONLY LOVE	Simply Red	*Elektra*	6
22	37	SHE DRIVES ME CRAZY	Fine Young Cannibals	*London*	9
25	38	THE LOVER IN ME	Sheena Easton	*MCA*	6
26	39	CUDDLY TOY	Roachford	*CBS*	8
-	40	CRYIN'	Vixen ●	*EMI Manhattan*	1

WEEK ENDING 11 MARCH 1989

LW	TW	Title	Artist	Label	Wks
9	1	TOO MANY BROKEN HEARTS	Jason Donovan	*PWL*	2
3	2	LOVE CHANGES EVERYTHING	Michael Ball	*Really Useful*	6
5	3	HELP!	Bananarama/La Na Nee Nee Noo Noo	*London*	3
4	4	STOP	Sam Brown	*A&M*	5
2	5	LEAVE ME ALONE	Michael Jackson	*Epic*	3
1	6	BELFAST CHILD	Simple Minds	*Virgin*	4
6	7	HEY MUSIC LOVER	S Express	*Rhythm King*	4
10	8	CAN'T STAY AWAY FROM YOU	Gloria Estefan and Miami Sound Machine	*Epic*	4
8	9	I DON"T WANT A LOVER	Texas	*Mercury*	5
17	10	BLOW THE HOUSE DOWN	Living In A Box	*Chrysalis*	3
30	11	THIS TIME I KNOW IT'S FOR REAL	Donna Summer	*Warner Bros*	2
16	12	TURN UP THE BASS	Tyree featuring Rock Steady	*ffrr*	3
14	13	EVERY ROSE HAS ITS THORN	Poison	*Enigma*	5
7	14	MY PREROGATIVE	Bobby Brown	*MCA*	8
34	15	STRAIGHT UP	Paula Abdul	*Siren*	2
20	16	NOTHING HAS BEEN PROVED	Dusty Springfield	*Parlophone*	3
32	17	I'D RATHER JACK	Reynolds Girls	*PWL*	2
26	18	WAGES DAY	Deacon Blue	*CBS*	2
11	19	HOLD ME IN YOUR ARMS	Rick Astley	*RCA*	5
12	20	SOMETHING'S GOTTEN HOLD OF MY HEART	Marc Almond featuring Gene Pitney	*Parlophone*	9
28	21	MEAN MAN	W.A.S.P.	*Capitol*	2
23	22	EVERYTHING COUNTS	Depeche Mode	*Mute*	3
15	23	LOOKING FOR LINDA	Hue And Cry	*Circa*	6
33	24	CELEBRATE THE WORLD	Womack and Womack	*Fourth + Broadway*	2
21	25	WILD THING/LOC'ED AFTER DARK	Tone Loc	*Fourth + Broadway*	4
13	26	LOVE TRAIN	Holly Johnson	*MCA*	8
40	27	CRYIN'	Vixen	*EMI Manhattan*	2
-	28	WHO WANTS TO BE THE DISCO KING	Wonder Stuff	*Far Out*	1
22	29	THE LIVING YEARS	Mike and the Mechanics	*WEA*	9
-	30	INTERNATIONAL RESCUE	We've Got A Fuzzbox And We're Gonna Use It	*WEA*	1
18	31	FINE TIME	Yazz	*Big Life*	6
-	32	ROUND AND ROUND	New Order	*Factory*	1
19	33	ROCKET	Def Leppard	*Bludgeon Riffola*	5
31	34	WHAT I AM	Edie Brickell and the New Bohemians	*Geffen*	4
27	35	YOU GOT IT	Roy Orbison	*Virgin*	9
-	36	ONE MAN	Chanelle ●	*Cooltempo*	1
25	37	THAT'S THE WAY LOVE IS	Ten City	*Atlantic*	8
-	38	VERONICA	Elvis Costello	*Warner Bros*	1
-	39	SLEEP TALK	Alyson Williams ●	*Def Jam*	1
-	40	VAGABONDS	New Model Army	*EMI*	1

WEEK ENDING 18 MARCH 1989

LW	TW	Title	Artist	Label	Wks
1	1	TOO MANY BROKEN HEARTS	Jason Donovan	*PWL*	3
-	2	LIKE A PRAYER	Madonna	*Sire*	1
3	3	HELP!	Bananarama/La Na Nee Nee Noo Noo	*London*	4
11	4	THIS TIME I KNOW IT'S FOR REAL	Donna Summer	*Warner Bros*	3
4	5	STOP	Sam Brown	*A&M*	6
15	6	STRAIGHT UP	Paula Abdul	*Siren*	3
8	7	CAN'T STAY AWAY FROM YOU	Gloria Estefan and Miami Sound Machine	*Epic*	5
2	8	LOVE CHANGES EVERYTHING	Michael Ball	*Really Useful*	7
7	9	HEY MUSIC LOVER	S Express	*Rhythm King*	5
10	10	BLOW THE HOUSE DOWN	Living In A Box	*Chrysalis*	4

March 1989

□ Highest position disc reached ● Act's first ever week on chart

LW	TW	Title	Artist	Label	Wks
5	11	LEAVE ME ALONE	Michael Jackson	*Epic*	4
17	12	I'D RATHER JACK	Reynolds Girls	*PWL*	3
6	13	BELFAST CHILD	Simple Minds	*Virgin*	5
9	14	I DON"T WANT A LOVER	Texas	*Mercury*	6
-	15	KEEP ON MOVIN'	Soul II Soul featuring Caron Wheeler ●	*10*	1
12	16	TURN UP THE BASS	Tyree featuring Rock Steady	*ffrr*	4
16	17	NOTHING HAS BEEN PROVED	Dusty Springfield	*Parlophone*	4
13	18	EVERY ROSE HAS ITS THORN	Poison	*Enigma*	6
24	19	CELEBRATE THE WORLD	Womack and Womack	*Fourth + Broadway*	3
18	20	WAGES DAY	Deacon Blue	*CBS*	3
-	21	PARADISE CITY	Guns N' Roses	*Geffen*	1
32	22	ROUND AND ROUND	New Order	*Factory*	2
30	23	INTERNATIONAL RESCUE	We've Got A Fuzzbox And We're Gonna Use It	*WEA*	2
22	24	EVERYTHING COUNTS	Depeche Mode	*Mute*	4
36	25	ONE MAN	Chanelle	*Cooltempo*	2
14	26	MY PREROGATIVE	Bobby Brown	*MCA*	9
21	27	MEAN MAN	W.A.S.P.	*Capitol*	3
39	28	SLEEP TALK	Alyson Williams	*Def Jam*	2
28	29	WHO WANTS TO BE THE DISCO KING	Wonder Stuff	*Far Out*	2
27	30	CRYIN'	Vixen	*EMI Manhattan*	3
38	31	VERONICA	Elvis Costello	*Warner Bros*	2
-	32	I BEG YOUR PARDON	Kon Kan ●	*Atlantic*	1
19	33	HOLD ME IN YOUR ARMS	Rick Astley	*RCA*	6
23	34	LOOKING FOR LINDA	Hue And Cry	*Circa*	7
25	35	WILD THING/LOC'ED AFTER DARK	Tone Loc	*Fourth + Broadway*	5
-	36	LOVE IN THE NATURAL WAY	Kim Wilde	*MCA*	1
40	37	VAGABONDS	New Model Army	*EMI*	2
-	38	INDESTRUCTIBLE	Four Tops	*Arista*	1
20	39	SOMETHING'S GOTTEN HOLD OF MY HEART	Marc Almond featuring Gene Pitney	*Parlophone*	10
26	40	LOVE TRAIN	Holly Johnson	*MCA*	9

WEEK ENDING 25 MARCH 1989

LW	TW	Title	Artist	Label	Wks
2	1	LIKE A PRAYER	Madonna	*Sire*	2
1	2	TOO MANY BROKEN HEARTS	Jason Donovan	*PWL*	4
4	3	THIS TIME I KNOW IT'S FOR REAL	Donna Summer	*Warner Bros*	4
6	4	STRAIGHT UP	Paula Abdul	*Siren*	4
15	5	KEEP ON MOVIN'	Soul II Soul featuring Caron Wheeler	*10*	2
3	6	HELP!	Bananarama/La Na Nee Nee Noo Noo	*London*	5
7	7	CAN'T STAY AWAY FROM YOU	Gloria Estefan and Miami Sound Machine	*Epic*	6
21	8	PARADISE CITY	Guns N' Roses	*Geffen*	2
5	9	STOP	Sam Brown	*A&M*	7
12	10	I'D RATHER JACK	Reynolds Girls	*PWL*	4
8	11	LOVE CHANGES EVERYTHING	Michael Ball	*Really Useful*	8
9	12	HEY MUSIC LOVER	S Express	*Rhythm King*	6
23	13	INTERNATIONAL RESCUE	We've Got A Fuzzbox And We're Gonna Use It	*WEA*	3
10	14	BLOW THE HOUSE DOWN	Living In A Box	*Chrysalis*	5
11	15	LEAVE ME ALONE	Michael Jackson	*Epic*	5
25	16	ONE MAN	Chanelle	*Cooltempo*	3
32	17	I BEG YOUR PARDON	Kon Kan	*Atlantic*	2
28	18	SLEEP TALK	Alyson Williams	*Def Jam*	3
14	19	I DON"T WANT A LOVER	Texas	*Mercury*	7
19	20	CELEBRATE THE WORLD	Womack and Womack	*Fourth + Broadway*	4
22	21	ROUND AND ROUND	New Order	*Factory*	3
13	22	BELFAST CHILD	Simple Minds	*Virgin*	6
16	23	TURN UP THE BASS	Tyree featuring Rock Steady	*ffrr*	5
-	24	PEOPLE HOLD ON	Coldcut featuring Lisa Stansfield	*Ahead Of Our Time*	1
18	25	EVERY ROSE HAS ITS THORN	Poison	*Enigma*	7
17	26	NOTHING HAS BEEN PROVED	Dusty Springfield	*Parlophone*	5
-	27	DON'T BE CRUEL	Bobby Brown	*MCA*	1

■*Indestructible* by the Four Tops also features Smokey Robinson (18.03.89) ■ Madonna's *Like A Prayer* is her first single release in over a year, and her first chart-topper for eighteen months (25.03.89)■

March 1989

□ Highest position disc reached ● Act's first ever week on chart

LW	TW	Title / Artist	Label	Wks
20	28	WAGES DAY Deacon Blue	CBS	4
-	29	FAMILY MAN Roachford	CBS	1
38	30	INDESTRUCTIBLE Four Tops	Arista	2
31	31	VERONICA Elvis Costello	Warner Bros	3
36	32	LOVE IN THE NATURAL WAY Kim Wilde	MCA	2
-	33	ETERNAL FLAME Bangles	CBS	1
-	34	I HAVEN'T STOPPED DANCING YET Pat and Mick	PWL	1
-	35	GOT TO GET YOU BACK Kym Mazelle ●	Syncopate	1
26	36	MY PREROGATIVE Bobby Brown	MCA	10
-	36	ONLY THE LONELY T'Pau	Siren	1
24	38	EVERYTHING COUNTS Depeche Mode	Mute	5
-	39	THE RATTLER Goodbye Mr Mackenzie ●	Capitol	1
-	40	MUSICAL FREEDOM (MOVING ON UP) Paul Simpson featuring Adeva ●	Cooltempo	1

LW	TW	*WEEK ENDING* **1 APRIL 1989**		Wks
1	1	LIKE A PRAYER Madonna	Sire	3
2	2	TOO MANY BROKEN HEARTS Jason Donovan	PWL	5
3	3	THIS TIME I KNOW IT'S FOR REAL Donna Summer	Warner Bros	5
4	4	STRAIGHT UP Paula Abdul	Siren	5
5	5	KEEP ON MOVIN' Soul II Soul featuring Caron Wheeler	10	3
8	6	PARADISE CITY Guns N' Roses	Geffen	3
7	7	CAN'T STAY AWAY FROM YOU Gloria Estefan and Miami Sound Machine	Epic	7
10	8	I'D RATHER JACK Reynolds Girls	PWL	5
6	9	HELP! Bananarama/La Na Nee Nee Noo Noo	London	6
17	10	I BEG YOUR PARDON Kon Kan	Atlantic	3
13	11	INTERNATIONAL RESCUE We've Got A Fuzzbox And We're Gonna Use It	WEA	4
9	12	STOP Sam Brown	A&M	8
33	13	ETERNAL FLAME Bangles	CBS	2
27	14	DON'T BE CRUEL Bobby Brown	MCA	1
24	15	PEOPLE HOLD ON Coldcut featuring Lisa Stansfield	Ahead Of Our Time	2
34	16	I HAVEN'T STOPPED DANCING YET Pat and Mick	PWL	2
18	17	SLEEP TALK Alyson Williams	Def Jam	4
11	18	LOVE CHANGES EVERYTHING Michael Ball	Really Useful	9
16	19	ONE MAN Chanelle	Cooltempo	4
15	20	LEAVE ME ALONE Michael Jackson	Epic	6
12	21	HEY MUSIC LOVER S Express	Rhythm King	7
-	22	FIRE WOMAN Cult	Beggars Banquet	1
14	23	BLOW THE HOUSE DOWN Living In A Box	Chrysalis	6
21	24	ROUND AND ROUND New Order	Factory	4
29	25	FAMILY MAN Roachford	CBS	2
-	26	THE BEAT(EN) GENERATION The The	Epic	1
20	27	CELEBRATE THE WORLD Womack and Womack	Fourth + Broadway	5
-	28	AMERICANOS Holly Johnson	MCA	1
35	29	GOT TO GET YOU BACK Kym Mazelle	Syncopate	2
40	30	MUSICAL FREEDOM (MOVING ON UP) Paul Simpson featuring Adeva	Cooltempo	2
19	31	I DON"T WANT A LOVER Texas	Mercury	8
22	32	BELFAST CHILD Simple Minds	Virgin	7
-	33	BABY I DON'T CARE Transvision Vamp	MCA	1
-	34	CAN YOU KEEP A SECRET Brother Beyond	Parlophone	1
36	35	ONLY THE LONELY T'Pau	Siren	2
25	36	EVERY ROSE HAS ITS THORN Poison	Enigma	8
39	37	THE RATTLER Goodbye Mr Mackenzie	Capitol	2
-	38	SHE'S A MYSTERY TO ME Roy Orbison	Virgin	1
26	39	NOTHING HAS BEEN PROVED Dusty Springfield	Parlophone	6
-	40	OF COURSE I'M LYING Yello	Mercury	1

LW	TW	*WEEK ENDING* **8 APRIL 1989**		Wks
1	1	LIKE A PRAYER Madonna	Sire	4
2	2	TOO MANY BROKEN HEARTS Jason Donovan	PWL	6
4	3	STRAIGHT UP Paula Abdul	Siren	6
3	4	THIS TIME I KNOW IT'S FOR REAL Donna Summer	Warner Bros	6
13	5	ETERNAL FLAME Bangles	CBS	3
5	6	KEEP ON MOVIN' Soul II Soul featuring Caron Wheeler	10	4
6	7	PARADISE CITY Guns N' Roses	Geffen	4
10	8	I BEG YOUR PARDON Kon Kan	Atlantic	4
16	9	I HAVEN'T STOPPED DANCING YET Pat and Mick	PWL	3
8	10	I'D RATHER JACK Reynolds Girls	PWL	6
11	11	INTERNATIONAL RESCUE We've Got A Fuzzbox And We're Gonna Use It	WEA	5
15	12	PEOPLE HOLD ON Coldcut featuring Lisa Stansfield	Ahead Of Our Time	3
14	13	DON'T BE CRUEL Bobby Brown	MCA	2
28	14	AMERICANOS Holly Johnson	MCA	2
22	15	FIRE WOMAN Cult	Beggars Banquet	2
33	16	BABY I DON'T CARE Transvision Vamp	MCA	2
7	17	CAN'T STAY AWAY FROM YOU Gloria Estefan and Miami Sound Machine	Epic	8
26	18	THE BEAT(EN) GENERATION The The	Epic	2
-	19	IF YOU DON'T KNOW ME BY NOW Simply Red	Elektra	1
17	20	SLEEP TALK Alyson Williams	Def Jam	5
-	21	MYSTIFY INXS	Mercury	1
34	22	CAN YOU KEEP A SECRET Brother Beyond	Parlophone	2
19	23	ONE MAN Chanelle	Cooltempo	5
9	24	HELP! Bananarama/La Na Nee Nee Noo Noo	London	7
30	25	MUSICAL FREEDOM (MOVING ON UP) Paul Simpson featuring Adeva	Cooltempo	3
12	26	STOP Sam Brown	A&M	9
38	27	SHE'S A MYSTERY TO ME Roy Orbison	Virgin	2
24	28	ROUND AND ROUND New Order	Factory	5
25	29	FAMILY MAN Roachford	CBS	3
18	30	LOVE CHANGES EVERYTHING Michael Ball	Really Useful	10
20	31	LEAVE ME ALONE Michael Jackson	Epic	7
40	32	OF COURSE I'M LYING Yello	Mercury	2
21	33	HEY MUSIC LOVER S Express	Rhythm King	8
35	34	ONLY THE LONELY T'Pau	Siren	3
29	35	GOT TO GET YOU BACK Kym Mazelle	Syncopate	3
23	36	BLOW THE HOUSE DOWN Living In A Box	Chrysalis	7
-	37	GOT TO KEEP ON Cookie Crew	ffrr	1
-	38	WHAT DOES IT TAKE Then Jerico	London	1
-	39	DEVOTION Ten City	Atlantic	1
-	40	BEAUTY'S ONLY SKIN DEEP Aswad	Mango	1

LW	TW	*WEEK ENDING* **15 APRIL 1989**		Wks
5	1	ETERNAL FLAME Bangles	CBS	4
19	2	IF YOU DON'T KNOW ME BY NOW Simply Red	Elektra	2
1	3	LIKE A PRAYER Madonna	Sire	5
3	4	STRAIGHT UP Paula Abdul	Siren	7
8	5	I BEG YOUR PARDON Kon Kan	Atlantic	5
2	6	TOO MANY BROKEN HEARTS Jason Donovan	PWL	7
16	7	BABY I DON'T CARE Transvision Vamp	MCA	3
4	8	THIS TIME I KNOW IT'S FOR REAL Donna Summer	Warner Bros	7
14	9	AMERICANOS Holly Johnson	MCA	3
6	10	KEEP ON MOVIN' Soul II Soul featuring Caron Wheeler	10	5
12	11	PEOPLE HOLD ON Coldcut featuring Lisa Stansfield	Ahead Of Our Time	4
-	12	WHEN LOVE COMES TO TOWN U2 with B.B. King	Island	1
7	13	PARADISE CITY Guns N' Roses	Geffen	5
9	14	I HAVEN'T STOPPED DANCING YET Pat and Mick	PWL	4
13	15	DON'T BE CRUEL Bobby Brown	MCA	3
21	16	MYSTIFY INXS	Mercury	2
10	17	I'D RATHER JACK Reynolds Girls	PWL	7
11	18	INTERNATIONAL RESCUE We've Got A Fuzzbox And We're Gonna Use It	WEA	6
-	19	GOOD THING Fine Young Cannibals	London	1
15	20	FIRE WOMAN Cult	Beggars Banquet	3
37	21	GOT TO KEEP ON Cookie Crew	ffrr	2
25	22	MUSICAL FREEDOM (MOVING ON UP) Paul Simpson featuring Adeva	Cooltempo	4
32	23	OF COURSE I'M LYING Yello	Mercury	3
22	24	CAN YOU KEEP A SECRET Brother Beyond	Parlophone	3

In these weeks ■ Legendary bluesman B.B. King had never featured in the UK singles chart until U2 released a track from their 'Rattle And Hum' album (15.04.89) ■ The Reynolds Girls sing *I'd Rather Jack Than Fleetwood Mac*. Singles buyers seemed to agree, as Fleetwood Mac are to have no more Top 40 singles to the end of 1991 (01.04.89)■

LW	TW	Title	Artist	Label	Wks
18	25	THE BEAT(EN) GENERATION	The The	Epic	3
17	26	CAN'T STAY AWAY FROM YOU	Gloria Estefan and Miami Sound Machine	Epic	9
27	27	SHE'S A MYSTERY TO ME	Roy Orbison	Virgin	3
34	28	ONLY THE LONELY	T'Pau	Siren	4
39	29	DEVOTION	Ten City	Atlantic	2
20	30	SLEEP TALK	Alyson Williams	Def Jam	6
40	31	BEAUTY'S ONLY SKIN DEEP	Aswad	Mango	2
23	32	ONE MAN	Chanelle	Cooltempo	6
-	33	BEDS ARE BURNING	Midnight Oil ●	Sprint	1
38	34	WHAT DOES IT TAKE	Then Jerico	London	2
-	35	ME MYSELF AND I	De La Soul ●	Big Life	1
-	36	REAL LOVE	Jody Watley	MCA	1
24	37	HELP!	Bananarama/La Na Nee Nee Noo Noo	London	8
-	38	REQUIEM	London Boys ●	Teldec	1
-	39	THIS IS YOUR LAND	Blow Monkeys	RCA	1
-	40	PLEASE DON'T BE SCARED	Barry Manilow	Arista	1

WEEK ENDING 22 APRIL 1989

LW	TW	Title	Artist	Label	Wks
1	1	ETERNAL FLAME	Bangles	CBS	5
2	2	IF YOU DON'T KNOW ME BY NOW	Simply Red	Elektra	3
7	3	BABY I DON'T CARE	Transvision Vamp	MCA	4
9	4	AMERICANOS	Holly Johnson	MCA	4
5	5	I BEG YOUR PARDON	Kon Kan	Atlantic	6
12	6	WHEN LOVE COMES TO TOWN	U2 with B.B. King	Island	2
4	7	STRAIGHT UP	Paula Abdul	Siren	8
3	8	LIKE A PRAYER	Madonna	Sire	6
19	9	GOOD THING	Fine Young Cannibals	London	2
8	10	THIS TIME I KNOW IT'S FOR REAL	Donna Summer	Warner Bros	8
6	11	TOO MANY BROKEN HEARTS	Jason Donovan	PWL	8
-	12	LULLABY	Cure	Fiction	1
-	13	THIS IS YOUR LAND	Simple Minds	Virgin	1
16	14	MYSTIFY	INXS	Mercury	3
11	15	PEOPLE HOLD ON	Coldcut featuring Lisa Stansfield	Ahead Of Our Time	5
10	16	KEEP ON MOVIN'	Soul II Soul featuring Caron Wheeler	10	6
21	17	GOT TO KEEP ON	Cookie Crew	ffrr	3
-	18	ONE	Metallica	Vertigo	1
13	19	PARADISE CITY	Guns N' Roses	Geffen	6
-	20	AIN'T NOBODY BETTER	Inner City	10	1
33	21	BEDS ARE BURNING	Midnight Oil	Sprint	2
14	22	I HAVEN'T STOPPED DANCING YET	Pat and Mick	PWL	5
-	23	WHO'S IN THE HOUSE	Beatmasters with Merlin	Rhythm King	1
38	24	REQUIEM	London Boys	Teldec	2
22	25	MUSICAL FREEDOM (MOVING ON UP)	Paul Simpson featuring Adeva	Cooltempo	5
35	26	ME MYSELF AND I	De La Soul	Big Life	2
15	27	DON'T BE CRUEL	Bobby Brown	MCA	4
23	28	OF COURSE I'M LYING	Yello	Mercury	4
28	29	ONLY THE LONELY	T'Pau	Siren	5
-	30	DO YOU BELIEVE IN SHAME	Duran Duran	EMI	1
36	31	REAL LOVE	Jody Watley	MCA	2
39	32	THIS IS YOUR LAND	Blow Monkeys	RCA	2
34	33	WHAT DOES IT TAKE	Then Jerico	London	3
31	34	BEAUTY'S ONLY SKIN DEEP	Aswad	Mango	3
40	35	PLEASE DON'T BE SCARED	Barry Manilow	Arista	2
-	36	YOU ON MY MIND	Swing Out Sister	Fontana	1
17	37	I'D RATHER JACK	Reynolds Girls	PWL	8
29	38	DEVOTION	Ten City	Atlantic	3
-	39	MISS YOU LIKE CRAZY	Natalie Cole	EMI USA	1
18	40	INTERNATIONAL RESCUE	We've Got A Fuzzbox And We're Gonna Use It	WEA	7

WEEK ENDING 29 APRIL 1989

May 1989

□ Highest position disc reached ● Act's first ever week on chart

LW	TW	Title	Artist	Label	Wks
1	1	ETERNAL FLAME	Bangles	CBS	6
2	2	IF YOU DON'T KNOW ME BY NOW	Simply Red	Elektra	4
3	3	BABY I DON'T CARE	Transvision Vamp	MCA	5
4	4	AMERICANOS	Holly Johnson	MCA	5
12	5	LULLABY	Cure	Fiction	2
5	6	I BEG YOUR PARDON	Kon Kan	Atlantic	7
9	7	GOOD THING	Fine Young Cannibals	London	3
23	8	WHO'S IN THE HOUSE	Beatmasters with Merlin	Rhythm King	2
-	9	INTERESTING DRUG	Morrissey	HMV	1
20	10	AIN'T NOBODY BETTER	Inner City	10	2
24	11	REQUIEM	London Boys	Teldec	3
21	12	BEDS ARE BURNING	Midnight Oil	Sprint	3
18	13	ONE	Metallica	Vertigo	2
6	14	WHEN LOVE COMES TO TOWN	U2 with B.B. King	Island	3
13	15	THIS IS YOUR LAND	Simple Minds	Virgin	2
7	16	STRAIGHT UP	Paula Abdul	Siren	9
17	17	GOT TO KEEP ON	Cookie Crew	ffrr	4
8	18	LIKE A PRAYER	Madonna	Sire	7
10	19	THIS TIME I KNOW IT'S FOR REAL	Donna Summer	Warner Bros	9
11	20	TOO MANY BROKEN HEARTS	Jason Donovan	PWL	9
14	21	MYSTIFY	INXS	Mercury	4
16	22	KEEP ON MOVIN'	Soul II Soul featuring Caron Wheeler	10	7
26	23	ME MYSELF AND I	De La Soul	Big Life	3
39	24	MISS YOU LIKE CRAZY	Natalie Cole	EMI USA	2
15	25	PEOPLE HOLD ON	Coldcut featuring Lisa Stansfield	Ahead Of Our Time	6
-	26	YOUR MAMA DON'T DANCE	Poison	Capitol	1
-	27	WHERE HAS ALL THE LOVE GONE	Yazz	Big Life	1
22	28	I HAVEN'T STOPPED DANCING YET	Pat and Mick	PWL	6
36	29	YOU ON MY MIND	Swing Out Sister	Fontana	2
-	30	I'LL BE THERE FOR YOU	Bon Jovi	Vertigo	1
30	31	DO YOU BELIEVE IN SHAME	Duran Duran	EMI	2
19	32	PARADISE CITY	Guns N' Roses	Geffen	7
-	33	ELECTRIC YOUTH	Debbie Gibson	Atlantic	1
28	34	OF COURSE I'M LYING	Yello	Mercury	5
31	35	REAL LOVE	Jody Watley	MCA	3
25	36	MUSICAL FREEDOM (MOVING ON UP)	Paul Simpson featuring Adeva	Cooltempo	6
35	37	PLEASE DON'T BE SCARED	Barry Manilow	Arista	3
27	38	DON'T BE CRUEL	Bobby Brown	MCA	5
32	39	THIS IS YOUR LAND	Blow Monkeys	RCA	3
-	40	THE LOOK	Roxette ●	EMI	1

WEEK ENDING 6 MAY 1989

LW	TW	Title	Artist	Label	Wks
1	1	ETERNAL FLAME	Bangles	CBS	7
-	2	HAND ON YOUR HEART	Kylie Minogue	PWL	1
2	3	IF YOU DON'T KNOW ME BY NOW	Simply Red	Elektra	5
3	4	BABY I DON'T CARE	Transvision Vamp	MCA	6
11	5	REQUIEM	London Boys	Teldec	4
4	6	AMERICANOS	Holly Johnson	MCA	6
24	7	MISS YOU LIKE CRAZY	Natalie Cole	EMI USA	3
8	8	WHO'S IN THE HOUSE	Beatmasters with Merlin	Rhythm King	3
12	9	BEDS ARE BURNING	Midnight Oil	Sprint	4
7	10	GOOD THING	Fine Young Cannibals	London	4
5	11	LULLABY	Cure	Fiction	3
9	12	INTERESTING DRUG	Morrissey	HMV	2
10	13	AIN'T NOBODY BETTER	Inner City	10	3
13	14	ONE	Metallica	Vertigo	3
6	15	I BEG YOUR PARDON	Kon Kan	Atlantic	8
26	16	YOUR MAMA DON'T DANCE	Poison	Capitol	2
27	17	WHERE HAS ALL THE LOVE GONE	Yazz	Big Life	2
30	18	I'LL BE THERE FOR YOU	Bon Jovi	Vertigo	2
17	19	GOT TO KEEP ON	Cookie Crew	ffrr	5
16	20	STRAIGHT UP	Paula Abdul	Siren	10
33	21	ELECTRIC YOUTH	Debbie Gibson	Atlantic	2
23	22	ME MYSELF AND I	De La Soul	Big Life	4
-	23	I'M EVERY WOMAN	Chaka Khan	Warner Bros	1
20	24	TOO MANY BROKEN HEARTS	Jason Donovan	PWL	10
18	25	LIKE A PRAYER	Madonna	Sire	8
40	26	THE LOOK	Roxette	EMI	2
14	27	WHEN LOVE COMES TO TOWN	U2 with B.B. King	Island	4
-	28	BRING ME EDELWEISS	Edelweiss ●	WEA	1

■T'Pau's *Only The Lonely* is not the classic song written and recorded by the man one place higher in the charts, Roy Orbison (15.04.89) ■ Only *I Beg Your Pardon* by Canadian act Kon Kan is not at its peak among the Top ten singles (29.04.89)■

May 1989

□ Highest position disc reached ● Act's first ever week on chart

LW	TW	Title / Artist	Label	Wks
19	29	THIS TIME I KNOW IT'S FOR REAL Donna Summer	*Warner Bros*	10
29	30	YOU ON MY MIND Swing Out Sister	*Fontana*	3
21	31	MYSTIFY INXS	*Mercury*	5
15	32	THIS IS YOUR LIFE Simple Minds	*Virgin*	3
22	33	KEEP ON MOVIN' Soul II Soul featuring Caron Wheeler	*10*	8
35	34	REAL LOVE Jody Watley	*MCA*	4
31	35	DO YOU BELIEVE IN SHAME Duran Duran	*EMI*	3
25	36	PEOPLE HOLD ON Coldcut featuring Lisa Stansfield	*Ahead Of Our Time*	7
-	37	ROOMS ON FIRE Stevie Nicks ●	*Modern*	1
28	38	I HAVEN'T STOPPED DANCING YET Pat and Mick	*PWL*	7
-	39	DON'T IT MAKE YOU FEEL GOOD Stefan Dennis ●	*Sublime*	1
32	40	PARADISE CITY Guns N' Roses	*Geffen*	8

WEEK ENDING 13 MAY 1989

LW	TW	Title / Artist	Label	Wks
2	[1]	HAND ON YOUR HEART Kylie Minogue	*PWL*	2
1	2	ETERNAL FLAME Bangles	*CBS*	8
-	[3]	I WANT IT ALL Queen	*Parlophone*	1
5	[4]	REQUIEM London Boys	*Teldec*	5
7	5	MISS YOU LIKE CRAZY Natalie Cole	*EMI USA*	4
9	[6]	BEDS ARE BURNING Midnight Oil	*Sprint*	5
28	7	BRING ME EDELWEISS Edelweiss	*WEA*	2
23	[8]	I'M EVERY WOMAN Chaka Khan	*Warner Bros*	2
4	9	BABY I DON'T CARE Transvision Vamp	*MCA*	7
6	10	AMERICANOS Holly Johnson	*MCA*	7
8	11	WHO'S IN THE HOUSE Beatmasters with Merlin	*Rhythm King*	4
3	12	IF YOU DON'T KNOW ME BY NOW Simply Red	*Elektra*	6
16	[13]	YOUR MAMA DON'T DANCE Poison	*Capitol*	3
26	14	THE LOOK Roxette	*EMI*	3
21	15	ELECTRIC YOUTH Debbie Gibson	*Atlantic*	3
17	[16]	WHERE HAS ALL THE LOVE GONE Yazz	*Big Life*	3
10	17	GOOD THING Fine Young Cannibals	*London*	5
18	[18]	I'LL BE THERE FOR YOU Bon Jovi	*Vertigo*	3
13	19	AIN'T NOBODY BETTER Inner City	*10*	4
14	20	ONE Metallica	*Vertigo*	4
37	21	ROOMS ON FIRE Stevie Nicks	*Modern*	2
39	22	DON'T IT MAKE YOU FEEL GOOD Stefan Dennis	*Sublime*	2
15	23	I BEG YOUR PARDON Kon Kan	*Atlantic*	9
11	24	LULLABY Cure	*Fiction*	4
22	25	ME MYSELF AND I De La Soul	*Big Life*	5
19	26	GOT TO KEEP ON Cookie Crew	*ffrr*	6
25	27	LIKE A PRAYER Madonna	*Sire*	9
30	28	YOU ON MY MIND Swing Out Sister	*Fontana*	4
-	29	VIOLENTLY (EP) Hue And Cry	*Circa*	1
33	30	KEEP ON MOVIN' Soul II Soul featuring Caron Wheeler	*10*	9
20	31	STRAIGHT UP Paula Abdul	*Siren*	11
12	32	INTERESTING DRUG Morrissey	*HMV*	3
-	33	WORKIN' OVERTIME Diana Ross	*EMI*	1
24	34	TOO MANY BROKEN HEARTS Jason Donovan	*PWL*	11
29	35	THIS TIME I KNOW IT'S FOR REAL Donna Summer	*Warner Bros*	11
-	36	LOVE ATTACK Shakin' Stevens	*Epic*	1
34	37	REAL LOVE Jody Watley	*MCA*	5
-	38	HELYOM HALIB Cappella ●	*Music Man*	1
-	39	MY LOVE IS SO RAW Alyson Williams Featuring Nikki-D	*Def Jam*	1
27	40	WHEN LOVE COMES TO TOWN U2 with B.B. King	*Island*	5

WEEK ENDING 20 MAY 1989

LW	TW	Title / Artist	Label	Wks
-	[1]	FERRY CROSS THE MERSEY Gerry Marsden, Paul McCartney, Holly Johnson and the Christians ●	*PWL*	1
1	2	HAND ON YOUR HEART Kylie Minogue	*PWL*	3
5	3	MISS YOU LIKE CRAZY Natalie Cole	*EMI USA*	5
4	[4]	REQUIEM London Boys	*Teldec*	6
3	5	I WANT IT ALL Queen	*Parlophone*	2
7	6	BRING ME EDELWEISS Edelweiss	*WEA*	3
2	7	ETERNAL FLAME Bangles	*CBS*	9
8	[8]	I'M EVERY WOMAN Chaka Khan	*Warner Bros*	3
6	9	BEDS ARE BURNING Midnight Oil	*Sprint*	6
14	10	THE LOOK Roxette	*EMI*	4
9	11	BABY I DON'T CARE Transvision Vamp	*MCA*	8
11	12	WHO'S IN THE HOUSE Beatmasters with Merlin	*Rhythm King*	5
10	13	AMERICANOS Holly Johnson	*MCA*	8
15	[14]	ELECTRIC YOUTH Debbie Gibson	*Atlantic*	4
12	15	IF YOU DON'T KNOW ME BY NOW Simply Red	*Elektra*	7
21	[16]	ROOMS ON FIRE Stevie Nicks	*Modern*	3
22	17	DON'T IT MAKE YOU FEEL GOOD Stefan Dennis	*Sublime*	3
13	18	YOUR MAMA DON'T DANCE Poison	*Capitol*	4
16	19	WHERE HAS ALL THE LOVE GONE Yazz	*Big Life*	4
-	20	EVERY LITTLE STEP Bobby Brown	*MCA*	1
29	[21]	VIOLENTLY (EP) Hue And Cry	*Circa*	2
-	22	MY BRAVE FACE Paul McCartney	*Parlophone*	1
38	23	HELYOM HALIB Cappella	*Music Man*	2
18	24	I'LL BE THERE FOR YOU Bon Jovi	*Vertigo*	4
-	25	FERGUS SINGS THE BLUES Deacon Blue	*CBS*	1
-	26	MANCHILD Neneh Cherry	*Circa*	1
17	27	GOOD THING Fine Young Cannibals	*London*	6
36	[28]	LOVE ATTACK Shakin' Stevens	*Epic*	2
28	29	YOU ON MY MIND Swing Out Sister	*Fontana*	5
-	30	ON THE INSIDE Lynne Hamilton ●	*A1*	1
-	31	CAN I GET A WITNESS Sam Brown	*A&M*	1
33	[32]	WORKIN' OVERTIME Diana Ross	*EMI*	2
23	33	I BEG YOUR PARDON Kon Kan	*Atlantic*	10
39	[34]	MY LOVE IS SO RAW Alyson Williams Featuring Nikki-D	*Def Jam*	2
-	35	CHANGE HIS WAYS Robert Palmer	*EMI*	1
20	36	ONE Metallica	*Vertigo*	5
19	37	AIN'T NOBODY BETTER Inner City	*10*	5
-	[38]	DISAPPOINTED Public Image Ltd	*Virgin*	1
30	39	KEEP ON MOVIN' Soul II Soul featuring Caron Wheeler	*10*	10
25	40	ME MYSELF AND I De La Soul	*Big Life*	6

WEEK ENDING 27 MAY 1989

LW	TW	Title / Artist	Label	Wks
1	[1]	FERRY CROSS THE MERSEY Gerry Marsden, Paul McCartney, Holly Johnson and the Christians	*PWL*	2
2	2	HAND ON YOUR HEART Kylie Minogue	*PWL*	4
3	3	MISS YOU LIKE CRAZY Natalie Cole	*EMI USA*	6
4	[4]	REQUIEM London Boys	*Teldec*	7
6	[5]	BRING ME EDELWEISS Edelweiss	*WEA*	4
20	[6]	EVERY LITTLE STEP Bobby Brown	*MCA*	2
10	[7]	THE LOOK Roxette	*EMI*	5
26	8	MANCHILD Neneh Cherry	*Circa*	2
5	9	I WANT IT ALL Queen	*Parlophone*	3
8	10	I'M EVERY WOMAN Chaka Khan	*Warner Bros*	4
7	11	ETERNAL FLAME Bangles	*CBS*	10
23	12	HELYOM HALIB Cappella	*Music Man*	3
30	13	ON THE INSIDE Lynne Hamilton	*A1*	2
25	[14]	FERGUS SINGS THE BLUES Deacon Blue	*CBS*	2
14	15	ELECTRIC YOUTH Debbie Gibson	*Atlantic*	5
17	[16]	DON'T IT MAKE YOU FEEL GOOD Stefan Dennis	*Sublime*	4
9	17	BEDS ARE BURNING Midnight Oil	*Sprint*	7
22	[18]	MY BRAVE FACE Paul McCartney	*Parlophone*	2
-	19	I DON'T WANNA GET HURT Donna Summer	*Warner Bros*	1
11	20	BABY I DON'T CARE Transvision Vamp	*MCA*	9
31	21	CAN I GET A WITNESS Sam Brown	*A&M*	2
16	22	ROOMS ON FIRE Stevie Nicks	*Modern*	4
21	23	VIOLENTLY (EP) Hue And Cry	*Circa*	3
13	24	AMERICANOS Holly Johnson	*MCA*	9
12	25	WHO'S IN THE HOUSE Beatmasters with Merlin	*Rhythm King*	6
-	26	FUNKY COLD MEDINA/ON FIRE Tone Loc	*Delicious*	1
-	27	THE REAL ME W.A.S.P.	*Capitol*	1
15	28	IF YOU DON'T KNOW ME BY NOW Simply Red	*Elektra*	8
28	29	LOVE ATTACK Shakin' Stevens	*Epic*	3
18	30	YOUR MAMA DON'T DANCE Poison	*Capitol*	5
35	31	CHANGE HIS WAYS Robert Palmer	*EMI*	2
19	32	WHERE HAS ALL THE LOVE GONE Yazz	*Big Life*	5
-	33	PINK SUNSHINE We've Got A Fuzzbox And We're Gonna Use It	*WEA*	1

In these weeks ■ Three 'Neighbours' stars in the chart: Kylie Minogue at number one, Stefan Dennis at number 22 and Jason Donovan at number 34 (13.05.89) ■ After the Hillsborough tragedy, another Gerry & the Pacemakers hit is re-recorded to create a number one charity single by four Liverpool acts. It is Paul McCartney's 21st number one (20.05.89)■

LW	TW	Title / Artist	Label	Wks
24	34	I'LL BE THERE FOR YOU Bon Jovi	*Vertigo*	5
-	[35]	PSYCHONAUT Fields Of The Nephilim	*Situation Two*	1
-	36	I DROVE ALL NIGHT Cyndi Lauper	*Epic*	1
-	37	NOTHIN' (THAT COMPARES 2 U) Jacksons	*Epic*	1
-	38	JUST KEEP ROCKIN' Double Trouble and the Rebel MC ●	*Desire*	1
38	39	DISAPPOINTED Public Image Ltd	*Virgin*	2
-	40	ONE BETTER WORLD ABC	*Neutron*	1

LW	TW	*WEEK ENDING* **3 JUNE 1989**		Wks
1	[1]	FERRY CROSS THE MERSEY Gerry Marsden, Paul McCartney, Holly Johnson and the Christians	*PWL*	3
3	[2]	MISS YOU LIKE CRAZY Natalie Cole	*EMI USA*	7
13	[3]	ON THE INSIDE Lynne Hamilton	*A1*	3
2	4	HAND ON YOUR HEART Kylie Minogue	*PWL*	5
8	[5]	MANCHILD Neneh Cherry	*Circa*	3
4	6	REQUIEM London Boys	*Teldec*	8
19	[7]	I DON'T WANNA GET HURT Donna Summer	*Warner Bros*	2
5	8	BRING ME EDELWEISS Edelweiss	*WEA*	5
6	9	EVERY LITTLE STEP Bobby Brown	*MCA*	3
-	10	EXPRESS YOURSELF Madonna	*Sire*	1
12	[11]	HELYOM HALIB Cappella	*Music Man*	4
7	12	THE LOOK Roxette	*EMI*	6
26	[13]	FUNKY COLD MEDINA/ON FIRE Tone Loc	*Delicious*	2
-	14	SWEET CHILD O' MINE Guns N' Roses	*Geffen*	1
21	[15]	CAN I GET A WITNESS Sam Brown	*A&M*	3
14	16	FERGUS SINGS THE BLUES Deacon Blue	*CBS*	3
10	17	I'M EVERY WOMAN Chaka Khan	*Warner Bros*	5
9	18	I WANT IT ALL Queen	*Parlophone*	4
-	19	RIGHT BACK WHERE WE STARTED FROM Sinitta	*Fanfare*	1
38	20	JUST KEEP ROCKIN' Double Trouble and the Rebel MC	*Desire*	2
16	21	DON'T IT MAKE YOU FEEL GOOD Stefan Dennis	*Sublime*	5
36	22	I DROVE ALL NIGHT Cyndi Lauper	*Epic*	2
27	[23]	THE REAL ME W.A.S.P.	*Capitol*	2
33	24	PINK SUNSHINE We've Got A Fuzzbox And We're Gonna Use It	*WEA*	2
-	25	IT IS TIME TO GET FUNKY D Mob featuring LRS	*London*	1
15	26	ELECTRIC YOUTH Debbie Gibson	*Atlantic*	6
11	27	ETERNAL FLAME Bangles	*CBS*	11
31	[28]	CHANGE HIS WAYS Robert Palmer	*EMI*	3
18	29	MY BRAVE FACE Paul McCartney	*Parlophone*	3
-	30	FOREVER YOUR GIRL Paula Abdul	*Siren*	1
17	31	BEDS ARE BURNING Midnight Oil	*Sprint*	8
40	[32]	ONE BETTER WORLD ABC	*Neutron*	2
37	[33]	NOTHIN' (THAT COMPARES 2 U) Jacksons	*Epic*	2
-	34	I WON'T BACK DOWN Tom Petty	*MCA*	1
-	35	SONG FOR WHOEVER Beautiful South ●	*Go! Discs*	1
35	36	PSYCHONAUT Fields Of The Nephilim	*Situation Two*	2
22	37	ROOMS ON FIRE Stevie Nicks	*Modern*	5
24	38	AMERICANOS Holly Johnson	*MCA*	10
-	39	WHO MADE ME Vixen	*EMI*	1
25	40	WHO'S IN THE HOUSE Beatmasters with Merlin	*Rhythm King*	7

LW	TW	*WEEK ENDING* **10 JUNE 1989**		Wks
-	[1]	SEALED WITH A KISS Jason Donovan	*PWL*	1
-	[2]	THE BEST OF ME Cliff Richard	*EMI*	1
1	3	FERRY CROSS THE MERSEY Gerry Marsden, Paul McCartney, Holly Johnson and the Christians	*PWL*	4
2	4	MISS YOU LIKE CRAZY Natalie Cole	*EMI USA*	8
10	[5]	EXPRESS YOURSELF Madonna	*Sire*	2
19	6	RIGHT BACK WHERE WE STARTED FROM Sinitta	*Fanfare*	2
3	7	ON THE INSIDE Lynne Hamilton	*A1*	4
14	8	SWEET CHILD O' MINE Guns N' Roses	*Geffen*	2
5	9	MANCHILD Neneh Cherry	*Circa*	4
7	10	I DON'T WANNA GET HURT Donna Summer	*Warner Bros*	3
4	11	HAND ON YOUR HEART Kylie Minogue	*PWL*	6
-	12	BACK TO LIFE (HOWEVER DO YOU WANT ME) Soul II Soul	*10*	1
6	13	REQUIEM London Boys	*Teldec*	9
9	14	EVERY LITTLE STEP Bobby Brown	*MCA*	4
8	15	BRING ME EDELWEISS Edelweiss	*WEA*	6

June 1989

□ Highest position disc reached ● Act's first ever week on chart

LW	TW	Title / Artist	Label	Wks
13	16	FUNKY COLD MEDINA/ON FIRE Tone Loc	*Delicious*	3
22	17	I DROVE ALL NIGHT Cyndi Lauper	*Epic*	3
20	18	JUST KEEP ROCKIN' Double Trouble and the Rebel MC	*Desire*	3
25	19	IT IS TIME TO GET FUNKY D Mob featuring LRS	*London*	2
11	20	HELYOM HALIB Cappella	*Music Man*	5
15	21	CAN I GET A WITNESS Sam Brown	*A&M*	4
24	22	PINK SUNSHINE We've Got A Fuzzbox And We're Gonna Use It	*WEA*	3
35	23	SONG FOR WHOEVER Beautiful South	*Go! Discs*	2
12	24	THE LOOK Roxette	*EMI*	7
-	25	THE ONLY ONE Transvision Vamp	*MCA*	1
30	26	FOREVER YOUR GIRL Paula Abdul	*Siren*	2
27	27	ETERNAL FLAME Bangles	*CBS*	12
16	28	FERGUS SINGS THE BLUES Deacon Blue	*CBS*	4
23	29	THE REAL ME W.A.S.P.	*Capitol*	3
21	30	DON'T IT MAKE YOU FEEL GOOD Stefan Dennis	*Sublime*	6
18	31	I WANT IT ALL Queen	*Parlophone*	5
17	32	I'M EVERY WOMAN Chaka Khan	*Warner Bros*	6
-	33	CRUEL SUMMER Bananarama	*London*	1
28	34	CHANGE HIS WAYS Robert Palmer	*EMI*	4
34	35	I WON'T BACK DOWN Tom Petty	*MCA*	2
39	[36]	WHO MADE ME Vixen	*EMI*	2
-	[37]	GREEN AND GREY New Model Army	*EMI*	1
-	38	JOY AND PAIN Donna Allen	*BCM*	1
-	39	ORANGE CRUSH REM ●	*Warner Bros*	1
33	40	NOTHIN' (THAT COMPARES 2 U) Jacksons	*Epic*	3

LW	TW	*WEEK ENDING* **17 JUNE 1989**		Wks
1	[1]	SEALED WITH A KISS Jason Donovan	*PWL*	2
2	[2]	THE BEST OF ME Cliff Richard	*EMI*	2
12	3	BACK TO LIFE (HOWEVER DO YOU WANT ME) Soul II Soul	*10*	2
6	[4]	RIGHT BACK WHERE WE STARTED FROM Sinitta	*Fanfare*	3
5	[5]	EXPRESS YOURSELF Madonna	*Sire*	3
8	[6]	SWEET CHILD O' MINE Guns N' Roses	*Geffen*	3
4	7	MISS YOU LIKE CRAZY Natalie Cole	*EMI USA*	9
17	8	I DROVE ALL NIGHT Cyndi Lauper	*Epic*	4
10	9	I DON'T WANNA GET HURT Donna Summer	*Warner Bros*	4
9	10	MANCHILD Neneh Cherry	*Circa*	5
23	11	SONG FOR WHOEVER Beautiful South	*Go! Discs*	3
19	12	IT IS TIME TO GET FUNKY D Mob featuring LRS	*London*	3
7	13	ON THE INSIDE Lynne Hamilton	*A1*	5
3	14	FERRY CROSS THE MERSEY Gerry Marsden, Paul McCartney, Holly Johnson and the Christians	*PWL*	5
25	[15]	THE ONLY ONE Transvision Vamp	*MCA*	2
18	16	JUST KEEP ROCKIN' Double Trouble and the Rebel MC	*Desire*	4
22	17	PINK SUNSHINE We've Got A Fuzzbox And We're Gonna Use It	*WEA*	4
11	18	HAND ON YOUR HEART Kylie Minogue	*PWL*	7
16	19	FUNKY COLD MEDINA/ON FIRE Tone Loc	*Delicious*	4
33	20	CRUE SUMMER Bananarama	*London*	2
13	21	REQUIEM London Boys	*Teldec*	10
38	22	JOY AND PAIN Donna Allen	*BCM*	2
14	23	EVERY LITTLE STEP Bobby Brown	*MCA*	5
26	[24]	FOREVER YOUR GIRL Paula Abdul	*Siren*	3
15	25	BRING ME EDELWEISS Edelweiss	*WEA*	7
20	26	HELYOM HALIB Cappella	*Music Man*	6
21	27	CAN I GET A WITNESS Sam Brown	*A&M*	5
39	[28]	ORANGE CRUSH REM	*Warner Bros*	2
35	29	I WON'T BACK DOWN Tom Petty	*MCA*	3
-	30	IN A LIFETIME Clannad, additional vocals: Bono	*RCA*	1
-	31	BE WITH YOU Bangles	*CBS*	1
24	32	THE LOOK Roxette	*EMI*	8
-	33	TILL I LOVED YOU Placido Domingo and Jennifer Rush ●	*CBS*	1
-	34	SUPERWOMAN Karyn White ●	*Warner Bros*	1
-	35	WALTZ DARLING Malcolm McLaren	*Epic*	1
36	[36]	WHO MADE ME Vixen	*EMI*	3
37	[37]	GREEN AND GREY New Model Army	*EMI*	2

■Cliff Richard's 100th single gives him his highest debut position since *The Young Ones* crashed straight in at number one 27 years and 150 days earlier (10.06.89) ■ Sam Brown's version of Marvin Gaye's classic *Can I Get A Witness* gives the song its only chart outing in Britain (03.06.89)■

June 1989

☐ Highest position disc reached ● Act's first ever week on chart

LW	TW	Title	Artist	Label	Wks
27	38	ETERNAL FLAME	Bangles	CBS	13
-	39	GATECRASHING	Living In A Box	Chrysalis	1
-	40	LICENCE TO KILL	Gladys Knight	MCA	1

WEEK ENDING 24 JUNE 1989

LW	TW	Title	Artist	Label	Wks
3	[1]	BACK TO LIFE (HOWEVER DO YOU WANT ME)	Soul II Soul	10	3
1	2	SEALED WITH A KISS	Jason Donovan	PWL	3
-	3	BATDANCE	Prince	Warner Brothers	1
4	[4]	RIGHT BACK WHERE WE STARTED FROM	Sinitta	Fanfare	4
-	5	ALL I WANT IS YOU	U2	Island	1
2	6	THE BEST OF ME	Cliff Richard	EMI	3
8	[7]	I DROVE ALL NIGHT	Cyndi Lauper	Epic	5
11	8	SONG FOR WHOEVER	Beautiful South	Go! Discs	4
6	9	SWEET CHILD O' MINE	Guns N' Roses	Geffen	4
5	10	EXPRESS YOURSELF	Madonna	Sire	4
12	11	IT IS TIME TO GET FUNKY	D Mob featuring LRS	London	4
7	12	MISS YOU LIKE CRAZY	Natalie Cole	EMI USA	10
16	13	JUST KEEP ROCKIN'	Double Trouble and the Rebel MC	Desire	5
17	[14]	PINK SUNSHINE	We've Got A Fuzzbox And We're Gonna Use It	WEA	5
22	15	JOY AND PAIN	Donna Allen	BCM	3
9	16	I DON'T WANNA GET HURT	Donna Summer	Warner Bros	5
15	17	THE ONLY ONE	Transvision Vamp	MCA	3
10	18	MANCHILD	Neneh Cherry	Circa	6
20	[19]	CRUE SUMMER	Bananarama	London	3
40	20	LICENCE TO KILL	Gladys Knight	MCA	2
30	21	IN A LIFETIME	Clannad, additional vocals: Bono	RCA	2
13	22	ON THE INSIDE	Lynne Hamilton	A1	6
19	23	FUNKY COLD MEDINA/ON FIRE	Tone Loc	Delicious	5
33	[24]	TILL I LOVED YOU	Placido Domingo and Jennifer Rush	CBS	2
34	25	SUPERWOMAN	Karyn White	Warner Bros	2
31	26	BE WITH YOU	Bangles	CBS	2
-	27	ATOMIC CITY	Holly Johnson	MCA	1
29	[28]	I WON'T BACK DOWN	Tom Petty	MCA	4
18	29	HAND ON YOUR HEART	Kylie Minogue	PWL	8
24	30	FOREVER YOUR GIRL	Paula Abdul	Siren	4
35	[31]	WALTZ DARLING	Malcolm McLaren	Epic	2
21	32	REQUIEM	London Boys	Teldec	11
28	33	ORANGE CRUSH	REM	Warner Bros	3
14	34	FERRY CROSS THE MERSEY	Gerry Marsden, Paul McCartney, Holly Johnson and the Christians	PWL	6
-	35	FIGHT THE POWER	Public Enemy	Motown	1
23	36	EVERY LITTLE STEP	Bobby Brown	MCA	6
39	37	GATECRASHING	Living In A Box	Chrysalis	2
-	38	POP MUZIK	M	Freestyle	1
-	39	LOOKING FOR A LOVE	Joyce Sims	Sleeping Bag	1
-	40	CRY	Waterfront ●	Polydor	1

WEEK ENDING 1 JULY 1989

LW	TW	Title	Artist	Label	Wks
1	[1]	BACK TO LIFE (HOWEVER DO YOU WANT ME)	Soul II Soul	10	4
3	[2]	BATDANCE	Prince	Warner Brothers	2
8	3	SONG FOR WHOEVER	Beautiful South	Go! Discs	5
5	4	ALL I WANT IS YOU	U2	Island	2
2	5	SEALED WITH A KISS	Jason Donovan	PWL	4
4	6	RIGHT BACK WHERE WE STARTED FROM	Sinitta	Fanfare	5
7	[7]	I DROVE ALL NIGHT	Cyndi Lauper	Epic	6
20	8	LICENCE TO KILL	Gladys Knight	MCA	3
11	9	IT IS TIME TO GET FUNKY	D Mob featuring LRS	London	5
15	[10]	JOY AND PAIN	Donna Allen	BCM	4
13	[11]	JUST KEEP ROCKIN'	Double Trouble and the Rebel MC	Desire	6
9	12	SWEET CHILD O'MINE	Guns N' Roses	Geffen	5
-	13	BREAKTHRU'	Queen	Parlophone	1
6	14	THE BEST OF ME	Cliff Richard	EMI	4
10	15	EXPRESS YOURSELF	Madonna	Sire	5
14	16	PINK SUNSHINE	We've Got A Fuzzbox And We're Gonna Use It	WEA	6
21	[17]	IN A LIFETIME	Clannad additional vocals: Bono	RCA	3
27	[18]	ATOMIC CITY	Holly Johnson	MCA	2
-	19	LONDON NIGHTS	London Boys	Teldec	1
38	20	POP MUZIK	M	Freestyle	2
16	21	I DON'T WANNA GET HURT	Donna Summer	Warner Bros	6
-	22	PATIENCE	Guns N' Roses	Geffen	2
26	[23]	BE WITH YOU	Bangles	CBS	3
12	24	MISS YOU LIKE CRAZY	Natalie Cole	EMI USA	11
25	25	SUPERWOMAN	Karyn White	Warner Bros	3
24	26	TILL I LOVED YOU	Placido Domingo and Jennifer Rush	CBS	3
19	27	CRUEL SUMMER	Bananarama	London	4
17	28	THE ONLY ONE	Transvision Vamp	MCA	4
18	29	MANCHILD	Neneh Cherry	Circa	7
35	30	FIGHT THE POWER	Public Enemy	Motown	2
31	[31]	WALTZ DARLING	Malcolm McLaren	Epic	3
23	32	FUNKY COLD MEDINA/ON FIRE	Tone Loc	Delicious	6
40	33	CRY	Waterfront	Polydor	2
28	34	I WON'T BACK DOWN	Tom Petty	MCA	5
29	35	HAND ON YOUR HEART	Kylie Minogue	PWL	9
37	[36]	GATECRASHING	Living In A Box	Chrysalis	3
-	37	GRANDPA'S PARTY	Monie Love	Cooltempo	2
-	38	YOU'LL NEVER STOP ME LOVING YOU	Sonia ●	Chrysalis	2
39	[39]	LOOKING FOR A LOVE	Joyce Sims	Sleeping Bag	3
-	40	VOODOO RAY	A Guy Called Gerald ●	Rham!	2

WEEK ENDING 8 JULY 1989

LW	TW	Title	Artist	Label	Wks
1	[1]	BACK TO LIFE (HOWEVER DO YOU WANT ME)	Soul II Soul	10	5
3	[2]	SONG FOR WHOEVER	Beautiful South	Go! Discs	6
19	3	LONDON NIGHTS	London Boys	Teldec	3
2	4	BATDANCE	Prince	Warner Brothers	3
-	[5]	IT'S ALRIGHT	Pet Shop Boys	Parlophone	1
8	[6]	LICENCE TO KILL	Gladys Knight	MCA	4
13	[7]	BREAKTHRU'	Queen	Parlophone	2
4	8	ALL I WANT IS YOU	U2	Island	3
7	9	I DROVE ALL NIGHT	Cyndi Lauper	Epic	7
22	[10]	PATIENCE	Guns N' Roses	Geffen	2
11	[11]	JUST KEEP ROCKIN'	Double Trouble and the Rebel MC	Desire	7
38	12	YOU'LL NEVER STOP ME LOVING YOU	Sonia	Chrysalis	2
6	13	RIGHT BACK WHERE WE STARTED FROM	Sinitta	Fanfare	6
5	14	SEALED WITH A KISS	Jason Donovan	PWL	5
20	[15]	POP MUZIK	M	Freestyle	3
9	16	IT IS TIME TO GET FUNKY	D Mob featuring LRS	London	6
10	17	JOY AND PAIN	Donna Allen	BCM	5
-	18	AIN'T NOBODY	Rufus and Chaka Khan	Warner Bros	1
17	19	IN A LIFETIME	Clannad additional vocals: Bono	RCA	4
12	20	SWEET CHILD O'MINE	Guns N' Roses	Geffen	6
25	21	SUPERWOMAN	Karyn White	Warner Bros	4
37	22	GRANDPA'S PARTY	Monie Love	Cooltempo	2
23	[23]	BE WITH YOU	Bangles	CBS	4
15	24	EXPRESS YOURSELF	Madonna	Sire	6
18	25	ATOMIC CITY	Holly Johnson	MCA	3
40	26	VOODOO RAY	A Guy Called Gerald	Rham!	2
33	27	CRY	Waterfront	Polydor	3
16	28	PINK SUNSHINE	We've Got A Fuzzbox And We're Gonna Use It	WEA	7
30	[29]	FIGHT THE POWER	Public Enemy	Motown	3
-	30	WIND BENEATH MY WINGS	Bette Midler ●	Atlantic	1
21	31	I DON'T WANNA GET HURT	Donna Summer	Warner Bros	7
-	32	THE SECOND SUMMER OF LOVE	Danny Wilson	Virgin	1
-	33	SAY NO GO	De La Soul	Tommy Boy	1
24	34	MISS YOU LIKE CRAZY	Natalie Cole	EMI USA	12
14	35	THE BEST OF ME	Cliff Richard	EMI	5
-	36	DAYS	Kirsty MacColl	Virgin	1
26	37	TILL I LOVED YOU	Placido Domingo and Jennifer Rush	CBS	4
-	38	WON'T TALK ABOUT IT/BLAME IT ON THE BASSLINE	Norman Cook ●	Go! Discs	1
-	39	GET LOOSE	LA Mix	Breakout	1
29	40	MANCHILD	Neneh Cherry	Circa	8

In these weeks ■ Two Housemartins' spin-off acts hit the chart - Beautiful South at number two contain Paul Heaton and Dave Hemmingway, while Norman Cook debuts at no. 38 (08.07.89) ■ Monie Love enjoys chart success with *Grandpa's Party*, but it is not the success that *Grandma's Party* was in 1976, when Paul Nicholas hit the top ten (01.07.89)■

LW	TW	WEEK ENDING 15 JULY 1989		Wks
1	1	BACK TO LIFE (HOWEVER DO YOU WANT ME) Soul II Soul	10	6
12	2	YOU'LL NEVER STOP ME LOVING YOU Sonia	Chrysalis	3
3	3	LONDON NIGHTS London Boys	Teldec	4
2	4	SONG FOR WHOEVER Beautiful South	Go! Discs	7
5	5	IT'S ALRIGHT Pet Shop Boys	Parlophone	2
18	6	AIN'T NOBODY Rufus and Chaka Khan	Warner Bros	2
6	7	LICENCE TO KILL Gladys Knight	MCA	5
-	8	ON OUR OWN Bobby Brown	MCA	1
30	9	WIND BENEATH MY WINGS Bette Midler	Atlantic	2
4	10	BATDANCE Prince	Warner Brothers	4
21	11	SUPERWOMAN Karyn White	Warner Bros	5
26	12	VOODOO RAY A Guy Called Gerald	Rham!	3
7	13	BREAKTHRU' Queen	Parlophone	3
10	14	PATIENCE Guns N' Roses	Geffen	3
9	15	I DROVE ALL NIGHT Cyndi Lauper	Epic	8
11	16	JUST KEEP ROCKIN' Double Trouble and the Rebel MC	Desire	8
15	17	POP MUZIK M	Freestyle	4
-	18	LIBERIAN GIRL Michael Jackson	Epic	1
22	19	GRANDPA'S PARTY Monie Love	Cooltempo	3
13	20	RIGHT BACK WHERE WE STARTED FROM Sinitta	Fanfare	7
14	21	SEALED WITH A KISS Jason Donovan	PWL	6
33	22	SAY NO GO De La Soul	Tommy Boy	2
8	23	ALL I WANT IS YOU U2	Island	4
17	24	JOY AND PAIN Donna Allen	BCM	6
27	25	CRY Waterfront	Polydor	4
16	26	IT IS TIME TO GET FUNKY D Mob featuring LRS	London	7
32	27	THE SECOND SUMMER OF LOVE Danny Wilson	Virgin	2
36	28	DAYS Kirsty MacColl	Virgin	2
39	29	GET LOOSE LA Mix	Breakout	2
-	30	DON'T WANNA LOSE YOU Gloria Estefan	Epic	1
38	31	WON'T TALK ABOUT IT/BLAME IT ON THE BASSLINE Norman Cook	Go! Discs	2
20	32	SWEET CHILD O'MINE Guns N' Roses	Geffen	7
-	33	A NEW FLAME Simply Red	WEA	1
24	34	EXPRESS YOURSELF Madonna	Sire	7
23	35	BE WITH YOU Bangles	CBS	5
19	36	IN A LIFETIME Clannad additional vocals: Bono	RCA	5
-	37	EDIE (CIAO BABY) Cult	Beggars Banquet	1
29	38	FIGHT THE POWER Public Enemy	Motown	4
28	39	PINK SUNSHINE We've Got A Fuzzbox And We're Gonna Use It	WEA	8
-	40	CHOICE Blow Monkeys featuring Sylvia Tella	RCA	1

LW	TW	WEEK ENDING 22 JULY 1989		Wks
2	1	YOU'LL NEVER STOP ME LOVING YOU Sonia	Chrysalis	4
3	2	LONDON NIGHTS London Boys	Teldec	5
1	3	BACK TO LIFE (HOWEVER DO YOU WANT ME) Soul II Soul	10	7
8	4	ON OUR OWN Bobby Brown	MCA	2
9	5	WIND BENEATH MY WINGS Bette Midler	Atlantic	3
6	6	AIN'T NOBODY Rufus and Chaka Khan	Warner Bros	3
5	7	IT'S ALRIGHT Pet Shop Boys	Parlophone	3
4	8	SONG FOR WHOEVER Beautiful South	Go! Discs	8
30	9	DON'T WANNA LOSE YOU Gloria Estefan	Epic	2
7	10	LICENCE TO KILL Gladys Knight	MCA	6
11	11	SUPERWOMAN Karyn White	Warner Bros	6
12	12	VOODOO RAY A Guy Called Gerald	Rham!	4
18	13	LIBERIAN GIRL Michael Jackson	Epic	2
10	14	BATDANCE Prince	Warner Brothers	5
28	15	DAYS Kirsty MacColl	Virgin	3
19	16	GRANDPA'S PARTY Monie Love	Cooltempo	4
25	17	CRY Waterfront	Polydor	5
22	18	SAY NO GO De La Soul	Tommy Boy	3
14	19	PATIENCE Guns N' Roses	Geffen	4
33	20	A NEW FLAME Simply Red	WEA	2
13	21	BREAKTHRU' Queen	Parlophone	4
16	22	JUST KEEP ROCKIN' Double Trouble and the Rebel MC	Desire	9
27	23	THE SECOND SUMMER OF LOVE Danny Wilson	Virgin	3
15	24	I DROVE ALL NIGHT Cyndi Lauper	Epic	9
29	25	GET LOOSE LA Mix	Breakout	3

August 1989

□ Highest position disc reached ● Act's first ever week on chart

LW	TW	WEEK ENDING 22 JULY 1989 (continued)		Wks
17	26	POP MUZIK M	Freestyle	5
40	27	CHOICE Blow Monkeys featuring Sylvia Tella	RCA	2
20	28	RIGHT BACK WHERE WE STARTED FROM Sinitta	Fanfare	8
31	29	WON'T TALK ABOUT IT/BLAME IT ON THE BASSLINE Norman Cook	Go! Discs	3
21	30	SEALED WITH A KISS Jason Donovan	PWL	7
-	31	SWING THE MOOD Jive Bunny and the Mastermixers ●	Music Factory Dance	1
37	32	EDIE (CIAO BABY) Cult	Beggars Banquet	2
24	33	JOY AND PAIN Donna Allen	BCM	7
23	34	ALL I WANT IS YOU U2	Island	5
26	35	IT IS TIME TO GET FUNKY D Mob featuring LRS	London	8
-	36	LET IT ROLL Raze presents Doug Lazy ●	Atlantic	1
34	37	EXPRESS YOURSELF Madonna	Sire	8
35	38	BE WITH YOU Bangles	CBS	6
-	39	CHA CHA HEELS Eartha Kitt and Bronski Beat ●	Arista	1
32	40	SWEET CHILD O'MINE Guns N' Roses	Geffen	8

LW	TW	WEEK ENDING 29 JULY 1989		Wks
1	1	YOU'LL NEVER STOP ME LOVING YOU Sonia	Chrysalis	5
-	2	TOO MUCH Bros	CBS	1
31	3	SWING THE MOOD Jive Bunny and the Mastermixers	Music Factory Dance	2
2	4	LONDON NIGHTS London Boys	Teldec	6
4	5	ON OUR OWN Bobby Brown	MCA	3
9	6	DON'T WANNA LOSE YOU Gloria Estefan	Epic	3
6	7	AIN'T NOBODY Rufus and Chaka Khan	Warner Bros	4
5	8	WIND BENEATH MY WINGS Bette Midler	Atlantic	4
3	9	BACK TO LIFE (HOWEVER DO YOU WANT ME) Soul II Soul	10	8
-	10	FRENCH KISS Lil Louis ●	ffrr	1
11	11	SUPERWOMAN Karyn White	Warner Bros	7
7	12	IT'S ALRIGHT Pet Shop Boys	Parlophone	4
10	13	LICENCE TO KILL Gladys Knight	MCA	7
15	14	DAYS Kirsty MacColl	Virgin	4
12	15	VOODOO RAY A Guy Called Gerald	Rham!	5
13	16	LIBERIAN GIRL Michael Jackson	Epic	3
20	17	A NEW FLAME Simply Red	WEA	3
17	18	CRY Waterfront	Polydor	6
8	19	SONG FOR WHOEVER Beautiful South	Go! Discs	9
18	20	SAY NO GO De La Soul	Tommy Boy	4
16	21	GRANDPA'S PARTY Monie Love	Cooltempo	5
27	22	CHOICE Blow Monkeys featuring Sylvia Tella	RCA	3
-	23	KICK IT IN Simple Minds	Virgin	1
14	24	BATDANCE Prince	Warner Brothers	6
25	25	GET LOOSE LA Mix	Breakout	4
23	26	THE SECOND SUMMER OF LOVE Danny Wilson	Virgin	4
36	27	LET IT ROLL Raze presents Doug Lazy	Atlantic	2
-	28	DO YOU LOVE WHAT YOU FEEL Inner City	10	1
22	29	JUST KEEP ROCKIN' Double Trouble and the Rebel MC	Desire	10
29	30	WON'T TALK ABOUT IT/BLAME IT ON THE BASSLINE Norman Cook	Go! Discs	4
19	31	PATIENCE Guns N' Roses	Geffen	5
39	32	CHA CHA HEELS Eartha Kitt and Bronski Beat	Arista	2
-	33	SICK OF IT Primitives	Lazy	1
-	34	POISON Alice Cooper	Epic	1
-	35	BETTER DAYS Gun ●	A&M	1
-	36	SHE BANGS THE DRUMS Stone Roses ●	Silvertone	1
-	37	THIS ONE Paul McCartney	Parlophone	1
30	38	SEALED WITH A KISS Jason Donovan	PWL	8
32	39	EDIE (CIAO BABY) Cult	Beggars Banquet	3
-	40	SATISFACTION Wendy and Lisa ●	Virgin	1

LW	TW	WEEK ENDING 5 AUGUST 1989		Wks
3	1	SWING THE MOOD Jive Bunny and the Mastermixers	Music Factory Dance	3

■Bobby Brown's records enjoyed more weeks on the chart in 1989 than any other artist, but number 4 is the highest chart placing he achieved (22.07.89) ■ Jive Bunny's *Swing The Mood* is the first medley to top the charts since Winifred Atwell's *Let's Have Another Party* at Christmas 1954 (05.08.89) ■ *Too Much* is Bros' first hit since the departure of Craig Logan (29.07.89)■

August 1989

□ Highest position disc reached ● Act's first ever week on chart

LW	TW	Title	Artist	Label	Wks
-	2	WOULDN'T CHANGE A THING	Kylie Minogue	*PWL*	1
1	3	YOU'LL NEVER STOP ME LOVING YOU	Sonia	*Chrysalis*	6
2	4	TOO MUCH	Bros	*CBS*	2
10	5	FRENCH KISS	Lil Louis	*ffrr*	2
6	6	DON'T WANNA LOSE YOU	Gloria Estefan	*Epic*	4
5	7	ON OUR OWN	Bobby Brown	*MCA*	4
4	8	LONDON NIGHTS	London Boys	*Teldec*	7
7	9	AIN'T NOBODY	Rufus and Chaka Khan	*Warner Bros*	5
8	10	WIND BENEATH MY WINGS	Bette Midler	*Atlantic*	5
9	11	BACK TO LIFE (HOWEVER DO YOU WANT ME)	Soul II Soul	*10*	9
14	12	DAYS	Kirsty MacColl	*Virgin*	5
34	13	POISON	Alice Cooper	*Epic*	2
11	14	SUPERWOMAN	Karyn White	*Warner Bros*	8
23	15	KICK IT IN	Simple Minds	*Virgin*	2
28	16	DO YOU LOVE WHAT YOU FEEL	Inner City	*10*	2
17	17	A NEW FLAME	Simply Red	*WEA*	4
13	18	LICENCE TO KILL	Gladys Knight	*MCA*	8
-	19	LANDSLIDE OF LOVE	Transvision Vamp	*MCA*	1
15	20	VOODOO RAY	A Guy Called Gerald	*Rham!*	6
12	21	IT'S ALRIGHT	Pet Shop Boys	*Parlophone*	5
22	22	CHOICE	Blow Monkeys featuring Sylvia Tella	*RCA*	4
24	23	BATDANCE	Prince	*Warner Brothers*	7
33	24	SICK OF IT	Primitives	*Lazy*	2
18	25	CRY	Waterfront	*Polydor*	7
-	26	YOU'RE HISTORY	Shakespear's Sister ●	*ffrr*	1
-	27	TOY SOLDIERS	Martika ●	*CBS*	1
20	28	SAY NO GO	De La Soul	*Tommy Boy*	5
21	29	GRANDPA'S PARTY	Monie Love	*Cooltempo*	6
37	30	THIS ONE	Paul McCartney	*Parlophone*	2
16	31	LIBERIAN GIRL	Michael Jackson	*Epic*	4
-	32	PURE	Lightning Seeds ●	*Ghetto*	1
35	33	BETTER DAYS	Gun	*A&M*	2
40	34	SATISFACTION	Wendy and Lisa	*Virgin*	2
-	35	SATELLITE KID	Dogs D'Amour ●	*China*	1
-	36	DO THE RIGHT THING	Redhead Kingpin and the FBI ●	*10*	1
19	37	SONG FOR WHOEVER	Beautiful South	*Go! Discs*	10
32	38	CHA CHA HEELS	Eartha Kitt and Bronski Beat	*Arista*	3
26	39	THE SECOND SUMMER OF LOVE	Danny Wilson	*Virgin*	5
-	40	ON AND ON	Aswad	*Mango*	1

WEEK ENDING 12 AUGUST 1989

LW	TW	Title	Artist	Label	Wks
1	1	SWING THE MOOD	Jive Bunny and the Mastermixers	*Music Factory Dance*	4
2	2	WOULDN'T CHANGE A THING	Kylie Minogue	*PWL*	2
5	3	FRENCH KISS	Lil Louis	*ffrr*	3
3	4	YOU'LL NEVER STOP ME LOVING YOU	Sonia	*Chrysalis*	7
13	5	POISON	Alice Cooper	*Epic*	3
6	6	DON'T WANNA LOSE YOU	Gloria Estefan	*Epic*	5
4	7	TOO MUCH	Bros	*CBS*	3
7	8	ON OUR OWN	Bobby Brown	*MCA*	5
27	9	TOY SOLDIERS	Martika	*CBS*	2
9	10	AIN'T NOBODY	Rufus and Chaka Khan	*Warner Bros*	6
10	11	WIND BENEATH MY WINGS	Bette Midler	*Atlantic*	6
8	12	LONDON NIGHTS	London Boys	*Teldec*	8
26	13	YOU'RE HISTORY	Shakespear's Sister	*ffrr*	2
19	14	LANDSLIDE OF LOVE	Transvision Vamp	*MCA*	2
12	15	DAYS	Kirsty MacColl	*Virgin*	6
32	16	PURE	Lightning Seeds	*Ghetto*	2
16	17	DO YOU LOVE WHAT YOU FEEL	Inner City	*10*	3
30	18	THIS ONE	Paul McCartney	*Parlophone*	3
11	19	BACK TO LIFE (HOWEVER DO YOU WANT ME)	Soul II Soul	*10*	10
15	20	KICK IT IN	Simple Minds	*Virgin*	3
17	21	A NEW FLAME	Simply Red	*WEA*	5
14	22	SUPERWOMAN	Karyn White	*Warner Bros*	9
36	23	DO THE RIGHT THING	Redhead Kingpin and the FBI	*10*	2
-	24	LOSING MY MIND	Liza Minnelli ●	*Epic*	1
-	25	BLAME IT ON THE BOOGIE	Big Fun ●	*Jive*	1
35	26	SATELLITE KID	Dogs D'Amour	*China*	2
34	27	SATISFACTION	Wendy and Lisa	*Virgin*	3
-	28	RIDE ON TIME	Black Box ●	*deConstruction*	1
20	29	VOODOO RAY	A Guy Called Gerald	*Rham!*	7
22	30	CHOICE	Blow Monkeys featuring Sylvia Tella	*RCA*	5
23	31	BATDANCE	Prince	*Warner Brothers*	8
40	32	ON AND ON	Aswad	*Mango*	2
18	33	LICENCE TO KILL	Gladys Knight	*MCA*	9
33	34	BETTER DAYS	Gun	*A&M*	3
-	35	HEY DJ I CAN'T DANCE TO THAT MUSIC YOU'RE PLAYING/ SKA TRAIN	Beatmasters featuring Betty Boo	*Rhythm King*	1
24	36	SICK OF IT	Primitives	*Lazy*	3
-	37	THIS IS THE RIGHT TIME	Lisa Stansfield ●	*Arista*	1
-	38	SELF!	We've Got A Fuzzbox And We're Gonna Use It	*WEA*	1
-	39	KISSES ON THE WIND	Neneh Cherry	*Circa*	1
21	40	IT'S ALRIGHT	Pet Shop Boys	*Parlophone*	6

WEEK ENDING 19 AUGUST 1989

LW	TW	Title	Artist	Label	Wks
1	1	SWING THE MOOD	Jive Bunny and the Mastermixers	*Music Factory Dance*	5
3	2	FRENCH KISS	Lil Louis	*ffrr*	4
2	3	WOULDN'T CHANGE A THING	Kylie Minogue	*PWL*	3
5	4	POISON	Alice Cooper	*Epic*	4
9	5	TOY SOLDIERS	Martika	*CBS*	3
24	6	LOSING MY MIND	Liza Minnelli	*Epic*	2
13	7	YOU'RE HISTORY	Shakespear's Sister	*ffrr*	3
25	8	BLAME IT ON THE BOOGIE	Big Fun	*Jive*	2
6	9	DON'T WANNA LOSE YOU	Gloria Estefan	*Epic*	6
4	10	YOU'LL NEVER STOP ME LOVING YOU	Sonia	*Chrysalis*	8
28	11	RIDE ON TIME	Black Box	*deConstruction*	2
8	12	ON OUR OWN	Bobby Brown	*MCA*	6
23	13	DO THE RIGHT THING	Redhead Kingpin and the FBI	*10*	3
35	14	HEY DJ I CAN'T DANCE TO THAT MUSIC YOU'RE PLAYING/ SKA TRAIN	Beatmasters featuring Betty Boo	*Rhythm King*	2
7	15	TOO MUCH	Bros	*CBS*	4
16	16	PURE	Lightning Seeds	*Ghetto*	3
37	17	THIS IS THE RIGHT TIME	Lisa Stansfield	*Arista*	2
14	18	LANDSLIDE OF LOVE	Transvision Vamp	*MCA*	3
11	19	WIND BENEATH MY WINGS	Bette Midler	*Atlantic*	7
10	20	AIN'T NOBODY	Rufus and Chaka Khan	*Warner Bros*	7
17	21	DO YOU LOVE WHAT YOU FEEL	Inner City	*10*	4
18	22	THIS ONE	Paul McCartney	*Parlophone*	4
39	23	KISSES ON THE WIND	Neneh Cherry	*Circa*	2
38	24	SELF!	We've Got A Fuzzbox And We're Gonna Use It	*WEA*	2
32	25	ON AND ON	Aswad	*Mango*	3
-	26	THE INVISIBLE MAN	Queen	*Parlophone*	1
12	27	LONDON NIGHTS	London Boys	*Teldec*	9
15	28	DAYS	Kirsty MacColl	*Virgin*	7
19	29	BACK TO LIFE (HOWEVER DO YOU WANT ME)	Soul II Soul	*10*	11
31	30	BATDANCE	Prince	*Warner Brothers*	9
-	31	FRIENDS	Jody Watley with Eric B and Rakim	*MCA*	1
-	32	MENTAL	Manic MC's featuring Sara Carlson ●	*RCA*	1
22	33	SUPERWOMAN	Karyn White	*Warner Bros*	10
21	34	A NEW FLAME	Simply Red	*WEA*	6
27	35	SATISFACTION	Wendy and Lisa	*Virgin*	4
-	36	WARNING	Adeva	*Cooltempo*	1
20	37	KICK IT IN	Simple Minds	*Virgin*	4
-	38	SUGAR BOX	Then Jerico	*London*	1
-	39	NUMERO UNO	Starlight ●	*Citybeat*	1
-	40	I NEED YOUR LOVIN'	Alyson Williams	*Def Jam*	1

WEEK ENDING 26 AUGUST 1989

LW	TW	Title	Artist	Label	Wks
1	1	SWING THE MOOD	Jive Bunny and the Mastermixers	*Music Factory Dance*	6
4	2	POISON	Alice Cooper	*Epic*	5
11	3	RIDE ON TIME	Black Box	*deConstruction*	3
2	4	FRENCH KISS	Lil Louis	*ffrr*	5
5	5	TOY SOLDIERS	Martika	*CBS*	4
3	6	WOULDN'T CHANGE A THING	Kylie Minogue	*PWL*	4
6	7	LOSING MY MIND	Liza Minnelli	*Epic*	3

In these weeks ■ Sixteen years after her first top ten hit album, stage and screen superstar Liza Minnelli enjoys her first hit single on either side of the Atlantic, thanks to producers The Pet Shop Boys (12.08.89) ■ The first of seven consecutive weeks with a different record at number two each week (12.08.89)■

September 1989

□ Highest position disc reached ● Act's first ever week on chart

LW	TW	Title	Artist	Label	Wks
8	8	BLAME IT ON THE BOOGIE	Big Fun	Jive	3
7	9	YOU'RE HISTORY	Shakespear's Sister	ffrr	4
-	10	I JUST DON'T HAVE THE HEART	Cliff Richard	EMI	1
14	11	HEY DJ I CAN'T DANCE TO THAT MUSIC YOU'RE PLAYING/ SKA TRAIN	Beatmasters featuring Betty Boo	Rhythm King	3
26	[12]	THE INVISIBLE MAN	Queen	Parlophone	2
17	[13]	THIS IS THE RIGHT TIME	Lisa Stansfield	Arista	3
13	14	DO THE RIGHT THING	Redhead Kingpin and the FBI	10	4
9	15	DON'T WANNA LOSE YOU	Gloria Estefan	Epic	7
10	16	YOU'LL NEVER STOP ME LOVING YOU	Sonia	Chrysalis	9
39	17	NUMERO UNO	Starlight	Citybeat	2
36	18	WARNING	Adeva	Cooltempo	2
40	19	I NEED YOUR LOVIN'	Alyson Williams	Def Jam	2
23	[20]	KISSES ON THE WIND	Neneh Cherry	Circa	3
31	[21]	FRIENDS	Jody Watley with Eric B and Rakim	MCA	2
12	22	ON OUR OWN	Bobby Brown	MCA	7
-	23	LAY YOUR HANDS ON ME	Bon Jovi	Vertigo	1
38	24	SUGAR BOX	Then Jerico	London	2
16	25	PURE	Lightning Seeds	Ghetto	4
24	26	SELF!	We've Got A Fuzzbox And We're Gonna Use It	WEA	3
15	27	TOO MUCH	Bros	CBS	5
-	28	LOVE'S ABOUT TO CHANGE MY HEART	Donna Summer	Warner Bros	1
20	29	AIN'T NOBODY	Rufus and Chaka Khan	Warner Bros	8
32	[30]	MENTAL	Manic MC's featuring Sara Carlson	RCA	2
18	31	LANDSLIDE OF LOVE	Transvision Vamp	MCA	4
25	32	ON AND ON	Aswad	Mango	4
19	33	WIND BENEATH MY WINGS	Bette Midler	Atlantic	8
-	34	SOMETHING'S JUMPIN' IN YOUR SHIRT	Malcolm McLaren	Epic	1
-	35	THE TIME WARP	Damian ●	Jive	1
30	36	BATDANCE	Prince	Warner Brothers	10
-	37	DON'T LOOK BACK	Fine Young Cannibals	London	1
21	38	DO YOU LOVE WHAT YOU FEEL	Inner City	10	5
-	39	WE COULD BE TOGETHER	Debbie Gibson	Atlantic	1
-	40	REVIVAL	Eurythmics	RCA	1

WEEK ENDING 2 SEPTEMBER 1989

LW	TW	Title	Artist	Label	Wks
1	[1]	SWING THE MOOD	Jive Bunny and the Mastermixers	Music Factory Dance	7
3	2	RIDE ON TIME	Black Box	deConstruction	4
10	[3]	I JUST DON'T HAVE THE HEART	Cliff Richard	EMI	2
2	4	POISON	Alice Cooper	Epic	6
5	[5]	TOY SOLDIERS	Martika	CBS	5
8	6	BLAME IT ON THE BOOGIE	Big Fun	Jive	4
11	[7]	HEY DJ I CAN'T DANCE TO THAT MUSIC YOU'RE PLAYING/ SKA TRAIN	Beatmasters featuring Betty Boo	Rhythm King	4
4	8	FRENCH KISS	Lil Louis	ffrr	6
-	9	SOWING THE SEEDS OF LOVE	Tears For Fears	Fontana	1
6	10	WOULDN'T CHANGE A THING	Kylie Minogue	PWL	5
17	11	NUMERO UNO	Starlight	Citybeat	3
19	12	I NEED YOUR LOVIN'	Alyson Williams	Def Jam	3
9	13	YOU'RE HISTORY	Shakespear's Sister	ffrr	5
7	14	LOSING MY MIND	Liza Minnelli	Epic	4
13	15	THIS IS THE RIGHT TIME	Lisa Stansfield	Arista	4
12	16	THE INVISIBLE MAN	Queen	Parlophone	3
18	[17]	WARNING	Adeva	Cooltempo	3
23	[18]	LAY YOUR HANDS ON ME	Bon Jovi	Vertigo	2
14	19	DO THE RIGHT THING	Redhead Kingpin and the FBI	10	5
28	[20]	LOVE'S ABOUT TO CHANGE MY HEART	Donna Summer	Warner Bros	2
35	21	THE TIME WARP	Damian	Jive	2
24	[22]	SUGAR BOX	Then Jerico	London	3
15	23	DON'T WANNA LOSE YOU	Gloria Estefan	Epic	8
16	24	YOU'LL NEVER STOP ME LOVING YOU	Sonia	Chrysalis	10
20	25	KISSES ON THE WIND	Neneh Cherry	Circa	4
-	26	NIGHTRAIN	Guns N' Roses	Geffen	1
39	27	WE COULD BE TOGETHER	Debbie Gibson	Atlantic	2
21	28	FRIENDS	Jody Watley with Eric B and Rakim	MCA	3
34	[29]	SOMETHING'S JUMPIN' IN YOUR SHIRT	Malcolm McLaren	Epic	2
40	30	REVIVAL	Eurythmics	RCA	2
-	31	THE BEST	Tina Turner	Capitol	1
-	32	RIGHT HERE WAITING	Richard Marx ●	EMI USA	1
22	33	ON OUR OWN	Bobby Brown	MCA	8
37	[34]	DON'T LOOK BACK	Fine Young Cannibals	London	2
-	35	MISS YOU MUCH	Janet Jackson	Breakout	1
32	36	ON AND ON	Aswad	Mango	5
30	37	MENTAL	Manic MC's featuring Sara Carlson	RCA	3
25	38	PURE	Lightning Seeds	Ghetto	5
27	39	TOO MUCH	Bros	CBS	6
26	40	SELF!	We've Got A Fuzzbox And We're Gonna Use It	WEA	4

WEEK ENDING 9 SEPTEMBER 1989

LW	TW	Title	Artist	Label	Wks
2	[1]	RIDE ON TIME	Black Box	deConstruction	5
1	2	SWING THE MOOD	Jive Bunny and the Mastermixers	Music Factory Dance	8
-	3	EVERY DAY (I LOVE YOU MORE)	Jason Donovan	PWL	1
6	[4]	BLAME IT ON THE BOOGIE	Big Fun	Jive	5
3	5	I JUST DON'T HAVE THE HEART	Cliff Richard	EMI	3
9	6	SOWING THE SEEDS OF LOVE	Tears For Fears	Fontana	2
7	[7]	HEY DJ I CAN'T DANCE TO THAT MUSIC YOU'RE PLAYING/ SKA TRAIN	Beatmasters featuring Betty Boo	Rhythm King	5
4	8	POISON	Alice Cooper	Epic	7
11	[9]	NUMERO UNO	Starlight	Citybeat	4
5	10	TOY SOLDIERS	Martika	CBS	6
12	11	I NEED YOUR LOVIN'	Alyson Williams	Def Jam	4
21	12	THE TIME WARP	Damian	Jive	3
8	13	FRENCH KISS	Lil Louis	ffrr	7
10	14	WOULDN'T CHANGE A THING	Kylie Minogue	PWL	6
32	15	RIGHT HERE WAITING	Richard Marx	EMI USA	2
31	16	THE BEST	Tina Turner	Capitol	2
26	[17]	NIGHTRAIN	Guns N' Roses	Geffen	2
18	[18]	LAY YOUR HANDS ON ME	Bon Jovi	Vertigo	3
17	19	WARNING	Adeva	Cooltempo	4
-	20	PARTYMAN	Prince	Warner Bros	1
13	21	YOU'RE HISTORY	Shakespear's Sister	ffrr	6
27	[22]	WE COULD BE TOGETHER	Debbie Gibson	Atlantic	3
15	23	THIS IS THE RIGHT TIME	Lisa Stansfield	Arista	5
20	24	LOVE'S ABOUT TO CHANGE MY HEART	Donna Summer	Warner Bros	3
-	25	PERSONAL JESUS	Depeche Mode	Mute	1
30	[26]	REVIVAL	Eurythmics	RCA	3
14	27	LOSING MY MIND	Liza Minnelli	Epic	5
19	28	DO THE RIGHT THING	Redhead Kingpin and the FBI	10	6
29	[29]	SOMETHING'S JUMPIN' IN YOUR SHIRT	Malcolm McLaren	Epic	3
35	30	MISS YOU MUCH	Janet Jackson	Breakout	2
16	31	THE INVISIBLE MAN	Queen	Parlophone	4
-	32	HOOKS IN YOU	Marillion	Capitol	1
-	33	LOVESONG	Cure	Fiction	1
-	34	LOVE IN AN ELEVATOR	Aerosmith ●	Geffen	1
22	35	SUGAR BOX	Then Jerico	London	4
-	36	IF ONLY I COULD	Sydney Youngblood ●	Circa	1
-	37	PUMP UP THE JAM	Technotronic featuring Felly ●	Swanyard	1
23	38	DON'T WANNA LOSE YOU	Gloria Estefan	Epic	9
-	39	MIXED EMOTIONS	Rolling Stones	Rolling Stones	1
24	40	YOU'LL NEVER STOP ME LOVING YOU	Sonia	Chrysalis	11

WEEK ENDING 16 SEPTEMBER 1989

LW	TW	Title	Artist	Label	Wks
1	[1]	RIDE ON TIME	Black Box	deConstruction	6
3	[2]	EVERY DAY (I LOVE YOU MORE)	Jason Donovan	PWL	2
15	3	RIGHT HERE WAITING	Richard Marx	EMI USA	3
2	4	SWING THE MOOD	Jive Bunny and the Mastermixers	Music Factory Dance	9
6	[5]	SOWING THE SEEDS OF LOVE	Tears For Fears	Fontana	3
4	6	BLAME IT ON THE BOOGIE	Big Fun	Jive	6
12	[7]	THE TIME WARP	Damian	Jive	4
11	[8]	I NEED YOUR LOVIN'	Alyson Williams	Def Jam	5
9	[9]	NUMERO UNO	Starlight	Citybeat	5

■Damian's *The Time Warp* has been re-issued and re-mixed, and finally becomes the first song from 'The Rocky Horror Show' to hit the top 40, almost two years after it was originally released (26.08.89) ■ Black Box become the first Italian act to top the charts, taking over from Marino Marini (number two in 1958) as the most successful Italian act in British chart history (09.09.89)■

September 1989

□ Highest position disc reached ● Act's first ever week on chart

LW	TW	Title	Artist	Label	Wks
16	10	THE BEST	Tina Turner	*Capitol*	3
7	11	HEY DJ I CAN'T DANCE TO THAT MUSIC YOU'RE PLAYING/ SKA TRAIN	Beatmasters featuring Betty Boo	*Rhythm King*	6
5	12	I JUST DON'T HAVE THE HEART	Cliff Richard	*EMI*	4
25	[13]	PERSONAL JESUS	Depeche Mode	*Mute*	2
20	[14]	PARTYMAN	Prince	*Warner Bros*	2
8	15	POISON	Alice Cooper	*Epic*	8
-	16	CHERISH	Madonna	*Sire*	1
36	17	IF ONLY I COULD	Sydney Youngblood	*Circa*	2
33	[18]	LOVESONG	Cure	*Fiction*	2
37	19	PUMP UP THE JAM	Technotronic featuring Felly	*Swanyard*	2
10	20	TOY SOLDIERS	Martika	*CBS*	7
18	21	LAY YOUR HANDS ON ME	Bon Jovi	*Vertigo*	4
17	22	NIGHTRAIN	Guns N' Roses	*Geffen*	3
34	23	LOVE IN AN ELEVATOR	Aerosmith	*Geffen*	2
22	24	WE COULD BE TOGETHER	Debbie Gibson	*Atlantic*	4
30	25	MISS YOU MUCH	Janet Jackson	*Breakout*	3
14	26	WOULDN'T CHANGE A THING	Kylie Minogue	*PWL*	7
13	27	FRENCH KISS	Lil Louis	*ffrr*	8
19	28	WARNING	Adeva	*Cooltempo*	5
24	29	LOVE'S ABOUT TO CHANGE MY HEART	Donna Summer	*Warner Bros*	4
32	[30]	HOOKS IN YOU	Marillion	*Capitol*	2
26	31	REVIVAL	Eurythmics	*RCA*	4
23	32	THIS IS THE RIGHT TIME	Lisa Stansfield	*Arista*	6
29	33	SOMETHING'S JUMPIN' IN YOUR SHIRT	Malcolm McLaren	*Epic*	4
21	34	YOU'RE HISTORY	Shakespear's Sister	*ffrr*	7
-	35	FOREVER FREE	W.A.S.P.	*Capitol*	1
39	[36]	MIXED EMOTIONS	Rolling Stones	*Rolling Stones*	2
-	37	HARLEM DESIRE	London Boys	*Teldec*	1
-	38	MANTRA FOR A STATE OF MIND	S Express	*Rhythm King*	1
28	39	DO THE RIGHT THING	Redhead Kingpin and the FBI	*10*	7
-	40	IT ISN'T IT WASN'T IT AIN'T NEVER GONNA BE	Aretha Franklin and Whitney Houston ●	*Arista*	1

WEEK ENDING 23 SEPTEMBER 1989

LW	TW	Title	Artist	Label	Wks
1	[1]	RIDE ON TIME	Black Box	*deConstruction*	7
3	[2]	RIGHT HERE WAITING	Richard Marx	*EMI USA*	4
16	[3]	CHERISH	Madonna	*Sire*	2
19	4	PUMP UP THE JAM	Technotronic featuring Felly	*Swanyard*	3
10	[5]	THE BEST	Tina Turner	*Capitol*	4
17	6	IF ONLY I COULD	Sydney Youngblood	*Circa*	3
7	[7]	THE TIME WARP	Damian	*Jive*	5
2	8	EVERY DAY (I LOVE YOU MORE)	Jason Donovan	*PWL*	3
5	9	SOWING THE SEEDS OF LOVE	Tears For Fears	*Fontana*	4
8	10	I NEED YOUR LOVIN'	Alyson Williams	*Def Jam*	6
4	11	SWING THE MOOD	Jive Bunny and the Mastermixers	*Music Factory Dance*	10
6	12	BLAME IT ON THE BOOGIE	Big Fun	*Jive*	7
9	13	NUMERO UNO	Starlight	*Citybeat*	6
13	14	PERSONAL JESUS	Depeche Mode	*Mute*	3
11	15	HEY DJ I CAN'T DANCE TO THAT MUSIC YOU'RE PLAYING/ SKA TRAIN	Beatmasters featuring Betty Boo	*Rhythm King*	7
14	16	PARTYMAN	Prince	*Warner Bros*	3
23	17	LOVE IN AN ELEVATOR	Aerosmith	*Geffen*	3
12	18	I JUST DON'T HAVE THE HEART	Cliff Richard	*EMI*	5
-	[19]	DON'T LET ME DOWN GENTLY	Wonder Stuff	*Polydor*	1
18	20	LOVESONG	Cure	*Fiction*	3
37	21	HARLEM DESIRE	London Boys	*Teldec*	2
25	[22]	MISS YOU MUCH	Janet Jackson	*Breakout*	4
15	23	POISON	Alice Cooper	*Epic*	9
38	24	MANTRA FOR A STATE OF MIND	S Express	*Rhythm King*	2
35	[25]	FOREVER FREE	W.A.S.P.	*Capitol*	2
24	26	WE COULD BE TOGETHER	Debbie Gibson	*Atlantic*	5
20	27	TOY SOLDIERS	Martika	*CBS*	8
-	[28]	LOVE AND REGRET	Deacon Blue	*CBS*	1
40	[29]	IT ISN'T IT WASN'T IT AIN'T NEVER GONNA BE	Aretha Franklin and Whitney Houston	*Arista*	2
-	30	OYE MI CANTO (HEAR MY VOICE)	Gloria Estefan	*Epic*	1
-	31	YOU KEEP IT ALL IN	Beautiful South	*Go! Discs*	1
-	[32]	BLUES FROM A GUN	Jesus And Mary Chain	*blanco y negro*	1
29	33	LOVE'S ABOUT TO CHANGE MY HEART	Donna Summer	*Warner Bros*	5
28	34	WARNING	Adeva	*Cooltempo*	6
21	35	LAY YOUR HANDS ON ME	Bon Jovi	*Vertigo*	5
26	36	WOULDN'T CHANGE A THING	Kylie Minogue	*PWL*	8
27	37	FRENCH KISS	Lil Louis	*ffrr*	9
36	38	MIXED EMOTIONS	Rolling Stones	*Rolling Stones*	3
-	39	NAME AND NUMBER	Curiosity Killed The Cat	*Mercury*	1
-	40	SECRET RENDEZVOUS	Karyn White	*Warner Bros*	1

WEEK ENDING 30 SEPTEMBER 1989

LW	TW	Title	Artist	Label	Wks
1	[1]	RIDE ON TIME	Black Box	*deConstruction*	8
2	[2]	RIGHT HERE WAITING	Richard Marx	*EMI USA*	5
4	3	PUMP UP THE JAM	Technotronic featuring Felly	*Swanyard*	4
6	4	IF ONLY I COULD	Sydney Youngblood	*Circa*	4
5	[5]	THE BEST	Tina Turner	*Capitol*	5
-	6	DRAMA!	Erasure	*Mute*	1
3	7	CHERISH	Madonna	*Sire*	3
7	8	THE TIME WARP	Damian	*Jive*	6
31	9	YOU KEEP IT ALL IN	Beautiful South	*Go! Discs*	2
9	10	SOWING THE SEEDS OF LOVE	Tears For Fears	*Fontana*	5
10	11	I NEED YOUR LOVIN'	Alyson Williams	*Def Jam*	7
-	[12]	THE SENSUAL WORLD	Kate Bush	*EMI*	1
17	[13]	LOVE IN AN ELEVATOR	Aerosmith	*Geffen*	4
-	14	SWEET SURRENDER	Wet Wet Wet	*Precious*	1
11	15	SWING THE MOOD	Jive Bunny and the Mastermixers	*Music Factory Dance*	11
8	16	EVERY DAY (I LOVE YOU MORE)	Jason Donovan	*PWL*	4
21	[17]	HARLEM DESIRE	London Boys	*Teldec*	3
13	18	NUMERO UNO	Starlight	*Citybeat*	7
14	19	PERSONAL JESUS	Depeche Mode	*Mute*	4
19	20	DON'T LET ME DOWN GENTLY	Wonder Stuff	*Polydor*	2
12	21	BLAME IT ON THE BOOGIE	Big Fun	*Jive*	8
24	22	MANTRA FOR A STATE OF MIND	S Express	*Rhythm King*	3
30	23	OYE MI CANTO (HEAR MY VOICE)	Gloria Estefan	*Epic*	2
15	24	HEY DJ I CAN'T DANCE TO THAT MUSIC YOU'RE PLAYING/ SKA TRAIN	Beatmasters featuring Betty Boo	*Rhythm King*	8
22	25	MISS YOU MUCH	Janet Jackson	*Breakout*	5
16	26	PARTYMAN	Prince	*Warner Bros*	4
39	27	NAME AND NUMBER	Curiosity Killed The Cat	*Mercury*	2
28	[28]	LOVE AND REGRET	Deacon Blue	*CBS*	2
-	29	WE DIDN'T START THE FIRE	Billy Joel	*CBS*	1
25	30	FOREVER FREE	W.A.S.P.	*Capitol*	3
18	31	I JUST DON'T HAVE THE HEART	Cliff Richard	*EMI*	6
20	32	LOVESONG	Cure	*Fiction*	4
29	33	IT ISN'T IT WASN'T IT AIN'T NEVER GONNA BE	Aretha Franklin and Whitney Houston	*Arista*	3
40	34	SECRET RENDEZVOUS	Karyn White	*Warner Bros*	2
-	35	IF I COULD TURN BACK TIME	Cher	*Geffen*	1
23	36	POISON	Alice Cooper	*Epic*	10
-	[37]	ROAD TO YOUR SOUL	All About Eve	*Mercury*	1
-	38	ROCK WIT'CHA	Bobby Brown	*MCA*	1
26	39	WE COULD BE TOGETHER	Debbie Gibson	*Atlantic*	6
-	40	ROOM IN YOUR HEART	Living In A Box	*Chrysalis*	1

WEEK ENDING 7 OCTOBER 1989

LW	TW	Title	Artist	Label	Wks
1	[1]	RIDE ON TIME	Black Box	*deConstruction*	9
3	[2]	PUMP UP THE JAM	Technotronic featuring Felly	*Swanyard*	5
4	[3]	IF ONLY I COULD	Sydney Youngblood	*Circa*	5
6	[4]	DRAMA!	Erasure	*Mute*	2
2	5	RIGHT HERE WAITING	Richard Marx	*EMI USA*	6
14	[6]	SWEET SURRENDER	Wet Wet Wet	*Precious*	2
5	7	THE BEST	Tina Turner	*Capitol*	6
9	[8]	YOU KEEP IT ALL IN	Beautiful South	*Go! Discs*	3
-	[9]	CHOCOLATE BOX	Bros	*CBS*	1
7	10	CHERISH	Madonna	*Sire*	4

In these weeks ■ Three 'Time' songs hit the Top ten within a few weeks: *Ride On Time, Time Warp* and Cher's first top ten hit for two years *If I Could Turn Back Time* (30.09.89) ■ Aerosmith's *Love In An Elevator* spends three weeks going up and three weeks going down, giving them their first UK Top 40 hit 13 years after their first American hit (30.09.89)■

October 1989

□ Highest position disc reached ● Act's first ever week on chart

LW	TW	Title	Artist	Label	Wks
29	11	WE DIDN'T START THE FIRE	Billy Joel	*CBS*	2
-	12	STREET TUFF	Rebel MC and Double Trouble	*Desire*	1
8	13	THE TIME WARP	Damian	*Jive*	7
27	14	NAME AND NUMBER	Curiosity Killed The Cat	*Mercury*	3
12	15	THE SENSUAL WORLD	Kate Bush	*EMI*	2
23	16	OYE MI CANTO (HEAR MY VOICE)	Gloria Estefan	*Epic*	3
13	17	LOVE IN AN ELEVATOR	Aerosmith	*Geffen*	5
35	18	IF I COULD TURN BACK TIME	Cher	*Geffen*	2
17	19	HARLEM DESIRE	London Boys	*Teldec*	4
11	20	I NEED YOUR LOVIN'	Alyson Williams	*Def Jam*	8
22	21	MANTRA FOR A STATE OF MIND	S Express	*Rhythm King*	4
34	22	SECRET RENDEZVOUS	Karyn White	*Warner Bros*	3
10	23	SOWING THE SEEDS OF LOVE	Tears For Fears	*Fontana*	6
-	24	GIRL I'M GONNA MISS YOU	Milli Vanilli	*Cooltempo*	1
18	25	NUMERO UNO	Starlight	*Citybeat*	8
15	26	SWING THE MOOD	Jive Bunny and the Mastermixers	*Music Factory Dance*	12
-	27	CAN'T FORGET YOU	Sonia	*Chrysalis*	1
-	28	LEAVE A LIGHT ON	Belinda Carlisle	*Virgin*	1
16	29	EVERY DAY (I LOVE YOU MORE)	Jason Donovan	*PWL*	5
19	30	PERSONAL JESUS	Depeche Mode	*Mute*	5
40	31	ROOM IN YOUR HEART	Living In A Box	*Chrysalis*	2
-	32	LOVE ON A MOUNTAIN TOP	Sinitta	*Fanfare*	1
38	33	ROCK WIT'CHA	Bobby Brown	*MCA*	2
-	34	KENNEDY	Wedding Present ●	*RCA*	1
20	35	DON'T LET ME DOWN GENTLY	Wonder Stuff	*Polydor*	3
24	36	HEY DJ I CAN'T DANCE TO THAT MUSIC YOU'RE PLAYING/ SKA TRAIN	Beatmasters featuring Betty Boo	*Rhythm King*	9
37	37	ROAD TO YOUR SOUL	All About Eve	*Mercury*	2
21	38	BLAME IT ON THE BOOGIE	Big Fun	*Jive*	9
25	39	MISS YOU MUCH	Janet Jackson	*Breakout*	6
-	40	WISHING ON A STAR	Fresh 4 featuring Lizz E ●	*10*	1

WEEK ENDING **14 OCTOBER 1989**

LW	TW	Title	Artist	Label	Wks
1	1	RIDE ON TIME	Black Box	*deConstruction*	10
2	2	PUMP UP THE JAM	Technotronic featuring Felly	*Swanyard*	6
3	3	IF ONLY I COULD	Sydney Youngblood	*Circa*	6
-	4	THAT'S WHAT I LIKE	Jive Bunny and the Mastermixers	*Music Factory Dance*	1
12	5	STREET TUFF	Rebel MC and Double Trouble	*Desire*	2
4	6	DRAMA!	Erasure	*Mute*	3
6	7	SWEET SURRENDER	Wet Wet Wet	*Precious*	3
11	8	WE DIDN'T START THE FIRE	Billy Joel	*CBS*	3
8	9	YOU KEEP IT ALL IN	Beautiful South	*Go! Discs*	4
24	10	GIRL I'M GONNA MISS YOU	Milli Vanilli	*Cooltempo*	2
5	11	RIGHT HERE WAITING	Richard Marx	*EMI USA*	7
7	12	THE BEST	Tina Turner	*Capitol*	7
18	13	IF I COULD TURN BACK TIME	Cher	*Geffen*	3
28	14	LEAVE A LIGHT ON	Belinda Carlisle	*Virgin*	2
9	15	CHOCOLATE BOX	Bros	*CBS*	2
14	16	NAME AND NUMBER	Curiosity Killed The Cat	*Mercury*	4
27	17	CAN'T FORGET YOU	Sonia	*Chrysalis*	2
31	18	ROOM IN YOUR HEART	Living In A Box	*Chrysalis*	3
16	19	OYE MI CANTO (HEAR MY VOICE)	Gloria Estefan	*Epic*	4
10	20	CHERISH	Madonna	*Sire*	5
21	21	MANTRA FOR A STATE OF MIND	S Express	*Rhythm King*	5
40	22	WISHING ON A STAR	Fresh 4 featuring Lizz E	10	2
32	23	LOVE ON A MOUNTAIN TOP	Sinitta	*Fanfare*	2
22	24	SECRET RENDEZVOUS	Karyn White	*Warner Bros*	4
13	25	THE TIME WARP	Damian	*Jive*	8
-	26	THE ROAD TO HELL (PART 2)	Chris Rea	*WEA*	1
17	27	LOVE IN AN ELEVATOR	Aerosmith	*Geffen*	6
-	28	LEAN ON YOU	Cliff Richard	*EMI*	1
15	29	THE SENSUAL WORLD	Kate Bush	*EMI*	3
20	30	I NEED YOUR LOVIN'	Alyson Williams	*Def Jam*	9
19	31	HARLEM DESIRE	London Boys	*Teldec*	5
26	32	SWING THE MOOD	Jive Bunny and the Mastermixers	*Music Factory Dance*	13
34	33	KENNEDY	Wedding Present	*RCA*	2
23	34	SOWING THE SEEDS OF LOVE	Tears For Fears	*Fontana*	7
25	35	NUMERO UNO	Starlight	*Citybeat*	9
-	36	I WANT THAT MAN	Deborah Harry	*Chrysalis*	1
33	37	ROCK WIT'CHA	Bobby Brown	*MCA*	3
29	38	EVERY DAY (I LOVE YOU MORE)	Jason Donovan	*PWL*	6
-	39	THE REAL WILD HOUSE	Raul Orellana ●	*BCM*	1
-	40	BED OF NAILS	Alice Cooper	*Epic*	1

WEEK ENDING **21 OCTOBER 1989**

LW	TW	Title	Artist	Label	Wks
4	1	THAT'S WHAT I LIKE	Jive Bunny and the Mastermixers	*Music Factory Dance*	2
1	2	RIDE ON TIME	Black Box	*deConstruction*	11
10	3	GIRL I'M GONNA MISS YOU	Milli Vanilli	*Cooltempo*	3
2	4	PUMP UP THE JAM	Technotronic featuring Felly	*Swanyard*	7
3	5	IF ONLY I COULD	Sydney Youngblood	*Circa*	7
5	6	STREET TUFF	Rebel MC and Double Trouble	*Desire*	3
8	7	WE DIDN'T START THE FIRE	Billy Joel	*CBS*	4
14	8	LEAVE A LIGHT ON	Belinda Carlisle	*Virgin*	3
13	9	IF I COULD TURN BACK TIME	Cher	*Geffen*	4
22	10	WISHING ON A STAR	Fresh 4 featuring Lizz E	*10*	3
18	11	ROOM IN YOUR HEART	Living In A Box	*Chrysalis*	4
7	12	SWEET SURRENDER	Wet Wet Wet	*Precious*	4
9	13	YOU KEEP IT ALL IN	Beautiful South	*Go! Discs*	5
6	14	DRAMA!	Erasure	*Mute*	4
26	15	THE ROAD TO HELL (PART 2)	Chris Rea	*WEA*	2
16	16	NAME AND NUMBER	Curiosity Killed The Cat	*Mercury*	5
28	17	LEAN ON YOU	Cliff Richard	*EMI*	2
11	18	RIGHT HERE WAITING	Richard Marx	*EMI USA*	8
12	19	THE BEST	Tina Turner	*Capitol*	8
23	20	LOVE ON A MOUNTAIN TOP	Sinitta	*Fanfare*	3
36	21	I WANT THAT MAN	Deborah Harry	*Chrysalis*	2
17	22	CAN'T FORGET YOU	Sonia	*Chrysalis*	3
15	23	CHOCOLATE BOX	Bros	*CBS*	3
-	24	EYE KNOW	De La Soul	*Tommy Boy*	1
19	25	OYE MI CANTO (HEAR MY VOICE)	Gloria Estefan	*Epic*	5
-	26	SCANDAL	Queen	*Parlophone*	1
32	27	SWING THE MOOD	Jive Bunny and the Mastermixers	*Music Factory Dance*	14
-	28	I THANK YOU	Adeva	*Cooltempo*	1
21	29	MANTRA FOR A STATE OF MIND	S Express	*Rhythm King*	6
20	30	CHERISH	Madonna	*Sire*	6
39	31	THE REAL WILD HOUSE	Raul Orellana	*BCM*	2
25	32	THE TIME WARP	Damian	*Jive*	9
-	33	I FEEL THE EARTH MOVE	Martika	*CBS*	1
-	34	DON'T MAKE ME OVER	Sybil	*Champion*	1
24	35	SECRET RENDEZVOUS	Karyn White	*Warner Bros*	5
-	36	C'MON AND GET MY LOVE	D. Mob introducing Cathy Dennis	*ffrr*	1
-	37	OH WELL	Oh Well ●	*Parlophone*	1
40	38	BED OF NAILS	Alice Cooper	*Epic*	2
27	39	LOVE IN AN ELEVATOR	Aerosmith	*Geffen*	7
31	40	HARLEM DESIRE	London Boys	*Teldec*	6

WEEK ENDING **28 OCTOBER 1989**

LW	TW	Title	Artist	Label	Wks
1	1	THAT'S WHAT I LIKE	Jive Bunny and the Mastermixers	*Music Factory Dance*	3
3	2	GIRL I'M GONNA MISS YOU	Milli Vanilli	*Cooltempo*	4
6	3	STREET TUFF	Rebel MC and Double Trouble	*Desire*	4
8	4	LEAVE A LIGHT ON	Belinda Carlisle	*Virgin*	4
2	5	RIDE ON TIME	Black Box	*deConstruction*	12
9	6	IF I COULD TURN BACK TIME	Cher	*Geffen*	5
11	7	ROOM IN YOUR HEART	Living In A Box	*Chrysalis*	5
4	8	PUMP UP THE JAM	Technotronic featuring Felly	*Swanyard*	8
7	9	WE DIDN'T START THE FIRE	Billy Joel	*CBS*	5
5	10	IF ONLY I COULD	Sydney Youngblood	*Circa*	8
10	11	WISHING ON A STAR	Fresh 4 featuring Lizz E	*10*	4
15	12	THE ROAD TO HELL (PART 2)	Chris Rea	*WEA*	3
-	13	ALL AROUND THE WORLD	Lisa Stansfield	*Arista*	1
21	14	I WANT THAT MAN	Deborah Harry	*Chrysalis*	3
33	15	I FEEL THE EARTH MOVE	Martika	*CBS*	2

■Jive Bunny becomes the fifth act (after Frankie Laine, Gerry and the Pacemakers, the Beatles and John Lennon) to have consecutive number ones with only one other chart-topper between them (21.09.89) ■ Love Affair may have taken their *Everlasting Love* to the very top, but Sinitta can only reach number 20 with Robert Knights' other UK hit song *Love On A Mountain Top* (21.10.89)■

October 1989

□ Highest position disc reached ● Act's first ever week on chart

LW	TW	Title	Artist	Label	Wks
24	**16**	EYE KNOW	De La Soul	*Tommy Boy*	2
28	**[17]**	I THANK YOU	Adeva	*Cooltempo*	2
12	**18**	SWEET SURRENDER	Wet Wet Wet	*Precious*	5
34	**[19]**	DON'T MAKE ME OVER	Sybil	*Champion*	2
13	**20**	YOU KEEP IT ALL IN	Beautiful South	*Go! Discs*	6
17	**21**	LEAN ON YOU	Cliff Richard	*EMI*	3
16	**22**	NAME AND NUMBER	Curiosity Killed The Cat	*Mercury*	6
36	**23**	C'MON AND GET MY LOVE	D. Mob introducing Cathy Dennis	*ffrr*	2
19	**24**	THE BEST	Tina Turner	*Capitol*	9
26	**[25]**	SCANDAL	Queen	*Parlophone*	2
20	**26**	LOVE ON A MOUNTAIN TOP	Sinitta	*Fanfare*	4
14	**27**	DRAMA!	Erasure	*Mute*	5
37	**[28]**	OH WELL	Oh Well	*Parlophone*	2
31	**[29]**	THE REAL WILD HOUSE	Raul Orellana	*BCM*	3
18	**30**	RIGHT HERE WAITING	Richard Marx	*EMI USA*	9
-	**31**	NEVER TOO MUCH	Luther Vandross	*Epic*	1
-	**32**	STATE OF MIND	Fish ●	*EMI*	1
27	**33**	SWING THE MOOD	Jive Bunny and the Mastermixers	*Music Factory Dance*	15
22	**34**	CAN'T FORGET YOU	Sonia	*Chrysalis*	4
25	**35**	OYE MI CANTO (HEAR MY VOICE)	Gloria Estefan	*Epic*	6
23	**36**	CHOCOLATE BOX	Bros	*CBS*	4
-	**37**	THE SUN RISING	Beloved ●	*WEA*	1
32	**38**	THE TIME WARP	Damian	*Jive*	10
-	**[39]**	TAKE CARE OF YOURSELF	Level 42	*Polydor*	1
-	**40**	THE MESSAGE IS LOVE	Arthur Baker and the Backbeat Disciples featuring Al Green ●	*Breakout*	1

WEEK ENDING 4 NOVEMBER 1989

LW	TW	Title	Artist	Label	Wks
1	**[1]**	THAT'S WHAT I LIKE	Jive Bunny and the Mastermixers	*Music Factory Dance*	4
2	**[2]**	GIRL I'M GONNA MISS YOU	Milli Vanilli	*Cooltempo*	5
13	**3**	ALL AROUND THE WORLD	Lisa Stansfield	*Arista*	2
3	**4**	STREET TUFF	Rebel MC and Double Trouble	*Desire*	5
7	**[5]**	ROOM IN YOUR HEART	Living In A Box	*Chrysalis*	6
4	**6**	LEAVE A LIGHT ON	Belinda Carlisle	*Virgin*	5
6	**7**	IF I COULD TURN BACK TIME	Cher	*Geffen*	6
9	**8**	WE DIDN'T START THE FIRE	Billy Joel	*CBS*	6
5	**9**	RIDE ON TIME	Black Box	*deConstruction*	13
12	**[10]**	THE ROAD TO HELL (PART 2)	Chris Rea	*WEA*	4
8	**11**	PUMP UP THE JAM	Technotronic featuring Felly	*Swanyard*	9
15	**12**	I FEEL THE EARTH MOVE	Martika	*CBS*	3
14	**[13]**	I WANT THAT MAN	Deborah Harry	*Chrysalis*	4
16	**[14]**	EYE KNOW	De La Soul	*Tommy Boy*	3
10	**15**	IF ONLY I COULD	Sydney Youngblood	*Circa*	9
11	**16**	WISHING ON A STAR	Fresh 4 featuring Lizz E	*10*	5
-	**17**	NEVER TOO LATE	Kylie Minogue	*PWL*	1
17	**18**	I THANK YOU	Adeva	*Cooltempo*	3
31	**19**	NEVER TOO MUCH	Luther Vandross	*Epic*	2
19	**20**	DON'T MAKE ME OVER	Sybil	*Champion*	3
23	**21**	C'MON AND GET MY LOVE	D. Mob introducing Cathy Dennis	*ffrr*	3
-	**22**	ANOTHER DAY IN PARADISE	Phil Collins	*Virgin*	1
-	**23**	GRAND PIANO	Mixmaster ●	*BCM*	1
21	**24**	LEAN ON YOU	Cliff Richard	*EMI*	4
18	**25**	SWEET SURRENDER	Wet Wet Wet	*Precious*	6
37	**[26]**	THE SUN RISING	Beloved	*WEA*	2
25	**27**	SCANDAL	Queen	*Parlophone*	3
28	**[28]**	OH WELL	Oh Well	*Parlophone*	3
33	**29**	SWING THE MOOD	Jive Bunny and the Mastermixers	*Music Factory Dance*	16
22	**30**	NAME AND NUMBER	Curiosity Killed The Cat	*Mercury*	7
-	**31**	BORN TO BE SOLD	Transvision Vamp	*MCA*	1
24	**32**	THE BEST	Tina Turner	*Capitol*	10
27	**33**	DRAMA!	Erasure	*Mute*	6
29	**34**	THE REAL WILD HOUSE	Raul Orellana	*BCM*	4
20	**35**	YOU KEEP IT ALL IN	Beautiful South	*Go! Discs*	7
32	**36**	STATE OF MIND	Fish	*EMI*	2
26	**37**	LOVE ON A MOUNTAIN TOP	Sinitta	*Fanfare*	5
40	**[38]**	THE MESSAGE IS LOVE	Arthur Baker and the Backbeat Disciples featuring Al Green	*Breakout*	2
39	**[39]**	TAKE CARE OF YOURSELF	Level 42	*Polydor*	2
-	**40**	DRIVE ON	Brother Beyond	*Parlophone*	1

WEEK ENDING 11 NOVEMBER 1989

LW	TW	Title	Artist	Label	Wks
3	**[1]**	ALL AROUND THE WORLD	Lisa Stansfield	*Arista*	3
2	**[2]**	GIRL I'M GONNA MISS YOU	Milli Vanilli	*Cooltempo*	6
1	**3**	THAT'S WHAT I LIKE	Jive Bunny and the Mastermixers	*Music Factory Dance*	5
17	**[4]**	NEVER TOO LATE	Kylie Minogue	*PWL*	2
4	**5**	STREET TUFF	Rebel MC and Double Trouble	*Desire*	6
5	**6**	ROOM IN YOUR HEART	Living In A Box	*Chrysalis*	7
12	**[7]**	I FEEL THE EARTH MOVE	Martika	*CBS*	4
22	**8**	ANOTHER DAY IN PARADISE	Phil Collins	*Virgin*	2
6	**9**	LEAVE A LIGHT ON	Belinda Carlisle	*Virgin*	6
7	**10**	IF I COULD TURN BACK TIME	Cher	*Geffen*	7
10	**11**	THE ROAD TO HELL (PART 2)	Chris Rea	*WEA*	5
23	**12**	GRAND PIANO	Mixmaster	*BCM*	2
19	**[13]**	NEVER TOO MUCH	Luther Vandross	*Epic*	3
9	**14**	RIDE ON TIME	Black Box	*deConstruction*	14
13	**15**	I WANT THAT MAN	Deborah Harry	*Chrysalis*	5
21	**16**	C'MON AND GET MY LOVE	D. Mob introducing Cathy Dennis	*ffrr*	4
14	**17**	EYE KNOW	De La Soul	*Tommy Boy*	4
8	**18**	WE DIDN'T START THE FIRE	Billy Joel	*CBS*	7
11	**19**	PUMP UP THE JAM	Technotronic featuring Felly	*Swanyard*	10
15	**20**	IF ONLY I COULD	Sydney Youngblood	*Circa*	10
18	**21**	I THANK YOU	Adeva	*Cooltempo*	4
31	**22**	BORN TO BE SOLD	Transvision Vamp	*MCA*	2
-	**23**	YOU GOT IT (THE RIGHT STUFF)	New Kids On The Block ●	*CBS*	1
16	**24**	WISHING ON A STAR	Fresh 4 featuring Lizz E	*10*	6
-	**25**	DON'T KNOW MUCH	Linda Ronstadt with Aaron Neville ●	*Elektra*	1
26	**[26]**	THE SUN RISING	Beloved	*WEA*	3
20	**27**	DON'T MAKE ME OVER	Sybil	*Champion*	4
-	**28**	RHYTHM NATION	Janet Jackson	*Breakout*	1
-	**29**	DON'T ASK ME WHY	Eurythmics	*RCA*	1
28	**30**	OH WELL	Oh Well	*Parlophone*	4
-	**[31]**	A NEW SOUTH WALES/THE ROCK	Alarm featuring the Morriston Orpheus Male Voice Choir	*IRS*	1
-	**[32]**	TELL ME WHEN THE FEVER ENDED	Electribe 101 ●	*Mercury*	1
-	**33**	GOLDEN GREEN/GET TOGETHER	Wonder Stuff	*Polydor*	1
25	**34**	SWEET SURRENDER	Wet Wet Wet	*Precious*	7
24	**35**	LEAN ON YOU	Cliff Richard	*EMI*	5
-	**[36]**	7 O'CLOCK	Quireboys ●	*Parlophone*	1
29	**37**	SWING THE MOOD	Jive Bunny and the Mastermixers	*Music Factory Dance*	17
-	**[38]**	RESTLESS DAYS (SHE SCREAMS OUT LOUD)	And Why Not? ●	*Island*	1
40	**[39]**	DRIVE ON	Brother Beyond	*Parlophone*	2
-	**40**	LAMBADA	Kaoma ●	*CBS*	1

WEEK ENDING 18 NOVEMBER 1989

LW	TW	Title	Artist	Label	Wks
1	**[1]**	ALL AROUND THE WORLD	Lisa Stansfield	*Arista*	4
8	**[2]**	ANOTHER DAY IN PARADISE	Phil Collins	*Virgin*	3
23	**3**	YOU GOT IT (THE RIGHT STUFF)	New Kids On The Block	*CBS*	2
4	**[4]**	NEVER TOO LATE	Kylie Minogue	*PWL*	3
2	**5**	GIRL I'M GONNA MISS YOU	Milli Vanilli	*Cooltempo*	7
25	**6**	DON'T KNOW MUCH	Linda Ronstadt with Aaron Neville	*Elektra*	2
7	**[7]**	I FEEL THE EARTH MOVE	Martika	*CBS*	5
3	**8**	THAT'S WHAT I LIKE	Jive Bunny and the Mastermixers	*Music Factory Dance*	6
12	**[9]**	GRAND PIANO	Mixmaster	*BCM*	3
5	**10**	STREET TUFF	Rebel MC and Double Trouble	*Desire*	7
6	**11**	ROOM IN YOUR HEART	Living In A Box	*Chrysalis*	8

In these weeks ■ Eleven years after his first hit, Chris Rea finally hits the Top ten. It is his fifth Top 40 hit, but he has also suffered through a record 13 singles which peaked between 41 and 75 (04.11.89) ■ Seventeen Top 40 weeks for *Swing The Mood* makes it the longest running chart hit of the year, a record equalled by *Ride On Time* three weeks later (11.11.89)■

December 1989

□ Highest position disc reached ● Act's first ever week on chart

LW	TW	Title	Artist	Label	Wks
-	12	INFINITE DREAMS (LIVE)	Iron Maiden	*EMI*	1
13	[13]	NEVER TOO MUCH	Luther Vandross	*Epic*	4
9	14	LEAVE A LIGHT ON	Belinda Carlisle	*Virgin*	7
16	[15]	C'MON AND GET MY LOVE	D. Mob introducing Cathy Dennis	*ffrr*	5
15	16	I WANT THAT MAN	Deborah Harry	*Chrysalis*	6
11	17	THE ROAD TO HELL (PART 2)	Chris Rea	*WEA*	6
14	18	RIDE ON TIME	Black Box	*deConstruction*	15
10	19	IF I COULD TURN BACK TIME	Cher	*Geffen*	8
-	20	PACIFIC	808 State ●	*ZTT*	1
18	21	WE DIDN'T START THE FIRE	Billy Joel	*CBS*	8
17	22	EYE KNOW	De La Soul	*Tommy Boy*	5
28	[23]	RHYTHM NATION	Janet Jackson	*Breakout*	2
-	24	HOMELY GIRL	Ub40	*DEP International*	1
29	[25]	DON'T ASK ME WHY	Eurythmics	*RCA*	2
19	26	PUMP UP THE JAM	Technotronic featuring Felly	*Swanyard*	11
40	27	LAMBADA	Kaoma	*CBS*	2
-	28	WHATCHA GONNA DO WITH MY LOVIN'	Inner City	*10*	1
20	29	IF ONLY I COULD	Sydney Youngblood	*Circa*	11
22	30	BORN TO BE SOLD	Transvision Vamp	*MCA*	3
31	[31]	A NEW SOUTH WALES/THE ROCK	Alarm featuring the Morriston Orpheus Male Voice Choir	*IRS*	2
32	[32]	TELL ME WHEN THE FEVER ENDED	Electribe 101	*Mercury*	2
-	33	COMMENT TE DIRE ADIEU	Jimmy Somerville featuring June Miles Kingston ●	*London*	1
-	34	I'M NOT THE MAN I USED TO BE	Fine Young Cannibals	*London*	1
-	35	THE ARMS OF ORION	Prince with Sheena Easton	*Warner Bros*	1
33	36	GOLDEN GREEN/GET TOGETHER	Wonder Stuff	*Polydor*	2
26	37	THE SUN RISING	Beloved	*WEA*	4
38	38	RESTLESS DAYS (SHE SCREAMS OUT LOUD)	And Why Not?	*Island*	2
-	[39]	SUN KING/EDIE (CIAO BABY)	Cult	*Beggars Banquet*	1
21	40	I THANK YOU	Adeva	*Cooltempo*	5

WEEK ENDING 25 NOVEMBER 1989

LW	TW	Title	Artist	Label	Wks
3	[1]	YOU GOT IT (THE RIGHT STUFF)	New Kids On The Block	*CBS*	3
1	2	ALL AROUND THE WORLD	Lisa Stansfield	*Arista*	5
6	3	DON'T KNOW MUCH	Linda Ronstadt with Aaron Neville	*Elektra*	3
2	4	ANOTHER DAY IN PARADISE	Phil Collins	*Virgin*	4
4	5	NEVER TOO LATE	Kylie Minogue	*PWL*	4
12	[6]	INFINITE DREAMS (LIVE)	Iron Maiden	*EMI*	2
24	7	HOMELY GIRL	UB40	*DEP International*	2
5	8	GIRL I'M GONNA MISS YOU	Milli Vanilli	*Cooltempo*	8
7	9	I FEEL THE EARTH MOVE	Martika	*CBS*	6
9	10	GRAND PIANO	Mixmaster	*BCM*	4
27	11	LAMBADA	Kaoma	*CBS*	3
20	12	PACIFIC	808 State	*ZTT*	2
-	13	FOOL'S GOLD/WHAT THE WORLD IS WAITING FOR	Stone Roses	*Silvertone*	1
8	14	THAT'S WHAT I LIKE	Jive Bunny and the Mastermixers	*Music Factory Dance*	7
15	[15]	C'MON AND GET MY LOVE	D. Mob introducing Cathy Dennis	*ffrr*	6
10	16	STREET TUFF	Rebel MC and Double Trouble	*Desire*	8
28	17	WHATCHA GONNA DO WITH MY LOVIN'	Inner City	*10*	2
-	18	OUIJA BOARD OUIJA BOARD	Morrissey	*HMV*	1
11	19	ROOM IN YOUR HEART	Living In A Box	*Chrysalis*	9
33	20	COMMENT TE DIRE ADIEU	Jimmy Somerville featuring June Miles Kingston	*London*	2
34	21	I'M NOT THE MAN I USED TO BE	Fine Young Cannibals	*London*	2
13	22	NEVER TOO MUCH	Luther Vandross	*Epic*	5
14	23	LEAVE A LIGHT ON	Belinda Carlisle	*Virgin*	8
-	24	EVE OF THE WAR	Jeff Wayne	*CBS*	1
16	25	I WANT THAT MAN	Deborah Harry	*Chrysalis*	7
18	26	RIDE ON TIME	Black Box	*deConstruction*	16
-	27	CAN'T SHAKE THE FEELING	Big Fun	*Jive*	1
25	28	DON'T ASK ME WHY	Eurythmics	*RCA*	3
-	29	RONI	Bobby Brown	*MCA*	1
-	30	MADCHESTER RAVE ON (EP)	Happy Mondays ●	*Factory*	1
35	31	THE ARMS OF ORION	Prince with Sheena Easton	*Warner Bros*	2
17	32	THE ROAD TO HELL (PART 2)	Chris Rea	*WEA*	7
23	33	RHYTHM NATION	Janet Jackson	*Breakout*	3
-	34	GET ON YOUR FEET	Gloria Estefan	*Epic*	1
19	35	IF I COULD TURN BACK TIME	Cher	*Geffen*	9
26	36	PUMP UP THE JAM	Technotronic featuring Felly	*Swanyard*	12
-	37	WOMAN IN CHAINS	Tears For Fears	*Fontana*	1
22	38	EYE KNOW	De La Soul	*Tommy Boy*	6
31	39	A NEW SOUTH WALES/THE ROCK	Alarm featuring the Morriston Orpheus Male Voice Choir	*IRS*	3
21	40	WE DIDN'T START THE FIRE	Billy Joel	*CBS*	9

WEEK ENDING 2 DECEMBER 1989

LW	TW	Title	Artist	Label	Wks
1	[1]	YOU GOT IT (THE RIGHT STUFF)	New Kids On The Block	*CBS*	4
3	[2]	DON'T KNOW MUCH	Linda Ronstadt with Aaron Neville	*Elektra*	4
2	3	ALL AROUND THE WORLD	Lisa Stansfield	Arista	6
24	4	EVE OF THE WAR	Jeff Wayne	*CBS*	2
4	5	ANOTHER DAY IN PARADISE	Phil Collins	*Virgin*	5
7	[6]	HOMELY GIRL	UB40	*DEP International*	3
11	7	LAMBADA	Kaoma	*CBS*	4
13	[8]	FOOL'S GOLD/WHAT THE WORLD IS WAITING FOR	Stone Roses	*Silvertone*	2
27	9	CAN'T SHAKE THE FEELING	Big Fun	*Jive*	2
12	[10]	PACIFIC	808 State	*ZTT*	3
5	11	NEVER TOO LATE	Kylie Minogue	*PWL*	5
17	[12]	WHATCHA GONNA DO WITH MY LOVIN'	Inner City	*10*	3
9	13	I FEEL THE EARTH MOVE	Martika	*CBS*	7
20	[14]	COMMENT TE DIRE ADIEU	Jimmy Somerville featuring June Miles Kingston	*London*	3
8	15	GIRL I'M GONNA MISS YOU	Milli Vanilli	*Cooltempo*	9
10	16	GRAND PIANO	Mixmaster	*BCM*	5
15	17	C'MON AND GET MY LOVE	D. Mob introducing Cathy Dennis	*ffrr*	7
14	18	THAT'S WHAT I LIKE	Jive Bunny and the Mastermixers	*Music Factory Dance*	8
30	[19]	MADCHESTER RAVE ON (EP)	Happy Mondays	*Factory*	2
21	[20]	I'M NOT THE MAN I USED TO BE	Fine Young Cannibals	*London*	3
29	[21]	RONI	Bobby Brown	*MCA*	2
16	22	STREET TUFF	Rebel MC and Double Trouble	*Desire*	9
34	[23]	GET ON YOUR FEET	Gloria Estefan	*Epic*	2
18	24	OUIJA BOARD OUIJA BOARD	Morrissey	*HMV*	2
6	25	INFINITE DREAMS (LIVE)	Iron Maiden	*EMI*	3
37	[26]	WOMAN IN CHAINS	Tears For Fears	*Fontana*	2
31	[27]	THE ARMS OF ORION	Prince with Sheena Easton	*Warner Bros*	3
23	28	LEAVE A LIGHT ON	Belinda Carlisle	*Virgin*	9
26	29	RIDE ON TIME	Black Box	*deConstruction*	17
-	30	THIS WOMAN'S WORK	Kate Bush	*EMI*	1
19	31	ROOM IN YOUR HEART	Living In A Box	*Chrysalis*	10
-	32	GOT TO GET	Rob 'n' Raz featuring Leila K ●	*Arista*	1
-	33	I DON'T WANNA LOSE YOU	Tina Turner	*Capitol*	1
-	34	IN PRIVATE	Dusty Springfield	*Parlophone*	1
22	35	NEVER TOO MUCH	Luther Vandross	*Epic*	6
-	36	DEEP HEAT 89	Latino Rave ●	*Deep Heat*	1
32	37	THE ROAD TO HELL (PART 2)	Chris Rea	*WEA*	8
28	38	DON'T ASK ME WHY	Eurythmics	*RCA*	4
36	39	PUMP UP THE JAM	Technotronic featuring Felly	*Swanyard*	13
25	40	I WANT THAT MAN	Deborah Harry	*Chrysalis*	8

WEEK ENDING 9 DECEMBER 1989

LW	TW	Title	Artist	Label	Wks
1	[1]	YOU GOT IT (THE RIGHT STUFF)	New Kids On The Block	*CBS*	5
2	[2]	DON'T KNOW MUCH	Linda Ronstadt with Aaron Neville	*Elektra*	5

■The Ben Liebrand re-mix of Jeff Wayne's *Eve Of The War* gives him a chart return eleven years after the single first charted (25.11.89) ■ A new lease of life for the over 40 ladies. Linda Ronstadt, Tina Turner, Dusty Springfield and Deborah Harry are all nearer their free bus passes than their 21st birthday parties, but they are all in the charts (02.12.89)■

December 1989

□ Highest position disc reached ● Act's first ever week on chart

LW	TW	Title	Artist	Label	Wks
4	[3]	EVE OF THE WAR	Jeff Wayne	CBS	3
7	[4]	LAMBADA	Kaoma	CBS	5
-	5	GET A LIFE	Soul II Soul	10	1
6	[6]	HOMELY GIRL	UB40	DEP International	4
-	7	WHEN YOU COME BACK TO ME	Jason Donovan	PWL	1
9	[8]	CAN'T SHAKE THE FEELING	Big Fun	Jive	3
8	9	FOOL'S GOLD/WHAT THE WORLD IS WAITING FOR	Stone Roses	Silvertone	3
3	10	ALL AROUND THE WORLD	Lisa Stansfield	Arista	7
33	11	I DON'T WANNA LOSE YOU	Tina Turner	Capitol	2
5	12	ANOTHER DAY IN PARADISE	Phil Collins	Virgin	6
10	13	PACIFIC	808 State	ZTT	4
32	14	GOT TO GET	Rob 'n' Raz featuring Leila K	Arista	2
12	15	WHATCHA GONNA DO WITH MY LOVIN'	Inner City	10	4
-	16	YOU SURROUND ME	Erasure	Mute	1
14	17	COMMENT TE DIRE ADIEU	Jimmy Somerville featuring June Miles Kingston	London	4
-	[18]	THE AMSTERDAM EP	Simple Minds	Virgin	1
34	19	IN PRIVATE	Dusty Springfield	Parlophone	2
20	[20]	I'M NOT THE MAN I USED TO BE	Fine Young Cannibals	London	4
-	[21]	THE MIRACLE	Queen	Parlophone	1
36	22	DEEP HEAT 89	Latino Rave	Deep Heat	2
23	[23]	GET ON YOUR FEET	Gloria Estefan	Epic	3
11	24	NEVER TOO LATE	Kylie Minogue	PWL	6
30	[25]	THIS WOMAN'S WORK	Kate Bush	EMI	2
13	26	I FEEL THE EARTH MOVE	Martika	CBS	8
-	27	SIT AND WAIT	Sydney Youngblood	Circa	1
19	28	MADCHESTER RAVE ON (EP)	Happy Mondays	Factory	3
26	29	WOMAN IN CHAINS	Tears For Fears	Fontana	3
-	30	DONALD WHERE'S YOUR TROOSERS	Andy Stewart	Stone	1
15	31	GIRL I'M GONNA MISS YOU	Milli Vanilli	Cooltempo	10
21	32	RONI	Bobby Brown	MCA	3
18	33	THAT'S WHAT I LIKE	Jive Bunny and the Mastermixers	Music Factory Dance	9
17	34	C'MON AND GET MY LOVE	D. Mob introducing Cathy Dennis	ffrr	8
-	35	WHENEVER GOD SHINES HIS LIGHT	Van Morrison with Cliff Richard ●	Polydor	1
16	36	GRAND PIANO	Mixmaster	BCM	6
22	37	STREET TUFF	Rebel MC and Double Trouble	Desire	10
-	38	HITMIX (OFFICIAL BOOTLEG MEGAMIX)	Alexander O'Neal	Tabu	1
-	39	BROKE AWAY	Wet Wet Wet	Precious	1
27	40	THE ARMS OF ORION	Prince with Sheena Easton	Warner Bros	4

WEEK ENDING 16 DECEMBER 1989

LW	TW	Title	Artist	Label	Wks
-	[1]	LET'S PARTY	Jive Bunny and the Mastermixers	Music Factory Dance	1
7	[2]	WHEN YOU COME BACK TO ME	Jason Donovan	PWL	2
5	[3]	GET A LIFE	Soul II Soul	10	2
1	4	YOU GOT IT (THE RIGHT STUFF)	New Kids On The Block	CBS	6
4	5	LAMBADA	Kaoma	CBS	6
3	6	EVE OF THE WAR	Jeff Wayne	CBS	4
2	7	DON'T KNOW MUCH	Linda Ronstadt with Aaron Neville	Elektra	6
11	[8]	I DON'T WANNA LOSE YOU	Tina Turner	Capitol	3
-	9	DEAR JESSIE	Madonna	Sire	1
30	10	DONALD WHERE'S YOUR TROOSERS	Andy Stewart	Stone	2
8	11	CAN'T SHAKE THE FEELING	Big Fun	Jive	4
6	12	HOMELY GIRL	UB40	DEP International	5
14	13	GOT TO GET	Rob 'n' Raz featuring Leila K	Arista	3
19	[14]	IN PRIVATE	Dusty Springfield	Parlophone	3
16	[15]	YOU SURROUND ME	Erasure	Mute	2
27	16	SIT AND WAIT	Sydney Youngblood	Circa	2
9	17	FOOL'S GOLD/WHAT THE WORLD IS WAITING FOR	Stone Roses	Silvertone	4
22	18	DEEP HEAT 89	Latino Rave	Deep Heat	3
18	19	THE AMSTERDAM EP	Simple Minds	Virgin	2
38	20	HITMIX (OFFICIAL BOOTLEG MEGAMIX)	Alexander O'Neal	Tabu	2
10	21	ALL AROUND THE WORLD	Lisa Stansfield	Arista	8
12	22	ANOTHER DAY IN PARADISE	Phil Collins	Virgin	7
-	23	GETTING AWAY WITH IT	Electronic ●	Factory	1
39	24	BROKE AWAY	Wet Wet Wet	Precious	2
35	25	WHENEVER GOD SHINES HIS LIGHT	Van Morrison with Cliff Richard	Polydor	2
15	26	WHATCHA GONNA DO WITH MY LOVIN'	Inner City	10	5
21	27	THE MIRACLE	Queen	Parlophone	2
17	28	COMMENT TE DIRE ADIEU	Jimmy Somerville featuring June Miles Kingston	London	5
13	29	PACIFIC	808 State	ZTT	5
24	30	NEVER TOO LATE	Kylie Minogue	PWL	7
25	31	THIS WOMAN'S WORK	Kate Bush	EMI	3
-	32	SISTER	Bros	CBS	1
20	33	I'M NOT THE MAN I USED TO BE	Fine Young Cannibals	London	5
23	34	GET ON YOUR FEET	Gloria Estefan	Epic	4
-	35	20 SECONDS TO COMPLY	Silver Bullet ●	Tam Tam	1
-	36	BURNING THE GROUND	Duran Duran	EMI	1
-	37	LISTEN TO YOUR HEART	Sonia	Chrysalis	1
33	38	THAT'S WHAT I LIKE	Jive Bunny and the Mastermixers	Music Factory Dance	10
26	39	I FEEL THE EARTH MOVE	Martika	CBS	9
-	40	GOING BACK TO MY ROOTS/RICH IN PARADISE	FPI Project ●	Rumour	1

WEEK ENDING 23 DECEMBER 1989

LW	TW	Title	Artist	Label	Wks
-	[1]	DO THEY KNOW IT'S CHRISTMAS	Band Aid II	PWL/Polydor	1
1	2	LET'S PARTY	Jive Bunny and the Mastermixers	Music Factory Dance	2
2	3	WHEN YOU COME BACK TO ME	Jason Donovan	PWL	3
3	4	GET A LIFE	Soul II Soul	10	3
5	5	LAMBADA	Kaoma	CBS	7
10	6	DONALD WHERE'S YOUR TROOSERS	Andy Stewart	Stone	3
9	7	DEAR JESSIE	Madonna	Sire	2
8	[8]	I DON'T WANNA LOSE YOU	Tina Turner	Capitol	4
7	9	DON'T KNOW MUCH	Linda Ronstadt with Aaron Neville	Elektra	7
4	10	YOU GOT IT (THE RIGHT STUFF)	New Kids On The Block	CBS	7
6	11	EVE OF THE WAR	Jeff Wayne	CBS	5
32	12	SISTER	Bros	CBS	2
23	13	GETTING AWAY WITH IT	Electronic	Factory	2
13	14	GOT TO GET	Rob 'n' Raz featuring Leila K	Arista	4
14	15	IN PRIVATE	Dusty Springfield	Parlophone	4
18	16	DEEP HEAT 89	Latino Rave	Deep Heat	4
11	17	CAN'T SHAKE THE FEELING	Big Fun	Jive	5
16	18	SIT AND WAIT	Sydney Youngblood	Circa	3
20	[19]	HITMIX (OFFICIAL BOOTLEG MEGAMIX)	Alexander O'Neal	Tabu	3
25	[20]	WHENEVER GOD SHINES HIS LIGHT	Van Morrison with Cliff Richard	Polydor	3
12	21	HOMELY GIRL	UB40	DEP International	6
15	22	YOU SURROUND ME	Erasure	Mute	3
24	23	BROKE AWAY	Wet Wet Wet	Precious	3
17	24	FOOL'S GOLD/WHAT THE WORLD IS WAITING FOR	Stone Roses	Silvertone	5
-	25	THE MAGIC NUMBER/BUDDY	De La Soul	Big Life	1
35	26	20 SECONDS TO COMPLY	Silver Bullet	Tam Tam	2
22	27	ANOTHER DAY IN PARADISE	Phil Collins	Virgin	8
19	28	THE AMSTERDAM EP	Simple Minds	Virgin	3
21	29	ALL AROUND THE WORLD	Lisa Stansfield	Arista	9
40	30	GOING BACK TO MY ROOTS/RICH IN PARADISE	FPI Project	Rumour	2
36	[31]	BURNING THE GROUND	Duran Duran	EMI	2
37	32	LISTEN TO YOUR HEART	Sonia	Chrysalis	2
-	33	WORDS	Christians	Island	1
-	34	DECEMBER	All About Eve	Mercury	1
30	35	NEVER TOO LATE	Kylie Minogue	PWL	8

In these weeks ■ Jive Bunny matches the achievements of Gerry and the Pacemakers and Frankie Goes To Hollywood by hitting number one with each of their first three singles. Jive Bunny do it in style, crashing straight into the top spot (16.12.89)■

□ Highest position disc reached ● Act's first ever week on chart

LW	TW		Wks
-	**36**	TOUCH ME 49ers ● .... *Fourth + Broadway*	1
26	**37**	WHATCHA GONNA DO WITH MY LOVIN' Inner City *10*	6
28	**38**	COMMENT TE DIRE ADIEU Jimmy Somerville featuring June Miles Kingston .... *London*	6
-	**39**	I'LL SAIL THIS SHIP ALONE Beautiful South .... *Go! Discs*	1
-	**40**	LIVING IN SIN Bon Jovi .... *Vertigo*	1

LW	TW	*WEEK ENDING* **30 DECEMBER 1989**	Wks
1	**1**	DO THEY KNOW IT'S CHRISTMAS Band Aid II .... *PWL/Polydor*	2
2	**2**	LET'S PARTY Jive Bunny and the Mastermixers .... *Music Factory Dance*	3
3	**3**	WHEN YOU COME BACK TO ME Jason Donovan .... *PWL*	4
6	**4**	DONALD WHERE'S YOUR TROOSERS Andy Stewart .... *Stone*	4
7	**5**	DEAR JESSIE Madonna .... *Sire*	3
4	**6**	GET A LIFE Soul II Soul 10 4	
5	**7**	LAMBADA Kaoma .... *CBS*	8
8	**8**	I DON'T WANNA LOSE YOU Tina Turner .... *Capitol*	5
9	**9**	DON'T KNOW MUCH Linda Ronstadt with Aaron Neville .... *Elektra*	8
12	**10**	SISTER Bros .... *CBS*	3
14	**11**	GOT TO GET Rob 'n' Raz featuring Leila K .... *Arista*	5
13	**12**	GETTING AWAY WITH IT Electronic .... *Factory*	3
25	**13**	THE MAGIC NUMBER/BUDDY De La Soul .... *Big Life*	2
10	**14**	YOU GOT IT (THE RIGHT STUFF) New Kids On The Block .... *CBS*	8
15	**15**	IN PRIVATE Dusty Springfield .... *Parlophone*	5
11	**16**	EVE OF THE WAR Jeff Wayne .... *CBS*	6
16	**17**	DEEP HEAT 89 Latino Rave .... *Deep Heat*	5
33	**18**	WORDS Christians .... *Island*	2
23	**19**	BROKE AWAY Wet Wet Wet .... *Precious*	4
20	**20**	WHENEVER GOD SHINES HIS LIGHT Van Morrison with Cliff Richard .... *Polydor*	4
18	**21**	SIT AND WAIT Sydney Youngblood .... *Circa*	4
17	**22**	CAN'T SHAKE THE FEELING Big Fun .... *Jive*	6
22	**23**	YOU SURROUND ME Erasure .... *Mute*	4
29	**24**	HITMIX (OFFICIAL BOOTLEG MEGAMIX) Alexander O'Neal .... *Tabu*	4
26	**25**	20 SECONDS TO COMPLY Silver Bullet .... *Tam Tam*	3
21	**26**	HOMELY GIRL UB40 .... *DEP International*	7
36	**27**	TOUCH ME 49ers .... *Fourthh + Broadway*	2
30	**28**	GOING BACK TO MY ROOTS/RICH IN PARADISE FPI Project .... *Rumour*	3
24	**29**	FOOL'S GOLD/WHAT THE WORLD IS WAITING FOR Stone Roses .... *Silvertone*	6
32	**30**	LISTEN TO YOUR HEART Sonia .... *Chrysalis*	3
39	**31**	I'LL SAIL THIS SHIP ALONE Beautiful South .... *Go! Discs*	2
29	**32**	ALL AROUND THE WORLD Lisa Stansfield .... *Arista*	10
27	**33**	ANOTHER DAY IN PARADISE Phil Collins .... *Virgin*	9
-	**34**	INNA CITY MAMMA Neneh Cherry .... *Circa*	1
40	**35**	LIVING IN SIN Bon Jovi .... *Vertigo*	2
31	**36**	BURNING THE GROUND Duran Duran .... *EMI*	3
28	**37**	THE AMSTERDAM EP Simple Minds .... *Virgin*	4
-	**38**	LA LUNA Belinda Carlisle .... *Virgin*	1
-	**39**	SMOKE ON THE WATER Rock Aid Armenia ● .... *Life Aid*	1
34	**40**	DECEMBER All About Eve .... *Mercury*	2

■*Do They Know It's Christmas* becomes the 13th song to be number one in two different versions, and the only song to go straight in at number one twice (23.12.89) ■ 29 years and 15 days after it sneaked into the chart at number 37, Andy Stewart's re-issued *Donald Where's Your Troosers* hits number 4, a real turn-up (30.12.89)■

1990

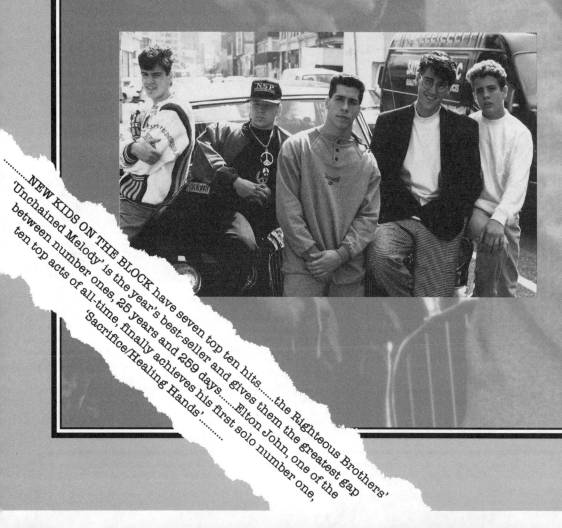

........NEW KIDS ON THE BLOCK have seven top ten hits.......the Righteous Brothers' 'Unchained Melody' is the year's best-seller and gives them the greatest gap between number ones, 25 years and 259 days.......Elton John, one of the ten top acts of all-time, finally achieves his first solo number one, 'Sacrifice/Healing Hands'........

January 1990

□ Highest position disc reached ● Act's first ever week on chart

LW	TW	WEEK ENDING 6 JANUARY 1990	Label	Wks
1	1	DO THEY KNOW IT'S CHRISTMAS? Band Aid II	PWL	3
3	2	WHEN YOU COME BACK TO ME Jason Donovan	PWL	5
6	3	GET A LIFE Soul II Soul	10	5
2	4	LET'S PARTY Jive Bunny & the Mastermixers	Music Factory Dance	4
5	5	DEAR JESSIE Madonna	Sire	4
4	6	DONALD WHERE'S YOUR TROOSERS? Andy Stewart	Stone	5
7	7	LAMBADA Kaoma	CBS	9
13	8	THE MAGIC NUMBER De La Soul	Big Life	3
-	9	HANGIN' TOUGH New Kids On The Block	CBS	1
14	10	YOU GOT IT (THE RIGHT STUFF) New Kids On The Block	CBS	9
11	11	GOT TO GET Rob'n'Raz featuring Leila K	Arista	6
17	12	DEEP HEAT '89 Latino Rave	Deep Heat	6
12	13	GETTING AWAY WITH IT Electronic	Factory	4
10	14	SISTER Bros	CBS	4
22	15	CAN'T SHAKE THE FEELING Big Fun	Jive	7
8	16	I DON'T WANNA LOSE YOU Tina Turner	Capitol	6
16	17	EVE OF THE WAR (BEN LIEBRAND REMIX) Jeff Wayne	CBS	11
25	18	20 SECONDS TO COMPLY Silver Bullet	Tam Tam	4
21	19	SIT AND WAIT Sydney Youngblood	Circa	5
30	20	LISTEN TO YOUR HEART Sonia	Chrysalis	4
23	21	YOU SURROUND ME Erasure	Mute	5
9	22	DON'T KNOW MUCH Linda Ronstadt with Aaron Neville	Elektra	9
27	23	TOUCH ME 49'ers	Fourth + Broadway	3
-	24	HEY YOU Quireboys	Parlophone	1
28	25	GOING BACK TO MY ROOTS FPI Project/Rich In Paradise	Rumour	4
-	26	BIG WEDGE Fish	EMI	1
24	27	HITMIX (THE OFFICIAL BOOTLEG MIX) Alexander O'Neal	Tabu	5
18	28	WORDS Christians	Island	3
19	29	BROKE AWAY Wet Wet Wet	Precious Organisation	5
-	30	QUEEN OF THE NEW YEAR Deacon Blue	CBS	1
15	31	IN PRIVATE Dusty Springfield	Parlophone	6
-	32	MADCHESTER RAVE ON (E.P.) Happy Mondays	Factory	1
-	33	GOT TO HAVE YOUR LOVE Mantronix featuring Wondress	Capitol	1
32	34	ALL AROUND THE WORLD Lisa Stansfield	Arista	11
29	35	WHAT THE WORLD IS WAITING FOR/FOOL'S GOLD Stone Roses	Silvertone	7
-	36	PUT YOUR HANDS TOGETHER D Mob	London	1
34	37	INNA CITY MAMMA Neneh Cherry	Circa	2
31	38	I'LL SAIL THIS SHIP ALONE Beautiful South	Go! Discs	3
26	39	HOMELY GIRL UB40	Dep International	8
20	40	WHENEVER GOD SHINES HIS LIGHT Van Morrison with Cliff Richard	Polydor	5

LW	TW	WEEK ENDING 13 JANUARY 1990	Label	Wks
9	1	HANGIN' TOUGH New Kids On The Block	CBS	2
2	2	WHEN YOU COME BACK TO ME Jason Donovan	PWL	6
3	3	GET A LIFE Soul II Soul	10	6
1	4	DO THEY KNOW IT'S CHRISTMAS? Band Aid II	PWL	4
5	5	DEAR JESSIE Madonna	Sire	5
23	6	TOUCH ME 49'ers	Fourth + Broadway	4
8	7	THE MAGIC NUMBER De La Soul	Big Life	4
11	8	GOT TO GET Rob'n'Raz featuring Leila K	Arista	7
7	9	LAMBADA Kaoma	CBS	10
20	10	LISTEN TO YOUR HEART Sonia	Chrysalis	5
18	11	20 SECONDS TO COMPLY Silver Bullet	Tam Tam	5
33	12	GOT TO HAVE YOUR LOVE Mantronix featuring Wondress	Capitol	2
12	13	DEEP HEAT '89 Latino Rave	Deep Heat	7
25	14	GOING BACK TO MY ROOTS FPI Project/Rich In Paradise	Rumour	5
13	15	GETTING AWAY WITH IT Electronic	Factory	5
36	16	PUT YOUR HANDS TOGETHER D Mob	London	2
-	17	BUTTERFLY ON A WHEEL Mission	Mercury	1
6	18	DONALD WHERE'S YOUR TROOSERS? Andy Stewart	Stone	6
4	19	LET'S PARTY Jive Bunny & the Mastermixers	Music Factory Dance	5
24	20	HEY YOU Quireboys	Parlophone	2
30	21	QUEEN OF THE NEW YEAR Deacon Blue	CBS	2
32	22	MADCHESTER RAVE ON (E.P.) Happy Mondays	Factory	2
19	23	SIT AND WAIT Sydney Youngblood	Circa	6
-	24	YOU MAKE ME FEEL (MIGHTY REAL) Jimmy Somerville	London	1
26	25	BIG WEDGE Fish	EMI	2
10	26	YOU GOT IT (THE RIGHT STUFF) New Kids On The Block	CBS	10
21	27	YOU SURROUND ME Erasure	Mute	6
14	28	SISTER Bros	CBS	5
16	29	I DON'T WANNA LOSE YOU Tina Turner	Capitol	7
-	30	COULD HAVE TOLD YOU SO Halo James ●	Epic	1
28	31	WORDS Christians	Island	4
17	32	EVE OF THE WAR (BEN LIEBRAND REMIX) Jeff Wayne	CBS	12
37	33	INNA CITY MAMMA Neneh Cherry	Circa	3
31	34	IN PRIVATE Dusty Springfield	Parlophone	6
-	35	I CALLED YOU Lil Louis and the World	London	1
-	36	NO MORE MR. NICE GUY Megadeth ●	SBK	1
22	37	DON'T KNOW MUCH Linda Ronstadt with Aaron Neville	Elektra	10
29	38	WORDS Christians	Island	6
-	39	MORE THAN YOU KNOW Martika	CBS	1
35	40	WHAT THE WORLD IS WAITING FOR/FOOL'S GOLD Stone Roses	Silvertone	8

LW	TW	WEEK ENDING 20 JANUARY 1990	Label	Wks
1	1	HANGIN' TOUGH New Kids On The Block	CBS	3
-	2	TEARS ON MY PILLOW Kylie Minogue	PWL	1
6	3	TOUCH ME 49'ers	Fourth + Broadway	5
12	4	GOT TO HAVE YOUR LOVE Mantronix featuring Wondress	Capitol	3
24	5	YOU MAKE ME FEEL (MIGHTY REAL) Jimmy Somerville	London	2
3	6	GET A LIFE Soul II Soul	10	7
16	7	PUT YOUR HANDS TOGETHER D Mob	London	3
8	8	GOT TO GET Rob'n'Raz featuring Leila K	Arista	8
2	9	WHEN YOU COME BACK TO ME Jason Donovan	PWL	7
14	10	GOING BACK TO MY ROOTS FPI Project/Rich In Paradise	Rumour	6
7	11	THE MAGIC NUMBER De La Soul	Big Life	5
17	12	BUTTERFLY ON A WHEEL Mission	Mercury	2
30	13	COULD HAVE TOLD YOU SO Halo James	Epic	2
10	14	LISTEN TO YOUR HEART Sonia	Chrysalis	6
9	15	LAMBADA Kaoma	CBS	11
5	16	DEAR JESSIE Madonna	Sire	6
11	17	20 SECONDS TO COMPLY Silver Bullet	Tam Tam	6
36	18	NO MORE MR. NICE GUY Megadeth	SBK	2
20	19	HEY YOU Quireboys	Parlophone	3
35	20	I CALLED YOU Lil Louis and the World	London	2
15	21	GETTING AWAY WITH IT Electronic	Factory	6
13	22	DEEP HEAT '89 Latino Rave	Deep Heat	8
39	23	MORE THAN YOU KNOW Martika	CBS	2
21	24	QUEEN OF THE NEW YEAR Deacon Blue	CBS	3
22	25	MADCHESTER RAVE ON (E.P.) Happy Mondays	Factory	3
-	26	WELCOME TO THE TERRORDOME Public Enemy	Def Jam	1
-	27	N-R-G Adamski ●	MCA	1
-	28	WELCOME Gino Latino ●	ffrr	1
34	29	IN PRIVATE Dusty Springfield	Parlophone	7
-	30	NOTHING COMPARES 2 U Sinead O'Connor	Ensign	1
33	31	INNA CITY MAMMA Neneh Cherry	Circa	4
4	32	DO THEY KNOW IT'S CHRISTMAS? Band Aid II	PWL	5
-	33	I'LL BE GOOD TO YOU Quincy Jones	Qwest	1
25	34	BIG WEDGE Fish	EMI	3
27	35	YOU SURROUND ME Erasure	Mute	7
23	36	SIT AND WAIT Sydney Youngblood	Circa	7

In these weeks ■ Band Aid II drop from four to 32, the biggest ever fall from the top five (20.01.90) ■ In the same week Jive Bunny and the Mastermixers' *Let's Party* becomes the first number one hit to spend only five weeks in the Top 40, a record equalled by *Do They Know It's Christmas* a week later (20.01.90)■

LW	TW	Title	Artist	Label	Wks
-	37	JUICY	Wrecks-N-Effect ●	*Motown*	1
31	38	WORDS	Christians	*Island*	5
26	39	YOU GOT IT (THE RIGHT STUFF)	New Kids On The Block	*CBS*	11
-	40	THE FACE	And Why Not?	*Island*	1

LW	TW	*WEEK ENDING* **27 JANUARY 1990**			Wks
2	1	TEARS ON MY PILLOW	Kylie Minogue	*PWL*	2
1	2	HANGIN' TOUGH	New Kids On The Block	*CBS*	4
30	3	NOTHING COMPARES 2 U	Sinead O'Connor	*Ensign*	2
3	4	TOUCH ME	49'ers	*Fourth + Broadway*	6
4	5	GOT TO HAVE YOUR LOVE	Mantronix featuring Wondress	*Capitol*	4
13	6	COULD HAVE TOLD YOU SO	Halo James	*Epic*	3
5	7	YOU MAKE ME FEEL (MIGHTY REAL)	Jimmy Somerville	*London*	3
7	8	PUT YOUR HANDS TOGETHER	D Mob	*London*	4
10	9	GOING BACK TO MY ROOTS	FPI Project/Rich In Paradise	*Rumour*	7
8	10	GOT TO GET	Rob'n'Raz featuring Leila K	*Arista*	9
6	11	GET A LIFE	Soul II Soul	*10*	8
27	12	N-R-G	Adamski	*MCA*	2
18	13	NO MORE MR. NICE GUY	Megadeth	*SBK*	3
19	14	HEY YOU	Quireboys	*Parlophone*	4
23	15	MORE THAN YOU KNOW	Martika	*CBS*	3
20	16	I CALLED YOU	Lil Louis and the World	*London*	3
9	17	WHEN YOU COME BACK TO ME	Jason Donovan	*PWL*	8
26	18	WELCOME TO THE TERRORDOME	Public Enemy	*Def Jam*	2
28	19	WELCOME	Gino Latino	*ffrr*	2
11	20	THE MAGIC NUMBER	De La Soul	*Big Life*	5
15	21	LAMBADA	Kaoma	*CBS*	12
14	22	LISTEN TO YOUR HEART	Sonia	*Chrysalis*	7
-	23	NOTHING EVER HAPPENS	Del Amitri ●	*A&M*	1
-	24	INSTANT REPLAY	Yell! ●	*Fanfare*	1
17	25	20 SECONDS TO COMPLY	Silver Bullet	*Tam Tam*	7
-	26	I WISH IT WOULD RAIN DOWN	Phil Collins	*Virgin*	1
33	27	I'LL BE GOOD TO YOU	Quincy Jones	*Qwest*	2
16	28	DEAR JESSIE	Madonna	*Sire*	7
12	29	BUTTERFLY ON A WHEEL	Mission	*Mercury*	3
37	30	JUICY	Wrecks-N-Effect	*Motown*	2
40	31	THE FACE	And Why Not?	*Island*	2
-	32	HAPPENIN' ALL OVER AGAIN	Lonnie Gordon ●	*Supreme*	1
-	33	WAS THAT ALL IT WAS	Kym Mazelle	*Syncopate*	1
25	34	MADCHESTER RAVE ON (E.P.)	Happy Mondays	*Factory*	4
21	35	GETTING AWAY WITH IT	Electronic	*Factory*	7
-	36	JUST LIKE JESSE JAMES	Cher	*Geffen*	1
22	37	DEEP HEAT '89	Latino Rave	*Deep Heat*	9
29	38	IN PRIVATE	Dusty Springfield	*Parlophone*	8
-	39	WALK ON BY	Sybil	*PWL*	1
-	40	ALL 4 LOVE (BREAK 4 LOVE 1990)	Raze featuring Lady J	*Champion*	1

February 1990

□ Highest position disc reached ● Act's first ever week on chart

LW	TW	*WEEK ENDING* **3 FEBRUARY 1990**			Wks
3	1	NOTHING COMPARES 2 U	Sinead O'Connor	*Ensign*	3
1	2	TEARS ON MY PILLOW	Kylie Minogue	*PWL*	3
-	3	GET UP (BEFORE THE NIGHT IS OVER)	Technotronic featuring Ya Kid K	*Swanyard*	1
5	4	GOT TO HAVE YOUR LOVE	Mantronix featuring Wondress	*Capitol*	5
4	5	TOUCH ME	49'ers	*Fourth + Broadway*	7
6	6	COULD HAVE TOLD YOU SO	Halo James	*Epic*	4
2	7	HANGIN' TOUGH	New Kids On The Block	*CBS*	5
7	8	YOU MAKE ME FEEL (MIGHTY REAL)	Jimmy Somerville	*London*	4
32	9	HAPPENIN' ALL OVER AGAIN	Lonnie Gordon	*Supreme*	2
26	10	I WISH IT WOULD RAIN DOWN	Phil Collins	*Virgin*	2
24	11	INSTANT REPLAY	Yell!	*Fanfare*	2
12	12	N-R-G	Adamski	*MCA*	3
9	13	GOING BACK TO MY ROOTS	FPI Project/Rich In Paradise	*Rumour*	8
8	14	PUT YOUR HANDS TOGETHER	D Mob	*London*	5
23	15	NOTHING EVER HAPPENS	Del Amitri	*A&M*	2
15	16	MORE THAN YOU KNOW	Martika	*CBS*	4
19	17	WELCOME	Gino Latino	*ffrr*	3
10	18	GOT TO GET	Rob'n'Raz featuring Leila K	*Arista*	10
39	19	WALK ON BY	Sybil	*PWL*	2
31	20	THE FACE	And Why Not?	*Island*	3
27	21	I'LL BE GOOD TO YOU	Quincy Jones	*Qwest*	3
-	22	SHINE ON	House Of Love ●	*Fontana*	1
-	23	18 AND LIFE	Skid Row ●	*Atlantic*	1
14	24	HEY YOU	Quireboys	*Parlophone*	5
36	25	JUST LIKE JESSE JAMES	Cher	*Geffen*	2
11	26	GET A LIFE	Soul II Soul	*10*	9
16	27	I CALLED YOU	Lil Louis and the World	*London*	4
13	28	NO MORE MR. NICE GUY	Megadeth	*SBK*	4
30	29	JUICY	Wrecks-N-Effect	*Motown*	3
40	30	ALL 4 LOVE (BREAK 4 LOVE 1990)	Raze featuring Lady J	*Champion*	2
18	31	WELCOME TO THE TERRORDOME	Public Enemy	*Def Jam*	3
-	32	SLEEP WITH ME	Birdland ●	*Lazy*	1
33	33	WAS THAT ALL IT WAS	Kym Mazelle	*Syncopate*	2
-	34	KING AND QUEEN OF AMERICA	Eurythmics	*RCA*	1
17	35	WHEN YOU COME BACK TO ME	Jason Donovan	*PWL*	9
-	36	HELLO	The Beloved	*WEA*	1
21	37	LAMBADA	Kaoma	*CBS*	13
-	38	COME BACK TO ME	Janet Jackson	*Breakout*	1
22	39	LISTEN TO YOUR HEART	Sonia	*Chrysalis*	8
20	40	THE MAGIC NUMBER	De La Soul	*Big Life*	6

LW	TW	*WEEK ENDING* **10 FEBRUARY 1990**			Wks
1	1	NOTHING COMPARES 2 U	Sinead O'Connor	*Ensign*	4
3	2	GET UP (BEFORE THE NIGHT IS OVER)	Technotronic featuring Ya Kid K	*Swanyard*	2
2	3	TEARS ON MY PILLOW	Kylie Minogue	*PWL*	4
9	4	HAPPENIN' ALL OVER AGAIN	Lonnie Gordon	*Supreme*	3
4	5	GOT TO HAVE YOUR LOVE	Mantronix featuring Wondress	*Capitol*	6
5	6	TOUCH ME	49'ers	*Fourth + Broadway*	8
10	7	I WISH IT WOULD RAIN DOWN	Phil Collins	*Virgin*	3
6	8	COULD HAVE TOLD YOU SO	Halo James	*Epic*	5
19	9	WALK ON BY	Sybil	*PWL*	3
11	10	INSTANT REPLAY	Yell!	*Fanfare*	3
15	11	NOTHING EVER HAPPENS	Del Amitri	*A&M*	3
23	12	18 AND LIFE	Skid Row	*Atlantic*	2
20	13	THE FACE	And Why Not?	*Island*	4
7	14	HANGIN' TOUGH	New Kids On The Block	*CBS*	6
-	15	DUB BE GOOD TO ME	Beats International ●	*GoBeat*	1
8	16	YOU MAKE ME FEEL (MIGHTY REAL)	Jimmy Somerville	*London*	5
17	17	WELCOME	Gino Latino	*ffrr*	4
25	18	JUST LIKE JESSE JAMES	Cher	*Geffen*	3
-	19	LIVE TOGETHER	Lisa Stansfield	*Arista*	1
22	20	SHINE ON	House Of Love	*Fontana*	2
13	21	GOING BACK TO MY ROOTS	FPI Project/Rich In Paradise	*Rumour*	9
12	22	N-R-G	Adamski	*MCA*	4
14	23	PUT YOUR HANDS TOGETHER	D Mob	*London*	6
36	24	HELLO	The Beloved	*WEA*	2
16	25	MORE THAN YOU KNOW	Martika	*CBS*	5
21	26	I'LL BE GOOD TO YOU	Quincy Jones	*Qwest*	4
38	27	COME BACK TO ME	Janet Jackson	*Breakout*	2
18	28	GOT TO GET	Rob'n'Raz featuring Leila K	*Arista*	11
34	29	KING AND QUEEN OF AMERICA	Eurythmics	*RCA*	2
29	30	JUICY	Wrecks-N-Effect	*Motown*	4
30	31	ALL 4 LOVE (BREAK 4 LOVE 1990)	Raze featuring Lady J	*Champion*	3
-	32	DOWNTOWN TRAIN	Rod Stewart	*Warner Brothers*	1
-	33	BAD LOVE	Eric Clapton	*Duck*	1
26	34	GET A LIFE	Soul II Soul	*10*	10

■ *I'll Be Good To You* is credited to Quincy Jones, but features the vocal talents of Ray Charles and Chaka Khan. For Ray Charles it is his first Top 40 entry since 1968 (03.02.90) ■ Kylie Minogue's *Tears On My Pillow* is not the same song that Johnny Nash took to number one. It is her version of the Little Anthony and the Imperials classic. It becomes the third title to be used by each of two different chart-toppers (27.01.90) ■

February 1990

□ Highest position disc reached ● Act's first ever week on chart

LW	TW	Title / Artist	Label	Wks
-	[35]	BIKINI GIRLS WITH MACHINE GUNS Cramps ●	Enigma	1
33	36	WAS THAT ALL IT WAS Kym Mazelle	Syncopate	3
24	37	HEY YOU Quireboys	Parlophone	6
-	38	EPIC Faith No More ●	Slash	1
27	39	I CALLED YOU Lil Louis and the World	London	5
28	40	NO MORE MR. NICE GUY Megadeth	SBK	5

LW	TW	*WEEK ENDING* 17 FEBRUARY 1990		Wks
1	[1]	NOTHING COMPARES 2 U Sinead O'Connor	Ensign	5
2	[2]	GET UP (BEFORE THE NIGHT IS OVER) Technotronic featuring Ya Kid K	Swanyard	3
15	3	DUB BE GOOD TO ME Beats International	GoBeat	2
4	[4]	HAPPENIN' ALL OVER AGAIN Lonnie Gordon	Supreme	4
-	5	I DON'T KNOW ANYBODY ELSE Black Box	deConstruction	1
9	[6]	WALK ON BY Sybil	PWL	4
7	[7]	I WISH IT WOULD RAIN DOWN Phil Collins	Virgin	4
5	8	GOT TO HAVE YOUR LOVE Mantronix featuring Wondress	Capitol	7
3	9	TEARS ON MY PILLOW Kylie Minogue	PWL	5
19	[10]	LIVE TOGETHER Lisa Stansfield	Arista	2
10	11	INSTANT REPLAY Yell!	Fanfare	4
6	12	TOUCH ME 49'ers	Fourth + Broadway	9
12	13	18 AND LIFE Skid Row	Atlantic	3
11	14	NOTHING EVER HAPPENS Del Amitri	A&M	4
18	15	JUST LIKE JESSE JAMES Cher	Geffen	4
13	16	THE FACE And Why Not?	Island	5
-	17	ENJOY THE SILENCE Depeche Mode	Mute	1
8	18	COULD HAVE TOLD YOU SO Halo James	Epic	6
24	[19]	HELLO The Beloved	WEA	3
27	[20]	COME BACK TO ME Janet Jackson	Breakout	3
32	21	DOWNTOWN TRAIN Rod Stewart	Warner Brothers	2
-	22	HOW AM I SUPPOSED TO LIVE WITHOUT YOU Michael Bolton ●	CBS	1
17	23	WELCOME Gino Latino	ffrr	5
-	[24]	BRASSNECK The Wedding Present	RCA	1
33	[25]	BAD LOVE Eric Clapton	Duck	2
14	26	HANGIN' TOUGH New Kids On The Block	CBS	7
-	27	STEAMY WINDOWS Tina Turner	Capitol	1
20	28	SHINE ON House Of Love	Fontana	3
25	29	MORE THAN YOU KNOW Martika	CBS	6
16	30	YOU MAKE ME FEEL (MIGHTY REAL) Jimmy Somerville	London	6
-	31	96 TEARS Stranglers	Epic	1
-	[32]	PUT IT THERE Paul McCartney	Parlophone	1
29	33	KING AND QUEEN OF AMERICA Eurythmics	RCA	3
26	34	I'LL BE GOOD TO YOU Quincy Jones	Qwest	5
-	35	TELL ME THERE'S A HEAVEN Chris Rea	East West	1
21	36	GOING BACK TO MY ROOTS FPI Project/Rich In Paradise	Rumour	10
38	[37]	EPIC Faith No More	Slash	2
-	38	ROOM AT THE TOP Adam Ant	MCA	1
-	39	PROBABLY A ROBBERY Renegade Soundwave ●	Mute	1
-	40	DIRTY LOVE Thunder ●	EMI	1

LW	TW	*WEEK ENDING* 24 FEBRUARY 1990		Wks
1	[1]	NOTHING COMPARES 2 U Sinead O'Connor	Ensign	6
3	2	DUB BE GOOD TO ME Beats International	GoBeat	3
2	3	GET UP (BEFORE THE NIGHT IS OVER) Technotronic featuring Ya Kid K	Swanyard	4
5	[4]	I DON'T KNOW ANYBODY ELSE Black Box	deConstruction	2
22	5	HOW AM I SUPPOSED TO LIVE WITHOUT YOU Michael Bolton	CBS	2
17	[6]	ENJOY THE SILENCE Depeche Mode	Mute	2
4	7	HAPPENIN' ALL OVER AGAIN Lonnie Gordon	Supreme	5
6	8	WALK ON BY Sybil	PWL	5
7	9	I WISH IT WOULD RAIN DOWN Phil Collins	Virgin	5
10	[10]	LIVE TOGETHER Lisa Stansfield	Arista	3
15	[11]	JUST LIKE JESSE JAMES Cher	Geffen	5
8	12	GOT TO HAVE YOUR LOVE Mantronix featuring Wondress	Capitol	8
27	[13]	STEAMY WINDOWS Tina Turner	Capitol	2
11	14	INSTANT REPLAY Yell!	Fanfare	5
9	15	TEARS ON MY PILLOW Kylie Minogue	PWL	6
21	16	DOWNTOWN TRAIN Rod Stewart	Warner Brothers	3
31	[17]	96 TEARS Stranglers	Epic	2
12	18	TOUCH ME 49'ers	Fourth + Broadway	10
-	19	STRONGER THAN THAT Cliff Richard	EMI	1
14	20	NOTHING EVER HAPPENS Del Amitri	A&M	5
20	21	COME BACK TO ME Janet Jackson	Breakout	4
38	22	ROOM AT THE TOP Adam Ant	MCA	2
13	23	18 AND LIFE Skid Row	Atlantic	4
35	[24]	TELL ME THERE'S A HEAVEN Chris Rea	East West	2
19	25	HELLO The Beloved	WEA	4
16	26	THE FACE And Why Not?	Island	6
-	27	INFINITY Guru Josh ●	deConstruction	1
25	28	BAD LOVE Eric Clapton	Duck	3
-	29	DUDE (LOOKS LIKE A LADY) Aerosmith	Geffen	1
18	30	COULD HAVE TOLD YOU SO Halo James	Epic	7
-	31	BLACK BETTY (BEN LIEBRAND REMIX) Ram Jam	Epic	1
40	[32]	DIRTY LOVE Thunder	EMI	2
-	33	TALKING WITH MYSELF Electribe 101	Mercury	1
24	34	BRASSNECK The Wedding Present	RCA	2
23	35	WELCOME Gino Latino	ffrr	6
-	36	WALK ON THE WILD SIDE Jamie J Morgan ●	Tabu	1
-	37	I MIGHT Shakin' Stevens	Epic	1
39	[38]	PROBABLY A ROBBERY Renegade Soundwave	Mute	2
26	39	HANGIN' TOUGH New Kids On The Block	CBS	8
30	40	YOU MAKE ME FEEL (MIGHTY REAL) Jimmy Somerville	London	7

LW	TW	*WEEK ENDING* 3 MARCH 1990		Wks
2	[1]	DUB BE GOOD TO ME Beats International	GoBeat	4
1	2	NOTHING COMPARES 2 U Sinead O'Connor	Ensign	7
5	[3]	HOW AM I SUPPOSED TO LIVE WITHOUT YOU Michael Bolton	CBS	3
3	4	GET UP (BEFORE THE NIGHT IS OVER) Technotronic featuring Ya Kid K	Swanyard	5
4	5	I DON'T KNOW ANYBODY ELSE Black Box	deConstruction	3
6	[6]	ENJOY THE SILENCE Depeche Mode	Mute	3
-	7	THE BRITS 1990 Various Artists	RCA	1
-	[8]	ELEPHANT STONE Stone Roses	Silvertone	1
27	9	INFINITY Guru Josh	deConstruction	2
16	[10]	DOWNTOWN TRAIN Rod Stewart	Warner Brothers	4
7	11	HAPPENIN' ALL OVER AGAIN Lonnie Gordon	Supreme	6
8	12	WALK ON BY Sybil	PWL	6
22	[13]	ROOM AT THE TOP Adam Ant	MCA	3
19	[14]	STRONGER THAN THAT Cliff Richard	EMI	2
31	15	BLACK BETTY (BEN LIEBRAND REMIX) Ram Jam	Epic	2
13	16	STEAMY WINDOWS Tina Turner	Capitol	3
11	17	JUST LIKE JESSE JAMES Cher	Geffen	6
9	18	I WISH IT WOULD RAIN DOWN Phil Collins	Virgin	6
17	19	96 TEARS Stranglers	Epic	3
29	[20]	DUDE (LOOKS LIKE A LADY) Aerosmith	Geffen	2
12	21	GOT TO HAVE YOUR LOVE Mantronix featuring Wondress	Capitol	9
-	22	MOMENTS IN SOUL JT and the Big Family ●	Champion	1
33	[23]	TALKING WITH MYSELF Electribe 101	Mercury	2
24	[24]	TELL ME THERE'S A HEAVEN Chris Rea	East West	3
10	25	LIVE TOGETHER Lisa Stansfield	Arista	4
14	26	INSTANT REPLAY Yell!	Fanfare	6
36	[27]	WALK ON THE WILD SIDE Jamie J Morgan	Tabu	2
15	28	TEARS ON MY PILLOW Kylie Minogue	PWL	7
37	29	I MIGHT Shakin' Stevens	Epic	2
18	30	TOUCH ME 49'ers	Fourth + Broadway	11
-	31	NATURAL THING Innocence ●	Cooltempo	1
-	32	A LOVER SPURNED Marc Almond	Some Bizzare	1
-	33	LOVE SHACK B52s	Reprise	1
-	34	LILY WAS HERE David A. Stewart featuring Candy Dulfer ●	Anxious	1

In these weeks ■ *The Brits 1990*, a mix of several of the records in the running for a 1990 Brit award, comes in at number seven, one place below the record that will win the Brit award for Best Single a year later, Depeche Mode's *Enjoy The Silence* (03.03.90) ■ David A. Stewart half of the Eurythmics, debuts with a new female partner, Dutch saxophonist Candy Duffer (03.03.90)■

LW	TW	Title	Artist	Label	Wks
20	35	NOTHING EVER HAPPENS	Del Amitri	A&M	6
-	36	ADVICE FOR THE YOUNG AT HEART	Tears For Fears	Fontana	1
-	37	HERE WE ARE	Gloria Estefan	Epic	1
28	38	BAD LOVE	Eric Clapton	Duck	4
25	39	HELLO	The Beloved	WEA	5
23	40	18 AND LIFE	Skid Row	Atlantic	5

WEEK ENDING 10 MARCH 1990

LW	TW	Title	Artist	Label	Wks
1	1	DUB BE GOOD TO ME	Beats International	GoBeat	5
7	2	THE BRITS 1990	Various Artists	RCA	2
3	3	HOW AM I SUPPOSED TO LIVE WITHOUT YOU	Michael Bolton	CBS	4
2	4	NOTHING COMPARES 2 U	Sinead O'Connor	Ensign	8
9	5	INFINITY	Guru Josh	deConstruction	3
6	6	ENJOY THE SILENCE	Depeche Mode	Mute	4
5	7	I DON'T KNOW ANYBODY ELSE	Black Box	deConstruction	4
22	8	MOMENTS IN SOUL	JT and the Big Family	Champion	2
4	9	GET UP (BEFORE THE NIGHT IS OVER)	Technotronic featuring Ya Kid K	Swanyard	6
8	10	ELEPHANT STONE	Stone Roses	Silvertone	2
10	11	DOWNTOWN TRAIN	Rod Stewart	Warner Brothers	5
-	12	BLUE SAVANNAH	Erasure	Mute	1
15	13	BLACK BETTY (BEN LIEBRAND REMIX)	Ram Jam	Epic	3
33	14	LOVE SHACK	B52s	Reprise	2
-	15	MADLY IN LOVE	Bros	CBS	1
13	16	ROOM AT THE TOP	Adam Ant	MCA	4
34	17	LILY WAS HERE	David A. Stewart featuring Candy Dulfer	Anxious	2
29	18	I MIGHT	Shakin' Stevens	Epic	3
11	19	HAPPENIN' ALL OVER AGAIN	Lonnie Gordon	Supreme	7
31	20	NATURAL THING	Innocence	Cooltempo	2
20	21	DUDE (LOOKS LIKE A LADY)	Aerosmith	Geffen	3
14	22	STRONGER THAN THAT	Cliff Richard	EMI	3
23	23	TALKING WITH MYSELF	Electribe 101	Mercury	3
37	24	HERE WE ARE	Gloria Estefan	Epic	2
12	25	WALK ON BY	Sybil	PWL	7
16	26	STEAMY WINDOWS	Tina Turner	Capitol	4
27	27	WALK ON THE WILD SIDE	Jamie J Morgan	Tabu	3
17	28	JUST LIKE JESSE JAMES	Cher	Geffen	7
32	29	A LOVER SPURNED	Marc Almond	Some Bizzare	2
-	30	DELIVERANCE	Mission	Mercury	1
19	31	96 TEARS	Stranglers	Epic	4
-	32	LOADED	Primal Scream ●	Creation	1
21	33	GOT TO HAVE YOUR LOVE	Mantronix featuring Wondress	Capitol	10
-	34	HOLD BACK THE RIVER	Wet Wet Wet	Precious	1
-	35	THE DEEPER THE LOVE	Whitesnake	EMI	1
36	36	ADVICE FOR THE YOUNG AT HEART	Tears For Fears	Fontana	2
18	37	I WISH IT WOULD RAIN DOWN	Phil Collins	Virgin	7
24	38	TELL ME THERE'S A HEAVEN	Chris Rea	East West	4
-	39	LOVE AND ANGER	Kate Bush	EMI	1
-	40	RUNAWAY HORSES	Belinda Carlisle	Virgin	1

WEEK ENDING 17 MARCH 1990

LW	TW	Title	Artist	Label	Wks
1	1	DUB BE GOOD TO ME	Beats International	GoBeat	6
2	2	THE BRITS 1990	Various Artists	RCA	3
3	3	HOW AM I SUPPOSED TO LIVE WITHOUT YOU	Michael Bolton	CBS	5
-	4	THAT SOUNDS GOOD TO ME	Jive Bunny & the Mastermixers	Music Factory Dance	1
9	5	INFINITY	Guru Josh	deConstruction	4
14	6	LOVE SHACK	B52s	Reprise	3
8	7	MOMENTS IN SOUL	JT and the Big Family	Champion	3
12	8	BLUE SAVANNAH	Erasure	Mute	2
4	9	NOTHING COMPARES 2 U	Sinead O'Connor	Ensign	9
17	10	LILY WAS HERE	David A. Stewart featuring Candy Dulfer	Anxious	3
-	11	I'LL BE LOVING YOU (FOREVER)	New Kids On The Block	CBS	1

March 1990

☐ Highest position disc reached ● Act's first ever week on chart

LW	TW	Title	Artist	Label	Wks
6	12	ENJOY THE SILENCE	Depeche Mode	Mute	5
7	13	I DON'T KNOW ANYBODY ELSE	Black Box	deConstruction	5
15	14	MADLY IN LOVE	Bros	CBS	2
9	15	GET UP (BEFORE THE NIGHT IS OVER)	Technotronic featuring Ya Kid K	Swanyard	7
20	16	NATURAL THING	Innocence	Cooltempo	3
13	17	BLACK BETTY (BEN LIEBRAND REMIX)	Ram Jam	Epic	4
-	18	STRAWBERRY FIELDS FOREVER	Candy Flip ●	Debut	1
11	19	DOWNTOWN TRAIN	Rod Stewart	Warner Brothers	6
-	20	MADE OF STONE	Stone Roses	Silvertone	1
18	21	I MIGHT	Shakin' Stevens	Epic	4
-	22	THIS IS HOW IT FEELS	Inspiral Carpets ●	Cow	1
24	23	HERE WE ARE	Gloria Estefan	Epic	3
32	24	LOADED	Primal Scream	Creation	2
10	25	ELEPHANT STONE	Stone Roses	Silvertone	3
16	26	ROOM AT THE TOP	Adam Ant	MCA	5
30	27	DELIVERANCE	Mission	Mercury	2
-	28	DON'T YOU LOVE ME	49ers	Fourth + Broadway	1
-	29	HANDFUL OF PROMISES	Big Fun	Jive	1
-	30	A GENTLEMAN'S EXCUSE ME	Fish	EMI	1
34	31	HOLD BACK THE RIVER	Wet Wet Wet	Precious	2
21	32	DUDE (LOOKS LIKE A LADY)	Aerosmith	Geffen	4
23	33	TALKING WITH MYSELF	Electribe 101	Mercury	4
-	34	BIRDHOUSE IN YOUR SOUL	They Might Be Giants ●	Elektra	1
19	35	HAPPENIN' ALL OVER AGAIN	Lonnie Gordon	Supreme	8
-	36	EVERYTHING STARTS WITH AN 'E'	E-Zee Posse ●	More Protein	1
36	37	ADVICE FOR THE YOUNG AT HEART	Tears For Fears	Fontana	3
39	38	LOVE AND ANGER	Kate Bush	EMI	2
35	39	THE DEEPER THE LOVE	Whitesnake	EMI	2
-	40	READ MY LIPS (ENOUGH IS ENOUGH)	Jimmy Somerville	London	1

WEEK ENDING 24 MARCH 1990

LW	TW	Title	Artist	Label	Wks
1	1	DUB BE GOOD TO ME	Beats International	GoBeat	7
6	2	LOVE SHACK	B52s	Reprise	4
3	3	BLUE SAVANNAH	Erasure	Mute	3
4	4	THAT SOUNDS GOOD TO ME	Jive Bunny & the Mastermixers	Music Factory Dance	2
11	5	I'LL BE LOVING YOU (FOREVER)	New Kids On The Block	CBS	2
18	6	STRAWBERRY FIELDS FOREVER	Candy Flip	Debut	2
10	7	LILY WAS HERE	David A. Stewart featuring Candy Dulfer	Anxious	4
3	8	HOW AM I SUPPOSED TO LIVE WITHOUT YOU	Michael Bolton	CBS	6
2	9	THE BRITS 1990	Various Artists	RCA	4
5	10	INFINITY	Guru Josh	deConstruction	5
7	11	MOMENTS IN SOUL	JT and the Big Family	Champion	4
-	12	THE POWER	Snap ●	Arista	1
9	13	NOTHING COMPARES 2 U	Sinead O'Connor	Ensign	10
28	14	DON'T YOU LOVE ME	49ers	Fourth + Broadway	2
22	15	THIS IS HOW IT FEELS	Inspiral Carpets	Cow	2
24	16	LOADED	Primal Scream	Creation	3
34	17	BIRDHOUSE IN YOUR SOUL	They Might Be Giants	Elektra	2
16	18	NATURAL THING	Innocence	Cooltempo	4
36	19	EVERYTHING STARTS WITH AN 'E'	E-Zee Posse	More Protein	2
12	20	ENJOY THE SILENCE	Depeche Mode	Mute	6
29	21	HANDFUL OF PROMISES	Big Fun	Jive	2
13	22	I DON'T KNOW ANYBODY ELSE	Black Box	deConstruction	6
21	23	I MIGHT	Shakin' Stevens	Epic	5
17	24	BLACK BETTY (BEN LIEBRAND REMIX)	Ram Jam	Epic	5
20	25	MADE OF STONE	Stone Roses	Silvertone	2
15	26	GET UP (BEFORE THE NIGHT IS OVER)	Technotronic featuring Ya Kid K	Swanyard	8
27	27	DELIVERANCE	Mission	Mercury	3

■Jive Bunny's fourth single, *That Sounds Good To Me* did not sound good enough to the record-buying public to make it their fourth number one. The other two acts who started with a hat-trick of number ones both took their fourth single to number two, so Jive Bunny cannot quite match Gerry and the Pacemakers or Frankie Goes To Hollywood (17.03.90)■

March 1990

□ Highest position disc reached ● Act's first ever week on chart

LW	TW	Title	Artist	Label	Wks
-	28	CHIME	Orbital ●	Oh'Zone	1
23	29	HERE WE ARE	Gloria Estefan	Epic	4
14	30	MADLY IN LOVE	Bros	CBS	3
30	31	A GENTLEMAN'S EXCUSE ME	Fish	EMI	2
40	32	READ MY LIPS (ENOUGH IS ENOUGH)	Jimmy Somerville	London	2
-	33	ALL I WANNA DO IS MAKE LOVE TO YOU	Heart	Capitol	1
-	34	MAMMA GAVE BIRTH TO THE SOUL CHILDREN	Queen Latifah & De La Soul ●	Tommy Boy	1
19	35	DOWNTOWN TRAIN	Rod Stewart	Warner Brothers	7
-	36	ANOTHER DAY IN PARADISE	Jam Tronik ●	Debut	1
31	37	HOLD BACK THE RIVER	Wet Wet Wet	Precious	3
-	38	TOO LATE TO SAY GOODBYE	Richard Marx	EMI	1
25	39	ELEPHANT STONE	Stone Roses	Silvertone	4
-	40	YOUR LOVE TAKES ME HIGHER	Beloved	East West	1

WEEK ENDING 31 MARCH 1990

LW	TW	Title	Artist	Label	Wks
12	1	THE POWER	Snap	Arista	2
2	2	LOVE SHACK	B52s	Reprise	5
6	3	STRAWBERRY FIELDS FOREVER	Candy Flip	Debut	3
3	4	BLUE SAVANNAH	Erasure	Mute	4
1	5	DUB BE GOOD TO ME	Beats International	GoBeat	8
7	6	LILY WAS HERE	David A. Stewart featuring Candy Dulfer	Anxious	5
5	7	I'LL BE LOVING YOU (FOREVER)	New Kids On The Block	CBS	3
17	8	BIRDHOUSE IN YOUR SOUL	They Might Be Giants	Elektra	3
4	9	THAT SOUNDS GOOD TO ME	Jive Bunny & the Mastermixers	Music Factory Dance	3
8	10	HOW AM I SUPPOSED TO LIVE WITHOUT YOU	Michael Bolton	CBS	7
10	11	INFINITY	Guru Josh	deConstruction	6
14	12	DON'T YOU LOVE ME	49ers	Fourth + Broadway	3
11	13	MOMENTS IN SOUL	JT and the Big Family	Champion	5
15	14	THIS IS HOW IT FEELS	Inspiral Carpets	Cow	3
19	15	EVERYTHING STARTS WITH AN 'E'	E-Zee Posse	More Protein	3
16	16	LOADED	Primal Scream	Creation	4
28	17	CHIME	Orbital	Oh'Zone	2
34	18	MAMMA GAVE BIRTH TO THE SOUL CHILDREN	Queen Latifah & De La Soul	Tommy Boy	2
9	19	THE BRITS 1990	Various Artists	RCA	5
13	20	NOTHING COMPARES 2 U	Sinead O'Connor	Ensign	11
36	21	ANOTHER DAY IN PARADISE	Jam Tronik	Debut	2
-	22	DON'T MISS THE PARTY LINE	Bizz Nizz ●	Cooltempo	1
33	23	ALL I WANNA DO IS MAKE LOVE TO YOU	Heart	Capitol	2
-	24	GHETTO HEAVEN	Family Stand ●	Atlantic	1
21	25	HANDFUL OF PROMISES	Big Fun	Jive	3
32	26	READ MY LIPS (ENOUGH IS ENOUGH)	Jimmy Somerville	London	3
-	27	BETTER WORLD	Rebel MC ●	Desire	1
-	28	PICTURES OF YOU	Cure	Fiction	1
18	29	NATURAL THING	Innocence	Cooltempo	5
-	30	KINGSTON TOWN	UB40	DEP International	1
-	31	ESCAPADE	Janet Jackson	Breakout	1
20	32	ENJOY THE SILENCE	Depeche Mode	Mute	7
-	33	BLACK VELVET	Alannah Myles ●	Atlantic	1
-	34	SHE BANGS THE DRUMS	Stone Roses	Silvertone	1
-	35	WHAT U WAITIN' 4	Jungle Brothers ●	Eternal	1
-	36	I REMEMBER YOU	Skid Row	Atlantic	1
22	37	I DON'T KNOW ANYBODY ELSE	Black Box	deConstruction	7
29	38	HERE WE ARE	Gloria Estefan	Epic	5
40	39	YOUR LOVE TAKES ME HIGHER	Beloved	East West	2
38	40	TOO LATE TO SAY GOODBYE	Richard Marx	EMI	2

WEEK ENDING 7 APRIL 1990

LW	TW	Title	Artist	Label	Wks
1	1	THE POWER	Snap	Arista	3
2	2	LOVE SHACK	B52s	Reprise	6
3	3	STRAWBERRY FIELDS FOREVER	Candy Flip	Debut	4
-	4	VOGUE	Madonna	Sire	1
4	5	BLUE SAVANNAH	Erasure	Mute	5
8	6	BIRDHOUSE IN YOUR SOUL	They Might Be Giants	Elektra	4
6	7	LILY WAS HERE	David A. Stewart featuring Candy Dulfer	Anxious	6
22	8	DON'T MISS THE PARTY LINE	Bizz Nizz	Cooltempo	2
-	9	HANG ON TO YOUR LOVE	Jason Donovan	PWL	1
5	10	DUB BE GOOD TO ME	Beats International	GoBeat	9
30	11	KINGSTON TOWN	UB40	DEP International	2
7	12	I'LL BE LOVING YOU (FOREVER)	New Kids On The Block	CBS	4
24	13	GHETTO HEAVEN	Family Stand	Atlantic	2
18	14	MAMMA GAVE BIRTH TO THE SOUL CHILDREN	Queen Latifah & De La Soul	Tommy Boy	3
23	15	ALL I WANNA DO IS MAKE LOVE TO YOU	Heart	Capitol	3
-	16	STEP ON	Happy Mondays	Factory	1
33	17	BLACK VELVET	Alannah Myles	Atlantic	2
14	18	THIS IS HOW IT FEELS	Inspiral Carpets	Cow	4
21	19	ANOTHER DAY IN PARADISE	Jam Tronik	Debut	3
27	20	BETTER WORLD	Rebel MC	Desire	2
31	21	ESCAPADE	Janet Jackson	Breakout	2
15	22	EVERYTHING STARTS WITH AN 'E'	E-Zee Posse	More Protein	4
-	23	THIS BEAT IS TECHNOTRONIC	Technotronic featuring MC Eric	Swanyard	1
12	24	DON'T YOU LOVE ME	49ers	Fourth + Broadway	4
11	25	INFINITY	Guru Josh	deConstruction	7
-	26	REAL REAL REAL	Jesus Jones ●	Food	1
17	27	CHIME	Orbital	Oh'Zone	3
28	28	PICTURES OF YOU	Cure	Fiction	2
10	29	HOW AM I SUPPOSED TO LIVE WITHOUT YOU	Michael Bolton	CBS	8
26	30	READ MY LIPS (ENOUGH IS ENOUGH)	Jimmy Somerville	London	4
9	31	THAT SOUNDS GOOD TO ME	Jive Bunny & the Mastermixers	Music Factory Dance	4
16	32	LOADED	Primal Scream	Creation	5
13	33	MOMENTS IN SOUL	JT and the Big Family	Champion	6
-	34	FAME 90 (GASS MIX)	David Bowie	EMI	1
35	35	WHAT U WAITIN' 4	Jungle Brothers	Eternal	2
-	36	OPPOSITES ATTRACT	Paula Abdul with the Wild Pair	Siren	1
-	37	I DON'T LOVE YOU ANYMORE	Quireboys	Parlophone	1
20	38	NOTHING COMPARES 2 U	Sinead O'Connor	Ensign	12
36	39	I REMEMBER YOU	Skid Row	Atlantic	2
25	40	HANDFUL OF PROMISES	Big Fun	Jive	4

WEEK ENDING 14 APRIL 1990

LW	TW	Title	Artist	Label	Wks
4	1	VOGUE	Madonna	Sire	2
1	2	THE POWER	Snap	Arista	4
17	3	BLACK VELVET	Alannah Myles	Atlantic	3
11	4	KINGSTON TOWN	UB40	DEP International	3
16	5	STEP ON	Happy Mondays	Factory	2
2	6	LOVE SHACK	B52s	Reprise	7
8	7	DON'T MISS THE PARTY LINE	Bizz Nizz	Cooltempo	3
9	8	HANG ON TO YOUR LOVE	Jason Donovan	PWL	2
3	9	STRAWBERRY FIELDS FOREVER	Candy Flip	Debut	5
6	10	BIRDHOUSE IN YOUR SOUL	They Might Be Giants	Elektra	5
15	11	ALL I WANNA DO IS MAKE LOVE TO YOU	Heart	Capitol	4
7	12	LILY WAS HERE	David A. Stewart featuring Candy Dulfer	Anxious	7
13	13	GHETTO HEAVEN	Family Stand	Atlantic	3
5	14	BLUE SAVANNAH	Erasure	Mute	6
23	15	THIS BEAT IS TECHNOTRONIC	Technotronic featuring MC Eric	Swanyard	2
14	16	MAMMA GAVE BIRTH TO THE SOUL CHILDREN	Queen Latifah & De La Soul	Tommy Boy	4
36	17	OPPOSITES ATTRACT	Paula Abdul with the Wild Pair	Siren	2
21	18	ESCAPADE	Janet Jackson	Breakout	3
19	19	ANOTHER DAY IN PARADISE	Jam Tronik	Debut	4
10	20	DUB BE GOOD TO ME	Beats International	GoBeat	10
20	21	BETTER WORLD	Rebel MC	Desire	3

In these weeks ■ Snap joins the select band of only six other acts to reach number one in their second week of chart life. Two more acts, Partners In Kryme and Vanilla Ice, will match Snap's feat before the year is out, making 1990 the best year ever for quick chart success (31.03.90)■

LW	TW	Title	Artist	Label	Wks
12	22	I'LL BE LOVING YOU (FOREVER)	New Kids On The Block	*CBS*	5
26	23	REAL REAL REAL	Jesus Jones	*Food*	2
28	[24]	PICTURES OF YOU	Cure	*Fiction*	3
18	25	THIS IS HOW IT FEELS	Inspiral Carpets	*Cow*	5
37	26	I DON'T LOVE YOU ANYMORE	Quireboys	*Parlophone*	2
22	27	EVERYTHING STARTS WITH AN 'E'	E-Zee Posse	*More Protein*	5
34	[28]	FAME 90 (GASS MIX)	David Bowie	*EMI*	2
25	29	INFINITY	Guru Josh	*deConstruction*	8
-	30	COUNTING EVERY MINUTE	Sonia	*Chrysalis*	1
-	31	EVERYBODY NEEDS SOMEBODY TO LOVE	Blues Brothers ●	*Atlantic*	1
-	[32]	PLAY (EP)	Ride ●	*Creation*	1
24	33	DON'T YOU LOVE ME	49ers	*Fourth + Broadway*	5
-	[34]	EASTER	Marillion	*EMI*	1
-	35	TOMORROW	Tongue 'n' Cheek ●	*Syncopate*	1
35	36	WHAT U WAITIN' 4	Jungle Brothers	*Eternal*	3
27	37	CHIME	Orbital	*Oh'Zone*	4
-	38	FROM OUT OF NOWHERE	Faith No More	*Slash*	1
-	39	KILLER	Adamski	*MCA*	1
-	40	BEATLES AND THE STONES	House Of Love	*Fontana*	1

WEEK ENDING 21 APRIL 1990

LW	TW	Title	Artist	Label	Wks
1	[1]	VOGUE	Madonna	*Sire*	3
3	[2]	BLACK VELVET	Alannah Myles	*Atlantic*	4
2	3	THE POWER	Snap	*Arista*	5
4	[4]	KINGSTON TOWN	UB40	*DEP International*	4
17	5	OPPOSITES ATTRACT	Paula Abdul with the Wild Pair	*Siren*	3
5	6	STEP ON	Happy Mondays	*Factory*	3
7	[7]	DON'T MISS THE PARTY LINE	Bizz Nizz	*Cooltempo*	4
11	[8]	ALL I WANNA DO IS MAKE LOVE TO YOU	Heart	*Capitol*	5
8	9	HANG ON TO YOUR LOVE	Jason Donovan	*PWL*	3
6	10	LOVE SHACK	B52s	*Reprise*	8
10	11	BIRDHOUSE IN YOUR SOUL	They Might Be Giants	*Elektra*	6
13	12	GHETTO HEAVEN	Family Stand	*Atlantic*	4
9	13	STRAWBERRY FIELDS FOREVER	Candy Flip	*Debut*	6
15	[14]	THIS BEAT IS TECHNOTRONIC	Technotronic featuring MC Eric	*Swanyard*	3
12	15	LILY WAS HERE	David A. Stewart featuring Candy Dulfer	*Anxious*	8
14	16	BLUE SAVANNAH	Erasure	*Mute*	7
18	[17]	ESCAPADE	Janet Jackson	*Breakout*	4
31	18	EVERYBODY NEEDS SOMEBODY TO LOVE	Blues Brothers	*Atlantic*	2
16	19	MAMMA GAVE BIRTH TO THE SOUL CHILDREN	Queen Latifah & De La Soul	*Tommy Boy*	5
39	20	KILLER	Adamski	*MCA*	2
30	21	COUNTING EVERY MINUTE	Sonia	*Chrysalis*	2
23	22	REAL REAL REAL	Jesus Jones	*Food*	3
22	23	I'LL BE LOVING YOU (FOREVER)	New Kids On The Block	*CBS*	6
20	24	DUB BE GOOD TO ME	Beats International	*GoBeat*	11
26	25	I DON'T LOVE YOU ANYMORE	Quireboys	*Parlophone*	3
21	26	BETTER WORLD	Rebel MC	*Desire*	4
19	27	ANOTHER DAY IN PARADISE	Jam Tronik	*Debut*	5
-	28	DIRTY CASH	Adventures Of Stevie V ●	*Mercury*	1
24	29	PICTURES OF YOU	Cure	*Fiction*	4
38	30	FROM OUT OF NOWHERE	Faith No More	*Slash*	2
25	31	THIS IS HOW IT FEELS	Inspiral Carpets	*Cow*	6
35	32	TOMORROW	Tongue 'n' Cheek	*Syncopate*	2
27	33	EVERYTHING STARTS WITH AN 'E'	E-Zee Posse	*More Protein*	6
28	34	FAME 90 (GASS MIX)	David Bowie	*EMI*	3
34	35	EASTER	Marillion	*EMI*	2
40	[36]	BEATLES AND THE STONES	House Of Love	*Fontana*	2
29	37	INFINITY	Guru Josh	*deConstruction*	9
32	38	PLAY (EP)	Ride	*Creation*	2
-	39	USE IT UP AND WEAR IT OUT	Pat & Mick	*PWL*	1
-	40	MUSICAL MELODY/WEIGHT FOR THE BASS	Unique Three ●	*10*	1

May 1990

□ Highest position disc reached ● Act's first ever week on chart

WEEK ENDING 28 APRIL 1990

LW	TW	Title	Artist	Label	Wks
1	[1]	VOGUE	Madonna	*Sire*	4
2	[2]	BLACK VELVET	Alannah Myles	*Atlantic*	5
5	3	OPPOSITES ATTRACT	Paula Abdul with the Wild Pair	*Siren*	4
3	4	THE POWER	Snap	*Arista*	6
4	5	KINGSTON TOWN	UB40	*DEP International*	5
6	6	STEP ON	Happy Mondays	*Factory*	4
20	7	KILLER	Adamski	*MCA*	3
8	[8]	ALL I WANNA DO IS MAKE LOVE TO YOU	Heart	*Capitol*	6
7	9	DON'T MISS THE PARTY LINE	Bizz Nizz	*Cooltempo*	5
12	[10]	GHETTO HEAVEN	Family Stand	*Atlantic*	5
28	11	DIRTY CASH	Adventures Of Stevie V	*Mercury*	2
18	[12]	EVERYBODY NEEDS SOMEBODY TO LOVE	Blues Brothers	*Atlantic*	3
9	13	HANG ON TO YOUR LOVE	Jason Donovan	*PWL*	4
10	14	LOVE SHACK	B52s	*Reprise*	9
15	15	THIS BEAT IS TECHNOTRONIC	Technotronic featuring MC Eric	*Swanyard*	4
21	[16]	COUNTING EVERY MINUTE	Sonia	*Chrysalis*	3
11	17	BIRDHOUSE IN YOUR SOUL	They Might Be Giants	*Elektra*	5
17	18	ESCAPADE	Janet Jackson	*Breakout*	5
13	19	STRAWBERRY FIELDS FOREVER	Candy Flip	*Debut*	7
22	20	REAL REAL REAL	Jesus Jones	*Food*	4
15	21	LILY WAS HERE	David A. Stewart featuring Candy Dulfer	*Anxious*	9
16	22	BLUE SAVANNAH	Erasure	*Mute*	8
30	[23]	FROM OUT OF NOWHERE	Faith No More	*Slash*	3
25	[24]	I DON'T LOVE YOU ANYMORE	Quireboys	*Parlophone*	4
39	25	USE IT UP AND WEAR IT OUT	Pat & Mick	*PWL*	2
-	26	SOMETHING HAPPENED ON THE WAY TO HEAVEN	Phil Collins	*Virgin*	1
19	27	MAMMA GAVE BIRTH TO THE SOUL CHILDREN	Queen Latifah & De La Soul	*Tommy Boy*	6
32	28	TOMORROW	Tongue 'n' Cheek	*Syncopate*	3
40	[29]	MUSICAL MELODY/WEIGHT FOR THE BASS	Unique Three	*10*	2
-	30	WILD WOMEN DO	Natalie Cole	*EMI*	1
23	31	I'LL BE LOVING YOU (FOREVER)	New Kids On The Block	*CBS*	7
24	32	DUB BE GOOD TO ME	Beats International	*GoBeat*	12
-	33	TATTOOED MILLIONAIRE	Bruce Dickinson ●	*EMI*	1
-	[34]	SCARLET	All About Eve	*Mercury*	1
-	35	THE SEX OF IT	Kid Creole & the Coconuts	*CBS*	1
26	36	BETTER WORLD	Rebel MC	*Desire*	5
27	37	ANOTHER DAY IN PARADISE	Jam Tronik	*Debut*	6
-	38	HITCHIN' A RIDE	Sinitta	*Fanfare*	1
-	[39]	SOMETHING YOU GOT	And Why Not?	*Island*	1
-	40	CRADLE OF LOVE	Billy Idol	*Chrysalis*	1

WEEK ENDING 5 MAY 1990

LW	TW	Title	Artist	Label	Wks
1	[1]	VOGUE	Madonna	*Sire*	5
3	[2]	OPPOSITES ATTRACT	Paula Abdul with the Wild Pair	*Siren*	5
2	3	BLACK VELVET	Alannah Myles	*Atlantic*	6
7	4	KILLER	Adamski	*MCA*	4
11	5	DIRTY CASH	Adventures Of Stevie V	*Mercury*	3
6	6	KINGSTON TOWN	UB40	*DEP International*	6
4	7	THE POWER	Snap	*Arista*	7
-	8	A DREAMS A DREAM	Soul II Soul	*10*	1
8	9	ALL I WANNA DO IS MAKE LOVE TO YOU	Heart	*Capitol*	7
10	[10]	GHETTO HEAVEN	Family Stand	*Atlantic*	6
6	11	STEP ON	Happy Mondays	*Factory*	5
-	[12]	NOVEMBER SPAWNED A MONSTER	Morrissey	*HMV*	1
9	13	DON'T MISS THE PARTY LINE	Bizz Nizz	*Cooltempo*	6
12	14	EVERYBODY NEEDS SOMEBODY TO LOVE	Blues Brothers	*Atlantic*	4
26	[15]	SOMETHING HAPPENED ON THE WAY TO HEAVEN	Phil Collins	*Virgin*	2

■The top three are by female vocalists, Madonna enjoying a record 7th number one, and Alannah Myles and Paula Abdul both enjoying their biggest chart hits (28.04.90 and 05.05.90) ■ *Easter* by Marillion is the seventh record to enter the Top 40 at number 34 in consecutive weeks■

May 1990

□ Highest position disc reached ● Act's first ever week on chart

LW	TW	Title / Artist	Label	Wks
30	[16]	WILD WOMEN DO Natalie Cole	*EMI*	2
16	17	COUNTING EVERY MINUTE Sonia	*Chrysalis*	4
33	[18]	TATTOOED MILLIONAIRE Bruce Dickinson	*EMI*	2
20	[19]	REAL REAL REAL Jesus Jones	*Food*	5
28	[20]	TOMORROW Tongue 'n' Cheek	*Syncopate*	4
14	21	LOVE SHACK B52s	*Reprise*	10
25	[22]	USE IT UP AND WEAR IT OUT Pat & Mick	*PWL*	3
23	[23]	FROM OUT OF NOWHERE Faith No More	*Slash*	4
13	24	HANG ON TO YOUR LOVE Jason Donovan	*PWL*	5
15	25	THIS BEAT IS TECHNOTRONIC Technotronic featuring MC Eric	*Swanyard*	5
38	26	HITCHIN' A RIDE Sinitta	*Fanfare*	2
18	27	ESCAPADE Janet Jackson	*Breakout*	6
-	[28]	SNAPPINESS BBG ●	*Urban*	1
35	[29]	THE SEX OF IT Kid Creole & the Coconuts	*CBS*	2
21	30	LILY WAS HERE David A. Stewart featuring Candy Dulfer	*Anxious*	10
29	31	MUSICAL MELODY/WEIGHT FOR THE BASS Unique Three	*10*	3
17	32	BIRDHOUSE IN YOUR SOUL They Might Be Giants	*Elektra*	6
-	33	HOLD ON En Vogue ●	*Atlantic*	1
40	[34]	CRADLE OF LOVE Billy Idol	*Chrysalis*	2
22	35	BLUE SAVANNAH Erasure	*Mute*	9
19	36	STRAWBERRY FIELDS FOREVER Candy Flip	*Debut*	8
24	37	I DON'T LOVE YOU ANYMORE Quireboys	*Parlophone*	5
-	38	HOW CAN WE BE LOVERS Michael Bolton	*CBS*	1
-	39	HEAVEN GIVE ME WORDS Propaganda	*Virgin*	1
-	[40]	EXPRESSION Salt-N-Pepa	*ffrr*	1

WEEK ENDING 12 MAY 1990

LW	TW	Title / Artist	Label	Wks
4	[1]	KILLER Adamski	*MCA*	5
5	[2]	DIRTY CASH Adventures Of Stevie V	*Mercury*	4
2	3	OPPOSITES ATTRACT Paula Abdul with the Wild Pair	*Siren*	6
1	4	VOGUE Madonna	*Sire*	6
-	5	BETTER THE DEVIL YOU KNOW Kylie Minogue	*PWL*	1
8	[6]	A DREAMS A DREAM Soul II Soul	*10*	2
3	7	BLACK VELVET Alannah Myles	*Atlantic*	7
-	8	COVER GIRL New Kids On The Block	*CBS*	1
6	9	KINGSTON TOWN UB40	*DEP International*	7
7	10	THE POWER Snap	*Arista*	8
9	11	ALL I WANNA DO IS MAKE LOVE TO YOU Heart	*Capitol*	8
10	12	GHETTO HEAVEN Family Stand	*Atlantic*	7
11	13	STEP ON Happy Mondays	*Factory*	6
33	14	HOLD ON En Vogue	*Atlantic*	2
15	[15]	SOMETHING HAPPENED ON THE WAY TO HEAVEN Phil Collins	*Virgin*	3
12	16	NOVEMBER SPAWNED A MONSTER Morrissey	*HMV*	2
16	17	WILD WOMEN DO Natalie Cole	*EMI*	3
-	18	WON'T TALK ABOUT IT Beats International	*Go Beat*	1
-	19	TAKE YOUR TIME Mantronix featuring Wondress	*Capitol*	1
-	[20]	CIRCLESQUARE Wonder Stuff	*Polydor*	1
13	21	DON'T MISS THE PARTY LINE Bizz Nizz	*Cooltempo*	7
38	22	HOW CAN WE BE LOVERS Michael Bolton	*CBS*	2
14	23	EVERYBODY NEEDS SOMEBODY TO LOVE Blues Brothers	*Atlantic*	5
26	[24]	HITCHIN' A RIDE Sinitta	*Fanfare*	3
-	[25]	BACKSTREET SYMPHONY Thunder	*EMI*	1
18	26	TATTOOED MILLIONAIRE Bruce Dickinson	*EMI*	3
20	27	TOMORROW Tongue 'n' Cheek	*Syncopate*	5
28	[28]	SNAPPINESS BBG	*Urban*	2
-	29	WHAT DID I DO TO YOU (EP) Lisa Stansfield	*Arista*	1
19	30	REAL REAL REAL Jesus Jones	*Food*	6
22	31	USE IT UP AND WEAR IT OUT Pat & Mick	*PWL*	4
-	32	LOVE THING Pasadenas	*CBS*	1
-	33	KISSING GATE Sam Brown	*A&M*	1
-	34	SOFTLY WHISPERING I LOVE YOU Paul Young	*Epic*	1
-	35	HOW WAS IT FOR YOU? James ●	*Fontana*	1
39	[36]	HEAVEN GIVE ME WORDS Propaganda	*Virgin*	2
17	37	COUNTING EVERY MINUTE Sonia	*Chrysalis*	5
21	38	LOVE SHACK B52s	*Reprise*	11
-	[39]	WITHOUT YOU Motley Crue	*Elektra*	1
-	40	GIVE A LITTLE LOVE BACK TO THE WORLD Emma ●	*Big Wave*	1

WEEK ENDING 19 MAY 1990

LW	TW	Title / Artist	Label	Wks
1	[1]	KILLER Adamski	*MCA*	*6*
5	[2]	BETTER THE DEVIL YOU KNOW Kylie Minogue	*PWL*	2
2	3	DIRTY CASH Adventures Of Stevie V	*Mercury*	5
8	[4]	COVER GIRL New Kids On The Block	*CBS*	2
3	5	OPPOSITES ATTRACT Paula Abdul with the Wild Pair	*Siren*	7
4	6	VOGUE Madonna	*Sire*	7
14	7	HOLD ON En Vogue	*Atlantic*	3
7	8	BLACK VELVET Alannah Myles	*Atlantic*	8
6	9	A DREAMS A DREAM Soul II Soul	*10*	3
18	10	WON'T TALK ABOUT IT Beats International	*Go Beat*	2
19	11	TAKE YOUR TIME Mantronix featuring Wondress	*Capitol*	2
9	12	KINGSTON TOWN UB40	*DEP International*	8
10	13	THE POWER Snap	*Arista*	9
22	14	HOW CAN WE BE LOVERS Michael Bolton	*CBS*	3
11	15	ALL I WANNA DO IS MAKE LOVE TO YOU Heart	*Capitol*	9
-	16	I STILL HAVEN'T FOUND WHAT I'M LOOKING FOR Chimes ●	*CBS*	1
12	17	GHETTO HEAVEN Family Stand	*Atlantic*	8
13	18	STEP ON Happy Mondays	*Factory*	7
15	19	SOMETHING HAPPENED ON THE WAY TO HEAVEN Phil Collins	*Virgin*	4
20	[20]	CIRCLESQUARE Wonder Stuff	*Polydor*	2
34	[21]	SOFTLY WHISPERING I LOVE YOU Paul Young	*Epic*	2
32	[22]	LOVE THING Pasadenas	*CBS*	*2*
17	23	WILD WOMEN DO Natalie Cole	*EMI*	4
21	24	DON'T MISS THE PARTY LINE Bizz Nizz	*Cooltempo*	8
29	[25]	WHAT DID I DO TO YOU (EP) Lisa Stansfield	*Arista*	2
25	26	BACKSTREET SYMPHONY Thunder	*EMI*	2
-	27	ANGEL Eurythmics	*RCA*	1
-	28	POLICY OF TRUTH Depeche Mode	*Mute*	1
33	29	KISSING GATE Sam Brown	*A&M*	2
-	30	VENUS Don Pablo's Animals ●	*Rumour*	1
-	31	GIVE IT UP Hothouse Flowers	*London*	1
35	[32]	HOW WAS IT FOR YOU? James	*Fontana*	2
40	[33]	GIVE A LITTLE LOVE BACK TO THE WORLD Emma	*Big Wave*	2
24	34	HITCHIN' A RIDE Sinitta	*Fanfare*	4
28	35	SNAPPINESS BBG	*Urban*	3
-	36	RADICAL YOUR LOVER Little Angels and the Big Bad Horns ●	*Polydor*	1
23	37	EVERYBODY NEEDS SOMEBODY TO LOVE Blues Brothers	*Atlantic*	6
-	38	ROAM B52s	*Reprise*	1
39	[39]	WITHOUT YOU Motley Crue	*Elektra*	2
30	40	REAL REAL REAL Jesus Jones	*Food*	7

WEEK ENDING 26 MAY 1990

LW	TW	Title / Artist	Label	Wks
1	[1]	KILLER Adamski	*MCA*	7
2	[2]	BETTER THE DEVIL YOU KNOW Kylie Minogue	*PWL*	3
3	3	DIRTY CASH Adventures Of Stevie V	*Mercury*	6
4	[4]	COVER GIRL New Kids On The Block	*CBS*	3
7	[5]	HOLD ON En Vogue	*Atlantic*	4
16	[6]	I STILL HAVEN'T FOUND WHAT I'M LOOKING FOR Chimes	*CBS*	2
5	7	OPPOSITES ATTRACT Paula Abdul with the Wild Pair	*Siren*	8
6	8	VOGUE Madonna	*Sire*	8
10	[9]	WON'T TALK ABOUT IT Beats International	*Go Beat*	3
11	[10]	TAKE YOUR TIME Mantronix featuring Wondress	*Capitol*	3
14	11	HOW CAN WE BE LOVERS Michael Bolton	*CBS*	4
30	12	VENUS Don Pablo's Animals	*Rumour*	2
8	13	BLACK VELVET Alannah Myles	*Atlantic*	9
9	14	A DREAMS A DREAM Soul II Soul	*10*	4
12	15	KINGSTON TOWN UB40	*DEP International*	9
28	[16]	POLICY OF TRUTH Depeche Mode	*Mute*	2
13	17	THE POWER Snap	*Arista*	10

In these weeks ■ Adamski's *Killer* features the vocal talents of Seal. This is the 1992 multi-Brit award winner's first chart action (12.05.90) ■ The Chimes' version of U2's *I Still Haven't Found What I'm Looking For* achieves the same chart peak as the original number six (26.05.90)■

LW	TW	Title / Artist	Label	Wks
15	18	ALL I WANNA DO IS MAKE LOVE TO YOU Heart	Capitol	10
17	19	GHETTO HEAVEN Family Stand	Atlantic	9
38	20	ROAM B52s	Reprise	2
21	21	SOFTLY WHISPERING I LOVE YOU Paul Young	Epic	3
22	22	LOVE THING Pasadenas	CBS	3
27	23	ANGEL Eurythmics	RCA	2
29	24	KISSING GATE Sam Brown	A&M	3
-	25	PAPA WAS A ROLLING STONE Was (Not Was)	Fontana	1
19	26	SOMETHING HAPPENED ON THE WAY TO HEAVEN Phil Collins	Virgin	5
25	27	WHAT DID I DO TO YOU (EP) Lisa Stansfield	Arista	3
20	28	CIRCLESQUARE Wonder Stuff	Polydor	3
18	29	STEP ON Happy Mondays	Factory	8
31	30	GIVE IT UP Hothouse Flowers	London	2
23	31	WILD WOMEN DO Natalie Cole	EMI	5
-	32	JOY AND HEARTBREAK Movement 98 featuring Carroll Thompson ●	Circa	1
-	33	DOIN' THE DO Betty Boo ●	Rhythm King	1
36	34	RADICAL YOUR LOVER Little Angels and the Big Bad Horns	Polydor	2
-	35	IT'S MY LIFE Talk Talk	Parlophone	1
-	36	DON'T WANNA FALL IN LOVE Jane Child ●	Warner Brothers	1
-	37	STILL GOT THE BLUES (FOR YOU) Gary Moore	Virgin	1
24	38	DON'T MISS THE PARTY LINE Bizz Nizz	Cooltempo	9
33	39	GIVE A LITTLE LOVE BACK TO THE WORLD Emma	Big Wave	3
-	40	IT'S HAPPENIN' Plus One featuring Sirron ●	MCA	1

WEEK ENDING 2 JUNE 1990

LW	TW	Title / Artist	Label	Wks
1	1	KILLER Adamski	MCA	8
-	2	WORLD IN MOTION... Englandneworder ●	Factory	1
2	3	BETTER THE DEVIL YOU KNOW Kylie Minogue	PWL	4
3	4	DIRTY CASH Adventures Of Stevie V	Mercury	7
5	5	HOLD ON En Vogue	Atlantic	5
6	6	I STILL HAVEN'T FOUND WHAT I'M LOOKING FOR Chimes	CBS	3
12	7	VENUS Don Pablo's Animals	Rumour	3
4	8	COVER GIRL New Kids On The Block	CBS	4
8	9	VOGUE Madonna	Sire	9
11	10	HOW CAN WE BE LOVERS Michael Bolton	CBS	5
9	11	WON'T TALK ABOUT IT Beats International	Go Beat	4
-	12	HEAR THE DRUMMER (GET WICKED) Chad Jackson ●	Big Wave	1
25	13	PAPA WAS A ROLLING STONE Was (Not Was)	Fontana	2
7	14	OPPOSITES ATTRACT Paula Abdul with the Wild Pair	Siren	9
33	15	DOIN' THE DO Betty Boo	Rhythm King	2
10	16	TAKE YOUR TIME Mantronix featuring Wondress	Capitol	4
20	17	ROAM B52s	Reprise	3
16	18	POLICY OF TRUTH Depeche Mode	Mute	3
-	19	STAR Erasure	Mute	1
35	20	IT'S MY LIFE Talk Talk	Parlophone	2
13	21	BLACK VELVET Alannah Myles	Atlantic	10
-	22	EVERYBODY EVERYBODY Black Box	deConstruction	1
24	23	KISSING GATE Sam Brown	A&M	4
-	24	THE ONLY ONE I KNOW Charlatans ●	Situation Two	1
36	25	DON'T WANNA FALL IN LOVE Jane Child	Warner Brothers	2
-	26	EXPRESS YOURSELF N.W.A. ●	Ruthless	1
32	27	JOY AND HEARTBREAK Movement 98 featuring Carroll Thompson	Circa	2
15	28	KINGSTON TOWN UB40	DEP International	10
18	29	ALL I WANNA DO IS MAKE LOVE TO YOU Heart	Capitol	11
17	30	THE POWER Snap	Arista	11
37	31	STILL GOT THE BLUES (FOR YOU) Gary Moore	Virgin	2
30	32	GIVE IT UP Hothouse Flowers	London	3
23	33	ANGEL Eurythmics	RCA	3
14	34	A DREAMS A DREAM Soul II Soul	10	5
-	35	INTO THE BLUE Mission	Mercury	1
-	36	HOLD ON Wilson Phillips ●	SBK	1
19	37	GHETTO HEAVEN Family Stand	Atlantic	10
-	38	IT MUST HAVE BEEN LOVE Roxette	EMI	1
21	39	SOFTLY WHISPERING I LOVE YOU Paul Young	Epic	4
-	40	YAAAH/TECHNO TRANCE D-Shake ●	Cooltempo	1

June 1990

□ Highest position disc reached ● Act's first ever week on chart

WEEK ENDING 9 JUNE 1990

LW	TW	Title / Artist	Label	Wks
2	1	WORLD IN MOTION... Englandneworder	Factory	2
1	2	KILLER Adamski	MCA	9
12	3	HEAR THE DRUMMER (GET WICKED) Chad Jackson	Big Wave	2
7	4	VENUS Don Pablo's Animals	Rumour	4
4	5	DIRTY CASH Adventures Of Stevie V	Mercury	8
3	6	BETTER THE DEVIL YOU KNOW Kylie Minogue	PWL	5
5	7	HOLD ON En Vogue	Atlantic	6
15	8	DOIN' THE DO Betty Boo	Rhythm King	3
6	9	I STILL HAVEN'T FOUND WHAT I'M LOOKING FOR Chimes	CBS	4
24	10	THE ONLY ONE I KNOW Charlatans	Situation Two	2
19	11	STAR Erasure	Mute	2
13	12	PAPA WAS A ROLLING STONE Was (Not Was)	Fontana	3
20	13	IT'S MY LIFE Talk Talk	Parlophone	3
8	14	COVER GIRL New Kids On The Block	CBS	5
9	15	VOGUE Madonna	Sire	10
22	16	EVERYBODY EVERYBODY Black Box	deConstruction	2
14	17	OPPOSITES ATTRACT Paula Abdul with the Wild Pair	Siren	10
17	18	ROAM B52s	Reprise	4
11	19	WON'T TALK ABOUT IT Beats International	Go Beat	5
10	20	HOW CAN WE BE LOVERS Michael Bolton	CBS	6
38	21	IT MUST HAVE BEEN LOVE Roxette	EMI	2
25	22	DON'T WANNA FALL IN LOVE Jane Child	Warner Brothers	3
36	23	HOLD ON Wilson Phillips	SBK	2
23	24	KISSING GATE Sam Brown	A&M	5
16	25	TAKE YOUR TIME Mantronix featuring Wondress	Capitol	5
-	26	SACRIFICE/HEALING HANDS Elton John	Rocket	1
26	27	EXPRESS YOURSELF N.W.A.	Ruthless	2
-	28	TOUCHED BY THE HAND OF CICCIOLINA Pop Will Eat Itself	RCA	1
40	29	YAAAH/TECHNO TRANCE D-Shake	Cooltempo	2
18	30	POLICY OF TRUTH Depeche Mode	Mute	4
-	31	THE ONLY RHYME THAT BITES MC Tunes vs 808 State ●	ZTT	1
35	32	INTO THE BLUE Mission	Mercury	2
21	33	BLACK VELVET Alannah Myles	Atlantic	11
31	34	STILL GOT THE BLUES (FOR YOU) Gary Moore	Virgin	3
-	35	GIRL TO GIRL 49ers	Fourth & Broadway	1
27	36	JOY AND HEARTBREAK Movement 98 featuring Carroll Thompson	Circa	3
30	37	THE POWER Snap	Arista	12
-	38	REPUTATION Dusty Springfield	Parlophone	1
-	39	THE FREE STYLE MEGA-MIX Bobby Brown	MCA	1
29	40	ALL I WANNA DO IS MAKE LOVE TO YOU Heart	Capitol	12

WEEK ENDING 16 JUNE 1990

LW	TW	Title / Artist	Label	Wks
1	1	WORLD IN MOTION... Englandneworder	Factory	3
-	2	STEP BY STEP New Kids On The Block	CBS	1
3	3	HEAR THE DRUMMER (GET WICKED) Chad Jackson	Big Wave	3
2	4	KILLER Adamski	MCA	10
26	5	SACRIFICE/HEALING HANDS Elton John	Rocket	2
21	6	IT MUST HAVE BEEN LOVE Roxette	EMI	3
8	7	DOIN' THE DO Betty Boo	Rhythm King	4
4	8	VENUS Don Pablo's Animals	Rumour	5
10	9	THE ONLY ONE I KNOW Charlatans	Situation Two	3
23	10	HOLD ON Wilson Phillips	SBK	3
5	11	DIRTY CASH Adventures Of Stevie V	Mercury	9
11	12	STAR Erasure	Mute	3
-	13	OOPS UP Snap	Arista	1
7	14	HOLD ON En Vogue	Atlantic	7
6	15	BETTER THE DEVIL YOU KNOW Kylie Minogue	PWL	6
13	16	IT'S MY LIFE Talk Talk	Parlophone	4
12	17	PAPA WAS A ROLLING STONE Was (Not Was)	Fontana	4
31	18	THE ONLY RHYME THAT BITES MC Tunes vs 808 State	ZTT	2

■Don Pablo's Animals' version of *Venus* is the third to hit the Top ten, after the original by Shocking Blue and the Bananarama hit of 1986. By reaching number four, Don Pablo does better than the earlier versions, which were both number one hits in America (09.06.90) ■ Elton John's first chart entry for almost two years is a re-issue of his last two singles, which separately missed the top 40. Together they will become Elton's most successful single of all (09.06.90)■

June 1990

□ Highest position disc reached ● Act's first ever week on chart

LW	TW	Title	Artist	Label	Wks
9	19	I STILL HAVEN'T FOUND WHAT I'M LOOKING FOR	Chimes	*CBS*	5
29	[20]	YAAAH/TECHNO TRANCE	D-Shake	*Cooltempo*	3
-	21	NESSUN DORMA	Luciano Pavarotti ●	*Decca*	1
39	22	THE FREE STYLE MEGA-MIX	Bobby Brown	*MCA*	2
16	23	EVERYBODY EVERYBODY	Black Box	*deConstruction*	3
22	24	DON'T WANNA FALL IN LOVE	Jane Child	*Warner Brothers*	4
18	25	ROAM	B52s	*Reprise*	5
20	26	HOW CAN WE BE LOVERS	Michael Bolton	*CBS*	7
15	27	VOGUE	Madonna	*Sire*	11
28	[28]	TOUCHED BY THE HAND OF CICCIOLINA	Pop Will Eat Itself	*RCA*	2
14	29	COVER GIRL	New Kids On The Block	*CBS*	6
24	30	KISSING GATE	Sam Brown	*A&M*	6
35	[31]	GIRL TO GIRL	49ers	*Fourth & Broadway*	2
-	32	WHOSE LAW (IS IT ANYWAY)	Guru Josh	*deConstruction*	1
17	33	OPPOSITES ATTRACT	Paula Abdul with the Wild Pair	*Siren*	11
34	34	STILL GOT THE BLUES (FOR YOU)	Gary Moore	*Virgin*	4
19	35	WON'T TALK ABOUT IT	Beats International	*Go Beat*	6
-	36	CLOSE TO YOU	Maxi Priest	*10*	1
27	37	EXPRESS YOURSELF	N.W.A.	*Ruthless*	3
-	38	THINKING OF YOU	Maureen ●	*Urban*	1
38	39	REPUTATION	Dusty Springfield	*Parlophone*	2
-	40	THE MASTERPLAN	Diana Brown & Barrie K Sharpe ●	*ffrr*	1

LW	TW	*WEEK ENDING* **23 JUNE 1990**			Wks
5	[1]	SACRIFICE/HEALING HANDS	Elton John	*Rocket*	3
1	2	WORLD IN MOTION...	Englandneworder	*Factory*	4
21	3	NESSUN DORMA	Luciano Pavarotti	*Decca*	2
6	4	IT MUST HAVE BEEN LOVE	Roxette	*EMI*	4
2	5	STEP BY STEP	New Kids On The Block	*CBS*	2
13	6	OOPS UP	Snap	*Arista*	2
3	7	HEAR THE DRUMMER (GET WICKED)	Chad Jackson	*Big Wave*	4
10	8	HOLD ON	Wilson Phillips	*SBK*	4
7	9	DOIN' THE DO	Betty Boo	*Rhythm King*	5
9	10	THE ONLY ONE I KNOW	Charlatans	*Situation Two*	4
4	11	KILLER	Adamski	*MCA*	11
18	12	THE ONLY RHYME THAT BITES	MC Tunes vs 808 State	*ZTT*	3
8	13	VENUS	Don Pablo's Animals	*Rumour*	6
22	[14]	THE FREE STYLE MEGA-MIX	Bobby Brown	*MCA*	3
36	15	CLOSE TO YOU	Maxi Priest	*10*	2
11	16	DIRTY CASH	Adventures Of Stevie V	*Mercury*	10
12	17	STAR	Erasure	*Mute*	4
38	18	THINKING OF YOU	Maureen	*Urban*	2
-	19	YOU'VE GOT A FRIEND	Big Fun and Sonia ●	*Jive*	1
-	20	MONA	Craig McLachlan and Check 1-2 ●	*Epic*	1
16	21	IT'S MY LIFE	Talk Talk	*Parlophone*	5
17	22	PAPA WAS A ROLLING STONE	Was (Not Was)	*Fontana*	5
14	23	HOLD ON	En Vogue	*Atlantic*	8
15	24	BETTER THE DEVIL YOU KNOW	Kylie Minogue	*PWL*	7
-	25	U CAN'T TOUCH THIS	M.C.Hammer ●	*Capitol*	1
32	[26]	WHOSE LAW (IS IT ANYWAY)	Guru Josh	*deConstruction*	2
19	27	I STILL HAVEN'T FOUND WHAT I'M LOOKING FOR	Chimes	*CBS*	6
20	28	YAAAH/TECHNO TRANCE	D-Shake	*Cooltempo*	4
-	29	TASTE THE PAIN	Red Hot Chili Peppers ●	*EMI USA*	1
-	30	TREAT ME GOOD	Yazz	*Big Life*	1
24	31	DON'T WANNA FALL IN LOVE	Jane Child	*Warner Brothers*	5
-	32	ALL THE YOUNG DUDES	Bruce Dickinson	*EMI*	1
28	33	TOUCHED BY THE HAND OF CICCIOLINA	Pop Will Eat Itself	*RCA*	3
25	34	ROAM	B52s	*Reprise*	6
-	35	ROCKIN' CHAIR	Magnum	*Polydor*	1
27	36	VOGUE	Madonna	*Sire*	12
-	37	VICTIMS OF SUCCESS	Dogs D'Amour	*China*	1
-	38	LOVING YOU	Massivo featuring Tracy ●	*Debut*	1
40	[39]	THE MASTERPLAN	Diana Brown & Barrie K Sharpe	*ffrr*	2
26	40	HOW CAN WE BE LOVERS	Michael Bolton	*CBS*	8

LW	TW	*WEEK ENDING* **30 JUNE 1990**			Wks
1	[1]	SACRIFICE/HEALING HANDS	Elton John	*Rocket*	4
3	[2]	NESSUN DORMA	Luciano Pavarotti	*Decca*	3
4	[3]	IT MUST HAVE BEEN LOVE	Roxette	*EMI*	5
2	4	WORLD IN MOTION...	Englandneworder	*Factory*	5
6	[5]	OOPS UP	Snap	*Arista*	3
8	[6]	HOLD ON	Wilson Phillips	*SBK*	5
20	7	MONA	Craig McLachlan and Check 1-2	*Epic*	2
15	8	CLOSE TO YOU	Maxi Priest	*10*	3
9	9	DOIN' THE DO	Betty Boo	*Rhythm King*	6
7	10	HEAR THE DRUMMER (GET WICKED)	Chad Jackson	*Big Wave*	5
12	11	THE ONLY RHYME THAT BITES	MC Tunes vs 808 State	*ZTT*	4
5	12	STEP BY STEP	New Kids On The Block	*CBS*	3
25	13	U CAN'T TOUCH THIS	M.C.Hammer	*Capitol*	2
19	[14]	YOU'VE GOT A FRIEND	Big Fun and Sonia	*Jive*	2
10	15	THE ONLY ONE I KNOW	Charlatans	*Situation Two*	5
11	16	KILLER	Adamski	*MCA*	12
18	17	THINKING OF YOU	Maureen	*Urban*	3
14	18	THE FREE STYLE MEGA-MIX	Bobby Brown	*MCA*	4
13	19	VENUS	Don Pablo's Animals	*Rumour*	7
30	[20]	TREAT ME GOOD	Yazz	*Big Life*	2
-	21	ANOTHER NIGHT	Jason Donovan	*PWL*	1
16	22	DIRTY CASH	Adventures Of Stevie V	*Mercury*	11
32	[23]	ALL THE YOUNG DUDES	Bruce Dickinson	*EMI*	2
-	24	UNSKINNY BOP	Poison	*Enigma*	1
-	25	GREAT SONG OF INDIFFERENCE	Bob Geldof	*Mercury*	1
17	26	STAR	Erasure	*Mute*	5
35	[27]	ROCKIN' CHAIR	Magnum	*Polydor*	2
21	28	IT'S MY LIFE	Talk Talk	*Parlophone*	6
38	29	LOVING YOU	Massivo featuring Tracy	*Debut*	2
22	30	PAPA WAS A ROLLING STONE	Was (Not Was)	*Fontana*	6
24	31	BETTER THE DEVIL YOU KNOW	Kylie Minogue	*PWL*	8
-	32	LOVE DON'T LIVE HERE ANYMORE	Double Trouble ●	*Desire*	1
26	33	WHOSE LAW (IS IT ANYWAY)	Guru Josh	*deConstruction*	3
23	34	HOLD ON	En Vogue	*Atlantic*	9
-	35	SHE AIN'T WORTH IT	Glenn Medeiros featuring Bobby Brown	*London*	1
37	[36]	VICTIMS OF SUCCESS	Dogs D'Amour	*China*	2
29	37	TASTE THE PAIN	Red Hot Chili Peppers	*EMI USA*	2
27	38	I STILL HAVEN'T FOUND WHAT I'M LOOKING FOR	Chimes	*CBS*	7
-	39	MOVE AWAY JIMMY BLUE	Del Amitri	*A&M*	1
-	40	SHE COMES IN THE FALL	Inspiral Carpets	*Cow*	1

LW	TW	*WEEK ENDING* **7 JULY 1990**			Wks
1	[1]	SACRIFICE/HEALING HANDS	Elton John	*Rocket*	5
2	[2]	NESSUN DORMA	Luciano Pavarotti	*Decca*	4
3	[3]	IT MUST HAVE BEEN LOVE	Roxette	*EMI*	6
7	4	MONA	Craig McLachlan and Check 1-2	*Epic*	3
5	[5]	OOPS UP	Snap!	*Arista*	4
4	6	WORLD IN MOTION...	Englandneworder	*Factory*	6
8	[7]	CLOSE TO YOU	Maxi Priest	*10*	4
6	8	HOLD ON	Wilson Phillips	*SBK*	6
13	9	U CAN'T TOUCH THIS	M.C.Hammer	*Capitol*	3
11	[10]	THE ONLY RHYME THAT BITES	MC Tunes vs 808 State	*ZTT*	5
17	[11]	THINKING OF YOU	Maureen	*Urban*	4
-	12	THUNDERBIRDS ARE GO	F.A.B. featuring MC Parker ●	*Brothers Organisation*	1
9	13	DOIN' THE DO	Betty Boo	*Rhythm King*	7
10	14	HEAR THE DRUMMER (GET WICKED)	Chad Jackson	*Big Wave*	6
25	[15]	GREAT SONG OF INDIFFERENCE	Bob Geldof	*Mercury*	2
14	16	YOU'VE GOT A FRIEND	Big Fun and Sonia	*Jive*	3
24	17	UNSKINNY BOP	Poison	*Enigma*	2
21	[18]	ANOTHER NIGHT	Jason Donovan	*PWL*	2
15	19	THE ONLY ONE I KNOW	Charlatans	*Situation Two*	6
16	20	KILLER	Adamski	*MCA*	13

In these weeks ■ The top three have a real footballing look. At number one, the ex-chairman of Watford F.C. enjoying his first number one after 19 years of trying; at number two, the England World Cup Squad with New Order and at number three the official theme of BBC-TV's World Cup coverage (23.06.90) ■ Luciano Pavarotti's *Nessun Dorma* becomes the most successful classical single ever, peaking at number two (30.06.90)■

LW	TW	Title / Artist	Label	Wks
35	21	SHE AIN'T WORTH IT Glenn Medeiros featuring Bobby Brown	London	2
18	22	THE FREE STYLE MEGA-MIX Bobby Brown	MCA	5
12	23	STEP BY STEP New Kids On The Block	CBS	4
20	24	TREAT ME GOOD Yazz	Big Life	3
32	25	LOVE DON'T LIVE HERE ANYMORE Double Trouble	Desire	2
23	26	ALL THE YOUNG DUDES Bruce Dickinson	EMI	3
29	27	LOVING YOU Massivo featuring Tracy	Debut	3
19	28	VENUS Don Pablo's Animals	Rumour	8
-	29	ALRIGHT Janet Jackson	A&M	1
40	30	SHE COMES IN THE FALL Inspiral Carpets	Cow	2
-	[31]	ALMOST HEAR YOU SIGH Rolling Stones	CBS	1
-	[32]	COME HOME James	Fontana	1
-	33	I'M STILL WAITING (PHILL CHILL REMIX) Diana Ross	Motown	1
22	34	DIRTY CASH Adventures Of Stevie V	Mercury	12
-	35	CARRY THE BLAME/CALIFORNIA DREAMIN' River City People ●	EMI	1
39	[36]	MOVE AWAY JIMMY BLUE Del Amitri	A&M	2
28	37	IT'S MY LIFE Talk Talk	Parlophone	7
27	38	ROCKIN' CHAIR Magnum	Polydor	3
-	[39]	MESSAGE IN THE BOX World Party ●	Ensign	1
31	40	BETTER THE DEVIL YOU KNOW Kylie Minogue	PWL	9

WEEK ENDING 14 JULY 1990

LW	TW	Title / Artist	Label	Wks
1	[1]	SACRIFICE/HEALING HANDS Elton John	Rocket	6
2	[2]	NESSUN DORMA Luciano Pavarotti	Decca	5
4	3	MONA Craig McLachlan and Check 1-2	Epic	4
-	[4]	ONE LOVE Stone Roses	Silvertone	1
3	5	IT MUST HAVE BEEN LOVE Roxette	EMI	7
9	6	U CAN'T TOUCH THIS M.C.Hammer	Capitol	4
12	7	THUNDERBIRDS ARE GO F.A.B. featuring MC Parker	Brothers Organisation	2
6	8	WORLD IN MOTION... Englandneworder	Factory	7
7	9	CLOSE TO YOU Maxi Priest	10	5
5	10	OOPS UP Snap!	Arista	5
8	11	HOLD ON Wilson Phillips	SBK	7
10	12	THE ONLY RHYME THAT BITES MC Tunes vs 808 State	ZTT	6
21	13	SHE AIN'T WORTH IT Glenn Medeiros featuring Bobby Brown	London	3
11	14	THINKING OF YOU Maureen	Urban	5
17	[15]	UNSKINNY BOP Poison	Enigma	3
13	16	DOIN' THE DO Betty Boo	Rhythm King	8
15	17	GREAT SONG OF INDIFFERENCE Bob Geldof	Mercury	3
20	18	KILLER Adamski	MCA	14
16	19	YOU'VE GOT A FRIEND Big Fun and Sonia	Jive	4
29	20	ALRIGHT Janet Jackson	A&M	2
25	[21]	LOVE DON'T LIVE HERE ANYMORE Double Trouble	Desire	3
33	22	I'M STILL WAITING (PHILL CHILL REMIX) Diana Ross	Motown	2
18	23	ANOTHER NIGHT Jason Donovan	PWL	3
14	24	HEAR THE DRUMMER (GET WICKED) Chad Jackson	Big Wave	7
27	[25]	LOVING YOU Massivo featuring Tracy	Debut	4
-	26	ROCKIN' OVER THE BEAT Technotronic featuring Ya Kid K	Swanyard	1
35	27	CARRY THE BLAME/CALIFORNIA DREAMIN' River City People	EMI	2
-	28	I'M FREE Soup Dragons featuring Junior Reid ●	Raw TV	1
30	29	SHE COMES IN THE FALL Inspiral Carpets	Cow	3
23	30	STEP BY STEP New Kids On The Block	CBS	5
19	31	THE ONLY ONE I KNOW Charlatans	Situation Two	7
32	[32]	COME HOME James	Fontana	2
31	33	ALMOST HEAR YOU SIGH Rolling Stones	CBS	2
-	34	NAKED IN THE RAIN Blue Pearl ●	WAU Mr Modo	1
-	35	SHAME ON YOU Gun	A&M	1
22	36	THE FREE STYLE MEGA-MIX Bobby Brown	MCA	6
24	37	TREAT ME GOOD Yazz	Big Life	4
-	38	GIMME SOME LOVIN' Thunder	EMI	1
-	39	OH GIRL Paul Young	CBS	1
26	40	ALL THE YOUNG DUDES Bruce Dickinson	EMI	4

July 1990

□ Highest position disc reached ● Act's first ever week on chart

WEEK ENDING 21 JULY 1990

LW	TW	Title / Artist	Label	Wks
1	[1]	SACRIFICE/HEALING HANDS Elton John	Rocket	7
3	[2]	MONA Craig McLachlan and Check 1-2	Epic	5
2	3	NESSUN DORMA Luciano Pavarotti	Decca	6
-	4	TURTLE POWER Partners In Kryme ●	SBK	1
7	[5]	THUNDERBIRDS ARE GO F.A.B. featuring MC Parker	Brothers Organisation	3
5	6	IT MUST HAVE BEEN LOVE Roxette	EMI	8
6	7	U CAN'T TOUCH THIS M.C.Hammer	Capitol	5
4	8	ONE LOVE Stone Roses	Silvertone	2
10	9	OOPS UP Snap!	Arista	6
8	10	WORLD IN MOTION... Englandneworder	Factory	8
9	11	CLOSE TO YOU Maxi Priest	10	6
13	[12]	SHE AIN'T WORTH IT Glenn Medeiros featuring Bobby Brown	London	4
28	13	I'M FREE Soup Dragons featuring Junior Reid	Raw TV	2
-	14	HANKY PANKY Madonna	Sire	1
26	15	ROCKIN' OVER THE BEAT Technotronic featuring Ya Kid K	Swanyard	2
11	16	HOLD ON Wilson Phillips	SBK	8
34	17	NAKED IN THE RAIN Blue Pearl	WAU Mr Modo	2
27	18	CARRY THE BLAME/CALIFORNIA DREAMIN' River City People	EMI	3
15	19	UNSKINNY BOP Poison	Enigma	4
12	20	THE ONLY RHYME THAT BITES MC Tunes vs 808 State	ZTT	7
22	[21]	I'M STILL WAITING (PHILL CHILL REMIX) Diana Ross	Motown	3
14	22	THINKING OF YOU Maureen	Urban	6
21	23	LOVE DON'T LIVE HERE ANYMORE Double Trouble	Desire	4
16	24	DOIN' THE DO Betty Boo	Rhythm King	9
20	25	ALRIGHT Janet Jackson	A&M	3
18	26	KILLER Adamski	MCA	15
29	[27]	SHE COMES IN THE FALL Inspiral Carpets	Cow	4
-	28	KNOCKED OUT (PETTIBONE REMIX) Paula Abdul	Virgin	1
25	29	LOVING YOU Massivo featuring Tracy	Debut	5
17	30	GREAT SONG OF INDIFFERENCE Bob Geldof	Mercury	4
-	31	WASH YOUR FACE IN MY SINK Dream Warriors ●	Fourth + Broadway	1
39	32	OH GIRL Paul Young	CBS	2
35	[33]	SHAME ON YOU Gun	A&M	2
33	34	ALMOST HEAR YOU SIGH Rolling Stones	CBS	3
24	35	HEAR THE DRUMMER (GET WICKED) Chad Jackson	Big Wave	8
38	[36]	GIMME SOME LOVIN' Thunder	EMI	2
-	37	LFO LFO ●	Warp	1
23	38	ANOTHER NIGHT Jason Donovan	PWL	4
-	39	POISON Bell Biv Devoe ●	MCA	1
19	40	YOU'VE GOT A FRIEND Big Fun and Sonia	Jive	5

WEEK ENDING 28 JULY 1990

LW	TW	Title / Artist	Label	Wks
4	[1]	TURTLE POWER Partners In Kryme	SBK	2
1	2	SACRIFICE/HEALING HANDS Elton John	Rocket	8
2	3	MONA Craig McLachlan and Check 1-2	Epic	6
14	4	HANKY PANKY Madonna	Sire	2
7	5	U CAN'T TOUCH THIS M.C.Hammer	Capitol	6
5	6	THUNDERBIRDS ARE GO F.A.B. featuring MC Parker	Brothers Organisation	4
6	7	IT MUST HAVE BEEN LOVE Roxette	EMI	9
17	8	NAKED IN THE RAIN Blue Pearl	WAU Mr Modo	3
15	[9]	ROCKIN' OVER THE BEAT Technotronic featuring Ya Kid K	Swanyard	3
13	10	I'M FREE Soup Dragons featuring Junior Reid	Raw TV	3
9	11	OOPS UP Snap!	Arista	7
12	[12]	SHE AIN'T WORTH IT Glenn Medeiros featuring Bobby Brown	London	5
-	13	TOM'S DINER DNA featuring Suzanne Vega ●	A&M	1

■The power of television is shown in the success of Craig McLachlan of 'Neighbours' and 'Home And Away', Luciano Pavarotti and *Thunderbirds Are Go*. Films made hits of *Turtle Power* (from 'Teenage Mutant Hero Turtles'), *It Must Have Been Love* (from 'Pretty Woman') and *Hanky Panky* (from 'Dick Tracy') (21.07.90)■

July 1990

☐ Highest position disc reached ● Act's first ever week on chart

LW	TW	Title	Artist	Label	Wks
8	14	ONE LOVE	Stone Roses	Silvertone	3
11	15	CLOSE TO YOU	Maxi Priest	10	7
18	16	CARRY THE BLAME/CALIFORNIA DREAMIN'	River City People	EMI	4
3	17	NESSUN DORMA	Luciano Pavarotti	Decca	7
10	18	WORLD IN MOTION...	Englandneworder	Factory	9
31	19	WASH YOUR FACE IN MY SINK	Dream Warriors	Fourth + Broadway	2
16	20	HOLD ON	Wilson Phillips	SBK	9
28	[21]	KNOCKED OUT (PETTIBONE REMIX)	Paula Abdul	Virgin	2
21	22	I'M STILL WAITING (PHILL CHILL REMIX)	Diana Ross	Motown	4
37	23	LFO	LFO	Warp	2
19	24	UNSKINNY BOP	Poison	Enigma	5
32	[25]	OH GIRL	Paul Young	CBS	3
22	26	THINKING OF YOU	Maureen	Urban	7
23	27	LOVE DON'T LIVE HERE ANYMORE	Double Trouble	Desire	5
-	[28]	VELOURIA	Pixies ●	4AD	1
39	29	POISON	Bell Biv Devoe	MCA	2
20	30	THE ONLY RHYME THAT BITES	MC Tunes vs 808 State	ZTT	8
-	[31]	THE EMPEROR'S NEW CLOTHES	Sinead O'Connor	Ensign	1
-	32	TRICKY DISCO	Tricky Disco ●	Warp	1
-	33	ONLY YOUR LOVE	Bananarama	London	1
-	34	DOUBLEBACK	ZZ Top	Warner Brothers	1
-	[35]	HOW MUCH LOVE	Vixen	EMI USA	1
26	36	KILLER	Adamski	MCA	16
-	[37]	SILENT VOICE	Innocence	Cooltempo	1
24	38	DOIN' THE DO	Betty Boo	Rhythm King	10
-	[39]	STARDATE 1990/RAINBOW CHILD	Dan Reed Network ●	Mercury	1
-	40	DOIN' OUR OWN DANG	Jungle Brothers	Eternal	1

LW	TW	*WEEK ENDING* **4 AUGUST 1990**			Wks
1	[1]	TURTLE POWER	Partners In Kryme	SBK	3
4	[2]	HANKY PANKY	Madonna	Sire	3
13	3	TOM'S DINER	DNA featuring Suzanne Vega	A&M	2
2	4	SACRIFICE/HEALING HANDS	Elton John	Rocket	9
5	5	U CAN'T TOUCH THIS	M.C.Hammer	Capitol	7
8	6	NAKED IN THE RAIN	Blue Pearl	WAU Mr Modo	4
3	7	MONA	Craig McLachlan and Check 1-2	Epic	7
10	8	I'M FREE	Soup Dragons featuring Junior Reid	Raw TV	4
9	[9]	ROCKIN' OVER THE BEAT	Technotronic featuring Ya Kid K	Swanyard	4
7	10	IT MUST HAVE BEEN LOVE	Roxette	EMI	10
-	11	THIEVES IN THE TEMPLE	Prince	Paisley Park	1
6	12	THUNDERBIRDS ARE GO	F.A.B. featuring MC Parker	Brothers Organisation	5
16	[13]	CARRY THE BLAME/CALIFORNIA DREAMIN'	River City People	EMI	5
23	14	LFO	LFO	Warp	3
11	15	OOPS UP	Snap!	Arista	8
19	[16]	WASH YOUR FACE IN MY SINK	Dream Warriors	Fourth + Broadway	3
-	17	TONIGHT	New Kids On The Block	CBS	1
12	18	SHE AIN'T WORTH IT	Glenn Medeiros featuring Bobby Brown	London	6
14	19	ONE LOVE	Stone Roses	Silvertone	4
29	20	POISON	Bell Biv Devoe	MCA	3
-	[21]	SHE'S A LITTLE ANGEL	Little Angels	Polydor	1
32	22	TRICKY DISCO	Tricky Disco	Warp	2
-	23	VIOLENCE OF SUMMER (LOVE'S TAKING OVER)	Duran Duran	Parlophone	1
-	24	HARDCORE UPROAR	Together ●	ffrr	1
-	25	ITSY BITSY TEENY WEENY YELLOW POLKA DOT BIKINI	Bombalurina ●	Carpet	1
-	[26]	THAT'S JUST THE WAY IT IS	Phil Collins	Virgin	1
33	[27]	ONLY YOUR LOVE	Bananarama	London	2
18	28	WORLD IN MOTION...	Englandneworder	Factory	10
34	[29]	DOUBLEBACK	ZZ Top	Warner Brothers	2
17	30	NESSUN DORMA	Luciano Pavarotti	Decca	8
15	31	CLOSE TO YOU	Maxi Priest	10	8
21	32	KNOCKED OUT (PETTIBONE REMIX)	Paula Abdul	Virgin	3
31	33	THE EMPEROR'S NEW CLOTHES	Sinead O'Connor	Ensign	2
20	34	HOLD ON	Wilson Phillips	SBK	10
40	[35]	DOIN' OUR OWN DANG	Jungle Brothers	Eternal	2
-	36	AMANDA	Craig McLachlan and Check 1-2	Epic	1
24	37	UNSKINNY BOP	Poison	Enigma	6
22	38	I'M STILL WAITING (PHILL CHILL REMIX)	Diana Ross	Motown	5
25	39	OH GIRL	Paul Young	CBS	4
-	40	I CAN SEE CLEARLY NOW	Hothouse Flowers	London	1

LW	TW	*WEEK ENDING* **11 AUGUST 1990**			Wks
1	[1]	TURTLE POWER	Partners In Kryme	SBK	4
3	[2]	TOM'S DINER	DNA featuring Suzanne Vega	A&M	3
5	[3]	U CAN'T TOUCH THIS	M.C.Hammer	Capitol	8
6	[4]	NAKED IN THE RAIN	Blue Pearl	WAU Mr Modo	5
8	[5]	I'M FREE	Soup Dragons featuring Junior Reid	Raw TV	5
2	6	HANKY PANKY	Madonna	Sire	4
11	[7]	THIEVES IN THE TEMPLE	Prince	Paisley Park	2
17	8	TONIGHT	New Kids On The Block	CBS	2
4	9	SACRIFICE/HEALING HANDS	Elton John	Rocket	10
9	10	ROCKIN' OVER THE BEAT	Technotronic featuring Ya Kid K	Swanyard	5
25	11	ITSY BITSY TEENY WEENY YELLOW POLKA DOT BIKINI	Bombalurina	Carpet	2
14	[12]	LFO	LFO	Warp	4
7	13	MONA	Craig McLachlan and Check 1-2	Epic	8
13	14	CARRY THE BLAME/CALIFORNIA DREAMIN'	River City People	EMI	6
22	15	TRICKY DISCO	Tricky Disco	Warp	3
16	[16]	WASH YOUR FACE IN MY SINK	Dream Warriors	Fourth + Broadway	4
24	17	HARDCORE UPROAR	Together	ffrr	2
10	18	IT MUST HAVE BEEN LOVE	Roxette	EMI	11
20	[19]	POISON	Bell Biv Devoe	MCA	4
23	[20]	VIOLENCE OF SUMMER (LOVE'S TAKING OVER)	Duran Duran	Parlophone	2
-	21	LISTEN TO YOUR HEART/DANGEROUS	Roxette	EMI	1
15	22	OOPS UP	Snap!	Arista	9
36	23	AMANDA	Craig McLachlan and Check 1-2	Epic	2
-	24	BLAZE OF GLORY	Jon Bon Jovi ●	Vertigo	1
12	25	THUNDERBIRDS ARE GO	F.A.B. featuring MC Parker	Brothers Organisation	6
-	26	ENGLISHMAN IN NEW YORK	Sting	A&M	1
18	27	SHE AIN'T WORTH IT	Glenn Medeiros featuring Bobby Brown	London	7
21	28	SHE'S A LITTLE ANGEL	Little Angels	Polydor	2
40	29	I CAN SEE CLEARLY NOW	Hothouse Flowers	London	2
26	30	THAT'S JUST THE WAY IT IS	Phil Collins	Virgin	2
29	31	DOUBLEBACK	ZZ Top	Warner Brothers	3
27	32	ONLY YOUR LOVE	Bananarama	London	3
35	[33]	DOIN' OUR OWN DANG	Jungle Brothers	Eternal	3
-	34	WHAT TIME IS LOVE?	KLF featuring Children Of The Revolution ●	KLF Communications	1
-	35	WHERE ARE YOU BABY?	Betty Boo	Rhythm King	1
-	36	WEAR YOU TO THE BALL	UB40	DEP International	1
-	37	STAY WITH ME HEARTACHE/I FEEL FINE	Wet Wet Wet	Precious	1
-	38	NOBODY	Tongue 'n' Cheek	Syncopate	1
-	[39]	LET LOVE RULE	Lenny Kravitz ●	Virgin	1
-	40	KING OF WISHFUL THINKING	Go West	Capitol	1

LW	TW	*WEEK ENDING* **18 AUGUST 1990**			Wks
1	[1]	TURTLE POWER	Partners In Kryme	SBK	5
2	[2]	TOM'S DINER	DNA featuring Suzanne Vega	A&M	4
11	3	ITSY BITSY TEENY WEENY YELLOW POLKA DOT BIKINI	Bombalurina	Carpet	3
4	[4]	NAKED IN THE RAIN	Blue Pearl	WAU Mr Modo	6

In these weeks ■ By climbing to number 18, Bell Biv Devoe overtake their former partner in New Edition, Bobby Brown, who is on his way down from number 12 with a new and unlikely partner, Glenn Medeiros (11.08.90) ■ One of the biggest bands of the early 90s, the KLF, enters the charts two years after their chart-topping success as the Timelords (11.08.90)■

LW	TW	Title	Artist	Label	Wks
3	5	U CAN'T TOUCH THIS	M.C.Hammer	Capitol	9
8	6	TONIGHT	New Kids On The Block	CBS	3
5	7	I'M FREE	Soup Dragons featuring Junior Reid	Raw TV	6
6	8	HANKY PANKY	Madonna	Sire	5
21	9	LISTEN TO YOUR HEART/DANGEROUS	Roxette	EMI	2
7	10	THIEVES IN THE TEMPLE	Prince	Paisley Park	3
9	11	SACRIFICE/HEALING HANDS	Elton John	Rocket	11
17	12	HARDCORE UPROAR	Together	ffrr	3
24	13	BLAZE OF GLORY	Jon Bon Jovi	Vertigo	2
15	14	TRICKY DISCO	Tricky Disco	Warp	4
10	15	ROCKIN' OVER THE BEAT	Technotronic featuring Ya Kid K	Swanyard	6
12	16	LFO	LFO	Warp	5
35	17	WHERE ARE YOU BABY?	Betty Boo	Rhythm King	2
26	18	ENGLISHMAN IN NEW YORK	Sting	A&M	2
23	19	AMANDA	Craig McLachlan and Check 1-2	Epic	3
14	20	CARRY THE BLAME/CALIFORNIA DREAMIN'	River City People	EMI	7
19	21	POISON	Bell Biv Devoe	MCA	5
16	22	WASH YOUR FACE IN MY SINK	Dream Warriors	Fourth + Broadway	5
29	23	I CAN SEE CLEARLY NOW	Hothouse Flowers	London	3
40	24	KING OF WISHFUL THINKING	Go West	Capitol	2
34	25	WHAT TIME IS LOVE?	KLF featuring Children Of The Revolution	KLF Communications	2
-	26	COME TOGETHER	Primal Scream	Creation	1
-	27	VISION OF LOVE	Mariah Carey ●	CBS	1
18	28	IT MUST HAVE BEEN LOVE	Roxette	EMI	12
-	29	SILLY GAMES	Lindy Layton featuring Janet Kay ●	Arista	1
37	30	STAY WITH ME HEARTACHE/I FEEL FINE	Wet Wet Wet	Precious	2
22	31	OOPS UP	Snap!	Arista	10
20	32	VIOLENCE OF SUMMER (LOVE'S TAKING OVER)	Duran Duran	Parlophone	3
13	33	MONA	Craig McLachlan and Check 1-2	Epic	9
-	34	LOOK ME IN THE HEART	Tina Turner	Capitol	1
36	35	WEAR YOU TO THE BALL	UB40	DEP International	2
33	36	DOIN' OUR OWN DANG	Jungle Brothers	Eternal	4
38	37	NOBODY	Tongue 'n' Cheek	Syncopate	2
-	38	HEART LIKE A WHEEL	Human League	Virgin	1
-	39	RELEASE ME	Wilson Phillips	SBK	1
39	40	LET LOVE RULE	Lenny Kravitz	Virgin	2

WEEK ENDING 25 AUGUST 1990

LW	TW	Title	Artist	Label	Wks
3	1	ITSY BITSY TEENY WEENY YELLOW POLKA DOT BIKINI	Bombalurina	Carpet	4
2	2	TOM'S DINER	DNA featuring Suzanne Vega	A&M	5
1	3	TURTLE POWER	Partners In Kryme	SBK	6
6	4	TONIGHT	New Kids On The Block	CBS	4
4	5	NAKED IN THE RAIN	Blue Pearl	WAU Mr Modo	7
9	6	LISTEN TO YOUR HEART/DANGEROUS	Roxette	EMI	3
5	7	U CAN'T TOUCH THIS	M.C.Hammer	Capitol	10
-	8	PRAYING FOR TIME	George Michael	Epic	1
17	9	WHERE ARE YOU BABY?	Betty Boo	Rhythm King	3
7	10	I'M FREE	Soup Dragons featuring Junior Reid	Raw TV	7
-	11	FOUR BACHARACH & DAVID SONGS (EP)	Deacon Blue	CBS	1
12	12	HARDCORE UPROAR	Together	ffrr	4
13	13	BLAZE OF GLORY	Jon Bon Jovi	Vertigo	3
-	14	CAN CAN YOU PARTY	Jive Bunny & the Mastermixers	Music Factory Dance	1
18	15	ENGLISHMAN IN NEW YORK	Sting	A&M	3
25	16	WHAT TIME IS LOVE?	KLF featuring Children Of The Revolution	KLF Communications	3
-	17	SILHOUETTES	Cliff Richard	EMI	1
24	18	KING OF WISHFUL THINKING	Go West	Capitol	3
8	19	HANKY PANKY	Madonna	Sire	6
14	20	TRICKY DISCO	Tricky Disco	Warp	5
19	21	AMANDA	Craig McLachlan and Check 1-2	Epic	4
27	22	VISION OF LOVE	Mariah Carey	CBS	2
29	23	SILLY GAMES	Lindy Layton featuring Janet Kay	Arista	2
11	24	SACRIFICE/HEALING HANDS	Elton John	Rocket	12
15	25	ROCKIN' OVER THE BEAT	Technotronic featuring Ya Kid K	Swanyard	7

September 1990

Highest position disc reached ● Act's first ever week on chart

LW	TW	Title	Artist	Label	Wks
16	26	LFO	LFO	Warp	6
10	27	THIEVES IN THE TEMPLE	Prince	Paisley Park	4
26	28	COME TOGETHER	Primal Scream	Creation	2
38	29	HEART LIKE A WHEEL	Human League	Virgin	2
23	30	I CAN SEE CLEARLY NOW	Hothouse Flowers	London	4
34	31	LOOK ME IN THE HEART	Tina Turner	Capitol	2
-	32	GROOVE IS IN THE HEART	Deee-Lite ●	Elektra	1
21	33	POISON	Bell Biv Devoe	MCA	6
-	34	THE JOKER	Steve Miller Band	Capitol	1
20	35	CARRY THE BLAME/CALIFORNIA DREAMIN'	River City People	EMI	8
39	36	RELEASE ME	Wilson Phillips	SBK	2
-	37	END OF THE WORLD	Sonia	Chrysalis	1
-	38	NEXT TO YOU	Aswad	Mango	1
-	39	NOW YOU'RE GONE (REMIX)	Whitesnake	EMI	1
30	40	STAY WITH ME HEARTACHE/I FEEL FINE	Wet Wet Wet	Precious	3

WEEK ENDING 1 SEPTEMBER 1990

LW	TW	Title	Artist	Label	Wks
1	1	ITSY BITSY TEENY WEENY YELLOW POLKA DOT BIKINI	Bombalurina	Carpet	5
11	2	FOUR BACHARACH & DAVID SONGS (EP)	Deacon Blue	CBS	2
4	3	TONIGHT	New Kids On The Block	CBS	5
9	4	WHERE ARE YOU BABY?	Betty Boo	Rhythm King	4
2	5	TOM'S DINER	DNA featuring Suzanne Vega	A&M	6
8	6	PRAYING FOR TIME	George Michael	Epic	2
6	7	LISTEN TO YOUR HEART/DANGEROUS	Roxette	EMI	4
14	8	CAN CAN YOU PARTY	Jive Bunny & the Mastermixers	Music Factory Dance	2
5	9	NAKED IN THE RAIN	Blue Pearl	WAU Mr Modo	8
17	10	SILHOUETTES	Cliff Richard	EMI	2
16	11	WHAT TIME IS LOVE?	KLF featuring Children Of The Revolution	KLF Communications	4
3	12	TURTLE POWER	Partners In Kryme	SBK	7
32	13	GROOVE IS IN THE HEART/WHAT IS LOVE	Deee-Lite	Elektra	2
34	14	THE JOKER	Steve Miller Band	Capitol	2
7	15	U CAN'T TOUCH THIS	M.C.Hammer	Capitol	11
22	16	VISION OF LOVE	Mariah Carey	CBS	3
10	17	I'M FREE	Soup Dragons featuring Junior Reid	Raw TV	8
13	18	BLAZE OF GLORY	Jon Bon Jovi	Vertigo	4
12	19	HARDCORE UPROAR	Together	ffrr	5
18	20	KING OF WISHFUL THINKING	Go West	Capitol	4
15	21	ENGLISHMAN IN NEW YORK	Sting	A&M	4
23	22	SILLY GAMES	Lindy Layton featuring Janet Kay	Arista	3
-	23	RHYTHM OF THE RAIN	Jason Donovan	PWL	1
37	24	END OF THE WORLD	Sonia	Chrysalis	2
38	25	NEXT TO YOU	Aswad	Mango	2
19	26	HANKY PANKY	Madonna	Sire	7
28	27	COME TOGETHER	Primal Scream	Creation	3
20	28	TRICKY DISCO	Tricky Disco	Warp	6
-	29	IN MY WORLD	Anthrax	Island	1
29	30	HEART LIKE A WHEEL	Human League	Virgin	3
39	31	NOW YOU'RE GONE (REMIX)	Whitesnake	EMI	2
21	32	AMANDA	Craig McLachlan and Check 1-2	Epic	5
31	33	LOOK ME IN THE HEART	Tina Turner	Capitol	3
-	34	DON'T BE A FOOL	Loose Ends	10	1
26	35	LFO	LFO	Warp	7
25	36	ROCKIN' OVER THE BEAT	Technotronic featuring Ya Kid K	Swanyard	8
36	37	RELEASE ME	Wilson Phillips	SBK	3
24	38	SACRIFICE/HEALING HANDS	Elton John	Rocket	13
-	39	LIFE'S WHAT YOU MAKE IT	Talk Talk	Parlophone	1
-	40	GROOVY TRAIN	Farm ●	Produce	1

WEEK ENDING 8 SEPTEMBER 1990

LW	TW	Title	Artist	Label	Wks
1	1	ITSY BITSY TEENY WEENY YELLOW POLKA DOT BIKINI	Bombalurina	Carpet	6

■Bombalurina's immortal remake of Brian Hyland's 1960 Top 10 hit becomes the longest song title (without brackets) to hit the top (25.08.90) ■ The most played song on Deacon Blue's EP is *I'll Never Fall In Love Again*, a chart-topper for Bobbie Gentry in 1969 (01.09.90) ■ Wilson Phillips enter at number 39 while the song that first brought fame to Mackenzie Phillips' Mama and Papa, *California Dreamin'* is still in the Top 20 (18.08.90)■

September 1990

□ Highest position disc reached ● Act's first ever week on chart

LW	TW	Title	Artist	Label	Wks
2	[2]	FOUR BACHARACH & DAVID SONGS (EP)	Deacon Blue	*CBS*	3
4	[3]	WHERE ARE YOU BABY?	Betty Boo	*Rhythm King*	5
13	4	GROOVE IS IN THE HEART/WHAT IS LOVE	Deee-Lite	*Elektra*	3
3	5	TONIGHT	New Kids On The Block	*CBS*	6
14	6	THE JOKER	Steve Miller Band	*Capitol*	3
11	7	WHAT TIME IS LOVE?	KLF featuring Children Of The Revolution	*KLF Communications*	5
9	8	NAKED IN THE RAIN	Blue Pearl	*WAU Mr Modo*	9
23	[9]	RHYTHM OF THE RAIN	Jason Donovan	*PWL*	2
6	10	PRAYING FOR TIME	George Michael	*Epic*	3
8	11	CAN CAN YOU PARTY	Jive Bunny & the Mastermixers	*Music Factory Dance*	3
10	12	SILHOUETTES	Cliff Richard	*EMI*	3
7	13	LISTEN TO YOUR HEART/DANGEROUS	Roxette	*EMI*	5
16	14	VISION OF LOVE	Mariah Carey	*CBS*	4
5	15	TOM'S DINER	DNA featuring Suzanne Vega	*A&M*	7
12	16	TURTLE POWER	Partners In Kryme	*SBK*	8
17	17	I'M FREE	Soup Dragons featuring Junior Reid	*Raw TV*	9
15	18	U CAN'T TOUCH THIS	M.C.Hammer	*Capitol*	12
24	19	END OF THE WORLD	Sonia	*Chrysalis*	3
20	20	KING OF WISHFUL THINKING	Go West	*Capitol*	5
34	21	DON'T BE A FOOL	Loose Ends	*10*	2
18	22	BLAZE OF GLORY	Jon Bon Jovi	*Vertigo*	5
-	23	THE SPACE JUNGLE	Adamski	*MCA*	1
25	[24]	NEXT TO YOU	Aswad	*Mango*	3
22	25	SILLY GAMES	Lindy Layton featuring Janet Kay	*Arista*	4
19	26	HARDCORE UPROAR	Together	*ffrr*	6
21	27	ENGLISHMAN IN NEW YORK	Sting	*A&M*	5
40	28	GROOVY TRAIN	Farm	*Produce*	2
-	29	LIVIN' IN THE LIGHT	Caron Wheeler ●	*RCA*	1
27	30	COME TOGETHER	Primal Scream	*Creation*	4
39	31	LIFE'S WHAT YOU MAKE IT	Talk Talk	*Parlophone*	2
-	32	BLACK CAT	Janet Jackson	*A&M*	1
31	33	NOW YOU'RE GONE (REMIX)	Whitesnake	*EMI*	3
-	[34]	GET ME OUT	New Model Army	*EMI*	1
-	35	EPIC	Faith No More	*Slash*	1
-	36	LA SERENISSIMA	DNA	*Raw Bass*	1
26	37	HANKY PANKY	Madonna	*Sire*	8
-	38	FASCINATING RHYTHM	Bass-O-Matic ●	*Virgin*	1
-	39	ICEBLINK LUCK	Cocteau Twins	*4AD*	1
37	40	RELEASE ME	Wilson Phillips	*SBK*	4

WEEK ENDING 15 SEPTEMBER 1990

LW	TW	Title	Artist	Label	Wks
6	[1]	THE JOKER	Steve Miller Band	*Capitol*	4
4	[2]	GROOVE IS IN THE HEART/WHAT IS LOVE	Deee-Lite	*Elektra*	4
1	3	ITSY BITSY TEENY WEENY YELLOW POLKA DOT BIKINI	Bombalurina	*Carpet*	7
2	4	FOUR BACHARACH & DAVID SONGS (EP)	Deacon Blue	*CBS*	4
7	[5]	WHAT TIME IS LOVE?	KLF featuring Children Of The Revolution	*KLF Communications*	6
3	6	WHERE ARE YOU BABY?	Betty Boo	*Rhythm King*	6
23	[7]	THE SPACE JUNGLE	Adamski	*MCA*	2
5	8	TONIGHT	New Kids On The Block	*CBS*	7
14	[9]	VISION OF LOVE	Mariah Carey	*CBS*	5
9	10	RHYTHM OF THE RAIN	Jason Donovan	*PWL*	3
28	11	GROOVY TRAIN	Farm	*Produce*	3
10	12	PRAYING FOR TIME	George Michael	*Epic*	4
21	[13]	DON'T BE A FOOL	Loose Ends	*10*	3
29	[14]	LIVIN' IN THE LIGHT	Caron Wheeler	*RCA*	2
32	[15]	BLACK CAT	Janet Jackson	*A&M*	2
-	16	SUICIDE BLONDE	INXS	*Mercury*	1
8	17	NAKED IN THE RAIN	Blue Pearl	*WAU Mr Modo*	10
19	[18]	END OF THE WORLD	Sonia	*Chrysalis*	4
12	19	SILHOUETTES	Cliff Richard	*EMI*	4
13	20	LISTEN TO YOUR HEART/DANGEROUS	Roxette	*EMI*	6
11	21	CAN CAN YOU PARTY	Jive Bunny & the Mastermixers	*Music Factory Dance*	4
38	22	FASCINATING RHYTHM	Bass-O-Matic	*Virgin*	2
31	[23]	LIFE'S WHAT YOU MAKE IT	Talk Talk	*Parlophone*	3
17	24	I'M FREE	Soup Dragons featuring Junior Reid	*Raw TV*	10
15	25	TOM'S DINER	DNA featuring Suzanne Vega	*A&M*	8
-	26	SHOW ME HEAVEN	Maria McKee ●	*Epic*	1
-	27	I'VE BEEN THINKING ABOUT YOU	Londonbeat	*Anxious*	1
20	28	KING OF WISHFUL THINKING	Go West	*Capitol*	6
35	29	EPIC	Faith No More	*Slash*	2
16	30	TURTLE POWER	Partners In Kryme	*SBK*	9
22	31	BLAZE OF GLORY	Jon Bon Jovi	*Vertigo*	6
-	32	FOOL'S GOLD/WHAT THE WORLD IS WAITING FOR	Stone Roses	*Silvertone*	1
18	33	U CAN'T TOUCH THIS	M.C.Hammer	*Capitol*	13
24	34	NEXT TO YOU	Aswad	*Mango*	4
36	35	LA SERENISSIMA	DNA	*Raw Bass*	2
25	36	SILLY GAMES	Lindy Layton featuring Janet Kay	*Arista*	5
-	[37]	THERE SHE GOES AGAIN/MISLED	Quireboys	*Parlophone*	1
39	[38]	ICEBLINK LUCK	Cocteau Twins	*4AD*	2
34	39	GET ME OUT	New Model Army	*EMI*	2
-	40	NOTHING TO LOSE	S'Express	*Rhythm King*	1

WEEK ENDING 22 SEPTEMBER 1990

LW	TW	Title	Artist	Label	Wks
1	[1]	THE JOKER	Steve Miller Band	*Capitol*	5
2	[2]	GROOVE IS IN THE HEART/WHAT IS LOVE	Deee-Lite	*Elektra*	5
-	[3]	HOLY SMOKE	Iron Maiden	*EMI*	1
26	4	SHOW ME HEAVEN	Maria McKee	*Epic*	2
4	5	FOUR BACHARACH & DAVID SONGS (EP)	Deacon Blue	*CBS*	5
5	6	WHAT TIME IS LOVE?	KLF featuring Children Of The Revolution	*KLF Communications*	7
3	7	ITSY BITSY TEENY WEENY YELLOW POLKA DOT BIKINI	Bombalurina	*Carpet*	8
7	8	THE SPACE JUNGLE	Adamski	*MCA*	3
11	9	GROOVY TRAIN	Farm	*Produce*	4
9	10	VISION OF LOVE	Mariah Carey	*CBS*	6
16	[11]	SUICIDE BLONDE	INXS	*Mercury*	2
27	12	I'VE BEEN THINKING ABOUT YOU	Londonbeat	*Anxious*	2
26	13	WHERE ARE YOU BABY?	Betty Boo	*Rhythm King*	7
22	14	FASCINATING RHYTHM	Bass-O-Matic	*Virgin*	3
15	[15]	BLACK CAT	Janet Jackson	*A&M*	3
-	16	THUNDERSTRUCK	AC/DC	*Atco*	1
13	17	DON'T BE A FOOL	Loose Ends	*10*	4
14	18	LIVIN' IN THE LIGHT	Caron Wheeler	*RCA*	3
-	19	THEN	Charlatans	*Situation Two*	1
8	20	TONIGHT	New Kids On The Block	*CBS*	8
-	21	CULT OF SNAP!	Snap!	*Arista*	1
18	22	END OF THE WORLD	Sonia	*Chrysalis*	5
32	23	FOOL'S GOLD/WHAT THE WORLD IS WAITING FOR	Stone Roses	*Silvertone*	2
10	24	RHYTHM OF THE RAIN	Jason Donovan	*PWL*	4
29	[25]	EPIC	Faith No More	*Slash*	3
17	26	NAKED IN THE RAIN	Blue Pearl	*WAU Mr Modo*	11
23	27	LIFE'S WHAT YOU MAKE IT	Talk Talk	*Parlophone*	4
-	28	I CAN'T STAND IT	Twenty4Seven featuring Captain Hollywood ●	*BCM*	1
12	29	PRAYING FOR TIME	George Michael	*Epic*	5
20	30	LISTEN TO YOUR HEART/DANGEROUS	Roxette	*EMI*	7
-	31	TUNES SPLITS THE ATOM	MC Tunes vs 808 State	*ZTT*	1
40	[32]	NOTHING TO LOSE	S'Express	*Rhythm King*	2
19	33	SILHOUETTES	Cliff Richard	*EMI*	5
35	[34]	LA SERENISSIMA	DNA	*Raw Bass*	3
-	35	IT'S A SHAME (MY SISTER)	Monie Love featuring True Image	*Cooltempo*	1
24	36	I'M FREE	Soup Dragons featuring Junior Reid	*Raw TV*	11
21	37	CAN CAN YOU PARTY	Jive Bunny & the Mastermixers	*Music Factory Dance*	5
37	38	THERE SHE GOES AGAIN/MISLED	Quireboys	*Parlophone*	2
25	39	TOM'S DINER	DNA featuring Suzanne Vega	*A&M*	9
-	[40]	(WHAT'S WRONG WITH) DREAMING	River City People	*EMI*	1

WEEK ENDING 29 SEPTEMBER 1990

LW	TW	Title	Artist	Label	Wks
4	[1]	SHOW ME HEAVEN	Maria McKee	*Epic*	3
1	2	THE JOKER	Steve Miller Band	*Capitol*	6

In these weeks ■ For the eighth consecutive week, the song at number two is at its peak (22.09.90) ■ The chart compilers could not separate the Steve Miller and Deee-Lite hits on sales figures, so *The Joker* was put at number one because it had shown the biggest increase in sales over the week. This caused such an uproar that the chart rules are changed to allow, in future, for records to hold equal chart positions (15.09.90)■

October 1990

□ Highest position disc reached ● Act's first ever week on chart

LW	TW	Title / Artist	Label	Wks
2	**3**	GROOVE IS IN THE HEART/WHAT IS LOVE Deee-Lite	*Elektra*	6
12	**4**	I'VE BEEN THINKING ABOUT YOU Londonbeat	*Anxious*	3
3	**5**	HOLY SMOKE Iron Maiden	*EMI*	2
9	**[6]**	GROOVY TRAIN Farm	*Produce*	5
6	**7**	WHAT TIME IS LOVE? KLF featuring Children Of The Revolution	*KLF Communications*	8
21	**[8]**	CULT OF SNAP! Snap!	*Arista*	2
14	**[9]**	FASCINATING RHYTHM Bass-O-Matic	*Virgin*	4
8	**10**	THE SPACE JUNGLE Adamski	*MCA*	4
28	**11**	I CAN'T STAND IT Twenty4Seven featuring Captain Hollywood	*BCM*	2
19	**[12]**	THEN Charlatans	*Situation Two*	2
16	**[13]**	THUNDERSTRUCK AC/DC	*Atco*	2
5	**14**	FOUR BACHARACH & DAVID SONGS (EP) Deacon Blue	*CBS*	6
-	**15**	NEVER ENOUGH Cure	*Fiction*	1
-	**16**	BLUE VELVET Bobby Vinton	*Epic*	1
10	**17**	VISION OF LOVE Mariah Carey	*CBS*	7
11	**18**	SUICIDE BLONDE INXS	*Mercury*	3
31	**19**	TUNES SPLITS THE ATOM MC Tunes vs 808 State	*ZTT*	2
7	**20**	ITSY BITSY TEENY WEENY YELLOW POLKA DOT BIKINI Bombalurina	*Carpet*	9
35	**21**	IT'S A SHAME (MY SISTER) Monie Love featuring True Image	*Cooltempo*	2
23	**[22]**	FOOL'S GOLD/WHAT THE WORLD IS WAITING FOR Stone Roses	*Silvertone*	3
13	**23**	WHERE ARE YOU BABY? Betty Boo	*Rhythm King*	8
-	**[24]**	HOLY WARS...THE PUNISHMENT DUE Megadeth	*Capitol*	1
15	**25**	BLACK CAT Janet Jackson	*A&M*	4
18	**26**	LIVIN' IN THE LIGHT Caron Wheeler	*RCA*	4
17	**27**	DON'T BE A FOOL Loose Ends	*10*	5
-	**28**	WORLD IN MY EYES Depeche Mode	*Mute*	1
-	**29**	THREE SONGS (EP) Wedding Present	*RCA*	1
20	**30**	TONIGHT New Kids On The Block	*CBS*	9
-	**31**	THE ANNIVERSARY WALTZ - PART ONE Status Quo	*Vertigo*	1
32	**[32]**	NOTHING TO LOSE S'Express	*Rhythm King*	3
25	**33**	EPIC Faith No More	*Slash*	4
-	**[34]**	FALL (EP) Ride	*Creation*	1
24	**35**	RHYTHM OF THE RAIN Jason Donovan	*PWL*	5
-	**36**	HEAVEN Chimes	*CBS*	1
34	**37**	LA SERENISSIMA DNA	*Raw Bass*	4
-	**38**	SHE'S SO FINE Thunder	*EMI*	1
-	**39**	BODY LANGUAGE Adventures Of Stevie V	*Mercury*	1
-	**40**	SPIN THAT WHEEL (TURTLES GET REAL) Hi Tek 3 featuring Ya Kid K ●	*Brothers Organisation*	1

LW	TW	*WEEK ENDING* **6 OCTOBER 1990**		Wks
1	**[1]**	SHOW ME HEAVEN Maria McKee	*Epic*	4
4	**[2]**	I'VE BEEN THINKING ABOUT YOU Londonbeat	*Anxious*	4
16	**3**	BLUE VELVET Bobby Vinton	*Epic*	2
-	**[4]**	SO HARD Pet Shop Boys	*Parlophone*	1
31	**5**	ANNIVERSARY WALTZ - PART ONE Status Quo	*Vertigo*	2
2	**6**	THE JOKER Steve Miller Band	*Capitol*	7
11	**[7]**	I CAN'T STAND IT Twenty4Seven featuring Captain Hollywood	*BCM*	3
3	**8**	GROOVE IS IN THE HEART/WHAT IS LOVE Deee-Lite	*Elektra*	7
9	**[9]**	FASCINATING RHYTHM Bass-O-Matic	*Virgin*	5
6	**10**	GROOVY TRAIN Farm	*Produce*	6
8	**11**	CULT OF SNAP! Snap!	*Arista*	3
-	**12**	MEGAMIX Technotronic	*Swanyard*	1
15	**[13]**	NEVER ENOUGH Cure	*Fiction*	2
7	**14**	WHAT TIME IS LOVE? KLF featuring Children Of The Revolution	*KLF Communications*	9
12	**15**	THEN Charlatans	*Situation Two*	3
21	**16**	IT'S A SHAME (MY SISTER) Monie Love featuring True Image	*Cooltempo*	3
10	**17**	THE SPACE JUNGLE Adamski	*MCA*	5
19	**[18]**	TUNES SPLITS THE ATOM MC Tunes vs 808 State	*ZTT*	3
-	**19**	HAVE YOU SEEN HER MC Hammer	*Capitol*	1
13	**20**	THUNDERSTRUCK AC/DC	*Atco*	3
28	**21**	WORLD IN MY EYES Depeche Mode	*Mute*	2
17	**22**	VISION OF LOVE Mariah Carey	*CBS*	8
5	**23**	HOLY SMOKE Iron Maiden	*EMI*	3
40	**24**	SPIN THAT WHEEL (TURTLES GET REAL) Hi Tek 3 featuring Ya Kid K	*Brothers Organisation*	2
29	**[25]**	THREE SONGS (EP) Wedding Present	*RCA*	2
14	**26**	FOUR BACHARACH & DAVID SONGS (EP) Deacon Blue	*CBS*	7
18	**27**	SUICIDE BLONDE INXS	*Mercury*	4
36	**28**	HEAVEN Chimes	*CBS*	2
-	**29**	I'VE GOT YOU UNDER MY SKIN Neneh Cherry	*Circa*	1
-	**30**	A LITTLE TIME Beautiful South	*Go! Discs*	1
39	**31**	BODY LANGUAGE Adventures Of Stevie V	*Mercury*	2
24	**32**	HOLY WARS...THE PUNISHMENT DUE Megadeth	*Capitol*	2
20	**33**	ITSY BITSY TEENY WEENY YELLOW POLKA DOT BIKINI Bombalurina	*Carpet*	10
38	**[34]**	SHE'S SO FINE Thunder	*EMI*	2
22	**35**	FOOL'S GOLD/WHAT THE WORLD IS WAITING FOR Stone Roses	*Silvertone*	4
23	**36**	WHERE ARE YOU BABY? Betty Boo	*Rhythm King*	9
-	**37**	RIGHT HERE, RIGHT NOW Jesus Jones	*Food*	1
34	**38**	FALL (EP) Ride	*Creation*	2
-	**39**	EVERYBODY (RAP) Criminal Element Orchestra ●	*deConstruction*	1
25	**40**	BLACK CAT Janet Jackson	*A&M*	5

LW	TW	*WEEK ENDING* **13 OCTOBER 1990**		Wks
1	**[1]**	SHOW ME HEAVEN Maria McKee	*Epic*	5
3	**[2]**	BLUE VELVET Bobby Vinton	*Epic*	3
2	**3**	I'VE BEEN THINKING ABOUT YOU Londonbeat	*Anxious*	5
5	**4**	ANNIVERSARY WALTZ - PART ONE Status Quo	*Vertigo*	3
4	**5**	SO HARD Pet Shop Boys	*Parlophone*	2
12	**[6]**	MEGAMIX Technotronic	*Swanyard*	2
7	**[7]**	I CAN'T STAND IT Twenty4Seven featuring Captain Hollywood	*BCM*	4
19	**[8]**	HAVE YOU SEEN HER MC Hammer	*Capitol*	2
30	**9**	A LITTLE TIME Beautiful South	*Go! Discs*	2
9	**10**	FASCINATING RHYTHM Bass-O-Matic	*Virgin*	6
8	**11**	GROOVE IS IN THE HEART/WHAT IS LOVE Deee-Lite	*Elektra*	8
6	**12**	THE JOKER Steve Miller Band	*Capitol*	8
10	**13**	GROOVY TRAIN Farm	*Produce*	7
16	**14**	IT'S A SHAME (MY SISTER) Monie Love featuring True Image	*Cooltempo*	4
11	**15**	CULT OF SNAP! Snap!	*Arista*	4
-	**16**	LET'S TRY AGAIN/DIDN'T I BLOW YOUR MIND THIS TIME New Kids On The Block	*CBS*	1
21	**[17]**	WORLD IN MY EYES Depeche Mode	*Mute*	3
24	**18**	SPIN THAT WHEEL (TURTLES GET REAL) Hi Tek 3 featuring Ya Kid K	*Brothers Organisation*	3
-	**19**	FROM A DISTANCE Cliff Richard	*EMI*	1
18	**20**	TUNES SPLITS THE ATOM MC Tunes vs 808 State	*ZTT*	4
-	**21**	MORE Sisters Of Mercy	*Merciful Release*	1
13	**22**	NEVER ENOUGH Cure	*Fiction*	3
15	**23**	THEN Charlatans	*Situation Two*	4
28	**[24]**	HEAVEN Chimes	*CBS*	3
29	**[25]**	I'VE GOT YOU UNDER MY SKIN Neneh Cherry	*Circa*	2
17	**26**	THE SPACE JUNGLE Adamski	*MCA*	6
-	**27**	CRYING IN THE RAIN a-ha	*Warner Brothers*	1
14	**28**	WHAT TIME IS LOVE? KLF featuring Children Of The Revolution	*KLF Communications*	10
31	**[29]**	BODY LANGUAGE Adventures Of Stevie V	*Mercury*	3
39	**[30]**	EVERYBODY (RAP) Criminal Element Orchestra	*deConstruction*	2
37	**[31]**	RIGHT HERE, RIGHT NOW Jesus Jones	*Food*	2
-	**[32]**	DANCE OF THE MAD Pop Will Eat Itself	*RCA*	1
-	**[33]**	CONTRIBUTION Mica Paris featuring Rakim	*Fourth + Broadway*	1
-	**[34]**	HANG IN LONG ENOUGH Phil Collins	*Virgin*	1
22	**35**	VISION OF LOVE Mariah Carey	*CBS*	9
-	**36**	GOOD MORNING BRITAIN Aztec Camera & Mick Jones ●	*WEA*	1
20	**37**	THUNDERSTRUCK AC/DC	*Atco*	4
-	**38**	LET'S PUSH IT Innocence	*Cooltempo*	1

■Maria McKee, writer of Feargal Sharkey's *A Good Heart* becomes the first and only woman to write a number one for herself and for someone else (29.09.90) ■ Bobby Vinton hits the Top 10 over 28 years after his chart debut, the longest wait for Top 10 glory, but he just misses the very top (13.10.90)■

October 1990

□ Highest position disc reached ● Act's first ever week on chart

LW	TW	Title / Artist	Label	Wks
-	39	BE TENDER WITH ME BABY Tina Turner	Capitol	1
-	40	WORKING MAN Rita MacNeil ●	Polydor	1

LW	TW	WEEK ENDING 20 OCTOBER 1990		Wks
1	1	SHOW ME HEAVEN Maria McKee	Epic	6
4	2	ANNIVERSARY WALTZ - PART ONE Status Quo	Vertigo	4
2	3	BLUE VELVET Bobby Vinton	Epic	4
9	4	A LITTLE TIME Beautiful South	Go! Discs	3
3	5	I'VE BEEN THINKING ABOUT YOU Londonbeat	Anxious	6
6	6	MEGAMIX Technotronic	Swanyard	3
7	7	I CAN'T STAND IT Twenty4Seven featuring Captain Hollywood	BCM	5
16	8	LET'S TRY AGAIN/DIDN'T I BLOW YOUR MIND THIS TIME New Kids On The Block	CBS	2
5	9	SO HARD Pet Shop Boys	Parlophone	3
8	10	HAVE YOU SEEN HER MC Hammer	Capitol	3
19	11	FROM A DISTANCE Cliff Richard	EMI	2
14	12	IT'S A SHAME (MY SISTER) Monie Love featuring True Image	Cooltempo	5
10	13	FASCINATING RHYTHM Bass-O-Matic	Virgin	7
21	14	MORE Sisters Of Mercy	Merciful Release	2
18	15	SPIN THAT WHEEL (TURTLES GET REAL) Hi Tek 3 featuring Ya Kid K	Brothers Organisation	4
-	16	I'M YOUR BABY TONIGHT Whitney Houston	Arista	1
11	17	GROOVE IS IN THE HEART/WHAT IS LOVE Deee-Lite	Elektra	9
-	18	PICCADILLY PALARE Morrissey	HMV	1
27	19	CRYING IN THE RAIN a-ha	Warner Brothers	2
-	20	KINKY AFRO Happy Mondays	London	1
13	21	GROOVY TRAIN Farm	Produce	8
17	22	WORLD IN MY EYES Depeche Mode	Mute	4
36	23	GOOD MORNING BRITAIN Aztec Camera & Mick Jones	WEA	2
40	24	WORKING MAN Rita MacNeil	Polydor	2
24	25	HEAVEN Chimes	CBS	4
-	26	(WE WANT) THE SAME THING Belinda Carlisle	Virgin	1
-	27	TAKE MY BREATH AWAY Berlin	CBS	1
39	28	BE TENDER WITH ME BABY Tina Turner	Capitol	2
12	29	THE JOKER Steve Miller Band	Capitol	9
-	30	BIRTHDAY Paul McCartney	Parlophone	1
15	31	CULT OF SNAP! Snap!	Arista	5
25	32	I'VE GOT YOU UNDER MY SKIN Neneh Cherry	Circa	3
38	33	LET'S PUSH IT Innocence	Cooltempo	2
-	34	MOTHER UNIVERSE Soup Dragons	Raw TV	1
-	35	DON'T ASK ME P.I.L.	Virgin	1
33	36	CONTRIBUTION Mica Paris featuring Rakim	Fourth + Broadway	2
20	37	TUNES SPLITS THE ATOM MC Tunes vs 808 State	ZTT	5
32	38	DANCE OF THE MAD Pop Will Eat Itself	RCA	2
31	39	RIGHT HERE, RIGHT NOW Jesus Jones	Food	3
-	40	THE OBVIOUS CHILD Paul Simon	Warner Brothers	1

LW	TW	WEEK ENDING 27 OCTOBER 1990		Wks
4	1	A LITTLE TIME Beautiful South	Go! Discs	4
1	2	SHOW ME HEAVEN Maria McKee	Epic	7
-	3	UNCHAINED MELODY Righteous Brothers	Verve	1
2	4	ANNIVERSARY WALTZ - PART ONE Status Quo	Vertigo	5
20	5	KINKY AFRO Happy Mondays	London	2
3	6	BLUE VELVET Bobby Vinton	Epic	5
16	7	I'M YOUR BABY TONIGHT Whitney Houston	Arista	2
27	8	TAKE MY BREATH AWAY Berlin	CBS	2
6	9	MEGAMIX Technotronic	Swanyard	4
5	10	I'VE BEEN THINKING ABOUT YOU Londonbeat	Anxious	7
7	11	I CAN'T STAND IT Twenty4Seven featuring Captain Hollywood	BCM	6
24	12	WORKING MAN Rita MacNeil	Polydor	3
19	13	CRYING IN THE RAIN a-ha	Warner Brothers	3
26	14	(WE WANT) THE SAME THING Belinda Carlisle	Virgin	2
10	15	HAVE YOU SEEN HER MC Hammer	Capitol	4
8	16	LET'S TRY AGAIN/DIDN'T I BLOW YOUR MIND THIS TIME New Kids On The Block	CBS	3
11	17	FROM A DISTANCE Cliff Richard	EMI	3
12	18	IT'S A SHAME (MY SISTER) Monie Love featuring True Image	Cooltempo	6
23	19	GOOD MORNING BRITAIN Aztec Camera & Mick Jones	WEA	3
15	20	SPIN THAT WHEEL (TURTLES GET REAL) Hi Tek 3 featuring Ya Kid K	Brothers Organisation	5
9	21	SO HARD Pet Shop Boys	Parlophone	4
35	22	DON'T ASK ME P.I.L.	Virgin	2
40	23	THE OBVIOUS CHILD Paul Simon	Warner Brothers	2
13	24	FASCINATING RHYTHM Bass-O-Matic	Virgin	8
33	25	LET'S PUSH IT Innocence	Cooltempo	3
34	26	MOTHER UNIVERSE Soup Dragons	Raw TV	2
14	27	MORE Sisters Of Mercy	Merciful Release	3
17	28	GROOVE IS IN THE HEART/WHAT IS LOVE Deee-Lite	Elektra	10
30	29	BIRTHDAY Paul McCartney	Parlophone	2
21	30	GROOVY TRAIN Farm	Produce	9
-	31	DRESSED FOR SUCCESS Roxette	EMI	1
-	32	WAITING FOR THAT DAY George Michael	Epic	1
-	33	YOU GOTTA LOVE SOMEONE Elton John	Rocket	1
28	34	BE TENDER WITH ME BABY Tina Turner	Capitol	3
-	35	I'M DOING FINE Jason Donovan	PWL	1
-	36	SOMETHING TO BELIEVE IN Poison	Enigma	1
-	37	LOVE WILL NEVER DO (WITHOUT YOU) Janet Jackson	A&M	1
25	38	HEAVEN Chimes	CBS	5
18	39	PICCADILLY PALARE Morrissey	HMV	2
29	40	THE JOKER Steve Miller Band	Capitol	10

LW	TW	WEEK ENDING 3 NOVEMBER 1990		Wks
3	1	UNCHAINED MELODY Righteous Brothers	Verve	2
1	2	A LITTLE TIME Beautiful South	Go! Discs	5
8	3	TAKE MY BREATH AWAY Berlin	CBS	3
2	4	SHOW ME HEAVEN Maria McKee	Epic	8
7	5	I'M YOUR BABY TONIGHT Whitney Houston	Arista	3
14	6	(WE WANT) THE SAME THING Belinda Carlisle	Virgin	3
5	7	KINKY AFRO Happy Mondays	London	3
4	8	ANNIVERSARY WALTZ - PART ONE Status Quo	Vertigo	6
-	9	STEP BACK IN TIME Kylie Minogue	PWL	1
6	10	BLUE VELVET Bobby Vinton	Epic	6
12	11	WORKING MAN Rita MacNeil	Polydor	4
9	12	MEGAMIX Technotronic	Swanyard	5
13	13	CRYING IN THE RAIN a-ha	Warner Brothers	4
10	14	I'VE BEEN THINKING ABOUT YOU Londonbeat	Anxious	8
-	15	CLOSE TO ME Cure	Fiction	1
-	16	DON'T WORRY Kim Appleby ●	Parlophone	1
11	17	I CAN'T STAND IT Twenty4Seven featuring Captain Hollywood	BCM	7
23	18	THE OBVIOUS CHILD Paul Simon	Warner Brothers	3
-	19	I'LL BE YOUR BABY TONIGHT Robert Palmer & UB40 ●	EMI	1
19	20	GOOD MORNING BRITAIN Aztec Camera & Mick Jones	WEA	4
-	21	FANTASY Black Box	deConstruction	1
31	22	DRESSED FOR SUCCESS Roxette	EMI	2
35	23	I'M DOING FINE Jason Donovan	PWL	2
16	24	LET'S TRY AGAIN/DIDN'T I BLOW YOUR MIND THIS TIME New Kids On The Block	CBS	4
15	25	HAVE YOU SEEN HER MC Hammer	Capitol	5
32	26	WAITING FOR THAT DAY George Michael	Epic	2
26	27	MOTHER UNIVERSE Soup Dragons	Raw TV	3
17	28	FROM A DISTANCE Cliff Richard	EMI	4
25	29	LET'S PUSH IT Innocence	Cooltempo	4
20	30	SPIN THAT WHEEL (TURTLES GET REAL) Hi Tek 3 featuring Ya Kid K	Brothers Organisation	6
22	31	DON'T ASK ME P.I.L.	Virgin	3
18	32	IT'S A SHAME (MY SISTER) Monie Love featuring True Image	Cooltempo	7
-	33	MY RISING STAR Northside ●	Factory	1
37	34	LOVE WILL NEVER DO (WITHOUT YOU) Janet Jackson	A&M	2
36	35	SOMETHING TO BELIEVE IN Poison	Enigma	2
21	36	SO HARD Pet Shop Boys	Parlophone	5

In these weeks ■ The Righteous Brothers hit the top over 25 years after their previous number one. However it is an old recording, the third re-issue of the year to hit the top, so Elvis Presley, Cliff Richard and the Bee Gees remain the only acts to top the charts with newly recorded hits over a span of 20 years (03.11.90) ■ Kim Appleby enjoys her first solo hit since the death of her sister Mel (03.11.90)■

LW	TW	Title	Artist	Label	Wks
33	37	YOU GOTTA LOVE SOMEONE	Elton John	Rocket	2
24	38	FASCINATING RHYTHM	Bass-O-Matic	Virgin	9
-	39	THERE SHE GOES	La's ●	Go!Discs	1
-	40	LITTLE BROTHER	Blue Pearl	Big Life	1

November 1990

□ Highest position disc reached ● Act's first ever week on chart

WEEK ENDING 10 NOVEMBER 1990

LW	TW	Title	Artist	Label	Wks
1	1	UNCHAINED MELODY	Righteous Brothers	Verve	3
2	2	A LITTLE TIME	Beautiful South	Go! Discs	6
3	3	TAKE MY BREATH AWAY	Berlin	CBS	4
9	4	STEP BACK IN TIME	Kylie Minogue	PWL	2
16	5	DON'T WORRY	Kim Appleby	Parlophone	2
6	6	(WE WANT) THE SAME THING	Belinda Carlisle	Virgin	4
5	7	I'M YOUR BABY TONIGHT	Whitney Houston	Arista	4
4	8	SHOW ME HEAVEN	Maria McKee	Epic	9
21	9	FANTASY	Black Box	deConstruction	2
19	10	I'LL BE YOUR BABY TONIGHT	Robert Palmer & UB40	EMI	2
-	11	FOG ON THE TYNE (REVISITED)	Gazza & Lindisfarne ●	Best	1
11	12	WORKING MAN	Rita MacNeil	Polydor	5
15	13	CLOSE TO ME	Cure	Fiction	2
7	14	KINKY AFRO	Happy Mondays	London	4
18	15	THE OBVIOUS CHILD	Paul Simon	Warner Brothers	4
8	16	ANNIVERSARY WALTZ - PART ONE	Status Quo	Vertigo	7
10	17	BLUE VELVET	Bobby Vinton	Epic	7
22	18	DRESSED FOR SUCCESS	Roxette	EMI	3
13	19	CRYING IN THE RAIN	a-ha	Warner Brothers	5
39	20	THERE SHE GOES	La's	Go!Discs	2
12	21	MEGAMIX	Technotronic	Swanyard	6
23	22	I'M DOING FINE	Jason Donovan	PWL	3
26	23	WAITING FOR THAT DAY	George Michael	Epic	3
14	24	I'VE BEEN THINKING ABOUT YOU	Londonbeat	Anxious	9
-	25	UNBELIEVABLE	EMF ●	Parlophone	1
20	26	GOOD MORNING BRITAIN	Aztec Camera & Mick Jones	WEA	5
17	27	I CAN'T STAND IT	Twenty4Seven featuring Captain Hollywood	BCM	8
-	28	TO LOVE SOMEBODY	Jimmy Somerville	London	1
-	29	CUBIK/OLYMPIC	808 State	ZTT	1
-	30	SPIT IN THE RAIN	Del Amitri	A&M	1
40	31	LITTLE BROTHER	Blue Pearl	Big Life	2
33	32	MY RISING STAR	Northside	Factory	2
-	33	NEW POWER GENERATION	Prince	Paisley Park	1
29	34	LET'S PUSH IT	Innocence	Cooltempo	5
27	35	MOTHER UNIVERSE	Soup Dragons	Raw TV	4
-	36	TIME TO MAKE THE FLOOR BURN	Megabass ●	Brothers Org	1
31	37	DON'T ASK ME	P.I.L.	Virgin	4
-	38	AFTERMATH/I'M FOR REAL	Nightmares On Wax ●	Warp	1
-	39	100 MILES AND RUNNIN'	N.W.A.	Ruthless	1
35	40	SOMETHING TO BELIEVE IN	Poison	Enigma	3

WEEK ENDING 17 NOVEMBER 1990

LW	TW	Title	Artist	Label	Wks
1	1	UNCHAINED MELODY	Righteous Brothers	Verve	4
11	2	FOG ON THE TYNE (REVISITED)	Gazza & Lindisfarne	Best	2
5	3	DON'T WORRY	Kim Appleby	Parlophone	3
2	4	A LITTLE TIME	Beautiful South	Go! Discs	7
9	5	FANTASY	Black Box	deConstruction	3
10	6	I'LL BE YOUR BABY TONIGHT	Robert Palmer & UB40	EMI	3
3	7	TAKE MY BREATH AWAY	Berlin	CBS	5
4	8	STEP BACK IN TIME	Kylie Minogue	PWL	3
6	9	(WE WANT) THE SAME THING	Belinda Carlisle	Virgin	5
7	10	I'M YOUR BABY TONIGHT	Whitney Houston	Arista	5
29	11	CUBIK/OLYMPIC	808 State	ZTT	2
28	12	TO LOVE SOMEBODY	Jimmy Somerville	London	2
15	13	THERE SHE GOES	La's	Go!Discs	3
8	14	SHOW ME HEAVEN	Maria McKee	Epic	10
25	15	UNBELIEVABLE	EMF	Parlophone	2
15	16	THE OBVIOUS CHILD	Paul Simon	Warner Brothers	5
13	17	CLOSE TO ME	Cure	Fiction	3
12	18	WORKING MAN	Rita MacNeil	Polydor	6
18	19	DRESSED FOR SUCCESS	Roxette	EMI	4
17	20	BLUE VELVET	Bobby Vinton	Epic	8
30	21	SPIT IN THE RAIN	Del Amitri	A&M	2
36	22	TIME TO MAKE THE FLOOR BURN	Megabass	Brothers Org	2
-	23	ISLAND HEAD (EP)	Inspiral Carpets	Cow	1
14	24	KINKY AFRO	Happy Mondays	London	5
-	25	LET'S SWING AGAIN	Jive Bunny & the Mastermixers	Music Factory Dance	1
33	26	NEW POWER GENERATION	Prince	Paisley Park	2
16	27	ANNIVERSARY WALTZ - PART ONE	Status Quo	Vertigo	8
-	28	HANDS ACROSS THE OCEAN	Mission	Mercury	1
22	29	I'M DOING FINE	Jason Donovan	PWL	4
-	30	MIRACLE	Jon Bon Jovi	Vertigo	1
19	31	CRYING IN THE RAIN	a-ha	Warner Brothers	6
31	32	LITTLE BROTHER	Blue Pearl	Big Life	3
24	33	I'VE BEEN THINKING ABOUT YOU	Londonbeat	Anxious	10
23	34	WAITING FOR THAT DAY	George Michael	Epic	4
-	35	FALLING	Julee Cruise ●	Warner Brothers	1
26	36	GOOD MORNING BRITAIN	Aztec Camera & Mick Jones	WEA	6
21	37	MEGAMIX	Technotronic	Swanyard	7
39	38	100 MILES AND RUNNIN'	N.W.A.	Ruthless	2
27	39	I CAN'T STAND IT	Twenty4Seven featuring Captain Hollywood	BCM	9
-	40	UK BLAK	Caron Wheeler	RCA	1

WEEK ENDING 24 NOVEMBER 1990

LW	TW	Title	Artist	Label	Wks
1	1	UNCHAINED MELODY	Righteous Brothers	Verve	5
3	2	DON'T WORRY	Kim Appleby	Parlophone	4
-	3	ICE ICE BABY	Vanilla Ice ●	SBK	1
2	4	FOG ON THE TYNE (REVISITED)	Gazza & Lindisfarne	Best	3
15	5	UNBELIEVABLE	EMF	Parlophone	3
5	6	FANTASY	Black Box	deConstruction	4
6	7	I'LL BE YOUR BABY TONIGHT	Robert Palmer & UB40	EMI	4
12	8	TO LOVE SOMEBODY	Jimmy Somerville	London	3
4	9	A LITTLE TIME	Beautiful South	Go! Discs	8
11	10	CUBIK/OLYMPIC	808 State	ZTT	3
35	11	FALLING	Julee Cruise	Warner Brothers	2
-	12	IT TAKES TWO	Rod Stewart & Tina Turner ●	Warner Brothers	1
8	13	STEP BACK IN TIME	Kylie Minogue	PWL	4
7	14	TAKE MY BREATH AWAY	Berlin	CBS	6
13	15	THERE SHE GOES	La's	Go!Discs	4
9	16	(WE WANT) THE SAME THING	Belinda Carlisle	Virgin	6
-	17	KING OF THE ROAD (EP)	Proclaimers	Chrysalis	1
22	18	TIME TO MAKE THE FLOOR BURN	Megabass	Brothers Org	3
25	19	LET'S SWING AGAIN	Jive Bunny & the Mastermixers	Music Factory Dance	2
10	20	I'M YOUR BABY TONIGHT	Whitney Houston	Arista	6
23	21	ISLAND HEAD (EP)	Inspiral Carpets	Cow	2
19	22	DRESSED FOR SUCCESS	Roxette	EMI	5
-	23	MY DEFINITION OF A BOOMBASTIC JAZZ STYLE	Dream Warriors	Fourth + Broadway	1
14	24	SHOW ME HEAVEN	Maria McKee	Epic	11
21	25	SPIT IN THE RAIN	Del Amitri	A&M	3
16	26	THE OBVIOUS CHILD	Paul Simon	Warner Brothers	6
-	27	MISSING YOU	Soul II Soul featuring Kym Mazelle	10	1
20	28	BLUE VELVET	Bobby Vinton	Epic	9
30	29	MIRACLE	Jon Bon Jovi	Vertigo	2
18	30	WORKING MAN	Rita MacNeil	Polydor	7
-	31	SEVEN LITTLE GIRLS SITTING IN THE BACK SEAT	Bombalurina	Carpet	1
17	32	CLOSE TO ME	Cure	Fiction	4
-	33	SUCKER DJ	Dimples D ●	FBI	1
26	34	NEW POWER GENERATION	Prince	Paisley Park	3
-	35	POWER OF LOVE/DEEE-LITE THEME	Deee-Lite	Elektra	1
-	36	BEING BORING	Pet Shop Boys	Parlophone	1
-	37	SUMERLAND (DREAMED)	Fields Of The Nephilim	Beggars Banquet	1
24	38	KINKY AFRO	Happy Mondays	London	6
-	39	ARE YOU DREAMING?	Twenty4Seven featuring Captain Hollywood	BCM	1
29	40	I'M DOING FINE	Jason Donovan	PWL	5

■This was the first of eight consecutive weeks in which the record at number seven fell the next week (10.11.90) ■ Vanilla Ice crashed into the chart for the first time ever at number three - the highest debut position in the history of the charts (24.11.90) ■ The new Pet Shop Boys hit is their least successful so far. Perhaps they really are *Being Boring* (24.11.90)■

December 1990

□ Highest position disc reached ● Act's first ever week on chart

LW	TW	WEEK ENDING 1 DECEMBER 1990		Wks
3	1	ICE ICE BABY Vanilla Ice	SBK	2
1	2	UNCHAINED MELODY Righteous Brothers	Verve	6
5	3	UNBELIEVABLE EMF	Parlophone	4
2	4	DON'T WORRY Kim Appleby	Parlophone	5
12	5	IT TAKES TWO Rod Stewart & Tina Turner	Warner Brothers	2
6	6	FANTASY Black Box	deConstruction	5
11	7	FALLING Julee Cruise	Warner Brothers	3
7	8	I'LL BE YOUR BABY TONIGHT Robert Palmer & UB40	EMI	5
17	9	KING OF THE ROAD (EP) Proclaimers	Chrysalis	2
8	10	TO LOVE SOMEBODY Jimmy Somerville	London	4
4	11	FOG ON THE TYNE (REVISITED) Gazza & Lindisfarne	Best	4
10	12	CUBIK/OLYMPIC 808 State	ZTT	4
23	13	MY DEFINITION OF A BOOMBASTIC JAZZ STYLE Dream Warriors	Fourth + Broadway	2
-	14	KINKY BOOTS Patrick Macnee & Honor Blackman ●	Deram	1
9	15	A LITTLE TIME Beautiful South	Go! Discs	9
18	16	TIME TO MAKE THE FLOOR BURN Megabass	Brothers Org	4
15	17	THERE SHE GOES La's	Go!Discs	5
31	18	SEVEN LITTLE GIRLS SITTING IN THE BACK SEAT Bombalurina	Carpet	2
14	19	TAKE MY BREATH AWAY Berlin	CBS	7
36	20	BEING BORING Pet Shop Boys	Parlophone	2
33	21	SUCKER DJ Dimples D	FBI	2
27	22	MISSING YOU Soul II Soul featuring Kym Mazelle	10	2
13	23	STEP BACK IN TIME Kylie Minogue	PWL	5
-	24	WICKED GAME Chris Isaak ●	London	1
35	25	POWER OF LOVE/DEEE-LITE THEME Deee-Lite	Elektra	2
19	26	LET'S SWING AGAIN Jive Bunny & the Mastermixers	Music Factory Dance	3
39	27	ARE YOU DREAMING? Twenty4Seven featuring Captain Hollywood	BCM	2
16	28	(WE WANT) THE SAME THING Belinda Carlisle	Virgin	7
21	29	ISLAND HEAD (EP) Inspiral Carpets	Cow	3
25	30	SPIT IN THE RAIN Del Amitri	A&M	4
-	31	DOWN TO EARTH Monie Love	Cooltempo	1
-	32	24 HOURS Betty Boo	Rhythm King	1
24	33	SHOW ME HEAVEN Maria McKee	Epic	12
20	34	I'M YOUR BABY TONIGHT Whitney Houston	Arista	7
29	35	MIRACLE Jon Bon Jovi	Vertigo	3
-	36	MONEY TALKS AC/DC	Atco	1
-	37	LOVE TAKES TIME Mariah Carey	CBS	1
26	38	THE OBVIOUS CHILD Paul Simon	Warner Brothers	7
22	39	DRESSED FOR SUCCESS Roxette	EMI	6
-	40	LOVE'S GOT ME Loose Ends	10	1

LW	TW	WEEK ENDING 8 DECEMBER 1990		Wks
1	1	ICE ICE BABY Vanilla Ice	SBK	3
2	2	UNCHAINED MELODY Righteous Brothers	Verve	7
3	3	UNBELIEVABLE EMF	Parlophone	5
4	4	DON'T WORRY Kim Appleby	Parlophone	6
14	5	KINKY BOOTS Patrick Macnee & Honor Blackman	Deram	2
-	6	SAVIOUR'S DAY Cliff Richard	EMI	1
5	7	IT TAKES TWO Rod Stewart & Tina Turner	Warner Brothers	3
7	8	FALLING Julee Cruise	Warner Brothers	4
-	9	JUSTIFY MY LOVE Madonna	Sire	1
6	10	FANTASY Black Box	deConstruction	6
24	11	WICKED GAME Chris Isaak	London	2
-	12	ALL TOGETHER NOW Farm	Produce	1
-	13	THIS ONE'S FOR THE CHILDREN New Kids On The Block	CBS	1
9	14	KING OF THE ROAD (EP) Proclaimers	Chrysalis	3
10	15	TO LOVE SOMEBODY Jimmy Somerville	London	5
13	16	MY DEFINITION OF A BOOMBASTIC JAZZ STYLE Dream Warriors	Fourth + Broadway	3
8	17	I'LL BE YOUR BABY TONIGHT Robert Palmer & UB40	EMI	6
21	18	SUCKER DJ Dimples D	FBI	3
18	19	SEVEN LITTLE GIRLS SITTING IN THE BACK SEAT Bombalurina	Carpet	3
-	20	PRAY MC Hammer	Capitol	1
16	21	TIME TO MAKE THE FLOOR BURN Megabass	Brothers Org	5
-	22	SITUATION Yazoo	Mute	1
11	23	FOG ON THE TYNE (REVISITED) Gazza & Lindisfarne	Best	5
-	24	MARY HAD A LITTLE BOY Snap!	Arista	1
27	25	ARE YOU DREAMING? Twenty4Seven featuring Captain Hollywood	BCM	3
20	26	BEING BORING Pet Shop Boys	Parlophone	3
32	27	24 HOURS Betty Boo	Rhythm King	2
12	28	CUBIK/OLYMPIC 808 State	ZTT	5
-	29	JUST THIS SIDE OF LOVE Malandra Burrows ●	YTV	1
22	30	MISSING YOU Soul II Soul featuring Kym Mazelle	10	3
25	31	POWER OF LOVE/DEEE-LITE THEME Deee-Lite	Elektra	3
31	32	DOWN TO EARTH Monie Love	Cooltempo	2
19	33	TAKE MY BREATH AWAY Berlin	CBS	8
15	34	A LITTLE TIME Beautiful South	Go! Discs	10
-	35	ALL MY TRIALS Paul McCartney	Parlophone	1
17	36	THERE SHE GOES La's	Go!Discs	6
37	37	LOVE TAKES TIME Mariah Carey	CBS	2
-	38	LOSE CONTROL James	Fontana	1
23	39	STEP BACK IN TIME Kylie Minogue	PWL	6
-	40	DISAPPEAR INXS	Mercury	1

LW	TW	WEEK ENDING 15 DECEMBER 1990		Wks
1	1	ICE ICE BABY Vanilla Ice	SBK	4
9	2	JUSTIFY MY LOVE Madonna	Sire	2
6	3	SAVIOUR'S DAY Cliff Richard	EMI	2
12	4	ALL TOGETHER NOW Farm	Produce	2
2	5	UNCHAINED MELODY Righteous Brothers	Verve	8
3	6	UNBELIEVABLE EMF	Parlophone	6
4	7	DON'T WORRY Kim Appleby	Parlophone	7
5	8	KINKY BOOTS Patrick Macnee & Honor Blackman	Deram	3
13	9	THIS ONE'S FOR THE CHILDREN New Kids On The Block	CBS	2
11	10	WICKED GAME Chris Isaak	London	3
20	11	PRAY MC Hammer	Capitol	2
24	12	MARY HAD A LITTLE BOY Snap!	Arista	2
-	13	YOU'VE LOST THAT LOVIN' FEELIN' Righteous Brothers	Verve	1
22	14	SITUATION Yazoo	Mute	2
29	15	JUST THIS SIDE OF LOVE Malandra Burrows	YTV	2
8	16	FALLING Julee Cruise	Warner Brothers	5
18	17	SUCKER DJ Dimples D	FBI	4
25	18	ARE YOU DREAMING? Twenty4Seven featuring Captain Hollywood	BCM	4
7	19	IT TAKES TWO Rod Stewart & Tina Turner	Warner Brothers	4
10	20	FANTASY Black Box	deConstruction	7
16	21	MY DEFINITION OF A BOOMBASTIC JAZZ STYLE Dream Warriors	Fourth + Broadway	4
-	22	TOTAL MIX Black Box	deConstruction	1
15	23	TO LOVE SOMEBODY Jimmy Somerville	London	6
40	24	DISAPPEAR INXS	Mercury	2
27	25	24 HOURS Betty Boo	Rhythm King	3
14	26	KING OF THE ROAD (EP) Proclaimers	Chrysalis	4
-	27	SADNESS PART 1 Enigma ●	Virgin	1
19	28	SEVEN LITTLE GIRLS SITTING IN THE BACK SEAT Bombalurina	Carpet	4
17	29	I'LL BE YOUR BABY TONIGHT Robert Palmer & UB40	EMI	7
-	30	FREEDOM! George Michael	Epic	1
-	31	MERRY CHRISTMAS DARLING/(THEY LONG TO BE) CLOSE TO YOU Carpenters	A&M	1
-	32	CRAZY Seal ●	ZTT	1
23	33	FOG ON THE TYNE (REVISITED) Gazza & Lindisfarne	Best	6
-	34	THE BEST CHRISTMAS OF THEM ALL Shakin' Stevens	Epic	1
-	35	ANNIVERSARY WALTZ - PART TWO Status Quo	Vertigo	1
21	36	TIME TO MAKE THE FLOOR BURN Megabass	Brothers Org	6
-	37	A MATTER OF FACT Innocence	Cooltempo	1
35	38	ALL MY TRIALS Paul McCartney	Parlophone	2
-	39	TURTLE RHAPSODY Orchestra On The Half Shell ●	SBK	1
-	40	GONNA MAKE YOU SWEAT C&C Music Factory featuring Freedom Williams ●	CBS	1

In these weeks ■ With the Righteous Brothers, Patrick Macnee and Honor Blackman, Cliff Richard and Tina Turner all aged 50 or more in the Top 10, it is one of the most elderly charts of all time (08.12.90) ■ George Michael's *Freedom* is not the same song as Wham!'s *Freedom* which topped the charts in 1984 (15.12.90)■

December 1990

□ Highest position disc reached ● Act's first ever week on chart

LW	TW	WEEK ENDING 22 DECEMBER 1990		Wks
1	[1]	ICE ICE BABY Vanilla Ice	*SBK*	5
3	2	SAVIOUR'S DAY Cliff Richard	*EMI*	3
2	3	JUSTIFY MY LOVE Madonna	*Sire*	3
13	4	YOU'VE LOST THAT LOVIN' FEELIN' Righteous Brothers	*Verve*	2
4	5	ALL TOGETHER NOW Farm	*Produce*	3
27	6	SADNESS PART 1 Enigma	*Virgin*	2
6	7	UNBELIEVABLE EMF	*Parlophone*	7
12	[8]	MARY HAD A LITTLE BOY Snap!	*Arista*	3
5	9	UNCHAINED MELODY Righteous Brothers	*Verve*	9
11	10	PRAY MC Hammer	*Capitol*	3
15	[11]	JUST THIS SIDE OF LOVE Malandra Burrows	*YTV*	3
10	12	WICKED GAME Chris Isaak	*London*	4
9	13	THIS ONE'S FOR THE CHILDREN New Kids On The Block	*CBS*	3
-	14	GREASE MEGAMIX John Travolta & Olivia Newton-John	*Polydor*	1
22	[15]	TOTAL MIX Black Box	*deConstruction*	2
8	16	KINKY BOOTS Patrick Macnee & Honor Blackman	*Deram*	4
7	17	DON'T WORRY Kim Appleby	*Parlophone*	8
14	18	SITUATION Yazoo	*Mute*	3
18	19	ARE YOU DREAMING? Twenty4Seven featuring Captain Hollywood	*BCM*	5
35	20	ANNIVERSARY WALTZ - PART TWO Status Quo	*Vertigo*	2
24	[21]	DISAPPEAR INXS	*Mercury*	3
17	22	SUCKER DJ Dimples D	*FBI*	5
32	23	CRAZY Seal	*ZTT*	2
34	24	THE BEST CHRISTMAS OF THEM ALL Shakin' Stevens	*Epic*	2
-	25	THE CRAZY PARTY MIXES Jive Bunny & the Mastermixers	*Music Factory Dance*	1
31	26	MERRY CHRISTMAS DARLING/(THEY LONG TO BE) CLOSE TO YOU Carpenters	*A&M*	2
-	27	ALL THE MAN THAT I NEED Whitney Houston	*Arista*	1
30	[28]	FREEDOM! George Michael	*Epic*	2
25	29	24 HOURS Betty Boo	*Rhythm King*	4
16	30	FALLING Julee Cruise	*Warner Brothers*	6
40	31	GONNA MAKE YOU SWEAT C&C Music Factory featuring Freedom Williams	*CBS*	2
19	32	IT TAKES TWO Rod Stewart & Tina Turner	*Warner Brothers*	5
20	33	FANTASY Black Box	*deConstruction*	8
21	34	MY DEFINITION OF A BOOMBASTIC JAZZ STYLE Dream Warriors	*Fourth + Broadway*	5
26	35	KING OF THE ROAD (EP) Proclaimers	*Chrysalis*	5
-	36	CRAZY Patsy Cline	*MCA*	1
23	37	TO LOVE SOMEBODY Jimmy Somerville	*London*	7
37	38	A MATTER OF FACT Innocence	*Cooltempo*	2
-	39	DOCTOR JEEP Sisters Of Mercy	*Merciful Release*	1
29	40	I'LL BE YOUR BABY TONIGHT Robert Palmer & UB40	*EMI*	8

LW	TW	WEEK ENDING 29 DECEMBER 1990		Wks
2	[1]	SAVIOUR'S DAY Cliff Richard	*EMI*	4
1	2	ICE ICE BABY Vanilla Ice	*SBK*	6
4	[3]	YOU'VE LOST THAT LOVIN' FEELIN' Righteous Brothers	*Verve*	3
6	4	SADNESS PART 1 Enigma	*Virgin*	3
14	5	GREASE MEGAMIX John Travolta & Olivia Newton-John	*Polydor*	2
5	6	ALL TOGETHER NOW Farm	*Produce*	4
3	7	JUSTIFY MY LOVE Madonna	*Sire*	4
8	[8]	MARY HAD A LITTLE BOY Snap!	*Arista*	4
10	[9]	PRAY MC Hammer	*Capitol*	4
7	10	UNBELIEVABLE EMF	*Parlophone*	8
12	11	WICKED GAME Chris Isaak	*London*	5
9	12	UNCHAINED MELODY Righteous Brothers	*Verve*	10
25	[13]	THE CRAZY PARTY MIXES Jive Bunny & the Mastermixers	*Music Factory Dance*	2
11	14	JUST THIS SIDE OF LOVE Malandra Burrows	*YTV*	4
23	15	CRAZY Seal	*ZTT*	3
20	[16]	ANNIVERSARY WALTZ - PART TWO Status Quo	*Vertigo*	3
19	[17]	ARE YOU DREAMING? Twenty4Seven featuring Captain Hollywood	*BCM*	6
15	18	TOTAL MIX Black Box	*deConstruction*	3
24	[19]	THE BEST CHRISTMAS OF THEM ALL Shakin' Stevens	*Epic*	3
13	20	THIS ONE'S FOR THE CHILDREN New Kids On The Block	*CBS*	4
18	21	SITUATION Yazoo	*Mute*	4
27	22	ALL THE MAN THAT I NEED Whitney Houston	*Arista*	2
21	23	DISAPPEAR INXS	*Mercury*	4
16	24	KINKY BOOTS Patrick Macnee & Honor Blackman	*Deram*	5
26	[25]	MERRY CHRISTMAS DARLING/(THEY LONG TO BE) CLOSE TO YOU Carpenters	*A&M*	3
36	26	CRAZY Patsy Cline	*MCA*	2
17	27	DON'T WORRY Kim Appleby	*Parlophone*	9
22	28	SUCKER DJ Dimples D	*FBI*	6
31	29	GONNA MAKE YOU SWEAT C&C Music Factory featuring Freedom Williams	*CBS*	3
29	30	24 HOURS Betty Boo	*Rhythm King*	5
30	31	FALLING Julee Cruise	*Warner Brothers*	7
28	32	FREEDOM! George Michael	*Epic*	3
32	33	IT TAKES TWO Rod Stewart & Tina Turner	*Warner Brothers*	6
-	34	GEORDIE BOYS (GAZZA RAP) Gazza ●	*Best*	1
33	35	FANTASY Black Box	*deConstruction*	9
35	36	KING OF THE ROAD (EP) Proclaimers	*Chrysalis*	6
39	[37]	DOCTOR JEEP Sisters Of Mercy	*Merciful Release*	2
-	38	TURTLE RHAPSODY Orchestra On The Half Shell	*SBK*	2
38	39	A MATTER OF FACT Innocence	*Cooltempo*	3
34	40	MY DEFINITION OF A BOOMBASTIC JAZZ STYLE Dream Warriors	*Fourth + Broadway*	6

■After 12 years as holders of the unique record of hitting number one with every release, John Travolta and Olivia Newton-John release a 'new' single, which eventually fails to top the charts (22.12.90) ■ Cliff Richard gets the Christmas number one for the second time in three years, and thus hits the top of the charts in a fifth decade (50s, 60s, 70s, 80s and 90s), a record which one cannot imagine being equalled (29.12.90)■

1991

..........BRYAN ADAMS sets a new record of sixteen consecutive weeks at number one with (Everything I Do) I Do It For You.......Queen have number ones before and after Freddie Mercury's death.......Britain raves on as dance music dominates the chart..........

January 1991

☐ Highest position disc reached ● Act's first ever week on chart

LW	TW	WEEK ENDING 5 JANUARY 1991		Wks
-	[1]	BRING YOUR DAUGHTER...TO THE SLAUGHTER Iron Maiden	EMI	1
2	2	ICE ICE BABY Vanilla Ice	SBK	7
1	3	SAVIOUR'S DAY Cliff Richard	EMI	5
4	4	SADNESS PART 1 Enigma	Virgin	4
5	5	GREASE MEGAMIX John Travolta & Olivia Newton-John	Polydor	3
3	6	YOU'VE LOST THAT LOVIN' FEELIN' Righteous Brothers	Verve	4
6	7	ALL TOGETHER NOW Farm	Produce	5
7	8	JUSTIFY MY LOVE Madonna	Sire	5
8	9	MARY HAD A LITTLE BOY Snap!	Arista	5
9	10	PRAY MC Hammer	Capitol	5
15	11	CRAZY Seal	ZTT	4
10	12	UNBELIEVABLE EMF	Parlophone	9
12	13	UNCHAINED MELODY Righteous Brothers	Verve	11
18	14	TOTAL MIX Black Box	deConstruction	4
20	15	THIS ONE'S FOR THE CHILDREN New Kids On The Block	CBS	5
16	[16]	ANNIVERSARY WALTZ - PART TWO Status Quo	Vertigo	4
14	17	JUST THIS SIDE OF LOVE Malandra Burrows	YTV	5
13	18	THE CRAZY PARTY MIXES Jive Bunny & the Mastermixers	Music Factory Dance	3
11	19	WICKED GAME Chris Isaak	London	6
17	20	ARE YOU DREAMING? Twenty4Seven featuring Captain Hollywood	BCM	7
26	21	CRAZY Patsy Cline	MCA	3
21	22	SITUATION Yazoo	Mute	5
-	23	GOT THE TIME Anthrax	Island	1
23	24	DISAPPEAR INXS	Mercury	5
29	25	GONNA MAKE YOU SWEAT C&C Music Factory featuring Freedom Williams	CBS	4
22	26	ALL THE MAN THAT I NEED Whitney Houston	Arista	3
24	27	KINKY BOOTS Patrick Macnee & Honor Blackman	Deram	6
28	28	SUCKER DJ Dimples D	FBI	7
30	29	24 HOURS Betty Boo	Rhythm King	6
25	30	MERRY CHRISTMAS DARLING/(THEY LONG TO BE) CLOSE TO YOU Carpenters	A&M	4
34	[31]	GEORDIE BOYS (GAZZA RAP) Gazza	Best	2
28	32	FREEDOM! George Michael	Epic	4
19	33	THE BEST CHRISTMAS OF THEM ALL Shakin' Stevens	Epic	4
-	34	(I'VE HAD) THE TIME OF MY LIFE Bill Medley & Jennifer Warnes	RCA	1
33	35	IT TAKES TWO Rod Stewart & Tina Turner	Warner Brothers	7
38	[36]	TURTLE RHAPSODY Orchestra On The Half Shell	SBK	3
40	37	MY DEFINITION OF A BOOMBASTIC JAZZ STYLE Dream Warriors	4th + Broadway	7
31	38	FALLING Julee Cruise	Warner Brothers	8
35	39	FANTASY Black Box	deConstruction	10
36	40	KING OF THE ROAD (EP) Proclaimers	Chrysalis	7

LW	TW	WEEK ENDING 12 JANUARY 1991		Wks
1	[1]	BRING YOUR DAUGHTER...TO THE SLAUGHTER Iron Maiden	EMI	2
4	2	SADNESS PART 1 Enigma	Virgin	5
5	[3]	GREASE MEGAMIX John Travolta & Olivia Newton-John	Polydor	4
11	4	CRAZY Seal	ZTT	5
2	5	ICE ICE BABY Vanilla Ice	SBK	8
7	6	ALL TOGETHER NOW Farm	Produce	6
6	7	YOU'VE LOST THAT LOVIN' FEELIN' Righteous Brothers	Verve	5
10	[8]	PRAY MC Hammer	Capitol	6
9	9	MARY HAD A LITTLE BOY Snap!	Arista	6
25	10	GONNA MAKE YOU SWEAT C&C Music Factory featuring Freedom Williams	CBS	5
8	11	JUSTIFY MY LOVE Madonna	Sire	6
14	[12]	TOTAL MIX Black Box	deConstruction	5
34	13	(I'VE HAD) THE TIME OF MY LIFE Bill Medley & Jennifer Warnes	RCA	2
21	[14]	CRAZY Patsy Cline	MCA	4
-	15	INTERNATIONAL BRIGHT YOUNG THING Jesus Jones	Food	1
23	[16]	GOT THE TIME Anthrax	Island	2
26	17	ALL THE MAN THAT I NEED Whitney Houston	Arista	4
-	18	X, Y AND ZEE Pop Will Eat Itself	RCA	1
16	19	ANNIVERSARY WALTZ - PART TWO Status Quo	Vertigo	5
3	20	SAVIOUR'S DAY Cliff Richard	EMI	6
20	21	ARE YOU DREAMING? Twenty4Seven featuring Captain Hollywood	BCM	8
19	22	WICKED GAME Chris Isaak	London	7
12	23	UNBELIEVABLE EMF	Parlophone	10
-	24	ALL TRUE MAN Alexander O'Neal	Tabu	1
22	25	SITUATION Yazoo	Mute	6
-	26	ALL THIS TIME Sting	A&M	1
-	27	I CAN'T TAKE THE POWER Off-Shore ●	Columbia	1
24	28	DISAPPEAR INXS	Mercury	6
-	29	PREACHERMAN Bananarama	London	1
-	30	MERCY MERCY ME - I WANT YOU Robert Palmer	EMI	1
13	31	UNCHAINED MELODY Righteous Brothers	Verve	12
-	32	ALWAYS THE SUN (REMIX) Stranglers	Epic	1
18	33	THE CRAZY PARTY MIXES Jive Bunny & the Mastermixers	Music Factory Dance	4
17	34	JUST THIS SIDE OF LOVE Malandra Burrows	YTV	6
-	[35]	JORDAN: THE E.P. Prefab Sprout	Kitchenware	1
-	36	BOX SET GO High	London	1
31	37	GEORDIE BOYS (GAZZA RAP) Gazza	Best	3
15	38	THIS ONE'S FOR THE CHILDREN New Kids On The Block	CBS	6
-	39	SUMMER RAIN Belinda Carlisle	Virgin	1
-	40	A LI'L AIN'T ENOUGH David Lee Roth ●	Warner Brothers	1

LW	TW	WEEK ENDING 19 JANUARY 1991		Wks
2	[1]	SADNESS PART 1 Enigma	Virgin	6
4	[2]	CRAZY Seal	ZTT	6
10	[3]	GONNA MAKE YOU SWEAT C&C Music Factory featuring Freedom Williams	CBS	6
3	4	GREASE MEGAMIX John Travolta & Olivia Newton-John	Polydor	5
-	5	3AM ETERNAL KLF featuring The Children Of The Revolution	KLF Communications	1
5	6	ICE ICE BABY Vanilla Ice	SBK	9
15	[7]	INTERNATIONAL BRIGHT YOUNG THING Jesus Jones	Food	2
6	8	ALL TOGETHER NOW Farm	Produce	7
1	9	BRING YOUR DAUGHTER...TO THE SLAUGHTER Iron Maiden	EMI	3
13	10	(I'VE HAD) THE TIME OF MY LIFE Bill Medley & Jennifer Warnes	RCA	3
27	11	I CAN'T TAKE THE POWER Off-Shore	Columbia	2
30	12	MERCY MERCY ME - I WANT YOU Robert Palmer	EMI	2
17	[13]	ALL THE MAN THAT I NEED Whitney Houston	Arista	5
14	[14]	CRAZY Patsy Cline	MCA	5
18	[15]	X, Y AND ZEE Pop Will Eat Itself	RCA	2
8	16	PRAY MC Hammer	Capitol	7
9	17	MARY HAD A LITTLE BOY Snap!	Arista	7
24	[18]	ALL TRUE MAN Alexander O'Neal	Tabu	2
7	19	YOU'VE LOST THAT LOVIN' FEELIN' Righteous Brothers	Verve	6
29	[20]	PREACHERMAN Bananarama	London	2
-	21	SENSITIVITY Ralph Tresvant ●	MCA	1
26	[22]	ALL THIS TIME Sting	A&M	2
12	23	TOTAL MIX Black Box	deConstruction	6
11	24	JUSTIFY MY LOVE Madonna	Sire	7
39	25	SUMMER RAIN Belinda Carlisle	Virgin	2
-	26	HIPPY CHICK Soho ●	S&M	1
-	27	CAN I KICK IT? A Tribe Called Quest ●	Jive	1
36	[28]	BOX SET GO High	London	2
32	[29]	ALWAYS THE SUN (REMIX) Stranglers	Epic	2
21	30	ARE YOU DREAMING? Twenty4Seven featuring Captain Hollywood	BCM	9

In these weeks ■ Five of the top six are past, present or future number ones, and the sixth is a megamix largely made up of two previous John Travolta and Olivia Newton-John number ones (05.01.91) ■ Two different songs called *Crazy* hit at the same time (12.01.91) ■ After Bobby Brown and Bell Biv Devoe, Ralph Tresvant completes the set of ex-New Edition members to hit the charts (19.01.91) ■ *Anniversary Waltz-Part Two* is Status Quo's 40th Top 40 hit (05.01.91)■

LW	TW	Title	Artist	Label	Wks
-	31	FORGET ME NOTS	Tongue 'N' Cheek	*Syncopate*	1
40	32	A LI'L AIN'T ENOUGH	David Lee Roth	*Warner Brothers*	2
16	33	GOT THE TIME	Anthrax	*Island*	3
-	34	GET HERE	Oleta Adams ●	*Fontana*	1
-	35	SATAN	Orbital	*ffrr*	1
-	36	I'M NOT IN LOVE	Will To Power	*Epic*	1
22	37	WICKED GAME	Chris Isaak	*London*	8
35	38	JORDAN: THE E.P.	Prefab Sprout	*Kitchenware*	2
25	39	SITUATION	Yazoo	*Mute*	7
-	40	MISS AMERICA	Big Dish ●	*East West*	1

WEEK ENDING 26 JANUARY 1991

LW	TW	Title	Artist	Label	Wks
-	1	INNUENDO	Queen	*Parlophone*	1
5	2	3AM ETERNAL	KLF featuring The Children Of The Revolution	*KLF Communications*	2
1	3	SADNESS PART 1	Enigma	*Virgin*	7
2	4	CRAZY	Seal	*ZTT*	7
3	5	GONNA MAKE YOU SWEAT	C&C Music Factory featuring Freedom Williams	*CBS*	7
-	6	WIGGLE IT	Two In A Room ●	*SBK*	1
11	7	I CAN'T TAKE THE POWER	Off-Shore	*Columbia*	3
10	8	(I'VE HAD) THE TIME OF MY LIFE	Bill Medley & Jennifer Warnes	*RCA*	4
12	9	MERCY MERCY ME - I WANT YOU	Robert Palmer	*EMI*	3
4	10	GREASE MEGAMIX	John Travolta & Olivia Newton-John	*Polydor*	6
-	11	DO THE BARTMAN	Simpsons ●	*Geffen*	1
8	12	ALL TOGETHER NOW	Farm	*Produce*	8
6	13	ICE ICE BABY	Vanilla Ice	*SBK*	10
-	14	CRY FOR HELP	Rick Astley	*RCA*	1
7	15	INTERNATIONAL BRIGHT YOUNG THING	Jesus Jones	*Food*	3
26	16	HIPPY CHICK	Soho	*S&M*	2
13	17	ALL THE MAN THAT I NEED	Whitney Houston	*Arista*	6
27	18	CAN I KICK IT?	A Tribe Called Quest	*Jive*	2
21	19	SENSITIVITY	Ralph Tresvant	*MCA*	2
14	20	CRAZY	Patsy Cline	*MCA*	6
20	21	PREACHERMAN	Bananarama	*London*	3
16	22	PRAY	MC Hammer	*Capitol*	8
25	23	SUMMER RAIN	Belinda Carlisle	*Virgin*	3
15	24	X, Y AND ZEE	Pop Will Eat Itself	*RCA*	3
18	25	ALL TRUE MAN	Alexander O'Neal	*Tabu*	3
31	26	FORGET ME NOTS	Tongue 'N' Cheek	*Syncopate*	2
34	27	GET HERE	Oleta Adams	*Fontana*	2
-	28	COMING OUT OF THE DARK	Gloria Estefan	*Epic*	1
36	29	I'M NOT IN LOVE	Will To Power	*Epic*	2
17	30	MARY HAD A LITTLE BOY	Snap!	*Arista*	8
35	31	SATAN	Orbital	*ffrr*	2
9	32	BRING YOUR DAUGHTER...TO THE SLAUGHTER	Iron Maiden	*EMI*	4
-	33	OUTSTANDING	Kenny Thomas ●	*Cooltempo*	1
19	34	YOU'VE LOST THAT LOVIN' FEELIN'	Righteous Brothers	*Verve*	7
-	35	DEDICATION	Thin Lizzy	*Vertigo*	1
-	36	SUMMERS MAGIC	Mark Summers ●	*4th + Broadway*	1
40	37	MISS AMERICA	Big Dish	*East West*	2
24	38	JUSTIFY MY LOVE	Madonna	*Sire*	8
22	39	ALL THIS TIME	Sting	*A&M*	3
23	40	TOTAL MIX	Black Box	*deConstruction*	7

February 1991

□ Highest position disc reached ● Act's first ever week on chart

WEEK ENDING 2 FEBRUARY 1991

LW	TW	Title	Artist	Label	Wks
2	1	3AM ETERNAL	KLF featuring The Children Of The Revolution	*KLF Communications*	3
1	2	INNUENDO	Queen	*Parlophone*	2
11	3	DO THE BARTMAN	Simpsons	*Geffen*	2
6	4	WIGGLE IT	Two In A Room	*SBK*	2
4	5	CRAZY	Seal	*ZTT*	8
3	6	SADNESS PART 1	Enigma	*Virgin*	8
14	7	CRY FOR HELP	Rick Astley	*RCA*	2
16	8	HIPPY CHICK	Soho	*S&M*	3
-	9	I BELIEVE	EMF	*Parlophone*	1
5	10	GONNA MAKE YOU SWEAT	C&C Music Factory featuring Freedom Williams	*CBS*	8
-	11	WHAT DO I HAVE TO DO	Kylie Minogue	*PWL*	1
7	12	I CAN'T TAKE THE POWER	Off-Shore	*Columbia*	4
9	13	MERCY MERCY ME - I WANT YOU	Robert Palmer	*EMI*	4
-	14	(I WANNA GIVE YOU) DEVOTION	*Nomad featuring* MC Mikee Freedom ●	*Rumour*	1
18	15	CAN I KICK IT?	A Tribe Called Quest	*Jive*	3
8	16	(I'VE HAD) THE TIME OF MY LIFE	Bill Medley & Jennifer Warnes	*RCA*	5
-	17	PLAY THAT FUNKY MUSIC	Vanilla Ice	*SBK*	1
19	18	SENSITIVITY	Ralph Tresvant	*MCA*	3
-	19	ONLY YOU	Praise ●	*Epic*	1
27	20	GET HERE	Oleta Adams	*Fontana*	3
12	21	ALL TOGETHER NOW	Farm	*Produce*	9
17	22	ALL THE MAN THAT I NEED	Whitney Houston	*Arista*	7
10	23	GREASE MEGAMIX	John Travolta & Olivia Newton-John	*Polydor*	7
23	24	SUMMER RAIN	Belinda Carlisle	*Virgin*	4
15	25	INTERNATIONAL BRIGHT YOUNG THING	Jesus Jones	*Food*	4
13	26	ICE ICE BABY	Vanilla Ice	*SBK*	11
21	27	PREACHERMAN	Bananarama	*London*	4
20	28	CRAZY	Patsy Cline	*MCA*	7
26	29	FORGET ME NOTS	Tongue 'N' Cheek	*Syncopate*	3
28	30	COMING OUT OF THE DARK	Gloria Estefan	*Epic*	2
33	31	OUTSTANDING	Kenny Thomas	*Cooltempo*	2
-	32	YOU GOT THE LOVE	Source featuring Candi Staton ●	*Truelove*	1
-	33	BONEYARD	Little Angels	*Polydor*	1
29	34	I'M NOT IN LOVE	Will To Power	*Epic*	3
36	35	SUMMERS MAGIC	Mark Summers	*4th + Broadway*	2
-	36	THE NIGHT FEVER MEGAMIX	Mixmasters ●	*IQ*	1
25	37	ALL TRUE MAN	Alexander O'Neal	*Tabu*	4
-	38	SOMEDAY	Mariah Carey	*Columbia*	1
22	39	PRAY	MC Hammer	*Capitol*	9
35	40	DEDICATION	Thin Lizzy	*Vertigo*	2

WEEK ENDING 9 FEBRUARY 1991

LW	TW	Title	Artist	Label	Wks
1	1	3AM ETERNAL	KLF featuring The Children Of The Revolution	*KLF Communications*	4
3	2	DO THE BARTMAN	Simpsons	*Geffen*	3
4	3	WIGGLE IT	Two In A Room	*SBK*	3
14	4	(I WANNA GIVE YOU) DEVOTION	Nomad featuring MC Mikee Freedom	*Rumour*	2
19	5	ONLY YOU	Praise	*Epic*	2
9	6	I BELIEVE	EMF	*Parlophone*	2
11	7	WHAT DO I HAVE TO DO	Kylie Minogue	*PWL*	2
8	8	HIPPY CHICK	Soho	*S&M*	4
7	9	CRY FOR HELP	Rick Astley	*RCA*	3
17	10	PLAY THAT FUNKY MUSIC	Vanilla Ice	*SBK*	2
5	11	CRAZY	Seal	*ZTT*	9
2	12	INNUENDO	Queen	*Parlophone*	3
6	13	SADNESS PART 1	Enigma	*Virgin*	9
10	14	GONNA MAKE YOU SWEAT	C&C Music Factory featuring Freedom Williams	*CBS*	9
18	15	GET HERE	Oleta Adams	*Fontana*	4
13	16	MERCY MERCY ME - I WANT YOU	Robert Palmer	*EMI*	5
-	17	GAMES	New Kids On The Block	*Columbia*	1
15	18	CAN I KICK IT?	A Tribe Called Quest	*Jive*	4
12	19	I CAN'T TAKE THE POWER	Off-Shore	*Columbia*	5
18	20	SENSITIVITY	Ralph Tresvant	*MCA*	4
-	21	G.L.A.D.	Kim Appleby	*Parlophone*	1
32	22	YOU GOT THE LOVE	Source featuring Candi Staton	*Truelove*	2
36	23	THE NIGHT FEVER MEGAMIX	Mixmasters	*IQ*	2
31	24	OUTSTANDING	Kenny Thomas	*Cooltempo*	3
30	25	COMING OUT OF THE DARK	Gloria Estefan	*Epic*	3
16	26	(I'VE HAD) THE TIME OF MY LIFE	Bill Medley & Jennifer Warnes	*RCA*	6
35	27	SUMMERS MAGIC	Mark Summers	*4th + Broadway*	3

■By falling from two to 12, Queen's *Innuendo* becomes the only number one hit to spend as few as two weeks in the Top Ten (09.02.91) ■ Iron Maiden's number one spends only four weeks in the Top 40, a record for a short chart life but a happy one which will be equalled by Queen in February (26.01.91)■

February 1991

□ Highest position disc reached ● Act's first ever week on chart

LW	TW	Title	Artist	Label	Wks
24	28	SUMMER RAIN	Belinda Carlisle	Virgin	5
21	29	ALL TOGETHER NOW	Farm	Produce	10
-	30	BLUE HOTEL	Chris Isaak	Reprise	1
23	31	GREASE MEGAMIX	John Travolta & Olivia Newton-John	Polydor	8
-	[32]	SMALLTOWN BOY (1991 REMIX)	Jimmy Somerville with Bronski Beat	London	1
22	33	ALL THE MAN THAT I NEED	Whitney Houston	Arista	8
29	34	FORGET ME NOTS	Tongue 'N' Cheek	Syncopate	4
33	35	BONEYARD	Little Angels	Polydor	2
26	36	ICE ICE BABY	Vanilla Ice	SBK	12
-	37	EVERY BEAT OF THE HEART	Railway Children	Virgin	1
-	38	GOOD TIMES	Jimmy Barnes and INXS ●	Atlantic	1
-	39	ALL RIGHT NOW	Free	Island	1
38	40	SOMEDAY	Mariah Carey	Columbia	2

WEEK ENDING 16 FEBRUARY 1991

LW	TW	Title	Artist	Label	Wks
2	[1]	DO THE BARTMAN	Simpsons	Geffen	4
3	2	3AM ETERNAL	KLF featuring The Children Of The Revolution	KLF Communications	5
4	3	(I WANNA GIVE YOU) DEVOTION	Nomad featuring MC Mikee Freedom	Rumour	3
5	[4]	ONLY YOU	Praise	Epic	3
3	5	WIGGLE IT	Two In A Room	SBK	4
7	[6]	WHAT DO I HAVE TO DO	Kylie Minogue	PWL	3
15	7	GET HERE	Oleta Adams	Fontana	5
6	8	I BELIEVE	EMF	Parlophone	3
8	9	HIPPY CHICK	Soho	S&M	5
21	[10]	G.L.A.D.	Kim Appleby	Parlophone	2
9	11	CRY FOR HELP	Rick Astley	RCA	4
22	12	YOU GOT THE LOVE	Source featuring Candi Staton	Truelove	3
10	13	PLAY THAT FUNKY MUSIC	Vanilla Ice	SBK	3
17	[14]	GAMES	New Kids On The Block	Columbia	2
11	15	CRAZY	Seal	ZTT	10
-	16	IN YER FACE	808 State	ZTT	1
39	17	ALL RIGHT NOW	Free	Island	2
24	18	OUTSTANDING	Kenny Thomas	Cooltempo	4
14	19	GONNA MAKE YOU SWEAT	C&C Music Factory featuring Freedom Williams	CBS	10
13	20	SADNESS PART 1	Enigma	Virgin	10
30	21	BLUE HOTEL	Chris Isaak	Reprise	2
18	22	CAN I KICK IT?	A Tribe Called Quest	Jive	5
16	23	MERCY MERCY ME - I WANT YOU	Robert Palmer	EMI	6
38	24	GOOD TIMES	Jimmy Barnes and INXS	Atlantic	2
23	25	THE NIGHT FEVER MEGAMIX	Mixmasters	IQ	3
19	26	I CAN'T TAKE THE POWER	Off-Shore	Columbia	6
27	[27]	SUMMERS MAGIC	Mark Summers	4th + Broadway	4
37	28	EVERY BEAT OF THE HEART	Railway Children	Virgin	2
-	[29]	TO HERE KNOWS WHEN	My Bloody Valentine ●	Creation	1
20	30	SENSITIVITY	Ralph Tresvant	MCA	5
12	31	INNUENDO	Queen	Parlophone	4
-	32	THINK ABOUT...	DJH featuring Stefy ●	RCA	1
-	33	LOVE REARS ITS UGLY HEAD	Living Color ●	Epic	1
32	34	SMALLTOWN BOY (1991 REMIX)	Jimmy Somerville with Bronski Beat	London	2
25	35	COMING OUT OF THE DARK	Gloria Estefan	Epic	4
-	36	AUBERGE	Chris Rea	East West	1
-	37	BEAUTIFUL LOVE	Julian Cope	Island	1
-	[38]	WHICH WAY SHOULD I JUMP?	Milltown Brothers ●	A&M	1
-	[39]	THE KING IS HALF UNDRESSED	Jellyfish ●	Charisma	1
-	40	HEAL THE PAIN	George Michael	Epic	1

WEEK ENDING 23 FEBRUARY 1991

LW	TW	Title	Artist	Label	Wks
1	[1]	DO THE BARTMAN	Simpsons	Geffen	5
3	[2]	(I WANNA GIVE YOU) DEVOTION	Nomad featuring MC Mikee Freedom	Rumour	4
2	3	3AM ETERNAL	KLF featuring The Children Of The Revolution	KLF Communications	6
7	[4]	GET HERE	Oleta Adams	Fontana	6
4	5	ONLY YOU	Praise	Epic	4
5	6	WIGGLE IT	Two In A Room	SBK	5
6	7	WHAT DO I HAVE TO DO	Kylie Minogue	PWL	4
12	8	YOU GOT THE LOVE	Source featuring Candi Staton	Truelove	4
16	[9]	IN YER FACE	808 State	ZTT	2
10	[10]	G.L.A.D.	Kim Appleby	Parlophone	3
17	11	ALL RIGHT NOW	Free	Island	3
8	12	I BELIEVE	EMF	Parlophone	4
18	13	OUTSTANDING	Kenny Thomas	Cooltempo	5
13	14	PLAY THAT FUNKY MUSIC	Vanilla Ice	SBK	4
9	15	HIPPY CHICK	Soho	S&M	6
15	16	CRAZY	Seal	ZTT	11
21	[17]	BLUE HOTEL	Chris Isaak	Reprise	3
24	[18]	GOOD TIMES	Jimmy Barnes and INXS	Atlantic	3
11	19	CRY FOR HELP	Rick Astley	RCA	5
14	20	GAMES	New Kids On The Block	Columbia	3
-	21	HERE COMES THE HAMMER	MC Hammer	Capitol	1
-	22	LOVE WALKED IN	Thunder	EMI	1
36	23	AUBERGE	Chris Rea	East West	2
28	[24]	EVERY BEAT OF THE HEART	Railway Children	Virgin	3
32	25	THINK ABOUT...	DJH featuring Stefy	RCA	2
-	[26]	OUR FRANK	Morrissey	HMV	1
20	27	SADNESS PART 1	Enigma	Virgin	11
-	28	MOVE YOUR BODY (ELEVATION)	Xpansions ●	Optimism	1
19	29	GONNA MAKE YOU SWEAT	C&C Music Factory featuring Freedom Williams	CBS	11
33	30	LOVE REARS ITS UGLY HEAD	Living Color	Epic	2
40	[31]	HEAL THE PAIN	George Michael	Epic	2
37	[32]	BEAUTIFUL LOVE	Julian Cope	Island	2
-	33	GO FOR IT! (HEART AND FIRE)	Joey B Ellis & Tynetta Hare ●	Bust It	1
25	34	THE NIGHT FEVER MEGAMIX	Mixmasters	IQ	4
-	35	BECAUSE I LOVE YOU (THE POSTMAN SONG)	Stevie B ●	Polydor	1
27	36	SUMMERS MAGIC	Mark Summers	4th + Broadway	5
23	37	MERCY MERCY ME - I WANT YOU	Robert Palmer	EMI	7
38	[38]	WHICH WAY SHOULD I JUMP?	Milltown Brothers	A&M	2
22	39	CAN I KICK IT?	A Tribe Called Quest	Jive	6
30	40	SENSITIVITY	Ralph Tresvant	MCA	6

WEEK ENDING 2 MARCH 1991

LW	TW	Title	Artist	Label	Wks
1	[1]	DO THE BARTMAN	Simpsons	Geffen	6
-	[2]	CRAZY FOR YOU (REMIX)	Madonna	Sire	1
2	3	(I WANNA GIVE YOU) DEVOTION	Nomad featuring MC Mikee Freedom	Rumour	5
8	[4]	YOU GOT THE LOVE	Source featuring Candi Staton	Truelove	5
-	5	SHOULD I STAY OR SHOULD I GO?	Clash	Columbia	1
4	6	GET HERE	Oleta Adams	Fontana	7
3	7	3AM ETERNAL	KLF featuring The Children Of The Revolution	KLF Communications	7
11	[8]	ALL RIGHT NOW	Free	Island	4
9	[9]	IN YER FACE	808 State	ZTT	3
28	10	MOVE YOUR BODY (ELEVATION)	Xpansions	Optimism	2
6	11	WIGGLE IT	Two In A Room	SBK	6
13	[12]	OUTSTANDING	Kenny Thomas	Cooltempo	6
7	13	WHAT DO I HAVE TO DO	Kylie Minogue	PWL	5
5	14	ONLY YOU	Praise	Epic	5
21	[15]	HERE COMES THE HAMMER	MC Hammer	Capitol	2
23	[16]	AUBERGE	Chris Rea	East West	3
10	17	G.L.A.D.	Kim Appleby	Parlophone	4
35	18	BECAUSE I LOVE YOU (THE POSTMAN SONG)	Stevie B	Polydor	2
30	19	LOVE REARS ITS UGLY HEAD	Living Color	Epic	3
18	20	GOOD TIMES	Jimmy Barnes and INXS	Atlantic	4
22	[21]	LOVE WALKED IN	Thunder	EMI	2
25	[22]	THINK ABOUT...	DJH featuring Stefy	RCA	3
33	23	GO FOR IT! (HEART AND FIRE)	Joey B Ellis & Tynetta Hare	Bust It	2
12	24	I BELIEVE	EMF	Parlophone	5

In these weeks ■ The Simpsons become the first cartoon characters since the Archies in 1969 to top the charts (16.02.91) ■ After 15 Top 40 hits without ever hitting the Top Ten, the Clash let the jeans do the talking to push the re-issue of their 13th Top 40 hit straight into the upper quartile (02.03.91) ■ Madonna's *Crazy For You* and Free's *All Right Now* are both enjoying their second spells of Top Ten action (02.03.91)■

LW	TW	Title / Artist	Label	Wks
17	25	BLUE HOTEL Chris Isaak	Reprise	4
15	26	HIPPY CHICK Soho	S&M	7
16	27	CRAZY Seal	ZTT	12
14	28	PLAY THAT FUNKY MUSIC Vanilla Ice	SBK	5
24	29	EVERY BEAT OF THE HEART Railway Children	Virgin	4
26	30	OUR FRANK Morrissey	HMV	2
-	31	UNFINISHED SYMPATHY Massive ●	Wild Bunch	1
-	32	ADRENALIN (EP) N-Joi	deConstruction	1
32	33	BEAUTIFUL LOVE Julian Cope	Island	3
-	34	WHO? WHERE? WHY? Jesus Jones	Food	1
-	35	FREE 'N' EASY Almighty ●	Polydor	1
19	36	CRY FOR HELP Rick Astley	RCA	6
31	37	HEAL THE PAIN George Michael	Epic	3
20	38	GAMES New Kids On The Block	Columbia	4
-	39	DON'T GO MESSIN' WITH MY HEART Mantronix	Capitol	1
-	40	IT'S TOO LATE Quartz introducing Dina Carroll ●	Mercury	1

WEEK ENDING **9 MARCH 1991**

LW	TW	Title / Artist	Label	Wks
5	1	SHOULD I STAY OR SHOULD I GO? Clash	Columbia	2
2	2	CRAZY FOR YOU (REMIX) Madonna	Sire	2
1	3	DO THE BARTMAN Simpsons	Geffen	7
4	4	YOU GOT THE LOVE Source featuring Candi Staton	Truelove	6
3	5	(I WANNA GIVE YOU) DEVOTION Nomad featuring MC Mikee Freedom	Rumour	6
18	6	BECAUSE I LOVE YOU (THE POSTMAN SONG) Stevie B	Polydor	3
10	7	MOVE YOUR BODY (ELEVATION) Xpansions	Optimism	3
8	8	ALL RIGHT NOW Free	Island	5
6	9	GET HERE Oleta Adams	Fontana	8
-	10	THE STONK Hale & Pace and the Stonkers ●	London	1
7	11	3AM ETERNAL KLF featuring The Children Of The Revolution	KLF Communications	8
9	12	IN YER FACE 808 State	ZTT	4
12	13	OUTSTANDING Kenny Thomas	Cooltempo	7
19	14	LOVE REARS ITS UGLY HEAD Living Color	Epic	4
-	15	OVER RISING Charlatans	Situation Two	1
-	16	HAPPY Ned's Atomic Dustbin ●	Furtive	1
31	17	UNFINISHED SYMPATHY Massive	Wild Bunch	2
-	18	JOYRIDE Roxette	EMI	1
15	19	HERE COMES THE HAMMER MC Hammer	Capitol	3
23	20	GO FOR IT! (HEART AND FIRE) Joey B Ellis & Tynetta Hare	Bust It	3
40	21	IT'S TOO LATE Quartz introducing Dina Carroll	Mercury	2
39	22	DON'T GO MESSIN' WITH MY HEART Mantronix	Capitol	2
32	23	ADRENALIN (EP) N-Joi	deConstruction	2
34	24	WHO? WHERE? WHY? Jesus Jones	Food	2
16	25	AUBERGE Chris Rea	East West	4
-	26	LOSING MY RELIGION REM	Warner Brothers	1
13	27	WHAT DO I HAVE TO DO Kylie Minogue	PWL	6
11	28	WIGGLE IT Two In A Room	SBK	7
22	29	THINK ABOUT... DJH featuring Stefy	RCA	4
21	30	LOVE WALKED IN Thunder	EMI	3
20	31	GOOD TIMES Jimmy Barnes and INXS	Atlantic	5
-	32	THE ONE AND ONLY Chesney Hawkes ●	Chrysalis	1
-	33	THIS IS YOUR LIFE Banderas ●	London	1
17	34	G.L.A.D. Kim Appleby	Parlophone	5
14	35	ONLY YOU Praise	Epic	6
-	36	PEOPLE ARE STRANGE Echo & the Bunnymen	East West	1
-	37	BOW DOWN MISTER Jesus Loves You ●	More Protein	1
-	38	SECRET LOVE Bee Gees	Warner Brothers	1
-	39	LUDI Dream Warriors	4th + Broadway	1
-	40	AROUND THE WAY GIRL LL Cool J	Def Jam	1

WEEK ENDING **16 MARCH 1991**

March 1991

□ Highest position disc reached ● Act's first ever week on chart

LW	TW	Title / Artist	Label	Wks
1	1	SHOULD I STAY OR SHOULD I GO? Clash	Columbia	3
10	2	THE STONK Hale & Pace and the Stonkers	London	2
3	3	DO THE BARTMAN Simpsons	Geffen	8
2	4	CRAZY FOR YOU (REMIX) Madonna	Sire	3
4	5	YOU GOT THE LOVE Source featuring Candi Staton	Truelove	7
6	6	BECAUSE I LOVE YOU (THE POSTMAN SONG) Stevie B	Polydor	4
7	7	MOVE YOUR BODY (ELEVATION) Xpansions	Optimism	4
18	8	JOYRIDE Roxette	EMI	2
21	9	IT'S TOO LATE Quartz introducing Dina Carroll	Mercury	3
5	10	(I WANNA GIVE YOU) DEVOTION Nomad featuring MC Mikee Freedom	Rumour	7
8	11	ALL RIGHT NOW Free	Island	6
14	12	LOVE REARS ITS UGLY HEAD Living Color	Epic	5
17	13	UNFINISHED SYMPATHY Massive	Wild Bunch	3
-	14	TODAY FOREVER (EP) Ride	Creation	1
15	15	OVER RISING Charlatans	Situation Two	2
9	16	GET HERE Oleta Adams	Fontana	9
16	17	HAPPY Ned's Atomic Dustbin	Furtive	2
32	18	THE ONE AND ONLY Chesney Hawkes	Chrysalis	2
26	19	LOSING MY RELIGION REM	Warner Brothers	2
-	20	RHYTHM OF MY HEART Rod Stewart	Warner Brothers	1
20	21	GO FOR IT! (HEART AND FIRE) Joey B Ellis & Tynetta Hare	Bust It	4
38	22	SECRET LOVE Bee Gees	Warner Brothers	2
24	23	WHO? WHERE? WHY? Jesus Jones	Food	3
-	24	I'M GOING SLIGHTLY MAD Queen	Parlophone	1
-	25	LOOSE FIT Happy Mondays	Factory	1
33	26	THIS IS YOUR LIFE Banderas	London	2
11	27	3AM ETERNAL KLF featuring The Children Of The Revolution	KLF Communications	9
22	28	DON'T GO MESSIN' WITH MY HEART Mantronix	Capitol	3
23	29	ADRENALIN (EP) N-Joi	deConstruction	3
-	30	HANGAR 18 Megadeth	Capitol	1
13	31	OUTSTANDING Kenny Thomas	Cooltempo	8
37	32	BOW DOWN MISTER Jesus Loves You	More Protein	2
12	33	IN YER FACE 808 State	ZTT	5
36	34	PEOPLE ARE STRANGE Echo & the Bunnymen	East West	2
19	35	HERE COMES THE HAMMER MC Hammer	Capitol	4
40	36	AROUND THE WAY GIRL LL Cool J	Def Jam	2
-	37	NOT A MINUTE TOO SOON Vixen	EMI	1
-	38	I'VE GOT NEWS FOR YOU Feargal Sharkey	Virgin	1
-	39	CHERRY PIE Warrant ●	Columbia	1
-	40	WEAR YOUR LOVE LIKE HEAVEN Definition Of Sound	Circa	1

WEEK ENDING **23 MARCH 1991**

LW	TW	Title / Artist	Label	Wks
2	1	THE STONK Hale & Pace and the Stonkers	London	3
1	2	SHOULD I STAY OR SHOULD I GO? Clash	Columbia	4
20	3	RHYTHM OF MY HEART Rod Stewart	Warner Brothers	2
8	4	JOYRIDE Roxette	EMI	3
18	5	THE ONE AND ONLY Chesney Hawkes	Chrysalis	3
6	6	BECAUSE I LOVE YOU (THE POSTMAN SONG) Stevie B	Polydor	5
-	7	WHERE THE STREETS HAVE NO NAME - CAN'T TAKE MY EYES OFF YOU/ HOW DO YOU EXPECT TO BE TAKEN SERIOUSLY Pet Shop Boys	Parlophone	1
9	8	IT'S TOO LATE Quartz introducing Dina Carroll	Mercury	4
5	9	YOU GOT THE LOVE Source featuring Candi Staton	Truelove	8
7	10	MOVE YOUR BODY (ELEVATION) Xpansions	Optimism	5
3	11	DO THE BARTMAN Simpsons	Geffen	9
22	12	SECRET LOVE Bee Gees	Warner Brothers	3
-	13	LET THERE BE LOVE Simple Minds	Virgin	1
4	14	CRAZY FOR YOU (REMIX) Madonna	Sire	4
12	15	LOVE REARS ITS UGLY HEAD Living Color	Epic	6
13	16	UNFINISHED SYMPATHY Massive	Wild Bunch	4
25	17	LOOSE FIT Happy Mondays	Factory	2
10	18	(I WANNA GIVE YOU) DEVOTION Nomad featuring MC Mikee Freedom	Rumour	8
19	19	LOSING MY RELIGION REM	Warner Brothers	3
26	20	THIS IS YOUR LIFE Banderas	London	3
23	21	WHO? WHERE? WHY? Jesus Jones	Food	4
24	22	I'M GOING SLIGHTLY MAD Queen	Parlophone	2
38	23	I'VE GOT NEWS FOR YOU Feargal Sharkey	Virgin	2
11	24	ALL RIGHT NOW Free	Island	7
14	25	TODAY FOREVER (EP) Ride	Creation	2

■ *The Stonk* is the first Comic Relief charity disc to get to number one since Cliff and the Young Ones did awful things to *Living Doll* in 1986 (23.03.91)

■ The Bee Gee's *Secret Love* is not the old Doris Day song, Simple Minds' *Let There Be Love* is not the Nat 'King' Cole song, but the Pet Shop Boys *Can't Take My Eyes Off You* is the Four Seasons/Andy Williams/Brystown Gang hit of previous years. The full title of the Pet Shop Boys hit is, at 77 letters, the longest ever to hit the UK singles charts (23.03.91)■

March 1991

□ Highest position disc reached ● Act's first ever week on chart

LW	TW	Title	Artist	Label	Wks
30	26	HANGAR 18	Megadeth	Capitol	2
32	27	BOW DOWN MISTER	Jesus Loves You	More Protein	3
21	28	GO FOR IT! (HEART AND FIRE)	Joey B Ellis & Tynetta Hare	Bust It	5
40	29	WEAR YOUR LOVE LIKE HEAVEN	Definition Of Sound	Circa	2
15	30	OVER RISING	Charlatans	Situation Two	3
16	31	GET HERE	Oleta Adams	Fontana	10
-	32	SHE'S A WOMAN	Scritti Politti featuring Shabba Ranks	Virgin	1
28	33	DON'T GO MESSIN' WITH MY HEART	Mantronix	Capitol	4
-	34	BEEN CAUGHT STEALING	Jane's Addiction ●	Warner Brothers	1
39	35	CHERRY PIE	Warrant	Columbia	2
-	36	OVER TO YOU JOHN (HERE WE GO AGAIN)	Jive Bunny & the Mastermixers	Music Factory Dance	1
36	37	AROUND THE WAY GIRL	LL Cool J	Def Jam	3
-	38	SAY HELLO WAVE GOODBYE '91	Soft Cell with Marc Almond	Mercury	1
-	39	CAN YOU DIG IT?	Mock Turtles ●	Siren	1
27	40	3AM ETERNAL	KLF featuring The Children Of The Revolution	KLF Communications	10

WEEK ENDING 30 MARCH 1991

LW	TW	Title	Artist	Label	Wks
5	1	THE ONE AND ONLY	Chesney Hawkes	Chrysalis	4
1	2	THE STONK	Hale & Pace and the Stonkers	London	4
3	3	RHYTHM OF MY HEART	Rod Stewart	Warner Brothers	3
7	4	WHERE THE STREETS HAVE NO NAME - CAN'T TAKE MY EYES OFF YOU/ HOW DO YOU EXPECT TO BE TAKEN SERIOUSLY	Pet Shop Boys	Parlophone	2
4	5	JOYRIDE	Roxette	EMI	4
13	6	LET THERE BE LOVE	Simple Minds	Virgin	2
-	7	SIT DOWN	James	Fontana	1
8	8	IT'S TOO LATE	Quartz introducing Dina Carroll	Mercury	5
2	9	SHOULD I STAY OR SHOULD I GO?	Clash	Columbia	5
12	10	SECRET LOVE	Bee Gees	Warner Brothers	4
6	11	BECAUSE I LOVE YOU (THE POSTMAN SONG)	Stevie B	Polydor	6
9	12	YOU GOT THE LOVE	Source featuring Candi Staton	Truelove	9
-	13	SNAP! MEGAMIX	Snap!	Arista	1
23	14	I'VE GOT NEWS FOR YOU	Feargal Sharkey	Virgin	3
10	15	MOVE YOUR BODY (ELEVATION)	Xpansions	Optimism	6
20	16	THIS IS YOUR LIFE	Banderas	London	3
15	17	LOVE REARS ITS UGLY HEAD	Living Color	Epic	6
11	18	DO THE BARTMAN	Simpsons	Geffen	10
19	19	LOSING MY RELIGION	REM	Warner Brothers	4
16	20	UNFINISHED SYMPATHY	Massive	Wild Bunch	7
17	21	LOOSE FIT	Happy Mondays	Factory	3
29	22	WEAR YOUR LOVE LIKE HEAVEN	Definition Of Sound	Circa	3
14	23	CRAZY FOR YOU (REMIX)	Madonna	Sire	5
32	24	SHE'S A WOMAN	Scritti Politti featuring Shabba Ranks	Virgin	2
-	25	HUMAN NATURE	Gary Clail On-U Sound System ●	Perfecto	1
21	26	WHO? WHERE? WHY?	Jesus Jones	Food	5
18	27	(I WANNA GIVE YOU) DEVOTION	Nomad featuring MC Mikee Freedom	Rumour	9
27	28	BOW DOWN MISTER	Jesus Loves You	More Protein	4
-	29	HIGHWIRE	Rolling Stones	Rolling Stones	1
22	30	I'M GOING SLIGHTLY MAD	Queen	Parlophone	3
-	31	LOVE AND KISSES	Dannii Minogue ●	MCA	1
36	32	OVER TO YOU JOHN (HERE WE GO AGAIN)	Jive Bunny & the Mastermixers	Music Factory Dance	2
-	33	HERE WE GO	C&C Music Factory featuring Freedom Williams	Columbia	1
34	34	BEEN CAUGHT STEALING	Jane's Addiction	Warner Brothers	2
39	35	CAN YOU DIG IT?	Mock Turtles	Siren	2
-	36	CARAVAN	Inspiral Carpets	Cow	1
26	37	HANGAR 18	Megadeth	Capitol	3
38	38	SAY HELLO WAVE GOODBYE '91	Soft Cell with Marc Almond	Mercury	2
-	39	WORD OF MOUTH	Mike & the Mechanics	Virgin	1
-	40	PRODUCT OF THE WORKING CLASS	Little Angels	Polydor	1

WEEK ENDING 6 APRIL 1991

LW	TW	Title	Artist	Label	Wks
1	1	THE ONE AND ONLY	Chesney Hawkes	Chrysalis	5
7	2	SIT DOWN	James	Fontana	2
3	3	RHYTHM OF MY HEART	Rod Stewart	Warner Brothers	4
5	4	JOYRIDE	Roxette	EMI	5
10	5	SECRET LOVE	Bee Gees	Warner Brothers	5
4	6	WHERE THE STREETS HAVE NO NAME - CAN'T TAKE MY EYES OFF YOU/ HOW DO YOU EXPECT TO BE TAKEN SERIOUSLY?	Pet Shop Boys	Parlophone	3
6	7	LET THERE BE LOVE	Simple Minds	Virgin	3
8	8	IT'S TOO LATE	Quartz introducing Dina Carroll	Mercury	6
2	9	THE STONK	Hale & Pace and the Stonkers	London	5
13	10	SNAP! MEGAMIX	Snap!	Arista	2
-	11	THE WHOLE OF THE MOON	Waterboys	Ensign	1
14	12	I'VE GOT NEWS FOR YOU	Feargal Sharkey	Virgin	4
9	13	SHOULD I STAY OR SHOULD I GO?	Clash	Columbia	6
25	14	HUMAN NATURE	Gary Clail On-U Sound System	Perfecto	2
31	15	LOVE AND KISSES	Dannii Minogue	MCA	2
16	16	THIS IS YOUR LIFE	Banderas	London	4
22	17	WEAR YOUR LOVE LIKE HEAVEN	Definition Of Sound	Circa	4
11	18	BECAUSE I LOVE YOU (THE POSTMAN SONG)	Stevie B	Polydor	7
-	19	ANTHEM	N-Joi ●	deConstruction	1
24	20	SHE'S A WOMAN	Scritti Politti featuring Shabba Ranks	Virgin	3
33	21	HERE WE GO	C&C Music Factory featuring Freedom Williams	Columbia	2
-	22	DEEP DEEP TROUBLE	Simpsons	Geffen	1
12	23	YOU GOT THE LOVE	Source featuring Candi Staton	Truelove	10
19	24	LOSING MY RELIGION	REM	Warner Brothers	5
18	25	DO THE BARTMAN	Simpsons	Geffen	11
-	26	STRIKE IT UP	Black Box	deConstruction	1
15	27	MOVE YOUR BODY (ELEVATION)	Xpansions	Optimism	7
32	28	OVER TO YOU JOHN (HERE WE GO AGAIN)	Jive Bunny & the Mastermixers	Music Factory Dance	3
29	29	HIGHWIRE	Rolling Stones	Rolling Stones	2
36	30	CARAVAN	Inspiral Carpets	Cow	2
20	31	UNFINISHED SYMPATHY	Massive	Wild Bunch	6
17	32	LOVE REARS ITS UGLY HEAD	Living Color	Epic	7
35	33	CAN YOU DIG IT?	Mock Turtles	Siren	3
23	34	CRAZY FOR YOU (REMIX)	Madonna	Sire	6
39	35	WORD OF MOUTH	Mike & the Mechanics	Virgin	2
-	36	RING MY BELL	Monie Love vs Adeva ●	Cooltempo	1
21	37	LOOSE FIT	Happy Mondays	Factory	4
-	38	HYPERREAL	Shamen ●	One Little Indian	1
-	39	WHERE LOVE LIVES (COME ON IN)	Alison Limerick ●	Arista	1
26	40	WHO? WHERE? WHY?	Jesus Jones	Food	6

WEEK ENDING 13 APRIL 1991

LW	TW	Title	Artist	Label	Wks
1	1	THE ONE AND ONLY	Chesney Hawkes	Chrysalis	6
2	2	SIT DOWN	James	Fontana	3
11	3	THE WHOLE OF THE MOON	Waterboys	Ensign	2
-	4	RESCUE ME	Madonna	Sire	1
3	5	RHYTHM OF MY HEART	Rod Stewart	Warner Brothers	5
-	6	THE SIZE OF A COW	Wonder Stuff	Polydor	1
4	7	JOYRIDE	Roxette	EMI	6
19	8	ANTHEM	N-Joi	deConstruction	2
22	9	DEEP DEEP TROUBLE	Simpsons	Geffen	2
15	10	LOVE AND KISSES	Dannii Minogue	MCA	3
5	11	SECRET LOVE	Bee Gees	Warner Brothers	6
14	12	HUMAN NATURE	Gary Clail On-U Sound System	Perfecto	3
12	13	I'VE GOT NEWS FOR YOU	Feargal Sharkey	Virgin	5
10	14	SNAP! MEGAMIX	Snap!	Arista	3
7	15	LET THERE BE LOVE	Simple Minds	Virgin	4
8	16	IT'S TOO LATE	Quartz introducing Dina Carroll	Mercury	7
6	17	WHERE THE STREETS HAVE NO NAME - CAN'T TAKE MY EYES OFF YOU/ HOW DO YOU EXPECT TO BE TAKEN SERIOUSLY?	Pet Shop Boys	Parlophone	4
26	18	STRIKE IT UP	Black Box	deConstruction	2
17	19	WEAR YOUR LOVE LIKE HEAVEN	Definition Of Sound	Circa	5
21	20	HERE WE GO	C&C Music Factory featuring Freedom Williams	Columbia	3
20	21	SHE'S A WOMAN	Scritti Politti featuring Shabba Ranks	Virgin	4

In these weeks ■ Chesney Hawkes is the son of Chip Hawkes of the Tremeloes. He thus becomes the first son of a chart-topping father to have a solo number one (30.03.91) ■ *Rhythm Of My Heart* is Rod Stewart's fourth Top Ten hit over sixteen years to have the word *Heart* in the title (06.04.91) ■ Two Jesus acts in the Top 40. Jesus Loves You is Boy George in disguise (30.03.91)■

33 22 CAN YOU DIG IT? Mock Turtles ... *Siren* 4
35 23 WORD OF MOUTH Mike & the Mechanics ... *Virgin* 3
13 24 SHOULD I STAY OR SHOULD I GO? Clash ... *Columbia* 7
16 25 THIS IS YOUR LIFE Banderas ... *London* 5
9 26 THE STONK Hale & Pace and the Stonkers ... *London* 6
36 27 RING MY BELL Monie Love vs Adeva ... *Cooltempo* 2
24 28 LOSING MY RELIGION REM ... *Warner Brothers* 6
39 29 WHERE LOVE LIVES (COME ON IN) Alison Limerick ... *Arista* 2
38 30 HYPERREAL Shamen ... *One Little Indian* 2
30 31 CARAVAN Inspiral Carpets ... *Cow* 3
- 32 ROCK THE CASBAH Clash ... *Columbia* 1
- [33] SING YOUR LIFE Morrissey ... *HMV* 1
- 34 SENZA UNA DONNA (WITHOUT A WOMAN) Zucchero featuring Paul Young ● ... *London* 1
- 35 UNDERCOVER ANARCHIST Silver Bullet ... *Parlophone* 1
- 36 SAILING ON THE SEVEN SEAS OMD ... *Virgin* 1
28 37 OVER TO YOU JOHN (HERE WE GO AGAIN) Jive Bunny & the Mastermixers ... *Music Factory Dance* 4
- 38 (I JUST WANNA) B WITH U Transvision Vamp ... *MCA* 1
- 39 SINFUL! (SCARY JIGGIN' WITH DOCTOR LOVE) Pete Wylie & the Farm ● ... *Siren* 1
27 40 MOVE YOUR BODY (ELEVATION) Xpansions ... *Optimism* 8

LW TW *WEEK ENDING* **20 APRIL 1991** Wks

1 [1] THE ONE AND ONLY Chesney Hawkes ... *Chrysalis* 7
2 [2] SIT DOWN James ... *Fontana* 4
4 [3] RESCUE ME Madonna ... *Sire* 2
3 4 THE WHOLE OF THE MOON Waterboys ... *Ensign* 3
6 [5] THE SIZE OF A COW Wonder Stuff ... *Polydor* 2
5 6 RHYTHM OF MY HEART Rod Stewart ... *Warner Brothers* 6
9 [7] DEEP DEEP TROUBLE Simpsons ... *Geffen* 3
10 [8] LOVE AND KISSES Dannii Minogue ... *MCA* 4
8 9 ANTHEM N-Joi ... *deConstruction* 3
7 10 JOYRIDE Roxette ... *EMI* 7
12 11 HUMAN NATURE Gary Clail On-U Sound System ... *Perfecto* 4
11 12 SECRET LOVE Bee Gees ... *Warner Brothers* 7
23 [13] WORD OF MOUTH Mike & the Mechanics ... *Virgin* 4
13 14 I'VE GOT NEWS FOR YOU Feargal Sharkey ... *Virgin* 6
32 [15] ROCK THE CASBAH Clash ... *Columbia* 2
18 [16] STRIKE IT UP Black Box ... *deConstruction* 3
16 17 IT'S TOO LATE Quartz introducing Dina Carroll ... *Mercury* 8
22 [18] CAN YOU DIG IT? Mock Turtles ... *Siren* 5
36 19 SAILING ON THE SEVEN SEAS OMD ... *Virgin* 2
27 [20] RING MY BELL Monie Love vs Adeva ... *Cooltempo* 3
20 21 HERE WE GO C&C Music Factory featuring Freedom Williams ... *Columbia* 4
34 22 SENZA UNA DONNA (WITHOUT A WOMAN) Zucchero featuring Paul Young ... *London* 2
- 23 SHOOP SHOOP SONG (IT'S IN HIS KISS) Cher ... *Epic* 1
19 24 WEAR YOUR LOVE LIKE HEAVEN Definition Of Sound ... *Circa* 6
14 25 SNAP! MEGAMIX Snap! ... *Arista* 4
15 26 LET THERE BE LOVE Simple Minds ... *Virgin* 5
29 [27] WHERE LOVE LIVES (COME ON IN) Alison Limerick ... *Arista* 3
39 [28] SINFUL! (SCARY JIGGIN' WITH DOCTOR LOVE) Pete Wylie & the Farm ... *Siren* 2
30 [29] HYPERREAL Shamen ... *One Little Indian* 3
38 [30] (I JUST WANNA) B WITH U Transvision Vamp ... *MCA* 2
17 31 WHERE THE STREETS HAVE NO NAME - CAN'T TAKE MY EYES OFF YOU/ HOW DO YOU EXPECT TO BE TAKEN SERIOUSLY? Pet Shop Boys ... *Parlophone* 5
- 32 QUADROPHONIA Quadrophonia ● ... *ARS* 1
35 [33] UNDERCOVER ANARCHIST Silver Bullet ... *Parlophone* 2
- 34 SEAL OUR FATE Gloria Estefan ... *Epic* 1
28 35 LOSING MY RELIGION REM ... *Warner Brothers* 7
21 36 SHE'S A WOMAN Scritti Politti featuring Shabba Ranks ... *Virgin* 5
- [37] MY HEAD'S IN MISSISSIPPI ZZ Top ... *Warner Brothers* 1
- 38 LONG TRAIN RUNNING Bananarama ... *London* 1
- 39 FOOTSTEPS FOLLOWING ME Frances Nero ● ... *Debut* 1
- 40 GET READY Roachford ... *Columbia* 1

LW TW *WEEK ENDING* **27 APRIL 1991** Wks

1 [1] THE ONE AND ONLY Chesney Hawkes ... *Chrysalis* 8

May 1991

□ Highest position disc reached ● Act's first ever week on chart

23 2 SHOOP SHOOP SONG (IT'S IN HIS KISS) Cher ... *Epic* 2
2 3 SIT DOWN James ... *Fontana* 5
4 4 THE WHOLE OF THE MOON Waterboys ... *Ensign* 4
3 5 RESCUE ME Madonna ... *Sire* 3
5 6 THE SIZE OF A COW Wonder Stuff ... *Polydor* 3
7 [7] DEEP DEEP TROUBLE Simpsons ... *Geffen* 4
19 8 SAILING ON THE SEVEN SEAS OMD ... *Virgin* 3
22 9 SENZA UNA DONNA (WITHOUT A WOMAN) Zucchero featuring Paul Young ... *London* 3
11 [10] HUMAN NATURE Gary Clail On-U Sound System ... *Perfecto* 5
8 11 LOVE AND KISSES Dannii Minogue ... *MCA* 5
9 12 ANTHEM N-Joi ... *deConstruction* 4
6 13 RHYTHM OF MY HEART Rod Stewart ... *Warner Brothers* 7
- 14 GET THE MESSAGE Electronic ... *Factory* 1
- 15 BORN FREE Vic Reeves & Roman Numerals ● ... *Sense* 1
- 16 RING RING RING (HA HA HEY) De La Soul ... *Big Life* 1
15 17 ROCK THE CASBAH Clash ... *Columbia* 3
18 [18] CAN YOU DIG IT? Mock Turtles ... *Siren* 6
13 19 WORD OF MOUTH Mike & the Mechanics ... *Virgin* 5
- 20 THERE'S NO OTHER WAY Blur ● ... *Food* 1
10 21 JOYRIDE Roxette ... *EMI* 8
- 22 CHILDREN EMF ... *Parlophone* 1
12 23 SECRET LOVE Bee Gees ... *Warner Brothers* 8
32 24 QUADROPHONIA Quadrophonia ... *ARS* 2
16 25 STRIKE IT UP Black Box ... *deConstruction* 4
34 26 SEAL OUR FATE Gloria Estefan ... *Epic* 2
14 27 I'VE GOT NEWS FOR YOU Feargal Sharkey ... *Virgin* 7
28 [28] SINFUL! (SCARY JIGGIN' WITH DOCTOR LOVE) Pete Wylie & the Farm ... *Siren* 3
20 29 RING MY BELL Monie Love vs Adeva ... *Cooltempo* 4
38 [30] LONG TRAIN RUNNING Bananarama ... *London* 2
27 31 WHERE LOVE LIVES (COME ON IN) Alison Limerick ... *Arista* 4
39 32 FOOTSTEPS FOLLOWING ME Frances Nero ... *Debut* 2
29 33 HYPERREAL Shamen ... *One Little Indian* 4
- [34] ARE YOU READY? AC/DC ... *Atco* 1
21 35 HERE WE GO C&C Music Factory featuring Freedom Williams ... *Columbia* 5
40 36 GET READY Roachford ... *Columbia* 2
37 [37] MY HEAD'S IN MISSISSIPPI ZZ Top ... *Warner Brothers* 2
17 38 IT'S TOO LATE Quartz introducing Dina Carroll ... *Mercury* 9
- 39 SILENT LUCIDITY Queensryche ● ... *EMI* 1
- 40 LOVE IS A WONDERFUL THING Michael Bolton ... *Columbia* 1

LW TW *WEEK ENDING* **4 MAY 1991** Wks

2 [1] SHOOP SHOOP SONG (IT'S IN HIS KISS) Cher ... *Epic* 3
1 2 THE ONE AND ONLY Chesney Hawkes ... *Chrysalis* 9
- 3 LAST TRAIN TO TRANCENTRAL The KLF featuring Children Of The Revolution ... *KLF Communications* 1
3 4 SIT DOWN James ... *Fontana* 6
8 5 SAILING ON THE SEVEN SEAS OMD ... *Virgin* 4
15 [6] BORN FREE Vic Reeves & Roman Numerals ... *Sense* 2
9 7 SENZA UNA DONNA (WITHOUT A WOMAN) Zucchero featuring Paul Young ... *London* 4
4 8 THE WHOLE OF THE MOON Waterboys ... *Ensign* 5
14 9 GET THE MESSAGE Electronic ... *Factory* 2
16 [10] RING RING RING (HA HA HEY) De La Soul ... *Big Life* 2
20 11 THERE'S NO OTHER WAY Blur ... *Food* 2
7 12 DEEP DEEP TROUBLE Simpsons ... *Geffen* 5
5 13 RESCUE ME Madonna ... *Sire* 4
24 [14] QUADROPHONIA Quadrophonia ... *ARS* 3
10 15 HUMAN NATURE Gary Clail On-U Sound System ... *Perfecto* 6
6 16 THE SIZE OF A COW Wonder Stuff ... *Polydor* 4
12 17 ANTHEM N-Joi ... *deConstruction* 5
11 18 LOVE AND KISSES Dannii Minogue ... *MCA* 6
22 [19] CHILDREN EMF ... *Parlophone* 2
13 20 RHYTHM OF MY HEART Rod Stewart ... *Warner Brothers* 8
- 21 FUTURE LOVE (EP) Seal ... *ZTT* 1
18 22 CAN YOU DIG IT? Mock Turtles ... *Siren* 7

■Vic Reeves becomes the first person to bring the much recorded *Born Free* into the charts (27.04.91) ■ Cher hits number one over 25 years after her chart debut, the longest wait ever by somebody who does not finally make it with a re-issue (04.05.91) ■ *The Size Of A Cow* is the first bovine Top Ten hit since Tommy Steele's *Little White Bull* in 1960 (20.04.91)■

May 1991

□ Highest position disc reached ● Act's first ever week on chart

LW	TW	Title	Artist	Label	Wks
32	23	FOOTSTEPS FOLLOWING ME	Frances Nero	*Debut*	3
26	[24]	SEAL OUR FATE	Gloria Estefan	*Epic*	3
-	25	TOUCH ME (ALL NIGHT LONG)	Cathy Dennis ●	*Polydor*	1
17	26	ROCK THE CASBAH	Clash	*Columbia*	4
-	27	JUST A GROOVE	Nomad	*Rumour*	1
19	28	WORD OF MOUTH	Mike & the Mechanics	*Virgin*	6
36	29	GET READY	Roachford	*Columbia*	3
30	[30]	LONG TRAIN RUNNING	Bananarama	*London*	3
40	31	LOVE IS A WONDERFUL THING	Michael Bolton	*Columbia*	2
25	32	STRIKE IT UP	Black Box	*deConstruction*	5
-	33	PROMISE ME	Beverley Craven ●	*Epic*	1
39	[34]	SILENT LUCIDITY	Queensryche	*EMI*	2
21	35	JOYRIDE	Roxette	*EMI*	9
-	[36]	DON'T LET ME DOWN	Farm	*Produce*	1
23	37	SECRET LOVE	Bee Gees	*Warner Brothers*	9
34	38	ARE YOU READY?	AC/DC	*Atco*	2
31	39	WHERE LOVE LIVES (COME ON IN)	Alison Limerick	*Arista*	5
-	40	GONNA CATCH YOU	Lonnie Gordon	*Supreme*	1

WEEK ENDING 11 MAY 1991

LW	TW	Title	Artist	Label	Wks
1	[1]	SHOOP SHOOP SONG (IT'S IN HIS KISS)	Cher	*Epic*	4
3	[2]	LAST TRAIN TO TRANCENTRAL	The KLF featuring Children Of The Revolution	*KLF Communications*	2
5	[3]	SAILING ON THE SEVEN SEAS	OMD	*Virgin*	5
7	[4]	SENZA UNA DONNA (WITHOUT A WOMAN)	Zucchero featuring Paul Young	*London*	5
2	5	THE ONE AND ONLY	Chesney Hawkes	*Chrysalis*	10
6	[6]	BORN FREE	Vic Reeves & Roman Numerals	*Sense*	3
25	7	TOUCH ME (ALL NIGHT LONG)	Cathy Dennis	*Polydor*	2
9	[8]	GET THE MESSAGE	Electronic	*Factory*	3
4	9	SIT DOWN	James	*Fontana*	7
11	10	THERE'S NO OTHER WAY	Blur	*Food*	3
10	11	RING RING RING (HA HA HEY)	De La Soul	*Big Life*	3
21	[12]	FUTURE LOVE (EP)	Seal	*ZTT*	2
8	13	THE WHOLE OF THE MOON	Waterboys	*Ensign*	6
14	[14]	QUADROPHONIA	Quadrophonia	*ARS*	4
33	15	PROMISE ME	Beverley Craven	*Epic*	2
27	[16]	JUST A GROOVE	Nomad	*Rumour*	2
23	[17]	FOOTSTEPS FOLLOWING ME	Frances Nero	*Debut*	4
12	18	DEEP DEEP TROUBLE	Simpsons	*Geffen*	6
13	19	RESCUE ME	Madonna	*Sire*	5
16	20	THE SIZE OF A COW	Wonder Stuff	*Polydor*	5
15	21	HUMAN NATURE	Gary Clail On-U Sound System	*Perfecto*	7
29	[22]	GET READY	Roachford	*Columbia*	4
19	23	CHILDREN	EMF	*Parlophone*	3
31	24	LOVE IS A WONDERFUL THING	Michael Bolton	*Columbia*	3
18	25	LOVE AND KISSES	Dannii Minogue	*MCA*	7
-	26	FADING LIKE A FLOWER	Roxette	*EMI*	1
-	27	ANASTHASIA	T-99 ●	*XL Recordings*	1
20	28	RHYTHM OF MY HEART	Rod Stewart	*Warner Brothers*	9
-	[29]	DALLIANCE	Wedding Present	*RCA*	1
-	[30]	A MESSAGE TO YOUR HEART	Samantha Janus ●	*Hollywood*	1
17	31	ANTHEM	N-Joi	*deConstruction*	6
40	[32]	GONNA CATCH YOU	Lonnie Gordon	*Supreme*	2
24	33	SEAL OUR FATE	Gloria Estefan	*Epic*	4
-	34	BABY BABY	Amy Grant	*A&M*	1
30	35	LONG TRAIN RUNNING	Bananarama	*London*	4
-	[36]	DEVIL'S TOY	Almighty	*Polydor*	1
36	37	DON'T LET ME DOWN	Farm	*Produce*	2
22	38	CAN YOU DIG IT?	Mock Turtles	*Siren*	8
-	39	YOU'RE IN LOVE	Wilson Phillips	*SBK*	1
26	40	ROCK THE CASBAH	Clash	*Columbia*	5

WEEK ENDING 18 MAY 1991

LW	TW	Title	Artist	Label	Wks
1	[1]	SHOOP SHOOP SONG (IT'S IN HIS KISS)	Cher	*Epic*	5
2	[2]	LAST TRAIN TO TRANCENTRAL	The KLF featuring Children Of The Revolution	*KLF Communications*	3
-	3	GYPSY WOMAN (LA DA DEE)	Crystal Waters ●	*A&M*	1
3	4	SAILING ON THE SEVEN SEAS	OMD	*Virgin*	6
7	[5]	TOUCH ME (ALL NIGHT LONG)	Cathy Dennis	*Polydor*	3
15	6	PROMISE ME	Beverley Craven	*Epic*	3
4	7	SENZA UNA DONNA (WITHOUT A WOMAN)	Zucchero featuring Paul Young	*London*	6
10	[8]	THERE'S NO OTHER WAY	Blur	*Food*	4
8	9	GET THE MESSAGE	Electronic	*Factory*	4
-	10	TAINTED LOVE	Soft Cell featuring Marc Almond	*Mercury*	1
5	11	THE ONE AND ONLY	Chesney Hawkes	*Chrysalis*	11
26	[12]	FADING LIKE A FLOWER	Roxette	*EMI*	2
12	13	FUTURE LOVE (EP)	Seal	*ZTT*	3
27	[14]	ANASTHASIA	T-99	*XL Recordings*	2
6	15	BORN FREE	Vic Reeves & Roman Numerals	*Sense*	4
11	16	RING RING RING (HA HA HEY)	De La Soul	*Big Life*	4
16	17	JUST A GROOVE	Nomad	*Rumour*	3
17	18	FOOTSTEPS FOLLOWING ME	Frances Nero	*Debut*	5
9	19	SIT DOWN	James	*Fontana*	8
-	20	CALL IT WHAT YOU WANT	New Kids On The Block	*Columbia*	1
-	21	SUCCESS	Dannii Minogue	*MCA*	1
14	22	QUADROPHONIA	Quadrophonia	*ARS*	5
24	[23]	LOVE IS A WONDERFUL THING	Michael Bolton	*Columbia*	4
13	24	THE WHOLE OF THE MOON	Waterboys	*Ensign*	7
-	25	R.S.V.P.	Jason Donovan	*PWL*	1
34	26	BABY BABY	Amy Grant	*A&M*	2
-	27	I WANNA SEX YOU UP	Color Me Badd ●	*Giant*	1
22	28	GET READY	Roachford	*Columbia*	5
39	[29]	YOU'RE IN LOVE	Wilson Phillips	*SBK*	2
30	[30]	A MESSAGE TO YOUR HEART	Samantha Janus	*Hollywood*	2
-	31	WHENEVER YOU NEED ME	T'Pau	*Siren*	1
19	32	RESCUE ME	Madonna	*Sire*	6
32	33	GONNA CATCH YOU	Lonnie Gordon	*Supreme*	3
-	[34]	TAKE IT	Flowered Up	*London*	1
-	35	SHINY HAPPY PEOPLE	R.E.M.	*Warner Brothers*	1
-	[36]	INTO TOMORROW	Paul Weller Movement ●	*Freedom High*	1
20	37	THE SIZE OF A COW	Wonder Stuff	*Polydor*	6
21	38	HUMAN NATURE	Gary Clail On-U Sound System	*Perfecto*	8
29	39	DALLIANCE	Wedding Present	*RCA*	2
23	40	CHILDREN	EMF	*Parlophone*	4

WEEK ENDING 25 MAY 1991

LW	TW	Title	Artist	Label	Wks
1	[1]	SHOOP SHOOP SONG (IT'S IN HIS KISS)	Cher	*Epic*	6
3	[2]	GYPSY WOMAN (LA DA DEE)	Crystal Waters	*A&M*	2
6	[3]	PROMISE ME	Beverley Craven	*Epic*	4
2	4	LAST TRAIN TO TRANCENTRAL	The KLF featuring Children Of The Revolution	*KLF Communications*	4
10	[5]	TAINTED LOVE	Soft Cell featuring Marc Almond	*Mercury*	2
5	6	TOUCH ME (ALL NIGHT LONG)	Cathy Dennis	*Polydor*	4
27	7	I WANNA SEX YOU UP	Color Me Badd	*Giant*	2
4	8	SAILING ON THE SEVEN SEAS	OMD	*Virgin*	7
26	9	BABY BABY	Amy Grant	*A&M*	3
7	10	SENZA UNA DONNA (WITHOUT A WOMAN)	Zucchero featuring Paul Young	*London*	7
21	[11]	SUCCESS	Dannii Minogue	*MCA*	2
20	[12]	CALL IT WHAT YOU WANT	New Kids On The Block	*Columbia*	2
35	13	SHINY HAPPY PEOPLE	R.E.M.	*Warner Brothers*	2
12	14	FADING LIKE A FLOWER	Roxette	*EMI*	3
14	15	ANASTHASIA	T-99	*XL Recordings*	3
8	16	THERE'S NO OTHER WAY	Blur	*Food*	5
25	[17]	R.S.V.P.	Jason Donovan	*PWL*	2
-	[18]	CAUGHT IN MY SHADOW	Wonder Stuff	*Polydor*	1
13	19	FUTURE LOVE (EP)	Seal	*ZTT*	4
31	20	WHENEVER YOU NEED ME	T'Pau	*Siren*	2
17	21	JUST A GROOVE	Nomad	*Rumour*	4
9	22	GET THE MESSAGE	Electronic	*Factory*	5
-	[23]	YOUR SWAYING ARMS	Deacon Blue	*Columbia*	1
18	24	FOOTSTEPS FOLLOWING ME	Frances Nero	*Debut*	6
11	25	THE ONE AND ONLY	Chesney Hawkes	*Chrysalis*	12
23	26	LOVE IS A WONDERFUL THING	Michael Bolton	*Columbia*	5
16	27	RING RING RING (HA HA HEY)	De La Soul	*Big Life*	5
-	28	HEADLONG	Queen	*Parlophone*	1
-	29	SEE THE LIGHTS	Simple Minds	*Virgin*	1
29	30	YOU'RE IN LOVE	Wilson Phillips	*SBK*	3

In these weeks ■ Crystal Waters first chart week at number three equals the record set a few months earlier by Vanilla Ice (18.05.91) ■ Paul Weller enters the chart under a fourth name. After Jam, Style Council and the Council Collective comes the Paul Weller Movement (18.05.91) ■ For a second week, four songs in the Top Ten have brackets in their title (25.05.91)■

LW	TW	Title / Artist	Label	Wks
-	31	MOVE THAT BODY Technotronic	*ARS*	1
22	32	QUADROPHONIA Quadrophonia	*ARS*	6
-	33	KISS THEM FOR ME Siouxsie & the Banshees	*Wonderland*	1
-	[34]	COAST IS CLEAR Curve ●	*Anxious*	1
19	35	SIT DOWN James	*Fontana*	9
-	[36]	SIMPLE TRUTH Chris de Burgh	*A&M*	1
24	37	THE WHOLE OF THE MOON Waterboys	*Ensign*	8
15	38	BORN FREE Vic Reeves & Roman Numerals	*Sense*	5
34	39	TAKE IT Flowered Up	*London*	2
36	40	INTO TOMORROW Paul Weller Movement	*Freedom High*	2

WEEK ENDING 1 JUNE 1991

LW	TW	Title / Artist	Label	Wks
1	[1]	SHOOP SHOOP SONG (IT'S IN HIS KISS) Cher	*Epic*	7
7	2	I WANNA SEX YOU UP Color Me Badd	*Giant*	3
2	3	GYPSY WOMAN (LA DA DEE) Crystal Waters	*A&M*	3
3	4	PROMISE ME Beverley Craven	*Epic*	5
9	5	BABY BABY Amy Grant	*A&M*	4
5	6	TAINTED LOVE Soft Cell featuring Marc Almond	*Mercury*	3
4	7	LAST TRAIN TO TRANCENTRAL The KLF featuring Children Of The Revolution	*KLF Communications*	5
6	8	TOUCH ME (ALL NIGHT LONG) Cathy Dennis	*Polydor*	5
13	9	SHINY HAPPY PEOPLE R.E.M.	*Warner Brothers*	3
-	10	SHOCKED Kylie Minogue	*PWL*	1
11	[11]	SUCCESS Dannii Minogue	*MCA*	3
31	[12]	MOVE THAT BODY Technotronic	*ARS*	2
8	13	SAILING ON THE SEVEN SEAS OMD	*Virgin*	8
28	[14]	HEADLONG Queen	*Parlophone*	2
10	15	SENZA UNA DONNA (WITHOUT A WOMAN) Zucchero featuring Paul Young	*London*	8
20	[16]	WHENEVER YOU NEED ME T'Pau	*Siren*	3
12	17	CALL IT WHAT YOU WANT New Kids On The Block	*Columbia*	3
18	[18]	CAUGHT IN MY SHADOW Wonder Stuff	*Polydor*	2
14	19	FADING LIKE A FLOWER Roxette	*EMI*	4
29	[20]	SEE THE LIGHTS Simple Minds	*Virgin*	2
-	21	YO!! SWEETNESS MC Hammer	*Capitol*	1
17	22	R.S.V.P. Jason Donovan	*PWL*	3
23	[23]	YOUR SWAYING ARMS Deacon Blue	*Columbia*	2
15	24	ANASTHASIA T-99	*XL Recordings*	4
-	25	92 DEGREES Pop Will Eat Itself	*RCA*	1
16	26	THERE'S NO OTHER WAY Blur	*Food*	6
-	27	ROBOTS Kraftwerk	*EMI*	1
-	28	ONLY FOOLS (NEVER FALL IN LOVE) Sonia	*IQ*	1
-	29	LIGHT MY FIRE Doors	*Elektra*	1
24	30	FOOTSTEPS FOLLOWING ME Frances Nero	*Debut*	7
19	31	FUTURE LOVE (EP) Seal	*ZTT*	5
33	[32]	KISS THEM FOR ME Siouxsie & the Banshees	*Wonderland*	2
22	33	GET THE MESSAGE Electronic	*Factory*	6
-	[34]	YOUNG GODS Little Angels	*Polydor*	1
-	35	RECIPE FOR LOVE/ IT HAD TO BE YOU Harry Connick Jr ●	*Columbia*	1
-	36	THINKING ABOUT YOUR LOVE Kenny Thomas	*Cooltempo*	1
-	37	DO YOU WANT ME Salt-N-Pepa	*ffrr*	1
21	38	JUST A GROOVE Nomad	*Rumour*	5
-	39	WALKING DOWN MADISON Kirsty MacColl	*Virgin*	1
26	40	LOVE IS A WONDERFUL THING Michael Bolton	*Columbia*	6

WEEK ENDING 8 JUNE 1991

LW	TW	Title / Artist	Label	Wks
2	[1]	I WANNA SEX YOU UP Color Me Badd	*Giant*	4
1	2	SHOOP SHOOP SONG (IT'S IN HIS KISS) Cher	*Epic*	8
5	3	BABY BABY Amy Grant	*A&M*	5
4	4	PROMISE ME Beverley Craven	*Epic*	6
3	5	GYPSY WOMAN (LA DA DEE) Crystal Waters	*A&M*	4
10	[6]	SHOCKED Kylie Minogue	*PWL*	2
6	7	TAINTED LOVE Soft Cell featuring Marc Almond	*Mercury*	4
9	8	SHINY HAPPY PEOPLE R.E.M.	*Warner Brothers*	4
7	9	LAST TRAIN TO TRANCENTRAL The KLF featuring Children Of The Revolution	*KLF Communications*	6
29	10	LIGHT MY FIRE Doors	*Elektra*	2
11	[11]	SUCCESS Dannii Minogue	*MCA*	4
-	12	HOLIDAY Madonna	*Sire*	1
8	13	TOUCH ME (ALL NIGHT LONG) Cathy Dennis	*Polydor*	6

June 1991

☐ Highest position disc reached ● Act's first ever week on chart

LW	TW	Title / Artist	Label	Wks
12	14	MOVE THAT BODY Technotronic	*ARS*	3
28	15	ONLY FOOLS (NEVER FALL IN LOVE) Sonia	*IQ*	2
21	[16]	YO!! SWEETNESS MC Hammer	*Capitol*	2
-	17	JEALOUSY Pet Shop Boys	*Parlophone*	1
17	18	CALL IT WHAT YOU WANT New Kids On The Block	*Columbia*	4
13	19	SAILING ON THE SEVEN SEAS OMD	*Virgin*	9
27	[20]	ROBOTS Kraftwerk	*EMI*	2
16	21	WHENEVER YOU NEED ME T'Pau	*Siren*	4
36	22	THINKING ABOUT YOUR LOVE Kenny Thomas	*Cooltempo*	2
25	[23]	92 DEGREES Pop Will Eat Itself	*RCA*	2
14	24	HEADLONG Queen	*Parlophone*	3
37	25	DO YOU WANT ME Salt-N-Pepa	*ffrr*	2
19	26	FADING LIKE A FLOWER Roxette	*EMI*	5
-	[27]	PLANET OF SOUND Pixies	*4AD*	1
15	28	SENZA UNA DONNA (WITHOUT A WOMAN) Zucchero featuring Paul Young	*London*	9
22	29	R.S.V.P. Jason Donovan	*PWL*	4
39	30	WALKING DOWN MADISON Kirsty MacColl	*Virgin*	2
20	31	SEE THE LIGHTS Simple Minds	*Virgin*	3
32	[32]	KISS THEM FOR ME Siouxsie & the Banshees	*Wonderland*	3
26	33	THERE'S NO OTHER WAY Blur	*Food*	7
-	34	I TOUCH MYSELF Divinyls ●	*Virgin*	1
35	35	RECIPE FOR LOVE/ IT HAD TO BE YOU Harry Connick Jr	*Columbia*	2
24	36	ANASTHASIA T-99	*XL Recordings*	5
23	37	YOUR SWAYING ARMS Deacon Blue	*Columbia*	3
-	38	REMEMBER ME WITH LOVE Gloria Estefan	*Epic*	1
-	[39]	SPACE New Model Army	*EMI*	1
-	40	SOLACE OF YOU Living Color	*Epic*	1

WEEK ENDING 15 JUNE 1991

LW	TW	Title / Artist	Label	Wks
1	[1]	I WANNA SEX YOU UP Color Me Badd	*Giant*	5
3	[2]	BABY BABY Amy Grant	*A&M*	6
2	3	SHOOP SHOOP SONG (IT'S IN HIS KISS) Cher	*Epic*	9
4	4	PROMISE ME Beverley Craven	*Epic*	7
12	[5]	HOLIDAY Madonna	*Sire*	2
8	[6]	SHINY HAPPY PEOPLE R.E.M.	*Warner Brothers*	5
10	[7]	LIGHT MY FIRE Doors	*Elektra*	3
5	8	GYPSY WOMAN (LA DA DEE) Crystal Waters	*A&M*	5
6	9	SHOCKED Kylie Minogue	*PWL*	3
22	10	THINKING ABOUT YOUR LOVE Kenny Thomas	*Cooltempo*	3
15	11	ONLY FOOLS (NEVER FALL IN LOVE) Sonia	*IQ*	3
17	[12]	JEALOUSY Pet Shop Boys	*Parlophone*	2
25	13	DO YOU WANT ME Salt-N-Pepa	*ffrr*	3
7	14	TAINTED LOVE Soft Cell featuring Marc Almond	*Mercury*	5
14	15	MOVE THAT BODY Technotronic	*ARS*	4
13	16	TOUCH ME (ALL NIGHT LONG) Cathy Dennis	*Polydor*	7
16	17	YO!! SWEETNESS MC Hammer	*Capitol*	3
9	18	LAST TRAIN TO TRANCENTRAL The KLF featuring Children Of The Revolution	*KLF Communications*	7
-	[19]	MONKEY BUSINESS Skid Row	*Atlantic*	1
34	20	I TOUCH MYSELF Divinyls	*Virgin*	2
11	21	SUCCESS Dannii Minogue	*MCA*	5
38	[22]	REMEMBER ME WITH LOVE Gloria Estefan	*Epic*	2
30	[23]	WALKING DOWN MADISON Kirsty MacColl	*Virgin*	3
-	24	PEOPLE ARE STILL HAVING SEX LaTour ●	*Polydor*	1
-	25	FROM A DISTANCE Bette Midler	*Atlantic*	1
-	26	GET THE FUNK OUT Extreme ●	*A&M*	1
-	27	MOTOWN SONG Rod Stewart	*Warner Brothers*	1
-	28	IT AIN'T OVER 'TIL IT'S OVER Lenny Kravitz	*Virgin*	1
19	29	SAILING ON THE SEVEN SEAS OMD	*Virgin*	10
20	30	ROBOTS Kraftwerk	*EMI*	3
21	31	WHENEVER YOU NEED ME T'Pau	*Siren*	5
35	[32]	RECIPE FOR LOVE/ IT HAD TO BE YOU Harry Connick Jr	*Columbia*	3
40	[33]	SOLACE OF YOU Living Color	*Epic*	2
-	[34]	COVER MY EYES (PAIN AND HEAVEN) Marillion	*EMI*	1
-	35	TRIBAL BASE Rebel MC, Tenor Fly & Barrington Levy ●	*Desire*	1

■The nearest two sisters have ever been to having simultaneous solo Top Ten hit is when Kylie and Dannii Minogue are both at their chart peaks at numbers six and 11 (08.06.91) ■ The female voice dominates. Of the top eleven singles only Color Me Badd and the re-issued *Tainted Love* do not feature female vocalists. Even R.E.M. have borrowed the talents of the B52s Kate Pierson for *Shining Happy People* (01.06.91) ■ In the first six months of the year, there are nine weeks in which no record has spent ten weeks on the chart. In the final six months, there are none (08.06.91)■

June 1991

□ Highest position disc reached ● Act's first ever week on chart

LW	TW	Title	Artist	Label	Wks
-	[36]	FAREWELL MR. SORROW	All About Eve	Mercury	1
-	37	SAFE FROM HARM	Massive Attack	Wild Bunch	1
27	38	PLANET OF SOUND	Pixies	4AD	2
-	[39]	NAKED LOVE (JUST SAY YOU WANT ME)	Quartz with Dina Carroll	Mercury	1
-	[40]	TAKE 5	Northside	Factory	1

WEEK ENDING 22 JUNE 1991

LW	TW	Title	Artist	Label	Wks
1	[1]	I WANNA SEX YOU UP	Color Me Badd	Giant	6
-	2	ANY DREAM WILL DO	Jason Donovan	Really Useful	1
2	3	BABY BABY	Amy Grant	A&M	7
3	4	SHOOP SHOOP SONG (IT'S IN HIS KISS)	Cher	Epic	10
10	5	THINKING ABOUT YOUR LOVE	Kenny Thomas	Cooltempo	4
13	6	DO YOU WANT ME	Salt-N-Pepa	ffrr	4
25	7	FROM A DISTANCE	Bette Midler	Atlantic	2
4	8	PROMISE ME	Beverley Craven	Epic	8
6	9	SHINY HAPPY PEOPLE	R.E.M.	Warner Brothers	6
11	[10]	ONLY FOOLS (NEVER FALL IN LOVE)	Sonia	IQ	4
7	11	LIGHT MY FIRE	Doors	Elektra	4
27	12	MOTOWN SONG	Rod Stewart	Warner Brothers	2
20	13	I TOUCH MYSELF	Divinyls	Virgin	3
28	14	IT AIN'T OVER 'TIL IT'S OVER	Lenny Kravitz	Virgin	2
24	[15]	PEOPLE ARE STILL HAVING SEX	LaTour	Polydor	2
5	16	HOLIDAY	Madonna	Sire	3
8	17	GYPSY WOMAN (LA DA DEE)	Crystal Waters	A&M	6
9	18	SHOCKED	Kylie Minogue	PWL	4
26	[19]	GET THE FUNK OUT	Extreme	A&M	2
35	[20]	TRIBAL BASE	Rebel MC, Tenor Fly & Barrington Levy	Desire	2
12	21	JEALOUSY	Pet Shop Boys	Parlophone	3
-	22	RUSH RUSH	Paula Abdul	Virgin	1
22	23	REMEMBER ME WITH LOVE	Gloria Estefan	Epic	3
23	24	WALKING DOWN MADISON	Kirsty MacColl	Virgin	4
37	[25]	SAFE FROM HARM	Massive Attack	Wild Bunch	2
16	26	TOUCH ME (ALL NIGHT LONG)	Cathy Dennis	Polydor	8
-	27	REAL LOVE	Driza Bone ●	4th + Broadway	1
15	28	MOVE THAT BODY	Technotronic	ARS	5
-	29	THERE'S NOTHING LIKE THIS	Omar ●	Talkin Loud	1
14	30	TAINTED LOVE	Soft Cell featuring Marc Almond	Mercury	6
19	31	MONKEY BUSINESS	Skid Row	Atlantic	2
-	32	SHERIFF FATMAN	Carter The Unstoppable Sex Machine ●	Big Cat	1
-	33	NIGHT IN MOTION	Cubic 22 ●	XL	1
34	[34]	COVER MY EYES (PAIN AND HEAVEN)	Marillion	EMI	2
17	35	YO!! SWEETNESS	MC Hammer	Capitol	4
-	[36]	WATCHER'S POINT OF VIEW	PM Dawn ●	Gee Street	1
-	37	I'M A MAN NOT A BOY	Chesney Hawkes	Chrysalis	1
18	38	LAST TRAIN TO TRANCENTRAL	The KLF featuring Children Of The Revolution	KLF Communications	8
32	39	RECIPE FOR LOVE/ IT HAD TO BE YOU	Harry Connick Jr	Columbia	4
-	[40]	HIGHER THAN THE SUN	Primal Scream	Creation	1

WEEK ENDING 29 JUNE 1991

LW	TW	Title	Artist	Label	Wks
2	[1]	ANY DREAM WILL DO	Jason Donovan	Really Useful	2
1	2	I WANNA SEX YOU UP	Color Me Badd	Giant	7
-	[3]	CHORUS	Erasure	Mute	1
5	[4]	THINKING ABOUT YOUR LOVE	Kenny Thomas	Cooltempo	5
6	[5]	DO YOU WANT ME	Salt-N-Pepa	ffrr	5
7	[6]	FROM A DISTANCE	Bette Midler	Atlantic	3
3	7	BABY BABY	Amy Grant	A&M	8
-	8	(EVERYTHING I DO) I DO IT FOR YOU	Bryan Adams	A&M	1
4	9	SHOOP SHOOP SONG (IT'S IN HIS KISS)	Cher	Epic	11
12	[10]	MOTOWN SONG	Rod Stewart	Warner Brothers	3
14	[11]	IT AIN'T OVER 'TIL IT'S OVER	Lenny Kravitz	Virgin	3
13	12	I TOUCH MYSELF	Divinyls	Virgin	4
10	13	ONLY FOOLS (NEVER FALL IN LOVE)	Sonia	IQ	5
22	14	RUSH RUSH	Paula Abdul	Virgin	2
15	[15]	PEOPLE ARE STILL HAVING SEX	LaTour	Polydor	3
27	[16]	REAL LOVE	Driza Bone	4th + Broadway	2
9	17	SHINY HAPPY PEOPLE	R.E.M.	Warner Brothers	7
29	18	THERE'S NOTHING LIKE THIS	Omar	Talkin Loud	2
8	19	PROMISE ME	Beverley Craven	Epic	9
19	20	GET THE FUNK OUT	Extreme	A&M	3
20	21	TRIBAL BASE	Rebel MC, Tenor Fly & Barrington Levy	Desire	3
33	22	NIGHT IN MOTION	Cubic 22	XL	2
18	23	SHOCKED	Kylie Minogue	PWL	5
11	24	LIGHT MY FIRE	Doors	Elektra	5
-	25	HEY STOOPID	Alice Cooper	Epic	1
-	26	ALWAYS THERE	Incognito featuring Jocelyn Brown ●	Talkin Loud	1
37	[27]	I'M A MAN NOT A BOY	Chesney Hawkes	Chrysalis	2
32	28	SHERIFF FATMAN	Carter The Unstoppable Sex Machine	Big Cat	2
17	29	GYPSY WOMAN (LA DA DEE)	Crystal Waters	A&M	7
16	30	HOLIDAY	Madonna	Sire	4
25	31	SAFE FROM HARM	Massive Attack	Wild Bunch	3
-	32	ROLLIN 'IN MY 5.0	Vanilla Ice	SBK	1
23	33	REMEMBER ME WITH LOVE	Gloria Estefan	Epic	4
-	34	UNFORGETTABLE	Natalie Cole & Nat 'King' Cole ●	Elektra	1
28	35	MOVE THAT BODY	Technotronic	ARS	6
36	[36]	WATCHER'S POINT OF VIEW	PM Dawn	Gee Street	2
24	37	WALKING DOWN MADISON	Kirsty MacColl	Virgin	5
-	38	GENERATIONS OF LOVE	Jesus Loves You ●	More Protein	1
26	39	TOUCH ME (ALL NIGHT LONG)	Cathy Dennis	Polydor	9
30	40	TAINTED LOVE	Soft Cell featuring Marc Almond	Mercury	7

WEEK ENDING 6 JULY 1991

LW	TW	Title	Artist	Label	Wks
1	[1]	ANY DREAM WILL DO	Jason Donovan	Really Useful	3
8	2	(EVERYTHING I DO) I DO IT FOR YOU	Bryan Adams	A&M	2
3	[3]	CHORUS	Erasure	Mute	2
2	4	I WANNA SEX YOU UP	Color Me Badd	Giant	8
4	5	THINKING ABOUT YOUR LOVE	Kenny Thomas	Cooltempo	6
5	6	DO YOU WANT ME	Salt-N-Pepa	ffrr	6
14	7	RUSH RUSH	Paula Abdul	Virgin	3
6	8	FROM A DISTANCE	Bette Midler	Atlantic	4
26	9	ALWAYS THERE	Incognito featuring Jocelyn Brown	Talkin Loud	2
12	[10]	I TOUCH MYSELF	Divinyls	Virgin	5
11	[11]	IT AIN'T OVER 'TIL IT'S OVER	Lenny Kravitz	Virgin	4
10	12	MOTOWN SONG	Rod Stewart	Warner Brothers	4
7	13	BABY BABY	Amy Grant	A&M	9
18	[14]	THERE'S NOTHING LIKE THIS	Omar	Talkin Loud	3
22	[15]	NIGHT IN MOTION	Cubic 22	XL	3
16	[16]	REAL LOVE	Driza Bone	4th + Broadway	3
-	17	7 WAYS TO LOVE	Cola Boy ●	Arista	1
9	18	SHOOP SHOOP SONG (IT'S IN HIS KISS)	Cher	Epic	12
13	19	ONLY FOOLS (NEVER FALL IN LOVE)	Sonia	IQ	6
15	20	PEOPLE ARE STILL HAVING SEX	LaTour	Polydor	4
25	[21]	HEY STOOPID	Alice Cooper	Epic	2
-	22	BRING THE NOISE	Anthrax featuring Chuck D	Island	1
28	[23]	SHERIFF FATMAN	Carter The Unstoppable Sex Machine	Big Cat	3
20	24	GET THE FUNK OUT	Extreme	A&M	4
17	25	SHINY HAPPY PEOPLE	R.E.M.	Warner Brothers	8
34	26	UNFORGETTABLE	Natalie Cole & Nat 'King' Cole	Elektra	2
32	[27]	ROLLIN 'IN MY 5.0	Vanilla Ice	SBK	2
19	28	PROMISE ME	Beverley Craven	Epic	10
21	29	TRIBAL BASE	Rebel MC, Tenor Fly & Barrington Levy	Desire	4
-	30	NOW THAT WE'VE FOUND LOVE	Heavy D & the Boyz ●	MCA	1
-	31	SEXUALITY	Billy Bragg	Go! Discs	1
-	32	MY NAME IS NOT SUSAN	Whitney Houston	Arista	1
-	33	THINGS THAT MAKE YOU GO HMMM...	C&C Music Factory featuring Freedom Williams	Columbia	1
27	34	I'M A MAN NOT A BOY	Chesney Hawkes	Chrysalis	3
-	35	MAMA	Kim Appleby	Parlophone	1
-	[36]	BEST I CAN	Queensryche	EMI	1
38	37	GENERATIONS OF LOVE	Jesus Loves You	More Protein	2
23	38	SHOCKED	Kylie Minogue	PWL	6
24	39	LIGHT MY FIRE	Doors	Elektra	6
-	[40]	WAVE OF THE FUTURE	Quadrophonia	ARS	1

In these weeks ■ Bryan Adams makes his chart debut in the only position no record had yet entered the chart in 1991, at number eight (29.06.91) ■ Jason Donovan becomes the only person ever to top the charts with a song from their own London stage show, while they are still starring in it. *Any Dream Will Do* is a number one hit for an Australian in Britain, giving the Aussies revenge for Max Bygraves' version, which was number one in Australia many years earlier (29.06.61)■

LW	TW	WEEK ENDING 13 JULY 1991		Wks
2	[1]	(EVERYTHING I DO) I DO IT FOR YOU Bryan Adams	*A&M*	3
1	2	ANY DREAM WILL DO Jason Donovan	*Really Useful*	4
-	[3]	YOU COULD BE MINE Guns N' Roses	*Geffen*	1
3	4	CHORUS Erasure	*Mute*	3
5	5	THINKING ABOUT YOUR LOVE Kenny Thomas	*Cooltempo*	7
9	[6]	ALWAYS THERE Incognito featuring Jocelyn Brown	*Talkin Loud*	3
7	7	RUSH RUSH Paula Abdul	*Virgin*	4
17	[8]	7 WAYS TO LOVE Cola Boy	*Arista*	2
30	9	NOW THAT WE'VE FOUND LOVE Heavy D & the Boyz	*MCA*	2
4	10	I WANNA SEX YOU UP Color Me Badd	*Giant*	9
6	11	DO YOU WANT ME Salt-N-Pepa	*ffrr*	7
-	[12]	ARE YOU MINE? Bros	*Columbia*	1
11	13	IT AIN'T OVER 'TIL IT'S OVER Lenny Kravitz	*Virgin*	5
22	[14]	BRING THE NOISE Anthrax featuring Chuck D	*Island*	2
14	15	THERE'S NOTHING LIKE THIS Omar	*Talkin Loud*	4
10	16	I TOUCH MYSELF Divinyls	*Virgin*	6
12	17	MOTOWN SONG Rod Stewart	*Warner Brothers*	5
33	18	THINGS THAT MAKE YOU GO HMMM... C&C Music Factory featuring Freedom Williams	*Columbia*	2
8	19	FROM A DISTANCE Bette Midler	*Atlantic*	5
26	20	UNFORGETTABLE Natalie Cole & Nat 'King' Cole	*Elektra*	3
15	21	NIGHT IN MOTION Cubic 22	*XL*	4
13	22	BABY BABY Amy Grant	*A&M*	10
16	23	REAL LOVE Driza Bone	*4th + Broadway*	4
23	24	SHERIFF FATMAN Carter The Unstoppable Sex Machine	*Big Cat*	4
35	25	MAMA Kim Appleby	*Parlophone*	2
-	26	PANDORA'S BOX Orchestral Manoeuvres In The Dark	*Virgin*	1
31	[27]	SEXUALITY Billy Bragg	*Go! Discs*	2
-	28	I LIKE IT D.J.H. featuring Stefy	*RCA*	1
32	[29]	MY NAME IS NOT SUSAN Whitney Houston	*Arista*	2
-	30	BITTER TEARS INXS	*Mercury*	1
-	31	LET THE BEAT HIT 'EM Lisa Lisa and Cult Jam	*Columbia*	1
21	32	HEY STOOPID Alice Cooper	*Epic*	3
19	33	ONLY FOOLS (NEVER FALL IN LOVE) Sonia	*IQ*	7
20	34	PEOPLE ARE STILL HAVING SEX LaTour	*Polydor*	5
37	[35]	GENERATIONS OF LOVE Jesus Loves You	*More Protein*	3
-	36	LOVE AND UNDERSTANDING Cher	*Geffen*	1
25	37	SHINY HAPPY PEOPLE R.E.M.	*Warner Brothers*	9
18	38	SHOOP SHOOP SONG (IT'S IN HIS KISS) Cher	*Epic*	13
27	39	ROLLIN 'IN MY 5.0 Vanilla Ice	*SBK*	3
24	40	GET THE FUNK OUT Extreme	*A&M*	5

August 1991

□ Highest position disc reached ● Act's first ever week on chart

LW	TW	WEEK ENDING 20 JULY 1991		Wks
1	[1]	(EVERYTHING I DO) I DO IT FOR YOU Bryan Adams	*A&M*	4
2	2	ANY DREAM WILL DO Jason Donovan	*Really Useful*	5
3	[3]	YOU COULD BE MINE Guns N' Roses	*Geffen*	2
9	4	NOW THAT WE'VE FOUND LOVE Heavy D & the Boyz	*MCA*	3
4	5	CHORUS Erasure	*Mute*	4
7	[6]	RUSH RUSH Paula Abdul	*Virgin*	5
18	7	THINGS THAT MAKE YOU GO HMMM... C&C Music Factory featuring Freedom Williams	*Columbia*	3
5	8	THINKING ABOUT YOUR LOVE Kenny Thomas	*Cooltempo*	8
6	9	ALWAYS THERE Incognito featuring Jocelyn Brown	*Talkin Loud*	4
8	10	7 WAYS TO LOVE Cola Boy	*Arista*	3
11	11	DO YOU WANT ME Salt-N-Pepa	*ffrr*	8
12	[12]	ARE YOU MINE? Bros	*Columbia*	2
26	13	PANDORA'S BOX Orchestral Manoeuvres In The Dark	*Virgin*	2
10	14	I WANNA SEX YOU UP Color Me Badd	*Giant*	10
36	15	LOVE AND UNDERSTANDING Cher	*Geffen*	2
28	[16]	I LIKE IT D.J.H. featuring Stefy	*RCA*	2
31	[17]	LET THE BEAT HIT 'EM Lisa Lisa and Cult Jam	*Columbia*	2
19	18	FROM A DISTANCE Bette Midler	*Atlantic*	6
20	[19]	UNFORGETTABLE Natalie Cole & Nat 'King' Cole	*Elektra*	4
-	[20]	(HAMMER HAMMER) THEY PUT ME IN THE MIX MC Hammer	*Capitol*	1
25	21	MAMA Kim Appleby	*Parlophone*	3
16	22	I TOUCH MYSELF Divinyls	*Virgin*	7
13	23	IT AIN'T OVER 'TIL IT'S OVER Lenny Kravitz	*Virgin*	6
17	24	MOTOWN SONG Rod Stewart	*Warner Brothers*	6
15	25	THERE'S NOTHING LIKE THIS Omar	*Talkin Loud*	5
-	[26]	I AIN'T GONNA CRY Little Angels	*Polydor*	1
14	27	BRING THE NOISE Anthrax featuring Chuck D	*Island*	3
-	28	JUST ANOTHER DREAM Cathy Dennis	*Polydor*	1
21	29	NIGHT IN MOTION Cubic 22	*XL*	5
27	30	SEXUALITY Billy Bragg	*Go! Discs*	3
23	31	REAL LOVE Driza Bone	*4th + Broadway*	5
22	32	BABY BABY Amy Grant	*A&M*	11
-	33	A BETTER LOVE Londonbeat	*Anxious*	1
30	34	BITTER TEARS INXS	*Mercury*	2
24	35	SHERIFF FATMAN Carter The Unstoppable Sex Machine	*Big Cat*	5
-	36	RIGHT HERE, RIGHT NOW Jesus Jones	*Food*	1
-	37	THE SOUND OF EDEN Shades Of Rhythm	*ZTT*	1
-	38	MONSTERS AND ANGELS Voice Of The Beehive	*London*	1
29	39	MY NAME IS NOT SUSAN Whitney Houston	*Arista*	3
-	40	INFILTRATE 202 Altern 8	*Network*	1

LW	TW	WEEK ENDING 27 JULY 1991		Wks
1	[1]	(EVERYTHING I DO) I DO IT FOR YOU Bryan Adams	*A&M*	5
4	[2]	NOW THAT WE'VE FOUND LOVE Heavy D & the Boyz	*MCA*	4
2	3	ANY DREAM WILL DO Jason Donovan	*Really Useful*	6
7	[4]	THINGS THAT MAKE YOU GO HMMM... C&C Music Factory featuring Freedom Williams	*Columbia*	4
3	5	YOU COULD BE MINE Guns N' Roses	*Geffen*	3
6	[6]	RUSH RUSH Paula Abdul	*Virgin*	6
13	[7]	PANDORA'S BOX Orchestral Manoeuvres In The Dark	*Virgin*	3
-	8	MORE THAN WORDS Extreme	*A&M*	1
-	9	MOVE ANY MOUNTAIN Shamen	*One Little Indian*	1
15	[10]	LOVE AND UNDERSTANDING Cher	*Geffen*	3
5	11	CHORUS Erasure	*Mute*	5
8	12	THINKING ABOUT YOUR LOVE Kenny Thomas	*Cooltempo*	9
28	[13]	JUST ANOTHER DREAM Cathy Dennis	*Polydor*	2
-	14	JUMP TO THE BEAT Dannii Minogue	*MCA*	1
9	15	ALWAYS THERE Incognito featuring Jocelyn Brown	*Talkin Loud*	5
16	[16]	I LIKE IT D.J.H. featuring Stefy	*RCA*	3
17	[17]	LET THE BEAT HIT 'EM Lisa Lisa and Cult Jam	*Columbia*	3
10	18	7 WAYS TO LOVE Cola Boy	*Arista*	4
21	19	MAMA Kim Appleby	*Parlophone*	4
12	20	ARE YOU MINE? Bros	*Columbia*	3
20	21	(HAMMER HAMMER) THEY PUT ME IN THE MIX MC Hammer	*Capitol*	2
11	22	DO YOU WANT ME Salt-N-Pepa	*ffrr*	9
33	[23]	A BETTER LOVE Londonbeat	*Anxious*	2
19	24	UNFORGETTABLE Natalie Cole & Nat 'King' Cole	*Elektra*	5
14	25	I WANNA SEX YOU UP Color Me Badd	*Giant*	11
-	26	THE WHISTLE SONG Frankie Knuckles	*Virgin America*	1
38	27	MONSTERS AND ANGELS Voice Of The Beehive	*London*	2
40	[28]	INFILTRATE 202 Altern 8	*Network*	2
-	29	PREGNANT FOR THE LAST TIME Morrissey	*HMV*	1
-	30	WINTER IN JULY Bomb The Bass	*Rhythm King*	1
36	[31]	RIGHT HERE, RIGHT NOW Jesus Jones	*Food*	2
18	32	FROM A DISTANCE Bette Midler	*Atlantic*	7
-	33	THE BEGINNING Seal	*ZTT*	1
-	34	TWIST AND SHOUT Deacon Blue	*Columbia*	1
37	[35]	THE SOUND OF EDEN Shades Of Rhythm	*ZTT*	2
26	36	I AIN'T GONNA CRY Little Angels	*Polydor*	2
-	37	I'M TOO SEXY Right Said Fred ●	*Tug*	1
23	38	IT AIN'T OVER 'TIL IT'S OVER Lenny Kravitz	*Virgin*	7
25	39	THERE'S NOTHING LIKE THIS Omar	*Talkin Loud*	6
-	40	HOLDING ON Beverley Craven	*Epic*	1

LW	TW	WEEK ENDING 3 AUGUST 1991		Wks
1	[1]	(EVERYTHING I DO) I DO IT FOR YOU Bryan Adams	*A&M*	6
8	[2]	MORE THAN WORDS Extreme	*A&M*	2

■1991 is the year of Sex. After Color Me Badd's number one, there are hits by Billy Bragg and LaTour, as well as Carter the Unstoppable Sex Machine. Number two hits by Salt-N-Pepa and Right Said Fred will continue the theme for the rest of the year (13.07.91) ■ Modern Technology enables Natalie Cole to duet with her long-dead but still *Unforgettable* father Nat (20.07.91)■

August 1991

□ Highest position disc reached ● Act's first ever week on chart

LW	TW	Title	Artist	Label	Wks
2	3	NOW THAT WE'VE FOUND LOVE	Heavy D & the Boyz	MCA	5
9	[4]	MOVE ANY MOUNTAIN	Shamen	One Little Indian	2
4	5	THINGS THAT MAKE YOU GO HMMM...	C&C Music Factory featuring Freedom Williams	Columbia	5
3	6	ANY DREAM WILL DO	Jason Donovan	Really Useful	7
7	[7]	PANDORA'S BOX	Orchestral Manoeuvres In The Dark	Virgin	4
14	[8]	JUMP TO THE BEAT	Dannii Minogue	MCA	2
5	9	YOU COULD BE MINE	Guns N' Roses	Geffen	4
10	[10]	LOVE AND UNDERSTANDING	Cher	Geffen	4
6	11	RUSH RUSH	Paula Abdul	Virgin	7
37	12	I'M TOO SEXY	Right Said Fred	Tug	2
13	[13]	JUST ANOTHER DREAM	Cathy Dennis	Polydor	3
30	14	WINTER IN JULY	Bomb The Bass	Rhythm King	2
34	15	TWIST AND SHOUT	Deacon Blue	Columbia	2
12	16	THINKING ABOUT YOUR LOVE	Kenny Thomas	Cooltempo	10
26	[17]	THE WHISTLE SONG	Frankie Knuckles	Virgin America	2
11	18	CHORUS	Erasure	Mute	6
16	19	I LIKE IT	D.J.H. featuring Stefy	RCA	4
15	20	ALWAYS THERE	Incognito featuring Jocelyn Brown	Talkin Loud	6
17	21	LET THE BEAT HIT 'EM	Lisa Lisa and Cult Jam	Columbia	4
19	22	MAMA	Kim Appleby	Parlophone	5
23	[23]	A BETTER LOVE	Londonbeat	Anxious	3
27	24	MONSTERS AND ANGELS	Voice Of The Beehive	London	3
29	[25]	PREGNANT FOR THE LAST TIME	Morrissey	HMV	2
-	26	SUMMERTIME	DJ Jazzy Jeff and Fresh Prince	Jive	1
-	27	ALL 4 LOVE	Color Me Badd	Giant	1
33	28	THE BEGINNING	Seal	ZTT	2
28	29	INFILTRATE 202	Altern 8	Network	3
18	30	7 WAYS TO LOVE	Cola Boy	Arista	5
25	31	I WANNA SEX YOU UP	Color Me Badd	Giant	12
24	32	UNFORGETTABLE	Natalie Cole & Nat 'King' Cole	Elektra	6
-	33	APPARENTLY NOTHIN'	Young Disciples	Talkin' Loud	1
31	34	RIGHT HERE, RIGHT NOW	Jesus Jones	Food	3
-	35	A ROLLER SKATING JAM NAMED SATURDAYS	De La Soul	Big Life	1
-	36	NO ONE CAN	Marillion	EMI	1
21	37	(HAMMER HAMMER) THEY PUT ME IN THE MIX	MC Hammer	Capitol	3
40	38	HOLDING ON	Beverley Craven	Epic	2
-	39	EVERY HEARTBEAT	Amy Grant	A&M	1
20	40	ARE YOU MINE?	Bros	Columbia	4

WEEK ENDING 10 AUGUST 1991

LW	TW	Title	Artist	Label	Wks
1	[1]	(EVERYTHING I DO) I DO IT FOR YOU	Bryan Adams	A&M	7
2	[2]	MORE THAN WORDS	Extreme	A&M	3
12	3	I'M TOO SEXY	Right Said Fred	Tug	3
4	[4]	MOVE ANY MOUNTAIN	Shamen	One Little Indian	3
-	[5]	ENTER SANDMAN	Metallica	Vertigo	1
3	6	NOW THAT WE'VE FOUND LOVE	Heavy D & the Boyz	MCA	6
14	[7]	WINTER IN JULY	Bomb The Bass	Rhythm King	3
5	8	THINGS THAT MAKE YOU GO HMMM...	C&C Music Factory featuring Freedom Williams	Columbia	6
7	9	PANDORA'S BOX	Orchestral Manoeuvres In The Dark	Virgin	5
15	[10]	TWIST AND SHOUT	Deacon Blue	Columbia	3
27	11	ALL 4 LOVE	Color Me Badd	Giant	2
6	12	ANY DREAM WILL DO	Jason Donovan	Really Useful	8
26	13	SUMMERTIME	DJ Jazzy Jeff and Fresh Prince	Jive	2
8	14	JUMP TO THE BEAT	Dannii Minogue	MCA	3
10	15	LOVE AND UNDERSTANDING	Cher	Geffen	5
13	16	JUST ANOTHER DREAM	Cathy Dennis	Polydor	4
9	17	YOU COULD BE MINE	Guns N' Roses	Geffen	5
11	18	RUSH RUSH	Paula Abdul	Virgin	8
33	19	APPARENTLY NOTHIN'	Young Disciples	Talkin' Loud	2
24	20	MONSTERS AND ANGELS	Voice Of The Beehive	London	4
16	21	THINKING ABOUT YOUR LOVE	Kenny Thomas	Cooltempo	11
35	[22]	A ROLLER SKATING JAM NAMED SATURDAYS	De La Soul	Big Life	2
17	23	THE WHISTLE SONG	Frankie Knuckles	Virgin America	3
28	[24]	THE BEGINNING	Seal	ZTT	3
19	25	I LIKE IT	D.J.H. featuring Stefy	RCA	5
-	26	BANG	Blur	Food	1
21	27	LET THE BEAT HIT 'EM	Lisa Lisa and Cult Jam	Columbia	5
39	28	EVERY HEARTBEAT	Amy Grant	A&M	2
20	29	ALWAYS THERE	Incognito featuring Jocelyn Brown	Talkin Loud	7
18	30	CHORUS	Erasure	Mute	7
23	31	A BETTER LOVE	Londonbeat	Anxious	4
38	[32]	HOLDING ON	Beverley Craven	Epic	3
-	33	SATISFACTION	Vanilla Ice	SBK	1
29	34	INFILTRATE 202	Altern 8	Network	4
-	35	LOVE'S UNKIND	Sophie Lawrence ●	IQ	1
-	36	TIME LOVE AND TENDERNESS	Michael Bolton	Columbia	1
22	37	MAMA	Kim Appleby	Parlophone	6
25	38	PREGNANT FOR THE LAST TIME	Morrissey	HMV	3
36	39	NO ONE CAN	Marillion	EMI	2
-	[40]	WORK	Technotronic featuring Reggie	ARS	1

WEEK ENDING 17 AUGUST 1991

LW	TW	Title	Artist	Label	Wks
1	[1]	(EVERYTHING I DO) I DO IT FOR YOU	Bryan Adams	A&M	8
3	[2]	I'M TOO SEXY	Right Said Fred	Tug	4
2	3	MORE THAN WORDS	Extreme	A&M	4
4	[4]	MOVE ANY MOUNTAIN	Shamen	One Little Indian	4
-	5	SET ADRIFT ON MEMORY BLISS	PM Dawn	Gee Street	1
11	6	ALL 4 LOVE	Color Me Badd	Giant	3
7	[7]	WINTER IN JULY	Bomb The Bass	Rhythm King	4
6	8	NOW THAT WE'VE FOUND LOVE	Heavy D & the Boyz	MCA	7
5	9	ENTER SANDMAN	Metallica	Vertigo	2
13	10	SUMMERTIME	DJ Jazzy Jeff and Fresh Prince	Jive	3
10	11	TWIST AND SHOUT	Deacon Blue	Columbia	4
8	12	THINGS THAT MAKE YOU GO HMMM...	C&C Music Factory featuring Freedom Williams	Columbia	7
19	[13]	APPARENTLY NOTHIN'	Young Disciples	Talkin' Loud	3
9	14	PANDORA'S BOX	Orchestral Manoeuvres In The Dark	Virgin	6
12	15	ANY DREAM WILL DO	Jason Donovan	Really Useful	9
17	16	YOU COULD BE MINE	Guns N' Roses	Geffen	6
-	17	GUARANTEED	Level 42	RCA	1
20	18	MONSTERS AND ANGELS	Voice Of The Beehive	London	5
16	19	JUST ANOTHER DREAM	Cathy Dennis	Polydor	5
15	20	LOVE AND UNDERSTANDING	Cher	Geffen	6
14	21	JUMP TO THE BEAT	Dannii Minogue	MCA	4
33	[22]	SATISFACTION	Vanilla Ice	SBK	2
22	23	A ROLLER SKATING JAM NAMED SATURDAYS	De La Soul	Big Life	3
26	[24]	BANG	Blur	Food	2
28	[25]	EVERY HEARTBEAT	Amy Grant	A&M	3
35	26	LOVE'S UNKIND	Sophie Lawrence	IQ	2
-	[27]	NEAR WILD HEAVEN	REM	Warner Brothers	1
36	[28]	TIME LOVE AND TENDERNESS	Michael Bolton	Columbia	2
18	29	RUSH RUSH	Paula Abdul	Virgin	9
-	30	ROMANTIC	Karyn White	Warner Brothers	1
-	31	COLD COLD HEART	Midge Ure	Arista	1
32	[32]	HOLDING ON	Beverley Craven	Epic	4
39	[33]	NO ONE CAN	Marillion	EMI	3
25	34	I LIKE IT	D.J.H. featuring Stefy	RCA	6
-	35	LOVE....THY WILL BE DONE	Martika	Columbia	1
24	36	THE BEGINNING	Seal	ZTT	4
-	[37]	FAMILY AFFAIR	BEF featuring Lalah Hathaway ●	Ten	1
-	[38]	IT'S ON/EGG RUSH	Flowered Up	London	1
21	39	THINKING ABOUT YOUR LOVE	Kenny Thomas	Cooltempo	12
-	[40]	STAY BEAUTIFUL	Manic Street Preachers ●	Columbia	1

WEEK ENDING 24 AUGUST 1991

LW	TW	Title	Artist	Label	Wks
1	[1]	(EVERYTHING I DO) I DO IT FOR YOU	Bryan Adams	A&M	9
2	[2]	I'M TOO SEXY	Right Said Fred	Tug	5
5	[3]	SET ADRIFT ON MEMORY BLISS	PM Dawn	Gee Street	2
3	4	MORE THAN WORDS	Extreme	A&M	5
6	[5]	ALL 4 LOVE	Color Me Badd	Giant	4
4	6	MOVE ANY MOUNTAIN	Shamen	One Little Indian	5

In these weeks ■ Yet another TV soap star hits the charts as Eastenders' Sophie Lawrence arrives in the Top 40 (10.08.91) ■ Three weeks in August at number seven for the Bomb The Bass single *Winter In July* (10.08.91) ■ For a fifth consecutive week, a new entry at number 26 (10.08.91) ■ Deacon Blue's *Twist And Shout* is not the song that brought success for the Isley Borthers and Brian Poole and the Tremeloes. *I Like It* is not the Gerry And The Pacemakers number one, but Vanilla Ice's *Satisfaction* is his version of the Rolling Stones classic (10.08.91)■

LW	TW	Title	Artist	Label	Wks
7	7	WINTER IN JULY	Bomb The Bass	Rhythm King	5
10	8	SUMMERTIME	DJ Jazzy Jeff and Fresh Prince	Jive	4
-	9	CHARLY	Prodigy ●	XL	1
8	10	NOW THAT WE'VE FOUND LOVE	Heavy D & the Boyz	MCA	8
11	11	TWIST AND SHOUT	Deacon Blue	Columbia	5
-	12	HAPPY TOGETHER	Jason Donovan	PWL	1
35	13	LOVE....THY WILL BE DONE	Martika	Columbia	2
-	14	SUNSHINE ON A RAINY DAY (REMIX)	Zoe ●	M&G	1
13	15	APPARENTLY NOTHIN'	Young Disciples	Talkin' Loud	4
12	16	THINGS THAT MAKE YOU GO HMMM...	C&C Music Factory featuring Freedom Williams	Columbia	8
18	17	MONSTERS AND ANGELS	Voice Of The Beehive	London	6
16	18	YOU COULD BE MINE	Guns N' Roses	Geffen	7
31	19	COLD COLD HEART	Midge Ure	Arista	2
17	20	GUARANTEED	Level 42	RCA	2
-	21	INSANITY	Oceanic ●	Dead Dead Good	1
26	21	LOVE'S UNKIND	Sophie Lawrence	IQ	3
30	23	ROMANTIC	Karyn White	Warner Brothers	2
14	24	PANDORA'S BOX	Orchestral Manoeuvres In The Dark	Virgin	7
25	25	EVERY HEARTBEAT	Amy Grant	A&M	4
-	26	WHAT CAN YOU DO FOR ME	Utah Saints ●	ffrr	1
15	27	ANY DREAM WILL DO	Jason Donovan	Really Useful	10
23	28	A ROLLER SKATING JAM NAMED SATURDAYS	De La Soul	Big Life	4
27	29	NEAR WILD HEAVEN	REM	Warner Brothers	2
9	30	ENTER SANDMAN	Metallica	Vertigo	3
22	31	SATISFACTION	Vanilla Ice	SBK	3
-	32	I'LL BE BACK	Arnee and the Terminaters ●	Epic	1
28	33	TIME LOVE AND TENDERNESS	Michael Bolton	Columbia	3
20	34	LOVE AND UNDERSTANDING	Cher	Geffen	7
-	35	MIND	Farm	Produce	1
24	36	BANG	Blur	Food	3
19	37	JUST ANOTHER DREAM	Cathy Dennis	Polydor	6
-	38	20TH CENTURY BOY	Marc Bolan & T. Rex	Marc On Wax	1
-	39	YOU BELONG IN ROCK N' ROLL	Tin Machine ●	London	1
-	40	LIFT/OPEN YOUR MIND	808 State	ZTT	1

WEEK ENDING 31 AUGUST 1991

LW	TW	Title	Artist	Label	Wks
1	1	(EVERYTHING I DO) I DO IT FOR YOU	Bryan Adams	A&M	10
2	2	I'M TOO SEXY	Right Said Fred	Tug	6
3	3	SET ADRIFT ON MEMORY BLISS	PM Dawn	Gee Street	3
9	4	CHARLY	Prodigy	XL	2
-	5	GETT OFF	Prince & the New Power Generation	Paisley Park	1
5	6	ALL 4 LOVE	Color Me Badd	Giant	5
4	7	MORE THAN WORDS	Extreme	A&M	6
14	8	SUNSHINE ON A RAINY DAY (REMIX)	Zoe	M&G	2
32	9	I'LL BE BACK	Arnee and the Terminaters	Epic	2
12	10	HAPPY TOGETHER	Jason Donovan	PWL	2
21	11	INSANITY	Oceanic	Dead Dead Good	2
13	12	LOVE....THY WILL BE DONE	Martika	Columbia	3
-	13	STAND BY LOVE	Simple Minds	Virgin	1
8	14	SUMMERTIME	DJ Jazzy Jeff and Fresh Prince	Jive	5
7	15	WINTER IN JULY	Bomb The Bass	Rhythm King	6
6	16	MOVE ANY MOUNTAIN	Shamen	One Little Indian	6
19	17	COLD COLD HEART	Midge Ure	Arista	3
26	18	WHAT CAN YOU DO FOR ME	Utah Saints	ffrr	2
10	19	NOW THAT WE'VE FOUND LOVE	Heavy D & the Boyz	MCA	9
38	20	20TH CENTURY BOY	Marc Bolan & T. Rex	Marc On Wax	2
-	21	CALLING ELVIS	Dire Straits	Vertigo	1
11	22	TWIST AND SHOUT	Deacon Blue	Columbia	6
18	23	YOU COULD BE MINE	Guns N' Roses	Geffen	8
-	24	LET'S TALK ABOUT SEX	Salt-N-Pepa	ffrr	1
17	25	MONSTERS AND ANGELS	Voice Of The Beehive	London	7
21	26	LOVE'S UNKIND	Sophie Lawrence	IQ	4
16	27	THINGS THAT MAKE YOU GO HMMM...	C&C Music Factory featuring Freedom Williams	Columbia	9
-	28	LIES	EMF	Parlophone	1
-	29	GOOD VIBRATIONS	Marky Mark & the Funky Bunch featuring Loleatta Holloway ●	Interscope	1
15	30	APPARENTLY NOTHIN'	Young Disciples	Talkin' Loud	5
35	31	MIND	Farm	Produce	2
23	32	ROMANTIC	Karyn White	Warner Brothers	3
39	33	YOU BELONG IN ROCK N' ROLL	Tin Machine	London	2

September 1991

□ Highest position disc reached ● Act's first ever week on chart

LW	TW	Title	Artist	Label	Wks
-	34	BE YOUNG BE FOOLISH BE HAPPY	Sonia	IQ	1
25	35	EVERY HEARTBEAT	Amy Grant	A&M	5
-	36	HOUSECALL	Shabba Ranks featuring Maxi Priest ●	Epic	1
-	37	REPUBLICAN PARTY REPTILE (EP)	Big Country	Vertigo	1
40	38	LIFT/OPEN YOUR MIND	808 State	ZTT	2
-	39	HARD TO HANDLE	Black Crowes ●	Def American	1
-	40	SOMETIMES IT'S A BITCH	Stevie Nicks	EMI	1

WEEK ENDING 7 SEPTEMBER 1991

LW	TW	Title	Artist	Label	Wks
1	1	(EVERYTHING I DO) I DO IT FOR YOU	Bryan Adams	A&M	11
2	2	I'M TOO SEXY	Right Said Fred	Tug	7
4	3	CHARLY	Prodigy	XL	3
5	4	GETT OFF	Prince & the New Power Generation	Paisley Park	2
9	5	I'LL BE BACK	Arnee and the Terminaters	Epic	3
8	6	SUNSHINE ON A RAINY DAY (REMIX)	Zoe	M&G	3
3	7	SET ADRIFT ON MEMORY BLISS	PM Dawn	Gee Street	4
11	8	INSANITY	Oceanic	Dead Dead Good	3
12	9	LOVE....THY WILL BE DONE	Martika	Columbia	4
6	10	ALL 4 LOVE	Color Me Badd	Giant	6
7	11	MORE THAN WORDS	Extreme	A&M	7
10	12	HAPPY TOGETHER	Jason Donovan	PWL	3
24	13	LET'S TALK ABOUT SEX	Salt-N-Pepa	ffrr	2
18	14	WHAT CAN YOU DO FOR ME	Utah Saints	ffrr	3
20	15	20TH CENTURY BOY	Marc Bolan & T. Rex	Marc On Wax	3
29	16	GOOD VIBRATIONS	Marky Mark & the Funky Bunch featuring Loleatta Holloway	Interscope	2
14	17	SUMMERTIME	DJ Jazzy Jeff and Fresh Prince	Jive	6
-	18	THE WORD IS OUT	Kylie Minogue	PWL	1
17	19	COLD COLD HEART	Midge Ure	Arista	4
16	20	MOVE ANY MOUNTAIN	Shamen	One Little Indian	7
13	21	STAND BY LOVE	Simple Minds	Virgin	2
15	22	WINTER IN JULY	Bomb The Bass	Rhythm King	7
19	23	NOW THAT WE'VE FOUND LOVE	Heavy D & the Boyz	MCA	10
34	24	BE YOUNG BE FOOLISH BE HAPPY	Sonia	IQ	2
-	25	HEARTHAMMER (EP)	Runrig ●	Chrysalis	1
-	26	THE BIG L	Roxette	EMI	1
21	27	CALLING ELVIS	Dire Straits	Vertigo	2
22	28	TWIST AND SHOUT	Deacon Blue	Columbia	7
-	29	MAKIN' HAPPY	Crystal Waters	A&M	1
28	30	LIES	EMF	Parlophone	2
-	31	PEACE	Sabrina Johnston ●	East West	1
-	32	PRIMAL SCREAM	Motley Crue	Elektra	1
36	33	HOUSECALL	Shabba Ranks featuring Maxi Priest	Epic	2
23	34	YOU COULD BE MINE	Guns N' Roses	Geffen	9
31	35	MIND	Farm	Produce	3
27	36	THINGS THAT MAKE YOU GO HMMM...	C&C Music Factory featuring Freedom Williams	Columbia	10
-	37	CAN'T GIVE YOU MORE	Status Quo	Vertigo	1
25	38	MONSTERS AND ANGELS	Voice Of The Beehive	London	8
-	39	JET CITY WOMAN	Queensryche	EMI	1
-	40	EVERYBODY'S FREE (TO FEEL GOOD)	Rozalla ●	Pulse-8	1

WEEK ENDING 14 SEPTEMBER 1991

LW	TW	Title	Artist	Label	Wks
1	1	(EVERYTHING I DO) I DO IT FOR YOU	Bryan Adams	A&M	12
2	2	I'M TOO SEXY	Right Said Fred	Tug	8
3	3	CHARLY	Prodigy	XL	4
6	4	SUNSHINE ON A RAINY DAY (REMIX)	Zoe	M&G	4
8	5	INSANITY	Oceanic	Dead Dead Good	4
4	6	GETT OFF	Prince & the New Power Generation	Paisley Park	3
13	7	LET'S TALK ABOUT SEX	Salt-N-Pepa	ffrr	3
5	8	I'LL BE BACK	Arnee and the Terminaters	Epic	4
9	9	LOVE....THY WILL BE DONE	Martika	Columbia	5
7	10	SET ADRIFT ON MEMORY BLISS	PM Dawn	Gee Street	5
14	11	WHAT CAN YOU DO FOR ME	Utah Saints	ffrr	4
10	12	ALL 4 LOVE	Color Me Badd	Giant	7
15	13	20TH CENTURY BOY	Marc Bolan & T. Rex	Marc On Wax	4

■After several near misses, David Bowie's Tin Machine finally reach the Top 40, but do not climb very far (31.08.91) ■ Two records at number 21 equal (24.08.91) ■ For three consecutive weeks, new entries peak at both 37 and 39 (31.08.91) ■ Two Top Ten hits for Prince, as he also has a hand in writing and producing Martika's *Love ... Thy Will Be Done* (07.09.91)■

September 1991

□ Highest position disc reached ● Act's first ever week on chart

LW	TW	Title / Artist	Label	Wks
16	[14]	GOOD VIBRATIONS Marky Mark & the Funky Bunch featuring Loleatta Holloway	Interscope	3
11	15	MORE THAN WORDS Extreme	A&M	8
18	[16]	THE WORD IS OUT Kylie Minogue	PWL	2
31	17	PEACE Sabrina Johnston	East West	2
29	[18]	MAKIN' HAPPY Crystal Waters	A&M	2
12	19	HAPPY TOGETHER Jason Donovan	PWL	4
-	[20]	I WANNA BE ADORED Stone Roses	Silvertone	1
26	[21]	THE BIG L Roxette	EMI	2
24	[22]	BE YOUNG BE FOOLISH BE HAPPY Sonia	IQ	3
-	[23]	MORE TO LIFE Cliff Richard	EMI	1
20	24	MOVE ANY MOUNTAIN Shamen	One Little Indian	8
-	25	CAN'T STOP THIS THING WE STARTED Bryan Adams	A&M	1
40	26	EVERYBODY'S FREE (TO FEEL GOOD) Rozalla	Pulse-8	2
25	27	HEARTHAMMER (EP) Runrig	Chrysalis	2
-	28	SUCH A FEELING Bizarre Inc ●	Vinyl Solution	1
19	29	COLD COLD HEART Midge Ure	Arista	5
22	30	WINTER IN JULY Bomb The Bass	Rhythm King	8
33	[31]	HOUSECALL Shabba Ranks featuring Maxi Priest	Epic	3
17	32	SUMMERTIME DJ Jazzy Jeff and Fresh Prince	Jive	7
-	33	SALTWATER Julian Lennon	Virgin	1
-	34	SUCH A GOOD FEELING Brothers In Rhythm ●	4th + Broadway	1
23	35	NOW THAT WE'VE FOUND LOVE Heavy D & the Boyz	MCA	11
-	[36]	DOMINATOR Human Resource ●	R&S	1
-	[37]	MAKE IT TONIGHT Wet Wet Wet	Precious	1
-	38	BRIDGE OVER TROUBLED WATER PJB featuring Hannah & her Sisters ●	Dance Pool	1
-	[39]	ONLY LOVE CAN BREAK YOUR HEART St. Etienne ●	Heavenly	1
-	[40]	WILD HEARTED SON Cult	Beggars Banquet	1

WEEK ENDING 21 SEPTEMBER 1991

LW	TW	Title / Artist	Label	Wks
1	[1]	(EVERYTHING I DO) I DO IT FOR YOU Bryan Adams	A&M	13
2	[2]	I'M TOO SEXY Right Said Fred	Tug	9
7	3	LET'S TALK ABOUT SEX Salt-N-Pepa	ffrr	4
5	4	INSANITY Oceanic	Dead Dead Good	5
4	5	SUNSHINE ON A RAINY DAY (REMIX) Zoe	M&G	5
3	6	CHARLY Prodigy	XL	5
-	7	LOVE TO HATE YOU Erasure	Mute	1
-	[8]	DON'T CRY Guns N' Roses	Geffen	1
17	9	PEACE Sabrina Johnston	East West	3
11	[10]	WHAT CAN YOU DO FOR ME Utah Saints	ffrr	5
6	11	GETT OFF Prince & the New Power Generation	Paisley Park	4
9	12	LOVE....THY WILL BE DONE Martika	Columbia	6
26	13	EVERYBODY'S FREE (TO FEEL GOOD) Rozalla	Pulse-8	3
8	14	I'LL BE BACK Arnee and the Terminaters	Epic	5
13	15	20TH CENTURY BOY Marc Bolan & T. Rex	Marc On Wax	5
-	16	SOMETHING GOT ME STARTED Simply Red	East West	1
14	17	GOOD VIBRATIONS Marky Mark & the Funky Bunch featuring Loleatta Holloway	Interscope	4
25	18	CAN'T STOP THIS THING WE STARTED Bryan Adams	A&M	2
-	19	CREAM Prince & the New Power Generation	Paisley Park	1
28	20	SUCH A FEELING Bizarre Inc	Vinyl Solution	2
-	[21]	TRUST Ned's Atomic Dustbin	Furtive	1
18	22	MAKIN' HAPPY Crystal Waters	A&M	3
10	23	SET ADRIFT ON MEMORY BLISS PM Dawn	Gee Street	6
23	24	MORE TO LIFE Cliff Richard	EMI	2
34	25	SUCH A GOOD FEELING Brothers In Rhythm	4th + Broadway	2
15	26	MORE THAN WORDS Extreme	A&M	9
21	27	THE BIG L Roxette	EMI	3
-	28	THE ONE I LOVE REM	IRS	1
33	29	SALTWATER Julian Lennon	Virgin	2
12	30	ALL 4 LOVE Color Me Badd	Giant	8
-	31	NUTBUSH CITY LIMITS (90s VERSION) Tina Turner	Capitol	1
38	32	BRIDGE OVER TROUBLED WATER PJB featuring Hannah & her Sisters	Dance Pool	2
16	33	THE WORD IS OUT Kylie Minogue	PWL	3
20	34	I WANNA BE ADORED Stone Roses	Silvertone	2
31	35	HOUSECALL Shabba Ranks featuring Maxi Priest	Epic	4
22	36	BE YOUNG BE FOOLISH BE HAPPY Sonia	IQ	4
36	37	DOMINATOR Human Resource	R&S	2
-	38	TRY Bros	Columbia	1
37	39	MAKE IT TONIGHT Wet Wet Wet	Precious	2
19	40	HAPPY TOGETHER Jason Donovan	PWL	5

WEEK ENDING 28 SEPTEMBER 1991

LW	TW	Title / Artist	Label	Wks
1	[1]	(EVERYTHING I DO) I DO IT FOR YOU Bryan Adams	A&M	14
3	[2]	LET'S TALK ABOUT SEX Salt-N-Pepa	ffrr	5
4	[3]	INSANITY Oceanic	Dead Dead Good	6
7	[4]	LOVE TO HATE YOU Erasure	Mute	2
2	5	I'M TOO SEXY Right Said Fred	Tug	10
5	6	SUNSHINE ON A RAINY DAY (REMIX) Zoe	M&G	6
13	7	EVERYBODY'S FREE (TO FEEL GOOD) Rozalla	Pulse-8	4
9	[8]	PEACE Sabrina Johnston	East West	4
6	9	CHARLY Prodigy	XL	6
10	[10]	WHAT CAN YOU DO FOR ME Utah Saints	ffrr	6
16	[11]	SOMETHING GOT ME STARTED Simply Red	East West	2
18	[12]	CAN'T STOP THIS THING WE STARTED Bryan Adams	A&M	3
29	13	SALTWATER Julian Lennon	Virgin	3
20	14	SUCH A FEELING Bizarre Inc	Vinyl Solution	3
19	[15]	CREAM Prince & the New Power Generation	Paisley Park	2
25	16	SUCH A GOOD FEELING Brothers In Rhythm	4th + Broadway	3
8	17	DON'T CRY Guns N' Roses	Geffen	2
11	18	GETT OFF Prince & the New Power Generation	Paisley Park	5
-	19	WIND OF CHANGE Scorpions	Vertigo	1
28	20	THE ONE I LOVE REM	IRS	2
12	21	LOVE....THY WILL BE DONE Martika	Columbia	7
15	22	20TH CENTURY BOY Marc Bolan & T. Rex	Marc On Wax	6
31	[23]	NUTBUSH CITY LIMITS (90s VERSION) Tina Turner	Capitol	2
-	24	JACKY Marc Almond	Some Bizzare	1
32	25	BRIDGE OVER TROUBLED WATER PJB featuring Hannah & her Sisters	Dance Pool	3
14	26	I'LL BE BACK Arnee and the Terminaters	Epic	6
17	27	GOOD VIBRATIONS Marky Mark & the Funky Bunch featuring Loleatta Holloway	Interscope	5
22	28	MAKIN' HAPPY Crystal Waters	A&M	4
21	29	TRUST Ned's Atomic Dustbin	Furtive	2
27	30	THE BIG L Roxette	EMI	4
24	31	MORE TO LIFE Cliff Richard	EMI	3
-	32	LIVE YOUR LIFE BE FREE Belinda Carlisle	Virgin	1
38	33	TRY Bros	Columbia	2
26	34	MORE THAN WORDS Extreme	A&M	10
-	35	NO MORE TEARS Ozzy Osbourne	Epic	1
23	36	SET ADRIFT ON MEMORY BLISS PM Dawn	Gee Street	7
-	[37]	INTERNAL EXILE Fish	Polydor	1
-	38	I THINK I LOVE YOU Voice Of The Beehive	London	1
-	[39]	FEEL EVERY BEAT Electronic	Factory	1
30	40	ALL 4 LOVE Color Me Badd	Giant	9

WEEK ENDING 5 OCTOBER 1991

LW	TW	Title / Artist	Label	Wks
1	[1]	(EVERYTHING I DO) I DO IT FOR YOU Bryan Adams	A&M	15
2	[2]	LET'S TALK ABOUT SEX Salt-N-Pepa	ffrr	6
3	[3]	INSANITY Oceanic	Dead Dead Good	7
4	[4]	LOVE TO HATE YOU Erasure	Mute	3
19	5	WIND OF CHANGE Scorpions	Vertigo	2
7	[6]	EVERYBODY'S FREE (TO FEEL GOOD) Rozalla	Pulse-8	5
5	7	I'M TOO SEXY Right Said Fred	Tug	11
8	[8]	PEACE Sabrina Johnston	East West	5
6	9	SUNSHINE ON A RAINY DAY (REMIX) Zoe	M&G	7
13	10	SALTWATER Julian Lennon	Virgin	4
11	[11]	SOMETHING GOT ME STARTED Simply Red	East West	3
10	12	WHAT CAN YOU DO FOR ME Utah Saints	ffrr	7
14	[13]	SUCH A FEELING Bizarre Inc	Vinyl Solution	4
16	[14]	SUCH A GOOD FEELING Brothers In Rhythm	4th + Broadway	4
12	15	CAN'T STOP THIS THING WE STARTED Bryan Adams	A&M	4
20	[16]	THE ONE I LOVE REM	IRS	3
24	[17]	JACKY Marc Almond	Some Bizzare	2
9	18	CHARLY Prodigy	XL	7
15	19	CREAM Prince & the New Power Generation	Paisley Park	3

In these weeks ■ Right Said Fred complete six weeks at number two, equalling the record set in the 70s by Father Abraham and the Smurfs and the Brighouse and Rastrick Brass Band (21.09.91) ■ This is the week in which Bryan Adams passes the previous record of 11 consecutive weeks at number one, set by Slim Whitman's *Rose Marie* in 1955 (28.09.91) ■ In the same week, Bryan Adams' follow-up peaks at number 12. *Everything I Do* remains his only Top Ten hit (28.09.91)■

LW	TW	Title	Artist	Label	Wks
32	20	LIVE YOUR LIFE BE FREE	Belinda Carlisle	*Virgin*	2
25	21	BRIDGE OVER TROUBLED WATER	PJB featuring Hannah & her Sisters	*Dance Pool*	4
-	22	BEST OF YOU	Kenny Thomas	*Cooltempo*	1
23	23	NUTBUSH CITY LIMITS (90s VERSION)	Tina Turner	*Capitol*	3
18	24	GETT OFF	Prince & the New Power Generation	*Paisley Park*	6
38	25	I THINK I LOVE YOU	Voice Of The Beehive	*London*	2
21	26	LOVE....THY WILL BE DONE	Martika	*Columbia*	8
33	27	TRY	Bros	*Columbia*	3
22	28	20TH CENTURY BOY	Marc Bolan & T. Rex	*Marc On Wax*	7
17	29	DON'T CRY	Guns N' Roses	*Geffen*	3
-	30	ALWAYS LOOK ON THE BRIGHT SIDE OF LIFE	Monty Python's Flying Circus ●	*Virgin*	1
-	31	I WANT YOU (FOREVER)	DJ Carl Cox ●	*Perfecto*	1
35	32	NO MORE TEARS	Ozzy Osbourne	*Epic*	2
-	33	LIVE FOR LOVING YOU	Gloria Estefan	*Epic*	1
-	34	DRY LAND	Marillion	*EMI*	1
-	35	WORLD IN UNION	Kiri Te Kanawa ●	*Columbia*	1
-	36	GET READY FOR THIS	2 Unlimited ●	*PWL Continental*	1
-	37	TOO MANY WALLS	Cathy Dennis	*Polydor*	1
-	38	LOVE'S A LOADED GUN	Alice Cooper	*Epic*	1
-	39	DON'T LET THE SUN GO DOWN ON ME	Oleta Adams	*Fontana*	1
39	40	FEEL EVERY BEAT	Electronic	*Factory*	2

WEEK ENDING 12 OCTOBER 1991

LW	TW	Title	Artist	Label	Wks
1	1	(EVERYTHING I DO) I DO IT FOR YOU	Bryan Adams	*A&M*	16
5	2	WIND OF CHANGE	Scorpions	*Vertigo*	3
3	3	INSANITY	Oceanic	*Dead Dead Good*	8
2	4	LET'S TALK ABOUT SEX	Salt-N-Pepa	*ffrr*	7
4	5	LOVE TO HATE YOU	Erasure	*Mute*	4
10	6	SALTWATER	Julian Lennon	*Virgin*	5
6	7	EVERYBODY'S FREE (TO FEEL GOOD)	Rozalla	*Pulse-8*	6
30	8	ALWAYS LOOK ON THE BRIGHT SIDE OF LIFE	Monty Python's Flying Circus	*Virgin*	2
7	9	I'M TOO SEXY	Right Said Fred	*Tug*	12
8	10	PEACE	Sabrina Johnston	*East West*	6
35	11	WORLD IN UNION	Kiri Te Kanawa	*Columbia*	2
9	12	SUNSHINE ON A RAINY DAY (REMIX)	Zoe	*M&G*	8
22	13	BEST OF YOU	Kenny Thomas	*Cooltempo*	2
20	14	LIVE YOUR LIFE BE FREE	Belinda Carlisle	*Virgin*	3
13	15	SUCH A FEELING	Bizarre Inc	*Vinyl Solution*	5
11	16	SOMETHING GOT ME STARTED	Simply Red	*East West*	4
14	17	SUCH A GOOD FEELING	Brothers In Rhythm	*4th + Broadway*	5
17	18	JACKY	Marc Almond	*Some Bizzare*	3
36	19	GET READY FOR THIS	2 Unlimited	*PWL Continental*	2
12	20	WHAT CAN YOU DO FOR ME	Utah Saints	*ffrr*	8
21	21	BRIDGE OVER TROUBLED WATER	PJB featuring Hannah & her Sisters	*Dance Pool*	5
-	22	CAN'T TRUSS IT	Public Enemy	*Def Jam*	1
16	23	THE ONE I LOVE	REM	*IRS*	4
31	24	I WANT YOU (FOREVER)	DJ Carl Cox	*Perfecto*	2
25	25	I THINK I LOVE YOU	Voice Of The Beehive	*London*	3
15	26	CAN'T STOP THIS THING WE STARTED	Bryan Adams	*A&M*	5
37	27	TOO MANY WALLS	Cathy Dennis	*Polydor*	2
19	28	CREAM	Prince & the New Power Generation	*Paisley Park*	4
-	29	MY LOVE LIFE	Morrissey	*HMV*	1
23	30	NUTBUSH CITY LIMITS (90s VERSION)	Tina Turner	*Capitol*	4
18	31	CHARLY	Prodigy	*XL*	8
-	32	EMOTIONS	Mariah Carey	*Columbia*	1
39	33	DON'T LET THE SUN GO DOWN ON ME	Oleta Adams	*Fontana*	2
33	34	LIVE FOR LOVING YOU	Gloria Estefan	*Epic*	2
-	35	WALKING IN MEMPHIS	Marc Cohn ●	*Atlantic*	1
-	36	DECADENCE DANCE	Extreme	*A&M*	1
-	37	FINALLY	Ce Ce Peniston ●	*A&M*	1
38	38	LOVE'S A LOADED GUN	Alice Cooper	*Epic*	2
24	39	GETT OFF	Prince & the New Power Generation	*Paisley Park*	7
27	40	TRY	Bros	*Columbia*	4

WEEK ENDING 19 OCTOBER 1991

October 1991

□ Highest position disc reached ● Act's first ever week on chart

LW	TW	Title	Artist	Label	Wks
1	1	(EVERYTHING I DO) I DO IT FOR YOU	Bryan Adams	*A&M*	17
2	2	WIND OF CHANGE	Scorpions	*Vertigo*	4
8	3	ALWAYS LOOK ON THE BRIGHT SIDE OF LIFE	Monty Python's Flying Circus	*Virgin*	3
11	4	WORLD IN UNION	Kiri Te Kanawa	*Columbia*	3
3	5	INSANITY	Oceanic	*Dead Dead Good*	9
19	6	GET READY FOR THIS	2 Unlimited	*PWL Continental*	3
6	7	SALTWATER	Julian Lennon	*Virgin*	6
4	8	LET'S TALK ABOUT SEX	Salt-N-Pepa	*ffrr*	8
5	9	LOVE TO HATE YOU	Erasure	*Mute*	5
7	10	EVERYBODY'S FREE (TO FEEL GOOD)	Rozalla	*Pulse-8*	7
13	11	BEST OF YOU	Kenny Thomas	*Cooltempo*	3
14	12	LIVE YOUR LIFE BE FREE	Belinda Carlisle	*Virgin*	4
9	13	I'M TOO SEXY	Right Said Fred	*Tug*	13
-	14	CHANGE	Lisa Stansfield	*Arista*	1
-	15	BABY LOVE	Dannii Minogue	*MCA*	1
15	16	SUCH A FEELING	Bizarre Inc	*Vinyl Solution*	6
27	17	TOO MANY WALLS	Cathy Dennis	*Polydor*	3
18	18	JACKY	Marc Almond	*Some Bizzare*	4
10	19	PEACE	Sabrina Johnston	*East West*	7
12	20	SUNSHINE ON A RAINY DAY (REMIX)	Zoe	*M&G*	9
16	21	SOMETHING GOT ME STARTED	Simply Red	*East West*	5
35	22	WALKING IN MEMPHIS	Marc Cohn	*Atlantic*	2
24	23	I WANT YOU (FOREVER)	DJ Carl Cox	*Perfecto*	3
17	24	SUCH A GOOD FEELING	Brothers In Rhythm	*4th + Broadway*	6
32	25	EMOTIONS	Mariah Carey	*Columbia*	2
-	26	GO	Moby ●	*Outer Rhythm*	1
-	27	CARIBBEAN BLUE	Enya	*WEA*	1
25	28	I THINK I LOVE YOU	Voice Of The Beehive	*London*	4
20	29	WHAT CAN YOU DO FOR ME	Utah Saints	*ffrr*	9
22	30	CAN'T TRUSS IT	Public Enemy	*Def Jam*	2
21	31	BRIDGE OVER TROUBLED WATER	PJB featuring Hannah & her Sisters	*Dance Pool*	6
37	32	FINALLY	Ce Ce Peniston	*A&M*	2
-	33	RADIO WALL OF SOUND	Slade	*Polydor*	1
-	34	AMERICAN PIE	Don McLean	*Liberty*	1
33	35	DON'T LET THE SUN GO DOWN ON ME	Oleta Adams	*Fontana*	3
-	36	NOCTURNE	T99	*Emphasis*	1
-	37	SAVE UP ALL YOUR TEARS	Cher	*Geffen*	1
23	38	THE ONE I LOVE	REM	*IRS*	5
-	39	SWING LOW (RUN WITH THE BALL)	Union featuring England World Cup Rugby Squad ●	*Columbia*	1
-	40	WOMAN TO WOMAN	Beverley Craven	*Epic*	1

WEEK ENDING 26 OCTOBER 1991

LW	TW	Title	Artist	Label	Wks
1	1	(EVERYTHING I DO) I DO IT FOR YOU	Bryan Adams	*A&M*	18
6	2	GET READY FOR THIS	2 Unlimited	*PWL Continental*	4
2	3	WIND OF CHANGE	Scorpions	*Vertigo*	5
4	4	WORLD IN UNION	Kiri Te Kanawa	*Columbia*	4
3	5	ALWAYS LOOK ON THE BRIGHT SIDE OF LIFE	Monty Python's Flying Circus	*Virgin*	4
-	6	DIZZY	Vic Reeves & the Wonder Stuff ●	*Sense*	1
5	7	INSANITY	Oceanic	*Dead Dead Good*	10
7	8	SALTWATER	Julian Lennon	*Virgin*	7
8	9	LET'S TALK ABOUT SEX	Salt-N-Pepa	*ffrr*	9
14	10	CHANGE	Lisa Stansfield	*Arista*	2
26	11	GO	Moby	*Outer Rhythm*	2
10	12	EVERYBODY'S FREE (TO FEEL GOOD)	Rozalla	*Pulse-8*	8
-	13	DJ CULTURE	Pet Shop Boys	*Parlophone*	1
15	14	BABY LOVE	Dannii Minogue	*MCA*	2
27	15	CARIBBEAN BLUE	Enya	*WEA*	2
-	16	AFTER THE WATERSHED	Carter The Unstoppable Sex Machine	*Big Cat*	1
9	17	LOVE TO HATE YOU	Erasure	*Mute*	6
17	18	TOO MANY WALLS	Cathy Dennis	*Polydor*	4
-	19	THE SHOW MUST GO ON	Queen	*Parlophone*	1
11	20	BEST OF YOU	Kenny Thomas	*Cooltempo*	4
33	21	RADIO WALL OF SOUND	Slade	*Polydor*	2
12	22	LIVE YOUR LIFE BE FREE	Belinda Carlisle	*Virgin*	5
25	23	EMOTIONS	Mariah Carey	*Columbia*	3

■19 records in the Top 40 at their chart peak (05.10.91) ■ Bryan Adams completes a record-shattering sixteen weeks at the top, the longest consecutive run ever recorded (26.10.91) ■ The Rugby Union World Cup, held in Britain and France, gives Dame Kiri Te Kanawa a number four hit with the ITV theme, and brings the England World Cup Squad chart glory to go with their runners-up medals (19.10.91)■

October 1991

□ Highest position disc reached ● Act's first ever week on chart

13 24 I'M TOO SEXY Right Said Fred .... *Tug* 14
16 25 SUCH A FEELING Bizarre Inc .... *Vinyl Solution* 7
- [26] 40 MILES Congress ● .... *Inner Rhythm* 1
22 27 WALKING IN MEMPHIS Marc Cohn .... *Atlantic* 3
34 28 AMERICAN PIE Don McLean .... *Liberty* 2
32 [29] FINALLY Ce Ce Peniston .... *A&M* 3
23 30 I WANT YOU (FOREVER) DJ Carl Cox .... *Perfecto* 4
20 31 SUNSHINE ON A RAINY DAY (REMIX) Zoe .... *M&G* 10
- 32 DON'T DREAM IT'S OVER Paul Young .... *Columbia* 1
36 [33] NOCTURNE T99 .... *Emphasis* 2
18 34 JACKY Marc Almond .... *Some Bizzare* 5
19 35 PEACE Sabrina Johnston .... *East West* 8
- 36 REAL LIFE Simple Minds .... *Virgin* 1
21 37 SOMETHING GOT ME STARTED Simply Red .... *East West* 6
24 38 SUCH A GOOD FEELING Brothers In Rhythm ..... *4th + Broadway* 7
37 39 SAVE UP ALL YOUR TEARS Cher .... *Geffen* 2
- [40] THIS HOUSE Alison Moyet .... *Columbia* 1

LW TW *WEEK ENDING* **2 NOVEMBER 1991** Wks

- [1] THE FLY U2 .... *Island* 1
6 2 DIZZY Vic Reeves & the Wonder Stuff .... *Sense* 2
2 3 GET READY FOR THIS 2 Unlimited .... *PWL Continental* 5
1 4 (EVERYTHING I DO) I DO IT FOR YOU Bryan Adams ...... *A&M* 19
4 5 WORLD IN UNION Kiri Te Kanawa .... *Columbia* 5
3 6 WIND OF CHANGE Scorpions .... *Vertigo* 6
5 7 ALWAYS LOOK ON THE BRIGHT SIDE OF LIFE Monty Python's Flying Circus .... *Virgin* 5
7 8 INSANITY Oceanic .... *Dead Dead Good* 11
- 9 NO SON OF MINE Genesis .... *Virgin* 1
11 [10] GO Moby .... *Outer Rhythm* 3
16 [11] AFTER THE WATERSHED Carter The Unstoppable Sex Machine .... *Big Cat* 2
10 12 CHANGE Lisa Stansfield .... *Arista* 3
15 [13] CARIBBEAN BLUE Enya .... *WEA* 3
9 14 LET'S TALK ABOUT SEX Salt-N-Pepa .... *ffrr* 10
8 15 SALTWATER Julian Lennon .... *Virgin* 8
19 [16] THE SHOW MUST GO ON Queen .... *Parlophone* 2
28 17 AMERICAN PIE Don McLean .... *Liberty* 3
23 18 EMOTIONS Mariah Carey .... *Columbia* 4
- 19 IF YOU WERE WITH ME NOW Kylie Minogue and Keith Washington ● .... *PWL* 1
32 [20] DON'T DREAM IT'S OVER Paul Young .... *Columbia* 2
14 21 BABY LOVE Dannii Minogue .... *MCA* 3
13 22 DJ CULTURE Pet Shop Boys .... *Parlophone* 2
21 23 RADIO WALL OF SOUND Slade .... *Polydor* 3
- 24 DJS TAKE CONTROL/WAY IN MY BRAIN SL2 ● .... *XL* 1
12 25 EVERYBODY'S FREE (TO FEEL GOOD) Rozalla *Pulse-8* 9
26 [26] 40 MILES Congress .... *Inner Rhythm* 2
18 27 TOO MANY WALLS Cathy Dennis .... *Polydor* 5
- 28 SHINING STAR INXS .... *Mercury* 1
17 29 LOVE TO HATE YOU Erasure .... *Mute* 7
29 30 FINALLY Ce Ce Peniston .... *A&M* 4
24 31 I'M TOO SEXY Right Said Fred .... *Tug* 15
22 32 LIVE YOUR LIFE BE FREE Belinda Carlisle .... *Virgin* 6
20 33 BEST OF YOU Kenny Thomas .... *Cooltempo* 5
36 [34] REAL LIFE Simple Minds .... *Virgin* 2
33 35 NOCTURNE T99 .... *Emphasis* 3
27 36 WALKING IN MEMPHIS Marc Cohn .... *Atlantic* 4
- [37] LIGHTNING Zoe .... *M&G* 1
25 38 SUCH A FEELING Bizarre Inc .... *Vinyl Solution* 8
37 39 SOMETHING GOT ME STARTED Simply Red .... *East West* 7
- 40 DANCE WITH ME (I'M YOUR ECSTASY) Control ● .... *All Around The World* 1

LW TW *WEEK ENDING* **9 NOVEMBER 1991** Wks

2 [1] DIZZY Vic Reeves & the Wonder Stuff .... *Sense* 3
1 2 THE FLY U2 .... *Island* 2
3 3 GET READY FOR THIS 2 Unlimited .... *PWL Continental* 6
4 4 (EVERYTHING I DO) I DO IT FOR YOU Bryan Adams ...... *A&M* 20
5 5 WORLD IN UNION Kiri Te Kanawa .... *Columbia* 6
9 [6] NO SON OF MINE Genesis .... *Virgin* 2
19 7 IF YOU WERE WITH ME NOW Kylie Minogue and Keith Washington .... *PWL* 2
- 8 RHYTHM IS A MYSTERY K-Klass ● .... *deConstruction* 1
7 9 ALWAYS LOOK ON THE BRIGHT SIDE OF LIFE Monty Python's Flying Circus .... *Virgin* 6
6 10 WIND OF CHANGE Scorpions .... *Vertigo* 7
24 [11] DJS TAKE CONTROL/WAY IN MY BRAIN SL2 .... *XL* 2
17 [12] AMERICAN PIE Don McLean .... *Liberty* 4
10 13 GO Moby .... *Outer Rhythm* 4
8 14 INSANITY Oceanic .... *Dead Dead Good* 12
13 15 CARIBBEAN BLUE Enya .... *WEA* 4
11 16 AFTER THE WATERSHED Carter The Unstoppable Sex Machine .... *Big Cat* 3
18 [17] EMOTIONS Mariah Carey .... *Columbia* 5
- 18 IT'S GRIM UP NORTH Justified Ancients Of Mu Mu ● .... *KLF Communications* 1
- 19 SWING LOW (RUN WITH THE BALL) Union featuring England World Cup Rugby Squad .... *Columbia* 2
12 20 CHANGE Lisa Stansfield .... *Arista* 4
14 21 LET'S TALK ABOUT SEX Salt-N-Pepa .... *ffrr* 11
20 22 DON'T DREAM IT'S OVER Paul Young .... *Columbia* 3
16 23 THE SHOW MUST GO ON Queen .... *Parlophone* 3
40 24 DANCE WITH ME (I'M YOUR ECSTASY) Control .... *All Around The World* 2
21 25 BABY LOVE Dannii Minogue .... *MCA* 4
- 26 FALL AT YOUR FEET Crowded House .... *Capitol* 1
28 [27] SHINING STAR INXS .... *Mercury* 2
- [28] ME, IN TIME Charlatans .... *Situation Two* 1
- 29 LOVE'S SWEET EXILE Manic Street Preachers .... *Columbia* 1
15 30 SALTWATER Julian Lennon .... *Virgin* 9
23 31 RADIO WALL OF SOUND Slade .... *Polydor* 4
- 32 WINTER SONG Chris Rea .... *East West* 1
30 33 FINALLY Ce Ce Peniston .... *A&M* 5
26 34 40 MILES Congress .... *Inner Rhythm* 3
- 35 THE UNFORGIVEN Metallica .... *Vertigo* 1
- [36] CLIPPED Curve .... *AnXious* 1
37 [37] LIGHTNING Zoe .... *M&G* 2
25 38 EVERYBODY'S FREE (TO FEEL GOOD) Rozalla *Pulse-8* 10
29 39 LOVE TO HATE YOU Erasure .... *Mute* 8
27 40 TOO MANY WALLS Cathy Dennis .... *Polydor* 6

LW TW *WEEK ENDING* **16 NOVEMBER 1991** Wks

1 [1] DIZZY Vic Reeves & the Wonder Stuff .... *Sense* 4
3 [2] GET READY FOR THIS 2 Unlimited .... *PWL Continental* 7
8 [3] RHYTHM IS A MYSTERY K-Klass .... *deConstruction* 2
7 [4] IF YOU WERE WITH ME NOW Kylie Minogue and Keith Washington .... *PWL* 3
2 5 THE FLY U2 .... *Island* 3
4 6 (EVERYTHING I DO) I DO IT FOR YOU Bryan Adams ...... *A&M* 21
5 7 WORLD IN UNION Kiri Te Kanawa .... *Columbia* 7
- 8 IS THERE ANYBODY OUT THERE Bassheads ● .. *deConstruction* 1
6 9 NO SON OF MINE Genesis .... *Virgin* 3
18 [10] IT'S GRIM UP NORTH Justified Ancients Of Mu Mu .... *KLF Communications* 2
- 11 ACTIV 8 (COME WITH ME) Altern 8 .... *Network* 1
11 12 DJS TAKE CONTROL/WAY IN MY BRAIN SL2 .... *XL* 3
12 13 AMERICAN PIE Don McLean .... *Liberty* 5
- 14 KILLER (EP) Seal .... *ZTT* 1
35 [15] THE UNFORGIVEN Metallica .... *Vertigo* 2
19 [16] SWING LOW (RUN WITH THE BALL) Union featuring England World Cup Rugby Squad .... *Columbia* 3
24 [17] DANCE WITH ME (I'M YOUR ECSTASY) Control .... *All Around The World* 3
13 18 GO Moby .... *Outer Rhythm* 5
17 19 EMOTIONS Mariah Carey .... *Columbia* 6
26 20 FALL AT YOUR FEET Crowded House .... *Capitol* 2
14 21 INSANITY Oceanic .... *Dead Dead Good* 13
- 22 FAITH (IN THE POWER OF LOVE) Rozalla *Pulse-8* 1
15 23 CARIBBEAN BLUE Enya .... *WEA* 5

In these weeks ■ For the first time since 23 March, a song from a film or a show is not on top of the charts (02.11.91) ■ *Dizzy* becomes the fifteenth song to be number one in two different versions (09.11.91) ■ Seal's *Killer* is his version of the Adamski record on which his vocals were a major factor in making it a number one (16.11.91)■

LW	TW	Title / Artist	Label	Wks
9	24	ALWAYS LOOK ON THE BRIGHT SIDE OF LIFE Monty Python's Flying Circus	*Virgin*	7
10	25	WIND OF CHANGE Scorpions	*Vertigo*	8
29	26	LOVE'S SWEET EXILE Manic Street Preachers	*Columbia*	2
32	27	WINTER SONG Chris Rea	*East West*	2
-	28	RADIO SONG REM	*Warner Brothers*	1
-	29	YOU TO ME ARE EVERYTHING Sonia	*IQ*	1
16	30	AFTER THE WATERSHED Carter The Unstoppable Sex Machine	*Big Cat*	4
-	31	WHEN A MAN LOVES A WOMAN Michael Bolton	*Columbia*	1
-	32	2/231 Anticapella ●	*PWL Continental*	1
-	33	DO YOU FEEL LIKE I FEEL Belinda Carlisle	*Virgin*	1
20	34	CHANGE Lisa Stansfield	*Arista*	5
-	35	SIN Nine Inch Nails ●	*Island*	1
-	36	HOW CAN I LOVE YOU MORE M People ●	*deConstruction*	1
37	37	LIGHTNING Zoe	*M&G*	3
28	38	ME, IN TIME Charlatans	*Situation Two*	2
-	39	DO WHAT YOU FEEL Joey Negro ●	*Ten*	1
-	40	MY TOWN Glass Tiger	*EMI*	1

WEEK ENDING 23 NOVEMBER 1991

LW	TW	Title / Artist	Label	Wks
-	1	BLACK OR WHITE Michael Jackson	*Epic*	1
1	2	DIZZY Vic Reeves & the Wonder Stuff	*Sense*	5
2	3	GET READY FOR THIS 2 Unlimited	*PWL Continental*	8
11	4	ACTIV 8 (COME WITH ME) Altern 8	*Network*	2
8	5	IS THERE ANYBODY OUT THERE Bassheads	*deConstruction*	2
3	6	RHYTHM IS A MYSTERY K-Klass	*deConstruction*	3
4	7	IF YOU WERE WITH ME NOW Kylie Minogue and Keith Washington	*PWL*	4
14	8	KILLER (EP) Seal	*ZTT*	2
-	9	PLAYING WITH KNIVES Bizarre Inc	*Vinyl Solution*	1
31	10	WHEN A MAN LOVES A WOMAN Michael Bolton	*Columbia*	2
22	11	FAITH (IN THE POWER OF LOVE) Rozalla	*Pulse-8*	2
6	12	(EVERYTHING I DO) I DO IT FOR YOU Bryan Adams	*A&M*	22
29	13	YOU TO ME ARE EVERYTHING Sonia	*IQ*	2
-	14	WAY OF THE WORLD Tina Turner	*Capitol*	1
-	15	HOLE HEARTED Extreme	*A&M*	1
13	16	AMERICAN PIE Don McLean	*Liberty*	6
20	17	FALL AT YOUR FEET Crowded House	*Capitol*	3
10	18	IT'S GRIM UP NORTH Justified Ancients Of Mu Mu	*KLF Communications*	3
7	19	WORLD IN UNION Kiri Te Kanawa	*Columbia*	8
-	20	WASTED TIME Skid Row	*East West*	1
-	21	SO REAL Love Decade ●	*All Around The World*	1
9	22	NO SON OF MINE Genesis	*Virgin*	4
-	23	SPENDING MY TIME Roxette	*EMI*	1
32	24	2/231 Anticapella	*PWL Continental*	2
-	25	SO TELL ME WHY Poison	*Capitol*	1
12	26	DJS TAKE CONTROL/WAY IN MY BRAIN SL2	*XL*	4
5	27	THE FLY U2	*Island*	4
17	28	DANCE WITH ME (I'M YOUR ECSTASY) Control	*All Around The World*	4
33	29	DO YOU FEEL LIKE I FEEL Belinda Carlisle	*Virgin*	2
15	30	THE UNFORGIVEN Metallica	*Vertigo*	3
36	31	HOW CAN I LOVE YOU MORE M People	*deConstruction*	2
-	32	THERE WILL NEVER BE ANOTHER TONIGHT Bryan Adams	*A&M*	1
40	33	MY TOWN Glass Tiger	*EMI*	2
16	34	SWING LOW (RUN WITH THE BALL) Union featuring England World Cup Rugby Squad	*Columbia*	4
-	35	WONDERFUL TONIGHT (LIVE) Eric Clapton	*Duck*	1
39	36	DO WHAT YOU FEEL Joey Negro	*Ten*	2
-	37	JUST A TOUCH OF LOVE (EVERYDAY) C&C Music Factory	*Columbia*	1
-	38	PROMISES Take That ●	*RCA*	1
23	39	CARIBBEAN BLUE Enya	*WEA*	6
-	40	DJ CULTURE Pet Shop Boys	*Parlophone*	3

WEEK ENDING 30 NOVEMBER 1991

December 1991

□ Highest position disc reached ● Act's first ever week on chart

LW	TW	Title / Artist	Label	Wks
1	1	BLACK OR WHITE Michael Jackson	*Epic*	2
2	2	DIZZY Vic Reeves & the Wonder Stuff	*Sense*	6
4	3	ACTIV 8 (COME WITH ME) Altern 8	*Network*	3
9	4	PLAYING WITH KNIVES Bizarre Inc	*Vinyl Solution*	2
3	5	GET READY FOR THIS 2 Unlimited	*PWL Continental*	9
-	6	RIDE LIKE THE WIND East Side Beat ●	*ffrr*	1
5	7	IS THERE ANYBODY OUT THERE Bassheads	*deConstruction*	3
10	8	WHEN A MAN LOVES A WOMAN Michael Bolton	*Columbia*	3
-	9	SMELLS LIKE TEEN SPIRIT Nirvana ●	*DGC*	1
-	10	WHEN YOU TELL ME THAT YOU LOVE ME Diana Ross	*Capitol*	1
6	11	RHYTHM IS A MYSTERY K-Klass	*deConstruction*	4
15	12	HOLE HEARTED Extreme	*A&M*	2
14	13	WAY OF THE WORLD Tina Turner	*Capitol*	2
21	14	SO REAL Love Decade	*All Around The World*	2
-	15	SOUND James	*Fontana*	1
8	16	KILLER (EP) Seal	*ZTT*	3
13	17	YOU TO ME ARE EVERYTHING Sonia	*IQ*	3
-	18	EXTACY Shades Of Rhythm	*ZTT*	1
7	19	IF YOU WERE WITH ME NOW Kylie Minogue and Keith Washington	*PWL*	5
-	20	STARS Simply Red	*East West*	1
11	21	FAITH (IN THE POWER OF LOVE) Rozalla	*Pulse-8*	3
23	22	SPENDING MY TIME Roxette	*EMI*	2
-	22	YOU SHOWED ME Salt-N-Pepa	*ffrr*	1
-	24	JUDGE FUDGE Happy Mondays	*Factory*	1
-	25	WICKED LOVE Oceanic	*Dead Dead Good*	1
24	26	2/231 Anticapella	*PWL Continental*	3
-	27	SEND ME AN ANGEL Scorpions	*Vertigo*	1
17	28	FALL AT YOUR FEET Crowded House	*Capitol*	4
31	29	HOW CAN I LOVE YOU MORE M People	*deConstruction*	3
35	30	WONDERFUL TONIGHT (LIVE) Eric Clapton	*Duck*	2
37	31	JUST A TOUCH OF LOVE (EVERYDAY) C&C Music Factory	*Columbia*	2
16	32	AMERICAN PIE Don McLean	*Liberty*	7
33	33	MY TOWN Glass Tiger	*EMI*	3
20	34	WASTED TIME Skid Row	*East West*	2
32	35	THERE WILL NEVER BE ANOTHER TONIGHT Bryan Adams	*A&M*	2
12	36	(EVERYTHING I DO) I DO IT FOR YOU Bryan Adams	*A&M*	23
-	37	MARTIKA'S KITCHEN Martika	*Columbia*	1
-	38	TENDER LOVE Kenny Thomas	*Cooltempo*	1
25	39	SO TELL ME WHY Poison	*Capitol*	2
38	40	PROMISES Take That	*RCA*	2

WEEK ENDING 7 DECEMBER 1991

LW	TW	Title / Artist	Label	Wks
-	1	DON'T LET THE SUN GO DOWN ON ME George Michael & Elton John ●	*Epic*	1
1	2	BLACK OR WHITE Michael Jackson	*Epic*	3
6	3	RIDE LIKE THE WIND East Side Beat	*ffrr*	2
10	4	WHEN YOU TELL ME THAT YOU LOVE ME Diana Ross	*Capitol*	2
-	5	JUSTIFIED AND ANCIENT KLF featuring Tammy Wynette	*KLF Communications*	1
3	6	ACTIV 8 (COME WITH ME) Altern 8	*Network*	4
9	7	SMELLS LIKE TEEN SPIRIT Nirvana	*DGC*	2
2	8	DIZZY Vic Reeves & the Wonder Stuff	*Sense*	7
15	9	SOUND James	*Fontana*	2
4	10	PLAYING WITH KNIVES Bizarre Inc	*Vinyl Solution*	3
20	11	STARS Simply Red	*East West*	2
5	12	GET READY FOR THIS 2 Unlimited	*PWL Continental*	10
-	13	ROCKET MAN Kate Bush	*Mercury*	1
-	14	DRIVEN BY YOU Brian May ●	*Parlophone*	1
-	15	AM I RIGHT? Erasure	*Mute*	1
18	16	EXTACY Shades Of Rhythm	*ZTT*	2
22	17	YOU SHOWED ME Salt-N-Pepa	*ffrr*	2
13	18	WAY OF THE WORLD Tina Turner	*Capitol*	3
7	19	IS THERE ANYBODY OUT THERE Bassheads	*deConstruction*	4
8	20	WHEN A MAN LOVES A WOMAN Michael Bolton	*Columbia*	4
-	21	WE SHOULD BE TOGETHER Cliff Richard	*EMI*	1
-	22	TOO BLIND TO SEE IT Kim Syms ●	*East West*	1

■Thanks to a bizarre limited release policy by their record company, Island, U2's *The Fly* becomes the third number one of the year to enter the charts at number one, and the third to spend only four weeks in the Top 40 (23.11.91) ■ For both George Michael and Elton John, *Don't Let The Sun Go Down On Me* is their second duet with another chart soloist to get to number one. It is only the fourth time that two number one hitmakers have combined to make a number one duet (after Frank and Nancy Sinatra, Queen and David Bowie, Kylie Minogue and Jason Donovan) (07.12.91)■

December 1991

□ Highest position disc reached ● Act's first ever week on chart

LW	TW	Title / Artist	Label	Wks
12	23	HOLE HEARTED Extreme	*A&M*	3
11	24	RHYTHM IS A MYSTERY K-Klass	*deConstruction*	5
-	[25]	DIAMONDS AND PEARLS Prince & the New Power Generation	*Paisley Park*	1
38	[26]	TENDER LOVE Kenny Thomas	*Cooltempo*	2
14	27	SO REAL Love Decade	*All Around The World*	3
37	28	MARTIKA'S KITCHEN Martika	*Columbia*	2
25	29	WICKED LOVE Oceanic	*Dead Dead Good*	2
30	[30]	WONDERFUL TONIGHT (LIVE) Eric Clapton	*Duck*	3
-	31	JOSEPH MEGA-REMIX Jason Donovan	*Really Useful*	1
29	32	HOW CAN I LOVE YOU MORE M People	*deConstruction*	4
-	33	BARE NECESSITIES MEGAMIX UK Mixmasters	*Connect*	1
-	34	THE SHOW MUST GO ON Queen	*Parlophone*	4
-	35	HOW CAN I KEEP FROM SINGING Enya	*Warner Brothers*	1
-	36	DON'T TALK JUST KISS Right Said Fred	*Tug*	1
17	37	YOU TO ME ARE EVERYTHING Sonia	*IQ*	4
24	38	JUDGE FUDGE Happy Mondays	*Factory*	2
19	39	IF YOU WERE WITH ME NOW Kylie Minogue and Keith Washington	*PWL*	6
16	40	KILLER (EP) Seal	*ZTT*	4

WEEK ENDING 14 DECEMBER 1991

LW	TW	Title / Artist	Label	Wks
1	[1]	DON'T LET THE SUN GO DOWN ON ME George Michael & Elton John	*Epic*	2
4	[2]	WHEN YOU TELL ME THAT YOU LOVE ME Diana Ross	*Capitol*	3
5	[3]	JUSTIFIED AND ANCIENT KLF featuring Tammy Wynette	*KLF Communications*	2
2	4	BLACK OR WHITE Michael Jackson	*Epic*	4
3	5	RIDE LIKE THE WIND East Side Beat	*ffrr*	3
14	[6]	DRIVEN BY YOU Brian May	*Parlophone*	2
22	7	TOO BLIND TO SEE IT Kim Syms	*East West*	2
11	[8]	STARS Simply Red	*East West*	3
-	[9]	IF YOU GO AWAY New Kids On The Block	*Columbia*	1
7	10	SMELLS LIKE TEEN SPIRIT Nirvana	*DGC*	3
6	11	ACTIV 8 (COME WITH ME) Altern 8	*Network*	5
13	[12]	ROCKET MAN Kate Bush	*Mercury*	2
-	[13]	MYSTERIOUS WAYS U2	*Island*	1
8	14	DIZZY Vic Reeves & the Wonder Stuff	*Sense*	8
17	[15]	YOU SHOWED ME Salt-N-Pepa	*ffrr*	3
9	16	SOUND James	*Fontana*	3
36	17	DON'T TALK JUST KISS Right Said Fred	*Tug*	2
15	18	AM I RIGHT? Erasure	*Mute*	2
21	19	WE SHOULD BE TOGETHER Cliff Richard	*EMI*	2
33	20	BARE NECESSITIES MEGAMIX UK Mixmasters	*Connect*	2
12	21	GET READY FOR THIS 2 Unlimited	*PWL Continental*	11
10	22	PLAYING WITH KNIVES Bizarre Inc	*Vinyl Solution*	4
28	23	MARTIKA'S KITCHEN Martika	*Columbia*	3
18	24	WAY OF THE WORLD Tina Turner	*Capitol*	4
31	25	JOSEPH MEGA-REMIX Jason Donovan	*Really Useful*	2
25	26	DIAMONDS AND PEARLS Prince & the New Power Generation	*Paisley Park*	2
34	27	THE SHOW MUST GO ON Queen	*Parlophone*	5
16	28	EXTACY Shades Of Rhythm	*ZTT*	3
26	29	TENDER LOVE Kenny Thomas	*Cooltempo*	3
19	30	IS THERE ANYBODY OUT THERE Bassheads	*deConstruction*	5
-	[31]	COVER FROM THE SKY Deacon Blue	*Columbia*	1
35	[32]	HOW CAN I KEEP FROM SINGING Enya	*Warner Brothers*	2
20	33	WHEN A MAN LOVES A WOMAN Michael Bolton	*Columbia*	5
-	34	HAZY SHADE OF WINTER/SILENT NIGHT Simon & Garfunkel	*Columbia*	1
30	35	WONDERFUL TONIGHT (LIVE) Eric Clapton	*Duck*	4
-	36	RUNNING OUT OF TIME Digital Orgasm ●	*Dead Dead Good*	1
-	37	EVERYBODY MOVE Cathy Dennis	*Polydor*	1
24	38	RHYTHM IS A MYSTERY K-Klass	*deConstruction*	6
-	[39]	IT'S THE END OF THE WORLD AS WE KNOW IT REM	*IRS*	1
-	[40]	YODELING SONG Frank Ifield & the Backroom Boys ●	*EMI*	1

WEEK ENDING 21 DECEMBER 1991

LW	TW	Title / Artist	Label	Wks
-	[1]	BOHEMIAN RHAPSODY/THESE ARE THE DAYS OF OUR LIVES Queen	*Parlophone*	1
1	2	DON'T LET THE SUN GO DOWN ON ME George Michael & Elton John	*Epic*	3
3	[3]	JUSTIFIED AND ANCIENT KLF featuring Tammy Wynette	*KLF Communications*	3
2	4	WHEN YOU TELL ME THAT YOU LOVE ME Diana Ross	*Capitol*	4
-	[5]	LIVE AND LET DIE Guns N' Roses	*Geffen*	1
6	[6]	DRIVEN BY YOU Brian May	*Parlophone*	3
7	7	TOO BLIND TO SEE IT Kim Syms	*East West*	3
4	8	BLACK OR WHITE Michael Jackson	*Epic*	5
17	9	DON'T TALK JUST KISS Right Said Fred	*Tug*	3
19	[10]	WE SHOULD BE TOGETHER Cliff Richard	*EMI*	3
8	11	STARS Simply Red	*East West*	4
5	12	RIDE LIKE THE WIND East Side Beat	*ffrr*	4
-	13	ROOBARB AND CUSTARD Shaft ●	*ffrreedom*	1
20	[14]	BARE NECESSITIES MEGAMIX UK Mixmasters	*Connect*	3
9	15	IF YOU GO AWAY New Kids On The Block	*Columbia*	2
-	16	ADDAMS GROOVE Hammer	*Capitol*	1
15	17	YOU SHOWED ME Salt-N-Pepa	*ffrr*	4
12	18	ROCKET MAN Kate Bush	*Mercury*	3
23	19	MARTIKA'S KITCHEN Martika	*Columbia*	4
25	20	JOSEPH MEGA-REMIX Jason Donovan	*Really Useful*	3
13	21	MYSTERIOUS WAYS U2	*Island*	2
14	22	DIZZY Vic Reeves & the Wonder Stuff	*Sense*	9
11	23	ACTIV 8 (COME WITH ME) Altern 8	*Network*	6
-	[24]	WAS IT WORTH IT Pet Shop Boys	*Parlophone*	1
10	25	SMELLS LIKE TEEN SPIRIT Nirvana	*DGC*	4
-	26	THE COMPLETE DOMINATOR Human Resource	*Outer Rhythm*	1
36	27	RUNNING OUT OF TIME Digital Orgasm	*Dead Dead Good*	2
16	28	SOUND James	*Fontana*	4
27	29	THE SHOW MUST GO ON Queen	*Parlophone*	6
37	30	EVERYBODY MOVE Cathy Dennis	*Polydor*	2
18	31	AM I RIGHT? Erasure	*Mute*	3
34	32	HAZY SHADE OF WINTER/SILENT NIGHT Simon & Garfunkel	*Columbia*	2
26	33	DIAMONDS AND PEARLS Prince & the New Power Generation	*Paisley Park*	3
21	34	GET READY FOR THIS 2 Unlimited	*PWL Continental*	12
-	35	ALL WOMAN Lisa Stansfield	*Arista*	1
24	36	WAY OF THE WORLD Tina Turner	*Capitol*	5
29	37	TENDER LOVE Kenny Thomas	*Cooltempo*	4
31	38	COVER FROM THE SKY Deacon Blue	*Columbia*	2
22	39	PLAYING WITH KNIVES Bizarre Inc	*Vinyl Solution*	5
32	40	HOW CAN I KEEP FROM SINGING Enya	*Warner Brothers*	3

WEEK ENDING 28 DECEMBER 1991

LW	TW	Title / Artist	Label	Wks
1	[1]	BOHEMIAN RHAPSODY/THESE ARE THE DAYS OF OUR LIVES Queen	*Parlophone*	2
4	[2]	WHEN YOU TELL ME THAT YOU LOVE ME Diana Ross	*Capitol*	5
2	3	DON'T LET THE SUN GO DOWN ON ME George Michael & Elton John	*Epic*	4
3	4	JUSTIFIED AND ANCIENT KLF featuring Tammy Wynette	*KLF Communications*	4
9	5	DON'T TALK JUST KISS Right Said Fred	*Tug*	4
5	6	LIVE AND LET DIE Guns N' Roses	*Geffen*	2
7	7	TOO BLIND TO SEE IT Kim Syms	*East West*	4
6	8	DRIVEN BY YOU Brian May	*Parlophone*	4
16	9	ADDAMS GROOVE Hammer	*Capitol*	2
13	10	ROOBARB AND CUSTARD Shaft	*ffrreedom*	2
8	11	BLACK OR WHITE Michael Jackson	*Epic*	6
10	12	WE SHOULD BE TOGETHER Cliff Richard	*EMI*	4
11	13	STARS Simply Red	*East West*	5
14	[14]	BARE NECESSITIES MEGAMIX UK Mixmasters	*Connect*	4
20	15	JOSEPH MEGA-REMIX Jason Donovan	*Really Useful*	4
12	16	RIDE LIKE THE WIND East Side Beat	*ffrr*	5
19	[17]	MARTIKA'S KITCHEN Martika	*Columbia*	5
26	[18]	THE COMPLETE DOMINATOR Human Resource	*Outer Rhythm*	2
18	19	ROCKET MAN Kate Bush	*Mercury*	4

In these weeks ■ In the wake of the death of Freddie Mercury *Bohemian Rhapsody* becomes the sixth single of the year to debut at number one, the second by Queen to do so, and the first record ever to be a number one hit on two totally separate occasions (21.12.91) ■ Diana Ross enjoys here first Top Ten hit since *Chain Reaction* was a number one in early 1986 (28.12.91)▶

December 1991

□ Highest position disc reached ● Act's first ever week on chart

17 **20** YOU SHOWED ME Salt-N-Pepa .... *ffrr* 5
27 **21** RUNNING OUT OF TIME Digital Orgasm .... *Dead Dead Good* 3
22 **22** DIZZY Vic Reeves & the Wonder Stuff .... *Sense* 10
35 **23** ALL WOMAN Lisa Stansfield .... *Arista* 2
15 **24** IF YOU GO AWAY New Kids On The Block .... *Columbia* 3
25 **25** SMELLS LIKE TEEN SPIRIT Nirvana .... *DGC* 5
23 **26** ACTIV 8 (COME WITH ME) Altern 8 .... *Network* 7
24 **27** WAS IT WORTH IT Pet Shop Boys .... *Parlophone* 2
21 **28** MYSTERIOUS WAYS U2 .... *Island* 3
30 **29** EVERYBODY MOVE Cathy Dennis .... *Polydor* 3
32 **[30]** HAZY SHADE OF WINTER/SILENT NIGHT Simon & Garfunkel .... *Columbia* 3
34 **31** GET READY FOR THIS 2 Unlimited .... *PWL Continental* 13
33 **32** DIAMONDS AND PEARLS Prince & the New Power Generation .... *Paisley Park* 4
28 **33** SOUND James .... *Fontana* 5
\- **[34]** I'LL BE HOME THIS CHRISTMAS Shakin' Stevens .... *Epic* 1
\- **[35]** COUNTING SHEEP Airhead .... *Korova* 1
31 **36** AM I RIGHT? Erasure .... *Mute* 4
36 **37** WAY OF THE WORLD Tina Turner .... *Capitol* 6
\- **38** FAIRYTALE OF NEW YORK Pogues featuring Kirsty MacColl .... *PM* 1
37 **39** TENDER LOVE Kenny Thomas .... *Cooltempo* 5
29 **40** THE SHOW MUST GO ON Queen .... *Parlophone* 7

■Only four songs with a Christmas theme in the Christmas chart, and two of them are re-issues (*Hazy Shade Of Winter/Silent Night* and *Fairytale Of New York*). Cliff fails to put his Christmas release on the top of the pile this year (28.12.91)■

Index by song title

Title – Act	Date of Chart Entry
A Ba Ni Bi - **Izhar Cohen & Alphabeta**	13.05.78
Abacab - **Genesis**	22.08.81
ABC - **Jackson 5**	23.05.70
Abide With Me - **Inspirational Choir with the Royal Choral Society**	28.12.85
Abracadabra - **Steve Miller Band**	19.06.82
Abraham, Martin and John - **Marvin Gaye**	9.05.70
Absolute - **Scritti Politti**	16.06.84
Absolute Beginners - **David Bowie**	15.03.86
Absolute Reality - **Alarm**	16.03.85
Acapulco 1922 - **Kenny Ball & his Jazzmen**	22.08.63
Accident Prone - **Status Quo**	2.12.78
Accidents Will Happen - **Elvis Costello**	26.05.79
Ace of Spades - **Motorhead**	1.11.80
Aces High - **Iron Maiden**	3.11.84
Acid Man - **Jolly Roger**	22.10.88
Act of War - **Elton John & Millie Jackson**	22.06.85
Action - **Sweet**	19.07.75
Activ 8 (Come With Me) - **Altern 8**	16.11.91
Addams Groove - **Hammer**	21.12.91
Addicted to Love - **Robert Palmer**	17.05.86
Adios Amigo - **Jim Reeves**	5.07.62
Adoration Waltz - **David Whitfield**	25.01.57
Adrenalin (EP) - **N-Joi**	2.03.91
Advice For the Young at Heart - **Tears for Fears**	3.03.90
Africa - **Toto**	5.02.83
African Waltz - **Johnny Dankworth**	2.03.61
After A Fashion - **Midge Ure and Mick Karn**	16.07.83
After the Gold Rush - **Prelude**	26.01.74
After the Goldrush - **Prelude**	29.05.82
After The Love Has Gone - **Earth Wind & Fire**	4.08.79
After The Love Has Gone - **Princess**	30.11.85
After The War - **Gary Moore**	21.01.89
After The Watershed - **Carter The Unstoppable Sex Machine**	26.10.91
Afterglow of Your Love - **Small Faces**	19.03.69
Aftermath/I'm For Real - **Nightmares on Wax**	10.11.90
Afternoon Delight - **Starland Vocal Band**	14.08.76
Agadoo - **Black Lace**	28.07.84
Again and Again - **Status Quo**	2.09.78
Against All Odds (Take A Look At Me Now) - **Phil Collins**	7.04.84
Ai No Corrida (I-No-Ko-Ree-Da) - **Quincy Jones**	18.04.81
Ain't Complaining - **Status Quo**	26.03.88
Ain't Gonna Bump No More - **Joe Tex**	23.04.77
Ain't Gonna Wash for A Week - **Brook Brothers**	31.08.61
Ain't Got No-I Got Life/Do What You Gotta Do - **Nina Simone**	30.10.68
Ain't Love A Bitch - **Rod Stewart**	10.02.79
Ain't Misbehavin' - **Johnnie Ray**	20.04.56
Ain't Misbehavin' - **Tommy Bruce**	9.06.60
Ain't No Pleasing You - **Chas and Dave**	20.03.82
Ain't No Stoppin' Us Now - **McFadden & Whitehead**	26.05.79
Ain't No Stopping - **Enigma**	23.05.81
Ain't No Sunshine - **Michael Jackson**	26.08.72
Ain't Nobody - **Rufus & Chaka Khan**	31.03.84
Ain't Nobody - **Rufus & Chaka Khan**	8.07.89
Ain't Nobody Better - **Inner City**	22.04.89
Ain't Nothin' But A Houseparty - **Showstoppers**	13.03.68
Ain't Nothin' Goin' On But The Rent - **Gwen Guthrie**	19.07.86
Ain't Nothing Like The Real Thing - **Marvin Gaye & Tammi Terrell**	19.06.68
Ain't Nothing But A Houseparty - **Showstoppers**	13.02.71
Ain't She Sweet - **Beatles**	18.06.64
Ain't That A Shame - **Pat Boone**	18.11.55
Ain't That A Shame - **Fats Domino**	25.01.57
Ain't That A Shame - **Four Seasons**	4.07.63
Ain't That Funny - **Jimmy Justice**	14.06.62
Ain't That Loving You Baby - **Elvis Presley**	29.10.64
Ain't Too Proud To Beg - **Temptations**	28.07.66
The Air That I Breathe - **Hollies**	9.02.74
Airport - **Motors**	17.06.78
Al Capone - **Prince Buster**	9.03.67
Al Di La - **Emilio Pericoli**	5.07.62
Alabama Song - **David Bowie**	1.03.80
Albatross - **Fleetwood Mac**	4.12.68
Albatross - **Fleetwood Mac**	19.05.73
Alexander Graham Bell - **Sweet**	30.10.71
Alfie - **Cilla Black**	31.03.66
Alice I Want You Just For Me - **Full Force**	28.12.85
Alive and Kicking - **Simple Minds**	12.10.85
All-American Boy - **Bill Parsons**	10.04.59
All-Star Hit Parade No.2 - **Various Artists**	26.07.57
All 4 Love (Break 4 Love 1990) - **Raze featuring Lady J**	27.01.90
All 4 Love - **Color Me Badd**	3.08.91
All Alone Am I - **Brenda Lee**	17.01.63
All Along The Watchtower - **Jimi Hendrix Experience**	30.10.68
All And All - **Joyce Sims**	26.04.86
All Around My Hat - **Steeleye Span**	22.11.75
All Around The World - **Jam**	23.07.77
All Around The World - **Jam**	29.01.83
All Around the World - **Lisa Stansfield**	28.10.89
All Because of You - **Geordie**	24.03.73
All By Myself - **Eric Carmen**	17.04.76
All Cried Out - **Alison Moyet**	13.10.84
All Day And All Of The Night - **Kinks**	5.11.64
All Day and All of The Night - **Stranglers**	9.01.88
All Fall Down - **Lindisfarne**	30.09.72
All Fall Down - **Five Star**	11.05.85
All Fall Down - **Ultravox**	22.11.86
All Fired Up - **Pat Benatar**	9.07.88
All For Leyna - **Billy Joel**	26.04.80
All I Ask of You - **Cliff Richard & Sarah Brightman**	11.10.86
All I Ever Need Is You - **Sonny & Cher**	22.01.72
All I Have To Do Is Dream - **Everly Brothers**	23.05.58
All I Have To Do Is Dream - **Bobbie Gentry & Glen Campbell**	6.12.69
All I Need Is Everything - **Aztec Camera**	8.09.84
All I Really Want to Do - **Byrds**	12.08.65
All I Really Want to Do - **Cher**	19.08.65
All I See Is You - **Dusty Springfield**	22.09.66
All I Wanna Do Is Make Love To You - **Heart**	24.03.90
All I Want - **Howard Jones**	4.10.86
All I Want For Christmas Is A Beatle - **Dora Bryan**	5.12.63
All I Want Is You - **Roxy Music**	19.10.74
All I Want Is You - **U2**	24.06.89
All Join Hands - **Slade**	17.11.84
All Kinds of Everything - **Dana**	4.04.70
All My Love - **Jackie Wilson**	13.10.60
All My Love - **Cliff Richard**	15.11.67
All My Loving - **Dowlands**	16.01.64
All My Trials - **Paul McCartney**	8.12.90
All Night Holiday - **Russ Abbott**	13.07.85
All Night Long - **Rainbow**	16.02.80
All Night Long - **Mary Jane Girls**	2.07.83
All Night Long (All Night) - **Lionel Ritchie**	8.10.83
All Night Long (All Night) - **Lionel Richie**	7.01.84
All of Me - **Sabrina**	8.10.88
All Of Me Loves All Of You - **Bay City Rollers**	12.10.74
All of My Heart - **ABC**	4.09.82
All of My Life - **Diana Ross**	12.01.74
All Of You - **Sammy Davis Jr.**	28.12.56
All Or Nothing - **Small Faces**	11.08.66
All Out of Love - **Air Supply**	11.10.80
All Over The World - **Francoise Hardy**	1.04.65
All Over The World - **Electric Light Orchestra**	9.08.80
All Right Now - **Free**	6.06.70
All Right Now - **Free**	21.07.73
All Right Now - **Free**	18.02.78
All Right Now - **Free**	9.02.91
All She Wants Is - **Duranduran**	7.01.89
All Shook Up - **Elvis Presley**	14.06.57
All Star Hit Parade - **Various Artists**	29.06.56
All Stood Still - **Ultravox**	13.06.81
All That I Am - **Elvis Presley**	13.10.66
All The Love In The World - **Consortium**	12.02.69
All The Love In The World - **Dionne Warwick**	18.12.82
All The Man That I Need - **Whitney Houston**	22.12.90
All The Things She Said - **Simple Minds**	12.04.86
All The Time and Everywhere - **Dickie Valentine**	13.03.53
All The Way - **Frank Sinatra**	22.11.57
All The Way From Memphis - **Mott the Hoople**	8.09.73
All The Young Dudes - **Mott the Hoople**	12.08.72
All The Young Dudes - **Bruce Dickinson**	23.06.90
All This Time - **Sting**	12.01.91
All Those Years Ago - **George Harrison**	30.05.81
All Together Now - **Farm**	8.12.90
All Tomorrow's Parties - **Japan**	19.03.83
All True Man - **Alexander O'Neal**	12.01.91
All Woman - **Lisa Stansfield**	21.12.91

All You Need Is Love - **Beatles** 12.07.67
The Alley Cat Song - **David Thorne** 31.01.63
Alley Oop - **Hollywood Argyles** 21.07.60
Ally's Tartan Army - **Andy Cameron** 4.03.78
Almaz - **Randy Crawford** 17.01.87
Almost Hear You Sigh - **Rolling Stones** 7.07.90
Almost There - **Andy Williams** 16.09.65
Alone - **Shepherd Sisters** 15.11.57
Alone - **Petula Clark** 15.11.57
Alone - **Southlanders** 22.11.57
Alone - **Heart** 4.07.87
Alone Again (Naturally) - **Gilbert O'Sullivan** 4.03.72
Alone Again Or - **Damned** 25.04.87
Alone Without You - **King** 17.08.85
Alphabet Street - **Prince** 7.05.88
Alright - **Janet Jackson** 7.07.90
Alright Alright Alright - **Mungo Jerry** 14.07.73
Alright Baby - **Stevenson's Rocket** 6.12.75
Also Sprach Zarathustra (2001) - **Deodato** 12.05.73
Alternate Title - **Monkees** 22.06.67
Always - **Sammy Turner** 13.11.59
Always - **Atlantic Starr** 20.06.87
Always and Forever/Mind Blowing Decisions - **Heatwave** 4.11.78
Always Look on The Bright Side of Life - **Monty Python's Flying Circus** 5.10.91
Always On My Mind - **Elvis Presley** 16.12.72
Always On My Mind - **Pet Shop Boys** 12.12.87
Always The Sun - **Stranglers** 25.10.86
Always the Sun (Remix) - **Stranglers** 12.01.91
Always There - **Marti Webb & the Simon May Orchestra** 20.09.86
Always There - **Incognito featuring Jocelyn Brown** 29.06.91
Always You And Me - **Russ Conway** 6.12.62
Always Yours - **Gary Glitter** 15.06.74
Am I A Toy or A Treasure - **Kay Starr** 15.10.54
Am I Right? - **Erasure** 7.12.91
Am I That Easy to Forget - **Engelbert Humperdinck** 10.01.68
Am I Wasting My Time? - **Frankie Vaughan** 10.10.58
Amanda - **Stuart Gillies** 31.03.73
Amanda - **Craig McLachlan & Check 1-2** 4.08.90
Amateur Hour - **Sparks** 27.07.74
Amazing Grace - **Judy Collins** 19.12.70
Amazing Grace - **Royal Scots Dragoon Guards Band** 1.04.72
America - **Nice** 10.07.68
America - **Simon & Garfunkel** 7.10.72
America - **David Essex** 18.05.74
American Girl - **Tom Petty & the Heartbreakers** 27.08.77
American Pie - **Don McLean** 29.01.72
American Pie - **Don McLean** 19.10.91
American Trilogy - **Elvis Presley** 17.06.72
American Woman - **Guess Who** 30.05.70
Americanos - **Holly Johnson** 1.04.89
Amigo - **Black Slate** 27.09.80
Amityville (The House On The Hill) - **Lovebug Starski** 7.06.86
Among My Souvenirs - **Connie Francis** 4.12.59
Amor - **Ben E King** 5.10.61
Amor - **Julio Iglesias** 16.10.82
Amoureuse - **Kiki Dee** 17.11.73
The Amsterdam EP - **Simple Minds** 9.12.89
An Affair to Remember - **Vic Damone** 6.12.57
An Everlasting Love - **Andy Gibb** 19.08.78
An Innocent Man - **Billy Joel** 18.02.84
An Olympic Record - **Barron Knights** 30.10.68
Anarchy In The UK - **Sex Pistols** 18.12.76
Anasthasia - **T-99** 11.05.91
And I Love You So - **Perry Como** 28.04.73
And I'm Telling You I'm Not Going - **Jennifer Holliday** 18.09.82
And She Was - **Talking Heads** 15.02.86
And The Bands Played On - **Saxon** 11.04.81
And The Beat Goes On - **Whispers** 2.02.80
And the Heavens Cried - **Anthony Newley** 16.03.61
(And the) Pictures in the Sky - **Medicine Head** 26.06.71
And The Sun Will Shine - **Jose Feliciano** 18.10.69
And Then She Kissed Me - **Gary Glitter** 24.10.81
And You Smiled - **Matt Monro** 1.12.73
Anfield Rap (Red Machine in Full Effect) - **Liverpool FC** 14.05.88
Angel - **Aretha Franklin** 22.09.73
Angel - **Madonna** 21.09.85
Angel - **Eurythmics** 19.05.90
Angel Eyes - **Roxy Music** 11.08.79
Angel Eyes (Home and Away) - **Wet Wet Wet** 12.12.87
Angel Eyes/Voulez Vous - **Abba** 21.07.79
Angel Face - **Glitter Band** 23.03.74
Angel Fingers - **Wizzard** 1.09.73
Angel of Harlem - **U2** 17.12.88
Angel of The Morning - **PP Arnold** 24.07.68
Angel of the Morning/Anyway You Want Me - **Mary Mason** 15.10.77
Angela Jones - **Michael Cox** 9.06.60
Angelo - **Brotherhood of Man** 9.07.77
Angels With Dirty Faces - **Sham 69** 20.05.78
Angel/What Made Milwaukee Famous - **Rod Stewart** 18.11.72
Angie - **Rolling Stones** 1.09.73
Angry At the Big Oak Tree - **Frank Ifield** 30.04.64
Animal - **Def Leppard** 1.08.87
Annabella - **John Walker** 26.07.67
Annie, I'm Not Your Daddy - **Kid Creole & the Coconuts** 9.10.82
Annie's Song - **John Denver** 17.08.74
Annie's Song - **James Galway** 3.06.78
Anniversary Waltz - **Anita Harris** 30.01.68
The Anniversary Waltz - Part One - **Status Quo** 29.09.90
Anniversary Waltz - Part Two - **Status Quo** 15.12.90
Another Brick In The Wall - **Pink Floyd** 1.12.79
Another Day - **Paul McCartney** 27.02.71
Another Day In Paradise - **Phil Collins** 4.11.89
Another Day In Paradise - **Jam Tronic** 24.03.90
Another Funny Honeymoon - **David Dundas** 23.04.77
Another Nail In My Heart - **Squeeze** 8.03.80
Another Night - **Jason Donovan** 30.06.90
Another One Bites the Dust - **Queen** 13.09.80
Another Part of Me - **Michael Jackson** 10.09.88
Another Rock and Roll Christmas - **Gary Glitter** 15.12.84
Another Saturday Night - **Sam Cooke** 16.05.63
Another Saturday Night - **Cat Stevens** 31.08.74
Another Star - **Stevie Wonder** 10.09.77
Another Step (Closer to You) - **Kim Wilde & Junior** 11.04.87
Another Suitcase In Another Hall - **Barbara Dickson** 5.03.77
Another Tear Falls - **Walker Brothers** 22.09.66
Another Time, Another Place - **Engelbert Humperdinck** 11.09.71
Another Weekend - **Five Star** 4.06.88
Anotherloverholenyohead - **Prince & the Revolution** 1.11.86
Answer Me - **David Whitfield** 9.10.53
Answer Me - **Frankie Laine** 30.10.53
Answer Me - **Barbara Dickson** 24.01.76
Ant Rap - **Adam & the Ants** 12.12.81
Anthem - **New Seekers** 5.08.78
Anthem - **N-Joi** 6.04.91
Antmusic - **Adam & the Ants** 6.12.80
Any Dream Will Do - **Jason Donovan** 22.06.91
Any Love - **Luther Vandross** 15.10.88
Any Old Iron - **Peter Sellers** 2.08.57
Anyone Can Fall In Love - **Anita Dobson** 9.08.86
Anyone For Tennis - **Cream** 12.06.68
Anyone Who Had A Heart - **Cilla Black** 6.02.64
Anything - **Damned** 22.11.86
Anything For You - **Gloria Estefan & Miami Sound Machine** 20.08.88
Anything Goes - **Harper's Bizarre** 4.10.67
Anything That's Rock & Roll - **Tom Petty & the Heartbreakers** 2.07.77
Anyway Anyhow Anywhere - **Who** 27.05.65
Anyway That You Want Me - **Troggs** 15.12.66
Anyway You Want It - **Dave Clark Five** 22.10.64
Apache - **Shadows** 21.07.60
Apache - **Bert Weedon** 11.08.60
Apache Dropout - **Edgar Broughton Band** 6.02.71
Apeman - **Kinks** 12.12.70
Apollo 9 - **Adam Ant** 22.09.84
Apparently Nothin' - **Young Disciples** 3.08.91
Apple Blossom Time - **Rosemary June** 23.01.59
Applejack - **Jet Harris & Tony Meehan** 12.09.63
April Love - **Pat Boone** 6.12.57
April Skies - **Jesus & Mary Chain** 2.05.87
Arabian Nights - **Siouxsie & the Banshees** 8.08.81
Are Friends Electric - **Tubeway Army** 2.06.79
Are You Being Served Sir - **John Inman** 1.11.75
Are You Dreaming? - **Twenty4Seven featuring Captain Hollywood** 24.11.90
Are You Getting Enough of What Makes You Happy - **Hot Chocolate** 26.07.80
Are You Lonesome Tonight? - **Elvis Presley** 19.01.61
Are You Lonesome Tonight - **Elvis Presley** 20.03.82
Are You Mine? - **Bros** 13.07.91
Are You Ready to Rock - **Wizzard** 4.01.75
Are You Ready - **Break Machine** 25.08.84

Are You Ready? - **AC/DC** 27.04.91
Are You Sure - **Allisons** 23.02.61
Argentine Melody - **San Jose** 1.07.78
Aria - **Acker Bilk** 28.08.76
Armageddon It - **Def Leppard** 9.04.88
Armed and Extremely Dangerous - **First Choice** 19.05.73
Arms of Mary - **Sutherland Brothers/Quiver** 10.04.76
The Arms of Orion - **Prince with Sheena Easton** 18.11.89
Army Dreamers - **Kate Bush** 11.10.80
Arnold Layne - **Pink Floyd** 6.04.67
Around The Way Gril - **LL Cool J** 9.03.91
Around The World - **Ronnie Hilton** 24.05.57
Around The World - **Bing Crosby** 24.05.57
Around the World - **Mantovani Orchestra** 31.05.57
Around The World - **Gracie Fields** 31.05.57
Arrivederci Darling - **Anne Shelton** 16.12.55
Arriverderci Darling - **Edna Savage** 13.01.56
Art For Art's Sake - **10 C.C.** 6.12.75
Arthur Daley (E's Alright) - **Firm** 24.07.82
Arthur's Theme (Best That Can Do) - **Christopher Cross** 16.1.82.
Aquarius/Let The Sunshine In - **Fifth Dimension** 23.04.69
As I Love You - **Shirley Bassey** 19.12.58
As Long As He Needs Me - **Shirley Bassey** 4.08.60
As Long As The Price Is Right - **Dr Feelgood** 12.05.79
As Tears Go By - **Marianne Faithfull** 13.08.64
As Time Goes By - **Dooley Wilson** 17.12.77
As Usual - **Brenda Lee** 9.01.64
As You Like It - **Adam Faith** 10.05.62
Ashes to Ashes - **Mindbenders** 1.09.66
Ashes to Ashes - **David Bowie** 16.08.80
Asia Minor - **Kokomo** 27.04.61
Ask - **Smiths** 1.11.86
Assassing - **Marillion** 12.05.84
At The Club - **Drifters** 15.04.65
At The Club - **Drifters** 25.03.72
At The Edge - **Stiff Little Fingers** 23.02.80
At the Hop - **Danny & the Juniors** 17.01.58
At the Hop - **Danny & the Juniors** 24.07.76
At The Palace (Parts 1 and 2) - **Wilfred Brambell & Harry H Corbett** 5.12.63
At The Top Of The Stairs - **Formations** 21.08.71
Athena - **Who** 9.10.82
Atlantis - **Shadows** 6.06.63
Atlantis - **Donovan** 11.12.68
Atmosphere - **Russ Abbot** 12.01.85
Atmosphere - **Joy Division** 25.06.88
Atomic - **Blondie** 23.02.80
Atomic City - **Holly Johnson** 24.06.89
Attack - **Toys** 27.01.66
Attention to Me - **Nolans** 21.03.81
Auberge - **Chris Rea** 16.02.91
Auf Wiederseh'n - **Vera Lynn** 14.11.52
Autobahn - **Kraftwerk** 10.05.75
Autodrive - **Herbie Hancock** 15.10.83
Automatic - **Pointer Sisters** 20.04.84
Automatic Lover - **Dee D. Jackson** 22.04.78
Automatic Lover - **Vibrators** 1.04.78
Automatically Sunshine - **Supremes** 15.07.72
Autumn Almanac - **Kinks** 25.10.67
Autumn Concerto - **George Melachrino Orchestra** 12.10.56
Avalon - **Roxy Music** 19.06.82
Ave Maria - **Shirley Bassey** 26.04.62
Avenues and Alleyways - **Tony Christie** 17.02.73
Axel F - **Harold Faltermeyer** 15.06.85
Ay Ay Ay Ay Moosey - **Modern Romance** 14.11.81
Ba-Na-Na-Bam-Boo - **Westworld** 9.05.87
Baal's Hymn (EP) - **David Bowie** 13.03.82
Babe - **Styx** 12.01.80
Babooshka - **Kate Bush** 12.07.80
The Baby - **Hollies** 26.02.72
Baby Baby - **Frankie Lymon & the Teenagers** 12.04.57
Baby Baby - **Amy Grant** 11.05.91
Baby Baby My Love Is All For You - **Deniece Williams** 19.11.77
Baby Come Back - **Equals** 15.05.68
Baby Come Back - **Player** 4.03.78
Baby Come To Me - **Patti Austin and James Ingram** 12.02.83
Baby Don't Change Your Mind - **Gladys Knight & the Pips** 28.05.77
Baby Don't Forget My Number - **Milli Vanilli** 14.01.89
Baby Don't Get Hooked On Me - **Mac Davis** 11.11.72
Baby Don't Go - **Sonny & Cher** 16.09.65
Baby Face - **Little Richard** 2.01.59
Baby Face - **Bobby Darin** 6.12.62
Baby Face - **Wing And A Prayer Fife & Drum Corps** 24.01.76
Baby I Don't Care - **Buddy Holly** 6.07.61
Baby I Don't Care - **Transvision Vamp** 1.04.89
Baby I Know - **Rubettes** 19.02.77
Baby I Love You - **Ronettes** 9.01.64
Baby I Love You - **Aretha Franklin** 6.09.67
Baby I Love You - **Dave Edmunds** 27.01.73
Baby I Love You, OK - **Kenny** 14.06.75
Baby I Love You - **Ramones** 2.02.80
Baby I Love Your Way-Freebird - **Will To Power** 7.01.89
Baby I Need Your Lovin' - **Fourmost** 3.12.64
Baby I Won't Let You Down - **Pickettywitch** 14.11.70
Baby I'm A Want You - **Bread** 15.01.72
Baby I'm Yours - **Peter & Gordon** 28.10.65
Baby I'm Yours - **Linda Lewis** 24.04.76
Baby It's You - **Dave Berry** 30.04.64
Baby Jane - **Rod Stewart** 04.06.83
Baby Jump - **Mungo Jerry** 6.02.71
Baby Let Me Take You Home - **Animals** 16.04.64
Baby Love - **Supremes** 22.10.64
Baby Love - **Diana Ross & the Supremes** 31.08.74
Baby Love - **Dannii Minogue** 19.10.91
Baby Lover - **Petula Clark** 28.02.58
Baby Make It Soon - **Marmalde** 11.06.69
Baby My Heart - **Crickets** 2.06.60
Baby Now That I've Found You - **Foundations** 4.10.67
Baby of Mine/Just For You - **Alan Price** 17.02.79
Baby Please Don't Go - **Them** 7.01.65
Baby Roo/Where the Boys Are - **Connie Francis** 16.03.61
Baby Sittin' - **Bobby Angelo** 17.08.61
Baby Sittin' Boogie - **Buzz Clifford** 9.03.61
Baby Stop Crying - **Bob Dylan** 29.07.78
Baby Take A Bow - **Adam Faith** 13.12.62
Baby We Better Try and Get It Together - **Barry White** 21.08.76
Baby We Can't Go Wrong - **Cilla Black** 9.02.74
(Baby) You Don't Have To Tell Me - **Walker Brothers** 14.07.66
Baby You're Dynamite - **Cliff Richard** 7.04.84
Babylon's Burning - **Ruts** 23.06.79
Baby's First Christmas - **Connie Francis** 28.12.61
Back and Forth - **Cameo** 2.05.87
Back Home - **England World Cup Squad** 18.04.70
Back In Love Again - **Donna Summer** 22.04.78
Back In My Arms Again - **Supremes** 10.06.65
Back In The U.S.S.R. - **Beatles** 10.07.76
The Back Of Love - **Echo and the Bunnymen** 29.05.82
Back of My Hand - **Jags** 22.09.79
Back Off Boogaloo - **Ringo Starr** 1.04.72
Back On My Feet Again - **Foundations** 30.01.68
Back on the Chain Gang - **Pretenders** 9.10.82
Back Seat of My Car - **Paul & Linda McCartney** 11.09.71
Back Stabbers - **O'Jays** 30.09.72
Back Street Luv - **Curved Air** 7.08.71
Back to Life (However Do You Want Me) - **Soul II Soul** 10.06.89
Back to Love - **Evelyn King** 27.11.82
Back to the Sixties - **Tight Fit** 25.07.81
Back to the Sixties Part 2 - **Tight Fit** 3.10.81
Back Together Again - **Roberta Flack & Donny Hathaway** 24.05.80
Backchat - **Queen** 28.08.82
Backfired - **Debbie Harry** 8.08.81
Backstage - **Gene Pitney** 24.02.66
Backstreet Symphony - **Thunder** 12.05.90
Bad - **Michael Jackson** 26.09.87
Bad Bad Boy - **Nazareth** 21.07.73
Bad Boy - **Marty Wilde** 11.12.59
Bad Boy - **Miami Sound Machine** 24.05.86
Bad Boys - **Wham!** 14.05.83
Bad Day - **Carmel** 20.08.83
Bad Girls - **Donna Summer** 7.07.79
Bad Love - **Eric Clapton** 10.02.90
Bad Medicine - **Bon Jovi** 24.09.88
Bad Moon Rising - **Creedence Clearwater Revival** 23.08.69
A Bad Night - **Cat Stevens** 9.08.67
Bad Old Days - **CoCo** 22.04.78
Bad Penny Blues - **Humphrey Lyttelton Band** 13.07.56
Bad To Me - **Billy J Kramer & the Dakotas** 1.08.63
Bad Weather - **Supremes** 5.05.73
Bad Young Brother - **Derek B** 7.05.88

Badge - **Cream** 16.04.69
Baggy Trousers - **Madness** 13.09.80
Baker Street - **Gerry Rafferty** 25.02.78
Ball Park Incident - **Wizzard** 16.12.72
Ballad of Bonnie and Clyde - **Georgie Fame** 13.12.67
Ballad of Davy Crockett - **Bill Hayes** 6.01.56
Ballad of Davy Crockett - **Tennessee Ernie Ford** 13.01.56
Ballad of Davy Crockett - **Max Bygraves** 17.02.56
The Ballad of John and Yoko - **Beatles** 4.06.69
Ballad of Paladin - **Duane Eddy** 23.08.62
Ballad of Spotty Muldoon - **Peter Cook** 15.07.65
Ballad of the Green Berets - **S/Sgt Barry Sadler** 31.03.66
Ballerina Girl - **Lionel Richie** 27.12.86
Ballroom Blitz - **Sweet** 22.09.73
Bama Boogie Woogie - **Cleveland Eton** 30.09.78
Bama Lama Bama Loo - **Little Richard** 11.06.64
Bambino - **Springfields** 16.11.61
Bamboo Houses/Bamboo Music - **Sylvian Sakamoto** 7.08.82
Banana Boat Song - **Shirley Bassey** 15.02.57
Banana Boat Song - **Harry Belafonte** 1.03.57
Banana Boat Song - **Tarriers** 1.03.57
Banana Republic - **Boomtown Rats** 22.11.80
Banana Rock - **Wombles** 29.06.74
Banana Splits - **Dickies** 28.04.79
Band of Gold - **Don Cherry** 10.02.56
Band of Gold - **Freda Payne** 5.09.70
Band on the Run - **Paul McCartney & Wings** 6.07.74
Band Played the Boogie - **CCS** 11.08.73
Bang - **Blur** 20.08.91
Bang Bang - **B.A. Robertson** 11.08.79
Bang Bang - **Cher** 31.03.66
(Bang Zoom) Let's Go - **Real Roxanne with Hitman Howie Tee** 28.06.86
Bangers and Mash - **Peter Sellers & Sophia Loren** 12.01.61
Bangin' Man - **Slade** 6.07.74
Bangla Desh - **George Harrison** 14.08.71
Banjo Boy - **Jan & Kjeld** 21.07.60
Banjo's Back In Town - **Alma Cogan** 23.09.55
Bank Robber - **Clash** 16.08.80
Banks of the Ohio - **Olivia Newton-John** 30.10.71
Banner Man - **Blue Mink** 29.05.71
Barabajagal - **Donovan & Jeff Beck** 16.07.69
Barbados - **Typically Tropical** 5.07.75
Barbara Ann - **Beach Boys** 17.02.66
Barcelona - **Freddie Mercury and Montserrat Caballe** 7.11.87
Bare Necessities Megamix - **UK Mixmasters** 7.12.91
Barefootin' - **Robert Parker** 11.08.66
Bark At The Moon - **Ozzy Osbourne** 26.11.83
Bass (How Low Can You Go) - **Simon Harris** 19.03.88
Bassline - **Mantronix** 24.05.86
Bat Out Of Hell - **Meat Loaf** 10.02.79
Batdance - **Prince** 24.06.89
Battle of New Orleans - **Lonnie Donegan** 26.06.59
Battle of New Orleans - **Johnny Horton** 26.06.59
The Battle's O'er - **Andy Stewart** 1.06.61
Be-Bop-A-Lula - **Gene Vincent** 13.07.56
Be Good to Yourself - **Frankie Miller** 11.06.77
Be Loud Be Proud Be Heard - **Toyah** 16.10.82
Be Mine - **Lance Fortune** 19.02.60
Be Mine - **Tremeloes** 8.11.67
Be My Baby - **Ronettes** 17.10.63
Be My Girl - **Jim Dale** 11.10.57
Be My Guest - **Fats Domino** 18.12.59
Be My Twin - **Brother Beyond** 21.01.89
Be Near Me - **ABC** 6.04.85
Be Tender With Me Baby - **Tina Turner** 13.10.90
Be Thankful For What You've Got - **William De Vaughan** 13.07.74
Be With You - **Bangles** 17.06.89
Be Young Be Foolish Be Happy - **Tams** 28.02.70
Be Young Be Foolish Be Happy - **Sonia** 31.08.91
Beach Baby - **The First Class** 22.06.74
Beach Boy Gold - **Gidea Park** 18.07.81
Bear Cage - **Stranglers** 29.03.80
Beat Dis - **Bomb the Bass** 20.02.88
Beat for Beatniks - **John Barry Orchestra** 5.05.60
Beat Goes On - **Sonny & Cher** 16.02.67
Beat It - **Michael Jackson** 9.04.83
Beat Surrender - **Jam** 4.12.82
Beat The Clock - **Sparks** 28.07.79
The Beat(en) Generation - **The The** 1.04.89
Beatles and the Stones - **House of Love** 14.04.90
Beatles Movie Medley - **Beatles** 12.06.82
Beatnik Fly - **Johnny & the Hurricanes** 17.03.60
Beautiful Lover - **Brotherhood of Man** 3.06.78
Beautiful Love - **Julian Cope** 16.02.91
Beautiful Noise - **Neil Diamond** 30.10.76
Beautiful Sunday - **Daniel Boone** 15.04.72
Beauty and The Beast - **David Bowie** 28.01.78
Beauty Is Only Skin Deep - **Temptations** 13.10.66
Beauty's Only Skin Deep - **Aswad** 8.04.89
Because - **Demis Roussos** 2.04.77
Because - **Julian Lennon** 28.12.85
Because I Love You - **Georgie Fame** 23.03.67
Because I Love You - **Shakin' Stevens** 1.11.86
Because I Love You (The Postman Song) - **Stevie B** 23.02.91
Because of Love - **Billy Fury** 25.10.62
Because of You 6.12.86
Because The Night - **Patti Smith Group** 29.04.78
Because They're Young - **Duane Eddy** 21.07.60
Because They're Young - **James Darren** 11.08.60
Because You're Mine - **Mario Lanza** 14.11.52
Because You're Mine - **Nat 'King' Cole** 19.12.52
Bed of Nails - **Alice Cooper** 14.10.89
Beds are Burning - **Midnight Oil** 15.04.89
The Bed's Too Big Without You - **Sheila Hylton** 7.02.81
Bedsitter - **Soft Cell** 14.11.81
Been Caught Stealing - **Jane's Addiction** 23.03.91
Beethoven (I Love to Listen To) - **Eurythmics** 24.10.87
Beg, Steal or Borrow - **New Seekers** 4.03.72
Beggin' - **Time Box** 31.07.68
Begin the Beguine (Volver A Empezar) - **Julio Iglesias** 24.10.81
The Beginning - **Seal** 27.07.91
Behind A Painted Smile - **Isley Brothers** 23.04.69
Behind Closed Doors - **Charlie Rich** 20.04.74
Behind the Groove - **Teena Marie** 7.06.80
Behind the Mask - **Eric Clapton** 24.01.87
Behind the Wheel - **Depeche Mode** 9.01.88
Being Boiled - **Human League** .... 16.1.82.
Being Boring - **Pet Shop Boys** 24.11.90
Being With You - **Smokey Robinson** 16.05.81
Belfast - **Boney M** 5.11.77
Belfast Boy - **Don Fardon** 2.05.70
Belfast Child - **Simple Minds** 18.02.89
Bell Bottom Blues - **Alma Cogan** 19.03.54
The Belle of St Mark - **Sheila E** 9.03.85
Bells of Avignon - **Maz Bygraves** 1.06.61
Ben - **Michael Jackson** 25.11.72
Ben - **Marti Webb** 15.06.85
Bend It! - **Dave Dee Dozy Beaky Mick & Tich** 15.09.66
Bend Me Shape Me - **Amen Corner** 17.01.68
Bend Me Shape Me - **American Breed** 7.02.68
Benny & the Jets - **Elton John** 9.10.76
Benny's Theme - **Paul Henry & Mayson Glen Orchestra** 14.01.78
Bermuda Triangle - **Barry Manilow** 18.04.81
Bernadette - **Four Tops** 30.03.67
Bernadette - **Four Tops** 25.03.72
Berserker - **Gary Numan** 3.11.84
Besame Mucho - **Jet Harris** 24.05.62
The Best - **Tina Turner** 2.09.89
The Best Christmas of Them All - **Shakin' Stevens** 15.12.90
The Best Disco in Town - **Ritchie Family** 18.09.76
Best Friend-Stand Down Margaret - **Beat** 23.08.80
Best I Can - **Queensryche** 6.07.91
Best Kept Secret - **China Crisis** 31.01.87
Best of Everything - **Johnny Mathis** 27.11.59
The Best of Me - **Cliff Richard** 10.06.89
Best of My Love - **Emotions** 10.09.77
Best of You - **Kenny Thomas** 5.10.91
The Best Part of Breaking Up - **Symbols** 17.01.68
Best Thing That Ever Happened - **Gladys Knight And The Pips** 2.08.75
Best Years of Our Lives - **Modern Romance** 20.11.82
Bet Yer Life I Do - **Herman's Hermits** 23.05.70
Betcha By Golly Wow - **Stylistics** 24.06.72
Bette Davis Eyes - **Kim Carnes** 16.05.81
Better Days - **Gun** 29.07.89
A Better Love - **Londonbeat** 20.07.91
Better Love Next Time - **Dr. Hook** 12.01.80
Better the Devil You Know - **Kylie Minogue** 12.05.90
Better World - **Rebel MC** 31.03.90

betweenThe Wars (EP) - **Billy Bragg** 16.03.85
Beyond the Pale - **Mission** 23.04.88
Beyond the Stars - **David Whitfield & the Mantovani Orchestra** 11.02.55
Bicycle Race/Fat Bottomed Girls - **Queen** 28.10.78
Big Apple - **Kajagoogoo** 17.09.83
Big Area - **Then Jerico** 28.01.89
Big Bad John - **Jimmy Dean** 26.10.61
The Big Bean - **Pigbag** 17.07.82
The Big Beat - **Fats Domino** 28.03.58
Big Beat Boogie - **Bert Weedon** 10.03.60
Big City/Think About That - **Dandy Livingstone** 13.01.81
Big Eight - **Judge Dread** 21.04.73
Big Fun - **Kool & the Gang** 14.08.82
Big Fun - **Gap Band** 13.12.86
Big Fun - **Inner City featuring Kevin Saunderson** 10.09.88
Big Girls Don't Cry - **Four Seasons** 24.01.63
Big Hunk O' Love - **Elvis Presley** 24.07.59
The Big Hurt - **Maureen Evans** 22.01.60
The Big Hurt - **Toni Fisher** 12.02.60
Big in Japan - **Alphaville** 1.09.84
The Big L - **Roxette** 7.09.91
Big Log - **Robert Plant** 30.07.83
Big Love - **Fleetwood Mac** 18.04.87
Big Man - **Four Preps** 13.06.58
Big Man in A Big House - **Leroy Van Dyke** 26.04.62
Big Mouth Strikes Again - **Smiths** 31.05.86
Big Seven - **Judge Dread** 16.12.72
Big Ship - **Cliff Richard** 28.05.69
Big Six - **Judge Dread** 2.09.72
The Big Sky - **Kate Bush** 10.05.86
Big Spender - **Shirley Bassey** 11.10.67
Big Ten - **Judge Dread** 4.10.75
Big Time - **Peter Gabriel** 28.03.87
Big Time Operator - **Zoot Money & the Big Roll Band** 25.08.66
Big Wedge - **Fish** 6.01.90
Big Yellow Taxi - **Joni Mitchell** 4.07.70
Bikini Girls With Machine Guns - **Cramps** 10.02.90
Biko - **Peter Gabriel** 23.08.80
Biljo - **Clodagh Rodgers** 8.11.69
Bill Bailey - **Bobby Darin** 30.06.60
Billie Jean - **Michael Jackson** 5.02.83
Billy, Don't Be A Hero - **Paper Lace** 23.02.74
Bimbo - **Ruby Wright** 16.04.54
Bionic Santa - **Chris Hill** 11.12.76
Bird Dog - **Everly Brothers** 12.09.58
Bird of Paradise - **Snowy White** 7.01.84
Bird Song - **Lene Lovich** 10.11.79
Birdhouse In Your Soul - **They Might Be Giants** 17.03.90
Birdie Song - **Tweets** 19.09.81
Birds and Bees - **Warm Sounds** 11.05.67
Birds And The Bees - **Alma Cogan** 13.07.56
Birds and the Bees - **Jewel Akens** 25.03.65
Birth - **Peddlers** 6.09.69
Birthday - **Paul McCartney** 20.10.90
The Bitch - **Olympic Runners** 4.08.79
The Bitch is Back - **Elton John** 14.09.74
Bite Your Lip/Chicago - **Elton John/Kiki Dee** 18.06.77
Bits and Pieces - **Dave Clark Five** 20.02.64
Bitter Sweet - **Marc Almond** 12.11.88
Bitter Tears - **INXS** 13.07.91
The Bitterest Pill (I Ever Had to Swallow) - **Jam** 18.09.82
Black and White - **Greyhound** 26.06.71
Black Betty - **Ram Jam** 10.09.77
Black Betty (Ben Liebrand Remix) - **Ram Jam** 24.02.90
Black Cat - **Janet Jackson** 8.09.90
The Black Eyes Boys - **Paper Lace** 31.08.74
Black Girl - **Four Pennies** 5.11.64
Black Hills of Dakota - **Doris Day** 27.08.54
Black Is Black - **Los Bravos** 30.06.66
Black Is Black - **La Belle Epoque** 10.09.77
Black Magic Woman - **Fleetwood Mac** 24.04.68
Black Man Ray - **China Crisis** 6.04.85
Black Night - **Deep Purple** 5.09.70
Black or White - **Michael Jackson** 23.11.91
Black Pudding Bertha - **Goodies** 28.06.75
Black Skin Blue Eyed Boys - **Equals** 9.01.71
Black Stockings - **John Barry Seven** 15.12.60
Black Superman (Muhammad Ali) - **John Wakelin & the Kinshasa Band** 25.01.75
Black Velvet - **Alannah Myles** 31.03.90
Black Velvet Band - **Dubliners** 6.09.67
Blackberry Way - **Move** 8.01.69
Blame It On The Bossa Nova - **Eydie Gorme** 7.02.63
Blame It On The Pony Express - **Johnny Johnson & his Bandwagon** 5.12.70
Blame It On The Boogie - **Jacksons** 30.09.78
Blame It On The Boogie - **Mick Jackson** 30.09.78
Blame It On The Boogie - **Big Fun** 12.08.89
Blanket On The Ground - **Billie Jo Spears** 19.07.75
Blaze of Glory - **Jon Bon Jovi** 11.08.90
Bless You - **Tony Orlando** 5.10.61
Bless You - **Martha Reeves & the Vandellas** 15.01.72
Blind Vision - **Blancmange** 7.05.83
Blinded By The Light - **Manfred Mann's Earth Band** 4.09.76
Blockbuster - **Sweet** 13.01.73
Blood that Moves the Body - **A-Ha** 18.06.88
Bloodnok's Rock 'N' Roll Call/Ying Tong Song - **Goons** 14.09.56
A Blossom Fell - **Dickie Valentine** 18.02.55
A Blossom Fell - **Nat 'King' Cole** 25.02.55
A Blossom Fell - **Ronnie Hilton** 11.03.55
Blow The House Down - **Living In A Box** 25.02.89
Blowin' In The Wind - **Stevie Wonder** 25.08.66
Blowin' Wild - **Frankie Laine** 8.01.54
Blowing In The Wind - **Peter Paul & Mary** 24.10.63
Blue Angel - **Gene Pitney** 30.11.74
Blue Bayou - **Linda Ronstadt** 4.02.78
Blue Bayou/Mean Woman Blues - **Roy Orbison** 26.09.63
Blue Blue Heartaches - **Johnny Duncan** 25.10.57
Blue Christmas - **Elvis Presley** 10.12.64
Blue Eyed Boy - **Al Saxon** 29.12.60
Blue Eyes - **Don Partridge** 29.05.68
Blue Eyes - **Elton John** 3.04.82
Blue Girl - **Bruisers** 8.08.63
Blue Guitar - **Justin Hayward/John Lodge** 25.10.75
Blue Hat For A Blue Day - **Nick Heyward** 1.10.83
Blue Hotel - **Chris Isaak** 9.02.91
Blue Is The Colour - **Chelsea Football Team** 26.02.72
Blue Jean - **David Bowie** 22.09.84
Blue Monday - **Fats Domino** 29.03.57
Blue Monday - **Fats Domino** 19.04.57
Blue Monday - **New Order** 19.03.83
Blue Monday - **New Order** 17.09.83
Blue Monday 1988 - **New Order** 7.05.88
Blue Moon - **Elvis Presley** 16.11.56
Blue Moon - **Marcels** 13.04.61
Blue Moon - **Showaddywaddy** 6.12.80
Blue Peter - **Mike Oldfield** 15.12.79
Blue River - **Elvis Presley** 24.02.66
Blue Savannah - **Erasure** 10.03.90
Blue Star (The Medic Theme) - **Charlie Applewhite** 23.09.55
Blue Star (The Medic Theme) - **Cyril Stapleton** 23.09.55
Blue Star (The Medic Theme) - **Ron Goodwin** 28.10.55
Blue Suede Shoes - **Carl Perkins** 18.05.56
Blue Suede Shoes - **Elvis Presley** 25.05.56
Blue Tango - **Ray Martin** 14.11.52
Blue Turns To Grey - **Cliff Richard** 24.03.66
Blue Velvet - **Bobby Vinton** 29.09.90
Blue Weekend - **Karl Denver** 27.09.62
Blue World - **Moody Blues** 27.08.83
Bluebell Polka - **Jimmy Shand** 23.12.55
Blueberry Hill - **Fats Domino** 30.11.56
Blueberry Hill - **John Barry Orchestra** 18.08.60
Bluebirds Over The Mountain - **Beach Boys** 8.01.69
Bluer Than Blue - **Rolf Harris** 30.04.69
Blues From A Gun - **Jesus and Mary Chain** 23.09.89
Bo Diddley - **Buddy Holly** 6.06.63
The Boat That I Row - **Lulu** 20.04.67
Bobby Tomorrow - **Bobby Vee** 27.06.63
Bobby's Girl - **Susan Maughan** 18.10.62
Body and Soul - **Mai Tai** 24.08.85
Body Heat - **James Brown** 5.02.77
Body Language - **Detroit Spinners** 31.05.80
Body Language - **Queen** 1.05.82
Body Language - **Adventures of Stevie V** 29.09.90
Body Rock - **Maria Vidal** 7.09.85
Body Talk - **Imagination** 13.06.81
Body Work - **Hot Streak** 17.09.83
Bohemian Rhapsody - **Queen** 15.11.75
Bohemian Rhapsody/These Are The Days of Our Lives - **Queen** 21.12.91
The Boiler - **Rhoda With The Specials AKA** 30.1.82.

Boll Weevil Song - **Brook Benton** 13.07.61
Bomber - **Motorhead** 15.12.79
Boneyard - **Little Angels** 2.02.91
Bonnie Came Back - **Duane Eddy** 19.02.60
Bony Moronie - **Larry Williams** 17.01.58
Boogaloo Party - **Flamingos** 4.06.69
Boogie Down - **Eddie Kendricks** 23.03.74
Boogie Down - **Real Thing** 28.07.79
Boogie Nights - **Heatwave** 29.01.77
Boogie on Reggae Woman - **Stevie Wonder** 11.01.75
Boogie On Up - **Rokotto** 5.11.77
Boogie Oogie Oogie - **A Taste of Honey** 1.07.78
Boogie Shoes - **K.C. & the Sunshine Band** 6.05.78
Boogie Wonderland - **Earth Wind & Fire** 12.05.79
The Book - **David Whitfield** 19.02.54
Book of Love - **Mudlarks** 6.06.58
Boom Bang-A-Bang - **Lulu** 12.03.69
Boops (Here To Go) - **Sly & Robbie** 18.04.87
Borderline - **Madonna** 25.01.86
Born A Woman - **Sandy Posey** 22.09.66
Born Again - **Christians** 30.04.88
Born Free - **Vic Reeves & Roman Numerals** 27.04.91
Born This Way (Let's Dance) - **Cookie Crew** 14.01.89
Born To Be Alive - **Patrick Hernandez** 30.06.79
Born To Be Sold - **Transvision Vamp** 4.11.89
Born To Be With You - **Chordettes** 31.08.56
Born To Be Wild - **Steppenwolf** 18.06.69
Born To Be With You - **Dave Edmunds** 16.06.73
Born to Run - **Bruce Springsteen** 23.05.87
Born Too Late - **Poni-Tails** 19.09.58
Born With A Smile On My Face - **Stephanie De Sykes & Rain** 20.07.74
Borne on the Wind - **Roy Orbison** 20.02.64
Borrowed Time - **John Lennon** 24.03.84
Borsalino - **Bobby Crush** 4.11.72
The Boss - **Diana Ross** 4.08.79
Boss Guitar - **Duane Eddy** 14.02.63
Bossa Nova Baby - **Elvis Presley** 24.10.63
The Boston Tea Party - **Sensation Alex Harvey Band** 26.06.76
Both Ends Burning - **Roxy Music** 27.12.75
Both Sides Now - **Judy Collins** 31.01.70
Bourgie Bourgie - **Gladys Knight & the Pips** 15.11.80
Bow Down Mister - **Jesus Loves You** 9.03.91
Box Set Go - **High** 12.01.91
The Boxer - **Simon & Garfunkel** 30.04.69
Boxerbeat - **JoBoxers** 19.03.83
Boy - **Lulu** 5.06.68
Boy From New York City - **Darts** 6.05.78
A Boy From Nowhere - **Tom Jones** 18.04.87
The Boy In The Bubble - **Paul Simon** 20.12.86
A Boy Named Sue 20.09.69
Boy Oh Boy - **Racey** 1.09.79
The Boy With the Thorn In His Side - **Smiths** 5.10.85
The Boys Are Back In Town - **Thin Lizzy** 5.06.76
Boys Cry - **Eden Kane** 6.02.64
Boys Don't Cry - **Cure** 3.05.86
Boys Keep Swingin' - **David Bowie** 5.05.79
The Boys of Summer - **Don Henley** 16.02.85
Boys (Summertime Love) - **Sabrina** 11.06.88
Brand New Friend - **Lloyd Cole & the Commotions** 14.09.85
Brand New Key - **Melanie** 1.01.72
Brand New Lover - **Dead or Alive** 20.09.86
Brandy - **Scott English** 16.10.71
Brandy - **O'Jays** 7.10.78
B.A.B.Y. - **Rachel Sweet** 23.12.78
Brass In Pocket - **Pretenders** 8.12.79
Brassneck - **The Wedding Present** 17.02.90
Brave New World - **Toyah** 29.05.82
Brazil - **Crispy And Company** 23.08.75
Brazilian Love Song - **Nat 'King' Cole** 29.03.62
Brazilian Love Affair - **George Duke** 26.07.80
Bread and Butter - **Newbeats** 10.09.64
Break 4 Love - **Raze** 21.01.89
Break Dance Party - **Break Machine** 12.05.84
Break My Stride - **Matthew Wilder** 21.01.84
Break the Rules - **Status Quo** 4.05.74
Break Up To Make Up - **Stylistics** 31.03.73
Breakaway - **Springfields** 7.09.61
Breakaway - **Beach Boys** 11.06.69
Breakaway - **Gallagher & Lyle** 25.09.76
Breakaway - **Tracey Ullman** 26.03.83
Breakfast In America - **Supertramp** 7.07.79
Breakfast in Bed - **UB40 with Chrissie Hynde** 18.06.88
Breakfast on Pluto - **Don Partridge** 26.02.69
Breakin' Down (Sugar Samba) - **Julia & Company** 3.03.84
Breakin' Up Is Breakin' My Heart - **Roy Orbison** 27.01.66
Breaking Away - **Jaki Graham** 9.08.86
Breaking Down The Walls of Heartache - **Bandwagon** 16.10.68
Breaking in A Brand New Broken Heart - **Connie Francis** 15.06.61
Breaking the Law - **Judas Priest** 7.06.80
Breaking Up Is Hard To Do - **Neil Sedaka** 19.07.62
Breaking Up Is Hard To Do - **Partridge Family** 8.07.72
Breaking Up My Heart - **Shakin' Stevens** 2.03.85
Breakin'...There's No Stopping Us - **Ollie & Jerry** 23.06.84
Breakout - **Swing Out Sister** 1.11.86
Breakthru' - **Queen** 1.07.89
Breathe Life Into Me - **Mica Paris** 12.11.88
Breathing - **Kate Bush** 3.05.80
Breathless - **Jerry Lee Lewis** 11.04.58
The Breeze and I - **Caterina Valente** 19.08.55
Brickhouse/Sweet Love - **Commodores** 15.10.77
Bridge of Sighs - **David Whitfield** 2.10.53
Bridge Over Troubled Water - **Simon and Garfunkel** 28.02.70
Bridge Over Troubled Water - **Linda Clifford** 12.05.79
Bridge Over Troubled Water - **PJB featuring Hannah & her Sister** 14.09.91
Bridge to Your Heart - **Wax** 15.08.87
Bridget the Midget - **Ray Stevens** 13.03.71
Bright Eyes - **Art Garfunkel** 24.03.79
Brilliant Disguise - **Bruce Springsteen** 3.10.87
Brilliant Mind - **Furniture** 28.06.86
Bring A Little Water, Sylvie - **Lonnie Donegan** 7.09.56
Bring It On Home To Me - **Animals** 8.04.65
Bring Me Closer - **Altered Images** 04.06.83
Bring Me Edelweiss - **Edelweiss** 6.05.89
Bring On Back The Good Times - **Love Affair** 23.07.69
Bring On The Dancing Horses - **Echo & the Bunnymen** 19.10.85
Bring the Noise - **Public Enemy** 16.01.88
Bring The Noise - **Anthrax featuring Chuck D** 6.07.91
Bring Your Daughter ... To The Slaughter - **Iron Maiden** 5.01.91
Bristol Stomp - **Late Show** 24.03.79
Britannia Rag - **Winifred Atwell** 12.12.52
British Hustle - **Hi Tension** 19.08.78
The Brits 1990 - **Various Artists** 3.03.90
Broke Away - **Wet Wet Wet** 9.12.89
Broken-Hearted Melody - **Sarah Vaughan** 11.09.59
Broken Doll - **Tommy Bruce** 8.09.60
Broken Down Angel - **Nazareth** 12.05.73
Broken Hearted - **Ken Dodd** 5.12.70
Broken Land - **Adventures** 30.04.88
Broken Wings - **Stargazers** 13.02.53
Broken Wings - **Art & Dottie Todd** 13.02.53
Broken Wings - **Dickie Valentine** 20.02.53
Broken Wings - **Mr Mister** 11.01.86
Brontosaurus - **Move** 25.04.70
Brother - **CCS** 11.03.72
Brother Louie - **Hot Chocolate** 14.04.73
Brother Louie - **Modern Talking** 16.08.86
Brothers In Arms - **Dire Straits** 2.11.85
Brown-Eyed Handsome Man - **Buddy Holly** 14.03.63
Brown Sugar/Bitch/Let It Rock - **Rolling Stones** 24.04.71
The Bucket of Water Song - **Four Bucketeers** 10.05.80
Buffalo Gals - **Malcolm McLaren & the World's Famous Supreme Team** 4.12.82
Buffalo Soldier - **Bob Marley and the Wailers** 14.05.83
Buffalo Stance - **Neneh Cherry** 17.12.88
Build - **Housemartins** 21.11.87
Build Me Up Buttercup - **Foundations** 27.11.68
Build Your Love - **Johnnie Ray** 6.09.57
The Bump - **Kenny** 7.12.74
A Bunch Of Thyme - **Foster and Allen** 13.02.82
Buona Sera - **Mr. Acker Bilk** 15.12.60
Buona Sera - **Louis Prima** 21.02.58
Buona Sera (Don't Be Angry) 28.11.81
Burb Baby Burn - **Hudson Ford** 23.02.74
Burlesque - **Family** 30.09.72
Burn - **Doctor & the Medics** 9.08.86
Burn It Up - **Beatmasters with PP Arnold** 8.10.88
(Burn It Up) Bring It Down! (This Insane Thing) - **Redskins** 22.06.85
Burn Rubber on Me - **Gap Band** 17.01.81
Burnin' Hot - **Jermaine Jackson** 2.08.80

Burning Bridges - **Jack Scott** 2.06.60
Burning Bridges (On and Off and On Again) - **Status Quo** 3.12.88
Burning Car - **John Foxx** 26.07.80
Burning Heart - **Survivor** 8.02.86
Burning Love - **Elvis Presley** 30.09.72
Burning Of The Midnight Lamp - **Jimi Hendrix Experience** 30.08.67
Burning the Ground - **Duran Duran** 16.12.89
Burundi Black - **Burundi Steiphenson Black** 20.11.71
Bus Stop - **Hollies** 23.06.66
Busted - **Ray Charles** 7.11.63
But I Do - **Clarence 'Frogman' Henry** 4.05.61
But Not For Me - **Ella Fitzgerald** 16.10.59
But You Love Me Daddy - **Jim Reeves** 13.12.69
But You're Mine - **Sonny & Cher** 28.10.65
Butterfingers - **Tommy Steele** 3.05.57
Butterfly - **Charlie Gracie** 19.04.57
Butterfly - **Andy Williams** 19.04.57
Butterfly - **Danyel Gerard** 25.09.71
Butterfly on A Wheel - **Mission** 13.01.90
Buzz Buzz A Diddle It - **Matchbox** 26.01.80
By The Devil - **Blue Mink** 3.03.73
By The Fountains of Rome - **Edmund Hockridge** 31.08.56
By The Fountains of Rome - **David Hughes** 21.09.56
By The Light of The Silvery Moon - **Little Richard** 3.04.59
By the Way - **Big Three** 18.07.63
By the Way - **Tremeloes** 21.03.70
By Your Side - **Peters & Lee** 10.11.73
Bye Bye Baby - **Johnny Otis Show featuring Marie Adams** 10.01.58
Bye Bye Baby - **Tony Jackson & the Vibrations** 15.10.64
Bye Bye Baby - **Bay City Rollers** 8.03.75
Bye Bye Blues - **Bert Kaempfert** 6.01.66
Bye Bye Love - **Everly Brothers** 12.07.57
C30 C60 C90 Go - **Bow Wow Wow** 16.08.80
Ca Plane Pour Moi - **Plastic Bertrand** 20.05.78
Cacharpaya (Andes Pumpsa Desi) - **Incantation** 18.12.82
Calendar Girl - **Neil Sedaka** 9.02.61
Calendar Song - **Trinidad Oil Company** 28.05.77
California Dreamin' - **Mamas & Papas** 5.05.66
California Girls - **Beach Boys** 9.09.65
California Here I Come - **Freddy Cannon** 10.03.60
California Man - **Move** 20.05.72
Call Her Your Sweetheart - **Frank Ifield** 5.01.67
Call It What You Want - **New Kids On The Block** 18.05.91
Call Me - **Blondie** 12.04.80
Call Me - **Go West** 11.05.85
Call Me - **Spagna** 1.08.87
(Call Me) Number One - **Tremeloes** 1.11.69
Call Me Round - **Pilot** 26.04.75
Call Of The Wild - **Midge Ure** 14.06.86
Call Rosie on The Phone - **Guy Mitchell** 11.10.57
The Call Up - **Clash** 6.12.80
Call Up The Groups - **Barron Knights** 9.07.64
Calling All The Heroes - **It Bites** 2.08.86
Calling America - **Electric Light Orchestra** 8.03.86
Calling Elvis - **Dire Straits** 31.08.91
Calling Occupants of Interplanetary Craft - **Carpenters** 15.10.77
Calling Your Name - **Marilyn** 12.11.83
Calypso Crazy - **Billy Ocean** 14.05.88
Cambodia - **Kim Wilde** 21.11.81
Camouflage - **Stan Ridgeway** 12.07.86
Can Can - **Bad Manners** 27.06.81
Can Can '62 - **Peter Jay & the Jaywalkers** 15.11.62
Can Can You Party - **Jive Bunny & the Mastermixers** 25.08.90
Can I - **Cashmere** 19.01.85
Can I Get A Witness - **Sam Brown** 20.05.89
Can I Kick It? - **A Tribe Called Quest** 19.01.91
Can I Play With Madness - **Iron Maiden** 26.03.88
Can I Take You Home Little Girl - **Drifters** 6.12.75
Can I Trust You - **Bachelors** 7.07.66
Can the Can - **Suzi Quatro** 19.05.73
Can U Dig It - **Pop Will Eat Itself** 18.02.89
Can You Dig It? - **Mock Turtles** 23.03.91
Can You Do It - **Geordie** 16.06.73
Can You Feel The Force? - **Real Thing** 24.02.79
Can You Feel It - **Jacksons** 7.03.81
Can You Feel the Force - **Real Thing** 9.08.86
Can You Forgive Me - **Karl Denver** 28.03.63
Can You Handle It - **Sharon Redd** 14.03.81
Can You Keep A Secret - **Brother Beyond** 1.04.89
Can You Party - **Royal House** 22.10.88
Can You Please Crawl Out Your Window - **Bob Dylan** 27.01.66
Candida - **Dawn** 16.01.71
Candle in the Wind - **Elton John** 2.03.74
Candle in The Wind (Live) - **Elton John** 23.01.88
Candy - **Cameo** 29.11.86
Candy Girl - **New Edition** 7.05.83
Candy Man - **Brian Poole & the Tremeloes** 6.02.64
Candyman - **Siouxsie & the Banshees** 8.03.86
Cannonball - **Duane Eddy** 2.01.59
Can't Be With You Tonight - **Judy Boucher** 4.04.87
Can't Buy Me Love - **Beatles** 26.03.64
Can't Buy Me Love - **Ella Fitzgerald** 7.05.64
Can't Fight This Feeling - **REO Speedwagon** 30.03.85
Can't Forget You - **Sonia** 7.10.89
Can't Get Along Without You/We Are Not Alone - **Frankie Vaughan** 7.03.58
Can't Get By Without You - **Real Thing** 24.05.86
Can't Get Enough - **Bad Company** 8.06.74
Can't Get Enough of Your Love Babe - **Barry White** 24.08.74
Can't Get Enough of You - **Eddy Grant** 18.04.81
Can't Get Used to Losing You - **Andy Williams** 28.03.63
Can't Get Used To Losing You - **Beat** 7.05.83
Can't Give You More - **Status Quo** 7.09.91
Can't Happen Here - **Rainbow** 27.06.81
Can't Help Falling In Love - **Andy Williams** 14.03.70
Can't Help Falling in Love - **Stylistics** 24.04.76
Can't I? - **Nat 'King' Cole** 14.07.53
Can't Keep It In - **Cat Stevens** 16.12.72
Can't Let You Go - **Barry Ryan** 15.01.72
Can't Live With You (Can't Live Without You) - **Mindbenders** 5.05.66
Can't Say How Much I Love You - **Demis Roussos** 20.03.76
Can't Shake The Feeling - **Big Fun** 25.11.89
Can't Stand Losing You - **Police** 14.07.79
Can't Stay Away From You - **Gloria Estefan & Miami Sound Machine** 18.02.89
Can't Stop the Music - **Village People** 16.08.80
Can't Stop This Thing We Started - **Bryan Adams** 14.09.91
Can't Take My Eyes Off You - **Andy Williams** 27.03.68
Can't Take My Eyes Off You - **Boystown Gang** 7.08.82
Can't Truss It - **Public Enemy** 12.10.91
Can't Wait Another Minute - **Five Star** 12.04.86
Can't You Hear My Heart - **Danny Rivers** 12.01.61
Can't You Hear The Beat of A Broken Heart - **Iain Gregory** 4.01.62
Can't You Hear My Heart Beat - **Goldie & the Gingerbreads** 25.02.65
Can't You See That She's Mine - **Dave Clark Five** 28.05.64
Cantonese Boy - **Japan** 22.05.82
Capstick Comes Home/The Sheffield Grinder - **Tony Capstick & the Carlton Main Frickley Colliery Band** 28.03.81
Captain Beaky - **Keith Michell** 2.02.80
Captain Kremmen - **Kenny Everett & Mike Vickers** 12.11.77
The Captain of Her Heart - **Double** 1.02.86
Captain of Your Ship - **Reparata & the Delrons** 20.03.68
Car 67 - **Driver 67** 6.01.79
Car Trouble - **Adam & the Ants** 7.02.81
Car Wash - **Rose Royce** 8.01.77
Car Wash/Is It Love You're After - **Rose Royce** 18.06.88
Cara Mia - **David Whitfield** 18.06.54
Caravan - **Inspiral Carpets** 30.03.91
Caravan of Love - **Housemartins** 6.12.86
Cardiac Arrest - **Madness -** 20.02.82
Careless Hands - **Des O'Connor** 8.11.67
Careless Memories - **Duran Duran** 16.05.81
Careless Whisper - **George Michael** 4.08.84
Caribbean Blue - **Enya** 19.10.91
The Caribbean Disco Show - **Lobo** 1.08.81
Caribbean Queen (No More Love on The Run) - **Billy Ocean** 27.10.84
The Carnival Is Over - **Seekers** 4.11.65
Caroline - **Status Quo** 15.09.73
Caroline (Live at the NEC) - **Status Quo** 30.10.82
Caroline Moon/Stupid Cupid - **Connie Francis** 22.08.58
'Carousel' Soundtrack (LP) - **Various Artists** 15.06.56
Carousel Waltz - **Ray Martin** 15.06.56
Carrie-Anne - **Hollies** 8.06.67
Carrie - **Cliff Richard** 9.02.80
Carrie - **Europe** 25.04.87
Carry the Blame/California Dreamin' - **River City People** 7.07.90
Cars - **Gary Numan** 1.09.79
Cars ('E' Reg Model) - **Gary Numan** 19.09.87
Casablanca - **Kenny Ball & his Jazzmen** 2.05.63
Casanova - **Coffee** 4.10.80

Casanova - **Levert** 29.08.87
Casanova/Chariot - **Petula Clark** 16.05.63
Casino Royale - **Herb Alpert** 11.05.67
Cast Your Fate To The Wind - **Sounds Orchestral** 10.12.64
Cat Among The Pigeons/Silent Night - **Bros** 3.12.88
The Cat Came Back - **Sonny James** 30.11.56
The Cat Crept In - **Mud** 13.04.74
Cat People (Putting Out Fire) - **David Bowie** 17.04.82
Cat People (Putting Out Fire) - **David Bowie** 17.04.82
Catch - **Cure** 11.07.87
Catch A Falling Star - **Perry Como** 7.03.58
Catch The Wind - **Donovan** 25.03.65
Catch Us If You Can - **Dave Clark Five** 15.07.65
Caterina - **Perry Como** 10.05.62
The Caterpillar - **Cure** 7.04.84
Cath/Will She Always Be Waiting - **Bluebells** 29.09.84
Cathy's Clown - **Everly Brothers** 14.04.60
Caught In My Shadow - **Wonder Stuff** 25.05.91
Causing A Commotion - **Madonna** 19.09.87
Cavatina (Original Soundtrack From Deer Hunter) - **John Williams** 2.06.79
Celebrate The World - **Womack & Womack** 4.03.89
Celebration - **Kool & the Gang** 8.11.80
The Celtic Soul Brothers - **Kevin Rowland and Dexy's Midnight Runners** 2.04.83
Central Park Arrest - **Thunderthighs** 29.06.74
Centre City - **Fat Larry's Band** 9.07.77
Centrefold - **J Geils Band** 13.02.82
Ceremony - **New Order** 14.03.81
Certain Smile - **Johnny Mathis** 26.09.58
C'Est La Vie - **Robbie Nevil** 3.01.87
C'Est Si Bon - **Conway Twitty** 2.03.61
Cha Cha Heels - **Eartha Kitt & Bronski Beat** 22.07.89
Chain Gang - **Jimmy Young** 16.03.56
Chain Gang - **Sam Cooke** 29.09.60
Chain Reaction - **Diana Ross** 8.02.86
Chains of Love (Remix) - **Erasure** 11.06.88
Chalk Dust-The Umpire Strikes Back - **Brat** 17.07.82
Chance - **Big Country** 3.09.83
Chances - **Hot Chocolate** 2.10.82
Change - **Tears For Fears** 5.02.83
Change - **Lisa Stansfield** 19.10.91
Change His Ways - **Robert Palmer** 20.05.89
Change of Heart - **Change** 9.06.84
Change With The Times - **Van McCoy** 8.11.75
Change Your Mind - **Sharpe & Numan** 16.02.85
Changes - **Imagination** 8.01.83
Changing Partners - **Bing Crosby** 19.03.54
Changing Partners - **Kay Starr** 19.03.54
Chanson D'Amour - **Manhattan Transfer** 5.02.77
Chant No. 1 (I Don't Need This Pressure on) - **Spandau Ballet** 18.07.81
Chantilly Lace - **Big Bopper** 26.12.58
Chantilly Lace - **Jerry Lee Lewis** 13.05.72
Chapel of Love - **Dixie Cups** 18.06.64
Chapel of The Roses - **Malcolm Vaughan** 10.05.57
Charade - **Skids** 6.10.79
Chariot - **Rhet Stoller** 12.01.61
Chariots of Fire - **Vangelis** 23.05.81
Charleston - **Temperance Seven** 7.12.61
Charlie Brown - **Coasters** 27.3.59
Charlotte Anne - **Julian Cope** 8.10.88
Charly - **Prodigy** 24.08.91
Charmaine - **Bachelors** 24.01.63
Charming Billy - **Johnny Preston** 8.12.60
Check Out The Groove - **Bobby Thurston** 12.04.80
Check This Out - **LA Mix** 21.05.88
Chemistry - **Nolans** 22.08.81
Cheri Babe - **Hot Chocolate** 7.12.74
Cherish - **Kool & the Gang** 1.06.85
Cherish - **Madonna** 16.09.89
Cherry Oh Baby - **UB40** 24.03.84
Cherry Pie - **Jess Conrad** 30.06.60
Cherry Pie - **Warrant** 16.03.91
Cherry Pink & Apple Blossom White - **Perez Prado** 25.03.55
Cherry Pink & Apple Blossom White - **Eddie Calvert** 8.04.55
Cherry Pink and Apple Blossom White - **Modern Romance featuring John Du Prez** 21.08.82
Chequered Love - **Kim Wilde** 9.05.81
Chestnut Mare - **Byrds** 13.02.71
Chi Mai (Theme from The Life and Times of David Lloyd George) - **Ennio Morricone** 11.04.81
Chick-A-Boom - **53rd And 3rd** 27.09.75
Chicka Boom - **Guy Mitchell** 6.11.53
The Chicken Song - **Spitting Image** 10.05.86
Children - **EMF** 27.04.91
Children of the Revolution - **T.Rex** 16.09.72
Children Say - **Level 42** 12.12.87
A Child's Prayer - **Hot Chocolate** 23.08.75
Chime - **Orbital** 24.03.90
China Doll - **Slim Whitman** 23.09.55
China Girl - **David Bowie** 11.06.83
China In Your Hand - **T'Pau** 31.10.87
China Tea - **Russ Conway** 21.08.59
China Town - **Move** 23.10.71
Chinatown - **Thin Lizzy** 31.05.80
The Chinese Way - **Level 42** 22.01.83
Chirpy Chirpy Cheep Cheep - **Middle of the Road** 5.06.71
Chiquitita - **Abba** 3.02.79
Chocolate Box - **Bros** 7.10.89
Choice - **Blow Monkeys featuring Sylvia Tella** 15.07.89
Chorus - **Erasure** 29.06.91
Chosen Few - **Dooleys** 6.10.79
Christian - **China Crisis** 5.02.83
Christine - **Miss X** 15.08.63
Christine - **Siouxsie & the Banshees** 7.06.80
Christmas Alphabet - **Dickie Valentine** 25.11.55
Christmas and You - **Dave King** 21.12.56
Christmas Countdown - **Frank Kelly** 24.12.83
Christmas In Dreadland/Come Outside - **Judge Dread** 13.12.75
Christmas In Smurfland - **Father Abraham** 9.12.78
Christmas Island - **Dickie Valentine** 7.12.56
Christmas on 45 - **Holly & the Ivys** 26.12.81
Christmas Song - **Gilbert O'Sullivan** 21.12.74
Christmas Song/Thank You For A Good Year - **Alexander O'Neal** 10.12.88
Christmas Spectre - **Jingle Belles** 24.12.83
Christmas Will Be Just Another Lonely Day - **Brenda Lee** 17.12.64
Christmas Wrappin' - **Kurtis Blow** 22.12.79
Chuck E's In Love - **Rickie Lee Jones** 7.07.79
Church Of The Poison Mind - **Culture Club** 9.04.83
Ciao Ciao Bambina - **Marino Marini** 20.3.59
Ciao Ciao Bambino - **Domenico Modugno** 27.3.59
Cinderella Rockefella - **Esther & Abi Ofarim** 14.02.68
Cindy Incidentally - **Faces** 17.02.73
Cindy Oh Cindy - **Eddie Fisher** 23.11.56
Cindy Oh Cindy - **Tony Brent** 30.11.56
Cindy Oh Cindy - **Vince Martin** 14.12.56
Cindy's Birthday - **Shane Fenton** 19.07.62
Circle in The Sand - **Belinda Carlisle** 14.05.88
Circles - **New Seekers** 17.06.72
Circlesquare - **Wonder Stuff** 12.05.90
The Circus - **Erasure** 3.10.87
Circus Games - **Skids** 23.08.80
Cities In Dust - **Siouxsie & the Banshees** 26.10.85
City Lights - **David Essex** 20.03.76
Clair - **Gilbert O'Sullivan** 21.10.72
The Clairvoyant - **Iron Maiden** 19.11.88
The Clapping Song - **Shirley Ellis** 6.05.65
The Clapping Song - **Belle Stars** 24.07.82
Clash City Rockers - **Clash** 4.03.78
Classic - **Adrian Gurvitz** 27.02.82
Classical Gas - **Mason Williams** 4.09.68
Classical Muddley - **Portsmouth Sinfonia** 29.09.81
Clean Clean - **Buggles** 19.04.80
Clean Up Your Own Back Yard - **Elvis Presley** 6.09.69
Clementine - **Bobby Darin** 31.03.60
Clipped - **Curve** 9.11.91
Clog Dance - **Violinski** 3.03.79
Close the Door - **Stargazers** 9.09.55
Close To Me - **Cure** 28.09.85
Close to Me - **Cure** 3.11.90
Close (To The Edit) - **Art of Noise** 19.01.85
Close To You - **Maxi Priest** 16.06.90
Close Your Eyes - **Tony Bennett** 16.09.55
Closer to The Heart - **Rush** 11.02.78
Closest Thing to Heaven - **Kane Gang** 21.07.84
Cloud 99 - **St. Andrews Chorale** 21.02.76
Cloud Lucky Seven - **Guy Mitchell** 18.12.53
Cloud Nine - **Temptations** 30.08.69
Cloudburst - **Don Lang** 4.11.55
Cloudburst - **Don Lang** 13.01.56

Cloudbusting - **Kate Bush** 26.10.85
Clouds Across the Moon - **Rah Band** 6.04.85
Clouds Will Soon Roll By - **Tony Brent** 28.02.58
Clown Shoes - **Johnny Burnette** 17.05.62
Club Country - **Associates** 8.05.82
Club Fantastic Megamix - **Wham!** 3.12.83
Club Tropicana - **Wham!** 30.07.83
C'Mon And Get My Love - **D. Mob introducing Cathy Dennis** 21.10.89
C'Mon! C'Mon - **Bronski Beat** 29.03.86
C'Mon Everybody - **Eddie Cochran** 13.03.59
C'Mon Everybody - **Sex Pistols** 30.06.79
C'Mon Everybody - **Eddie Cochran** 20.02.88
C'Mon Marianne - **Grapefruit** 28.08.68
Co-Co - **Sweet** 12.06.71
Coast Is Clear - **Curve** 25.05.91
Cocomotion - **El Coco** 21.01.78
Code of Love - **Mike Sarne** 4.04.63
The Coffee Song - **Frank Sinatra** 30.11.61
Cold As Christmas - **Elton John** 17.12.83
Cold As Ice - **Foreigner** 12.08.78
Cold Cold Heart - **Midge Ure** 17.08.91
Cold Light of Day - **Gene Pitney** 2.03.67
Cold Sweat - **Thin Lizzy** 12.02.83
Cold Turkey - **Plastic Ono Band** 1.11.69
Colette - **Billy Fury** 10.03.60
Colour Of My Love - **Jefferson** 16.04.69
Colours - **Donovan** 3.06.65
Combine Harvester - **The Wurzels** 15.05.76
Come Along Please - **Bob Wallis** 4.01.62
Come And Get It - **Badfinger** 10.01.70
Come and Stay With Me - **Marianne Faithfull** 18.02.65
Come Back - **Mighty Wah!** 14.07.84
Come Back and Shake Me - **Clodagh Rodgers** 2.04.69
Come Back And Finish What You Started - **Gladys Knight & the Pips** 15.07.78
Come Back And Stay - **Paul Young** 10.09.83
Come Back My Love - **Darts** 4.02.78
Come Back to Me - **Janet Jackson** 3.02.90
Come Dance With Me (LP) - **Frank Sinatra** 15.05.59
Come Dancing - **Kinks** 20.08.83
Come Home - **Dave Clark Five** 27.05.65
Come Home - **James** 7.07.90
Come Into My Life - **Joyce Sims** 9.01.88
Come Live With Me - **Heaven 17** 25.06.83
Come Next Spring - **Tony Bennett** 13.04.56
Come On - **Rolling Stones** 1.08.63
Come On Dance Dance - **Saturday Night Band** 8.07.78
Come on Eileen - **Dexy's Midnight Runners with the Emerald Express** 17.07.82
Come on Home - **Springfields** 25.07.63
Come On Home - **Wayne Fontana** 28.04.66
Come On Let's Go - **Tommy Steele** 14.11.58
Come on Let's Go - **Los Lobos** 10.10.87
Come On Over To My Place - **Drifters** 29.04.65
Come On Over To My Place - **The Drifters** 2.09.72
Come Outside - **Mike Sarne** 17.05.62
Come Prima - **Marino Marini** 10.10.58
Come Round Here - **Smokey Robinson & the Miracles** 30.01.71
Come See About Me - **Supremes** 28.01.65
Come See About Me - **Shakin' Stevens** 26.09.87
Come Softly to Me - **Fleetwoods** 24.04.59
Come Softly to Me - **Frankie Vaughan & the Kaye Sisters** 1.05.59
Come Softly To Me - **New Seekers** 16.12.72
Come to Me - **Julie Grant** 24.09.64
Come To Me - **Ruby Winters** 29.04.78
Come To Milton Keynes - **Style Council** 6.07.85
Come Together - **Primal Scream** 18.08.90
Come Tomorrow - **Manfred Mann** 14.01.65
Come What May - **Vicky Leandros** 8.04.72
Come With Me - **Jesse Green** 18.06.77
Comes A-Long A-Love - **Kay Starr** 5.12.52
Comin' Home - **Delaney & Bonnie & Friends** 20.12.69
Comin' On Strong - **Broken English** 13.06.87
Coming Around Again - **Carly Simon** 7.02.87
Coming Home - **David Essex** 23.10.76
Coming Home - **Marshall Hain** 21.10.78
Coming Home Baby - **Mel Torme** 10.01.63
Coming Out Of The Dark - **Gloria Estefan** 26.01.91
Coming Up - **Paul McCartney** 26.04.80
The Commancheros - **Lonnie Donegan** 18.01.62
Comment Te Dire Adieu - **Jimmy Somerville featuring June Miles Kingston** 18.11.89
Communication - **David McCallum** 28.04.66
Communication - **Spandau Ballet** 19.02.83
The Complete Dominator - **Human Resource** 21.12.91
Complex - **Gary Numan** 24.11.79
Computer Love/The Model - **Kraftwerk** 18.07.81
Concrete & Clay - **Randy Edelman** 6.03.76
Concrete and Clay - **Unit Four Plus Two** 4.03.65
Confessin' - **Frank Ifield** 27.06.63
Confusion - **Lee Dorsey** 19.05.66
Confusion - **New Order** 3.09.83
Confusion (Hits Us Every Time) - **Truth** 25.06.83
Confusion/Last Train to London - **Electric Light Orchestra** 17.11.79
Congratulations - **Cliff Richard** 20.03.68
Conquistador - **Procol Harum** 12.08.72
Conscience - **James Darren** 28.06.62
Constantly - **Cliff Richard** 30.04.64
Contact - **Edwin Starr** 3.02.79
The Continental - **Maureen McGovern** 12.06.76
Contribution - **Mica Paris featuring Rakim** 13.10.90
Conversations - **Cilla Black** 9.07.69
Convoy - **C.W. McCall** 21.02.76
Convoy GB - **Laurie Lingo & the Dipsticks** 24.04.76
Cool Baby - **Charlie Gracie** 10.01.58
Cool For Cats - **Squeeze** 24.03.79
Cool Meditation - **Third World** 13.01.79
Cool Out Tonight - **David Essex** 24.09.77
Cool Water - **Frankie Laine** 24.06.55
Coronation Rag - **Winifred Atwell** 15.05.53
Costafine Town - **Splinter** 9.11.74
Cottonfields - **Beach Boys** 23.05.70
Could Have Told You So - **Halo James** 13.01.90
Could It Be Forever - **David Cassidy** 8.04.72
Could It Be I'm Falling in Love - **Detroit Spinners** 21.04.73
Could It Be I'm Falling In Love (EP) - **Detroit Spinners** 7.05.77
Could It Be I'm Falling In Love - **David Grant & Jaki Graham** 23.03.85
Could It Be Magic - **Donna Summer** 19.06.76
Could It Be Magic - **Barry Manilow** 13.01.79
Could You Be Loved - **Bob Marley & the Wailers** 28.06.80
Couldn't Get It Right - **Climax Blues Band** 16.10.76
Could've Been - **Tiffany** 19.03.88
Count on Me - **Julie Grant** 4.04.63
Count Your Blessings - **Bing Crosby** 7.01.55
Countdown/New World Man - **Rush** 21.05.83
Counting Every Minute - **Sonia** 14.04.90
Counting Sheep - **Airhead** 28.12.91
Counting Teardrops - **Emile Ford & the Checkmates** 8.12.60
Country Boy - **Fats Domino** 31.03.60
Country Boy - **Heinz** 5.12.63
Cousin Norman - **Marmalade** 4.09.71
Cover From The Sky - **Deacon Blue** 14.12.91
Cover Girl - **New Kids On The Block** 12.05.90
Cover Me - **Bruce Springsteen** 13.10.84
Cover Me - **Bruce Springsteen** 23.03.85
Cover My Eyes (Pain and Heaven) - **Marillion** 15.06.91
Coward of The County - **Kenny Rogers** 26.01.80
Cowboy Jimmy Joe - **Alma Cogan** 11.05.61
Cowpuncher's Cantata - **Max Bygraves** 14.11.52
Coz I Luve You - **Slade** 30.10.71
Crackers International (EP) - **Erasure** 10.12.88
Crackin' Up - **Tommy Hunt** 25.10.75
Crackin' Up - **Nick Lowe** 16.06.79
Cracklin' Rose - **Neil Diamond** 7.11.70
Cradle of Love - **Johnny Preston** 28.04.60
Cradle of Love - **Billy Idol** 28.04.90
Crash - **Primitives** 27.02.88
Crawlin' Back - **Roy Orbison** 11.11.65
Crazy - **Mud** 17.03.73
Crazy - **Icehouse** 12.03.88
Crazy - **Seal** 15.12.90
Crazy - **Patsy Cline** 22.12.90
Crazy Crazy Nights - **Kiss** 3.10.87
Crazy Dream - **Jim Dale** 17.01.58
Crazy For You - **Madonna** 8.06.85
Crazy For You (Remix) - **Madonna** 2.03.91
Crazy Horses - **Osmonds** 11.11.72
Crazy Little Thing Called Love - **Queen** 20.10.79
Crazy Love - **Paul Anka** 30.05.58
Crazy Otto Rag - **Stargazers** 3.06.55

The Crazy Party Mixes - **Jive Bunny & the Mastermixers** 22.12.90
Crazy Water - **Elton John** 5.03.77
Cream - **Prince & the New Power Generation** 21.09.91
Creatures Of The Night - **Kiss** 7.05.83
The Creep - **Ken Mackintosh Orchestra** 15.01.54
Creeque Alley - **Mamas & Papas** 26.07.67
Criticize - **Alexander O'Neal** 14.11.87
Crockett's Theme - **Jan Hammer** 19.09.87
Crocodile Rock - **Elton John** 11.11.72
Crocodiles - **Echo & the Bunnymen** 18.04.81
Cross My Broken Heart - **Sinitta** 19.03.88
Cross My Heart - **Eighth Wonder** 2.07.88
Cross That Bridge - **Ward Brothers** 31.01.87
Cross Town Traffic - **Jimi Hendrix** 16.04.69
The Crowd - **Roy Orbison** 5.07.62
The Crown - **Gary Byrd and the GB Experience** 23.07.83
The Cruel Sea - **Dakotas** 18.07.63
Cruel Summer - **Bananarama** 9.07.83
Cruel Summer - **Bananarama** 10.06.89
Cruel To Be Kind - **Nick Lowe** 8.09.79
The Crunch - **Rah Band** 16.07.77
Crush on You - **Jets** 14.02.87
Crushed By The Wheels Of Industry - **Heaven 17** 10.09.83
Cry - **Godley & Creme** 27.04.85
Cry - **Waterfront** 24.06.89
Cry and Be Free - **Marilyn** 25.02.84
Cry Boy Cry - **Blue Zoo** 23.10.82
Cry For Help - **Rick Astley** 26.01.91
Cry Just A Little Bit - **Shakin' Stevens** 5.11.83
Cry Like A Baby - **Box Tops** 27.03.68
Cry Me A River - **Julie London** 5.04.57
Cry Me A River - **Mari Wilson** 26.03.83
Cry My Heart - **David Whitfield & the Mantovani Orchestra** 14.02.58
Cry Myself to Sleep - **Del Shannon** 13.09.62
Cry to Me - **Pretty Things** 15.07.65
Cry Wolf - **A-Ha** 6.12.86
Cryin' - **Roy Orbison** 28.09.61
Cryin' - **Vixen** 4.03.89
Cryin' In The Rain - **Everly Brothers** 18.01.62
Crying - **Don McLean** 17.05.80
The Crying Game - **Dave Berry** 13.08.64
Crying in The Chapel - **Lee Lawrence** 20.11.53
Crying in the Chapel - **Elvis Presley** 27.05.65
Crying In The Rain - **A-Ha** 13.10.90
Crying, Laughing, Loving, Lying - **Labi Siffre** 25.03.72
Crying Over You - **Ken Boothe** 4.01.75
Cuba/Better Do It Salsa - **Gibson Brothers** 1.03.80
Cubik/Olympic - **808 State** 10.11.90
Cuddly Toy - **Roachford** 14.01.89
Cuff of My Shirt - **Guy Mitchell** 19.02.54
Cult of Snap! - **Snap!** 22.09.90
Cum On Feel The Noize - **Slade** 3.03.73
Cumberland Gap - **Vipers** 22.03.57
Cumberland Gap - **Lonnie Donegan** 5.04.57
Cupboard Love - **John Leyton** 28.02.63
Cupid-I've Loved You For A Long Time - **Detroit Spinners** 5.07.80
Cupid - **Sam Cooke** 3.08.61
Cupid - **Johnny Nash** 2.04.69
Curly - **Move** 23.07.69
Cut Me Down - **Lloyd Cole & the Commotions** 25.01.86
Cut The Cake - **Average White Band** 3.05.75
The Cutter - **Echo and The Bunnymen** 22.01.83
Cutty Sark - **John Barry Seven** 26.04.62
D-A-A-Ance - **Lambrettas** 31.05.80
D-Darling - **Anthony Newley** 25.01.62
D-Days - **Hazel O'Connor** 28.03.81
Da Da Da - **Trio** 10.07.82
Da Doo Ron Ron - **Crystals** 20.06.63
Da Doo Ron Ron - **Crystals** 19.10.74
Daddy Cool - **Boney M.** 25.12.76
Daddy Cool - **Darts** 5.11.77
Daddy Don't You Walk So Fast - **Daniel Boone** 28.08.71
Daddy's Home - **Cliff Richard** 21.11.81
Dalliance - **Wedding Present** 11.05.91
Dambusters March - **Central Band of the Royal Air Force** 21.10.55
Damned Don't Cry - **Visage** 13.03.82
Dance Away - **Roxy Music** 5.05.79
Dance Dance Dance - **Beach Boys** 21.01.65
Dance Dance Dance - **Chic** 3.12.77
Dance (Disco Heat) - **Sylvester** 25.11.78
Dance Hall Days - **Wang Chung** 10.03.84
Dance Little Sister - **Terence Trent D'Arby** 17.10.87
Dance Me Up - **Gary Glitter** 30.06.84
Dance Of The Cuckoos - **Band Of The Black Witch** 20.12.75
Dance of the Mad - **Pop Will Eat Itself** 13.10.90
Dance On! - **Shadows** 13.12.62
Dance On - **Kathy Kirby** 22.08.63
Dance Stance - **Dexy's Midnight Runners** 9.02.80
Dance The Body Music - **Osibisa** 19.06.76
Dance the Kung Fu - **Carl Douglas** 30.11.74
Dance To the Music - **Sly & the Family Stone** 17.07.68
Dance With Me - **Drifters** 8.01.60
Dance With Me - **Carrie Lucas** 23.06.79
Dance With Me (I'm Your Ecstasy) - **Control** 2.11.91
Dance With The Guitar Man - **Duane Eddy** 8.11.62
Dance With The Devil - **Cozy Powell** 15.12.73
Dance Yourself Dizzy - **Liquid Gold** 8.03.80
Dancin' Easy - **Danny Williams** 6.08.77
Dancin' In The Moonlight - **Thin Lizzy** 13.08.77
Dancin' In The City - **Marshall Hain** 10.06.78
Dancin' In The Key of Life - **Steve Arrington** 13.07.85
Dancin' Party - **Chubby Checker** 16.08.62
Dancin' Party - **Showaddywaddy** 12.11.77
Dancing Girls - **Nik Kershaw** 14.04.84
Dancing In The Street - **Martha & the Vandellas** 5.11.64
Dancing In The Street - **Martha Reeves & the Vandellas** 15.01.69
Dancing In The Dark - **Bruce Springsteen** 26.05.84
Dancing In The Dark - **Bruce Springsteen** 19.01.85
Dancing In The Dark (EP) - **Big Daddy** 23.03.85
Dancing In The Street - **David Bowie & Mick Jagger** 7.09.85
Dancing On A Saturday Night - **Barry Blue** 4.08.73
Dancing on the Floor (Hooked on Love) - **Third World** 13.06.81
Dancing On The Ceiling - **Lionel Richie** 26.07.86
Dancing Queen - **Abba** 21.08.76
Dancing the Night Away - **Voggue** 1.08.81
Dancing Tight - **Galaxy featuring Phil Fearon** 23.04.83
Dancing With The Captain - **Paul Nicholas** 16.10.76
Dancing With Tears In My Eyes - **Ultravox** 19.05.84
Danger Games - **Pinkees** 2.10.82
The Danger of A Stranger - **Stella Parton** 5.11.77
Daniel - **Elton John** 20.01.73
Dare Me - **Pointer Sisters** 20.06.85
Dare to Dream/Both Sides Now - **Viola Wills** 22.03.86
Dark Is The Night - **Shakatak** 11.06.83
Dark Lady - **Cher** 2.03.74
Dark Moon - **Tony Brent** 28.06.57
Dark Town Strutter's Ball - **Joe Brown** 17.03.60
Darklands - **Jesus & Mary Chain** 7.11.87
Darlin' - **Beach Boys** 17.01.68
Darlin' - **David Cassidy** 1.11.75
Darlin' - **Frankie Miller** 14.10.78
Darlin' Darlin' Baby - **O'Jays** 12.02.77
Dat - **Pluto Shervington** 14.02.76
Daughter of Darkness - **Tom Jones** 18.04.70
David Watts/A Bomb In Wardour Street - **Jam** 26.08.78
Davy's On The Road Again - **Manfred Mann's Earth Band** 27.05.78
Dawn - **Flintlock** 12.06.76
Day After Day - **Badfinger** 5.02.72
The Day Before You Came - **Abba** 30.10.82
The Day Before You Came - **Blancmange** 21.07.84
Day By Day - **Holly Sherwood** 12.02.72
The Day I Met Marie - **Cliff Richard** 16.08.67
Day In Day Out - **David Bowie** 4.04.87
The Day That Curly Billy Shot Crazy Sam McGee - **Hollies** 20.10.73
Day the Rains Came - **Jane Morgan** 5.12.58
The Day The World Turned Dayglow - **X-Ray Spex** 6.05.78
Day Trip to Bangor - **Fiddler's Dream** 15.12.79
Day Tripper/We Can Work It Out - **Beatles** 9.12.65
A Day Without Love - **Love Affair** 18.09.68
Daydream - **Lovin' Spoonful** 14.04.66
Daydream Believer - **Monkees** 15.11.67
Daydreamer/Puppy Song - **David Cassidy** 13.10.73
Days - **Kinks** 24.07.68
Days - **Kirsty MacColl** 8.07.89
Days of No Trust - **Magnum** 19.03.88
Daytime Friends - **Kenny Rogers** 24.09.77
Daytime Friends - **Kenny Rogers** 1.10.77
Daytona Demon - **Suzi Quatro** 3.11.73

Dazz - **Brick** 12.02.77
Dazzle - **Siouxsie & the Banshees** 2.06.84
De Do Do Do De Da Da Da - **Police** 13.12.80
Dead Cities - **Exploited** 24.10.81
Dead End Street - **Kinks** 24.11.66
Dead Giveaway - **Shalamar** 11.06.83
Dead Ringer For Love - **Meat Loaf** 5.12.81
Deadlier Than The Male - **Walker Brothers** 15.12.66
The Deal - **Pat Campbell** 22.11.69
The Dean and I **10CC** 25.08.73
Dear Delilah - **Grapefruit** 21.02.68
Dear Elaine - **Roy Wood** 18.08.73
Dear Jessie - **Madonna** 16.12.89
Dear John - **Status Quo** 27.03.82
Dear Lonely Hearts - **Nat 'King' Cole** 27.12.62
Dear Miss Lonely Hearts - **Phil Lynott** 19.04.80
Dear Mrs. Applebee - **David Garrick** 29.09.66
Dear Prudence - **Siouxsie and the Banshees** 1.10.83
Death Disco - **Public Image Ltd** 7.07.79
Death of A Clown - **Dave Davies** 19.07.67
Debora - **Tyrannosaurus Rex** 15.05.68
Debora/One Inch Rock - **Tyrannosaurus Rex** 8.04.72
Decadence Dance - **Extreme** 12.10.91
December - **All About Eve** 23.12.89
December '63 - **Four Seasons** 31.01.76
Deck of Cards - **Wink Martindale** 4.12.59
Deck of Cards - **Wink Martindale** 25.04.63
Deck of Cards - **Max Bygraves** 6.10.73
Deck of Cards - **Wink Martindale** 27.10.73
Dedicated Follower of Fashion - **Kinks** 3.03.66
Dedicated To The One I Love - **Mamas & the Papas** 13.04.67
Dedication - **Thin Lizzy** 26.01.91
Deep Deep Trouble - **Simpsons** 6.04.91
Deep Heat 89 - **Latino Rave** 1.12.89
Deep In the Heart of Texas - **Duane Eddy** 31.05.62
Deep Purple - **Billy Ward** 29.11.57
Deep Purple - **Nino Tempo & April Stevens** 14.11.63
Deep Purple - **Donny & Marie Osmond** 17.01.76
Deeper and Deeper - **Freda - Payne** 5.12.70
The Deeper the Love - **Whitesnake** 10.03.90
Delaware - **Perry Como** 26.02.60
Delilah - **Tom Jones** 28.02.68
Delilah - **Sensational Alex Harvey Band** 26.07.75
Delilah Jones - **McGuire Sisters** 1.06.56
Deliverance - **Mission** 10.03.90
Delta Lady - **Joe Cocker** 4.10.69
Denis - **Blondie** 25.02.78
Desafinado - **Stan Getz & Charlie Byrd** 15.11.62
Desafinado - **Ella Fitzgerald** 22.11.62
Desiderata - **Les Crane** 4.03.72
Desire - **U2** 1.10.88
Desire Me - **Doll** 20.01.79
Desiree - **Neil Diamond** 24.12.77
Desperate But Not Serious - **Adam Ant** 4.12.82
Desperate Dan - **Lieutenant Pigeon** 16.12.72
Destination Zululand - **King Kurt** 29.10.83
Destiny - **Jacksons** 10.02.79
Detroit City - **Tom Jones** 16.02.67
Deutscher Girls - **Adam and the Ants** 27.02.82
Devil Gate Drive - **Suzi Quatro** 9.02.74
Devil in Disguise - **Elvis Presley** 4.07.63
The Devil Went Down To Georgia - **Charlie Daniels** 6.10.79
Devil Woman - **Marty Robbins** 4.10.62
Devil Woman - **Cliff Richard** 15.05.76
Devil's Answer - **Atomic Rooster** 10.07.71
Devil's Toy - **Almighty** 11.05.91
Devotion - **Ten City** 8.04.89
Diamond Dogs - **David Bowie** 22.06.74
Diamond Lights - **Glenn & Chris** 18.04.87
Diamond Smiles - **Boomtown Rats** 17.11.79
Diamonds - **Jet Harris & Tony Meehan** 17.01.63
Diamonds - **Herb Alpert** 13.06.87
Diamonds and Pearls - **Prince & The New Power Generation** 7.12.91
Diamonds Are Forever - **Shirley Bassey** 5.02.72
Diana - **Paul Anka** 9.08.57
Diane - **Bachelors** 23.01.64
The Diary of Horace Wimp - **Electric Light Orchestra** 28.07.79
Dick-A-Dum-Dum - **Des O'Connor** 14.05.69
Did You Ever - **Nancy & Lee** 21.08.71
Didn't I (Blow Your Mind This Time) - **Delfonics** 1.05.71
Didn't We Almost Have It All - **Whitney Houston** 22.08.87
A Different Corner - **George Michael** 5.04.86
Digging Your Scene - **Blow Monkeys** 8.03.86
Dignity - **Deacon Blue** 13.02.88
Dim All The Lights - **Donna Summer** 22.09.79
Dime and A Dollar - **Guy Mitchell** 30.04.54
Dimples - **John Lee Hooker** 18.06.64
Ding-A-Dong - **Teach-In** 12.04.75
Ding Dong - **George Harrison** 11.01.75
Dinner with Gershwin - **Donna Summer** 7.11.87
Dippety Day - **Father Abraham & the Smurfs** 14.10.78
Dirty Cash - **Adventures of Stevie V** 21.04.90
Dirty Diana - **Michael Jackson** 16.07.88
Dirty Love - **Thunder** 17.02.90
Disappear - **Inxs** 8.12.90
Disappearing Act - **Shalamar** 20.08.83
Disappointed - **Public Image Ltd** 20.05.89
D.I.S.C.O. - **Ottawan** 20.09.80
Disco Connection Movement - **Isaac Hayes** 3.04.76
Disco Duck - **Rick Dees & his Cast of Idiots** 18.09.76
Disco Inferno - **Trammps** 14.05.77
Disco Lady - **Johnny Taylor** 1.05.76
Disco Music (I Like It) - **J.A.L.N. Band** 25.09.76
Disco Queen - **Hot Chocolate** 24.05.75
Disco Stomp - **Hamilton Bohannon** 31.05.75
Disenchanted - **Communards** 31.05.86
Distant Drums - **Jim Reeves** 18.08.66
Divine Emotions - **Narada** 30.04.88
Dizzy - **Tommy Roe** 30.04.69
Dizzy - **Vic Reeves & the Wonder Stuff** 26.10.91
DJ Culture - **Pet Shop Boys** 26.10.91
DJS Take Control/Way In My Brain - **SL2** 2.11.91
Do Anything You Wanna Do - **Rods** 13.08.77
Do Anything You Want To - **Thin Lizzy** 23.06.79
Do I Do - **Stevie Wonder** 12.06.82
Do I Love You - **Ronettes** 15.10.64
Do It Again-Billie Jean - **Clubhouse** 23.07.83
Do It Again - **Beach Boys** 31.07.68
Do It Again - **Steely Dan** 6.09.75
Do It Anyway You Wanna - **People's Choice** 4.10.75
Do It Do It Again - **Raffaella Carra** 22.04.78
Do It To The Music - **Raw Silk** 23.10.82
Do Not Disturb - **Bananarama** 31.08.85
Do Nothing - **Specials** 20.12.80
Do That To Me One More Time - **Captain & Tennille** 23.02.80
(Do The) - **Spanish Hustle - Fatback Band** 21.02.76
Do The Bartman - **Simpsons** 26.01.91
Do The Bus Stop - **Fatback Band** 13.12.75
Do the Clam - **Elvis Presley** 11.03.65
Do the Conga - **Black Lace** 1.12.84
Do The Funky Chicken - **Rufus Thomas** 18.04.70
(Do) The Hucklebuck - **Coast to Coast** 14.02.81
Do The Right Thing - **Redhead Kingpin and the FBI** 5.08.89
Do They Know It's Christmas - **Band Aid** 15.12.84
Do They Know It's Christmas - **Band Aid** 7.12.85
Do They Know It's Christmas - **Band Aid II** 23.12.89
Do Wah Diddy Diddy - **Manfred Mann** 16.07.64
Do What You Do - **Jermaine Jackson** 2.03.85
Do What You Feel - **Joey Negro** 16.11.91
Do What You Gotta Do - **Four Tops** 4.10.69
Do What You Wanna Do - **T Connection** 25.06.77
Do Ya Do Ya (Wanna Please Me) - **Samantha Fox** 28.06.86
Do Ya Wanna Funk - **Sylvester with Patrick Cowley** 25.09.82
Do You Believe In The Westworld - **Theatre Of Hate** 6.02.82
Do You Believe In Shame - **Duran Duran** 22.04.89
Do You Feel - **Peter Frampton** 20.11.76
Do You Feel Like I Feel - **Belinda Carlisle** 16.11.91
Do You Feel My Love - **Eddy Grant** 22.11.80
Do You Know The Way To San Jose - **Dionne Warwick** 15.05.68
Do You Know Where You're Going To - **Diana Ross** 3.04.76
Do You Love Me? - **Brian Poole & the Tremeloes** 12.09.63
Do You Love Me? - **Dave Clark Five** 17.10.63
Do You Love Me - **Deep Feeling** 9.05.70
Do You Love What You Feel - **Inner City** 29.07.89
Do You Mind? - **Anthony Newley** 24.03.60
Do You Really Love Me Too - **Billy Fury** 2.01.64
Do You Really Want to Hurt Me - **Culture Club** 25.09.82
Do You Remember - **Scaffold** 3.04.68

Do You Think I'm Sexy? - **Rod Stewart** 18.11.78
Do You Wanna Touch Me (Oh Yeah) - **Gary Glitter** 20.01.73
Do You Wanna Dance - **Barry Blue** 3.11.73
Do You Want Me - **Salt-N-Pepa** 1.06.91
Do You Want To Dance/I'm Looking Out the Window - **Cliff Richard** 10.05.62
Do You Want To Know A Secret? - **Billy J Kramer & the Dakotas** 9.05.63
Do Your Dance - **Rose Royce** 1.10.77
Doctor! Doctor! - **Thompson Twins** 4.02.84
Doctor Doctor - **UFO** 3.02.79
Doctor Doctor - **UFO** 17.02.79
Doctor Jeep - **Sisters of Mercy** 22.12.90
Doctor My Eyes - **Jackson Five** 17.02.73
Doctorin' The House - **Coldcut featuring Yazz & the Plastic Population** 20.02.88
Doctorin' The Tardis - **Timelords** 4.06.88
Doctor's Orders - **Sunny** 6.04.74
Does She Have A Friend - **Gene Chandler** 19.07.80
Does Your Chewing Gum Lose It's Flavour? - **Lonnie Donegan** 6.02.59
Does Your Mother Know - **Abba** 5.05.79
Dog Eat Dog - **Adam & the Ants** 18.10.80
Dogs - **Who** 26.06.68
Doin' Our Own Dang - **Jungle Brothers** 28.07.90
Doin' the Do - **Betty Boo** 26.05.90
Dolce Vita - **Ryan Paris** 10.09.83
Doll House - **King Brothers** 12.01.61
Dolly My Love - **Moments** 26.07.75
Dominator - **Human Resource** 14.09.91
Dominion - **Sisters of Mercy** 27.02.88
Dominique - **Singing Nun** 5.12.63
Domino Dancing - **Pet Shop Boys** 24.09.88
Dominoes - **Robbie Nevil** 9.05.87
Don Juan - **Dave Dee, Dozy, Beaky, Mick & Tich** 12.03.69
Don Quixote - **Nik Kershaw** 3.08.85
Donald Where's Your Troosers? - **Andy Stewart** 15.12.60
Donald Where's Your Troosers - **Andy Stewart** 9.12.89
Donkey Cart - **Frank Chacksfield Orchestra** 31.08.56
Donna - **Marty Wilde** 6.03.59
Donna - **Richie Valens** 6.03.59
Donna - **10CC** 30.09.72
Don't - **Elvis Presley** 28.02.58
Don't Answer Me - **Cilla Black** 9.06.66
Don't Ask Me - **P.I.L.** 20.10.90
Don't Ask Me Why Eurythmics 11.11.89
Don't Be A Dummy - **John Du Cann** 6.10.79
Don't Be A Fool - **Loose Ends** 1.09.90
Don't Be Cruel - **Bill Black's Combo** 10.11.60
Don't Be Cruel - **Elvis Presley** 8.07.78
Don't Be Cruel - **Bobby Brown** 25.03.89
Don't Believe A Word - **Thin Lizzy** 15.01.77
Don't Believe the Hype - **Public Enemy** 2.07.88
Don't Blame It On That Girl/Wap-Bam-Boogie - **Matt Bianco** 11.06.88
Don't Blame Me - **Frank Ifield** 9.01.64
Don't Break My Heart Again - **Whitesnake** 18.04.81
Don't Break My Heart - **UB40** 26.10.85
Don't Break the Heart That Loves You - **Connie Francis** 3.05.62
Don't Bring Lulu - **Dorothy Provine** 14.12.61
Don't Bring Me Down - **Pretty Things** 29.10.64
Don't Bring Me Your Heartaches - **Paul & Barry Ryan** 11.11.65
Don't Bring Me Down - **Animals** 2.06.66
Don't Bring Me Down - **Electric Light Orchestra** 1.09.79
Don't Call Me Baby - **Voice of the Beehive** 28.05.88
Don't Come Close - **Ramones** 14.10.78
Don't Cry - **Asia** 20.08.83
Don't Cry - **Guns N' Roses** 21.09.91
Don't Cry Daddy - **Elvis Presley** 28.02.70
Don't Cry For Me Argentina - **Julie Covington** 25.12.76
Don't Cry For Me Argentina - **Shadows** 13.01.79
Don't Cry Out Loud - **Elkie Brooks** 18.11.78
Don't Dilly Dally/Waiting At The Church - **Muppets** 24.12.77
Don't Do It Baby - **Mac & Katie Kissoon** 10.05.75
Don't Do That - **Geordie** 9.12.72
Don't Dream It's Over - **Crowded House** 13.06.87
Don't Dream It's Over - **Paul Young** 26.10.91
Don't Ever Change - **Crickets** 21.06.62
Don't Fall In Love (I Said) - **Toyah** 4.05.85
(Don't Fear) The Reaper - **Blue Oyster Cult** 27.05.78
Don't Fight It - **Wilson Pickett** 9.12.65
Don't Forbid Me - **Pat Boone** 1.02.57
Don't Forget To Catch Me - **Cliff Richard & the Shadows** 4.12.68
Don't Forget to Remember - **Bee Gees** 23.08.69
Don't Forget Me (When I'm Gone) - **Glass Tiger** 8.11.86
Don't Get Me Wrong - **Pretenders** 18.10.86
Don't Give Up On Us - **David Soul** 18.12.76
Don't Give Up - **Peter Gabriel & Kate Bush** 1.11.86
Don't Go - **Yazoo** 17.07.82
Don't Go - **Hothouse Flowers** 21.05.88
Don't Go Breaking My Heart - **Elton John & Kiki Dee** 10.07.76
Don't Go Messin' With My Heart - **Mantronix** 2.03.91
Don't Hang Up - **Orlons** 17.01.63
Don't Hold Back - **Chanson** 20.01.79
Don't It Make My Brown Eyes Blue - **Crystal Gayle** 12.11.77
Don't It Make You Feel Good - **Stefan Dennis** 6.05.89
Don't Jump Off The Roof Dad - **Tommy Cooper** 6.07.61
Don't Kill The Whale - **Yes** 16.09.78
Don't Knock The Rock - **Bill Haley & his Comets** 8.02.57
Don't Know Much - **Linda Ronstadt with Aaron Neville** 11.11.89
Don't Laugh at Me - **Norman Wisdom** 19.02.54
Don't Leave Me This Way - **Harold Melvin & the Blue Notes** 22.01.77
Don't Leave Me This Way - **Thelma Houston** 5.02.77
Don't Leave Me This Way - **Communards** 23.08.86
Don't Let Go - **Manhattan Transfer** 4.06.77
Don't Let Him Touch You - **Angelettes** 20.05.72
Don't Let It Die - **Hurricane Smith** 19.06.71
Don't Let It Fade Away - **Darts** 18.11.78
Don't Let It Pass You By/Don't Slow Down - **UB40** 23.05.81
Don't Let Me Be Misunderstood - **Animals** 4.02.65
Don't Let Me Be Misunderstood - **Costello Show** 1.02.86
Don't Let Me Down Gently - **Wonder Stuff** 23.09.89
Don't Let Me Down - **Farm** 4.05.91
Don't Let The Stars Get In Your Eyes - **Perry Como** 16.01.53
Don't Let The Sun Catch You Crying - **Gerry & the Pacemakers** 16.04.64
Don't Let The Rain Come Down - **Ronnie Hilton** 21.05.64
Don't Let The Sun Go Down On Me - **Elton John** 1.06.74
Don't Let The Sun Go Down On Me - **Oleta Adams** 5.10.91
Don't Let The Sun Go Down on Me - **George Michael & Elton John** 7.12.91
Don't Like Mondays - **Boomtown Rats** 21.07.79
Don't Look Back - **Fine Young Cannibals** 26.08.89
Don't Look Down - The Sequel - **Go West** 30.11.85
Don't Love Me Too Hard - **Nolans** 13.03.82
Don't Make Me Over - **Swinging Blue Jeans** 27.01.66
Don't Make Me Wait Too Long - **Barry White** 13.11.76
Don't Make Me Over - **Sybil** 21.10.89
Don't Make My Baby Blue - **Shadows** 5.08.65
Don't Make Waves - **Nolans** 19.04.80
Don't Mess With Dr Dream - **Thompson Twins** 31.08.85
Don't Miss the Party Line - **Bizz Nizz** 31.03.90
Don't Need A Gun - **Billy Idol** 14.03.87
Don't Play That Song - **Aretha Franklin** 29.08.70
Don't Play Your Rock and Roll To Me - **Smokie** 11.10.75
Don't Push It Don't Force It - **Leon Haywood** 22.03.80
Don't Say I Told You So - **Tourists** 25.10.80
Don't Set Me Free - **Ray Charles** 28.03.63
Don't Sleep In The Subway - **Petula Clark** 8.06.67
Don't Stand So Close To Me - **Police** 27.09.80
Don't Stand So Close To Me 86 - **Police** 11.10.86
Don't Stay Away Too Long - **Peters & Lee** 20.04.74
Don't Stop - **Fleetwood Mac** 7.05.77
Don't Stop It Now - **Hot Chocolate** 27.03.76
Don't Stop Me Now - **Queen** 17.02.79
Don't Stop 'Til You Get Enough - **Michael Jackson** 22.09.79
Don't Stop The Carnival - **Alan Price Set** 30.01.68
Don't Stop the Music - **Yarborough & Peoples** 10.01.81
Don't Stop That Crazy Rhythm - **Modern Romance** 14.05.83
Don't Stop The Dance - **Bryan Ferry** 31.08.85
Don't Stop Twist - **Frankie Vaughan** 1.02.62
Don't Take Away the Music - **Tavares** 9.10.76
Don't Take No For An Answer - **Tom Robinson Band** 18.02.78
Don't Talk Just Kiss - **Right Said Fred** 7.12.91
Don't Talk to Him - **Cliff Richard** 7.11.63
Don't Talk To Me About Love - **Altered Images** 19.03.83
Don't Tell Me - **Blancmange** 14.04.84
Don't That Beat All - **Adam Faith** 6.09.62
Don't Throw Away All Those Teardrops - **Frankie Avalon** 5.05.60
Don't Throw It All Away - **Gary Benson** 16.08.75
Don't Throw Your Love Away - **Searchers** 16.04.64
Don't Treat Me Like a Child - **Helen Shapiro** 23.03.61
Don't Try To Change Me - **Crickets** 13.06.63
Don't Try To Stop It - **Roman Holiday** 2.07.83
Don't Turn Around - **Merseybeats** 23.04.64

Don't Turn Around - **Aswad** 5.03.88
Don't Walk Away - **Electric Light Orchestra** 22.11.80
Don't Walk Away - **Four Tops** 26.12.81
Don't Wanna Fall In Love - **Jane Child** 26.05.90
Don't Wanna Lose You - **Gloria Estefan** 15.07.89
Don't Waste My Time - **Paul Hardcastle** 8.02.86
Don't Worry - **Johnny Brandon** 1.07.55
Don't Worry - **Billy Fury** 4.05.61
Don't Worry - **Kim Appleby** 3.11.90
Don't Worry Be Happy - **Bobby McFerrin** 1.10.88
Don't You (Forget About Me) - **Simple Minds** 20.04.85
Don't You Just Know It - **Amazulu** 30.11.85
Don't You Know It? - **Adam Faith** 27.07.61
Don't You Know - **Butterscotch** 16.05.70
Don't You Love Me - **49ers** 17.03.90
Don't You Rock Me Daddy-O - **Lonnie Donegan** 18.01.57
Don't You Rock Me Daddy-O - **Vipers** 25.01.57
Don't You Think It's Time - **Mike Berry & the Outlaws** 3.01.63
Don't You Want Me - **Human League** 5.12.81
Doobedood'Ndoobe Doobedood'Ndoobe - **Diana Ross** 20.05.72
Doors of your Heart - **Beat** 27.06.81
Double Barrel - **Dave & Ansil Collins** 3.04.71
Double Dutch - **Fatback Band** 19.03.77
Double Dutch - **Malcolm McLaren** 9.07.83
Doubleback - **ZZ Top** 28.07.90
Down By The Lazy River - **Osmonds** 8.04.72
Down Deep Inside - **Donna Summer** 27.08.77
Down Down - **Status Quo** 7.12.74
Down in The Boondocks - **Billy Joe Royal** 7.10.65
Down In The Subway - **Soft Cell** 25.02.84
Down In The Tube Station at Midnight - **Jam** 21.10.78
Down In The Tube Station At Midnight - **Jam** 29.01.83
Down on the Beach Tonight - **Drifters** 19.10.74
Down on The Corner - **Creedence Clearwater Revival** 14.02.70
Down On the Street - **Shakatak** 14.07.84
Down The Dustpipe - **Status Quo** 16.05.70
Down The Hall - **Four Seasons** 3.09.77
Down to Earth - **Curiosity Killed the Cat** 17.01.87
Down to Earth - **Monie Love** 1.12.90
Down Under - **Men At Work** 8.01.83
Down Yonder - **Johnny & the Hurricanes** 16.06.60
Downhearted - **Eddie Fisher** 1.05.53
Downtown - **Petula Clark** 19.11.64
Downtown '88 - **Petula Clark** 3.12.88
Downtown Train - **Rod Stewart** 10.02.90
Dr Beat - **Miami Sound Machine** 18.08.84
Dr Heckyll And Mr Jive - **Men At Work** 17.09.83
Dr Mabuse - **Propaganda** 14.04.84
Dr Who - **Mankind** 9.12.78
Dragnet - **Ted Heath Orchestra** 23.10.53
Dragnet - **Ray Anthony Orchestra** 4.12.53
Drama! - **Erasure** 30.09.89
Dreadlock Holiday - **10 C.C.** 19.08.78
Dream A Little Dream of Me - **Mama Cass** 21.08.68
Dream A Little Dream of Me - **Anita Harris** 21.08.68
Dream Baby - **Roy Orbison** 8.03.62
Dream Baby - **Clen Campbell** 3.04.71
Dream Girl - **Mark Wynter** 16.03.61
Dream Lover - **Bobby Darin** 29.05.59
Dream To Sleep - **H_2O** 04.06.83
Dreamboat - **Alma Cogan** 27.05.55
Dreamboat - **Limmie & Family Cookin'** 27.10.73
Dreamer - **Supertramp** 22.02.75
Dreamer - **Jacksons** 20.08.77
Dreamer - **BB+Q** 20.09.86
Dreamin' - **Johnny Burnette** 6.10.60
Dreamin' - **Liverpool Express** 18.06.77
Dreamin' - **Cliff Richard** 23.08.80
Dreamin' - **Status Quo** 13.12.86
Dreaming - **Blondie** 29.09.79
Dreaming - **Glen Goldsmith** 26.03.88
Dreams - **Fleetwood Mac** 16.07.77
A Dreams A Dream - **Soul II Soul** 5.05.90
Dreams Can Tell A Lie - **Nat 'King' Cole** 27.01.56
Dreams of You - **Ralph McTell** 10.01.76
Dreamy Lady - **T. Rex Disco Party** 18.10.75
Dress You Up - **Madonna** 7.12.85
Dressed for Success - **Roxette** 27.10.90
Drinking Song - **Mario Lanza** 4.02.55
Drive-In Saturday - **David Bowie** 14.04.73
Drive - **Cars** 29.09.84
Drive - **Cars** 10.08.85
Drive On - **Brother Beyond** 4.11.89
Drive Safely Darlin' - **Tony Christie** 24.01.76
Driven By You - **Brian May** 7.12.91
Drivin' Home - **Duane Eddy** 14.09.61
Driving Away From Home - **It's Immaterial** 19.04.86
Driving in My Car - **Madness** 24.07.82
D.J. - **David Bowie** 21.07.79
Drop the Boy - **Bros** 19.03.88
Drop The Pilot - **Joan Armatrading** 5.03.83
Drowning In Berlin - **Mobiles** 16.1.82.
Drowning/All Out To Get You - **Beat** 25.04.81
Dr. Kiss Kiss - **5000 Volts** 31.07.76
Dr. Love - **Tina Charles** 11.12.76
Drummer Man - **Tonight** 28.01.78
Drummin' Up A Storm - **Sandy Nelson** 28.06.62
Drums Are My Beat - **Sandy Nelson** 29.03.62
Dry Land - **Marillion** 5.10.91
Dub Be Good To Me - **Beats International** 10.02.90
Duchess - **Stranglers** 25.08.79
Dude (Looks Like A Lady) - **Aerosmith** 24.02.90
Duel - **Propaganda** 1.06.85
Duelling Banjos - **Soundtrack 'Deliverance'** 31.03.73
Duke of Earl - **Darts** 28.07.79
Dum Dum - **Brenda Lee** 27.07.61
Dyna-Mite - **Mud** 27.10.73
Dynamite - **Cliff Richard & the Shadows** 9.10.59
Dynomite - **Tony Camillo's Bazuka** 7.06.75
D.I.V.O.R.C.E. - **Tammy Wynette -** 28.06.75
D.I.V.O.R.C.E. - **Billy Connolly** 1.11.75
D.W. Washburn - **Monkees** 26.06.68
Each And Every One - **Everything But the Girl** 19.05.84
Each Time You Break My Heard - **Nick Kamen** 15.11.86
Early In The Morning - **Buddy Holly** 29.08.58
Early In The Morning - **Vanity Fare** 23.07.69
Early to Bed - **Poni-Tails** 10.04.59
Earth Angel - **Crew Cuts** 15.04.55
The Earth Dies Screaming/Dream A Lie - **UB40** 1.11.80
Easier Said Than Done - **Shakatak** 16.1.82.
East of Eden - **Big Country** 29.09.84
East River - **Brecker Brothers** 18.11.78
East West - **Herman's Hermits** 22.12.66
Easter - **Marillion** 14.04.90
Easy - **Commodores** 9.07.77
Easy - **Commodores** 3.09.88
Easy Easy - **Scotland World Cup Squad** 22.06.74
Easy Going Me - **Adam Faith** 27.04.61
Easy Lover - **Philip Bailey (duet with Phil Collins)** 9.03.85
Eat It - **Weird Al Yankovic** 28.04.84
Ebb Tide - **Frank Chacksfield** 12.02.54
Ebony And Ivory - **Paul McCartney with Stevie Wonder** 10.04.82
Ebony Eyes - **Everly Brothers** 9.02.61
Echo Beach - **Martha & the Muffins** 8.03.80
Edelweiss - **Vince Hill** 9.02.67
The Edge of Heaven - **Wham!** 21.06.86
Edie (Ciao Baby) - **Cult** 15.07.89
Eeny Meeny - **Showstoppers** 20.11.68
Ego - **Elton John** 15.04.78
Egyptian Reggae - **J. Richman & the Modern Lovers** 12.11.77
Eight by Ten - **Ken Dodd** 6.02.64
18 and Life - **Skid Row** 3.02.90
18 Carat Love Affair/Love Hangover - **Associates** 7.08.82
Eighteen With A Bullet - **Pete Wingfield** 5.07.75
Eight Miles High - **Byrds** 19.05.66
Eighteen Yellow Roses - **Bobby Darin** 1.08.63
Eighth Day - **Hazel O'Connor** 23.08.80
Einstein A Go-Go - **Landscape** 14.03.81
El Paso - **Marty Robbins** 29.01.60
Eleanor Rigby - **Ray Charles** 7.08.68
Elected - **Alice Cooper** 7.10.72
Election Day - **Arcadia** 26.10.85
Electric Avenue - **Eddy Grant** 15.01.83
Electric Lady - **Geordie** 25.08.73
Electric Youth - **Debbie Gibson** 29.04.89
Elenore - **Turtles** 6.11.68
Elephant Stone - **Stone Roses** 3.03.90
Elephant Tango - **Cyril Stapleton Orchestra** 27.05.55

The Elephant's Graveyard (Guilty) - **Boomtown Rats** 31.01.81
Elizabethan Reggae - **Boris Gardner** 31.01.70
Elmo James - **Chairmen of the Board** 14.10.72
ELO EP - **Electric Light Orchestra** 16.12.78
Eloise - **Barry Ryan** 23.10.68
Eloise - **Damned** 8.02.86
Elusive Butterly - **Bob Lind** 17.03.66
Elusive Butterfly - **Val Doonican** 17.03.66
Embarrassment - **Madness** 22.11.80
E=MC² - **Big Audio Dynamite** 29.03.86
Emma - **Hot Chocolate** 16.03.74
Emotional Rescue - **Rolling Stones** 12.07.80
Emotions - **Samantha Sang** 11.02.78
Emotions - **Mariah Carey** 12.10.91
The Emperor's New Clothes - **Sinead O'Connor** 28.07.90
Empty Rooms - **Gary Moore** 27.07.85
Enchanted Lady - **Pasadenas** 3.12.88
End of The World - **Skeeter Davis** 21.03.63
End of the World - **Sonia** 25.08.90
Endless - **Dickie Valentine** 5.11.54
Endless Love - **Diana Ross & Lionel Richie** 12.09.81
Endless Sleep - **Marty Wilde** 11.07.58
Endlessly - **Brook Benton** 10.07.59
Engine Engine Number Nine - **Roger Miller** 3.06.65
England Swings - **Roger Miller** 6.01.66
English Civil War - **Clash** 3.03.79
English Country Garden - **Jimmy Rodgers** 14.06.62
Englishman in New York - **Sting** 11.08.90
Enjoy the Silence - **Depeche Mode** 17.02.90
Enola Gay - **Orchestral Manoeuvres In The Dark** 11.10.80
Enter Sandman - **Metallica** 10.08.91
The Entertainer - **Marvin Hamlisch** 6.04.74
Entry of the Gladiators - **Nero and the Gladiators** 6.04.61
Epic - **Faith No More** 10.02.90
Epic - **Faith No More** 8.09.90
Ernie (The Fastest Milkman in the West) - **Benny Hill** 13.11.71
Escapade - **Janet Jackson** 31.03.90
Escape (The Pina Colada Song) - **Rupert Holmes** 19.01.80
Especially For You - **Kylie Minogue & Jason Donovan** 10.12.88
Et Les Oiseaux Chantaient (And The Birds Were Singing) - **Sweet People** 11.10.80
Et Meme - **Francoise Hardy** 14.01.65
Eternal Flame - **Bangles** 25.03.89
Eternally - **Jimmy Young** 21.08.53
Eton Rifles - **Jam** 3.11.79
Europe (After the Rain) - **John Foxx** 5.09.81
European Female - **Stranglers** 8.01.83
European Son - **Japan** .... 30.1.82.
Eve of Destruction - **Barry McGuire** 9.09.65
Eve Of The War - **Jeff Wayne's War Of The Worlds** 30.09.78
Eve of The War - **Jeff Wayne** 25.11.89
Even More Party Pops - **Russ Conway** 1.12.60
Even The Bad Times Are Good - **Tremeloes** 2.08.67
Even Though You're Gone - **Jacksons** 18.02.78
Evening Falls - **Enya** 24.12.88
Ever Fallen in Love - **Fine Young Cannibals** 28.03.87
Ever Since You Said Goodbye - **Marty Wilde** 1.11.62
Ever So Lonley - **Monsoon** 10.04.82
Everlasting - **Natalie Cole** 25.06.88
Everlasting Love - **Love Affair** 3.01.68
Everlasting Love - **Robert Knight** 17.01.68
Everlasting Love - **Robert Knight** 9.03.74
Everlasting Love - **Rex Smith & Rachel Sweet** 5.09.81
Everlovin' - **Ricky Nelson** 16.11.61
Evermore - **Ruby Murray** 1.07.55
Every 1's A Winner - **Hot Chocolate** 4.03.78
Every Angel - **All About Eve** 16.04.88
Every Beat of My Heart 12.07.86
Every Beat of The Heart - **Railway Children** 9.02.91
Every Breath You Take - **Police** 28.05.83
Every Day Hurts - **Sad Cafe** 29.09.79
Every Day (I Love You More) - **Jason Donovan** 9.09.89
Every Day Is Like Sunday - **Morrissey** 11.06.88
Every Day of My Life - **Malcolm Vaughan** 1.07.55
Every Girl & Boy - **Spagna** 27.08.88
Every Heartbeat - **Amy Grant** 3.08.91
Every Little Teardrop - **Gallagher & Lyle** 29.01.77
Every Little Thing She Does Is Magic - **Police** 24.10.81
Every Little Step - **Bobby Brown** 20.05.89
Every Loser Wins - **Nick Berry** 11.10.86
Every Night - **Phoebe Snow** 20.01.79
Every Nite's A Saturday Night With You - **Drifters** 25.09.76
Every Rose Has Its Thorn - **Poison** 11.02.89
Every Time You Go Away - **Paul Young** 9.03.85
Everybody - **Tommy Roe** 26.09.63
Everybody Dance - **Chic** 1.04.78
Everybody Everybody - **Black Box** 2.06.90
Everybody Get Together - **Dave Clark Five** 7.03.70
Everybody Knows - **Dave Clark Five** 28.01.65
Everybody Knows - **Dave Clark Five** 8.11.67
Everybody Loves A Lover - **Doris Day** 15.08.58
Everybody Loves Somebody - **Dean Martin** 27.08.64
Everybody Move - **Cathy Dennis** 14.12.91
Everybody Needs Somebody to Love - **Blues Brothers** 14.04.90
Everybody (Rap) - **Criminal Element Orchestra** 6.10.90
Everybody Salsa - **Modern Romance** 22.08.81
Everybody Wants to Rule The World - **Tears for Fears** 30.03.85
Everybody Wants To Run The World - **Tears For Fears** 31.05.86
Everybody's Free (To Feel Good) - **Rozalla** 7.09.91
Everybody's Gonna Be Happy - **Kinks** 1.04.65
Everybody's Got To Learn Sometime - **Korgis** 31.05.80
Everybody's Happy Nowadays - **Buzzcocks** 17.03.79
Everybody's Laughing - **Phil Fearon & Galaxy** 14.07.84
Everybody's Somebody's Fool - **Connie Francis** 18.08.60
Everybody's Twisting - **Frank Sinatra** 19.04.62
Everybody's Talking - **Nilsson** 18.10.69
Everybody's Talkin' - **Nilsson** 21.03.70
Everybody's Talkin' 'Bout Love - **Silver Convention** 5.02.77
Everyday - **Don McLean** 28.04.73
Everyday - **Slade** 6.04.74
Everyday I Write The Book - **Elvis Costello** 9.07.83
Everyday People - **Sly & the Family Stone** 19.03.69
Everyone's Gone to The Moon - **Jonathan King** 29.07.65
Everything Counts - **Depeche Mode** 30.07.83
Everything Counts - **Depeche Mode** 25.02.89
(Everything I Do) I Do It For You - **Bryan Adams** 29.06.91
Everything I Have Is Yours - **Eddie Fisher** 23.01.53
Everything I Am - **Plastic Penny** 3.01.68
Everything I Own - **Bread** 6.05.72
Everything I Own - **Ken Boothe** 28.09.74
Everything I Own - **Boy George** 7.03.87
Everything Is Beautiful - **Ray Stevens** 16.05.70
Everything Is Great - **Inner Circle** 24.03.79
Everything Must Change - **Paul Young** 8.12.84
Everything Starts With An 'E' - **E-Zee Posse** 17.03.90
Everything Will Turn Out Fine - **Stealers Wheel** 8.09.73
Everything's Alright - **Mojos** 26.03.64
Everything's Tuesday - **Chairmen of the Board** 20.02.71
Everywhere - **Fleetwood Mac** 2.04.88
Evil Hearted You/Still I'm Sad - **Yardbirds** 14.10.65
The Evil That Men Do - **Iron Maiden** 13.08.88
Evil Woman - **Electric Light Orchestra** 17.01.76
Ev'ry Time We Say Goodbye - **Simply Red** 12.12.87
Ev'rywhere - **David Whitfield** 8.07.55
Excerpt from 'A Teenage Opera' - **Keith West** 9.08.67
Excitable - **Amazulu** 3.08.85
Exclusively Yours - **Mark Wynter** 15.06.61
Exodus - **Bob Marley & the Wailers** 2.07.77
Experiment IV - **Kate Bush** 8.11.86
Experiments with Mice - **Johnny Dankworth Orchestra** 22.06.56
Express - **B.T. Express** 5.04.75
Express Yourself - **Madonna** 3.06.89
Express Yourself - **N.W.A.** 2.06.90
Expression - **Salt-N-Pepa** 5.05.90
Expresso Bongo (EP) - **Cliff Richard & the Shadows** 15.01.60
Extacy - **Shades of Rhythm** 30.11.91
Extended Play - **Bryan Ferry** 7.08.76
Eye Know - **De La Soul** 21.10.89
Eye Level - **Simon Park Orchestra** 22.09.73
Eye of the Tiger - **Survivor** 7.08.82
Eye to Eye - **Chaka Khan** 20.04.85
Eyes Without A Face - **Billy Idol** 21.07.84
Fa-Fa-Fa-Fa-Fa (Sad Song) - **Otis Redding** 24.11.66
Fabulous - **Charlie Gracie** 14.06.57
The Face - **And Why Not?** 20.01.90
Fade to Grey - **Visage** 17.01.81
Fading Like A Flower - **Roxette** 11.05.91
Fairy Tale - **Dana** 23.10.76
Fairytale of New York - **Pogues featuring Kirsty MacColl** 5.12.87

Fairytale of New York - **Pogues featuring Kirsty MacColl** 28.12.91
Faith - **George Michael** 24.10.87
Faith Can Move Mountains - **Johnnie Ray & The Four Lads** 19.12.52
Faith Can Move Mountains - **Nat 'King' Cole** 2.01.53
Faith Can Move Mountains - **Jimmy Young** 9.01.53
Faith (In The Power of Love) - **Rozalla** 16.11.91
Faithful Hussar - **Ted Heath Orchestra** 6.07.56
Faithful Hussar - **Louis Armstrong** 13.07.56
Faithful Hussar - **Vera Lynn** 15.03.57
Fake - **Alexander O'Neal** 13.06.87
Fake 88 - **Alexander O'Neal** 24.09.88
Falcon - **Rah Band** 15.11.80
Fall At Your Feet - **Crowded House** 9.11.91
Fall (EP) - **Ride** 29.09.90
Fall In Love With You - **Cliff Richard & the Shadows** 24.03.60
Fallen Angel - **Frankie Valli** 17.04.76
Fallin' - **Connie Francis** 21.11.58
Fallin' In Love - **Hamilton Joe Frank and Reynolds** 20.09.75
Falling - **Roy Orbison** 30.05.63
Falling - **Julee Cruise** 17.11.90
Falling Angels Riding - **David Essex** 9.03.85
Falling Apart At the Seams - **Marmalade** 6.03.76
Fame - **David Bowie** 2.08.75
Fame - **Irene Cara** 3.07.82
Fame 90 (Gass Mix) - **David Bowie** 7.04.90
Family Affair - **Sly & the Family Stone** 8.01.72
Family Affair - **BEF featuring Lalah Hathaway** 17.08.91
Family Man - **Daryl Hall and John Oates** 7.05.83
Family Man - **Roachford** 25.03.89
Fancy Pants - **Kenny** 8.03.75
Fanfare For The Common Man - **Emerson Lake & Palmer** 11.06.77
Fanlight Fanny - **Clinton Ford** 15.03.62
Fantastic Day - **Haircut 100** 10.04.82
Fantasy - **Earth Wind & Fire** 18.02.78
Fantasy - **Gerard Kenny** 12.07.80
Fantasy - **Black Box** 3.11.90
Fantasy Island - **Tight Fit** 8.05.82
Far Away - **Shirley Bassey** 14.06.62
Far Far Away - **Slade** 19.10.74
Faraway Places - **Bachelors** 11.07.63
Farewell Angelina - **Joan Baez** 6.01.66
Farewell Is A Lonely Sound - **Jimmy Ruffin** 7.03.70
Farewell Is A Lonely Sound - **Jimmy Ruffin** 2.11.74
Farewell Mr Sorrow - **All About Eve** 15.06.91
Farewell My Summer Love - **Michael Jackson** 9.06.84
Farewell/Bring It On Home To Me - **Rod Stewart** 5.10.74
Farmer Bill's Cowman - **The Wurzels** 2.07.77
Fascinating Rhythm - **Bass-O-Matic** 8.09.90
Fashion - **David Bowie** 1.11.80
Fast Car - **Tracy Chapman** 25.06.88
Father Figure - **George Michael** 9.01.88
Fattie Bum Bum - **Carl Malcolm** 13.09.75
Fattie Bum Bum - **Diversions** 20.09.75
Favourite Shirts (Boy Meets Girl) - **Haircut 100** 24.10.81
Feel Every Beat - **Electronic** 28.09.91
Feel Like Calling Home - **Mr. Big** 4.06.77
Feel Like Making Love - **Roberta Flack** 7.09.74
Feel Like Makin' Love - **Bad Company** 6.09.75
Feel Like Makin' Love - **George Benson** 23.07.83
Feel So Fine - **Johnny Preston** 18.08.60
Feel So Real - **Steve Arrington** 27.04.85
Feel The Need In Me - **Detroit Emerals** 17.02.73
Feel The Need - **Detroit Emeralds** 25.06.77
Feel The Need - **Leif Garrett** 28.04.79
Feel The Need In Me - **Forrest** 21.05.83
Feel The Need In Me - **Shakin' Stevens** 23.07.88
Feelings - **Morris Albert** 27.09.75
(Feels Like) Heaven - **Fiction Factory** 21.01.84
Feels Like I'm In Love - **Kelly Marie** 9.08.80
Feels Like The First Time - **Foreigner** 6.05.78
Feet Up - **Guy Mitchell** 14.11.52
Fergus Sings the Blues - **Deacon Blue** 20.05.89
Fernando - **Abba** 3.04.76
The Ferris Wheel - **Everly Brothers** 16.07.64
Ferry Cross the Mersey - **Gerry & the Pacemakers** 17.12.64
Ferry Cross The Mersey - **Gerry Marsden, Paul McCartney, Holly Johnson & the Christians** 20.05.89
Festival Time - **San Remo Strings** 22.01.72
Fever - **Peggy Lee** 15.08.58
Fever - **Helen Shapiro** 23.01.64
Fields Of Fire (400 Miles) - **Big Country** 12.03.83
Fiesta - **Pogues** 16.07.88
A Fifth of Beethoven - **Walter Murphy** 17.07.76
Figaro - **Brotherhood of Man** 21.01.78
Fight for Ourselves - **Spandau Ballet** 26.07.86
Fight the Power - **Public Enemy** 24.06.89
5th Anniversary EP - **Judge Dread** 16.04.77
50 Ways To Leave Your Lover - Paul Simon 17.01.76
59th Street Bridge Song - **Harpers Bizarre** 6.04.67
The Final Countdown - **Europe** 8.11.86
Finally - **Ce Ce Peniston** 12.10.91
Finchley Central - **New Vaudeville Band** 18.05.67
Find My Love - **Fairground Attraction** 30.07.88
Find My Way Back Home - **Nashville Teens** 11.03.65
Find the Time - **Five Star** 26.07.86
Finders Keeper's - **Chairmen of the Board** 30.06.73
Fine Time - **New Order** 10.12.88
Fine Time - **Yazz** 4.02.89
The Finest - **SOS Band** 5.04.86
Fings Ain't Wot They Used T'Be - **Max Bygraves** 10.03.60
Fire - **Crazy World of Arthur Brown** 26.06.68
Fire - **Pointer Sisters** 31.03.79
Fire - **U2** 8.08.82
Fire Brigade - **Move** 7.02.68
Fire Down Below - **Jeri Southern** 21.06.57
Fire Down Below - **Shirley Bassey** 23.08.57
Fire Woman - **Cult** 1.04.89
Fireball - **Don Spencer** 11.04.63
Fireball - **Deep Purple** 20.11.71
Fireworks - **Siouxsie & the Banshees** 29.05.82
First Cut Is The Deepest - **P P Arnold** 11.05.67
First Impressions - **Impressions** 29.11.75
First of May - **Bee Gees** 19.02.69
The First Picture Of You - **Lotus Eaters** 16.07.83
First Taste of Love - **Ben E King** 2.02.61
First Thing In The Morning - **Kiki Dee** 26.02.77
The First Time - **Adam Faith** 26.09.63
The First Time - **Robin Beck** 29.10.88
The First Time Ever I Saw Your Face - **Roberta Flack** 27.05.72
Fisherman's Blues - **Waterboys** 28.01.89
The $5.98 EP - Garage Days Revisited - **Metallica** 22.08.87
5.15 - **Who** 13.10.73
5 4 3 2 1 - **Manfred Mann** 23.01.64
Five Get Over Excited - **Housemartins** 23.05.87
Five Little Fingers - **Frankie McBride** 23.08.67
Five Minutes - **Stranglers** 11.02.78
5-7-0-5 - **City Boy** 15.07.78
Flash - **Queen** 6.12.80
Flashback - **Imagination** 21.11.81
Flashdance...What A Feeling - **Irene Cara** 04.06.83
The Flasher - **Mistura with Lloyd Michels** 22.05.76
Flight of Icarus - **Iron Maiden** 23.04.83
Flip - **Jesse Green** 15.01.77
Flirt - **Jonathan King** 12.02.72
Flirtation Waltz - **Winifred Atwell** 25.09.53
Float On - **Floaters** 23.07.77
Floating in the Wind - **Hudson Ford** 29.06.74
Floral Dance - **Brighouse & Rastrick Band** 19.11.77
Floral Dance - **Terry Wogan** 7.01.78
Flowers In The Rain - **Move** 6.09.67
Flowers of Romance - **Public Image Ltd** 11.04.81
Flowers on The Wall - **Statler Brothers** 3.03.66
Floy Joy - **Supremes** 11.03.72
The Fly - **U2** 2.11.91
Fly Robin Fly - **Silver Convention** 22.11.75
Flying High - **Commodores** 8.07.78
Flying High - **Freeez** 2.05.81
Flying Machine - **Cliff Richard** 7.08.71
Foe-Dee-O-Dee - **Rubettes** 28.06.75
Fog on the Tyne (Revisisted) - **Gazza & Lindisfarne** 10.11.90
Foggy Mountain Breakdown - **Lester Flatt & Earl Scruggs** 6.12.67
The Folk Singer - **Tommy Roe** 21.03.63
Follow that Dream (EP) - **Elvis Presley** 21.06.62
Follow the Leader - **Eric B & Rakim** 2.07.88
Follow You Follow Me - **Genesis** 18.03.78
Fool - **Elvis Presley** 11.08.73
Fool - **Al Matthews** 30.08.75
A Fool Am I - **Cilla Black** 20.10.66

Fool For Your Loving - **Whitesnake** 3.05.80
Fool (If You Think It's Over) 21.10.78
Fool If You Think It's Over - **Elkie Brooks** 30.1.82.
A Fool Never Learns - **Andy Williams** 5.03.64
Fool Number One - **Brenda Lee** 16.11.61
A Fool Such As I/Need Your Love Tonight - **Elvis Presley** 24.04.59
Fool to Cry - **Rolling Stones** 8.05.76
Fooled Around & Fell In Love - **Elvin Bishop** 22.05.76
Foolish Beat - **Debbie Gibson** 9.07.88
Foolish Little Girl - **Shirelles** 30.05.63
Fool's Gold/What The World Is Waiting For - **Stone Roses** 25.11.89
Fool's Gold/What The World is Waiting For - **Stone Roses** 15.09.90
Fools Rush In - **Rick Nelson** 17.10.63
Foot Tapper - **Shadows** 7.03.63
Footloose - **Kenny Loggins** 5.05.84
Footprints In The Snow - **Johnny Duncan** 29.11.57
Footsee - **Wigan's Chosen Few** 25.01.75
Footsteps - **Ronnie Carroll** 31.03.60
Footsteps - **Steve Lawrence** 21.04.60
Footsteps - **Showaddywaddy** 5.12.81
Footsteps Following Me - **Frances Nero** 20.04.91
Footstompin' Music - **Hamilton Bohannon** 12.07.75
For A Few Dollars More - **Smokie** 28.01.78
For A Friend - **Communards** 5.03.88
For A Penny - **Pat Boone** 22.05.59
For All We Know - **Shirley Bassey** 21.08.71
For America - **Red Box** 1.11.86
(For God's Sake) Give More Power to the People - **Chi-Lites** 18.09.71
For Mama - **Matt Monro** 24.12.64
For Old Times Sake - **Millican & Nesbitt** 18.05.74
For Once In My Life - **Stevie Wonder** 18.12.68
For Once In My Life - **Dorothy Squires** 27.09.69
For The Good Times - **Perry Como** 1.09.73
For Those About to Rock (We Salute You) - **AC/DC** 3.07.82
For You - **Rick Nelson** 30.01.64
For Your Eyes Only - **Sheena Easton** 4.07.81
For Your Love - **Yardbirds** 18.03.65
Forbidden Colours - **David Sylvian and Riuichi Sakamoto** 2.07.83
A Forest - **Cure** 3.05.80
Forever - **Roy Wood** 8.12.73
Forever and Ever - **Slik** 17.01.76
Forever Autumn - **Justin Hayward** 15.07.78
Forever Came Today - **Diana Ross & the Supremes** 10.04.68
Forever Free - **W.A.S.P.** 16.09.89
Forever In Blue Jeans - **Neil Diamond** 10.03.79
A Forever Kind of Love - **Bobby Vee** 27.09.62
(Forever) Live and Die - **Orchestral Manoeuvres In The Dark** 13.09.86
Forever Your Girl - **Paul Abdul** 3.06.89
Forget-Me-Not - **Vera Lynn** 14.11.52
Forget About You - **Motors** 26.08.78
Forget Him - **Bobby Rydell** 30.05.63
Forget Me Not - **Eden Kane** 18.01.62
Forget Me Not - **Martha Reeves & the Vandellas** 13.02.71
Forget Me Nots - **Patrice Rushen** 1.05.82
Forget Me Nots - **Tongue 'N' Cheek** 19.01.91
Forgotten Dreams - **Leroy Anderson** 28.06.57
Forgotten Dreams - **Cyril Stapleton Orchestra** 19.07.57
Forgotten Town - **Christians** 14.02.87
Fort Worth Jail - **Lonnie Donegan** 8.05.59
48 Crash - **Suzi Quatro** 28.07.73
40 Miles - **Congress** 26.10.91
Forty Miles of Bad Road - **Duane Eddy** 4.09.59
Four Bacharach & David Songs (EP) - **Deacon Blue** 25.08.90
Four From Toyah (EO) - **Toyah** 28.02.81
Four Letter Word - **Kim Wilde** 10.12.88
Four Little Heels - **Brian Hyland** 20.10.60
Four More From Toyah - **Toyah** 28.11.81
Fox On The Run - **Manfred Mann** 1.01.69
Fox On The Run - **Sweet** 22.03.75
Foxhole - **Television** 22.04.78
Foxy Foxy - **Mott the Hoople** 29.06.74
Fraggle Rock Theme - **Fraggles** 3.03.84
Frankenstein - **Edgar Winter Group** 2.06.73
Frankie - **Sister Sledge** 8.06.85
Frankie and Johnny - **Elvis Presley** 7.04.66
Freak - **Bruce Foxton** 30.07.83
Freaks (Live) - **Marillion** 26.11.88
Free - **Deniece Williams** 2.04.77
Free Electric Band - **Albert Hammond** 7.07.73
Free Me - **Roger Daltrey** 9.08.80
Free 'N' Easy - **Almighty** 2.03.91
The Free Style Mega-Mix - **Bobby Brown** 9.06.90
Free Yourself - **Untouchables** 4.05.85
Freebird - **Lynyrd Skynyrd** 3.07.82
Freedom - **Wham!** 13.10.84
Freedom - **Wham!** 22.12.84
Freedom! - **George Michael** 15.12.90
Freedom Come, Freedom Go - **Fortunes** 18.09.71
Freeze-Frame - **J Geils Band** 17.04.82
The Freeze - **Spandau Ballet** 31.01.81
Freight Train - **Chas McDevitt Skiffle Group** 12.04.57
French Foreign Legion - **Frank Sinatra** 10.04.59
French Kiss - **Lil Louis** 29.07.89
French Kissin' In The USA - **Debbie Harry** 15.11.86
Fresh - **Kool & the Gang** 24.11.84
Friday Night (Live) - **Kids From Fame** 16.04.83
Friday On My Mind - **Easybeats** 3.11.66
Friday On My Mind - **Gary Moore** 23.05.87
Friend or Foe - **Adam Ant** 18.09.82
Friendly Persuasion - **Pat Boone** 7.12.56
Friendly Persuasion - **Four Aces** 4.01.57
Friends - **Beach Boys** 8.05.68
Friends - **Arrival** 17.01.70
Friends - **Shalamar** 4.12.82
Friends - **Amii Stewart** 12.01.85
Friends - **Jody Watley with Eric B & Rakim** 19.08.89
Friends and Neighbours - **Billy Cotton Band** 30.04.54
Friends Will Be Friends - **Queen** 21.06.86
Frightened City - **Shadows** 11.05.61
F.L.M. - **Mel & Kim** 11.07.87
From A Distance - **Cliff Richard** 13.10.90
From A Distance - **Bette Midler** 15.06.91
From A Jack To A King - **Ned Miller** 21.02.63
From A Window - **Billy J Kramer & the Dakotas** 23.07.64
From East to West/Scots Machine - **Voyage** 1.07.78
From Here to Eternity - **Giorgio** 24.09.77
From Me To You - **Beatles** 18.04.63
From Me To You - **Beatles** 30.04.83
From New York To LA - **Patsy Gallant** 17.09.77
From Out of Nowhere - **Faith no More** 14.04.90
From Russia With Love - **Matt Monro** 21.11.63
From Russia With Love - **John Barry Orchestra** 26.12.63
From The Bottom of My Heart - **Moody Blues** 10.06.65
From the Underworld - **Herd** 20.09.67
Frozen Orange Juice - **Peter Sarstedt** 11.06.69
Full Metal Jacket (I Wanna Be Your Drill Instructor) - **Abigail Mead & Nigel Goulding** 26.09.87
Full Time Job - **Doris Day and Johnnie Ray** 17.04.53
Funeral Pyre - **Jam** 6.06.81
Funkin' for Jamaica (N.Y.) - **Tom Browne** 26.07.80
Funky Cold Medina/On Fire - **Tone Loc** 27.05.89
The Funky Gibbon/Sick Man Blues - **Goodies** 15.03.75
Funky Moped/Magic Roundabout - **Jasper Carrott** 30.08.75
Funky Nassau - **Beginning of the End** 9.03.74
Funky Town - **Lipps Inc** 24.05.80
Funky Town - **Pseudo Echo** 8.08.87
Funky Weekend - **Stylistics** 21.02.76
Funny All Over - **Vernons Girls** 10.01.63
Funny Familiar Forgotten Feelings - **Tom Jones** 13.04.67
Funny Funny - **Sweet** 13.03.71
Funny How Love Can Be - **Ivy League** 4.02.65
Funny How Times Slip Away - **Dorothy Moore** 23.10.76
Funny Way of Laughin' - **Burl Ives** 24.05.62
Future Love (EP) - **Seal** 4.05.91
The Future's So Bright I Gotta Wear Shades - **Timbuk 3** 7.02.87
Gal With the Yaller Shoes - **Michael Holliday** 15.06.56
Galaxy - **War** 14.01.78
Galaxy of Love - **Crown Heights Affair** 26.08.78
Galloping Home - **London String Chorale** 2.02.74
Galveston - **Glen Campbell** 7.05.69
Gambler - **Madonna** 12.10.85
Gamblin' Bar Room Blues - **Sensational Alex Harvey Band** 6.12.75
Gamblin' Man - **Lonnie Donegan** 7.06.57
The Game - **Echo & the Bunnymen** 13.06.87
Game of Love - **Wayne Fontana & the Mindbenders** 4.02.65
Games - **New Kids On The Block** 9.02.91
Games People Play - **Joe South** 5.03.69

Games Without Frontiers - **Peter Gabriel** 16.02.80
Gangsters - **Specials** 11.08.79
Gangsters of the Groove - **Heatwave** 24.01.81
Garden of Eden - **Frankie Vaughan** 11.01.57
Garden of Eden - **Dick James** 11.01.57
Garden of Eden - **Gary Miller** 11.01.57
Garden of Eden - **Joe Valino** 18.01.57
Garden Party - **Mezzoforte** 12.03.83
Garden Party - **Marillion** 18.06.83
Gary Gilmour's Eyes - **The Adverts** 27.08.77
Gatecrashing - **Living In A Box** 17.06.89
Gather in the Mushrooms - **Benny Hill** 16.02.61
Gaudette - **Steeleye Span** 15.12.73
Gaye - **Clifford T. Ward** 7.07.73
Gee Baby - **Peter Shelley** 21.09.74
Gee But It's Lonely - **Pat Boone** 5.12.58
Gee Whiz It's You - **Cliff Richard** 30.03.61
Generals and Majors/Don't Lose Your Temper - **XTC** 13.09.80
Generations of Love - **Jesus Loves You** 29.06.91
Genetic Engineering - **Orchestral Manoeuvres In The Dark** 19.02.83
Genie - **Brooklyn Bronx & Queens** 13.07.85
Genie With The Light Brown Lamp - **Shadows** 3.12.64
Geno - **Dexy's Midnight Runners** 29.03.80
Gentle On My Mind - **Dean Martin** 5.02.69
A Gentleman's Excuse Me - **Fish** 17.03.90
Geordie Boys (Gazza Rap) - **Gazza** 29.12.90
Georgia On My Mind - **Ray Charles** 15.12.60
Georgina Bailey - **Noosha Fox** 19.11.77
Georgy Girl - **Seekers** 23.02.67
Germ Free Adolescence - **X-Ray Spex** 11.11.78
Geronimo - **Shadows** 5.12.63
Gertcha - **Chas & Dave** 9.06.79
Get A Life - **Soul II Soul** 9.12.89
Get Away - **George Fame & the Blue Flames** 23.06.66
Get Back - **Beatles with Billy Preston** 23.04.69
Get Back - **Beatles** 10.04.76
Get Back - **Rod Stewart** 27.11.76
Get Dancin' - **Bombers** 26.05.79
Get Dancing - **Disco Tex & the Sex-O-Lettes** 30.11.74
Get Down - **Gilbert O'Sullivan** 17.03.73
Get Down - **Gene Chandler** 10.02.79
Get Down and Get With It - **Slade** 3.07.71
Get Down On It - **Kool & the Gang** 26.12.81
Get Down Saturday Night - **Oliver Cheatham** 16.07.83
Get Down Tonight - **K.C. & the Sunshine Band** 5.04.75
Get Here - **Oleta Adams** 19.01.91
Get In The Swing - **Sparks** 2.08.75
Get It - **Darts** 17.02.79
Get It - **Stevie Wonder & Michael Jackson** 4.06.88
Get It On - **T.Rex** 10.07.71
Get It On - **Power Station** 18.05.85
Get It Right Next Time - **Gerry Rafferty** 25.08.79
Get It Together - **Crispy & Co** 27.12.75
Get It While You Can - **Olympic Runners** 21.10.78
Get Loose - **LA Mix** 8.07.89
Get Lost - **Eden Kane** 14.09.61
Get Lucky - **Jermaine Stewart** 9.04.88
Get Me Out - **New Model Army** 8.09.90
Get Off Of My Cloud - **Rolling Stones** 28.10.65
Get On The Dance Floor - **Rob Base & DJ E-Z Rock** 14.01.89
Get On Your Feet - **Gloria Estefan** 25.11.89
Get Out - **Harold Melvin And The Bluenotes** 14.06.75
Get Out Of My Life Woman - **Lee Dorsey** 10.02.66
Get Out of Your Lazy Bed - **Matt Bianco** 18.02.84
Get Outta My Dreams Get Into My Car - **Billy Ocean** 6.02.88
Get Ready - **Temptations** 5.03.69
Get Ready - **Roachford** 20.04.91
Get Ready For This - **2 Unlimited** 5.10.91
Get The Balance Right - **Depeche Mode** 12.02.83
Get The Funk Out - **Extreme** 15.06.91
Get The Message - **Electronic** 27.04.91
Get Up and Boogie - **Silver Convention** 10.04.76
Get Up (Before the Night Is Over) - **Technotronic featuring Ya Kid K** 3.02.90
Get Up I Feel Like Being A Sex Machine - **James Brown** 31.10.70
Get Up Offa That Thing - **James Brown** 25.09.76
Get Your Love Back - **Three Degrees** 2.11.74
Gett Off - **Prince & the New Power Generation** 31.08.91
Gettin' Ready for Love - **Diana Ross** 26.11.77
Getting A Drag - **Lynsey De Paul** 9.12.72
Getting Away With It - **Electronic** 16.12.89
Getting Mighty Crowded - **Betty Everett** 14.01.65
Getting Over You - **Andy Williams** 25.05.74
Ghetto Child - **Detroit Spinners** 29.09.73
Ghetto Heaven - **Family Stand** 31.03.90
The Ghost of Love - **Tavares** 25.03.78
Ghost Town - **Specials** 20.06.81
Ghostbusters - **Ray Parker Jnr** 1.09.84
Ghostdancing - **Simple Minds** 15.11.86
Ghosts - **Japan** 27.03.82
Giddy-Up-A-Ding-Dong - **Freddie Bell & the Bellboys** 28.09.56
Gigi - **Billy Eckstine** 13.02.59
Gigolo - **Damned** 7.02.87
Gilly Gilly Ossenfeffer Katzenellen Bogen by The Sea - **Max Bygraves** 10.09.54
Gimme All Your Lovin' - **ZZ Top** 27.10.84
Gimme Dat Banana - **Black Gorilla** 3.09.77
Gimme Dat Ding - **Pipkins** 28.03.70
Gimme Gimme Good Lovin' - **Crazy Elephant** 21.05.69
Gimme Gimme Gimme - **Abba** 20.10.79
Gimme Hope Jo'Anna - **Eddy Grant** 6.02.88
Gimme Little Sign - **Brenton Wood** 27.12.67
Gimme Some - **Brendon** 26.03.77
Gimme Some Loving - **Spencer Davis Group** 3.11.66
Gimme Some Lovin' - **Thunder** 14.07.90
Gimmix Playloud - **John Cooper Clark** 17.03.79
Gin Gan Goolie - **Scaffold** 6.12.69
Gin House Blues - **Amen Corner** 2.08.67
Ginchy - **Bert Weedon** 9.02.61
Ginger Bread - **Frankie Avalon** 10.10.58
Ginny Come Latley - **Brian Hyland** 10.05.62
Girl - **St. Louis Union** 20.01.66
Girl - **Truth** 10.02.66
The Girl Can't Help It - **Little Richard** 15.03.86
Girl Crazy - **Hot Chocolate** 24.04.82
Girl Don't Come - **Sandie Shaw** 10.12.64
The Girl From Ipanema - **Stan Getz & Joao Gilberto** 23.07.64
Girl I'm Gonna Miss You - **Milli Vanilli** 7.10.89
Girl In The Wood - **Frankie Laine** 20.03.53
The Girl is Mine - **Michael Jackson & Paul McCartney** 6.11.82
A Girl Like You - **Cliff Richard** 22.06.61
A Girl Like You - **Young Rascals** 23.08.67
Girl of My Best Friend - **Elvis Presley** 11.09.76
Girl of My Dreams - **Tony Brent** 5.09.58
Girl Sang The Blues - **Everly Brothers** 17.10.63
Girl to Girl - **49ers** 9.06.90
Girl You Know It's True - **Milli Vanilli** 15.10.88
Girl You're So Together - **Michael Jackson** 1.09.84
Girlfriend - **Pebbles** 2.04.88
Girlfriend In A Coma - **Smiths** 22.08.87
Girlie - **Peddlers** 31.01.70
Girlie Girlie - **Sophia George** 14.12.85
Girls - **Johnny Burnette** 10.08.61
Girls - **Moments And Whatnauts** 8.03.75
Girls Ain't Nothing But Trouble - **DJ Jazzy Jeff & Fresh Prince** 18.10.86
Girls and Boys - **Prince & the Revolution** 16.08.86
Girls Are Out to Get You - **Fascinations** 17.07.71
Girls Can Get It - **Dr Hook** 29.11.80
Girls! Girls! Girls! - **Fourmost** 6.01.66
Girls Girls Girls - **Sailor** 3.04.76
Girls Girls Girl - **Kandidate** 18.08.79
Girls Girls Girls - **Motley Crue** 1.08.87
Girls Just Want To Have Fun - **Cyndi Lauper** 21.01.84
Girls on Film - **Duran Duran** 25.07.81
Girls Talk - **Dave Edmunds** 7.07.79
Give A Little Love - **Bay City Rollers** 12.07.75
Give A Little Bit - **Supertramp** 2.07.77
Give A Little Love - **Aswad** 28.05.88
Give A Little Love Back to the World - **Emma** 12.05.90
Give and Take - **Pioneers** 22.01.72
Give! Give! Give! - **Tommy Steele** 28.08.59
Give Her My Love - **Johnston Brothers** 8.02.57
Give Ireland Back To The Irish - **Wings** 4.03.72
Give It Some Emotion - **Tracie** 23.07.83
Give It To Me - **Troggs** 23.02.67
Give It To Me Now - **Kenny** 7.07.73
Give It Up - **KC and the Sunshine Band** 23.07.83
Give It Up - **Hothouse Flowers** 19.05.90
Give Me All Your Love - **Whitesnake** 6.02.88
Give Me Back My Heart - **Dollar** 27.03.82

Give Me Just A Little More Time - **Chairmen of the Board** 22.08.70
Give Me Love (Give Me Peace on Earth) - **George Harrison** 2.06.73
Give Me More Time - **Whitesnake** 14.01.84
Give Me One More Chance - **Donald Peers & the Les Reed Orchestra** 8.07.72
Give Me Some Kinda Magic - **Dollar** 25.09.82
Give Me The Night - **George Benson** 2.08.80
Give Me The Reason - **Luther Vandross** 30.01.88
Give Me Time - **Dusty Springfield** 1.06.67
Give Me Tonight - **Shannon** 14.04.84
Give Me Your Word - **Tennessee Ernie Ford** 21.01.55
Give Me Your Word - **Billy Fury** 11.08.66
Give Me Your Heart Tonight - **Shakin' Stevens** 28.08.82
Give Peace A Chance - **Plastic Ono Band** 9.07.69
Give Peace A Chance - **Plastic Ono Band** 31.01.81
Givin' Up Givin' In - **Three Degrees** 14.10.78
G.L.A.D. - **Kim Appleby** 9.02.91
Giving It All Away - **Roger Daltrey** 14.04.73
Giving It Back - **Phil Hurtt** 18.11.78
Glad All Over - **Dave Clark Five** 21.11.63
Glad It's All Over/Damned on 45 - **Captain Sensible** 31.03.84
Glam Slam - **Prince** 23.07.88
Glass Of Champagne - **Sailor** 13.12.75
Glendora - **Perry Como** 28.09.56
Glendora - **Glen Mason** 28.09.56
Glittering Prize - **Simple Minds** 11.09.82
Globe-Trotter - **Tornados** 10.01.63
Gloria - **Laura Branigan** 15.01.83
Glory Days - **Bruce Springsteen** 3.08.85
Glory Glory Man. Utd - **Manchester United FC** 21.05.83
Glory of Love - **Peter Cetera** 16.08.86
Glow Worm - **Mills Brothers** 30.01.53
Go - **Gigliola Cinquetti** 11.05.74
Go - **Moby** 19.10.91
Go Away Little Girl - **Mark Wynter** 13.12.62
Go Deh Yaka (Go To The Top) - **Monyaka** 17.09.83
Go For It! (Heart and Fire) - **Joey B Ellis & Tynetta Hare** 23.02.91
Go Go Go - **Chuck Berry** 25.07.63
Go North - **Richard Barnes** 14.11.70
Go Now - **Moody Blues** 10.12.64
Go On By - **Alma Cogan** 14.10.55
Go West - **Village People** 16.06.79
Go Wild In The Country - **Bow Wow Wow** 27.02.82
Go Your Own Way - **Fleetwood Mac** 26.02.77
God Gave Rock and Roll To You - **Argent** 31.03.73
God Only Knows - **Beach Boys** 28.07.66
God Save The Queen - **Sex Pistols** 4.06.77
God Thank You Woman - **Culture Club** 7.06.86
Goin' For The One - **Yes** 3.12.77
Goin' Out Of My Head - **Dodie West** 14.01.65
Goin' Places - **Jacksons** 12.11.77
Going Back - **Dusty Springfield** 7.07.66
Going Back to My Roots - **Odyssey** 6.06.81
Going Back to Call/Jack the Ripper - **LL Cool J** 20.02.88
Going Back To My Roots/Rich In Paradise - **FPI Project** 16.12.89
Going Down the Road - **Roy Wood** 15.06.74
Going Down Town Tonight - **Status Quo** 19.05.84
Going Home - **Osmonds** 14.07.73
Going In With My Eyes Open - **David Soul** 26.03.77
Going to A Go Go - **Rolling Stones** 19.06.82
Going Underground/Dreams of Children - **Jam** 22.03.80
Going Underground/Dreams of Children - **Jam** 29.01.83
Going Up The Country - **Canned Heat** 8.01.69
Gold - **Spandau Ballet** 13.08.83
Golden Age of Rock & Roll - **Mott the Hoople** 30.03.74
Golden Brown - **Stranglers** .... 16.1.82.
Golden Green/Get Together - **Wonder Stuff** 11.11.89
Golden Lights - **Twinkle** 25.02.65
Golden Slumbers/Carry That Weight - **Trash** 25.10.69
Golden Years - **David Bowie** 29.11.75
Golden Years (EP) - **Motorhead** 3.05.80
Goldfinger - **Shirley Bassey** 15.10.64
Gone - **Shirley Bassey** 9.04.64
Gone Gone Gone - **Everly Brothers** 10.12.64
Gone Gone Gone - **Johnny Mathis** 18.08.79
Gonna Capture Your Heart - **Blue** 7.05.77
Gonna Catch You - **Lonnie Gordon** 4.05.91
Gonna Get Along Without Ya Now - **Patience & Prudence** 1.03.57
Gonna Get Along Without You Now - **Viola Wills** 20.10.79
Gonna Give Her All The Love I've Got - **Jimmy Ruffin** 4.05.67
Gonna Make You An Offer You Can't Refuse - **Jimmy Helms** 3.03.73
Gonna Make You A Star - **David Essex** 19.10.74
Gonna Make You Sweat - **C&C Music Factory featuring Freedom Williams** 15.12.90
Good-bye-ee - **14/18** 15.11.75
Good Golly Miss Molly - **Little Richard** 28.02.58
Good Golly Miss Molly - **Jerry Lee Lewis** 21.03.63
Good Golly Miss Molly - **Swinging Blue Jeans** 19.03.64
Good Golly Miss Molly/Rip It Up - **Little Richard** 9.07.77
Good Grief Christina - **Chicory Tip** 7.04.73
A Good Heart - **Feargal Sharkey** 26.10.85
The Good Life - **Tony Bennett** 18.07.63
Good Life - **Inner City** 10.12.88
Good Love Can Never Die - **Alvin Stardust** 1.02.75
Good Lovin' Ain't Easy To Come By - **Marvin Gaye & Tammi Terrell** 18.06.69
Good Lovin' Gone Bad - **Bad Company** 29.03.75
Good Luck Charm - **Elvis Presley** 10.05.62
Good Morning - **Leapy Lee** 10.01.70
Good Morning Judge - **10 C.C.** 23.04.77
Good Morning Starshine - **Oliver** 16.08.69
Good Morning Freedom - **Blue Mink** 28.03.70
Good Morning Britain - **Aztec Camera & Mick Jones** 13.10.90
Good Old Arsenal - **Arsenal 1st Team Squad** 15.05.71
Good Old Fashioned Loverboy - **Queen** 4.06.77
Good Old Rock 'N' Roll - **Dave Clark Five** 6.12.69
The Good, The Bad and The Ugly - **Hugo Montenegro** 18.09.68
Good Thing - **Fine Young Cannibals** 15.04.89
Good Thing Going - **Sugar Minott** 4.04.81
Good Times - **Eric Burdon & the Animals** 13.09.67
Good Times - **Cher** 7.07.79
Good Times - **Jimmy Barnes & INXS** 9.02.91
Good Times (Better Times) - **Cliff Richard** 26.02.69
Good Timin' - **Jimmy Jones** 16.06.60
Good To Go Lover/Outside in the Rain - **Gwen Guthrie** 21.02.87
Good Tradition - **Tanita Tikaram** 6.08.88
Good Vibrations - **Beach Boys** 3.11.66
Good Vibrations - **Beach Boys** 10.07.76
Good Vibrations - **Marky Mark & the Funky Bunch featuring Loleatta Holloway** 31.08.91
Good Year For The Roses - **Elvis Costello** 10.10.81
Goodbye - **Mary Hopkin** 2.04.69
Goodbye Cruel World - **James Darren** 28.12.61
Goodbye Girl - **Go West** 3.08.85
Goodbye Is Just Another Word - **New Seekers** 23.06.73
Goodbye Jimmy Goodbye - **Ruby Murray** 5.06.59
Goodbye My Love - **The Glitter Band** 25.01.7
Goodbye My Love - **Searchers** 11.03.65
Goodbye Nothing to Say - **Javells & Nosmo King** 16.11.74
Goodbye Sam Hello Samantha - **Cliff Richard** 6.06.70
Goodbye Stranger - **Pepsi & Shirlie** 30.05.87
Goodbye to Love - **Carpenters** 30.09.72
Goodbye Yellow Brick Road - **Elton John** 6.10.73
Goodbyee - **Peter Cook & Dudley Moore** 24.06.65
Goodgroove - **Derek B** 27.02.88
Goodness Gracious Me - **Peter Sellers & Sophia Loren** 10.11.60
Goodnight - **Roy Orbison** 11.02.65
Goodnight Midnight - **Clodagh Rodgers** 9.07.69
Goodnight Mrs Flintstone - **Piltdown Men** 16.03.61
Goodnight Saigon/Leave A Tender Moment Alone - **Billy Joel** 30.06.84
Goodnight Tonight - **Wings** 14.04.79
Goody Goody - **Frankie Lymon & the Teenagers** 20.09.57
Goody Two Shoes - **Adam Ant** 22.05.82
Google Eye - **Nashville Teens** 22.10.64
Gossip Calypso - **Bernard Cribbins** 20.12.62
Got A Feeling - **Patrick Juvet** 9.09.78
Got A Girl - **Four Preps** 26.05.60
Got A Lot O' Livin' To Do - **Elvis Presley** 18.10.57
Got A Match - **Russ Conway** 29.08.58
Got My Mind Set On You - **George Harrison** 31.10.87
Got The Time - **Anthrax** 5.01.91
Got To Be Certain - **Kylie Minogue** 14.05.88
Got To Be There - **Michael Jackson** 12.02.72
Got To Get - **Rob 'n' Raz featuring Leila K** 2.12.89
Got To Get You Into My Life - **Cliff Bennett & the Rebel Rousers** 18.08.66
Got To Get You Into My Life - **Earth Wind & Fire** 21.10.78
Got To Get You Back - **Kym Mazelle** 25.03.89
Got To Give It Up - **Marvin Gaye** 7.05.77
Got To Have Your Love - **Mantronix featuring Wondress** 6.01.90
Got To Keep On - **Cookie Crew** 8.04.89

Got You on My Mind - **Tony Brent** 23.01.53
Gotta Get You Home Tonight - **Eugene Wilde** 20.10.84
Gotta Go Home - **Boney M** 11.08.79
Gotta Go Home/El Lute - **Boney M** 29.09.79
Gotta Have Something In The Bank Frank - **Frankie Vaughan & the Kaye Sisters** 1.11.57
Gotta Pull Myself Together - **Nolans** 27.09.80
Gotta See Baby Tonight - **Mr. Acker Bilk** 2.08.62
Gotta See Jane - **R Dean Taylor** 26.06.68
Govinda - **Radha Krishna Temple** 4.04.70
G.T.O. - **Sinitta** 19.12.87
Granada - **Frankie Laine** 26.03.54
Granada - **Frank Sinatra** 28.09.61
Grand Coolie Dam - **Lonnie Donegan** 11.04.58
Grand Piano - **Mixmaster** 4.11.89
Grandad - **Clive Dunn** 5.12.70
Grandma's Party - **Paul Nicholas** 11.12.76
Grease - **Frankie Valli** 2.09.78
Grease Megamix - **John Travolta & Olivia Newton-John** 22.12.90
Greased Lightning - **John Travolta** 2.12.78
Great Balls of Fire - **Jerry Lee Lewis** 20.12.57
Great Pretender - **Jimmy Parkinson** 2.03.56
Great Pretender/Only You - **Platters** 7.09.56
The Great Pretender - **Freddie Mercury** 7.03.87
The Great Rock 'N' Roll Swindle/Rock Around - **Sex Pistols** 13.10.79
Great Song of Indifference - **Bob Geldof** 30.06.90
The Greatest Cockney Rip Off - **Cockney Rejects** 3.05.80
Greatest Love Of All - **George Benson** 1.10.77
The Greatest Love of All - **Whitney Houston** 19.04.86
Green and Grey - **New Model Army** 10.06.89
Green Back Dollar - **Chas McDevitt Skiffle Group** 14.06.57
Green Door - **Jim Lowe** 26.10.56
Green Door - **Frankie Vaughan** 9.11.56
Green Door - **Glen Mason** 16.11.56
Green Door - **Shakin' Stevens** 25.07.81
Green Fields - **Brothers Four** 7.07.60
Green Fields - **Beverley Sisters** 7.07.60
Green Green Grass of Home - **Tom Jones** 10.11.66
Green Green Grass Of Home - **Elvis Presley** 6.12.75
Green Jeans - **Flee-Rekkers** 19.05.60
Green Leaves of Summer - **Kenny Ball & his Jazzmen** 24.05.62
The Green Manalishi - **Fleetwood Mac** 30.05.70
Green Onions - **Booker T. & the MG's** 5.01.80
Green River - **Creedence Clearwater Revival** 22.11.69
Green Street Green - **New Vaudeville Band** 16.08.67
Green Tambourine - **Lemon Pipers** 7.02.68
Grey Day - **Madness** 25.04.81
Grimly Fiendish - **Damned** 30.03.85
Grip '89 (Get A) Grip (On Yourself) - **Stranglers** 28.01.89
The Groove - **Rodney Franklin** 26.04.80
Groove Is In The Heart - **Deee-Lite** 25.08.90
The Groove Line - **Heatwave** 14.01.78
Groover - **T.Rex** 16.06.73
Groovin' - **Young Rascals** 1.06.67
Groovin' With Mr Bloe - **Mr. Bloe** 9.05.70
Groovin' (You're The Best Thing)/Big Boss Groove - **Style Council** 26.05.84
Groovy Baby - **Microbe** 14.05.69
Groovy Kind of Love - **Mindbenders** 13.01.66
Groovy Kind of Love - **Les Gray** 5.03.77
Groovy Kind of Love - **Phil Collins** 3.09.88
Groovy Train - **Farm** 1.09.90
Groupie Girl - **Tony Joe White** 6.06.70
Guantanamera - **Sandpipers** 22.09.66
Guaranteed - **Level 42** 17.08.91
Gudbuy T'Jane - **Slade** 25.11.72
Guilty - **Jim Reeves** 24.10.63
Guilty - **Pearls** 8.06.74
Guilty - **Mike Oldfield** 28.04.79
Guilty - **Barbra Streisand & Barry Gibb** 17.01.81
Guilty Of Love - **Whitesnake** 13.08.83
Guitar Boogie Shuffle - **Bert Weedon** 15.05.59
Guitar Man - **Elvis Presley** 28.02.68
Guitar Man - **Bread** 30.09.72
Guitar Tango - **Shadows** 2.08.62
Guns For Hire - **AC/DC** 5.11.83
Guns of Navarone - **Skalites** 27.04.67
Gurney Slade - **Max Harris** 1.12.60
Gypsy Eyes/Remember - **Jimi Hendrix** 13.11.71
Gypsy Woman (La Da Dee) - **Crystal Waters** 18.05.91
Gypsys Tramps and Thieves - **Cher** 6.11.71
Ha Cha Cha - **Brass Construction** 19.02.77
Ha! Ha! Said The Clown - **Manfred Mann** 6.04.67
Haitian Divorce - **Steely Dan** 18.12.76
Half A Minute - **Matt Bianco** 17.11.84
Half As Much - **Rosemary Clooney** 14.11.52
Half Way Hotel - **Voyager** 23.06.79
Halfway Down The Stairs - **Muppets** 28.05.77
Halfway to Paradise - **Billy Fury** 25.05.61
Hallelujah - **Milk & Honey** 14.04.79
Hallelujah Day - **Jackson Five** 16.06.73
Hallelujah Freedom - **Junior Campbell** 14.10.72
Hallelujah I Love Her So - **Eddie Cochran** 22.01.60
(Hammer Hammer) They Put Me In The Mix - **MC Hammer** 20.07.91
Hammer to Fall - **Queen** 22.09.84
Hand Held In Black and White - **Dollar** 29.08.81
Hand In Glove - **Sandie Shaw** 28.04.84
Hand On Your Heart - **Kylie Minogue** 6.05.89
Handbags and Gladrags - **Chris Farlowe** 20.12.67
Handful of Promises - **Big Fun** 17.03.90
Handle With Care - **Traveling Wilburys** 12.11.88
Hands Across the Ocean - **Mission** 17.11.90
Hands Off She's Mine - **Beat** 1.03.80
Hands to Heaven - **Breathe** 6.08.88
Hands Up (Give Me Your Heart) - **Ottawan** 5.09.81
Handy Man - **Jimmy Jones** 17.03.60
Handy Man - **Del Shannon** 6.08.64
Hang In Long Enough - **Phil Collins** 13.10.90
Hang On In There Baby - **Johnny Bristol** 24.08.74
Hang On Now - **Kajagoogoo** 04.06.83
Hang on Sloopy - **McCoys** 9.09.65
Hang On Sloopy - **Sandpipers** 4.12.76
Hang On To Your Love - **Jason Donovan** 7.04.90
Hang Together - **Odyssey** 31.01.81
Hangar 18 - **Megadeth** 16.03.91
Hangin' On A String (Contemplating) - **Loose Ends** 9.03.85
Hangin' Tough - **New Kids On the Block** 6.01.90
The Hanging Garden - **Cure** 31.07.82
Hanging On The Telephone - **Blondie** 11.11.78
Hanky Panky - **Tommy James & the Shondells** 4.08.66
Hanky Panky - **Madonna** 21.07.90
Happenin' All Over Again - **Lonnie Gordon** 27.01.90
The Happening - **Supremes** 18.05.67
Happiness - **Ken Dodd** 30.07.64
Happiness Is Me and You - **Gilbert O'Sullivan** 16.02.74
Happy - **Ned's Atomic Dustbin** 9.03.91
Happy Anniversary - **Joan Regan** 5.02.60
Happy Anniversary - **Slim Whitman** 12.10.74
Happy Birthday Sweet Sixteen - **Neil Sedaka** 21.12.61
Happy Birthday - **Stevie Wonder** 25.07.81
Happy Birthday - **Altered Images** 10.10.81
Happy Christmas, War Is Over - **John Lennon & Yoko Ono with the Plastic Ono Band & the Harlem Community Choir** 9.12.72
Happy Christmas (War Is Over) - **John Lennon** 27.12.80
Happy Christmas (War Is Over) - **John Lennon** 26.12.81
Happy Days - **Pratt & McLain** 8.10.77
Happy Days & Lonely Nights - **Suzi Miller & the Johnston Brothers** 21.01.55
Happy Days & Lonely Nights - **Ruby Murray** 4.02.55
Happy Days and Lonely Nights - **Frankie Vaughan** 28.01.55
Happy Ever After - **Julia Fordham** 30.07.88
Happy Go Lucky Me/Banjo Boy - **George Formby** 28.07.60
Happy Guitar - **Tommy Steele** 25.04.58
Happy Heart - **Andy Williams** 21.05.69
Happy Hour - **Housemartins** 14.06.86
Happy House - **Siouxsie & the Banshees** 15.03.80
Happy Jack - **Who** 15.12.66
Happy Song - **Otis Redding** 29.05.68
Happy Talk - **Captain Sensible** 26.06.82
Happy To Be On An Island In The Sun - **Demis Roussos** 29.11.75
Happy Together - **Turtles** 30.03.67
Happy Together - **Jason Donovan** 24.08.91
Happy Wanderer - **Obernkirchen Children's Choir** 22.01.54
Happy Wanderer - **Stargazers** 9.04.54
Happy When It Rains - **Jesus & Mary Chain** 15.08.87
Happy Whistler - **Don Robertson** 11.05.56
Happy Whistler - **Cyril Stapleton Orchestra** 1.06.56
Harbour Lights - **Platters** 29.01.60
A Hard Day's Night - **Beatles** 16.07.64
Hard Habit to Break - **Chicago** 3.11.84

Hard Headed Woman - **Elvis Presley** 25.07.58
Hard Hearted Hannah - **Temperance Seven** 5.10.61
A Hard Rain's Gonna Fall - **Bryan Ferry** 6.10.73
Hard Road - **Black Sabbath** 21.10.78
Hard To Handle - **Otis Redding** 7.08.68
Hard to Handle - **Black Crowes** 31.08.91
Hard to Say I'm Sorry - **Chicago** 18.09.82
Hardcore Uproar - **Together** 4.08.90
The Harder I Try - **Brother Beyond** 6.08.88
The Harder They Come - **Rockers Revenge featuring Donnie Calvin** 5.02.83
Hare Krishna Mantra - **Radha Krishna Temple** 20.09.69
Harlem Desire - **London Boys** 16.09.89
Harlem Shuffle - **Bob & Earl** 19.03.69
Harlem Shuffle - **Rolling Stones** 15.03.86
Harmony In My Head - **Buzzcocks** 28.07.79
Harmour Love - **Syreeta** 19.07.75
Harper Valley PTA - **Jeannie C Riley** 23.10.68
Harvest For the World - **Isley Brothers** 10.07.76
Harvest for The World - **Christians** 15.10.88
Harvest of Love - **Benny Hill** 16.05.63
Harvester of Sorrow - **Metallica** 3.09.88
Hasta La Vista - **Sylvia** 3.05.75
Hats Off To Larry - **Del Shannon** 14.09.61
Hava Nagile - **Spotnicks** 7.02.63
Have A Drink on Me - **Lonnie Donegan** 11.05.61
Have I The Right? - **Honeycombs** 30.07.64
Have I The Right - **Dead End Kids** 2.04.77
Have Pity on The Boy - **Paul & Barry Ryan** 3.02.66
Have You Ever Seen the Rain - **Creedence Clearwater Revival** 20.03.71
Have You Ever Fallen In Love - **Buzzcocks** 30.09.78
Have You Ever Been In Love - **Leo Sayer** 20.03.82
Have You Ever Had It Blue - **Style Council** 5.04.86
Have You Ever Loved Somebody - **Freddie Jackson** 21.02.87
Have You Seen Your Mother Baby Standing In The Shadow - **Rolling Stones** ... 29.09.66
Have You Seen Her - **Chi-Lites** 15.01.72
Have You Seen Her/Oh Girl - **Chi-Lites** 21.06.75
Have You Seen Her - **MC Hammer** 6.10.90
Haven't Stopped Dancing Yet - **Gonzalez** 14.04.79
Having A Party - **Osmonds** 8.03.75
Hawaiian Wedding Song - **Julie Rogers** 8.04.65
Hawkeye - **Frankie Laine** 25.11.55
Hazell - **Maggie Bell** 22.04.78
Hazy Shade of Winter - **Bangles** 20.02.88
Hazy Shade of Winter/Silent Night - **Simon & Garfunkel** 14.12.91
He Ain't Heavy He's My Brother - **Hollies** 4.10.69
He Ain't Heavy He's My Brother - **Hollies** 3.09.88
He Ain't Heavy He's My Brother - **Bill Medley** 3.09.88
He Ain't No Competition - **Brother Beyond** 5.11.88
He Got What He Wanted - **Little Richard** 25.10.62
He Knows You Know - **Marillion** 12.02.83
He Was Beautiful (Cavatina) - **Iris Williams** 3.11.79
Head Over Heels In Love - **Kevin Keegan** 16.06.79
Head Over Heels - **Abba** 27.02.82
Head Over Heels - **Tears For Fears** 22.06.85
Headline News - **Edwin Starr** 25.08.66
Headlines - **Midnight Star** 28.06.86
Headlong - **Queen** 25.05.91
Heal The Pain - **George Michael** 16.02.91
Hear the Drummer (Get Wicked) - **Chad Jackson** 2.06.90
Heart - **Max Bygraves** 5.04.57
Heart - **Johnston Brothers** 19.04.57
Heart - **Rita Pavone** 5.01.67
Heart - **Pet Shop Boys** 2.04.88
Heart and Soul - **Jan & Dean** 7.09.61
Heart and Soul - **T'Pau** 29.08.87
Heart Beat - **England Sisters** 17.03.60
Heart Full of Soul - **Yardbirds** 17.06.65
Heart Like A Wheel - **Human League** 18.08.90
Heart of A Man - **Frankie Vaughan** 24.07.59
Heart of A Teenage Girl - **Craig Douglas** 5.05.60
Heart of Glass - **Blondie** 27.01.79
Heart of Gold - **Neil Young** 18.03.72
Heart of Gold - **Johnny Hates Jazz** 5.03.88
Heart of Lothian - **Marillion** 30.11.85
Heart of My Heart - **Max Bygraves** 14.05.54
Heart of Stone - **Kenny** 3.03.73
Heart On My Sleeve - **Gallagher & Lyle** 29.05.76
Heart (Stop Beating in Time) - **Leo Sayer** 26.06.82
Heartache - **Pepsi & Shirlie** 24.01.87
Heartache Avenue - **Maisonettes** 25.12.82
Heartaches - **Patsy Cline** 6.12.62
Heartaches - **Vince Hill** 17.03.66
Heartaches by the Number - **Guy Mitchell** 27.11.59
Heartache's Tonight - **Eagles** 27.10.79
Heartbeat - **Buddy Holly** 16.01.59
Heartbeat - **Buddy Holly** 28.04.60
Heartbeat - **Showaddywaddy** 6.09.75
Heartbreak Hotel - **Elvis Presley** 11.05.56
Heartbreak Hotel/Hound Dog - **Elvis Presley** 24.07.71
Heartbreaker - **Dionne Warwick** 30.10.82
Hearthammer (EP) - **Runrig** 7.09.91
Heartland - **The The** 30.08.86
Heartsong - **Gordon Giltrap** 21.01.78
The Heat Is On - **Agnetha Faltskog** 04.06.83
The Heat Is On - **Glenn Frey** 23.03.85
Heat It Up - **Wee Papa Girl Rappers** 9.07.88
Heather Honey - **Tommy Roe** 30.07.69
Heatseeker - **AC/DC** 16.01.88
Heaven - **Psychedelic Furs** 7.04.84
Heaven - **Bryan Adams** 1.06.85
Heaven - **Chimes** 29.09.90
Heaven Give Me Words - **Propaganda** 5.05.90
Heaven In My Hands - **Level 42** 3.09.88
Heaven Is A Place on Earth - **Belinda Carlisle** 19.12.87
Heaven Is In The Back Seat of My Cadillac - **Hot Chocolate** 28.08.76
Heaven Is My Woman's Love - **Val Doonican** 17.03.73
Heaven Knows - **Donna Summer** 24.02.79
Heaven Knows - **Robert Plant** 13.02.88
Heaven Knows I'm Miserable Now - **Smiths** 2.06.84
Heaven Must Be Missing An Angel - **Tavares** 10.07.76
Heaven Must Be Missing An Angel - **Tavares** 22.02.86
Heaven Must Have Sent You - **Elgins** 8.05.71
Heaven On The 7th Floor - **Paul Nicholas** 16.07.77
Heavenly - **Showaddywaddy** 22.11.75
Heavy Makes You Happy - **Bobby Blook** 16.01.71
Helen Wheels - **Wings** 3.11.73
Hell Hath No Fury - **Frankie Laine** 4.05.56
He'll Have To Go - **Jim Reeves** 24.03.60
Hell Raiser - **Sweet** 5.05.73
Hello - **Lionel Richie** 10.03.84
Hello - **The Beloved** 3.02.90
Hello Buddy - **Tremeloes** 17.07.71
Hello Darling - **Tippa Irie** 29.03.86
Hello Dolly - **Louis Armstrong** 4.06.64
Hello Dolly - **Kenny Ball & his Jazzmen** 11.06.64
Hello Dolly - **Frankie Vaughan** 11.06.64
Hello Dolly - **Bachelors** 13.01.66
Hello Goodbye - **Beatles** 29.11.67
Hello Happiness - **Drifters** 20.03.76
Hello Heartache Goodbye Love - **Little Peggy March** 19.09.63
Hello Hello I'm Back Again - **Gary Glitter** 7.04.73
Hello How Are You - **Easybeats** 10.04.68
Hello Hurray - **Alice Cooper** 17.02.73
Hello I Love You - **Doors** 11.09.68
Hello Little Girl - **Fourmost** 19.09.63
Hello Muddah! Hello Fadduh! - **Allan Sherman** 19.09.63
Hello Stranger - **Yvonne Elliman** 14.05.77
Hello Summertime - **Bobby Goldsboro** 10.08.74
Hello Susie - **Amen Corner** 25.06.69
Hello This Is Joannie - **Paul Evans** 23.12.78
Hello World - **Tremeloes** 19.03.69
Help! - **Beatles** 29.07.65
Help - **Beatles** 17.04.76
Help - **Tina Turner** 10.03.84
Help! - **Bananarama/La Na Nee Nee Noo Noo** 25.02.89
Help It Along/Tomorrow Rising - **Cliff Richard** 19.05.73
Help Me Girl - **Eric Burdon & the Animals** 27.10.66
Help Me Make It Through the Night - **Gladys Knight & the Pips** 25.11.72
Help Me Make It Through the Night - **John Holt** 21.12.74
Help Me Rhonda - **Beach Boys** 3.06.65
Help Yourself - **Tom Jones** 17.07.68
Helule Helule - **Tremeloes** 15.05.68
Helyom Halib - **Cappella** 13.05.89
Her Royal Majesty - **James Darren** 5.04.62
Here Come The Nice - **Small Faces** 8.06.67
Here Comes My Baby - **Tremeloes** 2.02.67
Here Comes Summer - **Jerry Keller** 28.08.59
Here Comes That Feeling - **Brenda Lee** 28.06.62

Here Comes The Night - **Them** 25.03.65
Here Comes The Judge - **Shorty Long** 17.07.68
Here Comes the Star - **Herman's Hermits** 15.11.69
Here Comes The Sun - **Steve Harley & Cockney Rebel** 7.08.76
Here Comes The Night - **Beach Boys** 21.04.79
Here Comes The Summer - **Undertones** 28.07.79
Here Comes The Rain Again - **Eurythmics** 21.01.84
Here Comes That Sound - **Simon Harris** 5.11.88
Here Comes The Hammer - **MC Hammer** 23.02.91
Here I Go Again - **Hollies** 28.05.64
Here I Go Again - **Archie Bell & the Drells** 21.10.72
Here I Go Again - **Guys and Dolls** 24.05.75
Here I Go Again - **Twiggy** 21.08.76
Here I Go Again/Bloody Luxury - **Whitesnake** 20.11.82
Here I Go Again - **Whitesnake** 31.10.87
Here in My Heart - **Al Martino** 14.11.52
Here Is The News/Ticket To The Moon - **Electric Light Orchestra** .... 16.1.82.
Here It Comes Again - **Fortunes** 14.10.65
Here There and Everywhere - **Emmylou Harris** 20.03.76
Here We Are - **Gloria Estefan** 3.03.90
Here We Go - **Everton 1985** 18.05.85
Here We Go - **C&C Music Factory featuring Freedom Williams** 30.03.91
Here We Go Again - **Ray Charles** 5.07.67
Here We Go Round the Mulberry Bush - **Traffic** 6.12.67
Here's To Love - **John Christie** 8.01.77
Hernando's Hideaway - **Johnnie Ray** 7.10.55
Hernando's Hideaway - **Johnston Brothers** 7.10.55
Heroes - **David Bowie** 15.10.77
Heroes and Villains - **Beach Boys** 23.08.67
Hersham Boys - **Sham 69** 4.08.79
He's A Rebel - **Crystals** 20.12.62
He's Gonna Step on You Again - **John Kongos** 5.06.71
He's Got No Love - **Searchers** 15.07.65
He's Got The Whole World In His Hands - **Laurie London** 8.11.57
He's In Town - **Rockin' Berries** 22.10.64
He's Misstra Know It All - **Stevie Wonder** 13.04.74
He's Old Enough to Know Better - **Brook Brothers** 25.01.62
He's So Fine - **Chiffons** 18.04.63
He's The Greatest Dancer - **Sister Sledge** 24.03.79
He's The One - **Billie Davis** 6.06.63
Hey! - **Julio Iglesias** 30.04.83
Hey Baby - **Bruce Channel** 22.03.62
Hey DJ I Can't Dance To That Music You're Playing/Ska Train - **Beatmasters featuring Betty Boo** 12.08.89
Hey Girl - **Small Faces** 12.05.66
Hey Girl Don't Bother Me - **Tams** 7.08.71
Hey Good Lookin' - **Bo Diddley** 18.03.65
Hey Joe - **Frankie Laine** 9.10.53
Hey Joe - **Jimi Hendrix** 12.01.67
Hey Jude - **Wilson Pickett** 15.01.69
Hey Jude - **Beatles** 3.04.76
Hey Jude 4.09.68
Hey Little Girl - **Del Shannon** 22.03.62
Hey Little Girl - **Icehouse** 12.02.83
Hey Lord Don't Ask Me Questions - **Graham Parker** 6.05.78
Hey Mama - **Frankie Vaughan** 27.06.63
Hey Mama - **Joe Brown** 21.04.73
Hey Matthew - **Karel Fialka** 12.09.87
Hey Miss Payne - **Chequers** 6.03.76
Hey Mister Christmas - **Showaddywaddy** 7.12.74
Hey Mr Heartache - **Kim Wilde** 21.05.88
Hey Mr. Dream Maker - **Cliff Richard** 4.12.76
Hey Mr. Music Man - **Peters & Lee** 13.03.76
Hey Music Lover - **S Express** 18.02.89
Hey Paula - **Paul & Paula** 14.02.63
Hey Rock and Roll - **Showaddywaddy** 25.05.74
Hey Senorita - **War** 15.04.78
Hey Stoopid - **Alice Cooper** 29.06.91
Hey There - **Rosemary Clooney** 30.09.55
Hey There - **Lita Roza** 7.10.55
Hey There - **Sammy Davis Jr.** 7.10.55
Hey There - **Johnnie Ray** 14.10.55
(Hey There) Lonely Girl - **Eddie Holman** 19.10.74
Hey Willy - **Hollies** 29.05.71
Hey You - **Tommy Steele** 22.11.57
Hey You - **Quireboys** 6.01.90
(Hey You) The Rocksteady Crew - **Rocksteady Crew** 8.10.83
Heykens Serenade/The Day Is Over - **Royal Scots Dragoon Guards Band** 19.08.72
Hi-De-Hi - **Paul Shane & the Yellowcoats** 23.05.81

Hi-Fidelity - **Kids from 'Fame' featuring Valerie Landsburg** 21.08.82
Hi-Heel Sneakers - **Tommy Tucker** 9.04.64
Hi-Ho Silver Lining - **Jeff Beck** 13.04.67
Hi-Lili-Hi-Lo - **Richard Chamberlain** 21.02.63
Hi-Lili Hi-Lo - **Alan Price Set** 21.07.66
Typical Male - **Tina Turner** 30.08.86
Hi De Hi-Hi De Ho - **Kool & the Gang** 11.12.82
Hi Fidelity - **Elvis Costello & the Attractions** 19.04.80
Hi Hi Hi/C. Moon - **Wings** 9.12.72
Hi Ho Silver - **Jim Diamond** 1.03.86
Hi Ho Silver Lining - **Jeff Beck** 4.11.72
Hi Tension - **Hi Tension** 13.05.78
Hide and Seek - **Howard Jones** 18.02.84
Hideaway - **Dave Dee Dozy Beaky Mick & Tich** 9.06.66
High Class Baby - **Cliff Richard & the Drifters** 21.11.58
High Energy - **Evelyn Thomas** 19.05.84
High Hopes - **Frank Sinatra** 28.08.59
High In The Sky - **Amen Corner** 7.08.68
High Life - **Modern Romance** 5.03.83
High Noone - **Frankie Laine** 14.11.52
High School Confidential - **Jerry Lee Lewis** 23.01.59
High Time - **Paul Jones** 13.10.66
Higher Ground - **Stevie Wonder** 20.10.73
Higher Love - **Steve Winwood** 5.07.86
Higher Than The Sun - **Primal Scream** 22.06.91
Highfly - **John Miles** 25.10.75
Highly Strung - **Spandau Ballet** 20.10.84
Highway Code - **Master Singers** 14.04.66
Highway of My Life - **Isley Brothers** 26.01.74
Highway Song - **Nancy Sinatra** 6.12.69
Highwire - **Linda Carr And The Love Squad** 19.07.75
Highwire - **Rolling Stones** 30.03.91
Him - **Rupert Holmes** 5.04.80
Hippy Chick - **Soho** 19.01.91
Hippy Hippy Shake - **Swinging Blue Jeans** 19.12.63
History - **Mai Tai** 1.06.85
Hit and Miss - **John Barry Seven** 10.03.60
Hit and Run - **Girlschool** 18.04.81
Hit Me With Your Rhythm Stick - **Ian Dury & the Blockheads** 16.12.78
Hit That Perfect Beat - **Bronski Beat** 7.12.85
Hit The Ground - **Darling Buds** 14.01.89
Hit the Road Jack - **Ray Charles** 26.10.61
Hitchin' A Ride - **Vanity Fare** 27.12.69
Hitchin' A Ride - **Sinitta** 28.04.90
Hitmix (Official Bootleg Megamix) - **Alexander O'Neal** 9.12.89
Hocus Pocus - **Focus** 20.01.73
The Hokey-Cokey - **Black Lace** 21.12.85
Hokey Cokey - **Snowmen** 18.12.81
Hold Back The Night - **Trammps** 18.10.75
Hold Back The Night/Sweet On You - **Graham Parker & Rumour** 19.03.77
Hold Back the River - **Wet Wet Wet** 10.03.90
Hold Back Tomorrow - **Miki & Griff** 2.10.59
Hold Me - **P.J. Proby** 4.06.64
Hold Me - **BA Robertson & Maggie Bell** 17.10.81
Hold Me Close - **David Essex** 20.09.75
Hold Me In Your Arms - **Rick Astley** 11.02.89
Hold Me Now - **Thompson Twins** 19.11.83
Hold Me Now - **Johnny Logan** 23.05.87
Hold Me Thrill Me Kiss Me - **Muriel Smith** 15.05.53
Hold Me Tight - **Johnny Nash** 14.08.68
Hold Me Tighter In The Rain - **Billy Griffin** 15.01.83
Hold My Hand - **Don Cornell** 3.09.54
Hold On - **En Vogue** 5.05.90
Hold On - **Wilson Phillips** 2.06.90
Hold on Tight - **Electric Light Orchestra** 1.08.81
Hold On Tight - **Samantha Fox** 6.09.86
Hold On To Love - **Peter Skellern** 5.04.75
Hold On To My Love - **Jimmy Ruffin** 3.05.80
Hold The Line - **Toto** 3.03.79
Hold Tight - **Dave Dee Dozy Beaky Mick & Tich** 10.03.66
Hold Your Head Up - **Argent** 11.03.72
Holdin' On - **Tony Rallo & the Midnight Band** 15.03.80
Holding Back The Years - **Simply Red** 24.05.86
Holding On - **Beverley Craven** 27.07.91
Holding Out For A Hero - **Bonnie Tyler** 31.08.85
Hole Hearted - **Extreme** 23.11.91
Hole In My Shoe - **Traffic** 13.09.67
Hole In My Shoe - **neil** 14.07.84
Hole in the Bucket - **Harry Belafonte & Odetta** 28.09.61

Hole in the Ground - **Bernard Cribbins** 15.02.62
Holiday - **Madonna** 21.01.84
Holiday - **Madonna** 3.08.85
Holiday - **Madonna** 8.06.91
Holiday Rap - **MC Miker G & DJ Sven** 6.09.86
Holidays In The Sun - **Sex Pistols** 22.10.77
Holliedaze - **Hollies** 5.09.81
Hollywood - **Boz Scaggs** 17.12.77
Holy Cow - **Lee Dorsey** 3.11.66
Holy Roller - **Nazareth** 22.11.75
Holy Smoke - **Iron Maiden** 22.09.90
Holy Wars...The Punishment Due - **Megadeth** 29.09.90
Homburg - **Procol Harum** 4.10.67
Home Is Where The Heart Is - **Gladys Knight & the Pips** 8.10.77
Home Lovin' Man - **Andy Williams** 28.11.70
Homely Girl - **Chi-Lites** 30.03.74
Homely Girl - **UB40** 18.11.89
Homeward Bound - **Simon & Garfunkel** 31.03.66
Homicide - **999** 25.11.78
Homing Waltz - **Vera Lynn** 14.11.52
Honaloochie Boogie - **Mott the Hoople** 16.06.73
Honey - **Bobby Goldsboro** 24.04.68
Honey - **Bobby Goldsboro** 5.04.75
Honey Chile - **Fats Domino** 1.02.57
Honey Chile - **Martha Reeves & the Vandellas** 30.01.68
Honey Come Back - **Glen Campbell** 9.05.70
Honey Honey - **Sweet Dreams** 27.07.74
Honey I - **George McCrae** 31.01.76
Honey I Need - **Pretty Things** 25.02.65
Honey I'm Lost - **Dooleys** 24.02.79
Honeycomb - **Jimmie Rodgers** 1.11.57
The Honeythief - **Hipsway** 8.03.86
Hong Kong Garden - **Siouxsie & the Banshees** 2.09.78
Honky Cat - **Elton John** 9.09.72
Honky Tonk Train Blues - **Keith Emerson** 17.04.76
Honky Tonk Women - **Rolling Stones** 9.07.69
Hooked on A Feeling - **Jonathan King** 27.11.71
Hooked on Classics - **Royal Philharmonic Orchestra** 25.07.81
Hooks in You - **Marillion** 9.09.89
Hooray Hooray It's A Holi Holiday - **Boney M** 28.04.79
Hoots Mon - **Lord Rockingham's XI** 24.10.58
Hooverville (And They Promised Us The World) - **Christians** 4.07.87
Hopelessly Devoted to You - **Olivia Newton-John** 4.11.78
Horse With No Name - **America** 8.01.72
Hot Diggity - **Perry Como** 25.05.56
Hot Diggity - **Michael Holliday** 22.06.56
Hot Diggity - **Stargazers** 22.06.56
Hot Dog - **Shakin' Stevens** 23.02.80
Hot In The City - **Billy Idol** 23.01.88
Hot Legs/I Was Only Joking - **Rod Stewart** 28.01.78
Hot Love - **T.Rex** 27.02.71
Hot Love - **Kelly Marie** 21.02.81
Hot Shot - **Barry Blue** 26.10.74
Hot Shot - **Karen Young** 2.09.78
Hot Shot Tottenham! - **Tottenham Hotspur FC/Chas & Dave** 16.05.87
Hot Stuff - **Donna Summer** 19.05.79
Hot Toddy - **Ted Heath Orchestra** 3.07.53
Hot Valves - **Be-Bop Deluxe** 20.11.76
Hot Water - **Level 42** 1.09.84
Hound Dog - **Elvis Presley** 21.09.56
Hounds of Love - **Kate Bush** 1.03.86
Hourglass - **Squeeze** 29.08.87
House Arrest - **Krush** 26.12.87
House Nation - **House Master Boyz & the Rude Boy of House** 12.09.87
House of Fun - **Madness** 22.05.82
House of The Rising Sun - **Animals** 25.06.64
House of The Rising Sun - **Frijid Pink** 4.04.70
House of The Rising Sun - **Animals** 14.10.72
The House of the Rising Sun - **Animals** 25.09.82
House On Fire - **Boomtown Rats** 3.04.82
The House That Jack Built - **Alan Price Set** 2.08.67
The House That Jack Built - **Tracie** 2.04.83
House With Love In It - **Vera Lynn** 26.10.56
Housecall - **Shabba Ranks featuring Maxi Priest** 31.08.91
How About That - **Adam Faith** 15.09.60
How Am I Supposed to Live Without You - **Michael Bolton** 17.02.90
How 'Bout Us - **Champaign** 23.05.81
How Can I Be Sure - **David Cassidy** 16.09.72
How Can I Keep From Singing - **Enya** 7.12.91
How Can I Love You More - **M People** 16.11.91
How Can I Meet Her - **Everly Brothers** 24.05.62
How Can I Tell Her - **Fourmost** 13.08.64
How Can This Be Love - **Andrew Gold** 15.07.78
How Can We Be Lovers - **Michael Bolton** 5.05.90
How Can You Tell - **Sandie Shaw** 25.11.65
How Come - **Ronnie Lane** 19.01.74
How Deep Is Your Love - **Bee Gees** 29.10.77
How Do You Do It? - **Gerry & the Pacemakers** 14.03.63
How Do You Know It's Love - **Teresa Brewer** 30.06.60
How Do You Speak To An Angel - **Dean Martin** 22.10.54
How Does It Feel - **Slade** 15.02.75
How Does That Grab You Darlin' - **Nancy Sinatra** 28.04.66
How Glad I Am - **Kiki Dee Band** 19.04.75
How High The Moon - **Gloria Gaynor** 24.01.76
How Long - **Ace** 16.11.74
How Many Lies - **Spandau Ballet** 21.02.87
How Many Tears - **Bobby Vee** 3.08.61
How Men Are - **Aztec Camera** 5.03.88
(How Much is) That Doggie In The Window - **Patti Page** 27.03.53
(How Much is) That Doggie In The Window - **Lita Roza** 13.03.53
How Much Love - **Leo Sayer** 16.04.77
How Much Love - **Vixen** 28.07.90
How Soon? - **Henry Mancini Orchestra** 24.09.64
How Soon Is Now - **Smiths** 9.02.85
How Sweet It Is - **Junior Walker & the All-Stars** 1.09.66
How Was It For You? - **James** 12.05.90
How Will I Know - **Whitney Houston** 25.01.86
How Wonderful to Know - **Pearl Carr & Teddy Johnson** 27.04.61
Howards' Way Theme - **Simon May Orchestra** 2.11.85
Howzat - **Sherbet** 2.10.76
H.A.P.P.Y. Radio - **Edwin Starr** 26.05.79
Hubble Bubble Toil and Trouble - **Manfred Mann** 16.04.64
Human - **Human League** 23.08.86
Human Nature - **Gary Clail On-U Sound System** 30.03.91
Human Racing - **Nik Kershaw** 15.09.84
Human Touch - **Rick Springfield** 21.01.84
Humming Bird - **Frankie Laine** 11.11.55
Humpin' - **Gap Band** 25.04.81
Hungry for Love - **Johnny Kidd & the Pirates** 28.11.63
Hungry Like The Wolf - **Duran Duran** 15.05.82
Hunt - **Barry Ryan** 4.10.69
Hunting High and Low - **A-Ha** 14.06.86
Hurdy Gurdy Man - **Donovan** 29.05.68
Hurry Home - **Wavelength** 31.07.82
Hurry Up Harry - **Sham 69** 14.10.78
Hurt - **Elvis Presley** 8.05.76
Hurt - **Manhattans** 2.10.76
Hurt By Love - **Inez Foxx** 30.07.64
Hurt So Good - **Susan Cadogan** 12.04.75
Hush Not A Word to Mary - **John Rowles** 19.06.68
The Hustle - **Van McCoy** 31.05.75
Hustle! (To The Music...) - **Funky Worm** 30.07.88
Hymn - **Ultravox** 27.11.82
Hymn to Her - **Pretenders** 20.12.86
Hyperactive! - **Thomas Dolby** 28.01.84
Hyperreal - **Shamen** 6.04.91
Hypnosis - **Mud** 30.06.73
Hysteria - **Def Leppard** 28.11.87
I Ain't Gonna Stand For It - **Stevie Wonder** 10.01.81
I Ain't Gonna Cry - **Little Angels** 20.07.91
I Ain't Got Time Any More - **Cliff Richard** 5.09.70
I Ain't Lyin' - **George McCrae** 25.10.75
I Almost Lost My Mind - **Pat Boone** 17.08.56
I Am A Cider Drinker - **Wurzels** 11.09.76
I Am A Rock - **Simon & Garfunkel** 16.06.66
I Am (I'm Me) - **Twisted Sister** 2.04.83
I Am The Beat - **Look** 10.01.81
I Am The Law - **Anthrax** 28.02.87
I Am What I Am - **Greyhound** 1.04.72
I Am What I Am - **Gloria Gaynor** 14.01.84
I Am...I Said - **Neil Diamond** 8.05.71
I Apologise - **P.J. Proby** 25.02.65
I Beg Your Pardon - **Kon Kan** 18.03.89
I Believe - **Frankie Laine** 3.04.53
I Believe - **Bachelors** 19.03.64
I Believe - **EMF** 2.02.91
I Believe (A Soulful Re-Recording) - **Tears for Fears** 12.10.85
I Believe I'm Gonna Love You - **Frank Sinatra** 27.12.75

I Believe (In Love) - **Hot Chocolate** 4.09.71
I Believe In Father Christmas - **Greg Lake** 6.12.75
I Believe You - **Dorothy Moore** 22.10.77
I Belong - **Kathy Kirby** 11.03.65
I Called You - **Lil Louis & the World** 13.01.90
I Can Dance - **Brian Poole & the Tremeloes** 5.12.63
I Can Do It - **Rubettes** 8.03.75
I Can Do This - **Monie Love** 4.02.89
I Can Dream About You - **Dan Hartman** 24.08.85
I Can Hear Music - **Beach Boys** 5.03.69
I Can Hear The Grass Grow - **Move** 6.04.67
I Can Help - **Billy Swan** 14.12.74
I Can Help - **Elvis Presley** 24.12.83
I Can Make You Feel Good - **Shalamar** 3.04.82
I Can Prove It - **Tony Etoria** 18.06.77
I Can Prove It - **Phil Phearon** 9.08.86
I Can See Clearly Now - **Jpohnny Nash** 1.07.72
I Can See Clearly Now - **Hothouse Flowers** 4.08.90
I Can See For Miles - **Who** 25.10.67
I Can Sing A Rainbow-Love Is Blue - **Dells** 23.07.69
I Can Take Or Leave Your Loving - **Herman's Hermits** 17.01.68
I Can't Ask For Anything More Than You Babe - **Cliff Richard** 28.08.76
I Can't Control Myself - **Troggs** 6.10.66
I Can't Explain - **Who** 25.02.65
(I Can't Get No) Satisfaction - **Rolling Stones** 26.08.65
(I Can't Get No) Satisfaction - **Bubble Rock** 2.02.74
I Can't Get By Without You - **Real Thing** 4.09.76
I Can't Get Next To You - **Temptations** 17.01.70
I Can't Get You Outa My Mind - **Yvonne Elliman** 20.08.77
I Can't Give You Anything (But My Love) - **Stylistics** - 26.07.75
I Can't Go For That (No Can Do) - **Daryl Hall And John Oates** .... 30.1.82.
I Can't Help Myself - **Four Tops** 15.07.65
I Can't Help Myself - **Four Tops** 28.03.70
I Can't Help Myself - **Donnie Elbert** 26.02.72
I Can't Help It - **Bananarama** 16.01.88
I Can't Leave You Alone - **George McCrae** 5.10.74
I Can't Let Go - **Hollies** 3.03.66
I Can't Let Maggie Go - **Honeybus** 3.04.68
I Can't Live A Dream - **Osmonds** 13.11.76
I Can't Make It Alone - **P.J. Proby** 17.11.66
I Can't Make It - **Small Faces** 16.03.67
I Can't Stand The Rain - **Eruption** 18.02.78
I Can't Stand Up For Falling Down - **Elvis Costello** 16.02.80
I Can't Stand It - **Twenty4Seven featuring Captain Hollywood** 22.09.90
I Can't Stop - **Osmonds** 27.04.74
I Can't Stop - **Gary Numan** 28.06.86
I Can't Stop Loving You - **Ray Charles** 21.06.62
I Can't Stop Lovin' You - **Leo Sayer** 23.09.78
I Can't Take the Power - **Off-Shore** 12.01.91
I Can't Tell the Bottom From The Top - **Hollies** 25.04.70
I Can't Turn You Loose - **Otis Redding** 1.09.66
I Can't Wait - **Nu Shooz** 24.05.86
I Close My Eyes and Count to Ten - **Dusty Springfield** 10.07.68
I Could Be Happy - **Altered Images** 18.12.81
I Could Be So Good For You - **Dennis Waterman** 1.11.80
I Could Easily Fall - **Cliff Richard** 10.12.64
I Could Never Take The Place of Your Man - **Prince** 28.11.87
I Couldn't Live Without Your Love - **Petula Clark** 30.06.66
I Count the Tears - **Drifters** 23.03.61
I Cried for You - **Ricky Stevens** 28.12.61
I Did What I Did for Maria - **Tony Christie** 15.05.71
I Didn't Know I Loved You (Till I Saw You Rock 'N' Roll) - **Gary Glitter** 23.09.72
I Didn't Mean To Turn You On - **Robert Palmer** 19.07.86
I Die: You Die - **Gary Numan** 30.08.80
I Dig You Baby - **Marvin Rainwater** 6.06.58
I Do I Do I Do - **Abba** 2.08.75
I Don't Believe In If Anymore - **Roger Whittaker** 18.04.70
I Don't Believe In Miracles - **Colin Blunstone** 18.11.72
I Don't Believe In Miracles - **Sinitta** 1.10.88
I Don't Blame You At All - **Smokey Robinson & the Miracles** 5.06.71
I Don't Care - **Liberace** 19.10.56
I Don't Care - **Los Bravos** 15.09.66
I Don't Care If The Sun Don't Shine - **Elvis Presley** 23.11.56
I Don't Know Why - **Eden Kane** 17.05.62
I Don't Know Why - **Stevie Wonder** 26.03.69
I Don't Know Why - **Andy & David Williams** 7.04.73
I Don't Know Anybody Else - **Black Box** 17.02.90
I Don't Love You But I Think I Love You - **Gilbert O'Sullivan** 21.06.75
I Don't Love You Anymore - **Quireboys** 7.04.90
I Don't Mind At All - **Bourgeois Tagg** 20.02.88
I Don't Need A Doctor - **W.A.S.P.** 14.11.87
I Don't Think That Man Should Sleep Alone - **Ray Parker Jnr.** 17.10.87
(I Don't Wanna Go To) Chelsea - **Elvis Costello & the Attraction** 18.03.78
I Don't Wanna Play House - **Tammy Wynette** 19.06.76
I Don't Wanna Lose You - **Kandidate** 7.04.79
I Don't Wanna Dance - **Eddy Grant** 23.10.82
I Don't Wanna Go On With You Like That - **Elton John** 25.06.88
I Don't Wanna Get Hurt - **Donna Summer** 27.05.89
I Don't Wanna Lose You - **Tina Turner** 1.12.89
I Don't Want To Go On Without You - **Moody Blues** 11.03.65
I Don't Want Our Loving to Die - **Herd** 17.04.68
I Don't Want To Put A Hold On You - **Berni Flint** 19.03.77
I Don't Want To Talk About It/First Cut Is The Deepest - **Rod Stewart** 30.04.77
I Don't Want To Lose Your Love - **Emotions** 24.12.77
I Don't Want To Be A Freak - **Dynasty** 3.11.79
I Don't Want To Be A Hero - **Johnny Hates Jazz** 5.09.87
I Don't Want To Talk About It - **Everything But The Girl** 9.07.88
I Don't Want Your Love - **Duran Duran** 1.10.88
I Don't Want A Lover - **Texas** 11.02.89
I Dreamed - **Beverley Sisters** 1.02.57
I Drove All Night - **Cyndi Lauper** 27.05.89
I Eat Cannibals Part I - **Toto Coelo** 14.08.82
I Feel A Cry Coming On - **Hank Locklin** 12.05.66
I Feel Fine Beatles 3.12.64
I Feel For You - **Chaka Khan** 20.10.84
I Feel Free - **Cream** 22.12.66
I Feel Like Buddy Holly - **Alvin Stardust** 19.05.84
I Feel Love - **Donna Summer** 9.07.77
I Feel Love - **Donna Summer** 11.12.82
I Feel Love (Medley) - **Bronski Beat & Marc Almond** 20.04.85
I Feel Love Coming On - **Felice Taylor** 1.11.67
I Feel The Earth Move - **Martika** 21.10.89
I Fought the Law - **Bobby Fuller Four** 21.04.66
I Fought The Law - **Clash** 19.05.79
I Fought the Law - **Clash** 19.03.88
I Found Lovin' - **Fatback Band** 3.10.87
I Found Lovin' - **Steve Walsh** 3.10.87
I Found Out The Hard Way - **Four Pennies** 16.07.64
I Found Someone - **Cher** 26.12.87
I Found Sunshine - **Chi-Lites** 3.08.74
I Gave It Up (When I Fell In Love) - **Luther Vandross** 23.04.88
I Gave You My Heart (Didn't I) - **Hot Chocolate** 18.02.84
I Get A Kick Out of You - **Gary Shearston** 5.10.74
I Get A Little Sentimental Over You - **New Seekers** 9.03.74
I Get Around - **Beach Boys** 16.07.64
I Get So Lonely - **Four Knights** 4.06.54
I Get The Sweetest Feeling - **Jackie Wilson** 5.08.72
I Get The Sweetest Feeling - **Jackie Wilson** 10.05.75
I Get The Sweetest Feeling - **Jackie Wilson** 28.02.87
I Go Ape - **Neil Sedaka** 24.04.59
I Go To Sleep - **Pretenders** 14.11.81
I Got A Feeling - **Ricky Nelson** 21.11.58
I Got Da Feelin'/It's Like That Y'All - **Sweet Tee** 30.01.88
I Got Rhythm - **Happenings** 25.05.67
I Got the Music In Me - **Kiki Dee Band** .... 14.09.74]
I Got To Sing - **J.A.L.N. Band** 10.09.77
I Got You - **James Brown** 10.03.66
I Got You - **Split Enz** 30.08.80
I Got You Babe - **Sonny and Cher** 12.08.65
I Got You Babe - **UB40 guest vocals by Chrissie Hynde** 3.08.85
I Guess I'll Always Love You - **Isley Brothers** 22.01.69
I Guess That's Why They Call It The Blues - **Elton John** 4.06.83
I Have A Dream - **Abba** 15.12.79
I Haven't Stopped Dancing Yet - **Pat & Mick** 25.03.89
I Hear A Symphony - **Supremes** 6.01.66
I Hear Talk - **Bucks Fizz** 19.01.85
I Hear You Knocking - **Dave Edmunds** 21.11.70
I Hear You Now - **Jon & Vangelis** 19.01.80
I Heard A Heart Break Last Night - **Jim Reeves** 6.12.67
I Heard A Rumour - **Bananarama** 18.07.87
I Heard It Through the Grapevine - **Marvin Gaye** 12.02.69
I Heard It Through The Grapevine - **Marvin Gaye** 26.04.86
I Honestly Love You - **Olivia Newton-John** 12.10.74
I Just Called to Say I Love You - **Stevie Wonder** 25.08.84
I Just Can't Help Believing - **Elvis Presley** 11.12.71
I Just Can't Stop Loving You - **Michael Jackson with Siedah Garrett** 8.08.87
(I Just) Died In Your Arms - **Cutting Crew** 30.08.86
I Just Don't Know What To Do With Myself - **Dusty Springfield** 2.07.64

I Just Don't Have the Heart - **Cliff Richard** 26.08.89
I Just Go For You - **Jimmy Jones** 8.09.60
(I Just Wanna) B With U - **Transvision Vamp** 13.04.91
I Just Wanna Be Your Everything - **Andy Gibb** 9.07.77
I Just Wanna (Spend Some Time With You) - **Alton Edwards** .... 16.1.82.
I Knew The Bride - **Dave Edmunds** 9.07.77
I Knew You Were Waiting (For Me) - **Aretha Franklin & George Michael** 31.01.87
I Know - **Perry Como** 10.07.59
I Know A Place - **Petula Clark** 11.03.65
I Know Him So Well - **Elaine Page & Barbara Dickson** 12.01.85
(I Know) I'm Losing You - **Temptations** 22.12.66
I Know What I Like (In Your Wardrobe) - **Genesis** 13.04.74
I Know Where I'm Going - **George Hamilton IV** 18.07.58
I Know You Got Soul - **Eric B & Rakim** 12.03.88
I Left My Heart In San Francisco - **Tony Bennett** 14.10.65
I Life For Your Love - **Natalie Cole** 24.12.88
I Like It - **Gerry & the Pacemakers** 30.05.63
I Like It - **D.J.H. featuring Stefy** 13.07.91
I Like (What You're Doing To Me) - **Young & Co** 8.11.80
I Like Your Kind of Love - **Andy Williams** 21.06.57
I Live For the Sun - **Vanity Fare** 4.09.68
I Lost My Heart to A Starship Trooper - **Sarah Brightman & Hot Gossip** 18.11.78
I Love America - **Patrick Juvet** 11.11.78
I Love Being In Love With You - **Adam Faith** 28.05.64
I Love Her - **Paul & Barry Ryan** 19.05.66
I Love How You Love Me - **Jimmy Crawford** 23.11.61
I Love How You Love Me - **Maureen Evans** 5.03.64
I Love How You Love Me - **Paul & Barry Ryan** 28.07.66
I Love Music - **The O'Jays** 7.02.76
I Love Music - **O'Jays** 8.04.78
I Love Music - **Enigma** 15.08.81
I Love My Dog - **Cat Stevens** 20.10.66
I Love My Radio - **Taffy** 17.01.87
I Love Rock 'N' Roll - **Joan Jett and the Blackhearts** 24.04.82
I Love The Night Life - **Alicia Bridges** 18.11.78
I Love The Sound of Breaking Glass - **Nick Lowe** 11.03.78
I Love The Way You Love - **Marv Johnson** 12.05.60
I Love To Boogie - **T.Rex** 26.06.76
I Love to Love - **Tina Charles** 14.02.76
I Love You - **Cliff Richard** 1.12.60
I Love You - **Donna Summer** 10.12.77
I Love You Baby - **Paul Anka** 8.11.57
I Love You Baby - **Freddie & the Dreamers** 21.05.64
I Love You Because - **Jim Reeves** 27.02.64
I Love You Because/He'll Have to Go/Moonlight & Roses - **Jim Reeves** 3.07.71
I Love You Love Me Love - **Gary Glitter** 17.11.73
I Love You So Much It Hurts/Wandering Eyes - **Charlie Gracie** 23.08.57
I Love You Yes I Do - **Merseybeats** 21.10.65
I Love You Yes I Love You - **Eddy Grant** 1.08.81
I Made It Through The Rain - **Barry Manilow** 14.02.81
I May Never Pass This Way Again - **Ronnie Hilton** 18.04.58
I May Never Pass This Way Again - **Robert Earl** 25.04.58
I May Never Pass This Way Again - **Perry Como** 30.05.58
I Met A Girl - **Shadows** 17.03.66
I Might - **Shakin' Stevens** 24.02.90
I Miss You Baby - **Marv Johnson** 8.11.69
I Missed Again - **Phil Collins** 14.03.81
I Must Be In Love - **Rutles** 29.04.78
I Must Be Seeing Things - **Gene Pitney** 18.02.65
I Need A Man - **Eurythmics** 9.04.88
I Need It - **Johnny Guitar Watson** 4.09.76
I Need Love - **LL Cool J** 19.09.87
I Need To Be In Love - **Carpenters** 10.07.76
I Need You - **Pointer Sisters** 18.08.84
I Need You - **B.V.S.M.P.** 30.07.88
I Need You Now - **Eddie Fisher** 29.10.54
I Need Your Lovin' - **Teena Marie** 18.10.80
I Need Your Lovin' - **Alyson Williams** 19.08.89
I Only Have Eyes For You - **Art Garfunkel** 20.09.75
I Only Live to Love You - **Cilla Black** 13.12.67
I Only Wanna Be With You - **Bay City Rollers** 11.09.76
I Only Wanna Be With You - **Samantha Fox** 28.01.89
I Only Want To Be With You - **Dusty Springfield** 28.11.63
I Only Want To Be With You - **Tourists** 24.11.79
I Owe You Nothing - **Bros** 18.06.88
I Owe You One - **Shalamar** 6.09.80
I Pretend - **Des O'Connor** 22.05.68
I Pretend - **Des O'Connor** 1.01.69
I Put A Spell On You - **Alan Price Set** 31.03.66
I Put A Spell On You - **Nina Simone** 22.01.69
I Really Didn't Mean It - **Luther Vandross** 18.07.87
I Recall A Gypsy Woman - **Don Williams** 26.06.76
I Remember Elvis Presley - **Danny Mirror** 24.09.77
I Remember Yesterday - **Donna Summer** 24.09.77
I Remember You 5.07.62
I Remember You - **Skid Row** 31.03.90
I Quit - **Bros** 17.09.88
I Saw Her Again - **Mamas & Papas** 28.07.66
I Saw Her Standing There - **Elton John Band featuring John Lennon & the Muscle Shoals Horns** 28.03.81
I Saw Him Standing There - **Tiffany** 4.06.88
I Saw Linda Yesterday - **Doug Sheldon** 14.02.63
I Saw Mommy Kissing Santa Claus - **Jimmy Boyd** 27.11.53
I Saw The Light - **Todd Rundgren** 14.07.73
I Say A Little Prayer - **Aretha Franklin** 7.08.68
I Say Nothing - **Voice of the Beehive** 30.07.88
I Second That Emotion - **Smokey Robinson & the Miracles** 10.01.68
I Second That Emotion - **Diana Ross & the Supremes & the Temptations** 20.09.69
I Second That Emotion - **Japan** 10.07.82
I See A Star - **Mouth & McNeal** 18.05.74
I See The Moon - **Stargazers** 19.02.54
I Shall Be Released - **Tremeloes** 18.12.68
I Shot the Sheriff - **Eric Clapton** 30.08.74
I Shot the Sheriff - **Light of the World** 24.01.81
I Should Be So Lucky - **Kylie Minogue** 30.01.88
I Should Care - **Frank Ifield** 23.07.64
I Should Have Known Better - **Naturals** 20.08.64
I Should Have Known Better - **Jim Diamond** 3.11.84
I Shoulda Loved Ya - **Narada Michael Walden** 26.04.80
I Specialise In Love - **Sharon Brown** 1.05.82
I Stand Accused - **Merseybeats** 20.01.66
I Started Something I Couldn't Finish - **Smiths** 14.11.87
I Still Haven't Found What I'm Looking For - **U2** 6.06.87
I Still Haven't Found What I'm Looking For - **Chimes** 19.05.90
I Still Love You All - **Kenny Ball & his Jazzmen** 11.05.61
I Surrender - **Rainbow** 31.01.81
I Surrender (To the Spirit of the Night) - **Samantha Fox** 25.07.87
I Thank You - **Sam & Dave** 20.03.68
I Thank You - **Adeva** 21.10.89
I Think I Love You - **Partridge Family** 13.02.71
I Think I Love You - **Voice of The Beehive** 28.09.91
I Think I'm Gonna Fall In Love With You - **Dooleys** 20.08.77
I Think of You - **Merseybeats** 23.01.64
I Think of You - **Perry Como** 15.05.71
I Think of You - **Detroit Emeralds** 18.08.73
I Think We're Alone Now - **Tiffany** 16.01.88
I Thought It Took A Little Time - **Diana Ross** 17.07.76
I Thought It Was You - **Herbie Hancock** 26.08.78
I Threw It All Away - **Bob Dylan** 21.05.69
I Told You So - **Jimmy Jones** 6.04.61
I Touch Myself - **Divinyls** 8.06.91
I Understand - **G-Clefs** 30.11.61
I Understand - **Freddie & the Dreamers** 12.11.64
I Wanna Be A Winner - **Brown Sauce** 26.12.81
I Wanna Be A Flintstone - **Screaming Blue Messiahs** 30.01.88
I Wanna Be Adored - **Stone Roses** 14.09.91
I Wanna Be Loved - **Ricky Nelson** 15.01.60
I Wanna Be Loved - **Elvis Costello & the Attractions** 16.06.84
I Wanna Be Your Man - **Rolling Stones** 21.11.63
I Wanna Dance Wit Choo - **Disco Tex & the Sex-O-Lettes** 26.04.75
I Wanna Dance With Somebody (Who Loves Me) - **Whitney Houston** 23.05.87
I Wanna Do It With You - **Barry Manilow** 16.10.82
I Wanna Get Next To You - **Rose Royce** 9.04.77
(I Wanna Give You) Devotion - **MC Mikee Freedom** 2.02.91
I Wanna Go Back - **New Seekers** 12.02.77
I Wanna Go Home - **Lonnie Donegan** 26.05.60
I Wanna Hold Your Hand - **Dollar** 22.12.79
I Wanna Hold Your Hand - **Dollar** 12.01.80
I Wanna Love My Life Away - **Gene Pitney** 6.04.61
I Wanna Sex You Up - **Color Me Badd** 18.05.91
I Wanna Stay Here - **Mike & Griff** 29.08.63
I Wanna Stay With You - **Gallagher & Lyle** 6.03.76
I Want Candy - **Brian Poole & the Tremeloes** 5.08.65
I Want Candy - **Bow Wow Wow** 5.06.82
I Want Her - **Keith Sweat** 12.03.88
I Want It All - **Queen** 13.05.89
I Want More - **Can** 11.09.76
I Want That Man - **Deborah Harry** 14.10.89

I Want To Be Wanted - **Brenda Lee** ... 27.10.60
I Want To Be Straight - **Ian Dury & the Blockheads** ... 30.08.80
I Want to Be Free - **Toyah** ... 16.05.81
I Want To Be Your Property - **Blue Mercedes** ... 21.11.87
I Want To Break Free - **Queen** ... 14.04.84
I Want to Give - **Perry Como** ... 25.05.74
I Want To Hold Your Hand - **Beatles** ... 5.12.63
I Want To Know What Love Is - **Foreigner** ... 22.12.84
I Want To Stay Here ... 22.08.63
I Want To Wake Up With You - **Boris Gardiner** ... 2.08.86
I Want to Walk You Home - **Fats Domino** ... 16.10.59
I Want You - **Bob Dylan** ... 21.07.66
I Want You Back - **Jackson 5** ... 7.02.70
I Want You Back - **Bananarama** ... 9.04.88
I Want You Back '88 - **Michael Jackson & the Jackson Five** ... 16.04.88
I Want You (Forever) - **DJ Carl Cox** ... 5.10.91
I Want You, I Need You, I Love You - **Elvis Presley** ... 13.07.56
I Want You To Be My Baby - **Billie Davis** ... 16.10.68
I Want You To Want Me - **Cheap Trick** ... 12.05.79
I Want Your Love - **Chic** ... 24.02.79
I Want Your Lovin' (Just A Little Bit) - **Curtis Hairston** ... 27.04.85
I Want Your Love - **Transvision Vamp** ... 9.07.88
I Want Your Sex - **George Michael** ... 13.06.87
I Was Born To Love You - **Freddie Mercury** ... 27.04.85
I Was Kaiser Bill's Batman - **Whistling Jack Smith** ... 9.03.67
I Was Made For Dancin' - **Leif Garrett** ... 27.01.79
I Was Made to Love Her - **Stevie Wonder** ... 26.07.67
I Was Tired of Being Alone - **Patrice Rushen** ... 17.07.82
I (Who Have Nothing) - **Tom Jones** ... 15.08.70
I Who Have Nothing - **Shirley Bassey** ... 3.10.63
I Will - **Billy Fury** ... 30.04.64
I Will - **Ruby Winters** ... 12.11.77
I Will Be With You - **T'Pau** ... 25.06.88
I Will Drink the Wine - **Frank Sinatra** ... 6.03.71
I Will Return - **Springwater** ... 23.10.71
I Will Survive - **Arrival** ... 6.06.70
I Will Survive - **Gloria Gaynor** ... 10.02.79
I Wish - **Stevie Wonder** ... 18.12.76
I Wish I Could Shimmy Like My Sister Kate - **Olympics** ... 19.01.61
I Wish it Could Be Christmas Everyday - **Wizzard** ... 8.12.73
I Wish It Could Be Christmas Everyday - **Wizzard** ... 22.12.84
I Wish It Would Rain Down - **Phil Collins** ... 27.01.90
I Wish U Heaven - **Prince** ... 5.11.88
I Wonder - **Dickie Valentine** ... 3.06.55
I Wonder - **Jane Froman** ... 17.06.55
I Wonder - **Brenda Lee** ... 18.07.63
I Wonder - **Crystals** ... 23.03.64
I Wonder If I Take You Home - **Lisa Lisa & Cult Jam with Full Force** ... 10.08.85
I Wonder Why - **Showaddywaddy** ... 25.03.78
I Won't Back Down - **Tom Petty** ... 3.06.89
I Won't Bleed For You - **Climie Fisher** ... 27.08.88
I Won't Close My Eyes - **UB40** ... 27.02.82
I Won't Come In While He's There - **Jim Reeves** ... 2.02.67
I Won't Cry - **Glen Goldsmith** ... 28.11.87
I Won't Forget You - **Jim Reeves** ... 18.06.64
I Won't Hold You Back - **Toto** ... 25.06.83
I Won't Last A Day Without You - **Carpenters** ... 15.06.74
I Won't Let The Sun Go Down On Me - **Nik Kershaw** ... 16.06.84
I Won't Let You Down - **PhD** ... 24.04.82
I Won't Run Away - **Alvin Stardust** ... 17.11.84
I Wouldn't Trade You For The World - **Bachelors** ... 20.08.64
I Write The Songs/For Love - **David Cassidy** ... 5.07.75
Ice Cream Man - **Tornados** ... 6.06.63
Ice Ice Baby - **Vanilla Ice** ... 24.11.90
Ice In The Sun - **Status Quo** ... 28.08.68
Iceblink Luck - **Cocteau Twins** ... 8.09.90
Icing On The Cake - **Stephen 'Tin Tin' Duffy** ... 25.05.85
I'd Be Surprisingly Good For You - **Linda Lewis** ... 16.06.79
I'd Do Anything - **Mike Preston** ... 1.09.60
I'd Love You To Want Me - **Lobo** ... 8.06.74
I'd Never Find Another You - **Billy Fury** ... 21.12.61
I'd Rather Go Blind - **Chicken Shack** ... 7.05.69
I'd Rather Go Blind - **Ruby Turner** ... 21.03.87
I'd Rather Jack - **Reynolds Girls** ... 4.03.89
I'd Really Love To See You Tonight - **England Dan & John Ford Coley** ... 9.10.76
Ideal World - **Christians** ... 19.12.87
Identity - **X-Ray Spex** ... 29.07.78
Idle Gossip - **Perry Como** ... 25.06.54
Idle on Parade (EP) - **Anthony Newley** ... 8.05.59

If - **Telly Savalas** ... 22.02.75
If - **Yin and Yan** ... 5.04.75
If A Man Answers - **Bobby Darin** ... 11.10.62
If Anyone Finds This I Love You - **Ruby Murray** ... 18.03.55
If Dreams Came True - **Pat Boone** ... 29.08.58
If Every Day Was Like Christmas - **Elvis Presley** ... 1.12.66
If I Can Dream - **Elvis Presley** ... 26.02.69
If I Can't Have You - **Yvonne Elliman** ... 13.05.78
If I Could - **David Essex** ... 13.12.75
If I Could (El Condor Pasa) - **Julie Felix** ... 25.04.70
If I Could Only Make You Care - **Mike Berry** ... 20.12.80
If I Could Turn Back Time - **Cher** ... 30.09.89
If I Didn't Care - **David Cassidy** ... 11.05.74
If I Give My Heart To You - **Doris Day** ... 1.10.54
If I Give My Heart To You - **Joan Regan** ... 1.10.54
If I Had A Hammer - **Trini Lopez** ... 12.09.63
If I Had Words - **Scott Fitzgerald & Yvonne Keely** ... 14.01.78
If I Had You - **Korgis** ... 14.07.79
If I Have To Go Away - **Jigsaw** ... 13.08.77
If I Knew Then What I Know Now - **Val Doonican** ... 30.10.68
If I Loved You - **Richard Anthony** ... 23.04.64
If I Needed Someone - **Hollies** ... 16.12.65
If I Only Had Time - **John Rowles** ... 13.03.68
If I Ruled The World - **Harry Secombe** ... 21.11.63
If I Ruled The World - **Tony Bennett** ... 27.05.65
If I Ruled The World - **Kurtis Blow** ... 25.01.86
If I Said You Had A Beautiful Body - **Bellamy Brothers** ... 18.08.79
If I Say Yes - **Five Star** ... 22.11.86
If I Thought You'd Change Your Mind - **Cilla Black** ... 13.12.69
If I Was - **Midge Ure** ... 14.09.85
If I Was Your Girlfriend - **Prince** ... 20.06.87
If I Were A Carpenter - **Bobby Darin** ... 20.10.66
If I Were A Carpenter - **Four Tops** ... 13.03.68
If I Were A Rich Man - **Topol** ... 27.04.67
If It Happens Again - **UB40** ... 22.09.84
If It Wasn't For the Reason That I Love You - **Miki Anthony** ... 3.02.73
If Leaving Me Is Easy - **Phil Collins** ... 13.06.81
If Loving You Is Wrong (I Don't Want To Be Right) - **Rod Stewart** ... 7.06.80
If Not For You - **Olivia Newton-John** ... 20.03.71
If Not You - **Dr. Hook** ... 6.11.76
If Only I Could Live My Life Again - **Jane Morgan** ... 22.05.59
If Only I Could - **Sydney Youngblood** ... 9.09.89
If Only Tomorrow - **Ronnie Carroll** ... 22.11.62
(If Paradise Is) Half As Nice - **Amen Corner** ... 29.01.69
If Paradise Was Half As Nice - **Amen Corner** ... 28.02.76
If She Knew What She Wants - **Bangles** ... 17.05.86
If She Should Come to You - **Anthony Newley** ... 14.07.60
If The Kids Are United - **Sham 69** ... 29.07.78
If The Whole World Stopped Loving - **Val Doonican** ... 25.10.67
If This Is It - **Huey Lewis & the News** ... 17.11.84
If You Believe - **Johnnie Ray** ... 8.04.55
If You Can't Give Me Love - **Suzi Quatro** ... 25.03.78
If You Can't Stand the Heat - **Bucks Fizz** ... 4.12.82
If You Could Read My Mind - **Gordon Lightfoot** ... 26.06.71
If You Don't Know Me By Now - **Harold Melvin & the Bluenotes** ... 13.01.81
If You Don't Know Me By Now - **Simply Red** ... 8.04.89
If You Go Away - **Terry Jacks** ... 6.07.74
If You Go Away - **New Kids On The Block** ... 14.12.91
If You Gotta Make A Fool of Somebody - **Freddie & the Dreamers** ... 9.05.63
If You Gotta Go Go Now - **Manfred Mann** ... 16.09.65
If You Know What I Mean - **Neil Diamond** ... 21.08.76
If You Leave Me Now - **Chicago** ... 9.10.76
If You Let Me Stay - **Terence Trent D'Arby** ... 21.03.87
If You Love Her - **Dick Emery** ... 26.02.69
If You Love Me - **Mary Hopkin** ... 27.03.76
If You Love Somebody Set Them Free - **Sting** ... 15.06.85
If You Really Love Me - **Stevie Wonder** ... 22.01.72
If You Talk In Your Sleep - **Elvis Presley** ... 20.07.74
If You Think You Know How To Love Me - **Smokie** ... 19.07.75
If You Wanna Be Happy - **Jimmy Soul** ... 18.07.63
If You Were Here Tonight - **Alexander O'Neal** ... 22.02.86
If You Were With Me Now - **Kylie Minogue & Keith Washington** ... 2.11.91
If You're Lookin' For A Way Out - **Odyssey** ... 20.09.80
If You're Ready (Come Go With Me) - **Staple Singers** ... 15.06.74
If You're Ready (Come Go With Me) - **Ruby Turner featuring Jonathan Butler** ... 1.02.86
Iko Iko - **Dixie Cups** ... 13.05.65
Iko Iko - **Natasha** ... 12.06.82
Iko Iko - **Belle Stars** ... 19.06.82

Il Silenzio - **Nini Rosso** 26.08.65
I'll Always Be In Love With You - **Michael Holliday** 11.07.58
I'll Always Love My Mama - **Intruders** 27.04.74
I'll Be Around - **Terri Wells** 12.05.84
I'll Be Back - **Arnee & the Terminaters** 24.08.91
I'll Be Good - **Rene & Angela** 14.09.85
I'll Be Good To You - **Quincy Jones** 20.01.90
I'll Be Home - **Pat Boone** 27.04.56
I'll Be Home This Christmas - **Shakin' Stevens** 28.12.91
I'll Be Loving You (Forever) - **New Kids on the Block** 17.03.90
I'll Be Satisfied - **Shakin' Stevens** 23.10.82
I'll Be There - **Gerry & the Pacemakers** 25.03.65
I'll Be There - **Jackie Trent** 9.04.69
I'll Be There - **Jackson 5** 21.11.70
I'll Be There For You - **Bon Jovi** 29.04.89
I'll Be Your Baby Tonight - **Robert Palmer & UB40** 3.11.90
I'll Come Running - **Cliff Richard** 15.06.67
I'll Come When You Call - **Ruby Murray** 14.10.55
I'll Cut Your Tail Off - **John Leyton** 15.08.63
I'll Do Anything You Want Me To - **Barry White** 24.05.75
I'll Find My Way Home - **Jon & Vangelis** 18.12.81
I'll Find You - **David Whitfield** 5.04.57
I'll Fly For You - **Spandau Ballet** 25.08.84
I'll Get By - **Connie Francis** 31.10.58
I'll Get By - **Shirley Bassey** 23.11.61
I'll Give You the Earth - **Keith Michell** 1.05.71
I'll Go on Hoping - **Des O'Connor** 14.03.70
I'll Go Where Your Music Takes Me - **Jimmy James & the Vagabonds** 1.05.76
I'll Go Where Your Music Takes Me - **Tina Charles** 25.03.78
I'll House You - **Richie Rich meets the Jungle Brothers** 22.10.88
I'll Keep On Loving You - **Princess** 19.04.86
I'll Keep You Satisfied - **Billy J Kramer & the Dakotas** 7.11.63
I'll Love You Forever Today - **Cliff Richard** 26.06.68
I'll Meet You At Midnight - **Smokie** 2.10.76
I'll Never Fall In Love Again - **Johnnie Ray** 4.12.59
I'll Never Fall In Love Again - **Tom Jones** 26.07.67
I'll Never Fall In Love Again - **Bobbie Gentry** 30.08.69
I'll Never Find Another You - **Seekers** 14.01.65
I'll Never Get Over You - **Johnny Kidd & the Pirates** 25.07.63
I'll Never Get Over You - **Everly Brothers** 2.09.65
I'll Never Quite Get Over You - **Billy Fury** 3.03.66
I'll Never Stop Loving You - **Doris Day** 21.10.55
I'll Pick A Rose For My Rose - **Marv Johnson** 29.01.69
I'll Put You Together Again - **Hot Chocolate** 9.12.78
I'll Remember Tonight - **Pat Boone** 16.01.59
I'll Sail This Ship Alone - **Beautiful South** 23.12.89
I'll Say Forever My Love - **Jimmy Ruffin** 11.07.70
I'll See You In My Dreams - **Pat Boone** 22.02.62
I'll Stay By You - **Kenny Lynch** 17.06.65
I'll Stay Single - **Jerry Lordan** 8.01.60
I'll Step Down - **Garry Mills** 20.07.61
I'll Stop at Nothing - **Sandie Shaw** 25.02.65
I'll Take You Home Again Kathleen - **Slim Whitman** 12.04.57
I'll Take You Home - **Drifters** 17.10.63
I'll Take You There - **Staple Singers** 10.06.72
I'll Try Anything - **Dusty Springfield** 2.03.67
I'll Walk With God - **Mario Lanza** 18.02.55
I'm A Believer - **Monkees** 12.01.67
I'm A Believer - **Robert Wyatt** 5.10.74
I'm A Better Man - **Engelbert Humperdinck** 9.08.69
I'm A Boy - **Who** 8.09.66
I'm A Clown/Some Kind of A Summer - **David Cassidy** 24.03.73
I'm A Fool - **Slim Whitman** 13.04.56
I'm A Man - **Spencer Davis Group** 26.01.67
I'm A Man - **Chicago** 10.01.70
I'm A Man Not A Boy - **Chesney Hawkes** 22.06.91
I'm A Midnight Mover - **Wilson Pickett** 18.09.68
I'm A Moody Guy - **Shane Fenton & the Fentones** 26.10.61
I'm A Tiger - **Lulu** 13.11.68
I'm A Wonderful Thing (Baby) - **Kid Creole and the Coconuts** 29.05.82
I'm Alive - **Hollies** 3.06.65
I'm Alive - **Electric Light Orchestra** 31.05.80
I'm Alright - **Young Steve & the Afternoon Boys** 4.12.82
(I'm Always Touched By Your) Presence Dear - **Blondie** 6.05.78
I'm An Upstart - **Angelic Upstarts** 28.04.79
I'm Born Again - **Boney M** 22.12.79
I'm Comin' Home Cindy - **Trini Lopez** 26.05.66
I'm Coming Home - **Tom Jones** 15.11.67
I'm Coming Out - **Diana Ross** 15.11.80
I'm Crying - **Animals** 17.09.64
I'm Doin' Fine Now - **New York City** 28.07.73
I'm Doing Fine - **Jason Donovan** 27.10.90
I'm Every Woman - **Chaka Khan** 9.12.78
I'm Every Woman - **Chaka Khan** 6.05.89
I'm Falling - **Bluebells** 14.04.84
I'm Forever Blowing Bubbles - **West Ham United 1st Team Squad** 10.05.75
I'm Forever Blowing Bubbles - **Cockney Rejects** 31.05.80
I'm Free - **Roger Daltrey/LSO & Chamber Choir** 11.08.73
I'm Free - **Soup Dragons featuring Junior Reid** 14.07.90
I'm Going Home - **Gene Vincent** 31.08.61
I'm Going Slightly Mad - **Queen** 16.03.91
I'm Gonna Be - **Proclaimers** 3.09.88
I'm Gonna Be Strong - **Gene Pitney** 12.11.64
I'm Gonna Be A Country Girl Again - **Buffy Sainte-Marie** 25.03.72
I'm Gonna Get Married - **Lloyd Price** 11.09.59
I'm Gonna Get There Somehow - **Val Doonican** 15.04.65
I'm Gonna Get Me A Gun - **Cat Stevens** 6.04.67
I'm Gonna Knock on Your Door - **Eddie Hodges** 28.09.61
I'm Gonna Knock on Your Door - **Little Jimmy Osmond** 30.03.74
I'm Gonna Love You Just A Little Bit More Baby - **Barry White** 16.06.73
I'm Gonna Make You Love Me - **Diana Ross & the Supremes & the Temptations** 29.01.69
I'm Gonna Make You Mine - **Lou Christie** 20.09.69
I'm Gonna Run Away From You - **Tami Lynn** 29.05.71
I'm Gonna Run Away From You - **Tami Lynn** 17.05.75
I'm Gonna Sit Right Down and Write Myself A Letter - **Billy Williams** 2.08.57
I'm Gonna Sit Right Down & Write Myself A Letter - **Barry Manilow** 18.12.82
I'm Gonna Tear Your Playhouse Down - **Paul Young** 13.10.84
I'm In A Different World - **Four Tops** 20.11.68
I'm In Favour of Friendship - **Five Smith Brothers** 22.07.55
I'm In Love - **Fourmost** 2.01.64
I'm In Love - **Evelyn King** 11.07.81
I'm In Love Again - **Fats Domino** 27.07.56
I'm In Love Again - **Sad Cafe** 17.01.81
I'm In Love With A German Film Star - **Passions** 7.02.81
I'm In The Mood For Dancing - **Nolans** 5.01.80
I'm Into Something Good - **Herman's Hermits** 20.08.64
I'm Just A Baby - **Louise Cordet** 12.07.62
I'm Just A Singer (In A Rock & Roll Band) - **Moody Blues** 17.02.73
I'm Leavin' - **Elvis Presley** 2.10.71
I'm Leaving It All Up To You - **Donny & Marie Osmond** 3.08.74
I'm Left You're Right She's Gone - **Elvis Presley** 17.01.58
I'm Living In Shame - **Diana Ross & the Supremes** 23.04.69
I'm Lost Without You - **Billy Fury** 14.01.65
I'm Mandy Fly Me - **10C.C.** 20.03.76
Im Nin'Alu - **Ofra Haza** 14.05.88
I'm Not A Juvenile Delinquent - **Frankie Lymon & the Teenagers** 29.03.57
I'm Not Going To Let You - **Colonel Abrams** 15.02.86
I'm Not In Love - **10CC** 7.06.75
I'm Not In Love - **Will To Power** 19.01.91
I'm Not Scared - **Eighth Wonder** 5.03.88
I'm Not The Man I Used To Be - **Fine Young Cannibals** 18.11.89
(I'm Not Your) Stepping Stone - **Sex Pistols** 21.06.80
I'm Nver Giving Up - **Sweet Dreams** 23.04.83
I'm On Fire - **5000 Volts** 6.09.75
I'm On Fire/Born In The USA - **Bruce Springsteen** 15.06.85
I'm On My Way To A Better Place - **Chairmen of the Board** 16.12.72
I'm On My Way - **Dean Parrish** 1.03.75
I'm Ready For Love - **Martha & the Vandellas** 8.12.66
I'm Real - **James Brown** 4.06.88
I'm Qualified To Satisfy - **Barry White** 19.03.77
I'm So Crazy - **K.C. And The Sunshine Band** 29.11.75
I'm So Excited - **Pointer Sisters** 3.11.84
I'm So Happy/Time - **Light of the World** 11.04.81
I'm Sorry - **Platters** 17.05.57
I'm Sorry - **Brenda Lee** 14.07.60
I'm Sorry I Made You Cry - **Connie Francis** 27.06.58
I'm Still Gonna Need You - **Osmonds** 29.11.75
I'm Still In Love With You - **Al Green** 2.09.72
I'm Still Standing - **Elton John** 6.08.83
I'm Still Waiting - **Diana Ross** 31.07.71
I'm Still Waiting (Phill Chill Remix) - **Diana Ross** 7.07.90
I'm Stone In Love With You - **Stylistics** 4.11.72
I'm Stone In Love With You - **Johnny Mathis** 1.02.75
I'm Telling You Now - **Freddie & the Dreamers** 8.08.63
I'm The Leader of the Gang (I Am) - **Gary Glitter** 21.07.73
I'm The Lonely One - **Cliff Richard** 6.02.64
I'm The Man - **Anthrax** 5.12.87

I'm The One - **Gerry & the Pacemakers** 16.01.64
I'm The Urban Spaceman - **Bonzo Dog Doo-Dah Band** 13.11.68
I'm Too Scared - **Steven Dante** 23.07.88
I'm Too Sexy - **Right Said Fred** 27.07.91
I'm Walkin' - **Fats Domino** 19.04.57
I'm Walking Behind You - **Eddie Fisher** 22.05.53
I'm Walking Behind You - **Dorothy Squires** 5.06.53
I'm Walking Backwards for Christmas - **Goons** 29.06.56
I'm Wondering - **Stevie Wonder** 1.11.67
I'm Your Baby Tonight - **Whitney Houston** 20.10.90
I'm Your Man - **Wham!** 23.11.85
I'm Your Puppet - **James & Bobby Purify** 1.05.76
Image of A Girl - **Mark Wynter** 25.08.60
Image of A Girl - **Nelson Keene** 25.08.60
Imagination - **Rockey Sharpe & the Replays** 14.04.79
Imagination - **Belouis Some** 25.01.86
Imagine - **John Lennon** 8.11.75
Imagine - **John Lennon** 27.12.80
Imagine Me, Imagine You - **Fox** 17.05.75
Imperial Wizard - **David Essex** 10.03.79
Importance of Your Love - **Vince Hill** 10.07.68
In A Big Country - **Big Country** 28.05.83
In A Broken Dream - **Python Lee Jackson** 7.10.72
In A Golden Coach - **Billy Cotton** 1.05.53
In A Golden Coach - **Dickie Valentine** 5.06.53
In A Lifetime - **Clannad additional vocals: Bono** 25.01.86
In A Lifetime - **Clannad, additional vocals: Bono** 17.06.89
In A Little Spanish Town - **Bing Crosby** 27.04.56
In A Persian Market - **Sammy Davis Jr.** 20.04.56
In and Out of Love - **Diana Ross & the Supremes** 29.11.67
In and Out Of Love - **Imagination** 12.09.81
In Between Days - **Cure** 27.07.85
The In Betweenies/Father Christmas Do Not Touch Me - **Goodies** 14.12.74
The 'In' Crowd - **Dobie Gray** 4.03.65
The 'In' Crowd - **Bryan Ferry** 25.05.74
In Dreams - **Roy Orbison** 7.03.63
In Dulce Jubilo/On Horseback - **Mike Oldfield** 27.12.75
In For A Penny - **Slade** 22.11.75
In Love - **Michael Holliday** 14.03.58
In My Chair - **Status Quo** 7.11.70
In My Dreams - **Will Downing** 9.07.88
In My Own Time - **Family** 17.07.71
In My World - **Anthrax** 1.09.90
In Old Lisbon - **Frank Chacksfield** 24.02.56
In Private - **Dusty Springfield** 1.12.89
In Summer - **Billy Fury** 1.08.63
In The Air Tonight - **Phil Collins** 17.01.81
In The Air Tonight - **Phil Collins** 18.06.88
In The Arms of Love - **Andy Williams** 22.09.66
In The Army Now - **Status Quo** 4.10.86
In The Bad Old Days - **Foundations** 12.03.69
In The Beginning - **Frankie Laine** 11.03.55
In The Brownies - **Billy Connolly** 8.09.79
In The Bush - **Musique** 25.11.78
In The Chapel In The Moonlight - **Bachelors** 4.11.65
In The City - **The Jam** 4.06.77
In The City - **Jam** 3.05.80
In The Country - **Cliff Richard & the Shadows** 15.12.66
In The Ghetto - **Elvis Presley** 11.06.69
In the Heat of the Night - **Imagination** 2.10.82
In the Meantime - **George Fame** 4.03.65
In The Middle Of A Dark Dark Night/Sweet Stuff - **Guy Mitchell** 26.07.57
In The Middle of An Island - **King Brothers** 9.08.57
In The Middle of Nowhere - **Dusty Springfield** 1.07.65
In The Midnight Hour - **Wilson Pickett** 30.09.65
In The Mood - **Ernie Fields** 25.12.59
In The Mood - **Ray Stevens** 12.03.77
In The Name Of Love - **Sharon Redd** 22.01.83
In The Navy - **Village People** 17.03.79
In The Summertime - **Mungo Jerry** 6.06.70
In The Year 2525 - **Zager & Evans** 9.08.69
In Thoughts of You - **Billy Fury** 22.07.65
In Too Deep - **Dead Or Alive** 29.06.85
In Too Deep - **Genesis** 30.08.86
In Yer Face - **808 State** 16.02.91
In Your Car - **Cool Notes** 13.07.85
In Your Eyes - **George Benson** 1.10.83
In Your Room - **Bangles** 19.11.88
In Zaire - **Johnny Wakelin** 31.07.76

Incommunicado - **Marillion** 23.05.87
Indescribably Blue - **Elvis Presley** 9.02.67
Indestructible - **Four Tops** 18.03.89
Indian Love Call - **Slim Whitman** 29.07.55
Indian Love Call - **Karl Denver** 20.06.63
Indian Love Call - **Ray Stevens** 4.10.75
Indian Reservation - **Don Fardon** 24.10.70
Indiana Wants Me - **R. Dean Taylor** 10.04.71
Infatuation - **Rod Stewart** 9.06.84
Infidelity - **Simply Red** 30.05.87
Infiltrate 202 - **Altern 8** 20.07.91
Infinished Sympathy - **Massive** 2.03.91
Infinite Dreams (Live) - **Iron Maiden** 18.11.89
Infinity - **Guru Josh** 24.02.90
Inherit the Wind - **Wilton Felder** 15.11.80
The Ink In The Well - **David Sylvian** 18.08.84
Inna City Mamma - **Neneh Cherry** 30.12.89
Innamorata - **Dean Martin** 27.04.56
Innuendo - **Queen** 26.01.91
Insanity - **Oceanic** 24.08.91
Inside - Looking Out - **Animals** 17.02.66
Inside America - **Juggy Jones** 28.02.76
Inside Looking Out - **Grand Funk Railroad** 6.02.71
Inside Out - **Odyssey** 19.06.82
Instant Karma - **John Lennon and Yoko Ono with the Plastic Ono Band** 21.02.70
Instant Replay - **Dan Hartman** 28.10.78
Instant Replay - **Yell!** 27.01.90
Instinction - **Spandau Ballet** 24.04.82
Interesting Drug - **Morrissey** 29.04.89
Internal Exile - **Fish** 28.09.91
International Rescue - **We've Got A Fuzzbox & We're Gonna Use It** 11.03.89
International Bright Young Thing - **Jesus Jones** 12.01.91
Into the Blue - **Mission** 2.06.90
Into the Groove - **Madonna** 27.07.85
Into The Valley - **Skids** 24.02.79
Into Tomorrow - **Paul Weller Movement** 18.05.91
Intuition - **Linx** 21.03.81
Invisible - **Alison Moyet** 1.12.84
The Invisible Man - **Queen** 19.08.89
Invisible Sun - **Police** 26.09.81
Invisible Touch - **Genesis** 31.05.86
Invitations - **Shakatak** 11.09.82
IOU - **Freeez** 25.06.83
Ire Feelings (Skanga) - **Rupie Edwards** 23.11.74
The Irish Rover - **Pogues & the Dubliners** 28.03.87
Iron Fist - **Motorhead** 3.04.82
I.O.U. Freeez 17.01.87
Is It A Dream - **Classix Nouveaux** 20.03.82
Is It A Dream - **Damned** 21.09.85
Is It Because? - **Honeycombs** 22.10.64
Is It Love You're After - **Rose Royce** 24.11.79
Is It Really Over? - **Jim Reeves** 18.11.65
Is It True? - **Brenda Lee** 10.09.64
Is She Really Going Out With Him - **Joe Jackson** 11.08.79
Is That Love - **Squeeze** 23.05.81
Is There Anybody There/Another Piece of Meat - **Scorpions** 2.06.79
Is There Anybody Out There - **Bassheads** 16.11.91
Is There Something I Should Know - **Duran Duran** 26.03.83
Is This A Love Thing - **Raydio** 22.07.78
Is This Love - **Bob Marley & the Wailers** 25.02.78
Is This Love - **Alison Moyet** 6.12.86
Is This Love - **Whitesnake** 6.06.87
Is This The Way to Amarillo - **Tony Christie** 27.11.71
Is Vic There - **Department S** 18.04.81
Is Your Love Strong Enough - **Bryan Ferry** 5.04.86
Island Girl - **Elton John** 11.10.75
Island Head (EP) - **Inspiral Carpets** 17.11.90
Island In The Sun - **Harry Belafonte** 14.06.57
Island In The Sun - **Righteous Brothers** 22.12.66
Island of Dreams - **Springfields** 20.12.62
Island of Lost Souls - **Blondie** 8.05.82
Islands In The Stream - **Kenny Rogers and Dolly Parton** 26.11.83
Isle of Innisfree - **Bing Crosby** 14.11.52
Isn't Life Strange - **Moody Blues** 6.05.72
Isn't She Lovely - **David Parton** 15.01.77
The Israelites - **Desmond Dekker & the Aces** 19.03.69
Israelites - **Desmond Dekker** 10.05.75
Istanbul - **Frankie Vaughan** 29.01.54
It Ain't Me Babe - **Johnny Cash** 3.06.65

It Ain't Necessarily So - **Bronski Beat** 15.12.84
It Ain't Over 'Til It's Over - **Lenny Kravitz** 15.06.91
It Ain't What You Do It's The Way That You Do It - **Fun Boy Three and Bananarama** 20.02.82
It Didn't Matter - **Style Council** 17.01.87
It Doesn't Have To Be This Way - **Blow Monkeys** 31.01.87
It Doesn't Have To Be - **Erasure** 28.02.87
It Doesn't Matter Any More - **Buddy Holly** 27.02.59
It Don't Come Easy - **Ringo Starr** 17.04.71
It Hurts So Much - **Jim Reeves** 11.02.65
It Hurts To Be In Love - **Gene Pitney** 22.10.64
It Is Time To Get Funky - **D Mob featuring LRS** 3.06.89
It Isn't It Wasn't It Ain't Never Gonna Be - **Aretha Franklin & Whitney Houston** 16.09.89
It Keeps Right On A Hurtin' - **Johnny Tillotson** 12.07.62
It Makes You Feel Like Dancin' - **Rose Royce** 6.05.78
It Maybe Winter Outside - **Love Unlimited** 1.02.75
It Miek - **Desmond Dekker & the Aces** 2.07.69
It Might As Well Rain Until September - **Carole King** 27.09.62
It Must Be Him (Seul Sur Son Etoile) - **Vikki Carr** 15.06.67
It Must Be Love - **Labi Siffre** 4.12.71
It Must Be Love - **Madness** 5.12.81
It Must Have Been Love - **Magnum** 2.07.88
It Must Have Been Love - **Roxette** 2.06.90
It Only Takes A Minute - **100 Ton & a Feather** 3.07.76
It Only Took A Minute - **Joe Brown** 15.11.62
It Oughta Sell A Million - **Lyn Paul** 12.07.75
It Should Have Been Me - **Yvonne Fair** 31.01.76
It Started All Over Again - **Brenda Lee** 20.09.62
It Started With A Kiss - **Hot Chocolate** 10.07.82
It Sure Brings Out The Love In Your Eyes - **David Soul** 27.05.78
It Takes All Night Long - **Gary Glitter** 29.01.77
It Takes Two - **Marvin Gaye & Kim Weston** 2.02.67
It Takes Two - **Rob Base & DJ E-Z Rock** 23.04.88
It Takes Two - **Rod Stewart & Tina Turner** 24.11.90
It Takes Two To Tango - **Richard Myhill** 8.04.78
It Won't Seem Like Christmas Without You - **Elvis Presley** 22.12.79
Italian Theme - **Cyril Stapleton Orchestra** 6.04.56
Itchycoo Park - **Small Faces** 16.08.67
Itchycoo Park - **Small Faces** 20.12.75
It'll Be Me - **Cliff Richard** 6.09.62
It's A Disco Night (Rock Don't Stop) - **Isley Brothers** 10.11.79
It's A Game - **Bay City Rollers** 14.05.77
It's A Hard Life - **Queen** 28.07.84
It's A Heartache - **Bonnie Tyler** 3.12.77
It's A Love Thing - **Whispers** 21.03.81
It's A Man's Man's Man's World - **James Brown** 16.06.66
It's A Miracle - **Culture Club** 24.03.84
It's A Mistake - **Men At Work** 9.07.83
It's A Raggy Waltz - **Dave Brubeck** 8.02.62
It's A Shame - **Motown Spinners** 14.11.70
It's A Shame (My Sister) - **Monie Love featuring True Image** 22.09.90
It's A Sin - **Pet Shop Boys** 27.06.87
It's A Sin to Tell A Lie - **Gerry Monroe** 17.04.71
It's All In the Game - **Tommy Edwards** 3.10.58
It's All In The Game - **Cliff Richard** 22.08.63
It's All In The Game - **Four Tops** 30.05.70
It's All Over Now - **Shane Fenton** 12.04.62
It's All Over Now - **Rolling Stones** 2.07.64
It's All Over Now Baby Blue - **Joan Baez** 9.09.65
It's All Over - **Cliff Richard** 23.03.67
It's All Up To You - **Jim Capaldi** 3.08.74
It's Almost Tomorrow - **Dream Weavers** 10.02.56
It's Almost Tomorrow - **Mark Wynter** 14.11.63
It's Alright - **Pet Shop Boys** 8.07.89
It's An Open Secret - **Joy Strings** 5.03.64
It's Been Nice - **Everly Brothers** 13.06.63
It's Been So Long - **George McCrae** 26.07.75
It's Better to Have - **Don Covay** 14.09.74
It's Called A Heart - **Depeche Mode** 28.09.85
It's Different For Girls - **Joe Jackson** 19.01.80
It's Ecstasy - **Barry White** 29.10.77
It's For You - **Cilla Black** 6.08.64
It's Four In The Morning - **Faron Young** 22.07.72
It's Getting Better - **Mama Cass** 30.08.69
It's Going to Happen - **Undertones** 9.05.81
It's Gonna Be All Right - **Gerry & the Pacemakers** 3.09.64
It's Gonna Be A Cold Cold Christmas - **Dana** 20.12.75
It's Good News Week - **Hedgehoppers Anonymous** 7.10.65
It's Grim Up North - **Justified Ancients Of Mu Mu** 9.11.91
It's Happenin' - **Plus One featuring Sirron** 26.05.90
It's Hard To Be Humble - **Mac Davis** 20.12.80
It's Impossible - **Perry Como** 30.01.71
It's In His Kiss - **Betty Everett** 6.11.68
It's In His Kiss - **Linda Lewis** 19.07.75
It's Late - **Ricky Nelson** 17.04.59
It's Late - **Shakin' Stevens** 23.07.83
(It's Like A) Sad Old Kinda Movie - **Pickettywitch** 4.07.70
It's Love - **Ken Dodd** 10.11.66
It's Love That Really Counts - **Merseybeats** 19.09.63
It's My House - **Diana Ross** 8.12.79
It's My House - **Storm** 15.12.79
It's My Life - **Animals** 28.10.65
It's My Life - **Talk Talk** 26.05.90
It's My Party - **Lesley Gore** 20.06.63
It's My Party - **Dave Stewart & Barbara Gaskin** 26.09.81
It's My Time - **Everly Brothers** 22.05.68
It's My Turn - **Diana Ross** 24.01.81
It's Not Unusual - **Tom Jones** 11.02.65
It's Not Unusual - **Tom Jones** 6.06.87
It's Now Or Never - **Elvis Presley** 3.11.60
It's Now Or Never - **Elvis Presley** 3.09.77
It's One of Those Nights - **Partridge Family** 4.03.72
It's On/Egg Rush - **Flowered Up** 17.08.91
It's Only Love/Beyond The Reef - **Elvis Presley** 30.08.80
It's Only Love - **Bryan Adams & Tina Turner** 9.11.85
It's Only Love - **Simply Red** 28.01.89
It's Only Make Believe - **Conway Twitty** 14.11.58
It's Only Make Believe - **Billy Fury** 23.07.64
It's Only Make Believe - **Glen Campbell** 21.11.70
It's Only Make Believe - **Child** 5.08.78
It's Only Rock and Roll - **Rolling Stones** 3.08.74
It's 'Orrible Being In Love (When You're 8½) - **Claire & Friends** 21.06.86
It's Over - **Roy Orbison** 30.04.64
It's Over - **Funk Masters** 25.06.83
It's Over - **Level 42** 12.09.87
It's Raining - **Darts** 12.08.78
It's Raining - **Shakin' Stevens** 10.10.81
It's Raining Again - **Supertramp** 6.11.82
It's Raining Men - **Weather Girls** 10.03.84
It's So Easy - **Andy Williams** 15.08.70
It's Still Rock 'N' Roll To Me - **Billy Joel** 16.08.80
It's The End of The World As We Know It - **REM** 14.12.91
It's The Same Old Song - **Four Tops** 23.09.65
It's the Same Old Song - **Weathermen** 23.01.71
It's Time For Love - **Chi-Lites** 20.09.75
It's Time to Cry - **Paul Anka** 26.02.60
It's Too Late Now - **Swinging Blue Jeans** 11.07.63
It's Too Late Now - **Long John Baldry** 5.02.69
It's Too Late - **Carole King** 14.08.71
It's Too Late - **Quartz introducing Dina Carroll** 2.03.91
It's Too Soon to Know - **Pat Boone** 11.04.58
It's Tricky - **Run-DMC** 6.06.87
It's Up To You - **Rick Nelson** 17.01.63
It's Yer Money I'm After Baby - **Wonder Stuff** 24.09.88
It's You - **Freddie Starr** 23.02.74
It's Your Day Today - **PJ Proby** 13.03.68
It's Your Life - **Smokie** 23.07.77
It's Your Thing - **Isley Brothers** 2.07.69
Itsy Bitsy Teeny Weeny Yellow Polka Dot Bikini - **Brian Hyland** 14.07.60
Itsy Bitsy Teeny Weeny Yellow Polka Dot Bikini - **Bombalurina** 4.08.90
I've Been A Bad Bad Boy - **Paul Jones** 19.01.67
I've Been Drinking - **Jeff Beck and Rod Stewart** 12.05.73
I've Been Hurt - **Guy Darrell** 25.08.73
I've Been In Love Before - **Cutting Crew** 22.11.86
I've Been In Love Before - **Cutting Crew** 28.11.87
I've Been Lonely For So Long - **Frederick Knight** 17.06.72
I've Been Losing You - **A-Ha** 4.10.86
I've Been Thinking About You - **Londonbeat** 15.09.90
I've Been Wrong Before - **Cilla Black** 29.04.65
I've Done Everything For You - **Sammy Hagar** 23.02.80
I've Got A Thing About You Baby - **Elvis Presley** 16.03.74
I've Got News For You - **Feargal Sharkey** 16.03.91
I've Got To Love Somebody - **Sister Sledge** 26.01.80
I've Got You Under My Skin - **Four Seasons** 6.10.66
I've Got You On My Mind - **Dorian Gray** 3.04.68
I've Got You On My Mind - **White Plains** 18.04.70
I've Got You Under My Skin - **Neneh Cherry** 6.10.90

I've Gotta Get A Message To You - **Bee Gees** 7.08.67
I've Had Enough - **Earth Wind and Fire** 20.02.82
(I've Had) The Time of My Life - **Bill Medley & Jennifer Warnes** 7.11.87
(I've Had) The Time of My Life - **Bill Medley & Jennifer Warnes** 5.01.91
I've Lost You - **Elvis Presley** 14.11.70
I've Never Been To Me - **Charlene** 22.05.82
I've Passed This Way Before - **Jimmy Ruffin** 9.02.67
I've Passed This Way Before - **Jimmy Ruffin** 6.09.69
I've Told Every Little Star - **Linda Scott** 25.05.61
I've Waited So Long - **Anthony Newley** 1.05.59
Ivory Tower - **Three Kayes** 25.05.56
JA-DA - **Johnny and the Hurricanes** 2.03.61
Jack & Jill - **Raydio** 15.04.78
Jack and Diane - **John Cougar** 30.10.82
Jack in the Box - **Clodagh Rodgers** 20.03.71
Jack In The Box - **Moments** 29.01.77
Jack Le Freak - **Chic** 19.09.87
Jack Mix II - **Mirage** 16.05.87
Jack Mix IV - **Mirage** 7.11.87
Jack O' Diamonds - **Lonnie Donegan** 20.12.57
The Jack That House Built - **Jack 'n' Chill** 23.01.88
Jack the Groove - **Raze** 17.01.87
Jack To the Sound of The Underground - **Hithouse** 19.11.88
Jack Your Body - **Steve 'Silk' Hurley** 3.01.87
Jackie - **Scott Walker** 13.12.67
Jackie Wilson Said - **Kevin Rowland & Dexy's Midnight Runners** 2.10.82
Jacky - **Marc Almond** 28.09.91
Jacqueline - **Bobby Helms** 1.08.58
Jailbreak - **Thin Lizzy** 14.08.76
Jailhouse Rock - **Elvis Presley** 24.01.58
Jailhouse Rock (EP) - **Elvis Presley** 31.01.58
Jailhouse Rock - **Elvis Presley** 12.02.83
Jam Jam Jam - **People's Choice** 21.01.78
Jambalaya - **Jo Stafford** 19.12.52
Jambalaya - **Carpenters** 9.03.74
The James Bond Theme - **John Barry Orchestra** 8.11.62
Jamming/Punky Reggae Party - **Bob Marley & the Wailers** 17.12.77
Jane - **Jefferson Starship** 2.02.80
January - **Pilot** 18.01.72
January February - **Barbara Dickson** 22.03.80
Japanese Boy - **Aneka** 15.08.81
Jarrow Song - **Alan Price** 1.06.74
Jaws - **Lalo Schifrin** 16.10.76
Jazz Carnival - **Azymuth** 19.01.80
Je Said Ne Pas Pourquoi - **Kylie Minogue** 22.10.88
Je Suis Music - **Cerrone** 27.01.79
Je T'Aime - **Judge Dread -** 5.07.75
Je T'Aime ... Moi Non Plus - **Jane Birkin & Serge Gainsbourg** 16.08.69
Je T'Aime ... Moi Non Plus - **Jane Birkin & Serge Gainsbourg** 4.10.69
Je T'Aime ... Moi Non Plus - **Jane Birkin & Serge Gainsbourg** 14.12.74
Jealous Guy - **Roxy Music** 21.02.81
Jealous Mind - **Alvin Stardust** 16.02.74
Jealousy - **Billy Fury** 14.09.61
Jealousy - **Pet Shop Boys** 8.06.91
The Jean Genie - **David Bowie** 9.12.72
Jeannie - **Danny Williams** 25.01.62
Jeannie Jeannie Jeannie - **Eddie Cochran** 7.12.61
Jeans On - **David Dundas** 24.07.76
Jeepster - **T.Rex** 13.11.71
Jennifer Eccles - **Hollies** 3.04.68
Jennifer Jennifer - **Donovan** 21.02.68
Jennifer She Said - **Lloyd Cole & the Commotions** 16.01.88
Jenny Jenny - **Little Richard** 13.09.57
Jenny Take A Ride - **Mitch Ryder & the Detroit Wheels** 24.02.66
Jesamine - **Casuals** 21.08.68
Jesus - **Cliff Richard** 11.03.72
Jet - **Paul McCartney & Wings** 2.03.74
Jet City Woman - **Queensryche** 7.09.91
Jezebel - **Marty Wilde** 24.05.62
Jig-A-Jig - **East of Eden** 24.04.71
Jilted John - **Jilted John** 12.08.78
Jimmy Jimmy - **Undertones** 5.05.79
Jimmy Mack - **Martha & the Vandellas** 13.04.67
Jimmy Mack - **Martha and the Vandellas** 5.09.70
Jimmy Unknown - **Lita Roza** 23.03.56
Jingle Bell Rock - **Max Bygraves** 18.12.59
Jingle Bell Rock - **Chubby Checker & Bobby Rydell** 27.12.62
Jingo - **Jellybean** 19.12.87
Jitterbuggin' - **Heatwave** 28.03.81
Jive Talkin' - **Bee Gees** 5.07.75
Jive Talkin' - **Boogie Box High** 11.07.87
Joan of Arc - **Orchestral Manoeuvres In The Dark** 24.10.81
Joanna - **Scott Walker** 1.05.68
Joanna/Tonight - **Kool & the Gang** 18.02.84
Joe Le Taxi - **Vanessa Paradis** 20.02.88
John & Julie - **Eddie Calvert** 29.07.55
John I'm Only Dancing - **David Bowie** 23.09.72
John I'm Only Dancing (Again) - **David Bowie** 15.12.79
John I'm Only Dancing/Big Green Car - **Polecats** 21.03.81
John Kettley (Is A Weatherman) - **A Tribe of Toffs** 24.12.88
John Wayne is Big Leggy - **Haysi Fantayzee** 7.08.82
Johnny Angel - **Patti Lynn** 10.05.62
Johnny B Goode - **Jimi Hendrix** 19.02.72
Johnny Come Home - **Fine Young Cannibals** 8.06.85
Johnny Friendly - **Jo Boxers** 3.09.83
Johnny Get Angry - **Carol Deene** 12.07.62
Johnny Reggae - **Piglets** 6.11.71
Johnny Remember Me - **John Leyton** 3.08.61
Johnny Rocco - **Marty Wilde** 10.03.60
Johnny Will - **Pat Boone** 14.12.61
Join In And Sing (No. 3) - **Johnston Brothers** 7.12.56
Join In And Sing - **Johnston Brothers** 30.12.55
Join the Party - **Honky** 4.06.77
Join Together - **Who** 24.06.72
The Joker - **Steve Miller Band** 25.08.90
Jolene - **Dolly Parton** 22.05.76
Jones vs Jones/Summer Madness/Funky Stuff - **Kool & the Gang** 28.02.81
Jordan: The E.P. - **Prefab Sprout** 12.01.91
Joseph Mega-Remix - **Jason Donovan** 7.12.91
Journey - **Duncan Browne** 19.08.72
Joy - **Band AKA** 12.03.83
Joy and Heartbreak - **Movement 98 featuring Carroll Thompson** 26.05.90
Joy and Pain - **Donna Allen** 10.06.89
Joy of Living - **Cliff and Hank** 28.02.70
Joy to the World - **Three Dog Night** 5.06.71
Joybringer - **Manfred Mann's Earthband** 8.09.73
Joyride - **Roxette** 9.03.91
Judge Fudge - **Happy Mondays** 30.11.91
Judy In Disguise (With Glasses) - **John Fred & the Playboy Band** 10.01.68
Judy Teen - **Cockney Rebel** 18.05.74
Juicy - **Wrecks-N-Effect** 20.01.90
Juicy Fruit - **Mtume** 28.05.83
Juke Box Baby - **Perry Como** 27.04.56
Juke Box Jive - **Rubettes** 16.11.74
Julie-Ann - **Kenny** 23.08.75
Julie Do Ya Love Me? - **White Plains** 24.10.70
Julie Do Ya Love Me - **Bobby Sherman** 14.11.70
Juliet - **Four Pennies** 2.04.64
Jumbo/The Singer Sang His Song - **Bee Gees** 3.04.68
Jump - **Van Halen** 25.02.84
Jump Back (Set Me Free) - **Dhar Braxton** 14.06.86
Jump (For My Love) - **Pointer Sisters** 23.06.84
Jump Start - **Natalie Cole** 27.08.88
Jump To The Beat - **Stacy Lattisaw** 21.06.80
Jump To The Beat - **Dannii Minogue** 27.07.91
Jumping Jack Flash - **Rolling Stones** 29.05.68
Jungle Fever - **Chakachas** 10.06.72
Jungle Rock - **Hank Mizell** 20.03.76
Junior's Farm - **Paul McCartney & Wings** 9.11.74
Just A Feeling - **Bad Manners** 4.04.81
Just A Groove - **Nomad** 4.05.91
Just A Little Too Much - **Ricky Nelson** 11.09.59
Just A Little Bit Too Late - **Wayne Fontana & the Mindbenders** 24.06.65
Just A Little Bit Better - **Herman's Hermits** 2.09.65
Just A Little Misunderstanding - **Contours** 31.01.70
Just A Mirage - **Jellybean featuring Adele Bertei** 26.03.88
Just A Shadow - **Big Country** 19.01.85
Just A Smile - **Pilot** 4.10.75
Just A Touch of Love (Everyday) - **C&C Music Factory** 23.11.91
Just An Illusion - **Imagination** 6.03.82
Just Another Broken Heart - **Sheena Easton** 26.09.81
Just Another Night - **Mick Jagger** 23.02.85
Just Another Dream - **Cathy Dennis** 20.07.91
Just As Much As Ever - **Nat 'King' Cole** 17.11.60
Just Be Good To Me - **SOS Band** 14.04.84
Just Born - **Jim Dale** 10.01.58
Just Call - **Sherrick** 8.08.87
Just Can't Get Enough - **Depeche Mode** 26.09.81

Just Can't Give You Up - **Mystic Merlin** 10.05.80
Just Don't Want to be Lonely - **Main Ingredient** 6.07.74
Just Don't Want To Be Lonely - **Freddie McGregor** 11.07.87
Just For Kicks - **Mike Sarne** 10.01.63
Just For Money - **Paul Hardcastle** 9.11.85
Just for You - **Glitter Band** 10.08.74
Just Got Lucky - **Jo Boxers** 21.05.83
Just Keep It Up - **Dee Clark** 2.10.59
Just Keep Rockin' - **Double Trouble and The Rebel MC** 27.05.89
Just Let Me Do My Thing - **Sine** 17.06.78
Just Like A Woman - **Manfred Mann** 4.08.66
Just Like Eddie - **Heinz** 8.08.63
Just Like Heaven - **Cure** 17.10.87
Just Like Jesse James - **Cher** 27.01.90
Just Like Me - **Hollies** 30.05.63
Just Like Paradise - **David Lee Roth** 12.03.88
(Just Like) Starting Over - **John Lennon** 8.11.80
Just Listen To My Heart - **Spotnicks** 2.05.63
Just Loving You - **Anita Harris** 5.07.67
Just My Imagination - **Temptations** 22.05.71
Just My Soul Responding - **Smokey Robinson** 9.03.74
Just One Look - **Hollies** 27.02.64
Just One Look - **Faith, Hope & Charity** 7.02.76
Just One More Night - **Yellow Dog** 11.02.78
Just One Smile - **Gene Pitney** 17.11.66
Just Out Of Reach (Of My Two Empty Arms) - **Ken Dodd** 2.12.72
Just Outside Of Heaven - **H_2O** 27.08.83
Just Say No - **Grange Hill Cast** 19.04.86
Just Seven Numbers - **Four Tops** 8.05.71
Just the Two of Us - **Grover Washington Jr** 30.05.81
Just The Way You Are - **Billy Joel** 11.02.78
Just The Way You Are - **Barry White** 23.12.78
Just The Way You Like It - **SOS Band** 11.08.84
Just This Side of Love - **Malandra Burrows** 8.12.90
Just Walk In My Shoes - **Gladys Knight & the Pips** 8.07.72
Just Walking In The Rain - **Johnnie Ray** 12.10.56
Just What I Always Wanted - **Mari Wilson** 18.09.82
Just When I Needed You Most - **Randy Vanwarmer** 11.08.79
Just When I Needed You Most - **Barbara Jones** 7.02.81
Just Who Is The 5 O'clock Hero - **Jam** 3.07.82
Justified and Ancient - **KLF featuring Tammy Wynette** 7.12.91
Justify My Love - **Madonna** 8.12.90
Kansas City - **Little Richard** 5.06.59
Kansas City - **Trini Lopez** 26.12.63
Karma Chameleon - **Culture Club** 10.09.83
Kate Bush Live On Stage - **Kate Bush** 15.09.79
Kayleigh - **Marillion** 18.05.85
Keep A Knockin' - **Little Richard** 29.11.57
Keep Away From Other Girls - **Helen Shapiro** 25.10.62
(Keep Feeling) Fascination - **Human League** 23.04.83
Keep It Comin's Love - **KC & Sunshine Band** 18.12.76
Keep It Dark - **Genesis** 7.11.81
Keep Me In Mind - **Boy George** 6.06.87
Keep On - **Bruce Channel** 3.07.68
Keep on Dancing - **Bay City Rollers** 18.09.71
Keep On Dancing - **Gary's Gang** 3.03.79
Keep on Loving You - **REO Speedwagon** 25.04.81
Keep on Movin' - **Soul II Soul featuring Caron Wheeler** 18.03.89
Keep On Running - **Spencer Davis Group** 9.12.65
Keep On Truckin' - **Eddie Kendricks** 3.11.73
Keep Searchin' - **Del Shannon** 14.01.65
Keep Your Eye on Me - **Herb Alpert** 28.03.87
Keep Your Hands Off My Baby - **Little Eva** 3.01.63
Keeper of the Castle - **Four Tops** 25.11.72
Keeping The Dream Alive - **Freiheit** 24.12.88
Kennedy - **Wedding Present** 7.10.89
Kentucky Rain - **Elvis Presley** 16.05.70
Kewpie Doll - **Perry Como** 9.05.58
Kewpie Doll - **Frankie Vaughan** 9.05.58
Kicking Up The Leaves - **Mark Wynter** 17.11.60
Kid - **The Pretenders** 21.07.79
The Kids Are Back - **Twisted Sister** 04.06.83
Kids In America - **Kim Wilde** 7.03.81
The Kid's Last Fight - **Frankie Laine** 16.04.54
Killer - **Adamski** 14.04.90
Killer (EP) - **Seal** 16.11.91
Killer On The Loose - **Thin Lizzy** 27.09.80
Killer Queen - **Queen** 26.10.74
Killers Live (EP) - **Thin Lizzy** 9.05.81
Killing Me Softly With His Song - **Roberta Flack** 24.02.73
The Killing Moon - **Echo & the Bunnymen** 28.01.84
The Killing of Georgie - **Rod Stewart** 21.08.76
A Kind of Magic - **Queen** 29.03.86
King and Queen of America - **Eurythmics** 3.02.90
King Creole - **Elvis Presley** 3.10.58
King For A Day - **Thompson Twins** 19.10.85
King In A Catholic Style (Wake Up) - **China Crisis** 15.06.85
The King Is Half Undressed - **Jellyfish** 16.02.91
King Kong - **Terry Lightfoot** 21.12.61
King Midas In Reverse - **Hollies** 4.10.67
King of Clowns - **Neil Sedaka** 19.04.62
King of Emotion - **Big Country** 20.08.88
King of Pain - **Police** 14.01.84
The King of Rock 'N' Roll - **Prefab Sprout** 7.05.88
King Of The Cops - **Billy Howard** 20.12.75
King of the Road - **Roger Miller** 18.03.65
King of the Road (EP) - **Proclaimers** 24.11.90
King of Wishful Thinking - **Go West** 11.08.90
King Rocker - **Generation X** 27.01.79
King/Food For Thought - **UB40** 22.03.80
King's Call - **Phil Lynott** 12.07.80
Kings of the Wild Frontier - **Adam & the Ants** 21.02.81
Kingston Town - **UB40** 31.03.90
Kinky Afro - **Happy Mondays** 20.10.90
Kinky Boots - **Patrick Macnee & Honor Blackman** 1.12.90
Kiss - **Dean Martin** 18.09.53
Kiss - **Prince** 8.03.86
Kiss - **Art of Noise featuring Tom Jones** 29.10.88
Kiss And Say Goodbye - **Manhattans** 26.06.76
Kiss Me - **Stephen Tin Tin' Duffy** 2.03.85
Kiss Me Another - **Georgia Gibbs** 13.07.56
Kiss Me Honey Honey Kiss Me - **Shirley Bassey** 26.12.58
Kiss Me Quick - **Elvis Presley** 19.12.63
Kiss On My List - **Daryl Hall & John Oates** 29.11.80
Kiss The Bride - **Elton John** 15.10.83
Kiss Them For Me - **Siouxsie & the Banshees** 25.05.91
Kiss You All Over - **Exile** 2.09.78
Kisses on the Wind - **Neneh Cherry** 12.08.89
Kisses Sweeter Than Wine - **Jimmie Rodgers** 20.12.57
Kisses Sweeter Than Wine - **Frankie Vaughan** 20.12.57
Kissin' Cousins - **Elvis Presley** 25.06.64
Kissin' In The Back Row - **Drifters** 15.06.74
Kissing A Fool - **George Michael** 3.12.88
Kissing Gate - **Sam Brown** 12.05.90
Kissing With Confidence - **Will Powers** 15.10.83
Kit It In - **Simple Minds** 29.07.89
Kites - **Simon Dupree & the Big Sound** 15.11.67
Kitsch - **Barry Ryan** 30.05.70
Knee Deep In The Blues - **Tommy Steele** 15.02.57
Knee Deep In The Blues - **Guy Mitchell** 15.02.57
Knock Knock Who's There - **Mary Hopkin** 28.03.70
Knock On Wood - **Eddie Floyd** 16.03.67
Knock on Wood - **Otis Redding & Carla Thomas** 1.11.67
Knock on Wood - **David Bowie** 28.09.74
Knock On Wood - **Amii Stewart** 14.04.79
Knock on Wood/Light My Fire - **Amii Stewart** 31.08.85
Knock Three Times - **Dawn** 10.04.71
Knocked It Off - **B.A. Robertson** 10.11.79
Knocked Out (Pettibone Remix) - **Paula Abdul** 21.07.90
Knockin' On Heaven's Door - **Bob Dylan** 6.10.73
Knockin' On Heaven's Door - **Eric Clapton** 23.08.75
Knowing Me Knowing You - **Abba** 5.03.77
Kokomo - **Beach Boys** 3.12.88
Kommotion - **Duane Eddy** 10.11.60
Kon-Tiki - **Shadows** 7.09.61
Kookie Kookie Lend Me Your Comb - **Eddie Byrnes & Connie Stevens** 12.05.60
Kookie Little Paradise - **Frankie Vaughan** 29.09.60
Kool In The Kaftan - **BA Robertson** 29.03.80
Kumbaya - **Sandpipers** 26.03.69
Kung Fu Fighting - **Carl Douglas** 24.08.74
Kyrie - **Mr Mister** 8.03.86
Kyrila - **Demis Roussos** 25.06.77
L-L-Lucy - **Mud** 4.10.75
La-La Means I Love You - **Delfonics** 10.07.71
La Bamba - **Los Lobos** 18.07.87
La Booga Rooga - **Surprise Sisters** 20.03.76
La Dee Dah - **Jackie Dennis** 14.03.58
La Derniere Valse - **Mireille Mathieu** 13.12.67

La Isla Bonita - **Madonna** 4.04.87
La La La - **Massiel** 24.04.68
La Luna - **Belinda Carlisle** 30.12.89
La Mer (Beyond the Sea) - **Bobby Darin** 29.01.60
La Plume de Ma Tante - **Hugo & Luigi** 24.07.59
La Serenissima - **DNA** 8.09.90
Labelled With Love - **Squeeze** 17.10.81
Labour of Love - **Hue & Cry** 18.07.87
Ladies Night - **Kool & the Gang** 3.11.79
Lady - **Kenny Rogers** 22.11.80
Lady Barbara - **Peter Noone & Herman's Hermits** 28.11.70
Lady D'Arbanville - **Cat Stevens** 27.06.70
Lady Eleanor - **Lindisfarne** 13.05.72
Lady Godiva - **Peter & Gordon** 29.09.66
The Lady In Red - **Chris De Burgh** 12.07.86
Lady Is A Tramp - **Buddy Greco** 21.07.60
Lady Jane - **David Garrick** 16.06.66
Lady Love Bug - **Clodagh Rodgers** 16.10.71
Lady Love Me (One More Time) - **George Benson** 28.05.83
Lady Lynda - **Beach Boys** 23.06.79
Lady Madonna - **Beatles** 20.03.68
Lady Marmalade - **Labelle** 22.03.75
Lady Rose - **Mungo Jerry** 29.05.71
Lady Willpower - **Union Gap** 14.08.68
Lambada - **Kaoma** 11.11.89
Lament - **Ultravox** 7.07.84
Lamplight - **David Essex** 10.11.73
Lana - **Roy Orbison** 16.06.66
Land of A Thousand Dances - **Wilson Pickett** 8.09.66
Land of Confusion - **Genesis** 22.11.86
The Land of Make Believe - **Bucks Fizz** 5.12.81
Landslide - **Olivia Newton-John** 22.1.82.
Landslide of Love - **Transvision Vamp** 5.08.89
The Language of Love - **John D. Loudermilk** 4.01.62
Las Palabras de Amor - **Queen** 19.06.82
Las Vegas - **Tony Christie** 16.01.71
Last Christmas/Everything She Wants - **Wham!** 15.12.84
Last Christmas - **Wham!** 14.12.85
The Last Farewell - **Roger Whittaker - 2.08.75**
Last Film - **Kissing The Pink** 9.04.83
The Last Kiss - **David Cassidy** 2.03.85
Last Night - **Merseybeats** 12.11.64
Last Night A DJ Saved My Life - **Indeep** 29.01.83
Last Night I Dreamt I Dreamt That Somebody Loved Me - **Smiths** 19.12.87
Last Night In Soho - **Dave Dee Dozy Beaky Mick & Tich** 10.07.68
Last Night on The Back Porch - **Alma Cogan** 23.01.59
Last Night Was Made For Love - **Billy Fury** 3.05.62
The Last of The Famous International Playboys - **Morrissey** 11.02.89
The Last Time - **Rolling Stones** 4.03.65
Last Time I Saw Him - **Diana Ross** 11.05.74
Last Train to San Fernando - **Johnny Duncan** 26.07.57
Last Train to Clarksville - **Monkees** 2.02.67
Last Train To Trancentral - **The KLF featuring Children of The Revolution** 4.05.91
The Last Waltz - **Engelbert Humperdinck** 23.08.67
Lately - **Stevie Wonder** 14.03.81
Laugh At Me - **Sonny** 26.08.65
Laughing Gnome - **David Bowie** 22.09.73
Laughter in the Rain - **Neil Sedaka** 29.06.74
Laurel and Hardy - **Equals** 21.08.68
Lavender - **Marillion** 7.09.85
Lawdy Miss Clawdy - **Elvis Presley** 8.11.57
Lay All Your Love on Me - **Abba** 18.07.81
Lay Back In The Arms of Someone - **Smokie** 26.03.77
Lay Down - **Strawbs** 28.10.72
Lay Down Sally - **Eric Clapton** 21.01.78
Lay Down Your Arms - **Anne Shelton** 24.08.56
Lay Lady Lay - **Bob Dylan** 13.09.69
Lay Love On You - **Luisa Fernandez** 18.11.78
Lay Your Hands on Me - **Thompson Twins** 8.12.84
Lay Your Hands On Me - **Bon Jovi** 26.08.89
Lay Your Love On Me - **Racey** 2.12.78
Layla - **Derek & the Dominos** 12.08.72
Layla - **Derek and the Dominoes** 13.03.82
Lazy Bones - **Jonathan King** 5.06.71
Lazy River - **Bobby Darin** 23.03.61
Lazy Sunday - **Small Faces** 17.04.68
Lazy Sunday - **Small Faces** 3.04.76
Le Freak - **Chic** 18.11.78
Leader of The Pack - **Shangri-Las** 21.01.65
Leader of the Pack - **Shangri-Las** 14.10.72
Leader of the Pack - **Shangri Las** 19.06.76
Lean On Me - **Bill Withers** 19.08.72
Lean On Me - **Mud** 27.11.76
Lean on Me - **Club Nouveau** 28.03.87
Lean On Me (Ah-Li-Ayo) - **Red Box** 14.09.85
Lean On You - **Cliff Richard** 14.10.89
Leap Up and Down (Wave Your Knickers in the Air) - **St Cecilia** 26.06.71
Learnin' The Blues - **Frank Sinatra** 5.08.55
Learning The Game - **Buddy Holly** 27.10.60
Leave A Light On - **Belinda Carlisle** 7.10.89
Leave A Little Love - **Lulu** 24.06.65
Leave in Silence - **Depeche Mode** 4.09.82
Leave It - **Mike McGear** 12.10.74
Leave Me Alone - **Michael Jackson** 25.02.89
Leavin' (Durham Town) - **Roger Whittaker** 22.11.69
Leavin' On A Jet Plane - **Peter, Paul and Mary** 17.01.70
Leaving Me Now - **Level 42** 14.12.85
The Lebanon - **Human League** 5.05.84
Leeds United - **Leeds United FC** 29.04.72
Left Bank - **Winifred Atwell** 20.07.56
Left of Centre - **Suzanne Vega** 5.07.86
Left To My Own Devices - **Pet Shop Boys** 26.11.88
A Legal Matter - **Who** 31.03.66
Legend of Xanadu - **Dave Dee Dozy Beaky Mick & Tich** 14.02.68
Lego Skanga - **Rupie Edwards** 15.02.75
Legs - **ZZ Top** 2.03.85
Les Bicyclettes de Belsize - **Engelbert Humperdinck** 25.09.68
Lesson One - **Russ Conway** 22.02.62
Lessons In Love - **Allisons** 22.02.62
Lessons In Love - **Level 42** 26.04.86
Let 'Em In - **Wings** 7.08.76
Let 'Em In - **Billy Paul** 7.05.77
Let It All Blow - **Dazz Band** 10.11.84
Let It All Hang Out - **Jonathan King** 10.01.70
Let It Be - **Beatles** 14.03.70
Let It Be - **Ferry Aid** 4.04.87
Let It Be Me - **Everly Brothers** 12.02.60
Let It Rock/Memphis Tennessee - **Chuck Berry** 10.10.63
Let It Roll - **Raze presents Doug Lazy** 22.07.89
Let Love Rule - **Lenny Kravitz** 11.08.90
Let Me Be The One - **Shadows** 15.03.75
Let Me Be The One - **Five Star** 20.06.85
Let Me Cry On Your Shoulder - **Ken Dodd** 26.01.67
Let Me Go Lover - **Teresa Brewer** 11.02.55
Let Me Go Lover - **Joan Weber** 18.02.55
Let Me Go Lover - **Dean Martin** 25.02.55
Let Me Go Lover - **Ruby Murray** 4.03.55
Let Me Go Lover - **Kathy Kirby** 20.02.64
Let Me In Again - **Osmonds** 27.10.73
Let Me Know (I Have A Right) - **Gloria Gaynor** 20.10.79
Let Me Talk - **Earth Wind & Fire** 18.10.80
Let Me Try Again - **Tammy Jones** 26.04.75
Let My People Go - **Rainmakers** 28.03.87
Let The Beat Hit 'Em - **Lisa Lisa & Cult Jam** 13.07.91
Let the Heartaches Begin - **Long John Baldry** 8.11.67
Let The Little Girl Dance - **Billy Bland** 19.05.60
Let The Music Play - **Barry White** 10.01.76
Let The Music Play - **Shannon** 4.02.84
Let The Water Run Down - **P.J. Proby** 8.07.65
Let There Be Drums - **Sandy Nelson** 14.12.61
Let There Be Love - **Nat 'King' Cole with George Shearing** 19.07.62
Let There Be Peace on Earth (Let It Begin with Me) - **Michael Ward** 29.09.73
Let There Be Love - **Simple Minds** 23.03.91
Let True Love Begin - **Nat 'King' Cole** 23.11.61
Let Your Body Go Down Town - **Martyn Ford Orchestra** 21.05.77
Let Your Heart Dance - **Secret Affair** 17.11.79
Let Your Love Flow - **Bellamy Brothers** 24.04.76
Let Your Yeah Be Yeah - **Pioneers** 14.08.71
Let Yourself Go - **Sybil** 2.05.87
Let's All Chant - **Michael Zager Band** 15.04.78
Let's All Chant - **Mick & Pat** 16.04.88
Let's Call It Quits - **Slade** 14.02.76
Let's Clean Up The Ghetto - **Philadelphia International All Stars** 27.08.77
Let's Dance - **Chris Montez** 11.10.62
Let's Dance - **Chris Montez** 21.10.72
Let's Dance - **David Bowie** 26.03.83
Let's Dance - **Chris Rea** 6.06.87
Let's Do Rock Steady - **Bodysnatchers** 22.03.80

Let's Do The Latin Hustle - **M&O Band** 28.02.76
Let's Do The Latin Hustle - **Eddie Drennon & B.B.S. Unlimited** 6.03.76
Let's Fly Away - **Voyage** 31.03.79
Let's Get Brutal - **Nitro Deluxe** 6.02.88
Let's Get It On - **Marvin Gaye** 29.09.73
Let's Get It Up - **AC/DC** 6.02.82
Let's Get Serious - **Jermaine Jackson** 17.05.80
Let's Get This Straight (From the Start)/Old - **Dexy's Midnight Runners** 4.12.82
Let's Get Together Again - **Big Ben Banjo Band** 9.12.55
Let's Get Together - **Hayley Mills** 19.10.61
Let's Get Together Again - **Glitter Band** 26.10.74
Let's Go - **Routers** 3.01.63
Let's Go All The Way - **Sly Fox** 21.06.86
Let's Go Crazy/Take Me With U - **Prince & the Revolution** 23.02.85
Let's Go Disco - **Real Thing** 17.06.78
Let's Go Round Again - **Average White Band** 3.05.80
Let's Go to San Francisco - **Flowerpot Men** 23.08.67
Let's Go Together - **Change** 30.03.85
Let's Groove - **Earth, Wind & Fire** 7.11.81
Let's Hang On - **Four Seasons** 18.11.65
Let's Hang On - **Bandwagon** 25.06.69
Let's Hang On - **Darts** 21.06.80
Let's Hang On - **Barry Manilow** 3.10.81
Let's Have A Party - **Winifred Atwell** 4.12.53
Let's Have A Ding Dong - **Winifred Atwell** 4.11.55
Let's Have A Ball - **Winifred Atwell** 6.12.57
Let's Have A Party - **Wanda Jackson** 1.09.60
Let's Have A Quiet Night In - **David Soul** 17.12.77
Let's Have Another Party - **Winifred Atwell** 26.11.54
Let's Hear It For The Boy - **Deniece Williams** 12.05.84
Let's Jump the Broomstick - **Brenda Lee** 2.02.61
Let's Jump The Broomstick - **Coast to Coast** 30.05.81
Let's Live It Up (Nite People) - **David Joseph** 4.06.83
Let's Make A Baby - **Billy Paul** 29.05.76
Let's Party - **Jive Bunny & the Mastermixers** 16.12.89
Let's Pretend - **Lulu** 5.07.67
Let's Push It - **Innocence** 13.10.90
Let's Put It All Together - **Stylistics** 19.10.74
Let's Rock and Roll - **Winifred Atwell** 22.02.57
Let's See the Action - **Who** 6.11.71
Let's Spend The Night Together - **Rolling Stones** 19.01.67
Let's Stay Together - **Al Green** 15.01.72
Let's Stay Together - **Tina Turner** 19.11.83
Let's Stick Together - **Bryan Ferry** 12.06.76
Let's Stick Together '88 - **Bryan Ferry** 5.11.88
Let's Swing Again - **Jive Bunny & the Mastermixers** 17.11.90
Let's Talk About Love - **Helen Shapiro** 3.05.62
Let's Talk About Sex - **Salt-N-Pepa** 31.08.91
Let's Think About Living - **Bob Luman** 8.09.60
Let's Try Again/Didn't I Blow Your Mind This Time - **New Kids on the Block** 13.10.90
Let's Turkey Trot - **Little Eva** 14.03.63
Let's Twist Again - **Chubby Checker** 31.08.61
Let's Twist Again - **John Asher** 22.11.75
Let's Twist Again/The Twist - **Chubby Checker** 6.12.75
Let's Wait Awhile - **Janet Jackson** 21.03.87
Let's Walk That A-Way - **Doris Day & Johnnie Ray** 24.07.53
Let's Womble To The Party Tonight - **Wombles** 27.12.75
Let's Work - **Mick Jagger** 3.10.87
Let's Work Together - **Canned Heat** 31.01.70
Let's/Serenata - **Sarah Vaughan** 5.01.61
The Letter - **Long And The Short** 10.09.64
The Letter - **Box Tops** 20.09.67
The Letter - **Joe Cocker** 11.07.70
Letter from America - **Proclaimers** 21.11.87
Letter Full of Tears - **Billy Fury** 15.03.62
Letter To A Soldier - **Barbara Lyon** 21.12.56
Letter to Lucille - **Tom Jones** 21.04.73
A Letter to You - **Shakin' Stevens** 15.09.84
Levi Stubbs Tears (EP) - **Billy Bragg** 5.07.86
LFO - **LFO** 21.07.90
Liberian Girl - **Michael Jackson** 15.07.89
Licence to Kill - **Gladys Knight** 17.06.89
Lick It Up - **Kiss** 5.11.83
Lido Shuffle - **Boz Scaggs** 21.05.77
Lies - **Status Quo** 6.12.80
Lies - **Jonathan Butler** 5.09.87
Lies - **EMF** 31.08.91
Lies In Your Eyes - **Sweet** 24.01.76
Life At A Top People's Health Farm - **Style Council** 28.05.88
Life In A Northern Town - **Dream Academy** 6.04.85
Life In One Day - **Howard Jones** 29.06.85
Life in Tokyo - **Japan** 16.10.82
Life Is A Long Song/Up the Pool - **Jethro Tull** 18.09.71
Life Is A Minestrone - **10CC** 12.04.75
Life Is A Rock (But The Radio Rolled Me) - **Reunion** 28.09.74
Life Is Too Short Girl - **Sheer Elegance** 10.04.76
Life On Mars - **David Bowie** 30.06.73
Life On Your Own - **Human League** 30.06.84
Lifeline - **Spandau Ballet** 9.10.82
Life's Been Good - **Joe Walsh** 15.07.78
Life's Just A Ballgame - **Womack & Womack** 19.11.88
Life's What You Make It - **Talk Talk** 25.01.86
Life's What You Make It - **Talk Talk** 1.09.90
Lifetime Love - **Joyce Sims** 20.06.87
Lift/Open Your Mind - **808 State** 24.08.91
Light My Fire - **Jose Feliciano** 25.09.68
Light My Fire/137 Disco Heaven - **Amii Stewart** 23.06.79
Light My Fire - **Doors** 1.06.91
(Light of Experience) Doina de Jale - **Gheorghe Zamfir** 28.08.76
Light of Love - **T.Rex** 13.07.74
Light Up The Fire - **Parchment** 23.09.72
Lightning - **Zoe** 2.11.91
Lightning Strikes - **Lou Christie** 24.02.66
The Lightning Tree - **Settlers** 23.10.71
Lights of Cincinatti - **Scott Walker** 18.06.69
Like A Baby - **Len Barry** 20.01.66
Like A Butterfly - **Mac And Katie Kissoon** 6.09.75
Like A Child - **Julie Rogers** 17.12.64
Like A Prayer - **Madonna** 18.03.89
Like A Rolling Stone - **Bob Dylan** 26.08.65
Like A Virgin - **Madonna** 24.11.84
Like Clockwork - **Boomtown Rats** 24.06.78
Like Dreamers Do - **Applejacks** 18.06.64
Like Dreamers Do - **Mica Paris featuring Courtney Pine** 30.07.88
Like I Do - **Maureen Evans** 6.12.62
Like I've Never Been Gone - **Billy Fury** 14.02.63
Like Sister and Brother - **Drifters** 11.08.73
Like Strangers - **Everly Brothers** 15.12.60
Like to Get to Know You Well - **Howard Jones** 11.08.84
Like We Used to Be - **Georgie Fame** 12.08.65
A Li'l Ain't Enough - **David Lee Roth** 12.01.91
Lil' Devil - **Cult** 2.05.87
Lilac Wine - **Elkie Brooks** 4.03.78
Lily the Pink - **Scaffold** 13.11.68
Lily Was There - **David A Stewart featuring Candy Dulfer** 3.03.90
Limbo Rock - **Chubby Checker** 15.11.62
Lines - **Planets** 1.09.79
The Lion Sleeps Tonight - **Tokens** 21.12.61
The Lion Sleeps Tonight - **Dave Newman** 13.05.72
The Lion Sleeps Tonight - **Tight Fit** 6.02.82
The Lion's Mouth - **Kajagoogoo** 17.03.84
Lip Up Fatty - **Bad Manners** 5.07.80
Lips Like Sugar - **Echo & the Bunnymen** 8.08.87
Lipsmackin' Rock & Rollin' - **Peter Blake** 15.10.77
Lipstick on Your Collar - **Connie Francis** 3.07.59
Lipstick Powder and Paint - **Shakin' Stevens** 12.10.85
The Liquidator - **Harry J. All Stars** 25.10.69
Listen - **Stiff Little Fingers** 22.1.82.
Listen to Me - **Buddy Holly** 14.03.58
Listen to Me - **Hollies** 2.10.68
Listen to the Music - **Doobie Brothers** 16.03.74
Listen To The Radio: Atmospherics - **Tom Robinson and Crew** 26.11.83
Listen to What The Man Said - **Wings** 31.05.75
Listen To Your Father - **Feargal Sharkey** 20.10.84
Listen To Your Heart - **Sonia** 16.12.89
Listen to Your Heart/Dangerous - **Roxette** 11.08.90
Little Arrows - **Leapy Lee** 28.08.68
Little Band of Gold - **James Gilreath** 9.05.63
Little Bernadette - **Harry Belafonte** 22.08.58
A Little Bit Me A Little Bit You - **Monkees** 6.04.67
A Little Bit More - **Dr. Hook** 3.07.76
Little Bit of Love - **Free** 3.06.72
A Little Bit of Soap - **Showaddywaddy** 1.07.78
Little Bitty Tear - **Burl Ives** 1.02.62
Little Bitty Tear - **Miki & Griff** 8.02.62
Little Black Book - **Jimmy Dean** 15.11.62
A Little Boogie Woogie In The Back of My Car - **Gary Glitter** 23.07.77
A Little Boogie Woogie (In The Back of My Mind) - **Shakin' Stevens** 11.07.87

Little Boy Sad - **Johnny Brunette** 13.04.61
Little Brother - **Blue Pearl** 3.11.90
Little By Little - **Dusty Springfield** 3.02.66
Little Children - **Billy J Kramer & the Dakotas** 27.02.64
Little Christine - **Dick Jordan** 23.06.60
Little Darlin' - **Diamonds** 31.05.57
Little Darling - **Rubettes** 29.11.75
Little Devil - **Neil Sedaka** 18.05.61
Little Does She Know - **Kursaal Flyers** 27.11.76
Little Donkey - **Gracie Fields** 6.11.59
Little Donkey - **Beverley Sisters** 20.11.59
Little Donkey - **Nina & Frederick** 17.11.60
Little Drops of Silver - **Gerry Monroe** 21.08.71
Little Drummer Boy - **Harry Simeone Chorale** 13.02.59
Little Drummer Boy - **Beverley Sisters** 13.02.59
Little Drummer Boy - **Michael Flanders** 27.02.59
Little Drummer Boy - **Royal Scots Dragoon Guards Band** 2.12.72
Little Girl - **Marty Wilde** 22.12.60
Little Girl - **Troggs** 13.03.68
Little Girl - **The Banned** 24.12.77
Little Green Apples - **Roger Miller** 3.04.68
Little Green Apples - **Roger Miller** 7.05.69
A Little in Love - **Cliff Richard** 24.01.81
Little Jeannie - **Elton John** 7.06.80
Little Lies - **Fleetwood Mac** 10.10.87
A Little Love A Little Kiss - **Karl Denver** 7.06.62
A Little Love and Understanding - **Gilbert Becaud** 5.04.75
A Little Lovin' - **Neil Sedaka** 16.02.74
A Little Loving - **Fourmost** 23.04.64
Little Man - **Sonny & Cher** 8.09.66
Little Miss Lonely - **Helen Shapiro** 19.07.62
A Little More Love - **Olivia Newton-John** 23.12.78
A Little Peace - **Nicole** 8.05.82
Little Piece of Leather - **Donnie Elbert** 29.04.72
Little Red Monkey - **Frank Chacksfield Orchestra** 3.04.53
Little Red Rooster - **Rolling Stones** 19.11.64
A Little Respect - **Erasure** 1.10.88
Little Serenade - **Eddie Calvert** 20.06.58
The Little Shoemaker - **Petula Clark** 11.06.54
Little Sister/His Latest Flame - **Elvis Presley** 2.11.61
Little Star - **Elegants** 26.09.58
Little Things Mean A Lot - **Kitty Allen** 2.07.54
Little Things Mean A Lot - **Alma Cogan** 27.08.54
Little Things - **Dave Berry** 25.03.65
A Little Time - **Beautiful South** 6.10.90
Little Town - **Cliff Richard** 11.12.82
Little Town Flirt - **Del Shannon** 24.01.63
Little Train/Gotta Have Rain - **Max Bygraves** 22.08.58
Little White Bull - **Tommy Steele** 4.12.59
Little White Berry - **Roy Castle** 22.12.60
Little Willy - **Sweet** 17.06.72
A Little You - **Freddie & the Dreamers** 22.04.65
Live and Let Die - **Wings** 9.06.73
Live and Let Die - **Guns N' Roses** 21.12.91
The Live EP - **Gary Numan** 25.05.85
Live For Loving You - **Gloria Estefan** 5.10.91
Live In The Sky - **Dave Clark Five** 4.12.68
Live In The Sky - **Dave Clark Five** 18.12.68
Live In Trouble - **Barron Knights** 5.11.77
Live Is Life - **Opus** 29.06.85
Live It Up - **Mental As Anything** 14.02.87
Live To Tell - **Madonna** 26.04.86
Live Together - **Lisa Stansfield** 10.02.90
Live Your Life Be Free - **Belinda Carlisle** 28.09.91
Lively - **Lonnie Donegan** 24.11.60
Liverpool Lou - **Scaffold** 1.06.74
Livin' In The Light - **Caron Wheeler** 8.09.90
Livin' Lovin' Doll - **Cliff Richard & the Drifters** 30.01.59
Livin' On A Prayer - **Bon Jovi** 25.10.86
Livin' Thing - **Electric Light Orchestra** 20.11.76
Living After Midnight - **Judas Priest** 29.03.80
Living By Numbers - **New Musik** 26.01.80
The Living Daylights - **A-Ha** 4.07.87
Living Doll - **Cliff Richard & the Drifters** 10.07.59
Living Doll - **Cliff Richard & the Young Ones** 22.03.86
Living for the City - **Stevie Wonder** 19.01.74
Living In A Box - **Living In A Box** 11.04.87
Living In America - **James Brown** 25.01.86
Living In Harmony - **Cliff Richard** 2.09.72
Living In Sin - **Bon Jovi** 23.12.89
Living In The Past - **Jethro Tull** 21.05.69
Living In The Plastic Age - **Buggles** 2.02.80
Living Next Door To Alice - **Smokie** 4.12.76
Living On An Island - **Status Quo** 1.12.79
Living On The Front Line - **Eddy Grant** 16.06.79
Living on the Ceiling - **Blancmange** 6.11.82
Living On Video - **Trans-X** 13.07.85
The Living Years - **Mike & the Mechanics** 14.01.89
Loaded - **Primal Scream** 10.03.90
Loadsamoney (Doin' Up the House) - **Harry Enfield** 7.05.88
Lock Up Your Daughters - **Slade** 3.10.81
The Loco-Motion - **Little Eva** 13.09.62
The Loco-Motion - **Kylie Minogue** 6.08.88
Loco In Acapulco - **Four Tops** 10.12.88
The Locomotion - **Little Eva** 5.08.72
Locomotion - **Orchestral Manoeuvres In The Dark** 14.04.84
The Lodgers - **Style Council** 28.09.85
The Logical Song - **Supertramp** 7.04.79
Lola - **Kinks** 4.07.70
Lollipop - **Chordettes** 18.04.58
Lollipop - **Mudlarks** 2.05.58
London Boys - **T.Rex** 13.03.76
London Calling - **Clash** 22.12.79
London Nights - **London Boys** 1.07.89
London Town - **Bucks Fizz** 8.10.83
The Lone Ranger - **Quantum Jump** 9.06.79
Lone Rider - **John Leyton** 22.03.62
The Loneliest Man In The World - **Tourists** 29.09.79
Loneliness - **Des O'Connor** 29.11.69
Lonely - **Mr. Acker Bilk** 27.09.62
Lonely Ballerina - **Mantovani Orchestra** 11.02.55
Lonely Boy - **Paul Anka** 10.07.59
Lonely Boy - **Andrew Gold** 9.04.77
Lonely Boy Lonely Guitar - **Duane Eddy** 13.06.63
The Lonely Bull - **Tijuana Brass** 10.01.63
Lonely City - **John Leyton** 10.05.62
Lonely Days - **Bee Gees** 12.12.70
Lonely Days Lonely Nights - **Don Downing** 17.11.73
The Lonely Man Theme - **Cliff Adams Orchestra** 28.04.60
Lonely Pup (In A Christmas Shop) - **Adam Faith** 17.11.60
Lonely This Christmas - **Mud** 30.11.74
Lonely Together - **Barry Manilow** 15.11.80
Lonesome - **Chris Barber** 9.10.59
Lonesome Traveller - **Lonnie Donegan** 26.09.58
Long After Tonight Is All Over - **Jimmy Radcliffe** 4.02.65
The Long And Winding Road - **Ray Morgan** 1.08.70
Long Cool Woman In A Black Dress - **Hollies** 9.09.72
Long Haired Lover From Liverpool - **Little Jimmy Osmond** 2.12.72
Long Hot Summer - **Style Council** 13.08.83
Long Legged Woman Dressed in Black - **Mungo Jerry** 13.04.74
Long Live Love - **Sandie Shaw** 13.05.65
Long Live Love - **Olivia Newton-John** 16.03.74
Long Live Rock & Roll - **Rainbow** 8.04.78
Long Lost Lover - **Three Degrees** 12.07.75
Long Shot Kick De Bucket - **Pioneers** 25.10.69
Long Tall Glasses - **Leo Sayer** 21.09.74
Long Tall Sally - **Pat Boone** 27.07.56
Long Tall Sally - **Little Richard** 8.02.57
Long Time - **Arrow** 27.07.85
Long Train Running - **Bananarama** 20.04.91
The Longest Time - **Billy Joel** 5.05.84
Lonnie Donegan Showcase (LP) - **Lonnie Donegan** 21.12.56
Lonnie's Skiffle Party - **Lonnie Donegan** 14.11.58
Loo-Be-Loo - **Chucks** 24.01.63
The Look - **Roxette** 29.04.89
Look Around - **Vince Hill** 9.10.71
Look At That Girl - **Guy Mitchell** 28.08.53
Look Away - **Big Country** 12.04.86
Look for A Star - **Gary Mills** 14.07.60
Look Mama - **Howard Jones** 20.04.85
Look Me In The Heart - **Tina Turner** 18.08.90
The Look Of Love - **ABC** 15.05.82
The Look of Love - **Madonna** 12.12.87
Look of Love - **Gladys Knight & the Pips** 10.03.73
Look Through Any Window - **Hollies** 2.09.65
Look Wot You Dun - **Slade** 5.02.72
Lookin' Through the Windows - **Jackson Five** 11.11.72
Looking After Number One - **Boomtown Rats** 3.09.77

Looking At Midnight - **Imagination** 11.06.83
Looking For A New Love - **Jody Watley** 30.05.87
Looking For A Love - **Joyce Sims** 24.06.89
Looking for Clues - **Robert Palmer** 6.12.80
Looking For Linda - **Hue & Cry** 4.02.89
Looking High High High - **Bryan Johnson** 10.03.60
Looking Through The Eyes of Love - **Gene Pitney** 10.06.65
Looking Thru' The Eyes of Love - **Partridge Family** 3.02.73
Looks Looks Looks - **Sparks** 11.10.75
Loop-De-Loop - **Frankie Vaughan** 31.01.63
Loop Di Love - **Shag** 21.10.72
Loose Fit - **Happy Mondays** 16.03.91
Lorelei - **Lonnie Donegan** 25.08.60
Lorraine - **Bad Manners** 13.12.80
Lose Control - **James** 8.12.90
Losing My Mind - **Liza Minnelli** 12.08.89
Losing My Religion - **REM** 9.03.91
Losing You - **Brenda Lee** 4.04.63
Losing You - **Dusty Springfield** 22.10.64
Lost in France - **Bonnie Tyler** 6.11.76
Lost In Music - **Sister Sledge** 18.08.79
Lost In Music - **Sister Sledge** 8.09.84
Lost In You - **Rod Stewart** 28.05.88
Lost In Your Eyes - **Debbie Gibson** 4.02.89
Lost Weekend - **Lloyd Cole & the Commotions** 9.11.85
Lost Without Your Love - **Bread** 15.01.77
Louie Louie - **Kingsmen** 30.01.64
Louise - **Human League** 17.11.84
Love Action (I Believe in Love) - **Human League** 8.08.81
Love All Day - **Nick Heyward** 9.06.84
Love and Affection - **Joan Armatrading** 16.10.76
Love and Anger - **Kate Bush** 10.03.90
Love and Kisses - **Dannii Minogue** 30.03.91
Love and Marriage - **Frank Sinatra** 13.01.56
Love and Pride - **King** 19.01.85
Love and Regret - **Deacon Blue** 23.09.89
Love and Understanding - **Cher** 13.07.91
Love At First Sight - **Sounds Nice** 20.09.69
Love Attack - **Shakin' Stevens** 13.05.89
Love Ballad - **George Benson** 21.04.79
Love Bites - **Def Leppard** 16.07.88
Love Blonde - **Kim Wilde** 6.08.83
Love Bug - **Tina Charles** 29.10.77
Love Can't Turn Around - **Farley 'Jackmaster' Funk** 23.08.86
Love Changes (Everything) - **Climie Fisher** 19.03.88
Love Changes Everything - **Michael Ball** 4.02.89
Love Child - **Diana Ross & the Supremes** 27.11.68
Love Come Down - **Evelyn King** 4.09.82
Love Comes Quickly - **Pet Shop Boys** 15.03.86
Love Don't Live Here Anymore - **Rose Royce** 23.09.78
Love Don't Live Here Anymore - **Jimmy Nail** 4.05.85
Love Don't Live Here Anymore - **Double Trouble** 30.06.90
Love Game - **Mudlarks** 27.02.59
Love Games - **Drifters** 15.02.75
Love Games - **Level 42** 2.05.81
Love Games - **Belle & the Devotions** 28.04.84
Love Grows - **Edison Lighthouse** 24.01.70
Love Hangover - **Diana Ross** 1.05.76
Love Her - **Walker Brothers** 29.04.65
Love Hit Me - **Maxine Nightingale** 19.03.77
Love House - **Samantha Fox** 26.11.88
Love How You Feel - **Sharon Redd** 29.10.83
Love Hurts - **Jim Capaldi** 1.11.75
Love Hurts - **Nazareth** 1.10.77
The Love I Lost - **Harold Melvin & the Bluenotes** 19.01.74
Love In An Elevator - **Aerosmith** 9.09.89
Love In C Minor - **Cerrone** 12.03.77
Love In Itself.2 - **Depeche Mode** 1.10.83
Love In the First Degree - **Bananarama** 17.10.87
Love In The Natural Way - **Kim Wilde** 18.03.89
Love In The Sun - **Glitter Band** 16.08.75
The Love In Your Eyes - **Vicky Leandros** 3.02.73
Love Is A Battlefield - **Pat Benatar** 30.03.85
Love Is A Golden Ring - **Frankie Laine** 26.04.57
Love Is A Many Splendored Thing - **Four Aces** 18.11.55
Love Is A Stranger - **Eurythmics** 16.04.83
Love Is A Wonderful Colour - **Icicle Works** 14.01.84
Love Is A Wonderful Thing - **Michael Bolton** 27.04.91
Love Is All - **Malcolm Roberts** 22.11.69
Love Is All Around - **Troggs** 25.10.67
Love Is All Is All Right - **UB40** 22.05.82
Love Is Blue - **Paul Mauriat** 21.02.68
Love Is Blue - **Jeff Beck** 6.03.68
Love is Contagious - **Taja Seville** 5.03.88
Love is Forever - **Billy Ocean** 24.01.87
Love Is Here And Now You're Gone - **Supremes** 9.03.67
Love Is In Control (Finger on the Trigger) - **Donna Summer** 17.07.82
Love Is In The Air - **John Paul Young** 6.05.78
Love Is Just The Great Pretender - **Animal Nightlife** 13.07.85
Love Is Life - **Hot Chocolate** 22.08.70
Love Is Like A Violin - **Ken Dodd** 7.07.60
Love Is Like Oxygen - **Sweet** 4.02.78
Love Is Love - **Barry Ryan** 19.02.69
Love Is Strange - **Everly Brothers** 28.10.65
Love Is The Drug - **Roxy Music** 11.10.75
Love Is The Drug - **Grace Jones** 8.03.86
Love Is The Slug - **We've Got a Fuzzbox & We're Gonna Use It** 15.11.86
Love Is The Tender Grap - **Frank Sinatra** 20.01.56
Love Kills - **Freddie Mercury** 22.09.84
Love Letters - **Ketty Lester** 19.04.62
Love Letters - **Elvis Presley** 7.07.66
Love Letters - **Alison Moyet** 5.12.87
Love Letters In The Sand - **Pat Boone** 5.07.57
Love Letters In the Sand - **Vince Hill** 4.10.67
Love Lies Lost - **Helen Terry** 26.05.84
Love Like A Man - **Ten Years After** 20.06.70
Love Like A River - **Climie Fisher** 7.01.89
Love Like Blood - **Killing Joke** 9.02.85
Love Like You & Me - **Gary Glitter** 3.05.75
A Love Like Yours - **Ike & Tina Turner** 27.10.66
Love Love Love - **Bobby Hebb** 2.09.72
Love Loves to Love Love - **Lulu** 15.11.67
Love Machine - **Miracles** 17.01.76
Love Makes The World Go Round - **Perry Como** 7.11.58
Love Makes The World Go Round - **Jets** 20.02.82
Love Me - **Diana Ross** 12.10.74
Love Me - **Yvonne Elliman** 13.11.76
Love Me As Though There Were No Tomorrow - **Nat 'King' Cole** 14.09.56
Love Me Baby - **Susan Cadogan** 26.07.75
Love Me Do - **Beatles** 1.11.62
Love Me Do - **Beatles** 16.10.82
Love Me For A Reason - **Osmonds** 24.08.74
Love Me Forever - **Marion Ryan** 24.01.58
Love Me Forever - **Eydie Gorme** 24.01.58
Love Me Forever - **Four Esquires** 31.01.58
Love Me Like I Love You - **Bay City Rollers** 10.04.76
Love Me Like A Lover - **Tina Charles** 8.05.76
Love Me Love My Dog - **Peter Shelley** 22.03.75
Love Me Or Leave Me - **Doris Day** 9.09.55
Love Me Or Leave Me - **Sammy Davis Jr.** 9.09.55
Love Me Tender - **Elvis Presley** 7.12.56
Love Me Tender - **Richard Chamberlain** 8.11.62
Love Me Tender - **Roland Rat Superstar** 12.05.84
Love Me Tonight - **Tom Jones** 14.05.69
Love Me Tonight - **Trevor Walters** 24.10.81
Love Me Warm & Tender - **Paul Anka** 22.03.62
Love Me With All of Your Heart - **Karl Denver** 2.07.64
Love Missile F1-11 - **Sigue Sigue Sputnik** 1.03.86
Love Needs No Disguise - **Gary Numan & Dramatis** 5.12.81
Love of My Life - **Dooleys** 19.11.77
Love of The Common People - **Nicky Thomas** 13.06.70
Love Of The Common People - **Paul Young** 19.11.83
Love of the Loved - **Cilla Black** 24.10.63
Love On A Mountain Top - **Robert Knight** 1.12.73
Love On A Mountain Top - **Sinitta** 7.10.89
Love on Delivery - **Billy Ocean** 17.07.76
Love On The Rocks - **Neil Diamond** 29.11.80
Love On Your Side - **Thompson Twins** 5.02.83
Love Patrol - **Dooleys** 15.03.80
Love Plus One - **Haircut 100** 30.1.82.
Love ... Thy Will Be Done - **Martika** 17.08.91
Love Really Hurts Without You - **Billy Ocean** 21.02.76
Love Rears Its Ugly Head - **Living Color** 16.02.91
Love Removal Machine - **Cult** 28.02.87
Love Resurrection - **Alison Moyet** 30.06.84
Love Shack - **B52s** 3.03.90
Love Song - **The Damned** 12.05.79
Love Songs Are Back Again (Medley) - **Band of Gold** 4.08.84

Love Story - **Jethro Tull** 8.01.69
A Love Supreme - **Will Downing** 16.04.88
Love Take Over - **Five Star** 21.09.85
Love Takes Time - **Mariah Carey** 1.12.90
Love the One You're With - **Stephen Stills** 13.03.71
Love Theme From 'The Thorn Birds' - **Juan Martin** 4.02.84
Love Thing - **Pasadenas** 12.05.90
Love To Hate You - **Erasure** 21.09.91
Love to Love You Baby - **Donna Summer** 17.01.76
Love Touch - **Rod Stewart** 24.05.86
Love Town - **Booker Newberry III** 28.05.83
Love Train - **O'Jays** 10.03.73
Love Train - **Holly Johnson** 21.01.89
Love Truth & Honesty - **Bananarama** 24.09.88
Love Walked In - **Thunder** 23.02.91
Love Wars - **Womack & Womack** 12.05.84
Love Will Find A Way - **David Grant** 8.10.83
Love Will Keep Us Together - **The Captain And Tennille** 2.08.75
Love Will Never Do (Without You) - **Janet Jackson** 27.10.90
Love Will Save The Day - **Whitney Houston** 28.05.88
Love Will Tear Us Apart - **Joy Division** 5.07.80
Love Will Tear Us Apart - **Joy Division** 12.11.83
Love Won't Let Me Wait - **Major Harris** 23.08.75
A Love Worth Waiting For - **Shakin' Stevens** 24.03.84
Love X Love - **George Benson** 11.10.80
Love You Inside Out - **Bee Gees** 21.04.79
Love You More - **Buzzcocks** 22.07.78
The Love You Save - **Jackson 5** 1.08.70
Lovely Day - **Bill Withers** 14.01.78
Lovely Day - **Bill Withers** 10.09.88
Lovely One - **Jacksons** 1.11.80
Lover Come Back To Me - **Dead or Alive** 20.04.85
The Lover In Me - **Sheena Easton** 28.01.89
Lover Please - **Vernons Girls** 17.05.62
A Lover Spurned - **Marc Almond** 3.03.90
Loverboy - **Billy Ocean** 19.01.85
The Lovers - **Alexander O'Neal** 28.05.88
A Lover's Concerto - **Toys** 4.11.65
A Lover's Holiday/Glow of Love - **Change** 5.07.80
Lovers of The World Unite - **David & Jonathan** 21.07.66
Love's A Loaded Gun - **Alice Cooper** 5.10.91
Love's About to Change My Heart - **Donna Summer** 26.08.89
Love's Been Good To Me - **Frank Sinatra** 11.10.69
Love's Comin' At Ya - **Melba Moore** 16.10.82
Love's Got Me - **Loose Ends** 1.12.90
Love's Gotta Hold On Me - **Dollar** 1.09.79
Love's Great Adventure - **Ultravox** 20.10.84
Love's Just A Broken Heart - **Cilla Black** 20.01.66
Love's Made A Fool of You - **Crickets** 24.04.59
Love's Made A Fool of You - **Buddy Holly** 17.09.64
Loves Me Like A Rock - **Paul Simon** 13.10.73
Love's Such A Wonderful Thing - **Real Thing** 6.08.77
Love's Sweet Exile - **Manic Street Preachers** 9.11.91
Love's Theme - **Love Unlimited Orchestra** 2.02.74
Love's Unkind - **Donna Summer** 3.12.77
Love's Unkind - **Sophie Lawrence** 20.08.91
Lovesick Blues - **Frank Ifield** 25.10.62
Lovesong - **Cure** 9.09.89
Lovin' Things - **Marmalade** 5.06.68
Lovin' Up A Storm - **Jerry Lee Lewis** 1.05.59
Loving and Free - **Kiki Dee** 18.09.76
Loving Just For Fun - **Kelly Marie** 25.10.80
Loving On The Losing Side - **Tommy Hunt** 21.08.76
Loving the Alien - **David Bowie** 8.06.85
Loving You - **Elvis Presley** 1.11.57
Loving You - **Minnie Riperton** 19.04.75
Loving You - **Feargal Sharkey** 13.07.85
Loving You - **Massivo featuring Tracy** 23.06.90
Loving You Ain't Easy - **Pagliaro** 4.03.72
Loving You Has Made Me Bananas - **Guy Marks** 27.05.78
Loving You Is Sweeter Than Ever - **Four Tops** 11.08.66
Loving You Is Swetter Than Ever - **Nick Kamen** 7.03.87
Low Rider - **War** 24.01.76
Lowdown - **Boz Scaggs** 6.11.76
L.A. Connection - **Rainbow** 7.10.78
L.A. Run - **Carvells** 3.12.77
L.O.V.E. - **Al Green** 22.03.75
Lucille - **Little Richard** 28.06.57
Lucille - **Kenny Rogers** 7.05.77
Lucille/So Sad - **Everly Brothers** 22.09.60
Lucky Devil - **Frank Ifield** 19.02.60
Lucky Five - **Russ Conway** 26.05.60
Lucky Lips - **Cliff Richard** 9.05.63
Lucky Number - **Lene Lovich** 24.02.79
Lucky Star - **Madonna** 24.03.84
Lucky Stars - **Dean Friedman** 23.09.78
Lucretia My Reflection - **Sisters of Mercy** 18.06.88
Lucy In The Sky With Diamonds - **Elton John** 23.11.74
Ludi - **Dream Warriors** 9.03.91
Luka - **Suzanne Vega** 30.05.87
Lullaby - **Cure** 22.04.89
The Lunatics (Have Taken Over the Asylum) - **Fun Boy Three** 14.11.81
Luton Airport - **Cats UK** 20.10.79
Lydia - **Dean Friedman** 25.11.78
Lyin' Eyes - **Eagles** 8.11.75
Ma-Ma-Belle - **Electric Light Orchestra** 16.03.74
Ma Baker - **Boney M** 25.06.77
Ma He's Making Eyes at Me - **Johnny Otis Show featuring Marie Adams** 22.11.57
Ma He's Making Eyes at Me - **Lena Zavaroni** 9.02.74
Ma Says Pa Says - **Johnnie Ray and Doris Day** 3.04.53
Macarthur Park - **Richard Harris** 26.06.68
MacArthur Park - **Richard Harris** 29.07.72
Macarthur Park - **Donna Summer** 14.10.78
Macdonald's Cave - **Piltdown Men** 22.09.60
Machine Gun - **Commodores** 7.09.74
Machinery - **Sheena Easton** 7.08.82
Mack the Knife - **Bobby Darin** 25.09.59
Mack the Knife - **Louis Armstrong** 6.11.59
Mack the Knife - **Ella Fitzgerald** 21.04.60
Mad About You - **Bruce Ruffin** 8.07.72
Mad Eyed Screamer - **Creatures** 3.10.81
Mad Passionate Love - **Bernard Bresslaw** 5.09.58
Mad World - **Tears for Fears** 16.10.82
Madam Butterfly (Un Bel Di Vedremo) - **Malcolm McLaren** 1.09.84
Madchester Rave On (EP) - **Happy Mondays** 25.11.89
Madchester Rave On (EP) - **Happy Mondays** 6.01.90
Made of Stone - **Stone Roses** 17.03.90
Made to Love (Girls Girls Girls) - **Eddie Hodges** 23.08.62
The Madison - **Ray Ellington** 27.12.62
Madly in Love - **Bros** 10.03.90
Maggie - **Foster and Allen** 12.03.83
Maggie May - **Rod Stewart** 11.12.76
Maggie's Farm - **Bob Dylan** 17.06.65
Magic - **Pilot** 2.11.74
Magic - **Olivia Newton-John** 30.08.80
Magic Bus - **Who** 30.10.68
Magic Fly - **Space** 20.08.77
Magic Moments - **Perry Como** 7.02.58
Magic Moments - **Ronnie Hilton** 21.02.58
The Magic Number/Buddy - **De La Soul** 23.12.89
Magic Smile - **Rosie Vela** 31.01.87
Magic Touch - **Loose Ends** 11.05.85
Magical Mystery Tour (EP) - **Beatles** 13.12.67
The Magnificent Seven - **Clash** 2.05.81
Mah Na Mah Na - **Piero Umiliani** 30.04.77
Maid Of Orleans (The Waltz Joan Of Arc) - **Orchestral Manoeuvres In The Dark** .... 22.1.82.
The Main Attraction - **Pat Boone** 22.11.62
Main Theme From 'The Thorn Birds' - **Henry Mancini & His Orchestra** 18.02.84
Main Title Theme From 'The Man With The Golden Arm' - **Billy May Orchestra** 27.04.56
Main Title Theme From 'The Man With the Golden Arm' - **Jet Hrris** 23.08.62
Mais Oui - **King Brothers** 28.07.60
Majorca - **Petula Clark** 18.02.55
Make A Daft Noise For Christmas - **Goodies** 20.12.75
Make Her Mine - **Nat 'King' Cole** 8.10.54
Make It A Party - **Winifred Atwell** 26.10.56
Make It Easy On Yourself - **Walker Brothers** 19.08.65
Make It Soon - **Tony Brent** 2.01.53
Make It Tonight - **Wet Wet Wet** 14.09.91
Make It With You - **Bread** 8.08.70
Make Love to Me - **Jo Stafford** 7.05.54
Make Me An Island - **Joe Dolan** 25.06.69
Make Me Laugh - **Anthrax** 10.09.88
Make Me Smile (Come Up and See Me) - **Steve Harley & Cockney Rebel** 8.02.75
Make That Move - **Shalamar** 11.04.81
Make The World Go Away - **Eddy Arnold** 17.02.66
Make The World Go Away - **Donny and Marie Osmond** 21.06.75

Makin' Happy - **Crystal Waters** 7.09.91
Makin' Love - **Floyd Robinson** 16.10.59
Making Plans For Nigel - **XTC** 13.10.79
Making Up Again - **Goldie** 3.06.78
Making Your Mind Up - **Bucks Fizz** 28.03.81
Male Stripper - **Man 2 Man meets Man Parrish** 7.02.87
Malt and Barley Blues - **McGuinness Flint** 8.05.71
Mama - **David Whitfield** 27.05.55
Mama - **Connie Francis** 19.05.60
Mama - **Dave Berry** 30.06.66
Mama - **Genesis** 3.09.83
Mama - **Kim Appleby** 6.07.91
Mama Mia - **Abba** 20.12.75
Mama Never Told Me - **Sister Sledge** 28.06.75
Mama Told Me Not To Come - **Three Dog Night** 15.08.70
Mama Used To Say - **Junior** 8.05.82
Mama Weer All Crazee Now - **Slade** 2.09.72
Mama's Boy - **Suzi Quatro** 2.02.80
Mama's Pearl - **Jackson 5** 10.04.71
Mambo Italiano - **Dean Martin** 4.02.55
Mambo Rock - **Billy Halley & his Comets** 15.04.55
Mamma Gave Birth to the Soul Children - **Queen Latifah & De La Soul** 24.03.90
Mammy Blue - **Roger Whittaker** 9.10.71
Mammy Blue - **Los Pop Tops** 16.10.71
Man - **Rosemary Clooney** 5.02.54
Man From Laramie - **Jimmy Young** 16.09.55
Man From Laramie - **Al Martino** 23.09.55
Man From Nazareth - **John Paul Jones** 16.01.71
The Man in Black - **Cozy Powell** 1.06.74
Man In The Mirror - **Michael Jackson** 20.02.88
Man of Mystery/The Stranger - **Shadows** 10.11.60
Man of The World - **Fleetwood Mac** 16.04.69
Man on Fire/Wandering Eyes - **Frankie Vaughan** 4.10.57
The Man That Got Away - **Judy Garland** 10.06.55
Man to Man - **Hot Chocolate** 3.07.76
Man Who Plays The Mandolino - **Dean Martin** 22.03.57
The Man Who Sold the World - **Lulu** 26.01.74
Man With The Child In His Eyes - **Kate Bush** 17.06.78
A Man Without Love - **Kenneth McKellar** 17.03.66
A Man Without Love - **Engelbert Humperdinck** 24.04.68
Manchild - **Neneh Cherry** 20.05.89
Mandinka - **Sinead O'Connor** 30.01.88
Mandolins in The Moonlight - **Perry Como** 21.11.58
Mandy - **Eddie Calvert** 7.02.58
Mandy - **Barry Manilow** 1.03.75
Maneater - **Daryl Hall & John Oates** 30.10.82
Mangos - **Rosemary Clooney** 29.03.57
Manhattan Skyline - **A-Ha** 28.02.87
Manhattan Spiritual - **Reg Owen** 27.02.59
Manic Monday - **Bangles** 22.02.86
Mantra For A State of Mind - **S Express** 16.09.89
Many Rivers To Cross - **UB40** 10.12.83
Many Tears Ago - **Connie Francis** 12.01.61
March of the Siamese Children - **Kenny Ball & his Jazzmen** 15.02.62
March of the Mods - **Joe Loss Orchestra** 12.11.64
Marcheta - **Karl Denver** 22.06.61
Margie - **Fats Domino** 22.05.59
Margot - **Billy Fury** 26.06.59
Marguerita Time - **Status Quo** 10.12.83
Maria - **P.J. Proby** 25.11.65
Maria Elena - **Los Indios Tabajaras** 7.11.63
Maria Elena - **Gene Pitney** 12.03.69
Mariana - **Gibson Brothers** 19.07.80
Marianne - **Hilltoppers** 5.04.57
Marianne - **Cliff Richard** 2.10.68
Marie - **Bachelors** 20.05.65
Marie Marie - **Shakin' Stevens** 23.08.80
Marlene on The Wall - **Suzanne Vega** 12.04.86
Maroc 7 - **Shadows** 20.04.67
Marrakesh Express - **Crosby, Stills & Nash** 30.08.69
Married Men - **Bonnie Tyler** 30.06.79
Marquee Moon - **Television** 16.04.77
Marquee Moon - **Television** 30.04.77
Marry Me - **Mike Preston** 9.03.61
Marta - **Bachelors** 5.07.67
Martha's Harbour - **All About Eve** 30.07.88
Martika's Kitchen - **Martika** 30.11.91
Mary Anne - **Shadows** 11.02.65
Mary Had A Little Lamb - **Wings** 27.05.72
Mary Had A Little Boy - **Snap!** 8.12.90
Mary Jane - **Del Shannon** 26.03.64
Mary of The Fourth Form - **Boomtown Rats** 26.11.77
Mary's Boy Child - **Harry Belafonte** 1.11.57
Mary's Boy Child - **Harry Belafonte** 28.11.58
Mary's Boy Child - **Harry Belafonte** 11.12.59
Mary's Boy Child - **Nina & Frederick** 18.12.59
Mary's Boy Child - **Boney M** 2.12.78
Mary's Prayer - **Danny Wilson** 16.04.88
Masquerade - **Skids** 26.05.79
Massachusetts - **Bee Gees** 20.09.67
Master and Servant - **Depeche Mode** 1.09.84
Masterblaster (Jammin') - **Stevie Wonder** 13.09.80
The Masterplan - **Diana Brown & Barrie K Sharpe** 16.06.90
Matchstalk Men & Matchstalk Cats & Dogs - **Brian & Michael** 4.03.78
Mated - **David Grant & Jaki Graham** 23.11.85
Material Girl - **Madonna** 2.03.85
A Matter of Fact - **Innocence** 15.12.90
Matthew and Son - **Cat Stevens** 12.01.67
May Each Day - **Andy Williams** 3.03.66
May I Have The Next Dream With You - **Malcolm Roberts** 6.11.68
May The Sun Shine - **Nazareth** 10.02.79
May You Always - **McGuire Sisters** 1.05.59
May You Always - **Joan Regan** 1.05.59
Maybe - **Thom Pace** 16.06.79
Maybe Baby - **Crickets** 14.03.58
Maybe I Know - **Lesley Gore** 24.09.64
Maybe I Know - **Seashells** 23.09.72
Maybe I'm Amazed - **Wings** 26.02.77
Maybe Tomorrow - **Billy Fury** 27.02.59
Maybe Tomorrow - **Chords** 16.02.80
Maybe Tomorrow - **UB40** 17.10.87
Maybe (We Should Call It A Day) 25.06.88
Me & Mr Sanchez - **Blue Rondo a la Turk** 21.11.81
Me & My Baby Brother - **War** 3.07.76
Me and Julio Down By the School Yard - **Paul Simon** 29.04.72
Me and Mrs Jones - **Billy Paul** 20.01.73
Me and My Girl (Night-Clubbing) - **David Essex** 10.07.82
Me and My Shadow - **Frank Sinatra & Sammy Davis Jnr** 20.12.62
Me and the Farmer - **Housemartins** 5.09.87
Me and You and A Dog Name Boo - **Lobo** 26.06.71
Me, In Time - **Charlatans** 9.11.91
Me Myself and I - **De La Soul** 15.04.89
Me Myself I - **Joan Armatrading** 5.07.80
Me No Pop I - **Kid Creole & the Coconuts present Coati Mundi** 4.07.81
Me The Peaceful Heart - **Lulu** 28.02.68
Mean Girl - **Status Quo** 21.04.73
Mean Man - **W.A.S.P.** 4.03.89
Mean Mean Man - **Wanda Jackson** 9.02.61
Mean Streak - **Cliff Richard & the Drifters** 8.05.59
Mean to Me - **Shaye Cogan** 24.03.60
The Meaning Of Love - **Depeche Mode** 8.05.82
Mecca - **Cheetahs** 1.10.64
The Medal Song - **Culture Club** 1.12.84
Medicine Show - **Big Audio Dynamite** 7.06.86
The Medicine Song - **Stephanie Mills** 22.09.84
Meet El Presidente - **Duran Duran** 25.04.87
Meet Me On The Corner - **Max Bygraves** 18.11.55
Meet Me On The Corner - **Lindisfarne** 26.02.72
Megablast/Don't Make Me Wait - **Bomb The Bass** 27.08.88
Megamix - **Technotronic** 6.10.90
Mellow Mellow Right On - **Lowrell** 8.12.79
Mellow Yellow - **Donovan** 9.02.67
Melody of Love - **Ink Spots** 29.04.55
Melting Pot - **Blue Mink** 22.11.69
Memo from Turner - **Mick Jagger** 21.11.70
Memories Are Made of This - **Dean Martin** 10.02.56
Memories Are Made of This - **Dave King** 17.02.56
Memories Are Made of This - **Val Doonican** 2.03.67
Memory - **Elaine Page** 13.06.81
Memory - **Barbra Streisand** 27.03.82
Memphis Tennessee - **Dave Berry & the Cruisers** 3.10.63
Mental - **Manic MC's featuring Sara Carlson** 19.08.89
Merci Cherie - **Vince Hill** 2.06.66
Mercy Mercy Me - I Want You - **Robert Palmer** 12.01.91
Merry Christmas Everyone - **Shakin' Stevens** 7.12.85
Merry Christmas Darling/(They Long To Be) Close to You - **Carpenters** 15.12.90
Merry Gentle Pops - **Barron Knights** 16.12.65
A Merry Jingle - **Greedies** 5.01.80

Merry Xmas Everybody - **Slade** 15.12.73
Merry Xmas Everybody - **Slade** 26.12.81
Merry Xmas Everybody - **Slade** 17.12.83
A Mess Of Blues - **Status Quo** 5.11.83
Mess of Blues - **Elvis Presley** 28.07.60
The Message - **Grandmaster Flash and the Furious Five** 28.08.82
Message In A Bottle - **Police** 22.09.79
Message in the Box - **World Party** 7.07.90
The Message Is Over - **Arthur Baker & the Backbeat Disciples featuring Al Green** 28.10.89
Message of Love - **Pretenders** 14.02.81
Message to Martha (Kentucky Bluebird) - **Lou Johnson** 26.11.64
Message to Martha (Kentucky Bluebird) - **Adam Faith** 26.11.64
Message to You Rudy/Nite Klub - **Specials/Rico** 3.11.79
A Message To Your Heart 11.05.91
Message Understood - **Sandie Shaw** 30.09.65
Messages - **Orchestral Manoeuvres In The Dark** 24.05.80
Metal Guru - **T.Rex** 13.05.72
Method of Modern Love - **Daryl Hall & John Oates** 2.03.85
Mexicali Rose - **Karl Denver** 19.10.61
Mexican Girl - **Smokie** 7.10.78
Mexico - **Long John Baldry** 23.10.68
Miami Vice Theme - **Jan Hammer** 12.10.85
Michael - **Highwaymen** 14.09.61
Michael - **Geno Washington** 16.02.67
Michael & The Slipper Tree - **Equals** 2.04.69
Michael Caine - **Madness** 11.02.84
Michael Row the Boat - **Lonnie Donegan** 31.08.61
Michelle - **David & Jonathan** 13.01.66
Michelle - **Overlands** 13.01.66
Mickey - **Toni Basil** 13.02.82
Micro Kid - **Level 42** 29.10.83
Midas Touch - **Midnight Star** 4.10.86
Middle of The House - **Alma Cogan** 2.11.56
Middle of The House - **Jimmy Parkinson** 9.11.56
Middle Of The House - **Johnston Brothers** 30.11.56
Midnight - **Paul Anka** 26.09.58
Midnight at the Oasis - **Maria Muldaur** 6.07.74
Midnight At The Lost And Found - **Meat Loaf** 1.10.83
Midnight Flyer - **Nat 'King' Cole** 4.09.59
Midnight in Moscow - **Kenny Ball & his Jazzmen** 16.11.61
Midnight Rider - **Paul Davidson** 10.01.76
Midnight Shift - **Buddy Holly** 31.07.59
Midnight Summer Dream - **Stranglers** 5.03.83
Midnight Train to Georgia - **Gladys Knight & the Pips** 15.05.76
Midnite Dynamos - **Matchbox** 17.05.80
Mighty Power of Love - **Tavares** 5.02.77
The Mighty Quinn - **Manfred Mann** 24.01.68
Mike Oldfield's Single - **Mike Oldfield** 20.07.74
Milk and Alcohol - **Dr Feelgood** 27.01.79
Milkyway - **Sheer Elegance** 10.01.76
Milly Molly Mandy - **Glyn Poole** 3.11.73
Milord - **Frankie Vaughan** 27.10.60
Milord - **Edith Piaf** 3.11.60
Mind - **Farm** 24.08.91
Mind Blowing Decisions - **Heatwave** 10.06.78
Mind Games - **John Lennon** 24.11.73
Mind of A Toy - **Visage** 14.03.81
Mind Up Tonight - **Melba Moore** 15.01.83
Mine All Mine/Party Freak - **Cashflow** 24.05.86
Minnie the Moocher - **Reggae Philharmonic Orchestra** 17.12.88
Minuetto Allegretto - **Wombles** 19.10.74
A Minute of Your Time - **Tom Jones** 4.12.68
The Minute You're Gone - **Cliff Richard** 11.03.65
The Miracle - **Queen** 9.12.89
Miracle - **Jon Bon Jovi** 17.11.90
The Miracle of Love - **Eurythmics** 29.11.86
Mirror In The Bathroom - **Beat** 10.05.80
Mirror Man - **Human League** 20.11.82
Mirror Mirror - **Pinkerton's Assorted Colours** 20.01.66
Mirror Mirror - **Dollar** 5.12.81
Mirror Mirror - **Diana Ross** 30.1.82.
Mirrors - **Sally Oldfield** 23.12.78
Misfit - **Curiosity Killed the Cat** 20.06.87
Misled - **Kool & the Gang** 16.02.85
Miss America - **Big Dish** 19.01.91
Miss Hit and Run - **Barry Blue** 10.08.74
Miss The Girl - **Creatures** 30.04.83
Miss You - **Jimmy Young** 17.10.63
Miss You - **Rolling Stones** 3.06.78
Miss You Like Crazy - **Natalie Cole** 22.04.89
Miss You Much - **Janet Jackson** 2.09.89
Miss You Nights - **Cliff Richard** 21.02.76
Missing Words - **Selecter** 5.04.80
Missing You - **John Waite** 6.10.84
Missing You - **Chris De Burgh** 5.11.88
Missing You - **Soul II featuring Kym Mazelle** 24.11.90
Missionary Man - **Eurythmics** 28.02.87
Mississippi - **Pussycat** 4.09.76
Mississippi - **Pussycat** 22.01.77
Mistletoe & Wine - **Cliff Richard** 3.12.88
Misty - **Johnny Mathis** 29.01.60
Misty - **Ray Stevens** 21.06.75
Misty Blue - **Dorothy Moore** 26.06.76
Mixed Emotions - **Rolling Stones** 9.09.89
M'Lady - **Sly & the Family Stone** 9.10.68
Mobile - **Ray Burns** 11.02.55
Mocking Bird Hill - **Migil Five** 9.04.64
Mockingbird - **Inex & Charlie Foxx** 19.02.69
Mockingbird - **Carly Simon & James Taylor** 23.03.74
The Model/Computer Love - **Kraftwerk** 9.1.82.
Modern Girl - **Sheena Easton** 16.08.80
Modern Girl - **Meat Loaf** 13.10.84
Modern Love - **David Bowie** 24.09.83
Modern World - **Jam** 5.11.77
Modern World - **Jam** 19.11.77
Moments in Soul - **JT & the Big Family** 3.03.90
Mona - **Craig McLachlan & Check 1-2** 23.06.90
Mona Lisa - **Conway Twitty** 21.08.59
Monday Monday - **Mamas & the Papas** 12.05.66
Money - **Bern Elliott & the Fenmen** 28.11.63
Money - **Flying Lizards** 18.08.79
Money For Nothing - **Dire Straits** 20.06.85
Money Go Round (Part 1) - **Style Council** 28.05.83
Money Honey - **Bay City Rollers** 22.11.75
Money In My Pocket - **Dennis Brown** 3.03.79
Money Money Money - **Abba** 20.11.76
Money Talks - **AC/DC** 1.12.90
Money's Too Tight to Mention - **Simply Red** 6.07.85
The Monkees (EP) - **Monkees** 29.03.80
Monkey - **George Michael** 16.07.88
Monkey Business - **Skid Row** 15.06.91
Monkey Chop - **Dan-I** 17.11.79
Monkey's Spanner - **Dave & Ansil Collins** 3.07.71
Monsieur Dupont - **Sandie Shaw** 12.02.69
Monster Mash - **Bobby Pickett & the Crypt Kickers** 8.09.73
Monsters and Angels - **Voice of The Beehive** 20.07.91
Montego Bay - **Bobby Bloom** 5.09.70
Montego Bay - **Amazulu** 20.09.86
Mony Mony - **Tommy James & the Shondells** 12.06.68
Mony Mony - **Billy Idol** 10.10.87
Mony Mony - **Amazulu** 24.10.87
Moody Blue - **Elvis Presley** 5.03.77
Moody River - **Pat Boone** 6.07.61
Moon River - **Danny Williams** 9.11.61
Moon River - **Greyhound** 15.01.72
Moon Shadow - **Cat Stevens** 11.09.71
Moon Talk - **Perry Como** 5.09.58
Moonchild - **Fields of the Nephilim** 4.06.88
Moonglow and Theme From 'Picnic' - **Morris Stoloff** 1.06.56
Moonlight & Muzak - **M** 22.12.79
Moonlight Gambler - **Frankie Laine** 28.12.56
Moonlight Serenade - **Glenn Miller Orchestra** 12.03.54
Moonlight Shadow - **Mike Oldfield** 18.06.83
Moonlighting - **Leo Sayer** 30.08.75
'Moonlighting' Theme - **Al Jarreau** 7.03.87
Moonlighting Serenade/Little Brown Jug/In The Mood - **Glenn Miller** 31.01.76
Moonshine Sally - **Mud** 21.06.75
More - **Perry Como** 21.09.56
More - **Jimmy Young** 28.09.56
More - **Sisters of Mercy** 13.10.90
More and More Party Pops - **Russ Conway** 20.11.59
More Good Old Rock 'N' Roll - **Dave Clark Five** 7.11.70
The More I See You - **Joy Marshall** 23.06.66
The More I See You - **Chris Montez** 30.06.66
More Like The Movies - **Dr. Hook** 1.04.78
More Money for You and Me - **Four Preps** 9.11.61
More More More - **Andrea True Connection** 24.04.76

More More More - **Carmel** 25.02.84
More Party Pops - **Russ Conway** 28.11.58
More Than A Feeling - **Boston** 29.01.77
More Than A Lover - **Bonnie Tyler** 26.03.77
More Than A Woman - **Tavares** 6.05.78
More Than Ever - **Malcolm Vaughan** 17.10.58
More Than Ever - **Robert Earl** 24.10.58
More Than I Can Say/Staying In - **Bobby Vee** 13.04.61
More Than I Can Say - **Leo Sayer** 12.07.80
More Than In Love - **Kate Robbins** 30.05.81
More Than Love - **Ken Dodd** 4.08.66
More Than This - **Roxy Music** 3.04.82
More Than Words - **Extreme** 27.07.91
More Than You Know - **Martika** 13.01.90
More To Life - **Cliff Richard** 14.09.91
The More You Live The More You Love - **A Flock of Seagulls** 11.08.84
Morgen - **Ivo Robic** 6.11.59
Mornin' - **Al Jarreau** 21.05.83
Morning Dance - **Spyro Gyra** 4.08.79
Morning Glory - **James & Bobby Purify** 14.08.76
Morning Has Broken - **Cat Stevens** 1.01.72
Morning of Our Lives - **Modern Lovers** 21.01.78
Morning Side of the Mountain - **Donny & Marie Osmond** 4.01.75
Morningtown Ride - **Seekers** 24.11.66
The Most Beautiful Girl - **Charlie Rich** 23.02.74
Mother-In-Law - **Ernie K-Doe** 18.05.61
Mother And Child Reunion - **Paul Simon** 19.02.72
Mother of Mine - **Neil Reid** 1.01.72
Mother Universe - **Soup Dragons** 20.10.90
Mothers Talk - **Tears for Fears** 18.08.84
The Motive - **Then Jerico** 22.08.87
Motor Biking - **Chris Spedding** 6.09.75
Motor Mania - **Roman Holiday** 22.10.83
Motorhead Live - **Motorhead** 11.07.81
Motown Song - **Rod Stewart** 15.06.91
Mouldy Old Dough - **Lieutenant Pigeon** 16.09.72
Mountain Greenery - **Mel Torme** 27.04.56
Mountain of Love - **Kenny Lynch** 14.07.60
The Mountain's High - **Dick & Deedee** 2.11.61
Move Any Mountain - **Shamen** 27.07.91
Move Away - **Culture Club** 15.03.86
Move Away Jimmy Blue - **Del Amitri** 30.06.90
Move Closer - **Phyllis Nelson** 23.03.85
Move In A Little Closer - **Harmony Grass** 5.02.69
Move It - **Cliff Richard & The Drifters** 12.09.58
Move It Baby - **Simon Scott** 27.08.64
Move On Up - **Curtis Mayfield** 7.08.71
Move Over Darling - **Doris Day** 23.03.64
Move Over Darling - **Tracey Ullman** 3.12.83
Move That Body - **Technotronic** 25.05.91
Move Your Body - **Gene Farrow** 29.04.78
Move Your Body (Elevation) - **Xpansions** 23.02.91
Moviestar - **Harpo** 24.04.76
Movin' - **Brass Construction** 3.04.76
Movin' 1988 - **Brass Construction** 28.05.88
Movin' Out (Anthony's Song) - **Billy Joel** 8.07.78
Mozart 40 - **Sovereign Collection** 10.04.71
Mozart Symphony No. 40 - **Waldo de Los Rios** 10.04.71
Mr DJ - **Concept** 14.12.85
Mr Sandman - **Four Aces** 7.01.55
Mr Sandman - **Max Bygraves** 21.01.55
Mr Second Class - **Spencer Davis Group** 17.01.68
Mr Solitaire - **Animal Nightlife** 15.09.84
Mr Telephone Man - **New Edition** 9.03.85
Mr. Bass Man - **Johnny Cymbal** 21.03.63
Mr. Blue - **Mike Preston** 30.10.59
Mr. Blue - **David Macbeth** 30.10.59
Mr. Blue Sky - **Electric Light Orchestra** 28.01.78
Mr. Custer - **Charlie Drake** 3.11.60
Mr. President - **Dozy, Beaky, Mick and Tich** 8.08.70
Mr. Raffles (Man It Was Mean) - **Steve Harley & Cockney Rebel** 7.06.75
Mr. Soft - **Cockney Rebel** 10.08.74
Mr. Success - **Frank Sinatra** 14.11.58
Mr. Tambourine Man - **Byrds** 17.06.65
Mr. Wonderful - **Peggy Lee** 24.05.57
Mrs Robinson - **Simon & Garfunkel** 17.07.68
Mrs Robinson (EP) - **Simon & Garfunkel** 8.01.69
Mrs. Mills Medley - **Mrs. Mills** 14.12.61
Ms. Grace - **Tymes** 21.12.74
Mule (Chant No. 2) - **Beggar & Co** 26.09.81
Mule Skinner Blues - **Rusty Draper** 11.08.60
Mule Skinner Blues - **Fendermen** 8.09.60
Mule Train - **Frank Ifield** 24.10.63
Mull of Kintyre/Girls School - **Wings** 26.11.77
Multiplication - **Bobby Darin** 21.12.61
Multiplication - **Showaddywaddy** 20.06.81
Murphy's Law - **Cheri** 19.06.82
Musclebound/Glow - **Spandau Ballet** 11.04.81
Muscles - **Diana Ross** 30.10.82
Music - **John Miles** 27.03.76
Music and Lights - **Imagination** 26.06.82
Music For Chameleons - **Gary Numan** 6.03.82
Music Makes You Feel Like Dancing - **Brass Construction** 9.02.80
The Music of the Night/Wishing You Were Somehow Here - **Michael Crawford/ Sarah Brightman** 31.01.87
The Music of Torvill and Dean (EP) - **Richard Hartley & the Michael Reed Orchestra** 3.03.84
Music (Part 1) - **D Train** 14.05.83
Music to Watch Girls By - **Andy Williams** 11.05.67
Musical Freedom (Moving On Up) - **Paul Simpson featuring Adeva** 25.03.89
Musical Melody/Weight for the Bass - **Unique Three** 21.04.90
Muskrat - **Everly Brothers** 5.10.61
Muskrat Ramble - **Freddie Cannon** 27.04.61
Must Be Madison - **Joe Loss Orchestra** 1.11.62
Must Be Santa - **Tommy Steele** 29.12.60
Mustang Sally - **Wilson Pickett** 22.12.66
Mustapha - **Bob Azzam & his Orchestra** 26.05.60
Mutually Assured Destruction - **Gillan** 14.02.81
My Baby Just Cares for Me - **Nina Simone** 7.11.87
My Baby Left Me - **Dave Berry** 20.02.64
My Best Friend's Girl - **Cars** 11.11.78
My Blue Heaven - **Frank Sinatra** 27.04.61
My Boomerang Won't Come Back - **Charlie Drake** 5.10.61
My Boy - **Elvis Presley** 16.11.74
My Boy Flat Top - **Frankie Vaughan** 3.02.56
My Boy Lollipop - **Millie** 26.03.64
My Brave Face - **Paul McCartney** 20.05.89
My Brother Jake - **Free** 8.05.71
My Camera Never Lies - **Bucks Fizz** 27.03.82
My Cherie Amour - **Stevie Wonder** 16.07.69
My Child - **Connie Francis** 10.06.65
My Coo-Ca-Choo - **Alvin Stardust** 10.11.73
My Definition of A Boombastic Jazz Style - **Dream Warriors** 24.11.90
My Ding-A-Ling - **Chuck Berry** 28.10.72
My Dixie Darlin' - **Lonnie Donegan** 11.10.57
My Ever Changing Moods - **Style Council** 18.02.84
My Eyes Adored You - **Frankie Valli** 1.02.75
My Favourite Waste of Time - **Owen Paul** 14.06.86
My Feet Keep Dancing - **Chic** 15.12.79
My Forbidden Lover - **Chic** 20.10.79
My Friend - **Frankie Laine** 13.08.54
My Friend - **Roy Orbison** 7.05.69
My Friend Stan - **Slade** 6.10.73
My Friend the Sea - **Petula Clark** 30.11.61
My Generation - **Who** 4.11.65
My Girl - **Otis Redding** 9.12.65
My Girl - **Otis Redding** 21.02.68
My Girl - **Madness** 12.01.80
My Girl - **Whispers** 19.07.80
My Girl - **Rod Stewart** 10.01.81
My Girl Bill - **Jim Stafford** 13.07.74
My Girl Josephine - **Fats Domino** 12.01.61
My Girl Lollipop (My Boy Lollipop) - **Bad Manners** 7.08.82
My Guy-My Girl - **Amii Stewart & Johnny Bristol** 2.08.80
My Guy - **Mary Wells** 21.05.64
My Guy - **Mary Wells** 15.07.72
My Guy - **Tracey Ullman** 10.03.84
My Happiness - **Connie Francis** 13.02.59
My Head's In Mississippi - **ZZ Top** 20.04.91
My Heart - **Gene Vincent** 17.03.60
My Heart Goes Bang (Get Me To The Doctor) - **Dead Or Alive** 28.09.85
My Heart Has A Mind of Its Own - **Connie Francis** 3.11.60
My Heart Sings - **Paul Anka** 30.01.59
My Heart's Symphony - **Gary Lewis & the Playboys** 22.02.75
My Kind of Girl - **Matt Monro** 9.03.61
My Kind of Girl - **Frank Sinatra with Count Basie** 7.03.63
My Kinda Life - **Cliff Richard** 12.03.77
My Last Night With You - **Arrows** 8.02.75

My Life - **Billy Joel** 16.12.78
My Little Baby - **Mike Berry & the Outlaws** 18.04.63
My Little Girl - **Crickets** 24.01.63
My Little Girl - **Autumn** 23.10.71
My Little Lady - **Tremeloes** 25.09.68
My Little One - **Marmalade** 3.04.71
My Love - **Petula Clark** 10.02.66
My Love - **Wings** 14.04.73
My Love - **Julio Iglesias** 13.08.88
My Love & Devotion - **Matt Monro** 15.11.62
My Love and Devotion - **Doris Day** 21.11.52
My Love For You - **Johnny Mathis** 6.10.60
My Love Is So Raw - **Alyson Williams featuring Nikki-D** 13.05.89
My Love Is Waiting - **Marvin Gaye** 15.01.83
My Love Life - **Morrissey** 12.10.91
My Lover's Prayer - **Otis Redding** 21.07.66
My Magic Man - **Rochelle** 1.02.86
My Mammy - **Happenings** 16.08.67
My Man and Me - **Lynsey De Paul** 29.03.75
My Marie - **Engelbert Humperdinck** 13.06.70
My Melancholy Baby - **Tommy Edwards** 7.08.59
My Mind's Eye - **Small Faces** 17.11.66
My Mum is One In A Million - **The Children of Tansley School** 4.04.81
My Name Is Jack - **Manfred Mann** 19.06.68
My Name Is Not Susan - **Whitney Houston** 6.07.91
My Oh My - **Sad Cafe** 29.03.80
My Oh My - **Slade** 26.11.83
My Old Man's A Dustman - **Lonnie Donegan** 24.03.60
My Old Piano - **Diana Ross** 20.09.80
My One Sin - **Nat 'King' Cole** 26.08.55
My One Temptation - **Mica Paris** 21.05.88
My Own Way - **Duran Duran** 28.11.81
My Perfect Cousin - **Undertones** 19.04.80
My Personal Possession - **Nat 'King' Cole** 18.10.57
My Prayer - **Platters** 2.11.56
My Prayer - **Gerry Monroe** 21.11.70
My Prerogative - **Bobby Brown** 21.01.89
My Pretty One - **Cliff Richard** 27.06.87
My Resistance is Low - **Robin Sarstedt** 15.05.76
My Rising Star - **Northside** 3.11.90
My Sentimental Friend - **Herman's Hermits** 23.04.69
My September Love - **David Whitfield** 2.03.56
My Sharona - **Knack** 14.07.79
My Ship Is Coming In - **Walker Brothers** 2.12.65
My Simple Heart - **Three Degrees** 1.12.79
My Son John - **David Whitfield** 24.08.56
My Son My Son - **Vera Lynn** 15.10.54
My Special Angel - **Malcolm Vaughan** 29.11.57
My Special Angel - **Bobby Helms** 29.11.57
My Special Dream - **Shirley Bassey** 30.01.64
My Sunday Baby - **Dale Sisters** 30.11.61
My Sweet Lord - **George Harrison** 23.01.71
My Sweet Rosalie - **Brotherhoold of Man** 3.07.76
My Toot Toot - **Denise LaSalle** 29.06.85
My Town - **Glass Tiger** 16.11.91
My True Love - **Jack Scott** 10.10.58
My Ukelele - **Max Bygraves** 2.01.59
My Unfinished Symphony - **David Whitfield** 31.08.56
My Way - **Eddie Cochran** 2.05.63
My Way - **Frank Sinatra** 16.04.69
My Way - **Dorothy Squires** 15.08.70
My Way - **Elvis Presley** 10.12.77
My Way of Thinking/I Think It's Going To Rain - **UB40** 21.06.80
My White Bicycle - **Nazareth** 14.06.75
My World - **Cupid's Inspiration** 9.10.68
My World - **Bee Gees** 29.01.72
My World - **Secret Affair** 15.03.80
My World of Blue - **Karl Denver** 12.03.64
Mysterious Ways - **U2** 14.12.91
Mystery - **Dio** 29.09.84
Mystery Girl - **Jess Conrad** 16.02.61
Mystery Song - **Status Quo** 17.07.76
Mystery Train - **Elvis Presley** 15.02.57
Mystify - **Inxs** 8.04.89
N-N-Nineteen Not Out - **Commentators** 29.06.85
N-R-G - **Adamski** 20.01.90
Na Na Hey Hey Kiss Him Goodbye - **Steam** 14.02.70
Na Na Hey Hey Kiss Him Goodbye - **Bananarama** 26.02.83
Na Na Is The Saddest Word - **Stylistics** 22.11.75
Na Na Na - **Cozy Powell** 17.08.74
Nadine - **Chuck Berry** 20.02.64
Nairobi - **Tommy Steele** 7.03.58
Naked in the Rain - **Blue Pearl** 14.07.90
Naked Love (Just Say You Want Me) - **Quartz with Dina Carroll** 15.06.91
Name and Number - **Curiosity Killed the Cat** 23.09.89
Name Of The Game - **Abba** 22.10.77
Nappy Love/Wild Thing - **Goodies** 27.09.75
Nashville Boogie - **Bert Weedon** 20.11.59
Nashville Cats - **Lovin' Spoonful** 12.01.67
Nasty - **Janet Jackson** 7.06.86
Nathan Jones - **Supremes** 28.08.71
Nathan Jones - **Bananarama** 19.11.88
Native New Yorker - **Odyssey** 7.01.78
Natural Born Bugie - **Humble Pie** 23.08.69
Natural High - **Bloodstone** 1.09.73
Natural Sinner - **Fair Weather** 18.07.70
Natural Thing - **Innocence** 3.03.90
Nature Boy - **Bobby Darin** 13.07.61
Nature Boy - **George Benson** 11.06.77
Nature Boy - **Central Line** 29.01.83
Nature's Time for Love - **Joe Brown** 4.07.63
Naughty Girls (Need Love Too) - **Samantha Fox** 28.05.88
Naughty Lady of Shady Lane - **Dean Martin** 28.01.55
Naughty Lady of Shady Lane - **Ames Brothers** 4.02.55
Naughty Naughty Naughty - **Joy Sarney** 14.05.77
Ne-Ne-Na-Na-Na-Na-Nu-Nu - **Bad Manners** 29.03.80
Neanderthal Man - **Hotlegs** 11.07.70
Near Wild Heaven - **REM** 17.08.91
Near You - **Migil Five** 18.06.64
Need You Tonight - **Inxs** 12.11.88
Need Your Love So Bad - **Fleetwood Mac** 14.08.68
Need Your Love So Bad - **Fleetwood Mac** 30.07.69
Needles and Pins - **Searchers** 16.01.64
Needles and Pins - **Smokie** 22.10.77
Neither One Of Us - **Gladys Knight & the Pips** 2.06.73
Nellie the Elephant - **Toy Dolls** 15.12.84
Nelson Mandela - **Special AKA** 24.03.84
Neon Knights - **Black Sabbath** 12.07.80
Nervous Shakedown - **AC/DC** 11.08.84
Nervous Wreck - **Radio Stars** 11.02.78
Nessun Dorma - **Luciano Pavarotti** 16.06.90
Neutron Dance - **Pointer Sisters** 19.01.85
Never Be Anyone Else But You - **Ricky Nelson** 15.05.59
Never Before - **Deep Purple** 1.04.72
Never Before - **Deep Purple** 22.04.72
Never Can Say Goodbye - **Jackson 5** 31.07.71
Never Can Say Goodbye - **Gloria Gaynor** 14.12.74
Never Can Say Goodbye - **Communards** 7.11.87
Never Do A Tango With An Eskimo - **Alma Cogan** 23.12.55
Never Ending Song of Love - **New Seekers** 17.07.71
Never Ending Story - **Limahl** 27.10.84
Never Enough - **Cure** 29.09.90
Never Give Up On A Good Thing - **George Benson** .... 22.1.82.
Never Give You Up - **Sharon Redd** 9.10.82
Never Gonna Fall In Love Again - **Dana** 13.03.76
Never Gonna Give You Up - **Musical Youth** 12.02.83
Never Gonna Give You Up - **Rick Astley** 8.08.87
Never Goodbye - **Karl Denver** 8.03.62
Never Had A Dream Come True - **Stevie Wonder** 4.04.70
Never Knew Love Like This Before - **Stephanie Mills** 25.10.80
Never Knew Love Likes This - **Alexander O'Neal featuring Cherelle** 13.02.88
Never Let Her Slip Away - **Andrew Gold** 25.03.78
Never Let Me Down Again - **Depeche Mode** 5.09.87
Never Let Me Down - **David Bowie** 12.09.87
Never Mind - **Cliff Richard & the Drifters** 15.05.59
Never Mind The Presents - **Barron Knights** 13.12.80
Never Never - **Assembly** 12.11.83
Never Never Gonna Give Ya Up - **Barry White** 2.02.74
Never Never Never - **Shirley Bassey** 10.03.73
Never On A Sunday - **Manuel & his Music of the Mountains** 13.10.60
Never on Sunday - **Makadopoulos & his Greek Serenaders** 20.10.60
Never on Sunday - **Don Costa** 20.10.60
Never on Sunday - **Lynn Cornell** 27.10.60
Never Say Die - **Black Sabbath** 10.06.78
Never Say Die (Give A Little Bit More) - **Cliff Richard** 3.09.83
Never Say Goodbye - **Bon Jovi** 15.08.87
Never Stop - **Echo and the Bunnymen** 16.07.83
Never Surrender - **Saxon** 18.07.81

Never Take Me Alive - **Spear of Destiny** 18.04.87
Never Tear Us Apart - **Inxs** 25.06.88
Never Too Late - **Kylie Minogue** 4.11.89
Never Too Much - **Luther Vandross** 28.10.89
Never Trust A Stranger - **Kim Wilde** 8.10.88
Never Turn Your Back on Mother Earth - **Sparks** 19.10.74
Nevertheless - **Frankie Vaughan** 6.03.68
Nevertheless (I'm In Love With You) - **Eve Graham/New Seekers** 14.04.73
Never/These Dreams - **Heart** 5.03.88
New Amsterdam - **Elvis Costello** 14.06.80
New Beginning (Mamba Seyra) - **Bucks Fizz** 14.06.86
A New England - **Kirsty MacColl** 26.01.85
A New Fashion - **Bill Wyman** 27.03.82
A New Flame - **Simply Red** 15.07.89
New Kid In Town - **Eagles** 22.01.77
New Life - **Depeche Mode** 4.07.81
New Live and Rare - **Deep Purple** 22.10.77
New Moon on Monday - **Duran Duran** 4.02.84
New Orleans - **US Bonds** 19.01.61
New Orleans - **Bern Elliott & the Fenmen** 26.03.64
New Orleans - **Harley Quinne** 14.10.72
New Orleans - **Gillan** 28.03.81
New Power Generation - **Prince** 10.11.90
New Sensation - **Inxs** 16.01.88
New Song - **Howard Jones** 1.10.83
A New South Wales/The Rock - **Alarm featuring the Morriston Orpheus Male Voice Choir** 11.11.89
New Year's Day - **U2** 22.01.83
New York City - **T. Rex** 12.07.75
New York Groove - **Hello** 25.10.75
New York Mining Disaster 1941 - **Bee Gees** 4.05.67
News Of The World - **Jam** 11.03.78
News Of The World - **Jam** 29.01.83
Next Door To An Angel - **Neil Sedaka** 29.11.62
The Next Time - **Cliff Richard** 6.12.62
Next to You - **Aswad** 25.08.90
Nice and Slow - **Jesse Green** 14.08.76
Nice In Nice - **Stranglers** 23.08.86
Nice Legs Shame About Her Face - **Monks** 5.05.79
Nice 'N' Easy - **Frank Sinatra** 8.09.60
Nice 'N' Sleazy - **Stranglers** 6.05.78
Nice One Cyril - **Cockerel Chorus** 3.03.73
Night - **Frankie Valli & the Four Seasons** 19.04.75
A Night At Daddy Gee's - **Showaddywaddy** 24.11.79
Night Birds - **Shakatak** 3.04.82
The Night Chicago Died - **Paper Lace** 4.05.74
Night Fever - **Fatback Band** 21.08.76
Night Fever - **Bee Gees** 15.04.78
The Night Fever Megamix - **Mixmasters** 2.02.91
Night Games - **Graham Bonnet** 4.04.81
The Night Has A Thousand Eyes - **Bobby Vee** 7.02.63
Night In Motion - **Cubic 22** 22.06.91
A Night In New York - **Elbow Bones & the Racketeers** 28.01.84
The Night is Young/There Goes That Song Again - **Gary Miller** 21.12.61
Night of Fear - **Move** 5.01.67
Night of the Long Grass - **Troggs** 1.06.67
Night Owl - **Gerry Rafferty** 2.06.79
The Night The Wine and The Roses - **Liquid Gold** 8.11.80
The Night They Drove Old Dixie Down - **Joan Baez** 9.10.71
A Night to Remember - **Shalamar** 19.06.82
Night Train - **Buddy Morrow** 20.03.53
Night Train - **Visage** 3.07.82
Night You Murdered Love - **ABC** 19.09.87
Nightmare - **Gillan** 17.10.81
Nightporter - **Japan** 27.11.82
Nightrain - **Guns N' Roses** 2.09.89
Nights In White Satin - **Moody Blues** 3.01.68
Nights In White Satin - **Moody Blues** 2.12.72
Nights In White Satin - **Dickies** 22.09.79
Nights In White Satin - **Moody Blues** 24.11.79
Nights in White Satin - **Elkie Brooks** 24.07.82
Nights On Broadway - **Candi Staton** 23.07.77
Nightshift - **Commodores** 2.02.85
Nikita - **Elton John** 19.10.85
9AM (The Comfort Zone) - **Londonbeat** 10.12.88
19 - **Paul Hardcastle** 4.05.85
1999/Little Red Corvette - **Prince** 19.01.85
Nineteenth Nervous Breakdown - **Rolling Stones** 10.02.66
Nine Times Out of Ten - **Cliff Richard** 22.09.60
9 To 5 - **Sheena Easton** 26.07.80
98.6 - **Keith** 26.01.67
Ninety-Nine Ways - **Tab Hunter** 12.04.57
99 Red Balloons - **Nena** 11.02.84
92 Degrees - **Pop Will Eat Itself** 1.06.91
96 Tears - **?(Question Mark & the Mysterians)** 24.11.66
96 Tears - **Stranglers** 17.02.90
No-One But You - **Billy Eckstine** 12.11.54
No-One Is Innocent/My Way - **Sex Pistols** 8.07.78
No-one To Cry To - **Ray Charles** 1.10.64
No Arms Could Ever Hold You - **Bachelors** 10.12.64
No Chance (No Charge) - **Billy Connolly** 17.07.76
No Doubt About It - **Hot Chocolate** 3.05.80
No Face No Name and No Number - **Traffic** 6.03.68
No Honestly - **Lynsey De Paul** 9.11.74
No Laughing in Heaven - **Gillan** 20.06.81
No Matter How I Try - **Gilbert O'Sullivan** 4.12.71
No Matter What Sign You Are - **Diana Ross & the Supremes** 23.07.69
No Matter What - **Badfinger** 9.01.71
No Memory - **Scarlet Fantastic** 24.10.87
No Mercy - **Stranglers** 8.12.84
No Milk Today - **Herman's Hermits** 6.10.66
No More - **McGuire Sisters** 1.04.55
No More Heroes - **Stranglers** 1.10.77
No More Lies - **Sharpe & Numan** 30.01.88
No More Lonely Nights (Ballad) - **Paul McCartney** 6.10.84
No More Mr Nice Guy - **Megadeth** 13.01.90
No More Mr. Nice Guy - **Alice Cooper** 21.04.73
No More Tears (Enough Is Enough) - **Donna Summer/Barbra Streisand** 10.11.79
No More Tears - **Ozzy Osbourne** 28.09.91
No More The Fool - **Elkie Brooks** 13.12.86
No Mule's Fool - **Family** 1.11.69
No One - **Ray Charles** 19.09.63
No One Can - **Marillion** 3.08.91
No One Can Break A Heart Like You - **Dave Clark Five** 6.03.68
No One Can Make My Sunshine Smile - **Everly Brothers** 25.10.62
No One Driving - **John Foxx** 29.03.80
No One Is To Blame - **Howard Jones** 15.03.86
No One Will Ever Know - **Frank Ifield** 23.06.66
No Other Baby - **Bobby Helms** 21.02.58
No Other Love - **Johnston Brothers** 13.04.56
No Other Love - **Ronnie Hilton** 20.04.56
No Other Love - **Edmund Hockridge** 11.05.56
No Particular Place To Go - **Chuck Berry** 14.05.64
No Regrets - **Shirley Bassey** 3.06.65
No Regrets - **Walker Brothers** 17.01.76
No Regrets - **Midge Ure** 19.06.82
No Rest - **New Model Army** 27.04.85
No Self Control - **Peter Gabriel** 31.05.80
No Sleep Till Brooklyn - **Beastie Boys** 30.05.87
No Son of Mine - **Genesis** 2.11.91
No Time To Be 21 - **Adverts** 11.02.78
No Woman No Cry - **Bob Marley And The Wailers** 27.09.75
No Woman No Cry - **Bob Marley & the Wailers** 20.06.81
Nobody - **Tongue 'n' Cheek** 11.08.90
Nobody But You - **Gladys Knight & the Pips** 22.01.77
Nobody Does It Better - **Carly Simon** 13.08.77
Nobody I Know - **Peter & Gordon** 4.06.64
Nobody Needs Your Love - **Gene Pitney** 9.06.66
Nobody Told Me - **John Lennon** 21.01.84
Nobody's Child - **Karen Young** 6.09.69
Nobody's Darlin' But Mine - **Frank Ifield** 11.04.63
Nobody's Diary - **Yazoo** 21.05.83
Nobody's Fool - **Jim Reeves** 21.03.70
Nobody's Fool - **Haircut 100** 21.08.82
Nobody's Hero/Tin Soldiers - **Stiff Little Fingers** 31.05.80
Nocturne - **T99** 19.10.91
Non Ho L'Eta Per Amarti - **Gigliola Cinquetti** 30.04.64
No. 9 Dream - **John Lennon** 15.02.75
Norah Malone - **Teresa Brewer** 10.05.57
Norman - **Carol Deene** 1.02.62
Norman Bates - **Landscape** 20.06.81
North to Alaska - **Johnny Horton** 19.01.61
Northern Lights - **Renaissance** 29.07.78
Not A Minute Too Soon - **Vixen** 16.03.91
Not As A Stranger - **Frank Sinatra** 2.09.55
Not Fade Away - **Rolling Stones** 27.02.64
Not Now John - **Pink Floyd** 7.05.83
Not Too Little - Not Too Much - **Chris Sandford** 12.12.63

Not Until The Next Time - **Jim Reeves** 15.04.65
Nothin' At All - **Heart** 29.10.88
Nothin' But A Good Time - **Poison** 14.05.88
Nothin' (That Compares 2 U) - **Jacksons** 27.05.89
Nothin' To Do - **Michael Holliday** 30.03.56
Nothing Can Divide Us - **Jason Donovan** 10.09.88
Nothing Comes Easy - **Sandie Shaw** 26.05.66
Nothing Compares 2 U - **Sinead O'Connor** 20.01.90
Nothing Ever Happens - **Del Amitri** 27.01.90
Nothing Has Been Proved - **Dusty Springfield** 25.02.89
Nothing Rhymed - **Gilbert O'Sullivan** 5.12.70
(Nothing Serious) Just Buggin' - **Whistle** 1.03.86
Nothing's Gonna Stop Us Now - **Starship** 18.04.87
Nothing's Gonna Stop Me Now - **Samantha Fox** 30.05.87
Nothing's Gonna Change My Love For You - **Glenn Medeiros** 25.06.88
Nothing to Lose - **S'Express** 15.09.90
Notorious - **Duran Duran** 1.11.86
November Spawned A Monster - **Morrissey** 5.05.90
Now - **Al Martino** 30.01.53
Now I'm Here - **Queen** 25.01.75
Now Is The Time - **Jimmy James & the Vagabonds** 24.07.76
Now That We've Found Love - **Third World** 30.09.78
Now That We've Found Love - **Third World** 23.03.85
Now That We've Found Love - **Heavy D & the Boys** 6.07.91
Now Those Days Are Gone - **Bucks Fizz** 26.06.82
Now We're Thru - **Poets** 29.10.64
Now You're Gone (Remix) - **Whitesnake** 25.08.90
Nowhere to Run - **Martha & the Vandellas** 1.04.65
Nuclear Device (Wizard of Aus) - **Stranglers** 20.10.79
The Number Of The Beast - **Iron Maiden** 15.05.82
The Number One Song In Heaven - **Sparks** 5.05.79
Numbers/Barriers - **Soft Cell** 5.03.83
Numero Uno - **Starlight** 19.08.89
Nut Rocker - **B. Bumble & the Stingers** 19.04.62
Nut Rocker - **B.Bumble & the Stingers** 17.06.72
007 - **Desmond Dekker & the Aces** 19.07.67
Nutbush City Limits - **Ike & Tina Turner** 15.09.73
Nutbush City Limits (90s version) - **Tina Turner** 21.09.91
O L'Amour - **Dollar** 16.01.88
O' My Father Had A Rabbit - **Ray Moore** 13.12.86
O Superman - **Laurie Anderson** 17.10.81
Ob-La-Di Ob-La-Da - **Marmalade** 11.12.68
Ob-La-Di Ob-La-Da - **Bedrocks** 18.12.68
Oblivious - **Aztec Camera** 12.11.83
Obsession - **Animotion** 18.05.85
The Obvious Child - **Paul Simon** 20.10.90
Ode to Billy Joe - **Bobbie Gentry** 20.09.67
Of Course I'm Lying - **Yello** 1.04.89
Off The Wall - **Michael Jackson** 1.12.79
Offshore Banking Business - **Members** 14.04.79
Oh-Oh I'm Falling In Love Again - **Jimmie Rodgers** 28.03.58
Oh Babe What Would You Say - **Hurricane Smith** 29.04.72
Oh Boy - **Crickets** 27.12.57
Oh Boy - **Mud** 26.04.75
Oh Boy - **Brotherhood of Man** 5.03.77
Oh! Carol - **Neil Sedaka** 13.11.59
Oh Carol - **Smokie** 27.05.78
Oh Carol/Breaking Up Is Hard to Do/Little Devil - **Neil Sedaka** 14.10.72
Oh Diane - **Fleetwood Mac** 15.01.83
Oh Girl - **Chi-Lites** 3.06.72
Oh Girl - **Paul Young** 14.07.90
Oh Happy Day - **Johnston Brothers** 3.04.53
Oh Happy Day - **Edwin Hawkins Singers** 21.05.69
Oh How I Miss You - **Bachelors** 20.04.67
Oh Julie - **Shakin' Stevens** 16.1.82.
Oh Lonesome Me - **Craig Douglas** 25.10.62
Oh Lori - **Alessi** 11.06.77
Oh Mein Papa - **Eddie Calvert** 18.12.53
Oh Mein Papa - **Eddie Fisher** 22.01.54
Oh No Not My Baby - **Manfred Mann** 15.04.65
Oh No Not My Baby - **Rod Stewart** 8.09.73
Oh Patti (Don't Feel Sorry for Loverboy) - **Scritti Politti** 21.05.88
Oh People - **Patti LaBelle** 9.08.86
Oh Pretty Woman - **Roy Orbison** 10.09.64
Oh Well - **Fleetwood Mac** 4.10.69
Oh Well - **Oh Well** 21.10.89
Oh What A Circus - **David Essex** 19.08.78
Oh What A Shame - **Roy Wood** 7.06.75
Oh Yeah (On the Radio) - **Roxy Music** 2.08.80
Oh Yes You're Beautiful - **Gary Glitter & Glitter Band** 23.11.74
Oh You Pretty Thing - **Peter Noone** 22.05.71
Okay! - **Dave Dee Dozy Beaky Mick & Tich** 25.05.67
Ol' Macdonald - **Frank Sinatra** 24.11.60
Ol' Rag Blues - **Status Quo** 10.09.83
The Old Fashioned Way - **Charles Aznavour** 27.10.73
Old Oaken Bucket - **Tommy Sands** 11.08.60
Old Payola Roll Blues - **Stan Freburg** 12.05.60
Old Pianna Rag - **Dickie Valentine** 16.12.55
Old Rivers - **Walter Brennan** 28.06.62
The Old Rugged Cross - **Ethna Campbell** 10.01.76
The Old Rugged Cross - **Ethna Campbell** 24.01.76
Old Shep - **Clinton Ford** 23.10.59
Old Siam Sir - **Wings** 23.06.79
Old Smokie/High Voltage - **Johnny & the Hurricanes** 13.07.61
The Oldest Swinger in Town - **Fred Wedlock** 7.02.81
Ole Ola - **Rod Stewart & the Scottish W.C. Squad** 27.05.78
Olive Tree - **Judith Durham** 22.06.67
Oliver's Army - **Elvis Costello & the Attractions** 17.02.79
On A Carousel - **Hollies** 16.02.67
On A Little Street In Singapore - **Manhattan Transfer** 20.05.78
On and On - **Aswad** 5.08.89
On Fire - **T. Connection** 14.01.78
On Mother Kelly's Doorstep - **Danny La Rue** 18.12.68
On My Own - **Patti LaBelle & Michael McDonald** 3.05.86
On My Radio - **Selecter** 27.10.79
On My Word - **Cliff Richard** 10.06.65
On Our Own - **Bobby Brown** 15.07.89
On The Beach - **Cliff Richard** 2.07.64
On The Beach - **Chris Rea** 13.08.88
On The Inside - **Lynne Hamilton** 20.05.89
On The Radio - **Donna Summer** 23.02.80
On the Rebound - **Floyd Cramer** 13.04.61
On The Road Again - **Canned Heat** 31.07.68
On The Street Where You Live - **Vic Damone** 9.05.58
On The Street Where You Live - **David Whitfield** 16.05.58
On The Wings of Love - **Jeffrey Osborne** 21.07.84
On With the Motley - **Harry Secombe** 9.12.55
Once Bitten Twice Shy - **Ian Hunter** 10.05.75
Once Bitten Twice Shy - **Vesta Williams** 17.01.87
Once In A Lifetime - **Talking Heads** 14.02.81
Once in Every Lifetime - **Ken Dodd** 22.06.61
Once There Was A Time/Not Responsible - **Tom Jones** 26.05.66
Once Upon A Dream - **Billy Fury** 26.07.62
Once Upon A Long Ago - **Paul McCartney** 28.11.87
Once Upon A Time - **Tom Jones** 6.05.65
One - **Metallica** 22.04.89
007 - **Musical Youth** 5.11.83
One and One Is One - **Medicine Head** 5.05.73
The One and Only - **Gladys Knight & the Pips** 15.04.78
The One and Only - **Chesney Hawkes** 9.03.91
One Better Day - **Madness** 2.06.84
One Better World - **ABC** 27.05.89
One Broken Heart For Sale - **Elvis Presley** 7.03.63
One Dance Won't Do - **Audrey Hall** 15.02.86
One Day At A Time - **Lena Martell** 6.10.79
One Day I'll Fly Away - **Randy Crawford** 6.09.80
One Day In Your Life - **Michael Jackson** 30.05.81
One Drink Too Many - **Sailor** 26.02.77
One Fine Day - **Chiffons** 18.07.63
One For You One For Me - **Jonathan King** 14.10.78
One Great Thing - **Big Country** 20.09.86
100 Miles And Runnin' - **N.W.A.** 10.11.90
100 Pounds Of Clay - **Craig Douglas** 20.04.61
The One I Love - **REM** 21.09.91
One In Ten - **UB40** 15.08.81
One Inch Rock - **Tyrannosaurus Rex** 18.09.68
One Love-People Get Ready - **Bob Marley & the Wailers** 20.04.84
One Love - **Stone Roses** 14.07.90
One Man - **Chanelle** 11.03.89
One Man Band - **Leo Sayer** 15.06.74
One Man Woman - **Sheena Easton** 25.10.80
One Moment In Time - **Whitney Houston** 24.09.88
One More Dance - **Esther & Abi Ofarim** 26.06.68
One More Night - **Phil Collins** 13.04.85
One More Sunrise - **Dickie Valentine** 23.10.59
One More Try - **George Michael** 23.04.88
One Nation Under A Groove - **Funkadelic** 16.12.78
One Night - **Mud** 2.08.75

One Night in Bangkok - **Murray Head** 17.11.84
One Night/I Got Stung - **Elvis Presley** 23.01.59
One Of These Nights - **Eagles** 16.08.75
One of Those Nights - **Bucks Fizz** 29.08.81
One of Us - **Abba** 12.12.81
One Of Us Must Know - **Bob Dylan** 28.04.66
10538 Overture - **Electric Light Orchestra** 5.08.72
One Piece At A Time - **Johnny Cash & the Tennessee Three** 10.07.76
One Road - **Love Affair** 26.02.69
One Rule For You - **After The Fire** 30.06.79
One Small Day - **Ultravox** 11.02.84
One Step Away - **Tavares** 2.07.77
One Step Beyond - **Madness** 17.11.79
1-2-3 - **Len Barry** 4.11.65
1-2-3 - **Gloria Estefan & Miami Sound Machine** 29.10.88
1-2-3 O'Leary - **Des O'Conner** 20.11.68
One Step Further - **Bardo** 17.04.82
One Vision - **Queen** 16.11.85
One Way Love - **Cliff Bennett & the Rebel Rousers** 8.10.64
One Way Ticket - **Eruption** 28.04.79
The Onion Song - **Marvin Gaye & Tammi Terrell** 15.11.69
Only Boy In the World - **Stevie Marsh** 4.12.59
Only Crying - **Keith Marshall** 11.04.81
Only Fools (Never Fall In Love) - **Sonia** 1.06.91
Only For Love - **Limahl** 5.11.83
Only In My Dreams - **Debbie Gibson** 19.03.88
Only Love - **Nana Mouskouri** 18.01.86
Only Love Can Break Your Heart - **St Etienne** 14.09.91
Only Love Remains - **Paul McCartney** 13.12.86
Only Man on the Island - **Tommy Steele** 18.07.58
Only Man On The Island - **Vic Damone** 1.08.58
The Only One - **Transvision Vamp** 10.06.89
The Only One I Know - **Charlatans** 2.06.90
Only One Woman - **Marbles** 2.10.68
The Only Rhyme That Bites - **MC Tunes vs 808 State** 9.06.90
Only Sixteen - **Craig Douglas** 7.08.59
Only Sixteen - **Sam Cooke** 14.08.59
Only Sixteen - **Al Saxon** 28.08.59
Only the Heartaches - **Houston Wells** 8.08.63
Only the Lonely - **Roy Orbison** 28.07.60
Only The Lonely - **T'Pau** 25.03.89
Only The Strong Survive - **Billy Paul** 26.11.77
The Only Way Is Up - **Yazz & the Plastic Population** 23.07.88
The Only Way Out - **Cliff Richard** 17.07.82
Only When You Leave - **Spandau Ballet** 9.06.84
Only Women Bleed - **Julie Covington** 10.12.77
Only Yesterday - **Carpenters** 19.04.75
Only You - **Hilltoppers** 27.01.56
Only You - **Mark Wynter** 9.04.64
Only You - **Jeff Collins** 2.12.72
Only You - **Ringo Starr** 30.11.74
Only You - **Child** 28.04.79
Only You - **Yazoo** 1.05.82
Only You - **Flying Pickets** 3.12.83
Only You - **Praise** 2.02.91
Only You Can - **Fox** 22.02.75
Only Your Love - **Bananarama** 28.07.90
Onward Christian Soldiers - **Harry Simeone Chorale** 22.12.60
Onward Christian Soldiers - **Harry Simeone Chorale** 28.12.61
Onward Christian Soldiers - **Harry Simeone Chorale** 27.12.62
Ooh-Wakka-Doo-Wakka-Day - **Gilbert O'Sullivan** 17.06.72
Ooh Baby - **Gilbert - O'Sullivan** 15.09.73
Ooh I Do - **Lynsey De Paul** 8.06.74
Ooh La La La (Let's Go Dancin') - **Kool & the Gang** 23.10.82
Ooh! My Soul - **Little Richard** 11.07.58
Ooh To Be Ah - **Kajagoogoo** 2.04.83
Ooh What A Life - **Gibson Brothers** 28.07.79
Oops Up - **Snap** 16.06.90
Oops Upside You Head - **Gap Band** 19.07.80
Oops Upside Your Head - **Gap Band** 18.07.87
Open Up - **Mungo Jerry** 29.04.72
Open Up Your Heart - **Joan Regan** 6.05.55
Open Your Heart - **Human League** 10.10.81
Open Your Heart - **Madonna** 13.12.86
Opportunities (Let's Make Lots of Money) - **Pet Shop Boys** 31.05.86
Opposites Attract - **Paula Abdul with the Wild Pair** 7.04.90
Opus 17 - **Four Seasons** 9.06.66
Orange Blossom Special - **Spotnicks** 14.06.62
Orange Crush - **REM** 10.06.89
Orchard Road - **Leo Sayer** 19.03.83
Ordinary Day - **Curiosity Killed the Cat** 4.04.87
The Original Bird Dance - **Electronicas** 26.09.81
Orinoco Flow - **Enya** 15.10.88
O.K. - **Rock Follies** 28.05.77
O.K. Fred - **Erroll Dunkley** 6.10.79
Orville's Song - **Keith Harris & Orville** 25.12.82
Ossie's Dream - **Tottenham Hotspur FA Cup Final Squad** 16.05.81
The Other Man's Grass - **Petula Clark** 20.12.67
The Other Side of Love - **Yazoo** 20.11.82
Ouija Board Ouija Board - **Morrissey** 25.11.89
Our Day Will Come - **Ruby & the Romantics** 4.04.63
Our Favourite Melodies - **Craig Douglas** 28.06.62
Our Frank - **Morrissey** 23.02.91
Our House - **Madness** 27.11.82
Our Last Song Together - **Neil Sedaka** 8.09.73
Our Lips Are Sealed - **Fun Boy Three** 30.04.83
(Our Love) Don't Throw It All Away - **Andy Gibb** 3.02.79
Out Demons Out - **Edgar Broughton Band** 2.05.70
Out In The Fields - **Gary Moore & Phil Lynott** 18.05.85
Out of My Mind - **Johnny Tillotson** 23.05.63
Out of Reach - **Primitives** 30.04.88
Out of The Blue - **Debbie Gibson** 14.05.88
Out of Time - **Chris Farlowe & the Thunderbirds** 23.06.66
Out of Town - **Max Bygraves** 25.05.56
Out With Her - **Blow Monkeys** 4.04.87
Outside of Heaven - **Eddie Fisher** 2.01.53
Outstanding - **Kenny Thomas** 26.01.91
Over and Over - **James Boys** 26.05.73
Over And Over - **Shalamar** 22.10.83
Over Rising - **Charlatans** 9.03.91
Over The Hills And Far Away - **Gary Moore** 20.12.86
Over The Rainbow/You Belong to Me - **Matchbox** 6.12.80
Over To You John (Here We Go Again) - **Jive Bunny & the Mastermixers** 23.03.91
Over Under Sideways Down - **Yardbirds** 2.06.66
Over You - **Freddie & the Dreamers** 27.02.64
Over You - **Roxy Music** 17.05.80
Overjoyed - **Stevie Wonder** 22.03.86
Overkill - **Motorhead** 24.03.79
Overkill - **Men At Work** 16.04.83
Owner Of A Lonely Heart - **Yes** 19.11.83
Oxygene Part IV - **Jean Michel Jarre** 27.08.77
Oye Mi Canto (Hear My Voice) - **Gloria Estefan** 23.09.89
Pacific - **808 State** 18.11.89
Paid In Full - **Eric B & Rakim** 7.11.87
Paint It, Black - **Rolling Stones** 19.05.66
Paint Me Down - **Spandau Ballet** 21.11.81
Painter Man - **Creation** 3.11.66
Painter Man - **Boney M** 3.03.79
Paisley Park - **Prince & the Revolution** 8.06.85
Pale Shelter - **Tears For Fears** 30.04.83
Palisades Park - **Freddy Cannon** 5.07.62
Paloma Blanca - **George Baker Selection** 13.09.75
Pamela Pamela - **Wayne Fontana** 15.12.66
Pandora's Box - **Procol Harum** 30.08.75
Pandora's Box - **Orchestral Manoeuvres In The Dark** 13.07.91
Panic - **Smiths** 2.08.86
Papa Don't Preach - **Madonna** 28.06.86
Papa Loves Mama - **Joan Regan** 28.07.60
Papa Ooh Mow Mow - **Sharonettes** 3.05.75
Papa Was A Rollin' Stone - **Temptations** 13.01.81
Papa Was A Rollin' Stone - **Temptations** 22.08.87
Papa Was A Rolling Stone - **Was (Not Was)** 26.05.90
Papa's Got A Brand New Bag - **James Brown** 30.09.65
Papa's Got A Brand New Pigbag - **Pigbag** 10.04.82
Paper Plane - **Status Quo** 13.01.81
Paper Roses - **Maureen Evans** 9.06.60
Paper Roses - **Kay Sisters** 7.07.60
Paper Roses - **Anita Bryant** 14.07.60
Paper Roses - **Marie Osmond** 17.11.73
Paper Sun - **Traffic** 8.06.67
Paper Tiger - **Sue Thompson** 11.02.65
Paperback Writer - **Beatles** 16.06.66
Paperback Writer - **Beatles** 3.04.76
Paradise - **Frank Ifield** 26.08.65
Paradise - **Black** 23.01.88
Paradise Bird/The Letter - **Amii Stewart** 26.01.80
Paradise City - **Guns N' Roses** 18.03.89
Paradise Lost - **Herd** 3.01.68

Paradise (Remix) - **Sade** 11.06.88
Paralysed - **Elvis Presley** 30.08.57
Paranoid - **Black Sabbath** 23.08.80
Paranoimia - **Art of Noise with Max Headroom** 28.06.86
Parisienne Walkways - **Gary Moore** 28.04.79
Part of the Union - **Strawbs** 27.01.73
Part Time Love - **Gladys Knight And The Pips** 22.11.75
Part Time Love - **Elton John** 28.10.78
Part Time Lover - **Stevie Wonder** 7.09.85
Party - **Elvis Presley** 4.10.57
The Party - **Kraze** 29.10.88
Party Doll - **Buddy Knox** 10.05.57
Party Fears Two - **Associates** 6.03.82
Party In Paris - **UK Subs** 1.11.80
Party Lights - **Gap Band** 11.10.80
Party Pops - **Russ Conway** 29.11.57
Partyman - **Prince** 9.09.89
The Party's Over - **Lonnie Donegan** 12.04.62
Pasadena - **Temperance Seven** 15.06.61
Pass the Dutchie - **Musical Youth** 25.09.82
Passengers - **Elton John** 18.08.84
Passing Breeze - **Russ Conway** 29.09.60
Passing Strangers - **Billy Eckstine & Sarah Vaughan** 27.09.57
Passing Strangers - **Sarah Vaughan & Billy Eckstine** 12.03.69
Passion - **Rod Stewart** 8.11.80
Passionate Friend - **Teardrop Explodes** 5.09.81
Paths of Paradise - **Johnnie Ray** 20.05.55
Patricia - **Perez Prado** 25.07.58
The Pay Off - **Kenny Ball & his Jazzmen** 18.10.62
Pay to The Piper - **Chairmen of the Board** 22.05.71
The Payback Mix Part One - **James Brown** 23.04.88
Peace - **Sabrina Johnston** 7.09.91
Peace In Our Time - **Big Country** 4.02.89
Peace on Earth-Little Drummer Boy - **David Bowie & Bing Crosby** 4.12.82
Peaceful - **Georgie Fame** 16.07.69
Peaches - **The Stranglers** 21.05.77
Pearl In The Shell - **Howard Jones** 26.05.84
Pearl's A Singer - **Elkie Brooks** 9.04.77
Pearly Dewdrops Drops - **Cocteau Twins** 28.04.84
Peek-A-Boo - **New Vaudeville Band** 2.02.67
Peek-A-Boo - **Stylistics** 7.07.73
Peek A Boo - **Siouxsie & the Banshees** 30.07.88
Peggy Sue - **Buddy Holly** 6.12.57
Peggy Sue Got Married - **Buddy Holly** 11.09.59
Peggy Sue/Rave On - **Buddy Holly** 10.04.68
Penny Arcade - **Roy Orbison** 27.09.69
Penny Lane/Strawberry Fields Forever - **Beatles** 23.02.67
Penny Lover - **Lionel Richie** 20.10.84
People - **Tymes** 22.01.69
People Are People - **Depeche Mode** 24.03.84
People Are Strange - **Echo & the Bunnymen** 27.02.88
People Are Strange - **Echo & the Bunnymen** 9.03.91
People Are Still Having Sex - **LaTour** 15.06.91
People Hold On - **Coldcut featuring Lisa Stansfield** 25.03.89
People Like You People Like Me - **Glitter Band** 28.02.76
Pepe - **Duane Eddy** 12.01.61
Pepe - **Russ Conway** 19.01.61
Pepper Box - **Peppers** 2.11.74
Peppermint Twist - **Danny Peppermit & the Jumping Jacks** 18.01.62
Peppermint Twist - **Joey Dee & Starliters** 8.02.62
Per-so-nal-ly - **Wigan's Ovation** 19.07.75
Perfect - **Fairground Attraction** 23.04.88
Perfect Skin - **Lloyd Cole & the Commotions** 23.06.84
Perfidia - **Ventures** 1.12.60
Personal Jesus - **Depeche Mode** 9.09.89
Personal Touch - **Errol Brown** 25.07.87
Personality - **Anthony Newley** 12.06.59
Personality - **Lloyd Price** 12.06.59
Personality - **Lena Zavaroni** 8.06.74
Personality/Let Her Feel It - **Eugene Wilde/Simplicious** 9.02.85
Peter and the Wolf - **Clyde Valley Stompers** 16.08.62
Peter Gunn - **Art of Noise featuring Duane Eddy** 22.03.86
Peter Gunn Theme - **Duane Eddy** 19.06.59
Petite Fleur - **Chris Barber** 13.02.59
The Phantom of the Opera - **Sarah Brightman & Steve Harley** 18.01.86
Philadelphia Freedom - **Elton John Band** 8.03.75
Photograph - **Ringo Starr** 27.10.73
Physical - **Olivia Newton-John** 24.10.81
Pianissimo - **Ken Dodd** 8.02.62
Piano In The Dark - **Brenda Russell** 2.04.88
Piano Party - **Winifred Atwell** 27.11.59
Piccadilly Palare - **Morrissey** 20.10.90
Pick A Bale of Cotton - **Lonnie Donegan** 23.08.62
Pick Up the Pieces - **Hudson Ford** 25.08.73
Pick Up The Pieces - **Average White Band** 22.02.75
Pickin' A Chicken - **Eve Boswell** 30.12.55
A Picture of You - **Joe Brown** 24.05.62
Picture This - **Blondie** 2.09.78
Pictures of Lily - **Who** 27.04.67
Pictures of Matchstick Men - **Status Quo** 30.01.68
Pictures of You - **Cure** 31.03.90
Pie Jesu - **Sarah Brightman & Paul Miles-Kingston** 23.03.85
Piece of the Action - **Bucks Fizz** 13.06.81
Pied Piper - **Crispian St. Peters** 7.04.66
Pied Piper - **Bob & Marcia** 19.06.71
Pied Piper (The Beeje) - **Steve Race** 28.02.63
Pillow Talk - **Sylvia** 30.06.73
Pills And Soap - **Imposter** 11.06.83
Piltdown Rides Again - **Piltdown Men** 19.01.61
Pinball - **Brian Protheroe** 7.09.74
Pinball Wizard - **Who** 19.03.69
Pinball Wizard/See Me Feel Me - **New Seekers** 24.02.73
Pinball Wizard - **Elton John** 20.03.76
Pink Cadillac - **Natalie Cole** 2.04.88
Pink Sunshine - **We've Got A Fuzzbox & We're Gonna Use It** 27.05.89
Pinky Blue - **Altered Images** 29.05.82
Pipeline - **Chantays** 2.05.63
Pipeline - **Bruce Johnston** 3.09.77
Pipes Of Peace - **Paul McCartney** 24.12.83
Pistol Packin' Mama - **Gene Vincent** 23.06.60
A Place In The Sun - **Shadows** 14.07.66
A Place In The Sun - **Stevie Wonder** 19.01.67
Planet Earth - **Duran Duran** 14.03.81
Planet of Sound - **Pixies** 8.06.91
Plastic Man - **Kinks** 16.04.69
Play (EP) - **Ride** 14.04.90
Play Me Like You Play Your Guitar - **Duane Eddy** 15.03.75
Play That Funky Music - **Wild Cherry** 9.10.76
Play That Funky Music - **Vanilla Ice** 2.02.91
Play the Game - **Queen** 14.06.80
Playground Twist - **Siouxsie & the Banshees** 14.07.79
Playing With Knives - **Bizarre Inc** 23.11.91
Pleasant Valley Sunday - **Monkees** 16.08.67
Please Come Home For Christmas - **Eagles** 23.12.78
Please Don't Go - **K.C. & the Sunshine Band** 15.12.79
Please Don't Touch - **Johnny Kidd & the Pirates** 12.06.59
Please Don't Tease - **Cliff Richard** 30.06.60
Please Don't Ask About Barbara - **Bobby Vee** 15.03.62
Please Don't Go - **Donald Peers** 25.12.68
Please Don't Make Me Cry - **UB40** 15.10.83
Please Don't Fall In Love - **Cliff Richard** 26.11.83
Please Don't Be Scared - **Barry Manilow** 15.04.89
Please Help Me I'm Falling - **Hank Locklin** 11.08.60
Please Mr. Postman - **Carpenters** 18.01.75
Please Please Me - **Beatles** 24.01.63
Please Please Me - **David Cassidy** 27.07.74
Please Please Me - **Beatles** 22.01.83
Please Stay - **Cryin' Shames** 14.04.66
Please Tell Him That I Said Hello - **Dana** 25.01.75
Pleasure Principle - **Janet Jackson** 13.06.87
Plenty Good Lovin' - **Connie Francis** 11.09.59
The Poacher - **Ronnie Lane & Slim Chance** 15.06.74
Pocket Calculator - **Kraftwerk** 23.05.81
Poetry in Motion - **Johnny Tillotson** 1.12.60
Poguetry In Motion - **Pogues** 8.03.86
Point of View - **Matumbi** 13.10.79
Poison - **Alice Cooper** 29.07.89
Poison - **Bell Biv Devoe** 21.07.90
Poison Arrow - **ABC** 6.03.82
Poison Ivy - **Coasters** 30.10.59
Poison Ivy - **Paramounts** 30.01.64
Poison Ivy - **Lambrettas** 15.03.80
Police and Thieves - **Junior Murvin** 10.05.80
Policy of Truth - **Depeche Mode** 19.05.90
The Politics of Dancing - **Re-Flex** 25.02.84
Polk Salad Annie - **Elvis Presley** 26.05.73
Pony Time - **Chubby Checker** 30.03.61
Pool Hall Richard/I Wish It Would Rain - **Faces** 8.12.73

Poor Jenny - **Everly Brothers** 29.05.59
Poor Little Fool - **Ricky Nelson** 22.08.58
Poor Man's Son - **Rockin' Berries** 13.05.65
Poor Me - **Adam Faith** 22.01.60
Poor People of Paris (Poor John) - **Winifred Atwell** 16.03.56
Pop Go The Workers - **Barron Knights** 1.04.65
Pop Goes My Love - **Freeez** 8.10.83
Pop Goes the Weasel/Bee Bom - **Anthony Newley** 15.06.61
Pop Muzik - **M** 14.04.79
Pop Muzik - **M** 24.06.89
Popcorn - **Hot Butter** 29.07.72
Poppa Joe - **Sweet** 12.02.72
Poppa Piccolino - **Diana Decker** 23.10.53
Port Au Prince - **Winifred Atwell & the Frank Chacksfield Orchestra** 18.05.56
Portrait of My Love - **Matt Monro** 15.12.60
Portsmouth - **Mike Oldfield** 27.11.76
Portuguese Washerwoman - **Joe 'Fingers' Carr** 29.06.56
Positively 4th Street - **Bob Dylan** 28.10.65
Pour Some Sugar on Me - **Def Leppard** 19.09.87
The Power - **Snap** 24.03.90
Power And The Glory - **Saxon** 30.04.83
The Power of Love - **Frankie Goes to Hollywood** 1.12.84
The Power of Love - **Huey Lewis & the News** 7.09.85
The Power of Love - **Jennifer Rush** 21.09.85
Power of Love/Do You Believe in Love - **Huey Lewis & the News** 22.02.86
Power of Love/Deee-Lite Theme - **Deee-Lite** 24.11.90
Power to All Our Friends - **Cliff Richard** 17.03.73
Power to the People - **John Lennon/Plastic Ono Band** 20.03.71
Pray - **MC Hammer** 8.12.90
Praying For Time - **George Michael** 25.08.90
Preacherman - **Bananarama** 12.01.91
Pregnant For The Last Time - **Morrissey** 27.07.91
Press - **Paul McCartney** 26.07.86
Pretend - **Nat 'King' Cole** 24.04.53
Pretend - **Alvin Stardust** 12.09.81
Pretty Blue Eyes - **Craig Douglas** 22.01.60
Pretty Brown Eyes - **Jim Reeves** 10.04.68
Pretty Flamingo - **Manfred Mann** 21.04.66
Pretty In Pink - **Psychedelic Furs** 6.09.86
Pretty Little Black Eyed Susie - **Guy Mitchell** 24.04.53
Pretty Little Angel Eyes - **Showaddywaddy** 4.11.78
Pretty Paper - **Roy Orbison** 19.11.64
Pretty Thing - **Bo Diddley** 17.10.63
Pretty Vacant - **Sex Pistols** 16.07.77
The Price of Love - **Everly Brothers** 20.05.65
Pride (In The Name of Love) - **U2** 15.09.84
Primal Scream - **Motley Crue** 7.09.91
Prime Mover - **Zodiac Mindwart & the Love Reacion** 9.05.87
Prime Times - **Tubes** 26.05.79
Primrose Lane - **Dickie Pride** 30.10.59
The Prince - **Madness** 15.09.79
Prince Charming - **Adam & the Ants** 12.09.81
Princess In Rags - **Gene Pitney** 11.11.65
Private Dancer - **Tina Turner** 24.11.84
Private Eyes - **Daryl Hall and John Oates** 24.04.82
Private Investigations - **Dire Straits** 4.09.82
Private Life - **Grace Jones** 2.08.80
Private Number - **Judy Clay & William Bell** 27.11.68
Prize of Gold - **Joan Regan** 25.03.55
Probably A Robbery - **Renegade Soundwave** 17.02.90
Problems - **Everly Brothers** 23.01.59
Procession/Everything's Gone Green - **New Order** 10.10.81
Prodigal Son - **Steel Pulse** 22.07.78
Product of The Working Class - **Little Angels** 30.03.91
The Promise - **Arcadia** 1.02.86
Promise Me - **Beverley Craven** 4.05.91
The Promise You Made - **Cock Robin** 5.07.86
Promised Land - **Chuck Berry** 21.01.65
Promised Land - **Elvis Presley** 18.01.75
Promised Land - **Style Council** 18.02.89
Promised You A Miracle - **Simple Minds** 17.04.82
Promised You a Miracle (Live) - **Simple Minds** 20.06.87
Promises - **Ken Dodd** 12.05.66
Promises - **Eric Clapton** 4.11.78
Promises - **Eric Clapton** 18.11.78
Promises - **Buzzcocks** 25.11.78
Promises - **Take That** 23.11.91
Proud Mary - **Creedence Clearwater Revival** 28.05.69
Proud Mary - **Checkmates Ltd** 22.11.69
The Proud One - **Osmonds** 24.05.75
Prove It - **Television** 30.07.77
Prove Your Love - **Taylor Dayne** 26.03.88
Psychedelic Shack - **Temptations** 20.06.70
Psychonaut - **Fields of The Nephilim** 27.05.89
Pub With No Beer - **Slim Dusty** 30.01.59
Public Image - **Public Image Ltd** 21.10.78
Puff - **Kenny Lynch** 20.09.62
Pull Up To The Bumper - **Grace Jones** 18.01.86
Pump It Up - **Elvis Costello** 20.05.78
Pump up the Bitter - **Star Turn on 45 (Pints)** 30.04.88
Pump Up The Jam - **Technotronic featuring Felly** 9.09.89
Pump Up the Volume/Anitina (The First Time I See She Dance) - **M/A/R/R/S** 5.09.87
Punch and Judy - **Marillion** 11.02.84
Puppet On A String - **Sandie Shaw** 16.03.67
Puppy Love - **Paul Anka** 21.04.60
Puppy Love - **Donny Osmond** 17.06.72
Pure - **Lightning Seeds** 5.08.89
Purely By Coincidence - **Sweet Sensation** 25.01.75
Purple Haze - **Jimi Hendrix Experience** 23.03.67
Purple People Eater - **Sheb Wooley** 20.06.58
Purple People Eater - **Jackie Dennis** 27.06.58
Purple Rain - **Prince & the Revolution** 22.09.84
Push It/Tramp - **Salt-N-Pepa** 25.06.88
Pushbike Song - **Mixtures** 16.01.71
Puss 'N Boots - **Adam Ant** 29.10.83
Put A Light in the Window 31.01.58
Put A Little Love In Your Heart - **Dave Clark Five** 1.11.69
Put A Little Love In Your Heart - **Annie Lennox & Al Green** 17.12.88
Put It There - **Paul McCartney** 17.02.90
Put Your Hands Together - **D Mob** 6.01.90
Put Your Head on My Shoulder - **Paul Anka** 30.10.59
Put Your Love In Me - **Hot Chocolate** 3.12.77
Put Yourself In My Place - **Isley Brothers** 6.09.69
Put Yourself in My Place - **Elgins** 9.10.71
Pyjamarama - **Roxy Music** 17.03.73
PYT (Pretty Young Thing) - **Michael Jackson** 31.03.84
Quadrophonia - **Quadrophonia** 20.04.91
Quando M'Innamoro - **Sandpipers** 5.06.68
Quarter to Three - **U.S. Bonds** 27.07.61
Que Sera Mi Vida - **Gibson Brothers** 17.11.79
Queen For Tonight - **Helen Shapiro** 14.02.63
The Queen of 1964 - **Neil Sedaka** 29.03.75
Queen of Clubs - **K.C. & the Sunshine Band** 24.08.74
Queen of Hearts - **Dave Edmunds** 29.09.79
Queen Of My Soul - **Average White Band** 16.10.76
Queen of the Hop - **Bobby Darin** 9.01.59
Queen Of The Rapping Scene (Nothing Ever Goes The Way You Plan) - **Modern Romance** 27.02.82
Queen of the New Year - **Deacon Blue** 6.01.90
The Queen's Birthday - **St John's College School Choir & the Band of the Grenadier Guards** 3.05.86
Question - **Moody Blues** 2.05.70
A Question of Lust - **Depeche Mode** 26.04.86
A Question of Time - **Depeche Mode** 23.08.86
Questions and Answers - **Sham 69** 31.03.79
Questions I Can't Answer - **Heinz** 15.10.64
Quick Joey Small - **Kasenetz-Katz Singing Orchestral Circus** 27.11.68
Quiereme Mucho (Yours) - **Julio Iglesias** 13.03.82
Quiet Life - **Japan** 26.09.81
Quit This Town - **Eddie & the Hot Rods** 28.01.78
Quite A Party - **Fireballs** 3.08.61
Rabbit - **Chase & Dave** 13.12.80
The Race - **Yello** 27.08.88
The Race Is On - **Dave Edmunds & the Stray Cats** 27.06.81
Race With the Devil - **Gene Vincent** 12.10.56
Race With the Devil - **Gun** 27.11.68
Rachel - **Al Martino** 10.07.53
Rachmaninoff's 18th Variaton on a Theme by Paganini (The Story of Three Loves) - **Winifred Atwell** 23.07.54
Radancer - **Marmalade** 8.04.72
Radar Love - **Golden Earring** 15.12.73
Radical Your Lover - **Little Angels & the Big Bad Horns** 19.05.90
Radio Africa - **Latin Quarter** 8.02.86
Radio Ga Ga - **Queen** 4.02.84
Radio Heart - **Radio Heart featuring Gary Numan** 11.04.87
Radio Radio - **Elvis Costello** 4.11.78
Radio Romance - **Tiffany** 19.11.88
Radio Song - **REM** 16.11.91

Radio Wall of Sound - **Slade** 19.10.91
Rag Doll - **Four Seasons** 27.08.64
Rag Mama Rag - **The Band** 11.04.70
Ragamuffin Man - **Manfred Mann** 30.04.69
Rage Hard - **Frankie Goes to Hollywood** 6.09.86
Rage to Love - **Kim Wilde** 4.05.85
Rags to Riches - **David Whitfield** 8.01.54
Rags to Riches - **Elvis Presley** 22.05.71
Ragtime Cowboy Joe - **Chipmunks** 24.07.59
Rain - **Bruce Ruffin** 8.05.71
Rain - **Status Quo** 14.02.76
Rain - **Cult** 5.10.85
The Rain - **Oran 'Juice' Jones** 29.11.86
Rain and Tears - **Aphrodite's Child** 13.11.68
Rain Forest - **Biddu Orchestra** 1.05.76
Rain in the Summertime - **Alarm** 17.10.87
Rain or Shine - **Five Star** 13.09.86
Rain Rain Rain - **Frankie Laine** 22.10.54
Rainbow - **Marmalade** 18.07.70
Rainbow - **Peters & Lee** 17.08.74
Rainbow Chaser - **Nirvana** 29.05.68
Rainbow Valley - **Love Affair** 1.05.68
Raindrops Keep Falling On My Head - **B.J. Thomas** 21.02.70
Raindrops Keep Falling On My Head - **Sacha Distel** 14.02.70
Raindrops Keep Fallin' On My Head - **Bobbie Gentry** 7.03.70
Rainin' Through My Sunshine - **Real Thing** 19.08.78
Raining In My Heart - **Leo Sayer** 9.12.78
Rainy Day Women Nos. 12 & 35 - **Bob Dylan** 12.05.66
Rainy Night in Georgia - **Randy Crawford** 15.08.81
Raised On Rock - **Elvis Presley** 1.12.73
Rama Lama Ding Dong - **Rockey Sharpe & the Replays** 13.01.79
Ramblin' Rose - **Nat 'King' Cole** 27.09.62
Ramona - **Bachelors** 4.06.64
Randy - **Blue Mink** 30.06.73
Rapp Payback - **James Brown** 17.01.81
Rapper's Delight - **Sugarhill Gang** 1.12.79
Rapture - **Blondie** 24.01.81
Raspberry Beret - **Prince & the Revolution** 3.08.85
Rasputin - **Boney M** 7.10.78
Rat In Mi Kitchen - **UB40** 17.01.87
Rat Race/Rude Boys Outa Jail - **Specials** 24.05.80
Rat Rapping (Brilliant Isn't It) - **Roland Rat Superstar** 26.11.83
Rat Trap - **Boomtown Rats** 14.10.78
The Rattler - **Goodbye Mr Mackenzie** 25.03.89
Raunchy - **Bill Justis** 10.01.58
Raunchy - **Ken Mackintosh Orchestra** 7.02.58
Rave On - **Buddy Holly** 20.06.58
Rawhide - **Frankie Laine** 13.11.59
Razzamatazz - **Quincy Jones** 27.06.81
Razzle Dazzle - **Bill Haley & his Comets** 14.09.56
Reach for the Stars/Climb Every Mountain - **Shirley Bassey** 27.07.61
Reach Out and Touch - **Diana Ross** 25.07.70
Reach Out For Me - **Dionne Warwick** 15.10.64
Reach Out I'll Be There - **Four Tops** 13.10.66
Reach Out I'll Be There - **Gloria Gaynor** 15.03.75
Reach Out I'll Be There - **Four Tops** 23.07.88
Reaching For The Best - **Exciters** 11.10.75
Read 'Em And Weep - **Barry Manilow** 10.12.83
Read My Lips (Enough is Enough) - **Jimmy Somerville** 17.03.90
Ready Willing and Able - **Doris Day** 8.04.55
Real Fashion Reggae Style - **Carey Johnson** 2.05.87
Real Gone Kid - **Deacon Blue** 22.10.88
Real Life - **Simple Minds** 26.10.91
Real Love - **Ruby Murray** 12.12.58
Real Love - **Jody Watley** 15.04.89
Real Love - **Driza Bone** 22.06.91
The Real Me - **W.A.S.P.** 27.05.89
Real Real Real - **Jesus Jones** 7.04.90
The Real Thing - **Jellybean featuring Steven Dante** 3.10.87
Real Wild Child (Wild One) - **Iggy Pop** 3.01.87
The Real Wild House - **Raul Orellana** 14.10.89
Really Free - **John Otway & Wild Willy Barrett** 10.12.77
Really Saying Something - **Bananarama with Funboy Three** 10.04.82
Reap the Wild Wind - **Ultravox** 2.10.82
Reason to Believe - **Rod Stewart** 4.09.71
Reason to Live - **Kiss** 19.12.87
Reasons To Be Cheerful - **Ian Dury & the Blockheads** 11.08.79
Rebel Rebel - **David Bowie** 23.02.74
Rebel Rouser - **Duane Eddy** 5.09.58
Rebel Run - **Toyah** 24.09.83
Rebel Without A Cause - **Public Enemy** 28.11.87
Rebel Yell - **Billy Idol** 14.09.85
Recipe for Love/It Had To Be You - **Harry Connick Jr** 1.06.91
Reckless - **Afrika Bambaataa & UB40** 5.03.88
Recovery - **Fontella Bass** 27.01.66
Red Balloon - **Dave Clark Five** 18.09.68
Red Dress - **Alvin Stardust** 11.05.74
Red Guitar - **David Sylvian** 2.06.84
Red Light Green Light - **Mitchel Torok** 11.01.57
Red Light Spells Danger - **Billy Ocean** 26.03.77
Red Red Wine - **Jimmy James & the Vagabonds** 2.10.68
Red Red Wine - **UB40** 20.08.83
Red River Rock - **Johnny & the Hurricanes** 9.10.59
Red Sails In The Sunset - **Fats Domino** 14.11.63
Red Sky - **Status Qup** 26.07.86
Reelin' and Rockin' - **Dave Clark Five** 18.03.65
Reelin' and Rockin' - **Chuck Berry** 3.02.73
Reet Petite - **Jackie Wilson** 15.11.57
Reet Petite - **Jackie Wilson** 6.12.86
Reflections - **Diana Ross & the Supremes** 6.09.67
Reflections of My Life - **Marmalade** 20.12.69
The Reflex - **Duran Duran** 28.04.84
Reggae For It Now - **Billy Lovelady** 25.08.79
Reggae Like It Used to Be - **Paul Nicholas** 24.04.76
Reggae Tune - **Andy Fairweather Low** 28.09.74
Reilly - **Olympic Orchestra** 22.10.83
Relax - **Frankie Goes to Hollywood** 7.01.84
Relay - **Who** 13.01.81
Release Me - **Engelbert Humperdinck** 26.01.67
Release Me - **Wilson Phillips** 18.08.90
Remember - **Rock Candy** 18.09.71
Remember Me - **Diana Ross** 10.04.71
Remember Me - **Cliff Richard** 31.10.87
Remember Me This Way - **Gary Glitter** 30.03.74
Remember Me With Love - **Gloria Estefan** 8.06.91
Remember (Sha-La-La-La) - **Bay City Rollers** 16.02.74
Remember Then - **Showaddywaddy** 7.04.79
Remember (Walkin' In The Sand) 15.10.64
Remember When - **Platters** 28.08.59
Remember Yesterday - **John Miles** 30.10.76
Remember You're Mine/There's A Goldmine In The Sky - **Pat Boone** 27.09.57
Remember You're A Womble - **Wombles** 6.04.74
Reminiscing - **Buddy Holly** 13.09.62
Rendezvous - **Tina Charles** 21.05.77
Renegades of Funk - **Afrika - Bambaataa & the Soul Sonic Force** 10.03.84
Rent - **Pet Shop Boys** 24.10.87
Renta Santa - **Chris Hill** 6.12.75
Republican Party Reptile (EP) - **Big Country** 31.08.91
Reputation - **Dusty Springfield** 9.06.90
Requiem - **Slik** 15.05.76
Requiem - **London Boys** 15.04.89
Rescue Me - **Fontella Bass** 2.12.65
Rescue Me - **Madonna** 13.04.91
Respect - **Aretha Franklin** 15.06.67
Respect - **Adeva** 14.01.89
Respect Yourself - **Kane Gang** 24.11.84
Respect Yourself - **Bruce Willis** 14.03.87
Respectable - **Rolling Stones** 30.09.78
Respectable - **Mel & Kim** 7.03.87
Restless - **Johnny Kidd & the Pirates** 13.10.60
Restless - **Gillan** .... 22.1.82.
Restless Days (She Screams Out Loud) - **And Why Not?** 11.11.89
Resurrection Shuffle - **Ashton, Gardner & Dyke** 23.01.71
Return of Django/Dollar In The Teeth - **Upsetters** 11.10.69
Return of the Red Baron - **Royal Guardsmen** 13.04.67
The Return of the Los Palmas Seven - **Madness** 24.01.81
Return to Me - **Dean Martin** 13.06.58
Return to Sender - **Elvis Presley** 29.11.62
Reunited - **Peaches & Herb** 28.04.79
Reveille Rock - **Johnny & the Hurricanes** 25.12.59
Revival - **Eurythmics** 26.08.89
Revolution - **Cult** 30.11.85
Revolution Baby - **Transvision Vamp** 17.09.88
Reward - **Teardrop Explodes** 28.02.81
Rhapsody - **Four Seasons** 25.06.77
Rhapsody In The Rain - **Lou Christie** 5.05.66
Rhinestone Cowboy - **Glen Campbell** 11.10.75
Rhythm and Greens - **Shadows** 3.09.64

Rhythm Is A Mystery - **K-Klass** 9.11.91
Rhythm Is Gonna Get You - **Gloria Estefan & Miami Sound Machine** 24.12.88
Rhythm Nation - **Janet Jackson** 11.11.89
Rhythm of My Heart - **Rod Stewart** 16.03.91
Rhythm Of The Rain - **Cascades** 7.03.63
Rhythm of The Night - **DeBarge** 27.04.85
Rhythm of the Rain - **Jason Donovan** 1.09.90
Rich Kids - **Rich Kids** 28.01.78
Rich Man, Poor Man - **Jimmy Young** 22.06.56
Ricochet - **Joan Regan** 11.12.53
The Riddle - **Nik Kershaw** 17.11.84
Ride A White Swan - **T.Rex** 31.10.70
Ride A Wild Horse - **Dee Clark** 18.10.75
Ride Away - **Roy Orbison** 16.09.65
Ride Like The Wind - **East Side Beat** 30.11.91
Ride On Baby - **Chris Farlowe & the Thunderbirds** 27.10.66
Ride on Time - **Black Box** 12.08.89
Riders in the Sky - **Ramrods** 23.02.61
Riders In The Sky - **Shadows** 9.02.80
Riders on the Storm - **Doors** 6.11.71
Riders On The Storm - **Doors** 27.03.76
Riders On The Storm - **Annabel Lamb** 3.09.83
Riding On A Train - **Pasadenas** 17.09.88
Right Back Where We Started From - **Maxine Nightingale** 8.11.75
Right Back Where We Started From - **Sinitta** 3.06.89
Right By Your Side - **Eurythmics** 12.11.83
Right Here, Right Now - **Jesus Jones** 6.10.90
Right Here, Right Now - **Jesus Jones** 20.07.91
Right Here Waiting - **Richard Marx** 2.09.89
Right Now - **Creatures** 23.07.83
Right Said Fred - **Bernard Cribbins** 12.07.62
The Right Stuff - **Bryan Ferry** 31.10.87
The Right Thing - **Simply Red** 21.02.87
The Right Thing To Do - **Carly Simon** 7.04.73
The Right to Love - **David Whitfield** 8.08.58
Ring My Bell - **Anita Ward** 2.06.79
Ring My Bell - **Monie Love vs Adeva** 6.04.91
Ring of Fire - **Duane Eddy** 22.06.61
Ring of Fire - **Eric Burdon & the Animals** 22.01.69
Ring of Ice - **Jennifer Rush** 21.12.85
Ring Out Solstice Bells - **Jethro Tull** 25.12.76
Ring Ring - **Abba** 20.07.74
Ring Ring Ring (Ha Ha Hey) - **De La Soul** 27.04.91
Ringo - **Lorne Greene** 24.12.64
Rio - **Michael Nesmith** 2.04.77
Rio - **Duran Duran** 13.11.82
Rip It Up - **Bill Haley & his Comets** 9.11.56
Rip It Up - **Little Richard** 14.12.56
Rip It Up - **Elvis Presley** 8.03.57
Rip It Up - **Orange Juice** 5.03.83
Rise - **Herb Alpert** 27.10.79
Rise - **Public Image Ltd** 1.02.86
Rise And Fall of Flingel Bunt - **Shadows** 7.05.64
Rise to the Occasion - **Climie Fisher** 26.12.87
Rising Sun - **Medicine Head** 4.08.73
The River - **Ken Dodd** 18.11.65
The River - **Bruce Springsteen** 27.06.81
River Deep, Mountain High - **Supremes/Four Tops** 26.06.71
River Deep Mountain High - **Ike & Tina Turner** 9.06.66
River Deep Mountain High - **Ike & Tina Turner** 19.02.69
River Stay 'Way From My Door - **Frank Sinatra** 16.06.60
Rivers of Babylon - **Boney M** 29.04.78
Road Runner - **Junior Walker & the All Stars** 9.04.69
The Road to Hell (Part 2) - **Chris Rea** 14.10.89
Road To Nowhere - **Talking Heads** 2.11.85
Road To Your Soul - **All About Eve** 30.09.89
Roadblock - **Stock Aitken Waterman** 1.08.87
Roadrunner - **Jonathan Richman** 16.07.77
Roam - **B52s** 19.05.90
Robert de Niro's Waiting - **Bananarama** 10.03.84
Robin Hood - **Gary Miller** 13.01.56
Robin Hood - **Dick James** 20.01.56
Robin's Return - **Neville Dickie** 25.10.69
Robot - **Tornados** 21.03.63
Robots - **Kraftwerk** 1.06.91
Rochdale Cowboy - **Mike Harding** 16.08.75
Rock-A-Beatin' Boogie - **Bill Haley & his Comets** 30.12.55
Rock-A-Billy - **Guy Mitchell** 26.04.57
Rock-A-Bye Your Baby - **Jerry Lewis** 8.02.57
Rock-A-Doodle-Doo - **Linda Lewis** 9.06.73
Rock-A-Hula Baby - **Elvis Presley** 1.02.62
Rock & Roll Damnation - **AC/DC** 24.06.78
Rock & Roll Music - **Beach Boys** 24.07.76
Rock & Roll Suicide - **David Bowie** 20.04.74
Rock & Roll Winter - **Wizzard** 27.04.74
Rock and Roll Waltz - **Kay Starr** 17.02.56
Rock and Roll Stage Show (LP) - **Bill Haley & his Comets** 9.11.56
Rock and Roll Part II - **Gary Glitter** 10.06.72
Rock and Roll (I Gave You The Best Years of My Life) - **Kevin Johnson** 18.01.75
Rock Around The Clock - **Bill Haley & his Comets** 7.01.55
Rock Around The Clock - **Bill Haley & his Comets** 14.10.55
Rock Around The Clock - **Bill Haley & his Comets** 10.04.68
Rock Around the Clock - **Billy Haley & the Comets** 16.03.74
Rock Around The Clock - **Telex** 4.08.79
Rock Island Line - **Lonnie Donegan** 6.01.56
Rock Island Line/Heartbreak Hotel - **Stan Freberg** 27.07.56
Rock Lobster - **B-52s** 18.08.79
Rock Lobster - **B-52s** 10.05.86
Rock Me Amadeus - **Falco** 29.03.86
Rock Me Baby - **David Cassidy** 25.11.72
Rock Me Gently - **Andy Kim** 31.08.74
Rock Me Tonight (For Old Time's Sake) - **Freddie Jackson** 8.03.86
Rock My World - **Five Star** 6.08.88
Rock 'N' Me - **Steve Miller Band** 6.11.76
Rock 'N' Roll Lady - **Showaddywaddy** 17.08.74
Rock 'N' Roll Ain't Noise Pollution - **AC/DC** 29.11.80
Rock 'N' Roll - **Status Quo** 5.12.81
Rock 'N' Roll Is King - **Electric Light Orchestra** 25.06.83
Rock 'N' Roll Children - **Dio** 17.08.85
Rock 'N' Roll Mercenaries - **Meat Loaf with John Parr** 13.09.86
Rock 'N' Soul - **Hues Corporation** 26.10.74
Rock On - **David Essex** 25.08.73
Rock On Brother - **Chequers** 18.10.75
Rock Steady - **Whispers** 13.06.87
Rock the Boat - **Hues Corporation** 27.07.74
Rock The Boat - **Forrest** 26.02.83
Rock the Casbah - **Clash** 10.07.82
Rock The Casbah - **Clash** 13.04.91
Rock The Joint - **Bill Haley & his Comets** 1.02.57
Rock the Night - **Europe** 7.02.87
Rock This Town - **Stray Cats** 7.02.81
Rock Wit'cha - **Bobby Brown** 30.09.89
Rock With the Cave Man - **Tommy Steele** 26.10.56
Rock With You - **Michael Jackson** 9.02.80
Rock Your Baby - **George McCrae** 6.07.74
Rockabilly Guy - **Polecats** 23.05.81
Rockabilly Rebel - **Matchbox** 17.11.79
Rockaria - **Electric Light Orchestra** 19.02.77
Rockbottom - **Lynsey de Paul & Mike Moran** 2.04.77
Rocket - **Mud** 27.07.74
Rocket - **Def Leppard** 11.02.89
The Rocket Man - **Spotnicks** 13.09.62
Rocket Man - **Elton John** 29.04.72
Rocket Man - **Kate Bush** 7.12.91
Rockin' All Over The World 8.10.77
Rockin' Around the Christmas Tree - **Brenda Lee** 29.11.62
Rockin' Around The Christmas Tree - **Kim Wilde & Mel Smith** 5.12.87
Rockin' Chair - **Magnum** 23.06.90
A Rockin' Good Way - **Shaky & Bonnie** 14.01.84
Rockin' Over The Beat - **Technotronic featuring Ya Kid K** 14.07.90
Rockin' Robin - **Bobby Day** 7.11.58
Rockin' Robin - **Michael Jackson** 27.05.72
Rockin' Roll Baby - **The Stylistics** 19.01.74
Rockin' Through the Rye - **Bill Haley & his Comets** 17.08.56
Rocking Goose - **Johnny & the Hurricanes** 6.10.60
Rocking Red Wing - **Sammy Masters** 9.06.60
Rockit - **Herbie Hancock** 6.08.83
Rocky - **Austin Roberts** 1.11.75
Rocky Mountain Way - **Joe Walsh** 30.07.77
Rok Da House - **Beatmasters featuring the Cookie Crew** 16.01.88
Roll Away The Stone - **Mott the Hoople** 24.11.73
Roll On Down The Highway - **Bachman-Turner Overdrive** 8.02.75
Roll Over Beethoven - **Electric Light Orchestra** 27.01.73
Roll Over Lay Down - **Status Quo** 17.05.75
A Roller Skating Jam Named Saturdays - **De La Soul** 3.08.91
Rollin' Home - **Status Quo** 17.05.86
Rollin' In My 5.0 - **Vanilla Ice** 29.06.91
Rollin' Stone - **David Essex** 12.07.75

Romantic - **Karyn White** 17.08.91
Romantica - **Jane Morgan** 21.07.60
Romeo - **Petula Clark** 13.07.61
Romeo - **Mr Big** 12.02.77
Romeo & Juliet - **Dire Straits** 24.01.81
Rondo - **Kenny Ball & his Jazzmen** 20.06.63
Roni - **Bobby Brown** 25.11.89
Roobarb and Custard - **Shaft** 21.12.91
Room At the Top - **Adam Ant** 17.02.90
Room In Your Heart - **Living In A Box** 30.09.89
Rooms on Fire - **Stevie Nicks** 6.05.89
Rosalie - **Thin Lizzy** 20.05.78
Rosanna - **Toto** 16.04.83
Rose Garden - **Lynn Anderson** 20.02.71
Rose Garden - **New World** 27.02.71
A Rose Has To Die - **Dooleys** 9.09.78
Rose Marie - **Slim Whitman** 15.07.55
Roses - **Haywoode** 5.07.86
Roses Are Red - **Ronnie Carroll** 9.08.62
Roses Are Red - **Mac Band featuring the McCampbell Brothers** 2.07.88
Roses of Picardy - **Vince Hill** 18.05.67
Rosetta - **Fame & Price Together** 17.04.71
Rosie - **Don Partridge** 7.02.68
Rough Boy - **ZZ Top** 10.05.86
Rough Boys - **Pete Townshend** 26.04.80
Rough Justice - **Bananarama** 9.06.84
Roulette - **Russ Conway** 15.05.59
Round and Around - **Jaki Graham** 6.07.85
Round and Round - **Jimmy Young** 3.05.57
Round and Round - **Spandau Ballet** 8.12.84
Round and Round - **New Order** 11.03.89
The Roussos Phenomenon - **Demis Roussos** 26.06.76
Roxanne - **The Police** 5.05.79
Royal Event - **Russ Conway** 10.03.60
R.S.V.P. - **Jason Donovan** 18.05.91
Rubber Ball - **Marty Wilde** 26.01.61
Rubber Ball - **Bobby Vee** 26.01.61
Rubber Ball - **Avons** 26.01.61
Rubber Band Man - **Detroit Spinners** 25.09.76
Rubber Bullets **10CC** 26.05.73
Ruby Ann - **Marty Robbins** 17.01.63
Ruby Don't Take Your Love To Town - **Kenny Rogers & the First Edition** 8.11.69
Rudi's In Love - **Locomotive** 23.10.68
Rudy's Rock - **Bill Haley & his Comets** 23.11.56
Ruff Mix - **Wonder Dogs** 11.09.82
Rumors - **Timex Social Club** 13.09.86
Rumour Has It - **Donna Summer** 25.02.78
Run - **Sandie Shaw** 15.09.66
Run Baby Run/Am I Not My Brother's Keeper - **Newbeats** 30.10.71
Run Back - **Carl Douglas** 10.12.77
Run For Home - **Lindisfarne** 24.06.78
Run For Your Life - **Bucks Fizz** 12.03.83
Run Rudolph Run - **Chuck Berry** 19.12.63
Run Run Run - **Jo Jo Gunne** 1.04.72
Run Runaway - **Slade** 11.02.84
Run to Him - **Bobby Vee** 26.12.61
Run to Me - **Bee Gees** 29.07.72
Run To My Lovin' Arms - **Billy Fury** 16.09.65
Run To The Door - **Clinton Ford** 9.02.67
Run To The Hills - **Iron Maiden** 20.02.82
Run To The Hills (Live) - **Iron Maiden** 14.12.85
Run To You - **Bryan Adams** 26.01.85
Runaround Sue - **Dion** 2.11.61
Runaround Sue - **Doug Sheldon** 16.11.61
Runaround Sue - **Racey** 27.12.80
Runaway - **Del Shannon** 4.05.61
Runaway Boys - **Stray Cats** 6.12.80
Runaway Horses - **Belinda Carlisle** 10.03.90
The Runner - **Three Degrees** 31.03.79
Runnin' Away - **Sly & the Family Stone** 22.04.72
Running All Over The World - **Status Quo** 20.08.88
Running Bear - **Johnny Preston** 12.02.60
Running Free - **Iron Maiden** 1.03.80
Running Free - **Iron Maiden** 5.10.85
Running in the Family - **Level 42** 14.02.87
Running Out of Time - **Digital Orgasm** 14.12.91
Running Scared - **Roy Orbison** 25.05.61
Running Up That Hill - **Kate Bush** 17.08.85
Running With The Night - **Lionel Richie** 7.01.84
Run's House - **Run DMC** 28.05.88
Rupert - **Jackie Lee** 9.01.71
Rush Hour - **Jane Wiedlin** 20.08.88
Rush Rush - **Paula Abdul** 22.06.91
Russians - **Sting** 21.12.85
S-S-S- Single Bed - **Fox** 17.04.76
Sabre Dance - **Love Sculpture** 27.11.68
Sacramento - **Middle of the Road** 8.04.72
Sacrifice/Healing Hands - **Elton John** 9.06.90
Sad Eyes - **Robert John** 3.11.79
Sad Songs (Say So Much) - **Elton John** 2.06.84
Sad Sweet Dreamer - **Sweet Sensation** 21.09.74
Saddle Up - **David Christie** 4.09.82
Sadie's Shawl - **Frank Cordell** 24.08.56
Sadness Part I - **Enigma** 15.12.90
Safe From Harm - **Massive Attack** 15.06.91
The Safety Dance - **Men Without Hats** 15.10.83
Sail On - **Commodores** 8.09.79
Sailing - **Rod Stewart** 16.08.75
Sailing - **Rod Stewart** 11.09.76
Sailing On The Seven Seas - **Orchestral Manoeuvres In The Dark** 13.04.91
Sailor - **Petula Clark** 26.01.61
Sailor - **Anne Shelton** 26.01.61
Saints Rock and Roll - **Bill Haley & his Comets** 25.05.56
Sally - **Gerry Monroe** 23.05.70
Sally Ann - **Joe Brown** 3.10.63
Sally Don't You Grieve/Betty Betty - **Lonnie Donegan** 11.07.58
Sal's Got A Sugar Lip - **Lonnie Donegan** 11.09.59
Saltwater - **Julian Lennon** 14.09.91
Sam - **Keith West** 29.11.67
Sam - **Olivia Newton-John** 11.06.77
Samantha - **Kenny Ball and his Jazz Band** 23.02.61
Samba Pa Ti - **Santana** 5.10.74
Same Old Scene - **Roxy Music** 8.11.80
Same Old Story - **Ultravox** 27.09.86
Samson and Delilah - **Middle of the Road** 5.08.72
San Antonio Rose - **Floyd Cramer** 10.08.61
San Bernadino - **Christie** 31.10.70
San Damiano (Heart and Soul) - **Sal Solo** 5.01.85
San Franciscan Nights - **Eric Burdon** 18.10.67
San Francisco (Be Sure to Wear Some Flowers In Your Hair) - **Scott McKenzie** 12.07.67
San Miguel - **Kingston Trio** 4.12.59
San Miguel - **Lonnie Donegan** 4.12.59
Sanctify Yourself - **Simple Minds** 1.02.86
Sanctuary - **Iron Maiden** 7.06.80
Sanctuary - **New Musik** 26.07.80
Sanctus - **Troubadours Due Roi Baudouin** 26.03.69
Sandy - **John Travolta** 7.10.78
Santa Bring My Baby Back to Me - **Elvis Presley** 15.11.57
Santa Claus Is Comin' To Town/My Hometown - **Bruce Springsteen** 14.12.85
Santa Claus Is On The Dole/First Atheist Tabernacle Choir - **Spitting Image** 20.12.86
Santa Clause Is Comin' To Town - **Carpenters** 27.12.75
Santo Natale - **David Whitfield** 12.11.54
Sarah - **Thin Lizzy** 10.11.79
Sarah - **Fleetwood Mac** 19.01.80
Sat In Your Lap - **Kate Bush** 11.07.81
Satan - **Orbital** 19.01.91
Satellite - **Hooters** 28.11.87
Satellite Kid - **Dogs D'Amour** 5.08.89
Satisfaction - **Aretha Franklin** 24.01.68
Satisfaction - **Wendy & Lisa** 29.07.89
Satisfaction - **Vanilla Ice** 20.08.91
Satisfaction Guaranteed - **Harold Melvin & the Bluenotes** 20.04.74
Satisfy My Soul - **Bob Marley & the Wailers** 17.06.78
Satsifaction - **Otis Redding** 7.04.66
Saturday Love - **Cherelle with Alexander O'Neal** 28.12.85
Saturday Night At The Duck Pond - **Cougars** 28.02.63
Saturday Night's Alright for Fighting - **Elton John** 7.07.73
Saturday Nite - **Earth Wind & Fire** 19.02.77
The Savage - **Shadows** 16.11.61
Save A Prayer - **Duran Duran** 21.08.82
Save Me - **Dave Dee Dozy Beaky Mick & Tich** 8.12.66
Save Me - **Silver Convention** 26.04.75
Save Me - **Queen** 2.02.80
Save The Last Dance For Me - **Drifters** 3.11.60
Save Up All Your Tears - **Cher** 19.10.91
Save Your Kisses For Me - **Brotherhood of Man** 13.03.76
Save Your Love - **Renee & Renato** 13.11.82

Saved By The Bell - **Robin Gibb** 9.07.69
Saving All My Love For You - **Whitney Houston** 23.11.85
Saviour's Day - **Cliff Richard** 8.12.90
Say A Little Prayer - **Bomb The Bass featuring Maureen** 26.11.88
Say, Has Anyone Seen My Sweet Gypsy Rose - **Dawn** 11.08.73
Say Hello Wave Goodbye - **Soft Cell** 6.02.82
Say Hello Wave Goodbye '91 - **Soft Cell with Marc Almond** 23.03.91
Say I Won't Be There - **Springfields** 28.03.63
Say I'm Your Number One - **Princess** 10.08.85
Say It Again - **Jermaine Stewart** 23.01.88
Say It With Flowers - **Dorothy Squires & Russ Conway** 24.08.61
Say No Go - **De La Soul** 8.07.89
Say Say Say - **Paul McCartney and Michael Jackson** 15.10.83
Say When - **Lene Lovich** 19.05.79
Say Wonderful Things - **Ronnie Carroll** 7.03.63
Say Yeah - **Limit** 12.01.85
Say You Don't Mind - **Colin Blunstone** 19.02.72
Say You Love Me - **Fleetwood Mac** 27.11.76
Say You Really Want Me - **Kim Wilde** 15.08.87
Say You Say Me - **Lionel Richie** 16.11.85
Say You'll Stay Until Tomorrow - **Tom Jones** 23.04.77
(Say) You're My Girl - **Roy Orbison** 29.07.65
Say You're Mine Again - **June Hutton** 7.08.53
Scales of Justice - **Living In A Box** 20.06.87
Scandal - **Queen** 21.10.89
Scarlet - **All About Eve** 28.04.90
Scarlet Ribbons - **Harry Belafonte** 6.09.57
Scarlett O'Hara - **Jet Harris & Tony Meehan** 25.04.63
Scary Monsters (And Super Creeps) - **David Bowie** 17.01.81
School Day - **Chuck Berry** 21.06.57
School Day - **Don Lang** 5.07.57
School Love - **Barry Blue** 9.03.74
Schools Out - **Alice Cooper** 22.07.72
Scotch On The Rocks - **Band Of The Black Watch** 6.09.75
A Scottish Soldier - **Andy Stewart** 19.01.61
The Scratch - **Surface Noise** 7.06.80
Scream Until You Like It - **W.A.S.P.** 5.09.87
Scullery - **Clifford T Ward** 16.02.74
Sea of Heartbreak - **Don Gibson** 31.08.61
Sea of Love - **Marty Wilde** 25.09.59
Seagull - **Rainbow Cottage** 13.03.76
Seagull - **Rainbow Cottage** 27.03.76
Seal Our Fate - **Gloria Estefan** 20.04.91
Sealed With A Kiss - **Brian Hyland** 9.08.62
Sealed With A Kiss - **Brian Hyland** 5.07.75
Sealed With A Kiss - **Jason Donovan** 10.06.89
Searchin' - **Coasters** 27.09.57
Searchin' - **Hollies** 5.09.63
Searchin' (I Gotta Find A Man) - **Hazell Dean** 12.05.84
Searching - **Change** 13.09.80
Seaside Shuffle - **Terry Dactyl & the Dinosaurs** 15.07.72
Seasons in the Sun - **Terry Jacks** 23.03.74
Seasons of Gold - **Gidea Park** 29.09.81
Second Hand Rose - **Barbra Streisand** 27.01.66
The Second Summer of Love - **Danny Wilson** 8.07.89
The Second Time - **Kim Wilde** 20.10.84
Secret - **Orchestral Manoeuvres In The Dark** 27.07.85
Secret Garden - **T'Pau** 1.10.88
Secret Love - **Doris Day** 2.04.54
Secret Love - **Kathy Kirby** 7.11.63
Secret Love - **Bee Gees** 9.03.91
Secret Lovers - **Atlantic Starr** 22.03.86
Secret Rendezvous - **Karyn White** 23.09.89
Secrets - **Sutherland Brothers & Quiver** 4.12.76
The Secrets That You Keep - **Mud** 15.02.75
See Emily Play - **Pink Floyd** 29.06.67
See My Baby Jive - **Wizzard** 21.04.73
See My Friend - **Kinks** 5.08.65
See The Day - **Dee C Lee** 16.11.85
See The Lights - **Simple Minds** 25.05.91
See Those Eyes - **Altered Images** 3.04.82
See You - **Depeche Mode** 13.02.82
See You Later, Alligator - **Billy Haley & his Comets** 9.03.56
The Seeker - **Who** 18.04.70
Self! - **We've Got A Fuzzbox & We're Gonna Use It** 12.08.89
Self Control - **Laura Branigan** 28.07.84
Semi-Detached Suburban Mr. James - **Manfred Mann** 27.10.66
Send In The Clowns - **Judy Collins** 17.05.75
Send Me An Angel - **Scorpions** 30.11.91
Send Me The Pillow You Dream On - **Johnny Tillotson** 11.10.62
Sending Out An S.O.S. - **Retta Young** 31.05.75
Senses Working Overtime - **XTC** 30.1.82.
Sensitivity - **Ralph Tresvant** 19.01.91
The Sensual World - **Kate Bush** 30.09.89
Senza Una Donna (Without A Woman) - **Zucchero featuring Paul Young** 13.04.91
Separate Lives - **Phil Collins & Marilyn Martin** 23.11.85
September - **Earth Wind & Fire** 16.12.78
September in the Rain - **Dinah Washington** 7.12.61
Serenade - **Mario Lanza** 22.04.55
Serenade - **Slim Whitman** 22.06.56
Serious - **Donna Allen** 16.05.87
Set Adrift on Memory Bliss - **PM Dawn** 17.08.91
Set Me Free - **Kinks** 27.05.65
Set Me Free - **Jaki Graham** 17.05.86
Seven Daffodils - **Cherokees** 17.09.64
Seven Daffodils - **Mojos** 17.09.64
Seven Days - **Anne Shelton** 13.04.56
Seven Drunken Nights - **Dubliners** 30.03.67
747 (Strangers In The Night) - **Saxon** 21.06.80
Seven Little Girls Sitting In The Back Seat - **Avons** 13.11.59
Seven Little Girls Sitting In the Back Seat - **Paul Evans & the Curls** 27.11.59
Seven Little Girls Sitting in The Back Seat - **Bombalurina** 24.11.90
Seven Lonely Days - **Gisele McKenzie** 17.07.53
7 O'clock - **Quireboys** 11.11.89
Seven Rooms of Gloom - **Four Tops** 15.06.67
Seven Seas - **Echo & the Bunnymen** 14.07.84
Seven Seas of Rhye - **Queen** 16.03.74
7,000 Dollars And You - **Stylistics** 9.04.77
7 Ways To Love - **Cola Boy** 6.07.91
7Teen - **Regents** 19.01.80
Seven Tears - **Goombay Dance Band** 6.03.82
Seventeen - **Frankie Vaughan** 2.12.55
Seventeen - **Boyd Bennett** 23.12.55
Seventh Son - **Georgie Fame** 20.12.69
76 Trombones - **King Brothers** 2.03.61
Severina - **Mission** 14.03.87
The Sex of It - **Kid Creole & the Coconuts** 28.04.90
Sex Talk (Live) - **T'Pau** 2.04.88
Sexcrime (Nineteen Eighty Four) - **Eurythmics** 17.11.84
(Sexual) Healing - **Marvin Gaye** 6.11.82
Sexuality - **Billy Bragg** 6.07.91
Sexy - **M.F.S.B.** 2.08.75
Sexy Eyes - **Dr. Hook** 29.03.80
Sexy Girl - **Lillo Thomas** 21.03.87
Sgt. Rock (Is Going to Help Me) - **XTC** 31.01.81
Sh-Boom - **Crew Cuts** 1.10.54
Sh-Boom - **Stan Freberg** 19.11.54
Sha-La-La (Make Me Happy) - **Al Green** 23.11.74
Sha La La - **Manfred Mann** 22.10.64
Sha La La La Lee - **Small Faces** 10.02.66
Sha La La La Lee - **Plastic Bertrand** 12.08.78
Shaddap You Face - **Joe Dolce Music Theatre** 7.02.81
The Shadow of Love - **Damned** 22.06.85
Shake - **Otis Redding** 22.06.67
Shake it Down - **Mud** 15.05.76
Shake Me I Rattle - **Kaye Sisters** 3.01.58
(Shake, Shake, Shake) Shake Your Booty - **KC & the Sunshine Band** 24.07.76
Shake The Disease - **Depeche Mode** 11.05.85
Shake You Down - **Gregory Abbott** 29.11.86
Shake Your Body (Down To The Ground) - **Jacksons** 31.03.79
Shake Your Foundations - **AC/DC** 18.01.86
Shake Your Groove Thing - **Peaches & Herb** 3.02.79
Shake Your Love - **Debbie Gibson** 23.01.88
Shake Your Thang (It's Your Thing) - **Salt-N-Pepa featuring EU** 10.09.88
Shakespeare's Sister - **Smiths** 30.03.85
The Shakin' Stevens EP - **Shakin' Stevens** 11.12.82
Shaking All Over - **Johnny Kidd & the Pirates** 23.06.60
Shame - **Evelyn 'Champagne' King** 22.07.78
Shame and Scandal In The Family - **Lance Percival** 4.11.65
Shame on You - **Gun** 14.07.90
Shame Shame Shame - **Shirley & Company** 8.02.75
Shang-A-Lang - **Bay City Rollers** 27.04.74
Shannon - **Henry Gross** 4.09.76
Shapes of Things - **Yardbirds** 3.03.66
Sharing You - **Bobby Vee** 14.06.62
Sharp Dressed Man - **ZZ Top** 12.01.85
Shattered Dreams - **Johnny Hates Jazz** 2.05.87
Shazam! - **Duane Eddy** 28.04.60

She - **Charles Aznavour** 22.06.74
She Ain't Worth It - **Glenn Medeiros featuring Bobby Brown** 30.06.90
She Bangs The Drums - **Stone Roses** 29.07.89
She Bangs The Drums - **Stone Roses** 31.03.90
She Comes In The Fall - **Inspiral Carpets** 30.06.90
She Don't Fool Me - **Status Quo** 19.06.82
She Drives Me Crazy - **Fine Young Cannibals** 7.01.89
She Loves You - **Beatles** 29.08.63
She Makes My Day - **Robert Palmer** 22.10.88
She Means Nothing To Me - **Phil Everly and Cliff Richard** 19.02.83
She Needs Love - **Wayne Fontana & the Mindbenders** 7.10.65
She Sells Sanctuary - **Cult** 29.06.85
She She Little Sheila - **Gene Vincent** 22.06.61
She Sold Me Magic - **Lou Christie** 27.12.69
She Wants to Dance With Me - **Rick Astley** 24.09.88
She Wears My Ring - **Solomon King** 3.01.68
She Wears Red Feathers - **Guy Mitchell** 13.02.53
She Won't Talk To Me - **Luther Vandross** 4.02.89
She Works Hard For The Money - **Donna Summer** 25.06.83
She'd Rather Be With Me - **Turtles** 15.06.67
Sheena Is A Punk Rocker - **Ramones** 21.05.77
Sheila - **Tommy Roe** 13.09.62
Sheila Take A Bow - **Smiths** 25.04.87
Shellshock - **New Order** 29.03.86
Sheriff Fatman - **Carter The Unstoppable Sex Machine** 22.06.91
Sherry - **Four Seasons** 11.10.62
Sherry - **Adrian Baker** 26.07.75
She's A Bad Mama Jama (She's Built She's Stacked) - **Carl Carlton** 25.07.81
She's A Lady - **Tom Jones** 23.01.71
She's A Little Angel - **Little Angels** 4.08.90
She's A Mystery To Me - **Roy Orbison** 1.04.89
She's A Windup - **Dr. Feelgood** 24.09.77
She's A Windup - **Dr. Feelgood** 8.10.77
She's A Winner - **Intruders** 13.07.74
She's A Woman - **Scritti Politti featuring Shabba Ranks** 23.03.91
She's About A Mover - **Sir Douglas Quintet** 17.06.65
She's Got Claws - **Gary Numan** 29.08.81
She's Got It - **Little Richard** 8.03.57
She's In Love With You - **Suzi Quatro** 27.10.79
She's In Parties - **Bauhaus** 16.04.83
She's Like the Wind - **Patrick Swayze featuring Wendy Fraser** 16.04.88
She's Mine - **Cameo** 24.10.87
She's Not There - **Zombies** 13.08.64
She's Not There - **Neil MacArthur** 12.02.69
She's Not There - **Santana** 29.10.77
She's Not There/Kicks EP - **UK Subs** 8.12.79
She's Not You - **Elvis Presley** 30.08.62
She's On It - **Beastie Boys** 25.07.87
She's Out Of My Life - **Michael Jackson** 10.05.80
(She's) Sexy And 17 - **Stray Cats** 27.08.83
She's So Beautiful - **Cliff Richard** 14.09.85
She's So Cold - **Rolling Stones** 18.10.80
She's So Fine - **Thunder** 29.09.90
She's So Modern - **Boomtown Rats** 15.04.78
She's Strange - **Cameo** 7.04.84
She's Strange - **Cameo** 7.12.85
Shifting Whispering Sands - **Eamonn Andrews** 20.01.56
Shifting Whispering Sands - **Billy Vaughn** 27.01.56
Shindig - **Shadows** 19.09.63
Shine - **Joe Brown & his Bruvvers** 2.02.61
Shine A Little Love - **Electric Light Orchestra** 19.05.79
Shine On - **House of Love** 3.02.90
Shine On Silver Sun - **Strawbs** 13.10.73
Shining Star - **INXS** 2.11.91
Shiny Happy People - **R.E.M.** 18.05.91
Shiny Shiny - **Haysi Fantayzee** 5.02.83
Ship of Fools - **Erasure** 5.03.88
Shipbuilding - **Robert Wyatt** 21.05.83
Ships In The Night - **Be-Bop Deluxe** 6.03.76
Shiralee - **Tommy Steele** 30.08.58
Shirley - **Shakin' Stevens** 24.04.82
Shiver - **George Benson** 29.11.86
Sho' You Right - **Barry White** 14.11.87
Shocked - **Kylie Minogue** 1.06.91
Shoo Doo Fu Fu Ooh - **Lenny Williams** 12.11.77
Shoop Shoop Song (It's In His Kiss) - **Cher** 20.04.91
Shoorah! Shoorah! - **Betty Wright** 25.01.75
Shooting Star - **Dollar** 18.11.78
Shoplifters of the World Unite - **Smiths** 7.02.87
Short Fat Fanny - **Larry Williams** 20.09.57
Shortnin' Bread - **Viscounts** 20.10.60
Shot In The Dark - **Ozzy Osbourne** 1.02.86
Shotgun Wedding - **Roy C.** 2.12.72
Shotgun Wedding - **Roy C** 28.04.66
Should I Stay Or Should I Go? - **Clash** 2.03.91
Shout - **Lulu & the Luvvers** 21.05.64
Shout - **Tears for Fears** 8.12.84
Shout - **Lulu** 2.08.86
Shout Shout (Knock Yourself Out) - **Rocky Sharpe and the Replays** 1.05.82
Shout to the Top - **Style Council** 13.10.84
The Show - **Rebecca Storm** 31.08.85
The Show - **Doug E Fresh & the Get Fresh Crew** 9.11.85
Show Me - **Dexy's Midnight Runners** 18.07.81
Show Me Girl - **Herman's Hermits** 19.11.64
Show Me Heaven - **Maria McKee** 15.09.90
Show Me The Way - **Peter Frampton** 15.05.76
Show Me You're A Woman - **Mud** 29.11.75
The Show Must Go On - **Leo Sayer** 15.12.73
The Show Must Go On - **Queen** 26.10.91
Show You The Way To Go - **The Jacksons** 4.06.77
Showdown - **Electric Light Orchestra** 13.10.73
Showing Out (Get Fresh At The Weekend) - **Mel & Kim** 25.10.86
Showroom Dummies - **Kraftwerk** 20.02.82
The Shuffle - **Van McCoy** 23.04.77
Shut Up - **Madness** 26.09.81
Shy Boy - **Bananarama** 10.07.82
Shy Girl - **Mark Wynter** 13.06.63
Si Si Je Suis Un Rock Star - **Bill Wyman** 1.08.81
Si Tu Dois Partir - **Fairport Convention** 9.08.69
Sick and Tired - **Fats Domino** 4.07.58
Sick Of It - **Primitives** 29.07.89
Side by Side - **Kay Starr** 24.04.53
Side Saddle - **Russ Conway** 20.02.59
Side Show - **Barry Biggs** 18.12.76
Sidewalking - **Jesus & Mary Chain** 9.04.88
Sign 'O' The Times - **Prince** 14.03.87
Sign Of The Times - **Bryan Ferry** 26.08.78
Sign Of The Times - **Belle Stars** 22.01.83
Sign Your Name - **Terence Trent D'Arby** 9.01.88
Signature Tune of 'The Army Game' - **Michael Medwin, Bernard Bresslaw, Alfie Bass & Leslie Fyson** 30.05.58
Signed, Sealed, Delivered, I'm Yours - **Stevie Wonder** 18.07.70
Silence Is Golden 27.04.67
Silent Lucidity - **Queensryche** 27.04.91
Silent Night - **Bing Crosby** 19.12.52
Silent Running (On Dangerous Ground) - **Mike & the Mechanics** 1.03.86
Silent Voice - **Innocence** 28.07.90
Silhouettes - **Herman's Hermits** 25.02.65
Silhouettes - **Cliff Richard** 25.08.90
Silly Games - **Janet Kay** 23.06.79
Silly Games - **Lindy Layton featuring Janet Kay** 18.08.90
Silly Love - **10cc** 14.09.74
Silly Love Songs - **Wings** 15.05.76
Silly Thing/Who Killed Bambi - **Sex Pistols/Ten Pole Tudor** 7.04.79
Silver - **Echo & the Bunnymen** 20.04.84
Silver Dream Machine - **David Essex** 5.04.80
Silver Lady - **David Soul** 27.08.77
Silver Machine - **Hawkwind** 8.07.72
Silver Machine - **Hawkwind** 28.10.78
Silver Star - **Four Seasons** 24.04.76
Silvery Rain - **Cliff Richard** 10.04.71
Simon Says - **1910 Fruitgum Co** 27.03.68
Simon Smith and the Amazing Dancing Bear - **Alan Price Set** 9.03.67
Simon Templar/Two Pints of Lager and A Packet of Crisps Please - **Spolodgenessa-bounds** 21.06.80
Simple Game - **Four Tops** 2.10.71
Simple Truth - **Chris De Burgh** 25.05.91
Sin - **Nine Inch Nails** 16.11.91
Since I Don't Have You - **Art Garfunkel** 28.07.79
Since Yesterday - **Strawberry Switchblade** 12.01.85
Since You're Gone - **Cars** 12.06.82
Since You've Been Gone - **Rainbow** 15.09.79
Sincerely - **McGuire Sisters** 15.07.55
Sinful - **Pete Wylie** 17.05.86
Sinful!(Scary Jiggin' With Doctor Love) - **Pete Wylie & the Farm** 13.04.91
Sing A Happy Song - **George McCrae** 29.03.75
Sing A Happy Song - **O'Jays** 13.10.79
Sing A Little Song - **Desmond Dekker** 30.08.75

Sing A Song of Freedom - **Cliff Richard** 20.11.71
Sing Baby Sing - **Stylistics** 10.05.75
Sing Don't Speak - **Blackfoot Sue** 13.01.81
Sing It Again With Joe - **Joe 'Mr. Piano' Henderson** 2.09.55
Sing It With Joe - **Joe 'Mr. Piano' Henderson** 3.06.55
Sing Like An Angel - **Jerry Lordan** 2.06.60
Sing Little Birdie - **Teddy Johnson & Pearl Carr** 20.3.59
Sing Me - **The Brothers** 29.01.77
Sing Me An Old Fashioned Song - **Billie Jo Spears** 25.12.76
Sing Our Own Song - **UB40** 12.07.86
Sing Your Life - **Morrissey** 13.04.91
Singalong-A-Santa - **Santa Claus & the Christmas Trees** 18.12.82
Singalong-A-Santa Again - **Santa Claus and the Christmas Trees** 24.12.83
Singin' In The Rain - **Sheila & B. Devotion** 25.03.78
Singing Dogs - **Singing Dogs** 25.11.55
Singing The Blues - **Guy Mitchell** 7.12.56
Singing The Blues - **Tommy Steele** 14.12.56
Singing The Blues - **Dave Edmunds** 16.02.80
Single Girl - **Sandy Posey** 12.01.67
Single Girl - **Sandy Posey** 13.09.75
Single Life - **Cameo** 21.09.85
Sins of The Family - **P.F. Sloan** 4.11.65
Sippin' Soda - **Guy Mitchell** 26.02.54
Sir Duke - **Stevie Wonder** 9.04.77
Sirdancealot - **Olympic Runners** 3.02.79
Sister - **Bros** 16.12.89
Sister Jane - **New World** 13.05.72
Sister of Mercy - **Thompson Twins** 7.07.84
Sister Surprise - **Gary Numan** 22.10.83
Sisters Are Doin' It For Themselves - **Eurythmics & Aretha Franklin** 2.11.85
Sit and Wait - **Sydney Youngblood** 9.12.89
Sit Down - **James** 30.03.91
(Sittin' On) The Dock of The Bay - **Otis Redding** 21.02.68
Sittin' On A Fence - **Twice As Much** 16.06.66
Sitting In The Park - **Georgie Fame** 5.01.67
Situation - **Yazoo** 8.12.90
Six Pack - **Police** 14.06.80
634-5789 - **Wilson Picket** 24.03.66
The Six Teens - **Sweet** 13.07.74
Sixteen - **Musical Youth** 21.01.84
16 Bars - **Stylistics** 14.08.76
Sixteen Reasons - **Connie Stevens** 19.05.60
Sixteen Tons - **Frankie Laine** 20.01.56
68 Guns - **Alarm** 1.10.83
Sixteen Tons - **Tennessee Ernie Ford** 6.01.56
Sixty Minute Man - **Trammps** 8.02.75
The Size of A Cow - **Wonder Stuff** 13.04.91
Skateaway - **Dire Straits** 11.04.81
Skiffle Session (EP) - **Lonnie Donegan** 6.07.56
Skiing In The Snow - **Wigans Ovation** 22.03.75
Skin Deep - **Ted Heath Orchestra** 12.02.54
Skin Deep - **Duke Ellington** 5.03.54
Skin Deep - **Stranglers** 6.10.84
Skin Trade - **Duran Duran** 21.02.87
Skweeze Me Pleeze Me - **Slade** 30.06.73
A Sky Blue Shirt and A Rainbow Tie - **Norman Brooks** 12.11.54
Sky High - **Jigsaw** 8.11.75
Sky Pilot - **Eric Burdon** 28.02.68
The Skye Boat Song - **Roger Whittaker & Des O'Connor** 22.11.86
Skywriter - **Jakcson Five** 8.09.73
Slabama Jubilee - **Ferko String Band** 12.08.55
Slap and Tickle - **Squeeze** 15.09.79
Slave to Love - **Bryan Ferry** 11.05.85
Slave to The Rhythm - **Grace Jones** 12.10.85
Sledgehammer - **Peter Gabriel** 3.05.86
Sleep Talk - **Alyson Williams** 11.03.89
Sleep Walk - **Santo & Johnny** 16.10.59
Sleep Walk - **Ultravox** 26.07.80
Sleep With Me - **Birdland** 3.02.90
Sleeping Bag - **ZZ Top** 19.10.85
Sleepy Joe - **Herman's Hermits** 1.05.68
The Slightest Touch - **Five Star** 18.04.87
Slip and Slide - **Medicine Head** 16.02.74
Slip Slidin' Away - **Paul Simon** 17.12.77
Sloop John B - **Beach Boys** 21.04.66
Slow Boat to China - **Emile Ford & the Checkmates** 5.02.60
Slow Down - **John Miles** 25.06.77
Slow Down - **Loose Ends** 20.09.86
Slow Hand - **Pointer Sisters** 29.08.81
Slow Motion - **Ultravox** 28.03.81
Slow Twistin' - **Chubby Checker** 12.04.62
Small Sad Sam - **Phil McLean** 18.01.62
Smalltown Boy - **Bronski Beat** 2.06.84
Smalltown Boy (1991 Remix) - **Jimmy Somerville with Bronski Beat** 9.02.91
Smarty Pants - **First Choice** 4.08.73
Smash It Up - **Damned** 27.10.79
Smells Like Teen Spirit - **Nirvana** 30.11.91
Smile - **Nat 'King' Cole** 10.9.54
Smile - **Pussycat** 15.01.77
Smile - **Audrey Hall** 12.07.86
Smoke Gets In Your Eyes - **Platters** 16.01.59
Smoke Gets In Your Eyes - **Blue Haze** 25.03.72
Smoke Gets In Your Eyes - **Bryan Ferry** 7.09.74
Smoke On The Water - **Deep Purple** 23.04.77
Smoke On The Water - **Rock Aid Armenia** 30.12.89
Smokey Blues Away - **New Generation** 10.07.68
Smokin' In The Boys Room - **Brownsville Station** 9.03.74
Smooth Criminal - **Michael Jackson** 26.11.88
Smooth Operator - **Sade** 22.09.84
Smuggler's Blues - **Glenn Frey** 29.06.85
Smurf Song - **Father Abraham & the Smurfs** 10.06.78
Snake In The Grass - **Dave Dee, Dozy, Beaky, Mick & Tich** 14.05.69
Snap! Megamix - **Snap!** 30.03.91
Snappiness - **BBG** 5.05.90
Snooker Loopy - **Matchroom Mob with Chas & Dave** 10.05.86
Snoopy Versus the Red Baron - **Hot Shots** 2.06.73
Snoopy vs The Red Baron - **Royal Guardsmen** 26.01.67
Snot Rap - **Kenny Everett** 2.04.83
Snow Coach - **Russ Conway** 13.11.59
Snowbird - **Anne Murray** 31.10.70
Snowbound for Christmas - **Dickie Valentine** 27.12.57
So Amazing - **Luther Vandross** 21.11.87
So Cold The Night - **Communards** 29.11.86
So Deep Is The Night - **Ken Dodd** 3.12.64
So Do I - **Kenny Ball & his Jazzmen** 23.08.62
So Emotional - **Whitney Houston** 14.11.87
So Far Away - **Dire Straits** 20.04.85
So Good - **Roy Orbison** 2.03.67
So Good To Be Back Home Again - **Tourists** 16.02.80
So Hard - **Pet Shop Boys** 6.10.90
So Here I am - **UB40** 4.09.82
So In Love - **Orchestral Manoeuvres In The Dark** 25.05.85
So In Love With You - **Spear of Destiny** 8.10.88
So It Will Always Be - **Everly Brothers** 28.03.63
So Lonely - **Police** 23.02.80
So Long Baby - **Del Shannon** 7.12.61
So Macho/Cruising - **Sinitta** 19.07.86
So Much In Love - **Tymes** 1.08.63
So Much Love - **Tony Blackburn** 30.01.68
So Near to Christmas - **Alvin Stardust** 22.12.84
So Real - **Love Decade** 23.11.91
So Sad The Song - **Gladys Knight & the Pips** 13.11.76
So Tell Me Why - **Poison** 23.11.91
So The Story Goes - **Living In A Box featuring Bobby Womack** 24.10.87
So This Is Romance - **Linx** 12.09.81
So Tired - **Frankie Vaughan** 15.11.67
So Tired - **Ozzy Osbourne** 2.06.84
So You Win Again - **Hot Chocolate** 18.06.77
Softly As I Leave You - **Matt Monro** 15.02.62
Softly Softly - **Ruby Murray** 28.01.55
Softly Whispering I Love You - **Congregation** 4.12.71
Softly Whispering I Love You - **Paul Young** 12.05.90
Solace of You - **Living Color** 8.06.91
Sold - **Boy George** 18.07.87
Sold My Soul for Rock 'N' Roll - **Linda And the Funky Boys** 19.06.76
Soldier Blue - **Buffy Sainte-Marie** 31.07.71
Soldier Boy - **Shirelles** 7.06.62
Soldier Boy - **Cheetahs** 28.01.65
Soldier of Love - **Donny Osmond** 27.08.88
Solid - **Ashford & Simpson** 19.01.85
A Solid Bond In Your Heart - **Style Council** 19.11.83
Solid Gold Easy Action - **T.Rex** 9.12.72
Solitaire - **Carpenters** 5.01.74
Solitaire - **Carpenters** 6.09.75
Solsbury Hill - **Peter Gabriel** 16.04.77
Some Candy Talking - **Jesus & Mary Chain** 26.07.86
Some Day We're Gonna Love Again - **Searchers** 16.07.64
Some Girls - **Racey** 31.03.79

Some Guys Have All The Luck - **Robert Palmer** 27.02.82
Some Guys Have All the Luck - **Rod Stewart** 4.08.84
Some Guys Have All The Luck - **Maxi Priest** 14.11.87
Some Kinda Earthquake - **Duane Eddy** 18.12.59
Some Kinda Fun - **Chris Montez** 24.01.63
Some Like It Hot - **Power Station** 16.03.85
Some of Your Lovin' - **Dusty Springfield** 23.09.65
Some Other Guy - **Big Three** 18.04.63
Some People - **Carol Deene** 30.08.62
Some People - **Belouis Some** 19.04.86
Some People - **Cliff Richard** 29.08.87
Some Things You Never Get Used To - **Diana Ross & the Supremes** 3.07.68
Somebody - **Stargazers** 4.03.55
Somebody - **Bryan Adams** 30.03.85
Somebody/Blasphemous Rumours - **Depeche Mode** 10.11.84
Somebody Else's Girl - **Billy Fury** 3.10.63
Somebody Else's Guy - **Jocelyn Brown** 20.04.84
Somebody Help Me - **Spencer Davis Group** 24.03.66
Somebody (Help Me Out) - **Beggar & Co.** 21.02.81
Somebody Stole My Gal - **Johnnie Ray** 10.04.53
Somebody to Love - **Queen** 27.11.76
Somebody's Watching Me - **Rockwell** 11.02.84
Someday - **Jodie Sands** 17.10.58
Someday - **Ricky Nelson** 7.11.58
Someday - **Kenny Ball & his Jazzmen** 31.08.61
Someday - **Gap Band** 7.04.84
Someday - **Mariah Carey** 2.02.92
Someday One Day - **Seekers** 24.03.66
Someday We'll Be Together - **Diana Ross & the Supremes** 20.12.69
Someone - **Johnny Mathis** 7.08.59
Someone Else's Roses - **Joan Regan** 14.05.54
Someone Else's Baby - **Adam Faith** 14.04.60
Someone On Your Mind - **Jimmy Young** 23.12.55
Someone Saved My Life Tonight - **Elton John** 5.07.75
Someone Someone - **Brian Poole & the Tremeloes** 14.05.64
Someone Somewhere (In Summertime) - **Simple Minds** 20.11.82
Someone's Looking At You - **Boomtown Rats** 2.02.80
Someone's Taken Maria Away - **Adam Faith** 8.07.65
Somethin' Else - **Eddie Cochran** 16.10.59
Somethin' Stupid - **Nancy Sinatra & Frank Sinatra** 23.03.67
Something - **Georgie Fame** 4.11.65
Something - **Shirley Bassey** 27.06.70
Something/Come Together - **Beatles** 8.11.69
Something About You - **Level 42** 5.10.85
Something Better Beginning - **Honeycombs** 29.04.65
Something Better Change - **Stranglers** 30.07.77
Something 'Bout You Baby I Like - **Tom Jones** 14.09.74
Something 'Bout You Baby I Like - **Status Quo** 28.02.81
Something Else/Friggin' In The Riggin' - **Sex Pistols** 3.03.79
Something For The Girl With Everything - **Sparks** 25.01.75
Something Got Me Started - **Simply Red** 21.09.91
Something Happened on the Way to Heaven - **Phil Collins** 28.04.90
Something Here In My Heart - **Paper Dolls** 27.03.68
Something In The Air - **Thunderclap Newman** 18.06.69
(Something Inside) So Strong - **Labi Siffre** 18.04.87
Something In My House - **Dead Or Alive** 17.01.87
Something Old Something New - **Fantastics** 27.03.71
Something Outa Nothing - **Letitia Dean & Paul Medford** 1.11.86
Something Tells Me (Something Is Gonna Happen Tonight) - **Cilla Black** 20.11.71
Something That I Said - **Ruts** 15.09.79
Something To Believe In - **Poison** 27.10.90
Something You Got - **And Why Not?** 28.04.90
Something's Burning - **Kenny Rogers/First Edition** 14.02.70
Something's Been Making Me Blue - **Smokie** 7.02.76
Something's Gotta Give - **Sammy Davis Jr.** 29.07.55
Something's Gotten Hold of My Heart - **Gene Pitney** 15.11.67
Something's Gotten Hold of My Heart - **Marc Almond featuring Gene Pitney** 14.01.89
Something's Happening - **Herman's Hermits** 18.12.68
Something's Jumpin' In Your Shirt - **Malcolm McLaren** 26.08.89
Sometimes - **Erasure** 15.11.86
Sometimes It's A Bitch - **Stevie Nicks** 31.08.91
Sometimes When We Touch - **Dan Hill** 11.03.78
Somewhere - **P.J. Proby** 10.12.64
Somewhere Along The Way - **Nat 'King' Cole** 14.11.52
Somewhere Down the Crazy River - **Robbie Robertson** 13.08.88
Somewhere In The Country - **Gene Pitney** 3.04.68
Somewhere In My Heart - **Aztec Camera** 14.05.88
Somewhere My Love - **Mike Sammes Singers** 29.09.66
Somewhere Out There - **Linda Ronstadt & James Ingram** 1.08.87
Somewhere Somebody - **Five Star** 5.12.87
Son of A Preacher Man - **Dusty Springfield** 11.12.68
Son of Hickory Holler's Tramp - **OC Smith** 5.06.68
Son of Mary - **Harry Belafonte** 12.12.58
Son of My Father - **Chicory Tip** 29.01.72
Son This Is She - **John Leyton** 4.01.62
Song For Guy - **Elton John** 16.12.78
Song For Whoever - **Beautiful South** 3.06.89
Song of Joy - **Miguel Rios** 18.07.70
Song of Mexico - **Tony Meehan** 23.01.65
Song of My Life - **Petula Clark** 13.02.71
Song of the Dreamer - **Johnnie Ray** 28.10.55
Song Sung Blue - **Neil Diamond** 20.05.72
The Song That I Sing (Theme From 'We'll Meet Again') - **Stutz Bearcats and the Denis King Orchestra** 1.05.82
Songbird - **Kenny G** 11.07.87
Songs for Christmas '87 (EP) - **Mini Pops** 2.01.88
Songs for Swinging Lovers (LP) - **Frank Sinatra** 15.06.56
Sonic Boom Boy - **Westworld** 21.02.87
Soothe Me - **Sam & Dave** 20.04.67
Sorrow - **Merseys** 5.05.66
Sorrow - **David Bowie** 20.10.73
Sorry Doesn't Always Make It Right - **Diana Ross** 12.04.75
Sorry I'm A Lady - **Baccara** 21.01.78
Sorry (I Ran All the Way Home) - **Impalas** 21.08.59
Sorry Robbie - **Bert Weedon** 3.11.60
Sorry Seems To Be The Hardest Word - **Elton John** 20.11.76
Sorry Suzanne - **Hollies** 5.03.69
SOS - **ABC** 28.01.84
Soul Cha Cha - **Van McCoy** 26.02.77
Soul City Walk - **Archie Bell & the Drells** 15.05.76
Soul Clap '69 - **Booker T & the MGs** 30.08.69
Soul Deep - **Box Tops** 23.08.69
Soul Deep (Part 1) - **Council Collective** 22.12.84
Soul Dracula - **Hot Blood** 16.10.76
Soul Finger - **Bar-Kays** 30.08.67
Soul Inside - **Soft Cell** 24.09.83
Soul Limbo - **Booker T & the MGs** 1.01.69
Soul Man - **Sam & Dave** 1.11.67
Soul Man - **Sam Moore & Lou Reed** 21.02.87
Soul Sister Brown Sugar - **Sam & Dave** 5.02.69
Soul Train - **Swans Way** 11.02.84
Sound - **James** 30.11.91
Sound and Vision - **David Bowie** 26.02.77
The Sound of Eden - **Shades of Rhythm** 20.07.91
The Sound of Philadephia - **MFSB** 4.05.74
Sound of Silence - **Bachelors** 17.03.66
The Sound of the Crowd - **Human League** 9.05.81
Sound Of The Suburbs - **Members** 3.02.79
Sound Your Funky Horn - **K.C. & the Sunshine Band** 30.11.74
South African Man - **Hamilton Bohannon** 15.02.75
Southern Freeez - **Freeez** 14.02.81
Southern Nights - **Glen Campbell** 2.04.77
Souvenir - **Orchestral Manoeuvres in the Dark** 5.09.81
Soweto - **Malcolm McLaren** 5.03.83
Sowing the Seeds of Love - **Tears for Fears** 2.09.89
Space - **New Model Army** 8.06.91
Space Age Love Song - **A Flock of Seagulls** 19.06.82
Space Bass - **Slick** 23.06.79
The Space Jungle - **Adamski** 8.09.90
Space Oddity - **David Bowie** 20.09.69
Space Oddity - **David Bowie** 11.10.75
A Spaceman Came Travelling/The Ballroom of Romance - **Chris de Burgh** 3.01.87
Spacer - **Sheila & B Devotion** 8.12.79
Spanish Eyes - **Al Martino** 21.07.73
Spanish Flea - **Herb Alpert & the Tijuana Brass** 16.12.65
Spanish Harlem - **Jimmy Justice** 30.08.62
Spanish Harlem - **Sounds Incorporated** 6.08.64
Spanish Harlem - **Aretha Franklin** 2.10.71
Spanish Stroll - **Mink DeVille** 13.08.77
Spanish Wine - **Chris White** 27.03.76
Spare Parts - **Bruce Springsteen** 24.09.88
The Sparrow - **Ramblers** 27.10.79
The Spartans - **Sounds Incorporated** 30.04.64
Speak Like A Child - **Style Council** 19.03.83
Speak to Me Pretty - **Brenda Lee** 12.04.62
Special Brew - **Bad Manners** 11.10.80
The Special Years - **Val Doonican** 21.01.65

Speed Your Love To Me - **Simple Minds** 28.01.84
Speedy Gonzales - **Pat Boone** 12.07.62
Spellbound - **Siouxsie & the Banshees** 30.05.81
Spend The Night - **Cool Notes** 23.03.85
Spending My Time - **Roxette** 23.11.91
Spice of Life - **Manhattan Transfer** 28.01.84
Spiders & Snakes - **Jim Stafford** 4.05.74
Spies Like Us - **Paul McCartney** 30.11.85
Spin That Wheel (Turltes Get Real) - **Hi Tek 3 featuring Ya Kid K** 29.09.90
Spinning Rock Boogie - **Hank C. Burnett** 6.11.76
Spiral Scratch - **Buzzcocks** 1.09.79
Spirit Body & Soul - **Nolan Sisters** 13.10.79
Spirit In The Sky - **Norman Greenbaum** 28.03.70
Spirit In The Sky - **Dr & the Medics** 10.05.86
Spirit Is Willing - **Peter Straker & the Hands of Dr Teleny** 4.03.72
Spirit of Radio - **Rush** 15.03.80
Spirit of 76 - **Alarm** 18.01.86
Spirits (Having Flown) - **Bee Gees** 12.01.80
Spirits in the Material World - **Police** 12.12.81
Spit In The Rain - **Del Amitri** 10.11.90
Splish Splash - **Bobby Darin** 1.08.58
Splish Splash - **Charlie Drake** 8.08.58
Spot the Pigeon - **Genesis** 4.06.77
Spread A Little Happiness - **Sting** 21.08.82
Spread Your Wings - **Queen** 25.02.78
Spy In The House of Love - **Was Not Was** 6.02.88
S.O.S. - **Abba** 27.09.75
Squeeze Box - **Who** 31.01.76
St Elmo's Fire (Man In Motion) - **John Parr** 28.09.85
Staccato's Theme - **Elmer Bernstein** 18.12.59
Stagger Lee - **Lloyd Price** 13.02.59
Stainsby Girls - **Chris Rea** 20.04.85
The Staircase - **Siouxsie & the Banshees** 31.03.79
Stairway of Love - **Michael Holliday** 16.05.58
Stairway of Love - **Terry Dene** 16.05.58
Stairway to Heaven - **Neil Sedaka** 14.04.60
Stairway to Heaven - **Far Corporation** 2.11.85
Stakker Humanoid - **Humanoid** 26.11.88
Stalemate - **Mac Band** 17.09.88
Stand and Deliver - **Adam & the Ants** 9.05.81
Stand By Love - **Simple Minds** 31.08.91
Stand By Me - **Ben E. King** 13.07.61
Stand By Me - **Kenny Lynch** 23.04.64
Stand by Me - **John Lennon** 10.05.75
Stand by Me - **Ben E. King** 14.02.87
Stand By Your Man - **Tammy Wynette** 3.05.75
Stand Up For Your Love Rights - **Yazz** 29.10.88
Stand Up For Your Love Rights - **Yazz** 7.01.89
Standing In The Road - **Blackfoot Sue** 19.08.72
Standing In The Shadows of Love - **Four Tops** 12.01.67
Standing On The Corner - **King Brothers** 14.04.60
Standing on The Corner - **Four Lads** 28.04.60
Standing on the Inside - **Neil Sedaka** 9.06.73
Star - **Stealers Wheel** 2.02.74
Star - **Earth Wind & Fire** 13.10.79
Star - **Kiki Dee** 28.02.81
Star - **Erasure** 2.06.90
A Star Is Born (Evergreen) - **Barbra Streisand** 16.04.77
Star On A TV Show - **The Stylistics** 25.01.75
Star Trekkin' - **Firm** 13.06.87
Star Wars Theme - **Meco** 8.10.77
Stardate 1990/Rainbow Child - **Dan Reed Network** 28.07.90
Stardust - **Billy Ward** 13.09.57
Stardust - **Nat 'King' Cole** 25.10.57
Stardust - **David Essex** 21.12.74
Staring at The Rude Boys - **Ruts** 26.04.80
Starmaker - **Kids from 'Fame'** 2.10.82
Starman - **David Bowie** 8.07.72
Starry Eyed - **Michael Holiday** 1.01.60
A Starry Night - **Joy Strings** 17.12.64
Stars - **Hear 'n' Aid** 26.04.86
Stars - **Simply Red** 30.11.91
Stars and Stripes/ Creole Jazz - **Mr. Acker Bilk** 2.11.61
Stars on 45 - **Starsound** 25.04.81
Stars on 45 (Volume 2) - **Starsound** 4.07.81
Stars on 45 (Volume 3) - **Starsound** 19.09.81
Stars On Stevie - **Starsound** 27.02.82
Stars Over 45 - **Chas & Dave** 18.12.81
Stars Shine In Your Eyes - **Ronnie Hilton** 26.08.55
Start - **Jam** 23.08.80
Start Me Up - **Rolling Stones** 29.08.81
Start Movin' - **Sal Mineo** 12.07.57
Start Movin' - **Terry Dene** 19.07.57
Start Talking Love - **Magnum** 7.05.88
Starting Together - **Su Pollard** 8.02.86
Startrax Club Disco - **Startrax** 8.08.81
Starvation/Tam Tam Pour L'Ethiopie - **Starvation** 16.03.85
State of Independence - **Donna Summer** 13.11.82
State of Mind - **Fish** 28.10.89
State of Shock - **Jacksons with Mick Jagger** 7.07.84
State of The Nation - **New Order** 27.09.86
Stay - **Maurice Williams & the Zodiacs** 5.01.61
Stay - **Hollies** 28.11.63
Stay - **Jackson Browne** 15.07.78
Stay - **Barry Manilow** 1.05.82
Stay Awhile - **Dusty Springfield** 20.02.64
Stay Beautiful - **Manic Street Preachers** 17.08.91
Stay on These Roads - **A-Ha** 26.03.88
Stay Out of My Life - **Five Star** 7.02.87
Stay With Me - **Walker Brothers** 16.02.67
Stay With Me - **Faces** 8.01.72
Stay With Me - **Blue Mink** 18.11.72
Stay With Me - **Mission** 18.10.86
Stay With Me Till Dawn - **Judie Tzuke** 21.07.79
Stay With Me Tonight - **Jeffrey Osborne** 5.05.84
Stay With Me Heartache/I Feel Fine - **Wet Wet Wet** 11.08.90
Stayin' Alive - **Bee Gees** 4.02.78
Steamy Windows - **Tina Turner** 17.02.90
Step Back In Time - **Kylie Minogue** 3.11.90
Step by Step - **Joe Simon** 23.06.73
Step by Step - **New Kids On The Block** 16.06.90
A Step In The Right Direction - **Truth** 10.09.83
Step Inside Love - **Cilla Black** 13.03.68
Step Into A Dream - **White Plains** 17.02.73
Step Into Christmas - **Elton John** 15.12.73
Step Off (Part 1) - **Grandmaster Melle Mel & the Furious Five** 29.12.84
Step On - **Happy Mondays** 7.04.90
Step Right Up - **Jaki Graham** 29.11.86
Steppin' Out - **Kool & the Gang** 7.11.81
Steppin' Out - **Joe Jackson** 15.01.83
Stereotype/International Jet Set - **Specials** 27.09.80
Stewball - **Lonnie Donegan** 20.04.56
Still - **Karl Denver** 22.08.63
Still - **Ken Dodd** 5.09.63
Still - **Commodores** 3.11.79
Still Got the Blues (For You) - **Gary Moore** 26.05.90
Still of the Night - **Whitesnake** 28.03.87
The Sting - **Ragtimers** 30.03.74
Stingray - **Shadows** 10.06.65
Stir It Up - **Johnny Nash** 15.04.72
Stomp - **Brothers Johnson** 8.03.80
Stone Cold - **Rainbow** 10.04.82
Stoned Love - **Supremes** 23.01.71
Stoney End - **Barbra Streisand** 13.02.71
Stoney Ground - **Guys & Dolls** 13.11.76
The Stonk - **Hale & Pace & the Stonkers** 9.03.91
Stood Up - **Ricky Nelson** 21.02.58
Stool Pigeon - **Kid Creole & the Coconuts** 24.07.82
Stop - **Sam Brown** 11.02.89
Stop And Go - **David Grant** 14.05.83
Stop Feeling Sorry for Yourself - **Adam Faith** 11.02.65
Stop Her On Sight (S.O.S.) - **Edwin Starr** 2.06.66
Stop Her On Sight/Headline News - **Edwin Starr** 11.12.68
Stop In The Name of Love - **Supremes** 1.04.65
Stop Look and Listen - **Wayne Fontana & the Mindbenders** 28.05.64
Stop Look Listen - **Diana Ross & Marvin Gaye** 27.07.74
Stop Me (If You've Heard It All Before) - **Billy Ocean** 20.11.76
Stop Stop Stop - **Hollies** 13.10.66
Stop That Girl - **Chris Andrews** 1.09.66
Stop the Cavalry - **Jona Lewie** 6.12.80
Stop the War Now - **Edwin Starr** 20.02.71
Stop This Crazy Thing - **Coldcut featuring Junior Reid** 10.09.88
Stop to Love - **Luther Vandross** 12.09.87
Stop Your Sobbing - **Pretenders** 3.03.79
Stories of Johnny - **Marc Almond** 24.08.85
Storm In A Tea Cup - **Fortunes**29.01.72
Story of My Life - **Gary Miller** 17.01.58
Story of My Life - **Michael Holliday** 17.01.58

Story of My Life - **Dave King** 24.01.58
Story of My Life - **Alma Cogan** 31.01.58
Story of My Love - **Conway Twitty** 27.3.59
The Story Of The Blues - **Wah!** 8.01.83
The Story of Tina - **Ronnie Harris** 24.09.54
The Story of Tina - **Al Martino** 1.10.54
Stowaway - **Barbara Lyon** 24.06.55
St. Valentine's Day Massacre (EP) - **Motorhead/Grilschool** 21.02.81
St. Therese of The Roses - **Malcolm Vaughan** 26.10.56
Straight Ahead - **Kool and the Gang** 17.12.83
Straight Up - **Paula Abdul** 4.03.89
Strange Band - **Family** 22.08.70
Strange Brew - **Cream** 15.06.67
Strange Kind of Woman - **Deep Purple** 27.02.71
Strange Lady in Town - **Frankie Laine** 15.07.55
Strange Little Girl - **Sad Cafe** 26.01.80
Strange Little Girl - **Stranglers** 24.07.82
Strange Magic - **Electric Light Orchestra** 10.07.76
Strange Town - **Jam** 17.03.79
Strangelove - **Depeche Mode** 9.05.87
Stranger In A Strange Land - **Iron Maiden** 22.11.86
Stranger in Paradise - **Tony Bennett** 15.04.55
Stranger in Paradise - **Don Cornell** 22.04.55
Stranger In Paradise - **Tony Martin** 22.04.55
Stranger In Paradise - **Bing Crosby** 29.04.55
Stranger in Paradise - **Eddie Calvert** 13.05.55
Stranger in Paradise - **Four Aces** 20.05.55
Stranger In Town - **Del Shannon** 18.03.65
Stranger on the Shore - **Mr. Acker Bilk** 30.11.61
Stranger on the Shore - **Andy Williams** 14.06.62
Strangers In The Night - **Frank Sinatra** 12.05.66
Stranglehold - **UK Subs** 30.06.79
Strawberry Blonde - **Frank D'Rone** 22.12.60
Strawberry Fair - **Anthony Newley** 1.12.60
Strawberry Fields - **Beatles** 10.04.76
Strawberry Fields Forever - **Candy Flip** 17.03.90
Strawberry Letter 23 - **Brothers Johnson** 16.07.77
Stray Cat Strut - **Stray Cats** 2.05.81
The Streak - **Ray Stevens** 25.05.74
Streamline Train - **Vipers** 31.05.57
A Street Called Hope - **Gene Pitney** 21.03.70
Street Dance - **Break Machine** 11.02.84
Street Fighting Man - **Rolling Stones** 10.07.71
Street Life - **Roxy Music** 24.11.73
Street Life - **Crusaders** 25.08.79
Street Tuff - **Rebel MC & Double Trouble** 7.10.89
Streets of London - **Ralph McTell** 7.12.74
Streetwalkin' - **Shakatak** 26.06.82
Strength - **Alarm** 5.10.85
Strictly Elvis (EP) - **Elvis Presley** 12.02.60
Strike It Up - **Black Box** 6.04.91
Stripped - **Depeche Mode** 22.02.86
Strollin' On - **Maxi Priest** 19.04.86
Strong As Steel - **Five Star** 10.10.87
Stronger Than That - **Cliff Richard** 24.02.90
Strut Your Funky Stuff - **Frantique** 25.08.79
Stuck In The Middle With You - **Stealers Wheel** 26.05.73
Stuck on You - **Elvis Presley** 7.04.60
Stuck on You - **Lionel Richie** 23.06.84
Stuck on You - **Trevor Walters** 11.08.84
Stuck With You - **Huey Lewis & the News** 30.08.86
Stuff Like That - **Quincy Jones** 5.08.78
Stupid Question - **New Model Army** 21.01.89
Stutter Rap (No Sleep Til Bedtime) - **Morris Minor & the Majors** 2.01.88
Substitute - **Who** 10.03.66
Substitute - **Who** 30.10.76
Substitute - **Clout** 1.07.78
Substitute - **Liquid Gold** 7.06.80
Subterranean Homesick Blues - **Bob Dylan** 29.04.65
Suburbia - **Pet Shop Boys** 4.10.86
Success - **Sigue Sigue Sputnik** 19.11.88
Success - **Dannii Minogue** 18.05.91
Such A Feeling - **Bizarre Inc** 14.09.91
Such A Good Feeling - **Brothers In Rhythm** 14.09.91
Such A Night - **Johnnie Ray** 9.04.54
Such A Night - **Elvis Presley** 20.08.64
Sucker DJ - **Dimples D** 24.11.90
Sucu Sucu - **Laurie Johnson Orchestra** 5.10.61
Sucu Sucu - **Ted Heath Orchestra** 12.10.61
Sucu Sucu - **Nina & Frederick** 12.10.61
Suddenly - **Olivia Newton-John & Cliff Richard** 1.11.80
Suddenly - **Billy Ocean** 25.05.85
Suddenly - **Angry Anderson** 26.11.88
Suddenly There's A Valley - **Petula Clark** 25.11.55
Suddenly There's A Valley - **Lee Lawrence** 2.12.55
Suddenly There's A Valley - **Jo Stafford** 9.12.55
Suddenly You Love Me - **Tremeloes** 24.01.68
Suedehead - **Morrissey** 27.02.88
Sue's Gonna Be Mine - **Del Shannon** 31.10.63
Sugar and Spice - **Searchers** 24.10.63
Sugar Baby Love - **Rubettes** 4.05.74
Sugar Box - **Then Jerico** 19.08.89
Sugar Bush - **Doris Day & Frankie Laine** 14.11.52
Sugar Candy Kisses - **Mac & Katie Kissoon** 25.01.75
Sugar Me - **Lynsey De Paul** 26.08.72
Sugar Mice - **Marillion** 25.07.87
Sugar Moon - **Pat Boone** 27.06.58
Sugar Sugar - **Archies** 18.10.69
Sugar Sugar - **Sakkarin** 24.04.71
Sugar Town - **Nancy Sinatra** 19.01.67
Sugartime - **McGuire Sisters** 14.02.58
Sugartime - **Alma Cogan** 14.02.58
Sugartime - **Jim Dale** 7.03.58
Suicide Blonde - **Inxs** 15.09.90
Sukiyaki - **Kenny Ball & his Jazzmen** 24.01.63
Sukiyaki - **Kyu Sakamoto** 4.07.63
Sultana - **Titanic** 2.10.71
Sultans of Swing - **Dire Straits** 17.03.79
Sumerland (Dreamed) - **Fields of the Nephilim** 24.11.90
Summer Breeze - **Isley Brothers** 1.06.74
Summer Fun - **Barracudas** 23.08.80
Summer Holiday - **Cliff Richard** 21.02.63
Summer In The City - **Lovin' Spoonful** 21.07.66
Summer is Over - **Frank Ifield** 1.10.64
Summer Night City - **Abba** 16.09.78
Summer Nights - **Marianne Faithfull** 29.07.65
Summer Nights - **John Travolta & Olivia Newton-John** 23.09.78
Summer Of '42 - **Biddu Orchestra** 2.08.75
Summer of My Life - **Simon May** 9.10.76
Summer of the Seventeenth Doll - **Winifred Atwell** 7.08.59
Summer Rain - **Belinda Carlisle** 12.01.91
Summer Set - **Mr. Acker Bilk & his Paramount Jazz Band** 22.01.60
Summer (The First Time) - **Bobby Goldsboro** 4.08.73
Summer Wind - **Frank Sinatra** 6.10.66
Summerlove Sensation - **Bay City Rollers** 27.07.74
Summers Magic - **Mark Summers** 26.01.91
Summertime - **Billy Stewart** 15.09.66
Summertime - **Fun Boy Three** 7.08.82
Summertime - **DJ Jazzy Jeff & Fresh Prince** 3.08.91
Summertime Blues - **Eddie Cochran** 7.11.58
Summertime Blues - **Eddie Cochran** 1.05.68
Summertime Blues - **Who** 8.08.70
Summertime City - **Mike Batt** 23.08.75
Sun Ain't Gonna Shine Anymore - **Walker Brothers** 3.03.66
The Sun Always Shines on TV - **A-Ha** 28.12.85
The Sun And The Rain - **Madness** 5.11.83
Sun Arise - **Rolf Harris** 1.11.62
Sun City - **Artists United Against Apartheid** 30.11.85
The Sun Goes Down (Living It Up) - **Level 42** 6.08.83
Sun King/Edie (Ciao Baby) - **Cult** 18.11.89
The Sun Rising - **Beloved** 28.10.89
Sun Street - **Katrina & the Waves** 19.07.86
Sunday Girl - **Blondie** 19.05.79
Sundown - **Gordon Lightfoot** 10.08.74
Sunglasses - **Tracey Ullman** 4.08.84
Sunny - **Bobby Hebb** 15.09.66
Sunny - **Georgie Fame** 22.09.66
Sunny - **Cher** 29.09.66
Sunny - **Boney M** 19.03.77
Sunny Afternoon - **Kinks** 9.06.66
Sunny Honey Girl - **Cliff Richard** 23.01.71
Sunset Now - **Heaven 17** 1.09.84
Sunshine After The Rain - **Elkie Brooks** 27.08.77
Sunshine Day - **Osibisa** 24.01.76
Sunshine Girl - **Herman's Hermits** 24.07.68
Sunshine of Your Love - **Cream** 9.10.68
The Sunshine of Your Smile - **Mike Berry** 9.08.80
Sunshine On A Rainy Day (Remix) - **Zoe** 24.08.91

Sunshine Superman - **Donovan** ... 8.12.66
Super Gran - **Billy Connolly** ... 6.04.85
Super Nature - **Cerrone** ... 5.08.78
Super Trouper - **Abba** ... 15.11.80
Super Womble - **Wombles** ... 2.08.75
Superfly Guy - **S Express** ... 23.07.88
Supergirl - **Graham Bonney** ... 31.03.66
Superman (Gioca Jouer) - **Black Lace** ... 1.10.83
Superman (Gioca Jouer) - **Black Lace** ... 7.01.84
Supership - **George Benson** ... 1.11.75
Supersonic Rocket Ship - **Kinks** ... 3.06.72
Superstar - **Temptations** ... 12.02.72
Superstar - **Lydia Murdock** ... 8.10.83
Superstar/For All We Know - **Carpenters** ... 2.10.71
Superstition - **Stevie Wonder** ... 3.02.73
Superstitious - **Europe** ... 27.08.88
Superwoman - **Karyn White** ... 17.06.89
Surf City - **Jan & Dean** ... 15.08.63
Surfin' USA - **Beach Boys** ... 15.08.63
Surrender - **Elvis Presley** ... 25.05.61
Surrender - **Diana Ross** ... 6.11.71
Surrender - **Swing Out Sister** ... 3.01.87
Surround Yourself With Sorrow - **Cilla Black** ... 19.02.69
Susanna - **Art Company** ... 9.06.84
Susannah's Still Alive - **Dave Davies** ... 13.12.67
Susie Darlin' - **Robin Luke** ... 17.10.58
Susie Darlin' - **Tommy Roe** ... 13.12.62
Suspicion - **Terry Stafford** ... 14.05.64
Suspicion - **Elvis Presley** ... 15.01.77
Suspicious Minds - **Elvis Presley** ... 29.11.69
Suspicious Minds - **Candi Staton** ... 15.05.82
Suspicious Minds - **Fine Young Cannibals** ... 11.01.86
Sussudio - **Phil Collins** ... 26.01.85
Suzanne Beware of the Devil - **Dandy Livingstone** ... 9.09.72
Swallow My Pride - **Ramones** ... 6.08.77
Sway - **Dean Martin** ... 1.10.54
Sway - **Bobby Rydell** ... 15.12.60
Swearin' To God - **Frankie Valli** ... 28.06.75
Swedish Rhapsody - **Mantovani Orchestra** ... 23.10.53
Swedish Rhapsody - **Ray Martin Orchestra** ... 4.12.53
Sweet Caroline - **Neil Diamond** ... 20.02.71
Sweet Cheatin' Rita - **Alvin Stardust** ... 19.07.75
Sweet Child O'Mine - **Guns N' Roses** ... 20.08.88
Sweet Child O' Mine - **Guns N' Roses** ... 3.06.89
Sweet Dream - **Jethro Tull** ... 1.11.69
Sweet Dreams - **Dave Sampson** ... 9.06.60
Sweet Dreams - **Roy Buchanan** ... 7.04.73
Sweet Dreams (Are Made Of This) - **Eurythmics** ... 19.02.83
Sweet Freedom - **Michael McDonald** ... 13.09.86
Sweet Hitch Hiker - **Creedence Clearwater Revival** ... 31.07.51
Sweet Home Alabama/Double Trouble - **Lynyrd Skynrd** ... 18.09.76
Sweet Illusion - **Junior Campbell** ... 2.06.73
Sweet Impossible You - **Brenda Lee** ... 31.10.63
Sweet Inspiration - **Johnny Johnson and Bandwagon** ... 1.08.70
Sweet Little Sixteen - **Chuck Berry** ... 25.04.58
Sweet Little Sixteen - **Jerry Lee Lewis** ... 13.09.62
Sweet Little Rock 'N' Roller - **Showaddywaddy** ... 4.08.79
Sweet Little Mystery - **Wet Wet Wet** ... 8.08.87
Sweet Love - **Anita Baker** ... 15.11.86
Sweet Memory - **Belle Stars** ... 7.05.83
Sweet Music - **Showaddywaddy** ... 1.03.75
Sweet Nothin's - **Brenda Lee** ... 7.04.60
Sweet Old Fashioned Girl - **Teresa Brewer** ... 13.07.56
Sweet Pea - **Manfred Mann** ... 1.06.67
Sweet Sixteen - **Billy Idol** ... 27.06.87
Sweet Somebody - **Shannon** ... 7.07.84
Sweet Soul Music - **Arthur Conley** ... 4.05.67
Sweet Surrender - **Rod Stewart** ... 24.12.83
Sweet Surrender - **Wet Wet Wet** ... 30.09.89
Sweet Sweet Smile - **Carpenters** ... 18.02.78
Sweet Talkin' Guy - **Chiffons** ... 16.06.66
Sweet Talkin' Woman - **Electric Light Orchestra** ... 7.10.78
Sweet Talking Guy - **Chiffons** ... 25.03.72
Sweet Understanding Love - **Four Tops** ... 10.11.73
Sweet William - **Millie** ... 2.07.64
Sweeter Than You - **Ricky Nelson** ... 4.09.59
Sweetest Girl - **Madness** ... 22.02.86
Sweetest Smile - **Black** ... 4.07.87
The Sweetest Taboo - **Sade** ... 19.10.85
Sweetie Pie - **Eddie Cochran** ... 13.10.60
Sweets For My Sweet - **Searchers** ... 4.07.63
Swimming Horses - **Siouxsie & the Banshees** ... 24.03.84
Swing Low (Run With The Ball) - **Union featuring England World Cup Rugby Squad** ... 19.10.91
Swing Low Sweet Chariot - **Eric Clapton** ... 17.05.75
Swing That Hammer - **Mike Cotton's Jazzmen** ... 27.06.63
Swing the Mood - **Jive Bunny & the Mastermixers** ... 22.07.89
Swing Your Daddy - **Jim Gilstrap** ... 22.03.75
Swingin' Shepherd Blues - **Ted Heath Orchestra** ... 14.03.58
Swingin' Shepherd Blues - **Moe Koffman** ... 28.03.58
Swingin' Shepherd Blues - **Ella Fitzgerald** ... 23.05.58
Swinging in the Rain - **Norman Vaughan** ... 31.05.62
Swinging On A Star - **Big Dee Irwin** ... 5.12.63
Swiss Maid - **Del Shannon** ... 18.10.62
Swords of A Thousand Men - **Ten Pole Tudor** ... 2.05.81
Sylvia - **Focus** ... 27.01.73
Sylvia's Mother - **Dr Hook & the Medicine Show** ... 1.07.72
Sympathy - **Rare Bird** ... 28.02.70
Synchronicity II - **Police** ... 5.11.83
System Addict - **Five Star** ... 18.01.86
Tahiti - **David Essex** ... 17.09.83
Tainted Love - **Soft Cell** ... 15.08.81
Tainted Love - **Soft Cell featuring Marc Almond** ... 18.05.91
Take 5 - **Northside** ... 15.06.91
Take A Chance On Me - **Abba** ... 4.02.78
Take A Chance With Me - **Roxy Music** ... 25.09.82
Take A Heart - **Sorrows** ... 23.09.65
Take A Look - **Level 42** ... 29.10.88
Take A Look Around - **Temptations** 15.04.72
Take A Message to Mary - **Everly Brothers** ... 22.05.59
Take Care of Yourself - **Level 42** ... 28.10.89
Take Five - **Dave Brubeck** ... 26.10.61
Take Good Care of Her - **Adam Wade** ... 8.06.61
Take Good Care of My Baby - **Bobby Vee** ... 26.10.61
Take Good Care of Yourself - **Three Degrees** ... 12.04.75
Take Good Care of My Baby - **Smokie** ... 3.05.80
Take It - **Flowered Up** ... 18.05.91
Take it Away - **Paul McCartney** ... 10.07.82
Take It On The Run - **REO Speedwagon** ... 11.07.81
Take It Or Leave It - **Searchers** ... 28.04.66
Take It Satch (EP) - **Louis Armstrong** ... 15.06.56
Take It To The Limit - **Eagles** ... 13.03.76
Take it To The Top - **Kool & the Gang** ... 6.06.81
Take Me Back 'Ome - **Slade** ... 3.06.72
Take Me For What I'm Worth - **Searchers** ... 23.12.65
Take Me Girl I'm Ready - **Junior Walker & the Allstars** ... 27.01.73
Take Me High - **Cliff Richard** ... 8.12.73
Take Me Home - **Phil Collins** ... 3.08.85
Take Me Home Country Roads - **Olivia Newton-John** ... 20.01.73
Take Me I'm Yours - **Squeeze** ... 15.04.78
Take Me In Your Arms - **Doobie Brothers** ... 14.06.75
Take Me In Your Arms and Love Me - **Gladys Knight & the Pips** ... 15.06.67
Take Me To The Mardi Gras - **Paul Simon** ... 16.06.73
Take Me To Your Heart Again - **Vince Hill** ... 13.01.66
Take Me To Your Heart - **Rick Astley** ... 26.11.88
Take My Breath Away (Love Theme From 'Top Gun') - **Berlin** ... 25.10.86
Take My Breath Away - **Berlin** ... 20.10.90
Take My Heart (You Can Have It If You Want It) - **Kool and the Gang**
Take My Heart - Al Martino ... 21.11.52
Take On Me - **A-Ha** ... 5.10.85
Take On The World - **Judas Priest** ... 3.02.79
Take That Look Off Your Face - **Marti Webb** ... 23.02.80
Take That Situation - **Nick Heyward** ... 18.06.83
Take That To The Bank - **Shalamar** ... 13.01.79
Take These Chains From My Heart - **Ray Charles** ... 16.05.63
Take to The Mountains - **Richard Barnes** ... 23.05.70
Take Your Mama For A Ride - **Lulu** ... 3.05.75
Take Your Time - **Mantronix featuring Wondress** ... 12.05.90
Takes A Little Time - **Total Contrast** ... 17.08.85
Takes Two to Tango - **Louis Armstrong** ... 19.12.52
Talk of The Town - **Pretenders** ... 5.04.80
Talk Talk - **Talk Talk** ... 20.11.82
Talking In Your Sleep - **Crystal Gayle** ... 9.09.78
Talking In Your Sleep - **Bucks Fizz** ... 1.09.84
Talking Loud and Clear - **Orchestral Manoeuvres In The Dark** ... 16.06.84
Talking With Myself - **Electribe 101** ... 24.02.90
Tall Dark Stranger - **Rose Brennan** ... 14.12.61
Tallahassee Lassie - **Freddy Cannon** ... 14.08.59

Tallahassee Lassie - **Tommy Steele** ... 14.08.59
Tallyman - **Jeff Beck** ... 9.08.67
Tammy - **Debbie Reynolds** ... 30.08.57
Tantalise (Wo Wo Ee Yeh Yeh) - **Jimmy The Hoover** ... 2.07.83
Tap Turns on the Water - **C.C.S.** ... 4.09.71
Tarzan Boy - **Baltimora** ... 17.08.85
A Taste of Aggro - **Barron Knights** ... 2.12.78
Taste of Bitter Love - **Gladys Knight & the Pips** ... 13.09.80
A Taste of Honey - **Mr. Acker Bilk** ... 24.01.63
The Taste of Your Tears - **King** ... 19.10.85
Taste the Pain - **Red Hot Chilli Peppers** ... 23.06.90
Tattooed Millionaire - **Bruce Dickinson** ... 28.04.90
Tchaikovsky One - **Second City Sound** ... 27.01.66
Tea for Two Cha Cha - **Tommy Dorsey Orchestra** ... 17.10.58
Teach Me Tonight - **deCastro Sisters** ... 11.02.55
Teach You To Rock/Short'nin' Bread - **Tony Crombie** ... 19.10.56
The Teacher - **Big Country** ... 21.06.86
Teacher Teacher - **Johnny Mathis** ... 23.05.58
A Tear Fell - **Teresa Brewer** ... 13.04.56
Tear Me Apart - **Suzi Quatro** ... 19.03.77
Teardrops - **Shakin' Stevens** ... 24.11.84
Teardrops - **Womack & Womack** ... 20.08.88
Tears - **Danny Williams** ... 5.07.62
Tears - **Ken Dodd** ... 2.09.65
Tears Are Not Enough - **ABC** ... 14.11.81
Tears From Heaven - **Heartbeat** ... 31.10.87
The Tears I Cried - **Glitter Band** ... 12.04.75
Tears In The Wind - **Chicken Shack** ... 6.09.69
Tears of A Clown - **Smokey Robinson & The Miracles** ... 1.08.70
Tears of A Clown - **Smokey Robinson & the Miracles** ... 16.10.76
Tears of A Clown/Ranking Full Stop - **Beat** ... 15.12.79
Tears On My Pillow - **Johnny Nash** ... 14.06.75
Tears On My Pillow - **Kylie Minogue** ... 20.01.90
Tears on the Telephone - **Claude Francois** ... 17.01.76
Tears On The Telephone - **Hot Chocolate** ... 1.10.83
Tears Run Rings - **Marc Almond** ... 3.09.88
Tears Won't Wash Away My Heartaches - **Ken Dodd** ... 9.08.69
Tease Me - **Keith Kelly** ... 19.05.60
Teddy Bear - **Elvis Presley** ... 12.07.57
Teddy Bear - **Red Sovine** ... 13.06.81
Teen Angel - **Mark Dinning** ... 17.03.60
Teen Beat - **Sandy Nelson** ... 6.11.59
Teenage - **UK Subs** ... 17.05.80
Teenage Depression - **Eddie & the Hot Rods** ... 20.11.76
Teenage Dream - **Marc Bolan & T.Rex** ... 9.02.74
Teenage Idol - **Rick Nelson** ... 6.09.62
Teenage Kicks - **Undertones** ... 28.10.78
Teenage Lament '74 - **Alice Cooper** ... 19.01.74
Teenage Warning - **Angelic Upstarts** ... 18.08.79
Teenager in Love - **Marty Wilde** ... 5.06.59
Teenager In Love - **Craig Douglas** ... 12.06.59
Teenager In Love - **Dion & the Belmonts** ... 26.06.59
Telegram Sam - **T.Rex** ... 29.01.72
The Telephone Always Rings - **Fun Boy Three** ... 15.05.82
Telephone Line - **Electric Light Orchestra** ... 28.05.77
Telephone Man - **Meri Wilson** ... 3.09.77
Tell Her About It - **Billy Joel** ... 10.12.83
Tell Him - **Billie Davis** ... 7.02.63
Tell Him - **Hello** ... 16.11.74
Tell It On The Mountain - **Peter Paul & Mary** ... 23.04.64
Tell It To My Heart - **Taylor Dayne** ... 30.01.88
Tell It To The Rain - **Four Seasons** ... 19.01.67
Tell Laura I Love Her - **Ricky Valance** ... 25.08.60
Tell Me - **Nick Kamen** ... 11.06.88
Tell Me A Story - **Frankie Laine & Jimmy Boyd** ... 8.05.53
Tell Me That You Love Me - **Paul Anka** ... 8.11.57
Tell Me There's A Heaven - **Chris Rea** ... 17.02.90
Tell Me Tomorrow - **Princess** ... 12.07.86
Tell Me What He Said - **Helen Shapiro** ... 15.02.62
Tell Me What You Want - **Jimmy Ruffin** ... 23.11.74
Tell Me When - **Applejacks** ... 12.03.64
Tell Me When The Fever Ended - **Electribe 101** ... 11.11.89
Tell Me Why - **Elvis Presley** ... 11.11.65
Tell Me Why - **Alvin Stardust** ... 30.11.74
Tell Me Why - **Musical Youth** ... 16.07.83
Telstar - **Tornados** ... 6.09.62
Temma Harbour - **Mary Hopkin** ... 31.01.70
Temptation - **Everly Brothers** ... 15.06.61
Temptation - **New Order** ... 22.05.82
Temptation - **Heaven 17** ... 23.04.83
Temptation - **Wet Wet Wet** ... 19.03.88
Ten Thousand Miles - **Michael Holliday** ... 5.10.56
Tender Love - **Force MD's** ... 3.05.86
Tender Love - **Kenny Thomas** ... 30.11.91
Tenderly - **Nat 'King' Cole** ... 16.04.54
Tennessee Wig Walk - **Bonnie Lou** ... 5.02.54
Teresa - **Joe Dolan** ... 8.11.69
Terry - **Twinkle** ... 26.11.64
Tequila - **Champs** ... 4.04.58
Tequila - **Ted Heath Orchestra** ... 11.04.58
Tesla Girls - **Orchestral Manoeuvres In The Dark** ... 15.09.84
Thank God It's Christmas - **Queen** ... 8.12.84
Thank U Very Much - **Scaffold** ... 15.11.67
Thank You For The Music - **Abba** ... 26.11.83
Thank You My Love - **Imagination** ... 12.01.85
Thanks for Saving My Life - **Billy Paul** ... 19.01.74
Thanks For the Memory - **Slade** ... 17.05.75
That Certain Smile - **Midge Ure** ... 16.11.85
That Girl - **Stevie Wonder** ... 6.02.82
That Girl Belongs to Yesterday - **Gene Pitney** ... 5.03.64
That Lady - **Isley Brothers** ... 29.09.73
That Means A Lot - **P.J. Proby** ... 30.09.65
That Noise - **Anthony Newley** ... 2.08.62
That Old Black Magic - **Sammy Davis Jr.** ... 30.09.55
That Ole Devil Called Love - **Alison Moyet** ... 16.03.85
That Same Old Feeling - **Pickettywitch** ... 28.02.70
That Sounds Good to Me - **Jive Bunny & the Mastermixers** ... 17.03.90
That Was Then But This Is Now - **ABC** ... 5.11.83
That Was Yesterday - **Foreigner** ... 13.04.85
That'll Be The Day - **Crickets** ... 27.09.57
That'll Be The Day - **Everly Brothers** ... 6.05.65
That's All - **Genesis** ... 19.11.83
That's Amore - **Dean Martin** ... 22.01.54
That's Entertainment - **Jam** ... 14.02.81
That's How A Love Song Was Born - **Ray Burns** ... 26.08.55
That's Just The Way It Is - **Phil Collins** ... 4.08.90
That's Living Alright (From 'Auf Wiedersehen Pet') - **Joe Fagin** ... 14.01.84
That's Love - **Billy Fury** ... 26.05.60
That's Love That It Is - **Blancmange** ... 3.12.83
That's My Doll - **Frankie Vaughan** ... 30.01.59
That's My Home - **Mr Acker Bilk** ... 20.07.61
That's Nice - **Neil Christian** ... 14.04.66
That's Right - **Deep River Boys** ... 7.12.56
That's The Way (I Like It) - **K.C. And The Sunshine Band** ... 2.08.75
That's The Way Love Goes - **Charles Dickens** ... 8.07.65
That's The Way - **Honeycombs** ... 12.08.65
That's The Way God Planned It - **Billy Preston** ... 9.07.69
That's The Way (I Like It) - **Dead Or Alive** ... 31.03.84
That's The Way It Is - **Mel & Kim** ... 27.02.88
That's The Way I Wanna Rock 'N' Roll - **AC/DC** ... 2.04.88
That's The Way Love Goes - **Ten City** ... 21.01.89
That's What Friends Are For - **Deniece Williams** ... 6.08.77
That's What Friends Are For - **Dionne Warwick & Friends** ... 16.11.85
That's What I Like - **Jive Bunny & the Mastermixers** ... 14.10.89
That's What Love Will Do - **Joe Brown** ... 14.02.63
That's When The Music Takes Me - **Neil Sedaka** ... 24.02.73
That's Why I'm Crying - **Ivy League** ... 6.05.65
That's You - **Nat 'King' Cole** ... 26.05.60
Them There Eyes - **Emile Ford & the Checkmates** ... 8.09.60
Theme for a Dream - **Cliff Richard** ... 2.03.61
Theme for Young Lovers - **Shadows** ... 5.03.64
Theme from 'A Summer Place' - **Percy Faith** ... 10.03.60
Theme from 'A Summer Place' - **Norrie Paramor Orchestra** ... 17.03.60
Theme From 'Dr. Kildare' - **Johnny Spence** ... 1.03.62
Theme from 'Dr. Kildare' (Three Stars Will Shine Tonight) - **Richard Chamberlain** ... 7.06.62
Theme From Deer Hunter ... 19.05.79
Theme from Dixie - **Duane Eddy** ... 20.04.61
Theme from 'Exodus' - **Ferrante and Teicher** ... 16.03.61
Theme from 'Exodus' - **Semprini** ... 16.03.61
Theme from 'ET (The Extra Terrestrial)' - **John Williams** ... 25.12.82
Theme from 'Honeymoon' - **Manuel & his Music of the Mountains** ... 28.08.59
Theme from 'Harry's Game' - **Clannad** ... 13.11.82
Theme From 'Hill Street Blues' - **Mike Post and Larry Carlton** ... 30.1.82.
Theme from 'Limelight' - **Ron Goodwin** ... 15.05.53
Theme from 'Limelight' - **Frank Chacksfield** ... 22.05.53
Theme from 'Moulin Rouge' - **Mantovani Orchestra** ... 29.05.53
Theme From 'Maigret' - **Joe Loss** ... 5.04.62

Theme From Mash (Suicide Is Painless) - **Mash** 17.05.80
Theme From New York New York - **Frank Sinatra** 1.03.86
Theme from 'Shaft' - **Isaac Hayes** 4.12.71
Theme From S Express - **S Express** 16.04.88
Theme From Shaft - **Eddy & the Soul Band** 23.02.85
Theme From Superman - **Original Soundtrack** 13.01.79
Theme From 'The Threepenny Opera' - **Dick Hyman Trio** 16.03.56
Theme From 'The Threepenny Opera' - **Billy Vaughn** 23.03.56
Theme From 'The Threepenny Opera' - **Louis Armstrong** 13.04.56
Theme from 'The Magnificent Seven' - **Al Caiola** 15.06.61
Theme From 'The Legion's Last Patrol' - **Ken Thorne** 25.07.63
Theme From The Hong Kong Beat - **Richard Denton & Martin Cook** 29.04.78
Theme From the Invaders - **Yellow Magic Orchestra** 28.06.80
Theme From Which Way Is Up - **Stargard** 4.02.78
Theme from 'Z Cars' - **Johnny Keating** 1.03.62
Theme from 'Z Cars' - **Norrie Paramor** 29.03.62
Then - **Charlatans** 22.09.90
Then Came You - **Dionne Warwicke & Detroit Spinners** 26.10.74
Then He Kissed Me - **Crystals** 19.09.63
Then I Kissed Her - **Beach Boys** 4.05.67
Then You Can Tell Me Goodbye - **Casinos** 2.03.67
There Ain't Nothing Like Shaggin' - **Tams** 28.11.87
There Are More Questions Than Answers - **Johnny Nash** 7.10.72
There But For Fortune - **Joan Baez** 8.07.65
There Goes My Everything - **Engelbert Humperdinck** 25.05.67
There Goes My Everything - **Elvis Presley** 20.03.71
There Goes My First Love - **Drifters** 13.09.75
There Is A Mountain - **Donovan** 1.11.67
There Is Always Something There To Remind Me - **Housemartins** 30.04.88
There It Is - **Shalamar** 4.09.82
There I've Said It Again - **Bobby Vinton** 9.01.64
There Must Be A Reason - **Frankie Laine** 8.10.54
There Must Be A Way - **Joni James** 30.01.59
There Must Be A Way - **Frankie Vaughan** 23.08.67
There Must Be An Angel (Playing With My Heart) - **Eurythmics** 6.07.85
There She Goes - **La's** 3.11.90
There She Goes Again/Misled - **Quireboys** 15.09.90
There There My Dear - **Dexy's Midnight Runners** 19.07.80
There Will Never Be Another You - **Chris Montez** 6.10.66
There Will Never Be Another Tonight - **Bryan Adams** 23.11.91
There Won't Be Many Coming Home - **Roy Orbison** 1.12.66
There'll Be Sad Songs To Make You Cry - **Billy Ocean** 26.04.86
There's A Ghost in My House - **R. Dean Taylor** 11.05.74
There's A Ghost In My House - **Fall** 16.05.87
There's A Guy Works Down The Chip Shop Swears He's Elvis - **Kirsty MacColl** 27.06.81
There's A Heartache Following Me - **Jim Reeves** 5.11.64
There's A Kind of Hush - **Herman's Hermits** 16.02.67
There's A Kind of Hush - **Carpenters** 3.04.76
There's A Whole Lot of Loving - **Guys and Dolls** 8.03.75
(There's) Always Something There To Remind Me - **Sandie Shaw** 8.10.64
There's Gonna Be A Showdown - **Archie Bell & the Drells** 10.02.73
There's More To Love - **Communards** 18.06.88
There's No One Quite Like Grandma - **St Winifred's School Choir** 29.11.80
There's No Other Way - **Blur** 27.04.91
There's Nothing Like This - **Omar** 22.06.91
There's Something Wrong In Paradise - **Kid Creole and the Coconuts** 17.09.83
There's the Girl - **Heart** 26.12.87
These Boots Are Made For Walkin' - **Nancy Sinatra** 27.01.66
These Things Will Keep Me Loving You - **Velvelettes** 7.08.71
(They Call Her) La Bamba - **Crickets** 9.07.64
They Don't Know - **Tracey Ullman** 1.10.83
(They Long To Be) Close to You - **Gwen Guthrie** 18.10.86
They Shoot Horses Don't They - **Racing Cars** 12.02.77
They're Coming To Take Me Away Ha-Haa - **Napoleon XIV** 11.08.66
Thieves In The Temple - **Prince** 4.08.90
Thieves Like Us - **New Order** 28.04.84
The Thin Wall - **Ultravox** 22.08.81
A Thing Called Love - **Johnny Cash & the Evangel Temple Choir** 15.04.72
Things - **Bobby Darin** 26.07.62
Things Can Only Get Better - **Howard Jones** 9.02.85
Things Get Better - **Eddie Floyd** 9.08.67
Things That Make You Go Hmmm - **C&C Music Factory featuring Freedom Williams** 06.07.91
Things We Do For Love - **10C.C.** 11.12.76
Think - **Brenda Lee** 16.04.64
Think - **Chris Farlowe & the Thunderbirds** 10.02.66
Think - **Aretha Franklin** 22.05.68
Think About ... - **DJH featuring Stefy** 16.02.91
Think About Your Chidren - **Mary Hopkin** 7.11.70
Think For A Minute - **Housemartins** 11.10.86
Think It Over - **Crickets** 25.07.58
(Think Of Me) Wherever You Are - **Ken Dodd** 13.12.75
Think Sometimes About Me - **Sandie Shaw** 24.11.66
Thinkin' Ain't For Me - **Paul Jones** 27.09.67
Thinking About Your Love - **Skipworth & Turner** 25.05.85
Thinking About Your Love - **Kenny Thomas** 1.06.91
Thinking of You - **Sister Sledge** 2.06.84
Thinking of You - **Colourfield** 2.02.85
Thinking of You - **Maureen** 16.06.90
Thinking of You Baby - **Dave Clark Five** 13.08.64
Third Finger Left Hand - **Pearls** 10.06.72
This Beat is Technotronic - **Technotronic featuring MC Eric** 7.04.90
This Charming Man - **Smiths** 19.11.83
This Corrosion - **Sisters of Mercy** 3.10.87
This Door Swings Both Ways - **Herman's Hermits** 23.06.66
This Flight Tonight - **Nazareth** 20.10.73
This Golden Ring - **Fortunes** 17.02.66
This Guy's In Love With You - **Herb Alpert** 10.07.68
This House - **Alison Moyet** 26.10.91
This House (Is Where Your Love Stands) - **Big Sound Authority** 2.02.85
This Is England - **Clash** 12.10.85
This Is How It Feels - **Inspiral Carpets** 17.03.90
This Is It - **Melba Moore** 22.05.76
This Is It - **Dan Hartman** 20.01.79
This Is It/Who Am I? - **Adam Faith** 9.02.61
This Is Love - **Gary Numan** 19.04.86
This Is Me - **Climie Fisher** 21.05.88
This Is Mine - **Heaven 17** 3.11.84
This Is My Night - **Chaka Khan** 19.01.85
This Is My Song - **Petula Clark** 9.02.67
This Is My Song - **Harry Secombe** 2.03.67
This Is Not A Love Song - **Public Image Ltd** 24.09.83
This Is Not America - **David Bowie & the Pat Metheny Group** 9.02.85
This Is The Right Time - **Lisa Stansfield** 12.08.89
This Is The World Calling - **Bob Geldof** 1.11.86
This Is Tomorrow - **Bryan Ferry** 12.02.77
This Is Your Land - **Blow Monkeys** 15.04.89
This Is Your Land - **Simple Minds** 22.04.89
This Is Your Life - **Banderas** 9.03.91
This Little Bird - **Marianne Faithfull** 6.05.65
This Little Bird - **Nashville Teens** 27.05.65
This Love I Have For You - **Lance Fortune** 5.05.60
This Old Heart of Mine - **Isley Brothers** 23.10.68
This Old Heart Of Mine - **Rod Stewart** 15.11.75
This Ole House - **Rosemary Clooney** 8.10.54
This Ole House - **Billie Anthony** 15.10.54
This Ole House - **Shakin' Stevens** 7.03.81
This One - **Paul McCartney** 29.07.89
This One's For the Children - **New Kids On the Block** 8.12.90
This Perfect Day - **The Saints** 23.07.77
This Strange Effect - **Dave Berry** 22.07.65
This Time - **Troy Shondell** 16.11.61
This Time I Know It's For Real - **Donna Summer** 4.03.89
This Time (We'll Get It Right) - **England World Cup Squad** 10.04.82
This Town Ain't Big Enough for Both of Us - **Sparks** 11.05.74
This Wheel's On Fire - **Julie Driscoll, Brian Auger & the Trinity** 24.04.68
This Wheel's On Fire - **Siouxsie & the Banshees** 17.01.87
This Will Be - **Natalie Cole** 18.10.75
This Woman's Work - **Kate Bush** 2.12.89
This World Is Not My Home - **Jim Reeves** 22.07.65
This World of Water - **New Musik** 3.05.80
This Wreckage - **Gary Numan** 20.12.80
Thorn In My Side - **Eurythmics** 6.09.86
Those Were The Days - **Mary Hopkin** 11.09.68
A Thousand Stars - **Billy Fury** 19.01.61
3AM Eternal - **KLF (featuring The Children of the Revolution)** 19.01.91
3 x 3 (EP) - **Genesis** 22.05.82
Three Bells - **Browns** 18.09.59
Three Bells - **Compagnons de la Chanson** 9.10.59
Three Bells - **Brian Poole & the Tremeloes** 7.01.65
Three Coins In The Fountain - **Frank Sinatra** 16.07.54
Three Coins In The Fountain - **Four Aces** 30.07.54
Three Little Words - **Applejacks** 15.10.64
Three Little Birds - **Bob Marley & the Wailers** 20.09.80
Three Minute Hero - **Selecter** 2.02.80
Three Ring Circus - **Barry Biggs** 16.07.77
Three Songs (EP) - **Wedding Present** 29.09.90

Three Stars - **Ruby Wright** 22.05.59
Three Steps to Heaven - **Eddie Cochran** 12.05.60
Three Steps to Heaven - **Showaddywaddy** 24.05.75
Three Times A Lady - **Commodores** 12.08.78
Thriller - **Michael Jackson** 19.11.83
Through the Barricades - **Spandau Ballet** 8.11.86
Throw Away the Key - **Linx** 20.06.81
Throw Down A Line - **Cliff & Hank** 13.09.69
Throwing It All Away - **Genesis** 27.06.87
Thunder And Lightning - **Thin Lizzy** 7.05.83
Thunder In My Heart - **Leo Sayer** 10.09.77
Thunder In The Mountains - **Toyah** 3.10.81
Thunderball - **Tom Jones** 20.01.66
Thunderbirds Are Go - **F.A.B. featuring MC Parker** 7.07.90
Thunderstruck - **AC/DC** 22.09.90
Thus Spake Zarathustra - **Philharmonia Orchestra conductor Lorin Maazel** 30.07.69
Ticket To Ride - **Beatles** 15.04.65
The Tide Is High - **Blondie** 8.11.80
Tie A Yellow Ribbon Round The Old Oak Tree - **Dawn** 10.03.73
Tie Me Kangaroo Down Sport - **Rolf Harris** 21.07.60
Tie Your Mother Down - **Queen** 26.03.77
Tiger Feet - **Mud** 19.01.74
Tighten Up (I Just Can't Stop Dancin') - **Wally Jump Jr & the Criminal Element** 19.12.87
Tijuana Taxi - **Herb Alpert & the Tijuana Brass** 24.03.66
'Til I Kissed You - **Everly Brothers** 11.09.59
Til I Loved You - **Barbra Streisand & Don Johnson** 12.11.88
Till - **Tony Bennett** 5.01.61
Till - **Dorothy Squires** 28.02.70
Till - **Tom Jones** 23.10.71
Till I Loved You - **Placido Domingo & Jennifer Rush** 17.06.89
Till The End of The Day - **Kinks** 2.12.65
Till There Was You - **Peggy Lee** 23.03.61
Time - **Craig Douglas** 6.07.61
Time - **Freddie Mercury** 24.05.86
Time After Time - **Cyndi Lauper** 23.06.84
Time and the River - **Nat 'King' Cole** 12.02.60
Time (Clock of the Heart) - **Culture Club** 27.11.82
Time Drags By - **Cliff Richard** 13.10.66
Time For Action - **Secret Affair** 8.09.79
Time For Living - **Association** 22.05.68
The Time Has Come - **Adam Faith** 26.10.61
The Time In Between - **Cliff Richard** 26.08.65
Time Is Tight - **Booker T & the MGs** 7.05.69
Time Love and Tenderness - **Michael Bolton** 20.08.91
Time Seller - **Spencer Davis Group** 9.08.67
Time To Make The Floor Burn - **Megabass** 10.11.90
The Time Warp - **Damian** 26.08.89
Time Will Crawl - **David Bowie** 27.06.87
The Times They Are A-Changin' - **Bob Dylan** 25.03.65
Tin Soldier - **Small Faces** 13.12.67
Tina Marie - **Perry Como** 30.12.55
Tired of Being Alone - **Al Green** 9.10.71
Tired of Getting Pushed Around - **2 Men A Drum Machine & A Trumpet** 23.01.88
Tired of Waiting For You - **Kinks** 21.01.65
To All The Girls I've Loved Before - **Julio Iglesias & Willie Nelson** 20.04.84
To Be A Lover - **Billy Idol** 11.10.86
To Be Loved - **Jackie Wilson** 14.03.58
To Be Loved - **Malcolm Vaughan** 21.03.58
To Be Or Not To Be - **BA Robertson** 14.06.80
To Be Or Not To Be (The Hitler Rap) - **Mel Brooks** 3.03.84
To Be Reborn - **Boy George** 21.11.87
To Be With You Again - **Level 42** 25.04.87
To Cut A Long Story Short - **Spandau Ballet** 22.11.80
To Have And To Hold - **Catherine Stock** 25.10.86
To Here Knows When - **My Bloody Valentine** 16.02.91
To Know Him Is To Love Him - **Teddy Bears** 19.12.58
To Know You Is To Love You - **Peter & Gordon** 1.07.65
To Love Somebody - **Nina Simone** 15.01.69
To Love Somebody - **Jimmy Somerville** 10.11.90
To Make A Big Man Cry - **P.J. Proby** 16.06.66
To Whom It Concerns - **Chris Andrews** 2.12.65
Toast of Love - **Three Degrees** 8.05.76
Toast/Hold On - **Streetband** 11.11.78
Tobacco Road - **Nashville Teens** 16.07.64
Toccata - **Sky** 19.04.80
Today - **Sandie Shaw** 14.02.68
Today - **Talk Talk** 31.07.82
Today Forever (EP) - **Ride** 16.03.91
Together - **Connie Francis** 14.09.61
Together - **P.J. Proby** 3.09.64
Together - **O.C. Smith** 2.04.77
Together Forever - **Rick Astley** 27.02.88
Together in Electric Dreams - **Giorgio Moroder & Philip Oakey** 29.09.84
Together We Are Beautiful - **Fern Kinney** 23.02.80
Tokoloshe Man - **John Kongos** 20.11.71
Tokyo Joe - **Bryan Ferry** 21.05.77
Tokyo Melody - **Helmut Zacharias** 29.10.64
Tom-Tom Turnaround - **New World** 3.07.71
Tom Dooley - **Lonnie Donegan** 21.11.58
Tom Dooley - **Kingston Trio** 21.11.58
Tom Hark - **Elias & his Zig Zag Jive Flutes** 25.04.58
Tom Hark - **Ted Heath Orchestra** 4.07.58
Tom Hark - **Piranhas** 9.08.80
Tom Pillibi - **Jacqueline Boyer** 28.04.60
Tom Sawyer - **Rush** 24.10.81
Tom the Peeper - **Act One** 18.05.74
Tomb of Memories - **Paul Young** 22.06.85
Tomboy - **Perry Como** 27.02.59
Tommy Gun - **Clash** 2.12.78
Tomorrow - **Johnny Brandon** 11.03.55
Tomorrow - **Sandie Shaw** 10.02.66
Tomorrow - **Communards** 12.09.87
Tomorrow - **Tongue 'n' Cheek** 14.04.90
Tomorrow Night - **Atomic Rooster** 6.02.71
Tomorrow People - **Ziggy Marley & the Melody Makers** 9.07.88
Tomorrow Tomorrow - **Bee Gees** 11.06.69
Tomorrow's Clown - **Marty Wilde** 16.11.61
Tomorrows Girls - **U.K. Subs** 15.09.79
Tomorrow's (Just Another Day)/Madness Is All In The Mind - **Madness** 19.02.83
Tom's Diner - **DNA featuring Suzanne Vega** 28.07.90
Tonight - **Shirley Bassey** 15.02.62
Tonight - **Move** 10.07.71
Tonight - **Rubettes** 13.07.74
Tonight - **New Kids on the Block** 4.08.90
Tonight I Celebrate My Love - **Peabo Bryson and Roberta Flack** 27.08.83
Tonight I'm Alright - **Narada Michael Walden** 8.03.80
Tonight I'm Yours (Don't Hurt Me) - **Rod Stewart** 24.10.81
Tonight in Tokyo - **Sandie Shaw** 12.07.67
Tonight Tonight Tonight - **Genesis** 14.03.87
Tonight You Belong To Me - **Patience & Prudence** 2.11.56
Tonight's the Night - **Rod Stewart** 12.06.76
Too Beautiful to Last - **Engelbert Humperdinck** 11.03.72
Too Big - **Suzi Quatro** 29.06.74
Too Blind To See It - **Kim Syms** 7.12.91
Too Busy Thinking About My Baby - **Marvin Gaye** 23.07.69
Too Busy Thinking About My Baby - **Mardi Gras** 12.08.72
Too Drunk to Fuck - **Dead Kennedys** 13.06.81
Too Good - **Little Tony** 15.01.60
Too Good to be Forgotten - **Chi-Lites** 2.11.74
Too Good To Be Forgotten - **Amazulu** 7.06.86
Too Hot - **Kool & the Gang** 26.01.80
Too Hot To Handle/Slip Your Disc To This - **Heatwave** 7.05.77
Too Hot to Trot/Zoom - **Commodores** 25.03.78
Too Late - **Junior** 17.07.82
Too Late for Goodbyes - **Julian Lennon** 20.10.84
Too Late to Say Goodbye - **Richard Marx** 24.03.90
Too Many Broken Hearts - **Jason Donovan** 4.03.89
Too Many Games - **Maze featuring Frankie Beverly** 27.07.85
Too Many Rivers - **Brenda Lee** 29.07.65
Too Many Walls - **Cathy Dennis** 5.10.91
Too Much - **Elvis Presley** 10.05.57
Too Much - **Bros** 29.07.89
Too Much Heaven - **Bee Gees** 25.11.78
Too Much Too Little Too Late - **Johnny Mathis & Deniece Williams** 25.03.78
Too Much Too Young (EP) - **Special AKA** 26.01.80
Too Nice to Talk To - **Beat** 20.12.80
Too Shy - **Kajagoogoo** 22.01.83
Too Soon To Know - **Roy Orbison** 18.08.66
Too Young - **Bill Forbes** 15.01.60
Too Young - **Donny Osmond** 16.09.72
Too Young To Go Steady - **Nat 'King' Cole** 11.04.56
Top Of The Pops - **Rezillos** 19.08.78
Top of the World - **Carpenters** 20.10.73
Top Teen Baby - **Gary Mills** 20.10.60
Topsy Parts I & II - **Cozy Cole** 5.12.58
Torch - **Soft Cell** 29.05.82

Torero - **Renato Carosone** 4.07.58
Torero - **Julius LaRosa** 4.07.58
Torn Between Two Lovers - **Mary MacGregor** 19.02.77
Torture - **Jacksons** 8.09.84
Torture - **King** 11.01.86
Tossing and Turning - **Ivy League** 1.07.65
Tossing and Turning - **Windjammer** 21.07.84
Total Eclipse Of The Heart - **Bonnie Tyler** 26.02.83
Total Mix - **Black Box** 15.12.90
Tottenham Tottenham - **Tottenham Hotspur FA Cup Final Squad** 8.05.82
Touch Me - **49ers** 23.12.89
Touch Me (All Night Long) - **Cathy Dennis** 4.05.91
Touch Me (I Want Your Body) - **Samantha Fox** 22.03.86
Touch Me In The Morning - **Diana Ross** 21.07.73
Touch Me Touch Me - **Dave Dee Dozy Beaky Mick & Tich** 16.03.67
Touch Too Much - **AC/DC** 16.02.80
A Touch Too Much - **Arrows** 1.06.74
Touched By The Hand of God - **New Order** 19.12.87
Touched by the Hand of Cicciolina - **Pop Will Eat Itself** 9.06.90
Touchy! - **A-Ha** 27.08.88
Tougher Than The Rest - **Bruce Springsteen** 18.06.88
Tour De France - **Kraftwerk** 13.08.83
Tour de France - **Kraftwerk** 8.09.84
Tous Les Garcons et Les Filles - **Francoise Hardy** 2.07.64
Tower of Strength - **Frankie Vaughan** 16.11.61
Tower of Strength - **Mission** 13.02.88
Towers of London - **XTC** 25.10.80
Town Called Malice/Precious - **Jam** 13.02.82
Town Crier - **Craig Douglas** 7.03.63
Town Without Pity - **Gene Pitney** 15.03.62
Toy - **Casuals** 4.12.68
Toy - **Casuals** 18.12.68
Toy Balloons - **Russ Conway** 7.12.61
Toy Boy - **Sinitta** 1.08.87
Toy Soldiers - **Martika** 5.08.98
Tracie - **Level 42** 21.01.89
The Tracks of My Tears - **Smokey Robinson & the Miracles** 7.05.69
Tracy - **Cufflinks** 29.11.69
Tragedy - **Argent** 1.07.72
Tragedy - **Bee Gees** 17.02.79
The Trail Of The Lonesome Pine - **Laurel And Hardy** 29.11.75
Train of Love - **Alma Cogan** 18.08.60
Train of Thought - **A-Ha** 5.04.86
Train to Skaville - **Ethiopians** 20.09.67
Train Tour to Rainbow City - **Pyramids** 15.11.67
Trains and Boats and Planes - **Billy J Kramer & the Dakotas** 20.05.65
Trains and Boats and Planes - **Burt Bacharach** 20.05.65
Trambone - **Krew Kats** 23.03.61
Tramp - **Otis Redding & Carla Thomas** 26.07.67
Trampolene - **Julian Cope** 17.01.87
Transfer Affection - **A Flock Of Seagulls** 9.07.83
Transistor Radio - **Benny Hill** 1.06.61
Trapped - **Colonel Abrams** 14.09.85
Trash - **Roxy Music** 10.03.79
Travellin' Band - **Creedence Clearwater Revival** 4.04.70
Travellin' Home - **Vera Lynn** 21.06.57
Travellin' Light - **Cliff Richard & the Shadows** 9.10.59
Travellin' Man/Hello Mary Lou - **Ricky Nelson** 1.06.61
Treason (It's Just A Story) - **Teardrop Explodes** 9.05.81
Treasure of Love - **Clyde McPhatter** 24.08.56
Treat Her Like A Lady - **Temptations** 17.11.84
Treat Her Right - **Roy Head** 11.11.65
Treat Me Good - **Yazz** 23.06.90
Treble Chance - **Joe Henderson** 23.10.59
Tribal Base - **Rebel MC, Tenor Fly & Barrington Levy** 15.06.91
Tribute (Right On) - **Pasadenas** 11.06.88
Tribute To A King - **William Bell** 5.06.68
Tribute to Buddy Holly - **Mike Berry** 12.10.61
Tribute to Jim Reeves - **Larry Cunningham & the Mighty Avons** 7.01.65
Trick of the Night - **Bananarama** 21.02.87
Tricky Disco - **Tricky Disco** 28.07.90
Trocadero - **Showaddywaddy** 5.06.76
The Trooper - **Iron Maiden** 2.07.83
Trouble - **Elvis Presley** 31.05.75
Trouble - **Gillan** 4.10.80
Trouble - **Lindsey Buckingham** 30.1.82
Trouble In Paradise - **Al Jarreau** 23.07.83
Trouble Is My Middle Name - **Brook Brothers** 28.02.63
Trouble Is My Middle Name - **Four Pennies** 24.02.66
The Trouble With Harry - **Alfi & Harry** 23.03.56
Truck On (Tyke) - **T.Rex** 24.11.73
Trudie - **Joe Henderson** 25.07.58
True - **Spandau Ballet** 23.04.83
True Blue - **Madonna** 4.10.86
True Colors - **Cyndi Lauper** 27.09.86
True Faith - **New Order** 1.08.87
True Love - **Bing Crosby & Grace Kelly** 23.11.56
True Love - **Terry Lightfoot & his New Orleans Jazzmen** 14.09.61
True Love - **Richard Chamberlain** 25.07.63
True Love - **Shakin' Stevens** 17.12.88
True Love For Evermore - **Bachelors** 8.04.65
True Love Ways - **Buddy Holly** 26.05.60
True Love Ways - **Peter & Gordon** 8.04.65
True Love Ways - **Cliff Richard and the London Philharmonic Orchestra** 16.04.83
Truly - **Lionel Richie** 20.11.82
Trust - **Ned's Atomic Dustbin** 21.09.91
Try - **Bros** 21.09.91
Try My World - **Georgie Fame** 27.09.67
Try to Understand - **Lulu** 16.09.65
Tryin' - **Hilltoppers** 14.09.56
Trying to Forget - **Jim Reeves** 2.08.67
Trying To Get to You - **Elvis Presley** 1.11.57
Tulane - **Steve Gibbons Band** 13.08.77
Tumbling Dice - **Rolling Stones** 29.04.72
Tumbling Tumbleweeds - **Slim Whitman** 9.03.56
Tunes Splits the Atom - **MC Tunes vs 808 State** 22.09.90
The Tunnel Of Love - **Fun Boy Three** 12.02.83
Turn Back the Clock - **Johnny Hates Jazz** 28.11.87
Turn It Into Love - **Hazell Dean** 24.09.88
Turn It On Again - **Genesis** 15.03.80
Turn It Up - **Conway Brothers** 22.06.85
Turn Me On Turn Me Off - **Honey Bane** 31.01.81
Turn The Music Up - **Players Association** 17.03.79
Turn to Stone - **Electric Light Orchestra** 5.11.77
Turn! Turn! Turn! - **Byrds** 18.11.65
Turn Up The Bass - **Tyree featuring Rock Steady** 25.02.89
Turn Up The Night - **Black Sabbath** 13.02.82
Turn Your Love Around - **George Benson** 21.11.81
Turn Your Radio On - **Ray Stevens** 1.04.72
Turning Away - **Shakin' Stevens** 8.02.86
Turning Japanese - **Vapors** 1.03.80
Turquoise - **Donovan** 18.11.65
Turtle Power - **Partners In Kryme** 21.07.90
Turtle Rhapsody - **Orchestra on the Half Shell** 15.12.90
Tusk - **Fleetwood Mac** 13.10.79
Tutti Frutti - **Little Richard** 22.02.57
Tuxedo Junction - **Manhattan Transfer** 7.02.76
TVC 15 - **David Bowie** 29.05.76
Tweedle Dee - **Georgia Gibbs** 22.04.55
Tweedle Dee - **Frankie Vaughan** 22.04.55
Tweedle Dee - **Little Jimmy Osmond** 31.03.73
Tweedle Dee Tweedle Dum - **Middle of the Road** 11.09.71
Twelfth of Never - **Cliff Richard** 8.10.64
The Twelfth of Never - **Donny Osmond** 10.03.73
Twelve Steps to Love - **Brian Poole & the Tremeloes** 27.08.64
20th Century Box - **Marc Bolan & T Rex** 24.08.91
20th Century Boy - **T. Rex** 10.03.73
21st Century Boy - **Sigue Sigue Sputnik** 7.06.86
25 Miles - **Edwin Starr** 20.09.69
25 Or 6 To 4 - **Chicago** 1.08.70
24 Hours - **Betty Boo** 1.12.90
Twenty Four Hours from Tulsa - **Gene Pitney** 5.12.63
24 Sycamore - **Gene Pitney** 12.05.73
20 Seconds To Comply - **Silver Bullet** 16.12.89
Twenty Tiny Fingers - **Alma Cogan** 16.12.55
Twenty Tiny Fingers - **Stargazers** 11.11.55
Twenty Tiny Fingers - **Coronets** 25.11.55
20/20 - **George Benson** 26.01.85
Twilight - **Electric Light Orchestra** 24.10.81
Twilight Cafe - **Susan Fassbender** 24.01.81
Twilight Time - **Platters** 16.05.58
Twilight World - **Swing Out Sister** 2.05.87
Twilight Zone-Twilight Tone - **Manhattan Transfer** 31.05.80
Twilight Zone/Wrathchild - **Iron Maiden** 21.03.81
Twinkie-Lee - **Gary Walker** 2.06.66
Twinkle Toes - **Roy Orbison** 7.04.66
The Twist - **Chubby Checker** 11.01.62

Twist and Shout - **Brian Poole & the Tremeloes** 11.07.63
Twist and Shout - **Salt-N-Pepa** 12.11.88
Twist and Shout - **Deacon Blue** 27.07.91
Twist In My Sobriety - **Tanita Tikaram** 22.10.88
Twist (Round And Round) - **Chill Fac-Torr** 16.04.83
The Twist (Yo, Twist) - **Fat Boys with Chubby Checker** 18.06.88
Twistin' The Night Away - **Sam Cooke** 8.03.62
Twisting By The Pool - **Dire Straits** 22.01.83
Twixt Twelve and Twenty - **Pat Boone** 31.07.59
Two Different Worlds - **Ronnie Hilton** 9.11.56
2.4.6.8. Motorway - **Tom Robinson** 22.10.77
Two Hearts - **Cliff Richard** 20.02.88
Two Hearts - **Phil Collins** 26.11.88
Two Hearts Beat As One - **U2** 2.04.83
Two Kinds of Teardrops - **Del Shannon** 25.04.63
Two Little Boys - **Rolf Harris** 22.11.69
Two Little Boys/Horse - **Splodgenessabounds** 13.09.80
2 Minutes To Midnight - **Iron Maiden** 18.08.84
Two Out of Three Ain't Bad - **Meat Loaf** 2.09.78
Two Silhouettes - **Del Shannon** 29.08.63
Two Streets - **Val Doonican** 8.06.67
2000 Miles - **Pretenders** 10.12.83
Two Tribes - **Frankie Goes to Hollywood** 16.06.84
2/231 - **Anticapella** 16.11.91
U Can't Touch This - **MC Hammer** 23.06.90
U Got The Look - **Prince** 15.08.87
The Ugly Duckling - **Mike Reid** 22.03.75
UK Blak - **Caron Wheeler** 17.11.90
'Ullo John! Gotta New Motor? - **Alexei Sayle** 3.03.84
Um Um Um Um Um Um - **Major Lance** 20.02.64
Um Um Um Um Um Um - **Wayne Fontana & the Mindbenders** 8.10.64
Un Banc, Un Arbre, Une Rue - **Severine** 1.05.71
Una Paloma Blanca - **Jonathan King** 13.09.75
Unbelievable - **EMF** 10.11.90
Unchained Melody - **Jimmy Young** 6.05.55
Unchained Melody - **Al Hibbler** 13.05.55
Unchained Melody - **Les Baxter** 13.05.55
Unchained Melody - **Liberace** 17.06.55
Unchained Melody - **Righteous Brothers** 12.08.65
Unchained Melody - **Righteous Brothers** 27.10.90
Uncle Sam - **Madness** 2.11.85
Unconditional Love - **Donna Summer** 22.10.83
Under Attack - **Abba** 18.12.82
Under My Thumb - **Wayne Gibson** 30.11.74
Under New Management - **Barron Knights** 8.12.66
Under One Roof - **Rubettes** 9.10.76
Under Pressure - **Queen & David Bowie** 14.11.81
Under the Boardwalk - **Tom Tom Club** 14.08.82
Under the Boardwalk - **Bruce Willis** 6.06.87
Under the Bridges of Paris - **Dean Martin** 1.04.55
Under The Bridges of Paris - **Eartha Kitt** 1.04.55
Under the Moon of Love - **Showaddywaddy** 6.11.76
Under Your Thumb - **Godley & Creme** 19.09.81
Undercover Anarchist - **Silver Bullet** 13.04.91
Undercover Of The Night - **Rolling Stones** 12.11.83
Underground - **David Bowie** 21.06.86
Underneath the Blanket Go - **Gilbert O'Sullivan** 3.04.71
Underpass - **John Foxx** 9.02.80
Unfinished Sympathy - **Massive** 2.03.91
Unforgettable - **Natalie Cole & Nat 'King' Cole** 29.06.91
The Unforgettable Fire - **U2** 4.05.85
The Unforgiven - **Metallica** 9.11.91
Union City Blue - **Blondie** 24.11.79
Union Of The Snake - **Duran Duran** 29.10.83
United - **Judas Priest** 6.09.80
United We Stand - **Brotherhood of Man** 14.02.70
Universal - **Small Faces** 10.07.68
Unskinny Bop - **Poison** 30.06.90
Unsquare Dance - **Dave Brubeck** 17.05.62
Until It's Time For You To Go - **Four Pennies** 21.10.65
Until It's Time For You To Go - **Elvis Presley** 1.04.72
Until You Come Back to Me - **Aretha Franklin** 23.02.74
Up Above My Head/Good Evening Friends - **Frankie Laine & Johnnie Ray** 4.10.57
Up Against The Wall - **Tom Robinson Band** 13.05.78
Up Around The Bend - **Creedence Clearwater Revival** 20.06.70
Up On The Catwalk - **Simple Minds** 24.03.84
Up On The Roof - **Kenny Lynch** 13.12.62
Up On The Roof - **Julie Grant** 3.01.63
Up the Hill Backwards - **David Bowie** 4.04.81
Up The Junction - **Squeeze** 9.06.79
Up The Ladder to The Roof - **Supremes** 9.05.70
Up Up and Away - **Johnny Mann Singers** 19.07.67
Up Where We Belong - **Joe Cocker and Jennifer Warnes** 22.01.83
Upside Down - **Diana Ross** 19.07.80
Uptight - **Stevie Wonder** 3.02.66
Uptown Festival - **Shalamar** 21.05.77
Uptown Girl - **Billy Joel** 22.10.83
Uptown Top Ranking - **Althia & Donna** 24.12.77
Uptown, Uptempo Woman - **Randy Edelman** 25.09.76
U.S. Male - **Elvis Presley** 15.05.68
Urban Guerilla - **Hawkwind** 25.08.73
The Urge - **Freddie Cannon** 26.05.60
Use It Up and Wear It Out - **Odyssey** 28.06.80
Use It Up and Wear It Out - **Pat & Mick** 21.04.90
Use Ta Be My Girl - **O'Jays** 24.06.78
Vacation - **Connie Francis** 2.08.62
Vado Via - **Drupi** 8.12.73
Vagabonds - **New Model Army** 11.03.89
Valentine - **T'Pau** 30.01.88
Valentino - **Connie Francis** 17.03.60
Valerie - **Steve Winwood** 3.10.87
Valleri - **Monkees** 3.04.68
Valley of Tears - **Fats Domino** 19.07.57
Valley of The Dolls - **Dionne Warwick** 13.03.68
Valley of The Dolls - **Generation X** 7.04.79
Vanessa - **Ted Heath Orchestra** 16.01.53
Vaya Con Dios - **Les Paul and Mary Ford** 20.11.53
Vaya Con Dios - **Millican & Nesbitt** 8.12.73
Vehicle - **Ides of March** 13.06.70
Velouria - **Pixies** 28.07.90
Venus - **Dickie Valentine** 13.03.59
Venus - **Frankie Avalon** 24.04.59
Venus - **Shocking Blue** 24.01.70
Venus - **Bananarama** 7.06.86
Venus - **Don Pablo's Animals** 19.05.90
Venus in Blue Jeans - **Mark Wynter** 11.10.62
Veronica - **Elvis Costello** 11.03.89
A Very Previous Love - **Doris Day** 13.06.58
Victim of Love - **Erasure** 30.05.87
Victims - **Culture Club** 10.12.83
Victims of Success - **Dogs D'Amour** 23.06.90
Victoria - **Kinks** 17.01.70
Victoria - **Fall** 6.02.88
Victory - **Kool & the Gang** 17.01.87
Video Killed The Radio Star - **Buggles** 29.09.79
Videotheque - **Dollar** 26.06.82
Vienna - **Ultravox** 24.01.81
Vienna Calling - **Falco** 31.05.86
View From A Bridge - **Kim Wilde** 24.04.82
A View To A Kill - **Duran Duran** 18.05.85
Village of St. Bernadette - **Anne Shelton** 20.11.59
Vincent - **Don McLean** 13.05.72
Violence Of Summer (Love's Taking Over) - **Duran Duran** 4.08.90
Violently (EP) - **Hue & Cry** 13.05.89
Virgin Mary - **Lonnie Donegan** 15.12.60
Virginia Plain - **Roxy Music** 26.08.72
Virginia Plain - **Roxy Music** 22.10.77
Visage - **Visage** 11.07.81
Vision of Love - **Mariah Carey** 18.08.90
Visions - **Cliff Richard** 21.07.66
Visions In Blue - **Ultravox** 19.03.83
Visions of China - **Japan** 14.11.81
Viva Bobby Joe - **Equals** 30.07.69
Viva Las Vegas - **Elvis Presley** 19.03.64
Vogue - **Madonna** 7.04.90
The Voice - **Ultravox** 14.11.81
Voice in the Wilderness - **Cliff Richard & the Shadows** 22.01.60
Voices In The Sky - **Moody Blues** 14.08.68
Volare - **Dean Martin** 29.08.58
Volare - **Domenico Modugno** 5.09.58
Volare - **Marino Marini** 3.10.58
Volare - **Charlie Drake** 24.10.58
Volare - **Bobby Rydell** 15.09.60
Voodoo Chile - **Jimi Hendrix Experience** 7.11.70
Voyage Voyage - **Desireless** 28.05.88
Wade In The Water - **Ramsey Lewis** 29.04.72
Wages Day - **Deacon Blue** 4.03.89
Wait - **Robert Howard & Kym Mazelle** 14.01.89

Wait For Me/Willingly - **Malcolm Vaughan** 27.02.59
Wait For Me Darling - **Joan Regan & the Johnston Brothers** 5.11.54
Wait For Me Mary-Anne - **Marmalade** 23.10.68
Wait Until Tonight (My Love) - **Galaxy featuring Phil Fearon** 6.08.83
Waiting For A Girl Like You - **Foreigner** 18.12.81
Waiting For A Train - **Flash and the Pan** 28.05.83
Waiting For A Star to Fall - **Boy Meets Girl** 31.12.88
Waiting For An Alibi - **Thin Lizzy** 10.03.79
Waiting For That Day - **George Michael** 27.10.90
(Waiting For) The Ghost Train 8.11.86
Waiting In Vain - **Bob Marley & the Wailers** 17.09.77
Waiting In Vain - **Bob Marley & the Wailers** 30.06.84
Wake Me Up Before You Go Go - **Wham!** 26.05.84
Wake Up Everybody - **Harold Melvin & the Blue Notes** 6.03.76
Wake Up Little Susie - **Everly Brothers** 8.11.57
Wake Up Little Susie - **King Brothers** 6.12.57
Wake Up Susan - **Detroit Spinners** 5.02.77
The Walk - **Inmates** 12.01.80
The Walk - **Cure** 9.07.83
Walk Away - **Shane Fenton & Fentones** 8.02.62
Walk Away - **Matt Monro** 17.09.64
Walk Away - **Joyce Sims** 30.04.88
Walk Away From Love - **David Ruffin** 24.01.76
Walk Away Renee - **Four Tops** 13.12.67
Walk Don't Run - **Ventures** 15.09.60
Walk Don't Run - **John Barry Seven** 22.09.60
Walk Hand In Hand - **Tony Martin** 13.07.56
Walk Hand In Hand - **Ronnie Carroll** 27.07.56
Walk Hand In Hand - **Jimmy Parkinson** 17.08.56
Walk Hand In Hand - **Gerry & the Pacemakers** 25.11.65
Walk In Love - **Manhattan Transfer** 11.03.78
Walk In The Black Forest - **Horst Jankowski** 29.07.65
Walk In The Night - **Jnr. Walker & the All Stars** 26.08.72
A Walk In The Park - **Nick Straker Band** 16.08.80
Walk Like A Man - **Four Seasons** 4.04.63
Walk Like An Egyptian - **Bangles** 4.10.86
Walk of Life - **Dire Straits** 11.01.86
Walk On - **Roy Orbison** 31.07.68
Walk On By - **Leroy Van Dyke** 11.01.62
Walk on By - **Dionne Warwick** 23.04.64
Walk On By - **Stranglers** 12.08.78
Walk on By - **Sybil** 27.01.90
Walk On The Wild Side - **Lou Reed** 12.05.73
Walk On The Wild Side - **Jamie J Morgan** 24.02.90
Walk Right Back - **Perry Como** 15.12.73
Walk Right In - **Rooftop Singers** 31.01.63
Walk Right Now - **Jacksons** 18.07.81
Walk Tall - **Val Doonican** 22.10.64
Walk the Dinosaur - **Was Not Was** 10.10.87
Walk This Way - **Run DMC** 6.09.86
Walk With Faith In Your Heart - **Bachelors** 8.12.66
Walk With Me - **Seekers** 8.09.66
Walk With Me My Angel - **Don Charles** 8.03.62
Walk With Me Talk With Me Darling - **Four Tops** 12.08.72
Walkin' - **C.C.S.** 27.02.71
Walkin' In The Rain With the One I Love - **Love Unlimited** 24.06.72
Walkin' In The Sunshine - **Bad Manners** 3.10.81
A Walkin' Miracle - **Limmie & the Family Cookin'** 6.04.74
Walkin' My Baby Back Home - **Johnnie Ray** 14.11.52
Walkin' Tall - **Frankie Vaughan** 18.09.59
Walkin' Tall - **Adam Faith** 11.07.63
Walkin' The Dog - **Dennisons** 21.05.64
Walkin' to Missouri - **Tony Brent** 19.12.52
Walking Alone - **Richard Anthony** 19.12.63
Walking Back to Happiness - **Helen Shapiro** 28.09.61
Walking Down Your Street - **Bangles** 17.01.87
Walking Down Madison - **Kirsty MacColl** 1.06.91
Walking In Memphis - **Marc Cohn** 12.10.91
Walking In Rhythm - **Blackbyrds** 7.06.75
Walking In The Air - **Aled Jones** 14.12.85
Walking In The Air - **Peter Auty & the Sinfonia of London** 2.01.88
Walking In The Rain - **Walker Brothers** 18.05.67
Walking In The Rain - **Partridge Family** 26.05.73
Walking In The Rain - **Modern Romance** 13.08.83
Walking My Cat Named Dog - **Norma Tanega** 14.04.66
Walking on Sunshine - **Rocker's Revenge featuring Donnie Calvin** 21.08.82
Walking On Sunshine - **Katrina & the Waves** 18.05.85
Walking On The Moon - **Police** 1.12.79
Walking on Thin Ice - **Yoko Ono** 7.03.81
Walking On The Chinese Wall - **Philip Bailey** 1.06.85
Walking the Floor Over You - **Pat Boone** 30.06.60
Walking to New Orleans - **Fats Domino** 4.08.60
Wall Street Shuffle - **10cc** 15.06.74
Walls Come Tumbling Down - **Style Council** 11.05.85
Walls Fell Down - **Marbles** 2.04.69
Waltz Darling - **Malcolm McLaren** 17.06.89
Wam Bam - **Handley Family** 14.04.73
The Wanderer - **Dion** 22.02.62
The Wanderer - **Dion** 29.05.76
The Wanderer - **Status Quo** 27.10.84
Wan'drin' Star/I Talk To The Trees - **Lee Marvin/Clint Eastwood** 7.02.70
Wanna Be Startin' Something - **Michael Jackson** 11.06.83
Wanted - **Al Martino** 4.06.54
Wanted - **Perry Como** 4.06.54
Wanted - **Dooleys** 30.06.79
Wanted - **Style Council** 31.10.87
Wanted Dead or Alive - **Bon Jovi** 11.04.87
War - **Edwin Starr** 24.10.70
War - **Bruce Springsteen** 29.11.86
War Baby - **Tom Robinson** 25.06.83
War Child - **Blondie** 31.07.82
War Lord - **Shadows** 2.12.65
War Paint - **Brook Brothers** 30.03.61
The War Song - **Culture Club** 6.10.84
Warhead - **UK Subs** 15.03.80
Warm and Tender Love - **Percy Sledge** 18.08.66
Warm Wet Circles - **Marillion** 7.11.87
Warmed Over Kisses - **Brian Hyland** 8.11.62
Warning - **Adeva** 19.08.89
Warning Sign - **Nick Heyward** 24.11.84
Warriors - **Gary Numan** 3.09.83
Warriors (Of The Wasteland) - **Frankie Goes to Hollywood** 22.11.86
Was It Worth It - **Pet Shop Boys** 21.12.91
Was That All It Was - **Kym Mazelle** 27.01.90
Wash Your Face In My Sink - **Dream Warriors** 21.07.90
Wasted Time - **Skid Row** 23.11.91
Wasted Years - **Iron Maiden** 6.09.86
Wasteland - **Mission** 17.01.87
Watch Me - **Labi Siffre** 5.08.72
Watchdogs - **UB40** 16.05.87
Watcher's Point of View - **PM Dawn** 22.06.91
Watchin' The Detectives - **Elvis Costello** 5.11.77
Watching - **Thompson Twins** 23.07.83
Watching the River Flow - **Bob Dylan** 17.07.71
Watching the Wheels - **John Lennon** 11.04.81
Watching The Wildlife - **Frankie Goes to Holywood** 7.03.87
Watching You Watching Me - **David Grant** 6.08.83
Water - **Geno Washington & his Ram Jam Band** 2.06.66
Water Margin - **Peter Mac Junior & Godiego** 29.10.77
Water on Glass/Boys - **Kim Wilde** 1.08.81
Water Water - **Tommy Steele** 16.08.57
Waterfalls - **Paul McCartney** 28.06.80
Waterfront - **Simple Minds** 26.11.83
Waterloo - **Stonewall Jackson** 17.07.59
Waterloo - **Abba** 20.04.74
Waterloo Sunset - **Kinks** 11.05.67
Wave of The Future - **Quadrophonia** 6.07.91
Waves - **Blancmange** 26.02.83
Way Back Home - **Jnr. Walker & the All Stars** 7.07.73
Way Behind Me - **Primitives** 3.09.88
Way Down - **Elvis Presley** 27.08.77
Way Down Yonder in New Orleans - **Freddie Cannon** 1.01.60
The Way I Walk - **Jack Scott** 25.09.59
The Way I Want to Touch You - **Captain & Tennille** 31.01.76
The Way It is - **Bruce Hornsby & the Range** 9.08.86
The Way It Used To Be - **Engelbert Humperdinck** 5.02.69
Way of Life - **Family Dogg** 11.06.69
Way of the World - **Tina Turner** 23.11.91
The Way We Were - **Barbra Streisand** 6.04.74
The Way We Were - **Gladys Knight & the Pips** 12.04.75
The Way You Are - **Tears For Fears** 3.12.83
The Way You Look Tonight - **Lettermen** 30.11.61
The Way You Make Me Feel - **Michael Jackson** 5.12.87
Wayward Wind - **Jimmy Young** 8.06.56
Wayward Wind - **Tex Ritter** 22.06.56
Wayward Wind - **Gogi Grant** 29.06.56
Wayward Wind - **Frank Ifield** 24.01.63
We All Follow Man Utd - **Manchester Utd Football Team** 18.05.85

We All Stand Together - **Paul McCartney & the Frog Chorus** ... 1.12.84
We All Stand Together - **Paul McCartney & the Frog Chorus** ... 28.12.85
We Are Detective - **Thomspon Twins** ... 16.04.83
We Are Family - **Sister Sledge** ... 2.06.79
We Are Family - **Sister Sledge** ... 24.11.84
We Are Glass - **Gary Numan** ... 24.05.80
We Are In Love - **Adam Faith** ... 19.12.63
We Are The Champions - **Queen** ... 22.10.77
We Are The World - **USA for Africa** ... 13.04.85
We Belong - **Pat Benatar** ... 26.01.85
We Built This City - **Starship** ... 30.11.85
We Call It Acieed - **D. Mob (featuring Gary Haisman)** ... 15.10.88
We Came To Dance - **Ultravox** ... 04.06.83
We Can Do It - **Liverpool Football Team** ... 28.05.77
We Can Do It - **Liverpool Football Team** ... 18.06.77
We Can Work It Out - **Stevie Wonder** ... 15.05.71
We Can Work It Out - **Four Seasons** ... 4.12.76
We Close Our Eyes - **Go West** ... 9.03.85
We Could Be Together - **Debbie Gibson** ... 26.08.89
We Didn't Start the Fire - **Billy Joel** ... 30.09.89
We Do It - **R & J Stone** ... 17.01.76
We Don't Have To - **Jermaine Stewart** ... 16.08.86
We Don't Need Another Hero (Thunderdome) - **Tina Turner** ... 20.06.85
We Don't Talk Anymore - **Cliff Richard** ... 21.07.79
We Got Love - **Alma Cogan** ... 18.12.59
We Got The Funk - **Positive Force** ... 12.01.80
We Gotta Get Out of This Place - **Animals** ... 22.07.65
We Have A Dream - **Scotland World Cup Squad** ... 1.05.82
We Kill The World (Don't Kill the World) - **Boney M** ... 28.11.81
We Love Each Other - **Charlie Rich** ... 8.02.75
We Love You/Dandelion - **Rolling Stones** ... 23.08.67
We Shall Overcome - **Joan Baez** ... 20.05.65
We Should Be Together - **Cliff Richard** ... 7.12.91
We Take Mystery (To Bed) - **Gary Numan** ... 19.06.82
(We Want) The Same Thing - **Belinda Carlisle** ... 20.10.90
We Will - **Gilbert O'Sullivan** ... 31.07.51
We Will Make Love - **Russ Hamilton** ... 24.05.57
Weak In The Presence of Beauty - **Alison Moyet** ... 7.03.87
Weak Spot - **Evelyn Thomas** ... 31.01.76
Wear My Ring - **Elvis Presley** ... 2.05.58
Wear You To the Ball - **UB40** ... 11.08.90
Wear Your Love Like Heaven - **Definition of Sound** ... 16.03.91
The Wedding - **Julie Rogers** ... 20.08.64
Wedding Bell Blues - **5th Dimension** ... 17.01.70
Wedding Bells - **Eddie Fisher** ... 18.03.55
Wedding Bells - **Godley & Creme** ... 28.11.81
Wedding Ring - **Russ Hamilton** ... 27.09.57
Wednesday Week - **Undertones** ... 12.07.80
Wee Rule - **Wee Papa Girl Rappers** ... 1.10.88
Wee Tom - **Lord Rockingham's XI** ... 6.02.59
Weekend - **Eddie Cochran** ... 15.06.61
Weekend - **Mick Jackson** ... 24.02.79
The Weight - **Band** ... 18.09.68
Welcome - **Gino Latino** ... 20.01.90
Welcome Home - **Peters & Lee** ... 2.06.73
Welcome Home Baby - **Brook Brothers** ... 23.08.62
Welcome to My World - **Jim Reeves** ... 20.06.63
Welcome To the Jungle/Nightrain - **Guns N' Roses** ... 29.10.88
Welcome to The Pleasure Dome - **Frankie Goes to Hollywood** ... 30.03.85
Welcome to the Terrordrome - **Public Enemy** ... 20.01.90
We'll Be With You - **Potters** ... 1.04.72
We'll Bring The House Down - **Slade** ... 7.02.81
We'll Find Our Day - **Stephanie de Sykes** ... 19.04.75
Well I Ask You - **Eden Kane** ... 8.06.61
We're All Alone - **Rita Coolidge** ... 2.07.77
We're Gonna Go Fishin' - **Hank Locklin** ... 29.11.62
We're Through - **Hollies** ... 24.09.64
West End Girls - **Pet Shop Boys** ... 30.11.85
West of Zanzibar - **Anthony Steel and the Radio Revellers** ... 10.09.54
Western Movies - **Olympics** ... 3.10.58
Wet Dream - **Max Romeo** ... 18.06.69
We've Got The Whole World - **Nottingham Forest & Paper Lace** ... 4.03.78
We've Got Tonight - **Kenny Rogers and Sheena Easton** ... 5.03.83
We've Only Just Begun - **Carpenters** ... 16.01.71
Wham Rap (Enjoy What You Do) - **Wham!** ... 29.01.83
What - **Soft Cell** ... 21.08.82
What A Crazy World We Live In - **Joe Brown** ... 18.01.62
What A Difference A Day Made - **Esther Phillips** ... 11.10.75
What A Fool Believes - **Doobie Brothers** ... 3.03.79
What A Mouth - **Tommy Steele** ... 30.06.60
What A Night - **City Boy** ... 11.11.78
What A Waste - **Ian Dury** ... 6.05.78
What A Wonderful World/Cabaret - **Louis Armstrong** ... 14.02.68
What A Wonderful World - **Johnny Nash** ... 19.06.76
What About Love - **Heart** ... 14.05.88
What Am I Gonna Do - **Emile Ford & the Checkmates** ... 9.03.61
What Am I Gonna Do With You - **Barry White** ... 8.03.75
What Am I Gonna Do - **Rod Stewart** ... 27.08.83
What Am I To You - **Kenny Lynch** ... 3.09.64
What Are We Gonna Get 'Er Indoors - **Dennis Waterman and George Cole** ... 24.12.83
What Are You Doing Sunday - **Dawn** ... 31.07.71
What Becomes of The Broken Hearted? - **Jimmy Ruffin** ... 17.11.66
What Becomes of the Broken Hearted - **Jimmy Ruffin** ... 30.08.74
What Becomes of the Broken Hearted - **Dave Stewart & Colin Blunstone** ... 21.03.81
What Can I Say - **Boz Scaggs** ... 29.01.77
(What Can I Say) To Make You Love Me - **Alexander O'Neal** ... 23.07.88
What Can You Do For Me - **Utah Saints** ... 24.08.91
What Did I Do To You (EP) - **Lisa Stansfield** ... 12.05.90
What Difference Does It Make - **Smiths** ... 28.01.84
What Do I Do - **Phil Fearon & Galaxy** ... 10.03.84
What Do I Get? - **Buzzcocks** ... 25.02.78
What Do I Have To Do - **Kylie Minogue** ... 2.02.91
What Do You Say - **Chubby Checker** ... 14.11.63
What Do You Want? - **Adam Faith** ... 20.11.59
What Do You Want To Make Those Eyes At Me For? - **Emile Ford & the Checkmates** ... 30.10.59
What Do You Want To Make Those Eyes At Me For - **Shakin' Stevens** ... 28.11.87
What Does It Take (To Win Your Love) - **Junior Walker & the All Stars** ... 25.10.69
What Does It Take - **Then Jerico** ... 8.04.89
What Ever You Want - **Status Quo** ... 22.09.79
What Good Am I - **Cilla Black** ... 15.06.67
What Have I Done to Deserve This - **Pet Shop Boys & Dusty Springfield** ... 22.08.87
What Have They Done to My Song Ma - **New Seekers** ... 16.01.71
What Have They Done To The Rain - **Searchers** ... 10.12.64
What Have You Done For Me Lately - **Janet Jackson** ... 12.04.86
What I Am - **Edie Bricknell & the New Bohemians** ... 18.02.89
What I Got Is What You Need - **Unique** ... 17.09.83
What in the World's Come Over You - **Jack Scott** ... 10.03.60
What In The World's Come Over You - **Rockin' Berries** ... 28.01.65
What In The World's Come Over You - **Tam White** ... 22.03.75
What Is A Man - **Four Tops** ... 4.06.69
What Is Life - **Olivia Newton John** ... 18.03.72
What Is Love - **Howard Jones** ... 3.12.83
What is Truth? - **Johnny Cash** ... 23.05.70
What I've Got In Mind - **Billie Jo Spears** ... 31.07.76
What Kind of Fool - **All About Eve** ... 12.11.88
What Kind of Fool Am I? - **Anthony Newley** ... 10.08.61
What Kind of Fool Am I/Gonna Build A Mountain - **Sammy Davis Jnr** ... 29.03.62
What Kinda Boy You Looking For (Girl) - **Hot Chocolate** ... 14.05.83
What More Do You Want - **Frankie Vaughan** ... 29.01.60
What Now - **Adam Faith** ... 31.01.63
What Now My Love - **Shirley Bassey** ... 30.08.62
What Now My Love - **Sonny & Cher** ... 24.02.66
What Time Is Love? - **KLF featuring Children of the Revolution** ... 11.08.90
What to Do - **Buddy Holly** ... 9.02.61
What To Do - **Buddy Holly** ... 19.12.63
What U Waitin' 4 - **Jungle Brothers** ... 31.03.90
What Would I Be - **Val Doonican** ... 10.11.66
What You Get Is What You See - **Tina Turner** ... 21.03.87
What You See Is What You Get - **Glen Goldsmith** ... 18.06.88
What You Waiting For - **Stargard** ... 23.09.78
What You're Proposing - **Status Quo** ... 11.10.80
What'cha Gonna Do About It - **Doris Troy** ... 26.11.64
Whatcha Gonna Do About It - **Small Faces** ... 9.09.65
Whatcha Gonna Do Now - **Chris Andrews** ... 2.06.66
Whatcha Gonna Do With My Lovin' - **Inner City** ... 18.11.89
What'd I Say - **Jerry Lee Lewis** ... 4.05.61
Whatever Gets You Thru' the Night - **John Lennon & Plastic Ono Nuclear Band** 2.11.74
Whatever Happened to You - **Highly Likely** ... 21.04.73
Whatever Happened To You - **Highly Likely** ... 5.05.73
Whatever I Do (Wherever I Go) - **Hazell Dean** ... 28.07.84
Whatever Lola Wants - **Alma Cogan** ... 29.03.57
Whatever Will Be Will Be - **Doris Day** ... 29.06.56
What's Another Year - **Johnny Logan** ... 3.05.80
What's In A Kiss - **Gilbert O'Sullivan** ... 4.10.80
What's Love Got to Do With It - **Tina Turner** ... 30.06.84
What's New Pussycat - **Tom Jones** ... 19.08.65

What's the Colour of Money - **Hollywood Beyond** 19.07.86
(What's Wrong With) Dreaming - **River City People** 22.09.90
What's Your Name - **Chicory Tip** 20.05.72
What's Your Name What's Your Number - **Andrea True Connection** 18.03.78
What's Your Problem - **Blancmange** 14.09.85
Wheels - **String-A-Longs** 23.02.61
Wheels Cha Cha - **Joe Loss** 6.07.61
Wheels of Steel - **Saxon** 12.04.80
When - **Kalin Twins** 18.07.58
When - **Showaddywaddy** 12.03.78
When A Child Is Born - **Johnny Mathis** 27.11.76
When A Heart Beats - **Nik Kershaw** 30.11.85
When A Man Loves A Woman - **Percy Sledge** 19.05.66
When A Man Loves A Woman - **Percy Sledge** 14.02.87
When A Man Loves A Woman - **Michael Bolton** 16.11.91
When Am I Going To Make A Living - **Sade** 2.06.84
When Doves Cry - **Prince** 7.07.84
When Forever Has Gone - **Demis Roussos** 2.10.76
When He Shines - **Sheena Easton** 9.05.81
When I Come Home - **Spencer Davis Group** 1.09.66
When I Fall In Love - **Donny Osmond** 10.11.73
When I Fall In Love - **Rick Astley** 12.12.87
When I Fall In Love - **Nat 'King' Cole** 19.12.87
When I Get Home - **Searchers** 21.10.65
When I Grow Up To Be A Man - **Beach Boys** 19.11.64
When I Need You - **Leo Sayer** 29.01.77
When I Think of You - **Janet Jackson** 16.08.86
When I'm Dead and Gone - **McGuinness Flint** 28.11.70
When It's Love - **Van Halen** 13.08.88
When Johnny Comes Marching Home - **Adam Faith** 30.06.60
When Julie Comes Around - **Cufflinks** 21.03.70
When Love Breaks Down - **Prefab Sprout** 23.11.85
When Love Comes To Town - **U2 with B.B. King** 15.04.89
When Love Comes Round Again - **Ken Dodd** 24.07.71
When Mexico Gave Up The Rhumba - **Mitchell Torok** 28.09.56
When My Little Girl Is Smiling - **Craig Douglas** 29.03.62
When My Little Girl Is Smiling - **Jimmy Justice** 5.04.62
When My Little Girl is Smiling - **Rick Nelson** 5.04.62
When Rock 'N' Roll Came to Trinidad - **Nat 'King' Cole** 5.07.57
When She Was My Girl - **Four Tops** 24.10.81
When Smokey Sings - **ABC** 6.06.87
When the Boys Talk About the Girls - **Valerie Carr** 4.07.58
When The Fingers Point - **Christians** 24.10.87
When the Girl In Your Arms is the Girl In Your Heart - **Cliff Richard** 19.10.61
When The Going Gets Tough The Tough Get Going - **Billy Ocean** 25.01.86
When the Summertime Is Over - **Jackie Trent** 1.07.65
When The Sun Comes Chining Thru' - **Long John Baldry** 11.09.68
When the Tigers Broke Free - **Pink Floyd** 14.08.82
When Tomorrow Comes - **Eurythmics** 14.06.86
When Two Worlds Collide - **Jim Reeves** 2.07.69
When We Was Fab - **George Harrison** 20.02.88
When We Were Young - **Solomon King** 8.05.68
When We Were Young - **Bucks Fizz** 18.06.83
When Will I Be Loved - **Everly Brothers** 14.07.60
When Will I Be Famous - **Bros** 16.01.88
When Will I See You Again - **Three Degrees** 13.07.74
When Will the Good Apples Fall - **Seekers** 27.09.67
When Will You Say I Love You - **Billy Fury** 16.05.63
When Will You Make My Telephone Ring - **Deacon Blue** 23.04.88
When You Are A King - **White Plains** 19.06.71
When You Are Young - **Jam** 25.08.79
When You Ask About Love - **Crickets** 15.01.60
When You Ask About Love - **Matchbox** 4.10.80
When You Lose The One You Love - **David Whitfield** 25.11.55
When You Say You Love Somebody (In The Heart) - **Kool & the Gang** 14.04.84
When You Tell Me That You Love Me - **Diana Ross** 30.11.91
When You Walk In The Room - **Searchers** 24.09.64
When You Walk In The Room - **Child** 13.05.78
When You Were Sweet Sixteen - **Fureys & Davey Arthur** 17.10.81
When You're In Love - **Dr Hook** 6.10.79
When You're Young and In Love - **Marvelettes** 29.06.67
When You're Young and In Love - **Flying Pickets** 20.04.84
Whenever God Shines His Light - **Van Morrison with Cliff Richard** 9.12.89
Whenever You're Ready - **Five Star** 22.08.87
Whenever You Want My Love - **Real Thing** 11.03.78
Whenever You Need Me - **T'Pau** 18.05.91
Whenever You Need Somebody - **Rick Astley** 31.10.87
Where Are You Baby? - **Betty Boo** 11.08.90
Where Are You Going To My Love - **Brotherhood of Man** 11.07.70
Where Are You Now (My Love) - **Jackie Trent** 22.04.65
Where Did All the Good Times Go - **Donny Osmond** 16.11.74
Where Did I Go Wrong - **UB40** 27.08.88
Where Did Our Love Go - **Supremes** 3.09.64
Where Did Our Love Go - **Donnie Elbert** 15.01.72
Where Did Our Love Go/Je Voulais Te Dire - **Manhatten Transfer** 23.09.78
Where Do Broken Hearts Go - **Whitney Houston** 12.03.88
(Where Do I Begin) Love Story - **Andy Williams** 20.03.71
(Where Do I Begin) Love Story - **Shirley Bassey** 27.03.71
Where Do You Go To My Lovely - **Peter Sarstedt** 5.02.69
Where Has All The Love Gone - **Yazz** 29.04.89
Where Is My Man - **Eartha Kitt** 14.01.84
Where Is The Love - **Roberta Flack & Donny Hathaway** 12.08.72
Where Is The Love - **Betty Wright** 19.04.75
Where Is The Love - **Delegation** 30.04.77
Where Is The Love - **Will Downing & Mica Paris** 21.01.89
Where Is Tomorrow - **Cilla Black** 12.06.68
Where Love Lives (Come On In) - **Alison Limerick** 6.04.91
Where the Happy People Go - **Trammps** 20.03.76
Where The Happy People Go - **Trammps** 10.04.76
Where the Heart Is - **Soft Cell** 4.12.82
Where The Rose Is Sown - **Big Country** 1.12.84
Where the Streets Have No Name - **U2** 12.09.87
Where The Streets Have No Name - Can't Take My Eyes Off You/How Do You Expect To Be Taken Seriously - **Pet Shop Boys** 23.03.91
Where the Wind Blows - **Frankie Laine** 4.09.53
Where Were You? - **Lloyd Price** 15.05.59
Where Were You Hiding When The Storm Broke - **Alarm** 21.01.84
Where Will The Dimple Be - **Rosemary Clooney** 20.05.55
Where Will You Be - **Sue Nicholls** 3.07.68
Wherever I Lay My Hat (That's My Home) - **Paul Young** 25.06.83
Which Way Should I Jump? - **Milltown Brothers** 16.02.91
Which Way You Goin' Billy? - **Poppy Family** 29.08.70
Whisky in The Jar - **Thin Lizzy** 27.01.73
The Whisper - **Selecter** 6.09.80
Whispering - **Bachelors** 29.08.63
Whispering - **Nino Tempo & April Stevens** 16.01.64
Whispering Grass - **Windsor Davies & Don Estelle** 17.05.75
Whistle Down The Wind - **Nick Heyward** 26.03.83
The Whistle Song - **Frankie Knuckles** 27.07.91
White Boys and Heroes - **Gary Numan** 28.08.82
White Christmas - **Mantovani** 19.12.52
White Christmas - **Pat Boone** 13.12.57
White Christmas - **Bing Crosby** 10.12.77
White Christmas - **Keith Harris & Orville** 4.01.86
White Cliffs of Dover - **Mr. Acker Bilk** 1.09.60
White Cliffs of Dover - **Righteous Brothers** 24.11.66
White Horses - **Jacky** 17.04.68
White Lines (Don't Don't Do It) - **Grandmaster Flash & Melle Mel** 16.06.84
(White Man) In Hammersmith Palais - **Clash** 1.07.78
White Punks On Dope - **Tubes** 26.11.77
White Riot - **The Clash** 9.04.77
White Room - **Cream** 22.01.69
White Sport Coat - **King Brothers** 31.05.57
White Sport Coat - **Terry Dene** 7.06.57
White Wedding - **Billy Idol** 20.06.85
A Whiter Shade of Pale - **Procol Harum** 25.05.67
A Whiter Shade of Pale - **Procol Harum** 29.04.72
Who Are We - **Vera Lynn** 8.06.56
Who Are We - **Ronnie Hilton** 29.06.56
Who Are You - **Who** 29.07.78
Who Comes to Boogie - **Little Benny & the Masters** 2.03.85
Who Could Be Bluer - **Jerry Lordan** 26.02.60
Who Do You Love - **Juicy Lucy** 21.03.70
Who Do You Think You Are - **Candlewick Green** 9.03.74
Who Found Who - **Jellybean featuring Elisa Fiorillo** 28.11.87
Who Gets The Love - **Status Quo** 28.05.88
Who Is It - **Mantronix** 28.02.87
Who Loves You - **Four Seasons** 27.09.75
Who Made Me - **Vixen** 3.06.89
Who Made Who - **AC/DC** 24.05.86
Who Pays The Ferry Man - **Yannis Markopoulos** 17.12.77
Who Put the Bomp - **Viscounts** 28.09.61
Who Put the Bomp (In the Bomp-A-Bomp-A-Bomp) - **Showaddywaddy** 11.09.82
Who Put the Lights Out - **Dana** 13.02.71
Who Wants the World - **Stranglers** 14.06.80
Who Wants To Be The Disco King - **Wonder Stuff** 11.03.89
Who Wants to Live Forever - **Queen** 27.09.86
Who Was It - **Hurricane Smith** 9.09.72

Who Were You With In The Moonlight - **Dollar** 26.05.79
Who? Where? Why? - **Jesus Jones** 2.03.91
Who Will You Run To - **Heart** 26.09.87
Whodunit - **Tavares** 9.04.77
Whole Lotta Love - **C.C.S.** 31.10.70
Whole Lotta Rosie - **AC/DC** 5.07.80
Whole Lotta Shakin' Goin' On - **Jerry Lee Lewis** 27.09.57
Whole Lotta Woman - **Marvin Rainwater** 7.03.58
The Whole of the Moon - **Waterboys** 9.11.85
The Whole of the Moon - **Waterboys** 6.04.91
Who's Gonna Love Me - **Imperials** 14.01.78
Who's Gonna Rock You - **Nolans** 13.12.80
Who's In the Strawberry Patch with Sally - **Tony Orlando & Dawn** 9.03.74
Who's In The House - **Beatmasters with Merlin** 22.04.89
Who's Leaving Who - **Hazell Dean** 2.04.88
Who's Sorry Now - **Johnnie Ray** 17.02.56
Who's Sorry Now - **Connie Francis** 4.04.58
Who's That Girl - **Eurythmics** 9.07.83
Who's That Girl - **Madonna** 18.07.87
Who's Zoomin' Who - **Aretha Franklin** 4.01.86
Whose Law (Is It Anyway) - **Guru Josh** 16.06.90
Why - **Anthony Newley** 15.01.60
Why - **Frankie Avalon** 22.01.60
Why - **Donny Osmond** 11.11.72
Why - **Carly Simon** 4.09.82
Why - **Bronski Beat** 22.09.84
Why Baby Why - **Pat Boone** 26.04.57
Why Can't It Be You - **Cure** 18.04.87
Why Can't This Be Love - **Van Halen** 26.04.86
Why Can't We Be Lovers - **Holland, Dozier** 28.10.72
Why Can't We Live Together - **Timmy Thomas** 24.02.73
Why Did You Do It - **Stretch** 15.11.75
Why Do Fools Fall In Love - **Teenagers featuring Frankie Lymon** 29.06.56
Why Do Fools Fall In Love - **Alma Cogan** 10.08.56
Why Do Fools Fall In Love - **Diana Ross** 7.11.81
Why Do Lovers Break Each Others Hearts - **Showaddywaddy** 18.10.80
Why Don't They Understand - **George Hamilton IV** 7.03.58
Why Don't You Believe Me - **Joni James** 6.03.53
Why (Must We Fall In Love) - **Diana Ross and the Supremes** 21.03.70
Why Not Now?/Can This Be Love? - **Matt Monro** 25.05.61
Why Not Tonight - **Mojos** 18.06.64
Why Oh Why Oh Why - **Gilbert O'Sullivan** 17.11.73
Why Should I Be Lonely? - **Tony Brent** 24.07.59
Wichita Lineman - **Glen Campbell** 5.02.69
Wicked Game - **Chris Isaak** 1.12.90
Wicked Love - **Oceanic** 30.11.91
Wide Boy - **Nik Kershaw** 16.03.85
Wide Eyed And Legless - **Andy Fairweather Low** 13.12.75
Wig-Wam Bam - **Sweet** 16.09.72
Wiggle It - **Two In A Room** 26.01.91
Wikka Wrap - **Evasions** 20.06.81
The Wild Boys - **Duran Duran** 3.11.84
Wild Cat - **Gene Vincent** 8.01.60
Wild Flower - **Cult** 22.08.87
Wild Frontier - **Gary Moore** 7.03.87
Wild Hearted Woman - **All About Eve** 23.01.88
Wild Hearted Son - **Cult** 14.09.91
Wild Honey - **Beach Boys** 15.11.67
Wild in the Country/I Feel So Bad - **Elvis Presley** 7.09.61
Wild Is The Wind - **David Bowie** 5.12.81
Wild Love - **Mungo Jerry** 17.11.73
Wild One - **Bobby Rydell** 10.03.60
The Wild One - **Suzi Quatro** 9.11.74
Wild Side of Life - **Tommy Quickly** 12.11.64
Wild Side of Life - **Status Quo** 11.12.76
Wild Thing - **Troggs** 12.05.66
Wild Thing/Loc'ed After Dark - **Tone Loc** 18.02.89
Wild West Hero - **Electric Light Orchestra** 24.06.78
Wild Wind - **John Leyton** 5.10.61
Wild Women Do - **Natalie Cole** 28.04.90
Wild World - **Jimmy Cliff** 15.08.70
Wild World - **Maxi Priest** 4.06.88
Will I What - **Mike Sarne** 30.08.62
Will You - **Hazel O'Connor** 30.05.81
Will You Love Me Tomorrow? - **Shirelles** 16.02.61
Will You Still Love Me Tomorrow - **Melanie** 2.03.74
William It Was Really Nothing - **Smiths** 1.09.84
Willie Can - **Alma Cogan** 30.03.56
Willie Can - **Beverley Sisters** 13.04.56
Wimoweh - **Karl Denver** 1.02.62
Winchester Cathedral - **New Vaudeville Band** 15.09.66
Wind Beneath My Wings - **Bette Midler** 8.07.89
The Wind Cries Mary - **Jimi Hendrix Experience** 11.05.67
Wind Me Up (Let Me Go) - **Cliff Richard** 11.11.65
Wind of Change - **Scorpions** 28.09.91
Windmill in Old Amsterdam - **Ronnie Hilton** 11.02.65
Windmills of Your Mind - **Noel Harrisson** 26.02.69
Window Shopping - **R.Dean Taylor** 7.09.74
Windpower - **Thomas Dolby** 4.09.82
Windsor Waltz - **Vera Lynn** 5.06.53
Wings Of A Dove - **Madness** 20.08.83
Winker's Song - **Ivor Biggun** 16.09.78
The Winkle Man - **Judge Dread** 8.05.76
Winner Takes It All - **Abba** 2.08.80
Winter in July - **Bomb The Bass** 27.07.91
Winter Melody - **Donna Summer** 15.01.77
Winter Song - **Chris Rea** 9.11.91
Winter Wonderland - **Johnny Mathis** 19.12.58
Winter World of Love - **Engelbert Humperdinck** 22.11.69
A Winter's Tale - **David Essex** 18.12.82
Wipe Out - **Surfaris** 25.07.63
Wipeout - **Fat Boys & the Beach Boys** 29.08.87
Wired for Sound - **Cliff Richard** 29.08.81
Wisdom of A Fool - **Norman Wisdom** 15.03.57
Wisdom of A Fool - **Ronnie Carroll** 29.03.57
Wish You Were Here - **Eddie Fisher** 6.11.53
Wishful Thinking - **China Crisis** 14.01.84
Wishin' and Hopin' - **Merseybeats** 9.07.64
Wishing - **Buddy Holly** 5.09.63
Wishing I Was Lucky - **Wet Wet Wet** 2.05.87
Wishing (If I Had A Photograph of You) - **A Flock of Seagulls** 20.11.82
Wishing On A Star - **Rose Royce** 21.01.78
Wishing On A Star - **Fresh 4 featuring Lizz E** 7.10.89
The Wishing Well - **G.O.S.H.** 2.01.88
Wishing Well - **Free** 13.01.73
Wishing Well - **Terence Trent D'Arby** 20.06.87
Witch Doctor - **David Seville** 23.05.58
Witch Doctor - **Don Lang** 23.05.58
Witch Queen of New Orleans - **Redbone** 2.10.71
Witchcraft - **Frank Sinatra** 7.02.58
Witch's Promise - **Jethro Tull** 24.01.70
With A Girl Like You - **Troggs** 14.07.66
With A Little Help From My Friends - **Young Idea** 5.07.67
With A Little Help From My Friends - **Joe Brown** 5.07.67
With A Little Help From My Friends - **Joe Cocker** 9.10.68
With A Little Help From My Friends/She's Leaving Home - **Wet Wet Wet/Billy Bragg with Cara Tivey** 14.05.88
With A Little Luck - **Wings** 8.04.78
With All My Heart - **Petula Clark** 26.07.57
With Or Without You - **U2** 28.03.87
With Pen In Hand - **Vikki Carr** 26.03.69
With the Eyes of A Child - **Cliff Richard** 13.12.69
With The Wind and The Rain In Your Hair - **Pat Boone** 10.04.59
With These Hands - **Shirley Bassey** 7.04.60
With These Hands - **Tom Jones** 15.07.65
With You I'm Born Again - **Billy Preston & Syreeta** 5.01.80
With Your Love - **Malcolm Vaughan** 27.01.56
Without Her - **Herb Alpert** 25.06.69
Without Love - **Tom Jones** 13.12.69
Without You - **Matt Monro** 25.03.65
Without You - **Nilsson** 12.02.72
Without You - **Nilsson** 23.10.76
Without You - **Motley Crue** 12.05.90
The Wizard - **Paul Hardcastle** 11.10.86
Woe Is Me - **Helen Shapiro** 2.05.63
Woman - **Peter & Gordon** 10.03.66
Woman - **John Lennon** 24.01.81
Woman from Liberia - **Jimmie Rodgers** 19.12.58
Woman In Chains - **Tears for Fears** 25.11.89
Woman In Love - **Frankie Laine** 7.09.56
Woman In Love - **Ronnie Hilton** 21.09.56
Woman In Love - **Four Aces** 19.10.56
Woman In Love - **Three Degrees** 20.01.79
Woman In Love - **Barbra Streisand** 11.10.80
Woman to Woman - **Beverley Craven** 19.10.91
Wombling Merry Christmas - **Wombles** 14.12.74
Wombling Song - **Wombles** 26.01.74
Wombling White Tie and Tails - **Wombles** 10.05.75

Women in Uniform - **Iron Maiden** 15.11.80
Wonder Boy - **Kinks** 17.04.68
The Wonder of You - **Ronnie Hilton** 21.08.59
The Wonder of You - **Ray Peterson** 4.09.59
Wonderful Christmas Time - **Paul McCartney** 8.12.79
Wonderful Copenhagen - **Danny Kaye** 27.02.53
Wonderful Dream - **Anne-Marie David** 28.04.73
Wonderful Land - **Shadows** 1.03.62
Wonderful Life - **Black** 22.08.87
Wonderful Secret of Love - **Robert Earl** 13.02.59
Wonderful Things - **Frankie Vaughan** 1.08.58
Wonderful Time Up There - **Pat Boone** 4.04.58
Wonderful Tonight (Live) - **Eric Clapton** 23.11.91
Wonderful Wonderful - **Gary Miller** 19.07.57
Wonderful Wonderful - **Ronnie Hilton** 2.08.57
Wonderful World - **Sam Cooke** 7.07.60
Wonderful World - **Herman's Hermits** 29.04.65
Wonderful World - **Sam Cooke** 22.03.86
Wonderful World Beautiful People - **Jimmy Cliff** 1.11.69
Wonderful World of the Young - **Danny Williams** 12.04.62
Wonderland - **Commodores** 26.01.80
Wonderland - **Big Country** 21.01.84
Wonderland - **Paul Young** 4.10.86
Wondrous Place - **Billy Fury** 29.09.60
Wondrous Stories - **Yes** 17.09.77
Won't Get Fooled Again - **Who** 17.07.71
Won't Somebody Dance With Me - **Lynsey De Paul** 27.10.73
Won't Talk About It/Blame It On The Bassline - **Norman Cook** 8.07.89
Won't Talk About It - **Beats International** 12.05.90
Won't You Hold My Hand Now - **King** 23.03.85
Wood Beez (Pray Like Aretha Franklin) - **Scritti Politti** 31.03.84
Wooden Heart - **Elvis Presley** 9.03.61
Wooly Bully - **Sam The Sham & the Pharaohs** 1.07.65
The Word Girl - **Scritti Politti** 18.05.85
The Word Is Out - **Kylie Minogue** 7.09.91
Word of Mouth - **Mike & the Mechanics** 30.03.91
Word Up - **Camco** 6.09.86
Words - **Allisons** 18.05.61
Words - **Bee Gees** 7.02.68
Words - **Rita Coolidge** 11.02.78
Words - **FR David** 2.04.83
Words - **Christians** 23.12.89
Wordy Rappinghood - **Tom Tom Club** 27.06.81
Work - **Technotronic featuring Reggie** 20.08.91
Work All Day - **Barry Biggs** 4.09.76
Work All Day - **Barry Biggs** 18.09.76
Work Rest and Play (EP) - **Madness** 5.04.80
Work that Body - **Diana Ross** 5.06.82
Workin' Overtime - **Diana Ross** 13.05.89
Working For The Yankee Dollar - **Skids** 24.11.79
Working In A Goldmine - **Aztec Camera** 13.08.88
Working In The Coal Mine - **Lee Dorsey** 18.08.66
Working Man - **Rita MacNeil** 13.10.90
Working My Way Back To You-Forgive Me Girl - **Detroit Spinners** 8.03.80
Working On A Building of Love - **Chairmen of the Board** 22.07.72
World - **Bee Gees** 15.11.67
World in Motion - **Englandneworder** 2.06.90
The World in my Arms - **Nat 'King' Cole** 16.02.61
World in My Eyes - **Depeche Mode** 29.09.90
World in Union - **Kiri Te Kanawa** 5.10.91
The World is Mine - **Malcolm Vaughan** 12.04.57
World of Broken Hearts - **Amen Corner** 18.10.67
World of Our Own - **Seekers** 22.04.65
The World Outside - **Ronnie Hilton** 9.01.59
The World Outside - **Four Aces** 23.01.59
The World Outside - **Russ Conway** 23.01.59
World Shut Your Mouth - **Julian Cope** 4.10.86
World We Knew - **Frank Sinatra** 30.08.67
World Without Love - **Peter & Gordon** 23.03.64
World Without You - **Belinda Carlisle** 17.09.88
Worzel's Song - **Jon Pertwee** 8.03.80
Wot - **Captain Sensible** 21.08.82
Would I Lie To You - **Whitesnake** 13.06.81
Would I Lie to You - **Eurythmics** 27.04.85
Wouldn't Change A Thing - **Kylie Minogue** 5.08.89
Wouldn't It Be Good - **Nik Kershaw** 4.02.84
Wow - **Kate Bush** 24.03.79
Wrap Her Up - **Elton John** 14.12.85
Wrapped Around Your Finger - **Police** 23.07.83
Wrapping Paper - **Cream** 27.10.66
W.O.L.D. - **Harry Chapin** 25.05.74
Wreck of the Antoinette - **Dave Dee Dozy Beaky Mick & Tich** 9.10.68
The Wreck of the Edmund Fitzgerald - **Gordon Lightfoot** 29.01.77
Writing on the Wall - **Tommy Steele** 24.08.61
Wunderbar - **Tenpole Tudor** 8.08.81
Wuthering Heights - **Kate Bush** 18.02.78
X, Y and Zee - **Pop Will Eat Itself** 12.01.91
Xanadu - **Olivia Newton-John & the Electric Light Orchestra** 21.06.80
Y Viva Espana - **Sylvia** 17.08.74
Y Viva Suspenders - **Judge Dread** 28.08.76
Ya Ya Twist - **Petula Clark** 5.07.62
Yaaah/Techno Trance - **D-Shake** 2.06.90
Yah Mo B There - **James Ingram with Michael McDonald** 19.01.85
Yakety Yak - **Coasters** 15.08.58
Ye Ke Ye Ke - **Mory Kante** 20.08.88
Yeah! Buddy - **Royal House** 14.01.89
Year of Decision - **Three Degrees** 13.04.74
Year of The Cat - **Al Stewart** 5.02.77
Years May Come and Years May Go - **Herman's Hermits** 7.02.70
Yeh Yeh - **Georgie Fame** 17.12.64
Yeh Yeh - **Matt Bianco** 12.10.85
Yellow Pearl - **Phil Lynott** .... 9.1.82.
Yellow River - **Christie** 9.05.70
Yellow Rose of Texas - **Mitch Miller** 7.10.55
Yellow Rose of Texas - **Gary Miller** 21.10.55
Yellow Rose of Texas - **Ronnie Hilton** 11.11.55
Yellow Submarine/Eleanor Rigby - **Beatles** 11.08.66
Yep! - **Duane Eddy** 24.07.59
Yes I Will - **Hollies** 28.01.65
Yes My Darling Daughter - **Eydie Gorme** 21.06.62
Yes Sir I Can Boogie - **Baccara** 1.10.77
Yes Tonight Josephine - **Johnnie Ray** 10.05.57
Yes Tonight Josephine - **Jets** 14.11.81
Yester-Me Yester-You Yesterday - **Stevie Wonder** 15.11.69
Yesterday - **Matt Monro** 21.10.65
Yesterday - **Marianne Faithfull** 4.11.65
Yesterday - **Beatles** 20.03.76
Yesterday Has Gone - **Cupid's Inspiration** 19.06.68
Yesterday Man - **Chris Andrews** 14.10.65
Yesterday Once More - **Carpenters** 14.07.73
Yesterday's Dreams - **Four Tops** 28.08.68
Yesterday's Gone - **Chad Stuart & Jeremy Clyde** 28.11.63
Yesterday's Men - **Madness** 31.08.85
Ying Tong Song - **Goons** 28.07.73
YMCA - **Village People** 2.12.78
Yo!! Sweetness - **MC Hammer** 1.06.91
Yodeling Song - **Frank Ifield & the Backroom Boys** 14.12.91
You - **Bandwagon** 12.02.69
You - **George Harrison** 18.10.75
You Ain't Livin' Till You're Lovin' - **Marvin Gaye & Tammi Terrell** 29.01.69
You Ain't Seen Nothing Yet - **Bachman-Turner Overdrive** 16.11.74
You Always Hurt The One You Love - **Connie Francis** 26.12.58
You Always Hurt The One You Love - **Clarence 'Frogman' Henry** 20.07.61
You and Me Tonight - **Aurra** 19.04.86
You Are Beautiful - **Johnny Mathis** 24.03.60
You Are Everything - **Diana Ross & Marvin Gaye** 23.03.74
You Are My Destiny - **Paul Anka** 31.01.58
You Are My First Love - **Ruby Murray** 31.08.56
You Are My Love - **Liverpool Express** 3.07.76
You Are My World - **Communards** 2.11.85
You Are My World ('87) - **Communards** 21.02.87
You Are the One - **A-Ha** 10.12.88
You Are the Sunshine of My Life - **Stevie Wonder** 19.05.73
You Belong In Rock 'N' Roll - **Tin Machine** 24.08.91
You Belong to Me - **Jo Stafford** 14.11.52
You Belong To Me - **Gary Glitter** 27.03.76
You Bet Your Love - **Herbie Hancock** 10.02.79
You Bet Your Love - **Herbie Hancock** 24.02.79
You Better You Bet - **Who** 7.03.81
You Came - **Kim Wilde** 16.07.88
You Came, You Saw, You Conquered - **Pearls** 30.09.72
You Can Call Me Al - **Paul Simon** 27.09.86
You Can Do It - **Al Hudson & the Soul Partners** 22.09.79
You Can Do Magic - **Limmie & the Family Cookin'** 28.07.73
You Can Get It If You Really Want It - **Desmond Dekker** 29.08.70
You Can Have Him - **Dionne Warwick** 8.04.65
You Can Have It All - **George McCrae** 4.01.75
You Can Make Me Dance, Sing or Anything - **Faces & Rod Stewart** 7.12.74

You Can Never Stop Me Loving You - **Kenny Lynch** ... 27.06.63
You Can't Be True to Two - **Dave King** ... 13.04.56
You Can't Hide (Your Love From Me) - **David Joseph** ... 5.03.83
You Can't Hurry Love - **Supremes** ... 8.09.66
You Can't Hurry Love - **Phil Collins** ... 11.12.82
You Can't Sit Down - **Phil Upchurch Combo** ... 12.05.66
You Caught My Eye - **Judy Boucher** ... 25.07.87
You Could Be Mine - **Guns N' Roses** ... 13.07.91
You Could've Been A Lady - **Hot Chocolate** ... 6.03.71
You Don't Bring Me Flowers - **Barbra & Neil** ... 2.12.78
You Don't Have To Be A Baby to Cry - **Caravelles** ... 8.08.63
You Don't Have To Be A Star - **Marilyn McCoo/Billy Davis** ... 26.03.77
You Don't Have to Be In the Army to Fight the War - **Mungo Jerry** ... 25.09.71
You Don't Have to Go - **Chi-Lites** ... 7.08.76
You Don't Have To Say You Love Me - **Dusty Springfield** ... 7.04.66
You Don't Have to Say You Love Me - **Elvis Presley** ... 9.01.71
You Don't Have To Say You Love Me - **Guys 'N' Dolls** ... 28.02.76
You Don't Know - **Helen Shapiro** ... 6.07.61
You Don't Know - **Berlin** ... 31.01.87
You Don't Know Me - **Ray Charles** ... 20.09.62
You Don't Know What You've Got - **Ral Donner** ... 28.09.61
You Don't Love Me - **Gary Walker** ... 24.02.66
You Don't Love Me - **Marilyn** ... 19.05.84
You Don't Owe Me A Thing - **Johnnie Ray** ... 18.01.57
You Drive Me Crazy - **Shakin' Stevens** ... 2.05.81
You Gave Me Love - **Crown Heights Affair** ... 10.05.80
You Gave Me Somebody To Love - **Manfred Mann** ... 14.07.66
You Give Love A Bad Name - **Bon Jovi** ... 23.08.86
You Go To My Head - **Bryan Ferry** ... 12.07.75
You Got It - **Roy Orbison** ... 14.01.89
You Got It (The Right Stuff) - **New Kids on The Block** ... 11.11.89
You Got Soul - **Johnny Nash** ... 8.01.69
You Got The Floor - **Arthur Adams** ... 7.11.81
You Got The Love - **Source featuring Candi Staton** ... 2.02.91
You Got What It Takes - **Johnny Kidd** ... 12.02.60
You Got What It Takes - **Marv Johnson** ... 12.02.60
You Got What It Takes - **Dave Clark Five** ... 23.03.67
You Got What It Takes - **Showaddywaddy** ... 30.07.77
You Gotta Be A Hustler If You Want to Get On - **Sue Wilkinson** ... 9.08.80
(You Gotta) Fight For Your Right (To Party) - **Beastie Boys** ... 28.02.87
You Gotta Have Love In Your Heart - **Supremes & the Four Tops** ... 27.11.71
You Gotta Love Someone - **Elton John** ... 27.10.90
You Gotta Stop/Love Machine - **Elvis Presley** ... 18.05.67
You Have Placed A Chill In My Heart - **Eurythmics** ... 11.06.88
You Haven't Done Nothin' - **Stevie Wonder** ... 19.10.74
You Just Might See Me Cry - **Our Kid** ... 5.06.76
You Keep It All In - **Beautiful South** ... 23.09.89
(You Keep Me) Hanging On - **Cliff Richard** ... 18.05.74
You Keep Me Hangin' On - **Supremes** ... 1.12.66
You Keep Me Hanging On - **Vanilla Fudge** ... 9.08.67
You Keep Me Hanging On/Stop In The Name of Love - **Roni Hill** ... 21.05.77
You Keep Me Hangin' On - **Kim Wilde** ... 25.10.86
You Keep Running Away - **Four Tops** ... 11.10.67
You Lay So Easy On My Mind - **Andy Williams** ... 14.06.75
You Little Thief - **Feargal Sharkey** ... 11.01.86
You Little Trust Maker - **Tymes** ... 28.09.74
You Made Me Believe In Magic - **Bay City Rollers** ... 6.08.77
You Made Me Love You - **Nat 'King' Cole** ... 29.05.59
You Make It Move - **Dave Dee Dozy Beaky Mick & Tich** ... 13.01.66
You Make Me Feel - **Sylvester** ... 19.08.78
You Make Me Feel Brand New - **Stylistics** ... 20.07.74
You Make Me Feel Like Dancing - **Leo Sayer** ... 30.10.76
You Make Me Feel (Mighty Real) - **Jimmy Somerville** ... 13.01.90
You Me and Us - **Alma Cogan** ... 18.01.57
You Might Need Somebody - **Randy Crawford** ... 20.06.81
You Must Have Been A Beautiful Baby - **Bobby Darin** ... 19.10.61
You My Love - **Frank Sinatra** ... 10.06.55
You Need Hands - **Max Bygraves** ... 2.05.58
You Need Wheels - **Merton Parkas** ... 18.08.79
You Needed Me - **Anne Murray** ... 6.01.79
You Never Can Tell - **Chuck Berry** ... 27.08.64
You Never Know What You've Got - **Me & You** ... 18.08.79
You On My Mind - **Swing Out Sister** ... 22.04.89
You Only Live Twice - **Nancy Sinatra** ... 5.07.67
You Only You - **Rita Pavone** ... 26.01.67
You Really Got Me - **Kinks** ... 13.08.64
You See the Trouble With Me - **Barry White** ... 13.03.76
You Send Me - **Sam Cooke** ... 17.01.58
You Sexy Sugar Plum - **Rodger Collins** ... 10.04.76
You Sexy Thing - **Hot Chocolate** ... 8.11.75
You Sexy Thing - **Hot Chocolate** ... 24.01.87
You Shook Me All Night Long - **AC/DC** ... 20.09.80
You Should Be Dancing - **Bee Gees** ... 31.07.76
You Showed Me - **Salt-N-Pepa** ... 30.11.91
You Spin Me Round (Like A Record) - **Dead Or Alive** ... 9.02.85
You Surround Me - **Erasure** ... 9.12.89
You Take Me Up - **Thompson Twins** ... 31.03.84
You Take My Heart Away - **DeEtta Little & Nelson Pigford** ... 20.08.77
You Think You're A Man - **Divine** ... 14.07.84
You to Me Are Everything - **The Real Thing** ... 5.06.76
You To Me Are Everything - **Real Thing** ... 15.03.86
You To Me Are Everything - **Sonia** ... 16.11.91
You Took The Words Right Out Of My Mouth - **Meat Loaf** ... 10.06.78
You Want It You Got It - **Detroit Emerals** ... 12.05.73
You Wear It Well - **Rod Stewart** ... 12.08.72
You Were Made For Me - **Freddie & the Dreamers** ... 7.11.63
You Were On My Mind - **Crispian St. Peters** ... 13.01.66
You Were There - **Heinz** ... 27.02.64
You Win Again - **Bee Gees** ... 3.10.87
You Won't Be Leavin' - **Hermit's Hermits** ... 24.03.66
You Won't Find Another Fool Like Me - **New Seekers** ... 24.11.73
You You Romeo - **Shirley Bassey** ... 6.09.57
You You You - **Alvin Stardust** ... 31.08.74
You'll Always Be A Friend - **Hot Chocolate** ... 28.10.72
You'll Always Find Me In The Kitchen at Parties - **Jona Lewie** ... 17.05.80
You'll Answer to Me - **Cleo Laine** ... 14.09.61
You'll Never Find Another Love Like Mine - **Lou Rawls** ... 7.08.76
You'll Never Get to Heaven - **Dionne Warwick** ... 6.08.64
You'll Never Get To Heaven - **Stylistics EP** ... 4.12.76
You'll Never Know - **Shirley Bassey** ... 18.05.61
You'll Never Know - **Hi Gloss** ... 29.08.81
You'll Never Know What You're Missing - **Emile Ford & the Checkmates** ... 26.05.60
You'll Never Know What You're Missing - **Real Thing** ... 19.02.77
You'll Never Never Know/It Isn't Right - **Platters** ... 25.01.57
You'll Never Walk Alone - **Gerry & the Pacemakers** ... 10.10.63
You'll Never Walk Alone - **Crowd** ... 8.06.85
Young Americans - **David Bowie** ... 1.03.75
Young and Foolish - **Ronnie Hilton** ... 10.02.56
Young and Foolish - **Edmund Hockridge** ... 17.02.56
Young and Foolish - **Dean Martin** ... 2.03.56
Young At Heart - **Frank Sinatra** ... 9.07.54
Young At Heart - **Bluebells** ... 30.06.84
Young Blood - **UFO** ... 19.01.80
Young Free And Single - **Sunfire** ... 2.04.83
Young, Gifted and Black - **Bob and Marcia** ... 14.03.70
Young Girl - **Union Gap** ... 24.04.68
Young Girl - **Gary Puckett & Union Gap** ... 22.06.74
Young Gods - **Little Angels** ... 1.06.91
Young Guns (Go For It) - **Wham!** ... 13.11.82
Young Hearts Run Free - **Candi Staton** ... 5.06.76
Young Love - **Sonny James** ... 8.02.57
Young Love - **Tab Hunter** ... 8.02.57
Young Love - **Donny Osmond** ... 18.08.73
Young Lovers - **Paul & Paula** ... 25.04.63
Young New Mexican Puppeteer - **Tom Jones** ... 1.04.72
The Young Ones - **Cliff Richard** ... 11.01.62
Young Parisians - **Adam & the Ants** ... 10.01.81
Young Turks - **Rod Stewart** ... 18.12.81
Young World - **Rick Nelson** ... 5.04.62
Younger Girl - **Critters** ... 21.07.66
Your Baby Ain't Your Baby Anymore - **Paul Da Vinci** ... 27.07.74
Your Cheating Heart - **Ray Charles** ... 20.12.62
Your Generation - **Generation X** ... 17.09.77
Your Honour - **Pluto** ... 13.02.82
Your Hurtin' Kind of Love - **Dusty Springfield** ... 18.02.65
Your Kiss Is Sweet - **Syreeta** ... 1.02.75
Your Latest Trick - **Dire Straits** ... 3.05.86
Your Love Is King - **Sade** ... 10.03.84
(Your Love Keeps Lifting Me) Higher and Higher - **Jackie Wilson** ... 14.05.69
(Your Love Keeps Lifting Me) Higher and Higher - **Jackie Wilson** ... 4.07.87
Your Love Takes Me Higher - **Beloved** ... 24.03.90
Your Ma Said You Cried In Your Sleep Last Night - **Doug Sheldon** ... 11.01.62
Your Magic Put A Spell On Me - **L.J. Johnson** ... 7.02.76
Your Mama Don't Dance - **Poison** ... 29.04.89
Your Mama Won't Like Me - **Suzi Quatro** ... 8.02.75
Your Personal Touch - **Evelyn 'Champagne' King** ... 16.11.85
Your Song - **Elton John** ... 23.01.71
Your Song - **Billy Paul** ... 13.08.77

Your Swaying Arms - **Deacon Blue** 25.05.91
Your Tender Look - **Joe Brown** 20.09.62
Your Time Hasn't Come Yet Baby - **Elvis Presley** 31.07.68
You're A Lady - **Peter Skellern**30.09.72
You're All I Need - **Motley Crue** 16.01.88
You're All I Need to Get By - **Marvin Gaye & Tammi Terrell** 2.10.68
You're Breakin' My Heart - **Keely Smith** 18.03.65
You're Driving Me Crazy - **Temperance Seven** 30.03.61
You're Everything To Me - **Boris Gardiner** 11.10.86
You're Fabulous Babe - **Kenny Williams** 26.11.77
You're Gonna Get Next To Me - **Bo Kirkland & Ruth Davis** 11.06.77
(You're) Having My Baby - **Paul Anka** 5.10.74
You're History - **Shakespear's Sister** 5.08.89
You're In Love - **Wilson Phillips** 11.05.91
You're In My Heart - **Rod Stewart** 15.10.77
You're Lying - **Linx** 4.10.80
You're More Than A Number In My Little Red Book - **Drifters** 25.12.76
You're Moving Out Today - **Carole Bayer Sager** 4.06.77
You're My Best Friend - **Queen** 3.07.76
You're My Best Friend - **Don Williams** 6.11.76
You're My Everything - **Temptations** 6.09.67
You're My Everything - **Max Bygraves** 12.03.69
You're My Everything - **Lee Garret** 5.06.76
You're My Girl - **Rockin' Berries** 2.09.65
You're My Life - **Barry Biggs** 30.04.77
(You're My) Soul and Inspiration - **Righteous Brothers** 14.04.66
You're My World - **Cilla Black** 7.05.64
You're No Good - **Swinging Blue Jeans** 4.06.64
You're Ready Now - **Frankie Valli** 12.12.70
You're Sixteen - **Johnny Burnette** 12.01.61
You're Sixteen - **Ringo Starr** 23.02.74
You're So Vain - **Carly Simon** 16.12.72
You're Such A Good Looking Woman - **Joe Dolan** 28.02.70
You're the First, The Last, My Everything - **Barry White** 2.11.74
You're The Inspiration - **Chicago** 9.02.85
You're the Only Good Thing - **Jim Reeves** 23.11.61
You're The One - **Kathy Kirby** 7.05.64
You're The One - **Petula Clark** 4.11.65
You're The Only One - **Val Doonican** 21.02.68
You're The One That I Want - **John Travolta & Olivia Newton-John** 27.05.78
You're The One That I Want - **Hylda Baker & Arthur Mullard** 16.09.78
You're The One For Me - **D-Train** 20.02.82
You're The One For Me - **D-Train** 10.08.85
You're The Reason Why - **Rubettes** 1.05.76
You're The Top Cha - **Al Saxon** 16.01.59
You're the Voice - **John Farnham** 16.05.87
Yours Until Tomorrow - **Gene Pitney** 4.12.68
Youth of Today - **Musical Youth** 20.11.82
You've Come Back - **P.J. Proby** 10.02.66
You've Got A Friend - **James Taylor** 28.08.71
You've Got A Friend - **James Taylor** 4.09.71
You've Got A Friend - **Big Fun & Sonia** 23.06.90
You've Got Love - **Buddy Holly & the Crickets** 28.05.64
You've Got Me Dangling on A String - **Chairmen of the Board** 14.11.70
You've Got My Number - **Undertones** 27.10.79
You've Got To Hid Your Love Away - **Silkie** 30.09.65
You've Got Your Troubles - **Fortunes** 8.07.65
You've Lost That Lovin' Feelin - **Cilla Black** 14.01.65
You've Lost That Lovin' Feelin' - **Righteous Brothers** 14.01.65
You've Lost That Lovin' Feeling - **Righteous Brothers** 12.02.69
You've Lost That Lovin' Feelin' - **Righteous Brothers** 15.12.90
You've Made Me So Very Happy - **Blood Sweat & Tears** 14.05.69
You've Never Been In Love Like This Before - **Unit Four Plus Two** 13.05.65
You've Not Changed - **Sandie Shaw** 11.10.67
Yum Yum (Gimme Some) - **Fatback Band** 20.09.75
Yummy Yummy Yummy - **Ohio Express** 12.06.68
Zabadak! - **Dave Dee Dozy Beaky Mick & Tich** 11.10.67
Zambesi - **Lou Busch** 27.01.56
Zambesi - **Eddie Calvert** 9.03.56
Zambezi - **Pirahnas featuring Boring Bob Grover** 23.10.82
Ziggy Stardust - **Bauhaus** 16.10.82
Zing A Little Zong - **Bing Crosby & Jane Wyman** 5.12.52
Zing Went the Strings of My Heart - **Trammps** 7.12.74
Zoom - **Fat Larry's Band** 18.09.82
Zorba's Dance - **Marcello Minerbi** 29.07.65

PAUL GAMBACCINI
TIM RICE
JONATHAN RICE